W9-BBT-490

THE NORTON ANTHOLOGY OF DRAMA

Second Edition

VOLUME 1: ANTIQUITY THROUGH THE EIGHTEENTH CENTURY

THE NORTON ANTHOLOGY OF DRAMA

Second Edition

J. ELLEN GAINOR
CORNELL UNIVERSITY

STANTON B. GARNER JR.
UNIVERSITY OF TENNESSEE

MARTIN PUCHNER
HARVARD UNIVERSITY

**VOLUME 1: ANTIQUITY THROUGH
THE EIGHTEENTH CENTURY**

W. W. NORTON & COMPANY

NEW YORK · LONDON

W. W. Norton & Company has been independent since its founding in 1923, when William Warder Norton and Mary D. Herter Norton first published lectures delivered at the People's Institute, the adult education division of New York City's Cooper Union. The firm soon expanded its program beyond the Institute, publishing books by celebrated academics from America and abroad. By midcentury, the two major pillars of Norton's publishing program— trade books and college texts—were firmly established. In the 1950s, the Norton family transferred control of the company to its employees, and today—with a staff of four hundred and a comparable number of trade, college, and professional titles published each year—W. W. Norton & Company stands as the largest and oldest publishing house owned wholly by its employees.

Editor: Peter Simon
Assistant Editor: Quynh Do
Managing Editor, College: Marian Johnson
Project Editor: Linda Feldman
Production Manager: Benjamin Reynolds
Electronic Media Editor: Eileen Connell
Marketing Manager, Literature: Kimberly Bowers
Photo Editor: Nelson Colón
Permissions Manager: Megan Jackson
Permissions Clearing: Nancy Rodwan
Text Design: Rubina Yeh
Art Director: Trish Marx

Composition: Westchester Book Composition
Manufacturing: R. R. Donnelley—Crawfordsville, IN

Library of Congress Cataloging-in-Publication Data

The Norton Anthology of Drama / [edited by] J. Ellen Gainor, Stanton B. Garner Jr., Martin Puchner.—Second edition.
    pages cm.
    Includes bibliographical references and index.
    ISBN 978-0-393-92151-9 (pbk., v. 1) — ISBN 978-0-393-92152-6 (pbk., v. 2)
    1. Drama—Collections. I. Gainor, J. Ellen, editor of compilation. II. Garner, Stanton B., 1955– editor of compilation. III. Puchner, H. Martin, editor of compilation.
    PN6112.N67 2014
    808.2—dc23

2013013971

W. W. Norton & Company, Inc., 500 Fifth Avenue, New York, NY 10110-0017
wwnorton.com
W. W. Norton & Company Ltd., Castle House, 75/76 Wells Street, London W1T 3QT

1 2 3 4 5 6 7 8 9 0

Contents

COLOR INSERT

*Plays in Performance: *Oedipus the King*
*Plays in Performance: *Everyman*
*Plays in Performance: *Hamlet*
*Plays in Performance: *Tartuffe*

Preface

Drama, one of the oldest of the arts, is also the most multifaceted. Grounded in the different mediums of writing and physical enactment, it offers pleasures both to the spectators of its theatrical realizations and to the solitary reader. In preparing the second edition of *The Norton Anthology of Drama*, the editors have remained mindful of this dual allegiance, and we have continued to follow our guiding principle that drama is at once a literary document, speaking to us across a vast expanse of time and space, and a live event, taking place in the here and now. Most of the plays collected here can be experienced in theaters today, or at least be seen in a filmed performance. But even those that are rarely performed in the contemporary era are presented in *The Norton Anthology of Drama* with considerable attention to their life on the stage.

With several new features—including a "Plays in Performance" section designed to enrich the student's understanding of plays in production—this second edition builds on the strengths that distinguish *The Norton Anthology of Drama* from other available drama anthologies. Its plays and their presentation reflect a commitment to the richness and internationality of the dramatic tradition and to the dialogues that mark dramatic performance across languages, borders, and periods. Most anthol-

ogies organize their plays into historical and geographical units with such headings as "Greek Drama," "Renaissance Drama," and "Contemporary Drama." One of the chief results of this kind of demarcation is the separation of Western traditions from non-Western ones, as if these existed in isolation from one another. We, on the other hand, rely on chronology to organize our plays (using actual or estimated dates of first performance, and substituting publication or composition dates for those plays not originally written for performance or plays whose performance was significantly delayed). This decision reflects our belief that theater is historically and geographically more fluid than unit "boxes" imply. We believe, too, that what we call "Western" and "non-Western" texts are marked by concurrent developments across cultures and by similarities of form, subject, and even performance conditions that traditional theatrical and dramatic histories neglect. Chronological presentation allows surprising juxtapositions: Zeami's noh masterpiece *Atsumori* with *The Second Shepherds' Play*, Racine's *Phèdre* with Sor Juana's *Loa for the Divine Narcissus*, and Arthur Miller's *Death of a Salesman* with Tawfiq al-Hakim's *Song of Death*. It also enhances flexibility of course development and organization—*The Norton Anthology of Drama* makes possible many different courses while mandating no specific approach. At the same time, those who desire a presentation of theatrical history that emphasizes historical periods and national traditions will find this structure in the anthology's Introduction.

In determining the table of contents for this anthology, the editors were guided by the desire to select the most thematically rich, performatively engaging, and pedagogically compelling plays available—plays that respond to the historical, cultural, literary, and theatrical contexts in which they were written in new, often groundbreaking, ways. The second edition continues to feature three masterpieces of the twentieth-century stage for which *The Norton Anthology of Drama* holds exclusive anthology publication rights. Two of these—Eugene O'Neill's *Long Day's Journey into Night* and Tennessee Williams's *A Streetcar Named Desire*—are numbered in the greatest plays from the modern American theater, while the third—Samuel Beckett's *Waiting for Godot*—is widely considered the century's most important and influential dramatic work. This last inclusion is particularly significant. Since its publication in 1952, Beckett's greatest play has been available in English only in editions from its American and British publishers. It had never before appeared in a general drama anthology prior to its publication in the first edition of *The Norton Anthology of Drama*, complete with annotation and critical introduction. Our presentation of twentieth-century drama is immeasurably enriched by its presence.

To ensure that reading classic plays written in languages other than English is a lively experience for students, we have selected vibrant translations that speak in a modern idiom while respecting the spirit and sense of the original. When no existing version satisfied us, we commissioned a new one. Whether commissioned specifically for *The Norton Anthology of Drama* or published previously, the translations in this anthology are all not only engaging and accessible on the page but also eminently *performable*. For example, our translation of Molière's *Tartuffe*, by the playwright Constance Congdon, premiered at the Two Rivers Theater in 2006 and has been performed on other stages throughout North America. New to this edition is Ted Hughes' tautly lyrical translation of Racine's *Phèdre*, which was brought to life in the acclaimed 1998 London production starring Diana Rigg.

In balancing the literary with the theatrical, we have designed an anthology that will work in both English and theater classrooms. For the instructor of dramatic literature courses at the introductory and advanced levels, the plays in *The Norton Anthology of Drama* reward textual attention of a literary kind while also encouraging analysis of the play's performance possibilities. For the theater instructor, the anthology provides theatrically vibrant texts in actable editions and translations. Students encountering drama for the first time will discover how powerfully the language of these plays comes alive on the tongue, and experienced and inexperienced students alike will find the versions here to be ideal for in-class performance as well as for line and scene reading. The teaching of drama can be conducted through a range of classroom activities, and *The Norton Anthology of Drama* has been designed to facilitate as many as possible.

Not only does this edition of *The Norton Anthology of Drama* offer more plays (sixty-six) than any other available drama anthology, but it also provides instructors with a fuller range of periods, texts, and playwrights from which to choose. Thus, in addition to the periods and movements usually covered by general anthologies, *The Norton Anthology of Drama* contains examples of Roman drama; classical Indian, Chinese, and Japanese drama; plays from the European and American theater between the years 1700 and 1880, including Part One of Goethe's *Faust* and William Wells Brown's abolitionist melodrama *The Escape; or, A Leap for Freedom*; French avant-garde drama, represented here by Alfred Jarry's *Ubu the King*; twentieth-century Arabic drama, represented by Tawfiq al-Hakim's *Song of Death*; and indigenous North American drama, represented in this edition by Daniel David Moses' *Almighty Voice and His Wife*. Our table of contents also provides a fuller presentation of the early modern period in Europe and the Americas, with four plays by English Renaissance playwrights other than Shakespeare and seven plays from the Spanish Golden Age (including the Spanish-speaking New World), the France of Louis XIV, and Restoration England.

Those familiar with the first edition of *The Norton Anthology of Drama* will notice a number of additions to the second. In response to comments from our readers, we have added three widely taught plays—Sophocles' *Antigone*, Euripides' *Medea*, and Henrik Ibsen's *A Doll House*—to the previously included plays by these dramatists, and we have replaced Harold Pinter's *Old Times* and Caryl Churchill's *The Number* with the more frequently requested selections *The Homecoming* and *Cloud Nine*. In addition to Moses' *Almighty Voice and His Wife*, which was recently revived to great acclaim in Canada, we have added Sophie Treadwell's 1928 play *Machinal*, which deepens the anthology's representation of plays written by women. All told, the second edition includes seven new plays.

Like the Norton anthologies of British, American, and world literatures; *The Norton Anthology of Theory and Criticism*; and the other anthologies with which Norton has shaped classroom teaching over the years, *The Norton Anthology of Drama* provides students and instructors with a wealth of introductory and editorial support. The substantial Introduction opens by exploring the relationship between dramatic literature and theatrical performance, and it concludes with a discussion of the challenges and opportunities of reading plays as scripts for performance. This final section—"Reading Drama, Imagining Theater"—is designed to give students approaching drama for the first time the tools they need to understand a uniquely hybrid form. The "Short History of Theater," which makes up the central part of the introduction, provides a detailed yet brisk overview of the political, social, and theatrical contexts within which drama has been embedded through the ages and across the globe.

We illustrate this history—and the headnotes that accompany each play—with vivid images of theaters, playwrights, actors, and audiences; manuscript pages, woodcuts, early printings, and other illustrations representing the importance of

manuscript and print culture to the development and dissemination of drama; pictures from acting manuals; and other images related to theatrical production. The performance dimension of the plays included in this anthology is further enlivened by thirty new headnote photographs of legendary or contemporary performances of the plays under discussion and by a new "Plays in Performance" feature, which highlights the issues involved in bringing eight classic plays to the contemporary stage. These color inserts (one set per volume) expand students' understanding of the complex decision-making that informs the production of a play, and they give students a glimpse of the creative work performed by actors and directors as they reframe and reimagine plays onstage. They also include examples of critical responses to the productions selected for discussion. We believe that these additions speak to the theatrical life of plays with greater vibrancy and immediacy.

Supplemented by the substantial yet concise historical survey that opens the anthology, the headnotes that accompany each selection offer detailed, accessible introductions to the plays. These headnotes include summaries of the author's life and career, the specific historical and cultural contexts of the play in question, production information (where pertinent), and consideration of the play's importance in terms of its historical period and the broader history of drama and theater. The headnotes also include a discussion of the plays themselves, though we have taken care not to "explain" the plays to students, instead raising issues that will enable them to interpret the works on their own. For those interested in delving more deeply into the subject matter, we provide a carefully chosen and annotated bibliography of books and articles on each play and author. Throughout the headnote and bibliography, the editors have emphasized usefulness, readability, and student interest.

Similar care has been taken with the dramatic texts and their annotations. We have done everything possible to ensure that the texts in *The Norton Anthology of Drama* are the most authoritative ones available; if competing versions of these texts exist, we have selected the ones that are endorsed by contemporary scholarly consensus. In cases in which there is more than one version of a play—Marlowe's *Doctor Faustus*, Shaw's *Pygmalion*, and Shepard's *Buried Child*, for instance—we have selected the text that reflects the playwright's earliest theatrical vision. Our edition of *Hamlet*—a play with one of the most complicated and contested textual histories in world drama—is accompanied by a brief summary of that textual history, an overview of recent attempts to establish or resist an "authoritative" text, and a rationale for the version of the text included here. At the levels of selection and copyediting, we have devoted an exceptional amount of attention to ensuring that the text as it appears here is the most correct published version available.

Whereas other drama anthologies occasionally present historically and linguistically challenging plays without any annotations at all, *The Norton Anthology of Drama* provides footnotes and marginal glosses whenever an unfamiliar word, phrase, or historical/cultural reference risks interfering with a student's understanding of the text. We have tried to avoid cluttering plays with such material—we assume that students have access to a dictionary—but we have worked to annotate those words and references whose significance is obscured or hidden by historical remoteness. A number of our plays—including *Godot*—are annotated here for the first time, and we hope that even those plays that have been annotated before have been given a fresh presentation through our footnotes and marginal glosses.

Comprehensive anthologies of drama, students and instructors have long agreed, are unwieldy affairs, encompassing as they do twenty-five centuries of drama in phone-book-size volumes. *The Norton Anthology of Drama*, by contrast, has been published in companion volumes that fit comfortably in the hand and on a lap, with the play-texts appearing on easy-to-read, single-column pages. Students can carry one volume at a time to class, and the anthology as a whole is an attractive addition to a bookshelf. There are pedagogical reasons for the two-volume choice as well. The first volume ("Antiquity through the Eighteenth Century") contains the periods that typically make up the first half of a two-semester history of theater or drama course, and the second volume ("The Nineteenth Century to the Present") lends itself to the second semester of such courses. Because of their rich historical coverage of specific periods, the two volumes can also be used—together or separately—for advanced courses in Renaissance drama, modern drama, American drama, contemporary drama, script analysis, dramaturgy, tragedy, comedy, and the like and for courses that include extended units in these and other areas. So that the users of the single volumes can have the fullest possible exposure to theatrical antecedents, crosscurrents, and historical developments, the Introduction has been included in full in each volume.

Finally, the many resources in *The Norton Anthology of Drama*—the Introduction, individual headnotes, bibliographies, and textual annotations—are complemented by resources outside the anthology itself. An Instructor's Manual by Zander Brietzke, written in consultation with the editors, provides valuable material for teaching both large survey courses and smaller lectures and seminars. This guide presents the most important topics that might be covered in a lecture on a given play; it also suggests creative classroom exercises for students who want to explore the complexities of a scene by performing it in class. Topics and exercises focus on particular passages and scenes, yet also cover larger themes, as do the handy paper topics provided for each play. Teachers will also find a list of prominent productions in this Instructor's Manual, along with a list of the best film adaptations that might be used in class or for further study. Of additional help is the second edition's improved companion website, wwnorton.com/drama, which provides students with a supplementary ebook reader containing texts exploring the criticism and theory of drama. For the present edition the editors have written short headnotes for these critical texts and annotated them where appropriate. Other resources on the extensive companion website offer students review materials, a comprehensive glossary of terms, and a guide to writing about drama.

Coming from performing arts and literature departments, the editors of *The Norton*

Anthology of Drama bring the perspectives of these overlapping disciplines to dramatic history and performance and to the project of compiling a comprehensive anthology of dramatic literature. We have been aided in our efforts by a number of contributing editors, who have taken responsibilities for plays and playwrights that require special expertise. Numerous other scholars have lent knowledge and experience to this project—reading drafts of the headnotes and Introduction; clarifying points of fact and interpretation; providing nuance, when needed, to prevent historical overgeneralization; and helping us track down and identify historical images for the anthology. *The Norton Anthology of Drama*, in short, has been a deeply collaborative process, in which scholars from a number of areas have pooled their expertise to produce the most complete, informative, and engaging anthology of its kind.

Acknowledgments

A project of this magnitude cannot reach its final form without the help and encouragement of many people beyond those whose names appear on the book's cover. Given our appreciation of and love for the collaborative art of theater, we editors of *The Norton Anthology of Drama* are especially sensitive to the countless ways in which we have been helped and inspired by others.

CONTRIBUTING EDITORS

First, we would like to acknowledge the following scholars, who lent us their expertise by editing and introducing specific plays:

Dina Ahmed Amin (University of Cairo), *Song of Death*

Art Borreca (University of Iowa), *The Homecoming; Angels in America: Millennium Approaches*

Karen Brazell (late of Cornell University), *Atsumori*

Thomas Cartelli (Muhlenberg College), *The Tragical History of Doctor Faustus*

Sudipto Chatterjee (Loughborough University), *The Little Clay Cart*

Heather Hirschfeld (University of Tennessee), *The Spanish Tragedy; The Duchess of Malfi*

Ivo Kamps (University of Mississippi), *Hamlet; Twelfth Night*

Evan Darwin Winet (Independent scholar, Berkeley, Ca.), *Snow in Midsummer*

Each of these scholars has played a critical role in making the anthology what it is, and we are grateful to have had the opportunity to collaborate with them.

TRANSLATORS

Some of the texts in *The Norton Anthology of Drama* are plays in translation that were commissioned specifically for the anthology. We thank the following translators whose skillful work has provided our readers with new translations that are both readable and performable:

Sudipto Chatterjee (Loughborough University), *The Little Clay Cart*

Constance Congdon (Amherst College), *Tartuffe*

Gregory Racz (Long Island University), *Life Is a Dream; Fuenteovejuna*

David Ball (Smith College), *Ubu the King*

We remain grateful to all those who offered support and assistance with the first edition of the anthology. We would like to acknowledge here the following people and institutions who provided us with advice, encouragement, administrative support, research assistance, and constructive critiques as we prepared the second edition: Andrew Bielski, Zander Brietzke, Amanda Claybaugh, Kerri Ann Considine, Jerry Dickey, Mary Dzon, David, St. John, and Loie Faulkner, Helene Foley, Mary Gainor, Alison Maerker Garner, Helen Elizabeth Garner, Amy Gillingham, Laura L. Howes, Rebecca Kastleman, Mechele Leon, Shilo McGiff, Meagan Michelson, Fred Muratori and the Reference and Interlibrary Loan Staff of Cornell University Libraries, Virginia H. Murphy, Sarah Powers Norman, Gregary Racz, Jeffrey Rusten, Sabine Sörgel, Victoria Swanson, Thomas Robert Travers, Judith Welch, Katherine Young, and the staff of the University of Tennessee Library Interlibrary Loan and Library Express departments.

Finally, the publisher and editors are grateful to all of the educators who responded to surveys, questionnaires, and review requests during the planning stages of both the first and second editions. The anthology continues to be a popular and useful text in large part because of the good suggestions offered by the following people: Michael Abbott, Mara Amster, Gordon S. Armstrong, Wendy Arons, M. G. Aune, Yashdip S. Bains, Beulah Baker, John I. Baker III, Margaret Ball, Claudia Barnett, Jane Barnette, Maria Beach, Keri Behre, Susan Bennett, Linda Ben-Zvi, Robin Bernstein, Scott Blanks, Dallas Boggs, Scott Boltwood, Kimberley A. Bouchard, Sandra M. Boynton, Adrienne Macki Braconi, Owen E. Brady, Kazimierz Braun, Sybil Brinberg, Chris Brooks, Sarah Bryant-Bertail, Jackson R. Bryer, Doug Buchanan, Matthew Buckley, Mike Burnett, Tom Butler, Ruth Cantrell, Anne Cattaneo, Dorothy Chansky, Renee Charlow, Nick Clary, Angus Cleghorn, Thomas F. Connolly, Kenneth Cox, Margaret Croskery, Marsha Cummins, Richard Cunningham, Keith Cushman, Koos Daley, Lynda Del Valle, William Demastes, Brian Desmond, Carlos Dews, Betty Diamond, Lyn Dohaney, Elizabeth Lee Dollar, Maria-Elena Doyle, Lofton Durham, Robert Duxbury, Bill Dynes, David W. Engel, Michael Erickson, Jay Farness, Anne Fearman, Mary Field, Phyllis Fields, Nancy Finn, Chris Fisher, Theresa Flowers, Terezinha Fonseca, Ivan Fuller, Valerie L. Gager, Donald P. Gagnon, Jure Gantar, Steven Gilbert, Gary Gisselman, Daniel Gonzalez, Rebecca Gorman, Fanni Green, Elissa Guralnick, Janet Haedicke, Paul Hansom, Jerry Harris, Kevin J. Harty, David Hay, Christopher Herr, Jessica Hillman, Woody Hood, David Hopes, D. J. Hopkins, Glenn Hopp, Elisabeth Schulz Hostetter, Helen M. Housley, Tonya Howe, Keith N. Hull, William Hutchings, Bill Jenkins, David Johnson, Peggy Rae Johnson, Walter H. Johnson, Mark Johnston, Greg Jones, P. Pennington Jones, Karen Rae Keck, Helen Killoran, Michael King, Matthew Kinservik, Cindy Kistenberg, Robert Knopf, Michael Kohler, David Kramer, David Kranes, Damon Kupper, James H. Lake, Penne J. Laubenthal, Lisa Leibering, Bruce Leland, Paul M. Levitt, John L'Heureux, Mark Lococo, Stanley V. Longman, Wayne Luckman, Thomas Luddy, William Luhr, Kevin M. Lynch, Bonnie Lyons, Sue Mach, William MacLennan, Philip Manwell, Deborah Martinson, Irene Martyniuk, Cary Mazer, Joseph McCadden, Adrienne McCormick, Janet E. McLean, Kirk Melnikoff, Lorraine Mercer, Naomi Miller, Lamata Mitchell, Kathleen Monahan, Deborah J. Montuori, Robert Moore, Annissa Morgensen-Lindsay, Jonathan Morse, Wayne Narey, Joan Navarre, Emmanuel N. Ngwang, Lance Norman, I. Nunnari, Kevin Oakes, Leslie O'Dell, Deirdre O'Leary, Pat Onion, Lary Opitz, Terry Otten, Howard Pearce, Todd Pettigrew, Jen Plants, Michael Pogach, Ann Price, Ray Pritchard, June Pulliam, Marjean D. Purinton, Jason Radalin, Paige Reynolds, Elise Robinson, Korey Rothman, Elizabeth Rowse, Gene Ruffini, Rebecca Rumbo, Neil Kristian Scharnick, Owen W. Schaub, Joel Schechter, Samuel T. Shanks, Johanna M. Smith, Mark Spergel, N. J. Stanley, Sally Story, William Streitberger, Sharon Sullivan, Sherman Sutherland, Wilbur Thomas, David Thompson, Dean Thompson, Jon Tuttle, Randolph Umberger, Mardi Valgemae, Martine Van Elk, Ronald Wainscott, Brian Warren, Albert Wertheim, J. Chris Westgate, Kevin Wetmore, David Wheeler, Lisa Whitney, Kayla Wiggins, Heather Williams, Don B. Wilmeth, Janet S. Wolf, Whitney Womack Smith, Leigh Woods, Joyce Wszalek, Kate Wulle, Trisha Yarbrough, Yvonne Yaw, Rick Yeatman, Mary Yost-Rushton, John T. Young, Kelly Younger, and Toby Zinman.

Thank you, one and all.

THE NORTON ANTHOLOGY OF DRAMA

Second Edition

VOLUME 1: ANTIQUITY THROUGH THE EIGHTEENTH CENTURY

Introduction

DRAMA AND THEATER

Audiences gather in a hillside amphitheater under the eastern Mediterranean sun to watch the impersonated figures of Greek myth play out their heroic, terrifying stories. In Kyoto, Japan, the sweep of robes on a railed wooden bridge announces the entry of a masked noh actor, who moves and gestures in front of his aristocratic audience with stylized precision. In London, a group of traveling players are given advice on acting by a Danish prince while the spectators who crowd the theater—aldermen, midwives, apprentices—enjoy the irony of actors meditating on their craft. In Paris, two tramps sitting by a tree on a country road share conversation and stage routines that barely conceal their anguish; an audience, seated in the dark, bears witness to their starkly contemporary situation.

The history of theater and dramatic performance is, in many ways, the history of moments such as these. The collaborative product of actors, playwrights, designers, directors, and spectators, theater achieves its magic in the live moment, rich with its sounds, sights, and feelings. The immediacy of the audience-stage encounter renders the act of theater-making magical and unique. Like other

art forms—such as novels, paintings, and movies—theater constructs imaginative worlds that we can marvel at, be moved by, and learn from. Unlike these other forms, however, theater puts its worlds into live motion, in real time. In a kind of alchemy, theater takes the realm of fiction and brings it to life with living beings whose interactions take place before our eyes. At the same time, it takes the experiences of everyday life and transforms them through the magic of performance into something more powerful, deeply felt, and artful than the daily exchanges we witness and participate in. The actor stands in for us, embodies our hopes and fears, boldly enacts what is forbidden or only dreamed of. And like the theater itself, the actor introduces us to the pleasures inherent in recognition, imitation, and the intensity of a life passionately observed and lived.

Theater is the art of the moment, and its ability to captivate us with its illusion is linked to its magical but always precarious sleight of hand. Theater is the most ephemeral of vehicles—a performance, once finished, is lost to time—and the unrepeatability of its accomplishments is a major source of its power. Unlike film,

1

which fixes action in celluloid or other media, theater takes place in the actual, in the here and now that it shares with its spectators, and its illusions are inseparable from its precariousness. Not surprisingly, the most memorable playgoing experiences are often those when something goes wrong—a stage chair collapses, a piece of stage machinery fails, an understudy is rushed on during the middle of a performance when the main actor falls ill—and the carefully constructed dramatic illusion hangs in the balance.

Central to the act of theater-making is the dramatic text, play-text, or script, which serves as the fictional and narrative foundation of the theatrical event. Whether these texts are loosely sketched, as in the improvisational performances of the Renaissance commedia dell'arte, or highly detailed in plot, setting, characterization, and dialogue, the use of scripted narratives is one of the principal features distinguishing theater from other performance types. With the invention of writing, these texts became artworks in and of themselves, and drama assumed its place as the first "literary" form, no longer exclusively dependent on performance for its realization. Plays were available in manuscript form to the educated elite of ancient Greece and Rome; classical India, China, and Japan; and medieval Europe; and after the invention of the printing press in the fifteenth century, they became available to an expanding popular readership. The plays of WILLIAM SHAKESPEARE and TENNESSEE WILLIAMS share space on twenty-first-century bookstore shelves with the novels of Jane Austen and Cormac McCarthy. But the literary dimension of dramatic works remains inseparable from performance—actual, possible, historical, imagined—with the result that drama has different aims and reference points than do more exclusively literary forms. To read a novel is to project characters, actions, and locations within an imaginative realm that is guided and limited by the words on the page; it is to undertake a mental and emotional activity that resembles dreaming more than it does the actions we engage in daily. To read a play, in contrast, is to encounter a text whose primary purpose, with rare exceptions, is to make something happen in real space and time with actors whose bodies and voices are the drama's principal instruments. In this sense, a play resembles a symphonic score, whose printed notations are directions for the production of musical sound. Even those plays that we refer to as "closet dramas," which were usually not performed when written—whether because of political, technical, or cultural barriers or because their authors preferred them to be read or recited rather than subjected to the stage's inherent limitations—often seem to have been created with some ideal performance in mind.

As the final section of this introduction ("Reading Drama, Imagining Theater") will discuss in more detail, drama invites the reader to put her- or himself in the position of a theater artist, alive to the possibilities and choices that bring a play to life, imagining the different ways that a scene, line, or gesture might look, sound, and feel when performed. Being attentive to the conditions of performance allows one to appreciate the features that characterize drama as a literary and theatrical form: the necessary economy of its action, setting, and characterization, which are denied the leisure of novelistic description; the centrality of spoken language, which provides access to offstage and subjective worlds; and the preoccupation with questions of role-playing, impersonation, and the many ways in which we perform for the benefit of others and ourselves. In the absence of an omniscient narrator or other guiding authorial consciousness, drama emerges through the interplay of its characters, who enact their stories in the theater and on the imagined stage of one's reading. The power of these stories resides in the immediacy of the actors and their interactions with the theater environment, which of course includes the audience.

Humans have always told each other stories. From the earliest times for which we have physical or documentary evidence, we have acted our stories for each other. We donned costumes and masks, wielded props, and later created designated places—theaters—where we use the immediacy of live performance to communicate the powerful experiences that have

Spectators watch a performance of Anton Chekhov's *Three Sisters* at the Guthrie Theater in Minneapolis, 1963.

shaped us. Like other forms of organized social performance—games, festivities, storytelling, athletic displays, civic ceremonies, political events, and rituals—these encounters are deeply embedded in specific historical, social, and cultural contexts. To study the history of theater and drama is to confront a range of historical junctures, social and institutional practices, and cultural forms. It is also to encounter one of the most enduring of human activities: make-believe, the act of making oneself other than oneself for purposes of entertainment, commemoration, communication, or devotion.

Through performance and its rituals, we confirm our shared humanity—we acknowledge the importance of each other's existence and suggest that our lives are of value. Collectively, we generate forms of community while articulating the meanings that lend shape to our lives. The sense of communion and reciprocal awareness engendered by live performance, and the dramatic texts written for it, transcends cultures and history; it is foundational to who we are as living beings. As prehistoric cave paintings indicate, imitation and ritual were part of the earliest human societies. We are performers by nature. Although theater and drama are relative latecomers to human history (having been around for a mere 2,500 years), the activities they draw on are as old as humanity itself.

A SHORT HISTORY OF THEATER

The origins of theater—and hence of drama—have long been a subject of scholarly debate. We possess little material evidence concerning the development of theatrical activity in most cultures, and what generalizations we might draw from it are complicated by the fact that the earliest forms of theater were the product of a variety of social, political, and religious forces. However, those studying different dramatic traditions have found theater to be closely connected to hunting, fertility, and other rituals in those early societies where it emerged. The nature of this connection has been debated by scholars, but the consensus view is that theatrical activity represented an extension of ritual's symbolic forms of representation into nonritual contexts. The rituals of early societies involved the enactment of religious and mythic narratives by privileged participants—shaman, priest, ruler, sacrificial victim—and these performances could become quite elaborate. In Egypt, rituals commemorating the death and resurrection of Osiris, a god associated with fertility, took place at the sacred site of Abydos as early as 2500 B.C.E. Evidence suggests that the dramatic events of Osiris's life may have been performed by priests and that these performances were accompanied by lavish spectacle.

Ritual differs from theater, of course, in that its prescribed actions, passed down from generation to generation, are designed to effect change in the natural or spiritual worlds. The ritual performances of Egypt remained tied to their religious and dynastic functions and never developed in the direction of theater. In those cultures in which theater did emerge, symbolic performance asserted itself as an object of interest in its own right, thereby paving the way for institutions, practitioners, and audiences who conceived of theater as a communal artistic activity. The earliest of these transitions—and one of the most important for the subsequent history of theater and drama—occurred in Greece in the fifth century B.C.E.

Greek Theater

ORIGINS OF GREEK THEATER

The theater of classical Greece looms large in the history of Western theater. Not only did the emergence of theater as an institution in Athens during the fifth century B.C.E. establish the world's first theatrical culture, but the characters who confronted their fate on the Greek stage—Orestes, Oedipus, Antigone, Medea—remain among the most imposing characters in the dramatic repertoire. Yet despite the importance of Greek theater to the history of Western drama, little is known about its origins. Scholars have depended, for the most part, on the scattered remarks of later classical writers who were themselves speculating about events hundreds of years in the past. Archaeological findings, the history of words associated with the theater, and vase paintings have since provided additional hints as to how the first Greek theaters came into existence. Most scholars subscribe to the notion that the origins of Greek theater lie in religious rituals. Ancient Greek religious life included many different types of ceremonies and public performances: funeral services, festivals celebrating the seasons or individual gods, processions and competitions. But which of these performances provided the decisive impulse is much harder to pinpoint. The Greek word for tragedy, *tragōidia*, originally meant "goat song" and therefore seems to associate tragedy with ritual practices involving the killing of a goat. Other theories hold that theater emerged from rituals performed at the tombs of heroes.

Though we know little about either the goat song or the ritual performances at tombs, other cultural practices that aided the development of theater are much better documented. Among them are the public performances of storytellers, or *rhapsōidoi*, who recited stories of gods and mythical humans to large audiences. The first theorist of theater, the philosopher Plato (ca. 427–ca. 347 B.C.E.), emphasized the similarities between public recitations of epic poetry and simple dramatic performances. What is still the most convincing theory about the origin of Greek theater was developed by Aristotle (384–322 B.C.E.), who wrote a generation after his teacher Plato. Aristotle claimed that theater emerged from a specific ceremony honoring Dionysus, a god associated with fertility, agriculture, wine, and (by extension) physical and spiritual intoxication. During the Attic ceremony honoring him, a chorus and a chorus leader (*koryphaios*) sang and danced a hymn composed in a particular form known as the *dithyrambos*. According to Aristotle, these ritual performances formed the basis for later dramatic performance. The Greek language reinforces Aristotle's claim, for

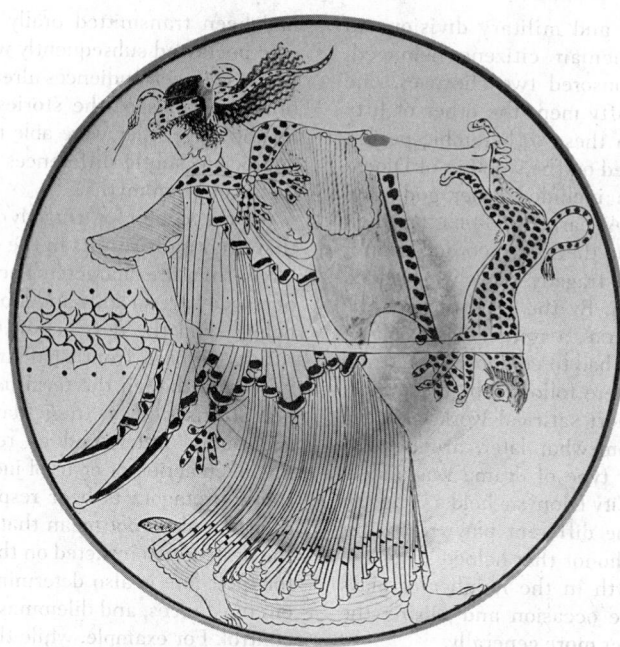

This image, a detail from a *kylix* (a wine cup) painted by the so-called Brygos Painter in the early fifth century B.C.E., depicts a devotee (a *bacchante* or *maenad*) of the god Dionysus performing a ritualized dance. In her right hand is a *thrysus*, an ivy-covered staff that was an important part of sacred rituals.

the choral performers of dithyrambs were called *tragōidoi*, pointing once again to the later word for tragedy.

The association of theater with the dithyrambs performed in the honor of Dionysus makes sense for many reasons. The first Greek playwright, Thespis (sixth century B.C.E.), whose plays have all been lost, is credited with adding an individual performer to the dithyrambic chorus and chorus leader, and thus enabling dramatic interaction to emerge. Because Thespis himself is said to have performed this newly individual role, he is considered by many to be the world's first actor, and his name has given us the word *thespian*. From this point on the chorus (or chorus leader) was not limited to reciting a hymn but could impersonate an imaginary figure by engaging in a dialogue with the newly introduced actor. The Greek word for actor, *hypokritēs*, by the way, still exists in the English word *hypocrite*, whose now largely negative meaning underscores that acting involves imitation

and pretense. Subsequent playwrights added more actors to increase the possibilities for dialogue between individuals, although the chorus remained an important component of Greek, and subsequently of Roman, theater.

Another reason for associating theater with the Dionysian dithyrambs is that the first known Greek plays were performed at the City Dionysia, one of four Athenian festivals (another was the Rural Dionysia) held during the winter in honor of the god. Over the course of the fifth century B.C.E., when Greek theater was at its height, other festivals incorporated dramatic performances, but the City Dionysia remained the most important event for theater. The City Dionysia, which attracted many visitors from other city-states and from outside Greece, was a multiday affair, whose focus was various competitions. The first was a competition of dithyrambs, first organized around 600 B.C.E., among the four (later ten) "tribes" (*phylai*)—the administrative and military divisions to which all Athenian citizens belonged. Each tribe sponsored two choruses, one consisting of fifty men, the other of fifty boys. Although these dithyrambic performances centered on the worship of Dionysus, they soon included other gods and myths as well. As early as 534 B.C.E., when Thespis became the first recorded winner of the prize for tragedy, plays were added to the program. By the beginning of the fifth century B.C.E, a system was in place: each dramatist had to compose three tragedies, which were followed by the performance of a short satirical work (called a *satyr play*). Somewhat later, around 486 B.C.E., another type of drama was added: comedy. The City Dionysia held a competition among the different playwrights for first prize, an honor that helped spark the explosive growth in the number of plays written for the occasion and raising the status of theater more generally.

GREEK TRAGEDY

One development necessary for drama to emerge from these various rituals and performances was the invention of writing and the spread of literacy. Greek rituals did not include written scripts but were instead based on formulaic and orally transmitted incantations, hymns, and performances. Likewise, dithyrambic and epic poems were originally memorized and improvised by the performers, but not composed as literature. The first epics to be preserved in writing were those attributed to Homer (ca. 750–700 B.C.E.), the *Iliad* and the *Odyssey*; and in the late seventh century B.C.E., Arion (active 628–625 B.C.E.) was apparently the first to write down his own dithyrambs (none of which have survived). Consequently, Homer and Arion are considered by some to be the first tragedians, though they did not actually write plays.

The earliest extant tragedies all date from the fifth century B.C.E. and were written by three playwrights: AESCHYLUS (ca. 525–456 B.C.E.), SOPHOCLES (ca. 496–406 B.C.E.), and EURIPIDES (ca. 480–406 B.C.E.). These plays are set in a mythical past (with one exception—Aeschylus's *Persians*, which takes place during the Persian Wars), using the stories of gods and heroic humans that had been transmitted orally by the early epic poets and subsequently written down. Because Greek audiences already knew the broad outlines of the stories dramatized on the stage, they were able to notice and appreciate subtle differences in the treatments of given myths.

At the center of tragedy is a conflict that eventually results in the downfall of a larger-than-life character. The protagonists of tragedy are socially and morally elevated beings, and the destruction they undergo results, in part, from what Aristotle called *hamartia*; though the term has sometimes been translated as "tragic flaw," it is more accurately understood as referring to a mistaken action or error of judgment. That tragic protagonists bear responsibility for their fate does not mean that they deserve the destruction inflicted on them, however, for their fate is also determined by forces, circumstances, and dilemmas outside their control. For example, while the decision of Antigone (in Sophocles' play of the same name) to bury her brother Polyneices follows the religious imperative, obeying that imperative brings her into conflict with her uncle Creon, the king of Thebes, who has declared him a traitor and therefore has forbidden his burial. Faced with this set of forces not of her making—one, a social and religious mandate; the other, a legal prohibition—Antigone has no alternative but to choose her tragic fate. Similarly, the protagonist of Sophocles' OEDIPUS THE KING (ca. 428 B.C.E.), who unknowingly killed his father and married his mother, must accept punishment for deeds performed not with malicious intent but with an overweening pride and belief in his own invulnerability. Ironically, the man of action and the solver of the Sphinx's riddle proves rash in his actions and blind to fate's riddle in his own life. Virtues and flaws, the notion of *hamartia* may also suggest, are intimately tied up in each other: we can trust our talents and strengths too much and learn, in the outcome of our actions, that they are both the reason for our good fortune and the cause of our demise.

As these tragic conflicts unfold, the protagonists find themselves in another contentious relation, namely with the chorus. Not surprisingly, given its origins in choral dithyrambs, tragedy retained the chorus as an important element. Reflecting the perspective of the community, this body observes and comments on the actions and entanglements of the protagonists, trying to rein in their excesses and restore order to the civic realm. The chorus also reminds the audience of the background story of a given myth and often engages the protagonists in a dialogue that draws out the motives of their actions. In keeping with the evolving nature of Greek tragedy during the fifth century B.C.E., the role of the chorus underwent changes. As dramatic characters grew in number, complexity, and importance, the role of the chorus lessened.

The complexity of the relations between individual actors and the chorus shaped the typical structure of Greek tragedy. Greek tragedies begin either with a prologue that sets the scene or with the entrance—*parodos*—of the chorus. The main body of the tragedy is then composed of a sequence of episodes—*epeisodia*, scenes in which the main actors talk to one another or to the chorus—and choral songs without dialogue, *stasima*. At the end of the play, the characters and the chorus leave the stage in what is called the *exodos*. Greek tragedy, in other words, was a highly structured and formalized art form in which dialogue between two individual actors, today the main component of drama, was relatively unimportant. Instead, choral lyrics and the dialogue between chorus and protagonist took up most of the play. Playwrights used different styles of language and meter to distinguish between the different sections of tragedy. Choral lyrics were a form of poetry highly elevated in diction and intricately composed, while the exchanges between the chorus and individual characters, though still quite stylized, were more conversational. The dialogues in iambic meter between the individual characters, though they too were artfully wrought, were closer still to everyday speech. Such differentiation can clearly be seen in the works of Euripides, who, writing slightly later than Aeschylus and Sophocles, attempted to bring the language of tragedy nearer to the language actually spoken by the audience.

As noted above, in its mature form the City Dionysia included a competition in

This detail from the so-called Pronomos Vase, painted in the late fifth century B.C.E., depicts actors preparing for a satyr play.

which each dramatist presented three tragedies followed by a satyr play. Unfortunately, because only one complete satyr play has survived—Euripides' *Cyclops*—it is difficult to generalize about the genre. The plays seem to have dealt with the same mythical and heroic figures and stories as tragedies but irreverently, as burlesque. Accordingly, their language was apparently more colloquial than that of tragedy. The satyr play remained closely connected to Dionysus, for in Greek mythology satyrs were half-human and half-bestial creatures who formed part of his retinue, and the leader of the chorus in satyr plays was Silenus, a satyr who was a constant companion of the god. The satyr play provided the audience with comic relief at the end of a daylong performance of tragedies.

GREEK COMEDY

The satyr play, despite its comic elements, belonged to a genre distinct from comedy. Although comedies had not originally been part of festival competitions, they were incorporated into the City Dionysia festival around 486 B.C.E. The origins of comedy also lie in ritual, most likely in rites that featured groups of men wearing representations of large *phalloi* (male sexual organs) and animal masks. A second source for Greek comedy was a form of mime—short, improvised sketches treating everyday situations humorously. These foundations are visible in what is called Old Comedy, which developed in the fifth century B.C.E.; its only remaining examples are the plays of ARISTOPHANES (ca. 450–ca. 385 B.C.E.), although the names of other comic playwrights are known to us, including Magnes (active 472 B.C.E.) and Aristophanes' main rival, Eupolis (ca. 445–ca. 411 B.C.E.). The choruses of comedy may well represent animals or inanimate objects—Aristophanes' plays have such titles as *The Frogs*, *The Wasps*, and *The Clouds*—and they often treat explicitly sexual themes. In contrast to both tragedy and the satyr play, comedies take as their subject matter not the gods and heroes of Greek mythology but rather the everyday life of contemporary Athenians, and the topics they engage range from the long Peloponnesian War with Sparta (which provides the background to *LYSISTRATA* [411 B.C.E.], Aristophanes' best-known play) to public personalities such as the philosopher Socrates. Like tragedy, Old Comedy begins with a prologue, which is followed by the entry of the chorus; it contains passages of dialogue; and it concludes with the exit of all the characters. It also features an added element: a section called the *parabasis* (literally, "digression") in which the chorus addresses the audience directly, discussing political and social problems and sometimes praising the playwright. In the *parabasis* and throughout each play, classical comedy engages with political and social issues much more directly than tragedy, although it does so comically, drawing on fantasy, humor that frequently is ribald, and farce.

THE GREEK STAGE

The main performance venue for Athenian theater was the Dionysus theater, located in the hill just below the Acropolis, an elevated area on which stood the Parthenon and which served as the city's religious and political center. Given the elaborate nature of later Greek and Roman theaters, the Dionysus theater in the fifth century B.C.E. was surprisingly simple. A large *amphitheatron*, holding between 14,000 to 17,000 audience members, was built into the hillside, with seating provided by temporary wooden benches. At the center of the amphitheater was the *orchēstra* (or "dancing place"), a semicircle in whose middle stood the *thymelē*, a raised stone used as an altar or a table. Behind the *orchēstra* stood a wooden structure, the *skēnē*, which served as a place where actors could change masks and costumes and, through one or more doors, appear and disappear from the stage. The area in front of the *skēnē* would later be known as the *paraskēnion*, a term from which the modern word *proscenium* derives. On either side of the *skēnē* were passageways.

This physical arrangement was used by the Greek dramatists in increasingly complex ways. The passageways aided the elaborate entrances and exits of the chorus, while the *orchēstra* was the place where the dances performed by the chorus and the interaction between chorus and individual actors took place. The altar or table could be used by individual actors to hide and suddenly appear. The *skēnē* at the back of the performance area provided even more theatrical possibilities. For example, playwrights placed messengers and other figures on its roof, where they could be on the lookout and describe battles and other scenes they pretended to see on its other side (a stage device called *teichoskopeia*, or "watching from a wall"). The doors in the *skēnē* were used not only to aid entrances and exits but also to suddenly reveal characters. To heighten the effect of the doors, a rolling platform, or *ekkyklēma*, was employed to roll the body of a killed character in front of the audience or to make other dramatic disclosures. Such a device was especially important since almost all physical violence—the blinding of Oedipus, for example, or Medea's murder of her children—occurred offstage, often (the audience was led to believe) within the scene building. A second mechanism became increasingly popular: a crane called a *mēchanē*, which could move characters through the air into the space in front of the scene building. Euripides, in particular, used such cranes to introduce gods, who would resolve the plot and mete out punishment at the end of his tragedies; this device became well-known by its Latin name, *deus ex machina* (god from a machine). Various forms of painted panels were probably employed on the stage as well, though little is known about their appearance and function.

Because theater was an integral part of civic and religious festivals, an elaborate system of rules and practices governed the production of plays. A leading figure of the Athenian government, an *archōn eponymos*, selected from among the wealthy citizens a *chorēgos*, or producer, who would provide the funds for the chorus, while the city government provided the funds for the playwright and the leading actors.

The playwrights were responsible for rehearsals and sometimes even performed in their own plays. The number of performers was strictly limited. The chorus probably contained twelve to fifteen members, although as many as fifty may have appeared in some early plays of Aeschylus. The number of individual actors was even more crucial, because it directly affected how many characters were available to the playwright. Aeschylus's early plays used two actors, who could take on different roles over the course of a play—but obviously, no more than two speaking parts could be present simultaneously. Either Aeschylus or, more likely, his younger rival Sophocles took the decisive step of introducing a third actor, thereby expanding the playwright's options considerably.

One reason why actors could change so easily from one role to the next was the relative simplicity of their costumes. A thick, richly colored garment covered their bodies; large, high boots made them appear larger than life; and a mask made from either fabric or wood covered their entire face. Given the size of the theater and the bulkiness of their costumes, the actors had

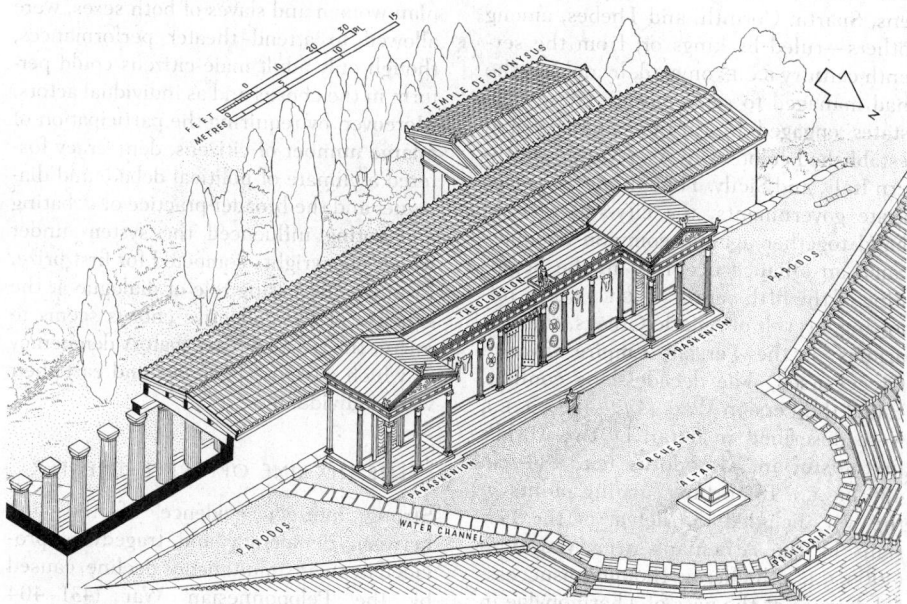

A reconstruction of the Dionysus theater by the theater and architectural scholar Richard Leacroft. An actor stands in the *orchēstra*, while another stands on the roof of the *skēnē*.

to rely on large gestures rather than on small, intimate reactions, and in masks they lacked any recourse to facial expressions. Scenes of dialogue alternated with the elaborate dances of the chorus. The performance of Greek plays was accompanied by music, provided mainly by the flute—it was a flute player who led the entrance of the chorus at the beginning of the play—but various other wind and percussion instruments were employed as well. Today's audiences and readers can easily overlook the significance of music, which is generally little used in contemporary revivals of Greek plays, but the scholars and artists who attempted to revive Greek tragedy during the European Renaissance were very conscious of its importance. Indeed, this awareness led to the creation of opera, a form of theater that relies primarily on music and song and only secondarily on spoken dialogue.

THEATER AND ATHENIAN DEMOCRACY

The emergence and rise of Greek theater is intimately tied to the political history of Greece. Greece was not a unified nation but rather a network of city-states—Athens, Sparta, Corinth, and Thebes, among others—ruled by kings or, from the seventh century B.C.E. onward, by nobles who had managed to seize power. These city-states engaged in various alliances and established colonies in Asia Minor, southern Italy, and Sicily. Though they had separate governments, the city-states could band together against common enemies. Such an alliance occurred in the beginning of the fifth century B.C.E., when, following a revolt of Asiatic Greeks, the vast armies of the Persian Empire invaded Greece itself. The decades-long conflict, called the Persian Wars (499–449 B.C.E.), were described in detail by the world's first historian, Herodotus (ca. 484–ca. 425 B.C.E.). Important turning points in the war included the defeat of the Persians by the Athenians near Marathon (490 B.C.E.), the heroic though unsuccessful defense of the pass of Thermopylae in central Greece by a small Spartan force (480 B.C.E.), and the destruction of the Persian fleet by Athens at Salamis (480

B.C.E.), a battle that was critical to Persia's subsequent defeat.

The crucial role of Athens in winning this victory led to its increasing dominance over the rest of Greece, and it built a largely seaborne empire consisting of allies, dependent states, and colonies. It was during this time of military dominance that Athens became a cosmopolitan center for the arts—the birthplace of Greek theater and the center of many other intellectual and cultural pursuits, such as philosophy (although many philosophers living in Athens were foreign-born). Equally important was the development in Athens of an early form of democracy that involved all adult male citizens in the governance of the Athenian empire, serving in the courts, military offices, and other administrative posts. Women, slaves, and foreigners, it is important to note, were not considered citizens. Moreover, though it was a predecessor of modern democracies, Athenian democracy included many features that might strike today's citizens as odd, such as the choosing of important positions by lot (to avoid favoritism). Many scholars consider the rise of Athenian theater and of democracy to be related developments. It is likely that most of the city's inhabitants, including Athenian women and slaves of both sexes, were allowed to attend theater performances, though only adult male citizens could perform in the chorus and as individual actors. Moreover, by requiring the participation of a large number of citizens, democracy fostered a climate of political debate and dialogue, and the broader practice of debating and voting influenced the system under which playwrights competed for first prize. Even the increasing role of dialogue at the expense of the collective chorus seems to mirror the rise of a participatory democracy in which citizens speak out and cast their votes individually.

THE DECLINE OF GREEK THEATER

Strong indirect evidence of the link between democracy and tragedy is provided by their simultaneous decline, caused by the Peloponnesian War (431–404 B.C.E.)—the long conflict between Athens and Sparta described by the Athenian historian Thucydides (ca. 455–ca. 400 B.C.E.).

The ruins of the theater at Epidaurus, Greece. The theater was built in the middle of the fourth century B.C.E.

By the war's end, Athens had lost its empire and, at least temporarily, its democracy. Though Greek theater continued to develop—chiefly through the emergence, in the following century, of New Comedy, whose main practitioner was the playwright Menander (ca. 342–ca. 292 B.C.E.) and whose plays depended much less on fantastic plots and conceits than had their Old Comedy predecessors—by the end of the fifth century B.C.E. the most important era of Greek theater had come to an end.

GREEK THEORIES OF DRAMA

The fourth century B.C.E.'s contribution to theater history was the work of two authors who together provided the first written theories of drama: Plato and Aristotle. Though Plato did not take up the subject separately, his philosophy as a whole is deeply engaged with the theater as medium and institution. All of his works were written as dialogues, and although there is no evidence of their performance before large audiences, they may have been recited by students in his Academy, the school that he founded (which took its name from its site, a park sacred to the legendary hero Academus). In these dialogues, Plato—or, more precisely, his main character, Socrates—is often critical of tragedy and comedy as well as of actors, arguing that drama and other works of art offer mere representations of the world and therefore stand in the way of the pursuit of truth, which consists of knowledge of the things themselves. Drawn to the exchange of ideas but suspicious of the seductions of theatrical performance, Plato offered his own philosophical dialogues as an alternative form of drama.

Plato's student Aristotle, by contrast, devoted an entire treatise to the subject of tragedy, describing its classifications, elements, and structure and examining its effect on spectators. In his widely influential *Poetics*, probably composed around 330 B.C.E., Aristotle discusses the origin of tragedy in dithyrambic hymns, the nature of the heroic protagonist, the function of the chorus, and what he considers to be the six crucial elements of theater: plot, character, thought, diction, music, and spectacle (the last is accorded a marginal position in his descriptive hierarchy). He also emphasizes certain plot elements, such as sudden reversals (*peripeteiai*) and the moment of recognition (*anagnōrisis*), and insists that unlike epic poetry, with its meandering plots, tragedy should present a single, unified action. This focus mandates that the action of tragedy be confined to short periods of time, typically one day, and to a single place. Renaissance commentators on the *Poetics* turned these recommendations into the three unities—of time, place, and action— that, according to the strictures of what became known as neoclassical theory, must be maintained by playwrights.

In response to Plato's attack on theatrical representation, Aristotle defended actors by arguing that the drive to imitate, *mimēsis*, was a common human trait and served as a source of pleasure. Perhaps the most influential term introduced in this treatise was *katharsis*, the purging or cleansing of emotions that was the desired effect of tragedy on the audience. Whereas Plato had argued that the extreme emotions depicted in tragedy could have adverse effects on the audience and therefore recommended that playwrights, like other artists, be banished from his ideal republic, Aristotle held that tragedy provided a release, a *katharsis*, of those stirred-up emotions—particularly fear and pity—and that dramatic art thus served a socially therapeutic function. The disagreement between Plato and Aristotle about the value of theater, the reaction of the audience, and the status of actors has persisted to the present—in our debates, for instance, about depictions of violence onstage and on the screen. Much as the playwrights of the fifth century B.C.E. have continued to influence theater history, so the philosophers of the fourth century still shape our thinking about theater.

Roman Theater

The decline of Athens, which at its height had dependent colonies in Italy (where Greeks from several city-states had settled as early as the eighth century B.C.E.), coincided with the rise and expanding influence of Rome. By the middle of the third century B.C.E., the city-state of Rome had managed to unify most of Italy under its leadership, and its victory over its North African rival, Carthage, in the First Punic War (264–241 B.C.E.) enabled Rome to extend its hegemony over Sicily as well as parts of Greece itself. One hundred years later, Rome had absorbed the entire Greek world, on its way to becoming one of the largest empires ever created.

Even though Rome was a rising military power, its art, literature, philosophy, and theater remained heavily influenced by those of Greece. Like Greek theater, Roman theater was performed in the context of civic festivals, here called *ludi*, which by 240 B.C.E. included both tragedies and comedies. The most important of these festivals were the *Ludi Romani*, which honored not Dionysus (or his Roman counterpart, Bacchus) but Jupiter, chief of the gods. This and other festivities differed from their Greek counterparts in significant ways. Influenced by the earlier performance practices of the Etruscans, who belonged to an earlier civilization (centered in present-day Tuscany and part of Umbria) that reached its height in the sixth century B.C.E., the festivities of early Rome included

Roman masks—one tragic, one comic—as depicted in a wall mosaic from the first century B.C.E.

a variety of nondramatic entertainments—chariot races, prizefighting, dance, farce—that vied with dramatic performance for the spectators' attention. Relatively few early Roman tragedies and comedies survive, although it is clear that most were adaptations of existing Greek plays, which were introduced to Rome in 240 B.C.E. The first known dramatists in Rome, Livius Andronicus (ca. 284–ca. 204 B.C.E.) and Gnaeus Naevius (ca. 270–201 B.C.E.), adapted both Greek tragedies and comedies into Latin, while later playwrights, including the tragedians Quintus Ennius (239–169 B.C.E.) and Lucius Accius (170–ca. 86 B.C.E.), specialized in one or the other genre. Even though Roman tragedies were mostly versions of Greek ones, Roman playwrights introduced considerable alterations, changes, and innovations; far from being a sign of unoriginality, adaptation thus became a special art form. Whereas the Greek playwrights had used known stories and characters in composing their plays, Roman playwrights perfected a more elaborate technique of imitation by working from established dramatic models.

ROMAN COMEDY

Though both tragedies and comedies were performed in Roman theaters, comedy was the genre in which Roman playwrights excelled. Roman comedians could look back at a long tradition of farce, and they drew especially on Atellan farce, a burlesque form based on improvisation and a small set of stock characters that took its name from Atella, a town near Naples in southern Italy. These improvised sketches and stock characters remained popular throughout the history of Rome and beyond, influencing such later theater traditions as Italy's commedia dell'arte. At the same time, a more literary form of comedy, based on Greek Old and New Comedy, was developing. The two most famous Roman playwrights—TITUS MACCIUS PLAUTUS (ca. 254–ca. 184 B.C.E.) and Terence (Publius Terentius Afer, ca. 190–159 B.C.E.)—were authors of such comedies. The most important changes Plautus and Terence made to their Greek models were eliminating the chorus and significantly expanding the use of music, thereby turning their comedies into a kind of musical theater.

EMPIRE AND SPECTACLE

The height of Roman drama, as represented by Plautus and Terence, occurred under the Roman Republic, a political system that allowed a limited number of citizens to participate in government and prevented any single individual from gaining supreme power. It was under the Republic that Rome established its dominance through the Second Punic War with Carthage (218–201

This detail from a Roman mosaic depicts a *venation*—a battle between a leopard and a gladiator.

B.C.E.) and finally defeated and destroyed Carthage in 146 B.C.E. at the end of the Third Punic War (149–146 B.C.E.). Rome now dominated not only Italy and Greece but also large parts of northern Africa. The resulting flow of wealth and power to Rome increasingly undermined republican institutions, and the Republic gave way to an empire with an absolute ruler. Under the emperors—beginning with Augustus (63 B.C.E.–14 C.E.)—Rome expanded its empire as far as England, Germany, France, Spain, and the Balkans and controlled the entire Mediterranean basin.

The increasing scale of the Roman Empire, and the unheard-of concentration of wealth and power in Rome itself, fueled a tendency toward expensive and lavish spectacles, comparable perhaps to blockbuster Hollywood action films today. These non-dramatic varieties of performance, most of them significantly more spectacular than anything seen on the dramatic stage, came to overshadow tragedy and comedy. Among these new public entertainments were chariot races held in sizable arenas, the largest of which, the Circus Maximus in Rome, accommodated more than 60,000 spectators. Other spectacles included elaborately orchestrated, and often lethal, sea battles, which sometimes involved thousands of participants; contests called *venationes,* in which wild animals fought against one another or against humans; and of course the most emblematic and notorious of Roman spectacles—gladiatorial contests, which featured hand-to-hand combat to the death. Although their appetite for staged (but real) violence was voracious, Romans weren't entirely bloodthirsty in their entertainment preferences; pantomime and short comic sketches of mime performances were also very popular.

CLOSET TRAGEDY

The overwhelming popularity of nondramatic entertainments led to a decline of traditional dramatic forms, especially tragedy and comedy. Writers with literary ambitions therefore began to create "closet dramas," plays designed to be recited at small, private gatherings or to be read in private. In fact, the most famous Roman tragic dramatist, LUCIUS ANNAEUS SENECA (4 B.C.E.–65 C.E.), wrote only closet dramas, and his plays were never performed on the great Roman stages of the time. Modeled on Greek tragedy, Seneca's tragedies are composed in an intricate, literary Latin that became a model for many subsequent writers. That these dramas were not written to be performed did not make them less violent. Indeed, unlike Greek tragedy, which had hidden most of its violence offstage, Seneca required that the audience or readers envision it as happening in their "sight." Though few in his own time would have known of his plays, they proved enormously influential on later playwrights, including the Elizabethan playwrights THOMAS KYD and WILLIAM SHAKESPEARE.

THE ROMAN STAGE

Although plays had been written in Latin since the third century B.C.E., the first permanent theater—erected at Pompeii—was not built until 55 B.C.E. Before that time, temporary stages (often quite stable and elaborate) were used for dramatic and other performances. Modeled on their Greek predecessors, Roman theaters included large amphitheaters for the audience; these could be built into hills, like Greek theaters, or erected on level ground. The amphitheater formed a semicircle similar to the Greek *orchēstra*, which was closed on one side by a building, the *scaena*, which was the counterpart of the Greek *skēnē*. In their adaptation from one society to another, however, the function and proportions of these elements changed significantly. For example, the *orchēstra* was used by the chorus, but its Roman equivalent was occupied—as it is in today's theaters—by the most privileged of the audience members. The action of the play took place on a raised stage, or *pulpitum,* located in front of the scene building, which was significantly larger and more elaborate than its Greek predecessor. Supported by several sets of columns and often ornately decorated, the scene building could be many stories high—a change that had profound implications. Unlike the audience of Greek theater, whose view of the stage was framed by landscape and sky, the Roman audience looked entirely at the artificial world created on a stage.

A digital reconstruction of the interior of the theater of Pompey in Rome. This image—based on a collaborative research project by Richard Beacham, James E. Packer, and John Burge—was generated by the King's Visualization Lab and is copyright © King's College London.

Even as playwrights such as Seneca withdrew from the stage, the Roman taste for spectacle—races, parades, festivals, and staged battles—led to the development of elaborate stage machinery. Roman theater producers not only instituted the stage curtain but also invented sliding panels, cranes, and a type of elevator with which actors or animals could be lifted onto the stage from below. They also introduced more complex, three-dimensional stage decorations, extensive stage props, and even live animals. The actors, called *histriones* in Latin, were not, as had originally been the case in Greece, talented citizen amateurs; instead, they were theater professionals, some of whom were slaves. Their acting style ranged from burlesque and conversational for comedy to more formal and declamatory for tragedy. Costumes and masks were mostly fashioned on Greek models.

THE DECLINE AND INFLUENCE OF ROMAN THEATER

Roman theater declined significantly with the rise of Christianity, which won official toleration in 313 C.E. when the emperor Constantine I issued the Edict of Milan; it soon became the dominant religion in the Roman Empire. Christian clergy were highly critical of theater and in particular its actors, declaring the attendance of theater cause for excommunication and denying actors the holy sacraments (a practice that remained in place in some parts of Europe well into the modern era). Yet despite the theater's waning under Christianity, the influence of classical theater would reverberate through the centuries. The architecture of Roman theater buildings helped shape Renaissance stage design, for example, and Roman comedy and tragedy were important models for English Renaissance playwrights, who often knew of Greek works only through their Roman adaptations and translations. Equally vital for Renaissance theater was Rome's most significant critic, the poet Quintus Horatius Flaccus, known as Horace (65–8 B.C.E.), whose *Ars Poetica* (*The Art of Poetry* [ca. 10 B.C.E.]) discusses the origins, forms, and ends of drama. Recommending such formal practices as the division of plays into five acts, Horace also offered a powerfully moral conception of drama's function. Not only should playwrights cater to their audiences, he asserted, they should also serve as moral instructors: their works, in other words, should prove useful (*utile*) as well as pleasing (*dulce*). In keeping with this conception of theater's social role, he argued against the more fantastic, spectacular, and violent aspects of Roman theater. Like those of Aristotle, his views on drama were taken up by later theorists of drama and theater.

Although Roman theater was in many ways derivative, the influence of its drama, architecture, and practice on subsequent theater history was even greater than that of its Greek predecessor and model. The plays of Plautus, Terence, and Seneca inspired the work of later playwrights, and Roman theater technology—much of it described in *De Architectura* (*On Architecture*), written in the first century B.C.E. by the architect and engineer Vitruvius—made important contributions to theater design during the European Renaissance. One of the most lasting legacies of Roman theater may be the division it opened up between drama as a literary genre and stage as a site of spectacle. In later centuries, in the great ages of world theater, drama and theater have often worked hand in hand; but at times they have become estranged, leading to forms of literary drama disconnected from a theater system mainly interested in extravagant spectacle. To the extent that this division still informs our theater today—when, for example, lavish Broadway spectacles divert attention from serious plays—we are still in the process of working through the inheritance of Roman theater.

Classical Indian Theater

During the millennium after Greece and Rome established the outlines of European theatrical culture, the foundations were being laid for separate traditions in Asia. The earliest, and arguably the most influential, form of Asian theater emerged in India, home to one of the world's oldest civilizations. By 2500 B.C.E. the Indus Valley civilization had introduced city-states and a technologically advanced agricultural society in northwestern and western India. Its decline was caused in part by internal weakness and in part by the incursions of the Aryans, a nomadic people from northern Iran or central Asia. By 1500 B.C.E., the Indian subcontinent had been settled by the Aryans, who developed the Vedic civilization that would subsequently shape Indian history and culture. Central to this culture were the Vedas, or scriptures, that constituted the founding texts of Hinduism (the earliest of these, the *Rig-Veda*, was composed between 1500 and 1000 B.C.E.). Written in Sanskrit, these texts inspired a number of further writings; among them were two epic poems, the *Mahabharata* and the *Ramayana* (both written between 500 and 200 B.C.E.), which exerted a vast influence on later literature and theater in India and Southeast Asia. The Aryans also introduced the system of caste, or social stratification, that divided Indian society into four groups: priests, warriors and rulers, traders and merchants, and workers and peasants. The caste system, which provided the social framework of classical Indian drama and the audience that attended it, remains influential in today's India despite laws mandating equality of treatment for all members of society.

ORIGINS OF INDIAN THEATER

The scarcity of available historical evidence prevents us from knowing much about the origins of Indian, or Sanskrit, theater. In some Vedic rituals priests performed symbolic gestures, and these actions occasionally involved impersonating a represented figure, but it is impossible to tell whether these rites were the seeds of a more purely theatrical tradition. The *Mahabharata* makes references to performers (*nata*), though it is not known if actors were among them. Unlike Greece, India has no surviving theater structures from this period. The earliest plays extant, which date from the first century C.E., display a sophistication that suggests a long period of prior development, but there is no way of determining when a literary theater was first established. What evidence we do have concerning the Sanskrit theater comes from the plays that have survived from later centuries and from the *Natyasastra* (*The Art of Theater*), a compendious treatise on the nature and purpose of dramatic performance ascribed to Bharata Muni and written sometime between 300 B.C.E. and 200 C.E. Longer and more detailed than Aristotle's *Poetics*, the *Natyasastra* includes information concerning acting, theater and stage structures, theater organization, music, dance, playwriting, and aesthetics.

AUDIENCE, PLAYHOUSE, AND ACTORS

Theatrical performances during the classical age of Sanskrit theater (100–900 C.E.) apparently were offered on occasions ranging from sacred festivals to the coronation of kings, marriages, births, or the return of travelers. Although Bharata writes that the ideal spectator for such performances was learned and of high birth, members of all four castes (seated separately) seem to have attended. The *Natyasastra* describes three types of playhouses (square, triangular, and rectangular) and three sizes that these buildings could assume (small, medium-sized, and large), but focuses mainly on a rectangular building measuring 96 by 48 feet. Such a playhouse should resemble a cave, so that the actors' voices would resonate. Its interior was divided into two equal areas, with one half (called the *prekshagriha*) devoted to seating an audience that would have probably included no more than 500 spectators. The other half was itself divided in two: its back half (the *nepathya*) served as a backstage and dressing room,

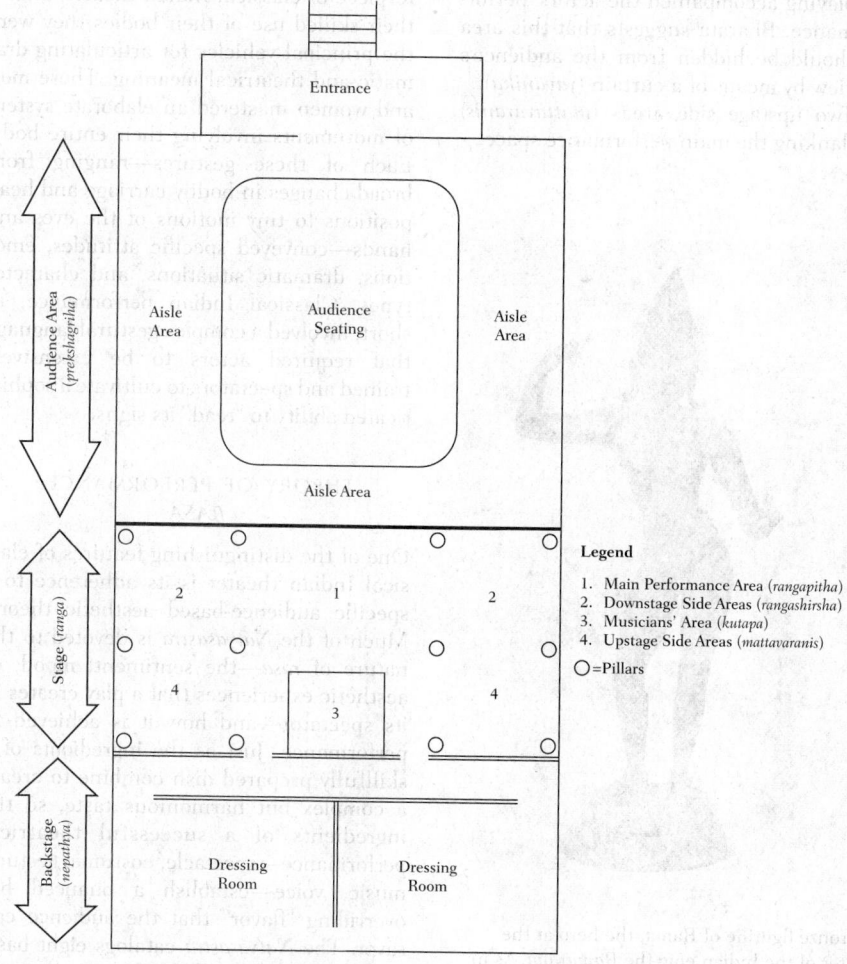

The Classical Indian Stage

A diagram of the Sanskrit stage, based on descriptions in the *Natyasastra* by Bharata.

and its front half (the *ranga*) represented the performance area. The performance area, in turn, contained a number of distinct zones:

1. The main performance space (*rangapitha*) at the center of the stage.
2. The upstage area (*rangashirsha*), which stretched across the width of the performance space, between the back wall and the front performance area. Demarcating the back of this area was an ornamented curtain, possibly held by two attendants, with two openings, one for entrances and the other for exits.
3. The space between these openings (the *kutapa*), an area for musicians, whose playing accompanied the actors' performance. Bharata suggests that this area should be hidden from the audience's view by means of a curtain (*yavanika*).
4. Two upstage side areas (*mattavaranis*) flanking the main performance space.

A bronze figurine of Rama, the hero at the center of the Indian epic the *Ramayana*. As in performance, the gestures and attitudes portrayed in Indian sculpture are highly stylized.

These separate but contiguous acting areas made possible the fluid narrative structure of Sanskrit drama, in which dramatic action shifts between different locations and events and encounters can be staged simultaneously.

Apart from general decorations, which could serve a symbolic function, there were few props and no scenery on the classical Indian stage. Location and specific actions were indicated through a fixed repertoire of highly stylized movements. Actors walked around the stage in a circle to indicate a journey, for example, and mimed actions such as stepping into and out of a carriage. To an even greater degree than most other theatrical traditions, actors were the centerpiece of classical Indian theater, and in their skilled use of their bodies they were the principal vehicles for articulating dramatic and theatrical meaning. These men and women mastered an elaborate system of movements involving their entire body. Each of these gestures—ranging from broad changes in bodily carriage and head positions to tiny motions of the eyes and hands—conveyed specific attitudes, emotions, dramatic situations, and character types. Classical Indian performance, in short, involved a complex gestural language that required actors to be extensively trained and spectators to cultivate a sophisticated ability to "read" its signs.

THEORY OF PERFORMANCE: *RASA*

One of the distinguishing features of classical Indian theater is its adherence to a specific audience-based aesthetic theory. Much of the *Natyasastra* is devoted to the nature of *rasa*—the sentiment, mood, or aesthetic experiences that a play creates in its spectator—and how it is achieved in performance. Just as the ingredients of a skillfully prepared dish combine to create a complex but harmonious taste, so the ingredients of a successful theatrical performance—spectacle, costume, gesture, music, voice—establish a nuanced but overriding "flavor" that the audience can savor. The *Natyasastra* catalogs eight basic *rasas* (a ninth was added by later commentators) and associates these with eight permanent (and thirty-three transitory) human emotions, or *bhavas*. As actors portray these emotions, the spectator experiences the corresponding *rasa*. The effect, akin to that of any good meal, is a sense of aesthetic fullness and satisfaction.

CLASSICAL INDIAN DRAMA

About two dozen Sanskrit plays have survived to the present day, and they demonstrate the formal richness of classical Indian drama. Though Bharata describes ten major categories of play, two types were dominant on the classical Indian stage: *nataka* plays, whose stories are drawn from mythology or history, deal with exploits of kings and heroes; and *prakarana* plays are characterized by invented stories and less exalted characters. All plays combine a central story with numerous subsidiary plots, interweaving the serious and the comic. Indian dramatists employed both verse and prose in their plays and a mixture of Sanskrit and the popular dialects collectively known as Prakrit. The former is reserved for characters of high social standing, whereas the latter is spoken by characters of lesser station.

Most of the finest Sanskrit plays were written during the Gupta dynasty (ca. 320–ca. 550 C.E.), a period that witnessed a golden age of science, mathematics, literature, and philosophy in India. Major playwrights during this period include Bhasa, the author of thirteen surviving plays; Kalidasa, whose epic romance *Shakuntala* is considered by many to be the finest Sanskrit play; and SHUDRAKA, whose lengthy masterpiece THE LITTLE CLAY CART (ca. 100–300 C.E.) is excerpted in this anthology. Important Sanskrit drama continued to be written through the seventh century. Subsequent Indian history was marked by political instability as the court culture that helped sustain Sanskrit drama was threatened by a series of invasions by Muslim armies from the north from the tenth century onward. Sanskrit theater had largely disappeared as a cultural form by 1000 C.E.

Classical Chinese Theater

ORIGINS OF CHINESE THEATER

China, another of the world's oldest civilizations, has one of its richest performance and theater histories. Ancient Chinese scholars described performances synthesizing dance, music, and poetry as early as the reign of the legendary sage-ruler Yi Shun (2300–2205 B.C.E.), and shamanistic and court rituals involving dance and music were attributed to the Shang dynasty (1600–1045 B.C.E.). There are records dating to the first millennium B.C.E. of court entertainments—performed by jesters and others—that included music, dance, and mime. The integration of various activities in these earliest Chinese performances anticipates the capacious scope of later Chinese theater. The Chinese word that would later be used for "play" (*xi*) also meant "game," and it could be used to describe acrobatics, sports, and other kinds of entertainment. This highly theatrical synthesis of performance forms has flourished in Chinese theater to the present day, as the popularity of Beijing opera—a style of theater combining dance, music, storytelling, acrobatics, and martial arts—demonstrates.

THEATER DURING THE TANG AND SONG DYNASTIES

Theater and other forms of entertainment thrived during the Tang and Song dynasties, whose rulers held power in China between the seventh and thirteenth centuries C.E. During the Tang dynasty (618–907 C.E.), dance stories, skits, shadow and puppet plays, and a popular genre of play satirizing corrupt officials thrived at court and in the marketplace, as did circuslike performances and other forms of staged spectacle. Storytelling flourished as well, in forms that included the oral presentation of religious and secular stories by preachers attempting to disseminate Buddhism to nonliterate audiences. It was during the Tang period that Emperor Minghuang—considered the patron of Chinese theater—established the Pear Orchard Conservatory, the first academy in China devoted to the training of actors and other performers.

During the Song dynasty (960–1279), a period that saw a rise in commerce and the growth and social diversification of Chinese urban centers, amusement centers called "tile districts" (*wazi*) were organized in major cities. These centers, which provided a wide variety of entertainment, included theaters—as many as fifty in the tile districts of the northern capital Bianliang (modern-day Kaifeng)—that could seat up to several thousand spectators. The most accomplished players also performed at the emperor's palace, while itinerant players performed in villages and elsewhere on temporary stages. In addition to viewing such activities as tightrope walking, storytelling, and puppetry, audiences in the tile districts of northern China (a region that was taken over from the Song emperor by invaders from Manchuria in 1127 and ruled thereafter by the Jin dynasty) were entertained by the performance of *zaju*: variety shows that featured dramatic sketches accompanied by musical performance, comic routines, dancing, and acrobatics. In the southern provinces (which remained under Song rule), a separate form of theater known as *nanxi* developed during this period. Longer than their counterparts presented in the north and more intricate in story lines, *nanxi* made use of folk music and an array of familiar character types that influenced subsequent Chinese drama.

YUAN DRAMA: ZAJU

Though *nanxi* and the *zaju* have clear dramatic elements, it was not until the Yuan dynasty (1234–1368), when first part and later all of China was under Mongol occupation, that drama flourished as a literary genre. As the Venetian explorer Marco Polo (1254–1324) reported during his travels to the court of Kublai Khan (1215–1294), greatest of the Mongol emperors, China during the Yuan dynasty was a land of prosperity and cultural achievement, enjoying the fruits of increased trade and cultural exchange with western Asia and Europe. Contemporary records mention the titles of some 700 plays written during this period—of which 163 have been preserved, many of them in collections compiled during the late Ming dynasty (1368–1644)—and the names of roughly 550 dramatists, including GUAN HANQING (ca. 1245–ca. 1322), the most prolific and best known of the Yuan playwrights. In its quantity and sophistication, Yuan drama has often been compared to

that of Elizabethan and Jacobean England. One of the reasons for its flourishing is that Chinese scholars, who had traditionally served in government posts, found themselves excluded from civil service under Mongol rule; they therefore turned their attention to other careers, such as writing. To appeal to a popular audience, these scholars abandoned the classical Chinese of Confucius (Kong Fuzi, ca. 551–479 B.C.E.)—whose ethical teachings constituted a pillar of traditional Chinese society—and helped develop the vernacular as a dramatic language. The result was a richly poetic drama, literary in conception yet deeply grounded in the performance traditions of Chinese theater.

Most of this drama is referred to as "Yuan *zaju*," to distinguish it from the earlier form of northern theater. These plays treated subjects ranging from the historical, legendary, and supernatural to the contemporary. They told stories of love, war, political intrigue, adventure, religious conversion, domestic drama, crime, and judicial punishment. Their characters—covering a broad spectrum, from gods, emperors, and generals to hermits, outlaws, concubines, and ordinary people—derive from an array of popular types. Yuan *zaju* plays are typically four acts long, though shorter wedge acts (*xiezi*) may be added when additional plot material is required, and they include from ten to twenty songs, all performed by the main character. These songs, often of great poetic beauty, are the lyrical center of *zaju* plays. The remainder of the dramatic action is conveyed through speech and dialogue. In keeping with the Confucian emphasis on right and wrong and on the importance of correct conduct, *zaju* plays end with justice served, even when (as in Guan Hanqing's SNOW IN MIDSUMMER) a play's hero or heroine dies.

ACTORS AND STAGE

Yuan acting troupes included men and women performers, and both men and women played male and female roles. From the scattered evidence we possess—including a fourteenth-century colored mural from a temple in the northern province of Shanxi that depicts a Yuan acting

Yuan troupe onstage, from a 1324 temple wall painting in the northern Chinese province of Shanxi.

troupe onstage—we know that actors wore ornate, colorful costumes and highly stylized makeup. Though the physical structure of the stage most likely varied with the venue and performance occasion, the stage depicted in the Shanxi mural—consisting of a bare tile floor with entrances on either side of a decorative wall painting in the rear—was probably typical. There was no formal scenery on the Yuan stage and props were minimal. Musicians performed onstage, and their instruments included the flute, gong, clapper, drum, and a lute-like instrument known as a *pipa*. The audience of these Yuan performers seems to have represented a wide range of Chinese society, from the Mongol emperors and their courts down to merchants, peasants, and poor laborers. Yuan *zaju* was a drama that appealed to educated and uneducated spectators alike.

THE RISE OF *NANXI*

Zaju continued to be popular into the Ming dynasty, which assumed power in 1368 after a rebellion drove the Yuan from power, but in the fourteenth century it was rivaled and eventually eclipsed by the reemergence of *nanxi* drama in the southern provinces and its development into a form markedly different from the theater found in the north. *Nanxi* plays are longer than *zaju* plays, and they contain a variable number of acts (as many as fifty or more, each with its own title). Singing is not restricted to a single character; instead, songs are performed by two or more singers, and sometimes by choruses. Acted to the accompaniment of a bamboo flute, *nanxi* plays drew on folk music, and their overall atmosphere in performance was elegiac. Although *zaju* is considered China's premier classical drama, the development of a "southern style" of drama proved to be more influential. A number of the distinctive character types of *nanxi* drama, in fact, remain popular on today's Chinese stage.

Classical Japanese Theater

When Westerners think of Asian theater, it is the theater of Japan that most often comes to mind. In part, this can be explained by the cultural distinctiveness of Japan's theatrical and dramatic traditions: the meditative dance theater of noh, the stylized acrobatics of kabuki, the sophisticated gestures of bunraku puppet theater. But it also has to do with the preservation of such theatrical traditions through centuries of political and social change. In a country devoted to ritual, ceremony, and other forms of tradition, theatrical practices have been handed down with the formal exactitude of the tea ceremony. As a result, we can come to understand the development of Japanese theater not only by reading histories of theater but by attending live performances.

ORIGINS OF JAPANESE THEATER

Although archaeologists have uncovered clay representations of singers, dancers, and musical instruments from as early as the third century B.C.E., the earliest manifestations of what we would consider theater in Japan were dance-based ritual celebrations collectively known as *kagura*. These performances were connected with Shintoism, a prehistoric religion devoted to the worship of gods and spirits who represented aspects of the natural world. Versions of *kagura* were performed at Shinto shrines by shamanistic priestesses, at the imperial court, and in villages during harvest and other annual festivals. Other theatrical forms emerged in the centuries after Buddhism was introduced to Japan between 538 and 552 C.E., a period during which continental Asian culture was embraced by the imperial court. In the seventh and eighth centuries, two forms of dance theater came from China via Korea: *gigaku*, a Buddhist dance play in which masked figures moved in procession, and *bugaku*, a stately court entertainment that eventually included dances from India, Tibet, and Vietnam in addition to those from China and Korea.

Other popular forms of entertainment also flourished during this time, involving music, dance, masked pantomime, and in some instances acrobatics, juggling, and tightrope walking. Several of these traditions had dramatic components, including *sarugaku* (monkey entertainment), a form of variety theater containing comic dialogues and short skits that came to be performed at Buddhist temples. By the thirteenth century, the dramatic and performance elements of these entertainments had become increasingly sophisticated, and the form was given the name *sarugaku noh*. The term *noh*, which means "skill" or "craft," eventually stood alone as a theatrical category.

THE EMERGENCE OF NOH THEATER: KANAMI AND ZEAMI

The emergence of noh theater reflected the political and social changes that Japan had undergone during the previous two centuries. In 1192 the Japanese emperor relinquished rule of the country to samurai generals, whose rising military and economic power had made them the country's dominant social class. These generals, who gave themselves the title *shogun*, presided over wealthy courts in Kamakura and later Kyoto and established a feudal society with rigidly demarcated social strata. Although many cultural forms that had found favor in the imperial court fell out of fashion, the shoguns patronized the arts, including the theater of *sarugaku noh*. In 1374, Kanami Kiyotsugu (1333–1384), head of one of the country's *sarugaku noh* troupes, performed before the young shogun Ashikaga Yoshimitsu (1358–1408). So impressed was the shogun that he became Kanami's patron and took the performer's son, ZEAMI MOTOKIYO (1363–1443), who was also an accomplished actor, as his companion and lover.

It was through the efforts of Kanami and Zeami that noh became an autonomous form. An innovator by temperament, Kanami combined elements of existing performance traditions into a dramatic form adapted to the tastes of the shogunate and lower warrior classes. Kanami amalgamated popular songs, dance, music, and poetry within an aesthetic of meditative deliberateness and restraint drawn from Zen Buddhism. Limiting his plays to a single protagonist, he advocated a style of acting based on authenticity of physical and vocal characterization. After Kanami's death, Zeami, who would become one of the most important figures in the history of Japanese theater, extended and refined his father's theatrical innovations. In a number of theoretical writings, including the seven-volume *Kadensho* (1400–02), Zeami discussed the intricacies of noh acting, the relationship of noh theater to its audience, and the aesthetic concepts underlying noh performance, such as *yugen*, which denotes suggestive beauty, gracefulness, and an awareness of life's impermanence. In addition to being noh's chief theoretician and one of its greatest actors, Zeami was also its most accomplished playwright, authoring nearly half of the 240 surviving plays that constitute the noh repertoire.

NOH DRAMA

The stories of noh plays are drawn from mythology, legend, and history, particularly (as in Zeami's *ATSUMORI* [ca. 1400]) the twelfth-century civil war between rival samurai clans. The main character (or *shite*) is often a ghost, demon, or tormented person who cannot find rest because of his or her past deeds. In the typical two-act structure, the central character appears disguised in the first act and is revealed in the second. He or she speaks an elevated, highly literary verse and frequently quotes classical Chinese and Japanese poetry. Other established roles include the main character's companion (*tsure*); a third party (*waki*), frequently a priest, who encounters the main character in the first act; and a servant or commoner (*kyogen*), whose language is colloquial and who often provides a narrative summary in the interlude between acts. An onstage chorus sings many of the characters' lines and narrates events within the dramatic action, while three or four onstage musicians accompany the play with drums and

The *shite*, or primary actor, in a contemporary performance of the noh drama *The Lady Aoi*. Note the mask, costume, folding fan, and stylized gesture of the performer. In the background sit the *hayashi-kata*, or musicians.

flute. The climax of a noh play takes the form of a ritualized dance.

Noh dramas fall into five categories: plays about gods; warrior plays; plays about women, or "wig plays"; miscellaneous plays, including plays about madness and plays about the present time; and demon plays, in which the main character is a good or evil supernatural being. In a traditional noh program, plays from each of these categories were performed, in the order given. Between the plays, farcical sketches known as *kyogen* (wild words) were performed by the same actors who took the colloquial roles in the noh drama. A *nohgaku* program (the term refers to the combination of *noh* and *kyogen* in performance) took seven or eight hours to complete.

ACTORS

The actors of noh drama, who were male—a tradition maintained in all but a few noh companies today—were dressed in elaborate, highly formal silk costumes. These costumes, which included kimonos for male characters, involved variously layered inner and outer garments. Actors were usually wigged. Among the most celebrated features of noh theater are the masks that the main character and his or her companion wore. Treasured for their craftsmanship and elegant yet simple design, these masks offered stylized representations of the established noh character types: male and female, old and young, human and supernatural. Actors in other roles wore masklike makeup. In contrast to the richness of visual presentation that characterized the actors thus attired, the physical setting and props in noh performance were minimal. Movable structures were used to represent a hut, boat, mountain, and other features, while handheld props served to represent emotional states and a range of other objects. A folding fan, for instance, one of the main props in noh theater, could be used to stand for a sword, a flute, or other item. The handling of physical objects formed part of the broader choreography of noh performance, which involved slow, deliberate movement and symbolic, meditative gestures. The acts of walking and dancing, for example, called for painstaking control of body posi-

tion and motion, and years of training were required for the actor to master such simple gestures as lifting an arm or raising a hand to the eyes, the symbol of weeping.

THE NOH STAGE

Drawn to its formal precision and ceremonial nature, later dramatists and theater artists have sought to appropriate elements of the noh for the modern theater (*Four Plays for Dancers*, published in 1921 by the Irish playwright and poet William Butler Yeats, represents one such attempt). To an extent unrivaled in world theater, however, traditional noh performance is inseparable from the stage for which it was written. The configuration, dimensions, and materials of this stage were standardized during the seventeenth century and have remained unchanged in noh theaters to the present day. The main stage, roughly 18 feet square and raised about $2\frac{1}{2}$ feet above the ground, consists of a polished surface of Japanese cypress with four pillars, roughly 15 feet high, that support a temple-like roof. The audience sits in front of and to the left of this stage. A visible backstage area, at the front of which the musicians sit, features a wooden wall with painted pine trees, while an area to the audience's right of the main acting area is occupied by the chorus, who sit in two rows facing the stage.

One of the most characteristic features of the noh stage is the *hashigakiri*, a railed passageway or bridge that extends from the side of the backstage area on the audience's left to a dressing (or "mirror") room, from which actors make their entrances and to which they exit. A secondary exit to the right of the backstage area is used by the chorus and stage attendants. Reverberating jars are placed under the main stage, backstage, and bridge to provide additional resonance and to amplify the sound of characters walking and stomping their feet. Specific areas of the stage are associated with individual characters and with conventionally assigned functions. The pillar that stands where the bridge meets the stage, for instance, known as the *shite* pillar, is where the main character stops to announce his name upon entering the stage area.

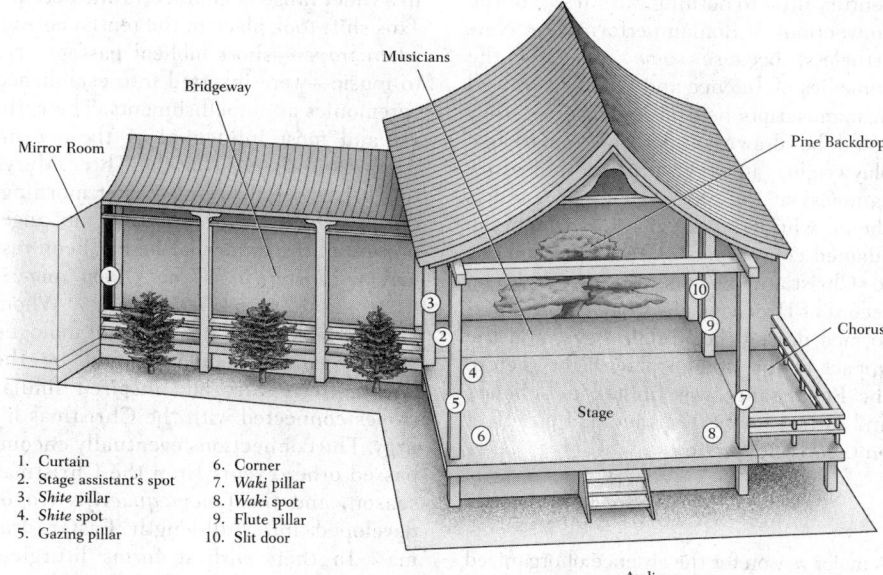

Mirror Room

Bridgeway

Musicians

Pine Backdrop

Chorus

Stage

Audience

1. Curtain
2. Stage assistant's spot
3. *Shite* pillar
4. *Shite* spot
5. Gazing pillar
6. Corner
7. *Waki* pillar
8. *Waki* spot
9. Flute pillar
10. Slit door

LATER NOH THEATER

The conventions of modern-day noh theater were standardized during the Tokugawa shogunate (1603–1867), a period when the center of government was moved to Edo (modern-day Tokyo) and the hierarchies of Japanese society were institutionalized to a greater extent. Noh theater companies assumed their modern form as hereditary heads (*iemoto*) were made responsible for preserving the traditions of the major schools of noh. Rooted in the practices and accomplishments of its early masters, noh became an art for connoisseurs; although amateur noh companies found support among the commoners, its principal audience was courtly and upper-class.

KABUKI AND BUNRAKU

By the early seventeenth century, other theatrical forms had emerged to satisfy the tastes of a rising urban middle class. Kabuki—a form of dramatic theater involving music, dance, and acrobatics; ornate costumes and makeup; extensive scenery; and spectacular tricks of stage technology—developed in the early decades of the 1600s from the lively, often erotic, dances that temple maidens performed at religious shrines. The performance of kabuki, which

was restricted to adult males in 1653, became a highly conventional and stylized art, and its practitioners—including the popular *onnagata*, or actor of female roles—require decades of training. Bunraku, an elaborate form of puppet (or doll) theater that developed out of earlier puppet and storytelling traditions, also became popular during this period. Like noh, which can be seen in specially built theaters throughout Japan, these centuries-old theater forms remain popular on today's stage.

Medieval European Theater

EUROPE AFTER THE ROMAN EMPIRE

The disintegration of the Roman Empire between the fifth and sixth centuries C.E. marked the end of organized theatrical activity in western and central Europe as it had been practiced in classical Rome. Itinerant groups of performers traveled through southern Europe offering such entertainments as storytelling, juggling, tumbling, and jesting; local popular festivals, many with origins in pagan rites surrounding the winter solstice and the earth's return to fertility in spring, contained a variety of performative elements. But although the abandoned amphitheaters across Europe gave evidence of an earlier theatrical culture, after the sixth century little to nothing was known of the conventions of Roman performance. Nevertheless, because some copies of the comedies of Terence and Plautus survived in manuscripts held in monasteries, they could be drawn on by one remarkable playwright: HROTSVIT, a tenth-century canoness at the Saxon abbey of Gandersheim, who wrote six plays in which she adapted conventions of Terentian comedy to Christian subjects. But there is no record of Hrotsvit's plays having been performed during the Middle Ages, and the impact of the Roman playwrights before the Renaissance was limited to scholars and to literary circles; they had no effect on theatrical practice.

EARLY CHURCH DRAMA

A major reason for the absence of organized theater during this era was the opposition of the Christian Church to all such activities. Throughout the Middle Ages (and much of the early modern period), church authorities and moralists denounced theater and other forms of spectacle and impersonation as idolatrous, obscene, and dangerous in their effects on the audience members' passions. Ironically, this same church served as the major site for the reemergence of theater in medieval Europe—but perhaps not surprisingly, since the Catholic liturgy is itself a performed spectacle. During the medieval mass, priests wearing ornate robes officiated before spectators gathered in designated locations within enclosed structures. Processions and other forms of ceremony marked holy days throughout the year, while each day's canonical "offices" or "hours" (such as matins and vespers) were marked by services of their own. Chanting during the liturgy was often antiphonal—with passages sung alternately by two choirs, much like dialogue—and singer-performers often gave voice to the words of Christ and others in the Bible. Individual dates throughout the Christian calendar commemorated biblical events and the figures who participated in them, and thus were inherently associated with a rich trove of narrative and potentially dramatic material.

But ritual and ceremony are not the same as drama, and the latter could emerge only when liturgical celebration gave way to a wider range of characters and actions. This shift took place in the tenth century, when *tropes*—short biblical passages set to music—were inserted into established ceremonies as embellishments. The earliest and most influential of these commemorated the visit by the Three Marys to Christ's sepulchre on Easter morning, during which they learn from an angel present at the tomb that he has been resurrected. Known as the *Quem quaeritis* trope after its opening line ("Whom are you seeking?"), this chanted dialogue rapidly gained popularity and by the late tenth century had inspired similar tropes connected with the Christmas liturgy. The connections eventually encompassed other events from the Christmas season, and the *Quem quaeritis* tropes developed into full-length Easter dramas. In their earliest forms liturgical tropes were performed in Benedictine monasteries for fellow monastics; but as cathedrals and other large church buildings were constructed in the eleventh

This engraving, a nineteenth-century copy of an original devotional miniature by Jean Fouquet (ca. 1415–1481), depicts the performance of a "miracle play" of the martyrdom of St. Apollonia of Alexandria.

and twelfth centuries, the lay congregations became audiences for these religious performances.

By the twelfth century, church drama had so expanded in scope and complexity that some works—the Christmas and Passion plays from the Benediktbeuern Abbey in Bavarian Germany, for example—were performed outside the context of the liturgy. Eventually, as part of this natural progression, the plays came to be performed outside the context of the church. The range of suitable dramatic subjects grew to include figures and events from the Old and the New Testament: the raising of Lazarus, Daniel in the lion's den, and the conversion of St. Paul, to name a few. Plays commemorating the lives of saints—often called "miracle plays" because they recounted the miracles or martyrdoms that led to the protagonist's conversion—mixed narratives of conflict and romantic adventure with moral exempla. Versions of these saints' plays were written and performed into the late Middle Ages.

CORPUS CHRISTI CYCLES

In a parallel development, religious plays began to be written in the national languages of central and western Europe (rather than the Latin of the church), and during the fourteenth and fifteenth centuries these vernacular forms developed into elaborate dramatic cycles of short plays, or pageants. The most notable of these cycle plays were performed in conjunction with the Feast of Corpus Christi (literally, "The Body of Christ"), a holy day—proposed by Pope Urban IV in 1264 and instituted by the church in 1311—celebrating the redemptive presence of the Holy Eucharist. This feast day, which occurred in late spring or early summer, included an outdoor procession in which the host was displayed; eventually, taking advantage of the generally favorable weather and the longer period of daylight, performers took an entire day and sometimes more to mount plays dramatizing events from biblical history. Though more limited versions of these cycles were performed on the Continent, the best-known achievements in this extended dramatic form were England's Corpus Christi plays, which dramatized the history of the world from the fall of the angels and the creation to the Last Judgment. Local records and the manuscripts of individual plays note performances in London, Coventry, Norwich, Newcastle-on-Tyne, and elsewhere in England, but the great majority of the surviving cycle plays come from just four towns, apparently all in the north: York, Wakefield, Chester, and N Town (where N stands for *nomen*—Latin for "name"—suggesting that this cycle was performed by touring players who would insert whatever name was appropriate as they traveled across the countryside). These cycles are quite extensive, containing between twenty-five pageants (the Chester cycle) to forty-eight (the York cycle). Although English cycle drama was performed as early as 1376, most Corpus Christi plays date from the fifteenth century. This distinctive form of drama continued to be performed—scholars have speculated that as a youth, WILLIAM SHAKESPEARE may have seen a performance of the Coventry cycle; by the late sixteenth century, however, it was effectively suppressed by the newly established Church of England.

The development of theatrical activity on such a scale was made possible by the growth of medieval towns and the formation of guilds: that is, associations governing the practice of individual crafts and trades, which participated in town government and played a major role in both the religious and nonreligious aspects of civic life. In northern England, guilds assumed primary responsibility for the production of the Corpus Christi plays, which therefore are also called "mystery cycles" (the word *mystery*, derived from the Latin *mysterium*, referred to a craft, trade, or profession known only to a few). This arrangement indicates that the cycle plays performed a civic as well as religious function. Given responsibility for individual pageants, guilds provided actors, scenery, costumes, props, and other theatrical elements and materials. In some cases guilds were assigned plays for which they seemed particularly suited: the shipwrights would be given the Noah plays, for instance, while the goldsmiths produced plays about the Three Kings.

STAGING

The manner in which individual Corpus Christi cycles were staged remains a matter of debate. Although practice varied from town to town, there is evidence of two forms of staging: processional and fixed. In certain cities, such as York and Coventry, plays were mounted on pageant wagons that performed, in procession, before spectators gathered at designated viewing sites throughout the town. Scholars disagree on the structure and appearance of these wagons: some speculate that they had two levels (the lower serving as a dressing room), while others argue for a single-platform structure. In addition to the acting area, performers occasionally acted in the street surrounding the pageant wagon; in the Nativity pageant, one of two surviving plays from Coventry, the actor playing Herod "rages in the pagond [pageant wagon] and in the street also." In the alternative staging method, all plays were performed at stationary locations. It is also possible that some combination of processional and fixed staging was practiced: for instance, pageant wagons may have paraded through the town with the actors arranged in tableaux, then gathered in a circle at an open place where they could serve as stages for an audience that stood within the circle's periphery and moved from play to play.

Whether presented on pageant wagons or at fixed locations, the Corpus Christi cycles drew on a staging convention that had characterized medieval drama since its liturgical beginnings. The acting area had two components: one or more structures called *sedes* (mansions) and a nonlocalized playing space adjacent to these that was known as the *platea* (courtyard, or place). The former, usually represented by decorative booths, oriented the dramatic action to specific locations (Heaven, Hell, palace, house, manger), while the latter allowed for extensions of the action into more indeterminate spaces beyond the *sedes*. Financed by prosperous guilds and engineered by skilled craftsmen, Corpus Christi performances could be awe-inspiring affairs,

This engraved illustration from Thomas Sharp's *Dissertation on the Pageants Anciently Performed at Coventry* (1825) presents an imaginative reconstruction of the performance of a pageant play in Coventry, England.

with special effects and elaborate technical devices. Cranes enabled characters to ascend, descend, and fly between locations, while the Hell's Mouth through which sinners were dragged relied on an elaborate contraption of pulleys and smoke-ejecting bellows. Costumes included everyday medieval garments, ecclesiastical vestments, and—in the case of heavenly beings, who wore gilded masks, and devils, who were given the features of grotesque animals—nonnaturalistic adornments.

DRAMATIC TEXTS

Individual plays, or pageants, within specific cycles vary in length, structure, and style. Some are very formal and rely heavily on long-standing conventions, while others combine biblical narratives with scenes and characters from medieval life. Because the authors of these plays often embellished the biblical accounts with more realistic incidents and characterizations, the Corpus Christi cycles established links between sacred history and the world of their audiences. Indeed, the plays reveal as much about the medieval world as they do about the biblical episodes they take as their subjects. Among the greatest of these works blending the sacred and everyday is by an author whom later scholars call the WAKEFIELD MASTER. This unidentified playwright, whose plays display a command of vernacular dialects, complex characterization, and realistic situations, wrote *THE SECOND SHEPHERDS' PLAY* (ca. 1475), which parallels and contrasts the scene of the Nativity with a rustic sheep-stealing episode. By counterpointing the mystery of Christ's Incarnation with the earthiness of fallen humanity, this widely known play demonstrates the use of comedy in Corpus Christi drama. Its folk elements remind us of popular forms of entertainment and celebration—folk festivals, songs and stories, mummers' plays (i.e., seasonal folk plays)—and of the drama that emerged from them in the later Middle Ages. In this tradition are the farces of the German poet and dramatist Hans Sachs (1494–1576), written for the festivities of Shrovetide, the three days preceding Lent.

MORALITY PLAYS

At the same time that the mystery cycles were being organized in the late fourteenth century, a different form of religious drama was emerging in England and France: the morality play. Like the Corpus Christi pageants, this drama was concerned with human salvation—but rather than exploring sin and redemption across the vast landscape of human and divine history, as did the cycles, morality plays focused on the moral life of the individual Christian. Written in the mode of allegory, in which abstract ideas and categories of individuals are given concrete form, morality drama featured a representative figure of humanity—Mankind, Everyman, Well-Advised, Ill-Advised—whose identity is universal rather than historical, biblical, or individual. This character interacts with figures personifying virtues and vices, who typically seek to win his soul in a battle between temptation and spiritual obedience. Whereas Corpus Christi plays occasionally employed allegorical characters, morality drama derived neither from these plays nor from the liturgical drama that preceded them. In addition to reflecting the general fondness for allegory in the Middle Ages—Prudentius's poem *Psychomachia* (fourth century C.E.), which introduced the competition of virtues and vices, was widely influential throughout the medieval period—morality drama likely drew on Pater Noster (or Lord's Prayer) plays; these were dramatizations of the seven deadly sins, performed in England during the fourteenth and fifteenth centuries. Since no Pater Noster plays have survived, specific relationships between the two dramatic forms cannot be established.

The oldest extant English morality play is a dramatic fragment titled *The Pride of Life* (ca. 1350). Only a few plays from the following 160 years have survived, but they indicate the drama's variety of forms and staging practices. The longest and most complex of the English moralities, *The Castle of Perseverance* (ca. 1405–25), presents the life of its protagonist Mankind from birth to death, the struggle over his soul by virtues and vices, a debate

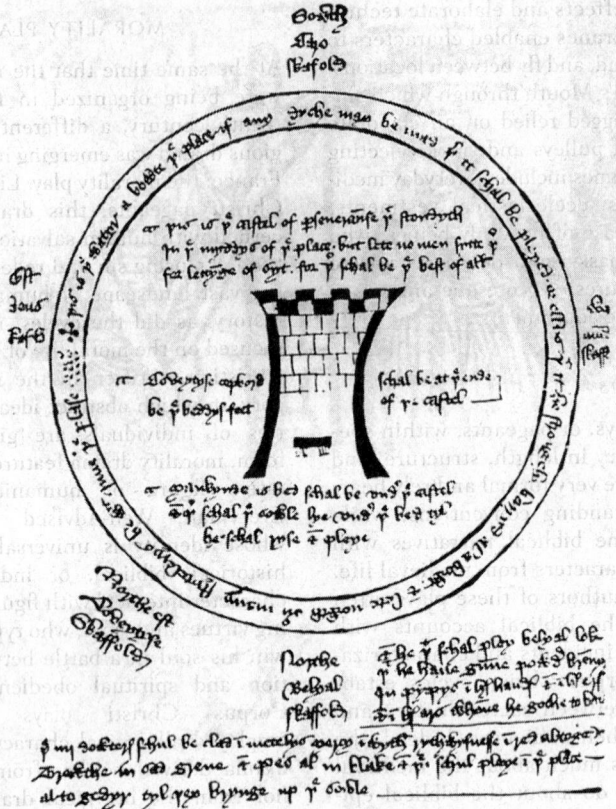

Diagram for staging *The Castle of Perseverance*, from a fifteenth-century manuscript.

between Body and Soul, the parliament of heaven, and the final judgment on Mankind's soul. The manuscript for this play, which includes a diagram, offers particular insight into its staging. Located outdoors, the performance area of *The Castle of Perseverance* consisted of a circular playing space with a structure indicating Mankind's castle in the center and five mansions on the periphery. The later *Mankind* (ca. 1465–70), by contrast, was performed before rural audiences by an itinerant group of professional or semiprofessional actors. The staging requirements were necessarily simple—a few props, a small booth for entrances and exits—and the play could be staged both in an open courtyard and indoors. The play itself combines the story of the farmer Mankind's temptation, fall, and repentance with wide-ranging comic business, most

having to do with the devil and his attendant mischief-figures. Finally, the best known of the moralities, *EVERYMAN* (ca. 1510, translated from a 1495 Dutch original), eschews the drama of temptation for the more somber story of Everyman's journey to death and final judgment. Although textual evidence suggests that the play was written for a playing area with fixed structures, there are no records of its actual performance.

During the sixteenth century, morality drama became broadly popular with audiences across the social spectrum. A growing number of morality plays were performed in public and private venues throughout England by troupes of professional actors—the direct precursors of the acting companies of Shakespeare's time. As the intellectual and religious climate of England changed in response to Renaissance humanism (a revival in the study of classical literature, science, and philosophy) and to the Reformation (a movement to reform the Catholic Church that led to the founding of Protestant religious denominations), morality drama evolved in its subject matter as well as its ideological function. In the hands of such Tudor humanist writers as Henry Medwall (1462–1501?) and John Skelton (ca. 1460–1529), morality plays engaged with increasingly secular subjects, addressing issues of philosophy, social relations, and politics in addition to moral and religious questions. In this form they frequently resembled Tudor interludes (indoor dramatic entertainments that were usually performed in noble households, guild halls, and schools). During the religious controversies of the English Reformation, morality drama was employed by Catholics and Protestants to dramatize their doctrinal and political divisions. Even more profoundly than the Corpus Christi cycles, which were cumbersome in structure and rooted in a medieval religious consensus that no longer applied in sixteenth-century England, morality plays helped shape subsequent English drama. Because their allegorical conventions were adaptable to a range of issues and ideologies, these plays provided a dramatic structure for such Elizabethan and Jacobean plays as CHRISTOPHER MARLOWE'S *DOCTOR FAUSTUS* (ca. 1588). Certainly, the legacy of the Vice characters, with their conniving but theatrically appealing horseplay, can be seen clearly in such later dramatic masterpieces as BEN JONSON'S *VOLPONE* (1606).

Theater in Early Modern Europe, 1500–1700

As European theater developed between 1500 and 1700, it was affected by a range of political, economic, social, artistic, and religious changes that were transforming the region and its relationship to the rest of the world. The term *early modern*, which is often used to designate the period in European history between the end of the Middle Ages and the beginning of the Industrial Revolution, focuses attention on those developments that inaugurated the world we know today: the rise of science and accelerating technological innovation, the growth of cities and the emergence of mercantile economies, New World exploration and colonization, and the transformations of church and state through reformation, absolutism, and revolution. But as the competing term *Renaissance*—applied to the fifteenth and sixteenth centuries—suggests, this period is also characterized by a powerful look backward to the classical era of Greece and Rome and to the social, artistic, and intellectual values that scholars, newly given access to many of its rediscovered texts, found there. As they combined the new and the old in fruitful, and also volatile, ways, the years 1500–1700 were a period of unprecedented discovery and rediscovery in the visual, plastic, architectural, and musical arts. But arguably it was theater—where audiences in England, Spain, France, and elsewhere in Europe saw their world represented in action—that witnessed the greatest accomplishments during this extraordinary period.

THE EUROPEAN RENAISSANCE: HUMANISM AND THE CLASSICAL PAST

The European Renaissance played a crucial role in the transformations that Europe underwent in the fifteenth and sixteenth centuries. The term *Renaissance,* which means "rebirth," was first used in 1550 by the artist and critic Giorgio Vasari (1511–1574) to refer to the rediscovery of classical values—which, he claimed, had been eclipsed during the Middle Ages by Christianity and the "barbarian" cultures of northern Europe—in the paintings of Giotto (ca. 1267–1337) and later Florentine artists. This view of medieval civilization as a dark age compared to the civilizations of Greece and Rome is, of course, inaccurate, as is any absolute demarcation between the later Middle Ages and the Renaissance. Europe in the 1500s remained in many ways medieval. But the turn to the classical world represented a driving force behind humanism, the dominant intellectual movement in Renaissance Europe, and it effected a profound shift of cultural direction. Convinced that the civilizations of Greece and Rome represented the highest point of human achievement and that modern Europe should cultivate their ideals and emulate their accomplishments, scholars devoted themselves to the rediscovery, translation, and textual study of classical works, many of which had been preserved in European monasteries and in the libraries of the Byzantine Empire and Islamic Spain. The invention of the printing press in 1450 by Johann Gutenberg (ca. 1400–1468) accelerated the process by which these texts and Renaissance commentaries on them were disseminated.

The deepening understanding of Greek and Roman writers, and of classical civilization as a whole, revolutionized the fields of literature and the arts. The Italian writers Petrarch (Francesco Petrarca, 1304–1374) and Giovanni Boccaccio (1313–1375) urged their peers to study Greek and Roman writers, and the influence of authors, literary forms, historical subjects, and mythological characters from the classical period was widespread in the literature of the next three centuries. Though it is a mistake to see this expanding interest as a departure from the religious concerns of medieval literature—most Renaissance writers explored classical materials in the context of Christian belief—an intensifying concern with human experience and the things of the world makes itself felt throughout the literature of this period, including its finest: the essays of Michel de Montaigne (1533–1592), for example, and the picaresque fiction of Miguel de Cervantes (1547–1616). A similar interest in the world as it is lived and observed is apparent in the work of Leonardo da Vinci (1452–1519), Michelangelo (1475–1564), and other Renaissance artists, who abandoned the flat, often ornamental surfaces of medieval art for more lifelike representations of the human figure and the visible world.

PATRONAGE

The Renaissance as a cultural phenomenon was closely linked to the increasing urbanization and the changing economic and political landscapes of European society. The movement began in the city-states of Italy, where rulers competed with each other to be patrons of scholarship, literature, and the other arts. Here, as elsewhere in Europe, wealth and power were increasingly concentrated in the hands of princes and other monarchs, civic authorities, and an expanding merchant class, and these groups sought to enhance their prestige by funding art, architecture, literature, music, and lavish spectacles. The most prominent of the Italian cultural centers was Florence, which served—under the rule of Lorenzo de' Medici (1449–1492), "the Magnificent"—as a home for humanists, artists, poets, and philosophers. Later centers of patronage included the courts of England's Elizabeth I and James I, Spain's Philip II, and France's Louis XIV. Acting companies, whose members had previously operated on the margins of society, also benefited from the patronage system during the sixteenth and seventeenth centuries. Even as it earned money from the London playgoing public, for instance, the company to which WILLIAM SHAKESPEARE belonged—the Lord Chamberlain's Men, later renamed the King's Men—enjoyed the support, protection, and legitimation conferred by courtly patronage.

SCIENCE AND THE "NEW PHILOSOPHY"

As Renaissance humanism reevaluated medieval learning in light of earlier classical traditions, it profoundly altered established fields of knowledge and inquiry. In the field of political philosophy, for instance, the Italian theorist Niccolò Machiavelli (1469–1527) proposed a view of politics and government in which the maintenance and exercise of power, not moral authority, were the ultimate justification for political action. So controversial were these ideas that his very name became synonymous with cunning and ruthless self-interest. The argument between older and newer conceptions of the world was a defining feature of the scientific revolution that took place during the sixteenth and seventeenth centuries. In 1543 Nicolaus Copernicus (1473–1543) published his treatise demonstrating that the earth orbited the sun, thereby refuting the geocentric model that had dominated classical and medieval understanding of the heavens.

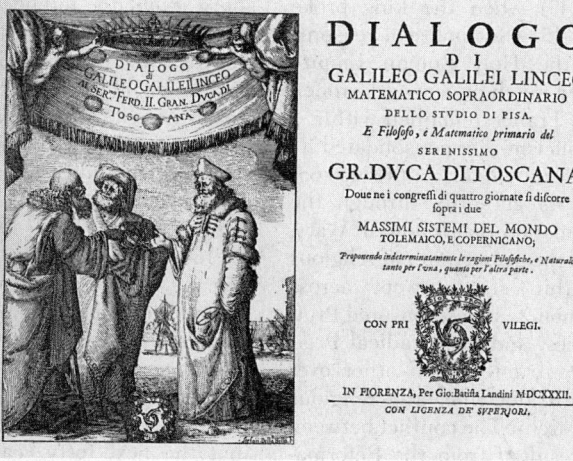

The title page and engraved frontispiece of Galileo's *Dialogue Concerning the Two Chief World Systems*, published in Florence in 1632. In the book, Galileo argued in favor of Copernicus's model of the solar system, in which the planets revolve around the sun, and against the older Ptolemaic system, which placed the earth at the center of the known universe. The engraving shows Aristotle (left), Ptolemy (center), and Copernicus (right).

Further astronomical discoveries were made by Galileo Galilei (1564–1642), who relied on an improved version of the recently invented telescope to make direct celestial observations. The use of empirical observation, experimentation, and inductive reasoning (i.e., drawing general conclusions from data) represented a shift from the more abstract procedures applied by medieval scholars of the natural world. While Aristotle and classical authorities continued to influence Renaissance science and its social practice—the theories of human physiology set forth by the Greek physician Galen (129–ca. 199 C.E.) remained popular during the period, for example—and while most early modern scientists reconciled their scientific methods and discoveries with a literal belief in the Bible, the scientific method worked to undermine traditional notions of authority. As the poet John Donne wrote of recent scientific discoveries in 1611, "[T]he new Philosophy calls all in doubt."

REFORMATION AND COUNTER-REFORMATION

By 1600, the spirits of inquiry and individualism had challenged the authority of the Catholic Church and, in the process, redrawn the political and religious map of Europe. The Protestant Reformation began as a call for reform within the church in 1517, when Martin Luther (1483–1546) wrote a series of theses protesting the sale of indulgences (the remission of temporal punishment for sins) on behalf of the pope. Luther's opposition to the abuses of the Catholic Church quickly expanded to include a broader challenge to its authority. Believing that the church had lost contact with the fundamental truths of Christianity, Luther rejected the doctrine that salvation required the intercession of a religious clergy, arguing instead that salvation was a function of faith alone and that the Bible was the sole authority on spiritual matters.

With the help of the newly invented printing press, Luther's ideas were widely disseminated throughout Europe, and other Protestant movements followed. Protestantism was adopted by states in Germany, Scandinavia, and elsewhere in northern Europe, many of which took advantage of this opportunity to assert their independence from Catholic Rome; the Church of England, for example, was established as a Protestant church under the head of Henry

VIII (1491–1547) when the king broke from Rome in 1534 for political reasons. Italy, Spain, the Holy Roman Empire (which included much of central Europe), and eventually France remained within a reviving Catholicism that consolidated its doctrine at the Council of Trent (1545–63) and extended its authority through the Counter-Reformation that followed. Wars, rebellions, and the persecution of religious minorities within states swept across Europe as Catholics, state-sponsored Protestant majorities, and more radical Protestant sects confronted each other over matters of faith, doctrine, and religious and social hierarchy. The conflict between nations that resulted from the Reformation would not begin to be resolved until the Peace of Westphalia, which ended Europe's devastating Thirty Years War (1618–48).

MONARCHY AND GOVERNMENT

Religious controversy and the political turmoil it precipitated contributed to the changing shapes of monarchy and government during the early modern period. In the late sixteenth and early seventeenth centuries, power was increasingly centralized in the hands of monarchs, who justified this movement toward absolutism by invoking the doctrine of the divine right of kings—the right to rule by virtue of birth, a right bestowed by God alone. France offers the most striking example of this development. Following the religious wars that divided the country in the 1500s and the continuation of civil disturbances and political intrigues in the first half of the 1600s, Louis XIV (1638–1715), the "Sun King," assumed the throne in 1643 and began a seventy-two-year reign that saw France and the French court achieve a position of dominance throughout Europe. The statement that is famously attributed to him—"L'état, c'est moi" ("I am the state")—reflects his power over the country's nobility, laws, military, and growing bureaucracy. His model was followed by other European monarchs such as Frederick William I (1688–1740) of Prussia and Peter the Great (1672–1725) of Russia; indeed, the latter built a palace in the recently founded city of St. Peters-

burg explicitly intended to rival Louis' monumental palace at Versailles.

Absolutism did not triumph everywhere in Europe, however. In England the moves toward centralized royal power undertaken by the Tudor monarchs Henry VII, Henry VIII, and Elizabeth I were checked by Parliament in the 1600s: the Stuart king Charles I (1600–1649) was beheaded in 1649 during the English Civil War, and for the following eleven years—a period divided into the Commonwealth and the Protectorate—England was subject to parliamentary and military rule. The Stuart monarchy was restored in 1660 with the crowning of Charles II (1630–1685), but the next forty years, known as the Restoration, witnessed the overthrow of his brother and successor, the Catholic James II (1633–1701), as a result of conflicts with his Protestant Parliament. Similar clashes awaited European monarchs in the eighteenth century.

NEW WORLD ENCOUNTERS

No overview of early modern Europe would be complete that failed to acknowledge the profound shift in European consciousness brought about by the encounter with the Western Hemisphere. In the Middle Ages Europeans had traveled through Asia by land as far east as Kublai Khan's China, and by 1500 the Portuguese had explored the west coast of Africa. But the "discovery" of an inhabited land across the ocean by the Italian-born Spanish explorer Christopher Columbus (1451–1506), who landed in the Caribbean in 1492 while seeking a western sea route to Asia, had consequences that reached much further. The success of this and subsequent expeditions prompted a race for conquest and settlement of the Americas by Spain and other European powers competing for resources, territorial possessions, and prestige. Over the next hundred years, the Spanish colonized an area stretching from eastern and southern South America to what is today Mexico and much of the United States, while Portugal, the Netherlands, France, and England also established colonies in the New World. The first permanent English settlement was Jamestown (located in the colony of Virginia) in 1607, and by the end of the seventeenth century England's colonial holdings encompassed a good deal of eastern North America.

The history of European colonialism in the Americas is, without doubt, a dark one. The indigenous peoples of South, Central, and North America suffered violence, exploitation, death by disease, and forced conversions, and the relationships between colonizer and colonized were shaped by military power, economic interests, and the religious fervor of missionaries. Europe's colonization of the New World inaugurated a transatlantic system of trade that would eventually bring African slaves to the Americas as part of a highly organized exchange of labor, resources, and commodities. At the same time, even as New World settlers may have sought to Europeanize the indigenous peoples and societies they encountered, their own world was transformed by the contact. Materially, Europe benefited from the introduction of new commodities, such as tobacco, corn, and previously unknown medications. But as Renaissance travel literature reveals, the encounter with the New World also fundamentally changed Europeans' awareness of their recently expanded world. When four delegates (or "kings," as they were called)

from the Iroquois Confederacy visited London and Queen Anne's court in 1710, they inspired a fascination whose intensity reveals how deeply their newly discovered hemisphere had penetrated the early modern imagination.

PROFESSIONAL THEATER, 1500–1700

Theater played an important part in the emergence of early modern Europe. As a medium of impersonation and display, theater spoke to a deeply theatricalized society where power was asserted through spectacles, performances, and rituals of display. The spirits of individualism and inquiry found a natural home in an art form in which characters grappled with their destinies on a public stage, and spectators who flocked to attend these performances saw the concerns of their world illuminated and explored. As defenders and critics debated its moral authority, European theater during this period exerted unprecedented social influence.

The years 1500–1700 saw wide-ranging developments in the institution and practices of theater. In addition to those performances that took place in court, private, and university settings, the first

An engraving from the mid-1600s showing actors onstage at the Hôtel de Bourgogne.

professional theaters, public and private, opened in Europe during the second half of the sixteenth century. Paris had the Hôtel de Bourgogne, built in 1548; London the short-lived Red Lion, in 1567; and Madrid the Corral de la Cruz, in 1579; and by 1600 these major cities—and several in Italy—had become thriving theatrical centers. Many of these early theater buildings employed staging arrangements used in courtyard and other outdoor performance venues—the major public theaters of London, such as the Globe, were open-air theaters and contained stages that extended into the audience. But the development of theater architecture and scenic practices during this period was also influenced by the rediscovery of the treatise on architecture by the Roman engineer and architect Vitruvius. Italian architects and theorists drew on it in determining the theater's shape, the relationship between stage and auditorium, and the design of tragic, comic, and pastoral scenes. During the seventeenth and eighteenth centuries, Italian stage design became influential throughout Europe, as such innovations were introduced as the use of perspective, a form of visual representation that creates the impression of three-dimensionality and distance. As it gained popularity, the simultaneous staging that characterized the medieval period and continued into early modern production was replaced by a spatially unified visual field. Italian designers also pioneered the use of the proscenium, an archway or a frame that would become characteristic of European stage design from the late sixteenth to nineteenth centuries.

As the sophistication of theater technology grew, stage design and scenic effects became increasingly elaborate. The spectacular staging for which the theaters of seventeenth-century Italy, France, and Spain became particularly well-known— multiple scenery changes, flying chariots, hidden grottoes, lavish pictorial effects— were manifestations of the baroque style that dominated European arts during this period. The baroque, which stresses exuberance, monumentality, and ornateness, achieved its highest realization in court performances, when royalty spent large sums for the work of Italy's leading designers and those who studied their innovations. This movement toward greater spectacle was accelerated by the development of opera during the 1600s.

COMMEDIA DELL'ARTE

The establishment of theater as a public, private, and courtly institution was paralleled by the professionalization of actors and others involved in theatrical productions. Acting companies operated in England and on the Continent throughout the sixteenth century, and these troupes often performed in other countries in addition to their own. The most widely known were the *commedia dell'arte* (literally, "comedy of art") players who emerged in Italy in the mid-1500s, performed throughout Europe, and occupied an important place in European theatrical history into the eighteenth century. These troupes—which consisted of ten to twelve actors, both male and female—presented comic scenarios centering on love and intrigue. While the narrative outlines of these scenarios were established in advance, their performance depended on improvisation and the use of comic routines or improvisational asides known as *lazzi*. Popular with audiences, *lazzi* were often ingenious bits of comic business that players used to enliven their performances, such as using a wooden arm to slip away from a beating or engaging in acrobatic contortions in order to catch a flea. Commedia dell'arte actors portrayed a range of stock characters—some masked and some unmasked—that included lovers, masters, and servants (known as *zanni*). Among the best known of the masked characters are Pantalone, a rich miser, and Arlecchino (or Harlequin), an acrobatic servant with a distinctive motley-colored costume.

Commedia dell'arte companies were organized on the sharing plan, an arrangement that enabled performers to share in the risks and profits of their companies. It was just one of the forms of economic organization that acting companies throughout Europe used as actors, managers, playwrights, and others participated in the expanding business of theater. Per-

Riciulina.   *Metzetin*

A sixteenth-century engraving of two commedia actors dancing.

forming at Europe's courts (often under the patronage of royalty and nobility) while also operating within a newly established network of public and private playhouses, theater companies in the late 1500s and 1600s began to enjoy some measure of economic security. At the same time, the life of theater professionals remained a hard one, with actors and playwrights often living on the edge of poverty and under the threat of debtors' prison. Theater and the profession of acting were regarded with the social ambivalence and antitheatrical prejudice that early modern Europe inherited from the medieval period. In Catholic and Protestant countries alike, the theater was regularly associated with immorality, and such charges came from secular as well as religious sources. Relationships with state and civic authorities were often equally fraught. Dramatic censorship was instituted in Spain and England, and the theater was subject to a range of restrictive laws throughout Europe. Although the licensing of theaters that took place during the 1600s conferred greater legitimacy on the companies that gained state approval, the implementation of such policies had the effect of bringing theatrical activity even more firmly under government control.

THE DRAMA OF EARLY MODERN EUROPE

The profound changes in Europe between 1500 and 1700 and the accompanying theatrical developments helped ensure that the era would become one of the most prominent in the creation of dramatic literature. The rediscovery, translation, and publication of Greek and Roman plays spurred widespread interest in classical drama, and the translation into Italian of Aristotle's *Poetics* in 1549 helped ignite a debate over Aristotelian dramatic theory that lasted into the eighteenth century. Through the efforts of sixteenth-century Italian and French commentators, Aristotle's treatise was interpreted and codified into neoclassical precepts concerning decorum, verisimilitude, dramatic probability, concentrated action, and uniformity of subject and tone. The dramatic unities of time, place, and action, for example, dictated that the playwright not strain a spectator's credulity by having events take place over more than one day and in more than one location and that the play be restricted to a single, focused plotline. Noble characters were appropriate to tragedy, while those of lower social station belonged to the domain of comedy. Neoclassical theory had its greatest impact on the drama of Italy and France; but even in England and Spain, where dramatists generally eschewed its precepts for more episodic, stylistically varied dramatic styles, debates over classical authority took place.

Early in the sixteenth century, comedy, tragedy, tragicomedy, pastoral, and dramatic satire were strongly influenced by classical models. But as the academic performance of plays in Latin gave way to plays written in the vernacular, the drama of early modern Europe began drawing more strongly on native performance traditions inherited from the Middle Ages. The result was a rich tapestry of dramatic styles, ranging from the multiple, episodic plots of Elizabethan and Jacobean English drama to the classical simplicity of the plays of JEAN RACINE (1639–1699). As part of a larger theatrical field that included religious performances, royal pageants, civic commemorations, and such popular forms as mumming, drama during the period 1500–1700 entertained a variety of spectators in numerous venues. Concentrated in Europe's major cities, this drama reflected a lively urban culture and the early stirrings of national self-awareness. And although many of its most enduring technological, performative, and theoretical innovations arose in Italy, the theater of early modern Europe found its highest dramatic achievement in England, Spain, and France.

English Theater, 1576–1642

In 1576, when the actor, manager, and theatrical entrepreneur James Burbage (1531–1597) built the Theatre in Shoreditch (an area to the northeast of the City of London), the commercial theater was in its infancy in England. The performance of plays and other theatrical activity had, of course, enjoyed popularity earlier in the sixteenth century. Dramatists influenced by Renaissance humanism wrote comedies, tragedies, and moral interludes that made use of classical and medieval models alike; they were performed in a variety of places, including at court and in noble households, schools, universities, and London's legal societies, the Inns of Court. Among the best known of these earlier plays are *Ralph Roister Doister* (ca. 1553) and *Gammer Gurton's Needle* (1552–53), two early English comedies, and Thomas Norton and Thomas Sackville's *Gorboduc* (1561), generally considered the first English tragedy. Traveling actors brought mummings, farces, and other forms of popular dramatic entertainment to local communities, and Corpus Christi plays continued to be staged throughout England until the 1570s, when their performance was effectively halted by royal edict. But the expansion of dramatic activity that would make London one of the most vibrant theatrical centers in Europe did not occur until the commercial theater was established during the century's final quarter.

PUBLIC AND PRIVATE THEATERS

In England, as elsewhere in Europe, the construction of theater buildings was essential to the institutionalization of theater. Theater buildings in London were of two kinds: public and private. Burbage's Theatre established the model for subsequent public theaters. Polygonal in shape, it contained three tiers of audience galleries surrounding a roughly circular, unroofed yard. We have sufficient information about this and other public theaters built between 1577 and 1623—notably the Swan, the Rose, the Fortune, and the Globe, which was built in Southwark (on the southern side of the Thames) with timber from the dismantled Theatre in 1599—to know that the stage for these theaters extended into the yard at a height of approximately 5 feet. Partly roofed, this stage featured a structure at the rear known as the *tiring house*, which included two doors for entrances and exits and one or two balcony levels that could be used for audience seating, music, and scenes requiring actors to perform above stage level (the so-called balcony scene in SHAKESPEARE's *Romeo and Juliet* [1595], for example). A trapdoor on the stage floor allowed ghosts and other characters to ascend from a darkened cellar (sometimes referred to as *hell*), while pulleys on

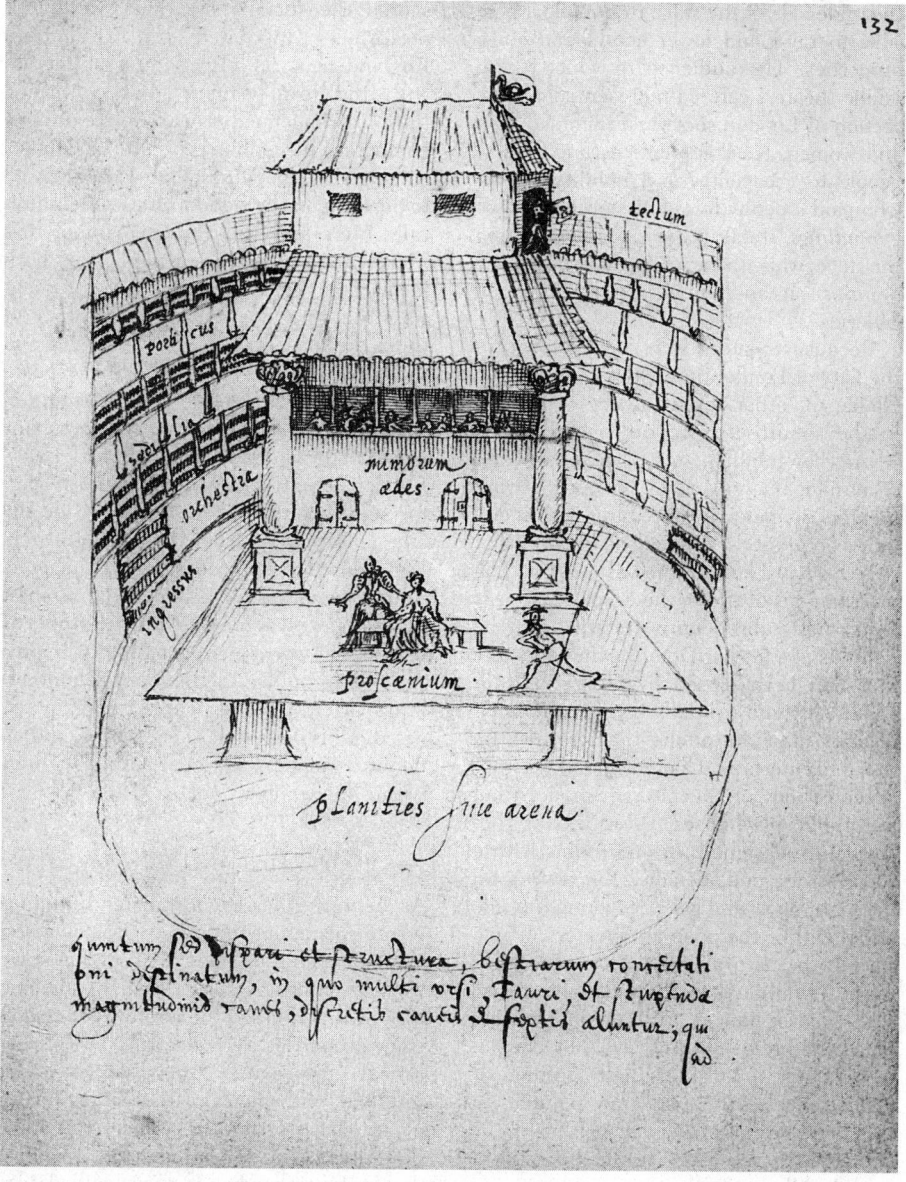

This sketch of the Swan Theater—a copy of an original by a late-sixteenth-century Dutch visitor to London named Johannes de Witt—is the only surviving contemporary likeness of the inside of an Elizabethan theater. Latin words or phrases identify the major parts of the theater: the *proscaenium* (the flat, open stage); the *mimorum aedes* (a dressing room for the actors); the *planities sive arena* (the "yard," in which spectators could stand in front of the stage); the *tectum* (the roof); the *porticus* (covered gallery); the *sedilia* (seats); the *orchestra* (seats for important spectators); and the *ingressus* (the entry into the various galleries).

the underside of the stage roof made it possible to raise and lower actors and stage properties. The audience to which these public theaters catered represented a cross section of London society; it included men and women, from apprentices and tradespeople to the gentry and nobility. Those who paid a penny for admission, known as *groundlings*, stood in the yard surrounding the stage, while those who paid two or three pennies sat on benches in the covered galleries.

Because theaters were banned within the City of London itself, the Theatre, the Globe, and other public theaters were built in the suburbs to the north and south, where they could operate beyond the reach of municipal law. Most of London's private theaters, in contrast, were built within city limits on properties known as *liberties* that were exempt from municipal control. The most famous of these, the Blackfriars, was built and subsequently rebuilt on the grounds of a former Dominican monastery that had been closed by Henry VIII in 1538. With substantially higher admission charges than the public theaters, private theaters entertained a more socially homogeneous body of spectators. Smaller than the public playhouses, these indoor theaters were designed as long rooms with a stage at one end, benches for seating on the main floor, and galleries along the side walls. Unlike the open-air theaters, which were lit by natural light, private theaters were illuminated by candlelight. Until 1609, performances at London's private theaters were given exclusively by companies of boy actors; originally formed at choir schools, they became popular at court and on the London stage during the late 1500s and early 1600s but subsequently fell out of favor.

ACTING COMPANIES

An essential contribution to the rise of professional theater in late-sixteenth-century England was a legal shift in the status of actors. In 1572 the government of Elizabeth I passed a law decreeing that itinerant actors and entertainers be arrested and punished as vagabonds if they could not demonstrate that they belonged to the household of a nobleman. The law under-scored the socially marginal world that performers inhabited in Elizabethan England, but its effect—in conjunction with the royal patents that confirmed these arrangements—was to legitimize companies through aristocratic patronage. Among the companies that were licensed to perform on the London stage, the Admiral's Men and the Lord Chamberlain's Men (later renamed the King's Men), both licensed in 1594, were the most influential; the former produced the plays of CHRISTOPHER MARLOWE (1564–1593) and the latter the plays of William Shakespeare (1564–1616). In addition to performing in specific theaters—Shakespeare's company played at the Globe and, later, Blackfriars—London theatrical companies also performed at court and on tours outside the city (a necessity when London theaters were closed during outbreaks of plague). Adult companies were structured as sharing plans, with actors sharing the profits as well as the work of running the company. As a shareholder in the Lord Chamberlain's Men, Shakespeare wrote plays, acted in his own and others' works, and no doubt assumed additional responsibilities within the company.

PROPERTIES AND COSTUMES

As befit the design of theater buildings where spectators surrounded the stage on three or even four sides, the London stage was presentational rather than illusionistic in how it addressed the audience. Though stage properties were clearly a part of theatrical performance, they tended to be minimal, with much of the action taking place on an undefined area of the stage reminiscent of the *platea* of medieval drama. Setting, when it was specified, was established more through verbal description than through stage properties. Costumes, on the other hand, were often quite elaborate, with visually luxurious pieces provided by the nobility or purchased by the companies themselves. Whereas actresses were allowed to perform on the Continent, only male actors performed on the London stage before the closing of the theaters in 1642. Women's roles were usually played by boy actors within the companies, a practice that Shakespeare's

Cleopatra (played by a boy) alludes to when she imagines her story being performed on a Roman stage: "I shall see / Some squeaking Cleopatra boy my greatness / I'th' posture of a whore." But what may seem like limitations to the modern eye were opportunities for exceptional displays of acting skill by the period's many renowned performers, including the most celebrated actor of his day, Richard Burbage (James Burbage's son, 1568–1619).

PLAYWRIGHTS AND PLAYS

The proliferation of theaters and the rising demand for theatrical entertainment created intense competition for new plays, and a professional class of playwrights emerged to meet this demand. Shakespeare earned enough money from his playwriting and other theatrical efforts to purchase a large house and property in Stratford-upon-Avon, but not all playwrights had equal success, and they often turned their hands to pamphleteering and other activities in London's booming print market. Forced to work under the eye of the Master of the Revels, who in 1581 was granted the power to license plays (and thereby to act as government censor), playwrights were subject to arrest, imprisonment, and even torture if they addressed controversial subjects in their plays. Because plays belonged to the companies that purchased them, playwrights had no rights over their production or publication. Nor were plays accorded the literary standing of poetry and other more strictly literary forms. Company-authorized and pirated versions of plays occasionally appeared in inexpensive quarto editions (on small-sized paper), but it wasn't until 1616, when BEN JONSON (1572–1637) published his plays under the title *The Works of Benjamin Jonson,* that a dramatist presumed to accord his works the status of literary art. Like most of his contemporary dramatists, Shakespeare showed little interest in the publication of his plays, and it was only in 1623, seven years after his death, that two of his colleagues published his plays in a large-format edition, subsequently known as the First Folio.

The drama of Renaissance England was rich and varied, combining the eloquence of dramatic poetry with the vibrant particularity of contemporary life. During the 1580s and 1590s, the London stage offered a wealth of plays in the genres of comedy, tragedy, dramatic pastoral, and history play. With *THE SPANISH TRAGEDY* (1587), THOMAS KYD (1558–1594) inaugurated the genre of revenge tragedy that was to prove popular during the reigns of Elizabeth and James, and before his premature death (in 1593) Marlowe wrote a half-dozen or so tragedies and history plays that remain among the finest of their age. Elizabethan comedy ranged from the pastoral and romantic plays of Robert Greene (1558–1592) to Jonson's early satiric comedies. The exuberance that characterizes much of this drama reflected the optimism of an England that was asserting itself as a European power (the English defeat of the Spanish Armada occurred in 1588). This attitude changed in the years preceding Elizabeth's death in 1603, and the drama of the early seventeenth century was marked by a darkening of tone and subject matter. Shakespeare's greatest tragedies were written during this period, as were the plays of JOHN WEBSTER (1579–1630s?) and other tragic dramatists. In the area of comedy, the closing years of the sixteenth century and the first quarter of the seventeenth saw the sharpening of dramatic satire; a proliferation of city comedies (plays whose characters are drawn from London's urban classes) in the drama of Thomas Middleton (1580–1627), Thomas Dekker (ca. 1572–1632), and others; and the popularity of a hybrid genre—tragicomedy—in the plays of Francis Beaumont (ca. 1584–1616) and John Fletcher (1579–1625). The years of Charles I's reign (1625–49) saw the tragedies of John Ford (1586–1639?) and the genteel comedies of James Shirley (1596–1666).

COURT THEATER: MASQUES

The early seventeenth century also witnessed a flowering of theatrical activity in the courts of James I and Charles I. The Stuart court masque was an elaborate form of entertainment that featured lavish spectacle, music, singing, dance, and allegorical or mythological plots celebrating monarchical authority. Jonson was the leading writer of masques during this

Costume design by Inigo Jones for Ben Jonson's *The Masque of Queens* (1609).

period, and he worked in collaboration with the architect and stage designer Inigo Jones (1573–1652), who introduced important aspects of Italian stage design to the English theater. Like the court ballets that were performed in France during the reign of Louis XIV later in the century, the Stuart masques reflect the profound relationship between theatricality and the performance of power in the early modern state.

CIVIL WAR, COMMONWEALTH, AND THE CLOSING OF THE THEATERS

This relationship came to an end during the English Civil War (1642–49), which was followed by the Commonwealth and the Protectorate (1649–60); those eighteen years witnessed the overthrow of the English monarchy by a Puritan-dominated Parliament and the closing of the theaters by parliamentary decree in 1642. The Globe was torn down in 1644 to make room for tenements, and other theaters were subsequently dismantled or allowed to fall into disrepair. Theatrical activity was not entirely eliminated during these years—dramatic performances were given at private houses and other nontheatrical venues, and in the 1650s the musical dramas of William Davenant (1606–1668) marked the beginning of English opera—but the great age of Tudor and Stuart theater had come to a decisive end.

Spanish Theater, 1580–1700

During the sixteenth and seventeenth centuries, a period known as the "Golden Age" of Spanish literature and art, dramatic theater in Spain achieved a level of excellence that rivaled that of SHAKE-SPEARE's England. The rise of theater and the distinctive shapes it assumed reflected the history of Spain's emergence as a European and global power. During the medieval period much of Spain was under Muslim rule, and the slow reconquest of the Iberian peninsula by Christian armies was not completed until the Battle of Granada in 1492. The kingdoms of Aragon and Castile were joined by the marriage of Ferdinand II (1452–1516) and Isabella I (1451–1504) in 1469, and the resultant unified Spain extended its power through further dynastic alliances and an overseas empire that included vast areas of North, Central, and South America.

While other areas of Europe were feeling the initial shocks of the Protestant Reformation, the Catholic Church consolidated its authority in Spain and, through the office of the Spanish Inquisition, kept religious division beyond its borders. Spain's unique history strongly affected its theatrical development. The centuries of Muslim occupation gave Spanish drama and Spanish literature as a whole their most distinctive theme— that of honor; at the same time, the pervasive Catholicism of Spanish life during the later period ensured that the religious and secular theaters, which were diverging elsewhere in Europe, remained unusually close.

RELIGIOUS DRAMA:
THE *AUTO SACRAMENTALE*

The most widely produced form of religious drama in sixteenth- and seventeenth-century Spain was the *auto sacramentale*. Performed, like the earlier mystery cycles throughout Europe, on the Feast of Corpus Christi, *autos sacramentales* celebrated the mystery of the Eucharist in stories mixing the human, the supernatural, and the allegorical. To put on the *autos*, the players used two-story *carros*, or wagons, which were first paraded through Madrid and other cities and towns as part of the Corpus Christi procession and then positioned behind a portable or fixed outdoor stage. Two *carros* were used for each performance until the mid-1600s, when the number was expanded to four (and later to eight). Early *autos* were produced by trade guilds, but by the mid-sixteenth century the responsibility had passed to municipal authorities, who often spent considerable amounts to stage them. Enormously popular events that brought together civic and church authority, *autos sacramentales* were performed by professional acting troupes hired specifically for these occasions, and they commanded the talents of Spain's leading dramatists.

PUBLIC THEATER: THE *CORRALES*

Although there was dramatic and theatrical activity—including the performance of secular plays for academic, aristocratic, and popular audiences—in the early and mid-sixteenth century, it was not until the 1570s that a professional public theater was fully established in Spain's major cities. Not surprisingly, the country's theatrical center was Madrid, which in 1561 became the capital under Philip II (1527–1598). The Corral de la Cruz, Madrid's first permanent theater, was built in 1579; it was followed by the Corral del Príncipe in 1583. Like the open-air theaters of Elizabethan England, the design of the *corrales*, or Spanish public theaters, derived from courtyard performances. The *corrales* were constructed within square or rectangular courtyards enclosed on three sides by buildings. A raised stage with permanent backdrop and upper levels was placed on one

The Corral de Comedias de Almagro, built in 1628 and restored in the 1950s, is the only surviving *corral*. Seats for the audience are positioned in an enclosed courtyard, while the rows of seats known as *gradas* ascend on either side.

end of the courtyard, and an open space, or *patio,* for standing spectators was located directly in front of it. In the seventeenth century several rows of benches or stools (called *taburetes*) were installed immediately in front of the stage on a raised platform. On either side of the patio, a section of seats in ascending rows known as the *gradas* extended to the second story. Above the *alojería* (refreshment booth) at the end of the courtyard facing the stage, galleries accommodated additional spectators. The first of these, the *cazuela,* provided seating for women, while higher galleries accommodated officials from the city of Madrid and the Council of Castile and (above them) clergymen and intellectuals. The windows of buildings above the *gradas* served as box seats (*aposentos*), and additional levels of box seats or open galleries were available at the third- and fourth-floor levels. The lively, sometimes unruly, audiences who attended performances in the *corrales* represented a cross section of Madrid society.

From its inception the public theater in Madrid was embedded in the city's institutional structures. The *corrales* were originally licensed to confraternities, or charitable organizations, which used theatrical performance as a means of raising money to support hospitals and aid the poor. This arrangement lasted until 1615, when the city of Madrid assumed control of the theaters and the distribution of their revenues for charitable purposes. The theatrical companies it hired—consisting of actor-managers (*autores*), actors, apprentices, and others involved in the productions—were subject to government regulation. After 1603 only licensed companies could operate in Spain, and the number of licenses was limited. Actors who were not hired by these companies joined *compañías de la legua* (companies of the road), which performed throughout the countryside. No company was allowed to perform in any one place for more than two months of the year, and only one could perform there at any one time (more were permitted in Madrid and Seville). As a result, even licensed companies regularly traveled between cities. Women actors were licensed to perform in 1587, but this practice sparked such controversy that a royal decree was issued in 1599 stipulating that only those women married to members of the company perform and that male and female actors not dress in the clothing of the opposite sex. Compromises in response to this final restriction were frequent, however, and actresses who played women disguised as men regularly wore male clothing down to the waist with a skirt below.

THEATER AT COURT

Court performances, which had been infrequent in Spain during the sixteenth century, began to be mounted in the seventeenth century with a splendor that rivaled that displayed in Italy and France. During the reign of Philip III (r. 1598–1621), professional productions and masquelike entertainments involving elaborate settings, costumes, and special effects were given in one of the halls in the Alcázar (the royal palace). When a new palace, the Buen Retiro, was completed on the outskirts of Madrid in 1633, it became the center for court entertainments, which reached their high point during the reign of Philip IV

(r. 1621–65). Under the supervision of Italian set designers who were brought to the Spanish court to oversee and engineer these performances, spectacular entertainments were staged both within the palace—a permanent theater, the Coliseo, was constructed there in 1640—and outdoors on the palace grounds. For a 1635 production of *Love Is the Greatest Enchantment* by PEDRO CALDERÓN DE LA BARCA (1600–1681), the Tuscan hydraulics engineer, scenographer, and landscape designer Cosimo (Cosme) Lotti (d. 1643) built a special stage above the waters of a lake, managed to have a silver chariot drawn across the water's surface by two large fish, and transformed a mountain into a palace.

SPANISH GOLDEN AGE DRAMA

The drama of Spain's Golden Age represents one of the period's greatest achievements. Those plays that were performed by early professional troupes in Spain were written by actor-managers for the companies they ran—hence, these versatile men of the theater were given the full title *autores de comedias*. By the 1590s, a class of professional dramatists had emerged to satisfy the increasing demand for original dramatic scripts. The *comedia nueva* (new drama)—or *comedia*, as it became known less formally—proved to be the most popular and enduring dramatic form written during the Spanish Golden Age. Consisting of three-act plays in varying verse forms, *comedia nueva* mixed high and low, tragedy and comedy, in plots that were drawn from history, mythology, legend, Italian *novelle* and other literary sources, the Bible, popular ballads, and the everyday life of country and town. Among its specialized subgenres were the *comedias de capa y espada* (cape and sword plays), which featured stories of romance and intrigue, and *comedias de costumbres* (comedies of manners). Popular character types in the *comedia* included the *cabellero* (gentleman), *galán* (cavalier or gallant), *dama* (lady), and *gracioso* (comic character, or fool, whose actions often parallel the actions of those of superior rank).

Of the many playwrights who contributed to the *comedia nueva*, none played a greater role in its development and success than LOPE DE VEGA (1562–1635), a towering figure in Spanish Golden Age drama and one of the most prolific dramatists ever to write for the stage. He wrote as many as 1,500 plays (of which 470 have survived), and his output included *comedias*, *autos sacramentales*, and *loas* (prologues) and *entremeses* (interludes), which were performed before and between the acts of plays, respectively. In *The New Art of Writing Plays* (1609), his treatise on dramatic theory, Lope defended his disregard for the classical rules of playwriting in favor of variety and "the likeness of truth." Other dramatists followed in his footsteps—including Tirso de Molina (Gabriel Téllez, ca. 1584–1648), whose play *The Trickster of Seville* is the earliest known version of the Don Juan story—but none achieved a more prominent position in seventeenth-century Spanish theater than Pedro Calderón de la Barca. Calderón—whose plays are marked by meticulous craftsmanship, linguistic complexity, and richness of metaphor—became a leading figure in the *corrales* and in the court of Philip IV, where much of his dramatic activity was concentrated. He also became the leading author of *autos sacramentales*; so exceptional was his mastery of this form that between 1647 and 1681 he wrote all of the *autos* produced in Madrid.

THE LEGACY OF GOLDEN AGE DRAMA

Calderón's death is generally considered to mark the end of Spanish Golden Age drama. Those dramatists who followed in his footsteps conformed to established models rather than pursuing innovation. While spectacular productions continued to be undertaken at court through the end of the century, the heyday of both the court theater and public *corrales* had passed. In their decline they mirrored the condition of Spain itself, which had been weakened and demoralized by a century of wars, declining wealth, and waning influence. Yet during its Golden Age, Spain had achieved one of Europe's most vibrant theatrical cultures, and its dramatic legacy was felt throughout the Continent (particularly in France) and in the world beyond its shores. Colonizing armies and Spanish missionaries brought drama and theatrical performance to the Philippines and the Americas, and the colo-

nial drama that appeared there retained its Spanish heritage (the Philippine vernacular drama known as *komedya*, for instance, derived from European romances brought to the islands by Spanish soldiers). The more developed colonial societies produced dramatists who worked within the forms and conventions of Golden Age drama. The Mexican scholar, poet, and nun SOR JUANA INÉS DE LA CRUZ (1648?–1695), one of the finest writers of the Spanish Golden Age, composed nearly thirty *autos sacramentales*, comedies, and *loas*. The theater of sixteenth- and seventeenth-century Spain, in other words, provided the world with its first truly global drama.

French Theater, 1630–1700

THEATER IN PARIS

During the second half of the seventeenth century, France established one of the most admired and emulated dramatic traditions in Europe. Yet the theatrical institutions needed to underpin this achievement developed significantly later there than they did in Italy, England, and Spain. The delay was largely attributable to external factors, most importantly the Wars of Religion between Catholics and French Protestants (known as Huguenots) that paralyzed the country from 1562 to 1598. The early history of the public theater in Paris certainly did not bode well for establishing an urban theatrical culture. The Hôtel de Bourgogne, Paris's first public theater, was built in 1548 by the Confrérie de la Passion, an association of Paris merchants and tradesmen that had been organized in 1402 to produce religious plays and thereafter held a monopoly on theatrical productions of all kinds in Paris. By the end of the century the Confrérie had ceased to perform plays and was leasing its theater for short periods to theater companies from outside Paris. But traveling companies often avoided Paris, because the cost of renting the Hôtel de Bourgogne was substantial, and because the Confrérie enforced its monopoly by charging a fee to companies who chose to perform elsewhere in the city. The capital lacked a resident theater company until 1629, when a permanent company was allowed to occupy the Hôtel de Bourgogne. In 1634 a second theater—the Théâtre de

Marais—opened in a converted tennis court (the sport, popular among the nobility, was played on enclosed courts with a gallery for spectators; these structures often served as theaters in the seventeenth century). It housed a second permanent company, and after a fire in 1644 the theater was rebuilt with many technical improvements. Though Paris had not been without theatrical entertainment during the early decades of the 1600s—commedia dell'arte troupes performed in the city, farce was widely popular, and the foundations of a French dramatic tradition were laid by Alexandre Hardy (ca. 1572–1632), who composed hundreds of tragedies, tragicomedies, and pastoral plays—it was not until the 1630s that the theater became a regular pastime for Paris's middle and upper classes.

STATE PATRONAGE

The growing status of French theater during this time owed much to the support of those in positions of power. Cardinal Riche-lieu (1585–1642), chief minister to Louis XIII (1601–1643) and one of the figures most responsible for the centralization of power in the French monarchy, was a strong supporter of the arts, and under his patronage the theater acquired a legitimacy it had previously lacked. Richelieu awarded a subsidy to the theater company that occupied the Marais, inaugurating the practice whereby all major French companies received government subsidies. In addition, he had a theater built in his private palace, the Palais Cardinal (renamed the Palais Royal when the palace came under the control of the crown); it was the first in France to include the proscenium arch and side wings characteristic of Italian stage design. The strong link between theater and the French state that Richelieu helped establish was a defining feature of the reigns of Louis XIII and Louis XIV—and this link achieved its clearest institutional expression in 1680, when the latter merged Paris's two leading theater companies to form Europe's first national theater, the Comédie Française.

An engraving from 1641 showing the stage, complete with proscenium arch and perspectival stage scenery in the background, of the Palais Cardinal.

THEATERS AND AUDIENCE

Like the indoor tennis courts that preceded them and continued to be used as venues for theatrical productions, the public theaters of Paris were rectangular structures, typically long and narrow, with an auditorium for the public and a stage that included room, as the century progressed, for increasingly sophisticated technical machinery. The main floor of the auditorium consisted of a pit (*parterre*) for standing spectators with benches along the wall. The side and rear walls contained three rows of galleries, the first two of which were divided into boxes (*loges*). At the rear of the *parterre* and below the boxes rose the *amphithéâtre*, a section whose rows were raked to provide a better angle for viewing the stage. Both stage and auditorium were illuminated by candlelight. For much of the first half of the seventeenth century, scenic practice followed the conventions of medieval drama, with dramatic locales represented by the separate scenic structures called *mansions*. But as Italian scene design was adopted in the public theaters, the Parisian stage incorporated the spatially unifying principles of perspective staging. Any increase in dramatic illusion that might have resulted from perspective staging, though, was offset by the lively presence of the spectators, whose appearance and behavior in the Paris theater often constituted a performance in their own right. Perhaps more distracting to the actors than the unruly occupants of the *parterre* were those spectators who were allowed to sit onstage during performances. A cross section of Paris society, including the nobility and, on occasion, the king himself, made up the audience.

NEOCLASSICISM AND FRENCH DRAMA

The triumph of Italian scene design, with its concentration on single locations, was aided by the growing influence of neoclassicism on seventeenth-century French drama. During the 1630s and 1640s a number of French authors and intellectuals championed the "rules" that earlier Renaissance commentators had drawn from Aristotle's *Poetics*, and the principles advocated by neoclassical theory (including

An engraving showing the performance of Molière's *The Imaginary Invalid*, in 1664, before Louis XIV and his court.

the dramatic unities) were given official sanction by the newly formed Académie Française. The authority and validity of neoclassicism were fiercely debated, particularly as its strictures might apply to the genre of tragedy. The most passionately argued of these debates concerned *Le Cid* (1636–37), a tragedy written by France's leading playwright at the time, Pierre Corneille (1606–1684). Those who attacked Corneille's play for not observing the principles of verisimilitude, decorum, and purity of genre were supported by the Académie, which entered the debate at the request of Richelieu. Although some writers continued to resist, the principles of neoclassical theory became widely adopted by French playwrights. That these principles could be artistically enabling as well as prescriptive is demonstrated by the formally elegant, psychologically complex plays of JEAN RACINE (1639–1699), France's greatest tragic dramatist.

French comedy also attained a pinnacle of excellence in the later seventeenth century, chiefly through the plays of JEAN-BAPTISTE POQUELIN (1621?–1673), better known by his stage name, MOLIÈRE. Like SHAKESPEARE, Molière was a man of the theater as well as a writer, and his career as a dramatist is intertwined with the professions of actor and company manager. After years touring the French provinces, the theatrical troupe that Molière had helped found in 1643 settled in the French capital. By the 1660s the company had established itself in the Palais Royal, had been awarded an annual subsidy from Louis XIV, and was performing to great acclaim at court and before the Parisian public. Much of this acclaim resulted from Molière's dramatic contributions: farces influenced by the commedia dell'arte, court spectacles, ballets, and, most of all, the comedies of manners in which Molière offered lively and satirical portraits of French society. These plays were not without their controversies—*TARTUFFE* (1664–69), Molière's comic investigation of religious hypocrisy, was attacked on religious grounds and banned from performance for five years—but they quickly became standards of the classical French repertoire.

THE DECLINE OF COURT INFLUENCE

By the end of the seventeenth century, Paris had established itself as the theatrical capital of Europe. The Comédie Française was the leading theatrical company of its time, and under the influence of Jean-Baptiste Lully (1632–1687) French opera had become equally renowned. The brilliance of the theatrical arts in seventeenth-century France owed much to the splendor of the French court, which displayed its power through the culture of spectacle. After Louis XIV moved his court and France's nobility outside Paris to the newly built Palace of Versailles in 1682, however, the role in French theater of the court and its literary tastes declined. As in England at the turn of the eighteenth century, in France public theater was left to thrive on its own terms. That Paris continued to exert a strong influence on European theater in the centuries that followed is powerful testimony to the theater that Corneille, Racine, and Molière helped build.

English Theater, 1660–1700

RESTORATION AND THEATER

When Charles II, eldest son of the executed Charles I, made his triumphant return in 1660 after eighteen years of parliamentary rule, both the monarchy and the public theater were reestablished in England. But the intervening years ensured that both institutions looked very different than they had before the Civil War. Restoration theater (1660–1700) was the product of a largely aristocratic culture, and it catered to a much narrower audience than had the theater of Elizabeth I and James I. Rejecting the Puritanism of the Commonwealth and Protectorate, upper-class Restoration London was an intensely social world, and the licentiousness, materialism, social competition, and love of wit for which the elite society of this period is notorious found ample representation onstage.

The emergence of this theater owes much to broader European theatrical developments. During their exile in France, Charles II and members of his court grew familiar with the theatrical

An early-nineteenth-century engraving of the interior of the Duke's Theatre in Lincoln's Inn Fields during the reign of Charles II.

culture that flourished under Louis XIV, and the theater that they helped establish upon their return reflected their taste for Continental stagecraft. Shortly after Charles II was restored to the throne, he issued royal patents to William Davenant (1606–1668) and Thomas Killigrew (1612–1683) to form theatrical companies and purchase or build theaters. Because the few theaters that survived the Civil War were unable to meet the technical requirements of Italian scenic innovations—sliding upstage shutters and side wings that made possible rapid scene changes, trapdoors, and flying machinery, for instance—new theaters were built to accommodate the new technology. The King's Company (managed by Killigrew and sponsored by Charles II himself) first used an indoor tennis court but soon was performing at the newly built Theatre Royal on Bridges Street; when this burned down in 1672 they performed at a new structure on the same site, the Drury Lane Theatre. The Duke's Company (managed by Davenant and sponsored by the duke of York, the future king James II) used the Lincoln's Inn Fields Theatre (a converted tennis court) and, after 1671,

the Dorset Garden Theatre. Given that the patented companies held a monopoly over theatrical production in London—merging in 1682 (after the King's Company fell into dire financial straits) to form the United Company, an arrangement that lasted until 1695—these buildings were the center of London's theatrical life.

PLAYHOUSES, AUDIENCE, AND ACTORS

Restoration playhouses were small structures when compared with the open-air theaters that were built in London in the late sixteenth century. The stage featured a proscenium arch with a curved apron (or open floor) extending into the audience and to the side. The main floor of the auditorium (or pit) contained benches, and these were surrounded on the side and rear by box seats and galleries. The play-watching experience in this setting was intimate. Restoration theaters accommodated no more than 600 spectators, and all were seated within 35 feet or so of the stage. Boxes allowed spectators to sit above the sides of the stage (and hence be prominently displayed to the rest of the audience), and by the end of the century spectators were routinely seated onstage. Auditorium and stage were both lit by candelabra, with the result that actors and their spectators were equally illuminated. Restoration actors often played on the forestage (near the audience), and they delivered their lines as much to the spectators as to the play's other characters. It was not uncommon for spectators, who could be quite unruly in the Restoration theater, to interrupt a play by addressing the actors themselves.

As these practices and behaviors begin to suggest, the relationship between Restoration spectators and the performances they attended was marked by mutual interaction and display. Attending the theater was a popular activity for the upper classes of London society and for the king, and the theater became a microcosm of this aristocratic world, its relationships (overt and covert), and its social distinctions. Men and women came to the theater arrayed in the latest fashions, and the theater became an arena for displaying symbols of social distinction. Women—some of them prostitutes—often wore masks (or *vizards*) to disguise their identities, and the rendezvous that were arranged through this and other stratagems mirrored the sexual intrigue being performed onstage. The introduction of women actors for the first time on the English stage contributed to the sexually charged atmosphere of Restoration theaters. Charles II, who had seen actresses perform on the Continent, justified their inclusion in the name of moral reformation, since their presence would eliminate transvestism—boys dressing as women. But the theatrical display of female bodies onstage became an erotic attraction in its own right, particularly when women actors dressed as men, donning tight-fitting, knee-length pants in what were called *breeches roles*. Contemporary moralists viewed actresses as a symbol of the theater's licentiousness; and while their general accusation was unfair, it was certainly true that some actresses did have affairs with theatergoers. Charles II, a well-known libertine, numbered the actress Nell Gwynn (1650–1687) among his many mistresses.

RESTORATION DRAMA

The drama of Restoration England assumed a number of characteristic forms. Even the revivals of English plays written before the Civil War—chiefly, the works of Beaumont and Fletcher, Shakespeare, and JONSON—were often adapted to reflect contemporary tastes and conventions. During this period heroic tragedy flourished; it featured larger-than-life characters, exotic locales, and elevated—occasionally ranting—dramatic verse. Other tragedies written during this time observed the principles of French neoclassicism, such as the concentration of dramatic action according to the dramatic "unities." Adherence to these principles was not as strict in England as it was in France, however, and Restoration tragedy continued to be influenced by Shakespeare and by earlier English dramatic conventions. In his 1668 *An Essay of Dramatic Poesy,* the period's most significant work of dramatic theory, John Dryden (1611–1700)—a

leading writer of tragic and other drama—defended "the honour of our *English* writers" against those who overvalued French dramatic models.

But it was in comedy that the Restoration's achievements were most dazzling. Set in contemporary London, the Restoration comedy of manners featured gallants (or rakes), ladies, jealous husbands, cast-off mistresses, unsophisticated country visitors, fops, and clever servants engaged in often predatory games of intrigue and seduction. The wit and wordplay that characterize these plays reflect the importance of language, innuendo, and verbal disguise to Restoration stage interactions. Many of the plays contain a secondary plot involving conventional lovers, but the theatrical energies of the finest Restoration comedies—THE COUNTRY WIFE (1675), by WILLIAM WYCHERLEY (1641–1716); *The Man of Mode* (1676), by George Etherege (1636–1692); THE ROVER (written in two parts, 1677, 1681), by APHRA BEHN (1640–1689), England's first professional woman playwright; and *The Way of the World* (1700), by William Congreve (1670–1729)—are located in the central, equally matched "wit" couple. The lens provided by these interactions enabled playwrights to investigate fashion, marriage as a social contract, authenticity, masculinity, and social difference. By the end of the century, however, Restoration comedy faced opposition from a growing middle-class audience that rejected its libertinism, amorality, and elitism. When Jeremy Collier (1650–1726), an English clergyman, published *A Short View of the Immorality and Profaneness of the English Stage* in 1698, his attack hastened the end of a comic form that had outlived the courtly world of Charles II.

Eighteenth-Century Theater

The eighteenth century in Europe was characterized by stability and change; it was a period when the new rubbed uncomfortably against the old, and the outlines of the modern world began to emerge with unprecedented clarity. Throughout the century many of the artistic forms that had traditionally been preferred by the social elite continued to thrive. However, the social and economic transformations that would lead, by century's end, to the beginning of the Industrial Revolution hastened the growth of a middle class with its own interests, moral expectations, and tastes. Neoclassicism retained considerable authority on the Continent throughout the century, and the influence of classical ideals was evident in movements in literature, art, architecture, and music late in the century, but these were countered by the growing middle-class demand for nonelite literary and cultural forms such as the novel, which—with the help of an expanding popular press—by 1800 had become a literary form in its own right.

THE ENLIGHTENMENT

The eighteenth century was also the period of the Enlightenment, a philosophical movement centered in France that stressed the authority of reason and universally valid principles in human affairs. While some of the age's thinkers approved of the authoritarian rule of such "enlightened despots" as Frederick the Great (1712–1786) of Prussia and Catherine the Great (1729–1796) of Russia, the Enlightenment's main proponents challenged arbitrary authority and advocated limits to state power. The writings of such theorists as Jean-Jacques Rousseau (1712–1778), who argued that a social contract between individuals constitutes the only legitimate form of political order, established the foundations of modern democracy and were an important influence on the American Revolution (1775–83), the French Revolution (1789–99), and the Latin American revolutions of the early nineteenth century.

THEATERS AND ACTORS

The public theaters of eighteenth-century Europe offered a variety of entertainments—pantomime, comic opera, burlesque, and other popular performance forms in

A painting by William Hogarth of a scene from John Gay's popular ballad opera *The Beggar's Opera*. Note the audience members onstage in boxes.

addition to serious and comic drama—to an audience whose numbers grew throughout the century. To accommodate this increase in spectators and keep up with the latest trends in stage design and technology, the major theaters of the period were expanded, renovated, and sometimes replaced by newer, larger buildings. Established theaters and theatrical companies continued to dominate theatrical life in Europe's capitals, usually as a result of government licensing, though theatrical activity beyond these theaters enjoyed periods of popularity. In London (the capital of what was now known as Great Britain, following the union of England and Scotland in 1707), a number of unlicensed theaters operating in the 1720s and 1730s contributed to a lively theatrical scene that produced the long-running ballad opera *The Beggar's Opera* (1728), by John Gay (1685–1732), and satirical burlesques directed at the government of Sir Robert Walpole (1676–1745), who was in effect Britain's prime minister (a title not yet in official usage). In part as a reaction to this satirical activity, the Theatrical Licensing Act, which confirmed the Drury Lane and Covent Garden as London's only licensed theaters and empowered the Lord Chamberlain to approve plays for performance, was passed in 1737. In Paris, the monopoly of the Comédie Française and the Opéra was challenged by nonlicensed troupes that performed as part of the city's seasonal fairs. These troupes, which presented comic operas, pantomimes, and (by the end of the century) comic and noncomic drama, eventually established themselves as year-round companies housed on the fashionable Boulevard du Temple.

Although theater as an institution changed less in the eighteenth century than in earlier centuries, scenic practice underwent a number of modifications designed to intensify the stage's visual realism. The symmetries of classical perspective were relinquished in favor of angled perspectives, which allowed the scene to be viewed from varying points of view, and mid- and late-century designers introduced picturesque landscapes, historical and exotic locales, and increasingly sophisticated atmospheric settings made possible, in part, by advances in lighting and sound effects.

Another development that reinforced the increasing illusionism of the eighteenth-century stage in London and Paris was the removal from it of spectators, a change that was complete by the middle of the century.

Although by modern standards eighteenth-century acting remained stylized in gesture and vocal delivery, in this area, too, practitioners shifted toward realism—and away from rhetorical modes of delivery. David Garrick (1717–1779), the century's greatest English actor, was praised for his natural style of acting, and similar advances in realistic performance took place on the Continent. To be sure, these efforts to bring the stage closer to life were limited in their aspirations and accomplishments. But though realism would not become a fully formed theatrical aesthetic until the nineteenth century, the first steps toward it were taken in the eighteenth.

EIGHTEENTH-CENTURY DRAMA

In the eighteenth century, the genres of tragedy and comedy underwent a number of important modifications that reflected the tastes of a growing middle-class audience and its largely conservative moral outlook. Tragedy, which had traditionally been concerned with actions of the ruling classes, set in historical and mythological locales, was expanded to include the events and scenes of ordinary life. The pioneering play in the subgenre of domestic tragedy was THE LONDON MERCHANT (1731), by the English playwright GEORGE LILLO (1693–1739), which centered on the downfall and moral reclamation of a London apprentice. Comedy was similarly modified as the values of wit, ingenuity, and sexual titillation gave way to noble feeling, moral elevation, and what Sir Richard Steele (1672–1729), one of the new subgenre's earliest champions, called "a joy too exquisite for laughter." Sentimental comedy (known in France as *comédie larmoyante*, or "tearful comedy") became popular throughout Europe during the eighteenth century.

Traditional tragedy and comedy had their supporters and practitioners as well. For example, the French philosopher and writer Voltaire (François-Marie Arouet, 1694–1778) wrote intricate tragedies in the elevated style, and the Irish-born London playwrights Oliver Goldsmith (ca. 1730–1774) and RICHARD BRINSLEY SHERIDAN (1751–1816) championed "laughing comedy" against the drama of sentimentality. In Italy Carlo Goldoni (1707–1793) reformed Italian comedy by transforming the improvisational drama of the commedia dell'arte into a literary genre. While eliminating the bawdiness and nonrealistic devices of the commedia, he nonetheless succeeded in preserving the tradition's comic spirit. Overall, though, sentimental drama and the century's other dramatic innovations crossed and, because of their popularity, undermined the boundaries between the traditional genres. In the 1750s Denis Diderot (1713–1784), one of the leading figures of the French Enlightenment, advocated a genre midway between tragedy and comedy: the *drame bourgeois*, which would take the social and familial problems of the middle class as its subject. Though it produced few plays of note during the late eighteenth century, the *drame bourgeois* was an important precursor to the social problem plays of HENRIK IBSEN (1828–1906) and later modern dramatists.

GERMAN THEATER AND DRAMA

One of the most important theatrical developments in the eighteenth century was the rise of established theater beyond its traditional centers in Italy, Spain, England, and France. This expansion was most striking in the German states of northern and central Europe. Although Vienna was one of the leading centers of opera in the late seventeenth century and troupes of professional actors performed at courts and in public settings throughout German-speaking Europe, an organized German theater did not develop until the eighteenth century. The Thirty Years War, which was fought largely on German soil, had devastated the region in the seventeenth century, and the territories that in the late nineteenth century would become modern Germany consisted of numerous small states within a declining Holy Roman Empire. With the region's resources scattered over a large area rather than concentrated in a capital or in other urban centers, it fell to the individual states to establish and support public theaters.

The Hamburg National Theater, established in 1767, was a short-lived venture that paved the way for state-subsidized theaters elsewhere in German-speaking Europe. The Gotha Court Theater was founded in 1775, the Imperial and National Theater of Vienna in 1776, and the Court and National Theater of Mannheim in 1779. Of the numerous state theaters that followed these, the most significant were the Royal National Theater, established in Berlin in 1786, and the Weimar Court Theater (1791), which produced plays by two of the century's greatest dramatists, JOHANN WOLFGANG VON GOETHE (1749–1832) and Friedrich von Schiller (1759–1805). Though these theaters operated independently of each other, their founding reflected a broad cultural concern with the expression of German national identity.

Despite being a relative newcomer to the European dramatic tradition, German drama of the mid- and late eighteenth century was significant in its experimentation and the range of its literary achievement. Gotthold Ephraim Lessing (1729–1781), an early advocate of sentimental drama, wrote plays that dealt with national, social, and philosophical themes and was instrumental in freeing German drama from the influence of French neoclassicism. His *Hamburg Dramaturgy,* a series of essays published in 1767 and 1768, was one of the century's most important works of dramatic theory. A more radical break with neoclassicism was achieved by the playwrights of the *Sturm und Drang* (storm and stress) movement, a revolt against Enlightenment rationalism that flourished between the late 1760s and early 1780s. The drama written as part of this movement—including early plays by Goethe and Schiller—explored intense emotion, nature, rebellion against society, and violent action in irregular, often episodic plots.

Goethe and Schiller eventually rejected *Sturm und Drang* for the "Weimar classicism" of their work created between the former's visit to Italy in 1786–88 and the latter's death in 1805. Ranging over modern European history, classical mythology, and philosophy, the plays of this period pursued the values of harmony, wholeness, and aesthetic distance. This desire to provide Germany with a classical tradition

An illustration of a scene from one of Schiller's *Sturm und Drang* dramas, *Kabale und Liebe* (1784).

reflected a revived interest in the classical world in late-eighteenth-century Europe—the ruins of Herculaneum and Pompeii, which offered Europeans a mesmerizing portrait of Roman life preserved in the ashes of Mount Vesuvius's eruption of 79 C.E., were discovered in Italy in 1709 and 1748. The resultant drama embodied the aesthetic values of beauty, harmony, and form rather than the prescriptive neoclassicism of earlier centuries. At the same time, this drama drew its subjects from a Europe facing a period of political and aesthetic changes. Indeed, Goethe's masterpiece, the poetic drama *FAUST* (written in two parts, 1808, 1831), owes as much to the Romanticism that flourished in the next century as it does to the classical past.

Romanticism and Melodrama, 1800–1880

THE AGE OF REVOLUTION

At the end of the eighteenth century, two events fundamentally changed the political and cultural landscape of the Western world: the American Revolution and the French Revolution. The American Revolution severed England from its most prosperous colony and launched a radical experiment in democracy in the New World. A few years later, the French Revolution showed that even in Europe the old order was not impervious to change. Begun as a relatively modest revolt against the excesses of a king seeking absolute power, the French Revolution became radical when the lower orders and their revolutionary leaders turned against the aristocracy with increasing violence. The twin revolutions had far-reaching consequences, as neighboring countries watched them and their aftermaths with astonishment, enthusiasm, and fear. Soon, they would be directly affected as well, when Napoleon Bonaparte (1769–1821) rose from the French revolutionary forces to conquer much of Europe, propelled by a powerful army and the promise of freedom from local tyranny. Even after Napoleon had been defeated and the political map of Europe reordered in 1815 at the Congress of Vienna, what historians now term the Age of Revolution would continue well into the second half of the nineteenth century.

ROMANTICISM AND THE THEATER

The two revolutions changed more than the political order of two countries: they also altered how Western societies thought about themselves, with marked effects on cultural institutions and the arts. The French and the American revolutions had been inspired by Enlightenment philosophers such as Voltaire (François-Marie Arouet, 1694–1778), Immanuel Kant (1724–1804), and Thomas Jefferson (1743–1826), who had advocated new social organizations based not on religious beliefs but on rational planning and thought. But as the social upheavals of these revolutions grew more and more violent and unsettling, the Enlightenment insistence on pure reason lost some of its currency. Reflecting these changing historical and intellectual currents, the generation of writers, artists, and thinkers following the revolutions articulated the movement known as Romanticism. The Romantics did not reject the Enlightenment and its social experiments entirely, but they considered its more extreme claims with skepticism. They consequently placed greater emphasis on subjective experience and even on irrational desires and beliefs, which had been rejected by the Enlightenment. By the same token, they turned against the restrained, rational movement in the arts known as classicism. Whereas artists adhering to classicism respected the boundaries between styles and poetic forms, the Romantics created unusual mixtures and sometimes left their works deliberately in fragments. Ruins of medieval architecture were prized over classical buildings, and folk arts such as fairy tales or rustic idylls over Greek and Roman models.

These developments changed the face of drama and theater as well. Indeed, the battles between the advocates of classicist theater and those of the new Romantic theater were often fierce. The French writer Victor Hugo (1802–1885), whose preface to the play *Cromwell* (1827) served as a manifesto of Romanticism, aroused the ire of traditionalists by rejecting the unities of time and place, advocating the use of historically accurate stage settings, and calling for a theatrical art that included the sublime and the grotesque. So intense were the passions of classicists

An illustration, by Jean Albert Grand-Carteret, of the audience disturbances that followed the final scene of Victor Hugo's *Hernani* at its premiere in 1830.

and romanticists over the future of French theater that the performances of Hugo's play *Hernani* (1830) at the Comédie Française were interrupted by sustained outbursts by supporters and detractors.

Like many of their contemporaries, Romantic playwrights developed an

This late-eighteenth-century engraving of King Lear in the storm indicates the passionate intensity with which Shakespeare was often performed on the Romantic stage.

ambivalent attitude toward the French Revolution. In the early nineteenth century GEORG BÜCHNER (1813–1837) wanted to bring the legacy of the French Revolution to Germany, where the political system was especially hierarchical and repressive. He even wrote a tragedy about one of the leaders of the French Revolution—*Danton's Death* (1835), a sympathetic portrait of Georges-Jacques Danton (1759–1774). Other Romantics, such as William Wordsworth (1770–1850) and Samuel Taylor Coleridge (1772–1834), became much more disenchanted with the French Revolution, foregrounding not its social gains but its violence. But though they were divided in their attitudes toward the political and social upheavals of their time, the Romantics could agree on many other things. One was the eminence of WILLIAM SHAKESPEARE, which led to a revival of the playwright across Europe; French and German Romantics treated the Elizabethan playwright as their most important predecessor. What the Romantics admired in Shakespeare was precisely what classicism had rejected: namely, the mixing of high and low characters and of comedy and tragedy, as well as the fantastic events depicted in Shakespeare's romances.

CLOSET DRAMA

Despite the fascination with theater in general and Shakespeare in particular, Romantic drama was characterized by an increasing distance from the theater audience. Although plays such as Hugo's *Hernani* enjoyed controversy and success on the popular stage, many dramas written by the great Romantic writers either were not performed during their lifetimes or received limited, private performances or readings. Such plays written for reading only, or *closet dramas*, form the most significant genre of dramatic literature during the Romantic era. Among them are *The Borderers* (1796), by Wordsworth; *The Death of Empedocles* (1798; unfinished), by Friedrich Hölderlin (1770–1843); *Remorse* (1813), by Coleridge; *Manfred* (1817), by Lord Byron (1788–1824); *The Cenci* (1819), by Percy Bysshe Shelley (1792–1822); and the plays of Alfred de Musset (1810–1857). The two plays from this era

collected in the *Norton Anthology of Drama*—GOETHE's *FAUST* (part 1, 1808) and BÜCHNER's *WOYZECK* (1836)—are closet dramas as well.

THEATERS AND ACTORS

The increasing division between dramatic literature and theatrical performance had to do both with the preferences of writers and with the state of the theater industry. Poets distrusted theater managers and actors, choosing instead to write for the reading public only. At the same time, theaters—which, throughout Europe, continued to expand in size during the nineteenth century—catered to the tastes of the general public by putting on lavish spectacles. (When a similar estrangement between dramatic authors and theater managers had occurred in imperial Rome, SENECA likewise wrote only for readers or small recitations and left the theater to the popular entertainments then dominating the stage.) The demand for such spectacles drove innovation, and thus nineteenth-century theater history is dominated by a series of technical developments—including the use of gaslights (first introduced around 1825) and limelights, an early form of spotlight that greatly enhanced designers' ability to create theatrical illusions and effects. The public also desired equestrian as well as nautical plays, as new traps, elevators, moving panoramas, and, later on, revolving stages expanded the range of theatrical possibilities. Other developments were more in tune with cultural tastes and ideas dominant in the Romantic era. As general interest in the distant past grew, audiences began to pay more attention to historically accurate costumes and sets. At the same time, celebrated actors such as England's Edmund Kean (1787–1833)—famous for his interpretation of Shakespeare—and France's Frédérick Lemaître (1800–1876) developed a Romantic acting style, based on the expression of strong emotions. Such performances may have seemed spontaneous and authentic, but in fact many Romantic actors, who were given little time for rehearsal, followed manuals of gesture and expression.

MELODRAMA

Though most poets refused to write plays for the stage, a second group of writers were only too willing to supply the theaters of Europe with the popular drama they needed. The most popular type of play during this period was melodrama, which suited the public's taste for spectacle, music, and easily digestible characters and plots. The term *melodrama* is taken from the French *melodrame*, which joins the Greek word for music (*melos*) to drama; it was first applied in the late eighteenth century to plays with musical interludes that employ an easily recognizable dramatic formula and unambiguous moral contrasts. Drawing on a set of stock characters—the villain, the hapless maiden in distress, and the hero—melodramatic plots involve extraordinary coincidences and hinge on sudden revelations and encounters. France was the birthplace of melodrama, and its king was René-Charles Guilbert de Pixérécourt (1773–1844). Another prominent author of melodrama was the Irish writer Dion Boucicault (1820?–1890). Boucicault not only wrote popular plays set in Ireland, such as *The Colleen Bawn* (1860), but after spending several years in the United States he set several notable plays there as well, including *The Octoroon; or, Life in Louisiana* (1859).

Both in England and in France, many melodramas were produced by adapting novels to the stage. It was a time when the novel experienced an unprecedented rise in status and appeal, and many of the era's most accomplished writers turned their hands to fiction. Prime candidates for adaptation were the immensely popular novels of Charles Dickens (1812–1870). In France, novels by Alexandre Dumas père (1802–1870) and his son, Alexandre Dumas fils (1824–1895), were adapted by the two authors themselves, among them the former's *The Three Musketeers* (1844) and *The Count of Monte Christo* (1845) and the latter's *La Dame aux camélias* (in English known as *Camille*; 1848), which also became the libretto for Giuseppe Verdi's opera *La Traviata* (1853). Because of Paris's dominant cultural position, nineteenth-century French melodramas were imported into many European countries and more distant lands.

THE WELL-MADE PLAY

Alongside melodrama, French playwrights perfected another, related form of drama, the so-called *well-made play* (a name borrowed from the French *pièce bien-fait*). The well-made play was based not on spectacle and music but on complicated, intricately constructed plots. Playwrights relied on well-known techniques such as overheard conversations, mistaken identities, sudden appearances and disappearances, and other forms of confusion that culminated in the main scene of the play—the confrontation of the main antagonists—followed by the final resolution. Because everything in a well-made play led up to such a scene, it was called *scène à faire*, the obligatory scene that "had to be done." Masters of the well-made play included Augustin-Eugène Scribe (1791–1861), who wrote more than 300 plays, and the even more popular Victorien Sardou (1831–1908), who composed several plays specifically for the greatest star of the French nineteenth-

Sarah Bernhardt in the title role of Victorien Sardou's *Theodora* (1884).

century stage, Sarah Bernhardt (1844–1923). Sardou so dominated the second half of the nineteenth century that GEORGE BERNARD SHAW (1856–1950), a radical reformer of the well-made play, referred to his drama as "sardoodledom." Like melodrama, the well-made play was an extremely popular export, imitated everywhere.

EUROPE AT MIDCENTURY

The ever-more-sophisticated spectacles, melodramas, and well-made plays were created in the context of Europe's larger economic and political developments. The Age of Revolution had come to a second climax with the Europe-wide revolution of 1848, during which the countries of Continental Europe suffered through protests, strikes, and overturned governments. The revolution of 1848 gave expression to the social consequences of rapid, though uneven, industrialization in various regions of Europe, including the large-scale movements of people to urban centers, the emergence of an industrial proletariat, and the triumph of a bourgeois class. What followed was a period of political reaction and a new focus on economic gains. It was a time when England and France in particular secured and expanded their empires, and from those holdings outside Europe they drew enormous resources. The financial speculation that attended such enterprises as the building of the railroads led a fortunate few to amass unheard-of fortunes, especially in the 1870s and 1880s. This new accumulation of wealth contributed to the development of extravagant and lavish spectacles, the expansion of theaters, and an emphasis on technical developments.

NATIONALISM AND THE THEATER

The nineteenth century was also the century of nationalism, as growing numbers of countries attempted to establish and affirm their own native traditions and values. Nationalists called for national theaters to showcase the new (or old) national self-consciousness, on the model of the Comédie Française, the foremost theater of France. Theatrically the most remarkable of those efforts was undertaken by

Richard Wagner (1813–1883) in Germany. Wagner sought to integrate dramatic literature, music, and acting, as well as all the other components of theater such as set design and lighting, into a new and complete synthesis—what he labeled the *Gesamtkunstwerk* (total work of art). Single-handedly, he wrote the libretti, composed the music, and influenced the staging of his operas, which he called music-dramas, at the opera house in Bayreuth newly built under his supervision, the Festspielhaus (Festival Theater). Because Wagner wanted to immerse his spectators in the power of theatrical illusion, he inaugurated what are today common theatrical methods such as dimming the light in the auditorium and hiding the orchestra to encourage the audience to focus exclusively on the stage. Though Wagner himself relied on Romantic plots and folktales, many later theater practitioners, such as the Swiss designer Adolphe Appia (1862–1928), took their inspiration from him as they attempted to create a new and modern theater.

THEATER IN THE UNITED STATES, 1800–1900

The quest for national identity was no less urgent in the United States, but it took a very different form. Theatrical activity in colonial America was recorded in the 1600s, and the first theater was built in Williamsburg, Virginia, in 1716. Even after the American Revolution was over and independence from England had been won, many economic and cultural ties between the newly formed United States of America and its former mother country remained in place. One particularly strong connection was their theaters. In the United States in the late eighteenth century, theatrical activity was largely restricted to the cities of Philadelphia, New York, Boston, and Charleston, South Carolina, and the small but growing number of resident professional companies was dominated by English-born actors and actors who had been trained in England. While the United States produced its own playwrights—including Mercy Otis Warren (1728–1814) and Royall Tyler (1757–1826)—English plays constituted most of

The Astor Place Riot, New York City, 1849.

the dramatic repertoire well into the nineteenth century.

During the nineteenth century, a new and genuinely American theater culture appeared, owing in no small part to the country's first native-born acting star. Edwin Forrest (1806–1872) established an American school of acting based on a heroic style that relied on grand, physical gestures and speech that appealed to popular audiences. While Forrest stayed in America, Charlotte Cushman (1816–1876), the first famous American actress, moved to England once she had become well known, proving that England still had greater cachet and rewards for an ambitious actor. In 1849 the relation between the United States and England, and more specifically the difference between the English and the more physical American acting schools, led to violence. In New York City, both Forrest and the visiting English actor William Charles Macready (1793–1873) were playing Macbeth. The two men were longtime rivals, and when thousands of followers of Forrest invaded the Astor Place Opera House to stop Macready's performance, with thousands more outside, the mayor called out the National Guard. Guardsmen fired into the crowd, and at least twenty-two died in what has become known as the Astor Place Riot.

STAGING RACE

While Americans were fighting for cultural independence, there emerged in the United States another type of theater not found in England or any other part of Europe: the minstrel show. Initially its players were white performers in blackface, their skins darkened with burnt cork or shoe polish, but African American minstrel troupes soon appeared as well. Musicians and singers would form a semicircle, and they would alternate between songs, dances, and short bits of dialogue, mostly between two characters—Tambo (a player of the tambourine) and Bones (a player of the bones, a clacking folk instrument made of bones or wood)—seated at either end of the semicircle, or between them and an interlocutor who sat in the middle. The minstrel show relied on racial stereotypes, for whether whites represented African Americans, as was most often the case, or African Americans made up the troupe, they had to conform to the stereotyped routines that were initially established by white performers and demanded by the predominantly white audiences. In this way, the minstrel show, America's most popular form of theatrical entertainment in the nineteenth century, was part of the fabric of American racism even as it established an American, and especially an African American, performance tradition.

America's most popular play of the nineteenth century also dealt with race relations. Harriet Beecher Stowe's (1811–1896) immensely influential novel *Uncle Tom's Cabin* (1851–52), which some have credited with having helped to start the U.S. Civil War (1861–65) through its moving depiction of the plight of slaves, inspired numerous dramatic adaptations; the most famous was an 1852 version by George L. Aiken (1830–1876), which had the longest run—more than 300 performances—of any single production in nineteenth-century America. Aiken's dramatization was largely faithful to Stowe's antislavery stance, but many other adaptations simply reverted to racial stereotypes. These adaptations, known as Tom shows, helped establish "Uncle Tom" as a derogatory label for African Americans who appeared to make their peace with slavery and suppression rather than rebelling against them. While minstrel shows and the dramatizations of *Uncle Tom's Cabin* played a central role in nineteenth-century American theater, other representations of black life or slavery rarely appeared onstage. As so often in the history of drama, dramatists at odds with popular taste had to write for a smaller reading public instead, as the African American writer and former slave WILLIAM WELLS BROWN (1814–1884) did with his play *THE ESCAPE; OR, A LEAP FOR FREEDOM* (1858).

Modern Theater, 1880–1945

THEATER AND THE MODERN WORLD

In the era of Romanticism, theatrical performance and dramatic literature had increasingly drifted apart. During the last two decades of the nineteenth century, however, serious writers were finally drawn to the theater once more. This did not mean that they sought to please the tastes of popular audiences. Indeed, modern drama was often characterized by a tension, even antagonism, between dramatists and audiences, an antagonism sometimes provoked by the playwrights themselves. Riling up audiences had been part of theater history for some time, as demonstrated by various nineteenth-century clashes in theaters, but now an adversarial relationship between producers and consumers became expected. The history of modern drama frequently involved confrontations between supporters of innovation and hostile audiences unprepared for new subjects, dramatic structures, and theatrical techniques. Whether by design or not, being controversial became the very condition for being modern.

Many modern dramatists earned their notoriety by engaging and often confronting audiences with challenging subjects and unusual forms. They wanted to restore theater's serious, moral function and to challenge, rather than please, their audience. To that end, they depicted the most vexing moral problems and dilemmas of their time. During the late nineteenth and early twentieth centuries, Europe and North America underwent a number of profound changes: new technologies, scientific advancement, urbanism, the proliferation of nationalist movements, changing class relationships, an accelerating economic transition from agriculture to industry, and new theories of human nature (including Marxism, Darwinism, and Freudianism).

Challenging the conventions and complacency of late nineteenth and early twentieth century society, modern playwrights addressed the impact of these and other changes. The Norwegian dramatist HENRIK IBSEN (1828–1906) depicted public hypocrisy, restrictive social conventions, and such taboo subjects as hereditary syphilis. His play *A DOLL HOUSE* (1879), which exposes the hypocrisies and inequalities of Victorian marriage, was denounced in newspapers, sermons, and books. GEORGE BERNARD SHAW (1856–1950), who championed his Norwegian contemporary in *The Quintessence of Ibsenism* (1891), wrote about prostitution and woman's emancipation in *Mrs. Warren's Profession* (1893) and expressed his idiosyncratic form of socialism in such plays as *Man and Superman* (1903). The German writer Gerhart Hauptmann (1862–1946) used his play *The Weavers* (1892) to call attention to the degrading conditions of weavers, while the Swedish playwright AUGUST STRINDBERG (1849–1912) depicted the ruthless battle between the sexes in *MISS JULIE* (1888). Even OSCAR WILDE (1854–1900), who delighted audiences with *THE IMPORTANCE OF BEING EARNEST* (1895) and

Eleonora Duse as Rebecca in the 1906 production of Ibsen's *Rosmersholm* at the National Theater of Christiana. Rebecca rejects not only the Christian religion but also the entire structure of Christian ethics.

other social comedies, violated conventional expectations with *Salomé* (1894), a play based on a sexually charged episode in the New Testament that describes the decapitation of St. John the Baptist. What united these playwrights was that all struggled with official censors; many of their plays could be presented only to small, private audiences because they were banned.

Though provocative themes and characters drew the most immediate hostile reaction, dramatists also deviated radically from the established rules governing dramatic forms. Many modernists criticized and ridiculed the most popular nineteenth-century dramas, such as melodramas and well-made plays. Ibsen and Shaw borrowed the conventions of the well-made play but interrupted its smooth, technically structured plots with lengthy dialogues, set speeches, and other devices that shifted dramatic attention from incidents to social and psychological issues. In such later plays as *The Dream Play* (1902) and *The Ghost Sonata* (1907), Strindberg abandoned dramatic rules for the logic of dreams. Seeking to capture the nuances of everyday life, ANTON CHEKHOV (1860–1904) rejected the stock characters and heightened dramatic incidents of the contemporary Russian theater for a drama of understatement, indirection, and psychological nuance. Traditional forms, when they were used, were adapted to new purposes, and new forms were developed to respond to a changing modern world.

THE INDEPENDENT THEATER MOVEMENT: NATURALISM

These modern playwrights could present their work to the public because of the opening of small, independent theaters intended to provide an alternative to the larger commercial theaters. Particularly important in this respect was André Antoine's (1858–1943) Théâtre Libre in Paris, which introduced the plays of Ibsen, among others. In London the Independent Theatre, founded by J. T. Grein (1862–1935), was devoted to the same task, and later Shaw and Harley Granville-Barker (1877–1946) would find a home at the Court Theatre. In Berlin it was the Freie Bühne of Otto Brahm (1856–1912) and in Moscow the Moscow Art Theater of Konstanin Stanislavsky (1863–1938) that made available performance venues for modern drama. All the theaters named above were associated with naturalism, a movement that originated in France in the 1860s and advocated that literature and art must faithfully present reality, with the writer and artist assuming the position of an objective scientist.

In its concern with the accurate portrayal of human beings and the external world, naturalism represented an extension of the realist movement that came to dominate European and North American art and literature during the middle of the nineteenth century and remains a powerful aesthetic current in today's theater. A reaction against the idealizing tendencies of Romanticism, realism seeks to depict contemporary life and society directly, unmediated by art's distorting conventions. The plays of Ibsen and Chekhov and the early plays of Shaw, which address social realities in recognizably contemporary settings, fall under this rubric. Naturalism differs from realism in that it relies on a more scientifically grounded understanding of the relation between individuals and their environment. Inspired by Charles Darwin (1809–1882) and his theory of natural selection, naturalists believed that humans are not free agents choosing their own destiny but rather are creatures determined by their environment, their physiology, and the social conditions under which they live. In the arts, the chief proponent of naturalism was Émile Zola (1840–1902), who influenced Antoine, Grein, Brahm, and other directors associated with naturalism in the theater. Dramatists who were strongly affected by naturalism include Strindberg and Hauptmann.

MODERN ACTING

Naturalism changed not only the nature of plays but also the modes of staging them. The movement led to an increased emphasis on realistic stage props and décor and a rejection of the histrionic acting practiced in the nineteenth-century commercial theater. The Russian actor and director Konstantin Stanislavsky, for example, pioneered a new acting system based on the actor's psychology and emotions. For performances of Ibsen, he even imported Norwegian furniture to help the actors merge with their roles. What Stanislavsky did for individual roles, George II, the duke of Saxe-Meiningen (1826–1914), did for groups, introducing new systems of ensemble acting and bringing vivid crowds to the stage. Modern plays, with their new and daring female roles, also made it possible for a new generation of female stars to emerge and contribute to a truly modern acting style. Among them were Eleonora Duse (1958–1924) in Italy, Elizabeth Robins (1862–1952) in England, and Eva Le Gallienne (1899–1991) in the United States. In developing their signature roles, many of these actresses chose characters from Ibsen's plays.

AESTHETICISM AND SYMBOLISM

Naturalism was not the only movement that sought to break with the conventions of nineteenth-century theater. Indeed, the rapidity with which such movements followed one another, and their strenuous and public efforts to present a distinctive rationale for artistic innovation, became a distinctive feature of modernism. Aestheticism, which advocated the primacy of beauty over values such as social or political utility, was particularly associated with Oscar Wilde (although Wilde himself was well aware of the importance of societal forces; he expressed a commitment to socialism and suffered prosecution as a homosexual). Symbolism focused on rarified meanings, subjectivity, and suggestion rather than common idioms or everyday speech. Symbolist playwrights

A set-design sketch by Adolphe Appia, ca. 1910. Note the abstract pattern of lines and angles.

included Maurice Maeterlinck (Belgium, 1862– 1949), Madame Rachilde (France, 1860–1953), William Butler Yeats (Ireland, 1865–1939), and Aleksandr Blok (Russia, 1880–1921). Symbolism also entailed a return to exalted and poetic speeches and a preference for simple, symbolic designs over the cluttered stage sets of naturalism. Symbolist design was championed especially in Paris, in Aurélien Lugné-Poe's (1869–1940) Théâtre de l'Œuvre. In England, the abstract sets of Edward Gordon Craig (1872–1966) had many affinities with symbolism, as did the monumental and abstract designs of Adolphe Appia (1862–1928).

THEATER AND THE AVANT-GARDE

The battles between different movements became more pronounced and complicated in the first decades of the twentieth century. A host of "isms," often announced through manifestos and declarations, emerged virtually overnight, and many disappeared as quickly. Among those that made a mark was expressionism, which arose in Germany at the start of the century. Expressionists, who advocated the externalization of psychic states instead of the realistic representation of life, critiqued the dehumanizing forces of industrialization in distorted, often nightmarish form. Prominent expressionistic dramatists included Georg Kaiser (1878–1945), Oskar Kokoshka (1886–1980), and Ernst Toller (1893–1939). These and other writers championed technological advances that supported their artistry, especially in scenic design and stage lighting, as well as through the expanding medium of cinema. *The Cabinet of Dr. Caligari* (1920) was an especially influential expressionistic film. In the late 1910s and 1920s, expressionism also had an influence on such American playwrights as EUGENE O'NEILL (1888–1953),

A photograph of the original 1935 production of Antonin Artaud's *Les Cenci*. Based on an Italian story of incest, torture, and patricide, the play embodies the Theater of Cruelty that Artaud espoused in *The Theater and Its Double*. Artaud, in the role of Count Cenci, stands in front.

SUSAN GLASPELL (1876–1948), and SOPHIE TREADWELL (1885–1970).

A very different movement was futurism, which was initiated by F. T. Marinetti (1876–1944) and flourished largely in Italy and Russia. Inspired by an enthusiasm for technology and machines—the products of a belated but rapid industrialization in northern Italy—Marinetti sought to banish the human actor from the theater, relying instead on puppets, machines, and other inanimate objects. He also rejected well-structured plays in favor of short episodes of discontinuous actions and effects. Futurism was followed by Dadaism, which pushed the anarchic provocations of the futurists to an extreme. In the Cabaret Voltaire, which flourished in Zurich during World War I (1914–18), Tristan Tzara (1896–1963) and other Dadaists presented nonsense poems, manifestos, musical pieces, and masked performances of various kinds, often simultaneously. Like futurism, Dadaism quickly became an international movement with followers in the major European cities and beyond. When Dadaism declined in Paris in the early twenties, many of its adherents joined the movement of surrealism, which was led by André Breton (1896–1966). Influenced by the psychoanalytic theory of Sigmund Freud (1865–1939), surrealism focused on spontaneous associations, drifting thoughts, and dream images. The surrealists were also interested in earlier writers who shared their concerns, including the provocateur ALFRED JARRY (1873–1907), who had written crude and funny plays violating almost all strictures of decency and proper form. His scatological, grotesque, and irreverent play *UBU THE KING* (1896) became an icon of the surrealist movement. The most influential theater maker associated with surrealism (even though he left the movement after a quarrel with Breton) was Antonin Artaud (1896–1948), who, under the name Theater of Cruelty, advocated a primal, physical theater inspired not just by ancient rituals but also by the slapstick comedy of the Marx Brothers. Artaud's writings on theater, which were published in 1938 under the title *The Theater and Its Double*, drew on images such as the plague, primitive myths, and the "animated hieroglyphics" of Balinese theater to establish theater as an antidote to the decadence of modern life.

The increasingly strident movements of the early twentieth century are often grouped together under the classification *avant-garde*. Originally a military term used to designate the advance corps of an army, in the early nineteenth century *avant-garde* became a political label applied to radical and advanced groups seeking social change. It was only in the second half of the nineteenth century that the notion of the avant-garde infiltrated the arts, allowing artists of various movements to present themselves as ahead of everyone else. Yet because the avant-garde groups maintained ties to their political roots, their formation must be understood in the context of the political history of the early twentieth century, and they often strongly promoted socialism, anarchism, or, as in the case of the Italian futurists, fascism. Indeed, the Futurists were extreme Italian nationalists, advocating war as an end in itself as well as a form of self-aggrandizement. The Dadaists, by contrast, formed in opposition to World War I and came to embrace an international socialism as a way to destroy the old class-based societies. They shared that aim with surrealists, many of whom joined various communist parties. Even more closely linked to socialism were the Russian futurists, who participated in the Russian October Revolution of 1917 and strove through artistic means to help it succeed.

POLITICAL THEATER: BRECHT

Socialism had an immense effect on many artists and thinkers of the first half of the twentieth century and later, including those not associated with the more extreme avant-garde movements. The most influential political playwright was BERTOLT BRECHT (1898–1956), who developed a new form of drama and performance called Epic Theater, which relied on a number of techniques meant to interrupt the flow of plot and acting. Brecht believed that such interruptions would ensure that audiences actively ponder, rather than passively consume, the theatrical spectacle. He had also learned from the director Erwin Piscator (1893–1966) the value of bringing many art forms, including film (still relatively new at the time), into the theater, and he collaborated with composers such as Kurt Weill (1900–1950) on new, presentational forms

A scene from the original 1928 production of *The Threepenny Opera*, a collaboration between the composer Kurt Weill and Bertolt Brecht.

of opera and other forms of musical theater. Brecht, Piscator, and Weill, together with many other European writers and theater makers, fled to the United States during the Nazi era and exerted considerable influence on theater and music there. Besides these émigrés, the best-known political writer in the United States was Clifford Odets (1906–1963), whose plays depicted the plight of working-class families and often included rousing calls for a socialist society.

CULTURAL RENEWAL: IRELAND AND THE UNITED STATES

Not all theaters in the early twentieth century were dominated by avant-garde and socialist plays. The Abbey Theatre (1904) in Dublin, for example, was devoted to gaining the cultural independence of Ireland, which for centuries had been under England's control; it thus followed the nineteenth-century movement for national theaters in European countries other than those—England, France, Spain, and Italy—that had traditionally dominated theater. One of its founding members, Lady Augusta Gregory (1852–1932), advocated a return to the Irish language, which had long been marginalized by English colonizers and settlers. The playwrights associated with the theater took varied approaches to drama. While Ireland's leading poet William Butler Yeats composed dense, difficult plays filled with highly poetic language and mostly set in a mythical past, JOHN MILLINGTON SYNGE (1871–1909) wrote in a more colloquial, highly lyrical idiom. His plays, which undercut romanticized views of the Irish peasantry, proved controversial with the theatergoing Dublin public; so jarring was his presentation of rural Ireland in *The Playboy of the Western World* (1907) that it sparked theatrical riots and a long dispute that threatened the existence of the Abbey Theatre and the Irish Theatre Movement of which it was part.

Cultural independence was also the purpose of the Provincetown Players in the United States, a small theater troupe devoted to presenting new and challenging plays by American playwrights such as Susan Glaspell and Eugene O'Neill. Founded in Cape Cod and then moved to

A photograph of the Provincetown Players' original production of Eugene O'Neill's *All God's Chill'un Got Wings* (1924). Paul Robeson, seated, played the lead role.

New York City, the company was part of the so-called Little Theatre Movement of the 1910s and 1920s in the United States. This movement, which was inspired by Europe's alternative theater movement of the late nineteenth century, provided the space for staging new and experimental plays without the financial constraints of the commercial theater, which by the late nineteenth century was dominated by New York's Broadway theaters and by touring productions of successful shows that took star performers to theaters in an extensive network across the United States. Some modern playwrights, such as O'Neill, both participated in the Little Theatre Movement and managed to have their plays performed on Broadway, where the largest and most elegant commercial theaters were located. Broadway still retains its unique status, as demonstrated by the distinction drawn today between Broadway, off-Broadway, and even off-off-Broadway theaters.

TRAGEDY, METATRAGEDY, METATHEATER

While the era of modern drama saw an unprecedented explosion of new forms of drama and theater, a number of playwrights also sought to return to one of the oldest dramatic forms: tragedy. In the eyes of Ibsen, the bourgeois family and its struggle against the overwhelming power of the past created the conditions for modern tragedy to take place. A similar view led Eugene O'Neill to adapt Greek tragedies to contemporary America, as in *Mourning Becomes Electra* (1931), and to write new tragedies based on his own family, as in LONG DAY'S JOURNEY INTO NIGHT (written 1941; produced 1956). Other playwrights in the United States followed his lead: such dramatists as TENNESSEE WILLIAMS (1911–1983), ARTHUR MILLER (1915–2005), SAM SHEPARD (b. 1943), DAVID MAMET (b. 1947), and EDWARD ALBEE (b. 1928) have all explored the intersection of the tragic and the everyday in American life, as characters grapple with the economic, social, and personal challenges of their modern world. Another set of playwrights turned to remote, rural settings in search for appropriate material for modern tragedies. The Spaniard FEDERICO GARCÍA LORCA (1898–1936), for example, set such tragedies as THE HOUSE OF BERNARDA ALBA (1936) in Andalusia, and Synge turned to the remote western coast of Ireland for RIDERS TO THE SEA (1904), a play that was later adapted by the Caribbean writer DEREK WALCOTT (b. 1930) in THE SEA AT DAUPHIN (1957).

A second group of modern playwrights were also drawn to tragedy but did not believe that it was suitable for the modern world. Instead, they wrote plays *about* tragedy—what they called metatragedy or *metatheater*—that focused on the nature of role-playing and the relationship between reality and theatrical illusion. The best-known writer of metatragedies was the Italian LUIGI PIRANDELLO (1867–1936), whose plays— such as the influential SIX CHARACTERS IN SEARCH OF AN AUTHOR (1921)—are mirrored cabinets in which characters adopt roles, pretend to be mad, or philosophize, in self-referential ways, about the nature of theater itself. Another prominent writer of metatragedies was the French JEAN GENET (1910–1986). Originally a novelist, Genet turned to the theater because of his fascination with costumes and role-playing, and his plays create intricate layers of pretense that are never entirely peeled back. The turn to metatheater proved influential throughout modern and contemporary drama— nontragic as well as tragic—and a self-conscious awareness of theatrical reality is an important part of the twentieth- and early twenty-first-century stage.

WAR, REVOLUTION, AND DEPRESSION: 1900–1945

The explosion of forms, the emergence of politically driven avant-gardes, the return to tragedy, and the rise of metatheater were all responses to the unprecedented turmoil of the first half of the twentieth century in Europe and elsewhere. Nineteenth-century industrialization had effected profound changes in how people lived and worked, leading scores of men and women who formerly had labored in agriculture or trades to join the urban proletariat. The revolutions and wars of the first half of the twentieth century were fueled by these changes. Social unrest was everywhere, even in the relatively stable United States, and the Russian Revolution of 1917 was only one of its most striking manifestations. The unforeseen horrors of World War I, in which the European nations brought on themselves incalculable loss of life, showed once and for all the destructive potential of advances in technology and industrialization. European self-confidence, as well as the belief in progress and the upward course of civilization more generally, was dashed. Peace brought only short-lived relief, as the worldwide stock market crash of 1929 and the depression that followed it threw the global economy into a crisis—one that, unlike the war, affected the United States as much as it did Europe. Faced with the Great Depression, President Franklin Delano Roosevelt (1882–1945) undertook, as part of his New Deal, an ambitious public works program, which included unprecedented sponsorship of the theater. During its brief existence (1935–39), the Federal Theatre Project rejuvenated theatrical activity across the country and pioneered such innovative forms as the "living

Figures silhouetted by the U.S. Constitution in a production of *Triple-A Plowed Under* sponsored by the Federal Theatre Project during the 1930s. This play, one of the earliest and best-known of the "living newspapers," addressed the plight of American farmers during the Depression.

newspaper," which addressed social and political issues in innovative, multimedia productions. Other changes affected the theater arts as well. Economic turmoil and racism in the South encouraged the great migration of African Americans to northern cities, which helped make New York's Harlem a cultural center for the arts in the 1910s and 1920s. African American musicians and jazz flourished, and so did such writers, intellectuals, and playwrights of the Harlem Renaissance as Zora Neale Hurston (1891–1960) and LANGSTON HUGHES (1902–1967).

In Europe of the twenties and thirties, fascism and Nazism were on the rise, and soon England and the Continent, the United States, and the world as a whole would be plunged into another and even bloodier war. The cataclysm of World War II (1939–45) brought to a close the era of modern drama that began with Ibsen and other groundbreaking figures of the later nineteenth century, and it cleared the way for new movements and playwrights who would explore the emerging outlines of the contemporary world. The period 1880–1945—which opened with Thomas Edison's first public demonstration of the

incandescent lightbulb on December 31, 1879, and ended with the atomic bombing of Hiroshima and Nagasaki in August 1945—was a time of profound and unsettling changes that inevitably affected playwrights. They participated in the political, ideological, and social movements and changes around them, contributing with their plays and performances to urgent debates, problems, and opportunities. They responded to these unsettling times in their stark and jagged plays, in which all the old forms, structures, and certainties seemed to have fallen apart. In the process, they gave rise to the most innovative and influential era of theatermaking since the Renaissance. The varied forms of dramatic art that they introduced would influence the shape of theater for generations.

Postwar Theater, 1945–1970

THE POSTWAR WORLD

In political, social, and cultural terms, the latter half of the twentieth century was shaped by the second of two global wars and by the geopolitical changes that followed in its wake. World War II, which was fought between the Axis powers (Germany, Italy, Japan) and the Allies (Britain, France, the Soviet Union, the United States, and China), claimed 60 million military and civilian lives, including 11 million who died in German-controlled concentration camps (6 million of them Jews killed in the Holocaust) and as many as 200,000 who died as a result of the atomic bombs that the United States dropped on the Japanese cities of Hiroshima and Nagasaki. With much of Europe and parts of Asia devastated by warfare, the United States emerged from World War II as the world's dominant military, industrial, and economic power, though its unilateral supremacy proved to be short-lived. The Soviet Union, which successfully tested its own atomic bomb in 1949, established its influence over the countries of Eastern Europe, while the revolution led by Mao Zedong (1893–1976) ended with a communist government ruling mainland China. By 1950 the international landscape had been redrawn between two competing economic and ideological blocs—a capitalist "West" and a communist "East"—and the cold war that would dominate the world for the next forty years was well under way. Although the United States and the Soviet Union avoided direct military confrontation during this period, their struggle for ideological supremacy played itself out in a series of regional wars—notably in Korea, Vietnam, and Afghanistan—and in the internal politics of countries throughout Asia, Africa, and Latin America. They competed as well in the fields of science, technology, culture, and sports. No symbol was more resonant of this bipolar world than the city of Berlin, which was divided into western and eastern sectors by the Berlin Wall, a literal version of the "Iron Curtain" that divided not just Germany but Europe as a whole.

The 1950s inaugurated a period of prosperity for North America, Western Europe, and Japan, and the middle class established itself more firmly as the arbiter of social values. After years of wartime austerity, many in the West began to enjoy the benefits of a thriving consumer-oriented economy that catered to domestic households and an emergent youth subculture. On the surface, the 1950s was a decade of materialism and conformity, a period during which social stability was reinforced—particularly in the United States, where a new "Red Scare," like the one that had followed the Russian Revolution, inflamed anticommunist sentiment in the late 1940s and early 1950s—by the fears of enemy infiltration and nuclear war. Yet many of the social problems that would erupt in the following decade were already visible. The civil rights movement on behalf of African Americans took definitive shape in the United States in the mid-1950s, and London was the site of clashes between white youths and West Indian immigrants in the Notting Hill race riots of 1958. In 1954 France became involved in a war in Algeria that ended eight years later with the independence of its oldest major colony. Decolonization was under way around the globe, as the former holdings of European empires became newly independent countries in what was soon being called the Third World. Even in those nations under Soviet control—the Warsaw Pact countries of Eastern Europe—there were disturbances, as citizens in client states sought more autonomy. In 1956 the Soviet Union brutally suppressed the Hungarian Revolution, as it would Czechoslovakia's "Prague Spring" in 1968.

Driven by these and other impulses for change, an increasing number of challenges arose in the 1960s to the social consensus that had largely prevailed in the United States and Western Europe since the end of World War II. A growing number of intellectuals and activists condemned the inequalities of Western capitalism from the points of view of Marxism/socialism and anarchism, and to their social critique were added the voices of radical trade unionists, an emerging youth subculture, Black Power advocates in the United States, and members of such issue-specific movements as the Campaign for Nuclear Disarmament in Britain and the international protests against the United States' war in Vietnam (1961–73). These movements came to a head in Paris in May 1968, when an escalating series of strikes by students and workers brought France to a standstill and nearly toppled the government of Charles de Gaulle (1890–1970). Similar uprisings took place elsewhere, and it seemed—for the moment, at least—as if capitalism itself was under siege.

POSTWAR THEATER: EXPANSION, CONTINUITY, AND INNOVATION

During the years 1945–70 theater and drama underwent their own changes, many of which intensified trends that had emerged earlier in the century—while others signaled important new directions for the late-twentieth-century stage. Even as London, Paris, Berlin, Moscow, New York, Toronto, and other major cities continued to serve and grow as important theatrical centers, more theaters were built and more residential theater companies formed outside these cities. Regional and provincial theaters were established, a number of annual theatrical festivals—such as those in Avignon, France; Edinburgh, Scotland; and Stratford, Ontario—were founded and expanded, and smaller theaters were opened in cities to provide opportunities for productions that the larger commercial theaters were unwilling or unable to undertake. The period also saw the founding of a number of state-sponsored theaters and theater companies, such as London's National Theatre, which was established in 1963. Like other new theaters and companies, these venues opened the way for new kinds of techniques, performance aesthetics outside the mainstream, and unconventional dramatic texts.

Though new theatrical theorists emerged, much of the innovation of these years reflected the influence of two earlier writers: BERTOLT BRECHT and Antonin Artaud. Brecht's Epic Theater—specifically, its presentational devices and acting style, as well as its view of theater as a medium for social analysis and intervention—maintained a powerful hold on European political theater, while Artaud's conception of a total theater that would surround its audience and address it on a visceral level had a profound impact on the environmental theater movements of the 1960s and the pioneering work of the Polish director Jerzy Grotowski (1933–1999). Both of these traditions helped the theater of the mid-

twentieth century to meet one of its greatest challenges: rediscovering its performative uniqueness during an age when competition from film, radio, and television was increasing.

POSTWAR FRENCH THEATER: ABSURDISM

The psychological and social impact of World War II on midcentury drama was felt most immediately in France, where the absurdists established themselves as one of the most important groups of postwar dramatists. The term *absurdism* was not coined until 1961, when the critic and scholar Martin Esslin (1918–2002) published his influential study *The Theater of the Absurd*, and the dramatists who were included under this label are as notable for their differences as for their similarities. But the word does underscore a shared rejection of conventional dramatic structures and a skepticism toward rationality, language, and the coherent subject of traditional philosophy and drama. As they confronted a universe apparently bereft of meaning, divine or otherwise, they echoed the assumptions of Jean-Paul Sartre (1905–1980), Albert Camus (1913–1960), and other proponents of philosophical existentialism, while the dramatic features that defined their plays—nonlinearity, antirealism, lack of traditional coherence, nonsensical language, metadramatic awareness, and the mixture of tragedy, comedy, and farce in a modern form of tragicomedy—owed much to the experiments of Dada, surrealism, and other avant-garde movements earlier in the century. Eugène Ionesco (1909–1994) and JEAN GENET (1910–1986) are among the most prominent of the playwrights whose works show the influence of absurdism, though no figure in this tradition had a greater impact on the drama that followed than the Irish-born playwright SAMUEL BECKETT (1906–1989), whose play *WAITING FOR GODOT* (1952)—first performed in Paris in 1953—changed the landscape of postwar theater. Although it originated in France, absurdism exerted a pronounced influence on international drama during the 1950s and 1960s. Its challenge to arbitrary forms of order lent

In Eugène Ionesco's *The Bald Soprano*, a classic example of Theater of the Absurd, characters engage in nonsensical banter that calls into question the nature of communication in modern society. Pictured here is the 1950 production at the Théâtre Noctambules in Paris, directed by Nicolas Bataille.

itself to social and political critique in the hands of Eastern European dissidents such as the Czech playwright Václav Havel (1936–2011) and dramatists living under repressive regimes throughout the Third World.

POSTWAR GERMAN THEATER: THE BRECHTIAN LEGACY

Postwar drama followed a different trajectory in Germany and the other German-speaking countries of central Europe. Most of Germany's theaters had been destroyed during the war, and the governments of both West Germany and East Germany embarked on major efforts to rebuild their countries' cultural infrastructure. The drama that was written for these theaters in the 1950s dealt mainly with social and political issues, and the subjects of guilt and responsibility loomed particularly large for a people confronting their collective role in World War II. Aiding the development of political theater were Bertolt Brecht's return to East Germany after his self-imposed exile during the Nazi period and the founding of the

Berliner Ensemble in 1949 by Brecht and his wife, the actress Helene Weigel (1900–1971). The Berliner Ensemble put Brecht's theories of rehearsal and production into practice and in performing to audiences at home and abroad established Brecht's plays and the "Brechtian style" as major forces in the contemporary theater. In the German-speaking theater Brecht's influence was manifest in the drama of a new generation of playwrights, many of whom adopted the Brechtian focus on social and political issues and employed Brechtian techniques, though usually without the doctrinaire and, at times, utopian Marxism that often shaped Brecht's plays. The Swiss playwright Friedrich Dürrenmatt (1921–1990) made Brechtian and absurdist techniques part of his pessimistic dramatic vision of humanity in the postwar world, while the German playwright Peter Weiss (1916–1982) brought elements of Artaud's Theater of Cruelty to a Brechtian concern with history. Weiss's dramas of the mid- and late 1960s—such as *The Investigation* (1965), which examines the Holocaust through the theatrical re-creation of war crimes testimony—were written in the style of documentary theater, a genre that other dramatists embraced during the decade.

POSTWAR BRITISH THEATER: THE WELFARE STATE AND ITS DISCONTENTS

In the ten years immediately following the war, the theater in Britain gave little evidence of the important role it would play in the history of contemporary drama. The country itself was undergoing historic changes: in 1945 Clement Attlee's (1883–1967) Labour Party achieved a landslide victory over the incumbent prime minister and wartime hero Winston Churchill (1874–1965), and the following six years saw the establishment of the British welfare state. One sign of the increasing role of government in society was the creation of the Arts Council of Great Britain, an independent, government-funded body that—for the first time in Britain—provided state subsidies for the arts. But these changes in society left little mark on the London theater, which for the most part was sustaining itself on an uninspiring diet of West End productions. Two events caused a seismic shift. In 1955 Beckett's *Waiting for Godot* was given its London premiere, and in the following year *Look Back in Anger*, by the playwright John Osborne (1929–1994), electrified the theater world; it was produced by the London Stage Company, a noncommercial company specifically formed to support new playwrights. Osborne's play expressed the restlessness and anger of a generation at odds with the materialism and oppressive class structure of Britain in the mid-1950s, and it reflected the disillusionment permeating an imperial power in the twilight of its ascendancy. Along with the work of the Theatre Workshop—a company in a working-class area in East London that, under the leadership of Joan Littlewood (1914–2002), produced plays by such working-class playwrights as Shelagh Delaney (1939–2011)—*Look Back in Anger* opened the door for a new generation of dramatists grappling with social class and other issues central to British national identity.

The subsequent development of social and political theater in Britain was influenced by Brecht's theories and practices; indeed, over the next two decades Brechtian dramaturgy and stagecraft found their widest application outside Germany in British theater. The Berliner Ensemble visited London in 1956 (the year of Brecht's death) and 1965, and its epic style influenced a number of left-wing directors, designers, and play-

Jimmy Porter (played by Kenneth Haigh) plays his trumpet to distract himself from his cramped quarters and the complacency of postwar Britain in the original 1956 Royal Court production of John Osborne's *Look Back in Anger*.

wrights. John Arden (1930–2012) and Edward Bond (b. 1934) belong to the first generation of British dramatists who employed the strategies and techniques of Brechtian theater to strikingly original ends. The Brechtian turn in British drama received greater impetus in the aftermath of 1968, when a new generation of socialist playwrights—inspired by the revolutionary events in Paris and elsewhere and aided by the abolition of government censorship, which had been in effect since the Theatrical Licensing Act of 1737—made Brechtian devices a cornerstone of their more radical political drama. John McGrath (1935–2002), Howard Brenton (b. 1942), and David Hare (b. 1947) are only a few of the many dramatists who drew on Brecht in the 1970s and early 1980s. Among the women playwrights who sought to adapt Brecht within the politics of an emerging feminist movement, CARYL CHURCHILL (b. 1938)—whose plays range with deliberate abandon through space and time in treating their historical and contemporary subjects—is the most accomplished and widely known. This intensification of political playwriting after the events of 1968 was matched by a proliferation of radical (or "fringe") theater groups throughout Britain and Northern Ireland.

PINTER, STOPPARD, ORTON

Other playwrights and dramatic currents helped define postwar British theater. The influence of Samuel Beckett was apparent in the drama of HAROLD PINTER (1930–2008) and Tom Stoppard (b. 1937), two of the country's leading contemporary playwrights. Pinter combined the indeterminacy and linguistic evasions of Beckettian drama with the often gritty realism of interactions within the lower, middle, and upper strata of Britain's class-based society. Stoppard, who was born in Czechoslovakia, drew on Beckett in a technically virtuoso, philosophically sophisticated drama that also has more than a passing kinship to GEORGE BERNARD SHAW's "drama of ideas." Joining Stoppard in reworking the English comic tradition was Joe Orton (1933–1967), whose plays of the mid-1960s exploited the farcical, the macabre, and the surface gentility of English drawing-room comedy within an anarchic drama of sexual desire pursued across boundaries of gender, sexual identity, and class.

POSTWAR AMERICAN THEATER: EXPRESSIVE REALISM, METHOD ACTING

Theater in the United States achieved one of its greatest flowerings in the years immediately following World War II. While Europe found it necessary to revive—and in many cases, rebuild—its theatrical institutions, the Broadway theaters that represented the center of theatrical life in the United States had been left relatively untouched by the war. But with few exceptions—the plays of Thornton Wilder (1897–1975), for instance—this theater had produced little of substance since the mid-1930s. The rebirth of American theater that followed the end of the war resulted from the collaboration between a group of visionary theatrical practitioners and two emerging dramatists—TENNESSEE WILLIAMS (1911–1983) and ARTHUR MILLER (1915–2005)—whose innovative dramaturgy was put to work in plays that captured the aspirations and

Director Elia Kazan and playwright Arthur Miller sitting on Jo Mielziner's set for the 1949 Broadway production of *Death of a Salesman*.

anxieties of postwar America. The designer Jo Mielziner (1901–1976) pioneered an expressive or "subjective" stage realism that presented the theatrical categories of present and past, here and there, exterior and interior with poetic fluidity. Using the stage designs of Mielziner and under the direction of Elia Kazan (1909–2003), such plays as Williams's *A STREETCAR NAMED DESIRE* (1947) and Miller's *DEATH OF A SALESMAN* (1949) explored the shifting landscapes of memory and desire on a stage where the external world was at once materially real and evanescent. Such plays created a need for performers to convey greater psychological complexity, and it was met by contemporary developments in American acting. Continuing the interest in Konstantin Stanislavsky's psychological approach to acting that had marked the work of the Group Theater in the 1930s, the Actors Studio (founded in 1947 by members of the earlier company) promoted method acting, a performance style that emphasized psychological motivation, intention, and the importance of subtext in the presentation of dramatic characters. This approach, perhaps most famously realized in the theatrical and film performances of Marlon Brando (1924–2004), dominated American acting through the 1950s.

OFF-BROADWAY AND OFF-OFF-BROADWAY THEATER

Even as Broadway played a central role in presenting a revitalized American drama, its historically dominant role in American theater was challenged during the postwar years. In an attempt to diversify and expand theatrical activity outside the city of New York, a number of regional theaters were formed with resident companies presenting an annual season of plays. Among the most prominent of these are the Alley Theatre (Houston, 1947), the Arena Stage (Washington, 1950), and the Guthrie Theater (Minneapolis, 1963). Within New York, the increasing conservatism of Broadway theaters in the face of rising production costs led to the opening of off-Broadway theaters. Like the Little Theater Movement of the 1910s, off-Broadway theater involved smaller buildings that often were some distance from the main commercial theater district, and because these spaces served smaller audiences—between 100 and 499 spectators—they could be used to produce plays that the larger

Playwright Luis Valdez, right, founder of El Teatro Campesino, with the United Farm Workers president, Cesar Chavez, in front of New York's Winter Garden Theater in 1979. *Zoot Suit*, by Valdez, was the first Chicano play to be performed on Broadway.

Broadway houses found too risky. European writers such as Beckett and Ionesco saw the first New York productions of their plays in off-Broadway theaters, as did a number of new American playwrights, including EDWARD ALBEE (b. 1928). Off-Broadway also played a significant role in the careers of more established American playwrights. The 1956 production of *The Iceman Cometh* by Circle in the Square, one of the decade's most important off-Broadway theaters, revived interest in the plays of EUGENE O'NEILL (1888–1953) and thus helped lead to the Broadway premiere of *LONG DAY'S JOURNEY INTO NIGHT* that same year.

But by the end of the 1950s, off-Broadway theaters were themselves dealing with rising costs; they therefore became more reluctant to gamble on experimental plays or on unproven writers and increasingly reliant on productions whose commercial success seemed guaranteed. In response, off-off-Broadway theaters were founded throughout New York. These low-budget theaters—which were located in coffeehouses, church buildings, various basements, and wherever else space was available—provided opportunities for a generation of younger dramatists with strong antiestablishment leanings and experimental creative interests. During the 1960s—in Caffe Cino (1958), La MaMa Experimental Theatre Club (1961), Judson Poets' Theater (1961), and elsewhere—they launched the careers of such prominent contemporary playwrights as MARIA IRENE FORNES (b. 1930) and SAM SHEPARD (b. 1943). The often radical plays produced in these venues took part in the experimentation more broadly under way in 1960s American theater. For example, under the leadership of Joseph Chaikin (1935–2003), the Open Theater rejected the psychological realism of method acting for a form of acting rooted in improvisation, role-playing, and transformation. Communal theater groups, such as the Living Theater (which had been founded as an off-Broadway company in 1947), explored a radically participatory theater in which the division between performer and audience became almost imperceptible. Other theater groups—the Free Southern Theater, the Bread and Puppet Theater, and El Teatro Campesino, to name a few—used agitprop techniques, puppetry, and populist theater traditions to engage with social issues such as civil rights, the conditions of migrant farmworkers, and the Vietnam War.

AFRICAN AMERICAN THEATER

The years 1945–70 also saw the rise of contemporary African American drama. Drama and theater, of course, had played a central role in the Harlem Renaissance during the 1920s and 1930s, most notably in the plays of LANGSTON HUGHES (1902–1967), and the government-funded Federal Theatre Project of the 1930s had provided work for African American theater professionals through the "Negro units" that were established in New York and other cities. But it was not until Lorraine Hansberry's (1930–1965) play *A Raisin in the Sun*, which had an acclaimed run on Broadway in 1959, that serious African American drama claimed the attention of mainstream audiences. A product of the 1950s civil rights movement, the play also anticipated the more radical political and cultural movements of the decade that followed. African American theater of the 1960s reflected a deepening militancy; the plays of Amiri Baraka (b. 1934), for instance, reveal the author's growing separatism and revolutionary convictions, while the Black Arts Repertory Theatre (1965) that Baraka helped establish in Harlem was at the forefront of the militant Black Arts Movement. These and other dramatists of the 1950s and 1960s laid the groundwork for such later African American playwrights as Ntozake Shange (b. 1948), AUGUST WILSON (1945–2005), and SUZAN-LORI PARKS (b. 1964).

Contemporary Theater
THE CONTEMPORARY WORLD

The term *contemporary,* always imprecise, is particularly elusive when applied to today's historical moment. In a world of accelerated change—where international events, technological developments, and cultural trends follow each other with dizzying speed—the past of even a few years ago can seem like another age. Much has transpired during the period from the end of the 1960s through the first decade of the twenty-first century, and these years could be subdivided into smaller segments, each with its defining issues and preoccupations. Over the time since 1970, a world has emerged markedly different from that of the postwar years, and the overall trends and transformations of those decades have led to a present whose outlines we are still coming to understand.

In the past forty years a number of pivotal events have remapped the international geopolitical landscape, and two have been particularly important in their immediate and long-range consequences. As the result of intensifying pressure from the outside and the weaknesses of their own economic and social systems, which were unable to adapt to a changing global economy, the Soviet Union and its satellite states rejected communism in favor of Western-style capitalist economies in the years 1989–91, thereby bringing an end to the cold war that had defined international relations since the end of World War II. The fall of the Berlin Wall in November 1989 was the most visual symbol of this rapid change that took the form of peaceful and violent revolutions throughout the former Eastern Bloc, the unification of Germany, the dissolution of the Soviet Union in 1991, and the wars among the newly independent states of the former Yugoslavia. The second major shift was the rise of Islamist militancy as a social and political force. Islamic fundamentalists in Iran overthrew the monarchy of the shahs in 1979, replacing it with a revolutionary Islamic republic; in the 1980s, foreign volunteers joined an Afghan national resistance movement in what they viewed as a fight for Islam and drove the Soviet Union out of Afghanistan (1979–89). Such successes helped foster the growth of organized terrorist organizations, leading to the attacks on the World Trade Center and the Pentagon on September 11, 2001, and the subsequent wars in Afghanistan and Iraq.

THEATER AND GLOBALIZATION

Even more important in shaping the contemporary world than these geopolitical and ideological changes have been developments in the transnational spheres of capital and finance, corporate organization, information, communications, and culture. The world's economy has become

The 1987 production at the Theatre des Bouffes du Nord of *Mahabharata*, directed by Peter Brook.

literally global: the flow of goods, services, money, and information is increasingly unfettered, as traders move currencies and corporations reconfigure labor forces, production networks, management operations, and marketing strategies without respect to national borders. This process of globalization has been supported by innovations in information and communications technology—most notably, personal and network computing, cellular and electronic communications, and the rapid expansion of the Internet, which has made possible unprecedented access to information. Culture and the arts also show the effects of the global economy, as the products of high, popular, and mass (or commercial) culture reflect an ever-richer dialogue between the local and global. American teenagers read graphic novels that borrow from the latest in Japanese anime, while fans in Asia, Europe, and South America follow the steadily internationalizing game of American basketball. Music and other cultural products circulate between societies, and these encounters generate hybrid forms that draw on and transform both national and more localized styles and traditions.

Not surprisingly, the field of theater has adapted itself to—and been shaped by—this globalizing, technological world. Though one can still speak of national theaters, the activities of theater and drama have become increasingly internationalized over the twentieth and early twenty-first centuries. The 1913 Nobel Prize in Literature was won by the Indian poet and playwright Rabindranath Tagore (1861–1941), whose play *The Post Office* had been performed by Dublin's Abbey Theatre earlier that year; the 2000 prize was awarded to the Chinese playwright and novelist Gao Xingjian (b. 1940). Playwrights, theatrical companies, and productions cross borders with ease, and the encounter of cultural traditions has become both a subject and a collaborative aesthetic of theatrical production. The 1985 theatrical adaptation of the Hindu epic the *Mahabharata* by the British director Peter Brook (b. 1925) was produced at the Avignon Festival in France with actors from sixteen countries; over the next four years it toured internationally. More recently, the French Canadian direc-

tor, writer, and performer Robert Lepage (b. 1957) has produced a number of theatrical pieces that combine international performance styles in narratives about history, migration, and cultural identity that span the globe. These, too, have been performed around the world. Other prominent contemporary directors—such as Ariane Mnouchkine (b. 1939) and Robert Wilson (b. 1941)—similarly are international theater figures.

THEATER AND MEDIA

One reason for the internationalism of contemporary theater is the shifting relationship of the performing arts to the expanding field of media technologies. For much of the twentieth century, theater was forced to compete with a series of emerging media: film, radio, tape recording, and television. In a number of cases, it responded by incorporating these technologies into its repertoire of staging practices: onstage projections in Brechtian theater, for example, and the disembodied voices of BECKETT's late plays. In the century's final decades, the line separating theater from film and other media continued to blur. The American playwright SAM SHEPARD's (b. 1943) reputation owes as much to his work as a film actor as it does to his theater work, while DAVID MAMET (b. 1947) writes as frequently for cinema as he does for the stage. Plays are regularly adapted for film and television—vastly more people saw TONY KUSHNER's (b. 1956) *ANGELS IN AMERICA* (1991–92) on HBO in 2003 (and subsequently on videotape) than saw it in the theater—and noteworthy productions of such plays as CHEKHOV's *Uncle Vanya* are available for video libraries. As it becomes less reliant on specific performance sites, in other words, theater is more transportable than it has ever been.

The shifting boundary between theater and other media—and the resultant blurring of the distinction between elite and mass culture—is also reflected in the influence of postmodernism on contemporary theater and drama. *Postmodernism*, a term most frequently applied to developments in architecture, the visual arts, and literature in the second half of the twentieth century, denotes a style (or set of styles) that challenges the Enlightenment and modernist belief in metanarratives (i.e., overarching frameworks of meaning) and abandons historical analysis in favor of juxtaposing historical and contemporary elements in the mode of quotation or pastiche.

The theater has also responded to competing media technologies by asserting its uniqueness in the actuality of the theatrical moment and the proximity of live actor to spectator. This impulse, which marked the activities of theater groups influenced by Artaud and the performances of the Living Theater and other communal theater groups of the 1960s, manifested itself in the work of performance artists who began presenting their work in the United States during the 1970s. These artists, often working solo, appeared at a range of locations inside and outside the theater; their performances, which could be scripted or unscripted, often involved the performer's body in situations or encounters that addressed various issues pertaining to social representation, politics, and other matters. By the 1980s, though, even these artists were engaging with contemporary media culture in their performances.

INTERNATIONAL THEATER

In keeping with the overall trend of globalization, in the twentieth and early twenty-first centuries the importance of theater outside Europe and the United States has increased. The rise of national theaters outside Italy, Britain, France, Spain, and Germany is connected to the political and cultural nationalisms that gathered force in Europe and other areas of the world in the late nineteenth and twentieth centuries. From Mexico to Ireland to Egypt, plays were produced that embraced newly emerging cultural identities, often within theaters that were built and designated as national sites. The dramatists who helped drive these movements frequently were influenced by traditional and modern European dramatic forms, and in this sense their dramatic writing represented an attempt to bring Western modernity to local theatrical cultures. This pattern can be observed in Japan, China, and India, where Western-influenced plays entered ancient theatrical traditions. Many of the most influential figures in international theater during the past century brought Western traditions into dialogue with indigenous theatrical, dramatic, and narrative forms. The Egyptian playwright TAWFIQ AL-HAKIM (1898–1987), for instance—who lived in Paris for several years during the 1920s—helped establish an Arabic literary dramatic tradition by applying Western dramatic forms and techniques to traditional Arabic story material (such as *The Thousand and One Nights*). Al-Hakim's plays after 1950, like those of playwrights who followed in his footsteps, addressed the political and social issues of the contemporary Arab world.

POSTCOLONIAL THEATER

The internationalization of drama after the end of World War II received a strong impetus from the decolonization movements that led to the dismantling of Europe's global empires. India achieved its independence from Great Britain in 1947, and by 1970 all but a few of the British, French, and other European colonies in Africa, Asia, and the Caribbean had followed suit. In most cases independence followed intense campaigns by nationalist groups, such as the Viet Minh (the full form of its name means "League for the Independence of Vietnam") of Ho Chi Minh (1890–1969) in French Indochina and the Mouvement National Congolais of Patrice Lumumba (1925–1961) in the Belgian Congo. The newly independent countries faced their own formidable challenges: poverty and underdevelopment; corrupt, often repressive governments; outside political interference; economic exploitation; and tribal, ethnic, and sectarian divisions, in addition to the pervasive political, social, and economic legacies of colonial rule. The unbalanced power relations between indigenous peoples and long-established populations of white settlers caused wide economic disparities, which had political consequences. For example, in South Africa, which became independent of Great Britain in 1910, a system known as *apartheid* (an Afrikaans word that means "separate") restricted political power to citizens of

British and Dutch ancestry and legally classified all persons within the country into one of four racial groups. Until it was abolished in 1994, black citizens were forced to live and work in so-called homelands (only those with a work permit could live in a city), were forced into a separate education system, and were compelled to carry government-issued passes for identification. Other former colonies, as well as those nation-states that achieved independence when the Soviet Union dissolved in 1991, have had to deal with their own legacies of colonial suppression.

The term *postcolonial* is frequently used in discussions of national identity in a world still coming to terms with the effects of colonialism—or, according to some, now living under a neocolonial system of new economic and cultural dependencies. The term is often applied to literature and other cultural forms—such as theater—within those nations previously subjected to colonial rule. *Postcolonial*, in this sense, refers less to the historical period after colonialism than it does to the inheritance of a system whose tensions and contradictions—social, psychological, and cultural—remain

very much alive. Postcolonial writers and other artists address the metropolitan centers that historically dominated their nations and societies (most prominently, London and Paris), but they do so as subjects who have been partly formed by those centers and their language, educational system, social structures, and culture. Literature, theater, and other postcolonial art forms establish relationships between native and colonial traditions; explore the influence of imperial ideologies, power structures, and discourses on contemporary perceptions and relations; and look for ways in which those who live in postcolonial societies can achieve new forms of identity and cultural resistance.

Postcolonial dramatists, whose work represents one of the most vibrant and important currents in contemporary theater, have been at the forefront of those seeking to rewrite the received traditions of Western culture from a postcolonial point of view. The Nigerian playwright WOLE SOYINKA (b. 1934), who studied in England and worked with the Royal Court Theatre in London before returning to his native country in the late 1950s, draws on

Actor-playwrights Percy Mtwa and Mbongeni Ngema in *Woza Albert!*, a play about apartheid performed in 1983 at the Market Theater in Johannesburg.

the rituals and festivals of Nigeria's Yoruba culture as well as on European dramatic models in plays that address the impact of colonialism and the tyranny of oppressive regimes that followed in its wake. The West Indian playwright DEREK WALCOTT (b. 1930) has also sought fusions of Western and indigenous performance forms, drawing on Caribbean folklore, dance, storytelling, and linguistic patois while celebrating the hybridization of the region's multiple cultures. Because language was central to the dynamics of colonial subjugation—local languages were usually subordinated to an "official" tongue and, in some countries, were even outlawed— the politics of language is an important subject of postcolonial drama. Many of these plays include non-European languages—Gaelic, Zulu, Bengali—within a broadened field of linguistic interaction.

The term *postcolonial* is also used to refer to playwrights who live in the former "settlement colonies," predominantly English-speaking countries where white settlers adopted their own version of British culture and whose relations with London, for most of the colonial period, were largely autonomous. In Canada, which became a dominion in 1867 and achieved legislative independence in 1931, drama challenging the dominant Anglo-Canadian culture has been produced by the country's French-speaking minority— including the leading Quebecois playwright, Michel Tremblay (b. 1942)—and such Native American playwrights as Tomson Highway (Cree, b. 1951) and DANIEL DAVID MOSES (Delaware, b. 1952). In Australia, which was settled as a British penal colony in the late eighteenth century, a national history that includes the displacement of the indigenous population has been explored by such writers as the Aboriginal playwright Jack Davis (1917–2000) and the white Australian Louis Nowra (b. 1950). And no postcolonial drama is more socially urgent than that which was produced within apartheid South Africa by writers such as ATHOL FUGARD (b. 1932), Zakes Mda (b. 1948), and Maishe Maponya (b. 1951), many of them associated with the pioneering multiracial Market Theatre in Johannesburg (established 1976).

THEATER AND DIVERSITY

The social, cultural, and psychological changes associated with postcolonialism, it is important to note, extend beyond the nations that had been imperial holdings. Many former colonial subjects were among the immigrants who streamed into Europe to work in the decades after World War II, and this growing population of naturalized citizens—South Asians, West Indians, and Africans in Britain; North Africans in France; Turks in West Germany—has redrawn the racial profile of societies that once were homogeneous. Throughout western Europe, cities have become more cosmopolitan—a cosmopolitanism deepened at the end of the twentieth century and the beginning of the twenty-first by the economic integration of nations within the European Union and the liberalization of economies in eastern Europe. The effects on the contemporary theater of Britain, Ireland, and the Continent have been profound. Second- and third-generation writers from immigrant populations—Hanif Kureishi (b. 1954) and Ayub Khan-Din (b. 1961) in Britain, for instance—who find themselves between two cultures and belonging completely to neither, have created plays that explore their often conflicted position, while playwrights from culturally dominant racial groups have produced a drama increasingly concerned with the changing face of nationhood.

A different version of this cultural evolution is evident in the United States, where immigration has been central to national self-definition since the metaphor of the "melting pot" was first used in 1782. Though it has traditionally been assumed that immigrants and their descendents would surrender their particular racial and ethnic differences for a dominant, shared "Americanness," this stance has been replaced in recent decades by an embrace of cultural uniqueness and ethnic/racial identity. Following the development of a contemporary African American drama in the 1950s and 1960s, the American theater has seen the emergence of Asian American drama in the work of DAVID HENRY HWANG (b. 1957) and others, Chicano/a drama, and—since the 1990s—Arab American drama. The growing political and cultural assertiveness of the continent's original inhabitants has also produced an impressive body of Native American drama. This drama is sometimes the product of theater groups, such as the U.S.-based Spiderwoman Theater, that draw on Native American storytelling and performance traditions.

More broadly, the theater has begun to include a wider range of voices and experiences that traditionally have been marginalized within, or excluded from, the stage. The roots of this expansion lie in the "identity" or "liberation" movements that have gathered strength in recent decades in Europe, North America, and other areas of the world. The contemporary women's movement, for example, which burgeoned in the 1970s, has produced a rich body of drama concerned with women's experience, the meaning of "woman" in traditional representations, and the changing manifestations of gender in the late twentieth and early twenty-first centuries. This drama has often formed part of an explicit feminist project to challenge male-directed theatrical practices, institutions, and notions of authorship, and it has sometimes been produced by companies employing newer, more collaborative forms of theatrical practice.

Gay and lesbian drama has also gained a prominent voice in the contemporary theater. Though homosexual rights groups existed in Europe and the United States earlier in the century, agitation for the rights and recognition of gay, lesbian, bisexual, and transgendered individuals did not come to the attention of the general public until the late 1960s. The Sexual Offenses Act of 1967 decriminalized most sexual acts between adults in Britain, and the 1969 Stonewall riots in New York galvanized the gay liberation movement in the United States. Perhaps because of its interest in role-playing and its tolerance for unconventional identities, the modern theater has attracted an impressive number of homosexual and bisexual playwrights, including OSCAR WILDE (1854–1900), Gertrude Stein (1874–1946), FEDERICO GARCÍA LORCA (1898–1936), TENNESSEE WILLIAMS (1911–1983), JEAN GENET (1910–1986), Lorraine Hansberry (1930–

1965), EDWARD ALBEE (b. 1928), and Joe Orton (1933–1967). Yet only in the 1970s did an openly gay and lesbian drama emerge in its own right. Among the leading writers of this drama is the American playwright Tony Kushner, whose two-part dramatic fantasia *Angels in America* was one of a number of plays during the 1980s and 1990s that addressed the AIDS epidemic. Important authors of lesbian drama include the contemporary American playwright and performance artist Holly Hughes (b. 1955).

THEATER IN THE TWENTY-FIRST CENTURY

As the works of these and other contemporary playwrights indicate, theater remains deeply responsive to social movements, cultural developments, and historical shifts and transformations. As the twenty-first century unfolds, theater—a medium at once traditional and new—offers a unique perspective on the issues and preoccupations of a changing world. One of the oldest of the arts, theater brings nearly 2,500 years of performance forms and dramatic texts to the current historical moment. At the same time, theater is one of the most immediate of the representational arts, grounded in the physical presence of the actor's body and the irreproducible occasion of live performance. Old plays are performed in new contexts, and the resulting dialogue frames both present and past in mutually illuminating ways. HAMLET (1600–01) has been performed thousands of times, but every time the Danish prince picks up Yorick's skull—a stage prop—he does it for different audiences in a performance interaction that changes from moment to moment. Its sensitivity to audience and occasion makes theater exceptionally responsive to the complex web of issues, relationships, and interactions that make up the present moment. For this reason, many of the contemporary theater's most important activities have taken place not in traditional theater buildings but in the squares, community centers, and other sites where people gather and work. Health and theater workers have used theater as a vehicle for vaccination campaigns in South America, AIDS education in Africa, and trauma therapy for those victimized by violence around the world. In these and other forms, theater remains deeply important in regions that may not have access to other media, in cultures that rely for education less on print than on oral modes of transmitting information, and with marginalized social groups in other societies.

Theater is more international than it has ever been, and in its emerging and time-honored forms it constitutes an important part of the global cultural landscape. As the expansion and proliferation of media continue in this digitalizing age of multiple entertainment sources, theater and drama carry on traditions that have been handed down for centuries, reworking these conventions in often striking ways and making them responsive to a new century's changing realities.

READING DRAMA, IMAGINING THEATER

For those of us who are used to reading novels and short stories, opening the text of a play can come as something of a surprise. Characters are identified before the story ever begins, in a listing (often labeled *dramatis personae*) that seems more like the entries in an address book than the stuff of literature. Instead of the designations "he said" or "she said" that embed what these characters say within a novel's or short story's unfolding narrative, dialogue is presented directly, with the speakers' names indicated on the left-hand margin. Stage directions indicate when characters enter or exit the dramatic scene, how they move around in relation to each other, and how they handle the objects of their material world. The very world they inhabit feels constrained—even claustrophobic—next to the expansive, shifting settings of *Don Quixote* or *War and Peace*.

Features such as these point to the essential difference between drama and more strictly literary forms such as fiction and poetry. While the term *playwright* means "maker of plays," the written text that we pick up to read provides only a part of the larger phenomenon we call *performance*. Its meanings, in other words, are not limited to the private worlds created by readers as they encounter words on a page. Rather, the printed play is a blueprint for something that happens in real time and space before an audience. The dramatic text in performance thus depends not on a single literary author but on the collective artistry of actors, designers, directors, and others involved in theatrical production. Even those plays—known as "closet dramas"— that were written with the expectation that they would never (or could never) be performed in an actual theater generate imaginative scenarios that have more in common with an audience's experience of watching a play than with a solitary reader's enjoyment. The fact that plays are written with some form of theater in mind—that they exist as dramatic scripts as well as literary works—ensures that the pleasures associated with dramatic art are rich and complex.

As a consequence, to read drama well requires a theatrical imagination attuned to the possible realizations of the dramatic script onstage. The first time we encounter an unfamiliar play, we seek and respond to its narrative—the story it is telling us. But we cannot fully appreciate the impact of such a play unless we consider *how* that story is told and what kind of performance it suggests. Reading plays is an active process—a creative collaboration with the dramatist that takes place in the mind of the reader. As a way of conceiving the dramatic world of a play, it may be helpful to start by envisioning its physical environment, or setting. Where and when is the play set? What and where are the key markers in that location (a door, for example, or a throne)? Some playwrights— particularly those who write under the influence of theatrical realism—include a great deal of information about the play's physical environment, making the stage materialize by supplying a wealth of particular detail. Other dramatic texts provide minimal, or no, setting specifications; for example, SAMUEL BECKETT'S *WAITING FOR GODOT* (1952) includes the famously minimalist direction "A country road. A tree. Evening." Plays written before the nineteenth century often lack place descriptions and depend on the dramatic action and dialogue to establish what is onstage. The settings of Sanskrit drama, for instance, are suggested through dialogue and mimed actions, as when the courtesan Vasantasena mimes stepping into a carriage in SHUDRAKA'S *THE LITTLE CLAY CART* (ca. 100–300 C.E.), while the plays of SHAKESPEARE and his contemporaries establish location through economical, highly evocative verbal description. Knowing something about the production conventions in use during specific periods can help you re-create how a play might have looked to its original audience, but it should not limit your imagination. As the history of theatrical performance indicates, plays are adaptable to other kinds of theaters, stage resources, and production practices.

When visualizing this physical environment, you may wish to make a rough sketch of the scenic environment (or environments) indicated within the dramatic text, so that you can visualize how the characters and locale interact in each scene. Some theatrical terminology is useful here. In many theatrical traditions, locations and movement onstage are designated by a gridlike pattern. The section farthest away from the audience is considered *upstage*, while the area closest to them is *downstage*. Unless otherwise indicated, the sides of the stage are noted from the actor's perspective; hence, *stage right* will be to the actor's right, and *stage left* will be to the actor's left. The midpoint of the stage is called its *center*. Thus, for example, an actor might be told to enter through a door up right and to move (or "cross") to sit on a chair down left. When imagining the layout of a particular scene, it is important to be aware of who is onstage and where, at all times, even when these characters participate only silently in what is going on. Though the presence of such characters may be easy to forget, they may prove pivotal to the action of individual scenes.

Try to envision each character's appearance, as well as how much flexibility there may be in matching the bodily reality of a given actor to the physical description of the character. At some times and in some places, the correspondence between bodily appearance and role has been fairly conventionalized, with recognizable "types" recurring in similar dramatic performances. But even such roles can be taken by actors who vary in appearance, bearing, age, and manner, or even play against type. Throughout theater history, for example, what we now call cross-gender casting and cross-racial casting have been important elements of performance. As part of your effort to visualize the play in performance, you might cast known actors in your imaginary staging to make it more vivid, then substitute others to see how different personalities and styles of acting might shape a role differently. Here, too, the text can be your guide. Is the performance required by the text naturalistic or stylized, comic or serious? In some cases—the stylized theater of Japanese noh, for example—the answer is clear, and by imposing antithetical acting styles you may violate the play's aesthetic underpinnings. In most cases, however, access to a range of acting styles can liberate possibilities within the dramatic text, offering new perspectives and opening it up to new theatrical energies.

In addition, it is useful to pay close attention to what characters say and how they say it. Language is the playwright's principal means for revealing characters and their dramatic world, and the play relies mainly on the spoken word to communicate with its audience. Dramatic speech often reveals important information about the characters, including their class position, geographic origin (especially through dialect), and personality. In the absence of a narrator who might make known to us a character's inner thoughts and feelings, speech is the conduit through which the play's figures disclose their hopes, fears, and intentions. Such characterization rests not simply on what a specific character says but also on what is said about him or her. Indeed, the richness of a dramatic portrait is often the product of multiple—and differing—accounts, observations, and perspectives offered by a play's characters.

Language, of course, is more than information, and nowhere is this truer than in the theater, where language exists not to be read but to be spoken. The words on the page of a dramatic text are designed for the mouth, and as chosen by the best dramatists their sounds fill and guide the mouth, position the body in specific attitudes, and occupy the stage with their acoustic power. When the playwright JOHN MILLINGTON SYNGE wrote that "in a good play every speech should be as fully flavored as a nut or apple," he was referring not just to his own use of Irish dialect but to the linguistic and syntactical richness that makes all great dialogue a kind of vocal music. When bringing a play to theatrical life in your mind, read its lines aloud, feel the emotions they stir in your body, and enjoy the music that they create within your room. By yourself or with a friend, read some of the dialogue, noticing the contrapuntal rhythms that characters establish when they speak together. Even when reading translations—such as the ones included in this anthology, which were selected with vocal and other forms of performability in mind—you can feel such cadences and musicality. Along with the other sounds that a play may require— the ritualized foot stamping of the noh actor, the swish of regal costumes, Feste's lute in Shakespeare's TWELFTH NIGHT (1600–01)—the spoken word makes up the soundscape of dramatic performance. Reading with an awareness of this aural power can enhance your understanding and appreciation of drama.

While noting that the spoken language is a primary determinant of dramatic and theatrical meaning, we must not ignore the other elements that reinforce or complicate the acts of expression, communication, and signification. Three texts, in fact, work together in performance: the spoken text, the action text, and the subtext. Whereas the *spoken text*, or dialogue, is what the characters say to each other (or to the audience) during the play, the *action text*— whether scripted by the playwright or created by the director, the actors, or both—is the physical language of the play: the gestures and movements that signifi-

cantly shape our understanding of the story. In highly conventionalized theater cultures, such as those of classical India and Japan, the actors' movements and gestures become intricate languages in their own right, signifying to an audience that understands their meaning specific relationships, emotions, and attitudes. But directors and actors of all eras have used the action text as a way of communicating meaning, even when the effect of such gestures and movements may be to undermine the sentiments expressed in the spoken text (as when the villain of nineteenth-century melodrama winks at the audience while professing his sincerity to an onstage character). *Subtext* consists of the unspoken thoughts, feelings, and intentions of the characters that underlie and prompt the action and spoken texts. The relationship between the subtext and its manifestation in word and action is as variable in the theater as it is in life. Sometimes language and gesture express the inner life directly and fully. "Language most shows the man; speak that I may see thee," wrote BEN JONSON in a prose collection published shortly after his death. But as *VOLPONE* (1606) and other plays by Jonson demonstrate, drama concerns itself more frequently with the discrepancy between private intention and public expression. Characters hide their meanings from others (and occasionally from themselves), feign indifference when they feel love, say only part of what they mean, pursue their designs under the unsuspecting eyes of those they interact with. Even silence—the choice not to speak—plays an important role in conveying contextual meaning.

The dynamic interplay of these three texts—and their interaction with set design, lighting, and the other elements of production—creates the depth and complexity of live theater. When we speak of an actor's interpretation of a role, or a director's concept for a production, we are thinking about the myriad choices that artists make, using these intersecting texts, to develop fully realized characters and to communicate with the audience through the play and its performance. The key word here is "interpretation," for the dramatic text as it exists on its own is fundamentally incomplete, suspended between possible realizations. Because plays are designed for performance, they depend on the activities of actors, directors, designers, stage managers, musicians, and the other theatrical practitioners who have served in different periods to usher them into life. And every choice that is made by these practitioners helps to realize, or interpret, the play in light of its possible range of meanings. Because the combinations of such choices are infinite, no two productions of a play are ever the same, and a great work of dramatic art has an endless capacity to surprise us with new experiences and insights whenever it is performed.

Because reading drama can and should resemble the process of actual production, you should approach the dramatic text as if you were a theater professional. Instead of reading a play to discern preexisting meanings, look for the places where a role, a scene, or a verbal exchange may be performed in different ways, and make choices as to how such components might be interpreted in the theater of your mind. What happens if an actor dwells on certain words in a speech as opposed to others? Where might he or she pause when delivering the lines, and what would be the effect of such vocal punctuation? What subtextual meanings do you see behind words and actions, and how might your actors bring them out? Consider the other elements of production as well. How would you light a production of your play, and what would be the effect of your decisions? How do the meaning and dynamics of a scene change if you focus your light on certain characters rather than others? What costumes do you imagine for your actors, and what would these tell us about the characters they play? Where would you position actors on the stage, and how would they move in relation to each other? Is the stage busy or relatively still during individual scenes? In those plays that lack detailed set descriptions, what theatrical environment do you envision for the action that takes place? Conversely, with plays that have extensive directions, what specific fixtures and objects might you choose to realize the desired effect? Although some dramatists have indicated that they expect their directions be followed exactly in production, would you want to modify the given directions in any way, either to accommodate different kinds of stages or to offer a more radical vision of the play and its dramatic possibilities? As you imagine your play in the theater, you can also consider how much—if any—of the direction provided by the playwright to employ and what possible impact on an audience such changes in direction might have. Finally, what stage might you choose for a production of your play: a traditional stage, with the audience seated directly in front of the action (the proscenium stage, for instance), or a different stage arrangement, such as one in which the audience is seated on three sides (i.e., "in the round")? How do the meanings and implications of your play change when the spectators are so close to the actors and can see each other as they look at the stage?

Though reading a play in this way does not require extensive familiarity with the theater, your ability to appreciate the theatrical possibilities of a given play will be greatly enriched by the experience of seeing plays performed onstage. Go to the theater when you can; immerse yourself in the moment when the audience grows quiet, the actors enter, and the stage is taken over by a spectacle that is illusory but feels, in its most powerful moments, more real than life itself. And while attending the theater will enhance your reading of dramatic texts, the reverse is also true. Readers who imagine the theater as part of their reading become more informed and responsive audience members, actively aware of the choices the artists have made in interpreting dramatic texts and better able to evaluate their effectiveness. One of the many pleasures of reading drama is measuring your interpretation against actual performances of the play and comparing those individual performances with each other. Like the aficionados of other arts, you may develop, over a lifetime, your own repertoire of remembered performances and texts. And as you deepen your awareness of the relationship between what is written and what takes place onstage, you may fall under the spell of drama, which—whether enacted in the theater or in your own mind—is timeless yet always new.

THE PLAYS

AESCHYLUS

ca. 525–456 B.C.E.

T HE author of the earliest existing
Greek tragedies, Aeschylus is the inau-
gurator of Western drama. His plays set the
standard against which subsequent playwrights have measured their works. Fifty
years after Aeschylus's death, the comic
playwright aristophanes wrote a play, *The
Frogs*, in which he acknowledged—even as
he parodied Aeschylus's sometimes pompous language and relentlessly elevated
style—that Aeschylus not only created tragedy as we know it but also created its most
perfect examples. Many subsequent writers
have agreed with Aristophanes, singling
out Aeschylus's surviving trilogy, the *Oresteia*, as the high-water mark of tragedy to
this day.

As a member of the aristocratic elite of
the city-state of Athens, Aeschylus participated in some of the most important
events in its history. He fought against the
huge Persian army at Marathon in 490
B.C.E., a momentous battle that was a crucial turning point in the war between
Greece and Persia, which lasted fifty-one
years. Ten years later, he played a role in
the battle of Salamis, a legendary conflict
that pitted an overwhelming Persian fleet
against many fewer but also more agile
Greek ships. Tactics required Athenians
to abandon their city, leaving it to be plundered and partially destroyed by the Persian army. Retreating to the island of

Salamis, the Greeks, led by the Athenian
commander, Themistocles, lured their
enemy into a brutal naval battle that devastated the Persian forces. The victory
forced the Persians to retreat from Greece,
and it established Athens as the preeminent power among all Greek city-states.
Not surprisingly, because he was a witness to and participant in these Athenian
victories, Aeschylus's plays express the
confidence and authority of an emerging
empire.

Although Aeschylus is considered the
first great innovator of Western drama, it
is sometimes difficult to judge the full
extent of the innovations he introduced,
since no plays by his predecessor, Thespis,
have been preserved. What we know about
drama prior to Aeschylus suggests that it
had developed gradually out of choral lyrics, occasionally interrupted by short dialogues between the chorus and a single
speaker or singer representing an individual character. Aeschylus took the decisive
step of introducing a second actor, thus
enabling for the first time a dialogue or
conflict between two individuals to take
place on the stage and in front of an audience. In addition, an actor could leave the
stage and reappear in the guise of another
character, thus permitting an increase in
the overall number of persons represented.
In his later plays, Aeschylus used three

actors, allowing him to feature a large number of characters—as in *The Libation Bearers*, the second play of the *Oresteia* trilogy—in his dramas.

The innovations made possible by Aeschylus's introduction of a second character are significant enough, but he also used the chorus in a distinctive manner. While the choruses in Aeschylus's plays sing (and dance) formal odes, they also engage in conversation with individual characters using the less formal iambic meter. This variation in the chorus's tone was mirrored by modulations in characters' diction. Individual characters spoke in different modes, ranging from almost colloquial dialogue to long reports or lamentations in a higher register. Aeschylus thus displayed skillful variation not only between chorus and character but also between different forms of verse. These literary subtleties of his dramatic poetry are difficult to capture in English and have posed a particular challenge for translators.

In addition to introducing his own genuine changes, Aeschylus also took advantage of structural renovations made during his lifetime to the Dionysus theater, where Athenian tragedy was performed. Thanks to a newly erected wooden shed toward the back of the stage, called the *skēnē*, Aeschylus could now have characters enter and exit through a door and, by throwing open this door, suddenly reveal scenes staged inside the shed. In addition, he could place characters on the top of the shed to report events putatively taking place elsewhere. Aeschylus used this new device to great effect in the *Oresteia* and other plays. At the same time, he continued composing plays in the older style, without the use of the scene building and its new theatrical possibilities. Although Aeschylus was certainly a man of the theater—he even acted in his own plays—he also held on to a literary conception of theater, based as much on different literary modes as on theatrical effects.

The seven extant plays by Aeschylus are a small remnant of a corpus that may have included more than ninety plays, of which thirteen won first prizes at the Dionysus festival, but the range of his drama can be surmised even from these relatively few plays. The earliest tragedy, *The Persians* (ca. 472), stands out in that it was based not on mythology, as were almost all other Greek tragedies, but on a historical event: the defeat of the Persian fleet at Salamis in which Aeschylus had personally participated. Surprisingly, perhaps, Aeschylus represents the war from the perspective of the defeated Persians and not of the Athenian victors, creating a play that avoids bellicose patriotism and instead is a harrowing meditation on war and defeat. *Seven Against Thebes* (467), based on the mythological battle between the two sons of Oedipus, is known mostly for its evocative description of the symbolic shields of the seven attackers, which has become a famous literary set piece on a par with Homer's description of Achilles' shield in the *Iliad*. *The Suppliants* (468), a play about a group of women seeking asylum at Argos, is remarkable in that it is centered on a chorus of women. *Prometheus Unbound* (460) shows the literary side of Aeschylus's drama once more, since it lacks almost all visible stage action, being based instead on the rebellious speeches of Prometheus against Zeus (its literary qualities captured the imagination of the English Romantic poets, especially Percy Bysshe Shelley).

All Greek tragedies presented at the Dionysus festival were performed in groups of three (followed by a humorous "satyr play"), but the *Oresteia* is the only extant example we have of such a trilogy. The *Oresteia*'s influence and importance is at least partly the result of this accident of fate, and our understanding of Greek drama is much richer than it would have been had the *Oresteia* not survived. Unfortunately, *Proteus*, the satyr play that followed the performance of the *Oresteia*, has been lost along with almost all other satyr plays. From our few isolated examples of the type we can surmise that *Proteus* presented a farcical dramatization of mythology. But because no existing satyr plays can be linked to any extant tragedies, it is difficult to assess the relationship between *Proteus* and the trilogy that preceded it. Most commentators, beginning with Aristotle, have confined their remarks to the tragedies themselves.

The *Oresteia* was based on a well-known myth, the multigenerational saga of the house of Atreus. The Atrides, or descendants of Atreus, are members of a cursed family. Their ancestor Pelops had bribed the charioteer Myrtilus in order to triumph in the race that would win the hand of Hippodamia—and then had thrown him into the sea as a reward. Before dying, Myrtilus uttered the curse that would bring woe to Pelops's descendants, beginning with Atreus and Thyestes, two of his sons. After Thyestes seduces Atreus's wife, Atreus retaliates by killing two of Thyestes' three sons, chopping them up, and serving them to their father in a dish. In response to this heinous act, Thyestes utters a new curse on the house of Atreus. Aeschylus's *Oresteia* picks up the story in the next generation, with the sons of Atreus, Menelaus, and Agamemnon, and their difficult return home from the Trojan War. The trilogy is one of many works devoted to those returns, or *nostoi*, the most famous of which is Homer's *Odyssey*. Aeschylus focuses on the return of Agamemnon and his subsequent murder by his wife, Clytaemnestra, a murder she commits to retaliate for the death of their daughter Iphigeneia, whom Agamemnon had sacrificed to secure safe passage to Troy. *The Libation Bearers*, the second play of the trilogy, shows the murder of Clytaemnestra by her son, Orestes, who has returned from exile to take revenge for the murder of his father. The last play of the trilogy, *The Eumenides*, depicts Orestes being driven mad by Furies particularly aroused by matricide. After showing the consequences of the curse Thyestes had laid upon the house of Atreus, the *Oresteia* ends with a kind of resolution brought about by the judicious intervention of Athena, who appeases the Furies and replaces the bloody cycle of revenge with a new system of law. By having the myth thus end with the institution of law, Aeschylus was undoubtedly influenced by various legal reforms taking place during his lifetime. Those reforms made Athens famous throughout Greece for its impartial judiciary. The end of the *Oresteia* would have certainly pleased the Athenian audience, which could see their present political and legal system confirmed and their own achievements celebrated in the play.

Athenians would have seen themselves, too, in the chorus, the part of tragedy that most directly represents the people assembled in the theater. As it engages in moral commentary, responding to and weighing the arguments put forth by the various characters to justify their misdeeds, the chorus calls to mind the democratic deliberations of Athenian citizens. Individual actions and justifications are confronted with the views of the group throughout *Agamemnon*, and often the rulers themselves become beholden to the will of the people. But Aeschylus does not treat the chorus as a single block. The climax of the play occurs when the chorus hears the death cries of Agamemnon and is thrown into disarray, with different members recommending different actions, leading to general confusion and disunion. Throughout the play, the chorus, which represents the old men of Argos, remains divided about the morality of Clytaemnestra's action. But even when it is scattered or in disarray, the chorus reminds the audience that individual rulers must justify themselves before the people and, as in the end of the trilogy, before a court of law. In Aeschylus's hands, the mythological tale of the house of Atreus has been transformed into a story about the transition of Greece from a mythical and heroic past to a historical and more democratic present.

AGAMEMNON, the first play in the trilogy and the play reprinted here, not only depicts the brutal murder of its protagonist but also harks back to the Trojan War, the final defeat of the Trojans, the capture of Helen, and the difficult return home. It is a play packed with action. As in many Greek tragedies, however, very little of this action is presented on the stage. Instead, the play contains long and evocative descriptions of offstage action by the Herald and later by Agamemnon, and equally long descriptions by Clytaemnestra about the sacrifice of her daughter. Indeed, the entire play draws its power from a varied use of language. The descriptions of battles and sacrifices are followed by more confrontational dialogues between individuals, first between Clytaemnestra and the returning Agamemnon

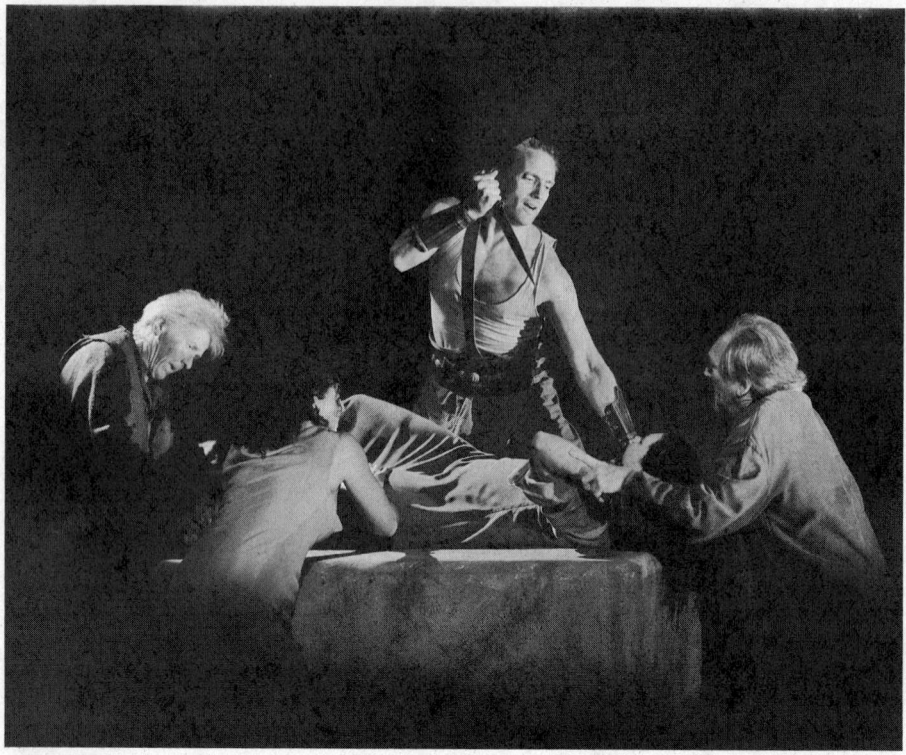

The sacrifice of Iphigenia, as portrayed in a 2008 production of *Agamemnon* at the Getty Villa in Los Angeles.

and then between Clytaemnestra and Cassandra, the daughter of the king of Troy whom Agamemnon has brought as his trophy. The latter dialogue is especially remarkable because it is based entirely on miscommunication. Cassandra fails to respond to anything Clytaemnestra says, including her direct threats, and the chorus vainly seeks to mediate between the two figures. If Cassandra does not, or does not want to, understand Clytaemnestra, Cassandra herself is even more difficult to comprehend. Her utterances take the form of prophecies whose dense images are comparable to the language associated with the oracle at Delphi; indeed, Cassandra draws her prophetic power from Apollo, the source also of the oracle's soothsaying abilities. Cassandra's frantic utterances provide a fragmentary preview of Agamemnon's murder shortly before the deed itself occurs, offstage. Only the second account of the murder, after the fact, is controlled and clear, rendered by the triumphant and defiant Clytaemnestra herself.

Even though *Agamemnon* does not, ultimately, resolve the divisions between radically different points of view, between different types of murder and their justifications, it concludes with a pointed debate between Clytaemnestra and the chorus over the justice of her acts. With the help of the chorus, we are finally back in the realm of moral argument; and even though the chorus and, presumably, the audience cannot find an adequate solution and judgment, the play ends with clear alternatives, pitting the murder of a daughter against the murder of a husband.

The most striking feature of the poetic style employed in the *Oresteia* is the series of extended images and comparisons that give this text its rich and vivid character. One such image occurs in the description of Paris and his capture of Helen, which led to the Trojan War and the downfall of Troy (lines 713–43). Extending over thirty lines, the passage compares Helen to a lion cub that is being cuddled and spoiled only to grow up and devour those who spoiled it, bringing destruction to all. More startling still is the moment when Clytaemnestra describes her murder of Agamemnon by comparing his blood to a rain fertilizing gardens. The most famous image of the play, however, is the red carpet that Clytaemnestra spreads before Agamemnon upon his return. This is the first time we see Agamemnon, and it is also the first (and last) dialogue between husband and wife. Agamemnon does not want to step on the precious carpet, deeming such an act appropriate only for a god, but Clytaemnestra persuades him to march across it toward the palace, where he will soon find his death. For an audience—such as the Athenians watching the original performance—who knows the outcome of the story, this scene anticipates the red blood that will be spilled, unseen, inside the palace doors.

The red carpet is a reminder that the images used by Aeschylus do not always dwell in the domain of language alone. Here, they become material reality in the theater, a striking stage prop used on an otherwise bare stage. Even the large audience in the Dionysus theater of Athens, numbering up to 17,000, would have been able to see the red carpet from afar. The carpet is but one example of Aeschylus's effective use of the theatrical means available to him. The carpet traces Agamemnon's path toward the wooden shed at the back of the stage, where the king will find his death. And once the murder is committed, Clytaemnestra will throw open its doors to reveal the body together with the net and sword, the tools of her deed. The wooden shed is central to the play from the beginning. The play famously opens with a watchman positioned on the roof of the shed, looking out for a signal light that will indicate the victory and return of the Greek army. This opening also anticipates Clytaemnestra's ingenuity and control, giving her time to prepare her premeditated deed. In the end, perhaps, *Agamemnon* derives its power from the way in which it utilizes the setup of the theater, while taking full advantage of a highly poetic and visual language.

Ever since its first performance, the *Oresteia* has held playwrights and audiences in its thrall. The most ambitious playwrights of the past 2,500 years have tried their own versions of its material, beginning with Aeschylus's immediate successors, SOPHOCLES and EURIPIDES. The Roman tragedian SENECA offered his own version as well. In more recent history, the eighteenth-century philosopher and playwright Voltaire composed a version (*Oreste*, 1750), as did the twentieth-century playwright and philosopher Jean-Paul Sartre (*Les Mouches*, 1943) as well as the playwright EUGENE O'NEILL, in his *Mourning Becomes Electra* (1931). These and many other playwrights and philosophers were drawn to Aeschylus out of a desire to understand the origin of Western theater and to strengthen the connection between those roots and their own time.

Aeschylus continues to compel readers, directors, actors, and audiences not only because he was the first Greek playwright whose plays survived. His plays, and not those of his now-forgotten rivals, were preserved precisely because of their unique combination of theatrical imagination, literary subtlety, and bold characterization. They display an enduring grandeur, a boldly conceived majesty that has given them an aura of true classics. Through new translations, adaptations, and theatrical productions they, more than most plays in the history of the theater, have been able to speak to audiences across the centuries.   M.P.

Agamemnon[1]

CHARACTERS

WATCHMAN
CLYTAEMNESTRA
HERALD
AGAMEMNON
CASSANDRA
AEGISTHUS

CHORUS, the Old Men of Argos
and their LEADER
Attendants of Clytaemnestra
and of Agamemnon,
bodyguard of Aegisthus

[TIME AND SCENE: *A night in the tenth and final autumn of the Trojan war. The house of Atreus in Argos.*[2] *Before it, an altar stands unlit; a watchman on the high roofs fights to stay awake.*]

WATCHMAN   Dear gods, set me free from all the pain,
the long watch I keep, one whole year awake . . .
propped on my arms, crouched on the roofs of Atreus
like a dog.
　　　　　I know the stars by heart,
5　the armies of the night, and there in the lead
the ones that bring us snow or the crops of summer,
bring us all we have—
our great blazing kings of the sky,
I know them, when they rise and when they fall . . .
10　and now I watch for the light, the signal-fire
breaking out of Troy, shouting Troy is taken.
So she commands, full of her high hopes.
That woman—she manoeuvres like a man.

And when I keep to my bed, soaked in dew,
15　and the thoughts go groping through the night
and the good dreams that used to guard my sleep . . .
not here, it's the old comrade, terror, at my neck.
I mustn't sleep, no—
　　　　　[*Shaking himself awake.*]
　　　　　　　　　Look alive, sentry.
And I try to pick out tunes, I hum a little,

1. Translated by Robert Fagles.
2. A city in Argolis, in the northeast of the Peloponnesian peninsula, or sometimes Argolis itself; in Homer and in most accounts, Atreus was the ruler of Mycenae, about 5 miles northeast of Argos. Conventionally, later poets referred to his kingdom as Argos, which by Aeschylus's time was the more powerful polity. Shortly before this play was written, Argos destroyed Mycenae and became an ally of Athens (an alliance to which the trilogy's final play alludes).

20   a good cure for sleep, and the tears start,
      I cry for the hard times come to the house,
      no longer run like the great place of old.

      Oh for a blessed end to all our pain,
      some godsend burning through the dark—
            [*Light appears slowly in the east; he struggles to his feet and scans it.*]
                                          I salute you!
25   You dawn of the darkness, you turn night to day—
      I see the light at last.
      They'll be dancing in the streets of Argos
      thanks to you, thanks to this new stroke of—
                              Aieeeeee!
      There's your signal clear and true, my queen!
30   Rise up from bed—hurry, lift a cry of triumph
      through the house, praise the gods for the beacon,
      if they've taken Troy . . .
                        But there it burns,
      fire all the way. I'm for the morning dances.
      Master's luck is mine. A throw of the torch
35   has brought us triple-sixes[3]—we have won!
      My move now—
            [*Beginning to dance, then breaking off, lost in thought.*]
                        Just bring him home. My king,
      I'll take your loving hand in mine and then . . .
      the rest is silence. The ox is on my tongue.[4]
      Aye, but the house and these old stones,
40   give them a voice and what a tale they'd tell.
      And so would I, gladly . . .
      I speak to those who know; to those who don't
      my mind's a blank. I never say a word.
            [*He climbs down from the roof and disappears into the palace through a
            side entrance. A* CHORUS, *the old men of Argos who have not learned the
            news of victory, enters and marches round the altar.*]

CHORUS   Ten years gone, ten to the day
45   our great avenger went for Priam—
         Menelaus and lord Agamemnon,
      two kings with the power of Zeus,[5]
      the twin throne, twin sceptre,
      Atreus' sturdy yoke of sons
50   launched Greece in a thousand ships,
      armadas cutting loose from the land,
      armies massed for the cause, the rescue—
            [*From within the palace* CLYTAEMNESTRA *raises a cry of triumph.*]

3. The best throw in a dice game popular in   4. That is, he will keep silent.
ancient Greece.   5. King of the gods in Greek mythology.

the heart within them screamed for all-out war!⁶
Like vultures robbed of their young,
55   the agony sends them frenzied,
soaring high from the nest, round and
round they wheel, they row their wings,
stroke upon churning thrashing stroke,
but all the labour, the bed of pain,
60   the young are lost forever.
Yet someone hears on high—Apollo,
Pan or Zeus—the piercing wail
these guests of heaven raise,
and drives at the outlaws, late
65   but true to revenge, a stabbing Fury!⁷

[CLYTAEMNESTRA *appears at the doors and pauses with her entourage.*]

So towering Zeus the god of guests
drives Atreus' sons at Paris,
all for a woman manned by many
the generations wrestle, knees
70   grinding the dust, the manhood drains,
the spear snaps in the first blood rites
        that marry Greece and Troy.
And now it goes as it goes
and where it ends is Fate.
75   And neither by singeing flesh
nor tipping cups of wine⁸
nor shedding burning tears can you
enchant away the rigid Fury.

[CLYTAEMNESTRA *lights the altar-fires.*]

We are the old, dishonoured ones,
80   the broken husks of men.
Even then they cast us off,
the rescue mission left us here
to prop a child's strength upon a stick.
What if the new sap rises in his chest?
85   He has no soldiery in him,
        no more than we,
and we are aged past ageing,
gloss of the leaf shrivelled,
three legs at a time we falter on.
90   Old men are children once again,
        a dream that sways and wavers
into the hard light of day.

---

6. That is, the Trojan War, triggered when Paris, son of the Trojan king, Priam, abducted Helen, wife of Menelaus, the Greek king of Sparta. After ten years of indecisive combat, the Greek forces led by Menelaus's brother and fellow king, Agamemnon, sacked the city of Troy and killed Priam.

7. One of the Eumenides, monstrous female personifications of vengeance. *Apollo:* Greek god of prophecy, light, and healing; son of Zeus. *Pan:* Greek god of pastures, flocks, and wild places.

8. That is, by offering wine and animal sacrifices to the gods.

                                    But you,
      daughter of Leda,[9] queen Clytaemnestra,
      what now, what news, what message
95   drives you through the citadel
            burning victims? Look,
      the city gods, the gods of Olympus,[1]
      gods of the earth and public markets—
      all the altars blazing with your gifts!
100   Argos blazes! Torches
      race the sunrise up her skies—
      drugged by the lulling holy oils,
            unadulterated,
      run from the dark vaults of kings.
105   Tell us the news!
      What you can, what is right—
      Heal us, soothe our fears!
      Now the darkness comes to the fore,
      now the hope glows through your victims,
110   beating back this raw, relentless anguish
            gnawing at the heart.

            [CLYTAEMNESTRA *ignores them and pursues her rituals; they assemble*
            for the opening chorus.]

      O but I still have power to sound the god's command at the roads
      that launched the kings. The gods breathe power through my song,
            my fighting strength, Persuasion grows with the years—
115   I sing how the flight of fury hurled the twin command,
                  one will that hurled young Greece
      and winged the spear of vengeance straight for Troy!
      The kings of birds to kings of the beaking prows, one black,
            one with a blaze of silver
120   skimmed the palace spearhand right
            and swooping lower, all could see,
                  plunged their claws in a hare, a mother
            bursting with unborn young—the babies spilling,
      quick spurts of blood—cut off the race just dashing into life!
125   Cry, cry for death, but good win out in glory in the end.

      But the loyal seer of the armies[2] studied Atreus' sons,
      two sons with warring hearts—he saw two eagle-kings
            devour the hare and spoke the things to come,
      'Years pass, and the long hunt nets the city of Priam,
130   the flocks beyond the walls,
      a kingdom's life and soul—Fate stamps them out.
      Just let no curse of the gods lour on us first,
            shatter our giant armour

9. Queen of Sparta who was seduced by Zeus   1. A mountain in Thessaly, in northern
in the form of a swan and gave birth to both   Greece, believed to be the home of the gods.
Helen, over whom the Trojan War was   2. Calchas (see line 158), a seer in the Greek
fought, and Clytaemnestra, who became wife   army.
of Agamemnon.

forged to strangle Troy. I see
135   pure Artemis³ bristle in pity—
              yes, the flying hounds of the Father
        slaughter for armies . . . their own victim . . . a woman
    trembling young, all born to die—She loathes the eagles' feast!'
    Cry, cry for death, but good win out in glory in the end.
140   'Artemis, lovely Artemis, so kind
    to the ravening lion's tender, helpless cubs,
    the suckling young of beasts that stalk the wilds—
         bring this sign for all its fortune,
             all its brutal torment home to birth!
145   I beg you, Healing Apollo, soothe her before
    her crosswinds hold us down and moor the ships too long,
    pressing us on to another victim . . .
         nothing sacred, no
             no feast to be eaten
150   the architect of vengeance
             [*Turning to the palace.*]
         growing strong in the house
    with no fear of the husband
    here she waits
    the terror raging back and back in the future
155   the stealth, the law of the hearth, the mother—
                 Memory womb of Fury child-avenging Fury!'
    So as the eagles wheeled at the crossroads,
    Calchas clashed out the great good blessings mixed with doom
        for the halls of kings, and singing with our fate
160   we cry, cry for death, but good win out in glory in the end.

                 Zeus, great nameless all in all,
                      if that name will gain his favour,
                          I will call him Zeus.
                  I have no words to do him justice,
165   weighing all in the balance,
                          all I have is Zeus, Zeus—
                 lift this weight, this torment from my spirit,
                          cast it once for all.

                  He who was so mighty once,
170   storming for the wars of heaven,
                          he has had his day.
                  And then his son who came to power
                      met his match in the third fall
                      and he is gone,⁴ Zeus, Zeus—
175   raise your cries and sing him Zeus the Victor!
                      You will reach the truth:

3. Daughter of Zeus and twin sister of Apollo;   which Uranus was emasculated and det-
goddess of the hunt.   hroned by his son Cronos, who was later
4. The chorus alludes to the myth according to   overthrown by his son Zeus.

Zeus has led us on to know,
the Helmsman lays it down as law
that we must suffer, suffer into truth.
180 We cannot sleep, and drop by drop at the heart
the pain of pain remembered comes again,
and we resist, but ripeness comes as well.
From the gods enthroned on the awesome rowing-bench
there comes a violent love.

185 So it was that day the king,
the steersman at the helm of Greece,
would never blame a word the prophet said—
swept away by the wrenching winds of fortune
he conspired! Weatherbound we could not sail,[5]
190 our stores exhausted, fighting strength hard-pressed,
and the squadrons rode in the shallows off Chalkis
where the riptide crashes, drags,

and winds from the north pinned down our hulls at Aulis,
port of anguish . . . head winds starving,
195 sheets and the cables snapped
and the men's minds strayed,
the pride, the bloom of Greece
was raked as time ground on,
ground down, and then the cure for the storm
200 and it was harsher—Calchas cried,
'My captains, Artemis must have blood!'—
so harsh the sons of Atreus
dashed their sceptres on the rocks,
could not hold back the tears,

205 and I still can hear the older warlord saying,
'Obey, obey, or a heavy doom will crush me!—
Oh but doom *will* crush me
once I rend my child,
the glory of my house—
210 a father's hands are stained,
blood of a young girl streaks the altar.
Pain both ways and what is worse?
Desert the fleets, fail the alliance?
No, but stop the winds with a virgin's blood,
215 feed their lust, their fury?—feed their fury!—
Law is law!—
Let all go well.'

And once he slipped his neck in the strap of Fate,
his spirit veering black, impure, unholy,

5. Because Agamemnon had offended Artemis, the Greek fleet was trapped by unfavorable winds
in the port of Aulis, located (like Chalkis) on the Gulf of Euboea.

once he turned he stopped at nothing,
220   seized with the frenzy
            blinding driving to outrage—
wretched frenzy, cause of all our grief!
Yes, he had the heart
         to sacrifice his daughter,
225   to bless the war that avenged a woman's loss,[6]
            a bridal rite that sped the men-of-war.

'My father, father!'—she might pray to the winds;
no innocence moves her judges mad for war.
Her father called his henchmen on,
230   on with a prayer,
            'Hoist her over the altar
like a yearling, give it all your strength!
She's fainting—lift her,
            sweep her robes around her,
235   but slip this strap in her gentle curving lips . . .
            here, gag her hard, a sound will curse the house'—

and the bridle chokes her voice . . . her saffron robes
pouring over the sand
                        her glance like arrows showering
wounding every murderer through with pity
240   clear as a picture, live,
she strains to call their names . . .
I remember often the days with father's guests
when over the feast her voice unbroken,
            pure as the hymn her loving father
245   bearing third libations, sang to Saving Zeus—
transfixed with joy, Atreus' offspring
            throbbing out their love.

What comes next? I cannot see it, cannot say.
The strong techniques of Calchas do their work.
250   But Justice turns the balance scales,
            sees that we suffer
and we suffer and we learn.
And we will know the future when it comes.
Greet it too early, weep too soon.
255   It all comes clear in the light of day.
Let all go well today, well as she could want,
            [*Turning to* CLYTAEMNESTRA.]
our midnight watch, our lone defender,
            single-minded queen.
LEADER   We've come,
Clytaemnestra. We respect your power.

6. Following the recommendation of Calchas, Agamemnon had sacrificed Iphigeneia, his daughter, in order to appease Artemis and win favorable passage to Troy to retrieve Helen.

260 Right it is to honour the warlord's woman
     once he leaves the throne.
                                    But why these fires?
     Good news, or more good hopes? We're loyal,
     we want to hear, but never blame your silence.

CLYTAEMNESTRA   Let the new day shine—as the proverb says—
265 glorious from the womb of Mother Night.

        [*Lost in prayer, then turning to the* CHORUS.]

     You will hear a joy beyond your hopes.
     Priam's citadel—the Greeks have taken Troy!

LEADER   No, what do you mean? I can't believe it.

CLYTAEMNESTRA   Troy is ours. Is that clear enough?

LEADER   The joy of it,
270 stealing over me, calling up my tears—

CLYTAEMNESTRA   Yes, your eyes expose your loyal hearts.

LEADER   And you have proof?

CLYTAEMNESTRA   I do,
     I must. Unless the god is lying.

LEADER   That,
     or a phantom spirit sends you into raptures.

275 CLYTAEMNESTRA   No one takes me in with visions—senseless dreams.

LEADER   Or giddy rumour, you haven't indulged yourself—

CLYTAEMNESTRA   You treat me like a child, you mock me?

LEADER   Then when did they storm the city?

CLYTAEMNESTRA   Last night, I say, the mother of this morning.

280 LEADER   And who on earth could run the news so fast?

CLYTAEMNESTRA   The god of fire—rushing fire from Ida![7]
     And beacon to beacon rushed it on to me,
     my couriers riding home the torch.
                                    From Troy
     to the bare rock of Lemnos, Hermes' Spur,
285 and the Escort winged the great light west
     to the Saving Father's face, Mount Athos hurled it
     third in the chain and leaping Ocean's back
     the blaze went dancing on to ecstasy—pitch-pine
     streaming gold like a new-born sun—and brought
290 the word in flame to Mount Makistos' brow.
     No time to waste, straining, fighting sleep,
     that lookout heaved a torch glowing over
     the murderous straits of Euripos to reach
     Messapion's watchmen craning for the signal.
295 Fire for word of fire! tense with the heather
     withered gray, they stack it, set it ablaze—
     the hot force of the beacon never flags,
     it springs the Plain of Asôpos, rears
     like a harvest moon to hit Kithairon's crest

---

7. A mountain of Asia Minor (present-day
Turkey), near Troy. The following place-
names trace the path of the signal fires from
there to Argos, where the play is set. *God of
fire:* Haephestus.

300 and drives new men to drive the fire on.
    That relay pants for the far-flung torch,
    they swell its strength outstripping my commands
    and the light inflames the marsh, the Gorgon's Eye,
    it strikes the peak where the wild goats range—
305 my laws, my fire whips that camp!
    They spare nothing, eager to build its heat,
    and a huge beard of flame overcomes the headland
    beetling down the Saronic Gulf, and flaring south
    it brings the dawn to the Black Widow's face—
310 the watch that looms above your heads—and now
    the true son of the burning flanks of Ida
    crashes on the roofs of Atreus' sons!

    And I ordained it all.
    Torch to torch, running for their lives,
315 one long succession racing home my fire.
                                          One,
    first in the laps and last, wins out in triumph.
    There you have my proof, *my* burning sign, I tell you—
    the power my lord passed on from Troy to me!
    LEADER   We'll thank the gods, my lady—first this story,
320 let me lose myself in the wonder of it all!
    Tell it start to finish, tell us all.
    CLYTAEMNESTRA   The city's ours—in our hands this very day!
    I can hear the cries in crossfire rock the walls.
    Pour oil and wine in the same bowl,
325 what have you, friendship? A struggle to the end.
    So with the victors and the victims—outcries,
    you can hear them clashing like their fates.

    They are kneeling by the bodies of the dead,
    embracing men and brothers, infants over
330 the aged loins that gave them life, and sobbing,
    as the yoke constricts their last free breath,
    for every dear one lost.
                              And the others,
    there, plunging breakneck through the night—
    the labour of battle sets them down, ravenous,
335 to breakfast on the last remains of Troy.
    Not by rank but chance, by the lots they draw,
    they lodge in the houses captured by the spear,
    settling in so soon, released from the open sky,
    the frost and dew. Lucky men, off guard at last,
340 they sleep away their first good night in years.
    If only they are revering the city's gods,
    the shrines of the gods who love the conquered land,
    no plunderer will be plundered in return.[8]

8. In the traditional account, the Greeks showed no such reverence.

Just let no lust, no mad desire seize the armies
345   to ravish what they must not touch—
overwhelmed by all they've won!
                                          The run for home
and safety waits, the swerve at the post,
the final lap of the gruelling two-lap race.
And even if the men come back with no offence
350   to the gods, the avenging dead may never rest—
Oh let no new disaster strike! And here
you have it, what a woman has to say.
Let the best win out, clear to see.
A small desire but all that I could want.
355 LEADER   Spoken like a man, my lady, loyal,
full of self-command. I've heard your sign
and now your vision.
               [*Reaching towards her as she turns and re-enters the palace.*]
                              Now to praise the gods.
The joy is worth the labour.
       CHORUS   O Zeus my king and Night, dear Night,
360   queen of the house who covers us with glories,
you slung your net on the towers of Troy,
neither young nor strong could leap
the giant dredge net of slavery,
          all-embracing ruin.
365   I adore you, iron Zeus of the guests[9]
and your revenge—you drew your longbow
year by year to a taut full draw
till one bolt, not falling short
or arching over the stars,
370   could split the mark of Paris![1]

The sky stroke of god!—it is all Troy's to tell,
but even I can trace it to its cause:
god does as god decrees.
          And still some say
375   that heaven would never stoop to punish men
who trample the lovely grace of things
untouchable. How wrong they are!
          A curse burns bright on crime—
               full-blown, the father's crimes will blossom,
380   burst into the son's.
Let there be less suffering . . .
give us the sense to live on what we need.

               Bastions of wealth
               are no defence for the man

---

9. As patron of hospitality, Zeus would punish
anyone who harmed a visiting stranger.
1. That is, hit the target of Paris (a skilled

archer), whose abduction of Helen sparked
the Trojan War. Here the chorus describes
the fall of Troy.

385   who treads the grand altar of Justice
                    down and out of sight.

        Persuasion, maddening child of Ruin
        overpowers him—Ruin plans it all.
        And the wound will smoulder on,
390   there is no cure,
        a terrible brilliance kindles on the night.
        He is bad bronze scraped on a touchstone:
        put to the test, the man goes black.
               Like the boy who chases
395   a bird on the wing, brands his city,
                       brings it down and prays,
        but the gods are deaf
        to the one who turns to crime, they tear him down.

                    So Paris learned:
400   he came to Atreus' house
                    and shamed the tables spread for guests,
                       he stole away the queen.²

        And she left her land *chaos*, clanging shields,
        companions tramping, bronze prows, men in bronze,
405   and she came to Troy with a dowry, death,
        strode through the gates
                    defiant in every stride,
        as prophets of the house looked on and wept,
        'Oh the halls and the lords of war,
410   the bed and the fresh prints of love.
        I *see* him, unavenging, unavenged,
        the stun of his desolation is so clear—
               he longs for the one who lies across the sea
        until her phantom seems to sway the house.

415   Her curving images,
                    her beauty hurts her lord,
                       the eyes starve and the touch
                          of love is gone,

        'and radiant dreams are passing in the night,
420   the memories throb with sorrow, joy with pain . . .
               it is pain to dream and see desires
        slip through the arms,
                    a vision lost for ever
        winging down the moving drifts of sleep.'
425   So he grieves at the royal hearth

        2. Because Paris came to the house of Atreus   Since Zeus is the god guaranteeing hospital-
        as a guest and stole Menelaus's wife, Helen,   ity, Paris brought the wrath of Zeus upon
        he violated the sacred rules of hospitality.   himself and Troy.

yet others' grief is worse, far worse.
All through Greece for those who flocked to war
they are holding back the anguish now,
    you can feel it rising now in every house;
430 I tell you there is much to tear the heart.

        They knew the men they sent,
        but now in place of men
        ashes and urns come back
            to every hearth.

435 War, War, the great gold-broker of corpses
holds the balance of the battle on his spear!
Home from the pyres he sends them,
    home from Troy to the loved ones,
heavy with tears, the urns brimmed full,
440   the heroes return in gold-dust,
dear, light ash for men; and they weep,
they praise them, 'He had skill in the swordplay,'
    'He went down so tall in the onslaught,'
'All for another's woman.' So they mutter
445 in secret and the rancour steals
towards our staunch defenders, Atreus' sons.

        And there they ring the walls, the young,
        the lithe, the handsome hold the graves
        they won in Troy; the enemy earth
450   rides over those who conquered.

The people's voice is heavy with hatred,
now the curses of the people must be paid,
and now I wait, I listen . . .
    there—there is something breathing
455 under the night's shroud. God takes aim
    at the ones who murder many;
the swarthy Furies stalk the man
gone rich beyond all rights—with a twist
    of fortune grind him down, dissolve him
460 into the blurring dead—there is no help.
The reach for power can recoil,
the bolt of god can strike you at a glance.

        Make me rich with no man's envy,
        neither a raider of cities, no,
465   nor slave come face to face with life
            overpowered by another.
        [Speaking singly.]
    —Fire comes and the news is good,
        it races through the streets

but is it true? Who knows?
470   Or just another lie from heaven?

—Show us the man so childish, wonderstruck,
      he's fired up with the first torch,
   then when the message shifts
   he's sick at heart.

                  —Just like a woman
475   to fill with thanks before the truth is clear.

—So gullible. Their stories spread like wildfire,
      they fly fast and die faster;
   rumours voiced by women come to nothing.
LEADER   Soon we'll know her fires for what they are,
480   her relay race of torches hand-to-hand—
   know if they're real or just a dream,
   the hope of a morning here to take our senses.
   I see a herald running from the beach
   and a victor's spray of olive shades his eyes
485   and the dust he kicks, twin to the mud of Troy,
   shows he has a voice—no kindling timber
   on the cliffs, no signal-fires for him.
   He can shout the news and give us joy,
   or else . . . please, not that.
                     Bring it on,
490   good fuel to build the first good fires.
   And if anyone calls down the worst on Argos
   let him reap the rotten harvest of his mind.
         [*The* HERALD *rushes in and kneels on the ground.*]
HERALD   Good Greek earth, the soil of my fathers!
   Ten years out, and a morning brings me back.
495   All hopes snapped but one—I'm home at last.
   Never dreamed I'd die in Greece, assigned
   the narrow plot I love the best.
                  And now
   I salute the land, the light of the sun,
   our high lord Zeus and the king of Pytho[3]—
500   no more arrows, master, raining on our heads!
   At Scamander's[4] banks we took our share,
   your longbow brought us down like plague.
   Now come, deliver us, heal us—lord Apollo!
   Gods of the market, here, take my salute.
505   And you, my Hermes,[5] Escort,
   loving Herald, the herald's shield and prayer!—

3. Apollo had slain the Python, a huge serpent
that guarded Delphi, and thus taken control
of the Delphic oracle. He sided with the Trojans against the Greeks in the Trojan War.
4. A river near Troy. In the *Iliad*, Homer

describes Achilles' fight against the river god
Scamander.
5. Greek god of boundaries and travelers, as
well as invention, commerce, and cunning;
Zeus's messenger and the gods' herald.

And the shining dead of the land who launched the armies,
warm us home . . . we're all the spear has left.

You halls of the kings, you roofs I cherish,
510   sacred seats—you gods that catch the sun,
if your glances ever shone on him in the old days,
greet him well—so many years are lost.
He comes, he brings us light in the darkness,
free for every comrade, Agamemnon lord of men.

515   Give him the royal welcome he deserves!
He hoisted the pickaxe of Zeus who brings revenge,
he dug Troy down, he worked her soil down,
the shrines of her gods and the high altars, gone!—
and the seed of her wide earth he ground to bits.
520   That's the yoke he claps on Troy. The king,
the son of Atreus comes. The man is blest,
the one man alive to merit such rewards.

Neither Paris nor Troy, partners to the end,
can say their work outweighs their wages now.
525   Convicted of rapine, stripped of all his spoils,
and his father's house and the land that gave it life—
he's scythed them to the roots. The sons of Priam[6]
pay the price twice over.
LEADER   Welcome home
from the wars, herald, long live your joy.
HERALD   Our joy—
530   now I could die gladly. Say the word, dear gods.
LEADER   Longing for your country left you raw?
HERALD   The tears fill my eyes, for joy.
LEADER   You too,
down with the sweet disease that kills a man
with kindness . . .
HERALD   Go on, I don't see what you—
LEADER   Love
535   for the ones who love you—that's what took you.
HERALD   You mean
the land and the armies hungered for each other?
LEADER   There were times I thought I'd faint with longing.
HERALD   So anxious for the armies, why?
LEADER   For years now,
only my silence kept me free from harm.
HERALD   What,
540   with the kings gone did someone threaten you?
LEADER   So much . . .
now as you say, it would be good to die.

6. Priam's sons included not only Paris but also the heroic warriors Hector and Troilus. "Sons of
Priam" can also be understood to mean all of Priam's Trojan subjects.

HERALD   True, we *have* done well.
          Think back in the years and what have you?
          A few runs of luck, a lot that's bad.
545   Who but a god can go through life unmarked?

          A long, hard pull we had, if I would tell it all.
          The iron rations, penned in the gangways
          hock by jowl like sheep. Whatever miseries
          break a man, our quota, every sun-starved day.

550   Then on the beaches it was worse. Dug in
          under the enemy ramparts—deadly going.
          Out of the sky, out of the marshy flats
          the dews soaked us, turned the ruts we fought from
          into gullies, made our gear, our scalps
555   crawl with lice.
                          And talk of the cold,
          the sleet to freeze the gulls, and the big snows
          come avalanching down from Ida. Oh but the heat,
          the sea and the windless noons, the swells asleep,
          dropped to a dead calm . . .

560   But why weep now?
          It's over for us, over for them.
          The dead can rest and never rise again;
          no need to call their muster. We're alive,
          do we have to go on raking up old wounds?
565   Good-bye to all that. Glad I am to say it.

          For us, the remains of the Greek contingents,
          the good wins out, no pain can tip the scales,
          not now. So shout this boast to the bright sun—
          fitting it is—wing it over the seas and rolling earth:

570   'Once when an Argive[7] expedition captured Troy
          they hauled these spoils back to the gods of Greece,
          they bolted them high across the temple doors,
          the glory of the past!'
                                And hearing that,
          men will applaud our city and our chiefs,
575   and Zeus will have the hero's share of fame—
          he did the work.
                          That's all I have to say.
LEADER   I'm convinced, glad that I was wrong.
          Never too old to learn; it keeps me young.
               [CLYTAEMNESTRA *enters with her women.*]

---

7. The term for a citizen of Argos, used more generally by Homer and others to refer to any Greek.

First the house and the queen, it's their affair,
580   but I can taste the riches.

CLYTAEMNESTRA   I cried out long ago!—
for joy, when the first herald came burning
through the night and told the city's fall.
And there were some who smiled and said,
'A few fires persuade you Troy's in ashes.
585   Women, women, elated over nothing.'

You made me seem deranged.
For all that I sacrificed—a woman's way,
you'll say—station to station on the walls
we lifted cries of triumph that resounded
590   in the temples of the gods. We lulled and blessed
the fires with myrrh and they consumed our victims.

          [*Turning to the* HERALD.]
But enough. Why prolong the story?
From the king himself I'll gather all I need.
Now for the best way to welcome home
595   my lord, my good lord . . .
                              No time to lose!
What dawn can feast a woman's eyes like this?
I can see the light, the husband plucked from war
by the Saving God and open wide the gates.

Tell him that, and have him come with speed,
600   the people's darling—how they long for him.
And for his wife,
may he return and find her true at hall,
just as the day he left her, faithful to the last.
A watchdog gentle to him alone,
          [*Glancing towards the palace.*]
                              savage
605   to those who cross his path. I have not changed.
The strains of time can never break our seal.
In love with a new lord, in ill repute I am
as practised as I am in dyeing bronze.[8]

That is my boast, teeming with the truth.
610   I am proud, a woman of my nobility—
I'd hurl it from the roofs!
          [*She turns sharply, enters the palace.*]
LEADER   She speaks well, but it takes no seer to know
she only says what's right.
          [*The* HERALD *attempts to leave; the leader takes him by the arm.*]
                              Wait, one thing.
Menelaus, is he home too, safe with the men?

_____

8. That is, not practiced at all. In ancient Greece, only men worked as metalsmiths.

615   The power of the land—dear king.
       HERALD   I doubt that lies will help my friends,
          in the lean months to come.
       LEADER   Help us somehow, tell the truth as well.
          But when the two conflict it's hard to hide—
620   out with it.
       HERALD   He's lost, gone from the fleets!
          He and his ship, it's true.
       LEADER   After you watched him
          pull away from Troy? Or did some storm
          attack you all and tear him off the line?
       HERALD   There,
          like a marksman, the whole disaster cut to a word.
625   LEADER   How do the escorts give him out—dead or alive?
       HERALD   No clear report. No one knows . . .
          only the wheeling sun that heats the earth to life.
       LEADER   But then the storm—how did it reach the ships?
          How did it end? Were the angry gods on hand?
630   HERALD   This blessed day, ruin it with *them*?
          Better to keep their trophies far apart.

          When a runner comes, his face in tears,
          saddled with what his city dreaded most,
          the armies routed, two wounds in one,
635   one to the city, one to hearth and home . . .
          our best men, droves of them, victims
          herded from every house by the two-barb whip
          that Ares⁹ likes to crack,
                                    that charioteer
          who packs destruction shaft by shaft,
640   careering on with his brace of bloody mares—
          When he comes in, I tell you, dragging that much pain,
          wail your battle-hymn to the Furies, and high time!

          But when he brings salvation home to a city
          singing out her heart—
645   how can I mix the good with so much bad
          and blurt out this?—
                                'Storms swept the Greeks,
          and not without the anger of the gods!'

          Those enemies for ages, fire and water,
          sealed a pact and showed it to the world—
650   they crushed our wretched squadrons.
                                            Night looming,
          breakers lunging in for the kill
          and the black gales come brawling out of the north—
          ships ramming, prow into hooking prow, gored

          _____
          9. Greek god of war, especially savage warfare and bloodlust.

by the rush-and-buck of hurricane pounding rain
655   by the cloudburst—
                              ships stampeding into the darkness,
         lashed and spun by the savage shepherd's hand!

         But when the sun comes up to light the skies
         I see the Aegean[1] heaving into a great bloom
         of corpses . . . Greeks, the pick of a generation
660   scattered through the wrecks and broken spars.

         But not us, not our ship, our hull untouched.
         Someone stole us away or begged us off.
         No mortal—a god, death grip on the tiller,
         or lady luck herself, perched on the helm,
665   she pulled us through, she saved us. Aye,
         we'll never battle the heavy surf at anchor,
         never shipwreck up some rocky coast.

         But once we cleared that sea-hell, not even
         trusting luck in the cold light of day,
670   we battened on our troubles, they were fresh—
         the armada punished, bludgeoned into nothing.
         And now if one of them still has the breath
         he's saying *we* are lost. Why not?
         We say the same of him. Well,
675   here's to the best.
                              And Menelaus?
         Look to it, he's come back, and yet . . .
         if a shaft of the sun can track him down,
         alive, and his eyes full of the old fire—
         thanks to the strategies of Zeus, Zeus
680   would never tear the house out by the roots—
         then there's hope our man will make it home.

         You've heard it all. Now you have the truth.
                 [*Rushing out.*]
CHORUS   Who—what power named the name that drove your fate?—
         what hidden brain could divine your future,
685   steer that word to the mark,
         to the bride of spears,
              the whirlpool churning armies,
                   Oh for all the world a Helen!
         Hell at the prows, hell at the gates
690   hell on the men-of-war,
         from her lair's sheer veils she drifted
              launched by the giant western wind,
                   and the long tall waves of men in armour,

---

1. The Aegean Sea, between Greece and Asia Minor.

huntsmen trailing the oar-blades' dying spoor
695   slipped into her moorings,
      Simois'[2] mouth that chokes with foliage,
        bayed for bloody strife,
for Troy's Blood Wedding Day—she drives her word,
her burning will to the birth, the Fury
700   late but true to the cause,
to the tables shamed
      and Zeus who guards the hearth—
        the Fury makes the Trojans pay!
Shouting their hymns, hymns for the bride
705   hymns for the kinsmen doomed
to the wedding march of Fate.
      Troy changed her tune in her late age,
        and I think I hear the dirges mourning
'Paris, born and groomed for the bed of Fate!'
710   They mourn with their life breath,
      they sing their last, the sons of Priam
        born for bloody slaughter.

      So a man once reared
a lion cub at hall, snatched
715   from the breast, still craving milk
      in the first flush of life.
A captivating pet for the young,
and the old men adored it, pampered it
      in their arms, day in, day out,
720   like an infant just born.
Its eyes on fire, little beggar,
fawning for its belly, slave to food.

      But it came of age
and the parent strain broke out
725   and it paid its breeders back.
      Grateful it was, it went
through the flock to prepare a feast,
an illicit orgy—the house swam with blood,
      none could resist that agony—
730   massacre vast and raw!
From god there came a priest of ruin,
adopted by the house to lend it warmth.

And the first sensation Helen brought to Troy . . .
call it a spirit
735   shimmer of winds dying
      glory light as gold
        shaft of the eyes dissolving, open bloom
that wounds the heart with love.

---

2. A small river in Asia Minor, near Troy, that is a tributary of the Scamander.

But veering wild in mid-flight
740   she whirled her wedding on to a stabbing end,
slashed at the sons of Priam—hearthmate, friend to the death,
        sped by Zeus who speeds the guest,
a bride of tears, a Fury.

There's an ancient saying, old as man himself:
745   men's prosperity
            never will die childless,
                    once full-grown it breeds.
            Sprung from the great good fortune in the race
        comes bloom on bloom of pain—
750   insatiable wealth! But not I,
I alone say this. Only the reckless act
can breed impiety, multiplying crime on crime,
        while the house kept straight and just
is blessed with radiant children.

755   But ancient Violence longs to breed,
                            new Violence comes
                when its fatal hour comes, the demon comes
                to take her toll—no war, no force, no prayer
                        can hinder the midnight Fury stamped
760   with parent Fury moving through the house.

                    But Justice shines in sooty hovels,
                            loves the decent life.
            From proud halls crusted with gilt by filthy hands
                she turns her eyes to find the pure in spirit—
765   spurning the wealth stamped counterfeit with praise,
                she steers all things towards their destined end.

[AGAMEMNON *enters in his chariot, his plunder borne before him
by his entourage; behind him, half hidden, stands* CASSANDRA.
The old men press towards him.]

Come, my king, the scourge of Troy,
        the true son of Atreus—
How to salute you, how to praise you
770   neither too high nor low, but hit
the note of praise that suits the hour?
So many prize some brave display,
they prefer some flaunt of honour
        once they break the bounds.
775   When a man fails they share his grief,
but the pain can never cut them to the quick.
When a man succeeds they share his glory,
torturing their faces into smiles.
But the good shepherd knows his flock.
780   When the eyes seem to brim with love
        and it is only unction, fawning,
he will know, better than we can know.

That day you marshalled the armies
all for Helen—no hiding it now—
785   I drew you in my mind in black;
you seemed a menace at the helm,
      sending men to the grave
to bring her home, that hell on earth.
But now from the depths of trust and love
790   I say Well fought, well won—
      the end is worth the labour!
Search, my king, and learn at last
who stayed at home and kept their faith
      and who betrayed the city.

AGAMEMNON   First,
795   with justice I salute my Argos and my gods,
my accomplices who brought me home and won
my rights from Priam's Troy—the just gods.
No need to hear our pleas. Once for all
they consigned their lots to the urn of blood,
800   they pitched on death for men, annihilation
for the city. Hope's hand, hovering
over the urn of mercy, left it empty.
Look for the smoke—it is the city's seamark,
building even now.
                        The storms of ruin live!
805   Her last dying breath, rising up from the ashes
sends us gales of incense rich in gold.

For that we must thank the gods with a sacrifice
our sons will long remember. For their mad outrage
of a queen we raped their city—we were right.
810   The beast of Argos, foals of the wild mare,
thousands massed in armour rose on the night
the Pleiades[3] went down, and crashing through
their walls our bloody lion lapped its fill,
gorging on the blood of kings.
                              Our thanks to the gods,
815   long drawn out, but it is just the prelude.

      [CLYTAEMNESTRA approaches with her women; they are carrying
      dark red tapestries. AGAMEMNON turns to the leader.]

And your concern, old man, is on my mind.
I hear you and agree, I will support you.
How rare, men with the character to praise
a friend's success without a trace of envy,
820   poison to the heart—it deals a double blow.
Your own losses weigh you down but then,
look at your neighbour's fortune and you weep.
Well I know. I understand society,

---

3. A cluster of stars in the constellation Taurus, which sets in the winter; in mythology, the
daughters of the Titan Atlas and Pleione, daughter of Oceanus.

the flattering mirror of the proud.

My comrades . . .

825 they're shadows, I tell you, ghosts of men
who swore they'd die for me. Only Odysseus:[4]
I dragged that man to the wars but once in harness
he was a trace-horse, he gave his all for me.
Dead or alive, no matter, I can praise him.

830 And now this cause involving men and gods.
We must summon the city for a trial,
found a national tribunal. Whatever's healthy,
shore it up with law and help it flourish.
Wherever something calls for drastic cures
835 we make our noblest effort: amputate or wield
the healing iron, burn the cancer at the roots.

Now I go to my father's house—
I give the gods my right hand, my first salute.
The ones who sent me forth have brought me home.

[*He starts down from the chariot, looks at* CLYTAEMNESTRA,
stops, and offers up a prayer.]

840 Victory, you have sped my way before,
now speed me to the last.

[CLYTAEMNESTRA *turns from the king to the* CHORUS.]

CLYTAEMNESTRA   Old nobility of Argos
gathered here, I am not ashamed to tell you
how I love the man. I am older,
and the fear dies away . . . I am human.
845 Nothing I say was learned from others.
This is my life, my ordeal, long as the siege
he laid at Troy and more demanding.

First,
when a woman sits at home and the man is gone,
the loneliness is terrible,
850 unconscionable . . .
and the rumours spread and fester,
a runner comes with something dreadful,
close on his heels the next and his news worse,
and they shout it out and the whole house can hear;
855 and wounds—if he took one wound for each report
to penetrate these walls, he's gashed like a dragnet,
more, if he had only died . . .
for each death that swelled his record, he could boast
like a triple-bodied Geryon[5] risen from the grave,

---

4. King of Ithaca and one of Agamemnon's principal lieutenants; initially feigned madness in an unsuccessful effort to avoid his obligation to join the expedition to Troy.

5. A giant with three heads and three bodies; he was killed by the great hero Heracles, whose tenth labor was to steal the cattle of Geryon.

860 'Three shrouds I dug from the earth, one for every body
that went down!'
                        The rumours broke like fever,
broke and then rose higher. There were times
they cut me down and eased my throat from the noose.
I wavered between the living and the dead.
            [*Turning to* AGAMEMNON.]

                                            And so
865 our child is gone, not standing by our side,
the bond of our dearest pledges, mine and yours;
by all rights our child should be here . . .
Orestes.[6] You seem startled.
You needn't be. Our loyal brother-in-arms
870 will take good care of him, Strophios the Phocian.
He warned from the start we court two griefs in one.
You risk all on the wars—and what if the people
rise up howling for the king, and anarchy
should dash our plans?
                        Men, it is their nature,
875 trampling on the fighter once he's down.
Our child is gone. That is my self-defence
and it is true.
                        For me, the tears that welled
like springs are dry. I have no tears to spare.
I'd watch till late at night, my eyes still burn,
880 I sobbed by the torch I lit for you alone.
            [*Glancing towards the palace.*]
I never let it die . . . but in my dreams
the high thin wail of a gnat would rouse me,
piercing like a trumpet—I could see you
suffer more than all
885 the hours that slept with me could ever bear.

I endured it all. And now, free of grief,
I would salute that man the watchdog of the fold,
the mainroyal,[7] saving stay of the vessel,
rooted oak that thrusts the roof sky-high,
890 the father's one true heir.
Land at dawn to the shipwrecked past all hope,
light of the morning burning off the night of storm,
the cold clear spring to the parched horseman—
O the ecstasy, to flee the yoke of Fate!

895 It is right to use the titles he deserves.

---

6. Son of Agamemnon and Clytaemnestra; at
the time of the action of *Agamemnon*, he was
a ward of Strophios, king of Phocis, in central
Greece. Orestes is the protagonist of the other
two plays of Aeschylus's *Oresteia* trilogy.
7. The upper sail of a ship's principal mast.

Let envy keep her distance. We have suffered
long enough.
              [*Reaching towards* AGAMEMNON.]
                    Come to me now, my dearest,
down from the car of war, but never set the foot
that stamped out Troy on earth again, my great one.

900   Women, why delay? You have your orders.
Pave his way with tapestries.
              [*They begin to spread the crimson tapestries between the king
              and the palace doors.*]
                          Quickly.
Let the red stream flow and bear him home
to the home he never hoped to see—Justice,
lead him in!
                    Leave all the rest to me.
905   The spirit within me never yields to sleep.
We will set things right, with the god's help.
We will do whatever Fate requires.
AGAMEMNON   There
is Leda's daughter, the keeper of my house.
And the speech to suit my absence, much too long.
910   But the praise that does us justice,
let it come from others, then we prize it.
                          This—
you treat me like a woman. Grovelling, gaping up at me—
what am I, some barbarian peacocking out of Asia?
Never cross my path with robes and draw the lightning.[8]
915   Never—only the gods deserve the pomps of honour
and the stiff brocades of fame. To walk on them . . .
I am human, and it makes my pulses stir
with dread.
                    Give me the tributes of a man
and not a god, a little earth to walk on,
920   not this gorgeous work.
There is no need to sound my reputation.
I have a sense of right and wrong, what's more—
heaven's proudest gift. Call no man blest
until he ends his life in peace, fulfilled.
925   If I can live by what I say, I have no fear.
CLYTAEMNESTRA   One thing more. Be true to your ideals and tell me—
AGAMEMNON   True to my ideals? Once I violate them I am lost.
CLYTAEMNESTRA   Would you have sworn this act to god in a time of terror?
AGAMEMNON   Yes, if a prophet called for a last, drastic rite.
930   CLYTAEMNESTRA   But Priam—can you see him if he had your success?
AGAMEMNON   Striding on the tapestries of god, I see him now.

---

8. That is, draw the wrath of Zeus by stepping on the crimson tapestries, an act of profound
hubris offensive to Greek sensibilities.

CLYTAEMNESTRA   And *you* fear the reproach of common men?
AGAMEMNON   The voice of the people—aye, they have enormous power.
CLYTAEMNESTRA   Perhaps, but where's the glory without a little gall?
935 AGAMEMNON   And where's the woman in all this lust for glory?
CLYTAEMNESTRA   But the great victor—it becomes him to give way.
AGAMEMNON   Victory in this . . . war of ours, it means so much to you?
CLYTAEMNESTRA   O give way! The power is yours if you surrender,
all of your own free will, to me!
AGAMEMNON   Enough.
940 If you are so determined—

> [*Turning to the women, pointing to his boots.*]

Let someone help me off with these at least.
Old slaves, they've stood me well.
                                                    Hurry,
and while I tread his splendours dyed red in the sea,[9]
may no god watch and strike me down with envy
945 from on high. I feel such shame—
to tread the life of the house, a kingdom's worth
of silver in the weaving.

> [*He steps down from the chariot to the tapestries and reveals* CASSANDRA,[1]
> *dressed in the sacred regalia, the fillets, robes, and sceptre of Apollo.*]

                              Done is done.
Escort this stranger in, be gentle.
Conquer with compassion. Then the gods
950 shine down upon you, gently. No one chooses
the yoke of slavery, not of one's free will—
and she least of all. The gift of the armies,
flower and pride of all the wealth we won,
she follows me from Troy.
                                      And now,
955 since you have brought me down with your insistence,
just this once I enter my father's house,
trampling royal crimson as I go.

> [*He takes his first steps and pauses.*]

CLYTAEMNESTRA   There is the sea
and who will drain it dry? Precious as silver,
inexhaustible, ever-new, it breeds the more we reap it—
960 tides on tides of crimson dye our robes blood-red.
Our lives are based on wealth, my king,
the gods have seen to that.
Destitution, our house has never heard the word.
I would have sworn to tread on legacies of robes,
965 at one command from an oracle, deplete the house—
suffer the worst to bring that dear life back!

> [*Encouraged,* AGAMEMNON *strides to the entrance.*]

9. The robes have been dyed with Tyrian purple, a rare and costly pigment obtained from a
marine mollusk most commonly found, in ancient times, near the city of Tyre in Phoenicia.
1. Daughter of Priam, now Agamemnon's

slave and prize. Before the Trojan War, the
god Apollo desired her for her beauty and
gave her the gift of prophesy; but when she
would not return his love, he added the curse
that no one would believe her prophesies.

When the root lives on, the new leaves come back,
spreading a dense shroud of shade across the house
to thwart the Dog Star's[2] fury. So you return
970 to the father's hearth, you bring us warmth in winter
like the sun—
                    And you are Zeus when Zeus
tramples the bitter virgin grape for new wine
and the welcome chill steals through the halls, at last
the master moves among the shadows of his house, fulfilled.

> [AGAMEMNON *goes over the threshold; the women gather up the*
> *tapestries while* CLYTAEMNESTRA *prays.*]

975 Zeus, Zeus, master of all fulfilment, now fulfil our prayers—
speed our rites to their fulfilment once for all!

> [*She enters the palace, the doors close, the old men huddle in terror.*]

CHORUS   Why, why does it rock me, never stops,
this terror beating down my heart,
        this seer that sees it all—
980 it beats its wings, uncalled unpaid
thrust on the lungs
the mercenary song beats on and on
singing a prophet's strain—
        and I can't throw it off
985 like dreams that make no sense,
and the strength drains
that filled the mind with trust,
and the years drift by and the driven sand
        has buried the mooring lines
990 that churned when the armoured squadrons cut for Troy . . .
and now I believe it, I can prove he's home,
        my own clear eyes for witness—
                                        Agamemnon!
Still it's chanting, beating deep so deep in the heart
this dirge of the Furies, oh dear god,
995 not fit for the lyre, its own master
        it kills our spirit
kills our hopes
and it's real, true, no fantasy—
        stark terror whirls the brain
1000   and the end is coming
                    Justice comes to birth—
I pray my fears prove false and fall
and die and never come to birth!
Even exultant health, well we know,
1005   exceeds its limits, comes so near disease
it can breach the wall between them.

---

2. Sirius, the brightest star in the Northern Hemisphere, associated by the ancients with the heat
of summer.

Even a man's fate, held true on course,
 in a blinding flash rams some hidden reef;
but if caution only casts the pick of the cargo—
1010 one well-balanced cast—
the house will not go down, not outright;
labouring under its wealth of grief
the ship of state rides on.

Yes, and the great green bounty of god,
1015 sown in the furrows year by year and reaped each fall
can end the plague of famine.

But a man's life-blood
 is dark and mortal.
Once it wets the earth
1020 what song can sing it back?
Not even the master-healer
 who brought the dead to life[3]—
Zeus stopped the man before he did more harm.

Oh, if only the gods had never forged
1025 the chain that curbs our excess,
 one man's fate curbing the next man's fate,
my heart would outrace my song, I'd pour out all I feel—
  but no, I choke with anguish,
  mutter through the nights.
1030 Never to ravel out a hope in time
and the brain is swarming, burning—

 [CLYTAEMNESTRA *emerges from the palace and goes to* CASSANDRA, *impassive in the chariot.*]

CLYTAEMNESTRA Won't you come inside? I mean you, Cassandra.
Zeus in all his mercy wants you to share
some victory libations with the house.
1035 The slaves are flocking. Come, lead them
up to the altar of the god who guards
our dearest treasures.
    Down from the chariot,
this is no time for pride. Why even Heracles,[4]
they say, was sold into bondage long ago,
1040 he had to endure the bitter bread of slaves.
But if the yoke descends on you, be grateful
for a master born and reared in ancient wealth.
Those who reap a harvest past their hopes
are merciless to their slaves.
    From us

---

3. Asclepius or Aesculapius, son of Apollo and Greek god of medicine; Zeus killed him with a thunderbolt.
4. A son of Zeus and greatest of the divine heroes in classical mythology (known to the Romans as Hercules). In one myth, Heracles commits a murder and is punished by being made a slave to Omphale, queen of Lydia.

1045   you will receive what custom says is right.

[CASSANDRA *remains impassive.*]

LEADER   It's *you* she is speaking to, it's all too clear.
You're caught in the nets of doom—obey
if you can obey, unless you cannot bear to.

CLYTAEMNESTRA   Unless she's like a swallow, possessed

1050   of her own barbaric song, strange, dark.
I speak directly as I can—she must obey.

LEADER   Go with her. Make the best of it, she's right.
Step down from the seat, obey her.

CLYTAEMNESTRA   Do it *now*—
I have no time to spend outside. Already

1055   the victims crowd the hearth, the Navelstone,[5]
to bless this day of joy I never hoped to see!—
our victims waiting for the fire and the knife,
and you,
if you want to taste our mystic rites, come now.

1060   If my words can't reach you—

[*Turning to the* LEADER.]

Give her a sign,
one of her exotic handsigns.

LEADER   I think
the stranger needs an interpreter, someone clear.
She's like a wild creature, fresh caught.

CLYTAEMNESTRA   She's mad,
her evil genius murmuring in her ears.

1065   She comes from a *city* fresh caught.
She must learn to take the cutting bridle
before she foams her spirit off in blood—
and that's the last I waste on her contempt!

[*Wheeling, re-entering the palace. The* LEADER *turns to* CASSANDRA,
who remains transfixed.]

LEADER   Not I, I pity her. I will be gentle.

1070   Come, poor thing. Leave the empty chariot—
Of your own free will try on the yoke of Fate.

CASSANDRA   Aieeeeee! Earth—Mother—
Curse of the Earth—Apollo Apollo!

LEADER   Why cry to Apollo?
He's not the god to call with sounds of mourning.

1075   CASSANDRA   Aieeeeee! Earth—Mother—
Rape of the Earth—Apollo Apollo!

LEADER   Again, it's a bad omen.
She cries for the god who wants no part of grief.

[CASSANDRA *steps from the chariot, looks slowly towards the
rooftops of the palace.*]

---

5. An altar to Zeus, guardian of the hearth.

CASSANDRA   God of the long road,
    Apollo *Apollo* my destroyer[6]—
1080 you destroy me once, destroy me twice—
LEADER   She's about to sense her own ordeal, I think.
    Slave that she is, the god lives on inside her.
CASSANDRA   God of the iron marches,
    Apollo *Apollo* my destroyer—
1085 where, where have you led me now? what house—
LEADER   The house of Atreus and his sons. Really—
    don't you know? It's true, see for yourself.
CASSANDRA   No . . . the house that hates god,
    an echoing womb of guilt, kinsmen
1090   torturing kinsmen, severed heads,
    slaughterhouse of heroes, soil streaming blood—
LEADER   A keen hound, this stranger.
    Trailing murder, and murder she will find.
CASSANDRA   See, my witnesses—
1095   I trust to them, to the babies
      wailing, skewered on the sword,
    their flesh charred, the father gorging on their parts[7]—
LEADER   We'd heard your fame as a seer,
    but no one looks for seers in Argos.
1100 CASSANDRA   Oh no, what horror, what new plot,
    new agony this?—
    it's growing, massing, deep in the house,
      a plot, a monstrous—*thing*
        to crush the loved ones, no,
1105   there is no cure, and rescue's far away and—
LEADER   I can't read these signs; I knew the first,
    the city rings with them.
CASSANDRA   You, you godforsaken—you'd do *this*?
    The lord of your bed,
1110 you bathe him . . . his body glistens, then—
      how to tell the climax?—
        comes so quickly, see,
      hand over hand shoots out, hauling ropes—
                  then lunge!
LEADER   Still lost. Her riddles, her dark words of god—
1115 I'm groping, helpless.
CASSANDRA   No no, look *there*!—
    what's that? some net flung out of hell—
      No, *she* is the snare,
    the bedmate, deathmate, murder's strong right arm!
      Let the insatiate discord in the race
1120 rear up and shriek 'Avenge the victim—stone them dead!'
LEADER   What Fury is this? Why rouse it, lift its wailing
    through the house? I hear you and lose hope.

---

6. The Greek word "destroyer" (*apollōn*) echoes   7. A reference to "Thyestes' feast" (see note at
the god's name.   line 1254).

CHORUS   Drop by drop at the heart, the gold of life ebbs out.
         We are the old soldiers . . . wounds will come
1125   with the crushing sunset of our lives.
         Death is close, and quick.
CASSANDRA   Look out! *look out!*—
         Ai, drag the great bull from the mate!—
            a thrash of robes, she traps him—
         writhing—
                     black horn glints, twists—
                              she gores him through!
1130   And now he buckles, look, the bath swirls red—
         There's stealth and murder in the cauldron, do you hear?
LEADER   I'm no judge, I've little skill with the oracles,
         but even I know danger when I hear it.
CHORUS   What good are the oracles to men? Words, more words,
1135   and the hurt comes on us, endless words
         and a seer's techniques have brought us
         terror and the truth.
CASSANDRA   The agony—O I am breaking!—Fate's so hard,
         and the pain that floods my voice is mine alone.
1140   Why have you brought me here, tormented as I am?
         Why, unless to die with him, why else?
LEADER AND CHORUS   Mad with the rapture—god speeds you on
            to the song, the deathsong,
         like the nightingale that broods on sorrow,
1145   mourns her son, her son,
         her life inspired with grief for him,
         she lilts and shrills, dark bird that lives for night.
CASSANDRA   The nightingale—O for a song, a fate like hers!
         The gods gave her a life of ease, swathed her in wings,[8]
1150   no tears, no wailing. The knife waits for me.
         They'll splay me on the iron's double edge.
LEADER AND CHORUS   Why?—what god hurls you on, stroke on stroke
            to the long dying fall?
         Why the horror clashing through your music,
1155   terror struck to song?—
         why the anguish, the wild dance?
         Where do your words of god and grief begin?
CASSANDRA   Ai, the wedding, wedding of Paris,
         death to the loved ones. Oh Scamander,
1160   you nursed my father . . . once at your banks
            I nursed and grew, and now at the banks
         of Acheron,[9] the stream that carries sorrow,
         it seems I'll chant my prophecies too soon.
LEADER AND CHORUS   What are you saying? Wait, it's clear,
1165   a child could see the truth, it wounds within,

8. In Greek mythology, the gods turned   and feeding him their son.
Procne into a nightingale after she took ven- 9. One of the rivers in Hades (the under-
geance on her husband (who had raped and   world), a tributary of the river Styx.
cut out the tongue of her sister) by cooking

like a bloody fang it tears—
I hear your destiny—breaking sobs,
cries that stab the ears.

CASSANDRA   Oh the grief, the grief of the city
1170   ripped to oblivion. Oh the victims,
the flocks my father burned at the wall,
rich herds in flames . . . no cure for the doom
that took the city after all, and I,
her last ember, I go down with her.

1175   LEADER AND CHORUS   You cannot stop, your song goes on—
some spirit drops from the heights and treads you down
and the brutal strain grows—
your death-throes come and come and
I cannot see the end!

1180   CASSANDRA   Then off with the veils that hid the fresh young bride—
we will see the truth.
Flare up once more, my oracle! Clear and sharp
as the wind that blows towards the rising sun,
I can feel a deeper swell now, gathering head
1185   to break at last and bring the dawn of grief.

No more riddles. I will teach you.
Come, bear witness, run and hunt with me.
We trail the old barbaric works of slaughter.

These roofs—look up—there is a dancing troupe
1190   that never leaves. And they have their harmony
but it is harsh, their words are harsh, they drink
beyond the limit. Flushed on the blood of men
their spirit grows and none can turn away
their revel breeding in the veins—the Furies!
1195   They cling to the house for life. They sing,
sing of the frenzy that began it all,
strain rising on strain, showering curses
on the man who tramples on his brother's bed.[1]

There. Have I hit the mark or not? Am I a fraud,
1200   a fortune-teller babbling lies from door to door?
Swear how well I know the ancient crimes
that live within this house.

LEADER   And if I did?
Would an oath bind the wounds and heal us?
But you amaze me. Bred across the sea,
1205   your language strange, and still you sense the truth
as if you had been here.

---

1. A reference to the adultery committed by Thyestes against his brother Atreus, king of Mycenae and father of Agamemnon and Menelaus. The ensuing cycle of murderous vengeance (see lines 1254–55) was part of the curse on their house, caused by the crimes of their father (Pelops) and grandfather (Tantalus).

CASSANDRA   Apollo the Prophet
   introduced me to his gift.
LEADER   A *god*—and moved with love?
CASSANDRA   I was ashamed to tell this once,
1210   but now . . .
LEADER   We spoil ourselves with scruples,
   long as things go well.
CASSANDRA   He came like a wrestler,
   magnificent, took me down and breathed his fire
   through me and—
LEADER   You bore him a child?
CASSANDRA   I yielded,
   then at the climax I recoiled—I deceived Apollo!
1215 LEADER   But the god's skills—they seized you even then?
CASSANDRA   Even then I told my people all the grief to come.
LEADER   And Apollo's anger never touched you?—is it possible?
CASSANDRA   Once I betrayed him I could never be believed.
LEADER   We believe you. Your visions seem so true.
CASSANDRA   Aieeeee!—
1220 the pain, the terror! the birth-pang of the seer
   who tells the truth—
                  it whirls me, oh,
   the storm comes again, the crashing chords!
   Look, you see them nestling at the threshold?
   Young, young in the darkness like a dream,
1225 like children really, yes, and their loved ones
   brought them down . . .
                  their hands, they fill their hands
   with their own flesh, they are serving it like food,
   holding out their entrails . . . now it's clear,
   I can see the armfuls of compassion, see the father
1230 reach to taste and—
               For so much suffering,
   I tell you, someone plots revenge.
   A lion who lacks a lion's heart,
   he sprawled at home in the royal lair
   and set a trap for the lord on his return.
1235 My lord . . . I must wear his yoke, I am his slave.
   The lord of the men-of-war, he obliterated Troy—
   he is so blind, so lost to that detestable hellhound
   who pricks her ears and fawns and her tongue draws out
   her glittering words of welcome—
                  No, he cannot see
1240 the stroke that Fury's hiding, stealth, and murder.
   What outrage—the woman kills the man!
                   What to call
   that . . . monster of Greece, and bring my quarry down?
   Viper coiling back and forth?
                Some sea-witch?—

Scylla[2] crouched in her rocky nest—nightmare of sailors?
1245   Raging mother of death, storming deathless war against
the ones she loves!

                   And how she howled in triumph,
boundless outrage. Just as the tide of battle
broke her way, she seems to rejoice that he
is safe at home from war, saved for her.

1250   Believe me if you will. What will it matter
if you won't? It comes when it comes,
and soon you'll see it face to face
and say the seer was all too true.
You will be moved with pity.

LEADER   Thyestes' feast,[3]
1255   the children's flesh—that I know,
and the fear shudders through me. It's true,
real, no dark signs about it. I hear the rest
but it throws me off the scent.

CASSANDRA   Agamemnon.
You will see him dead.

LEADER   Peace, poor girl!
1260   Put those words to sleep.

CASSANDRA   No use,
the Healer[4] has no hand in this affair.

LEADER   Not if it's true—but god forbid it is!

CASSANDRA   You pray, and they close in to kill!

LEADER   What man prepares this, this dreadful—

CASSANDRA   Man?
1265   You *are* lost, to every word I've said.

LEADER   Yes—
I don't see who can bring the evil off.

CASSANDRA   And yet I know my Greek, too well.

LEADER   So does the Delphic oracle,
but he's hard to understand.

CASSANDRA   His *fire*!—
1270   sears me, sweeps me again—the torture!
Apollo Lord of the Light, you burn,
you blind me—

               Agony!

                 She is the lioness,
she rears on her hind legs, she beds with the wolf
when her lion king goes ranging—

                  she will kill me—

---

2. A six-headed sea monster, whom tradition
locates in the Straits of Messina, between
Italy and Sicily.
3. After Thyestes, the brother of King Atreus,
seduced Atreus's wife and challenged his
claim to the throne, Atreus took revenge by

tricking him into eating his own sons. Thyestes then cursed the house of Atreus. It is this
curse that is being played out in the *Oresteia*
(see lines 1612–43).
4. An epithet of Apollo, god of medicine.

1275   Ai, the torture!
                        She is mixing her drugs,
        adding a measure more of hate for me.
        She gloats as she whets the sword for him.
        He brought me home and we will pay in carnage.

        Why mock yourself with these—trappings, the rod,
1280   the god's wreath, his yoke around my throat?
        Before I die I'll tread you—
                [*Ripping off her regalia, stamping it into the ground.*]
                                        Down, out,
        die die die!
        Now you're down. I've paid you back.
        Look for another victim—I am free at last—
1285   make her rich in all your curse and doom.
                [*Staggering backwards as if wrestling with a spirit tearing at her robes.*]
                                        See,
        Apollo himself, his fiery hands—I feel him again,
        he's stripping off my robes, the Seer's robes!
        And after he looked down and saw me mocked,
        even in these, his glories, mortified by friends
1290   I loved, and they hated me, they were so blind
        to their own demise—
                                I went from door to door,
        I was wild with the god, I heard them call me
        'Beggar! Wretch! Starve for bread in hell!'

        And I endured it all, and now he will
1295   extort me as his due. A seer for the Seer.
        He brings me here to die like this,
        not to serve at my father's altar. No,
        the block is waiting. The cleaver steams
        with my life blood, the first blood drawn
1300   for the king's last rites.
                [*Regaining her composure and moving to the altar.*]
                                        We will die,
        but not without some honour from the gods.
        There will come another to avenge us,
        born to kill his mother, born
        his father's champion. A wanderer, a fugitive
1305   driven off his native land, he will come home
        to cope the stones of hate that menace all he loves.[5]
        The gods have sworn a monumental oath: as his father lies
        upon the ground he draws him home with power like a prayer.

        Then why so pitiful, why so many tears?
1310   I have seen my city faring as she fared,

---

5. Cassandra prophesies that Orestes will   *Libation Bearers*, the second play in the
return to Argos and murder his mother, Cly-   *Oresteia* trilogy.
taemnestra. This murder is the subject of *The*

and those who took her, judged by the gods,
faring as they fare. I must be brave.
It is my turn to die.

      [*Approaching the doors.*]

I address you as the Gates of Death.
1315   I pray it comes with one clear stroke,
no convulsions, the pulses ebbing out
in gentle death. I'll close my eyes and sleep.

LEADER   So much pain, poor girl, and so much truth,
you've told so much. But if you *see* it coming,
1320   clearly—how can you go to your own death,
like a beast to the altar driven on by god,
and hold your head so high?

CASSANDRA   No escape, my friends,
not now.

LEADER   But the last hour should be savoured.

CASSANDRA   My time has come. Little to gain from flight.

1325 LEADER   You're brave, believe me, full of gallant heart.

CASSANDRA   Only the wretched go with praise like that.

LEADER   But to go nobly lends a man some grace.

CASSANDRA   My noble father—you and your noble children.

      [*She nears the threshold and recoils, groaning in revulsion.*]

LEADER   What now? what terror flings you back?
1330   Why? Unless some horror in the brain—

CASSANDRA   Murder.
The house breathes with murder—bloody shambles![6]

LEADER   No, no, only the victims at the hearth.

CASSANDRA   I know that odour. I smell the open grave.

LEADER   But the Syrian myrrh,[7] it fills the halls with splendour,
1335   can't you sense it?

CASSANDRA   Well, I must go in now,
mourning Agamemnon's death and mine.
Enough of life!

      [*Approaching the doors again and crying out.*]

          Friends—I cried out,
not from fear like a bird fresh caught,
but that you will testify to *how* I died.
1340   When the queen, woman for woman, dies for me,
and a man falls for the man who married grief.
That's all I ask, my friends. A stranger's gift
for one about to die.

LEADER   Poor creature, you
and the end you see so clearly. I pity you.

1345 CASSANDRA   I'd like a few words more, a kind of dirge,
it is my own. I pray to the sun,
the last light I'll see,

---

6. Literally, a slaughterhouse.
7. A rare and costly incense obtained from tree resin.

that when the avengers[8] cut the assassins down
they will avenge me too, a slave who died,
1350   an easy conquest.
                              Oh men, your destiny.
When all is well a shadow can overturn it.
When trouble comes a stroke of the wet sponge,
and the picture's blotted out. And that,
I think that breaks the heart.
                    [*She goes through the doors.*]
1355 CHORUS   But the lust for power never dies—
             men cannot have enough.
      No one will lift a hand to send it
      from his door, to give it warning,
      'Power, never come again!'
1360 Take this man: the gods in glory
      gave him Priam's city to plunder,
      brought him home in splendour like a god.
      But now if he must pay for the blood
             his fathers shed, and die for the deaths
1365 he brought to pass, and bring more death
      to avenge his dying, show us one
             who boasts himself born free
      of the raging angel, once he hears—
                    [*Cries break out within the palace.*]
AGAMEMNON   Aagh!
Struck deep—the death-blow, deep—
LEADER   Quiet. Cries,
1370 but who? Someone's stabbed—
AGAMEMNON   Aaagh, again . . .
second blow—struck home.
LEADER   The work is done,
you can feel it. The king, and the great cries—
Close ranks now, find the right way out.
                    [*But the old men scatter, each speaks singly.*]
CHORUS   —I say send out heralds, muster the guard,
1375 they'll save the house.

                    —And I say rush in now,
catch them red-handed—butchery running on their blades.

—Right with you, do something—now or never!

—Look at them, beating the drum for insurrection.

                                              —Yes,
we're wasting time. They rape the name of caution,
1380 their hands will never sleep.
                    —Not a plan in sight.

---

8. In *The Libation Bearers*, Orestes returns with Pylades, the son of Strophius.

Let men of action do the planning, too.
—I'm helpless. Who can raise the dead with words?

—What, drag out our lives? bow down to the tyrants,
    the ruin of the house?

                                    —Never, better to die
1385 on your feet than live on your knees.

                            —Wait,
do we take the cries for signs, prophesy like seers
and give him up for dead?

                            —No more suspicions,
not another word till we have proof.

                            —Confusion
on all sides—one thing to do. See how it stands
1390 with Agamemnon, once and for all we'll see—

> [He rushes at the doors. They open and reveal a silver cauldron that holds
> the body of AGAMEMNON shrouded in bloody robes, with the body of CAS-
> SANDRA to his left and CLYTAEMNESTRA standing to his right, sword in
> hand. She strides towards the chorus.]

CLYTAEMNESTRA Words, endless words I've said to serve the moment—
now it makes me proud to tell the truth.
How else to prepare a death for deadly men
who seem to love you? How to rig the nets
1395 of pain so high no man can overleap them?
I brooded on this trial, this ancient blood feud
year by year. At last my hour came.
Here I stand and here I struck
and here my work is done.
1400 I did it all. I don't deny it, no.
He had no way to flee or fight his destiny—

> [Unwinding the robes from AGAMEMNON's body, spreading them before
> the altar where the old men cluster around them, unified as a chorus
> once again.]

our never-ending, all embracing net, I cast it
wide for the royal haul, I coil him round and round
in the wealth, the robes of doom, and then I strike him
1405 once, twice, and at each stroke he cries in agony—
he buckles at the knees and crashes here!
And when he's down I add the third, last blow,
to the Zeus who saves the dead beneath the ground
I send that third blow home in homage like a prayer.

1410 So he goes down, and the life is bursting out of him—
great sprays of blood, and the murderous shower
wounds me, dyes me black and I, I revel
like the Earth when the spring rains come down,

the blessed gifts of god, and the new green spear
1415 splits the sheath and rips to birth in glory!

So it stands, elders of Argos gathered here.
Rejoice if you can rejoice—I glory.
And if I'd pour upon his body the libation
it deserves, what wine could match my words?
1420 It is right and more than right. He flooded
the vessel of our proud house with misery,
with the vintage of the curse and now
he drains the dregs. My lord is home at last.

LEADER   You appal me, you, your brazen words—
1425 exulting over your fallen king.

CLYTAEMNESTRA   And you,
you try me like some desperate woman.
My heart is steel, well you know. Praise me,
blame me as you choose. It's all one.
Here is Agamemnon, my husband made a corpse
1430 by this right hand—a masterpiece of Justice.
Done is done.

CHORUS   Woman!—what poison cropped from the soil
or strained from the heaving sea, what nursed you,
drove you insane? You brave the curse of Greece.
You have cut away and flung away and now
1435 the people cast you off to exile,
broken with our hate.

CLYTAEMNESTRA   And now you sentence me?—
you banish *me* from the city, curses breathing
down my neck? But *he*—
name one charge you brought against him then.
1440 He thought no more of it than killing a beast,
and his flocks were rich, teeming in their fleece,
but he sacrificed his own child, our daughter,
the agony I laboured into love
to charm away the savage winds of Thrace.[9]
1445 Didn't the law demand you banish him?—
hunt him from the land for all his guilt?
But now you witness what I've done
and you are ruthless judges.
                              Threaten away!
I'll meet you blow for blow. And if I fall
1450 the throne is yours. If god decrees the reverse,
late as it is, old men, you'll learn your place.

CHORUS   Mad with ambition,
            shrilling pride!—some Fury
crazed with the carnage rages through your brain—

9. Region bordering on the Aegean Sea,
encompassing portions of present-day northeastern Greece, southern Bulgaria, and European Turkey. On the sacrifice of Iphigenia,
see lines 189–247.

1455   I can see the flecks of blood inflame your eyes!
     But vengeance comes—you'll lose your loved ones,
     stroke for painful stroke.
     CLYTAEMNESTRA   Then learn this, too, the power of my oaths.
     By the child's Rights I brought to birth,
1460   by Ruin, by Fury—the three gods to whom
     I sacrificed this man—I swear my hopes
     will never walk the halls of fear so long
     as Aegisthus[1] lights the fire on my hearth.
     Loyal to me as always, no small shield
1465   to buttress my defiance.
                          Here he lies.
     He brutalized me. The darling of all
     the golden girls who spread the gates of Troy.
     And here his spear-prize . . . what wonders she beheld!—
     the seer of Apollo shared my husband's bed,
1470   his faithful mate who knelt at the rowing-benches,
     worked by every hand.
                        They have their rewards.
     He as you know. And she, the swan of the gods
     who lived to sing her latest, dying song—
     his lover lies beside him.
1475   She brings a fresh, voluptuous relish to my bed!
     CHORUS   Oh quickly, let me die—
     no bed of labour, no, no wasting illness . . .
     bear me off in the sleep that never ends,
          now that he has fallen,
1480   now that our dearest shield lies battered—
        Woman made him suffer,
           woman struck him down.

     Helen the wild, maddening Helen,
     one for the many, the thousand lives
1485   you murdered under Troy, Now you are crowned
     with this consummate wreath, the blood
     that lives in memory, glistens age to age.
     Once in the halls she walked and she was war,
     angel of war, angel of agony, lighting men to death.
1490 CLYTAEMNESTRA   Pray no more for death, broken
     as you are. And never turn
        your wrath on her, call her
     the scourge of men, the one alone
     who destroyed a myriad Greek lives—
1495   Helen the grief that never heals.
     CHORUS   The *spirit*!—you who tread

---

1. Son of Thyestes and his daughter, Pelopia, whom he raped after an oracle told Thyestes that this son would kill Atreus and seize power in revenge for Atreus's murder of Thyestes' sons. After all this came to pass, Atreus's sons Menelaus and Agamemnon overthrew Thyestes and Aegisthus. During the Trojan War, Aegisthus took advantage of Agamemnon's absence and seduced Clytaemnestra to help him return to power.

the house and the twinborn sons of Tantalus[2]—
you empower the sisters, Fury's twins
    whose power tears the heart!
1500   Perched on the corpse your carrion raven
    glories in her hymn,
        her screaming hymn of pride.

CLYTAEMNESTRA Now you set your judgement straight,
    you summon *him*! Three generations
1505   feed the spirit in the race.
Deep in the veins he feeds our bloodlust—
aye, before the old wound dies
it ripens in another flow of blood.

CHORUS The great curse of the house, the spirit,
1510   dead weight wrath—and you can praise it!
Praise the insatiate doom that feeds
relentless on our future and our sons.
Oh all through the will of Zeus,
the cause of all, the one who works it all.
1515   What comes to birth that is not Zeus?
Our lives are pain, what part not come from god?

Oh my king, my captain,
how to salute you, how to mourn you?
What can I say with all my warmth and love?
1520   Here in the black widow's web you lie,
gasping out your life
in a sacrilegious death, dear god,
reduced to a slave's bed,
my king of men, yoked by stealth and Fate,
1525   by the wife's hand that thrust the two-edged sword.

CLYTAEMNESTRA You claim the work is mine, call me
Agamemnon's wife—you are so wrong.
Fleshed in the wife of this dead man,
    the spirit lives within me,
1530   our savage ancient spirit of revenge.
In return for Atreus' brutal feast
he kills his perfect son—for every
murdered child, a crowning sacrifice.

CHORUS And *you*, innocent of his murder?
1535   And who could swear to that? and how? . . .
and still an avenger could arise,
bred by the fathers' crimes, and lend a hand.
He wades in the blood of brothers,
stream on mounting stream—black war erupts
1540   and where he strides revenge will stride,
clots will mass for the young who were devoured.

2. The father of Pelops, who in turn is father
of Atreus and Thyestes. He drew the gods'
anger by revealing their secrets and attempting to feed them his slaughtered son Pelops
(whom they revived).

Oh my king, my captain,
how to salute you, how to mourn you?
What can I say with all my warmth and love?

1545 Here in the black widow's web you lie,
gasping out your life
in a sacrilegious death, dear god,
reduced to a slave's bed,
my king of men, yoked by stealth and Fate,

1550 by the wife's hand that thrust the two-edged sword.

CLYTAEMNESTRA   No slave's death, I think—
no stealthier than the death he dealt
our house and the offspring of our loins,
    Iphigeneia, girl of tears.

1555 Act for act, wound for wound!
Never exult in Hades, swordsman,
here you are repaid. By the sword
you did your work and by the sword you die.

CHORUS   The mind reels—where to turn?

1560   All plans dashed, all hope! I cannot think . . .
    the roofs are toppling, I dread the drumbeat thunder
        the heavy rains of blood will crush the house
            the first light rains are over—
        Justice brings new acts of agony, yes,

1565 on new grindstones Fate is grinding sharp the sword of Justice.

Earth, dear Earth,
if only you'd drawn me under
long before I saw him huddled
in the beaten silver bath.

1570 Who will bury him, lift his dirge?
    [Turning to CLYTAEMNESTRA.]
You, can you dare this?
To kill your lord with your own hand
then mourn his soul with tributes, terrible tributes—
do his enormous works a great dishonour.

1575 This god-like man, this hero. Who at the grave
will sing his praises, pour the wine of tears?
Who will labour there with truth of heart?

CLYTAEMNESTRA   This is no concern of yours.
The hand that bore and cut him down

1580 will hand him down to Mother Earth.
This house will never mourn for him.
    Only our daughter Iphigeneia,
by all rights, will rush to meet him
first at the churning straits,[3]

1585 the ferry over tears—
she'll fling her arms around her father,
pierce him with her love.

---

3. The river (variously identified as the Styx or Acheron) across which the souls of the dead are ferried to the underworld.

CHORUS   Each charge meets counter-charge.
    None can judge between them. Justice.
1590   The plunderer plundered, the killer pays the price.
    The truth still holds while Zeus still holds the throne:
       the one who acts must suffer—
    that is law. Who can tear from the veins
    the bad seed, the curse? The race is welded to its ruin.

1595 CLYTAEMNESTRA   At last you see the future and the truth!
    But I will swear a pact with the spirit
    born within us. I embrace his works,
    cruel as they are but done at last,
      if he will leave our house
1600   in the future, bleed another line
    with kinsmen murdering kinsmen.
    Whatever he may ask. A few things
    are all I need, once I have purged
    our fury to destroy each other—
1605   purged it from our halls.

        [AEGISTHUS *has emerged from the palace with his bodyguard and*
        stands triumphant over the body of AGAMEMNON.]

AEGISTHUS   O what a brilliant day
    it is for vengeance! Now I can say once more
    there are gods in heaven avenging men,
    blazing down on all the crimes of earth.
    Now at last I see this man brought down
1610   in the Furies' tangling robes. It feasts my eyes—
    he pays for the plot his father's hand contrived.

    Atreus, this man's father, was king of Argos.
    My father, Thyestes—let me make this clear—
    Atreus' brother challenged him for the crown,
1615   and Atreus drove him out of house and home
    then lured him back, and home Thyestes came,
    poor man, a suppliant to his own hearth,
    to pray that Fate might save him.
                     So it did.
    There was no dying, no staining our native ground
1620   with *his* blood. Thyestes was the guest,
    and this man's godless father—

        [*Pointing to* AGAMEMNON.]

    the zeal of the host outstripping a brother's love,
    made my father a feast that seemed a feast for gods,
    a love feast of his children's flesh.
                     He cuts
1625   the extremities, feet and delicate hands
    into small pieces, scatters them over the dish
    and serves it to Thyestes throned on high.
    He picks at the flesh he cannot recognize,
    the soul of innocence eating the food of ruin—
1630   look,

        [*Pointing to the bodies at his feet.*]

that feeds upon the house! And then,
when he sees the monstrous thing he's done, he shrieks,
he reels back head first and vomits up that butchery,
tramples the feast—brings down the curse of Justice:
'Crash to ruin, all the race of Pleisthenes,[4] crash down!'

1635   So you see him, down. And I, the weaver of Justice,
plotted out the kill. Atreus drove us into exile,
my struggling father and I, a babe-in-arms,
his last son, but I became a man
and Justice brought me home. I was abroad
1640   but I reached out and seized my man,
link by link I clamped the fatal scheme
together. Now I could die gladly, even I—
now I see this monster in the nets of Justice.

LEADER   Aegisthus, you revel in pain—you sicken me.
1645   You say you killed the king in cold blood,
single-handed planned his pitiful death?
I say there's no escape. In the hour of judgement,
trust to this, your head will meet the people's
rocks and curses.

AEGISTHUS   You say! you slaves at the oars—
1650   while the master on the benches cracks the whip?
You'll learn, in your late age, how much it hurts
to teach old bones their place. We have techniques—
chains and the pangs of hunger,
two effective teachers, excellent healers.
1655   They can even cure old men of pride and gall.
Look—can't you see? The more you kick
against the pricks, the more you suffer.

LEADER   You, pathetic—
the king had just returned from battle.
1660   You waited out the war and fouled his lair,
you planned my great commander's fall.

AEGISTHUS   Talk on—
you'll scream for every word, my little Orpheus.[5]
We'll see if the world comes dancing to your song,
your absurd barking—snarl your breath away!
1665   I'll make you dance, I'll bring you all to heel.

LEADER   *You* rule Argos? You who schemed his death
but cringed to cut him down with your own hand?

AEGISTHUS   The treachery was the woman's work, clearly.
I was a marked man, his enemy for ages.
1670   But I will use his riches, stop at nothing
to civilize his people. All but the rebel:
him I'll yoke and break—

4. A son of Atreus. In some versions of the myth, he is the father of Agamemnon and Menelaus, whom Atreus later adopted.
5. In classical mythology, the greatest poet and singer, whose music not only entranced animals and humans but also made rocks and trees dance.

no cornfed colt, running free in the traces.[6]
Hunger, ruthless mate of the dark torture-chamber,
trains her eyes upon him till he drops!
LEADER   Coward, why not kill the man yourself?
Why did the woman, the corruption of Greece
and the gods of Greece, have to bring him down?
Orestes—
                    If he still sees the light of day,
bring him home, good Fates, home to kill
this pair at last. Our champion in slaughter!
AEGISTHUS   Bent on insolence? Well, you'll learn, quickly.
At them, men—you have your work at hand!

[*His men draw swords; the old men take up their sticks.*]

LEADER   At them, fist at the hilt, to the last man—
AEGISTHUS   Fist at the hilt, I'm not afraid to die.
LEADER   It's death you want and death you'll have—
we'll make that word your last.

[CLYTAEMNESTRA *moves between them, restraining* AEGISTHUS.]

CLYTAEMNESTRA   No more, my dearest,
no more grief. We have too much to reap
right here, our mighty harvest of despair.
Our lives are based on pain. No bloodshed now.

Fathers of Argos, turn for home before you act
and suffer for it. What we did was destiny.
If we could end the suffering, how we would rejoice.
The spirit's brutal hoof has struck our heart.
And that is what a woman has to say.
Can you accept the truth?

[CLYTAEMNESTRA *turns to leave.*]

AEGISTHUS   But these . . . mouths
that bloom in filth—spitting insults in my teeth.
You tempt your fates, you insubordinate dogs—
to hurl abuse at me, your master!
LEADER   No Greek
worth his salt would grovel at your feet.
AEGISTHUS   I—I'll stalk you all your days!
LEADER   Not if the spirit brings Orestes home.
AEGISTHUS   Exiles feed on hope—well I know.
LEADER   More,
gorge yourself to bursting—soil justice, while you can.
AEGISTHUS   I promise you, you'll pay, old fools—in good time, too!
LEADER   Strut on your own dunghill, you cock beside your mate.
CLYTAEMNESTRA   Let them howl—they're impotent. You and I have power now.
We will set the house in order once for all.

[*They enter the palace; the great doors close behind them; the old men
disband and wander off.*]

6. The trace-horse, attached to the side of the yoked pair by a harness, bore no collar or yoke.

SOPHOCLES

ca. 496–406 B.C.E.

A GENERATION younger than AESCHY-
LUS, Sophocles is often regarded as the
most accomplished author of Greek tragedy. He was certainly the most successful.
Up to twenty-four victories at the Dionysus festival in Athens are recorded for him
(in contrast to thirteen for Aeschylus and
five for EURIPIDES), and it is said that he
never finished lower than second. Aristotle, the first philosopher to write an
extended work on Greek tragedy, singled
out Sophocles' OEDIPUS THE KING as a
model of what tragedy should look like.
The Oedipus myth inspired Sophocles to
write not just one but three masterpieces:
ANTIGONE, a play about Oedipus's daughter;
Oedipus the King; and Oedipus at Colonos,
a searching tragedy about the aging
Oedipus. In Oedipus and his descendants,
Sophocles recognized the subject most perfectly suited to the art of tragedy.

Although only scant information is
available about Sophocles' life, we know
that he was born into a wealthy family of
Colonus and that he occupied some of the
highest political positions in Athens. He
served as treasurer of the Delian League,
a network of allied and dependent states
built by Athens after its victory over the
Persians. Moreover, together with Pericles, the famed leader of Athens, he commanded the Athenian fleet in its campaign
against Samos. During his adult life,

Sophocles watched Athens evolve from a
small city-state to the greatest empire of
the region, projecting its power far into
Persia. The last decades of his life were
dominated by a second war—the Peloponnesian War with a rival Greek city-state,
Sparta. Toward the end of his life, he
became a *proboulos*, one of ten advisors
endowed with special powers of governance. Sophocles died at the age of ninety
as a respected and admired citizen and civic
leader, a few years before the Peloponnesian War would end in the final defeat of
Athens and the demise of its empire.

Sophocles launched his career as a
playwright in 468 B.C.E., when he won his
first victory at the Dionysus festival in
Athens by defeating the acknowledged
master of tragedy, Aeschylus. He was
enormously productive, writing more than
one hundred plays, although only seven
have been preserved: *Ajax* (ca. 450), *Antigone* (ca. 441), *Oedipus the King* (ca. 428),
Electra (ca. 419), *The Trachian Women*
(ca. 413), *Philoctetes* (ca. 409), and *Oedipus at Colonus* (ca. 406), as well as one
comical satyr play, *The Trackers* (date
unknown). Sophocles shaped the course
of theater not only through his plays but
also through his theatrical innovations.
The philosopher Aristotle praised Sophocles for having established new techniques
of scene painting; for having introduced a

third actor (hitherto, only two actors had been permitted), thereby significantly expanding the possibilities for interaction among individual characters; and for having enlarged the tragic chorus from twelve to fifteen. At the same time, Sophocles accorded the chorus less room in his plays than the older playwright Aeschylus had done, foregrounding instead the conflicts among individual characters. As a consequence, his plays are much closer to the form of contemporary drama than any previous Greek tragedies extant.

Like his predecessor Aeschylus and his younger contemporary Euripides, Sophocles took the material for his plays from Greek myth. However, he used this material in his own distinct manner. Sophocles placed much more emphasis than did Aeschylus on turning the individual characters into complex, three-dimensional humans with conflicting motives and passions. One example is his version of the Electra myth—the sole myth whose dramatic adaptations by all three major Greek tragedians survive (though different playwrights often treated the same myth). Comparing Sophocles' version with Aeschylus's, *The Libation Bearers* (the middle part of the *Oresteia* trilogy; see the headnote on Aeschylus, above) is particularly instructive. Sophocles' version is much more dynamic, and it shifts emphasis from Orestes' act of matricide to the solitary suffering of his sister, Electra. Sophocles also uses much more suspense, postponing and drawing out the recognition scenes as long as possible, even though the audience was of course familiar with the basic outlines of the plot.

Emphasizing the individual was an innovation that allowed for a more nuanced form of characterization. But it also had a cultural and political dimension. The very structure of Greek tragedy—with individual characters, often the rulers, engaging in conflict with a chorus, usually composed of elders or representative citizens—dramatized for the Athenian audience the political history of their own city. During the emergence of Athenian tragedy, Athens had gone from autocratic rule to a democracy that involved a growing number of male citizens in the political process. The rule of the one versus the rule of the many

was therefore a topic of immense political importance. Sophocles' tragedies, depicting complex individuals, thus reflected the struggle over the new political form of democracy.

Of all the characters Sophocles used to populate his plays, none fascinated him more than Oedipus, a tragic figure perfectly suited to Sophocles' interest in conflicted persons. From one perspective, the myth of Oedipus is that of an individual doomed by outside forces. The son of the king and queen of Thebes, Oedipus is condemned to death to avoid the terrible prediction of an oracle that he would kill his father. But a servant takes pity on the child, and the young Oedipus is simply cast out. He grows up in the city of Corinth, ignorant of his true parents, and as an adult he returns to Thebes, unwittingly killing his father at a crossroads after having been provoked by one of the attendants. The next set piece of the myth is the encounter with the Sphinx, which is holding the city in her thrall. Oedipus submits to her test, correctly answering the riddle. Hailed as liberator of Thebes, he now marries the widowed queen and becomes a good ruler. It is only when a pestilence devastates the city and the oracle declares the murderer of the late king to be still at large that Oedipus turns to the crime and begins a methodical manhunt that constitutes most of the play. Only gradually does the truth come out, and Oedipus must finally recognize himself as the murderer he has been hunting. He blinds himself and submits to a life in exile, enduring perpetual wandering until he finds a final resting place near Athens.

Sophocles first treated the Oedipus myth with an early play about Oedipus's daughter, *Antigone*; he then returned to the myth in his middle period with *Oedipus the King*. Toward the end of his life, he felt himself drawn to the figure of Oedipus once more, composing his very last play, *Oedipus at Colonus*, on the aging Oedipus. Containing almost no external action, it depicts the old, blinded Oedipus searching for a final resting place, which is finally granted to him by the liberal city of Athens. It is a ruminative and meditative play about an Oedipus reconciled to his fate and looking for a place to die. Rather than being conceived as interrelated, the three Oedipus plays are unconnected works, each exemplary in its own way.

ANTIGONE

Antigone, Sophocles' first play on the Oedipus myth, takes place after Oedipus has died and depicts how his children and the city of Thebes deal with his terrible legacy. Before the action of the play begins, Oedipus's two sons, Eteokles and Polyneikes, have quarreled over the throne of Thebes. When Eteokles manages to seize control of the city, Polyneikes forms an alliance with the king of Argos and attacks the city. The drawn-out battle culminates in a man-to-man fight between the two brothers, leaving both of them dead. Kreon, brother of Oedipus's wife,

Jocasta, takes the empty throne and has Eteokles, who defended the city, buried with honors. His brother, who went in liege with a foreign power and attacked the city, is left unburied, in disgrace. No one is allowed to give the traitor his last honors. His body will be torn to pieces by birds and dogs, a warning to all.

This is the situation with which the play begins, and the drama of burial will continue to dominate to the bitter end. Funeral rites are among the most important cultural institutions, dating back to the very origins of human society. We believe that we owe it to the dead to honor their bodies. The action of the play is set in motion when Antigone, following this ancient and religious practice, tries to bury her disgraced brother. What makes *Antigone* such an explosive play is that Sophocles con-

This 2005 production of *Antigone* at the Teatro Greco in Syracuse, Sicily, directed by Irene Papas, features giant replicas of Cycladic statues along the stage periphery and a large chorus.

fronts this obligation with another, more political, one: to defend one's city. In burying her brother, Antigone violates Kreon's edict. Thus *Antigone* becomes the starkest example of a tragedy depicting an unsolvable conflict between two equally legitimate moral values and positions.

The two antagonists could not be more unequally matched. Antigone, offspring of the disgraced union of Oedipus and his wife/mother, whose only companion is her timid sister, is the epitome of a social outcast. The king of Thebes, by contrast, wields political power and has, for the time

being, the support of the community, which has entrusted him with restoring order to the city.

Antigone may be weak and alone, but she is tenacious, determined to maintain her right. She claims that burying her brother is not only an obligation owed to the dead, but specifically an obligation of kinship: she must bury her own brother. Kinship, of course, is the curse that hangs over her family, since Oedipus's murder of his father and betrothal to his mother are the starkest violations of the rules of kinship. Kinship is Antigone's curse, but she

A 2012 modern-dress production of *Antigone* by the National Theatre in London, directed by Polly Findlay and featuring Jodie Whittaker as Antigone and Christopher Eccleston as Kreon.

now claims it as a right as well, specifically with respect to her brother. A husband or a child might be replaced, but never a brother, especially now that none are left alive.

Antigone's rebellion against King Kreon has inspired the weak in their struggles against the mighty all over the world, making *Antigone* one of the modern era's favorite Greek tragedies. But Kreon is not only a tyrant who oppresses the people with his strict laws. He has come to power after a civil war and must make sure that the law is obeyed. The right of the city to defend itself against its enemies and to punish traitors is indisputable.

Both Antigone and Kreon have right on their side, but both overreach. Kreon is overly concerned about upholding his power, always worried at the smallest sign of resistance. In particular he feels his authority threatened by a woman resisting his decree. His rigid stance will undo not only himself but also his family. Antigone is perhaps even more single-minded, claiming that she owes more to the dead than to the living. It is fitting that she, whose mind had been set on burial from the beginning, will end up being buried alive—"My tomb," she says, "my bridal bedroom, my home."

Audiences have debated whose side to take and have seen the conflict as one between woman and man, between the weak and the strong, kinship and state. Moral philosophers have weighed in, generating a long tradition of philosophical commentary on the play, and playwrights have adapted it to modern political situations. But at heart, *Antigone* is a play about death and burial, and as such it taps into one of our most fundamental practices. This is a fitting topic for a tragedy that presents us with the descendants of Oedipus, the most quintessentially tragic figure of antiquity.

OEDIPUS THE KING

Oedipus the King—composed seventeen years after *Antigone* and ten years before *Oedipus at Colonus*—is Sophocles' most haunting play about the Oedipus myth, and for many it is among the most haunting plays of all time. Its power arises in part from its extraordinary structure and form. In a bold move that distinguishes this play from most other Greek tragedies, Sophocles set the entire action of the play in its past, thus presenting onstage a gradual revelation of events—conveyed by speeches and dialogue—that happened long before the onstage "present." The past dominates the lives of the characters, holding them firmly in its grip.

The emphasis on the revelation of the past also means that *Oedipus the King* directs attention mostly to the realm of language rather than to the action presented on the stage. At the beginning of the play, King Oedipus has consulted the oracle at Delphi, seeking a way to halt the plague devastating the city. The oracle declares that the reason for the pestilence is the continued presence in Thebes of the murderer of the former king, Laius, who must be cast out. Oedipus is most eager to find the murderer and to expel him. As various witnesses and messengers are brought before him, the play turns into a veritable detective story—a search for traces and clues of a past crime through the cross-examination of witnesses and the careful interpretation of various prophecies and oracles. Oedipus leaps at this challenge, not only because his own rule and power depend on his success but also because he is supremely confident in his skill at untangling puzzles and riddles. As the foreign visitor who freed Thebes from the clutches of the Sphinx by solving its famous riddle, Oedipus had previously demonstrated his talent for sharp and analytical thinking. And because he owes his current position as venerated tyrant of Thebes to this skillful feat, his pride in his intellect seems warranted. Faced with a new threat to his adopted home, he is ready to exercise his skill again, once again deciphering riddles to free the city from its plight.

This time, however, things are different. Despite his self-confidence, he has in fact become something of a riddle himself. The whole play revolves around this paradox: on the one hand Oedipus is the ideal ruler, a patient and responsive king who speaks to his people directly and listens intently to their pleas; but on the other hand, he is the very pestilence that has ruined the city. Oedipus is a riddle or puzzle in another sense as well: by having unwittingly killed his father and married his mother, he becomes, as the chorus points out repeatedly, both son and husband and, to the offspring of this incestuous union, both father and sibling. These are paradoxes Oedipus cannot fathom or solve; they are the web spun around him, leading to the final, cruel revelation at the end of the play.

The riddle of a person who is both husband and son, brother and father is ultimately based on kinship. Kinship is central to Greek mythology, with its family curses passed down from parents to children. In *Oedipus the King* this theme is pursued to its extreme. In its largest dimensions, kinship helps distinguish between citizens and foreigners. Oedipus had come to Thebes as a voluntary exile, fleeing the couple whom he thought were his real parents in the city of Corinth in order to escape the prophecy that he would kill his father and marry his mother. Only at the end of the play, as part of its tragic turn, does it become clear that he is in fact a citizen of Thebes, son of the late King Laius and his wife (and now Oedipus's wife), Jocasta. Oedipus is thus doubly ignorant: he knows neither what city-state he belongs to nor who his kin are. This, precisely, is his crime, or his failure, and for this he is punished.

Dominated by messengers, reports, rumors, oracles, and prophecies, *Oedipus the King* is also unusually rich in puns and plays on names. Oedipus is named after his swollen (*oidos*) foot, an injury caused when he was cast out by his parents in their attempt to thwart the prophecy attached to their child. But his name also contains the word *oida*, which means "I know." The play is full of references to and echoes of both meanings, punning on the word for swelling and the concept of knowledge as well as its opposite, ignorance. The most famous metaphor for the play's attention to knowledge and ignorance is light. From the beginning, Oedipus vows to shed light on the mysterious murder of the former king and insists that he will force the obscure truth out into the open, no matter at what cost. Well into the play, his wife begins to fathom the grim reality of his identity and begs him to halt his single-minded search for his own past. But Oedipus wants nothing to remain hidden and does not stop until he has brought the bitter truth into the bright daylight. Given the role of light and darkness played in the entire tragedy, it is only fitting that Oedipus would punish himself not only with exile but also with blinding, so that he may no longer set eyes on the terrible deeds he has done. That the blind seer Tiresias has been right all along underscores the play's singular fixation on this one assemblage of images and metaphors.

Oedipus the King, with its pestilence and foreign ruler, is also embedded in the cultural and political history of Athens. The historian Thucydides famously described the plague that devastated Athens during the Peloponnesian War, which the plague in Thebes inevitably brings to mind. The play is also remarkable in its attention to medical language, registering the emergence of medicine as a specialized discipline in the fifth century B.C.E. Finally, it should be remembered that the play was performed before Athenian audiences, which would naturally compare their own city to Thebes. This point is brought home in Sophocles' last play, *Oedipus at Colonus*, where the magnanimous Athenians protect the outcast Oedipus, thus gratifying the Athenian audience at the expense of their rival.

Modern audiences have been disturbed that Oedipus is punished for a deed he had not intended and which he had in fact done everything to avoid. But Oedipus is not merely a victim of fate. For one thing, he is overconfident in his own powers, in his ability to protect the city and to excise its pestilence. We see him pass rash judgment on those who want the truth to remain hidden in order to protect themselves and Oedipus. Yet he is not an unfair ruler. Rather, the play is a meditation on the concept of luck, *tuchē*, so central to Greek tragedy and morality. Oedipus had been an extraordinarily lucky man, as he himself admits. But he is revealed to be the unluckiest of all. That forces larger than human powers dominate these characters' lives is no reason to absolve them from responsibility and moral judgment, however. Indeed, Oedipus takes responsibility for all of it—for his actions, for his changing luck, for what he did not know, and also for what he had to learn.

Few plays have provoked the imagination and conscience of audiences as powerfully as this one, and few have inspired as many adaptations and interpretations. Julius Caesar wrote a version of *Oedipus the King*, as did the Roman playwright SENECA. A celebrated version by the French playwright Corneille (1659) was followed by that of the Enlightenment philosopher and playwright Voltaire (1718). Sigmund Freud coined the term "Oedipus complex," based in part on his interpretation of Sophocles' play, to describe one of his core psychological theories. Cultural anthropologists have used the play to explain features shared in different societies. The twentieth century brought an influential adaptation by Jean Cocteau (1934). *Oedipus the King* has also been set to music by Carl Orff (1959) and filmed by the influential Italian filmmaker Pier Paulo Pasolini (1967). Numerous performances and interpretations of Sophocles' play have ensured that the story of a man who killed his father and married his mother still captures our fears today.

In the end, however, what ensured the power of this play across centuries may not be its various adaptations or its focus on incest, a taboo across cultures and eras. Incest was in fact only one element in Sophocles' campaign to use the theater in a way that was startlingly new at the time: namely, as a vehicle for truth. The play depicts an uncompromising, even self-destructive, search for truth at all cost. Everything else—the well-being of Jocasta, of Kreon, and of Oedipus himself—is ignored. If you want the truth, the play says, you must be ready to sacrifice everything for it. Rarely has a play formulated this fundamental insight and shown its consequences with greater clarity than does Sophocles' unique and radical tragedy. To learn more about the staging of *Oedipus the King* and to view photographs from select performances of the play, see the "Plays in Performance" color insert near the center of this volume.

M.P.

Oedipus the King[1]

CHARACTERS

OEDIPUS, king of Thebes
A PRIEST of Zeus
KREON, brother of Jocasta
A CHORUS of Theban citizens
   and their LEADER
TIRESIAS, a blind prophet
JOCASTA, the queen, wife of Oedipus

A MESSENGER from Corinth
A SHEPHERD
A MESSENGER from inside the palace
ANTIGONE, ISMENE, daughters of
   Oedipus and Jocasta
GUARDS and attendants
PRIESTS of Thebes

[TIME AND SCENE: *The royal house of Thebes.[2] Double doors dominate the façade; a stone altar stands at the center of the stage.*

Many years have passed since OEDIPUS *solved the riddle of the Sphinx[3] and ascended the throne of Thebes, and now a plague has struck the city. A procession of priests enters;*

1. Translated by Robert Fagles.
2. Capital city of the region of Boeotia, in east-central Greece, famed throughout the ancient world for the seven gates in its fortifications.
3. A monster that had terrorized Thebes as long as no one could answer her riddle: "What walks on

four feet in the morning, two at noon, and three in the evening?" When Oedipus correctly answered "Man," the monster killed herself, and Oedipus was rewarded with both the Theban kingship and the hand of Thebes' queen, Jocasta, in marriage.

*suppliants, broken and despondent, they carry branches wound in wool and lay them
on the altar.*

The doors open. Guards assemble. OEDIPUS *comes forward, majestic but for a telltale limp, and slowly views the condition of his people.*]

OEDIPUS   Oh my children, the new blood of ancient Thebes,
why are you here? Huddling at my altar,
praying before me, your branches wound in wool.[4]
Our city reeks with the smoke of burning incense,
5   rings with cries for the Healer[5] and wailing for the dead.
I thought it wrong, my children, to hear the truth
from others, messengers. Here I am myself—
you all know me, the world knows my fame:
I am Oedipus.
        [*Helping a* PRIEST *to his feet.*]
                    Speak up, old man. Your years,
10   your dignity—you should speak for the others.
Why here and kneeling, what preys upon you so?
Some sudden fear? some strong desire?
You can trust me. I am ready to help,
I'll do anything. I would be blind to misery
15   not to pity my people kneeling at my feet.

PRIEST   Oh Oedipus, king of the land, our greatest power!
You see us before you now, men of all ages
clinging to your altars. Here are boys,
still too weak to fly from the nest,
20   and here the old, bowed down with the years,
the holy ones—a priest of Zeus[6] myself—and here
the picked, unmarried men, the young hope of Thebes.
And all the rest, your great family gathers now,
branches wreathed, massing in the squares,
25   kneeling before the two temples of queen Athena
or the river-shrine where the embers glow and die
and Apollo sees the future in the ashes.[7]
                        Our city—
look around you, see with your own eyes—
our ship pitches wildly, cannot lift her head
30   from the depths, the red waves of death . . .
Thebes is dying. A blight on the fresh crops
and the rich pastures, cattle sicken and die,
and the women die in labor, children stillborn,
and the plague, the fiery god of fever hurls down
35   on the city, his lightning slashing through us—
raging plague in all its vengeance, devastating

4. Emblems of supplication, laid on the altar
and then taken up again after the suppliant's
request is granted.
5. Apollo, god of medicine as well as light and
prophecy.

6. Ruler of the Greek gods.
7. That is, the ashes of sacrificed animals: the
priests of Apollo divined the future through
the patterns found in them. *Athena:* goddess
of wisdom and war.

the house of Cadmus![8] And black Death luxuriates
in the raw, wailing miseries of Thebes.
Now we pray to you. You cannot equal the gods,
40   your children know that, bending at your altar.
But we do rate you first of men,
both in the common crises of our lives
and face-to-face encounters with the gods.
You freed us from the Sphinx, you came to Thebes
45   and cut us loose from the bloody tribute we had paid
that harsh, brutal singer. We taught you nothing,
no skill, no extra knowledge, still you triumphed.
A god was with you, so they say, and we believe it—
you lifted up our lives.
                                    So now again,
50   Oedipus, king, we bend to you, your power—
we implore you, all of us on our knees:
find us strength, rescue! Perhaps you've heard
the voice of a god or something from other men,
Oedipus . . . what do you know?
55   The man of experience—you see it every day—
his plans will work in a crisis, his first of all.

Act now—we beg you, best of men, raise up our city!
Act, defend yourself, your former glory!
Your country calls you savior now
60   for your zeal, your action years ago.
Never let us remember of your reign:
you helped us stand, only to fall once more.
Oh raise up our city, set us on our feet.
The omens were good that day you brought us joy—
65   be the same man today!
Rule our land, you know you have the power,
but rule a land of the living, not a wasteland.
Ship and towered city are nothing, stripped of men
alive within it, living all as one.

OEDIPUS   My children,
70   I pity you. I see—how could I fail to see
what longings bring you here? Well I know
you are sick to death, all of you,
but sick as you are, not one is sick as I.
Your pain strikes each of you alone, each
75   in the confines of himself, no other. But my spirit
grieves for the city, for myself and all of you.
I wasn't asleep, dreaming. You haven't wakened me—
I've wept through the nights, you must know that,
groping, laboring over many paths of thought.

8. The mythical founder of Thebes.

80 After a painful search I found one cure:
     I acted at once. I sent Kreon,
     my wife's own brother, to Delphi[9]—
     Apollo the Prophet's oracle—to learn
     what I might do or say to save our city.

85 Today's the day. When I count the days gone by
     it torments me . . . what is he doing?
     Strange, he's late, he's gone too long.
     But once he returns, then, then I'll be a traitor
     if I do not do all the god makes clear.

90 PRIEST Timely words. The men over there
     are signaling—Kreon's just arriving.
     OEDIPUS [Sighting KREON, then turning to the altar.]
                                              Lord Apollo,
     let him come with a lucky word of rescue,
     shining like his eyes!
     PRIEST Welcome news, I think—he's crowned, look,
95 and the laurel wreath is bright with berries.[1]
     OEDIPUS We'll soon see. He's close enough to hear—
          [Enter KREON from the side; his face is shaded with a wreath.]
     Kreon, prince, my kinsman, what do you bring us?
     What message from the god?
     KREON   Good news.
     I tell you even the hardest things to bear,
100 if they should turn out well, all would be well.
     OEDIPUS Of course, but what were the god's *words*? There's no hope
     and nothing to fear in what you've said so far.
     KREON If you want my report in the presence of these . . .
          [Pointing to the priests while drawing OEDIPUS toward the palace.]
     I'm ready now, or we might go inside.
     OEDIPUS   Speak out,
105 speak to us all. I grieve for these, my people,
     far more than I fear for my own life.
     KREON   Very well,
     I will tell you what I heard from the god.
     Apollo commands us—he was quite clear—
     "Drive the corruption from the land,
110 don't harbor it any longer, past all cure,
     don't nurse it in your soil—root it out!"
     OEDIPUS How can we cleanse ourselves—what rites?
     What's the source of the trouble?
     KREON Banish the man, or pay back blood with blood.

---

9. Site of the shrine on the slope of Mount Parnassus, in central Greece, where Apollo prophesies through his priestess. *Kreon*: a direct descendant of Cadmus, Thebes' founder; it was Kreon who offered to share the Theban throne with anyone who could solve the riddle of the Sphinx.

1. The laurel crown is a sign that Kreon bears good news.

115 Murder sets the plague-storm on the city.

OEDIPUS   Whose murder?
Whose fate does Apollo bring to light?

KREON   Our leader,
my lord, was once a man named Laius,[2]
before you came and put us straight on course.

OEDIPUS   I know—
or so I've heard. I never saw the man myself.

120 KREON   Well, he was killed, and Apollo commands us now—
he could not be more clear,
"Pay the killers back—whoever is responsible."

OEDIPUS   Where on earth are they? Where to find it now,
the trail of the ancient guilt so hard to trace?

125 KREON "Here in Thebes," he said.
Whatever is sought for can be caught, you know,
whatever is neglected slips away.

OEDIPUS   But where,
in the palace, the fields or foreign soil,
where did Laius meet his bloody death?

130 KREON   He went to consult an oracle, Apollo said,
and he set out and never came home again.

OEDIPUS   No messenger, no fellow-traveler saw what happened?
Someone to cross-examine?

KREON   No,
they were all killed but one. He escaped,
135 terrified, he could tell us nothing clearly,
nothing of what he saw—just one thing.

OEDIPUS   What's that?
one thing could hold the key to it all,
a small beginning give us grounds for hope.

KREON   He said thieves attacked them—a whole band,
140 not single-handed, cut King Laius down.

OEDIPUS   A thief,
so daring, so wild, he'd kill a king? Impossible,
unless conspirators paid him off in Thebes.

KREON   We suspected as much. But with Laius dead
no leader appeared to help us in our troubles.

145 OEDIPUS   Trouble? Your *king* was murdered—royal blood!
What stopped you from tracking down the killer
then and there?

KREON   The singing, riddling Sphinx.
She . . . persuaded us to let the mystery go
and concentrate on what lay at our feet.

OEDIPUS   No,
150 I'll start again—I'll bring it all to light myself!
Apollo is right, and so are you, Kreon,

---

2. Former king of Thebes and husband of Jocasta; he was on his way to Delphi to consult the oracle of Apollo when he was killed.

to turn our attention back to the murdered man.
Now you have *me* to fight for you, you'll see:
I am the land's avenger by all rights,
155   and Apollo's champion too.
But not to assist some distant kinsman, no,
for my own sake I'll rid us of this corruption.
Whoever killed the king may decide to kill me too,
with the same violent hand—by avenging Laius
160   I defend myself.

                    [*To the priests.*]

                         Quickly, my children.
Up from the steps, take up your branches now.

                    [*To the guards.*]

One of you summon the city here before us,
tell them I'll do everything. God help us,
we will see our triumph—or our fall.

                    [OEDIPUS *and* KREON *enter the palace, followed by the guards.*]

165   PRIEST   Rise, my sons. The kindness we came for
Oedipus volunteers himself.
Apollo has sent his word, his oracle—
Come down, Apollo, save us, stop the plague.

                    [*The priests rise, remove their branches and exit to the side. Enter a*
                    CHORUS, *the citizens of Thebes, who have not heard the news that*
                    KREON *brings. They march around the altar, chanting.*]

CHORUS   Zeus!
Great welcome voice of Zeus,[3] what do you bring?
170   What word from the gold vaults of Delphi
comes to brilliant Thebes? Racked with terror—
          terror shakes my heart
and I cry your wild cries, Apollo, Healer of Delos[4]
I worship you in dread . . . what now, what is your price?
175   some new sacrifice? some ancient rite from the past
come round again each spring?—
          what will you bring to birth?
Tell me, child of golden Hope
          warm voice that never dies!

180   You are the first I call, daughter of Zeus
deathless Athena—I call your sister Artemis,[5]
heart of the market place enthroned in glory,
          guardian of our earth—
I call Apollo, Archer astride the thunderheads of heaven—
185   O triple shield against death, shine before me now!
If ever, once in the past, you stopped some ruin

3. That is, Apollo, who could speak for Zeus,
his father.
4. Apollo's birthplace, an island in the Aegean

Sea that was central to his cult.
5. Goddess of the moon and the hunt; twin
sister of Apollo.

launched against our walls
    you hurled the flame of pain
far, far from Thebes—you gods
190   come now, come down once more!
                                 No, no
the miseries numberless, grief on grief, no end—
too much to bear, we are all dying
O my people . . .
    Thebes like a great army dying
195 and there is no sword of thought to save us, no
and the fruits of our famous earth, they will not ripen
no and the women cannot scream their pangs to birth—
screams for the Healer, children dead in the womb
      and life on life goes down
200   you can watch them go
    like seabirds winging west, outracing the day's fire
down the horizon, irresistibly
      streaking on to the shores of Evening
                              Death
so many deaths, numberless deaths on deaths, no end—
205 Thebes is dying, look, her children
stripped of pity . . .
    generations strewn on the ground
unburied, unwept, the dead spreading death
and the young wives and gray-haired mothers with them
210 cling to the altars, trailing in from all over the city—
Thebes, city of death, one long cortege
      and the suffering rises
        wails for mercy rise
    and the wild hymn for the Healer blazes out
215 clashing with our sobs our cries of mourning—
    O golden daughter of god, send rescue
    radiant as the kindness in your eyes!

Drive him back!—the fever, the god of death
    that raging god of war[6]
220 not armored in bronze, not shielded now, he burns me,
battle cries in the onslaught burning on—
O rout him from our borders!
Sail him, blast him out to the Sea-queen's chamber
    the black Atlantic gulfs
225 or the northern harbor, death to all
where the Thracian[7] surf comes crashing.
Now what the night spares he comes by day and kills—
the god of death.

6. Ares, son of Zeus and Hera, the god of savage warfare.
7. Ares was associated with Thrace, northeast
of Greece, whose inhabitants the Greeks
viewed as savage. *Sea-queen:* Amphitrite, consort of Poseidon, god of the sea.

                    O lord of the stormcloud,
        you who twirl the lightning, Zeus, Father,
230   thunder Death to nothing!

        Apollo, lord of the light, I beg you—
            whip your longbow's golden cord
        showering arrows on our enemies—shafts of power
        champions strong before us rushing on!

235   Artemis, Huntress,
            torches flaring over the eastern ridges—
                    ride Death down in pain!

        God of the headdress gleaming gold, I cry to you—
        your name and ours are one, Dionysus—
240   come with your face aflame with wine
                your raving women's[8] cries
            your army on the march! Come with the lightning
        come with torches blazing, eyes ablaze with glory!
        Burn that god of death[9] that all gods hate!

            [OEDIPUS enters from the palace to address the CHORUS, as if
            addressing the entire city of Thebes.]

245 OEDIPUS   You pray to the gods? Let me grant your prayers.
        Come, listen to me—do what the plague demands:
        you'll find relief and lift your head from the depths.
        I will speak out now as a stranger to the story,[1]
        a stranger to the crime. If I'd been present then,
250   there would have been no mystery, no long hunt
        without a clue in hand. So now, counted
        a native Theban years after the murder,
        to all of Thebes I make this proclamation:
        if any one of you knows who murdered Laius,
255   the son of Labdacus, I order him to reveal
        the whole truth to me. Nothing to fear,
        even if he must denounce himself,
        let him speak up
        and so escape the brunt of the charge—
260   he will suffer no unbearable punishment,
        nothing worse than exile, totally unharmed.

            [OEDIPUS pauses, waiting for a reply.]

                                            Next,
        if anyone knows the murderer is a stranger,
        a man from alien soil, come, speak up.
        I will give him a handsome reward, and lay up
265   gratitude in my heart for him besides.

---

8. The Maenads—frenzied women who wor-   princess.
ship Dionysus, the god of wine and of drama.   9. That is, Ares.
He is identified with Thebes (see line 239)   1. Oedipus was raised in Corinth, a Greek
because his mother was Semele, a Theban   city-state south of Thebes.

[*Silence again, no reply.*]

But if you keep silent, if anyone panicking,
trying to shield himself or friend or kin,
rejects my offer, then hear what I will do.
I order you, every citizen of the state
270   where I hold throne and power: banish this man—
whoever he may be—never shelter him, never
speak a word to him, never make him partner
to your prayers, your victims burned to the gods.
Never let the holy water touch his hands
275   Drive him out, each of you, from every home.
He is the plague, the heart of our corruption,
as Apollo's oracle has just revealed to me.
So I honor my obligations:
I fight for the god and for the murdered man.

280   Now my curse on the murderer. Whoever he is,
a lone man unknown in his crime
or one among many, let that man drag out
his life in agony, step by painful step—
I curse myself as well . . . if by any chance
285   he proves to be an intimate of our house,
here at my hearth, with my full knowledge,
may the curse I just called down on him strike me!

These are your orders: perform them to the last.
I command you, for my sake, for Apollo's, for this country
290   blasted root and branch by the angry heavens.
Even if god had never urged you on to act,
how could you leave the crime uncleansed so long?
A man so noble—your king, brought down in blood—
you should have searched. But I am the king now,
295   I hold the throne that he held then, possess his bed
and a wife who shares our seed[2] . . . why, our seed
might be the same, children born of the same mother
might have created blood-bonds between us
if his hope of offspring hadn't met disaster—
300   but fate swooped at his head and cut him short.
So I will fight for him as if he were my father,
stop at nothing, search the world
to lay my hands on the man who shed his blood,
the son of Labdacus descended of Polydorus,
305   Cadmus of old and Agenor, founder of the line:[3]
their power and mine are one.
                         Oh dear gods,
my curse on those who disobey these orders!

2. Jocasta, queen of Thebes, was the widow
of Laius.
3. Here Oedipus traces the lineage of his

predecessor, King Laius, back to Cadmus,
the city's founder, and Agenor, father of
Cadmus.

Let no crops grow out of the earth for them—
shrivel their women, kill their sons,
310 burn them to nothing in this plague
that hits us now, or something even worse.
But you, loyal men of Thebes who approve my actions,
may our champion, Justice, may all the gods
be with us, fight beside us to the end!

315 LEADER   In the grip of your curse, my king, I swear
I'm not the murderer, I cannot point him out.
As for the search, Apollo pressed it on us—
he should name the killer.

OEDIPUS   Quite right,
but to force the gods to act against their will—
320 no man has the power.

LEADER   Then if I might mention
the next best thing . . .

OEDIPUS   The third best too—
don't hold back, say it.

LEADER   I still believe . . .
Lord Tiresias[4] sees with the eyes of Lord Apollo.
Anyone searching for the truth, my king,
325 might learn it from the prophet, clear as day.

OEDIPUS   I've not been slow with that. On Kreon's cue
I sent the escorts, twice, within the hour.
I'm surprised he isn't here.

LEADER   We need him—
without him we have nothing but old, useless rumors.

330 OEDIPUS   Which rumors? I'll search out every word.

LEADER   Laius was killed, they say, by certain travelers.

OEDIPUS   I know—but no one can find the murderer.

LEADER   If the man has a trace of fear in him
he won't stay silent long,
335 not with your curses ringing in his ears.

OEDIPUS   He didn't flinch at murder,
he'll never flinch at words.

> [*Enter* TIRESIAS, *the blind prophet, led by a boy with escorts in
> attendance. He remains at a distance.*]

LEADER   Here is the one who will convict him, look,
they bring him on at last, the seer, the man of god.
340 The truth lives inside him, him alone.

OEDIPUS   O Tiresias,
master of all the mysteries of our life,
all you teach and all you dare not tell,
signs in the heavens, signs that walk the earth!
Blind as you are, you can feel all the more
345 what sickness haunts our city. You, my lord,
are the one shield, the one savior we can find.

---

4. The blind prophet of Thebes.

We asked Apollo—perhaps the messengers
haven't told you—he sent his answer back:
"Relief from the plague can only come one way.
350 Uncover the murderers of Laius,
put them to death or drive them into exile."
So I beg you, grudge us nothing now, no voice,
no message plucked from the birds, the embers
or the other mantic ways within your grasp.
355 Rescue yourself, your city, rescue me—
rescue everything infected by the dead.
We are in your hands. For a man to help others
with all his gifts and native strength:
that is the noblest work.

TIRESIAS   How terrible—to see the truth
360 when the truth is only pain to him who sees!
I knew it well, but I put it from my mind,
else I never would have come.

OEDIPUS   What's this? Why so grim, so dire?

TIRESIAS   Just send me home. You bear your burdens,
365 I'll bear mine. It's better that way,
please believe me.

OEDIPUS   Strange response . . . unlawful,
unfriendly too to the state that bred and reared you—
you withhold the word of god.

TIRESIAS   I fail to see
that your own words are so well-timed.
370 I'd rather not have the same thing said of me . . .

OEDIPUS   For the love of god, don't turn away,
not if you know something. We beg you,
all of us on our knees.

TIRESIAS   None of you knows—
and I will never reveal my dreadful secrets,
375 not to say your own.

OEDIPUS   What? You know and you won't tell?
You're bent on betraying us, destroying Thebes?

TIRESIAS   I'd rather not cause pain for you or me.
So why this . . . useless interrogation?
380 You'll get nothing from me.

OEDIPUS   Nothing! You,
you scum of the earth, you'd enrage a heart of stone!
You won't talk? Nothing moves you?
Out with it, once and for all!

TIRESIAS   You criticize my temper . . . unaware
385 of the one you live with, you revile me.

OEDIPUS   Who could restrain his anger hearing you?
What outrage—you spurn the city!

TIRESIAS   What will come will come.
Even if I shroud it all in silence.

390 OEDIPUS   What will come? You're bound to tell me that.

TIRESIAS   I'll say no more. Do as you like, build your anger

to whatever pitch you please, rage your worst—
OEDIPUS   Oh I'll let loose, I have such fury in me—
now I see it all. You helped hatch the plot,
395   you did the work, yes, short of killing him
with your own hands—and given eyes I'd say
you did the killing single-handed!
TIRESIAS   Is that so!
I charge you, then, submit to that decree
you just laid down: from this day onward
400   speak to no one, not these citizens, not myself.
You are the curse, the corruption of the land!
OEDIPUS   You, shameless—
aren't you appalled to start up such a story?
You think you can get away with this?
TIRESIAS   I have already.
405   The truth with all its power lives inside me.
OEDIPUS   Who primed you for this? Not your prophet's trade.
TIRESIAS   You did, you forced me, twisted it out of me.
OEDIPUS   What? Say it again—I'll understand it better.
TIRESIAS   Didn't you understand, just now?
410   Or are you tempting me to talk?
OEDIPUS   No, I can't say I grasped your meaning.
Out with it, again!
TIRESIAS   I say you are the murderer you hunt.
OEDIPUS   That obscenity, twice—by god, you'll pay.
415 TIRESIAS   Shall I say more, so you can really rage?
OEDIPUS   Much as you want. Your words are nothing—futile.
TIRESIAS   You cannot imagine . . . I tell you,
you and your loved ones live together in infamy,
you cannot see how far you've gone in guilt.
420 OEDIPUS   You think you can keep this up and never suffer?
TIRESIAS   Indeed, if the truth has any power.
OEDIPUS   It does
but not for you, old man. You've lost your power,
stone-blind, stone-deaf—senses, eyes blind as stone!
TIRESIAS   I pity you, flinging at me the very insults
425   each man here will fling at you so soon.
OEDIPUS   Blind,
lost in the night, endless night that cursed you!
You can't hurt me or anyone else who sees the light—
you can never touch me.
TIRESIAS   True, it is not your fate
to fall at my hands. Apollo is quite enough,
430   and he will take some pains to work this out.
OEDIPUS   Kreon! Is this conspiracy his or yours?
TIRESIAS   Kreon is not your downfall, no, you are your own.
OEDIPUS   O power—
wealth and empire, skill outstripping skill
in the heady rivalries of life,
435   what envy lurks inside you! Just for this,

the crown the city gave me—I never sought it,
they laid it in my hands—for this alone, Kreon,
the soul of trust, my loyal friend from the start
steals against me . . . so hungry to overthrow me
440   he sets this wizard on me, this scheming quack,
this fortune-teller peddling lies, eyes peeled
for his own profit—seer blind in his craft!

Come here, you pious fraud. Tell me,
when did you ever prove yourself a prophet?
445   When the Sphinx, that chanting Fury kept her deathwatch here,
why silent then, not a word to set our people free?
There was a riddle, not for some passer-by to solve[5]—
it cried out for a prophet. Where were you?
Did you rise to the crisis? Not a word,
450   you and your birds, your gods—nothing.
No, but I came by, Oedipus the ignorant,
I stopped the Sphinx! With no help from the birds,
the flight of my own intelligence hit the mark.

And this is the man you'd try to overthrow?
455   You think you'll stand by Kreon when he's king?
You and the great mastermind—
you'll pay in tears, I promise you, for this,
this witch-hunt. If you didn't look so senile
the lash would teach you what your scheming means!
460   LEADER   I would suggest his words were spoken in anger,
Oedipus . . . yours too, and it isn't what we need.
The best solution to the oracle, the riddle
posed by god—we should look for that.
TIRESIAS   You are the king no doubt, but in one respect,
465   at least, I am your equal: the right to reply.
I claim that privilege too.
I am not your slave. I serve Apollo.
I don't need Kreon to speak for me in public.
                                             So,
you mock my blindness? Let me tell you this.
470   You with your precious eyes,
you're blind to the corruption of your life,
to the house you live in, those you live with—
who *are* your parents? Do you know? All unknowing
you are the scourge of your own flesh and blood,
475   the dead below the earth and the living here above,
and the double lash of your mother and your father's curse
will whip you from this land one day, their footfall
treading you down in terror, darkness shrouding
your eyes that now can see the light!

---

5. Oedipus was on his way to Apollo's oracle at Delphi when he came upon the Sphinx.

                                        Soon, soon
480   you'll scream aloud—what haven won't reverberate?
      What rock of Cithaeron[6] won't scream back in echo?
      That day you learn the truth about your marriage,
      the wedding-march that sang you into your halls,
      the lusty voyage home to the fatal harbor!
485   And a crowd of other horrors you'd never dream
      will level you with yourself and all your children.

      There. Now smear us with insults—Kreon, myself,
      and every word I've said. No man will ever
      be rooted from the earth as brutally as you.
490   OEDIPUS   Enough! Such filth from him? Insufferable—
      what, still alive? Get out—
      faster, back where you came from—vanish!
      TIRESIAS   I would never have come if you hadn't called me here.
      OEDIPUS   If I thought you would blurt out such absurdities,
495   you'd have died waiting before I'd had you summoned.
      TIRESIAS   Absurd, am I! To you, not to your parents:
      the ones who bore you found me sane enough.
      OEDIPUS   Parents—who? Wait . . . who is my father?
      TIRESIAS   This day will bring your birth and your destruction.
500   OEDIPUS   Riddles—all you can say are riddles, murk and darkness.
      TIRESIAS   Ah, but aren't you the best man alive at solving riddles?
      OEDIPUS   Mock me for that, go on, and you'll reveal my greatness.
      TIRESIAS   Your great good fortune, true, it was your ruin.
      OEDIPUS   Not if I saved the city—what do I care?
505   TIRESIAS   Well then, I'll be going.
                  [To his attendant.]

                                        Take me home, boy.
      OEDIPUS   Yes, take him away. You're a nuisance here.
      Out of the way, the irritation's gone.
                  [Turning his back on TIRESIAS, moving toward the palace.]
      TIRESIAS   I will go,
      once I have said what I came here to say.
      I'll never shrink from the anger in your eyes—
510   you can't destroy me. Listen to me closely:
      the man you've sought so long, proclaiming,
      cursing up and down, the murderer of Laius—
      he is here. A stranger,
      you may think, who lives among you,
515   he soon will be revealed a native Theban
      but he will take no joy in the revelation.
      Blind who now has eyes, beggar who now is rich,
      he will grope his way toward a foreign soil,
      a stick tapping before him step by step.
                  [OEDIPUS enters the palace.]

---

6. The mountain range, south of Thebes, where the infant Oedipus was abandoned.

520   Revealed at last, brother and father both
         to the children he embraces, to his mother
         son and husband both—he sowed the loins
         his father sowed, he spilled his father's blood!
         Go in and reflect on that, solve that.
525   And if you find I've lied
         from this day onward call the prophet blind.
              [TIRESIAS *and the boy exit to the side.*]

CHORUS   Who—
         who is the man the voice of god denounces
         resounding out of the rocky gorge of Delphi?
              The horror too dark to tell,
530   whose ruthless bloody hands have done the work?
         His time has come to fly
              to outrace the stallions of the storm
                   his feet a streak of speed—
         Cased in armor, Apollo son of the Father
535   lunges on him, lightning-bolts afire!
         And the grim unerring Furies[7]
              closing for the kill.
                             Look,
         the word of god has just come blazing
         flashing off Parnassus'[8] snowy heights!
540   That man who left no trace—
         after him, hunt him down with all our strength!
         Now under bristling timber
              up through rocks and caves he stalks
                   like the wild mountain bull—
545   cut off from men, each step an agony, frenzied, racing blind
         but he cannot outrace the dread voices of Delphi
              ringing out of the heart of Earth,
                   the dark wings beating around him shrieking doom
                        the doom that never dies, the terror—
550   The skilled prophet scans the birds and shatters me with terror!
         I can't accept him, can't deny him, don't know what to say,
         I'm lost, and the wings of dark foreboding beating—
         I cannot see what's come, what's still to come . . .
         and what could breed a blood feud between
555   Laius' house and the son of Polybus?[9]
         I know of nothing, not in the past and not now,
         no charge to bring against our king, no cause
         to attack his fame that rings throughout Thebes—
              not without proof—not for the ghost of Laius,
560   not to avenge a murder gone without a trace.

---

7. Monstrous female personifications of
vengeance.
8. Site of Delphi, where the oracular shrine
was a deep cave or chasm (see lines 546–47).

9. A reference to the rivalry between the cities of Thebes (formerly ruled by King Laius)
and Corinth (ruled by Polybus, Oedipus's
adoptive father).

Zeus and Apollo know, they know, the great masters
      of all the dark and depth of human life.
But whether a mere man can know the truth,
whether a seer can fathom more than I—
565   there is no test, no certain proof
      though matching skill for skill
a man can outstrip a rival. No, not till I see
these charges proved will I side with his accusers.
We saw him then, when the she-hawk[1] swept against him,
570   saw with our own eyes his skill, his brilliant triumph—
      there was the test—he was the joy of Thebes!
      Never will I convict my king, never in my heart.

        [Enter KREON *from the side.]*

KREON   My fellow-citizens, I hear King Oedipus
levels terrible charges at me. I had to come.
575   I resent it deeply. If, in the present crisis
he thinks he suffers any abuse from me,
anything I've done or said that offers him
the slightest injury, why, I've no desire
to linger out this life, my reputation in ruins.
580   The damage I'd face from such an accusation
is nothing simple. No, there's nothing worse:
branded a traitor in the city, a traitor
to all of you and my good friends.

LEADER   True,
but a slur might have been forced out of him,
585   by anger perhaps, not any firm conviction.

KREON   The charge was made in public, wasn't it?
I put the prophet up to spreading lies?

LEADER   Such things were said . . .
I don't know with what intent, if any.

590 KREON   Was his glance steady, his mind right
when the charge was brought against me?

LEADER   I really couldn't say. I never look
to judge the ones in power.

        [The doors open. OEDIPUS *enters.]*

                        Wait,
here's Oedipus now.

OEDIPUS   You—here? You have the gall
595   to show your face before the palace gates?
You, plotting to kill me, kill the king—
I see it all, the marauding thief himself
scheming to steal my crown and power!

                       Tell me,
in god's name, what did you take me for,
600   coward or fool, when you spun out your plot?

---

1. That is, the Sphinx, which had the paws of a lion, the tail of a serpent, and the wings of an eagle.

Your treachery—you think I'd never detect it
creeping against me in the dark? Or sensing it,
not defend myself? Aren't you the fool,
you and your high adventure. Lacking numbers,

605   powerful friends, out for the big game of empire—
you need riches, armies to bring that quarry down!

KREON   Are you quite finished? It's your turn to listen
for just as long as you've . . . instructed me.
Hear me out, then judge me on the facts.

610 OEDIPUS   You've a wicked way with words, Kreon,
but I'll be slow to learn—from you.
I find you a menace, a great burden to me.

KREON   Just one thing, hear me out in this.

OEDIPUS   Just one thing,
don't tell *me* you're not the enemy, the traitor.

615 KREON   Look, if you think crude, mindless stubbornness
such a gift, you've lost your sense of balance.

OEDIPUS   If you think you can abuse a kinsman,
then escape the penalty, you're insane.

KREON   Fair enough, I grant you. But this injury

620   you say I've done you, what is it?

OEDIPUS   Did you induce me, yes or no,
to send for that sanctimonious prophet?

KREON   I did. And I'd do the same again.

OEDIPUS   All right then, tell me, how long is it now

625   since Laius . . .

KREON   Laius—what did *he* do?

OEDIPUS   Vanished,
swept from sight, murdered in his tracks.

KREON   The count of the years would run you far back . . .

OEDIPUS   And that far back, was the prophet at his trade?

KREON   Skilled as he is today, and just as honored.

630 OEDIPUS   Did he ever refer to me then, at that time?

KREON   No,
never, at least, when I was in his presence.

OEDIPUS   But you did investigate the murder, didn't you?

KREON   We did our best, of course, discovered nothing.

OEDIPUS   But the great seer never accused me then—why not?

635 KREON   I don't know. And when I don't, *I* keep quiet.

OEDIPUS   You do know this, you'd tell it too—
if you had a shred of decency.

KREON   What?
If I know, I won't hold back.

OEDIPUS   Simply this:
if the two of you had never put heads together,

640   we would never have heard about *my* killing Laius.

KREON   If that's what he says . . . well, you know best.
But now I have a right to learn from you
as you just learned from me.

OEDIPUS   Learn your fill,
 you never will convict me of the murder.
645 KREON   Tell me, you're married to my sister, aren't you?
 OEDIPUS   A genuine discovery—there's no denying that.
 KREON   And you rule the land with her, with equal power?
 OEDIPUS   She receives from me whatever she desires.
 KREON   And I am the third, all of us are equals?
650 OEDIPUS   Yes, and it's there you show your stripes—
 you betray a kinsman.
 KREON   Not at all.
 Not if you see things calmly, rationally,
 as I do. Look at it this way first:
 who in his right mind would rather rule
655 and live in anxiety than sleep in peace?
 Particularly if he enjoys the same authority.
 Not I, I'm not the man to yearn for kingship,
 not with a king's power in my hands. Who would?
 No one with any sense of self-control.
660 Now, as it is, you offer me all I need,
 not a fear in the world. But if I wore the crown . . .
 there'd be many painful duties to perform,
 hardly to my taste.
      How could kingship
 please me more than influence, power
665 without a qualm? I'm not that deluded yet,
 to reach for anything but privilege outright,
 profit free and clear.
 Now all men sing my praises, all salute me,
 now all who request your favors curry mine.
670 I am their best hope: success rests in me.
 Why give up that, I ask you, and borrow trouble?
 A man of sense, someone who sees things clearly
 would never resort to treason.
 No, I've no lust for conspiracy in me,
675 nor could I ever suffer one who does.

 Do you want proof? Go to Delphi yourself,
 examine the oracle and see if I've reported
 the message word-for-word. This too:
 if you detect that I and the clairvoyant
680 have plotted anything in common, arrest me,
 execute me. Not on the strength of one vote,
 two in this case, mine as well as yours.
 But don't convict me on sheer unverified surmise.
 How wrong it is to take the good for bad,
685 purely at random, or take the bad for good.
 But reject a friend, a kinsman? I would as soon
 tear out the life within us, priceless life itself.
 You'll learn this well, without fail, in time.

Time alone can bring the just man to light—
690 the criminal you can spot in one short day.

LEADER   Good advice,
my lord, for anyone who wants to avoid disaster.
Those who jump to conclusions may go wrong.

OEDIPUS   When my enemy moves against me quickly,
plots in secret, I move quickly too, I must,
695 I plot and pay him back. Relax my guard a moment,
waiting his next move—he wins his objective,
I lose mine.

KREON   What do you want?
You want me banished?

OEDIPUS   No, I want you dead.

KREON   Just to show how ugly a grudge can . . .

OEDIPUS   So,
700 still stubborn? you don't think I'm serious?

KREON   I think you're insane.

OEDIPUS   Quite sane—in my behalf.

KREON   Not just as much in mine?

OEDIPUS   You—my mortal enemy?

KREON   What if you're wholly wrong?

OEDIPUS   No matter—I must rule.

KREON   Not if you rule unjustly.

OEDIPUS   Hear him, Thebes, my city!

705 KREON   My city too, not yours alone!

LEADER   Please, my lords.

          [Enter JOCASTA from the palace.]

                              Look, Jocasta's coming,
and just in time too. With her help
you must put this fighting of yours to rest.

JOCASTA   Have you no sense? Poor misguided men,
710 such shouting—why this public outburst?
Aren't you ashamed, with the land so sick,
to stir up private quarrels?

          [To OEDIPUS.]

Into the palace now. And Kreon, you go home.
Why make such a furor over nothing?

715 KREON   My sister, it's dreadful . . . Oedipus, your husband,
he's bent on a choice of punishments for me,
banishment from the fatherland or death.

OEDIPUS   Precisely. I caught him in the act, Jocasta,
plotting, about to stab me in the back.

720 KREON   Never—curse me, let me die and be damned
if I've done you any wrong you charge me with.

JOCASTA   Oh god, believe it, Oedipus,
honor the solemn oath he swears to heaven.
Do it for me, for the sake of all your people.

          [The CHORUS begins to chant.]

725 CHORUS   Believe it, be sensible
        give way, my king, I beg you!
    OEDIPUS   What do you want from me, concessions?
    CHORUS   Respect him—he's been no fool in the past
        and now he's strong with the oath he swears to god.
730 OEDIPUS   You know what you're asking?
    CHORUS   I do.
    OEDIPUS   Then out with it!
    CHORUS   The man's your friend, your kin, he's under oath—
        don't cast him out, disgraced
        branded with guilt on the strength of hearsay only.
    OEDIPUS   Know full well, if that is what you want
735   you want me dead or banished from the land.
    CHORUS   Never—
        no, by the blazing Sun, first god of the heavens!
          Stripped of the gods, stripped of loved ones,
        let me die by inches if that ever crossed my mind.
        But the heart inside me sickens, dies as the land dies
740   and now on top of the old griefs you pile this,
        your fury—both of you!
    OEDIPUS   Then let him go,
        even if it does lead to my ruin, my death
        or my disgrace, driven from Thebes for life.
        It's you, not him I pity—your words move me.
745   He, wherever he goes, my hate goes with him.
    KREON   Look at you, sullen in yielding, brutal in your rage—
        you'll go too far. It's perfect justice:
        natures like yours are hardest on themselves.
    OEDIPUS   Then leave me alone—get out!
    KREON   I'm going.
750   You're wrong, so wrong. These men know I'm right.
              [Exit to the side. The CHORUS turns to JOCASTA.]
    CHORUS   Why do you hesitate, my lady
        why not help him in?
    JOCASTA   Tell me what's happened first.
    CHORUS   Loose, ignorant talk started dark suspicions
755   and a sense of injustice cut deeply too.
    JOCASTA   On both sides?
    CHORUS   Oh yes.
    JOCASTA   What did they say?
    CHORUS   Enough, please, enough! The land's so racked already
        or so it seems to me . . .
        End the trouble here, just where they left it.
760 OEDIPUS   You see what comes of your good intentions now?
        And all because you tried to blunt my anger.
    CHORUS   My king,
        I've said it once, I'll say it time and again—
          I'd be insane, you know it,
        senseless, ever to turn my back on you.
765   You who set our beloved land—storm-tossed, shattered—

straight on course. Now again, good helmsman,
steer us through the storm!

    [*The* CHORUS *draws away, leaving* OEDIPUS *and* JOCASTA *side by side.*]

JOCASTA   For the love of god,
Oedipus, tell me too, what is it?
Why this rage? You're so unbending.

770 OEDIPUS   I will tell you. I respect you, Jocasta,
much more than these . . .

    [*Glancing at the* CHORUS.]

Kreon's to blame, Kreon schemes against me.

JOCASTA   Tell me clearly, how did the quarrel start?

OEDIPUS   He says I murdered Laius—I am guilty.

775 JOCASTA   How does he know? Some secret knowledge
or simple hearsay?

OEDIPUS   Oh, he sent his prophet in
to do his dirty work. You know Kreon,
Kreon keeps his own lips clean.

JOCASTA   A prophet?
Well then, free yourself of every charge!

780 Listen to me and learn some peace of mind:
no skill in the world,
nothing human can penetrate the future.
Here is proof, quick and to the point.

An oracle came to Laius one fine day
785 (I won't say from Apollo himself
but his underlings, his priests) and it said
that doom would strike him down at the hands of a son,
our son, to be born of our own flesh and blood. But Laius,
so the report goes at least, was killed by strangers,
790 thieves, at a place where three roads meet . . . my son—
he wasn't three days old and the boy's father
fastened his ankles, had a henchman fling him away
on a barren, trackless mountain.

                        There, you see?
Apollo brought neither thing to pass. My baby
795 no more murdered his father than Laius suffered—
his wildest fear—death at his own son's hands.
That's how the seers and all their revelations
mapped out the future. Brush them from your mind.
Whatever the god needs and seeks
800 he'll bring to light himself, with ease.

OEDIPUS   Strange,
hearing you just now . . . my mind wandered,
my thoughts racing back and forth.

JOCASTA   What do you mean? Why so anxious, startled?

OEDIPUS   I thought I heard you say that Laius
805 was cut down at a place where three roads meet.

JOCASTA   That was the story. It hasn't died out yet.

OEDIPUS   Where did this thing happen? Be precise.

JOCASTA   A place called Phocis, where two branching roads,
    one from Daulia,[2] one from Delphi,
810   come together—a crossroads.

OEDIPUS   When? How long ago?

JOCASTA   The heralds no sooner reported Laius dead
    than you appeared and they hailed you king of Thebes.

OEDIPUS   My god, my god—what have you planned to do to me?

815 JOCASTA   What, Oedipus? What haunts you so?

OEDIPUS   Not yet.
    Laius—how did he look? Describe him.
    Had he reached his prime?

JOCASTA   He was swarthy,
    and the gray had just begun to streak his temples,
    and his build . . . wasn't far from yours.

OEDIPUS   Oh no no,
820   I think I've just called down a dreadful curse
    upon myself—I simply didn't know!

JOCASTA   What are you saying? I shudder to look at you.

OEDIPUS   I have a terrible fear the blind seer can see.
    I'll know in a moment. One thing more—

JOCASTA   Anything,
825   afraid as I am—ask, I'll answer, all I can.

OEDIPUS   Did he go with a light or heavy escort,
    several men-at-arms, like a lord, a king?

JOCASTA   There were five in the party, a herald among them,
    and a single wagon carrying Laius.

OEDIPUS   Ai—
830   now I can see it all, clear as day.
    Who told you all this at the time, Jocasta?

JOCASTA   A servant who reached home, the lone survivor.

OEDIPUS   So, could he still be in the palace—even now?

JOCASTA   No indeed. Soon as he returned from the scene
835   and saw you on the throne with Laius dead and gone,
    he knelt and clutched my hand, pleading with me
    to send him into the hinterlands, to pasture,
    far as possible, out of sight of Thebes.
    I sent him away. Slave though he was,
840   he'd earned that favor—and much more.

OEDIPUS   Can we bring him back, quickly?

JOCASTA   Easily. Why do you want him so?

OEDIPUS   I'm afraid,
    Jocasta, I have said too much already.
    That man—I've got to see him.

JOCASTA   Then he'll come.
845   But even I have a right, I'd like to think,
    to know what's torturing you, my lord.

---

2. A Boeotian town not far from Thebes. *Phocis*: the region where Delphi is located, west of
Boeotia.

OEDIPUS   And so you shall—I can hold nothing back from you,
   now I've reached this pitch of dark foreboding.
   Who means more to me than you? Tell me,
850   whom would I turn toward but you
   as I go through all this?

   My father was Polybus, king of Corinth.
   My mother, a Dorian,[3] Merope. And I was held
   the prince of the realm among the people there,
855   till something struck me out of nowhere,
   something strange . . . worth remarking perhaps,
   hardly worth the anxiety I gave it.
   Some man at a banquet who had drunk too much
   shouted out—he was far gone, mind you—
860   that I am not my father's son. Fighting words!
   I barely restrained myself that day
   but early the next I went to mother and father,
   questioned them closely, and they were enraged
   at the accusation and the fool who let it fly.
865   So as for my parents I was satisfied,
   but still this thing kept gnawing at me,
   the slander spread—I had to make my move.
                                And so,
   unknown to mother and father I set out for Delphi,
   and the god Apollo spurned me, sent me away
870   denied the facts I came for,
   but first he flashed before my eyes a future
   great with pain, terror, disaster—I can hear him cry,
   "You are fated to couple with your mother, you will bring
   a breed of children into the light no man can bear to see—
875   you will kill your father, the one who gave you life!"
   I heard all that and ran. I abandoned Corinth,
   from that day on I gauged its landfall only
   by the stars, running, always running
   toward some place where I would never see
880   the shame of all those oracles come true.
   And as I fled I reached that very spot
   where the great king, you say, met his death.

   Now, Jocasta, I will tell you all.
   Making my way toward this triple crossroad
885   I began to see a herald, then a brace of colts
   drawing a wagon, and mounted on the bench . . . a man,
   just as you've described him, coming face-to-face,
   and the one in the lead and the old man himself
   were about to thrust me off the road—brute force—
890   and the one shouldering me aside, the driver,
   I strike him in anger!—and the old man, watching me

---

3. From Doris, a region of central Greece.

coming up along his wheels—he brings down
his prod, two prongs straight at my head!
I paid him back with interest!
895   Short work, by god—with one blow of the staff
in this right hand I knock him out of his high seat,
roll him out of the wagon, sprawling headlong—
I killed them all—every mother's son!

Oh, but if there is any blood-tie
900   between Laius and this stranger . . .
what man alive more miserable than I?
More hated by the gods? I am the man
no alien, no citizen welcomes to his house,
law forbids it—not a word to me in public,
905   driven out of every hearth and home.
And all these curses I—no one but I
brought down these piling curses on myself!
And you, his wife, I've touched your body with these,
the hands that killed your husband cover you with blood.

910   Wasn't I born for torment? Look me in the eyes!
I am abomination—heart and soul!
I must be exiled, and even in exile
never see my parents, never set foot
on native ground again. Else I am doomed
915   to couple with my mother and cut my father down . . .
Polybus who reared me, gave me life.
                                        But why, why?
Wouldn't a man of judgment say—and wouldn't he be right—
some savage power has brought this down upon my head?

Oh no, not that, you pure and awesome gods,
920   never let me see that day! Let me slip
from the world of men, vanish without a trace
before I see myself stained with such corruption,
stained to the heart.
LEADER   My lord, you fill our hearts with fear.
925   But at least until you question the witness,
do take hope.
OEDIPUS   Exactly. He is my last hope—
I am waiting for the shepherd. He is crucial.
JOCASTA   And once he appears, what then? Why so urgent?
OEDIPUS   I will tell you. If it turns out that his story
930   matches yours, I've escaped the worst.
JOCASTA   What did I say? What struck you so?
OEDIPUS   You said thieves—
he told you a whole band of them murdered Laius.
So, if he still holds to the same number,
I cannot be the killer. One can't equal many.
935   But if he refers to one man, one alone,

clearly the scales come down on me:
I am guilty.
    JOCASTA   Impossible. Trust me,
    I told you precisely what he said,
    and he can't retract it now;
940   the whole city heard it, not just I.
    And even if he should vary his first report
    by one man more or less, still, my lord,
    he could never make the murder of Laius
    truly fit the prophecy. Apollo was explicit:
945   my son was doomed to kill my husband . . . my son,
    poor defenseless thing, he never had a chance
    to kill his father. They destroyed him first.

    So much for prophecy. It's neither here nor there.
    From this day on, I wouldn't look right or left.
950 OEDIPUS   True, true. Still, that shepherd,
    someone fetch him—now!
    JOCASTA   I'll send at once. But do let's go inside.
    I'd never displease you, least of all in this.

        [OEDIPUS *and* JOCASTA *enter the palace.*]

    CHORUS   Destiny guide me always
955   Destiny find me filled with reverence
        pure in word and deed.
    Great laws tower above us, reared on high
    born for the brilliant vault of heaven—
        Olympian Sky their only father,[4]
960   nothing mortal, no man gave them birth,
    their memory deathless, never lost in sleep:
    within them lives a mighty god, the god does not grow old.

    Pride breeds the tyrant
    violent pride, gorging, crammed to bursting
965   with all that is overripe and rich with ruin—
    clawing up to the heights, headlong pride
    crashes down the abyss—sheer doom!
        No footing helps, all foothold lost and gone.
    But the healthy strife that makes the city strong—
970   I pray that god will never end that wrestling:
    god, my champion, I will never let you go.

    But if any man comes striding, high and mighty
        in all he says and does,
    no fear of justice, no reverence
975   for the temples of the gods—
        let a rough doom tear him down,
    repay his pride, breakneck, ruinous pride!

4. Mount Olympus in Thessaly, in northern Greece, was believed to be the home of the gods.

If he cannot reap his profits fairly
   cannot restrain himself from outrage—
980 mad, laying hands on the holy things untouchable!

    Can such a man, so desperate, still boast
   he can save his life from the flashing bolts of god?
     If all such violence goes with honor now
      why join the sacred dance?

985 Never again will I go reverent to Delphi,
   the inviolate heart of Earth
  or Apollo's ancient oracle at Abae
  or Olympia[5] of the fires—
   unless these prophecies all come true
990 for all mankind to point toward in wonder.
  King of kings, if you deserve your titles
   Zeus, remember, never forget!
  You and your deathless, everlasting reign.

    They are dying, the old oracles sent to Laius,
995   now our masters strike them off the rolls.
     Nowhere Apollo's golden glory now—
      the gods, the gods go down.

[*Enter* JOCASTA *from the palace, carrying a suppliant's branch
wound in wool.*]

JOCASTA   Lords of the realm,[6] it occurred to me,
  just now, to visit the temples of the gods,
1000 so I have my branch in hand and incense too.

  Oedipus is beside himself. Racked with anguish,
  no longer a man of sense, he won't admit
  the latest prophecies are hollow as the old—
  he's at the mercy of every passing voice
1005 if the voice tells of terror.
  I urge him gently, nothing seems to help,
  so I turn to you, Apollo, you are nearest.

[*Placing her branch on the altar, while an old herdsman enters
from the side, not the one just summoned by the King but an
unexpected* MESSENGER *from Corinth.*]

  I come with prayers and offerings . . . I beg you,
  cleanse us, set us free of defilement!
1010 Look at us, passengers in the grip of fear,
  watching the pilot of the vessel go to pieces.

MESSENGER [*Approaching* JOCASTA *and the* CHORUS.]
  Strangers, please, I wonder if you could lead us

5. Site in the western Peloponnesus of a
major temple of Zeus (location of the qua-
drennial Olympic games). *Abae*: a town in

Phocis, whose oracle of Apollo was older than
that at Delphi.
6. That is, the chorus.

to the palace of the king . . . I think it's Oedipus.
Better, the man himself—you know where he is?
1015 LEADER   This is his palace, stranger. He's inside.
But here is his queen, his wife and mother
of his children.
MESSENGER   Blessings on you, noble queen,
queen of Oedipus crowned with all your family—
blessings on you always!
1020 JOCASTA   And the same to you, stranger, you deserve it . . .
such a greeting. But what have you come for?
Have you brought us news?
MESSENGER   Wonderful news—
for the house, my lady, for your husband too.
JOCASTA   Really, what? Who sent you?
MESSENGER   Corinth.
1025 I'll give you the message in a moment.
You'll be glad of it—how could you help it?—
though it costs a little sorrow in the bargain.
JOCASTA   What can it be, with such a double edge?
MESSENGER   The people there, they want to make your Oedipus
1030 king of Corinth, so they're saying now.
JOCASTA   Why? Isn't old Polybus still in power?
MESSENGER   No more. Death has got him in the tomb.
JOCASTA   What are you saying? Polybus, dead?—dead?
MESSENGER   If not,
if I'm not telling the truth, strike me dead too.
1035 JOCASTA [To a servant.]   Quickly, go to your master, tell him this!
You prophecies of the gods, where are you now?
This is the man that Oedipus feared for years,
he fled him, not to kill him—and now he's dead,
quite by chance, a normal, natural death,
1040 not murdered by his son.
OEDIPUS [Emerging from the palace.]
                         Dearest,
what now? Why call me from the palace?
JOCASTA [Bringing the MESSENGER closer.]
Listen to him, see for yourself what all
those awful prophecies of god have come to.
OEDIPUS   And who is he? What can he have for me?
1045 JOCASTA   He's from Corinth, he's come to tell you
your father is no more—Polybus—he's dead!
OEDIPUS [Wheeling on the MESSENGER.]
What? Let me have it from your lips.
MESSENGER   Well,
if that's what you want first, then here it is:
Make no mistake, Polybus is dead and gone.
1050 OEDIPUS   How—murder? sickness?—what? what killed him?
MESSENGER   A light tip of the scales can put old bones to rest.
OEDIPUS   Sickness then—poor man, it wore him down.

MESSENGER   That,
  and the long count of years he'd measured out.
OEDIPUS   So!
  Jocasta, why, why look to the Prophet's hearth,
1055 the fires of the future? Why scan the birds
  that scream above our heads? They winged me on
  to the murder of my father, did they? That was my doom?
  Well look, he's dead and buried, hidden under the earth,
  and here I am in Thebes, I never put hand to sword—
1060 unless some longing for me wasted him away,
  then in a sense you'd say I caused his death.
  But now, all those prophecies I feared—Polybus
  packs them off to sleep with him in hell!
  They're nothing, worthless.
JOCASTA   There.
1065 Didn't I tell you from the start?
OEDIPUS   So you did. I was lost in fear.
JOCASTA   No more, sweep it from your mind forever.
OEDIPUS   But my mother's bed, surely I must fear—
JOCASTA   Fear?
  What should a man fear? It's all chance,
1070 chance rules our lives. Not a man on earth
  can see a day ahead, groping through the dark.
  Better to live at random, best we can.
  And as for this marriage with your mother—
  have no fear. Many a man before you,
1075 in his dreams, has shared his mother's bed.
  Take such things for shadows, nothing at all—
  Live, Oedipus,
  as if there's no tomorrow!
OEDIPUS   Brave words,
  and you'd persuade me if mother weren't alive.
1080 But mother lives, so for all your reassurances
  I live in fear, I must.
JOCASTA   But your father's death,
  that, at least, is a great blessing, joy to the eyes!
OEDIPUS   Great, I know . . . but I fear *her*—she's still alive.
MESSENGER   Wait, who is this woman, makes you so afraid?
1085 OEDIPUS   Merope, old man. The wife of Polybus.
MESSENGER   The queen? What's there to fear in her?
OEDIPUS   A dreadful prophecy, stranger, sent by the gods.
MESSENGER   Tell me, could you? Unless it's forbidden
  other ears to hear.
OEDIPUS   Not at all.
1090 Apollo told me once—it is my fate—
  I must make love with my own mother,
  shed my father's blood with my own hands.
  So for years I've given Corinth a wide berth,
  and it's been my good fortune too. But still,

1095   to see one's parents and look into their eyes
        is the greatest joy I know.
        MESSENGER   You're afraid of that?
        That kept you out of Corinth?
        OEDIPUS   My *father*, old man—
        so I wouldn't kill my father.
        MESSENGER   So that's it.
        Well then, seeing I came with such good will, my king,
1100   why don't I rid you of that old worry now?
        OEDIPUS   What a rich reward you'd have for that!
        MESSENGER   What do you think I came for, majesty?
        So you'd come home and I'd be better off.
        OEDIPUS   Never, I will never go near my parents.
1105   MESSENGER   My boy, it's clear, you don't know what you're doing.
        OEDIPUS   What do you mean, old man? For god's sake, explain.
        MESSENGER   If you ran from *them*, always dodging home . . .
        OEDIPUS   Always, terrified Apollo's oracle might come true—
        MESSENGER   And you'd be covered with guilt, from both your parents.
1110   OEDIPUS   That's right, old man, that fear is always with me.
        MESSENGER   Don't you know? You've really nothing to fear.
        OEDIPUS   But why? If I'm their son—Merope, Polybus?
        MESSENGER   Polybus was nothing to you, that's why, not in blood.
        OEDIPUS   What are you saying—Polybus was not my father?
1115   MESSENGER   No more than I am. He and I are equals.
        OEDIPUS   My father—
        how can my father equal nothing? You're nothing to me!
        MESSENGER   Neither was he, no more your father than I am.
        OEDIPUS   Then why did he call me his son?
        MESSENGER   You were a gift,
        years ago—know for a fact he took you
1120   from my hands.
        OEDIPUS   No, from another's hands?
        Then how could he love me so? He loved me, deeply . . .
        MESSENGER   True, and his early years without a child
        made him love you all the more.
        OEDIPUS   And you, did you . . .
        buy me? find me by accident?
        MESSENGER   I stumbled on you,
1125   down the woody flanks of Mount Cithaeron.
        OEDIPUS   So close,
        what were you doing here, just passing through?
        MESSENGER   Watching over my flocks, grazing them on the slopes.
        OEDIPUS   A herdsman, were you? A vagabond, scraping for wages?
        MESSENGER   Your savior too, my son, in your worst hour.
        OEDIPUS   Oh—
1130   when you picked me up, was I in pain? What exactly?
        MESSENGER   Your ankles . . . they tell the story. Look at them.
        OEDIPUS   Why remind me of that, that old affliction?
        MESSENGER   Your ankles were pinned together. I set you free.
        OEDIPUS   That dreadful mark—I've had it from the cradle.

1135 MESSENGER   And you got your name from that misfortune too,
the name's still with you.[7]
OEDIPUS   Dear god, who did it?—
mother? father? Tell me.
MESSENGER   I don't know.
The one who gave you to me, he'd know more.
OEDIPUS   What? You took me from someone else?
1140 You didn't find me yourself?
MESSENGER   No sir,
another shepherd passed you on to me.
OEDIPUS   Who? Do you know? Describe him.
MESSENGER   He called himself a servant of . . .
if I remember rightly—Laius.

[JOCASTA turns sharply.]

1145 OEDIPUS   The king of the land who ruled here long ago?
MESSENGER   That's the one. That herdsman was *his* man.
OEDIPUS   Is he still alive? Can I see him?
MESSENGER   They'd know best, the people of these parts.

[OEDIPUS and the MESSENGER turn to the CHORUS.]

OEDIPUS   Does anyone know that herdsman,
1150 the one he mentioned? Anyone seen him
in the fields, in the city? Out with it!
The time has come to reveal this once for all.
LEADER   I think he's the very shepherd you wanted to see,
a moment ago. But the queen, Jocasta,
1155 she's the one to say.
OEDIPUS   Jocasta,
you remember the man we just sent for?
Is *that* the one he means?
JOCASTA   That man . . .
why ask? Old shepherd, talk, empty nonsense,
don't give it another thought, don't even think—
1160 OEDIPUS   What—give up now, with a clue like this?
Fail to solve the mystery of my birth?
Not for all the world!
JOCASTA   Stop—in the name of god,
if you love your own life, call off this search!
My suffering is enough.
OEDIPUS   Courage!
1165 Even if my mother turns out to be a slave,
and I a slave, three generations back,
you would not seem common.
JOCASTA   Oh no,
listen to me, I beg you, don't do this.
OEDIPUS   Listen to you? No more. I must know it all,
1170 must see the truth at last.

7. "Oedipus" literally means "swollen foot."

JOCASTA   No, please—
for your sake—I want the best for you!
OEDIPUS   Your best is more than I can bear.
JOCASTA   You're doomed—
may you never fathom who you are!
OEDIPUS [*To a servant.*]   Hurry, fetch me the herdsman, now!
1175   Leave her to glory in her royal birth.
JOCASTA   Aieeeeee—
                   man of agony—
that is the only name I have for you,
that, no other—ever, ever, ever!
        [*Flinging through the palace doors. A long, tense silence follows.*]
LEADER   Where's she gone, Oedipus?
1180   Rushing off, such wild grief . . .
I'm afraid that from this silence
something monstrous may come bursting forth.
OEDIPUS   Let it burst! Whatever will, whatever must!
I must know my birth, no matter how common
1185   it may be—I must see my origins face-to-face.
She perhaps, she with her woman's pride
may well be mortified by my birth,
but I, I count myself the son of Chance,
the great goddess, giver of all good things—
1190   I'll never see myself disgraced. She is my mother!
And the moons have marked me out, my blood-brothers,
one moon on the wane, the next moon great with power.
That is my blood, my nature—I will never betray it,
never fail to search and learn my birth!
1195   CHORUS   Yes—if I am a true prophet
            if I can grasp the truth,
        by the boundless skies of Olympus,
    at the full moon of tomorrow, Mount Cithaeron
    you will know how Oedipus glories in you—
1200   you, his birthplace, nurse, his mountain-mother!
    And we will sing you, dancing out your praise—
    you lift our monarch's heart!
        Apollo, Apollo, god of the wild cry
            may our dancing please you!
                            Oedipus—
1205   son, dear child, who bore you?
    Who of the nymphs who seem to live forever
    mated with Pan,[8] the mountain-striding Father?
    Who was your mother? who, some bride of Apollo
    the god who loves the pastures spreading toward the sun?
1210   Or was it Hermes,[9] king of the lightning ridges?
    Or Dionysus, lord of frenzy, lord of the barren peaks—

8. Son of Hermes and a nymph; the god of woods and pastures and the companion of Dionysus. *Nymphs*: female nature spirits, long-lived but not immortal.

9. Greek god of boundaries and travelers, Zeus's messenger and the gods' herald; like Dionysus, he was associated with wild places, especially mountains.

did he seize you in his hands, dearest of all his lucky finds?—
   found by the nymphs, their warm eyes dancing, gift
to the lord who loves them dancing out his joy!

   [OEDIPUS *strains to see a figure coming from the distance. Attended by palace guards, an old* SHEPHERD *enters slowly, reluctant to approach the King.*]

1215 OEDIPUS   I never met the man, my friends . . . still,
   if I had to guess, I'd say that's the shepherd,
   the very one we've looked for all along.
   Brothers in old age, two of a kind,
   he and our guest here. At any rate
1220 the ones who bring him in are my own men,
   I recognize them.

         [*Turning to the* LEADER.]

                  But you know more than I,
   you should, you've seen the man before.
   LEADER   I know him, definitely. One of Laius' men,
   a trusty shepherd, if there ever was one.
1225 OEDIPUS   You, I ask you first, stranger,
   you from Corinth—is this the one you mean?
   MESSENGER   You're looking at him. He's your man.
   OEDIPUS [*To the* SHEPHERD.]   You, old man, come over here—
   look at me. Answer all my questions.
1230 Did you ever serve King Laius?
   SHEPHERD   So I did . . .
   a slave, not bought on the block though,
   born and reared in the palace.
   OEDIPUS   Your duties, your kind of work?
   SHEPHERD   Herding the flocks, the better part of my life.
1235 OEDIPUS   Where, mostly? Where did you do your grazing?
   SHEPHERD   Well,
   Cithaeron sometimes, or the foothills round about.
   OEDIPUS   This man—you know him? ever see him there?
   SHEPHERD [*Confused, glancing from the* MESSENGER *to the King.*]
   Doing what?—what man do you mean?
   OEDIPUS [*Pointing to the* MESSENGER.]   This one here—ever have
1240 dealings with him?
   SHEPHERD   Not so I could say, but give me a chance,
   my memory's bad . . .
   MESSENGER   No wonder he doesn't know me, master.
   But let me refresh his memory for him.
1245 I'm sure he recalls old times we had
   on the slopes of Mount Cithaeron;
   he and I, grazing our flocks, he with two
   and I with one—we both struck up together,
   three whole seasons, six months at a stretch
1250 from spring to the rising of Arcturus[1] in the fall,

---

1. One of the brightest stars in the northern sky; its "rising" before dawn in September is a sign
of summer's end.

then with winter coming on I'd drive my herds
to my own pens, and back he'd go with his
to Laius' folds.

    [*To the* SHEPHERD.]

          Now that's how it was,
wasn't it—yes or no?

SHEPHERD   Yes, I suppose . . .

1255 it's all so long ago.

MESSENGER   Come, tell me,
you gave me a child back then, a boy, remember?
A little fellow to rear, my very own.

SHEPHERD What? Why rake up that again?

MESSENGER Look, here he is, my fine old friend—

1260 the same man who was just a baby then.

SHEPHERD Damn you, shut your mouth—quiet!

OEDIPUS Don't lash out at him, old man—
you need lashing more than he does.

SHEPHERD   Why,
master, majesty—what have I done wrong?

1265 OEDIPUS You won't answer his question about the boy.

SHEPHERD He's talking nonsense, wasting his breath.

OEDIPUS So, you won't talk willingly—
then you'll talk with pain.

    [*The guards seize the* SHEPHERD.]

SHEPHERD No, dear god, don't torture an old man!

1270 OEDIPUS Twist his arms back, quickly!

SHEPHERD   God help us, why?—
what more do you need to know?

OEDIPUS Did you give him that child? He's asking.

SHEPHERD I did . . . I wish to god I'd died that day.

OEDIPUS You've got your wish if you don't tell the truth.

1275 SHEPHERD The more I tell, the worse the death I'll die.

OEDIPUS Our friend here wants to stretch things out, does he?

    [*Motioning to his men for torture.*]

SHEPHERD No, no, I gave it to him—I just said so.

OEDIPUS Where did you get it? Your house? Someone else's?

SHEPHERD It wasn't mine, no, I got it from . . . someone.

1280 OEDIPUS Which one of them?

    [*Looking at the citizens.*]

OEDIPUS   Whose house?

SHEPHERD   No—
god's sake, master, no more questions!

OEDIPUS You're a dead man if I have to ask again.

SHEPHERD Then—the child came from the house . . . of Laius.

OEDIPUS A slave? or born of his own blood?

SHEPHERD   Oh no,

1285 I'm right at the edge, the horrible truth—I've got to say it!

OEDIPUS And I'm at the edge of hearing horrors, yes, but I must hear!

SHEPHERD   All right! His son, they said it was—his son!
          But the one inside, your wife,
          she'd tell it best.
1290 OEDIPUS   My wife—
          she gave it to you?
      SHEPHERD   Yes, yes, my king.
      OEDIPUS   Why, what for?
      SHEPHERD   To kill it.
1295 OEDIPUS   Her own child,
          how could she?
      SHEPHERD   She was afraid—
          frightening prophecies.
      OEDIPUS   What?
1300 SHEPHERD   They said—
          he'd kill his parents.
      OEDIPUS   But you gave him to this old man—why?
      SHEPHERD   I pitied the little baby, master,
          hoped he'd take him off to his own country,
1305 far away, but he saved him for this, this fate.
          If you are the man he says you are, believe me,
          you were born for pain.
      OEDIPUS   O god—
          all come true, all burst to light!
          O light—now let me look my last on you!
1310 I stand revealed at last—
          cursed in my birth, cursed in marriage,
          cursed in the lives I cut down with these hands!

          [*Rushing through the doors with a great cry. The Corinthian* MESSENGER,
          the SHEPHERD *and attendants exit slowly to the side.*]

      CHORUS   O the generations of men
          the dying generations—adding the total
1315 of all your lives I find they come to nothing . . .
              does there exist, is there a man on earth
          who seizes more joy than just a dream, a vision?
          And the vision no sooner dawns than dies
          blazing into oblivion.
1320 You are my great example, you, your life
          your destiny, Oedipus, man of misery—
          I count no man blest.

                    You outranged all men!
              Bending your bow to the breaking-point
          you captured priceless glory, O dear god,
1325 and the Sphinx came crashing down,
                  the virgin, claws hooked
          like a bird of omen singing, shrieking death—
          like a fortress reared in the face of death
          you rose and saved our land.

1330   From that day on we called you king
       we crowned you with honors, Oedipus, towering over all—
       mighty king of the seven gates of Thebes.

       But now to hear your story—is there a man more agonized?
       More wed to pain and frenzy? Not a man on earth,
1335   the joy of your life ground down to nothing
       O Oedipus, name for the ages—
           one and the same wide harbor served you
              son and father both
       son and father came to rest in the same bridal chamber.
1340   How, how could the furrows your father plowed
       bear you, your agony, harrowing on
       in silence O so long?

                    But now for all your power
       Time, all-seeing Time has dragged you to the light,
       judged your marriage monstrous from the start—
1345   the son and the father tangling, both one—
       O child of Laius, would to god
          I'd never seen you, never never!
          Now I weep like a man who wails the dead
       and the dirge comes pouring forth with all my heart!
1350   I tell you the truth, you gave me life
       my breath leapt up in you
       and now you bring down night upon my eyes.
          [*Enter a* MESSENGER *from the palace.*]

     MESSENGER   Men of Thebes, always first in honor,
       what horrors you will hear, what you will see,
1355   what a heavy weight of sorrow you will shoulder . . .
       if you are true to your birth, if you still have
       some feeling for the royal house of Thebes.
       I tell you neither the waters of the Danube
       nor the Nile[2] can wash this palace clean.
1360   Such things it hides, it soon will bring to light—
       terrible things, and none done blindly now,
       all done with a will. The pains
       we inflict upon ourselves hurt most of all.
     LEADER   God knows we have pains enough already.
1365   What can you add to them?
     MESSENGER   The queen is dead.
     LEADER   Poor lady—how?
     MESSENGER   By her own hand. But you are spared the worst,
       you never had to watch . . . I saw it all,
       and with all the memory that's in me
1370   you will learn what that poor woman suffered.

---

2. The Greek original reads "Phasis," a river in Asia Minor; like the Danube, Europe's second-longest river, it empties into the Black Sea.

Once she'd broken in through the gates,
dashing past us, frantic, whipped to fury,
ripping her hair out with both hands—
straight to her rooms she rushed, flinging herself
1375 across the bridal-bed, doors slamming behind her—
once inside, she wailed for Laius, dead so long,
remembering how she bore his child long ago,
the life that rose up to destroy him, leaving
its mother to mother living creatures
1380 with the very son she'd borne.
Oh how she wept, mourning the marriage-bed
where she let loose that double brood—monsters—
husband by her husband, children by her child.

And then—
but how she died is more than I can say. Suddenly
1385 Oedipus burst in, screaming, he stunned us so
we couldn't watch her agony to the end,
our eyes were fixed on him. Circling
like a maddened beast, stalking, here, there,
crying out to us—

Give him a sword. His wife,
1390 no wife, his mother, where can he find the mother earth
that cropped two crops at once, himself and all his children?
He was raging—one of the dark powers pointing the way,
none of us mortals crowding around him, no,
with a great shattering cry—someone, something leading him on—
1395 he hurled at the twin doors and bending the bolts back
out of their sockets, crashed through the chamber.
And there we saw the woman hanging by the neck,
cradled high in a woven noose, spinning,
swinging back and forth. And when he saw her,
1400 giving a low, wrenching sob that broke our hearts,
slipping the halter from her throat, he eased her down,
in a slow embrace he laid her down, poor thing . . .
then, what came next, what horror we beheld!

He rips off her brooches, the long gold pins
1405 holding her robes—and lifting them high,
looking straight up into the points,
he digs them down the sockets of his eyes, crying, "You,
you'll see no more the pain I suffered, all the pain I caused!
Too long you looked on the ones you never should have seen,
1410 blind to the ones you longed to see, to know! Blind
from this hour on! Blind in the darkness—blind!"
His voice like a dirge, rising, over and over
raising the pins, raking them down his eyes.
And at each stroke blood spurts from the roots,
1415 splashing his beard, a swirl of it, nerves and clots—
black hail of blood pulsing, gushing down.

These are the griefs that burst upon them both,
coupling man and woman. The joy they had so lately,
the fortune of their old ancestral house
1420 was deep joy indeed. Now, in this one day,
wailing, madness and doom, death, disgrace
all the griefs in the world that you can name,
all are theirs forever.

LEADER   Oh poor man, the misery—
has he any rest from pain now?

        [*A voice within, in torment.*]

MESSENGER   He's shouting,
1425 "Loose the bolts, someone, show me to all of Thebes!
My father's murderer, my mother's—"
No, I can't repeat it, it's unholy.
Now he'll tear himself from his native earth,
not linger, curse the house with his own curse.
1430 But he needs strength, and a guide to lead him on.
This is sickness more than he can bear.

        [*The palace doors open.*]

                                        Look,
he'll show you himself. The great doors are opening—
you are about to see a sight, a horror
even his mortal enemy would pity.

        [*Enter* OEDIPUS, *blinded, led by a boy. He stands at the palace steps,
        as if surveying his people once again.*]

CHORUS   O the terror—
1435 the suffering, for all the world to see,
the worst terror that ever met my eyes.
What madness swept over you? What god,
what dark power leapt beyond all bounds,
beyond belief, to crush your wretched life?—
1440 godforsaken, cursed by the gods!
I pity you but I can't bear to look.
I've much to ask, so much to learn,
so much fascinates my eyes,
but you . . . I shudder at the sight.

OEDIPUS   Oh, Ohh—
1445 the agony! I am agony—
where am I going? where on earth?
        where does all this agony hurl me?
where's my voice?—
        winging, swept away on a dark tide—
1450 My destiny, my dark power, what a leap you made!

CHORUS To the depths of terror, too dark to hear, to see.

OEDIPUS Dark, horror of darkness
        my darkness, drowning, swirling around me
        crashing wave on wave—unspeakable, irresistible
1455   headwind, fatal harbor! Oh again,
        the misery, all at once, over and over

the stabbing daggers, stab of memory
raking me insane.
CHORUS   No wonder you suffer
twice over, the pain of your wounds,
1460   the lasting grief of pain.
OEDIPUS   Dear friend, still here?
Standing by me, still with a care for me,
the blind man? Such compassion,
    loyal to the last. Oh it's you,
I know you're here, dark as it is
1465   I'd know you anywhere, your voice—
it's yours, clearly yours.
CHORUS   Dreadful, what you've done . . .
how could you bear it, gouging out your eyes?
What superhuman power drove you on?
OEDIPUS   Apollo, friends, Apollo—
1470   he ordained my agonies—these, my pains on pains!
But the hand that struck my eyes was mine,
    mine alone—no one else—
    I did it all myself!
What good were eyes to me?
1475   Nothing I could see could bring me joy.
CHORUS   No, no, exactly as you say.
OEDIPUS   What can I ever see?
What love, what call of the heart
can touch my ears with joy? Nothing, friends.
    Take me away, far, far from Thebes,
1480   quickly, cast me away, my friends—
this great murderous ruin, this man cursed to heaven,
    the man the deathless gods hate most of all!
CHORUS   Pitiful, you suffer so, you understand so much . . .
I wish you'd never known.
OEDIPUS   Die, die—
1485   whoever he was that day in the wilds
who cut my ankles free of the ruthless pins,
    he pulled me clear of death, he saved my life
    for this, this kindness—
    Curse him, kill him!
1490   If I'd died then, I'd never have dragged myself,
my loved ones through such hell.
CHORUS   Oh if only . . . would to god.
OEDIPUS   I'd never have come to this,
    my father's murderer—never been branded
mother's husband, all men see me now! Now,
1495   loathed by the gods, son of the mother I defiled
            coupling in my father's bed, spawning lives in the loins
that spawned my wretched life. What grief can crown this grief?
        It's mine alone, my destiny—I am Oedipus!
CHORUS   How can I say you've chosen for the best?
1500   Better to die than be alive and blind.

OEDIPUS   What I did was best—don't lecture me,
     no more advice, I, with *my* eyes,
     how could I look my father in the eyes
     when I go down to death? Or mother, so abused . . .
1505   I have done such things to the two of them,
     crimes too huge for hanging.
                             Worse yet,
     the sight of my children, born as they were born,
     how could I long to look into their eyes?
     No, not with these eyes of mine, never.
1510   Not this city either, her high towers,
     the sacred glittering images of her gods—
     I am misery! I, her best son, reared
     as no other son of Thebes was ever reared,
     I've stripped myself, I gave the command myself.
1515   All men must cast away the great blasphemer,
     the curse now brought to light by the gods,
     the son of Laius—I, my father's son!

     Now I've exposed my guilt, horrendous guilt,
     could I train a level glance on you, my countrymen?
1520   Impossible! No, if I could just block off my ears,
     the springs of hearing, I would stop at nothing—
     I'd wall up my loathsome body like a prison,
     blind to the sound of life, not just the sight.
     Oblivion—what a blessing . . .
1525   for the mind to dwell a world away from pain.

     O Cithaeron, why did you give me shelter?
     Why didn't you take me, crush my life out on the spot?
     I'd never have revealed my birth to all mankind.
     O Polybus, Corinth, the old house of my fathers,
1530   so I believed—what a handsome prince you raised—
     under the skin, what sickness to the core.
     Look at me! Born of outrage, outrage to the core.
     O triple roads—it all comes back, the secret,
     dark ravine, and the oaks closing in
1535   where the three roads join . . .
     You drank my father's blood, my own blood
     spilled by my own hands—you still remember me?
     What things you saw me do? Then I came here
     and did them all once more!
                       Marriages! O marriage,
1540   you gave me birth, and once you brought me into the world
     you brought my sperm rising back, springing to light
     fathers, brothers, sons—one murderous breed—
     brides, wives, mothers. The blackest things
     a man can do, I have done them all!
                          No more—
1545   it's wrong to name what's wrong to do. Quickly,

for the love of god, hide me somewhere,
kill me, hurl me into the sea
where you can never look on me again.
        [*Beckoning to the* CHORUS *as they shrink away.*]
                                    Closer,
    it's all right. Touch the man of grief.
1550   Do. Don't be afraid. My troubles are mine
    and I am the only man alive who can sustain them.
        [*Enter* KREON *from the palace, attended by palace guards.*]
    LEADER   Put your requests to Kreon. Here he is,
    just when we need him. He'll have a plan, he'll act.
    Now that he's the sole defense of the country
    in your place.
1555 OEDIPUS   Oh no, what can I say to him?
    How can I ever hope to win his trust?
    I wronged him so, just now, in every way.
    You must see that—I was so wrong, so wrong.
    KREON   I haven't come to mock you, Oedipus,
1560   or to criticize your former failings.
        [*Turning to the guards.*]
                            You there,
    have you lost all respect for human feelings?
    At least revere the Sun, the holy fire
    that keeps us all alive. Never expose a thing
    of guilt and holy dread so great it appalls
1565   the earth, the rain from heaven, the light of day!
    Get him into the halls—quickly as you can.
    Piety demands no less. Kindred alone
    should see a kinsman's shame. This is obscene.
    OEDIPUS   Please, in god's name . . . you wipe my fears away,
1570   coming so generously to me, the worst of men.
    Do one thing more, for your sake, not mine.
    KREON   What do you want? Why so insistent?
    OEDIPUS   Drive me out of the land at once, far from sight,
    where I can never hear a human voice.
1575 KREON   I'd have done that already, I promise you.
    First I wanted the god to clarify my duties.
    OEDIPUS   The god? His command was clear, every word:
    death for the father-killer, the curse—
    he said destroy me!
1580 KREON   So he did. Still, in such a crisis
    it's better to ask precisely what to do.
    OEDIPUS   So miserable—
    you'd consult the god about a man like me?
    KREON   By all means. And this time, I assume,
    even you will obey the god's decrees.
    OEDIPUS   I will,
1585   I will. And you, I command you—I beg you . . .
    the woman inside, bury her as you see fit.

It's the only decent thing,
to give your own the last rites. As for me,
never condemn the city of my fathers
1590   to house my body, not while I'm alive, no,
let me live on the mountains, on Cithaeron,
my favorite haunt, I have made it famous.
Mother and father marked out that rock
to be my everlasting tomb—buried alive.
1595   Let me die there, where they tried to kill me.

Oh but this I know: no sickness can destroy me,
nothing can. I would never have been saved
from death—I have been saved
for something great and terrible, something strange.
1600   Well let my destiny come and take me on its way!
About my children, Kreon, the boys at least,
don't burden yourself. They're men,
wherever they go, they'll find the means to live.
But my two daughters, my poor helpless girls,
1605   clustering at our table, never without me
hovering near them . . . whatever I touched,
they always had their share. Take care of them,
I beg you. Wait, better—permit me, would you?
Just to touch them with my hands and take
1610   our fill of tears. Please . . . my king.
Grant it, with all your noble heart.
If I could hold them, just once, I'd think
I had them with me, like the early days
when I could see their eyes.

> [ANTIGONE *and* ISMENE, *two small children, are led in from
> the palace by a nurse.*]

                                        What's that
1615   O god! Do I really hear you sobbing?—
my two children. Kreon, you've pitied me?
Sent me my darling girls, my own flesh and blood!
Am I right?
KREON   Yes, it's my doing.
I know the joy they gave you all these years,
1620   the joy you must feel now.
OEDIPUS   Bless you, Kreon!
May god watch over you for this kindness,
better than he ever guarded me.
                                        Children, where are you?
Here, come quickly—

> [*Groping for* ANTIGONE *and* ISMENE, *who approach their father
> cautiously, then embrace him.*]

                                        Come to these hands of mine,
your brother's hands, your own father's hands
1625   that served his once bright eyes so well—
that made them blind. Seeing nothing, children,

knowing nothing, I became your father,
I fathered you in the soil that gave me life.
How I weep for you—I cannot see you now . . .
1630   just thinking of all your days to come, the bitterness,
the life that rough mankind will thrust upon you.
Where are the pubic gatherings you can join,
the banquets of the clans? Home you'll come,
in tears, cut off from the sight of it all,
1635   the brilliant rites unfinished.
And when you reach perfection, ripe for marriage,
who will he be, my dear ones? Risking all
to shoulder the curse that weighs down my parents,
yes and you too—that wounds us all together.
1640   What more misery could you want?
Your father killed his father, sowed his mother,
one, one and the selfsame womb sprang you—
he cropped the very roots of his existence.

Such disgrace, and you must bear it all!
1645   Who will marry you then? Not a man on earth.
Your doom is clear: you'll wither away to nothing,
single, without a child.
            [*Turning to* KREON.]
                        Oh Kreon,
you are the only father they have now . . .
we who brought them into the world
1650   are gone, both gone at a stroke—
Don't let them go begging, abandoned,
men without men. Your own flesh and blood!
Never bring them down to the level of my pains.
Pity them. Look at them, so young, so vulnerable,
1655   shorn of everything—you're their only hope.
Promise me, noble Kreon, touch my hand!
            [*Reaching toward* KREON, *who draws back.*]
You, little ones, if you were old enough
to understand, there is much I'd tell you.
Now, as it is, I'd have you say a prayer.
1660   Pray for life, my children,
live where you are free to grow and season.
Pray god you find a better life than mine,
the father who begot you.
KREON   Enough.
You've wept enough. Into the palace now.
1665 OEDIPUS   I must, but I find it very hard.
KREON   Time is the great healer, you will see.
OEDIPUS   I am going—you know on what condition?
KREON   Tell me. I'm listening.
OEDIPUS   Drive me out of Thebes, in exile.
1670 KREON   Not I. Only the gods can give you that.

OEDIPUS   Surely the gods hate me so much—
KREON   You'll get your wish at once.
OEDIPUS   You consent?
KREON   I try to say what I mean; it's my habit.
OEDIPUS   Then take me away. It's time.
1675 KREON   Come along, let go of the children.
OEDIPUS   No—
don't take them away from me, not now! No no no!

> [*Clutching his daughters as the guards wrench them loose and take
> them through the palace doors.*]

KREON   Still the king, the master of all things?
No more: here your power ends.
None of your power follows you through life.

> [*Exit* OEDIPUS *and* KREON *to the palace. The* CHORUS *comes forward
> to address the audience directly.*]

1680 CHORUS   People of Thebes, my countrymen, look on Oedipus.
He solved the famous riddle with his brilliance,
he rose to power, a man beyond all power.
Who could behold his greatness without envy?
Now what a black sea of terror has overwhelmed him.
1685   Now as we keep our watch and wait the final day,
count no man happy till he dies, free of pain at last.

> [*Exit in procession.*]

Antigone[1]

CHARACTERS

ANTIGONE, *daughter of Oedipus*
ISMENE, *daughter of Oedipus*
CHORUS *of Theban Elders*
LEADER (*of the Chorus*)
KREON, *King of Thebes, uncle of
    Antigone and Ismene*
GUARD

Kreon's Men (*silent*)
HAIMON, *son of Kreon*
TIRESIAS, *prophet of Thebes*
Lad (*silent*)
MESSENGER
EURYDIKE, *wife of Kreon*

SCENE: *Dawn in front of Kreon's palace in Thebes, the day after the battle in which the
Theban defenders repelled an attack on the city by an Argive coalition that included the
rebel Polyneikes, elder son of Oedipus. Polyneikes and his younger brother Eteokles, who
has remained loyal to Thebes, have killed each other simultaneously in face-to-face com-*

1. Translated by Robert Bagg.

bat at one of Thebes' seven gates. Kreon has suddenly seized the throne. * * * *Antig-*
one and Ismene enter through the central doors.[2]

ANTIGONE   Ismene, love! My own kind! Born
            like me from that same womb!
            Can you think of one evil—
            of all those Oedipus started—
5   that Zeus hasn't used *our own lives*
            to finish? There's *nothing*—no pain
            no shame, no terror, no humiliation!—
            you and I haven't seen and shared.
            Now there's this new command
10   our commander in chief[3]
            imposes on the whole city—
            do you know about it?
            Have you heard? *You don't know,*
            do you? It threatens our loved ones
15   as if they were our enemies!
ISMENE   No word of our family has reached *me*,
            Antigone, welcome or painful,
            not since we sisters lost our brothers
            in one day, when their hands struck
20   the double blow that killed them both.
            And since the Argive army fled last night
            I've heard nothing that could improve our luck—
            or make it any worse.
ANTIGONE   That's what I thought.
            That's why I've brought you out past the gates—
25   where no one but you can hear what I say.
ISMENE   What's wrong?
            It's plain something you've heard makes you livid.
ANTIGONE   It's Kreon. The way he's treated our brothers.
            Hasn't he buried one with honor?
            But he's shamed the other. Disgraced him!
30   Eteokles, they say, was laid to rest
            according to law and custom.
            The dead will respect him in Hades.
            But Polyneikes' sorry body can't be touched.

            The city is forbidden to mourn him or bury him
35   —no tomb, no tears. Convenient forage
            for cruising birds to feast their fill.
            That's the clear order our good general
            gives you and me—yes, I said me!
            They say he's coming here to proclaim it
40   in person to those who haven't heard it.
            This is not something he takes lightly.
            Violate any provision—the sentence is

2. All stage directions (in italics), as well as   3. Kreon.
the list of characters, are by the translator.

you're stoned to death in your own city.
Now you know.
                          And soon you'll prove
45   how nobly born you really are.
        Or did our family breed a coward?

ISMENE   If that's the bind we're in, you poor thing,
            what good can *I* do by yanking the knot
            tighter—*or* by trying to pry it loose?

50 ANTIGONE Make up your mind. Will you join me?
            Share the burden?

ISMENE   At what risk? What are you asking?

ANTIGONE   (*Raising up her hands.*)
            Will you help these hands lift his body?

ISMENE   You want to bury him? Break the law?

ANTIGONE   I'm going to bury my brother—your brother!—
55   with or without your help. I won't betray him.

ISMENE   You scare me, sister. Kreon's forbidden this.

ANTIGONE   He's got *no right* to keep me from what's mine!

ISMENE   He's mine too!
                          Just think what our father's
            destruction meant for us both.
60   Because of those horrible deeds—
            all self-inflicted, all self-detected
            he died hated and notorious,[4]
            his eyes battered into blindness
            by his own hands. And then
65   his wife and mother—two roles
            for one woman—disposed
            of her life with a noose
            of twisted rope. And now
            our poor brothers die the same day
70   in a mutual act of kin murder!
            Think how much worse
            our own deaths will be—abandoned
            as we are—if we defy the king's
            proclamation and his power.
75   Remember, we're women. How
            can we fight men. They're stronger.
            We must accept these things—and worse to come.
            I want the Spirits of the Dead

4. This play was written before *Oedipus the*   *Oedipus at Colonus*, the king ends his life
King and *Oedipus at Colonus*. Each of the   with redemption and triumph.
plays uses a different version of the myth. In

to understand this: I'm not free.
80   I must obey whoever's in charge.
It's crazy to attempt the impossible!

ANTIGONE   Then I'll stop asking you! And if you change
your mind, I won't accept your help.
Go be the person you've chosen to be.

85   I'll bury Polyneikes myself. I'll do
what's honorable, and then I'll die.
I who love him will lie down
next to him who loves me—
my criminal conduct blameless!—

90   for I owe more to the dead, with whom
I will spend a much longer time,
than I will ever owe to the living.
Go ahead, please yourself—defy
laws the gods expect us to honor.

95 ISMENE   I'm not insulting them! But how can I
defy the city? I don't have the strength.

ANTIGONE   Then make that your excuse. I'll heal
with earth the body of the brother I love.

ISMENE   I feel so sorry for you. And afraid.

100 ANTIGONE   Don't waste your fear. Straighten out your own life.

ISMENE   At least tell nobody what you're planning!
Say nothing about it. And neither will I.

ANTIGONE   No! Go on, tell them all!
I will hate you much more for your silence—
105   if you don't shout it everywhere.

ISMENE   You're burning to do what should stop you cold.

ANTIGONE   One thing I do know: I'll please those who matter.

ISMENE   *As if* you could! You love fights you can't win.

ANTIGONE   When my strength is exhausted, I'll quit.

110 ISMENE   Hopeless passion is wrong from the start.

ANTIGONE   Say that again and I'll despise you.
So will the dead—and they'll hate you
far longer. But go! Let me and my
recklessness deal with this alone.

115   No matter what I suffer
I won't die dishonored.

[*Exit* ANTIGONE *toward open country;* ISMENE *calls out her next
lines as her sister leaves, then she enters the palace through the great
central doors.*]

ISMENE   If you're determined, go ahead.
And know this much: you are a fool
to attempt this, but you're loved all
120   the more by the family you love.

[CHORUS *of Theban Elders enters singing.*]

CHORUS   Morning sunlight, loveliest ever
to shine on seven-gated Thebes!

Day's golden eye, risen at last
over Dirke's[5] glittering waters!
125 You stampede the Argive!
Invading in full battle gear,
his white shield flashing, he's wrenched
by your sharp piercing bit
into headlong retreat!
130 This attacker who championed
quarrelsome Polyneikes
skimmed through our farmland—
a white-feathered Eagle[6]
screeching, horse-hair
135 flaring from the helmets
of well-armed troops.

He had circled our houses, threatening
all seven gates, his spearpoints
out for blood, but he was thrown back
140 before his jaws could swell
with our gore, before the Firegod's
incendiary pinetar
engulfed the towers ringing our walls.
He cannot withstand the harsh blare
145 of battle that roars up
around him—and our Dragon[7]
wrestles him down.

How Zeus hates a proud tongue![8]
And when this river of men
150 surged forward, with arrogance
loud as its flash of gold,
he struck—with his own lightning—
that firebrand shouting in triumph
from the battlements!
155 Free-falling from the mad
fury of his charge, torch
still in his hand,
he crashed to earth, the man
who'd turned on us the raving
160 blast of his loathsome words.
But threats stuck in his throat:
To each enemy soldier
Ares the brute wargod,[9]

5. A river in Thebes.
6. The eagle is the emblem of the white-shielded Argives.
7. The dragon symbolizes Thebes. According to myth, the Thebans were born from dragon's teeth, sown by Kadmos.

8. Zeus struck down with a lightning bolt the most arrogant of the Argive invaders, Capaneus.
9. Ares, god of war, was an ancestor of the Theban royalty and patron of Thebes.

our surging wheelhorse,
165   assigned a separate doom,
shattering every attack.

Now seven captains facing seven gates,
our captains matching theirs,
throw down their arms as trophies
170   for Zeus—all but the doomed pair[1]
born to one father, one mother—
who share even their death
when their twin spears drive home.

Victory is now ours!
175   Her name is pure glory,[2]
her joy resounds
through Thebes' own joy—Thebes
swarming with chariots!
Let us now banish
180   this war from our minds
and visit each god's temple,
singing all night long! May
Bakkhos,[3] the god whose dancing
rocks Thebes, be there to lead us!

[*Enter* KREON.]

185 LEADER   Enter our new king,
Kreon, the son of Menoikeus,
who came to power
abruptly, when the gods changed our luck.
What plans does he turn over
190   in his mind—what will he ponder
with the Council of Elders
summoned in his new role?

KREON   Men, we have just survived some rough weather.
Monstrous waves have battered our city,
195   but now the gods have steadied the waters.
I sent my servants to gather you here
because, of all my people, I know
your veneration for Laios' royal
power has never wavered. When Oedipus
200   ruled our city, and then was struck down, you
stood by his sons. Now both of them fall
together, killed in one lethal exchange.

1. Polyneikes and Eteokles. The victors in Greek battle set up the armor of one of the dead as a trophy, to mark their place of triumph.
2. *Nike* ("Victory") is a feminine noun in Greek. Nike was represented in art as a winged woman.
3. Bakkhos (Dionysos), god of wine and revelry, is associated with Thebes, since his mother, Semele, was a Theban princess.

Because each struck the other's deathblow, each
was defiled by his own brother's blood.
205   As nearest kin to the men killed,
I've taken power and assumed the throne.

You cannot measure a man's character,
policies, or his common sense—until
you see him in action, enforcing old laws
210   and making new ones. To me, there's nothing
worse than a man, while he's running a city,
who fails to act on sound advice—but fears
something so much his mouth clamps shut.
Nor have I any use for a man whose friend
215   means more to him than his country.
Believe me, Zeus, for you miss nothing,
I'll always speak out when I see Thebes choosing
destruction rather than deliverance.
I'll never think our country's enemy
220   can be my friend. Keep this in mind:
Our *country* is the ship that must keep us safe.
It's only on board her, among the men
who sail her upright, that we make true friends.

Such are the principles I will follow
225   to preserve Thebes' greatness. Akin to these
are my explicit orders concerning
Oedipus' sons: Eteokles, who died
fighting for our city, and who excelled
in combat, will be given the rituals
230   and burial proper to the noble dead.

But his brother—I mean Polyneikes, who
returned from exile utterly determined
to burn down his own city, incinerate
the gods we worship, revel in kinsmen's blood,
235   enslave everyone left alive—
as for him, it is now a crime for Thebans
to bury him or mourn him. Dogs and birds
will savage and outrage his corpse—
an ugly and a visible disgrace.
240   That is my thinking. And I will never
tolerate giving a bad man more respect
than a good one. Only those faithful to Thebes
will I honor—in this life and after death.

LEADER   That is your pleasure, Kreon: Punish Thebes'
245   betrayers and reward her defenders.
You have all the authority you need
to discipline the living and the dead.

KREON	Are you willing to help enforce this law?
LEADER	Ask someone younger to shoulder that burden.
250 KREON	But I've already posted men at the corpse.
LEADER	Then what instructions do you have for me?
KREON	Don't join the cause of those who break this law.
LEADER	Who but a fool would want to die?
KREON	Exactly. He'd be killed. But easy money
255	frequently kills those it deludes.

[*Enter* GUARD. *He tends to mime the actions he describes.*]

GUARD I didn't run here at such a breakneck
pace, King, that I'm winded. Pausing to think
stopped me, wheeled me around, headed me back
more than once. My mind kept yelling at me:
260 "Reckless fool—why go where you'll be punished?"
Then: "Lazy clod! Dawdling, are you? What if
Kreon hears this news from somebody else?—
you'll pay for it."
                    I made myself dizzy,
hurrying slowly, stretching out a short road.
265 I finally realized I had to come.
If I'm talking annihilation here,
I'll still say it, since I'm of the opinion
nothing but my own fate can cause me harm.

KREON What's making you so agitated?
270 GUARD I've got to explain my role in this matter.
I didn't do it, I didn't see who did.
So it wouldn't be right to punish me.

KREON You're obsessed with protecting yourself.
That's a nice fortified wall you've thrown up
275 around your news—which must be odd indeed.

GUARD You bet. And bad news must be broken slowly.

KREON Why not just tell it? Then you can vanish.

GUARD But I *am* telling you! That corpse—someone's
buried it and run off. They sprinkled thirsty
280 dust on it. Then did all the rituals.

KREON What are you saying? What man would dare do this?

GUARD I've no idea. No marks from a pickaxe,
no dirt thrown up by a shovel. The ground's
all hard and dry, unbroken—no wheel ruts.
285 Whoever did this left no trace.
When the man on dawn-watch showed it to us,
we all got a nasty surprise. The dead man
had dropped out of sight. He wasn't entombed,
but dusted over, as though someone had tried
290 to stave off defilement. There was no sign
dogs or wild animals had chewed the corpse.
Then we all started yelling rough words, threats,
blaming each other, every guard ready

to throw punches—nobody to stop us.
295   Every man under suspicion—but none
of us convicted. We all denied it—
swearing to god we'd handle red-hot iron
or walk through fire to back up our oaths.

After interrogation got us nowhere,
300   one man spoke up and made us hang our heads
toward the ground in terror. We couldn't do
what he said—or avoid trouble if we did.
He advised us to tell you what happened,
not try to hide it. That seemed our best move.
305   So we drew lots to choose the messenger.
I lost—I'm no happier to be here
than you are to see me. Don't I know that.
Nobody loves the man who brings bad news.

LEADER   King, something has been bothering me: Suppose
310   this business was inspired by the gods?

KREON   Stop! Before your words fill me with rage.
Now, besides sounding old, you sound senile.
How could anyone possibly believe
the gods protect this corpse? Did *they* cover
315   his nakedness to reward him for loyal
service—this man who came here to burn
their colonnaded temples and treasuries,
to wipe out their country and tear up its laws?
Do you think that the gods honor rebels?
320   They don't. But for a good while now
men who despise me have been muttering
under their breaths—my edict bruised their necks.
They were rebelling against a just yoke—
unlike you good citizens who support me.
325   I'm sure these malcontents bribed my sentries
to do what they did.
                          Mankind's most deadly
invention is money—it plunders cities,
encourages men to abandon their homes,
tempts honest people to do shameful things.
330   It instructs them in criminal practice,
drives them to act on every godless impulse.
By doing this for silver, these men have
guaranteed that, sooner or later,
they'll pay the price.
                          But you who worship Zeus—
335   since Zeus enforces his own will through mine—
be sure of this, it is my solemn oath:
If you don't find the man who carried out
this burial and drag him before me,
a quick trip to Hades won't be your fate.

340   You will all be strung up—and you'll hang
           for a while, your insolence on display.
           From then on, you may calculate exactly
           how much profit to expect from your crimes.
           More men are destroyed by ill-gotten wealth
345   than such "wealth" ever saved from destruction.
    GUARD May I speak further? Or shall I just leave?
    KREON Don't you realize that your words pain me?
    GUARD Do your ears ache, or does the pain go deeper?
    KREON Why does the source of my pain interest you?
350 GUARD I just sting your ears. The man
           who did this stabs your gut.
    KREON You've run off at the mouth since you were born.
    GUARD Maybe so. But I had no part in this crime.
    KREON I think you did. Sold your life for some silver.
355 GUARD It's a sad thing when a judge gets it wrong.
    KREON You'll soon be on the wrong end of a judgment
           yourself.
                    If you don't find the guilty one,
           you'll find your greed buys you nothing but grief.
    GUARD I hope he's caught, but Fate will decide that.
360   And you'll never see me coming back here.
           Now that I have been spared—when everything
           seemed so desperate—all I can think about
           is how much gratitude I owe the gods.
           [*Exit* GUARD *to open country;* KREON *enters his palace.*]
    ELDERS Wonders[4] abound, but none
365   more astounding than man!
           He crosses to the far side
           of white seas, blown
           by winter gales, sailing
           below huge waves;
370   he wears Earth down—
           our primal, eternal,
           inexhaustible god—
           his stallion-sired mules
           plowing her soil
375   back and forth
           year after year.

           All breeds of carefree
           bird, savage beast
           and deep-sea creature,
380   ingenious man
           snares in his woven nets;
           he drives the mountain herds

---

4. The word for "wonders" (*ta deina*) can connote either "strange" or "terrible."

from wild lairs down to his folds;
he coaxes rough-maned horses
385   to thrust their necks through his yoke;
he tames the tireless mountain bull.

He has taught himself speech,
wind-quick thought,
and all the talents
390   that govern a city;
how to take shelter
from cold skies or pelting rain;
never baffled,
always resourceful,
395   he accepts every challenge;
but from Hades alone
has he found no way out—
though from hopeless disease
he has found a defense.

400   Exceeding all expectation,
his robust power to create
sometimes brings evil,
at other times, excellence.
When he follows the laws
405   Earth teaches him—
and Justice, which he's sworn
the gods he will enforce—
he soars with his city.
But reckless and corrupt,
410   a man will be driven
from his nation disgraced.

Let no man guilty of such things
share my hearth or invade my thoughts.
[*Enter* GUARD, *from countryside, leading* ANTIGONE.]

LEADER   I'm stunned—what's this? A warning from the gods?
415   I know this girl. She is Antigone.
Don't we all recognize her?
Unlucky Oedipus was her father,
now her own luck runs out.
What's happening? You—under guard?
420   Are you a prisoner? Did you break
the king's law? Commit some thoughtless act?
GUARD   There's your perpetrator. We caught her
burying the corpse. Where's Kreon?
[*Enter* KREON.]

LEADER   Here he comes. Just in time.
425   KREON   What makes my arrival so timely?

GUARD   Sir, never promise something won't happen;
           second thoughts can make your first one a lie.
           I vowed I'd never come back here,
           after you tongue-lashed me with those threats.
430   Then came a pleasure like no other,
           because it's a total surprise, something
           we hope for but can't believe will happen.
           So I came back—though I swore I wouldn't—
           to bring you the girl we caught sprinkling dust
435   on the dead body. No need to throw dice—
           this time the good fortune was all mine.
           Now she's all yours. Question and convict her—
           do as you see fit. But I have the right
           to go free of trouble once and for all.
440 KREON   Your prisoner—where was she when captured?
     GUARD   Covering up the dead body. There you have it.
     KREON   Do you know what you just said? No mistake?
     GUARD   I saw her bury the man you said no one
           could bury. How can I say it plainer?
445 KREON   How did you see her? Was she caught in the act?
     GUARD   Here's what happened. We went back there
           after those ugly threats of yours, to brush
           the dirt off the body and strip it down
           to its rotting flesh. Afterwards, we hunkered
450   upwind under some hills to spare us any stench
           the body might have sent our way. Each man
           kept alert, and kept his neighbor alert,
           by raking him with outbursts of abuse
           if he seemed to neglect his watch.
455   We kept at it until the round sun had climbed
           the heavens and baked us in the noon heat.
           Then, rising from the earth, a whirlwind
           whipped up the dust, and terror filled the sky,
           choking the grasslands, tearing leaves off trees,
460   churning up grit all around us.
                             Our eyes squeezed shut,
           we waited out this god-sent pestilence.
           After a bit the dust cleared, and we saw her
           cry out in anguish, a piercing scream
           like a bird homing to find her nest robbed.
465   When she saw the body stripped naked,
           she wailed one more time, then yelled a string
           of curses at those who'd done it. She scooped up
           powdery dust and, from a graceful bronze
           urn, poured out three cool swallows[5] for the dead.
470   Soon as we saw this, we moved in to stop her.
           She wasn't a bit shocked, when we charged her

5. She pours the dust as a "libation," a liquid sacrificial offering.

with the earlier crime, and now this one—
didn't deny a thing. That pleased,
but also troubled me. Escaping blame
475   oneself is always a relief; still, it hurts
to cause your own people grief. But all that
matters much less to me than my own safety.

KREON   (*To* ANTIGONE.)
You! Don't stand there nodding your head.
Out with it! Admit this or deny it.

480   ANTIGONE   I swear I did. And I don't deny it.
KREON   (*To* GUARD.)
You are excused from this grim business.
You're now free to go anywhere you please.
[*Exit* GUARD. *To* ANTIGONE.]
Explain something to me without elaborating.
Were you aware of my decree forbidding this?

485   ANTIGONE   Of course I knew. We all knew.
KREON   And still you dared to violate the law?
ANTIGONE   I did. It wasn't *Zeus* who issued me
this order. And Justice—who lives below—
was not involved. They'd never condone it!
490   I deny that your edicts—since *you*, a mere man,
imposed them—have the force to trample on
the gods' unwritten and infallible laws.
Their laws are not ephemeral, they weren't
made yesterday, and they will last forever.
495   No man knows how far back in time they go.
I'd never let any man's arrogance
bully me into breaking the gods' laws.
I'll die someday—how could I not know that?
I knew it without your proclamation.
500   If I do die young, that's an advantage,
for doesn't a person like me, who lives
besieged by trouble, escape by dying?
My own death isn't going to bother me,
but I would be devastated to see
505   my mother's son die and rot unburied.
I've no regrets for what I've done. And if you
consider my acts foolhardy, I say:
Look at the fool charging me with folly.

LEADER   It's apparent this girl's nature is savage
510   like her father's. She hasn't got the sense
to back off when she gets into trouble.

KREON   Stubborn spirits are the first to crack.
It's always the iron tool hardened by fire
that snaps and shatters. And headstrong horses
515   can be tamed by a small iron bit.
There's no excuse for a slave

to preen when her master's home.
This girl learned insolence long before
she broke this law. What's more, she keeps on
520 insulting us, and then gloats about it.
There is no doubt that if she emerges
victorious, and is never punished,
I am no man, *she* will be the man here.

I don't care if she is my sister's child,
525 a blood relative, closer than all those
who worship Zeus in my household,
she—and her sister—still must die.
I charge her sister too with conspiring
to bury Polyneikes. Bring her out.
530 I observed her inside just now,
screaming, hysterical, deranged.
Someone who intends to commit a crime
can lose control of a guilty conscience.
Her furtive treason gives itself away.
[*Two of Kreon's Men enter the palace.* KREON *turns to* ANTIGONE.]
535 But I also hate it when someone caught
red-handed tries to glorify her crime.

ANTIGONE Take me and kill me—is that your whole plan?
KREON That's it. When that's done I'll be satisfied.
ANTIGONE Then what stops you? Are you waiting for me
540 to accept what you've said? I never will.
And nothing I say will ever please you.
Yet, since you did mention glory, how
could I do anything more glorious
than build my own brother a tomb?
545 These men here would approve my actions—
if fear didn't seal their lips.   Tyranny
is fortunate in many ways: it can,
for instance, say and do anything it wants.
KREON These Thebans don't see it your way.
550 ANTIGONE But they do. To please you they bite their tongues.
KREON Aren't you ashamed not to follow their lead?
ANTIGONE Since when is it shameful to honor a brother?
KREON You had another brother who died fighting him?
ANTIGONE That's right. Born to the same mother and father.
555 KREON Then why do you honor Polyneikes
when doing so desecrates Eteokles?
ANTIGONE Eteokles wouldn't agree with you.
KREON Oh, but he would—because you've honored
treason as though it were patriotism.
560 ANTIGONE It was his *brother* who died, not his *slave*!

KREON	That brother died ravaging our country!
	Eteokles fell fighting to protect it.
ANTIGONE	Hades will still expect his rituals.
KREON	The brave deserve better than the vile.
565 ANTIGONE	Who knows what matters to the dead?
KREON	Not even death reconciles enemies.
ANTIGONE	I made no enemies by being born!
	I made my lifelong friends at birth.
KREON	Then go down to them! Love your dead brothers!
570	While I'm alive, no woman governs me.

[*Enter* ISMENE, *led in by Kreon's Men.*]

LEADER	Ismene's coming from the palace.
	She cries the loving tears of a sister;
	her eyes fill up, her flushed face darkens;
	tears pour down her cheeks.
KREON	Now you—a viper
575	who slithered through my house, quietly
	drinking my blood! I never knew
	I nurtured *two* insurrections,
	both attacking my throne.
	Go ahead,
	confess your role in this burial
580	party. Or do you claim ignorance?
ISMENE	I confess it—if she'll let me.
	I accept my full share of the blame.
ANTIGONE	Justice won't let you make that claim, sister!
	You refused to help me. You took no part.
585 ISMENE	You're leaving on a grim voyage. I'm not
	ashamed to suffer with you the whole way.
ANTIGONE	The dead in Hades know who buried him.
	I don't want love that just shows up in words.
ISMENE	You'll disgrace me, sister! Don't keep me
590	from honoring our dead! Let me come with you!
ANTIGONE	Don't try to share my death! Don't try to claim
	you helped me bury him! My death's enough.
ISMENE	With you dead, why would I want to live?
ANTIGONE	Ask Kreon that! You sprang to his defense.
595 ISMENE	Why do you wound me? It does you no good.
ANTIGONE	I'm sorry if my scorn for him hurts you.
ISMENE	I can still help you. Tell me what to do.
ANTIGONE	Go on living. I'd rather you survived.
ISMENE	Then you want to exclude me from your fate?
600 ANTIGONE	You made the choice to live. I chose to die.
ISMENE	And I've told you how much I hate that choice.
ANTIGONE	Some think you're right. *Others* think I am.
ISMENE	Then aren't we both equally wrong?
ANTIGONE	Gather your strength. Your life goes on. Long ago
605	I dedicated mine to the dead.

KREON	One woman only now shows her madness—
	the other's been out of her mind since birth.
ISMENE	King, when you are shattered by grief
	your native wit vanishes. It just goes.
610 KREON	You surely lost your wits when you teamed up
	with a criminal engaged in a crime.
ISMENE	What would my life be like without her?
KREON	You're living that life now. Hers is over.
ISMENE	Then you're willing to kill your own son's bride?
615 KREON	Oh yes. He'll find other fields to plow.
ISMENE	No other woman would suit him so well.
KREON	I want no pernicious wives for my son.
ANTIGONE	Dearest Haimon! How your father hates you!
KREON	Enough! No more talk about this marriage.
620 ISMENE	You're going to rob your son of his bride?
KREON	Hades will cancel their marriage for me.
LEADER	Then you've made up your mind she will die?
KREON	Both *my* mind and *your* mind. No more delay,
	men, take them in. Make sure they behave
625	like women. Don't let either slip away.
	Even the brave will try to run
	when they see death closing in.

(Kreon's Men take ANTIGONE *and* ISMENE *inside.)*

ELDERS	Lucky are those
	whose lives
630	never taste evil!
	For once the gods
	attack a family,
	their curse never relents.
	It sickens life after life,
635	rising like a deep
	sea swell, a darkness
	boiling from below, driven
	by the wild stormwinds
	of Thrace that churn up
640	black sand from the sea floor—
	the battered headlands
	moan as the storm pounds in.

	I see sorrows that struck
	the dead Labdakids long ago
645	break over their children,
	wave on wave of sorrows!
	Each generation fails
	to protect its own youth—
	because a god always hacks
650	at their roots, draining
	strength that could set them free.

Now the hope that brightened
over the last rootstock
alive in the house
655   of Oedipus, in its turn
is struck down—
by the blood-drenched dust
the death-gods demand,
by reckless talk,
660   by Furies[6] in the mind.

O Zeus,
what human arrogance
can rival your power?
Neither Sleep,
665   who beguiles us all,
nor the tireless, god-driven months
overcome it.
            O Monarch
whom time cannot age—
you live in the magical
670   sunrays of Olympos!
One law of yours rules
our own and future time,
just as it ruled the past:
Nothing momentous man
675   achieves will go unpunished.

For Hope is a wanderer
who profits multitudes
but tempts just as many
with light-headed longings—
680   and a man's failure
dawns on him only
when blazing coals
scald his feet.

The man was wise
685   who said these words:
"Evil seems noble—
early and late—to minds
unbalanced by the gods,
but only for a moment
690   will such men
hold off catastrophe."
    (*Enter* HAIMON.)

LEADER   There's Haimon,
the youngest of your sons.
Does he come here enraged

6. Spirits of vengeance.

695   that you have sentenced Antigone,
           the bride he's been promised,
           or in shock that his hopes
           for marriage have been crushed?
KREON   We'll soon have an answer
700   better than any prophet's.
           My son, now that you've heard
           my formal condemnation
           of your bride, have you come here
           to attack your father?
705   Or will I be dear to you still,
           no matter what I do?
HAIMON   I'm yours, father. I respect your wisdom.
           Show me the straight path, and I'll take it.
           I couldn't value any marriage more
710   than the excellent guidance you give me.
KREON   Son, that's exactly how you need to think:
           Follow your father's orders in all things.
           It's the reason men pray for loyal sons
           to be born and raised in their houses—
715   so they can harm their father's enemies
           and show his friends respect to match his own.
           If a man produces worthless children,
           what has he spawned? His grief, his rivals' glee.

           Don't throw away your judgment, son,
720   for the pleasure this woman offers.
           You'll feel her turn ice cold in your arms—
           you'll feel her scorn in the bedroom. No wound
           cuts deeper than poisonous love. So spit
           this girl out like the enemy she is.
725   Let her find a mate in Hades.
           I caught her in open defiance—
           she alone in the whole city—and I will take
           her life, just as I promised. I will not
           show myself as a liar to my people.
730   It is useless for her to harp on the Zeus
           of family life:[7] If I indulge my own
           family in rebelliousness,
           I must indulge it everywhere.

           A man who keeps his own house in order
735   will be perceived as righteous by his city.
           But if anyone steps out of line, breaks
           our laws, thinks he can dictate to his king,
           he shouldn't expect any praise from me.

---

7. Zeus was the defender of bonds between family members.

740	Citizens must obey men in office appointed by the city, both in minor matters and in the great questions of what is just— even when they think an action unjust. Obedient men lead ably and serve well.
745	Caught in a squall of spears, they hold their ground. They make brave soldiers you can trust. Insubordination is our worst crime. It wrecks cities and empties homes. It breaks and routs even allies who fight beside us.
750	Discipline is what saves the lives of all good people who stay out of trouble. And to make sure we enforce discipline— never let a woman overwhelm a king. Better to be driven from power, if it comes to that, by a man. Then nobody
755	can say you were beaten by some female.

LEADER   Unless the years have sapped my wits, King,
          what you have just said was wisely said.

HAIMON   Father, the gods instill reason in men.
          It's the most valuable thing we possess.

760   I don't have the skill—nor do I want it—
          to contradict all the things you have said.
          Though someone else's perspective might help.
          Look, it's not in your nature to notice
          what people say what they're condemning.

765   That harsh look on your face makes men afraid—
          no one tells you what you'd rather not hear.
          But I hear, unobserved, what people think.
          Listen. Thebes aches for this girl. *No person
          ever*, they're saying, *less deserved to die—*

770   *no one's ever been so unjustly killed*
          for actions as magnificent as hers.
          When her own brother died in that bloodbath
          she kept him from lying out there unburied,
          fair game for flesh-eating dogs and vultures.

775   *Hasn't she earned*, they ask, *golden honor?*
          Those are the words they whisper in the shadows.

          There's nothing I prize more, father,
          than your welfare.
                    What makes a son prouder
          than a father's thriving reputation?

780   Don't fathers feel the same about their sons?

          Attitudes are like clothes; you can change them.
          Don't think that what you say is always right.
          Whoever thinks that he alone is wise,

785

that he's got a superior tongue and brain,
open him up and you'll find him a blank.
It's never shameful for even a wise man
to keep on learning new things all his life.
Be flexible, not rigid. Think of trees
caught in a raging winter torrent: those

790

that bend will survive with all their limbs
intact; those that resist are swept away.
Or take a captain who cleats his mainsheet
down hard, never easing off in a blow;
he'll capsize his ship and go right on sailing,

795

his rowing benches where his keel should be.
Step back from your anger, let yourself change.

If I, as a younger man, can offer
a thought, it's this: Yes, it would be better
if men were born with perfect understanding.

800

But things don't work that way. The best response
to worthy advice is to learn from it.

LEADER

King, if he has said anything to ease
this crisis, you had better learn from it.
Haimon, you do the same. You both spoke well.

805 KREON
So men my age should learn from one of yours?

HAIMON
If I happen to be right, yes! Don't look
at my youth, look at what I've accomplished.

KREON
What? Backing rebels makes you proud?

HAIMON
I'm not about to condone wrongdoing.

810 KREON
Hasn't *she* been attacked by that disease?

HAIMON
Your fellow citizens would deny it.

KREON
Shall Thebans dictate how I should govern?

HAIMON
Listen to yourself: You talk like a boy.

KREON
Should I yield to them—or rule Thebes myself?

815 HAIMON
It's not a *city* if one man owns it.

KREON
Don't we say men in power *own* their cities?

HAIMON
You'd make a first-rate king of a wasteland.

KREON
It seems this *boy* fights on the woman's side.

HAIMON
Only if you're the woman. You're my concern.

820 KREON
Then why do you make open war on me?

HAIMON
What I attack is your abuse of power.

KREON
Is protecting my interest an abuse?

HAIMON
What is it you protect by scorning the gods?

KREON
Look at yourself! A woman overpowers you.

825 HAIMON
But no disgraceful impulse ever will.

KREON
Your every word supports that woman.

HAIMON
And you, and me, and the gods of this earth.

KREON
You will not marry her while she's on this earth.

HAIMON
Then she will die, and dead, kill someone else.

830 KREON
You are brazen enough to threaten me?

HAIMON
What threatens you is hearing what I think.

	KREON	Your mindless attack on me threatens you.
	HAIMON	I'd question your mind if you weren't my father.
	KREON	Stop your snide deference! You are her slave.
835	HAIMON	You're talking at me, but you don't hear me.
	KREON	Really? By Olympos above, I hear you.
		And I can assure you, you're going to
		suffer the consequences of your attacks.
		(KREON *speaks to his Men.*)
		Bring out the odious creature. Let her
840		die at once in his presence. Let him watch,
		this bridegroom, as she's killed beside him.
		(*Two Men enter palace.*)
	HAIMON	Watch her die next to me? You think I'd do that?
		Your eyes won't see my face, ever again.
		Go on raving to friends who can stand you.
		(*Exit* HAIMON.)
845	LEADER	King, the young man's fury hurls him out.
		Rage makes a man his age utterly reckless.
	KREON	Let him imagine he's superhuman.
		He'll never save the lives of those two girls.
	LEADER	Then you intend to execute them both?
850	KREON	Not the one with clean hands.
		I think you're right about her.
	LEADER	The one you're going to kill—how will you do it?
	KREON	I will lead her along a deserted road,
		and hide her, alive, in a hollow cave.
855		I'll leave her just enough food to evade
		defilement—so the city won't be infected.[8]
		She can pray there to Hades, the one god
		whom she respects. Maybe he will spare her!
		Though she's more likely to learn, in her last hours,
860		that she's thrown her life away on the dead.
		[KREON *remains on stage during the next choral ode, presumably retiring into the background.*]
	ELDERS	Love, you win all
		your battles!—raising
		havoc with our herds,
		dwelling all night
865		on a girl's soft cheeks,
		cruising the oceans,
		invading homes
		deep in the wilds!
		No god can outlast you,
870		no mortal outrun you.

8. Kreon imagines that if Antigone dies from starvation after the food runs out, the city will not incur "blood guilt" from her death.

And those you seize go mad.

You wrench even good men's minds
so far off course they crash in ruins.
Now you ignite hatred in men
875   of the same blood—but allure flashing
from the keen eyes of the bride
always wins, for Desire wields
all the power of ancient law:
Aphrodite[9] the implacable
880   plays cruel games with our lives.

(*Enter* ANTIGONE, *dressed in purple as a bride, guarded
by Kreon's Men.*)

LEADER   This sight also drives *me*
outside the law. I can't stop
my own tears flowing when I see
Antigone on her way
885   to the bridal chamber,
where we all lie down in death.

ANTIGONE Citizens of our fatherland, you see me
begin my last journey. I take one last look
at sunlight that I'll never see again.
890   Hades, who chills each one of us to sleep,
will guide me down to Acheron's[1] shore.
I'll go hearing no wedding hymn
to carry me to my bridal chamber, or songs
girls sing when flowers crown a bride's hair;
895   I'm going to marry the River of Pain.[2]

LEADER   Don't praise and glory go with you
to the deep caverns of the dead?
You haven't been wasted by disease;
you've helped no sword earn its keep.
900   No, you have chosen of your own free will
to enter Hades while you're still alive.
No one else has ever done that.

ANTIGONE I once heard that a Phrygian stranger,
Niobe, the daughter of Tantalos,
905   died a hideous death on Mt. Sipylos.[3]
Living rock, like relentless ivy,
crushed her. Now, people say, she slowly
erodes; rain and snow
never leave her, they constantly
910   pour like tears from her eyes,

9. Goddess associated with sexual desire; she
is the mother of Desire (*Eros*).
1. A river in the underworld.
2. Acheron.
3. Niobe, wife of Amphion (King of Thebes),
boasted that she had more children than Leto,
the mother of the twin gods Apollo and Artemis. In revenge, they killed all her children.
Niobe fled to Phrygia and was turned into a
rock on Mount Sipylos. A real rock formation
there looks like a woman's face, and the snow
melting down its surface resembles tears.

                    drenching the clefts of her body.
                    My death will be like hers,
                    when the god at last lets me sleep.
    LEADER   You forget, child, she was a goddess,[4]
915   with gods for parents, not a mortal
                    begotten by mortals like ourselves.
                    It's no small honor for a mere woman
                    to suffer so godlike a fate—in both
                    how she has lived, and the way she will die.
920 ANTIGONE   Now I'm being laughed at!
                    In the name of our fathers' gods,
                    wait till I'm gone, don't mock me
                    while I stand here in plain sight—
                    all you rich citizens of this town!

925   At least I can trust you,
                    headwaters of the river
                    Dirke,[5] and you, holy
                    plains around Thebes, home
                    of our great chariot-fleet,
930   to bear me witness: Watch them
                    march me off to my strange tomb,
                    my heaped-up rock-bound prison,
                    without a friend to mourn me
                    or any law to protect me—

935   me, a miserable woman
                    with no home here on earth
                    and none down with the dead,
                    not quite alive, not yet a corpse.

    LEADER   You took the ultimate risk when you smashed
940   yourself against the throne of Justice.
                    But the stiff price you're paying, daughter,
                    is one you inherit from your father.
    ANTIGONE   You've touched my worst grief,
                    the fate of my father, which I
945   keep turning over in my mind.
                    We all were doomed, the whole
                    grand house of Labdakos,
                    by my mother's horrendous,
                    incestuous, coupling with her son.
950   From what kind of parents was I born?

                    I'm going to them now,
                    I'm dying unmarried.

---

4. Tantalus, Niobe's father, was (in some versions of the myth) a son of Zeus; her mother
was also a goddess.
5. In Thebes.

And brother Polyneikes,
wasn't yours too a deadly
955   marriage?[6] And when you
were slaughtered, so was I.

LEADER   Your pious conduct might deserve some praise,
but no assault on power will ever
be tolerated by him who wields it.
960   It was your own hot-headed
willfulness that destroyed you.

ANTIGONE   No friends, no mourners, no wedding songs
go with me, they push me down a road
that runs through sadness;
965   they have prepared it for me, alone.
Soon I will lose sight of the sun's holy eye,
wretched, with no one to love me,
no one to grieve.

[KREON *moves forward, speaking first to* ANTIGONE, *then to his Men.*]

KREON   You realize, don't you, that singing
970   and wailing would go on forever
if they did the dying any good?

Hurry up now, take her away.
And when you've finished
enclosing her, just as I've ordered,
975   inside the cave's vault,
leave her there—absolutely
isolated—to decide whether
she wants to die at once, or go
on living in that black hole.
980   So we'll be pure as far as she's concerned.
In either case, today will be the last
she'll ever spend above the ground.

ANTIGONE   My tomb, my bridal bedroom, my home
dug from rock, where they'll keep me forever—
985   I'll join my family there, so many of us dead,
already welcomed by Persephone.[7]
I'll be the last to arrive, and the worst off,
going down with most of my life unlived.
I hope my coming will please my father,
990   comfort my mother, and bring joy
to you, brother, because I washed your dead
bodies, dressed you with my hands, and poured
blessèd offerings of drink on your graves.

---

6. Polyneikes married the daughter of Adras-   him to march against Thebes.
tus of Argos, to seal the alliance that enabled   7. Queen of the underworld.

Now, because I honored your corpse,
995   Polyneikes, *this* is how I'm repaid!
         I honored you as wise men would think right
         But I wouldn't have taken that task on
         had I been a mother who lost her child,
         or if my husband were rotting out there.
1000   For them, I would never defy my city.
         You want to know what law lets me say this?
         If my husband were dead, I could remarry.
         A new husband could give me a new child.
         But with my father and mother in Hades,
1005   a new brother could never bloom for me.
         That is the law that made me die for you,
         Polyneikes. But Kreon says I'm wrong,
         terribly wrong. And now I'm his captive,
         he pulls me by the wrist to no bride's bed;
1010   I won't hear bridal songs, or feel the joy
         of married love, and I will have no share
         in raising children. No, I will go grieving,
         friendless, and alive to a hollow tomb.
         Tell me, gods, which of *your* laws did I break?

1015   I'm too far gone to expect your help.
         But whose strength can I count on, when acts
         of blessing are considered blasphemy?
         If the gods are happy I'm sentenced to die
         I hope one day I'll discover
1020   what divine law I have broken.
         But if my judges are at fault, I want *them*
         to suffer the pain they inflict on me now.

LEADER   She's still driven by raw gusts
         raging through her mind.
1025 KREON   I have no patience with such outbursts.
         And none for men who drag their feet.
ANTIGONE I think you're saying that my death is near.
KREON   It will be carried out. Don't think otherwise.
ANTIGONE I leave you, Thebes, city of my fathers.
1030   I leave you, ancient gods.[8] This very moment,
         I'm being led away. They cannot wait!
         Look at me, princely citizens of Thebes:
         I'm the last daughter of the kings who ruled you.
         Look at what's done to me, and by whom
1035   it's done, to punish me for keeping faith.
         [*Kreon's Men lead* ANTIGONE *offstage.*]

---

8. The Theban royal house was descended from the gods Ares and Aphrodite.

ELDERS   Like you, lovely Danae[9] endured her loss
of heavenly sunlight
in a brass-bound cell—
1040   a prison secret as a tomb.
Night and day she was watched.
Like yours, my daughter,
her family was a great one.
The seed of Zeus, which fell
1045   on her as golden rain,
she treasured in her womb.
Fate is strange and powerful;
wealth cannot protect us,
nor can war, high city towers,
1050   or storm-beaten black ships.

Impounded too was Lycurgos,
short-tempered son of Dryas,
King of Edonia:[1] To pay
him back for insulting
1055   defiance, Dionysos shut
him up in a rocky cell;
there his surging madness ebbed.
He learned too late how mad
he was to taunt this god
1060   with derisive laughter:
When he tried to suppress
Bakkhanalian torches
and women fired by their god,
he angered the Muses
1065   who love the oboe's song.

By waters off the Black Rocks,
a current joins two seas;
the Bosphoros' channel
follows the Thracian
1070   coast of Salmydessos.
Ares from his nearby city
saw this wild assault—
the savage wife of Phineus
attacking his two sons:[2]

9. Daughter of Acrisius, king of Argos. It was prophesied that he would be killed by his daughter's son, so he shut his daughter up in a bronze tower, hoping she would never have a lover or son. But Zeus came to her in the form of a golden rain shower, and she had a son, Perseus, who did in the end accidentally kill his grandfather.
1. Thrace. Lycurgos opposed the introduction of Dionysiac religion into his kingdom and was imprisoned by Dionysos.
2. This stanza refers to a story that Cleopatra, daughter of the Athenian princess Orithyia, whom Boreas, the North Wind, carried off to his home in Thrace, was married to Phineus, the Thracian king, and bore him two sons. He later abandoned her and married Eidothea, who put out the eyes of Cleopatra's sons, while Ares, god of war, watched. The application of the story to Antigone's situation is unclear.

1075   Her stab-wounds darkened
        their vengeance-craving eyes,
        burst with a pointed shuttle
        gripped in her blood-drenched hands.

        Broken spirits, they howled
1080   in their pain—these sons
        of a woman unhappy
        in her marriage, this daughter
        descended from the ancient
        Erektheids.[3] Nursed in caves
1085   among her father's stormwinds,
        this daughter of the gods,
        this child of Boreas,
        rode swift horses over the mountains—
        yet Fate broke her brutally, my child.

        [*Enter* TIRESIAS *and the Lad who guides him.*]

1090 TIRESIAS   Theban lords, we walk here side by side,
               one pair of eyes looking out for us both.
               Blind men must travel with somebody's help.

     KREON   What news do you bring, old man Tiresias?

     TIRESIAS   I'll tell you. Then you must trust this prophet.

1095 KREON   I've never questioned the advice you've given.

     TIRESIAS   And it helped you keep Thebes on a straight course?

     KREON   I know your value. I learned it first-hand.

     TIRESIAS   Take care.
               You're standing on the razor's edge of fate.

1100 KREON   What do you mean? That makes me shudder.

     TIRESIAS   You'll comprehend when you hear the warnings
               issued by my art. When I took my seat
               at my accustomed post of augury,
               birds from everywhere fluttering nearby,
1105   I heard a strange sound coming from their midst.
               They screeched with such mindless ferocity,
               any meaning their song possessed was drowned out.
               I knew the birds were tearing at each other
               with lethal talons; the hovering beats
1110   of thrashing wings could have meant nothing else.
               Alarmed, I lit a sacrificial fire,
               but the god failed to keep his flames alive.
               Then from charred thighbones came a rancid slime,
               smoking and sputtering, oozing out
1115   into the ashes; the gall-bladder burst open;
               liquefying thighs slid free from the strips
               of fat enfolding them.
                              But my attempt
               at prophecy failed; the signs I had sought

3. Royal house of Athens.

never appeared—this I learned from my lad.
1120 He's my guide, just as I'm the guide for others.

Kreon, your mind has sickened Thebes.
Our city's altars, and our city's braziers,
have been defiled, all of them, by dogs
and birds, with flesh torn from the wretched
1125 corpse of Oedipus' fallen son.
Because of this, the gods will not accept
our prayers or the offerings of burnt meat
that come from our hands. No bird now sings
a clear omen—their keen cries have been garbled
1130 by the taste of a slain man's thickened blood.
Think about these facts, son.
                                        All men go wrong;
but when a man blunders, he won't be stripped
of his wits and his strength if he corrects
the error he's committed and then ends
1135 his stubborn ways. Stubbornness, you well know,
will provoke charges of stupidity.

Respect the dead. Don't spear the fallen.
How much courage does it take
to kill a dead man?
                              Let me
1140 help you. My counsel is sound and well meant.
No advice is sweeter than that from a wise
source who has only your interests at heart.

KREON   Old man, like archers at target practice,
you all aim arrows at me. And now you
1145 stoop to using prophecy against me.
For a long time I have been merchandise
sold far and wide by you omen-mongers.
Go, make your money, strike your deals, import
silver from Sardis, gold from India,
1150 if it suits you. But you won't hide that corpse
under the earth! Never—even if Zeus'
own eagles fly scraps of flesh to his throne.

Defilement isn't something I fear—it won't
persuade me to order this burial.
1155 I don't accept that men can defile gods.
But even the cleverest of mortals,
venerable Tiresias, will be brought
down hard if, hoping to turn a profit,
they clothe ugly ideas in handsome words.
1160 TIRESIAS   Does any man grasp . . . does he realize . . .
KREON   Realize . . . what? What point are you making?

TIRESIAS	. . . that no possession is worth more than good sense?
KREON	Just as its absence is our worst disease.
TIRESIAS	But hasn't that disease infected you?
1165 KREON	I won't trade insults with you, prophet.
TIRESIAS	You do when you call my prophecies false.
KREON	Your profession has always loved money.
TIRESIAS	And tyrants have a penchant for corruption.
KREON	You know you're abusing a king in power?
1170 TIRESIAS	You hold power because I helped you save Thebes.
KREON	You're a shrewd prophet. But you love to cause harm.
TIRESIAS	You'll force me to say what's clenched in my heart.
KREON	Say it. Unless you've been paid to say it.
TIRESIAS	I don't think it will pay you to hear it.
1175 KREON	Get one thing straight: My conscience can't be bought.
TIRESIAS	Then tell your conscience this: You will not live

for many circuits of the chariot sun
before you trade a child born from your loins
for all the corpses whose deaths you have caused.
1180 You have thrown children from the sunlight
down to the shades of Hades, ruthlessly
housing a living person in a tomb,
while you detain here, among us, something
that belongs to the gods who live below
1185 our world—the naked unwept corpse you've robbed
of the solemn grieving we owe our dead.
None of this should have been any concern
of yours—or of the Olympian gods—
but you have involved them in your outrage!
1190 Therefore, avengers wait to ambush you—
the Furies sent by Hades and its gods
will punish you for the crimes I have named.

Do you think someone hired me to tell you this?

It won't be long before wailing breaks out
1195 from the women and men in your own house.
And hatred against you will surge in all
the countries whose sons, in mangled pieces,
received their rites of burial
from dogs, wild beasts, or flapping birds
1200 who have carried the stench of defilement
to the homelands and the hearths of the dead.

Since you've provoked me, these are the arrows
I have shot in anger, like a bowman,
straight at your heart—arrows you cannot dodge,
1205 and whose pain you will feel.
                                    Lad, take me home—
let this man turn his anger on younger

people. That might teach him to hold his tongue,
and to think more wisely than he does now.

[*Exit* TIRESIAS *led by the Lad.*]

LEADER   This old man leaves stark prophecies behind.
1210   Never once, while my hair has gone from black
to white, has this prophet told Thebes a lie.

KREON   I'm well aware of that! It unnerves me.
Surrender would be devastating,
but if I stand firm, I could be destroyed.

1215 LEADER   What you need is some very clear advice,
son of Menoikeus.

KREON   What must I do?
If you have such advice, give it to me.

LEADER   Free the girl from her underground prison.
Build a tomb for the corpse you have let rot.

1220 KREON   That's your advice? I should surrender?

LEADER   Yes, King. Do it now. For the gods
act quickly to abort human folly.

KREON   I can hardly say this. But I'll give up
convictions I hold passionately—

1225   and do what you ask. We can't fight
the raw power of destiny.

LEADER   Then go!
Yourself. Delegate this to no one.

KREON   I'll go just as I am. Move out, men. Now!
All of you, bring axes and run toward
1230   that rising ground. You can see it from here.
Because I'm the one who has changed, I who
locked her away will go there to free her.
My heart is telling me we must obey
established law until the day we die.

[*Exit* KREON *and his Men toward open country.*]

1235 ELDERS   God with myriad names—
lustrous child
of Kadmos' daughter,
son of thundering Zeus—
you govern fabled Italy;
1240   you preside at Eleusis,
secluded Valley of Demeter
that welcomes all pilgrims.[4]
O Bakkhos! Thebes
is your homeland,
1245   mother-city of maenads[5]
on the quietly flowing

---

4. Kadmos's daughter is Semele, mother of
Dionysos (Bakkhos). Eleusis, the site of a mystery cult to Demeter, goddess of the harvest, is
near Athens.
5. Female worshippers of Dionysos.

Ismenos, where the dragon's
teeth were sown.[6]

Now you stand on the ridges rising
1250   up the twin peaks of Parnassos.[7]
There through the wavering
smoke-haze your torches flare;
there walk your devotees,
the nymphs of Korykia,
1255   beside Kastalia's fountains.
Thick-woven ivy on Nysa's sloping hills,
grape-clusters ripe on verdant shorelines
propel you here, while voices
of more than human power
1260   sing "Evohoi!"[8]—your name divine
when the streets of Thebes
are your final destination.

By honoring Thebes
beyond all cities,
1265   you honor your mother
whom the lightning killed.[9]
Now a plague
ravages our city. Come home
on healing footsteps—down
1270   the slopes of Parnassos,
or over the howling channel.
Stars breathing their gentle fire
shine joy on you as they rise,
O master of nocturnal voices!
1275   Take shape before our eyes, Bakkhos,
son of Zeus our king, let the Thyiads[1]
come with you, let them climb
the mad heights of frenzy
as you, Iakkhos,[2] the bountiful,
1280   watch them
dance through the night.

[*Enter* MESSENGER.]

MESSENGER   Neighbors, who live not far from the grand
old houses of Amphion and Kadmos,[3]
you can't trust anything in a person's life—
1285   praiseworthy or shameful—never to change.

---

6. The population of Thebes was supposed to have grown from dragon's teeth, sown by Kadmos.
7. The two cliffs above Delphi, where Dionysus was thought to reside in the winter months.
8. A cry associated with Dionysiac ecstasy.
9. Semele was killed when she saw her lover, Zeus, god of lightning, in his full glory, which was too much for a human.
1. Maenads.
2. Alternative name for Dionysus.
3. Builder and founder of Thebes.

Fate lifts up—and fate cuts down—both the lucky
and the unlucky, day in and day out.
No prophet can tell us what happens next.
Kreon always seemed someone to envy,
1290   to me at least. He saved from attack
the homeland where we sons of Kadmos live;
this won him absolute power. He was
the brilliant father of patrician children.
Now it has all slipped away. For when things
1295   that give pleasure and meaning to our lives
desert a man, he's not a human being
any more—he becomes a breathing corpse.
Amass wealth if you can, show off your house;
display the panache of a great monarch.
1300   But if joy disappears from your life
I wouldn't give the shadow cast by smoke
for all you possess. Only happiness matters.

LEADER   Should our masters expect more grief? What's happened?
MESSENGER   Death. And the killer is alive.
1305 LEADER   Name the murderer. Name the dead. Tell us.
MESSENGER   Haimon is dead. The hand that killed him was his own . . .
LEADER   . . . father's? Or do you mean he killed himself?
MESSENGER   He killed himself. Raging at his killer father.
LEADER   Tiresias, you spoke the truth.
1310 MESSENGER   You know the facts, now you must cope with them.

                 [*Enter* EURYDIKE.]

LEADER   I see Eurydike, soon to be crushed,
                 approaching from inside the house.
                 She may have heard what's happened to her son.

EURYDIKE   I heard all of you speaking as I came out—
1315   on my way to offer prayers to Athena.
                 I happened to unlatch the gate,
                 to open it, when words of our disaster
                 carried to my ears. I fainted, terrified
                 and dumbstruck, in the arms of my servants.
1320   Please tell me your news. Tell me all of it.
                 I'm someone who has lived through misfortune.

MESSENGER   O my dear Queen, I will spare you nothing.
                 I'll tell you truthfully what I've just seen.
                 Why should I say something to soothe you
1325   that will later prove me a liar?
                 Straight talk is always best.
                 I traveled with your husband to the far
                 edge of the plain where Polyneikes' corpse,
                 mangled by wild dogs, lay still uncared-for.

1330   We prayed for mercy to the Goddess
                 of Roadways; and to Pluto, asking them

to restrain their anger.[4] We washed his remains
with purified water. Using boughs stripped
from nearby bushes, we burned what was left,
then mounded a tomb from his native earth.

1335

After that we turned toward the girl's deadly
wedding cavern—with its bed of cold stone.
Still far off, we heard an enormous wail
coming from somewhere near the unhallowed
portico—so we turned back to tell Kreon.
As the king arrived, these incoherent
despairing shouts echoed all around him.
First he groaned, then he yelled out in raw pain,

1340

"Am I a prophet? Will my worst fears come true?
Am I walking down the bitterest street
of my life? That's my son's voice greeting me!

1345

"Move quickly, men, run through that narrow gap
where the stones have been pulled loose from the wall,
go where the cavern opens out. Tell me
the truth—is that Haimon's voice I'm hearing,
or have the gods played some trick on my ears?"

1350

Following orders from our despondent
master, we stared in. At the tomb's far end
there she was, hanging by the neck, a noose
of finely woven linen holding her aloft.
He fell against her, arms hugging her waist,
grieving for the bride he'd lost to Hades,
for his father's acts, for his own doomed love.

1355

When Kreon saw all this he stepped inside,
groaned horribly, and called out to his son:
"My desperate child! What have you done? What
did you think you were doing? When did the gods
destroy your reason? Come out of there, son.
I beg you."
                    His son then glared straight at him
with savage eyes, spat in his face, spoke not
one word in answer, but drew his two-edged sword.
His father leapt back, Haimon missed his thrust.
Then this raging youth—with no warning—turned
on himself, tensed his body to the sword,
and drove half its length deep into his side.

1360

1365

1370

---

4. The Goddess of the Roadways is Hecate, associated with crossroads, ghosts, and witchcraft.
Pluto is god of the underworld.

Still conscious, he clung to her with limp arms,
gasping for breath, spurts of his blood pulsing
onto her white cheek.
                              Then he lay there, his dead
body embracing hers, married at last,
1375   poor man not—up here, but somewhere
in Hades—proving that of all mankind's
evils, thoughtless violence is the worst.
[*Exit* EURYDIKE.]

LEADER   What do you make of that? She turns and leaves
without saying one word, brave or bitter.

1380 MESSENGER   I don't like it. I hope that having heard
the sorry way her son died, she won't grieve
for him in public. Maybe she's gone
to ask her maids to mourn him in the house.
This woman never loses her composure.

1385 LEADER   I'm not so sure. To me this strange silence
seems ominous as an outburst of grief.

MESSENGER   I'll go in and find out.
She could have disguised the real
intent of her impassioned heart.
1390   But I agree: Her silence is alarming.

[*Exit* MESSENGER *into the palace;* KREON *enters carrying the body of*
HAIMON *wrapped in cloth; his Men follow, bringing a bier on which*
KREON *will lay his son in due course.*]

LEADER   Here comes our king, burdened
with a message all too clear:
This wasn't caused by anyone's vengeance—
may I say it?—but by his own father's blunders.

1395 KREON   Oh, what errors of the mind I have made!
Deadly, bull-headed blunders.
You all see it—the man
who murdered, and the son
who's dead. What I did
1400   was blind and wrong!
You died so young, my son,
your death happened so fast!
Your life was cut short
not through your mad acts,
1405   but through mine.

LEADER   You saw the right course of action
but took it far too late.

KREON   I've learned that lesson now—
in all its bitterness.
1410   Sometime back, a god struck
my head an immense blow,
it drove me
to act in brutal ways,

1415	ways that stamped out all my happiness. What burdens and what pain men suffer and endure. [*Enter* MESSENGER *from palace.*]
MESSENGER	Master, your hands are full of sorrow, you bear its full weight.
1420	But other sorrows are in store— you'll face them soon, inside your house.
KREON	Can any new calamity make what's happened worse?
1425 MESSENGER	Your wife is dead—so much a loving mother to your son, poor woman, that she died of wounds just now inflicted.
KREON	Oh Hades, you are hard
1430	to appease! We flood your harbor, you want more. Why are you trying to destroy me? [*Turning to Messenger.*]
	What have you to tell me
1435	this time?—you who bring nothing but deadly news. I was hardly alive, and now, my young friend, you've come back to kill me again. Son, what are you telling me?
1440	What is this newest message [*The palace doors open;* EURYDIKE's *corpse is revealed.*] that buries me? My wife is dead. Slaughter after slaughter.
LEADER	Now you see it. Your house no longer hides it.
KREON	I see one more violent death. With what
1445	else can fate punish me? I have just held my dead son in my arms— now I see another dear body. Oh unhappy mother, oh my son.
MESSENGER	There, at the altar, she pierced
1450	herself with a sharp blade. Her eyes went quietly dark and she closed them. She had first mourned aloud the empty marriage bed
1455	of her dead son Megareus.[5]

5. Another son of Kreon and Eurydike, killed during the siege of the city. Tiresias had prophesied that his death would save the city.

		Then with her last breath
		she cursed you, Kreon,
		killer of your own son.
1460	KREON	Ahhh! That sends fear
		surging through me.
		Why hasn't someone
		driven a two-edged
		sword through my heart?
		I'm a wretched coward,
1465		awash with terror.
	MESSENGER	The woman whose corpse you see
		condemns you for the deaths of her sons.
	KREON	Tell me how she did it.
	MESSENGER	She drove the blade below her liver,
1470		so she could suffer the same wound
		that killed Haimon, for whom she mourns.
	KREON	There's no one I can blame,
		no other mortal.
		I am the only one.

[KREON *looks at and touches the body of* HAIMON *as his Men assemble to escort him offstage.*]

1475		I killed you, that's the reality.
		Men, take me inside,
		I'm less than nothing now.
	LEADER	You are doing what's right,
		if any right can be found
1480		among all these misfortunes.
		It's best to say little
		in the face of evil.
	KREON	Let it come, let it happen now—
		let my own kindest fate
1485		make this my final day on earth.
		That would be kindness itself.
		Let it happen, let it come.
		Never let me see
		tomorrow's dawn.
1490	LEADER	That's in the future. We
		must deal with the present.
		The future will be shaped
		by those who control it.
	KREON	My deepest desires are in that prayer.
1495	LEADER	Stop your prayers.
		No human being
		evades calamity
		once it has struck.

[KREON *puts his hand on* HAIMON's *corpse.*]

	KREON	Take me from this place.
1500		A foolish, impulsive man

who killed you, my son, mindlessly,
killed you as well, my wife.
I'm truly cursed! I don't know
where to rest my eyes,

1505   or on whose shoulders
I can lean my weight.
My hands warp
all they touch;

[KREON, *still touching* HAIMON's *corpse, looks toward* EURYDIKE's, *then lifts his hand and moves off toward the palace.*]

and over there,

1510   fate's avalanche
pounds my head.

LEADER   Good sense is crucial
to human happiness.
Never fail to respect the gods,

1515   for the huge claims of proud men
are always hugely punished—
by blows that, as the proud grow old,
pound wisdom through their minds.

[*All leave.*]

EURIPIDES

ca. 480–406 B.C.E.

T HE last of the three important Greek tragedians, Euripides was also the most daring innovator of the classical stage. His startling and powerful plays quickly made him one of the most successful playwrights of Athens, a rival to the older and more established AESCHYLUS and SOPHOCLES, and after his death, his fame continued to grow. Euripides managed to push the drama he had inherited to new extremes and to inaugurate a new form of tragedy, one attuned to a growing skepticism toward inherited truths. Although still based on mythic figures and events, Euripides' tragedies treat gods and heroes with suspicion, making them more human, exposing their frailties, and bringing them closer to everyday reality. Euripides' skepticism spoke not only to contemporaries but to later audiences. While some commentators, particularly in the nineteenth and twentieth centuries, celebrated Euripides as the great modernizer of tragedy, others blamed him for its demise—most famously the nineteenth-century philosopher Friedrich Nietzsche, who accused Euripides of having killed tragedy. But no matter whether one wishes to praise Euripides as innovator or fault him for excessive irreverence, there can be no doubt that he changed the course of drama, leaving an imprint on the form of tragedy that can be felt even today.

Although born into a wealthy family, Euripides did not participate in public life. He began to write tragedies when he was eighteen, but did not win first prize at the Dionysia until he was around forty years old; the titles of these winning plays are unknown. Euripides' oldest extant play is *Alcestis* (438 B.C.E.), a tragicomedy that took second place at the competition. *MEDEA*, his oldest tragedy, was presented in 431 B.C.E. Even though his tragedies found a following in Athens, they also made him enemies, who objected to his irreverent depiction of the gods. Probably because of the growing influence of these enemies, at an advanced age Euripides emigrated to Macedonia at the invitation of its king, Archelaus, and died there one year later. He won only four prizes at Athens during his lifetime, but the posthumous performance of his last play, *THE BACCHAE*, gained him a fifth; and soon his popularity was to surpass that of all other Greek tragedians—a status he still holds today, especially in the theater.

Euripides' popularity was due to a number of innovations. The most important is that his tragedies are much more realistic than those of his predecessors, both in their depiction of character and in their language. Expanding on the changes introduced by Sophocles, his older contemporary, Euripides further reduced the importance of the chorus, placing more emphasis on dramatic interaction and confrontation. Doing so enabled him to make his plots more complicated and his characterization more nuanced. In part to bring his complex plots to a final conclusion, Euripides often relied on the *deus ex machina* (literally, "god from a machine"), the conventional recourse to a god brought onto the stage by means of a crane at the end of the play to intervene in hopeless situations, to resolve dilemmas, and to deal out punishment. This dramaturgical strategy, especially as it appears in *Medea*, earned him a rebuke from Aristotle in *Poetics* (ca. 360–355 B.C.E.), who maintained that "the denouements of plots . . . should come out of the character . . . and not from the 'machine.'"[1] Critics have subsequently argued, however, that the *dea ex machina* in *Medea* reveal how we should ultimately understand this character as semi-divine and her horrific acts of violence as divine retribution. Shortly after Euripides' death, ARISTOPHANES' comedy *The Frogs* (405 B.C.E.) shows Euripides in competition with the first master of tragedy, Aeschylus. Even though Aeschylus finally wins, because his language and topics are weightier than those of Euripides, Aristophanes acknowledges Euripides' greater skill in developing plots and his more realistic approach.

Through a series of historical accidents, Euripides' is the largest existing corpus of plays of any Greek playwright. A number of his plays, like other Greek tragedies, survived through acting copies, which in turn became the basis for the collection of Greek tragedy at the Library of Alexandria during the second century B.C.E. But we are fortunate to have as well a portion of what may have been Euripides' collected works in alphabetical order: plays beginning with the Greek letters epsilon, eta, iota, or kappa.

Even a cursory look at Euripides' plays shows both the variety of his styles and his most typical techniques. His version of *Electra*, for example, was conceived in direct response to Aeschylus's treatment and probably also with Sophocles'. Of the three,

Euripides' *Orestes* is the least heroic by far and most prone to hesitation and doubt. All the characters are drawn more realistically; they are more rooted in common, everyday reality, even though the play is still set in the mythical past. Euripides' *Helen* follows the same pattern. Based on a common variant of the myth, according to which Helen resided in Egypt during the Trojan War while her double—created by the gods—caused all the trouble in Troy, Euripides' *Helen* depicts the secret arrival of Menelaus in Egypt, clad in rags and unimpressive in many other ways as well. Another innovation is also visible in this play: it ends not tragically but with the happy escape of Menelaus and Helen. Tragedy here becomes romance.

Euripides made tragedy more realistic, more concerned with individual character, and more flexible in its endings. But this approach did not render his tragedies less stark or brutal. On the contrary, he created some of the most extreme situations and events ever depicted on the Greek stage. He became notorious for treatments of sensational subject matter—such as the doomed passion of a woman for her stepson (in *Hippolytus*) or the murder of two children by their own mother in a desperate act of revenge on their father (in *Medea*)—that often culminated in lurid violence. Euripides was never one to compromise, and he constantly sought to find new avenues to take and new areas to explore even if they seemed to go against custom and common decency.

MEDEA

This strategy may well have cost him the prize in 431 B.C.E., when *Medea* shocked and dismayed audiences and judges alike with its grisly, murderous conclusion. Yet Euripides' uncompromising dramaturgy is arguably also responsible for the play's ongoing fascination. The character of Medea and the narratives of which she is a part have figured prominently in the performing arts for centuries. SENECA wrote his own dramatic version in the first century C.E.; the first ballet version was created in France in the mid-sixteenth century; and the first operatic version emerged a century later in Italy. Numerous addi-

---

1. Aristotle, *Poetics*, trans. Gerald F. Else (Ann Arbor: University of Michigan Press, 1970), p. 44.

tional dramatic, operatic, balletic, and filmic renditions, each famous in its own right, have followed. These include French playwright Jean Anouilh's 1953 adaptation; Italian composer Luigi Cherubini's 1787 opera, revived by opera diva Maria Callas in the mid-twentieth century; American choreographer Martha Graham's 1946 ballet; and Danish director Lars von Trier's 1988 film. In both classical and modern Greek, *Medea* remains a fixture in its native theater, and over the last century alone, leading actresses of each generation have tackled this demanding role in English translation, including Sybil Thorndike in 1919, Judith Anderson in 1947, Diana Rigg in 1992, and Fiona Shaw in 2000.

We know that Euripides had previously dramatized other episodes of the myth (now lost) before he crafted *Medea*, and his fifth-century B.C.E. audiences would certainly have had some familiarity with these stories, which had also been dramatized by SOPHOCLES and AESCHYLUS. The tale of Jason and the Golden Fleece, which the Nurse recounts at the opening of *Medea*, had long held a central place in Greek mythology. When Jason was a boy, his uncle Pelias usurped the throne of Iolcos from Jason's father, and the youth went into exile. Trained as a hero, Jason later returned to his homeland to reclaim his patrimony. Pelias agreed that he would give Jason the throne if he could capture the Golden Fleece, a treasure held in Colchis, across the Black Sea, and guarded by a fearful serpent. Jason, favored by the goddess Hera, arrives safely aboard the *Argo*. He receives critical help in his quest from Medea, daughter of the king of Colchis, who has fallen in love with him. To secure their escape with the Fleece, they kill her brother, and upon their return to Iolcos, Medea also arranges the unwitting murder of Pelias by his daughters. But instead of gaining his rightful throne, Jason and Medea are exiled, and they find refuge in Corinth, where Euripides sets his play.

While these core components of the myth were well established, it appears that there were multiple variants to the later Corinthian episodes in the Jason and Medea story. Euripides could thus exercise more originality and creativity with the plot of *Medea*, and it is clear that he took full advantage of this opportunity to call into question received notions of character and morality embedded in the ancient tales. Specifically, he interrogates Jason's heroic stature by imagining for him motives and actions that seem to be only self-interested. Jason's decision to abandon Medea to marry the Corinthian princess and secure his standing in his new homeland, his relative inaction following his new father-in-law Creon's decree of exile for Medea and their children, and his unwillingness now to acknowledge Medea's pivotal role in the successful quest for the Golden Fleece all reveal a figure less admirable than the older versions of the legends might have us believe. Moreover, Euripides contrasts Jason's recent behavior to his earlier promises to Medea—the oaths of loyalty he swore to her in acknowledgment of her aid and her love that, by ancient custom, he should have held sacred. Jason's violation of these vows is akin to an act of *hubris* and thus merits punishment by the gods. These oaths are particularly significant because they bound together people from two nations, Jason the Greek prince and Medea the "barbarian" (meaning "foreign") princess. For an Athenian audience, potentially aware of the imminence of hostilities with Sparta and the onset of what became known as the Peloponnesian War (431–404 B.C.E.), these figures from two different cultures, locked in conflict, may well have taken on larger symbolic meanings.

Euripides underscores the importance of such oaths by putting one at the very center of the play—in the scene between Medea and Aegeus, mythic king of Athens. While his appearance at this middle point in the narrative may at first seem odd—he has not heretofore been a part of the immediate story—Athenian audiences would have understood that this episode ties the strands of the legend together and links it directly to them. Within the world of the play, it is not sufficient that Aegeus simply agrees to protect Medea in exchange for her assurance of his longed-for paternity; she explains that "[a] promise in words only . . . might not be strong enough" (lines 757–58). Instead, she insists that

Aegeus "Swear by the Earth we stand on, and by Helios—my father's father—and the whole race of gods . . . Never to expel me from your land yourself, and never, as long as you live, to give me up willingly to any enemy" (lines 768–73). Medea, of course, does not divulge her larger plan to Aegeus while extracting this oath, and like so many other figures in the drama, Aegeus too plays an unwitting role in Medea's vengeful triumph.

Euripides' decision to question received notions of Jason's morality and heroic status through his broken oaths parallels the implicit requirement that we reexamine our ideas about Medea, the woman who demands such sacred vows. This "most theatrical of all Greek tragic characters"

(Macintosh) and the figure most responsible for renewed interest in the performance of Greek tragedy, Medea remains a challenge for artists and scholars alike, who continue to grapple with the contradictions and complexities of her character. Her ongoing fascination is clearly linked to the range of emotional states she exhibits and the variety of tactics and personae she employs to realize her goals. As the Nurse tells us in the prologue, Medea has been "dishonored," but she is also "a terror" (lines 25, 50). Indeed, Euripides defines Medea through such binaries: she is mortal yet also divine; accepted by the Chorus as like them yet also considered a barbarian; ferocious as an animal yet also deeply human; wronged and sympathetic

Fiona Shaw as Medea and Jonathan Cake as Jason in the 2001 Abbey Theatre production of *Medea*, directed by Deborah Warner.

yet also frightening and unfathomable in her resolve to kill again and again.

Some critics have suggested that Medea's semidivine status as the granddaughter of Helios, god of the sun, sets her apart from other women, while others look to her acts throughout the legends and identify her as a sorceress or witch. Medea certainly appears to have some special powers; we know they played a role in Jason's quest for the Golden Fleece, in the death of Pelias before the action begins, and crucially in the deaths of King Creon and his daughter during the play. Critic B. M. W. Knox, however, deems her simply a *pharmakis*, a woman with expertise in love potions, drugs, and poisons but not necessarily in witchcraft. Regardless of label, she destabilizes our received understanding of female identity, and we may well ask why Euripides ultimately ascribes such horrific behavior to a woman.

Critics have often noted that thirteen of Euripides' eighteen extant plays, including *The Bacchae*, feature a central female figure. Yet even as Euripides depicts the struggles of these figures to define their roles in Greek society, they do so within a cultural context focused on male selfhood. Theater in the classical era was part of the public sphere, the *polis*, defined and dominated by men. The *oikos*, women's domestic realm, was also shaped by patriarchal forces. Thus we may think of *Medea* as depicting the tensions between public and private life, as well as the more personal struggle between reason and emotion, rather than as a discourse on marriage per se or on relations between men and women in the classical era. We must not lose sight of the fact that Euripides, a male playwright, created Medea for a male actor to perform before a largely male audience.

THE BACCHAE

Unlike *Medea*, *The Bacchae* proved to be an immediate success when Euripides' son, also a playwright, staged it with *Iphigenia at Aulis* and the now lost *Alcmeon in Corinth*, in Athens. The play, Euripides' undisputed masterpiece, ends abruptly with a *deus ex machina*, Dionysus, who is hauled onto the stage by means of a crane

to punish most of the characters still alive. The play culminates with the dismemberment of Pentheus by his temporarily deluded mother—an extreme turn of events even by Euripides' standards. Euripides wrote this play in exile and never saw it performed. In fact, he may not have meant it for immediate performance, although it exploited the existing possibilities of the Greek stage with ingenuity.

Even though the concluding violence in *The Bacchae* is shocking, the play is also much more reflective, argumentative, and intellectual than the tragedies of previous playwrights. It is based on an opposition not only between two figures, Dionysus and Pentheus, but also between two philosophical positions, two conceptions of religion, and two views of political organization. Dionysus approaches the city from Asia as a figure whose natural habitat is the mountains, not the Greek city; Pentheus, in turn, wants to guard the Greek city or polis, the bastion of Greek civilization and political organization, and therefore attempts to keep this outsider and his cult from gaining a foothold in Thebes. Pentheus sees the foreign, rural cult of Dionysus as a threat to the urban order he has sworn to uphold, while Dionysus demands that his cult be established in the city alongside the existing ones. Pentheus thinks of himself as masculine and of Dionysus as effeminate, of his own clothes as proper and of Dionysus's garb as improper. In basing his play on a single opposition, Euripides was probably influenced by a new cast of traveling intellectuals, called sophists, who taught rhetoric and argument to enable citizens to represent themselves more effectively in court (Plato would soon criticize these early philosophers as being interested only in rhetorical prowess and not in truth, causing the term *sophist* to acquire the pejorative meaning it retains today). These philosophers left their mark on the language of Euripides, whose arguments are often constructed around reversals, subtle distinctions, and counterintuitive conclusions.

Although *The Bacchae* is in many ways typical of Euripides' style, it is also a unique play, a late work in which the playwright looks back over his long dramatic career, reflecting on his style and

Two bacchae tear Pentheus apart in this detail from a Greek vase painting.

choices—and perhaps offering a response to contemporaries who criticized his portraits of gods and heroes as lacking in proper respect. While his previous plays were notorious in this regard, *The Bacchae* turns irreverence itself into the predominant theme: Pentheus, king of Thebes, refuses to recognize Dionysus as a god, and Dionysus therefore seeks to prove his divinity. The entire play is devoted to furnishing this proof; once Dionysus is revealed as a god at the end, Pentheus and the entire city of Thebes are punished for their doubt.

One reason for the extraordinary power of this play is Euripides' use of theatrical techniques, particularly masks and disguises. Greek actors had always worn masks and costumes, but Euripides turned these props into central dramatic elements. Dionysus is the main protagonist throughout the play, but he appears always disguised in various costumes, shapes,

and forms. For Euripides, Dionysus becomes an ever-changing character who is impossible to pin down. The play uses many pseudonyms to refer to the god, who thus remains, until the end, incognito.

The different names serve to conceal the true identity of Dionysus, for the secrets of his cult must be carefully guarded. The Dionysus cult is a cult of initiates, and the chorus of followers refuses to divulge any of its secrets to Pentheus, who is eager to find out its true nature but is always thwarted. The play carefully leaves open several options. Though Pentheus believes that Dionysus drives the groups of reveling women into a sexual frenzy, the messengers sent to spy on them witness no sexual acts and instead tell of natural miracles and a life led in a strange harmony with nature. Euripides here makes good use of another convention of Greek tragedy: rather than showing these events directly to the audience, he evokes them before the audience through messengers and reporters—through language, not performance. In this way, the play keeps the audience in the same position as Pentheus, guessing what really goes on in the secret rituals devoted to the god. The task of guarding the secrets of the Dionysus cult had to be respected even by Euripides. According to some sources, however, Euripides may have gotten into trouble with members of the Dionysus cult, who felt that despite his precautions he had revealed too much about the most secretive of Greek rituals.

Whether Euripides successfully hid the secrets from his original audience or inadvertently revealed some of them, these mysterious rituals are more or less shielded from the eyes of the audience. The traces of the Dionysian ritual that we can discern from the play are evoked by signs and shapes, such as the special costumes worn by Dionysus's followers or their distinctive staffs and not by language or action. Costuming and dress thus play a central role in *The Bacchae*, from the very beginning of the play—which presents two revered older men, Cadmus and Tiresias, dressed in the distinctive feminine garments of the Dionysus cult, on their way to the mountains to participate in the rituals—to its conclusion, in which Pentheus himself dons the despised woman's attire to spy on the Bacchae in order to finally discover what they do.

Because of its attention to external shapes, appearances, masks, disguises, and props, *The Bacchae* is also a play about the theater itself. Chiefly, it is a play about seeing and being seen. The bloody climax of the play, when Pentheus is torn to pieces by the Bacchae, is brought about by his desire to watch the revelers engage in their secret ritual. His desire to see is simply too strong; he is even ready to don the Bacchic dress for the purpose. Watching is precisely the primary activity of the theater audience—the Greek word for theater, *theatron*, identifies it as a place for seeing. Thus, every time the play's action turns on costumes, disguises, acting, and watching, the audience is invited to think about the theater—and about itself.

The Bacchae also signals that it is not only a tragedy but also a tragedy about tragedy through its devotion to Dionysus, the god of theater. Greek tragedy first emerged as part of the Dionysus ritual, and all Greek tragedies were performed as part of the City Dionysia, a festival devoted to Dionysus. The central question of the play, whether Dionysus will be given his due, is therefore also the question of whether theater will be given its due. *The Bacchae* in addition concerns the origin of the theater more specifically, as it explores the relation between theater and ritual, in particular ritual sacrifice. The word *tragedy* comes from the Greek *tragoidia*, which means "goat song," presumably to accompany animal sacrifice, the killing of a goat (a "scapegoat"). Ritual sacrifice is precisely what happens in *The Bacchae*: Pentheus is ritually ripped to pieces by the Bacchae, including his mother, who are acting under the delusion that they are killing an animal. To be sure, ritual sacrifice is a punishment for Pentheus's misdeeds, but it also serves as a reminder of theater's dark origins. In this sense, too, *The Bacchae* is a characteristic late work, an occasion for the aging playwright to present a searching examination of his chosen art form, the theater.

At the same time that *The Bacchae* reaches far back into the history and prehistory of tragedy, it is also responding to the cultural changes of contemporary Athens. Over the course of the fifth century B.C.E., Athens had experienced an unprecedented rise in power, developing from a minor city-state to a sea-based empire dominating the Aegean and stretching east into Asia Minor and west to Sicily. Imperialism turned Athens into one of the most international of cities, with citizens of dependent or allied states living alongside Greeks. This new diversity undoubtedly contributed to the intellectual brilliance of the city—many of the philosophers, for example, were not originally from Athens—but it also forced traditional Greek culture to adapt to new customs and ways of life. This change forms the cultural background for *The Bacchae*, which presents the Dionysus cult as a specifically Asian and foreign cult whose acceptance in the Greek city of Thebes is anything but an easy matter.

The 1969 Yale Repertory Theatre production of *The Bacchae*, directed by Andre Gregory and designed by Santo Loquasto, featured a radically modern set design.

In addition to being foreign, Dionysus worship was rural. Pentheus is suspicious of the cult because it incites the women of Thebes to leave the ordered space of the city, which is under his firm control, and to revel instead in the mountains over which he has no dominion. Finally, the Dionysus cult was also a cult that appealed to the lower orders of Greece, not the elite. This division, too, is part of the texture of the play, which pits Pentheus against an unruly mass, represented by the chorus. The chorus of Greek tragedy had always, implicitly and explicitly, represented the people against the individual ruler, and in *The Bacchae*, Euripides uses this convention to great effect and to present a warning: if the ruler disregards the many, they will tear him to shreds. Like many other plays set in the rival city of Thebes, *The Bacchae* also served to gratify the democratic

audience of Athens, which had long accepted the Dionysus cult and had made it part of the city's civic and religious life. Euripides essentially congratulates Athens for having been more open-minded than Pentheus's Thebes.

The unusual construction of *The Bacchae*, simultaneously archaic and modern, philosophical and ritualistic, political and religious, has intrigued audiences from its first performance on. The play underwent a remarkable revival in the twentieth century, when playwrights and scholars developed a new interest in the ritualistic origins of theater. In recent decades, many leading playwrights and directors have produced versions of the *The Bacchae*, including the Nigerian Nobel Prize winner WOLE SOYINKA, whose adaptation (1973) emphasizes the multicultural dimension of the play, and the American playwright Charles L. Mee.

Among contemporary U.S. directors who have tackled the play is Richard Schechner, whose production *Dionysus in 69* (1968) was a central event for experimental theater in the 1960s. In 1978 the Japanese director Tadashi Suzuki created a compelling adaptation, mixing Japanese acting traditions with Western techniques.

These varied interpreters were drawn to Euripides because he had turned Greek tragedy into a form that reflected the political and cultural conflicts of his age. By bringing these conflicts to the fore, Euripides created plays that could be more easily adapted to new and different conflicts. Indeed, often no adaptation was necessary. The central conflicts depicted in his plays—attitudes toward the gods, responses to foreign influences, relations between the sexes—are as pressing and pertinent today as they were in the fifth century B.C.E. His contemporaries saw Euripides as modern, innovative, and daring, and he has remained so ever since.

M.P., J.E.G

Medea[1]

CHARACTERS

NURSE

TUTOR, *of Medea and Jason's sons*

MEDEA

CHORUS, *of Corinthian women*

CREON, *king of Corinth*

JASON

AEGEUS, *king of Athens*

MESSENGER

TWO BOYS, *sons of Medea and Jason*

SCENE: *A normal house on a street in Corinth. The elderly* NURSE *steps out of its front door.*

NURSE   I wish the *Argo*[2] never had set sail,
    had never flown to Colchis[3] through the dark
    Clashing Rocks; I wish the pines had never
    been felled along the hollows on the slopes
5   of Pelion[4] to fit their hands with oars—
    those heroes who went off to seek the golden
    pelt for Pelias[5] My mistress then,
    Medea, never would have sailed away

1. Translated by Diane Arnson Svarlien.
2. Jason's ship for his quest of the Golden Fleece; see introduction.
3. Medea's birthplace, across the Black Sea from Jason's homeland of Iolcos, now called

Volo.
4. Mountain in northeastern Greece near Iolcos.
5. Jason's uncle, usurper of the throne of Iolcos.

to reach the towers of Iolcus' land;
10   the sight of Jason never would have stunned
her spirit with desire. She would have never
persuaded Pelias' daughters to kill their father,[6]
never had to come to this land—Corinth.[7]
Here she's lived in exile with her husband
15   and children, and Medea's presence pleased
the citizens. For her part, she complied
with Jason in all things. There is no greater
security than this in all the world:
when a wife does not oppose her husband.
20   But now, there's only hatred. What should be
most loved has been contaminated, stricken
since Jason has betrayed them—his own children,
and my lady, for a royal bed.
He's married into power: Creon's daughter.
25   Poor Medea, mournful and dishonored,
shrieks at his broken oaths, the promise sealed
with his right hand (the greatest pledge there is)—
she calls the gods to witness just how well
Jason has repaid her. She won't touch food;
30   surrendering to pain, she melts away
her days in tears, ever since she learned
of this injustice. She won't raise her face;
her eyes are glued to the ground. Friends talk to her,
try to give her good advice; she listens
35   the way a rock does, or an ocean wave.
At most, she'll turn her pale neck aside,
sobbing to herself for her dear father,
her land, her home, and all that she betrayed
for Jason, who now holds her in dishonor.
40   This disaster made her realize:
a fatherland is no small thing to lose.
She hates her children, feels no joy in seeing them.
I'm afraid she might be plotting something.
Her mind is fierce, and she will not endure
45   ill treatment. I know her. I'm petrified
to think what thoughts she might be having now:
a sharpened knife-blade thrust right through the liver—
she could even strike the royal family, murder
the bridegroom too, make this disaster worse.
50   She's a terror. There's no way to be
her enemy and come out as the victor.
Here come the children, resting from their games,
with no idea of their mother's troubles.
A child's mind is seldom filled with pain.

[*Enter the* TUTOR *from the house with the two children of* JASON *and* MEDEA.]

6. See introduction.   7. City in southern Greece.

55 TUTOR   Timeworn stalwart of my mistress' household,
              why do you stand here by the gates, alone,
              crying out your sorrows to yourself?
              You've left Medea alone. Doesn't she need you?
   NURSE   Senior attendant to the sons of Jason,
60   decent servants feel their masters' griefs
              in their own minds, when things fall out all wrong.
              As for me, my pain was so intense
              that a desire crept over me to come out here
              and tell the earth and sky my mistress' troubles.
65 TUTOR   Poor thing. Is she not done with weeping yet?
   NURSE   What blissful ignorance! She's barely started.
   TUTOR   The fool—if one may say such things of masters—
              she doesn't even know the latest outrage.
   NURSE   What is it, old man? Don't begrudge me that.
70 TUTOR   Nothing. I'm sorry that I spoke at all.
   NURSE   By your beard, don't hide this thing from *me*,
              your fellow servant. I can keep it quiet.
   TUTOR   As I approached the place where the old men
              sit and play dice, beside the sacred spring
75   Peirene, I heard someone say—he didn't
              notice I was listening—that Creon,
              the ruler of this land, intends to drive
              these children and their mother out of Corinth.
              I don't know if it's true. I hope it isn't.
80 NURSE   Will Jason let his sons be so abused,
              even if he's fighting with their mother?
   TUTOR   He has a new bride; he's forgotten them.
              He's no friend to this household anymore.
   NURSE   We are destroyed, then. Before we've bailed our boat
85   from the first wave of sorrow, here's a new one.
   TUTOR   But please, don't tell your mistress. Keep it quiet.
              It's not the time for her to know of this.
   NURSE   Children, do you hear the way your father
              is treating you? I won't say, *May he die!*
90   —he is my master—but it's obvious
              he's harming those whom he should love. He's guilty.
   TUTOR   Who isn't? Are you just now learning this,
              that each man loves himself more than his neighbor?
              If their father doesn't cherish them, because
95   he's more preoccupied with his own bed—
   NURSE   Go inside now, children. Everything
              will be all right.
                    [*The* TUTOR *turns the children toward the house.*]
                          And you, keep them away—
              don't let them near their mother when she's like this.
              I've seen her: she looks fiercer than a bull;
100   she's giving them the eye, as if she means
              to do something. Her rage will not let up,
              I know, until she lashes out at someone.

May it be enemies she strikes, and not her loved ones!

[*In the following passage,* MEDEA *sings and the* NURSE *chants.*]

MEDEA   [*From within the house, crying out in rage.*]
Aaaah!
Oh, horrible, horrible, all that I suffer,
105   *my unhappy struggles. I wish I could die.*[8]

NURSE   You see, this is it. Dear children, your mother
has stirred up her heart, she has stirred up her rage.
Hurry up now and get yourselves inside the house—
but don't get too close to her, don't let her see you:
110   her ways are too wild, her nature is hateful,
her mind is too willful.
                    Go in. Hurry up!

[*Exit the* TUTOR *and the boys.*]

It's clear now, it's starting: a thunderhead rising,
swollen with groaning, and soon it will flash
as her spirit ignites it—then what will she do?
115   Her heart is so proud, there is no way to stop her;
her soul has been pierced by these sorrows.

MEDEA   *Aaaah!*
The pain that I've suffered, I've suffered so much,
worth oceans of weeping. O children, accursed,
may you die—with your father! Your mother is hateful.
120   *Go to hell, the whole household! Every last one.*

NURSE   Oh, lord. Here we go. What have *they* done—the children?
Their father's done wrong—why should you hate *them*?
Oh, children, my heart is so sore, I'm afraid
you will come to some harm.
                         Rulers are fierce
125   in their temperament; somehow, they will not be governed;
they like to have power, always, over others.
They're harsh, and they're stubborn. It's better to live
as an equal with equals. I never would want
to be grand and majestic—just let me grow old
130   in simple security. Even the *word*
"moderation" sounds good when you say it. For mortals
the middle is safest, in word and in deed.
Too much is too much, and there's always a danger
a god may get angry and ruin your household.

[*Enter the* CHORUS *of Corinthian women from the right, singing.*]

135   CHORUS   *I heard someone's voice, I heard someone shout:*
the woman from Colchis: poor thing, so unhappy.
Is her grief still unsoftened? Old woman, please tell us—
I heard her lament through the gates of my hall.
Believe me, old woman, I take no delight
140   *when this house is in pain. I have pledged it my friendship.*

---

8. Passages in italics indicate lyric sections that would have been sung with musical accompaniment.

NURSE   This house? It no longer exists. It's all gone.
    He's taken up with his new royal marriage.
    She's in her bedroom, my mistress, she's melting
    her life all away, and her mind can't be eased
145   by a single kind word from a single dear friend.
MEDEA   *Aaaah!*
    May a fire-bolt from heaven come shoot through my skull!
    What do I gain by being alive?
    Oh, god. How I long for the comfort of death.
    I hate this life. How I wish I could leave it.

[Strophe]

150 CHORUS   Do you hear, O Zeus, O sunlight and earth,
    this terrible song, the cry
    of this unhappy bride?
    Poor fool, what a dreadful longing,
    this craving for final darkness.
155   You'll hasten your death. Why do it?
    Don't pray for this ending.
    If your husband reveres a new bed, a new bride,
    don't sharpen your mind against him.
    You'll have Zeus himself supporting
160   your case. Don't dissolve in weeping
    for the sake of your bedmate.
MEDEA   *Great goddess Themis and Artemis, holy one:*[9]
    do you see what I suffer, although I have bound
    my detestable husband with every great oath?
165   *May I see him, along with his bride and the palace*
    scraped down to nothing, crushed into splinters.
    He started it. He was the one with the nerve
    to commit this injustice. Oh father, oh city,
    I left you in horror—I killed my own brother.[1]
170 NURSE   You hear what she says, and the gods that she prays to:
    Themis, and Zeus, the enforcer of oaths?
    There's no way my mistress' rage will die down
    into anything small.

[Antistrophe]

CHORUS   How I wish she'd come outside, let us see
175   her face, let her hear our words
    and the sound of our voice.
    If only she'd drop her anger,
    unburden her burning spirit,
    let go of this weight of madness.

9. Themis presided over petitions to the gods to ensure their reasonableness; Artemis, the Greek name for Diana, abjured marriage and protected women in childbirth.
1. See introduction.

180 I'll stand by our friendship.
Hurry up, bring her here, get her out, go inside,
and bring her to us. Go tell her
that we are her friends. Please hurry!
She's raging—the ones inside may
185 feel the sting of her sorrow.
       NURSE   I'll do as you ask, but I fear that my mistress
won't listen to me.
I will make the effort—what's one more attempt?
But her glare is as fierce as a bull's, let me tell you—
190 she's wild like a lion who's just given birth
whenever a servant tries telling her anything.

You wouldn't go wrong, you'd be right on the mark,
if you called them all half-wits, the people of old:
they made lovely songs for banquets and parties,
195 but no one took time to discover the music
that might do some good, the chords or the harmony
people could use to relieve all the hateful
pain and distress that leads to the downfall
of houses, the deaths and the dreadful misfortunes.
200 Let me tell you, there would be some gain in that—music
with the power to heal. When you're having a sumptuous
feast, what's the point of a voice raised in song?
Why bother with singing? The feast is enough
to make people happy. That's all that they need.
       [Exit the NURSE into the house.]
205 CHORUS   I heard a wail, a clear cry of pain;
she rails at the betrayer of her bed,
the bitter bridegroom.
For the injustice she suffers, she calls on the gods:
Themis of Zeus, protectress of oaths,
210 who brought her to Hellas,[2] over the salt water dark as night,
through the waves of Pontus' forbidding gate.[3]
       [Enter MEDEA from the house, attended by the NURSE and other female
       servants.[4] Here spoken dialogue resumes.]
   MEDEA   Women of Corinth, I have stepped outside
so you will not condemn me. Many people
act superior—I'm well aware of this.
215 Some keep it private; some are arrogant
in public view. Yet there are other people
who, just because they lead a quiet life,
are thought to be aloof. There is no justice
in human eyesight: people take one look
220 and hate a man, before they know his heart,

2. Greece.
3. Another name for the Black Sea, the "gate"
of which is the narrow strait known as the
Bosporus.
4. Nonspeaking roles, and thus not part of
the character list.

though no injustice has been done to them.
A foreigner must adapt to a new city,
certainly. Nor can I praise a citizen
who's willful, and who treats his fellow townsmen
225   harshly, out of narrow-mindedness.

My case is different. Unexpected trouble
has crushed my soul. It's over now; I take
no joy in life. My friends, I want to die.
My husband, who was everything to me—
230   how well I know it—is the worst of men.

Of all the living creatures with a soul
and mind, we women are the most pathetic.
First of all, we have to buy a husband:[5]
spend vast amounts of money, just to get
235   a master for our body—to add insult
to injury. And the stakes could not be higher:
will you get a decent husband, or a bad one?
If a woman leaves her husband, then she loses
her virtuous reputation. To refuse him
240   is just not possible. When a girl leaves home
and comes to live with new ways, different rules,
she has to be a prophet—learn somehow
the art of dealing smoothly with her bedmate.
If we do well, and if our husbands bear
245   the yoke without discomfort or complaint,
our lives are admired. If not, it's best to die.
A man, when he gets fed up with the people
at home, can go elsewhere to ease his heart
—he has friends, companions his own age.
250   We must rely on just one single soul.
They say that we lead safe, untroubled lives
at home while they do battle with the spear.
They're wrong. I'd rather take my stand behind
a shield three times than go through childbirth once.

255   Still, my account is quite distinct from yours.
This is your city. You have your fathers' homes,
your lives bring joy and profit. You have friends.
But I have been deserted and outraged—
left without a city by my husband,
260   who stole me as his plunder from the land
of the barbarians. Here I have no mother,
no brother, no blood relative to help
unmoor me from this terrible disaster.
So, I will need to ask you one small favor.

5. Ancient Greek custom dictated that the bride's family pay a dowry to the groom.

265   If I should find some way, some strategy
        to pay my husband back, bring him to justice,
        keep silent. Most of the time, I know, a woman
        is filled with fear. She's worthless in a battle
        and flinches at the sight of steel. But when
270   she's faced with an injustice in the bedroom,
        there is no other mind more murderous.
    CHORUS   I'll do as you ask. You're justified, Medea,
        in paying your husband back. I'm not surprised
        you grieve at your misfortunes.
                                    Look! I see Creon,
275   the lord of this land, coming toward us now.
        He has some new decision to announce.

        [*Enter* CREON *from the right, with attendants.*]

    CREON   You with the grim face, fuming at your husband,
        Medea, I hereby announce that you
        must leave this land, an exile, taking with you
280   your two children. You must not delay.
        This is my decision. I won't leave
        until I've thrown you out, across the border.
    MEDEA   Oh, god. I'm crushed; I'm utterly destroyed.
        My enemies, their sails unfurled, attack me,
285   and there's no land in sight, there's no escape
        from ruin. Although I suffer, I must ask:
        Creon, why do you send me from this land?
    CREON   I'll speak plainly: I'm afraid of you.
        You could hurt my daughter, even kill her.
290   Every indication points that way.
        You're wise by nature, you know evil arts,
        and you're upset because your husband's gone
        away from your bedroom. I have heard reports
        that you've made threats, that you've devised a plan
295   to harm the bride, her father, and the bridegroom.
        I want to guard against that. I would rather
        have you hate me, woman, here and now,
        than treat you gently and regret it later.
    MEDEA   Oh, god.
        Creon, this is not the first time: often
300   I've been injured by my reputation.
        Any man who's sensible by nature
        will set a limit on his children's schooling
        to make sure that they never grow too wise.
        The wise are seen as lazy, and they're envied
305   and hated. If you offer some new wisdom
        to half-wits, they will only think you're useless.
        And those who are considered experts hate you
        when the city thinks you're cleverer than they are.
        I myself have met with this reaction.
310   Since I am wise, some people envy me,

some think I'm idle, some the opposite,
and some feel threatened. Yet I'm not all that wise.

And you're afraid of me. What do you fear?
Don't worry, Creon. I don't have it in me
315 to do wrong to a man with royal power.
What injustice have you done to me?
Your spirit moved you, and you gave your daughter
as you saw fit. My husband is the one
I hate. You acted well, with wise restraint.
320 And now, I don't begrudge your happiness.
My best to all of you—celebrate the wedding.
Just let me stay here. I know when I'm beaten.
I'll yield to this injustice. I'll submit
in silence to those greater than myself.
325 CREON Your words are soothing, but I'm terrified
of what's in your mind. I trust you less than ever.
It's easier to guard against a woman
(or man, for that matter) with a fiery spirit
than one who's wise and silent. You must leave
330 at once—don't waste my time with talk. It's settled.
Since you are my enemy, and hate me,
no ruse of yours can keep you here among us.

> [MEDEA *kneels before* CREON *and grasps his hand and knees in*
> *supplication.*]

 MEDEA No, by your knees! By your new-married daughter!
 CREON You're wasting words. There's no way you'll persuade me.
335 MEDEA You'll drive me out, with no reverence for my prayers?
 CREON I care more for my family than for you.
 MEDEA How clearly I recall my fatherland.
 CREON Yes, that's what *I* love most—after my children.
 MEDEA Oh, god—the harm Desire does to mortals!
340 CREON Depending on one's fortunes, I suppose.
 MEDEA Zeus, do not forget who caused these troubles.
 CREON Just leave, you fool. I'm tired of struggling with you.
 MEDEA Struggles. Yes. I've had enough myself.
 CREON My guards will force you out in just a moment.
345 MEDEA Oh, please, not that! Creon, I entreat you!
 CREON You intend to make a scene, I gather.
 MEDEA I'll leave, don't worry. That's not what I'm asking.
 CREON Why are you forcing me? Let go of my hand!
 MEDEA Please, let me stay just one more day, that's all.
350 I need to make arrangements for my exile,
find safe asylum for my children, since
their father doesn't give them any thought.
Take pity on them. You yourself have children.
It's only right for you to treat them kindly.
355 If we go into exile, I'm not worried
about myself—I weep for their disaster.

CREON   I haven't got a ruler's temperament;
reverence has often led me into ruin.
Woman, I realize this is all wrong,
360   but you shall have your wish. I warn you, though:
if the sun god's lamp should find you and your children
still within our borders at first rising,
it means your death. I've spoken; it's decided.
Stay for one day only, if you must.
365   You won't have time to do the things I fear.

[*Exit* CREON *and attendants to the right.* MEDEA *rises to her feet.*]

CHORUS   Oh, god! This is horrible, unhappy woman,
the grief that you suffer. Where will you turn?
Where will you find shelter? What country, what home
will save you from sorrow? A god has engulfed you,
370   Medea—this wave is now breaking upon you,
there is no way out.

MEDEA   Yes, things are all amiss. Who could deny it?
Believe me, though, that's not how it will end.
The newlyweds have everything at stake,
375   and struggles await the one who made this match.
Do you think I ever could have fawned
on him like that without some gain in mind,
some ruse? I never would have spoken to him,
or touched him with my hands. He's such an idiot.
380   He could have thrown me out, destroyed my plans;
instead he's granted me a single day
to turn three enemies to three dead bodies:
the father, and the bride, and my own husband.
I know so many pathways to their deaths,
385   I don't know which to turn to first, my friends.
Shall I set the bridal home on fire,
creeping silently into their bedroom?

There's just one threat. If I am apprehended
entering the house, my ruse discovered,
390   I'll be put to death; my enemies
will laugh at me. The best way is the most
direct, to use the skills I have by nature
and poison them, destroy them with my drugs.

Ah, well.

All right, they die. What city will receive me?
395   What host will offer me immunity,
what land will take me in and give me refuge?
There's no one. I must wait just long enough
to see if any sheltering tower appears.
Then I will kill in silence, by deceit.
400   But if I have no recourse from disaster,
I'll take the sword and kill them, even if

it means my death. I have the utmost nerve.
Now, by the goddess whom I most revere,
Hecate,[6] whom I choose as my accomplice,
405   who dwells within my inmost hearth, I swear:
no one can hurt my heart and then fare well.
I'll turn their marriage bitter, desolate—
they'll regret the match, regret my exile.

And now, spare nothing that is in your knowledge,
410   Medea: make your plan, prepare your ruse.
Do this dreadful thing. There is so much
at stake. Display your courage. Do you see
how you are suffering? Do not allow
these Sisyphean snakes[7] to laugh at you
415   on Jason's wedding day. Your father is noble;
your grandfather is Helios. You have
the knowledge, not to mention woman's nature:
for any kind of noble deed, we're helpless;
for malice, though, our wisdom is unmatched.

CHORUS

[Strophe 1]

420   The streams of the holy rivers are flowing backward.
Everything runs in reverse—justice is upside down.
Men's minds are deceitful, and nothing is settled,
not even oaths that are sworn by the gods.
The tidings will change, and a virtuous reputation
425   will grace my name. The race of women will reap
honor, no longer the shame of disgraceful rumor.

[Antistrophe 1]

The songs of the poets of old will no longer linger
on my untrustworthiness. Women were never sent
the gift of divine inspiration by Phoebus
430   Apollo, lord of the elegant lyre,[8]
the master of music—or I could have sung my own song
against the race of men. The fullness of time
holds many tales: it can speak of both men and women.

[Strophe 2]

You sailed away from home and father,
435   driven insane in your heart; you traced a path
between the twin cliffs of Pontus.[9]

---

6. Goddess of magic or enchantment.
7. Derogatory reference to the Corinthians.
Sisyphus was an early king of Corinth known
for his cruelty; to be linked to Sisyphus was
thus an insult. See also note 8, p. 266.

8. Apollo, god of the sun, was often figured
with this stringed instrument.
9. An ancient region along the southern coast
of the Black Sea.

The land you live in is foreign.
Your bed is empty, your husband
gone. Poor woman, dishonored,
440   sent into exile.

[Antistrophe 2]

The Grace of oaths is gone, and Reverence
flies away into the sky, abandoning
great Hellas. No father's dwelling
unmoors you now from this heartache.
445   Your bed now yields to another:
now a princess prevails,
greater than you are.

[*Enter* JASON *from the right.*]

JASON   This is not the first time—I have often
observed that a fierce temper is an evil
450   that leaves you no recourse. You could have stayed
here in this land, you could have kept your home
by simply acquiescing in the plans
of those who are greater. You are now an exile
because of your own foolish words. To me
455   it makes no difference. You can keep on calling
Jason the very worst of men. However,
the words you spoke against the royal family—
well, consider it a gain that nothing worse
than exile is your punishment. As for me,
460   I wanted you to stay. I always tried
to calm the king, to soothe his fuming rage.
But you, you idiot, would not let up
your words against the royal family. That's why
you are now an exile. All the same,
465   I won't let down my loved ones. I have come here
looking out for your best interests, woman,
so you won't be without the things you need
when you go into exile with the children.
You'll need money—banishment means hardship.
470   However much you hate me, I could never
wish you any harm.
    MEDEA   You are the worst!
You're loathsome—that's the worst word I can utter.
You're not a man. You've come here—most detested
by the gods, by me, by all mankind.
475   That isn't courage, when you have the nerve
to harm your friends, then look them in the face.
No, that's the worst affliction known to man:
shamelessness.
                And yet, I'm glad you've come.
Speaking ill to you will ease my soul,
480   and listening will cause you pain. I'll start

at the beginning. First, I saved your life—
as every single man who sailed from Hellas
aboard the *Argo* knows—when you were sent
to yoke the fire-breathing bulls, and sow
485   the deadly crop.[1] I killed the dragon, too:
the sleepless one, who kept the Golden Fleece
enfolded in his convoluted coils;[2]
I was your light, the beacon of your safety.
For my part, I betrayed my home, my father,
490   and went with you to Pelion's slopes, Iolcus
with more good will than wisdom—and I killed
Pelias, in the cruelest possible way:
at his own children's hands. I ruined their household.

And you—you *are* the very worst of men—
495   betrayed me, after all of that. You wanted
a new bed, even though I'd borne you children.
If you had still been childless, anyone
could understand your lust for this new marriage.

All trust in oaths is gone. What puzzles me
500   is whether you believe those gods (the ones
who heard you swear) no longer are in power,
or that the old commandments have been changed?
You realize full well you broke your oath.

Ah, my right hand, which you took so often,
505   clinging to my knees.[3] What was the point
of touching me? You are despicable.
My hopes have all gone wrong. Well, then! You're here:
I have a question for you, friend to friend.
(What good do I imagine it will do?
510   Still, I'll ask, since it makes you look worse.)
Where do I turn now? To my father's household
and fatherland, which I betrayed for you?
Or Pelias' poor daughters? Naturally
they'll welcome me—the one who killed their father!

515   Here is my situation. I've become
an enemy to my own family, those
whom I should love, and I have gone to war
with those whom I had no reason at all
to hurt, and all for your sake. In exchange,
520   you've made me the happiest girl in all of Hellas.

---

1. Aeetes, king of Colchis, challenged Jason
with a series of tasks during his quest for the
Golden Fleece; among these were the requirements that he harness two fire-breathing
bulls, plow with them, and sow dragons' teeth
that sprouted warriors he then had to kill.
2. The Golden Fleece was guarded by a powerful serpent; see introduction.
3. Thus in a position of supplication.

I have you, the perfect spouse, a marvel,
so trustworthy—though I must leave the country
friendless and deserted, taking with me
my friendless children! What a charming scandal
525   for a newlywed: your children roam
as beggars, with the one who saved your life.

Zeus! For brass disguised as gold, you sent us
reliable criteria to judge.
But when a man is base, how can we know?
530   Why is there no sign stamped upon his body?
CHORUS   This anger is a terror, hard to heal,
when loved ones clash with loved ones in dispute.
JASON   It seems that I must have a way with words
and, like a skillful captain, reef my sails
535   in order to escape this gale that blows
without a break—your endless, tired harangue.
The way I see it, woman (since you seem
to feel that I must owe you some huge favor),
it was Cypris,[4] no other god or mortal,
540   who saved me on my voyage. Yes, your mind
is subtle. But I must say—at the risk
of stirring up your envy and your grudges—
Eros[5] was the one who forced your hand:
his arrows, which are inescapable,
545   compelled you to rescue me. But I won't put
too fine a point on that. You *did* support me.
You saved my life, in fact. However, you
received more than you gave, as I shall prove.
First of all, you live in Hellas now
550   instead of your barbarian land. With us,
you know what justice is, and civil law:
not mere brute force. And every single person
in Hellas knows that you are wise. You're famous.
You'd never have that kind of reputation
555   if you were living at the edge of nowhere.
As for me, I wouldn't wish for gold
or for a sweeter song than Orpheus'[6]
unless I had the fame to match my fortune.

Enough about my struggles—you're the one
560   who started this debate. As for my marriage
to the princess, which you hold against me,
I shall show you how I acted wisely
and with restraint, and with the greatest love
toward you and toward our children—Wait! Just listen!

4. Another name for the Greek goddess
Aphrodite.
5. God of love.

6. Orpheus received a lyre from Apollo, upon
which he played music of unparalleled beauty.

565 When I moved here from Iolcus, bringing with me
    disaster in abundance, with no recourse,
    what more lucky windfall could I find
    (exile that I was) than marrying
    the king's own child? It's not that I despised
570 your bed—the thought that irritates you most—
    nor was I mad with longing for a new bride,
    or trying to compete with anyone—
    to win the prize for having the most children.
    I have enough—no reason to complain.
575 My motive was the best: so we'd live well
    and not be poor. I know that everyone
    avoids a needy friend. I wanted to raise
    sons in a style that fits my family background,
    give brothers to the ones I had with you,
580 and treat them all as equals. This would strengthen
    the family, and I'd be blessed with fortune.
    What do *you* need children for? For me, though,
    it's good if I can use my future children
    to benefit my present ones. Is that
585 bad planning? If you weren't so irritated
    about your bed, you'd never say it was.
    But you're a woman—and you're all the same!
    If everything goes well between the sheets
    you think you have it all. But let there be
590 some setback or disaster in the bedroom
    and suddenly you go to war against
    the things that you should value most. I mean it—
    men should really have some other method
    for getting children. The whole female race
595 should not exist. It's nothing but a nuisance.
  CHORUS   Jason, you've composed a lovely speech.
    But I must say, though you may disagree:
    you have betrayed your wife. You've been unjust.
  MEDEA   Now, this is where I differ from most people.
600 In my view, someone who is both unjust
    and has a gift for speaking—such a man
    incurs the greatest penalty. He uses
    his tongue to cover up his unjust actions,
    and this gives him the nerve to stop at nothing
605 no matter how outrageous. Yet he's not
    all that wise. Take your case, for example.

    Spare me this display of cleverness;
    a single word will pin you to the mat.
    If you weren't in the wrong, you would have told me
610 your marriage plans, not kept us in the dark—
    your loved ones, your own family!
  JASON   Yes, of course
    you would have been all for it! Even now

you can't control your rage against the marriage.

MEDEA   That's not what you were thinking. You imagined

615   that for an older man, a barbarian wife
       was lacking in prestige.

JASON   No! Please believe me:
       It wasn't for the woman's sake I married
       into the king's family. As I have said,
       I wanted to save you, and give our children

620   royal brothers, a safeguard for our household.

MEDEA   May I not have a life that's blessed with fortune
       so painful, or prosperity so irritating.

JASON   Your prayer could be much wiser: don't consider
       what's useful painful. When you have good fortune,

625   don't see it as a hardship.

MEDEA   Go ahead—
       you have somewhere to turn!—commit this outrage.
       I am deserted, exiled from this land.

JASON   You brought that on yourself. Don't blame another.

MEDEA   Did I remarry? How did I betray you?

630 JASON   You blasphemously cursed the royal family.

MEDEA   And I'm a curse to your family as well.

JASON   I won't discuss this with you any further.
       If you'd like me to help you and the children
       with money for your exile, then just say so.

635   I'm prepared to give with an open hand,
       and make arrangements with my friends to show you
       hospitality. They'll treat you well.
       You'd be an idiot to refuse this offer.
       You'll gain a lot by giving up your anger.

640 MEDEA   I wouldn't stay with your friends, and I would never
       accept a thing from you. Don't even offer.
       There is no profit in a bad man's gift.

JASON   All the same, I call the gods to witness:
       I only want to help you and the children.

645   But you don't want what's good; you push away
       your friends; you're willful. And you'll suffer for it.

MEDEA   Get out of here. A craving for your new bride
       has overcome you—you've been away so long.
       Go, celebrate your wedding. It may be

650   (the gods will tell) a marriage you'll regret.

       [*Exit* JASON *to the right.*]

CHORUS

                    [Strophe 1]

       Desire, when it comes on too forcefully, never bestows
       excellence, never makes anyone prestigious.
       When she comes with just the right touch, there's no goddess
            more gracious
       than Cypris.

655   Mistress, never release from your golden bow
    an inescapable arrow, smeared with desire
    and aimed at my heart.

[Antistrophe 1]

    Please, let me be cherished by Wisdom, be loved by Restraint,
    loveliest gift of the gods. May dreadful Cypris
660   never stun my spirit with love for the bed of another
    and bring on
    anger, battles of words, endless fighting, strife.
    Let her be shrewd in her judgment; let her revere
    the bedroom at peace.

[Strophe 2]

665   O fatherland, O home, never allow
    me to be without a city:
    a grief without recourse, life that's hard to live through,
    most distressing of all fates.
    May I go to my death, my death
670   before I endure that; I'd rather face
    my final day. There's no worse heartache
    than to be cut off from your fatherland.

[Antistrophe 2]

    We've seen it for ourselves; nobody else
    gave me this tale to consider.
675   No city, no friend will treat you with compassion
    in your dreadful suffering.
    May he die, the ungracious man
    who won't honor friends, who will not unlock
    his mind to clear, calm thoughts of kindness.
680   I will never call such a man my friend.

        [*Enter* AEGEUS *from the left.*][7]

AEGEUS   Medea, I wish all the best to you.
    There is no finer way to greet a friend.
MEDEA   All the best to you, Aegeus, son
    of wise Pandion. Where are you traveling from?
685 AEGEUS   I've come from Phoebus' ancient oracle.[8]
MEDEA   What brought you to the earth's prophetic navel?
AEGEUS   Seeking how I might beget a child.
MEDEA   By the gods, are you still childless?
AEGEUS   Still childless. Some god must be to blame.

---

7. While the unanticipated arrival of the king of Athens at this part in the play may appear odd, Athenian audiences would have understood this episode as part of the larger Medea myth; see introduction.

8. The shrine of Phoebus Apollo, located in Delphi, was known as the "navel stone," where east and west meet, and was thus considered the center of the world.

690 MEDEA   Do you have a wife, or do you sleep alone?

AEGEUS   I'm married, and we share a marriage bed.

MEDEA   Well, what did Phoebus say concerning children?

AEGEUS   His words were too profound for human wisdom.

MEDEA   May I hear the oracle? Is it permitted?

695 AEGEUS   Yes, why not? This calls for a wise mind.

MEDEA   Then tell me, if indeed it is permitted.

AEGEUS   He said, "Don't loose the wineskin's hanging foot . . ."⁹

MEDEA   Before you do what thing? Or reach what place?

AEGEUS   Before returning to my paternal hearth.

700 MEDEA   And why have you sailed here? What do you need?

AEGEUS   There is a man named Pittheus, lord of Troezen . . .¹

MEDEA   Pelops' son.² They say he's very pious.

AEGEUS   I want to bring this prophecy to him.

MEDEA   Yes. He's wise, and well-versed in such things.

705 AEGEUS   And most beloved of my war companions.

MEDEA   Good luck to you. May you get what you desire.

AEGEUS   But you—your eyes are melting. What's the matter?

MEDEA   My husband is the very worst of men.

AEGEUS   What are you saying? Why the low spirits? Tell me.

710 MEDEA   Jason treats me unjustly. I've done him no harm.

AEGEUS   What has he done? Explain to me more clearly.

MEDEA   He has another wife, who takes my place.

AEGEUS   No. He wouldn't dare. It's much too shameful.

MEDEA   It's true. His former loved ones are dishonored.

715 AEGEUS   Did he desire another? Or tire of you?

MEDEA   Oh yes, he felt desire. We cannot trust him.

AEGEUS   Let him go, if he's as bad as you say.

MEDEA   He desired a royal marriage-bond.

AEGEUS   Who's giving away the bride? Go on, continue.

720 MEDEA   Creon, the ruler of this land of Corinth.

AEGEUS   Woman, your pain is understandable.

MEDEA   I am destroyed. And that's not all—I'm exiled.

AEGEUS   By whom? This is new trouble on top of trouble.

MEDEA   By Creon. He is driving me from Corinth.

725 AEGEUS   And Jason is allowing it? Shame on him.

MEDEA   He claims to be against it, but he'll manage
          to endure it somehow.

          [MEDEA *again assumes the supplicant position.*]

                    Listen, I entreat you;
          by your beard and by your knees, I beg you:
          Have pity on me; pity my misfortune.

---

9. An ambiguous prophecy based on the image of wine stored in the shank portion of an animal skin; see also next note.

1. In this Athenian legend, Pittheus knows that the prophecy means that Aegeus is not to drink wine until he returns to Athens. Pittheus, however, withholds this information,

allows Aegeus to drink to excess, and then allows him to sleep with his daughter Aethra. The Athenian hero Theseus is the product of this encounter.

2. The hero Pelops founded the Peloponnese, the peninsula in the south of Greece.

730   Don't let me go deserted into exile;
       receive me in your home and at your hearth.
       If you do it, may the gods grant your desire
       for children; may you die a prosperous man.
       You don't know what a windfall you have found!
735   I'll cure your childlessness, make you a father.
       I know the drugs required for such things.
       AEGEUS   For many reasons, woman, I am eager
       to grant this favor to you: first, the gods;
       and secondly, the children that you promise.
740   I'm at a total loss where that's concerned.
       But this is how it is. When you arrive,
       I'll treat you justly, try to shelter you.
       However, you must know this in advance:
       I'm not willing to escort you from this land.
745   If you can come to my house on your own,
       I'll let you stay there—it will be your refuge.
       I will not give you up to anyone.
       But you must leave this land all by yourself.
       My hosts here must have no complaint with me.
750   MEDEA   So be it. But if I had some assurance
       that I could trust you, I'd have all I need.
       AEGEUS   You don't believe me? Tell me, what's the problem?
       MEDEA   Oh, I believe you. But I have enemies:
       Creon, and the house of Pelias.
755   If they come for me, and you're not bound
       by any oath, then you might let them take me.
       A promise in words only, never sworn
       by any gods, might not be strong enough
       to keep you from befriending them, from yielding
760   to their delegations. I'm completely helpless;
       they have prosperity and royal power.
       AEGEUS   Your words show forethought. If you think it's best,
       I'll do it without any hesitation.
       In fact, this is the safest course for me:
765   I'll have a good excuse to turn away
       your enemies. And things are settled well
       for you, of course. I'll swear: just name the gods.
       MEDEA   Swear by the Earth we stand on, and by Helios[3]—
       my father's father—and the whole race of gods.
770   AEGEUS   To do or not do what? Just say the word.
       MEDEA   Never to expel me from your land yourself,
       and never, as long as you live, to give me up
       willingly to any enemy.
       AEGEUS   I swear by Earth, by Helios' sacred light,
775   by all the gods: I'll do just as you say.

3. The sun.

MEDEA   Fine. And if you don't? What would you suffer?

AEGEUS   Whatever an unholy man deserves.

      [MEDEA *rises.*]

MEDEA   Farewell, then, on your voyage. This is good.
    I'll find you in your city very soon,
780   once I've done my will, and had my way.

      [*Exit* AEGEUS *to the left. The* CHORUS *address him as he leaves.*]

CHORUS   May lord Hermes, the child of Maia,[4] escort you
    and bring you back home. May you do as you please,
    and have all you want. In my judgment, Aegeus,
    you're a good, noble man.

785 MEDEA   O Zeus, and Zeus's Justice, and the light
    of Helios, I now shall be the victor
    over my enemies. My friends, I've set my foot
    upon the path. My enemies will pay
    what justice demands—I now have hope of this.
790   This man, when I was at my lowest point,
    appeared, the perfect harbor for my plans.
    When I reach Pallas' city,[5] I shall have
    a steady place to tie my ship. And now
    I'll tell you what my plans are. Hear my words;
795   they will not bring you pleasure. I will send
    a servant to bring Jason here to see me.
    When he comes, I'll soothe him with my words:
    I'll say that I agree with him, that he
    was right to marry into the royal family,
800   betraying me—well done, and well thought out!
    "But let my children stay here!" I will plead—
    not that I would leave them in this land
    for my enemies to outrage—my own children.
    No: this is my deceit, to kill the princess.
805   I'll send them to her, bearing gifts in hand
    —a delicate robe, and a garland worked in gold.
    If she takes these fine things and puts them on,
    she, and anyone who touches her,
    will die a painful death. Such are the drugs
810   with which I will smear them.
                    But enough of that.
    Once that's done, the next thing I must do
    chokes me with sorrow. I will kill the children—
    my children. No one on this earth can save them.
    I'll ruin Jason's household, then I'll leave
815   this land, I'll flee the slaughter of the children
    I love so dearly. I will have the nerve
    for this unholy deed. You see, my friends,
    I will not let my enemies laugh at me.

---

4. The nymph Maia bore Hermes, who became
the gods' messenger.

5. Another name for Athens, protected by
Pallas Athene.

Let it go. What do I gain by being alive?
820 I have no fatherland, no home, no place
to turn from troubles. The moment I went wrong
was when I left my father's house, persuaded
by the words of that Greek man. If the gods will help me,
he'll pay what justice demands. He'll never see
825 them alive again, the children that I bore him.
Nor will he ever father another child:
his new bride, evil woman, she must die
an evil death, extinguished by my drugs.
Let no one think that I'm a simpleton,
830 or weak, or idle—I am the opposite.
I treat my friends with kindness, and come down hard
on the heads of my enemies. This is the way to live,
the way to win a glorious reputation.
CHORUS   Since you have brought this plan to us, and since
835 I want to help you, and since I support
the laws of mankind, I ask you not to do this.
MEDEA   There is no other way. It's understandable
that you would say this—you're not the one who's suffered.
CHORUS   Will you have the nerve to kill your children?
840 MEDEA   Yes: to wound my husband the most deeply.
CHORUS   And to make yourself the most miserable of women.
MEDEA   Let it go. Let there be no more words
until it's done.
        [*To her attendant.*]
You: go now, and bring Jason.
When I need to trust someone, I turn to you.
845 If you're a woman and mean well to your mistress,
do not speak of the things I have resolved.
        [*Exit the attendant to the right.*]
CHORUS

[Strophe 1]

The children of Erechtheus[6] have always prospered,
descended from blessèd gods.
They graze, in their sacred stronghold, on glorious
    wisdom,
850 with a delicate step through the clear and brilliant air.
They say that there
the nine Pierian Muses[7] once gave birth
to Harmony with golden hair.

6. Legendary king of Athens; metaphorically,   7. The Muses inspire creativity, especially in
his children are the Athenians.   poetry and music.

[Antistrophe 1]

They sing that Cypris dipped her pitcher in the waters
855   of beautiful Cephisus;[8]
      she sighed, and her breaths were fragrant
          and temperate breezes.
      With a garland of sweet-smelling roses in her hair
      she sends Desires
      to take their places alongside Wisdom's throne
860   and nurture excellence with her.

[Strophe 2]

      How can this city
      of holy rivers,
      receiver of friends and loved ones,
      receive you—when you've murdered your own children,
865   most unholy woman—among them?
      Just think of this deathblow aimed at the helpless,
      think of the slaughter you'll have on your hands.
      Oh no, by your knees, we beg you,
      we beg you, with every plea
870   we can plead: do not kill your children.

[Antistrophe 2]

      Where will you find it,
      the awful courage?
      The terrible nerve—how can you?
      How can your hand, your heart, your mind go through with
875   this slaughter? How will you be able
      to look at your children, keep your eyes steady,
      see them beseech you, and not fall apart?
      Your tears will not let you kill them;
      your spirit, your nerve will fail:
880   you will not soak your hands in their blood.
          [Enter JASON from the right.]
    JASON   I've come because you summoned me. Despite
      the hate between us, I will hear you out.
      What is it this time, woman? What do you want?
    MEDEA   Jason, I beg you, please forgive the things
885   I said. Your heart should be prepared, receptive
      like a seed bed. We used to love each other.
      It's only right for you to excuse my anger.
      I've thought it over, and I blame myself.
      Pathetic! Really, I must have been insane
890   to stand opposed to those who plan so well,
      to be an enemy to those in power
      and to my husband, who's done so well by me:

---

8. River in Athens.

marrying the royal princess, to beget
brothers for my children. Isn't it time
895   to drop my angry spirit, since the gods
have been so bountiful? What's wrong with me?
Don't I have children? Aren't we exiles? Don't we
need whatever friendship we can get?
That's what I said to myself. I realize
900   that I've been foolish, that there is no point
to all my fuming rage. I give you credit
for wise restraint, for making this connection,
this marriage that's in all our interests. Now
I understand that you deserve my praise.
905   I was such a moron. I should have supported
your plans, I should have made arrangements with you,
I should have stood beside the bridal bed,
rejoiced in taking care of your new bride.

We women—oh, I won't say that we're bad,
910   but we are what we are. You shouldn't sink
down to our level, trading childish insults.
I ask for your indulgence. I admit
I wasn't thinking straight, but now my plans
are much improved where these things are concerned.
        [MEDEA *turns toward the house to call the children.*]
915   Oh, children! Come out of the house, come here,
come out and greet your father, speak to him.
Come set aside, together with your mother,
the hatred that we felt toward one we love.
        [*The children come out from the house, escorted
        by the* TUTOR *and attendants.*]
We've made a treaty. My rage has gone away.
920   Take his right hand.
                              Oh, god, my mind is filled
with bad things, hidden things. Oh, children, look—
your lovely arms, the way you stretch them out.
Will you look this way your whole long lives?
I think I'm going to cry. I'm filled with fear.
925   After all this time, I'm making up
my quarrel with your father. This tender sight
is washed with tears; my eyes are overflowing.
CHORUS   In my eyes too fresh tears are welling up.
May this evil not go any further.
930   JASON   Woman, I approve your new approach—
not that I blame you for the way you felt.
It's only right for a female to get angry
if her husband smuggles in another wife.
But this new change of heart is for the best.
935   After all this time, you've recognized
the winning plan. You're showing wise restraint.

And as for you, my children, you will see
your father is no fool. I have provided
for your security, if the gods will help me.
940   Yes, I believe that you will be the leaders
here in Corinth, with your future brothers.
Grow up strong and healthy. All the rest
your father, with the favor of the gods,
will take care of. I pray that I may see you
945   grown up and thriving, holding sway above
my enemies.

       [JASON *turns to* MEDEA.]

          You! Why have you turned
your face away, so pale? Why are fresh tears
pouring from your eyes? Why aren't you happy
to hear what I have had to say?
MEDEA   It's nothing.
950   I was only thinking of the children.
JASON   Don't worry now. I'll take good care of them.
MEDEA   I'll do as you ask. I'll trust in what you say.
I'm female, that's all. Tears are in my nature.
JASON   So—why go on? Why moan over the children?
955   MEDEA   They're mine. And when you prayed that they would live,
pity crept over me. I wondered: would they?
As for the things you came here to discuss,
we've covered one. I'll move on to the next.
Since the royal family has seen fit
960   to exile me (and yes, I realize
it's for the best—I wouldn't want to stay
to inconvenience you, or this land's rulers,
who see me as an enemy of the family),
I will leave this land, go into exile,
965   but you must raise your children with your own hand:
ask Creon that they be exempt from exile.
JASON   Though I may not persuade him, I must try.
MEDEA   And ask your wife to ask her father: please
let the children be exempt from exile.
970   JASON   Certainly. I think I will persuade her.
MEDEA   No doubt, if she's a woman like all others.
And for this work, I'll lend you my support.
I'll send her gifts, much lovelier, I know,
than any living person has laid eyes on:
975   a delicate robe, and a garland worked in gold.
The children will bear them. Now, this very minute,
let one of the servants bring these fine things here.

      [*An attendant goes into the house to carry out this request.*
      She, or another servant, returns with the finery.]

She will be blessed a thousandfold with fortune:
with you, an excellent man to share her bed,
980   and these possessions, these fine things that once

my father's father, Helios, passed down
to his descendants. Take these wedding gifts
in your arms, my children; go and give them
to the lucky bride, the royal princess.
985   These are gifts that no one could find fault with.
       [*The attendant puts the gifts in the children's arms.*]
   JASON   You fool! Why let these things out of your hands?
       Do you think the royal household needs more robes,
       more gold? Hold on to these. Don't give them up.
       If my wife thinks anything of me,
990   I'm sure that I mean more to her than wealth.
   MEDEA   Don't say that. Even the gods can be persuaded
       by gifts. And gold is worth a thousand words.
       She has the magic charm; the gods are helping
       her right now: she's young, and she has power.
995   To save my children from exile, I'd give my life,
       not merely gold. You, children, when you've entered
       that wealthy house, must supplicate your father's
       young wife, my mistress. You must plead with her
       and ask her that you be exempt from exile.
1000   Give her these fine things. That is essential:
       she must receive these gifts with her own hands.
       Go quickly now, and bring back to your mother
       the good news she desires—that you've succeeded.
       [*The children, bearing the gifts, leave with the* TUTOR *to the right.*]
   CHORUS

[Strophe 1]

       Now I no longer have hope that the children will live,
1005   no longer. They walk to the slaughter already.
       The bride will receive the crown of gold;
       she'll receive her horrible ruin.
       Upon her golden hair, with her very own hands,
       she'll place the fine circlet of Hades.[9]

[Antistrophe 1]

1010   She'll be persuaded; the grace and the heavenly gleam
       will move her to try on the robe and the garland.
       The bride will adorn herself for death,
       for the shades below. She will fall
       into this net; her death will be horrible. Ruin
1015   will be inescapable, fated.

[Strophe 2]

       And you, poor thing, bitter bridegroom, in-law to
           royalty:

9. Death.

you don't know you're killing your children,
bringing hateful death to your bride.
How horrible: how unaware you are of your fate.

[Antistrophe 2]

1020   I cry for your pain in turn, poor thing; you're a
                mother, yet
        you will slaughter them, your own children,
        for the sake of your bridal bed,
        the bed that your husband now shares with somebody else.

        [The TUTOR returns, at the right, from the palace with the
        children.]

TUTOR   Mistress, your children are released from exile.
1025   The princess happily received the gifts
       with her own hands. As far as she's concerned,
       the children's case is settled; they're at peace.

       Ah!
       Why are you upset by your good fortune?
MEDEA   Oh, god.
TUTOR   Your cry is out of tune. This is good news!
1030 MEDEA   Oh god, oh god.
TUTOR   Have I made some mistake?
       Is what I've said bad news, and I don't know it?
MEDEA   You've said what you have said. I don't blame you.
TUTOR   So—why are you crying? Why are your eyes cast down?
MEDEA   Old man, I am compelled. The gods and I
1035   devised this strategy. What was I thinking?
TUTOR   Don't worry now. Your children will bring you home.
MEDEA   I'll send others home before that day.
TUTOR   You're not the only woman who's lost her children.
       We're mortals. We must bear disasters lightly.
1040 MEDEA   I'll do as you ask. Now, go inside the house
       and see to the children's needs, as usual.

       [Exit TUTOR into the house.]

       Oh, children, children, you two have a city
       and home, in which you'll live forever parted
       from your mother. You'll leave poor me behind.
1045   I'll travel to another land, an exile,
       before I ever have the joy of seeing
       you blessed with fortune—before your wedding days,
       before I prepare your beds and hold the torches.[1]
       My willfulness has cost me all this grief.
1050   I raised you, children, but it was no use;
       no use, the way I toiled, how much it hurt,
       the pain of childbirth, piercing like a thorn.

---

1. Weddings were traditionally held at night, hence the need for lit torches in the ceremony.

And I had so much hope when you were born:
you'd tend to my old age, and when I died,
1055　you'd wrap me in my shroud with your own hands:
an admirable fate for anyone.
That sweet thought has now been crushed. I'll be parted
from both of you, and I will spend my years
in sorrow and in pain. Your eyes no longer
1060　will look upon your mother. You'll move on
to a different life.
　　　　　　　　　Oh god, your eyes, the way
you look at me. Why do you smile, my children,
your very last smile? Aah, what will I do?
The heart goes out of me, women, when I look
1065　at my children's shining eyes. I couldn't do this.
Farewell to the plans I had before.
I'll take my children with me when I leave.
Why should I, just to cause their father pain,
feel twice the pain myself by harming them?
1070　I will not do it. Farewell to my plans.
But wait—what's wrong with me? What do I want?
To allow my enemies to laugh at me?
To let them go unpunished?
　　　　　　　　　　What I need
is the nerve to do it. I was such a weakling,
1075　to let a soothing word enter my mind.
Children, go inside the house.

> [*The children start to go toward the house, but as* MEDEA
> *continues to speak, they continue to watch and listen
> to her, delaying their entry inside.*]

　　　　　　　　　　　　　Whoever
is not permitted to attend these rites,
my sacrifice, let that be his concern.
I won't hold back the force that's in my hand.

Aah!
1080　Oh no, my spirit, please, not that! Don't do it.
Spare the children. Leave them alone, poor thing.
They'll live with me there. They will bring you joy.

By the avenging ones[2] who live below
in Hades, no, I will not leave my children
1085　at the mercy of my enemies' outrage.
Anyway, the thing's already done.
She won't escape. The crown is on her head.
The royal bride's destroyed, wrapped in her robes.
I know it. Now, since I am setting foot
1090　on a path that will break my heart, and sending them

---

2. The Eumenides, or Furies.

on one more heartbreaking still, I want to speak
to my children.

[MEDEA *reaches toward her children; they come back to her.*]

        Children, give me your right hands,
give them to your mother, let me kiss them.
Oh, how I love these hands, how I love these mouths,
1095   the way the children stand, their noble faces!
May fortune bless you—in the other place.
Your father's taken all that once was here.
Oh, your sweet embrace, your tender skin,
your lovely breath, oh children.
                 Go now—go.

[*The children go inside.*]

1100   I cannot look at them. Grief overwhelms me.
I know that I am working up my nerve
for overwhelming evil, yet my spirit
is stronger than my mind's deliberations:
this is the source of mortals' deepest grief.

1105 CHORUS   Quite often I've found myself venturing deeper
than women do normally into discussions
and subtle distinctions, and I would suggest
that we have our own Muse, who schools us in wisdom—
not every woman, but there are a few,
1110   you'll find one among many, a woman who doesn't
stand entirely apart from the Muses.

Here's my opinion: the childless among us,
the ones who have never experienced parenthood,
have greater good fortune than those who have children.
1115   They don't know—how could they?—if children
      are pleasant
or hard and distressing. Their lack of experience
saves them from heartache.
But those who have children, a household's sweet
      offshoot—
I see them consumed their whole lives with concern.
1120   They fret from the start: are they raising them well?
And then: will they manage to leave them enough?
Then finally: all of this toil and heartache,
is it for children who'll turn out to be
worthless or decent? That much is unclear.

1125   There's one final grief that I'll mention. Supposing
your children have grown up with plenty to live on,
they're healthy, they're decent—if fortune decrees it,
Death comes and spirits their bodies away
down to the Underworld. What is the point, then,
1130   if the gods, adding on to the pains that we mortals
endure for the sake of our children, send death,
most distressing of all? Tell me, where does that leave us?

MEDEA   My friends, I have been waiting for some time,
         keeping watch to see where this will lead.
1135   Look now: here comes one of Jason's men
         breathing hard—he seems to be about
         to tell us of some new and dreadful act.
         [*Enter the* MESSENGER *from the right.*]

MESSENGER   Medea, run away! Take any ship
         or wagon that will carry you. Leave now!
1140 MEDEA   Why should I flee? What makes it necessary?

MESSENGER   The royal princess and her father Creon
         have just now died—the victims of your poison.

MEDEA   This news is excellent. From this day forth
         I'll count you as a friend and benefactor.
1145 MESSENGER   What are you saying? Are you sane at all,
         or raving? You've attacked the royal hearth—
         how can you rejoice, and not be frightened?

MEDEA   I could tell my own side to this story.
         But calm down, friend, and please describe to me
1150   how they were destroyed. If you can say
         that they died horribly, I'll feel twice the pleasure.

MESSENGER   When we saw that your two boys had come
         together with their father to the bride's house,
         all of us—we servants who have felt
1155   the pain of your misfortunes—were delighted;
         the talk was that you'd settled your differences,
         you and your husband. We embraced the boys,
         kissing their hands, their golden hair. And I,
         overjoyed as I was, accompanied
1160   the children to the women's quarters. She—
         the mistress we now honor in your place—
         before she caught sight of your pair of boys
         was gazing eagerly at Jason. Then
         she saw the children, and she covered up
1165   her eyes, as if the sight disgusted her,
         and turned her pale cheek aside. Your husband
         tried to cool down the girl's bad temper,
         saying, "Don't be hateful toward your loved ones!
         Please, calm your spirit, turn your head this way,
1170   and love those whom your husband loves. Receive
         these gifts, and ask your father, for my sake,
         not to send these children into exile."
         Well, when she saw the fine things, she gave in
         to everything the man said. They had barely
1175   set foot outside the door—your children and
         their father—when she took the intricate
         embroidered robe and wrapped it round her body,
         and set the golden crown upon her curls,
         and smiled at her bright image—her lifeless double—
1180   in a mirror, as she arranged her hair.
         She rose, and with a delicate step her lovely

white feet traversed the quarters. She rejoiced
beyond all measure in the gifts. Quite often
she extended her ankle, admiring the effect.

1185 What happened next was terrible to see.
Her skin changed color, and her legs were shaking;
she reeled sideways, and she would have fallen
straight to the ground if she hadn't collapsed in
    her chair.
Then one of her servants, an old woman,
1190 thinking that the girl must be possessed
by Pan³ or by some other god, cried out—
a shriek of awe and reverence—but when
she saw the white foam at her mouth, her eyes
popping out, the blood drained from her face,
1195 she changed her cry to one of bitter mourning.
A maid ran off to get the princess' father;
another went to tell the bride's new husband
of her disaster. Everywhere the sound
of running footsteps echoed through the house.
1200 And then, in less time than it takes a sprinter
to cover one leg of a stadium race,
the girl, whose eyes had been shut tight, awoke,
poor thing, and she let out a terrible groan,
for she was being assaulted on two fronts:
1205 the golden garland resting on her head
sent forth a marvelous stream of all-consuming
fire, and the delicate robe, the gift
your children brought, was starting to corrode
the white flesh of that most unfortunate girl.
1210 She jumped up, with flames all over her,
shaking her hair, tossing her head around,
trying to throw the crown off. But the gold
gripped tight, and every movement of her hair
caused the fire to blaze out twice as much.
1215 Defeated by disaster, she fell down
onto the ground, unrecognizable
to anyone but a father. She had lost
the look her eyes had once had, and her face
had lost its beauty. Blood was dripping down,
1220 mixed with fire, from the top of her head
and from her bones the flesh was peeling back
like resin, shorn by unseen jaws of poison,
terrible to see. We all were frightened
to touch the corpse. We'd seen what had just
    happened.

---

3. God of shepherds, huntsmen, and country dwellers, usually represented with horns and
a lower body like a goat's.

1225   But her poor father took us by surprise:
he ran into the room and threw himself—
not knowing any better—on her corpse.
He moaned, and wrapped her in his arms,
    and kissed her,
crying, "Oh, my poor unhappy child,
1230   what god dishonors you? What god destroys you?
Who has taken you away from me,
an old man who has one foot in the grave?
Let me die with you, child." When he was done
with his lament, he tried to straighten up
1235   his aged body, but the delicate robe
clung to him as ivy clings to laurel,
and then a terrible wrestling match began.
He tried to flex his knee; she pulled him back.
If he used force, he tore the aged flesh
1240   off of his bones. He finally gave up,
unlucky man; his soul slipped away
when he could fight no longer. There they lie,
two corpses, a daughter and her aged father,
side by side, a disaster that longs for tears.

1245   About your situation, I am silent.
You realize what penalty awaits you.
About our mortal lives, I feel the way
I've often felt before: we are mere shadows.
I wouldn't hesitate to say that those
1250   who seem so wise, who deal in subtleties—
they earn the prize for being the greatest fools.
For really, there is no man blessed with fortune.
One man might be luckier, more prosperous
than someone else, but no man's ever blessed.

               [*Exit the* MESSENGER *to the right.*]

1255 CHORUS On this day fortune has bestowed on Jason
much grief, it seems, as justice has demanded.
Poor thing, we pity you for this disaster,
daughter of Creon, you who have descended
to Hades' halls because of your marriage to Jason.
1260 MEDEA My friends, it is decided: as soon as possible
I must kill my children and leave this land
before I give my enemies a chance
to slaughter them with a hand that's moved by
    hatred.
They must die anyway, and since they must,
1265   I will kill them. I'm the one who bore them.
Arm yourself, my heart. Why am I waiting
to do this terrible, necessary crime?
Unhappy hand, act now. Take up the sword,
just take it; approach the starting post of pain

1270   to last a lifetime; do not weaken, don't
    remember that you love your children dearly,
    that you gave them life. For one short day
    forget your children. Afterward, you'll grieve.
    For even if you kill them, they were yours;
1275   you loved them. I'm a woman cursed by fortune.

        [MEDEA *enters the house.*]

    CHORUS

                      [Strophe 1]

    O Earth, O radiant beam
    of Helios, look down and see her—
    this woman, destroyer, before she can lay
    her hand stained with blood,
1280   her kin-killing hand
    upon her own children
    descended from you
    the gods' golden race;
    for such blood to spill
1285   at the hands of a mortal
    fills us with fear.
    Light born from Zeus,
    stop her, remove
    this bloodstained Erinys;[4]
1290   take her away
    from this house cursed with vengeance.

                 [Antistrophe 1]

    Your toil has all been in vain,
    in vain, all the heartache of raising
    your children, your dearest, O sorrowful one
1295   who once left behind
    the dark Clashing Rocks
    most hostile to strangers.
    What burden of rage
    descended upon
1300   your mind? Why does wild
    slaughter follow on slaughter?
    Blood-spatter, stain,
    slaughter of kin,
    murder within
1305   the family brings grief
    tuned to the crime
    from the gods to the household.

---

4. Another name for a Fury.

CHILD   [*From within the house.*]
  Oh no!
CHORUS

[Strophe 2]

  Do you hear the shouts, the shouts of her children?
1310 Poor woman: she's cursed, undone by her fortune.
  CHILD 1   Oh, how can I escape my mother's hand?
  CHILD 2   Dear brother, I don't know. We are destroyed.
  CHORUS   Shall I go inside?
  I ought to prevent this,
  the slaughter of children.
1315 CHILD 1   Yes, come and stop her! That is what we need.
  CHILD 2   We're trapped; we're caught! The sword is at our throats.
  CHORUS   Poor thing: after all
  you were rock, you were iron:
  to reap with your own hand
1320 the crop that you bore;
  to cut down your kin
  with a fate-dealing hand.

[Antistrophe 2]

  I've heard of just one, just one other woman
  who dared to attack, to hurt her own children:

1325 Ino, whom the gods once drove insane
  and Zeus's wife sent wandering from her home.[5]

  The poor woman leapt
  to sea with her children:
  an unholy slaughter.

1330 She stepped down from a steep crag's rocky edge
  and died with her two children in the waves.
  What terrible deed
  could surpass such an outrage?
  O bed of their marriage,
1335 O woman's desire:
  such harm have you done,
  so much pain have you caused.
    [*Enter* JASON *from the right.*]

JASON   Women, you who stand here near the house—
  is she at home, Medea, the perpetrator
1340 of all these terrors, or has she gone away?

5. Ino was one of the women who, in Dionysiac frenzy, participates in the ritual killing of
Pentheus. Later, she wanders from home and
leaps to her death in the sea. Euripides
depicts the story of Pentheus in *The
Bacchae*.

Oh yes, she'll have to hide beneath the earth
or lift her body into the sky with wings
to escape the royal family's cry for justice.
Does she think she can murder this land's rulers
1345   then simply flee this house, with no requital?
I'm worried about the children more than her—
the ones she's hurt will pay her back in kind.
I've come to save my children, save their lives.
The family might retaliate, might strike
1350   the children for their mother's unholy slaughter.
CHORUS   Poor man. Jason, if you realized
    how bad it was, you wouldn't have said that.
JASON   What is it? Does she want to kill *me* now?
CHORUS   Your children are dead, killed by their mother's hand.
1355 JASON   What are you saying, women? You have destroyed me.
CHORUS   Please understand: your children no longer exist.
JASON   Where did she kill them? Inside the house, or outside?
CHORUS   Open the gates; you'll see your children's slaughter.
JASON   Servants, quick, open the door, unbar it;
1360   undo the bolts, and let me see this double
    evil: their dead bodies, and the one
    whom I will bring to justice.
        [MEDEA *appears above the roof in a flying chariot,*
        with the bodies of the children.][6]
    MEDEA   Why are you trying
    to pry those gates? Is it their corpses you seek,
    and me, the perpetrator? Stop your struggle.
1365   If you need something, ask me. Speak your mind.
    But you will never touch us with your hand.
    My father's father, Helios, gives me safety
    from hostile hands. This chariot protects me.
    JASON   You hateful thing, O woman most detested
1370   by the gods, by me, by all mankind—
    you dared to strike your children with a sword,
    children you bore yourself. You have destroyed me,
    left me childless. And yet you live, you look
    upon the sun and earth, you who had the nerve
1375   to do this most unholy deed. I wish
    you would die. I have more sense now than I had
    the day I took you from your barbarian land
    and brought you to a Greek home—you're a plague,
    betrayer of your father and the land
1380   that raised you. But the gods have sent the vengeance
    that *you* deserve to crash down on *my* head.
    You killed your brother right at home, then climbed
    aboard the *Argo* with its lovely prow.
    That's how your career began. You married

6. For a discussion of this staging, see the introduction.

1385   me, and bore me children. For the sake
            of passion, of your bed, you have destroyed them.
            No Greek woman would have had the nerve
            to do this, but I married you instead:
            a hateful bond. You ruined me. You're not
1390   a woman; you're a lion, with a nature
            more wild than Scylla's, the Etruscan freak.[7]
            I couldn't wound you with ten thousand insults;
            there's nothing you can't take. Get out of here,
            you filth, you child-murderer. For me,
1395   all that's left is tears for my misfortune.
            I'll never have the joy of my bride's bed,
            nor will I ever again speak to my children,
            my children, whom I raised. And now I've lost them.
      MEDEA   I would have made a long speech in reply
1400   to yours, if father Zeus were unaware
            of what I've done for you, and how you've acted.
            You dishonored my bed. There was no way
            you could go on to lead a pleasant life,
            to laugh at me—not you, and not the princess;
1405   nor could Creon, who arranged your marriage,
            exile me and walk away unpunished.
            So go ahead, call me a lion, call me
            a Scylla, skulking in her Etruscan cave.
            I've done what I had to do. I've jabbed your heart.
1410 JASON   You feel the pain yourself. This hurts you, too.
      MEDEA   The pain is good, as long as you're not laughing.
      JASON   O children, you were cursed with an evil mother.
      MEDEA   O sons, you were destroyed by your father's sickness.
      JASON   *My* right hand is not the one that killed them.
1415 MEDEA   Your outrage, and your newfound bride, destroyed them.
      JASON   The bedroom was enough to make you kill?
      MEDEA   Does that pain mean so little to a woman?
      JASON   Yes,
            to one with wise restraint. To you, it's everything.
      MEDEA   *They* exist no longer. That will sting you.
1420 JASON   They exist. They live to avenge your crime.
      MEDEA   The gods know who was first to cause this pain.
      JASON   Oh yes. They know your mind. They spit on it.
      MEDEA   Go on and hate me. I detest your voice.
      JASON   I feel the same. That makes it easy to leave you.
1425 MEDEA   What shall I do, then? I'd like nothing better.
      JASON   Let me bury their bodies. Let me grieve.
      MEDEA   Forget it. I will take them away myself
            and bury them with this hand, in the precinct
            sacred to Hera of the rocky heights.

---

7. The sea monster who threatens Odysseus in *The Odyssey.*

1430 No enemy will treat their graves with outrage.
To this land of Sisyphus[8] I bequeath
a holy festival, a ritual
to expiate in times to come this most
unholy slaughter. I myself will go
1435 to live together with Pandion's son
Aegeus, in Erechtheus's city.[9]
And you, an evil man, as you deserve,
will die an evil death, struck on the head
by a fragment of the *Argo*. You will see
1440 how bitter was the outcome of my marriage.

[*Here the meter changes from spoken dialogue to chanted anapests.*][1]

JASON May you be destroyed by the children's Erinys
and bloodthirsty Justice!
MEDEA   What spirit, what god
listens to you, you liar, you breaker
of oaths, you deceiver of guests?
JASON   You are loathsome.
1445 You murdered your children.
MEDEA   Get out of here, go—
go bury your wife.
JASON   I'm leaving, bereft
of my sons.
MEDEA   Do you think that you're mourning them now?
Just wait till you're old.
JASON Oh, dearest children.
MEDEA   To me, not to you.
1450 JASON And yet you still did this?
MEDEA   To make you feel pain.
JASON I wish I could hold them and kiss them, my children.
MEDEA You long for them now and you want to embrace them,
but you are the one who pushed them away.
JASON By the gods, let me touch the soft skin of my children.
1455 MEDEA No. What's the point? You are wasting your words.

[*The chariot flies away with* MEDEA *and the bodies of the children.*]

JASON Zeus, do you hear how I'm driven away,
do you see what I suffer at her loathsome hands,
this lion, this child-killer!
                              With all my strength
I mourn for them now and I call on the gods
1460 and spirits to witness that you killed my children
and now won't allow me to touch them or bury them.
I wish now that I'd never fathered them, only
to see them extinguished, to see what you've done.

[*Exit* JASON *to the right, accompanied by the* CHORUS.]

---

8. Corinth; in punishment for his crimes,
Sisyphus was doomed to the eternal torture
of having to push a rock uphill and having it
always roll back down.

9. Athens.
1. This change of rhythm signals to the audience that the play is nearing its conclusion.

CHORUS   Zeus on Olympus enforces all things;
1465   the gods can accomplish what no one would hope for.
           What we expect may not happen at all,
           while the gods find a way, against all expectation,
           to do what they want, however surprising.
           And that is exactly how this case turned out.

The Bacchae[1]

CHARACTERS

DIONYSUS (also called Bromius,   PENTHEUS
    Evius, and Bacchus)   ATTENDANT
CHORUS of Asian Bacchae   FIRST MESSENGER
    (followers of DIONYSUS)   SECOND MESSENGER
TEIRESIAS   AGAVE
CADMUS   CORYPHAEUS (chorus leader)

[SCENE: *Before the royal palace at Thebes. On the left is the way to Cithaeron; on the right, to the city. In the center of the orchestra stands, still smoking, the vine-covered tomb of Semele, mother of Dionysus.*[2]
    Enter DIONYSUS. *He is of soft, even effeminate, appearance. His face is beardless; he is dressed in a fawn-skin and carries a thyrsus (i.e., a stalk of fennel tipped with ivy leaves). On his head he wears a wreath of ivy, and his long blond curls ripple down over his shoulders. Throughout the play he wears a smiling mask.*]

DIONYSUS   I am Dionysus, the son of Zeus,
           come back to Thebes, this land where I was born.
           My mother was Cadmus' daughter, Semele by name,
           midwived by fire, delivered by the lightning's
5   blast.[3]
               And here I stand, a god incognito,
           disguised as man, beside the stream of Dirce[4]
           and the waters of Ismenus. There before the palace
           I see my lightning-married mother's grave,

---

1. Translated by William Arrowsmith.
2. Greek god of wine and fertility, patron of agriculture and theater. *Cithaeron*: a mountain sacred to Dionysus, between Thebes (to the north) and Athens (to the southeast).
3. After Semele had been impregnated by Zeus, the king of the gods, the jealous Hera

(his wife and sister) tricked her into asking Zeus to come to her as a god. His thunderbolts killed her, but he saved Dionysus (see lines 101–12). *Cadmus*: founder of Thebes.
4. Wife of Lycus, king of Thebes, and a devotee of Dionysus; she turned into a spring that feeds Thebes' river, the Ismenus.

and there upon the ruins of her shattered house
10 the living fire of Zeus still smolders on
in deathless witness of Hera's violence and rage
against my mother. But Cadmus wins my praise:
he has made this tomb a shrine, sacred to my mother.
It was I who screened her grave with the green
15 of the clustering vine.

Far behind me lie
those golden-rivered lands, Lydia and Phrygia,[5]
where my journeying began. Overland I went,
across the steppes of Persia where the sun strikes hotly
down, through Bactrian fastness and the grim waste
20 of Media.[6] Thence to rich Arabia I came;
and so, along all Asia's swarming littoral
of towered cities where Greeks and foreign nations,
mingling, live, my progress made. There
I taught my dances to the feet of living men,
25 establishing my mysteries and rites
that I might be revealed on earth for what I am:
a god.
And thence to Thebes.

This city, first
in Hellas,[7] now shrills and echoes to my women's cries,
their ecstasy of joy. Here in Thebes
30 I bound the fawn-skin to the women's flesh and armed
their hands with shafts of ivy.[8] For I have come
to refute that slander spoken by my mother's sisters—
those who least had right to slander her.
They said that Dionysus was no son of Zeus,
35 but Semele had slept beside a man in love
and fathered off her shame on Zeus—a fraud, they sneered,
contrived by Cadmus to protect his daughter's name.
They said she lied, and Zeus in anger at that lie
blasted her with lightning.
Because of that offense
40 I have stung them with frenzy, hounded them from home
up to the mountains where they wander, crazed of mind,
and compelled to wear my orgies' livery.
Every woman in Thebes—but the women only—
I drove from home, mad. There they sit,

---

5. Areas in Asia Minor (present-day Anatolia in Turkey). From the earliest times, Dionysus was viewed by the Greeks as a foreigner from the East.
6. A country of south Asia, corresponding to much of modern Iran and Iraq. *Bactrian fastness*: a remote, mountainous region of present-

day Afghanistan.
7. Greece.
8. The thyrsi (staffs made of fennel stalks, tipped with pinecones and wound with ivy and grape vines) that, together with deerskin clothes, distinguished the members of the Dionysus cult.

45 rich and poor alike, even the daughters of Cadmus,
   beneath the silver firs on the roofless rocks.
   Like it or not, this city must learn its lesson:
   it lacks initiation in my mysteries;
   that I shall vindicate my mother Semele
50 and stand revealed to mortal eyes as the god
   she bore to Zeus.
                         Cadmus the king has abdicated,
   leaving his throne and power to his grandson Pentheus;
   who now revolts against divinity, in *me*;
   thrusts *me* from his offerings; forgets *my* name
55 in his prayers. Therefore I shall *prove* to him
   and every man in Thebes that I am god
   indeed. And when my worship is established here,
   and all is well, then I shall go my way
   and be revealed to other men in other lands.
60 But if the men of Thebes attempt to force
   my Bacchae from the mountainside by threat of arms,
   I shall marshal my Maenads[9] and take the field.
   To these ends I have laid my deity aside
   and go disguised as man.
                    [*He wheels and calls offstage.*]
                                   On, my women,
65 women who worship me, women whom I led
   out of Asia where Tmolus[1] heaves its rampart
   over Lydia!
                    On, comrades of my progress here!
   Come, and with your native Phrygian drum—
   Rhea's drum[2] and mine—pound at the palace doors
70 of Pentheus! Let the city of Thebes behold you,
   while I return among Cithaeron's forest glens
   where my Bacchae wait and join their whirling dances.

            [*Exit* DIONYSUS *as the* CHORUS *of Asian Bacchae comes dancing in from
            the right. They are dressed in fawn-skins, crowned with ivy, and carry
            thyrsi, timbrels, and flutes.*]

CHORUS   Out of the land of Asia,
         down from holy Tmolus,
75   speeding the service of god,
         for Bromius[3] we come!
         Hard are the labors of god;
         hard, but his service is sweet.
         Sweet to serve, sweet to cry:
                    Bacchus!   *Evohé!*[4]

---

9. Another name for the Bacchae, the group
of ecstatic women following Dionysus.
1. A mountain range in Asia Minor (see lines
498–99).
2. Rhea, daughter of the sky god Uranus and

mother of Zeus, was worshipped with tambourines and drums.
3. Another name for Dionysus (literally,
"noisy").
4. A cry of joy.

80   —You on the streets!
                    —You on the roads!
                                    —Make way!
      —Let every mouth be hushed. Let no ill-omened words
          profane your tongues.
                          —Make way! Fall back!
                                            —Hush.
      —For now I raise the old, old hymn to Dionysus.

      —Blessèd, blessèd are those who know the mysteries of god.
85   —Blessèd is he who hallows his life in the worship of god,
          he whom the spirit of god possesseth, who is one
          with those who belong to the holy body of god.
      —Blessèd are the dancers and those who are purified,
          who dance on the hill in the holy dance of god.
90   —Blessèd are they who keep the rite of Cybele[5] the Mother.
      —Blessèd are the thyrsus-bearers, those who wield in their hands
          the holy wand of god.
      —Blessèd are those who wear the crown of the ivy of god.
      —Blessèd, blessèd are they: Dionysus is their god!

95   —On, Bacchae, on, you Bacchae,
          bear your god in triumph home!
          Bear on the god, son of god,
          escort your Dionysus home!
          Bear him down from Phrygian hill,
100   attend him through the streets of Hellas!

      —So his mother bore him once
          in labor bitter; lightning-struck,
          forced by fire that flared from Zeus,
          consumed, she died, untimely torn,
105   in childbed dead by blow of light!
          Of light the son was born!

      —Zeus it was who saved his son;
          with speed outrunning mortal eye,
          bore him to a private place,
110   bound the boy with clasps of gold;
          in his thigh as in a womb,
          concealed his son from Hera's eyes.

      —And when the weaving Fates fulfilled the time,
          the bull-horned[6] god was born of Zeus. In joy
115   he crowned his son, set serpents on his head—

---

5. Goddess of the earth, identified by the Greeks
with Rhea, her worship spread from Phrygia,
where she was said to have taught Dionysus
the mysteries.

6. An epithet of Dionysus. *Fates:* three goddesses who spin, measure, and cut the
threads of destiny.

wherefrom, in piety, descends to us
the Maenad's writing crown, her *chevelure*[7] of snakes.

—O Thebes, nurse of Semele,
    crown your hair with ivy!
120   Grow green with bryony!
    Redden with berries! O city,
    with boughs of oak and fir,
    come dance the dance of god!
    Fringe your skins of dappled fawn
125   with tufts of twisted wool!
    Handle with holy care
    the violent wand of god!
    And let the dance begin!
    He is Bromius who runs
130   *to the mountain!*
                to the mountain!
    where the throng of women waits,
    driven from shuttle and loom,
    possessed by Dionysus!

—And I praise the holies of Crete,
135   the caves of the dancing Curetes,[8]
    there where Zeus was born,
    where helmed in triple tier
    around the primal drum
    the Corybantes[9] danced. They,
140   they were the first of all
    whose whirling feet kept time
    to the strict beat of the taut hide
    and the squeal of the wailing flute.
    Then from them to Rhea's hands
145   the holy drum was handed down;
    but, stolen by the raving Satyrs,[1]
    fell at last to me and now
    accompanies the dance
    which every other year
150   celebrates your name:
        Dionysus!

—He is sweet upon the mountains. He drops to the earth
        from the running packs.
    He wears the holy fawn-skin. He hunts the wild goat

7. Hair (French).
8. Divinities who protected the infant Zeus.
Crete: largest Greek island, whose Minoan
civilization was the cultural center of the
Aegean before the rise of mainland Greece; it
was characterized by goddess worship.

9. Dancing votaries of the goddess Cybele,
with whom the Curetes are often identified.
1. Male attendants of Dionysus, creatures of
the forest whose appetites for wine and sex
are boundless.

155 and kills it.
     He delights in the raw flesh.
     He runs to the mountains of Phrygia, to the mountains
       of Lydia he runs!
     He is Bromius who leads us! *Evohé!*

160 —With milk the earth flows! It flows with wine!
     It runs with the nectar of bees!

     —Like frankincense in its fragrance
     is the blaze of the torch he bears.
     Flames float out from his trailing wand
165   as he runs, as he dances,
       kindling the stragglers,
       spurring with cries,
     and his long curls stream to the wind!

     —And he cries, as they cry, *Evohé!*—
170   On, Bacchae!
       On, Bacchae!
     Follow, glory of golden Tmolus,
       hymning god
       with a rumble of drums,
175 with a cry, *Evohé!* to the Evian god,[2]
     with a cry of Phrygian cries,
     when the holy flute like honey plays
     the sacred song of those who go
     to the mountain!
                    to the mountain!

180 —Then, in ecstasy, like a colt by its grazing mother,
     the Bacchante[3] runs with flying feet, she leaps!
       [*The* CHORUS *remains grouped in two semicircles about the orchestra as*
       TEIRESIAS[4] *makes his entrance. He is incongruously dressed in the bac-*
       chant's fawn-skin and is crowned with ivy. Old and blind, he uses his
       thyrsus to tap his way.]

     TEIRESIAS   Ho there, who keeps the gates?
                                    Summon Cadmus—
     Cadmus, Agenor's son, the stranger from Sidon[5]
     who built the towers of our Thebes.
                                    Go, someone.
185 Say Teiresias wants him. He will know what errand
     brings me, that agreement, age with age, we made
     to deck our wands, to dress in skins of fawn

---

2. That is, Dionysus (*Euios* is another of his
names).
3. A female worshipper of Dionysus; a
Maenad.

4. The blind prophet, adviser to Cadmus.
5. Major port city of Phoenicia (present-day
Lebanon).

and crown our heads with ivy.

[*Enter* CADMUS *from the palace. Dressed in Dionysiac costume and bent almost double with age, he is an incongruous and pathetic figure.*]

CADMUS   My old friend,
I knew it must be you when I heard your summons.
190   For there's a wisdom in his voice that makes
the man of wisdom known.
                              But here I am,
dressed in the costume of the god, prepared to go.
Insofar as we are able, Teiresias, we must
do honor to this god, for he was born
195   my daughter's son, who has been revealed to men,
the god, Dionysus.
                              Where shall we go, where
shall we tread the dance, tossing our white heads
in the dances of god?
                              Expound to me, Teiresias.
For in such matters you are wise.
                                        Surely
200   I could dance night and day, untiringly
beating the earth with my thyrsus! And how sweet it is
to forget my old age.

TEIRESIAS   It is the same with me.
I too feel young, young enough to dance.

CADMUS   Good. Shall we take our chariots to the mountain?

205 TEIRESIAS   Walking would be better. It shows more honor
to the god.

CADMUS   So be it. I shall lead, my old age
conducting yours.

TEIRESIAS   The god will guide us there
with no effort on our part.

CADMUS   Are we the only men
who will dance for Bacchus?

TEIRESIAS   They are all blind.
210   Only we can see.

CADMUS   But we delay too long.
Here, take my arm.

TEIRESIAS   Link my hand in yours.

CADMUS   I am a man, nothing more. I do not scoff
at heaven.

TEIRESIAS   We do not trifle with divinity.
No, we are the heirs of customs and traditions
215   hallowed by age and handed down to us
by our fathers. No quibbling logic can topple *them*,
whatever subtleties this clever age invents.
People may say: "Aren't you ashamed? At your age,
going dancing, wreathing your head with ivy?"
220   Well, I am *not* ashamed. Did the god declare
that just the young or just the old should dance?

No, he desires his honor from all mankind.
He wants no one excluded from his worship.
   CADMUS   Because you cannot see, Teiresias, let me be
225   interpreter for you this once. Here comes
the man to whom I left my throne, Echion's son,
Pentheus, hastening toward the palace. He seems
excited and disturbed. Yes, listen to him.

> [*Enter* PENTHEUS *from the right. He is a young man of athletic build,
> dressed in traditional Greek dress; like* DIONYSUS, *he is beardless. He enters
> excitedly, talking to the attendants who accompany him.*]

   PENTHEUS   I happened to be away, out of the city,
230   but reports reached me of some strange mischief here,
stories of our women leaving home to frisk
in mock ecstasies among the thickets on the mountain,
dancing in honor of the latest divinity,
a certain Dionysus, whoever he may be!
235   In their midst stand bowls brimming with wine.
And then, one by one, the women wander off
to hidden nooks where they serve the lusts of men.
Priestesses of Bacchus they claim they are,
but it's really Aphrodite[6] they adore.
240   I have captured some of them; my jailers
have locked them away in the safety of our prison.
Those who run at large shall be hunted down
out of the mountains like the animals they are—
yes, my own mother Agave, and Ino
245   and Autonoë, the mother of Actaeon.[7]
In no time at all I shall have them trapped
in iron nets and stop this obscene disorder.
     I am also told a foreigner has come to Thebes
from Lydia, one of those charlatan magicians,
250   with long yellow curls smelling of perfumes,
with flushed cheeks and the spells of Aphrodite
in his eyes. His days and nights he spends
with women and girls, dangling before them the joys
of initiation in his mysteries.
255   But let me bring him underneath that roof
and I'll stop his pounding with his wand and tossing
his head. By god, I'll have his head cut off!
And *this* is the man who claims that Dionysus
is a god and was sewn into the thigh of Zeus,
260   when, in point of fact, that same blast of lightning
consumed him and his mother both for her lie
that she had lain with Zeus in love. Whoever

---

6. Goddess of love.
7. Theban hero who saw the goddess Artemis
naked while she bathed; as punishment, she
turned him into a stag and he was killed by his
own dogs (see lines 362–67). His mother, like
Agave and Ino, was a daughter of Cadmus.

this stranger is, aren't such impostures,
such unruliness, worthy of hanging?

> [*For the first time he sees* TEIRESIAS *and* CADMUS *in their Dionysiac costumes.*]

265   *What!*

But this is incredible! Teiresias the seer
tricked out in a dappled fawn-skin!

>   And *you,*

you, my own grandfather, playing at the bacchant
with a wand!

>   Sir, I shrink to see your old age

270   so foolish. Shake that ivy off, grandfather!
Now drop that wand. Drop it, I say.

> [*He wheels on* TEIRESIAS.]

>   Aha,

I see: this is *your* doing, Teiresias.
Yes, you want still another god revealed to men
so you can pocket the profits from burnt offerings
275   and bird-watching.[8] By heaven, only your age
restrains me now from sending you to prison
with those Bacchic women for importing here to Thebes
these filthy mysteries. When once you see
the glint of wine shining at the feasts of women,
280   then you may be sure the festival is rotten.

CORYPHAEUS   What blasphemy! Stranger, have you no respect
for heaven? For Cadmus who sowed the dragon teeth?[9]
Will the son of Echion disgrace his house?

TEIRESIAS   Give a wise man an honest brief to plead
285   and his eloquence is no remarkable achievement.
But you are glib; your phrases come rolling out
smoothly on the tongue, as though your words were wise
instead of foolish. The man whose glibness flows
from his conceit of speech declares the thing he is:
290   a worthless and a stupid citizen.

>   I tell you,

this god whom you ridicule shall someday have
enormous power and prestige throughout Hellas.
Mankind, young man, possesses two supreme blessings.
First of these is the goddess Demeter,[1] or Earth—
295   whichever name you choose to call her by.
It was she who gave to man his nourishment of grain.
But after her there came the son of Semele,
who matched her present by inventing liquid wine

---

8. An ancient method of divination.
9. After choosing a place to found his city, Cadmus killed the dragon of Ares, which was guarding a nearby spring. He then sowed the dragon's teeth, which turned into warriors said to be the ancestors of the Theban aristocracy.
1. Goddess of grain and fertility, a sister of Zeus.

as his gift to man. For filled with that good gift,
300　suffering mankind forgets its grief; from it
comes sleep; with it oblivion of the troubles
of the day. There is no other medicine
for misery. And when we pour libations
to the gods, we pour the god of wine himself
305　that through his intercession man may win
the favor of heaven.
                              You sneer, do you, at that story
that Dionysus was sewed into the thigh of Zeus?
Let me teach you what that really means. When Zeus
rescued from the thunderbolt his infant son,
310　he brought him to Olympus. Hera, however,
plotted at heart to hurl the child from heaven.
Like the god he is, Zeus countered her. Breaking off
a tiny fragment of that ether which surrounds the world,
he molded from it a dummy Dionysus.
315　This he *showed* to Hera, but with time men garbled
the word and said that Dionysus had been *sewed*
into the thigh of Zeus. This was their story,
whereas, in fact, Zeus *showed* the dummy to Hera
and gave it as a hostage for his son.
                                          Moreover,
320　this is a god of prophecy. His worshippers,
like madmen, are endowed with mantic powers.
For when the god enters the body of a man
he fills him with the breath of prophecy.
                                              Besides,
he has usurped even the functions of warlike Ares.[2]
325　Thus, at times, you see an army mustered under arms
stricken with panic before it lifts a spear.
This panic comes from Dionysus.
                                      Someday
you shall even see him bounding with his torches
among the crags at Delphi,[3] leaping the pastures
330　that stretch between the peaks, whirling and waving
his thyrsus: great throughout Hellas.
                                          Mark my words,
Pentheus. Do not be so certain that power
is what matters in the life of man; do not mistake
for wisdom the fantasies of your sick mind.
335　Welcome the god to Thebes; crown your head;
pour him libations and join his revels.
Dionysus does not, I admit, *compel* a woman
to be chaste. Always and in every case
it is her character and nature that keeps

2. Greek god of war, especially savage warfare
and bloodlust.

3. Site, northwest of Thebes, where Apollo's
principal oracle is located.

340   a woman chaste. But even in the rites of Dionysus,
       the chaste woman will not be corrupted.
                                                   Think:
       you are pleased when men stand outside your doors
       and the city glorifies the name of Pentheus.
       And so the god: he too delights in glory.
345   But Cadmus and I, whom you ridicule, will crown
       our heads with ivy and join the dances of the god—
       an ancient foolish pair perhaps, but dance
       we must. Nothing you have said would make me
       change my mind or flout the will of heaven.
350   You are mad, grievously mad, beyond the power
       of any drugs to cure, for you are drugged
       with madness.
       CORYPHAEUS   Apollo[4] would approve your words.
       Wisely you honor Bromius: a great god.
       CADMUS   My boy,
       Teiresias advises well. Your home is here
355   with us, with our customs and traditions, not
       outside, alone. Your mind is distracted now,
       and what you think is sheer delirium.
       Even if this Dionysus is no god,
       as you assert, persuade yourself that he is.
360   The fiction is a noble one, for Semele will seem
       to be the mother of a god, and this confers
       no small distinction on our family.
                                     You saw
       that dreadful death your cousin Actaeon died
       when those man-eating hounds he had raised himself
365   savaged him and tore his body limb from limb
       because he boasted that his prowess in the hunt surpassed
       the skill of Artemis.[5]
                            Do not let his fate be yours.
       Here, let me wreathe your head with leaves of ivy.
       Then come with us and glorify the god.
370   PENTHEUS   Take your hands off me! Go worship your Bacchus,
       but do not wipe your madness off on me.
       By god, I'll make him pay, the man who taught you
       this folly of yours.
            [He turns to his attendants.]
                            Go, someone, this instant,
       to the place where this prophet prophesies.
375   Pry it up with crowbars, heave it over,
       upside down; demolish everything you see.
       Throw his fillets out to wind and weather.

4. Son of Zeus and god of light, healing, and   5. Apollo's twin sister, the goddess of the
prophecy.   hunt.

That will provoke him more than anything.
As for the rest of you, go and scour the city
380 for that effeminate stranger, the man who infects our women
with this strange disease and pollutes our beds.
And when you take him, clap him in chains
and march him here. He shall die as he deserves—
by being stoned to death. He shall come to rue
385 his merrymaking here in Thebes.
            [*Exeunt*[6] *attendants.*]

TEIRESIAS   Reckless fool,
you do not know the consequences of your words.
You talked madness before, but this is raving
lunacy!
            Cadmus, let us go and pray
for this raving fool and for this city too,
390 pray to the god that no awful vengeance strike
from heaven.
            Take your staff and follow me.
Support me with your hands, and I shall help you too
lest we stumble and fall, a sight of shame,
two old men together.
            But go we must,
395 acknowledging the service that we owe to god,
Bacchus, the son of Zeus.
            And yet take care
lest someday your house repent of Pentheus
in its sufferings. I speak not prophecy
but fact. The words of fools finish in folly.

        [*Exeunt* TEIRESIAS *and* CADMUS. PENTHEUS *retires into the palace.*]

400 CHORUS   —Holiness, queen of heaven,
            Holiness on golden wing
            who hover over earth,
            do you hear what Pentheus says?
            Do you hear his blasphemy
405   against the prince of the blessèd,
            the god of garlands and banquets,
            Bromius, Semele's son?
            These blessings he gave:
            laughter to the flute
410   and the loosing of cares
            when the shining wine is spilled
            at the feast of the gods,
            and the wine-bowl casts its sleep
            on feasters crowned with ivy.

415   —A tongue without reins,
            defiance, unwisdom—
            their end is disaster.

6. Exit (Latin, "they go out").

But the life of quiet good,
the wisdom that accepts—
420   these abide unshaken,
preserving, sustaining
the houses of men.
Far in the air of heaven,
the sons of heaven live.
425   But they watch the lives of men.
And what passes for wisdom is not;
unwise are those who aspire,
who outrange the limits of man.
Briefly, we live. Briefly,
430   then die. Wherefore, I say,
he who hunts a glory, he who tracks
some boundless, superhuman dream,
may lose his harvest here and now
and garner death. Such men are mad,
435   their counsels evil.

—O let me come to Cyprus,
island of Aphrodite,
homes of the loves that cast
their spells on the hearts of men!
440   Or Paphos[7] where the hundred-
mouthed barbarian river
brings ripeness without rain!
To Pieria, haunt of the Muses,
and the holy hill of Olympus![8]
445   O Bromius, leader, god of joy,
Bromius, take me there!
There the lovely Graces[9] go,
and there Desire, and there
the right is mine to worship
450   as I please.

—The deity, the son of Zeus,
in feast, in festival, delights.
He loves the goddess Peace,
generous of good,
455   preserver of the young.
To rich and poor he gives
the simple gift of wine,
the gladness of the grape.
But him who scoffs he hates,
460   and him who mocks his life,

7. City on the island of Cyprus that was the site of one of Aphrodite's most important cults.
8. The highest mountain in Greece, located in Pieria (an area of Thessaly, in northern Greece), was believed to be the home of the gods. *Muses:* nine daughters of Memory and Zeus who preside over the arts and all intellectual pursuits.
9. Daughters of Zeus, the personifications of beauty and grace.

the happiness of those
for whom the day is blessed
but doubly blessed the night;
whose simple wisdom shuns the thoughts
465   of proud, uncommon men and all
their god-encroaching dreams.
But what the common people do,
the things that simple men believe,
      I too believe and do.

> [As PENTHEUS *reappears from the palace, enter from the left several*
> *attendants leading* DIONYSUS *captive.*]

470   ATTENDANT   Pentheus, here we are; not empty-handed either.
We captured the quarry you sent us out to catch.
But our prey here was tame: refused to run
or hide, held out his hands as willing as you please,
completely unafraid. His ruddy cheeks were flushed
475   as though with wine, and he stood there smiling,
making no objection when we roped his hands
and marched him here. It made me feel ashamed.
"Listen, stranger," I said, "I am not to blame.
We act under orders from Pentheus. He ordered
480   your arrest."

         As for those women you clapped in chains
and sent to the dungeon, they're gone, clean away,
went skipping off to the fields crying on their god
Bromius. The chains on their legs snapped apart
by themselves. Untouched by any human hand,
485   the doors swung wide, opening of their own accord.
Sir, this stranger who has come to Thebes is full
of many miracles. I know no more than that.
The rest is your affair.

PENTHEUS   Untie his hands.
We have him in our net. He may be quick,
490   but he cannot escape us now, I think.

> [*While the servants untie* DIONYSUS' *hands,* PENTHEUS *attentively*
> *scrutinizes his prisoner. Then the servants step back, leaving*
> PENTHEUS *and* DIONYSUS *face to face.*]

                                                    So,
you *are* attractive, stranger, at least to women—
which explains, I think, your presence here in Thebes.
Your curls are long. You do not wrestle,[1] I take it.
And what fair skin you have—you must take care of it—
495   no daylight complexion; no, it comes from the night
when you hunt Aphrodite with your beauty.

                              Now then,
who are you and from where?

DIONYSUS   It is nothing
to boast of and easily told. You have heard, I suppose,

---

1. Wrestlers customarily cut their hair short to deny their opponents an easy handhold.

of Mount Tmolus and her flowers?

PENTHEUS   I know the place.
500   It rings the city of Sardis.

DIONYSUS   I come from there.
My country is Lydia.

PENTHEUS   Who is this god whose worship
you have imported into Hellas?

DIONYSUS   Dionysus, the son of Zeus.
He initiated me.

PENTHEUS   You have some local Zeus
who spawns new gods?

DIONYSUS   He is the same as yours—
505   the Zeus who married Semele.

PENTHEUS   How did you see him?
In a dream or face to face?

DIONYSUS   Face to face.
He gave me his rites.

PENTHEUS   What form do they take,
these mysteries of yours?

DIONYSUS   It is forbidden
to tell the uninitiate.

PENTHEUS   Tell me the benefits
510   that those who know your mysteries enjoy.

DIONYSUS   I am forbidden to say. But they are worth knowing.

PENTHEUS   Your answers are designed to make me curious.

DIONYSUS   No:
our mysteries abhor an unbelieving man.

PENTHEUS   You say you saw the god. What form did he assume?
515 DIONYSUS   Whatever form he wished. The choice was his,
not mine.

PENTHEUS   You evade the question.

DIONYSUS   Talk sense to a fool
and he calls you foolish.

PENTHEUS   Have you introduced your rites
in other cities too? Or is Thebes the first?

DIONYSUS   Foreigners everywhere now dance for Dionysus.
520 PENTHEUS   They are more ignorant than Greeks.

DIONYSUS   In this matter
they are not. Customs differ.

PENTHEUS   Do you hold your rites
during the day or night?

DIONYSUS   Mostly by night.
The darkness is well suited to devotion.

PENTHEUS   Better suited to lechery and seducing women.
525 DIONYSUS   You can find debauchery by daylight too.

PENTHEUS   You shall regret these clever answers.

DIONYSUS   And you,
your stupid blasphemies.

PENTHEUS   What a bold bacchant!
You wrestle well—when it comes to words.

DIONYSUS   Tell me,
what punishment do you propose?
PENTHEUS   First of all,
530   I shall cut off your girlish curls.
DIONYSUS   My hair is holy.
My curls belong to god.
        [PENTHEUS *shears away the god's curls.*]
PENTHEUS   Second, you will surrender
your wand.
DIONYSUS   *You* take it. It belongs to Dionysus.
        [PENTHEUS *takes the thyrsus.*]
PENTHEUS   Last, I shall place you under guard and confine you
in the palace.
DIONYSUS   The god himself will set me free
535   whenever I wish.
PENTHEUS   You will be with your women in prison
when you call on him for help.
DIONYSUS   He is here now
and sees what I endure from you.
PENTHEUS   Where is he?
I cannot see him.
DIONYSUS   With me. Your blasphemies
have made you blind.
PENTHEUS [*to attendants*]   Seize him. He is mocking me
540   and Thebes.
DIONYSUS   I give you sober warning, fools:
place no chains on *me*.
PENTHEUS   But *I* say: chain him.
And I am the stronger here.
DIONYSUS   You do not know
the limits of your strength. You do not know
what you do. You do not know who you are.
545 PENTHEUS   I am Pentheus, the son of Echion and Agave.
DIONYSUS   Pentheus: you shall repent that name.
PENTHEUS   Off with him.
Chain his hands; lock him in the stables by the palace.
Since he desires the darkness, give him what he wants.
Let him dance down there in the dark.
        [*As the attendants bind* DIONYSUS' *hands, the* CHORUS *beats on its drums
        with increasing agitation as though to emphasize the sacrilege.*]
                            As for these women,
550   your accomplices in making trouble here,
I shall have them sold as slaves or put to work
at my looms. That will silence their drums.
        [*Exit* PENTHEUS.]
DIONYSUS   I go,
though not to suffer, since that cannot be.
But Dionysus whom you outrage by your acts,
555   who you deny is god, will call you to account.

When you set chains on me, you manacle the god.

[*Exeunt attendants with* DIONYSUS *captive.*]

CHORUS   —O Dirce, holy river,
    child of Achelöus' water,[2]
    yours the springs that welcomed once
560   divinity, the son of Zeus!
    For Zeus the father snatched his son
    from deathless flame, crying:
    Dithyrambus,[3] *come!*
    Enter my male womb.
565   *I name you Bacchus and to Thebes*
    proclaim you by that name.
    But now, O blessèd Dirce,
    you banish me when to your banks I come,
    crowned with ivy, bringing revels.
570   O Dirce, why am I rejected?
    By the clustered grapes I swear,
    by Dionysus' wine,
    someday you shall come to know
      the name of *Bromius!*

575   —With fury, with fury, he rages,
    Pentheus, son of Echion,
    born of the breed of Earth,
    spawned by the dragon, whelped by Earth!
    Inhuman, a rabid beast,
580   a giant in wildness raging,
    storming, defying the children of heaven.
    He has threatened me with bonds
    though my body is bound to god.
    He cages my comrades with chains;
585   he has cast them in prison darkness.
    O lord, son of Zeus, do you see?
    O Dionysus, do you see
    how in shackles we are held
    unbreakably, in the bonds of oppressors?
590   Descend from Olympus, lord!
    Come, whirl your wand of gold
    and quell with death this beast of blood
    whose violence abuses man and god
      outrageously.

595   —O lord, where do you wave your wand
    among the running companies of god?

---

2. The largest river in Greece; its presiding deity, Achelöus, is the chief of all the river deities, including Dirce (see line 6 with note).

3. That is, Dionysus. Dionysus was worshipped with exuberant choral lyrics called dithyrambs, a form of poetry incorporated early into Greek drama.

There on Nysa,[4] mother of beasts?
There on the ridges of Corycia?[5]
Or there among the forests of Olympus
600   where Orpheus[6] fingered his lyre
and mustered with music the trees,
mustered the wilderness beasts?
O Pieria, you are blessed!
Evius honors you. He comes to dance,
605   bringing his Bacchae, fording the race
where Axios runs, bringing his Maenads
whirling over Lydias,[7]
generous father of rivers
and famed for his lovely waters
610   that fatten a land of good horses.

> [*Thunder and lightning. The earth trembles. The* CHORUS *is crazed with fear.*]

DIONYSUS [*from within*]   Ho!
   Hear me! Ho, Bacchae!
   Ho, Bacchae! Hear my cry!
CHORUS   Who cries?
615   Who calls me with that cry
   of Evius? Where are you, lord?
DIONYSUS   Ho! Again I cry—
   the son of Zeus and Semele!
CHORUS   O lord, lord Bromius!
620   Bromius, come to us now!
DIONYSUS   *Let the earthquake come! Shatter the floor of the world!*
CHORUS   —Look there, how the palace of Pentheus totters.
   —Look, the palace is collapsing!
   —Dionysus is within. Adore him!
625   —We adore him!
   —Look there!
          —Above the pillars, how the great stones
   gape and crack!
          —Listen. Bromius cries his victory!
DIONYSUS   *Launch the blazing thunderbolt of god! O lightnings,*
   come! Consume with flame the palace of Pentheus!

> [*A burst of lightning flares across the façade of the palace and tongues of flame spurt up from the tomb of Semele. Then a great crash of thunder.*]

630 CHORUS   Ah,
   look how the fire leaps up
   on the holy tomb of Semele,
   the flame of Zeus of Thunders,
   his lightnings, still alive,

---

4. A mythical mountain in Egypt or Ethiopia reputed to be the place where the infant Dionysus was raised (and the source of his name, interpreted as "Zeus of Nysa").
5. A cave on Mount Parnassus named for the nymph of a nearby spring.
6. In classical mythology, the greatest poet and singer, whose music not only entranced animals and humans but also made rocks and trees dance.
7. A river in Macedonia (northern Greece). *Axios:* a river ("race") in Macedonia and Paionia.

635   blazing where they fell!
        Down, Maenads,
        fall to the ground in awe! He walks
        among the ruins he has made!
        He has brought the high house low!
640   He comes, our god, the son of Zeus!

        [*The* CHORUS *falls to the ground in oriental fashion, bowing their heads*
        in the direction of the palace. A hush; then DIONYSUS *appears, lightly*
        picking his way among the rubble. Calm and smiling still, he speaks to
        the CHORUS *with a solicitude approaching banter.*]

DIONYSUS   What, women of Asia? Were you so overcome with fright
    you fell to the ground? I think then you must have seen
    how Bacchus jostled the palace of Pentheus. But come, rise.
    Do not be afraid.
CORYPHAEUS   O greatest light of our holy revels,
645   how glad I am to see your face! Without you I was lost.
DIONYSUS   Did you despair when they led me away to cast me down
    in the darkness of Pentheus' prison?
CORYPHAEUS   What else could I do?
    Where would I turn for help if something happened to you?
    But how did you escape that godless man?
DIONYSUS   With ease.
650   No effort was required.
CORYPHAEUS   But the manacles on your wrists?
DIONYSUS   There I, in turn, humiliated him, outrage for outrage.
    He seemed to think that he was chaining me but never once
    so much as touched my hands. He fed on his desires.
    Inside the stable he intended as my jail, instead of me,
655   he found a bull and tried to rope its knees and hooves.
    He was panting desperately, biting his lips with his teeth,
    his whole body drenched with sweat, while I sat nearby,
    quietly watching. But at that moment Bacchus came,
    shook the palace and touched his mother's grave with tongues
660   of fire. Imagining the palace was in flames,
    Pentheus went rushing here and there, shouting to his slaves
    to bring him water. Every hand was put to work: in vain.
    Then, afraid I might escape, he suddenly stopped short,
    drew his sword, and rushed to the palace. There, it seems,
665   Bromius had made a shape, a phantom which resembled me,
    within the court. Bursting in, Pentheus thrust and stabbed
    at that thing of gleaming air as though he thought it me.
    And then, once again, the god humiliated him.
    He razed the palace to the ground where it lies, shattered
670   in utter ruin—his reward for my imprisonment.
    At that bitter sight, Pentheus dropped his sword, exhausted
    by the struggle. A man, a man, and nothing more,
    yet he presumed to wage a war with god.
                      For my part,
    I left the palace quietly and made my way outside.
675   For Pentheus I care nothing.

But judging from the sound
of tramping feet inside the court, I think our man
will soon be here. What, I wonder, will he have to say?
But let him bluster. I shall not be touched to rage.
Wise men know constraint: our passions are controlled.

[*Enter* PENTHEUS, *stamping heavily, from the ruined palace.*]

680 PENTHEUS   But this is mortifying. That stranger, that man
I clapped in irons, has escaped.

[*He catches sight of* DIONYSUS.]

                                    What! *You?*
Well, what do you have to say for yourself?
How did you escape? Answer me.

DIONYSUS   Your anger
walks too heavily. Tread lightly here.

685 PENTHEUS   *How did you escape?*

DIONYSUS   Don't you remember?
Someone, I said, would set me free.

PENTHEUS   Someone?
But who? Who is this mysterious someone?

DIONYSUS   [He who makes the grape grow its clusters
for mankind.][8]

PENTHEUS   A splendid contribution, that.

690 DIONYSUS   You disparage the gift that is his chiefest glory.

PENTHEUS   [If I catch him here, he will not escape my anger.]
I shall order every gate in every tower
to be bolted tight.

DIONYSUS   And so? Could not a god
hurdle your city walls?

PENTHEUS   You are clever—very—

695 but not where it counts.

DIONYSUS   Where it counts the most,
there I *am* clever.

[*Enter a* MESSENGER, *a herdsman from Mount Cithaeron.*]

                          But hear this messenger
who brings you news from the mountain of Cithaeron.
We shall remain where we are. Do not fear:
we will not run away.

MESSENGER   Pentheus, king of Thebes,

700 I come from Cithaeron where the gleaming flakes of snow
fall on and on forever—

PENTHEUS   Get to the point.
What is your message, man?

MESSENGER   Sir, I have seen
the holy Maenads, the women who ran barefoot
and crazy from the city, and I wanted to report

705 to you and Thebes what weird fantastic things,
what miracles and more than miracles,

---

8. In this passage, the Greek text, as well as the attribution of some lines, is uncertain.

these women do. But may I speak freely
in my own way and words, or make it short?
I fear the harsh impatience of your nature, sire,
710   too kingly and too quick to anger.
PENTHEUS   Speak freely.
You have my promise: I shall not punish you.
Displeasure with a man who speaks the truth is wrong.
However, the more terrible this tale of yours,
that much more terrible will be the punishment
715   I impose upon that man who taught our womenfolk
this strange new magic.
MESSENGER   About that hour
when the sun lets loose its light to warm the earth,
our grazing herds of cows had just begun to climb
the path along the mountain ridge. Suddenly
720   I saw three companies of dancing women,
one led by Autonoë, the second captained
by your mother Agave, while Ino led the third.
There they lay in the deep sleep of exhaustion,
some resting on boughs of fir, others sleeping
725   where they fell, here and there among the oak leaves—
but all modestly and soberly, not, as you think,
drunk with wine, nor wandering, led astray
by the music of the flute, to hunt their Aphrodite
through the woods.
                         But your mother heard the lowing
730   of our hornèd herds, and springing to her feet,
gave a great cry to waken them from sleep.
And they too, rubbing the bloom of soft sleep
from their eyes, rose up lightly and straight—
a lovely sight to see: all as one,
735   the old women and the young and the unmarried girls.
First they let their hair fall loose, down
over their shoulders, and those whose straps had slipped
fastened their skins of fawn with writhing snakes
that licked their cheeks. Breasts swollen with milk,
740   new mothers who had left their babies behind at home
nestled gazelles and young wolves in their arms,
suckling them. Then they crowned their hair with leaves,
ivy and oak and flowering bryony. One woman
struck her thyrsus against a rock and a fountain
745   of cool water came bubbling up. Another drove
her fennel in the ground, and where it struck the earth,
at the touch of god, a spring of wine poured out.
Those who wanted milk scratched at the soil
with bare fingers and the white milk came welling up.
750   Pure honey spurted, streaming, from their wands.
If you had been there and seen these wonders for yourself,
you would have gone down on your knees and prayed
to the god you now deny.

We cowherds and shepherds
gathered in small groups, wondering and arguing
755 among ourselves at these fantastic things,
the awful miracles those women did.
But then a city fellow with the knack of words
rose to his feet and said: "All you who live
upon the pastures of the mountain, what do you say?
760 Shall we earn a little favor with King Pentheus
by hunting his mother Agave out of the revels?"
Falling in with his suggestion, we withdrew
and set ourselves in ambush, hidden by the leaves
among the undergrowth. Then at a signal
765 all the Bacchae whirled their wands for the revels
to begin. With one voice they cried aloud:
"O Iacchus![9] Son of Zeus!" "O Bromius!" they cried
until the beasts and all the mountain seemed
wild with divinity. And when they ran,
770 everything ran with them.
                                   It happened, however,
that Agave ran near the ambush where I lay
concealed. Leaping up, I tried to seize her,
but she gave a cry: "Hounds who run with me,
men are hunting us down! Follow, follow me!
775 Use your wands for weapons."
                                   At this we fled
and barely missed being torn to pieces by the women.
Unarmed, they swooped down upon the herds of cattle
grazing there on the green of the meadow. And then
you could have seen a single woman with bare hands
780 tear a fat calf, still bellowing with fright,
in two, while others clawed the heifers to pieces.
There were ribs and cloven hooves scattered everywhere,
and scraps smeared with blood hung from the fir trees.
And bulls, their raging fury gathered in their horns,
785 lowered their heads to charge, then fell, stumbling
to the earth, pulled down by hordes of women
and stripped of flesh and skin more quickly, sire,
than you could blink your royal eyes. Then,
carried up by their own speed, they flew like birds
790 across the spreading fields along Asopus'[1] stream
where most of all the ground is good for harvesting.
Like invaders they swooped on Hysiae
and on Erythrae[2] in the foothills of Cithaeron.
Everything in sight they pillaged and destroyed.
795 They snatched the children from their homes. And when
they piled their plunder on their backs, it stayed in place,

---

9. Another epithet for Dionysus.   2. Like Hysiae, a town in Boeotia, south of
1. A river of Boeotia, the region surrounding   Thebes.
Thebes.

untied. Nothing, neither bronze nor iron,
fell to the dark earth. Flames flickered
in their curls and did not burn them. Then the villagers,
800   furious at what the women did, took to arms.
And *there*, sire, was something terrible to see.
For the men's spears were pointed and sharp, and yet
drew no blood, whereas the wands the women threw
inflicted wounds. And then the men *ran*,
805   routed by women! Some god, I say, was with them.
The Bacchae then returned where they had started,
by the springs the god had made, and washed their hands
while the snakes licked away the drops of blood
that dabbled their cheeks.
                     Whoever this god may be,
810   sire, welcome him to Thebes. For he is great
in many other ways as well. It was he,
or so they say, who gave to mortal men
the gift of lovely wine by which our suffering
is stopped. And if there is no god of wine,
815   there is no love, no Aphrodite either,
nor other pleasure left to men.
         [*Exit* MESSENGER.]

CORYPHAEUS   I tremble
to speak the words of freedom before the tyrant.
But let the truth be told: there is no god
greater than Dionysus.

PENTHEUS   Like a blazing fire
820   this Bacchic violence spreads. It comes too close.
We are disgraced, humiliated in the eyes
of Hellas. This is no time for hesitation.
        [*He turns to an attendant.*]
You there. Go down quickly to the Electran gates[3]
and order out all heavy-armored infantry;
825   call up the fastest troops among our cavalry,
the mobile squadrons and the archers. We march
against the Bacchae! Affairs are out of hand
when we tamely endure such conduct in our women.
        [*Exit attendant.*]

DIONYSUS   Pentheus, you do not hear, or else you disregard
830   my words of warning. You have done me wrong,
and yet, in spite of that, I warn you once
again: do not take arms against a god.
Stay quiet here. Bromius will not let you
drive his women from their revels on the mountain.

835 PENTHEUS   Don't you lecture me. You escaped from prison.
Or shall I punish you again?

DIONYSUS   If I were you,

---

3. One of the seven gates in the fortified wall surrounding the city of Thebes.

I would offer him a sacrifice, not rage
and kick against necessity, a man defying
god.

840 PENTHEUS   I shall give your god the sacrifice
that he deserves. His victims will be his women.
I shall make a great slaughter in the woods of Cithaeron.

DIONYSUS   You will all be routed, shamefully defeated,
when their wands of ivy turn back your shields of bronze.

845 PENTHEUS   It is hopeless to wrestle with this man.
Nothing on earth will make him hold his tongue.

DIONYSUS   Friend,
you can still save the situation.

PENTHEUS   How?
By accepting orders from my own slaves?

DIONYSUS   No.
I undertake to lead the women back to Thebes.

850   Without bloodshed.

PENTHEUS   This is some trap.

DIONYSUS   A trap?
How so, if I save you by my own devices?

PENTHEUS   I know.
You and they have conspired to establish your rites
forever.

DIONYSUS True, I *have* conspired—with god.

855 PENTHEUS   Bring my armor, someone. And *you* stop talking.

[PENTHEUS *strides toward the left, but when he is almost offstage,*
DIONYSUS *calls imperiously to him.*]

DIONYSUS   *Wait!*
Would you like to *see* their revels on the mountain?

PENTHEUS   I would pay a great sum to see that sight.

DIONYSUS   Why are you so passionately curious?

PENTHEUS   Of course
860   I'd be sorry to see them drunk—

DIONYSUS   But for all your sorrow,
you'd like very much to see them?

PENTHEUS   Yes, very much.
I could crouch beneath the fir trees, out of sight.

DIONYSUS   But if you try to hide, they may track you down.

PENTHEUS   Your point is well taken. I will go openly.

865 DIONYSUS   Shall I lead you there now? Are you ready to go?

PENTHEUS   The sooner the better. The loss of even a moment
would be disappointing now.

DIONYSUS   First, however,
you must dress yourself in women's clothes.

PENTHEUS   What?
You want *me*, a man, to wear a woman's dress. But why?

870 DIONYSUS   If they knew you were a man, they would kill you instantly.

PENTHEUS   True. You are an old hand at cunning, I see.

DIONYSUS   Dionysus taught me everything I know.

PENTHEUS   Your advice is to the point. What I fail to see
  is what we do.
DIONYSUS   I shall go inside with you
875 and help you dress.
PENTHEUS   Dress? In a *woman's* dress,
  you mean? I would die of shame.
DIONYSUS   Very well.
  Then you no longer hanker to see the Maenads?
PENTHEUS   What is this costume I must wear?
DIONYSUS   On your head
  I shall set a wig with long curls.
PENTHEUS   And then?
880 DIONYSUS   Next, robes to your feet and a net for your hair.
PENTHEUS   Yes? Go on.
DIONYSUS   Then a thyrsus for your hand
  and a skin of dappled fawn.
PENTHEUS   I could not bear it.
  I *cannot* bring myself to dress in women's clothes.
DIONYSUS   Then you must fight the Bacchae. That means bloodshed.
885 PENTHEUS   Right. First we must go and reconnoiter.
DIONYSUS   Surely a wiser course than that of hunting bad
  with worse.
PENTHEUS   But how can we pass through the city
  without being seen?
DIONYSUS   We shall take deserted streets.
  I will lead the way.
PENTHEUS   Any way you like,
890 provided those women of Bacchus don't jeer at me.
  First, however, I shall ponder your advice,
  whether to go or not.
DIONYSUS   Do as you please.
  I am ready, whatever you decide.
PENTHEUS   Yes.
  Either I shall march with my army to the mountain
895 or act on your advice.
          [*Exit* PENTHEUS *into the palace.*]
DIONYSUS   Women, our prey now thrashes
  in the net we threw. He shall see the Bacchae
  and pay the price with death.
              O Dionysus,
  now action rests with you. And you are near.
  Punish this man. But first distract his wits;
900 bewilder him with madness. For sane of mind
  this man would never wear a woman's dress;
  but obsess his soul and he will not refuse.
  After those threats with which he was so fierce,
  I want him made the laughingstock of Thebes,
905 paraded through the streets, a woman.
                Now

I shall go and costume Pentheus in the clothes
which he must wear to Hades[4] when he dies, butchered
by the hands of his mother. He shall come to know
Dionysus, son of Zeus, consummate god,
910   most terrible, and yet most gentle, to mankind.

        [*Exit* DIONYSUS *into the palace.*]

CHORUS   —When shall I dance once more
      with bare feet the all-night dances,
      tossing my head for joy
      in the damp air, in the dew,
915   as a running fawn might frisk
      for the green joy of the wide fields,
      free from fear of the hunt,
      free from the circling beaters
      and the nets of woven mesh
920   and the hunters hallooing on
      their yelping packs? And then, hard pressed,
      she sprints with the quickness of wind,
      bounding over the marsh, leaping
      to frisk, leaping for joy,
925   gay with the green of the leaves,
      to dance for joy in the forest,
      to dance where the darkness is deepest,
      where no man is.

      —What is wisdom? What gift of the gods
930   is held in honor like this:
      to hold your hand victorious
      over the heads of those you hate?
      Honor is precious forever.

      —Slow but unmistakable
935   the might of the gods moves on.
      It punishes that man,
      infatuate of soul
      and hardened in his pride,
      who disregards the gods.
940   The gods are crafty:
      they lie in ambush
      a long step of time
      to hunt the unholy.
      Beyond the old beliefs,
945   no thought, no act shall go.
      Small, small is the cost
      to believe in this:
      whatever is god is strong;
      whatever long time has sanctioned,

---

4. The Greek underworld, the abode of the dead.

950   that is a law forever;
         the law tradition makes
         is the law of nature.
         —What is wisdom? What gift of the gods
         is held in honor like this:
955   to hold your hand victorious
         over the heads of those you hate?
         Honor is precious forever.

         —Blessèd is he who escapes a storm at sea,
         who comes home to his harbor.
960   —Blessèd is he who emerges from under affliction.
         —In various ways one man outraces another in the
         race for wealth and power.
         —Ten thousand men possess ten thousand hopes.
         —A few bear fruit in happiness; the others go awry.
965   —But he who garners day by day the good of life,
         he is happiest. Blessèd is he.

                    [Re-enter DIONYSUS from the palace. At the threshold he turns and calls
                    back to PENTHEUS.]

DIONYSUS   Pentheus, if you are still so curious to see
         forbidden sights, so bent on evil still,
         come out. Let us see you in your woman's dress,
970   disguised in Maenad clothes so you may go and spy
         upon your mother and her company.

                    [Enter PENTHEUS from the palace. He wears a long linen dress which
                    partially conceals his fawn-skin. He carries a thyrsus in his hand; on his
                    head he wears a wig with long blond curls bound by a snood. He is dazed
                    and completely in the power of the god who has now possessed him.]

                                         Why,
         you look exactly like one of the daughters of Cadmus.
PENTHEUS   I seem to see two suns blazing in the heavens.
         And now two Thebes, two cities, and each
975   with seven gates.[5] And you—you are a bull
         who walks before me there. Horns have sprouted
         from your head. Have you always been a beast?
         But now I see a bull.
DIONYSUS   It is the god you see.
         Though hostile formerly, he now declares a truce
980   and goes with us. You see what you could not
         when you were blind.
PENTHEUS [coyly primping]   Do I look like anyone?
         Like Ino or my mother Agave?
DIONYSUS   So much alike
         I almost might be seeing one of them. But look:
         one of your curls has come loose from under the snood
985   where I tucked it.
PENTHEUS   It must have worked loose

5. Thebes was famed throughout the ancient world for the seven gates in the fortifications surrounding the city.

when I was dancing for joy and shaking my head.

DIONYSUS   Then let me be your maid and tuck it back.
Hold still.

PENTHEUS   Arrange it. I am in your hands
completely.

[DIONYSUS *tucks the curl back under the snood.*]

DIONYSUS   And now your strap has slipped. Yes,
990   and your robe hangs askew at the ankles.

PENTHEUS [*bending backward to look*]   I think so.
At least on my right leg. But on the left the hem
lies straight.

DIONYSUS   You will think me the best of friends
when you see to your surprise how chaste the Bacchae are.

PENTHEUS   But to be a real Bacchante, should I hold
995   the wand in my right hand? Or this way?

DIONYSUS   No.
In your right hand. And raise it as you raise
your right foot. I commend your change of heart.

PENTHEUS   Could I lift Cithaeron up, do you think?
Shoulder the cliffs, Bacchae and all?

DIONYSUS   If you wanted.
1000   Your mind was once unsound, but now you think
as sane men do.

PENTHEUS   Should we take crowbars with us?
Or should I put my shoulder to the cliffs
and heave them up?

DIONYSUS   What? And destroy the haunts
of the nymphs, the holy groves where Pan[6] plays
1005   his woodland pipe?

PENTHEUS   You are right. In any case,
women should not be mastered by brute strength.
I will hide myself beneath the firs instead.

DIONYSUS   You will find all the ambush you deserve,
creeping up to spy on the Maenads.

PENTHEUS   Think.
1010   I can see them already, there among the bushes,
mating like birds, caught in the toils of love.

DIONYSUS   Exactly. This is your mission: you go to watch.
You may surprise them—or they may surprise you.

PENTHEUS   Then lead me through the very heart of Thebes,
1015   since I, alone of all this city, dare to go.

DIONYSUS   You and you alone will suffer for your city.
A great ordeal awaits you. But you are worthy
of your fate. I shall lead you safely there;
someone else shall bring you back.

PENTHEUS   Yes, my mother.

1020 DIONYSUS   An example to all men.

PENTHEUS   It is for that I go.

---

6. The god of wild places and pastures, with horns and goat's feet; he joined together reeds of
different lengths to invent the panpipe.

DIONYSUS You will be carried home—

PENTHEUS   O luxury!

DIONYSUS cradled in your mother's arms.

PENTHEUS   You will spoil me.

DIONYSUS I *mean* to spoil you.

PENTHEUS   I go to my reward.

DIONYSUS You are an extraordinary young man, and you go
1025   to an extraordinary experience. You shall win
        a glory towering to heaven and usurping
        god's.

                [*Exit* PENTHEUS.]

        Agave and you daughters of Cadmus,
    reach out your hands! I bring this young man
    to a great ordeal. The victor? Bromius.
1030   Bromius—and I. The rest the event shall show.

                [*Exit* DIONYSUS.]

CHORUS   —Run to the mountain, fleet hounds of madness!
        Run, run to the revels of Cadmus' daughters!
        Sting them against the man in women's clothes,
        the madman who spies on the Maenads, who peers
1035   from behind the rocks, who spies from a vantage!
        His mother shall see him first. She will cry
        to the Maenads: "Who is this spy who has come
        to the mountains to peer at the mountain-revels
        of the women of Thebes? What bore him, Bacchae?
1040   This man was born of no woman. Some lioness
        gave him birth, some one of the Libyan gorgons!"[7]

    —O Justice, principle of order, spirit of custom,
        come! Be manifest; reveal yourself with a sword!
        Stab through the throat that godless man,
1045   the mocker who goes, flouting custom and outraging god!
        O Justice, stab the evil earth-born spawn of Echion!

    —Uncontrollable, the unbeliever goes,
        in spitting rage, rebellious and amok,
        madly assaulting the mysteries of god,
1050   profaning the rites of the mother of god.
        Against the unassailable he runs, with rage
        obsessed. Headlong he runs to death.
        For death the gods exact, curbing by that bit
        the mouths of men. They humble us with death
1055   that we remember what we are who are not god,
        but men. We run to death. Wherefore, I say,
        accept, accept:
        humility is wise; humility is blest.

---

7. Medusa and her two sisters, snake-haired monsters who turned to stone all who looked at
them. In some traditions, Gorgons were savage female warriors living in Libya.

But what the world calls wise I do not want.
1060 Elsewhere the chase. I hunt another game,
       those great, those manifest, those certain goals,
       achieving which, our mortal lives are blest.
       Let these things be the quarry of my chase:
       purity; humility; an unrebellious soul,
1065 accepting all. Let me go the customary way,
       the timeless, honored, beaten path of those who walk
       with reverence and awe beneath the sons of heaven.

       —O Justice, principle of order, spirit of custom,
       come! Be manifest; reveal yourself with a sword!
1070 Stab through the throat that godless man,
       the mocker who goes, flouting custom and outraging god!
       O Justice, destroy the evil earth-born spawn of Echion!

       —O Dionysus, reveal yourself a bull! Be manifest,
       a snake with darting heads, a lion breathing fire!
1075 O Bacchus, come! Come with your smile!
       Cast your noose about this man who hunts
       your Bacchae! Bring him down, trampled
       underfoot by the murderous herd of your Maenads!

       [*Enter a* MESSENGER *from Cithaeron.*]

MESSENGER   How prosperous in Hellas these halls once were,
1080 this house founded by Cadmus, the stranger from Sidon
       who sowed the dragon seed in the land of the snake!
       I am a slave and nothing more, yet even so
       I mourn the fortunes of this fallen house.

CORYPHAEUS   What is it?
       Is there news of the Bacchae?

MESSENGER   This is my news:
1085 Pentheus, the son of Echion, is dead.

CORYPHAEUS   All hail to Bromius! Our god is a great god!

MESSENGER   What is this you say, women? You dare to rejoice
       at these disasters which destroy this house?

CORYPHAEUS   I am no Greek. I hail my god
1090 in my own way. No longer need I
       shrink with fear of prison.

MESSENGER   If you suppose this city is so short of men—

CORYPHAEUS   Dionysus, Dionysus, not Thebes,
       has power over me.

1095 MESSENGER   Your feelings might be forgiven, then. But this,
       this exultation in disaster—it is not right.

CORYPHAEUS   Tell us how the mocker died.
       How was he killed?

MESSENGER   There were three of us in all: Pentheus and I,
1100 attending my master, and that stranger who volunteered
       his services as guide. Leaving behind us
       the last outlying farms of Thebes, we forded
       the Asopus and struck into the barren scrubland

of Cithaeron.
                    There in a grassy glen we halted,
1105   unmoving, silent, without a word,
so we might see but not be seen. From the vantage,
in a hollow cut from the sheer rock of the cliffs,
a place where water ran and the pines grew dense
with shade, we saw the Maenads sitting, their hands
1110   busily moving at their happy tasks. Some
wound the stalks of their tattered wands with tendrils
of fresh ivy; others, frisking like fillies
newly freed from the painted bridles, chanted
in Bacchic songs, responsively.
                                        But Pentheus—
1115   unhappy man—could not quite see the companies
of women. "Stranger," he said, "from where I stand,
I cannot see these counterfeited Maenads.
But if I climbed that towering fir that overhangs
the banks, then I could see their shameless orgies
1120   better."
                    And now the stranger worked a miracle.
Reaching for the highest branch of a great fir,
he bent it down, down, down to the dark earth,
till it was curved the way a taut bow bends
or like a rim of wood when forced about the circle
1125   of a wheel. Like that he forced that mountain fir
down to the ground. No mortal could have done it.
Then he seated Pentheus at the highest tip
and with his hands let the trunk rise straightly up,
slowly and gently, lest it throw its rider.
1130   And the tree rose, towering to heaven, with my master
huddled at the top. And now the Maenads saw him
more clearly than he saw them. But barely had they seen,
when the stranger vanished and there came a great voice
out of heaven—Dionysus', it must have been—
1135   crying: "Women, I bring you the man who has mocked
at you and me and at our holy mysteries.
Take vengeance upon him." And as he spoke
a flash of awful fire bound earth and heaven.
The high air hushed, and along the forest glen
1140   the leaves hung still; you could hear no cry of beasts.
The Bacchae heard that voice but missed its words,
and leaping up, they stared, peering everywhere.
Again that voice. And now they knew his cry,
the clear command of god. And breaking loose
1145   like startled doves, through grove and torrent,
over jagged rocks, they flew, their feet maddened
by the breath of god. And when they saw my master
perching in his tree, they climbed a great stone
that towered opposite his perch and showered him
1150   with stones and javelins of fir, while the others

hurled their wands. And yet they missed their target,
poor Pentheus in his perch, barely out of reach
of their eager hands, treed, unable to escape.
Finally they splintered branches from the oaks
1155 and with those bars of wood tried to lever up the tree
by prying at the roots. But every effort failed.
Then Agave cried out: "Maenads, make a circle
about the trunk and grip it with your hands.
Unless we take this climbing beast, he will reveal
1160 the secrets of the god." With that, thousands of hands
tore the fir tree from the earth, and down, down
from his high perch fell Pentheus, tumbling
to the ground, sobbing and screaming as he fell,
for he knew his end was near. His own mother,
1165 like a priestess with her victim, fell upon him
first. But snatching off his wig and snood
so she would recognize his face, he touched her cheeks,
screaming, "*No, no, Mother! I am Pentheus,*
your own son, the child you bore to Echion!
1170 *Pity me, spare me, Mother! I have done a wrong,*
but do not kill your own son for my offense."
But she was foaming at the mouth, and her crazed eyes
rolling with frenzy. She was mad, stark mad,
possessed by Bacchus. Ignoring his cries of pity,
1175 she seized his left arm at the wrist; then, planting
her foot upon his chest, she pulled, wrenching away
the arm at the shoulder—not by her own strength,
for the god had put inhuman power in her hands.
Ino, meanwhile, on the other side, was scratching off
1180 his flesh. Then Autonoë and the whole horde
of Bacchae swarmed upon him. Shouts everywhere,
he screaming with what little breath was left,
they shrieking in triumph. One tore off an arm,
another a foot still warm in its shoe. His ribs
1185 were clawed clean of flesh, and every hand
was smeared with blood as they played ball with scraps
of Pentheus' body.
                    The pitiful remains lie scattered,
one piece among the sharp rocks, others
lying lost among the leaves in the depths
1190 of the forest. His mother, picking up his head,
impaled it on her wand. She seems to think it is
some mountain lion's head which she carries in triumph
through the thick of Cithaeron. Leaving her sisters
at the Maenad dances, she is coming here, gloating
1195 over her grisly prize. She calls upon Bacchus:
he is her "fellow-huntsman," "comrade of the chase,
crowned with victory." But all the victory
she carries home is her own grief.

                              Now,
        before Agave returns, let me leave
1200   this scene of sorrow. Humility,
        a sense of reverence before the sons of heaven—
        of all the prizes that a mortal man might win,
        these, I say, are wisest; these are best.
                [*Exit* MESSENGER.]
        CHORUS   —We dance to the glory of Bacchus!
1205   We dance to the death of Pentheus,
            the death of the spawn of the dragon!
                He dressed in woman's dress;
                he took the lovely thyrsus;
                it waved him down to death,
1210   led by a bull to Hades.
            Hail, Bacchae! Hail, women of Thebes!
            Your victory is fair, fair the prize,
                    this famous prize of grief!
            Glorious the game! To fold your child
1215   in your arms, streaming with his blood!
        CORYPHAEUS   But look: there comes Pentheus' mother, Agave,
        running wild-eyed toward the palace.
                                    —Welcome,
            welcome to the reveling band of the god of joy!
                [*Enter* AGAVE *with other Bacchantes. She is covered with blood and
                carries the head of* PENTHEUS *impaled upon her thyrsus.*]
        AGAVE   Bacchae of Asia—
        CHORUS   Speak, speak.
1220   AGAVE   We bring this branch to the palace,
            this fresh-cut spray from the mountains.
            Happy was the hunting.
        CHORUS   I see.
            I welcome our fellow-reveler of god.
        AGAVE   The whelp of a wild mountain lion,
1225   and snared by me without a noose.
            Look, look at the prize I bring.
        CHORUS   Where was he caught?
        AGAVE   On Cithaeron—
        CHORUS   On Cithaeron?
        AGAVE   Our prize was killed.
        CHORUS   Who killed him?
        AGAVE   I struck him first.
1230   The Maenads call me "Agave the blest."
        CHORUS   And then?
        AGAVE   Cadmus'—
        CHORUS   Cadmus'?
        AGAVE   Daughters.
            After me, they reached the prey.
            After me. Happy was the hunting.

CHORUS   Happy indeed.
AGAVE   Then share my glory,
1235   share the feast.
CHORUS   Share, unhappy woman?
AGAVE   See, the whelp is young and tender.
       Beneath the soft mane of its hair,
       the down is blooming on the cheeks.
CHORUS   With that mane he *looks* a beast.
1240 AGAVE   Our god is wise. Cunningly, cleverly,
       Bacchus the hunter lashed the Maenads
       against his prey.
CHORUS   Our king is a hunter.
AGAVE   You praise me now?
CHORUS   I praise you.
AGAVE   The men of Thebes—
CHORUS   And Pentheus, your son?
1245 AGAVE   Will praise his mother. She caught
       a great quarry, this lion's cub.
CHORUS   Extraordinary catch.
AGAVE   Extraordinary skill.
CHORUS   You are proud?
AGAVE   Proud and happy.
       I have won the trophy of the chase,
1250 a great prize, manifest to all.
CORYPHAEUS   Then, poor woman, show the citizens of Thebes
       this great prize, this trophy you have won
       in the hunt.

       [AGAVE *proudly exhibits her thyrsus with the head of* PENTHEUS
       impaled upon the point.]

AGAVE   You citizens of this towered city,
       men of Thebes, behold the trophy of your women's
1255 hunting! *This* is the quarry of our chase, taken
       not with nets nor spears of bronze but by the white
       and delicate hands of women. What are they worth,
       your boastings now and all that uselessness
       your armor is, since we, with our bare hands,
1260 captured this quarry and tore its bleeding body
       limb from limb?
                        —But where is my father Cadmus?
       He should come. And my son. Where is Pentheus?
       Fetch him. I will have him set his ladder up
       against the wall and, there upon the beam,
1265 nail the head of this wild lion I have killed
       as a trophy of my hunt.

       [*Enter* CADMUS, *followed by attendants who bear upon a bier the
       dismembered body of* PENTHEUS.]

CADMUS   Follow me, attendants.
       Bear your dreadful burden in and set it down,
       there before the palace.

[*The attendants set down the bier.*]

This was Pentheus

whose body, after long and weary searchings
1270 I painfully assembled from Cithaeron's glens
where it lay, scattered in shreds, dismembered
throughout the forest, no two pieces
in a single place.

Old Teiresias and I

had returned to Thebes from the orgies on the mountain
1275 before I learned of this atrocious crime
my daughters did. And so I hurried back
to the mountain to recover the body of this boy
murdered by the Maenads. There among the oaks
I found Aristaeus'[8] wife, the mother of Actaeon,
1280 Autonoë, and with her Ino, both
still stung with madness. But Agave, they said,
was on her way to Thebes, still possessed.
And what they said was true, for there she is,
and not a happy sight.

AGAVE   Now, Father,

1285 yours can be the proudest boast of living men.
For you are now the father of the bravest daughters
in the world. All of your daughters are brave,
but I above the rest. I have left my shuttle
at the loom; I raised my sight to higher things—
1290 to hunting animals with my bare hands.

You see?

Here in my hands I hold the quarry of my chase,
a trophy for our house. Take it, Father, take it.
Glory in my kill and invite your friends to share
the feast of triumph. For you are blest, Father,
1295 by this great deed I have done.

CADMUS   This is a grief

so great it knows no size. I cannot look.
This is the awful murder your hands have done.
This, this is the noble victim you have slaughtered
to the gods. And to share a feast like this
1300 you now invite all Thebes and me?

O gods,

how terribly I pity you and then myself.
Justly—too, too justly—has lord Bromius,
this god of our own blood, destroyed us all,
every one.

AGAVE   How scowling and crabbed is old age

1305 in men. I hope my son takes after his mother

---

8. Son of Apollo; he was worshipped as a protector of flocks and olive trees, and he taught bee-
keeping to mortals.

and wins, as she has done, the laurels of the chase
when he goes hunting with the younger men of Thebes.
But all my son can do is quarrel with god.
He should be scolded, Father, and you are the one
1310 who should scold him. Yes, someone call him out
so he can see his mother's triumph.

CADMUS   Enough. No more.
When you realize the horror you have done,
you shall suffer terribly. But if with luck
your present madness lasts until you die,
1315 you will seem to have, not having, happiness.

AGAVE   Why do you reproach me? Is there something wrong?

CADMUS   First raise your eyes to the heavens.

AGAVE   There.
But why?

CADMUS   Does it look the same as it did before?
Or has it changed?

AGAVE   It seems—somehow—clearer,
1320 brighter than it was before.

CADMUS   Do you still feel
the same flurry inside you?

AGAVE   The same—flurry?
No, I feel—somehow—calmer. I feel as though—
my mind were somehow—changing.

CADMUS   Can you still hear me?
Can you answer clearly?

AGAVE   No. I have forgotten
1325 what we were saying, Father.

CADMUS   Who was your husband?

AGAVE   Echion—a man, they said, born of the dragon seed.

CADMUS   What was the name of the child you bore your husband?

AGAVE   Pentheus.

CADMUS   And whose head do you hold in your hands?

AGAVE [averting her eyes]   A lion's head—or so the hunters told me.

1330 CADMUS   Look directly at it. Just a quick glance.

AGAVE   What is it? What am I holding in my hands?

CADMUS   Look more closely still. Study it carefully.

AGAVE   No! O gods, I see the greatest grief there is.

CADMUS   Does it look like a lion now?

AGAVE   No, no. It is—
1335 Pentheus' head—I hold—

CADMUS   And mourned by me
before you ever knew.

AGAVE   But who killed him?
Why am I holding him?

CADMUS   O savage truth,
what a time to come!

AGAVE   For god's sake, speak.
My heart is beating with terror.

CADMUS   *You* killed him.

1340 You and your sisters.

AGAVE   But where was he killed?

Here at home? Where?

CADMUS   He was killed on Cithaeron,

there where the hounds tore Actaeon to pieces.

AGAVE   But why? Why had Pentheus gone to Cithaeron?

CADMUS   He went to your revels to mock the god.

AGAVE   But *we*—

1345 what were we doing on the mountain?

CADMUS   You were mad.

The whole city was possessed.

AGAVE   Now, now I see:

Dionysus has destroyed us all.

CADMUS   You outraged him.

You denied that he was truly god.

AGAVE   Father,

where is my poor boy's body now?

CADMUS   There it is.

1350 I gathered the pieces with great difficulty.

AGAVE   Is his body entire? Has he been laid out well?

CADMUS   [All but the head. The rest is mutilated

horribly.]

AGAVE   But why should Pentheus suffer for my crime?

CADMUS   He, like you, blasphemed the god. And so

1355 the god has brought us all to ruin at one blow,

you, your sisters, and this boy. All our house

the god has utterly destroyed and, with it,

me. For I have no sons left, no male heir;

and I have lived only to see this boy,

1360 this branch of your own body, most horribly

and foully killed.

                    [*He turns and addresses the corpse.*]

                        —To you my house looked up.

Child, you were the stay of my house; you were

my daughter's son. Of you this city stood in awe.

No one who once had seen your face dared outrage

1365 the old man, or if he did, you punished him.

Now I must go, a banished and dishonored man—

I, Cadmus the great, who sowed the soldiery

of Thebes and harvested a great harvest. My son,

dearest to me of all men—for even dead,

1370 I count you still the man I love the most—

never again will your hand touch my chin;

no more, child, will you hug me and call me

"Grandfather" and say, "Who is wronging you?

Does anyone trouble you or vex your heart, old man?

1375 Tell me, Grandfather, and I will punish him."

No, now there is grief for me; the mourning

for you; pity for your mother; and for her sisters,
sorrow.
               If there is still any mortal man
who despises or defies the gods, let him look
1380 on this boy's death and believe in the gods.
       CORYPHAEUS Cadmus, I pity you. Your daughter's son
       has died as he deserved, and yet his death
       bears hard on you.
              [*At this point there is a break in the manuscript of nearly fifty lines. The
              following speeches of Agave and Coryphaeus and the first part of Diony-
              sus' speech have been conjecturally reconstructed from fragments and
              later material which made use of* The Bacchae. *Lines which can plausi-
              bly be assigned to the lacuna are otherwise not indicated. My own inven-
              tions are designed not to complete the speeches, but to effect a transition
              between the fragments, and are bracketed.—*TRANS.]

       AGAVE   O Father, now you can see
       how everything has changed. I am in anguish now,
1385 tormented, who walked in triumph minutes past,
       exulting in my kill. And that prize I carried home
       with such pride was my own curse. Upon these hands
       I bear the curse of my son's blood. How then
       with these accursed hands may I touch his body?
1390 How can I, accursed with such a curse, hold him
       to my breast? O gods, what dirge can I sing
       [that there might be] a dirge [for every]
       broken limb?
. . . .
                Where is a shroud to cover up his corpse?
       O my child, what hands will give you proper care
1395 unless with my own hands I lift my curse?
              [*She lifts up one of* PENTHEUS' *limbs and asks the help of* CADMUS *in piec-
              ing the body together. She mourns each piece separately before replacing
              it on the bier.*]
       Come, Father. We must restore his head
       to this unhappy boy. As best we can, we shall make
       him whole again.
                     —O dearest, dearest face!
       Pretty boyish mouth! Now with this veil
1400 I shroud your head, gathering with loving care
       these mangled bloody limbs, this flesh I brought
       to birth.
. . . .
       CORYPHAEUS Let this scene teach those [who see these things:
       Dionysus is the son] of Zeus.
              [*Above the palace* DIONYSUS *appears in epiphany.*]
       DIONYSUS   [I am Dionysus,
       the son of Zeus, returned to Thebes, revealed,
1405 a god to men.] But the men [of Thebes] blasphemed me.
       They slandered me; they said I came of mortal man,

and not content with speaking blasphemies,
[they dared to threaten my person with violence.]
These crimes this people whom I cherished well
1410 did from malice to their benefactor. Therefore,
I now disclose the sufferings in store for them.
Like [enemies], they shall be driven from this city
to other lands; there, submitting to the yoke
of slavery, they shall wear out wretched lives,
1415 captives of war, enduring much indignity.

> [He turns to the corpse of PENTHEUS.]

This man has found the death which he deserved,
torn to pieces among the jagged rocks.
You are my witnesses: he came with outrage;
he attempted to chain my hands, abusing me
1420 [and doing what he should least of all have done.]
And therefore he has rightly perished by the hands
of those who should the least of all have murdered him.
What he suffers, he suffers justly.
                                    Upon you,
Agave, and on your sisters I pronounce this doom:
1425 you shall leave this city in expiation
of the murder you have done. You are unclean,
and it would be a sacrilege that murderers
should remain at peace beside the graves [of those
whom they have killed].

> [He turns to CADMUS.]

. . . .
                              Next I shall disclose the trials
1430 which await this man. You, Cadmus, shall be changed
to a serpent, and your wife, the child of Ares,
immortal Harmonia, shall undergo your doom,
a serpent too. With her, it is your fate
to go a journey in a car drawn on by oxen,
1435 leading behind you a great barbarian host.
For thus decrees the oracle of Zeus.
With a host so huge its numbers cannot be counted,
you shall ravage many cities; but when your army
plunders the shrine of Apollo, its homecoming
1440 shall be perilous and hard. Yet in the end
the god Ares shall save Harmonia and you
and bring you both to live among the blest.
    So say I, born of no mortal father,
Dionysus, true son of Zeus. If then,
1445 when you would not, you had muzzled your madness,
you should have an ally now in the son of Zeus.

CADMUS We implore you, Dionysus. We have done wrong.

DIONYSUS Too late. When there was time, you did not know me.

CADMUS We have learned. But your sentence is too harsh.

1450 DIONYSUS I am a god. I was blasphemed by you.

CADMUS   Gods should be exempt from human passions.

DIONYSUS   Long ago my father Zeus ordained these things.

AGAVE   It is fated, Father. We must go.

DIONYSUS   Why then delay?
    For you must go.

CADMUS   Child, to what a dreadful end
1455   have we all come, you and your wretched sisters
    and my unhappy self. An old man, I must go
    to live a stranger among barbarian peoples, doomed
    to lead against Hellas a motley foreign army.
    Transformed to serpents, I and my wife,
1460   Harmonia, the child of Ares, we must captain
    spearsmen against the tombs and shrines of Hellas.
    Never shall my sufferings end; not even
    over Acheron[9] shall I have peace.

AGAVE   [embracing CADMUS]   O Father,
    to be banished, to live without you!

CADMUS   Poor child,
1465   like a white swan warding its weak old father,
    why do you clasp those white arms about my neck?

AGAVE   But banished! Where shall I go?

CADMUS   I do not know,
    my child. Your father can no longer help you.

AGAVE   Farewell, my home! City, farewell.
1470   O bridal bed, banished I go,
    in misery, I leave you now.

CADMUS   Go, poor child, seek shelter in Aristaeus' house.

AGAVE   I pity you, Father.

CADMUS   And I pity you, my child,
    and I grieve for your poor sisters. I pity them.

1475 AGAVE   Terribly has Dionysus brought
    disaster down upon this house.

DIONYSUS   I was terribly blasphemed,
    my name dishonored in Thebes.

AGAVE   Farewell, Father.

CADMUS   Farewell to you, unhappy child.
1480   Farewell. But you shall find your faring hard.
       [Exit CADMUS.]

AGAVE   Lead me, guides, where my sisters wait,
    poor sisters of my exile. Let me go
    where I shall never see Cithaeron more,
    where that accursed hill may not see me,
1485   where I shall find no trace of thyrsus!
    That I leave to other Bacchae.
       [Exit AGAVE with attendants.]

CHORUS   The gods have many shapes.
    The gods bring many things

---

9. That is, in death; Acheron is one of the rivers of the underworld.

to their accomplishment.
1490 And what was most expected
has not been accomplished.
But god has found his way
for what no man expected.
    So ends the play.

ARISTOPHANES

ca. 450–ca. 385 B.C.E.

COMEDY (a word derived from the Greek *kōmōidia*, "song of the *kōmos*," or band of revelers) officially joined its predecessor, tragedy, as part of the dramatic competitions in Athens in the fifth century B.C.E., first at the City Dionysia (ca. 486) and then at the Lenaea (ca. 442). While scholars estimate that several hundred plays that we now categorize as "Old Comedy" may have been produced at the festivals in the fifth century B.C.E. alone, only eleven relatively complete texts by Aristophanes remain to provide evidence of this important form of classical theater. Aristophanes' track record of success as a dramatist, with at least six first-place and four second-place awards in the competitions, may account in part for the preservation of his comedies across the centuries. Exuding energy and wit, his plays career from the depths of vulgarity to the heights of poetic sophistication. Although in some eras he has been faulted for the inconsistencies in his narratives and the implausibility of his scenarios, Aristophanes more recently has regained critical favor for his nuanced interplay of theme and action. *LYSISTRATA* stands out in this regard and has attracted sustained interest since the early twentieth century for its focus on women's roles at times of war.

Born in a region near Athens, Aristophanes appears to have been a landowner and also a political representative to the Athenian Council of 500, the group that helped establish the government's agenda. Plato's *Symposium* (ca. 384 B.C.E.) depicts Aristophanes as fitting in with the social and intellectual elite of Athens, and his plays certainly reflect familiarity with Attic politics and culture. Aristophanes is believed to have written more than forty plays, the first of which was produced in 427 B.C.E. and the last around 386 B.C.E. These works reflect the comparative freedom of expression granted to the comic playwrights of the era and are known for their pointed political critique, their frank sexuality, and their close engagement with the myths and social conventions of Attic culture. They blend the fantastic and the quotidian, often making the impossible seem plausible—as do the anthropomorphized choruses in *The Birds* (Dionysia, 414) and *The Frogs* (Lenaea, 405).

Produced at the Lenaea in 411, *Lysistrata* dealt directly with recent events in the Peloponnesian War, by then a twenty-year struggle between Athens (and its island and mainland dependencies) and Sparta (and its allies). The war would continue until 404, when the ultimate defeat of Athens' navy led to the end of its empire. This conflict spanned much of Aristophanes' career and recurred thematically in many of his plays. In *Lysistrata*, he was responding specifically to the disastrous loss of the

Athenian fleet in 413 at Sicily and its after-math, including the appointment by the Athenian government of a board of executive councillors called "Probouloi" who could act quickly and could officially manage the city-state's finances without being subject to the usual democratic process.

With the men of Athens and Sparta at war, Aristophanes depicts the ongoing conflict's impact on the daily lives of others, especially women and the elderly men left in charge of the government. Lysistrata, an Athenian woman, decides that the best way to bring the hostilities to a quick end is for the women to refuse to have sex with the warriors. Calling together the women on both sides of the war, she persuades them to leave their homes and, in the case of the Athenians, to occupy the Acropolis—the main meeting place and market of Athens, as well as the site of the city's treasury. In this way, Lysistrata believes, the women will gain control over both the financial and the human resources integral to the war effort, forcing a declaration of peace and the return to the communities of domestic order, tranquillity, and economic security.

The dramatic structure of Lysistrata exemplifies the standard form of Old Comedy. The opening scene, or prologue, introduces us to the central concerns of the play: in this instance, the sex-strike plot for which the work is most remembered. During the entrance (parados) of the chorus, Aristophanes chooses to divide the standard group of twenty-four into two halves—twelve old men and twelve old women—whose antagonism contributes both to the humor of the work and to its themes of domestic and political upheaval; moreover, the parados sets up the grounds for the debate, or agōn, to follow. This rhetorical contest between Lysistrata and the Commissioner of Public Safety, a satiric portrait of one of the Probouloi, reflects the spirit of formal competition that pervaded classical Greek culture; it also enables Aristophanes to expand the scope of the play to incorporate additional social and political issues, including Lysistrata's heartfelt depiction of women's grief at the loss of their sons in war. In such moments, we see that Aristophanes distinguishes his title character from his satiric portraits of

other figures, possibly because he modeled her on Lysimache, priestess of Athena Polias, the most important of such positions in Athenian religious culture. The parabasis, or interlude, that follows the agōn again showcases the chorus and provides a transition to the series of episodes that will resolve the action. Notable among these is the highly comic scene with the Athenian couple Myrrhine and Kinesias that bawdily demonstrates, through the oversized, erect phallus the latter sports, the effectiveness of the women's deprivation tactics.

At such a great remove from the classical era, audiences and readers today may find both the structure and style of ancient comedy challenging. Moreover, although we have some general knowledge of how these plays were performed, we lack the specific understanding necessary to envision them with historical authenticity. We know, for example, that the plays combined spoken verse, recitative (verse declaimed rhythmically), and song; music and dance also contributed significantly to the overall theatrical effect. Our uncertainty about the exact nature of any of these performative elements has frustrated some interpreters of Lysistrata, but others have capitalized on it to create exciting and innovative productions. The absence of stage directions, the corruptions in ancient manuscripts, and lingering doubts about the exact meaning of topical references or allusions all complicate the work of translators and scholars, but they also extend the range of possibilities for contemporary performances.

Despite the gaps in our knowledge about Greek comedy generally and Lysistrata specifically, we know enough to recognize that some aspects of the play that seem strange to us would have been considered routine, or at least not unusual, to fifth-century Athenians. First, because the City Dionysia and the Lenaea were both civic and religious festivals, replete with ritual sacrifices to the gods in addition to the theatrical competition, the mingling of religious and political themes in Lysistrata not only would have been highly appropriate for the festival context but also would have mirrored the tenor of Athenian daily life. Second, although the frank representation of

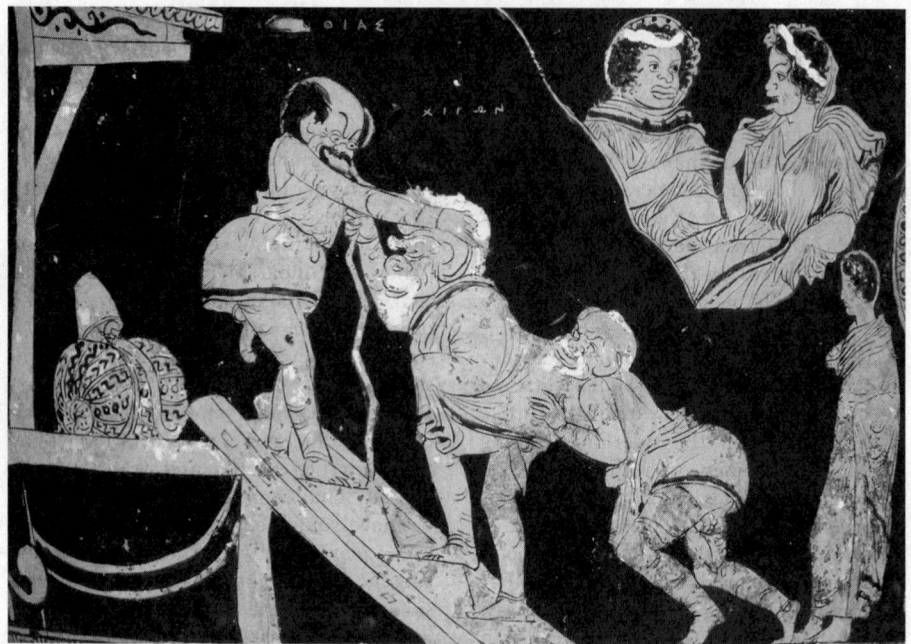

This detail from a painted bell-krater (large wine bowl) dating from the fourth century B.C.E. shows three actors performing in a comedy about the centaur Cheiron.

sexuality, especially the prominence of the phallus, might strike some contemporary readers as antithetical to a religious ceremony, it was perfectly in keeping with Greek cultural traditions; such explicitness is even less surprising if we consider that comedy most likely is partly rooted in the rituals of cults that honored the fertility gods Dionysus and Demeter (among other deities). Finally, the play's sexually explicit banter and innuendo would have been matched by equally explicit costumery—not only the phalluses padded to indicate various degrees of erection but also the stuffed bodysuit worn by the character Reconciliation, overemphasizing the proportions of the female anatomy to render them visible to a large outdoor audience. *Lysistrata* thus illustrates vividly how comic writers perceptively capture, often through exaggeration, distinctive cultural practices as well as individuals' foibles.

An awareness of this connection between comedy and its original context is especially important to a clear understanding of the central role of female characters in *Lysistrata*. Although *Lysistrata* is believed to be the first Western comedy featuring a female heroine and incorporating varied images of women's lives and attributes, we should also remember that this title character and all the other women in the play would have been portrayed by male performers, in a society in which the activities of well-off women were circumscribed and revolved exclusively around the home. Only male citizens participated in public endeavors, and Lysistrata's entry into the public sphere, although appearing potentially realistic to contemporary readers and audiences, should be seen in its Greek context as fantastical—as implausible as choruses of singing and dancing birds and frogs. Thus we should not interpret the play as proto-feminist, or as a critique of the "separate spheres" ideology that informed classical Greek society. Indeed, Lysistrata wants nothing more than to restore the status quo, with all citizens—male and female—returning to their established roles.

The implausibilities and inconsistencies in Aristophanes' dramaturgy have proven alienating to some contemporary readers and audiences, who are more comfortable with the conventions of dramatic realism that have dominated the theater since the nineteenth century. Yet if we can keep in mind that ideas about narrative cohesion and realistic action—our notions of what makes a play "good"—are themselves historical constructs, we may better appreciate Aristophanes' shifts between, for example, the farcical sex-strike plot of the *parados* and the *agōn*'s more serious treatment of financial concerns. Similarly, we might suspend our disbelief at the apparent contradiction between the warriors' absence from home and the women's plan to deny them sex.

More importantly, our openness to these unique qualities of Aristophanic dramaturgy may enable us to discern the metaphors he used to structure his fantasy of women's political intervention. First, the disjunctions in the "logical" flow of dramatic action parallel the war's disruption of civic and family life. The two-pronged strategy proposed by Lysistrata—withholding sex and blocking access to state funds— also helps make evident the foundational elements of marriage: the sexual relationship between husband and wife, and the economic transactions that similarly support the home environment. Lysistrata then works to establish the links between the women's world and the state, describing how domestic management mirrors core elements of governmental practices. Aristophanes further develops these associations

through the implied staging, which visually ties these domestic and civic worlds together. We assume that Lysistrata and her friend Kalonike first encounter each other outside their homes, but soon the central door in the *scaenae frons* (the wooden stage building used for entrances and exits) is also serving as the entrance to the Acropolis. Later, Myrrhine transforms the space just outside the Acropolis into a bedroom, furthering the linkage, and the play concludes with the women's hosting a banquet on the Acropolis to celebrate the peace. Aristophanes' utopian vision of harmony at home and abroad thus shapes a comedy that could at best work to influence the state's future strategies or at least temporarily divert an Athenian audience otherwise consumed by its increasingly grim political prospects.

Centuries later, Aristophanes' concept of women's leading the initiative for peace spurred a group of women actors to launch the *Lysistrata* Project, a global protest against the United States' invasion of Iraq. On March 3, 2003, artists around the world held more than 1,000 public readings of the play in fifty-nine countries to voice their opposition to this military action. That these artists and their audiences saw such relevance in a work almost 2,500 years old expresses volumes about the ongoing power of theater to speak of and to humanity.

—J.E.G.

Lysistrata[1]

CHARACTERS

LYSISTRATA, an Athenian woman
KALONIKE, Lysistrata's friend
MYRRHINE, an Athenian wife
LAMPITO, a Spartan wife
MAGISTRATE, one of the ten Probouloi
OLD WOMEN (three), allies of Lysistrata

WIVES (four), Lysistrata's conspirators
KINESIAS, Myrrhine's husband
BABY, son of Kinesias and Myrrhine
SPARTAN HERALD
SPARTAN AMBASSADOR
ATHENIAN AMBASSADORS (two)

1. Translated by Jeffrey Henderson.

MUTE CHARACTERS

ATHENIAN WOMEN
ISMENIA, a Theban woman
KORINTHIAN WOMAN
SPARTAN WOMEN
SKYTHIAN GIRL, Lysistrata's slave
MAGISTRATE'S SLAVES
SKYTHIAN POLICEMEN
OLD WOMEN, allies of Lysistrata

MANES, Kinesias' slave
SPARTAN DELEGATES
SPARTAN SLAVES, with the
  Spartan delegation
ATHENIAN DELEGATES
RECONCILIATION
DOORKEEPER

CHORUS

OLD ATHENIAN MEN (twelve)

OLD ATHENIAN WOMEN (twelve)

Prologue

[SCENE: *A neighborhood street in Athens, after dawn. The stage-building has a large central door and two smaller, flanking doors. From one of these* LYSISTRATA *emerges and looks expectantly up and down the street.*]

LYSISTRATA   Now if someone had invited the women to a revel for Bacchos, or to Pan's shrine, or to Genetyllis's at Kolias,[2] they'd be jamming the streets with their tambourines. But now there's not a single woman here. [*The far door opens.*] Except for my own neighbor there. Good morning, Kalonike.[3]

5 KALONIKE   You too, Lysistrata.[4] What's bothering you? Don't frown, child. Knitted brows are no good for your looks.

LYSISTRATA   But my heart's on fire, Kalonike, and I'm terribly annoyed about us women. You know, according to the men we're capable of all sorts of mischief—

10 KALONIKE   And that we are, by Zeus![5]

LYSISTRATA   but when they're told to meet here to discuss something that really matters, they're sleeping in and don't show up!

KALONIKE   Honey, they'll be along. For wives to get out of the house is a lot of trouble, you know: we've got to look after the husband or wake up a 15 slave or put the baby to bed, or give it a bath or feed it a snack.

LYSISTRATA   Sure, but there's other business they ought to take more seriously than that stuff.

KALONIKE   Well, Lysistrata dear, what exactly *is* this business you're calling us women together for? What's the deal? Is it a big one?

20 LYSISTRATA   Big!

KALONIKE   Not hard as well?

LYSISTRATA   It's big *and* hard, by Zeus.

KALONIKE   Then how come we're not all here?

LYSISTRATA   That's not what I meant! If it were, we'd all have shown up fast

2. Promontory near Athens where stood a statue of Aphrodite, the goddess of beauty and carnal love. *Bacchos*: also known as Dionysus, the god of wine and fertility. *Pan*: goat-footed god of woods and pastures, often worshipped with Dionysus. *Genetyllis*: pro-

tectress of childbirth (in some accounts, another name for Aphrodite; in others, her companion).
3. A name meaning "beautiful victory."
4. A name meaning "disbander of armies."
5. King of the Greek gods.

25 enough. No, it's something I've been thinking hard *about*, kicking it around, night after sleepless night.

KALONIKE   All those kicks must have made it really smart.

LYSISTRATA   Smart enough that the salvation of all Greece lies in the women's hands!

30 KALONIKE   In the *women's* hands? That's hardly reassuring!

LYSISTRATA   It's true: our country's future depends on *us*: whether the Peloponnesians[6] become extinct—

KALONIKE   Well, that would be just fine with me, by Zeus!

LYSISTRATA   and all the Boiotians[7] get annihilated—

35 KALONIKE   Not *all* of them, though: please spare the eels![8]

LYSISTRATA   I won't say anything like that about the Athenians, but you know what I *could* say. But if the women gather together here—the Boiotian women, the Peloponnesian women, and ourselves—together we'll be able to rescue Greece!

40 KALONIKE   But what can mere *women* do that's intelligent or noble? We sit around the house looking pretty, wearing saffron dresses and makeup and Kimberic gowns and canoe-sized slippers.

LYSISTRATA   Exactly! That's exactly what I think will rescue Greece: our fancy little dresses, our perfumes and our slippers, our rouge and our see-through 45 underwear!

KALONIKE   How do you mean? I'm lost.

LYSISTRATA   They'll guarantee that not a single one of the men who are still alive will raise his spear against another—

KALONIKE   Then, by the Two Goddesses,[9] I'd better get my party dress dyed 50 saffron!

LYSISTRATA   nor hoist his shield—

KALONIKE   I'll wear a Kimberic gown!

LYSISTRATA   nor even pull a knife!

KALONIKE   I've got to buy some slippers!

55 LYSISTRATA   So shouldn't the women have gotten here by now?

KALONIKE   By *now*? My god, they should have taken wing and flown here ages ago!

LYSISTRATA   My friend, you'll see that they're typically Athenian: everything they do, they do too late. There isn't even a single woman here from the Paralia, nor from Salamis.[1]

60 KALONIKE   Oh, them: I just *know* they've been up since dawn, straddling their mounts.

LYSISTRATA   And the women I reckoned would be here first, and counted on, the women from Acharnai,[2] they're not here either.

KALONIKE   Well, Theogenes' wife, for one, was set to make a fast getaway. 65 [*Groups of women begin to enter from both sides.*] But look, here come some of your women now!

---

6. Inhabitants of Peloponnesos, the peninsula that forms the southern Greek mainland, with whom Athens was at war; they were led by Sparta.
7. That is, the Thebans in Boiotia, northwest of Athens, its other main opponents in the Peloponnesian War.
8. A delicacy native to Boiotia.
9. Demeter, goddess of agriculture, and her

daughter Persephone or Kore (the Maiden), queen of the underworld; both were associated with fertility and women.
1. Island in the Aegean Sea near Athens. *Paralia*: a district on the coast of Attica, the region in which Athens is located (literally, "seacoast").
2. A district near Athens.

LYSISTRATA   And here come some others, over there!

KALONIKE   Phew! Where are *they* from?

LYSISTRATA   From Dungstown.

70   KALONIKE   It seems they've got some sticking to their shoes.

MYRRHINE   I hope we're not too late, Lysistrata. What do you say? Why don't you say something?

LYSISTRATA   Myrrhine,[3] I've got no medal for anyone who shows up late for important business.

75   MYRRHINE   Look, I couldn't find my girdle; it was dark. But now we're here, so tell us what's so important.

LYSISTRATA   No, let's wait a little while, until the women from Boiotia and the Peloponnesos come.

MYRRHINE   That's a much better plan. And look, there's Lampito coming now!

[*Enter* LAMPITO, *accompanied by a group of other Spartan women, a Theban woman (*ISMENIA*) and a Korinthian woman.*]

80   LYSISTRATA   Greetings, my very dear Spartan Lampito! My darling, how dazzling is your beauty! What rosy cheeks, what firmness of physique! You could choke a bull!

LAMPITO   Is true, I think, by Twain Gods. Much exercise, much leaping to harden buttocks.[4]

85   KALONIKE   And what a beautiful pair of boobs you've got!

LAMPITO   Hey, you feel me up like sacrificial ox!

LYSISTRATA   And this other young lady here, where's *she* from?

LAMPITO   By Twain Gods, she come as representative of Boiotia.

MYRRHINE   She's certainly *like* Boiotia, by Zeus, with all her lush bottomland.

90   KALONIKE   Yes indeed, her bush has been most elegantly pruned.

LYSISTRATA   And who's this other girl?

LAMPITO   Lady of substance, by Twain Gods, from Korinth.[5]

KALONIKE   She's substantial all right, both frontside and backside.

LAMPITO   Who convenes this assembly of women here?

95   LYSISTRATA   I'm the one.

LAMPITO   Then please to tell what you want of us.

KALONIKE   That's right, dear lady, speak up. What's this important business of yours?

LYSISTRATA   I'm ready to tell you. But before I tell you, I want to ask you a small question; it won't take long.

100   KALONIKE   Ask away.

LYSISTRATA   Don't you all pine for your children's fathers when they're off at war? I'm sure that every one of you has a husband who's away.

KALONIKE   My husband's been away five months, my dear, at the Thracian front; he's guarding Eukrates.[6]

105   MYRRHINE   And *mine's* been at Pylos[7] *seven* whole months.

---

3. A name meaning "myrtle," which was also a slang term for the vulva.

4. Spartan women, unlike their counterparts in other polities, received an education similar to that of men, including physical training. Throughout, Aristophanes caricatures the Doric dialect of the Spartans, which differed notably from the Attic-Ionic Greek of the Athenians. *Twain Gods*: the twins Kastor and

Pollux, sons of Leda, Zeus, and Tyndareos, king of Sparta, and patrons of the Spartans.

5. A city-state in the northern Peloponnesos; like Sparta and Thebes, a rival of Athens.

6. An Athenian general; Thrace, a region in northeastern Greece, was an ally of Athens, and many battles were fought there during the war.

7. A district in the southern Peloponnesos, occupied by the Athenians since 425 B.C.E.

LAMPITO   And *mine*, soon as he come home from regiment, is strapping on
the shield and flying off.

KALONIKE   Even *lovers* have disappeared without a trace, and ever since the
Milesians[8] revolted from us, I haven't even seen a six-inch dildo, which
110   might have been a consolation, however small.

LYSISTRATA   Well, if I could devise a plan to end the war, would you be ready
to join me?

KALONIKE   By the Two Goddesses, I would, even if I had to pawn this dress
and on the very same day—drink up the proceeds!

115   MYRRHINE   And *I* think I would even cut myself in two like a flounder and
donate half to the cause!

LAMPTIO   And I would climb up to summit of Taÿgeton,[9] if I'm able to see
where peace may be from there.

LYSISTRATA   Here goes then; no need to beat around the bush. Ladies, if
120   we're going to force the men to make peace, we're going to have to give up—

KALONIKE   Give up what? Tell us.

LYSISTRATA   You'll do it, then?

KALONIKE   We'll do it, even if it means our death!

LYSISTRATA   All right. We're going to have to give up—cock. Why are you
125   turning away from me? Where are you going? Why are you all pursing your
lips and shaking your heads? What means thine altered color and tearful
droppings?[1] Will you do it or not? What are you waiting for?

KALONIKE   Count me out; let the war drag on.

MYRRHINE   Me too, by Zeus; let the war drag on.

130   LYSISTRATA   This from you, Ms. Flounder? Weren't you saying just a moment
ago that you'd cut yourself in half?

KALONIKE   Anything else you want, anything at all! I'm even ready to walk
through fire; *that* rather than give up cock. There's nothing like it, Lysistrata dear.

135   LYSISTRATA   And what about you?

WOMAN   I'm ready to walk through fire too.

LYSISTRATA   Oh what a low and horny race are we! No wonder men write
tragedies about us: we're nothing but Poseidon and a bucket.[2] Dear Spartan, if you alone would side with me we might still salvage the plan; give
140   me your vote!

LAMPITO   By Twain Gods, is difficult for females to sleep alone without the
hard-on. But anyway, I assent; is need for peace.

LYSISTRATA   You're an absolute dear, and the only real woman here!

KALONIKE   Well, what if we *did* abstain from, uh, what you say, which heaven
145   forbid: would peace be likelier to come on account of *that*?

LYSISTRATA   Absolutely, by the Two Goddesses. If we sat around at home all
made up, and walked past them wearing only our see-through underwear

---

8. The inhabitants of Miletus, a Greek city-
state on the coast of Asia Minor (present-day
Turkey) that revolted from Athens in 412 B.C.E.
9. A mountain range near Sparta.
1. The elevated language characteristic of
tragedy is here (as often in Greek comedy)

used for comic effect.
2. An allusion to the myth of Tyro; after being
seduced by Poseidon, god of the sea, she gave
birth to twin boys whom she left in a tub by
the edge of a river.

and with our pubes plucked in a neat triangle, and our husbands got hard
and hankered to ball us, but we didn't go near them and kept away, they'd
150 sue for peace, and pretty quick, you can count on that!

LAMPITO   Like Menelaos! Soon as he peek at Helen's bare melons, he throw
his sword away, I think.[3]

KALONIKE   But what if our husbands pay us no attention?

LYSISTRATA   As Pherekrates said, skin the skinned dog.[4]

155 KALONIKE   Facsimiles are nothing but poppycock. And what if they grab us
and drag us into the bedroom by force?

LYSISTRATA   Hold on to the door.

KALONIKE   And what if they beat us up?

LYSISTRATA   Submit, but disagreeably: men get no pleasure in sex when they
160 have to force you. And make them suffer in other ways as well. Don't worry,
they'll soon give in. No husband can have a happy life if his wife doesn't
want him to.

KALONIKE   Well, if the two of you agree to this, then we agree as well.

LAMPITO   And we shall bring *our* menfolk round to making everyway fair and
165 honest peace. But how do you keep Athenian rabble from acting like lunatics?

LYSISTRATA   Don't worry, we'll handle the persuasion on *our* side.

LAMPITO   Not so, as long as your battleships are afoot and your Goddess'
temple have bottomless fund of money.[5]

LYSISTRATA   In fact, that's also been well provided for: we're going to occupy
170 the Akropolis this very day. The older women are assigned that part: while
we're working out our agreement down here, they'll occupy the Akropolis,
pretending to be up there for a sacrifice.

LAMPITO   Sounds perfect, like rest of your proposals.

LYSISTRATA   Then why not ratify them immediately by taking an oath,
175 Lampito, so that the terms will be binding?

LAMPITO   Reveal an oath, then, and we all swear to it.

LYSISTRATA   Well said. Where's the Skythian[6] girl? [*A* SLAVE-GIRL *comes out of
the stage-building with a shield.*] What are you gawking at? Put that shield
down in front of us—no, the other way—and someone give me the
180 severings.

KALONIKE   Lysistrata, what kind of oath are you planning to make us swear?

LYSISTRATA   What kind? The kind they say Aischylos once had people swear:
slaughtering an animal over a shield.[7]

KALONIKE   Lysistrata, you don't take an oath about peace over a shield!

185 LYSISTRATA   Then what kind of oath will it be?

KALONIKE   What if we got a white stallion somewhere and cut a piece off *him*?[8]

LYSISTRATA   White stallion? Get serious.

KALONIKE   Well, how *are* we going to swear the oath?

3. After the Greeks had captured Troy,
Menelaos, king of Sparta, was about to kill
his wife Helen for adultery when he was overcome by her beauty.
4. That is, use a dildo. *Pherekrates*: Athenian
comic poet (slightly earlier than Aristophanes).
5. Athens' treasury—filled with tribute carried back by its navy—was in the Parthenon,

the temple of Athena on the Akropolis.
6. From Skythia, a vast region north and
northeast of the Black Sea that was a source
of slaves.
7. An allusion to Aeschylus's play *Seven
against Thebes* (467 B.C.E.).
8. A rare and costly sacrifice ("a piece" probably refers to the penis).

LYSISTRATA   By Zeus, if you'd like to know, I can tell you. We put a big black
190   wine-bowl hollow-up right here, we slaughter a magnum of Thasian wine
into it, and we swear not to pour any water into the bowl![9]

LAMPITO   Oh da, I cannot find words to praise that oath!

LYSISTRATA   Somebody go inside and fetch a bowl and a magnum. [*The* SLAVE-
GIRL *takes the shield inside and returns with a large wine-bowl and a large cup.*]

MYRRHINE   Dearest ladies, what a conglomeration of pottery!

195 KALONIKE   [*Grabbing at the bowl*]   Just touching this could make a person glad!

LYSISTRATA   Put it down! And join me in laying hands upon this boar. [*All the
women put a hand on the magnum.*] Mistress Persuasion and Bowl of Fellowship, graciously receive this sacrifice from the women. [*She opens the
magnum and pours wine into the bowl.*]

KALONIKE   The blood's a good color and spurts out nicely.

200 LAMPITO   It smell good too, by Kastor!

MYRRHINE   Ladies, let me be the first to take the oath!

KALONIKE   Hold on, by Aphrodite! Not unless you draw the first lot!

LYSISTRATA   *All* of you lay your hands upon the bowl; you too Lampito. Now
one of you, on behalf of you all, must repeat after me the terms of the oath,
205   and the rest of you will then swear to abide by them. No man of any kind,
lover or husband—

KALONIKE   No man of any kind, lover or husband—

LYSISTRATA   shall approach me with a hard-on. I can't hear you!

KALONIKE   shall approach me with a hard-on. Oh god, my knees are buck-
210   ling, Lysistrata!

LYSISTRATA   At home in celibacy shall I pass my life—

KALONIKE   At home in celibacy shall I pass my life—

LYSISTRATA   wearing a party-dress and makeup—

KALONIKE   wearing a party-dress and makeup—

215 LYSISTRATA   so that my husband will get as hot as a volcano for me—

KALONIKE   so that my husband will get as hot as a volcano for me—

LYSISTRATA   but never willingly shall I surrender to my husband.

KALONIKE   but never willingly shall I surrender to my husband.

LYSISTRATA   If he should use force to force me against my will—

220 KALONIKE   If he should use force to force me against my will—

LYSISTRATA   I will submit coldly and not move my hips.

KALONIKE   I will submit coldly and not move my hips.

LYSISTRATA   I will not raise my oriental slippers toward the ceiling.

KALONIKE   I will not raise my oriental slippers toward the ceiling.

225 LYSISTRATA   I won't crouch down like the lioness on a cheesegrater.[1]

KALONIKE   I won't crouch down like the lioness on a cheesegrater.

LYSISTRATA   If I live up to these vows, may I drink from this bowl.

KALONIKE   If I live up to these vows, may I drink from this bowl.

LYSISTRATA   But if I break them, may the bowl be full of water.

230 KALONIKE   But if I break them, may the bowl be full of water.

---

9. Greeks viewed drinking wine mixed with
water as a sign of refinement; the preference
of women for unadulterated wine was a comic
stereotype. *Thasian:* from Thasos, an island in
the northern Aegean Sea that was famous in

antiquity for its apple-scented wine.
1. That is, to be mounted. The Greeks often
made the handles of household utensils in
the shape of animals.

LYSISTRATA   So swear you one and all?

ALL   So swear we all!

LYSISTRATA   All right, then, I'll consecrate the bowl. [*She takes a long drink.*]

KALONIKE   Only your share, my friend; lets make sure we're all on friendly
235   terms right from the start.

[*After they drink, a women's joyful cry is heard offstage.*]

LAMPITO   What's that hurrah?

LYSISTRATA   It's just what I was telling you before: the women have occupied
the Akropolis and the Goddess' temple. Now, Lampito: you take off and
arrange things in Sparta, but leave these women here with us as hostages.
240   [*Exit* LAMPITO.] Meanwhile, we'll go inside with the other women on the
Akropolis and bolt the gates behind us.

KALONIKE   But don't you think the men will launch a concerted attack on us,
and very soon?

LYSISTRATA   I'm not worried about *them*. They can't come against us with
245   enough threats or fire to get these gates open, except on the terms we've
agreed on.

KALONIKE   No they can't, by Aphrodite! Otherwise we women wouldn't
deserve to be called rascals you can't win a fight with!

[*All exit into the central door of the scene-building, which now represents the Akropolis.*]

Parodos[2]

[*A semichorus composed of twelve old men, poorly dressed, slowly makes its way
along one of the wings into the orchestra. Each carries a pair of logs, an unlit torch
and a bucket of live coals.*]

MEN'S LEADER   Onward, Drakes, lead the way, even if your shoulder *is* sore;
you've got to keep toting that load of green olive-wood, no matter how
heavy it is.

MEN (*strophe*)

   If you live long enough you'll get many surprises, yes sir!
5   Strymodoros: who in the world ever thought we'd hear
   that women, the very creatures we've kept in our homes,
   an obvious nuisance, now control the Sacred Image[3]
   and occupy *my* Akropolis, and not only that,
   they've locked the citadel gates with bolts and bars!

10   MEN'S LEADER   Let's hurry to the Akropolis, Philourgos, full speed ahead, so
we can lay these logs in a circle all around them, around all the women
who have instigated or abetted this business! We'll erect a single pyre and
condemn them all with a single vote, then throw them on top with our own
hands, starting with Lykon's wife!

MEN (*antistrophe*)

15   By Demeter, while I still live they'll never laugh at me!
   Not even Kleomenes,[4] the first to occupy this place,

---

2. Passage sung or recited when the chorus
enters the orchestra, the circular space in
front of the stage building.
3. A lifesize olive-wood statue of Athena,

housed in the Erechtheum on the Akropolis.
4. A Spartan king who, while attempting to
aid one Athenian faction, briefly occupied the
Akropolis in 508 B.C.E.

left here intact. No, for all he breathed the Spartan spirit,
he left without his weapons—surrendered to *me!*—
with only a little bitty jacket on his back, starving,
20   filthy, unshaven and unwashed for six whole years.

MEN'S LEADER   That's the way I laid siege to *that* fellow—savagely! We kept
watch on these gates in ranks seventeen deep. So: am I to stand by *now* and
do nothing to put down the effrontery of these *women*, enemies of all the gods
and of Euripides? If so, take down my trophy that stands at Marathon![5]

MEN (*strophe*)
25   I'm almost at the end of my trek;
all that remains is the steep stretch
up to the Akropolis; can't wait to get there!
How in the world are we going to haul
these loads up there without a donkey?
30   This pair of logs is utterly crushing my shoulder!
But I've got to soldier on,
and keep my fire alight.
It mustn't go out on me before I've reached my goal.
        [*They blow into their buckets of coals.*]
Ouch, ugh! The smoke!

(*antistrophe*)
35   How terribly, Lord Herakles,[6] this smoke
jumped from the bucket and attacked me!
It bit both my eyes like a rabid bitch!
And as for this fire, it's Lemnian[7]
in every possible way; otherwise
40   it wouldn't have buried its teeth in my eyeballs that way!
Hurry forth to the citadel,
run to the Goddess' rescue!
If this isn't the time to help her, Laches, when will that time be?
        [*They blow on their buckets of coals again.*]
Ouch, ugh! The smoke!

45   MEN'S LEADER   Praise the gods, this fire's awake and plenty lively too. Let's
place our logs right here, then dip our torches into the buckets, and when
they're lighted we'll charge the gates like rams. If the women don't unbolt
the gates when we invite their surrender, we'll set the portals afire and
smoke them into submission. Very well, let's put the logs down. Phew, that
50   smoke! Damn! Would any of the generals at Samos[8] care to help us with
this wood? [*He laboriously wrestles his pair of logs to the ground.*] They've
finally stopped crushing my back! Now it's *your* job, bucket, to rouse your
coals to flame and thus supply me, first of all, with a lighted torch! Lady

5. Plain about 25 miles northeast of Athens,
where Athenians defeated a large invading
Persian army in 490 B.C.E. Euripides (480–
406 B.C.E.), tragedian typically portrayed by
Aristophanes as a misogynist.
6. Son of Zeus, a demigod and the greatest of
the classical heroes.

7. From Lemnos, a volcanic island sacred to
Hephaestus, the blacksmith god, that was
controlled by Athens (possibly alluding to the
myth of the Lemnian women, who killed
their husbands).
8. An island in the eastern Aegean that was
serving as a critical Athenian military base.

Victory,[9] be our ally, help us win a trophy over the women on the Akropolis
55 and their present audacity!

> [As the men crouch down to light their torches the second semichorus
> enters on the run. It is composed of twelve old women, nicely dressed and
> carrying pitchers of water on their heads.]

WOMEN'S LEADER   I think I can see sparks and smoke, fellow women, as if a
fire were ablaze. We must hurry all the faster!

WOMEN (strophe)
Fly, fly, Nikodike,
before Kalyke and Kritylla are incinerated,
60 blown from all directions
by nasty winds and old men who mean death!
I'm filled with dread: am I too late to help?
I've just come from the well with my pitcher;
it was hard to fill by the light of dawn,
65 in the throng and crash and clatter of pots,
fighting the elbows of housemaids and branded slaves.
I hoisted it onto my head with zeal, and carry the water here
to assist the women, my fellow citizens faced with burning.

(antistrophe)
I've heard that some frantic old men
70 are on the loose with three talents[1] of logs,
like furnace-men at the public bathhouse.
They're coming to the Akropolis, screaming
the direst threats, that they mean to use their fire
"to turn these abominable women into charcoal."
75 Goddess, may I never see these women in flames;
instead let them rescue Greece and her citizens from war and madness!
O golden-crested Guardian of the citadel, that is why
they occupy your shrine. I invite thee to be our ally, Tritogeneia,[2]
defending it with water, should any man set it afire.

80 WOMEN'S LEADER   Hold on! Hey! What's this? Men! Awful, nasty men! No
gentlemen, no god-fearing men would ever be caught doing this!

MEN'S LEADER   This here's a complication we didn't count on facing: this
swarm of women outside the gates is here to help the others!

WOMEN'S LEADER   Fear and trembling, eh? Don't tell me we seem a lot to
85 handle: you haven't even seen the tiniest fraction of our forces yet!

MEN'S LEADER   Phaidrias, are we going to let these women go on jabbering
like this? Why hasn't somebody busted a log over their heads?

WOMEN'S LEADER   Let's ground our pitchers then; if anyone attacks us they
won't get in our way.

90 MEN'S LEADER   By Zeus, if someone had socked them in the mouth a couple
of times, like Boupalos,[3] they wouldn't still be talking!

---

9. Probably a reference to Athena Nike (Victory), whose temple also stood on the
Akropolis.
1. About 175 pounds.

2. An ancient name of Athena.
3. A sculptor (6th c. B.C.E.), born on the
island of Chios, who was subjected to severe
satire and invective by the poet Hipponax.

WOMEN'S LEADER OK, here's my mouth; someone take a sock at it; I'll stand here and take it. But then I'm the bitch who gets to grab you by the balls!

MEN'S LEADER If you don't shut up, I'll knock you right out of your old hide!

95 WOMEN'S LEADER Come over here and just touch Stratyllis with the tip of your finger.

MEN'S LEADER What if I give you the one-two punch? Got anything scary to counter with?

WOMEN'S LEADER I'll rip out your lungs and your guts with my fangs.

100 MEN'S LEADER There isn't a wiser poet than Euripides: no beast exists so shameless as women!

WOMEN'S LEADER Let's pick up our pitchers of water, Rhodippe.

MEN'S LEADER Why did you bring water here, you witch?

WOMEN'S LEADER And why have *you* got fire, you tomb? To burn yourself up?

105 MEN'S LEADER *I'm* here to build a pyre and burn up your friends.

WOMEN'S LEADER And *I've* come to put it out with this.

MEN'S LEADER *You're* going to put out *my* fire?

WOMEN'S LEADER That's what you soon will see.

MEN'S LEADER I think I might barbecue you with this torch of mine.

110 WOMEN'S LEADER Got any soap with you? I'll give you a bath.

MEN'S LEADER *You* give *me* a bath, you crone?

WOMEN'S LEADER A bath fit for a bridegroom!

MEN'S LEADER What insolence!

WOMEN'S LEADER I'm a free woman!

115 MEN'S LEADER I'll put a stop to your bellowing.

WOMEN'S LEADER You're not on a jury now, you know.[4]

MEN'S LEADER Torch her hair! [*The men advance.*]

WOMEN'S LEADER Acheloos,[5] do your thing! [*The women douse them.*]

MEN'S LEADER Oh! Damn!

120 WOMEN'S LEADER It wasn't too hot, was it?

MEN'S LEADER Hot? Stop it! What do you think you're doing?

WOMEN'S LEADER I'm watering you, so you'll bloom.

MEN'S LEADER But I'm already dried out from shivering!

WOMEN'S LEADER You've got fire there; why not sit by it and get warm?

Episode[6]

[*Enter the* MAGISTRATE, *an irascible old man, accompanied by two slaves carrying crowbars and four Skythian policemen.*]

MAGISTRATE So the women's depravity bursts into flame again: beating drums, chanting "Sabazios!", worshiping Adonis on the rooftops.[7] I heard it all once before while sitting in Assembly. Demostratos[8] (bad luck to him!) was moving that we send an armada to Sicily, while his wife was dancing 5 and yelling "Poor young Adonis!" Then Demostratos moved that we sign up

---

4. Paid jury duty provided old men with some financial support.
5. A large river in central Greece.
6. In ancient Greek drama, a scene of action between choral sections.
7. The cults of Sabazios and Adonis, which had come to Athens relatively recently from the east, were especially favored by women.
8. An Athenian orator and proponent of the expedition launched against Syracuse, on the island of Sicily, in 415 B.C.E.; the outcome was a disastrous loss for Athens.

some Zakynthian[9] infantry, but his wife up on the roof was getting drunk
and going "Beat your breast for Adonis!" But he just went on making his
motions, that godforsaken, disgusting Baron Bluster! From women, I say,
you get this kind of riotous extravagance!

10 MEN'S LEADER [*Pointing to the* CHORUS OF WOMEN]   Save your breath till you hear
about *their* atrocities! They've committed every kind, even doused us with those
pitchers. Now we get to shake water out of our clothes as if we'd peed in them!

MAGISTRATE   By the salty sea-god it serves us right! When we ourselves are
15   accomplices in our wives' misbehavior and teach them profligacy, these are
the sort of schemes they bring to flower! Aren't *we* the ones who go to the
shops and say stuff like, "Goldsmith, about that necklace you made me: my
wife was having a ball the other night, and now the prong's slipped out of its
hole. Me, I've got to cruise over to Salamis. So if you've got time, by all means
20   visit her in the evening and fit a prong in her hole." Another husband says this
to a teenage shoemaker with a very grown-up cock, "Shoemaker, my wife's
pinky-toe hurts. It seems the top-strap is cramping the bottom, where she's
tender. So why don't you drop in on her some lunchtime and loosen it up so
there's more play down there?" That's the sort of thing that's led to *this*, when
25   I, a Magistrate, have lined up timber for oars and now come to get the necessary funds, and find myself standing at the gate, locked out by women! But
I'm not going to stand around. [*To the two slaves*] Bring the crowbars; I'll put
a stop to their arrogance. What are *you* gaping at, you sorry fool? And where
are *you* staring? I said crowbar, not winebar! Come on, put those crowbars
under the gates and start jimmying on that side; I'll help out on this side.

30 LYSISTRATA [*Emerging from the gates*]   Don't jimmy the gates; I'm coming out
on my very own. Why do you need crowbars? It's not crowbars you need;
it's rather brains and sense.

MAGISTRATE   Really! You witch! Where's a policeman? Grab her and tie both
hands behind her back! [*One of the policemen advances on* LYSISTRATA.]

35 LYSISTRATA   If he so much as touches me with his fingertip, by Artemis[1] he'll
go home crying, public servant or not! [*The policeman retreats.*]

MAGISTRATE   What, are you scared? [*To a second policeman*] You there, help
him out; grab her around the waist and tie her up, on the double!

[*A large* OLD WOMAN *emerges from the gates.*]

FIRST OLD WOMAN   If you so much as lay a hand on her, by Pandrosos[2] I'll
40   beat the shit out of you! [*Both policemen retreat.*]

MAGISTRATE   Beat the shit out of me! Where's another policeman? [*A third
policeman steps forward.*] Tie *her* up first, the one with the dirty mouth!

[*A* SECOND OLD WOMAN *emerges from the gates.*]

SECOND OLD WOMAN   If you raise your fingertip to her, by our Lady of Light[3]
you'll be begging for an eye-cup! [*The third archer retreats.*]

45 MAGISTRATE   What's going on? Where's a policeman? [*The fourth policeman
steps forward.*] Arrest her. I'll foil *one* of these sallies of yours!

[*A* THIRD OLD WOMAN *emerges from the gates.*]

---

9. From Zakynthos, an island in the Ionian Sea
(west of the Peloponnesos) allied to Athens.
1. Virgin goddess of the hunt and the wilds,
twin sister of Apollo; she also brings release

to women in childbirth.
2. Daughter of the legendary first king of Athens; she was worshipped on the Akropolis.
3. Hekate, goddess of the moon and childbirth.

THIRD OLD WOMAN   If you come near her, by Eastern Artemis[4] I'll rip out your
hair till it screams! [*The fourth policeman retreats.*]
MAGISTRATE   What a terrible setback! I'm out of policemen. But men must
50 never, ever be worsted by women! Skythians, let's charge them *en masse;*
form up ranks!
[*The four policemen prepare to charge.*]
LYSISTRATA   By the Two Goddesses, you'll soon discover that we also have
four squadrons of fully armed combat-women, waiting inside!
MAGISTRATE   Skythians, twist their arms behind their backs!
[*The policemen advance.*]
55 LYSISTRATA [*Calling into the Akropolis like a military commander*]   Women of
the reserve, come out double-time! Forward, you spawn of the marketplace, you soup and vegetable mongers! Forward, you landladies, you
hawkers of garlic and bread! [*Four squadrons of tough old market-women
rush out of the Akropolis and, together with the women already onstage,
attack the four policemen.*] Tackle them! Hit them! Smash them! Call them
60 names, the nastier the better! [*The policemen run away howling.*] That's
enough! Withdraw! Don't strip the bodies!
[*The women of the reserve go back into the Akropolis.*]
MAGISTRATE   Terrible! What a calamity for my men!
LYSISTRATA   Well, what did you expect? Did you think you were going up
against a bunch of slave-girls? Or did you think women lack gall?
65 MAGISTRATE   They've got it aplenty, by Apollo, provided there's a wineshop
nearby.
MEN'S LEADER   You've little to show for all your talk, Magistrate of this country! What's the point of fighting a battle of words with these beasts? Don't
you comprehend the kind of bath they've given us just now—when we were
70 still in our clothes, and without soap to boot?
WOMEN'S LEADER   Well, sir, you shouldn't lift your hand against your neighbors just anytime you feel like it. If you do, you're going to end up with a
black eye. I'd rather be sitting at home like a virtuous maiden, making no
trouble for anyone here, stirring not a single blade of grass. But if anyone
75 annoys me and rifles my nest, they'll find a wasp inside!

Onstage Debate

MEN (*strophe*)
Zeus, how in the world are we going to deal with these monsters?
They've gone beyond what I can bear! Now it's time for a trial:
together let's find out
what they thought they were doing
5 when they occupied Kranaos'[5] citadel
and the great crag of the Akropolis,
a restricted, holy place.
MEN'S LEADER   Question her and don't give in; cross-examine what she says.
It's scandalous to let this sort of behavior go unchallenged.

4. Artemis was worshipped throughout the Greek world. To the east, in Tauris (the present-day Crimean Peninsula), that wor- / ship involved orgiastic rites.
5. A mythical king of Athens.

10 MAGISTRATE   Here's the first thing I'd like to know, by Zeus: what do you mean by barricading our Akropolis?

LYSISTRATA   To keep the money safe and to keep *you* from using it to finance the war.

MAGISTRATE   So we're at war on account of the money?

15 LYSISTRATA   Yes, and the money's why everything else got messed up too. Peisandros[6] and the others aiming to hold office were always fomenting some kind of commotion so that they'd be able to steal it. So let them keep fomenting to their hearts' content: they'll be withdrawing no more money from *this* place.

20 MAGISTRATE   But what do you plan to do?

LYSISTRATA   Don't you see? We'll manage it for you!

MAGISTRATE   *You'll* manage the money?

LYSISTRATA   What's so strange in that? Don't we manage the household finances for you already?

25 MAGISTRATE   That's different!

LYSISTRATA   How so?

MAGISTRATE   These are *war* funds!

LYSISTRATA   But there shouldn't even *be* a war.

MAGISTRATE   How else are we to protect ourselves?

30 LYSISTRATA   We'll protect you.

MAGISTRATE   *You?*

LYSISTRATA   Yes, us.

MAGISTRATE   What brass!

LYSISTRATA   You'll be protected whether you like it or not!

35 MAGISTRATE   You're going too far!

LYSISTRATA   Angry, are you? We've got to do it anyway.

MAGISTRATE   By Demeter, you've got no right!

LYSISTRATA   You must be saved, dear fellow.

MAGISTRATE   Even if I don't ask to be?

40 LYSISTRATA   All the more so!

MAGISTRATE   And where do *you* get off taking an interest in war and peace?

LYSISTRATA   We'll tell you.

MAGISTRATE   Well, make it snappy, unless you want to get hurt.

LYSISTRATA   Listen then, and try to control your fists.

45 MAGISTRATE   I can't; I'm so angry I can't keep my hands to myself.

FIRST OLD WOMAN   Then *you're* the one'll get hurt!

MAGISTRATE   Croak those curses at yourself, old bag! [*To* LYSISTRATA] Start talking.

LYSISTRATA   Gladly. All along, being proper women, we used to suffer in
50 silence no matter what you men did, because you wouldn't let us make a sound. But you weren't exactly all we could ask for. No, we knew only too well what you were up to, and too many times we'd hear in our homes about a bad decision you'd made on some great issue of state. Then, masking the pain in our hearts, we'd put on a smile and ask you, "How did the
55 Assembly go today? Any decision about a rider to the peace treaty?" And my husband would say, "What's that to you? Shut up!" And I'd shut up.

---

6. Athenian politician, often attacked in comedy for corruption. Soon after the first performance of *Lysistrata*, Peisandros joined an oligarchic faction that seized power, with widespread violence and confiscations (by 410 B.C.E., democracy was restored).

FIRST OLD WOMAN   *I* wouldn't have shut up!

MAGISTRATE   If you hadn't shut up you'd have got a beating!

LYSISTRATA   Well, that's why I *did* shut up. Later on we began to hear about
60   even worse decisions you'd made, and then we would ask, "Husband, how
      come you're handling this so stupidly?" And right away he'd glare at me and
      tell me to get back to my sewing if I didn't want major damage to my head:
      "War shall be the business of menfolk,"[7] unquote.

MAGISTRATE   He was right on the mark, by Zeus.

65   LYSISTRATA   How could he be right, you sorry fool, when we were forbidden
      to offer advice even when your policy was *wrong?* But *then*—when we began
      to hear you in the streets openly crying, "There isn't a man left in the land,"
      and someone else saying, "No, by Zeus, not a one"—after *that* we women
      decided to lose no more time and to band together to save Greece. What
70   was the point of waiting any longer? So, if you're ready to take your turn at
      listening, we have some good advice, and if you shut up, as we used to, we
      can put you back on the right track.

MAGISTRATE   *You* put *us*—outrageous! I won't stand for it!

LYSISTRATA   Shut up!

75   MAGISTRATE   *Me* shut up for *you?* A damned woman, with a veil on your face
      too?[8] I'd rather die!

LYSISTRATA   If the veil's an obstacle, here, take mine, it's yours, put it on *your* face
      [*She removes her veil and puts it on the* MAGISTRATE's *head*], and *then* shut up!

FIRST OLD WOMAN   And take this sewing-basket too.

80   LYSISTRATA   Now hitch up your clothes and start sewing; chew some beans[9]
      while you work. War shall be the business of womenfolk!

WOMEN'S LEADER   Come away from your pitchers, women: it's our turn to
      pitch in with a little help for our friends!

WOMEN (*antistrophe*)
      Oh yes! I'll dance with unflagging energy;
85   the effort won't weary my knees.
      I'm ready to face anything
      with women courageous as these:
      they've got character, charm and guts,
      they've got intelligence and heart
90   that's both patriotic and smart!

WOMEN'S LEADER   Now, most valiant of prickly mommies and spikey gran-
      nies, attack furiously and don't let up: you're still running with the wind!

LYSISTRATA   If Eros of the sweet soul and Cyprian Aphrodite imbue our thighs
      and breasts with desire, and infect the men with sensuous rigidity and club-
95   cock, then I believe all Greece will one day call us Disbanders of Battles.[1]

MAGISTRATE   What's your plan?

LYSISTRATA   First of all, we can stop people going to the market fully armed
      and acting crazy.

7. Words spoken by Hector to his wife,
Andromache, in the *Iliad* (6.492).
8. Respectable women wore veils in public.
9. The ancient equivalent of gum chewing.
1. In Greek, *Lusimachas*, an allusion to Lysimache (literally, "Battle Settler"), then priestess of Athena in Athens; possibly also a pun

on the title character's name. *Eros:* son of
Aphrodite and, like his mother, a deity of carnal love. *Cyprian:* of Cyprus, the island onto
which the newly born Aphrodite emerged
from the sea and an important center of her
cult.

FIRST OLD WOMAN   Paphian[2] Aphrodite be praised!

100 LYSISTRATA   At this very moment, all around the market, in the pottery shops and the grocery stalls, they're walking around in arms like Korybantes![3]

MAGISTRATE   By Zeus, a man's got to act like a man!

LYSISTRATA   But it's totally ridiculous when he takes a shield with a Gorgon-blazon[4] to buy sardines!

105 FIRST OLD WOMAN   Yes, by Zeus, I saw a long-haired fellow,[5] a cavalry captain, on horseback, getting porridge from an old women and sticking it into his brass hat. Another one, a Thracian, was shaking his shield and spear like Tereus;[6] he scared the fig-lady out of her wits and gulped down all the ripe ones!

110 MAGISTRATE   So how will you women be able to put a stop to such a complicated international mess, and sort it all out?

LYSISTRATA   Very easily.

MAGISTRATE   How? Show me.

[LYSISTRATA *uses the contents of the basket which the* MAGISTRATE *was given to illustrate her demonstration.*]

LYSISTRATA   It's rather like a ball of yarn when it gets tangled up. We hold it this way, and carefully wind out the strands on our spindles, now this way, 115 now that way. That's how we'll wind up this war, if allowed, unsnarling it by sending embassies, now this way, now that way.

MAGISTRATE   You really think your way with wool and yarnballs and spindles can stop a terrible crisis? How brainless!

LYSISTRATA   I do think so, and if *you* had any brains you'd handle *all* the polis' 120 business the way we handle our wool!

MAGISTRATE   Well, how then? I'm all ears.

LYSISTRATA   Imagine the polis as fleece just shorn. First, put it in a bath and wash out all the sheep-dung; spread it on a pallet and beat out the riff-raff with a stick and pluck out the thorns; as for those who clump and knot them-125 selves together to snag government positions, card them out and pluck off their heads. Next, card the wool into a basket of unity and goodwill, mixing in everyone. The resident aliens and any other foreigner who's your friend, and anyone who owes money to the people's treasury, mix them in there too. And by Zeus, don't forget the cities that are colonies of this land: they're like 130 flocks of your fleece, each one separated from the others. So take all these flocks and bring them together here, joining them all and making one big bobbin. And from this weave a fine new cloak for the people!

MAGISTRATE   Isn't it awful how these women go like this with their sticks and like this with their bobbins, when they share none of the war's burdens!

135 LYSISTRATA   None? You monster! We bear more than our fair share, first of all by giving birth to sons and sending them off to the army—

MAGISTRATE   Enough of that! Let's not open old wounds.

---

2. Of Paphos, a city on Cyprus that was the site of a famous temple of Aphrodite.

3. Eastern worshippers of the Phrygian goddess Cybele, known for ecstatic dancing.

4. Emblem depicting one of the three snake-haired sisters (common on warriors' shields); the sight of a Gorgon turned all who looked at her to stone.

5. That is, a Spartan; Spartan men traditionally wore their hair long.

6. A mythical Thracian king whose story was told in a tragedy by Sophocles. He raped his sister-in-law Philomela and cut out her tongue, but his wife, Prokne, still learned of the deed and fed him their own son in revenge. All three were turned into birds.

LYSISTRATA   Then, when we ought to be having fun and enjoying our bloom of
        youth, we sleep alone because of the campaigns. And to say no more about
140   *our* case, it pains me to think of the maidens growing old in their rooms.
    MAGISTRATE   Men grow old too, don't they?
    LYSISTRATA   That's quite a different story. When a man comes home he can
        quickly find a girl to marry, even if he's a greybeard. But a woman's prime is
        brief; if she doesn't seize it no one wants to marry her, and she sits at home
145   looking for good omens.
    MAGISTRATE   But any man who can still get a hard-on—
    LYSISTRATA   Why don't you just drop dead? Here's a grave-site; buy a coffin;
        I'll start kneading you a honeycake.[7] [*Taking off her garland*] Use these as a
        wreath.
    FIRST OLD WOMAN [*Handing him ribbons*]   You can have these from me.
150 SECOND OLD WOMAN   And this garland from me.
    LYSISTRATA   All set? Need anything else? Get on the boat, then. Charon[8] is
        calling your name and you're holding him up!
    MAGISTRATE   Isn't it shocking that I'm being treated like this? By Zeus, I'm
        going straight to the other magistrates to display myself just as I am![9]
155 LYSISTRATA [*As* MAGISTRATE *exits with his slaves*]   I hope you won't complain
        about the funeral we gave you. I tell you what: the day after tomorrow, first
        thing in the morning, we'll perform the third-day offerings at your grave!
        [*The women exit into the Akropolis.*]

Choral Debate

    MEN'S LEADER   No free man should be asleep now! Let's strip for action,
        men, and meet this emergency! [*The men remove their jackets.*]
    MEN (*strophe a*)
        I think I smell much bigger trouble in this
        a definite whiff of Hippias[1] tyranny!
5   I'm terrified that certain men from Sparta
        have gathered at the house of Kleisthenes[2]
        and scheme to stir up our godforsaken women
        to seize the Treasury and my jury-pay,
        my very livelihood.
10 MEN'S LEADER   It's shocking, you know, that they're lecturing the citizens now,
        and running their mouths—mere women!—about brazen shields. And to top
        it all off they're trying to make peace between us and the men of Sparta, who
        are no more trustworthy than a starving wolf. Actually, this plot they weave
        against us, gentlemen, aims at tyranny! Well, they'll never tyrannize over *me*:
15   from now on I'll be on my guard, I'll "carry my sword in a myrtle-branch" and
        go to market fully armed right up beside Aristogeiton.[3] I'll stand beside him
        like this [*assuming the posture of Aristogeiton's statue*]: that way I'll be ready to

7. Traditionally given to the dead as an offering to Cerberus, the three-headed dog that
guarded the entrance to the underworld.
8. The boatman who ferried dead souls across
the river Styx to the underworld.
9. That is, dressed as both a woman and a
corpse.
1. A tyrant expelled from Athens in 510 B.C.E.,

with the help of the Spartan king Kleomenes.
2. A contemporary of Aristophanes, frequently ridiculed in his plays as effeminate.
3. One of the assassins of Hipparchos (d. 514
B.C.E.), brother of Hippias; their statues
stood in the Agora, or marketplace. The Men's
Leader quotes a popular drinking song celebrating this killing.

smack this godforsaken old hag right in the jaw! [*He advances on the* WOM-
EN'S LEADER *with fist raised*.]

WOMEN'S LEADER   Just try it, and your own mommy won't recognize you
20   when you get home! Come on, fellow hags, let's start by putting *our* jackets
on the ground. [*The women remove their jackets*.]

WOMEN (*antistrophe a*)
   Citizens of Athens, we want to start
   by offering the polis some good advice,
   and rightly, for she raised me in splendid luxury.
25   As soon as I turned seven I was an Arrephoros;
   then I was a Grinder; when I was ten I shed
   my saffron robe for the Foundress at the Brauronia.
   And once, when I was a beautiful girl, I carried the Basket,
   wearing a necklace of dried figs.[4]

30 WOMEN'S LEADER   Thus I *owe* it to the polis to offer some good advice. And
   even if I *was* born a woman, don't hold it against me if I manage to suggest
   something better than what we've got now. I have a stake in our community: my contribution is *men*. You miserable geezers have *no* stake, since
   you've squandered your paternal inheritance, won in the Persian Wars,[5]
35   and now pay no taxes in return. On the contrary, we're all headed for bank-
   ruptcy on account of you! Have you anything to grunt in rebuttal? Any
   more trouble from you and I'll clobber you with this rawhide boot right in
   the jaw! [*She raises her foot at the Men's Leader*.]

MEN (*strophe b*)
   This behavior of theirs amounts to extreme hubris,
40   and I do believe it's getting aggravated.
   No man with any balls can let it pass.

MEN'S LEADER   Let's doff our shirts, 'cause a man's gotta smell like a man
   from the word go and shouldn't be all wrapped up like souvlaki.
      [*The men remove their shirts*.]

MEN   Come on, Whitefeet!
45   We went against Leipsydrion[6]
   when we still were something;
   now we've got to rejuvenate, grow wings
   all over, shake off these old skins of ours!

MEN'S LEADER   If any man among us gives these women the tiniest thing to
50   grab on to, there's no limit to what their nimble hands will do. Why, they'll
   even be building frigates and launching naval attacks, cruising against us
   like Artemisia.[7] And if they turn to horsemanship, you can scratch our cavalry: there's nothing like a woman when it comes to mounting and riding;
   even riding hard she won't slip off. Just look at the Amazons in Mikon's[8]
55   painting, riding chargers in battle against men. Our duty is clear: grab each

4. A symbol of fertility. The women list the
religious duties of upper-class Athenian girls,
serving Athena and, in the case of the Brauronia, honoring Artemis.
5. The conclusion of the wars with Persia by
448 B.C.E. left Athens in control of an empire,
from which it exacted tribute.
6. A stronghold in northern Attica, used by
those who sought unsuccessfully to over-

throw the tyrant Hippias in 513 B.C.E.
7. Ruler of Caria (in present-day Turkey), an
ally of the Persians; she led five ships against
the Greeks at Salamis in 480 B.C.E.
8. Athenian sculptor and painter (5th c. B.C.E.);
his frescoes included one in the temple of Theseus that represented Athenians fighting Amazons, a nation of warrior women believed to live
on the southeastern shore of the Black Sea.

woman's neck and lock it in the wooden stocks! [*He moves toward the*
WOMEN'S LEADER.]

WOMEN (*antistrophe b*)
    By the Two Goddesses, if you fire me up
    I'll come at you like a wild sow and clip you bare,
    and this very day you'll go bleating to your friends for help!

60 WOMEN'S LEADER   Quickly, women, let's also take off our tunics; a woman's gotta
    smell like a woman, mad enough to bite! [*The women remove their shirts.*]

WOMEN   All right now, someone attack me!
    He'll eat no more garlic
    and chew no more beans.
65   If you so much as curse at me, I boil over with such rage,
    I'll be the beetle-midwife to your eagle's eggs.[9]

WOMEN'S LEADER   You men don't worry me a bit, not while my Lampito's
    around and my Ismenia, the noble Theban girl. You'll have no power to do
    anything about us, not even if you pass seven decrees: that's how much every
70   one hates you, you good-for-nothing, and especially our neighbors. Why, just
    yesterday I threw a party for the girls in honor of Hekate, and I invited my
    friend from next door, a fine girl who's very special to me: an eel from Boiotia.
    But they said she couldn't come because of *your* decrees. And you'll *never*
    stop passing these decrees until someone grabs you by the leg and throws you
75   away and breaks your neck! [*She makes a grab for the* MEN'S LEADER'S *leg.*]

Episode

[LYSISTRATA *comes out of the Akropolis and begins to pace.*]

WOMEN'S LEADER
    O mistress of this venture and strategem,
    why com'st thou from thy halls so dour of mien?

LYSISTRATA
    The deeds of ignoble women and the female heart
    do make me pace dispirited to and fro.

WOMEN'S LEADER
5   What say'st thou? What say'st thou?

LYSISTRATA
    'Tis true, too true!

WOMEN'S LEADER
    What dire thing? Pray tell it to thy friends.

LYSISTRATA
    'Twere shame to say and grief to leave unsaid.

WOMEN'S LEADER
    Hide not from me the damage we have taken.

LYSISTRATA
10   The story in briefest compass: we need to fuck!

WOMEN'S LEADER
    Ah, Zeus!

LYSISTRATA
    Why rend the air for Zeus? You see our plight.

9. That is, testicles. In a fable by Aesop, a dung beetle avenges itself on an eagle by repeatedly
breaking the bird's eggs.

The truth is, I can't keep the wives away from their husbands any longer; they're running off in all directions. The first one I caught was over there
15   by Pan's Grotto,[1] digging at her hole, and another was trying to escape by clambering down a pulley-cable. And yesterday another one mounted a sparrow and was about to fly off to Orsilochos' house when I pulled her off by her hair. They're coming up with every kind of excuse to go home. [*A wife comes out of the Akropolis, looks around, and begins to run offstage.*] Hey you! What's your hurry?

20 FIRST WIFE   I want to go home. I've got some Milesian wool in the house, and the moths are chomping it all up.

LYSISTRATA   Moths! Get back inside.

FIRST WIFE   By the Two Goddesses, I'll be right back; just let me spread it on the bed!

25 LYSISTRATA   You won't be spreading anything, nor be going anywhere.

FIRST WIFE   So I'm supposed to let my wool go to waste?

LYSISTRATA   If that's what it takes. [*As the first wife walks back toward* LYSISTRATA *a second runs out of the Akropolis.*]

SECOND WIFE   Oh my god, my god, the flax! I forgot to shuck it when I left the house!

30 LYSISTRATA   Here's another one off to shuck her flax. March right back here.

SECOND WIFE   By our Lady of Light, I'll be back in a flash; just let me do a little shucking.

LYSISTRATA   No! No shucking! If *you* start doing it, some other wife will want to do the same. [*While the second wife walks back toward* LYSISTRATA *a third runs out of the Akropolis, holding her bulging belly.*]

35 THIRD WIFE   O Lady of Childbirth, hold back the baby till I can get to a more profane spot![2]

LYSISTRATA   What are you raving about?

THIRD WIFE   I'm about to deliver a child!

LYSISTRATA   But you weren't pregnant yesterday.

40 THIRD WIFE   But today I am. Please, Lysistrata, send me home to the midwife, and right away!

LYSISTRATA   What's the story? [*She feels the wife's belly.*] What's this? It's hard.

THIRD WIFE   It's a boy.

LYSISTRATA [*Knocking on it*]   By Aphrodite, it's obvious you've got something
45   metallic and hollow in there. Let's have a look. [*She lifts up the wife's dress, exposing a large bronze helmet.*] Ridiculous girl! You're big with the sacred helmet, not with child!

THIRD WIFE   But I *am* with child, by Zeus!

LYSISTRATA   Then what were you doing with this?

50 THIRD WIFE   Well, if I began to deliver here in the citadel, I could get into the helmet and have my baby there, like a pigeon.

LYSISTRATA   What kind of story is that? Excuses! It's obvious what's going on. You'll have to stay here till your—helmet has its naming-day.

THIRD WIFE   But I can't even *sleep* on the Akropolis, ever since I saw the
55   snake[3] that guards the temple.

---

1. A cave on the Akropolis containing a shrine to Pan, goat-footed god of woods, pastures, and wild places.
2. Sacred locations such as the Akropolis

would be polluted by birth or death.
3. The snake sacred to Athena, believed to live in the foundations of the Erechtheum, had never been seen.

FOURTH WIFE   And what about poor me—listening to the owls⁴ go *woo woo*
all night is killing me!

LYSISTRATA   You nutty girls, enough of your horror stories! I guess you do miss
your husbands; but do you think they don't miss *you*? They're spending
60 some very rough nights, I assure you. Just be patient, good ladies, and put
up with this, just a little bit longer. There's an oracle predicting victory for
us, *if* we stick together. Here's the oracle right here. [*She produces a scroll.*]

THIRD WIFE   Tell us what it says.

LYSISTRATA   Be quiet, then.

65   Yea, when the swallows hole up in a single home,
       fleeing the hoopoes⁵ and leaving the penis alone,
       then are their problems solved, what's high is low:
       so says high-thundering Zeus—

THIRD WIFE   You mean *we'll* be lying on top?

70 LYSISTRATA   But:
       if the swallows begin to argue and fly away
       down from the citadel holy, all will say,
       no bird more disgustingly horny lives today!

THIRD WIFE   A pretty explicit oracle. Ye gods!

75 LYSISTRATA   So let's hear no more talk of caving in. Let's go inside. Dear comrades, it would be a real shame if we betray the oracle. [*All enter the Akropolis.*]

Choral Songs

MEN (*strophe*)
       I want to tell you all a tale
       that once I heard when but a lad.
       In olden times there lived a young man,
       his name was Melanion.⁶
5   He fled from marriage until
       he got to the wilderness.
       And he lived in the mountains
       and he had a dog,
       and he wove traps and hunted rabbits,
10   but never went home again
       because of his hatred.
       That's how much *he* loathed women.
       And, being wise, *we* loathe them just
       as much as Melanion did.

15 MEN'S LEADER   How about a kiss, old bag?

WOMEN'S LEADER   Try it, and you've eaten your last onion!

MEN'S LEADER   How about I haul off and kick you? [*He kicks up his leg.*]

WOMEN'S LEADER [*Laughing*]   That's quite a bush you've got down there!

MEN'S LEADER   Well, Myronides too was rough down there,
20   and hairy-assed to all his enemies;
       so too was Phormion.⁷

---

4. Birds sacred to Athena.
5. The bird into which Tereus was transformed, known for its erectile crest.
6. In the myth featuring Melanion, the young
man wins and marries Atalanta through a

trick; she is the one fleeing marriage, having
sworn to accept only the man who could
defeat her in a footrace.
7. A successful Athenian general, as was
Myronides (both 5th c. B.C.E.).

WOMEN (*antistrophe*)
   I also want to tell you all a tale,
   a reply to your Melanion.
   There once was a drifter named Timon,
25   who fenced himself off with impregnable thorns,
   as implacable as a Fury.[8]
   So this Timon too
   left home because of his hatred
   <and lived in the mountains,>[9]
30   constantly cursing and railing
   against the wickedness of men.
   That's how much *he* loathed *you*,
   wicked men, ever and always.
   But he was a dear friend to women.
35 WOMEN'S LEADER   How would you like a punch in the mouth?
MEN'S LEADER   No way! You're really scaring me!
WOMEN'S LEADER   Then how about a good swift kick?
MEN'S LEADER   If you do you'll be flashing your twat!
WOMEN'S LEADER   Even so you'll never see
40   any hair down there on me:
   I may be getting antiquated
   but I keep myself well depilated.

> [*The* WOMEN'S CHORUS *picks up their and the men's discarded clothing and both semichoruses withdraw from the center of the orchestra to sit along its edges; during the ensuing episode the women put their clothing back on.*]

Episode

[LYSISTRATA *appears on the roof of the stage-building, which represents the Akropolis ramparts, and walks to and fro, looking carefully in all directions; suddenly she stops and peers into the distance.*]

LYSISTRATA   All right! Yes! Ladies, come here, quick!

> [MYRRHINE *and several other wives join* LYSISTRATA.]

WIFE   What is it? What's all the shouting?
LYSISTRATA   A man! I see a man coming this way, stricken, in the grip of
   Aphrodite's mysterious powers. Lady Aphrodite, mistress of Cyprus and
5   Kythera[1] and Paphos, make thy journey straight and upright!
WIFE   Where is he, whoever he is?
LYSISTRATA   He's by Chloe's[2] shrine.
WIFE   By Zeus, I see him now! But who is he?
LYSISTRATA   Take a good look. Anyone recognize him?
10 MYRRHINE   Oh God, I do. He's my own husband Kinesias![3]

---

8. One of the Eumenides, monstrous female personifications of vengeance. *Timon:* a legendary misanthrope, depicted by Shakespeare in *Timon of Athens* (1607–8); nowhere else is he portrayed as a friend to women (see line 34, below).
9. The words inside angled brackets are supplied by the translator for a line missing in the Greek text.

1. The island, off the southern tip of the Peloponnesos, near which Aphrodite was born in the sea foam.
2. An epithet of the goddess Demeter (literally, "Verdant").
3. Common Greek name; in this play, also a sexual pun on the Greek verb *kinein*, "to move, to arouse."

LYSISTRATA   All right, it's your job to roast him, to torture him, to bamboozle him, to love him and not to love him, and to give him anything he wants—except what you swore over the bowl not to.

MYRRHINE   Don't you worry, I'll do it!

15 LYSISTRATA   Great! I'll stick around here and help you bamboozle him and roast him. Now everyone get out of sight!

> [*All the wives go back inside except* LYSISTRATA. *Enter* KINESIAS, *wearing a huge erect phallus and accompanied by a male slave holding a baby. He is in obvious pain.*]

KINESIAS [*To himself*]   Oh, oh, evil fate! I've got terrible spasms and cramps. It's like I'm being broken on the rack!

LYSISTRATA [*Leaning down from the ramparts*]   Who's that who's standing up
20 within our defense perimeter?

KINESIAS   Me.

LYSISTRATA   A man?

KINESIAS [*Brandishing his phallus*]   Of course a man!

LYSISTRATA   In that case please depart.

25 KINESIAS   And who are *you* to throw me out?

LYSISTRATA   The daytime guard.

KINESIAS   Then in the gods' name call Myrrhine out here to me.

LYSISTRATA   Listen to him, "call Myrrhine"! And who might *you* be?

KINESIAS   Her husband, Kinesias, from Paionidai.[4]

30 LYSISTRATA   Well, hello, dear chum! Among us *your* name is hardly unknown or without celebrity. Your wife always has you on her lips; she'll be eating an egg or an apple and she'll say, "This one's for Kinesias."

KINESIAS   Oh gods!

LYSISTRATA   Yes, by Aphrodite. And whenever the conversation turns to men,
35 your wife speaks up forthwith and says, "Compared to Kinesias, everything else is trash!"

KINESIAS   Come on now, call her out!

LYSISTRATA   Well? Got anything for me?

KINESIAS [*Indicating his phallus*]   Indeed I do, if you want it. [LYSISTRATA
40 *looks away.*] What about this? [*He tosses her a purse.*] It's all I've got, and you're welcome to it.

LYSISTRATA   OK then, I'll go in and call her for you. [*She leaves the ramparts.*]

KINESIAS   Make it quick, now! [*Alone*] I've had no joy or pleasure in my life since the day Myrrhine left the house. I go into the house and feel agony;
45 everything looks empty to me; I get no pleasure from the food I eat. Because I'm horny!

MYRRHINE [*Still out of sight, speaking to* LYSISTRATA]   I love that man, I love him! But he doesn't *want* my love. Please don't make me go out to him!

KINESIAS   Myrrhinikins, dearest, why are you doing this? Get down here!

50 MYRRHINE [*Appearing at the ramparts*]   By Zeus I'm not going down there!

KINESIAS   You won't come down even when I ask you, Myrrhine?

MYRRHINE   You're asking me, but you don't want me at all.

KINESIAS   Me not want you? Why, I'm desolate!

MYRRHINE   I'm leaving.

---

4. A deme or village in Attica.

55 KINESIAS   No, wait! At least listen to the baby! [*He grabs the baby from the slave and holds it up towards* MYRRHINE.] Come on you, yell for mommy!

BABY   Mommy! Mommy! Mommy!

KINESIAS [*To* MYRRHINE]   Hey, what's wrong with you? Don't you feel sorry for the baby, unwashed and unsuckled for six days now?

60 MYRRHINE   *Him* I feel sorry for. Too bad his *father* doesn't care about him!

KINESIAS: Get down here, you screwy woman, and see to your child!

MYRRHINE   How momentous is motherhood! I've got no choice but to go down there. [*She leaves the ramparts.* KINESIAS *returns the baby to the slave.*]

KINESIAS   <Absence really does make the heart grow fonder!> She seems much
65   younger than I remember, and she has a sexier look in her eyes. She acted prickly and very stuck-up too, but that just makes me want her even more!

[MYRRHINE *enters from the Akropolis gates and goes over to the baby, ignoring* KINESIAS.]

MYRRHINE   Poor sweetie pie, with such a lousy father, let me give you a kiss, mommy's little dearest!

KINESIAS [*To* MYRRHINE's *back*]   What do you think you're doing, you naughty
70   girl, listening to those other women and giving me a hard time and hurting yourself as well? [*He puts a hand on her shoulder.*]

MYRRHINE [*Wheeling around*]   Don't you lay your hands on me!

KINESIAS   You know you've let our house, your things and mine, become an utter mess?

75 MYRRHINE   It doesn't bother me.

KINESIAS   It doesn't bother you that the hens are pulling your woollens apart?

MYRRHINE   Not a bit.

KINESIAS   And what a long time it's been since you've celebrated Aphrodite's holy mysteries.[5] Won't you come home?

80 MYRRHINE   Not me, by Zeus; I'm going nowhere until you men agree to a settlement and stop the war.

KINESIAS   Well, if that's what's decided, then that's what we'll do.

MYRRHINE   Well, if that's what's decided, I'll be going home. But for the time being I've sworn to stay here.

85 KINESIAS   But at least lie down here with me; it's been so long.

MYRRHINE   No way. But I'm not saying I don't love you.

KINESIAS   Love me? So why won't you lie down, Myrrhine?

MYRRHINE   Right here in front of the baby? You must be joking!

KINESIAS   Zeus no! Boy, take him home. [*Exit slave.*] There you are, the kid's
90   out of our way. Now, why don't you just lie down?

MYRRHINE   Lie down *where,* you silly man?

KINESIAS [*Looking around*]   Where? Pan's Grotto will do fine.

MYRRHINE   But I need to be pure before I can go back up to the Akropolis.

KINESIAS   Very easily done: just wash off in the Klepsydra.[6]

95 MYRRHINE   You're telling me, dear, that I should go back on the oath I swore?

KINESIAS   Don't worry about any oath; let me take the consequences.

MYRRHINE   All right then, I'll get us a bed.

KINESIAS   No, don't; the ground's OK for us.

---

5. That is, had sexual intercourse.   6. A spring on the slope of the Akropolis.

MYRRHINE   Apollo no! I wouldn't dream of letting you lie on the ground, no
100   matter what kind of man you are. [MYRRHINE *goes into one of the flanking
     doors, which represents Pan's Grotto.*]

KINESIAS   She really loves me, that's quite obvious!

MYRRHINE [*Returning with a cot*]   There you are! Lie right down while I
     undress. [KINESIAS *lies on the cot.*] But wait, I forgot, what is it, yes, a mat-
     tress! Got to get one.

105 KINESIAS   A mattress? Not for me, thanks.

MYRRHINE   By Artemis, it's shabby on cords.

KINESIAS   Well, give me a kiss.

MYRRHINE [*Kissing him*]   There. [*She returns to the Grotto.*]

KINESIAS   Oh lordy! Get the mattress quick!

110 MYRRHINE [*Returning with a mattress*]   There we are! Lie back down and I'll
     get my clothes off. But wait, what is it, a pillow, you haven't got a pillow!

KINESIAS   I don't need a pillow!

MYRRHINE   I do. [*She returns to the Grotto.*]

KINESIAS   Is this cock of mine supposed to be Herakles waiting for his dinner?[7]

115 MYRRHINE [*Returning with a pillow*]   Lift up now, upsy daisy. There, is that
     everything?

KINESIAS   Everything *I* need. Come here, my little treasure!

MYRRHINE   Just getting my breastband off. But remember: don't break your
     promise about a peace-settlement.

120 KINESIAS   May lightning strike me, by Zeus!

MYRRHINE   You don't have a blanket.

KINESIAS   It's not a blanket I want—I want to fuck!

MYRRHINE   That's just what you're going to get. Back in a flash. [*She returns
     to the Grotto.*]

KINESIAS   That woman drives me nuts with all her bedding!

125 MYRRHINE [*Returning with a blanket*]   Get up.

KINESIAS [*Pointing to his phallus*]   I've already got it up! [MYRRHINE *carefully
     arranges the blanket while* KINESIAS *fidgets.*]

MYRRHINE   Want some scent?

KINESIAS   Apollo[8] no, none for me.

MYRRHINE   But *I* will, by Aphrodite, whether you like it or not.

130 KINESIAS [*As* MYRRHINE *returns to the Grotto*]   Then let the scent flow! Lord
     Zeus!

MYRRHINE [*Returning with a round bottle of perfume*]   Hold out your hand.
     Take some and rub it in.

KINESIAS   I don't like this scent, by Apollo; it takes a long time warming up
135   and it doesn't smell like conjugal pleasures.

MYRRHINE   Oh silly me, I brought the Rhodian[9] brand!

KINESIAS   No, wait, I like it! Let it go, you screwy woman!

MYRRHINE   What are you talking about? [*She returns to the Grotto.*]

KINESIAS   Goddamn the man who first decocted scent!

140 MYRRHINE [*Returning with a long, cylindrical bottle*]   Here, try this tube.

KINESIAS [*Pointing to his phallus*]   Got one already! Now lie down, you slut,
     and don't bring me anything more.

7. The hero was routinely portrayed as having   8. Greek god of prophecy, light, and healing.
great appetites.   9. From the Aegean island of Rhodes.

MYRRHINE   By Artemis I will. Just getting my shoes off. But remember, darling,
    you're going to vote for peace. [*At this,* KINESIAS *averts his eyes from* MYRRHINE
    and fiddles with the blanket; MYRRHINE *dashes off into the Akropolis.*]

145 KINESIAS   I'll give it serious consideration. [*He looks up again, only to find*
    MYRRHINE *gone.*] The woman's destroyed me, annihilated me! Not only
    that: she's pumped me up and dropped me flat!

        [*During the ensuing duet both semichoruses return to the center of the*
        orchestra; the women carry the shirts that the men had removed earlier.]

    Now what shall I do? Whom shall I screw?
    I'm cheated of the sexiest girl I knew!
150   How will I raise and rear this orphaned cock?
    Is Fox Dog[1] out there anywhere?
    I need to rent a practical nurse!
  MEN'S LEADER   Yea frightful agony, thou wretch,
    dost rack the soul of one so sore bediddled.
155   Sure I do feel for thee, alack!
    What kidney could bear it,
    what soul, what balls,
    what loins, what crotch,
    thus stretched on the rack
160   and deprived of a morning fuck?
  KINESIAS   Ah Zeus! The cramps attack anew!
  MEN'S LEADER   And *this* is what she's done to you,
    the detestable, revolting shrew!
  WOMEN'S LEADER   No, she's totally sweet and dear!
165 MEN'S LEADER   Sweet, you say! She's wicked, wicked!
  KINESIAS   You're right: wicked is what she is!
    O Zeus, Zeus, raise up a great tornado,
    with lightning bolts and all,
    to sweep her up like a heap of grain
170   and twirl her into the sky,
    and then let go and let her fall
    back down to earth again,
    and let her point of impact be
    this dick of mine right here!

Episode

[*Enter a Spartan* HERALD, *both arms hidden beneath a long travelling cloak and*
pushing it out in front.]

HERALD [*To* KINESIAS]   Where be the Senate of Athens or the Prytanies?[2]
    Have some news to tell them.
  KINESIAS   And what might you be? Are you human? Or a Konisalos?[3]
  HERALD   Am Herald, youngun, by the Twain, come from Sparta about
5   settlement.
  KINESIAS   And that's why you've come hiding a spear in your clothes?

1. Nickname of the famous pimp Philostratos.
2. That portion of the Athenian council responsible for the day-to-day business of the
state; its membership rotated.
3. A phallic fertility spirit associated with a Spartan dance.

HERALD   Not I, by Zeus, no spear!

KINESIAS   Why twist away from me? And why hold your coat out in front of
you? You've got a swollen groin from the long ride, maybe?

10 HERALD   By Kastor, this guy crazy! [*He accidently reveals his erect phallus.*]

KINESIAS   Hey, that's hard-on, you rascal!

HERALD   No, by Zeus, is not! Don't be silly!

KINESIAS   Then what do you call *that*?

HERALD   Is Spartan walking-stick.

15 KINESIAS [*Pointing to his own phallus*]   Then *this* is a Spartan walking-stick
too. Listen, I know what's up; you can level with me. How are things going
in Sparta?

HERALD   All Sparta rise, also allies. All have hard-on. Need Pellana.[4]

KINESIAS   What caused this calamity to hit you? Was it Pan?

20 HERALD   Oh no. Was Lampito started it, yes, and then other women in
Sparta, they all start together like in footrace, keep men away from their
hair-pies.

KINESIAS   So how are you faring?

HERALD   Hard! Walk around town bent over, like men carrying oil-lamp in
25 wind. The women won't permit even to touch the pussy till all of us unani-
mously agree to make peace-treaty with rest of Greeks.

KINESIAS   So this business is a global conspiracy by all the women! Now I get
it! OK, get back to Sparta as quick as you can and arrange to send ambassadors here with full powers to negotiate a treaty. And I'll arrange for *our* Coun
30 cil to choose their own ambassadors; this cock of mine will be Exhibit A.

HERALD   I fly away. You offer capital advice. [*He exits by the way he entered;*
KINESIAS *exits in the opposite direction.*]

MEN'S LEADER   A woman's harder to conquer than any beast,
than fire, and no panther is quite so ferocious.

WOMEN'S LEADER   You understand that, but then you still resist us?
35 It's possible, you rascal, to have our lasting friendship.

MEN'S LEADER   I'll never cease to loathe women!

WOMEN'S LEADER   Well, whenever you like. But meanwhile I'll not stand
for you to be undressed like that. Just look how ridiculous you are!
I'm coming over to put your shirt back on.

[*She walks over and replaces his shirt, and the other women each follow
suit for one of the men.*]

40 MEN'S LEADER   By god, that's no mean thing you've done for us.
And now I'm sorry I got mad and took it off.

WOMEN'S LEADER   And now you look like a man again, not so ridiculous.
And if you weren't so hostile I'd have removed
that bug in your eye, that's still in there, I see.

45 MEN'S LEADER   So *that's* what's been driving me nuts! Here, take my ring;
please dig it out of my eye, then show it to me;
by god, it's been biting my eye for quite some time.

WOMEN'S LEADER   All right, I will, though you're a grumpy man.
Great gods, what a humongous gnat you've got in there!
50 There, take a look. Isn't it positively Trikorysian?[5]

---

4. A city south of Sparta; here, the name
appears to have obscure sexual connotations.

5. From Trikorythos, a marshy district in
Attica.

MEN'S LEADER   By god, you've helped me; that thing's been digging wells,
   and now it's out my eyes are streaming tears.
WOMEN'S LEADER   Then I'll wipe them away, though you're a genuine rascal,
   and kiss you.
55 MEN'S LEADER   Don't kiss me!
WOMEN'S LEADER   I'll kiss you whether you like it or not!
          [She does so, and the other women follow suit as before.]
MEN'S LEADER   The worst of luck to you! You're born sweet-talkers.
   The ancient adage gets it in a nutshell:
   "Can't live *with* the pests or without 'em either."
   But now I'll make peace, and promise nevermore
60   to mistreat you or to take mistreatment *from* you.
   Let's get together, then, and start our song.
          [The semichoruses become one and for the remainder of the play perform
          as a single chorus.]

CHORUS (strophe)
   We don't intend to say anything
   the least bit slanderous about
   any citizen, you gentlemen out there,
65   but quite the opposite: to say and do
   only what's nice, because the troubles
   you've got already are more than enough.

   So let every man and woman tell us
   if they need to have a little cash,
70   say two or three minas;[6] we've got it at home
   and we've got some purses for it too.
   And if peace should ever break out,
   everyone that we lent money to
   can forget to repay—if they got anything!

(antistrophe)
75   We're getting set to entertain
   some visitors from Karystos[7] today;
   they're fine and handsome gentlemen.
   There'll be a special soup, and that piglet
   of mine, I've sacrificed it on the grill,
80   and it's turning out to be fine and tender meat.
   So come on over to my house today:
   get up early and take a bath,
   and bathe the kids, and walk right in.
   You needn't ask anyone's permission,
85   just go straight on inside like it was yours,
   because the door will be locked!

---

6. A substantial sum of money. *So let every man and woman tell us*: a line unique in suggesting that women attended the performances of ancient comedy.
7. A small town on the Aegean island of Euboea, north of Athens, that was an ally of Athens.

Episode

[*The* SPARTAN AMBASSADORS *enter, their clothes concealing conspicuous bulges. They are accompanied by slaves.*]

CHORUS-LEADER   Hey! Here come ambassadors from Sparta, dragging long
  beards and wearing something around their waists that looks like a pig-
  pen. [*To the Spartans*] Gentlemen of Sparta: first, our greetings! Then tell
  us how you all are doing?

5 SPARTAN AMBASSADOR   No use to waste a lot of time describing. Is best to
  show how we're doing. [*The Spartans open their cloaks to reveal their erect
  phalli.*]

CHORUS-LEADER   Gosh! Your problem's grown very hard, and it seems to be
  even more inflamed than before.

SPARTAN AMBASSADOR   Unspeakable! What can one say? We wish for some
10 one to come, make peace for us on any terms he like.

    [ATHENIAN AMBASSADORS *enter from the opposite direction, with cloaks
    bulging.*]

CHORUS-LEADER   Look, I see a party of native sons approaching, like men
  wrestling, holding their clothes away from their bellies like that! Looks like
  a bad case of prickly heat.

FIRST ATHENIAN AMBASSADOR   [*To the* CHORUS-LEADER.]   Who can tell us
15 where Lysistrata is? The men are here, and we're . . . as you see. [*They
  reveal their own erect phalli.*]

CHORUS-LEADER   *Their* syndrome seems to be the same as *theirs*. These
  spasms: do they seize you in the wee hours?

FIRST ATHENIAN AMBASSADOR   Yes, and what's worse, we're worn totally raw
  by being in this condition! If someone doesn't get us a treaty pretty soon,
20 there's no way we won't be fucking Kleisthenes!

CHORUS-LEADER   If you've got any sense, you'll cover up there: you don't
  want one of the Herm-Dockers[8] to see you like this.

FIRST ATHENIAN AMBASSADOR   By god, that's good advice. [*The Athenians
  rearrange their cloaks to cover their phalli.*]

SPARTAN AMBASSADOR   By the Twain Gods, yes indeed. Come, put cloaks
25 back on! [*The Spartans follow suit.*]

FIRST ATHENIAN AMBASSADOR   Greetings, Spartans! We've had an awful time.

SPARTAN AMBASSADOR   Dear colleague, we've had a *fearful* time, if those men
  saw us fiddling with ourselves.

FIRST ATHENIAN AMBASSADOR   Come on, then, Spartans, let's talk details. The
30 reason for your visit?

SPARTAN AMBASSADOR   Are ambassadors, for settlement.

FIRST ATHENIAN AMBASSADOR   That's very good; us too. So why not invite Lysistrata to our meeting, since she's the only one who can settle our differences?

SPARTAN AMBASSADOR   Sure, by the Twain Gods, Lysistrata, and Lysistratos[9]
35 too if ye like!

    [LYSISTRATA *emerges from the Akropolis gate.*]

8. The unknown individuals who, just before
the great expedition was to leave for Sicily (in
415 B.C.E.), broke the erect phalluses off statues of Hermes. These representations of the
messenger god, the patron of travelers, stood
outside houses and public buildings throughout the city.
9. The masculine form of the name Lysistrata,
perhaps also mocking the Spartans as
homosexuals.

FIRST ATHENIAN AMBASSADOR   It looks as if we don't have to invite her: she must have heard us, for here she comes herself.

CHORUS-LEADER   Hail, manliest of all women! Now is your time: be forceful and flexible, high-class and vulgar, haughty and sweet, a woman for all sea
40   sons; because the head men of Greece, caught by your charms, have gathered together with all their mutual complaints and are turning them over to you for settlement.

LYSISTRATA   Well, it's an easy thing to do if you get them when they're hot for it and not testing each other for weaknesses. I'll soon know how ready they
45   are. Where's Reconciliation? [A naked girl comes out of the Akropolis.] Take hold of the Spartans first and bring them here; don't handle them with a rough or mean hand, or crudely, the way our husbands used to handle us, but use a wife's touch, like home sweet home. [The SPARTAN AMBASSADOR refuses to give his hand.] If he won't give you his hand, lead him by his
50   weenie. [The SPARTAN AMBASSADOR complies, and she leads him and his colleagues to LYSISTRATA, where they stand to her left.] Now go and fetch those Athenians too; take hold of whatever they give you and bring them here. [RECONCILIATION escorts the Athenians to LYSISTRATA's right.] Spartans, move in closer to me, and you Athenians too; I want you to listen to what I have to
55   say. I am a woman, but still I've got a mind: I'm pretty intelligent in my own right, and because I've listened many a time to the conversations of my father and the older men I'm pretty well educated too. Now that you're a captive audience I'm ready to give you the tongue-lashing you deserve—both of you.

Don't both of you sprinkle altars from the same cup like kinsmen, at the
60   Olympic Games, at Thermopylai, at Delphi,[1] and so many other places I could mention if I had to make a long list? Yet with plenty of enemies available with their barbarian armies, it's Greek men and Greek cities you're determined to destroy! That's the first point I wanted to make.

FIRST ATHENIAN AMBASSADOR [Gazing at RECONCILIATION]   My cock is burst
65   ing out of its skin and killing me!

LYSISTRATA   Next I'm going to turn to you, Spartans. Don't you remember the time when Perikleidas the Spartan came here on bended knee and sat at Athenian altars, white-faced in his scarlet uniform, begging for a military contingent? That time when Messenia was up in arms against you and the
70   god was shaking you with an earthquake? And Kimon came with four thousand infantrymen and rescued all Lakedaimon?[2] And after that sort of treatment from the Athenians, you're now out to ravage their country, who've treated you so well?

FIRST ATHENIAN AMBASSADOR   By Zeus they are guilty, Lysistrata!

75   SPARTAN AMBASSADOR   We're guilty—[looking at RECONCILIATION] but what an unspeakably fine ass!

---

1. Sites revered by all Greeks. At the Olympic Games, held quadrennially in Olympia, on the Peloponnesian Peninsula, a truce was observed; Thermopylae, in central Greece, was the site of the Spartans' heroic stand against the Persians in 480 B.C.E.; Delphi, in central Greece, was the site of the most important oracle of Apollo and of the Panhellenic games.

2. That is, Sparta. Kimon, an Athenian general and statesman, brought aid to Sparta in 464 B.C.E. after a devastating earthquake was followed by a rebellion of their serfs. (Lysistrata refrains from adding that the Spartans abruptly sent the Athenians away, an affront to Athenian pride that resulted in Kimon's exile.)

LYSISTRATA   Do you Athenians think I'm going to let *you* off? Don't you
remember the time when you were dressed in slaves' rags and the Spartans
came in force and wiped out many Thessalian fighters, many friends and
80   allies of Hippias?[3] That day when they were the only ones helping you to
drive him out? How they liberated you, and replaced your slaves' rags with
a warm cloak, as suits a free people?

SPARTAN AMBASSADOR   [*Still gazing at* RECONCILIATION]   I never saw such a
classy woman!

85   FIRST ATHENIAN AMBASSADOR   *I've* never seen a lovelier cunt!

LYSISTRATA   So after so many good deeds done, why are you at war? Why not
stop this terrible behavior? Why not make peace? Come on, what's in the way?

[*During the following negotiations* RECONCILIATION's *body serves as a
map of Greece.*]

SPARTAN AMBASSADOR   We are ready, if they are ready to return to us this
abutment.

90   LYSISTRATA   Which one, sir?

SPARTAN AMBASSADOR   Back Door[4] here, that we for long time count on having, and grope for.

FIRST ATHENIAN AMBASSADOR   By Poseidon, that you *won't* get!

LYSISTRATA   Give it to them, good sir.

95   FIRST ATHENIAN AMBASSADOR   Then who will *we* be able to harrass?

LYSISTRATA   Just ask for some other place in return for that one.

FIRST ATHENIAN AMBASSADOR   Well, let's see now. First of all give us Echinous
here and the Malian Gulf behind it and both Legs.[5]

SPARTAN AMBASSADOR   By Twain Gods, we will not give *everything*, dear fellow!

100   LYSISTRATA   Let it go: don't be squabbling about legs.

FIRST ATHENIAN AMBASSADOR   Now I'm ready to strip down and do some
ploughing!

SPARTAN AMBASSADOR   Me first, by Twain Gods: before one ploughs one
spreads manure!

105   LYSISTRATA   You may do that when you've ratified the settlement. If, after due
deliberation, you do decide to settle, go back and confer with your allies.

FIRST ATHENIAN AMBASSADOR   *Allies,* dear lady? We're too hard up for that!
Won't our allies, all of them, come to the same decision *we* have, namely, to
fuck?

110   SPARTAN AMBASSADOR   *Ours* will, by Twain Gods!

FIRST ATHENIAN AMBASSADOR   And so will the Karystians,[6] by Zeus!

LYSISTRATA   You make a strong case. For the time being see to it you remain
pure, so that we women can host you on the Akropolis with what we
brought in our boxes. There you may exchange pledges of mutual trust,
115   and after that each of you may reclaim his wife and go home.

FIRST ATHENIAN AMBASSADOR   What are we waiting for?

SPARTAN AMBASSADOR   [*To* LYSISTRATA]   Lead on wherever you wish.

---

3. The Spartans came to the aid of Athenian
democrats and expelled the tyrant Hippias
in 510 B.C.E. (Again, Lysistrata leaves out
the acrimonious end of the story—the Spartans' later attempt to overthrow the democracy.) *Thessalian*: from Thessaly, in northern
Greece.

4. Pylos; also a joke at the Spartans' supposed
preference for anal sex.
5. Echinous is a town in Thessaly; the Malian
Gulf is near Thermopylae; the "Legs" here
are the walls that connected the city of Meg-
ara, west of Athens, and its seaport, Nisaia.
6. The inhabitants of Karystos.

FIRST ATHENIAN AMBASSADOR By Zeus yes, as quick as you can!

[LYSISTRATA *escorts* RECONCILIATION *inside, followed by the* SPARTAN *and* ATHENIAN AMBASSADORS; *the Spartans' slaves sit down outside the door, which is attended by a doorkeeper.*]

CHORUS (*strophe*)
    Intricate tapestries,
120   nice clothes and fine gowns
    and gold jewellery: all that I own
    is yours for the asking
    for your sons and for your daughter too,
    when she's picked to march with the basket.[7]
125   I declare my home open to everyone
    to take anything you want.
    Nothing is sealed up so tight
    that you won't be able to break the seals
    and take away what you find inside.
130   But you won't see anything
    unless your eyes are sharper than mine.
(*antistrophe*)
    If anyone's out of bread
    but has slaves and lots of little kids to feed,
    you can get flour from my house:
135   puny grains, but a pound of them
    grow up to be a loaf
    that looks very hearty.
    Any of you poor people are welcome
    to come to my house with sacks and bags
140   to carry the flour away; my houseboy will load them up.
    A warning though: don't knock at my door—
    beware of the watchdog there!

Episode

FIRST ATHENIAN AMBASSADOR [*Still inside, knocking at the door and yelling to the doorkeeper*] Open the door, you! [*He bursts through the door, sending the doorkeeper tumbling down the steps. He wears a garland and carries a torch, as from a drinking-party.*] You should have got out of the way. [*Other Athenians emerge, similarly equipped. To the slaves*] You there, why are you sitting around? Want me to singe you with this torch?
5   What a stale routine! I refuse to do it. [*Encouragement from the spectators.*] Well, if it's absolutely necessary we'll go the extra mile, to do you all a favor. [*He begins to chase the slaves with his torch.*]
SECOND ATHENIAN AMBASSADOR [*Joining the* FIRST] And we'll help you go that extra mile! [*To the slaves*] Get lost! You'll cry for your hair if you don't!
10 FIRST ATHENIAN AMBASSADOR Yes, get lost, so the Spartans can come out after their banquet without being bothered. [*The slaves are chased off.*]
SECOND ATHENIAN AMBASSADOR I've never been at a better party! The Spartans were really great guys, and we made wonderful company ourselves over the drinks.

7. That is, during a religious festival.

15 FIRST ATHENIAN AMBASSADOR   Stands to reason: when we're sober we're not
  ourselves. If the Athenians will take my advice, from now on we'll do all our
  ambassadorial business drunk. As it is, whenever we go to Sparta sober, we
  start right in looking for ways to stir up trouble. When they say something
  we don't hear it, and when they don't say something we're convinced that
20 they did say it, and we each return with completely different reports. But
  this time everything turned out fine. When somebody sang the Telamon
  Song when he should have been singing the Kleitagora Song,[8] everybody
  would applaud and even swear up and down what a fine choice it was.
  [*Some of the slaves approach the door again.*] Hey, those slaves are back!
25 Get lost, you whip-fodder! [*They chase the slaves away.*]
  SECOND ATHENIAN AMBASSADOR   Yes, by Zeus, here they come out of the door.
  [*The* SPARTAN AMBASSADORS *file out; their leader carries bagpipes.*]
  SPARTAN AMBASSADOR [*To the stage-piper or to a piper who accompanies the
  Spartans*]   Take pipes, my good man, and I dance two-step and sing nice
  song for Athenians and ourselves.
  FIRST ATHENIAN AMBASSADOR   God yes, take the pipes: I love to watch you
30 people dance!
  SPARTAN AMBASSADOR   Memory, speed to this lad
  your own Muse, who knows
  about us and the Athenians,
  about that day at Artemision
35 when *they* spread sail like gods
  against the armada
  and whipped the Medes,
  while Leonidas[9] led *us*,
  like wild boars we were, yes,
40 gnashing our tusks, our jaws running
  streams of foam, and our legs too.
  The enemy, the Persians,
  outnumbered the sand on the shore.

  Goddess of the Wilds, Virgin Beast-Killer,[1]
45 come this way, this way to the treaty,
  and keep us together for a long long while.
  Now let friendship in abundance
  attend our agreement always,
  and may we ever abandon
50 foxy strategems.
  Come this way, this way,
  Virgin Huntress!
      [*A mute* LYSISTRATA *comes out of the Akropolis, followed by the Athenian
      and Spartan wives.*]

---

8. Evidently songs of war and of love (Telamon
was a legendary hero of the generation before
the Trojan War, and Kleitagora was a Spartan
woman poet).
9. The Spartan king and general who led the
small band against the Persians ("the Medes")

at Thermopylae in 480 B.C.E.; at the same
time, an indecisive naval battle took place
nearby at Cape Artemision. *Muse:* a goddess
of art and learning, conventionally invoked
for inspiration.
1. Artemis.

FIRST ATHENIAN AMBASSADOR   Well! Now that everything else has been wrapped
   up so nicely, it's time for you Spartans to reclaim these wives of yours; and
55   you Athenians, these here. Let's have husband stand by wife and wife by
   husband; then to celebrate our great good fortune let's have a dance for the
   gods. And let's be sure never again to make the same mistakes! [*The couples
   descend into the orchestra to dance to the* AMBASSADOR'S *song; around them
   dance the members of the chorus, who are also paired in couples.*]
      Bring on the dance, include the Graces,
      and invite Artemis,
60   and her twin brother, the benign Healer,[2]
      and the Nysian whose eyes flash
      bacchic among his maenads,
      and Zeus alight with flame
      and the thriving Lady his consort;[3]
65   and invite the divine powers
      we would have as witnesses
      to remember always
      this humane peace,
      which the goddess Kypris[4] has fashioned.
70 CHORUS   Alalai, yay Paian![5]
      Shake a leg, iai!
      Dance to victory, iai!
      Evoi evoi,[6] evai evai!

FIRST ATHENIAN AMBASSADOR Now, my dear Spartan, *you* give us some music:
75   a new song to match the last one!

SPARTAN AMBASSADOR   Come back again from fair Taÿgetos,
      Spartan Muse, and distinguish this occasion
      with a hymn to the God of Amyklai[7]
      and Athena of the Brazen House[8]
80   and Tyndareos' fine sons,
      who gallop beside the Eurotas.[9]
      Ho there, hop!
      Hey there, jump!
      Let's sing a hymn to Sparta,
85   home of dance divine
      and stomping feet,
      where by the Eurotas' banks
      young girls frisk like fillies,
      raising dust-clouds underfoot
90   and tossing their tresses
      like maenads waving their wands and playing,

2. Apollo. *Graces:* the incarnations of beauty
and grace, daughters of Zeus.
3. The goddess Hera, sister and wife of Zeus.
Maenads: the women who worship Dionysus,
god of wine and of an emotional cult who was
raised on Mount Nysa (whose location was a
matter of dispute).
4. Aphrodite.

5. A title of Apollo ("Healer").
6. The ecstatic cry of worshippers of Dionysus.
7. Site south of Sparta of a major shrine to
Apollo.
8. Sparta's bronze-plated temple to Athena.
9. The river that runs by Sparta. *Tyndareos'
fine sons:* Kastor and Pollux.

led by Leda's daughter,[1]
their chorus-leader pure and pretty.
[*To the* CHORUS] Come on now, hold your hair in your hand, get your feet
95   hopping like a deer and start making some noise to spur the dance! And
sing for the goddess who's won a total victory, Athena of the Brazen House!
[*All exit dancing, the* CHORUS *singing a traditional hymn to Athena.*]

1. Helen, the daughter of Leda and Zeus; she was worshipped as a goddess in Sparta.

TITUS MACCIUS PLAUTUS

ca. 254–184 B.C.E.

THE career of the Roman comic play-wright Plautus represents several significant "firsts" for the Western theatrical tradition. Plautus is the first man known to be a professional dramatist—in other words, the first who relied on writing plays for his income. He is the first Latin author for whom we possess a significant body of extant work, and his scripts serve as an invaluable resource in literary history. These texts may also be considered the first Latin writings that truly represent popular culture, since Plautus crafted plays for a mass audience that also had access to many other forms of entertainment with which his comedies were in direct competition. The success of these plays, as documented by classical authors and perhaps confirmed by the volume of scripts surviving for posterity, thus opens an important window onto ancient Roman society.

Despite his achievements, we know almost nothing definitive about Plautus's life and professional development. Contemporary scholars believe he was born around 254 B.C.E. in Sarsina, a rural part of Umbria, in what is now northeastern Italy. At some point, either during his lifetime or in later antiquity, he came to be known by the mock Roman name Titus Maccius Plautus. The latter parts of this sobriquet may take a parodic meaning from the mime and farce traditions of his day, roughly translating to "Titus the flat-footed clown" (possibly an allusion to the bare feet of mimes). A native speaker of Umbrian, he somehow mastered both Latin and Greek. Many scholars believe that his thorough grasp of theatrical practices, reflected in both the composition and the content of his plays, supports the hypothesis that he worked in the theater professionally before he took up playwriting. In Umbria, he may have been a performer in Atellan farces (short, popular pieces often featuring disguise and coarse jokes, named for the small town near Naples where they were believed to have originated), or he may have worked as an actor or a stagehand once he moved to Rome. We do not know when he began to write plays or how many he wrote in his lifetime. Twenty-one of his comedies have survived, some as mere fragments and others as almost complete scripts, yet we can only guess at their dates and order of composition. We do know, however, that PSEUDOLUS was commissioned for the dedication of the Temple of Magna Mater (the Great Mother Goddess) in 191 B.C.E. More than a century later, the great Roman statesman and orator Cicero claimed, in his De Senectute (On Old Age, ca. 45 B.C.E.), that Plautus particularly favored this work, and many scholars consider it his masterpiece.

Comparatively little is known about theatrical production in the second century B.C.E. Historians speculate that Roman military campaigns into what is now southern Italy in the First Punic War (264–241 B.C.E.) introduced Greek texts and theatrical culture into Rome, thereby inaugurating the transition from improvisation alone into a tradition that embraced both improvisatory and scripted performances. Since the first permanent theater in Rome was not built until 55 B.C.E., historians assume that plays in Plautus's era were staged in temporary structures, probably erected for the festivals that occurred at intervals throughout the year. High-ranking state officials called *aediles* paid for the productions. The Romans may also have employed staging techniques used in Greek theater, probably including the use of masks, but they perhaps incorporated performance elements from Atellan farce and mime as well. Roman comedy, understood primarily through the work of Plautus and his contemporary Terence (195?–159 B.C.E.), provides important evidence of Greek New Comedy, from which the Roman scripts were partially derived (though only one relatively complete example, by Menander, has survived). Through a process that Plautus called *"vortere barbare"*—the turning of Greek into "barbarian" Latin— Roman comedy transformed the plays of Greek New Comedy into a unique theatrical form that has significantly influenced the subsequent development of Western comedy. We thus may see in a work like *Pseudolus* the emergence of a new kind of drama, drawing both on the improvisatory structure of Atelan farce and on Greek New Comedy.

In tracing the initial evolution of this comic tradition, we find a shift from the pointed, political satire of the Greek Old Comedy, known to us primarily through the extant plays of ARISTOPHANES, to a more generalized form of humor that relies on familiar character types and situational tropes, often with a domestic rather than a public focus. In the aftermath of the Second Punic War (218–201 B.C.E.), Roman law prohibited dramatic references to specific individuals, and therefore the theater could not be a place for direct political comment. Playwrights may also not have wanted to risk loss of production and income by including content that could offend the *aediles*.

Despite its political reticence, Roman comedy retained the spirit of satire and critique of its Greek predecessors. Through his use of character types and familiar situations, Plautus could represent opposing perspectives on subjects of topical interest. These included public attitudes toward Rome's ongoing militarism and imperialism and the government's use of funds, especially in connection with these campaigns. In *Pseudolus*, for example, Pseudolus's discourse on the profits of his trickery implicitly comments on the distribution of the spoils of war. Equally central to the

This bas-relief found in Naples depicts a comic scene. Although neither the date nor the provenance of the relief is certain, some details in the image—such as the low-heeled shoes and masks worn by the performers and the elaborate scenic doorway to the left—are typical of classical comedy.

thrust of social commentary in Roman comedy is the calculated deployment of Greek source material and Greek references. Just as WILLIAM SHAKESPEARE and BERTOLT BRECHT many centuries later would use locations such as Milan or Chicago to critique their own places and times, so the Roman comic dramatists used Greece and the Greeks to safely parody aspects of domestic culture. Plautus employs a generic urban setting for his plays (a location critics have called "Plautinopolis") that appears to be Greek, yet is populated by characters who refer to Roman locations and embrace Roman customs and values.

Plautus's adaptations of Greek texts, his *fabulae palliatae* (literally, "cloak plays," an allusion to contemporary Greek dress), reflect cultural tensions between the very different classical civilizations of Greece and Rome, but they also raise stylistic questions about his process of transforming these New Comedies. The loss of all but one of his source dramas makes it impossible to generalize about Plautus's reworkings of the Greek originals. However, the one example we do have from Greek New Comedy—a fragment of Menander's *Dis Exapaton* (*The Double Deceiver*), on which Plautus based his *Two Bacchises*—reveals key distinctions between the dramatists. Whereas Menander's writing appears more "serious" and more concerned with psychological and situational realism, Plautus employs devices such as asides, eavesdropping, and extended monologues to give his play a less mimetic structure and an ironic tone. Similarly, his interpolation of scenes purely for comic effect—such as a lengthy exchange of insults between Pseudolus, his master Simo's son Calidorus, and the pimp Ballio in the third scene—distinguishes his works from Menander's. Indeed, this superabundance of language was a hallmark of the Plautine style, the closest English equivalent to which might be the patter songs so popular with the late Victorian audiences of Gilbert and Sullivan's comic operettas. Roman audiences were probably similarly entertained by Plautus's linguistic tours de force.

Audiences also responded to Plautus's narrative creativity—his ability to rework conventional stories with clever plot twists, with comic action, and with distinctive dialogue exhibiting metrical variety and musicality. Plautus's creative manipulation of familiar narratives prefigured such traditions as the well-made play, whose inventive variants of standardized plot lines captivated nineteenth-century audiences. Yet the messiness of Plautine narratives also distinguishes his works from the refined products of later dramatists. *Pseudolus* contains one of the clearest examples of this stylistic trait in its treatment of the impending sale of the courtesan Phoenicium, the object of Calidorus's desire, to a Macedonian soldier. We learn in the first scene that the courtesan has sent the youth a tablet containing all the background information, and yet Pseudolus and Calidorus appear surprised to hear the same story from the pimp Ballio later in the first act. What explains this seeming error in the play's story line? Perhaps the rowdy Roman audiences watching the play needed to be reminded of important plot elements. Perhaps Pseudolus and Calidorus are simply feigning surprise at Ballio's revelations as part of their initial plot to trick him. Or perhaps (as the scholar A. R. Sharrock argues), Plautus was doing something much more interesting and complex, using these moments of narrative disjunction to make audiences aware of, and to lead them to enjoy, the complexity of the work. This metacompositional quality of Plautus's plays may have been a technique calculated to reveal that writing—and the playwright doing the writing—is the force guiding even the most chaotic and seemingly improvisational moments in the play.

The word *metacompositional* is derived from the more common interpretive term *metatheatrical*, which has also been used to describe Plautus's plays generally and *Pseudolus* in particular. Theorists of metatheater, a concept developed in Lionel Abel's groundbreaking 1963 book, *Metatheatre: A New View of Dramatic Form*, posit that many dramatic texts have embedded within them the representation of key theatrical functions. Thus characters in plays may serve as directors, playwrights, and so on, in addition to their roles in the narrative of the play. Pseudolus takes on many such theatrical duties, including those of playwright, actor, and critic. On one level, then, *Pseudolus* is about the process of playmaking.

Whether his plays are metacompositional, metatheatrical, or straightforwardly clever, all is not just as it appears on the surface of Plautus's drama. At first glance, the ultimate triumph of the slave over his master would seem to imply that *Pseudolus* rests on a radical, or at least subversive, foundation. However, like other forms of art that the Russian critic Mikhail Bakhtin would later describe as "carnivalesque," *Pseudolus* inverts the social order in part to provide playgoers from the lower ranks with an acceptable, temporary safety valve for their frustrations with or resentments toward established societal hierarchies. Yet in the Plautine era, all individuals—citizens and noncitizens alike—could at times feel the burden of Roman law, and some of the wider appeal of *Pseudolus* may well derive from the shared but unacknowledged identification of all audience members with the central character and his ability to turn the tables on those in authority.

If this subtler social function for the play was one of Plautus's primary concerns, that focus may also help account for his relative lack of attention to developing the thwarted love plot. Once Calidorus is established as the prototypical helpless youth, he disappears from the action. The object of his desire, Phoenicium, is only fleetingly glimpsed, and she never speaks in the play. Thus the comedy is not really about the young lovers, even though they initiate the action. Nor is it a work that disrupts the patriarchal or moral structure of Roman society, because the son is not pitted directly against his father. Rather, the play concerns the relationship of money and power. That relationship is refracted through all the characters' interactions, whether between figures central to the narrative or those incorporated primarily for comic effect. Even the incidental interplay of Ballio, arguably Plautus's greatest comic villain, and the self-important cook helps to develop this theme. The setting, too—

the environs around a brothel—underlines the play's most fundamental truth: the fulfillment of any pleasure in life rests on one's access to, and use of, money.

We can trace the impact of Plautus (and, secondarily, the legacy of the New Greek Comedy that influenced him) both in specific texts and more generally in the forms, themes, narratives, and characters of Western comedy from the classical period to the present day. The rediscovery in 1429 of sixteen Plautine comedies had a great impact on the development of Italy's *commedia erudita* (or "learned" comedy, a counterpart to the popular form *commedia dell'arte*), which in turn influenced the evolution of Renaissance drama more generally. Adaptations of Plautus's plays after the fifteenth century are numerous and varied: Shakespeare's *Comedy of Errors* (1592–94) derives from Plautus's *Menaechmi*; MOLIÈRE's *The Miser* (1668) reworks *Aulularia*; Jean Giraudoux's *Amphitryon 38* (1929) directly reveals its source in *Amphitryon*; the musical *The Boys from Syracuse* (1938), with music by Richard Rodgers, lyrics by Lorenz Hart, and book by George Abbott, draws on *A Comedy of Errors* and thus also on *Menaechmi*; while the perennially popular *A Funny Thing Happened on the Way to the Forum* (1962; music and lyrics by Stephen Sondheim, book by Burt Shevelove and Larry Gelbart) puts Pseudolus and his colleagues center stage. Such character types as the braggart soldier, the miser, and the overbearing patriarch, developed in Roman comedy, have also proven highly influential. We can see in the allegorical figures of medieval morality plays a direct line of descent from Roman comedy, and Plautus's servant characters lead to a series of legendary figures, including Molière's Dorine and P. G. Wodehouse's Jeeves. Even contemporary situation comedies on television, as well as Hollywood films, rely heavily on classical dramatic structures, narratives, and character types developed by Plautus and refined through the centuries. The historical and dramaturgical importance of Plautus's writing cannot be overestimated.   J.E.G.

Pseudolus[1]

CHARACTERS

PSEUDOLUS, servant of Simo (slave)
CALIDORUS, a young man about town,
  son of Simo
BALLIO, a pimp
SIMO, an elderly gentleman, father
  of Calidorus
CALLIPHO, an elderly gentleman,
  neighbor of Simo

HARPAX, orderly of an officer in the
  Macedonian army (slave)
CHARINUS, friend of Calidorus
A SLAVE BOY of Ballio
A COOK
MONKEY (SIMIA), servant belonging
  to Charinus' family (slave)
SERVANTS and COURTESANS

[SCENE: *A street in Athens. Three houses front on it: stage left* SIMO's, *center* CALLI-
PHO's, *right* BALLIO's. *The exit on stage left leads downtown, that on stage right to
the country.*]

Prologue

You'd better get up and stretch your legs. There's a play by Plautus coming
on, and it's a long one.[2]

Act 1

[*The door of Calidorus' house opens, and* CALIDORUS *and* PSEUDOLUS *walk out.*

CALIDORUS, *"Beauty's Gift," is ancient comedy's traditional rich man's son:
handsome, well-dressed, empty-headed, and unemployable. At the moment he
is in a ludicrously blank state of despair, staring wordlessly at a set of waxed
wooden tablets bound with cord (the ancient equivalent of folded sheets of
paper) which he clutches with both hands.*

If CALIDORUS *has no brains,* PSEUDOLUS, *"Tricky," the family servant, has
enough for both. These are encased in an enormous head, which, along with a
bulging belly and a pair of oversize feet, give* PSEUDOLUS *a most deceptively
clownlike appearance.*]

PSEUDOLUS If I could figure out from this silence of yours what's the misery
    that's making you miserable, I'd have the pleasure of saving two men trou-
    ble: me of asking you questions and you of answering them. But I can't, so
    I've got to put the question. Tell me, what's the matter? For days now
5   you've been going around more dead than alive, holding that letter in your
    hands, washing it down with tears, and not confiding in anyone. Talk, will
    you! I'm in the dark; share the light with me.

1. Translated by Lionel Casson.
2. Roman comedies usually featured length-
ier prologues. The brevity of this prologue

suggests that the original, longer version may
have been lost.

CALIDORUS   I'm miserable. Miserably miserable.

PSEUDOLUS   Jupiter[3] forbid!

10 CALIDORUS   Jupiter has no jurisdiction in my case. I'm serving a sentence from Love, not Jupiter.

PSEUDOLUS   Am I allowed to know what it's all about? After all, up to now I was Accessory-in-Chief to all your projects.

CALIDORUS   I haven't changed.

15 PSEUDOLUS   Then let me in on what's ailing you. Resources, services, or good advice at your disposal.

CALIDORUS [handing him the tablets]   Take this letter. Then you can recite yourself the story of the worry and woe that's wasting me away.

PSEUDOLUS [taking the tablets]   Anything to make you happy. [Turning them
20 every which way and holding them at various distances from his eyes] Hey, what's this?

CALIDORUS   What's what?

PSEUDOLUS   If you ask me, the letters here want to have babies: each one's mounting the other.

25 CALIDORUS   Got to have your joke, don't you?

PSEUDOLUS   Maybe our Lady of the Riddles[4] can read them, but I swear nobody else can.

CALIDORUS   Why are you so cruel to the lovely letters of this lovely letter written in such a lovely hand?

30 PSEUDOLUS   Damn it all, I ask you now: do hens have hands? Because, believe me, some hen scribbled these letters.

CALIDORUS   You make me sick! Either read it or hand it back.

PSEUDOLUS   Oh no. I'll read it to the bitter end. Listen, and keep your mind on what I say.

35 CALIDORUS   I can't—it left me.

PSEUDOLUS   Call it back.

CALIDORUS   No, I'll keep quiet. You call it back. From that letter there. Because that's where my mind is now; it's not inside me.

PSEUDOLUS [slyly]   I see your girlfriend, Calidorus.

40 CALIDORUS   Pseudolus, please, I beg you! Tell me where she is!

PSEUDOLUS [holding up the tablets and pointing to the signature]   Here. Stretched out in this letter here. Lying on the lines.

CALIDORUS [throwing a punch at him]   I swear by all that's holy, I hope you go straight—

45 PSEUDOLUS [ducking nimbly and grinning]   —to heaven.

CALIDORUS [tragically]   I was like grass in summer, a minute ago: suddenly sprang up, and just as suddenly died down.

PSEUDOLUS   Quiet now while I read the letter.

CALIDORUS   Get going, will you!

50 PSEUDOLUS   "Dear sweetheart Calidorus. With tears in my eyes and tremors in my mind and heart and soul, through these waxed boards and piece of line and lines of communication, I send you my best wishes for your well-being—and my prayers for your help with mine."

CALIDORUS   Pseudolus! I'm lost! I'll never get what I need to help with hers!

3. In Roman mythology, king of the gods (equivalent to the Greek Zeus), also known as Jove.

4. That is, the Sibyl, a female prophet; the most famous was at Cumae, in Italy (on the coast west of modern Naples).

55 PSEUDOLUS What do you need?

CALIDORUS Gold.

PSEUDOLUS [*sticking the tablets in front of* CALIDORUS' *nose*] She sends best wishes in wood, and you want to answer in gold? Watch what you're doing, will you!

60 CALIDORUS Just go on reading. You'll find out soon enough how urgent it is that I get my hands on some gold.

PSEUDOLUS "The pimp has sold me for two thousand drachmas to a foreigner, a major from Macedon.[5] He's already left for home, after putting up a deposit of fifteen hundred; all that's holding matters up is a mere five

65 hundred. To arrange payment of this, the major left behind as means of identification his own picture stamped by his seal ring on a wax seal; the pimp is to hand me over to whoever arrives with an identical seal. And the date fixed for my departure is this coming Dionysus Day."[6]

CALIDORUS That's tomorrow. My end is practically upon me—unless you

70 can help.

PSEUDOLUS Let me finish reading.

CALIDORUS Go ahead. It makes me feel I'm talking with her. Read on; now you'll mix in some sweet for me along with the bitter.

PSEUDOLUS "Now our love, our life, the things we shared, our jokes and play

75 and talks and soft-sweet kisses, the tight embrace of impassioned bodies in love, the soft pressure of parted lips meeting tenderly, the burgeoning of my breasts under the sweet caress of your hand—all these joys will be taken away, torn away, trampled away—for you as well as for me—if you do not come to my rescue and I to yours. I have done my share: now you know all that I know.

80 I shall soon find out whether your love is real or pretended. Your loving Rosy."

CALIDORUS A piece of writing to make a man miserable, Pseudolus.

PSEUDOLUS [*glancing at the handwriting again*] Oh yes. Absolutely miserable.

CALIDORUS Then why aren't you crying?

PSEUDOLUS My eyes are made out of sand. I can't get them to squirt a single

85 tear.

CALIDORUS How come?

PSEUDOLUS Chronic dryness of the eyes. Runs through the whole family.

CALIDORUS You don't have the heart to help me?

PSEUDOLUS What do you expect from me?

90 CALIDORUS [*groaning*] Ai!

PSEUDOLUS Ai's? Good gods, don't spare *them*. I'll be your supplier.

CALIDORUS I'm in a bad way. I can't borrow a sou from a soul—

PSEUDOLUS [*grinning*] Ai!

CALIDORUS —and I don't have any money of my own—

95 PSEUDOLUS Ai!

CALIDORUS —and tomorrow that man's going to take my girl away.

PSEUDOLUS Ai!

CALIDORUS Is this the way you help me?

---

5. The northernmost kingdom of ancient Greece, bordering on the Aegean Sea to the south and Thrace (parts of present-day Bulgaria and Turkey) to the east. *Two thousand drachmas*: a considerable amount of money (a skilled worker might earn a drachma in a day).

6. Probably either the Lenaea, an early winter festival to honor Dionysus—the god of wine and fertility, a patron of agriculture and theater—or the Great Dionysia, a late winter festival that honored him with drama and music.

PSEUDOLUS   I'm giving you what I've got to give. It's the one item I have a
100   vast accumulation of in our house.

CALIDORUS   Then it's all over with me today. Could you please lend me a
drachma? I'll pay you back tomorrow.

PSEUDOLUS   I couldn't raise that much even if I put my own self in hock.
What are you going to do with a drachma anyway?

105   CALIDORUS   Buy myself a rope.

PSEUDOLUS   What for?

CALIDORUS   To turn myself into a pendulum. I've decided to darken my eyes
before dark today.

PSEUDOLUS   Then who'll pay me back my drachma if I lend it to you? Are you
110   deliberately planning to hang yourself just to do me out of a drachma if I
lend it to you?

CALIDORUS   I simply can't go on living if she's taken away from me and carried far, far away.

PSEUDOLUS   Stop crying, you dumb cluck! You'll live.

115   CALIDORUS   Why shouldn't I cry? I don't have any money in my pocket and
not the slightest prospect of borrowing anything from anybody.

PSEUDOLUS   As I gather from this letter, unless you can cry some cash for
her, all this shedding of tears to demonstrate your affections does about as
much good as using a sieve for a cistern. But stop worrying, fond lover: I
120   won't desert you. I'm a good operator; I have high hopes of finding salvation for you somewhere—financial salvation. Where am I going to get it? I
can't tell you where; I don't know where. But I'll get it all right: I have a
hunch today's my lucky day.

CALIDORUS   You say you can do it—if only you can do what you say!

125   PSEUDOLUS   Why, you know darn well the kind of ruckus I can raise once I
start my hocus-pocus.

CALIDORUS   My life depends on you! You're my only hope!

PSEUDOLUS   I'll arrange either to get you the girl or the two thousand. Will
that satisfy you?

130   CALIDORUS   [doubtfully]   Yes—if you'll do it.

PSEUDOLUS   Now put in a formal request for two thousand so I can prove I
perform what I promise. In the name of Jupiter, ask, will you! I'm dying to
make you a promise.

CALIDORUS   Do you hereby agree to give me two thousand in cash today?

135   PSEUDOLUS   I hereby agree. And now stop bothering me. And, just so you
won't tell me later that I didn't tell you, I'm telling you in advance: if I can't
get it from anyone else, I'll hit your father up for it.

CALIDORUS   Bless you! But I want to be a dutiful son, so, if possible, put the
touch on my mother too.

140   PSEUDOLUS   You're all set. Go to bed. Close your little ears.

CALIDORUS   Ears? Don't you mean eyes?

PSEUDOLUS   Less hackneyed the way I said it. [Turning to the audience; in
the tones of a town crier] And now, so no one will say I didn't warn him, I
hereby give public notice to everybody, voters, citizens, all my friends and
145   acquaintances: watch out for me all day long! Don't trust me!

CALIDORUS   Shh! Keep quiet! Please!

PSEUDOLUS   What's up?

CALIDORUS   The pimp's door handle just twisted.

PSEUDOLUS I wish it was his neck.

150 **CALIDORUS** And there he is, the dirty double-crosser. He's coming out.

> [*The two move to an unobtrusive spot off to the side. The door swings open, and* BALLIO, *"Tosser Around," the pimp, steps out, hefting a mean-looking whip.*
>
> BALLIO *is a businessman in a thoroughly unpleasant business: he owns a bevy of slave girls whom he supplies to those with the wherewithal to hire them or buy them outright. A straggly beard on his chin, a permanent snarl on his lips, an avaricious glint in his eye, and a filthy miserly get-up make him as unappetizing in appearance as in métier.*]

SONG

BALLIO [*turning and shouting through the open door*]
Come out of the house, good-for-nothings, come out!
What a mistake to have bought you and kept you about!

> [*Six terrified slave boys—miserable, underfed specimens in rags— scamper out of the door and huddle in front of it; one holds a shopping basket and a purse, another a jug, another an ax.* BALLIO *eyes them distastefully, then turns to the audience.*]

Not a one in the lot ever got the idea
To do anything good.

> [*Brandishing the whip.*]

          Without using this here,
155 They're all useless. To put them to use takes abuse.
And I've never seen hides more like donkeys', I swear:
They've been drubbed so, they've even grown calluses there;
Why, to thrash them takes less out of them than of you.
To be wear-the-whip-outers comes natural to
160   The whole breed. The one thought in their heads
      Is to snatch, steal,
      Grab, make hay,
      Gorge, swill,
      And run away.
165 It's their one, single purpose in life. Why, I say
I'd as soon let a wolf guard my sheep any day,
As let these watch my house any time I'm away.

> [BALLIO *glares at them. They summon up sickly smiles. He turns back to the audience.*]

Oh, their faces look fine; you can't go by their looks.
It's at work that they pull every trick in the books.

> [*He swings around abruptly and starts flailing with the whip.*]

170 Get the sleep from your eyes! Get the sloth from your brain!
Pay attention. I'll shortly begin to explain
      The orders of the day.
Listen hard or I'll batter your butts till they turn
      Every color, as gay
175 As a highly embroidered Neapolitan shawl
Or a Persian brocade with its beasties and all.

[*Shifts to a deadly menacing tone.*]

I issued orders yesterday assigning each of you
A station and official list of things he had to do.
You're such a bunch of loafers, though, such inborn stinkers that
180   You've forced me to remind you of your duties with this cat![7]
My whip and I admit defeat; the victory's yours instead.
And it's all because of the way you're made—so hard in hide and head!

[*As the slaves visibly relax, he suddenly flails about madly with the whip,
and they all make a wild scramble for safety. He addresses the audience
with mock exasperation.*]

Now look at that, if you please! You see the way their minds will stray?

[*Turning back to the slaves.*]

You mind me now, you hear! You tune those ears to what I say.
185   You stinkers, born and bred with special whip-proof back and side,
Remember that my rawhide's always harder than your hide.

[*Lunges suddenly and lands a blow on the nearest one, who lets out a howl.*]

What's up? It hurts? It's what I give a slave who's snotty to
His master. Now come here; face me, and hear what you're to do.

[*The slaves line up.*]

First you who's got the jug. Get water and fill the cooking pot.
190   And you with the ax I appoint my Chief of Fuel Supply.

SLAVE   But it's not
Got an edge, it's too dull to use!

BALLIO   So what?
                                              The whip's dulled your edge too.
Doesn't make the slightest difference to me—I keep using all of you.

[BALLIO *turns to the third.*]

195   You make that whole house shine. You've got your job, now hop, you lout!

[*To the fourth.*]

And you're Official Chair-Man.

[*To the fifth.*]

                              And you clean silver and lay it out.

[*To all of them.*]

Once I'm back from shopping, mind I find that everything's done—
Sweeping, setting, cleaning, shining—no chore undone, not one!
It's my birthday today. You must help celebrate.
200   Put the pig in the pot, from the trotters to pate.
Is that clear? I'm inviting big names; a big splash
Is the thing—make them think that I squander the cash.
Now go in and get going so there'll be no delay
When the chef makes it here. Because *I'm* on my way
205   To the market; I'm off on a fish-buying jag.

[*To the slave carrying a basket under one arm and a purse over one shoulder.*]

Go in front. I'm back here to keep thieves from that bag.

[*They start walking off, while the others race inside.* BALLIO *suddenly stops
short.*]

7. That is, cat-o'-nine-tails.

Wait a second. I almost forgot. I'm not through.

[*Goes to the doorway and calls through it.*]

Can you hear me, you girls? I've an announcement for you.

[*Four flashily dressed girls step out and line up sullenly in front of him.*]

You're all living in clover, my sweet little sprites.

210 You're all girls with a name, and the town's leading lights
Are your clients. Today I'll find out what you're at.
Do you work to get free? Or to gorge and get fat?
To acquire a nest egg? Or sleep until three?
Yes, today I'll work out who I think will get free

215 Or I think will wind up being sold for a whore.[8]
Have your clients bring in birthday presents galore!
For today we lay in one year's bread, drink, and meat,
Or tomorrow I'll have you out walking the street.
Now, you know it's my birthday. Well, have them kick in,

220 All the boyfriends for whom you've been "Doll," "Bunny-kin,"
"Cutie-pie," "Honeybunch," "Sweetheart," and "Pet,"
"Snookle-puss," "Babykins," "Ducky," et cet.
Make their slaves, bearing gifties, come by in brigades!
All the jewelry, money, the clothes and brocades

225 That I've had to provide—what's it got me, I say?
Little cash, only woe, from you bitches today!
All your passion's for drink, to tank up, whereas I
Have to live my whole life with a gullet bone dry!
And now I'll call you up by name and give you each the word.

230 This plan's the best since no one then can claim she hadn't heard.
So, all of you,
Here's what you do.
I'll start with Sweetsie, darling of the men who market grain.
Since each one stocks a good-sized hill, you're please to make them rain

235 Enough on me to give our house a year's supply to eat,
A flood so big my name will change from "Pimp" to "King of Wheat."

PSEUDOLUS [*sotto voce, to* CALIDORUS]   Do you hear the rat talk? Like a pretty
big dealer, Don't you think?

CALIDORUS [*sotto voce, to* PSEUDOLUS]   He sure is! And a pretty big stealer.
240 Now shut up. Pay attention to what he says next.

BALLIO   Now listen, Golddig. You're the girl the butchers all adore.
(They're like us pimps: they take their cut—their pound of flesh and more!)
You bring me in three meathooks loaded down with beef today
Or tomorrow you play Dirce[9]—and her story goes this way:

245 Her stepsons squared accounts with her by hitching her to a bull.
Well, you I'll stretch on a meathook, see—and *that's* a bull with pull!

---

8. Prostitutes who had to provide housing, food, and clothes for themselves in addition to paying a portion of their earnings to their owner had a worse arrangement than those who were maintained by a pimp in a domestic setting.

9. Wife of Lycus, king of Thebes, who had divorced Antiope. After Antiope was impregnated by Jupiter, Dirce imprisoned and tormented her, in the belief that Lycus was the father. Antiope's children punished Dirce by tying her to the tail of a wild bull, which dragged her over rocks and mountains, until the gods took pity on her and transformed her into a spring.

PSEUDOLUS [*aside, raging*] You hear him talk? I'm burning up—he's got me
    hopping mad!
How *can* you, Youth of Athens, patronize a man this bad?
Come out here, all you youngsters who've been buying love from pimps,
250   Let's gather altogether, boys, and everyone take part
To rid the citizen body of this canker at its heart!
          Pseudolus, you've got to learn,
          Pseudolus, you've got no brains.
          Why, sex makes youngsters all behave
255   Toward any pimp just like his slave
          And rush to do his every whim.
          And *you* want them to be so brave
          They'll up and do away with *him!*
CALIDORUS [*sotto voce*] Oh, shut your trap! You give me a pain—you're
260   drowning out what he's saying!
PSEUDOLUS   All right, I will.
CALIDORUS [*sotto voce*]
                  Well, don't just say so. Do it! Stop your braying.
BALLIO [*turning to the third girl*] Your turn. Now listen, Olive, sweetheart of
    the oil-trade crew.
When it comes to ready stock on hand, your lovers keep beaucoup.
I want a load of jugs of oil, and you'll produce tout' suite,[1]
265   Or tomorrow *you'll* get boiled in oil and dumped out on the street;
I'll set a bed for you out there, where *you* won't get much rest
Though you'll be plenty tired—why say more? By now you've guessed.
You've got a mob of boyfriends who just roll in oil, but you
Couldn't give your fellow slaves today a drop for their shampoo
270   Or give your lord and master some for juicing up his stew.
          I know the reason too:
          You don't have very much use for oil—
          Your anointing's done with alcohol!
    [*Glaring at all of them.*]
All right! You carry out the orders that I've given you today,
    [*Shaking the whip.*]
275   Or, gad, I'll let you have it, all at once and in one way!
    [*He turns to the last girl, by far the best looking of the four. It is
    Phoenicium, "Rosy," CALIDORUS' inamorata.*]
And now the girl always just about to buy her freedom and dash.
You're good at promising payment—but no good at raising cash.
Now, heartthrob of the upper crust, to you I've this to say.
Your boyfriends, Rosy, own big farms; so you produce today
280   A load of all the stuff they raise or tomorrow *you* will pay:
          I'll have you walking streets, my dame,
          Your hide tanned brighter than your name.
    [BALLIO *and his marketing attendant remain where they are. The girls,
    shuffling despondently, start filing into the house under* BALLIO's *baleful
    gaze. He does not hear the following conversation which* CALIDORUS *and*
    PSEUDOLUS *hold sotto voce.*]

1. Immediately (French, *tout de suite*).

CALIDORUS [*agonized*]   Pseudolus! Hear what he says?
PSEUDOLUS   Calidorus! I heard.
   And I'm thinking it out.
CALIDORUS   What ideas have you got
285   Of a gift I can send so he'll weaken and not
   Make a whore of my girl.
PSEUDOLUS   Don't you worry. Don't be blue.
   Because *I'll* do the worrying for me and for you.
   We've been swapping good wishes for years, he and I;
   We're old friends. Since today is his birthday, let's try
290   To prepare as a gift, which we'll send very soon,
   A whole potful of trouble, one big as the moon!
CALIDORUS   What's the use?
PSEUDOLUS [*taking him by the arm and starting to haul him off*]
                        Won't you please run along? You just go
   And get thinking about something else.
CALIDORUS   Whoa there, whoa!
PSEUDOLUS [*tugging harder*]   No there, no!
CALIDORUS   But I'm heartbroken!
PSEUDOLUS [*still hauling, though without much effect*]   Harden your heart.
295 CALIDORUS   No, impossible.
PSEUDOLUS   Do the impossible. Start.
CALIDORUS [*dumbly*]   I'm to start the impossible? How?
PSEUDOLUS [*as before*]   Fight your heart.
   Turn your mind to what's good. Heart's in tears? Close your ears!
CALIDORUS   Oh, that's nonsense. A lover must act like a fool.
   Otherwise it's no fun.
PSEUDOLUS   Since you won't stop this drool—
300 CALIDORUS   My dear Pseudolus, please! Let me stay just a fool!
PSEUDOLUS   Will you *please* let me go?
CALIDORUS   Let me be, let me be—
PSEUDOLUS [*turning on his heel and stalking off*]
   All right, *I'll* let you be. In return you let *me*
   Go on home.
CALIDORUS   No, no, wait!
        [*As* PSEUDOLUS *stops, unenthusiastically.*]
                        I'll be just as you wish.
PSEUDOLUS [*swiveling about and clapping him on the back*]
   Now you're using your head!
        [*At this moment the last of the girls shuffles inside, and* BALLIO *turns around.*]
BALLIO [*to his marketing attendant*]
                        We should go for that fish.
305   Time's awasting. Lead on.
CALIDORUS [*catching sight of them going off, frantically*]
                        Hey, he's off! Call him back!
        [*He wheels about to go after* BALLIO. PSEUDOLUS *grabs him.*]
PSEUDOLUS [*calmly*]   Easy, boy! What's the hurry?

CALIDORUS [*frantically*]   Because, if we're slack
    He'll be gone!
BALLIO [*to his slave boy, kicking him brutally*]
          So you're taking it easy, boy, eh?
PSEUDOLUS [*calling in dulcet tones*]   May I speak with you, birthday boy?
    Birthday boy! Hey!
    Turn around and look back, will you please? Yes, we know
310   That you're rushed but we *must* hold you up, even so.
        [*As* BALLIO *keeps walking.*]
    Hey there, stop, will you! Look, there's some people here who
    Are most anxious to talk over matters with you.
BALLIO [*stopping—but not turning; exasperated*]
    It's just when I'm rushed that these goddam yahoos
    Hold me up! What's the matter? Who is it?
PSEUDOLUS   One who's
315   Spent his life making sure that you prosper and thrive!
BALLIO   Spent his life? Then he's dead. I prefer one who's alive.
PSEUDOLUS   Don't be snooty, there, you!
BALLIO   Don't annoy me, there, you!
        [BALLIO, *still without turning around, starts walking again.*]
CALIDORUS [*to* PSEUDOLUS, *frantically*]   Hurry up! Hold him back!
BALLIO [*over his shoulder to his slave who is standing goggle-eyed*]
                  Get a move on, you, too!
PSEUDOLUS [*to* CALIDORUS]   Hey, come this way! Don't let him through!
    [*The two race around and stand blocking Ballio's way.*]
320 BALLIO [*to* PSEUDOLUS]   Whoever you are, I'll see you in hell!
PSEUDOLUS [*his voice carefully maintaining the ambiguity*]
    I'd like to see you.
BALLIO [*to* CALIDORUS]   And you as well.
    [*Over his shoulder to his slave as he charges off on a different tack.*]
    This way!
PSEUDOLUS [*nimbly barring the way again*]
        There's some things I'd like to clear.
BALLIO   But *I* wouldn't.
PSEUDOLUS   Things you'll like to hear.
BALLIO   Will you let me go or not?
PSEUDOLUS [*grabbing his arm*]   At ease!
325 BALLIO   Hands off!
CALIDORUS [*grabbing the other arm, desperately*]
        But, Ballio, listen, please!
BALLIO   I'm deaf to boys who talk hot air.
CALIDORUS   I gave while I had.
BALLIO   And I took. That's fair.
CALIDORUS   When I get, I'll give.
BALLIO   When you do, I'll give too.
CALIDORUS   Oh, yes, yes! All the money and gifts that I gave!
330   And to think how I lost it! All gone to the grave!
BALLIO   With your cash dead and buried, you're just talking for fun.
    You're a fool if you try to go over what's done.

PSEUDOLUS [*to* BALLIO, *trying bluster and pointing importantly to* CALIDORUS]
    Let me tell you, at least, who he happens to be—

BALLIO   Oh, I've known all along who he was. And now he
335   Can just know who he is by himself, without me.
    [*He wheels about and starts to stomp off, calling over his shoulder to his
    slave.*]
    Shake a leg, will you!

PSEUDOLUS   Ballio, turn around, please;
    Turn around just this once, and you'll pocket some fees!

BALLIO [*to the audience*]   For that price I'll turn around. I could be praying to
    Jupiter on high, I could have the holy offerings in my hand ready to give to
340   him, and if a chance to make a buck came along, I'd forget all about religion.
    No matter what, the almighty drachma's one religion there's no resisting.

PSEUDOLUS [*to the audience*]   We bend the knees to worship—and he snaps
    his finger at the gods.

BALLIO [*to the audience*]   I'll have a talk with them. [*To* PSEUDOLUS] Greet
345   ings, stinkingest slave in Athens!

PSEUDOLUS   May the gods put their blessing upon you and give you what
    [*winking to* CALIDORUS] this boy and I wish for you. But, if you deserve
    otherwise, may they put their curse upon you!

BALLIO   How're you doing, Calidorus?

350 CALIDORUS   I'm dying. Perishing for love—and dead broke.

BALLIO   I'd have some pity—if I could feed my household on pity.

PSEUDOLUS   Look, we know what you're like, so you can skip the speeches.
    Do you know what we're here for?

BALLIO   Just about. To see me in hell.

355 PSEUDOLUS   That plus what we just called you back for. Now listen carefully.

BALLIO   I'm listening. But whatever it is you're after, make it short. I'm busy now.

PSEUDOLUS   This boy here promised you two thousand for his girl, he promised
    it for a certain day, he hasn't paid it yet, and he feels terribly sorry about it all.

BALLIO   Feeling sorry is a lot easier for a fellow than feeling sore. He feels
360   sorry because he didn't pay; I feel sore because I didn't get paid.

PSEUDOLUS   He'll pay; he'll find a way. Just hold everything these next few
    days. You see, he's afraid you'll sell his girl because you have it in for him.

BALLIO   He had the chance to give me my money a long time ago—*if* he had
    really wanted to.

365 CALIDORUS   What if I didn't have it?

BALLIO   If you were really in love you'd have negotiated a loan—gone to a
    moneylender, given him his pittance of interest, and then stolen it all back
    from your father.

PSEUDOLUS   He steal from his father? You have a nerve! No chance of *your*
370   ever giving lessons in honesty.

BALLIO   I'm a pimp. That's not my job.

CALIDORUS   How could I steal anything from my father? He's always so care-
    ful! [*Suddenly remembering himself, in ringing tones*] What's more, even if
    I could, I wouldn't. Filial duty, you know.

375 BALLIO   I hear you. Then snuggle up to that filial duty of yours at night
    instead of Rosy. So filial duty is more important to you than your love life,
    is it? All right, then: is every man in the world your father? Isn't there any-
    one you can hit up for a loan?

CALIDORUS   Loan? There's no such word any more.

380 PSEUDOLUS   Listen, ever since that gang of fakers finished tanking up at the till—the ones who always guard their own pockets but take from others' and never pay back—all the moneylenders have been playing it safe, they're not trusting anyone.

CALIDORUS   I'm in a bad way. I can't scrape up any money anywhere. I'm so 385 bad off I'm dying twice, from love and insufficient funds.

BALLIO   Why don't you buy olive oil on credit and sell for cash? Believe me, you could end up fifty thousand to the good in no time.

CALIDORUS   Damn! I'm damned by that damned law against minors.[2] Everyone's scared to give me credit.

390 BALLIO   I come under the same law, you know. I'm scared to give you credit too.

PSEUDOLUS   Scared to give him credit? After all you've taken him for? Are you still not satisfied?

BALLIO   All decent, upright lovers never let their largess lapse. Clients should give and keep on giving. When there's nothing left to give, they should quit 395 being in love.

CALIDORUS   So you won't take pity on me?

BALLIO   Money talks—and you're here with empty pockets. Yet I'd have liked to see you alive and well.

PSEUDOLUS   Hey! He's not dead yet!

400 BALLIO   Whatever he is, when he talks the way he's been talking, believe me, to me he's dead. The minute a lover begins to plead with a pimp, life's over for him. [*To* CALIDORUS] When you come running to me, come with tears that clink. For example, this sob story of yours about not having any money. You're weeping on a stepmother's shoulder, boy!

405 PSEUDOLUS   Well! And just when did *you* marry his father?

BALLIO   Spare me that!

PSEUDOLUS   Do what we're asking, Ballio, please! If you're afraid to give *him* credit, trust me. Somewhere, on land or sea, I'll excavate the cash for you.

BALLIO   I trust *you?*

410 PSEUDOLUS   Why not?

BALLIO   Ye gods, I'd sooner tie up a runaway dog with a string of sausages than trust you.

CALIDORUS   Is this the thanks I deserve from you? I act nice and you act nasty?

BALLIO   What do you want now, anyway?

415 CALIDORUS   Just hold everything for the next six days or so. Don't sell her. Don't destroy the man who loves her!

BALLIO   Don't worry. I'll even hold off for the next six months.

CALIDORUS   That's wonderful! Ballio, you're terrific!

BALLIO   Now that you're so happy, would you like me to make you even happier?

420 CALIDORUS   What do you mean?

BALLIO   Rosy's not even for sale now.

CALIDORUS   She's not?

BALLIO   Nosirree!

CALIDORUS   Pseudolus! Quick! Get fatted calves and lambs! Get slaughterers! 425   I want to make an offering to Jupiter Almighty. [*Pointing to* BALLIO] Because this god here is lots more almighty in my book than Jupiter Almighty.

---

2. Roman law prohibited those under twenty-five from borrowing money or engaging in business.

BALLIO   No fatted calves. I want the sacramental meats of the sacrificial lamb!

CALIDORUS [to PSEUDOLUS, *as before*]   Hurry! What are you standing there for? Go get lambs! Didn't you hear what Jupiter Almighty said?

430   PSEUDOLUS [to CALIDORUS]   Be back in a flash. [*Gesturing in the direction of the city gate, beyond which lie the public execution grounds*] But first I'll have to run down past the city gate.

CALIDORUS   Why there?

PSEUDOLUS [to CALIDORUS—*but eying* BALLIO]   To bring back slaughterers
435   from *there*. Two of them. With bells for the victim—the kind that clank. And I'll drive back two whole herds—of birch rods. Then we'll have plenty for a successful sacrifice today to Jupiter Almighty here.

BALLIO [to PSEUDOLUS]   You go to hell.

PSEUDOLUS   That's where our Patron God of Pimps is going.

440   BALLIO   Do you know it's to your advantage if I die?

PSEUDOLUS   How's that?

BALLIO   I'll tell you. Because you'll never be an honest man as long as I live. [*Roars at his joke, recovers, and resumes his gravity.*] Do you know it's to your advantage if I stay alive?

445   PSEUDOLUS   How's that?

BALLIO   Because, if *I* die, *you'll* be the worst stinker in Athens. [*Second roar.*]

CALIDORUS   Listen, I've got a question to ask you, and I want a serious answer. Do I understand that Rosy is not for sale?

BALLIO   She most certainly is not. You see, I've already sold her.

450   CALIDORUS   How?

BALLIO   Garments excluded; just the carcass, guts and all.

CALIDORUS   You sold *my* girl?

BALLIO   That's right. For two thousand drachmas.

CALIDORUS   Two thousand?

455   BALLIO [*as before*]   Let's say two times one thousand, if you prefer. To a major from Macedon. And I've already collected fifteen hundred.

CALIDORUS   What's this you're telling me?

BALLIO   That your girlfriend's had a transformation. Into cash.

CALIDORUS   And you dared do a thing like that?

460   BALLIO   I felt like it. She was my property.

CALIDORUS   Pseudolus! Get my sword!

PSEUDOLUS   What do you need a sword for?

CALIDORUS   To kill him. And myself.

PSEUDOLUS   Why don't you just kill yourself? After all, starvation's going to
465   take care of him before long.

CALIDORUS   Listen here, you dirtiest double-crosser that ever walked the face of the earth, didn't you give me your solemn word you'd sell her to nobody but me?

BALLIO   I admit it.

470   CALIDORUS   Didn't you even cross your heart?

BALLIO   I crossed my fingers *too*.

CALIDORUS   You filthy liar, you went back on your word!

BALLIO   But I came into my money. I'm a filthy liar, but now I've got money to burn tucked away. You're a model son, you come from the right family—
475   and you're broke.

CALIDORUS   Pseudolus! Stand on the other side of him and cuss him out!

PSEUDOLUS   Right! I'm covering ground faster than I would en route to City
 Hall for my emancipation proclamation.

> [*The two take up positions on either side of* BALLIO. CALIDORUS, *breath-*
> *ing fire, and* PSEUDOLUS, *champing at the bit, face each other;* BALLIO,
> *standing unconcerned between them, faces the audience.*]

CALIDORUS   Give it to him! Pile it on!

480 PSEUDOLUS [*to* BALLIO]   Now I'm going to tear you to tatters. With my tongue.
 Good-for-nothing!

BALLIO   That's right.

PSEUDOLUS   Dirty rat!

BALLIO   It's the truth.

485 PSEUDOLUS   Jailbait!

BALLIO   Naturally.

PSEUDOLUS   Grave robber!

BALLIO   Of course.

PSEUDOLUS   Skunk!

490 BALLIO   Very good!

PSEUDOLUS   You'd rob your best friend!

BALLIO   Yes, I'd do that.

PSEUDOLUS   And kill your father!

BALLIO [*to* CALIDORUS]   Now you take a turn.

495 CALIDORUS   Church-robber!

BALLIO   I admit it.

CALIDORUS   Dirty double-crosser!

BALLIO   Old hat. You sang that song before.

CALIDORUS   Criminal!

500 BALLIO   Absolutely.

PSEUDOLUS   Corrupter of the young!

BALLIO   That's the stuff!

CALIDORUS   Housebreaker!

BALLIO   Voilà!

505 PSEUDOLUS   Jailbreaker!

BALLIO   Voici!³

CALIDORUS   Lawbreaker!

BALLIO   Obviously.

PSEUDOLUS   Crook!

510 CALIDORUS   Lousy—

PSEUDOLUS   —pimp!

CALIDORUS   Scum!

BALLIO   In fine voice, both of you!

CALIDORUS   You beat your father and mother.

515 BALLIO   What's more, I killed them sooner than pay for their upkeep. Nothing wrong in that, was there?

PSEUDOLUS [*to* CALIDORUS]   We're pouring into a punctured pot. We're wasting our breath.

BALLIO   Any further comments you two would like to make?

520 CALIDORUS   Aren't you ashamed of anything?

BALLIO   Aren't *you* ashamed of turning out to be a lover as broke as a nutshell?

---

3. Here you are (French; *voilà*, in contrast, means "there you are").

In spite of all the nasty names you've called me, I'll do this for you. Today's the last day for payment; if before tonight that major hasn't handed over the five hundred he owes, I think I'll be in a position to do my duty.

525 CALIDORUS What's that?

BALLIO If you pay me first, I'll break my promise to him. That's doing my duty. Well, if there was anything in it for me, I'd go on with this chat, but, without any cash, you're just kidding yourself if you think I'll have any pity on you. That's my considered opinion, so you can start figuring out what
530 you're going to do next.

[BALLIO *turns and stalks off, stage left, his attendant at his heels.*]

CALIDORUS Leaving already?

BALLIO I'm busy every minute right now.

PSEUDOLUS You'll be even busier a little later! [*To himself*] That fellow's my meat, unless the gods and men both desert me. I'll fillet him just the way a
535 cook fillets an eel. Calidorus, I want your help now.

CALIDORUS At your orders, sir!

PSEUDOLUS I want this town besieged and taken by storm before tonight. For this we need a cagey, clever, careful, competent man capable of carrying out orders, who won't go to sleep on his feet.

540 CALIDORUS Tell me—what are you up to?

PSEUDOLUS I'll let you know when the time comes. I don't want to go over it twice. [*To the audience*] Plays are long enough as is.

CALIDORUS Absolutely and perfectly right.

PSEUDOLUS Get going! Bring your man back here fast.

545 CALIDORUS Out of a whole group of friends, there are very few you can really rely on.

PSEUDOLUS I know that. So do it in two steps: first make a rough selection; then pick the one man you're sure of.

CALIDORUS I'll have him here right away.

550 PSEUDOLUS Can't you get going? All this talk is holding you up.

[CALIDORUS *dashes off, stage left.*] ·

PSEUDOLUS Well, Pseudolus, he's gone off, and you're here on your own. What are you going to do now after all the big talk you handed him? What's going to happen to those promises of yours? You haven't even the shred of a plot in mind. You'd like to weave one, but you don't have a beginning to start from or
555 an end to finish at. It's like being a playwright: once he's picked up his pen, he's on the hunt for something that exists nowhere on the face of the earth, yet he finds it anyway, he makes fiction sound like fact. I'll play playwright: that two thousand exists nowhere on the face of the earth, yet I'll find it anyway. I told the boy a long time ago that I'd come up with the money for him. I wanted to
560 get it out of the old man but somehow or other he always caught wise first. [*Looking toward the wings, stage left*] But I've got to turn off the talk and shut up! Look who I see coming—our Simo and his neighbor, Callipho. [*Gesturing toward* SIMO] This is the grave I'm going to rob today for the two thousand I need for his son. I'll just move over here where I can listen in on what they say.

[*Two graybeards, deep in conversation, totter in, leaning heavily on their sticks.*

SIMO, CALIDORUS' *father and* PSEUDOLUS' *owner, has the face you would expect on a man who all his life has been a canny, tightfisted*

businessman. CALLIPHO *is the exact opposite; his round, innocent countenance exudes goodness and implicit faith in his fellow man.*
    From the waggling of the head and other gesticulating, it is clear that SIMO *is in a foul mood.*]

565 SIMO If we decided to pick a spendthrift or a rake for Governor of Athens, no one, I swear, would be any competition for that son of mine. He's the one topic of conversation in the whole town, how he's got his heart set on freeing his girlfriend and is hunting for the money to do it. I've been getting reports from all sides. But I had smelled something fishy and knew all

570 about it a long time ago; I just pretended I didn't.

PSEUDOLUS [*aside*] So his son smelled fishy! The campaign's collapsed, the offensive's stuck in a rut. There's a tight roadblock across the route I wanted to take to the cash depot. He found out! No looting any loot there.

CALLIPHO If I had my way, people who babble gossip or listen to it would all

575 hang—babblers by the tongue and listeners by the ears. Why, these reports that you're getting, that your son has a love affair and wants to steal from you, may be all just talk, a pack of lies. But even if every word is true, the way people behave these days, what's he done that's so out of the ordinary? What's so odd about a young fellow falling in love and setting his girlfriend free?

580 PSEUDOLUS [*aside*] What a nice old man!

SIMO Well, I'm an old fellow, and I don't want it!

CALLIPHO It won't do you the slightest good not to want it. It *might* have, if you hadn't behaved the same way when you were young. Only a parent who was a paragon can expect his son to be better than he was. And you—the

585 money you threw away and the affairs you had could have taken care of every single solitary male in the city, barring none! Is it any wonder that the son takes after the father?

PSEUDOLUS [*to himself—but good and loud*] *Mon dieu!*[4] How few of you decent people there are in this world. Now, *there's* the kind of father a

590 father should be to a son!

SIMO Who's that talking? It's my servant Pseudolus. He's the archcriminal who's corrupted my son; he's his guide and mentor. I'd like to see him at the end of a rope!

CALLIPHO Now that's very silly of you, to show how angry you are. You'll get

595 much further by being nice to him and finding out whether those reports you're getting are true. "Trouble's double for the hasty heart."

SIMO All right. I'll take your advice.

PSEUDOLUS [*to himself*] The offensive's under way, Pseudolus! Have some fast talk ready for the old man. Greetings to you first, master, as is only

600 right and proper. And, if any are left over, greetings to the neighbors.

SIMO Greetings. Well, now, how are we doing?

PSEUDOLUS Oh, we're just standing here this way.

SIMO Look at that pose, will you? His lordship!

CALLIPHO I think his pose is very nice. Self-confident.

605 PSEUDOLUS If a servant is honest and his conscience is clear, he *should* hold his head high, especially in front of his master.

CALLIPHO We have a few things we'd like to ask you about. Some rumors we've been hearing that we're a bit vague about.

4. My god! (French).

SIMO   He'll talk you to death. You'll think it's Socrates[5] and not Pseudolus
610   you're talking to.
PSEUDOLUS   Yes, you haven't thought very well of me for quite some time now,
   I can see it. I know—you don't have very much faith in me. *You'd* like to see
   me bad and wicked, but, in spite of you, I'm going to be honest and decent!
SIMO   Pseudolus, will you kindly vacate the rooms in your ears so some
615   things I have to say can move in?
PSEUDOLUS   Even though I'm very annoyed with you, you go right ahead, say
   whatever you like.
SIMO   You annoyed with me? The servant annoyed with the master?
PSEUDOLUS   And does that seem so strange to you?
620   SIMO   Ye gods, the way you talk, I'd better watch out you don't get angry with
   me. You're thinking of giving me a beating, aren't you? And *not* the kind I'm
   accustomed to give you! [*To* CALLIPHO] What's your idea?
CALLIPHO   I really think he has every right to be angry. After all, you *don't*
   have much faith in him.
625   SIMO   Well, let him be angry. I'll see to it he does me no damage. Listen, you.
   What about the things I want to find out?
PSEUDOLUS   Anything you want to know, just ask. And consider whatever you
   hear from me an oracle from Delphi.[6]
SIMO   Then pay attention and don't forget your promise. Listen, are you
630   aware that my son is having an affair with a certain chorus girl?
PSEUDOLUS [*like an oracle from Delphi*]   Yea, verily.
SIMO   And that he wants to set her free?
PSEUDOLUS   Yea, verily to that too.
SIMO   And that you're getting your stunts and smart schemes set to steal a
635   certain two thousand drachmas from me?
PSEUDOLUS   *I* steal from *you*?
SIMO   That's right. To give to my son so he can set the girl free. Admit it, just
   say "Yea, verily to that too."
PSEUDOLUS   Yea, verily to that too.
640   CALLIPHO   He admits it!
SIMO [*to* CALLIPHO]   I told you so, all along.
CALLIPHO [*sadly*]   Yes, I remember.
SIMO [*to* PSEUDOLUS, *angrily*]   Why didn't you tell me the minute you heard
   instead of hiding it from me? Why didn't *I* hear about it?
645   PSEUDOLUS   I'll tell you why. I didn't want to be the one to start a bad
   precedent—this business of a servant carrying tales about one master to
   another.
SIMO [*to* CALLIPHO]   He should have been hauled off by the heels to the mill
   wheel![7]
650   CALLIPHO   He didn't do anything wrong, did he?
SIMO   Anything? Everything!
PSEUDOLUS   Don't, Callipho. I know how to handle my own affairs. I deserve
   the blame. [*To* SIMO] Now listen carefully. Why did I keep you in the dark

5. Athenian teacher and philosopher (469–
399 B.C.E.), known for seeking the truth
through talk (dialogue).
6. Shrine to Apollo that was the ancient
world's most important oracle, located near

Mount Parnassus in central Greece.
7. Being sent to work in a mill to grind wheat
was a proverbial punishment for recalcitrant
town slaves.

about your son's love affair? Because he had the mill wheel all set for me if
655 I talked.

SIMO   And you didn't know *I'd* have it all set for you if you kept quiet?

PSEUDOLUS   I knew that.

SIMO   Then why wasn't I told?

PSEUDOLUS   Because one evil was in front of me and the other a little farther
660 on. His was right there; with yours I had a teensy breathing spell.

SIMO   What are you two going to do now? After all, you can't get any money
out of me; I know everything. And I'm going to pass the word right now to
everyone in town not to lend you any.

PSEUDOLUS   Believe me, I'm not going to go begging. Not as long as *you're*
665 alive. Because, by Jupiter, *you're* going to give me the money. I'm going to
get it from you.

SIMO   So you're going to get it from me, eh?

PSEUDOLUS   And how!

SIMO   Well, by Jupiter, you can poke my eyes out if I ever give you that money!

670 PSEUDOLUS   You will. I'm telling you about it right now so you'll be on your
guard.

SIMO   One thing I'm sure of: if you do pull it off, you deserve a citation for
the sensation of the century.

PSEUDOLUS   I will.

675 SIMO   Suppose you don't?

PSEUDOLUS   Whip me to shreds. But suppose I do?

SIMO   As the gods are my witness, I won't lay a finger on you and you can
keep the money all your life.

PSEUDOLUS   And not just for one day. For every day of my life as long as I live.
680 But, if I do, will you, of your own free will, give me money for the pimp,
pronto?

CALLIPHO   That's a fair proposition. Tell him you will.

SIMO   You know what I just thought of? Supposing those two have a deal on!
Suppose they're in cahoots and have a scheme cooked up to do me out of
685 the money?

PSEUDOLUS   Even *I* wouldn't have the nerve to pull a stunt like that! No, Simo,
it's not that way at all. If he and I have any deal on, or if we ever had a single
meeting or discussion about any deal, you can take a rawhide pen and scrib-
ble over my whole hide just as if you were filling up a page with writing.

690 SIMO   You can announce your act now, whenever you want.

PSEUDOLUS   Callipho, would you please help me and not get tied up in any
other business? It's just for today.

CALLIPHO   But I've had everything set up since yesterday to go off to the
country . . .

695 PSEUDOLUS   Well, please dismantle the setup, will you?

CALLIPHO   All right, I've decided to stay, for your sake. I'm dying to watch your
act, Pseudolus. And, if I hear that [*gesturing toward* SIMO] he won't pay you
the money he promised, I'll pay it myself rather than see you lose out.

SIMO   I won't go back on my word.

700 PSEUDOLUS [*to* SIMO]   Darned right—because, if you don't come across, I'll
dun you, and the din will be long and loud. Now out of here, both of you;
get inside and leave the field clear for my hocus-pocus.

CALLIPHO [*moving off toward his house*]   Right. Anything you say.

PSEUDOLUS   Don't you forget that.

705   SIMO   How can you possibly catch me off guard, now that I've been forewarned?

PSEUDOLUS   I gave you fair warning to be on your guard. And I'm telling you now, in so many words: be on your guard. BE ON YOUR GUARD! Watch out—today, with those two hands, you're going to give me the money.

710   CALLIPHO   The man's a virtuoso, a maestro, if he keeps his word!

PSEUDOLUS   [to CALLIPHO]   Carry me off and make me your slave if I don't!

SIMO   Very nice and friendly of you—but don't you happen to be *my* slave at the moment?

PSEUDOLUS   Would you like to hear something that'll amaze the both of you
715   even more?

CALLIPHO   Oh yes! I'm dying to hear it. I love listening to you.

PSEUDOLUS   [turning to SIMO]   Before I conduct my campaign against you, I'm going to fight still another glorious and memorable campaign.

SIMO   What campaign?

720   PSEUDOLUS   Against the pimp who lives next door. You watch—with my stunts and smart schemes I'm going to pluck that chorus girl your son's pining for plunk from under his pimpish nose.

SIMO   What's that you say?

PSEUDOLUS   And I'll have both jobs done by tonight!

725   SIMO   Well, if you make good on all this big talk, you're a better man than Alexander the Great.[8] But, if you don't, is there any reason why I shouldn't have you shut up in the mill, pronto?

PSEUDOLUS   Now I don't want you to leave the house, you hear?

CALLIPHO   Of course. Glad to oblige.

730   SIMO   [to PSEUDOLUS]   But I have to go downtown. I'll be back right away.

PSEUDOLUS   Then hurry.

[CALLIPHO *goes into his house, and* SIMO *leaves, stage left.* PSEUDOLUS *walks downstage and addresses the audience.*]

PSEUDOLUS   I suspect that you suspect that I've made all these big promises just to keep you entertained until I get through this play, and that I'm not going to do the things I said I'd do. [*Mimicking* SIMO'S *tones*] "I won't go
735   back on my word." So far as I can see, I can't see how I'm going to do it— but, if there's one thing I *can* see, it's that I *will* do it. After all, when a character comes on stage, he ought to bring something fresh and new in a fresh and new way. And, if he can't, let him make way for someone who can. [*Moving off toward* SIMO'S *house*] And now I'd like to step inside here
740   for a minute while I carry out a mental mobilization of my underhand forces. I won't keep you long; I'm coming right out. Our flutist will entertain you with a selection in the meantime.[9]

[PSEUDOLUS *races into Simo's house, leaving the stage empty. A second later the flutist comes on to play an entr'acte.*]

8. Alexander III of Macedon (356–323 B.C.E.); the greatest of all Greek generals, he united Greece and conquered much of Asia.

9. Such use of instrumental music to mark a major break in the action was common in Roman comedy.

Act 2

[*The door of* SIMO's *house flies open.* PSEUDOLUS *bursts out and races downstage to address the audience.*]

SONG

PSEUDOLUS   Holy mackerel! It's marvelous! Everything I try
                Works out just like a charm.
      [*Tapping his brow.*]
Up in here is a scheme I can certify
                Is guaranteed free of harm.

5 When your eye's on the big things, it's madness, I say,
To proceed in a timid or half-hearted way.
           The way that things work out
           Is completely up to you.
           You want to do big things?
10   Then think and act big too!

    You take *me*. Why, up here in this head,
      Standing by for the fray,
  Are my armies—plus ambush, intrigue,
      Dirty deals, and foul play.

15 With the courage inherited from a long line of heroes,
  With the double-cross serving as shining shield,
The enemy's mine wherever I'll meet him—
  I'll phony my foemen from the field!

    Just watch me now. I'm set to go,
20   To fight the man who's our common foe,
    To rally-oh,
    And sally-oh
      'Gainst Ballio!
      [*Pointing to* BALLIO's *house.*]
Here's the fortress I want to lay siege to today.
25 So I'll draw up my forces in battle array,
And I'll take it by storm—to the joy of the nation—
And then quickly re-form for the next operation,
      [*Pointing to* SIMO's *house.*]
To lay siege to the doddering fort over here.
Here I'll load my allies and myself with such plunder
30 I'll be hailed as the scourge of my foes, as a wonder.
            I was born to be great;
            It's a family trait—
          To fight battles victorious,
         Memorable, glorious.
      [*Suddenly looking toward the wings, stage right.*]
35 Someone's coming this way. Who's this man that I spy?
Who's this stranger so suddenly in the way of my eye?

What's he want with that cutlass there, *I'd* like to know.
What's his business here? Pseudolus! Ambush the foe!

> [PSEUDOLUS *moves to an unobtrusive spot off to the side, and, a second later,* HARPAX, *"Snatcher," enters. He is an officer's orderly; he wears a uniform and carries a sword. In one hand he clutches a purse, obviously well-filled.*
>
> *The hesitant way in which he walks along, stopping to peer at the doorways, reveals immediately that he is a stranger in town.*]

HARPAX [*to himself*] The report of my eyes confirms, I can see,
40   The report my commander imparted to me,
Here's the district and quarter he meant.
Seven blocks from the entrance to town I should spot
The pimp's house, where the master said leave the whole lot,
Both this cash and the seal that he sent.
45   But I'd like to see someone come by who'd make clear
If a pimp, name of Ballio, lives around here.
PSEUDOLUS [*to himself*] Not a sound! Not a word! Unless heaven and men
All desert me, this man is my meat!
But I need a new gambit since all of a sudden
50   A new path has appeared at my feet.
All the plans I worked out must be jettisoned now;
In my new start I'll concentrate here [*pointing to* HARPAX].
So you've come as an errand boy, *mon général?*[1]
Watch me soon stand you up on your ear!

55   HARPAX I'll knock on the door and get someone to come out.
PSEUDOLUS Hey, whoever you are, I wish you'd cut out that knocking. You see, I'm patron protecter of portals. Popped out here for a precautionary peep.
HARPAX Are you Ballio?
PSEUDOLUS Not exactly. I'm Vice-Ballio.
60   HARPAX What's that mean?
PSEUDOLUS Chief layer-outer and layer-inner. Lord of the larder.
HARPAX You mean to say you're the major-domo?
PSEUDOLUS Me? I give orders to the major-domo!
HARPAX [*puzzled, unable to square* PSEUDOLUS' *tones with his slave's getup*] Are you a slave or aren't you?
65   PSEUDOLUS Well, for the moment, still a slave.
HARPAX You look it. You don't look the type to be anything but.
PSEUDOLUS Ever take a look at yourself before making cracks about others?
HARPAX [*to the audience, gesturing toward* PSEUDOLUS] Must be a bad egg, this one here.
70   PSEUDOLUS [*to the audience, gesturing toward* HARPAX] Well, look what heaven sent me! A nest all my own—I'll hatch plenty of schemes in it today!
HARPAX What's he talking to himself about?
PSEUDOLUS Hey, mister!
HARPAX What?
75   PSEUDOLUS Are you from that Macedonian major? Servant of the fellow who bought a girl from us and paid my master fifteen hundred and still owes him five hundred?

1. My general (French).

HARPAX   That's right. But where in the world do you know me from? Where did you ever see me or talk to me, anyway? I never set foot in Athens before

80   and never laid eyes on you till this minute.

PSEUDOLUS   You looked as if you came from him. After all, when he left he agreed on today as the last day for payment, and he hasn't yet made good.

HARPAX   [*hefting the purse*]   Oh, no. It's here.

PSEUDOLUS   You brought it?

85   HARPAX   I certainly did.

PSEUDOLUS   What are you waiting for? Hand it over.

HARPAX   Hand it over to who? You?

PSEUDOLUS   Certainly to me. I'm in charge of Ballio's books. I handle the cash—receive all receivables, pay all payables.

90   HARPAX   Certainly *not* to you. You could be cashier for Jupiter on high and all the treasures of heaven, but I'm not trusting you with a drachma.

PSEUDOLUS   Why, in two shakes of a lamb's tail, we could have the whole thing done.

HARPAX   I'd rather keep it *undone.*

95   PSEUDOLUS   You go to hell! So you've come here to blacken my good name, eh? As if people don't trust me personally with a thousand times that much money!

HARPAX   Others can think that way. Doesn't mean *I* have to trust you.

PSEUDOLUS   You mean to say I'm trying to do you out of your money?

100   HARPAX   Oh, no. *You* mean to say it. I mean to say I have my suspicions. What's your name, anyway?

PSEUDOLUS   [*to the audience*]   The pimp has a servant named Syrus. That's who I'll say I am. [*To* HARPAX] Syrus.

HARPAX   Syrus, eh?

105   PSEUDOLUS   That's my name.

HARPAX   Enough talk. Listen, whatever your name is, if your master's home, call him out so I can do what I was sent here to do.

PSEUDOLUS   If he *were* here, I'd call him out. But don't you want to give it to me? You'll be relieved of the whole business—more so than if you gave it to

110   him in person.

HARPAX   You don't get the point. The commander gave it to me to pay with, not play with. Oh, I can see you're practically running a fever because you can't dig your claws into it. I don't hand over any money to a soul except to Ballio in person.

115   PSEUDOLUS   He's tied up right now. In court on a case.

HARPAX   Well, I hope he wins. I'll come back when I figure he'll be at home. [*Pulling out a letter and handing it to* PSEUDOLUS] Here, take this letter and give it to him. It's got the identification seal my master agreed on with yours in this deal for the girl.

120   PSEUDOLUS   Yes, I know. The major told us what he wanted: we're to send the girl off with a fellow who'd bring the money and a seal with his picture. He left a duplicate with us, you know.

HARPAX   You know everything, don't you?

PSEUDOLUS   Why shouldn't I?

125   HARPAX   [*pointing to the letter*]   So you give him that identification.

PSEUDOLUS   Right. What's your name, anyway?

HARPAX   Snatcher.

PSEUDOLUS   On your way, Snatcher boy, I don't like you. You're not coming
inside this house, believe me; I want none of your snatching there.

130 HARPAX   I take my enemies alive, right out of the front line. That's how I got
the name.

PSEUDOLUS   If you ask me, you take the silverware right out of the front rooms.

HARPAX   No, sir! Say, Syrus, you know what I'd like to ask you to do?

PSEUDOLUS   Tell me and I'll know.

135 HARPAX   I'm staying at the third inn outside the city gate. The one run by
that old buttertub, Chrysis, the lame dame.

PSEUDOLUS   What do you want?

HARPAX   Come and pick me up there when your master gets back.

PSEUDOLUS   Sure. Anything you say.

140 HARPAX   I'm tired from the trip. Want to get some rest.

PSEUDOLUS   Very smart. Good idea. But don't make me go looking all over
the place when I come to get you.

HARPAX   Oh, no. After a bite to eat, a nap is all I'm interested in.

PSEUDOLUS   I'll bet.

145 HARPAX   Well, anything I can do for you?

PSEUDOLUS   You go take that nap.

HARPAX   I'm going.

PSEUDOLUS   Snatcher! Listen! Use plenty of blankets. You get a good sweat
up, and you'll feel tiptop.

> [HARPAX leaves. The minute he is out of earshot, PSEUDOLUS races down-
> stage and addresses the audience.]

150 PSEUDOLUS   Ye gods! That fellow saved my life by turning up, I swear!
I was heading wrong, he set me right—and *he's* to pay the fare!
Lady Luck herself could never have come at a luckier time, you see,
Than when I had this lucky letter luckily left with me.

> [Brandishing the letter.]

He's handed me a horn of plenty, in here's what I want and more:

155 Embezzlement, swindle, double-cross, dirty tricks, shady deals galore,
The cash we're after plus that girl the boy is crazy for.
And now I'll show my generous soul; my name and fame shall soar!
My army of plans had been mobilized, was at stations, was all set—
The way I'd go about the job, approach the pimp and get

160 The girl away from him. It all was in my head, but it seems
Lady Luck by herself can overturn a hundred wise men's schemes.
The fact is that, when we're doing well, and people say we're smart,
We owe it all to just how much Lady Luck has taken our part.
We hear that someone's plans have worked out; "He's a genius!" all of us
chime.

165 We hear that someone's plans went wrong; "What a fool!" we chime this time.
Why, we're the fools—we're unaware how wasted is our whole
Benighted, greedy struggle toward any particular goal,
As if the right path's ever known to any human soul!
The bird in hand we always leave to go for those in the bush;

170 And then 'mid all our sweat and strain, enter Death to give his push!

But enough of this philosophizing. I've been talking too much and too long.
Ye gods! That brainstorm I suddenly got a little while ago, to bluff and say I

belonged to the pimp, is worth a fortune! Now, with this letter, I'll double-cross the three of them, master, pimp, and letter-giver. [*His*

175 *attention suddenly caught, looks toward the wings, stage left.*] Well, look at that! Something else I wanted is happening, just as good as this. Here comes Calidorus, and he's got somebody with him.

[CALIDORUS *and his friend* CHARINUS (*pronounced ka-RYE-nus*), *"Chari-table," enter, so deep in conversation they don't notice* PSEUDOLUS.]

CALIDORUS   So I've told you everything, the sweet and the bitter. You know my toils, my troubles, my financial tribulations.

180 CHARINUS   I have everything in mind. Now just tell me what you want me to do.

CALIDORUS   Pseudolus gave me orders to bring someone who can get things done and who'd be willing to do me a good turn.

CHARINUS   You carry out orders to the letter: you're bringing a good friend ready to do you a good turn. But who's this Pseudolus? He's new to me.

185 CALIDORUS   The greatest virtuoso alive, my maestro of miracles. He's the one who told me he was going to do all the things I told you about.

PSEUDOLUS   I'll go up and greet him in the grand manner.

CALIDORUS   Whose voice is that?

PSEUDOLUS [*adopting the tones and gestures of a character in grand opera*]
      'Tis thee I seek, Your Majesty, yea thee

190   Whom thy servant Pseudolus serves. 'Tis thee I seek
      To give thee thrice, in triplewise, in form
      Threefold, three thrice-deserved delights derived
      From dumbbells three and by devices three:
      Deceit, deception, and double-cross.
         [*Waving the letter.*]

195   Delights that I bring thee signed and sealed
      In this here paltry piece of paper.

CALIDORUS [*to* CHARINUS]   That's the fellow!

CHARINUS   The scoundrel's better than an opera star!

PSEUDOLUS [*walking toward them, as before*]
      Advance thy step as I do mine and boldly

200   Extend to me thy hand and welcome words.

CALIDORUS   To welcome rescue true—or welcome *words*?

PSEUDOLUS   Both!

CALIDORUS   Welcome, words and rescue!
      What happened?

205 PSEUDOLUS   What are you so nervous about?

CALIDORUS [*pointing to* CHARINUS]   I've produced your man.

PSEUDOLUS   What's this "produced" business?

CALIDORUS   I mean I've brought him here.

PSEUDOLUS   Who is he?

210 CALIDORUS   Charinus.

PSEUDOLUS   Bravo!
            No man named Charinus
            Will ever malign us.

CHARINUS   What do you need done? Step up and give me my orders.

215 PSEUDOLUS   Thanks just the same and all the best to you, Charinus, but we really don't want to put you to any trouble.

CHARINUS   You won't put me to any trouble. Not a bit.

PSEUDOLUS Then stick around. [*Ostentatiously examines the letter.*]
CALIDORUS What's that?
220 PSEUDOLUS I've just intercepted this letter and this identification!
CALIDORUS Identification? What identification?
PSEUDOLUS The one the major just sent. His servant, the fellow who came
    to take your girl away, brought it along with the five hundred drachmas and
    did I make a monkey out of him just now!
225 CALIDORUS How?
PSEUDOLUS [*gesturing toward the audience*] Look, this play's being given
    for the benefit of these people. And they were here, they know all about it.
    I'll tell you two later.
CALIDORUS What do we do now?
230 PSEUDOLUS By tonight you'll have your girlfriend in your arms—and she'll
    be a free woman!
CALIDORUS I?
PSEUDOLUS Yes, you, I say—if I manage to stay alive. Provided, however, you
    two find me a man in a hurry.
235 CHARINUS What kind of man?
PSEUDOLUS A good-for-nothing. But one who's slick and smart enough, once
    he's been given a start, to figure out what to do next on his own. And it
    mustn't be anyone too well known around here.
CHARINUS Does it matter if he's a slave?
240 PSEUDOLUS On the contrary, I prefer a slave.
CHARINUS I think I have the man for you. He's a good-for-nothing, he's
    smart, and my father just sent him here from overseas. He came to Athens
    only yesterday, and he hasn't been out of the house yet.
PSEUDOLUS That'll be a great help. Now I've got to borrow five hundred
245   drachmas which I'll need just till tonight. His father owes me money.
CHARINUS Oh, I'll give it to you. Don't bother going to anyone else.
PSEUDOLUS My lifesaver! But I also need a uniform and a sword.
CHARINUS I've got some to spare.
PSEUDOLUS Ye gods! This Charinus is all plus and no minus! Now, about
250   that servant of yours who's just arrived—is he strong in the head?
CHARINUS No, just under the armpits.
PSEUDOLUS He ought to wear long sleeves. Is he tough? Does he have the
    old vinegar in the veins?
CHARINUS As sour as it comes.
255 PSEUDOLUS Suppose he has to give out with the old sweetness, instead? Has
    he got it in him?
CHARINUS Has he! Honey, sugar, syrup—he once tried to run a grocery in
    his guts.
260 PSEUDOLUS Touché, Charinus: beat me at my own game. But what's this
    servant of yours called?
CHARINUS Monkey.
PSEUDOLUS Can he do a good turn?
CHARINUS Like a top.
PSEUDOLUS Does he grasp things easily?
265 CHARINUS All the time—other people's things.
PSEUDOLUS Suppose he's caught in the act?
CHARINUS He slips out. He's an eel.

PSEUDOLUS   Has he got any sense?

CHARINUS   More sense than the Board of Censors.

270 PSEUDOLUS   Well, from what you say he sounds like a good man.

CHARINUS   You have no idea how good! Why, the minute he sees you he'll tell
you what you want him for. What have you got in mind, anyway?

PSEUDOLUS   I'll tell you. When I'm done dressing your man up, I want him to
impersonate the major's orderly. He'll take this identification along with
275 five hundred drachmas to the pimp and make off with the girl. There, now
you know the whole plot. The mechanics of how to do it I'll save for our
impersonator.

CALIDORUS   Well, what are we standing around for?

PSEUDOLUS   I'm off to the Aeschinus Loan Company. You two dress your
280 man in dress uniform and bring him to me there. But hurry!

CHARINUS   We'll be there before you will.

PSEUDOLUS   Then you'd better shake a leg! [*As* CALIDORUS *and* CHARINUS *dash
off, stage left, he turns and addresses the audience.*]
It's left my mind, it's gone away, the last shred of doubt and fear
I'd had before. My mind's been scoured, the road ahead is clear.
285 With flying flags I'm leading out the troops in my command;
The sky is blue, all dark clouds gone, and everything goes as planned;
Morale is high: I can—I know it!—wipe out the enemy band.
But first downtown to hand a load of sage advice to Monk:
Tell him what to do so he plays it smart and doesn't go kerplunk.
290 And then to storm Castle Pimp itself—and the enemy's cause is sunk!

[PSEUDOLUS *dashes off triumphantly, stage left, and the stage is empty.*]

Act 3

[*The door of* BALLIO's *house opens, and* BALLIO's *catamite steps out. He addresses the
audience.*]

BOY   When Fate makes a boy a slave in a pimp's home and, on top of that,
makes him homely, believe me, as I can tell from my feelings right now,
she's made him plenty of toil and trouble. Take me—that's the kind of slavery that came my way; I'm the sole support of all sorts of sorrows, small and
5 large. And I can't find any lover boy to love me and care for me so that for
once in my life things would be a teeny bit brighter.

Today is this pimp's birthday, and he's laid down the law to everyone in
the house from the lowest to the highest: whoever doesn't get him a gift
today gets the life tortured out of him tomorrow. In the position I'm in,
10 what in heaven's name can I do? *I* can't give what people who can give usually give. And, if I don't give the pimp a gift today, tomorrow he'll empty the
chamber pots down my throat. I'm still too small for things like that!

Golly, poor me, I'm so scared of swilling slops, [*leering*] if someone
slipped something into my palm to give it a little weight, I think I could
15 somehow grit my teeth and bear it even though it makes a person cry
hard—[*innocently*] so they tell me.

But right now I have to shut my mouth and bear it—there's Ballio coming back bringing a cook with him.

[*The* BOY *hurries into the house. A second later* BALLIO *enters, at his heels
his* SLAVE BOY, *and at his side an enormously fat* COOK *behind whom trails
a long line of young assistants.*]

BALLIO   And people, the damn fools, say the market is where you hire cooks!
20   It's where you hire crooks, not cooks! I tell you, if I had actually taken an
oath to find a worse cook than the one I've got here, I couldn't have done
it. Useless, brainless, a blowhard and a blabbermouth! I know why he
never died and went below: so he could be on hand here to cater funeral
feasts: he's the only one who can cook what a corpse would eat.

25   COOK   If you really think I'm the type you tell me I am, why did you hire me?

BALLIO   Shortage. There was no one else. If you're such a great cook, why
were all the others already gone from the square and you were still sitting
there all by yourself?

COOK   I'll tell you. I'm considered a poorer cook. Not through any fault of my
30   own, mind you. Through human greed.

BALLIO   How's that?

COOK   I'll tell you. It's because, when people come to hire a cook, they never
go after the best who'll cost the most; they'd rather hire the cook who costs
the least. That's why I was sitting in sole possession of the square today.
35   Let those other poor devils cook their one-drachma feeds. Nobody gets me
off my seat for less than two. I don't do a dinner like other cooks. They pile
up plates with potted pasture, that's what they do. They make cattle out of
the guests—feed 'em fodder! And even the fodder they season with still
more fodder. Inside they put coriander, fennel, garlic, celery. Outside they
40   put cabbage, beets, sorrel, spinach. On top of it all, they throw in a pound
of asafetida.[2] Then they'll grate in that damned mustard, which has the
graters' eyes going at a great rate before they're done grating. When these
cooks cook a meal and it comes to the seasoning, they don't season with
seasonings, they season with vultures—gives 'em a chance to get at the
45   easy livers around the table while still alive. That's why people hereabouts
don't live very long: they bloat their bellies with all this fodder that's horrible to mention, let alone eat. Fodder a cow wouldn't eat, a person will.

BALLIO   What about yourself? If you sneer at these seasonings, what do you
use? Seasonings from the gods to make people live longer?

50   COOK   You can say that again. If people ate regularly the meals I prepare, they
could live to even two hundred. Once I drop some clovidoopus in a pan, or
some dillipoopus, or a dash of fathead or cutathroat, right away the pan starts
sizzling on its own. [Becoming the maître d'hôtel] Now, these seasonings are for
your dishes made from the finny tribe. For your dishes made from the earthy
55   tribes I season with nutmegoopus. Or tenus tenerus or even muvius fluvius.

BALLIO   You and your seasoning can go plumb to hell! And take all your
damned lies with you!

COOK   Will you kindly allow me to continue?

BALLIO   Continue—and then go to hell!

60   COOK   When every pot is hot, I uncover every one, and the aroma flies to
heaven with feet outspread.

BALLIO   The aroma with feet outspread, eh?

COOK   Made a slip. Didn't realize it.

BALLIO   How's that?

65   COOK   With arms outspread, I meant to say. Jupiter on high sups nightly on
this aroma.

2. A bitter and foul-smelling dried gum resin, derived from the roots of certain west Asian plants,
used in small quantities both in preparing herbal medicines and in cooking.

BALLIO [*sarcastically*] And if you don't happen to be cooking anywhere, what in the world does Jupiter on high sup on?

COOK He goes to bed unsupped.

70 BALLIO And you go to hell! So for all this I'm supposed to pay you two drachmas today, am I?

COOK Oh, I admit I'm a very expensive cook. But I make sure the people get their money's worth in any house I go to cook in.

BALLIO To rob in, you mean.

75 COOK You think you can find a cook who doesn't have a pair of claws like a vulture?

BALLIO And you think you can go just anywhere to cook and not pull those claws in while you're cooking? [*Turning to his* SLAVE BOY] Now listen, you, you're on my side, so I'm giving you orders right now to get everything
80 that belongs to us out of sight in a hurry. And after that you keep your eyes on [*gesturing toward the* COOK] his. Wherever he looks, you look too. If he takes a step in any direction, you take a step in the same direction. If he reaches a hand in any direction, you reach a hand in the same direction. If he takes hold of anything that's his, you let him. If he takes hold of
85 anything that's ours, you take hold of the other end. If he moves, you move. If he stands, you stand. If he squats, you squat. And I'm appointing personal watchmen for these assistants of his too.

COOK Now you just stop worrying.

BALLIO I ask you, just show me how I can stop worrying when I'm bringing
90 *you* into my house?

COOK Because I'll make a concoction for you today that'll do for you what Medea did for Pelias when she cooked the old fellow up.[3] They say that by using her poisonous potions she turned the old fellow back into a young one. Well, I'll do the same for you.

95 BALLIO So you poison people, do you?

COOK No sir. On the contrary, I cure them.

BALLIO Look here, how much will you charge to teach me that one recipe?

COOK Which?

BALLIO The one that'll cure me from your stealing.

100 COOK If you trust me, two drachmas; if you don't, even fifty's not enough. This dinner you're giving, is it for friends or enemies?

BALLIO Ye gods! For my friends, of course.

COOK Why don't you invite your enemies instead? I'll do your diners such a dinner, make such deliciously delicious dishes, that, as soon as they pick
105 up something and taste it, they'll chomp off their fingers in the process.

BALLIO Please do me a favor, will you? Before you serve anything to any of my guests, you first take a taste and let your assistants taste too—so all of you can chomp off those thieving hands of yours.

COOK Maybe you don't believe what I'm telling you?

110 BALLIO Now don't be a nuisance, please! I've had enough of your cackling. Shut up! [*Gesturing toward his house*] Look, there's where I live. Go on in and cook dinner. And get a move on!

---

3. The sorceress Medea, seeking vengeance on behalf of her husband, Jason—because Pelias had caused the death of his parents and brother and denied him the rule of Iolcus—convinced Pelias's daughters that they could make their elderly father young again by cutting him up and boiling him with her drugs. They did so, without success.

[*The* COOK *stalks in,* BALLIO's SLAVE BOY *scampers in in his wake, and the line of assistants follows. The last boy in line turns and calls out to* BALLIO.]

ASSISTANT [*like a butler making an announcement*]   Kindly take your place at the table and call your guests. Dinner's now being—spoiled! [*Disappears into the house.*]

115 BALLIO [*to the audience*]   Look at that, will you! What a breed! [*Gesturing toward the* BOY *who has just gone in*] That Chief Dishlicker there is already a full-fledged good-for-nothing. I honestly don't know which to keep an eye on first: I've got thieves inside my house and [*gesturing toward* PSEUDOLUS' *house*] a bandit next door. You see, just a few minutes ago while downtown,

120 my neighbor here, Calidorus' father, warned me over and over to watch out for his servant Pseudolus, not to trust him. Says Pseudolus is out to pull a fast one and get the girl away from me if he can. Claims Pseudolus swore up and down that he was going to sneak Rosy away from me. I'll go in now and warn the household that none of them is to trust that Pseudolus one bit.

[BALLIO *enters his house, and the stage is now empty.*]

Act 4

[*Enter* PSEUDOLUS, *stage left.*]

SONG

PSEUDOLUS [*as if to* MONKEY *who he assumes is at his heels*]
   If Fate has ever felt an urge to help a mortal out,
   She feels it now for the boy and me, of that I have no doubt:
   If she's produced an assistant like you, with brains and education,
   Then she wants to see the saving of us, and the pimp's extermination.
      [*Turns to face* MONKEY—*and discovers there is no* MONKEY *to face.*]
5   Where is he? I'm talking to myself
         Like someone not all there!
      By Jove, he's put one over on me
         And left me flat, I'll swear.
      For one crook dealing with another,
10   I've been caught off guard for fair.
   If Monk's made off, my goose is cooked. The job I wanted done
   I'll never be able to do today. But wait, I see someone—
   There he is. He's coming now, our answer to a hangman's prayer.
   And look at the way he steps along. Quite a strut our boy has there!
      [*Enter* MONKEY, *resplendent in a uniform somewhat like* HARPAX's.]

15 PSEUDOLUS   Hey, I've been looking all over for you,
      Damned scared you'd run out on me.
   MONKEY   And if I'd been acting the way that I should
      I damned well would, I agree.
   PSEUDOLUS   Well, where did you stop?
   MONKEY   Where I wanted to be.
20 PSEUDOLUS   I know that.
   MONKEY   You do? Then why ask me?

PSEUDOLUS   I wanted to give you this warning to—

MONKEY   Don't you warn me, I'm warning *you!*

PSEUDOLUS   Now you look here. You're treating me
Like dirt, and I don't like it, see?

25 MONKEY   A holder of the *croix de guerre*[4]
Be nice to you? I wouldn't dare!

PSEUDOLUS   We've started something, and now I'd like
To do the job.

MONKEY [*drawing his sword and trying a few practice thrusts*]
For the love of Mike,
Just what do you think I'm doing, eh?

30 PSEUDOLUS   Then shake a leg. Don't take all day!

MONKEY [*ambling along with maddening slowness*]
I do things in a leisurely way.

PSEUDOLUS [*urgently, gesturing toward* BALLIO's *house*]
Here's our chance! While our soldier boy snores,
I want *you* to be first through those doors.

MONKEY   What's your hurry?

35 Take it easy, don't worry.
Lord Jupiter can let
That soldier be set
On *this* same spot, right here with me.
Whatever's the name

40 Of this fellow who came,
I'll make a better Snatcher than he!
So don't worry, I'll see
That it's done, one two three.
I'll bamboozle him so,

45 With my lying, I'll throw
Such a scare in our foe
He'll deny that he really is he
And declare that he really is me!

PSEUDOLUS   Yes, but how?

MONKEY   All these questions I get!

50 Oh, you *will* be the death of me yet!

PSEUDOLUS   You're so gracious and charming, my pet.

MONKEY   Now there's something I'd like you to know:
I admit you're my boss in this show,
But in cheating and double-cross you

55 Can't come close to the things I can do.

PSEUDOLUS   The gods bless you! For my sake.

MONKEY   No, *mine.*
Look me over now, please. Does the line
Of this uniform suit me this way?

PSEUDOLUS   Oh, it's perfect, it's great!

MONKEY   Then okay.

60 PSEUDOLUS   May the gods on high hear your prayers and grant them all, my
hero—
For if he listens to mine instead, he'll grant your worth, and that's zero.

4. Military award (French, "cross of war").

[*To the audience, gesturing toward* MONKEY.]

The lowest, sneakiest good-for-nothing I ever laid eyes upon.

MONKEY You'd say a thing like that to me?

PSEUDOLUS   My lips are sealed from now on.

You do a careful job for me and what gifts you'll get!

MONKEY   Shut up!

65 Remind a man who remembers things, and you'll make the man forget

The things he has to remember. I've got it all by heart, it's set

[*Tapping his head.*]

In here. My tricks are all worked out—and worked out trickily.

PSEUDOLUS [*to the audience*]   This man is good.

MONKEY [*to the audience, gesturing toward* PSEUDOLUS]

And this one's not—and the same is true for me.

70 PSEUDOLUS   Now watch your step.

MONKEY   Oh, shut your mouth.

PSEUDOLUS   I swear, so help me Jove

MONKEY   Help you? Not he! You're set to spout the lies and spout them hard!

PSEUDOLUS   —by my love and fear and vast respect for your consummate
treachery—

MONKEY   I teach that sort of thing to others. *You* can't soft-soap *me*.

75 PSEUDOLUS   —You pull this job successfully, and I'll see you have things
nice—

MONKEY   Some joke!

PSEUDOLUS   —nice wine, hors d'oeuvres and food, a regular paradise, plus a
nice little girl to make things nice with kiss upon kiss upon kiss.

MONKEY   You're too nice to me.

80 PSEUDOLUS   You pull this job, and the word you'll use is bliss!

[MONKEY *stares at him for a full ten seconds, deadpan.* **Suddenly he slaps
him resoundingly on the back.**]

MONKEY   If *I* don't do

This job for you,

Tell the torturer to

Give me rack and screw!

85 MONKEY   All right, hurry and show me where I enter the jaws of the pimp's
house.

PSEUDOLUS   The third this way.

[BALLIO *appears on the threshold.*]

MONKEY   Shh! They've opened wide.

PSEUDOLUS   If you ask me, the house has a bellyache.

90 MONKEY   Why?

PSEUDOLUS   It's throwing up the pimp.

MONKEY   Is that the fellow?

PSEUDOLUS   That's the fellow.

MONKEY   Rotten piece of merchandise, that.

95 PSEUDOLUS   Look, will you? He walks sideways, not frontwards. Like a crab!

[PSEUDOLUS *and* MONKEY *move off to the side where they can overhear
without being seen.* BALLIO *sidles downstage and addresses the audience.*]

BALLIO   He wasn't as bad as I thought, that cook I hired. All he's made off
with so far is a cup and a jug.

PSEUDOLUS [*to* MONKEY, *sotto voce*]   Hey! Now's our chance!

MONKEY [*to* PSEUDOLUS, *sotto voce*]   My feelings exactly.

100 PSEUDOLUS [*to* MONKEY, *sotto voce*]   On your way and play it smart. I'll stay
here in ambush.

> [MONKEY *steps into the street while* BALLIO's *back is turned, and walks
> slowly along, acting as if he is looking for some house.*]

MONKEY [*to himself—but good and loud*]   I kept count carefully: this is the
sixth street from the town gate, and this is where he told me to turn in. But
how many houses he said, I can't for the life of me remember.

105 BALLIO [*swiveling about at the sound of a voice, to himself*]   Who's this fellow
in uniform? Where does he come from?
Who's he looking for? Looks like a stranger; I don't recognize the face.

MONKEY [*turning and assuming an expression of pleased surprise at seeing* BAL-
LIO; *to the world at large*]   Well, here's someone who certainly can relieve
my uncertainty.

BALLIO   He's heading straight for me. Now where in the world could he be from?

110 MONKEY [*like a top sergeant*]   Hey, you standing there, you with the beard
like a billy goat, I have a question for you.

BALLIO   Just like that, eh, without even a "Good afternoon"?

MONKEY   Anything good I don't give away.

BALLIO   Then, damn it all, the same goes for me!

115 PSEUDOLUS [*aside, shaking his head despairingly*]   Doing just great, right from
the start!

MONKEY   Know anybody who lives in this street?
How about it, you?

BALLIO   Me? Sure, myself.

120 MONKEY   Aren't many who can say that. Downtown there isn't one in ten
who really knows himself.

PSEUDOLUS [*aside*]   I'm safe—now he's become a philosopher![5]

MONKEY   I'm looking for someone around here—a nasty, filthy, low-down,
lawbreaking liar.

125 BALLIO [*aside*]   He's looking for me. Those are all my titles. Now, if he'd only
mention the name—[*To* MONKEY] What's the fellow's name?

MONKEY   Ballio. A pimp.

BALLIO [*aside*]   I knew it! [*To* MONKEY] Mister, the man you're looking for is
right here.

130 MONKEY   You're Ballio?

BALLIO   Sure I'm Ballio.

MONKEY   From the clothes I'd say you're a pickpocket.

BALLIO   So when *you* hold me up some dark night, you won't bother to put
your thieving hands on them.

135 MONKEY   My master wants me to give you his best regards. [*Taking out the
letter*] Here, take this letter; I have orders to give it to you.

BALLIO   Orders from whom?

PSEUDOLUS   I'm a goner! My man's in a jam—he doesn't know the name!
We're stuck!

140 BALLIO   Who do you say sent this to me?

---

5. That is, Monkey has unwittingly quoted a famous inscription found at the oracle's shrine at
Delphi, "Know thyself."

MONKEY   Identify that picture, and then *you* tell me his name. I want to
make sure you're really Ballio.

BALLIO   Give me the letter.

MONKEY   Here. Now identify the seal.

145 BALLIO [*taking a quick look, to himself*]   Major I. Kutall Hedzoff to the life. I
recognize him. [*To* MONKEY] Hey, his name is I. Kutall Hedzoff.

MONKEY   Well, now that you've told me his name is I. Kutall Hedzoff, I know
I gave the letter to the right man.

BALLIO   What's he doing these days, anyway?

150 MONKEY   What any brave, honest soldier does, by Jove! Now get a move on and
read the letter through—that's first on the docket—then take the money and
deliver the girl, and make it snappy. Because if I'm not in Sicyon[6] by today,
I'm in my coffin by tomorrow. That's the way the major operates.

BALLIO   Don't I know! You're talking to someone who knows him.

155 MONKEY   Then get a move on and read the letter.

BALLIO   Just keep quiet and I will. [*Opens the letter and starts reading*] "Letter of Major I. Kutall Hedzoff to Pimp Ballio sealed with picture as provided by previous mutual agreement."

MONKEY   It's the seal on the letter.

160 BALLIO   I see it, I recognize it. But does he always write letters this way?
With no salutation?

MONKEY   Standard military procedure, Ballio. They send greetings to friends
[*saluting*] with the hand—and [*going through the motions of a saber cut*]
destruction to enemies with ditto. But keep on with the reading. Go ahead,
165 find out what the letter says.

BALLIO   Then listen. [*Reading*] "This is my orderly Harpax who has come to
you—" [*Looking up*] Are you Harpax?

MONKEY   That's me—the Snatcher in the flesh.

BALLIO [*resuming his reading*]   "—and who is delivering this letter. I want
170 you to accept payment of the money from him and at the same time send
the girl off with him. Deserving people deserve a letter with a salutation. If
I thought you were deserving, I'd have sent one."

MONKEY   What do we do now?

BALLIO   You hand over the money and take the girl.

175 MONKEY   Well, who's holding up who?

BALLIO   Follow me in, then.

MONKEY   I'm following.

[*The two go into* BALLIO's *house. The minute the door closes behind
them,* PSEUDOLUS *bursts out of his hiding place.*]

PSEUDOLUS [*to the audience*]   I swear by the gods, never in all my life have I
seen a dirty rat as fiendishly clever as that fellow! I'm afraid of him. I'm
180 really scared of him. He might pull the same sort of dirty trick on me he
pulled [*gesturing toward* BALLIO's *house*] on him. With things going so well,
he might lower his horns and charge *me*, if he ever gets the chance to do
me dirt. And that's something I would not like—because I like the guy!

Right now I've got three good reasons to be scared stiff. First of all, I'm
185 scared that that colleague of mine will desert me and defect to the enemy.
Next, I'm scared that Simo will be back any minute from downtown: we'll

6. A Greek city in the northeast of the Peloponnesian peninsula.

capture the loot, and *he'll* capture the looters. And, along with all these scares, I'm scared [*gesturing in the direction of the town gate*] that *that* Harpax will get here before *this* Harpax gets out of here with the girl.

190 This is killing me! They're taking so long to come out! My heart's all ready with its bags packed: if he doesn't come out of there with the girl, it's saying good-bye to my chest and taking off for good. [*The door opens and* MONKEY *and Rosy step out.*] I win! My guards were all on their guard, and I beat them all!

[MONKEY *walks from the door dragging a reluctant Rosy.*]

MONKEY Please don't cry, Rosy. You don't understand what's happening. I
195 promise you, you'll find out very soon, at the party. I'm not taking you to that snaggle-toothed monster of a major from Macedon, who's making you cry this way. I'm taking you to the one man you want to belong to most of all. I promise you, in a little while you'll be giving Calidorus a big hug.

PSEUDOLUS What were you hanging around inside there for? My heart's
200 been pounding in my chest so long, it's all bruised!

MONKEY Damn you, a fine time you pick to cross-examine me, in the middle of an enemy ambush! Out of here on the double!

PSEUDOLUS You're a good-for-nothing but, so help me, you have good ideas. Hip, hip, hooray! Forward march! Straight for that jug, men!

[*They dash off, stage left, dragging the bewildered Rosy after them. A second later the door of* BALLIO'S *house opens, and* BALLIO *sidles out.*]

205 BALLIO [*to the audience*] Whew! My mind's finally at rest, now that that fellow's gone and taken the girl away. Now let that dirty rat of a Pseudolus come and try to sneak her away from me! There's one thing I know for sure: I'd sooner commit perjury under oath a thousand times than have him pull a fast one and get the laugh on me. Now I'll have the laugh on him, if I ever meet
210 him. You ask me, though, the only thing he'll be meeting is his deserts—on a mill wheel. I wish Simo would come along so he could enjoy some of my joy.

[*At this point* SIMO *conveniently enters, stage left.*]

SIMO [*to himself*] I've come to see what that Ulysses[7] of mine has accomplished. Whether he's stolen the statue from Fort Ballio yet.

BALLIO Hey, lucky fellow, let me shake that lucky hand.

215 SIMO What's the matter?

BALLIO There is no longer—

SIMO No longer what?

BALLIO —anything for you to be afraid of.

SIMO What's happened? Has he been to your house?

220 BALLIO Nope.

SIMO Then what's happened that's so good?

BALLIO [*as before*] That two thousand Pseudolus solemnly swore he'd get out of you today is safe and sound.

SIMO Ye gods, do I wish it!

225 BALLIO If he gets his hands on that girl today or gives her to your son today, the way he said he would, you get the two thousand from *me*. Do me a favor: let's make it official. I'm dying to do it that way just to prove that there's absolutely no chance for a slipup anywhere. I'll even throw in the girl as a gift, too.

---

7. That is, Odysseus, legendary king of the Greek island of Ithaca, famed for his cunning; during the Trojan War, he stole from the citadel of Troy an ancient statue of Athena, the possession of which made the city impregnable.

SIMO I can't see a thing I've got to lose by taking you up. All right—do you
230 hereby agree to give me two thousand drachmas on those terms?

BALLIO I hereby agree.

SIMO Well, this isn't a bad turn of affairs at all. Did you run into him?

BALLIO Into the both of them, as a matter of fact.

SIMO What did he say? What did he tell you? What kind of story did he give
235 you?

BALLIO The nonsense you hear on the stage. The stuff they always say about
pimps in comedies, stuff any schoolboy knows by heart. He told me I was a
dirty, filthy double-crosser.

SIMO Believe me, he wasn't lying.

240 BALLIO I wasn't the least bit sore. What difference do insults make to a fellow who doesn't give a damn or bother to deny them?

SIMO But why don't I have to be afraid of him? That's what I want to hear.

BALLIO Because he'll never get the girl away from me. He can't! Remember
I told you a little while ago that I had sold her to a major from Macedon?

245 SIMO Yes.

BALLIO Well, his orderly brought me the money plus a sealed letter with
identification—

SIMO Yes, yes.

BALLIO —which he and I had agreed on between us. Well, just a few minutes
250 ago, the orderly took the girl away with him!

SIMO Is this the truth you're telling me? On your honor?

BALLIO Where would I get any honor?

SIMO Just watch out that he hasn't pulled some fancy stunt on you.

BALLIO The letter and the picture make me absolutely certain. I tell you, he
255 just left the city with her. He's headed for Sicyon.

SIMO Well done, by the gods! Why don't I have Pseudolus put his name
down for immigration to Treadmill Town this minute? [His attention
caught, looks toward the wings, stage right.] Who's this fellow in uniform?

BALLIO I don't know. Let's watch where he goes and what he does.

[Enter HARPAX looking a bit worried. He walks downstage and addresses
the audience.]

SONG

260 HARPAX The servant who doesn't give a damn for the orders a master's issued
Is a dirty good-for-nothing, that's a fact.
And I don't give a damn for the kind whose memory's so short
They need a second warning before they'll act.
And those who think they're emancipated
265 The minute they find themselves located
Out of the master's sight, and drink and whore
And go through every drachma they've saved and more,
Will bear the name of slave
To the grave.
270 There's nothing good in them—unless you add
The knack to stay alive by being bad.
Now I won't mix or be seen with this ilk; I cut them dead on the spot.

When *I* get orders, and the master's away, I act as if he's not.
    It's when he's gone I start to fear—
275   In order not to when he's near.

    [*Holds up the purse and continues more agitatedly.*]

    Here's a job that I'd better begin.
    Up till now I've been out at the inn,
    Where that Syrus—the fellow that I
    Gave the documents to—let me lie.
280   There I stayed, since he told me to stay:
    He'd come back and he'd fetch me away,
    So he said, when the pimp had come home.
    When he didn't show up, on my own
   I came here to find out what the matter could be,
285   And not give him a chance to get funny with me!
  The best I can do is knock right here and find someone who's free;
  I want the pimp to take this cash, and send the girl with me.

BALLIO [*to* SIMO *sotto voce*]   Hey, Simo!
SIMO [*sotto voce*]   What?
BALLIO   He's mine!
SIMO   How's that?
BALLIO   Because this man's my meat.
290 He wants a wench, he's got the cash—I'm dying to start to eat!
SIMO   You'll eat him up this minute?
BALLIO   Fresh and hot and nicely brown
  And served you on a platter thus, that's the time to gulp them down.
  All decent people let me starve, but the sinners don't, you see;
  The solid citizen slaves for the state—and the sinner slaves for me!
295 SIMO   You're such a rat, when the good gods act, what tortures they'll decree!
HARPAX   I'm wasting time. I'll knock on the door this minute and find out
    whether Ballio's in or not.
BALLIO [*to* SIMO, *sotto voce*]   These blessings come to me from Lady Love.
    She brings them here, these people who run away from profit to chase after
300   loss by spending their lives having a good time. They eat, they drink, they
    whore, they have different ideas from the likes of you, who won't let your-
    self have a good time and begrudge those who do.
HARPAX [*banging on the door and shouting*]   Hey, where is everybody?
BALLIO [*to* SIMO, *sotto voce*]   The fellow's coming straight at me by the
305   straightest route.
HARPAX   Hey, where are you people?
BALLIO   Hey, mister, someone in there owe you money? [*To* SIMO, *sotto voce*]
    I'll get a good haul out of him. I can tell: this is my lucky day.
HARPAX   Isn't anyone going to open this door?
310 BALLIO   Hey, soldier, someone in there owe you money?
HARPAX [*finally looking up and seeing the two of them*]   I'm looking for the
    master of the house. Ballio, the pimp.
BALLIO   Mister, you can cut your looking short, whoever you are.
HARPAX   Why?
315 BALLIO   Because you are personally in the flesh looking at him personally in
    the flesh.

HARPAX [*pointing to* SIMO] You're Ballio?

SIMO Soldier, you watch your step or you'll be in trouble from this stick. Point that finger at *him*; he's your pimp.

320 BALLIO [*to* HARPAX, *with a contemptuous gesture in* SIMO's *direction*] Oh yes, *he's* an honest man. [*To* SIMO, *sneering*] And you, my honest man, every time you go downtown you get plenty of dunning from your creditors since you don't have any money outside of what said pimp helps you out with.

325 HARPAX Would you mind talking to *me*?

BALLIO [*leaving* SIMO's *side and walking up to* HARPAX] I am. What's on your mind?

HARPAX [*holding out the purse*] Take this money.

BALLIO I've had my hand out for hours ready for you to hand over.

330 HARPAX Take it: exactly five hundred drachmas, every coin full weight. Major I. Kutall Hedzoff, my master, gave me orders to deliver it—it's the balance he owes—and take Rosy away with me.

BALLIO Your master?

HARPAX That's right.

335 BALLIO A major?

HARPAX That's correct.

BALLIO From Macedon maybe?

HARPAX Exactly.

BALLIO I. Kutall Hedzoff sent you to me, eh?

340 HARPAX Precisely.

BALLIO To give me this money?

HARPAX If you're Ballio the pimp.

BALLIO And to take the girl away with you?

HARPAX Right.

345 BALLIO Rosy he said her name was?

HARPAX You've got a good memory.

BALLIO Wait a second. I'll be right back. [*Turns and rushes over to* SIMO.]

HARPAX But hurry, because *I'm* in a hurry. You can see for yourself how late it is.

BALLIO I see, all right. I want to consult with this man here. You just wait

350 there. I'll be right with you. [*To* SIMO, *sotto voce, gleefully*] What's next, Simo? What do we do now? This fellow who's brought the money—I've caught him in the act!

SIMO [*sotto voce*] What do you mean?

BALLIO [*sotto voce*] Don't you know what this is all about?

355 SIMO I haven't the slightest idea.

BALLIO That Pseudolus of yours has sent this fellow to make believe he's from the major!

[BALLIO *grins delightedly. An answering grin gradually spreads over* SIMO's *face as the import sinks in. They continue talking, sotto voce.*]

SIMO Did you get the money from him?

BALLIO Do you have to ask? Can't you see?

360 SIMO Just remember to hand over half of that loot to me. It's only right we share it.

BALLIO Why the hell not? It all comes from you!

HARPAX When are you going to take care of me?

BALLIO I am right now! [*To* SIMO] What do you suggest I do now?

365 SIMO   Let's have some fun with our spy, the faker! And let's keep it up till he
catches on we're making fun of him.

BALLIO   Let's go. [*The two walk up together to* HARPAX.] So you're the major's
orderly, eh?

HARPAX   Of course.

370 BALLIO   How much did you cost him?

HARPAX   Every ounce of strength he had, to win me in battle. I'll have you
know I was commander in chief of the armed forces back in my homeland.

BALLIO   Your homeland? When did the major ever capture a jail?

HARPAX   You pass any nasty cracks and you'll hear some yourself.

375 BALLIO   How long did it take you to get here from Sicyon?

HARPAX   Day and a half.

BALLIO   Pretty fast traveling, that.

SIMO   Oh this fellow's quick, all right. One look at those legs and you can see
they're just the kind for—carrying shackles, extra-heavy shackles.

380 BALLIO   Tell me, when you were a boy, did you used to play around with girls?

SIMO   Of course he did.

BALLIO   And did you used to—[*leering*] you know what I'm going to say?

SIMO   Of course he did.

HARPAX [*looking from one to the other blankly*]   Are you two in your right mind?

385 BALLIO   Answer me this. When the major stood watch at night and you used
to go along with him, [*making an obscene gesture*] did his sword fit in your
scabbard?

HARPAX   You go to hell!

BALLIO   You can go there yourself. Today. Very soon today.

390 HARPAX [*grimly*]   Are you going to give me the girl? If not, hand back the
money.

BALLIO   Wait a second.

HARPAX   Why should I?

BALLIO   Tell me, how much did it cost to hire that uniform?

395 HARPAX   What are you talking about?

SIMO   And how much for the sword?

HARPAX   These fellows need a dose of hellebore![8]

BALLIO [*to* HARPAX, *reaching for his cap*]   Hey—

HARPAX   Hands off!

400 BALLIO   —how much is that headpiece earning for its owner?

HARPAX   What do you mean, owner? What are you two dreaming about?
Everything I'm wearing belongs to me, bought with my own money.

BALLIO   Sure—earned by the sweat of your thighs.

HARPAX [*to himself*]   This pair has had the steam bath. Now what they're

405 asking for is a good old-fashioned massage.

BALLIO   In all seriousness now, I ask you: how much are you getting out of
this? What's the pittance Pseudolus is paying you?

HARPAX   Pseudolus? Who's Pseudolus?

BALLIO   Your trainer, the fellow who coached you in this swindle so you

410 could swindle the girl away from me.

HARPAX   What Pseudolus? What's this swindle you're talking about? I don't
know the man, never saw hide nor hair of him.

8. An herb used in ancient times to treat mental illness.

BALLIO Why don't you just be on your way. There's no pickings for any
crooks around here today. You tell Pseudolus that someone else made off
415 with the loot, that Harpax beat him to it.

HARPAX Damn it, *I'm* Harpax!

BALLIO Damn it, you mean you wish you were! This man's a crook, plain as
the nose on your face.

HARPAX Listen, I just now gave you the money and a little while ago, the
420 minute I arrived, right in front of this door I handed your servant the identification, the letter sealed with the major's picture.

BALLIO You handed a letter to my servant? What servant?

HARPAX Syrus.

BALLIO He lacks confidence. Not very good at being a crook, this fellow
425 here: hasn't even thought up a good story. Damn that good-for-nothing
Pseudolus! He sure figured out a smart stunt: he gave this fellow the exact
amount of money the major owed and dressed him all up so he could do
me out of the girl. As a matter of fact, this letter he's talking about was
delivered to me by the real Harpax himself.

430 HARPAX *I'm* Harpax! *I'm* the major's orderly! I'm not trying any tricks or pulling any swindles! I haven't the faintest idea who that Pseudolus of yours is,
I never heard of him in my life!

[*There is a dead silence as* BALLIO *and* SIMO *stare at each other.*]

SIMO Pimp, unless I am very much mistaken, you are out one girl.

BALLIO Damn it all, the more I hear, the more I'm afraid of just that. Damn
435 it all, I got cold shivers a second ago from that there Syrus who took this
fellow's identification. I wouldn't be at all surprised if it was Pseudolus. [*To*
HARPAX] Listen, that fellow you gave the identification to before, what did
he look like?

HARPAX Red hair, pot belly, piano legs, big head, pointy eyes, darkish skin,
440 red face, and whopping big feet.

BALLIO The minute you mentioned those feet, you did for me! It was Pseudolus, all right. Simo, it's all over with me. I'm a dead man!

HARPAX I'm not letting you do any dying until I get my money back—two
thousand drachmas.

445 SIMO And another two thousand for me.

BALLIO You mean you'd actually take a bonus like that from me when I
promised it just for a joke?

SIMO It's a man's duty to take bonuses—or booty—from crooks.

BALLIO At least hand Pseudolus over to me.

450 SIMO I hand Pseudolus over to you? What crime did he commit? Didn't I
tell you a thousand times to watch out for him?

BALLIO He's killed me!

SIMO And hit me for a forfeit of a measly two thousand.

BALLIO What do I do now?

455 HARPAX Pay *me* back my money, and you can go hang yourself.

BALLIO Damn your hide! All right, follow me downtown and I'll settle up.

HARPAX I'm following.

SIMO What about me?

BALLIO Aliens today, citizens tomorrow. [*To the audience*] Pseudolus practically
460 held a session of the Supreme Court and got a death sentence against me
when he sent that fellow today to sneak off my girl. [*To* HARPAX] Follow me,

you. [*To the audience*] Don't think I'm coming back by this street here. The way things have worked out, I've decided to use the back alleys.

HARPAX   If you did as much walking as talking, you'd be downtown by now.

465 BALLIO   I've decided to change today from my birthday to my deathday. [*He exits, stage left, with* HARPAX *at his heels.*]

SIMO [*to the audience*]   I made a monkey out of him for fair—and my servant made a monkey out of his worst enemy for fair.

I've decided not to spring on Pseudolus what they always do in come- 470 dies. No whips, no canes. I'm going in now to get the two thousand I prom- ised him if he pulled off this stunt. I'll hand it over to him without waiting to be dunned. There's a fellow who's really smart, really tricky, a real scoun- drel. He did better than Ulysses and the Trojan Horse,[9] that Pseudolus. I'll go in now, bring out the money, and spring my surprise on him.

[SIMO *enters his house, and the stage is now empty.*]

Act 5

[*Enter* PSEUDOLUS, *stage left. He has just left a wild party at* CHARINUS' *house—and looks it.*]

SONG

PSEUDOLUS   What's goin' on? What a way to act!
　　　　Hey, feet, will *you* stand up or not?
　　　　You want to leave me lying here
　　　　Till someone heaves me from the spot?
5　　　　If *I* go into a somersault,
　　　　Believe you me, it's all your fault!
　　　　[*Makes a wild lurch.*]
　　　　Insist on keeping at it, eh?
　　　　I'll have to tell you off today!
　　　　[*Finally makes the center of the stage and stands there weaving.*]
　　'At's the trouble with wine. Always wrestles unfair;
10　　First thing in the ring, has your feet in the air.
　　I'm as drunk as a lord, I'm loaded, I'm high!
　　What with elegance fit for the gods in the sky,
　　　　And the choicest of foods for us all,
　　And a spot just as gala as a room for a ball,
15　　　　Boy, oh boy, did *we* have a ball!
　　Now, why should I beat about the bush?
　　　　This is why we stay alive,
　　　　This is where all pleasure lies,
　　　　This is where all joys derive—
20　　　　And *my* view is—it's paradise!

---

9. According to legend, the Trojan War was finally brought to an end when a large wooden horse filled with the best Greek warriors—led by Ulysses, who devised the stratagem—was pulled by the Trojans within the walls of Troy.

When a man takes a girl in his arms,
When he presses his mouth against hers,
When the two, without trying to hide,
Hold on fast, tongue on tongue—neither stirs,
25   When her bosom is pressed to his breast,
Or their bodies, if they choose, become one—
Ah, that's when the time is the best
To take from a dainty white hand
A full glass, and to drink—it's just grand!
30   It's the time when we're all out for fun,
And the feelings are good all around,
And the talk isn't just empty sound . . .
Let's not spare the bouquets or perfume!
Or the stuff for the looks of the room!
35   And the cooking and all of the rest—
No need asking: only the best!

> [*Breaks off and smiles blissfully. Then continues a little more
> matter-of-factly.*]

That's how we spent the rest of the day,
The boy and I; we were *gai, très gai*,[1]
When once I'd done my job as planned
40   And driven off the enemy band.
I left them gorging, guzzling, whoring,
(Left my own girl too), all getting roaring
Drunk and happy. When I stood up,
They asked me please to do a dance.
45   I gave them this, performed, of course,
With all my usual elegance.
The steps I did were the very best kinds—
I've had lessons, you know, in bumps and grinds.
Then I put on my coat and gave them one
50   That goes like this—but just for fun.
They stamped, they clapped, they yelled "encore,"
And called me back to give them more.
I start again and give them this,
(Didn't want to do the same thing twice)
55   I play it up to the girl I'm with,
(Make sure that later she'd treat me nice)
I whirl, I skid—and down I go,
And that was the swan song for my show.
So then I try to get on my feet,
60   And—whoops—all over my coat!

---

1. Happy, very happy (French).

I hand them a laugh with that—and get
    The jug as antidote.
I take a drink, I change my coat,
    I leave the old one there,
65   I come out here to clear my head
        By getting a breath of air.
        [*Lurching up to* SIMO's *door.*]
  I've left the son to see the father, and put a word in his ear about our deal.
        [*Shouting.*]
    Open up! Tell Simo, Pseudolus is here!
        [*He pounds like a madman, then lurches a few feet away. A second later*
        the door opens, and SIMO *appears clutching a purse.*]
SIMO [*as he comes out*] It's the voice of that scoundrel that's brought me out
here.
        [*Catching sight of* PSEUDOLUS *advancing boozily.*]
70   But what's *this* that I see? And how come? Very queer!
PSEUDOLUS It's your Pseudolus, fresh from a party—and tight.
SIMO From loose living, by god. Look at that! What a sight!
That your master's right here doesn't scare you one bit.
        [*To himself.*]
What's this call for? Sweet reason or throwing a fit?
        [*Caressing the purse, ruefully.*]
75   Ah, but *this* which I'm holding rules out being rough,
        [*Gesturing contemptuously toward* PSEUDOLUS.]
If I have any hopes out of *that* for this stuff.
PSEUDOLUS [*in the grand manner*] Common sinner comes calling on saint
nonpareil.
SIMO Hearty greetings, dear Pseudolus—
        [*As* PSEUDOLUS *belches resoundingly*]
                            you go to hell!
PSEUDOLUS [*trying hard to keep his balance, as* SIMO *gives him a shove.*]
  Hey, what's that for?
SIMO   Just what do you mean, you disgrace,
80   By belching your drunken breath in my face?
PSEUDOLUS Take it easy! Hey, hold me and spare me more spills—
Can't you see that I'm tight? I'm soused to the gills!
SIMO You sure have a nerve going around in this way—
As drunk as a lord in the broad light of day!
85 PSEUDOLUS I just felt I'd like doing it.
SIMO   Felt like it, eh?
        [*As* PSEUDOLUS *drags up another roaring belch*]
What again? What's all this? You still belching at me?
PSEUDOLUS Aw, my belches smell sweet, so you *just* let me be.
SIMO I swear, you could swill in an hour
All the alcohol Italy's manpower,
90   Using bumper crops only, could press
In four years.
PSEUDOLUS   Not an hour. Much less.

SIMO   Guess you're right. Here's a point I've ignored:
   At what dock was this load put aboard?
PSEUDOLUS   With your son. We've been boozing away.
95   I sure gave it to Ballio, eh?
   I did what I told you I would!
SIMO   You're a model of stinkerhood.
PSEUDOLUS   It's the girl's fault, you know. She's been freed,
   And she's there with your son at the feed.
100 SIMO   Oh, I've heard a complete résumé.
PSEUDOLUS   Then what's holding things up? Where's my pay?
SIMO   [holding out the purse]
   It's your right. I agree. Here you are.
PSEUDOLUS   You said you'd never come across—and here I get my pay!

   [Like a master ordering his slave, he points to his shoulder.]

   Well, load it on this shoulder, boy, and follow me this way.
105 SIMO   You're asking me to put this there?
PSEUDOLUS   You will, and I know why.
SIMO   He takes my money and then gets funny—what can I do with this guy?
PSEUDOLUS   The victor gets the spoils, they say.
SIMO   Then bend that shoulder down.
PSEUDOLUS   Okay.
SIMO   I'd never thought I'd see the day
110   That I'd be on my knees to you.
   Oh my god, my god!
PSEUDOLUS   Now that's taboo!
SIMO   It hurts!
PSEUDOLUS   If you didn't hurt right now,
   Then I would have the hurt—and how!
SIMO   Now my boy, would you rob your old master of this treasure?
115 PSEUDOLUS   You're darned right. There's nothing would give me more
   pleasure.
SIMO   Won't you please, as a favor, leave me some little part?
PSEUDOLUS   I will not! Go on, call me a miser at heart,
   But you'll never be richer by a drachma from me.
   Had my plans not worked out so successfully, I'd
120   Have got damned little pity out of you for my hide.
SIMO   Just as sure as I live, I'll get even, you'll see!
PSEUDOLUS   With the hide that I've got, do you think you scare me?
SIMO   All right, then. Good-bye!
PSEUDOLUS   Hey, come back!
SIMO   I come back? And what for?
PSEUDOLUS   Just come back.
125   I won't fool you.
SIMO   I'm back.
PSEUDOLUS   Well, just think—
   Here's the two of us off for a drink!
SIMO   For a drink?
PSEUDOLUS   You just do as I say
   And I promise you half of this pay—
   Maybe more.

SIMO   Show the way and I'll go
130   Any place that you want.
PSEUDOLUS   Is that so?
      You're not angry at me or your son
      On account of these things that I've done?
SIMO   Not at all.
PSEUDOLUS [*starting to walk off*]
                       Come this way.
SIMO   I'm behind.
            [*Stopping and pointing to the audience*]
      Let's invite the whole crowd. Do you mind?
PSEUDOLUS [*stopping and eying the audience*]
135   Well, they and I have never exchanged
      A single invitation.
            [*To the audience*]
      But if you're willing to give a hand,
          A loud and warm ovation,
      To all our actors and their play—
140   I invite you all—but not today!

LUCIUS ANNAEUS SENECA

4 B.C.E.–65 C.E.

PHILOSOPHER, playwright, and politician Lucius Annaeus Seneca is the only Roman writer of tragedies whose work has survived. Drawing on the same mythic material as Greek tragedy, Seneca managed to find a new style in which to cast familiar figures and plots, one steeped in his distinct philosophical thought and political experience. Whereas his Greek predecessors had written tragedies staged outdoors before audiences numbering up to 17,000, Seneca wrote for small indoor performances and declamation. After having fallen out of favor for centuries, Seneca's work was rediscovered in the Renaissance, when it had a decisive influence on such dramatists as WILLIAM SHAKESPEARE, who encountered antiquity not through Greek tragedy but through its Roman successors. The most recent revival of Seneca's plays occurred in the final decades of the twentieth century, with new productions and a new scholarly interest in Seneca bringing his plays before audiences once more.

Born in Cordoba, Spain, on the periphery of the Roman Empire, Seneca received an excellent education in rhetoric and philosophy, first at home and then in Rome. His father, Lucius Annaeus Seneca (known as Seneca the Elder), was a well-known figure in the field of rhetoric and public speaking, the author of several works that still survive. The younger Seneca initially followed in his father's footsteps, but soon got caught up in the political and cultural developments in Rome. Having made a name for himself there as an orator and a writer, he attracted the jealousy of the dangerous and unpredictable emperor Caligula. It was only after Caligula's death in 41 C.E. that Seneca managed to rise to power under the new emperor Claudius (who reigned from 41 to 52). But his position and his political career were never secure. His fortunes took a dangerous turn when he found himself banished for seven years at the instigation of Claudius's wife, Messalina, after being accused (probably falsely) of an affair with the emperor's niece. In 49, however, Seneca was recalled by Claudius's new wife, the powerful Agrippina, and placed in the important position of tutor to her willful son, Nero. It was during Nero's reign that Seneca achieved his greatest political influence. From the beginning, he tried to exert a moderating force on the young emperor and later had a hand in running the daily affairs of state. But this period of influence and wealth did not last long. Seneca withdrew from most of his positions in 62, although he remained in the orbit of the emperor. After the uncovering of a conspiracy against Nero in which several of Seneca's friends were involved, Nero ordered Seneca to take his own life.

Though Seneca's extensive philosophical and dramatic work occasionally reflects his biography, it often also seems to be curiously at odds with it. He was trained by philosophers belonging to the Stoic school, which preached withdrawal from public affairs and ridiculed the struggle to gain worldly possessions. Critics have been quick to note discrepancies between that philosophy and Seneca's active involvement in politics. Yet Seneca himself never advocated radical self-denial; he instead wrote about various human passions with the hope that a philosophical education might have a moderating influence on them. Indeed, his involvement in politics, in particular his close association with the increasingly volatile emperor Nero, must have confirmed in his mind the need for a life based on moderation. Prominent among Seneca's writings on the passions are letters of consolation—including the *Consolation to Helvia*, the *Consolation of Martocia*, and the *Consolation to Polybius*—which all make light of the various causes of suffering, such as the thwarting of ambition or the hardship of exile, and recommend a life devoted to the cultivation of inner resources. A more general theory of the "good life" (*vita beata*), to which all Stoic philosophy is ultimately devoted, can be found in his *On Tranquillity of Mind* and *On the Shortness of Life*. Other letters, dialogues, and treatises discuss specific qualities or passions, such as *On Clemency* and *On Anger*. Seneca analyzes each of these affects, seeking to explain their root causes and how they might be better controlled.

Seneca's Stoic philosophy as well as his eventful life shaped his understanding of tragedy. His versions of Greek tragedies show their protagonists in the grip of specific emotions and political ambitions that are anathema to a Stoic. *Raging Hercules* (*Hercules Furens*) is even titled after one such emotion. In his other tragedies, Seneca chose those myths that allowed him to present varied depictions of emotional extremes. His *Medea*, for example, is not constructed, as the *Medea* by EURIPIDES had been, around tragic conflicts between characters; rather, it focuses on a single character whose uncontrolled rage leads to utter self-destruction. Seneca's depiction of Phaedra is another case study in extremes, this time of a physical desire beyond all bounds. While the *Phaedra* of Euripides had depicted the ascetic Hippolytus as a misguided purist, for Seneca he becomes an exemplary Stoic, adhering to rational restraint and preferring a simple life away from the intrigues of the court. Seneca's version of *Oedipus* emphasizes the political ambition of its title character and his obsession with power, rather than the unfair cruelty of his fate. This philosophical interest in individual passions and extreme affects is nowhere clearer than in THYESTES, a tragedy about the ancestors of Agamemnon and the woes of the house of Atreus (a myth that is also the source of AESCHYLUS's *Agamemnon*). Like Hercules or Medea, Atreus is driven by a singular wrath and Thyestes by a blinding desire for power.

Stoic philosophy not only was responsible for Seneca's warning against destructive passions and political ambitions, but also led to a profound shift in the conception of tragedy itself. Greek tragedy had been based on conflict and struggle, culminating in the brutal destruction of the protagonists. Stoic philosophy, however, was based on an entirely different worldview. Rather than equating death with painful destruction and therefore considering it something to be avoided by all means possible, Stoicism saw it as something to be expected and the ultimate escape from pain, perhaps to be invited without struggle. Stoic philosophers pointed to the example of Socrates, who had taken his own life, rejecting the conflicts and passions of Greek tragedy. In this sense, Seneca's plays offer a new conception of tragedy: a philosophically inflected warning against extreme passions and the fear of death.

Thyestes draws on Greek mythology as it depicts the prehistory of Aeschylus's *Oresteia*, whose constituent plays are among the most successful and influential of Greek tragedies. The later Roman playwright here seeks to outdo his Greek predecessor by going back to the origins of the Greek myth. At the same time, *Thyestes* is deeply informed by Seneca's Stoicism. From the beginning, Atreus is driven by anger and a singular desire for revenge. The target of these two emotions is his brother, Thyestes, who has seduced Atreus's wife and now lives in exile. Seneca shows that Atreus acts out his passion to an extreme: not content simply to kill Thyestes and his children, he tries to invent the cruelest revenge imaginable and comes up with the idea of serving Thyestes his own children in a meal. Atreus is not a pure villain: he has a just grievance against Thyestes, who has seduced his wife and challenged his power. But Atreus's desire for revenge is disproportionate to Thyestes' offense. It is a passion without a tinge of rational reflection or moral concerns.

Thyestes is a much more divided character than his brother. On the one hand he is driven by the fear of Atreus's retribution and knows that it would be safest to remain in exile. When engaged in such reflections, he uses the language of Stoic philosophy and its recommendation to shun power and wealth. On the other hand, it is precisely the thirst for power

and wealth that fuels his desire to return to court and thus drives him into his brother's trap. In other words, Thyestes could have been and should have been a Stoic philosopher, but he was ensnared by the glamour of the court. He returns to it, believing his brother's false assurances, only to find himself caught in an unthinkably cruel plot. It is difficult to imagine a starker example of Stoic philosophy, a better warning that giving in to the seductions of power will lead only to a bitter end.

Thyestes is written as a case study in Stoicism, but it also reflects Seneca's own struggle with the attractions of power. We might recognize in Atreus the cruel and willful emperor Nero, unwilling to exercise any restraint or moderation. Thyestes, by contrast, can be seen as Seneca, someone struggling to endure exile but unable to renounce power. In a way, Seneca seems to have anticipated here his own death at the hands of a willful tyrant. Although no publication dates have survived for any of Seneca's plays, some scholars have speculated that Thyestes was written in exile, before Seneca became tutor and then

A tragic mask, from a Roman mosaic in the "House of the Faun" in Pompeii.

adviser of Nero. No matter when exactly the play was composed, Seneca had already seen the unrestrained tyranny of the previous emperor, Claudius. The dilemma of the choice between isolated exile and dangerous power dramatized in *Thyestes* was very familiar to Seneca and continued to shape his life until he received the order to commit suicide.

The influence of philosophy on Seneca's tragedies is connected to their intended audience. Scholars have long debated the role of performance in Seneca's plays. Following the model of large Greek outdoor theaters, the Romans had built impressive amphitheaters for mass audiences. However, the dramas performed in them were primarily the various kinds of comedies— works by such authors as PLAUTUS and adaptations from Greek playwrights—that the Roman public favored. Seneca's tragedies seem to have been destined instead for small, private performances and declamation. At first they may appear more sensational than their Greek predecessors— for example, in their willingness to depict gruesome murders and other acts of violence, whereas in Greek tragedy such events occurred discreetly offstage. But Seneca could bring these events onstage precisely because his plays were not meant for large-scale performance; their action took place within the realm of language. This difference in approach had many consequences. Individual speeches in Seneca's plays are much longer than in Greek tragedies and therefore far better suited for detailed analysis of the individual passions on which he is focusing. Moreover, Seneca changed the function of the chorus. In Greek tragedies, it had played an active role, often representing a group of citizens but sometimes becoming the main protagonist. In Seneca's tragedies, the chorus takes no part in the action; it is entirely removed from the drama and the conflicts between individual characters. Seneca was also unconstrained by the rules for staging that limited Greek tragedians, who, for example, could use only two or three actors, each of whom had to be allowed sufficient time to put on a different costume and mask before reentering in a different role.

A second major influence on Seneca's drama, after Stoic philosophy, was the tradition of oratory and declamation revered by Romans. Seneca himself had excelled as an orator and probably had written many speeches for Nero and other statesmen. In addition, semiprivate recitation was a common means of presenting treatises, dialogues, and other pieces of writing in an age when it was costly and cumbersome to reproduce texts. Most likely, the performances of Seneca's plays resembled such recitations, as the long speeches of his characters, recited in dramatic language, echoed oratorical set pieces of the type put forth in his father's treatises.

Like Seneca's other tragedies, *Thyestes* has a form that corresponds to its performance before small audiences. The chorus, composed of citizens of Argos, is disconnected from the dramatic situation and interacts little with the other characters. Mostly, it watches with astonishment the violent deeds committed by Atreus. Nevertheless, it plays an important role, as Seneca gives it significant speeches imbued with Stoic philosophy, containing many warnings about the harm done by passions such as fear or anger and much praise for a simple, tranquil life. The chorus also provides the mythological background, explaining connections and drawing comparisons to similar events.

That *Thyestes* is constructed from a string of performed speeches does not mean that the play is untheatrical. Indeed, more than many of Seneca's other tragedies, *Thyestes* is written with an eye toward theatrical effects, whether they were to be actually staged or only evoked poetically in recitation. The audience would be familiar with stage conventions in any case and thus able to imagine the vividly described action. Whereas some of Seneca's tragedies begin with long speeches, *Thyestes* opens dramatically with the ghost of Tantalus, grandfather of Atreus and Thyestes, being dragged by a Fury from his place in Hades. This opening scene not only is highly dramatic, it also portrays the driving force behind subsequent events. Compelled to appear before the palace of Atreus, Tantalus infects Atreus with his violent history, his passion, and his fate. In another vivid scene—which exemplifies Seneca's willingness to put even the most horrifying events onstage, whether imagined or real—Thyestes eats his sons; their killing is merely described, in detail, by a messenger. Even at such moments of grim violence, however, Seneca takes the opportunity to charge violent action with philosophy, for the messenger recounts the stoical death of one of Thyestes' sons, young Tantalus, who displays no panic or fear of death. Violent passion is met with exemplary self-control.

Seneca's plays have received a mixed reception. In classical times, the Roman rhetorician Quintilian and the historian Tacitus criticized Seneca's style for its excess. In the sixteenth century, Seneca's plays enjoyed renewed attention: a translation of Thyestes into English appeared in 1560, and a complete edition of Seneca's plays was published in 1581. This edition had an important influence on Renaissance drama, in particular the Renaissance revenge tragedies of such authors as THOMAS KYD and JOHN WEBSTER, who were fascinated not just by Seneca's sensationalism but also by his roots in rhetoric and oratory. The best-known author to draw on Seneca was undoubtedly William Shakespeare, whose early revenge tragedies were indebted to Seneca. Even the famous opening of Hamlet, centered on the appearance of Hamlet's father's ghost, has been attributed to Seneca's influence. His reputation then fell, and it was not until the early twentieth century that Seneca enjoyed another revival, this time led by T. S. Eliot. The French avant-garde playwright and theater visionary Antonin Artaud, advocate of a "theater of cruelty," was also fascinated by Seneca's sensational tragedies. Later in the twentieth century the English poet Ted Hughes wrote a famous adaptation of Seneca's Oedipus (1968), which received a full staging (directed by Peter Brook) to critical acclaim; productions of other plays followed.

Seneca has continued to inspire poets and directors, the ultimate proof, perhaps, that his plays are remarkable displays both of poetic language and of theatrical imagination. But his most important legacy was the new conjunction of tragedy and philosophy that he forged. In his plays, even the most extreme and violent scenes and actions are embedded in philosophical thought. When later playwrights attempted similar combinations, they invariably turned to Seneca as the master of a genuinely philosophical tragedy.   M.P.

Thyestes[1]

CHARACTERS

GHOST OF TANTALUS,
  grandfather of
  Atreus and
  Thyestes
FURY
ATREUS, king of Argos
MINISTER

THYESTES, Atreus' brother
TANTALUS, Thyestes' son (called
  after his great-grandfather)
  and two other sons who
  don't speak
MESSENGER
CHORUS

1. Translated by Emily Wilson.

Act One

GHOST OF TANTALUS   Who draws me from the cursed realm of Hell
    where I must gape my greedy mouth for food
    that flees my grasp? Who shows the homes of gods
    to Tantalus again—despite that past disaster? Is anything worse
5   than to be always wet and always thirsty, worse than hunger
    yearning without end? Can the slippery stone of Sisyphus
    be coming for me, must my shoulders bear it?
    Or the wheel which whirls the limbs in all directions?
    Or the sufferings of spreadeagled Tityos,[2] whose belly is an empty cave,
10   who feeds black birds on his own eviscerated flesh,
    and since night heals whatever day destroyed,
    his horizontal body gives fresh food for every beak?
    I am doomed to some new torture. What will it be?
    O cruel judge, whoever you are, that give new punishments
15   to those already dead: now try to increase the pain
    at which even the guard[3] of this terrible jail trembles,
    which makes grim Acheron shudder[4] and terrifies
    even me. Now from my family line a swarm of children
    creeps out, who will surpass their ancestors.
20   They will make me look innocent. No one has dared such deeds.
    If any space lies empty in the world of sin,
    I claim it. Minos[5] has work to do
    as long as Pelops'[6] house still stands.
FURY   Go on,
    horrible Ghost, torment the wicked gods with all your rage.
25   Let every crime participate, and let the sword
    be drawn by each in turn. Let anger know no limit,
    no shame, while darkening passion whips their hearts.
    Long live the father's fury, and let eternal sin
    enter the hearts of his offspring. Let nobody have the time
30   to hate a bygone sin. Let new ones always rise,
    with more than one in every one, and let crime grow
    until it is avenged. Let the arrogant brothers lose
    their power, and get it back from exile.[7] While kings falter,
    let Fortune's shifting wheel turn from that troubled house.
35   Let power turn to grief, and grief to power,
    and wash away the kingdom in the eternal tide of chance.
    When god says: 'Now go home,' let those exiled
    for crime, return for new crimes; let them be hated
    by everyone—as much as by themselves. Let there be nothing
40   out-of-bounds for anger. Let brother fear brother,

---

2. A giant who was condemned to the underworld after having raped the goddess Leto. He was staked to the ground, with two vultures forever eating at his liver, which would regenerate itself to receive new punishments.

3. Cerberus, the terrifying dog guarding the underworld.

4. A river in the underworld used here to signify the entire underworld.

5. King of Crete who became one of the judges of the dead in the underworld.

6. Son of Tantalus.

7. Both Atreus and Thyestes were exiled and then returned to claim power.

parent child, child parent; let children's deaths be terrible,
but even worse their births;[8] let wife be enemy
to husband, plotting against him;[9] let war cross the sea,
let blood drench every land, and let Desire
45 conquer the mighty leaders of the people;
let sexual wickedness be the least of sins;
let moral righteousness, and faithfulness,
and all law perish. Let even heaven be touched
by human wickedness; why do the stars still shine,
50 and give their usual fiery glory to the world?
Let deep night come, let day fall from the sky.
No more household gods! Bring hatred, murder, death;
Let the whole house be filled with Tantalus.
Adorn the pillars, let the doors look green and merry,
55 bedecked with laurel leaves; and light a fire
fitting for your return. Repeat that Thracian crime,[1]
but with more victims. Uncle[2] why so slow?
[Is Thyestes not yet grieving for his children?][3]
Will he ever strike? Now let the fires be lit,
60 to boil the cauldrons; chop up the bodies in pieces,
let children's blood pollute the ancestral hearth,
let the tables be set. You will come as a guest to a crime,
but one you[4] already know well. Today you will have a vacation,
to free yourself from hunger at that table.
65 Fill up your empty belly; watch as he drinks that cocktail
of blood and wine. I have found a type of feast
which even you would avoid. Stop, where are you going?
TANTALUS   Down to the lakes, the rivers, the waters which flee me,
the tree whose laden branches escape my hungry lips.
70 If only I could escape to the black bed of my prison,
and if my punishment seems too light, I would change
to a different river: may I be plunged in fire,
trapped in the middle of Phlegethon's boiling water.[5]
I call to all who suffer punishments
75 decreed by fate: to you, who lie in fear,
beneath the hollow cavern, always frightened
the mass will fall upon you; you who shudder
at the gaping jaws of the ravening lions, and the awful Furies
who tangle you in their nets; and you, half-burnt,
80 trying to ward off the approaching torches.
Listen to what I have to say: believe me, I learnt the hard way:

8. The murder of Thyestes' children is not as terrible as the incestuous conception of Aegisthus by the union of Thyestes and his daughter.
9. Clytemnestra plotted the murder of her husband, Agamemnon, with her lover, Aegisthus, just as Aerope plotted against her husband, Atreus, with Thyestes.
1. Procne killed her son Itys to punish her husband, Tereus, for having raped her sister Philomela. This crime will be repeated in subsequent generations, only with three children being killed.
2. Atreus.
3. This line was probably added later.
4. Addressed to Tantalus.
5. One of the rivers of the underworld, consisting of fire instead of water.

love your punishments. When will I achieve
escape from those above?

FURY   First you must cause chaos,
bring evil to the house, create in the kings
85 the urge to fight and kill; stir up the heart
into a crazy commotion.

TANTALUS   Punishment is something
I must accept, not become. Is it my mission to go
like deadly gas from a vent in the earth, or a plague
infecting the world? Will I bring my very own grandsons
90 to such a horror? Great Father of Gods—and my father[6]
    as well,
though you blush to admit it—you may judge that my tongue
talks too much and deserves the cruellest torture;
still I must speak of this: I warn you all, do not
pollute your hands with blasphemous murder, do not
95 infect the altars with a Fury's curse. I will stand by,
I will prevent this evil.—Why are you lashing your whip
in my face? Why the threat of these circling snakes? Why pierce
my belly with desperate hunger? My heart is burning,
alight with thirst; my half-charred stomach smokes.
100 I follow you.

FURY   Good! Spread out your madness through the house.
Make them resemble you, make them hate, make them thirst
to drink their own blood. Now the palace feels
your coming and it trembles with your touch.
105 Well done! Now go back to your hellish lakes,
your old familiar water. Now earth grieves
to feel the burden of your feet. Do you not see
how water is pushed back into the ground, and how the banks
stand dry, as a fiery wind drives the clouds away?
110 The trees grow white, the fruit falls from the branches,
and near at hand the Isthmus, roaring with the sound
of breaking waves dashing on both its sides,
as its slim strip of land divides the neighbouring waters,
now widens and hears the sound of distant tides.
115 Lerna[7] now moves back, and river Inachus
lies hidden, nor does sacred Alpheus
reveal its waters. Mount Cithaeron's heights
have shed their snow and all their white is gone.
The famous town of Argos fears its ancient thirst.[8]
120 See, even the Sun wonders whether to order the day,
whether to goad to life a day which is doomed to die.

CHORUS   If any of the gods loves Argos, in Achaea,
or Pisa famous for its chariot-race,
or the Corinthian realm around the Isthmus,
125 which divides the twin gates and the sea;

---

6. Jupiter.
7. A swamp, abode of the monster Hydra.

Alpheus is a river in the Peloponnese.
8. Argos used to be short of water.

if any cares for the snows of Mount Taygetus,
frozen by Boreas in the winter-time
on the topmost mountain peaks, melted again
in summer by the winds that guide the sails;
130   or if Alpheus' icy stream, that shines
as it glides past the Olympic stadium
is loved by any god, let him smile on us, and stop
this endless cycle of catastrophe.
Do not allow each generation to get worse,
135   each son more evil than his father was.
Let thirsty Tantalus' wicked children grow
weary at last, and put aside their rages.
Enough wrong has been done. Goodness has done no good,
and those alike in evil hurt each other. Myrtilus[9]
140   deceived his master, was betrayed, and died,
driven with treachery like his own, and giving
his name to that infamous Myrtoan sea.
No tale is more familiar to Ionian sailors.
The little boy[1] was run through with a sword—what wickedness!—
145   while he ran eagerly to his father's arms:
he fell, an unripe victim at the altar,
and Tantalus, you carved him up, to serve
as a feast for the visiting gods. Eternal hunger
follows as reward for such a meal;
150   eternal thirst, too—proper punishment
for such a savage kind of dinner-party.
Tantalus lingers, empty-mouthed and weary.
Abundance hovers over his evil head,
snatched from his grasp more swiftly than by Harpies.[2]
155   The tree is weighted down with heavy leaves,
and bent by its own fruit; its swaying motion
mocks the gaping jaws of Tantalus.
But for all his desperate yearning hunger,
he refuses to reach for the tree. He has had already
160   so many disappointments. He turns away,
clamps shut his mouth, and binds his hunger with locked teeth.
But then the whole wood moves its riches closer,
ripe fruit surrounded by the heavy leaves
jumps just above his head, and sets on fire
165   his hunger. Hunger tells his hands: 'Wake up,
and get to work.' But when he stretches them out
he sets himself up for failure. All the harvest
and all the nimble grove is snatched into the air.
Then thirst comes over him, as bad as hunger;
170   his blood grows hot, the fire sets him alight;
poor man, he stands there hoping for the water,

9. Pelops promised Myrtilus half a kingdom
for killing his master, Oenomaeus, but he
later betrayed and killed him.

1. Tantalus tried to serve Pelops to the gods.
2. Dangerous birds with women's faces.

which seems to flow towards his mouth; but it twists away,
leaving a barren, empty channel. The stream
abandons him; he tries in vain to follow.
175 He drinks the thick dust left from the rushing river.

Act Two

ATREUS   You have no courage, will, or spirit! What is worse,
in my view, for a tyrant in a crisis,
you have not taken revenge. After such crimes, such lies,
such brotherly betrayals, can you do nothing in your anger,
180 Atreus, but whine? The whole world ought already
to be ringing with your clashing arms, your fleet
should be lined up on both sides of the Isthmus,
country and town should blaze with fire, and swords
flash everywhere. Let the whole land of Argos
185 sound with the clatter of horsemen; let the forests
and mountain citadels provide the enemy
no safety. Come forth, people of Mycenae,
and blow the trumpet of war. If anyone tries to protect
that hated brother of mine, I will have him slaughtered.
190 I do not care if this great and glorious house
falls to ruin and kills me, as long as it kills him too.
Come on, my soul! Do deeds that history will condemn
but never cease to speak of. The crime that I must dare
is black and bloody—the kind of thing my brother
195 would wish he had done himself. To revenge a crime
you must go one better. Can any brutality outdo
the crimes of Thyestes? Does he ever give up?
His ambition knows no bounds when times are good;
no rest, when times are bad. I know the man:
200 persuasion and advice have no effect. He can be broken.
So now, before he has had time to gather his strength,
a pre-emptive strike is needed, to stop him attacking me
when I am off my guard. He will kill me, or I him;
the winner is the one who gets there first.
SERVANT   Are you not afraid
205 the people will speak against you?
ATREUS   The best thing about being king
is making folks accept whatever you do,
and even praise it.
SERVANT   If you force praise by fear,
hatred and fear come back around to you.
True glory, true respect, come from the heart
210 not from the lips.
ATREUS   Even a low-born peasant
can get true praise. But only the powerful
can get false praise. Let them want what they do not want.
SERVANT   A king should want the good, his wishes match his
          people's.
ATREUS   If rulers can only do good things, their rule

215 depends on the people's consent.

SERVANT   If there is no honour,
no reverence for law, no trust, no faith, no goodness,
the kingdom cannot stand.

ATREUS   Trust, faith, goodness,
are merely private goals; kings follow their own way.

SERVANT   Remember that harming a brother, even a bad one,
is wrong.

220 ATREUS   Any wrong is right against a brother like that.
What crime has he left undone, what has he spared
to touch with sin? He seduced my wife, he stole her
and stole my kingdom too; he used deceit
to get the ancient mark of rule and to wreak havoc

225 upon our family. In Pelops' lofty stables
there is a famous magic ram, lord of a wealthy flock.
A golden fleece flows over all his body.
Every new king in turn from the race of Tantalus
bears a sceptre gilded by that wool.

230 The owner of the ram is king, he has the power
over this mighty house. Safe in a distant meadow
the holy animal grazes; the meadow is surrounded
by a stone wall to protect the fateful beast.
With brazen daring he made my wife his partner,

235 betrayed my bed and stole away the ram.
That was the source of all our pain, inflicted
by each upon the other. In fear I wandered, an exile,
through my own kingdom, threatened by all my family:
my wife was corrupted, my throne shaken by betrayal,

240 my house was sick, my blood in doubt.[3] I was sure of nothing
except my brother's enmity. Why hesitate? Begin,
at last, to raise up your spirits. Look to Tantalus and Pelops:
my actions must be made to fit their model.
    Tell me how to slaughter this terrible man.

245 SERVANT   Let your enemy die by the sword, and breathe his last.

ATREUS   Death is the end of suffering. I want him to suffer.
Only weak kings kill. Under my rule, people beg
for the favour of death.

SERVANT   But are you not moved by morality?

ATREUS   Away, morality!—if in fact you ever came

250 to our house. Let come the gang of ravening Furies,
with violent Erinys, and Megaera, shaking
fire in each hand. The rage that burns my heart
needs to become more savage. I want to be filled
with greater horror.

SERVANT   You are mad! What is your plan?

255 ATREUS   Nothing that could accept the normal limits of pain;
I will leave no crime undone, and none will be enough.

SERVANT   Death by the sword?

---

3. Atreus fears that his children may have been fathered by his brother.

ATREUS	Far too little.
SERVANT	Burning?
ATREUS	Still too little.
SERVANT	Then what means can your huge resentment use?
ATREUS	The man himself: Thyestes.
SERVANT	Too much! even for your rage.

260 ATREUS   Yes, I agree. A trembling frenzy shakes my heart,
and stirs it deep inside; I am swept away—to where
I do not know, but I am. Earth bellows from below,
the day is calm but I hear thunder; through all its towers
the palace crashes and seems to break. Shaken,
265   the Lares[4] turn away. Let it be, let this evil come about,
despite your terror, gods.

SERVANT   So what are you planning to do?

ATREUS   My heart is swollen with some greater thing,
something extraordinary, more than human.
It stirs my idle hands. I know not what it is,
270   but it is something huge. And let it be. Heart, take it up.
Crime suits Thyestes, suits Atreus too;
let both perform it.—The house of Thrace has seen
feasts unspeakable—of course, it is an atrocity,
but rather too cliché. My resentment needs to find
275   something more. Procne, inspire my heart,
with Philomel—our motives are alike.[5] Help me,
urge on my hands. Let the father carve and eat
his children, and do it with greed, and even joy.
Good, that is plenty; I like this type of punishment—
280   for the moment. But where is it? Why is Atreus
innocent so long? A vision appears before me,
of a bloodbath, of a father's bereavement, his loss devoured
by the father's mouth. My heart, why shrink again,
why sink before the thing itself? Come on, you have to be brave.
285   As to the worst obscenity in my evil plan,
it is: he will do it himself.

SERVANT   But how will you deceive him
to put his foot into our net and be trapped?
He knows you hate him; he suspects you.

ATREUS   He could not be caught
unless he wished to be. He hopes to get my kingdom.
290   That hope will make him brave the threats of the stormy sea,
cross over the dangerous straits of Libyan Syrtis,
that hope will make him meet Jove's thunderbolt,
that hope will even make him face the worst of all:
his brother.

SERVANT   But who can make him trust you? Who
295   can make him believe it?

ATREUS   Evil hope will swallow anything.

---

4. Household gods.
5. Atreus points to the parallel between his

story and that of Procne and Philomela (see
note to line 56).

But I will send my sons to tell their uncle
his days of wandering in exile are finally over,
he can change misfortune for a kingdom, and rule Argos
sharing the power. If at first Thyestes stubbornly refuses
300   to listen, then his children—being naive, and tired
from all their troubles, easy to win over—
will yield first. Then his old ambition,
the bitterness of poverty and hardship,
will soften him, however hardened from misfortune.
305 SERVANT   But time has surely made his pain seem light by now.
ATREUS   Wrong! Every day he feels his suffering more.
It is easy to bear misfortune, hard to go on doing it.
SERVANT   Pick other agents for your savage plan.
ATREUS   Young people are more obedient to bad orders.
SERVANT   If you teach them to turn on their uncle, they will turn
310   on their father.
Crime often comes back round again to its teacher.
ATREUS   Even if nobody teaches the ways of crime and deceit,
power itself will teach it. Are you worried they will grow bad?
They were born that way. The plan you call so wicked,
315   which you think savage, brutal, blasphemous—
maybe Thyestes is plotting it already.
SERVANT   Will the boys
be told of the plot?
ATREUS   Children of tender years
cannot keep a secret; they could reveal my scheme.
Bitter experience teaches one to keep quiet.
320 SERVANT   Then you will trick the boys through whom you plan
to trick Thyestes?
ATREUS   Yes; then they will be innocent.
Just think: why should I implicate my children
in my own crime? Our hatred is between us, let us solve it.
No, my heart! You are shrinking back. If you spare your boys,
325   you will spare his too. Let Agamemnon be
a knowing instrument of my plot; let Menelaus
be conscious of the crime. Let me get proof
of their paternity from this bad deed. If they refuse
to fight for hatred, if they call him, 'Uncle,'
330   he is their father. Let them go.—But a fearful face
often reveals the truth; large plots betray
people against their will. Let them not know
the size of the scheme they serve.—And you must not tell.
SERVANT   I need no warning. Loyalty and fear—
335   but loyalty mostly—keeps your secret safe with me.
CHORUS   Now this noble house,
descended from ancient Inachus,[6]
has finally fixed the brothers' quarrel.
        What rage incites you

6. A river god and first king of Argos.

340   to shed each other's blood
     and get the throne by crime?
     In your greed for power, you do not know
     where kingship really lies.
     Wealth does not make the king,
345   nor robes of Tyrian purple,
     nor the diadem on the brow,
     nor ceilings bright with gold.
     A king is one who can set fear aside,
     who has no wickedness inside his heart.
350   Neither the rashness of ambition, nor
     the fickle favour of the populace
     can ever sway him.
     Not all the gold-mines of the west,
     or all the wealth of Tagus
355   whose riverbed shines golden;
     nor all the wheat, ground by the threshing-floors
     in the blaze of the Libyan harvest.
     The zigzag of the lightning's path
     will never touch him, nor the wind
360   from the east, seizing hold of the sea;
     nor the savage swelling of the wild
     Adriatic Sea.
     No soldier's spear
     nor drawn swords can subdue him.
365   From a place of safety,
     he looks down on everything,
     and willingly meets his fate.
     He does not complain at dying.
       Let the rulers band together:
370   those who rouse the nomadic Dahae,
     those who control the Indian Ocean,
     whose waters are stained the colour of blood
     by so many shining jewels;
     or those who fight on the Caspian Mountains
375   the strong Sarmatian invaders.
     War is for those who dare to walk
     on the frozen Danube, and those who wear
     distinguished robes of silk:
     the Seres, who live beyond our maps.
380   A strong mind is more powerful.
     There is no need of horses,
     there is no need of arms and feeble weapons,
     such as those the Parthian
     shoots from a distance when he pretends to flee,
385   no need to flatten cities
     by bringing in siege weapons
     to whirl the boulders through the air.
     A king is a man without fear,
     a king is a man without desire.

390   Everyone makes this kingdom for himself.
      Stand, if you wish, on the slippery
pinnacle of power.
But I am satisfied with sweet peace.
Let my place be humble, let me enjoy
395   quiet free time forever.
Let my life flow by in silence,
unmarked by the people of Rome.
When my days have passed in this way,
without noise, let me grow old,
400   but never rise in class, and let me die.
Death weighs more heavily on those
who are all too well known to everyone
but who do not know themselves.

Act Three

THYESTES   How I longed for my homeland, my house, and the wealth
405   of Argos! This is the greatest happiness for exiles, after pain,
to see their native earth and their ancestral gods—
if there are really gods—and the high and holy walls
built by the Cyclopes, on larger-than-human scale.
I see it all at last—the racetrack thronged with boys,
410   where I often used to win the prize, in my father's chariot.
All Argos will rush to meet me, all the people—
but that includes Atreus. Go back to your exile in the woods,
the thickly tangled groves, and the life you led in the wild,
with animals, and like them. No reason to be dazzled
415   by the false, flashy brightness of royal power.
When you look at the gift, look at the giver too.
Just now, I had the kind of life that everyone would pity;
but I was brave and happy. Now, on the other hand,
I am dizzy with fear. My heart is stuck, and longs
420   to carry my body back. I find myself moving, unwillingly.

TANTALUS JUNIOR[7]   What is this? My father hesitates,
he looks around, unsure of himself, uncertain.

THYESTES   My heart, why all this pondering? Why do you twist around
such an obvious course of action? When everything is in doubt—
425   the kingdom, and your brother—why would you fear more suffering?
Evil is conquered and tamed now: why run from misfortune?
Your pain has been well invested. Unhappiness now feels good.
Turn back and tear yourself away, while you still can.

TANTALUS J.   Father, why are you driven to turn back from your home
430   as soon as you glimpse it? Why wrap your garments close
to avoid such marvellous benefits? Your brother is no longer angry;
he returns and restores to you part of the kingdom.
He sets the bones of the broken house, and gives you back yourself.

THYESTES   Even I do not know quite why I am frightened.

---

7. Thyestes' son, named after his grandfather.

435   I see nothing to fear, but I am still afraid.
       I want to go, but my knees feel wobbly and weak,
       I get carried somewhere different from where I meant.
       Even if sails and oars spur on a ship,
       a current may confront them and carry the ship away.

440 TANTALUS J.   Overcome the obstacles that clutter up your mind,
       and look at all the prizes you can get if you turn back.
       Father, you can be king.

THYESTES   I can, since I can die.

TANTALUS J.   Absolute power is—

THYESTES   Nothing, if you have no desires.

TANTALUS J.   Your children will inherit.

THYESTES   The kingdom cannot hold two.

445 TANTALUS J.   Can someone choose unhappiness when happiness
       is possible?

THYESTES   Believe me, it is only language misapplied
       that makes us want to be 'great,' and fear to 'suffer.'
       Lofty position brought me constant fear; I was afraid
       even of my own sword. Ah, what a wonderful thing
450   to get in no one's way, to have a carefree picnic
       relaxing on the ground! Crime does not enter hovels:
       those who live in tiny homes can drain their cups in safety.
       Poison is drunk from gold. I know of what I speak.
       It makes good sense to choose bad fortune over good.
455   The little low-lying town does not tremble at the house
       that stands up high above it on the mountain peak,
       nor does the ivory shine on the lofty ceilings;
       no sentry guards my bedroom while I sleep.
       I need no fleet to catch my fish, I do not need
460   to drive the sea away with piles of rocks,
       nor glut my greedy belly with imported goods.
       No distant field in Parthia or Geta need be ploughed
       to feed me; I need no worship with incense or altars,
       replacing Jupiter with myself. No treetops sway
465   up high upon my roof; no steaming baths that take
       many hands to heat. My days are not passed in sleep,
       I do not stay awake to drink all night.
       Nobody fears me; I have no need of weapons to keep
       my house safe:
       deep peace comes to those in modest circumstances.
470   The ability to do without a kingdom is a kingdom.

TANTALUS J.   If god gives power you should not turn it down,
       nor try to get it. Your brother asks you to rule.

THYESTES   He asks? There must be trickery of some kind.

TANTALUS J.   Family loyalty usually comes back again,
475   the love we ought to feel will heal its long-lost strength.

THYESTES.   Could my brother love me? Before that happens,
       the sea will rise to drench the stars, the raging waves
       of the stormy Sicilian strait will stand stock still,
       ripe corn will grow on the Ionian waters, and black night

480   will light the earth. A loyal pact will sooner
       join fire to water, death to life, or wind to sea.
    TANTALUS J.   But why are you afraid? What do you suspect?
    THYESTES   Everything. What limit should I put to my fear?
       His power is as great as his hatred.
    TANTALUS J.   What power does he have
       against you?
485   THYESTES   I fear nothing for myself now; but you, sons,
       make me fear Atreus.
    TANTALUS J.   But you are on guard; why fear?
    THYESTES   When trouble comes it is too late to be careful.—
       Let it go. But I declare to you, my son, just this one thing:
       I follow you, it was not my idea.
    TANTALUS J.   God will
490   smile on good thinking. Go, no hesitation.
    ATREUS   The beast is tangled in the nets I laid.
       I see his offspring with him, all that hateful family
       joined together. Now my hatred lives
       safely; at last Thyestes is in my hands,
495   he comes to me, he comes, and all of him.
       I can hardly control my feelings, my vengeance strains
          at the leash:
       just like an Umbrian hound held on a long rope,
       as he tracks his prey with his keen nose, his face
       close to the ground; while he sniffs the lingering scent of the boar
500   from a distance, he runs quietly, and listens,
       but when the prey gets nearer, then he strains
       with his whole neck, and shouts with all his lungs:
       'Hurry, Master!' and he tears himself from the collar's grip.
       While my anger hopes for blood it cannot hide:
505   but I must hide it. Look how his hair is matted
       with dirt and long enough to cover his sad face.
       Look at his horrid beard. My loyalty must be perfect:
       How nice to see my brother! Come to my arms!
       I missed you. Whatever quarrels we had are over now.
510   From this day forward let us pay respect for family;
       let us say no to hatred! No more being enemies!
    THYESTES   If you were not like this, I could have refuted
       all charges.
       But Atreus, I confess. I committed all the crimes
       you thought I did. My case looks black in the light
515   of your brotherly love today. A man who could hurt
       so good a brother seems a total scoundrel.
       It is time for tears. For the first time you see me a suppliant;
       never before have I begged, but now I kneel before you.
       Let all our anger be set aside, all rage
520   be wiped clean from our hearts. Take these sweet children
       as pledges of my good faith.
    ATREUS   Stop hanging on to my knees!
       Stand up and come into my arms instead! And you,

protectors of our old age, all you boys,
come and embrace me!—Take off these dirty clothes;
525 it hurts me to see you like this. Dress up in garments
as rich as my own. Be ready to take your share
of your brother's kingdom. This is my greatest glory:
returning my father's crown to my brother safe and sound.
Having a kingdom is only luck; to give it away is virtue.
530 THYESTES   Brother, may the gods reward you fairly,
with blessings to match such kindness. But the royal crown
would not suit my rough appearance, and my hands
are too tainted to take the sceptre. I would prefer
to be lost in the midst of the crowd.
ATREUS   This kingdom allows
       two rulers.
535 THYESTES   I see all that is yours as mine, dear brother.
ATREUS   When Fortune pours out gifts, who would refuse?
THYESTES   The man who knows how fast they flow away.
ATREUS   Do you forbid your brother to get glory?
THYESTES   Your glory is achieved, mine is to come;
540 my mind is set, I will reject the kingdom.
ATREUS   I will leave my share unless you take yours.
THYESTES   I will accept it. I will bear the name of kingship;
but you will have the law, the army and myself.
ATREUS   Accept and bear the bindings on your noble head;
545 I will sacrifice the designated offerings to the gods.
CHORUS   Would anyone believe this? Fierce Atreus,
so wild and violent, so lacking self-control,
stopped dead, stunned, at his brother's face.
There is no greater power than true devotion;
550 strangers' quarrels may endure long years,
but true love always holds those it has held.
When major grievances stir anger up,
to rupture friendship and sound the sign for war,
when light-armed troops are clattering their reins,
555 and shining swords swing out from all directions,
wielded by Mars who longs for more fresh blood,
raging as he swipes again and again—
loving duty overcomes the sword
and joins the fighters' hands in peace, to their chagrin.
560   What god has made this sudden truce, after
so great a conflict? Just now throughout Mycenae
rang out the dreadful noise of civil war.
The mothers, faces pale, clutched hold of their babies,
the wives were fearful for their armoured husbands;
565 their swords unwillingly obeyed their hands,
rusty and ruined from the time of peace.
One struggles to restore the falling walls,
another to rebuild the shaken turrets,
another locks the gates with iron bolts,
570 and terrified, up on the battlements,

the guardsman keeps awake the whole long, anxious night.
For fear of war is even worse than war.
But now the threats of cruel swords subside;
now the deep rumble of the trumpets sounds no more;
575   now the shrill bugle's screech no longer rings;
deep peace has been restored to the happy town.
    So, when the waves are swelling from the deep,
when the north wind whips up the Sicilian sea,
the monster Scylla roars as her caves are battered,
580   and sailors in the harbour fear the sea,
vomited out by ravenous Charybdis.[8]
The savage Cyclopes, who live on top
of molten Etna, fear their father's[9] work:
in case the waters poured on top put out
585   the fire that sizzles in the ever-burning furnace.
Ithaca trembles and Laertes fears
his own poor kingdom will be under water.
But if the winds grow weak and lose their strength,
the sea subsides more gently on its bed,
590   the waters which the fleet had feared to cross—
even the splendid ships with sails unfurled—
lie calm and open to the playful skiff.
You can pause and count the swimming fish
where recently beneath the giant storm
595   the shaken Cyclades[1] were trembling at the sea.
    No situation lasts. Pleasure and pain
give way in turn; but pleasure is more brief.
A fleeting hour exchanges high and low.
The man who can give crowns to other men,
600   before whom people kneel on trembling knees,
whose nod can make the sun-dark Indians,
the Medes, and the Dahae, whose horsemen fight the Parthians,
all at an instant lay aside their wars—
that man is worried as he wields his sceptre,
605   fearfully trying to tell the future, the chances
which whirl the world around, and fickle time.
    You to whom the lord of sea and land
has given the great power of life and death,
set aside your proud and puffed-up face.
610   Whatever your subordinates fear from you,
your master may in turn inflict upon you:
for every kingdom lies beneath another.
If daybreak when it comes sees someone proud,
that day's departure will see him lie low.
615   No one should trust too much in his good fortune,
no one should give up hope of better luck.
Clotho mixes good with bad and stops

---

8. Scylla is a sea monster and Charybdis, a
whirlpool.
9. The father of the one-eyed Cyclopes is

Poseidon, god of the seas.
1. A group of islands.

Fortune from standing still; each man's fate rolls round.
No one has supporters rich enough
620 that he can guarantee himself tomorrow.
God moves our lives around on his swift spindle
and turns them upside-down.

Act Four

MESSENGER   What wind can whirl me sky-high through the air,
and wrap me in dark clouds, to tear my eyes away
625 from such abomination? This house would make blush
even Pelops and Tantalus.

CHORUS   What is your news?

MESSENGER   What place is this? Is it Argos, Sparta,
inheritance of two good brothers,[2] bordering
the twin sea-spouts of Corinth? Or is this where
630 the savage nomads run in flight on the frozen Hister;
or Hyrcania, deep with snow, or Scythia, home to wanderers?
What place is witness to so great a horror?

CHORUS   Tell us, reveal the evil, whatever it is.

MESSENGER   If my heart stops fluttering, if my body, stiff with fear,
635 can let my limbs be free. The vision of that crime
will not go from my eyes. Storm-winds, carry me
to where the day is taken far away.

CHORUS   Do not keep us suffering in suspense!
Tell us what you shudder at! Reveal the criminal!
640 I ask not 'Who?' but 'Which of them?' it was. Out with it!

MESSENGER   On top of the citadel, one side of Pelops' castle
is turned towards the south. Its farthest side
rears high as the mountain, shadowing over the city.
If the people grow rebellious, kings can reach
645 to strike them. An enormous hall inside
shines bright, its woodwork all adorned with gold,
its marvellous columns spotted with different colours.
After this public area, known and revered by all,
the palace spreads out into many rooms:
650 a hidden space lies in the farthest part,
an ancient grove buried in a deep valley,
at the centre of the kingdom, where no tree
blossomed or put forth fruit; no gardener pruned them.
The yew and cypress and the black holm-oak
655 swayed in that shadowy wood. Above them all
the oak tree dominates the grove from its great height.
From here the sons of Tantalus begin their reigns
from here they ask for help when things look bleak or doubtful.
Gifts hang from the trees; there is the trumpet,
660 the broken chariot,[3] spoils of the Myrtoan Sea;

2. The two inseparable brothers Castor and
Pollux are the opposite of Thyestes and Atreus,
who hate each other.

3. Pelops betrayed the charioteer Myrtilus
after inducing him to murder his master (see
note to line 139).

the wheels hang down from the pole that deceived the king.
All the family's history is here. Here Pelops
attached his turban to the tree, and the enemy spoils,
and a cloak embroidered with triumphs over foreigners.

665   Under the shadows is set a dismal fountain,
stuck in a black and stagnant pool; most like
the ugly water of terrible Styx,[4] by which the gods swear faith.
They say the spirits groan here in the dead of night,
the grove resounds with the clattering of chains,

670   and the ghosts howl. All things that make one shudder
even to hear, are there made visible. Old tombs break open,
releasing hordes of wandering dead. Everywhere spring
unprecedented wonders. Indeed, throughout the wood,
flames sparkle, and the tallest trunks shine, without fire.

675   Often the wood rings out with triple barking,
often great phantoms terrify the house.
Fear is not soothed by dawn: night-time belongs to that grove;
even in full daylight, the place is ruled by awe.
True oracles are given here to those who ask,

680   when from the inmost place, with a great crash,
fates are set free, the whole wood gives a roar
when god unfurls his voice. This was the place
where angry Atreus dragged his brother's children.
The altars are adorned—how can I say this?—

685   the little princes have their hands tied back;
he binds their poor little heads with a purple band.
Incense was not forgotten, or the holy juice of Bacchus,[5]
and with the knife he daubed the victims with salted grains.
All due ritual was observed, in case such a horrible crime

690   be done improperly.

CHORUS   Who held the sword?

MESSENGER   He was the priest himself, he was the one
who gabbled out the deadly prayers, the rites of murder.
He stood there at the altar, he checked the victims' bodies,
and he himself arranged them for the knife,

695   and acted as the audience. No part of the rite was lost.
The woods were trembling, the whole ground was shaken,
making the courtyard totter: it seems to hesitate,
unsure where it can set its weight. A shooting star
rushes with a black trail on the left part of the sky;

700   the dedicated wine is changed to blood
and flows into the fire. His royal crown
kept falling down. In the temples the statues wept.
All were aghast, but Atreus himself
alone remained unmoved, and was the one

705   to scare the gods that tried to threaten him.
Without delay he stood at the altar and scowled.
Just as in the forests of the Ganges

---

4. River of the underworld.   5. The god of wine.

a hungry tigress prowls between two bullocks,
wanting to seize them both, but wonders which
710 to pounce on and bite first; she turns her jaws
this way and that, keeping her hunger waiting—
so dreadful Atreus watches the boys whose lives are due
to his unholy rage. He wonders which
to slaughter first, and which to butcher second.
715 It makes no difference, but he ponders, and enjoys
order in brutality.

CHORUS   So which did he strike?

MESSENGER   Do not imagine he lacked family feeling:
first to be killed was his father's namesake, Tantalus.

CHORUS   How did the boy behave or look as he was killed?

720 MESSENGER   He stood there unconcerned and he refused
to waste his voice on prayers. But the wild murderer
buried his sword in a deep thrust, and pressing down
he fixed his hand on his throat; when he drew out the sword
the corpse still stood; it was unclear for a while
725 where it should fall, but it fell on the uncle.
Then that barbarian dragged Plisthenes to the altar,
and added him to his brother. He cut through his neck;
the body without its head flopped to the ground,
while the head rolled down, protesting indistinctly.

730 CHORUS   After the double murder what did he do?
Did he spare the little one, or heap more crime on crime?

MESSENGER   Just as the long-maned lion in Armenia
lies on his heap of victims after slaughter,
his jaws dripping with blood, his hunger assuaged,
735 he does not set aside his anger, everywhere
he still pursues the cattle, snarling with tired teeth—
so Atreus rages and swells with his rage,
holding out the sword drenched in the two boys' blood,
careless where his fury leads him, cruelly,
740 he drives the blade in the chest of the child, right through,
and all at once it pokes out from his back.
He fell and put the fires out with his blood,
wounded on both sides, he died.

CHORUS   What savagery!

MESSENGER   Are you horrified? If the crime stopped there,
745 Atreus would be holy.

CHORUS   But can nature allow
a worse atrocity?

MESSENGER   You think this the end of his crime?
It was the first step.

CHORUS   What more could he do? Did he throw
the bodies to wild beasts to tear, refuse cremation?

MESSENGER   If only he had! If only they lay unburied,
750 uncremated corpses, dragged away
to be a dismal dinner for wild beasts.
This man makes normal pain desirable:

if only the father could see his children unburied!
Incredible evil! Historians will deny it.
755 The entrails ripped from the living children's bellies
quiver, their veins throb, the heart still beats in fear;
but he sorts through the innards, checks the omens,
and scans the still-hot markings of the veins.
Once he was happy with the victims, he devoted himself
760 to his brother's dinner. He himself carved up
the body into segments, chopped the broad shoulders
down to the trunk, sawed through the biceps, laid bare
the limbs and chopped the bones—the cruel monster!
He only left the heads and hands—hands given in good faith.
765 He sticks the organs to the spits, and over the furnace
they slowly burn and drip; the boiling water
tosses them as the pot glows hot. The fire jumps over
the meat he gives it, and repeatedly
throws it back to the trembling hearth, resisting
770 its orders to stay still; it burns against its will.
The liver hisses on the spit; I can hardly say
whether the bodies or the flame groaned louder. The fire turned
to pitch-black smoke, and the smoke itself, heavy with smog,
could not drift upwards, could not move up high;
775 the malformed cloud covered even the household gods.
O all-enduring Sun, though you retreated
and drowned the broken day in the middle sky,
you set too late! The father rips apart his sons,
putting into his murderous mouth his own dear flesh and blood.
780 His hair is wet and shiny with perfume, his body heavy
with wine; his mouth is overstuffed, his jaws
can hardly hold new morsels. O Thyestes,
your only blessing is your ignorance.
But you will lose that too. If only Titan
785 could turn his chariot, meeting his own face,
and heavy night sent from the dawn usurp the day,
to cover up this black deed with new darkness.
But we must see this evil; all is now revealed.
CHORUS   Why, Lord of Earth and Sky?
790 Why is all beauty gone, why is dark night
risen at noon? Why this change of yours,
why destroy day in the middle of day?
Why, Phoebus, do you rob us of your face?
The messenger of night, the Evening Star,
795 has not yet called the night-light out;
the turning of the western wheel
has not yet set to rest its tired horses;
day had not yet switched to afternoon,
the trumpeter had not sounded the ninth hour;
800 the oxen were not weary yet—the ploughman
stopped, astonished, at the sudden dinner-time.
What drove you from your heavenly path?

Why were your horses flung away
from their usual track? Is Hell's dungeon opened
805   to reveal the conquered Giants, in a new
attempt at war? Is Tityos, though his torso
is weary of wounds, renewing his ancient rage?
Is Typhoeus throwing the mountain off his body,
and stretching out his bulk? Have the enemies
810   from the Phlegraean Field built up a highway
and is Pelion pressed by Thracian Ossa?[6]
Are the usual cycles of the sky all gone?
Will there be no more dawn and no more dusk?
The rosy mother of first light, the Dawn,
815   who normally hands the horses' reins to Phoebus,
stops in bewilderment:
her kingdom's entryway
is all gone wrong; she does not know
how to damp the tired horses or to soak
820   their manes, which smoke with sweat, into the sea.
The setting Sun is quite surprised to see
Aurora, an unusual guest to him;[7]
he tells the shadows to grow long although
night is not ready yet:
825   the stars have not inherited the sky,
no fire lights up the heavens,
the heavy Moon does not arrange the shadows.
    But whatever it is, let it be night!
Our hearts go pitter-patter, struck with such dread
830   fearing that everything is shaken and may topple
into disaster, chaos come again,
to overwhelm humanity and gods; Nature
again may cover up the earth and circling sea
and all the spangles of the painted sky.
835   No longer will the Sun, leader of stars,
raise his eternal torch and usher in
the seasons, pointing out the proper times
for summer and winter. The Moon, whose light reflects
the flames of Phoebus, will no longer take
840   terror from night, beating her brother's horses
as she runs her shorter race.
The mass of gods
will be heaped away into a single chasm.
The Zodiac, bearing the constellations,
845   the pathway of the sacred orbs, dividing
zones at a sideways angle, as it turns the years
now will slip and see its stars have fallen.
Aries, who brings back the gentle winds

---

6. The giants piled the mountain Pelion onto the mountain Ossa when they tried to conquer Olympus.

7. The usual arrangement between Phoebus, the god of the sun, and Aurora, goddess of dawn, has gone wrong.

to ships, when spring has not yet become kind,
850　will plunge down headlong underneath the waves,
through which he carried Helle,[8] terrified.
The Bull too will be lost, whose shining horns
display the Hyads; after him fall the Twins
and the curving claws of the Crab.
855　The Herculean Lion, burning and flaming with heat,
will fall from heaven now a second time;
the Virgin will fall down to the abandoned earth,
as will the weights of the level, truthful Scales,
taking with them cruel Scorpio.
860　Old Chiron[9] holding feather-tipped arrows
to his Thessalian bow
will break his string and the arrows will be lost.
The icy Goat, who brings numb winter back,
will fall, and break your urn, Aquarius—
865　whoever you are.[1] With you will disappear
the last stars of the sky,
Pisces the Fish.
The wonders never washed in waves before
will be drowned in the whirlpool which will cover the world.
870　The slimy Snake which divides the Bears in half
like a river, and cold Ursa Minor
covered with hard ice, and joined to the larger Snake,
and the slow guardian of the Great Bear,
Arctophylax will topple and rush to ruin.
875　　Were we from all humanity the ones
who earned destruction, crushed by the overturning
of the hinges of the world?
Will the last days come in our time?
We were born for a cruel lot,
880　whether we, poor things, have lost the sun,
or forced him into exile.—
Enough complaints, enough of fear;
one would have to be greedy for life not to want
to die when the world is dying.

Act Five

885　ATREUS　My steps are level with the stars, I rise above the world
touching heaven's axis with my exalted head.
Now royal power and my father's throne are mine.
No need of gods! Now all my prayers are answered.
It is good, it is plenty, it is enough, even for me—
890　but why, enough? I will go on, and fill the father up
with his children's death. Shame need not stand in my way:
the day is over: go on while the sky is empty.

---

8. The Golden Ram carried Helle through the
waves of the Hellespont.
9. A Feared centaur.

1. The identity of Aquarius was disputed.

If only I could prevent the gods from leaving,
drag them down and force them all to watch
895   this vengeance feast!—But let the father see it, that is enough.
Though day resists, I will shake off the shadows,
under which your misery is hidden.
You have been lying there eating, looking safe and cheerful,
for far too long. You have had enough food, enough wine.
900   I need Thyestes sober for this horror.
Slaves! All of you! Undo the doors of the palace!
I want the whole house open; party time!
     How sweet to watch him looking at his children's heads,
how sweet to see his altered face, to hear him
905   as his first grief gushes out. Look, he is dazed;
he stands there stiff and breathless. This is my work's harvest:
I want to watch the onset of his pain.
The open halls are bright with many torches;
he flops around on the gold and purple sofa,
910   propping his head on his left hand, befuddled with wine.
He belches. Yes! I am God! Highest of all the powers,
and King of Kings! This is better than I dreamed of.
He is full up. Now he sips from the silver cup.
Drink! No holding back! There is still plenty of blood;
915   there were so many victims. The vintage wine
camouflages the blood. May this drink, right here, right now,
round off his meal—a cocktail of his children's blood.
He would have drunk my children otherwise. Look, now
he calls for festive music. He is wasted, out of his mind!

920 **THYESTES**   Long suffering has numbed my heart.
Now set aside your cares!
Away with grief, away with fear,
away with that companion of my exile:
bitter poverty, and shame which weighs
925   heavily on the poor. The sense of loss
is worse than suffering.—Good for me!
I fell from a great height, but fixed my feet
firmly on the ground. Good for me!
I was oppressed by such calamities,
930   but bore the burden of my shattered power;
I did not break. I was faithful to my royal blood:
unconquered, upright in the midst of pain,
I bore the imposition of disaster.
But now—cast off the clouds of cruel fate,
935   away with all the marks of my bad times;
time for a happy face to greet my joy.
The old Thyestes is no longer here.
     Unhappy people tend to have this fault:
never believing happiness has come.
940   But good luck can come back again, although
those who have suffered distrust celebrations.—
Pain, you rise up inside me for no reason!

Why call me back and tell me not to revel
in this happy day, why say that I should weep?
945 Why do you stop me from binding up my hair
with lovely flowers? It stops me, stop now, stop!
    The spring-time roses topple from my head,
my hair, so wet from all this spicy perfume,
stands up on end with sudden shock.
950 I had not meant to weep; I find my cheeks are wet.
My words are interrupted by my cries.
Sorrow loves tears—she is used to them.
Unhappy people have a strange desire to cry:
I feel like letting out unlucky groans,
955 I feel like tearing up my fancy clothes, deep-dipped
in Tyrian purple dye. I feel like screaming.
    The mind gives indications of a grief to come,
prophet of its future pain.
Sailors know a major storm is coming
960 when the calm waters swell without a wind.
Madman, what are you imagining?
What griefs or storms? Be trustful in your heart
towards your brother. At this point, whatever happens,
either your fears are groundless, or too late.
965   Poor me! I do not want to feel this way:
but terror wanders in me and my eyes
gush with sudden tears. There is no cause.
Is it grief or fear? Or does great pleasure
make me cry?
970 ATREUS   Brother, let us celebrate together
this happy day. Today my throne is solid,
    and we are bound in solid trust, sure peace.
    THYESTES   I am full of food and full of wine.
The only thing that could increase my pleasure
975 is if my boys could join me in my joy.
    ATREUS   Your boys are here, believe me—held by their father.
They are here and always will be; no part of your children
can ever be taken from you. I will give you the faces
you long to see, I will fill you full of them all.
980 Do not worry, you will be satisfied. They are mingling
with my own boys, and enjoying a holy meal.
But they will be summoned. Have a drink.
This is a family cup.
    THYESTES   Thank you for the gift,
and here's to brotherhood. Pour a libation first
985 to the gods of our fathers; then drink. But what is this?
My hands refuse me, the cup is too heavy to hold;
the wine slips from my very lips and pours
away from my open mouth. How very frustrating!
Look, even the table is shaking, the ground trembles;
990 the fire flickers out; even the heavy sky
is empty, stupefied: not night or day.

What is this? The mighty dome of heaven slips;
struck over and over; darkness grows more dense;
night hides herself in night. All stars are gone.
995 Whatever it is, I pray the storm may spare
my brother and my children. Let it strike
only my wretched head. Now give my children back!
ATREUS I will. And they can never be taken from you.
THYESTES My stomach feels upset. What is this rumbling inside
1000 What is trembling? I feel a restless weight:
my belly moans with someone else's moan.
Come here, children! Your poor father wants you.
Come here! When I see you, I will be fine.
Where are their voices coming from?
ATREUS   Get ready to hug your
        children.
1005 They are here already. Do you not recognize them?
THYESTES I recognize my brother. Earth, can you allow
such an atrocity? Will you not break and sink
into the Styx and shadows of Hell, rip open and tear away
the kingdom and the king down into empty chaos?
1010 Will you not uproot this Mycenean palace
from its foundations? We should both already
have been with Tantalus. If anything lies lower
than Tartarus—and our grandfather—then, Earth, break your bonds,
create a massive chasm, cast us down there,
1015 bury us and cover us both up
with all of Hell. May the souls of the damned
wander above our heads, and the river of fire,
Phlegethon, burning, burning, roasting its toasted sands,
surge roughly over my place of exile.
1020 Earth, why do you lie there, still, a useless lump?
The gods have gone away.
ATREUS   Now be happy! You missed
your children; here they are! Brother, no need to wait.
Enjoy them, kiss them, multiply your hugs by three.
THYESTES Is this trust? Is this friendship? Is this a brother's word?
1025 Is this how you end your hatred? I do not even ask
to get my children safely back. I only want
something which cannot hurt your hatred or your crime.
I ask you as a brother: let me bury them.
Let them be cremated, right away. Give me my children,
1030 not to keep, but lose.
ATREUS   You have all that remains
of your children—and even what does not.
THYESTES Are their bodies food for birds of prey?
Are wild beasts ripping them apart and eating them?
ATREUS You are the one who feasted on your sons.
1035 THYESTES This is what made the gods ashamed, this drove
the day back to the east. Ah, what can I say,
how can I even mourn? What words could fit?

I see their heads cut off, their hands dismembered,
their feet torn from their broken bodies.
1040 These are the parts that even their greedy father
did not have room for. Inside my belly they heave,
the horror struggles to escape; there is no exit.
Brother give me your sword—it has already
gorged on my blood. That way, I can journey to my children.—
1045 But the sword refuses. I will beat my chest,
batter my body with grief—but now stop, poor hands:
be gentle to the dead. Who has seen such horror?
What pirate in the rocky, barren land
of Caucasus? What menacing highwayman
1050 in Attica? Look, my children and I
weigh down one another. The crime at least is balanced.
ATREUS Balance the books of crime when you commit it,
not when you pay it back. Even this is too little for me.
I should have poured hot blood into your mouth
1055 direct from their wounds, to make you drink them alive.
My impatience cheated my rage. I used my sword
to stab them. I rushed at the altars. I satisfied
the holy fires with slaughter. Chopping up
their lifeless bodies, I pared their limbs
1060 to little scraps, which I plunged in the boiling pots,
and had them simmered on a gentle heat.
I cut the arms and legs and muscles off
while they were still alive, and skewered them
on nice slim spits. I saw them groan, and brought
1065 fresh fires with my own hands.—But all of this
could have been better done by their own father.
My vengeance is a failure. The wicked father
munched up his sons, but did not know it; nor did they.
THYESTES Listen to this sin, seas shut in your winding shores,
1070 and you, gods, listen too—wherever you have hidden.
Listen, Lower World, and listen, Earth; and Night,
heavy with darkness: pay attention to my words.
Only you, Night, are left to comfort me;
you too have been abandoned by the stars.
1075 My prayers will be good and unselfish—in fact now—
what could I ask for myself? I pray only for you.
Great King of the Sky, Lord of the Hall
of Heaven, wrap the universe in clouds,
make all the winds wage war, and bellow thunder
1080 from every part of earth; and do not use
the gentle hand with which you touch the homes
of innocent men. Strike as you did when the mass
of the triple mountain fell, along with the Giants
who stood as high as mountains. So prepare
1085 to fight and hurl your fires; avenge this ruined day,
shoot flames; make up the light robbed from the sky
with lightning. Do not pause to judge the case:

we both deserve damnation.—Or do it for my sins:
come find me, let your trident pierce
1090 my heart with fire. My last hope for my sons
is that I may cremate them with due rites.
Then I myself must burn.—If nothing moves the gods,
if there are no powers above to hunt for sinners,
let night remain eternal, covering up
1095 my giant sins with growing darkness. Sun,
if you stay back I have no more complaints.

ATREUS   Hurrah for me! Now I have my real prize.
Without this pain, my crime would have been wasted.
Now I believe I have my sons, I have my marriage back.[2]

1100 THYESTES   What had my sons done to deserve this?

ATREUS   They were yours.

THYESTES   But giving children, to a father . . .

ATREUS   Yes! And best of all,
legitimate sons.

THYESTES   I call the gods, the guardians of the good!

ATREUS   And the gods of marriage?

THYESTES   Who pays back crime with crime?

ATREUS   I know your complaint: you mind me doing it first!
1105 You are not hurt because you gulped that ghastly meal,
but because you did not serve it. You had the plan
to lay out the same menu for your credulous brother,
to make their mother help attack the children
and kill them the same way. Only this stopped you:
1110 you thought they were yours.

THYESTES   The gods will take revenge;
I give you to their care for punishment.

ATREUS   And for your punishment, I give you to your children.

---

2. Atreus believes that through his revenge he has undone his wife's adultery with Thyestes.

SHUDRAKA

ca. 2nd or 3rd century C.E.

RCCHAKATIKA, or *THE LITTLE CLAY CART*, is one of the most frequently translated Sanskrit plays, closely rivaling the other masterpiece of Sanskrit drama, Kalidasa's *Shakuntala*. A love story verging on the tragic but restored at the very last minute to a happy ending, *The Little Clay Cart* offers an entertaining view of Indian society as it may have been almost two thousand years ago. It is masterfully crafted in its structure, plot management, and character delineation. At the same time, the poetic quality of the dialogue is of the highest order, deftly blending within a single text as many as seven different languages and dialects (a feature that, unfortunately, largely eludes translation). *The Little Clay Cart* remains one of the exemplary plays in the oeuvre of classical Indian drama.

Sanskrit drama, like Greek drama, is not available to us in its entirety, as many of the physical manuscripts have not survived. The plays were first written down centuries ago on palm-leaf pages that were stored mostly in temples and royal collections. Only a few of these survived—by chance, through periodic retranscriptions; many have been lost forever. Most scholars of ancient Sanskrit literature believe that *The Little Clay Cart* was written sometime between the second and third centuries in the Common Era. This play is ascribed to King Shudraka, who may in fact have been a king of Ujjayini (modern-day Ujjain). His name literally means "little Shudra," a member of the lowest caste, suggesting that like Aryaka, the insurgent monarch-to-be in *The Little Clay Cart*, he may not have been born into a royal family. Perhaps this is also why *The Little Clay Cart* emphasizes that irrespective of caste, an individual may be able to rise to high stations in life and society.

The play's events occur in and around Ujjayini, a city of great importance in ancient India and one of the seven holy cities of the Hindus. Known to the ancient Hellenic geographer and astronomer Ptolemy (second century C.E.) as Ozene, it has been identified by archaeologists as the capital of the semi-legendary kingdom of Avanti (ca. fifth century B.C.E.). Ujjayini was located close to the geographic center of the Indian subcontinent, and Buddhist chronicles call it one of the greatest seats of Sanskrit learning. On the evidence of *The Little Clay Cart*, it appears to have been a culturally diverse city, populated by professionals from all walks of life, with its social relationships and interactions defined by the caste system.

Castes were (and in contemporary India continue to be) an important hereditary mode of determining an individual's social station, tied to occupation and social class. There are four main castes: Brahmins, the most learned, who are usually priests and teachers; Khshatriyas, the warriors and rulers of the nobility; Vaishyas, the traders, merchants, and farmers; and Shudras, peasants and manual laborers. Within these four divisions are many subgroups, which depend on geographic areas, ethnicity, and so on. Intermarriage between castes is usually not permissible, although exceptions are possible, especially among the higher orders.

The Little Clay Cart borrows from an earlier play by the celebrated Bhasa titled *Charudatta,* the name of its male protagonist; that work survives only as a four-act fragment. However, unlike Bhasa and most other Sanskrit dramatists, Shudraka populates his play not with gods, goddesses, and demigods, or even characters culled out of legends, but with real-life people of flesh and blood. Its central plot concerns the thwarted love between Charudatta, a sad and recently impoverished Brahmin merchant, and Vasantasena, a courtesan who, abandoning her professional indifference, has fallen in love. Their path to union is not easy, especially since Vasantasena has also drawn the attention of the villainous Samsthanaka, brother-in-law of the king, who tries everything (from threats and false accusations to attempted murder) to keep the two lovers apart. In the background of this tortuous plot of frustrated love is the subplot of a political coup d'état in which Aryaka, a revolutionary leader, deposes a corrupt king; as tyranny gives way to a more democratic and socially enlightened state, events ultimately dovetail with the main plot to facilitate the lovers' union. As a result, The Little Clay Cart is not merely a love story or a simple parable of good winning over evil; Shudraka's narrative adds to a romantic tale the excitement of political intrigue. Its artful merger of several layers of narrative makes The Little Clay Cart a masterpiece of world as well as Sanskrit drama.

The play opens with a prologue, an important feature of Sanskrit theater. After an invocation to Shiva—the destroyer-god, the god of Time, and one of the Hindu "Great Trinity" of gods—the Sutradhara comes forward to talk to the audience and introduce the play. The word sutra (pronounced "sootra") in Sanskrit literally means "thread" (and is etymologically related to the Latin sutura, meaning "a sewing together," "a seam"); dhara (pronounced "dhaara") means "the one who holds." Standing both inside and outside the play, therefore, the Sutradhara acts as the thread that holds the play together. In The Little Clay Cart the Sutradhara, a poor Brahmin, sings the praises of the playwright, introduces the plot of the play, and is approached by his wife, one of the actresses. They talk about his hunger and her fast, which must be blessed by another Brahmin. The Sutradhara sets off to find him—and he is none other than Maitreya, another hungry Brahmin and a major character in the play. Thereafter all references to the prologue cease, and the play is officially launched.

As the poverty of these Brahmins makes clear, the image of the Indian caste system presented in Shudraka's play is of a fluid social structure, with movement between strata possible (though not always easy). It reflects how real status was determined by the economic advantages and privileges of a person and her or his family. In fact, one of the persistent themes in The Little Clay Cart is that those in any station of life can change their fate by means of their deeds. The examples are many: Charudatta, the hero of the play, continues to behave as a noble Brahmin (of the highest caste), despite his extreme impoverishment. Aryaka, son of the deposed King Gopala, returns to the throne. A dejected gambler finds freedom by piously following the path of the Buddha. Another impoverished Brahmin, Sharvilaka, driven to burglary by economic hardship, is able to rescue his lover, Madanika, from the bondage of slavery and to resume a righteous life. And finally, Vasantasena, the courtesan, through her love for and dedication to Charudatta, transcends her lowly social status and becomes one of his wives.

Vasantasena's case is particularly interesting. Unlike the prostitutes of today, the courtesans of ancient India were expected to be highly educated and trained in the fine arts. They therefore enjoyed respect and some status for their learning, even as they were held in contempt for providing sexual services. This ambiguous position put courtesans both outside and inside the caste system. However, if accepted by honorable members of one of the higher castes, they could leave the life of a public woman and have their own private homes. The Little Clay Cart helps us understand that in Shudraka's Ujjayini, it was possible for a courtesan not just to change her caste but to climb to the top of the caste ladder—marry a Brahmin and earn the right to live harmoniously with his original wife.

The Little Clay Cart is a play in ten acts; performed uncut, it could easily run for more than four or five hours—perhaps an inordinate length by modern standards, but normal for Sanskrit drama. The Natyasastra, a Sanskrit treatise on theater and dance ascribed to Bharata Muni (probably composed in the third century B.C.E. though the earliest manuscript dates only to the seventh or eighth century C.E.), strongly recommends that a full-length play must be at least ten acts for its complete and

Cristofer Jean plays Charudatta and Miriam A. Laube plays Vasantasena in the 2008 Oregon Shakespeare Festival production of *The Little Clay Cart*, directed by Bill Rauch.

satisfactory development. Within those acts there are distinct scenes, but Indian dramatists, unlike their classical European counterparts, made no effort to mark them out separately. In fact, the proper staging of these run-on scenes has long puzzled translators and scholars. They often seem to suggest actions occurring at the same time but in different places, reminiscent both of cinematic montage and of SHAKESPEARE's scene divisions. The original audiences must have swiftly shifted their focus between the distinct but continuous performance areas of the classical Indian stage. While scholars have offered intriguing proposals about how individual scenes might have been staged, these are merely guesswork; we should trust directors to find their own innovative ways to stage the dramas.

In the *Dasharupa*, a tenth-century treatise, the influential Sanskrit scholar Dhananjaya ranks ten kinds of plays. The highest form—the *nataka*—deals with royal heroes and heroines, gods and goddesses, or incarnations of the divine. Protagonists of plays in the second category, the *prakarana*, need not be royals, but they must still be noble in character and ethically strong, in a plot drawn from the imagination of the poet, not necessarily from myths or history. *The Little Clay Cart* perfectly represents this genre.

According to Dhananjaya, a playwright must name the play after its main character or characters, and most Sanskrit dramatists comply. But in breaking this rule, the author of *The Little Clay Cart* underscores the play's unity despite its exceedingly complicated plot, meandering through ten dense acts. The title is taken from act 6, in which Charudatta's little son, Rohasena, weeps because the boy next door can play with a golden cart while he has only a little clay cart—a symbol of his family's dire situation. Vasantasena, moved by the sight, stuffs the cart with pearls. Thus, a little boy's toy comes to bear the play's main philosophical and thematic question: what is true wealth, and where can it be found? Throughout the entire play, Shudraka points toward the same answer: in simplicity, honesty, sincerity, and unwavering dedication to the path of truth.

The Little Clay Cart, like most Sanskrit plays, weaves numerous languages into its dialogue. At the time these plays were being written, Sanskrit had fallen out of common use in daily speech; instead, it was largely reserved to signify formality and dignity both in the court and in literary creations. As a result, most "Sanskrit" plays combine Sanskrit (used mostly by the protagonists, who tend to speak in verse) and several dialects derived from Sanskrit. *The Little Clay Cart* surpasses all other Sanskrit dramas in its use of linguistic diversity to delineate characters and their social standing. The dialogue arguably employs as many as seven dialects or forms of the Prakrit, or vernacular (literally, the "natural" or "normal"), depending on the speaker. Charudatta always speaks Sanskrit, unless (as rarely happens) he addresses those who do not understand formal Sanskrit. The other characters all speak some variety of the Prakrit. Scholars have praised Shudraka's grasp of social detail and his knowledge of the languages then spoken by Ujjayini's multiethnic populace.

The text of *The Little Clay Cart* alternates between verse and prose, according to the occasion. In general, all characters—especially those who speak Sanskrit—switch to poetry whenever it is arguably appropriate, whether to voice an appreciation of beauty, to make a philosophic observation on life, or to express emotion in moments of utter despair. This is the general practice in all Sanskrit drama, in which the skill of the individual dramatist is revealed in the kind of poetry assigned to each character. Shudraka is masterful, creating characters whose linguistic worlds are consistent and well-defined. Charudatta's poetry is always highly romantic, representing the very best of Sanskrit versification and imagery, with Vasantasena's a close second; Samsthanaka's poetry is coarse and inappropriate; and Maitreya's poetry, epigrammatic at best, is usually misapplied for comic effect.

To fully appreciate Shudraka's achievement in *The Little Clay Cart*, it is important to have some understanding of Sanskrit aesthetics. Unlike much of Western drama, which seeks (in the words of Shakespeare's *Hamlet*) to hold "the mirror up to nature," Sanskrit drama is metaphorical rather than imitative, pointing toward reality by means of artistic representation. This notion of drama as an analogy to life is grounded in the rasa theory, as defined in Bharata's

NEIGHBORHOOD PLAYBILL

A Leaflet Issued with Each New Production at the Neighborhood Playhouse—Season 1924-5 No. 2

First Play of the Eleventh Season 1924-25
Opening Friday Evening, December 5th, 1924

THE LITTLE CLAY CART
A Hindu Drama

ATTRIBUTED TO KING SHUDRAKA

Translated from the original Sanskrit by
Arthur William Ryder
Directed by Agnes Morgan and Irene Lewisohn
Settings and Costumes by Aline Bernstein

Detail from a Rajput Painting

Program from the 1924–25 Neighborhood Playhouse production of *The Little Clay Cart*.

Natyasastra. The word *rasa* literally means "sap," "essence," "flavor," or "taste": here it becomes an adjective, applied to the aesthetic experience that a performance generates. In Sanskrit theory there are eight rasas: *shringara* (erotic), *hasya* (comic), *karuna* (sorrowful), *raudra* (angry), *veera* (heroic), *bhayanaka* (fearful), *vibhatsa* (odious), and *adbhuta* (wondrous). *Shanta* (peace), added in the tenth century by Abhinavagupta, a Buddhist scholar, has since been universally accepted, raising the total number of rasas to nine. The rasa is produced by the interaction between forty-one emotional types or psychological states—the universal emotional characteristics, according to Indian philosophy—and the specific conditions of the stage and the play being performed. The rasa, in other words, signifies the point at which the spectators' expectations, the performers' skill in enacting the play text, and the actual performance meet. Bharata used a culinary analogy to explain this theory. The performers, performance, and audience are in the same relation as cook, food, and diners. And just as at the end of a banquet only the utensils and crumbs remain, so a drama leaves behind only the rasa or taste—in effect, the memory of the performance.

Even a cursory exploration of *The Little Clay Cart* reveals that, like a sumptuous meal offering a range of tastes, it is capable of generating a wide variety of rasas. The *shringara* (erotic) rasa dominates the play, especially in the love scenes between Charudatta and Vasantasena, whereas the *hasya* (comic) is invariably ascendant in the scenes featuring Maitreya. *Hasya* combines with the *bhayanaka* (fearful) and *vibhatsa* (odious) when Samsthanaka and his foolish, sadistic humor are on stage, while *karuna* (sorrowful) rules when we witness Charudatta's poverty and when we anticipate his execution in the final scene. *Raudra* (angry) and *veera* (heroic) combine in the characters of Aryaka and Sharvilaka when the play's political subplot comes to the fore. *The Little Clay Cart* also evokes these emotions in audiences and readers unfamiliar with the theory underlying such drama, however. For although the rasa system took shape within a specific culture, the rasas themselves are based on universal human emotions.

After its first English translation from the Sanskrit in 1826 by Horace Hayman Wilson, versions of *The Little Clay Cart* appeared in French, German, Italian, Dutch, and Russian. It was staged in Paris, in 1850 and 1895, and in Germany in 1892–93. In June 1907, the play arrived in the United States when students at the University of California at Berkeley mounted a production of *The Little Clay Cart* in their 7,000-seat Greek Theatre. In December 1924, the play was staged professionally at the Neighborhood Playhouse in New York City. Thereafter, the play has been performed in various venues in the United States and Europe, professional as well as educational. In India, *The Little Clay Cart* has been translated and produced in most of the subcontinent's regional languages. In 1984 it was even turned into a Bollywood film, renamed *Utsav* (*Festival*), under the direction of the well-known Indian playwright and actor Girish Karnad. The translation by Sudipto Chatterjee used in this anthology formed the basis of a 1991 off-off-Broadway production by the Greek director Vasilios Calitsis at New York's Ohio Theatre.

SUDIPTO CHATTERJEE

PRONUNCIATION GUIDE

It is hard to transliterate Sanskrit names into the Latin alphabet, particularly for English-language speakers, because Sanskrit uses a far wider range of sounds than English. For example, there are at least four kinds of *d* and five variations of *t*, as well as various forms of *n*, *l*, and *k*. And if differences between short and long vowels are not observed exactly, the intended meaning may not be conveyed. Following is a rough guide to pronouncing the important names in the play in order of appearance, showing the length of the vowels. The underlining marks the only syllables that are stressed. Syllable breaks are indicated by slashes. Names without underlined syllables must be pronounced with equal stress on each syllable. In other words, the usual practice of accentuation in English must be resisted.

NAME	PRONUNCIATION	NAME	PRONUNCIATION
Sutradhara	Soot/ra/dhaar/a	Aryaka	Aar/ya/ka
Charudatta	Chaa/ru/datt/a	Gopala	Go/paa/la
Vasantasena	Va/san/ta/se/naa	Palaka	Paa/la/ka
Maitreya	Mai/tre/ya	Rohasena	Ro/ha/se/na
Samsthanaka	Sams/thaa/na/ka	Dhuta	Dhoo/taa
Sthavaraka	Sthaa/va/ra/ka	Sharvilaka	Shar/vi/la/ka
Karnapuraka	Kar/na/poo/ra/ka	Mathura	Maa/thu/ra
Vardhamanaka	Var/dha/maa/na/ka	Darduraka	Dar/du/ra/ka
Kumbhilaka	Kum/bhee/la/ka	Chandanaka	Chan/da/na/ka
Radanika	Ra/da/ni/kaa	Bandhula	Ban/dhu/la
Madanika	Ma/da/ni/kaa	Ujjayini	U/jja/yi/nee
Viraka	Vee/ra/ka	Pushpakarandaka	Push/pa/ka/run/da/ka

The Little Clay Cart[1]

CHARACTERS

SUTRADHARA, in the role of the Director[2]
   AN ACTRESS
CHARUDATTA, a Brahmin,[3] impoverished
   heir of a merchant
MAITREYA, a Brahmin, Charudatta's
   friend
ROHASENA, Charudatta's young son
[DHUTA, Charudatta's wife][4]
RADANIKA, Charudatta's attendant slave
   girl
VARDHAMANAKA, slave and driver of
   Charudatta
SAMSTHANAKA, brother-in-law to King
   Palaka, suitor of Vasantasena
VITA,[5] a libertine and poet,
   Samsthanaka's attendant wit
VASANTASENA, a courtesan in love with
   Charudatta
[MADANIKA, Vasantasena's attendant
   slave girl]
VITA 2, a libertine and poet, Vasantasena's
   attendant wit
[VASANTASENA'S MOTHER]
[The BANDHULAS, male inmates in
   Vasantasena's house]

KUMBHILAKA, slave of Vasantasena
[KARNAPURAKA, slave of Vasantasena]
SLAVE GIRL of Vasantasena
ARYAKA, nephew to King Palaka and
   claimant to the throne
SHARVILAKA, a Brahmin-turned-burglar,
   Madanika's lover, Aryaka's chief
   follower
MONK/MASSEUR, a masseur turned
   gambler, later a Buddhist monk
   (bhikshu)
STHAVARAKA, slave and driver of
   Samsthanaka
SLAVE of Samsthanaka
[MATHURA, keeper of a gambling house]
[A GAMBLER, winner in a game with
   Masseur]
[DARDURAKA, an educated gambler]
CHANDANAKA, police captain, later
   Aryaka's follower
VIRAKA, police captain
Two GROUPS OF MEN
[JUDGE, highest court official]
[PROVOST, trade guild leader, second-
   rank court official]

---

1. Translated by Sudipto Chatterjee. The translator would like to acknowledge previous translators of the play—Arthur William Ryder, R. Pendleton Oliver, J. A. B. van Buitenen, P. Lal, A. L. Basham, and M. R. Kale, who rendered the work into English; Ramashankar Tripathi, into Hindi; and Jyotirindranath Tagore, Sukumari Bhattacharya, and Jyotibhushan Chaki, into Bengali—without whose pathbreaking scholarly forays the present translation would not have been possible. I am also indebted to Vasilios Calitsis for having invited me to translate the play in 1991, and to B. V. Karanth and Suresh Awasthi for their initial guidance.
2. In Sanskrit drama, the Sutradhara (or "thread holder") opens the play and sets its action in motion.

3. A member of the educated, priestly caste (or social class) in traditional Hindu society. In the caste system, Brahmins are at the top of the social hierarchy, followed by the warrior caste (Khshatriyas), whose members include kings and members of the nobility; the trader or merchant caste (Vaishyas); and the laborer caste (Shudras), whose members perform the most menial of jobs in society. Beneath the laborers, and outside the formal caste system, are the Untouchables (Harijans), whose ranks included the aboriginal inhabitants of India (disparagingly referred to as Chandalas) as well as religious and social outcasts.
4. Brackets indicate characters who do not appear in the acts included here.
5. A stock figure in Sanskrit drama (literally, "a dissolute man").

[RECORDER, recorder of court minutes, third-rank court official]
[BAILIFF, lowest-rank court official]
EXECUTIONER 1, Goha, a *chandala* (of the lowest, Untouchable caste)

EXECUTIONER 2, Ahanta, a *chandala* (also of the lowest, Untouchable caste)
A CROWD
VOICES OFFSTAGE

[SETTING: *In and around Ujjayini, an ancient city in central India.*]

The Prologue

INVOCATION

May Shiva's meditation to Brahma[6] protect you,
When coiling up the snake that covers his knees
He folds his legs in the *paryanka* posture[7]—
May Shiva's meditation support you,
5   When he has held his breath so that all the senses
Stop working and awareness is suspended—
May Shiva's meditation protect you,
When with the eye of Truth within himself, he,
Free from all acts, sees the self within himself—
10   May Shiva's meditation seeing through
The Void, sunk in the Supreme Soul, support you!

And,

May the throat of the blue-throated[8] Shiva—
Upon which, dark as a thundercloud, flash the lightning-like
15   Vine-like arms of Gauri[9]—protect you!

[*Enter* SUTRADHARA.]

SUTRADHARA   No more of this tiresome wordiness. Waste of time! It only tries
the patience of our audience. I salute you gentlemen and beg to announce
that we have decided to present before this learned assembly a play with
human heroes and heroines by the name *The Little Clay Cart*. It was written
20   by the renowned King Shudraka—a leader of the Brahmins, celebrated poet,
and a man of profound character.[1] He was a paragon of theologians as well as
a great ascetic; valiant in war that could take on the elephants of his enemies
with his bare arms, yet was endowed with great prudence. His eyes were like

6. One of the three avatars, or personifications of God (Ishvara) in Hinduism. Shiva, who is both destroyer and creator, is worshipped as the Supreme God; Brahma is the creator of the universe; and Vishnu is the preserver of all being. The invocation (spoken by the Sutradhara) invokes Shiva as the source of protection for the unhindered performance of the play.
7. Seated yoga position in which Shiva is gen-
erally represented, meditating; the upper body is erect and the legs are crossed with each foot resting on the opposite thigh.
8. In Sanskrit *Neelkantha*, a common epithet of Shiva (usually depicted with a blue band around his neck).
9. Another name for Shiva's consort, Parvati.
1. Shudraka's historical existence cannot be verified.

those of the *chakora* bird.[2] He was blessed once by Shiva and returned from
blindness. He performed the horse-sacrifice to secure his empire and,
having seen his son ascend to the throne, he passed away at the ripe age
of one hundred years and ten days.

But to return to his play—in it you shall meet:

One poor merchant from Ujjayini, a young man
By name Charudatta, by caste Brahmin;
And, a courtesan, lovely as the spring, by name
Vasantasena: she feels love for him, he feels the same.

King Shudraka has shown here how their love progresses,
Then provokes against them a conspiracy, vile;
How crooks conduct themselves and justice defile
While Providence rules and Destiny disposes.

[*He walks around the stage*[3] *and glances around him.*]

But hey! Our stage is entirely empty! Where could the actors have all gone?
[*Thinks.*]

Ah! Of course!

"Empty is the house of a man without a son,
Empty the hours of a man whose friends are gone,
Empty to a fool the road beyond,
Empty to the poor the world around."

All right, enough of declamation! I have been talking so long my eyes are
popping like dry seeds in the summer sunshine, crackling from hunger. So
I'll call my wife and ask if there is any breakfast left. Hello!

[*Walks about the stage and looks around.*]

I am home now. Let's go inside.

["*Enters*" *house and looks around again.*]

What on earth is happening here? A river of starch-water flows down the
yard into the streets; the floor is covered with round black spots where the
metal pots were kept upside down. It looks like a girl's face with beauty
spots! Oh, I am getting terribly hungry now. Has someone uncovered hidden treasure in this house? I am starving to death! But everything here
seems so changed. That girl over there is making ointments; the other one
is stringing flower garlands.

[*Thinks.*]

Well, I'll have to call my lady and find out. Hello! Madam—will you come
out, please?

[*Enter the* ACTRESS.]

ACTRESS Here I am, sir. What are your orders?

SUTRADHARA Madam, my incessant speaking has left my body weak—as
tired as the dried stems of a withered lotus. Is there anything to eat? I am
ravenously . . .

---

2. A legendary partridge in Hindu mythology, which feeds on moonbeams.
3. In Sanskrit drama, a conventional indication of a journey.

60 ACTRESS   There are all kinds of things, sir.

SUTRADHARA   All kinds of things?

ACTRESS   Oh, yes. Sweetened rice or whole rice, fresh butter, ghee, and curds. In fact, dishes as tasty as the elixir of immortality!

SUTRADHARA   Everything? In our house? Are you joking?

65 ACTRESS   [to herself]   Of course I am joking! [aloud] Everything! Everything, sir . . . in the shops, that is.

SUTRADHARA   [angrily]   You whore! May your hopes be dashed as you have dashed mine! You threw me up in the air, like a bundle of hay, only to drop me down again!

70 ACTRESS   Forgive me, sir, please. I was only joking.

SUTRADHARA   Anyway, what are these special preparations for? The women with the ointment and garland and—

ACTRESS   I am starting a fast for a good husband.

SUTRADHARA   A good husband? In this life, or the next?

75 ACTRESS   In my next life, of course.

SUTRADHARA   [piqued]   Now look at this, noble gentlemen! I have to pay for the food so she will find herself a good husband again in her next life!

ACTRESS   Please, sir! Don't be angry with me. I am fasting so that in other lives I have no husband . . . other than you.

80 SUTRADHARA   Who suggested this fast?

ACTRESS   Your own great friend Churnavriddha.

SUTRADHARA   [addressing an imaginary Churnavriddha]   You son of a whore! I'll see to it that our King Palaka has you bound up like the braided tresses of a young bride.

85 ACTRESS   Please, be calm now! I observe this fast only to have you as my husband in my next lives.

[Throws herself at his feet.]

SUTRADHARA   There, there . . . get up now. But who is going to preside over this ceremony of yours?

ACTRESS   We must find a Brahmin whose station in life is close to ours.

90 SUTRADHARA   Very well. You can go back to your preparations, while I look for the Brahmin of our kind.

ACTRESS   Just as you say, sir. [Exit.]

SUTRADHARA   [pacing up and down]   Ujjayini is so rich! How can I, in this city, find a Brahmin of our class?

[Looks around and sees someone offstage.]

95 There's Charudatta's friend, Maitreya, coming! I'll ask him. Hello, Master— will you come and preside at a ceremony in my home?

[End of Prologue.]

Act 1

[Enter MAITREYA, a cloak over his arm.]

MAITREYA   "Ask another Brahmin, fellow, I'm busy today," that's what I told him. But nonetheless, Maitreya, the Brahmin has to accept invitations, even of strangers, if he has to eat at all. Ah, what a situation! Just compare. When Charudatta was rich I would sit at the gate of his big house, stuffing myself

5   with the delicacies his servants prepared day in, day out with meticulous care; sweets that smelled so good you could belch even from imagining the

taste! Aha—those were the days! I was surrounded by hundreds of little
dishes, like a painter among his color-bowls, from which I'd pick and toss. I
hogged away like a fat bull set free in the market place! And now, Charudatta

10   is poor and I have to wander around. If I have to return here, it is only for a
corner to sleep in, like a returning pigeon. [*Pause.*] This cloak . . . umh . . .
reeking of jasmine, is a gift for Charudatta. From his dear friend Churnavriddha. He told me to give it to him as soon as Charudatta was done
worshipping the gods. I must find him.

  [*Advances, looking around.*]

15   Ah, there he comes. Done with his worshipping, scattering offerings to the
house gods.

  [*Enter* CHARUDATTA, *as described, followed by* RADANIKA, *a maid.*]

CHARUDATTA [*raising his eyes to heaven, sighing hopelessly*]
  Once swans and cranes came swooping down in swarms
  To snatch from my doorstep the gifts I threw;
  And now, on weed-grown steps, a wretched few

20   Dry seeds lie ignored, waiting for worms . . .

  [*Very slowly he walks about the stage and sits.*]

MAITREYA   That is Charudatta. I'll join him. [*approaching* CHARUDATTA] Good
  day, sir, and good wishes!

CHARUDATTA   Ah, Maitreya, my friend of all times. Welcome. Sit down.

25   MAITREYA   Your wish, sir. [*Seats himself.*] Churnavriddha sends you this
  cloak—it is jasmine scented—as a gift and asks you to wear it after prayers.

  [*Hands it over.* CHARUDATTA *takes it but remains pensive.*]

  What are you thinking about? You look serious.

CHARUDATTA   Oh, my friend—
  Prosperity after bad luck is sheer joy,
  The light at the end of a dark night.

30   But the one who's poor after prosperity's joy
  Is the living dead of the darkest night.

MAITREYA   Come on now, friend, what would you really prefer—being poor
  or being dead?

CHARUDATTA   To choose between death and poverty?

35   I'd settle for death—painless brevity,
  To escape a "poor" life's longevity.

MAITREYA   Stop torturing yourself! The gods eat the nectar-light of the moon
  as it goes into eclipse, but it collects itself again and is soon back in full
  shine. Your loss has its brighter side too.

40   CHARUDATTA   No, I do not mourn for my lost riches—
  What hurts me is that guests leave, go by
  My house because my wealth is gone,
  Like bees after the mating season, that shun
  The elephant whose forehead is dry.[4]

45   MAITREYA   Greedy sons of bitches! That's what they are! They ate on your
  money and now, like cowherd boys that are scared of wasps and poisonous
  weeds, they look for fresh pastures.

CHARUDATTA   Fortune shines and fades with the wheel of Destiny,

---

4. In the aggressive state known as *musth,* associated with rutting, male elephants secrete a tarlike fluid
from glands in their temples; it is said to attract insects, including bees.

But friends desert a rich man who's fallen to poverty.
50   And more than that—
    Poverty reduces a man to total shame,
    Like losing his dignity (all the same).
    Without his dignity he is prey to scorn;
    Once scorned he must despair (being forlorn);
55   Disconsolate, he is put to much grief;
    The grief's so much, good sense takes its leave.
    Thus out of mind he is wrecked and feeble.
    Thus poverty brings on all evil.

MAITREYA   Cut that out! You know, money, after all, is only a trifle. So dump
60   your sorrows and be cheerful.

CHARUDATTA   Poverty is the wellspring, the source of all kinds of sorrow.
    He who's a friend (even wife or kin) will be your enemy tomorrow.
    Till the day you decide to leave, depart for the wilderness,
    That scorching flame in the heart will give you no recess.
65   Oh, it's the pain that never, never leads to death,
    The sorrow that tortures with every drawing breath.

Well, I am done with my offerings. Why don't *you* go now to the Mother god-
    desses[5] at the crossroads and throw an offering?

MAITREYA   Definitely not!

70 CHARUDATTA   May I know why?

MAITREYA   Worshipping the gods makes no sense; they don't help you anyway.

CHARUDATTA   That is no way to talk! It's a time-honored rule—
    The pious-at-heart who worship the gods
    (With humility, calm and sincerity)
75   Win divine blessings against all odds!

So . . . come on, go.

MAITREYA   No, I am not going. Ask someone else. And anyway, for a Brahmin
    everything happens in reverse: the left for the right and the right for the
    left, like in a mirror; the bad for the good and the good for the worst and so
80   on. . . . Besides, the royal highway at this late hour is infested with courte-
    sans, slaves, and many of the king's men. I'll be as vulnerable as a mouse
    running straight into a cobra hunting for frogs!

CHARUDATTA   All right, then. Stay. I shall go ahead with my meditation.

    [*On another part of the stage.*]

VOICES OFFSTAGE   Stop, Vasantasena, stop!

    [*Enter* VASANTASENA *on another part of the stage, pursued by the* VITA,
    SAMSTHANAKA, *and a* SLAVE.]

85 VITA   Vasantasena, stop! Stop at once!
    Don't let your elegance be spoilt by fear,
    Those feet are dancing feet—look where they go!
    And those seductive eyes—fright hurts them so!
    Why run as if chased by hunters—like a scared deer?

90 SAMSTHANAKA   Dear little Vasantasena, stop now!
    Where are you going, running, rushing, tripping?
    Stop, little morsel, please—you are not dying!

5. Representations of the anonymous divine Mothers who attend on Shiva. Offerings made at
crossroads were believed to be particularly effective.

Oh, my poor heart's on fire with love, and dripping
Like a fat chunk of meat on glowing coal—it's frying.

95 SLAVE   Madam—stop!
Why fly, all terrified? What? Are you a scared peahen
As she flashes her plumes in the summer, the colors of heaven?
As for my master? Look! How mightily, like a brave little pup,
He gallops, as though in a forest, bounding down and up!

100 VITA   Stop! Vasantasena! Stop!
Why, trembling like a slim banana tree,
Your red skirt flying in the breeze, do you flee?
Red lotus petals fall off your garland here and yonder;
And you're even redder than your cosmetic realgar powder![6]

105 SAMSTHANAKA   Vasantasena, stop at once!
You raised my love to frenzy, my passion you fed,
And drove sleep away from my nocturnal bed.
And though you flee, in fear you cower:
For I am Ravana, you are Kunti,[7] to be imprisoned by my power!

110 VITA   Vasantasena!
How come your paces outstrip mine, how come you fly
As from the King of Birds[8] the serpent shies?
You know I could run up a storm and pass it by,
But I don't—so on your rear I can feast my eyes!

115 SAMSTHANAKA   Vita! did you listen how I prayed to her? I called her by ten
names: Whip of Love Who Robs My Bucks, Woman Always in Heat, Dancing Whore, Unnosed Harlot, Breaker of Families, Fallen Woman, Treasure
Box of Lust, Brothel Hostess, Brothel Haunter, Brothel Huntress, and
Brothel Boarder. Ten names! And still she doesn't want me!

120 VITA   You are like a lute that the likes of me could play;
Why then in such terror do you run in disarray—
Hurting, scraping your cheeks as those earrings swing?
You tremble like a crane that's heard the thunder ring.

SAMSTHANAKA   Like the running Draupadi pursued by great Rama[9]
125   You run, your ornaments jingling in that trauma.
But soon I shall get you like Hanuman the brave
Got Subhadra,[1] the woman he craved.

SLAVE   Accept my master, the king's favorite; he's tender like loin meat.
And, in any case, dogs that are fed, why would they hunt to eat?

130 VITA   My dear Vasantasena—
Why must you run, clutching up the girdle that slips,
That glitters like stars and jingles in tune, down your hips?

---

6. Rouge made from a red-orange mineral
(arsenic sulfide).
7. Here and throughout the play, Samsthanaka
alludes erroneously to characters in the *Mahabharata* and the *Ramayana*, India's two principal
religious epics. The tyrant Ravana, who is often
depicted with ten heads and is known for his
conquests of women, plays a central role in the
Ramayana; Kunti in the *Mahabharata* gave
birth to three of the five Pandava brothers
(including Arjuna, its main warrior).

8. That is, the Garudas, mythological birds
who hunted down the Nagas, a race of intelligent serpent- or dragonlike creatures.
9. The title character of the *Ramayana*. Draupadi: the main female character of the *Mahabharata*; she served as a wife to Arjuna and the
other four Pandava brothers.
1. Another of Arjuna's wives in the *Mahabharata*. Hanuman: the monkey god, a character in the *Ramayana*.

And look at your face: your rouge melting, trickling down,
Like the Guardian Goddess's[2] face under the solar frown!

135 SAMSTHANAKA   This is a chase in the forest: you the jackal, I the dog;
But you have stolen a love-laden heart, heavy as a log.

VASANTASENA   Pallavaka, Pallavaka! Parabhritika, Parabhritika!

SAMSTHANAKA   Vita! A man! She's called for a man!

VITA   There is nothing to fear—

140 VASANTASENA   Malavika, Malavika!

VITA   —she's only looking for her attendants, you . . . er . . . simpleton!

SAMSTHANAKA   Vita! Is she calling a woman?

VITA   Yes, of course!

SAMSTHANAKA   Ah! Only a woman! I can kill a hundred of them. Am I not a
145   hero?

VASANTASENA [finding herself deserted]   O God! My servants have all run away!
Now if I have to escape it'll have to be on my own.

VITA   Go! Look for her now. Careful!

SAMSTHANAKA   Scream away, Vasantasena! Scream for your pallava flower
150   and your maadhavika[3] creeper! They can't help you. Scream for the whole
month of . . . er . . . vasanta, the season of Spring, Vasantasena! No one
can save you.
    What of Bhima, what of Rama-with-the-Hatchet.[4]
    Who cares about Arjuna or ten-faced Ravana?
155   My ideal model is the great Duhshasana.[5]
    Wherever you go with your flowing hair, I'll catch it!
And then you'll see what happens!
    Swish goes my sharp sword, whoosh goes your head;
    You're alive when you live, not when you're dead!
160   So give up this game, come running into my chest—
    Before you lose your head—that's where you'll rest.

VASANTASENA   Sir, I am only a woman!

SAMSTHANAKA   That's exactly why you aren't dead yet.

VASANTASENA [to herself]   Oh! His reassurance is terrifying!
165   [aloud] My lord, do you want my jewels? Is that what you want?

VITA   Oh no! God forbid such shameful crimes! Tell me: does it make sense
to uproot the very flowers that bedeck a lovely garden? Oh no, it's not the
jewels we're after!

VASANTASENA   Then what do you want?

170 SAMSTHANAKA   I want you to open your arms to me. Me—Samsthanaka! A
man—a man divine! Vasudeva, that is, Krishna himself.[6]

VASANTASENA [angrily]   Shantam! You have come too far! [to herself] Barbarian!

---

2. Perhaps the goddess protecting Ujjayini; in
central India's hot summers, the paint on her
statue might run.
3. A creeping vine. Pallava: lotus bud, often
depicted at the feet of the god Krishna.
4. Parashurama, the sixth incarnation of the
god Vishnu, who received his hatchet from
Shiva after learning the art of warfare from
him. Bhima: another of the Pandava brothers
in the Mahabharata and a warrior of great
strength.

5. One of the villains of the Mahabharata; he
attempted to disrobe Draupadi and rape her in
public but was prevented when the god
Krishna made the sari she was wearing infinitely long.
6. In Indian mythology, Vasudeva is the biological father of Krishna. Although Krishna is
sometimes referred to by his father's
name, this is most likely another erroneous
allusion.

SAMSTHANAKA [*laughing and clapping his hands*] Vita! did you hear that? In
a second, the girl has fallen for me! Heard what she said? "*Shrantam!*" She
175 thinks I am tired! "You have come *so far!*"—she says. But, believe me, pretty
little chick, I didn't leave my town to come here! No, no, I swear—by the
head of my Vita and by my own sore feet—it is just this chase for you that
fatigues me. That's all!

VITA [*to himself*] Ugh, the fool! She said *shantam*—"quiet!" And he heard
180 *shrantam*—"tired!" [*Aloud*] Come, come Vasantasena—your words don't
become your profession! Didn't you know—

A courtesan's home is a home for anyone, an abode
For every man; a flower that blossoms by the road!
Your body, your caresses are wares to be bought by gold,
185 So be available, sell to all, for pleasure-displeasure untold.

Right? And also—

The streams—bathe both the Brahmin and the lowest caste.
The blooming vine—a perch for both peacock and crow.
The boat—carries all castes, the high along with the low.
190 So the courtesan—caters to all, the first as well as the last!

VASANTASENA But it is only goodness that inspires love.

SAMSTHANAKA Vita! Vita! This . . . this slave-girl itches for that penniless
Charudatta ever since they met in the gardens of the Kama-temple.[7] That's
why she doesn't want me. Charudatta's house, by the way, is just over there
195 to the left, so be careful—don't let her slip through our fingers!

VITA [*to himself*] This fool always blurts out what he should hide. So . . .
Vasantasena is in love with the noble Charudatta! Yes, there's wisdom in
the proverb: "Pearls go with pearls!" Let her go, I'll say. I've had enough of
this idiot! [*Aloud*] Charudatta's house, is it there over to the left? Is that
200 what you said?

SAMSTHANAKA That's just what I said. There, to the left.

VASANTASENA [*to herself*] What? Charudatta's house, and I am right beside it?
The scoundrel, in trying to hurt me, has arranged a meeting with my love!

SAMSTHANAKA Vita! Eh, Vita! The night is dark indeed. I can't see clearly.
205 Just now I saw Vasantasena, and now I don't. She vanished like an ink-drop
in a bowl of black beans.

VITA It *is* very dark tonight—

Powerful eyes, wide open, straining in the dark,
Are sealed now with blindness; the night's made its mark.
210 True!

Liquid darkness anoints my arms, like black mascara raining down the sky.
Trying to see in this dark is like helping an ingrate, who'll everything deny.

SAMSTHANAKA Vita! Where did Vasantasena go?

VITA Do you see any sign of her?

215 SAMSTHANAKA What sign, Vita?

VITA Any sign—like the jingling of her ornaments, or, the scent of her
garland mixed with the perfume she's wearing?

SAMSTHANAKA Yes, yes! I can clearly hear her scent, but I really can't see her
ornaments jingle. My nose, you see, is stuffed with the darkness.

220 VITA [*aside*] Vasantasena!

7. A meeting place for lovers (Kamadeva is the Hindu god of love).

The night hides you like clouds that envelop the lightning's streak;
Cover your ornaments, for they will ring! Beware, your fragrance reeks!
Do you hear me, Vasantasena?

VASANTASENA [to herself]   Yes, yes I hear you. I'll take your advice.

[She mimes taking off her ornaments, takes off her garland and gropes in the "dark."]

225   I am feeling my way along the wall. . . . Yes, this must be the side door. But it is locked!

[On another part of the stage.]

CHARUDATTA   Maitreya, I am done with my meditation. So go now to the Mother goddesses and throw your offerings.

MAITREYA   I won't. I told you already.

230 CHARUDATTA   Ah!

When a man becomes poor his kin cease to obey;
His relatives, the best of his friends turn away.
Bad luck grows on him, his character loses its crown;
His honor wanes, like the moon as it goes down!

235   Maitreya—

The crimes of others will be upon you blamed;
None will ever consort with you; you'll be ashamed.

Moreover—

None will seek your company, no consideration to show;

240   Your poor attire, at a rich man's banquet, will bring you below
Your dignity. You'll do everything to avoid the public censure.
I've learnt that poverty is a deadly sin they forgot to measure.

So—

I pity you, Poverty. Where will you go, when I

245   Your indulgent, hospitable host, shall die?

MAITREYA [uneasily]   All right, all right! I'll go, since you insist. But do let Radanika come with me.

CHARUDATTA   Radanika, go with Maitreya.

RADANIKA   As you please, sir.

250 MAITREYA   Here, hold the offering and the lamp, Radanika. I'll open the side door.

[He does so.]

VASANTASENA   Look! The door has opened—as though to welcome me. I must go right in.

[She looks.]

Watch out! A lamp!

[She blows out RADANIKA's lamp by a wave of her dress and "enters."]

255 CHARUDATTA   Maitreya, what was that?

MAITREYA   As I opened the door, a gust of wind came and blew out the lamp. Radanika, dear, go out the door. Let me run in to light the lamp again. I'll be right back.

[Exits.]

[Across the stage.]

SAMSTHANAKA   Vita! I am still looking for Vasantasena.

260   VITA   Keep up the good work. Go ahead.

SAMSTHANAKA [doing so]   Vita! I've caught her! I've caught her!

VITA   It's me, you fool!

SAMSTHANAKA   Get out my way then—and stay out!

> [Searches again and grabs hold of the SLAVE.]

This time I've got her, Vita! It's her!

265   SLAVE   My lord, it's me, your slave!

SAMSTHANAKA   Vita, stay where you are! Slave, you stay where you are! So: here's the Vita and here's the Slave; here's the Slave and here's the Vita. Now, both of you—stay out of my way!

> [Searches again and this time grabs RADANIKA by her hair.]

Vita! This time I've really gotten her! I've got Vasantasena!

270   Although it is pitch dark, I worked through it.
    She was doing fine, but the scent of her garland blew it.
    And now I hold her by the hair, in strong custody,
    As Chanakya[8] once chased and caught Draupadi.

VITA   Ah, how you could have won the heart of a highborn youth,

275   With your charms and guiles, your flower-bedecked hair to boot.
    But alas! What a nasty end: that very hair has led to your loot.

SAMSTHANAKA   Shriek, scream, weep, and call; no God will come to your aid!
    I've got you by your hair, your tresses, your great long braid.

RADANIKA   Sirs, what are you up to?

280   VITA   This is not her voice, you bastard![9]

SAMSTHANAKA   Vita—this slave-girl has changed her voice! Just like a cat when it begs for milk.

VITA   What? A vocal transformation? But, of course, this is no surprise. These courtesans are trained actors, dancers, well versed in disguise.

> [Enter MAITREYA.]

285   MAITREYA   Look at this lamp! The flame's flickering in the evening breeze. It's trembling like the heart of a goat being dragged to the sacrifice.

> [Advancing, he finds RADANIKA.]

Here I am, Radanika!

SAMSTHANAKA   Vita! A man, a man!

MAITREYA   What? This is not right! Not right! Charudatta is poor; that doesn't

290   give you the right to just walk into his house.

RADANIKA   Master Maitreya, see how they are mistreating me!

MAITREYA   Just you? Both of us, I should say!

RADANIKA   You too?

MAITREYA   Of course! We are being assaulted!

295   RADANIKA   Exactly.

MAITREYA   Truly?

RADANIKA   Truly!

---

8. A historical figure instrumental in the founding of the Maurya Empire (322 B.C.E.) and author of the well-known political treatise *Arthashastra*; Samsthanaka means to say Duhshasana, not Chanakya.

9. The Sanskrit word used here, an insulting term for an unmarried woman with children, may also have been an honorific, which would explain why Samsthanaka doesn't take offense.

MAITREYA [*raising his stick in anger*]   Enough of this! Even a dog is a king in
his kennel—and I am a Brahmin! With this stick—as crooked as the fate
300   of people like me—I'll crack the head of this scoundrel. Like dry bamboo!
VITA   O great Brahmin, forgive us!
MAITREYA [*taking a good look at the* VITA]   No, you don't seem to be the culprit.
[*Studies* SAMSTHANAKA.]

That's him! That's the crook! Good God, it's Samsthanaka, the king's
brother-in-law—a beast! Is this how you behave? It may be that Charudatta
305   is a poor man now, but his virtues still make him the "Jewel of Ujjayini."
And you break into his house? You dare to lay your hands on his servants?
Hear this: never insult a man for poverty, for—
      A poor man's rich in his spirit, though poor in terms of opulence;
      A rich man has riches, but virtueless, he's poor before Providence!
310 VITA   Good Brahmin, please pardon us. We didn't mean to insult you. It is an
accident; we mistook you and your maid here for someone else.
      We chased a woman here, propelled by desire—
MAITREYA   This one?
VITA   No! Heaven forbid!
315   An unchaste dame, who nevertheless, set our hearts on fire.
      We lost her in the darkness; she vanished into thin air.
      And thus mistaken we took *her* instead—a very sordid affair.
      And to prove my apology—
      [*Casts away his sword, falls on his knees, raising clasped hands.*]
320 MAITREYA   You are an honest man. Get up, get up! I treated you badly because
I didn't know better. My apologies.
VITA   For what? It's we who owe you apologies! I shall get up on one condition.
MAITREYA   And what is that?
VITA   You won't mention this to the noble Charudatta.
MAITREYA   All right, I won't.
325 VITA   With respect, sir, do I acknowledge your magnanimity.
      Your virtue's humbled our swords. We'll part in amity.
      [*Moves away with* SAMSTHANAKA.]
SAMSTHANAKA [*annoyed*]   Vita, why did you humiliate yourself before that
clown?
VITA   Simple: I am scared.
330 SAMSTHANAKA   Scared? Scared of what?
VITA   Of Charudatta's virtues.
SAMSTHANAKA   What virtues? A man who doesn't even feed his guests—what
virtues does he have?
VITA   That is no way to talk!
335   The man was wrecked by keeping men like me.
      He never used his wealth to hurt anybody:
      Wealth to him was like a well in summer, full at first
      But dried at the end by quenching everyone's thirst.
SAMSTHANAKA   Son-of-a-slave! Who in the world does he think he is?
340   A great brave hero? Shvetaketu the Pandava?
      Or Ravana, Radha's son that Indra begot?
      A son of Kunti, the father being Rama?

Jatayu, Ashvatthaman, the whole of that lot?[1]

VITA   Are you crazy? I am speaking of the noble Charudatta, who is

345   The All-Giving Tree,[2] bent from the weight of its virtuous fruits.

Mirror to the learned, protector of the good against brutes,

A touchstone of honor, an ocean of the rivers of integrity,

Manly and righteous, a benefactor without a shade of vanity;

Courteous and noble, he practices all the virtues we revere.

350   Compared to him men merely breathe.—Well, let's get out of here.

SAMSTHANAKA   Without our prize? Without Vasantasena?

VITA   She has vanished.

SAMSTHANAKA   How?

VITA   Gone! Like the health of the sick, mind of the mad, sight of the blind,

355   Success of the lazy, or wisdom of the slow-witted (lecherously inclined).

Having seen you she vanished, like Love, when an enemy it finds.

SAMSTHANAKA   I won't move until we've caught her.

VITA   Have you never heard that

For a horse you need a bridle, for an elephant a post;

360   For a woman a loving heart, else the cause is lost?

SAMSTHANAKA   Go, if you want to. I am not going.

VITA   All right. I'll go then.

      [*Exits.*]

SAMSTHANAKA   Well, the Vita vanishes! [*to* MAITREYA] You! Bald-headed rogue! Sit down! Hit bottom!

365 MAITREYA   I have already hit bottom.

SAMSTHANAKA   Who made you do so?

MAITREYA   Fate.

SAMSTHANAKA   Then stand up.

MAITREYA   We all shall.

370 SAMSTHANAKA   When?

MAITREYA   When we are back in favor with Fate.

SAMSTHANAKA   Cry then!

MAITREYA   I have done my bit of crying.

SAMSTHANAKA   Who made you cry?

375 MAITREYA   Poverty.

SAMSTHANAKA   All right. Then laugh!

MAITREYA   We shall, at some point.

SAMSTHANAKA   When?

MAITREYA   When the noble Charudatta is rich again.

380 SAMSTHANAKA   Well, villainous Brahmin, go tell that beggar in my name that a courtesan called Vasantasena—decked with gold like an actress on opening night—has escaped into his house while I was courting her . . .

---

1. Samsthanaka again connects incongruous figures. Shvetaketu, a character in the Chandogya Upanishad, one of India's most ancient philosophical tracts, has nothing to do with the Pandavas. Ravana was not the son of Indra, king of the Hindu gods (and god of war), and Radha, fabled lover of Krishna. Kunti and Rama, who appear in different epics, had no children. In the *Ramayana* Jatayu, a demigod in the shape of an eagle, is slain by Ravana as he attempts to save Sita from being kidnapped. The warrior Asvathaman, because he killed all the children of the Pandavas in their sleep, was cursed to live for three thousand years in a leper's rotting body.

2. The "wish-fulfilling tree" (*kalpataru*) of Hindu mythology.

somewhat forcefully. Since she and your friend met in the gardens of the
Kama-temple, she has been in love with him. If he hands her over to me
quickly, without my having to sue him first, I'll be his friend. If not . . .
well, he has an enemy till death. Please remind him:

> Certain things will never break—a pumpkin with its stalk in dung,
> number one;
> Dried vegetables; stewed meat; and a winter meal, after the setting of the
> sun.
> Add to the list two things more: Debt and Enmity, neither of which can
> be undone.

You will tell him in nice, easy, clear words—clear enough for me to hear
them while I am sitting in the dovecot on the roof of my palace. And if you
don't I'll crack your head, like the elephant nut[3] between door and doorstep! Got it?

MAITREYA   I'll tell him.

SAMSTHANAKA [*aside to* SLAVE]   Slave—has the Vita really left?

SLAVE   Yes, sir, he has.

SAMSTHANAKA   In that case, let's run off!

SLAVE   Master, you've forgotten your sword!

SAMSTHANAKA   You carry it.

SLAVE   But should not the master carry the sword?

SAMSTHANAKA   [*Takes it by the wrong end.*]

> Radish red, on my shoulder, the sword sleeps in its sheath.
> I rush, like a jackal among howling dogs, hard on retreat.

[*Circling the stage, exit* SAMSTHANAKA *and the* SLAVE.]

MAITREYA   Radanika, be careful. Never discuss this terrible incident with your
master. He has had enough sufferings already, there's no need for more.

RADANIKA   You know me, Master. I can hold my tongue.

MAITREYA   Very good.

[*Across the stage.*]

CHARUDATTA [*to* VASANTASENA]   Radanika, I think it's time you brought the
boy home. Rohsena likes playing in the wind, but the evening is quite cold.
So please bring him home. And here, wrap him up with this cloak.

[*Holds out the cloak for her.*]

VASANTASENA [*to herself*]   He thinks I am the maid!

[*Takes the cloak, sniffs the fragrance.*]

Umh . . . it's scented with jasmine. He doesn't seem to be indifferent to the
pleasures of youth!

[*Stealthily she wraps herself with the cloak.*]

CHARUDATTA   Go on, Radanika! Bring Rohsena and come back inside the house!

VASANTASENA [*to herself*]   It is inside your *heart* that I would like to go! If only
I could . . .

CHARUDATTA   Come on, Radanika! Even you won't answer me? Ha!

> When Fate turns you miserable with the pains of poverty,
> Friends turn into enemies, old servants demand liberty.

[MAITREYA *and* RADANIKA *approach.*]

---

3. The round seed of the *kapittha* (wood-apple) tree.

MAITREYA   Here's Radanika, my friend. You called for her?

420 CHARUDATTA   This is Radanika? Who is the other woman then?

Though it was unintended—a mere accident—

The woman is now impure, touched by my garment.

VASANTASENA [*to herself*]   No, she's been made pure by that touch!

CHARUDATTA   She's beautiful, even while the cloak surrounds her—

425 Like the moon with the autumnal clouds all around her.

But no, I mustn't! It is not proper to look upon another's wife.

MAITREYA   Well, you can stop accusing yourself of sins not committed! She is
Vasantasena, and she's been in love with you ever since you met her in the
garden of the Kama-temple.

430 CHARUDATTA   Vasantasena? [*to himself*]

I fell in love with her; but when one's wealth is dissolved,

Love becomes a coward's rage, left in the mind unresolved.

MAITREYA   Friend, the king's brother-in-law has left a message for you.

CHARUDATTA   What is it?

435 MAITREYA   Well, he says a courtesan called Vasantasena—decked in gold like
an actress on opening night—who has been in love with you, has escaped
into your house while he was courting her *somewhat forcefully.*

VASANTASENA [*to herself*]   "Somewhat forcefully." That's flattering!

MAITREYA   If you hand her over to him quickly, before he's prompted to sue

440 you, he'll be your friend—if not, an enemy till death.

CHARUDATTA [*with contempt*]   He is mad! [*to himself*] She is a woman to be
worshipped like a goddess!

When he asked her to go with him, she rejected the proposition,

Although she well knows Fortune has given him a high position

445 And wealth. She knows, too, how men in high society operate;

Even then she held herself, though he did much more than insinuate.

[*aloud*] My lady Vasantasena, I have insulted you, though unintentionally,
by treating you as my maid. I didn't recognize you. I bow my head to beg
your forgiveness.

450 VASANTASENA   But it is I, sir, who was wrong: I entered your house without
permission. I bow my head to seek your pardon.

MAITREYA   Great! Now you are both nicely bowing like two paddy fields
nodding to each other. Well, now I'll bow my head, as a camel bends its
knee, and most humbly suggest that both of you get up.

455 CHARUDATTA   Yes, indeed. Let's dispense with formalities.

VASANTASENA [*to herself*]   How cleverly and graciously proposed! But it would
not be right to spend the night here. Especially because of the way I got in.
Then I should say—this: [*aloud*] If sir, you will grant me a small favor,
please allow me to leave these, my jewels, with you. Those bandits were

460 after me because of them.

CHARUDATTA   This poor house does not deserve such trust.

VASANTASENA   You are mistaken, sir. It is hands one trusts, not houses.

CHARUDATTA   Maitreya, take the jewels.

VASANTASENA   I am favored!

[*Hands over her jewels.*]

465 MAITREYA [*accepting them*]   So very kind of you!

CHARUDATTA   You blockhead, it is for custody—

MAITREYA [*to himself*]   In that case, let the thieves come and get them.

CHARUDATTA   —only for a few days—

MAITREYA   The deposit becomes our property.

470 CHARUDATTA   —after which I shall return them.

VASANTASENA   Sir, I wish to go home. And, if you will, can the Brahmin escort me?

CHARUDATTA   Maitreya, escort the lady.

MAITREYA   You do it yourself. Beside her you'll look like a regal swan walking
475   its mate. But I am only a poor Brahmin. They'll tear me to pieces like dogs
   that eat the offerings at the crossroads.

CHARUDATTA   Very well. Then I myself will accompany you, my lady. We must
   have torches lighted, so we can walk the royal highway with assurance.

MAITREYA   Vardhamanaka! Light torches.

480 VARDHAMANAKA [*aside to* MAITREYA]   How am I to light torches without oil?

MAITREYA [*aside to* CHARUDATTA]   Our torches are like courtesans: they won't
   burn for penniless lovers.

CHARUDATTA   Very well, Maitreya. No torches then. Look—
   The moon shines like a torch with its cosmic-maids, shining
485   On the road as though it were the pale cheeks of a woman pining
   For love. Its soft rays are dripping on the crowding darkness,
   As though with its milky drops it would rid the land of its dryness.

   [*He accompanies* VASANTASENA, *as they walk about the stage.* MAITREYA
   follows them. They stop when they arrive at the doorstep of VASANTASENA'S
   house.]

CHARUDATTA [*with tenderness*]   My lady Vasantasena, here is your house. Do
   you wish to enter?

   [VASANTASENA *looks at him with longing as she "enters" the house and
   exits the stage.*]

490 CHARUDATTA   Friend, Vasantasena has gone, and we must return.
   The highway is deserted, only guardsmen make their rounds;
   Men must stay alert at this hour for, at night, evil abounds.

   [*They walk about.*]

   You shall guard the jewel casket by night, while Vardhamanaka looks after
   it during the day.

495 MAITREYA   As you wish.

   [*End of Act.*]

SUMMARY OF ACT 2

Vasantasena confesses to her handmaiden, Madanika, the love she feels for Charudatta.
While they talk, we are introduced to a masseur-turned-gambler who is being chased by
debtors: a funny scene ensues. The Masseur makes his escape into Vasantasena's
household; after the debtors find him there, Vasantasena comes to his rescue by paying
off his debt. Moved by her generosity, the Masseur decides to leave his sinful life to become a Buddhist monk. Shortly after the Masseur/Monk exits, a great commotion is
heard offstage, and Vasantasena's manservant, Karnapuraka, runs in excitedly to tell
his mistress how he has saved the same Masseur/Monk from being trampled by one of
Vasantasena's elephants. He also tells her that a mysterious unknown passerby rewarded
him by giving him his shawl. Vasantasena finds Charudatta's name embroidered on the
shawl, a discovery that fuels her attraction to Charudatta by making her respect him
even more.

SUMMARY OF ACT 3

In a comic interlude, Sharvilaka, a Brahmin-turned-burglar, describes the refined art of burglary and mimes for the audience digging a tunnel into a rich household. The household he has burrowed his way into is Charudatta's, and all he finds there is the jewel box left by Vasantasena in the first act. Charudatta, who has been sleeping, wakes up and discovers that his house has been broken into. He is sad at first that the thief wasted his efforts on digging into a household where there is nothing to steal, but then he discovers, to his dismay, that the jewels are gone. Charudatta feels ashamed that he has unwittingly betrayed Vasantasena's trust and fears that his poverty will now make him an object of suspicion. In a generous gesture, Charudatta's wife Dhuta decides to give away the last remaining valuable in the house—a precious pearl necklace, probably worth more than the stolen jewels—to Vasantasena as compensation for her loss. Dhuta asks Maitreya to deliver the necklace to Vasantasena.

SUMMARY OF ACT 4

In a scene within her house, Vasantasena further expresses to Madanika her love for Charudatta. Sharvilaka enters and the audience learns that in addition to being an expert thief, he is also Madanika's lover and wants to buy Madanika's freedom from slavery. Vasantasena, who has been eavesdropping on their conversation, reveals herself, accepts the jewel box, and sets Madanika free. Though delighted, Sharvilaka expresses his concern about his friend Aryaka, who has been imprisoned by King Palaka on charges of sedition. Determined to free Aryaka from his captivity, Sharvilaka leaves his newly emancipated bride-to-be. Maitreya arrives to give Vasantasena the pearl necklace in place of the jewel box. Vasantasena accepts the compensation and decides to visit Charudatta in the evening.

Act 5

[CHARUDATTA is discovered[4] seated and pensive.]

CHARUDATTA [looking at the sky] A thunderstorm—how untimely!
The house-peacocks spread their jeweled plumes.
They've seen the dark sky, heard the thunder booms.
The swans were set to fly, but overhead a storm looms
5   That to more yearning a lover's heart dooms!

The rain streaming down like melted silver—in lightning
Flashes revealed for a moment, then in the dark disappearing;
Like tattered, trailing fringes, torn off heaven's clothing!
[Pauses to think.] It has been some time since Maitreya went to
10   Vasantasena, and still no sign of him.
[Enter MAITREYA at another part of the stage.]

MAITREYA God! That whore is so greedy and stingy! She hardly said anything. Just grabbed the pearl-necklace, with utter disregard. She's stinking rich. Yet never, not for once, did she ask me: "Master Maitreya, rest awhile. Let me offer you some sweet beverage in this crystal goblet." I do not ever want to see
15   that slave girl of a whore's face again! [cynically] They're right, those who say—
A lotus without a root; a merchant who'll never quibble to cheat;
A goldsmith who doesn't steal; villagers who'll peacefully meet;

4. In classical Sanskrit theater, characters would most likely have been "discovered" at the opening of an act or scene behind a temporary, handheld curtain, removed with a dramatic flourish.

And a whore without greed—five things that are impossible feats!
Therefore, I'll find my good friend and stop him from having an affair with
20 this courtesan!

[MAITREYA *walks around and finds* CHARUDATTA.]

MAITREYA [*approaching*] May all be well with you! May fortune shine anew!
CHARUDATTA [*seeing him*] There you are, my friend Maitreya. You're back!
Welcome, my friend. Sit.
MAITREYA That I shall.
25 CHARUDATTA Now tell me—how did everything go?
MAITREYA Everything went wrong.
CHARUDATTA Wrong? She didn't accept the necklace?
MAITREYA Are we that lucky? No, she folded her delicate lotus-bud-like
hands, touched them on her forehead and . . . took it.
30 CHARUDATTA Then why did you say everything went wrong?
MAITREYA Is everything all right then? How can you say that? For that cheap
little jewel box, which we could neither eat nor drink, which was stolen by
a thief—you gave away a pearl necklace, the prize of all the four oceans!
CHARUDATTA No, my friend, that is not right.
35 For the faith with which she had left the box in our dependence,
This was but a small repayment, a meager recompense.
MAITREYA I have a second complaint, friend. She gestured to her maid and
hid her face behind her shawl—to make fun of me! And even though I am
a Brahmin, I bow my head before you. I implore you to stop going any
40 further with this dangerous affair with a courtesan.
A courtesan is like a pebble inside your shoe;
Trying to get rid of it will only hurt you.
And above all, my friend, I am sure you know:
Where a courtesan, an elephant, a scribe,
45 A monk, a swindler, and a donkey thrive,
Not even weeds will grow!
CHARUDATTA Friend, I see no point in your slanderous jabs. My present
situation itself is prevention enough! For see:
To run fast, the horse would like a galloping start,
50 But his feet will refuse him if his breath runs out.
So man's fleeting desires make his mind fly about,
But, disappointed, they all come back into the heart.
Moreover, my friend—
Women are yours if you are wealthy,
55 For money can buy them all.
[*to himself*] Virtue is no good at all!
[*aloud*] But wealth has now forsaken me,
So she won't heed my call.
MAITREYA [*to himself, looking down*] The way he's looking up and sighing
60 tells me that the more I tell him not to proceed with the courtesan, the
more anxious he's getting to go ahead with it. The proverb is quite right—
Love blinds you, it always leaves you reason-bereft;
Sparing the strong right, it gets you on the weak left.
[*aloud*] Well, friend—I must say this: she is coming here to visit you this
65 evening. She told me to tell you. I guess the necklace wasn't enough. She
wants to ask for more.

CHARUDATTA   Let her come, friend. She'll return satisfied.

[*Enter* KUMBHILAKA, *a slave, on another part of the stage.*]

KUMBHILAKA   Listen up everybody—

    The more the clouds are drizzling,
70   The more my back is dripping,
    The more the cold wind's ripping,
    The more my heart is trembling.
[*Laughs.*] The sweet flute of the seven holes I will blow,
    The lovely *veena* of the seven strings I will play,
75   I will sing just as beautifully as a donkey will bray,
    Neither Tumburu nor Sage Narada[5] can do it so!
My mistress Vasantasena said to me: "Kumbhilaka, go! Tell Master Charudatta that I am coming." So, off to Master Charudatta's house I go!

[*He walks around, sees* CHARUDATTA.]

There's Charudatta in his orchard! And with him that blockheaded Brah
80   min brat. I'll go up to him. What? The orchard gate is shut! I'll give that
rascal Brahmin a hint.

[*Throws a clod of clay.*]

MAITREYA   Who's throwing clods at me? On my head that's like a wood-apple
with a fence around it.

CHARUDATTA   Must be those pigeons playing there, on the roof of the
85   garden-house.

MAITREYA   You son-of-a-slave pigeon! Wait! Just wait till I've brought you
down from the roof to the ground with this stick of mine, like a ripe mango.

[*Starts to run with his stick raised.*]

CHARUDATTA [*pulling him back by his Brahmin's thread[6]*]   Sit down, friend.
What are you doing? Leave the poor pigeon alone with his lover.

90 KUMBHILAKA   What? He sees the pigeon, but doesn't see me? All right, I'll hit
him again.

[*He does so.*]

MAITREYA [*looking about*]   Ouch! It's Kumbhilaka! I must go to him.

[*Walks over and opens the gate.*]

Come on in, Kumbhilaka! So, how are you?

KUMBHILAKA   Master, my respects to you.

95 MAITREYA   What are you doing here, in this bad weather?

KUMBHILAKA   It's her, er . . . her!

MAITREYA   Who "her?" What "her?" Who, who is this "her?"

KUMBHILAKA   Her, sir. Her!

5. A singer of sacred hymns, mantras, and prayers and the fabled inventor of the *veena*, a seven-stringed instrument whose large body and neck are hollowed out of a block of wood. *Tumburu*: a monster who had been granted invulnerability by the god Brahma. After he was buried alive during a battle with Rama and his brother Lakshmana, a *gandharva* (one of the male nature spirits known as extraordinary musicians) emerged from the ground where he had been imprisoned as the result of a curse.

6. The sacred thread, given to each male Brahmin during his boyhood initiation by his spiritual master, is made up of three strands running in a loop from the left shoulder diagonally across the chest and down to the waist. The true Brahmin should never part with his thread or let it be contaminated by unholy matter, objects, or persons of lower castes.

MAITREYA You son-of-a-slave! Why in the world are you puffing away *her-er-sir-her* like a half-starved beggar in a famine?

KUMBHILAKA And why are you hooting away *who-who-who-who* like the crows that come to peck at the offerings to Lord Indra?

MAITREYA That's enough. Now tell me why you are here.

KUMBHILAKA [*to himself*] Well, let me put it this way . . . [*aloud*] Here—let me ask you a question.

MAITREYA And let me put my foot in your face!

KUMBHILAKA No. Not till you get the answers right! In what season does the mango blossom?

MAITREYA In the summer, son-of-a-slave!

KUMBHILAKA [*laughing*] Wrong! Wrong!

MAITREYA [*to himself*] What should I do now? [*Thinks.*] Well . . . I'll go ask Charudatta. [*Aloud*] Wait a moment.

[*Goes to* CHARUDATTA.]

My friend, I need to ask you something. Er . . . in what season does the mango blossom?

CHARUDATTA Spring. In the season of *vasanta,* fool!

MAITREYA [*returning to* KUMBHILAKA] In the season of Spring—*vasanta,* fool!

KUMBHILAKA I'll ask another question. Who guards the rich cities?

MAITREYA The city guards, of course.

KUMBHILAKA [*laughing*] No, no, no!

MAITREYA [*to himself*] Well, I am stuck yet again. [*Thinks.*] I'll have to ask Charudatta again.

[*Goes to* CHARUDATTA.]

CHARUDATTA It's the army—the *séna*—that guards a rich city.

MAITREYA It's the *séna* that guards the city, you son-of-a-slave!

KUMBHILAKA Now quickly say the two together.

MAITREYA Army-spring! *Séna-vasanta!*

KUMBHILAKA No, the other way around.

MAITREYA [*turning around*] *Séna-vasanta!*

KUMBHILAKA You stupid Brahmin! Turn the two feet around!

MAITREYA [*turning his feet*] *Séna-vasanta!*

KUMBHILAKA I am talking about metrical "feet"! Two feet meaning the two words!

MAITREYA [*thinking*] *Vasanta-séna* . . . Yikes! Vasantasena!

KUMBHILAKA It's she who's coming.

MAITREYA Well, Charudatta ought to know about it.

[*Goes to* CHARUDATTA.]

Charudatta, a creditor has come.

CHARUDATTA A creditor? In our house?

MAITREYA Not exactly *in* the house. Rather, *at* the door. It's Vasantasena!

CHARUDATTA Are you pulling the wool over my eyes?

MAITREYA If you don't trust my words, ask Kumbhilaka. Kumbhilaka! Come here, you son-of-a-slave!

KUMBHILAKA [*coming over*] Accept my regards, sir.

CHARUDATTA You are welcome, my good man. Tell me, is Vasantasena really here?

KUMBHILAKA Well, sir, almost.

145 CHARUDATTA [*with pleasure*]   A bearer of good news has never left without a reward from me! Here—take it, this is your reward.

[*Gives* KUMBHILAKA *his shawl.*]

KUMBHILAKA [*Takes it and bows with joy.*]   I'll tell my mistress about it!

[*Leaves.*]

MAITREYA   Do you have any idea why she has risked this bad weather to come here?

150 CHARUDATTA   No, friend, I haven't the slightest.

MAITREYA   I do. The pearl necklace was cheaper than her jewels. She's coming here to ask for more.

CHARUDATTA [*to himself*]   She shall not leave unsatisfied.

[*Enter* VASANTASENA *at another part of the stage, flamboyantly dressed to meet her lover, quite lovesick. With her are the* SECOND VITA, *and a* SLAVE GIRL *holding an umbrella over her.*]

VITA 2   This is Lakshmi the beautiful the goddess personified
155   (Though without her lotus); Madana's[7] floral arrow of love;
      The sorrow of wives; bloom of the Love-tree in the heavens above;
      Blushing at the thought of lovemaking, but ever dignified;
      Gracefully alluring, she enters the stage of Amour
      Followed by the train of her fond, loving paramours.
160   Look, Vasantasena, look!
      The clouds that roar and cast shadows over the mountain peaks
      Are like the heart of the woman who her lover seeks.
      And when those rain-bearing clouds boom,
      The peacocks fan the air with jeweled plumes.
165   The muddy-faced, rain-soaked frogs are drinking deep.
      The peacock cries out in love! The *neepa* flower[8] blooms.
      Shining like bright torches, while the dark clouds keep
      The moon shrouded, the way a rascal his family name dooms.
      Lightning bolts sear across the sky, with flippancy,
170   Like a lowborn woman who knows no constancy.

VASANTASENA   You spoke very well, master. But listen to this—
      Like a rival in fury, Night blocks me in every way.
      She says, sounding her thunder, trying to make me delay:
      "Fool! He'll rest on my bosom, not yours. So stay!"

175 VITA 2   You are right! So, now take your turn. Rebuke the Night in return.

VASANTASENA   That would be useless, master. She is a woman, and like a woman, she is jealous, too. So what's the point?
      Though the clouds roar, though the rains pour, though the thunders bolt—
      A woman, journeying to meet her lover, doesn't care for heat or cold.

180 VITA 2   Watch those clouds, Vasantasena!
      Riding the winds the Clouds are advancing fast.
      The heavy raindrops they shoot are like arrows;

---

7. The god of love in Hindu mythology (also named Kamadeva). Like Cupid or Eros in classical mythology, he is represented as winged, armed with bow and arrows. *Lakshmi*: divine mother of the universe as well as Vishnu's consort and female counterpart,

traditionally represented sitting on a lotus flower.
8. The favorite flower of Krishna, usually yellow but occasionally in shades of pink; it symbolizes immortality and is one of the most celebrated flowers in India.

Like the drums of war do their thunders blast;
Their lightning is the banner that the monarch, who harrows
185   Another kingdom, flies. So, like a victorious king,
The Clouds stalk the realm of the Moon, the weakling.

VASANTASENA   True, true! But there's more to it:
Those clouds, dark as elephants, from whose bloated wombs
Bounce the streaks of lightning, their thunderous booms—
190   Wound the heart like barbed shafts. Then why does the crane
Rub in the pain of the lonely lover's heart, crying in vain?
Why does it have to sing its lament: "Rain, rain, rain?"

VITA 2   Excellent, Vasantasena! You mentioned elephants? Now look:
The sky looks so like a rutting elephant, in heat, aroused—
195   As if its faded headdress were the cranes that the heavens browse;
As if its plumed fans were the lightning streaks that skies carouse.

VASANTASENA   Shameless cloud! First you delay me
While I am speeding to my love;
Now roaring down from high above
200   With wet hands you dare to touch me?

Oh, Indra—King of the Gods, Giver of Thunder!
Have you then been in love with me before
That now you roar and threaten to hold me?
And while I long for him, should you pour
205   Your showers on my way and delay me?

Go! Throw your bolt a hundred times, and let it rain!
A woman going to her lover you never can detain.

Thunder, you may roar, for men are cruel, I am aware;
But maiden Lightning, don't you feel womanly despair?
210 VITA 2   Enough, good lady. Don't blame her too much. She's actually a friend!
This same lightning, that swings like the golden chain
On Indra's elephant Airavata's[9] chest, it does not in vain,
Like a banner planted atop a mountain peak, flicker ablaze;
It flashes to show your lover's house from Indra's heavenly place.

215 VASANTASENA   And here, master, is his house!

VITA 2   Well, you are trained in all the arts. There is nothing more you still
need to be taught. But my affection makes me offer a few words of advice.
Once you have entered this house, keep yourself reserved. But at the same
time, keep in mind: don't overdo it.
220   If you are without reserve, love will be reduced to inaction.
If you hold yourself back too much, what happens to passion?
So, you'll have to know to arouse both yourself and your lover;
Appease him to make him appease you, so love lives on forever.
That should be enough. Hello! Is there anybody there? Let Charudatta know—
225   At this hour, when the earth is fragrant with the scent
Of the *kadamba*[1] and *neepa* flowers—the rain's made its descent
On the tresses of this loving, joyful woman who has come to see

---

9. A celestial white elephant, often represented with five heads, that was ridden by Lord Indra.
1. An Indian shade tree.

Her beloved. Frightened by lightning and roaring thunder is she;
But still she sighs for him, even while, gently, she dismantles
230   The mud that clings to her feet and the *nupura*-bells[2] on her ankles.

CHARUDATTA [*listening*]   Friend, will you go and see what the matter is?

MAITREYA   I will.

[*Finds* VASANTASENA, *approaches, speaks respectfully.*]

May all be well with you, madam!

VASANTASENA   Accept my respects, Master Maitreya. Are you well? [*to her*
235 VITA] Master—my umbrella girl is all yours.

VITA 2 [*to himself*]   What a polite, effective way to dismiss someone! [*aloud*] I
accept. My dear Vasantasena—
A brothel is a cradle of tricks, pride, and lies,
The playground of lust, the very spirit of vice.
240   But now you're bartering yourself out of mere courtesy.
I wish you success: may Love bless you with ecstasy.

[*Leaves.*]

VASANTASENA   Master Maitreya, where is your gambler?

MAITREYA [*to himself*]   What? Is that a compliment she gives him? [*aloud*]
There he is, in that dry orchard.

245 VASANTASENA   What could you mean by a dry orchard, sir?

MAITREYA   Madam, it's a place where there's nothing to eat or drink.

[VASANTASENA *smiles.*]

MAITREYA   Please go in, my lady.

VASANTASENA [*to her* SLAVE GIRL]   What do I say, once I am inside?

SLAVE GIRL   Try, "Have you had a pleasant evening, gambler?"

250 VASANTASENA   Will I be able to?

SLAVE GIRL   Of course. And the occasion will help.

VASANTASENA

[*Enters, approaches* CHARUDATTA, *and playfully hits him with flowers.*]

Have you had a pleasant evening, gambler?

CHARUDATTA [*seeing her*]   Vasantasena has come! [*rising in joy*] My beloved—
Sleep does not come to me in the night,
255   My nightly hours are spent with sighs;
But now that I see you, woman-with-wide-eyes,
It seems that this evening ends my plight.
Is everything well with you? Sit down, please. Here's a seat.

MAITREYA   Here it is. Please, sit down, my lady.

[VASANTASENA *sits, the others after her.*]

260 CHARUDATTA   Look, friend:
From the *kadamba* blossom that droops from her ear,
Droplets of rain have fallen on one of her breasts.
It seems the breast has been anointed like a royal heir,
Consecrated to be a young king with a regal crest.
265 My friend, Vasantasena's garments are drenched. Go, get some choice
clothes right away!

---

2. Anklet bells, worn by dancers (a favorite image in Sanskrit romantic and erotic poetry).

MAITREYA   Right away.

SLAVE GIRL   Master Maitreya, there's no need for you to go. I will take care of my lady's needs.

[*She does so.*]

270   MAITREYA [*aside*]   My friend, do you think I could ask her a question?

CHARUDATTA   Of course.

MAITREYA [*aloud*]   What, may I ask, has caused my lady to come here on such a bad, dark, moonless night?

SLAVE GIRL   My, the Brahmin is outspoken, madam!

275   VASANTASENA   In fact, you might call him clever.

SLAVE GIRL   My lady actually came to find out the price of that pearl necklace—

MAITREYA [*aside*]   There! Didn't I tell you? She thinks the necklace is cheap, compared to the jewel box. She isn't happy and wants to ask for more.

280   SLAVE GIRL   —because she mistook it for her own and lost it in a gambling game. The games master has left on an errand for the king. Nobody knows where he is—

MAITREYA   Didn't *I* say this before?

SLAVE GIRL   —therefore take this jewel box in exchange, while we continue
285   to look for him.

[*She shows the jewel box.* MAITREYA *examines it and looks worried.*]

You are studying it too closely. Have you seen it before somewhere?

MAITREYA   No. The . . . er . . . craftsmanship catches my eye.

SLAVE GIRL   Well, master, your eye deceives you. It is the same jewel box.

MAITREYA [*happily*]   Friend, it is the same jewel box that the thief took from
290   our house!

CHARUDATTA   My friend,

They are beating us at our own game, by playing exactly the same;
The trick we played to return the deposit, it's that very stratagem!
The embarrassment, however, remains, for all our excuses are now lame.

295   MAITREYA   But, my friend, I can swear by my Brahminhood—the thing is real!

CHARUDATTA   I am glad. Indeed, this is a welcome piece of news!

MAITREYA [*aside*]   Should I ask how they found it?

CHARUDATTA   I see no harm in that.

MAITREYA   [*Whispers into the* SLAVE GIRL'*s ear, of which we hear only the last
word.*] . . . there!

300   SLAVE GIRL   [*Whispers back, of which we hear the last words, too.*] . . . that's where!

CHARUDATTA   May we know what's going on? Are we outsiders?

MAITREYA [*whispers into Charudatta's ear*]   . . . and that's it!

CHARUDATTA   My good woman, is this the same jewel box?

SLAVE GIRL   Yes, sir. It is.

305   CHARUDATTA   Never have I left happy news unrewarded. Here, take this ring.
This is now . . .

[*He looks at his hand only to find that all his rings are gone; he is
embarrassed.*]

VASANTASENA [*to herself*]   That is why I love you!

CHARUDATTA [*aside*]   Gratitude from a poor man makes no sense;

His anger and favor, both turn into nonsense.
310　　Poverty reduces life to utter insignificance.

Like man-deserted houses, blasted trees,
Like empty wells: the poor are like these.
No more can they be hospitable to good ends;
They are forgotten by their sometime friends.

315 MAITREYA　Come, come. No point lamenting. [*aloud and joking*] Madam, won't you return the towel that went with the jewel box?

VASANTASENA　Master Charudatta, it wasn't right of you to send the necklace and try my trust.

CHARUDATTA [*with an embarrassed smile*]　Vasantasena, would you have
320　　believed the truth? Think:

No one would've believed it. None would've taken my opinion.
In this world Poverty is honorless and deserves only suspicion.

MAITREYA　Umh . . . do you think you'd like to sleep over?

SLAVE GIRL [*laughing*]　You *do* seem to be a very outspoken man, Master
325　Maitreya!

MAITREYA　Friend, the Rain-god doesn't seem to like us sitting here. He's preparing to visit us again with his large raindrops.

CHARUDATTA　You are right—

Raindrops, like lotus stalks that the lake's muddy bottom pierce,
330　　Pierce the clouds. To the vanished moon they are the sky's tears.
Look there, my Love:
The clouds are anointed with the color of the *tamala*[3] flower.
As though the sky's being fanned cool with a scented evening breeze.
And thinking of love, Lightning has come on its own, before the shower,
335　　To hold her lover, the Cloud, in a passionate embrace, before release!

[VASANTASENA, *betraying her passion, embraces* CHARUDATTA; *and he, feeling her touch, returns the embrace.*]

CHARUDATTA　Roar with an even greater voice, Cloud—boom!
I'm eager to receive the offerings of your shower!
In that desire let goose bumps on my limbs bloom,
Like the bristly petals of the *kadamba* flower!

340 MAITREYA　Son-of-a-slave-girl you are—Thunder! You brat! How dare you frighten the lady with your lightning?

CHARUDATTA　Don't blame him, friend.
May the thunder rage, let the lightning flash for a hundred years!
Now she has me in her arms, the woman I never thought would be here!
345　Moreover, my friend:
He only knows what life's blessings are,
Whose beloved comes to him from afar,
Whose arms that dearest body enfold,
While yet with rain it's wet and cold.
350　Vasantasena, my beloved, look at this house!
The masonry is shaken, it's so old;
I truly wonder how the roof still holds.

3. A variety of gardenia with white or pale yellow flowers, celebrated in Indian traditional poetry for its scent.

Heavy with water is the painted wall,
From which melting bits of mortar fall.

[*He looks at the sky.*]

355 Look at the rainbow, beloved! Look!
See how the sky yawns! The cloudy jaws of heaven,
Its tongue, the streaked lightning, cloven—
Its gigantic arms, spread out, wide open.
Come. We must go inside.

[*He rises and walks around.*]

360 On palm trees shrill,
On thickets base and still,
On boulders dashing,
On waters splashing,
Like a *veena* strummed, the rain sings,
365 Falls in rhythm, in harmony rings.

[*They leave.*]

[*End of Act.*]

Act 6

[*Enter* SLAVE GIRL.]

SLAVE GIRL   My lady is still not awake? Let me go and wake her up. [*Walks around.*]

[*She discovers* VASANTASENA, *sleeping with her body covered.*]

SLAVE GIRL [*seeing her*]   Wake up, wake up madam! It's dawn.

VASANTASENA [*awakening*]   What! Is the night over? Is it morning already?

SLAVE GIRL   Morning for us. For my lady, it seems the night is far from over!

5 VASANTASENA   My dear, where is your "Gambler"?

SLAVE GIRL   Madam, he went to Pushapakarandaka, the old garden, after leaving his orders with Vardhamanaka.

VASANTASENA   What orders did he leave?

SLAVE GIRL   "Yoke the bullock to the cart while it's still dark. Vasantasena
10   shall go in it."

VASANTASENA   And where am I supposed to go?

SLAVE GIRL   To where Charudatta has gone.

VASANTASENA [*embracing her*]   I couldn't get a good look at him in the dark yesterday. But today, I shall see him face to face! Tell me, dear—has he
15   brought me to the innermost part of the house?

SLAVE GIRL   Not only to the innermost part of the house, my lady—to the innermost part of everyone's heart, everyone who lives here.

VASANTASENA   Do the people of the household feel sad?

SLAVE GIRL   They soon will.

20 VASANTASENA   When?

SLAVE GIRL   When my lady shall leave.

VASANTASENA   Then I shall be first to feel sad. [*Showing decided courtesy*] My dear, take this necklace and go to Lady Dhutta—now my sister—and give her a message. Tell her: "Charudatta's virtues have won me. I am his slave, and
25   therefore, your slave too. Therefore let this pearl necklace adorn *your* neck."

SLAVE GIRL   Madam, Master Charudatta will be angry.

VASANTASENA   Go. He won't be angry.

SLAVE GIRL [taking the necklace]   As you wish.

[Leaves and comes back in a few moments.]

Madam, Lady Dhutta says: "It would not be right for me to accept what he
30   gave you from his pleasure. Please know that he himself is my ornament."

[Enter RADANIKA with ROHASENA, a little boy.]

RADANIKA   Come, my dear. We'll play with your little cart.

ROHASENA [in a hurt voice]   What will I do with this clay cart, Radanika?
Give me that golden cart!

35   RADANIKA [sighing, depressed]   Where do we have gold in this house, little
one? You will play with a golden cart when your father is rich again. [to
herself] I'll have to take his mind off this. [Aloud] Let's go see Lady
Vasantasena. [To VASANTASENA] My respects to you, madam.

VASANTASENA   You are welcome, Radanika. But whose little boy is this? He
has no ornaments on him, but his moonlike face warms my heart!

40   RADANIKA   This is Master Charudatta's son—Rohasena.

VASANTASENA [stretching out her arms]   Come, darling—sit on my lap!

[Sets him on her lap.]

He looks just like his father.

RADANIKA   Not just by his looks—he's very much like his father in character,
too. He helps Master Charudatta keep his worries off.

45   VASANTASENA   Why is he crying?

RADANIKA   He was playing with the little golden cart that belongs to the boy
next door, and the boy took it away. When he kept on asking for it, I made
him a little clay cart to play with. And now he says: "What'll I do with a clay
cart? I want that golden cart!"

50   VASANTASENA   What a pity! Even he has to suffer from seeing the wealth of
others. O All-knowing Destiny—Man's fate, unsteady as water-drops upon
a lotus leaf, is your plaything. [She weeps.] Don't cry, my darling—you will
have a golden cart to play with.

ROHASENA   Who is this, Radanika?

55   VASANTASENA   I am your father's slave, bought by his goodness.

RADANIKA   She is also your mother, little one.

ROHASENA   You're lying, Radanika! If she really is my mother, how come she's
wearing all those jewels?

60   VASANTASENA   In your child's words, you've said the most painful thing, my
sweetheart!

[Weeping, she takes her ornaments off.]

There! Now I am your mother. Here, take them. Make your golden cart out
of these.

ROHASENA   Go! I won't take them. You're crying.

VASANTASENA [wiping her eyes]   No, son, I won't cry anymore! Go, play.

[She piles her jewelry on the little clay cart.]

65   Take these jewels. Make yourself a little golden cart.

[RADANIKA leaves with ROHASENA.]

[Enter VARDHAMANAKA at a different area of the stage, driving a covered
bullock-cart.]

VARDHAMANAKA   Radanika, Radanika! Tell Mistress Vasantasena—her covered cart waits by the side door.

[*Re-enter* RADANIKA *at the previous area of the stage.*]

RADANIKA Madam, Vardhamanaka sends word that your cart is ready. It
waits by the side door.

70 VASANTASENA Ask him to wait a moment, dear. I need to put on my makeup.

[RADANIKA *crosses over to* VARDHAMANAKA's *area on the stage.*]

RADANIKA Vardhamanaka, you'll have to wait a bit. She's getting ready.

75 VARDHAMANAKA Look at this! I forgot to get the cushions for the cart. I'll
have to go and get them. [*Looks at the bullocks.*] But these bullocks are getting jumpy. They don't like the reins in their noses, I suppose. Well, I'll take
the cart along, up and down.

[*Leaves.*]

VASANTASENA Get my toiletries, dear. Let me dress up. [*She busies herself,
dressing up.*]

[STHAVARAKA, *a coachman driving a covered bullock-cart, enters at
another area of the stage.*]

STHAVARAKA Samsthanaka, the king's brother-in-law, ordered me:
"Sthavaraka, quickly bring the bullock cart to the old Pushpakarandaka
garden." Come on now! Move it, bullock, move it!

[*Drives, looks around and says to himself.*]

80 Darn! The road is jammed with carts of the whole village! What am I
supposed to do? [*Haughtily*] Come on, come on! Get out of my way!
Out . . . out! [*Listening*] What's that? Whose cart is this? [*Aloud*] This is
the cart of Samsthanaka, the king's brother-in-law, himself! Now out of
my way and quick! [*Looking*] Who was that guy? The moment he saw me
85 he darted off, like he was the runaway gambler and I the games master at
his heels! Who could that be? Hell with it! What do I care? Must hurry.
Hey, you village people! Get out of my way, out! What was that again?
Wait a minute? Your wheels got stuck and you want me to lend you a
90 hand? *Me!* Do you realize, I am Samsthanaka, the king's brother-in-law's
coachman! But the poor guy's all by himself—let me help him out. I'll
stop the cart at the side door of Master Charudatta's house. [*Stops the
cart.*] All right, I'm coming! I'm coming!

[*Leaves.*]

SLAVE GIRL My lady, I think I hear wheels. The cart must have arrived.

VASANTASENA Come on, dear, let's go. My heart hurries me! Show me the
95 side door.

SLAVE GIRL This way, madam.

[VASANTASENA *walks around and crosses over to* STHAVARAKA's *area.*]

VASANTASENA [*to the* SLAVE GIRL] You can go and take rest.

SLAVE GIRL Your wish, my lady.

[*Leaves.*]

VASANTASENA My right eye is twitching![4] But all bad omens will be wiped
100 away, once I see Charudatta. [*Climbs in the cart.*]

[STHAVARAKA *returns to his cart.*]

STHAVARAKA I've cleared the carts out of the way. Finally, now, I can move on.

---

4. Twitching muscles were (and, in many parts of India, still are) believed to be an omen of bad
things to come for women, good things to come for men.

[*Mounts the cart and drives away. To himself.*]

Strange, the cart seems heavier! I guess it only seems so because I am tired from helping that guy change his wheel. Let's move on then. Come on, bullocks! Move it, move it!

105 VOICE OFFSTAGE Gatekeepers! Guards! To your stations! Every one of you! Alert! Look sharp! Gopala's son, Aryaka, has escaped! He's broken out of jail, killed his jailer, broken his chains and is on the run right now! Get him! Capture him! Catch him!

> [*Enter* ARYAKA, *suddenly, at yet another area of the stage. He drags broken shackles on one foot, keeps his face covered and walks around furtively.*]

STHAVARAKA [*to himself*] What an uproar in the city! Well, I must get out of
110 here as soon as I can.

> [*Leaves with the cart.*]

ARYAKA Imprisoned by the king's command I was, as though
  Immersed in the great of ocean of misery and sorrow.
  Now like an elephant, the broken end still on my feet,
  The severed chain I drag along on my retreat.

115 Frightened by a prophecy, King Palaka had me picked up from my village, put me in chains and threw me inside a solitary cell meant for those doomed to death. Thanks to the efforts of my dear friend Sharvilaka, I have made my escape from there. [*Sheds tears.*]

  The prophecy was not my fault, it was Fate being provident.
120 Was that reason enough, to chain me up like a wild elephant?
  But can a lone man fight a king? Can a king with Destiny fray?
  Destiny, the greater king, whose rule we must all obey?
But where can I go in my utter misfortune?

> [*Looking around and arriving near* CHARUDATTA's *house.*]

What is this? A house with an open side door!
125 The door has no locks on it; it sags on a broken hinge.
  The owner, like me, seems to have been by misfortune infringed.
I'll go in there and hide.

VOICE OFFSTAGE Hup-hup! Move, bullocks, move!

ARYAKA [*listening*] There's a cart coming this very way!
130 Maybe it's a bunch of upstarts, going out to party.
  Maybe it's out to fetch the bride, on marriage duty.
  Maybe it's taking some elite to his house in the country.
  Or, maybe, if I am lucky, it's going vacant and empty.

> [*Enter* VARDHAMANAKA *with the cart.*]

VARDHAMANAKA Yes, folks, I've got the cushions. Radanika—tell the mistress
135 Vasantasena, "The cart's ready for her to ride to the old Pushpakarandaka garden."

ARYAKA [*listening*] This is a courtesan's cart and it's going out of town. I simply can't let this chance go.

> [*Approaches the cart cautiously.*]

VARDHAMANAKA [*listening*] I hear her ringing anklets. The lady must've
140 come. The new nose reins have made these bullocks jumpy. Madam, please get in from the back.

> [ARYAKA *gets in from the back.*]

VARDHAMANAKA   The ringing of the anklets has stopped and the cart seems heavy. I suppose the lady has boarded the cart. I'll move on. Up, up, bullocks! Move it, move it.

[*Drives around the stage with* ARYAKA *in the cart.*]

[*Enter* VIRAKA *with a group of men.*]

145   VIRAKA   Hey, there! Jaya, Jayamana, Chandanaka, Mangala, Phullabhadra—and the rest of you!

Hush, you guys! Listen now: the son of Gopala has cut his tether.

He makes his escape, breaking both jail and the king's heart together.

You there, stand at the gate on the east road. You, at the west gate. You—

150   south. And you—take the north. I'll climb up this broken wall here with Chandanaka and take a look. Come on! This way, Chandanaka!

[*Enter* CHANDANAKA *hastily, with another group of men.*]

CHANDANAKA   Hey, you guys! Viraka, Vishalya, Bhimangada, Dandakala, Dandashira—and the rest of you!

Come on, my reliables! To action! Be quick! Be brisk!

155   The Royal Fortune may pass on to other hands; it's at risk!

Look! Search! Investigate! Whatever arises your suspicion:

Gardens, crowds, roads, suburbs, shops! Any insinuation!

Well, what do you think, Viraka? Be frank, exact, and open.

Who helped Gopala's son break out of prison? Be outspoken.

160   Who's this wretched creature: born with the Sun in the eighth position,

The Moon in the fourth, Venus in the sixth, Mars in the fifth station,

Jupiter in the sixth house, and Saturn in the ninth mansion?[5]

Who dares, with me alive, help Gopala's son avoid apprehension?

VIRAKA   Fellow soldier Chandanaka!

165   I swear upon your life, someone must've helped him out of prison,

For Aryaka had broken his chains even before the sun was half risen.

VARDHAMANAKA   Hup-hup! Move, bullocks, move!

CHANDANAKA   Look, man, look!

A covered cart is trailing down the middle of the road.

170   Find out whose it is! Who's in it, where it's taking its load?

VIRAKA   Hey, you—coachman! Freeze! Stop where you are. Tell me, whose cart is it? Who's in it? And where do you think you're going?

VARDHAMANAKA   This cart belongs to Master Charudatta. Vasantasena's the passenger and I am taking her to the old Pushpakarandaka garden where

175   she'll "meet" with him.

VIRAKA   [*approaching* CHANDANAKA]   The coachman says the cart belongs to Charudatta, that Vasantasena's in it, and that he's taking her to the old Pushpakarandaka garden.

---

5. All celestial positions indicating misfortune, in Indian astrology: the Sun in the eighth house signifies death; the Moon in the fourth, a severe stomach ailment; Venus in the sixth, mental degeneracy; Mars in the fifth, destruction or loss; Jupiter in the sixth, grief and trouble from an enemy; and Saturn in the ninth, loss of wealth and destitution.

CHANDANAKA   Then let him pass.

180 VIRAKA   Without an inspection?

CHANDANAKA   Yes, of course!

VIRAKA   On whose responsibility?

CHANDANAKA   Master Charudatta's.

VIRAKA   Who in the world do you think Charudatta and Vasantasena are that
185   we should let their cart pass unsearched?

CHANDANAKA   What! Seriously? You don't know Charudatta? Not even Vasantasena? Well, if you don't, then I'll say you don't know the moon and its beams.

   Who doesn't know this Moon of virtue, generosity's lotus flower;
   This pearl of the four oceans, this savior in man's luckless hour?

190   They are two citizens we all worship; they're Ujjayini's pride!
   Charudatta and Vasantasena—they are both known far and wide!

VIRAKA   I do know Charudatta and Vasantasena, but when I am on royal duty,
   I'll refuse to recognize anything—even my dad's paternity!

ARYAKA [to himself]   In my former life, one of those men must've been a
195   friend, the other an enemy.

   Of rank same, in ways different: these men are like two fires—
   One lit for marriage ceremonies, the other for funeral pyres.

CHANDANAKA   Well, my vigilant officer! You are the king's trustworthy captain.
   I'll hold the bullocks; why don't you go and search. How about that?

200 VIRAKA   Well, the king trusts you, and you are a captain as well. You may
   search the cart.

CHANDANAKA   My searching—will it be as good as yours?

VIRAKA   As good as the king searching himself, man!

CHANDANAKA   Lower the yoke, coachman.

   [VARDHAMANAKA obeys.]

205 ARYAKA [to himself]   The guards are going to find me. And even worse, I am
   unarmed! But—

   Let me do what Bhima the Pandava[6] did, and make my two arms
   My swords! Better to die fighting than to surrender without qualms!

   But, wait! This may not be the place to be violent.

   [CHANDANAKA mounts the cart and begins to search.]

210 ARYAKA   I seek your protection.

CHANDANAKA   Protected you will be that seeks, I assure.

ARYAKA   The Goddess of Victory will abandon, kith and kin will abjure
   The one who will falsely the promise of Protection assure.

CHANDANAKA   What! Aryaka, son of Gopala! A bird frightened only by the hawk,
215   fallen now into the hands of the birdcatcher! [thinking] He is innocent. And,
   above all, I've given him the assurance of my protection. Moreover, he rides
   Charudatta's cart, and on top of that, he's my friend Sharvilaka's friend. But,
   on the other hand, I have my royal duty. . . . What will I do? Well, what shall
   be, shall be. And, to start with, didn't I promise him my protection?

220   He who dies to keep his promise to protect true:
   The world will consider his action to be virtue.

   [Descends from the cart, frightened.]

---

6. Bhima often avenged insults to himself and his family by killing his opponents with his bare
hands.

I saw him—[*Stops in mid-sentence.*]—er . . . her . . . our lady, Vasantasena.
She said: "So this is propriety, this is sobriety: to insult me in the middle of
the road and—that too—when I am on my way to see Master Charudatta!"

225 VIRAKA   Chandanaka, I am having doubts.

CHANDANAKA   Doubts? Why?

VIRAKA   You sound scared, you stammer.
First you said "him," then "her"!
And that's exactly why I doubt and don't feel so sure.

230 CHANDANAKA   Is that it? That's the only reason why you don't "feel so sure"?
Well, I guess you know, I am from the south and our speech is not really
very clear! We know a thousand dialects spoken by the barbarians:
*Khashas-Khattis-Kadas-Kadatthobilas-Karnatas-Karnas-Praavaranas-
Dravidas-Cholas-Chanas-Barbars-Khéras-Khanas-Mukhas-Madhughatas*[7]—

235 and so on and so forth. We say whatever pops up on our lips: "he" for "she,"
"her" for "him"—and so on and so forth.

VIRAKA   Whatever you say, I have a right to inspect, as well. This is a royal
command and the king trusts me.

CHANDANAKA   And I am not trusted?

240 VIRAKA   It is His Majesty's command.

CHANDANAKA [*to himself*]   If the word gets around that Aryaka was trying to
escape in Charudatta's cart, then Charudatta is going to suffer at the king's
hand. What's to be done? [*Thinks*] Got it! Let me stir up a quarrel, in my
southern style. [*Aloud*] Who the hell do you think you are, Viraka? I,

245 Chandanaka, have searched the cart and now you want to search it again!

VIRAKA   Who the hell do you think *you* are?

CHANDANAKA   Maybe you are an honored and respected man, but, my friend,
you forget your caste!

VIRAKA   What then is my caste, sir?

250 CHANDANAKA   Who wants to say it?

VIRAKA   Go ahead, say it.

CHANDANAKA   No. It's better unsaid!
I know your caste by birth, but I don't with such things dabble;
You see, there is no point at all in cracking a wood-apple.

255 VIRAKA   Out with it! Come on, say it.

[CHANDANAKA *makes a gesture indicating the barber's profession.*]

VIRAKA   Now what's that supposed to mean?

CHANDANAKA   You had scissors in one hand that on men's heads would graze;
The sharp stone razor in your other hand men's beards would erase.
That very same barber is now an army captain. Hey, quite a raise!

260 VIRAKA   Well, Chandanaka, you are an honorable man, too, I believe. But
still you forget your caste?

CHANDANAKA   I am Chandanaka, as pure as *chandana*, sandalwood! And you
are talking about my caste?

VIRAKA   Right. Maybe I shouldn't. It doesn't deserve to be spoken about.

265 CHANDANAKA   No, no—go ahead, say it!

[VIRAKA *makes a gesture indicating the tanner's profession.*]

CHANDANAKA   What does that mean?

7. Languages and dialects spoken in classical India.

VIRAKA   Your mother was a kettledrum, your father a tabor-drum,
    And you are the brother of a filthy brother, a stinky bum!
    A tanner turned captain. Give me a break! Oh, come, come!

270 CHANDANAKA [angrily]   Me? Chandanaka—a tanner? And you dare say that?
    Go—search that cart.

VIRAKA   Hey, coachman! Turn the cart. I'll inspect it.

        [VARDHAMANAKA obeys. But just as VIRAKA is about to begin his "search,"
        CHANDANAKA pulls him down by his hair and starts kicking him.]

275 VIRAKA [getting up in a rage]   You dare to grab me by my hair and kick at me,
    while I am performing my royal duty! Then listen to this: if I do not take
    you to the court and quarter you there, my name is not Viraka!

CHANDANAKA   Come on, go! Go to the court. Better still, try the king's palace.
    Go wherever you wish. What do I care about a dog like you?

VIRAKA   We'll see!
        [Leaves.]

CHANDANAKA [looking in all directions]   Get going, coachman, move! If
280 anybody questions you, tell him that Chandanaka and Viraka have searched
    your cart. And my lady, keep this as a token to remember me.
        [Hands ARYAKA his sword.]

ARYAKA [Takes it. Joyfully, to himself]
    Good! I have a sword now. I can use it for self-defense!
    And my right arm muscles are quivering—a happy significance!

CHANDANAKA   My lady—
285   Chandanaka helped you. Do not put him out of your mind.
    I say this in friendship, to gain only in love, never in kind.

ARYAKA   Chandanaka, your honor is as pure as the moon;
    I'll remember, when the prophecy turns true—soon!

CHANDANAKA   May the gods protect you: the Sun, the Moon, Shiva, Vishnu,
290   and Brahma!
    May you kill your enemies, as Kali killed the demons Shumbha and
    Nishumbha![8]
        [VARDHAMANAKA drives off with the cart.]

CHANDANAKA [looking towards the back of the stage]   What? I see Sharvilaka,
    my good friend, following Aryaka, even as he goes. Well, that's done! And
295 now, I have made an enemy of Viraka, the trusted constable of the king.
    Therefore, it's time for me to run, too, following Aryaka. And not without
    my sons and my brothers.
        [He leaves.]
        [End of Act.]

SUMMARY OF ACT 7

Charudatta and Maitreya intercept Vardhamanaka's cart. The bashful Charudatta
asks Maitreya to help Vasantasena out of the cart. In the process, Maitreya discovers
the cart's passenger to be not "Ms. Vasanatasena" but a "Mr. Vasantasen"—a man with
chains on his feet. When Charudatta confronts him, Aryaka immediately asks for the

---

8. Two asuras, or demons, who warred against
the gods. They were finally slain by Kali (in the
form of Durga), an incarnation of the Great

Goddess Shakti (or Parvati), the female counterpart of Shiva and (in this incarnation) a figure of terror and destruction.

Brahmin's protection and the generous Charudatta lets him go, thereby winning his friendship.

Act 8

[*Enter a* MONK (*Bhikshu*), *carrying a wet garment in his hand.*]

MONK   Save, acquire *dharma*,[9] you ignorant people!
    Control your bellies, keep yourselves up and awake
    With the drums of meditation, for *dharma*'s sake!
    For the five senses rob *dharma*'s collection
5   Of goodness, the pious life's accumulation.
    Further, I have seen life in all its transitoriness. That is why I have taken refuge in the path of *dharma* with all my heart.
    He who has succeeded in vanquishing the Five Men (the Five Faculties),
    The woman (Ignorance) and the weak lowborn Chandala (his Personality),
10   Has saved the Village (his Soul) and found Svarga[1] (ultimate Liberty).

    Why shave your cheeks and head, if you haven't shaved clean the mind?
    One whose head is shaven must have a soul that has left evil behind.
    I've dyed my clothes *kashaya*, monk-red.[2] And now I'll rush into the king's brother-in-law's garden, wash these in the pond there, and be off as soon as
15   I can.

[*Walks around, "washes" his clothes.*]

VOICE OFFSTAGE   Stop, you wretched *bhikshu*,[3] stop!

MONK   [*looking about, scared*]   Help! It is that very Samsthanaka—the king's brother-in-law—coming here! A *bhikshu* had offended him once. Ever since, whenever he sees *bhikshus*, he ties them up and drags them off
20   like cows are dragged by their nose-reins! I am helpless. Where can I get help? Yes, the Lord Buddha shall be my refuge!

[*Enter* SAMSTHANAKA, *the* VITA *following, sword in hand.*]

SAMSTHANAKA,   Stop! Wretched *bhikshu*! Stop, I say! Or I'll break your head!
    Like they break the tip of the red radish appetizer in a tavern.

[*Beats the* MONK.]

VITA   It is not right to beat a poor *bhikshu* who has given up worldly life to
25   wear the ascetic's colors, my dear Bastard. What do you care about him?
    Look at the trees—
    To homeless men, the forest trees
    Mercifully bring joy and ease.
    The garden before you unguarded lies
30   (Unconcealed as the evil mind's vice).
    The garden's pleasures are freely yours,
    Like a kingdom that's won without wars.

---

9. Truth as taught by the Buddha.

1. The temporary paradise, located on the mythical Mount Meru, where those who have lived a virtuous life but have not yet attained union with God reside before being reborn. *Chandala*: a pejorative term used in Sanskrit literature to refer to the lowest and most despised group of indigenous people. Segregated from mainstream society as Untouchables,

the Chandalas performed undesirable tasks such as killing animals, executing criminals, and cremating corpses.

2. Ascetics traditionally wore red clothing.

3. Literally, "beggar," "someone who lives on alms given to him" (Sanskrit), a *bhikshu* is also a fully ordained monastic maintaining the basic Buddhist precepts and monastic discipline.

MONK   I welcome you, Servant of the Blessed One.

SAMSTHANAKA   Vita, Vita! He's calling me names!

35 VITA   What names?

SAMSTHANAKA   He calls me a "servant!" Does he think I am of the low barber caste, or what?

VITA   No. He praises you by calling you the servant of Buddha.

MONK   *Dhanya* are you! *Punya* are you!

40 SAMSTHANAKA   *Dhanya*—he's calling me a "skeptic!" *Punya*—he's calling me a "water-pot for cattle!"

VITA   *Dhanya* also means "blessed." And *punya* means "virtuous," too. My dear Bastard, he is praising you.

SAMSTHANAKA   Vita—why has he come here?

45 MONK   To wash my clothes.

SAMSTHANAKA   What? You wretched *bhikshu!* My sister's husband has given me this finest garden of all, this Pushpakarandaka garden. Jackals and dogs drink from its pond. Not even I, the noblest of noblemen, can bathe in it. And you dare to bring your stinking clothes, all stained with rotten bean soup, and wash them here? I will finish you off with one nice stroke!

VITA   Wait a minute, Bastard. It doesn't seem like this man's been a *bhikshu* for long.

SAMSTHANAKA   How do you know, Vita?

VITA   What is there to know? It's so obvious! See—

55   His head has been newly shaven: the scalp's still white;
     The coarse cloth of the cloak hasn't calloused his shoulder yet;
     Not used to his habit, he hasn't tied the knots right;
     The fabric's stiff, the cloak's a bad fit, not properly set.

MONK   You are right, Servant of the Lord. It hasn't been long since I decided to become a wandering *bhikshu.*

SAMSTHANAKA   Why didn't you decide the moment you were born?

     [*Beats him.*]

VITA   What's the point in beating this poor fellow? Leave him alone, and let him go.

SAMSTHANAKA   Wait! First I must consult, and then decide.

65 VITA   Consult? With whom?

SAMSTHANAKA   With my heart.

VITA [*aside*]   He still has one?

SAMSTHANAKA [*to himself*]   Dear little heart of mine, dear sir—should this *bhikshu* go? Or, should he stay? [*Decides.*] Neither go, nor stay. [*aloud*]

70   Vita, I consulted with my heart, and it—

VITA   What does it say?

SAMSTHANAKA   He should neither go, nor stay, neither breathe in, nor breathe out. In fact, he should drop dead on the spot.

MONK   My homage to you, Buddha! I seek your protection.

75 VITA   Let him go.

SAMSTHANAKA   On one condition.

VITA   What condition?

SAMSTHANAKA   He has to sling mud in such a way that the water does not get stirred—or, even better, let him pile up the water on one side and then

80   sling mud.

VITA   What stupidity!

The earth is burdened with such fools, chunks of wood and blocks of rock
Turned flesh and bones, but whose thoughts and acts have run amok!

[*The* MONK *mocks* SAMSTHANAKA *with gestures.*]

SAMSTHANAKA   What does he mean?

85 VITA   He is praising you.

SAMSTHANAKA   Yes! More praise, more praise! Go on—more praise!

[*Doing so, the* MONK *leaves.*]

VITA   Dear Bastard, look at the splendors of the garden—
The trees, with bright fruits and flowers, prosperously thrive
(The gardeners, under royal command, helping them survive).

90   Vine-embraced, they're happy like husbands in union with wives.

SAMSTHANAKA   Excellent, Vita! Right! The ground is covered with flower-drops;
The trees, heavy with fruits, groundward flop;
Like jackfruits, monkeys hang from treetops.

VITA   Here's a flat rock, my Bastard. Let's sit down.

95 SAMSTHANAKA   Here. I have seated myself.

[*They sit.*]

SAMSTHANAKA   Vita, I cannot forget that Vasantasena. She stays in my mind
like the insults of an evil person.

VITA [*to himself*]   Even after those rebukes he still dreams of her!
A gentleman's desire recedes when a woman gives it disdain;

100   A coward's desire, however, flares up, if only in vain.

SAMSTHANAKA   Vita, it's been a while now since I told that servant Sthavaraka
to bring the cart here. And he is still not here! I've been hungry a long time,
and how can one keep walking at midday? Look—
Like an angry monkey the sun is burning

105   Smack in the middle, the center of the sky;
The Earth is dried and cracked in mourning
Like Gandhari, who saw her hundred sons die.[4]

VITA   So it is.
The cows in the shade doze;

110   Their mouths full of cud ooze.
Thirsty deer the hot pond water drink;
People from the streets in fear slink.
The driver, I am sure, instead of driving,
Halts on the burning road, avoids arriving.

115 SAMSTHANAKA   Vita—
The sun beats down upon my head.
The birds aren't singing—are they dead?
People sit at home—the heat they dread—
Heaving hot sighs; the roads they've fled.

120   Why isn't that servant here yet, Vita? Well, I'm going to sing something to
pass the time.

[*He sings.*]

Vita, did you hear me sing?

VITA   You are as melodious as the heavenly choristers, the *gandharvas!* What
more can I say?

4. As recounted in the *Mahabharata,* the hundred sons of Gandhari, collectively known as the
Kauravas, were killed in battle by their cousins, the Pandavas.

125 SAMSTHANAKA   Of course, I *am* a *gandharva*! And why not?
With the sweetest herbs, my throat have I been anointing:
Heeng,[5] cumin seed, cypress, knot-vine, ginger, molasses, ginseng!
All that should, for sure, make my voice soar and ring!
Vita, here, let me sing again.
[*He sings again.*]
130   There! Did you hear that?
VITA   As I said, you must be a *gandharva*! What more can I say?
SAMSTHANAKA   Of course, I am a *gandharva*! Why shouldn't I?
I've eaten the meat of the cuckoo:
Scented with the spirit of *hingu*,[6]
135   Pepper-dusted, dripped in oil of sesame—
It was cooked in pure, buttery ghee
All this makes my voice sweet, you'll agree.
Why isn't that servant here yet, Vita?
VITA   Don't get too excited, he'll be here soon.
[*Enter the cart carrying* VASANTASENA, *with* STHAVARAKA. *It crosses the stage to where* SAMSTHANAKA *and the* VITA *are.*]
140 STHAVARAKA   I'm scared. The midday sun's beating down. Hope Samsthanaka isn't furious. Hey, hup-hup, bullocks! Move it!
VASANTASENA   Disaster! This not what Vardhamanaka sounds like! What has happened? Has Charudatta sent another cart to rest the bullocks that pull his own cart? My right eye twitches ominously, my heart's beating wild,
145   everything's blank, everything's reeling!
[*As* STHAVARAKA's *cart approaches.*]
SAMSTHANAKA [*hearing the wheels creak*]   Vita, Vita! The cart is here!
VITA   How do you know?
SAMSTHANAKA   Don't you see, Vita? I hear it grrrunting, like an old pig!
VITA [*looking*]   You saw it right. It's come, indeed.
150 SAMSTHANAKA   Sthavaraka, my boy, my slave, is that you?
STHAVARAKA   Yes, sir.
SAMSTHANAKA   And the cart, too?
STHAVARAKA   Yes, sir.
SAMSTHANAKA   And the bullocks, as well?
155 STHAVARAKA   Yes, sir.
SAMSTHANAKA   And you, also?
STHAVARAKA [*laughing*]   Yes, sir. Me, too!
SAMSTHANAKA   Bring it in.
STHAVARAKA   Er, by which way?
160 SAMSTHANAKA   Over that wall—where it has collapsed.
STHAVARAKA   But that would kill the bullocks, Master. It'd wreck the cart and break my neck!
SAMSTHANAKA   What? I am the king's brother-in-law—if the bullocks are killed, I'll buy others. If the cart breaks down, I'll get myself another. If you
165   die, I'll get another driver.
STHAVARAKA   Yes, sir. Everything will be fine. Except me—I'll be no more.
SAMSTHANAKA   Who cares? You drive over the wall!

5. Asafetida, a resinous gum from a Central Asian plant, used in medicine and in cooking.   6. That is, *heeng* (asafetida).

STHAVARAKA Break down, cart! Break down with your master. There'll be another cart, so says the Master.

    [*Drives in.*]

170 What? You made it without breaking! Master, the cart's here.

SAMSTHANAKA The bullocks didn't tear. The ropes weren't killed. And you've survived, too?

STHAVARAKA Yes, sir.

SAMSTHANAKA Come here, Vita. First, we'll inspect our cart. Vita, you are my
175 one and only chief guru. I look upon you with so much esteem. You are to be treated well. You are close to my heart. You'll have to be ahead of me in everything. So, please enter the cart first!

VITA So be it.

    [*Starts to enter the cart.*]

180 SAMSTHANAKA No! Wait! Do you think this is your father's cart and that you'll step into it first? I am the owner, I'll get in first.

VITA But you told me yourself!

SAMSTHANAKA Even if I did tell you myself, why didn't you have the courtesy to say "After you, Master?"

VITA After you, Master.

185 SAMSTHANAKA I will ascend now. Sthavaraka, my boy, turn the cart.

STHAVARAKA [*turning the cart*] Please get in, Master.

SAMSTHANAKA [*ascends, looks in, then—fear-stricken—gets off quickly and throws his arms around the* VITA's *neck*] Vita! Vita! Dead! You're dead! There's a demoness inside the cart, or, maybe a thief! If it's a demoness, she's going to rob both of us! If it's a thief, we'll both be eaten alive!

190 VITA Don't be scared. How can there be a demoness inside a bullock-cart? I think the midday sun has blinded you. You're hallucinating. You saw the shadow of Sthavaraka's robes and took them for something else.

SAMSTHANAKA Sthavaraka, my boy, my slave—are you still alive?

STHAVARAKA Yes, sir.

195 SAMSTHANAKA Vita! There's a woman in the cart! Go, take a look!

VITA A woman?

    Then like oxen that, in the rain, cower their heads low,
    Let us quietly remove ourselves from here and go.
    For though I can in public places show my dignity,
200   I'd hesitate to bare my eyes before a woman of nobility.

VASANTASENA [*to herself, in astonishment*] What? It is that thorn of my eye, the king's brother-in-law! Then, unfortunate that I am, I am in deep trouble. Coming here has been as useless, as fruitless, as throwing a handful of seeds on salty soil. What shall I do now?

205 SAMSTHANAKA This old slave of mine is a coward. He won't look inside the cart. Vita, you'll have to look.

VITA I see no harm. I'll do it.

SAMSTHANAKA My goodness! Do I see the jackals flying on their wings and the crows walking on four feet? Let me run for my life, as the demoness
210 chews him up with her eyes and looks at him with her teeth.

VITA [*seeing* VASANTASENA, *to himself, in despair*] Is it possible? The deer comes to meet the tiger. This is sad.

    While her mate, radiant in his silver plumes,
    Sleeps, on the seashore, lit by the autumn moon,

215   The swan steals away, leaves him forsaken—
    Only to rush into the arms of a raven!
  Vasantasena, this is not right, this is not worthy of you.
    Your pride made you reject him at first, so great was your love's ardor.
    And now you accept him, because of money, your mother's order?
220 VASANTASENA [*shaking her head*] No.
  VITA   You honor him again with the baseness of a courtesan's character?
    Didn't I tell you before, "Those you like and those you dislike: serve them
    both from an equal standpoint?"
  VASANTASENA   I am here because I got into the wrong cart. And now I seek
225   your protection.
  VITA   Don't worry, don't worry. I'll give him the dupe.
    [*Goes back to* SAMSTHANAKA.]
  Dear Bastard, you were right, after all. There *is* a demoness in there!
  SAMSTHANAKA   But, Vita, if there is a demoness in there, how come it hasn't
  robbed you? Or, if it is a robber, how come it hasn't eaten you up?
230 VITA   Well, let's not worry about that for now. Why don't we just go down
  those gardens and walk into Ujjayini.
  SAMSTHANAKA   Why will we do that?
  VITA   Why? Well, we'll get to exercise our legs a bit and rest those bullocks
  as well.
235 SAMSTHANAKA   All right, we'll do that. Sthavaraka, my slave, my son, take
  the cart away. Or, wait a minute. Am I going to the gods or to the Brahmins, that I'll have to walk? No! No, I say. I want to go in the cart, so that
  when the people see me from a distance they'll say: "There's Mister
  Brother-in-Law-of-the-King!"
240 VITA [*to himself*]   It's impossible to make medicine out of this poison! Well, then,
  so be it. [*Aloud*] Bastard dear, it is actually Vasantasena, come to visit you.
  VASANTASENA   Heaven forbid! What a shame!
  SAMSTHANAKA [*joyously*]   Vita! Vita! She's come to visit *me*, the great man?
  Lord Krishna himself?
245 VITA   Yes, indeed.
  SAMSTHANAKA   What an amazing stroke of luck! The last time, I made her
  mad. This time I'll fall on her feet and beg for forgiveness, to please her.
  VITA   Well said.
  SAMSTHANAKA   I'll throw myself at her feet. [*Approaching* VASANTASENA.] O
250   Mother of mine, listen to my prayer—
    I fall at your feet, you wide-eyed dame with glistening teeth.
    Here's the offering of my hands to the ten nails of your feet.
    I am your slave! Forgive my love-mad sins, which I shan't repeat.
  VASANTASENA [*angrily*]   Get out of my sight! Your words are filthy!
    [*Kicks at him.*]
255 SAMSTHANAKA   You dare to kick the head which grannies and mothers kiss?
    Which bends only for the gods (to revere, not to be remiss)?
    You dare to dump me, the way a jackal would corpses dismiss?
    Sthavaraka, you slave, where did you pick her up?
  STHAVARAKA   The main road was blocked by villagers' carts, sir. So I left it by
260   Charudatta's garden door and got out to help a fellow with his cart. I guess
  that's when she got into this cart by mistake.

SAMSTHANAKA   So, she got here by mistake? Not by choice, to court me? Get
out! Get out of my cart! You were tiring my bullocks to drive over and court
that pauper merchant of yours, that Charudatta! Get out, get out, you
265   daughter-of-a-slave-woman!

VASANTASENA   "To court Charudatta!" It's a compliment that shines on me
like an ornament. Now whatever has to happen, let it happen.

SAMSTHANAKA   These ten lotus-shaped fingers that'd touch you with care,
Will now be used to drag you off my cart by the hair
270   As Jatayu dragged Vali's wife, in spite of her despair.[7]

VITA   You can't drag women of such virtuous beauty by their hair;
Just as the tendrils of a garden-vine you should not impair.

SAMSTHANAKA [to himself]   The fire of anger that was lit by her insults has
now doubled from her kick. Now I'll kill her! And this is what I'll do.
275   [aloud] Vita, Vita—
A thick-woven, wide-fringed, big cloak—if that's what you require;
Rare dishes to eat, chew-chew-slurp-slurp—if that's what you aspire.

VITA   Then what?

SAMSTHANAKA   Will you grant me a favor, that I dearly desire?

280 VITA   Certainly I will, unless it is a crime.

SAMSTHANAKA   There's not even a scent of crime in this. Not a sign.

VITA   Out with it, then.

SAMSTHANAKA   Kill Vasantasena.

VITA [placing his hands on his ears]
Kill this young woman? The ornament of our city?
285   This rare courtesan who loves like a woman of nobility?
What raft will then ferry me over the river of Eternity?

SAMSTHANAKA   I'll get you a raft. Besides, who's going to see you kill her? The
garden is deserted.

VITA   Ten quarters of the world will see it, the nymphs of the forest,
290   The moon, the radiant sun, the sky, the winds and all the rest,
My inner soul, the Earth (who has all good and evil witnessed).

SAMSTHANAKA   Well, cover her up with your cloak and then kill her.

VITA   Fool! You've lost your head!

SAMSTHANAKA [to himself]   This old fox is scared of sinning. Well, let him be.
295   Let me ask this slave boy of mine, Sthavaraka. Sthavaraka, my boy, I'll get
you golden bracelets.

STHAVARAKA   I'll wear 'em!

SAMSTHANAKA   I'll have a golden bench made for you.

STHAVARAKA   I'll sit on it!

300 SAMSTHANAKA   I'll give you food from my own plate.

STHAVARAKA   I'll lap it up!

SAMSTHANAKA   You'll be the overseer of all the other slaves.

STHAVARAKA   I'll oversee!

SAMSTHANAKA   Then you must do what I say.

305 STHAVARAKA   Anything, Master, unless it's a crime.

SAMSTHANAKA   There's not a scent of crime in it.

STHAVARAKA   Tell me, master.

7. Vali, son of Indra and king of Kishkindha,   appeared in the same epic, he had nothing to
was a member of a monkeylike race in the   do with Vali or his wife.
Ramayana. Though Jatayu, a vulture god,

SAMSTHANAKA   Kill Vasantasena.

STHAVARAKA   Pardon me, Master! Mercy! It is me, this idiot, who brought the
310   lady here by mistake.

SAMSTHANAKA   You slave, do you think I have no power over you?

STHAVARAKA   Yes, sir, you do have power over my body, sir, but not over my
character. Have pity! Be merciful, Master! I am scared!

SAMSTHANAKA   You are *my* slave! What are you scared of?

315 STHAVARAKA   Of the other world, Master!

SAMSTHANAKA   What other world?

STHAVARAKA   The world that you are given as a result of your good and bad
deeds, Master.

SAMSTHANAKA   What results will good deeds bring you?

320 STHAVARAKA   Good deeds will give me a world like yours, with plenty of gold.

SAMSTHANAKA   And what world will bad deeds give you?

STHAVARAKA   A world like mine, sir, where one has to live off food others give.
No, Master, I won't commit a crime.

SAMSTHANAKA   You won't kill her?

[*Beats him.*]

325 STHAVARAKA   Beat me, Master! Murder me! But I won't commit a crime.
    The faults in my Fate have kept me a slave for a lifetime;
    I don't need to buy more faults. I won't commit a crime.

VASANTASENA   Master, I seek your protection!

VITA   Bastard dear, pardon her! Cool down. Well done, Sthavaraka.
330   Even the slave wants a place in the other world that's secure;
    But not his master! So, those who with bad deeds injure
    The path of virtue, why are they not by Fate abjured?
Moreover, it is true—
    Fate knows no justice: it enters through the smallest rupture,
335   But makes him the slave and you his master.
    So, just as he will never enjoy your wealth,
    You don't have to obey the order he has dealt.

SAMSTHANAKA [*to himself*]   The old fox is afraid of sinning. And this son-of-a-
slave's scared of his "other world"! But I am the king's brother-in-law!
340   Great man! Epitome of manhood! [*Aloud*] You! Son-of-a-slave! Go away.
Go home and rest. And keep out of my way.

STHAVARAKA   As you please, Master. [*to* VASANTASENA] My lady, that's the best
I could do.

[*Leaves.*]

SAMSTHANAKA [*looping his girdle*]   Wait, Vasantasena, stay right where you
345   are. I am going to kill you.

VITA   What! Not while I am around!

[*Grabs* SAMSTHANAKA *by the throat.*]

SAMSTHANAKA [*falling to the ground*]   Vita, you're beating up your master!

[*Faints and regains consciousness again.*]

    Haven't I always fed you with the best of butter and meat?
    And now in my time of need, you turn an enemy and it's me you beat.
350 [*Thinking, to himself*] There! I've hit upon an idea. The old fox is signaling
Vasantasena by shaking his head. So, I'll send him away and kill Vasantasena
while he's gone. Yes, that'll do it! [*Aloud*] Vita—do you really think that a

man like me would actually commit a crime just because I said I would? I am from a family of great fighting men. I said it only to make her say yes to
350   my proposition.

VITA   Why do you boast of your noble birth?
        Even thorny bushes flourish on fertile earth.
        It's virtue that makes you a man of worth.

SAMSTHANAKA   Vita, with you around, she is too shy and cannot acknowl
360   edge me. So, please go. Sthavaraka, my slave, has left because I gave him a good hiding. In fact, he's on the run. Go, catch him and bring him back here.

VITA [to himself]   Vasantasena is way too proud to own,
        With me around, her love for someone so crude.
365   So I'll leave her here with him alone;
        The pleasures of love work best in solitude.
        [Aloud] Very well, I'll go.

VASANTASENA [holding him by the hem of his cloak]   Didn't I ask for your protection?

370   VITA   Don't be scared, Vasantasena, don't be scared! Bastard dear, I leave Vasantasena in your custody.

SAMSTHANAKA   Agreed. And I shall "execute" your trust!

VITA   Truly?

SAMSTHANAKA   Truly.

375   VITA [starting to move, but stopping after a few steps]   No! As soon as I am gone, he'll turn around and kill her. Well, let me hide myself here and see exactly what he has in mind.
        [Hides himself in a corner.]

SAMSTHANAKA   Good! Now I'll kill her. But wait! That Brahmin is a shrewd old fox, maybe he's hiding somewhere and trying to cheat me. And like a
380   true fox he may even howl. There must be a way to trick him. Yes, that's what I'll do.
        [Plucks flowers and pretties himself up.]
        Vasantasena! My little girl, come, come here!

VITA   Ah! He's turned into a gallant lover now. Well, that's a relief. I'll go now.
        [Leaves.]

SAMSTHANAKA   I'm giving you gold, I'm talking so sweet;
385   With my head in turban I roll at your feet;
        Still you so refuse to enslave me, girl with teeth so bright,
        To have me for a servant. Oh, men suffer such plight!

VASANTASENA   Do you think I would ever doubt that?
        [Recites the next two verses with a bowed head.]
        Evil, filthy creature! Wealth you think will me allure?
390   The bee shall not leave its lotus, graceful and pure!

        What though he is poor. If he is a well-born, virtuous man,
        In giving herself to such a man, she honors a courtesan!
        Besides, having known the mango tree, do you think I'll consider a *palasha*?[8]

___

8. A flowering plant known for its bright red color; its resin was used in ancient India in cosmetics and medicine. The contrast is between the superficially attractive *palasha* and the sustenance of the fruit-bearing mango tree.

SAMSTHANAKA   Daughter-of-a-slave! You compare that beggar Charudatta to
395   a mango tree and me to a dry, odorless *palasha*? Even while insulting me,
all you think of is Charudatta?

VASANTASENA   He lives in the middle of my heart. How can I not remember him?

SAMSTHANAKA   Then I'll crush both you and that man "in the middle of your
400   heart," two together! Just you wait! You lover of a penniless trader, stay there!

VASANTASENA   Say it again. Please say it again. Those words honor me!

SAMSTHANAKA   Let that son-of-a-slave Charudatta come and save you now!

VASANTASENA   He would, if he could see me.

SAMSTHANAKA   Who is he? Indra? Vali's son, Mahendra? Rambha's son
405   Kalanemi? Subandhu? Shiva? Drona's son Jatayu? Chanakya? Dhundhumara? Trishanku?[9] Even they couldn't save you! And as Chanakya murdered Sita in the Bharata age,

As Jatayu slew Draupadi,[1] I'll gag you, have you ravaged!

[*Reaches out to grab her.*]

VASANTASENA   Oh Mother, where are you? Oh Charudatta, I die before our
410   heart's longing is met! I'll scream for help. But, no! I'll be shamed if people
say Vasantasena screamed. I bow to the noble Charudatta.

SAMSTHANAKA   The slave girl still speaks the scoundrel's name?

[*Pressing her throat.*]

Think of him, slave girl! Remember him now!

VASANTASENA   I bow to the noble Charudatta.

415   SAMSTHANAKA   Die, slave girl, die!

[*Strangles her.*]

[*Vasantasena falls to the ground and lies motionless.*]

SAMSTHANAKA   There she lies, the vessel of sin,
A vessel with wholesome pride within.
On time she had come for her lover to meet;
He didn't come, and Death brought her defeat.
420   But why do I boast of my arms, strong and stout?
She died simply because her breath gave out.
She died well, like Sita in *Mahabharata*,[2] the epic;
She cried, "Mother!"—the word my ears did pick.

She didn't want me, but I did want her!
425   Her refusal, in turn, led to my anger.
Angered thus, and finding her by herself, solitary,
I scared and then gagged her in this old sanctuary!

9. Again, Samsthanaka's references are a confused jumble of Indian mythology and history. Vali had no son named Mahendra; Kalanemi is an uncle by marriage of Rambha, Queen of the Apsarases, entertainers who danced in heaven before Indra's throne; Subandhu was a Sanskrit writer, and thus, like Chanakya (mentioned above) a historical figure; Jatayu was son of Aruna, who drove the chariot of the sun god, not Drona, a teacher and warrior of Hindu mythology; Dhundhumara is another name for the mythical King Kuvalayaswa, who killed the demon Dhundhu; and Trishanku, another mythical king, was granted his own heaven when he tried unsuccessfully to ascend to heaven as a mortal.

1. Neither the goddess Sita (Rama's wife and the heroine of the *Ramayana*) nor Draupadi was murdered or had any connection with the "murderers" named here.

2. Sita does not appear in the *Mahabharata*.

My brother, father, and my mother, like Draupadi,[3]
Missed my valorous act, my stupendous gallantry.

430 Well, what has happened has happened. The old fox may come back at any
moment. I'll step aside and wait.

[Does so.]

[Enter the VITA with STHAVARAKA.]

VITA I have managed to convince Sthavaraka to come back with me. Now I
must find where the Bastard is.

[Walks around, looking.]

What! Isn't that a tree fallen down across the road? And when it crashed it
435 crushed a woman beneath it. You murderer tree, why did you commit this
crime? Seeing that my heart has fallen, too. This is a bad omen, and my heart
fears for Vasantasena. Let the gods be good in every way. [going to Samst-
hanaka] Hello there, my Bastard! I've brought Sthavaraka back with me.

SAMSTHANAKA I am happy you came back, Vita. Sthavaraka, my slave-son, I
440 am happy you're back, too.

STHAVARAKA Your mercy, my Master.

VITA Give me back my custody.

SAMSTHANAKA Custody? What custody?

VITA Vasantasena.

445 SAMSTHANAKA She's gone.

VITA Where?

SAMSTHANAKA After you.

VITA [suspiciously] After me? She did not go that way.

SAMSTHANAKA Which way did you go?

450 VITA East.

SAMSTHANAKA I think she went south.

VITA I went south myself.

SAMSTHANAKA Well, then she went north.

VITA You sound confused. I cannot understand. And my heart is not at
455 peace. Tell me the truth!

SAMSTHANAKA Vita, I swear by your head, and by my feet: set your heart at
peace. I killed her.

VITA [in despair] You really killed her?

SAMSTHANAKA If you don't believe my word, see for yourself. The first heroic
460 deed of the king's brother-in-law!

[He shows him.]

VITA What disaster! To see this was written in my Fate!

[He swoons.]

SAMSTHANAKA The Vita has died!

STHAVARAKA Courage, learned Master, rest your heart! I killed her first when
I brought the cart here without thinking.

465 VITA [regaining consciousness, sadly] The flowing river of generosity has at
last dried up.

The goddess of love returns to the heavens above.
Lovely faced, so full of life, you were the gem of gems.

3. A possible reference to an episode in the
Mahabharata in which the eldest of the Pandava brothers gambles away everything—even
staking Draupadi, their common wife, who is
then dragged into the room.

Your expertise was brilliant when it came to amorous games.
470 You were a river of courtesy, your smiles were its islands.
You protected men like me; your love-store now disbands.
[*Weeping*] What did you gain from this, you vile, evil sinner?
She was the goddess of the city, and you dared to kill her?
[*To himself*] Who knows, maybe the scoundrel will put the blame on me.
475 I'd better run from here!

> [*He starts to walk off;* SAMSTHANAKA *catches up.*]

Don't you touch me, murderer! I am finished with you. I leave.

SAMSTHANAKA   Stop! First you kill Vasantasena and now you try to blame me
for it? Are you abandoning a person of my standing?

VITA   Scoundrel!

480 SAMSTHANAKA   I'll give you gold, money, and a turban—all to be taken;
Let this crime be shared, not me alone left forsaken!

VITA   This crime is yours and only you should it rake.

SAMSTHANAKA   Heaven help me!

> [*He laughs.*]

VITA   I've lost all affection for you! Stop laughing, fiend!
485 Curse on that friendship that insults the friend!
I'll have nothing to do with you and this you must know:
I discard you like an unstrung, broken bow!

SAMSTHANAKA   Don't be angry, Vita dear. Come, let's go and amuse ourselves
in the city.

490 VITA   If again people see me with you, if with you I go—
I am still an honorable man, but I wouldn't remain so,
For you have killed a woman, you're a killer without disguise;
The city women look at you with fear, and lower their eyes.
[*sadly*] Vasantasena—
495 I'll pray so that in your next life you're not born a courtesan;
But by your virtue, you're reborn as the daughter of a noble man!

SAMSTHANAKA   Where do you think you are going? You've murdered Vasantasena! And that, too, in my garden, the old Pushpakarandaka. Come on.
I'll take you to the court of my sister's husband, the king.

> [*Grabs him.*]

500 VITA   Just you wait, you miserable crook!

> [*Draws his sword.*]

SAMSTHANAKA [*stepping away in fear*]   What? Are you scared? So, go—run!

VITA [*to himself*]   I'd better not stay here anymore. Yes! I'll join the forces of
the noble Sharvilaka and Chandanaka.

> [*Leaves.*]

SAMSTHANAKA   Go to hell! Sthavaraka—my slave-boy. So, how did I do?

505 STHAVARAKA   You committed a great crime, Master.

SAMSTHANAKA   What, slave? You said "great crime?" I've committed a crime?
Well, let me put it this way.

> [*Takes off some of his ornaments.*]

Take these jewels. I give them to you. They are mine while I wear them.
The rest of the time they're yours.

510 STHAVARAKA   They look best on you, Master. What will I do with them?

SAMSTHANAKA You'd better go back to the palace with the bullocks and wait for me in the pigeon house on my palace roof.

STHAVARAKA As you command, Master.

[Leaves.]

515 SAMSTHANAKA The Vita disappeared to save his own skin. As for this slave, I'll chain him up and leave him in my pigeon house. In that way the word shall never spread. So, let's get out of here. But . . . maybe I ought to take a look at the corpse to see if it's really dead or whether I'll need to kill it all over again.

[Looks at her.]

Oh, she's dead, all right. Well dead! Good. Let me hide her under the cloak. But wait—hold it! An educated person might read my name on it.
520 Well, I'll cover her up then with this pile of dry leaves that the wind has blown over here.

[Does so and pauses to think.]

Good, that's settled. And now this is what I'll do: I'll go to the court and file a case against Charudatta the merchant, saying that he trespassed on my old Pushpakarandaka garden and murdered Vasantasena for her money.
525   I have devised a new plot to destroy Charudatta now;
    A sacrifice, in a sacred city, of a sanctimonious cow.
Good! It's time to make a move.

[Spots the MONK while exiting. Stops.]

This is incredible luck! Wherever I go, this accursed bhikshu always runs into me. There he is again, with a kashaya-colored robe. I had led him by
530 the nose and I am sure he hates me for that. If he sees me he'll inform others that I may have killed her. How can I get away? [Looking around] I'll climb over that half-broken wall over there!
    Like Mahendra from atop Mount Hanuman will I fly,
    Over the city of Lanka, soaring high in the sky![4]

[Leaves.]

[Enter the MONK, hurriedly.]

535 MONK Now that I'm done washing my robes, will I hang them from a branch to dry? The monkeys would run away with them. Shall I spread them out on the ground? They'll get dirty from the dust. Where can I put them out to dry? [looking around] Here, let me spread it out on this pile of windblown leaves.

[Does so.]

Glory to Buddha!

[Sits down.]

540 Now I shall chant a hymn from my faith.
    He who has succeeded in vanquishing the Five Men (the Five Faculties),
    The Woman (Ignorance) and the weak lowborn Chandala (his Personality),
    Has saved the Village (his Soul) and found Svarga (ultimate Liberty).
I have occupied myself a bit too much, I think, with ultimate liberty. But it
545 won't mean much unless I have expressed my gratitude to Vasantasena,

---

4. Mahendra is the mountain, a holy site mentioned in many ancient texts and the Mahabharata; Hanuman, an avatar of Shiva and a central character in the Ramayana, uprooted Mount Dronagiri and transported it hundreds of miles to the battlefield at Lanka, where Rama was engaged in war with Ravana.

that blessed servant of Buddha. Ever since she freed me from those gamblers, I feel like I've become her slave.

[*He looks around.*]

What's that? Did I hear a sigh from under the leaves? But no!
550   The wetted garment has moistened the leaves;
And they're heated by the hot breeze too, I believe.
As a result, like a bird's unfolding wings, they heave.

[VASANTASENA, *reviving, puts out a hand.*]

MONK   The hand of a woman! With beautiful bracelets and rings! What is this? And there's the other hand, too!

[*Studies them intently.*]

I think I recognize the hand. Of course! I am quite sure. It is this very hand
555   that granted me protection. Moreover, let's see—

[*Removes the leaves, sees and recognizes her.*]

Yes! This is she, the servant of Buddha herself!

[VASANTASENA *gestures that she wants water.*]

MONK   What? Do you want water? The pond is far off. What should I do now? Yes! I'll wring out water from these wet clothes on top of her.

[*Does so.*]

[VASANTASENA *is fully conscious now. She sits up. The* MONK *fans her with the edge of his robe.*]

VASANTASENA   Who are you, sir?
560   MONK   The servant of Buddha does not remember me? You bought me for ten gold pieces.

VASANTASENA   I seem to remember, but not what you say. I wish I had died!

MONK   What happened, servant of Buddha?

VASANTASENA [*regretfully*]   Whatever ends up happening to a prostitute.

565   MONK   Get up, servant of Buddha, arise! Hold on to this creeper here, close to this tree—

[*He brings the creeper within her reach;* VASANTASENA *gets up with its help.*]

In the monastery over there, I have a sister-in-faith. There you can stay awhile to calm your mind, before going home. Walk slowly, servant of Buddha. [*Walking, watchfully*] Move away, gentlemen, clear the way. It is a
570   young woman and a *bhikshu* pure of faith.
He is a man who can control his hands, mouth, and his senses;
What is a kingdom to him? He holds eternity in his defenses!

[*They leave.*]

[*End of Act.*]

SUMMARY OF ACT 9

In a courtroom Samsthanaka accuses Charudatta of murdering Vasantasena, although her body is never produced. A parade of witnesses follow, and Charudatta is implicated in an improbable conspiracy. On the basis of circumstantial evidence the old and confused Judge, who is not an admirer of the king's brother-in-law, is forced to sentence Charudatta to exile. In the last minutes of the trial, however, King Palaka overturns the Judge's lenient sentence and imposes an order of execution: Charudatta is to be impaled to death.

Act 10

[*Enter* CHARUDATTA, *with two* EXECUTIONERS *following him.*]

EXECUTIONERS   You ask for logic and reason in vain,
  For we shall shortly remove your pain
  By impaling you, perhaps chopping your head;
  We are both experts in turning the living dead.
5 Make way, make way, sirs! This is the noble Charudatta.
  Garlanded with oleanders he will with us, the executioners, march;
  He's like the flickering, fading, shimmering wick of a torch!
CHARUDATTA [*remorsefully*]   Limbs covered with dust, my face is wet with tears;
  My body is covered with the burning-ground flowers.[5]
10 Seeing me the ravens there croak hoarsely and pine;
  I'll be the bloody offering on which they shall dine.
EXECUTIONERS   Move out, move out, sirs!
  What is there to see?
  A good man drawing his last breath,
15 About to be axed by the god of death?
  He was like a tree
  To honest men who in him found rest,
  Like birds on a branch finding nests.
  Come, Master Charudatta, come.
20 CHARUDATTA   The ways of man's fate are beyond all imagination, that I should come to such a state!
  Red hand-marks and streaks of sandal paste
  All over my limbs and body have been placed;
  I'm covered with flour-paste and sesame,[6] so that they can
25 Turn me into a sacrificial beast, that was once a man.
  [*Looking in front of him*] Ah, see the differences among men!
  [*Compassionately*] "Curse Fate," some say, seeing me,
  Crying sorrow-cloven;
  Others, failing to save me, say, "He
30 Shall go to heaven."
EXECUTIONERS   Move away, sirs, move away! What's there to see? Don't you know—
  Indra's banner (the lightning in the sky),[7]
  A cow giving birth, a falling star,
35 A good man being taken to die
  Are four things not to see, not even from afar.
EXECUTIONER 1   Look, Ahanta, look—
  Because the god of death orders our noblest citizen to die,
  Do you see lightning and weeping rain in a cloudless sky?

---

5. Flowers traditionally used to decorate bodies on their final journey to the special areas, usually on the outskirts of a city or village and often on the banks of a river, reserved for the ritual burning of the dead.

6. These edible substances symbolize that convicts would become food for the gods upon their execution.

7. That is, like Indra's glorious banner, a bolt of lightning can hurt the eye if seen directly.

40 EXECUTIONER 2 No, Goha.

There's neither lightning nor weeping rain in the cloudless sky;
The cloud's a throng of women, the rain—the tears in their eyes!
Also, look—
As we take this good man to die,

45 The citizens ceaselessly cry;
Their tears wet the road that was dry;
It is so wet, not even dust would fly.

CHARUDATTA [looking about, pitiably] The women cry, craning their necks
from their palace windows,
"Alas, Charudatta!" And their weeping in rivulets flows.

50 EXECUTIONERS Come, Charudatta, come. We've now got to the first proclamation point.[8] Sound the drum! Pronounce the proclamation! (together)
"Listen, good people, listen! This is Charudatta, son of Sagaradatta,
grandson of Provost Vinayadatta. He committed a crime: he lured Vasantasena into the deserted Pushpakarandaka garden and strangled her

55 with his own hands for a trifling sum of money. He was caught with the
loot and confessed his crime. Therefore, King Palaka has ordered us to
execute him. As any person who commits a crime is accursed in this
world and the next, our King Palaka would have him executed in the very
same accursed manner!"

60 CHARUDATTA [despairingly, to himself] My family name, in a hundred fire
ceremonies purified,
Repeated along with Vedic mantras[9] and thus glorified,
A name once spoken with pride in crowded temples of fame,
Is now being publicly announced by lowborn men. Shame!
[Clapping his hands over his ears, in despair] Oh, Vasantasena, my love!

65 Your teeth are as bright as the moon's pure light,
Your lips are as crimson as the coral's red;
How can I, who on your face's divine nectar fed,
Helplessly drink the poison of shame and slight?

EXECUTIONERS Out of the way, sirs, out of the way!

70 Like a mine of gems, he is virtue's quarry,
A bridge for suffering men to cross beyond misery.
And now he is led out of town without a piece of jewelry.
It's true—
People think only of those who are well off and comfortable;

75 Who cares about the poor and those with luck unfavorable?

CHARUDATTA [looking around] I see ex-friends hide their faces in their gar-
ments and run;
Even a stranger is a friend when you are rich—for it's fun!
But when evil days arrive, alas, friends there are none.

EXECUTIONERS The people have been cleared out. The main road is clear.

80 And, since the criminal has already been marked with the signs of death,
let's take him down.

CHARUDATTA Ah, Maitreya, what bad luck has struck me today!

---

8. A designated site at which an execution was announced to the public while the condemned person was paraded through the city on the way to the burning grounds.

9. Ritual incantations in Vedic, an ancient form of Sanskrit and the language of the Vedas. Hinduism's oldest texts.

My innocent wife of Brahmin birth—what dismay!
Rohasena, you see nothing of this—with others you play.

85 VOICES OFFSTAGE   —"Oh Father!"—"My friend!"

CHARUDATTA [*having heard, with emotion*]   You are the noblest of your caste.
I beg you to do me a favor.

EXECUTIONERS   A favor! Will you accept it from *us*?

CHARUDATTA   What a shame! Even you executioners have a greater sense of
90   propriety than the evil Palaka. He is the real *chandala*. For my happiness in
the other world, I wish to look once more upon the face of my son.

EXECUTIONERS   That can be done.

VOICE OFFSTAGE   Father, Father!

CHARUDATTA [*mournfully*]   You are the noblest of your caste.

95 EXECUTIONERS   Citizens! Make way, make way, for Master Charudatta to
catch a glimpse of his son's face. [*Looking backstage*] This way, sir, this
way! Come over here, boy, this way.

[*Enter* MAITREYA *with* ROHASENA.]

MAITREYA   Hurry, hurry, my boy! They're taking your father. To kill him!

ROHASENA   Father, father!

100 MAITREYA   My friend, must I see you like this!

CHARUDATTA [*looking at his son and friend*]   My son! Maitreya! [*Pitifully*]
What pain!
In the other world, thirst shall keep me in blight;
For the food and water of my last rites will be slight.
But what have I to leave my son?

[*Looks on himself and sees his Brahminical thread.*]

105   Yes, I still have this.
The Brahmin's ornament, though not of pearls or gold,
May satisfy the gods and spirits of our forefathers old.

[*Gives Rohasena the thread.*]

EXECUTIONER 1   Come, Charudatta, move along!

EXECUTIONER 2   Hey! You dare call Master Charudatta by name, without a
110   title? Look:
Fate—galloping away like a young, riderless, fugitive mare,
In prosperity or ruin, by day or night—goes the way it'll dare!
You have called him without respect, do you think he'll care?
But still, we should bow before him to prove we're honest and fair.
115   Even if Rahu[1] eclipses the moon, do people stop their prayers?

ROHASENA   Executioners, where are you taking my father?

CHARUDATTA   My child,
On my shoulders, an oleander garland and a stake-pole I carry;
Like a sacrificial goat following a priest, I walk to the crematory.

120 EXECUTIONER 1   Know this, son—
We may be lowborn executioners by birth, but we are not the bad guys;
They who torture good men are the true executioners, in disguise.

ROHASENA   Then why are you going to kill my father?

EXECUTIONER 1   May your life be long! It's the king's order that's to be blamed,
125   son, not us.

---

1. In Indian mythology, a snake or dragon that brings about lunar eclipses by attempting to eat the moon; also one of the nine planets in Hindu astronomy, generally considered inauspicious.

ROHASENA   Kill me then, and let my father go.

EXECUTIONER 1   Blessed one, say more of such words and live long.

CHARUDATTA [*embracing his son, in tears*]   This is the true wealth of love that
    rich and poor both share;
    A balm to the heart that does not for fancy ingredients care!

130   MAITREYA   Good men, let go my dear friend. Kill me, instead!

CHARUDATTA   Heaven forbid!

EXECUTIONER 1   Make way, make way, sirs! What are you staring at?
    Slander has murdered all his hopes of living; can you not tell?
    He's like a golden pitcher with its rope broken that sinks in the well.

135   CHARUDATTA [*thinking of* VASANTASENA]   Your teeth are as bright as the
    moon's pure light,
    Your lips are as crimson as the coral's red;
    How can I, who on your face's divine nectar fed,
    Helplessly drink this poison of shame and slight?

EXECUTIONER 2   Come on, you must repeat the proclamation.

140   EXECUTIONER 1 [*repeats*]   "Listen, good people, listen! This is Charudatta, son
of Sagaradatta, grandson of Provost Vinayadatta. He committed a crime: he
lured Vasantasena into the deserted Pushpakarandaka garden and strangled
her with his own hands for a trifling sum of money. He was caught with the
loot and confessed his crime. Therefore, King Palaka has ordered us to
145   execute him. As any person who commits a crime is accursed in this world
and the next, our King Palaka would have him executed in the very same
accursed manner!"

CHARUDATTA   Misfortune's spell drags me to this shameful station;
    Which like a tree shall give the fruit of death,
150   But—"He killed her!"—the ringing proclamation,
    Is what's hurting my heart with every drawing breath.

    [*On another part of the stage* STHAVARAKA *is discovered in fetters, inside
    the palace.*]

STHAVARAKA [*having heard the proclamation, in despair*]   What? Must the
innocent Charudatta die? And I have been chained by my master. So what? I
will shout, "Listen, folks, listen! It is I, this sinner, who drove Vasantasena to
155   the old Pushpakarandaka garden, because she mistook the cart I drove to be
hers. And there my master strangled her with his own hands because she
wouldn't love him. Charudatta didn't do it at all!" My voice is not reaching
them. They're much too far away. What should I do? I'll jump to the ground.

    [*Thinks.*]

If I do that, they won't kill Master Charudatta. Right. I'll hurl myself through
160   this old circle-window, beside the staircase to the attic. It's better that I die
than Master Charudatta, the nesting tree that shelters birds, the savior of
wellborn sons. Even if I die in this, I have the assurance of a good deliverance to the next world.

    [*Throws himself down.*]

Amazing! I didn't die! But my chains have broken. I'll find out where the
165   drums of those executioners are coming from.

    [*Finds them and approaches.*]

You, executioners! Let me through!

EXECUTIONERS   Who is this, that wants to get through?

STHAVARAKA   Listen, folks, listen! It is I, this who drove Vasantasena to the
old Pushpakarandaka garden, because she mistook the cart I drove to be hers.
170   And there my master strangled her with his own hands because she wouldn't
love him. Charudatta didn't do it at all!

CHARUDATTA   Who is this, when I am about to wear the deathly Kala's[2] noose,
Like clouds, over a drought-stricken field, bringing rain-news?
Have you heard him?
175   It is besmeared reputation, not death, that truly frightens me;
Death would be as dear as a newborn son, if I lived shame-free.
But,
That debased sinner, Death, whom I never hated,
Stains me now with an arrow, poison-baited.
180   EXECUTIONERS   Sthavaraka, are you telling the truth?

STHAVARAKA   I am telling the truth. And to stop me from telling his story, my
master kept me chained in the attic pigeon house of his palace.

[*Enter* SAMSTHANAKA *at a different area of the stage.*]

SAMSTHANAKA [*joyfully*]   Today at home I had my lunch on sour and bitter
dishes:
Greens, lentil, treacled rice . . . meat and a couple of fishes!
185   [*Listens*] I can hear those executioners chattering, clattering like busted
brass cymbals. Are those the drums of execution? They're taking that pauper Charudatta to the killing field. Let me have a look. The death of an
enemy is a huge satisfaction. Besides, I have heard, he who sees an enemy
being killed won't suffer from eye trouble in his next life. And yes, like a
190   worm trapped inside the knot of a lotus root, I searched and searched for a
hole to crawl out, and found it finally by bringing about that pauper Charudatta's death. Now I shall go up to my very own pigeon house attic and
witness my heroic achievement!

[*He does so and looks out.*]

Well, well! What a thronging crowd has gathered to see poor Charudatta's
195   execution! I wonder how big a crowd would gather if a person like me, a
preeminent prominent personage, were being led to his death?

[*Looks closely.*]

Prettied up like a new bullock he is taken south. And now what? The sound
of the proclamation, loud enough to carry to my pigeon house attic, suddenly stops!

[*Looks around.*]

200   What? Sthavaraka gone! I hope he hasn't run away and told my secret—I
have to find him!

[*He goes down and enters the main action area.*]

STHAVARAKA [*seeing him*]   There he comes, gentlemen!
EXECUTIONERS   Move out! Make way! Bolt your door!
Be very quiet! Say nothing more!
205   There he comes like a raging bull,
With pointed horns, sharp and full.

SAMSTHANAKA   Hey, make way for me, make way! [*Approaching*] Sthavaraka,
my son, come along, slave. Let's go.

2. God of death (also known as Yama). The word *kala* also means "time."

STHAVARAKA   You scoundrel! Aren't you happy with murdering Vasantasena?
210   Are you now up in arms to kill Charudatta as well? That heavenly wishing-
tree to all seekers?

SAMSTHANAKA   I am like a pitcher made of gems and jewels. I do not kill
women.

STHAVARAKA   It is you who killed her, not Charudatta.

215   SAMSTHANAKA   Says who?

ALL [*pointing at* STHAVARAKA]   This honest man!

SAMSTHANAKA [*afraid, using his hand to hide his face, to himself*]   My goodness!
Didn't I chain Sthavaraka strongly enough? He's a witness to my crime!
[*Thinking*] This is what I'll do . . . [*Aloud*] It's a lie, gentlemen! This slave
220   was caught stealing my gold, so I beat him up and chained him down.
That's why he hates me. How can you believe what he says in his anger
towards me? [*Aside to* STHAVARAKA, *secretly offering him a bracelet*] Here,
Sthavaraka, my little son, have this and change your story.

STHAVARAKA [*taking it*]   Look, look, gentlemen—he's trying to tempt me with
225   gold!

SAMSTHANAKA [*snatching the bracelet back*]   There is my gold. Which is why
I tied him up! [*Angrily*] Executioners, I had given this one the charge of my
gold locker. When he stole from it, I beat him up. If you don't believe me,
take a look at his back.

230   EXECUTIONERS [*looking*]   He's right. When a slave is mad, he can say anything.

STHAVARAKA   This is what it means to be a slave. No one will believe me,
even when I speak the truth! [*Pitifully*] Master Charudatta—I have done
all I could within my power.

[*Throws himself at* CHARUDATTA'*s feet.*]

CHARUDATTA [*compassionately*]   My upright, virtuous friend, arise.
235   Unselfishly, with me you sympathize.
You tried in every way to set me free,
But Destiny with you could not agree.

EXECUTIONERS   Sir, give this slave another beating and drive him away.

SAMSTHANAKA   Get away from here.

[*Drives* STHAVARAKA *away.*]

240   You executioners—what are you waiting for? Kill him!

ROHASENA   Kill me, executioners, but let my father go!

SAMSTHANAKA   Kill him and his boy too!

CHARUDATTA   This fool can do anything. You must go now, my son, go back to
your mother.

245   ROHASENA   And what will I do after I go back?

CHARUDATTA   You'll go to a hermitage[3] with your mother today;
Let not what happened to your father come your way.
Maitreya, take him and leave.

MAITREYA   Friend, is this what you've understood? That I will continue to live
250   without you?

CHARUDATTA   It is not right, Maitreya, to give up living when your life is in
your own hands.

---

3. A place of refuge for the needy and the homeless (upon Charudatta's death, his house would be
confiscated and his family left penniless).

MAITREYA [*to himself*]   Yes, it would be sinful. But it is impossible for me to live without my dear friend. So, I shall deliver the boy to his mother and then
255   follow my friend into death. [*Aloud*] My friend, I'll take him away at once.

[*Embraces* CHARUDATTA *and falls at his feet.*]

[ROHASENA *prostrates himself before* CHARUDATTA, *weeping.*]

SAMSTHANAKA   What's this? Didn't I tell you to kill him with the boy?

[CHARUDATTA *shows fear.*]

EXECUTIONERS   The king's order is very specific; it doesn't say we are to kill his son as well. Run along, boy. Get going.

[MAITREYA *leaves with* ROHASENA.]

EXECUTIONERS   We've reached the third proclamation point. Beat the drum!
260   [*repeating*] "Listen, good people, listen! This is Charudatta, son of Sagaradatta, grandson of Provost Vinayadatta. He committed a crime: he lured Vasantasena into the deserted Pushpakarandaka garden and strangled her with his own hands for a trifling sum of money. He was caught with the loot and confessed his crime. Therefore, King Palaka has ordered us to execute him. As any
265   person who commits a crime is accursed in this world and the next, our King Palaka would have him executed in the very same accursed manner!"

SAMSTHANAKA [*to himself*]   What's going on? The townspeople still don't believe it? [*Aloud*] You, Charudatta, brat of a Brahmin, the townspeople still don't believe you did it. Tell them with your own tongue: you killed Vasantasena.

[CHARUDATTA *remains silent.*]

270   SAMSTHANAKA   Look, executioners, this young man won't talk. Make him talk! Thrash him, over and over again, with that bamboo drumstick of yours.

EXECUTIONER 1 [*preparing to hit*]   Talk, Charudatta.

CHARUDATTA [*sorrowfully*]   I have been hurled so deep into Sorrow's ocean,
        My mind feels no terror, no despairing emotion;
275   But I am by the flames of disgrace being seared,
        To say: "I've killed the one my heart had endeared!"

SAMSTHANAKA   Make him talk! Thrash him, over and over again with that bamboo drumstick!

CHARUDATTA   Listen, townspeople—
280   Being cruel and careless of things that in the other world await;
        A woman as lovely and pure as Rati[4] did I . . . let him the rest relate.

SAMSTHANAKA   ". . . I murdered!"

CHARUDATTA   You said it.

EXECUTIONER 1   You're in charge of the execution today.
285   EXECUTIONER 2   No, you are.

EXECUTIONER 1   All right, let's calculate in writing.

[*They make complicated calculations, writing or drawing lines in many combinations.*]

EXECUTIONER 1   All right, all right, it is my execution today. But then, it'll have to wait a little.

EXECUTIONER 2   What for?

290   EXECUTIONER 1   Well, before he died my father said: "My brave son, when you are in charge of an execution, never be in a hurry to kill."

---

4. Goddess of desire and consort of Kamadeva, god of love.

EXECUTIONER 2   Why not?

EXECUTIONER 1   Well, you know, a good man may suddenly appear and buy the condemned man's freedom. Or, a son is born to the king and he grants amnesty to all the condemned. Or, an elephant may break free and in the commotion the condemned man may run away. Or, maybe, there's a change of kings and everyone on death row is set free.

SAMSTHANAKA   What, what was that? A change of kings?

EXECUTIONER 2   Oh, we're just trying to figure out whose turn it is to do the execution.

SAMSTHANAKA   Oh, come on now. Hurry up and execute Charudatta!

[He withdraws to the side with STHAVARAKA.]

EXECUTIONER 1   Master Charudatta, blame the king's order, do not blame us executioners. Now think your last thoughts.

CHARUDATTA   If my love has any power, my beloved will deliver me
     (Whether in Indra's heavenly abode or not she be)
     By the sheer merit of her own virtuous quality;
     Falsely slandered, though, I am crushed by Fate,
     By men of powerful and exalted estate.
   Where would you like me to go, friend?

EXECUTIONER 1 [pointing ahead]   Look, you see the southern burning-ground there? Where the condemned lose their lives in no time? Over there at that stake—
     The lower half of an impaled corpse the jackal drags and mangles;
     While the other half stares like a laughing mask, even as it dangles!

CHARUDATTA   All is lost. Unfortunate that I am!

     [Falls on the ground.]

SAMSTHANAKA   I am not moving. Not before I have seen Charudatta being killed.

     [Walks about and looks.]

   What? He's sitting down?

EXECUTIONER 1   Are you afraid, Charudatta?

CHARUDATTA [rising at once]   Fools!
     It is besmeared reputation, not death, that frightens me;
     Death would be as dear as a newborn son, if I were shame-free!

EXECUTIONER 2   Master Charudatta, it is not just people who are scared of death and their own kind; even the sun and the moon, in the heavens, have to die in their eclipses. He who rises has to fall, just as he who falls can rise again: so he who dies lives again. It is like changing garments, this fall and rise of the body. Think that over in your mind and you'll be composed and strong. [to EXECUTIONER 1] This is the place for the fourth proclamation.

EXECUTIONERS [together]   "Listen, good people, listen! This is Charudatta, son of Sagaradatta, grandson of Provost Vinayadatta. He committed a crime: he lured Vasantasena into the deserted Pushpakarandaka garden and strangled her with his own hands for a trifling sum of money. He was caught with the loot and confessed his crime. Therefore, King Palaka has ordered us to execute him. As any person who commits a crime is accursed in this world and the next, our King Palaka would have him executed in the very same accursed manner!"

CHARUDATTA   Vasantasena, my love!

Your teeth are as bright as the moon's pure light,
Your lips are as crimson as the coral's red;
340   How can I, who on your face's divine nectar fed,
Helplessly drink the poison of shame and slight?

    [Enter VASANTASENA and the MONK, excitedly, at another area of the stage.]

MONK   My ascetic life has been blessed, to be able to comfort Vasantasena after her untimely collapse and bring her here. Servant of the Lord, where shall I escort you?

345 VASANTASENA   To Master Charudatta's house. Make me happy with the sight of him, like the night-lotus when it sees the moon!

MONK [to himself]   What road shall I take? [Thinking] I'll take the royal highway. Come, servant of the Lord. Here's the main road, the royal highway. [Listening] But what's that great racket I hear?

350 VASANTASENA [looking ahead]   There's a huge crowd! Do you know what's going on there, sir? It seems as though Ujjayini's tipping to one side like a ship whose cargo has been rocked!

EXECUTIONER 1   Here we are at the place for the final proclamation. Beat the drum. Pronounce the proclamation!

355 EXECUTIONERS [together]   "Listen, good people, listen! This is Charudatta, son of Sagaradatta, grandson of Provost Vinayadatta. He committed a crime: he lured Vasantasena into the deserted Pushpakarandaka garden and strangled her with his own hands for a trifling sum of money. He was caught with the loot and confessed his crime. Therefore, King Palaka has
360   ordered us to execute him. As any person who commits a crime is accursed in this world and the next, our King Palaka would have him executed in the very same accursed manner!"

CHARUDATTA   O Mother goddesses!

    [VASANTASENA and the MONK have moved closer to the main acting area.]

MONK [listening, panicked]   They're taking Charudatta to be executed because
365   he has killed you!

VASANTASENA [terrified]   Oh, horror! Catastrophe! Unfortunate that I am, they're killing Master Charudatta for me? Hurry, hurry, sir, show me the way!

MONK   Run! Run, servant of the Buddha! Bring Charudatta back to life! Let us through, folks, let us through!

370 EXECUTIONER 1   Master Charudatta, the king's orders are to blame. Remember whatever you need to remember.

CHARUDATTA   What more can I have to say?
    If my love has any power, my beloved will deliver me
    (Whether in Indra's heavenly abode or not she be)
375   By the sheer merit of her own virtuous quality;
    Falsely slandered, though, I am crushed by Fate,
    By men of powerful and exalted estate.

EXECUTIONER 1 [drawing his sword]   Lie down on your back and don't move. We'll deliver you to Indra's paradise with one clean stroke.

    [CHARUDATTA lies down.]

380 EXECUTIONER 1 [about to strike; the sword falls from his hand]   What is that?
    I drew my sword, vigorously swung it;
    In my two hands I literally wrung it;
    Yet the deadly weapon I couldn't hold;
    It fell on the ground like a thunderbolt!

385   This seems to be a definite sign: the noble Charudatta should not die.
O great goddess Durga, dweller of the Mount Sahya[5]—have mercy! If
Charudatta really doesn't have to die, it will mean well for us executioners.

EXECUTIONER 2   But we must carry out our orders.

EXECUTIONER 1   Yes. Of course. Let us do this, then.

    [They prepare to impale CHARUDATTA.*]*

390 CHARUDATTA   If my love has any power, my beloved will deliver me
    (Whether in Indra's heavenly abode or not she be)
    By the sheer merit of her own virtuous quality;
    Falsely slandered, though, I am crushed by Fate,
    By men of powerful and exalted estate.

    [The MONK *and* VASANTASENA *arrive at the main acting area.]*

395 MONK *and* VASANTASENA *[seeing the preparations]*   Don't, sirs, don't!

VASANTASENA   It is I, the unfortunate wretch, for whom he is about to die!

EXECUTIONER 1 *[looking in their direction]*   Who is she? On her shoulders
    spreads her abundant hair;
    And crying with hands raised, doesn't she this way fare?

400 VASANTASENA   Noble Charudatta, what has happened?

    [Falls on his chest.]

MONK   What is this, Master Charudatta?

    [Falls on his feet.]

EXECUTIONER 1 *[approaches, trembling.]*   What? Vasantasena! How lucky—I
    didn't kill an innocent man!

MONK *[rising]*   Thank heaven, Charudatta lives!

405 EXECUTIONER 1   May he live for a hundred years!

VASANTASENA *[joyfully]*   Then I live again!

EXECUTIONER 1   We must go and inform the king. He's at the sacrifice grounds.

    [They start off.]

SAMSTHANAKA *[trembling, as he stares at* VASANTASENA*]*   The impossible has
happened. Who has brought this slave girl back to life? My life's running
410   away from me. I must get away from here!

    [He flees.]

EXECUTIONER 1 *[returning]*   The king's order asks us to execute the molester
of Vasantasena. We must chase him down, the brother-in-law of the king!

    [They leave.]

CHARUDATTA *[astounded]*   Just as the sword was raised and I stood before
    Death's gate,
    Who are you, like rain on a parched field, that my pains abate?
415   *[Staring at her]* Is this another Vasantasena, or has she from heaven
    descended?
    Is she really not dead, or has she from my imagination ascended?

VASANTASENA *[in tears, prostrating herself at* CHARUDATTA's *feet]*   It's I. Yes, the
    sinner, for whom you fell to such unworthy disgrace.

BYSTANDERS   Miracle! A miracle! Vasantasena lives!

---

5. The place where Shiva appeared at the request of the gods to kill the demon Tripurasura. *Durga:*
one of the many incarnations in which Parvati (Shakti) appears as Shiva's consort.

CHARUDATTA

    [*Rises quickly, hearing the bystanders, and touches* VASANTASENA, *closing his eyes, ecstatically.*]

420   My love! You are Vasantasena!

VASANTASENA   Yes, that same ill-fated woman.

CHARUDATTA [*looking at her with delight*]   Vasantasena it is!

    [*With extreme happiness*] From where did you come, with your breasts
      bathed in tears;

    With knowledge to rouse the dead, wherefrom did you appear?

425   Beloved Vasantasena!

    I was about to die for you, but you saved me in the end;

    The power of lovers' uniting can make the dead ascend!

    And look, my beloved:

    This crimson robe is like the one worn by a bridegroom;

430   And this garland is quite like the one worn by a bride;

    And that drum, the one that so long sounded death's doom;

    Will boom like marriage drums, to add to the festive tide!

VASANTASENA   But tell me, what was it that you, with your overt generosity, did?

CHARUDATTA   Beloved, he said that I had murdered you.

435   My die-hard princely enemy with this lie, that he the world would tell,

    Almost dragged me to my doom! But he is himself now almost in hell!

VASANTASENA [*stopping her ears*]   Heaven forbid! That brother-in-law of the king was the one who tried to kill me!

CHARUDATTA [*noticing the* MONK]   But who is this?

440 VASANTASENA   While that ignoble man tried to kill me, this noble man brought me back to life.

CHARUDATTA   Who are you, selfless friend?

MONK   Don't you recognize me, Master? I am the masseur, the *samvihaka*, who massaged your feet! I had fallen into the hands of gamblers, and she bought
445 me free, repaying my debts with her jewels, because I was once in your service. I was so disgusted with gambling that I became a Buddhist *bhikshu*. This noble lady took the wrong cart and came to the Pushpakarandaka garden. And that scoundrel strangled her with his own hands because she refused to give in to him. And I found her there.

    [*Loud tumult offstage.*]

450 A VOICE   Hail to the bull-bannered Shiva, who destroyed Daksha's[6] insulting oblation;

    Hail to the six-faced Kartikeya,[7] who cleaved the Krauncha Pass by demolition;

    And hail unto Aryaka, who by putting a formidable enemy to eternal rest

    Has won the whole world, whose blazing banner is Mount Kailasha's[8] crest!

    [*Enter* SHARVILAKA, *suddenly, into another part of the stage.*]

6. Father of Sati, who disapproved of her marriage to Shiva. After Daksha insulted Shiva during a ritual sacrifice, Sati committed suicide out of shame and Shiva had Daksha killed by Virabhadra, a terrifying superwarrior. Shiva later restored Daksha to life, his missing head replaced with that of a goat.
7. Younger son of Shiva and Parvati. Unable to settle their dispute about who was more pow-

erful, Kartikeya and Indra asked Mount Kailasha. Enraged that it favored Indra, Kartikeya hurled his spear at the mountain, cleaving the Krauncha Pass out of it.
8. Favorite residence of Shiva and Parvati. Hindus view Kailasha as the location of paradise, the desired final destination of all departed souls.

SHARVILAKA   I've slain the evil Palaka, consecrating Aryaka in his stead,
455   And now I bear, like a wreath of flowers, upon my head,
         The command of our new king, his first directive:
         To free Charudatta from this unfair invective!

         The enemy whose ministers and soldiers had fled, he slew;
         And having, by his grand display, won the people's confidence,
460   He has now acquired the enemy's land, with sovereignty, anew;
         Like Indra drove the *asuras*[9] from their heavenly residence!
[*Looking ahead*] Yes, that's where he should be, where those crowds are
gathered. May the first enterprise of our new King Aryaka be crowned with
the renewed life of the noble Charudatta. [*Quickening his steps*] Out of the
465 way, out, loiterers! [*Looking, with joy*] Ah! Charudatta is still alive and so is
Vasantasena! The king's wishes shall be fulfilled.
         Thanks to heaven, from sorrow's shoreless sea
         I see him relieved, by his beloved, set free—
         As if by a ship of virtue and goodness carried ashore,
470   Like the Moon, freed from Rahu's jaws, glittering galore!
But how can I approach him? I who have sinned so against him? But
honesty is the best policy! [*Approaching* CHARUDATTA *openly, with joined
palms*] Master Charudatta!
CHARUDATTA   Who are you, sir?
475 SHARVILAKA   I am he who broke into your house and stole the jewel's custody;
         I committed a mortal sin and I beg before you, please, pardon me.
CHARUDATTA   Of course, my friend! In fact, by stealing the jewels you did me
a great service.
         [*Embraces him.*]
SHARVILAKA   One thing more:
480   To save his family's pride, the noble prince Aryaka,
         Like a sacrificial animal, has slain the evil Palaka!
CHARUDATTA   What?
SHARVILAKA   The same man who rode your cart and found your preservation,
         Sacrificed Palaka like a beast while he was doing another oblation.
485 CHARUDATTA   Sharvilaka, then you were the one who set Aryaka free after
Palaka had him arrested from his village and thrown into a dungeon without cause?
SHARVILAKA   That is right.
CHARUDATTA   This is good news, very good news for me!
490 SHARVILAKA   As soon as he was established on the throne of Ujjayini, your
friend Aryaka announced that you would be the ruler of the kingdom of
Kushavati-upon-Vena[1] from now on. Please honor this first request from
your friend. [*Turning around*] You there. Bring that scoundrel here, the late
king's brother-in-law!
495 BYSTANDERS   Do as Sharvilaka orders!
SHARVILAKA   King Aryaka also sends you this message, Master Charudatta: "I
have obtained this kingdom through your virtue. Therefore you ought to
enjoy it!"

9. Demonic creatures who unsuccessfully bat-
tled the *devas* (gods) for dominance.
1. Also known as Kushasthali, a polity founded

by Kusha, one of King Rama's twins. The Vena
is a tributary of the Wardha River in south-
central India.

CHARUDATTA   Obtained this kingdom through my virtue?

500 BYSTANDERS   Come, Mister Royal Brother-in-Law, come on over! Reap the
harvest of your crimes.

[*Enter* SAMSTHANAKA *with his hands fettered, led in by several men.*]

SAMSTHANAKA   Incredible!
I had run away like a donkey that had broken away from its rope;
Now they drag me back, leashed like a mad dog, as if I'm a dope!
[*Looking all around him*] The new king's henchmen are all around me. I

505 am totally alone! Who will help me in this unfavorable state? [*Thinking*]
Yes. I'll go to him, the ever obliging Protector of the Seeker! [*Drawing near*]
Master Charudatta—save me, save me!

[*Falls at his feet.*]

BYSTANDERS   Master Charudatta, leave him to us. We'll kill him!

SAMSTHANAKA   Protector of the Unprotected, deliver me!

510 CHARUDATTA [*compassionately*]   Yes! Whoever seeks my protection shall not
be denied.

SHARVILAKA [*angrily*]   Get that creature away from Charudatta! [*to* CHARU-
DATTA] Tell us, what should we do with this sinner?
Should we bind him and have him dragged until he dies?

515 Or should dogs devour him as the scoundrel lies?
Or should we, rather, make him sit atop a stake?
Or maybe we should saw him apart, two from one make?

CHARUDATTA   Will what I say be done?

SHARVILAKA   Who doubts it?

520 SAMSTHANAKA   Master Charudatta, I have sought your protection! Save me,
save me! Do what you would normally do. What is worthy of you. I'll never
do it again!

BYSTANDERS   Kill him, kill him! Why let that sinner live?

[VASANTASENA *takes the condemned man's wreath off* CHARUDATTA's
shoulders and throws it over SAMSTHANAKA's.]

SAMSTHANAKA   Forgive me, dame-of-a-slave, have mercy! I'll never murder

525 you again! Save me!

SHARVILAKA   Come on, take him away. Master Charudatta, tell us what shall
be done with the wretch.

CHARUDATTA   Will what I say be done?

SHARVILAKA   As I said, who doubts it?

530 CHARUDATTA   Truly?

SHARVILAKA   Truly.

CHARUDATTA   If that is so, then he should be right away—

SHARVILAKA   Executed?

CHARUDATTA   —allowed to go.

535 SHARVILAKA   But why?

CHARUDATTA   Even if he has wronged you, the enemy who asks for clemency,
Should not be executed—

SHARVILAKA   He should be thrown to the dogs!

CHARUDATTA   —he should rather be punished with mercy.

SHARVILAKA   Amazing! But do tell us what should be done with him.

540 CHARUDATTA   He should be released.

SHARVILAKA   Set him free!

SAMSTHANAKA Astonishing! I am alive again!

    [*Leaves with his captors.*]

SHARVILAKA My lady Vasantasena, the king is pleased to confer upon you the legal title of a "wedded wife."

545 VASANTASENA I am immensely honored, sir.

SHARVILAKA [*Veils* VASANTASENA; *turns to* CHARUDATTA.] Master, what shall we do for the *bhikshu*?

CHARUDATTA *Bhikshu*, what is your desire?

MONK Having seen this example of the uncertainty of all things, my desire
550 to remain a *bhikshu* has redoubled.

CHARUDATTA Friend, he seems resolute. So, let us make him the head of all Buddhist monasteries in the land!

SHARVILAKA As you say, Master.

VASANTASENA Now I feel really restored to life!

555 SHARVILAKA And, what should we do for Sthavaraka?

CHARUDATTA My good man, I free you from slavery. And let those executioners be the chiefs of all other executioners. Make Chanadanaka the chief of police in the kingdom. And, let the former king's brother-in-law have the same office he had before.

560 SHARVILAKA It will be as you say. But only let go of that last one. Let me kill him!

CHARUDATTA Protect him who seeks refuge—

    Even if he has wronged you, the enemy who asks for forgiveness,
    Should not be executed, but should be punished with thankfulness.

SHARVILAKA Now tell me, Master, what else can I do that'll please you?

565 CHARUDATTA What more can I ask for?

    My character's virtue has finally been proven;
    To my destroyed enemy a pardon I have given;
    King Aryaka has crushed his enemies to rule the earth;
    I regained my loved one; saw in you a friend's birth;
570   What else can I pray for, that is of more worth?

    For Destiny ignores one, only to fulfill another;
    She would uplift one, only another one to smother;
    Or, if she wants, she can hold a third at bay—
    Fortune and misfortune switch like night and day!
575   Destiny's games on the Laws of Opposites dwell:
    Like two water buckets going up and down in a well.
    I will, nevertheless, make this wish:
    May the cows give milk, may the earth yield the best grain,
    May the winds soothe our hearts, may the clouds timely rain,
580   May all be happy, may all Brahmins earn their due reverence,
    May virtuous kings tame their foes and rule with deference.

    [*All leave.*]

    [THE END.]

HROTSVIT OF GANDERSHEIM

935?–1002?

Hrotsvit, a canoness in the tenth-century abbey of Gandersheim, in north-central Germany, lays claim to several significant firsts in the history of Western literature. She is the first known Christian dramatist, the first Saxon poet, and the first female historian of Europe. Her plays are the first performable plays of the Middle Ages, and her epic poems are the only extant Latin epics composed by a woman. Her sophisticated output has been a puzzle and anomaly for literary scholars and historians for centuries, and opinions about the works have often been shaped by an unwillingness to acknowledge that a medieval woman could possibly know as much or write with as much skill as Hrotsvit did. Only during the last decades of the twentieth century were Hrotsvit's achievements given the sort of attention that they deserve; and even now, there is much that we don't know and can't fully appreciate about this remarkable woman.

What little we do know of Hrotsvit's life comes from clues in her own writing. Scholars suspect that she was born around 935. Although nothing is certain about her activities before she entered the abbey at Gandersheim in 955, we can say a few things confidently about the nature of her education and religious service once she chose to live in that Christian community. First, she would have had access to many classical Latin texts. During the medieval period, the major centers of learning in Europe were the monastic and cathedral schools, whose libraries amassed major collections of philosophical and theological writings. The Benedictine nunnery at Gandersheim was one of the most prominent of these centers. Such libraries collected manuscripts drawn not only from the Christian era but also from the classical Roman era that had preceded it. Because early Christian theologians believed that the pagan Latin texts were useful preparation for the more difficult challenge of reading Holy Scripture in Latin, students in monastic settings had access to much of the classical canon as well as to writings on church doctrine and biblical texts. Judging from clues in her own writings, it appears that Hrotsvit read Virgil, Ovid, and Terence among classical authors; she was also familiar with such early Christian philosophers as Augustine and Boethius. She was particularly well versed in saints' lives—the hagiographic texts that underlie many of her legends and dramas.

We also assume that Hrotsvit, like most canonesses who entered Gandersheim and other monasteries, was of noble birth. We know that she joined the community at about the same time that Gerberga II, a niece of Otto I (the German king and Holy Roman Emperor), came to the monastery.

In her writings, Hrotsvit credits Gerberga with much of her education. This connection to one of the most powerful families in Saxony suggests that either before or during her years at Gandersheim, Hrotsvit may have spent time at court, which would have given her further access to broad cultural influences.

Hrotsvit's oeuvre remained completely unknown to scholars for nearly five hundred years after her death; then, in 1494, the German humanist Conrad Celtis found what is now known as the Emmeram-Munich Codex, which he published in 1501. While German scholars, in a spirit of cultural nationalism, were quick to embrace Hrotsvit, critics elsewhere found her writing so advanced compared to other manuscripts from that period that they questioned its authenticity. In 1867, the Viennese scholar Joseph von Aschbach asserted that Celtis had forged the codex, arguing that no medieval woman could possibly have possessed Hrotsvit's knowledge of either the world or of classical literature. Aschbach's theories have subsequently been definitively refuted by the discovery of additional copies of Hrotsvit's writing, in their original Latin as well as in early vernacular translation. But the confirmation of the legitimacy of her oeuvre—which comprises eight verse legends; six plays in rhymed, rhythmic prose; two verse epics; and a short poem—has not resolved fundamental questions, particularly in the case of the plays, surrounding their genesis or historical significance.

Although we cannot definitively date Hrotsvit's work, most recent scholarship posits that she was at the height of her creative powers from 965 to 975. Scholars believe she began writing legends based on saints' lives soon after her arrival at the abbey, and her collection of plays followed. If these assumptions are true, then she may well have written her dramas at about the same time that the *Quem quaeritis* (Whom do you seek?) trope came to be added to the Easter Mass. This precursor to full-fledged medieval liturgical drama consisted of a short series of simple questions and answers between an angel and the women who come to Christ's tomb following the resurrection, sung by two halves of a church choir. Hrotsvit's work could thus predate the first extant mystery plays, or dramas based on scriptural incidents, by about seventy-five years. This revised history would then throw into question the long-held theory about how drama "reemerged" in the West after the end of the classical era.

In the standard explanation, dramatic arts declined precipitously after the collapse of Rome—essentially lying dormant for six centuries, only to be reborn in the tenth century. This rebirth was the product of growing theatricality in the rituals of the Catholic Mass, starting with the *Quem quaeritis* trope. Liturgical drama eventually broke free of the confines of the Mass, evolving into the mystery cycles that were sponsored and performed by professional guilds. From that point, scholars have generally believed, it was merely a matter of time before the drama would fully reflower, as it eventually did during the Renaissance.

Hrotsvit's dramas disrupt the prevailing narrative of medieval theater history because her plays are much more sophisticated than the rudimentary seed from which the revived Western drama was traditionally thought to have grown. In addition, the plays of Hrotsvit, which the playwright herself describes as imitations of the Roman comic dramatist Terence, demonstrate a continuity between classical and medieval theater, not the revival of a dead form.

Even among scholars who recognize that Hrotsvit's work complicates the standard history, there is considerable disagreement about the influence of her plays on medieval drama generally. Some have characterized Hrotsvit's work as an "isolated experiment," or a mere "literary exercise," implying that her plays were neither widely known nor intended for performance. While the discovery of copies of her manuscripts in different locations suggests that her works were known within the Christian community in Europe and thus could indeed have had some impact on medieval drama, the current evidence allows no more than conjecture about what, and how extensive, that impact might have been. Whether her plays were works of theater or just literary exercises has proven a more vexing question. We cannot conclude from the form of these six works that they were composed for theatrical performance. Like SENECA's plays in late antiquity, Hrotsvit's plays may simply have been examples of closet drama—pieces never staged, or never intended to be staged. But regardless of Hrotsvit's intentions, the plays themselves are undeniably theatrical, and can be performed.

The extent of Hrotsvit's understanding of theatrical performance is difficult to gauge, as many historians believe that Europeans in the tenth century had little knowledge of classical stage practice. In this era, written dialogues with speech prefixes (sometimes names of real people) were considered valuable pedagogical tools, but it is unclear whether they were meant to be read silently or aloud. Nor is it certain that such texts that we now understand to be dramatic or theatrical were distinguished from others in any way. Some scholars have speculated that dialogues may have been read aloud, either by a single person or by a number voicing the different "characters," with the suggested action silently dramatized by a mime, but there is little evidence to support or disprove this theory. What we can say is that of all of Hrotsvit's plays, DULCITIUS most strongly suggests its author's sense of performance. For this reason, it has emerged as a crucial text for historians seeking to explore the possible conjunction of dialogue and action in medieval drama.

Further complicating our interpretation of Hrotsvit's intentions is the self-deprecating tone of the prefaces and epistles that introduce many of her works. Initially, Hrotsvit's own prose was taken as evidence of her negligibility as a writer, but scholars have more recently acknowledged that it simply adheres to a common medieval Christian convention that gives God, not the writer, credit for whatever genius might be found in the work. A better clue to her sense of self and of her earthly mission may reside in the Latin nom de plume she adopted: Clamor Validus Gandeshemensis, or "the strong voice of Gandersheim." Perhaps, like some modern critics, she saw her own strength in a bold and daring design in her writings that was unmatched by any efforts of her contemporaries, either in literature or visual art. Or perhaps she was thinking that representing wise, strong, and virtuous Christian women in texts to be shared within communities like her own would have the power to transform cultural stereotypes.

In the preface to her dramas, Hrotsvit explains her goals, declaring a debt to and a quarrel with the Latin playwright Terence:

> Many Catholics one may find, and we are also guilty of charges of this kind, who for the beauty of their eloquent style, prefer the use of pagan guile to the usefulness of Sacred Scripture. There are also others, who, devoted to sacred reading and scorning the works of other pagans, yet frequently read Terence's fiction, and as they delight in the sweetness of his style and diction, they are stained by learning of wicked things in his depiction. Therefore I, the strong voice of Gandersheim, have not refused to imitate him in writing whom others laud in reading, so that in that selfsame form of composition in which the shameless acts of lascivious women were phrased the laudable chastity of sacred virgins may be praised within the limits of my little talent.

From this brief statement, Hrotsvit's plan is clear: she will revise Terence for Christendom. While borrowing his compositional style, she will correct his misogynistic portrayal of women and instead promote images of female virtue and chastity.

Although critics are divided about the extent and nature of Hrotsvit's debt to Terence, they generally agree that *Dulcitius* is the most Terentian of her plays. The influence of classical comedy may be seen in the play's lighter moments, such as the scene in which the Roman governor Dulcitius makes a lunge at pots and pans, thinking they are the young Christian virgins whom he wishes to ravish, ends up with soot all over his face, and is then mistaken for a demon. Comparisons can likewise be made between Terence's use of established classical character types, such as bombastic fathers, and Hrotsvit's adaptation of them as Roman figures of

COMEDIA SECVNDA DVLCICVS

An illustration from the 1501 edition of Hrotsvit's complete works showing the virgins Agape (love), Chionia (purity), and Hirena (peace) being burned alive.

authority. We may also observe a shared predilection for love conflicts as plot devices, and such motifs as scheming and disguise figuring in the works of both dramatists. Some critics, however, argue that these resemblances are isolated parallels, and that the spirit and content of Hrotsvit's plays much more thoroughly reflect medieval sensibilities. In their view, the comic scene and the conflicts between typed characters illustrate the use of Christian symbolism, as Hrotsvit pits the pagan forces of evil against the blessedness of Christian virtue and martyrdom.

Hrotsvit is remarkably faithful in *Dulcitius* to her source material, which is taken from the *Acta Sanctorum* (*Acts of the Saints*), a sixty-eight-volume compendium of exemplary tales of Christian saints' lives. The story that serves as the basis for *Dulcitius* describes the martyr-dom of the holy virgins Agape (love), Chionia (purity), and Hirene (peace), all put to death by order of the Roman emperor Diocletian in Thessalonica in the year 290. In her careful schema, Hrotsvit opposes the idealized women to the pagan male authorities Dulcitius (who represents lust), Diocletian (arrogance), and Sissinus (cruelty). The virgins' death at the hands of torturers ensures their Christian salvation, while their pagan persecutors secure eternal damnation—made literal by Dulcitius's representation as the soot-faced devil—for their evil deeds. Like Christ, the women are tempted to abandon their religious beliefs and sense of mission, but they resist. They withstand torture and death, thereby overpowering their male aggressors, whom they show to be impotent in the face of Christian faith. Through these trials, Hrotsvit throws into question the image of women as the weaker sex. Moreover, by celebrating female chastity she strongly links women not with Eve—the dominant association—but with the idealized Virgin Mary.

These themes of female fortitude and faith recur in Hrotsvit's other dramas, *Gallicanus*, *Calimachus*, *Abraham*, *Pafnutius*, and especially *Sapientia*, her last drama, which also depicts the martyrdom of three young virgins. The works not only were thematically innovative but also reflected an astounding facility with Latin rhetorical structures, including *stichomythia*, the use of alternating lines of dialogue to dramatize a dispute. By including doxologies (short hymns of praise to God) at the close of most of her works and in other ways, Hrotsvit demonstrated her clear understanding of the role her works might play in the broader arena of Christian education, as well as her knowledge of the liturgy. And her skill at characterization remains unprecedented in early medieval dramaturgy.

While scholars may never be able fully to determine how Hrotsvit's work may have influenced the development of the medieval drama, her growing significance in the modern period is indisputable. Her plays have been translated and performed steadily from the late nineteenth century forward. Especially noteworthy is the 1914 production of *Pafnutius* in London by the Pioneer Players, which showcased the talents of three prominent women of the Edwardian theater. Edith Craig directed, using the English translation of Christabel Marshall (under the pseudonym Christopher St. John), and the performance featured the legendary actor Ellen Terry in the role of the Nun. The study of Hrotsvit's plays from the mid-twentieth century onward has forced scholars both to carefully reexamine foundational assumptions in theater history and to reconsider dismissive attitudes toward women's writing throughout the Western tradition. The rediscovery of other medieval women authors—most notably the twelfth-century dramatist and musician-composer Hildegard of Bingen, writer of the earliest extant liturgical morality play, *Ordo virtutum*—will surely help fuel this important critical dialogue.   J.E.G.

The Martyrdom of the Holy Virgins Agape, Chionia, and Hirena[1]

DULCITIUS

CHARACTERS

DIOCLETIAN, a Roman emperor
AGAPE, a holy virgin
CHIONIA, a holy virgin
HIRENA, a holy virgin
DULCITIUS, a Roman governor

DULCITIUS'S WIFE
SISSINUS, a Roman count
SOLDIERS
GUARDS

The martyrdom of the holy virgins Agape, Chionia, and Hirena whom, in the silence of the night, Governor Dulcitius secretly visited, desiring to delight in their

1. Translated by Katharina M. Wilson.

embrace.[2] *But as soon as he entered, he became demented and kissed and hugged the pots and pans, mistaking them for the girls until his face and his clothes were soiled with disgusting black dirt. Afterward Count Sissinus, acting on orders, was given the girls so he might put them to tortures. He, too, was deluded miraculously but finally ordered that Agape and Chionia be burnt and Hirena be slain by an arrow.*

DIOCLETIAN[3]   The renown of your free and noble descent and the brightness of your beauty demand that you be married to one of the foremost men of my court. This will be done according to our command if you deny Christ and comply by bringing offerings to our gods.

5 AGAPE   Be free of care, don't trouble yourself to prepare our wedding because we cannot be compelled under any duress to betray Christ's holy name, which we must confess, nor to stain our virginity.

DIOCLETIAN   What madness possesses you? What rage drives you three?

AGAPE   What signs of our madness do you see?

10 DIOCLETIAN   An obvious and great display.

AGAPE   In what way?

DIOCLETIAN   Chiefly in that renouncing the practices of ancient religion you follow the useless, newfangled ways of the Christian superstition.

AGAPE   Heedlessly you offend the majesty of the omnipotent God. That is

15 dangerous . . .

DIOCLETIAN   Dangerous to whom?

AGAPE   To you and to the state you rule.

DIOCLETIAN   She is mad; remove the fool!

CHIONIA   My sister is not mad; she rightly reprehended your folly.

20 DIOCLETIAN   She rages even more madly; remove her from our sight and arraign the third girl.

HIRENA   You will find the third, too, a rebel and resisting you forever.

DIOCLETIAN   Hirena, although you are younger in birth, be greater in worth!

HIRENA   Show me, I pray, how?

25 DIOCLETIAN   Bow your neck to the gods, set an example for your sisters, and be the cause for their freedom!

HIRENA   Let those worship idols, Sire, who wish to incur God's ire. But I won't defile my head, anointed with royal unguent by debasing myself at the idols' feet.

30 DIOCLETIAN   The worship of gods brings no dishonor but great honor.

HIRENA   And what dishonor is more disgraceful, what disgrace is any more shameful than when a slave is venerated as a master?

DIOCLETIAN   I don't ask you to worship slaves but the mighty gods of princes and greats.

---

2. The story of the martyrdom of the holy virgins in 290 C.E. derives from the *Acta Sanctorum* (*Acts of the Saints*), an encyclopedia of the saints recognized by the Roman Catholic Church. The virgins' Greek names mean Love, Purity, and Peace, respectively. Although there was an actual Dulcitius, a Roman military leader who in 369 C.E. was appointed *Dux Britanniarum* (commander of Britain; Latin), he lived nearly a century after the events depicted in the play. Hrotsvit may have chosen the name simply for the irony of its link to the Latin *dulcis*, which means "sweet, charming."

3. Gaius Aurelius Valerius Diocletianus (ca. 245–316 C.E.), Roman emperor from 284 to 305 C.E. He was zealous in the persecution of Christians.

35 HIRENA   Is he not anyone's slave who, for a price, is up for sale?

DIOCLETIAN   For her speech so brazen, to the tortures she must be taken.

HIRENA   This is just what we hope for, this is what we desire, that for the love of Christ through tortures we may expire.

DIOCLETIAN   Let these insolent girls who defy our decrees and words be put
40   in chains and kept in the squalor of prison until Governor Dulcitius can examine them.[4]

*

DULCITIUS   Bring forth, soldiers, the girls whom you hold sequestered.

SOLDIERS   Here they are whom you requested.

DULCITIUS   Wonderful, indeed, how beautiful, how graceful, how admirable
45   these little girls are!

SOLDIERS   Yes, they are perfectly lovely.

DULCITIUS   I am captivated by their beauty.

SOLDIERS   That is understandable.

DULCITIUS   To draw them to my heart, I am eager.

50 SOLDIERS   Your success will be meager.

DULCITIUS   Why?

SOLDIERS   Because they are firm in faith.

DULCITIUS   What if I sway them by flattery?

SOLDIERS   They will despise it utterly.

55 DULCITIUS   What if with tortures I frighten them?

SOLDIERS   Little will it matter to them.

DULCITIUS   Then what should be done, I wonder?

SOLDIERS   Carefully you should ponder.

DULCITIUS   Place them under guard in the inner room of the pantry, where
60   they keep the servants' pots.

SOLDIERS   Why in that particular spot?

DULCITIUS   So that I may visit them often at my leisure.

SOLDIERS   At your pleasure.

DULCITIUS   What do the captives do at this time of night?

65 SOLDIERS   Hymns they recite.

DULCITIUS   Let us go near.

SOLDIERS   From afar we hear their tinkling little voices clear.

DULCITIUS   Stand guard before the door with your lantern but I will enter and satisfy myself in their longed-for embrace.

70 SOLDIERS   Enter. We will guard this place.

*

AGAPE   What is that noise outside the door?

HIRENA   That wretched Dulcitius coming to the fore.

CHIONIA   May God protect us!

AGAPE   Amen.

75 CHIONIA   What is the meaning of this clash of the pots and the pans?

HIRENA   I will check. Come here, please, and look through the crack!

AGAPE   What is going on?

---

4. The asterisks have been added by the translator to denote changes in locale or the passage of time;
Hrotsvit's extant manuscripts contain no such scene divisions.

HIRENA   Look, the fool, the madman base, he thinks he is enjoying our embrace.

AGAPE   What is he doing?

80   HIRENA   Into his lap he pulls the utensils, he embraces the pots and the pans, giving them tender kisses.

CHIONIA   Ridiculous!

HIRENA   His face, his hands, his clothes, are so soiled, so filthy, that with all the soot that clings to him, he looks like an Ethiopian.

85   AGAPE   It is only right that he should appear in body the way he is in his mind: possessed by the Devil.

HIRENA   Wait! He prepares to leave. Let us watch how he is greeted, and how he is treated by the soldiers who wait for him.

*

SOLDIERS   Who is coming out? A demon without doubt. Or rather, the Devil
90   himself is he; let us flee!

DULCITIUS   Soldiers, where are you taking yourselves in flight? Stay! Wait! Escort me home with your light!

SOLDIERS   The voice is our master's tone but the look the Devil's own. Let us not stay! Let us run away; the apparition will slay us!

95   DULCITIUS   I will go to the palace and complain, and reveal to the whole court the insults I had to sustain.

*

DULCITIUS   Guards, let me into the palace; I must have a private audience.

GUARDS   Who is this vile and detestable monster covered in torn and despicable rags? Let us beat him, from the steps let us sweep him; he must not
100   be allowed to enter.

DULCITIUS   Alas, alas, what has happened? Am I not dressed in splendid garments? Don't I look neat and clean? Yet anyone who looks at my mien loathes me as a foul monster. To my wife I shall return, and from her learn what has happened. But there is my spouse, with disheveled hair she leaves
105   the house, and the whole household follows her in tears.

WIFE   Alas, alas, my Lord Dulcitius, what has happened to you? You are not sane; the Christians have made a laughingstock out of you.

DULCITIUS   Now I know at last. I owe this mockery to their witchcraft.

WIFE   What upsets me so, what makes me more sad, is that you were igno-
110   rant of all that happened to you.

DULCITIUS   I command that those insolent girls be led forth, and that they be publicly stripped of all their clothes, so that they experience similar mockery in retaliation for ours.

*

SOLDIERS   We labor in vain; we sweat without gain. Behold, their garments
115   stick to their virginal bodies like skin, and he who urged us to strip them snores in his seat, and he cannot be awakened from his sleep. Let us go to the Emperor and report what has happened.

*

DIOCLETIAN   It grieves me very much to hear that Governor Dulcitius has been so greatly deluded, so greatly insulted, so utterly humiliated. But
120   these vile young women shall not boast with impunity of having made a

mockery of our gods and those who worship them. I shall direct Count Sissinus to take due vengeance.

*

SISSINUS Soldiers, where are those insolent girls who are to be tortured?
SOLDIERS They are kept in prison.
125 SISSINUS Leave Hirena there, bring the others here.
SOLDIERS Why do you except the one?
SISSINUS Sparing her youth. Perchance, she may be converted easier, if she is not intimidated by her sisters' presence.
SOLDIERS That makes sense.

*

130 SOLDIERS Here are the girls whose presence you requested.
SISSINUS Agape and Chionia, give heed, and to my council accede!
AGAPE We will not give heed.
SISSINUS Bring offerings to the gods.
AGAPE We bring offerings of praise forever to the true Father eternal, and to
135 His Son co-eternal, and also to the Holy Spirit.
SISSINUS This is not what I bid, but on pain of penalty prohibit.
AGAPE You cannot prohibit it; neither shall we ever sacrifice to demons.
SISSINUS Cease this hardness of heart, and make your offerings. But if you persist, then I shall insist that you be killed according to the Emperor's
140 orders.
CHIONIA It is only proper that you should obey the orders of your Emperor, whose decrees we disdain, as you know. For if you wait and try to spare us, then you could be rightfully killed.
SISSINUS Soldiers, do not delay, take these blaspheming girls away, and
145 throw them alive into the flames.
SOLDIERS We shall instantly build the pyre you asked for, and we will cast these girls into the raging fire, and thus we'll put an end to these insults at last.
AGAPE O Lord, nothing is impossible for Thee; even the fire forgets its nature and obeys Thee; but we are weary of delay; therefore, dissolve the
150 earthly bonds that hold our souls, we pray, so that as our earthly bodies die, our souls may sing your praise in Heaven.

*

SOLDIERS Oh, marvel, oh stupendous miracle! Behold their souls are no longer bound to their bodies, yet no traces of injury can be found; neither their hair, nor their clothes are burnt by the fire, and their bodies are not at all harmed by the pyre.
155 SISSINUS Bring forth Hirena.

*

SOLDIERS Here she is.
SISSINUS Hirena, tremble at the deaths of your sisters and fear to perish according to their example.
HIRENA I hope to follow their example and expire, so with them in Heaven
160 eternal joy I may acquire.
SISSINUS Give in, give in to my persuasion.
HIRENA I will never yield to evil persuasion.

SISSINUS   If you don't yield, I shall not give you a quick and easy death, but multiply your sufferings.

165 HIRENA   The more cruelly I am tortured, the more gloriously I'll be exalted.

SISSINUS   You fear no tortures, no pain? What you abhor, I shall ordain.

HIRENA   Whatever punishment you design, I will escape with help Divine.

SISSINUS   To a brothel you will be consigned, where your body will be shamefully defiled.

170 HIRENA   It is better that the body be dirtied with any stain than that the soul be polluted with idolatry.

SISSINUS   If you are so polluted in the company of harlots, you can no longer be counted among the virginal choir.

HIRENA   Lust deserves punishment, but forced compliance the crown. With
175 neither is one considered guilty, unless the soul consents freely.

SISSINUS   In vain have I spared her, in vain have I pitied her youth.

SOLDIERS   We knew this before; for on no possible score can she be moved to adore our gods, nor can she be broken by terror.

SISSINUS   I shall spare her no longer.

180 SOLDIERS   Rightly you ponder.

SISSINUS   Seize her without mercy, drag her with cruelty, and take her in dishonor to the brothel.

HIRENA   They will not do it.

SISSINUS   Who can prohibit it?

185 HIRENA   He whose foresight rules the world.

SISSINUS   I shall see . . .

HIRENA   Sooner than you wish, it will be.

SISSINUS   Soldiers, be not afraid of what this blaspheming girl has said.

SOLDIERS   We are not afraid, but eagerly follow what you bade.

*

190 SISSINUS   Who are those approaching? How similar they are to the men to whom we gave Hirena just then. They are the same. Why are you returning so fast? Why so out of breath, I ask?

SOLDIERS   You are the one for whom we look.

SISSINUS   Where is she whom you just took?

195 SOLDIERS   On the peak of the mountain.

SISSINUS   Which one?

SOLDIERS   The one close by.

SISSINUS   Oh you idiots, dull and blind. You have completely lost your mind!

SOLDIERS   Why do you accuse us, why do you abuse us, why do you threaten
200 us with menacing voice and face?

SISSINUS   May the gods destroy you!

SOLDIERS   What have we committed? What harm have we done? How have we transgressed against your orders?

SISSINUS   Have I not given the orders that you should take that rebel against
205 the gods to a brothel?

SOLDIERS   Yes, so you did command, and we were eager to fulfill your demand, but two strangers intercepted us saying that you sent them to us to lead Hirena to the mountain's peak.

SISSINUS   That's new to me.

210 SOLDIERS   We can see.

SISSINUS   What were they like?

SOLDIERS   Splendidly dressed and an awe-inspiring sight.

SISSINUS   Did you follow?

SOLDIERS   We did so.

215 SISSINUS   What did they do?

SOLDIERS   They placed themselves on Hirena's left and right, and told us to be forthright and not to hide from you what happened.

SISSINUS   I see a sole recourse, that I should mount my horse and seek out those who so freely made sport with us.

*

220 SISSINUS   Hmm, I don't know what to do. I am bewildered by the witchcraft of these Christians. I keep going around the mountain and keep finding this track, but I neither know how to proceed nor how to find my way back.

SOLDIERS   We are all deluded by some intrigue; we are afflicted with a great fatigue; if you allow this insane person to stay alive, then neither you nor 225 we shall survive.

SISSINUS   Anyone among you, I don't care which, string a bow, and shoot an arrow, and kill that witch!

SOLDIERS   Rightly so.

HIRENA   Wretched Sissinus, blush for shame, and proclaim your miserable 230 defeat because without the help of weapons, you cannot overcome a tender little virgin as your foe.

SISSINUS   Whatever the shame that may be mine, I will bear it more easily now because I know for certain that you will die.

HIRENA   This is the greatest joy I can conceive, but for you this is a cause to 235 grieve, because you shall be damned in Tartarus[5] for your cruelty, while I shall receive the martyr's palm and the crown of virginity; thus I will enter the heavenly bridal chamber of the Eternal King, to whom are all honor and glory in all eternity.

---

5. In Greek and Roman mythology, a realm of punishment and torment beneath the underworld; in the Christian context of *Dulcitius*, Tartarus refers to hell.

GUAN HANQING

ca. 1245–ca. 1322

HAILED as the most original pioneer of the form of dramatic theater called zaju (Northern variety drama), Guan Hanqing holds a position similar to that of SHAKESPEARE: a prolific writer during a pivotal historical era whose writings have been accorded unrivaled cultural status. While the critical reputations of his contemporaries have waxed and waned over the centuries, Guan's literary and theatrical standing remains unchallenged even today. Chinese critics and audiences alike have praised his works for their sympathetic portrayals of ordinary human life and suffering, their skillful balance of realism and dramatic poetry, and their remarkably powerful women characters. These qualities are exemplified in *Dou E Yuan*— literally *Injustice to Dou E*, but sometimes (as here) published in English as *SNOW IN MIDSUMMER*, the title of a well-known later adaptation—which remains one of the best-loved of Guan's zaju plays. In the centuries since it was written it has become one of the most frequently performed and adapted works in Chinese theater.

Guan was born in the mid-thirteenth century and lived out his life in the northern district of Yen-ching, which in 1267 became Kublai Khan's "great capital," Ta-tu, on the site of modern-day Beijing. He began writing around 1260 and did not stop until his death in the late thirteenth or early fourteenth century. His long career spanned the entire period of Kublai Khan's reign as Khan from 1260 to 1294 and as first ruler of the Mongol (or Yuan) dynasty (1271–1368). Official court records of the time make no specific reference to Guan, suggesting that he did not hold an official post there. Though this may at first seem surprising, given his celebrity as a respected writer, playwrights were rarely granted positions at court under Kublai Khan. It is also unlikely that

Guan had sympathetic ties with the old Han Chinese aristocracy. He would never have known the court of the Song dynasty (960–1279), which the Mongol khans overthrew; and during his lifetime, north China under Kublai Khan was relatively peaceful and prosperous. A more probable explanation is that Guan favored more mundane pleasures over those of the court. Because Guan lived in a physician's household (where he himself may have worked as a practicing physician), he was protected from mandatory public service and taxation and enjoyed considerable freedom to live as he pleased. Indeed, he was known as the "Playboy of the Grand Capital" and focused his attention on gambling, drinking, and romance. By all accounts, he preferred the teahouse to the palace and would rather spend time with public entertainers and their commoner clientele than with courtly entertainers and their aristocratic patrons.

Although the performance traditions and techniques of Chinese theater have developed and changed considerably since the fourteenth century, Chinese still tend to view zaju plays as their "classical" drama, a corpus of works of higher poetic and literary quality than the drama of other eras. This lofty status is even more remarkable when we consider that there are more than three millennia of recorded theater history in China prior to the Yuan era. Accounts from court histories of the first millennium B.C.E. describe early theatrical performances in the time of the mythical King Yu Shun (2300–2205 B.C.E.). According to the scholars of the East Zhou dynasty (770–256 B.C.E.), theatrical rituals and musical performances occurred in China from the Shang dynasty (1760–1066 B.C.E.) onward. Imperial patronage during the first millennium B.C.E. supported jesters, puppeteers, storytellers, and other theatrical entertainers; Chinese actors today trace their art back to these various performative traditions, as well as to the famous Pear Orchard Conservatory, China's first known academy of music, which was established during the Tang dynasty (618–907 C.E.). Building on the various theatrical and musical forms that preceded them, early *zaju* of the Song dynasty in northern China arranged acrobatics, musical performances, and other entertainments around a short theatrical sketch, usually of a satirical nature. The growing popularity of theatrical entertainments coincided with the emergence of a vibrant middle class. To meet the increased demand for staged performances, numerous permanent theaters were built, some of them in the form of grand entertainment venues similar to today's film megaplexes.

This long tradition of performing arts in China might have been abruptly cut short had the Han intellectuals at the center of power during the Song dynasty held theatrical entertainments in high esteem, for the Mongol khans were keen to reject the cultural values of their predecessors and to keep the Han Chinese out of court. They therefore dismantled many crucial Chinese institutions after their conquest, casting many artists and intellectuals—who favored literary and philosophical pursuits dedicated to elucidating and

The ghost of Dou E appears to her father in this woodblock illustration from a Ming Dynasty publication of *Snow in Midsummer*.

expanding on the Confucian classics—out of positions of power and respect. Theatrical entertainers, who had enjoyed little respect from the Han elite, actually found their fortunes improved under Mongol rule: because they were officially classified with skilled technicians, they were protected from some of the more brutal state policies that affected intellectuals previously rewarded during the Song dynasty. It was the genius of Guan Hanqing and his contemporaries to take this cultural opportunity to transform the dramatic elements from various theatrical traditions, including early *zaju*, into cohesive dramatic texts—into a new form of *zaju* drama—much as the first great Greek theater artists, Thespis and AESCHYLUS, crafted tragedies from the looser frameworks of Dionysian rituals. As a result, during the Yuan dynasty *zaju* performances finally became high culture, and their scripts gained new literary respectability.

Guan's most admired *zaju* play, *Dou E Yuan*, concerns Dou E, who as a seven-year-old girl is given by her father, a poor Confucian scholar, to the widow Cai as payment for a debt. Ten years later, Dou E marries Cai's son but soon finds herself a widow. When another debtor, Doctor Lu, attempts to strangle Cai instead of repaying what he owes, she is rescued by Old Zhang and his son Donkey, who seek to marry the women. Dou E refuses Donkey's proposal out of loyalty to her dead husband, and the spurned suitor attempts to poison Cai, believing that the older woman's death will force Dou E to accept him. When instead Old Zhang drinks the poisoned soup and dies, Donkey accuses Dou E of murder and presents her with the choice of marrying him or going to court. Taken before the Prefect and beaten, Dou E maintains her innocence; but to spare her mother-in-law a beating, she falsely confesses to the crime and is sentenced to death. Dou E promises that her death will be followed by several signs that she has suffered an injustice, including a snowfall during the hottest part of the summer. Three years after her execution, her father returns as a court-appointed judicial official. Dou E's ghost appears to him, and when he hears her story he vows to avenge the wrong done to her.

Snow in Midsummer consists of four sequences of song sets (marked here as acts), each of which—as in Yuan *zaju* generally—contains about a dozen songs or verse passages connected by prose dialogue and action. In keeping with the dramatic convention of Yuan *zaju*, one major character—in this case, Dou E—sings the most morally and emotionally sympathetic lines of the play in lyric poetry. The other characters convey their feelings and opinions in various forms of spoken verse, while those passages whose principal function is to advance the story are spoken in simple prose. Because the Yuan stage had no formal scenery and minimal props, Guan's play relies heavily on language to underscore onstage movements, the passage of time, and the arc of its dramatic action. Characters identify and reidentify themselves, repeatedly recounting the events that have taken place. For example, Act 2 opens with an actor declaring: "I am Dr. Lu. I lured Mistress Cai outside the town and was just going to strangle her when two men rescued her. Today I am opening shop. I wonder who will turn up." This technique creates a story that is as much narrative as dramatic, and the sketch of past and present acquires an almost ceremonial clarity of presentation. It is the outline of moral illustration, but it is also the outline of a tragedy at once individual, social, and—in the face of death—cosmological.

Unifying these levels of meaning is the play's concern with justice in human affairs. *Snow in Midsummer* belongs to the popular genre of Chinese crime and detective fiction known in the sixteenth century as *kung-an*. *Zaju* plays written in this mode involve the commission of a crime and its prosecution under the legal system of the period. Within the courtroom, a judge or clerk ultimately solves the crime and dispenses justice. In almost all "courtroom" plays, the crime is murder, and the conflict is presented as a metaphysical struggle between good and evil. *Snow in Midsummer* also falls into a more specialized category: the "judgment-reversal" *zaju*, in which the verdict of a first judge is discovered to be erroneous and overturned by a second judge. The main points of interest in this subgenre are the difference between the corrupt judge and the honest judge and the process by which the latter undoes the damage caused by the former. Any Yuan courtroom play requires a villain, and the judgment-reversal plays call for two: the person who actually commits the crime and the dishonest judge. In *Snow in Midsummer* and other plays of this type, the victim is initially given a choice between a private and court settlement. The victim always chooses the court, confident that justice will prevail, but is proved terribly wrong. So it plays out in *Snow in Midsummer*, as the Prefect completes the cycle of injustice by sentencing Dou E to death.

The notion of justice portrayed in courtroom *zaju* is broadly in accordance with the principles of Confucius (551–479 B.C.E.), a philosopher whose teachings on government, justice, social relationships, and individual ethical conduct exerted a powerful influence on Chinese thought and literature for millennia. During the Song dynasty, which preceded the Mongol occupation, the *Analects* and other writings of the *Ru* philosophical school that Confucius founded were required study for those, like Dou E's father, who took the imperial civil service examinations. The principles of Confucianism—loyalty, proper observance of ritual, duty, justice, and benevolence—permeated every aspect of Chinese intellectual and cultural life. In the area of social relationships, Confucius stressed that cruelty should be redressed with justice, and all Yuan courtroom dramas, including *Snow in Midsummer*, meet that requirement in their conclusions. The judgment-reversal plays portray an especially stark imbalance in what a Confucian would view as the just equilibrium of human society, an imbalance epitomized in the disgraceful figure of the first judge and set right by his replacement in the second trial. From a Confucian perspective, the results are morally satisfying: the social, natural, and divine order is restored and an injustice redressed. Guan complicates these moral polarities that underlie Confucian thought and conventional judgment-reversal drama, however. In *Snow in Midsummer*, the second judge—Dou E's father—is not simply the inverse of the first judge. His methods appear no less brutal than those of his predecessor, and his powers of investigation little better. Moreover, it takes the otherworldly intercession of Dou E's ghost for her father even to pay attention to the case, and he discovers nothing that she does not explain to him.

Confucian principles also underlie the play's characterizations, though here, too, Guan's dramatic writing imbues Confucian models with human realism and complexity. Confucianism places a high value on filial duty and piety, for instance, and Dou E is clearly motivated by duty to her father (and, later, Cai). Yet rather than being a Confucian archetype, she is clearly an individual, motivated by passion and subject to historical social conditions. Throughout the play, she is the victim of misfortune and exploitation, and the social dimensions of her life's sorrows are recapitulated several times throughout the play, first by Cai and later with more personal bitterness by herself. The young widow's fierce denunciation of Cai's acceptance of a husband is fueled at least partly by her knowledge that fate has denied her the pleasures and protections of marriage. Medieval Chinese women were often powerless in the face of male desires, as demonstrated in the play by Cai's inability to fend off Zhang's advances despite her economic independence. Unmarried women and widows were especially vulnerable to such abuses, and Dou E's calamities are closely related to her status as a woman without a husband.

The personal difficulties of widowhood, of course, do not obscure the fact that Dou E acts at every turn in accordance with Confucian family values. Given the bitterness of her attack on Cai's inappropriate marriage, her willingness to sacrifice herself for her adoptive mother in court is stunning. But what appears in the abstract to be a noble act in the name of filial piety can also be understood as a welcome release from the tribulations of a miserable life. Similarly, while the miracles granted by Heaven at Dou E's execution and the circumstances of her return as a ghost to demand justice frame her story as a divine restoration of the natural Confucian order, the dramatic emphasis is on the final appeal from a daughter to her father to redress her personal tragedy.

Justice may triumph at the end of *Snow in Midsummer*, but Guan's play remains haunted by Dou E's earlier protest and lament, sung before her execution:

> The good are poor, and die before their
>   time;
> The wicked are rich, and live to a great
>   old age.
> The gods are afraid of the mighty and
>   bully the weak;
> They let evil take its course.
> Ah, Earth! You will not distinguish
>   good from bad,
> And, Heaven! You let me suffer this
>   injustice!
> Tears pour down my cheeks in vain!

By calling into question Confucian notions of divine justice, lines such as these challenge the certainties of Confucian belief. Indeed, Dou E's redemption at the conclu-sion of the play seems as much a product of her will, indomitable even after death, as it is of heavenly or earthly justice.

Later adaptations of *Dou E Yuan* by the literati of the Ming dynasty (1368–1644) altered the work in ways that deepened its adherence to Confucian thought. But Guan's original play, which appealed to a wider, populist audience, emphasizes the ordinary passions and frustrations of Dou E and the other characters. Thus Dou E, who might be seen as a universal representation of conservative Confucian moral values, is at the same time a compellingly individual character, forceful in personality and artic-ulate in her protests against the injustice she faces. Such complexity has led critics to variously interpret *Snow in Midsummer* as a Chinese tragedy, a piece of historical social realism, a parable of Confucian justice, and a proto-feminist work.

EVAN DARWIN WINET

Snow in Midsummer[1]

CHARACTERS

MISTRESS CAI, a widow
DOU TIANZHANG, a poor scholar,
   later a government inspector
DOU E, Dou Tianzhang's daughter
  DUANYUN
DOCTOR LU

OLD ZHANG
DONKEY, his son
PREFECT
ATTENDANT
The OFFICER in charge of executions
EXECUTIONER

Act 1

[*Enter* MISTRESS CAI.]

MRS. CAI   A flower may blossom again,
    But youth never returns.

I am Mistress Cai of Chuzhou.[2] There were three of us in my family; but unluckily my husband died, leaving me just one son who is eight years old.
5   We live together, mother and son, and are quite well off. A scholar named Dou of Shanyang Prefecture borrowed five taels[3] of silver from me last year. Now the interest and capital come to ten taels,[4] and I've asked several times for the money; but Mr. Dou cannot pay it. He has a daughter, and I've a good mind to make her my daughter-in-law;[5] then he won't have to
10   pay back the ten taels. Mr. Dou chose today as a lucky day, and is bringing the girl to me; so I won't ask him to pay me back, but wait for him at home. He should be here soon.

[*Enter* DOU TIANZHANG, *leading his daughter* DUANYUN.]

DOU   I am master of all the learning in the world,
    But my fate is worse than that of other men.

15   My name is Dou Tianzhang, and the home of my ancestors is Chang-an.[6] I have studied the classics since I was a child and read a good deal; but I

---

1. Translated by Yang Xianyi and Gladys Yang.
2. A city in Anhui province, southeast China. In the original Chinese, Cai identifies herself here as an older woman with a humble term meaning "mother-in-law."
3. Chinese unit of weight, slightly more than an English ounce. *Scholar*: the original Chinese term here was used during the Tang dynasty (618–907 C.E.) to specify one who had passed the state examination to become a civil servant; later, under the Song (907–1279) and Yuan (1271–1368) dynasties, it referred more generally to a scholar or candidate for the examination. *Shanyang Prefecture*:

an administrative subdivision of Liaoning province in northeast China.
4. An interest rate that doubles the original loan is outrageously usurious, a recurring theme in the play.
5. It was customary for a family to take in a girl, usually from a poor family, to raise as a future daughter-in-law. Before marriage, she would be referred to as a "child-daughter-in-law" (in this translation, "child-bride").
6. Several times the capital of ancient China. Dou Tianzhang identifies himself humbly here with a traditional self-reference for a young man.

haven't yet taken the examinations.[7] Unfortunately my wife has died, leaving me this only daughter, Duanyun. She lost her mother when she was three, and now she is seven. Living from hand to mouth, I moved to Shanyang Pre
20 fecture in Chuzhou and took lodgings here. There is a widow in this town named Cai, who lives alone with her son and is fairly well off, and as I had no money for traveling I borrowed five taels from her. Now, with the interest, I owe her ten taels; but though she has asked several times for the money, I haven't been able to pay her. And recently she has sent to say she would like
25 my daughter to marry her son. Since the spring examinations will soon be starting, I should be going to the capital; but I have no money for the road. So I am forced to take Duanyun to Widow Cai as her future daughter-in-law. I'm not marrying my daughter but selling her! For this means the widow will cancel my debt and give me some cash for my journey. This is all I can hope
30 for. Ah, child, your father does this against his will! While talking to myself I've reached her door. Mistress Cai! Are you at home?

       [*Enter* MISTRESS CAI.]

MRS. CAI   So it's Mr. Dou! Come in, please. I've been waiting for you.

       [*They greet each other.*]

DOU   I've brought you my daughter, ma'am, not to be your daughter-in-law— that would be asking too much—but to serve you day and night. I must be
35 going to take the examination. I hope you will look after her.

MRS. CAI   Well, you owed me ten taels including interest. Here is your promissory note back and another two taels for your journey. I hope you don't think it too little.

DOU   Thank you, ma'am! Instead of asking for what I owe you, you have
40 given me money for the road. Someday I shall repay your kindness in full. My daughter is a foolish child. Please take care of her, ma'am, for my sake.

MRS. CAI   Don't worry, Mr. Dou. I shall look after your daughter as if she were my own.

DOU [*kneeling to her*]   If the child deserves a beating, ma'am, for my sake
45 just scold her! And if she deserves a scolding, for my sake speak gently to her! As for you, Duanyun, this isn't like at home, where your father used to put up with your whims. If you're naughty here, you'll be beaten and cursed. When shall I see you again, child? [*He sighs.*]

    I drum sadly on my sheath;
50   I have studied the Confucian classics;
    My unhappy wife died young,
    And now I am parted from my only daughter.

       [*Exit.*]

MRS. CAI   Now Mr. Dou has left me his daughter, and gone to the capital for the examination. I must see to the house.

       [*Exeunt.*[8]]

       [*Enter* DOCTOR LU.]

---

7. That is, the state examinations to demonstrate literary proficiency; successful candidates were admitted to the civil bureaucracy, a primary means of climbing the social ladder. *The classics*: the works of Confucius (551–449 B.C.E.), which were the basis of a Chinese classical education.
8. They exit (Latin).

55 DOCTOR   I diagnose all diseases with care,
    And prescribe as the Herbal[9] dictates;
    But I cannot bring dead men back to life,
    And the live ones I treat often die.[1]
I am Doctor Lu. I own a drug shop[2] here. I've borrowed ten taels of silver
60 from Mistress Cai of this town, and with interest now owe her twenty taels.
She keeps coming for the money; but I haven't got it. If she doesn't come
back, so much the better. If she does, I have a plan. I'll sit in my shop now,
and wait to see who turns up.

       [*Enter* MISTRESS CAI.]

MRS. CAI   I am Mistress Cai. Thirteen years ago Mr. Dou Tianzhang left his
65 daughter Duanyun with me to marry my son, and I changed her name to
Dou E. But after their marriage my son died, so now she's a widow. That
was nearly three years ago, and she'll soon be out of mourning.[3] I've told
her that I'm going to town to collect a debt from Doctor Lu. Now I've
reached his house. Is Doctor Lu in?

70 DOCTOR   Yes, ma'am, come in.

MRS. CAI   You've kept my money for a long time, doctor. You must pay me back.

DOCTOR   I've no money at home, ma'am. If you'll come with me to the village, I'll get money for you.

MRS. CAI   Very well. I'll go with you.

       [*They start walking.*]

75 DOCTOR   Now we are outside the city. Here's a good spot, with no one about.
Why not do it here? I've got the rope ready. Who's that calling you, ma'am?

MRS. CAI   Where?

       [*The* DOCTOR *strangles the widow with the rope. Enter* OLD ZHANG *and
his son* DONKEY. *As they rush forward the* DOCTOR *takes to his heels.* OLD
ZHANG *revives* MISTRESS CAI.]

DONKEY   It's an old woman, dad, nearly strangled to death.

ZHANG   Hey, you! Who are you? What's your name? Why did that fellow try
80 to strangle you?

MRS. CAI   My name is Cai and I live in town with my widowed daughter-in-law.
Doctor Lu owes me twenty taels so he lured me here and tried to strangle
me. If not for you and this young man,[4] it would have been all up with me!

DONKEY   Did you hear that, dad? She has a daughter-in-law at home!
85 Suppose you take her as your wife and I take the daughter-in-law? Propose
it to her, dad!

ZHANG   Hey, widow! You've no husband and I've no wife. How about the two
of us getting married?

MRS. CAI   What an idea! I shall give you a handsome sum of money to thank
you.

90 DONKEY   So you refuse! I'd better strangle you after all.

MRS. CAI   Wait! Let me think a moment, brother!

---

9. An early Chinese pharmaceutical treatise.
1. Some translators interpret these ambiguous lines to mean "I uselessly treat the dead,
and kill the living."
2. That is, a pharmacy, where raw medicinal
herbs are sold.

3. That is, Dou E has faithfully observed the
protocols of widowhood and will soon be able
to stop wearing mourning clothes (and thus
will become eligible for remarriage).
4. Mrs. Cai uses a courteous form of address
that literally means "older brother."

DONKEY What do you need to think for? You take my dad, and I'll take your daughter-in-law.

MRS. CAI [*aside*] If I don't agree he'll strangle me! [*To them.*] Very well.
95 Come home with me, both of you.

DONKEY Let's go.

[*Exeunt.*]

[*Enter* DOU E.]

DOU E I am Duanyun,[5] and my home was in Chuzhou. When I was three I lost my mother; and when I was seven I had to leave my father, for he sent me to Mistress Cai as her son's child-bride, and she changed my name to
100 Dou E. At seventeen I married; but unluckily my husband died three years ago. Now I am twenty. There is a Doctor Lu in town who owes my mother-in-law twenty taels including interest; and though she has asked him several times for the money, he hasn't paid her back. She's gone today to try to collect the debt. Ah, when shall I escape from my misery?

105   My heart is full of grief,
        I have suffered for so many years!
        Morning or evening it is all the same:
        From dawn to dusk I can neither eat nor sleep,
        Racked by sad dreams at night, sad thoughts by day,
110   Unending sorrow which I cannot banish,
        Unceasing reasons for fresh misery.
        Wretchedness makes me weep, grief makes me frown;
      Will this never come to an end?
        Is it my fate to be wretched all my life?
115   Who else knows grief like mine?
        For my sorrow, like flowing water, never ceases.
        At three I lost my mother, at seven was torn from my father;
        Then the life of the husband I married was cut short;
        So my mother-in-law and I are left as widows,
120   With no one to care for us or see to our needs.
        Did I burn too little incense in my last life[6]
        That my marriage was unlucky?
        We should all do good betimes;
        So I mourn for my husband and serve my mother-in-law,
125   Obedient to all her bidding.
      My mother-in-law has been gone a long time to collect that debt. What can be keeping her?

[*Enter* MISTRESS CAI *with* OLD ZHANG *and* DONKEY.]

MRS. CAI Wait here at the door while I go in.

DONKEY All right, mother. Go in and tell her her husband is at the door.

[MISTRESS CAI *sees* DOU E.]

130 DOU E So you're back, mother. Have you had a meal?

MRS. CAI [*crying*] Ah, poor child! How am I going to break this to you?

DOU E I see her in floods of tears,

---

5. Dou E identifies herself with a humble self-reference for a young woman.
6. A reference to the Buddhist belief in

karma, the doctrine that one's actions determine one's destiny in future incarnations.

Hiding some grief in her heart;
Greeting her quickly, I beg her to tell me the reason.

135 MRS. CAI   How can I say this?

DOU E   She's shilly-shallying and looks ashamed.
What has upset you, mother? Why are you crying?

MRS. CAI   When I asked Doctor Lu for the silver, he lured me outside the
town, then tried to strangle me; but an old man called Zhang and his son
140   Donkey saved my life. Now Old Zhang is going to marry me: that's why I'm
upset.

DOU E   That would never do, mother! Please think again! We're not short of
money. Besides, you are growing old—how can you take another husband?

MRS. CAI   Child, I couldn't do anything else!

145 DOU E   Mother, listen to me!
What will become of you
If you choose a day and solemnize a wedding?[7]
Now your hair is as white as snow,
How can you wear the bright silk veil of a bride?
150   No wonder they say it is hard to keep women at home,[8]
If at sixty, when all thought of love should be over,
You've forgotten your former husband,
And taken a fancy to another man!
This will make others split their sides with laughter!
155   Yes, split their sides with laughter!
Like the widow who fanned her husband's tomb,
You're no tender bamboo shoot, no tender shoot.
How can you paint your eyebrows and remarry?
Your husband left you his property,
160   Made provision for the future,
For daily food and a good livelihood,
So that you and your son could remain beholden to no one,
And live to a ripe old age.
Did he go to such trouble for nothing?

165 MRS. CAI   Since it has come to this, I think you'd better take a husband too,
and today can be the wedding day.

DOU E   You take a husband if you must. I won't!

MRS. CAI   The date is fixed, and they are already here.

DONKEY   Now we shall marry into their family. Our hats are brushed as good
170   as new, and have narrow brims like bridegrooms'! Good! Fine!

DOU E   Stand back, you fellows!
Women should not believe all men say;
Such a marriage could not last.
Where did she find this old yokel,
175   And this other ruffian here?
Have you no feeling left for the dead?
You must think this over again.
Your husband worked in different cities and counties
To amass a well-earned fortune, and lack nothing.

---

7. That is, by burning incense in ancestral
halls.
8. According to a Chinese proverb, "A grown
girl is not to be kept at home; if you try, you
only make an enemy out of her."

180   How can you let his estate go to Donkey Zhang?
       He tilled the land, but others are reaping the harvest.

             [*Exit.*]

ZHANG [*to* MRS. CAI]   Let us go and drink, ma'am.

             [*Exeunt.*]

DONKEY   Dou E refuses to have me, but I shan't let her get away: she will
       have to be my wife. Now I'll drink with my old man! [*Exit.*]

Act 2

             [*Enter* DOCTOR LU.]

DOCTOR   I am Doctor Lu. I lured Mistress Cai outside the town and was just
       going to strangle her when two men rescued her. Today I am opening shop.
       I wonder who will turn up.

             [*Enter* DONKEY.]

DONKEY   I am Donkey Zhang. Dou E still refuses to marry me. Now the old
5   woman is ill, I'm going to poison her; for once the old one is dead, the young
       one will have to be my wife.[9] Ah, here is a drug shop. Doctor! I want a drug!

DOCTOR   What drug do you want?

DONKEY   I want some poison.

DOCTOR   Who dares sell you poison? How can you ask such a thing?

10 DONKEY   You won't let me have it then?

DOCTOR   I won't. What are you going to do about it?

DONKEY [*seizing him*]   Fine! Fine! Aren't you the man who tried to murder
       Mistress Cai? Do you think I don't recognize you? I'll take you to court.

DOCTOR [*in panic*]   Let me go, brother! I've got it! I've got it!

             [*Gives him the poison.*]

15 DONKEY   Now that I've got the poison, I'm going home.

             [*Exit.*]

DOCTOR   So that man who came to buy poison was one of the men who res-
       cued the widow. Since I've given him poison, he may get me into further
       trouble later. I'd better close my shop and go to Zhuozhou[1] to sell drugs.

             [*Exit.*]

             [*Enter* MISTRESS CAI, *supported by* OLD ZHANG *and* DONKEY.]

20 ZHANG   I came to Mistress Cai's house hoping to be her second husband.
       Who would have thought that the widow would fall ill? I am really too
       unlucky. If there's anything you fancy to eat, ma'am, just let me know.

MRS. CAI   I'd like some mutton tripe soup.

ZHANG   Son, go and tell Dou E to make some mutton tripe soup for her
       mother-in-law.

25 DONKEY   Dou E! Your mother-in-law wants some mutton tripe soup. Look
       sharp about it!

             [*Enter* DOU E.]

DOU E   I am Dou E. My mother-in-law is unwell and wants some mutton tripe
       soup, so I've made her some. When you think of it, some women are too fickle!
       She wants to lie with a husband all her life,

---

9. That is, social and economic necessity will
force Dou E to accept him as a husband.

1. A city in Hebei province, northeastern
China.

30 Unwilling to sleep alone;
  First she married one, and now she has picked another.
  Some women never speak of household matters,
  But pick up all the gossip,
  Describe their husbands' adventures,
35 And are always up to some low tricks themselves.
  Is there one like Lady Zhuo[2] who stooped to serve in a tavern?
  Or like Meng Guang[3] who showed such respect to her husband?
  The women today are different:
  You can neither tell their character from their speech,
40 Nor judge them by their actions.
  They're all of them faithless, all run after new lovers;
  And before their husband's graves are dry
  They set aside their mourning for new clothes.
  Where is the woman whose tears for her husband
45 Caused the Great Wall to crumble?[4]
  Where is she who left her washing
  And drowned herself in the stream?[5]
  Where is she who changed into stone
  Through longing for her husband?[6]
50 How shameful that women today are so unfaithful,
  So few of them are chaste, so many wanton!
  All, all are gone, those virtuous women of old;
  For wives will not cleave to their husbands!
 Now the soup is ready. I had better take it in.

DONKEY Let me take it to her. [*He takes the bowl.*] This hasn't much flavor.
55 Bring some salt and vinegar.

    [DOU E *goes out.* DONKEY *puts poison in the soup.* DOU E *comes back.*]

DOU E Here are the salt and vinegar.

DONKEY Put some in.

DOU E You say that it lacks salt and vinegar,
60 Adding these will improve the flavor.
  I hope my mother will be better soon,
  And the soup will serve as a cordial.
  Then the three of you can live happily together.

ZHANG Son, is the soup ready?

---

2. Zhuo Wenjun, the daughter of a rich man, who eloped with Sima Xiangru (179–117 B.C.E.), a famous Han Dynasty scholar. Since they were poor, they kept a small tavern in Chengdu where she served as barmaid [translator's note].

3. Wife of Liang Hung of the Later Han dynasty. She showed her respect and love for her husband by raising the dinner tray as high as her eyebrows when she brought it to him.

4. According to a folktale, Meng Jiang-nu's husband, a conscript laborer, died while building the Great Wall during the reign of the First Emperor of Qin. She went to the wall to find her missing husband and wept so bitterly that part of it collapsed, revealing his dead body.

5. During the Spring and Autumn Period (770–475 B.C.E.), Wu Zixu, a minister of Chu, fled to Wu. He came upon a woman doing her laundry by a river, who fed him and then drowned herself in the river—both to prove that she would not betray him to his pursuers and because she had compromised her chastity by taking in a man who was a stranger.

6. A reference to a legend about a faithful wife who, during her husband's absence from home, climbed a hill every day to watch for his return. Finally she turned into a boulder, which was called *wang-fu shi* (watching-for-husband stone).

65 DONKEY   Here it is. Take it.

ZHANG [*taking the soup*]   Have some soup, ma'am.

MRS. CAI   I am sorry to give you so much trouble. You have some first.

ZHANG   Won't you try it?

MRS. CAI   No, I want *you* to drink it first.

      [OLD ZHANG *drinks the soup.*]

70 DOU E   One says: "Won't you try it?"
      The other says: "You have it!"
      What a shameful way to talk!
      How can I help being angry?
      The new couple is in transports;
75   Forgetting her first husband,
      She listens to this new man's lightest word.
      Now her heart is like a willow seed in the breeze,
      Not steadfast as a rock.
      Old love is nothing to new love;
80   She wants to live with this new man forever,
      Without a thought for the other man far away.

ZHANG   Why has this soup made me dizzy?

      [*He falls to the ground.*]

MRS. CAI   Why should you feel unwell after that soup? [*Panic-stricken.*] Take
   a grip on yourself, old man! Don't give up so easily! [*Wails.*]

85 DOU E   It's no use grieving for him;
      All mortal men must die when their time is up.
      Some fall ill, some meet with accidents;
      Some catch a chill, some are struck down by heat;
      Some die of hunger, surfeit, or overwork;
90   But every death has its cause,
      Human life is ruled by fate,[7]
      And no man can control it,
      For our span of life is predestined.
      He has been here a few days only;
95   He is not of your family,
      And he never sent you wedding gifts:
      Sheep, wine, silk, or money.
      For a time you stayed together,
      But now he is dead and gone!
100   I am not an unfilial daughter,
      But I fear what the neighbors may say;
      So stop your moaning and wailing:
      He is not the man you married as a girl.

      [OLD ZHANG *dies.*]

MRS. CAI   What shall we do? He's dead!

105 DOU E   He's no relation—I have no tears for him.
      There's no need to be so overcome with grief,
      Or to cry so bitterly and lose your head!

---

7. Human affairs are subject to the authority of Heaven and Earth, which is often invoked in this play when human judgment falters.

DONKEY   Fine! You've poisoned my father! What are you going to do about it?

MRS. CAI   Child, you had better marry him now.

110 DOU E   How can you say such a thing, mother?

This fellow forced my mother-in-law to keep him;

Now he's poisoned his father,

But whom does he think he can frighten?

MRS. CAI   You'd better marry him, child.

115 DOU E   A horse can't have two saddles;[8]

I was your son's wife when he was alive,

Yet now you are urging me to marry again.

This is unthinkable!

120 DONKEY   Dou E, you murdered my old man. Do you want to settle this in private or settle it in public?

DOU E   What do you mean?

DONKEY   If you want it settled in public, I'll drag you to the court, and you'll have to confess to the murder of my father! If you want it settled in private, agree to be my wife. Then I'll let you off.

125 DOU E   I am innocent. I'll go with you to the prefect.[9]

[DONKEY *drags* DOU E *and* MISTRESS CAI *out.*]

Act 3

[*Enter the* PREFECT *with an* ATTENDANT.]

PREFECT   I am a hard-working official;

I make money out of my lawsuits;

But when my superiors come to investigate,

I pretend to be ill and stay at home in bed.

5   I am prefect of Chuzhou. This morning I am holding court.

Attendant, summon the court!

[*The* ATTENDANT *gives a shout.*]

[*Enter* DONKEY, *dragging in* DOU E *and* MISTRESS CAI.]

DONKEY   I want to lodge a charge.

ATTENDANT   Come over here.

[DONKEY *and* DOU E *kneel to the* PREFECT, *who kneels to them.*][1]

PREFECT [*kneeling*]   Please rise.

10 ATTENDANT   Your Honor, this is a citizen who's come to ask for justice. Why should you kneel to him?

PREFECT   Why? Because such citizens are food and clothes to me!

[*The* ATTENDANT *assents.*]

PREFECT   Which of you is the plaintiff, which the defendant? Out with the truth now!

15 DONKEY   I am the plaintiff. I accuse this young woman, Dou E, of poisoning my father with soup. Let justice be done, Your Honor!

PREFECT   Who poisoned the soup?

DOU E   Not I!

---

8. A proverb meaning that a wife cannot serve two husbands.

9. The presiding judicial magistrate.

1. A stylized self-presenting gesture of humility that is appropriate for Donkey and Dou E, but ironic for a prefect.

MRS. CAI   Not I!

20 DONKEY   Not I!

PREFECT   If none of you did it, I wonder if I could have done it?

DOU E   Your Honor is as discerning as a mirror,
    And can see my innermost thoughts.
    There was nothing wrong with the soup,
25   I know nothing about the poison;
    He made a pretense of tasting it,
    Then his father drank it and fell down dead.
    It is not that I want to deny my guilt in court;
    But I cannot confess to a crime I have not committed!

30 PREFECT   Low characters like that: they'll only confess when put to
    torture. Attendant! Bring the bastinado to beat her.

    [*The* ATTENDANT *beats* DOU E. *Three times she faints and he has to sprinkle
    her with water to bring her round.*]

DOU E   This terrible beating is more than I can bear.
    You brought this on yourself, mother. Why complain?
    May all women in the world who marry again
35   Be warned by me!
    Why are they shouting so fiercely?
    I groan with pain;
    I come to myself, then faint away again.
    A thousand strokes: I am streaming with blood!
40   At each blow from the bastinado
    My blood spurts out and my skin is torn from my flesh;
    My spirit takes flight in fear,
    Approaching the nether regions.[2]
    Who knows the bitterness in my heart?
45   It was not I who poisoned the old man;
    I beg Your Honor to find out the truth!

PREFECT   Will you confess now?

DOU E   I swear it was not I who put in the poison.

PREFECT   In that case, beat the old woman.

50 DOU E [*hastily*]   Stop, stop! Don't beat my mother-in-law!
    Rather than that, I'll say I poisoned the old man.

PREFECT   Fasten her in the cangue[3] and throw her into the gaol for the con-
    demned. Tomorrow she shall be taken to the marketplace to be executed.

MRS. CAI [*weeping*]   Dou E, my child! It's because of me you are losing your
55   life. Oh, this will be the death of me!

DOU E   When I am a headless ghost, unjustly killed,
    Do you think I will spare that scoundrel?
    Men cannot be deceived forever,
    And Heaven will see this injustice.
60   I struggled as hard as I could, but now I am helpless;
    I was forced to confess that I poisoned the old man;
    How could I let you be beaten, mother?
    How could I save you except by dying myself?

    [*She is led off.*]

---

2. That is, nearing death.
3. A frame used to confine the neck and hands in a portable pillory or stocks.

DONKEY   If she's to be killed tomorrow, I'll hang around.
   [*Exit.*]

65 MRS. CAI   Poor child! Tomorrow she will be killed in the marketplace. This
   will be the death of me! [*Exit.*]

PREFECT   Tomorrow Dou E will be executed. Today's work is done. Bring me
   my horse; I am going home to drink.
      [*Exeunt.*]
      [*Enter the* OFFICER *in charge.*]

OFFICER   I am the officer in charge of executions. Today we are putting a
70   criminal to death. We must stand guard at the end of the road, to see that
   no one comes through.
      [*Enter the* ATTENDANTS. *They beat the drum and the gong three times;
      then the* EXECUTIONER *enters, sharpens his sword, and waves a flag.* DOU
      E *is led on in a cangue. The gong and drum are beaten.*]

EXECUTIONER   Get a move on! Let no one pass this way.

DOU E   Through no fault of mine I am called a criminal,
      And condemned to be beheaded—
75   I cry out to Heaven and Earth of this injustice!
      I reproach both Earth and Heaven
      For they would not save me.
      The sun and moon give light by day and by night,
      Mountains and rivers watch over the world of men;
80   Yet Heaven cannot tell the innocent from the guilty;
      And confuses the wicked with the good!
      The good are poor, and die before their time;
      The wicked are rich, and live to a great old age.
      The gods are afraid of the mighty and bully the weak;
85   They let evil take its course.
      Ah, Earth! you will not distinguish good from bad,
      And, Heaven! you let me suffer this injustice!
      Tears pour down my cheeks in vain!

EXECUTIONER   Get a move on! We are late.

90 DOU E   The cangue round my neck makes me stagger this way and that,
      And I'm jostled backward and forward by the crowd.
      Will you do me a favor, brother?

EXECUTIONER   What do you want?

DOU E   If you take me the front way, I shall bear you a grudge;
95   If you take me the back way, I shall die content.
      Please do not think me willful!

EXECUTIONER   Now that you're going to the execution ground, are there any
   relatives you want to see?

DOU E   I am going to die. What relatives do I need?

100 EXECUTIONER   Why did you ask me just now to take you the back way?

DOU E   Please don't go by the front street, brother,
      But take me by the back street.
      The other way my mother-in-law might see me.

EXECUTIONER   You can't escape death, so why worry if she sees you?

105 DOU E   If my mother-in-law were to see me in chains being led to the
   execution ground—
      She would burst with indignation!

She would burst with indignation!
Please grant me this comfort, brother, before I die!

[*Enter* MISTRESS CAI.]

110 MRS. CAI   Ah, Heaven! Isn't that my daughter-in-law? This will be the death
of me!

EXECUTIONER   Stand back, old woman!

DOU E   Let her come closer so that I can say a few words to her.

EXECUTIONER   Hey, old woman! Come here. Your daughter-in-law wants to

115   speak to you.

MRS. CAI   Poor child! This will be the death of me!

DOU E   Mother, when you were unwell and asked for mutton tripe soup, I prepared some for you. Donkey Zhang made me fetch more salt and vinegar so
that he could poison the soup, and then told me to give it to you. He didn't

120   know his old man would drink it. Donkey Zhang poisoned the soup to kill you,
so that he could force me to be his wife. He never thought his father would
die instead. To take revenge, he dragged me to court. Because I didn't want
you to suffer, I had to confess to murder, and now I am going to be killed. In
future, mother, if you have gruel to spare, give me half a bowl; and if you have

125   paper money to spare, burn some for me, for the sake of your dead son![4]
Take pity on one who is dying an unjust death;
Take pity on one whose head will be struck from her body;
Take pity on one who has worked with you in your home;
Take pity on one who has neither mother nor father;

130   Take pity on one who has served you all these years;
And at festivals offer my spirit a bowl of cold gruel.

MRS. CAI [*weeping*]   Don't worry. Ah, this will be the death of me!

DOU E   Burn some paper coins to my headless corpse,
For the sake of your dead son.

135   We wail and complain to Heaven:
There is no justice! Dou E is wrongly slain!

EXECUTIONER   Now then, old woman, stand back! The time has come.

[DOU E *kneels, and the* EXECUTIONER *removes the cangue from her neck.*]

DOU E   I want to say three things, officer. If you will let me, I shall die content. I want a clean mat and a white silk streamer twelve feet long to hang

140   on the flagpole. When the sword strikes off my head, not a drop of my
warm blood will stain the ground. It will all fly up instead to the white silk
streamer. This is the hottest time of summer, sir. If injustice has indeed
been done, three feet of snow will cover my dead body. Then this district
will suffer from drought for three whole years.

145 EXECUTIONER   Be quiet! What a thing to say!

[*The* EXECUTIONER *waves his flag.*]

DOU E   A dumb woman was blamed for poisoning herself;
A buffalo is whipped while it toils for its master.

EXECUTIONER   Why is it suddenly so overcast? It is snowing!

[*He prays to Heaven.*]

---

4. By the time of the play's composition, the
ancient Chinese custom of offering burnt
sacrifices for the newly dead had been superseded by the burning of paper symbols of
worldly wealth—coins, livestock, luxury
goods, etc.—to help ensure prosperity in the
afterlife.

DOU E Once Zou Yan[5] caused frost to appear

150   Now snow will show the injustice done to me!

[*The* EXECUTIONER *beheads her, and the* ATTENDANT *sees to her body.*]

EXECUTIONER A fine stroke! Now let us go and have a drink.

[*The* ATTENDANTS *assent, and carry the body off.*]

Act 4

[*Enter* DOU TIANZHANG.][6]

DOU I am Dou Tianzhang. It is thirteen years since I left my child Duanyun. I went to the capital, passed the examination and was made a counsellor.[7] And because I am able, just, and upright, the emperor appointed me Inspector of the Huai River Area.[8] I have traveled from place to place investigating cases,

5 and I have the sword of authority and golden tally[9] so that I can punish corrupt officials without first reporting to the throne. My heart is torn between grief and happiness. I am glad because I am a high official responsible for seeing that justice is done. I am sad, though, because when Duanyun was seven I gave her to Mistress Cai; and after I became an official and sent for

10 news of the widow to Chuzhou, the neighbors said she had moved away—to what place they did not know—and there has been no word since. I have wept for my child till my eyes are dim and my hair is white. Now I have come south of the Huai River, and am wondering why this district has had no rain for three years. I shall rest in the district office, boy. Tell the local officers

15 they need not call today. I shall see them early tomorrow.

SERVANT [*calling out*] The officers and secretaries are not to call on His Excellency today. He will see them early tomorrow.

DOU Tell the secretaries of the different departments to send all their cases here for my inspection. I shall study some under the lamp.

[*The* SERVANT *brings him the files.*]

20 DOU Light the lamp for me. You have been working hard, and you may rest now. But come when I call you.

[*The* SERVANT *lights the lamp and leaves.*]

DOU I shall go through a few cases. Here is one concerning Dou E, who poisoned her father-in-law. Curious that the first culprit's surname should be the same as mine! To murder one's father-in-law is one of the unpardonable

25 crimes;[1] so it seems there are lawless elements among my clan. Since this case has been dealt with, I need not read it. I'll put it at the bottom of the pile

5. A loyal official serving the prince of Yan during the Warring States period (475–221 B.C.E.). When the prince imprisoned him on the strength of an enemy's accusation, Zou Yan cried out to heaven, which exhibited displeasure by bringing frost in midsummer.

6. His new status is indicated by a cap and a sash. He is accompanied by his servant (a role that would be played as a clown).

7. Specifically, a counsellor for state affairs in the Imperial Secretariat.

8. That is, a provincial surveillance commissioner for two adjacent judicial circuits north of the Yangtze River: one to the west of the Huai River, and the other to the east of the Huai River.

9. Symbols of authority, given by the emperor. The sword empowered the receiver to deliver the death penalty without the usual mandatory review by a central authority (an extraordinary sanction); the golden tablet was worn by high-ranking Yuan officials.

1. The Criminal Law Section in the *History of Yuan* lists ten unpardonable crimes: to contemplate rebellion, to contemplate a greatly subversive act, to contemplate treason, to commit a detestable or subversive act (Dou E's crime), to lack moral rules, to be extremely disrespectful, to lack filial piety, to abuse one for whom one would be obliged to mourn, to behave unrighteously, and to commit incest.

and look at another. Wait, I suddenly feel drowsy. I suppose I am growing old, and am tired after traveling. I will take a short nap on the desk. [*He sleeps.*]

[*Enter* DOU E's *ghost.*]

DOU E   Day after day I weep in the underworld,[2]
30   Waiting impatiently for my revenge.
          I pace on slowly in darkness,
          Then am borne along by the whirlwind;
          Enveloped by mist I come swiftly in ghostly form.
[*She looks about her.*] Now the door-gods[3] will not let me pass. I am the
35   daughter of Inspector Dou. Though I died unjustly, my father does not
        know it; so I have come to visit him in his dreams.

[*She enters the room and weeps.*]

DOU [*shedding tears*]   Duanyun, my child! Where have you been?

[DOU E's *spirit leaves,*[4] *and* DOU *wakes up.*]

How odd! I fell asleep and dreamed that I saw my daughter coming towards me; but where is she now? Let me go on with these cases.

[DOU E's *spirit enters and makes the lamp burn low.*]

40   Strange! I was just going to read a case when the light flickered and dimmed. My servant is asleep; I must trim the wick myself. [*As he trims the lamp,* DOU E's *spirit rearranges the file.*] Now the light is brighter, I can read again. "This concerns the criminal Dou E, who poisoned her father-in-law." Strange! I read this case first, and put it under the others. How has it come to the top?
45   Since this case has already been dealt with let me put it at the bottom again and study a different one. [*Once more* DOU E's *spirit makes the lamp burn low.*] Strange! Why is the light flickering again? I must trim it once more. [*As* DOU *trims the light,* DOU E's *spirit once more turns over the file.*] Now the lamp is brighter, I can read another case. "This concerns the criminal Dou E, who
50   poisoned her father-in-law." How extraordinary! I definitely put this at the bottom of the pile just before I trimmed the lamp. How has it come to the top again? Can there be ghosts in this office? Well, ghost or no ghost, an injustice must have been done. Let me put this underneath and read another. [DOU E's *spirit makes the lamp burn low again.*] Strange! The lamp is flickering again.
55   Can there actually be a ghost here tampering with it? I'll trim it once more. [*As he trims the wick,* DOU E's *spirit comes up to him and he sees her. He strikes his sword on the desk.*] Ah, there's the ghost! I warn you, I am the emperor's inspector of justice. If you come near, I'll cut you in two. Hey, boy! How can you sleep so soundly? Get up at once! Ghosts! Ghosts! This is terrifying!

DOU E   Fear is making him lose his head;
60   The sound of my weeping has frightened him more than ever.
          Here, Dou Tianzhang, my old father,
          Will you let your daughter Dou E bow to you?

DOU   You say I am your father, ghost, and offer to bow to me as my daughter. Aren't you mistaken? My daughter's name is Duanyun. When she was

---

2. That is, she weeps at "the Home-gazing Terrace" to which, according to Chinese folklore, the dead ascend in order to watch their families in the human world.
3. At New Year's, pictures of the gods of the left and right doors are hung to ward off spirits.

4. A "false exit," as it is known in classical Chinese theater: the actor turns his or her back toward the audience to indicate an absence, and then simply turns around again to "reenter."

65　seven she was given to Mistress Cai as a child-bride. You call yourself by a different name, Dou E. How can you be my child?

DOU E　After you gave me to Mistress Cai, father, she changed my name to Dou E.

DOU　So you say you are my child Duanyun. Let me ask you this: Are you the
70　woman accused of murdering her father-in-law and executed?

DOU E　I am.

DOU　Hush, girl! I've wept for you till my eyes grew dim, and worried for you till my hair turned white. How did you come to be condemned for this most heinous of crimes? I am a high official now, whose duty it is to see
75　that justice is done. I have come here to investigate cases and discover corrupt officials. You are my child, but you are guilty of the worst crime of all. If I could not control you, how can I control others? When I married you to the widow's son, I expected you to observe the Three Duties and Four Virtues.[5] The Three Duties are obedience to your father before marriage,
80　obedience to your husband after marriage, and obedience to your son after your husband's death. The Four Virtues are to serve your parents-in-law, to show respect to your husband, to remain on good terms with your sisters-in-law, and to live in peace with your neighbors. But regardless of your duties, you have committed the gravest crime of all! The proverb says: Look
85　before you leap, or you may be sorry too late. For three generations no son of our clan has broken the law; for five generations no daughter has married again. As a married woman, you should have studied propriety and morality; but instead you perpetrated the most terrible crime. You have disgraced our ancestors and injured my good name. Tell me the whole
90　truth at once, and nothing but the truth! If you utter one false word, I shall send you to the tutelary god; then your spirit will never reenter human form, but remain a hungry ghost forever in the shades.[6]

DOU E　Don't be so angry, father. Don't threaten me like an angry wolf or tiger! Let me explain this to you. At three, I lost my mother; at seven, I was
95　parted from my father, when you sent me to Mistress Cai as her future daughter-in-law, and my name was changed to Dou E. At seventeen, I married; but unhappily two years later my husband died, and I stayed as a widow with my mother-in-law. In Chuzhou there lived a certain Doctor Lu, who owed my mother-in-law twenty taels of silver. One day when she went
100　to ask him for the money, he lured her outside the town and tried to strangle her; but Donkey Zhang and his father came by and saved her life. Old Zhang asked: "Whom do you have in your family, ma'am?" My mother-in-law said: "No one but a widowed daughter-in-law." Old Zhang said: "In that case, I will marry you. What do you say?" When my mother-in-law refused,
105　the two men said: "If you don't agree, we shall strangle you again!" So she was frightened into marrying him. Donkey tried to seduce me several times, but I always resisted him. One day my mother-in-law was unwell and wanted some mutton tripe soup. When I prepared it, Donkey told me to let him taste it. "It's good," he said. "But there's not enough salt and vinegar." When I

5. Fundamental Confucian principles. For a gentleman, the Three Duties are to cultivate nonviolence and gravity of bearing, to serve the truth, and to speak only what is worthy and just; the Four Virtues are sincerity, benevolence, filial piety, and propriety.

6. In Chinese folklore, ghosts are restless souls that wander forever in a perpetual state of unfulfilled desire. *To the tutelary god*: that is, to the temple of the city's guardian god.

110　went to fetch more, he secretly poisoned the soup and told me to take it to
　　her. But my mother-in-law gave it to Old Zhang. Then blood spurted from
　　the old man's mouth, nose, ears and eyes, and he died. At that Donkey said,
　　"Dou E, you poisoned my father. Do you want to settle this in public or in
　　private?" "What do you mean?" I asked. "If you want it settled in public," he
115　said, "I shall take the case to court, and you will pay for my father's death—
　　with your life. If you want it settled in private, then be my wife." "A good
　　horse won't have two saddles," I told him. "A good woman won't remarry. For
　　three generations no son of our clan has broken the law; for five generations
　　no daughter has married again. I'd rather die than be your wife. I am inno-
120　cent. I'll go to court with you." Then he dragged me before the prefect. I was
　　tried again and again, stripped and tortured; but I would rather have died
　　than make a false confession. When the prefect saw that I wouldn't confess,
　　he threatened to have my mother-in-law tortured; and because she was too
　　old to stand the torture, I made a false confession. Then they took me to the
125　execution ground to kill me. I made three vows before my death. First, I
　　asked for a twelve-foot white silk streamer and swore that, if I was innocent,
　　when the sword struck off my head no drop of my blood would stain the
　　ground—it would all fly up to the streamer. Next I vowed that, though it was
　　midsummer, Heaven would send down three feet of snow to cover my body.
130　Last, I vowed that this district would suffer three years' drought. All these
　　vows have come true, because of the crime against me.

　　　　I complained not to any official but to Heaven,
　　　　For I could not express the injustice that was done me;
　　　　And to save my mother from torture
135　　　I confessed to a crime of which I was innocent,
　　　　And remained true to my dead husband.
　　　　Three feet of snow fell on my corpse;
　　　　My hot blood gushed to the white silk streamer;
　　　　Zou Yan called down frost,
140　　　And snow showed the injustice done me.
　　　　Your child committed no crime,
　　　　But suffered a great wrong:
　　　　For resisting seduction I was executed!
　　　　I would not disgrace my clan, so I lost my life!
145　　　Day after day in the shades
　　　　My spirit mourns alone.
　　　　You are sent by the emperor with authority;
　　　　Consider this case and this man's wickedness;
　　　　Cut him in pieces and avenge my wrong!

150　DOU [weeping]　Ah, my wrongly slain daughter, how this wrings my heart!
　　Let me ask you this: Is it because of you that this district has suffered for
　　three years from drought?

　　DOU E　It is.

　　DOU　So! This reminds me of a story. In the Han Dynasty[7] there was a virtu-
155　ous widow whose mother-in-law hanged herself, and whose sister-in-law
　　accused her of murdering the old woman. The governor of Donge[8] had her

───────────

7. 206 B.C.E.–220 C.E.
8. Unclear reference; Shih Chung-wen trans-　　lates this title instead as the governor of
　　Tung-hai, or the prefect of the East Sea.

executed, but because of her unjust death there was no rain in that district for three years. When Lord Yu came to investigate, he saw the dead woman's ghost carrying a plea and weeping before the hall; and after he changed

160 the verdict, killed a bull, and sacrificed at her grave there was a great downpour of rain. This case is rather similar to that. Tomorrow I shall right this wrong for you.

    I bow my white head in sorrow
    Over the innocent girl who was wrongly slain.

165   Now dawn is breaking, you had better leave me;
    Tomorrow I shall set right this miscarriage of justice.

DOU E [*bowing*] With sharp sword of authority and tally of gold,
    You will kill all evil and corrupt officials,
    To serve your sovereign and relieve the people!

170 [*She turns back.*] There's one thing I nearly forgot, father. My mother-in-law is old now, and has no one to look after her.

DOU This is dutiful, my child.

DOU E I ask my father to care for my mother-in-law,
    For she is growing old. My father now

175   Will reopen my case and change the unjust verdict.

       [*Exit.*]

DOU Dawn is breaking. Call the local officers, and all those concerned in the case of Dou E.

SERVANT Yes, Your Excellency.

    [*The* PREFECT, MISTRESS CAI, DONKEY ZHANG *and* DOCTOR LU *are sent in. They kneel before* DOU.]

DOU Mistress Cai, do you recognize me?

180 MRS. CAI No, Your Excellency.

DOU I am Dou Tianzhang. Listen, all of you, to the verdict! Donkey Zhang murdered his father and blackmailed good citizens. He shall be executed in public. Let him be taken to the marketplace to be killed. The prefect passed a wrong sentence. He shall be given one hundred strokes and have

185 his name struck off the official list.[9] Doctor Lu is guilty of selling poison. Let him be beheaded in the marketplace. Mistress Cai shall be lodged in my house. The wrong sentence passed on Dou E shall be rescinded.

    Let the Donkey be killed in public,
    The prefect dismissed from office;

190   Then let us offer a great sacrifice
    So that my daughter's spirit may go to heaven.

---

9. That is, he will never again be eligible for government employment; hence, he will never be able to improve his social standing.

ZEAMI MOTOKIYO

1363–1443

AMONG the numerous theatrical forms and dramatic genres developed in Japan, none has been more revered than the stately yet elusive noh theater that became a high art form in the fourteenth century. While kabuki theater would later dazzle the senses with extravagant costumes, acrobatic movements, and elaborate scenic effects, noh achieved its dramatic and theatrical effects through understatement, ritualistic gesture, and a poetic conception of language, character, and the stage. In the evolution of noh from earlier forms of theater to a courtly entertainment of the samurai, or warrior, class, Zeami Motokiyo is a celebrated and central figure. Actor, head of an acting troupe, and playwright, Zeami refined the art of noh into a theatrical form combining songs, dance, music, and poetry. During his long and productive career, Zeami articulated the aesthetics of this newly crafted art and its performance in a series of treatises that rank among the world's most important works of dramatic theory.

Born in 1363, Zeami was the son of Kanami Kiyotsugu (1333–1384), who was an accomplished actor and playwright and the head of an acting troupe specializing in *sarugaku* (or *sarugaku noh*, as the theatrical form was then called). In 1374, Kanami and his eleven-year-old son performed at the Imakumano Shrine in Kyoto, the imperial capital of medieval Japan. As the result of this performance, they won the patronage of the young shogun (or military ruler) Ashikaga Yoshimitsu (1358–1408), who, as part of his successful attempt to enhance his legitimacy, aided the arts as the earlier nobility had always done. With Yoshimitsu's support and with the benefit of a highly cultured audience, Kanami brought a number of innovations to *sarugaku* that furthered its development

into the sophisticated art we recognize as noh.

His son became a favorite of the shogun, serving him as both artist and companion/lover, and upon Kanami's death the young Zeami took over as head of his father's troupe. Consolidating and extending his father's theatrical innovations, Zeami became one of the noh theater's most accomplished actors, playwrights, and theorists. In a number of studies—including *Fushikadensho* (*Teachings on Style and the Flower*, 1400–02), *Shikado* (*The True Path to the Flower*, 1420), and *Nosakusho* (*On Writing Noh Plays*, 1423)—Zeami discussed the origins of noh and its defining features, the intricacies of acting, and the principles of noh composition. About fifty plays are now ascribed to him, including some that are extensive revisions of earlier texts, and the greatest of these—such plays as *Komachi at Sekidera* and *ATSUMORI*—stand as crowning achievements in the canon of noh drama. With the death of Yoshimitsu in 1408, however, Zeami lost his privileged position at court; and though he continued to act and write for the noh theater, the shoguns who followed Yoshimitsu extended their patronage to other individuals and rival theatrical traditions. In 1422, Zeami passed the leadership of his acting troupe to his eldest son, Motomosa, and became a Buddhist monk. Greater disappointment and hardship awaited him. Under the shogun Yoshinori, who assumed power in 1429, Zeami and Motomosa were relieved of their official responsibilities; and in 1434 Zeami was banished to the remote island of Sado, where he composed *Kintōsho* (*Book of the Golden Island*) about his exile. When he returned—most likely following the general amnesty declared after the assassination of Yoshinori in 1441—he probably lived until

A philosophy

his death at eighty in the care of his son-in-law and artistic successor Komparu Zenchiko (1405–ca. 1470).

In his theoretical and dramatic writings, Zeami completed the development of noh from its roots in folk theater to a performance form marked by narrative concentration and verbal intensity. Whereas his father had conceived of noh through the aesthetics of imitation, Zeami took the form in a poetic direction. Drawing their plots from myth, legend, and history, Zeami's plays are dense in their allusions to poetry, court and military narratives, religious tales, and other established forms of Japanese and Chinese literature. But Zeami's poetic conception of noh went well beyond literary citation. Expanding traditional poetic techniques from verbal devices into theatrical ones, Zeami combined poetry, music, movement, and stage effects into a poetry for all the senses. Crafted with a jeweler's precision, many of his plays exemplify the ideal of *yūgen*—elegant, mysterious beauty—that was central to Zeami's aesthetic treatises. In Zeami's earliest writing *yūgen* refers to the achievement of refinement in movement, bearing, and action—especially when such accomplishments involve unexpected grace

or beauty. But over the course of Zeami's career the term acquired deeper, more elusive meanings that reflect the spiritual vision of Buddhism, including Zen, which was introduced to Japan at the end of the twelfth century and became popular with the samurai class. In this sense, *yūgen* arises from an awareness of the transitoriness of the world; it reflects both the ephemerality of material phenomena and the timelessness of the reality that underlies them.

Zeami's greatest plays achieve the quality of *yūgen* not by concentrating on plot or personality but by presenting ideas and emotions, emphasizing spiritual and aesthetic concerns, and depicting the texture of existence, which unlike life, extends beyond the grave. One of his strategies for attaining this perspective on life was to feature ghosts as his leading characters. These ghosts are not seen through the eyes of the living, as they are in SHAKE-SPEARE's *Hamlet* and elsewhere in Western drama; rather, life in all its intensity is recalled and re-created by the ghosts themselves in evocative, highly poetic acts of memory. Not surprisingly, many of Zeami's most powerful characters were the ghosts of members of the military class for whom he so often performed. These "ghost-of-warrior plays" (*shura mono*), a form that Zeami largely introduced, constitute the second of five categories of plays that came to be performed in sequence as part of a formal noh program. The others are deity plays (*waki nō*); woman or "wig" plays (*kazura mono*); miscellaneous plays, including those about madness (*kyōran mono*) and those about individuals alive in the dramatic present (*genzai mono*); and plays featuring a supernatural being or demon (*kiri nō*). In *Atsumori*, one of the finest of these ghost-of-warrior plays, Zeami established a powerful counterpoint between the past as a site of heroic action and the dramatic present as a site of recollection, transcendent awareness, and reconciliation.

Taira Atsumori, a young warrior who died bravely in battle, had already been the subject of numerous Japanese tales and plays. Zeami's source for *Atsumori* was *The Tale of the Heike*, a fictionalized narrative of the civil wars between supporters of the Taira

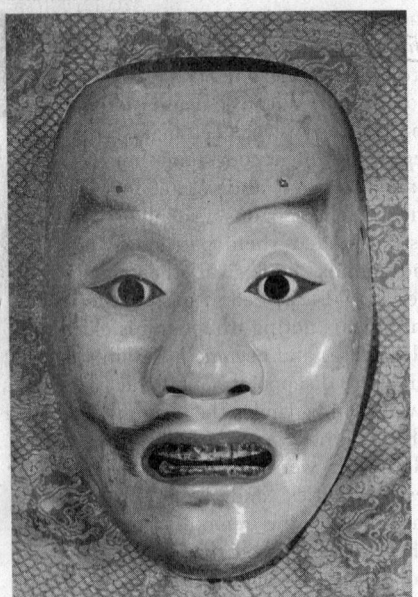

This noh mask, dating from the late fourteenth century, depicts a samurai character.

clan (also called the Heike) and the Mina-moto clan (also called the Genji) in the late twelfth century. In its most popular, fourteenth-century version, *The Tale of the Heike* was recited by players of the *biwa* (a kind of lute) who roamed the countryside. In this account, the fleeing Atsumori turns back to face the challenge of the mature Kumagae; they struggle, and Kumagae emerges victorious only to realize that his opponent is a youth his own son's age. Kumagae wishes to spare Atsumori, but because his own troops are fast approaching, he has no choice but to behead Atsumori quickly to save him further suffering and, sometime after the battle, take religious vows and pray for Atsumori's soul. The dramatic potentials of this story are legion, and some of them are developed at length in an eighteenth-century puppet play titled *The Chronicle of the Battle of Ichinotani*, which depicts the conflicts of love and duty. In the puppet play, duty wins: the social structure is outwardly affirmed, although the cost is Kumagae's sacrifice of his own son in place of Atsumori.

Zeami, however, was interested in neither the drama of physical battle nor the tension between love and duty. In his play, Atsumori's ghost appears some years after his death and confronts Kumagae, who has become the monk Renshō. In this ghost-of-warrior play, dramatic conflict is minimized; very little happens. The military events recorded in *The Tale of the Heike* are presented not only through brief sections of dramatic reenactment but through recited narration and stylized dance. Like the twenty-three-year rule of the Heike themselves, these events exist—to quote one of Zeami's most resonant lines—"in the space of a dream." But less, in this case, is more. The absence of extended external action in *Atsumori* makes possible a deeper exploration of time, self-knowledge, and the fleetingness of human life. Through his focus on interior experience, emotion, and reflection, Zeami creates a play of poignant beauty.

In keeping with his source, Zeami depicts Atsumori as both a brave warrior and an artist—an accomplished flutist. He also compares him with the ninth-century poet Ariwara no Yukihira and the fictional shining prince of *The Tale of Genji*, both of whom were exiled at Suma, the noh play's setting. Like other ghost-of-warrior plays by Zeami, *Atsumori* aids in legitimizing the ruling class by helping to create and propagate the figure of the military aristocrat as both cultural and military hero, excelling in aesthetic creativity and sensibility as well as in military skills and virtues. At the same time, the play acknowledges the stature of the lower classes (within the text the grass cutters, but also the lowly actors) by arguing that humble people may also possess artistic talent. An effective parallel is drawn between the grass cutters in act 1 and the Taira clansmen in act 2. *Atsumori* directly advocates a social message: don't envy your superiors or despise your inferiors, for in this topsy-turvy world, those at the top may end up at the bottom and vice versa. It also expresses the classic Buddhist concept of nondualism: opposites are equivalents; enemies indeed are friends.

In medieval Japanese thought, which was deeply influenced both by the teachings of Buddhism and by the Japanese religion known as Shinto or "the way of the gods," human passions and desires do not cease with one's death. Ghosts continue to interact with living beings, usually because of some attachment to life that interferes with the attainment of enlightenment. The structure of Zeami's ghost plays reflects these assumptions. A priest (played by the secondary actor, who is called the *waki*) travels to a well-known place, where he meets and questions a local inhabitant (the main actor, or *shite*). The local figure describes a famous person connected with the place, hints that he is indeed that person, and disappears. In the second act, the ghost of the famous person (played by the recostumed *shite*) appears in his or her earthly form and presents crucial moments of that life. As dawn breaks the phantom disappears, often requesting that the traveler pray for his or her soul.

From its opening lines—"Awake to awareness, the world's but a dream, / . . . one may cast it aside—is this what is Real?"—the play sets up a complex relationship between reality and dream. The priest Renshō has cast aside secular life, but he is still attached to this illusory world through his desire to assuage his guilt over killing Atsumori by praying for his dead enemy's soul. Thus his good works bind him to life as an unenlightened being. Atsumori, whose ghost enters in act 2, is dead; however, he too exists in an unenlightened state, returning to earth "To clear the karma left from this waking world"—that is, to wash away the sins he committed while alive. When Renshō encounters Atsumori's ghost, he assumes that he must be dreaming. Atsumori puts Renshō's assumption into question by explaining that one gains nothing by distinguishing between dream and reality. Life is a dream and dreams are real, for both states are illusory and must be transcended. This transcendence is enlightenment, the state that both Atsumori and Renshō are seeking. They do not explicitly achieve it at the end of the play; all that is promised is the hope "that in the end they will be reborn together / on a single lotus petal" in paradise.

Shortly after the *shite*, garbed as a grass cutter, enters the stage, one of Ariwara no Yukihira's poems, written when the poet was exiled at Suma Bay, is quoted and expanded upon:

> "If anyone should ask after me,
> my reply would speak of lonely grief
> here at Suma Bay
> where brine drips from seaweed."
> Should anyone learn who I am,
> . . . .
> then I too would have a friend.

Here Zeami employs a strategy successfully used in many of his plays, presenting the basic plot of the play in an early lyric passage; that is, the action of the poem becomes the action of the play. The speaker of the poem (the grass cutter) is living at Suma Bay; someone (the priest Renshō) comes to ask after him, and Atsumori's ghost (in its "true" form in act 2) replies by describing how the Taira clan passed dismal days on the Suma seacoast. Moreover, once the visitor Renshō learns Atsumori's identity, the two become friends "in Buddha's Law." By ascribing Yukihira's poem to Atsumori and incorporating its delivery, the play not only serves as a requiem for the souls of the warriors but also legitimizes the social status of the warrior class by identifying them with earlier noble exiles at Suma.

One other notable characteristic of this noh play, which it shares with the *Tale of the Heike,* is Atsumori's love of music. His return to the Taira encampment to retrieve his precious flute caused him to lose the opportunity to board one of the fleeing Taira ships and leads directly to his death. In act 1, Renshō hears and admires the flute playing of the grass cutter, just as Kumagae had heard and admired Atsumori's flute playing from the opposing military camp the night before their fatal encounter. In act 2, the lyrical tone of that earlier evening is presented through a gentle, medium-tempo dance—an unusual choice for a warrior play, but well-suited to this play's depiction of Atsumori as a cultured man. It is especially appropriate because the dance is performed to strains of flute music. Immediately after this graceful dance, the play turns to a more forceful enactment of the brave Atsumori's death in battle. Whereas most of the text is chanted in the melodic mode, a musical style associated with feminine and aristocratic characters, the battle scene at the play's conclusion is chanted in the dynamic mode, a style associated with warriors and ferocious characters. This deeply musical quality makes *Atsumori* one of Zeami's most elegant ghost-of-warrior plays.

Today noh is almost always performed on a special stage or a facsimile of it placed over a different structure. The noh stage is now most often a roofed area within an auditorium, with the audience seated at stage right and in front of it. A curtained bridgeway leads from far stage right to the main stage, a 19-foot square with a small back area for the attendants and instrumentalists; the chorus is at stage left. Backstage to the left is a small door through which the chorus and attendants enter and exit, and minor characters killed in the course of the play exit. All noh plays are accompanied by a flute and two or three drums, and much of the text (including lines attributed to the main character) is chanted by the chorus. The music is scripted and all movements are minutely choreographed. There is no need for a director; the performers each learn their roles individually and the

Contemporary performances of noh continue to retain traditional staging and costuming, as this woodcut image of a performance at the Kasuga Shrine, ca. 1980, shows.

shite chooses any variations to the standard text and performance practices. One or two stage props may be present, although *Atsumori* uses none; otherwise there is no scenery. Museum-quality costumes and masks provide visual interest, and the actors manipulate fans, bundles of grass (for the grass cutters), swords (for warriors), and other hand props appropriate to the characters. A two-act noh play requires a minimum of three actors. The *shite* represents the main character, usually in two different forms, and the *waki* represents a priest or secondary male figure. Both of these actors may describe the scenery or the action as well as speak the lines of their character. In the interlude between acts, a *kyōgen* (or comic actor) often retells the story behind the play in more colloquial language (usually that of the eighteenth century) both to clarify the plot for the audience and to give the *shite* time to change his costume. All roles are traditionally played by male actors, although one occasionally sees women on the professional stage today, and both in its early days and in modern times female groups have performed noh. The texts of noh are relatively short, but most plays take about one and a half hours to perform.

Noh plays, especially Zeami's, became a focus of attention in the West in the early twentieth century. They were admired by such poets as Ezra Pound and W. B. Yeats, who were drawn to the poetic concentration and formal beauty of noh theater, and such modern stage designers as Edward Gordon Craig. Since that time, noh drama has continued to influence a wide variety of poets, playwrights, performers, filmmakers, and theater theorists. In Japan, noh has been performed without interruption by professional and amateur actors, but its audience has changed over time. In 1879, Japanese diplomats entertained the former American president Ulysses S. Grant with a noh performance, and Tokyo audiences in the early twenty-first century include many hip young Japanese. From noh's early days amateurs have learned to chant, dance, and perform it; the texts have been illustrated in a number of artistic styles; and beginning in early modern times, excerpts from noh texts were taught in the schools. The texts'

many allusions and quotations, part of the cultural currency of the medieval elite, have been explained in detail over the centuries, and high school courses on Japanese literature now rely on heavily annotated texts.

KAREN BRAZELL

Atsumori[1]

CHARACTERS

SHITE,[2] in act 1, a grass cutter without a mask; in act 2, the masked ghost of Atsumori

COMPANIONS, two or three other maskless grass cutters

WAKI,[3] Renshō (or Rensei), the priestly name of Kumagae (or Kumagai) no Jirō Naozane, the man who killed Atsumori in battle

KYŌGEN,[4] a local man

CHORUS of eight or ten members seated at stage left

Musicians with a flute and two hand drums seated at the back of the stage

Two attendants seated at the back of the stage, stage right of instruments

Act 1

[To the music of the hand drums and the flute, the WAKI, dressed as a priest, enters the bridgeway[5] and moves slowly to back stage right, turns to face the pine tree painted on the back wall of the stage, and chants in the melodic mode.]

WAKI Awake to awareness, the world's but a dream,
    awake to awareness, the world's but a dream,
    one may cast it aside—is this what is Real?[6]
CHORUS Awake to awareness, the world's but a dream,
5 one may cast it aside—is this what is Real?

[Intoned speech with no accompaniment; the WAKI faces front.]

1. Translated by Karen Brazell.
2. Principal actor and character; protagonist.
3. Supporting actor and character (often a traveling priest).
4. Comic actor who performed in noh drama during the interlude between acts.

5. *Hashigakari*, the narrow passageway from which characters enter and exit the noh stage.
6. Here, the *waki* questions whether simply taking religious vows is enough to enable one to attain enlightenment.

WAKI   I am Kumagae no Jirō Naozane, a resident of Musashi, who has re-
nounced this world and taken the priestly name Renshō. I did this because
of the deep remorse I felt at having killed Atsumori. Now I am going to
Ichinotani[7] to pray for the repose of his soul.

> [*He continues to face front, chanting in the melodic mode with drum
> accompaniment.*]

10   WAKI   Departing the capital as clouds part
departing the capital as clouds part,
the moon too travels southward,
a small wheel rolling toward
Yodo; Yamazaki soon passed;
15   then the ponds of Koya, Ikuta River,

> [*Takes a few steps to indicate travel.*]

Suma Bay, where "waves surge beside us";[8]
at Ichinotani I have arrived,

> [*Takes a few steps to indicate his arrival.*]

I have arrived at Ichinotani.

How quickly I've reached Ichinotani in the province of Tsu. Scenes from
20   the past come to mind as if present. [*Hands together in a prayer gesture*]
Hail, Amida[9] Buddha. [*Turns slightly to the right*] What's that? I hear the
sound of a flute coming from that high meadow. I think I'll wait for the
flutist and ask him to tell me something about this place.

> [*The* SHITE *and two or three* COMPANIONS *costumed as humble grass cut-
> ters enter along the bridgeway. They are unmasked, and each carries a
> bamboo pole with grass attached. They proceed to the front of the stage
> and form two lines perpendicular to the front and facing each other.*]

SHITE and COMPANIONS   The grass cutter's flute adds its voice,
25   the grass cutter's flute adds its voice
to the wind blowing over the meadows.

> [*The* SHITE *faces front.*]

SHITE   The "man who cuts grass on that hill"[1] makes his way through the
fields
in the gathering dusk; it's time to go home.

SHITE and COMPANIONS [*facing each other again*]
30   Was his way home, too, beside the Suma Sea?
How limited the path we tread
entering the hills, returning to the shore;
how miserable the lowly lives we lead.

---

7. The place on the Japan Sea, near Suma,
where Kumagae killed Atsumori (in present-
day Kobe). *Musashi*: province in eastern
Japan that contains Tokyo. In the following
passage, Kumagae lists some of the intervening locations.
8. The first of many phrases in this play taken
from the "Suma" chapter of *The Tale of
Genji*, a classic 11th-century work attributed
to Murasaki Shikibu (ca. 973–ca. 1031), a
Japanese noblewoman.

9. A major manifestation of Buddha, in whose
Pure Land the characters at the end of the
play hope to achieve rebirth.
1. This is a line from a poem by the poet Hito-
maro (ca. 662–710), in which the speaker
asks that the grass not be cut so that it can
serve as feed for the horse of a lover whose
arrival is expected.

"If anyone should ask after me,
35 my reply would speak of lonely grief
here at Suma Bay
where brine drips from seaweed."[2]
Should anyone learn who I am,

> [*Brief instrumental interlude.*]

should anyone learn who I am,
40 then I, too, would have a friend.
Such wretched seafolk we've become that
"even dear ones are grown estranged."[3]

We live our lives, such as they are,
yielding to misery, we exhaust our days,

> [*The* SHITE *goes to the shite spot*[4] *while the* COMPANIONS *line up in front of the* CHORUS.]

45 yielding to misery, we exhaust our days,

> [*The* WAKI *stands at the waki spot,*[5] *faces the* SHITE, *and speaks.*]

WAKI Hello there! There's something I'd like to ask you grass cutters.

SHITE Are you speaking to us? What is it you want?

WAKI Was one of you playing the flute just now?

SHITE Yes. One of us was playing.

50 WAKI It was exquisite! And all the more exquisite because such music is not expected from men in your position.

SHITE You say it's unexpected from men in our position. People should neither envy superiors nor despise inferiors, or so it is said.

COMPANIONS [*chanting*] "Foresters' songs, shepherds' pipes"[6] is a set phrase;
55 grass cutters' flutes and woodsmen's songs

SHITE and COMPANIONS are well-known topics in poetry;
bamboo flutes have widespread fame.
Do not think it strange.

> [*Song in the melodic mode to quiet drum accompaniment.*]

WAKI Indeed there is sense in what you say.
60 Those "foresters' songs and shepherds' pipes"

SHITE are the flutes of grass cutters

WAKI and the songs of woodsmen

SHITE "passing through this bitter world, a melody"[7]

WAKI to sing

65 SHITE to dance,

WAKI to blow,

SHITE to play.

---

2. A poem by the well-known poet Ariwara no Narihira (825–880).

3. An allusion to the preface to the *Kokinshū*, the early 10th-century anthology in which Ariwara's poem was first anthologized; it states that even close friends desert those who fall in status.

4. The spot on the noh stage closest to the passageway where the *shite* often stands.

5. The place at front stage left of the noh stage where the *waki* usually stands or sits.

6. Quoted from a poem written in Chinese by the Japanese poet Ki no Tadana (959– 999): "When the sun sets on mountain roads / the sounds of foresters' songs and shepherds' pipes fill the ear. / When the birds return to valley nests / the tints of bamboo smoke and pine mist obstruct the vision." "Grass cutters" and "woodsmen" are Japanese references.

7. A phrase used in a medieval song/dance form (*kusemai*) called "Traveling to the West" to describe the songs of female entertainers.

CHORUS   We lead our lives
                    [*The* SHITE *faces front and spreads his arms.*]
         guided by discerning hearts that fancy,
                    [*Brief instrumental interlude; the* WAKI *sits at the waki spot.*]
70   guided by discerning hearts that fancy
         bamboo flutes: Tender Branch, Broken Cicada,
         such names as these are numerous.[8]

         The flute the grass cutter plays
         also has a name:
75   know it as Green Leaf.
         At water's edge near Sumiyoshi
                    [*The* SHITE *circles the stage to the left, and the three* COMPANIONS *quietly
                    exit up the bridgeway.*]
         one would find Korean flutes;[9]
         here at Suma one might say
         seafolk play Charred Stick,
80   seafolk play Charred Stick.[1]
                    [*Intoned speech, no accompaniment.*]
WAKI   How strange. All the other grass cutters have left, yet you remain. Why
         is that?
SHITE   Even you ask why? Drawn by the power of your voice above the eve-
         ning waves, I have come to request ten Hail Amidas. Say them for me,
85   please.
WAKI   Ten Hail Amidas is an easy thing to grant. For whom should I pray?
SHITE   To be honest, I am related to Atsumori.
WAKI   You're related, you say? How nostalgic that makes me,
SHITE   he says, putting his palms together [*clasps his rosary between his
90   hands*], Hail, Amida Buddha.
SHITE   [*The* SHITE *kneels, and they chant together.*]   "Should I attain enlight-
         enment, no being in all the world
WAKI   who calls my name shall be cast aside."[2]
                    [*The* SHITE *looks at the* WAKI *and lowers his hands.*]
CHORUS   Please cast me not aside.
95   Though a single cry should suffice,
         each day, each night, you pray.
         How fortunate I am, my name
                    [*Looking down, he stands and then goes toward the shite spot.*]
         unspoken, yet clear, at dawn and at dusk too
         you hold services for the soul of one

---

8. Flutes and other valuable instruments
were often named. According to *The Tale of
the Heike,* Tender Branch was the flute Atsumori carried with him to his death; other
sources give the name Green Leaf.
9. Used in court music. *Sumiyoshi:* a port frequented by ships from Korea, in present-day
Osaka.

1. That is, burned wood to gain salt from
brine. There is a reference in a 13th-century
anthology of short tales (*Jikkinshō*) to a flute
called Charred Head.
2. Quoted from a passage in a basic sutra of
Pure Land Buddhism that describes meditations centering on Amida Buddha.

[*He turns and looks intently at the* WAKI.]

100 whose name is mine, he says

as his figure fades from sight,

[*Facing front, he spreads his arms to indicate his disappearance.*]

as his figure fades from sight.

[*He walks quietly up the bridgeway and out under the raised curtain.*]

Kyōgen Interlude

[*The* KYŌGEN, *who has entered inconspicuously and seated himself at the back of the bridgeway, now rises and moves to the shite spot.*]

KYŌGEN I am a person who lives at Suma Bay. Today I've come to amuse myself by watching the boats go by. Hm! There's a priest I've never seen before. Where are you from?

5 WAKI I'm a priest from the capital. Do you live nearby?

KYŌGEN Yes, indeed I do.

WAKI Then please come over here. I've something I'd like to ask you.

KYŌGEN [*Goes to center stage and sits.*] Certainly. What is it you want to know?

10 WAKI It's a bit unusual. I've heard that this is the harbor where the battle between the Heike and the Genji[3] was fought. Could you please tell me what you know about the death of the Heike nobleman Atsumori?

KYŌGEN That's certainly an unexpected request. Those of us who live around here don't know much about such things; however, since you've come out of your way to inquire, what can I do? I don't really know much, but I'll tell

15 what I've heard.

WAKI Thank you.

KYŌGEN Sometime in the autumn of Jūei 2 [1183] when the Heike were forced from the capital by Kiso Yoshinaka, they retreated to this spot. However, the Genji, dividing their sixty thousand cavalry into two groups,

20 attacked fiercely from both left and right. The Heike fled, scattering here and there. Among them was the young Atsumori, son of Tsunemori, chief of the Office of Palace Repairs. Atsumori had reached the shore, intending to board a ship, only to realize that he had left his precious flute, known as Little Branch, in the main camp. Not wanting it to fall into enemy hands,

25 he went back to fetch it.

Upon retrieving his flute, Atsumori raced again to the shore, only to discover that all the boats, the imperial barque and the troopships, had already put out to sea. Atsumori's horse was strong, so he urged it into the sea. Just then, however, a resident of Musashi Province, Kumagae no Jirō

30 Naozane, beckoned Atsumori with his fan, and he turned back to face this enemy. They fought in the waves, then grappled on the shore, finally falling from their horses. Kumagae, who was unusually strong, managed to come out on top and was about to cut off Atsumori's head when he glimpsed the face beneath the helmet. He saw the powdered brow and blackened teeth

35 of a youth of fifteen or sixteen.[4]

---

3. That is, the Battle of Ichinotani (1184), late in the Genpei War, which pitted the Taira clan (the Heike) against the Minamoto clan (the Genji) in a struggle over imperial succession.

4. His use of cosmetics identifies the youth as a member of an aristocratic family.

"A pity! What an elegant warrior. If only I could spare him." He looked around. Doi and Kajiwara were fast approaching with a dozen other warriors.

"I would like to spare you," he explained, "however, as you can see, a
40 group of my allies is almost upon us. I will kill you and then pray for your soul." Thus he took Atsumori's head.

Examining the corpse, he found a flute in a brocade bag. When he made his presentation before the general, people remarked on how cultivated the dead man must have been. Even among the nobility, few would concern
45 themselves with a flute in such a crisis. The victors' armored sleeves were dampened by their tears. Eventually the youth was identified as Atsumori, the young son of Tsunemori.

Kumagae is said to have retired from the world to pray for Atsumori's enlightenment. Since he didn't spare Atsumori when he might have, this
50 seems like a pack of lies to me. If that Kumagae should come here, we would kill him to prove our loyalty to Atsumori.

That's about all that I've heard. Why do you ask me about it? It seems a bit strange.

WAKI   You were kind to tell me this tale. Why should I conceal anything? I
55 was Kumagae no Jirō Naozane. Now I have become a priest and taken the name Renshō. I have come here to pray for the repose of Atsumori's soul.

KYŌGEN   What! You're that lord Kumagae? Unwittingly I've told you these things. Please forgive me. A force for good is said to be a force for evil too. Maybe it works both ways. I hope that you will pray for Atsumori's soul.

60 WAKI   Don't be upset. I have come only to pray for his soul. I would like to remain a while and read some efficacious sutras. I shall pray diligently.

KYŌGEN   If that's the case, I can give you lodging.

WAKI   Thank you. That would be helpful.

KYŌGEN   At your service.

[*He goes to the bridgeway and sits. After the* SHITE *has made his entrance, the* KYŌGEN *walks quietly up the bridgeway.*]

Act 2

[*Chanted in the melodic mode as he kneels at front stage left.*]

WAKI   Spreading dew-drenched grass to make a bed,
spreading dew-drenched grass to make a bed,
now that the sun has set and night fallen
I'll pray to Amida that Atsumori
5 may yet achieve enlightenment, that he
may yet achieve enlightenment, I'll pray.

[*The* SHITE, *now costumed as the warrior Atsumori, enters to instrumental music and stands at backstage right facing front.*]

SHITE   "Back and forth to Awaji plovers
fly; their cries awaken one
who guards the pass at Suma."[5]

5. Quoted from an early 12th-century poem by Minamoto Kanemasa (d. 1112). In the "Suma" chapter of *The Tale of Genji*, too, the cries of plovers awaken the exiled hero.

10   What is your name?

      [*Sung with the* SHITE *standing at the shite spot and the* WAKI *sitting at the waki spot.*]

SHITE   Look here, Renshō,
Atsumori has arrived.

WAKI   How very strange!
Beating on the gong, performing holy rites,
15   I have not had a moment to doze, and yet
Atsumori appears before me.
Surely this must be a dream.

SHITE   Why need it be a dream?
To clear the karma left from this waking world
20   I make my appearance here.

WAKI   This can't be. It's said,
"A single Hail Amida erases countless sins."
I've offered ceaseless prayers
to clear away all sinful hindrances.
25   What karma can remain from this rough sea of life,

SHITE   so deep my sins, please wash them away,

WAKI   and in doing so, my own salvation seek.

SHITE   Your prayers affecting both our future lives—

WAKI   once enemies

30 SHITE   now instead

WAKI   in Buddha's Law

SHITE   made friends [*takes a step toward the* WAKI].

      [*The* SHITE *spreads his arms facing front; the melodic song matches the accompanying drum rhythms.*]

CHORUS   Now I see!
"Cast aside an evil friend,

      [*The* SHITE *points at the* WAKI *with his left hand and moves toward him.*]

35   beckon near an enemy who's good";

      [*The* SHITE *flips his sleeve over his left arm and stares intently at the* WAKI.]

that refers to you!
How fortunate, how very fortunate!

      [*Changing the mood, the* SHITE *circles left to the shite spot.*]

And now, with my confessional tale
let us while the night away,
40   let us while the night away,

      [*The* SHITE *goes to center stage and sits on a stool provided by the stage attendant. The song is elaborately embellished.*]

Spring blossoms mounting tips of trees
inspire ascent toward enlightenment;
the autumn moon sinking to ocean's depths
symbolizes grace descending to mankind.

      [*All remain seated.*]

45 SHITE   Even though the clan put forth new sprouts,
kinsmen branching out in all directions,

CHORUS　"our glory was that of the short-lived rose of sharon."[6]
　　　How difficult to find encouragement toward good—
　　　good hard flintstones engender sparks
50　　whose lights are gone before one knew they were—
　　　the lives of humans flash by like this.
SHITE　Yet those high up inflict pain on people down below;
　　　those living lives of luxury are unaware of arrogance.

> *[The SHITE stands and dances during the following segment sung in the melodic mode with the drum accompaniment. The flute enters midway.]*

CHORUS　It happened that the Heike
55　　ruled the world some twenty years,
　　　truly a fleeting generation,
　　　passed in the space of a dream.
　　　"That famous autumn, leaves"[7]

> *[Moves forward slightly.]*

　　　lured by "winds from the four directions,"[8]
60　　scattered here and there in leaflike

> *[Moves his fan in a sweeping gesture and looks to the right.]*

　　　boats bobbing on the waves, we sleep,
　　　not even in our dreams returning home—
　　　"caged birds longing for cloudy realms,
　　　ranks of homing geese broken, scattered,"[9]
65　　uncertain skies, aimless travel gowns tied

> *[Looks up at the sky and circles left.]*

　　　and layered sunsets, moonrises, months, a year
　　　journeys by, returns to spring
　　　here at Ichinotani secluded for a while
　　　here at Suma Shore we live.
70 SHITE　From the hills behind, winds roar down

> *[Opens his fan and raises it before his face.]*

CHORUS　to coastal fields keenly cold
　　　our boats draw up, no day or night without
　　　the cries of plovers,
　　　our sleeves too

> *[Twirls his sleeve over his arm to make a pillow and kneels.]*

6. A paraphrase of the second line of a well-known couplet by the Chinese poet Po Chu-i (772–846): "The pine has a thousand years, yet in the end, it dies: / the rose of sharon a single day to enjoy its glory."

7. An allusion to the Kakuichi version of *The Tale of the Heike*: "Now it is evident to every eye that adversity and happiness follow identical paths, that prosperity and decline are like a flip of the hand. Who of us could but feel pity? Once in the past they flourished like springtime blossoms; now in the present they fall like autumn leaves." *A fleeting generation*: an allusion to the Nagato version of *The Tale of the Heike*: "A generation used to last thirty-three years, but now it's only twenty-one."

8. The first of nine phrases in this section listed by Yoshimoto Nijō (Zeami's poetry mentor) as phrases that one should quote from the "Suma" chapter of *The Tale of Genji*.

9. More phrases from the Kakuichi version of *The Tale of the Heike*, where they refer to a Heike clansman, Shigehira, who was captured by the Genji: "Perhaps his thoughts, fretful as caged birds longing for the sky, find themselves afloat on the southern seas, a thought miles from home. Perhaps his feelings are as sad as those of a lone goose headed homeward, separated from his fellows."

75 dampened by the waves that
  drench our rocky pillows,
  in seaside shacks we huddle together
  befriended only by Suma folk—
  bent like wind-bent pines on the strands
    [*Circles left to the* shite *spot.*]
80 of evening smoke rising from the fires—
    [*Waving his fan in his left hand, the* SHITE *moves forward.*]
  brushwood, it's called,
    [*Holding out his fan parallel to the floor.*]
  this stuff piled up to sleep upon.
  Our worries, too, pile up in rustic Suma,
  where we're forced to play out our lives
    [*Pointing his fan to the right, he looks up.*]
85 becoming simple Suma folk—
    [*Circles to the left.*]
  such is our clan's fate; how forlorn we are!
    [*Stops at backstage center.*]
    [*The chanting changes from the melodic to the dynamic mode.*]
 SHITE And then, on the night of the sixth day of the second month,
  Tsunemori, my father, gathered us together
  to enjoy ourselves with song and dance.
90 WAKI And your entertainment that night,
  the elegant flute music from your encampment,
  was clearly heard by us on the opposing side.
 SHITE It was indeed Atsumori,
  awaiting the end, his bamboo flute
95 WAKI accompanying a variety of
 SHITE ballads and songs,
 WAKI many voices
    [*The* SHITE *circles right to the shite spot.*]
 CHORUS arise, creating steady cadences.
    [*Medium tempo dance. The* SHITE *performs a sprightly yet elegant dance to
    the music of the flute and hand drums. This dance, unusual in a warrior
    play, emphasizes Atsumori's artistic sensitivity. The context also foregrounds
    the flute music, which is the normal accompaniment to the dance.*]
 SHITE [*Raising his fan*] And so it is,
100 the royal barque sets forth
    [*The dynamic song becomes strongly rhythmical, matching the steady beats of
    the drums.*]
 CHORUS and all the members of the clan
    [*The* SHITE *stamps his feet.*]
  board their ships to sail.
    [*Making a sweeping point with his fan, he turns to the right.*]
  Not wanting to be late
    [*Goes to the front of the stage.*]

Atsumori races to the shore;
105   the royal barque and troopships, too,
have already put out to sea.
      [Raises his fan over his head and looks out into the distance.]
SHITE   It's hopeless! Reining in his horse
      [Mimes pulling on the reins with his left hand.]
amidst the breakers, he stands bewildered.
      [Waves his fan to indicate agitation.]
CHORUS   At that very moment
      [The SHITE stamps his feet.]
110   from behind comes
      [He turns and faces the bridgeway.]
Kumagae no Jirō Naozane.
"Don't flee!"
      [Hurries to the shite spot.]
he shouts and charges.
Atsumori too
      [Moves quickly to center front.]
115   turns about his horse, and
      [Mimes reining in his horse and races backstage.]
in the breakers they draw swords
      [Mimes drawing a sword (represented by his fan) and goes to the front right corner.]
and exchange blows, twice, thrice,
      [Strikes with his fan.]
they are seen to strike;
on horseback they grapple,
      [Wraps his arms around himself.]
120   then fall onto the wave-swept shore,
      [Twirls around and kneels.]
one atop the other; finally
struck down, Atsumori dies;
      [Points his fan at his head and looks down.]
the wheel of fate turns, and they meet.
      [Stands, goes to center back, and draws his sword.]
"The enemy's right here!"
      [Hurries toward the WAKI.]
125   he cries and is about to strike.
      [Raises his sword to strike.]
Returning good for evil,
      [Kneels.]
the priest performs services and prays
      [Stands and returns to backstage.]
that in the end they will be reborn together
      [Spreads his arms, moves toward the WAKI again, and drops his sword.]

on a single lotus petal,

    [*Circles to the front right corner.*]

130   and Renshō the priest
is an enemy no more.

    [*Returns to the shite spot.*]

Please pray for my soul,

    [*Makes a prayer gesture toward the* WAKI.]

please pray for my soul.

    [*Turns to face the bridgeway and performs closing stamps;
then exits slowly.*]

THE WAKEFIELD MASTER

O NE of the most popular forms of theater in England between the late fourteenth and mid-sixteenth centuries was
the Corpus Christi plays, cycles of short
plays—or pageants—that dramatized biblical history from the Fall of the Angels
and the Creation of the World to the Last
Judgment. Performed in conjunction with
the Feast of Corpus Christi (literally, "Body
of Christ," a feast day commemorating the
institution of the Eucharist, or the consumption of consecrated bread and wine in
the Holy Communion), these plays were
produced by local guilds as part of the religious and civic celebrations that marked
the growth of towns in the late medieval
period. Staging practice varied from town
to town, but generally Corpus Christi plays
were performed either at stationary locations or on pageant wagons that moved in
procession between fixed viewing sites.
Particularly in the north of England,
where most extant Corpus Christi plays
were written and performed, the cycles
provided a rich tapestry of character and
incident, and in their panoramic narrative
of creation, fall, redemption, and judgment,
they explored the relationship between
divine history and contemporary human
life. Of the many plays that make up the
English Corpus Christi cycles, none is
more widely known and admired than the
Wakefield SECOND SHEPHERDS' PLAY. Bold
in its use of comedy and theatrical realism, it is considered not just one of the
finest artistic achievements of the late
medieval period but one of the masterpieces of the English stage.

The *Second Shepherds' Play* is part of
the Towneley cycle (named after the Lan-
cashire family that long owned the manuscript), which contains thirty-two pageants.
The Towneley cycle was almost certainly
written and performed in Wakefield, a
manorial town in West Yorkshire that by
the mid-fifteenth century had become a
prosperous center of the wool trade. Insufficient historical evidence exists to date the
cycle at Wakefield with any certainty, and
scholars have proposed dates ranging from
the early to late fifteenth century for its
emergence. As they have noted, it was not
until the final third of the century that
Wakefield possessed sufficient people,
resources, and civic pride to mount a project as ambitious as a Corpus Christi cycle.
Information concerning the staging of the
cycle is likewise scarce. Because of the difficulties that production on pageant wagons
would have presented in a town the size of
Wakefield, most scholars believe that the
cycle was performed at a single site over a
span of one to three consecutive days.

The appearance of an angel to shepherds
watching their flocks on the night of the
Nativity and their subsequent visit to the
newly born Christ child (the biblical
account of which can be found in Luke 2)
was a popular episode in English and Continental drama throughout the Middle
Ages. The Visit of the Shepherds (*Officium
pastorum*) was one of the early non-Easter
liturgical tropes—dramatic scenes that
developed in the tenth century out of liturgical services and represent the earliest
form of public medieval drama—and it
appeared in the liturgical drama that developed from these tropes. The French city of
Rouen had a version by the late 1100s, and
a shepherds' play was performed at the
Cathedral at York in the mid-1200s. Despite
the popularity of the episode, separate
shepherds' plays were a rarity on the
Continent. Because Christmas Day was
crowded with other liturgical ceremonies, the episode was more typically performed in Europe on the feast of the
Epiphany (celebrated on January 6) in a

play commemorating the Visit of the Three Kings. In England, by contrast, all four extant English Corpus Christi cycles—York, Chester, Wakefield, and N-town—feature individual shepherds' plays, and in two of the cycles (Chester and Wakefield) this episode provides the inspiration for plays of considerable stylistic imagination.

That the representatives of common humanity who witness this birth were shepherds would have been of particular interest to audiences in the rural north of England, where the surviving cycles originated. The contemporary touches that often characterize these shepherds—the realism for which the Chester and Wakefield shepherds' plays, in particular, are justly famous—allowed the cycle dramatists to bring the biblical and fifteenth-century worlds close to each other.

The Towneley manuscript is unusual, of course, in that it includes two shepherds' plays, not one. Both works—their Latin titles in the manuscript are *Prima Pastorum* and *Secunda Pastorum*—come from the hand of an anonymous but skilled writer identified since the early twentieth century as the "Wakefield Master." In addition to a number of references to settings in Wakefield and the surrounding areas, the work of the Wakefield Master is recognizable in the Towneley manuscript by its linguistic variety, including a command of vernacular dialects; complex characterization; vigorous comic writing; and use of a distinctive stanza found nowhere else in medieval English literature. The Wakefield Master was most likely a cleric, though his plays reveal a familiarity with the practical spheres of medieval life (the law, music, animal husbandry, and cookery, to name

The Adoration of the Shepherds by Bernadino Butinone, ca. 1480–85.

just a few) as well as biblical, classical, and Latin theological texts. In addition to *Noah*, the two shepherd plays, *Herod the Great*, and *The Buffeting*, he is credited with revising at least nine other plays in the Wakefield cycle, several of which came originally from the York cycle. The traditional scholarly view is that the Wakefield Master began working on the cycle during the latter stages of its development, expanding and polishing a number of existing plays while also contributing his own. Some have recently argued that the Wakefield Master was the principal compiler of the Wakefield cycle and should be regarded as its guiding intelligence. But this view should be embraced with caution, since the notion of authorship in the Middle Ages was different than it has been in more recent centuries, particularly as it concerns dramatic texts designed for performance. Like the other surviving cycles, the Towneley plays as a group were probably the product of a number of hands.

Why two shepherds' plays? Their relationship is clarified little by the Latin sentence that introduces the second in the Towneley manuscript: *Incipit Alia eorundem,* or "Here begins another of the same." Were the plays intended for performance in alternate years? Were they alternative versions available to a producer of the cycle in any given year? Was the first intended to end the first day and the second to open the following morning on those occasions when the cycle was performed over the course of more than one day? Similarities between the two plays suggest that the second was both a revision and expansion of the narrative structure offered in the first. Both plays include an opening sequence in which the shepherds lament the hardship of their lives, an extended section marked by comic material (an argument over imaginary sheep and a mock feast in the *First Shepherds' Play;* the famous sheep-stealing scene in the *Second Shepherds' Play*), the annunciation of Christ's birth and a comic attempt by the shepherds to imitate the angels' celestial song, and a visit to the manger in which the shepherds present gifts to the newborn child. In both plays the biblical outlines of the story are fleshed out with the details of rural northern English life, establishing a dramatic landscape that is true to the established Nativity tradition while also recognizably grounded in the late medieval here and now.

The relationship between past and present is particularly striking in the *Second Shepherds' Play.* In the play's opening sequence all three shepherds lament that their world is one of hardship and woe. The harshness of the weather—"Lord, these weathers are spiteous [spiteful], / And the winds full keen, / And the frosts so hideous / They water mine een [eyes]"—symbolizes the broader inhospitability of a world in need of God's grace. Poverty and injustice here are man-made as well as natural. With the eye toward social satire that gives the writing of the Wakefield Master much of its contemporaneity, the First Shepherd (Coll) accuses the "gentlerymen," the well-off retainers in the employment of the manorial lord, of exploiting the poor for their own ends. But even in the midst of this catalogue of life's woes, there are ironic and direct anticipations of the redemptive birth that will provide the hope of salvation. In his long complaint on behalf of henpecked husbands who are shackled with children they cannot afford to raise, the Second Shepherd (Gib) introduces the theme of nativity that will powerfully come to the fore by the play's end. And even as he bemoans a world that is now "worse than it was," the Third Shepherd (Daw) refers anachronistically to the salvation that the Nativity will bring about: "Christ's cross me speed / And Saint Nicholas!" The shepherds conclude their opening interaction by singing; and while their performance is rude, the theme of music that they introduce anticipates Christ's harmonizing entrance into human history.

Mak's entrance at this point introduces the extended comic subplot—a sheep-stealing interlude—that distinguishes the *Second Shepherds' Play* from other pageants in the surviving English Corpus Christi cycles. These scenes, in which Mak and his wife, Gill, disguise a sheep that he has stolen from the shepherds as a baby in a crib, occupy 632 of the play's 1,087 lines. The length and comic vigor of this episode, which has analogues in folklore, has raised questions among critics concerning the play's unity. In *A Literary History of England* (1948), Albert C. Baugh wrote: "The length of the Mak episode is hopelessly out of proportion to the proper matter of the play. The *Second Shepherds' Play* as a shepherds' play is an artistic absurdity; as a farce of Mak the sheep-stealer it is the masterpiece of the English religious drama." In *English Drama from Early Times to the Elizabethans* (1950), A. P. Rossiter rejected the notion of unity entirely. The *Second Shepherds' Play*, according to Rossiter, is an example of the "Gothic" ambivalence evident elsewhere in late medieval art, in which the transcendental and the grotesque are set in unresolvable tension with each other: "Clowning and adoration are laid together, like the mystery and the boorishness in Bruegel's *Adoration of the Magi*." More typically, though, critics have argued that the comic and religious plots are integrated through complex narrative and thematic parallels and that the sheep-stealing episode and Nativity scene exist in mutually illuminating contrast.

The characterization of Mak, for instance, establishes important parallels and contrasts within the play's larger religious and moral framework. Arriving unannounced at the point when an audience would expect the Angel to appear, he is a bearer of false news as opposed to the good tidings that represent this pageant's central revelation. Assuming the dress and dialect of a southern retainer (the very figure that Coll disparages in his opening speech), he is a dissembler, a comic Satan who misleads humanity with falsehoods, a parodic version of the "fiend" later mentioned by the Angel. When Mak identifies himself to Gill outside the door to their cottage, his wife provides one of the play's many thematic associations between him and the beguiler of men: "Then may we see here / The devil in a band, / Sir Guile!"

The most daring parallel between the two plots concerns the themes of nativity and visitation. The sheep that Mak and Gill disguise as a baby is a comic version of the Christ child—the Lamb of God (*Agnus Dei*) recently born in Bethlehem—and the shepherds' visit to Mak's cottage anticipates their subsequent journey to the manger that houses the Holy Family. Although we have little evidence as to how the *Second Shepherds' Play* was originally staged, what we do know about medieval stage practice suggests that the cottage and the manger would likely have been represented by the same structure (or "mansion") or by two structures located in visually contrasting parts of the playing area. Textually, the scene with the disguised sheep is rife with ironic allusions to the true Nativity. Daw uses the same phrase to refer to the couple's unseen "baby" ("little day-starn [star]") that Gib will later use to greet the Christ child; and Gill's promise that she will "eat this child / That lies in this cradle" ironically foreshadows the Eucharistic sacrament commemorated by the Feast of Corpus Christi.

With the Angel's entrance divine time reveals itself within human time, and the imminence of Christ's salvation makes itself known to the common "herdmen" who will bear witness to the Nativity on behalf of the play's audience. Nowhere is the Wakefield Master's control of tone, his ability to integrate the transcendental and the homely, more in evidence than in the manger scene. The three shepherds, who have hailed the fulfillment of Old Testament prophesy, address the newborn child with a mixture of reverence and gentle endearment: "Hail, little tiny mop! / Of our creed thou art crop [head]." Their gifts—cherries, a bird, and a tennis ball—reflect the spiritual and everyday worlds that intersect so powerfully. On the one hand, as Lawrence J. Ross has demonstrated, the cherries that appear miraculously out of season derive, as do the other two gifts, from symbols associated with Christ in medieval religious art. The tennis ball, on the other hand, humorously (and touchingly) given to this helpless baby, refers to a sport of the better-off, a social stratum far removed from the "rude" herdsmen who are given the honor of witnessing the savior's birth.

Charged by Mary to "Tell forth as ye go, / And min on [remember] this morn," the shepherds go out singing, reminding us that these tenders of sheep would have been seen by their medieval spectators as figures of the clergy. The English word *pastor* derives from the Latin word for shepherd, of course, and it is the function of a proper ministry to spread the gospel, or "good tidings of great joy" (Luke 2.10), to those who toil in a fallen world. With its skillful blending of humor, social observation, and awe, the *Second Shepherds' Play* shares this celebration. S.G.

The Second Shepherds' Play[1]

CHARACTERS

COLL	GILL
GIB	ANGEL
DAW	MARY
MAK	

[SCENE: *A field.*]

    [*Enter* COLL.]

COLL   Lord, what° these weathers are cold,   *how*
    And I am ill happed;°   *clothed*
    I am nearhand dold,°   *nearly numb*
    So long have I napped;
5   My legs they fold,°   *give way*
    My fingers are chapped.
    It is not as I wold,°   *would (wish)*
    For I am all lapped°   *wrapped*
      In sorrow:
10 In storms and tempest,
    Now in the east, now in the west,
    Woe is him that has never rest
      Midday nor morrow.

    But we sely° husbands°   *poor / farmworkers*
15 That walks on the moor,
    In faith we are nearhands°   *nearly*
    Out of the door.°   *homeless*
    No wonder, as it stands
    If we be poor,
20 For the tilth° of our lands   *arable part*
    Lies fallow as the floor,[2]
      As ye ken.°   *know*
    We are so hammed,°   *hamstrung*

---

1. The present text is based on *The Towneley Plays* (1994), edited by A. C. Cawley and Martin Stevens. Spelling has been modernized except where doing so would interfere with rhyme, and scene directions have been added to the four included in Latin in the manuscript (translated here after lines 273, 290,

386, and 918).
2. Fifteenth-century landowners frequently allowed arable land to lie fallow ("as flat as the floor") in preparation for converting it to pasture. The process, termed *enclosure*, led many farmers to become shepherds.

Fortaxed,° and rammed,°   *Overtaxed / beaten down*
25 We are made hand-tamed
     With these gentlery-men.[3]

Thus they reave us° our rest—   *rob us of*
Our Lady them wary!°   *curse*
These men that are lord-fest,°   *bound to lords*
30 They cause the plow tarry.
That, men say, is for the best—
We find it contrary.
Thus are husbands oppressed
In point to miscarry
35   On live.[4]
Thus hold they us under,
Thus they bring us in blunder,°   *trouble*
It were a great wonder
     And° ever should we thrive.   *If*

40 There shall come a swain
As proud as a po.[5]
He must borrow my wain,°   *wagon*
My plow also;
Then I am full fain°   *glad*
45 To grant ere he go.
Thus live we in pain,
Anger, and woe,
     By night and by day.
He must have if he lang it,
50 If I should forgang it.[6]
I were better be hanged
     Than once say him nay.

For may he get a paint-sleeve[7]
Or brooch nowadays,
55 Woe is him that him grieve
Or once again-says.°   *gainsays*
Dare no man him reprieve,°   *reprove*
What mastery he maes.[8]
And yet may no man lieve°   *believe*
60 One word that he says,
     No letter.
He can make purveyance[9]

---

3. By these gentry folks (here the retainers, or
supervisors, employed by absentee landlords
to manage an estate).
4. Thus are farmworkers oppressed to the
point of perishing.
5. There shall come a retainer, as proud as a
peacock. Here (and in the following lines)
Coll refers to the ostentatious livery worn by
the "gentlery-men."

6. If he desires (something) he must have it,
even if I have to do without (forgo) it.
7. Painted sleeve. This and the brooch in line
54 refer to the badges of authority worn by
the landlord's officers.
8. No matter what force he uses.
9. The requisitioning of food or vehicles in
the name of the lord or king.

With boast and bragance,°   *bragging*
And all is through maintenance°   *protection*
65   Of men that are greater.

It does me good, as I walk
Thus by mine one,°   *myself*
Of this world for to talk
In manner of moan.
70   To my sheep I will stalk,
And hearken anon,
There abide on a balk,[1]
Or sit on a stone,
        Full soon;
75   For I trow,° pardie,°   *believe / by God*
True men if they be,[2]
We get more company
        Ere it be noon.

          [*Enter* GIB, *who at first does not see* COLL.]

    GIB   Benste and Dominus,[3]
80   What may this bemean?°   *mean*
Why fares this world thus?
Such have we not seen.
Lord, these weathers are spiteous°   *spiteful*
And the winds full keen,
85   And the frosts so hideous
They water mine een,°   *eyes*
        No lie.
Now in dry, now in wet,
Now in snow, now in sleet,
90   When my shoon° freeze to my feet   *shoes*
        It is not all easy.

But as far as I ken,
Or yet as I go,[4]
We sely wedmen°   *poor married men*
95   Dree° mickle° woe;   *Suffer / much*
We have sorrow then and then°—   *time and time again*
It falls oft so.
Sely Copple,[5] our hen,
Both to and fro
100   She cackles;
But begin she to croak,
To groan or to cluck,

---

1. A ridge of rough grassland dividing two plowed portions of a common field.
2. That is, if the other shepherds, whom Coll has arranged to meet, keep their promise.
3. Bless us and Lord (a corruption of the Latin blessing *Benedicite Dominus*, "Bless us, Lord").
4. That is, as I know from experience.
5. Literally, the crest on a bird's head.

Woe is him is our cock,
　　For he is in the shackles.

105　These men that are wed
　　Have not all their will:
　　When they are full hard stead°　　　　　　　　　*hard put to it*
　　They sigh full still;°　　　　　　　　　　　　*unceasingly*
　　God wot° they are led　　　　　　　　　　　　*knows*
110　Full hard and full ill;
　　In bower nor in bed
　　They say nought theretill.°　　　　　　　　　*thereto*
　　　This tide°　　　　　　　　　　　　　　　　*time*
　　My part have I fun;°　　　　　　　　　　　*found, learned*
115　I know my lesson:
　　Woe is him that is bun,°　　　　　　　　*bound (in marriage)*
　　　For he must abide.

　　But now late in our lives—
　　A marvel to me,
120　That I think my heart rives°　　　　　　　　*breaks*
　　Such wonders to see;
　　What that destiny drives
　　It should so be[6]—
　　Some men will have two wives,
125　And some men three
　　　In store.[7]
　　Some are woe° that has any,　　　　　　　　*miserable*
　　But so far can° I,　　　　　　　　　　　　*know*
　　Woe is him that has many,
130　　For he feels sore.

　　But young men a-wooing,
　　For God that you bought,°　　　　　　　　　*redeemed*
　　Be well ware of wedding
　　And think in your thought:
135　"Had I wist"° is a thing　　　　　　　　　*known*
　　That serves of nought.
　　Mickle° still° mourning　　　　　　　　*Much / constant*
　　Has wedding home brought,
　　　And griefs,
140　With many a sharp shower,°　　　　　　　　　*pang*
　　For thou may catch in an hour
　　That° shall sow° thee full sour°　　*That which / vex / bitterly*
　　　As long as thou lives.

　　For as ever read I 'pistle,[8]
145　I have one to my fere°　　　　　　　　　*for my mate*

6. What destiny compels must come to pass.
7. That is, because they remarry after being
widowed.

8. That is, epistle—a scriptural reading in the
Mass, often from the epistles of St. Paul.

As sharp as a thistle,
As rough as a brere;°   *briar*
She is browed like a bristle,
With a sour-loten cheer,⁹
150 Had she once wet her whistle
She could sing full clear
    Her Pater Noster.¹
She is great as a whale;
She has a gallon of gall:
155 By him that died for us all,
    I would I had run to° I lost her.   *until*

COLL   God look over the raw!²
[to GIB] Full deafly ye stand!
GIB   Yea, the devil in thy maw°   *belly*
160 So tariand!°   *For tarrying so*
Saw thou awhere of Daw?³
COLL   Yea, on a lea-land°   *fallow ground*
Heard I him blaw.°   *blow (his horn)*
He comes here at hand,
165   Not far.
Stand still.
GIB   Why?
COLL   For he comes, hope° I.   *think*
GIB   He will make us both a lie
But if° we be ware.   *Unless*
    [Enter DAW,⁴ who does not see the others.]
170 DAW   Christ's cross me speed°   *help me*
And Saint Nicholas!⁵
Thereof had I need:
It is worse than it was.
Whoso could take heed
175 And let the world pass,
It is ever in dread°   *fear*
And brickle° as glass,   *brittle*
    And slithes.°   *slides away*
This world foor° never so,   *fared*
180 With marvels mo° and mo,   *more*
Now in weal, now in woe,
And all thing writhes.°   *everything changes*

Was never sin° Noah's flood   *since*
Such floods seen,

9. She has bristly brows and a sour-looking expression.
1. Our Father (Latin); that is, the Lord's prayer, which begins with this phrase (see Matthew 6.9–13 and Luke 11.2–4).
2. God watch over the audience (row)! As the next line suggests, Coll accuses Gib of lectur-
ing the audience while he has tried to get his attention.
3. Have you seen Daw anywhere?
4. Daw, whose name is both a nickname for *David* and a word meaning "simpleton," is a boy who works for one of the older shepherds.
5. The patron saint of young people.

185 Winds and rains so rude
And storms so keen:
Some stammered,° some stood   *staggered*
In doubt,° as I ween.°   *fear / suppose*
Now God turn all to good!
190 I say as I mean.
    For ponder:°   *consider this*
These floods so they drown
Both in fields and in town,
And bears all down,
195 And that is a wonder.

We that walk on the nights
Our cattle to keep,
We see sudden° sights   *unexpected*
When other men sleep.
200 Yet methink my heart lights:°   *lightens*
I see shrews peep.⁶
    [*He sees the others, but does not hail them.*]
Ye are two all-wights.°   *monsters*
I will give my sheep
    A turn.
205 But full ill have I meant:⁷
As I walk on this bent°   *field*
I may lightly° repent,   *readily*
    My toes if I spurn.°   *stub*

Ah, sir, God you save,
210 And master mine!
A drink fain° would I have,   *gladly*
And somewhat to dine.
    COLL Christ's curse, my knave,
    Thou art a lither° hine!°   *lazy / servant*
215 GIB What, the boy list rave!
Abide unto sine.⁸
    We have made it.⁹
Ill thrift° on thy pate!°   *luck / head*
Though the shrew° came late   *rascal*
220 Yet is he in state
    To dine—if he had it.

    DAW Such servants as I,
    That sweats and swinks,°   *toil*
    Eats our bread full dry,
225 And that me forthinks.°   *displeases*

---

6. I see rascals peeping. Daw, who has witnessed monstrous apparitions while tending his sheep in the past, is relieved to recognize the other two shepherds. He keeps up the pretense that they are monsters in the following two lines.
7. But that's a very poor idea.
8. What, the boy is in a raving mood! Wait until later.
9. We have already eaten.

We are oft wet and weary
When master-men winks,°   *sleep*
Yet comes full lately°   *very slowly*
Both dinners and drinks.
230   But nately°   *thoroughly*
Both our dame and our sire,
When we have run in the mire,
They can nip° at our hire,°   *reduce / wages*
    And pay us full lately.

235   But here my troth, master,
For the fare° that ye make°   *food / provide*
I shall do thereafter:
Work as I take.[1]
I shall do a little, sir,
240   And among ever lake,
For yet lay my supper
Never on my stomach
    In fields.[2]
Whereto should I threap?°   *wrangle*
245   With my staff can I leap,°   *run away*
And men say, "Light cheap
    Litherly foryields."[3]

COLL   Thou were an ill lad
To ride a-wooing
250   With a man that had
But little of spending.[4]
GIB   Peace, boy, I bade—
No more jangling,°   *wrangling*
Or I shall make thee full rad,[5]
255   By the heaven's King!
    With thy gauds°—   *tricks*
Where are our sheep, boy?—we scorn.
DAW   Sir, this same day at morn
I left them in the corn°   *grain*
260   When they rang Lauds.[6]

They have pasture good,
They cannot go wrong.
COLL   That is right. By the rood,°   *cross*
These nights are long!
265   Yet I would, ere we yode,°   *went*

1. Work (as little) as I am paid.
2. I shall do a little work, sir, and play the rest of the time, for never has my supper lain heavily on my stomach (i.e., interfered with my activity) when I've been in the field.
3. A cheap bargain repays badly (proverbial).
4. You would be the wrong servant to accompany a man with little money to spend who was going wooing.
5. Or I shall quickly make you (stop your wrangling).
6. The first church service of the day, conducted while it is still dark.

One gave us a song.

GIB So I thought as I stood,
To mirth° us among.°   *cheer / in the meantime*

DAW I grant.

270 COLL Let me sing the tenory.°   *tenor*

GIB And I the treble so hee.°   *high*

DAW Then the mean° falls to me.   *middle part*
Let see how you chant.   *[They sing.]*

[Enter MAK *with a cloak over his clothes.]*

MAK Now, Lord, for thy names seven,

275 That made both moon and starns°   *stars*
Well mo than I can neven,°   *name*
Thy will, Lord, of me tharns.[7]
I am all uneven°—   *out of sorts*
That moves oft my harns.[8]

280 Now would God I were in heaven,
For there weep no barns°   *children*
So still.°   *incessantly*

COLL Who is that pipes so poor?

MAK *[aside]* Would God ye wist° how I foor!°   *knew / fared*

285 *[aloud]* Lo, a man that walks on the moor
And has not all his will.

GIB Mak, where has thou gone?
Tell us tiding.

DAW Is he come? Then ilkone°   *everyone*

290 Take heed to his thing.°   *things*

[Snatches the cloak from him.]

MAK What! Ich[9] be a yeoman,
I tell you, of the king,
The self and the same,
Sond° from a great lording   *Messenger*

295 And sich.°   *the like*
Fie on you! Goth° hence   *Go*
Out of my presence:
I must have reverence.
Why, who be ich?

300 COLL Why make ye it so quaint?[1]
Mak, ye do wrang.°   *wrong*

GIB But Mak, list ye saint?
I trow° that ye lang.[2]   *believe*

DAW I trow the shrew° can paint°—   *rascal / deceive*

7. Thy will concerning me, Lord, is lacking (i.e., thy will is unclear to me).
8. That often perplexes my brain.
9. By employing "Ich" for "I" (and "goth" and "doth" in subsequent lines), Mak uses southern dialect, associated with royalty and privilege, instead of the rural northern dialect spoken by the shepherds.
1. Why are you putting on such manners?
2. Do you want to play the saint? I believe you long to do so.

305   The devil might him hang!
    MAK   Ich shall make complaint
       And make you all to thwang°   *be flogged*
          At a word,
       And tell even how ye doth.°   *do*
310 COLL   But Mak, is that sooth?
       Now take out that Southern tooth,[3]
          And set° in a turd!   *put*

    GIB   Mak, the devil in your ee!°   *eye*
       A stroke would I lean° you!   *give*
315 DAW   Mak, know ye not me?
       By God, I could teen° you.   *hurt*
    MAK   God look° you all three: *watch over*
       Methought I had seen you.
          Ye are a fair company.
320 COLL   Can ye now mean you?[4]
    GIB   Shrew, peep![5]
       Thus late as thou goes,
       What will men suppose?
       And thou has an ill nose°   *reputation*
325   Of stealing sheep.

    MAK   And I am true as steel,
       All men wate.°   *know*
       But a sickness I feel
       That holds me full hate:°   *violently*
330 My belly fares not weel,°   *well*
       It is out of estate.
    DAW   Seldom lies the de'el
       Dead by the gate[6]
    MAK   Therefore
335 Full sore am I and ill.
       If I stand stone-still,
       I eat not a needill[7]
          This month and more.

    COLL   How fares thy wife? By my hood,
340 How fares sho?°   *she*
    MAK   Lies waltering,° by the rood,°   *sprawling / cross*
       By the fire, lo!
       And a house full of brood.°   *children*
       She drinks well, too:
345 Ill speed other good

---

3. Now knock off that southern talk!
4. Can you now remember yourself? (i.e., can
you give up your false airs?)
5. Rascal, look around!
6. Seldom lies the devil dead by the roadside

(proverbial); that is, when it comes to the
devil, appearances can be deceiving.
7. As sure as I stand here stone-still, I haven't
eaten a needle's worth (i.e., a morsel).

That she will do!⁸
    But sho
Eats as fast as she can;
And ilk° year that comes to man   *each*
350   She brings forth a lakan°—   *baby*
    And some years two.

But were I now more gracious°   *prosperous*
And richer by far,
I were eaten out of house
355   And of harbar.°   *home*
Yet is she a foul douce,°   *wench*
If ye come nar:⁹
There is none that trows°   *imagines*
Nor knows a war°   *worse*
360   Than ken° I.   *know*
Now will ye see what I proffer:
To give all in my coffer
Tomorn at next to offer
    Her head-masspenny.¹

365 GIB   I wot° so forwaked²   *know*
Is none in this shire.
I would sleep if° I taked   *even if*
Less to my hire.³
DAW   I am cold and naked
370 And would have a fire.
COLL   I am weary forraked°   *from walking*
And run in the mire.
    Wake thou.⁴   [*Lies down.*]
  GIB   Nay, I will lie down by,
375 For I must sleep, truly.   [*Lies down beside him.*]
DAW   As good a man's son was I
    As any of you.
      [*Lies down and motions to* MAK *to lie between them.*]
But Mak, come hither, between
Shall thou lie down.
380 MAK   Then might I let you bedeen
Of that ye would rown,⁵
    No dread.°   *No doubt*
From my top to my toe,   [*Lies down and prays.*]
Manus tuas commendo

---

8. Ill success to any other good that she does (i.e., she's not good for anything other than drinking).
9. That is, near the truth.
1. To give everything I own—tomorrow, at the latest—as a payment to have masses sung for her soul (i.e., Mak would give anything to have his wife dead).
2. Wearied from lack of sleep.
3. I would sleep even if I earned less money.
4. You keep watch.
5. Then might I hinder you if you want to whisper to each other.

385   *Pontio Pilato.*[6]

        Christ's cross me speed!°   *help*

            [He gets up as the others sleep and speaks.]

        Now were time for a man

        That lacks what he wold°   *would (have)*

        To stalk privily than°   *then*

390   Unto a fold,°   *sheepfold*

        And nimbly to work than,

        And be not too bold,

        For he might abuy° the bargan°   *pay for / bargain*

          At the ending.

395   Now were time for to reel:°   *move quickly*

        But he needs good counseel°   *counsel*

        That fain would fare weel

        And has but little spending.°   *money*

          [He draws a magic circle around the shepherds
                and recites a spell.]

        But about you a circill,°   *circle*

400   As round as a moon,

        To° I have done that° I will,   *Until / what*

        Till that it be noon,

        That ye lie stone-still

        To° that I have done;°   *Until / finished*

405   And I shall say theretill°   *thereto*

        Of good words a foon:°   *few*

        "On hight,°   *high*

        Over your heads my hand I lift.

        Out go your eyes! Fordo your sight!"[7]

410   But yet I must make better shift°   *efforts*

         And it be right.[8]

        Lord, what° they sleep hard—   *how*

        That may ye all hear.

        Was I° never a shephard,   *I was*

415   But now will I lear.°   *learn*

        If the flock be scar'd,

        Yet shall I nip near.[9]

        How! Draws hitherward![1]   *[He catches one.]*

        Now mends our cheer

420   From sorrow.

        A fat sheep, I dare say!

        A good fleece, dare I lay!°   *wager*

        Eft-quit° when I may,   *Repay*

---

6. "I commend thy hands to Pontius Pilate," a misquotation of Christ's last words on the cross in the vulgate (Latin) Bible, as given in Luke: "Father, into thy hands I commend my spirit" (23.46).

7. May your sight be destroyed (i.e., rendered powerless).

8. If things are to turn out right.

9. Even if the flock is alarmed, I'll grab (a sheep) tightly.

1. Hey! Come here!

But this will I borrow.
[*Moves with the sheep to his cottage and calls from outside.*]
425 How, Gill, art thou in?
Get us some light.
GILL [*inside*] Who makes such a din
This time of the night?
I am set for to spin;
430 I hope not I might
Rise a penny to win[2]—
I shrew° them on height!   curse
So fares
A housewife that has been
435 To be raised thus between:[3]
Here may no note° be seen   work
For° such small chares.°   Because of / chores

MAK   Good wife, open the hek!°   inner door
Sees thou not what I bring?
440 GILL   I may thole° thee draw the sneck.°   let / latch
Ah, come in, my sweeting.
MAK   Yea, thou thar not reck
Of my long standing.[4]
[*She opens the door.*]
GILL   By the naked neck
445 Art thou like for to hing.°   hang
MAK   Do way!°   Enough
I am worthy° my meat,°   worthy of / food
For in a strait° I can get   in a fix
More than they that swink° and sweat   toil
450 All the long day.

Thus it fell to my lot,
Gill, I had such grace.°   luck
GILL   It were a foul blot
To be hanged for the case.°   deed
455 MAK   I have 'scaped,° Jelot,[5]   escaped
Of as hard a glase.°   blow
GILL   But "So long goes the pot
To the water," men says,
"At last
460 Comes it home broken."
MAK   Well know I the token,°   portent

2. I don't see how I can earn a penny (from
my spinning) by so much getting up like this.
3. This is what it's like for any woman who
has been a housewife: to be gotten up (i.e.,
interrupted) continually.
4. Yes, you needn't mind about keeping me
standing here so long.
5. An affectionate nickname for Gill.

But let it never be spoken!
   But come and help fast.

I would he were flain,°   skinned
465   I list° well eat: wish (to)
This twelvemonth was I not so fain°   glad
   Of one sheep-meat.
GILL   Come they° ere he be slain,   If they come
And hear the sheep bleat—
470 MAK   Then might I be ta'en°—   taken
That were a cold sweat!
   Go spar°   fasten
The gate-door.°   outer door
GILL   Yes, Mak,
For and° they come at thy back—   if
475 MAK   Then might I buy, for all the pack,
   The devil of the war.[6]

GILL   A good bourd° have I spied,   trick
Sin° thou can° none.   Since / know
Here shall we him hide
480   To° they be gone,   Until
In my cradle. Abide!
Let me alone,
And I shall lie beside
In childbed and groan.
485 MAK   Thou red,°   get ready
And I shall say thou was light°   delivered
   Of a knave-child° this night.   male child
GILL   Now well is me day bright
   That ever I was bred.[7]

490   This is a good guise°   method
And a far-cast:°   cunning trick
Yet a woman's advice
Helps at the last.
I wot° never who spies: know
495   Again° go thou fast.   Back
MAK   But° I come ere they rise,   Unless
Else blows a cold blast.
   I will go sleep.   [Returns to the shepherds.]
Yet° sleeps all this meny,°   Still / company
500 And I shall go stalk privily,
As it had never been I
   That carried their sheep.   [Lies down among them.]
     [The shepherds are waking.]

---

6. Then I might receive a devil of a hard time   7. Now lucky for me the bright day on which
from the pack of them.   I was born.

COLL   *Resurrex a mortruus!*[8]
      Have hold my hand!
505   *Judas carnas dominus!*[9]
      I may not well stand.
      My foot sleeps, by Jesus,
      And I walter° fastand.°   *stagger / (from) hunger*
      I thought we had laid us
510   Full near England.
    GIB   Ah, yea?
      Lord, what° I have slept weel!   *how*
      As fresh as an eel,
      As light I me feel
515   As leaf on a tree.

DAW   Benste° be herein!   *A blessing*
      So my body quakes,
      My heart is out of skin,
      What-so it makes.[1]
520   Who makes all this din?
      So my brows blakes,[2]
      To the door will I win.[3]
      Hark, fellows, wakes!
        We were four:
525   See ye aywhere of Mak now?
    COLL   We were up ere thou.
    GIB   Man, I give God avow
      Yet yede° he naw're.°   *went / nowhere*

DAW   Methought he was lapped°   *wrapped*
530   In a wolfskin.
    COLL   So are many happed°   *covered*
      Now, namely° within.   *especially*
    DAW   When we had long napped,
      Methought with a gin°   *snare*
535   A fat sheep he trapped,
      But he made no din.
    GIB   Be still!
      Thy dream makes thee wood.°   *mad*
      It is but phantom, by the rood.
540 COLL   Now God turn all to good,
      If it be his will.

     [*They wake up* MAK, *who pretends to have been asleep.*]

    GIB   Rise, Mak, for shame!
      Thou lies right lang.°   *long*
    MAK   Now Christ's holy name

---

8. Corruption of *resurrexit a mortuis* (He rose from the dead), from the Latin Creed.
9. "Judas flesh lord," possibly a corruption of *laudes canas Domino* (sing praises to the Lord).

1. Whatever (may) cause it.
2. My brow grows pale (with fear).
3. I'll head to the door. (Daw is so disoriented by his nightmare he forgets that he is sleeping outdoors.)

545   Be us amang!°   *among*
     What is this? For Saint Jame,
     I may not well gang.°   *walk*
     I trow° I be the same.   *suppose*
     Ah, my neck has lain wrang.°   *wrong, crookedly*
     [*One of them twists his neck.*]
550   Enough!
     Mickle° thank! Sin° yestereven   *Much / Since*
     Now, by Saint Stephen,
     I was flayed with a sweven—
      My heart out of slough.[4]

555   I thought Gill began to croak
     And travail° full sad,°   *labor / heavily*
     Well-near at the first cock,[5]
     Of a young lad,
     For to mend° our flock—   *increase*
560   Then be I never glad:
     I have tow on my rock[6]
     More than ever I had.
      Ah, my head!
     A house full of young tharms!°   *bellies*
565   The devil knock out their harns!°   *brains*
     Woe is him has many barns,°   *children*
      And thereto little bread.

     I must go home, by your leave,
     To Gill, as I thought.°   *intended*
570   I pray you look° my sleeve,   *inspect*
     That I steal nought.
     I am loath you to grieve
     Or from you take aught.
    DAW   Go forth! Ill might thou chieve!°   *fare*
575   Now would I we sought
      This morn,
     That we had all our store.[7]
    COLL   But I will go before.
     Let us meet.
    GIB   Whore?°   *Where*
580 DAW At the crooked thorn.
      [*They go off in search of their sheep.*]
      [MAK's *house.* MAK *arrives at the door.*]
    MAK   Undo this door!
    GILL   Who is here?
    MAK   How long shall I stand?
    GILL   Who makes such a bere?°   *noise*

4. I was terrified by a dream—My heart (jumped) out of my skin.
5. When the cock first crows (i.e., midnight).
6. I have flax on my distaff (i.e., I'm in trouble).
7. I'd like us to check this morning (to be sure) that we have all our stock.

Now walk in the weniand![8]

585 MAK   Ah, Gill, what cheer?
It is I, Mak, your husband.
GILL   Then may we see here
The devil in a band,°   *noose*
Sir Guile!
590 Lo, he comes with a lote°   *noise*
As° he were holden in° the throat: *As if / held by*
I may not sit at my note°   *work (weaving)*
A hand-long° while.   *brief*

MAK   Will ye hear what fare° she makes   *commotion*
595 To get her a glose?°   *excuse (for not working)*
And does nought but lakes°   *plays*
And claws° her toes?   *scratches*
GILL   Why, who wanders? Who wakes?
Who comes? Who goes?
600 Who brews? Who bakes?
What makes me thus hose?°   *hoarse*
And than°   *then*
It is ruth° to behold,   *pity*
Now in hot, now in cold,
605 Full woeful is the household
That wants° a woman.   *lacks*

But what end has thou made
With the herds,° Mak?   *shepherds*
MAK   The last word that they said
610 When I turned my back,
They would look that they had
Their sheep all the pack.
I hope° they will not be well paid°   *expect / pleased*
When they their sheep lack.
615 Pardie!°   *By God*
But how-so the game goes,
To me they will suppose,[9]
And make a foul nose,°   *noise*
And cry out upon me.
620 But thou must do as thou hight.°   *promised*
GILL   I accord me theretill.[1]
I shall swaddle him right
In my cradle

[*She wraps up the sheep and puts it in the cradle.*]

If it were a greater sleight,
625 Yet could I help till.[2]

---

8. The waning of the moon, thought to be a
time of bad luck. (Gill is cursing.)
9. However the game goes, they'll suspect me.

1. I agree to that.
2. Even if it were a greater trick, I could still
help with it.

	I will lie down straight.°	*at once*
	Come hap° me.	*cover*
MAK	I will.	[*Covers her.*]
GILL	Behind!	
	Come Coll and his marrow,°	*mate*
630	They will nip us full narrow.°	*hard*
MAK	But I may cry "Out, harrow,"[3]	
	The sheep if they find.	

GILL	Hearken ay when they call—	
	They will come anon.	
635	Come and make ready all,	
	And sing by thine one.°	*self*
	Sing "lullay"° thou shall,	*lullaby*
	For I must groan	
	And cry out by the wall	
640	On Mary and John	
	For sore.°	*pain*
	Sing "lullay" on fast	
	When thou hears at the last,[4]	
	And but I play a false cast,[5]	
645	Trust me no more.	

[*The shepherds meet again.*]

DAW	Ah, Coll, good morn.	
	Why sleeps thou not?	
COLL	Alas, that ever I was born!	
	We have a foul blot:	
650	A fat wether° have we lorn.°	*ram / lost*
DAW	Marry, God's forbot!°	*God forbid*
GIB	Who should do us that scorn?	
	That were a foul spot!°	*disgrace*
COLL	Some shrew.°	*rascal*
655	I have sought with my dogs	
	All Horbury[6] shrogs,°	*thickets*
	And of fifteen hogs	
	Found I but one ewe.[7]	

DAW	Now trow me, if ye will,
660	By Saint Thomas of Kent,
	Either Mak or Gill
	Was at that assent.[8]
COLL	Peace, man, be still!
	I saw when he went.

---

3. A cry of distress or alarm.
4. When you finally hear (them).
5. And if I don't play a false trick.
6. A village near Wakefield.
7. And among fifteen hogs (i.e., young sheep),
I found only an ewe. (That is, the ram, or "fat wether," is missing.)
8. Was a party to it. *Saint Thomas of Kent:* Thomas à Becket (ca. 1118–1170), the martyred archbishop of Canterbury.

665 Thou slanders him ill—
     Thou ought to repent
        Good speed.°   *speedily*
     GIB   Now as ever might I thee,°   *thrive*
     If I should even here dee,°   *die*
670 I would say it were he
        That did that same deed.

     DAW   Go we thither, I read,°   *advise*
     And run on our feet.
     Shall I never eat bread
675 The sooth to I weet.[9]
     COLL   Nor drink in my head,[1]
     With him till I meet.
     GIB   I will rest in no stead°   *place*
     Till that I him greet,
680   My brother.
     One I will hight:[2]
     Till I see him in sight
     Shall I never sleep one night
        There I do another.[3]

     [*The shepherds approach* MAK's *house.* MAK *and* GILL *within,*
        she in bed, groaning, he singing a lullaby.]

685 DAW   Will ye hear how they hack?[4]
     Our sire list° croon.   *is pleased to*
     COLL   Heard I never none crack°   *bawl*
     So clear out of tune.
     Call on him.
     GIB   Mak!
690 Undo your door soon!°   *immediately*
     MAK   Who is that spake,
     As° it were noon,   *As if*
        On loft?°   *Loudly*
     Who is that, I say?
695 DAW   Good fellows, were it day.[5]
     MAK   As far as ye may,
     [*opening*] Good,° speaks soft   *Good sirs*

     Over a sick woman's head
     That is at malease.[6]
700 I had liefer° be dead   *rather*
     Ere she had any disease.°   *disturbance*
     GILL   Go to another stead!

---

9. Until I know the truth.
1. That is, in my mouth.
2. One thing I will promise.
3. I'll never sleep two nights in the same place.

4. Trill (used sarcastically).
5. Good friends, if it were daylight (i.e., they are not good friends, since it is night).
6. Who is unwell.

I may not well wheeze:°   *breathe*
Each foot that ye tread
705   Goes through my nese°   *nose*
         So hee!°   *loudly*
COLL   Tell us, Mak, if you may,
      How fare ye, I say?
MAK   But are ye in this town today?
710   Now how fare ye?

      Ye have run in the mire
      And are wet yit.
      I shall make you a fire
      If you will sit.
715   A nurse would I hire.
      Think ye on yit?[7]
      Well quit is my hire—
      My dream this is it—
         A season.[8]
720   I have barns,° if ye knew,   *children*
      Wel mo than enew:°   *enough*
      But we must drink as we brew,
         And that is but reason.

      I would ye dined ere ye yode.°   *go*
725   Methink that ye sweat.
   GIB   Nay, neither mends our mood,
      Drink nor meat.[9]
   MAK   Why sir, ails you aught but good?[1]
   DAW   Yea, our sheep that we get°   *tend*
730   Are stolen as they yode:°   *wandered*
      Our loss is great.
   MAK   Sirs, drinks!
      Had I been thore,°   *there*
      Some should have bought° it full sore.   *paid for*
735 COLL   Marry, some men trows° that ye wore,°   *believe / were*
         And that us forthinks.°   *displeases*

   GIB   Mak, some men trows,
      That it should be ye.
   DAW   Either ye or your spouse,
740   So say we.
   MAK   Now if you have suspouse°   *suspicion*
      To Gill or to me,
      Come and ripe° the house   *ransack*

7. Do you remember it (i.e., my dream about childbirth)?
8. My wages have been well paid for a while (i.e., I've got what was coming to me). My dream has come true.
9. Neither drink nor food will mend our mood.
1. Does anything not good trouble you? (i.e., is something wrong?)

And then may ye see
745   Who had her[2]
If I any sheep fot,°   *fetched, stole*
Either cow or stot°   *heifer*
And Gill my wife rose not
Here sin° she laid her.°   *since / lay down*

750   As I am true and leal,°   *honest*
To God here I pray
That this be the first meal
That I shall eat this day.
    COLL   Mak, as I have sele,[3]
755   Advise thee, I say:
He learned timely to steal
That could not say nay.[4]   *[They begin to search.]*
    GILL   I swelt!°   *die*
Out, thieves, from my wones!°   *dwelling*
760   Ye come to rob us for the nones.[5]
    MAK   Hear ye not how she groans?
Your hearts should melt.

    GILL   Out, thieves, from my barn!°   *child*
Nigh him not thore![6]
765   MAK   Wist ye how she had farn,[7]
Your hearts would be sore.
You do wrong, I you warn,
That thus comes before°   *in the presence*
To° a woman that has farn°—   *Of / been in labor*
770   But I say no more.
    GILL   Ah, my middle!
I pray to God so mild,
If ever I you beguiled,
That I eat this child
775   That lies in this cradle
    MAK   Peace, woman, for God's pain,
And cry not so!
Thou spills° thy brain   *You injure*
And makes me full woe.
780   GIB   I trow our sheep be slain.
What find ye two?
    DAW   All work we in vain;
As well may we go.
But hatters![8]
785   I can find no flesh,
Hard nor nesh,°   *soft*

---

2. Who took the sheep.
3. As I hope to have the happiness (of salvation).
4. He who could not say no (to another's property) learned early to steal (proverbial).

5. You come for the purpose of robbing us.
6. Don't come near him there!
7. If you knew how she had labored.
8. Confound it! (an oath of unclear origin).

Salt nor fresh,
    But two tome° platters.   *empty*

    Quick cattle but this,
790 Tame nor wild,
    None, as I have bliss,
    As loud as he smiled.[9]   [*Approaches the cradle.*]
  GILL   No, so God me bliss,°   *bless*
    And give me joy of my child!
795 COLL We have marked° amiss—   *aimed*
    I hold° us beguiled.   *consider*
  GIB Sir, don!°   *completely*
    [*to* MAK] Sir—Our Lady him save!—
    Is your child a knave?°   *boy*
800 MAK Any lord might him have,
    This child, to° his son.   *as*

    When he wakens he kips,°   *snatches, grabs*
    That joy is to see.
  DAW In good time to his hips,
805 And in sely.[1]
    But who were his gossips,°   *godparents*
    So soon ready?
  MAK So fair fall their lips[2]
  COLL Hark, now, a lee,°   *lie*
810 MAK So God them thank,
    Perkin, and Gibbon Waller, I say,
    And gentle John Horne, in good fay°—   *faith*
    He made all the garray°   *commotion*
    With the great shank.[3]

815 GIB Mak, friends will we be,
    For we are all one.°   *at one, agreed*
  MAK We? Now I hold for me,
    For mends get I none.[4]
    Farewell all three,
820 All glad were ye gone.[5]
  DAW Fair words may there be,
    But love is there none
    This year.   [*They go out the door.*]
  COLL Gave ye the child anything?
825 GIB I trow not one farthing.

---

9. (I can find) no livestock but this (i.e., the baby), neither tame nor wild, that smelled—as I (hope to) have bliss—as strong as he (i.e., the missing ram).
1. Good luck to him, and happiness.
2. May good luck come to them.
3. Long legs; an allusion to a dispute among the shepherds in the *First Shepherds' Play*.
4. I'll look out for myself, for I'll get no amends.
5. I'd be very glad if you were gone (probably spoken as an aside).

DAW   Fast again will I fling.°   *run*
      Abide ye me there.   [*He runs back.*]

    Mak, take it no grief
    If I come to thy barn.°   *child*

830 MAK   Nay, thou does me great reprief,°   *shame*
      And foul has thou farn.°   *done*

DAW   The child it will not grief,
      That little day-starn.°   *day star*
      Mak, with your leaf,°   *leave, permission*

835   Let me give your barn
      But sixpence.

MAK   Nay, do way! He sleeps.

DAW   Methinks he peeps.

MAK   When he wakens he weeps.

840   I pray you go hence.

              [*The other shepherds reenter.*]

DAW   Give me leave him to kiss,
      And lift up the clout.°   *cloth*
    [*lifts the cover*]
    What the devil is this?
    He has a long snout!

845 COLL   He is marked amiss.
    We wot ill about.[6]

GIB   Ill-spun weft, ywis,°   *certainly*
      Ay comes foul out.[7]
      Aye, so!

850   He is like to our sheep.

DAW   How, Gib, may I peep?

COLL   I trow kind will creep
    Where it may not go.[8]

    GIB   This was a quaint gaud°   *cunning trick*

855   And a far-cast.°   *clever device*
    It was high fraud.

DAW   Yea, sirs, was't.°   *it was*
    Let bren° this bawd   *Let's burn*
    And bind her fast.

860   A false scaud°   *scold*
    Hang at the last.[9]
      So shall thou.
    Will you see how they swaddle
    His four feet in the middle?

865   Saw I never in the cradle
    A horned lad[1] ere now.

---

6. He's deformed. We do wrong to pry around.
7. Ill-spun threads always make bad cloth (proverbial); that is, evil always reveals itself in its results.
8. Nature will creep where it can't walk (pro-

verbial); that is, nature will reveal itself one way or another.
9. Will hang at the end.
1. That is, the devil.

MAK   Peace bid I! What,
 Let be your fare!°   *commotion*
 I am he that him gat.°   *begot*
870 And yond woman him bare.
 COLL What devil shall he hat?²
 Lo, God, Mak's heir!
 GIB Let be all that!
 Now God give him care°—   *sorrow*
875 I sawgh!³
 GILL A pretty child is he
 As sits on a woman's knee,
 A dillydown,° pardie,   *darling*
  To gar° a man laugh.   *make*

880 DAW I know him by the earmark—
 That is a good token.
 MAK I tell you, sirs, hark,
 His nose was broken.
 Sithen° told me a clerk⁴   *Afterward*
885 That he was forspoken.°   *bewitched*
 COLL This is a false wark.°   *work, deed*
 I would fain be wroken.°   *avenged*
  Get wapen.°   *(a) weapon*
 GILL He was taken with° an elf   *by*
890 I saw it myself—
 When the clock struck twelf
  Was he forshapen.°   *transformed*

 GIB Ye two are well feft
 Sam in a stead.⁵
895 DAW Sin° they maintain their theft,   *Since*
 Let do° them to dead.°   *Let's put / death*
 MAK If I trespass eft,°   *again*
 Gird° off my head.   *Strike*
 With you will I be left.⁶
900 COLL Sirs, do° my read:°   *follow / advice*
 For this trespass
 We will neither ban° ne flite,°   *curse / quarrel*
 Fight nor chite,°   *chide*
 But have done as tite,°   *quickly*
905 And cast him in canvas.
    [*They toss* MAK *in a blanket.*]

---

2. What in the devil will he be named?
3. I saw (the sheep).
4. A literate, learned person, possibly a local church or government official (in England pronounced "clark," as the rhyme scheme requires).
5. You two are well provided for in the same way; that is, you are as clever a pair of rogues as ever lived.
6. I leave myself with you (as a judge); that is, I put myself at your mercy.

[*The fields.*]

COLL Lord, what° I am sore,   *how*
 In point for to brist!°   *burst*
 In faith, I may no more—
 Therefore will I rist.°   *rest*
910 GIB As a sheep of seven score[7]
 He weighed in my fist:
 For to sleep aywhore°   *anywhere*
 Methink that I list.°   *desire*
 DAW Now I pray you
915 Lie down on this green.
 COLL On these thieves yet I mean.°   *think*
 DAW Whereto should ye teen?°   *be angry*
 Do as I say you.   [*They lie down.*]

 [*An* ANGEL *sings* Gloria in Excelsis[8] *and then speaks.*]

 ANGEL Rise, herdmen hend,°   *gentle*
920 For now is he born
 That shall take fro the fiend
 That Adam had lorn;[9]
 That warlock° to shend,°   *devil / destroy*
 This night is he born.
925 God is made your friend
 Now at this morn,
 He behestys.°   *promises*
 At Bedlem° go see: *Bethlehem*
 There lies that free,°   *noble one*
930 In a crib full poorly,
 Betwixt two bestys.°   *beasts*

 [*The* ANGEL *withdraws.*]

 COLL This was a quaint° steven°   *exquisite / voice*
 That ever yet I hard.°   *heard*
 It is a marvel to neven°   *speak of*
935 Thus to be scar'd.°   *scared*
 GIB Of God's Son of heaven
 He spake upward.°   *from above*
 All the wood on a leven
 Methought that he gard
940 Appear.[1]
 DAW He spake of a barn°   *child*
 In Bedlem, I you warn.°   *tell*
 COLL That betokens yond starn.[2]
 Let us seek him there.

7. That is, 140 pounds.
8. Glory [to God] in the highest (Latin), the title and first words of the "great doxology," used in the Roman Catholic Mass (a variation of the words in the Vulgate Bible with which angels announce the birth of Jesus to shepherds; see Luke 2.14).
9. What Adam lost.
1. I thought he made the woods appear as if lit up in a flash of lightning.
2. That's what yonder star signifies.

945   GIB   Say, what was his song?
        Heard ye not how he cracked° it?   *sang*
        Three breves° to a long?   *short notes*
  DAW   Yea, marry, he hacked° it.   *trilled*
        Was no crochet° wrong,   *note*
950   Nor nothing that lacked it.°   *that it lacked*
  COLL   For to sing us among,
        Right as he knacked° it,   *sang*
        I can.°   *know how*
  GIB   Let see how ye croon!
955   Can ye bark at the moon?
  DAW   Hold your tongues! Have done!
  COLL   Hark after, than!   **[*Sings.*]**

  GIB   To Bedlem he bade
        That we should gang:°   *go*
960   I am full fard°   *afraid*
        That we tarry too lang.°   *long*
  DAW   Be merry and not sad;
        Of mirth is our sang:
        Everlasting glad°   *joy*
965   To meed° may we fang.°   *As reward / get*
  COLL   Without nose°   *noise*
        Hie we thither forthy°   *therefore*
        To that child and that lady;
        If° we be wet and weary,   *Even if*
970   We have it not to lose.[3]

  GIB   We find by the prophecy—
        Let be your din!—
        Of David and Isay,°   *Isaiah*
        And mo° than I min,°   *more / remember*
975   That prophesied by clergy°   *learnedly*
        That in a virgin
        Should he light° and lie,   *alight*
        To sloken° our sin   *quench*
        And slake° it,   *relieve*
980   Our kind,° from woe,   *humankind*
        For Isay said so:
        Ecce virgo
        Concipiet[4] a child that is naked.

  DAW   Full glad may we be
985   And abide° that day   *look forward to*
        That lovely to see,
        That all mights may.[5]

---

3. We must not forget it.
4. Behold, a virgin shall conceive (Vulgate;   Isaiah 7.14).
5. To see that lovely one who is almighty.

Lord, well were me
For once and for ay
990   Might I kneel on my knee,
Some word for to say
    To that child.
But the angel said
In a crib was he laid,
995   He was poorly arrayed,
      Both meaner° and mild.   *lowly*

COLL   Patriarchs that has been,
And prophets beforn,°   *in the past*
That desired to have seen
1000   This child that is born,
They are gone full clean°—   *completely*
That have they lorn.[6]
We shall see him, I ween,°   *think*
Ere it be morn,
1005   To token.[7]
When I see him and feel,
Then wot I full weel
It is true as steel
    That° prophets have spoken: *What*

1010   To so poor as we are
That he would appear,
First find and declare[8]
By his messenger.
GIB   Go we now, let us fare,
1015   The place is us near.
DAW   I am ready and yare;°   *eager*
Go we in fere°   *together*
    To that bright.°   *bright one*
Lord, if thy wills be—
1020   We are lewd° all three—   *unlearned*
Thou grant us some kins glee
    To comfort thy wight.[9]
    [*They go to Bethlehem and enter the stable.*]
COLL   Hail, comely and clean!°   *pure*
1025   Hail, young child!
Hail Maker, as I mean,°   *believe*
Of° a maiden so mild!   *Born of*
Thou has waried,° I ween,° *cursed / believe*
The warlock° so wild.   *devil*
The false guiler of teen,[1]

---

6. That opportunity have they lost.
7. As a sign.
8. Find (us) first and declare (his coming).

9. Grant us some joyful means of comforting thy child.
1. The false and malevolent beguiler.

1030   Now goes he beguiled.
          Lo, he merries!°   is merry
       Lo, he laughs, my sweeting!
       A well fair meeting!
       I have holden° my heting:°   kept / promise
1035   Have a bob° of cherries.   bunch

GIB   Hail, sovereign Saviour,
       For thou has us sought!
       Hail freely food° and flour,°   noble child / flower
       That all thing has wrought!
1040   Hail, full of favour,
       That made all of nought!
       Hail! I kneel and I cower.
       A bird have I brought
          To my barn.°   child
1045   Hail, little tiny mop!°   baby
       Of our creed thou art crop.°   head
       I would drink on thy cup,
          Little day-starn.

DAW   Hail, darling dear,
1050   Full of Godhead!
       I pray thee be near
       When that I have need.
       Hail, sweet is thy cheer°—   face
       My heart would bleed
1055   To see thee sit here
       In so poor weed,°   clothing
          With no pennies.
       Hail, put forth thy dall!°   hand
       I bring thee but a ball:
1060   Have and play thee withal,
          And go to the tennis.[2]
MARY   The Father of heaven,
       God omnipotent,
       That set all on seven,[3]
1065   His Son has he sent.
       My name could he neven,
       And light ere he went.[4]
       I conceived him full even°   indeed
       Through might as he meant.[5]
1070   And now is he born.
       He° keep you from woe!   May he
       I shall pray him so.
       Tell forth as ye go,
          And min on° this morn.   remember

2. The sport of tennis was identified with the   4. He named my name and alighted (in me)
court and nobility in the late Middle Ages.   before he went.
3. Who created everything in seven (days).   5. Through (God's) might, as he intended.

1075 COLL   Farewell, lady,
           So fair to behold,
           With thy child on thy knee.
       GIB   But he lies full cold.
           Lord, well is me.
1080   Now we go, thou behold.
       DAW   Forsooth, already
           It seems to be told
           Full oft.
       COLL   What grace we have fun!°
1085 GIB   Come forth, now are we won!°
       DAW   To sing are we bun:°
           Let take on loft.[6]
               [*They sing.*]

found

redeemed

bound

6. Let us begin (to sing) loudly.

EVERYMAN

ca. 1510

*E*VERYMAN, the most widely read and frequently produced play written in English before the Elizabethan age, forms part of the tradition of morality drama that flourished in England during the fifteenth and early sixteenth centuries. A play about sin, repentance, and death, it reflects the religious and moral worldview of the late Middle Ages. Appearing at the turn of the sixteenth century, however, *Everyman* is also a transitional play in the history of English dramatic literature. As one of the first plays to be published in England, *Everyman* owes much of its popularity during its time to a new reading public that emerged after the invention of the printing press by the German Johannes Gutenberg around 1450. Such a readership had been unavailable to the dramatists of earlier centuries, whose plays were available only in manuscript. In addition, while this drama of Everyman's final reckoning reflects the theology of orthodox Catholicism, its insistence on certain doctrinal points suggests an awareness of the burgeoning reform movement that would profoundly divide Christian Europe during the Protestant Reformation. The allegorical structure of *Everyman* and other morality plays—in which characters, objects, and actions represent abstract concepts or principles in a narrative that conveys a moral lesson—provided English playwrights with a useful framework for examining these and other social and philosophical issues in the turbulent years that followed.

Everyman survives in four different editions, two of them incomplete, which appeared between 1510 and 1535. No manuscript of the play exists. The play bears close similarities to an earlier Dutch play titled *Elckerlijc*, which was written by a Petrus Diesthemius, or Peter from the [Flemish city of] Diest, frequently identified as the theologian and Carthusian priest Peter of Doorlandt. *Elckerlijc* was printed in 1495 in Delft; it was subsequently published in Antwerp, where it was awarded first prize at a *landjuweel*, or rhetorical contest. For a number of decades, scholars argued over which play came first, but the weight of recent evidence—textual and otherwise—has established beyond reasonable doubt that the English *Everyman* was a translation of the Dutch original. As A. C. Cawley points out, Antwerp was an important printing center at the turn of the sixteenth century, regularly publishing English translations of books originally written in Dutch for sale in the English market. In London, foreign printers enjoyed privileges not granted to their domestic counterparts and were frequently accorded royal patronage. One of these printers, a Norman named Richard Pynson, published the first extant edition of *Everyman*; though we do not know the identity of the translator, we can infer the play's popularity from the number of surviving editions.

It has become a critical commonplace that while *Everyman* is the most famous of English morality plays, it is in many ways the least typical. In earlier moralities, such as *The Castle of Perseverence* (ca. 1405–25) and *Mankind* (ca. 1465–70), figures representing Virtue and Vice contend for the soul of humankind in often elaborate allegorical settings rife with incident and encounter. Moral conflict in these plays is frequently dramatized through comic horseplay, as the Vice figures demonstrate the distractions posed by earthly temptation. By focusing on words over action, in contrast, *Everyman* concentrates on the closing moments of life and on the moral crisis that occurs when Death calls the sinner to account. As Everyman undergoes his final journey, learning that the earthly things in which he had put his faith will fail him in his hour of extremity and that the path to salvation lies through good deeds and repentance, the distractions of earthly temptation and the diversions of horseplay are relegated to the past. No Vice figures prance across the stage in *Everyman*; instead, the play's moral allegory unfolds with a simplicity verging on parable. This theatrical asceticism may owe something to its sources, for scholars have determined that one of *Everyman*'s core narrative elements—the testing of friends in an hour of need—is Buddhist rather than Western in origin. This story was introduced to medieval Europe through the eleventh-century Greek text *Barlaam and Josaphat*, a collection of Christianized tales from the East.

In its focus on mortality, *Everyman* reflects a broader literary and social preoccupation with death in the fifteenth century. In his 1924 study *The Waning of the Middle Ages*, Johan Huizinga wrote: "No other epoch has laid so much stress as the expiring Middle Ages on the thought of death." *Memento mori* (remember that you must die) was a regular theme in the sermons of mendicant preachers since the thirteenth century, and its lesson resonated in a Europe that lost one-third of its population to the Black Death in the mid-1300s. Personifications of Death were common in fifteenth-century woodcuts, and the spectacle of Death choosing his victims indiscriminately from all stations of life formed the subject of the Dance of Death (or *Danse Macabre*), a dramatic form that originated in Germany and was performed in England in the fifteenth century. Of even greater relevance to *Everyman* were the treatises on the art of holy dying or *Ars moriendi*, widely known throughout Europe in the 1400s. The *Ars moriendi* dealt with the process of death and the techniques (meditations, prayers, questions) that would help one die in a state of holiness. Particular attention was given to the temptations that threaten to divert the virtuous mind at the hour of death: heresy, despair, rage, spiritual pride, and an attachment to the things of the world.

This last temptation, elaborated in William Caxton's 1490 translation (from a French work) *The Art and Craft to Know Well to Die*—"the over-great occupation of outward things and temporal, as toward his wife his children and his friends carnal, toward his riches or toward other things which he hath most loved in his life"—finds particularly strong echoes in *Everyman*. To find strength in the face of death, the dying individual is instructed to meditate on the death of Christ.

Like Moriens (literally, "The Dying One"), the protagonist at the center of the *Ars moriendi*, Everyman stands as the representative of a broader humanity that must come to terms with the inevitability of death and the impermanence of earthly life. The Messenger's speech that opens the play underscores the identification between Everyman on stage and Everyman in the audience—"Here shall you see how fellowship and jollity, / Both strength, pleasure, and beauty, / Will fade from thee as flower in May." God's speech, which follows it, extends this allegorical identification. As V. A. Kolve has noted, Everyman is spoken of as both singular and plural in number in God's opening speech: as a consequence of this linguistic slippage, "We are implicated collectively as well as individually." Like Death's victims in the Dance of Death, the character Everyman is caught unawares by calls of mortality and judgment. Immersed in a life of pleasure and possessions, he has elevated the temporal order over the spiritual; and as he embarks on this final journey, or "pilgrimage," he must revalue his life according to its higher moral law. *Everyman*'s many references to "reckoning" and to rendering "account," which recall the parable of the talents in Matthew 25.14–30, emphasize the need for spiritual industry and proper discernment of what is transitory and what is eternal.

As he prepares to undertake Death's journey, Everyman seeks the company and support of his friends, kindred, and material possessions from which he derived pleasure in more carefree days. That Fellowship, Kindred, Cousin, and Goods abandon him in his hour of greatest need despite their earlier promises never to for-

This woodcut from the fifteenth-century, *Ars moriendi*, shows
Moriens, at the end of his struggle with earthly temptations, being
welcomed into paradise.

sake him comes as no surprise to the audience; their departures are both inevitable and accompanied by a certain humor, as when Cousin protests that he cannot accompany Everyman because he has a cramp in his toe. The popular sayings that Everyman repeats in soliciting their help—"For it is said ever among / That money maketh all right that is wrong," for instance—are shown to be empty. When Everyman turns to his Good Deeds, he finds her willing to accompany him but too enfeebled by his sins to rise from the ground and do so. His encounter with her is a turning point both in the play's narrative and in his theological development, for

he learns the steps by which he may render his spiritual account clean and adequate. He is introduced to Knowledge, whose name denoted a number of related understandings to the play's medieval audience: knowledge of God, acknowledgment of sin, and an awareness of its remedies. Knowledge, in turn, introduces him to Confession, who instructs him in contrition and encourages him to punish his offending flesh with the scourge of Penance. When Everyman has purified himself through these penitential acts, Good Deeds rises from the ground, restored, to accompany him on the remainder of his pilgrimage. The morally rejuvenated Everyman is also joined on his final pilgrimage by four "persons of great might": Discretion, Strength, Beauty, and Five-Wits (the personification of the five physical senses). Unlike Everyman's unreliable earlier companions, who signify the attachments of the external world, the allegorical figures in this last group represent the individual's personal attributes redeemed by grace.

Before he reaches his grave, Everyman departs to receive the sacraments of Holy Communion and extreme unction, or last rites, and his brief exit affords Knowledge and Five-Wits the opportunity for an extended digression on the importance of priesthood. Because they administer the seven sacraments, these two insist, priests stand even "above angels in degree." Though some priests violate their divine responsibilities, priesthood offers the only "remedy we find under God." The emphasis on sacraments is important to the play's doctrinal foundations, for in Roman Catholic belief and observance, they represent the vehicles by which God's grace is manifested in human life. Everyman has expressed contrition for his sins, but it is not until he receives the sacraments that his reconciliation with God is complete.

The closing sequence, in which Everyman meets his death and is received into heaven, achieves a surprisingly emotional effect in a play that is otherwise marked by the contemplative distance and processional formality of allegory. As Everyman stands before his grave—so weak he "may not stand"—he is successively abandoned by Beauty, Strength, Discretion, and Five-Wits. Unlike his earlier abandonment by his companions and worldly goods, which this scene mirrors, this last-minute departure comes as something of a jolt to the play's audience as well as to its protagonist. Although Strength may promise Everyman that "we will not from you go / Till ye have done this voyage long," the support of Everyman's attributes and faculties necessarily but painfully fail at the moment of death. Even Knowledge, whose support proved crucial to Everyman's transition into a state of grace, must abandon the dying individual in the end. When Everyman exclaims "O all thing faileth save God alone," he expresses the anguish that marks the loss of these deeply per-

Frontispiece of the 1528–29 edition of *Everyman* printed by John Skot.

sonal companions. But this anguish also affirms a faith in the constancy embodied in God's promise of salvation. Accompanied by Good Deeds, his lone companion into the afterlife, Everyman echoes Christ's dying words: *"In manus tuas . . . commendo spiritum meum"* ("Into thy hands I commend my spirit"; Luke 23.46). As reward for his moral regeneration he is welcomed by an Angel to heaven and eternal life. His reckoning, which was earlier described as "blotted and blind," is now "crystal clear."

The epilogue of *Everyman*, which is delivered by a theological Doctor, underscores the play's moral lesson: "And he that hath his account whole and sound, / High in heaven he shall be crowned." As he redirects the play's attention from Everyman onstage to Everyman in the audience—"Ye hearers"—he reminds us that this play about dying right is equally, in the end, about the importance of living right. Like other visual and literary works in the *memento mori* tradition, *Everyman* seeks to impress upon its audience an awareness of life's impermanence, an ability to discern the eternal in the midst of the transitory, and a commitment to live life as if every day might be one's last.

No evidence has survived concerning sixteenth-century performances of *Everyman*; indeed, there is no record of performance before the nineteenth century. Because the title page of the 1528–29 edition of the play printed by John Skot (upon which the present text is based) opens with the words "HERE BEGINNETH A TREATISE . . . IN MANNER OF A MORAL PLAY," some critics have concluded that—in contrast with its Dutch counterpart, for which performance records exist—*Everyman* was translated and printed primarily for a reading public. But while the number of editions in which it appeared supports the claim that *Everyman* had a wide readership, the play's success in twentieth-century theaters, churches, and schools attests to its theatrical qualities, and the simplicity of its theatrical requirements encourages the belief that it was known to audiences as well as readers.

Whether *Everyman* was performed outdoors, like the earlier English moralities, or indoors, like the Tudor interludes it also resembles, is open to conjecture, and the absence of stage directions from the printed text makes precise reconstruction of a sixteenth-century performance impossible. But some of the play's central theatrical features are evident from textual indications, and others can be inferred from contemporary theatrical practice. The play's setting observes the dual structure characteristic of other medieval drama, in which a localized structure (or *sedes*) is contrasted with an unlocalized acting area (or *platea*). The House of Salvation—Confession's abode—looms over the action of *Everyman* as the site of the allegorical protagonist's pivotal transformations. As Cawley suggests, it is reasonable to assume that this structure had a battlement height from which God addresses sinful humanity at the start of the play and into which Everyman's soul is received at its conclusion. Placement of Everyman's grave in front of this structure would allow Everyman to exit his grave and ascend to heaven with requisite speed. Distinguished as they are by their initial immobility, both Goods and Good Deeds no doubt require their own acting areas. The text of *Everyman* provides evidence of additional theatrical elements. Props, while few in number, figure prominently in the play's dramatic and theological action: Everyman's account book, the penitential scourge, the crucifix that Everyman presents after receiving the sacraments. Costume also contributes to the play's meaning. Everyman, who is dressed "gaily" at the beginning of the play, exchanges these clothes for a penitential robe in the play's second half. He certainly would not have been the only character whose allegorical significance is marked by dress: if productions of *Everyman* followed Tudor theatrical practice, its costumes would have been vividly emblematic—most notably in the case of Death, whose representation would have drawn from an extensive repertoire of medieval woodcuts and other illustrations.

The history of Everyman's emergence in our own time as a classic of the early English theater is almost as striking as the play itself. After several centuries' absence from the stage, *Everyman* became the first medieval play to appear on the modern stage in July 1901, when William Poel, founder of the Elizabethan Stage Society, mounted a production of this supposedly "primitive" drama in the courtyard of a former London monastery. The production was an immediate sensation: by the following season it had reached the commercial theaters, and it subsequently toured abroad. An observation by one of the play's initial reviewers suggests both the success of Poel's production and the power that *Everyman* must have held for its Tudor audience as well: "In the open air in a courtyard and enclosed with antiquated buildings with no distinction of lighting to differentiate between performers and auditors . . . the essential human vitality of the whole thing was what most strongly appeared." To learn more about the staging of *Everyman* and to view photographs from select performances of the play, see the "Plays in Performance" color insert near the center of this volume.

S.G.

Everyman[1]

CHARACTERS

MESSENGER	KNOWLEDGE
GOD	CONFESSION
DEATH	BEAUTY
EVERYMAN	STRENGTH
FELLOWSHIP	DISCRETION
KINDRED	FIVE-WITS
COUSIN	ANGEL
GOODS	DOCTOR
GOOD DEEDS	

HERE BEGINNETH A TREATISE HOW THE HIGH FATHER OF HEAVEN SENDETH DEATH
TO SUMMON EVERY CREATURE TO COME AND GIVE ACCOUNT OF THEIR
LIVES IN THIS WORLD, AND IS IN MANNER OF A MORAL PLAY.

[*Enter* MESSENGER.]

MESSENGER   I pray you all give your audience,
　　　And hear this matter with reverence,
　　　By figure° a moral play.   *In its form*
　　　The Summoning of Everyman called it is,
5　　That of our lives and ending shows
　　　How transitory we be all day.°   *always*
　　　The matter is wonder precious,
　　　But the intent of it is more gracious
　　　And sweet to bear away.
10　The story saith: Man, in the beginning
　　　Look well, and take good heed to the ending,
　　　Be you never so gay.
　　　You think sin in the beginning full sweet,
　　　Which in the end causeth the soul to weep,
15　When the body lieth in clay.
　　　Here shall you see how fellowship and jollity,
　　　Both strength, pleasure, and beauty,
　　　Will fade from thee as flower in May.
　　　For ye shall hear how our Heaven-King
20　Calleth Everyman to a general reckoning.
　　　Give audience and hear what he doth say.
　　　　　[*Exit* MESSENGER.—*Enter* GOD.]

---

1. The text is based on the earliest printing of
the play (no manuscript is known) by John
Skot, about 1530, as reproduced by W. W.
Greg (1904). The spelling has been modernized except where modernization would spoil
the rhyme, and modern punctuation has
been added. The stage directions have been
amplified.

GOD   I perceive, here in my majesty,
          How that all creatures be to me unkind,[2]
          Living without dread in worldly prosperity.
25   Of ghostly sight[3] the people be so blind,
          Drowned in sin, they know me not for their God.
          In worldly riches is all their mind:
          They fear not of my righteousness the sharp rod;
          My law that I showed when I for them died
30   They forget clean, and shedding of my blood red.
          I hanged between two,[4] it cannot be denied:
          To get them life I suffered to be dead.
          I healed their feet, with thorns hurt was my head.
          I could do no more than I did, truly—
35   And now I see the people do clean forsake me.
          They use the seven deadly sins damnable,
          As pride, coveitise,° wrath, and lechery[5]   *covetousness*
          Now in the world be made commendable.
          And thus they leave of angels the heavenly company.
40   Every man liveth so after his own pleasure,
          And yet of their life they be nothing sure.
          I see the more that I them forbear,
          The worse they be from year to year:
          All that liveth appaireth° fast.   *degenerates*
45   Therefore I will, in all the haste,
          Have a reckoning of every man's person.
          For, and° I leave the people thus alone   *if*
          In their life and wicked tempests,
          Verily they will become much worse than beasts;
50   For now one would by envy another up eat.
          Charity do they all clean forgeet.
          I hoped well that every man
          In my glory should make his mansion,°   *dwelling place*
          And thereto I had them all elect.°   *chosen*
55   But now I see, like traitors deject,°   *debased*
          They thank me not for the pleasure that I to° them meant,   *for*
          Nor yet for their being that I them have lent.
          I proffered the people great multitude of mercy,
          And few there be that asketh it heartily.°   *sincerely*
60   They be so cumbered° with worldly riches   *encumbered*
          That needs on them I must do justice—
          On every man living without fear.
          Where art thou, Death, thou mighty messenger?
                    [*Enter* DEATH.]
     DEATH   Almighty God, I am here at your will,
65   Your commandment to fulfill.
     GOD   Go thou to Everyman,

---

2. Lacking in natural filial affection or duty.   Jesus was crucified.
3. In spiritual vision.   5. The other deadly sins are gluttony, sloth,
4. That is, the two thieves between whom   and envy.

And show him, in my name,
A pilgrimage he must on him take,
Which he in no wise may escape;
70 And that he bring with him a sure reckoning
Without delay or any tarrying.

DEATH   Lord, I will in the world go run over all,°   *throughout*
And cruelly° out-search both great and small.   *rigorously*
[*Exit* GOD.]

Everyman will I beset that liveth beastly
75 Out of God's laws, and dreadeth not folly.
He that loveth riches I will strike with my dart,
His sight to blind, and from heaven to depart°   *cut off*
Except that Almsdeeds be his good friend—
In hell for to dwell, world without end.
80 Lo, yonder I see Everyman walking:
Full little he thinketh on my coming;
His mind is on fleshly lusts and his treasure,
And great pain it shall cause him to endure
Before the Lord, Heaven-King.
[*Enter* EVERYMAN.]

85 Everyman, stand still! Whither art thou going
Thus gaily? Hast thou thy Maker forgeet?°   *forgotten*
EVERYMAN   Why askest thou?
Why wouldest thou weet?°   *know*
DEATH   Yea, sir, I will show you:
90 In great haste I am sent to thee
From God out of his majesty.
EVERYMAN   What! sent to me?
DEATH   Yea, certainly.
Though thou have forgot him here,
95 He thinketh on thee in the heavenly sphere,
As, ere we depart, thou shalt know.
EVERYMAN   What desireth God of me?
DEATH   That shall I show thee:
A reckoning he will needs have
100 Without any longer respite.
EVERYMAN   To give a reckoning longer leisure I crave.
This blind° matter troubleth my wit.°   *obscure / understanding*
DEATH   On thee thou must take a long journay:
Therefore thy book of count° with thee thou bring,   *accounts*
105 For turn again thou cannot by no way.
And look thou be sure of thy reckoning,
For before God thou shalt answer and shew
Thy many bad deeds and good but a few—
How thou hast spent thy life and in what wise,
110 Before the Chief Lord of Paradise.
Have ado that we were in that way,[6]
For weet thou well thou shalt make none attornay.[7]

6. That is, let's get going.   7. No one (your) advocate.

EVERYMAN   Full unready I am such reckoning to give.
　　I know thee not. What messenger art thou?
115 DEATH   I am Death that no man dreadeth,[8]
　　For every man I 'rest,° and no man spareth;　　　　　　　　*arrest*
　　For it is God's commandment
　　That all to me should be obedient.
EVERYMAN   O Death, thou comest when I had thee least in mind.
120 　In thy power it lieth me to save:
　　Yet of my good° will I give thee, if thou will be kind,　　*goods*
　　Yea, a thousand pound shalt thou have—
　　And defer this matter till another day.
DEATH   Everyman, it may not be, by no way.
125 　I set nought by[9] gold, silver, nor riches,
　　Nor by pope, emperor, king, duke, nor princes,
　　For, and° I would receive gifts great,　　　　　　　　　　　*if*
　　All the world I might get.
　　But my custom is clean contrary:
130 　I give thee no respite. Come hence and not tarry!
EVERYMAN   Alas, shall I have no longer respite?
　　I may say Death giveth no warning.
　　To think on thee it maketh my heart sick,
　　For all unready is my book of reckoning.
135 　But twelve year and I might have a biding,[1]
　　My counting-book I would make so clear
　　That my reckoning I should not need to fear.
　　Wherefore, Death, I pray thee, for God's mercy,
　　Spare me till I be provided of remedy.
140 DEATH   Thee availeth not to cry, weep, and pray;
　　But haste thee lightly° that thou were gone that journay　　*quickly*
　　And prove° thy friends, if thou can.　　　　　　　*put to the test*
　　For weet° thou well the tide° abideth no man,　　　*know / time*
　　And in the world each living creature
145 　For Adam's sin must die of nature.[2]
EVERYMAN   Death, if I should this pilgrimage take
　　And my reckoning surely make,
　　Show me, for saint° charity,　　　　　　　　　　　　　　*holy*
　　Should I not come again shortly?
150 DEATH   No, Everyman. And thou be once there,
　　Thou mayst never more come here,
　　Trust me verily.
EVERYMAN   O gracious God in the high seat celestial,
　　Have mercy on me in this most need!
155 　Shall I have company from this vale terrestrial
　　Of mine acquaintance that way me to lead?
DEATH   Yea, if any be so hardy
　　That would go with thee and bear thee company.
　　Hie thee that thou were gone[3] to God's magnificence,

8. Who is afraid of no man.　　　　　　　2. In the course of nature.
9. I set no store by.　　　　　　　　　　3. Hurry up and go.
1. If I might have a respite for twelve years.

160   Thy reckoning to give before his presence.
       What, weenest° thou thy life is given thee,   *suppose*
       And thy worldly goods also?
       EVERYMAN   I had weened so, verily.
       DEATH   Nay, nay, it was but lent thee.
165   For as soon as thou art go,°   *gone*
       Another a while shall have it and then go therefro,
       Even as thou hast done.
       Everyman, thou art mad! Thou hast thy wits° five,   *senses*
       And here on earth will not amend thy live!⁴
170   For suddenly I do come.
       EVERYMAN   O wretched caitiff!° Whither shall I flee   *unfortunate wretch*
       That I might 'scape this endless sorrow?
       Now, gentle Death, spare me till tomorrow,
       That I may amend me
175   With good advisement.⁵
       DEATH   Nay, thereto I will not consent,
       Nor no man will I respite,
       But to the heart suddenly I shall smite,
       Without any advisement.
180   And now out of thy sight I will me hie:
       See thou make thee ready shortly,
       For thou mayst say this is the day
       That no man living may 'scape away.
                   [*Exit* DEATH.]
       EVERYMAN   Alas, I may well weep with sighs deep:
185   Now have I no manner of company
       To help me in my journey and me to keep.°   *protect*
       And also my writing° is full unready—   *account*
       How shall I do now for to excuse me?
       I would to God I had never be geet!°   *been born*
190   To my soul a full great profit it had be.
       For now I fear pains huge and great.
       The time passeth: Lord, help, that all wrought!
       For though I mourn, it availeth nought.
       The day passeth and is almost ago:°   *gone*
195   I wot° not well what for to do.   *know*
       To whom were I best my complaint to make?
       What and° I to Fellowship thereof spake,   *if*
       And showed him of this sudden chance?
       For in him is all mine affiance,°   *trust*
200   We have in the world so many a day
       Be good friends in sport and play.
       I see him yonder, certainly.
       I trust that he will bear me company.
       Therefore to him will I speak to ease my sorrow.
                   [*Enter* FELLOWSHIP.]

4. In your life.   5. With proper reflection.

205   Well met, good Fellowship, and good morrow!
       FELLOWSHIP   Everyman, good morrow, by this day!
          Sir, why lookest thou so piteously?
          If anything be amiss, I pray thee me say,
          That I may help to remedy.
210   EVERYMAN   Yea, good Fellowship, yea:
          I am in great jeopardy.
       FELLOWSHIP   My true friend, show to me your mind.
          I will not forsake thee to my life's end
          In the way of good company.
215   EVERYMAN   That was well spoken, and lovingly!
       FELLOWSHIP   Sir, I must needs know your heaviness.°   sorrow
          I have pity to see you in any distress.
          If any have you wronged, ye shall revenged be,
          Though I on the ground be slain for thee,
220   Though that I know before that I should die.
       EVERYMAN   Verily, Fellowship, gramercy.°   many thanks
       FELLOWSHIP   Tush! by thy thanks I set not a stree.°   straw
          Show me your grief and say no more.
       EVERYMAN   If I my heart should to you break,°   open
225   And then you to turn your mind fro me,
          And would not me comfort when ye hear me speak,
          Then should I ten times sorrier be.
       FELLOWSHIP   Sir, I say as I will do, indeed.
       EVERYMAN   Then be you a good friend at need.
230   I have found you true herebefore.
       FELLOWSHIP   And so ye shall evermore.
          For, in faith, and° thou go to hell,   if
          I will not forsake thee by the way.
       EVERYMAN   Ye speak like a good friend. I believe you well.
235   I shall deserve° it, and° I may.   repay / if
       FELLOWSHIP   I speak of no deserving, by this day!
          For he that will say and nothing do
          Is not worthy with good company to go.
          Therefore show me the grief of your mind,
240   As to your friend most loving and kind.
       EVERYMAN   I shall show you how it is:
          Commanded I am to go a journay,
          A long way, hard and dangerous,
          And give a strait° count,° without delay,   strict / account
245   Before the high judge Adonai.[6]
          Wherefore I pray you bear me company,
          As ye have promised, in this journay.
       FELLOWSHIP   This is matter indeed! Promise is duty—
          But, and° I should take such a voyage on me,   if
250   I know it well, it should be to my pain.
          Also it maketh me afeard, certain.
          But let us take counsel here, as well as we can—

6. A Hebrew name for God.

	For your words would fear° a strong man.	*frighten*
	EVERYMAN Why, ye said if I had need,	
255	Ye would me never forsake, quick ne° dead,	*alive nor*
	Though it were to hell, truly.	
	FELLOWSHIP So I said, certainly,	
	But such pleasures° be set aside, the sooth° to say.	*pleasantries / truth*
	And also, if we took such a journay,	
260	When should we again come?	
	EVERYMAN Nay, never again, till the day of doom.[7]	
	FELLOWSHIP In faith, then will not I come there!	
	Who hath you these tidings brought?	
	EVERYMAN Indeed, Death was with me here.	
265	FELLOWSHIP Now by God that all hath bought,°	*redeemed*
	If Death were the messenger,	
	For no man that is living today	
	I will not go that loath° journay—	*loathsome*
	Not for the father that begat me!	
270	EVERYMAN Ye promised otherwise, pardie.°	*by God*
	FELLOWSHIP I wot well I said so, truly.	
	And yet, if thou wilt eat and drink and make good cheer,	
	Or haunt to women the lusty company,[8]	
	I would not forsake you while the day is clear,	
275	Trust me verily!	
	EVERYMAN Yea, thereto ye would be ready—	
	To go to mirth, solace,° and play:	*enjoyment*
	Your mind to folly will sooner apply°	*attend*
	Than to bear me company in my long journay.	
280	FELLOWSHIP Now in good faith, I will not that way.	
	But, and° thou will murder or any man kill,	*if*
	In that I will help thee with a good will.	
	EVERYMAN O that is simple° advice, indeed!	*foolish*
	Gentle fellow, help me in my necessity:	
285	We have loved long, and now I need—	
	And now, gentle Fellowship, remember me!	
	FELLOWSHIP Whether ye have loved me or no,	
	By Saint John, I will not with thee go!	
	EVERYMAN Yet I pray thee take the labor and do so much for me,	
290	To bring me forward,° for saint charity,	*escort me*
	And comfort me till I come without° the town.	*outside*
	FELLOWSHIP Nay, and° thou would give me a new gown,	*even if*
	I will not a foot with thee go.	
	But, and° thou had tarried, I would not have left thee so.	*if*
295	And as° now, God speed thee in thy journay!	*as for*
	For from thee I will depart as fast as I may.	
	EVERYMAN Whither away, Fellowship? Will thou forsake me?	
	FELLOWSHIP Yea, by my fay!° To God I betake° thee.	*faith / commend*
	EVERYMAN Farewell, good Fellowship! For thee my heart is sore.	
300	Adieu forever—I shall see thee no more.	

---

7. That is, Judgment Day.   8. Or frequent the lusty company of women.

FELLOWSHIP   In faith, Everyman, farewell now at the ending:
    For you I will remember that parting is mourning.
       [*Exit* FELLOWSHIP.]
EVERYMAN   Alack, shall we thus depart° indeed—   *part*
    Ah, Lady,[9] help!—without any more comfort?
305   Lo, Fellowship forsaketh me in my most need!
    For help in this world whither shall I resort?
    Fellowship herebefore with me would merry make,
    And now little sorrow for me doth he take.
    It is said, "In prosperity men friends may find
310   Which in adversity be full unkind."
    Now whither for succor shall I flee,
    Sith° that Fellowship hath forsaken me?   *Since*
    To my kinsmen I will, truly,
    Praying them to help me in my necessity.
315   I believe that they will do so,
    For kind will creep where it may not go.[1]
    I will go 'say°—for yonder I see them—   *assay, try*
    Where° be ye now my friends and kinsmen.   *Whether*
       [*Enter* KINDRED *and* COUSIN.]
KINDRED   Here be we now at your commandment:
320   Cousin, I pray you show us your intent
    In any wise, and not spare.
COUSIN   Yea, Everyman, and to us declare
    If ye be disposed to go anywhither.
    For, weet° you well, we will live and die togither.   *know*
325 KINDRED   In wealth and woe we will with you hold,
    For over his kin a man may be bold.[2]
EVERYMAN   Gramercy, my friends and kinsmen kind.
    Now shall I show you the grief of my mind.
    I was commanded by a messenger
330   That is a high king's chief officer:
    He bade me go a pilgrimage, to my pain—
    And I know well I shall never come again.
    Also I must give a reckoning strait,°   *strict*
    For I have a great enemy that hath me in wait,[3]
335   Which intendeth me to hinder.
KINDRED   What account is that which ye must render?
    That would I know.
EVERYMAN   Of all my works I must show
    How I have lived and my days spent;
340   Also of ill deeds that I have used
    In my time sith life was me lent,
    And of all virtues that I have refused.
    Therefore I pray you go thither with me

---

9. The Virgin Mary.
1. For kinship will crawl where it cannot walk
(proverbial); that is, kinsmen will find a way to
help each other no matter what the circumstance.
2. That is, for a man may count on his
kinsmen.
3. That is, Satan, who lies in wait for me.

To help me make mine account, for saint charity.
345 COUSIN   What, to go thither? Is that the matter?
Nay, Everyman, I had liefer° fast° bread and water   *rather / fast on*
All this five year and more!
EVERYMAN   Alas, that ever I was bore!°   *born*
For now shall I never be merry
350 If that you forsake me.
KINDRED   Ah, sir, what? Ye be a merry man:
Take good heart to you and make no moan.
But one thing I warn you, by Saint Anne,[4]
As for me, ye shall go alone.
355 EVERYMAN   My Cousin, will you not with me go?
COUSIN   No, by Our Lady! I have the cramp in my toe:
Trust not to me. For, so God me speed,
I will deceive° you in your most need.   *betray*
KINDRED   It availeth you not us to 'tice.°   *entice*
360 Ye shall have my maid with all my heart:
She loveth to go to feasts, there to be nice,°   *wanton*
And to dance, and abroad to start.[5]
I will give her leave to help you in that journey,
If that you and she may agree.
365 EVERYMAN   Now show me the very effect° of your mind: *tenor*
Will you go with me or abide behind?
KINDRED   Abide behind? Yea, that will I and I may!
Therefore farewell till another day.
        [*Exit* KINDRED.]
EVERYMAN   How should I be merry or glad?
370 For fair promises men to me make,
But when I have most need they me forsake.
I am deceived. That maketh me sad.
COUSIN   Cousin Everyman, farewell now,
For verily I will not go with you;
375 Also of mine own an unready reckoning
I have to account—therefore I make tarrying.°   *stay behind*
Now God keep thee, for now I go.
        [*Exit* COUSIN.]
EVERYMAN   Ah, Jesus, is all come hereto?°   *to this*
Lo, fair words maketh fools fain:°   *glad*
380 They promise and nothing will do, certain.
My kinsmen promised me faithfully
For to abide with me steadfastly,
And now fast away do they flee.
Even so Fellowship promised me.
385 What friend were best me of to provide?[6]
I lose my time here longer to abide.
Yet in my mind a thing there is:

4. The mother of the Virgin Mary.
5. And to run around.

6. To provide myself with.

All my life I have loved riches;
If that my Good° now help me might,   *Goods*
390   He would make my heart full light.
I will speak to him in this distress.
Where art thou, my Goods and riches?
GOODS [*within*]   Who calleth me? Everyman? What, hast thou haste?
I lie here in corners, trussed and piled so high,
395   And in chests I am locked so fast—
Also sacked in bags—thou mayst see with thine eye
I cannot stir, in packs low where I lie.
What would ye have? Lightly° me say.   *Quickly*
EVERYMAN   Come hither, Good, in all the haste thou may,
400   For of counsel I must desire thee.
                [*Enter* GOODS.]
GOODS   Sir, and° ye in the world have sorrow or adversity,   *if*
That can I help you to remedy shortly.
EVERYMAN   It is another disease° that grieveth me: *trouble*
In this world it is not, I tell thee so.
405   I am sent for another way to go,
To give a strait count general
Before the highest Jupiter° of all.   *God*
And all my life I have had joy and pleasure in thee:
Therefore I pray thee go with me,
410   For, peradventure, thou mayst before God Almighty
My reckoning help to clean and purify.
For it is said ever among[7]
That money maketh all right that is wrong.
GOODS   Nay, Everyman, I sing another song:
415   I follow no man in such voyages.
For, and° I went with thee,   *if*
Thou shouldest fare much the worse for me;
For because on me thou did set thy mind,
Thy reckoning I have made blotted and blind,°   *illegible*
420   That thine account thou cannot make truly—
And that hast thou for the love of me.
EVERYMAN   That would grieve me full sore
When I should come to that fearful answer.
Up, let us go thither together.
425   GOODS   Nay, not so, I am too brittle, I may not endure.
I will follow no man one foot, be ye sure.
EVERYMAN   Alas, I have thee loved and had great pleasure
All my life-days on good and treasure.
GOODS   That is to thy damnation, without leasing,[8]
430   For my love is contrary to the love everlasting.
But if thou had me loved moderately during,[9]
As to the poor to give part of me,
Then shouldest thou not in this dolor° be,   *distress*

7. For it is commonly said.   9. That is, during your lifetime.
8. Without a lie (i.e., truly).

Nor in this great sorrow and care.

435 EVERYMAN   Lo, now was I deceived ere I was ware,
        And all I may wite° misspending of time.   *blame on*
     GOODS   What, weenest° thou that I am thine?   *suppose*
     EVERYMAN   I had weened so.
     GOODS   Nay, Everyman, I say no.
440 As for a while I was lent thee;
        A season thou hast had me in prosperity.
        My condition° is man's soul to kill;   *nature*
        If I save one, a thousand I do spill.°   *destroy*
        Weenest thou that I will follow thee?
445 Nay, from this world, not verily.
     EVERYMAN   I had weened otherwise.
     GOODS   Therefore to thy soul Good is a thief;
        For when thou art dead, this is my guise°—   *custom*
        Another to deceive in the same wise
450 As I have done thee, and all to his soul's repreef.°   *shame*
     EVERYMAN   O false Good, cursed thou be,
        Thou traitor to God, that hast deceived me
        And caught me in thy snare!
     GOODS   Marry, thou brought thyself in care,[1]
455 Whereof I am glad:
        I must needs laugh, I cannot be sad.
     EVERYMAN   Ah, Good, thou hast had long my heartly° love;   *heartfelt*
        I gave thee that which should be the Lord's above.
        But wilt thou not go with me, indeed?
460 I pray thee truth to say.
     GOODS   No, so God me speed!
        Therefore farewell and have good day.
                    [*Exit* GOODS.]
     EVERYMAN   Oh, to whom shall I make my moan
        For to go with me in that heavy° journey?   *sorrowful*
465 First Fellowship said he would with me gone:°   *go*
        His words were very pleasant and gay,
        But afterward he left me alone.
        Then spake I to my kinsmen, all in despair,
        And also they gave me words fair—
470 They lacked no fair speaking,
        But all forsake me in the ending.
        Then went I to my Goods that I loved best,
        In hope to have comfort; but there had I least
        For my Goods sharply did me tell
475 That he bringeth many into hell.
        Then of myself I was ashamed,
        And so I am worthy to be blamed:
        Thus may I well myself hate.
        Of whom shall I now counsel take?

---

1. That is, you brought sorrow on yourself.

480 I think that I shall never speed
Till that I go to my Good Deed.
But alas, she is so weak
That she can neither go° nor speak.   *walk*
Yet will I venture° on her now.   *gamble*
485 My Good Deeds, where be you?
GOOD DEEDS [*speaking from the ground*]   Here I lie, cold in the ground:
Thy sins hath me sore bound
That I cannot stear.°   *stir*
EVERYMAN   O Good Deeds, I stand in fear:
490 I must you pray of counsel,
For help now should come right well.[2]
GOOD DEEDS   Everyman, I have understanding
That ye be summoned, account to make,
Before Messiah of Jer'salem King.
495 And you do by me,[3] that journey with you will I take.
EVERYMAN   Therefore I come to you my moan to make:
I pray you that ye will go with me.
GOOD DEEDS   I would full fain,° but I cannot stand, verily.   *gladly*
EVERYMAN   Why, is there anything on you fall?°   *fallen*
500 GOOD DEEDS   Yea, sir, I may thank you of all:
If ye had perfectly cheered me,
Your book of count full ready had be.
               [GOOD DEEDS *shows him the account book.*]
Look, the books of your works and deeds eke,°   *also*
As how they lie under the feet,
505 To your soul's heaviness.°   *distress*
EVERYMAN   Our Lord Jesus help me!
For one letter here I cannot see.
GOOD DEEDS   There is a blind° reckoning in time of distress![4]   *illegible*
EVERYMAN   Good Deeds, I pray you help me in this need,
510 Or else I am forever damned indeed.
Therefore help me to make reckoning
Before the Redeemer of all thing
That King is and was and ever shall.
GOOD DEEDS   Everyman, I am sorry of° your fall   *for*
515 And fain would help you and° I were able.   *if*
EVERYMAN   Good Deeds, your counsel I pray you give me.
GOOD DEEDS   That shall I do verily,
Though that on my feet I may not go;
I have a sister that shall with you also,
520 Called Knowledge, which shall with you abide
To help you to make that dreadful reckoning.
               [*Enter* KNOWLEDGE.]
KNOWLEDGE   Everyman, I will go with thee and be thy guide,
In thy most need to go by thy side.

---

2. For help would be most welcome now.   4. That is, for the sinful person, the book of
3. If you do as I advise.   reckoning is hard to read in the hour of distress.

EVERYMAN   In good condition I am now in everything,
525   And am whole content with this good thing,
       Thanked be God my Creator.
       GOOD DEEDS   And when she hath brought you there
       Where thou shalt heal thee of thy smart,°   pain
       Then go you with your reckoning and your Good Deeds together
530   For to make you joyful at heart
       Before the blessed Trinity.⁵
       EVERYMAN   My Good Deeds, gramercy!
       I am well content, certainly,
       With your words sweet.
535   KNOWLEDGE   Now go we together lovingly
       To Confession, that cleansing river.
       EVERYMAN   For joy I weep—I would we were there!
       But I pray you give me cognition,°   knowledge
       Where dwelleth that holy man Confession?
540   KNOWLEDGE   In the House of Salvation:
       We shall find him in that place,
       That shall us comfort, by God's grace.
          [KNOWLEDGE *leads* EVERYMAN *to* CONFESSION.]
       Lo, this is Confession: kneel down and ask mercy,
       For he is in good conceit° with God Almighty.   esteem
545   EVERYMAN [*kneeling*]   O glorious fountain that all
               uncleanness doth clarify,°   purify
       Wash from me the spots of vice unclean,
       That on me no sin may be seen.
       I come with Knowledge for my redemption,
       Redempt° with heart and full contrition,   Redeemed
550   For I am commanded a pilgrimage to take
       And great accounts before God to make.
       Now I pray you, Shrift,° mother of Salvation,   Confession
       Help my Good Deeds for my piteous exclamation.
       CONFESSION   I know your sorrow well, Everyman:
555   Because with Knowledge ye come to me,
       I will you comfort as well as I can,
       And a precious jewel I will give thee,
       Called Penance, voider° of adversity.   expeller
       Therewith shall your body chastised be—
560   With abstinence and perseverance in God's service.
       Here shall you receive that scourge of me,
       Which is penance strong that ye must endure,
       To remember thy Saviour was scourged for thee
       With sharp scourges, and suffered it patiently.
565   So must thou ere thou 'scape that painful pilgrimage.
       Knowledge, keep° him in this voyage,   guard
       And by that time Good Deeds will be with thee.
       But in any wise be secure° of mercy—   certain
       For your time draweth fast—and ye will saved be.

5. That is, God as existing in three persons: the Father, Son, and Holy Spirit.

570 Ask God mercy and he will grant, truly.
When with the scourge of penance man doth him° bind,   *himself*
The oil of forgiveness then shall he find.
EVERYMAN   Thanked be God for his gracious work,
For now I will my penance begin.
575 This hath rejoiced and lighted my heart,
Though the knots be painful and hard within.[6]
KNOWLEDGE   Everyman, look your penance that ye fulfill,
What pain that ever it to you be;
And Knowledge shall give you counsel at will
580 How your account ye shall make clearly.
EVERYMAN   O eternal God, O heavenly figure,
O way of righteousness, O goodly vision,
Which descended down in a virgin pure
Because he would every man redeem,
585 Which Adam forfeited by his disobedience;
O blessed Godhead, elect and high Divine,°   *divinity*
Forgive my grievous offense!
Here I cry thee mercy in this presence:[7]
O ghostly Treasure, O Ransomer and Redeemer,
590 Of all the world Hope and Conduiter,°   *Conductor, Guide*
Mirror of joy, Foundator° of mercy,   *Founder*
Which enlumineth° heaven and earth thereby,   *illuminates*
Hear my clamorous complaint, though it late be;
Receive my prayers, of thy benignity.
595 Though I be a sinner most abominable,
Yet let my name be written in Moses' table.[8]
O Mary, pray to the Maker of all thing°   *things*
Me for to help at my ending,
And save me from the power of my enemy,
600 For Death assaileth me strongly.
And Lady, that I may by mean of thy prayer
Of your Son's glory to be partner—
By the means of his passion I it crave.
I beseech you help my soul to save.
605 Knowledge, give me the scourge of penance:
My flesh therewith shall give acquittance.°   *satisfaction for sins*
I will now begin, if God give me grace.
KNOWLEDGE   Everyman, God give you time and space!°   *opportunity*
Thus I bequeath you in the hands of our Saviour:
610 Now may you make your reckoning sure.
EVERYMAN   In the name of the Holy Trinity
My body sore punished shall be:
Take this, body, for the sin of the flesh!
Also° thou delightest to go gay and fresh,°   *As / finely dressed*

---

6. Though the knots (of the scourge) are hard
and painful to my senses.
7. That is, in the presence of Knowledge and
Confession.

8. That is, the tablets that God gave Moses on
Mount Sinai on which the Ten Commandments
were written. In the Middle Ages these tablets
were associated with baptism and penance.

615 And in the way of damnation thou did me bring,
Therefore suffer now strokes of punishing!
Now of penance I will wade the water clear,
To save me from purgatory, that sharp fire.

GOOD DEEDS   I thank God, now can I walk and go,
620 And am delivered of my sickness and woe.
Therefore with Everyman I will go, and not spare:
His good works I will help him to declare.

KNOWLEDGE   Now, Everyman, be merry and glad:
Your Good Deeds cometh now, ye may not be sad.
625 Now is your Good Deeds whole and sound,
Going° upright upon the ground.   *Walking*

EVERYMAN   My heart is light, and shall be evermore.
Now will I smite faster than I did before.

GOOD DEEDS   Everyman, pilgrim, my special friend,
630 Blessed be thou without end!
For thee is preparate° the eternal glory.   *prepared*
Ye have me made whole and sound
Therefore I will bide by thee in every stound.°   *trial*

EVERYMAN   Welcome, my Good Deeds! Now I hear thy voice,
635 I weep for very sweetness of love.

KNOWLEDGE   Be no more sad, but ever rejoice:
God seeth thy living in his throne above.
Put on this garment to thy behove,°   *advantage*
Which is wet with your tears—
640 Or else before God you may it miss
When ye to your journey's end come shall.

EVERYMAN   Gentle Knowledge, what do ye it call?

KNOWLEDGE   It is a garment of sorrow;
From pain it will you borrow:°   *protect*
645 Contrition it is
That getteth forgiveness;
It pleaseth God passing° well.   *exceedingly*

GOOD DEEDS   Everyman, will you wear it for your heal?°   *well-being*

EVERYMAN   Now blessed be Jesu, Mary's son,
650 For now have I on true contrition.
And let us go now without tarrying.
Good Deeds, have we clear our reckoning?

GOOD DEEDS   Yea, indeed, I have it here.

EVERYMAN   Then I trust we need not fear.
655 Now friends, let us not part in twain.

KNOWLEDGE   Nay, Everyman, that will we not, certain.

GOOD DEEDS   Yet must thou lead with thee
Three persons of great might.

EVERYMAN   Who should they be?

660 GOOD DEEDS   Discretion and Strength they hight,°   *are called*
And thy Beauty may not abide behind.

KNOWLEDGE   Also ye must call to mind
Your Five-Wits° as for your counselors.   *senses*

GOOD DEEDS   You must have them ready at all hours.

₆₆₅ EVERYMAN   How shall I get them hither?
KNOWLEDGE   You must call them all togither,
  And they will be here incontinent.°   *immediately*
EVERYMAN   My friends, come hither and be present,
  Discretion, Strength, my Five-Wits, and Beauty!
    [*They enter.*]
₆₇₀ BEAUTY   Here at your will we be all ready.
  What will ye that we should do?
GOOD DEEDS   That ye would with Everyman go
  And help him in his pilgrimage.
  Advise you:° will ye with him or not in that voyage?   *Consider*
₆₇₅ STRENGTH   We will bring him all thither,
  To his help and comfort, ye may believe me.
DISCRETION   So will we go with him all togither.
EVERYMAN   Almighty God, loved° might thou be!   *praised*
  I give thee laud that I have hither brought
₆₈₀ Strength, Discretion, Beauty, and Five-Wits—lack I nought—
  And my Good Deeds, with Knowledge clear,
  All be in my company at my will here:
  I desire no more to my business.
STRENGTH   And I, Strength, will by you stand in distress,
₆₈₅ Though thou would in battle fight on the ground.
FIVE-WITS   And though it were through the world round,
  We will not depart for sweet ne sour.
BEAUTY   No more will I, until death's hour,
  Whatsoever thereof befall.
₆₉₀ DISCRETION   Everyman, advise you first of all:
  Go with a good advisement° and deliberation.   *reflection*
  We all give you virtuous° monition°   *confident / prediction*
  That all shall be well.
EVERYMAN   My friends, hearken what I will tell;
₆₉₅ I pray God reward you in his heaven-sphere;
  Now hearken all that be here,
  For I will make my testament,
  Here before you all present:
  In alms half my good° I will give with my hands twain,   *goods*
₇₀₀ In the way of charity with good intent;
  And the other half, still° shall remain,   *which still*
  I 'queath° to be returned there° it ought to be.   *bequeath / where*
  This I do in despite of the fiend of hell,
  To go quit out of his perel,
₇₀₅ Ever after and this day.⁹
KNOWLEDGE   Everyman, hearken what I say:
  Go to Priesthood, I you advise,
  And receive of him, in any wise,°   *at all costs*
  The holy sacrament and ointment¹ togither;

9. To be free of his power today and ever after.   unction (anointing of the sick).
1. The Eucharist (see line 724) and extreme

710 Then shortly see ye turn again hither:
      We will all abide you here.

      FIVE-WITS Yea, Everyman, hie you that ye ready were.
      There is no emperor, king, duke, ne baron,
      That of God hath commission

715 As hath the least priest in the world being:
      For of the blessed sacraments pure and bening°   *benign*
      He beareth the keys,[2] and thereof hath the cure°   *care*
      For man's redemption—it is ever sure—
      Which God for our souls' medicine

720 Gave us out of his heart with great pine,°   *suffering*
      Here in this transitory life for thee and me.
      The blessed sacraments seven there be:
      Baptism, confirmation, with priesthood° good,   *ordination*
      And the sacrament of God's precious flesh and blood,

725 Marriage, the holy extreme unction, and penance:
      These seven be good to have in remembrance,
      Gracious sacraments of high divinity.

      EVERYMAN Fain° would I receive that holy body,   *Gladly*
      And meekly to my ghostly° father I will go.   *spiritual*

730 FIVE-WITS Everyman, that is the best that ye can do:
      God will you to salvation bring.
      For priesthood exceedeth all other thing:°   *things*
      To us Holy Scripture they do teach,
      And converteth man from sin, heaven to reach;

735 God hath to them more power given
      Than to any angel that is in heaven.
      With five words[3] he may consecrate
      God's body in flesh and blood to make,
      And handleth his Maker between his hands.

740 The priest bindeth and unbindeth all bands,[4]
      Both in earth and in heaven.
      Thou ministers° all the sacraments seven;   *administers*
      Though we kiss thy feet, thou were worthy;
      Thou art surgeon that cureth sin deadly;

745 No remedy we find under God
      But all° only priesthood.   *Except*
      Everyman, God gave priests that dignity
      And setteth them in his stead among us to be.
      Thus be they above angels in degree.

            [*Exit* EVERYMAN.]

750 KNOWLEDGE If priests be good, it is so, surely.
      But when Jesu hanged on the cross with great smart,°   *pain*
      There he gave out of his blessed heart
      The same sacrament in great torment,
      He sold them not to us, that Lord omnipotent:

---

2. Spiritual power or authority. See Matthew
16.19.
3. *Hoc est enim corpus meum* ("For this is my

body"; Latin), words for the consecration of
bread in the Roman Catholic liturgy.
4. Bonds (of sin). See Matthew 16.19.

755 Therefore Saint Peter the Apostle doth say
That Jesu's curse hath all they
Which God their Saviour do buy or sell[5]
Or they for any money do take or tell.[6]
Sinful priests giveth the sinners example bad:
760 Their children sitteth by other men's fires, I have heard;[7]
And some haunteth women's company
With unclean life, as lusts of lechery.
These be with sin made blind.
FIVE-WITS   I trust to God no such may we find.
765 Therefore let us priesthood honor,
And follow their doctrine for our souls' succor.
We be their sheep and they shepherds be
By whom we all be kept in surety.
Peace, for yonder I see Everyman come,
770 Which hath made true satisfaction.
GOOD DEEDS   Methink it is he indeed.

[*Re-enter* EVERYMAN.]

EVERYMAN   Now Jesu be your alder speed![8]
I have received the sacrament for my redemption,
And then mine extreme unction.
775 Blessed be all they that counseled me to take it!
And now, friends, let us go without longer respite.
I thank God that ye have tarried so long.
Now set each of you on this rood° your hond°   *cross / hand*
And shortly follow me:
780 I go before there I would be.[9] God be our guide!
STRENGTH   Everyman, we will not from you go
Till ye have done this voyage long.
DISCRETION   I, Discretion, will bide by you also.
KNOWLEDGE   And though this pilgrimage be never so strong,°   *wearisome*
785 I will never part you fro.
STRENGTH   Everyman, I will be as sure by thee
As ever I did by Judas Maccabee.[1]
EVERYMAN   Alas, I am so faint I may not stand—
My limbs under me doth fold!
790 Friends, let us not turn again to this land,
Not for all the world's gold.
For into this cave must I creep
And turn to earth, and there to sleep.
BEAUTY   What, into this grave, alas?
795 EVERYMAN   Yea, there shall ye consume,° more and lass.[2]   *decay*
BEAUTY   And what, should I smother here?

---

5. An allusion to simony, the buying or selling of sacraments, sacred objects, or ecclesiastical offices. See Acts 8.18–21.
6. Or who for (any sacrament) take or pay money. *Tell:* to count out.
7. That is, they have illegitimate children.
8. Now may Jesus favor you all.
9. I lead (the way to) where I wish to be.
1. The leader of the Jews in their successful revolt against the Syrians in the 2nd century B.C.E.
2. More and less (i.e., all of you).

EVERYMAN   Yea, by my faith, and nevermore appear.
    In this world live no more we shall,
    But in heaven before the highest Lord of all.
800 BEAUTY   I cross out all this!³ Adieu, by Saint John—
    I take my tape in my lap and am gone.⁴
EVERYMAN   What, Beauty, whither will ye?
BEAUTY   Peace, I am deaf—I look not behind me,
    Not and° thou wouldest give me all the gold in thy chest.   *if*
        [*Exit* BEAUTY.]
805 EVERYMAN   Alas, whereto may I trust?
    Beauty goeth fast away fro me—
    She promised with me to live and die!
STRENGTH   Everyman, I will thee also forsake and deny.
    Thy game liketh° me not at all.   *pleases*
810 EVERYMAN   Why then, ye will forsake me all?
    Sweet Strength, tarry a little space.°   *while*
STRENGTH   Nay, sir, by the rood of grace,
    I will hie me from thee fast,
    Though thou weep till thy heart tobrast.°   *break into pieces*
815 EVERYMAN   Ye would ever bide by me, ye said.
STRENGTH   Yea, I have you far enough conveyed!
    Ye be old enough, I understand,
    Your pilgrimage to take on hand:⁵
    I repent me that I hither came.
820 EVERYMAN   Strength, you to displease I am to blame,⁶
    Yet promise is debt, this ye well wot.°   *know*
STRENGTH   In faith, I care not:
    Thou art but a fool to complain;
    You spend your speech and waste your brain.
825   Go, thrust thee into the ground.
        [*Exit* STRENGTH.]
EVERYMAN   I had weened° surer I should you have found.   *supposed*
    He that trusteth in his Strength
    She him deceiveth at the length.
    Both Strength and Beauty forsaketh me—
830   Yet they promised me fair and lovingly.
DISCRETION   Everyman, I will after Strength be gone:
    As for me, I will leave you alone.
EVERYMAN   Why Discretion, will ye forsake me?
DISCRETION   Yea, in faith, I will go from thee.
835   For when Strength goeth before,
    I follow after evermore.
EVERYMAN   Yet I pray thee, for the love of the Trinity,
    Look in my grave once piteously.

---

3. I cancel all this (i.e., my promise to stay with you).
4. I'll gather up my knitting or spinning and be on my way (proverbial).
5. To take responsibility for your own pilgrimage.
6. I am to blame for displeasing you.

DISCRETION   Nay, so nigh° will I not come.   *near*
840   Farewell everyone!

   [*Exit* DISCRETION.]

EVERYMAN   O all thing faileth save God alone—
   Beauty, Strength, and Discretion.
   For when Death bloweth his blast
   They all run fro me full fast.
845 FIVE-WITS   Everyman, my leave now of thee I take.
   I will follow the other, for here I thee forsake.
EVERYMAN   Alas, then may I wail and weep,
   For I took you for my best friend.
FIVE-WITS   I will no longer thee keep.°   *watch over*
850   Now farewell, and there an end!

   [*Exit* FIVE-WITS.]

EVERYMAN   O Jesu, help, all hath forsaken me!
GOOD DEEDS   Nay, Everyman, I will bide with thee:
   I will not forsake thee indeed;
   Thou shalt find me a good friend at need.
855 EVERYMAN   Gramercy, Good Deeds! Now may I true friends see.
   They have forsaken me every one—
   I loved them better than my Good Deeds alone.
   Knowledge, will ye forsake me also?
KNOWLEDGE   Yea, Everyman, when ye to Death shall go,
860   But not yet, for no manner of danger.
EVERYMAN   Gramercy, Knowledge, with all my heart!
KNOWLEDGE   Nay, yet will I not from hence depart
   Till I see where ye shall become.[7]
EVERYMAN   Methink, alas, that I must be gone
865   To make my reckoning and my debts pay,
   For I see my time is nigh spent away.
   Take example, all ye that this do hear or see,
   How they that I best loved do forsake me,
   Except my Good Deeds that bideth truly.
870 GOOD DEEDS   All earthly things is but vanity.
   Beauty, Strength, and Discretion do man forsake,
   Foolish friends and kinsmen that fair spake—
   All fleeth save Good Deeds, and that am I.
EVERYMAN   Have mercy on me, God most mighty,
875   And stand by me, thou mother and maid, holy Mary!
GOOD DEEDS   Fear not: I will speak for thee.
EVERYMAN   Here I cry God mercy!
GOOD DEEDS   Short° our end, and 'minish° our pain.   *Shorten / diminish*
   Let us go, and never come again.
880 EVERYMAN   Into thy hands, Lord, my soul I commend:
   Receive it, Lord, that it be not lost.
   As thou me boughtest,° so me defend,   *redeemed*
   And save me from the fiend's boast,

---

7. What shall become of you.

That I may appear with that blessed host
885   That shall be saved at the day of doom.
       In manus tuas, of mights most,
       Forever *commendo spiritum meum.*[8]
              [EVERYMAN *and* GOOD DEEDS *descend into the grave.*]

   KNOWLEDGE   Now hath he suffered that° we all shall endure,   *that which*
       The Good Deeds shall make all sure.
890   Now hath he made ending,
       Methinketh that I hear angels sing
       And make great joy and melody
       Where Everyman's soul received shall be.

   ANGEL [*within*]   Come, excellent elect° spouse to Jesu![9]   *chosen*
895   Here above thou shalt go
       Because of thy singular virtue.
       Now the soul is taken the body fro,
       Thy reckoning is crystal clear:
       Now shalt thou into the heavenly sphere—
900   Unto the which all ye shall come
       That liveth well before the day of doom.
              [*Enter* DOCTOR.[1]]

   DOCTOR   This moral men may have in mind:
       Ye hearers, take it of worth,° old and young,   *prize it highly*
       And forsake Pride, for he deceiveth you in the end.
905   And remember Beauty, Five-Wits, Strength, and Discretion,
       They all at the last do Everyman forsake,
       Save° his Good Deeds there doth he take—   *Only*
       But beware, for and° they be small,   *if*
       Before God he hath no help at all—
910   None excuse may be there for Everyman.
       Alas, how shall he do than?°   *then*
       For after death amends may no man make,
       For then mercy and pity doth him forsake.
       If his reckoning be not clear when he doth come,
915   God will say, "*Ite, maledicti, in ignem eternum!*"[2]
       And he that hath his account whole and sound,
       High in heaven he shall be crowned,
       Unto which place God bring us all thither,
       That we may live body and soul together.
920   Thereto help, the Trinity!
       Amen, say ye, for saint° charity.   *holy*

8. Into thy hands, greatest of powers, I commend my spirit forever; the Latin directly quotes the last words of Jesus on the cross, according to Luke 23.46 (in the Vulgate).
9. Marriage was a common medieval metaphor for the soul's union with Christ.
1. A doctor of theology.
2. Go, ye cursed, into everlasting fire (slightly misquoting Matthew 25.41).

THOMAS KYD

1558–1594

"*VINDICTA mihi!*" cries *THE SPANISH TRAG-EDY*'s protagonist Hieronimo, whose son has been cruelly slain. "Vengeance is mine!" Hieronimo is citing biblical passages that assign retribution to God alone. But in Hieronimo's mouth the words quickly take on a very different meaning; the protagonist speaks them only as a precursor to his vow to avenge his son himself. Vengeance in *The Spanish Tragedy* is Hieronimo's, and his single-minded pursuit of retribution against a corrupt court brings him to the very edge of sanity. Such a pursuit, which would have appealed to a Renaissance audience concerned about the limits of justice and the righteousness of retaliation, speaks to us today in its portrayal of cycles of violence and the passionate desire for revenge that keeps them turning.

Thomas Kyd was born in London, the son of a scrivener, or scribe. In 1565, he entered the Merchant Taylors' School, a respected grammar school where he learned classical and Continental languages and literatures. Kyd appears not to have gone on to study at a university, remaining instead in London, where he may have followed his father's example in a suitable trade before or while pursuing his literary interests. The London of Kyd's day was uniquely suited for aspiring writers, partly because the market for printed texts was expanding but also, and more significantly, because a stable theater industry had been established in the city. Professional acting companies, installed in permanent playhouses by the late 1570s, required a regular supply of fresh plays to please their growing audiences, and Kyd belonged to a generation of dramatists—SHAKESPEARE among them—whose work it was to satisfy this need.

Much of Kyd's biography and literary corpus remains shadowy. His name was associated with the prestigious Queen's Company, a troupe culled from the best actors of the day, between 1583 and 1585. In 1588, his translation of an Italian guidebook, *The Housholders Philosophie,* was published; his translation of a French closet drama (i.e., a play not intended for public performance), Robert Garnier's *Cornelia,* appeared in 1594. *The Spanish Tragedy* was published, anonymously, in 1592; a fellow playwright's reference to "M. Kid, in his Spanish Tragedy," in a 1612 treatise establishes his authorship. Kyd is credited by some with the anonymous *Soliman and Perseda* (1592), which focuses on characters that appear in the play-within-the-play that ends *The Spanish Tragedy*. A number of scholars also believe that sometime before 1589 Kyd wrote a now lost "Ur-Hamlet," which served as the model for Shakespeare's *Hamlet.* More controversially, some assign to Kyd *I Jeronimo,* first published in 1605 but mentioned in the financial records of the theater entrepreneur Philip Henslowe between 1591 and 1592.

What does not remain shadowy about Kyd is the final year of his life, which seems to follow a revenge tragedy plot. In 1593 Kyd was arrested during a government investigation of libels circulating in London against foreigners living in the city. Charged specifically with possessing "heretical" writings that denied the deity of Jesus— writings discovered during a search of his rooms following his arrest—Kyd was imprisoned, interrogated, and tortured. In an effort to defend his honor and reputation, Kyd wrote letters to high-ranking members of Queen Elizabeth's government, attacking his fellow dramatist, CHRISTO-PHER MARLOWE, with whom he had once shared lodgings. According to Kyd, the heretical documents were Marlowe's, "shufled wth some of myne (vnknown to me) by some occasion of o^r wrytinge in one chamber twoe yeares synce." He accused his former roommate of being a blasphemous traitor, an atheist who believed that Jesus Christ was a homosexual. Whether these letters, written after Marlowe's death on May 30, 1593, represent Kyd's desperation or his vengeful energies, they provide a glimpse into the complicated world of the Elizabethan playwright, which could be filled with political intrigues as well as professional rivalries and friendships. Kyd's death in August 1594, within a year of his release from prison, may have been hastened by his torture.

The plot of *The Spanish Tragedy*, Kyd's signature achievement, echoes the brutal events governing his life. The play was a success and recognized in its own time—though sometimes mocked—for its popular appeal. Its setting in Catholic Spain would have inspired the nationalistic sensibilities of the predominantly Protestant English audience, since the countries were at war during most of the latter part of the sixteenth century, divided by political as well as religious disagreements. Depicting the Spanish court as a haven for corruption capitalized on popular anti-Spanish sentiment, but the play also served as a

The Spanish Tragedie:
OR,
Hieronimo is mad agains.

Containing the lamentable end of *Don Horatio*, and
Belimperia; with the pittifull death of *Hieronimo*.

Newly corrected, amended, and enlarged with new
Additions of the *Painters* part, and others, as
it hath of late been divers times acted.

LONDON,
Printed by W. White, for I. White and T Langley,
and are to be fold at their Shop ouer againft the
Sarazens head without New-gate. 1615.

The title page of the 1615 quarto of *The Spanish Tragedy*. Horatio, left, hangs lifeless in the arbor; Hieronomo, holding a torch, prepares to cut him down; Bel-imperia exclaims, "Murder, helpe Hieronimo"; and Lorenzo, right, responds with "Stop her mouth."

warning to English viewers as it portrayed what their country might become if their magistrates were not vigilant about issues of law and religion. Its setting has led to much debate over the date of the play's original composition and performance, with some scholars arguing that its anti-Spanish sensibilities would have been more appropriate for audiences *before* 1588—the year of England's victory over the Spanish Armada—and others maintaining that the play's pro-English tone was possible only *after* the triumph. But the play would also have appealed to audiences as a marvel of dramatic synthesis, for it combines elements of the classical tragedy of SENECA—political decay, extravagant rhetoric—with native traditions of the English stage such as the dumb show and comic interlude. Most important, its theme of revenge demanded a mixture of volatile emotions, ethical questions, and violent activity. These ingredients, which give *The Spanish Tragedy* a timeless interest, were of particular importance to Kyd's audience, whom the conflict between the public and private justice deeply engaged.

The play's focus on vengeance is evident from its opening scene, when the ghost of Don Andrea, a Spanish knight killed in battle, makes his entrance alongside the allegorical figure of Revenge. Andrea and Revenge serve as the play's Chorus: they provide essential background information, including an account of Andrea's death and journey to Hades (the classical underworld), and comment on events at the end of each act. Their conversations, in which Revenge's comic nonchalance is pitted against Andrea's urgent need to get back at the soldiers who slew him, highlight the play's central conflicts between love and war, honor and disgrace, obligation to self and obligation to the state. In their position on a balcony above the stage, the two figures assume the role of masters of the action that unfolds below them.

That action takes a surprising turn. The audience has been led to believe that the play will show how Don Andrea's comrade, Horatio, and his fiancée, Bel-imperia, niece to the king of Spain, avenge Andrea's death at the hands of Balthazar, a Portuguese prince. But Bel-imperia's strategy for revenge is to fall in love with Horatio. "Yes, second love shall further my revenge. / I'll love Horatio, my Andrea's friend, / The more to spite the Prince that wrought his end" she says, bestowing on Horatio the handkerchief she had once given to Andrea. When Bel-imperia's brother, who wants to match Bel-imperia with Balthazar, learns of the wooing he becomes furious and plots to murder Horatio. The cunning, self-serving Lorenzo—one of the earliest "Machiavellian" (or ethically unscrupulous) characters on the English Renaissance stage—persuades Bel-imperia's own servant, Pedringano, to betray the couple during a romantic encounter in an arbor near Horatio's home. Lorenzo and Balthazar brutally hang Horatio.

This murder, in the second act, shifts the focus of the play. Almost immediately, Hieronimo—Horatio's father, Knight Marshal of Spain—and his wife, Isabella, discover the dead body of their son. Both parents mourn Horatio, but Hieronimo's shock and grief turn into a pledge to revenge: taking the scarf from Horatio's lifeless body, he vows:

> See'st thou this handkercher
> besmeared with blood?
> It shall not from me till I take
> revenge.
> See'st thou those wounds that yet are
> bleeding fresh?
> I'll entomb them till I have
> revenged.
> Then will I joy amidst my
> discontent;
> Till then my sorrow never shall be
> spent.

While Hieronimo's delivery here may seem overly stylized to us today, Kyd's use of rhetorical devices such as the repetition of the same words at the beginning and ends of lines was meant to convey real suffering. Performed well, Hieronimo's various outbursts over the course of the play are deeply moving expressions of his fury and sense of loss. As his country's chief legal officer, Hieronimo first defers the retaliation he pledges when he encounters Horatio's body. But as both he and Isabella come to recognize that adequate redress for their son will be impossible in the Spanish court, they become convinced that revenge is necessary as well as right. Their convictions are accompanied by waves of despair and suicidal thinking, moments of insanity that eventually overwhelm Isabella but that Hieronimo uses to disguise his vengeful plans.

These plans, as Hieronimo insists, have to be special: "Not as the vulgar wits of men, / With open, but inevitable ills, / As by a secret, yet a certain, mean, / Which under kindship will be cloakèd best." Hieronimo's unique strategy is to mount a play at court, in which he, Lorenzo, Balthazar, and Bel-imperia will participate, for an audience that includes the king of Spain as well as Lorenzo's father and Balthazar's father (the king of Portugal). As Hieronimo explains, the play, a tragedy modeled on the ill-fated story of the lovers Erasto and Perseda and the Turkish sultan Soliman, will involve the deaths of the characters played by Lorenzo and Balthazar. What he reveals only to Bel-imperia is that during the performance their killing of the two men will be no act. Hieronimo's vengeance, accomplished in a play-within-the-play, is an exceptionally dramatic one that, like the presence of the Chorus, blurs the line between what is theatrical and what is real.

The retribution is also excessive. Hieronimo's vengeful desire encompasses not just righting an uncorrected wrong and punishing the evildoers but harming the relatives of those evildoers. He wants the suffering of the fathers of Lorenzo and Balthazar to equal his own (which has increased, as Isabella has killed herself). Thus the play-within-the-play is deliberately chaotic, with the characters performing in "unknown languages." Whether or not Latin, Greek, and French were actually used in performance—a question still debated among critics—Hieronimo's demand for different tongues is designed to give the audience a taste of the confusion of thought and feeling that he has been experiencing. The jarring suicides of Bel-imperia and Hieronimo, which are not specifically scripted, only add to the chaos of the inset play.

Kyd attempts to control the confusion in the last Chorus, in which Andrea summarizes the entire play. But even here a sense of uncertainty remains, as the play ends not with words of closure but with Andrea's calls for more punishment and Revenge's promise that in the underworld, "though death hath end their misery, / I'll there begin their endless tragedy." Their comments suggest that what we thought complete action is in fact a prologue to another, otherworldly, drama. Revenge, the play both warns and teaches us, never really sleeps.   HEATHER HIRSCHFELD

The Spanish Tragedy

CHARACTERS

The ghost of Don° ANDREA ⎫ figures in the frame   *Spanish noble title*
REVENGE   ⎭

The KING of Spain
Don Cyprian, Duke of CASTILE, the King's brother
Don LORENZO, the Duke's son and Bel-imperia's brother
BEL-IMPERIA, the Duke's daughter and Lorenzo's sister
GENERAL of the Spanish army

The VICEROY of Portugal
Prince BALTHAZAR, his son
Don PEDRO, the Viceroy's brother
ALEXANDRO ⎱
VILLUPPO ⎰ Portuguese noblemen
AMBASSADOR of Portugal to the court of Spain

Don HIERONIMO, Knight Marshal[1] of Spain
ISABELLA, his wife
Don HORATIO, their son

PEDRINGANO, servant to Bel-imperia
SERBERINE, servant to Balthazar
CHRISTOPHIL, servant to Lorenzo
Don BAZULTO, an old man
PAGE ("boy") to Lorenzo
Three WATCHMEN
A MESSENGER
A DEPUTY
A HANGMAN
A MAID to Isabella
Two PORTUGUESE (Portingales)
A SERVANT to Hieronimo
[see Three CITIZENS] Three CITIZENS
Two NOBLEMEN of Portugal
Soldiers of the Spanish army, officers, trumpeters,
    attendants, halberdiers°   soldiers with spears
Three knights, three kings, and a drummer in the first
    dumb show
Hymen and two torchbearers in the second dumb show

In Hieronimo's play:
Soliman, Sultan of Turkey (played by Balthazar)
Erasto ("Erastus"), Knight of Rhodes (played by Lorenzo)
Bashaw (played by Hieronimo)
Perseda (played by Bel-imperia)

[SCENE: *The courts of Spain and Portugal.*]

1.1

[SCENE: *The opening chorus.*]
        [*Enter the ghost of* ANDREA, *and with him* REVENGE.]
ANDREA   When this eternal substance of my soul
      Did live imprisoned in my wanton° flesh,   *sinful, lewd*
      Each in their function serving other's need,
      I was a courtier in the Spanish court.
5   My name was Don Andrea; my descent,
      Though not ignoble, yet inferior far

---

1. Military officer and legal official of the royal household.

To gracious fortunes of my tender youth.[2]
For there, in prime° and pride° of all my years,   *springtime / lust*
By duteous service and deserving love

10 In secret I possessed a worthy dame
Which hight° sweet Bel-imperia by name.   *Who was called*
But in the harvest of my summer joys
Death's winter nipped the blossoms of my bliss,
Forcing divorce° betwixt my love and me.   *separation*

15 For in the late° conflict with Portingale°   *recent / Portugal*
My valor drew me into danger's mouth,
Till life to death made passage through my wounds.[3]
When I was slain, my soul descended straight°   *immediately*
To pass the flowing stream of Acheron;[4]

20 But churlish Charon,° only boatman there,   *ferryman of the dead*
Said that my rites of burial not° performed,[5]
I might not sit amongst his passengers.
Ere Sol had slept three nights in Thetis' lap,[6]
And slaked his smoking° chariot in her flood,   *fiery*

25 By Don Horatio, our knight marshal's son,
My funerals and obsequies° were done.   *burial rites*
Then was the ferryman of hell content
To pass me over to the slimy strand°   *shore*
That leads to fell° Avernus'[7] ugly waves.   *fatal, deadly*

30 There pleasing° Cerberus[8] with honeyed speech,   *after I pleased*
I passed the perils of the foremost porch.
Not far from hence, amidst ten thousand souls,
Sat Minos, Aeacus, and Rhadamanth,°   *judges of the underworld*
To whom no sooner 'gan I make approach

35 To crave a passport for my wandr'ing ghost,
But Minos, in graven leaves of lottery,
Drew forth the manner of my life and death.[9]
"This knight," quoth he, "both lived and died in love,
And for his love tried fortune of the wars,

40 And by war's fortune lost both love and life."
"Why, then," said Aeacus, "convey him hence
To walk with lovers in our fields of love,
And spend the course of everlasting time
Under green myrtle trees and cypress shades."

45 "No, no," said Rhadamanth, "it were not well°   *would not be fitting*
With loving souls to place a martialist;°   *warrior*

2. My rank and parentage were inferior to my good fortune in being the lover of the high-born Bel-imperia.
3. At death, the soul was thought to leave the body by the mouth or through wounds.
4. A river in the classical underworld. The description of Hades in lines 18–85 is based loosely on Virgil's *Aeneid*, book 6.
5. That since my burial rites had not been performed.
6. That is, the sun had set three times in the sea. (Thetis is a sea nymph). The sun god drove his chariot across the sky.
7. The lake through which Aeneas entered the underworld (Virgil, *Aeneid* 6.115–295).
8. The three-headed dog who guards the gate to the underworld.
9. Minos, former king of Crete, drew forth a lottery slip meant to settle where Andrea will spend the afterlife; here the slip also gives an account of Andrea's past.

He died in war, and must to martial fields,
Where wounded Hector lives in lasting pain,
And Achilles' Myrmidons[1] do scour° the plain." range rapidly across
50 Then Minos, mildest censor° of the three, judge
Made this device to end the difference:
"Send him," quoth he, "to our infernal king,
To doom[2] him as best seems His Majesty."
To this effect my passport straight was drawn.
55 In keeping on my way to Pluto's court,
Through dreadful shades of ever-glooming night,
I saw more sights than thousand tongues can tell,
Or pens can write, or mortal hearts can think.
Three ways there were. That on the right-hand side
60 Was ready way unto the foresaid fields
Where lovers live, and bloody martialists,
But either sort contained within his° bounds. its
The left-hand path, declining fearfully,
Was ready downfall° to the deepest hell, sudden descent
65 Where bloody Furies[3] shakes° their whips of steel, shake
And poor Ixion turns an endless wheel;[4]
Where usurers[5] are choked with melting gold,
And wantons° are embraced with ugly snakes, lecherous persons
And murderers groan with never-killing wounds,
70 And perjured wights° scalded in boiling lead, people
And all foul sins with torments overwhelmed.
'Twixt these two ways, I trod the middle path,
Which brought me to the fair Elysian green,[6]
In midst whereof there stands a stately tower,
75 The walls of brass, the gates of adamant.° diamond
Here finding Pluto with his Proserpine,° queen of Hades
I showed my passport, humbled on my knee,
Whereat fair Proserpine began to smile,
And begged that only she might give my doom.° sentence
80 Pluto was pleased and sealed it with a kiss.
Forthwith, Revenge, she rounded° thee in th'ear, whispered to
And bade thee lead me through the gates of horn,
Where dreams have passage in the silent night.[7]
No sooner had she spoke but we were here—
85 I wot° not how—in twinkling of an eye. know
REVENGE Then know, Andrea, that thou art arrived
Where thou shalt see the author of thy death,

1. Followers of Achilles, the greatest of the Greek warriors at Troy, who killed Hector, the greatest among the Trojans.
2. That is, send Andrea to Pluto, king of the underworld, who will judge him.
3. The Eumenides, monstrous female personifications of vengeance.
4. Because of the ingratitude he had shown Zeus (who had purified him of blood guilt) by making sexual advances to Hera, Zeus's wife,

Ixion was bound to a fiery wheel that turned endlessly.
5. Those who lend money at interest.
6. Elysium, or the Elysian fields, in classical mythology the dwelling place of the blessed.
7. According to Virgil (Aeneid 6.893–96), spirits send dreams through one of two gates: true dreams pass through the gate of horn; false dreams, through the gate of ivory.

Don Balthazar, the Prince of Portingale,
Deprived of life by Bel-imperia.
90　Here sit we down to see the mystery,[8]
And serve for chorus in this tragedy.

[*They sit and watch the play.*]

1.2

[SCENE: *The Spanish royal court.*]

[*Enter Spanish* KING, GENERAL, CASTILE, [*and*] HIERONIMO.]

KING　Now say, Lord General, how fares our camp?°   *army (in the field)*
GENERAL　All well, my sovereign liege, except some few
　　That are deceased by fortune of the war.
KING　But what portends thy cheerful countenance,
5　And posting° to our presence thus in haste?   *speeding, hastening*
　　Speak, man, hath fortune given us victory?
GENERAL　Victory, my liege, and that with little loss.
KING　Our Portingals° will pay us tribute, then?   *Portuguese*
GENERAL　Tribute and wonted° homage therewithal.   *customary*
10　KING　Then blest be heaven, and guider of the heavens,
　　From whose fair influence such justice flows!
CASTILE　*O multum dilecte Deo, tibi militat aether,*
　　Et conjuratae curvato poplite gentes
　　Succumbunt; recti soror est victoria juris.[9]
15　KING　Thanks to my loving brother of Castile.
　　But, General, unfold in brief discourse
　　Your form of battle and your war's success,
　　That, adding all the pleasure of thy news
　　Unto the height of former happiness,
20　With deeper wage° and greater dignity   *larger reward*
　　We may reward thy blissful chivalry.°   *skill in arms*
GENERAL　Where Spain and Portingale do jointly knit
　　Their frontiers, leaning on each other's bound,°   *boundaries*
　　There met our armies in their proud array,
25　Both furnished well, both full of hope and fear,
　　Both menacing alike with daring shows,
　　Both vaunting sundry colors of device,°   *heraldic banner*
　　Both cheerly sounding trumpets, drums, and fifes,
　　Both raising dreadful clamors to the sky,
30　That° valleys, hills, and rivers made rebound,   *So that*
　　And heaven itself was frighted with the sound.
　　Our battles both were pitched in squadron form,
　　Each corner strongly fenced with wings of shot.[1]
　　But ere we joined and came to push of pike,°   *close-order combat*

---

8. Play, enigma, or puzzle with the potential of revealing a hidden truth.
9. O man much loved of God, for you the heavens fight, and the conspiring people fall on bended knee; victory is the sister of just right (Latin; adapted from Claudian, *De tertio*

consulatu Honorii, ca. 400 C.E.).
1. That is, both our armies were deployed in a square formation, each corner reinforced by armed soldiers placed on the outer edges of the formation.

35 I brought a squadron of our readiest shot
From out our rearward to begin the fight;
They° brought another wing to encounter us.   *(The Portuguese)*
Meanwhile our ordnance played° on either side,   *volleyed*
And captains strove to have their valors tried.°   *tested, challenged*
40 Don Pedro, their chief horsemen's colonel,
Did with his cornet° bravely make attempt   *cavalry company*
To break the order of our battle ranks.
But Don Rogero, worthy man of war,
Marched forth against him with our musketeers,
45 And stopped the malice of his fell° approach.   *fierce*
While they maintain hot skirmish to and fro,
Both battles° join and fall to handy° blows,   *armies / hand-to-hand*
Their violent shot resembling th'ocean's rage,
When, roaring loud and with a swelling tide,
50 It beats upon the rampiers° of huge rocks,   *ramparts*
And gapes to swallow neighbor-bounding° lands.   *Sea-bordering*
Now while Bellona° rageth here and there,   *Roman goddess of war*
Thick storms of bullets rain like winter's hail,
And shivered lances dark° the troubled air.   *darken*
55   *Pede pes et cuspide cuspis;*
                 Arma sonant armis, vir petiturque viro.[2]
On every side drop captains to the ground,
And soldiers, some ill maimed,° some slain outright;   *seriously wounded*
Here falls a body scindered° from his head,   *sundered*
60 There legs and arms lie bleeding on the grass,
Mingled with weapons and unboweled steeds,
That scattering overspread the purple° plain.   *bloodred*
In all this turmoil, three long hours and more,
The victory to neither part inclined,
65 Till Don Andrea with his brave lanciers°   *cavalry with lances*
In their main battle made so great a breach
That, half dismayed, the multitude retired;
But Balthazar, the Portingales' young prince,
Brought rescue and encouraged them to stay.
70 Herehence° the fight was eagerly renewed,   *As a result*
And in that conflict was Andrea slain—
Brave man-at-arms, but weak to° Balthazar.   *compared with*
Yet while the Prince, insulting° over him,   *exulting*
Breathed out proud vaunts, sounding to° our reproach,   *indicating*
75 Friendship and hardy valor, joined in one,
Pricked° forth Horatio, our knight marshal's son,   *Spurred*
To challenge forth that prince in single fight.
Not long between these twain the fight endured,
But straight the Prince was beaten from his horse
80 And forced to yield him° prisoner to his foe.   *himself*
When he was taken, all the rest they fled,

2. Foot against foot and lance against lance; arms clash with arms, and man is attacked by man
(Latin).

And our carbines° pursued them to the death,   *armed soldiers*
Till, Phoebus° waning to the western deep,   *the sun (god)*
Our trumpeters were charged to sound retreat.
85 KING   Thanks, good Lord General, for these good news,
And, for some argument° of more to come,   *token, sign*
Take this and wear it for thy sovereign's sake.
    [*Give him his chain.*]
But tell me now, hast thou confirmed a peace?
GENERAL   No peace, my liege, but° peace conditional,   *except*
90 That if with homage tribute be well paid
The fury of your forces will be stayed;°   *restrained*
And to this peace their viceroy hath subscribed,
    [*Give the* KING *a paper.*]
And made a solemn vow that during life
His tribute shall be truly paid to Spain.
95 KING   These words, these deeds become thy person well.—
But now, Knight Marshal, frolic° with thy king,   *celebrate*
For 'tis thy son that wins this battle's prize.
HIERONIMO   Long may he live to serve my sovereign liege,
And soon decay° unless he serve my liege!   *decline in fortune*
    [*A tucket° afar off.*]   *trumpet flourish*
100 KING   Nor° thou nor he shall die without reward.   *Neither*
What means the warning of this trumpet's sound?
GENERAL   This tells me that Your Grace's men of war—
Such as war's fortune hath reserved° from death—   *preserved*
Come marching on towards your royal seat
105 To show themselves before Your Majesty,
For so I gave in charge° at my depart;°   *I ordered / departure*
Whereby by demonstration shall appear,
That all (except three hundred or few more)
Are safe returned and by their foes enriched.°   *(with ransom fees)*
    [*The army enters;* BALTHAZAR, *between* LORENZO
    and HORATIO, *captive.*]
110 KING   A gladsome sight! I long to see them here.
    [*They enter and pass by.*]
Was that the warlike prince of Portingale
That by our nephew was in triumph led?
GENERAL   It was, my liege, the Prince of Portingale.
KING   But what was he that on the other side
115 Held him by th'arm as partner of the prize?
HIERONIMO   That was my son, my gracious sovereign,
Of whom, though from his tender infancy
My loving thoughts did never hope but well,
He never pleased his father's eyes till now,
120 Nor filled my heart with overcloying° joys.   *overabundant*
KING   Go let them march once more about these walls,
That, staying° them, we may confer and talk   *stopping*
With our brave prisoner and his double guard.—
Hieronimo, it greatly pleaseth us

125   That in our victory thou have a share,
        By virtue of thy worthy son's exploit.
                  [*Enter the army again.*]
        Bring hither the young prince of Portingale.
        The rest march on; but ere they be dismissed,
        We will bestow on every soldier
130   Two ducats,° and on every leader ten,   *gold coins*
        That they may know our largesse° welcomes them.   *bountiful gift-giving*
          [*Exeunt all the army but* BALTHAZAR, LORENZO,
            and HORATIO. *The* KING, CASTILE, *and the*
                   GENERAL *remain onstage.*]
        Welcome, Don Balthazar! Welcome, nephew!
        And thou, Horatio, thou art welcome too.
        Young prince, although thy father's hard misdeeds,
135   In keeping back the tribute that he owes,
        Deserve but evil measure at our hands,
        Yet shalt thou know that Spain is honorable.
    BALTHAZAR   The trespass that my father made in peace
        Is now controlled° by fortune of the wars,   *checked; ended*
140   And, cards once dealt, it boots not° ask why so.   *does no good to*
        His men are slain—a weakening to his realm;
        His colors° seized—a blot unto his name;   *military standards*
        His son distressed—a corsive° to his heart: *corrosive*
        These punishments may clear° his late offense.   *erase*
145 KING   Ay, Balthazar, if he observe this truce
        Our peace will grow the stronger for these wars.
        Meanwhile live thou, though not in liberty,
        Yet free from bearing any servile yoke,
        For in our hearing thy deserts were great,
150   And in our sight thyself art gracious.
    BALTHAZAR   And I shall study° to deserve this grace.   *strive*
    KING   But tell me—for their holding° makes me doubt—   *the way they hold you*
        To which of these twain art thou prisoner.
    LORENZO   To me, my liege.
    HORATIO   To me, my sovereign.
155 LORENZO   This hand first took his courser° by the reins.   *battle horse*
    HORATIO   But first my lance did put him from his horse.
    LORENZO   I seized his weapon and enjoyed° it first.   *possessed*
    HORATIO   But first I forced him lay his weapons down.
    KING   Let go his arm, upon our privilege.[3]   [*Let him go.*]
160   Say, worthy Prince, to whether° didst thou yield?   *which*
    BALTHAZAR   To him in courtesy, to this perforce.
        He spake me fair, this other gave me strokes;
        He promised life, this other threatened death;
        He wan my love, this other conquered me;
165   And truth to say I yield myself to both.[4]

---

3. That is, my royal prerogative. Monarchs customarily speak of themselves in the plural, using the so-called royal "we."
4. Balthazar explains the terms according to which he yielded to both Horatio and Lorenzo. Lorenzo was courteous, spoke gently, and won Balthazar's love. Horatio was forceful and threatening, and thus conquered Balthazar.

HIERONIMO   But° that I know Your Grace for° just and wise,   *Were it not / to be*
  And° might seem partial in this difference,°   *And that I / dispute*
  Enforced by nature° and by law of arms,   *Moved by blood ties*
  My tongue should plead for young Horatio's right.
170 He hunted well that was a lion's death,
  Not he that in a garment wore his skin;[5]
  So hares may pull dead lions by the beard.
KING   Content thee, Marshal, thou shalt have no wrong,
  And for thy sake thy son shall want° no right.—   *lack*
175 Will both abide the censure of my doom?°   *judgment*
LORENZO   I crave no better than Your Grace awards.
HORATIO   Nor I, although I sit beside my right.[6]
KING   Then by my judgment thus your strife shall end:
  You both deserve and both shall have reward.
180 Nephew, thou took'st his weapon and his horse;
  His weapons and his horse are thy reward.
  Horatio, thou didst force him first to yield;
  His ransom therefore is thy valor's fee.
  Appoint the sum as you shall both agree.
185 But, nephew, thou shalt have the Prince in guard,°   *your custody*
  For thine estate° best fitteth such a guest;   *social rank*
  Horatio's house were small for all his train.°   *retinue*
  Yet in regard thy substance° passeth his,   *because your wealth*
  And that just guerdon may befall desert,[7]
190 To him° we yield the armor of the Prince.   *(Horatio)*
  How likes Don Balthazar of this device?
BALTHAZAR   Right well, my liege, if this proviso were,
  That Don Horatio bear us company,
  Whom I admire and love for chivalry.
195 KING   Horatio, leave him not that loves thee so.
  Now let us hence to see our soldiers paid,
  And feast our prisoner as our friendly guest.   [*Exeunt.°*]   *They exit (Latin)*

1.3

[SCENE: *The Portuguese royal court.*]

   [*Enter* VICEROY, ALEXANDRO, VILLUPPO, *and attendants.*]

VICEROY   Is our ambassador dispatched for Spain?
ALEXANDRO   Two days, my liege, are passed since his depart.
VICEROY   And tribute payment gone along with him?
ALEXANDRO   Ay, my good lord.
5 VICEROY   Then rest we here awhile in our unrest,
  And feed our sorrows with some inward sighs,
  For deepest cares break never into tears.
  But wherefore sit I in a regal throne?

---

5. That is, the real hero is the man who kills
the lion, not the one who wears the lion's hide
(a reference to Aesop's fable "The Ass in the
Lion's Skin").

6. Neither do I, even if I must forgo my just
rewards.
7. And so that merit is rewarded.

This better fits a wretch's endless moan.

[*Falls to the ground.*]

10   Yet this is higher than my fortunes reach,[8]
And therefore better than my state° deserves.   condition, situation
Ay, ay, this earth, image of melancholy,[9]
Seeks him whom fates adjudge to misery.
Here let me lie, now am I at the lowest.
15   *Qui jacet in terra non habet unde cadat.*
                In me consumpsit vires fortuna nocendo,
                Nil superest ut iam possit obesse magis.[1]
Yes, Fortune may bereave me of my crown.
Here, take it now! Let Fortune do her worst.

[*He takes off his crown.*]

20   She will not rob me of this sable weed;°   black mourning garment
Oh, no, she envies° none but pleasant things.   feels ill will toward
Such is the folly of despiteful° chance!   spiteful
Fortune is blind and sees not my deserts;
So is she deaf and hears not my laments;
25   And could she hear, yet is she willful mad,
And therefore will not pity my distress.
Suppose that she could pity me, what then?
What help can be expected at her hands,
Whose foot is standing on a rolling stone,
30   And mind more mutable than fickle winds?
Why wail I, then, where's hope of no redress?
Oh, yes, complaining makes my grief seem less.
My late ambition hath distained my faith;[2]
My breach of faith occasioned bloody wars;
35   Those bloody wars have spent my treasure,
And with my treasure my people's blood,
And with their blood, my joy and best beloved,
My best beloved, my sweet and only son.
Oh, wherefore went I not to war myself?
40   The cause was mine; I might have died for both.°   (myself and Balthazar)
My years were mellow, his but young and green;
My death were° natural, but his was forced.   would have been
ALEXANDRO   No° doubt, my liege, but° still the Prince survives.   There's no / but that
VICEROY   Survives? Ay, where?
45 ALEXANDRO   In Spain, a prisoner by mischance of war.

8. My circumstances are even worse than can
be symbolized by my being on the ground.
9. A reference to the humoral theory that
dominated early modern accounts of human
emotion. Imbalances among the four humors,
or bodily fluids, were believed to determine
personality. An excess of black bile, a cold,
dry substance in the body corresponding to
the earth, made people melancholic; blood
and air were associated with the sanguine,
yellow bile; fire with the choleric; and phlegm

and water a with the phlegmatic.
1. He who lies on the ground has no further to
fall. In me, Fortune has exhausted her power
to injure; nothing now remains that can harm
me anymore (Latin; the first line quotes Ala-
nus de Insulis, a medieval French theologian;
the second echoes line 698 of the Roman play
Agamemnon by Seneca; the third is Kyd's own
invention).
2. My recent ambition (to conquer Spain) has
sullied my honor.

VICEROY   Then they have slain him for his father's fault.

ALEXANDRO   That were a breach to common law of arms.

VICEROY   They reck° no laws that° meditate revenge.   *heed / who*

ALEXANDRO   His ransom's worth will stay° from foul revenge.   *restrain (his captors)*

50 VICEROY   No, if he lived the news would soon be here.

ALEXANDRO   Nay, evil news fly faster still° than good.   *always*

VICEROY   Tell me no more of news, for he is dead.

VILLUPPO   [*kneeling*] My sovereign, pardon the author of ill news,
   And I'll bewray° the fortune of thy son.   *reveal*

55 VICEROY   Speak on; I'll guerdon° thee whate'er it be.   *reward*
   Mine ear is ready to receive ill news,
   My heart grown hard 'gainst mischief's battery.°   *assault*
   Stand up, I say, and tell thy tale at large.°   *at length*

VILLUPPO   [*standing*] Then hear that truth which these mine
      eyes have seen.

60 When both the armies were in battle joined,
   Don Balthazar, amidst the thickest troops,
   To win renown did wondrous feats of arms.
   Amongst the rest I saw him hand to hand
   In single fight with their lord general;

65 Till Alexandro, that here counterfeits
   Under the color of° a duteous friend,   *pretense of being*
   Discharged his pistol at the Prince's back,
   As though he would have slain their general;
   But therewithal Don Balthazar fell down,

70 And when he fell then we began to fly;
   But had he lived the day had sure been ours.

ALEXANDRO   Oh, wicked forgery!° O traitorous miscreant!   *falsehood*

VICEROY   Hold thou thy peace!—But now, Villuppo, say,
   Where then became° the carcass of my son?   *What then happened to*

75 VILLUPPO   I saw them drag it to the Spanish tents.

VICEROY   Ay, ay, my nightly dreams have told me this.—
   Thou false, unkind,° unthankful traitorous beast,   *unnatural*
   Wherein had Balthazar offended thee,
   That thou shouldst thus betray him to our foes?

80 Was't Spanish gold that bleared° so thine eyes   *dazzled*
   That thou couldst see no part of our deserts?
   Perchance because thou art Terceira's° lord,   *(an island in the Azores)*
   Thou hadst some hope to wear this diadem
   If first my son and then myself were slain;

85 But thy ambitious thought shall break thy neck.
   Ay, this was it that made thee spill his blood,
         [*Take the crown and put it on again.*]
   But I'll now wear it till thy blood be spilt.

ALEXANDRO   Vouchsafe, dread sovereign, to hear me speak.

VICEROY   Away with him! His sight is second hell.

90 Keep him till we determine of his death.
         [*Exeunt attendants, guarding* ALEXANDRO.]
   If Balthazar be dead, he° shall not live.   *(Alexandro)*
   villuppo, follow us for thy reward.   [*Exit* VICEROY.]

VILLUPPO   Thus have I with an envious forged° tale   *fabricated*
     Deceived the King, betrayed mine enemy,
95   And hope for guerdon of my villainy.   [*Exit.*]

1.4

[SCENE: *The Spanish royal court.*]

[*Enter* HORATIO *and* BEL-IMPERIA.]

BEL-IMPERIA   Signor Horatio, this is the place and hour
     Wherein I must entreat thee to relate
     The circumstance of Don Andrea's death,
     Who, living, was my garland's sweetest flower,
5   And in his death hath buried my delights.
HORATIO   For love of him and service to yourself,
     I nill° refuse this heavy, doleful charge.   *will not*
     Yet tears and sighs, I fear, will hinder me.
     When both our armies were enjoined° in fight,   *joined*
10   Your worthy chevalier amidst the thick'st,
     For glorious cause still aiming at the fairest,[3]
     Was at the last by young Don Balthazar
     Encountered hand to hand. Their fight was long,
     Their hearts were great, their clamors menacing,
15   Their strength alike, their strokes both dangerous.
     But wrathful Nemesis,[4] that wicked power,
     Envying at Andrea's praise and worth,
     Cut short his life to end his praise and worth.
     She, she herself, disguised in armor's mask
20   (As Pallas was before proud Pergamus),[5]
     Brought in a fresh supply of halberdiers,°   *soldiers with pikes*
     Which paunched° his horse and dinged° him to the ground.   *stabbed / thrust*
     Then young Don Balthazar, with ruthless° rage,   *pitiless*
     Taking advantage of his foe's distress,
25   Did finish what his halberdiers begun,
     And left° not till Andrea's life was done.   *ceased*
     Then, though too late, incensed with just remorse,°   *indignation, pity*
     I with my band set forth against the Prince,
     And brought him prisoner from his halberdiers.
30 BEL-IMPERIA   Would thou hadst slain him that so slew my love!
     But then was Don Andrea's carcass lost?
HORATIO   No, that was it for which I chiefly strove,
     Nor stepped I back till I recovered him.
     I took him up and wound him in mine arms,
35   And, wielding° him unto my private tent,   *carrying*
     There laid him down and dewed him with my tears,

3. That is, continually striving to excel in order to be worthy of Bel-imperia.
4. Greek goddess of divine retribution.
5. Pallas Athena, Greek goddess of wisdom and warfare, fought on the side of the Greeks at Troy (sometimes called by poets Pergamon, the name of its citadel).

And sighed and sorrowed as became a friend.
But neither friendly sorrow, sighs, nor tears
Could win pale Death from his° usurped right.   (Death's)
40   Yet this I did, and less I could not do:
I saw him honored with due funeral.
This scarf I plucked from off his lifeless arm,
And wear it in remembrance of my friend.

BEL-IMPERIA   I know the scarf; would he had kept it still!
45   For had he lived he would have kept it still,
And worn it for his Bel-imperia's sake,
For 'twas my favor° at his last depart.   love token
But now wear thou it both for him and me,
For after him thou hast deserved it best.
50   But, for thy kindness in his life and death,
Be sure, while Bel-imperia's life endures,
She will be Don Horatio's thankful friend.

HORATIO   And, madam, Don Horatio will not slack°   fail in duty
Humbly to serve fair Bel-imperia.
55   But now if your good liking stand thereto,°   if you approve
I'll crave your pardon to go seek the Prince,
For so the Duke your father gave me charge. [Exit.]

BEL-IMPERIA   Ay, go, Horatio, leave me here alone,
For solitude best fits my cheerless mood.
60   Yet what avails to wail Andrea's death,
From whence Horatio proves my second love?
Had he not loved Andrea as he did,
He could not sit in Bel-imperia's thoughts.
But how can love find harbor in my breast
65   Till I revenge the death of my beloved?
Yes, second love shall further my revenge.
I'll love Horatio, my Andrea's friend,
The more to spite the Prince that wrought his end;
And where Don Balthazar, that slew my love,
70   Himself now pleads for favor at my hands,
He shall, in rigor of my just disdain,
Reap long repentance for his murderous deed.
For what was't else but murderous cowardice,
So many to oppress one valiant knight
75   Without respect of honor in the fight?
And here he comes that murdered my delight.

[Enter LORENZO and BALTHAZAR.]

LORENZO   Sister, what means this melancholy walk?
BEL-IMPERIA   That for awhile I wish no company.
LORENZO   But here the Prince is come to visit you.
80   BEL-IMPERIA   That argues that he lives in liberty.
BALTHAZAR   No, madam, but in pleasing servitude.°   service to a lady
BEL-IMPERIA   Your prison then belike is your conceit.[6]

6. Your prison, then, is perhaps only a figment of your imagination.

BALTHAZAR Ay, by conceit my freedom is enthralled.[7]

BEL-IMPERIA Then with conceit enlarge° yourself again.   *free*

85 BALTHAZAR What if conceit have laid my heart to gage?[8]

BEL-IMPERIA Pay that° you borrowed and recover it.°   *what / (your heart)*

BALTHAZAR I die if it return from whence it lies.

BEL-IMPERIA A heartless man and live? A miracle!

BALTHAZAR Ay, lady, love can work such miracles.

90 LORENZO Tush, tush, my lord, let go these ambages,°   *circumlocutions*

And in plain terms acquaint her with your love.

BEL-IMPERIA What boots° complaint, when there's no remedy?   *is the use of*

BALTHAZAR Yes, to your gracious self must I complain,

In whose fair answer lies my remedy,

95 On whose perfection all my thoughts attend,

On whose aspect° mine eyes find beauty's bower,   *appearance*

In whose translucent breast my heart is lodged.

BEL-IMPERIA Alas, my lord, these are but words of course,°   *conventional phrases*

And but device° to drive me from this place.   *merely a way*

[*She, in going in, lets fall her glove, which* HORATIO,
coming out,° takes up.]   *entering onstage*

100 HORATIO Madam, your glove.

BEL-IMPERIA Thanks, good Horatio. Take it for thy pains.

[*Exit, leaving the glove with him.*]

BALTHAZAR Signor Horatio stooped in happy time.°   *opportunely*

HORATIO I reaped more grace than I deserved or hoped.

LORENZO [*to* BALTHAZAR] My lord, be not dismayed for what is passed.

105 You know that women oft are humorous.°   *temperamental*

These clouds will overblow with little wind;

Let me alone,° I'll scatter them myself.   *Leave it to me*

Meanwhile let us devise to spend the time

In some delightful sports and reveling.

110 HORATIO The King, my lords, is coming hither straight,°   *immediately*

To feast the Portingale ambassador;

Things were in readiness before I came.

BALTHAZAR Then here it fits° us to attend the King,   *befits*

To welcome hither our ambassador,

115 And learn my father° and my country's health.   *father's*

[*Enter the banquet,° trumpets,° the* KING,   *tables and food / trumpeters*
CASTILE, *and* AMBASSADOR.]

KING See, Lord Ambassador, how Spain entreats°   *treats*

Their prisoner Balthazar, thy viceroy's son.

We pleasure° more in kindness than in wars.   *take pleasure*

AMBASSADOR Sad is our king, and Portingale laments,

120 Supposing that Don Balthazar is slain.

BALTHAZAR So am I slain, by beauty's tyranny.

You see, my lord, how Balthazar is slain:

I frolic with the Duke of Castile's son,

Wrapped every hour in pleasures of the court,

---

7. Yes, a fancy of being enthralled and imprisoned (by your beauty).

8. But what if, in my fancy, I have pledged my heart?

125 And graced with favors of His Majesty.
    KING   Put off your greetings till our feast be done.
    Now come and sit with us and taste our cheer.
        [*Sit to the banquet.*]
    Sit down, young Prince, you are our second guest.
    Brother, sit down, and, nephew, take your place.
130 Signor Horatio, wait thou upon our cup,°   *serve as cupbearer*
    For well thou hast deserved to be honored.
    Now, lordings,° fall to. Spain is Portugal,   *lords*
    And Portugal is Spain; we both are friends,
    Tribute is paid, and we enjoy our right.
135 But where is old Hieronimo, our marshal?
    He promised us, in honor of our guest,
    To grace our banquet with some pompous jest.°   *elaborate display*
        [*Enter* HIERONIMO *with a drum, three knights, each his*
        scutcheon. Then he fetches three kings; they take their
        crowns and them captive.[9]]
    Hieronimo, this masque contents mine eye,
    Although I sound° not well the mystery.   *understand*
140 HIERONIMO   The first armed knight that hung his scutcheon up
        [*He takes the scutcheon and gives it to the* KING.]
    Was English Robert, Earl of Gloucester,
    Who, when King Stephen° bore sway in Albion,°   *r. 1135–54 / England*
    Arrived with five-and-twenty thousand men
    In Portingale, and by success of war
145 Enforced the King, then but a Saracen,°   *Muslim; Arab*
    To bear the yoke of English monarchy.[1]
    KING   My lord of Portingale, by this you see
    That which may comfort both your king and you,
    And make your late discomfort seem the less.—
150 But say, Hieronimo, what was the next?
    HIERONIMO   The second knight that hung his scutcheon up
        [*He doth as he did before.*]
    Was Edmund, Earl of Kent in Albion,
    When English Richard° wore the diadem.   *Richard II (r. 1377–99)*
    He came likewise and razed Lisbon walls,
155 And took the King of Portingale in fight,
    For which, and other suchlike service done,
    He after was created Duke of York.
    KING   This is another special° argument   *appropriate, pertinent*
    That Portingale may deign to bear our yoke,
160 When it by little England hath been yoked.
    But now, Hieronimo, what were the last?

---

9. In this dumb show, the knights, representing England, capture and dethrone the three Iberian kings—a pro-English display. *Drum:* drummer. *Each:* each (with). *Scutcheon:* heraldic shield.

1. While it is true that Portugal, like Spain, became part of a Muslim state in the 8th century (the reconquests occurred in the 12th and 15th centuries, respectively), Hieronimo's (or Kyd's) assertion that the English invaded Portugal during this period is fanciful.

HIERONIMO   The third and last, not least in our account,
  [*Doing as before.*]
 Was, as the rest, a valiant Englishman,
 Brave John of Gaunt, the Duke of Lancaster,
165 As by his scutcheon plainly may appear.
 He with a puissant° army came to Spain,   *powerful*
 And took our King of Castile prisoner.
AMBASSADOR   This is an argument for our viceroy
 That Spain may not insult for° her success,   *exult in*
170 Since English warriors likewise conquered Spain
 And made them bow their knees to Albion.
KING   Hieronimo, I drink to thee for this device,°   *show, masque*
 Which hath pleased both the ambassador and me.
 Pledge me,° Hieronimo, if thou love thy king.   *Drink to me*
  [*Takes the cup of*° HORATIO.]   *from*
175 [*To the* AMBASSADOR] My lord, I fear we sit but overlong,
 Unless our dainties were more delicate;²
 But welcome are you to the best we have.
 Now let us in, that you may be dispatched;
 I think our council is already set.³ [*Exeunt omnes.*°] *All exit (Latin)*

1.5

[SCENE: *The chorus figures remain onstage.*]

ANDREA   Come we for this from depth of underground
 To see him feast that gave me my death's wound?
 These pleasant sights are sorrow to my soul—
 Nothing but league, and love, and banqueting!
5 REVENGE   Be still, Andrea. Ere we go from hence
 I'll turn their friendship into fell° despite,   *fierce, cruel*
 Their love to mortal° hate, their day to night,   *deadly*
 Their hope into despair, their peace to war,
 Their joys to pain, their bliss to misery.

2.1

[SCENE: CASTILE'S *palace*; LORENZO'S *apartments.*]
 [*Enter* LORENZO *and* BALTHAZAR.]
LORENZO   My lord, though Bel-imperia seem thus coy,
 Let reason hold you in your wonted° joy.   *accustomed*
 In time the savage bull sustains° the yoke,   *accepts*
 In time all haggard° hawks will stoop to lure,   *wild, untrained*
5 In time small wedges cleave the hardest oak,
 In time the flint is pierced with softest shower,
 And she in time will fall from her disdain

---

2. Unless we were able to provide you with
more delicate fare.

3. Our council is already in session to negotiate terms of peace.

And rue the sufferance of your friendly pain.[4]

BALTHAZAR   No, she is wilder and more hard withal

10   Than beast, or bird, or tree, or stony wall.
        But wherefore blot° I Bel-imperia's name?   *tarnish*
        It is my fault, not she, that merits blame.
        My feature° is not° to content her sight;   *appearance / not able*
        My words are rude and work her no delight.
15   The lines I send her are but harsh and ill,
        Such as do drop from Pan and Marsyas' quill.[5]
        My presents are not of sufficient cost,
        And, being worthless, all my labor's lost.
        Yet might she love me for my valiancy;
20   Ay, but that's slandered° by captivity.   *discredited*
        Yet might she love me to content her sire;
        Ay, but her reason masters his desire.
        Yet might she love me as her brother's friend;
        Ay, but her hopes aim at some other end.
25   Yet might she love me to uprear her state;°   *social status*
        Ay, but perhaps she hopes some nobler mate.
        Yet might she love me as her beauty's thrall;[6]
        Ay, but I fear she cannot love at all.

LORENZO   My lord, for my sake leave these ecstasies,°   *passions*
30   And doubt not but we'll find some remedy.
        Some cause there is that lets you not be loved;°   *hinders your being loved*
        First that must needs be known and then removed.
        What if my sister love some other knight?

BALTHAZAR   My summer's day will turn to winter's night.

35 LORENZO   I have already found a stratagem
        To sound the bottom° of this doubtful theme.   *plumb*
        My lord, for once° you shall be ruled by me;   *on this occasion*
        Hinder me not, whate'er you hear or see.
        By force or fair means will I cast about
40   To find the truth of all this question out.—
        Ho, Pedringano!

PEDRINGANO   [*from offstage*] Signor?

LORENZO   *Vien qui presto.*[7]

        [*Enter* PEDRINGANO.]

PEDRINGANO   Hath Your Lordship any service to command me?

LORENZO   Ay, Pedringano, service of import.
        And, not to spend the time in trifling words,
45   Thus stands the case: it is not long, thou know'st,
        Since I did shield thee from my father's wrath
        For thy conveyance° in Andrea's love,   *secret contrivance*

4. And pity the pain you endure in loving her.
5. Both Pan, the Greek god of pastures and wild places (and inventor of the panpipe) and the flute player Marsyas unsuccessfully challenged the god Apollo to musical contests;

Marsyas was flayed alive. The quill here is both a pen for writing and a plectrum for plucking a musical instrument.
6. As one enthralled by her beauty.
7. Come here quickly (Italian).

For which thou wert adjudged to punishment.
I stood betwixt thee and thy punishment;
50 And since,° thou knowest how I have favored thee.   *since then*
Now to these favors will I add reward,
Not with fair words, but store° of golden coin,   *abundance*
And lands and living° joined with dignities,°   *property / paying offices*
If thou but satisfy my just demand.°   *answer my question*
55 Tell truth and have me for thy lasting friend.

PEDRINGANO   Whate'er it be Your Lordship shall demand,
My bounden duty bids me tell the truth,
If case it lie in me° to tell the truth.   *I am able*

LORENZO   Then, Pedringano, this is my demand:
60 Whom loves my sister Bel-imperia?
For she reposeth all her trust in thee.
Speak, man, and gain both friendship and reward.
I mean, whom loves she in Andrea's place?

PEDRINGANO   Alas, my lord, since Don Andrea's death
65 I have no credit with° her as before,   *am no longer trusted by*
And therefore know not if she love or no.

LORENZO   [*drawing his sword*] Nay, if thou dally, then I am thy foe,
And fear shall force what friendship cannot win.
Thy death shall bury what thy life conceals.
70 Thou diest for more esteeming her than me.

PEDRINGANO   Oh, stay,° my lord!   *wait*

LORENZO   Yet speak the truth and I will guerdon thee,
And shield thee from whatever can ensue,
And will conceal whate'er proceeds from thee;
75 But if thou dally once again, thou diest.

PEDRINGANO   If Madam Bel-imperia be in love—

LORENZO   What, villain, ifs and ands?
         [*He threatens* PEDRINGANO.]

PEDRINGANO   Oh, stay, my lord! She loves Horatio.
         [BALTHAZAR *starts back.*]

LORENZO   What, Don Horatio, our knight marshal's son?
80 PEDRINGANO   Even him, my lord.

LORENZO   Now say but how° knowest thou he is her love,   *only say how*
And thou shalt find me kind and liberal.°   *generous*
Stand up, I say, and fearless tell the truth.

PEDRINGANO   She sent him letters which myself perused,
85 Full fraught° with lines and arguments of love,   *Fully laden*
Preferring him before Prince Balthazar.

LORENZO   Swear on this cross° that what thou sayest is true,   *(sword hilt)*
And that thou wilt conceal what thou hast told.

PEDRINGANO   I swear to both, by Him that made us all.

90 LORENZO   In hope thine oath is true, here's thy reward;
         [*He gives money.*]
But if I prove thee perjured and unjust,°   *dishonest*
This very sword whereon thou took'st thine oath
Shall be the worker of thy tragedy.

PEDRINGANO   What I have said is true, and shall for me°   *for my part*
95   Be still° concealed from Bel-imperia.   *always*
        Besides, Your Honor's liberality
        Deserves my duteous service, even till death.
    LORENZO   Let this be all that thou shalt do for me:
        Be watchful when, and where, these lovers meet,
100   And give me notice in some secret sort.°   *means, manner*
    PEDRINGANO   I will, my lord.
    LORENZO   Then shalt thou find that I am liberal.
        Thou know'st that I can more advance thy state
        Than she; be therefore wise and fail me not.
105   Go and attend her as thy custom is,
        Lest absence make her think thou dost amiss.
                                    [*Exit* PEDRINGANO.]
        Why so: *Tam armis quam ingenio;*[8]
        Where words prevail not, violence prevails,
        But gold doth more than either of them both.
110   How likes Prince Balthazar this stratagem?
    BALTHAZAR   Both well and ill. It makes me glad and sad:
        Glad, that I know the hinderer of my love,
        Sad, that I fear she hates me whom I love;
        Glad, that I know on whom to be revenged,
115   Sad, that she'll fly me if I take revenge.
        Yet must I take revenge or die myself,
        For love resisted grows impatient.
        I think Horatio be my destined plague!
        First in his hand he brandishèd a sword,
120   And with that sword he fiercely wagèd war,
        And in that war he gave me dangerous wounds,
        And by those wounds he forcèd me to yield,
        And by my yielding I became his slave.
        Now in his mouth he carries pleasing words,
125   Which pleasing words do harbor sweet conceits,°   *figures of speech*
        Which sweet conceits are limed[9] with sly deceits,
        Which sly deceits smooth° Bel-imperia's ears,   *flatter*
        And through her ears dive down into her heart,
        And in her heart set him where I should stand.
130   Thus hath he ta'en my body by his force,
        And now by sleight° would captivate my soul;   *cunning*
        But in his fall I'll tempt the Destinies,[1]
        And either lose my life or win my love.
    LORENZO   Let's go, my lord; your staying stays° revenge.   *hinders*
135   Do you but follow me and gain your love;
        Her favor must be won by his remove.°   [*Exeunt.*]   *removal (by death)*

---

8. As much by force as by guile (Latin).
9. Made into traps (like branches coated with sticky lime to snare birds).

1. To bring about his downfall, I'll tempt the Fates.

2.2

[SCENE: *Scene continues.*]

[*Enter* HORATIO *and* BEL-IMPERIA.]

HORATIO   Now, madam, since by favor of your love
    Our hidden smoke is turned to open flame,
    And that° with looks and words we feed our thoughts   *since*
    (Two chief contents,° where more cannot be had),   *sources of contentment*
5   Thus in the midst of love's fair blandishments°   *flatteries*
    Why show you sign of inward languishments?°   *feebleness*

      [*Entering above,*° PEDRINGANO *showeth all*   *onto upper acting area*
      to the PRINCE *and* LORENZO, *placing them in secret.*]

BEL-IMPERIA   My heart, sweet friend, is like a ship at sea:
    She wisheth port, where, riding all at ease,
    She may repair what stormy times have worn,
10 And, leaning on the shore, may sing with joy
    That pleasure follows pain, and bliss annoy.°   *bliss (follows) sorrow*
    Possession of thy love is th'only port
    Wherein my heart, with fears and hopes long tossed,
    Each hour doth wish and long to make resort,
15 There to repair° the joys that it hath lost,   *restore*
    And, sitting safe, to sing in Cupid's° quire°   *Roman god of love / choir*
    That sweetest bliss is° crown of love's desire.   *which is*
BALTHAZAR [*above*]   Oh, sleep, mine eyes! See not my love profaned.
    Be deaf, my ears! Hear not my discontent.
20 Die, heart! Another joys° what thou deservest.   *enjoys*
LORENZO [*aside*]   Watch still, mine eyes, to see this love disjoined;
    Hear still, mine ears, to hear them both lament;
    Live, heart, to joy at fond° Horatio's fall.   *foolish, besotted*
BEL-IMPERIA   Why stands Horatio speechless all this while?
25 HORATIO   The less I speak, the more I meditate.
BEL-IMPERIA   But whereon dost thou chiefly meditate?
HORATIO   On dangers past and pleasures to ensue.
BALTHAZAR [*aside*]   On pleasures past and dangers to ensue.
BEL-IMPERIA   What dangers and what pleasures dost thou mean?
30 HORATIO   Dangers of war, and pleasures of our love.
LORENZO [*aside*]   Dangers of death, but pleasures none at all.
BEL-IMPERIA   Let dangers go. Thy war shall be with me,
    But such a war as breaks no bond of peace.
    Speak thou fair words, I'll cross them with fair words;
35 Send thou sweet looks, I'll meet them with sweet looks;
    Write loving lines, I'll answer loving lines;
    Give me a kiss, I'll countercheck thy kiss.
    Be this our warring peace, or peaceful war.
HORATIO   But, gracious madam, then appoint the field
40 Where trial of this war shall first be made.
BALTHAZAR [*aside*]   Ambitious villain, how his boldness grows!
BEL-IMPERIA   Then be thy father's pleasant bower° the field,   *arbor*
    Where first we vowed a mutual amity;
    The court were° dangerous, that place is safe.   *would be*

45 Our hour shall be when Vesper° 'gins to rise,   *the evening star (Venus)*
    That summons home distressful travelers.°   *weary laborers*
    There none shall hear us but the harmless birds;
    Happily° the gentle nightingale   *Perhaps*
    Shall carol us asleep ere we be ware,°   *aware*
50 And, singing with the prickle at her breast,[2]
    Tell° our delight and mirthful dalliance.   *sing of*
    Till then each hour will seem a year and more.
  HORATIO   But, honey-sweet and honorable love,
    Return we now into your father's sight;
55 Dangerous suspicion waits on° our delight.   *attends, follows*
  LORENZO [*aside*]   Ay, danger mixed with jealous° despite   *jealous*
    Shall send thy soul into eternal night.   [*Exeunt.*]

2.3

[SCENE: *The Spanish royal court.*]

[*Enter* KING *of Spain, Portingale* AMBASSADOR, *Don Cyprian*
(Duke of CASTILE), *attendants, etc.*]

  KING   Brother of Castile, to the Prince's love
    What says your daughter Bel-imperia?
  CASTILE   Although she coy it as becomes her kind,
    And yet dissemble that she loves the Prince,[3]
5 I doubt not, I, but she will stoop in time.[4]
    And were she froward,° which she will not be,   *stubborn, perverse*
    Yet herein shall she follow my advice,
    Which is to love him or forgo my love.
  KING   Then, Lord Ambassador of Portingale,
10 Advise thy king to make this marriage up,
    For strengthening of our late-confirmèd league;
    I know no better means to make us friends.
    Her dowry shall be large and liberal:
    Besides that she is daughter and half heir
15 Unto our brother here, Don Cyprian,
    And shall enjoy the moiety° of his land,   *half*
    I'll grace her marriage with an uncle's gift,
    And this it is: in case the match go forward,
    The tribute which you pay shall be released,
20 And if by Balthazar she have a son,
    He shall enjoy the kingdom after us.
  AMBASSADOR   I'll make the motion° to my sovereign liege,   *proposal*
    And work it if my counsel may prevail.
  KING   Do so, my lord, and, if he give consent,
25 I hope his presence here will honor us

2. In Greek mythology, the nightingale was originally a woman, Procne, whose husband raped and cut out the tongue of her sister; in revenge, she fed him their son, and in mourning she sings and leans her breast against a thorn.

3. Although she feigns disinterest as it is a woman's nature to do and does not admit that she loves Balthazar.

4. Eventually, she will become obedient. "Stoop" is a term from falconry (see 2.1.4).

In celebration of the nuptial day;
And let himself determine of the time.
AMBASSADOR   Will't please Your Grace command me aught beside?
KING   Commend me to the King, and so farewell.
30   But where's Prince Balthazar, to take his leave?
AMBASSADOR   That is performed already, my good lord.
KING   Amongst the rest of what you have in charge,
   The Prince's ransom must not be forgot;
   That's none of mine, but his that took him prisoner,
35   And well his forwardness° deserves reward.   zeal
   It was Horatio, our knight marshal's son.
AMBASSADOR   Between us there's a price already pitched,°   agreed on
   And shall be sent with all convenient speed.
KING   Then once again farewell, my lord.
40   AMBASSADOR   Farewell, my lord of Castile and the rest. [*Exit.*]
KING   Now, brother, you must take some little pains
   To win fair Bel-imperia from her will;°   willfulness
   Young virgins must be rulèd by their friends.°   kinfolk
   The Prince is amiable and loves her well;
45   If she neglect him and forgo his love
   She both will wrong her own estate and ours.
   Therefore, whiles I do entertain the Prince
   With greatest pleasure that our court affords,
   Endeavor you to win your daughter's thought;
50   If she give back,° all this will come to naught. [*Exeunt.*]   refuse

2.4

[SCENE: *The bower in* HIERONIMO'S *garden.*]

[*Enter* HORATIO, BEL-IMPERIA, *and* PEDRINGANO.]

HORATIO   Now that the night begins with sable wings
   To overcloud the brightness of the sun,
   And that in darkness pleasures may be done,
   Come, Bel-imperia, let us to the bower,
5   And there in safety pass a pleasant hour.
BEL-IMPERIA   I follow thee, my love, and will not back,
   Although my fainting heart controls° my soul.   masters, oppresses
HORATIO   Why, make you doubt of Pedringano's faith?
BEL-IMPERIA   No, he is as trusty as my second self.—
10   Go, Pedringano, watch without° the gate,   outside
   And let us know if any make approach.
PEDRINGANO [*aside*]   Instead of watching I'll deserve more gold
   By fetching Don Lorenzo to this match. [*Exit* PEDRINGANO.]
HORATIO   What means my love?
BEL-IMPERIA   I know not what, myself;
15   And yet my heart foretells me some mischance.
HORATIO   Sweet, say not so; fair Fortune is our friend,
   And heavens have shut up day to pleasure us.
   The stars, thou see'st, hold back their twinkling shine,
   And Luna° hides herself to pleasure us.   the moon

20 BEL-IMPERIA Thou hast prevailed; I'll conquer my misdoubt,
  And in thy love and counsel drown my fear.
  I fear no more; love now is all my thoughts.
  Why sit we not? For pleasure asketh ease.
HORATIO The more thou sit'st within these leafy bowers,
25 The more will Flora° deck it with her flowers.   *goddess of flowers*
BEL-IMPERIA Ay, but if Flora spy Horatio here,
  Her jealous eye will think I sit too near.
HORATIO Hark, madam, how the birds record° by night,   *sing*
  For joy that Bel-imperia sits in sight.
30 BEL-IMPERIA No, Cupid counterfeits the nightingale,
  To frame° sweet music to Horatio's tale.   *compose, arrange*
HORATIO If Cupid sing, then Venus[5] is not far.
  Ay, thou art Venus, or some fairer star.
BEL-IMPERIA If I be Venus, thou must needs be Mars,[6]
35 And where Mars reigneth there must needs be wars.
HORATIO Then thus begin our wars: put forth thy hand,
  That it may combat with my ruder° hand.   *rougher, coarser*
BEL-IMPERIA Set forth thy foot to try the push of mine.
HORATIO But first my looks shall combat against thine.
40 BEL-IMPERIA Then ward° thyself. I dart this kiss at thee.   *guard*
HORATIO Thus I retort the dart thou threw'st at me.
      [*They kiss.*]
BEL-IMPERIA Nay, then, to gain the glory of the field,
  My twining arms shall yoke and make thee yield.
HORATIO Nay, then, my arms are large and strong withal;°   *as well*
45 Thus elms by vines are compassed° till they fall.   *encircled*
BEL-IMPERIA Oh, let me go! For in my troubled eyes
  Now mayst thou read that life in passion dies.
HORATIO Oh, stay awhile and I will die with thee;[7]
  So shalt thou yield, and yet have conquered me.
50 BEL-IMPERIA Who's there? Pedringano? We are betrayed!
      [*Enter* LORENZO, BALTHAZAR, SERBERINE, *and*
      PEDRINGANO, *disguised.*]
LORENZO [*to* BALTHAZAR] My lord, away with her! Take her aside.
  [*To* HORATIO] Oh, sir, forbear, your valor is already tried.°   *tested*
  [*To* SERBERINE *and* PEDRINGANO] Quickly dispatch,
      my masters.° [*They hang him in the arbor.*]   *my good sirs*
HORATIO What, will you murder me?
55 LORENZO Ay, thus, and thus! These are the fruits of love.
      [*They stab him.*]
BEL-IMPERIA Oh, save his life and let me die for him!
  Oh, save him, brother, save him, Balthazar!
  I loved Horatio, but he loved not me.

---

5. Roman goddess of love and Cupid's mother.
6. Roman god of war and Venus's lover. (Vulcan was her husband).
7. This exchange puns on a meaning of "die" common in Kyd's time, "come to orgasm."

BALTHAZAR   But Balthazar loves Bel-imperia.

60 LORENZO   Although his life were still ambitious proud,
　　Yet is he at the highest[8] now he is dead.

BEL-IMPERIA   Murder, murder! Help, Hieronimo, help!

LORENZO   Come, stop her mouth. Away with her!

　　　　　　[*Exeunt forcibly taking off* BEL-IMPERIA. HORATIO's
　　　　　　　body remains hanging in the arbor.]

2.5

[SCENE: *Scene continues.*]

　　　　　　[*Enter* HIERONIMO *in his shirt,*° *etc.*]　　　　　　　　　*nightshirt*

HIERONIMO   What outcries pluck me from my naked bed,
　　And chill my throbbing heart with trembling fear,
　　Which never danger yet could daunt before?
　　Who calls Hieronimo? Speak, here I am.
5　　I did not slumber, therefore 'twas no dream.
　　No, no, it was some woman cried for help,
　　And here within this garden did she cry,
　　And in this garden must I rescue her.—
　　But stay, what murd'rous spectacle is this?
10　　A man hanged up and all the murderers gone,
　　And in my bower, to lay the guilt on me?
　　This place was made for pleasure, not for death.
　　　　　　[*He cuts him down.*]
　　Those garments that he wears I oft have seen—
　　Alas, it is Horatio, my sweet son!
15　　Oh, no, but he that whilom° was my son.　　　　　　　　*until now*
　　Oh, was it thou that called'st me from my bed?
　　Oh, speak if any spark of life remain.
　　I am thy father. Who hath slain my son?
　　What savage monster, not of human kind,
20　　Hath here been glutted with thy harmless blood,
　　And left thy bloody corpse dishonored here,
　　For me amidst this° dark and deathful shades　　　　　　　*these*
　　To drown thee with an ocean of my tears?
　　O heavens, why made you night to cover sin?
25　　By day this deed of darkness had not been.
　　O earth, why didst thou not in time° devour　　　*at the proper moment*
　　The vile profaner of this sacred bower?
　　O poor Horatio, what hadst thou misdone,
　　To leese° thy life ere life was new begun?°　　　　　*lose / in youth*
30　　O wicked butcher whatsoe'er thou wert,
　　How could thou strangle virtue and desert?°　　　　　　*worthiness*
　　Ay me, most wretched, that have lost my joy,

---

8. Although during his life he was ambitious for a high position, it is at his death that he is the highest (because he is literally hanging).

In leesing my Horatio, my sweet boy!
    [*Enter* ISABELLA.]
ISABELLA   My husband's absence makes my heart to throb.—
35 Hieronimo!
HIERONIMO   Here, Isabella, help me to lament,
For sighs are stopped,° and all my tears are spent.   *stopped up*
ISABELLA   What world of grief—My son Horatio!
Oh, where's the author of this endless woe?
40 HIERONIMO   To know the author were° some ease of grief,   *would be*
For in revenge my heart would find relief.
ISABELLA   Then is he gone? And is my son gone too?
Oh, gush out, tears, fountains and floods of tears!
Blow, sighs, and raise an everlasting storm!
45 For outrage° fits our cursèd wretchedness.   *passionate behavior*
HIERONIMO   Sweet lovely rose, ill-plucked before thy time,
Fair worthy son, not conquered but betrayed,
I'll kiss thee now, for words with° tears are stayed.°   *by / stopped*
ISABELLA   And I'll close up the glasses of his sight,
50 For once these eyes were only my° delight,   *my only*
HIERONIMO   See'st thou this handkercher besmeared with blood?
It shall not from me till I take revenge.
See'st thou those wounds that yet are bleeding fresh?
I'll not entomb them till I have revenged.
55 Then will I joy amidst my discontent;
Till then my sorrow never shall be spent.°   *used up*
ISABELLA   The heavens are just; murder cannot be hid;
Time is the author both of truth and right,
And time will bring this treachery to light.
60 HIERONIMO   Meanwhile, good Isabella, cease thy plaints,°   *laments*
Or at the least dissemble them awhile;
So shall we sooner find the practice° out,   *plot*
And learn by whom all this was brought about.
Come, Isabel, now let us take him up,
    [*They take him up.*]
65 And bear him in from out this cursèd place.
I'll say his dirge; singing fits not this case.
O aliquis mihi quas pulchrum ver educat herbas
    [HIERONIMO *sets his breast unto his sword.*]
Misceat, et nostro detur medicina dolori;
Aut, si qui faciunt animis oblivia, succos
70 *Praebeat. Ipse metam magnum quaecunque per orbem*
Gramina Sol pulchras effert in luminis oras.
Ipse bibam quicquid meditatur saga veneni,
Quicquid et herbarum vi caeca nenia nectit.
Omnia perpetiar, lethum quoque, dum semel omnis
75 *Noster in extincto moriatur pectore sensus.*
Ergo tuos oculos nunquam, mea vita, videbo,
Et tua perpetuus sepelivit lumina somnus?
Emoriar tecum, sic, sic juvat ire sub umbras.

At tamen absistam properato cedere letho,

80 *Ne mortem vindicta tuam tum nulla sequatur.*[9]

[*Here he throws it° from him and*   (*the sword*)
bears the body away. Exeunt.]

2.6

[SCENE: *The chorus figures have been onstage from the start and remain so.*]

ANDREA   Brought'st thou me hither to increase my pain?
I looked° that Balthazar should have been slain,   *expected*
But 'tis my friend Horatio that is slain,
And they abuse fair Bel-imperia,

5   On whom I doted more than all the world,
Because she loved me more than all the world.

REVENGE   Thou talkest of harvest when the corn° is green.   *grain*
The end is crown of every work well done;
The sickle comes not till the corn be ripe.

10   Be still, and ere I lead thee from this place
I'll show thee Balthazar in heavy case.°   *sad state*

3.1

[SCENE: *The Portuguese royal court.*]

[*Enter* VICEROY *of Portingale,* NOBLES, *and* VILLUPPO.]

VICEROY   Infortunate condition of kings,
Seated amidst so many helpless doubts!°   *fears*
First we are placed upon extremest height,
And oft supplanted with exceeding heat,°   *fury*

5   But ever subject to the wheel of chance;°   *wheel of Fortune*
And at our highest never joy we so
As° we both doubt° and dread our overthrow.   *But that / fear*
So striveth not the waves with sundry winds
As Fortune toileth in the affairs of kings,[1]

10   That would° be feared, yet fear to be beloved,   *Who wish to be*
Sith° fear or love to kings is flattery.[2]   *Since*
For instance, lordings,° look upon your king,   *lords*
By hate deprivèd of his dearest son,
The only hope of our successive line.°   *line of succession*

---

9. Let someone mix me herbs that the beautiful spring brings forth, and let a medicine be given for our sorrows; or if there are any juices that will induce oblivion in our minds, let that person offer them. I, for my part, will gather whatever herbs the sun brings forth, throughout all the world, into the fair realms of light. I will drink whatever poison the sorceress contrives and also whatever herbs the goddess of funeral songs weaves together by her secret power. I will attempt all things, even death, until all feeling dies at once in my dead heart. Shall I never again see your face, you who are my life, and has perpetual sleep entombed your light? I will die with you; thus, thus, will I rejoicingly go to the shades below. Nonetheless, I will hold back from a hasty death, lest revenge not follow your death (Latin; a mixture of Latin phrases from classical poetry and original writing by Kyd).

1. The battle between sea and wind is as nothing compared to Fortune's violent interference in the lives of kings.

2. Lines 1–11 are based on Seneca, *Agamemnon* 57–73.

15 FIRST NOBLEMAN   I had not thought that Alexandro's heart
    Had been envenomed with such extreme hate;
    But now I see that words have several works,°   *accompany various acts*
    And there's no credit in the countenance.³
    VILLUPPO   No; for, my lord, had you beheld the train°   *treachery*
20 That feignèd love had colored° in his looks   *depicted*
    When he in camp consorted° Balthazar,   *associated with*
    Far more inconstant had you thought the sun,
    That hourly coasts° the center of the earth,   *circles around*
    Than Alexandro's purpose to the Prince.
25 VICEROY   No more, Villuppo. Thou hast said enough,
    And with thy words thou slayest our wounded thoughts.
    Nor shall I longer dally with the world,
    Procrastinating Alexandro's death.—
    Go, some of you, and fetch the traitor forth,
30 That, as he is condemnèd, he may die.

          [*One goes to the door.*]

          [*Enter* ALEXANDRO *with a* NOBLEMAN *and halberds.*°   *halberdiers (see 1.4.21)*
          ALEXANDRO *and the* NOBLEMEN *converse among*
          themselves.]

    SECOND NOBLEMAN   In such extremes, will naught but patience serve.
    ALEXANDRO   But in extremes, what patience shall I use?
    Nor discontents it me to leave the world,⁴
    With whom° there nothing can prevail but wrong.   *In which (world)*
35 SECOND NOBLEMAN   Yet hope the best.
    ALEXANDRO   'Tis heaven is my hope.
    As for the earth, it is too much infect°   *too corrupt*
    To yield me hope of any of her mold.⁵
    VICEROY   Why linger ye? Bring forth that daring fiend,
    And let him die for his accursèd deed.
40 ALEXANDRO   Not that I fear the extremity of death,
    For nobles cannot stoop to servile fear,
    Do I, O King, thus discontented live.
    But this, oh, this torments my laboring soul:
    That thus I die suspected of a sin
45 Whereof, as heavens have known my secret thoughts,
    So am I free from this suggestion.°   *false accusation*
    VICEROY   No more, I say! To the tortures! When!°   *Get on with it!*
    Bind him, and burn his body in those flames

          [*They bind him to the stake.*]

    That shall prefigure those unquenchèd fires
50 Of Phlegethon⁶ preparèd for his soul.
    ALEXANDRO   My guiltless death will be avenged on thee,
    On thee, Villuppo, that hath maliced° thus,   *slandered (me)*
    Or for thy meed° hast falsely me accused.   *reward*

---

3. No trustworthiness in a person's appearance.
4. Alexandro asks if he should endure his fate in the world or renounce the world entirely.
5. For me to expect anything good from anyone composed of her dust (i.e., humans; see Genesis 2.7, 3.19).
6. The river of fire in the underworld.

VILLUPPO   Nay, Alexandro, if thou menace me,

55   I'll lend a hand to send thee to the lake[7]

Where those thy words shall perish with thy works,

Injurious° traitor, monstrous homicide!   *Libelous*

       [*Enter* AMBASSADOR *attended.*]

AMBASSADOR   Stay! Hold awhile,

And here, with pardon of His Majesty,

60   Lay hands upon Villuppo.

VICEROY   Ambassador,

What news hath urged this sudden entrance?

AMBASSADOR   Know, sovereign lord, that Balthazar doth live.

VICEROY   What sayest thou? Liveth Balthazar, our son?

AMBASSADOR   Your Highness' son, Lord Balthazar, doth live,

65   And, well entreated° in the court of Spain,   *treated*

Humbly commends him° to Your Majesty.   *sends his greeting*

These eyes beheld, and these my followers,

With these, the letters of the King's commends,°   *greetings*

       [*Gives him letters.*]

Are happy witnesses of His Highness'° health.   *(Balthazar's)*

       [*The* KING *looks on the letters and proceeds.*°]   *reads aloud*

70 VICEROY   "Thy son doth live, your tribute is received,

Thy peace is made, and we are satisfied.

The rest resolve upon[8] as things proposed

For both our honors and thy benefit."

AMBASSADOR   These are His Highness'° farther articles.   *(the Spanish King's)*

       [*He gives him more letters.*]

75 VICEROY [*to* VILLUPPO]   Accursèd wretch, to intimate these ills

Against the life and reputation

Of noble Alexandro! [*To* ALEXANDRO] Come, my lord,

Let him unbind thee that is bound to death,

To make a quital for thy discontent.[9] [*They unbind him.*]

80 ALEXANDRO   Dread lord, in kindness° you could do no less,   *by your (kingly) nature*

Upon report of such a damnèd fact;°   *deal*

But thus we see our° innocence hath saved   *my*

The hopeless life which thou, Villuppo, sought

By thy suggestions° to have massacred.   *false suggestions*

85 VICEROY   Say, false Villuppo, wherefore° didst thou thus   *why*

Falsely betray Lord Alexandro's life,

Him whom thou knowest that no unkindness° else,   *unnatural deed*

But even the slaughter of our dearest son,

Could once have moved us to have misconceived?°   *suspected, misjudged*

90 ALEXANDRO   Say, treacherous Villuppo, tell the King,

Wherein hath Alexandro used thee ill?

---

7. That is, Acheron, in the underworld (see 1.1.19 and note).

8. Examine and decide upon (the articles in the letters).

9. Let Villupo's being bound and sentenced to death serve as compensation for your wrongs.

VILLUPPO Rent° with remembrance of so foul a deed,   *Torn*
 My guilty soul submits me to thy doom;°   *judgment*
 For, not for Alexandro's injuries,[1]
95 But for reward, and hope to be preferred,°   *of advancement*
 Thus have I shamelessly hazarded his life.
VICEROY Which, villain, shall be ransomed° with thy death,   *paid for*
 And not so mean° a torment as we here   *moderate*
 Devised for him, who thou said'st slew our son,
100 But with the bitterest torments and extremes
 That may be yet invented for thine end.
   [ALEXANDRO *seems to*° *entreat.*]   *is seen to*
 Entreat me not.—Go, take the traitor hence.
     [*Exit* VILLUPPO *guarded.*]
 And, Alexandro, let us honor thee
 With public notice of thy loyalty.
105 To end those things articulated° here   *written*
 By our great lord the mighty king of Spain,
 We with our council will deliberate.
 Come, Alexandro, keep us company.   [*Exeunt.*]

3.2

[SCENE: *Near* CASTILE'*s palace.*]

   [*Enter* HIERONIMO.]

HIERONIMO O eyes, no eyes, but fountains fraught with tears!
 O life, no life, but lively° form of death!   *lifelike*
 O world, no world, but mass of public wrongs,
 Confused and filled with murder and misdeeds!
5 O sacred heavens, if this unhallowed deed,
 If this inhuman and barbarous attempt,
 If this incomparable murder thus
 Of mine—but now no more—my son
 Shall unrevealed and unrevengèd pass,
10 How should we term your dealings to be just,
 If you unjustly deal with those that in your justice trust?
 The night, sad secretary° to my moans,   *confidant*
 With direful visions wake° my vexèd soul,   *wakes*
 And with the wounds of my distressful son
15 Solicit me for notice of° his death.   *to cry out against*
 The ugly fiends do sally forth of hell,
 And frame° my steps to unfrequented paths,   *direct*
 And fear° my heart with fierce inflamèd thoughts.   *frighten*
 The cloudy day my discontents records,
20 Early begins to register my dreams
 And drive me forth to seek the murderer.
 Eyes, life, world, heavens, hell, night, and day,
 See, search, show, send, some man, some mean,° that may—   *means*
   [*A letter falleth.*]

---

1. (1) Not to harm Alexandro; (2) not because of any harm that Alexandro might have done to me.

What's here? A letter? Tush, it is not so.
25 A letter written to Hieronimo! [*Red ink.*²]
"For want of ink, receive this bloody writ.
Me hath my hapless° brother hid from thee;   *deserving of bad luck*
Revenge thyself on Balthazar and him,
For these were they that murderèd thy son.
30 Hieronimo, revenge Horatio's death,
And better fare than Bel-imperia doth."
What means this unexpected miracle?
My son slain by Lorenzo and the Prince?
What cause had they Horatio to malign?°   *hate*
35 Or what might move thee, Bel-imperia,
To accuse thy brother, had he° been the mean?   *even if he had*
Hieronimo, beware, thou art betrayed,
And to entrap thy life this train° is laid.   *trap*
Advise thee, therefore; be not credulous;
40 This is devisèd to endanger thee,
That thou by this Lorenzo shouldst accuse,
And he, for thy dishonor done, should draw
Thy life in question and thy name in hate.
Dear was the life of my belovèd son,
45 And of his death behooves me be revenged;
Then hazard not thine own,° Hieronimo,   *your own life*
But live t'effect thy resolution.
I therefore will by circumstances³ try
What I can gather to confirm this writ,
50 And, heark'ning near the Duke of Castile's house,
Close° if I can with Bel-imperia,   *Meet*
To listen more, but nothing to bewray.°   *reveal*
          [*Enter* PEDRINGANO.]
     Now, Pedringano!
PEDRINGANO   Now, Hieronimo!
HIERONIMO   Where's thy lady?
PEDRINGANO   I know not. Here's my lord.
          [*Enter* LORENZO.]
55 LORENZO   How now, who's this? Hieronimo?
HIERONIMO   My lord.
PEDRINGANO [*to* LORENZO]   He asketh for my lady Bel-imperia.
LORENZO   What to do, Hieronimo? The Duke, my father, hath
     Upon some disgrace awhile removed her hence,
     But if it be aught I may inform her of,
60 Tell me, Hieronimo, and I'll let her know it.
HIERONIMO   Nay, nay, my lord, I thank you, it shall not need;°   *is not necessary*
     I had a suit unto her, but too late,
     And her disgrace makes me unfortunate.

---

2. To signify blood, as Hieronimo explains   3. By gathering circumstantial evidence.
below.

LORENZO   Why so, Hieronimo? Use me.°   *Put your suit to me.*
65 HIERONIMO   Oh, no, my lord, I dare not, it must not be.
     I humbly thank Your Lordship.
   LORENZO   Why, then, farewell.
   HIERONIMO [*aside*]   My grief no heart, my thoughts no
       tongue can tell.   [*Exit.*]
   LORENZO   Come hither, Pedringano. See'st thou this?[4]
   PEDRINGANO   My lord, I see it, and suspect it too.
70 LORENZO   This is that damnèd villain Serberine,°   (see 2.4.50 ff)
     That hath, I fear, revealed Horatio's death.
   PEDRINGANO   My lord, he could not, 'twas so lately done,
     And since° he hath not left my company.   *since then (the murder)*
   LORENZO   Admit he have not, his condition's such[5]
75   As fear or flattering words may make him false.
     I know his humor,° and therewith repent   *temperament*
     That e'er I used him in this enterprise.
     But, Pedringano, to prevent the worst,
     And 'cause I know thee secret as my soul,
80   Here for thy further satisfaction take thou this,
         [*Gives him more gold.*]
     And hearken to me. Thus it is devised:
     This night thou must—and prithee so resolve—
     Meet Serberine at Saint Luigi's Park;
85   Thou knowest 'tis here hard by behind the house.
     There take thy stand, and see thou strike him sure,
     For die he must, if we do mean to live.
   PEDRINGANO   But how shall Serberine be there, my lord?
   LORENZO   Let me alone.° I'll send to him to meet   *Leave it to me.*
90   The Prince and me, where thou must do this deed.
   PEDRINGANO   It shall be done, my lord, it shall be done,
     And I'll go arm myself to meet him there.
   LORENZO   When things shall alter, as I hope they will,
     Then shalt thou mount° for this. Thou knowest my mind.   *rise in rank*
                                     [*Exit* PEDRINGANO.]
95 *Che le, Ieron!*[6]
         [*Enter* PAGE.]
   PAGE   My lord?
   LORENZO   Go, sirrah,[7] to Serberine,
     And bid him forthwith meet the Prince and me
     At Saint Luigi's Park, behind the house,
100   This evening, boy.
   PAGE   I go, my lord.
   LORENZO   But, sirrah, let the hour be eight o'clock.
     Bid him not fail.
   PAGE   I fly, my lord.   [*Exit.*]

---

4. That is, Hieronimo's suspicious behavior.
5. Even if he hasn't reported the murder, his
state is such.

6. Unexplained; possibly a corruption of a
summons or form of address to the page.
7. A form of address to male social inferiors.

105 LORENZO Now, to confirm the complot thou hast cast°   *plot I devised*
Of all these practices,° I'll spread° the watch,   *schemes / station*
Upon° precise commandment from the King,   *As if upon*
Strongly to guard the place where Pedringano
This night shall murder hapless Serberine.
110 Thus must we work that will avoid distrust;[8]
Thus must we practice to prevent mishap,
And thus one ill another must expulse.°   *drive out*
This sly inquiry of Hieronimo
For Bel-imperia breeds suspicion,
115 And this suspicion bodes a further ill.
As for myself, I know my secret fault,°   *crime*
And so do they,[9] but I have dealt for them.
They that for coin their souls endangerèd,
To save my life, for coin shall venture theirs,[1]
120 And better 'tis that base companions° die   *lowbred fellows*
Than by their life to hazard our good haps.°   *fortune*
Nor shall they live for me to fear their faith.[2]
I'll trust myself; myself shall be my friend;
For die they shall. Slaves° are ordained to no other end.   *Servants, wretches*
                                                                [*Exit.*]

3.3

[SCENE: *Saint Luigi's Park, behind* CASTILE'S *palace.*]

[*Enter* PEDRINGANO *with a pistol.*]

PEDRINGANO Now, Pedringano, bid thy pistol hold,°   *not misfire*
And hold on,° Fortune! Once more favor me;   *be steady*
Give but success to mine attempting spirit,
And let me shift for taking of mine aim.[3]
5 Here is the gold, this is the gold proposed;°   *offered as reward*
It is no dream that I adventure for,
But Pedringano is possessed thereof.
And he° that would not strain his conscience   *anyone*
For him° that thus his liberal purse hath stretched,   *(one like Lorenzo)*
10 Unworthy such a favor may he fail,
And, wishing, want,° when such as I prevail.   *be in want*
As for the fear of apprehension,
I know, if need should be, my noble lord
Will stand between me and ensuing harms.
15 Besides, this place is free from all suspect.°   *suspicion*
Here therefore will I stay and take my stand.
                [*Enter the Watch.*]

FIRST WATCHMAN I wonder much to what intent it is
That we are thus expressly charged to watch?

---

8. Thus must schemers work who want to avoid suspicion.
9. That is, Pedringano and Serberine.
1. Pedringano and Serberine, who risked their souls by committing murder for money,

will now have to pay with (the coin of) their lives to save mine.
2. Neither shall they live so that I have to worry continually whether they will betray me.
3. Leave it to me to take aim.

SECOND WATCHMAN   'Tis by commandment in the King's
      own name.
20 THIRD WATCHMAN   But we were never wont° to watch and   *accustomed*
      ward°   *guard*
   So near the Duke his brother's house before.
SECOND WATCHMAN   Content yourself. Stand close; there's
      somewhat in't.°   *something brewing*
      [*Enter* SERBERINE.]
SERBERINE [*to himself*]   Here, Serberine, attend and stay thy
      pace,°   *stop walking*
   For here did Don Lorenzo's page appoint
25 That thou by his command shouldst meet with him.
   How fit a place, if one were so disposed,
   Methinks this corner is to close with one!°   *to attack someone*
PEDRINGANO [*aside*]   Here comes the bird that I must seize upon.
   Now, Pedringano, or never play the man!°   *or renounce your manhood*
30 SERBERINE [*to himself*]   I wonder that His Lordship⁴ stays so
      long,
   Or wherefore should he send for me so late?
PEDRINGANO   For this, Serberine, and thou shalt ha't.°   *have it*
      [*Shoots the dag.*° SERBERINE *falls.*]   *heavy pistol*
   So, there he lies. My promise is performed.
      [*The Watch come forward.*]
FIRST WATCHMAN   Hark, gentlemen, this is a pistol shot.
35 SECOND WATCHMAN   And here's one slain. Stay° the murderer.   *Arrest*
PEDRINGANO   Now by the sorrows of the souls in hell,
      [*He strives° with the Watch.*]   *fights, struggles*
   Who° first lays hand on me, I'll be his priest.⁵   *Whoever*
THIRD WATCHMAN   Sirrah, confess, and therein play the priest.⁶
   Why hast thou thus unkindly° killed the man?   *unnaturally*
40 PEDRINGANO   Why, because he walked abroad° so late.   *out of doors*
THIRD WATCHMAN   Come, sir, you had been better kept your bed
   Than have committed this misdeed so late.°   *recently; at night*
SECOND WATCHMAN   Come to the Marshal's with the murderer!
FIRST WATCHMAN   On to Hieronimo's! Help me here
45 To bring the murdered body with us too.
PEDRINGANO   Hieronimo? Carry me before whom you will.
   Whate'er he be, I'll answer him and you;
   And do your worst, for I defy you all.
                              [*Exeunt with* SERBERINE'*s body.*]

3.4

[SCENE: CASTILE'*s palace.*]

      [*Enter* LORENZO *and* BALTHAZAR.]
BALTHAZAR   How now, my lord, what makes you rise so soon?

---

4. That is, Lorenzo (see 3.2.88–89).   6. That is, be your own confessor in telling
5. A euphemism for "I'll murder him," since a   the crime.
priest attends a dying person.

LORENZO Fear of preventing our mishaps too late.[7]

BALTHAZAR What mischief is it that we not mistrust?° *do not anticipate*

LORENZO Our greatest ills we least mistrust, my lord,

5   And inexpected° harms do hurt us most. *unexpected*

BALTHAZAR Why, tell me, Don Lorenzo, tell me, man,

If aught concerns our honor and your own?

LORENZO Nor you nor me,° my lord, but both in one. *Neither of us singly*

For I suspect—and the presumption's great—

10   That by those base confederates in our fault,° *crime*

Touching° the death of Don Horatio, *Relating to*

We are betrayed to old Hieronimo.

BALTHAZAR Betrayed, Lorenzo! Tush, it cannot be.

LORENZO A guilty conscience,[8] urgèd with the thought

15   Of former evils,° easily cannot err. *crimes*

I am persuaded—and dissuade me not—

That all's revealèd to Hieronimo.

And therefore know that I have cast° it thus— *devised*

[*Enter the* PAGE.]

But here's the page.—How now, what news with thee?

20 PAGE My lord, Serberine is slain.

BALTHAZAR Who? Serberine, my man?° *servant*

PAGE Your Highness' man, my lord.

LORENZO Speak, page, who murdered him?

PAGE He that is apprehended for the fact.° *deed*

25 LORENZO Who?

PAGE Pedringano.

BALTHAZAR Is Serberine slain, that loved his lord so well?

Injurious villain, murderer of his friend!

LORENZO Hath Pedringano murdered Serberine?

30   My lord, let me entreat you to take the pains

To exasperate° and hasten his° revenge *make harsher / on him*

With your complaints unto my lord the King.

This their dissension breeds a greater doubt.[9]

BALTHAZAR Assure thee, Don Lorenzo, he shall die,

35   Or else His Highness hardly° shall deny. *with difficulty; harshly*

Meanwhile, I'll haste the marshal sessions,[1]

For die he shall for this his damnèd deed.

[*Exit* BALTHAZAR.]

LORENZO [*to himself*] Why so, this fits our former policy,° *my earlier plans*

And thus experience bids the wise to deal.

40   I lay the plot, he prosecutes the point;° *executes it*

I set the trap, he breaks the worthless twigs,

And sees not that wherewith the bird was limed.[2]

Thus hopeful men that mean to hold their own° *prosper*

Must look like fowlers° to their dearest friends. *innocent bird-catchers*

---

7. Fear of not preventing troubles in time.
8. That is, the conscience of Lorenzo's partners in crime.
9. Pedringano and Serberine's fighting generates further worry about our being betrayed.

1. I'll speed up the process of bringing the
matter to trial.
2. Lorenzo plots the trap in which Balthazar
participates while not recognizing the plot's
full extent (see 2.1.126 and note).

45 He runs to kill whom I have holp to catch,[3]
And no man knows it was my reaching fetch.°   *farseeing plan*
'Tis hard to trust unto a multitude,
Or anyone, in mine opinion,
When men themselves their secrets will reveal.
    [*Enter a* MESSENGER *with a letter.*]

50 Boy!
PAGE   My lord?
LORENZO   What's he?°   *Who's there?*
MESSENGER   I have a letter to Your Lordship.
LORENZO   From whence?
55 MESSENGER   From Pedringano that's imprisoned.
    [*He hands* LORENZO *the letter.*]
LORENZO   So, he is in prison, then?
MESSENGER   Ay, my good lord.
LORENZO   What would he with us? [*He reads.*] He writes us here
    To stand good lord° and help him in distress.—   *act as a patron*
60 Tell him I have his letters, know his mind,
And what we may, let him assure him of.[4]
Fellow, begone. My boy shall follow thee.
    [*Exit* MESSENGER.]
This works like wax;° yet once more try thy wits.—   *is easily shaped*
Boy, go convey this purse to Pedringano.
    [LORENZO *gives a purse.*]
65 Thou knowest the prison. Closely° give it him,   *Secretly*
And be advised° that none be thereabout.   *take care*
Bid him be merry still, but secret;
And though the marshal sessions be today,
Bid him not doubt of his delivery.
70 Tell him his pardon is already signed,
And thereon bid him boldly be resolved;°   *resolute*
For, were he ready to be turnèd off[5]—
As 'tis my will the uttermost be tried[6]—
Thou with his pardon shalt attend him still.
75 Show him this box, tell him his pardon's in't,
    [*He gives a box.*]
But open't not, an if° thou lovest thy life,   *if*
But let him wisely keep his hopes unknown;
He shall not want while Don Lorenzo lives.
Away!
80 PAGE   I go, my lord, I run.
LORENZO   But, sirrah, see that this be cleanly° done.   *efficiently*
    [*Exit* PAGE.]
Now stands our fortune on a tickle° point,   *ticklish, critical*

---

3. That is, Balthazar goes to kill him (Pedringano) whom I set up.
4. Let him rest assured that I (Lorenzo) will
do all I may.

5. Thrust from the gallows ladder and thus
hanged (see also 3.6.107 SD).
6. Every attempt be made to save him.

And now or never ends Lorenzo's doubts.
One only thing is uneffected yet,
85 And that's to see the executioner.
But to what end? I list not° trust the air   *have no wish to*
With utterance of our pretense° therein,   *my design*
For fear the privy° whisp'ring of the wind   *secret*
Convey our words amongst unfriendly ears,
90 That lie too open to advantages.[7]
E quel che voglio io, nessun lo sa;
Intendo io, quel mi basterà .[8]   [*Exit.*]

3.5

[SCENE: *Outside* CASTILE'S *palace.*]

[*Enter boy* PAGE, *with the box.*]

PAGE My master hath forbidden me to look in this box;
and by my troth, 'tis likely, if he had not warned me,
I should not have had so much idle time,[9] for we men's-
kind in our minority[1] are like women in their uncer-
5 tainty:° that° they are most forbidden, they will soon-   *perversity / that which*
est attempt. So I now. [*He opens the box.*] By my bare°   *simple*
honesty, here's nothing but the bare empty box! Were it
not sin against secrecy, I would say it were a piece of gen-
tlemanlike knavery. I must go to Pedringano, and tell him
10 his pardon is in this box; nay, I would have sworn it, had
I not seen the contrary. I cannot choose but smile to think
how the villain will flout° the gallows, scorn the audience,   *jest at*
and descant on° the hangman, and all presuming of his   *mock*
pardon from hence. Will't not be an odd jest for me to stand
15 and grace every jest he makes, pointing my finger at this
box, as who would say,° "Mock on, here's thy war rant"?   *as if to say*
Is't not a scurvy° jest, that a man should jest himself to   *base, shabby*
death? Alas, poor Pedringano, I am in a sort° sorry for thee,   *way*
but if I should be hanged[2] with thee, I cannot weep. [*Exit.*]

3.6

[SCENE: *Knight Marshal's courtroom.*]

[*Enter* HIERONIMO *and the* DEPUTY. *A gallows is provided onstage.*]

HIERONIMO Thus must we toil in other men's extremes,°   *hardships*
That know not how to remedy our own,
And do them justice, when unjustly we,

7. Too ready to take advantage of such
opportunities.
8. And what I want, no one knows; I understand, and that suffices for me (Italian;
unknown source).
9. If he had not told me not to, I would not
have looked.
1. Underage males.
2. The Page plays on the proverbial sense of
this phrase—"if my life depended on it"—and
its literal meaning.

For all our wrongs, can compass° no redress.   *find*
5   But shall I never live to see the day
That I may come, by justice of the heavens,
To know the cause that may my cares allay?
This toils° my body, this consumeth age,°   *burdens / wears me out*
That only I to all men just must be,
10 And neither gods nor men be just to me.
DEPUTY Worthy Hieronimo, your office asks
A care° to punish such as do transgress.   *concern, regard*
HIERONIMO So is't my duty to regard his° death   *care about Horatio's*
Who, when he lived, deserved my dearest blood.
15 But come, for that° we came for, let's begin,   *that which*
For here lies that³ which bids me to be gone.

> [*Enter officers (one of them the* HANGMAN*), boy (*PAGE*, with
> the box), and* PEDRINGANO, *with a letter in his hand, bound.*]

DEPUTY Bring forth the prisoner, for the court is set.
PEDRINGANO [*aside to the* PAGE] Gramercy,° boy, but it was   *Many thanks*
   time to come,
For I had written to my lord anew
20 A nearer° matter that concerneth him,   *more intimate, serious*
For fear His Lordship had forgotten me;
But sith° he hath remembered me so well—   *since*
[*Aloud*] Come, come, come on, when shall we to this gear?°   *business*
HIERONIMO Stand forth, thou monster, murderer of men,
25 And here, for satisfaction of the world,
Confess thy folly and repent thy fault,
For [*indicating the gallows*] there's thy place of execution.
PEDRINGANO This is short work. Well, to Your Marshalship
First I confess—nor fear I death therefore—
30 I am the man; 'twas I slew Serberine.
But, sir, then you think this shall be the place
Where we shall satisfy you for this gear?
DEPUTY Ay, Pedringano.
PEDRINGANO   Now I think not so.
HIERONIMO Peace,° impudent! For thou shalt find it so.   *Hold your peace, shut up*
35 For blood with blood shall, while I sit as judge,
Be satisfied, and the law discharged.°   *fulfilled, satisfied*
And though myself cannot receive the like,°   *(i.e., similar justice)*
Yet will I see that others have their right.
Dispatch! The fault's approvèd° and confessed,   *proven*
40 And by our law he is condemned to die.
HANGMAN Come on, sir, are you ready?
PEDRINGANO To do what, my fine officious knave?
HANGMAN To go to this gear.
PEDRINGANO Oh, sir, you are too forward. Thou wouldst
45 fain° furnish me with a halter,° to disfurnish me of my   *wish to / noose*

---

3. Hieronimo likely touches his heart ("here"), where he hides the bloody handkerchief (see
2.5.51–52).

habit;[4] so I should go out of this gear, my raiment, into that
gear, the rope. But, hangman, now° I spy your knavery,°   *now that / trickery*
I'll not change without boot,° that's flat.°   *compensation / certain*

HANGMAN   Come, sir.

50 PEDRINGANO   So, then I must up?

HANGMAN   No remedy.

PEDRINGANO   Yes, but there shall be for my coming down.

HANGMAN   Indeed, here's a remedy for that.

PEDRINGANO   How? Be turned off?°   *hanged*

55 HANGMAN   Ay, truly. Come, are you ready? I pray, sir,
   dispatch;° the day goes away.   *make haste*

PEDRINGANO   What, do you hang by the hour? If you do,
   I may chance to break your old custom.

HANGMAN   Faith, you have reason,° for I am like° to break   *you're right / likely*
60   your young neck.

PEDRINGANO   Dost thou mock me, hangman? Pray God I
   be not preserved to break your knave's pate° for this.   *head*

HANGMAN   Alas, sir, you are a foot too low to reach it, and I
   hope you will never grow so high while I am in the office.[5]

65 PEDRINGANO   Sirrah,° dost see yonder boy with the box in   *(see 3.2.97n)*
   his hand?

HANGMAN   What, he that points to it with his finger?

PEDRINGANO   Ay, that companion.°   *fellow*

HANGMAN   I know him not, but what of him?

70 PEDRINGANO   Dost thou think to live till his old doublet° will   *waistcoat, jacket*
   make thee a new truss?°   *garment*

HANGMAN   Ay, and many a fair year after, to truss up°   *stirring up*
   many an honester man than either thou or he.

PEDRINGANO   What hath he in his box, as thou think'st?

75 HANGMAN   Faith,° I cannot tell, nor I care not greatly.   *By my faith*
   Methinks you should rather hearken to your soul's health.   *(mild oath)*

PEDRINGANO   Why, sirrah hangman? I take it that that°   *what*
   is good for the body is likewise good for the soul; and, it
   may be, in that box is balm for both.

80 HANGMAN   Well, thou art even the merriest piece of man's
   flesh° that e'er groaned at my office door.   *specimen of humanity*

PEDRINGANO   Is your roguery become an office,° with a   *official function*
   knave's name?[6]

HANGMAN   Ay, and that shall all they witness that see you
85   seal° it with a thief's name.   *confirm (by hanging)*

PEDRINGANO   I prithee request this good company° to pray   *the witnesses*
   with me.

HANGMAN   Ay, marry,° sir, this is a good motion.°—My   *by Mary / proposal*
   masters,° you see here's a good fellow.   *good sirs*

90 PEDRINGANO   Nay, nay, now I remember me, let them alone
   till some other time, for now I have no great need.

---

4. Clothes. Hangmen customarily received
the clothing of the hanged criminal.
5. The Hangman must be a foot taller than

Pedringano.
6. Despite your lowly reputation (as a
hangman).

HIERONIMO   I have not seen a wretch so impudent.
      Oh, monstrous times, where murder's set so light,
      And where the soul, that should be shrined° in heaven,   *enshrined*
95   Solely delights in interdicted° things,   *forbidden*
      Still wand'ring in the thorny passages
      That intercepts itself of° happiness!   *thwarts its own*
      Murder, oh, bloody monster! God forbid
      A fault so foul should scape unpunishèd.—
100   Dispatch, and see this execution done.
      This makes me to remember thee, my son. [*Exit* HIERONIMO.]

      [PEDRINGANO *is readied for the hanging.*]

PEDRINGANO   Nay, soft,° no haste.   *wait a minute*
DEPUTY   Why, wherefore stay you? Have you hope of life?
PEDRINGANO   Why, ay.
105   HANGMAN   As how?
PEDRINGANO   Why, rascal, by my pardon from the King.
HANGMAN   Stand[7] you on that? Then you shall off with this.°   *(the noose)*

      [*He turns him off.*°]   *hangs him*

DEPUTY   So, executioner, convey him hence,
      But let his body be unburièd.
110   Let not the earth be chokèd or infect
      With that which heaven contemns° and men neglect.°   *scorns / shun*
                               [*Exeunt.*]

3.7

[SCENE: *Scene continues.*]

      [*Enter* HIERONIMO.]

HIERONIMO   Where shall I run to breathe abroad° my woes—   *cry aloud*
      My woes, whose weight hath wearièd the earth—
      Or mine exclaims,° that have surcharged the air   *my exclamations*
      With ceaseless plaints° for my deceasèd son?   *laments*
5   The blust'ring winds, conspiring with my words,
      At my lament have moved the leafless trees,[8]
      Disrobed the meadows of their flowered green,
      Made mountains marsh with spring tides of my tears,
      And broken through the brazen gates of hell.
10   Yet still tormented is my tortured soul
      With broken sighs and restless passions,
      That, wingèd, mount, and, hovering in the air,
      Beat at the windows of the brightest heavens,
      Soliciting for justice and revenge.
15   But they° are placed in those empyreal° heights   *(the gods) / heavenly*
      Where, countermured° with walls of diamond,   *doubly walled*
      I find the place impregnable, and they
      Resist my woes, and give my words no way.

---

7. Depend (with a pun on the fact that Pedringano is standing on the scaffold).

8. Have stripped the trees of their leaves.

[*Enter* HANGMAN *with a letter.*]

HANGMAN   Oh, lord, sir, God bless you, sir, the man,
20   sir, Petergade,° sir, he that was so full of merry conceits°— *Pedringano / jests*
HIERONIMO   Well, what of him?
HANGMAN   Oh, lord, sir, he went the wrong way; the fellow had *proper written*
a fair commission° to the contrary. Sir, here is his passport.° *authority /*
I pray you, sir, we have done him wrong. *discharge permit*
25   HIERONIMO   I warrant thee, give it me.

[*He takes the letter.*]

HANGMAN   You will stand between the gallows and me?
HIERONIMO   Ay, ay.
HANGMAN   I thank Your Lord Worship.   [*Exit* HANGMAN.]
HIERONIMO   And yet, though somewhat nearer me concerns,[9]
30   I will, to ease the grief that I sustain,
Take truce with sorrow while I read on this.   [*He reads.*]
"My lord, I writ as mine extremes required,
That you would labor my delivery.° *work to free me*
If you neglect, my life is desperate,
35   And in my death I shall reveal the truth.° *truth*
You know, my lord, I slew him° for your sake, *(Serberine)*
And was confederate with the Prince and you,
Won by rewards and hopeful promises;
I holp° to murder Don Horatio, too." *helped*
40   Holp he to murder mine Horatio?
An actor in th'accursèd tragedy
Wast thou, Lorenzo—Balthazar, and thou—
Of whom my son, my son, deserved so well?
What have I heard? What have mine eyes beheld?
45   O sacred heavens, may it come to pass
That such a monstrous and detested deed,
So closely smothered° and so long concealed, *kept secret*
Shall thus by this° be vengèd° or revealed? *this letter /avenged*
Now see I what I durst° not then suspect: *dared*
50   That Bel-imperia's letter was not feigned,
Nor feignèd she, though falsely they° have wronged *(Lorenzo and Balthazar)*
Both her, myself, Horatio, and themselves.
Now may I make compare, 'twixt hers and this,° *(this letter)*
Of every accident.° I ne'er could find° *event / understand*
55   Till now, and now I feelingly perceive,
They did what heaven unpunished would not leave.[1]
O false Lorenzo, are these thy flattering looks?
Is this the honor that thou didst my son?
And Balthazar, bane° to thy soul and me, *poison, ruin*
60   Was this the ransom he reserved thee° for? *spared you from death*
Woe to the cause of these constrainèd° wars, *forced*
Woe to thy baseness° and captivity, *cowardice in battle*

9. Though something more urgent and per-   1. What heaven would not leave unpunished.
sonal concerns me.

Woe to thy birth, thy body and thy soul,
Thy cursèd father, and thy conquered self!
65 And banned° with bitter execrations be   *accursed*
The day and place where he° did pity° thee!   *(Horatio) / spare*
But wherefore waste I mine unfruitful words,
When naught but blood will satisfy my woes?
I will go plain me° to my lord the King,   *complain*
70 And cry aloud for justice through the court,
Wearing the flints² with these my withered feet,
And either purchase° justice by entreats   *obtain*
Or tire° them all with my revenging threats. [*Exit.*] *weary*

3.8

[SCENE: HIERONIMO's *house.*]

[*Enter* ISABELLA *and her* MAID.]

ISABELLA So that you say this herb will purge° the eye, *cleanse, heal*
And this the head?
Ah, but none of them will purge the heart.
No, there's no medicine left for my disease,
5 Nor any physic° to recure° the dead. [*She runs lunatic.*] *medicine / revive*
Horatio, oh, where's Horatio?
MAID Good madam, affright not thus yourself
With outrage° for your son Horatio.   *passionate grief*
He sleeps in quiet in the Elysian fields.°   *(see 1.1.73n)*
10 ISABELLA Why, did I not give you gowns and goodly things,
Bought you a whistle and a whip-stalk³ too,
To be revengèd on their villainies?
MAID Madam, these humors° do torment my soul.   *fancies*
ISABELLA "My soul"? Poor soul, thou talks° of things *talk'st*
15 Thou know'st not what. My soul hath silver wings,
That mounts me up unto the highest heavens,
To heaven; ay, there sits my Horatio,
Backed with° a troop of fiery cherubins⁴   *surrounded by*
Dancing about his newly healèd wounds,
20 Singing sweet hymns and chanting heavenly notes—
Rare harmony to greet his innocence,
That died, ay, died, a mirror° in our days.   *model of excellence*
But say, where shall I find the men, the murderers,
That slew Horatio? Whither shall I run
25 To find them out that murderèd my son?   [*Exeunt.*]

---

2. Wearing down the pavement stones.
3. Whip handle used in a child's game.
4. Cherubins (the Hebrew plural of *cherub*),
angelic beings that dwell in the highest
heaven, or empyrean (see 3.7.15).

3.9

[SCENE: BEL-IMPERIA's *room in* CASTILE's *palace*.]

[BEL-IMPERIA *at a window*.[5]]

BEL-IMPERIA What means this outrage that is offered° me? *done to*
    Why am I thus sequestered from the court?
    No notice?° Shall I not know the cause *Kept in ignorance*
    Of this my secret and suspicious ills?
5   Accursèd brother, unkind° murderer, *unnatural*
    Why bends thou° thus thy mind to martyr me? *do you apply*
    Hieronimo, why writ I° of thy wrongs, *why did I bother to write*
    Or why art thou so slack in thy revenge?
    Andrea, O Andrea, that thou sawest[6]
10   Me for thy friend Horatio handled thus,
    And him for me thus causeless murderèd!
    Well, force perforce,° I must constrain myself *of necessity*
    To patience, and apply me to the time,° *accept the circumstances*
    Till heaven, as I have hoped, shall set me free.

[*Enter* CHRISTOPHIL.]

15 CHRISTOPHIL Come, Madam Bel-imperia, this may not be.

[*Exeunt*.]

3.10

[SCENE: CASTILE's *palace*.]

[*Enter* LORENZO, BALTHAZAR, *and the* PAGE.]

LORENZO Boy, talk no further; thus far things go well.
    Thou art assurèd that thou sawest him° dead? *(Pedringano)*
PAGE Or else, my lord, I live not.
LORENZO   That's enough.
    As for his resolution in his end,° *the state of his soul*
5   Leave that to him° with whom he sojourns now. *(i.e., the devil)*
    Here, take my ring,° and give it Christophil, *(as proof of authority)*
    And bid him let my sister be enlarged,° *freed*
    And bring her hither straight. [*Exit* PAGE.]
    This that I did was for a policy° *stratagem*
10   To smooth and keep the murder secret,[7]
    Which as a nine days' wonder being o'erblown,[8]
    My gentle° sister will I now enlarge. *wellborn*
BALTHAZAR And time,° Lorenzo, for my lord the Duke, *in good time*
    You heard, inquirèd for her yesternight.
15 LORENZO Why, and, my lord, I hope you heard me say
    Sufficient reason why she kept away.
    But that's all one.° My lord, you love her? *(i.e., let it go)*

---

5. That is, on an upper acting level or a balcony.
6. If you could only see (a stage irony, since the ghost of Andrea witnesses all that occurs).
7. To hide or to hush up the murder.
8. Which, as a celebrated but transient event that has now blown over.

BALTHAZAR   Ay.

LORENZO   Then in your love beware; deal cunningly;
  Salve° all suspicions; only soothe me up;°   *Soothe / agree with me*
20 And if she hap to stand on terms° with us,   *should make conditions*
  As for her sweetheart, and concealment so,
  Jest with her gently; under feignèd jest
  Are things concealed that else would breed unrest.
  But here she comes.

                    [*Enter* BEL-IMPERIA.]

                    Now, sister—

BEL-IMPERIA   Sister? No,
25 Thou art no brother, but an enemy!
  Else wouldst thou not have used thy sister so,
  First, to affright me with thy weapons drawn,
  And with extremes abuse my company,°   *companion (i.e., Horatio)*
  And then to hurry me, like whirlwind's rage,
30 Amidst a crew of thy confederates,
  And clap° me up where none might come at me,   *shut*
  Nor I at any to reveal my wrongs.
  What madding fury did possess thy wits?
  Or wherein is't that I offended thee?

35 LORENZO   Advise you better,° Bel-imperia,   *Be more careful*
  For I have done you no disparagement,
  Unless,° by more discretion than deserved,   *Unless in that*
  I sought to save your honor and mine own.

BEL-IMPERIA   Mine honor? Why, Lorenzo, wherein is't
40 That I neglect my reputation so
  As you, or any, need to rescue it?

LORENZO   His Highness and my father were resolved
  To come confer with old Hieronimo
  Concerning certain matters of estate
45 That by the Viceroy was determinèd.[9]

BEL-IMPERIA   And wherein was mine honor touched in that?

BALTHAZAR   Have patience, Bel-imperia, hear the rest.

LORENZO   Me next in sight° as messenger they sent,   *standing nearby*
  To give him° notice that they were so nigh.   *(Hieronimo)*
50 Now, when I came, consorted with° the Prince,   *accompanied by*
  And unexpected in an arbor there
  Found Bel-imperia with Horatio—

BEL-IMPERIA   How then?

LORENZO   Why, then, rememb'ring that old disgrace°   *the secret love affair*
55 Which you for Don Andrea had endured,
  And now were likely longer to sustain,[1]
  By being found so meanly accompanied,[2]
  Thought rather—for I knew no readier mean°—   *means*
  To thrust Horatio forth° my father's way.   *out of*

9. Concerning a dowry that the Viceroy of   1. Continue (by loving Horatio).
Portugal was proposing to settle on Balthazar 2. Found with someone of lower rank.
if he should marry Bel-imperia.

60 BALTHAZAR   And carry you obscurely somewhere else,
Lest that His Highness should have found you there.
BEL-IMPERIA   Even so, my lord? And you are witness
That this is true which he entreateth of?°   *relates*
You, gentle brother, forged this for my sake,
65 And you, my lord,° were made his instrument—   *(Balthazar)*
A work of worth, worthy the noting too!
But what's the cause that you concealed me since?
LORENZO   Your melancholy, sister, since the news
Of your first favorite Don Andrea's death
70 My father's old wrath hath exasperate.°   *made more violent*
BALTHAZAR   And better was't for you, being in disgrace,
To absent yourself and give his fury place.°   *proper distance*
BEL-IMPERIA   But why had I no notice of his ire?
LORENZO   That were to add more fuel to your fire,
75 Who burnt like Etna° for Andrea's loss.   *a volcano in Sicily*
BEL-IMPERIA   Hath not my father then inquired for me?
LORENZO   Sister, he hath, and thus excused I thee.

[*He whispereth in her ear.*]

But, Bel-imperia, see the gentle prince;
Look on thy love, behold young Balthazar,
80 Whose passions by thy presence are increased,
And in whose melancholy thou mayest see
Thy hate, his love; thy flight, his following thee.[3]
BEL-IMPERIA   Brother, you are become an orator—
I know not, I, by what experience—
85 Too politic° for me, past all compare,   *cunning*
Since last I saw you. But content yourself;
The Prince is meditating higher things.
BALTHAZAR   'Tis of thy beauty, then, that conquers kings;
Of those thy tresses, Ariadne's twines,[4]
90 Wherewith my liberty thou hast surprised;°   *captured*
Of that thine ivory front,° my sorrow's map,   *forehead*
Wherein I see no haven to rest my hope.
BEL-IMPERIA   To love, and fear, and both at once, my lord,
In my conceit, are things of more import
95 Than women's wits are to be busied with.
BALTHAZAR   'Tis I that love.
BEL-IMPERIA   Whom?
BALTHAZAR   Bel-imperia.
BEL-IMPERIA   But I that fear.
BALTHAZAR   Whom?
BEL-IMPERIA   Bel-imperia.

---

3. See how his melancholy is brought on by
the hatred with which you repay his love and
by your fleeing from his pursuit.
4. Balthazar compares Bel-imperia's hair to
the skein of thread given by the Cretan princess Ariadne to Theseus to enable him to

make his way out of King Minos's labyrinth.
Balthazar may also be referring to Arachne, a
woman who challenged Athena to a weaving
contest and was punished by being turned
into a spider.

LORENZO Fear yourself?

BEL-IMPERIA Ay, brother.

LORENZO How?

BEL-IMPERIA As those

That what they love are loath and fear to lose.[5]

100 BALTHAZAR Then, fair, let Balthazar your keeper be.

BEL-IMPERIA No, Balthazar doth fear as well as we.

Et tremulo metui pavidum junxere timorem,

Et vanum stolidae proditionis opus.[6] [*Exit.*]

LORENZO Nay, an° you argue things so cunningly, *if*

105 We'll go continue this discourse at court.

BALTHAZAR Led by the lodestar° of her heavenly looks *guiding star*

Wends poor oppressèd Balthazar

As o'er the mountains walks the wanderer,

Incertain to effect° his pilgrimage. [*Exeunt.*] *accomplish*

3.11

[SCENE: *Near* CASTILE's *palace.*]

[*Enter two Portingales* (PORTUGUESE), *and* HIERONIMO *meets them.*]

FIRST PORTUGUESE By your leave, sir.

HIERONIMO Good leave have you. Nay, I pray you, go,

For I'll leave you, if you can leave me so.

SECOND PORTUGUESE Pray you,

5 Which is the next° way to my lord the Duke's? *nearest*

HIERONIMO The next way° from me. *By getting far away*

FIRST PORTUGUESE To his house, we mean.

HIERONIMO Oh, hard by;° 'tis yon house that you see. *close by*

SECOND PORTUGUESE You could not tell us if his son were there?

HIERONIMO Who, my lord Lorenzo?

FIRST PORTUGUESE Ay, sir.

[*He goeth in at one door and comes out at another.*[7]]

HIERONIMO Oh, forbear,

10 For other talk for us far fitter were.° *would be more appropriate*

But if you be importunate° to know *persistent*

The way to him, and where to find him out,

Then list° to me, and I'll resolve your doubt. *listen*

There is a path upon your left-hand side° *(i.e., the path to hell)*

15 That leadeth from a guilty conscience

Unto a forest of distrust and fear—

A darksome place and dangerous to pass.

There shall you meet with melancholy thoughts,

Whose baleful humors if you but uphold,° *continue in*

20 It will conduct you to despair and death,

Whose rocky cliffs when you have once beheld,

---

5. Because Bel-imperia is afraid that she will lose her self (her identity), she fears herself.
6. And they joined timidity to quaking fear, a futile work of stupid betrayal (a mixture of classical sources and Kyd's own Latin).
7. This stage business signals that the first Portuguese goes into Castile's house to find Lorenzo but is unsuccessful.

Within a hugy° dale of lasting° night   *huge / everlasting*
That, kindled with the world's iniquities,
Doth cast up filthy and detested fumes.
25   Not far from thence, where murderers have built
A habitation for their cursèd souls,
There in a brazen caldron fixed by Jove
In his fell° wrath upon a sulfur flame,   *fierce*
Yourselves shall find Lorenzo bathing him°   *himself*
30   In boiling lead and blood of innocents.
FIRST PORTUGUESE   Ha, ha, ha!
HIERONIMO   Ha, ha, ha!
Why, ha, ha, ha! Farewell, good, ha, ha, ha!   [*Exit.*]
SECOND PORTUGUESE   Doubtless this man is passing° lunatic,   *exceedingly*
Or imperfection of his age doth make him dote.°   *deranged*
35   Come, let's away to seek my lord the Duke.   [*Exeunt.*]

3.12

[SCENE: *The Spanish royal court.*]

[*Enter* HIERONIMO *with a poniard in one hand and
a rope in the other.*[8]]

HIERONIMO   Now, sir,° perhaps I come and see the King;   (*an imaginary listener*)
The King sees me, and fain would hear my suit.
Why, is not this a strange and seld-seen° thing,   *seldom-seen*
5   That standers-by with toys° should strike me mute?   *trifles, idle tales*
Go to, I see their shifts,° and say no more.   *tricks*
Hieronimo, 'tis time for thee to trudge.°   *be on your way*
Down by the dale that flows with purple° gore   *bloodred*
Standeth a fiery tower; there sits a judge
10   Upon a seat of steel and molten brass,
And 'twixt his teeth he holds a firebrand
That leads unto the lake where hell doth stand.
Away, Hieronimo! To him° be gone!   (*Pluto, king of hell*)
He'll do thee justice for Horatio's death.
15   Turn down this path, thou shalt be with him straight,
Or this, and then thou need'st not take thy breath.[9]
This way, or that way? Soft and fair,° not so;   *Wait a moment*
For if I hang or kill myself, let's know°   *consider*
Who will revenge Horatio's murder then?
No, no, fie, no! Pardon me; I'll none of that.
20   [*He flings away the dagger and halter.*°]   *noose*
This way I'll take, and this way comes the King,
      [*He takes them up again.*]
And here I'll have a fling at him, that's flat.°   *certain*
And, Balthazar, I'll be with thee to bring,°   *I'll get even with you*
And thee, Lorenzo! Here's the King; nay, stay,

8. Hieronimo carries the traditional gear of
the suicide: a dagger and a rope, which can
be made into a noose.

9. Hieronimo considers two paths for ending
his life: the poniard or the noose. *Need'st not
take thy breath*: need not live any longer.

And here, ay, here, there goes the hare away.° *the prey escapes*

25   [*Enter* KING, AMBASSADOR, CASTILE, *and* LORENZO.]

KING   Now show, Ambassador, what our viceroy° saith.   *the viceroy of Portugal*
    Hath he received the articles° we sent?   *terms*

HIERONIMO   Justice, oh, justice to Hieronimo!

LORENZO   Back! See'st thou not the King is busy?

30 HIERONIMO   Oh, is he so?

KING   Who is he that interrupts our business?

HIERONIMO   Not I. [*Aside*] Hieronimo, beware! Go by,° go by.   *Beware*

AMBASSADOR   Renownèd King, he hath received and read
    Thy kingly proffers and thy promised league,

35   And, as a man extremely overjoyed
    To hear his son so princely entertained,
    Whose death he had so solemnly bewailed,
    This, for thy further satisfaction
    And kingly love, he kindly lets thee know:

40   First, for° the marriage of his princely son   *as for*
    With Bel-imperia, thy belovèd niece,
    The news are more delightful to his soul
    Than myrrh or incense to the offended heavens.
    In person therefore will he come himself

45   To see the marriage rites solemnized;
    And, in the presence of the court of Spain,
    To knit a sure inexplicable band°   *indissoluble bond*
    Of kingly love and everlasting league
    Betwixt the crowns of Spain and Portingale,

50   There will he give his crown to Balthazar
    And make a queen of Bel-imperia.

KING   Brother, how like you this our Viceroy's love?

CASTILE   No doubt, my lord, it is an argument°   *proof*
    Of honorable care to keep° his friend,   *keep you as*

55   And wondrous zeal to Balthazar, his son;
    Nor am I least indebted to His Grace,
    That bends° his liking to my daughter thus.   *directs*

AMBASSADOR   Now last, dread lord, here hath His Highness sent—
    Although he send not that his son return[1]—

60   His ransom due to Don Horatio.

      [*The ransom is brought forward.*]

HIERONIMO   Horatio? Who calls Horatio?

KING   And well remembered; thank His Majesty.—
    Here, see it given to Horatio.

HIERONIMO   Justice, oh, justice, justice, gentle King!

65 KING   Who is that? Hieronimo?

HIERONIMO   Justice, oh, justice! Oh, my son, my son,
    My son whom naught can ransom or redeem!

LORENZO   Hieronimo, you are not well advised.°   *not behaving properly*

HIERONIMO   Away, Lorenzo, hinder me no more,

---

1. The Viceroy no longer needs to request the return of Balthazar.

70　For thou hast made me bankrupt of my bliss.
　　Give me my son! You shall not ransom him.
　　Away! I'll rip the bowels of the earth
　　　　[*He diggeth with his dagger.*]
　　And ferry over to th'Elysian plains,°　　　　　　　　　　*(see 1.1.73n)*
　　And bring my son to show his deadly wounds.
75　Stand from about° me!　　　　　　　　　　　　　　　*away from*
　　I'll make a pickax of my poniard,
　　And here surrender up my marshalship;
　　For I'll go marshal up the fiends in hell
　　To be avengèd on you all for this.
80　KING　What means this outrage?°　　　　　　　　　　　*outburst*
　　Will none of you restrain his fury?
　　HIERONIMO　Nay, soft and fair;° you shall not need to strive.　*gently*
　　Needs must he go that the devils drive.[2]　　[*Exit.*]
　　KING　What accident hath happed° Hieronimo?　　*What has happened to*
85　I have not seen him to demean him so.°　　　　　　*behave this way*
　　LORENZO　My gracious lord, he is with extreme pride—
　　Conceived of young Horatio, his son,
　　And covetous of having to himself
　　The ransom of the young Prince Balthazar—
90　Distract and in a manner lunatic.
　　KING　Believe me, nephew, we are sorry for't.
　　This is the love that fathers bear their sons.
　　[*To* CASTILE] But, gentle brother, go give to him this gold,
　　The Prince's ransom; let him have his due;
95　For what he hath, Horatio shall not want.
　　Happily Hieronimo hath need thereof.[3]
　　LORENZO　But if he be thus helplessly distract,
　　'Tis requisite his office be resigned
　　And given to one of more discretion.
100　KING　We shall increase his melancholy so.
　　'Tis best that we see° further in it first,　　　　　　　*examine*
　　Till when, ourself will not exempt the place.[4]
　　And, brother, now bring in° the ambassador,　　　　　*escort in*
　　That he may be a witness of the match
105　'Twixt Balthazar and Bel-imperia,
　　And that we may prefix° a certain time　　　　　*decide in advance*
　　Wherein the marriage shall be solemnized,
　　That we may have thy lord the Viceroy here.
　　AMBASSADOR　Therein Your Highness highly shall content
110　His Majesty, that longs to hear from hence.
　　KING　On, then, and hear you,[5] Lord Ambassador. [*Exeunt.*]

---

2. That is, when the devil chases you, you
must keep moving.
3. Perhaps Hieronimo needs the reward.

4. Until which time, I will not remove Hieronimo from his office.
5. Come and hear what you will.

3.13

[SCENE: *The Knight Marshal's courtroom*]

[*Enter* HIERONIMO *with a book*° *in his hand.*]　　　　　(*of Seneca's plays*)

HIERONIMO　*Vindicta mihi!*[6]

　　Ay, heaven will be revenged of° every ill,　　　　　　　*on*
　　Nor will they° suffer murder unrepaid.　　　　　　(*the heavens*)
　　Then stay, Hieronimo, attend their will,
5　　For mortal men may not appoint their time.
　　Per scelus semper tutum est sceleribus iter.[7]
　　Strike, and strike home,° where wrong is offered thee,　　*all the way*
　　For evils unto ills conductors be,
　　And death's the worst of resolution.[8]
10　For he that thinks with patience to contend°　　　　　　*strive for*
　　To quiet life, his life shall easily° end.　　　　　　*contentedly*
　　Fata si miseros juvant, habes salutem;
　　Fata si vitam negant, habes sepulchrum.[9]
　　If destiny thy miseries do ease,
15　Then hast thou health, and happy shalt thou be;
　　If destiny deny thee life, Hieronimo,
　　Yet shalt thou be assurèd of a tomb.
　　If neither,° yet let this thy comfort be:　　　　　(*happiness or tomb*)
　　Heaven covereth him that hath no burial.[1]
20　And to conclude, I will revenge his death!
　　But how? Not as the vulgar wits of men,
　　With open, but inevitable ills,
　　As by a secret, yet a certain, mean,
　　Which under kindship will be cloakèd best.[2]
25　Wise men will take their opportunity,
　　Closely and safely fitting things to time;°　　　　*finding the right moment*
　　But in extremes advantage hath no time,[3]
　　And therefore all times fit not for revenge.
　　Thus therefore will I rest me in unrest,
30　Dissembling quiet in unquietness,
　　Not seeming that I know their villainies,
　　That my simplicity° may make them think　　　　　　*naïveté*
　　That ignorantly I will let all slip;
　　For ignorance, I wot,° and well they know,　　　　　*know*
35　*Remedium malorum iners est.*[4]

6. Vengeance is mine! (Latin; see Deuteronomy 32.35 and Romans 12.19, where similar language is used by God).

7. The safe way for crime is always through crime (Latin; slightly altered from Seneca, *Agamemnon* 115).

8. For evil deeds lead to further evil, and death is the worst thing that can happen to a resolute man.

9. From Seneca, *Troades* 510–12 (freely translated here in lines 14–17).

1. The heavens cover the dead who have no burial urn; that is, the heavens bless the virtuous dead even if they do not have proper burial rites (Lucan, *Pharsalia* 7.819).

2. Hieronimo will not pursue revenge like the common sort, with open violence, but through cunning, secrecy, and feigned kindness.

3. In extreme situations, there is no such thing as a perfect time to act.

4. [Ignorance] is a futile remedy for all evils (slightly altered from Seneca, *Oedipus* 515).

Nor aught avails it° me to menace them,   *Nor does it avail*
Who, as a wintry storm upon a plain,
Will bear me down with their nobility.°   *seniority in rank*
No, no, Hieronimo, thou must enjoin
40 Thine eyes to observation, and thy tongue
To milder speeches than thy spirit affords,
Thy heart to patience, and thy hands to rest,
Thy cap to curtsey,° and thy knee to bow,   *doffing (as a salute)*
Till to revenge thou know when, where, and how.
   [*A noise within.*]
45 How now, what noise? What coil is that you keep?°   *What fuss is this?*
   [*Enter a* SERVANT.]
SERVANT   Here are a sort,° of poor petitioners,   *group*
That are importunate, an° it shall please you, sir,   *if*
That you should plead their cases to the King.
HIERONIMO   That I should plead their several actions?°   *various petitions*
50 Why, let them enter, and let me see them.
   [*Enter three* CITIZENS *and an old man (Don* BAZULTO).]
FIRST CITIZEN [*to his companions*]   So I tell you this: for
   learning and for law,
There's not any advocate in Spain
That can prevail, or will take half the pain,°   *pains, efforts*
That he will in pursuit of equity.
55 HIERONIMO   Come near, you men that thus importune me.
   [*Aside*] Now must I bear a face of gravity,
For thus I used, before my marshalship,
To plead in causes as corregidor.°—   *advocate*
Come on, sirs, what's the matter?
SECOND CITIZEN   Sir, an action.
60 HIERONIMO   Of battery?
FIRST CITIZEN   Mine of debt.
HIERONIMO   Give place.°   *Stand back*
SECOND CITIZEN   No, sir, mine is an action of the case.°   *special appeal*
THIRD CITIZEN   Mine an *ejectione firmae*° by a lease.   *eviction notice (Latin)*
HIERONIMO   Content you, sirs. Are you determinèd
That I should plead your several actions?
65 FIRST CITIZEN   Ay, sir, and here's my declaration.
SECOND CITIZEN   And here is my band.°   *bond*
THIRD CITIZEN   And here is my lease.
   [*They give him papers.*]
HIERONIMO   But wherefore stands yon silly° man so mute,   *pitiable*
With mournful eyes and hands to heaven upreared?
Come hither, father,° let me know thy cause.   *old man*
70 BAZULTO   O worthy sir, my cause but° slightly known   *although*
May move the hearts of warlike Myrmidons,°   *(see 1.1.49n)*
And melt the Corsic° rocks with ruthful° tears.   *Corsican / pitying*
HIERONIMO   Say, father, tell me, what's thy suit?
BAZULTO   No, sir, could my woes
75 Give way unto my most distressful words,
Then should I not in paper, as you see,

With ink bewray what blood began in me.[5]

HIERONIMO [*reading*]   What's here? "The humble supplication
Of Don Bazulto for his murdered son."

80 BAZULTO Ay, sir.

HIERONIMO   No, sir, it was my murdered son,
Oh, my son, my son, oh, my son Horatio!
But mine, or thine, Bazulto, be content.
Here, take my handkercher and wipe thine eyes,
Whiles wretched I in thy mishaps may see

85   The lively° portrait of my dying self.   lifelike

                [*He draweth out a bloody napkin.*]

Oh, no, not this! Horatio, this was thine,
And when I dyed it in thy dearest blood,
This was a token 'twixt thy soul and me
That of thy death revengèd I should be.

                [*He draws out more objects.*]

90   But here, take this, and this—what, my purse?—
Ay, this and that, and all of them are thine,
For all as one° are our extremities.°   the same / sufferings

FIRST CITIZEN   Oh, see the kindness of Hieronimo!

SECOND CITIZEN   This gentleness shows him a gentleman.

95 HIERONIMO   See, see, oh, see thy shame, Hieronimo!
See here a loving father to his son!
Behold the sorrows and the sad laments
That he delivereth for his son's decease!
If love's effects so strives in lesser things,

100   If love enforce such moods in meaner wits,°   lower intelligences
If love express such power in poor estates,°   lower classes
Hieronimo, whenas° a raging sea,   when
Tossed with the wind and tide, o'erturneth then
The upper billows, course of waves to keep,

105   Whilest lesser waters labor in the deep,[6]
Then shamest thou not, Hieronimo, to neglect
The sweet revenge of thy Horatio?
Though on this earth justice will not be found,
I'll down to hell, and in this passion

110   Knock at the dismal gates of Pluto's court,
Getting by force, as once Alcides[7] did,
A troop of Furies and tormenting hags
To torture Don Lorenzo and the rest.
Yet lest the triple-headed porter° should   Cerberus

115   Deny my passage to the slimy strand,°   shore

5. If I could speak my miseries, I wouldn't
have to write down in ink what blood and passion have stirred up in me.
6. Hieronimo accuses himself of neglecting
his duty to his son, contrasting the blustering
(but ineffective) surface of the sea with the

more forceful waters of the deep, as seen in
the mute but profound grief of a "lesser" man
such as Don Bazulto.
7. That is, Heracles (Hercules), the greatest
of the heroes in classical mythology; his final
labor was to carry Cerberus away from Hades.

The Thracian poet[8] thou shalt counterfeit:
Come on, old father, be my Orpheus,
And if thou canst no notes° upon the harp,   cannot play
Then sound the burden[9] of thy sore heart's grief,
120   Till we do gain° that Proserpine may grant   obtain
Revenge on them that murderèd my son.
Then will I rend and tear them thus and thus,
Shivering their limbs in pieces with my teeth.
          [*Tear the papers.*]
      FIRST CITIZEN   Oh, sir, my declaration!
          [*Exit* HIERONIMO, *and they after.*]
125   SECOND CITIZEN   Save my bond!
          [*Enter* HIERONIMO *followed still by the* CITIZENS.]
      Save my bond!
      THIRD CITIZEN   Alas, my lease! It cost me ten pound,
      And you, my lord, have torn the same.
      HIERONIMO   That cannot be; I gave it never a wound.
130   Show me one drop of blood fall from the same.
      How is it possible I should slay it, then?
      Tush, no. Run after; catch me if you can.
          [*Exeunt all but the old man,* BAZULTO.]

          [BAZULTO *remains till* HIERONIMO *enters again, who,*
          staring him in the face, speaks.]
      And art thou come, Horatio, from the depth,
      To ask for justice in this upper earth?
135   To tell thy father thou art unrevenged?
      To wring more tears from Isabella's eyes,
      Whose lights are dimmed with overlong laments?
      Go back, my son; complain to Aeacus,°   judge of the dead
      For here's no justice. Gentle boy, begone,
140   For justice is exilèd from the earth.
      Hieronimo will bear thee company.
      Thy mother cries on righteous Rhadamanth°   judge of the dead
      For just revenge against the murderers.
      BAZULTO   Alas, my lord, whence springs this troubled speech?
145   HIERONIMO   But° let me look on my Horatio.   Only
      Sweet boy, how art thou changed in death's black shade!
      Had Proserpine no pity on thy youth,
      But suffered thy fair crimson-colored spring
      With withered winter to be blasted° thus?   blighted, stricken
150   Horatio, thou art older than thy father.
      Ah, ruthless fate, that favor thus transforms!°   alters the face
      BAZULTO   Ah, my good lord, I am not your young son.
      HIERONIMO   What, not my son? Thou, then, a Fury art,
      Sent from the empty kingdom of black night

----

8. Orpheus, the greatest poet and singer in classical mythology, who journeyed to the underworld in an attempt to bring back to the living his dead wife, Eurydice.
9. Heavy load, with a pun on "burden" meaning the refrain or chorus of a song.

155   To summon me to make appearance
      Before grim Minos and just Rhadamanth,
      To plague Hieronimo, that° is remiss   *who*
      And seeks not vengeance for Horatio's death.

     BAZULTO   I am a grievèd man, and not a ghost,
160   That came for justice for my murdered son.

     HIERONIMO   Ay, now I know thee, now thou namest my son:
      Thou art the lively image of my grief.
      Within thy face, my sorrows I may see.
      Thy eyes are gummed with tears, thy cheeks are wan,
165   Thy forehead troubled, and thy mutt'ring lips
      Murmur sad words abruptly broken off;
      By force of windy sighs thy spirit breathes,
      And all this sorrow riseth for thy son;
      And selfsame sorrow feel I for my son.
170   Come in, old man; thou shalt to Isabel.
      Lean on my arm; I thee, thou me shalt stay,°   *support*
      And thou, and I, and she will sing a song,
      Three parts in one, but all of discords framed.°   *composed*
      Talk not of cords,° but let us now be gone,   *chords; ropes*
175   For with a cord Horatio was slain.   *[Exeunt.]*

3.14

[SCENE: *The Spanish royal court.*]

> [*Enter* KING *of Spain, the Duke of* CASTILE, VICEROY, *and*
> LORENZO, BALTHAZAR, *Don* PEDRO, *and* BEL-IMPERIA *attended by*
> *servants. The Spanish and Portuguese parties, entering from*
> *opposite sides, meet and formally greet one another.*]

     KING   Go, brother, it is the Duke of Castile's cause;[1]
      Salute the Viceroy in our name.

     CASTILE   I go.

> [*He embraces the* VICEROY.]

     VICEROY   Go forth, Don Pedro, for thy nephew's° sake,   *(Bathazar's)*
      And greet the Duke of Castile.

     PEDRO   It shall be so.

> [*He embraces* CASTILE.]

5   KING   And now to meet these Portuguese,
      For as we now are, so sometimes° were these,   *formerly*
      Kings and commanders of the western Indies.

> [*The* KING *embraces the* VICEROY.]

      Welcome, brave Viceroy, to the court of Spain,
      And welcome, all his honorable train.°   *entourage*
10   'Tis not unknown to us forwhy° you come,   *why*
      Or have so kingly° crossed the seas.   *in royal splendor*
      Sufficeth it in this we note the troth°   *fealty, obligation*
      And more than common love you lend° to us.   *give*

---

1. Castile, as father of the bride-to-be, is deeply involved in the marriage treaty.

So is it that mine honorable niece

15 (For it beseems° us now that it be known)   *suits*
Already is betrothed to Balthazar,
And by appointment and our condescent°   *consent*
Tomorrow are they to be married.
To this intent we entertain thyself,

20 Thy followers, their pleasure, and our peace.[2]
Speak, men of Portingale, shall it be so?
If ay, say so; if not, say flatly no.

VICEROY   Renownèd King, I come not as thou think'st,
With doubtful followers, unresolvèd men,

25 But such as have upon thine articles
Confirmed thy motion° and contented me.   *proposal*
Know, sovereign, I come to solemnize
The marriage of thy belovèd niece,
Fair Bel-imperia, with my Balthazar—

30 With thee, my son, whom, sith° I live to see,   *since*
Here, take my crown; I give it her and thee—
And let me live a solitary life,
In ceaseless prayers,
To think how strangely° heaven hath thee preserved.   *miraculously*
    [He weeps.]

35 KING [*to* CASTILE]   See, brother, see, how nature° strives in him!—   *natural feeling*
Come, worthy Viceroy, and accompany
Thy friend° with thine extremities;°   *Me / extremes of emotion*
A place more private fits this princely mood.

VICEROY   Or° here or where Your Highness thinks it good.   *Either*
    [Exeunt all but CASTILE *and* LORENZO *and servants.]*

40 CASTILE   Nay, stay, Lorenzo, let me talk with you.
See'st thou this entertainment° of these kings?   *reception*

LORENZO   I do, my lord, and joy to see the same.

CASTILE   And knowest thou why this meeting is?

LORENZO   For her, my lord, whom Balthazar doth love,

45 And to confirm their promised marriage.

CASTILE   She is thy sister.

LORENZO   Who, Bel-imperia?
Ay, my gracious lord, and this is the day
That I have longed so happily to see.

CASTILE   Thou wouldst be loath that any fault of thine

50 Should intercept° her in her happiness.   *obstruct*

LORENZO   Heavens will not let Lorenzo err so much.

CASTILE   Why, then, Lorenzo, listen to my words:
It is suspected, and reported too,
That thou, Lorenzo, wrong'st Hieronimo,

55 And in his suits towards His Majesty
Still keep'st him back, and seeks to cross° his suit.   *prevent*

LORENZO   That I, my lord?

---

2. The King connects the young couple's happiness with peace between the two countries.

CASTILE   I tell thee, son, myself have heard it said,
         When to my sorrow I have been ashamed
60   To answer for thee, though thou art my son.
         Lorenzo, knowest thou not the common° love   *widespread*
         And kindness that Hieronimo hath won
         By his deserts° within the court of Spain?   *merits*
         Or see'st thou not the King my brother's care
65   In his behalf, and to procure his health?°   *well-being*
         Lorenzo, shouldst thou thwart his passions,°   *complaints*
         And he exclaim against thee to the King,
         What honor were't in this assembly,
         Or what a scandal were't among the kings
70   To hear Hieronimo exclaim on° thee!   *denounce*
         Tell me—and look thou° tell me truly too—   *see to it*
         Whence grows the ground° of this report in court?   *basis*
LORENZO   My lord, it lies not in Lorenzo's power
         To stop the vulgar,° liberal of° their tongues.   *commoners / too free with*
75   A small advantage makes a water-breach,[3]
         And no man lives that long contenteth all.
CASTILE   Myself have seen thee busy to keep back
         Him and his supplications from the King.
LORENZO   Yourself, my lord, hath seen his passions,
80   That ill beseemed the presence of a king,
         And, for° I pitied him in his distress,   *because*
         I held him thence with kind and courteous words,
         As free from malice to Hieronimo
         As to my soul, my lord.
85 CASTILE   Hieronimo, my son, mistakes thee then.
LORENZO   My gracious father, believe me, so he doth.
         But what's a silly man, distract in mind,
         To think upon the murder of his son?
         Alas, how easy is it for him to err!
90   But, for his satisfaction and the world's,
         'Twere good, my lord, that Hieronimo and I
         Were reconciled, if he misconster° me.   *misconstrue*
CASTILE   Lorenzo, thou hast said;° it shall be so.—   *spoken wisely*
         Go, one of you, and call Hieronimo.   [*Exit a* SERVANT.]
             [*Enter* BALTHAZAR *and* BEL-IMPERIA.]
95 BALTHAZAR   Come, Bel-imperia, Balthazar's content,
         My sorrow's ease and sovereign of my bliss,
         Sith° heaven hath ordained thee to be mine: *Since*
         Disperse those clouds and melancholy looks,
         And clear them up with those thy sun-bright eyes
100   Wherein my hope and heaven's fair beauty lies.
BEL-IMPERIA   My looks, my lord, are fitting for my love,
         Which, new begun, can show° no brighter yet.   *look*
BALTHAZAR   New-kindled flames should burn as morning sun.

---

3. A small leak, if unchecked, becomes a flood.

BEL-IMPERIA   But not too fast, lest heat and all be done.°   *consumed*
105   I see my lord my father.
BALTHAZAR   Truce,[4] my love.
      I will go salute him.
CASTILE   Welcome, Balthazar,
      Welcome, brave Prince, the pledge of Castile's peace![5]
      And welcome, Bel-imperia. How now, girl?
      Why comest thou sadly to salute us° thus?   *greet me*
110   Content thyself, for I am satisfied.
      It is not now as when Andrea lived;
      We have forgotten and forgiven that,
      And thou art gracèd with a happier love.—
      But, Balthazar, here comes Hieronimo.
115   I'll have a word with him.

               [*Enter* HIERONIMO *and a* SERVANT.]

HIERONIMO   And where's the Duke?
SERVANT   Yonder.
HIERONIMO [*aside*]   Even so.
      What new device have they devisèd, trow?°   *do you suppose*
      Pocas palabras,° mild as the lamb.   *Few words (Spanish)*
      Is't I will be revenged? No, I am not the man.[6]
120   CASTILE   Welcome, Hieronimo.
LORENZO   Welcome, Hieronimo.
BALTHAZAR   Welcome, Hieronimo.
HIERONIMO   My lords, I thank you for Horatio.
CASTILE   Hieronimo, the reason that I sent
125   To speak with you is this.
HIERONIMO   What, so short?
      Then I'll be gone, I thank you for't.[7]   [*He starts to leave.*]
CASTILE   Nay, stay, Hieronimo.—Go call him, son.
LORENZO   Hieronimo, my father craves a word with you.
HIERONIMO   With me, sir? Why, my lord, I thought you had done.
130   LORENZO [*aside*]   No, would he had.
CASTILE   Hieronimo, I hear
      You find yourself aggrievèd at my son,
      Because you have not access unto the King,
      And say 'tis he that intercepts your suits.
HIERONIMO   Why, is not this a miserable thing, my lord?
135   CASTILE   Hieronimo, I hope you have no cause,
      And would be loath° that one of your deserts   *I would hate*
      Should once have reason to suspect my son,
      Considering how I think of you myself.
HIERONIMO   Your son Lorenzo? Whom,° my noble lord?   *Is that whom*
140   The hope of Spain, mine honorable friend?

---

4. That is, let's call a truce to our contest of
words.
5. Castile sees Balthazar as the assurance of
peace for the two countries and for himself.

6. Hieronimo assumes the disguise of patient
forbearance in order to deceive his enemies.
7. Hieronimo continues to feign madness,
here by leaving too hastily.

Grant me the combat of them,[8] if they dare.

    [*Draws out his sword.*]

I'll meet him face to face to tell me so.
These be the scandalous reports of such
As loves° not me, and hate my lord° too much.   *love / you, my lord*
145 Should I suspect Lorenzo would prevent
Or cross my suit, that loved my son so well?
My lord, I am ashamed it should be said.
LORENZO   Hieronimo, I never gave you cause.
HIERONIMO   My good lord, I know you did not.
CASTILE   There then pause,
150 And for the satisfaction of the world,
Hieronimo, frequent my homely° house,   *welcoming; humble*
The Duke of Castile, Cyprian's ancient seat,
And when thou wilt, use° me, my son, and it;   *make use of*
But here, before Prince Balthazar and me,
155 Embrace each other, and be perfect friends.
HIERONIMO   Ay, marry,° my lord, and shall.   *by Mary*
Friends, quoth he? See, I'll be friends with you all,
[*To* BALTHAZAR] Specially with you, my lovely lord.
For divers causes it is fit for us
160 That we be friends; the world is suspicious,
And men may think what we imagine not.
BALTHAZAR   Why, this is friendly done, Hieronimo.
LORENZO   And thus, I hope, old grudges are forgot.
HIERONIMO   What else?° It were a shame it should not be so.   *But of course*
165 CASTILE   Come on, Hieronimo, at my request,
Let us entreat your company today.
HIERONIMO   Your Lordship's to command.

            [*Exeunt all but* HIERONIMO.]

            Pha! Keep your way.

Chi mi fa più carezze che non suole,
Tradito mi ha, o tradir mi vuole.[9]   [*Exit.*]

3.15

[SCENE: *The chorus to act 3.*]

    [*Ghost of* ANDREA *and* REVENGE *remain onstage.*]

ANDREA   Awake, Erictho!° Cerberus, awake!   *a sorceress*
Solicit Pluto, gentle Proserpine!
To combat, Acheron and Erebus!°   *Hades*
For ne'er by Styx and Phlegethon° in hell   *rivers of the underworld*
5 . . . .[1]
Nor ferried Charon to the fiery lakes

---

8. Allow me to challenge those who suggest
this of me.
9. He who caresses me more than usual either
has betrayed me or wishes to do so (Italian).

1. The grammatical difficulty here suggests
that a line—"Was I distressed with outrage sore
as this," or words to that effect—is missing.

Such fearful sights as poor Andrea sees!
Revenge, awake!
REVENGE   Awake? Forwhy?°   *Why?*
10 ANDREA   Awake, Revenge, for thou art ill-advised
To sleep away what thou art warned° to watch.   *urged*
REVENGE   Content thyself, and do not trouble me.
ANDREA   Awake, Revenge, if love,° as love hath had,   *my cause of love*
Have yet the power or prevalence in hell!
15 Hieronimo with Lorenzo is joined in league
And intercepts° our passage to revenge.   *interferes with*
Awake, Revenge, or we are woebegone!
REVENGE   Thus worldlings ground what they have dreamed upon.[2]
Content thyself, Andrea. Though I sleep,
20 Yet is my mood soliciting° their souls.   *inciting, drawing on*
Sufficeth° thee that poor Hieronimo   *Let it satisfy*
Cannot forget his son Horatio.
Nor dies Revenge, although he sleep awhile;
For in unquiet, quietness is feigned,[3]
25 And slumb'ring is a common worldly wile.
Behold, Andrea, for an instance how
Revenge hath slept, and then imagine thou
What 'tis to be subject to destiny.
          [*Enter a dumb show of two torchbearers and Hymen.*°]   *god of marriage*
ANDREA   Awake, Revenge! Reveal this mystery.[4]
30 REVENGE   The two first the nuptial torches bore
As brightly burning as the midday's sun;
But after them doth Hymen hie° as fast,   *hasten*
Clothèd in sable° and a saffron° robe,   *black / yellow*
And blows them out and quencheth them with blood,
35 As° discontent that things continue so.   *As if*
ANDREA   Sufficeth me thy meaning's understood,
And thanks to thee and those infernal powers
That will not tolerate a lover's woe.
Rest thee, for I will sit to see the rest.
40 REVENGE   Then argue not, for thou hast thy request.
                    [*Exeunt dumb show.*]

4.1

[SCENE: *A room in* CASTILE's *palace.*]

[*Enter* BEL-IMPERIA *and* HIERONIMO.]

BEL-IMPERIA   Is this the love thou bear'st Horatio?
Is this the kindness that thou counterfeits?
Are these the fruits of thine incessant tears?
Hieronimo, are these thy passions,°   *passionate outcries*

---

2. Thus mortal men take their dreams for reality.
3. For in a state of turmoil, quietness can be feigned (in order to accomplish vengeance).
4. Explain (1) this dramatic spectacle; (2) this enigma, puzzle.

5   Thy protestations, and thy deep laments
     That thou wert wont to weary men withal?
     O unkind° father! O deceitful world!   *unnatural; unloving*
     With what excuses canst thou show thyself?
     With what devices seek thyself to save
10 From this dishonor and the hate of men,
     Thus to neglect the loss and life of him
     Whom both my letters and thine own belief
     Assures thee to be causeless slaughterèd?
     Hieronimo, for shame, Hieronimo,
15 Be not a history° to aftertimes   *an example*
     Of such ingratitude unto thy son.
     Unhappy mothers of such children then,
     But monstrous fathers, to forget so soon
     The death of those whom they with care and cost
20 Have tendered° so, thus careless should be lost!   *cared for*
     Myself, a stranger in respect of thee,[5]
     So loved his life as still° I wish their° deaths,   *constantly / (his enemies')*
     Nor shall his death be unrevenged by me,
     Although I bear it out° for fashion's sake.   *pretend to accept it*
25 For here I swear, in sight of heaven and earth,
     Shouldst thou neglect the love thou shouldst retain,
     And give it over° and devise° no more,   *give up / plot*
     Myself should send their hateful souls to hell
     That wrought his downfall with extremest death.
30 HIERONIMO   But may it be that Bel-imperia
     Vows such revenge as she hath deigned to say?
     Why, then, I see that heaven applies our drift,°   *aids our intents*
     And all the saints do sit soliciting
     For vengeance on those cursèd murderers.
35 Madam, 'tis true, and now I find it so,°   *confirmed*
     I found a letter, written in your name,
     And in that letter how Horatio died.
     Pardon, oh, pardon, Bel-imperia,
     My fear and care° in not believing it,   *caution*
40 Nor think I thoughtless think upon a mean
     To let his death be unrevenged at full![6]
     And here I vow, so° you but give consent   *provided that*
     And will conceal my resolution,
     I will ere long determine of° their deaths,   *bring about*
45 That causeless thus have murderèd my son.
    BEL-IMPERIA   Hieronimo, I will consent, conceal,
     And aught that may effect for thine avail°   *that can help you*
     Join with thee to revenge Horatio's death.
    HIERONIMO   On, then. Whatsoever I devise,
50 Let me entreat you grace° my practices,   *support*
     Forwhy° the plot's already in mine head.—   *Why*

---

5. I, who have only a distant relation with Horatio compared to you.

6. Do not think that I am not contemplating a way to revenge Horatio's death to the utmost!

Here they are.

[*Enter* BALTHAZAR *and* LORENZO.]

BALTHAZAR   How now, Hieronimo,
What, courting Bel-imperia?

HIERONIMO   Ay, my lord,
Such courting as, I promise you,
55 She hath my heart;° but you, my lord, have hers.   *affection; secret*

LORENZO   But now, Hieronimo, or never,
We are to entreat your help.

HIERONIMO   My help?
Why, my good lords, assure yourselves of me,
For you have given me cause,
60 Ay, by my faith have you.

BALTHAZAR   It pleased you
At the entertainment of the ambassador
To grace the King so much as with a show.[7]
Now, were your study° so well furnished   *learning*
As, for the passing° of the first night's sport,°   *conducting / diversion*
65 To entertain my father with the like,
Or any suchlike pleasing motion,°   *entertainment*
Assure yourself it would content them well.

HIERONIMO   Is this all?

BALTHAZAR   Ay, this is all.

70 HIERONIMO   Why, then, I'll fit you;[8] say no more.
When I was young, I gave my mind
And plied myself to fruitless° poetry,   *impractical*
Which, though it profit the professor° naught,   *poet, practitioner*
Yet is it passing° pleasing to the world.   *exceedingly*

75 LORENZO   And how for that?°   *What of it?*

HIERONIMO   Marry, my good lord, thus—
And yet methinks you are too quick with us—
When in Toledo there I studied,
It was my chance to write a tragedy—
See here, my lords—   [*He shows them a book.*]
80 Which, long forgot, I found this° other day.   *the*
Now, would Your Lordships favor me so much
As but to grace me with your acting it—
I mean, each one of you to play a part—
Assure you it will prove most passing strange,°   *wonderful*
85 And wondrous plausible° to that assembly.   *worthy of applause*

BALTHAZAR   What, would you have us play a tragedy?

HIERONIMO   Why, Nero thought it no disparagement,[9]
And kings and emperors have ta'en delight
To make experience° of their wits in plays!   *trial*
90 LORENZO   Nay, be not angry, good Hieronimo;

---

7. Honor him with a performance (see 1.4.136–74).
8. (1) I'll accommodate your request; (2) I'll get you back.

9. The Roman emperor Nero (r. 54–68 C.E.), widely viewed as a dissipated tyrant, delighted in acting in and watching plays.

The Prince but asked a question.

BALTHAZAR   In faith, Hieronimo, an° you be in earnest,   *if*
I'll make one.°   *play a part*

LORENZO   And I another.

95 HIERONIMO   Now, my good lord, could you entreat
Your sister Bel-imperia to make one—
For what's a play without a woman in it?

BEL-IMPERIA   Little entreaty shall serve° me, Hieronimo,   *be needed to persuade*
For I must needs be employed in your play.

100 HIERONIMO   Why, this is well. I tell you, lordings,
It was determinèd° to have been acted   *intended; written*
By gentlemen and scholars too,
Such as could tell what° to speak.   *would have the skill*

BALTHAZAR   And now it shall be played by princes and courtiers

105 Such as can tell how to speak,
If, as it is our country manner,°   *custom*
You will but let us know the argument.°   *plot*

HIERONIMO   That shall I roundly.° The chronicles of Spain   *immediately*
Record this written of a knight of Rhodes:

110 He was betrothed and wedded at the length
To one Perseda, an Italian dame,
Whose beauty ravished all that her beheld,
Especially the soul of Suleiman,[1]
Who at the marriage was the chiefest guest.

115 By sundry means sought Suleiman to win
Perseda's love, and could not gain the same.
Then 'gan he break° his passions to a friend,   *make known*
One of his bashaws° whom he held full dear.   *pashas, nobles*
Her had this bashaw long solicited,

120 And saw she was not otherwise to be won
But by her husband's death, this knight of Rhodes,
Whom presently by treachery he slew.
She, stirred with an exceeding hate therefor,
As cause° of this slew Suleiman,   *Because*

125 And, to escape the bashaw's tyranny,
Did stab herself; and this the tragedy.

LORENZO   Oh, excellent!

BEL-IMPERIA   But say, Hieronimo,
What then became of him that was the bashaw?

HIERONIMO   Marry, thus: moved with remorse of his misdeeds,

130 Ran to a mountaintop and hung himself.

BALTHAZAR   But which of us is to perform that part?

HIERONIMO   Oh, that will I, my lords, make no doubt of it;
I'll play the murderer, I warrant you,
For I already have conceited° that.   *imagined, designed*

135 BALTHAZAR   And what shall I?

HIERONIMO   Great Suleiman, the Turkish emperor.

LORENZO   And I?

---

1. Suleiman I, known as "the Magnificent" (r. 1520–66), sultan of the Ottoman Empire.

HIERONIMO	Erastus, the Knight of Rhodes.	
BEL-IMPERIA	And I?	

140 HIERONIMO Perseda, chaste and resolute.

And here, my lords, are several abstracts° drawn, *individual parts*

For each of you to note° your parts *observe; memorize*

And act it as occasion's offered you.

You must provide a Turkish cap,

145   A black mustachio, and a fauchion;° *falchion, curved sword*

[*Gives a paper to* BALTHAZAR.]

You with a cross like to a knight of Rhodes;

[*Gives another to* LORENZO.]

And, madam, you must attire yourself

[*He giveth* BEL-IMPERIA ANOTHER.]

Like Phoebe, Flora, or the Huntress,[2]

Which to your discretion shall seem best.

150   And as for me, my lords, I'll look to one,° *prepare my part*

And, with the ransom that the Viceroy sent,

So furnish and perform this tragedy

As all the world shall say Hieronimo

Was liberal in gracing of° it so. *generous in presenting*

155 BALTHAZAR Hieronimo, methinks a comedy were better.

HIERONIMO A comedy?

Fie, comedies are fit for common wits;

But to present a kingly troop withal,° *to royal spectators*

Give me a stately written tragedy,

160   *Tragedia cothurnata*,[3] fitting kings,

Containing matter,° and not common things. *serious content*

My lords, all this must be performed

As fitting for the first night's reveling.

The Italian tragedians were so sharp of wit

165   That in one hour's meditation° *rehearsal*

They would perform anything in action.[4]

LORENZO And well it may,° for I have seen the like *may be so*

In Paris, 'mongst the French tragedians.

HIERONIMO In Paris? Mass,° and well remembered! *By the Mass*

170   There's one thing more that rests° for us to do. *remains*

BALTHAZAR What's that, Hieronimo? Forget not anything.

HIERONIMO Each one of us must act his part

In unknown languages,

That it may breed the more variety,

175   As you, my lord, in Latin, I in Greek,

You° in Italian; and forbecause° I know *(Lorenzo) / because*

That Bel-imperia hath practicèd the French,

---

2. Three classical divinities: Phoebe, a Titan who possessed the Delphic oracle before Apollo (and a name of Artemis, in her capacity as goddess of the moon); Flora, the Roman goddess of flowers and spring; and Artemis (the Roman Diana), goddess of the hunt.
3. Literally, "booted tragedy" (Italian). In clas-

sical Greece (and Rome), actors wore *cothornoi*, or high boots, that signaled that they were performing a tragedy, the most serious kind of drama.
4. Hieronimo describes the improvisational style of commedia dell'arte, a form of 16th- to 18th-century Italian comedy.

In courtly French shall all her phrases be.

BEL-IMPERIA   You mean to try my cunning° then, Hieronimo.   *learning; deceit*

180   BALTHAZAR   But this will be a mere° confusion,   *total*
And hardly shall we all be understood.

HIERONIMO   It must be so, for the conclusion
Shall prove the invention° and all was good;   *make good on the fiction*
And I myself, in an oration,

185   And with a strange and wondrous show besides
That I will have there behind a curtain,
Assure yourself, shall make the matter known.°   *explain the play*
And all shall be concluded in one scene,
For there's no pleasure ta'en in tediousness.

190   BALTHAZAR [*aside to* LORENZO]   How like you this?

LORENZO [*aside to* BALTHAZAR]   Why, thus, my lord:
We must resolve to soothe his humors up.°   *indulge him*

BALTHAZAR   On, then, Hieronimo. Farewell till soon.

HIERONIMO   You'll ply this gear?°   *undertake this*

LORENZO   I warrant you.

[*Exeunt all but* HIERONIMO.]

HIERONIMO   Why, so.

195   Now shall I see the fall of Babylon,
Wrought by the heavens in this confusion.[5]
And if the world like not this tragedy,
Hard is the hap of° old Hieronimo.   [*Exit.*]   *Bad luck for*

4.2

[SCENE: *The garden of* HIERONIMO's *house.*]

[*Enter* ISABELLA *with a weapon.*]

ISABELLA   Tell me no more! Oh, monstrous homicides!
Since neither piety nor pity moves
The King to justice or compassion,
I will revenge myself upon this place

5   Where thus they murdered my belovèd son.

[*She cuts down the arbor.*]

Down with these branches and these loathsome boughs
Of this unfortunate and fatal pine!
Down with them, Isabella, rend them up,
And burn the roots from whence the rest is sprung!

10   I will not leave a root, a stalk, a tree,
A bough, a branch, a blossom, nor a leaf,
No, not an herb within this garden plot.
Accursèd complot of my misery![6]
Fruitless forever may this garden be,

15   Barren the earth, and blissless whosoever

5. A possible reference both to the fall of the corrupt city of Babylon, as described in Revelation 18, and to the "confusion" of tongues that followed the destruction of the Tower of Babel (Genesis 11.1–9).

6. (1) Accursed garden; (2) accursed trickery of the murderers. Both are sources of her misery.

Imagines not to keep it unmanured![7]
An eastern wind, commixed with noisome° airs,   *foul, pestilent*
Shall blast° the plants and the young saplings;   *blight*
The earth with serpents shall be pesterèd,
20 And passengers,° for fear to be infect,   *passersby*
Shall stand aloof, and, looking at it, tell,
"There murdered died the son of Isabel."
Ay, here he died, and here I him embrace.
See where his ghost solicits with his wounds
25 Revenge on her that should revenge his death![8]
Hieronimo, make haste to see thy son,
For sorrow and despair hath cited° me   *summoned*
To hear Horatio plead with Rhadamanth.
Make haste, Hieronimo, to hold excused°   *offer excuses for*
30 Thy negligence in pursuit of their deaths
Whose hateful wrath bereavèd him of his breath.
Ah, nay, thou dost delay their deaths,
Forgives° the murderers of thy noble son,   *Thou forgivest*
And none but I bestir me—to no end.
35 And as I curse this tree from further fruit,
So shall my womb be cursèd for his sake,
And with this weapon will I wound the breast,
      [*She stabs herself.*]
The hapless breast that gave Horatio suck.   [*Exit.*][9]

4.3

[SCENE: *A hall in the Spanish royal court.*]

    [*Enter* HIERONIMO; *he knocks up*° *the curtain.*   *fastens up*
    Enter the Duke of CASTILE].

CASTILE   How now, Hieronimo, where's your fellows,
    That you take all this pain?°   *these pains, efforts*
HIERONIMO   Oh, sir, it is for the author's credit
    To look° that all things may go well.   *see to it*
5   But, good my lord, let me entreat Your Grace
    To give the King the copy of the play.
    This is the argument° of what we show.   *plot*
      [*He hands* CASTILE *a book.*]
CASTILE   I will, Hieronimo.
HIERONIMO   One thing more, my good lord.
10 CASTILE   What's that?
HIERONIMO   Let me entreat Your Grace
    That when the train° are passed into the gallery,°   *retinue / hall*
    You would vouchsafe to throw me down the key.
CASTILE   I will, Hieronimo.   [*Exit* CASTILE.]

7. May the person who plans to cultivate it be damned.
8. The wounds of Horatio's ghost call down revenge on any woman (especially me) who fails to avenge his death. *Should:* that is, should but does not.
9. Either Isabella stumbles offstage as she stabs herself or her body is removed from the stage before the start of the next scene.

15 HIERONIMO [*calling*]   What, are you ready, Balthazar?
  Bring a chair and a cushion for the King.

  [*Enter* BALTHAZAR *with a chair.*]

  Well done, Balthazar. Hang up the title;[1]
  Our scene is Rhodes. What, is your beard on?
  BALTHAZAR   Half on; the other is in my hand.
20 HIERONIMO   Dispatch, for shame! Are you so long?°   *slow*

  [*Exit* BALTHAZAR.]

  Bethink thyself, Hieronimo;
  Recall thy wits, recount thy former wrongs
  Thou hast received by murder of thy son,
  And lastly, not least, how Isabel,
25 Once his mother and thy dearest wife,
  All woebegone for him, hath slain herself.
  Behooves thee, then, Hieronimo, to be revenged!
  The plot is laid of dire revenge.
  On, then, Hieronimo, pursue revenge,
30 For nothing wants° but acting of revenge.   *is lacking*

  [*Exit* HIERONIMO.]

4.4

[SCENE: *Scene continues.*]

  [*Enter Spanish* KING, VICEROY, *the Duke of* CASTILE,
  and their train, including Don PEDRO.]

  KING   Now, Viceroy, shall we see the tragedy
  Of Suleiman, the Turkish emperor,
  Performed of pleasure by° your son the Prince,   *at the pleasure of*
  My nephew Don Lorenzo, and my niece.
5 VICEROY   Who, Bel-imperia?
  KING   Ay, and Hieronimo, our marshal,
  At whose request they deign to do't themselves.
  These be our pastimes in the court of Spain.—
  Here, brother, you shall be the bookkeeper.°   *prompter*
10 This is the argument of that they show.

  [*He giveth him*° *a book.*]   *(Castile)*

  (Gentlemen, this play of Hieronimo in sundry languages was thought
  good to be set down in English more largely for the easier understanding to every public reader.)[2]

  [*Enter* BALTHAZAR *as Suleiman,* BEL-IMPERIA *as Perseda,*
  and HIERONIMO *as the Bashaw.*]

  BALTHAZAR   *Bashaw, that Rhodes is ours, yield heavens the honor,*
  And holy Mahomet,° *our sacred prophet;*   *Muhammad*
  And be thou graced with every excellence

---

1. A board or other device to display for the
audience the name of the drama or the location of a scene.
2. A publisher's note to the reader of the text,
though it is possible that Castile reads this
from the playbook. It is accordingly impossible to determine whether or not the playlet
was performed for its Elizabethan audience
in multiple languages or in English.

15   *That Suleiman can give or thou desire.*
    But thy desert in conquering Rhodes is less
    Than in reserving° this fair Christian nymph,   *sparing the life of*
    Perseda, blissful lamp of excellence,
    Whose eyes compel, like powerful adamant,°   *a strong magnet*
20   *The warlike heart of Suleiman to wait.°*   *attend on her*
    KING   See, Viceroy, that is Balthazar, your son,
    That represents the Emperor Suleiman.
    How well he acts his amorous passion!
    VICEROY   Ay, Bel-imperia hath taught him that.
25 CASTILE   That's because his mind runs all on Bel-imperia.
    HIERONIMO   *Whatever° joy earth yields betide° Your Majesty!*   *May whatever / befall*
    BALTHAZAR   *Earth yields no joy without Perseda's love.*
    HIERONIMO   *Let then Perseda on Your Grace attend.*
    BALTHAZAR   *She shall not wait on me, but I on her;*
30   *Drawn by the influence of her lights,³ I yield.*
    But let my friend the Rhodian knight come forth,
    Erasto,° dearer than my life to me,   *Erastus (see 4.1.138)*
    That he may see Perseda, my beloved.
        [*Enter* LORENZO *as Erasto.*]
    KING   Here comes Lorenzo. Look upon the plot⁴
35   And tell me, brother: what part plays he?
    BEL-IMPERIA   *Ah, my Erasto, welcome to Perseda!*
    LORENZO   *Thrice happy is Erasto that thou livest.*
    Rhodes' loss is nothing to° Erasto's joy;   *compared with*
    Sith his Perseda lives, his life survives.
        [*Suleiman confers privately with the Bashaw.*]
40 BALTHAZAR   *Ah, Bashaw, here is love between Erasto*
    And fair Perseda, sovereign of my soul!
    HIERONIMO   *Remove Erasto, mighty Suleiman,*
    And then Perseda will be quickly won.
    BALTHAZAR   *Erasto is my friend, and while he lives*
45   *Perseda never will remove her love.*
    HIERONIMO   *Let not Erasto live to grieve great Suleiman.*
    BALTHAZAR   *Dear is Erasto in our princely eye.*
    HIERONIMO   *But if he be your rival, let him die.*
    BALTHAZAR   *Why, let him die; so love commandeth me.*
50   *Yet grieve I that Erasto should so die.*
        [*The Bashaw approaches Erasto.*]
    HIERONIMO   *Erasto, Suleiman saluteth thee,*
    And lets thee wit° by me His Highness' will,   *know*
    Which is, thou shouldst be thus employed.
        [*Stab him.*]
    BEL-IMPERIA   *Ay me!*
    Erasto! See, Suleiman, Erasto's slain!

---

3. Eyes. Active emanations or projections were believed to come from the eyes and exert influence or power.

4. The summary of the playlet provided for the court audience; that is, the book given by the King to the Viceroy (see 4.4.9–10).

BALTHAZAR   *Yet liveth Suleiman to comfort thee.*

55   *Fair queen of beauty, let not favor die,*[5]
  But with a gracious eye behold his grief°   *my lovesickness*
  That with Perseda's beauty is increased,
  If by Perseda his grief be not released.

BEL-IMPERIA   *Tyrant, desist soliciting vain suits!*

60   *Relentless*° *are mine ears to thy laments*   *As unyielding*
  As thy butcher° *is pitiless and base*   *(the Bashaw)*
  Which seized on my Erasto, harmless knight.
  Yet by thy power thou thinkest to command,
  And to thy power Perseda doth obey;

65   *But were she able, thus she would revenge*
  Thy treacheries on thee, ignoble prince,

            [Stab him.]

  And on herself she would be thus revenged.

            [Stab herself.]

KING   Well said!° Old Marshal, this was bravely° done!   *Well done / excellently*
HIERONIMO   But Bel-imperia plays Perseda well.

70 VICEROY   Were this in earnest, Bel-imperia,
  You would be better to my son than so.°   *in this play*

KING   But now what follows for Hieronimo?

HIERONIMO   Marry, this follows for Hieronimo:
  Here break we off our sundry languages,

75   And thus conclude I in our vulgar° tongue.   *vernacular*
  Haply° you think—but bootless° are your thoughts—   *Perhaps / useless*
  That this is fabulously counterfeit,°   *fictional*
  And that we do as all tragedians do:
  To die today, for fashioning our scene°—   *as part of the fiction*

80   The death of Ajax,[6] or some Roman peer—
  And in a minute, starting up again,
  Revive to please tomorrow's audience.
  No, princes, know I am Hieronimo,
  The hopeless father of a hapless son,

85   Whose tongue is tuned to tell his latest° tale,   *final*
  Not to excuse gross errors in the play.
  I see your looks urge instance° of these words.   *explanations*
  Behold the reason urging me to this.

      [*He draws back the curtain and shows his dead son.*°]   *(see 4.1.185–87,*
                                           4.3.0 SD)

  See here my show. Look on this spectacle!

90   Here lay my hope, and here my hope hath end;
  Here lay my heart, and here my heart was slain;
  Here lay my treasure, here my treasure lost;
  Here lay my bliss, and here my bliss bereft;
  But hope, heart, treasure, joy, and bliss

95   All fled, failed, died, yea, all decayed with this.

---

5. (1) Do not let love go unrequited; (2) do not let the love you had for Erastus be wasted.
6. The great Greek warrior; following the Trojan War, he killed himself in shame after realizing that in madness he had attacked cattle, believing that they were his enemies (a story told in Sophocles' *Ajax*, ca. 450 B.C.E.).

From forth these wounds came breath that gave me life;[7]
They murdered me that made these fatal marks.
The cause° was love, whence grew this mortal hate: *cause of Horatio's murder*
The hate, Lorenzo and young Balthazar,
100 The love, my son to Bel-imperia.
But night, the coverer of accursèd crimes,
With pitchy° silence hushed these traitors' harms,°   *dark / evil deeds*
And lent them leave,° for they had sorted leisure,[8]   *occasion*
To take advantage in my garden plot
105 Upon my son, my dear Horatio.
There, merciless, they butchered up my boy,
In black dark night, to pale, dim, cruel death.
He shrieks;° I heard—and yet methinks I hear—   *shrieked*
His dismal outcry echo in the air.
110 With soonest° speed I hasted to the noise,   *quickest*
Where, hanging on a tree, I found my son,
Through-girt° with wounds, and slaughtered as you see.   *Pierced*
And grieved I, think you, at this spectacle?
Speak, Portuguese, whose loss resembles mine.
115 If thou canst weep upon thy Balthazar,
'Tis like I wailed for my Horatio.
[*To* CASTILE] And you, my lord, whose reconcilèd° son   *(see 3.14.148–73)*
Marched in a net,° and thought himself unseen,   *as if invisible*
And rated° me for brainsick lunacy,   *berated*
120 With "God amend that mad Hieronimo!"
How can you brook° our play's catastrophe?   *endure*
And here behold this bloody handkercher,
    [*He draws forth the handkerchief from his breast.*]
Which at Horatio's death I weeping dipped
Within the river of his bleeding wounds.
125 It, as propitious,° see, I have reserved,°   *favorable / kept*
And never hath it left my bloody heart,
Soliciting remembrance of my vow
With these,° oh, these accursèd murderers,   *To be revenged on these*
Which, now performed, my heart is satisfied.
130 And to this end the Bashaw I became,
That might revenge me on Lorenzo's life,
Who therefore was appointed to the part
And was to represent the Knight of Rhodes,
That I might kill him more conveniently.
135 So, Viceroy, was this Balthazar, thy son,
That Suleiman which Bel-imperia,
In person of Perseda, murderèd,
Solely appointed to that tragic part
That she might slay him that offended her.
140 Poor Bel-imperia missed° her part in this,   *strayed from*
For, though the story saith she should have died,

7. From out of these wounds came the spirit   note).
on which my life depended (see 1.1.17 and   8. For they had found an opportunity.

Yet I of kindness and of care to her
Did otherwise determine of her end;
But love of him° whom they did hate too much   *(Horatio)*
145 Did urge her resolution to be such.
And, princes, now behold Hieronimo,
Author and actor in this tragedy,
Bearing his latest fortune in his fist,
And will as resolute conclude his part
150 As any of the actors gone before.
And, gentles,° thus I end my play.   *gentlemen and ladies*
Urge no more words; I have no more to say.
     [*He runs to hang himself.*]
KING   Oh, hearken, Viceroy!—Hold, Hieronimo!—
Brother, my nephew and thy son are slain.
155 VICEROY   We are betrayed! My Balthazar is slain.
Break ope the doors!⁹ Run, save Hieronimo!
     [*Attendants break in and restrain* HIERONIMO.]
Hieronimo, do but inform the King of these events.
Upon mine honor, thou shalt have no harm.
HIERONIMO   Viceroy, I will not trust thee with my life,
160 Which I this day have offered° to my son.   *(i.e., as a sacrifice)*
[*To an attendant*] Accursèd wretch,
Why stayest° thou him that was resolved to die?   *hinder*
KING   Speak, traitor! Damnèd, bloody murderer, speak!
For, now I have thee, I will make thee speak.
165 Why hast thou done this undeserving° deed?   *undeserved*
VICEROY   Why hast thou murderèd my Balthazar?
CASTILE   Why hast thou butchered both my children thus?
HIERONIMO   Oh, good words!°   *well said*
As dear to me was my Horatio
170 As yours, or yours, or yours, my lord, to you.
My guiltless son was by Lorenzo slain,
And by° Lorenzo and that Balthazar   *by the deaths of*
Am I at last revengèd thoroughly,
Upon whose souls may heavens be yet avenged
175 With greater far than these afflictions!
CASTILE   But who were thy confederates in this?
VICEROY   That was thy daughter Bel-imperia,
For by her hand my Balthazar was slain.
I saw her stab him.
KING [*to* HIERONIMO]   Why speakest thou not?
180 HIERONIMO   What lesser liberty can kings afford
Than harmless silence? Then afford it me.
Sufficeth I may not, nor I will not, tell thee.
KING   Fetch forth the tortures!—
Traitor as thou art, I'll make thee tell.
185 HIERONIMO   Indeed,

---

9. At 4.3.11–13, Hieronimo arranged to have the doors locked so that no one might escape.

Thou mayest torment me, as his wretched son
Hath done in murd'ring my Horatio,
But never shalt thou force me to reveal
The thing which I have vowed inviolate;[1]
190 And therefore, in despite of all thy threats,
Pleased with their deaths and eased with their revenge,
First take my tongue and afterwards my heart.
       [*He bites out his tongue.*]
KING Oh, monstrous resolution of a wretch!
See, Viceroy, he hath bitten forth his tongue
195 Rather than to reveal what we required.
CASTILE Yet can he write.
KING And if in this he satisfy us not,
We will devise th'extremest kind of death
That ever was invented for a wretch.
    [*Then he° makes signs for a knife to mend his pen.*[2]]   (Hieronimo)
200 CASTILE Oh, he would have a knife to mend his pen.
VICEROY Here, and advise thee° that thou write the truth.°   see to it / truth
    [*He° with a knife stabs the* DUKE *and himself.*]   (Hieronimo)
KING Look to my brother! Save Hieronimo!
What age hath ever heard such monstrous deeds?
My brother and the whole succeeding hope
205 That Spain expected after my decease!
Go bear his° body hence, that we may mourn   (Castile's)
The loss of our belovèd brother's death,
That he may be entombed whate'er befall.
I am the next, the nearest,° last of all.   closest in blood
210 VICEROY And thou, Don Pedro, do the like for us.
Take up our hapless son, untimely slain;
Set me with him, and he with woeful me,
Upon the mainmast of a ship unmanned,
And let the wind and tide haul me along
215 To Scylla's barking and untamèd gulf,[3]
Or to the loathsome pool of Acheron,°   (see 1.1.19n)
To weep my want for° my sweet Balthazar.   loss of
Spain hath no refuge for a Portingale.
    [*The trumpets sound a dead march, the* KING *of Spain*
      mourning after his brother's body, and the KING°*of*   (i.e., the viceroy)
      Portingale bearing the body of his son. Exeunt.]

4.5

[SCENE: *The final chorus.*]

[*Ghost of* ANDREA *and* REVENGE.]

ANDREA Ay, now my hopes have end in their effects,

1. Since Hieronimo has revealed all, it is hard to know what further information the King might want to know.
2. A quill pen requires constant maintenance with a penknife.
3. That is, the narrow Strait of Messina between Italy and Sicily, the location traditionally ascribed to the mythical sea monsters Scylla, who had dogs joined to her body, and Charybdis, who three times daily swallowed and spouted forth the water of the sea, forming a whirlpool.

When blood and sorrow finish my desires:
Horatio murdered in his father's bower,
Vile Serberine by Pedringano slain,
5   False Pedringano hanged by quaint° device,   *ingenious*
Fair Isabella by herself misdone,°   *done in*
Prince Balthazar by Bel-imperia stabbed,
The Duke of Castile and his wicked son
Both done to death by old Hieronimo,
10   My Bel-imperia fall'n as Dido fell,[4]
And good Hieronimo slain by himself—
Ay, these were spectacles to please my soul.
Now will I beg at lovely Proserpine,°   *queen of Hades*
That by the virtue of her princely doom°   *judgment*
15   I may consort° my friends in pleasing sort,   *accompany*
And on my foes work just and sharp revenge.
I'll lead my friend Horatio through those fields
Where never-dying wars are still inured;°   *carried on*
I'll lead fair Isabella to that train°   *company; way of life*
20   Where pity weeps but never feeleth pain;
I'll lead my Bel-imperia to those joys
That vestal virgins and fair queens possess;
I'll lead Hieronimo where Orpheus plays,°   *(see 3.13.116–17 and note)*
Adding sweet pleasure to eternal days.
25   But say, Revenge, for thou must help or none,
Against the rest how shall my hate be shown?
    REVENGE   This hand shall hale° them down to deepest hell,   *drag*
Where none but Furies, bugs,° and tortures dwell.   *bugbears, demons*
    ANDREA   Then, sweet Revenge, do this at my request:
30   Let me be judge and doom them to unrest.
Let loose poor Tityus from the vulture's gripe,[5]
And let Don Cyprian supply his room;°   *take his place*
Place Don Lorenzo on Ixion's wheel,°   *(see 1.1.66 and note)*
And let the lover's[6] endless pains surcease°   *cease*
35   (Juno forgets old wrath and grants him° ease);   *(Ixion)*
Hang Balthazar about Chimera's° neck,
And let him there bewail his bloody love,°   *deadly passion*
Repining at our joys that are above;
Let Serberine go roll the fatal stone,
40   And take from Sisyphus his endless moan;[7]
False Pedringano, for his treachery,
Let him be dragged through boiling Acheron,
And there live, dying still° in endless flames,   *eternally*

---

4. That is, by stabbing herself. Dido, the queen of Carthage, took her own life in despair at being deserted by Aeneas (see Virgil's *Aeneid*, book 4).
5. Grip. Tityus, a giant, attempted to rape the goddess Leto; he was killed by her children, Apollo and Artemis, and as punishment in Hades his liver was constantly eaten by vultures.

6. A fire-breathing monster that combined a lion, a goat, and a dragon.
7. Sisyphus, legendary king of Corinth, dealt treacherously with the gods and betrayed Zeus's secrets; he was punished in the underworld by forever having to roll uphill a huge stone that always rolled back down.

Blaspheming gods and all their holy names.

45 REVENGE   Then haste we down to meet thy friends and foes,
    To place thy friends in ease, the rest in woes.
    For here, though death hath end° their misery,   *ended*
    I'll there begin their endless tragedy.   [*Exeunt.*]

[FINIS.]

CHRISTOPHER MARLOWE

1564–1593

A LANDMARK event in the development of the Faust myth, Christopher Marlowe's *DOCTOR FAUSTUS* also served, at its moment of production (ca. 1590–93), as a legend of its own time. The play's representation of a consummate scholar's embrace of necromancy (or black magic) to gain a "world of profit and delight," the sale of his soul to the devil, and the consequent loss of both body and soul placed it at the heart of the age's religious controversies and debates. However, Marlowe's casting of his protagonist in the role of a Renaissance *magus*—a blend of scientist, physician, dabbler in the occult, and seeker of spiritual truths—also evoked that age's fascination with gaining mastery over the material world, probing the secrets of nature, and extending human experience to the frontiers of the globe. At a time when Spanish ships were returning from the Americas freighted down with gold and silver, travelers on new trade routes to the East were bringing back daily reports of exotic places and people, and great wealth was being created that could serve new tastes and desires, Marlowe's audience would understandably be drawn to a scholar born of "parents base of stock" who decided to employ forbidden means to realize his most extravagant dreams and ambitions.

Born the son of a shoemaker in 1564 in the cathedral city of Canterbury, Christo-

pher Marlowe could surely be compared to such a character. Unlike most sons of tradesmen, who could at best expect to follow in their fathers' footsteps after a few years of schooling, Marlowe not only attended the King's School, having won a place set aside for gifted children of the poor, but was also awarded a prestigious scholarship to study at Corpus Christi College, Cambridge, where he joined a mix of the wealthiest and most "forward wits" of his time. Marlowe took up residence there in December 1580, earned his B.A. in 1584, and, despite notable unexplained absences, received his M.A. in 1587 at the special urging of Queen Elizabeth's Privy Council for having "done her Majesty good service . . . in matters touching the benefit of his country." This "service" almost surely involved spying on English Catholics in France on behalf of the Elizabethan secret service. Yet the very same year he received his M.A., Marlowe also emerged as the author of *Tamburlaine the Great*—one of the most successful, provocative, and influential plays to be performed on the Elizabethan stage.

Although Marlowe was one of several Cambridge graduates to turn their study of the classics, and their painstaking emulation of Latin verse forms, to positive artistic and commercial advantage in London, he was the first to make the leap from mannered imitation to the creation of an English blank-verse line answerable to the challenges of public playhouse performance. In *Tamburlaine*, Marlowe dramatizes the rise to unlimited worldly power of a former shepherd, who struts across the stage celebrating his successive triumphs with conquering looks and words, unconstrained by any moral misgiving or religious qualm. Urged on by the "strong enchantments" of what BEN JONSON would later call Marlowe's "mighty line," the London audience clamored for more; and Marlowe supplied it in an equally successful sequel to *Tamburlaine*, with Edward Alleyn, the leading actor of the time, again playing the featured role. Marlowe would go on to write four more plays—*The Jew of Malta*, *Edward II*, *Doctor Faustus*, and *The Massacre at Paris*—each one of which could have earned him the early death that in fact befell him had he directly identified himself with the pronouncements and

Title page of the 1616 B-text of *Doctor Faustus*.

professions of his protagonists: a "bottle-nosed" Jew bent on murder and mayhem; a lovesick English monarch, willing to trade his kingdom in order to "frolic" with his male lover; a renowned scholar who sells his soul to the devil; and a ruthless Machiavellian Catholic responsible for fomenting the notorious St. Bartholomew's Day massacre of French Protestants in 1572. Uncertain as the chronology of these plays' composition is, their intention to court controversy could not be clearer.

A study in mystery and contradiction from first to last, this remarkably gifted, mercurial poet-playwright—who was accounted "the Muses' darling" soon after his death—would meet his end in the town of Deptford on the evening of May 29, 1593, when one Ingram Frizer plunged a knife into his forehead. Marlowe was in the company of the same shady customers—debtors, money brokers, intriguers, spies—with whom he had been consorting for some time. No one knows whether Frizer acted in drunkenness, in self-defense, or in furtherance of a well-laid plan, or if Marlowe was a victim of his own violent temperament or scandalous opinions. Those opinions, including his supposed denial of Christ's divinity, had prompted the Privy Council on May 18 to issue a warrant for Marlowe's arrest. Nine days later, they featured prominently in a deposition from Richard Baines, another of Marlowe's suspect companions, claiming that Marlowe had denied Christ's divinity and made other blasphemous statements. The clock appears to have been counting down for Marlowe much as it did in the last minutes of Doctor Faustus's life, though a number of scholars argue that his former sponsors on the Privy Council are far more likely to have been responsible for his demise than the devil or despair.

Tempting as it is to bring Marlowe's notorious life and death to bear on that of his most famous protagonist, *Doctor Faustus* diverged considerably from the unerringly heterodox direction he pursued in his other plays. In a seeming departure from the "atheist lecture" he was reported to have delivered, Marlowe had Faustus entertain a series of grandiose fantasies only to bring the full weight of the medieval Christian cosmos—with its angels and devils whispering messages of mercy and despair in the wavering soul's ear—down upon the magus's head for daring to do "more than heavenly power permits." And he did so by situating Faustus within the framework of a medieval morality play presided over by a Chorus that influences the audience's impressions of Faustus from first to last, conflating Faustus's daring with the foolhardiness of the mythical Icarus and the presumption of Lucifer in the very first speech of the play. The plot, as Marlowe's Chorus proclaims it, could not be simpler. A brilliant scholar becomes so "swoll'n" with pride at his attainments that "Nothing so sweet as magic is to him, / Which he prefers before [what should be] his chiefest bliss." The stages of Faustus's conversion to the black arts are detailed in the play's first act and almost immediately consummated in his first transactions with Lucifer's agent, Mephistopheles. The rest of the play dramatizes how little Faustus receives in return for his investment and how fiercely he strives to repent before the clock runs out on the twenty-four years of pleasure he has bargained for and Mephistopheles comes to claim him.

The dramatic foreshortening of Faustus's necromantic career is much more pronounced in the 1604 A-text of Doctor Faustus (reprinted here) than it is in the considerably longer 1616 B-text. Since neither version was published during Marlowe's lifetime, neither has the kind of authority scholars look for in making determinations about authorship. But since the disproportionate number of tricks and other comic business found in the B-text are symptomatic of the additions that the theatrical impresario Philip Henslowe commissioned after Marlowe's death, most scholars believe that the A-text is closer to the author's intentions. Like most cinematic remakes, the B-text lacks both the bite and integrity of its supposed original, which often bears the imprint of a dramatist composing in the white heat of artistic concentration. Marlowe seems to have written the haunting postscript—*"Terminat hora diem, terminat Author opus"* ("The hour ends the day, the author ends his work")—to his career-defining play just as the clock struck twelve.

Marlowe's comparatively orthodox treatment of his subject matter likely owes much to the critical tone taken toward Faustus's exploits by his source, *The History of the Damnable Life and Deserved Death of Doctor John Faustus,* a recent English translation (ca. 1589–92) of what has come to be known as the *Faustbook,* which was first published in German in 1587. However, Marlowe also took pains to transform the itinerant magician of his English and German sources into a universally accomplished scholar who makes the tragically momentous decision to risk everything to achieve godlike power. Marlowe signals at every turn the fatal (and foolish) mistakes Faustus makes. Indeed, nature itself rebels against Faustus's bargain, as when his blood congeals and refuses to flow long enough to allow him to deed his body and soul to Lucifer. In the end Faustus attempts to revolt against his devil's reckoning and tries to repent, but he is bullied back into submission by Mephistopheles. He concludes that his transgressions have rendered him unforgivable, forever incapable of sincerely asking for, much less receiving, God's saving grace.

Doctor Faustus is a study in paradox and contradiction, the product not only of colliding medieval and early modern worldviews but of competing religious professions and doctrinal debates. Though a strong case has been made for Calvinism—with its strict division of humanity into the elect and the damned—as the religious system of belief that informs Faustus's conception of himself as unredeemable and of God as vengeful and remote, the play presents a shifting array of religious signs and markers, making it difficult to determine which specific Christian ordering of nature presides over the scholar's fall. Faustus is, for example, told by Mephistopheles in the space of eight lines that hell lies "Within the bowels of these elements, / Where we are tortured and remain forever," as well as that "Hell hath no limits, nor is circumscribed / In one self place, for where we are is hell / And where hell is must we ever be." He is subsequently invited by Lucifer himself to view hell, as if it were a geo-

Paul Hilton as Doctor Faustus (left) and Arthur Darvill as Mephistopheles in the 2011 production of *Doctor Faustus* at Shakespeare's Globe, London.

graphically demarcated place on a tour map. To delight his mind, he's even given a command performance of a parade of the seven deadly sins: a standard piece of the medieval theological and iconographic repertory that had fallen out of fashion by Marlowe's time. Other seeming contradictions present themselves with a devilishly deadly irony that the savvy Faustus should have anticipated from the very first appearance of the devil at his door when summoned, an indication that the worlds of good and evil, heaven and hell, angels on one side and demons on the other are both intact and fixed in opposition to one another. This dichotomy is clearly exemplified when Mephistopheles denies Faustus's seemingly modest request for a wife, claiming that "marriage is but a ceremonial toy"; what he really means is that marriage has a sacramental status that places it beyond the pale of the devil's control or authority.

Ironically, given the price he has paid for it, the twenty-four years of Faustus's supernatural power turn out to be uneventful, even tedious. For someone who dreamed of becoming "great emperor of the world," Faustus spends a disproportionate amount of time conjuring spirits, playing jokes, and trading quips. The end of the play finds him in the same place as its beginning: at home in Wittenberg with his servant Wagner and his fellow scholars. Whereas Robin, the clownish but practical fool, says he would never bargain his soul for a joint of lamb unless it were well roasted, Faustus appears to have traded "eternal joy" for a banquet that never gets served, much less eaten. In the end he finds himself alone, facing the ultimate penalty laid out in his signed agreement. Imagine the last hour of Faustus's life, abbreviated in Marlowe's play to the time it takes an actor to speak 58 lines—no more than two or three minutes. In a play in which so much else is rendered uncertain or ambiguous, death and damnation are facts that Faustus knows will arrive on schedule. The penalty for his life has been set: "the clock will strike; / The devil will come, and Faustus must be damned." Faustus tries to hope, tries to make time stop and the planets "stand still," tries to beg Christ for mercy. He asks the earth to "gape" so that he may run into it, asks that his body dissolve "like a foggy mist" into the clouds, and imagines his soul transmigrating into that of "some brutish beast" or metamorphosing "into little waterdrops / [That] fall into the ocean, ne'er [to] be found." All to no avail. God "bends his ireful brows," the devil pulls him down, and his last expedient, a promise to burn his books, falls on deaf ears. If it is true that there is nothing like the prospect of death to concentrate the mind, then it may well be said that nothing in dramatic literature concentrates the mind on the imminence of death as intensely as does the last scene of *Doctor Faustus*.

Yet what sin has Faustus committed that he must be damned? Is it pride, the deadliest of the seven deadly sins? Is it the unforgivable sin of despair, which prevents an individual from harboring any hope of redemption? Or is it Faustus's conviction that he has been singled out as one of the reprobates who, unlike the "elect," can do nothing to make himself worthy of God's grace? Apart from playing several crude practical jokes and asking Mephistopheles to torment the Old Man (who apparently has been sent on a mission of mercy from God), Faustus does nothing in the course of the drama to harm others; and on his last night on earth, he appears to be well-loved and regarded by those who know him best, Wagner and his students. Could (or should) God have made Faustus stronger, more capable of resisting the temptations and power of the devil? Or has God spoken through the words and ministrations of the Good Angel and Old Man, and given Faustus as much of a chance to redeem himself as he gives anyone?

As Faustus is spirited offstage by Mephistopheles and his crew of devils at the end of the play, it may well seem that the odds have worked against Faustus from the start and that while conscientiously cultivating his damnation, he has gotten precious little help or protection from on high. Indeed, the last image of God provided by Faustus is of a punishing, wrathful deity to whom he desperately pleads, "My God, my God, look not so fierce on me!" Faustus, the foolish, deluded, profoundly overmatched victim, as opposed to the arrogant, overreaching Faustus of the play's first two acts, is the final version of the character we see before the Chorus reenters to shut off controversy with the authority of a slammed door:

> Cut is the branch that might have
>   grown full straight,
> And burnèd is Apollo's laurel bough
> That sometime grew within this
>   learnèd man.
> Faustus is gone. Regard his hellish fall,
> Whose fiendful fortune may exhort
>   the wise
> Only to wonder at unlawful things,
> Whose deepness doth entice such
>   forward wits
> To practice more than heavenly
>   power permits.

A branch that might have grown straight has been cut, a laurel bough bespeaking divinely appointed inspiration has been burned, and the fault is Faustus's own for failing to take advantage of "learning's golden gifts." A hard verdict, no doubt, but one that may, in retrospect, remind us of another "Muses' darling" cut down in his prime.

THOMAS CARTELLI

The Tragical History of Doctor Faustus

CHARACTERS

The CHORUS
Doctor John FAUSTUS
WAGNER, his servant
The GOOD ANGEL
The EVIL ANGEL
VALDES ⎫
CORNELIUS ⎬ famous magicians
Three SCHOLARS
MEPHISTOPHELES
ROBIN, the clown, a stableman
Devils
RAFE, a stableman, another clown
LUCIFER
Beelzebub
PRIDE ⎫
COVETOUSNESS ⎪
WRATH ⎪
ENVY ⎬ the Seven Deadly Sins
GLUTTONY ⎪
SLOTH ⎪
LECHERY ⎭

The POPE
The Cardinal of LORRAINE
FRIARS
A VINTNER
The EMPEROR of Germany, Charles V
A KNIGHT
Attendants
Alexander the Great ⎫
His paramour ⎬ spirits
A HORSE-COURSER
The DUKE of Vanholt
The DUCHESS of Vanholt
Helen of Troy, a spirit
An OLD MAN

SCENE: *Doctor Faustus's study at Wittenberg, and on his travels.*

Prologue

[*Enter* CHORUS.]

CHORUS Not marching now in fields of Trasimene,[1]
    Where Mars° did mate° the Carthaginians,   *Roman god of war / defeat*
    Nor sporting in the dalliance of love
    In courts of kings where state is overturned,
5   Nor in the pomp of proud audacious deeds,
    Intends our muse to vaunt his heavenly verse.[2]

---

1. The lake in Italy where the Carthaginian general Hannibal destroyed two Roman legions in 217 B.C.E.
2. "Our muse" appears to refer to Marlowe himself, with the preceding lines alluding to earlier plays of his, including *Edward II* and the first and second parts of *Tamburlaine the Great*. The reference to a play about Hannibal remains obscure.

Only this, gentlemen: we must perform
The form of Faustus' fortunes, good or bad.
To patient judgments we appeal our plaud,°   *seek approval*
10   And speak for Faustus in his infancy.
Now is he born, his parents base of stock,
In Germany, within a town called Rhode.
Of riper years to Wittenberg he went,
Whereas° his kinsmen chiefly brought him up.   *Where*
15   So soon he profits in divinity,
The fruitful plot of scholarism graced,
That shortly he was graced with doctor's name,
Excelling all whose sweet delight disputes
In heavenly matters of theology;
20   Till, swoll'n with cunning° of a self-conceit,   *learning; cleverness*
His waxen wings did mount above his reach,[3]
And, melting, heavens conspired his overthrow.
For, falling to a devilish exercise,
And glutted more with learning's golden gifts,
25   He surfeits upon cursèd necromancy;
Nothing so sweet as magic is to him,
Which he prefers before his chiefest bliss.[4]
And this the man that in his study sits.   [*Exit.*]

1.1

[*Enter* FAUSTUS *in his study.*]

FAUSTUS   Settle thy studies, Faustus, and begin
To sound the depth of that° thou wilt profess.   *that which*
Having commenced, be a divine in show,[5]
Yet level at the end° of every art,   *aim at the goal*
5   And live and die in Aristotle's works.
Sweet *Analytics*,[6] 'tis thou hast ravished me!
[*He reads.*] "*Bene disserere est finis logices.*"[7]
Is to dispute well logic's chiefest end?
Affords this art no greater miracle?
10   Then read no more; thou hast attained the end.
A greater subject fitteth Faustus' wit.
Bid *On kai me on*[8] farewell. Galen,[9] come!
Seeing *ubi desinit philosophus, ibi incipit medicus,*[1]
Be a physician, Faustus. Heap up gold,

---

3. An allusion to the mythological figure Icarus, whose "waxen wings" (devised by his father, Daedalus), melted when he flew too close to the sun.
4. That is, the hope of salvation.
5. A theologian in appearance.
6. Two of the treatises on logic by the Greek philosopher Aristotle (384–322 B.C.E.) are the *Prior Analytics* and the *Posterior Analytics*.

7. Quoted (Latin) from Peter Ramus's *Dialectica* (1576) and translated in the following line.
8. Being and not being (Greek).
9. Greek physician (129–ca. 199 C.E.), the standard authority on medicine for centuries.
1. Where the philosopher ends, there the physician begins (Latin).

15 And be eternized° for some wondrous cure.   *made forever famous*
   [*He reads.*] *"Summum bonum medicinae sanitas"*:[2]
   "The end of physic° is our body's health."   *medicine*
   Why, Faustus, hast thou not attained that end?
   Is not thy common talk sound aphorisms?°   *established wisdom*
20 Are not thy bills° hung up as monuments,   *prescriptions*
   Whereby whole cities have escaped the plague
   And thousand desp'rate maladies been eased?
   Yet art thou still but Faustus, and a man.
   Wouldst thou make man to live eternally,
25 Or, being dead, raise them to life again,
   Then this profession were to be esteemed.
   Physic, farewell. Where is Justinian?[3]
   [*He reads.*] *"Si una eademque res legatur duobus,*
   Alter rem, alter valorem rei,"[4] etc.
30 A pretty° case of paltry legacies!   *petty*
   [*He reads.*] *"Exhaereditare filium non potest pater nisi*[5]—"
   Such is the subject of the Institute
   And universal body of the church.°   *canon law*
   His study fits a mercenary drudge
35 Who aims at nothing but external trash—
   Too servile and illiberal° for me.   *ungentlemanly*
   When all is done, divinity is best.
   Jerome's Bible,[6] Faustus, view it well.
   [*He reads.*] *"Stipendium peccati mors est."*° Ha!   *(see Romans 6.23)*
40 *"Stipendium,"* etc.
   "The reward of sin is death." That's hard.
   [*He reads.*] *"Si peccasse negamus, fallimur,*
   Et nulla est in nobis veritas."°   *(see 1 John 1.8)*
   "If we say that we have no sin,
45 We deceive ourselves, and there's no truth in us."
   Why then belike we must sin,
   And so consequently die.
   Ay, we must die an everlasting death.
   What doctrine call you this? Che serà, serà,°   *(Spanish)*
50 "What will be, shall be"? Divinity, adieu!
          [*He picks up a book of magic.*]
   These metaphysics° of magicians   *This occult lore*
   And necromantic books are heavenly,
   Lines, circles, signs, letters, and characters°—   *astrological signs*
   Ay, these are those that Faustus most desires.
55 Oh, what a world of profit and delight,
   Of power, of honor, of omnipotence

2. An Aristotelian claim (see *Nicomachean Ethics* 1.7, 1097a).
3. Roman emperor (r. 527–65 C.E.); he codified Roman law in a series of publications, including the *Institutes* (533), the textbook quoted below.
4. If one thing is willed to two persons, one gets the thing, the other the value of the thing (Latin).
5. A father cannot disinherit his son unless (Latin).
6. The Latin (or Vulgate) version of the Bible, translated by Saint Jerome (ca. 347–419/420 C.E.).

Is promised to the studious artisan!°   *cultivator of the arts*
All things that move between the quiet° poles   *unmoving*
Shall be at my command. Emperors and kings
60   Are but obeyed in their several provinces,
Nor can they raise the wind or rend the clouds;
But his dominion that exceeds° in this   *excels*
Stretcheth as far as doth the mind of man.
A sound magician is a mighty god.
65   Here, Faustus, try° thy brains to gain a deity.°   *test / godhood*
   [*Calling*] Wagner!
        [*Enter* WAGNER.]
              Commend me to my dearest friends,
   The German Valdes and Cornelius.
   Request them earnestly to visit me.
WAGNER   I will, sir.   [*Exit.*]
70 FAUSTUS   Their conference will be a greater help to me
   Than all my labors, plod I ne'er so fast.
      [*Enter the* GOOD ANGEL *and the* EVIL ANGEL.]
GOOD ANGEL   O Faustus, lay that damnèd book aside
   And gaze not on it, lest it tempt thy soul
   And heap God's heavy wrath upon thy head!
75   Read, read the Scriptures. That° is blasphemy.   (*the book of magic*)
EVIL ANGEL   Go forward, Faustus, in that famous art
   Wherein all nature's treasury is contained.
   Be thou on earth as Jove° is in the sky,   *Jupiter (i.e., God)*
   Lord and commander of these elements.
            [*Exeunt*° ANGELS.]   *They exit (Latin)*
80 FAUSTUS   How am I glutted with conceit° of this!   *the idea*
   Shall I make spirits fetch me what I please,
   Resolve me of° all ambiguities,   *Free me from*
   Perform what desperate° enterprise I will?   *reckless*
   I'll have them fly to India° for gold,   *the Indies*
85   Ransack the ocean for orient pearl,
   And search all corners of the newfound world°   *(i.e., America)*
   For pleasant fruits and princely delicates.°   *delicacies*
   I'll have them read° me strange philosophy   *teach*
   And tell the secrets of all foreign kings.
90   I'll have them wall all Germany with brass
   And make swift Rhine circle fair Wittenberg.
   I'll have them fill the public schools° with silk,   *university lecture halls*
   Wherewith the students shall be bravely° clad.   *smartly*
   I'll levy soldiers with the coin they bring
95   And chase the Prince of Parma[7] from our land,
   And reign sole king of all our provinces;
   Yea, stranger engines° for the brunt° of war   *machines / assault*
   Than was the fiery keel at Antwerp's bridge[8]

7. The Spanish governor-general in the Netherlands from 1579 to 1592 and commander
of the Spanish Armada in 1588.

8. Those defending Antwerp against the
Spanish in 1585 used a fireship to destroy
Parma's bridge over the Scheldt River.

I'll make my servile spirits to invent.
100 Come, German Valdes and Cornelius,
And make me blest with your sage conference!

[*Enter* VALDES *and* CORNELIUS.]

Valdes, sweet Valdes, and Cornelius,
Know that your words have won me at the last
To practice magic and concealèd arts.
105 Yet not your words only, but mine own fantasy,
That will receive no object,° for my head   *other idea; objection*
But° ruminates on necromantic skill.   *Only*
Philosophy is odious and obscure;
Both law and physic are for petty wits;
110 Divinity is basest of the three,
Unpleasant, harsh, contemptible, and vile.
'Tis magic, magic that hath ravished me.
Then, gentle° friends, aid me in this attempt,   *wellborn*
And I, that have with concise syllogisms
115 Graveled° the pastors of the German church   *Floored, confounded*
And made the flow'ring pride of Wittenberg
Swarm to my problems° as the infernal spirits   *disputations, lectures*
On sweet Musaeus when he came to hell,[9]
Will be as cunning as Agrippa[1] was,
120 Whose shadows° made all Europe honor him.   *spirits*
VALDES   Faustus, these books, thy wit, and our experience
Shall make all nations to canonize us.
As Indian Moors[2] obey their Spanish lords,
So shall the subjects° of every element   *servant-spirits*
125 Be always serviceable to us three.
Like lions shall they guard us when we please,
Like Almaine rutters° with their horsemen's staves,°   *German cavalry / lances*
Or Lapland giants, trotting by our sides;
Sometimes like women, or unwedded maids,
130 Shadowing more beauty in their airy° brows   *heavenly*
Than in the white breasts of the Queen of Love.°   *Venus*
From Venice shall they drag huge argosies,°   *large merchant ships*
And from America the golden fleece[3]
That yearly stuffs old Philip's treasury,
135 If learnèd Faustus will be resolute.
FAUSTUS   Valdes, as resolute am I in this
As thou to live. Therefore object it not.°   *do not object*
CORNELIUS   The miracles that magic will perform
Will make thee vow to study nothing else.

9. Marlowe is apparently confusing the mythical poet Musaeus (described as standing in
the midst of a large number of spirits in the
underworld; Virgil, *Aeneid* 6.666–68) with
his predecessor Orpheus, who descended to
Hades in an unsuccessful attempt to retrieve
his dead wife, Eurydice.
1. Henry Cornelius Agrippa (1486–1535),
famous German physician and alchemist.

2. That is, the indigenous residents of the
Americas, such as the Aztecs of Mexico and
Incas of Peru.
3. That is, the huge amounts of gold the
Spanish were transporting over the Atlantic
to the king of Spain, Philip II (r. 1556–98). In
classical mythology, a literal golden fleece
was the object of the quest by Jason and the
Argonauts.

140 He that is grounded in astrology,
Enriched with tongues,° well seen° in minerals,　　　　*languages / versed*
Hath all the principles magic doth require.
Then doubt not, Faustus, but to be renowned
And more frequented° for this mystery°　　　　*resorted to / art*
145 Than heretofore the Delphian oracle.[4]
The spirits tell me they can dry the sea
And fetch the treasure of all foreign wrecks—
Ay, all the wealth that our forefathers hid
Within the massy entrails of the earth.
150 Then tell me, Faustus, what shall we three want?°　　　　*lack*
FAUSTUS Nothing, Cornelius. Oh, this cheers my soul!
Come, show me some demonstrations magical,
That I may conjure in some lusty° grove　　　　*pleasant*
And have these joys in full possession.
155 VALDES Then haste thee to some solitary grove,
And bear wise Bacon's and Albanus' works,[5]
The Hebrew Psalter, and New Testament;
And whatsoever else is requisite
We will inform thee ere our conference cease.
160 CORNELIUS Valdes, first let him know the words of art,°　　　　*magical incantations*
And then, all other ceremonies learned,
Faustus may try his cunning by himself.
VALDES First I'll instruct thee in the rudiments,
And then wilt thou be perfecter than I.
165 FAUSTUS Then come and dine with me, and after meat°　　　　*food*
We'll canvass every quiddity° thereof,　　　　*scrutinize every detail*
For ere I sleep I'll try what I can do.
This night I'll conjure, though I die therefore. [*Exeunt.*]

1.2

[*Enter two* SCHOLARS.]

FIRST SCHOLAR I wonder what's become of Faustus, that
was wont to make our schools ring with "*sic probo.*"°　　　　*I prove it thus (Latin)*
SECOND SCHOLAR That shall we know, for see, here comes
his boy.°　　　　*servant*

[*Enter* WAGNER *carrying wine.*]

5 FIRST SCHOLAR How now, sirrah,[6] where's thy master?
WAGNER God in heaven knows.
SECOND SCHOLAR Why, dost not thou know?
WAGNER Yes, I know, but that follows not.
FIRST SCHOLAR Go to, sirrah! Leave your jesting, and tell
10 us where he is.
WAGNER That follows not necessary by force of argument

---

4. Apollo's shrine at Delphi, in lower central
Greece, was the site of the most authoritative
oracle in the ancient world.
5. The English scientist Roger Bacon (ca.

1220–1292) and the Italian physician Pietro
d'Abano (ca. 1250–1316) were both philosophers accused of heresy and black magic.
6. A form of address to male social inferiors.

that you, being licentiate,° should stand upon't. There   *advanced scholars*
fore, acknowledge your error, and be attentive.

SECOND SCHOLAR   Why, didst thou not say thou knew'st?

15 WAGNER   Have you any witness on't?

FIRST SCHOLAR   Yes, sirrah, I heard you.

WAGNER   Ask my fellow if I be a thief.

SECOND SCHOLAR   Well, you will not tell us.

WAGNER   Yes, sir, I will tell you. Yet if you were not dunces,
20   you would never ask me such a question. For is not he
corpus naturale?° And is not that *mobile?* Then, where   *a natural body (Latin)*
fore should you ask me such a question? But that I
am° by nature phlegmatic,[7] slow to wrath, and prone to   *Were I not*
lechery—to love, I would say—it were not for you to
25   come within forty foot of the place of execution,°   *dining room, gallows*
although I do not doubt to see you both hanged
the next sessions.° Thus, having triumphed over you,   *sitting of the court*
I will set my countenance like a precisian° and begin to   *Puritan*
speak thus: Truly, my dear brethren, my master is
30   within at dinner with Valdes and Cornelius, as this
wine, if it could speak, it would inform Your Worships.
And so the Lord bless you, preserve you, and keep you,
my dear brethren, my dear brethren.   *[Exit.]*

FIRST SCHOLAR   Nay, then, I fear he is fall'n into that
35   damned art for which they two are infamous through the
world.

SECOND SCHOLAR   Were he a stranger, and not allied° to me,   *a companion*
yet should I grieve for him. But come, let us go and
inform the rector,° and see if he, by his grave counsel, can   *head of the university*
40   reclaim him.

FIRST SCHOLAR   Oh, but I fear me nothing can reclaim him.

SECOND SCHOLAR   Yet let us try what we can do.   *[Exeunt.]*

1.3

[Enter FAUSTUS to conjure.]

FAUSTUS   Now that the gloomy shadow of the earth,
Longing to view Orion's drizzling look,[8]
Leaps from th'Antarctic world unto the sky
And dims the welkin° with her pitchy breath,   *sky*
5   Faustus, begin thine incantations,
And try if devils will obey thy hest,°   *behest, command*
Seeing thou hast prayed and sacrificed to them.
Within this circle is Jehovah's name,
Forward and backward anagrammatized,
10   The breviated names of holy saints,
Figures of every adjunct to the heavens,

---

7. Sluggish or dull. According to early modern
accounts of human emotion, imbalances in the
four bodily humors (fluids)—black bile (melancholic), blood (sanguine), yellow bile (choleric), and phlegm—determined one's

personality.
8. Because in the Northern Hemisphere the
constellation Orion rises in November, it was
associated with winter storms.

And characters of signs° and erring stars°   *the zodiac / planets*
By which the spirits are enforced to rise.
Then fear not, Faustus, but be resolute,
15 And try the uttermost magic can perform.
Sint mihi dei Acherontis propitii! Valeat numen triplex
Jehovae! Ignei, aerii, aquatici, terreni, spiritus, salvete! Ori-
entis princeps Lucifer, Beelzebub, inferni ardentis monar-
cha, et Demogorgon, propitiamus vos, ut appareat et surgat
20 *Mephistopheles. Quid tu moraris? Per Jehovam, Gehennam,*
et consecratam aquam quam nunc spargo, signumque cru-
cis quod nunc facio, et per vota nostra, ipse nunc surgat
nobis dicatus Mephistopheles![9]

    [FAUSTUS *sprinkles holy water and makes a sign of the*
    cross.]

    [*Enter a devil* (MEPHISTOPHELES).]

I charge thee to return and change thy shape.
25 Thou art too ugly to attend on me.
Go, and return an old Franciscan friar;
That holy shape becomes a devil best.

    [*Exit devil* (MEPHISTOPHELES).]

I see there's virtue° in my heavenly words.   *power*
Who would not be proficient in this art?
30 How pliant is this Mephistopheles,
Full of obedience and humility!
Such is the force of magic and my spells.
Now, Faustus, thou art conjurer laureate,
That canst command great Mephistopheles.
35 *Quin redis, Mephistopheles, fratris imagine!*[1]

    [*Enter* MEPHISTOPHELES *dressed as a friar.*]

MEPHISTOPHELES   Now, Faustus, what wouldst thou have me do?
FAUSTUS   I charge thee wait upon me whilst I live,
To do whatever Faustus shall command,
Be it to make the moon drop from her sphere
40 Or the ocean to overwhelm the world.
MEPHISTOPHELES   I am a servant to great Lucifer
And may not follow thee without his leave.
No more than he commands must we perform.
FAUSTUS   Did not he charge thee to appear to me?
45 MEPHISTOPHELES   No, I came now hither of mine own accord.
FAUSTUS   Did not my conjuring speeches raise thee? Speak.
MEPHISTOPHELES   That was the cause, but yet *per accidens.*°   *incidentally (Latin)*
For when we hear one rack° the name of God,   *torture, tear*

9. May the gods of Acheron be propitious to me. Away with the threefold godhead of Jehovah! Hail, spirits of fire, air, water, and earth! Lucifer, Prince of the East, Beelzebub, monarch of burning hell, and Demogorgon, we invoke you, that Mephistopheles may appear and rise. Why do you delay? By Jehovah, Gehenna, and the holy water that I now sprin- kle, by the sign of the cross that I now make, and by our vows, may Mephistopheles himself, invoked by us, now rise! (Latin). *Acheron*: a river of the underworld. *Beelzebub, Demogorgon*: devils. *Gehenna*: hell.
1. Why not return in the image of a friar, Mephistopheles! (Latin).

Abjure the Scriptures and his Savior Christ,
50   We fly in hope to get his glorious soul,
        Nor will we come unless he use such means
        Whereby he is in danger to be damned.
        Therefore, the shortest cut for conjuring
        Is stoutly to abjure the Trinity[2]
55   And pray devoutly to the prince of hell.

FAUSTUS   So Faustus hath
        Already done, and holds this principle:
        There is no chief but only Beelzebub,
        To whom Faustus doth dedicate himself.
60   This word "damnation" terrifies not him,
        For he confounds hell in Elysium.[3]
        His ghost be with the old philosophers![4]
        But leaving these vain trifles of men's souls,
        Tell me what is that Lucifer thy lord?

65 MEPHISTOPHELES   Archregent and commander of all spirits.

FAUSTUS   Was not that Lucifer an angel once?

MEPHISTOPHELES   Yes, Faustus, and most dearly loved of God.

FAUSTUS   How comes it then that he is prince of devils?

MEPHISTOPHELES   Oh, by aspiring pride and insolence,
70   For which God threw him from the face of heaven.

FAUSTUS   And what are you that live with Lucifer?

MEPHISTOPHELES   Unhappy spirits that fell with Lucifer,
        Conspired against our God with Lucifer,
        And are forever damned with Lucifer.

75 FAUSTUS   Where are you damned?

MEPHISTOPHELES   In hell.

FAUSTUS   How comes it then that thou art out of hell?

MEPHISTOPHELES   Why, this is hell, nor am I out of it.
        Think'st thou that I, who saw the face of God
80   And tasted the eternal joys of heaven,
        Am not tormented with ten thousand hells
        In being deprived of everlasting bliss?
        O Faustus, leave these frivolous demands,
        Which strike a terror to my fainting soul!

85 FAUSTUS   What, is great Mephistopheles so passionate
        For being deprived of the joys of heaven?
        Learn thou of° Faustus manly fortitude,   *from*
        And scorn those joys thou never shalt possess.
        Go bear these tidings to great Lucifer:
90   Seeing Faustus hath incurred eternal death
        By desp'rate thoughts against Jove's deity,
        Say he surrenders up to him his soul,
        So° he will spare him four-and-twenty years,   *Provided that*
        Letting him live in all voluptuousness,
95   Having thee ever to attend on me,

2. That is, God as existing in three persons: Elysian fields, the abode of the blessed in the
the Father, the Son, and the Holy Spirit.   underworld in Greek and Roman mythology.
3. He conflates the Christian Hell with the   4. That is, pre-Christian philosophers.

To give me whatsoever I shall ask,
To tell me whatsoever I demand,
To slay mine enemies and aid my friends,
And always be obedient to my will.
100 Go and return to mighty Lucifer,
And meet me in my study at midnight,
And then resolve me of° thy master's mind.   *explain to me*
MEPHISTOPHELES   I will, Faustus.   [*Exit.*]
FAUSTUS   Had I as many souls as there be stars,
105 I'd give them all for Mephistopheles.
By him I'll be great emperor of the world
And make a bridge through the moving air
To pass the ocean with a band of men;
I'll join the hills that bind° the Afric shore   *surround, encircle*
110 And make that land continent to° Spain,   *contiguous with*
And both contributory to my crown.
The emp'ror shall not live but by my leave,
Nor any potentate of Germany.
Now that I have obtained what I desire,
115 I'll live in speculation° of this art   *contemplation*
Till Mephistopheles return again.   [*Exit.*]

1.4

[*Enter* WAGNER *and* ROBIN *the clown.*]

WAGNER   Sirrah boy, come hither.
ROBIN   How, "boy"? 'Swounds,° "boy"! I hope you have seen   *By God's wounds (oath)*
many boys with such pickedevants° as I have. "Boy,"   *pointed beards*
quotha?[5]
5 WAGNER   Tell me, sirrah, hast thou any comings in?°   *income*
ROBIN   Ay, and goings out[6] too, you may see else.
WAGNER   Alas, poor slave,° see how poverty jesteth in his   *rogue, servant*
nakedness! The villain is bare and out of service,[7] and so
hungry that I know he would give his soul to the devil for
10 a shoulder of mutton, though it were blood raw.
ROBIN   How? My soul to the devil for a shoulder of mutton, though 'twere blood raw? Not so, good friend. By'r
Lady,[8] I had need have it well roasted, and good sauce to
it, if I pay so dear.
15 WAGNER   Well, wilt thou serve me, and I'll make thee go
like *Qui mihi discipulus*?[9]
ROBIN   How, in verse?
WAGNER   No, sirrah, in beaten silk and stavesacre.[1]
ROBIN   How, how, knave's acre?[2] [*Aside*] Ay, I thought that

---

5. That is, "You call *me* 'boy'?"
6. Expenses (with a possible reference to what
can be seen through Robin's tattered clothing).
7. The wretch is poor and unemployed.
8. By our Lady—that is, the Virgin Mary (an
oath).

9. You who are my pupil (Latin).
1. In embroidered silk anointed with larkspur
(whose seeds were used to make a delousing
concoction).
2. The name of a poor, narrow street in
London.

20   was all the land his father left him. [*To* WAGNER] Do ye
      hear? I would be sorry to rob you of your living.

    WAGNER   Sirrah, I say in stavesacre.

    ROBIN   Oho, oho, "stavesacre"! Why then, belike,° if I were   *probably*
    your man,° I should be full of vermin.   *servant*

25 WAGNER   So thou shalt, whether thou be'st with me or
    no. But, sirrah, leave your jesting, and bind° yourself   *apprentice*
    presently° unto me for seven years, or I'll turn all the lice   *now*
    about thee into familiars,³ and they shall tear thee in
    pieces.

30 ROBIN   Do you hear, sir? You may save that labor. They are
    too familiar with me already. 'Swounds, they are as bold
    with my flesh as if they had paid for my meat and drink.

    WAGNER   Well, do you hear, sirrah? [*Offering money*] Hold,
    take these guilders.°   *Dutch coins*

35 ROBIN   Gridirons?° What be they?   *Griddles*

    WAGNER   Why, French crowns.°   *coins*

    ROBIN   Mass,° but for the name of French crowns a man were   *By the Mass (oath)*
    as good have as many English counters.⁴ And what should I
    do with these?

40 WAGNER   Why now, sirrah, thou art at an hour's warning°   *notice*
    whensoever or wheresoever the devil shall fetch thee.

    ROBIN   No, no, here, take your gridirons again.

        [*He attempts to return the money.*]

    WAGNER   Truly, I'll none of them.

    ROBIN   Truly, but you shall.

45 WAGNER [*to the audience*]   Bear witness I gave them him.

    ROBIN   Bear witness I gave them you again.

    WAGNER   Well, I will cause two devils presently to fetch
    thee away. [*Calling*] Balioll and Belcher!

    ROBIN   Let your Balio and your Belcher come here and I'll
50   knock them. They were never so knocked since they
    were devils. Say I should kill one of them, what would
    folks say? "Do ye see yonder tall° fellow in the round   *valiant*
    slop?° He has killed the devil." So I should be called "Kill   *baggy breeches*
    devil" all the parish over.

        [*Enter two devils, and* ROBIN *the clown runs up and
        down crying.*]

55 WAGNER   Balioll and Belcher! Spirits, away!

                [*Exeunt devils.*]

    ROBIN   What, are they gone? A vengeance on them! They
    have vile long nails. There was a he-devil and a she-
    devil. I'll tell you how you shall know them:° all he-devils   *tell them apart*
    has horns,⁵ and all she-devils has clefts° and cloven feet.   *cleft hooves; vulvas*

60 WAGNER   Well, sirrah, follow me.

    ROBIN   But do you hear? If I should serve you, would you
    teach me to raise up Banios and Belcheos?

---

3. Attendant evil spirits, which take the shape   exchange.
of animals.   5. Devils' horns; cuckolds' horns.
4. Valueless tokens used in computation and

WAGNER   I will teach thee to turn thyself to anything, to
    a dog, or a cat, or a mouse, or a rat, or anything.
65 ROBIN   How? A Christian fellow to a dog or a cat, a mouse
    or a rat? No, no, sir. If you turn me into anything, let it
    be in the likeness of a little, pretty, frisking flea, that I
    may be here and there and everywhere. Oh, I'll tickle the
    pretty wenches' plackets!° I'll be amongst them, i'faith!   *slits in petticoats*
70 WAGNER   Well, sirrah, come.
    ROBIN   But do you hear, Wagner?
    WAGNER   How? [*Calling*] Balioll and Belcher!
    ROBIN   Oh, Lord, I pray sir, let Banio and Belcher go sleep.
    WAGNER   Villain, call me Master Wagner, and let thy left
75   eye be diametarily° fixed upon my right heel, with *quasi*   *diametrically*
    vestigiis nostris insistere.[6]   [*Exit.*]
    ROBIN   God forgive me, he speaks Dutch fustian.° Well, I'll   *bombast*
    follow him, I'll serve him, that's flat.°   [*Exit.*]   *for certain*

2.1

[*Enter* FAUSTUS *in his study.*]

FAUSTUS   Now, Faustus, must thou needs be damned,
    And canst thou not be saved.
    What boots° it then to think of God or heaven?   *avails*
    Away with such vain fancies, and despair!
5   Despair in God and trust in Beelzebub.
    Now go not backward. No, Faustus, be resolute.
    Why waverest thou? Oh, something soundeth in mine ears:
    "Abjure this magic, turn to God again!"
    Ay, and Faustus will turn to God again.
10 To God? He loves thee not.
    The god thou servest is thine own appetite,
    Wherein is fixed the love of Beelzebub.
    To him I'll build an altar and a church,
    And offer lukewarm blood of newborn babes.

[*Enter* GOOD ANGEL *and* EVIL ANGEL.]

15 GOOD ANGEL   Sweet Faustus, leave that execrable art.
    FAUSTUS   Contrition, prayer, repentance—what of them?
    GOOD ANGEL   Oh, they are means to bring thee unto heaven.
    EVIL ANGEL   Rather illusions, fruits of lunacy,
    That makes men foolish that do trust them most.
20 GOOD ANGEL   Sweet Faustus, think of heaven and heavenly things!
    EVIL ANGEL   No, Faustus, think of honor and wealth.

[*Exeunt* ANGELS.]

FAUSTUS   Of wealth?
    Why, the seigniory of Emden° shall be mine.   *(port in north Germany)*
    When Mephistopheles shall stand by me,
25 What god can hurt thee, Faustus? Thou art safe;

6. As if to walk in our (my) footsteps (Latin).

Cast° no more doubts. Come, Mephistopheles,   *Entertain*
And bring glad tidings from great Lucifer.
Is't not midnight? Come, Mephistopheles!
Veni, veni,° *Mephistophile!*   *Come, come (Latin)*
    [*Enter* MEPHISTOPHELES.]
30 Now tell, what says Lucifer, thy lord?

MEPHISTOPHELES   That I shall wait on Faustus whilst he lives,
So° he will buy my service with his soul.   *Provided that*

FAUSTUS   Already Faustus hath hazarded that for thee.

MEPHISTOPHELES   But, Faustus, thou must bequeath it solemnly
35 And write a deed of gift with thine own blood,
For that security° craves great Lucifer.   *guarantee*
If thou deny it, I will back to hell.

FAUSTUS   Stay, Mephistopheles, and tell me, what good Will
my soul do thy lord?

MEPHISTOPHELES   Enlarge his kingdom.

40 FAUSTUS   Is that the reason he tempts us thus?

MEPHISTOPHELES   *Solamen miseris socios habuisse doloris.*[7]

FAUSTUS   Have you any pain, that tortures° others?   *you who torture*

MEPHISTOPHELES   As great as have the human souls of men.
But tell me, Faustus, shall I have thy soul?
45 And I will be thy slave, and wait on thee,
And give thee more than thou hast wit to ask.

FAUSTUS   Ay, Mephistopheles, I give it thee.

MEPHISTOPHELES   Then stab thine arm courageously,
And bind thy soul that at some certain day
50 Great Lucifer may claim it as his own,
And then be thou as great as Lucifer.

FAUSTUS [*cutting his arm*]   Lo, Mephistopheles, for love of thee
I cut mine arm, and with my proper° blood   *own*
Assure my soul to be great Lucifer's,
55 Chief lord and regent of perpetual night.
View here the blood that trickles from mine arm,
And let it be propitious for my wish.

MEPHISTOPHELES   But, Faustus, thou must
Write it in manner of a deed of gift.

60 FAUSTUS   Ay, so I will. [*He writes.*] But Mephistopheles,
My blood congeals, and I can write no more.

MEPHISTOPHELES   I'll fetch thee fire to dissolve it straight.°   *immediately*
                        [*Exit.*]

FAUSTUS   What might the staying of my blood portend?
Is it unwilling I should write this bill?°   *legal document*
65 Why streams it not, that I may write afresh?
"Faustus gives to thee his soul"—ah, there it stayed!
Why shouldst thou? Is not thy soul thine own?
Then write again: "Faustus gives to thee his soul."
    [*Enter* MEPHISTOPHELES *with a chafer*° *of coals.*]   *chafing dish*

MEPHISTOPHELES   Here's fire. Come, Faustus, set it on.

---

7. It is a comfort to the wretched to have companions in their sorrows (i.e., misery loves company; Latin).

70 FAUSTUS   So. Now the blood begins to clear again.
　　Now will I make an end immediately.   [*He writes.*]
MEPHISTOPHELES [*aside*]   Oh, what will not I do to obtain his soul?
FAUSTUS   *Consummatum est.*[8] This bill is ended,
　　And Faustus hath bequeathed his soul to Lucifer.
75　But what is this inscription on mine arm?
　　"*Homo, fuge!*"° Whither should I fly?　　　　　　　　　　　*Flee, o man! (Latin)*
　　If unto God, he'll throw thee down to hell.—
　　My senses are deceived; here's nothing writ.—
　　I see it plain. Here in this place is writ
80　"*Homo, fuge!*" Yet shall not Faustus fly.
MEPHISTOPHELES [*aside*]   I'll fetch him somewhat° to delight　　*something*
　　his mind.　　　　　　　　　　　　　　　　[*Exit.*]
　　　　[*Enter* MEPHISTOPHELES *with devils, giving crowns and
　　　　rich apparel to* FAUSTUS, *and dance and then depart.*]
FAUSTUS   Speak, Mephistopheles. What means this show?
MEPHISTOPHELES   Nothing, Faustus, but to delight thy mind withal°　　*with*
　　And to show thee what magic can perform.
85 FAUSTUS   But may I raise up spirits when I please?
MEPHISTOPHELES   Ay, Faustus, and do greater things than these.
FAUSTUS   Then there's enough for° a thousand souls.　　　　　*to pay for*
　　Here, Mephistopheles, receive this scroll,
　　A deed of gift of body and of soul—
90　But yet conditionally that thou perform
　　All articles prescribed between us both.
MEPHISTOPHELES   Faustus, I swear by hell and Lucifer
　　To effect all promises between us made.
FAUSTUS   Then hear me read them.
95　"On these conditions following:
　　　　First, that Faustus may be a spirit in form and substance.
　　　　Secondly, that Mephistopheles shall be his servant,
　　and at his command.
　　　　Thirdly, that Mephistopheles shall do for him and bring
100　him whatsoever.°　　　　　　　　　　　　　　　　*anything at all*
　　　　Fourthly, that he shall be in his chamber or house invisible.
　　　　Lastly, that he shall appear to the said John Faustus at
　　all times in what form or shape soever he please.
　　　　I, John Faustus of Wittenberg, Doctor, by these pres-
105　ents° do give both body and soul to Lucifer, Prince of the　　*this document*
　　East, and his minister Mephistopheles; and furthermore
　　grant unto them that, four-and-twenty years being ex-
　　pired, the articles above written inviolate,° full power to　　*not violated*
　　fetch or carry the said John Faustus, body and soul, flesh,
110　blood, or goods, into their habitation wheresoever.
　　　　　　　　　　By me, John Faustus."
MEPHISTOPHELES   Speak, Faustus. Do you deliver this as
　　your deed?

---

8. It is finished (Latin), the last words of Jesus on the cross, according to John 19.30 (Vulgate).

FAUSTUS [*giving the deed*] Ay. Take it, and the devil give
115   thee good on't.
MEPHISTOPHELES Now, Faustus, ask what thou wilt.
FAUSTUS First will I question with thee about hell.
   Tell me, where is the place that men call hell?
MEPHISTOPHELES Under the heavens.
FAUSTUS   Ay, but whereabout?
120 MEPHISTOPHELES Within the bowels of these elements,
   Where we are tortured and remain forever.
   Hell hath no limits, nor is circumscribed
   In one self° place, for where we are is hell,   *one and the same*
   And where hell is must we ever be.
125   And, to conclude, when all the world dissolves,
   And every creature shall be purified,
   All places shall be hell that is not heaven.
FAUSTUS Come, I think hell's a fable.
MEPHISTOPHELES Ay, think so still, till experience change thy mind.
130 FAUSTUS Why, think'st thou then that Faustus shall be damned?
MEPHISTOPHELES Ay, of necessity, for here's the scroll
   Wherein thou hast given thy soul to Lucifer.
FAUSTUS Ay, and body too. But what of that?
   Think'st thou that Faustus is so fond°   *foolish*
135   To imagine that after this life there is any pain?
   Tush, these are trifles and mere old wives' tales.
MEPHISTOPHELES But, Faustus, I am an instance to prove the
   contrary,
   For I am damned and am now in hell.
FAUSTUS How? Now in hell? Nay, an° this be hell,   *if*
140   I'll willingly be damned here. What? Walking, disputing,
   etc.?[9] But leaving off this, let me have a wife, the fairest
   maid in Germany, for I am wanton and lascivious and cannot live without a wife.
MEPHISTOPHELES How, a wife? I prithee, Faustus, talk not
145   of a wife.
FAUSTUS Nay, sweet Mephistopheles, fetch me one, for I
   will have one.
MEPHISTOPHELES Well, thou wilt have one. Sit there till I
   come. I'll fetch thee a wife, in the devil's name.   [*Exit.*]
       [*Enter* MEPHISTOPHELES *with a devil dressed like*
       a woman, with fireworks.]
150 MEPHISTOPHELES Tell, Faustus, how dost thou like thy wife?
FAUSTUS A plague on her for a hot whore!
MEPHISTOPHELES Tut, Faustus, marriage is but a ceremonial toy.° *amusement*
   If thou lovest me, think no more of it.   [*Exit devil.*]
   I'll cull thee out the fairest courtesans
155   And bring them ev'ry morning to thy bed.
   She whom thine eye shall like thy heart shall have,
   Be she as chaste as was Penelope,

---

9. "Etc." signals a moment of improvisation.

As wise as Saba,[1] or as beautiful
As was bright Lucifer before his fall.
160   [*Presenting a book*] Hold, take this book. Peruse it thoroughly.
The iterating° of these lines brings gold;   *repeating, reciting*
The framing° of this circle on the ground   *inscribing*
Brings whirlwinds, tempests, thunder, and lightning.
Pronounce this thrice devoutly to thyself,
165 And men in armor shall appear to thee,
Ready to execute what thou desir'st.
     FAUSTUS   Thanks, Mephistopheles. Yet fain° would I have   *gladly*
a book wherein I might behold all spells and incanta-
tions, that I might raise up spirits when I please.
170 MEPHISTOPHELES   Here they are in this book.
                                [*There turn to them.*]
     FAUSTUS   Now would I have a book where I might see all
characters° and planets of the heavens, that I might   *astrological symbols*
know their motions and dispositions.
MEPHISTOPHELES   Here they are too.   [*Turn to them.*]
175 FAUSTUS   Nay, let me have one book more—and then I
have done—wherein I might see all plants, herbs, and
trees that grow upon the earth.
MEPHISTOPHELES   Here they be.   [*Turn to them.*]
     FAUSTUS   Oh, thou art deceived.
180 MEPHISTOPHELES   Tut, I warrant thee.   [*Exeunt.*]

2.2

     [*Enter* ROBIN *the ostler° with a book in his hand.*]   *stable boy*
     ROBIN   Oh, this is admirable! Here I ha' stol'n one of
Doctor Faustus' conjuring books, and, i'faith, I mean
to search some circles[2] for my own use. Now will I
make all the maidens in our parish dance at my plea-
5   sure stark naked before me, and so by that means I
shall see more than e'er I felt or saw yet.
     [*Enter* RAFE, *calling* ROBIN.]
     RAFE   Robin, prithee, come away. There's a gentleman
tarries to have his horse, and he would have his things[3]
rubbed and made clean; he keeps such a chafing with
10   my mistress about it, and she has sent me to look thee
out.° Prithee, come away.   *look for you*
     ROBIN   Keep out, keep out, or else you are blown up,
you are dismembered, Rafe! Keep out, for I am about a
roaring piece of work.
15 RAFE   Come, what dost thou with that same book?° Thou   *that book there*
canst not read?

---

1. The queen of Sheba, who greatly admired
Solomon's wisdom (Kings 10.1–9). *Penelope:*
the wife of Odysseus and in classical myth a
model of faithfulness.

2. Conjuring circles; vaginas.
3. His leather riding gear (with sexual
suggestion).

ROBIN   Yes, my master and mistress shall find that I can
read—he for his forehead, she for her private study.[4] She's
born to bear with me,[5] or else my art fails.

20   RAFE   Why, Robin, what book is that?

ROBIN   What book? Why the most intolerable[6] book for
conjuring that e'er was invented by any brimstone devil.

RAFE   Canst thou conjure with it?

ROBIN   I can do all these things easily with it: first, I can
25   make thee drunk with hippocras° at any tavern in Europe   °spiced wine
for nothing. That's one of my conjuring works.

RAFE   Our Master Parson says that's nothing.

ROBIN   True, Rafe; and more, Rafe, if thou hast any mind
to° Nan Spit,[7] our kitchen maid, then turn her and   °any liking for
30   wind her to thy own use as often as thou wilt, and at midnight.

RAFE   Oh, brave,° Robin! Shall I have Nan Spit, and to   °splendid
mine own use? On that condition I'll feed thy devil with
horse-bread° as long as he lives, of free cost.   °horse feed, fodder

35   ROBIN   No more, sweet Rafe. Let's go and make clean our
boots, which lie foul upon our hands, and then to our conjuring, in the devil's name.   [Exeunt.]

2.3

[Enter FAUSTUS in his study, and MEPHISTOPHELES.]

FAUSTUS   When I behold the heavens, then I repent
And curse thee, wicked Mephistopheles,
Because thou hast deprived me of those joys.

MEPHISTOPHELES   Why, Faustus,
5   Think'st thou heaven is such a glorious thing?
I tell thee, 'tis not half so fair as thou
Or any man that breathes on earth.

FAUSTUS   How provest thou that?

MEPHISTOPHELES   It was made for man; therefore is man
10   more excellent.

FAUSTUS   If it were made for man, 'twas made for me.
I will renounce this magic and repent.

[Enter GOOD ANGEL and EVIL ANGEL.]

GOOD ANGEL   Faustus, repent yet, God will pity thee.

EVIL ANGEL   Thou art a spirit. God cannot pity thee.

15   FAUSTUS   Who buzzeth in mine ears I am a spirit?
Be I a devil,[8] yet God may pity me;

---

4. That is, in sex with her, which will put a
cuckold's horns on his forehead.
5. Put up with me; support my body in sex;
bear my child.
6. Malapropism for "incomparable."

7. Named for the spit on which cooking meat
is turned.
8. A notoriously ambiguous phrase, which
may mean "Even if I *am* a devil" or "Even if I
were a devil."

Ay, God will pity me if I repent.
EVIL ANGEL   Ay, but Faustus never shall repent.

[*Exeunt* ANGELS.]

FAUSTUS   My heart's so hardened I cannot repent.
20   Scarce can I name salvation, faith, or heaven
But fearful echoes thunders in mine ears:
"Faustus, thou art damned!" Then swords and knives,
Poison, guns, halters° and envenomed steel°   *nooses / swords*
Are laid before me to dispatch myself;
25   And long ere this I should have slain myself
Had not sweet pleasure conquered deep despair.
Have not I made blind Homer sing to me
Of Alexander's love and Oenone's death?[9]
And hath not he that built the walls of Thebes
30   With ravishing sound of his melodious harp[1]
Made music with my Mephistopheles?
Why should I die, then, or basely despair?
I am resolved Faustus shall ne'er repent.
Come, Mephistopheles, let us dispute again
35   And argue of divine astrology.
Tell me, are there many heavens above the moon?
Are all celestial bodies but one globe,
As is the substance of this centric earth?[2]
MEPHISTOPHELES   As are the elements, such are the spheres,
40   Mutually folded in each others' orb;
And, Faustus, all jointly move upon one axletree,°   *axle, pole*
Whose terminine° is termed the world's wide pole.   *limit*
Nor are the names of Saturn, Mars, or Jupiter
Feigned, but are erring stars.°   *wandering planets*
45 FAUSTUS   But tell me, have they all one motion, both *situ*
et tempore?°   *in space and time (Latin)*
MEPHISTOPHELES   All jointly move from east to west in
four-and-twenty hours upon the poles of the world,
but differ in their motion upon the poles of the zodiac.°   *i.e., along the zodiac*
50 FAUSTUS   Tush, these slender trifles Wagner can decide.
Hath Mephistopheles no greater skill?
Who knows not the double motion of the planets?
The first is finished in a natural day,
The second thus, as Saturn in thirty years, Jupiter in
55   twelve, Mars in four,° the Sun, Venus, and Mercury in a   *(in fact, two)*
year, the moon in twenty-eight days. Tush, these are
freshmen's suppositions.° But tell me, hath every sphere   *arguing points*
a dominion or intelligentia?°   *controlling spirit*

---

9. The story of the love of Paris (Alexander) for Helen, whom the Greeks waged the Trojan War to retrieve, forms the backdrop of Homer's *Iliad*; and Oenone, the daughter of a river god who was Paris's first love, killed herself after his death.

1. In Greek mythology Amphion, a son of Zeus, was famous for his musical talent; after he became king of Thebes, he built the city walls by playing his lyre to move their stones.
2. That is, this earth at the center of the universe (the Ptolemaic view).

MEPHISTOPHELES   Ay.

60 FAUSTUS   How many heavens or spheres are there?

MEPHISTOPHELES   Nine: the seven planets, the firmament,
and the empyreal° heaven.   *highest*

FAUSTUS   Well, resolve me in this question: why have we
not conjunctions, oppositions, aspects, eclipses all at one

65   time,° but in some years we have more, in some less?   *at regular intervals*

MEPHISTOPHELES   *Per inaequalem motum respectu totius.*[3]

FAUSTUS   Well, I am answered. Tell me who made the world.

MEPHISTOPHELES   I will not.

FAUSTUS   Sweet Mephistopheles, tell me.

70 MEPHISTOPHELES   Move° me not, for I will not tell thee.   *Anger*

FAUSTUS   Villain, have I not bound thee to tell me anything?

MEPHISTOPHELES   Ay, that is not against our kingdom, but
this is. Think thou on hell, Faustus, for thou art damned.

FAUSTUS   Think, Faustus, upon God, that made the world.

75 MEPHISTOPHELES   Remember this.°   [*Exit.*]   *You will pay for this*

FAUSTUS   Ay, go, accursèd spirit, to ugly hell!
'Tis thou hast damned distressèd Faustus' soul.
Is't not too late?

[*Enter* GOOD ANGEL *and* EVIL ANGEL.]

EVIL ANGEL   Too late.

80 GOOD ANGEL   Never too late, if Faustus can repent.

EVIL ANGEL   If thou repent, devils shall tear thee in pieces.

GOOD ANGEL   Repent, and they shall never raze thy skin.

[*Exeunt* ANGELS.]

FAUSTUS   Ah, Christ, my Savior,
Seek to save distressèd Faustus' soul!

[*Enter* LUCIFER, BEELZEBUB, *and* MEPHISTOPHELES.]

85 LUCIFER   Christ cannot save thy soul, for he is just.
There's none but I have int'rest in the same.

FAUSTUS   Oh, who art thou that look'st so terrible?

LUCIFER   I am Lucifer,
And this is my companion prince in hell.

90 FAUSTUS   O Faustus, they are come to fetch away thy soul!

LUCIFER   We come to tell thee thou dost injure us.
Thou talk'st of Christ, contrary to thy promise.
Thou shouldst not think of God. Think of the devil,
And of his dame,[4] too.

95 FAUSTUS   Nor will I henceforth. Pardon me in this,
And Faustus vows never to look to heaven,
Never to name God or to pray to him,
To burn his Scriptures, slay his ministers,
And make my spirits pull his churches down.

100 LUCIFER   Do so, and we will highly gratify° thee. Faustus,   *reward, satisfy*

---

3. Because of unequal motion in respect to
the whole (Latin).
4. Dam, wife. Witchcraft manuals attribute

to the devil (Lucifer) many sexual partners
and, occasionally, a long-term female consort
or wife.

we are come from hell to show thee some pastime.
Sit down, and thou shalt see all the Seven Deadly
Sins appear in their proper° shapes.   *own*
FAUSTUS   That sight will be as pleasing unto me as Para-
105   dise was to Adam the first day of his creation.
LUCIFER   Talk not of Paradise nor creation, but mark this
show. Talk of the devil, and nothing else.—Come away!

[FAUSTUS *sits.*]

[*Enter the Seven Deadly Sins.*]

Now, Faustus, examine them of° their several° names   *about / different*
and dispositions.
110   FAUSTUS   What art thou, the first?
PRIDE   I am Pride. I disdain to have any parents. I am like
to Ovid's flea:[5] I can creep into every corner of a wench.
Sometimes like a periwig I sit upon her brow, or like a
fan of feathers I kiss her lips. Indeed I do. What do I
115   not? But fie, what a scent is here! I'll not speak another
word except° the ground were perfumed and covered with   *unless*
cloth of arras.°   *rich tapestry*
FAUSTUS   What art thou, the second?
COVETOUSNESS   I am Covetousness, begotten of an old
120   churl in an old leathern bag;° and might I have my   *money bag*
wish, I would desire that this house and all the people
in it were turned to gold, that I might lock you up in
my good chest. O my sweet gold!
FAUSTUS   What art thou, the third?
125   WRATH   I am Wrath. I had neither father nor mother. I
leaped out of a lion's mouth when I was scarce half an
hour old, and ever since I have run up and down the
world with this case of rapiers,° wounding myself when I   *pair of swords*
had nobody to fight withal.° I was born in hell, and   *with*
130   look to it,° for some of you shall be my father.   *be advised*
FAUSTUS   What art thou, the fourth?
ENVY   I am Envy, begotten of a chimney sweeper and an
oyster-wife.° I cannot read, and therefore wish all   *oyster seller*
books were burnt. I am lean with seeing others eat.
135   Oh, that there would come a famine through all the
world, that all might die, and I live alone! Then thou
shouldst see how fat I would be. But must thou sit and
I stand? Come down, with a vengeance!°   *with a curse (on you)*
FAUSTUS   Away, envious rascal!—What are thou, the fifth?
140   GLUTTONY   Who, I, sir? I am Gluttony. My parents are all
dead, and the devil a penny° they have left me but   *not even a penny*
a bare pension, and that is thirty meals a day, and
ten bevers°—a small trifle to suffice nature.° Oh, I come   *snacks / bodily nature*
of a royal parentage. My grandfather was a gammon
145   of bacon,° my grandmother a hogshead° of claret   *ham / large cask*

5. The medieval "Elegy of a Flea" was wrongly attributed to the Roman poet Ovid (43 B.C.E.–17
C.E.).

wine. My godfathers these: Peter Pickle-herring° and *pickled herring*
Martin Martlemas-beef.[6] Oh, but jolly gentlewoman,
and well beloved in every good town and city; her name
was Mistress Margery March-beer.° Now, Faustus, *strong beer*
150 thou hast heard all my progeny, wilt thou bid me to
supper?

FAUSTUS No, I'll see thee hanged. Thou wilt eat up all my
victuals.

GLUTTONY Then the devil choke thee!

155 FAUSTUS Choke thyself, glutton!—What art thou, the
sixth?

SLOTH I am Sloth. I was begotten on a sunny bank, where
I have lain ever since, and you have done me great injury
to bring me from thence. Let me be carried thither again
160 by Gluttony and Lechery. I'll not speak another word for a
king's ransom.

FAUSTUS What are you, Mistress Minx, the seventh and
last?

LECHERY Who, I, sir? I am one that loves an inch of raw
165 mutton better than an ell of fried stockfish,[7] and the first
letter of my name begins with lechery.

LUCIFER Away, to hell, to hell! [*Exeunt the Sins.*]
Now, Faustus, how dost thou like this?

FAUSTUS Oh, this feeds my soul!

170 LUCIFER Tut, Faustus, in hell is all manner of delight.

FAUSTUS Oh, might I see hell and return again, how happy
were I then!

LUCIFER Thou shalt. I will send for thee at midnight. [*He
presents a book.*] In meantime, take this book. Peruse it
175 throughly,° and thou shalt turn thyself into what shape *thoroughly*
thou wilt.

FAUSTUS [*taking the book*] Great thanks, mighty Lucifer. This
will I keep as chary° as my life. *carefully*

LUCIFER Farewell, Faustus, and think on the devil.

180 FAUSTUS Farewell, great Lucifer. Come, Mephistopheles.

[*Exeunt omnes*° FAUSTUS *and* MEPHISTOPHELES *by one* *all (Latin)*
way, LUCIFER *and* BEELZEBUB *by another.*]

3. Chorus

[*Enter* WAGNER *solus.*°] *alone (Latin)*

WAGNER Learnèd Faustus,
To know the secrets of astronomy
Graven° in the book of Jove's high firmament, *Engraved*
Did mount himself to scale Olympus'[8] top,
5 Being seated in a chariot burning bright

6. Beef slaughtered on the Feast of St. Martin (November 11).
7. One who prefers raw meat to dried cod—
that is, hot sex to cold chastity.
8. A mountain in northern Greece and, in classical mythology, the home of the gods.

Drawn by the strength of voky° dragons' necks. *yoked*
He now is gone to prove° cosmography, *make trial of*
And, as I guess, will first arrive at Rome
To see the Pope and manner of his court
10 And take some part of° holy Peter's feast[9] *in*
That to this day is highly solemnized.   [*Exit* WAGNER.]

3.1

[*Enter* FAUSTUS *and* MEPHISTOPHELES.]

FAUSTUS   Having now, my good Mephistopheles
Passed with delight the stately town of Trier° *(in western Germany)*
Environed round with airy mountaintops,
With walls of flint and deep intrenchèd lakes° *moats*
5 Not to be won by any conquering prince;
From Paris next, coasting° the realm of France, *skirting*
We saw the river Maine fall into Rhine,
Whose banks are set with groves of fruitful vines.
Then up to Naples, rich Campania,
10 Whose buildings, fair and gorgeous to the eye,
The streets straight forth° and paved with finest brick, *perfectly straight*
Quarters the town in four equivalents.
There saw we learned Maro's[1] golden tomb,
The way he cut an English mile in length
15 Thorough° a rock of stone in one night's space[2] *through*
From thence to Venice, Padua, and the rest,
In midst of which a sumptuous temple[3] stands
That threats° the stars with her aspiring top. *threatens, challenges*
Thus hitherto hath Faustus spent his time.
20 But tell me now, what resting place is this?
Hast thou, as erst° I did command, *earlier*
Conducted me within the walls of Rome?
MEPHISTOPHELES   Faustus, I have. And because° we will *in order that*
not be unprovided, I have taken up His Holiness's privy° *private*
25 chamber for our use.
FAUSTUS   I hope His Holiness will bid us welcome.
MEPHISTOPHELES   Tut, 'tis no matter, man. We'll be bold
with his good cheer.
And now, my Faustus, that thou mayst perceive
30 What Rome containeth to delight thee with,
Know that this city stands upon seven hills
That underprops the groundwork of the same.
Just° through the midst runs flowing Tiber's stream, *Right*
With winding banks that cut it in two parts,

9. In the Roman Catholic Church, the main
feast (or festival) of St. Peter and St. Paul
takes place on June 29.
1. The Roman poet Virgil (70–19 B.C.E.),
whose full name was Publius Vergilius Maro.
2. This tunnel through volcanic tufa, about a

half mile long, was probably constructed in
the 1st century C.E.; in the Middle Ages, it
was credited to Virgil and his magic.
3. That is, St. Mark's Basilica in Venice, consecrated in 1094.

35   Over the which four stately bridges lean,
      That makes safe passage to each part of Rome.
      Upon the bridge called Ponte Angelo
      Erected is a castle passing° strong,   *surpassingly*
      Within whose walls such store of ordnance are,
40   And double cannons, framed° of carvèd brass   *made*
      As match the days within one complete year[4]
      Besides the gates and high pyramides°   *obelisks*
      Which Julius Caesar[5] brought from Africa.
  FAUSTUS   Now, by the kingdoms of infernal rule,
45   Of Styx, Acheron, and the fiery lake
      Of ever-burning Phlegethon[6] I swear
      That I do long to see the monuments
      And situation of bright splendent Rome.
      Come, therefore, let's away!
50 MEPHISTOPHELES   Nay, Faustus, stay. I know you'd fain see
      the Pope
      And take some part of holy Peter's feast,
      Where thou shalt see a troupe of bald-pate friars
      Whose *summum bonum*° is in belly cheer.   *highest good (Latin)*
55 FAUSTUS   Well, I am content to compass° then some sport,   *devise*
      And by their folly make us merriment.
      Then charm° me, that I may be invisible, to do what I   *put a spell on*
      please unseen of any whilst, stay in Rome.
  MEPHISTOPHELES [*placing a robe on* FAUSTUS]   So, Faustus,
60   now do what thou wilt, thou shalt not be discerned.
         [*Sound a sennet.*° *Enter the* POPE *and the Cardinal of*   *trumpet call*
         LORRAINE *to the banquet, with* FRIARS *attending.*]
  POPE   My lord of Lorraine, will't please you draw near?
  FAUSTUS   Fall to, and the devil choke you an you spare.°   *if you hold back*
  POPE   How now, who's that which spake?—Friars, look
      about.
         [*Some* FRIARS *attempt to search.*]
65 FRIAR   Here's nobody, if it like° Your Holiness.   *please*
  POPE [*presenting a dish*]   My lord, here is a dainty dish was°   *that was*
      sent me from the Bishop of Milan.
  FAUSTUS [*snatching it*]   I thank you, sir.
  POPE   How now, who's that which snatched the meat from
70   me? Will no man look? [*Some* FRIARS *search about.*] My
      lord, this dish was sent me from the Cardinal of Florence.
  FAUSTUS [*snatching the dish*]   You say true. I'll ha't.
  POPE   What, again?—My lord, I'll drink to Your Grace.
75 FAUSTUS [*snatching the cup*]   I'll pledge Your Grace.
  LORRAINE   My lord, it may be some ghost, newly crept out of
      purgatory, come to beg a pardon of Your Holiness.

---

4. That is, there are 365 cannons.
5. During the civil war precipitated by Caesar (100–44 B.C.E.), the Roman general fought in Egypt and Africa; however, the first ruler to bring Egyptian obelisks to Rome was his successor, Augustus.
6. A river of fire in the classical underworld; Styx and Acheron are also rivers in Hades.

POPE It may be so.—Friars, prepare a dirge to lay° the fury   *allay*
      of this ghost.—Once again, my lord, fall to.°   *partake of the feast*

      [*The* POPE *crosseth himself.*]

80 FAUSTUS What, are you crossing of yourself?
        Well, use that trick no more, I would advise you.

        [*The* POPE *crosses himself again.*]

        Well, there's a second time. Aware° the third,   *Beware*
        I give you fair warning.

              [*The* POPE *crosses himself again, and* FAUSTUS *hits
              him a box of the ear, and they all (except* FAUSTUS
              and MEPHISTOPHELES*) run away.*]

        Come on, Mephistopheles. What shall we do?

85 MEPHISTOPHELES Nay, I know not. We shall be cursed
        with bell, book, and candle.[7]

  FAUSTUS How? Bell, book, and candle, candle, book, and
        bell, Forward and backward, to curse Faustus to hell.
        Anon you shall hear a hog grunt, a calf bleat, and an ass
90   bray, Because it is Saint Peter's holy day.

        [*Enter all the* FRIARS *to sing the dirge.*]

  FRIAR Come, brethren, let's about our business with good
        devotion.

        [*The* FRIARS *sing this.*]

        Cursèd be he that stole away His Holiness's meat from
        the table.
95   *Maledicat Dominus!*[8]
        Cursèd be he that struck His Holiness a blow on the
        face.
        Maledicat Dominus!
        Cursèd be he that took° Friar Sandelo a blow on the pate.°   *gave / head*
100   *Maledicat Dominus!*
        Cursèd be he that disturbeth our holy dirge.
        Maledicat Dominus!
        Cursèd be he that took away His Holiness's wine.
        Maledicat Dominus!
105 *Et omnes sancti.*[9] Amen.

              [FAUSTUS *and* MEPHISTOPHELES *beat the* FRIARS,
              and fling fireworks among them, and so exeunt.]

3.2

        [*Enter* ROBIN *with a conjuring book and* RAFE *with
        a silver goblet.*]

  ROBIN Come, Rafe, did not I tell thee we were forever
        made by this Doctor Faustus' book? *Ecce signum.*° Here's   *Behold the proof (Latin)*
        a simple purchase° for horse-keepers! Our horses shall   *acquisition*

---

7. A form of excommunication that involved
ringing a bell, closing a holy book, and snuffing out a candle.

8. May the Lord curse him! (Latin).
9. And all the saints (Latin); that is, may all
the saints curse him too.

eat no hay[1] as long as this lasts.

           [*Enter the* VINTNER.°]   *innkeeper*

5 RAFE   But, Robin, here comes the Vintner.

    ROBIN   Hush, I'll gull° him supernaturally.—Drawer,° I hope   *trick / Bartender*

      all is paid. God be with you. Come, Rafe. [*They start to go.*]

    VINTNER [*to* ROBIN]   Soft,° sir, a word with you. I must yet   *Wait*

      have a goblet paid from you ere you go.

10 ROBIN   I, a goblet? Rafe, I, a goblet? I scorn you, and you are

      but a etc. I, a goblet? Search me.

    VINTNER   I mean so, sir, with your favor.°   *permission*

           [*The* VINTNER *searches* ROBIN.]

    ROBIN   How say you now?

    VINTNER   I must say somewhat° to your fellow.—You, sir.   *something*

15 RAFE   Me, sir? Me, sir? Search your fill.

           [*He tosses the goblet to* ROBIN; *then the* VINTNER

           searches RAFE.]

    Now, sir, you may be ashamed to burden honest men with

    a matter of truth.°   *question of honesty*

    VINTNER   Well, t'one of you hath this goblet about you.

    ROBIN   You lie, drawer, 'tis afore° me. Sirrah, you, I'll teach   *in front of*

20 ye to impeach° honest men. Stand by. I'll scour° you   *accuse / beat*

      for a goblet. Stand aside, you had best, I charge you in the

      name of Beelzebub.   [*He tosses the goblet to* RAFE.]

    [*Aside to* RAFE] Look to the goblet, Rafe.

    VINTNER   What mean you, sirrah?

25 ROBIN   I'll tell you what I mean. [*He reads.*] "*Sanctobulorum*

      Periphrasticon!"°—Nay, I'll tickle you, Vintner. [*Aside to*   *(Latin gibberish)*

      Rafe] Look to the goblet, Rafe.—"*Polypragmos Belseborams*

      framanto pacostiphos tostu Mephistopheles!" etc.°   *(Latin gibberish)*

           [*Enter to them* MEPHISTOPHELES.]

                    [*Exit the* VINTNER, *running.*]

    MEPHISTOPHELES   Monarch of hell, under whose black survey

30 Great potentates do kneel with awful° fear,   *awe-filled*

    Upon whose altars thousand souls do lie,

    How am I vexèd with these villains' charms!°   *spells*

    From Constantinople am I hither come

    Only for pleasure of these damnèd slaves.

35 ROBIN   How, from Constantinople? You have had a great

      journey. Will you take sixpence in your purse to pay for

      your supper and be gone?

    MEPHISTOPHELES   Well, villains, for your presumption I

      transform thee [*to* ROBIN] into an ape, and thee [*to* RAFE]

40 into a dog. And so, begone!

           [*They are transformed in shape.*]

                      [*Exit* MEPHISTOPHELES.]

    ROBIN   How, into an ape? That's brave.° I'll have fine sport   *excellent*

    with the boys; I'll get nuts and apples enough.

---

1. That is, they will eat like kings.

RAFE And I must be a dog.

ROBIN I'faith, thy head will never be out of the pottage° pot.   porridge

[*Exeunt.*]

4. Chorus

[*Enter* CHORUS.]

CHORUS When Faustus had with pleasure ta'en the view
   Of rarest things and royal courts of kings,
   He stayed his course° and so returnèd home,   stopped traveling
   Where such as bear his absence but with grief—
5   I mean his friends and nearest companions—
   Did gratulate° his safety with kind words.   rejoice at
   And in their conference of what befell,
   Touching° his journey through the world and air,   Regarding
   They put forth questions of astrology,
10   Which Faustus answered with such learnèd skill
   As° they admired and wondered at his wit.   That
   Now is his fame spread forth in every land.
   Amongst the rest the Emperor[2] is one,
   Carolus the Fifth, at whose palace now
15   Faustus is feasted 'mongst his noblemen.
   What there he did in trial° of his art°   demonstration / skill
   I leave untold, your eyes shall see performed.   [*Exit.*]

4.1

[*Enter* EMPEROR, FAUSTUS, MEPHISTOPHELES, *and*
a KNIGHT, *with attendants.*]

EMPEROR Master Doctor Faustus, I have heard strange° re-   unusual,
port of thy knowledge in the black art—how that none in   wondrous
my empire, nor in the whole world, can compare with thee
for the rare effects of magic. They say thou hast a familiar
5 spirit by whom thou canst accomplish what thou list.° This,   desire, want
therefore, is my request: that thou let me see some proof of
thy skill, that mine eyes may be witnesses to confirm what
mine ears have heard reported. And here I swear to thee,
by the honor of mine imperial crown, that whatever thou
10 dost, thou shalt be no ways prejudiced or endamaged.

KNIGHT [*aside*] I'faith, he looks much like a conjurer.°   (ironic)

FAUSTUS My gracious sovereign, though I must confess
myself far inferior to the report men have published,° and   spread abroad
nothing answerable° to the honor of Your Imperial Majesty,   suitable
15 yet, for that° love and duty binds me there unto, I am   because
content to do whatsoever Your Majesty shall command me.

---

2. Charles (Carolus) V (1500–1558), king of Spain (r. 1516–56) and emperor of the Holy
Roman Empire (r. 1519–56).

EMPEROR   Then, Doctor Faustus, mark what I shall say.
As I was sometime° solitary set   *recently*
Within my closet,° sundry thoughts arose   *private room*
20 About the honor of mine ancestors—
How they had won by prowess such exploits,
Got such riches, subdued so many kingdoms
As we that do succeed or they that shall
Hereafter possess our throne shall,
25 I fear me, never attain to that degree
Of high renown and great authority.
Amongst which kings is Alexander the Great,[3]
Chief spectacle of the world's preeminence,
The bright shining of whose glorious acts
30 Lightens the world with his reflecting beams—
As° when I hear but motion° made of him,   *so that / mention*
It grieves my soul I never saw the man.
If, therefore, thou by cunning of thine art
Canst raise this man from hollow vaults below
35 Where lies entombed this famous conqueror,
And bring with him his beauteous paramour,
Both in their right shapes, gesture, and attire
They used to wear during their time of life,
Thou shalt both satisfy my just desire
40 And give me cause to praise thee whilst I live.

FAUSTUS   My gracious lord, I am ready to accomplish your
request, so far forth as by art and power of my spirit I am
able to perform.

KNIGHT [*aside*] I'faith, that's just nothing at all.

45 FAUSTUS   But if it like° Your Grace, it is not in my ability to   *please*
present before your eyes the true substantial bodies of those
two deceased princes, which long since are consumed to
dust.

KNIGHT [*aside*] Ay, marry,° Master Doctor, now there's a sign   *by Mary (an oath)*
of grace in you, when you will confess the truth.

50 FAUSTUS   But such spirits as can lively° resemble Alexander   *in a lifelike*
and his paramour shall appear before Your Grace in that   *manner*
manner that they best lived in, in their most flourishing
estate—which I doubt not shall sufficiently content Your
Imperial Majesty.

55 EMPEROR   Go to,° Master Doctor. Let me see them presently.°   *Proceed / at once*

KNIGHT   Do you hear, Master Doctor? You bring Alexander
and his paramour before the Emperor?

FAUSTUS   How then, sir?

KNIGHT   I'faith, that's as true as Diana[4] turned me to a stag.

---

3. Alexander III of Macedon (356–323
B.C.E.); the greatest of all Greek generals, he
unified Greece and conquered much of Asia.

4. The Roman huntress goddess (the Greek
Artemis).

60 FAUSTUS   No, sir, but when Actaeon died,[5] he left the horns
for you. [*Aside to* MEPHISTOPHELES] Mephistopheles,
begone!

[*Exit* MEPHISTOPHELES.]

KNIGHT   Nay, an you go to conjuring,° I'll be gone.   *if you play mere tricks*

[*Exit* KNIGHT.]

FAUSTUS [*aside*]   I'll meet with° you anon for interrupting   *get even with*
me so.—Here they are, my gracious lord.

[*Enter* MEPHISTOPHELES *with Alexander and his
paramour.*]

65 EMPEROR   Master Doctor, I heard this lady while she lived
had a wart or mole in her neck. How shall I know
whether it be so or no?

FAUSTUS   Your Highness may boldly go and see.

[*The* EMPEROR *makes an inspection, and then exit
Alexander with his paramour.*]

EMPEROR   Sure these are no spirits, but the true substantial
70 bodies of those two deceased princes.

FAUSTUS   Will't please Your Highness now to send for the
knight that was so pleasant° with me here of late?   *humorous*

EMPEROR   One of you call him forth.

[*An attendant goes to summon the* KNIGHT.]

[*Enter the* KNIGHT *with a pair of horns on his head.*]

How now, Sir Knight? Why, I had thought thou hadst been a
75 bachelor, but now I see thou hast a wife, that not only gives
thee horns but makes thee wear them.[6] Feel on thy head.

KNIGHT [*to* FAUSTUS]   Thou damnèd wretch and execrable dog,
Bred in the concave° of some monstrous rock,   *hollow*
How dar'st thou thus abuse a gentleman?

80 Villain, I say, undo what thou hast done.

FAUSTUS   Oh, not so fast, sir. There's no haste but good.°   *Don't be too hasty*
Are you remembered° how you crossed me in my confer-   *Do you remember*
ence with the Emperor? I think I have met with you for it.

EMPEROR   Good Master Doctor, at my entreaty release
85 him. He hath done penance sufficient.

FAUSTUS   My gracious lord, not so much for the injury° he   *insult*
offered me here in your presence as to delight you
with some mirth hath Faustus worthily requited this
injurious knight; which being all I desire, I am con-
90 tent to release him of his horns.—And, Sir Knight,
hereafter speak well of scholars. [*Aside to* MEPHISTOPH-
ELES] Mephistopheles, transform him straight.° [*The   *at once*
horns are removed.*] Now, my good lord, having
done my duty, I humbly take my leave.

EMPEROR   Farewell, Master Doctor. Yet, ere you go,

---

5. Because Acteon saw the goddess naked,
Artemis/Diana turned him into a stag, and he
was torn to pieces by his own dogs.

6. Cuckolds were traditionally represented as
wearing horns.

95 Expect from me a bounteous reward.
    [Exeunt EMPEROR, KNIGHT, *and attendants.]*
FAUSTUS Now, Mephistopheles, the restless course
 That time doth run with calm and silent foot,
 Short'ning my days and thread of vital life,
 Calls for the payment of my latest° years.   *last, final*
100 Therefore, sweet Mephistopheles, let us make haste
 To Wittenberg.
MEPHISTOPHELES What, will you go on horseback or on foot?
FAUSTUS Nay, till I am past this fair and pleasant green,
 I'll walk on foot.
    [Enter a HORSE-COURSER.[7]*]*
105 HORSE-COURSER I have been all this day seeking one Master
 Fustian.° Mass,° see where he is.—God save you, Master *Bombast / By the Mass*
 Doctor.
FAUSTUS What, Horse-courser! You are well met.[8]
HORSE-COURSER *[offering money]* Do you hear, sir? I have
110 brought you forty dollars for your horse.
FAUSTUS I cannot sell him so. If thou lik'st him for fifty, take
 him.
HORSE-COURSER Alas, sir, I have no more.
 [To MEPHISTOPHELES*]* I pray you, speak for me.
115 MEPHISTOPHELES *[to* FAUSTUS*]* I pray you, let him have him.
 He is an honest fellow, and he has a great charge,° neither *financial burden*
 wife nor child.
FAUSTUS Well, come, give me your money. *[He takes the*
 money.] My boy° will deliver him to you. But I must tell *servant*
120 you one thing before you have him: ride him not into the
 water, at any hand.°   *on any account*
HORSE-COURSER Why, sir, will he not drink of all waters?[9]
FAUSTUS Oh, yes, he will drink of all waters. But ride him
 not into the water. Ride him over hedge, or ditch, or where
125 thou wilt, but not into the water.
HORSE-COURSER Well, sir. *[Aside]* Now am I made man forever! I'll not leave my horse for forty. If he had but the
 quality of hey, ding, ding, hey, ding, ding, I'd make a
 brave living on him; he has a buttock as slick as an eel.[1]
130 *[To* FAUSTUS*]* Well, good-bye, sir. Your boy will deliver him
 me? But hark ye, sir: if my horse be sick or ill at ease, if I
 bring his water[2] to you, you'll tell me what it is?
FAUSTUS Away, you villain! What, dost think I am a horse
 doctor?
           [Exit HORSE-COURSER.*]*
135 What art thou, Faustus, but a man condemned to die?
 Thy fatal time doth draw to final end.

---

7. A horse dealer (stereotypically a shrewd or dishonest bargainer).
8. An expression of greeting.
9. That is, go anywhere (proverbial).

1. That is, he is sleek and well-formed. *Hey, ding, ding:* a virile quality (to generate stud fees).
2. That is, his urine (to diagnose the illness).

Despair doth drive distrust unto my thoughts.
Confound° these passions with a quiet sleep.   *Allay, alleviate*
Tush! Christ did call the thief upon the cross;[3]
140   Then rest thee, Faustus, quiet in conceit.°   *in thought*

[FAUSTUS *sleeps in his chair.*]

[*Enter* HORSE-COURSER *all wet, crying.*]

HORSE-COURSER   Alas, alas! "Doctor" Fustian, quotha!° Mass,   *indeed*
Doctor Lopus[4] was never such a doctor. He's given me a
purgation, he's purged me of forty dollars. I shall never
see them more. But yet, like an ass as I was, I would not
145   be ruled by him, for he bade me I should ride him into no
water. Now I, thinking my horse had had some rare
quality that he would not have had me known of, I, like
a venturous youth, rid him into the deep pond at the
town's end. I was no sooner in the middle of the pond
150   but my horse vanished away and I sat upon a bottle° of   *bundle*
hay, never so near drowning in my life. But I'll seek out
my doctor and have my forty dollars again, or I'll make
it the dearest horse! Oh, yonder is his snippersnapper.°—   *mouthy fellow*
Do you hear? You, hey-pass,[5] where's your master?
155   MEPHISTOPHELES   Why, sir, what would you? You cannot
speak with him.
HORSE-COURSER   But I will speak with him.
MEPHISTOPHELES   Why, he's fast asleep. Come some
other time.
160   HORSE-COURSER   I'll speak with him now, or I'll break his
glass windows° about his ears.   *eyeglasses*
MEPHISTOPHELES   I tell thee he has not slept this eight nights.
HORSE-COURSER   An° he have not slept this eight weeks,   *Even if*
I'll speak with him.
165   MEPHISTOPHELES   See where he is, fast asleep.
HORSE-COURSER   Ay, this is he.—God save ye, Master
Doctor. Master Doctor, Master Doctor Fustian! Forty
dollars, forty dollars for a bottle of hay!
MEPHISTOPHELES   Why, thou see'st he hears thee not.
170   HORSE-COURSER [*hollers in his ear*]   So-ho, ho! So-ho, ho! No?
Will you not wake? I'll make you wake ere I go.

[*The* HORSE-COURSER *pulls him by the leg, and
pulls it away.*]

Alas, I am undone! What shall I do?
FAUSTUS   Oh, my leg, my leg! Help, Mephistopheles!
Call the officers! My leg, my leg!
175   MEPHISTOPHELES [*seizing the* HORSE-COURSER]   Come,
villain, to the constable.

---

3. Jesus said to the thief who feared the judgment of God, "Verily I say unto thee, Today shalt
thou be with me in paradise" (Luke 23.43).
4. Roderigo Lopez (ca. 1525–1594), Queen
Elizabeth's private physician; a Portuguese

Jew, he was implicated in a plot to poison her
and was executed.
5. An exclamation of conjurors or jugglers
commanding objects to move.

HORSE-COURSER   Oh, Lord, sir, let me go, and I'll give you
    forty dollars more.
MEPHISTOPHELES   Where be they?
180 HORSE-COURSER   I have none about me. Come to my hostry°   *hostelry, inn*
    and I'll give them you.
MEPHISTOPHELES   Begone, quickly. [HORSE-COURSER *runs away.*]
FAUSTUS   What, is he gone? Farewell, he!° Faustus has his leg   *Good riddance to him*
    again, and the Horse-courser, I take it, a bottle of hay for
185   his labor. Well, this trick shall cost him forty dollars more.
        [*Enter* WAGNER.]
    How now, Wagner, what's the news with thee?
WAGNER   Sir, the Duke of Vanholt° doth earnestly entreat   *Anhalt (in Germany)*
    your company.
190 FAUSTUS   The Duke of Vanholt! An honorable gentleman, to
    whom I must be no niggard of° my cunning.° Come,   *unsparing with / skill*
    Mephistopheles, let's away to him.   [*Exeunt.*]

4.2

        [*Enter* FAUSTUS *with Mephistopheles. Enter to them*
        the DUKE *of Vanholt and the pregnant* DUCHESS. *The*
        DUKE *speaks.*]
DUKE   Believe me, Master Doctor, this merriment hath
    much pleased me.
FAUSTUS   My gracious lord, I am glad it contents you so
    well.—But it may be, madam, you take no delight in this.
5   I have heard that great-bellied women do long for some
    dainties or other. What is it, madam? Tell me, and you
    shall have it.
DUCHESS   Thanks, good Master Doctor. And, for° I see your   *because*
    courteous intent to pleasure me, I will not hide from you
10   the thing my heart desires. And were it now summer, as it
    is January and the dead time of the winter, I would desire
    no better meat° than a dish of ripe grapes.   *food*
FAUSTUS   Alas, madam, that's nothing. [*Aside to* MEPHISTOPHE-
    LES] Mephistopheles, begone!   [*Exit* MEPHISTOPHELES.]
15   Were it a greater thing than this, so° it would content   *provided that*
    you, you should have it.
        [*Enter* MEPHISTOPHELES *with the grapes.*]
    Here they be, madam. Will't please you taste on them?
        [*The* DUCHESS *tastes the grapes.*]
DUKE   Believe me, Master Doctor, this makes me wonder
    above the rest, that, being in the dead time of winter and in
20   the month of January, how you should come by these grapes.
FAUSTUS   If it like Your Grace, the year is divided into two cir-
    cles over the whole world, that when it is here winter with
    us, in the contrary circle it is summer with them, as in
    India, Saba,[6] and farther countries in the East; and by

6. Sheba, an ancient kingdom on the Red Sea.

25 means of a swift spirit that I have, I had them brought
hither, as ye see.—How do you like them, madam? Be they
good?

DUCHESS   Believe me, Master Doctor, they be the best grapes
that e'er I tasted in my life before.

30 FAUSTUS   I am glad they content you so, madam.

DUKE   Come, madam, let us in,
Where you must well reward this learnèd man
For the great kindness he hath showed to you.

DUCHESS   And so I will, my lord, and whilst I live

35 Rest beholding° for this courtesy.   *Remain beholden*

FAUSTUS   I humbly thank Your Grace.

DUKE   Come, Master Doctor, follow us and receive your reward.
[*Exeunt.*]

5.1

[*Enter* WAGNER *solus.*]

WAGNER   I think my master means to die shortly,
For he hath given to me all his goods.
And yet methinks if that death were near
He would not banquet and carouse and swill

5 Amongst the students, as even now he doth,
Who are at supper with such belly-cheer
As Wagner ne'er beheld in all his life.
See where they come. Belike° the feast is ended.   [*Exit.*]   *Apparently*
[*Enter* FAUSTUS *with two or three* SCHOLARS *and*
MEPHISTOPHELES.]

FIRST SCHOLAR   Master Doctor Faustus, since our confer-

10 ence about fair ladies—which was the beautifull'st in all
the world—we have determined with° ourselves that   *among*
Helen of Greece was the admirablest lady that ever
lived. Therefore, Master Doctor, if you will do us that
favor as to let us see that peerless dame of Greece,

15 whom all the world admires for majesty, we should
think ourselves much beholding unto you.

FAUSTUS   Gentlemen,
For that° I know your friendship is unfeigned,   *Because*
And Faustus' custom is not to deny

20 The just requests of those that wish him well,
You shall behold that peerless dame of Greece,
No otherways° for pomp and majesty   *otherwise*
Than when Sir Paris crossed the seas with her
And brought the spoils to rich Dardania.°   *Troy*

25 Be silent then, for danger is in words.
[*Music sounds and Helen led in by* MEPHISTOPHE-
LES *passeth over the stage.*]

SECOND SCHOLAR   Too simple is my wit to tell her praise,

Whom all the world admires for majesty.

THIRD SCHOLAR   No marvel though the angry Greeks pursued°   *avenged*
     With ten years' war the rape° of such a queen,   *abduction*
30   Whose heavenly beauty passeth all compare.°   *comparison*
FIRST SCHOLAR   Since we have seen the pride of nature's works
     And only paragon of excellence,
                    [*Enter an* OLD MAN.]
     Let us depart; and for this glorious deed
     Happy and blest be Faustus evermore!
35 FAUSTUS   Gentlemen, farewell. The same I wish to you.
                                   [*Exeunt* SCHOLARS.]

OLD MAN   Ah, Doctor Faustus, that I might prevail
     To guide thy steps unto the way of life,
     By which sweet path thou mayst attain the goal
     That shall conduct thee to celestial rest!
40   Break heart, drop blood, and mingle it with tears—
     Tears falling from repentant heaviness
     Of thy most vile and loathsome filthiness,
     The stench whereof corrupts the inward soul
     With such flagitious° crimes of heinous sins   *wicked*
45   As no commiseration may expel
     But mercy, Faustus, of thy Savior sweet,
     Whose blood alone must wash away thy guilt.
FAUSTUS   Where art thou, Faustus? Wretch, what hast thou done?
     Damned art thou, Faustus, damned! Despair and die!
50   Hell calls for right, and with a roaring voice
     Says, "Faustus, come! Thine hour is come."
          [MEPHISTOPHELES *gives him a dagger.*]
     And Faustus will come to do thee right.
          [FAUSTUS *prepares to stab himself.*]
OLD MAN   Ah, stay, good Faustus, stay thy desperate steps!
     I see an angel hovers o'er thy head,
55   And with a vial full of precious grace
     Offers to pour the same into thy soul.
     Then call for mercy and avoid despair.
FAUSTUS   Ah, my sweet friend, I feel thy words
     To comfort my distressèd soul.
60   Leave me awhile to ponder on my sins.
OLD MAN   I go, sweet Faustus, but with heavy cheer,°   *frame of mind*
     Fearing the ruin of thy hopeless soul.   [*Exit.*]
FAUSTUS   Accursèd Faustus, where is mercy now?
     I do repent, and yet I do despair.
65   Hell strives with grace for conquest in my breast.
     What shall I do to shun the snares of death?
MEPHISTOPHELES   Thou traitor, Faustus, I arrest thy soul
     For disobedience to my sovereign lord.
     Revolt,° or I'll in piecemeal tear thy flesh.   *Recant, turn back*
70 FAUSTUS   Sweet Mephistopheles, entreat thy lord
     To pardon my unjust presumption,

And with my blood again I will confirm
My former vow I made to Lucifer.
MEPHISTOPHELES   Do it then quickly, with unfeignèd heart,
75   Lest greater danger do attend thy drift.

[FAUSTUS *cuts his arm and writes with his blood.*]

FAUSTUS   Torment, sweet friend, that base and crooked age°   old man
That durst dissuade me from thy Lucifer,
With greatest torments that our hell affords.
MEPHISTOPHELES   His faith is great. I cannot touch his soul.
80   But what I may afflict his body with
I will attempt, which is but little worth.
FAUSTUS   One thing, good servant, let me crave of thee
To glut the longing of my heart's desire:
That I might have unto° my paramour   as
85   That heavenly Helen which I saw of late,
Whose sweet embracings may extinguish clean°   entirely
These thoughts that do dissuade me from my vow,
And keep mine oath I made to Lucifer.
MEPHISTOPHELES   Faustus, this, or what else thou shalt desire,
90   Shall be performed in twinkling of an eye.

[*Enter Helen brought in by* MEPHISTOPHELES.]

FAUSTUS   Was this the face that launched a thousand ships
And burnt the topless° towers of Ilium?°   immensely high / Troy
Sweet Helen, make me immortal with a kiss.   [*They kiss.*]
Her lips sucks forth my soul. See where it flies!
95   Come, Helen, come, give me my soul again.

[*They kiss again.*]

Here will I dwell, for heaven be in these lips,
And all is dross° that is not Helena.   impurity; rubbish

[*Enter* OLD MAN.]

I will be Paris, and for love of thee
Instead of Troy shall Wittenberg be sacked,
100   And I will combat with weak Menelaus,[7]
And wear thy colors° on my plumèd crest.   emblems, device
Yea, I will wound Achilles in the heel[8]
And then return to Helen for a kiss.
Oh, thou art fairer than the evening air,
105   Clad in the beauty of a thousand stars.
Brighter art thou than flaming Jupiter
When he appeared to hapless Semele,[9]

---

7. King of Sparta and Helen's cuckolded
husband.
8. According to one legend, the mother of the
Greek hero Achilles dipped her infant son
into the river Styx, rendering him invulnerable except for the heel by which she held him.

At Troy, he was fatally wounded by an arrow
shot by Paris.
9. When Zeus (Roman Jupiter) complied with
Semele's wish that he appear to her as he did
to his wife, the goddess Hera, she was consumed by lightning.

More lovely than the monarch of the sky
In wanton Arethusa's azured° arms;[1]   sky-blue
110   And none but thou shalt be my paramour.

      [*Exeunt* FAUSTUS *and Helen, with* MEPHISTOPHELES.]

OLD MAN   Accursèd Faustus, miserable man,
That from thy soul exclud'st the grace of heaven
And fliest the throne of His tribunal seat!

      [*Enter the devils with* MEPHISTOPHELES. *They
      menace the* OLD MAN.]

Satan begins to sift me with his pride.
115   As in this furnace God shall try my faith,
My faith, vile hell, shall triumph over thee.
Ambitious fiends, see how the heavens smiles
At your repulse and laughs your state to scorn!
Hence, hell! For hence I fly unto my God.   [*Exeunt.*]

5.2

      [*Enter* FAUSTUS *with the* SCHOLARS.]

FAUSTUS   Ah, gentlemen!
FIRST SCHOLAR   What ails Faustus?
FAUSTUS   Ah, my sweet chamber-fellow! Had I lived with
  thee, then had I lived still, but now I die eternally. Look,
5   comes he not? Comes he not?

      [*The* SCHOLARS *speak among themselves.*]

SECOND SCHOLAR   What means Faustus?
THIRD SCHOLAR   Belike he is grown into some sickness by
  being oversolitary.
10   FIRST SCHOLAR   If it be so, we'll have physicians to cure him.
  [*To* FAUSTUS] 'Tis but a surfeit.°   Never fear, man.   excessive indulgence

FAUSTUS   A surfeit of deadly sin that hath damned both body
  and soul.
SECOND SCHOLAR   Yet, Faustus, look up to heaven. Remember
  God's mercies are infinite.
15   FAUSTUS   But Faustus' offense can ne'er be pardoned. The
  serpent that tempted Eve° may be saved, but not Faustus.   (see Gen. 3.1–6)
  Ah, gentlemen, hear me with patience, and tremble not at
  my speeches. Though my heart pants and quivers to
  remember that I have been a student here these thirty
20   years, oh, would I had never seen Wittenberg, never read
  book! And what wonders I have done, all Germany can witness, yea, all the world, for which Faustus hath lost both
  Germany and the world, yea, heaven itself—heaven, the seat
  of God, the throne of the blessed, the kingdom of joy—and

---

1. The nymph Arethusa, an attendant of the virgin goddess Artemis, fled the sexual advances of the river god Alpheus (not Jupi-ter, monarch of the sky). When she was trans-formed by the goddess into a stream, the river god sought to mingle his waters with hers.

25 must remain in hell forever. Hell, ah, hell forever! Sweet
friends, what shall become of Faustus, being in hell forever?

THIRD SCHOLAR   Yet, Faustus, call on God.

FAUSTUS   On God, whom Faustus hath abjured? On God,
30 whom Faustus hath blasphemed? Ah, my God, I would weep,
but the devil draws in my tears. Gush forth blood instead of
tears! Yea, life and soul! Oh, he stays my tongue! I would lift
up my hands, but see, they hold them, they hold them!

ALL [THE SCHOLARS]   Who, Faustus?

FAUSTUS   Lucifer and Mephistopheles. Ah, gentlemen! I
35 gave them my soul for my cunning.

ALL [THE SCHOLARS]   God forbid!

FAUSTUS   God forbade it indeed, but Faustus hath done it.
For vain pleasure of four-and-twenty years hath Faustus
40 lost eternal joy and felicity. I writ them a bill with mine
own blood. The date is expired, the time will come, and
he will fetch me.

FIRST SCHOLAR   Why did not Faustus tell us of this
before, that divines might have prayed for thee?

FAUSTUS   Oft have I thought to have done so, but the devil
45 threatened to tear me in pieces if I named God, to fetch
both body and soul if I once gave ear to divinity. And now
'tis too late. Gentlemen, away, lest you perish with me.

SECOND SCHOLAR   Oh, what shall we do to save Faustus?

FAUSTUS   Talk not of me, but save yourselves and depart.

50 THIRD SCHOLAR   God will strengthen me. I will stay with
Faustus.

FIRST SCHOLAR [to the THIRD SCHOLAR]   Tempt not° God, sweet   *Don't*
friend, but let us into the next room and there pray for him.   *presumptuously test*

FAUSTUS   Ay, pray for me, pray for me! And what noise
55 soever ye hear, come not unto me, for nothing can rescue me.

SECOND SCHOLAR   Pray thou, and we will pray that God
may have mercy upon thee.

FAUSTUS   Gentlemen, farewell. If I live till morning, I'll
visit you; if not, Faustus is gone to hell.

60 ALL [THE SCHOLARS]   Faustus, farewell!

[*Exeunt* SCHOLARS. *The clock strikes eleven.*]

FAUSTUS   Ah, Faustus,
Now hast thou but one bare hour to live,
And then thou must be damned perpetually.
Stand still, you ever-moving spheres of heaven,
65 That time may cease and midnight never come!
Fair Nature's eye,° rise, rise again, and make   *i.e., the sun*
Perpetual day; or let this hour be but
A year, a month, a week, a natural day,
That Faustus may repent and save his soul!
70 *O lente, lente currite noctis equi!*[2]

2. Oh, run slowly, slowly, horses of the night! (Latin; slightly misquoted from Ovid, *Amores* 1.13.40).

The stars move still; time runs; the clock will strike;
The devil will come, and Faustus must be damned.
Oh, I'll leap up to my God! Who pulls me down?
See, see where Christ's blood streams in the firmament!
75 One drop would save my soul, half a drop. Ah, my Christ!
Ah, rend not my heart for naming of my Christ!
Yet will I call on him. Oh, spare me, Lucifer!
Where is it now? 'Tis gone; and see where God
Stretcheth out his arm and bends his ireful brows!
80 Mountains and hills, come, come and fall on me,
And hide me from the heavy wrath of God!
No, no!
Then will I headlong run into the earth.
Earth, gape! Oh, no, it will not harbor me.
85 You stars that reigned at my nativity,
Whose influence hath allotted death and hell,
Now draw up Faustus like a foggy mist
Into the entrails of yon laboring cloud,
That when you vomit forth into the air,°   *hurl a thunderbolt*
90 My limbs may issue from your smoky mouths,
So that my soul may but ascend to heaven.
        [*The watch strikes.*]
Ah, half the hour is past!
'Twill all be past anon.
O God,
95 If thou wilt not have mercy on my soul,
Yet for Christ's sake, whose blood hath ransomed me,
Impose some end to my incessant pain.
Let Faustus live in hell a thousand years,
A hundred thousand, and at last be saved!
100 Oh, no end is limited to damnèd souls.
Why wert thou not a creature wanting° soul?   *lacking a*
Or why is this immortal that thou hast?
Ah, Pythagoras' metempsychosis,[3] were that true,
This soul should fly from me and I be changed
105 Unto some brutish beast.
All beasts are happy, for, when they die,
Their souls are soon dissolved in elements;
But mine must live still° to be plagued in hell.   *always*
Curst be the parents that engendered me!
110 No, Faustus, curse thyself. Curse Lucifer,
That hath deprived thee of the joys of heaven.
        [*The clock striketh twelve.*]
Oh, it strikes, it strikes! Now, body, turn to air,
Or Lucifer will bear thee quick° to hell.   *alive*
        [*Thunder and lightning.*]

---

3. The passage of the soul at death into another body (human or animal), a theory espoused by
the Greek philosopher Pythagoras (6th c. B.C.E.).

O soul, be changed into little waterdrops,
115 And fall into the ocean, ne'er be found!
My God, my God, look not so fierce on me!

    [*Enter* LUCIFER, MEPHISTOPHELES, *and other devils.*]

Adders and serpents, let me breathe awhile!
Ugly hell, gape not. Come not, Lucifer!
I'll burn my books. Ah, Mephistopheles!

        [*The devils exeunt with him.*]

Epilogue

  [*Enter* CHORUS.]

CHORUS   Cut is the branch that might have grown full straight,
    And burnèd is Apollo's laurel bough[4]
    That sometime° grew within this learnèd man.   *formerly*
    Faustus is gone. Regard his hellish fall,
5   Whose fiendful fortune may exhort the wise
    Only to wonder at[5] unlawful things,
    Whose deepness doth entice such forward° wits   *daring, presumptuous*
    To practice more than heavenly power permits.   [*Exit.*]

Terminat hora diem; terminat author opus.[6]

---

4. The laurel, sacred to Apollo, the god of wisdom, is associated with poetry and victory.
5. That is, to wonder at without partaking of.

6. The hour ends the day; the author ends his work (Latin).

WILLIAM SHAKESPEARE

1564–1616

"HE was not of an age, but for all time" —so wrote BEN JONSON, William Shakespeare's contemporary and rival playwright, in a commendatory poem included in the first collected edition of Shakespeare's plays, the so-called First Folio (published in 1623). Almost 400 years later, these words must seem prophetic to us. Shakespeare's plays and poetry have been translated into every conceivable language, his plays have been performed on stages the world over, and his influence on generations of writers and poets, on popular culture and media, and on the English language itself has been incalculable. What accounts for Shakespeare's enormous and lasting success? Is it the rich density and complexity of his verse, his keen insight into human nature, or his talent for capturing in words the energies, hopes, and anxieties of his time? One factor stands out above all others: from his earliest plays—the farcical *Comedy of Errors* (1589–93), the sprawling historical tetralogy about the English Wars of the Roses (1589–94), and the bloody Roman tragedy *Titus Andronicus* (1589–91)—Shakespeare demonstrated an unfailing sense of theater, both its ability to hold an audience and its power as a medium for social and psychological exploration. Shakespeare's plays have remained at the center of the theatrical repertoire through periods of changing dramatic tastes, and they have adapted themselves to different cultures and theatrical traditions. The success of such contemporary Hollywood movies as Kenneth Branagh's *Henry V* (1989), Baz Luhrmann's *Romeo + Juliet* (1996), Richard Loncraine's *Richard III* (1995), and Josh Madden's *Shakespeare in Love* (1998)—the Oscar-winning film about Shakespeare's life—demonstrates how fully this man of the theater has been embraced by new audiences and media.

William Shakespeare was born in 1564 in the small market town of Stratford-upon-Avon, to a glove maker named John Shakespeare and Mary Arden, a member of a distinguished Warwickshire family. Though a commoner and a craftsman, John Shakespeare must have been an ambitious man. He acquired real estate and held a series of increasingly important positions in local government, culminating in the office of bailiff (mayor) in 1569. Companies of traveling actors visited Stratford on a number of occasions during William's childhood, and it is almost certain that the young Shakespeare, perhaps because of his father's standing in the community, witnessed his first dramatic performances in the town's Guild Hall. The young boy's imagination may have been sparked by Corpus Christi or morality plays, or by early Tudor humanist plays, all of which left traces of influence in Shakespeare's dramas. In the late 1570s, however, when William was six years old, his father's financial and political fortunes took a steep downward turn, and the coat of arms for which he had applied, and which would have granted him the appellation of "gentleman," was held up (until William paid the remaining balance on the application in 1596).

It is likely that William Shakespeare attended Stratford's grammar school, where Latin and the classics were taught. He married at the age of eighteen. His bride, Anne Hathaway, was his senior by some eight years. Their first child, Susanna, was born in May 1583, about six months after the wedding. Two more children, the twins Judith and Hamnet, were born in 1585. After that the picture of Shakespeare's activities gets murky. There are apocryphal stories about him working as a schoolmaster, a lawyer's aide, a sailor, and a soldier, but there is no firm evidence to support any of them. A traveling company of actors, the Earl of Leicester's Men (which later was to become the Lord Chamberlain's Men), came through Stratford in 1587. It is tempting to imagine that the young Shakespeare, taken with the acting craft, found employment with them and accompanied them back to London, where he was to make his fortune as a dramatist. Unfortunately, there is nothing in the historical record to validate such musings.

The next thing we know for certain is that Shakespeare was a working playwright in London by 1592. The rival dramatist Robert Greene refers to him in that year as an "upstart crow" and parodies a line from Shakespeare's early history play *Henry VI, Part 3*. Around 1594, Shakespeare joined the Lord Chamberlain's Men (the same troupe that had visited Stratford in 1587). Shakespeare was to stay with the Lord Chamberlain's Men, renamed the King's Men in 1603 when King James I assumed patronage over the company, until his retirement from the theater and return to Stratford around 1613. The Lord Chamberlain's Men had been the proud owners of the first permanent London playhouse, the Theatre, located in the district of Shoreditch—just northeast of the city walls and outside the jurisdiction of the city fathers, whose Puritan leanings made them aggressive opponents of stage plays. Following a financial dispute with their landlord, the Lord Chamberlain's Men pulled down their playhouse and reassembled it on the south bank of the river Thames; they named their new home, which opened for business in 1599, the Globe. It is in this theater that the comedy *TWELFTH NIGHT; OR, WHAT YOU WILL* and *THE TRAGEDY OF HAMLET, PRINCE OF DENMARK*, both anthologized here, were first presented to the public.

The conditions of performance at the Globe theater differed substantially from those on today's stages. First, all performances had to take place during daytime, as they were illuminated only by the sunlight pouring in through the open roof. The stage, a rectangular wooden scaffold some 5.5 feet high and believed to have measured roughly 43 feet wide by 27 feet deep, did not have a proscenium arch (as many stages do today), was covered by a roof, and protruded into the audience area of the theater known as the pit. The underside of the stage's roof, which was painted with the signs of the zodiac and was referred to as "the heavens," gave some protection to the actors during bad weather, a comfort not afforded to the "groundlings" who stood packed in the pit, exposed to the elements. Customers who paid more had seats in the covered, multitiered galleries surrounding the pit and the stage. The stage itself had a gallery above (which was used for such occasions as Romeo and Juliet's "balcony" scene), as well as a small inner stage or discovery space (used, for example, to reveal Miranda and Ferdinand playing chess in Shakespeare's late play *The Tempest*). The stage also had a trapdoor that could serve as the exit into hell (as in CHRISTOPHER MARLOWE's *Doctor Faustus*) or as the point of entry for the ghost of Hamlet's father. With "the heavens" above and the netherworld below, Shakespeare's Globe symbolically encompassed the entire cosmos within the "wooden O" (*Henry V*) that was the theater. The manner of performance itself was in some ways deeply symbolic in that the actors did not employ elaborate scenery or complicated special effects to

A detail from Claes Jansz Visscher's engraved panorama of London, *Londinum Florentissima Britanniae Urbs* (1616). The Globe theater is in the center foreground.

create a sense of realism, though they did don sumptuous costumes.

Audiences of Shakespeare's *Hamlet*, for instance, were asked to accept that the Ghost appeared on the castle walls "in the dead waste and middle of the night," while the actor before them stood on a wooden stage, surrounded by spectators, on a bright, sunny afternoon. What is more, a prohibition against the appearance of female actors on the stage (which was not repealed until shortly after the restoration of the monarchy in 1660) meant that all female roles were acted by boys. Whether such cross-dressing undermined the "realism" of the performance, or exactly how Elizabethan audiences experienced it, is a matter of some controversy. More than anything, however, it is fair to say that actors relied heavily on Shakespeare's amazingly rich and allusive language to spark the imagination and hold the attention of their paying spectators.

HAMLET

By the time Shakespeare wrote *The Tragedy of Hamlet, Prince of Denmark* (1600–1601) he had reached the height of his powers as a dramatist. During the 1590s, Shakespeare had written a sonnet sequence, carefully crafted narrative poems, and a number of highly successful comedies, tragedies, and history plays, including *The Taming of the Shrew* (1592), *Richard II* (1595), *Romeo and Juliet* (1595), *A Midsummer Night's Dream* (1594–96), *The Merchant of Venice* (1596–97), *Henry IV, Part 1* (1596–97), *Henry V* (1598–99), *Julius Caesar* (1599), *Much Ado about Nothing* (1598), and *As You Like It* (1599–1600). With the composition of *Hamlet* he initiated a period of less than ten years during which he composed his greatest tragedies. Among these, *Hamlet* has probably captivated our interest the most; for more than four centuries, its titular hero has been a magnetic figure for actors, critics, and audiences alike. The Romantic poet Samuel Taylor Coleridge so deeply admired Hamlet's courage, skill, and ability for abstract and rational thought that he proclaimed, "I have a smack of Hamlet myself." Hamlet has been hailed not only as the quintessential Renaissance courtier and prince, but also as the first literary character who is like us: that is, one who dramatizes what Harold Bloom calls the "internalization of the self" so strikingly that it rivals or even exceeds the complex inner life we encounter in the thought of such early modern giants as Martin Luther, Desiderius Erasmus, and Michel de Montaigne. For some, Hamlet has become such an iconic figure that he has outgrown the play in which he appears. Whether or not this is true, many of us find ourselves attracted to and fascinated by Hamlet, even though we seem so far to have been unable to "pluck out the heart of [his] mystery."

Composed near the end of Elizabeth I's reign, *Hamlet* tells a story that is not original with Shakespeare. It may be based on a number of sources, the so-called *Ur-Hamlet* (a play that no longer exists), Saxo Grammaticus's *Historia Danica* (1180–1208), and François de Belleforest's *Histories Tragiques* (1576, a French translation of Grammaticus) chief among them. Although

Shakespeare's play differs in many significant aspects from Grammaticus's narrative history, there are also similarities that appear too striking to be accidental. Grammaticus's account describes a fratricide (which, as in *Hamlet,* is also a regicide), an incestuous marriage, feigned madness (Hamlet's "antic disposition"), a spying courtier, the use of a woman (*Hamlet's* Ophelia) as a lure, and a voyage to England.

A number of these elements are also vital to a group of Elizabethan revenge plays to which *Hamlet* certainly belongs, and which includes THOMAS KYD's *The Spanish Tragedy* and works by JOHN WEBSTER, Thomas Middleton, John Marston,

Frontispiece illustration for Christiern Pedersen's 1514 edition of Saxo Grammaticus's *Historia Danica*.

and others. Harkening back to the "tragedies of blood" created by the Roman playwright SENECA, Elizabethan revenge plays typically contain an act of murder that cannot be redressed by the authorities (usually because the highest authority in the play is complicit in the crime), an appearance of a ghost who demands just revenge (usually from a son or father), madness (feigned or actual), a great deal of intrigue, a hesitation or delay on the part of the avenger, and a set of actions that leads to the death of the murderer but simultaneously contaminates the avenger and typically results in his death. Shakespeare's *Hamlet* certainly puts most of these elements on display, but it handles them creatively in ways that enrich the genre and deeply complicate our understanding of the play.

The question of Hamlet's "delay" has long vexed critics and audiences. Why does Hamlet not simply kill Claudius after his initial meeting with his father's ghost? Hamlet is adamant that the specter is a trustworthy, "honest ghost," and he surely seems to have opportunities to kill Claudius. Yet considerable time passes, and Hamlet neither slays his uncle nor develops a plan to do so. The truth is that, like the critics who have tried to solve the riddle of his delay, Hamlet himself seems confused and perturbed by his inaction. Watching with admiration and bewilderment an impromptu performance of the fall of Troy by a troupe of traveling players who visit Elsinore, Hamlet wonders why it is that an actor can muster such intense passion in acting out a fiction—for "What's Hecuba to him, or he to Hecuba, / That he should weep for her?" —while he, who has a real "cue for passion," does nothing, "not for a king / Upon whose property and most dear life / A damned defeat was made." Hamlet never provides us with a satisfactory answer to his own question, which is all the more puzzling given that he despises Claudius and would not for a moment regret his death. Even when Hamlet appears to settle on a course of action by putting on "The Murder of Gonzago" to "catch the conscience of the King," his actions appear erratic and confused. This play-within-a-play sequence, as devised by Hamlet, has attracted critical interest as a prime example of metatheatricality, a dramaturgical device in which a play's characters take on various theatrical functions. In this scene, as well as in the "nunnery" scene with Ophelia, Hamlet embodies both directorial and playwriting roles in his orchestration of others' words and actions. Yet these scenes also demonstrate that actors and directors cannot completely control their audiences' reactions. While watching a loose reenactment of the murder of King Hamlet, Claudius does have a response that could be construed as guilt, but his calling an abrupt halt to the performance occurs not when the king is killed by a brother but when Lucianus, his nephew, pours poison into the sleeping king's ear. We may expect that Hamlet will now finally "sweep to [his] revenge," but instead he answers a summons from his mother. When, on his way to Gertrude's chambers, he comes upon Claudius at prayer, he fails to seize this opportunity to dispatch the king and instead takes his anger out on his mother in an unstoppable flood of words.

The depth and subtlety of Hamlet's trauma over the revenge question stand in sharp contrast with Shakespeare's handling of two other young princes, Laertes and Fortinbras, who also suffer the loss of a father. Fortinbras's father was killed in single combat by Hamlet's father before the start of the play, and Laertes' father, Polonius, is stabbed to death by Hamlet. Neither Fortinbras nor Laertes lacks the necessary passion for swift vengeance. In the first scene, we hear that Fortinbras is readying a military invasion of Denmark, and when Laertes learns of his father's death he rushes back from France to kill whoever is responsible, even if it turns out to be King Claudius. "That drop of blood that's calm proclaims me bastard," Laertes says, suggesting that avenging a father's death is an instinctive act for an honorable son. Such an act requires no deliberation or concern for consequences, and it is this reckless liberty that Hamlet longs for but, as a result of his self-reflective nature, is unable to achieve.

Yet Hamlet finds it impossible to be more like Laertes or Fortinbras, and it is precisely in his inability to be a one-dimensional man of action that we encounter the depth and complexity of his character. He lacks the passion and single-ness of purpose to act on his father's command. Maybe it is because he perceives too great a disjunction between the straightfor-wardness of the Ghost's call for justice and the widespread disorder and corruption that render Denmark an "unweeded garden / That grows to seed." Maybe Hamlet real-izes that killing Claudius would be nothing more than an isolated and ambiguous act of revenge in a fundamentally unjust world. But whatever his reasons, Hamlet's inabil-ity to balance the Ghost's command with the corrupt world of Elsinore is precisely what intensifies and expands the inner life of his character. His inability to live in and accept the world as he finds it drives him inward, rendering him significantly more introspective and self-conscious, and there-fore more recognizably modern, than other characters who walked across the Elizabe-than public stage. It is as if the character of Hamlet allows Shakespeare to explore recesses of the human mind of which other poets and dramatists had at best only been dimly aware.

But the depth of Hamlet's interiority, insofar as it is promoted by his frustration over not killing the king, comes at a heavy price. When the play comes to a close, not only Claudius but also Gertrude, Rosen-crantz, Guildenstern, Laertes, Polonius, Ophelia, and Hamlet himself are dead, and one could argue that the swift execu-tion of justice on Claudius by Hamlet in the first act would have saved the lives of all of them. The madness and death of Ophelia are particularly distressing to audiences because the young woman is wholly a victim of others' machinations, including those of Hamlet.

Ophelia's plight and the gender dynam-ics that shape it draw attention to the lim-ited number of options aristocratic young women had available to them in the early modern period. During her premarriage days, Ophelia would have been expected to guard her reputation and chastity zealously, to be an obedient daughter to her father and an obedient sister to her brother. Her identity in Danish aristo-cratic society is defined largely in relation to the men in her life and in terms of her exchangeability on the marriage market.

As limiting as this life trajectory may seem to us, it was a reality for most aristo-cratic women of the time, and Ophelia apparently does not possess the inner strength to resist this model (as some of Shakespeare's other heroines attempt to do). What is more, it is the vital responsi-bility of the men who control Ophelia's destiny to facilitate her transition from one position to the next. Laertes' strong admonition to Ophelia to rebuff Hamlet's courtship reflects his guardianship of his sister's chastity as well as his recognition of the importance of her purity to the state. In practical terms, Laertes is guarding his sis-ter's reputation; yet his action also hinders her transition from the role of sister and daughter to that of wife. Her father, Polo-nius, is equally anxious about Hamlet's intentions, and he forbids her from seeing Hamlet any further. Claudius, who, like Elizabeth I, has a fundamental interest in shaping aristocratic marriages, completely fails in his role as kingly guardian of one of his noble subjects when he goes along with Polonius's plan to use Ophelia as a pawn in a spying game to learn more about the cause of Hamlet's odd behavior. None of the men show any concern for how their words and actions destroy Ophelia's future in Danish society.

Hamlet also contributes significantly to Ophelia's anguish when he elects to inflict his "antic disposition" on her. The genu-ine distress that this performance causes Ophelia seems of no concern to Hamlet. Betrayed by her father, brother, king, and potential husband, there is literally noth-ing for Ophelia to be anymore. The "nun-nery" to which a cruel Hamlet tries to consign her at one point might be a socially acceptable choice for Ophelia, but the option is never pursued.

Critics have long argued over whether Ophelia's madness speech gives us clues that she and Hamlet might have con-summated their relationship. While her song about love betrayed and loss of maidenhead (4.5) need not imply physical consummation, her emotional and psy-chological commitment to a life with Hamlet is so complete that she is unable to imagine or reconstitute another role for herself in the world of Elsinore, whether she is physically a virgin or not.

The dismantling of Ophelia's identity has led to the dissolution of her psychological coherence, and it results, following a cruel logic, in the loss of her very being in death.

It is possible that Hamlet's dying endorsement of the Norwegian warrior Prince Fortinbras as Denmark's new ruler is an acknowledgment that action, even reckless and violent action, is preferable to Hamlet's own propensity for delay and indecision. The rise of Fortinbras can be read as a return to power of Hamlet's father, a return of the feudal warrior-king. It functions as a rejection not only of the Machiavellian Claudius but also of Hamlet himself; indeed, it is difficult to imagine Hamlet as an effective ruler, given his style of decision making. But even so, despite the human cost associated with Hamlet's delay, it is precisely this delay, and more specifically Hamlet's anxious

pondering of its meaning, that yields us a character of uncommon psychological depth, self-scrutiny, and complexity.

To learn more about the staging of *Hamlet* and to view photographs from select performances of the play, see the "Plays in Performance" color insert near the center of this volume.

TWELFTH NIGHT

Twelfth Night; or, What You Will (1600–1601) is one of Shakespeare's most provocative, captivating, and complex romantic comedies, and yet it appears to be the last that he composed in this form. Around 1601, at the height of his dramatic powers, Shakespeare entered an artistic phase that produced his so-called problem plays (or "dark comedies") and his mature tragedies,

The King Drinks (ca. 1640), by David Teniers the Younger, depicts a popular ritual associated with Twelfth Night throughout Europe: the person who finds a dried bean in his serving of the "Three Kings cake" is pronounced king for the evening.

including *Hamlet*. The explanations of why Shakespeare abandoned romantic comedy at this time are necessarily speculative, but it appears likely that the dramatist was growing increasingly dissatisfied with the form's inability to accommodate the complexities of real life. In the midst of its festive spirit, *Twelfth Night* reveals the beginning of this dissatisfaction.

We know that *Twelfth Night* was performed at the Inns of Court (the residences in London of the city's legal societies) on the occasion of Candlemas Day, February 2, 1602. A witness to the performance noted a similarity between *Twelfth Night* and one of the mistaken-identity farces of the Roman playwright PLAUTUS (which had also influenced an earlier Shakespeare play, *The Comedy of Errors*). The year 1602 marks the earliest *recorded* performance of the play, but it is possible that Shakespeare's acting company, the Lord Chamberlain's Men, had already staged it at the Globe. It has been suggested that a performance took place in 1601 at the court of Queen Elizabeth to coincide with the visit to England of the duke of Bracciano, Don Virginio Orsino. But as tempting as it is to tease out possible analogies between *Twelfth Night*'s Duke Orsino and the historical Don Virginio Orsino, there is no indication that Shakespeare wrote *Twelfth Night* or any of his plays for special court occasions.

Twelfth Night—which is based on Barnabe Riche's story "Of Apolonius and Silla" (1581) and, indirectly, on the anonymous Italian comedy *Gl'Ingannati* (1537)—offers a compelling tale of look-alike twins separated by shipwreck. Characterized by a festive atmosphere and a preoccupation with love, romantic comedies exhibit a drive toward social unity, marriage, and happiness. Typically, Shakespeare starts his romantic comedies by presenting us with a group of young, single men and women who are eligible for marriage but who encounter obstacles to the fulfillment of their personal desires. What is more, the obstacles stand in the way not only of personal happiness but, more importantly, of socially acceptable unions that enable the orderly reproduction of existing social classes and family structures (both of which are of vital concern to the genre of romantic comedy). The impediment can take a variety of forms, including obstructionist parents, an antagonist who wishes the lovers ill, misguided desire, grief over the loss of a loved one, or fear of the opposite sex. The middle acts of romantic comedies are commonly taken up with the younger generation's clumsy but sometimes endearing attempts to overcome these obstacles, an endeavor in which they ultimately succeed, though sometimes only because of good fortune, outside aid from their elders, or supernatural intervention. The resolution of the story's dramatic conflicts is generally harmonious, mostly satisfying (to the characters as well as the audience), and life-affirming. *Twelfth Night*—perhaps reflecting the growing strain between realism and romance in Shakespearean comedy—withholds some of that satisfaction and admits disturbances to that harmony.

Shakespeare signals his interest in the social energies associated with those disturbances in the title of his play. Loosely connected to the Roman festival of Saturnalia—which marked the winter solstice with feasting, revelry, playful disrespect for authority, and sensual indulgences—"twelfth night," also known as Epiphany, marks the end of the holiday season that lasts from Christmas through January 6. The carnivalesque spirit that prevailed during these days was sometimes channeled into ritualized lampoonings of Elizabethan civil and church authorities. The Feast of Fools and such figures as the Boy Bishop, the Lords of Misrule, and the Boy King inverted the established social order and allowed ordinary men and women to release (in a controlled fashion) any resentments and hostilities that might have accrued from living and working in an oppressive, hierarchical society with sharp divisions between the haves and have nots. Although Shakespeare neither mentions "twelfth night" in the body of his text nor dramatizes any of the popular rituals associated with it, the play is permeated on all levels with a carnivalesque spirit and energy that produces significant upheaval and reversal in the traditional social order.

The second part of the play's title—*What You Will*—connects the theme of disorder through *mis*directed desire more specifically to individual events and characters. According to the *Oxford English Dictionary,* the word *will* can mean "desire, wish, [or] longing," with a sexual connotation. Virtually all the characters in the play engage in forms of desire that conflict for one reason or another with the established social order and therefore impede the proper and orderly reproduction of the play's social structure, which is an essential element of a successful romantic comedy.

The hard-drinking Sir Toby Belch and the professional jester Feste, whose name implies festivity and who declares himself to be a deliberate "corrupter of words," are of course the most obvious representatives of a type of Saturnalian disorder; but the aristocrats themselves, because they insist on following their "will" or desire, appear equally at odds with the normative social order. Duke Orsino, for instance, wallows in an obsessive and self-indulgent love for the Countess Olivia, even though we quickly gather that she will never have him. His misdirected desire prevents him from marrying and producing an heir, thereby putting the processes of generational renewal and social reproduction, as well as the future governance of Illyria, in limbo. Olivia, in turn, decides to mourn her recently deceased brother and father for the uncommonly long period of seven years, thus endangering the future of her estate and blocking the timely reproduction of the aristocratic class of Illyria. She further complicates things by unwittingly falling in love with an unobtainable partner, a woman named Viola who has disguised herself as a man (named Cesario). Viola herself falls in love with her employer, Duke Orsino, but her male disguise makes it impossible for her to pursue her desire in overt ways. Adding to the confusion, Toby and Maria (Olivia's gentlewoman) trick Malvolio into believing that Olivia is in love with him, prompting the sour but ambitious steward who dreams of becoming "Count Malvolio" to behave ridiculously and upend the very principles of decorum and propriety he is supposed to uphold. Sir Andrew Aguecheek, a foolish knight who spends his time in the company of Sir Toby, also has his heart set on the Countess Olivia, but it becomes clear almost immediately that he has no chance of winning her. His desire is fruitless; all he is good for is paying Toby's liquor bills.

Antonio the sea captain, who saves Viola's twin brother, Sebastian, after the shipwreck, has very strong, homoerotic feelings for Sebastian, but the latter does not seem interested in reciprocating, giving rise to another instance of misdirected desire within a comic world where heterosexuality is the norm.

The expectation—created by the genre of romantic comedy—is that disorder gives way to order and harmony by play's end. These are ordinarily achieved by a repositioning of characters to their proper place within the social fabric of the play, either by confirming their proper social rank or gender or by having them enter into socially acceptable marriages. *Twelfth Night* certainly attempts to achieve such harmony through a repositioning of characters, but the effort is not entirely successful—a failure that is surely deliberate. On the surface, matters appear resolved. Viola is reunited with her look-alike twin brother, Sebastian. Viola's female gender is confirmed, and she will become Orsino's wife. The Countess Olivia realizes that she inadvertently fell for another woman, but this mistake is rectified when she equally inadvertently marries Sebastian (whom she believes to be Cesario at the time the couple exchanges their vows). Even the riotous Toby appears to leave behind his self-indulgent ways when he enters into a union with the sensible Maria. After all the disorder, it appears that the ruling class of Illyria may be settling down to a calmer family life and the business of biological and social reproduction.

But when we look just below its surface, we recognize that this newfound harmony may be only superficial. Olivia is now married to a man she has known for only a few hours, and their compatibility could well become an issue later. What is more, Olivia's same-sex desire for Viola cannot have magically evaporated. When Orsino describes Cesario's physical appearance, he stresses "his" feminine qualities: "Diane's lip / Is not more smooth and rubious; thy small pipe / Is as the maiden's organ, shrill and sound, / And all is semblative a woman's part." In other words, you sound like a woman, you look like a woman, and you resemble a woman in every way. Because the part of Viola was played by a boy actor in Shakespeare's theater, there is

Indira Varma (left) as Olivia and Victoria Hamilton (right) as Viola in the 2011 Donmar Warehouse (London) production of *Twelfth Night*.

no doubt that the "woman's part" could have been removed from the performance. A boy could simply act as a boy would. But Shakespeare appears determined that Olivia shall fall madly in love with a character whose "woman's part" breaks through the masculine disguise. No matter how surprised Olivia is when she finally learns that Cesario is a woman, we cannot discount that she fell in love with "him" in part because of those female qualities. Sebastian tries to explain to Olivia what has transpired, saying, "lady, you have been mistook. / But nature to her bias drew in that. / You would have been contracted to a maid." Sebastian's metaphor is taken from the game of bowls, which was played with a ball with an off-center weight that made it curve from a straight path. These lines are generally interpreted as intended to quiet fears of Olivia's homoeroticism by suggesting that "nature" redirected her affections from Cesario to Sebastian. But if we take "that" to refer to what is "mistook," then nature's "bias" in fact drew Olivia to her mistake, to another woman.

An element of homoeroticism also remains part of the Orsino-Viola relation-

ship. Viola's female gender has been verbally established at the time that Orsino proposes marriage, but Viola never removes her masculine disguise, meaning that we are visually presented with a union between two men. No doubt Viola will soon again don her "maiden weeds," but who is to say that Orsino will not one day remember the time he fell in love with "her" and ask, "Would you like to try on again those breeches and doublet you used to wear?" This question and the broader issue of how these couples will fare in the future are not openly addressed amid the festiveness of the play's conclusion, but they are implied or encouraged by the "o'erhasty marriage[s]"—to borrow a phrase from *Hamlet*.

We may not care very much that the marriage between Toby and Maria is equally hasty and unprepared for, nor may we feel very sorry that the foolish Sir Andrew is left without a mate at play's end, but we may be disturbed by Illyria's inability to find a place for Captain Antonio. Elizabethan culture strongly disapproved of sodomy, but writers often idealized male-male friendship, especially between aristocratic males, and described it in passionate and erotic language. We cannot be certain that Antonio is what we would today call a homosexual, but his complete devotion to Sebastian leaves him without an obvious partner when Sebastian marries. Yet Shakespeare makes it clear that Antonio does not deserve to be excluded from a newly harmonious Illyrian society. Antonio is a thoroughly noble and admirable character who unselfishly risks his life for Sebastian (and Viola) on more than one occasion. If anything, Shakespeare gives us reason to lament that a character as worthy as Antonio cannot find a place for himself within the society's social structure. It is as if in 1601 or 1602, when Shakespeare writes Twelfth Night, he no longer feels that the comedic resolution—which calls for heterosexual marriages—can adequately contain the complexities of human desire and social reality. And even the marriages that do occur seem somehow less plausible than we would want them to be. Of course it would be misleading to suggest that Shakespeare's earlier romantic comedies tie up all the loose ends neatly—they do not—but Twelfth Night seems to anticipate the even more problematic endings of his "dark comedies" to follow.

Audiences may be less troubled by the fate of Olivia's steward Malvolio, who, like Antonio and Andrew, is left unintegrated into the play's multiple unions, but his vow to "be revenged on the whole pack of you" strikes a jarring note at play's end. Such a tone does not seem to fit the supposedly conciliatory spirit of comedy. There is no doubt that Malvolio is an unpleasant person, and his rigid opposition to the spirit of carnival embraced by Toby, Andrew, and Maria makes him a killjoy, but we cannot forget that he is ultimately only doing the bidding of his employer, the Countess Olivia. To an English audience living in a class-based society, it may indeed have seemed mad for the commoner Malvolio to think he could marry a countess; but such marriages were becoming increasingly common in Shakespeare's time, as many aristocratic families could not sustain themselves and their estates in the new economy and wealthy merchants and traders were increasingly willing to part with vast sums of money for the privilege of marrying into the upper class. Audiences may have disliked Malvolio as a man, but his ambition may well have been their fantasy.

The trend toward a darker, more pessimistic view of life, glimpsed at in Twelfth Night and fully realized in Hamlet, becomes increasingly persistent in the plays written in the first decade of the seventeenth century. Critics have speculated that the death of Shakespeare's father in 1601 may have led the playwright to contemplate his own mortality. The "problem" plays Troilus and Cressida (1602), Measure for Measure (1603), and All's Well That Ends Well (1604–05) contain elements of such earlier romantic comedies as A Midsummer Night's Dream, Much Ado about Nothing, and As You Like It, but they do not offer the same satisfying, life-affirming resolutions as those prior plays. The writing of Hamlet marks the beginning of a period in which Shakespeare wrote his greatest tragedies: Othello (1603–04), King Lear (1605), Macbeth (1606), and Anthony and Cleopatra (1606). In the final years of his career as a playwright, Shakespeare wrote four plays that are listed among the comedies in the First Folio but are more commonly referred to today as "romances": Pericles (1607–08), Cymbeline (1609–10), The Winter's Tale (1609), and The Tempest (1610–11). As we might expect from an aging author who harbors no illusions about the ways of the world yet is not without hope, these final plays tackle some of the same issues that dominate the tragedies—family crisis, destructive jealousy, political betrayal—but they rely on magical or miraculous interventions to produce endings that, while not unequivocally happy, avoid outright tragedy. In their self-conscious allusions to characters and dramatic situations from earlier in Shakespeare's career, these late plays reveal a playwright, on the eve of his retirement from the theater, looking back over his own artistic achievement and recombining elements from it in new, often magical configurations. Indeed, many critics have seen Prospero—the magician who stage-manages the events and transformations of The Tempest—as a figure of Shakespeare himself. In Prospero's decision to "abjure" his "rough magic" at the play's end, audiences, readers, and scholars have sometimes seen Shakespeare's farewell to his own dramatic art and to the stage—"this insubstantial pageant"—that he

TEXTUAL NOTE FOR *HAMLET*

The earliest versions of Shakespeare's *Hamlet* exist in three printed forms: a quarto dated 1603, another quarto dated 1604, and the text printed in the First Folio of 1623. The consensus is that the 1603 text (known as Q1) is what scholars call a "bad quarto." It is most likely a reconstruction based on the memories of one or more of the actors who performed in the play. For that reason it may give us valuable insights into stage directions, and it may also offer accurate versions of speeches as delivered by the particular actor(s) in question, but it tends to be unreliable in most other ways. The second quarto is probably based on Shakespeare's own manuscript or on a scribal version of that manuscript. The Folio text is presumably based on a prompt-book (a version of the play authorized for performance by the Master of the Revels, the government's censor). The promptbook, rather than the author's manuscript, was the basis for the play's performance and therefore the version of the play that Shakespeare's audiences actually witnessed.

The survival of the second quarto (Q2) and the First Folio (F1) texts creates a dilemma for today's editors of Shakespeare's text. While the two texts are identical in many respects, they are also different in important ways. F1 deletes about 230 lines that appear in Q2, but F1 adds 83 different lines that are not present in Q2. F1, for instance, does not have Hamlet's famous final soliloquy, "How all occasions do inform against me." The crux, of course, lies in the reasons that account for the differences between the two texts. Are these differences the product of interventions by actors or by the printer, or do they represent Shakespeare's own revision of the play? Textual scholars have offered a range of answers to this question, but none is conclusive.

What is more, we have to decide what our objective is in editing the play: do we want to get as close as possible to the

brought to life with such dazzling power. It is a measure of this power that centuries later, his plays continue to define the theater he took as his own.　　IVO KAMPS

Shakespearean "original," or do we want to reconstruct the text as it was performed in Shakespeare's theater in his time? If we seek the former, we should focus on Q2 as our primary text; if we want the theater-based text, we must turn to F1.

Some editors have addressed the textual instability of *Hamlet* by providing all three texts rather than resolving their discrepancies and producing a composite version. In their 2003 edition, Bernice W. Kliman and Benjamin Bertram printed Q1, Q2, and F1 in parallel columns, while Ann Thompson and Neil Taylor published separate editions of the three versions in two volumes (2006). Other editors have produced digital versions of *Hamlet* that allow users to navigate among different versions. Bernice W. Kliman's *Enfolded Hamlet* (1996), for instance, presents Q2 and F1 embedded on the same screen; users can click on one version or the other, or both, as a way of exploring the textual variants.

The current edition, which consists of the text edited by Robert S. Miola for the Norton Critical Edition of *Hamlet*, takes a more conservative editorial approach. Miola uses Q2, the text closest to Shakespeare's manuscript, or "foul papers," as its copy text and makes changes to it only when a reading doesn't make sense or makes less sense than a variant reading present in one of the other texts. The explanatory notes and the introduction to the current edition are new.

TEXTUAL NOTE FOR *TWELFTH NIGHT*

Because the only authoritative text of *Twelfth Night* is the one that appears in F1, all editions of this play derive from this source. The current edition consists of the text edited by Barbara A. Mowat and Paul Werstine, which appears in the *Norton Anthology of English Literature*. The explanatory notes and the introduction to the current edition are new.

The Tragedy of Hamlet, Prince of Denmark

THE PERSONS OF THE PLAY

GHOST of Hamlet, the late King of
  Denmark
KING CLAUDIUS, his brother
QUEEN GERTRUDE of Denmark, widow
  of King Hamlet, now
  wife of Claudius
Prince HAMLET, son of King Hamlet
  and Queen Gertrude
POLONIUS, a lord
LAERTES, son of Polonius
OPHELIA, daughter of Polonius
REYNALDO, servant of Polonius
HORATIO ⎫
ROSENCRANTZ ⎬ friends of Prince
GUILDENSTERN ⎭ Hamlet
FRANCISCO ⎫
BARNARDO ⎬ soldiers
MARCELLUS ⎭

VALTEMAND
CORNELIUS ⎫
OSRIC ⎬ courtiers
GENTLEMEN ⎭
A SAILOR
Two CLOWNS, a gravedigger and his
  companion
A PRIEST
FORTINBRAS, Prince of Norway
A CAPTAIN in his army
AMBASSADORS from England
PLAYERS, who play the parts of
  the PROLOGUE, PLAYER KING,
  PLAYER QUEEN, and LUCIANUS, in
  The Mousetrap
Lords, messengers, attendants, guards,
  soldiers, followers of Laertes, sailors

1.1

Enter [separately] BARNARDO *and* FRANCISCO, *two sentinels*
[at several° doors].　　　　　　　　　　　　　　　　　　　　　　　*separate*

BARNARDO　Who's there?
FRANCISCO　Nay, answer me.[1] Stand and unfold yourself.°　　*make yourself known*
BARNARDO　Long live the King!
FRANCISCO　Barnardo?
5 BARNARDO　He.
FRANCISCO　You come most carefully° upon your hour.　　*precisely*
BARNARDO　'Tis now struck twelve. Get thee to bed, Francisco.
FRANCISCO　For this relief much thanks. 'Tis bitter cold,
  And I am sick at heart.
10 BARNARDO　Have you had quiet guard?
FRANCISCO　Not a mouse stirring.
BARNARDO　Well, good night.
  If you do meet Horatio and Marcellus,
  The rivals° of my watch, bid them make haste.　　*partners*

1.1 Location: The guard platform of Elsinore Castle at midnight.
1. As the sentry on duty, Francisco has the right to challenge anyone who approaches.

Enter HORATIO *and* MARCELLUS.

15 FRANCISCO   I think I hear them.—Stand, ho! Who is there?

HORATIO   Friends to this ground.°   *i.e, this country*

MARCELLUS   And liegemen to the Dane.°   *the Danish King*

FRANCISCO   [*Leaving*] Give° you good night.   *May God give*

MARCELLUS   O, farewell, honest soldier. Who hath relieved you?

FRANCISCO   Barnardo hath my place. Give you good night.

Exit.

20 MARCELLUS   Holla, Barnardo.

BARNARDO   Say, what, is Horatio there?

HORATIO   A piece of him.[2]

BARNARDO   Welcome, Horatio. Welcome, good Marcellus.

HORATIO   What, has this thing appeared again tonight?

BARNARDO   I have seen nothing.

25 MARCELLUS   Horatio says 'tis but our fantasy,

And will not let belief take hold of him

Touching° this dreaded sight twice seen of° us.   *Regarding / by*

Therefore I have entreated him along

With us to watch the minutes of this night,

30 That if again this apparition come

He may approve° our eyes and speak to it.[3]   *confirm*

HORATIO   Tush, tush, 'twill not appear.

BARNARDO   Sit down awhile,

And let us once again assail your ears,

That are so fortified against our story,

What we have two nights seen.

35 HORATIO   Well, sit we down,

And let us hear Barnardo speak of this.

BARNARDO   Last night of all,°   *this very last night*

When yond same star that's westward from the pole°   *the North Star*

Had made his° course t'illume that part of heaven   *its*

40 Where now it burns, Marcellus and myself,

The bell then beating one—

Enter GHOST [*in armor*].

MARCELLUS   Peace, break thee off! Look where it comes again!

BARNARDO   In the same figure like the King that's dead.

MARCELLUS   Thou art a scholar; speak to it, Horatio.

45 BARNARDO   Looks 'a° not like the King? Mark it, Horatio.   *he*

HORATIO   Most like. It harrows me with fear and wonder.

BARNARDO   It would° be spoke to.   *wants to*

MARCELLUS   Speak to it, Horatio.

HORATIO   What art thou that usurp'st[4] this time of night,

Together with that fair and warlike form

---

2. Horatio may mean that the only part of him that is visible in the dark is the hand he offers in greeting.

3. It was popularly held that a ghost could not speak unless spoken to. Marcellus thinks that Horatio, a man of learning, is the appropriate

person to address the ghost (see line 48).

4. As a creature belonging to another realm, the ghost has entered the natural world and seized a shape belonging to the King of Denmark.

50 In which the majesty of buried Denmark[5]
Did sometimes° march? By heaven, I charge thee, speak!   *formerly*
MARCELLUS   It is offended.
BARNARDO   See, it stalks away.
HORATIO   Stay, speak, speak! I charge thee speak!

Exit GHOST.

MARCELLUS   'Tis gone and will not answer.
55 BARNARDO   How now, Horatio, you tremble and look pale.
Is not this something more than fantasy?
What think you on't?°   *of it*
HORATIO   Before my God I might not this believe
Without the sensible° and true avouch°   *sensory / guarantee*
Of mine own eyes.
60 MARCELLUS   Is it not like the King?
HORATIO   As thou art to thyself.
Such was the very armor he had on
When he the ambitious Norway° combated;   *King of Norway*
So frowned he once when, in an angry parle,°   *discussion*
65 He smote the sledded Polacks[6] on the ice.
'Tis strange.
MARCELLUS   Thus twice before and jump at this dead hour,
With martial stalk hath he gone by our watch.
HORATIO   In what particular thought to work[7] I know not,
70 But in the gross and scope of mine opinion,[8]
This bodes some strange eruption° to our state.   *disruption*
MARCELLUS   Good now,° sit down, and tell me, he that   *(an entreaty; "Please")*
knows,
Why this same strict and most observant watch
So nightly toils the subject of the land,[9]
75 And why such daily cost of brazen cannon
And foreign mart° for implements of war,   *trade*
Why such impress° of shipwrights, whose sore task   *forced service*
Does not divide the Sunday from the week.
What might be toward,° that this sweaty haste   *imminent*
80 Doth make the night joint-laborer with the day?
Who is't that can inform me?
HORATIO   That can I.
At least the whisper goes so: our last King,
Whose image even but now appeared to us,
Was, as you know, by Fortinbras of Norway,
85 Thereto pricked° on by a most emulate° pride,   *urged / competitive*
Dared to the combat; in which our valiant Hamlet[1]—
For so this side of our known world esteemed him—
Did slay this Fortinbras; who, by a sealed compact°   *contract, agreement*

---

5. That is, the recently deceased King of
Denmark.
6. Poles (who traveled by sled).
7. Exactly how to comprehend this.
8. But in the general sense of my opinion (in

contrast with my "particular thought" [line
69]).
9. Causes the subjects of this country to toil.
1. That is, the recently deceased king, not the
young prince.

Well ratified by law and heraldry,°   *practices pertaining to rank,*
90   Did forfeit with his life all these his lands   *pedigree, and precedence*
Which he stood seized[2] of to the conqueror.
Against the which a moiety competent°   *an equal portion*
Was gagèd° by our King, which had return°   *pledged / would have reverted*
To the inheritance° of Fortinbras,   *possession*
95   Had he been vanquisher, as by the same cov'nant
And carriage of the article designed,°   *drawn up*
His fell to Hamlet. Now, sir, young Fortinbras,[3]
Of unimprovèd° mettle hot and full,   *untested, unrestrained*
Hath in the skirts° of Norway here and there   *outlying territories*
100   Sharked up a list[4] of lawless resolutes
For food and diet to some enterprise
That hath a stomach in't;° which is no other—   *appetite for it*
As it doth well° appear unto our state—   *clearly*
But to recover of us, by strong hand
105   And terms compulsatory, those foresaid lands
So by his father lost. And this, I take it,
Is the main motive of our preparations,
The source of this our watch, and the chief head°   *source*
Of this post-haste and rummage° in the land.   *turmoil*
110 BARNARDO   I think it be no other but e'en so.
Well may it sort that this portentous figure
Comes armèd through our watch so like the King
That was and is the question° of these wars.   *cause*
HORATIO   A mote° it is to trouble the mind's eye.   *speck of dust*
115   In the most high and palmy° state of Rome,   *triumphant*
A little ere the mightiest Julius[5] fell,
The graves stood tenantless, and the sheeted° dead   *shrouded*
Did squeak and gibber in the Roman streets
At stars with trains of fire[6] and dews of blood,
120   Disasters[7] in the sun; and the moist star,°   *the moon*
Upon whose influence Neptune's empire stands,[8]
Was sick almost to doomsday with eclipse.[9]
And even the like precurse° of feared events,   *precursor*
As harbingers° preceding still° the Fates   *heralds / always*
125   And prologue to the omen[1] coming on,
Have heaven and earth together demonstrated
Unto our climatures° and countrymen.   *regions*
        Enter GHOST.

---

2. Which he held in possession.
3. Son of the slain King of Norway.
4. Hastily and indiscriminately collected a band.
5. Julius Caesar (100–44 B.C.E.), Roman general and statesman, stabbed to death by a band of conspirators.
6. That is, comets, traditionally seen as ominous portents.
7. Signs of ill omen.
8. The seas depend (as by the currents and tides). *Neptune*: Roman god of the sea.
9. In 1598, England witnessed both solar and lunar eclipses. Many believed that the Second Coming and Final Judgment were close at hand, citing prophesies in the biblical Book of Revelation (6.12) of the sun "as black as dark sackcloth" and the moon "like blood."
1. Usually, an "omen" is a sign that presages of a future good or evil event, but here it appears to refer to the event itself.

But, soft,° behold, lo, where it comes again!   *be quiet*
I'll cross² it though it blast° me.—Stay, illusion!   *injure; curse*
　　　[*The* GHOST *spreads his arms.*]
130　If thou hast any sound or use of voice,
　　　Speak to me!
　　　If there be any good thing to be done,
　　　That may to thee do ease and grace to me,
　　　Speak to me!
135　If thou art privy to thy country's fate,
　　　Which, happily,° foreknowing may avoid,   *perhaps*
　　　Oh, speak!
　　　Or if thou hast uphoarded° in thy life   *heaped up*
　　　Extorted treasure in the womb of earth,
140　For which, they say, your spirits oft walk in death,
　　　Speak of it!　　　　　　　　*The cock crows.*
　　　　　　　　Stay, and speak!—Stop it, Marcellus!
　　MARCELLUS　Shall I strike it with my partisan?°   *long-handled spear*
　　HORATIO　Do, if it will not stand. [*They strike at it.*]
　　BARNARDO　'Tis here!
145　HORATIO　'Tis here!　　　　　　　　　　　[*Exit* GHOST.]
　　MARCELLUS　'Tis gone.
　　　We do it wrong, being so majestical,
　　　To offer it the show of violence,
　　　For it is as the air invulnerable,
150　And our vain blows malicious mockery.°   *pretended violence*
　　BARNARDO　It was about to speak when the cock crew.
　　HORATIO　And then it started like a guilty thing
　　　Upon a fearful summons. I have heard
　　　The cock, that is the trumpet to the morn,
155　Doth with his lofty and shrill-sounding throat
　　　Awake the god of day,° and at his warning,   *the sun god Apollo*
　　　Whether in sea or fire, in earth or air,
　　　Th'extravagant and erring³ spirit hies°   *hastens*
　　　To his confine;° and of the truth herein   *territory*
160　This present object° made probation.°   *sight / proof*
　　MARCELLUS　It faded on the crowing of the cock.
　　　Some say that ever 'gainst° that season comes   *just before*
　　　Wherein our Savior's birth is celebrated,
　　　This bird of dawning singeth all night long.
165　And then they say no spirit dare stir abroad,
　　　The nights are wholesome, then no planets strike,°   *exert evil influence*
　　　No fairy takes,° nor witch hath power to charm—   *bewitches*
　　　So hallowed and so gracious° is that time.   *full of grace, blessed*
　　HORATIO　So have I heard, and do in part believe it.
170　But look, the morn in russet mantle clad
　　　Walks o'er the dew of yon high eastward hill.

---

2. Encounter; also, make the sign of the cross
(as a defense against its potentially evil
power).

3. That is, wandering outside of its proper
boundaries.

Break we our watch up and by my advice
Let us impart what we have seen tonight
Unto young Hamlet, for upon my life
175 This spirit, dumb to us, will° speak to him.   *wishes to*
Do you consent we shall acquaint him with it,
As needful in our loves,[4] fitting our duty?
MARCELLUS Let's do't, I pray, and I this morning know
Where we shall find him most convenient.

                                        Exeunt.°   *(They) exit. (Latin)*

1.2

Flourish. Enter CLAUDIUS, *King of Denmark,* GERTRUDE
the Queen, COUNCIL, *as°* POLONIUS *and his son* LAERTES,   *including*
HAMLET, *cum aliis* [*including* CORNELIUS, VOLTEMAND,
and ATTENDANTS].

KING Though yet of Hamlet our[5] dear brother's death
The memory be green, and that it us befitted
To bear our hearts in grief, and our whole kingdom
To be contracted in one brow of woe,
5 Yet so far hath discretion fought with nature[6]
That we with wisest sorrow think on him,
Together with remembrance of ourselves.
Therefore our sometime° sister, now our queen,   *former*
Th'imperial jointress° to this warlike state,   *joint owner*
10 Have we—as 'twere with a defeated joy,
With an auspicious° and a dropping° eye,   *joyful / tearful*
With mirth in funeral, and with dirge in marriage,
In equal scale weighing delight and dole°—   *sorrow*
Taken to wife. Nor have we herein barred
15 Your better wisdoms, which have freely gone
With this affair along. For all, our thanks.
Now follows that you know° young Fortinbras,   *be informed that*
Holding a weak supposal° of our worth,   *estimation*
Or thinking by our late dear brother's death
20 Our state to be disjoint and out of frame,°   *order*
Colleagued° with this dream of his advantage,   *Coupled*
He hath not failed to pester us with message
Importing° the surrender of those lands   *Regarding*
Lost by his father, with all bands° of law,   *binding terms*
25 To our most valiant brother—so much for him.
Now for ourself and for this time of meeting,
Thus much the business is: we have here writ
To Norway, uncle of young Fortinbras—
Who, impotent and bedrid, scarcely hears
30 Of this his nephew's purpose—to suppress
His further gait° herein, in that the levies,   *course*

4. As necessitated by the love we bear him.   5. My (Claudius often uses the royal "we").
1.2 Location: Elsinore Castle.   6. Natural inclination (to mourn the dead king).

The lists, and full proportions are all made
Out of his subject.[7] And we here dispatch
You, good Cornelius, and you, Voltemand,
35 For bearers of this greeting to old Norway,
Giving to you no further personal power
To business with the King more than the scope
Of these dilated° articles allow. [*He gives them a paper.*] *detailed*
Farewell, and let your haste commend your duty.[8]

COR. ⎫
40 VOL. ⎬ In that and all things will we show our duty.

KING We doubt it nothing.° Heartily farewell. *not at all*

[*Exeunt* CORNELIUS *and* VOLTEMAND.]

And now, Laertes, what's the news with you?
You told us of some suit; what is't, Laertes?
You cannot speak of reason to the Dane[9]
45 And lose your voice.° What wouldst thou beg, Laertes, *i.e., waste your words*
That shall not be my offer, not thy asking?[1]
The head is not more native[2] to the heart,
The hand more instrumental to the mouth,
Than is the throne of Denmark to thy father.
What wouldst thou have, Laertes?

50 LAERTES   My dread lord,
Your leave° and favor° to return to France, *consent / approval*
From whence, though willingly, I came to Denmark
To show my duty in your coronation.
Yet now I must confess, that duty done,
55 My thoughts and wishes bend again toward France,
And bow them to your gracious leave and pardon.° *permission to depart*

KING Have you your father's leave? What says Polonius?

POLONIUS He hath, my lord, wrung from me my slow leave
By laborsome petition, and at last
60 Upon his will° I sealed my hard° consent. *wish / grudging*
I do beseech you, give him leave to go.

KING Take thy fair hour,[3] Laertes. Time be thine,
And thy best graces spend it at thy will.
But now, my cousin[4] Hamlet, and my son—

65 HAMLET A little more than kin and less than kind.[5]

KING How is it that the clouds still hang on you?

HAMLET Not so, my lord. I am too much in the sun.[6]

QUEEN Good Hamlet, cast thy nighted color[7] off,

---

7. That is, because the expenses and troops are drawn from his subjects.
8. Let your haste in this matter be worthy of your duty (to Denmark).
9. The King of Denmark; that is, Claudius himself.
1. That I will not grant you before you even ask it.
2. Closely and naturally related (an allusion to the "body politic").
3. Seize the moment (of your youth).

4. Kinsman (a term used for relatives more distant than one's brother or sister).
5. As Claudius's stepson, Hamlet is now more than "kin"; but because he is Claudius's nephew he is also less than "kind" (son). Hamlet is also punning that he feels less than kindly toward Claudius.
6. In the sunlight of Claudius's favor (with a pun on "son").
7. His melancholy behavior as well as his black mourning attire.

And let thine eye look like a friend on Denmark.
70 Do not forever with thy vailèd° lids   *downcast*
Seek for thy noble father in the dust.
Thou know'st 'tis common—all that lives must die,
Passing through nature to eternity.
HAMLET   Ay, madam, it is common.[8]
QUEEN   If it be,
75 Why seems it so particular° with thee?   *personal, special*
HAMLET   "Seems," madam, nay, it is. I know not "seems."
'Tis not alone my inky cloak, good mother,°   *stepmother*
Nor customary suits of solemn black,
Nor windy suspiration° of forced breath,   *sighing*
80 No, nor the fruitful° river in the eye,   *productive (of tears)*
Nor the dejected havior° of the visage,   *expression*
Together with all forms, moods, shapes of grief,
That can denote me truly. These indeed "seem,"
For they are actions that a man might play;
85 But I have that within which passes show,
These but the trappings and the suits of woe.
KING   'Tis sweet and commendable in your nature, Hamlet,
To give these mourning duties to your father,
But you must know your father lost a father,
90 That father lost, lost his, and the survivor bound
In filial obligation for some term
To do obsequious sorrow.[9] But to persever
In obstinate condolement° is a course   *lamentation*
Of impious stubbornness; 'tis unmanly grief.
95 It shows a will most incorrect to° heaven,   *defiant of*
A heart unfortified or mind impatient,
An understanding simple° and unschooled.   *childish, ignorant*
For what we know must be and is as common
As any the most vulgar thing to sense,[1]
100 Why should we in our peevish opposition
Take it to heart? Fie, 'tis a fault to heaven,
A fault against the dead, a fault to nature,
To reason most absurd, whose common theme
Is death of fathers, and who still° hath cried   *always*
105 From the first corpse[2] till he that died today,
"This must be so." We pray you, throw to earth
This unprevailing° woe and think of us   *ineffective*
As of a father. For, let the world take note,
You are the most immediate° to our throne,   *next in succession*
110 And with no less nobility of love
Than that which dearest father bears his son,

---

8. Generally true; Hamlet may also be implying that it is vulgar.
9. To mourn in a manner appropriate to
funeral rites.
1. As common as any of the ordinary things

we perceive through our senses.
2. An infelicitous reference to the biblical
character Abel, who, like Hamlet's father, was
killed by his brother.

Do I impart toward you. For your intent
In going back to school in Wittenberg,[3]
It is most retrograde° to our desire,   *contrary*
115 And we beseech you bend you° to remain   *submit yourself*
Here in the cheer and comfort of our eye,
Our chiefest courtier, cousin, and our son.
QUEEN   Let not thy mother lose her prayers, Hamlet.
I pray thee, stay with us; go not to Wittenberg.
120 HAMLET   I shall in all my best obey you, madam.
KING   Why, 'tis a loving and a fair reply.
Be as ourself in Denmark. Madam, come,
This gentle and unforced accord of Hamlet
Sits smiling° to my heart; in grace° whereof   *Pleases / honor*
125 No jocund health that Denmark° drinks today   *the King of Denmark*
But the great cannon to the clouds shall tell,°   *proclaim, sound*
And the King's rouse[4] the heaven shall bruit° again,   *loudly sound*
Respeaking earthly thunder. Come away.

Flourish. Exeunt all but HAMLET.

HAMLET   Oh, that this too, too solid[5] flesh would melt,
130 Thaw, and resolve° itself into a dew,   *dissolve*
Or that the Everlasting had not fixed
His canon° gainst self-slaughter. O God, God,   *law*
How weary, stale, flat, and unprofitable
Seem to me all the uses° of this world!   *employments; customs*
135 Fie on't, ah, fie. 'Tis an unweeded garden
That grows to seed; things rank and gross in nature
Possess it merely.° That it should come thus,   *utterly*
But two months dead—nay, not so much, not two!
So excellent a king that was to this,°   *(Claudius)*
140 Hyperion to a satyr,[6] so loving to my mother,
That he might not beteem° the winds of heaven   *permit*
Visit her face too roughly. Heaven and earth,
Must I remember? Why, she would hang on him
As if increase of appetite had grown
145 By what it fed on, and yet within a month—
Let me not think on't. Frailty, thy name is woman!
A little month, or ere° those shoes were old   *before*
With which she followed my poor father's body,
Like Niobe, all tears,[7] why she—
150 O God, a beast that wants discourse of reason[8]
Would have mourned longer!—married with my uncle,
My father's brother, but no more like my father

---

3. A university town in Germany.
4. A bout of drinking or a toast.
5. Instead of "solid," Q1 has "sallied," which is probably an obsolete form of "sullied": contaminated, soiled, polluted.
6. In classical myth, a woodland creature part man and part goat, known for lechery and

love of wine. *Hyperion:* the sun god (a Titan).
7. In Greek myth, Niobe wept so ceaselessly for her children, killed by the gods Apollo and Artemis to punish her for boasting, that she was turned into a stone from which water endlessly flows.
8. That is, that lacks the capacity to reason.

Than I to Hercules.[9] Within a month,
Ere yet the salt of most unrighteous° tears   *hypocritical*
155   Had left the flushing° in her gallèd° eyes,   *redness / inflamed*
She married. Oh, most wicked speed, to post°   *hasten*
With such dexterity° to incestuous sheets![1]   *nimbleness, eagerness*
It is not, nor it cannot come to good.
But break,° my heart, for I must hold my tongue.   *stop*

          Enter HORATIO, MARCELLUS, *and* BARNARDO.

160   HORATIO   Hail to your lordship.
HAMLET   I am glad to see you well. Horatio!—or I do forget myself.
HORATIO   The same, my lord, and your poor servant ever.
HAMLET   Sir, my good friend. I'll change° that name with   *exchange*
          you.
And what make you from[2] Wittenberg, Horatio?
165   —Marcellus!
MARCELLUS   My good lord.
HAMLET   I am very glad to see you. [*To* BARNARDO] Good
          even, sir.
—But what, in faith, make you from Wittenberg?
HORATIO   A truant° disposition, good my lord.   *idle*
170   HAMLET   I would not hear your enemy say so,
Nor shall you do my ear that violence
To make it truster of your own report
Against yourself. I know you are no truant.
But what is your affair in Elsinore?
175   We'll teach you for to drink ere you depart.
HORATIO   My lord, I came to see your father's funeral.
HAMLET   I prithee, do not mock me, fellow-student;
I think it was to see my mother's wedding.
HORATIO   Indeed, my lord, it followed hard upon.°   *soon after*
180   HAMLET   Thrift, thrift, Horatio. The funeral baked meats
Did coldly° furnish forth the marriage tables.   *when coldly*
Would I had met my dearest° foe in heaven   *most bitter*
Or ever I had seen that day, Horatio.
My father, methinks I see my father.
HORATIO   Where, my lord?
185   HAMLET   In my mind's eye, Horatio.
HORATIO   I saw him once. 'A° was a goodly king.   *He*
HAMLET   'A was a man. Take him for all in all,
I shall not look upon his like again.
HORATIO   My lord, I think I saw him yesternight.
HAMLET   Saw who?
190   HORATIO   My lord, the King your father.
HAMLET   The King my father?
HORATIO   Season your admiration[3] for a while

---

9. In classical mythology, the greatest of all heroes.
1. Both the Catholic Church and the Church of England condemned as incest the marriage between a man and his deceased brother's wife.
2. That is, what are you doing away from.
3. Temper your astonishment.

With an attent° ear till I may deliver   *attentive*
Upon the witness of these gentlemen
This marvel to you.
195 HAMLET   For God's love, let me hear!
     HORATIO   Two nights together had these gentlemen,
        Marcellus and Barnardo, on their watch
        In the dead waste and middle of the night,
        Been thus encountered: a figure like your father,
200   Armèd at point° exactly, cap-à-pie,[4]   *in readiness*
        Appears before them, and with solemn march
        Goes slow and stately by them. Thrice he walked
        By their oppressed and fear-surprisèd eyes
        Within his truncheon's length, whilst they, distilled°   *melted*
205   Almost to jelly with the act° of fear,   *effect*
        Stand dumb and speak not to him. This to me
        In dreadful secrecy impart they did,
        And I with them the third night kept the watch.
        Where, as they had delivered, both in time,
210   Form of the thing, each word made true and good,
        The apparition comes. I knew your father;
        These hands are not more like.[5]
     HAMLET   But where was this?
     MARCELLUS   My lord, upon the platform where we watch.
     HAMLET   Did you not speak to it?
     HORATIO   My lord, I did,
215   But answer made it none. Yet once methought
        It lifted up its head and did address
        Itself to motion, like as it would speak;[6]
        But even° then the morning cock crew loud,   *just*
        And at the sound it shrunk in haste away
        And vanished from our sight.
220 HAMLET   'Tis very strange.
     HORATIO   As I do live, my honored lord, 'tis true.
        And we did think it writ down° in our duty   *stipulated*
        To let you know of it.
     HAMLET   Indeed, sirs, but this troubles me.
        Hold you the watch tonight?
225 ALL   We do, my lord.
     HAMLET   Armed, say you?
     ALL   Armed, my lord.
     HAMLET   From top to toe?
     ALL   My lord, from head to foot.
     HAMLET   Then saw you not his face.
     HORATIO   O, yes, my lord, he wore his beaver° up.   *faceguard of a helmet*
230 HAMLET   What looked he, frowningly?
     HORATIO   A countenance more in sorrow than in anger.

---

4. Head to foot (French).
5. That is, my hands resemble each other as
much as the apparition resembled your father.

6. That is, it made a gesture as if it wanted to
speak.

HAMLET Pale or red?

HORATIO Nay, very pale.

HAMLET   And fixed his eyes upon you?

HORATIO Most constantly.

HAMLET   I would I had been there.

HORATIO It would have much amazed you.

235 HAMLET   Very like.
    Stayed it long?

HORATIO While one with moderate haste might tell°   *count to*
    ahundred.

MAR.⎤
BAR. ⎦ Longer, longer.

HORATIO Not when I saw't.

HAMLET   His beard was grizzled°—no?   *gray*

240 HORATIO It was as I have seen it in his life,
    A sable silvered.[7]

HAMLET   I will watch tonight.
    Perchance 'twill walk again.

HORATIO   I warr'nt° it will.   *guarantee*

HAMLET If it assume my noble father's person,
    I'll speak to it, though hell itself should gape
245 And bid me hold my peace. I pray you all,
    If you have hitherto concealed this sight,
    Let it be tenable° in your silence still;   *withheld*
    And whatsoever else shall hap° tonight,   *happen*
    Give it an understanding but no tongue.
250 I will requite your loves. So, fare you well.
    Upon the platform twixt eleven and twelve,
    I'll visit you.

ALL   Our duty to your honor.

HAMLET Your loves, as mine to you; farewell.

      Exeunt [HORATIO, MARCELLUS, *and* BARNARDO].

    My father's spirit in arms? All is not well;
255 I doubt° some foul play. Would the night were come.   *susupect*
    Till then sit still, my soul. Foul deeds will rise,
    Though all the earth o'erwhelm them, to men's eyes.   *Exit.*

1.3

Enter LAERTES *and* OPHELIA, *his sister.*

LAERTES My necessaries are embarked.° Farewell.   *aboard ship*
    And, sister, as the winds give benefit
    And convey is assistant,[8] do not sleep
    But let me hear from you.

OPHELIA   Do you doubt that?

5 LAERTES For Hamlet, and the trifling of his favor,
    Hold it a fashion and a toy in blood,[9]

---

7. Black and gray (or white).   8. That is, a means of transport is available.
1.3 Location: Unlocalized, perhaps the home   9. That is, consider it a passing enthusiasm
of Polonius.   and an amorous flirtation.

A violet in the youth of primy nature,
Forward,° not permanent, sweet, not lasting,   *Precocious*
The perfume and suppliance° of a minute—   *diversion*
No more.
OPHELIA   No more but so.
10 LAERTES   Think it no more.
For nature crescent° does not grow alone   *growing*
In thews° and bulks, but as this temple° waxes,   *muscles / body*
The inward service° of the mind and soul   *duty*
Grows wide withal.° Perhaps he loves you now,   *along with it*
15 And now no soil° nor cautel° doth besmirch   *blemish / trickery*
The virtue of his will,° but you must fear,   *desires*
His greatness weighed,° his will is not his own.   *considered*
He may not, as unvalued persons° do,   *commoners*
20 Carve for himself,¹ for on his choice depends
The safety and health of this whole state,
And therefore must his choice be circumscribed
Unto the voice° and yielding° of that body²   *vote / consent*
Whereof he is the head. Then if he says he loves you,
It fits° your wisdom so far to believe it   *befits*
25 As he in his particular act and place³
May give his saying deed,⁴ which is no further
Than the main° voice of Denmark goes withal.   *general*
Then weigh what loss your honor may sustain
If with too credent° ear you list° his songs,   *credulous / listen to*
30 Or lose your heart, or your chaste treasure open
To his unmastered° importunity.   *unrestrained*
Fear it, Ophelia, fear it, my dear sister,
And keep you in the rear of your affection,⁵
Out of the shot° and danger of desire.   *range*
35 "The chariest° maid is prodigal enough   *most circumspect*
If she unmask her beauty to the moon;"⁶
"Virtue itself scapes not calumnious strokes";
"The canker galls the infants⁷ of the spring"
Too oft before their buttons be disclosed,°   *are open*
40 And in the morn and liquid dew of youth
Contagious blastments° are most imminent.   *blights*
Be wary then; best safety lies in fear.
Youth to itself rebels though none else near.
OPHELIA   I shall th'effect of this good lesson keep
45 As watchman to my heart. But, good my brother,
Do not, as some ungracious° pastors do,   *graceless; ungodly*
Show me the steep and thorny way to heaven
Whiles, a puffed° and reckless libertine,   *bloated, proud*

1. That is, choose for himself.
2. The body politic, the state.
3. His particular rank and power.
4. That is, may turn his words into actions.
5. That is, stay behind the front line of your
feelings (a military metaphor).

6. The moon (identified in classical mythology with the virgin huntress goddess Artemis / Diana) here symbolizes chastity.
7. That is, the cankerworm damages the young plants.

Himself the primrose path of dalliance treads,
And recks° not his own rede.°   *heeds / advice*
50 LAERTES   Oh, fear me not.°   *don't worry about me*
    I stay too long.

        Enter POLONIUS.

            But here my father comes.
    A double blessing is a double grace;
    Occasion smiles upon a second leave.[8]
    POLONIUS   Yet here, Laertes? Aboard, aboard, for shame!
55 The wind sits in the shoulder° of your sail,   *billow*
    And you are stayed° for. There—my blessing with thee.   *waited*
    And these few precepts in thy memory
    Look thou character.° Give thy thoughts no tongue,   *inscribe*
    Nor any unproportioned° thought his act.   *disorderly*
60 Be thou familiar,° but by no means vulgar.[9]   *friendly*
    Those friends thou hast, and their adoption tried,[1]
    Grapple them unto thy soul with hoops of steel,
    But do not dull thy palm with entertainment[2]
    Of each new-hatched, unfledged courage.° Beware   *high-spirited youth*
65 Of entrance to a quarrel, but, being in,
    Bear't° that th'opposèd may beware of thee.   *Handle it so*
    Give every man thy ear, but few thy voice.
    Take each man's censure,° but reserve thy judgment.   *opinion*
    Costly thy habit° as thy purse can buy,   *clothing*
70 But not expressed in fancy;° rich not gaudy,   *frivolous fashion*
    For the apparel oft proclaims the man,
    And they in France of the best rank and station
    Are of a most select and generous chief in that.[3]
    Neither a borrower nor a lender be,
75 For loan oft loses both itself and friend,
    And borrowing dulls the edge of husbandry.°   *thrift*
    This above all—to thine own self be true,
    And it must follow, as the night the day,
    Thou canst not then be false to any man.
80 Farewell. My blessing season° this in thee.   *ripen, mature*
    LAERTES   Most humbly do I take my leave, my lord.
    POLONIUS   The time invests° you. Go, your servants tend.°   *presses / await*
    LAERTES   Farewell, Ophelia, and remember well
    What I have said to you.
    OPHELIA   'Tis in my memory locked,
85 And you yourself shall keep the key of it.
    LAERTES   Farewell.   *Exit* LAERTES.
    POLONIUS   What is't, Ophelia, he hath said to you?
    OPHELIA   So please you, something touching the Lord
    Hamlet.

---

8. That is, it is a happy opportunity that affords a second farewell.
9. Indiscriminate in friendship.
1. Their friendship tested.

2. That is, do not make the palm of your hand callous by shaking the hand.
3. The nobles of France are first in displaying their rank through their fine apparel.

POLONIUS   Marry,[4] well bethought.
90   'Tis told me he hath very oft of late
     Given private time to you, and you yourself
     Have of your audience° been most free and bounteous.   *attention*
     If it be so—as so 'tis put on° me,   *to*
     And that in way of caution—I must tell you
95   You do not understand yourself so clearly
     As it behooves my daughter and your honor.
     What is between you? Give me up the truth.
OPHELIA   He hath, my lord, of late made many tenders°   *offers*
     Of his affection to me.
100 POLONIUS   "Affection"? Pooh, you speak like a green girl,
     Unsifted° in such perilous circumstance.   *Inexperienced*
     Do you believe his "tenders," as you call them?
OPHELIA   I do not know, my lord, what I should think.
POLONIUS   Marry, I will teach you. Think yourself a baby
105   That you have ta'en these tenders for true pay,
     Which are not sterling.° Tender° yourself more dearly,   *genuine / Price*
     Or—not to crack the wind of the poor phrase,
     Wronging it thus—you'll tender me a fool.[5]
OPHELIA   My lord, he hath importuned me with love
110   In honorable fashion.
POLONIUS   Ay, "fashion" you may call it. Go to,[6] go to.
OPHELIA   And hath given countenance° to his speech, my   *authority*
          lord,
     With almost all the holy vows of heaven.
POLONIUS   Ay, springes° to catch woodcocks.[7] I do know,   *snares*
115   When the blood burns, how prodigal° the soul   *generously; wastefully*
     Lends the tongue vows. These blazes, daughter,
     Giving more light than heat, extinct° in both,   *extinguished*
     Even in their promise as it is a-making,
     You must not take for fire. From this time
120   Be something scanter of your maiden presence;
     Set your entreatments at a higher rate
     Than a command to parle.[8] For Lord Hamlet,
     Believe so much in° him, that he is young,   *about*
     And with a larger tether may he walk
125   Than may be given you. In few,° Ophelia,   *short*
     Do not believe his vows, for they are brokers,°   *go-betweens*
     Not of that dye which their investments[9] show,
     But mere implorators° of unholy suits,   *implorers*
     Breathing° like sanctified and pious bawds,   *Whispering*
130   The better to beguile. This is for all:

---

4. By the Virgin Mary (a mild oath).
5. You will make me look like a fool; you will present me with a grandchild ("fool" was often used as a synonym for "child"). *Crack . . . thus*: wear out the phrase by overusing it.
6. Come now (i.e., "don't be so naïve"). *Fashion*: flattery resulting from a passing and

youthful fancy (see line 6).
7. Proverbially stupid birds.
8. That is, value your favors more highly than to grant every request for an interview.
9. Clerical vestments (i.e., they are not what they seem).

I would not, in plain terms, from this time forth
Have you so slander° any moment leisure   disgrace
As to give words or talk with the Lord Hamlet.
Look to't, I charge you. Come your ways.°   Come along
135 OPHELIA   I shall obey, my lord.

Exeunt.

1.4

Enter HAMLET, HORATIO, *and* MARCELLUS.

HAMLET   The air bites shrewdly;° it is very cold.   sharply
HORATIO   It is a nipping and an eager° air.   biting
HAMLET   What hour now?
HORATIO   I think it lacks of twelve.
MARCELLUS   No, it is struck.
HORATIO   Indeed? I heard it not.
5   It then draws near the season°   time
      Wherein the spirit held his wont° to walk.   was accustomed ·
            A flourish of trumpets, and two pieces go off.°   (cannons fire offstage)
      What does this mean, my lord?
HAMLET   The King doth wake tonight and takes his rouse,°   drinks
      Keeps wassail, and the swagg'ring upspring reels,¹
10   And as he drains his drafts of Rhenish° down,   Rhine wine
      The kettledrum and trumpet thus bray out
      The triumph of his pledge.²
HORATIO   Is it a custom?
HAMLET   Ay, marry, is't,
      But to my mind, though I am native here
15   And to the manner° born, it is a custom   custom
      More honored in the breach than the observance.
      This heavy-headed revel east and west
      Makes us traduced and taxed of° other nations;   criticized by
      They clepe° us drunkards and with swinish phrase°   call / calling us pigs
20   Soil our addition;° and indeed it takes   reputation
      From our achievements, though performed at height,°   most excellently
      The pith° and marrow of our attribute.°   heart / reputation
      So, oft it chances in particular men
      That for some vicious mole of nature³ in them,
25   As in their birth°—wherein they are not guilty,   Inherited at birth
      Since nature cannot choose his° origin—   its
      By their o'ergrowth of some complexion,⁴
      Oft breaking down the pales° and forts of reason,   fences, boundaries
      Or by some habit that too much o'erleavens
30   The form of plausive manners⁵—that these men,

1.4 Location: The guard platform of Elsinore
Castle at midnight.
1. Staggers through a vigorous dance. *Wassail:* carousal, health drinking.
2. The triumph of his toast (achieved by emptying his cup at a single draught).
3. A blemish in some men's nature that leads
to vice.

4. That is, by the domination of one of the
four humors, thought to determine character:
black bile was held responsible for a melancholy disposition; blood, sanguine; yellow
bile, choleric; and phlegm, phlegmatic.
5. That is, exerts its negative influence over
pleasing manners (as too much leavening can
ruin a batch of bread dough).

Carrying, I say, the stamp of one defect,
Being nature's livery or fortune's star,[6]
His virtues else,° be they as pure as grace,   *other virtues*
As infinite as man may undergo,°   *sustain*
35 Shall in the general censure° take corruption   *public opinion*
From that particular fault. The dram of evil[7]
Doth all the noble substance often dout
To his own scandal.°   *disgrace*

        Enter GHOST.

HORATIO   Look, my lord, it comes!
HAMLET Angels and ministers of grace defend us!
40 Be thou a spirit of health or goblin° damned,   *demon*
Bring with thee airs from heaven or blasts[8] from hell,
Be thy intents wicked or charitable,
Thou com'st in such a questionable° shape   *question-provoking*
That I will speak to thee. I'll call thee Hamlet,
45 King, father, royal Dane. Oh, answer me!
Let me not burst in ignorance, but tell
Why thy canonized° bones, hearsèd° in death,   *sanctified / coffined*
Have burst their cerements,° why the sepulcher,   *grave clothes*
Wherein we saw thee quietly interred,
50 Hath oped his ponderous and marble jaws
To cast thee up again. What may this mean,
That thou, dead corpse, again in complete steel°   *full armor*
Revisits thus the glimpses of the moon,°   *shimmering moonlight*
Making night hideous, and we fools of nature[9]
55 So horridly to shake our disposition°   *state of mind*
With thoughts beyond the reaches of our souls?
Say, why is this? Wherefore? What should we do?

        [GHOST] *beckons* [HAMLET].

HORATIO It beckons you to go away with it,
As if it some impartment° did desire   *communication*
To you alone.
60 MARCELLUS   Look with what courteous action
It waves you to a more removèd ground.
But do not go with it.
HORATIO   No, by no means.
HAMLET It will not speak; then I will follow it.
HORATIO Do not, my lord.
HAMLET   Why, what should be the fear?
65 I do not set my life at a pin's fee,°   *the worth of a pin*
And for my soul, what can it do to that,
Being a thing immortal as itself?
It waves me forth again. I'll follow it.
HORATIO What if it tempt you toward the flood,° my lord,   *sea*

6. Either by a defect in their nature or the influence of ill fortune.
7. Minuscule amount of evil, punning on "evil" and "eale," or yeast (see line 29).
8. Foul, malignant airs that spread infection.

Airs: wholesome breezes.
9. Accustomed to the natural order of things (and therefore shaken by supernatural phenomena).

70 Or to the dreadful summit of the cliff
That beetles o'er° his base into the sea,   overhangs
And there assume some other horrible form
Which might deprive your sovereignty of reason,[1]
And draw you into madness? Think of it.
75 The very place puts toys of desperation,°   desperate fancies
Without more motive, into every brain
That looks so many fathoms to the sea
And hears it roar beneath.

HAMLET   It waves me still.—Go on. I'll follow thee.
MARCELLUS   You shall not go, my lord. [*They hold him.*]
80 HAMLET   Hold off your hands!
HORATIO   Be ruled. You shall not go.
HAMLET   My fate cries out,
And makes each petty artery in this body
As hardy as the Nemean lion's[2] nerve.
    [GHOST *beckons.*]
Still am I called. Unhand me, gentlemen!
85 By heaven, I'll make a ghost of him that lets° me!   hinders
[*Breaking free*] I say, away!—Go on. I'll follow thee.

                Exeunt GHOST *and* HAMLET.

HORATIO   He waxes desperate with imagination.
MARCELLUS   Let's follow. 'Tis not fit thus to obey him.
HORATIO   Have after.° To what issue° will this come?   Go on / end
90 MARCELLUS   Something is rotten in the state of Denmark.
HORATIO   Heaven will direct it.°   (the outcome)
MARCELLUS   Nay, let's follow him.

                            Exeunt.

1.5

Enter GHOST *and* HAMLET.

HAMLET   Whither wilt thou lead me? Speak, I'll go no
    further.
GHOST   Mark me.
HAMLET   I will.
GHOST   My hour is almost come,
When I to sulf'rous and tormenting flames
Must render up myself.
HAMLET   Alas, poor ghost!
5 GHOST   Pity me not, but lend thy serious hearing
To what I shall unfold.
HAMLET   Speak. I am bound to hear.
GHOST   So art thou to revenge, when thou shalt hear.
HAMLET   What?

---

1. Deprive reason of its sovereignty over your
mind.
2. In classical mythology, a lion whose skin
was impervious to weapons; killing it was the

first of Hercules' twelve labors.
1.5 Location: The battlements of Elsinore
Castle.

GHOST   I am thy father's spirit,

10   Doomed for a certain term to walk the night,
      And for the day confined to fast° in fires,   *do penance*
      Till the foul crimes done in my days of nature°   *my natural life*
      Are burnt and purged away.[3] But that I am forbid
      To tell the secrets of my prison house,
15   I could a tale unfold whose lightest word
      Would harrow up° thy soul, freeze thy young blood,   *lacerate, tear*
      Make thy two eyes like stars start from their spheres,
      Thy knotted and combinèd locks to part,
      And each particular hair to stand an end
20   Like quills upon the fearful porpentine.
      But this eternal blazon[4] must not be
      To ears of flesh and blood. List,° list, oh, list!   *Listen*
      If thou didst ever thy dear father love—

HAMLET   O God!

25 GHOST   Revenge his foul and most unnatural murder.

HAMLET   Murder?

GHOST   Murder most foul, as in the best it is,
      But this most foul, strange, and unnatural.

HAMLET   Haste me to know't, that I with wings as swift
30   As meditation or the thoughts of love
      May sweep to my revenge.

GHOST   I find thee apt;
      And duller shouldst thou be than the fat° weed   *gross*
      That roots itself in ease on Lethe wharf,[5]
      Wouldst thou not stir in this. Now, Hamlet, hear:
35   'Tis given out that, sleeping in my orchard,°   *garden*
      A serpent stung me; so the whole ear of Denmark
      Is by a forgèd process° of my death   *false account*
      Rankly abused.° But know, thou noble youth,   *deceived*
      The serpent that did sting thy father's life
40   Now wears his crown.

HAMLET   O my prophetic soul! My uncle!

GHOST   Ay, that incestuous, that adulterate° beast,   *adulterous*
      With witchcraft of his wit, with traitorous gifts°—   *talents*
      O wicked wit and gifts that have the power
45   So to seduce—won to his shameful lust
      The will of my most seeming-virtuous queen.
      O Hamlet, what falling off was there
      From me, whose love was of that dignity
      That it went hand in hand even with the vow
50   I made to her in marriage, and to decline
      Upon a wretch whose natural gifts were poor
      To° those of mine.   *Compared to*
      But virtue, as it never will be moved,

---

3. A description that suggests purgatory, the place, mainly associated with Catholicism, where the dead expiate their sins by suffering.

4. Revelation of eternal things.
5. The bank of Lethe, the river in the classical underworld whose waters cause forgetfulness.

Though lewdness court it in a shape of heaven,
55 So lust, though to a radiant angel linked,
Will sate itself in a celestial bed
And prey on garbage.
But soft.° Methinks I scent the morning air;   *wait*
Brief let me be. Sleeping within my orchard,
60 My custom always of the afternoon,
Upon my secure hour thy uncle stole,
With juice of cursèd hebona⁶ in a vial,
And in the porches° of my ears did pour   *entrances*
The leperous distilment,° whose effect   *extracted essence*
65 Holds such an enmity with blood of man
That swift as quicksilver it courses through
The natural gates and alleys of the body,
And with a sudden vigor it doth possess
And curd, like eager° droppings into milk,   *sour, acid*
70 The thin and wholesome blood. So did it mine,
And a most instant tetter barked about,⁷
Most lazar-like,° with vile and loathsome crust,   *like a leper*
All my smooth body.
Thus was I, sleeping, by a brother's hand,
75 Of life, of crown, of queen, at once dispatched,°   *dispossessed*
Cut off even in the blossoms of my sin,⁸
Unhouseled, disappointed, unaneled,⁹
No reck'ning° made, but sent to my account   *settling of spiritual accounts*
With all my imperfections on my head.   *(by confession of sins)*
80 O horrible, O horrible, most horrible!
If thou hast nature° in thee, bear it not;   *natural feeling*
Let not the royal bed of Denmark be
A couch for luxury° and damned incest.   *lust*
But, howsoever thou pursues this act,
85 Taint not thy mind,¹ nor let thy soul contrive
Against thy mother aught.° Leave her to heaven,   *anything whatsoever*
And to those thorns that in her bosom lodge
To prick and sting her. Fare thee well at once.
The glow-worm shows the matin° to be near,   *morning*
90 And 'gins° to pale his uneffectual fire.   *begins*
Adieu, adieu, adieu. Remember me.   [*Exit.*]
HAMLET   O all you host of heaven! O earth! What else?
And shall I couple° hell? Oh, fie! Hold, hold, my heart,   *add*
And you, my sinews, grow not instant old,
95 But bear me swiftly up. Remember thee?
Ay, thou poor ghost, whiles memory holds a seat

---

6. A poison; possibly a confusion for "henbane," a plant with poisonous properties.
7. That is, a pustular eruption of the skin ("tetter") covered the body as bark covers a tree.
8. That is, before there was an opportunity to confess and repent sins.

9. Without the Eucharist ("unhouseled"); unprepared ("disappointed"), because unconfessed and unrepentant; and without receiving extreme unction or anointing ("unaneled").
1. Do not become corrupted yourself.

In this distracted globe.[2] Remember thee?
Yea, from the table° of my memory   *tablet*
I'll wipe away all trivial, fond° records,   *foolish*
100 All saws of books, all forms, all pressures past[3]
That youth and observation copied there,
And thy commandment all alone shall live
Within the book and volume of my brain,
Unmixed with baser matter. Yes, by heaven.
105 O most pernicious woman!
O villain, villain, smiling, damnèd villain!
My tables°—meet° it is I set it down   *writing tablets / fitting*
That one may smile and smile and be a villain.
At least, I am sure, it may be so in Denmark.
110 So, uncle, there you are. Now to my word.[4]
It is "Adieu, adieu. Remember me."
I have sworn't.

    Enter HORATIO *and* MARCELLUS [*calling*].

HORATIO   My lord, my lord!
MARCELLUS   Lord Hamlet!
115 HORATIO   Heavens secure him.
HAMLET   [*Aside*] So be it.
MARCELLUS   Illo,[5] ho, ho, my lord!
HAMLET   Hillo, ho, ho, boy! Come and come.
MARCELLUS   How is't, my noble lord?
120 HORATIO   What news, my lord?
HAMLET   Oh, wonderful!°   *astonishing*
HORATIO   Good my lord, tell it.
HAMLET   No, you will reveal it.
HORATIO   Not I, my lord, by heaven.
125 MARCELLUS   Nor I, my lord.
HAMLET   How say you, then? Would heart of man once
    think it?
  But you'll be secret?
HOR. }
MAR. } Ay, by heaven.
HAMLET   There's never a villain dwelling in all Denmark
130 But he's an arrant° knave.   *out-and-out*
HORATIO   There needs no ghost, my lord, come from the
    grave
  To tell us this.
HAMLET   Why, right, you are in the right.
And so without more circumstance° at all,   *ceremony*
I hold it fit that we shake hands and part,
135 You, as your business and desire shall point you—
For every man hath business and desire,

---

2. Troubled earth; perhaps, confused head; also perhaps a reference to the Globe theater in which *Hamlet* was performed.
3. That is, all wise sayings from books, all shape or customs, all past impressions.
4. Perhaps, watchword; or the ghost's command; or oath.
5. A falconer's cry to his hawk.

Such as it is—and for my own poor part,
I will go pray.

HORATIO   These are but wild and whirling words, my lord.

140 HAMLET   I am sorry they offend you, heartily;
Yes, faith, heartily.

HORATIO   There's no offense, my lord.

HAMLET   Yes, by Saint Patrick, but there is, Horatio,
And much offense too. Touching this vision here,
It is an honest° ghost, that let me tell you.   *truthful, reliable*
145 For your desire to know what is between us,
O'ermaster't as you may. And now, good friends,
As you are friends, scholars, and soldiers,
Give me one poor request.

HORATIO   What is't, my lord? We will.

HAMLET   Never make known what you have seen tonight.

HOR. ⎤
150 MAR. ⎰ My lord, we will not.

HAMLET   Nay, but swear't.

HORATIO   In faith, my lord, not I.[6]

MARCELLUS   Nor I, my lord, in faith.

HAMLET   [*Holding out his sword*] Upon my sword.

155 MARCELLUS   We have sworn, my lord, already.

HAMLET   Indeed, upon my sword, indeed.

GHOST (*Cries under the stage*)   Swear.

HAMLET   Ha, ha, boy, sayst thou so? Art thou there,
truepenny?°—   *honest fellow*
Come on, you hear this fellow in the cellarage;
Consent to swear.

160 HORATIO   Propose the oath, my lord.

HAMLET   Never to speak of this that you have seen,
Swear by my sword.

GHOST [*Beneath*]   Swear.

HAMLET   *Hic et ubique*?[7] Then we'll shift our ground.
[*He moves to another place.*]
165 Come hither, gentlemen,
And lay your hands again upon my sword.
Swear by my sword
Never to speak of this that you have heard.

GHOST   [*Beneath*] Swear by his sword.

170 HAMLET   Well said, old mole! Canst work i' th' earth so fast?
A worthy pioner.°—Once more remove,° good friends.   *miner / move*
[*He moves again.*]

HORATIO   O day and night, but this is wondrous strange!

HAMLET   And therefore as a stranger give it welcome.[8]
There are more things in heaven and earth, Horatio,
175 Than are dreamt of in your philosophy.[9] But come.
Here, as before, never, so help you mercy,

6. Indeed, I will not reveal it.
7. Here and everywhere (Latin).
8. That is, welcome it with the courtesy due
to a stranger.
9. Natural philosophy (i.e., science).

How strange or odd soe'er I bear myself—
As I, perchance, hereafter shall think meet
To put an antic disposition on[1]—
180 That you, at such times seeing me, never shall,
With arms encumbered° thus, or this headshake,   *folded*
Or by pronouncing of some doubtful° phrase   *ambiguous*
As "Well, well, we know," or "We could an if° we would,"   *if only*
Or "If we list° to speak," or "There be, an if they might,"[2]   *liked*
185 Or such ambiguous giving out, to note
That you know aught° of me—this do swear,   *anything*
So grace and mercy at your most need help you.
        GHOST [Beneath] Swear. [They swear.]
        HAMLET   Rest, rest, perturbèd spirit.—So, gentlemen,
190 With all my love I do commend me to you,
And what so poor a man as Hamlet is
May do t'express his love and friending° to you,   *friendship*
God willing, shall not lack.° Let us go in together;   *be deficient*
And still° your fingers on your lips, I pray.   *always*
195 The time is out of joint.° O cursèd spite,   *in complete disorder*
That ever I was born to set it right!
Nay, come, let's go together.[3]
                                        Exeunt.

2.1

Enter old POLONIUS *with his man* [REYNALDO].

        POLONIUS   Give him this money and these notes, Reynaldo.
        [*He gives money and papers.*]
        REYNALDO   I will, my lord.
        POLONIUS   You shall do marvelous wisely, good Reynaldo,
Before you visit him, to make inquire
Of his behavior.
5 REYNALDO   My lord, I did intend it.
        POLONIUS   Marry, well said, very well said. Look you, sir,
Inquire me° first what Danskers° are in Paris,   *for me / Danes*
And how, and who, what means,° and where they keep,°   *means of income / reside*
What company, at what expense; and finding
10 By this encompassment and drift of question[4]
That they do know my son, come you more nearer
Than your particular demands will touch it.[5]
Take you,° as 'twere, some distant knowledge of him,   *Pretend*
As thus, "I know his father and his friends,
15 And in part him"—do you mark this, Reynaldo?
        REYNALDO   Ay, very well, my lord.

---

1. To behave fantastically, to act like a madman.
2. There are those who would say this or that if they could so do safely.
3. Hamlet tells the others to depart with him (rather than to follow him, as befitting his rank).
2.1 Location: Polonius's chambers
4. By this roundabout manner of questioning.
5. You will come nearer to the truth than if you make direct inquiries.

POLONIUS   "And in part him, but," you may say, "not well.
    But if't be he I mean, he's very wild,
    Addicted so and so," and there put on him°   *accuse him of*
20   What forgeries[6] you please—marry, none so rank°   *heinous*
    As may dishonor him, take heed of that—
    But, sir, such wanton,° wild, and usual slips   *unrestrained*
    As are companions noted and most known
    To youth and liberty.
REYNALDO   As gaming, my lord.
25 POLONIUS   Ay, or drinking, fencing, swearing,
    Quarreling, drabbing°—you may go so far.   *whoring*
REYNALDO   My lord, that would dishonor him.
POLONIUS   Faith, no, as you may season° it in the charge.   *moderate*
    You must not put another scandal on him,
30   That he is open° to incontinency;°   *given to / sexual excess*
    That's not my meaning. But breathe his faults so quaintly°   *delicately*
    That they may seem the taints of liberty,[7]
    The flash and outbreak of a fiery mind,
    A savageness in unreclaimèd° blood,   *untamed*
35   Of general assault.[8]
REYNALDO   But, my good lord—
POLONIUS   Wherefore° should you do   *Why*
    this?
REYNALDO   Ay, my lord, I would know that.
POLONIUS   Marry, sir, here's my drift,
    And I believe it is a fetch of wit:
40   You laying these slight sullies° on my son   *stain*
    As 'twere a thing a little soiled wi' the working,[9]
    Mark you, your party° in converse, him you would sound,°   *partner / sound out*
    Having° ever seen in the prenominate crimes[1]   *If he has*
    The youth you breathe of guilty, be assured
45   He closes with° you in this consequence:[2]   *discloses to*
    "Good sir," or so, or "friend," or "gentleman,"
    According to the phrase° or the addition[3]   *expression*
    Of man and country—
REYNALDO   Very good, my lord.
POLONIUS   And then, sir, does 'a° this—'a does—What was I   *he*
    about to say?
50   By the mass,° I was about to say something. Where did I   *(a mild oath)*
    leave?
REYNALDO   At "closes in the consequence."
POLONIUS   At "closes in the consequence"—ay, marry.
    He closes thus: "I know the gentleman;
    I saw him yesterday," or "th'other day"
55   —Or then or then with such or such—and, "as you say,

---

6. False accusations.
7. The blemishes that result from freedom without discipline.
8. To which all young men are prone.
9. Shopworn (i.e., slightly soiled while com-

ing to maturity).
1. Aforementioned transgressions.
2. In the following manner.
3. Title; customary style of address.

	There was 'a° gaming," "there o'ertook in's rouse,"°	he / drunk from his carousal
	"There falling out° at tennis," or perchance,	quarreling
	"I saw him enter such a house of sale,"	
	Videlicet,° a brothel, or so forth. See you now	That is to say (Latin)
60	Your bait of falsehood takes this carp° of truth,	fish
	And thus do we of wisdom and of reach,°	understanding
	With windlasses, and with assays of bias,⁴	
	By indirections find directions out.⁵	
	So, by my former° lecture and advice	previous
65	Shall you my son. You have me,° have you not?	have my meaning

REYNALDO   My lord, I have.

POLONIUS   God be wi'ye; fare ye well.

REYNALDO   Good my lord.

	POLONIUS Observe his inclination in° yourself.	for
	REYNALDO I shall, my lord.	
70	POLONIUS And let him ply° his music.	practice

REYNALDO   Well, my lord.

POLONIUS   Farewell.

                                        Exit REYNALDO.

        Enter OPHELIA.

                    How now, Ophelia, what's the matter?

OPHELIA   Oh, my lord, my lord, I have been so affrighted!

POLONIUS   With what, i'the name of God?

75	OPHELIA My lord, as I was sewing in my closet,	
	Lord Hamlet, with his doublet all unbraced,°	his jacket unlaced
	No hat upon his head, his stockings fouled,	
	Ungartered, and down-gyvèd to his ankle,⁶	
	Pale as his shirt, his knees knocking each other,	
80	And with a look so piteous in purport	
	As if he had been loosèd out of hell	
	To speak of horrors—he comes before me.	

POLONIUS   Mad for thy love?

OPHELIA   My lord, I do not know,

    But truly I do fear it.

POLONIUS   What said he?

85	OPHELIA He took me by the wrist and held me hard,	
	Then goes he to the length of all his arm,	
	And with his other hand thus o'er his brow,	
	He falls to such perusal of my face	
	As 'a° would draw it. Long stayed he so.	As if he
90	At last, a little shaking of mine arm,	
	And thrice his head thus waving up and down,	
	He raised a sigh so piteous and profound	
	As it did seem to shatter all his bulk°	body
	And end his being. That done, he lets me go,	
95	And, with his head over his shoulder turned,	

---

4. That is, indirect efforts: a "windlass" is a roundabout approach to intercept the game in hunting; "bias" is the curve taken by the ball toward its target in the game of bowls.

5. That is, by indirect means find out the truth.
6. Fallen down around his ankles like shackles (gyves).

He seemed to find his way without his eyes,
For out o' doors he went without their helps,
And to the last bended their light[7] on me.

POLONIUS   Come, go with me: I will go seek the King.
100   This is the very ecstasy° of love,   insanity
Whose violent property fordoes° itself   destroys
And leads the will to desperate undertakings,
As oft as any passion under heaven
That does afflict our natures. I am sorry.
105   What, have you given him any hard words of late?

OPHELIA   No, my good lord, but, as you did command,
I did repel his letters and denied
His access to me.

POLONIUS   That hath made him mad.
I am sorry that with better heed and judgment
110   I had not quoted° him: I feared he did but trifle,   observed
And meant to wrack thee. But beshrew my jealousy![8]
By heaven, it is as proper to our age
To cast beyond ourselves[9] in our opinions
As it is common for the younger sort
115   To lack discretion. Come, go we to the King.
This must be known, which, being kept close,° might move   secret
More grief to hide than hate to utter love.[1]
Come.

                                                    Exeunt.

2.2

Flourish. Enter KING *and* QUEEN, ROSENCRANTZ *and*
GUILDENSTERN [*and* ATTENDANTS].

KING   Welcome, dear Rosencrantz and Guildenstern.
Moreover° that we much did long to see you,   Besides
The need we have to use you did provoke
Our hasty sending.° Something have you heard   summons
5   Of Hamlet's transformation—so call it,
Sith° nor th'exterior nor the inward man   Since
Resembles that° it was. What it should be,   what
More than his father's death, that thus hath put him
So much from th'understanding of himself,
10   I cannot dream of. I entreat you both
That, being of so young days° brought up with him,   from childhood
And sith so neighbored to[2] his youth and havior,°   behavior
That you vouchsafe your rest° here in our court   agree to remain
Some little time, so by your companies
15   To draw him on to pleasures, and to gather,
So much as from occasion° you may glean,   opportunities

7. That is, the light that eyes were thought to
emit.
8. Curse my suspicious nature. *Wrack thee:*
take your virginity.
9. Go too far (by way of caution). *Proper to
our age:* i.e., characteristic of men of Poloni-

us's own (advanced) age.
1. That is, might cause more grief if kept
secret than it would incur hatred (or disapproval) if revealed.
2.2 Location: The castle.
2. Familiar with.

Whether aught° to us unknown afflicts him thus   *anything*
That, opened,° lies within our remedy.   *if revealed*

QUEEN   Good gentlemen, he hath much talked of you,

20 And sure I am two men there is not living
To whom he more adheres.° If it will please you   *is more attached*
To show us so much gentry° and good will   *courtesy*
As to expend your time with us awhile,
For the supply and profit³ of our hope,

25 Your visitation shall receive such thanks
As fits a king's remembrance.

ROSENCRANTZ   Both Your Majesties
Might, by the sovereign power you have of° us,   *over*
Put your dread° pleasures more into command   *revered*
Than to entreaty.

GUILDENSTERN   But we both obey,

30 And here give up ourselves in the full bent°   *to our utmost*
To lay our service freely at your feet,
To be commanded.

KING   Thanks, Rosencrantz and gentle Guildenstern.

QUEEN   Thanks, Guildenstern and gentle Rosencrantz.

35 And I beseech you instantly to visit
My too much changèd son.—Go, some of you,
And bring these gentlemen where Hamlet is.

GUILDENSTERN   Heavens make our presence and our   *doings; stratagems*
     practices°
Pleasant and helpful to him.

QUEEN   Ay, amen.

     Exeunt ROSENCRANTZ, GUILDENSTERN
     [*and some* ATTENDANTS].

     Enter POLONIUS.

40 POLONIUS   Th'ambassadors from Norway, my good lord,
Are joyfully returned.

KING   Thou still° hast been the father of good news.   *always*

POLONIUS   Have I, my lord? I assure my good liege
I hold my duty as I hold my soul,

45 Both to my God and to my gracious king;
And I do think—or else this brain of mine
Hunts not the trail of policy° so sure   *statecraft*
As it hath used to do—that I have found
The very cause of Hamlet's lunacy.

50 KING   Oh, speak of that; that do I long to hear.

POLONIUS   Give first admittance to th'ambassadors;
My news shall be the fruit° to that great feast.   *dessert*

KING   Thyself do grace to them and bring them in.

     [*Exit* POLONIUS.]

He tells me, my dear Gertrude, he hath found

55 The head° and source of all your son's distemper.   *chief reason*

QUEEN   I doubt° it is no other but the main,°   *suspect / main cause*
His father's death and our hasty marriage.

---

3. Support and advancement.

KING Well, we shall sift him.°   *question (Polonius)*

Enter AMBASSADORS [VOLTEMAND *and* CORNELIUS, *with*
POLONIUS].

—Welcome, my good friends.

Say, Voltemand, what from our brother° Norway?   *fellow monarch*

60 VOLTEMAND   Most fair return of greetings and desires.°   *good wishes*
Upon our first,[4] he sent out to suppress
His nephew's levies, which to him appeared
To be a preparation 'gainst the Polack,°   *the King of Poland*
But, better looked into, he truly found

65 It was against Your Highness; whereat grieved
That so his sickness, age, and impotence
Was falsely borne in hand,[5] sends out arrests
On Fortinbras;[6] which he, in brief, obeys,
Receives rebuke from Norway, and, in fine,°   *conclusion*

70 Makes vow before his uncle never more
To give th'assay of arms[7] against Your Majesty.
Whereon old Norway, overcome with joy,
Gives him three-score° thousand crowns in annual fee,°   *sixty / payment*
And his commission to employ those soldiers,

75 So levied as before, against the Polack,
With an entreaty, herein further shown, [*He gives a paper.*]
That it might please you to give quiet pass
Through your dominions for this enterprise,
On such regards of safety and allowance[8]
As therein are set down.

80 KING   It likes° us well,   *pleases*
And at our more considered time[9] we'll read,
Answer, and think upon this business.
Meantime we thank you for your well-took labor.
Go to your rest; at night we'll feast together.
Most welcome home!

Exeunt AMBASSADORS.

85 POLONIUS   This business is well ended.
My liege, and madam, to expostulate°   *reason earnestly*
What majesty should be, what duty is,
Why day is day, night, night, and time is time,
Were nothing but to waste night, day, and time.

90 Therefore, since brevity is the soul of wit,°   *wisdom*
And tediousness the limbs and outward flourishes,°   *rhetorical flourishes*
I will be brief. Your noble son is mad,
"Mad" call I it, for to define true madness,
What is't but to be nothing else but mad?
But let that go.

---

4. When we first broached the matter (of
young Fortinbras's military preparations).
5. That is, was deceitfully taken advantage of.
6. Orders to Fortinbras to stop his military

action against Denmark.
7. To undertake military action.
8. With such safeguards and stipulations.
9. A convenient time for further consideration.

95 QUEEN　　　　　　More matter with less art.°   *rhetorical art*

POLONIUS　Madam, I swear I use no art at all.
　That he's mad, 'tis true; 'tis true, 'tis pity,
　And pity 'tis, 'tis true—a foolish figure,°   *figure of speech*
　But farewell it,° for I will use no art.   *to it*
100　Mad let us grant him then, and now remains
　That we find out the cause of this effect,
　Or rather say, the cause of this defect,
　For this effect defective comes by cause.[1]
　Thus it remains, and the remainder thus.
105　Perpend.°   *Consider*
　I have a daughter—have while she is mine°—   *until she marries*
　Who, in her duty and obedience, mark,
　Hath given me this. Now gather and surmise.
　　　[*He reads a letter.*]
　"To the celestial, and my soul's idol, the most beautified°   *beautiful*
110　Ophelia"—that's an ill phrase, a vile phrase, "beautified" is
　a vile phrase; but you shall hear. Thus: [*He reads.*]
　"In her excellent white bosom,[2] these," etc.
QUEEN　Came this from Hamlet to her?
POLONIUS　Good madam, stay° awhile; I will be faithful.°   *wait/read faithfully*
　　　[*He reads the letter.*]

115　　　　　"Doubt thou the stars are fire,
　　　　　　Doubt that the sun doth move,
　　　　　Doubt° truth to be a liar,   *Suspect*
　　　　　　But never doubt I love.

　Oh, dear Ophelia, I am ill at these numbers.[3] I have not
120　art to reckon my groans.[4] But that I love thee best, oh,
　most best, believe it. Adieu.
　Thine evermore, most dear lady, whilst this machine is to°   *body belongs*
　him, Hamlet."
　This in obedience hath my daughter shown me,
125　And, more above,° hath his solicitings,   *moreover*
　As they fell out° by time, by means, and place,   *came to pass*
　All given to mine ear.
　KING　　　　　　But how hath she
　Received his love?
POLONIUS　　　　　What do you think of me?
KING　As of a man faithful and honorable.
130 POLONIUS　I would fain° prove so. But what might you think,   *gladly*
　When I had seen this hot love on the wing—
　As I perceived it, I must tell you that,
　Before my daughter told me—what might you,
　Or my dear Majesty your queen here, think,
135　If I had played the desk or table book,[5]
　Or given my heart a winking,° mute and dumb,   *closing of the eyes*

1. That is, this effect, which in Hamlet is a
defect (i.e., his madness), has a cause.
2. Where love letters should be kept.
3. Bad at writing verses.
4. Count my groans (in metrical verse).
5. That is, if I had kept this knowledge secret.

Or looked upon this love with idle sight?
What might you think? No, I went round° to work,   *straightaway*
And my young mistress thus I did bespeak:°   *address*
140   "Lord Hamlet is a prince out of thy star.[6]
This must not be." And then I prescripts gave her
That she should lock herself from his resort,°   *company*
Admit no messengers, receive no tokens.
Which done, she took the fruits of my advice;
145   And he, repellèd—a short tale to make—
Fell into a sadness, then into a fast,
Thence to a watch,° thence into a weakness,   *insomnia*
Thence to lightness,° and by this declension°   *light-headedness / decline*
Into the madness wherein now he raves,
And all we° mourn for.   *of us*
150   KING   Do you think this?
     QUEEN   It may be very like.°   *likely*
     POLONIUS   Hath there been such a time—I would fain
        know that—
     That I have positively said " 'Tis so,"
     When it proved otherwise?
     KING   Not that I know.
155   POLONIUS   Take this from this, if this be otherwise.
     If circumstances lead me, I will find
     Where truth is hid, though it were hid indeed
     Within the center.[7]
     KING   How may we try° it further?   *test*
     POLONIUS   You know sometimes he walks four hours
        together
     Here in the lobby.
160   QUEEN   So he does indeed.
     POLONIUS   At such a time I'll loose my daughter to him.
     [*To the* KING] Be you and I behind an arras° then.   *a hanging tapestry*
     Mark the encounter. If he love her not,
     And be not from his reason fall'n thereon,°   *for that reason*
165   Let me be no assistant for a state,
     But keep a farm and carters.°   *cart drivers*
     KING   We will try it.
        Enter HAMLET [*reading a book*].
     QUEEN   But look where sadly the poor wretch comes
        reading.
     POLONIUS   Away, I do beseech you, both away.
     I'll board him presently.[8] Oh, give me leave.
        Exeunt KING *and* QUEEN [*with* ATTENDANTS].
170   How does my good Lord Hamlet?
     HAMLET   Well, God-a-mercy.[9]
     POLONIUS   Do you know me, my lord?
     HAMLET   Excellent well. You are a fishmonger.°   *fish dealer*

---

6. Above your sphere (a reference to the concentric spheres of the Ptolemaic universe).
7. The center of the earth (which, in the Ptolemaic system, is also the center of the universe).
8. I'll approach him immediately.
9. God have mercy (on you); a courteous response to a greeting.

POLONIUS   Not I, my lord.

175 HAMLET   Then I would you were so honest a man.

POLONIUS   Honest, my lord?

HAMLET   Ay, sir. To be honest, as this world goes, is to be
one man picked out of ten thousand.

POLONIUS   That's very true, my lord.

180 HAMLET   For if the sun breed maggots in a dead dog, being
a good kissing carrion[1]—Have you a daughter?

POLONIUS   I have, my lord.

HAMLET   Let her not walk i'the sun. Conception[2] is a bless-
ing, but as your daughter may conceive, friend, look to't.°   *be careful about that*

185 POLONIUS [*Aside*]   How say you by that? Still harping on my
daughter. Yet he knew me not at first; 'a° said I was a fish   *he*
monger. 'A is far gone. And truly in my youth I suffered
much extremity for love, very near this. I'll speak to him
again.—What do you read, my lord?

190 HAMLET   Words, words, words.

POLONIUS   What is the matter,[3] my lord?

HAMLET   Between who?

POLONIUS   I mean the matter that you read, my lord.

HAMLET   Slanders, sir; for the satirical rogue says here
195 that old men have gray beards, that their faces are wrin-
kled, their eyes purging° thick amber° and plum-tree   *discharging / resin*
gum, and that they have a plentiful lack of wit, together
with most weak hams.° All which, sir, though I most   *thighs*
powerfully and potently believe, yet I hold it not hon-
200 esty° to have it thus set down; for yourself, sir, shall grow   *proper, honorable*
old as I am, if, like a crab, you could go backward.

POLONIUS [*Aside*]   Though this be madness, yet there is
method in't.—Will you walk out of the air,[4] my lord?

HAMLET   Into my grave.

205 POLONIUS   Indeed, that's out of the air. [*Aside*] How
pregnant° sometimes his replies are—a happiness° that   *full of meaning / An aptness*
often madness hits on, which reason and sanity could not
so prosperously° be delivered of. I will leave him and my   *successfully*
daughter.—My lord, I will take my leave of you.

210 HAMLET   You cannot take from me anything that I will not
more willingly part withal°—except my life, except my   *with*
life, except my life.

POLONIUS   Fare you well, my lord.

HAMLET   These tedious old fools.

Enter GUILDENSTERN *and* ROSENCRANTZ.

215 POLONIUS   You go to seek the Lord Hamlet. There he is.

ROSENCRANTZ [*To* POLONIUS]   God save you, sir.

[*Exit* POLONIUS.]

1. Flesh good enough for the sun to "kiss."
"Carrion" most often refers to a dead carcass,
but it can also refer contemptuously to living
flesh, with a sexual connotation.
2. The power to form ideas; pregnancy. *Let . . .
sun*: have her avoid public spaces; keep her

away from me (with a pun on "sun" / "son," and
the use of the sun as an emblem of royalty).
3. Subject (but Hamlet takes it as a conflict
between two parties).
4. Fresh air was thought harmful to the sick.

GUILDENSTERN   My honored lord.

ROSENCRANTZ   My most dear lord.

HAMLET   My excellent good friends! How dost thou, Guil-
220   denstern? Ah, Rosencrantz. Good lads, how do you both?

ROSENCRANTZ   As the indifferent children° of the earth.   *ordinary men*

GUILDENSTERN   Happy° in that we are not overhappy. On   *Fortunate*
   Fortune's cap we are not the very button.°   *top*

HAMLET   Nor the soles of her shoe?

225 ROSENCRANTZ   Neither, my lord.

HAMLET   Then you live about her waist, or in the middle of
   her favors?

GUILDENSTERN   Faith, her privates[5] we.

HAMLET   In the secret parts of Fortune? Oh, most true, she
230   is a strumpet.° What news?   *whore*

ROSENCRANTZ   None, my lord, but the world's grown honest.

HAMLET   Then is doomsday near. But your news is not
   true. But in the beaten way[6] of friendship, what make
   you at° Elsinore?   *brings you to*

235 ROSENCRANTZ   To visit you, my lord; no other occasion.

HAMLET   Beggar that I am, I am ever poor in thanks; but I
   thank you, and sure, dear friends, my thanks are too dear
   a halfpenny.[7] Were you not sent for? Is it your own
   inclining? Is it a free° visitation? Come, come, deal justly   *voluntary*
240   with me; come, come. Nay, speak.

GUILDENSTERN   What should we say, my lord?

HAMLET   Anything but to the purpose. You were sent for,
   and there is a kind of confession in your looks, which
   your modesties have[8] not craft enough to color.° I know   *conceal*
245   the good King and Queen have sent for you.

ROSENCRANTZ   To what end, my lord?

HAMLET   That you must teach me. But let me conjure° you,   *implore*
   by the rights of our fellowship, by the consonancy° of our *concord, friendship*
   youth, by the obligation of our ever-preserved love, and
250   by what more dear a better proposer° can charge you   *speaker*
   withal,° be even° and direct with me whether you were   *besides / honest*
   sent for or no.

ROSENCRANTZ [*To* GUILDENSTERN] What say you?

HAMLET   Nay, then, I have an eye of° you. If you love me,   *on*
255   hold not off.°   *speak freely*

GUILDENSTERN   My lord, we were sent for.

HAMLET   I will tell you why. So shall my anticipation prevent your discovery,[9] and your secrecy to the King and
   Queen molt no feather.° I have of late, but wherefore I   *i.e., remain intact*
260   know not, lost all my mirth, forgone all custom of°   *customary*
   exercises, and indeed it goes so heavily with my disposition that this goodly frame,° the earth, seems to me a   *structure*

---

5. Private parts; close friends; ordinary subjects (without title or office).
6. Well-worn, familiar way.
7. That is, too expensively priced at a half-

penny (i.e., my gratitude is of little worth).
8. Your personal integrity has.
9. Your having to betray the confidence (of
the king and queen).

sterile promontory,° this most excellent canopy, the air, look   *land jutting out into water*
you, this brave o'erhanging[1] firmament, this majestical roof
265　fretted° with golden fire, why, it appeareth nothing to me   *decorated*
but a foul and pestilent congregation of vapors. What a
piece of work° is a man! How noble in reason, how infinite   *masterpiece*
in faculties,° in form and moving how express[2] and   *natural aptitude*
admirable, in action how like an angel, in apprehension
270　how like a god! The beauty of the world, the paragon of
animals! And yet to me, what is this quintessence[3] of
dust? Man delights not me; nor women neither, though
by your smiling you seem to say so.
　　ROSENCRANTZ　My lord, there was no such stuff in my
275　thoughts.
　　HAMLET　Why did ye laugh then, when I said "man delights
not me"?
　　ROSENCRANTZ　To think, my lord, if you delight not in
man, what Lenten entertainment[4] the players shall
280　receive from you. We coted them° on the way, and hither   *passed them by*
are they coming to offer you service.
　　HAMLET　He that plays the king shall be welcome. His
Majesty shall have tribute of me, the adventurous knight
shall use his foil and target,[5] the lover shall not sigh gra-
285　tis,° the humorous man shall end his part in peace,[6] and   *without payment*
the lady shall say her mind freely—or the blank verse
shall halt for't.[7] What players are they?
　　ROSENCRANTZ　Even those you were wont to take such
delight in, the tragedians° of the city.   *actors*
290　HAMLET　How chances it they travel? Their residence,[8]
both in reputation and profit, was better both ways.
　　ROSENCRANTZ　I think their inhibition[9] comes by the
means of the late innovation.[1]
　　HAMLET　Do they hold the same estimation° they did   *good reputation*
295　when I was in the city? Are they so followed?
　　ROSENCRANTZ　No, indeed, are they not.

1. This splendid overhang; that is, the roof or
"heavens" overhanging the Elizabethan stage,
decorated with stars or the signs of the zodiac.
2. Well framed, well designed.
3. The most essential part of a substance; literally, the "fifth essence" of which the heavenly bodies were supposedly composed,
thought to be actually latent in the four elements (air, water, earth, fire).
4. Meager reception (with an allusion to the
prohibition of plays during Lent).
5. Sword and shield.
6. That is, the man who is governed by one of
the four humors shall be allowed to play his
part without interruption. (The "humorous
Man," the "adventurous knight," and the
other figures mentioned in this speech are
stock characters in Elizabethan plays.)
7. That is, she shall be allowed to speak her

mind (without censoring her words?), or else
her blank verse (unrhymed iambic pentameter) will not scan properly.
8. That is, residence in the city, presumably
in their permanent theater.
9. Ban on the performance of stage plays
(perhaps a reference to a Privy Council order
of 1600 limiting performances to two a week,
in only two theaters.
1. If "the late innovation" means "recent
political insurrection," then this could refer
to a ban on stage plays possibly resulting from
the performance of *Richard II* during the earl
of Essex's rebellion in 1601 against Elizabeth I.
"Innovation" may also refer to the emergence
of the very popular company of boy actors
that performed at the private Blackfriars theater and provided stiff competition for the
adult companies.

HAMLET   It is not very strange; for my uncle is King of Den-
mark, and those that would make mouths° at him while my   *faces*
father lived give twenty, forty, fifty, a hundred ducats apiece
300   for his picture in little.° 'Sblood,[2] there is something in this   *miniature*
more than natural,° if philosophy° could find it out.   *unnatural / science*
A flourish.

GUILDENSTERN   There are the players.

HAMLET   Gentlemen, you are welcome to Elsinore. Your
hands, come then. Th'appurtenance° of welcome is   *accessory*
305   fashion and ceremony. Let me comply with you in this
garb,[3] lest my extent° to the players, which I tell you must   *what I show*
show fairly° outwards, should more appear like enter-   *plainly*
tainment° than yours.° You are welcome. But my uncle-   *more welcoming /*
father and aunt-mother are deceived.   *to you*

310   GUILDENSTERN   In what, my dear lord?

HAMLET   I am but mad north-north-west;[4] when the wind
is southerly I know a hawk from a handsaw.[5]
Enter POLONIUS.

POLONIUS   Well be with you, gentlemen.

HAMLET   Hark you, Guildenstern, and you too, at each ear
315   a hearer: that great baby you see there is not yet out of
his swaddling clouts.

ROSENCRANTZ   Haply° he is the second time come to them,   *Perhaps*
for they say an old man is twice° a child.   *for the second time*

HAMLET   I will prophesy he comes to tell me of the play-
320   ers; mark it. [*Loudly*] You say right, sir; o' Monday
morning, 'twas then indeed.

POLONIUS   My lord, I have news to tell you.

HAMLET   My lord, I have news to tell you. When Roscius[6]
was an actor in Rome—

325   POLONIUS   The actors are come hither, my lord.

HAMLET   Buzz, buzz.

POLONIUS   Upon my honor—

HAMLET   Then came each actor on his ass.

POLONIUS   The best actors in the world, either for tragedy,
330   comedy, history, pastoral, pastoral-comical, historical-
pastoral, scene individable, or poem unlimited.[7] Seneca
cannot be too heavy nor Plautus too light.[8] For the law of
writ and the liberty,[9] these are the only men.

2. By God's blood (a common oath).
3. Use courteous action with you in the
appropriate fashion (by shaking hands).
4. That is, I am mad only when the wind
blows from the north-northwest; or, I am
only a little bit mad (because the north-
northwesterly direction on a compass is only
a little bit removed from true north).
5. That is, one tool from another (a "hawk" is
a pickaxe in addition to being a bird of prey).
6. Quintus Roscius Gallus (d. ca. 62 B.C.E.), a

famous Roman actor.
7. That is, scenes and plays that observe the
unities of time, place, and action (individable) and those that ignore them (unlimited).
8. Lucius Annaeus Seneca (ca. 4 B.C.E.–65
C.E.), Roman writer of tragedy and philosophy; Titus Macchius Plautus (ca. 254–184
B.C.E.), Roman writer of comedies.
9. For plays that are written according to the
rules and those that are not.

HAMLET O Jephthah, judge of Israel,[1] what a treasure hadst
335   thou!
POLONIUS What a treasure had he, my lord?
HAMLET Why,

> "One fair daughter, and no more,
> The which he lovèd passing° well."   *surpassing*

340 POLONIUS [*Aside*] Still on my daughter.
HAMLET Am I not i'the right, old Jephthah?
POLONIUS If you call me Jephthah, my lord, I have a
  daughter that I love passing well.
HAMLET Nay, that follows not.
345 POLONIUS What follows, then, my lord?
HAMLET Why,

> "As by lot,° God wot"°   *chance / knows*

and then, you know,

> "It came to pass, as most like° it was"—   *likely*

350 the first row° of the pious chanson° will show you more, for   *stanza / song*
  look where my abridgment[2] comes.

    Enter the PLAYERS.

You are welcome, masters, welcome all.—I am glad to
see thee well. Welcome, good friends.—Oh, old friend!
Why, thy face is valanced[3] since I saw thee last. Com'st
355 thou to beard° me in Denmark?—What, my young lady   *oppose (with pun)*
and mistress![4] By'r lady, your ladyship is nearer to heaven
than when I saw you last by the altitude of a chopine.°   *i.e., a thick cork sole*
Pray God, your voice, like a piece of uncurrent gold, be
not cracked within the ring.[5]—Masters, you are all wel-
360 come. We'll e'en to't° like French falconers, fly at any-   *go at it*
thing we see.[6] We'll have a speech straight.° Come, give   *immediately*
us a taste of your quality.° Come, a passionate speech.   *abilities*
FIRST PLAYER What speech, my good lord?
HAMLET I heard thee speak me a speech once, but it was
365 never acted, or if it was, not above once, for the play, I
remember, pleased not the million; 'twas caviar to the
general.° But it was—as I received it, and others, whose   *common people*
judgments in such matters cried in the top of° mine—an   *superseded*
excellent play, well digested° in the scenes, set down   *shaped*
370 with as much modesty° as cunning. I remember one said   *restraint*
there were no sallets[7] in the lines to make the matter
savory, nor no matter in the phrase that might indict the

---

1. Title of a popular ballad (quoted by Hamlet
in later lines). Jephthah vowed that if he
defeated the Ammonites, he would sacrifice
the first living thing that met him on his return
home—which was his daughter (Judges
11.30–40).
2. Those who interrupt me; also, entertainments.
3. Fringed (with facial hair).
4. The boy who played female characters.

5. That is, your voice is still suitable for acting female roles. Coins that were clipped
(cracked) so deeply around the edges (to
obtain small amounts of metal) that the circle
around the monarch's head was broken were
"uncurrent" (no longer legal tender).
6. That is, undertake anything, no matter
how difficult and without much forethought.
7. Literally, salads, something mixed or
savory; that is, spicy or vulgar words.

author of affection, but called it an honest method, as
wholesome as sweet, and by very much more handsome
375   than fine.[8] One speech in't I chiefly loved: 'twas
Aeneas's talk to Dido and thereabout of it, especially
when he speaks of Priam's slaughter.[9] If it live in your
memory, begin at this line—let me see, let me see—

"The rugged° Pyrrhus, like th'Hyrcanian beast"[1]—   *savage*

380   'Tis not so. It begins with Pyrrhus—

"The rugged Pyrrhus, he whose sable° arms,   *black*
Black as his purpose, did the night resemble
When he lay couchèd° in th'ominous horse,[2]   *hidden*
Hath now this dread and black complexion° smeared   *appearance*
385   With heraldry° more dismal. Head to foot   *heraldic colors*
Now is he total gules,° horridly tricked°   *red / sketched*
With blood of fathers, mothers, daughters, sons,
Baked and impasted with° the parching° streets   *encrusted by / blazing*
That lend a tyrannous and a damnèd light
390   To their lord's murder. Roasted in wrath and fire,
And thus o'ersized[3] with coagulate gore,
With eyes like carbuncles,[4] the hellish Pyrrhus
Old grandsire Priam seeks."
So, proceed you.

395   POLONIUS   'Fore God, my lord, well spoken, with good
accent and good discretion.

FIRST PLAYER   "Anon° he finds him,   *Soon*
Striking too short at Greeks. His antique sword,
Rebellious to his arm, lies where it falls,
Repugnant° to command. Unequal matched,   *Resistant*
400   Pyrrhus at Priam drives, in rage strikes wide.
But with the whiff and wind of his fell° sword   *fierce; deadly*
Th'unnervèd° father falls. Then senseless Ilium,[5]   *unmanned*
Seeming to feel this blow, with flaming top
Stoops to his° base, and with a hideous crash   *its*
405   Takes prisoner Pyrrhus' ear. For lo, his sword,
Which was declining° on the milky° head   *descending / white*
Of reverend Priam, seemed i'th'air to stick;
So as a painted tyrant[6] Pyrrhus stood,
And, like a neutral to his will and matter,[7]
410   Did nothing.
But as we often see against° some storm   *before*

8. More graceful than ostentatious.
9. In book 2 of Virgil's *Aeneid* (19 B.C.E.), the
Trojan Aeneas tells Dido, queen of Carthage,
stories of the fall of Troy, including the death
of its king, Priam.
1. The tiger (the region of Hyrcania in the Caucasus was associated in the *Aeneid* with tigers).
Pyrrhus: the son of the Greek warrior Achilles,
who came to Troy to avenge his father's death.
2. The wooden horse within which Greek sol-

diers hid to gain entry into Troy.
3. Covered with size, a glutinous substance
used to prepare a porous surface for painting.
4. Red jewels believed to shine in the dark.
5. The citadel of Troy.
6. That is, as a tyrant in a painting, unable to
move.
7. As one indifferent to his intention and
circumstance.

A silence in the heavens, the rack° stand still,   *mass of clouds*
The bold winds speechless, and the orb° below   *sphere (earth)*
As hush as death, anon the dreadful thunder
415   Doth rend the region,° so, after Pyrrhus' pause,   *sky*
A rousèd vengeance sets him new a-work,
And never did the Cyclops'[8] hammers fall
On Mars's armor, forged for proof eterne,[9]
With less remorse° than Pyrrhus' bleeding sword   *pity*
420   Now falls on Priam.
Out, out, thou strumpet, Fortune! All you gods
In general synod,° take away her power!   *assembly*
Break all the spokes and fellies from her wheel,[1]
And bowl the round nave° down the hill of heaven,[2]   *hub*
425   As low as to the fiends!"

POLONIUS   This is too long.

HAMLET   It shall to the barber's with your beard.—Prithee,
say on. He's for a jig[3] or a tale of bawdry, or he sleeps.
Say on; come to Hecuba.[4]

430 FIRST PLAYER   "But who—ah woe!—had seen the moblèd°   *muffled*
queen"—

HAMLET   "The moblèd queen"?

POLONIUS   That's good.

FIRST PLAYER   "Run barefoot up and down, threat'ning the
435   flames
With bisson rheum,° a clout° upon that head   *blinding tears / cloth*
Where late the diadem° stood, and for a robe,   *crown*
About her lank and all o'erteemèd[5] loins,
A blanket, in the alarm of fear caught up—
440   Who this had seen, with tongue in venom steeped,
'Gainst Fortune's state° would treason have pronounced.   *rule*
But if the gods themselves did see her then,
When she saw Pyrrhus make malicious sport
In mincing with his sword her husband's limbs,
445   The instant burst of clamor that she made,
Unless things mortal move them not at all,
Would have made milch° the burning eyes of heaven,   *moist*
And passion° in the gods."   *strong emotion*

POLONIUS   Look whe'er° he has not turned his color and   *whether*
450   has tears in's eyes.—Prithee, no more.

HAMLET   'Tis well. I'll have thee speak out the rest of this
soon.—Good my lord, will you see the players well
bestowed?° Do you hear, let them be well used° for they   *lodged / treated*
are the abstract° and brief chronicles of the time.   *summary account*

8. In classical mythology, one-eyed giants who forged weapons for the gods.
9. To be eternally impenetrable. *Mars his:* Mars's (the Roman god of war).
1. The goddess Fortune is often pictured with a wheel whose turning controls human fate. *Fellies:* segments of the wheel's rim.
2. Perhaps Mount Olympus, by tradition the home of the classical gods.
3. A comic song and dance (usually performed at the end of a play).
4. The wife of Priam, queen of Troy.
5. Worn out with bearing children (more than a dozen, according to traditional accounts).

455 After your death you were better have a bad epitaph
than their ill report while you live.

POLONIUS My lord, I will use them according to their
desert.

HAMLET God's bodikins,[6] man, much better. Use every
460 man after° his desert, and who shall scape whipping?   °according to
Use them after your own honor and dignity; the less they
deserve, the more merit is in your bounty. Take them in.

POLONIUS Come, sirs.

HAMLET Follow him, friends. We'll hear a play tomorrow.

[As they start to leave, HAMLET *speaks aside to the* FIRST
PLAYER.]

465 Dost thou hear me, old friend? Can you play *The Murder
of Gonzago?*

FIRST PLAYER Ay, my lord.

HAMLET We'll ha't° tomorrow night. You could, for need,°   °have it / °if necessary
study a speech of some dozen lines, or sixteen lines,
470 which I would set down and insert in't, could you not?

FIRST PLAYER Ay, my lord.

HAMLET Very well. Follow that lord, and look you mock
him not.

Exeunt POLONIUS *and* PLAYERS.

My good friends, I'll leave you till night. You are wel-
475 come to Elsinore.

ROSENCRANTZ Good my lord.

Exeunt [ROSENCRANTZ *and* GUILDENSTERN].

HAMLET Ay, so, good-bye to you.—Now I am alone.
Oh, what a rogue and peasant slave am I!
Is it not monstrous that this player here,
480 But° in a fiction, in a dream of passion,   °Merely
Could force his soul so to his own conceit[7]
That from her° working all the visage wanned,°   °(his soul's) / °grew pale
Tears in his eyes, distraction in his aspect,
A broken voice, and his whole function° suiting   °all his gestures
485 With forms to his conceit?° And all for nothing.   °imagination
For Hecuba.
What's Hecuba to him, or he to her,
That he should weep for her? What would he do,
Had he the motive and the cue for passion
490 That I have? He would drown the stage with tears
And cleave the general ear[8] with horrid speech,
Make mad the guilty and appall the free,°   °innocent
Confound the ignorant, and amaze,° indeed,   °perplex
The very faculties of eyes and ears. Yet I,
495 A dull and muddy-mettled° rascal, peak°   °dull-spirited / °mope
Like John-a-dreams,[9] unpregnant of° my cause,   °not quickened by

---

6. By God's little body (a mild oath).   8. The ears of all who heard him.
7. That is, could conform his very being to   9. A proverbial name for a dreamy fellow.
the character he was playing.

And can say nothing—no, not for a king
Upon whose property[1] and most dear life
A damned defeat[2] was made. Am I a coward?
500 Who calls me villain, breaks my pate° across,   head
Plucks off my beard and blows it in my face,
Tweaks me by the nose, gives me the lie i'the throat
As deep as to the lungs?[3] Who does me this,
Ha? 'Swounds,° I should take it; for it cannot be   By God's wounds (an oath)
505 But I am pigeon-livered, and lack gall[4]
To make oppression bitter, or ere this
I should ha'fatted all the region kites[5]
With this slave's offal. Bloody, bawdy villain!
Remorseless, treacherous, lecherous, kindless° villain!   unnatural
510 Why, what an ass am I. This is most brave,°   splendid
That I, the son of a dear father murdered,
Prompted to my revenge by heaven and hell,
Must like a whore unpack my heart with words
And fall a-cursing like a very drab,°   whore
515 A scullion.° Fie upon't, foh!   kitchen servant
About,[6] my brains! Hum, I have heard
That guilty creatures sitting at a play
Have by the very cunning° of the scene   artfulness
Been struck so to the soul that presently°   instantly
520 They have proclaimed their malefactions;°   crimes
For murder, though it have no tongue, will speak
With most miraculous organ. I'll have these players
Play something like the murder of my father
Before mine uncle. I'll observe his looks;
525 I'll tent° him to the quick. If 'a° do blench,   probe / he
I know my course. The spirit that I have seen
May be the devil, and the devil hath power
T'assume a pleasing shape; yea, and perhaps
Out of my weakness and my melancholy,
530 As he is very potent with such spirits,[7]
Abuses° me to damn me. I'll have grounds   Tricks
More relative° than this. The play's the thing   pertinent
Wherein I'll catch the conscience of the King.   *Exit.*

3.1

Enter KING, QUEEN, POLONIUS, OPHELIA, ROSENCRANTZ,
GUILDENSTERN, LORDS.

KING   And can you, by no drift of conference,[8]
    Get from him why he puts on this confusion,

1. Crown and queen; also, Claudius's essential character qualities.
2. A destructive crime worthy of damnation.
3. Calls me an egregious liar.
4. Pigeons or doves were thought to be mild
because they did not secrete gall (believed to
cause anger).

5. All the kites (birds of prey) in the air.
6. Get going; turn about.
7. It was thought that those given to melancholy and despair were more easily manipu-
lated by the devil.
3.1 Location: The castle.
8. By no carefully directed conversation.

Grating so harshly all his days of quiet
With turbulent and dangerous lunacy?

5 ROSENCRANTZ   He does confess he feels himself distracted,
But from what cause 'a° will by no means speak.   *he*

GUILDENSTERN   Nor do we find him forward° to be   *willing*
sounded,°   *questioned*
But, with a crafty madness, keeps aloof
When we would bring him on to some confession
10   Of his true state.

QUEEN   Did he receive you well?

ROSENCRANTZ   Most like a gentleman.

GUILDENSTERN   But with much forcing of his disposition.°   *mood*

ROSENCRANTZ   Niggard of question,9 but of° our demands   *to*
Most free in his reply.

15 QUEEN   Did you assay° him to any pastime?   *try to win*

ROSENCRANTZ   Madam, it so fell out that certain players
We o'erraught° on the way. Of these we told him,   *overtook*
And there did seem in him a kind of joy
To hear of it. They are here about the court,
20   And, as I think, they have already order
This night to play before him.

POLONIUS   'Tis most true.
And he beseeched me to entreat Your Majesties
To hear and see the matter.

KING   With all my heart, and it doth much content me
25   To hear him so inclined.
Good gentlemen, give him a further edge,°   *encouragement*
And drive his purpose into these delights.

ROSENCRANTZ   We shall, my lord.

          Exeunt ROSENCRANTZ *and* GUILDENSTERN [*and* LORDS].

KING   Sweet Gertrude, leave us two,
30   For we have closely° sent for Hamlet hither,   *privately*
That he, as 'twere by accident, may here
Affront° Ophelia. Her father and myself,   *Meet*
We'll so bestow ourselves that, seeing, unseen,
We may of their encounter frankly judge,
35   And gather by him, as he is behaved,
If 't be th'affliction of his love or no
That thus he suffers for.

QUEEN   I shall obey you.
And for your part, Ophelia, I do wish
That your good beauties be the happy cause
40   Of Hamlet's wildness. So shall I hope your virtues
Will bring him to his wonted° way again,   *usual*
To both your honors.

OPHELIA   Madam, I wish it may.

                    [*Exit* QUEEN.]

POLONIUS   Ophelia, walk you here.—Gracious,° so please   *Your Grace*
you,

9. Sparing of conversation.

We will bestow ourselves.
[*To* OPHELIA, *giving a book*] Read on this book,
45 That show of such an exercise[1] may color
Your loneliness.[2] We are oft to blame in this—
'Tis too much proved°—that with devotion's visage   too often made plain
And pious action we do sugar o'er
The devil himself.
50 KING [*Aside*] Oh, 'tis too true!
How smart° a lash that speech doth give my conscience.   stinging
The harlot's cheek, beautied with plast'ring° art,   cosmetic
Is not more ugly to° the thing that helps it[3]   compared to
Than is my deed to my most painted word.
55 Oh, heavy burden!
POLONIUS   I hear him coming. Withdraw, my lord.
[*They withdraw.*]

Enter HAMLET. [OPHELIA *pretends to read.*]

HAMLET   To be or not to be—that is the question.
Whether 'tis nobler in the mind to suffer
The slings and arrows of outrageous fortune,
60 Or to take arms against a sea of troubles
And by opposing end them. To die, to sleep—
No more—and by a sleep to say we end
The heartache and the thousand natural shocks
That flesh is heir to. 'Tis a consummation°   final ending
65 Devoutly to be wished. To die, to sleep,
To sleep, perchance to dream—ay, there's the rub,[4]
For in that sleep of death what dreams may come
When we have shuffled° off this mortal coil°   cast / turmoil; flesh
Must give us pause. There's the respect°   consideration
70 That makes calamity of so long life.°   so long-lived
For who would bear the whips and scorns of time,
Th'oppressor's wrong, the proud man's contumely,°   insolent abuse
The pangs of despised love, the law's delay,
The insolence of office,[5] and the spurns°   insults
75 That patient merit of th'unworthy takes,[6]
When he himself might his quietus make[7]
With a bare bodkin?° Who would fardels° bear,   dagger / burdens
To grunt and sweat under a weary life,
But that the dread of something after death,
80 The undiscovered country, from whose bourn°   boundary
No traveler returns, puzzles° the will,   perplexes
And makes us rather bear those ills we have
Than fly to others that we know not of?
Thus conscience° does make cowards of us all,   moral judgment; knowledge

1. Act of devotion (the book is a prayer book).
2. That is, may give a credible appearance to your solitude.
3. That is, the cosmetic.
4. In the game of bowls, an obstacle that hinders or diverts a bowl from its intended course.
5. That is, of officeholders; bureaucrats.
6. That is, that the worthy have to endure patiently from the unworthy.
7. Gain his discharge—here, death. Paid-off debts were marked *quietus est,* "he is quit" (Latin).

85 And thus the native hue° of resolution   *natural (sanguine) color*
Is sicklied o'er with the pale cast° of thought,   *tinge, shade*
And enterprises of great pitch[8] and moment,°   *importance*
With this regard,° their currents° turn awry,   *respect / courses*
And lose the name of action.—Soft you now,
90 The fair Ophelia.—Nymph, in thy orisons°   *prayers*
Be all my sins remembered.

OPHELIA   Good my lord,
How does your honor for this many a day?

HAMLET   I humbly thank you; well.

OPHELIA   My lord, I have remembrances of yours
95 That I have longèd long to redeliver.
I pray you, now receive them.

HAMLET   No, not I. I never gave you aught.

OPHELIA   My honored lord, you know right well you did,
And with them words of so sweet breath composed
100 As made these things more rich. Their perfume lost,
Take these again, for to the noble mind
Rich gifts wax° poor when givers prove unkind.   *grow*
There, my lord. [*She returns gifts.*]

HAMLET   Ha, ha, are you honest?°   *chaste; truthful*
105 OPHELIA   My lord?

HAMLET   Are you fair?

OPHELIA   What means your lordship?

HAMLET   That if you be honest and fair, your honesty
should admit no discourse to° your beauty.   *conversation with*
110 OPHELIA   Could beauty, my lord, have better commerce°   *dealings*
than with honesty?

HAMLET   Ay, truly, for the power of beauty will sooner
transform honesty from what it is to a bawd than the
force of honesty can translate beauty into his° likeness.   *its*
115 This was sometime a paradox, but now the time° gives it   *the present time*
proof. I did love you once.

OPHELIA   Indeed, my lord, you made me believe so.

HAMLET   You should not have believed me; for virtue
cannot so inoculate our old stock but we shall relish of
120 it.[9] I loved you not.

OPHELIA   I was the more deceived.

HAMLET   Get thee to a nunnery.[1] Why wouldst thou be a
breeder of sinners? I am myself indifferent honest,° but   *reasonably virtuous*
yet I could accuse me of such things that it were better
125 my mother had not borne me. I am very proud, revengeful, ambitious, with more offenses at my beck° than I   *command*
have thoughts to put them in, imagination to give them
shape, or time to act them in. What should such fellows

8. That is, height (the high point of a bird's flight).
9. That is, we will always taste ("relish") our original sin because a graft of virtue, no matter how strong in us, is unable to overcome it (a metaphor from horticulture).
1. A convent (requiring Ophelia to take a vow of chastity); also, in slang, a brothel.

as I do crawling between earth and heaven? We are
130 arrant° knaves; believe none of us. Go thy ways to a　　　　　*out-and-out*
nunnery. Where's your father?

OPHELIA　At home, my lord.

HAMLET　Let the doors be shut upon him that he may play
the fool nowhere but in's own house. Farewell.

135 OPHELIA　Oh, help him, you sweet heavens!

HAMLET　If thou dost marry, I'll give thee this plague for
thy dowry: be thou as chaste as ice, as pure as snow,
thou shalt not escape calumny.° Get thee to a nunnery,　　　*slander*
farewell. Or if thou wilt needs marry, marry a fool, for
140 wise men know well enough what monsters[2] you° make of　　*you women*
them. To a nunnery, go, and quickly too. Farewell.

OPHELIA　Heavenly powers, restore him!

HAMLET　I have heard of your paintings well enough. God
hath given you one face, and you make yourselves another.
145 You jig and amble, and you lisp,° you nickname God's　　　*speak affectedly*
creatures[3] and make your wantonness ignorance.[4] Go
to, I'll no more on't;° it hath made me mad. I say we will　　　*of it*
have no more marriage. Those that are married already—
all but one—shall live. The rest shall keep as they are. To
150 a nunnery, go!　　　　　　　　　　　　　　　*Exit.*

OPHELIA　Oh, what a noble mind is here o'erthrown!
The courtier's, soldier's, scholar's, eye, tongue, sword,
Th'expectation and rose of the fair state,
The glass° of fashion and the mold of form,[5]　　　　　*mirror image*
155 Th'observed of all observers—quite, quite down!
And I, of ladies most deject and wretched,
That sucked the honey of his music vows,
Now see that noble and most sovereign reason
Like sweet bells jangled out of time and harsh,
160 That unmatched form and stature of blown° youth　　　　*in full bloom*
Blasted° with ecstasy.° Oh, woe is me,　　　　*Blighted / madness*
T'have seen what I have seen, see what I see!

　　　Enter KING *and* POLONIUS.

KING　Love—his affections° do not that way tend;　　　　*feelings*
Nor what he spake, though it lacked form a little,
165 Was not like madness. There's something in his soul
O'er which his melancholy sits on brood,
And I do doubt° the hatch and the disclose°　　　　*fear / disclosure*
Will be some danger; which for to prevent,
I have in quick determination
170 Thus set it down:° he shall with speed to England　　　*determined it*
For the demand of our neglected tribute.[6]
Haply the seas and countries different

---

2. Cuckolds, who were said to grow horns on
their forehead.
3. That is, as if the true names of God's creatures are not good enough.
4. Excuse your illicit and seductive behavior

as ignorance.
5. The pattern of courtly decorum.
6. Between 886 and 1066, considerable parts
of England were under Danish control.

With variable objects[7] shall expel
This something settled° matter in his heart,   *somewhat established*
175 Whereon his brains still° beating puts him thus   *always*
From fashion of himself.[8] What think you on't?

POLONIUS   It shall do well. But yet do I believe
The origin and commencement of his grief
Sprung from neglected° love.—How now, Ophelia?   *unrequited*
180 You need not tell us what Lord Hamlet said;
We heard it all.—My lord, do as you please,
But if you hold it fit, after the play
Let his queen-mother all alone entreat him
To show his grief. Let her be round° with him;   *frank*
185 And I'll vbe placed, so please you, in the ear°   *within earshot*
Of all their conference. If she find him not,[9]
To England send him, or confine him where
Your wisdom best shall think.

KING   It shall be so.
Madness in great ones° must not unwatched go.   *those of high rank*

                                      Exeunt.

3.2

Enter HAMLET *and three of the* PLAYERS.

HAMLET   Speak the speech, I pray you, as I pronounced it
to you, trippingly on the tongue. But if you mouth it[1] as
many of our players do, I had as lief° the town crier spoke   *soon*
my lines. Nor do not saw the air too much with your
5 hand, thus, but use all gently, for in the very torrent, tempest, and, as I may say, whirlwind of your passion, you
must acquire and beget a temperance that may give it
smoothness. Oh, it offends me to the soul to hear a robus-
tious° periwig-pated° fellow tear a passion to tatters,   *bombastic / wig-wearing*
10 to very rags, to split the ears of the ground lings,[2] who for
the most part are capable of° nothing but inexplicable   *able to understand*
dumb shows[3] and noise. I would have such a fellow
whipped for o'erdoing Termagant. It out-Herods Herod;[4]
pray you, avoid it.

15 PLAYER   I warrant your honor.[5]

HAMLET   Be not too tame neither, but let your own discretion be your tutor. Suit the action to the word, the word
to the action, with this special observance, that you
o'erstep not the modesty° of nature. For anything so   *moderation*
20 o'erdone is from° the purpose of playing, whose end,   *contrary to*

---

7. With various (new) objects of interest.
8. Puts him out of his normal conduct.
9. If she fails to uncover the truth.
3.2 Location: The castle.
1. If you speak in a pompously oratorical style.
2. Those who paid the least to see plays; they
stood in the yard of the theater (in front of the
stage).

3. Pantomime episodes that perform the plot
of the next scene.
4. The Herod of the New Testament was portrayed in medieval mystery plays as a raging
tyrant. *Termagant:* an imaginary deity, presented in mystery plays as a violent and raging character worshipped by Muslims.
5. I promise your lordship (that we will avoid it).

both at the first and now, was and is to hold, as 'twere, the mirror up to nature, to show virtue her feature, scorn her own image, and the very age and body of the time his form and pressure.[6] Now this overdone or come tardy
25   off,° though it makes the unskillful° laugh, cannot but   *done poorly / ignorant*
make the judicious grieve—the censure of which one[7] must in your allowance o'erweigh a whole theater of others. Oh, there be players that I have seen play and heard others praise—and that highly—not to speak it profanely, that,
30   neither having th'accent of Christians, nor the gait of Christian, pagan, nor man, have so strutted and bel-lowed that I have thought some of Nature's journeymen[8] had made men, and not made them well, they imitated humanity so abominably.
35 PLAYER   I hope we have reformed that indifferently° with us.   *tolerably*
HAMLET   Oh, reform it altogether. And let those that play your clowns speak no more than is set down for them, for there be of° them that will themselves laugh to set   *some of*
on° some quantity of barren° spectators to laugh too,   *provoke / witless*
40   though in the meantime some necessary question of the play be then to be considered. That's villainous, and shows a most pitiful ambition in the fool that uses it. Go make you ready.

[*Exeunt* PLAYERS.]

Enter POLONIUS, GUILDENSTERN, *and* ROSENCRANTZ.

How now, my lord, will the King hear this piece of work?
45 POLONIUS   And the Queen too, and that presently.°   *immediately*
HAMLET   Bid the players make haste.

[*Exit* POLONIUS.]

Will you two help to hasten them?
ROSENCRANTZ   Ay, my lord.

Exeunt they two.

HAMLET   What, ho, Horatio!
Enter HORATIO.
50 HORATIO   Here, sweet lord, at your service.
HAMLET   Horatio, thou art e'en as just a man
As e'er my conversation coped withal.[9]
HORATIO   Oh, my dear lord—
HAMLET   Nay, do not think I flatter,
For what advancement may I hope from thee,
55   That no revenue hast but thy good spirits
To feed and clothe thee? Why should the poor be
    flattered?
No, let the candied° tongue lick absurd pomp,   *flattering*

6. That is, a play shows the imprint of the truth of the present time in the same way that a stamp imprints itself on wax.
7. The judgment of even one of them (the judicious).
8. Hirelings, not yet masters of their trade.
9. As ever I encountered in my dealings ("conversation") with people.

And crook the pregnant° hinges of the knee   *ready (to bend)*
Where thrift may follow fawning.[1] Dost thou hear?
60   Since my dear soul was mistress of her choice[2]
And could of° men distinguish her election,   *between*
Sh'hath sealed° thee for herself, for thou hast been   *set a mark on; claimed*
As one, in suffering all, that° suffers nothing,   *who*
A man that Fortune's buffets and rewards
65   Hast ta'en with equal thanks; and blest are those
Whose blood° and judgment are so well commeddled°   *passions / commingled*
That they are not a pipe for Fortune's finger
To sound what stop[3] she please. Give me that man
That is not passion's slave, and I will wear him
70   In my heart's core, ay, in my heart of heart,
As I do thee.—Something too much of this.—
There is a play tonight before the King.
One scene of it comes near the circumstance
Which I have told thee of my father's death.
75   I prithee, when thou seest that act afoot,
Even with the very comment of thy soul[4]
Observe my uncle. If his occulted° guilt   *hidden*
Do not itself unkennel[5] in one speech,
It is a damnèd ghost that we have seen,
80   And my imaginations are as foul
As Vulcan's stithy.[6] Give him heedful note,
For I mine eyes will rivet to his face,
And after we will both our judgments join
In censure of his seeming.[7]
85 HORATIO   Well, my lord.
If 'a steal aught the whilst this play is playing
And scape detecting, I will pay the theft.[8]

    [*Flourish.*] *Enter trumpets and kettledrums,* KING,
    QUEEN,POLONIUS, OPHELIA[, ROSENCRANTZ, GUILDEN-
    STERN, *and others*].

HAMLET   They are coming to the play. I must be idle.° Get   *unoccupied; incoherent*
you a place.
90 KING   How fares[9] our cousin° Hamlet?   *kinsman*
HAMLET   Excellent, i'faith, of the chameleon's dish: I eat
the air,[1] promise-crammed. You cannot feed capons[2] so.
KING   I have nothing with this answer, Hamlet. These
words are not mine.

---

1. Where profit may result from flattery.
2. Was able to discriminate.
3. Finger hole in a wind instrument.
4. With your most acute critical faculty.
5. That is, reveal (as a fox is driven from its hole).
6. Blacksmith's shop. Vulcan was the Roman god of fire and metalworking.
7. To judge his appearance or reaction.
8. That is, make restitution for the stolen goods.
9. Does. *Fare* also means "food" or "to feed," a meaning on which Hamlet plays in his response.
1. Chameleons were believed to feed on air.
2. Castrated roosters, fattened or "crammed" for eating; also, dull men. *Promise-crammed*: possibly a reference to Claudius's promise that Hamlet will succeed to the throne, perhaps with a play on "air" / "heir."

95 HAMLET No, nor mine now, my lord. [*To* POLONIUS] You
     played once i'th'university, you say?

POLONIUS That did I, my lord, and was accounted a good
     actor.

HAMLET What did you enact?

100 POLONIUS I did enact Julius Caesar. I was killed i'the
     Capitol; Brutus killed me.

HAMLET It was a brute part of him to kill so capital a calf°   fool
     there.—Be the players ready?

ROSENCRANTZ Ay, my lord. They stay° upon your patience.   wait

105 QUEEN Come hither, my dear Hamlet, sit by me.

HAMLET [*Approaching* OPHELIA] No, good mother,° here's   stepmother
     metal more attractive.[3]

POLONIUS [*To the* KING] Oho, do you mark that?

HAMLET Lady, shall I lie in your lap?

110 OPHELIA No, my lord.

HAMLET Do you think I meant country matters?[4]

OPHELIA I think nothing, my lord.

HAMLET That's a fair thought to lie between maids' legs.

OPHELIA What is, my lord?

115 HAMLET Nothing.

OPHELIA You are merry, my lord.

HAMLET Who, I?

OPHELIA Ay, my lord.

HAMLET O God, your only jig-maker.[5] What should a man
120 do but be merry? For look you how cheerfully my mother
     looks, and my father died within's° two hours.   within this

OPHELIA Nay, 'tis twice two months, my lord.

HAMLET So long? Nay then, let the devil wear black, for
     I'll have a suit of sables.[6] O heavens, die two months
125 ago, and not forgotten yet? Then there's hope a great
     man's memory may outlive his life half a year. But, by'r
     Lady, 'a° must build churches then or else shall 'a suffer   he
     not thinking on,[7] withthe hobby-horse,[8] whose epitaph
     is "For O, for O, the hobby-horse is forgot."

          The trumpets sound. Dumb show follows.

          Enter a KING *and a* QUEEN, *the* QUEEN *embracing him
          and he her. He takes her up, and declines his head upon
          her neck. He lies him down upon a bank of flowers. She,
          seeing him asleep, leaves him. Anon comes in another
          man, takes off his crown, kisses it, pours poison in the
          sleeper's ears, and leaves him. The* QUEEN *returns, finds*

3. Metal (also "temperament") with greater
magnetic powers.
4. Vulgar doings (with a pun on "cunt").The
sexual puns continue with "nothing" (vagina)
and "thing" (penis).
5. The performer or creator of a farcical song
and dance, frequently performed right after
the end of a play. *Only:* peerless, best.
6. A suit trimmed with (black) sable fur (not

an appropriate garment for a mourner).
7. Endure not being thought of.
8. The performer in morris dances and May
Day festivities who wore the figure of a horse
(also called a hobbyhorse) around his waist.
The "epitaph" for the hobbyhorse—which
disapproving Puritans sought to ban—is probably a line from a song.

the KING *dead, makes passionate action. The* POISONER
*with some three or four come in again, seem to condole
with her. The dead body is carried away. The* POISONER
woos the QUEEN *with gifts; she seems harsh awhile, but in
the end accepts love.*

[*Exeunt* PLAYERS.]

130 OPHELIA   What means this, my lord?

HAMLET   Marry, this is mitching malicho;⁹ it means
mischief.

OPHELIA   Belike this show imports the argument° of the   *plot*
play.

Enter PROLOGUE.

135 HAMLET   We shall know by this fellow. The players can-
not keep counsel;° they'll tell all.   *a secret*

OPHELIA   Will 'a° tell us what this show meant?   *he*

HAMLET   Ay, or any show that you will show him. Be not you
ashamed to show, he'll not shame to tell you what it means.

140 OPHELIA   You are naught,° you are naught. I'll mark the   *indecent*
play.

PROLOGUE   For us and for our tragedy,
Here stooping to your clemency,
We beg your hearing patiently.   [*Exit.*]

145 HAMLET   Is this a prologue or the posy of a ring?¹

OPHELIA   'Tis brief, my lord.

HAMLET   As woman's love.

Enter [*two players as*] KING *and* QUEEN.

PLAYER KING   Full thirty times hath Phoebus' cart² gone
round

Neptune's salt wash and Tellus' orbèd ground,³

150 And thirty dozen moons with borrowed° sheen   *reflected*
About the world have times twelve thirties been,
Since love our hearts and Hymen° did our hands   *god of marriage*
Unite commutual in most sacred bands.

PLAYER QUEEN   So many journeys may the sun and moon

155 Make us again count o'er ere love be done.
But, woe is me, you are so sick of late,
So far from cheer and from our former state,
That I distrust° you. Yet, though I distrust,   *am worried about*
Discomfort° you, my lord, it nothing must,   *Disturb*

160 For women fear too much, even as they love,
And women's fear and love hold quantity,°   *are of equal proportion*
Either none, in neither aught, or in extremity.⁴
Now what my love is, proof° hath made you know,   *experience*
And as my love is sized,° my fear is so.   *proportioned*

165 Where love is great, the littlest doubts are fear;
Where little fears grow great, great love grows there.

---

9. Sneaking misdeed ("*malicho*" is Spanish).
1. The motto inscribed in a ring.
2. The chariot of the sun god Apollo (i.e., the sun).

3. Tellus is the Roman goddess of the earth
("orbè ground"); Neptune is the Roman god
of the sea.
4. Either not existing at all or extremely strong.

PLAYER KING   Faith, I must leave thee, love, and shortly too;

My operant° powers their functions leave° to do,   *active / cease*

And thou shalt live in this fair world behind,

170   Honored, beloved; and haply° one as kind   *perhaps*

For husband shalt thou—

PLAYER QUEEN   Oh, confound° the rest!   *bring to nought*

Such love must needs be treason in my breast.

In second husband let me be accurst!

None wed the second but who killed the first.

175 HAMLET   That's wormwood.[5]

PLAYER QUEEN   The instances° that second marriage move°   *reasons / motivate*

Are base respects of thrift,° but none of love.   *desires for profit*

A second time I kill my husband dead

When second husband kisses me in bed.

180 PLAYER KING   I do believe you think what now you speak,

But what we do determine oft we break.

Purpose is but the slave to memory,[6]

Of violent birth, but poor validity,°   *durability*

Which now, like fruit unripe, sticks on the tree,

185   But fall unshaken when they mellow be.

Most necessary 'tis that we forget

To pay ourselves what to ourselves is debt.[7]

What to ourselves in passion we propose,

The passion ending, doth the purpose lose.

190   The violence of either grief or joy

Their own enactures with themselves destroy.[8]

Where joy most revels, grief doth most lament,

Grief joys, joy grieves, on slender accident.[9]

This world is not for aye, nor 'tis not strange

195   That even our loves should with our fortunes change;

For 'tis a question left us yet to prove

Whether love lead fortune or else fortune love.

The great man down, you mark his favorite flies;

The poor, advanced,° makes friends of enemies;   *promoted*

200   And hitherto° doth love on fortune tend,°   *thus for / attend*

For who not needs shall never lack a friend,

And who in want a hollow friend doth try,°   *test*

Directly seasons him° his enemy.   *trains him (to be)*

But, orderly to end where I begun,

205   Our wills and fates do so contrary run

That our devices still° are overthrown;   *our plans always*

Our thoughts are ours, their ends° none of our own.   *outcomes*

So think thou wilt no second husband wed,

But die thy thoughts when thy first lord is dead.

210 PLAYER QUEEN   Nor earth to me give food, nor heaven light,

Sport and repose lock from me day and night,

---

5. A proverbially bitter-tasting plant whose oil was used in medicine.

6. That is, (carrying out) an intention depends on memory.

7. That is, it is natural that we forget the promises that we made to ourselves.

8. Extreme grief or joy destroy themselves in their fulfillment.

9. Because of a small, unanticipated event.

To desperation turn my trust and hope,
And anchor's cheer in prison be my scope,[1]
Each opposite[2] that blanks° the face of joy   *makes pale*
215 Meet what I would have well, and it destroy,
Both here and hence pursue me lasting strife,
If, once I be a widow, ever I be a wife.

HAMLET   If she should break it° now—   *her oath*

PLAYER KING   'Tis deeply sworn. Sweet, leave me here awhile.
220 My spirits grow dull, and fain° I would beguile   *gladly*
The tedious day with sleep.

PLAYER QUEEN   Sleep rock thy brain,
And never come mischance between us twain.

                [He sleeps.] Exit [PLAYER QUEEN].

HAMLET   Madam, how like you this play?

QUEEN   The lady doth protest too much, methinks.
225 HAMLET   Oh, but she'll keep her word.

KING   Have you heard the argument?° Is there no offense   *plot*
    in't?

HAMLET   No, no, they do but jest, poison in jest; no offense
    i'the world.
230 KING   What do you call the play?

HAMLET   *The Mousetrap.* Marry, how? Tropically.[3] This play
    is the image of a murder done in Vienna. Gonzago is the
    Duke's name, his wife, Baptista. You shall see anon. 'Tis a
    knavish piece of work, but what of that? Your Majesty
235   and we that have free° souls, it touches° us not. Let   *innocent / concerns*
    the galled jade winch, our withers are unwrung.[4]

        Enter LUCIANUS.

    This is one Lucianus, nephew to the King.

OPHELIA   You are as good as a chorus,[5] my lord.

HAMLET   I could interpret between you and your love, if I
240   could see the puppets dallying.[6]

OPHELIA   You are keen,° my lord, you are keen.   *sharp-witted*

HAMLET   It would cost you a groaning to take off mine edge.[7]

OPHELIA   Still better, and worse.[8]

HAMLET   So you mis-take your husbands.[9]—Begin, mur-
245   derer. Leave thy damnable faces[1] and begin. Come, "the
    croaking raven doth bellow for revenge."[2]

---

1. The extent of my happiness. *Anchor's cheer:* a hermit's (anchorite's) fare.
2. Each adverse event.
3. Figuratively (i.e., as a trope).
4. Let the inferior horse ("jade") whose hide is sore from chafing wince, our shoulders (literally, the portion of the horse's back between the shoulder blades) are not rubbed sore ("unwrung").
5. A character (named "Chorus") who describes or interprets the action of the play (see Shakespeare's *Henry V* and *Romeo and Juliet*).
6. Flirting. In a puppet show, the actor who

narrates the dialogue was known as the "interpreter."
7. To satisfy my sexual desire (Hamlet puns on "keen" as "sexually aroused") leading to "groaning" in sexual intercourse, childbirth, or both.
8. More sharp-witted and less well-mannered.
9. So you take husbands under false pretenses ("for better and for worse") and subsequently betray them.
1. Facial expressions.
2. Misquoted from the anonymous *The True Tragedy of Richard III* (ca. 1591).

LUCIANUS   Thoughts black, hands apt, drugs fit, and time
    agreeing,
    Confederate° season, else no creature seeing,   *Conniving*
    Thou mixture rank° of midnight weeds collected,   *foul*
250 With Hecate's ban³ thrice blasted, thrice infected,
    Thy natural magic and dire property°   *quality*
    On wholesome life usurps immediately.

        [*He pours the poison into the* SLEEPER'*s ear.*]

HAMLET   'A° poisons him i'the garden for his estate.° His   *He* / *state, kingdom*
    name's Gonzago. The story is extant and written in very
255 choice Italian; you shall see anon how the murderer gets
    the love of Gonzago's wife.

        [CLAUDIUS *stands.*]

OPHELIA   The King rises.
QUEEN   How fares my lord?
POLONIUS   Give o'er° the play.   *Stop*
260 KING   Give me some light. Away!
POLONIUS   Lights, lights, lights!

         Exeunt all but HAMLET *and* HORATIO.

HAMLET   "Why, let the strucken deer go weep,⁴
      The hart ungallèd° play;   *unwounded*
    For some must watch,° while some must sleep,   *stay awake*
265   Thus runs the world away."⁵
    Would not this, sir, and a forest of feathers⁶—if the rest of
    my fortunes turn Turk⁷ with me—with Provincial roses on
    my razed shoes,⁸ get me a fellowship in a cry of players?⁹
HORATIO   Half a share.
270 HAMLET   A whole one, ay.
    "For thou dost know, O Damon¹ dear,
      This realm dismantled° was   *stripped*
    Of Jove² himself, and now reigns here
      A very, very—pajock."³
275 HORATIO   You might have rhymed.
HAMLET   O good Horatio, I'll take the ghost's word for a
    thousand pound. Didst perceive?
HORATIO   Very well, my lord.
HAMLET   Upon the talk of the poisoning?
280 HORATIO   I did very well note him.
HAMLET   Aha! Come, some music, come, the recorders!
    "For if the King like not the comedy,

---

3. Curse of Hecate, Greek goddess of child-birth and later witchcraft.
4. A deer was thought to weep when mortally hurt. Lines 262–65 are probably from a lost ballad.
5. That's the way things go (in the world).
6. Plumes, often worn by Elizabethan actors onstage. *This:* the play just performed.
7. Become a renegade (literally, convert to Islam).
8. Shoes with decorative slashes. *Provincial*

roses: rosettes of ribbon (resembling French roses).
9. Part ownership in a theatrical company (literally, a pack of players).
1. A figure in Greek mythology, legendary for his friendship with Pythias.
2. Jupiter, the king of the Roman gods.
3. Peacock (here used as a term of contempt). "Pajock" appears in the place of the expected rhyme word, "ass."

Why then, belike, he likes it not, perdy."° *by God; indeed*
Come, some music!

Enter ROSENCRANTZ *and* GUILDENSTERN.

285 GUILDENSTERN   Good my lord, vouchsafe me a word with
you.

HAMLET   Sir, a whole history.

GUILDENSTERN   The King, sir—

HAMLET   Ay, sir, what of him?

290 GUILDENSTERN   Is in his retirement° marvelous distem- *withdrawal*
pered.

HAMLET   With drink, sir?

GUILDENSTERN   No, my lord, with choler.[4]

HAMLET   Your wisdom should show itself more richer° to sig- *of greater value*
295 nify this to the doctor, for for me to put him to his purgation[5] would perhaps plunge him into more choler.

GUILDENSTERN   Good my lord, put your discourse into some
frame,° and start° not so wildly from my affair. *order / leap away*

HAMLET   I am tame, sir. Pronounce.

300 GUILDENSTERN   The Queen, your mother, in most great
affliction of spirit, hath sent me to you.

HAMLET   You are welcome.

GUILDENSTERN   Nay, good my lord, this courtesy is not of
the right breed.° If it shall please you to make me a whole- *kind*
305 some° answer, I will do your mother's commandment; if *sane; beneficial*
not, your pardon° and my return shall be the end of *permission to depart*
business.

HAMLET   Sir, I cannot.

ROSENCRANTZ   What, my lord?

310 HAMLET   Make you a wholesome answer; my wit's diseased. But, sir, such answer as I can make, you shall
command, or rather, as you say, my mother. Therefore
no more, but to the matter: my mother, you say—

ROSENCRANTZ   Then thus she says: your behavior hath
315 struck her into amazement and admiration.° *astonishment*

HAMLET   Oh, wonderful son that can so stonish° a mother! *astonish*
But is there no sequel at the heels of this mother's admiration? Impart.

ROSENCRANTZ   She desires to speak with you in her closet° *private chamber*
320 ere you go to bed.

HAMLET   We shall obey were she ten times our mother.
Have you any further trade with us?

ROSENCRANTZ   My lord, you once did love me.

HAMLET   And do still, by these pickers and stealers.[6]

325 ROSENCRANTZ   Good my lord, what is your cause of distemper? You do surely bar the door upon your own liberty if you deny your griefs to your friend.

---

4. Anger; also, a bilious disorder requiring the
attentions of a physician (the meaning to
which Hamlet responds).
5. Bloodletting; spiritual purging.

6. Hands. (The catechism in the Book of
Common Prayer contains the promise "to
keep my hands from picking and stealing.")

HAMLET   Sir, I lack advancement.

ROSENCRANTZ   How can that be, when you have the voice
330   of the King himself for your succession in Denmark?

HAMLET   Ay, sir, but "While the grass grows"[7]—the prov-
erb is something° musty.   *somewhat*

    Enter the PLAYERS *with recorders.*

Oh, the recorders. Let me see one. [*He takes a recorder.*]
To withdraw° with you, why do you go about to recover   *speak privately*
335   the wind[8] of me, as if you would drive me into a toil?°   *trap*

GUILDENSTERN   O my lord, if my duty be too bold, my love
is too unmannerly.[9]

HAMLET   I do not well understand that. Will you play
upon this pipe?°   *(the recorder)*
340   GUILDENSTERN   My lord, I cannot.

HAMLET   I pray you.

GUILDENSTERN   Believe me, I cannot.

HAMLET   I do beseech you.

GUILDENSTERN   I know no touch of it, my lord.

345   HAMLET   It is as easy as lying: govern these ventages° with   *finger holes*
your fingers and thumb, give it breath with your mouth,
and it will discourse most eloquent music. Look you,
these are the stops.

GUILDENSTERN   But these cannot I command to any
350   utt'rance of harmony; I have not the skill.

HAMLET   Why, look you now how unworthy a thing you
make of me. You would play upon me, you would seem
to know my stops, you would pluck out the heart of my
mystery. You would sound me[1] from my lowest note to
355   my compass,° and there is much music, excellent voice,   *range (of musical pitch)*
in this little organ,° yet cannot you make it speak.   *musical instrument*
'Sblood, do you think I am easier to be played on than a
pipe? Call me what instrument you will, though you fret[2]
me, you cannot play upon me.

    Enter POLONIUS.

360   God bless you, sir.

POLONIUS   My lord, the Queen would speak with you, and
presently.°   *immediately*

HAMLET   Do you see yonder cloud that's almost in shape
of a camel?

365   POLONIUS   By the mass, and 'tis like a camel indeed.

HAMLET   Methinks it is like a weasel.

POLONIUS   It is backed like a weasel.

HAMLET   Or like a whale.

POLONIUS   Very like a whale.

---

7. "While the grass grows, the horse starves."
Hamlet means that he may not live long
enough to gain the crown of Denmark.
8. Move to the leeward side.
9. That is, if I am too presumptuous (with

you) it is only because of my love (for you).
1. Ascertain my depth; play on me.
2. Vex. Also, to furnish with frets, the bars on
the fingerboard of stringed instruments that
regulate the fingering.

370 HAMLET   Then I will come to my mother by and by.° [*Aside*]   *right away*
They fool me to the top of my bent.³—I will come by and
by. Leave me, friends. I will. Say so. "By and by" is easily
said.

[*Exeunt all but* HAMLET.]

'Tis now the very witching time of night,
375   When churchyards yawn, and hell itself breathes out
Contagion to this world. Now could I drink hot blood,
And do such business as the bitter day
Would quake to look on. Soft, now to my mother.
O heart, lose not thy nature!° Let not ever   *natural affection*
380   The soul of Nero⁴ enter this firm° bosom.   *resolute*
Let me be cruel, not unnatural.
I will speak daggers to her but use none.
My tongue and soul in this be hypocrites,⁵
How in my words soever she be shent,⁶
385   To give them seals⁷ never my soul consent.   *Exit.*

3.3

Enter KING, ROSENCRANTZ, *and* GUILDENSTERN.

KING   I like him not, nor stands it safe with us
To let his madness range. Therefore prepare you.
I your commission will forthwith dispatch,°   *prepare*
And he to England shall along with you.
5   The terms of our estate° may not endure   *My position as king*
Hazard so near's as doth hourly grow
Out of his brows.
GUILDENSTERN   We will ourselves provide.°   *make ready*
Most holy and religious fear° it is   *care*
To keep those many many bodies safe
10   That live and feed upon Your Majesty.
ROSENCRANTZ   The single and peculiar° life is bound   *individual and private*
With all the strength and armor of the mind
To keep itself from noyance°, but much more   *harm*
That spirit upon whose weal° depends and rests   *well-being*
15   The lives of many. The cess° of majesty   *decease*
Dies not alone, but like a gulf° doth draw   *whirlpool*
What's near it with it; or it is a massy° wheel⁸   *massive*
Fixed on the summit of the highest mount,
To whose huge spokes ten thousand lesser things
20   Are mortised° and adjoined, which,° when it falls,   *attached / so that*
Each small annexment, petty consequence,
Attends° the boist'rous ruin. Never alone   *Accompanies*

---

3. They make me play the madman to the
limits of my skill.
4. The Roman emperor Nero (r. 54–68 C.E.)
murdered his mother, Agrippina.
5. That is, let my words and appearance mis-
leadingly suggest that I mean to do her

violence.
6. However my words put her to shame.
7. To validate them with actions.
3.3 Location: The castle.
8. That is, Fortune's wheel (usually depicted
with the king at its top).

Did the king sigh, but with a general groan.

KING   Arm you,° I pray you, to this speedy voyage,   *Prepare yourself*
25   For we will fetters put about this fear
    Which now goes too free-footed.

ROSENCRANTZ   We will haste us.

Exeunt GENTLEMEN [ROSENCRANTZ *and*
GUILDENSTERN].

Enter POLONIUS.

POLONIUS   My lord, he's going to his mother's closet.
    Behind the arras° I'll convey myself   *wall tapestry*
    To hear the process;° I'll warrant she'll tax him home.[9]   *proceedings*
30   And, as you said, and wisely was it said,
    'Tis meet° that some more audience than a mother,   *proper*
    Since nature makes them partial, should o'erhear
    The speech, of vantage.[1] Fare you well, my liege.
    I'll call upon you ere you go to bed
    And tell you what I know.
35   KING   Thanks, dear my lord.

Exit [POLONIUS].

    Oh, my offense is rank, it smells to heaven;
    It hath the primal eldest curse[2] upon't,
    A brother's murder. Pray can I not,
    Though inclination be as sharp as will;[3]
40   My stronger guilt defeats my strong intent,
    And like a man to double business bound[4]
    I stand in pause where I shall first begin,
    And both neglect. What if this cursèd hand
    Were thicker than itself with brother's blood?[5]
45   Is there not rain enough in the sweet heavens
    To wash it white as snow? Whereto serves mercy
    But to confront the visage of offense?[6]
    And what's in prayer but this twofold force,
    To be forestallèd° ere we come to fall,   *prevented (from sinning)*
50   Or pardoned being down? Then I'll look up.
    My fault is past. But, oh, what form of prayer
    Can serve my turn? "Forgive me my foul murder"?
    That cannot be since I am still possessed
    Of those effects for which I did the murder—
55   My crown, mine own ambition, and my queen.
    May one be pardoned and retain th'offense?
    In the corrupted currents of this world
    Offense's gilded° hand may shove by justice,   *bribing*
    And oft 'tis seen the wicked prize[7] itself

9. Scold him sternly.
1. To (our) profit or benefit.
2. The curse God put on Cain for committing the first murder, of his brother, Abel (Genesis 4.11–12).
3. Though my desire is as strong as my resolve.

4. That is, committed to divergent goals.
5. What if this hand had on it a layer of blood thicker than the hand itself.
6. That is, what function does mercy have other than to confront sin face-to-face?
7. The fruits of wickedness.

60 Buys out the law; but 'tis not so above.
   There is no shuffling,° there the action lies   *evasive conduct*
   In his° true nature,[8] and we ourselves compelled,   *its*
   Even to the teeth and forehead of° our faults,   *face-to-face with*
   To give in evidence.[9] What then? What rests?°   *remains*
65 Try what repentance can. What can it not?
   Yet what can it when one cannot repent?
   Oh, wretched state, oh, bosom black as death!
   Oh, limèd[1] soul that, struggling to be free,
   Art more engaged!° Help, angels, make assay.°   *restricted / an attempt*
70 Bow, stubborn knees, and heart with strings of steel,
   Be soft as sinews of the new-born babe.
   All may be well. [*He kneels.*]

     Enter HAMLET.

HAMLET   Now might I do it. But now 'a° is a-praying.   *he*
   And now I'll do't. [*He draws his sword.*]
         And so 'a goes to heaven,
75 And so am I revenged. That would be scanned:[2]
   A villain kills my father and for that,
   I, his sole son, do this same villain send
   To heaven.
   Why, this is hire and salary, not revenge.
80 'A took my father grossly, full of bread,[3]
   With all his crimes broad blown,[4] as flush as May,
   And how his audit stands who knows save heaven?
   But in our circumstance and course of thought,[5]
   'Tis heavy with him. And am I then revenged,
85 To take him in the purging of his soul,
   When he is fit and seasoned° for his passage?   *suitably prepared*
   No.
   Up, sword, and know thou a more horrid hent.°   *occasion*
     [*He sheathes his sword.*]
   When he is drunk asleep, or in his rage,
90 Or in th'incestuous pleasure of his bed,
   At game a-swearing, or about some act
   That has no relish° of salvation in't—   *tinge*
   Then trip him that his heels may kick at heaven,
   And that his soul may be as damned and black
95 As hell, whereto it goes. My mother stays.°   *awaits*
   This physic[6] but prolongs thy sickly days.   *Exit.*
KING   My words fly up, my thoughts remain below.
   Words without thoughts never to heaven go.   *Exit.*

---

8. The deed (literally, the legal proceeding) is truly revealed.
9. To testify. Unlike in an English court, in heaven one is compelled to give evidence against oneself.
1. Caught as with birdlime, a sticky substance used for snaring birds.
2. That needs to be examined.
3. In full enjoyment of worldly pleasures.

"Behold, this was the iniquity of thy sister Sodom, pride, fullness of bread, and abundance of idleness was in her and in her daughters" (Ezekiel 16.49).
4. With all his sins in full bloom.
5. That is, in the context of our limited understanding here on earth.
6. Medicine (i.e., both Hamlet's delay in revenging and Claudius's prayer).

3.4

Enter [QUEEN] GERTRUDE *and* POLONIUS.

POLONIUS 'A° will come straight.° Look you lay home to   *He / right away*
  him.[7]
  Tell him his pranks have been too broad° to bear with,   *unrestrained; indecent*
  And that Your Grace hath screened and stood between
  Much heat° and him. I'll silence me even here.   *anger*
  Pray you, be round.°   *blunt*
5 QUEEN   I'll warrant you. Fear° me not.   *Doubt*
  Withdraw, I hear him coming.
                    [POLONIUS *hides behind the arras.*]

  Enter HAMLET.

HAMLET   Now, Mother, what's the matter?
QUEEN   Hamlet, thou hast thy father° much offended.   *(stepfather, Claudius)*
HAMLET   Mother, you have my father° much offended.   *(old Hamlet)*
10 QUEEN   Come, come, you answer with an idle° tongue.   *foolish*
HAMLET   Go, go, you question with a wicked tongue.
QUEEN   Why, how now,° Hamlet?   *what's this*
HAMLET   What's the matter now?
QUEEN   Have you forgot me?[8]
HAMLET   No, by the rood,° not so.   *cross (of Christ)*
  You are the Queen, your husband's brother's wife,
15 And, would it were not so, you are my mother.
QUEEN   Nay, then, I'll set those to you that can speak.[9]
HAMLET   Come, come, and sit you down; you shall not
  budge.
  You go not till I set you up a glass°   *mirror*
  Where you may see the inmost part of you.
20 QUEEN   What wilt thou do? Thou wilt not murder me?
  Help, ho!
POLONIUS [*Behind the arras*] What ho! Help!
HAMLET [*Drawing*] How now, a rat?
  [*He thrusts his rapier through the arras.*]
                    Dead for a ducat, dead![1]
POLONIUS   Oh, I am slain!   [*He falls and dies.*]
25 QUEEN   O me, what hast thou done?
HAMLET   Nay, I know not. Is it the King?
QUEEN   Oh, what a rash and bloody deed is this!
HAMLET   A bloody deed—almost as bad, good Mother,°   *stepmother*
  As kill a king and marry with his brother.
30 QUEEN   As kill a king!
HAMLET   Ay, lady, it was my word.
  [*He discovers* POLONIUS.]
  Thou wretched, rash, intruding fool, farewell.

3.4 Location: The Queen's private chamber.
7. Be sure you admonish him ("lay" means
"thrust").
8. Have you forgotten to whom you are
speaking?

9. That is, who can speak to someone as ill-
mannered as you.
1. I'll wager a ducat he is dead; or, I'll kill him
for a ducat.

I took thee for thy better;° take thy fortune.   *(i.e., Claudius)*
Thou find'st to be too busy° is some danger.   *prying*
35 —Leave wringing of your hands. Peace, sit you down,
And let me wring your heart, for so I shall,
If it be made of penetrable stuff,
If damnèd custom° have not brazed[2] it so   *habitual sinfulness*
That it be proof and bulwark against sense.[3]
40 QUEEN What have I done, that thou dar'st wag thy tongue
In noise so rude against me?

HAMLET   Such an act
That blurs the grace and blush of modesty,
Calls virtue hypocrite, takes off the rose[4]
From the fair forehead of an innocent love
45 And sets a blister there,[5] makes marriage vows
As false as dicers' oaths. Oh, such a deed
As from the body of contraction° plucks   *the marriage contract*
The very soul, and sweet religion makes
A rhapsody[6] of words. Heaven's face does glow°   *blush*
50 O'er this solidity and compound mass[7]
With heated visage, as against the doom,[8]
Is thought-sick at the act.

QUEEN   Ay me, what act
That roars so loud, and thunders in the index?[9]

HAMLET   [*Showing her two likenesses*]
Look here upon this picture, and on this,
55 The counterfeit presentment° of two brothers.   *painted representation*
See what a grace was seated on this brow,
Hyperion's curls, the front° of Jove himself,   *brow*
An eye like Mars to threaten and command,
A station° like the herald Mercury[1]   *stance*
60 New-lighted° on a heaven-kissing hill—   *Newly alighted*
A combination and a form indeed
Where every god did seem to set his seal°   *to authenticate*
To give the world assurance of a man.
This was your husband. Look you now what follows:
65 Here is your husband, like a mildewed ear°   *ear of grain*
Blasting° his wholesome brother. Have you eyes?   *Infecting*
Could you on this fair mountain leave° to feed   *cease*
And batten on this moor?[2] Ha, have you eyes?
You cannot call it love, for at your age
70 The heyday in the blood° is tame, it's humble,   *sexual desire*
And waits upon° the judgment, and what judgment   *is subservient to*
Would step from this to this? Sense,[3] sure, you have,

---

2. Brazened, hardened.
3. Armed and fortified against natural feeling.
4. The emblem of ideal love.
5. Prostitutes were branded on the forehead.
6. A disconnected string.
7. The earth itself (a compound of the four
elements believed to constitute all matter).

8. As if doomsday were at hand.
9. Table of contents; preface.
1. The winged messenger of the Roman gods.
2. Gorge yourself on this barren wasteland.
3. Perception through the five senses (sight,
smell, hearing, taste, and touch).

Else could you not have motion,° but sure that sense   *locomotion*
Is apoplexed,° for madness would not err,   *paralyzed*
75 Nor sense to ecstasy° was ne'er so thrilled   *madness*
But it reserved some quantity of choice
To serve in such a difference.[4] What devil was't
That thus hath cozened you at hoodman-blind?°   *blindman's buff*
Eyes without feeling, feeling without sight,
80 Ears without hands or eyes, smelling sans all,[5]
Or but a sickly part of one true sense
Could not so mope.° Oh, shame! Where is thy blush?   *be so stupefied*
Rebellious hell,
If thou canst mutine° in a matron's bones,   *mutiny*
85 To flaming youth let virtue be as wax,
And melt in her° own fire. Proclaim no shame   *(youth's)*
When the compulsive ardor gives the charge,°   *orders the attack*
Since frost itself as actively doth burn,
And reason pardons will.[6]
QUEEN   O Hamlet, speak no more.
90 Thou turn'st my very eyes into my soul.
And there I see such black and grainèd° spots   *ingrained*
As will leave there their tinct.°   *color*
HAMLET   Nay, but to live
In the rank sweat of an enseamèd° bed,   *a greasy*
Stewed[7] in corruption, honeying and making love
Over the nasty sty—
95 QUEEN   Oh, speak to me no more.
These words like daggers enter in my ears;
No more, sweet Hamlet.
HAMLET   A murderer and a villain,
A slave that is not twentieth part the tithe°   *tenth part*
Of your precedent° lord, a vice[8] of kings,   *former*
100 A cutpurse° of the empire and the rule,   *pickpocket*
That from a shelf the precious diadem stole
And put it in his pocket—
QUEEN   No more!
HAMLET   A king of shreds and patches[9]—
         Enter GHOST.
Save me and hover o'er me with your wings,
105 You heavenly guards!—What would your gracious figure?
QUEEN   Alas, he's mad!
HAMLET   Do you not come your tardy son to chide,
That, lapsed in time and passion,[1] lets go by

---

4. That is, the difference between Hamlet's father and Claudius.
5. Without the other senses.
6. When mature passion ("frost") burns as intensely as does youthful passion, and when reason, which is supposed to counsel the will with restraint, instead acts as a pimp to desire.
7. Boiled (with a pun on *stew*, meaning "brothel").
8. The comic character in a morality play presenting a vice.
9. The multicolored outfit of the vice character.
1. Having allowed time to elapse and my passion (for revenge) to cool.

Th'important° acting of your dread command?   *urgent*
110   Oh, say!
    GHOST   Do not forget. This visitation
      Is but to whet thy almost blunted purpose.
      But look, amazement° on thy mother sits.   *bewilderment*
      Oh, step between her and her fighting° soul.   *struggling, conflicted*
115   Conceit° in weakest bodies strongest works.   *Imagination*
      Speak to her, Hamlet.
    HAMLET   How is it with you, lady?
    QUEEN   Alas, how is't with you,
      That you do bend your eye on vacancy,
      And with th'incorporal° air do hold discourse?   *immaterial*
120   Forth at your eyes your spirits wildly peep,
      And, as the sleeping soldiers in th'alarm,°   *call to arms*
      Your bedded hair, like life in excrements,[2]
      Start up and stand an end. O gentle son,
      Upon the heat and flame of thy distemper°   *disordered mind*
125   Sprinkle cool patience. Whereon do you look?
    HAMLET   On him, on him! Look you how pale he glares!
      His form and cause conjoined,[3] preaching to stones
      Would make them capable.° [*To* GHOST] Do not look upon   *receptive*
      me,
      Lest with this piteous action you convert°   *turn aside*
130   My stern effects.° Then what I have to do   *purpose*
      Will want true color—tears perchance for blood.[4]
    QUEEN   To whom do you speak this?
    HAMLET   Do you see nothing there?
    QUEEN   Nothing at all, yet all that is I see.
135   HAMLET   Nor did you nothing hear?
    QUEEN   No, nothing but ourselves.
    HAMLET   Why, look you there, look how it steals away,
      My father in his habit as he lived.[5]
      Look where he goes even now out at the portal!

                           Exit GHOST.

140   QUEEN   This is the very coinage of your brain.
      This bodiless creation ecstasy
      Is very cunning in.[6]
    HAMLET   My pulse as yours doth temperately keep time,
      And makes as healthful music. It is not madness
145   That I have uttered. Bring me to the test,
      And I the matter will reword,° which madness   *repeat verbatim*
      Would gambol° from. Mother, for love of grace,   *leap away*
      Lay not that flattering unction[7] to your soul

---

2. In outgrowths (such as hair and nails). *Bedded*: laid flat.

3. His appearance joined with his purpose for appearing.

4. That is, then my purpose (i.e., revenge) will lack true passion or motivation; I will instead produce colorless tears and not shed red blood.

5. In his typical attire and appearance as if (or when) he lived.

6. Madness is especially crafty in the creation of hallucinations like this.

7. An ointment that appears to heal (by lessening or removing discomfort) but does not cure the disease.

That not your trespass but my madness speaks.
150 It will but skin° and film the ulcerous place,   *thinly cover*
Whiles rank corruption, mining° all within,   *undermining*
Infects unseen. Confess yourself to heaven,
Repent what's past, avoid what is to come,
And do not spread the compost on the weeds,
155 To make them ranker. Forgive me this my virtue,°   *my virtuous entreaty*
For in the fatness° of these pursy° times   *grossness / fat*
Virtue itself of vice must pardon beg,
Yea, curb° and woo for leave° to do him good.   *bow / permission*
QUEEN   O Hamlet, thou hast cleft my heart in twain.
160 HAMLET   Oh, throw away the worser part of it,
And live the purer with the other half.
Good night. But go not to my uncle's bed.
Assume° a virtue, if you have it not.   *Act out*
That monster, Custom, who all sense doth eat,
165 Of habits devil, is angel yet in this,
That to the use° of actions fair and good   *habit*
He likewise gives a frock or livery
That aptly° is put on. Refrain tonight,   *fittingly*
And that shall lend a kind of easiness
170 To the next abstinence, the next more easy;
For use almost can change the stamp of nature,
And either shame the devil, or throw him out
With wondrous potency. Once more, good night.
And when you are desirous to be blessed,
I'll blessing beg of you. [*He gestures to* POLONIUS.]
175   For this same lord,°   *(Polonius)*
I do repent; but heaven hath pleased it so
To punish me with this, and this with me,
That I must be their scourge and minister.[8]
I will bestow° him and will answer well[9]   *dispose of*
180 The death I gave him. So again, good night.
I must be cruel only to be kind.
This bad begins, and worse remains behind.°   *to come*
One word more, good lady.
QUEEN   What shall I do?
HAMLET   Not this by no means that I bid you do:
185 Let the bloat° king tempt you again to bed,   *bloated*
Pinch wanton on your cheek, call you his mouse,
And let him, for a pair of reechy° kisses   *filthy*
Or paddling° in your neck with his damned fingers,   *playing fondly*
Make you to ravel° all this matter out   *unwind (i.e., reveal)*
190 That I essentially am not in madness,

8. "Scourge" and "minister" were sometimes used interchangeably to refer to one who punishes sin on God's behalf. "Scourge" is also applied to tyrants, who may still be serving God's justice when they kill, but who appear to contaminate or condemn them-selves in the process because they kill cruelly or for personal reasons. God's "minister," by contrast, acts as God's servant and does not become an independent agent of revenge.
9. Assume responsibility for.

But mad in craft.° 'Twere good you let him know,   *by design*
For who that's but° a queen—fair, sober, wise—   *only*
Would from a paddock,° from a bat, a gib,°   *toad / tomcat*
Such dear concerning° hide? Who would do so?   *important matters*
195   No, in despite of sense and secrecy,
Unpeg the basket on the house's top,
Let the birds fly, and, like the famous ape,
To try conclusions,° in the basket creep   *To experiment*
And break your own neck down.[1]
200 QUEEN   Be thou assured, if words be made of breath,
And breath of life, I have no life to breathe
What thou hast said to me.
HAMLET   I must to England. You know that?
QUEEN   Alack,
I had forgot. 'Tis so concluded on.
205 HAMLET   There's letters sealed, and my two schoolfellows,
Whom I will trust as I will adders° fanged,   *venomous snakes*
They bear the mandate; they must sweep my way
And marshal me to knavery.[2] Let it work.
For 'tis the sport to have the enginer[3]
210   Hoist with his own petard,[4] and't shall go hard
But I will delve one yard below their mines°   *military tunnels*
And blow them at the moon. Oh, 'tis most sweet,
When in one line two crafts directly meet.[5]
This man shall set me packing.
215   I'll lug the guts into the neighbor room.
Mother, good night. Indeed, this counselor
Is now most still, most secret, and most grave,
Who was in life a most foolish, prating knave.
—Come, sir, to draw toward an end with you.[6]
220   —Good night, Mother.   *Exit* [HAMLET *dragging* POLONIUS].

4.1

Enter KING *to* QUEEN, *with* ROSENCRANTZ *and*
GUILDENSTERN.

KING   There's matter in these sighs, these profound heaves,
You must translate. 'Tis fit we understand them.
Where is your son?
QUEEN   Bestow this place on us a little while.
[*Exeunt* ROSENCRANTZ *and* GUILDENSTERN.]
5   Ah, mine own lord, what have I seen tonight!
KING   What, Gertrude? How does Hamlet?
QUEEN   Mad as the sea and wind when both contend

---

1. In a story now lost, an ape apparently enters a cage on top of a house that has been opened (unpegged), allowing birds to escape. The ape falls to its death, perhaps because it tries to fly.
2. Prepare the way for me and lead me into a trap.
3. The designer of military devices.
4. Blown up by his own explosive.
5. When two cunning plots come together.
6. To conclude matters between us (with a pun on "draw," pull).
4.1 Location: The castle.

Which is the mightier. In his lawless fit,
Behind the arras hearing something stir,
10　Whips out his rapier, cries "A rat, a rat!"
　　And in this brainish apprehension° kills　　　　　　　　　　*headstrong delusion*
　　The unseen good old man.
　KING　　　　　　　　　　　　Oh, heavy deed!
　　It had been so with us,° had we been there.　　　　　　　　　*me (the royal "we")*
　　His liberty is full of threats to all—
15　To you yourself, to us, to everyone.
　　Alas, how shall this bloody deed be answered?°　　　　　*explained satisfactorily*
　　It will be laid to° us, whose providence°　　　　　　　　*blamed on / foresight*
　　Should have kept short,° restrained, and out of haunt[7]　　　*controlled*
　　This mad young man. But so much was our love,
20　We would not understand what was most fit,
　　But, like the owner° of a foul disease,　　　　　　　　　　*carrier*
　　To keep it from divulging,° let it feed　　　　　　　　　　*being known*
　　Even on the pith° of life. Where is he gone?　　　　　　　*vital substance*
　QUEEN　To draw apart the body he hath killed,
25　O'er whom his very madness, like some ore°　　　　　　　*vein of gold*
　　Among a mineral° of metals base,　　　　　　　　　　　　*mine*
　　Shows itself pure: 'a° weeps for what is done.　　　　　　　*he*
　KING　O Gertrude, come away!
　　The sun no sooner shall the mountains touch
30　But we will ship him hence, and this vile deed
　　We must with all our majesty and skill
　　Both countenance° and excuse.　　　　　　　　　　　　　*authorize*
　　　　Enter ROSENCRANTZ *and* GUILDENSTERN.
　　　　　　　　　　　　—Ho, Guildenstern!
　　Friends both, go join you with some further aid.
　　Hamlet in madness hath Polonius slain,
35　And from his mother's closet hath he dragged him.
　　Go seek him out, speak fair, and bring the body
　　Into the chapel. I pray you, haste in this.
　　　　[*Exeunt* ROSENCRANTZ *and* GUILDENSTERN.]
　　Come, Gertrude, we'll call up our wisest friends
　　And let them know both what we mean to do
40　And what's untimely done. So, haply, slander,[8]
　　Whose whisper o'er the world's diameter°　　　　　　　*whole extent*
　　As level as the cannon to his blank[9]
　　Transports his poisoned shot, may miss our name
　　And hit the woundless° air. Oh, come away.　　　　　　　*invulnerable*
45　My soul is full of discord and dismay.
　　　　　　　　　　　　　　　　　　　　Exeunt.

7. Away from places frequented by others.
8. The phrase "So, haply, slander" is supplied
by earlier editors because half a verse line is
missing from Q2.
9. As straight as the cannon to its target (i.e.,
point-blank).

4.2

Enter HAMLET.

HAMLET Safely stowed. But soft, what noise? Who calls
on Hamlet? Oh, here they come.

[*Enter* ROSENCRANTZ, GUILDENSTERN, *and others.*]

ROSENCRANTZ What have you done, my lord, with the
dead body?

5 HAMLET Compound° it with dust, whereto 'tis kin.   *United*

ROSENCRANTZ Tell us where 'tis, that we may take it
thence, and bear it to the chapel.

HAMLET Do not believe it.

ROSENCRANTZ Believe what?

10 HAMLET That I can keep your counsel and not mine own.[1]
Besides, to be demanded of° a sponge! What replication°   *questioned by / reply*
should be made by the son of a king?

ROSENCRANTZ Take you me for a sponge, my lord?

HAMLET Ay, sir, that soaks up the King's countenance,° his   *favor*
15 rewards, his authorities. But such officers do the King
best service in the end. He keeps them, like an ape, in the
corner of his jaw, first mouthed to be last swallowed.
When he needs what you have gleaned, it is but squeezing you, and, sponge, you shall be dry again.

20 ROSENCRANTZ I understand you not, my lord.

HAMLET I am glad of it. A knavish speech sleeps in a foolish ear.

ROSENCRANTZ My lord, you must tell us where the body is
and go with us to the King.

25 HAMLET The body is with the King, but the King is not with
the body.[2] The King is a thing.

GUILDENSTERN A thing, my lord?

HAMLET Of nothing. Bring me to him.

Exeunt.

4.3

Enter KING, *and two or three.*

KING I have sent to seek him and to find the body.
How dangerous is it that this man goes loose!
Yet must not we put the strong law on him;
He's loved of° the distracted° multitude,   *by / fickle*
5 Who like not in their judgment, but their eyes,[3]
And where 'tis so, th'offender's scourge° is weighed,   *punishment*
But never the offense. To bear° all smooth and even,   *manage*
This sudden sending him away must seem

4.2 Location: The castle.
1. That I can follow your advice ("counsel")
and keep my secret ("counsel").
2. The theory of "the king's two bodies" distinguished the monarch's mortal body from

the sacred and eternal body of his royal office.
4.3 Location: The castle.
3. Who judge not with their rational faculties
but by outward appearance.

Deliberate pause.[4] Diseases desperate grown
10 By desperate appliance° are relieved,   *remedy*
Or not at all.

          Enter ROSENCRANTZ, [GUILDENSTERN,] *and all the rest.*

          How now, what hath befall'n?
ROSENCRANTZ Where the dead body is bestowed, my lord,
We cannot get from him.
KING   But where is he?
ROSENCRANTZ Without, my lord, guarded, to know your
pleasure.
KING Bring him before us.
15 ROSENCRANTZ   Ho! Bring in the lord.

          They enter [with HAMLET].

KING Now, Hamlet, where's Polonius?
HAMLET At supper.
KING At supper? Where?
HAMLET Not where he eats, but where 'a° is eaten. A   *he*
20 certain convocation of politic[5] worms are e'en° at him.   *now*
Your worm is your only emperor for diet.[6] We fat all crea-
tures else to fat us, and we fat ourselves for maggots.
Your fat king and your lean beggar is but variable
service°—two dishes, but to one table. That's the end.   *different courses*
25 KING Alas, alas!
HAMLET A man may fish with the worm that hath eat of
a king, and eat of the fish that hath fed of that worm.
KING What dost thou mean by this?
HAMLET Nothing but to show you how a king may go a
30 progress[7] through the guts of a beggar.
KING Where is Polonius?
HAMLET In heaven. Send thither to see. If your messenger
find him not there, seek him i'th'other place yourself.
But, indeed, if you find him not within this month, you
35 shall nose him as you go up the stairs into the lobby.
KING [*To some* ATTENDANTS] Go seek him there.
HAMLET 'A will stay till you come.

          [*Exeunt* ATTENDANTS.]

KING Hamlet, this deed, for thine especial safety—
Which we do tender,° as we dearly grieve   *value*
40 For that which thou hast done—must send thee hence.
Therefore prepare thyself.
The bark is ready, and the wind at help,
Th'associates tend,° and everything is bent°   *companions wait / ready*
For England.
45 HAMLET For England?

---

4. A carefully considered decision (to interrupt the action).
5. Crafty; skilled in statecraft.
6. Food; perhaps also a pun on the Diet (council) at the German city of Worms in 1521, at

which the reform-minded theologian Martin
Luther, in the presence of Emperor Charles V,
was condemned for religious heresy.
7. On a state journey made by a royal or noble.

KING   Ay, Hamlet.

HAMLET   Good.

KING   So is it, if thou knew'st our purposes.

HAMLET   I see a cherub[8] that sees them. But come, for
50   England. Farewell, dear Mother.

KING   Thy loving father, Hamlet.

HAMLET   My mother. Father and mother is man and wife;
man and wife is one flesh,[9] so, my mother. Come, for
England.

Exit.

55   KING   Follow him at foot;° tempt him with speed aboard.   *at his heels*
Delay it not. I'll have him hence tonight.
Away, for everything is sealed and done
That else leans° on th'affair. Pray you, make haste.   *bears*

[*Exeunt all but the* KING.]

And, England,[1] if my love thou hold'st at aught°—   *at any value*
60   As my great power thereof may give thee sense,[2]
Since yet thy cicatrice° looks raw and red   *scar*
After the Danish sword, and thy free awe[3]
Pays homage to us—thou mayst not coldly set°   *regard with indifference*
Our sovereign process,° which imports at full,[4]   *royal command*
65   By letters congruing° to that effect,   *appealing earnestly*
The present° death of Hamlet. Do it, England,   *immediate*
For like the hectic° in my blood he rages,   *consumptive fever*
And thou must cure me. Till I know 'tis done,
Howe'er my haps,° my joys will ne'er begin.   *Exit.*   *fortunes*

4.4

Enter FORTINBRAS *with his army over the stage.*

FORTINBRAS   Go, Captain, from me greet the Danish king.
Tell him that by his license° Fortinbras   *permission*
Craves the conveyance of° a promised march   *escort*
Over his kingdom. You know the rendezvous.
5   If that His Majesty would aught with us,
We shall express our duty° in his eye;°   *respect / presence*
And let him know so.

CAPTAIN   I will do't, my lord.

FORTINBRAS   Go softly on.

[*Exeunt all but the* CAPTAIN.]

Enter HAMLET, ROSENCRANTZ, [GUILDENSTERN,] *etc.*

HAMLET   Good sir, whose powers° are these?   *forces*
10   CAPTAIN   They are of Norway, sir.

HAMLET   How purposed, sir, I pray you?

---

8. A member of the second-highest rank in
the angelic hierarchy, associated by the early
Catholic Church with divine knowledge.
9. A reference to the biblical injunction that
"a man . . . shall cleave unto his wife: and
they shall be one flesh" (Genesis 2.24).

1. King of England.
2. That is, as my great power may give you
reason to value my love.
3. Voluntary show of reverence.
4. Communicates in detailed instructions.
4.4 Location: The coast of Denmark.

CAPTAIN   Against some part of Poland.

HAMLET   Who commands them, sir?

CAPTAIN   The nephew to old Norway, Fortinbras.

15 HAMLET   Goes it against the main° of Poland, sir,   *the main part*
Or for some frontier?

CAPTAIN   Truly to speak, and with no addition,°   *exaggeration*
We go to gain a little patch of ground
That hath in it no profit but the name.

20 To pay five ducats, five, I would not farm° it.   *lease*
Nor will it yield to Norway or the Pole
A ranker rate,° should it be sold in fee.°   *higher return / outright*

HAMLET   Why, then the Polack never will defend it.

CAPTAIN   Yes, it is already garrisoned.

25 HAMLET   Two thousand souls and twenty thousand ducats
Will not debate the question of this straw.°   *trifling matter*
This is th'imposthume° of much wealth and peace   *abscess*
That inward breaks and shows no cause without°   *on the outside*
Why the man dies. I humbly thank you, sir.

30 CAPTAIN   God be wi'you, sir.   [*Exit.*]

ROSENCRANTZ   Will't please you go, my lord?

HAMLET   I'll be with you straight. Go a little before.

[*Exeunt all but* HAMLET.]

How all occasions do inform against° me   *accuse*
And spur my dull revenge! What is a man,

35 If his chief good and market° of his time   *profit*
Be but to sleep and feed? A beast, no more.
Sure he that made us with such large discourse,°   *powers of reasoning*
Looking before and after,[5] gave not
That capability° and godlike reason   *intelligence*

40 To fust° in us unused. Now, whether it be   *Became moldy*
Bestial oblivion,[6] or some craven scruple°   *cowardly qualm*
Of° thinking too precisely on th'event—   *From*
A thought which, quartered, hath but one part wisdom
And ever three parts coward—I do not know

45 Why yet I live to say "This thing's to do,"
Sith° I have cause, and will, and strength, and means   *Since*
To do't. Examples gross° as earth exhort me: *obvious*
Witness this army of such mass and charge,°   *expense*
Led by a delicate and tender° prince,   *skillful and young*

50 Whose spirit with divine ambition puffed°   *swollen*
Makes mouths at the invisible event,[7]
Exposing what is mortal and unsure
To all that fortune, death, and danger dare,
Even for an eggshell. Rightly to be great

55 Is not to stir without great argument,
But greatly to find quarrel in a straw

---

5. With an understanding of the past and the future.
6. Animal-like forgetfulness.

7. Makes disdainful faces at unforeseeable consequences.

When honor's at the stake.[8] How stand I then,
That have a father killed, a mother stained,
Excitements of° my reason and my blood,   *Events that excite*
60   And let all sleep, while to my shame I see
Th'imminent death of twenty thousand men
That for a fantasy and trick° of fame,   *trifle; sham*
Go to their graves like beds, fight for a plot
Whereon the numbers cannot try the cause,[9]
65   Which is not tomb enough and continent°   *container*
To hide the slain? Oh, from this time forth,
My thoughts be bloody or be nothing worth!   *Exit.*

4.5

Enter HORATIO, [QUEEN] GERTRUDE, *and a* GENTLEMAN.

QUEEN   I will not speak with her.
GENTLEMAN   She is importunate,
Indeed distract. Her mood will needs be pitied.
QUEEN   What would she have?
GENTLEMAN   She speaks much of her father, says she hears
5   There's tricks° i'the world, and hems, and beats her heart,°   *dishonesty / breast*
Spurns enviously at straws,[1] speaks things in doubt°   *obscurely*
That carry but half sense. Her speech is nothing,
Yet the unshapèd use° of it doth move   *confused manner*
The hearers to collection;° they yawn° at it,   *inference / gape*
10   And botch° the words up fit to their own thoughts,   *patch*
Which,° as her winks, and nods, and gestures yield them,   *(i.e., the words)*
Indeed would make one think there might be thought,
Though nothing sure, yet much unhappily.
HORATIO   'Twere good she were spoken with, for she may
strew
15   Dangerous conjectures in ill-breeding minds.
Let her come in.

[*Exit* GENTLEMAN.]

QUEEN   [*Aside*] To my sick soul, as sin's true nature is,
Each toy° seems prologue to some great amiss.°   *trifle / misfortune*
So full of artless jealousy° is guilt,   *crude suspicion*
20   It spills itself in fearing to be spilt.

Enter OPHELIA.

OPHELIA   Where is the beauteous majesty of Denmark?
QUEEN   How now, Ophelia?
OPHELIA   (*She sings.*) "How should I your true love know
From another one?
25   By his cockle hat and staff

___

8. That is, to be truly great is not to start a
war without outstanding reasons, but nobly
("greatly") to find conflict in a trifling matter
when honor hangs in the balance.

9. That is, not large enough for the armies to
fight on.
4.5 Location: The castle.
1. Takes offense angrily at trifles.

And his sandal shoon."[2]

QUEEN   Alas, sweet lady, what imports° this song?   *means*

OPHELIA   Say you? Nay, pray you, mark.°   *listen*

"He is dead and gone, lady,   *Song.*

30   He is dead and gone;

At his head a grass green turf,

At his heels a stone."

Oho!

QUEEN   Nay, but Ophelia—

35 OPHELIA   Pray you, mark.

[*Sings*] "White his shroud as the mountain snow"—

Enter KING.

QUEEN   Alas, look here, my lord.

OPHELIA   "Larded° all with sweet flowers;   *Song.*   *Bedecked*

Which bewept to the ground did not[3] go

40   With true-love showers."°   *tears*

KING   How do you, pretty lady?

OPHELIA   Well, God 'ild° you. They say the owl was a baker's   *God yield (repay)*

daughter.[4] Lord, we know what we are, but know not

what we may be. God be at your table.

45 KING   Conceit° upon her father.   *Morbid thoughts*

OPHELIA   Pray, let's have no words of this; but when they

ask you what it means, say you this:

"Tomorrow is Saint Valentine's day,[5]   *Song.*

All in the morning betime,°   *early*

50 And I a maid at your window,

To be your Valentine.

Then up he rose and donned his clothes,

And dupped° the chamber door,   *opened*

Let in the maid, that out a maid°   *a virgin*

55   Never departed more."

KING   Pretty Ophelia.

OPHELIA   Indeed, without an oath, I'll make an end on't:°   *of it*

[*Sings*] "By Gis° and by Saint Charity,[6]   *Jesus*

Alack, and fie for shame!

60 Young men will do't° if they come to't;   *i.e., have sex*

By Cock,[7] they are to blame.

Quoth she, 'Before you tumbled me,

You promised me to wed.'"

He answers:

---

2. The "sandal shoon" (shoes) and the "cockle hat" were typical attributes of a pilgrim (the cockleshell was attached to the hats of those who had returned from the shrine of St. James in Compostella, Spain).

3. The insertion of "not" interrupts the meter and changes the expected meaning.

4. In an old folktale, a baker's daughter who gave ungenerously when Christ asked for bread was turned into an owl. In Wales, the owl's cry was thought to signify an unmarried girl's loss of virginity.

5. The song hints at the notion that the first girl seen by a man on Valentine's day will be his true love.

6. That is, Holy Charity (not an actual saint).

7. A common corruption of "God" in mild oaths (with an obvious pun on "penis").

65   "'So would I ha' done, by yonder sun,
       An° thou hadst not come to my bed.'"   *If*
KING   How long hath she been thus?
OPHELIA   I hope all will be well. We must be patient, but I
    cannot choose but weep to think they would lay him
70   i'the cold ground. My brother shall know of it. And so I
    thank you for your good counsel.—Come, my coach!
    Good night, ladies, good night. Sweet ladies, good night,
    good night.

                                     [*Exit.*]

KING   Follow her close; give her good watch, I pray you.

                              [*Exit* HORATIO.]

75   Oh, this is the poison of deep grief; it springs
    All from her father's death—and now behold!
    O Gertrude, Gertrude,
    When sorrows come, they come not single spies,°   *scouts*
    But in battalions. First, her father slain;
80   Next, your son gone, and he most violent author
    Of his own just remove; the people muddied,°   *confused*
    Thick and unwholesome in thoughts and whispers
    For good Polonius' death—and we have done but greenly°   *foolishly*
    In hugger-mugger° to inter him; poor Ophelia,   *Secretly*
85   Divided from herself and her fair judgment,
    Without the which we are pictures or mere beasts;
    Last, and as much containing° as all these,   *as pertinent*
    Her brother is in secret come from France,
    Feeds on this wonder, keeps himself in clouds,[8]
90   And wants° not buzzers° to infect his ear   *lacks / rumormongers*
    With pestilent speeches of his father's death,
    Wherein necessity, of matter beggared,°   *lacking facts*
    Will nothing stick our person to arraign
    In ear and ear.[9] O my dear Gertrude, this,
95   Like to a murdering piece,[1] in many places
    Gives me superfluous[2] death.
      A noise within.
KING   Attend!
    Where is my Switzers?[3] Let them guard the door.
      Enter a MESSENGER.
    What is the matter?
MESSENGER   Save yourself, my lord!
100   The ocean, overpeering of his list,[4]
    Eats not the flats° with more impiteous° haste   *flatlands / ruthless; unpifying*
    Than young Laertes, in a riotous head,°   *armed force*
    O'erbears your officers. The rabble call him lord,

---

8. Obscure, hidden; or, perhaps, in clouds of suspicion.
9. That is, will not fail to accuse me in every ear.
1. A cannon that scattered its shot.

2. Superfluous because one death would be enough.
3. Swiss mercenaries (employed as royal guards at a number of European courts).
4. Rising above its shore (boundary).

And, as the world were now but[5] to begin,
105 Antiquity forgot, custom not known,
The ratifiers and props of every word,[6]
They cry, "Choose we! Laertes shall be king!"
Caps, hands, and tongues applaud it to the clouds,
"Laertes shall be king! Laertes king!" *A noise within.*
110 QUEEN   How cheerfully on the false trail they cry.[7]
Oh, this is counter,[8] you false Danish dogs!

Enter LAERTES *with* OTHERS.

KING   The doors are broke.
LAERTES   Where is this king?—Sirs, stand you all without.
ALL   No, let's come in.
115 LAERTES   I pray you, give me leave.
ALL   We will, we will.
LAERTES   I thank you. Keep the door. [OTHERS *retire.*]
O thou vile king,
Give me my father!
QUEEN [*Holding him*]   Calmly, good Laertes.
LAERTES   That drop of blood that's calm proclaims me
bastard,
120 Cries cuckold to my father, brands the harlot
Even here, between the chaste unsmirchèd brows
Of my true mother.
KING   What is the cause, Laertes,
That thy rebellion looks so giant-like?
Let him go, Gertrude; do not fear our° person.   fear for my
125 There's such divinity doth hedge° a king,   protect
That treason can but peep to what it would,[9]
Acts little of his° will. Tell me, Laertes,   its
Why thou art thus incensed. Let him go, Gertrude.
Speak, man.
LAERTES   Where is my father?
KING   Dead.
130 QUEEN   But not by him.
KING   Let him demand his fill.
LAERTES   How came he dead? I'll not be juggled with.°   deceived
To hell, allegiance! Vows, to the blackest devil!
Conscience and grace, to the profoundest pit!
I dare damnation. To this point I stand,[1]
135 That both the worlds I give to negligence.[2]
Let come what comes, only I'll be revenged
Most throughly° for my father.   thoroughly
KING   Who shall stay° you?   stop

5. That is, as if the world were only now
beginning.
6. The ancient traditions and customs, which
ratify the meaning of every word, have been
forgotten (by the rabble).
7. That is, as if they were hounds baying after
their prey.

8. Following the trail of game in the reverse
(here, the wrong) direction.
9. That is, that treason can only glimpse at
what it would like to do.
1. This I insist on.
2. That I do not care about the consequences
in this world or the ones after death.

LAERTES   My will, not all the world's.
    And for my means, I'll husband them so well,
140   They shall go far with little.
    KING   Good Laertes,
    If you desire to know the certainty
    Of your dear father, is't writ in your revenge
    That, swoopstake,[3] you will draw° both friend and foe,   *take from*
    Winner and loser?
    LAERTES   None but his enemies.
145 KING   Will you know them, then?
    LAERTES   To his good friends thus wide I'll ope my arms,
    And like the kind life-rend'ring pelican
    Repast them with my blood.[4]
    KING   Why, now you speak
    Like a good child and a true gentleman.
150   That I am guiltless of your father's death,
    And am most sensibly° in grief for it,   *intensely*
    It shall as level° to your judgment 'pear   *plain*
    As day does to your eye. *A noise within.*
        Enter OPHELIA [*singing, meeting* LAERTES' *followers*].
    LAERTES   Let her come in.
    How now, what noise is that?
155   O heat, dry up my brains![5] Tears seven times salt,
    Burn out the sense and virtue° of mine eye!   *power*
    By heaven, thy madness shall be paid with weight,
    Till our scale turn the beam.[6] O rose of May,
    Dear maid, kind sister, sweet Ophelia!
160   O heavens, is't possible a young maid's wits
    Should be as mortal as a poor man's life?
    OPHELIA   "They bore him barefaced on the bier   *Song.*
            And in his grave rained many a tear"—
    Fare you well, my dove.
165 LAERTES   Hadst thou thy wits, and didst persuade° revenge,   *argue for*
    It could not move thus.
    OPHELIA   You must sing "A-down, a-down,"[7] and you "call
    him a-down-a." Oh, how the wheel[8] becomes it! It is the
    false steward that stole his master's daughter.
170 LAERTES   This nothing's more than matter.[9]
    OPHELIA   There's rosemary, that's for remembrance; pray you,
    love, remember. And there is pansies, that's for thoughts.[1]

3. Indiscriminately (literally, taking all the stakes in a game of chance).
4. The pelican mother was thought to feed ("repast") its young with blood from a wound she pecked in her own breast.
5. According to the humoral theory of physiology, the brain was a cold and moist organ. In this line and the next, Laertes expresses the wish that his rational and sensory abilities perish so that he would not have to bear witness to Ophelia's madness.
6. The image is of the scales of justice, in which madness will be outweighed by vengeance.
7. A common refrain in popular ballads.
8. Refrain; possibly also a reference to Fortune's wheel.
9. That is, this nonsense means more than coherent speech does.
1. Rosemary was thought to strengthen memory, and it was commonly associated with remembrance at weddings and at funerals. Pansies symbolize love; Ophelia puns on *pensées* (thoughts; French), from which the flower's name derives.

LAERTES A document° in madness, thoughts and remem-   *lesson*
brance fitted.°   *conferred fittingly*

175 OPHELIA There's fennel for you, and columbines.[2]
There's rue for you, and here's some for me; we may
call it "herb of grace" o' Sundays. You may wear your
rue with a difference.[3] There's a daisy. I would give you
some violets,[4] but they withered all when my father
180 died. They say 'a° made a good end.   *he*
[*Sings*] "For bonny sweet Robin is all my joy."

LAERTES Thought and afflictions, passion,° hell itself   *suffering*
She turns to favor° and to prettiness.   *grace*

OPHELIA "And will 'a not come again?   *Song.*
185   And will 'a not come again?
        No, no, he is dead,
        Go to thy deathbed,
    He never will come again.
    "His beard was as white as snow,
190   Flaxen° was his poll.°   *white / head*
        He is gone, he is gone,
        And we cast away moan,
    God ha' mercy on his soul."
And of all Christians' souls. God be wi'you.   [*Exit.*]

195 LAERTES Do you see this, O God?

KING Laertes, I must commune with° your grief,   *share in*
    Or you deny me right. Go but apart,
    Make choice of whom° your wisest friends you will,   *whichever of*
    And they shall hear and judge twixt you and me.
200 If by direct or by collateral° hand   *indirect*
    They find us touched,° we will our kingdom give,   *touched with guilt*
    Our crown, our life, and all that we call ours
    To you in satisfaction;° but if not,   *compensation*
    Be you content to lend your patience to us,
205 And we shall jointly labor with your soul
    To give it due content.

LAERTES   Let this be so.
    His means of death, his obscure funeral—
    No trophy,° sword, nor hatchment[5] o'er his bones,   *memorial*
    No noble rite, nor formal ostentation°—   *display, ceremony*
210 Cry to be heard, as 'twere from heaven to earth,
    That I must call't in question.

KING   So you shall.
    And where th'offense is, let the great axe fall.
    I pray you, go with me.
                                        Exeunt.

---

2. Fennel signifies flattery; columbine was
known for its horned shape and here may
signify cuckoldry. Rue (an aromatic herb)
suggests regret and repentance.
3. Perhaps Ophelia means that she and the
recipient (the King or Queen?) of the imagi-

nary rue have different reasons for wearing it.
4. The daisy may signify dissembling or faith-
lessness; the violets, faithfulness.
5. A square or lozenge-shaped tablet exhibiting the armorial bearings of the deceased.

4.6

Enter HORATIO[, *a* GENTLEMAN,] *and others.*

HORATIO   What are they that would speak with me?

GENTLEMAN   Seafaring men, sir. They say they have letters for you.

HORATIO   Let them come in.

[*Exit* GENTLEMAN.]

5   I do not know from what part of the world I should be
greeted, if not from Lord Hamlet.

Enter SAILORS.

SAILOR   God bless you, sir.

HORATIO   Let him bless thee too.

SAILOR   'A° shall, sir, an't° please him. There's a letter for you,   He / if it

10   sir—it came from th'ambassador that was bound for England—if your name be Horatio, as I am let to know it is.

[*He gives a letter.*]

HORATIO   [*Reads*] "Horatio, when thou shalt have over-
looked° this, give these fellows some means° to the King;   read / access
they have letters for him. Ere we were two days old at

15   sea, a pirate of very warlike appointment° gave us chase.   equipment
Finding ourselves too slow of sail, we put on a compelled
valor, and in the grapple I boarded them. On the instant
they got clear of our ship, so I thieves of mercy, but they
knew what they did;[6] I am to do a turn for them. Let the

20   King have the letters I have sent and repair° thou to me   come
with as much speed as thou wouldst fly° death. I have   flee
words to speak in thine ear will make thee dumb, yet are
they much too light for the bore of the matter.[7] These good
fellows will bring thee where I am. Rosencrantz and Guil-

25   denstern hold their course for England; of them I have
much to tell thee. Farewell.

He that thou knowest
thine, Hamlet."

Come, I will give you way° for these your letters,   a means of delivery

30   And do't the speedier that you may direct me
To him from whom you brought them.

Exeunt.

4.7

Enter KING *and* LAERTES.

KING   Now must your conscience my acquittance seal,[8]
And you must put me in your heart for friend,

4.6 Location: The castle.
6. That is, the pirates showed mercy to Hamlet
with the expectation of some reward or compensation. *Thieves of mercy*: merciful thieves.
7. A firearms metaphor: the caliber or importance ("bore") of this subject ("the matter")

requires more than the light-gauge shot
("words") Hamlet has at his disposal.
4.7 Location: The castle.
8. That is, your conscience must confirm my
innocence.

Sith° you have heard, and with a knowing ear,   *Since*
That he which hath your noble father slain
Pursued my life.
5 LAERTES   It well appears. But tell me
Why you proceed not against these feats,°   *acts*
So criminal and so capital° in nature,   *punishable by death*
As by your safety, greatness, wisdom, all things else,
You mainly° were stirred up.   *greatly*
10 KING   Oh, for two special reasons,
Which may to you, perhaps, seem much unsinewed,°   *very feeble*
But yet to me they're strong. The Queen his mother
Lives almost by his looks, and for myself—
My virtue or my plague, be it either which—
15 She is so conjunctive° to my life and soul,   *closely joined*
That, as the star moves not but in his sphere,[9]
I could not but by her. The other motive
Why to a public count° I might not go   *accounting*
Is the great love the general gender° bear him,   *common people*
20 Who, dipping all his faults in their affection,
Work like the spring that turneth wood to stone,[1]
Convert his gyves° to graces, so that my arrows,   *shackles*
Too slightly timbered° for so loud° a wind,   *light / strong*
Would have reverted to my bow again,
25 But not where I have aimed them.
LAERTES   And so have I a noble father lost,
A sister driven into desp'rate terms,°   *circumstances*
Whose worth, if praises may go back again,[2]
Stood challenger on mount of all the age
30 For her perfections.[3] But my revenge will come.
KING   Break not your sleeps for that. You must not think
That we are made of stuff so flat and dull°   *tame and spiritless*
That we can let our beard be shook with danger[4]
And think it pastime. You shortly shall hear more.
35 I loved your father, and we love ourself,
And that, I hope, will teach you to imagine—
    Enter a MESSENGER *with letters.*
MESSENGER   [*Giving letters*] These to Your Majesty, this to
    the Queen.
KING   From Hamlet! Who brought them?
MESSENGER   Sailors, my lord, they say. I saw them not:
40 They were given me by Claudio. He received them
Of him that brought them.
KING   Laertes, you shall hear them.
—Leave us.   [*Exit* MESSENGER.]

---

9. According to Ptolemaic astronomy, planets (stars) circled around the earth, each confined to a specific sphere.
1. The spring whose water contains so much lime that it petrifies fallen branches or exposed roots.
2. May refer to the past (i.e., to Ophelia's former virtues).
3. Challenged the world, in the sight of all ("on mount"), to match her virtues.
4. That I will let myself be affronted by someone powerful.

[*Reads*] "High and mighty, you shall know I am set naked° on   *destitute; defenseless*
your kingdom. Tomorrow shall I beg leave to see your
45 kingly eyes, when I shall, first asking you pardon,°   *permission*
thereunto recount the occasion of my sudden return."
What should this mean? Are all the rest come back?
Or is it some abuse,° and no such thing?   *trickery*
LAERTES Know you the hand?
KING   'Tis Hamlet's character.° "Naked,"   *handwriting*
50 And in a postscript here, he says "alone."
Can you devise° me?   *explain to*
LAERTES I am lost in it, my lord. But let him come.
It warms the very sickness in my heart
That I shall live and tell him to his teeth,
"Thus didst thou."
55 KING   If it be so, Laertes—
As how should it be so, how otherwise?[5]—
Will you be ruled by me?
LAERTES   Ay, my lord,
So you will not o'errule me to a peace.
KING To thine own peace. If he be now returned,
60 As checking at[6] his voyage, and that° he means   *if*
No more to undertake it—I will work him
To an exploit, now ripe in my device,°   *planning*
Under the which he shall not choose but fall,
And for his death no wind of blame shall breathe,
65 But even his mother shall uncharge° the practice°   *not accuse / scheme*
And call it accident.
LAERTES   My lord, I will be ruled,
The rather° if you could devise it so   *All the more quickly*
That I might be the organ.°   *instrument*
KING   It falls right.
You have been talked of since your travel much,
70 And that in Hamlet's hearing, for a quality
Wherein they say you shine. Your sum of parts°   *abilities combined*
Did not together pluck such envy from him
As did that one, and that, in my regard,
Of the unworthiest siege.°   *lowest rank*
75 LAERTES What part is that, my lord?
KING A very ribbon in the cap of youth,
Yet needful too, for youth no less becomes°   *is suited by*
The light and careless livery that it wears
Than settled age his sables° and his weeds,°   *furred gowns / garments*
80 Importing health and graveness.° Two months since°   *seriousness, sobriety / ago*
Here was a gentleman of Normandy—
I have seen myself, and served against, the French,
And they can well° on horseback, but this gallant   *are skilled*
Had witchcraft in't; he grew unto his seat,
85 And to such wondrous doing brought his horse,

5. That is, how can Hamlet have returned (despite the order for his execution), but how else to explain the letter?

6. Turning away from (as a falcon abandons the prey it was sent to pursue).

As had he been incorpsed and demi-natured[7]
With the brave beast. So far he topped° my thought   *surpassed*
That I in forgery of shapes and tricks[8]
Come short of what he did.

90   LAERTES   A Norman was't?

  KING   A Norman.

  LAERTES   Upon my life, Lamord.

  KING   The very same.

  LAERTES   I know him well. He is the brooch° indeed   *ornament*
And gem of all the nation.

  KING   He made confession° of you,   *acknowledgment*
95   And gave you such a masterly report
For art and exercise in your defense,
And for your rapier most especial,
That he cried out 'twould be a sight indeed
If one could match you. Th'escrimers° of their nation   *fencers*
100   He swore, had neither motion, guard, nor eye,
If you opposed them. Sir, this report of his
Did Hamlet so envenom with his envy
That he could nothing do but wish and beg
Your sudden° coming o'er, to play° with you.   *prompt / fence*
Now, out of this—

105   LAERTES   What out of this, my lord?

  KING   Laertes, was your father dear to you?
Or are you like the painting of a sorrow,
A face without a heart?

  LAERTES   Why ask you this?

  KING   Not that I think you did not love your father,
110   But that I know love is begun by time,°   *by circumstances*
And that I see in passages of proof°   *actual instances*
Time qualifies° the spark and fire of it.   *tempers*
There lives within the very flame of love
A kind of wick or snuff[9] that will abate it,
115   And nothing is at a like° goodness still,°   *an identical / always*
For goodness, growing to a pleurisy,[1]
Dies in his own too much.[2] That we would do,
We should do when we would; for this "would" changes,
And hath abatements° and delays as many   *decreases*
120   As there are tongues, are hands, are accidents,°   *occurrences*
And then this "should" is like a spendthrift sigh,
That hurts by easing.[3] But to the quick° o' th'ulcer   *life, core*
Hamlet comes back. What would you undertake
To show yourself in deed your father's son
More than in words?

125   LAERTES   To cut his throat i'the church.

---

7. As if he had been made into one body and had half the nature (like a centaur).
8. That my ability to imagine his maneuvers and feats of skill.
9. The burned part of the wick (which must be removed to allow the candle to burn brightly).

1. An excess (the inflammatory lung disease pleurisy was believed to be caused by an excess of humors).
2. Of its own overabundance.
3. Each sigh was believed to cost a drop of blood.

KING   No place, indeed, should murder sanctuarize;[4]
    Revenge should have no bounds. But good Laertes,
    Will you do this, keep close within your chamber.
    Hamlet returned shall know you are come home.
130   We'll put on° those shall praise your excellence   *encourage*
    And set a double varnish on the fame
    The Frenchman gave you, bring you in fine° together,   *conclusion*
    And wager o'er your heads. He, being remiss,°   *inattentive*
    Most generous,° and free from all contriving,   *noble in nature*
135   Will not peruse the foils, so that with ease,
    Or with a little shuffling, you may choose
    A sword unbated,° and in a pass of practice[5]   *unblunted*
    Requite him for your father.
LAERTES   I will do't.
    And for that purpose I'll anoint my sword.
140   I bought an unction° of a mountebank°   *ointment / quack doctor*
    So mortal that, but dip a knife in it,
    Where it draws blood no cataplasm° so rare,   *poultice*
    Collected from all simples° that have virtue°   *herbs / healing powers*
    Under the moon,[6] can save the thing from death
145   That is but scratched withal.° I'll touch my point   *with it*
    With this contagion, that if I gall° him slightly,   *wound*
    It may be death.
KING   Let's further think of this.
    Weigh what convenience both of time and means
    May fit us to our shape.[7] If this should fail,
150   And that our drift look° through our bad performance,   *purpose become visible*
    'Twere better not assayed.° Therefore this project   *attempted*
    Should have a back or second° that might hold   *back-up position*
    If this did blast in proof.[8] Soft, let me see.
    We'll make a solemn wager on your cunnings°—   *skills*
155   I ha't!
    When in your motion° you are hot and dry—   *exercise*
    As make your bouts more violent to that end—
    And that he calls for drink, I'll have prepared him
    A chalice for the nonce,° whereon but sipping,   *occasion*
160   If he by chance escape your venomed stuck,°   *thrust*
    Our purpose may hold there. [*A noise within*] But stay,
      what noise?

        Enter QUEEN.

QUEEN   One woe doth tread upon another's heel,
    So fast they follow. Your sister's drowned, Laertes.
LAERTES   Drowned! Oh, where?
165 QUEEN   There is a willow[9] grows askant the brook,
    That shows his hoary° leaves in the glassy stream;   *gray; white*

---

4. Shield a murderer from punishment. In England, criminals who took refuge in a church were protected from arrest for all crimes except sacrilege and treason.
5. With a treacherous sword thrust.
6. Herbs picked by moonlight were believed to be especially potent.
7. May make us ready for the roles we will assume (in our plan).
8. Should blow up in our faces (like a cannon).
9. The willow is an emblem of forsaken love and of mourning.

Therewith fantastic garlands did she make
Of crowflowers, nettles, daisies, and long purples,°   *purple orchids*
That liberal° shepherds give a grosser[1] name,   *free-spoken*
170   But our cold° maids do dead men's fingers call them.   *chaste*
There on the pendent boughs her crownet° weeds   *made into a crown*
Clamb'ring to hang,[2] an envious sliver° broke,   *a malicious branch*
When down her weedy trophies and herself
Fell in the weeping brook. Her clothes spread wide,
175   And mermaid-like awhile they bore her up,
Which time she chanted snatches of old lauds,°   *hymns*
As one incapable° of her own distress,   *unaware*
Or like a creature native and endued°   *adopted*
Unto that element. But long it could not be
180   Till that her garments, heavy with their drink,
Pulled the poor wretch from her melodious lay°   *song*
To muddy death.

LAERTES   Alas, then she is drowned.

QUEEN   Drowned, drowned.

LAERTES   Too much of water hast thou, poor Ophelia,
185   And therefore I forbid my tears. But yet
It is our trick;° nature her custom holds,   *natural tendency*
Let shame say what it will. [*He weeps.*] When these are
        gone,
The woman will be out.[3] Adieu, my lord.
I have a speech o' fire that fain° would blaze,   *eagerly*
But that this folly drowns it.   *Exit.*
190   KING   Let's follow, Gertrude.
How much I had to do to calm his rage!
Now fear I this will give it start again.
Therefore let's follow.

                                        Exeunt.

5.1

Enter two CLOWNS[4] [*one a* GRAVEDIGGER].

GRAVEDIGGER   Is she to be buried in Christian burial when
she willfully seeks her own salvation?[5]

OTHER   I tell thee she is; therefore make her grave straight.°   *immediately*
The crowner° hath sat on her and finds it Christian burial.[6]   *coroner*

5   GRAVEDIGGER   How can that be, unless she drowned herself in her own defense?

OTHER   Why, 'tis found so.

---

1. More lewd (e.g., "priest's-pintle" [penis];
"dog's cullions" [testicles]).
2. Forsaken lovers were said to hang garlands
in willow trees.
3. That is, when I am done crying the woman
in me will also be gone.
5.1 Location: A churchyard.
4. Men from the country, rustics.
5. Possibly a mistake for "damnation"; suicide
was considered a mortal sin that disqualified

one from a "Christian burial" in consecrated
ground. Or the clown may be suggesting that
Ophelia is speeding her "salvation" by going to
her reward "willfully" rather than by waiting
for nature to take its course.
6. The coroner has investigated the case of
her death and concluded that it merits a
Christian burial (i.e., that her drowning was
not a suicide).

GRAVEDIGGER   It must be *se offendendo*;[7] it cannot be else.
For here lies the point: if I drown myself wittingly, it argues
10   an act, and an act hath three branches—it is to act, to
do, to perform. Argal,[8] she drowned herself wittingly.

OTHER   Nay, but hear you, goodman delver°—   *Master Digger*

GRAVEDIGGER   Give me leave. Here lies the water—good.
Here stands the man—good. If the man go to this water
15   and drown himself, it is, will he, nill he,° he goes. Mark   *willy-nilly*
you that. But if the water come to him and drown him, he
drowns not himself. Argal, he that is not guilty of his own
death shortens not his own life.

OTHER   But is this law?

20 GRAVEDIGGER   Ay, marry, is't—crowner's quest° law.   *inquest*

OTHER   Will you ha' the truth on't? If this had not been a
gentlewoman, she should have been buried out o' Christian burial.

GRAVEDIGGER   Why, there thou sayst.° And the more pity   *that's right*
25   that great folk should have countenance° in this world to   *privilege*
drown or hang themselves more than their even°-   *fellow*
Christian. Come, my spade. There is no ancient gentlemen but gardeners, ditchers, and grave-makers. They hold
up° Adam's profession.   *continue in*

30 OTHER   Was he a gentleman?

GRAVEDIGGER   'A° was the first that ever bore arms.[9] I'll   *He*
put another question to thee. If thou answerest me not
to the purpose, confess thyself—[1]

OTHER   Go to.[2]

35 GRAVEDIGGER   What is he that builds stronger than either
the mason, the shipwright, or the carpenter?

OTHER   The gallows-maker, for that outlives a thousand
tenants.

GRAVEDIGGER   I like thy wit well, in good faith. The gallows
40   does well.° But how does it well? It does well to those   *is a good answer*
that do ill. Now thou dost ill to say the gallows is built
stronger than the church. Argal, the gallows may do well
to thee. To't again, come.

OTHER   Who builds stronger than a mason, a shipwright,
45   or a carpenter?

GRAVEDIGGER   Ay, tell me that, and unyoke.[3]

OTHER   Marry,° now I can tell.   *By the Virgin Mary*

GRAVEDIGGER   To't.

OTHER   Mass,° I cannot tell.   *By the Mass*

50 GRAVEDIGGER   Cudgel thy brains no more about it, for
your dull ass will not mend° his pace with beating. And   *quicken*

7. In self-offense; an error for the Latin
legal phrase *se defendendo*, "[killing] in self-
defense."
8. A corruption of the Latin *ergo* (therefore).
9. Was given the heraldic insignia that entitled a man to call himself a "gentleman"

(punning on "arms," meaning "limbs").
1. Proverbial: "Confess thyself and be hanged."
2. An exclamation of impatience.
3. Cease (your joking), as an ox stops working
at the end of the day when unyoked.

when you are asked this question next, say "a grave-
maker." The houses he makes lasts till doomsday. Go get
thee in and fetch me a stoup° of liquor.   *flagon*

[*Exit* OTHER.]

[GRAVEDIGGER *digs.*]

55 "In youth when I did love, did love,   *Song.*
        Methought it was very sweet,
    To contract°—oh—the time for—a—my behove,°   *shorten / advantage*
        Oh, methought there—a—was nothing—a—meet."[4]

Enter HAMLET *and* HORATIO.

HAMLET   Has this fellow no feeling of his business? 'A°   *He*
60 sings in grave-making.

HORATIO   Custom hath made it in him a property of
easiness.[5]

HAMLET   'Tis e'en so. The hand of little employment
hath the daintier sense.[6]

65 GRAVEDIGGER   "But age, with his stealing steps,   *Song.*
        Hath clawed me in his clutch,
    And hath shipped me into the land,
        As if I had never been such."[7]

[*He throws up a skull.*]

HAMLET   That skull had a tongue in it and could sing
70 once. How the knave jowls° it to the ground, as if 'twere   *dashes*
Cain's jawbone, that did the first murder. This might be
the pate of a politician°—which this ass now   *schemer*
o'erreaches[8]—one that would circumvent God, might it
not?

75 HORATIO   It might, my lord.

HAMLET   Or of a courtier, which could say, "Good morrow,
sweet lord. How dost thou, sweet lord?" This might be
my Lord Such-a-one, that praised my Lord Such-a-one's
horse when 'a° went to beg it, might it not?   *he*

80 HORATIO   Ay, my lord.

HAMLET   Why, e'en so, and now my Lady Worm's, chapless,°   *without a lower jaw*
and knocked about the mazard° with a sexton's spade.   *head*
Here's fine revolution, an we had the trick[9] to see't. Did
these bones cost no more the breeding but to play at
85 loggets with them?[1] Mine ache to think on't.

GRAVEDIGGER   "A pickaxe and a spade, a spade,   *Song.*
        For and° a shrouding sheet;   *And also*
    Oh, a pit of clay for to be made

---

4. That is, nothing so suitable. The clown's
song is a garbled version of lines from Lord
Thomas Vaux's poem "The Aged Lover
Renounceth Love," which appears in *Tottel's
Miscellany* (1557).
5. Something he can do easily, without emotional distress.
6. Is more sensitive (because it is not
calloused).

7. Perhaps, been such in youth.
8. Lords it over (as if he were of superior rank).
9. If we had the ability. *Revolution:* a turning
of Fortune's wheel.
1. That is, did these bones mature for no
other purpose than to be used in loggets (a
game played by throwing sticks as closely as
possible to a stake)?

For such a guest is meet."

[*He throws up another skull.*]

90 HAMLET   There's another. Why may not that be the skull
of a lawyer? Where be his quiddities° now, his quillities,°   *subtleties / quibbles*
his cases, his tenures,° and his tricks? Why does he suffer   *property titles*
this mad knave now to knock him about the sconce°   *head*
with a dirty shovel, and will not tell him of his action of
95   battery?° Hum, this fellow might be in's time a great   *prosecution for assault*
buyer of land, with his statutes, his recognizances, his
fines, his double vouchers, his recoveries.[2] To have his fine°   *excellent*
pate full of fine dirt! Will vouchers vouch° him no more of   *assure*
his purchases and doubles than the length and breadth of
100   a pair of indentures?° The very conveyances of his lands   *contracts*
will scarcely lie in this box,° and must th'inheritor°   *coffin / owner*
himself have no more, ha?
HORATIO   Not a jot more, my lord.
HAMLET   Is not parchment made of sheepskins?
105 HORATIO   Ay, my lord, and of calves' skins too.
HAMLET   They are sheep and calves° which seek out   *simpletons and dolts*
assurance[3] in that. I will speak to this fellow.—Whose
grave's this, sirrah?[4]
GRAVEDIGGER   Mine, sir.
110   [*Sings.*] "Oh, a pit of clay for to be made"—
HAMLET   I think it be thine, indeed, for thou liest in't.
GRAVEDIGGER   You lie out on't, sir, and therefore 'tis not
yours. For my part, I do not lie in't, yet it is mine.
HAMLET   Thou dost lie in't, to be in't and say it is thine.
115   'Tis for the dead not for the quick;° therefore thou liest.   *living*
GRAVEDIGGER   'Tis a quick° lie, sir; 'twill away again from   *lively*
me to you.
HAMLET   What man dost thou dig it for?
GRAVEDIGGER   For no man, sir.
120 HAMLET   What woman then?
GRAVEDIGGER   For none neither.
HAMLET   Who is to be buried in't?
GRAVEDIGGER   One that was a woman, sir, but, rest her
soul, she's dead.
125 HAMLET   How absolute° the knave is! We must speak by   *precise, literal*
the card[5] or equivocation will undo us. By the Lord,
Horatio, this three years I have took note of it: the age is
grown so picked° that the toe of the peasant comes so   *refined*
near the heel of the courtier he galls his kibe.°—How   *chafes his heel*
130   long hast thou been grave-maker?

2. All legal terms: "statutes" and "recognizances" are documents in which portions of
land or properties were pledged as surety in a
contractual agreement; "double vouchers"
are summons of two persons into court to
attest to the title to a property; "recoveries"
are processes by which an entailed estate is

transferred from one party to another.
3. Who seek security (in legal documents).
4. Term of address to a social inferior.
5. With utmost clarity (Hamlet may be referring to the mariner's card, on which were
marked the points of a compass).

GRAVEDIGGER   Of the days i'the year, I came to't that day
     that our last king Hamlet overcame Fortinbras.
HAMLET   How long is that since?
GRAVEDIGGER   Cannot you tell that? Every fool can tell
135   that. It was that very day that young Hamlet was born,
     he that is mad and sent into England.
HAMLET   Ay, marry, why was he sent into England?
GRAVEDIGGER   Why, because 'a° was mad. 'A shall recover   *he*
     his wits there, or if 'a do not, 'tis no great matter there.
140 HAMLET   Why?
GRAVEDIGGER   'Twill not be seen in him there. There the
     men are as mad as he.
HAMLET   How came he mad?
GRAVEDIGGER   Very strangely, they say.
145 HAMLET   How strangely?
GRAVEDIGGER   Faith, e'en with losing his wits.
HAMLET   Upon what ground?°   *For what reason*
GRAVEDIGGER   Why, here in Denmark. I have been sexton
     here, man and boy, thirty years.
150 HAMLET   How long will a man lie i'the earth ere he rot?
GRAVEDIGGER   Faith, if 'a be not rotten before 'a die—as
     we have many pocky⁶ corpses that will scarce hold the
     laying in⁷—'a° will last you some eight year or nine year.   *he*
     A tanner will last you nine year.
155 HAMLET   Why he more than another?
GRAVEDIGGER   Why, sir, his hide is so tanned with his
     trade that 'a will keep out water a great while, and your
     water is a sore decayer of your whoreson⁸ dead body.
     Here's a skull now hath lien you i'th'earth three-and-
160   twenty years.
HAMLET   Whose was it?
GRAVEDIGGER   A whoreson mad fellow's it was. Whose do
     you think it was?
HAMLET   Nay, I know not.
165 GRAVEDIGGER   A pestilence on him for a mad rogue! 'A
     poured a flagon of Rhenish° on my head once. [*He picks*   *Rhine wine*
     up a skull.] This same skull, sir, was, sir, Yorick's skull,
     the King's jester.
HAMLET   This?
170 GRAVEDIGGER   E'en that.
HAMLET   [*He takes the skull.*] Alas, poor Yorick. I knew
     him, Horatio, a fellow of infinite jest, of most excellent
     fancy. He hath bore me on his back a thousand times,
     and now how abhorred in my imagination it is! My gorge
175   rises at it. Here hung those lips that I have kissed I know
     not how oft. Where be your gibes now, your gambols,°   *tricks*

---

6. Infected with the pox (a term that usually
referred to syphilis).
7. That is, that will scarcely hold together
during the burial ceremony.
8. Vile (a general term of contempt).

your songs, your flashes of merriment that were wont to
set the table on a roar? Not one now, to mock your own
grinning? Quite chopfallen?[9] Now, get you to my lady's
180 table and tell her, let her paint° an inch thick, to this   *wear makeup*
favor° she must come. Make her laugh at that. Prithee,   *appearance*
Horatio, tell me one thing.

HORATIO   What's that, my lord?

HAMLET   Dost thou think Alexander[1] looked o' this fashion
185 i'th'earth?

HORATIO   E'en so.

HAMLET   And smelt so? Pah! [*He puts down the skull.*]

HORATIO   E'en so, my lord.

HAMLET   To what base uses we may return, Horatio! Why
190 may not imagination trace the noble dust of Alexander
till 'a find it stopping a bunghole?

HORATIO   'Twere to consider too curiously° to consider so.   *minutely*

HAMLET   No, faith, not a jot, but to follow him thither with
modesty° enough, and likelihood to lead it: Alexander   *moderation*
195 died, Alexander was buried, Alexander returneth to dust,
the dust is earth, of earth we make loam,[2] and why of
that loam whereto he was converted might they not stop
a beer barrel?

Imperious Caesar, dead and turned to clay,
200 Might stop a hole to keep the wind away.
Oh, that that earth which kept the world in awe
Should patch a wall t'expel the winter's flaw!°   *gust of wind*

    Enter KING, QUEEN, LAERTES, *and the corpse* [*of* OPHE-
    LIA, *with a* DOCTOR OF DIVINITY, *and* ATTENDANTS.]

But soft, but soft awhile. Here comes the King,
The Queen, the courtiers. Who is this they follow?
205 And with such maimed rites?[3] This doth betoken
The corpse they follow did with desp'rate hand
Fordo° its own life. 'Twas of some estate.°   *Destroy / rank*
Couch we° awhile and mark.   *Let us hide*

    [*They withdraw.* OPHELIA's *body is taken to the grave.*]

LAERTES   What ceremony else?

210 HAMLET [*To* HORATIO]   That is Laertes, a very noble youth.
Mark.

LAERTES   What ceremony else?

DOCTOR   Her obsequies have been as far enlarged
As we have warranty.° Her death was doubtful,[4]   *authority*
And but that great command o'ersways the order[5]
215 She should in ground unsanctified been lodged
Till the last trumpet.° For° charitable prayers,   *Judgment Day / Instead of*

---

9. Dejected; with lower jaw fallen away.
1. Alexander the Great (356–323 B.C.E.), King
of Macedon, who conquered a great empire.
2. A mixture of clay, sand, and other materials
used to make bricks and plaster.
3. A curtailed ceremony (rather than an elab-

orate court funeral).
4. Questionable (because it may have been a
suicide.)
5. If the power of the court had not overruled
church practice.

Flints and pebbles should be thrown on her.
Yet here she is allowed her virgin crants,°   *garland*
Her maiden strewments,° and the bringing home   *strewn flowers*
220 Of bell and burial.[6]

LAERTES   Must there no more be done?

DOCTOR   No more be done.
We should profane the service of the dead
To sing a requiem and such rest to her
As to peace-parted° souls.   *peacefully departed*

LAERTES   Lay her i'th'earth,
225 And from her fair and unpolluted flesh
May violets spring. I tell thee, churlish priest,
A minist'ring angel shall my sister be
When thou liest howling.°   *(in hell)*

HAMLET [*To* HORATIO]   What, the fair Ophelia?

QUEEN [*Strewing flowers*]   Sweets to the sweet. Farewell.
230 I hoped thou shouldst have been my Hamlet's wife.
I thought thy bride-bed to have decked, sweet maid,
And not have strewed thy grave.

LAERTES   Oh, treble woe
Fall ten times double on that cursèd head
Whose wicked deed thy most ingenious sense°   *keen intellect*
235 Deprived thee of!—Hold off the earth awhile,
Till I have caught her once more in mine arms.

[*He leaps into the grave and embraces* OPHELIA.]

Now pile your dust upon the quick and dead,
Till of this flat a mountain you have made,
T'o'ertop old Pelion[7] or the skyish head
240 Of blue Olympus.

HAMLET [*Advancing*]   What is he whose grief
Bears such an emphasis, whose phrase° of sorrow *particular expression*
Conjures the wand'ring stars,° and makes them stand   *planets*
Like wonder-wounded° hearers? This is I,   *awestruck*
Hamlet the Dane![8]

LAERTES [*Grappling with him*]   The devil take thy soul!
245 HAMLET   Thou pray'st not well.
I prithee, take thy fingers from my throat,
For though I am not splenitive° and rash,   *hot-tempered*
Yet have I in me something dangerous,
Which let thy wisdom fear. Hold off thy hand.
250 KING   Pluck them asunder.

QUEEN   Hamlet, Hamlet!

ALL   Gentlemen!

HORATIO   Good my lord, be quiet.

[*The* ATTENDANTS *part them.*]

---

6. The burial procession and interment to the sound of church bells.
7. The highest mountain of a range in Thessaly, in northern Greece; in Greek mythology, the Titans piled Mount Ossa on Pelion in an attempt to scale Mount Olympus and defeat the gods.
8. The title normally given to the King of Denmark.

HAMLET   Why, I will fight with him upon this theme
255   Until my eyelids will no longer wag.°   *blink*
QUEEN   O my son, what theme?
HAMLET   I loved Ophelia. Forty thousand brothers
       Could not with all their quantity of love
       Make up my sum.—What wilt thou do for her?
260 KING   Oh, he is mad, Laertes.
QUEEN   For love of God, forbear him.°   *leave him alone*
HAMLET   'Swounds,° show me what thou'lt do.   *By God's wounds*
       Woo't° weep? Woo't fight? Woo't fast? Woo't tear thyself?   *Wilt thou*
       Woo't drink up eisel?° Eat a crocodile?   *vinegar*
265   I'll do't. Dost come here to whine,
       To outface me with leaping in her grave?
       Be buried quick° with her, and so will I.   *alive*
       And if thou prate of mountains, let them throw
       Millions of acres on us till our ground,
270   Singeing his pate against the burning zone,⁹
       Make Ossa like a wart! Nay, an° thou'lt mouth,°   *if / rant, rage*
       I'll rant as well as thou.
QUEEN   This is mere madness,
       And this awhile the fit will work on him.
       Anon,° as patient as the female dove,   *Soon*
275   When that her golden couplets¹ are disclosed,°   *hatched*
       His silence will sit drooping.
HAMLET   Hear you, sir.
       What is the reason that you use me thus?
       I loved you ever. But it is no matter.
       Let Hercules himself do what he may,
280   The cat will mew, and dog will have his day.²   *Exit.*
KING   I pray thee, good Horatio, wait upon° him.   *accompany*
                                                [*Exit* HORATIO.]
[*To* LAERTES]   Strengthen your patience in° our last night's   *with*
       speech;
       We'll put the matter to the present push.°   *to immediate trial*
       —Good Gertrude, set some watch over your son.—
285   This grave shall have a living° monument.   *lasting*
       An hour of quiet thereby shall we see;
       Till then in patience our proceeding be.
                                                Exeunt.

                                      5.2

       Enter HAMLET *and* HORATIO.

HAMLET   So much for this, sir; now shall you see the other.°   *other matter*
       You do remember all the circumstance?
HORATIO   Remember it, my lord!
HAMLET   Sir, in my heart there was a kind of fighting

---

9. In the Ptolemaic system, the sphere of the sun.
1. Two yellow chicks.

2. That is, even if mighty Hercules were to stand in the way, each will do what he must.
5.2 Location: The castle.

5   That would not let me sleep. Methought I lay
    Worse than the mutines in the bilboes.³ Rashly,°   *Impulsively*
    And praised be rashness for it—let us know°   *acknowledge*
    Our indiscretion sometime serves us well,
    When our deep plots do pall° and that should learn us   *weaken*
10 There's a divinity that shapes our ends,
    Rough-hew° them how we will—   *Roughly form*
    HORATIO   That is most certain.
    HAMLET   Up from my cabin,
    My sea-gown scarfed about me, in the dark
    Groped I to find out them, had my desire,
15 Fingered° their packet, and in fine° withdrew   *Filched / finally*
    To mine own room again, making so bold,
    My fears forgetting manners, to unfold
    Their grand commission, where I found, Horatio,
    A royal knavery, an exact command,
20 Larded° with many several° sorts of reasons,   *Enriched / different*
    Importing° Denmark's health and England's too,   *Relating to*
    With—ho!—such bugs and goblins in my life,⁴
    That on the supervise,° no leisure bated,°   *reading / delay permitted*
    No, not to stay° the grinding of the axe,   *await*
    My head should be struck off.
25 HORATIO   Is't possible?
    HAMLET [*Giving a paper*] Here's the commission. Read it
        at more leisure.
    But wilt thou hear now how I did proceed?
    HORATIO   I beseech you.
    HAMLET   Being thus benetted round° with villains—   *hemmed in*
30 Ere I could make a prologue to my brains,
    They had begun the play⁵—I sat me down,
    Devised a new commission, wrote it fair.⁶
    I once did hold it, as our statists° do,   *states men, politicians*
    A baseness° to write fair, and labored much   *lower-class skill*
35 How to forget that learning, but, sir, now
    It did me yeoman's service.° Wilt thou know   *served me well*
    Th'effect of what I wrote?
    HORATIO   Ay, good my lord.
    HAMLET   An earnest conjuration° from the King,   *request*
    As England was his faithful tributary,
40 As love between them like the palm might flourish,
    As peace should still her wheaten garland⁷ wear
    And stand a comma° 'tween their amities,   *link*
    And many suchlike "as"es of great charge,⁸
    That on the view and knowing of these contents,
45 Without debatement further more or less,
    He should those bearers put to sudden death,

3. The mutineers in the shackles.
4. Such things to be dreaded if I were allowed
to live. *Bugs:* bugbears.
5. That is, Hamlet began to devise a plan
before he consciously intended to do so.

6. That is, in the clear handwriting of the
clerks who prepared official documents.
7. A symbol of agricultural prosperity and peace.
8. Important clauses beginning with "as"
(with a pun on "asses").

Not shriving time[9] allowed.

HORATIO   How was this sealed?

HAMLET   Why, even in that was heaven ordinant.°   *guiding*
    I had my father's signet in my purse,
50   Which was the model of that Danish seal,
    Folded the writ up in the form of th'other,
    Subscribed° it, gave't th'impression,[1] placed it safely,   *Signed*
    The changeling[2] never known. Now, the next day
    Was our sea fight, and what to this was sequent°   *subsequent*
55   Thou knowest already.

HORATIO   So Guildenstern and Rosencrantz go to't.

HAMLET   They are not near my conscience; their defeat°   *destruction*
    Does by their own insinuation° grow.   *interference*
    'Tis dangerous when the baser nature comes
60   Between the pass and fell incensèd points
    Of mighty opposites.[3]

HORATIO   Why, what a king is this!

HAMLET   Does it not, think thee, stand me now upon?[4]
    He that hath killed my king and whored my mother,
    Popped in between th'election[5] and my hopes,
65   Thrown out his angle° for my proper° life,   *fishing hook / own*
    And with such coz'nage°—is't not perfect conscience?   *deceit*

        Enter [OSRIC], *a courtier.*

OSRIC   Your lordship is right welcome back to Denmark.

HAMLET   I humbly thank you, sir. [*Aside to* HORATIO] Dost
    know this water-fly?

70 HORATIO [*Aside*] No, my good lord.

HAMLET [*Aside*] Thy state is the more gracious,° for 'tis a vice   *blessed*
    to know him. He hath much land and fertile. Let a beast
    lord of beasts, and his crib shall stand at the King's mess.[6]
    'Tis a chough,° but, as I say, spacious in the possession of   *crow or jackdaw*
75   dirt.   *(noisy bird)*

OSRIC   Sweet lord, if your lordship were at leisure, I
    should impart a thing to you from His Majesty.

HAMLET   I will receive it, sir, with all diligence of spirit.
    Your bonnet° to his right use; 'tis for the head.   *hat*

80 OSRIC   I thank your lordship; it is very hot.

HAMLET   No, believe me, 'tis very cold; the wind is northerly.

OSRIC   It is indifferent° cold, my lord, indeed.   *somewhat*

HAMLET   But yet methinks it is very sultry and hot for my
    complexion.°   *constitution*

85 OSRIC   Exceedingly, my lord. It is very sultry, as 'twere—I
    cannot tell how. My lord, His Majesty bade me signify

---

9. No time for confession and absolution (as ordinarily granted to the condemned).
1. Imprinted the seal in wax.
2. The substituted letter (literally, an elf child substituted for a human child by fairies).
3. Between the thrust and fiercely angry rapiers ("points") of mighty adversaries.

4. Rest incumbent on me.
5. In Denmark, the king was elected.
6. A man of wealth and property (possessing many herds) shall find himself at the king's table, even if he is no better than his animals. *Crib:* feed box, manger.

to you that 'a° has laid a great wager on your head. Sir,   *he*
this is the matter—
HAMLET I beseech you, remember.[7]

    [HAMLET *gestures to* OSRIC *to put on his hat.*]

90 OSRIC Nay, good my lord, for my ease, in good faith. Sir,
here is newly come to court Laertes—believe me, an
absolute gentleman, full of most excellent differences,°   *superior qualities*
of very soft society and great showing.[8] Indeed, to speak
feelingly° of him, he is the card° or calendar of gentry,[9]   *discerningly / map*
95 for you shall find in him the continent of what part[1] a
gentleman would see.
HAMLET Sir, his definement suffers no perdition in you,[2]
though I know to divide him inventorially° would dozy°   *by way of inventory /*
th'arithmetic of memory, and yet but yaw neither in respect   *make dizzy*
100 of his quick sail.[3] But, in the verity of extolment,° I take   *future praise*
him to be a soul of great article,[4] and his infusion° of such   *inborn essence*
dearth° and rareness as, to make true diction° of him, his   *dearness / to speak truly*
semblable° is his mirror, and who else would trace him, his   *likeness*
umbrage, nothing more.[5]
105 OSRIC Your lordship speaks most infallibly of him
HAMLET The concernancy,° sir? Why do we wrap the gentle-   *relevance*
man in our more rawer breath?°   *words*
OSRIC Sir?
HORATIO Is't not possible to understand in another
110 tongue? You will do't, sir, really.[6]
HAMLET What imports the nomination° of this gentleman?   *mention*
OSRIC Of Laertes?
HORATIO [*To* HAMLET] His purse is empty already; all's
golden words are spent.
115 HAMLET Of him, sir.
OSRIC I know, you are not ignorant—
HAMLET I would you did, sir. Yet, in faith, if you did, it
would not much approve° me. Well, sir?   *recommend*
OSRIC You are not ignorant of what excellence Laertes is—
120 HAMLET I dare not confess that, lest I should compare
with him in excellence.[7] But to know a man well were to
know himself.

---

7. That is, remember your courtesy (i.e., put
your hat back on).
8. Of pleasing manners and noble appearance.
9. That is, the model of gentlemanly behavior.
Calendar: guide, register.
1. Embodiment of all qualities. ("Continent"
continues the geographical metaphor begun
in line 93.)
2. He loses nothing in your definition of him.
Hamlet mimics Osric's affected style of
speech to acknowledge that Osric's description does Laertes justice.
3. Still mocking Osric's mode of speech,
Hamlet employs a nautical metaphor: any

such tediously verbose attempt to list all of
Laertes' virtues would tend to swerve ("yaw")
off course in comparison with Laertes' rapid
forward motion ("quick sail").
4. Of great moment.
5. That is, anyone who imitates him becomes
only his shadow, nothing more.
6. That is, is it not possible to understand
your own (Osric's) manner of speech when
spoken by another (Hamlet)? You can if you
will try, sir, splendidly.
7. That is, I dare not confirm his excellence,
because I would have to assert my own equal
excellence to recognize his.

OSRIC   I mean, sir, for his weapon. But in the imputation
laid on him by them in his meed,° he's unfellowed.°   *merit / unequaled*

125 HAMLET   What's his weapon?

OSRIC   Rapier and dagger.

HAMLET   That's two of his weapons—but well.

OSRIC   The King, sir, hath wagered with him six Barbary
horses, against the which he has impawned,° as I take it, six   *wagered*

130 French rapiers and poniards, with their assigns,[8] as girdle,
hanger,[9] and so. Three of the carriages, in faith, are very
dear to fancy,[1] very responsive to the hilts, most delicate°   *charming*
carriages, and of very liberal conceit.°   *elaborate design*

HAMLET   What call you the "carriages"?

135 HORATIO   [*To* HAMLET] I knew you must be edified by the
margent[2] ere you had done.

OSRIC   The carriages, sir, are the hangers.

HAMLET   The phrase would be more germane to the matter if we could carry a cannon by our sides.[3] I would it

140 might be "hangers" till then. But, on: six Barbary horses
against six French swords, their assigns, and three
liberal-conceited carriages; that's the French bet against
the Danish. Why is this all "impawned," as you call it?

OSRIC   The King, sir, hath laid,° sir, that in a dozen passes   *wagered*

145 between yourself and him, he shall not exceed you three
hits.[4] He hath laid on twelve for nine,[5] and it would come
to immediate trial if your lordship would vouchsafe the
answer.°   *accept the challenge*

HAMLET   How if I answer no?

150 OSRIC   I mean, my lord, the opposition of your person in
trial.

HAMLET   Sir, I will walk here in the hall. If it please His
Majesty, it is the breathing time of day[6] with me; let the
foils be brought. The gentleman willing, and the King

155 hold his purpose, I will win for him an I can; if not, I will
gain nothing but my shame and the odd hits.

OSRIC   Shall I deliver you so?

HAMLET   To this effect, sir, after what flourish your nature
will.

160 OSRIC   I commend my duty° to your lordship.   *offer my service*

HAMLET   Yours.

[*Exit* OSRIC.]

'A° does well to commend° it himself; there are no tongues   *He / recommend*
else for's turn.[7]

8. With their paraphernalia ("assigns"), such
as sword belt ("girdle") and the loop or strap
on a sword belt from which the sword was
hung (often richly ornamented).

9. A pretentious way of saying "hangers."

1. That is beautifully made.

2. That is, by a gloss, as in the margin of a
book.

3. Hamlet refers to a gun carriage (the
wheeled frame on which a cannon is

mounted).

4. That is, the King has wagered that in
twelve bouts Laertes will outscore Hamlet by
no more than three hits.

5. The meaning of this phrase is unclear. Perhaps Osric is saying that in the twelve bouts
Laertes must score twelve hits against Hamlet's nine to win.

6. That is, the time for exercise.

7. That is, no one else will do it for him.

HORATIO   This lapwing runs away with the shell on his head.[8]

165 HAMLET   'A did comply so, sir, with his dug[9] before 'a
sucked it. Thus has he—and many more of the same
breed that I know the drossy° age dotes on—only got the   *worthless*
tune of the time and, out of an habit of encounter,[1] a kind
of yeasty collection,° which carries them through and   *set of frothy phrases*
170 through the most profane and winnowed opinions;[2] and
do but blow them to their trial, the bubbles are out.[3]

    Enter a LORD.

LORD   My lord, His Majesty commended him to you by
young Osric, who brings back to him that you attend
him in the hall. He sends to know if your pleasure hold
175 to play with Laertes, or that you will take longer time.

HAMLET   I am constant to my purposes; they follow the
King's pleasure. If his fitness speaks, mine is ready,[4] now
or whensoever, provided I be so able as now.

LORD   The King and Queen and all are coming down.

180 HAMLET   In happy time.[5]

LORD   The Queen desires you to use some gentle entertainment to Laertes[6] before you fall to play.

HAMLET   She well instructs me.

                                 [*Exit* LORD.]

HORATIO   You will lose, my lord.

185 HAMLET   I do not think so. Since he went into France, I
have been in continual practice. I shall win at the odds.°   *(see 5.2.140–43)*
Thou wouldst not think how ill all's here about my heart,
but it is no matter.

HORATIO   Nay, good my lord.

190 HAMLET   It is but foolery, but it is such a kind of gaingiv-
ing° as would perhaps trouble a woman.   *misgiving*

HORATIO   If your mind dislike anything, obey it. I will forestall their repair° hither and say you are not fit.   *arrival*

HAMLET   Not a whit, we defy augury. There is special provi-
195 dence in the fall of a sparrow.[7] If it be now, 'tis not to
come; if it be not to come, it will be now; if it be not now,
yet it will come. The readiness is all. Since no man of
aught he leaves knows, what is't to leave betimes?[8] Let be.

8. Elizabethans frequently alluded to the
notion that the newly hatched plover lapwing
(plover) runs from the nest with its shell on
its head. The suggestion here is that Osric
has finally replaced his bonnet. Also, his gait
may resemble the lapwing's wavering flight.
9. He did bow politely to his mother's breast.
1. The style of speech ("tune") of the time
and the conventions ("habit") of polite social
intercourse.
2. The most well-aired and well-sifted
opinions.
3. Put them to the test ("blow them") and their
ignorance will be exposed (the "bubbles" will
burst).

4. That is, if this is a good time for him, it is
also for me.
5. At an opportune time (a polite phrase).
6. To receive Laertes with some sign of
respect or courtesy.
7. Elizabethans distinguished between general providence (God's overarching plan for
human history) and special providence (God's
guidance in particular events, such as the fall
of a single sparrow, which, according to Matthew 10.29, shall not happen without God's
knowledge).
8. That is, because no man truly owns what he
leaves behind (i.e., earthly possessions), what
does it matter if he leaves this world early?

A table prepared. [ENTER] *trumpets, drums, and officers*
with cushions, KING, QUEEN, *and all the state, foils,*
daggers, [*cups of wine,* OSRIC,] *and* LAERTES

KING   Come, Hamlet, come, and take this hand from me.
[*The* KING *puts* LAERTES*'s hand into* HAMLET*'s.*]

200 HAMLET   Give me your pardon, sir. I have done you wrong,
But pardon't, as you are a gentleman.
This presence° knows,   royal assembly
And you must needs have heard, how I am punished
With a sore distraction. What I have done
205 That might your nature, honor, and exception°   displeasure
Roughly awake, I here proclaim was madness.
Was't Hamlet wronged Laertes? Never Hamlet.
If Hamlet from himself be ta'en away,
And when he's not himself does wrong Laertes,
210 Then Hamlet does it not. Hamlet denies it.
Who does it, then? His madness. If't be so,
Hamlet is of the faction that is wronged;
His madness is poor Hamlet's enemy.
Let my disclaiming from° a purposed evil   disavowing any part in
215 Free me so far in your most generous thoughts
That I have shot my arrow o'er the house
And hurt my brother.
LAERTES   I am satisfied in nature,[9]
Whose motive in this case should stir me most
To my revenge. But in my terms of honor
220 I stand aloof, and will no reconcilement
Till by some elder masters of known honor
I have a voice° and precedent of peace   authoritative declaration
To keep my name ungored.° But till that time   unblemished
I do receive your offered love like love,
And will not wrong it.
225 HAMLET   I embrace it freely,
And will this brother's wager frankly° play.   freely
—Give us the foils.
LAERTES   Come, one for me.
HAMLET   I'll be your foil,[1] Laertes. In mine ignorance
Your skill shall, like a star i'the darkest night,
Stick° fiery off indeed.   Stand out; thrust
230 LAERTES   You mock me, sir.
HAMLET   No, by this hand.
KING   Give them the foils, young Osric. Cousin Hamlet,
You know the wager?
HAMLET   Very well, my lord;
Your Grace has laid the odds o' the weaker side.
235 KING   I do not fear it; I have seen you both.

9. That is, according to natural personal
feeling.
1. Flattering contrast (from the metal foil

placed under a gem to add to its brilliance),
with a pun on fencing foils.

But since he is better,° we have therefore odds.²	*favored*

LAERTES   This is too heavy. Let me see another.

HAMLET This likes° me well. These foils have all a° length?	*pleases / the same*

[*They prepare to play.*]

OSRIC   Ay, my good lord.

240 KING Set me the stoups° of wine upon that table.	*flagons*

If Hamlet give the first or second hit,
Or quit in answer of the third exchange,³
Let all the battlements their ordnance fire.

The King shall drink to Hamlet's better breath,°	*improved energy*
245 And in the cup an union° shall he throw,	*a pearl*

Richer than that which four successive kings
In Denmark's crown have worn. Give me the cups,

And let the kettle° to the trumpet speak,	*kettledrum*

The trumpet to the cannoneer without,
250   The cannons to the heavens, the heaven to earth,
"Now the King drinks to Hamlet." Come, begin.

     Trumpets the while.

And you, the judges, bear a wary eye.

HAMLET   Come on, sir.

LAERTES   Come, my lord.

     [*They play.* HAMLET *scores a hit.*]

255   HAMLET   One.

LAERTES   No.

HAMLET   Judgment?

OSRIC   A hit, a very palpable hit.

     Drum, trumpets, and shot. Flourish. A piece goes off.

LAERTES   Well, again.

260 KING Stay,° give me drink. Hamlet, this pearl is thine.	*Stop*

Here's to thy health. [*He drinks.*] Give him the cup.

HAMLET   I'll play this bout first. Set it by awhile.
Come. [*They play.*] Another hit; what say you?

LAERTES   I do confess't.

KING   Our son shall win.

265 QUEEN He's fat° and scant of breath.	*sweaty; out of shape*
Here, Hamlet, take my napkin,° rub thy brows.	*handkerchief*
The Queen carouses° to thy fortune, Hamlet.	*drinks a toast*

HAMLET   Good madam.

KING   Gertrude, do not drink.

270   QUEEN   I will, my lord. I pray you pardon me. [*She drinks.*]

KING [*Aside*]   It is the poisoned cup; it is too late.

HAMLET   I dare not drink yet, madam; by-and-by.

QUEEN   Come, let me wipe thy face.

LAERTES [*Aside*]   My lord, I'll hit him now.

KING [*Aside*]   I do not think't.

275   LAERTES [*Aside*] And yet it is almost against my conscience.

HAMLET   Come, for the third, Laertes; you do but dally.

---

2. That is, I have arranged the terms in your favor (referring to Hamlet's advantage of three hits).

3. Repay ("quit") Laertes with a hit in the third bout (presumably having lost the first two).

I pray you pass° with your best violence;   *thrust*
I am sure you make a wanton of me.[4]

LAERTES   Say you so? Come on.

    [*They play.*]

280 OSRIC   Nothing neither way.

LAERTES   Have at you now!

    [LAERTES *wounds* HAMLET; *then, in scuffling, they*
    change rapiers, and HAMLET *wounds* LAERTES.]

KING   Part them! They are incensed.

HAMLET   Nay, come again!

    [*The* QUEEN *falls.*]

OSRIC   Look to the Queen there, ho!

HORATIO   They bleed on both sides. How is it, my lord?

285 OSRIC   How is't, Laertes?

LAERTES   Why, as a woodcock[5] to my own springe,° Osric;   *trap*
I am justly killed with mine own treachery.

HAMLET   How does the Queen?

KING   She swoons to see them bleed.

QUEEN   No, no, the drink, the drink—O my dear Hamlet!—

290 The drink, the drink! I am poisoned. [*She dies.*]

HAMLET   O villainy! Ho, let the door be locked!
Treachery! Seek it out!

                    [LAERTES *falls. Exit* OSRIC.]

LAERTES   It is here, Hamlet, thou art slain.
No med'cine in the world can do thee good;

295 In thee there is not half an hour's life;
The treacherous instrument is in thy hand,
Unbated° and envenomed. The foul practice   *Not blunted*
Hath turned itelf on me. Lo, here I lie,
Never to rise again. Thy mother's poisoned.

300 I can no more. The King, the King's to blame.

HAMLET   The point envenomed too? Then, venom, to thy work!

    [*He stabs the* KING.]

ALL   Treason! treason!

KING   Oh, yet defend me, friends! I am but hurt.

HAMLET   [*Forcing the* KING *to drink*]
Here, thou incestuous, damnèd Dane,

305 Drink off this potion! Is thy union[6] here?
Follow my mother.

    [*The* KING *dies.*]

LAERTES   He is justly served;
It is a poison tempered° by himself.   *mixed*
Exchange forgiveness with me, noble Hamlet.
Mine and my father's death come not upon thee,[7]

310 Nor thine on me. [*He dies.*]

---

4. You play with me as if I were a spoiled child.
5. A proverbially stupid bird.
6. Pearl (with a pun on "marriage").

7. That is, you are not responsible for our deaths.

HAMLET   Heaven make thee free of it. I follow thee.
I am dead, Horatio. Wretched Queen, adieu.
You that look pale and tremble at this chance,
That are but mutes° or audience to this act,   *silent witnesses*
315   Had I but time—as this fell sergeant,[8] Death,
Is strict in his arrest—oh, I could tell you—
But let it be. Horatio, I am dead;
Thou livest. Report me and my cause aright
To the unsatisfied.
HORATIO   Never believe it.
320   I am more an antique Roman than a Dane.[9]
Here's yet some liquor left.

   [*He attempts to drink from the poisoned cup but* HAMLET
   restrains him.]

HAMLET   As thou'rt a man,
Give me the cup! Let go! By heaven, I'll ha't.
O God, Horatio, what a wounded name,
Things standing thus unknown, shall I leave behind me.
325   If thou didst ever hold me in thy heart,
Absent thee from felicity awhile,
And in this harsh world draw thy breath in pain,
To tell my story.   *A march afar off* [*and shot within*].
                    What warlike noise is this?

   Enter OSRIC.

OSRIC   Young Fortinbras, with conquest come from Poland,
330   To th'ambassadors of England gives
This warlike volley.°   *military salute*
HAMLET   Oh, I die, Horatio.
The potent poison quite o'ercrows° my spirit.   *triumphs over*
I cannot live to hear the news from England,
But I do prophesy th'election lights
335   On Fortinbras. He has my dying voice.°   *vote*
So tell him, with th'occurrents° more and less,   *events*
Which have solicited[1]—the rest is silence. [*He dies.*]
HORATIO   Now cracks a noble heart. Good night, sweet
   prince,
And flights of angels sing thee to thy rest. [*March within.*]
340   Why does the drum come hither?

   Enter FORTINBRAS, *with the* [*English*] AMBASSADORS
   [*with drums, colors, and* ATTENDANTS].

FORTINBRAS   Where is this sight?
HORATIO   What is it you would see?
If aught of woe or wonder, cease your search.
FORTINBRAS   This quarry cries on havoc.[2] O proud Death,
What feast is toward° in thine eternal cell,   *in preparation*

---

8. This dread sheriff's officer.
9. The ancient Romans (unlike the Christian Danes) viewed suicide as sometimes honorable.
1. Incited (this sentence seems to be incomplete, possibly broken off as Hamlet realizes he is about to die).
2. This heap of game ("quarry") proclaims a massacre.

345 That thou so many princes at a shot
  So bloodily hast struck?
AMBASSADOR   The sight is dismal,
  And our affairs from England come too late.
  The ears are senseless that should give us hearing
350 To tell him° his commandment is fulfilled,   *(Claudius)*
  That Rosencrantz and Guildenstern are dead.
  Where should we have our thanks?
HORATIO   Not from his mouth,
  Had it th'ability of life to thank you.
  He never gave commandment for their death.
  But since, so jump° upon this bloody question,° *immediately / quarrel*
355 You from the Polack wars, and you from England,
  Are here arrived, give order that these bodies
  High on a stage be placèd to the view,
  And let me speak to th'yet unknowing world
  How these things came about. So shall you hear
360 Of carnal, bloody, and unnatural acts,
  Of accidental judgments,° casual° slaughters, *retributions / chance*
  Of deaths put on° by cunning, and for no cause,   *instigated*
  And, in this upshot, purposes mistook
  Fall'n on th'inventors' heads. All this can I
  Truly deliver.
365 FORTINBRAS Let us haste to hear it,
  And call the noblest to the audience.
  For me, with sorrow I embrace my fortune.
  I have some rights of memory in this kingdom,
  Which now to claim my vantage doth invite me.
370 HORATIO Of that I shall have also cause to speak,
  And from his mouth whose voice will draw on more.[3]
  But let this same be presently performed,
  Even while men's minds are wild, lest more mischance
  On° plots and errors happen.   *On top of*
FORTINBRAS   Let four captains
375 Bear Hamlet like a soldier to the stage,
  For he was likely, had he been put on,[4]
  To have proved most royal; and for his passage,
  The soldiers' music and the rite of war
  Speak loudly for him.
380 Take up the bodies. Such a sight as this
  Becomes the field,[5] but here shows° much amiss. *appears*
  Go bid the soldiers shoot.

     Exeunt [marching, with the bodies;
    after which a peal of ordnance is shot off].

       FINIS.

---

3. Whose vote will draw more votes (in Fortinbras's favor).

4. Put to the test (as King of Denmark).
5. Is fitting for a battlefield.

Twelfth Night;
or, What You Will

THE PERSONS OF THE PLAY

ORSINO, duke of Illyria

VALENTINE
CURIO } attending on Orsino

FIRST OFFICER

SECOND OFFICER

VIOLA, a lady, later disguised as
  Cesario

A CAPTAIN

SEBASTIAN, Viola's twin brother

ANTONIO, another sea-captain

OLIVIA, a countess

MARIA, Olivia's waiting-gentlewoman

SIR TOBY Belch, Olivia's kinsman

SIR ANDREW Aguecheek, companion of
  Sir Toby

MALVOLIO, Olivia's steward

FABIAN, a member of Olivia's
  household

FESTE the clown, Olivia's jester

A PRIEST

A SERVANT of Olivia

Musicians, sailors, lords, attendants

1.1

Enter ORSINO, *Duke of Illyria,*[1] CURIO, *and other
lords, with musicians playing.*

ORSINO   If music be the food of love, play on.
  Give me excess of it, that, surfeiting,
  The appetite may sicken and so die.
  That strain° again! It had a dying fall.°   *(of music) / cadence*
5 O, it came o'er my ear like the sweet sound
  That breathes upon a bank of violets,
  Stealing and giving odor. Enough; no more.
  'Tis not so sweet now as it was before.
  O spirit of love, how quick and fresh[2] art thou,
10 That, notwithstanding thy capacity,
  Receiveth as the sea,° naught enters there,   *without limit*
  Of what validity° and pitch[3] soe'er,   *value*
  But falls into abatement° and low price   *decreased value*
  Even in a minute. So full of shapes° is fancy°   *fanciful forms / love*
15 That it alone is high fantastical[4]
CURIO   Will you go hunt, my lord?
ORSINO   What, Curio?
CURIO   The hart.

1.1 Location: Orsino's palace.
1. An imaginary dukedom on the eastern
coast of the Adriatic Sea.
2. Lively and eager to devour.

3. High worth (in falconry, "pitch" is the
highest point in a hawk's flight).
4. That is, love reigns supreme in the imagination of the lover.

ORSINO Why, so I do, the noblest that I have.⁵
  O, when mine eyes did see Olivia first,
  Methought she purged the air of pestilence.⁶
20 That instant was I turned into a hart,
  And my desires, like fell° and cruel hounds,   *fierce*
  E'er since pursue me.⁷

  Enter VALENTINE

            How now, what news from her?
VALENTINE So please my lord, I might not be admitted,°   *was not granted entry*
  But from her handmaid do return this answer:
25 The element itself, till seven years' heat,⁸
  Shall not behold her face at ample° view,   *full*
  But like a cloistress° she will veilèd walk,   *nun*
  And water once a day her chamber round
  With eye-offending brine°—all this to season°   *salty tears / preserve*
30 A brother's dead love,⁹ which she would keep fresh
  And lasting in her sad remembrance.
ORSINO O, she that hath a heart of that fine frame¹
  To pay this debt of love but to a° brother,   *to a mere*
  How will she love when the rich golden shaft²
35 Hath killed the flock of all affections else°   *all other feelings*
  That live in her; when liver, brain, and heart,³
  These sovereign thrones, are all supplied, and filled
  Her sweet perfections⁴ with one self° king!   *one and the same*
  Away before me to sweet beds of flowers!
40 Love thoughts lie rich when canopied with bowers.

                                      Exeunt.°   *They exit (Latin)*

1.2

  Enter VIOLA, *a* CAPTAIN, *and sailors.*

VIOLA What country, friends, is this?
CAPTAIN   This is Illyria, lady.
VIOLA And what should I do in Illyria?
  My brother he is in Elysium.⁵
  Perchance° he is not drowned. What think you, sailors?   *Perhaps*
5 CAPTAIN It is perchance° that you yourself were saved.   *by chance*
VIOLA O my poor brother! And so perchance may he be.
CAPTAIN True, madam. And to comfort you with chance,°   *that possibility*
  Assure yourself, after our ship did split,°   *break up*
  When you and those poor number saved with you

---

5. Orsino puns on "hart" and "heart."
6. Serious epidemic diseases were thought to be caused by bad air.
7. Orsino compares himself to Actaeon, a hunter in classical mythology who was turned into a stag and torn apart by his own dogs after he saw the goddess Diana (Artemis) bathing naked.
8. The sky ("element") itself for seven hot summers.
9. That is, her love for her dead brother.

1. Such excellent construction.
2. The arrow of Cupid, Roman god of love.
3. In the Renaissance, the liver, brain, and heart were often identified as the seats of, respectively, love, the rational soul, and feeling or emotion.
4. And her sweet perfections are filled.
1.2 Location: The coast of Illyria.
5. In classical mythology, the abode of the blessed after death.

10   Hung on our driving boat,[6] I saw your brother,
      Most provident in peril, bind himself—
      Courage and hope both teaching him the practice—
      To a strong mast that lived° upon the sea,   *floated*
      Where, like Arion[7] on the dolphin's back,
15   I saw him hold acquaintance with the waves[8]
      So long as I could see.
      VIOLA [*giving him money*]   For saying so, there's gold.
      Mine own escape unfoldeth to° my hope,   *encourages*
      Whereto thy speech serves for authority,°   *corroboration*
      The like° of him. Know'st thou this country?   *The same (news)*
20   CAPTAIN   Ay, madam, well, for I was bred and born
      Not three hours' travel from this very place.
      VIOLA   Who governs here?
      CAPTAIN   A noble duke, in nature as in name.
      VIOLA   What is his name?
25   CAPTAIN   Orsino.
      VIOLA   Orsino. I have heard my father name him.
      He was a bachelor then.
      CAPTAIN   And so is now, or was so very late;°   *recently*
      For but a month ago I went from hence,
30   And then 'twas fresh in murmur°—as, you know,   *rumor*
      What great ones do the less will prattle of—
      That he did seek the love of fair Olivia.
      VIOLA   What's she?
      CAPTAIN   A virtuous maid, the daughter of a count
35   That died some twelvemonth since, then leaving her
      In the protection of his son, her brother,
      Who shortly° also died, for whose dear love,   *shortly thereafter*
      They say, she hath abjured° the sight   *renounced*
      And company of men.
      VIOLA   O, that I served that lady,
40   And might not be delivered° to the world   *made known*
      Till I had made mine own occasion mellow,°   *ripe (to be known)*
      What my estate° is.   *rank, social position*
      CAPTAIN   That were hard to compass,°   *achieve*
      Because she will admit no kind of suit,°   *petition*
      No, not the Duke's.
45   VIOLA   There is a fair behavior[9] in thee, captain,
      And though that nature with a beauteous wall
      Doth oft close in pollution,[1] yet of thee
      I will believe thou hast a mind that suits
      With this thy fair and outward character.
50   I prithee°—and I'll pay thee bounteously—   *pray thee*
      Conceal me what I am, and be my aid
      For such disguise as haply° shall become   *possibly*

---

6. Our boat being driven before the wind.
7. Greek poet and singer (late 7th c. B.C.E.).
According to legend, to avoid being murdered
by pirates, he jumped into the sea and was
rescued by dolphins enchanted by his music.

8. That is, stay above water.
9. Manner of conduct; external appearance.
1. Though nature often conceals a person's
inward corruption with outward beauty.

The form of my intent.[2] I'll serve this duke.
Thou shalt present me as an eunuch[3] to him.

55 It may be worth thy pains,° for I can sing   *troubles*
And speak to him in many sorts of music
That will allow me very worth his service.[4]
What else may hap, to time I will commit.
Only shape thou thy silence to my wit.°   *plan*

60 CAPTAIN   Be you his eunuch, and your mute° I'll be.   *silent servant*
When my tongue blabs, then let mine eyes not see.

VIOLA   I thank thee. Lead me on.   *Exeunt.*

1.3

Enter SIR TOBY [*Belch*] *and* MARIA.[5]

SIR TOBY   What a plague° means my niece to take the   *(an oath)*
death of her brother thus? I am sure care's an enemy
to life.

MARIA   By my troth, Sir Toby, you must come in earlier o'
5 nights. Your cousin,° my lady, takes great exceptions to   *kinswoman*
your ill hours.

SIR TOBY   Why, let her except before excepted![6]

MARIA   Ay, but you must confine yourself within the
modest limits of order.

10 SIR TOBY   Confine? I'll confine myself no finer[7] than I
am. These clothes are good enough to drink in, and so
be these boots too. An° they be not, let them hang them-   *If*
selves in their own straps!

MARIA   That quaffing and drinking will undo you. I heard
15 my lady talk of it yesterday, and of a foolish knight that
you brought in one night here to be her wooer.

SIR TOBY   Who, Sir Andrew Aguecheek?[8]

MARIA   Ay, he.

SIR TOBY   He's as tall[9] a man as any's in Illyria.

20 MARIA   What's that to th' purpose?

SIR TOBY   Why, he has three thousand ducats a year!

MARIA   Ay, but he'll have but a year in all these ducats.[1]
He's a very° fool and a prodigal.   *an absolute*

SIR TOBY   Fie that you'll say so! He plays o' th' viol-de-
25 gamboys,[2] and speaks three or four languages word for

2. The outward appearance of my plan.
3. A castrato, a male soprano. While this disguise would explain Viola's feminine voice, she ultimately chooses the disguise of a young (male) page whose voice has not yet changed.
4. That will prove me very worthy to serve him.
1.3 Location: The Countess Olivia's residence.
5. Usually pronounced "Ma-RYE-uh."
6. A play on a Latin legal phrase (*exceptis excipiendis*) meaning "with the necessary exceptions having been made." Thus Toby

sidesteps Olivia's criticism.
7. A pun: he will dress ("confine") himself neither more strictly (because of his girth) nor more elegantly.
8. Usually pronounced "AY-gyoo-cheek."
9. Brave (Maria understands the word in its usual modern sense).
1. That is, he will spend his money in a year.
2. The viola da gamba, a bowed stringed instrument played while held between the legs (as is the modern cello).

word without book,° and hath all the good gifts of   *from memory*
nature.

MARIA He hath indeed, almost natural,[3] for besides
that he's a fool, he's a great quarreler, and but that he
30   hath the gift° of a coward to allay the gust° he hath in   *talent / relish*
quarreling, 'tis thought among the prudent he would
quickly have the gift of a grave.

SIR TOBY By this hand, they are scoundrels and sub-
stractors° that say so of him. Who are they?   *i.e., detractors*
35   MARIA They that add, moreover, he's drunk nightly in
your company.

SIR TOBY With drinking healths to my niece. I'll drink
to her as long as there is a passage in my throat and
drink in Illyria. He's a coward and a coistrel° that will   *horse groom, knave*
40   not drink to my niece till his brains turn o'th' toe, like
a parish top.[4] What, wench! *Castiliano, vulgo,*[5] for here
comes Sir Andrew Agueface.[6]

Enter SIR ANDREW *[Aguecheek].*

SIR ANDREW Sir Toby Belch! How now, Sir Toby Belch?

SIR TOBY Sweet Sir Andrew!

45   SIR ANDREW *[to* MARIA*]* Bless you, fair shrew.[7]

MARIA And you too, sir.

SIR TOBY Accost, Sir Andrew, accost![8]

SIR ANDREW What's that?

SIR TOBY My niece's chambermaid.°   *lady-in-waiting*

50   SIR ANDREW Good Mistress Accost, I desire better
acquaintance.

MARIA My name is Mary, sir.

SIR ANDREW Good Mistress Mary Accost—

SIR TOBY You mistake, knight. "Accost" is front her,
55   board her, woo her, assail[9] her.

SIR ANDREW By my troth, I would not undertake[1] her in
this company.° Is that the meaning of "accost"?   *this audience*

MARIA Fare you well, gentlemen. *[begins to exit]*

SIR TOBY An° thou let part so, Sir Andrew, would thou   *If*
60   mightst never draw sword again.[2]

SIR ANDREW An you part so, mistress, I would I might
never draw sword again. Fair lady, do you think you
have fools in hand?°   *are dealing with fools*

---

3. Naturally deficient in intellect. (Idiots were called "naturals.")
4. A large top that parishioners could whip into spinning for their entertainment and exercise.
5. The meaning of this phrase is unknown; perhaps "speak of the devil," because Castilians were considered devilish.
6. With a face pale and thin, as if he were suffering from the cold stage of an ague.
7. A woman given to scolding; here, probably used in a benign and playful sense.

8. Greet (Maria), possibly with a kiss as was Elizabethan fashion.
9. A series of nautical terms with double meanings, beginning with "accost," or sail alongside (which is also a meaning of "board"). *Front*: meet face-to-face; *board*: make advances to; *assail*: make trial of, woo.
1. Attempt her (with sexual implication).
2. That is, to part with her in this fashion is unworthy of a knight (but also with sexual implication).

MARIA   Sir, I have not you by th' hand.

65   SIR ANDREW   Marry,[3] but you shall have, and here's my
hand.

MARIA   [taking his hand]   Now sir, thought is free.[4] I pray
you, bring your hand to th' butt'ry-bar,[5] and let it drink.

SIR ANDREW   Wherefore,° sweetheart? What's your meta-   Why
70   phor?

MARIA   It's dry,[6] sir.

SIR ANDREW   Why, I think so. I am not such an ass but I
can keep my hand dry.[7] But what's your jest?

MARIA   A dry jest,[8] sir.

75   SIR ANDREW   Are you full of them?

MARIA   Ay, sir, I have them at my fingers' ends.[9] Marry,
now I let go your hand, I am barren.°   Exit.   (of jokes)

SIR TOBY   O knight, thou lack'st° a cup of canary![1] When   are in need of
did I see thee so put down?[2]

80   SIR ANDREW   Never in your life, I think, unless you see
canary put me down.° Methinks sometimes I have no   lay me low
more wit than a Christian° or an ordinary man has. But   an ordinary human
I am a great eater of beef,[3] and I believe that does
harm to my wit.

85   SIR TOBY   No question.

SIR ANDREW   An I thought that, I'd forswear it. I'll ride
home tomorrow, Sir Toby.

SIR TOBY   Pourquoi,° my dear knight?   Why (French)

SIR ANDREW   What is "pourquoi"? Do, or not do? I would
90   I had bestowed that time in the tongues[4] that I have in
fencing, dancing, and bear-baiting. O, had I but followed the arts!°   i.e., liberal arts

SIR TOBY   Then hadst thou had an excellent head of hair.

SIR ANDREW   Why, would that have mended° my hair?   improved

95   SIR TOBY   Past question, for thou seest it will not curl by
nature.

SIR ANDREW   But it becomes me well enough, does't not?

SIR TOBY   Excellent! It hangs like flax on a distaff,[5] and I
hope to see a housewife take thee between her legs and
100   spin it off.[6]

---

3. By the Virgin Mary (a mild oath).

4. I may think whatever I like (proverbial).

5. The ledge on top of the half-door to the buttery, a storeroom for liquor and provisions, over which such items were served.

6. Unproductive of its intended meaning. Dryness of the palm of Sir Andrew's hand (which Maria is holding) is also a sign of sexual impotence.

7. A reference to the proverb "fools have wit enough to keep themselves out of the rain."

8. A joke about dryness; a joke that displays a dry or sharp wit; a joke that partially fails because of Sir Andrew's obtuseness.

9. Ready at hand; she also refers to Sir

Andrew, whom she holds at her fingers' ends.

1. A sweet wine (originally from the Canary Islands).

2. Defeated verbally, made a fool of.

3. Eating too much beef was believed to lower intelligence.

4. The study of languages; Sir Toby answers as if he had meant (curling) tongs.

5. A staff that holds the wool or flax being spun into thread.

6. That is, remove his hair both by using it as if it were flax to be spun and by infecting him with venereal disease (which will result in baldness). One meaning of "housewife" (hus-wife) is prostitute.

SIR ANDREW Faith,° I'll home tomorrow, Sir Toby. Your *By my faith*
niece will not be seen, or if she be, it's four to one she'll
none of me. The Count[7] himself here hard by° woos her. *nearby*
SIR TOBY She'll none o' th' Count. She'll not match above
105 her degree,° neither in estate,° years, nor wit. I *social rank / status*
have heard her swear't. Tut, there's life in't,[8] man.
SIR ANDREW I'll stay a month longer. I am a fellow o' th'
strangest mind i' th' world. I delight in masques and
revels sometimes altogether.
110 SIR TOBY Art thou good at these kickshawses,[9] knight?
SIR ANDREW As any man in Illyria, whatsoever he be,
under the degree of my betters; and yet I will not compare with an old man.° *expert*
SIR TOBY What is thy excellence in a galliard,[1] knight?
115 SIR ANDREW Faith, I can cut a caper.[2]
SIR TOBY And I can cut the mutton° to't. *cooked sheep; whore*
SIR ANDREW And I think I have the back-trick[3] simply as
strong as any man in Illyria.
SIR TOBY Wherefore are these things hid? Wherefore
120 have these gifts a curtain[4] before 'em? Are they like to
take dust, like Mistress Mall's[5] picture? Why dost thou
not go to church in a galliard and come home in a cor-
anto?[6] My very walk should be a jig. I would not so
much as make water but in a cinquepace.[7] What dost
125 thou mean? Is it a world to hide virtues in? I did think,
by the excellent constitution of thy leg, it was formed
under the star of a galliard.[8]
SIR ANDREW Ay, 'tis strong, and it does indifferent° well in *reasonably*
a flame-colored stock.° Shall we set about some revels? *multicolored stockings*
130 SIR TOBY What shall we do else? Were we not born under
Taurus?[9]
SIR ANDREW Taurus? That's sides and heart.
SIR TOBY No, sir, it is legs and thighs. Let me see thee
caper.
[SIR ANDREW *dances.*]
135 Ha, higher! Ha, ha, excellent. *Exeunt.*

---

7. That is, Duke Orsino (sometimes referred
to as "Count" in the play).
8. Where there's life, there's hope (proverbial).
9. Trifles (from the French *quelque chose*).
1. A quick, lively dance in triple time.
2. Dance or leap in a frolicsome way. Also,
capers (the buds or berries of a plant used as
a condiment) were employed in mutton
sauces.
3. Backward step in the galliard.
4. Paintings were sometimes hidden behind
curtains to protect them from dust and
sunlight.
5. "Mall" was a nickname for "Mary." It has
been suggested that this is a reference to

Queen Elizabeth's lady-in-waiting, Mary Fit-
ton, who was pregnant with Sir William Knol-
lys's illegitimate child at the time Shakespeare
wrote *Twelfth Night*.
6. A "running dance" (*courante*) of French
origin.
7. A galliard-like dance whose steps were regulated by the number five.
8. That is, under a star conducive to dancing.
9. The second sign of the zodiac, the Bull,
was associated with the neck and the throat
and, less commonly, with the legs and thighs,
but never with the sides and the heart (as Sir
Andrew suggests).

1.4

Enter VALENTINE, *and* VIOLA *in man's attire [as Cesario].*

VALENTINE   If the Duke continue these favors towards
you, Cesario, you are like to be much advanced. He
hath known you but three days, and already you are no
stranger.

5 VIOLA   You either fear his humor° or my negligence, that   *changeable mood*
you call in question the continuance of his love. Is he
inconstant, sir, in his favors?

VALENTINE   No, believe me.

VIOLA   I thank you. Here comes the Count.

Enter ORSINO, CURIO, *and attendants*

10 ORSINO   Who saw Cesario, ho?

VIOLA   On your attendance,° my lord, here.   *At your service*

ORSINO   *[to* CURIO *and attendants]*   Stand you a while
aloof.° *[to* VIOLA*]* Cesario,   *to the side*
Thou know'st no less but all.° I have unclasped   *i.e., everything*
To thee the book even of my secret soul.

15 Therefore, good youth, address thy gait unto her.°   *go to (Olivia)*
Be not denied access, stand at her doors
And tell them, there thy fixèd foot shall grow°   *take root*
Till thou have audience.

VIOLA   Sure, my noble lord,
If she be so abandoned to her sorrow

20 As it is spoke, she never will admit me.

ORSINO   Be clamorous and leap all civil bounds[1]
Rather than make unprofited° return.   *unsuccessful*

VIOLA   Say I do speak with her, my lord, what then?

ORSINO   O, then unfold the passion of my love.

25 Surprise her with discourse of my dear° faith.[2]   *heartfelt*
It shall become thee well to act my woes—
She will attend it better in thy youth
Than in a nuncio's° of more grave aspect.°   *messenger's / appearance*

VIOLA   I think not so, my lord.

ORSINO   Dear lad, believe it;

30 For they shall yet° belie thy happy years   *thus far*
That say thou art a man. Diana's lip
Is not more smooth and rubious,° thy small pipe°   *ruby red / treble voice*
Is as the maiden's organ, shrill° and sound,°   *high-pitched / uncracked*
And all is semblative° a woman's part.   *similar to*

35 I know thy constellation[3] is right apt
For this affair. *[to* CURIO *and attendants]* Some four or
five attend him,
All, if you will, for I myself am best
When least in company. *[to* VIOLA*]* Prosper well in this

1.4 Location: Orsino's palace.
1. Exceed the norms of courtesy.
2. Take her unawares with speech of my

heartfelt love.
3. That is, your nature (as determined by the stars).

And thou shalt live as freely as thy lord,
To call his fortunes thine.

40 VIOLA   I'll do my best
To woo your lady. [*aside*] Yet a barful strife!⁴
Whoe'er I woo, myself would be his wife.   *Exeunt.*

1.5

Enter MARIA *and* [FESTE,⁵ *the*] *clown.*

MARIA Nay, either tell me where thou hast been or I will
not open my lips so wide as a bristle may enter in° way of   *by*
thy excuse. My lady will hang thee for thy absence.

FESTE Let her hang me. He that is well hanged⁶ in this
5   world needs to fear no colours.⁷

MARIA Make that good.°   *Explain that*

FESTE He shall see none to fear.

MARIA A good Lenten⁸ answer. I can tell thee where
that saying was born, of "I fear no colors."

10 FESTE Where, good Mistress Mary?

MARIA In the wars; and that may you be bold to say in
your foolery.

FESTE Well, God give them wisdom that have it, and
those that are fools, let them use their talents.⁹

15 MARIA Yet you will be hanged for being so long absent, or
to be turned away°—is not that as good as a hanging to   *dismissed*
you?

FESTE Many a good hanging¹ prevents a bad marriage,
and, for turning away, let summer bear it out.²

20 MARIA You are resolute, then?

FESTE Not so, neither, but I am resolved on two points.°   *issues; laces*

MARIA That if one break, the other will hold, or, if both
break, your gaskins° fall.   *wide breeches*

FESTE Apt, in good faith, very apt. Well, go thy way. If
25   Sir Toby would leave drinking, thou wert as witty a
piece of Eve's flesh° as any in Illyria.³   *a woman*

MARIA Peace, you rogue. No more o' that. Here comes my
lady. Make your excuse wisely, you were best.°   [*Exit*] *it would be best for you*

Enter Lady OLIVIA *with* MALVOLIO⁴ [*and attendants*]

FESTE [*aside*] Wit,° an't° be thy will, put me into good   *Intelligence / if it*
30   fooling! Those wits that think they have thee do very oft
prove fools, and I that am sure I lack thee may pass for a

---

4. A task full of hindrances.
1.5 Location: Orsino's residence.
5. Usually pronounced "FESS-tee."
6. Hanged to death. Feste also implies that he
is "well hung" (i.e., well-endowed sexually), a
trait regularly attributed to fools (as supposed
to accompany mental deficiency).
7. Fear no foe (literally, military flags); punning on "collars," the hangman's noose.
8. Lean or meager (i.e., appropriate to Lent).
9. Abilities, with a punning allusion to the

parable of the talents (coins) in Matthew
25.14–30.
1. A reference to both capital punishment
and sexual endowment.
2. That is, let mild weather make it bearable
(for the newly homeless).
3. Feste appears to say that Toby is as likely to
give up drinking as Maria is to be witty.
4. Usually pronounced "Mal-VOE-lee-o" (a
name meaning "ill will").

wise man. For what says Quinapalus?[5] "Better a witty
Fool than a foolish wit." God bless thee, lady.

OLIVIA [*to attendants*]   Take the fool away.

35 FESTE   Do you not hear, fellows? Take away the lady.

OLIVIA   Go to,[6] you're a dry° fool. I'll no more of you.   dull
Besides, you grow dishonest.[7]

FESTE   Two faults, madonna,° that drink and good counsel   my lady (Italian)
will amend. For give the dry fool drink, then is the fool
40 not dry. Bid the dishonest man mend° himself: if he   reform
mend, he is no longer dishonest; if he cannot, let the
botcher° mend him. Anything that's mended is but   mender of old clothes
patched; virtue that transgresses is but patched with
sin, and sin that amends is but patched with virtue.[8] If
45 that this simple syllogism will serve, so; if it will not,
what remedy? As there is no true cuckold but calamity,
so beauty's a flower.[9] The lady bade take away the fool.
Therefore, I say again, take her away.

OLIVIA   Sir, I bade them take away you.

50 FESTE   Misprision[1] in the highest degree! Lady, *cucullus
non facit monachum.*[2] That's as much to say as, I wear
not motley[3] in my brain. Good madonna, give me leave
to prove you a fool.

OLIVIA   Can you do it?

55 FESTE   Dexteriously,° good madonna.   Dexterously

OLIVIA   Make your proof.

FESTE   I must catechize you for it, madonna. Good my
mouse° of virtue, answer me.   (term of endearment)

OLIVIA   Well, sir, for want of other idleness° I'll bide° your   diversion / await
60 proof.

FESTE   Good madonna, why mournest thou?

OLIVIA   Good fool, for my brother's death.

FESTE   I think his soul is in hell, madonna.

OLIVIA   I know his soul is in heaven, fool.

65 FESTE   The more fool, madonna, to mourn for your
brother's soul, being in heaven. Take away the fool,
gentlemen.

OLIVIA   What think you of this fool, Malvolio? Doth he
not mend?[4]

70 MALVOLIO   Yes, and shall do till the pangs of death
shake him. Infirmity, that decays the wise, doth ever
make the better fool.

---

5. An invented philosopher whose wisdom
Feste pretends to quote.
6. An expression of impatience.
7. Unreliable (because unaccountably absent
from the house).
8. In this passage, Feste caricatures formal
logic (the syllogism).
9. That is, the cuckold is the misfortune that
Olivia has wed, to which she must be unfaithful so that her beauty can bloom and find love

(before it fades).
1. Misunderstanding; wrongful arrest.
2. The cowl does not make the monk (Latin
proverb).
3. The multicolored tunic of professional
jesters.
4. Improve (by becoming more entertaining);
Malvolio takes the improvement to lie in
becoming more foolish.

FESTE   God send you, sir, a speedy infirmity, for the better increasing your folly! Sir Toby will be sworn that I
75 am no fox, but he will not pass his word for twopence
that you are no fool.

OLIVIA   How say you to that, Malvolio?

MALVOLIO   I marvel your ladyship takes delight in such a
barren rascal. I saw him put down[5] the other day with an
80 ordinary fool that has no more brain than a stone. Look
you now, he's out of his guard° already. Unless you laugh   *defenseless*
and minister occasion[6] to him, he is gagged. I protest I
take these wise men that crow so at these set kind of
fools no better than the fools' zanies.[7]

85 OLIVIA   O, you are sick of° self-love, Malvolio, and taste   *from*
with a distempered° appetite. To be generous, guiltless,   *unhealthy*
and of free° disposition is to take those things for bird-   *magnanimous*
bolts[8] that you deem cannon bullets. There is no slan-
der in an allowed fool, though he do nothing but rail;
90 nor no railing in a known discreet man, though he do
nothing but reprove.

FESTE   Now Mercury indue thee with leasing,[9] for thou
speakest well of fools.

Enter MARIA

MARIA   Madam, there is at the gate a young gentleman
95 much desires to speak with you.

OLIVIA   From the Count Orsino, is it?

MARIA   I know not, madam. 'Tis a fair young man, and
well attended.

OLIVIA   Who of my people hold him in delay?

100 MARIA   Sir Toby, madam, your kinsman.

OLIVIA   Fetch him off, I pray you. He speaks nothing but
madman.° Fie on him! [MARIA *exits.*] Go you, Malvolio. If   *madman's speech*
it be a suit from the Count, I am sick, or not at home,
what you will, to dismiss it. [*Malvolio exits.*] Now you
105 see, sir, how your fooling grows old, and people dislike it.

FESTE   Thou hast spoke for us, madonna, as if thy eldest
son should be a fool, whose skull Jove[1] cram with
brains, for—here he comes—one of thy kin has a most
weak *pia mater.*[2]

Enter SIR TOBY

110 OLIVIA   By mine honor, half-drunk. What is he at the
gate, cousin?°   *kinsman*

SIR TOBY   A gentleman.

OLIVIA   A gentleman? What gentleman?

---

5. Defeated in a battle of wits.
6. Provide opportunity.
7. The subordinate fools who imitate the
main comic performers ("zany" is a term from
the Italian commedia dell'arte). Set: deliberate, artificial.
8. Blunt-headed arrows for shooting birds.

9. That is, may Mercury, the Roman god of
traders, thieves, and tricksters, grant you the
gift of lying.
1. Jupiter, the king of the Roman gods.
2. The brain (literally, the membrane enclosing it; "tender mother," in Latin).

SIR TOBY   'Tis a gentleman here. [*He belches.*] A plague o'
115   these pickle herring!—How now, sot?°   *fool, drunkard*
FESTE   Good Sir Toby.
OLIVIA   Cousin, cousin, how have you come so early by
   this lethargy?
SIR TOBY   Lechery? I defy lechery. There's one° at the gate.   *someone*
120 OLIVIA   Ay, marry, what is he?
SIR TOBY   Let him be the devil an° he will, I care not. Give   *if*
   me faith,[3] say I. Well, it's all one.   [*Exit*]
OLIVIA   What's a drunken man like, fool?
FESTE   Like a drowned man, a fool, and a madman. One
125   draught above heat[4] makes him a fool, the second
   mads him, and a third drowns him.
OLIVIA   Go thou and seek the coroner and let him sit o'°   *hold an inquest on*
   my coz,° for he's in the third degree of drink: he's   *cousin (Toby)*
   drowned. Go look after him.
130 FESTE   He is but mad yet, madonna, and the fool shall
   look to the madman.   [*Exit*]
       Enter MALVOLIO

MALVOLIO   Madam, yond young fellow swears he will
   speak with you. I told him you were sick; he takes on
   him to understand so much, and therefore comes to
135   speak with you. I told him you were asleep; he seems to
   have a foreknowledge of that too, and therefore comes
   to speak with you. What is to be said to him, lady? He's
   fortified against any denial.
OLIVIA   Tell him he shall not speak with me.
140 MALVOLIO   He's been told so, and he says he'll stand at
   your door like a sheriff's post[5] and be the supporter to
   a bench, but he'll speak with you.
OLIVIA   What kind o' man is he?
MALVOLIO   Why, of mankind.
145 OLIVIA   What manner of man?
MALVOLIO   Of very ill manner. He'll speak with you, will
   you or no.
OLIVIA   Of what personage° and years is he?   *appearance*
MALVOLIO   Not yet old enough for a man, nor young
150   enough for a boy—as a squash[6] is before 'tis a peascod,
   or a codling° when 'tis almost an apple. 'Tis with him in   *unripe apple*
   standing water[7] between boy and man. He is very well-
   favored,° and he speaks very shrewishly.° One would   *handsome / sharply*
   think his mother's milk were scarce out of him.
155 OLIVIA   Let him approach. Call in my gentlewoman.
MALVOLIO   Gentlewoman, my lady calls.   *Exit*
       Enter MARIA

---

3. That is, faith to resist the devil.
4. One more drink than it takes to make him feel warm.
5. The painted post outside the sheriff's office to which proclamations were affixed.
6. An unripe pea pod.
7. The time between the incoming and outgoing tides.

OLIVIA   Give me my veil. Come, throw it o'er my face.
We'll once more hear Orsino's embassy.°   *ambassador's message*

Enter VIOLA [*as Cesario*]

VIOLA   The honorable lady of the house, which is she?
160 OLIVIA   Speak to me. I shall answer for her. Your will?
VIOLA   Most radiant, exquisite, and unmatchable
beauty—I pray you, tell me if this be the lady of the
house, for I never saw her. I would be loath to cast
away° my speech, for, besides that it is excellently well   *waste*
165   penned, I have taken great pains to con° it. Good beau-   *memorize*
ties, let me sustain° no scorn. I am very comptible,°   *endure / sensitive*
even to the least sinister usage.[8]
OLIVIA   Whence came you, sir?
VIOLA   I can say little more than I have studied,° and   *committed to memory*
170   that question's out of my part. Good gentle one, give
me modest° assurance if you be the lady of the house,   *reasonable*
that I may proceed in my speech.
OLIVIA   Are you a comedian?°   *an actor*
VIOLA   No, my profound heart.[9] And yet, by the very fangs
175   of malice, I swear I am not that I play.° Are you the lady   *what I act*
of the house?
OLIVIA   If I do not usurp° myself, I am.   *impersonate*
VIOLA   Most certain, if you are she, you do usurp yourself,
for what is yours to bestow is not yours to reserve.[1] But
180   this is from° my commission.° I will on with my speech   *beyond / instructions*
in your praise, and then show you the heart of my
message.
OLIVIA   Come to what is important in't, I forgive you° the   *excuse you from reciting*
praise.
185 VIOLA   Alas, I took great pains to study it, and 'tis poetical.
OLIVIA   It is the more like to be feigned. I pray you keep
it in. I heard you were saucy° at my gates, and allowed   *impertinent*
your approach rather to wonder at you than to hear
you. If you be not mad, be gone. If you have reason, be
190   brief. 'Tis not that time of moon with me to make one
in so skipping a dialogue.[2]
MARIA   Will you hoist sail, sir? Here lies your way.
VIOLA   No, good swabber, I am to hull[3] here a little longer. —Some mollification for your giant,[4] sweet lady.
195   Tell me your mind, I am a messenger.
OLIVIA   Sure you have some hideous matter to deliver,
when the courtesy[5] of it is so fearful. Speak your office.°   *commission*

---

8. The smallest discourtesy.
9. My most wise lady.
1. That is, a woman usurps a husband's rightful role if she bestows herself not on a man
but on herself (by "reserving" herself).
2. That is, I am not so under the moon's influence (literally, so lunatic) that I am willing to

participate in such a fantastic conversation.
3. Lie at anchor, with furled sails. *Swabber:*
one who mops the decks of a ship.
4. Maria, who is small of stature, is here
mockingly identified as one of the giants who
protected ladies in medieval romances.
5. The courteous preamble.

VIOLA   It alone concerns your ear. I bring no overture° of   declaration
war, no taxation of homage.[6] I hold the olive° in my hand.   olive branch
200 My words are as full of peace as matter.°   meaning
OLIVIA   Yet you began rudely. What are you? What would
you?
VIOLA   The rudeness that hath appeared in me have I
learned from my entertainment.° What I am and what I   reception
205 would are as secret as maidenhead:° to your ears, divin-   virginity
ity; to any other's, profanation.
OLIVIA [to MARIA and attendants]   Give us the place alone.
We will hear this divinity.°   MARIA and attendants exit.   religious discourse
Now sir, what is your text?[7]
210 VIOLA   Most sweet lady—
OLIVIA   A comfortable° doctrine, and much may be said   comforting
of it. Where lies your text?
VIOLA   In Orsino's bosom.
OLIVIA   In his bosom? In what chapter of his bosom?
215 VIOLA   To answer by the method,° in the first of his heart.   in the same style
OLIVIA   O, I have read it; it is heresy. Have you no more
to say?
VIOLA   Good madam, let me see your face.
OLIVIA   Have you any commission from your lord to nego-
220 tiate with my face? You are now out of° your text. But we   straying from
will draw the curtain and show you the picture. [She
removes her veil.] Look you, sir, such a one I was this
present.[8] Is't not well done?
VIOLA   Excellently done, if God did all.[9]
225 OLIVIA   'Tis in grain,° sir; 'twill endure wind and weather.   It is dyed fast
VIOLA   'Tis beauty truly blent,° whose red and white   blended
Nature's own sweet and cunning° hand laid on.   skillful
Lady, you are the cruel'st she° alive   woman
If you will lead these graces to the grave
230 And leave the world no copy.[1]
OLIVIA   O sir, I will not be so hard-hearted! I will give out
divers schedules° of my beauty. It shall be inventoried   inventory
and every particle and utensil labeled[2] to my will: as,
item, two lips, indifferent° red; item, two gray eyes,   moderately
235 with lids to them; item, one neck, one chin, and so
forth. Were you sent hither to praise° me?   appraise
VIOLA   I see you what you are. You are too proud.
But if° you were the devil, you are fair.   Even if
My lord and master loves you. O, such love
240 Could be but recompensed though[3] you were crowned

6. Demand for payment of tribute.
7. That is, the passage on which "Cesario's"
sermon will expound.
8. That is, this is a current ("present") likeness of me (as though she were revealing a
portrait of herself).

9. If it is your natural face, without cosmetics.
1. That is, no child; Olivia, however, takes
"copy" to mean "written record."
2. Every individual part and article described
and added as a codicil.
3. Should be equally returned even if.

The nonpareil of beauty.°   *An unsurpassed beauty*

OLIVIA   How does he love me?

VIOLA   With adorations, fertile° tears,   *plentiful*
With groans that thunder love, with sighs of fire.⁴

OLIVIA   Your lord does know my mind. I cannot love him.

245   Yet I suppose him virtuous, know him noble,
Of great estate, of fresh and stainless youth;
In voices well divulged,° free,° learned, and valiant,   *well spoken of / noble*
And in dimension and the shape of nature°   *physical appearance*
A gracious° person. But yet I cannot love him.   *An attractive*

250   He might have took his answer long ago.

VIOLA   If I did love you in° my master's flame,°   *with / passion*
With such a suff'ring, such a deadly° life,   *deathlike*
In your denial I would find no sense,
I would not understand it.

OLIVIA   Why, what would you?

255   VIOLA   Make me a willow⁵ cabin at your gate
And call upon my soul° within the house,   *(i.e., Olivia)*
Write loyal cantons° of contemnèd° love   *songs / despised*
And sing them loud even in the dead of night,
Hallow° your name to the reverberate° hills   *Shout / echoing*

260   And make the babbling gossip of the air⁶
Cry out "Olivia!" O, you should not rest
Between the elements of air and earth
But you should pity me.

OLIVIA   You might do much.

265   What is your parentage?

VIOLA   Above my fortunes,⁷ yet my state° is well.   *social standing*
I am a gentleman.

OLIVIA   Get you to your lord.
I cannot love him. Let him send no more—
Unless perchance you come to me again

270   To tell me how he takes it. Fare you well.
I thank you for your pains. Spend this for me.

[*She offers money.*]

VIOLA   I am no fee'd post,° lady. Keep your purse.   *hired messenger*
My master, not myself, lacks recompense.
Love make his heart of flint that you shall love.⁸

275   And let your fervor, like my master's, be
Placed in contempt. Farewell, fair cruelty.   *Exit.*

OLIVIA   "What is your parentage?"
"Above my fortunes, yet my state is well.
I am a gentleman." I'll be sworn thou art.

---

4. The "tears," "groans," and "sighs of fire"
are all clichés of romantic melancholy, fashionable in Elizabethan sonnet writing.
5. The willow was a symbol of grief for unrequited love.
6. Echo, in classical mythology. In love with

but rejected by Narcissus, the nymph Echo
was eventually reduced to nothing but a voice.
7. My (current) circumstances.
8. That is, may love harden the heart of the
man you fall in love with.

280 Thy tongue, thy face, thy limbs, actions, and spirit
Do give thee fivefold blazon.[9] Not too fast! Soft,° soft—   *Wait*
Unless the master were the man.° How now?   *servant*
Even so quickly may one catch the plague?
Methinks I feel this youth's perfections
With an invisible and subtle stealth
285 To creep in at mine eyes. Well, let it be.—
What ho, Malvolio!

    Enter MALVOLIO

MALVOLIO   Here, madam, at your service.
OLIVIA   Run after that same peevish messenger,
The County's° man. He left this ring behind him,   *Count's (i.e., Duke's)*
290 Would I° or not. Tell him I'll none of it.   *Whether I wished it*
Desire him not to flatter with° his lord,   *encourage*
Nor hold him up with hopes. I am not for him.
If that the youth will come this way tomorrow,
I'll give him reasons for't. Hie thee,° Malvolio.   *Hurry*
295 MALVOLIO   Madam, I will.   *Exit.*
OLIVIA   I do I know not what, and fear to find
Mine eye too great a flatterer for my mind.[1]
Fate, show thy force. Ourselves we do not owe.°   *own*
What is decreed must be, and be this so.

                    [*Exit at another door.*]

2.1

    Enter ANTONIO *and* SEBASTIAN.

ANTONIO   Will you stay no longer? Nor will° you not that   *wish*
   I go with you?
SEBASTIAN   By your patience, no. My stars shine darkly
   over me. The malignancy of my fate[2] might perhaps
5 distemper° yours. Therefore I shall crave of you your   *disturb; infect*
   leave that I may bear my evils alone. It were a bad
   recompense for your love to lay any of them on you.
ANTONIO   Let me yet know of you whither you are bound.
SEBASTIAN   No, sooth,° sir. My determinate° voyage is   *truly / determined-on*
10 mere extravagancy.° But I perceive in you so excellent a   *aimless wandering*
   touch of modesty° that you will not extort from me   *civility; reserve*
   what I am willing to keep in. Therefore it charges me
   in manners° the rather to express myself. You must   *in courteous fashion*
   know of me then, Antonio, my name is Sebastian, which
15 I called Roderigo. My father was that Sebastian of Messaline[3] whom I know you have heard of. He left behind
   him myself and a sister, both born in an hour.° If the   *in the same hour*

9. That is, your natural attributes—tongue,
face, limbs, etc.—proclaim you a gentleman
as well as any coat of arms would.
1. That is, my eye has seduced my reason.
2.1 Location: Somewhere near the Illyrian
coast.

2. The malevolent influence of the stars
(which shape my future); "malignancy" also
has its medical sense.
3. Possibly Messina (in Sicily) or Massila
(modern-day Marseille), or a fictional town.

heavens had been pleased, would we had so ended!
But you, sir, altered that, for some hour before you took
20 me from the breach° of the sea was my sister drowned.   *surf*
ANTONIO Alas the day!
SEBASTIAN A lady, sir, though it was said she much resembled me, was yet of many accounted beautiful. But
though I could not with such estimable wonder° overfar   *appreciative judgment*
25 believe that, yet thus far I will boldly publish° her: she   *declare*
bore a mind that envy° could not but call fair. She is   *envy itself; the envious*
drowned already, sir, with salt water, though I seem to
drown her remembrance again with more.
ANTONIO Pardon me, sir, your bad entertainment.[4]
30 SEBASTIAN O good Antonio, forgive me your trouble.[5]
ANTONIO If you will not murder me[6] for my love, let me
be your servant.
SEBASTIAN If you will not undo what you have done—
that is, kill him whom you have recovered°—desire it   *rescued*
35 not. Fare ye well at once. My bosom is full of kind-
ness,° and I am yet° so near the manners of my mother   *tender feelings / still*
that, upon the least occasion more, mine eyes will tell
tales of me.[7] I am bound to the Count Orsino's court.
Farewell.   *Exit.*
40 ANTONIO The gentleness of all the gods go with thee!
I have many enemies in Orsino's court,
Else would I very shortly see thee there.
But come what may, I do adore thee so
That danger shall seem sport, and I will go.   *Exit.*

2.2

Enter VIOLA *and* MALVOLIO, *at several° doors.*   *different*

MALVOLIO Were not you even° now with the Countess   *just*
Olivia?
VIOLA Even now, sir. On° a moderate pace I have since   *At*
arrived but hither.°   *traveled only this far*
5 MALVOLIO She returns this ring to you, sir. You might have
saved me my pains to have taken it away yourself. She
adds, moreover, that you should put your lord into a des-
perate assurance° she will none of him. And one thing   *hopeless certainty*
more, that you be never so hardy° to come again in his   *bold*
10 affairs, unless it be to report your lord's taking of this.[8]
Receive it so.
VIOLA She took the ring of me.[9] I'll none of it.
MALVOLIO Come, sir, you peevishly threw it to her, and
her will is it should be so returned.

4. That is, the inadequate hospitality I have
offered you.
5. The trouble I have put you through (by
being your guest).
6. That is, cause my death by insisting that I
depart.

7. That is, my tears will betray my feelings.
2.2 Location: Somewhere between Olivia's
estate and Orsino's palace.
8. Reaction to Olivia's rejection.
9. From me (Viola plays along with Olivia's
story).

[He throws down the ring.]

15 If it be worth stooping for, there it lies, in your eye;° if   *within your view*
    not, be it his that finds it.   *Exit.*

VIOLA   I left no ring with her. What means this lady?

[She picks up the ring.]

Fortune forbid my outside° have not charmed her!   *outward appearance*
She made good view of° me, indeed so much   *examined me closely*
20 That sure methought her eyes had lost° her tongue,   *had made her lose*
For she did speak in starts distractedly.
She loves me, sure! The cunning of her passion
Invites me in° this churlish messenger.   *by means of*
None of my lord's ring? Why, he sent her none!
25 I am the man.[1] If it be so, as 'tis,
Poor lady, she were better love a dream.
Disguise, I see thou art a wickedness
Wherein the pregnant° enemy° does much.   *resourceful / (Satan)*
How easy is it for the proper false[2]
30 In women's waxen hearts to set their forms![3]
Alas, our frailty is the cause, not we,
For such as we are made of, such we be.[4]
How will this fadge?° My master loves her dearly,   *turn out*
And I, poor monster,[5] fond° as much on him,   *dote*
35 And she, mistaken, seems to dote on me.
What will become of this? As I am man,
My state is desperate for my master's love.
As I am woman (now, alas the day!),
What thriftless° sighs shall poor Olivia breathe!   *unprofitable*
40 O Time, thou must untangle this, not I.
It is too hard a knot for me t'untie.   *[Exit]*

2.3

Enter SIR TOBY *and* SIR ANDREW.

SIR TOBY   Approach, Sir Andrew. Not to be abed after
    midnight is to be up betimes,° and "*diliculo surgere*,"[6]   *early*
    thou knowest.

SIR ANDREW   Nay, by my troth,° I know not. But I know to   *by my faith (a mild oath)*
5   be up late is to be up late.

SIR TOBY   A false conclusion. I hate it as an unfilled can.°   *drinking vessel, tankard*
    To be up after midnight and to go to bed then is early, so
    that to go to bed after midnight is to go to bed betimes.
    Does not our lives consist of the four elements?[7]

10 SIR ANDREW   Faith, so they say, but I think it rather con-
    sists of eating and drinking.

---

1. That is, the man of Olivia's affections.
2. Men who are handsome and duplicitous.
3. To make strong impressions in women's
soft hearts (the seat of their passions).
4. That is, we are frail because we are made
of frail flesh.
5. That is, both a man and a woman.

2.3 Location: Olivia's house.
6. An abbreviated form of the Latin phrase
Diliculo surgere saluberrimum est (To rise at
dawn is most healthful).
7. The four elements—fire, water, earth, and
air—thought to constitute all matter.

SIR TOBY Thou'rt a scholar. Let us therefore eat and
drink. Marian, I say, a stoup° of wine!   *drinking vessel*

   Enter [FESTE, the] clown.

SIR ANDREW Here comes the fool, i'faith.

15 FESTE How now, my hearts? Did you never see the picture of "We Three"?[8]

SIR TOBY Welcome, ass. Now let's have a catch.°   *sing a round*

SIR ANDREW By my troth, the fool has an excellent breast.°   *voice*
I had rather than forty shillings I had such a leg,° and so   *(for dancing)*

20 sweet a breath to sing, as the fool has.—In sooth, thou
wast in very gracious fooling last night when thou
spokest of Pigrogromitus, of the Vapians passing the
equinoctial of Queubus.[9] 'Twas very good, i'faith. I sent
thee sixpence for thy leman.° Hadst it?   *sweetheart*

25 FESTE I did impeticos thy gratillity,[1] for Malvolio's nose
is no whipstock,° my lady has a white hand, and the Myr-   *whip handle*
midons[2] are no bottle-ale houses.°   *low-class taverns*

SIR ANDREW Excellent! Why, this is the best fooling,
when all is done. Now a song.

30 SIR TOBY [to FESTE] Come on, there is sixpence for you.
Let's have a song.

SIR ANDREW [to FESTE] There's a testril[3] of me, too. If
one knight give a——

FESTE Would you have a love song or a song of good° life?   *virtuous*

35 SIR TOBY A love song, a love song.

SIR ANDREW Ay, ay, I care not for good life.

FESTE *sings*

O mistress mine, where are you roaming?
O, stay and hear! Your truelove's coming,
   That can sing both high and low.

40 Trip° no further, pretty sweeting.   *Go*
Journeys end in lovers meeting,
   Every wise man's son doth know.

SIR ANDREW Excellent good, i'faith.

SIR TOBY Good, good.

45 FESTE What is love? 'Tis not hereafter.
Present mirth hath present laughter.
   What's to come is still° unsure.   *always*
In delay there lies no plenty,
Then come kiss me, sweet and twenty.[4]

50 Youth's a stuff will not endure.

SIR ANDREW A mellifluous voice, as I am true knight.

SIR TOBY A contagious breath.[5]

8. A picture, inscribed "we three," of two
fools or ass heads, the third being the viewer.
9. Examples of Feste's mock learning.
1. That is, impetticoat (pocket) your gratuity
(a small tip).
2. Followers of the Greek warrior Achilles at
Troy; here, possibly the name of a tavern (the

obscurity of Feste's meaning is probably
intentional).
3. That is, a tester, a sixpence coin.
4. Sweet and twenty more times sweet.
5. A catchy voice; also, foul or infectious
breath.

SIR ANDREW   Very sweet and contagious, i' faith.

SIR TOBY   To hear by the nose, it is dulcet in contagion.[6]

55   But shall we make the welkin° dance indeed? Shall we   *heavens*
rouse the night owl in a catch that will draw three
souls out of one weaver?[7] Shall we do that?

SIR ANDREW   An° you love me, let's do't. I am dog° at a   *If / expert*
catch.

60   FESTE   By'r Lady, sir, and some dogs will catch well.

SIR ANDREW   Most certain. Let our catch be "Thou Knave."

FESTE   "Hold thy peace, thou knave," knight? I shall be
constrained in't to call thee "knave," knight.

SIR ANDREW   'Tis not the first time I have constrained
65   one to call me "knave." Begin, Fool. It begins "Hold thy
peace."

FESTE   I shall never begin if I hold my peace.

SIR ANDREW   Good, i' faith. Come, begin. [*They sing the
catch.*]

          Enter MARIA.

MARIA   What a caterwauling do you keep here! If my
70   lady have not called up her steward Malvolio and bid
him turn you out of doors, never trust me.

SIR TOBY   My lady's a Cathayan,[8] we are politicians,° Mal-   *connivers*
volio's a Peg-a'-Ramsey,[9] and [*sings*] "Three merry men
be we." Am not I consanguineous?[1] Am I not of her
75   blood? Tillyvally!° "Lady"! [*sings*] "There dwelt a man in   *Fiddlesticks*
Babylon, lady, lady."[2]

FESTE   Beshrew° me, the knight's in admirable fooling.   *Curse me (a mild oath)*

SIR ANDREW   Ay, he does well enough if he be disposed,
and so do I, too. He does it with a better grace, but I do
80   it more natural.[3]

SIR TOBY [*sings*]   "O' the twelfth day of December"[4]—

MARIA   For the love o' God, peace!

          Enter MALVOLIO

MALVOLIO   My masters, are you mad? Or what are you?
Have you no wit,° manners, nor honesty° but to gabble   *sense / decency*
85   like tinkers at this time of night? Do ye make an ale-
house of my lady's house, that you squeak out your
coziers'° catches without any mitigation or remorse° of   *cobblers' / intermission*
voice? Is there no respect of place, persons, nor time in
you?

90   SIR TOBY   We did keep time, sir, in our catches. Sneck up!°   *Go hang yourself*

---

6. If we heard with our noses, the sound
would be sweetly infectious.
7. Weavers, commonly associated with the
singing of psalms, would presumably be resistant to most simple catches. Music was
believed able to draw the soul from the body.
8. Chinese; but also a slang term for "cheat."
9. A line from an old song. *Peg-a'-Ramsey*: a
character in a popular ballad (here used

scornfully).
1. That is, a blood relative of Olivia.
2. The first line ("There dwelt a man in Babylon") and the refrain ("Lady, lady") of the ballad "Constant Susanna."
3. Effortlessly; "natural" also means "idiot."
4. Probably the first line of another ballad or
possibly a version of "the twelfth day of
Christmas," hence *Twelfth Night*.

MALVOLIO Sir Toby, I must be round° with you. My lady	*direct*
bade me tell you that, though she harbors you as her	
kinsman, she's nothing allied° to your disorders. If you	*no kin*
can separate yourself and your misdemeanors, you are	
95 welcome to the house; if not, an° it would please you to	*if*
take leave of her, she is very willing to bid you farewell.	

SIR TOBY [*sings*] "Farewell, dear heart, since I must needs
be gone."[5]

MARIA Nay, good Sir Toby.

100 FESTE "His eyes do show his days are almost done."

MALVOLIO Is't even so?

SIR TOBY "But I will never die."

FESTE "Sir Toby, there you lie."

MALVOLIO This is much credit to you.

105 SIR TOBY "Shall I bid him go?"

FESTE "What an if° you do?" — *an if=if*

SIR TOBY "Shall I bid him go, and spare not?"

FESTE "O no, no, no, no, you dare not."

SIR TOBY Out o' tune, sir? Ye lie. Art° any more than a — *Are you*
110 steward? Dost thou think because thou art virtuous
there shall be no more cakes and ale?[6]

FESTE Yes, by Saint Anne, and ginger[7] shall be hot i' th'
mouth, too.

SIR TOBY Thou'rt i' th' right.—Go, sir, rub your chain
115 with crumbs.[8]—A stoup of wine, Maria!

MALVOLIO Mistress Mary, if you prized my lady's favor at
anything more than contempt you would not give
means° for this uncivil rule.° She shall know of it, by this — *drink / uncivilized behavior*
hand.   *Exit.*

120 MARIA Go shake your ears!° — *(i.e., your ass's ears)*

SIR ANDREW 'Twere as good a deed as to drink when a
man's a-hungry to challenge him the field° and then to — *to a duel*
break promise with him and make a fool of him.

SIR TOBY Do't, knight. I'll write thee a challenge. Or I'll
125 deliver thy indignation to him by word of mouth.

MARIA Sweet Sir Toby, be patient for tonight. Since the
youth of the Count's was today with my lady, she is
much out of quiet. For Monsieur Malvolio, let me
alone with him. If I do not gull him into a nayword and
130 make him a common recreation,[9] do not think I have
wit enough to lie straight in my bed. I know I can do it.

SIR TOBY Possess° us, possess us, tell us something of him. — *Inform*

---

5. A line from the ballad "Corydon's Farewell to Phyllis."
6. That is, good things. Cakes and ale were often served at church fairs, a practice frowned on by the Puritans (with whom Malvolio is associated by Maria in line 133, below).
7. A root used to flavor drinks such as ale. *Saint*

Anne: mother of the Virgin Mary (the veneration of whom was offensive to Puritans).
8. That is, mind your own business (literally, "go shine your steward's chain").
9. One who provides recreation or entertainment for all (by becoming a laughingstock). *Nayword:* a byword (for "gull" or "fool").

MARIA   Marry, sir, sometimes he is a kind of puritan.[1]

SIR ANDREW   O, if I thought that, I'd beat him like a dog!

135 SIR TOBY   What, for being a puritan? Thy exquisite° rea-   *ingenious*
     son, dear knight?

SIR ANDREW   I have no exquisite reason for't, but I have
     reason good enough.

MARIA   The devil a puritan that he is, or anything con-

140 stantly but a time-pleaser;° an affectioned° ass that cons   *flatterer / affected*
     state without book[2] and utters it by great swathes;° the   *in long stretches*
     best persuaded of himself,[3] so crammed, as he thinks,
     with excellencies, that it is his grounds of faith° that all   *unyielding belief*
     that look on him love him. And on that vice in him will

145 my revenge find notable cause to work.

SIR TOBY   What wilt thou do?

MARIA   I will drop in his way some obscure epistles of
     love, wherein by the color of his beard, the shape of his
     leg, the manner of his gait, the expressure° of his eye,   *expression*

150 forehead, and complexion,° he shall find himself most   *appearance*
     feelingly personated.° I can write very like my lady your   *represented*
     niece; on a forgotten matter, we can hardly make dis-
     tinction of our hands.°   *handwriting*

SIR TOBY   Excellent! I smell a device.°   *scheme, plot*

155 SIR ANDREW   I have't in my nose, too.

SIR TOBY   He shall think, by the letters that thou wilt
     drop, that they come from my niece, and that she's in
     love with him.

MARIA   My purpose is indeed a horse of that color.

160 SIR ANDREW   And your horse now would make him an ass.

MARIA   Ass° I doubt not.   *(punning on "as")*

SIR ANDREW   O, 'twill be admirable!

MARIA   Sport° royal, I warrant you. I know my physic° will   *Amusement / medicine*
     work with him. I will plant you two, and let the fool

165 make a third, where he shall find the letter. Observe his
     construction° of it. For this night, to bed, and dream on   *interpretation*
     the event.° Farewell.   *Exit.*   *outcome*

SIR TOBY   Good night, Penthesilea.[4]

SIR ANDREW   Before me,[5] she's a good wench.

170 SIR TOBY   She's a beagle true bred, and one that adores
     me. What o' that?

SIR ANDREW   I was adored once, too.

SIR TOBY   Let's to bed, knight. Thou hadst need send for
     more money.

175 SIR ANDREW   If I cannot recover° your niece, I am a foul   *win*
     way out.°   *at a financial loss*

---

1. That is, he is puritanical in his strictness
and moral conduct (though not necessarily a
member of a Puritan sect).
2. Memorizes high-flown language.

3. Having the highest opinion of himself.
4. Queen of the Amazons (another playful
allusion to Maria's small size).
5. A play on the common oath "before God."

SIR TOBY   Send for money, knight. If thou hast her not i'
th' end, call me "Cut."[6]
SIR ANDREW   If I do not, never trust me, take it how you
180   will.
SIR TOBY   Come, come, I'll go burn some sack.° 'Tis too   *warm some Spanish wine*
late to go to bed now. Come, knight; come, knight.
                                                    Exeunt.[7]

2.4

Enter ORSINO, VIOLA, CURIO, *and others.*

ORSINO   Give me some music. Now good morrow,° friends.   *morning*
   Now good Cesario, but° that piece of song,   *(give us) just*
   That old and antique° song we heard last night.   *quaint*
   Methought it did relieve my passion° much,   *suffering*
5   More than light airs and recollected° terms   *studied; artificial*
   Of these most brisk and giddy-pacèd times.
   Come, but one verse.
CURIO   He is not here, so please your lordship, that
   should sing it.
10 ORSINO   Who was it?
CURIO   Feste the jester, my lord, a fool that the Lady Oliv-
   ia's father took much delight in. He is about the house.
ORSINO   Seek him out, and play the tune the while.
                                                    [*Exit* CURIO]
   Music plays.
   [*To* VIOLA] Come hither, boy. If ever thou shalt love,
15   In the sweet pangs of it remember me,
   For such as I am, all true lovers are,
   Unstaid° and skittish in all motions° else   *Unsteady / emotions*
   Save in the constant image of the creature
   That is beloved. How dost thou like this tune?
20 VIOLA   It gives a very echo to the seat
   Where love is throned.°   *(i.e., the heart)*
ORSINO   Thou dost speak masterly.°   *masterfully*
   My life upon't, young though thou art, thine eye
   Hath stayed upon some favor° that it loves.   *face*
   Hath it not, boy?
VIOLA   A little, by your favor.°   *leave; face*
ORSINO   What kind of woman is't?
25 VIOLA   Of your complexion.
ORSINO   She is not worth thee, then. What years, i' faith?
VIOLA   About your years, my lord.
ORSINO   Too old, by heaven. Let still° the woman take   *always*
   An elder than herself. So wears° she to him;   *she slowly adapts*
30   So sways she level° in her husband's heart.   *she holds steady*

---

6. Dock-tailed, as a workhorse; also, slang
term for a gelding.
7. Feste has no lines after line 113; thus, he

may exit with Maria above, or even earlier.
2.4 Location: Orsino's palace.

For, boy, however we do praise ourselves,
Our fancies° are more giddy and unfirm,   *affections*
More longing, wavering, sooner lost and worn,°   *spent, exhausted*
Than women's are.
VIOLA   I think° it well, my lord.   *believe*
35 ORSINO   Then let thy love be younger than thyself,
Or thy affection cannot hold the bent.°   *remain steady*
For women are as roses, whose fair flower,
Being once displayed, doth fall that very hour.
VIOLA   And so they are. Alas, that they are so,
40   To die even° when they to perfection grow!   *just*
       Enter CURIO *and* [FESTE, *the*] *clown.*
ORSINO   O, fellow, come, the song we had last night.—
Mark it, Cesario. It is old and plain;
The spinsters° and the knitters in the sun   *spinners*
And the free° maids that weave their thread with bones[8]   *carefree*
45 Do use° to chant it. It is silly sooth,   *Are accustomed*
And dallies with° the innocence of love   *lingers lovingly on*
Like the old age.[9]
FESTE   Are you ready, sir?
ORSINO   Ay, prithee, sing.
       Music.
50 FESTE [*sings*]   Come away,° come away, death,   *hither*
                        And in sad cypress[1] let me be laid.
                   Fly away, fly away, breath,
                        I am slain by a fair cruel maid.
                   My shroud of white, stuck all with yew,°   *yew sprigs*
55   O prepare it.
                   My part of death, no one so true
                        Did share it.[2]

                   Not a flower, not a flower sweet
                   On my black coffin let there be strewn;
60   Not a friend, not a friend greet
                        My poor corpse, where my bones shall
                             be thrown.
                   A thousand thousand sighs to save,
                        Lay me, O, where
                   Sad true lover never find my grave,
65   To weep there.
ORSINO [*giving money*]   There's for thy pains.°   *efforts*
FESTE   No pains, sir. I take pleasure in singing, sir.
ORSINO   I'll pay thy pleasure, then.
FESTE   Truly, sir, and pleasure will be paid,[3] one time or
70   another.
ORSINO   Give me now leave to leave° thee.   *permission to dismiss*

8. Use bone bobbins (to weave "bone lace").
9. As in the good old days.
1. A coffin made of cypress wood, or a bier
covered with cypress boughs. The cypress,
like the yew (line 54), symbolized mourning

and death.
2. That is, no one died so true to love as I.
3. That is, pleasure must be paid for
(proverbial).

FESTE   Now the melancholy god[4] protect thee, and the
          tailor make thy doublet° of changeable taffeta,[5] for thy   *jacket*
75   mind is a very opal.[6] I would have men of such con-
          stancy put to sea, that their business might be every-
          thing and their intent° everywhere, for that's it that   *destination*
          always makes a good voyage of nothing.[7] Farewell.

                                                        Exit.

ORSINO   Let all the rest give place.°   *leave us*
              [*Exeunt all but* ORSINO *and* VIOLA.]
                                              Once more, Cesario,
          Get thee to yond same sovereign cruelty.
80   Tell her my love, more noble than the world,
          Prizes not quantity of dirty lands.
          The parts° that fortune hath bestowed upon her,   *rank and riches*
          Tell her, I hold as giddily° as fortune.   *lightly*
          But 'tis that miracle and queen of gems°   *(i.e., her beauty)*
85   That nature pranks° her in attracts my soul.   *dresses*
VIOLA   But if she cannot love you, sir—
ORSINO   I cannot be so answered.
VIOLA   Sooth,° but you must.   *In truth*
          Say that some lady, as perhaps there is,
          Hath for your love as great a pang of heart
90   As you have for Olivia. You cannot love her;
          You tell her so. Must she not then be answered?
ORSINO   There is no woman's sides
          Can bide° the beating of so strong a passion   *endure*
          As love doth give my heart; no woman's heart
95   So big, to hold so much; they lack retention.°   *capacity, constancy*
          Alas, their love may be called appetite,
          No motion° of the liver, but the palate,[8]   *impulse*
          That suffer surfeit, cloyment,° and revolt;°   *satiety / revulsion*
          But mine is all as hungry as the sea,
100   And can digest as much. Make no compare
          Between that love a woman can bear me
          And that I owe° Olivia.   *have for*
VIOLA   Ay, but I know—
ORSINO   What dost thou know?
105 VIOLA Too well what love women to men may owe.
          In faith, they are as true of heart as we.
          My father had a daughter loved a man
          As it might be, perhaps, were I a woman,
          I should your lordship.
ORSINO   And what's her history?

---

4. Saturn, the god and planet associated by
astrology with melancholy.
5. A thin silk, whose color appears to change
when viewed from different perspectives.
6. An iridescent gemstone that appears to
change color when viewed from different
perspectives.

7. That is, an aimless sea voyage is a good
experience for the fickle lover because he has
no specific goal.
8. That is, their love originates not in the liver
(the seat of real, lasting love) but in the palate
(and thus is a matter of casual taste).

110 VIOLA   A blank, my lord. She never told her love,
But let concealment, like a worm i' th' bud,
Feed on her damask° cheek. She pined in thought,   *pink and white*
And with a green and yellow⁹ melancholy
She sat like Patience on a monument,¹
115   Smiling at grief. Was not this love indeed?
We men may say more, swear more, but indeed
Our shows are more than will;² for still° we prove   *always*
Much in our vows but little in our love.
   ORSINO   But died thy sister of her love, my boy?
120 VIOLA   I am all the daughters of my father's house,
And all the brothers, too—and yet I know not.
Sir, shall I to this lady?
   ORSINO   Ay, that's the theme.
To her in haste. Give her this jewel. Say
My love can give no place, bide no denay.°   *cannot abide denial*

                              Exeunt [severally].

                              2.5

                    Enter SIR TOBY, SIR ANDREW, *and* FABIAN.

   SIR TOBY   Come thy ways,° Signior Fabian.   *Come along*
   FABIAN   Nay, I'll come. If I lose a scruple° of this sport let   *the least bit*
      me be boiled to death with melancholy.³
   SIR TOBY   Wouldst thou not be glad to have the niggardly
5   rascally sheep-biter⁴ come by some notable shame?
   FABIAN   I would exult, man. You know he brought me out
      o' favor with my lady about a bearbaiting⁵ here.
   SIR TOBY   To anger him, we'll have the bear again, and we
      will fool° him black and blue, shall we not, Sir Andrew?   *mock*
10 SIR ANDREW   An° we do not, it is pity of our lives.   *If*

                    Enter MARIA [*with a letter*].

   SIR TOBY   Here comes the little villain.—How now, my
      metal of India?⁶
   MARIA   Get ye all three into the boxtree.° Malvolio's com-   *boxwood hedge*
      ing down this walk. He has been yonder i' the sun prac-
15   ticing behavior to his own shadow this half hour. Observe
      him, for the love of mockery, for I know this letter will
      make a contemplative⁷ idiot of him. Close,° in the name   *Hide*
      of jesting! [*The men hide.*] Lie thou there, [*putting
      down the letter*] for here comes the trout that must be
20   caught with tickling.⁸   *Exit.*

---

9. Pale and sallow in complexion.
1. That is, like a sculpted figure of Patience atop a gravestone.
2. Our displays of passion are greater than the love we feel.
2.5 Location: Olivia's garden.
3. In the humoral theory of physiology, melancholy was a cold humor, caused by a preponderance of bile, on which "boiled" may pun.
4. A sneaking fellow (literally, a dog that bites

sheep); also, a whoremonger (someone who chases after "mutton" or whores).
5. A pursuit frowned on by Puritans.
6. Gold (implying that Maria is worth her weight in gold).
7. Meditative (a word with religious overtones).
8. That is, flattery; trout can be caught by gently stroking beneath them until they back into one's hand.

Enter MALVOLIO.

MALVOLIO 'Tis but fortune, all is fortune. Maria once told
me she did affect° me, and I have heard herself come   *(Olivia) was fond of*
thus near, that should she fancy,° it should be one of my   *fall in love*
complexion. Besides, she uses me with a more exalted
25   respect than anyone else that follows her. What should
I think on't?

SIR TOBY   Here's an overweening rogue.

FABIAN   O, peace! Contemplation makes a rare turkey-
cock of him. How he jets° under his advanced° plumes!   *struts / pulled up*

30 SIR ANDREW   'Slight,° I could so beat the rogue!   *By God's light (an oath)*

SIR TOBY   Peace, I say.

MALVOLIO   To be Count Malvolio!

SIR TOBY   Ah, rogue!

SIR ANDREW   Pistol him, pistol him!

35 SIR TOBY   Peace, peace!

MALVOLIO   There is example° for't. The Lady of the   *precedent*
Strachy married the yeoman of the wardrobe.[9]

SIR ANDREW   Fie on him, Jezebel![1]

FABIAN   O, peace, now he's deeply in. Look how imagi-
40   nation blows him.°   *puffs him up*

MALVOLIO   Having been three months married to her,
sitting in my state°—   *chair of state*

SIR TOBY   O, for a stone-bow,[2] to hit him in the eye!

MALVOLIO   Calling my officers° about me, in my branched[3]   *household staff*
45   velvet gown, having come from a daybed,° where I have   *sofa*
left Olivia sleeping—

SIR TOBY   Fire and brimstone!

FABIAN   O, peace, peace!

MALVOLIO   And then to have the humor of state;[4] and
50   after a demure travel of regard,[5] telling them I know
my place, as I would they should do theirs, to ask for
my kinsman Toby—

SIR TOBY   Bolts and shackles!

FABIAN   O, peace, peace, peace! Now, now.

55 MALVOLIO   Seven of my people, with an obedient start,
make out° for him. I frown the while, and perchance   *go forth*
wind up my watch, or play with my—some rich jewel.[6]
Toby approaches; curtsies° there to me—   *bows*

SIR TOBY   Shall this fellow live?

60 FABIAN   Though our silence be drawn from us with
cars,[7] yet peace.

---

9. The person in charge of the linen and
clothing in a wealthy household (this Lady
has not been identified).
1. A proud, immoral woman (from the wife of
King Ahab of Israel; see especially 1 Kings
21).
2. A crossbow used to shoot stones.
3. Embroidered in a figured pattern.
4. To adopt the manner of the great.
5. Casting my eye about the room with proper

gravity.
6. Malvolio probably begins to say "my chain"
(the symbol of his rank as steward in the
household), but then remembers that as Olivia's husband he will have replaced it with a
more appropriate ornament, a jewel.
7. That is, by torture (a prisoner might be tied
to two carts, or "cars," which then pulled in
opposite directions).

MALVOLIO   I extend my hand to him thus, quenching my
   familiar° smile with an austere regard of control—   *friendly*
SIR TOBY   And does not Toby take° you a blow o' the lips   *give*
65   then?
MALVOLIO   Saying "Cousin Toby, my fortunes, having
   cast me on your niece, give me this prerogative of
   speech"—
SIR TOBY   What, what?
70 MALVOLIO   "You must amend your drunkenness."
SIR TOBY   Out, scab!
FABIAN   Nay, patience, or we break the sinews of our plot.
MALVOLIO   "Besides, you waste the treasure of your time
   with a foolish knight"—
75 SIR ANDREW   That's me, I warrant you.
MALVOLIO   "One Sir Andrew."
SIR ANDREW   I knew 'twas I, for many do call me fool.
MALVOLIO [*seeing the letter*]   What employment° have we   *business*
   here?
80 FABIAN   Now is the woodcock near the gin.[8]
SIR TOBY   O, peace, and the spirit of humors intimate[9]
   reading aloud to him.
MALVOLIO [*taking up the letter*]   By my life, this is my lady's
   hand. These be her very c's, her u's, and her t's,[1] and thus
85   makes she her great P's. It is in contempt of° question   *beyond*
   her hand.
SIR ANDREW   Her c's, her u's, and her t's? Why that?
MALVOLIO [*reads*]   "To the unknown beloved, this, and my
   good wishes."—Her very phrases! By your leave, wax.°   *sealing wax*
90   Soft.° And the impressure her Lucrece,[2] with which she   *Wait*
   uses to seal—'tis my lady! [*He opens the letter.*] To
   whom should this be?
FABIAN   This wins him, liver[3] and all.
MALVOLIO [*reads*]   "Jove knows I love,
95   But who?
          Lips, do not move;
          No man must know."
   "No man must know." What follows? The numbers°   *meter*
   altered.
   "No man must know." If this should be thee, Malvolio!
100 SIR TOBY   Marry, hang thee, brock![4]
MALVOLIO [*reads*]   "I may command where I adore,
          But silence, like a Lucrece knife,
          With bloodless stroke my heart doth gore;
          M.O.A.I. doth sway my life."

8. Snare. The woodcock is a proverbially stupid and easily caught bird.
9. May the spirit of whimsy suggest.
1. Malvolio unwittingly spells "cut," slang for
the vagina.
2. The image of Lucretia, the Roman model

of chastity (who stabbed herself to death after
being raped), was printed in the wax.
3. The seat of love (see 1.1.36n).
4. Badger, conventionally labeled "stinky"; so
dirty fellow, skunk.

105 FABIAN A fustian° riddle! *pompous*

SIR TOBY Excellent wench, say I.

MALVOLIO "M.O.A.I. doth sway my life." Nay, but first let me see, let me see, let me see.

FABIAN What dish o' poison has she dressed° him! *prepared for*

110 SIR TOBY And with what wing the staniel checks at it!⁵

MALVOLIO "I may command where I adore." Why, she may command me; I serve her, she is my lady. Why, this is evident to any formal capacity.⁶ There is no obstruction° *difficulty* in this. And the end—what should that alphabetical posi-

115 tion° portend? If I could make that resemble something *ordering of letters* in me! Softly! "M.O.A.I."—

SIR TOBY O, ay make up that.—He is now at a cold scent.

FABIAN Sowter will cry upon't for all this, though it be as rank as a fox.⁷

120 MALVOLIO "M"—Malvolio. "M"—why, that begins my name!

FABIAN Did not I say he would work it out? The cur is excellent at faults.⁸

MALVOLIO "M." But then there is no consonancy in the

125 sequel.⁹ That suffers under probation.° "A" should *close scrutiny* follow, but "O" does.

FABIAN And "O"¹ shall end, I hope.

SIR TOBY Ay, or I'll cudgel him and make him cry "O."

MALVOLIO And then "I" comes behind.

130 FABIAN Ay, an° you had any eye behind you, you might *if* see more detraction° at your heels than fortunes before *defamation* you.

MALVOLIO "M.O.A.I." This simulation° is not as the *riddle* former, and yet to crush° this a little, it would bow² to *force*

135 me, for every one of these letters are in my name. Soft, here follows prose. [*He reads.*] "If this fall into thy hand, revolve.° In my stars° I am above thee, but be *consider / fortunes* not afraid of greatness. Some are born great, some achieve greatness, and some have greatness thrust

140 upon 'em. Thy fates open their hands.° Let thy blood *offer their bounty* and spirit embrace them. And, to inure° thyself to what *accustom* thou art like° to be, cast thy humble slough³ and appear *likely* fresh. Be opposite° with a kinsman, surly with servants. *contrary, quarrelsome* Let thy tongue tang arguments of state.⁴ Put thyself

145 into the trick of singularity.° She thus advises thee that *act eccentrically*

---

5. That is, with what speed does this inferior hawk fly after it.
6. Normal understanding.
7. "Sowter" (the name of a hound) will cry out when it loses the scent of its quarry, even though that scent is as strong ("rank") as a fox's.
8. That is, good at following his quarry (literally, excellent at lost scents, or "faults").

9. No pattern to the letters that follow.
1. That is, the hangman's noose (perhaps also a cry of pain or lamentation).
2. Yield (its meaning).
3. Cast off your humble deportment, as a snake sheds (sloughs) its old skin.
4. Let your tongue ring loudly with arguments about politics or statecraft.

sighs for thee. Remember who commended thy yellow
stockings and wished to see thee ever cross-gartered.[5] I
say, remember. Go to,° thou art made, if thou desirest   *Get going*
to be so. If not, let me see thee a steward still, the fel-
150 low of servants, and not worthy to touch Fortune's fingers. Farewell. She that would alter services[6] with thee.
                    The Fortunate-Unhappy.''
Daylight and champaign discovers[7] not more! This is
open.° I will be proud, I will read politic° authors, I will   *clear / political*
155 baffle° Sir Toby, I will wash off gross acquaintance,[8] I   *disgrace*
will be point-device the very man.[9] I do not now fool
myself, to let imagination jade° me; for every reason   *trick*
excites to this, that my lady loves me. She did commend my yellow stockings of late, she did praise my
160 leg being cross-gartered, and in this she manifests
herself to my love and, with a kind of injunction, drives
me to these habits° of her liking. I thank my stars, I am   *this attire*
happy. I will be strange,° stout,° in yellow stockings,   *aloof / proud*
and cross-gartered, even with the swiftness of putting
165 on. Jove and my stars be praised! Here is yet a postscript. [*He reads.*] "Thou canst not choose but know
who I am. If thou entertainest° my love, let it appear in   *accept*
thy smiling; thy smiles become thee well. Therefore in
my presence still° smile, dear my sweet, I prithee.'' Jove,   *always*
170 I thank thee. I will smile, I will do everything that thou
wilt have me.   *Exit.*
FABIAN   I will not give my part of this sport for a pension of thousands to be paid from the Sophy.°   *Shah of Persia*
SIR TOBY   I could marry this wench for this device.
175 SIR ANDREW   So could I, too.
SIR TOBY   And ask no other dowry with her but such
another jest.
SIR ANDREW   Nor I neither.
          Enter MARIA
FABIAN   Here comes my noble gull-catcher.°   *fool catcher*
180 SIR TOBY   Wilt thou set thy foot o' my neck?[1]
SIR ANDREW   Or o' mine either?
SIR TOBY   Shall I play° my freedom at tray-trip[2] and   *gamble*
become thy bondslave?
SIR ANDREW   I' faith, or I either?
185 SIR TOBY   Why, thou hast put him in such a dream that
when the image of it leaves him he must run mad.
MARIA   Nay, but say true, does it work upon him?

---

5. The fashion (possibly outmoded by the
time of the play) of wearing the garters so
that in front they pass above as well as below
the knee.
6. Exchange places (of mistress and servant).
7. Open country reveals.
8. Rid myself of acquaintances of low social

rank.
9. That is, I will become, to the smallest
detail, the man described in the letter.
1. An act symbolizing a conquerer's triumph.
2. A game of dice in which three (trey) was a
winning roll.

SIR TOBY   Like aqua vitae° with a midwife.   *strong liquor*

MARIA   If you will then see the fruits of the sport, mark
190   his first approach before my lady. He will come to her
   in yellow stockings, and 'tis a color she abhors, and
   cross-gartered, a fashion she detests; and he will smile
   upon her, which will now be so unsuitable to her disposition, being addicted to a melancholy as she is, that it
195   cannot but turn him into a notable contempt.[3] If you
   will see it, follow me.

SIR TOBY   To the gates of Tartar,[4] thou most excellent
   devil of wit!

SIR ANDREW   I'll make one,° too.   *Exeunt.*   *go along*

3.1

Enter VIOLA *and* [FESTE, *the*] *clown* [*with pipe and*
tabor].°   *small drum*

VIOLA   Save° thee, friend, and thy music. Dost thou live   *God save*
   by thy tabor?

FESTE   No, sir, I live by° the church.   *near*

VIOLA   Art thou a churchman?°   *clergyman*

5 FESTE   No such matter, sir. I do live by the church, for I do
   live at my house, and my house doth stand by the church.

VIOLA   So thou mayst say the king lies by[5] a beggar if a
   beggar dwell near him, or the church stands° by thy   *is maintained*
   tabor if thy tabor stand by the church.

10 FESTE   You have said, sir. To see this age! A sentence° is   *saying*
   but a chev'ril° glove to a good wit. How quickly the   *kidskin*
   wrong side may be turned outward!

VIOLA   Nay, that's certain. They that dally nicely° with   *play cleverly*
   words may quickly make them wanton.[6]

15 FESTE   I would therefore my sister had had no name, sir.

VIOLA   Why, man?

FESTE   Why, sir, her name's a word, and to dally with
   that word might make my sister wanton. But, indeed,
   words are very rascals since bonds[7] disgraced them.

20 VIOLA   Thy reason, man?

FESTE   Troth, sir, I can yield you none without words,
   and words are grown so false I am loath to prove reason with them.

VIOLA   I warrant thou art a merry fellow and carest for
25   nothing.

FESTE   Not so, sir. I do care for something. But in my
   conscience, sir, I do not care for you. If that be to care
   for nothing, sir, I would it would make you invisible.

VIOLA   Art not thou the Lady Olivia's fool?

---

3. A notable object of contempt.
4. Tartarus (that part of the classical underworld where the wicked were punished).
3.1 Location: Olivia's garden.
5. Dwells near; also, lies with sexually.

6. Equivocal; also, lewd.
7. Written contracts, which replaced a man's
simple promise; Feste puns on the meaning
"fetters."

30 FESTE   No indeed, sir. The Lady Olivia has no folly. She
will keep no fool, sir, till she be married, and fools are
as like husbands as pilchards° are to herrings: the   *small fish*
husband's the bigger. I am indeed not her fool but her
corrupter of words.

35 VIOLA   I saw thee late° at the Count Orsino's.   *recently*

FESTE   Foolery, sir, does walk about the orb[8] like the
sun; it shines everywhere. I would be sorry, sir, but°   *unless*
the fool should be as oft with your master as with my
mistress. I think I saw your wisdom[9] there.

40 VIOLA   Nay, an thou pass upon me,[1] I'll no more with thee.
Hold, there's expenses for thee. [*giving a coin*]

FESTE   Now Jove in his next commodity° of hair send   *parcel, supply*
thee a beard!

VIOLA   By my troth I'll tell thee, I am almost sick° for   *eager; lovesick*
45 one, [*aside*] though I would not have it grow on *my*   *(for Orsino)*
chin.—Is thy lady within?

FESTE   Would not a pair of these° have bred,° sir?   *(coins) / multiplied*

VIOLA   Yes, being kept together and put to use.[2]

FESTE   I would play Lord Pandarus[3] of Phrygia, sir, to
50 bring a Cressida to this Troilus.

VIOLA   I understand you, sir. 'Tis well begged. [*giving
another coin*]

FESTE   The matter I hope is not great, sir, begging but a
beggar: Cressida was a beggar.[4] My lady is within, sir.
I will conster° to them whence you come. Who you   *explain*
55 are and what you would are out of my welkin°—I might   *sky; air (an element)*
say "element," but the word is overworn.   *Exit.*

VIOLA   This fellow is wise enough to play the fool,
And to do that well craves° a kind of wit.°   *requires / intelligence*
He must observe their mood on whom he jests,
60 The quality° of persons, and the time,   *social rank; character*
And, like the haggard,° check at every feather[5]   *wild hawk*
That comes before his eye. This is a practice°   *skill*
As full of labor as a wise man's art,
For folly that he wisely shows is fit,°   *appropriate*
65 But wise men, folly-fall'n, quite taint their wit.[6]

        Enter SIR TOBY *and* SIR ANDREW

SIR TOBY   Save you, gentleman.

VIOLA   And you, sir.

SIR ANDREW   *Dieu vous garde, monsieur.*[7]

8. The earth (around which, in the Ptolemaic
system, all heavenly bodies orbited).
9. "Your wisdom" is a form of address, here
sarcastic.
1. If you attack me (literally, make a fencing
pass at me).
2. Invested; lent out at interest.
3. The go-between in the love story of Troilus
and Cressida. Feste will bring two coins
together, as Pandarus would lovers, and have

them reproduce.
4. In Robert Henryson's version of the story,
Testament of Cresseid (though not in Shakespeare's own *Troilus and Cressida*), Cressida
becomes a leprous beggar.
5. Fly after every bird.
6. That is, wise men, having fallen into folly,
tarnish their innate intelligence or wisdom.
7. God protect you, sir (French).

VIOLA *Et vous aussi. Votre serviteur!*[8]

70 SIR ANDREW I hope, sir, you are, and I am yours.

SIR TOBY Will you encounter° the house? My niece is   *approach; enter*
desirous you should enter, if your trade be to her.

VIOLA I am bound to° your niece, sir; I mean, she is the   *for*
list° of my voyage.   *limit; destination*

75 SIR TOBY Taste° your legs, sir; put them to motion.   *Try, test*

VIOLA My legs do better understand° me, sir, than I under-   *stand under*
stand what you mean by bidding me taste my legs.

SIR TOBY I mean, to go, sir, to enter.

VIOLA I will answer you with gait and entrance.[9]

Enter OLIVIA *and* [MARIA, *her*] *gentlewoman*

80 But we are prevented.° Most excellent accomplished   *anticipated*
lady, the heavens rain odors on you!

SIR ANDREW [*to* SIR TOBY] That youth's a rare° courtier.   *an excellent*
"Rain odors," well.

VIOLA My matter hath no voice,° lady, but to your own   *must not be spoken*

85 most pregnant° and vouchsafed[1] ear.   *receptive*

SIR ANDREW [*to* SIR TOBY] "Odors," "pregnant," and
"vouchsafed." I'll get 'em all three all ready.°   *committed to memory*

OLIVIA Let the garden door be shut, and leave me to my
hearing.   [*Exeunt* SIR TOBY, SIR ANDREW, *and* MARIA.]

90 Give me your hand, sir.

VIOLA My duty, madam, and most humble service.

OLIVIA What is your name?

VIOLA Cesario is your servant's name, fair princess.

OLIVIA My servant, sir? 'Twas never merry world

95 Since lowly feigning was called compliment.[2]
You're servant to the Count Orsino, youth.

VIOLA And he is yours, and his must needs be yours.
Your servant's servant is *your* servant, madam.

OLIVIA For° him, I think not on him. For his thoughts,   *As for*

100 Would they were blanks rather than filled with me.

VIOLA Madam, I come to whet your gentle thoughts
On his behalf.

OLIVIA   O, by your leave,[3] I pray you.
I bade you never speak again of him;
But would you undertake another suit,

105 I had rather hear you to solicit that
Than music from the spheres.[4]

VIOLA   Dear lady—

OLIVIA Give me leave, beseech you. I did send,
After the last enchantment you did here,
A ring in chase of you. So did I abuse°   *dishonor*

---

8. And you, also; (I am) your servant (French).
9. Going and entering, with a pun on "gate."
1. Graciously offered.
2. That is, the world has not been a happy place since flattery came to be called courtesy.
3. Permit me to interrupt (a courteous expres-

sion, as is "give me leave," line 108).
4. In the Ptolemaic system, the planets and other heavenly bodies were thought to be affixed to concentric spheres, whose turning made glorious music inaudible to human ears.

110 Myself, my servant, and, I fear me, you.
Under your hard construction must I sit,[5]
To force° that on you in a shameful cunning   *For forcing*
Which you knew none of yours. What might you think?
Have you not set mine honor at the stake,
115 And baited it with all th' unmuzzled thoughts[6]
That tyrannous heart can think? To one of your
receiving°   *perceptiveness*
Enough is shown. A cypress,[7] not a bosom,
Hides my heart. So let me hear you speak.
VIOLA   I pity you.
OLIVIA   That's a degree to° love.   *step toward*
120 VIOLA   No, not a grize,° for 'tis a vulgar proof°   *step / common experience*
That very oft we pity enemies.
OLIVIA   Why then methinks 'tis time to smile again.[8]
O world, how apt° the poor are to be proud!   *ready*
If one should be a prey, how much the better
125 To fall before the lion than the wolf.[9]
          Clock strikes.
The clock upbraids me with the waste of time.
Be not afraid, good youth, I will not have you.
And yet when wit and youth is come to harvest,
Your wife is like to reap a proper° man.   *handsome; worthy*
There lies your way, due west.
130 VIOLA   Then westward ho![1]
Grace and good disposition° attend your ladyship.   *frame of mind*
You'll nothing, madam, to my lord by me?
OLIVIA   Stay. I prithee, tell me what thou think'st of me.
VIOLA   That you do think you are not what you are.
135 OLIVIA   If I think so, I think the same of you.[2]
VIOLA   Then think you right. I am not what I am.
OLIVIA   I would you were as I would have you be.
VIOLA   Would it be better, madam, than I am?
I wish it might, for now I am your fool.[3]
140 OLIVIA   [*aside*]   O, what a deal of scorn looks beautiful
In the contempt and anger of his lip!
A murd'rous guilt shows not itself more soon
Than love that would seem hid. Love's night is noon.—[4]
Cesario, by the roses of the spring,
145 By maidhood, honor, truth, and everything,
I love thee so, that, maugre° all thy pride,   *despite*
Nor° wit nor reason can my passion hide.   *Neither*

5. I must be judged harshly by you.
6. An allusion to bearbaiting, in which a bear is chained to a stake and attacked by hungry dogs.
7. A piece of light, transparent material, often used (when black) for mourning.
8. That is, to leave melancholy behind (because we are not enemies).
9. That is, to fall before a noble foe like Ors-

ino rather than unyielding Cesario.
1. The cry of Thames boatmen as they depart from London toward Westminster.
2. Here, apparently rebuffed by "Cesario," Olivia switches back to the polite "you" after having used the familiar "thou" (line 134).
3. That is, you made a fool of me.
4. That is, love shines out brightly at all times.

Do not extort thy reasons from this clause,
For that I woo, thou therefore hast no cause;[5]
150 But rather reason thus with reason fetter:[6]
Love sought is good, but given unsought is better.
VIOLA   By innocence I swear, and by my youth,
I have one heart, one bosom, and one truth,
And that no woman has, nor never none
155 Shall mistress be of it, save I alone.
And so adieu, good madam. Nevermore
Will I my master's tears to you deplore.°   *lament*
OLIVIA   Yet come again, for thou perhaps mayst move
That heart, which now abhors, to like his love.

Exeunt [severally].

3.2

Enter SIR TOBY, SIR ANDREW, *and* FABIAN.

SIR ANDREW   No, faith, I'll not stay a jot longer.
SIR TOBY   Thy reason, dear venom,° give thy reason.   *venomous one*
FABIAN   You must needs yield your reason, Sir Andrew.
SIR ANDREW   Marry, I saw your niece do more favors to the
5   Count's servingman than ever she bestowed upon me.
I saw't i' th' orchard.°   *garden*
SIR TOBY   Did she see thee the while, old boy? Tell me
that.
SIR ANDREW   As plain as I see you now.
10 FABIAN   This was a great argument° of love in her toward   *proof*
you.
SIR ANDREW   'Slight, will you make an ass o' me?
FABIAN   I will prove it legitimate, sir, upon the oaths of
judgment and reason.
15 SIR TOBY   And they have been grand-jurymen[7] since
before Noah was a sailor.
FABIAN   She did show favor to the youth in your sight
only to exasperate you, to awake your dormouse[8] valor,
to put fire in your heart and brimstone° in your liver.   *heat*
20 You should then have accosted her, and with some
excellent jests, fire-new from the mint,° you should   *newly minted*
have banged the youth into dumbness. This was looked
for at your hand, and this was balked.[9] The double gilt°   *gold plating*
of this opportunity you let time wash off, and you are
25 now sailed into the north of my lady's opinion,[1] where
you will hang like an icicle on a Dutchman's[2] beard,

5. That is, do not extract reasons from what I
have just said to argue that because ("for that")
I woo, you need not reciprocate my love.
6. But instead restrain your reasoning with
the following reason.
3.2 Location: Olivia's house.
7. Experts at evaluating evidence.
8. Sleeping (dormice are small rodents known

for their long periods of hibernation).
9. This opportunity was ignored.
1. That is, out of the warmth of her favor.
2. An allusion to the Dutch Arctic explorer Wil-
lem Barents (ca. 1550–1597), who made several attempts to discover a navigable passage to
the East along the northern coast of Russia.

unless you do redeem it by some laudable attempt
either of valor or policy.°   *crafty device*

SIR ANDREW   An't° be any way, it must be with valor, for   *If it*
30 policy I hate. I had as lief° be a Brownist as a politician.[3]   *soon*

SIR TOBY   Why then, build me thy fortunes upon the basis
of valor. Challenge me° the Count's youth to fight with   *for me*
him. Hurt him in eleven places. My niece shall take note
of it, and assure thyself, there is no love-broker° in the   *go-between*
35 world can more prevail in man's commendation with
woman than report of valor.

FABIAN   There is no way but this, Sir Andrew.

SIR ANDREW   Will either of you bear me a challenge to
him?

40 SIR TOBY   Go, write it in a martial hand. Be curst° and brief.   *abusive*
It is no matter how witty, so it be eloquent and full of
invention.° Taunt him with the license of ink.[4] If thou   *imagination*
"thou'st" him[5] some thrice, it shall not be amiss, and as
many lies as will lie in thy sheet of paper, although the
45 sheet were big enough for the bed of Ware[6] in
England, set 'em down. Go, about it. Let there be gall
enough in thy ink, though thou write with a goose-
pen,[7] no matter. About it.°   *Get on with it*

SIR ANDREW   Where shall I find you?

50 SIR TOBY   We'll call thee at the cubiculo.° Go.   *little chamber*

Exit SIR ANDREW.

FABIAN   This is a dear manikin° to you, Sir Toby.   *puppet*

SIR TOBY   I have been dear° to him, lad, some two thou-   *costly*
sand strong, or so.

FABIAN   We shall have a rare letter from him. But you'll
55 not deliver't?

SIR TOBY   Never trust me, then. And by all means stir on
the youth to an answer. I think oxen and wainropes°   *wagon ropes*
cannot hale° them together. For Andrew, if he were   *pull*
opened and you find so much blood in his liver[8] as
60 will clog° the foot of a flea, I'll eat the rest of th'   *burden*
anatomy.°   *cadaver*

FABIAN   And his opposite,° the youth, bears in his visage   *rival*
no great presage of cruelty.

Enter MARIA

SIR TOBY   Look where the youngest wren of nine[9] comes.

---

3. An intriguer. *Brownist:* a follower of the
Puritan sect founded by Robert Browne (ca.
1550–1633).
4. With the freedom that writing allows
(when compared to conversation).
5. That is, address him discourteously (to use
the familiar "thou" to a relative stranger was
an insult).
6. A famous bedstead built in 1590, almost

11 feet square (twice the normal size of beds
of the period).
7. A quill pen made from the feather of a
goose, a proverbially foolish bird. *Gall:* an
ingredient of ink; bitterness, acrimony.
8. Cowards were believed to have little or no
blood in their liver.
9. The smallest wren in a nest of nine; that is,
the smallest of the small.

65 MARIA   If you desire the spleen,[1] and will laugh yourselves into stitches, follow me. Yond gull° Malvolio is   *dupe*
turned heathen, a very renegado;[2] for there is no Christian that means to be saved by believing rightly can
ever believe such impossible passages of grossness.[3]

70 He's in yellow stockings.

SIR TOBY   And cross-gartered?

MARIA   Most villainously,° like a pedant° that keeps a   *atrociously / teacher*
school i' th' church.[4] I have dogged him like his mur-
derer. He does obey every point of the letter that I

75 dropped to betray him. He does smile his face into
more lines than is in the new map with the augmenta-
tion of the Indies.[5] You have not seen such a thing as
'tis. I can hardly forbear hurling things at him. I know
my lady will strike him. If she do, he'll smile and take't

80 for a great favor.

SIR TOBY   Come, bring us, bring us where he is. *Exeunt.*

3.3

Enter SEBASTIAN *and* ANTONIO.

SEBASTIAN   I would not by my will have troubled you,
But, since you make your pleasure of your pains,
I will no further chide you.

ANTONIO   I could not stay behind you. My desire,

5 More sharp than filèd steel, did spur me forth;
And not all° love to see you—though so much   *not entirely (out of)*
As might have drawn one to a longer voyage—
But jealousy° what might befall your travel,   *anxiety about*
Being skill-less in° these parts, which to a stranger,   *unfamiliar with*

10 Unguided and unfriended, often prove
Rough and unhospitable. My willing love,
The rather° by these arguments of fear,   *All the more*
Set forth in your pursuit.

SEBASTIAN   My kind Antonio,
I can no other answer make but thanks,

15 And thanks, and ever [thanks; and] oft° good turns   *very often*
Are shuffled off° with such uncurrent[6] pay.   *shrugged off*
But were my worth, as is my conscience,° firm,   *awareness of my debt*
You should find better dealing. What's to do?
Shall we go see the relics° of this town?   *antiquities; memorials*

20 ANTONIO   Tomorrow, sir. Best first go see your lodging.

SEBASTIAN   I am not weary, and 'tis long to night.

---

1. Thought to be the seat of immoderate
laughter.
2. Renegade (Spanish); apostate.
3. Such obvious absurdities (as the planted
letter contains; see 2.5).
4. The practice of holding classes in church
buildings was disappearing in Shakespeare's
time.

5. Possibly a reference to a new map (published ca. 1599) that showed the Earth's surface crisscrossed by rhumb lines and that was
"augmented" with recent discoveries in both
the Americas and the East Indies.
3.3 Location: A street.
6. No longer current; that is, worthless.

I pray you let us satisfy our eyes
With the memorials and the things of fame
That do renown this city.

ANTONIO   Would you'd pardon me.
25 I do not without danger walk these streets.
    Once in a sea fight 'gainst the Count his° galleys   (the Count's)
    I did some service, of such note indeed
    That were I ta'en° here it would scarce be answered.[7]   captured

SEBASTIAN   Belike° you slew great number of his people?   Perhaps

30 ANTONIO   Th' offense is not of such a bloody nature,
    Albeit the quality° of the time and quarrel   circumstances
    Might well have given us bloody argument.°   reason for bloodshed
    It might have since been answered in repaying
    What we took from them, which, for traffic's° sake,   trade's
35 Most of our city did. Only myself stood out,°   refused to go along
    For which if I be latchèd° in this place,   captured
    I shall pay dear.

SEBASTIAN   Do not then walk too open.

ANTONIO   It doth not fit° me. Hold, sir, here's my purse.   is not fitting for
    In the south suburbs at the Elephant°   (an inn)
40 Is best to lodge. I will bespeak our diet°   order our food
    Whiles you beguile° the time and feed your knowledge   pass
    With viewing of the town. There shall you have me.

SEBASTIAN   Why I your purse?

ANTONIO   Haply° your eye shall light upon some toy°   Perhaps / trifle
45 You have desire to purchase, and your store,°   supply of money
    I think, is not for idle markets,[8] sir.

SEBASTIAN   I'll be your purse-bearer and leave you
    For an hour.

ANTONIO   To th' Elephant.

SEBASTIAN   I do remember.

                              Exeunt [severally].

                         3.4

Enter OLIVIA and MARIA.

OLIVIA [aside]   I have sent after him. He says he'll come.
    How shall I feast him? What bestow of° him?   on
    For youth is bought more oft than begged or borrowed.
    I speak too loud.—
5   [To MARIA]   Where's Malvolio? He is sad° and civil°   serious / respectful
    And suits well for a servant with my fortunes.
    Where is Malvolio?

MARIA   He's coming, madam, but in very strange manner.
    He is sure possessed,[9] madam.

---

7. That is, it would be hard for me to defend myself or make reparations.
8. Sufficient to buy unnecessary luxuries.
3.4 Location: Olivia's garden.

9. That is, insane; possession by a demon or the devil was a common explanation for madness.

10 OLIVIA   Why, what's the matter? Does he rave?

MARIA   No, madam, he does nothing but smile. Your
  ladyship were best to have some guard about you if he
  come, for sure the man is tainted in's° wits.   *in his*

OLIVIA   Go call him hither.   [*Exit* MARIA.]

  I am as mad as he,

15   If sad and merry madness equal be.

      Enter [MARIA *with*] MALVOLIO [*cross-gartered and
      wearing yellow stockings*].

  How now, Malvolio?

MALVOLIO   Sweet lady, ho, ho!

OLIVIA   Smil'st thou? I sent for thee upon a sad occasion.°   *serious matter*

MALVOLIO   Sad, lady? I could be sad. This does make
20   some obstruction in the blood, this cross-gartering, but
  what of that? If it please the eye of one, it is with me as
  the very true sonnet° is: "Please one, and please all."[1]   *short poem; song*

OLIVIA   Why, how dost thou, man? What is the matter
  with thee?

25 MALVOLIO   Not black in my mind, though yellow in my
  legs.[2] It did come to his hands, and commands shall be
  executed. I think we do know the sweet Roman hand.[3]

OLIVIA   Wilt thou go to bed,[4] Malvolio?

MALVOLIO   [*kissing his hand*] To bed? "Ay, sweetheart,
30   and I'll come to thee."[5]

OLIVIA   God comfort thee! Why dost thou smile so, and
  kiss thy hand so oft?

MARIA   How do you, Malvolio?

MALVOLIO   At your request? Yes, nightingales answer daws![6]

35 MARIA   Why appear you with this ridiculous boldness
  before my lady?

MALVOLIO   "Be not afraid of greatness." 'Twas well writ.

OLIVIA   What meanest thou by that, Malvolio?

MALVOLIO   "Some are born great"—

40 OLIVIA   Ha?

MALVOLIO   "Some achieve greatness"—

OLIVIA   What sayst thou?

MALVOLIO   "And some have greatness thrust upon them."

OLIVIA   Heaven restore thee!

45 MALVOLIO   "Remember who commended thy yellow
  stockings"—

OLIVIA   Thy yellow stockings?

MALVOLIO   "And wished to see thee cross-gartered."

OLIVIA   Cross-gartered?

---

1. That is, "If I please you, then I please
everyone I care to please" (a line from a popular ballad).
2. Black indicated melancholy; yellow, both
jealousy and choler.
3. The Italian-style handwriting then coming

into use.
4. That is, to cure your madness with sleep.
5. A line from a popular song.
6. That is, should I answer you? A nightingale
(whose song is proverbially beautiful) does
not respond to a crow.

50 MALVOLIO "Go to, thou art made, if thou desirest to be
so"—

OLIVIA Am I made?

MALVOLIO "If not, let me see thee a servant still."

OLIVIA Why, this is very midsummer madness!⁷

Enter a SERVANT.

55 SERVANT Madam, the young gentleman of the Count
Orsino's is returned. I could hardly entreat him
back. He attends° your ladyship's pleasure.   *awaits*

OLIVIA I'll come to him.   [*Exit* SERVANT.]
Good Maria, let this fellow be looked to. Where's my

60 cousin Toby? Let some of my people have a special
care of him. I would not have him miscarry° for the   *come to harm*
half of my dowry.

[*Exeunt* OLIVIA *and* MARIA, *severally.*]

MALVOLIO O ho, do you come near° me now? No worse   *understand*
man than Sir Toby to look to me. This concurs directly

65 with the letter. She sends him on purpose that I may
appear stubborn to him, for she incites me to that in
the letter: "Cast thy humble slough," says she. "Be
opposite with a kinsman, surly with servants; let thy
tongue tang with arguments of state; put thyself the

70 into trick of singularity," and consequently° sets   *thereafter*
down the manner how: as, a sad face, a reverend car-
riage, a slow tongue,° in the habit° of some sir of *deliberate speech / clothing*
note,° and so forth. I have limed her,⁸ but it is Jove's   *a gentleman*
doing, and Jove make me thankful! And when she

75 went away now, "Let this fellow be looked to." "Fellow."⁹ Not "Malvolio," nor after my degree, but "fellow." Why, everything adheres together, that no dram
of a scruple, no scruple of a scruple,¹ no obstacle, no
incredulous° or unsafe circumstance—what can be   *incredible*

80 said? Nothing that can be can come between me and
the full prospect of my hopes. Well, Jove, not I, is the
doer of this, and he is to be thanked.

Enter SIR TOBY, FABIAN, *and* MARIA.

SIR TOBY Which way is he, in the name of sanctity?° If all   *of all that is sacred*
the devils of hell be drawn in little,° and Legion²   *in miniature*

85 himself possessed him, yet I'll speak to him.

FABIAN Here he is, here he is.—How is't with you, sir?
How is't with you, man?

MALVOLIO Go off, I discard you. Let me enjoy my private.° Go off.   *privacy*

---

7. The midsummer moon was thought to
cause insanity.
8. Caught her, like a bird trapped by sticky
birdlime spread on a branch.
9. Malvolio gives "fellow" the meaning (unintended by Olivia) "consort" or "counterpart."

1. That is, no bit of doubt; as apothecaries'
weights, a dram is 60 grains and a scruple is
one-third of a dram.
2. The name of an "unclean spirit" exorcised
by Jesus (Mark 5.8–9).

90 MARIA [*to* SIR TOBY]   Lo, how hollow° the fiend speaks   *resoundingly*
      within him! Did not I tell you? Sir Toby, my lady prays
      you to have a care of him.

   MALVOLIO   Aha, does she so?

   SIR TOBY   Go to, go to! Peace, peace. We must deal gently
95   with him. Let me alone.°—How do you, Malvolio? How   *Leave him to me*
      is't with you? What, man, defy the devil! Consider, he's
      an enemy to mankind.

   MALVOLIO   Do you know what you say?

   MARIA   La° you, an° you speak ill of the devil, how he   *Look / if*
100   takes it at heart! Pray God he be not bewitched!

   FABIAN   Carry his water to th' wise woman.[3]

   MARIA   Marry, and it shall be done tomorrow morning if I
      live. My lady would not lose him for more than I'll say.

   MALVOLIO   How now, mistress?

105 MARIA   O Lord!

   SIR TOBY   Prithee, hold thy peace. This is not the way.
      Do you not see you move° him? Let me alone with him.   *excite; anger*

   FABIAN   No way but gentleness, gently, gently. The fiend
      is rough° and will not be roughly used.   *violent*

110 SIR TOBY   Why, how now, my bawcock?[4] How dost thou,
      chuck?°   *chick (endearment)*

   MALVOLIO   Sir!

   SIR TOBY   Ay, biddy,° come with me.—What, man, 'tis not   *hen; chicken*
      for gravity to play at cherry-pit[5] with Satan. Hang him,
115   foul collier![6]

   MARIA   Get him to say his prayers, good Sir Toby; get
      him to pray.

   MALVOLIO   My prayers, minx?°   *insolent girl*

   MARIA   No, I warrant you, he will not hear of godliness.

120 MALVOLIO   Go hang yourselves all! You are idle,° shallow   *foolish*
      things. I am not of your element.° You shall know more   *social sphere*
      hereafter.   *Exit.*

   SIR TOBY   Is't possible?

   FABIAN   If this were played upon a stage now, I could
125   condemn it as an improbable fiction.

   SIR TOBY   His very genius° hath taken the infection of   *spirit; soul*
      the device,° man.   *scheme*

   MARIA   Nay, pursue him now, lest the device take air and
      taint.[7]

130 FABIAN   Why, we shall make him mad indeed.

   MARIA   The house will be the quieter.

   SIR TOBY   Come, we'll have him in a dark room and bound.[8]

---

3. The female healer, herbalist. *Water:* urine
(used to diagnose illness).
4. Fine fellow (from the French *beau coq*,
"fine bird").
5. It is not fitting for a dignified man to play a
children's game (pitching cherry stones into a
small hole).

6. Coal miner or carrier (the devil was commonly portrayed as pitch black).
7. Be exposed to the effects of the air (i.e.,
become public knowledge) and therefore
spoil.
8. A standard treatment of the insane.

My niece is already in the belief that he's mad. We may
carry it thus, for our pleasure and his penance, till our
135   very pastime, tired out of breath, prompt us to have
merc on him, at which time we will bring the device to
the bar[9] and crown thee for a finder of madmen. But
see, but see!

       Enter SIR ANDREW.

FABIAN   More matter for a May morning.[1]
140 SIR ANDREW [*presenting a paper*] Here's the challenge.
    Read it. I warrant there's vinegar and pepper in't.
FABIAN   Is't so saucy?
SIR ANDREW   Ay, is't? I warrant him. Do but read.
SIR TOBY   Give me. [*He reads.*] "Youth, whatsoever thou
145   art, thou art but a scurvy fellow."
FABIAN   Good, and valiant.
SIR TOBY,   "Wonder not, nor admire° not in thy mind, why   *marvel*
    I do call thee so, for I will show thee no reason for't."
FABIAN   A good note, that keeps you from the blow of
150   the law.[2]
SIR TOBY   "Thou comest to the Lady Olivia, and in my sight
    she uses thee kindly. But thou liest in thy throat;° that is   *deeply; egregiously*
    not the matter I challenge thee for."
FABIAN   Very brief, and to exceeding good sense—less.
155 SIR TOBY   "I will waylay thee going home, where if it be
    thy chance to kill me"—
FABIAN   Good.
SIR TOBY   "Thou killest me like a rogue and a villain."
FABIAN   Still you keep o' th' windy side[3] of the law. Good.
160 SIR TOBY   "Fare thee well, and God have mercy upon
    one of our souls. He may have mercy upon mine, but
    my hope is better, and so look to thyself. Thy friend,
    as thou usest him, and thy sworn enemy,

                         Andrew Aguecheek."
165   If this letter move° him not, his legs cannot. I'll give't him.   *incite*
MARIA   You may have very fit occasion for't. He is now in
    some commerce° with my lady, and will by and by depart.   *dealings*
SIR TOBY   Go, Sir Andrew. Scout me° for him at the   *Look out*
    corner of the orchard like a bum-baily.[4] So soon as
170   ever thou seest him, draw, and as thou drawest, swear
    horrible, for it comes to pass oft that a terrible oath,
    with a swaggering accent sharply twanged off, gives
    manhood more approbation° than ever proof° itself   *confirmation /*
    would have earned him. Away!   *demonstration; deed*
175 SIR ANDREW   Nay, let me alone for swearing.[5]   *Exit.*

---

9. That is, the bar of judgment; to a court.
1. Entertainment for May Day (i.e., a holiday).
2. That safeguards you from legal action (for
slander or disturbing the peace).
3. To windward and thus out of the reach of

the law.
4. A contemptuous term for a bailiff, an officer charged with making arrests.
5. That is, I am unsurpassed at swearing.

SIR TOBY   Now will not I deliver his letter, for the behavior of the young gentleman gives him out to be of good
capacity° and breeding; his employment between his   ability
lord and my niece confirms no less. Therefore, this let-
180   ter, being so excellently ignorant, will breed no terror in
the youth. He will find it comes from a clodpoll.° But,   blockhead
sir, I will deliver his challenge by word of mouth, set
upon Aguecheek a notable report of valor, and drive
the gentleman—as I know his youth will aptly receive
185   it[6]—into a most hideous° opinion of his rage, skill, fury,   terrifying
and impetuosity. This will so fright them both that they
will kill one another by the look, like cockatrices.[7]

Enter OLIVIA *and* VIOLA.

FABIAN   Here he comes with your niece. Give them way°   *Stay out of their way*
till he take leave, and presently° after him.   *immediately go*
190   SIR TOBY   I will meditate the while upon some horrid
message for a challenge.

[*Exeunt* SIR TOBY, FABIAN, *and* MARIA.]

OLIVIA   I have said too much unto a heart of stone
And laid mine honor too unchary[8] on't.
There's something in me that reproves my fault,
195   But such a headstrong potent fault it is
That it but mocks reproof.
VIOLA   With the same 'havior that your passion bears
Goes on my master's griefs.[9]
OLIVIA   Here, wear this jewel[1] for me. 'Tis my picture.
200   Refuse it not, it hath no tongue to vex you.
And I beseech you come again tomorrow.
What shall you ask of me that I'll deny,
That honor, saved, may upon asking give?[2]
VIOLA   Nothing but this: your true love for my master.
205   OLIVIA   How with mine honor may I give him that
Which I have given to you?
VIOLA   I will acquit you.[3]
OLIVIA   Well, come again tomorrow. Fare thee well.
A fiend like thee might bear my soul to hell.   [*Exit.*]

Enter [SIR] TOBY *and* FABIAN.

SIR TOBY   Gentleman, God save thee.
210   VIOLA   And you, sir.
SIR TOBY   That defense thou hast, betake thee to't. Of
what nature the wrongs are thou hast done him, I
know not, but thy intercepter, full of despite,° bloody   defiance
as the hunter,[4] attends° thee at the orchard end.   awaits

---

6. That is, his inexperience will cause him to
believe the report of Sir Andrew's valor.
7. Basilisks, mythical monsters that killed
with a look.
8. Risked my honor too incautiously.
9. With the same behavior that marks your

passion, my master's griefs persist.
1. That is, a jeweled locket.
2. That honor, uncompromised, may give
when asked.
3. Release you (from your promise to me).
4. Bloodthirsty as a hunting dog or a huntsman.

215　Dismount thy tuck,° be yare° in thy preparation, for thy　　*Draw your rapier / quick*
　　　assailant is quick, skillful, and deadly.

VIOLA　You mistake, sir, I am sure no man hath any quarrel
　　　to° me. My remembrance° is very free and clear from any　　*with / memory*
　　　image of offense done to any man.

220　SIR TOBY　You'll find it otherwise, I assure you. There-
　　　fore, if you hold your life at any price, betake you to
　　　your guard, for your opposite° hath in him what youth,　　*opponent*
　　　strength, skill, and wrath can furnish man withal.°　　*with*

VIOLA　I pray you, sir, what is he?

225　SIR TOBY　He is knight dubbed with unhatched[5] rapier
　　　and on carpet consideration,[6] but he is a devil in pri-
　　　vate brawl. Souls and bodies hath he divorced three,
　　　and his incensement at this moment is so implacable
　　　that satisfaction can be none but by pangs of death and

230　sepulcher. "Hob, nob"[7] is his word;° "give't or take't."　　*motto*

VIOLA　I will return again into the house and desire some
　　　conduct° of the lady. I am no fighter. I have heard of　　*protective escort*
　　　some kind of men that put quarrels purposely on oth-
　　　ers, to taste° their valor. Belike° this is a man of that　　*test / Perhaps*

235　quirk.

SIR TOBY　Sir, no. His indignation derives itself out of a
　　　very competent° injury. Therefore get you on and give　　*sufficient*
　　　him his desire. Back you shall not to the house, unless
　　　you undertake that° with me which with as much　　*(a duel)*

240　safety you might answer him. Therefore on, or strip
　　　your sword stark naked, for meddle° you must, that's　　*fight a duel*
　　　certain, or forswear to wear iron about you.[8]

VIOLA　This is as uncivil as strange. I beseech you, do me
　　　this courteous office, as to know of° the knight what my　　*from*

245　offense to him is. It is something of my negligence,
　　　nothing of my purpose.

SIR TOBY　I will do so.—Signior Fabian, stay you by this
　　　gentleman till my return.　　　　　　　　　　　*Exit.*

VIOLA　Pray you, sir, do you know of this matter?

250　FABIAN　I know the knight is incensed against you even to
　　　a mortal arbitrement,° but nothing of the circumstance　　*fight to the death*
　　　more.

VIOLA　I beseech you, what manner of man is he?

FABIAN　Nothing of that wonderful promise, to read° him　　*judge*

255　by his form° as you are like to find him in the proof of his　　*appearance*
　　　valor. He is indeed, sir, the most skillful, bloody, and
　　　fatal opposite that you could possibly have found in
　　　any part of Illyria. Will you° walk towards him, I will　　*If you will*
　　　make your peace with him if I can.

---

5. Unused in battle.　　　　　　　　　　7. Have or have not; that is, give it or take it,
6. "Carpet knights" won their titles not in　　or kill or be killed.
battle but in the carpeted ease of the court.　　8. Or give up your right to wear a sword.

260 VIOLA I shall be much bound to you for't. I am one
that had rather go with Sir Priest than Sir Knight, I
care not who knows so much of my mettle.° *Exeunt.*   temperament; courage

Enter SIR TOBY *and* SIR ANDREW.

SIR TOBY Why, man, he's a very devil. I have not seen such
a virago.[9] I had a pass[1] with him, rapier, scabbard, and
265 all, and he gives me the stuck-in[2] with such a mortal
motion that it is inevitable; and on the answer,° he pays   return hit
you as surely as your feet hits the ground they step on.
They say he has been fencer to the Sophy.°   Shah of Persia

SIR ANDREW Pox on't! I'll not meddle with him.

270 SIR TOBY Ay, but he will not now be pacified. Fabian can
scarce hold him yonder.

SIR ANDREW Plague on't! An° I thought he had been val-   If
iant and so cunning in fence, I'd have seen him damned
ere I'd have challenged him. Let him let the matter
275 slip, and I'll give him my horse, gray Capilet.

SIR TOBY I'll make the motion.° Stand here, make a good   offer
show on't. This shall end without the perdition of souls.°   loss of lives
[*aside*] Marry, I'll ride your horse as well as I ride
you.

Enter FABIAN *and* VIOLA.

280 [*aside to* FABIAN] I have his horse to take up° the quarrel.   settle
I have persuaded him the youth's a devil.

FABIAN [*aside to* SIR TOBY] He is as horribly conceited[3]
of him, and pants and looks pale as if a bear were at
his heels.

285 SIR TOBY [*to* VIOLA] There's no remedy, sir; he will fight
with you for's° oath' sake. Marry, he hath better bethought   for his
him of his quarrel, and he finds that now scarce to be
worth talking of. Therefore, draw for the supportance
of his vow.[4] He protests° he will not hurt you.   solemnly declares

290 VIOLA [*aside*] Pray God defend me. A little thing[5] would
make me tell them how much I lack of a man.

FABIAN [*to* SIR ANDREW] Give ground if you see him
furious.

SIR TOBY Come, Sir Andrew, there's no remedy. The gen-
295 tleman will, for his honor's sake, have one bout with
you. He cannot by the duello° avoid it. But he has prom-   code of dueling
ised me, as he is a gentleman and a soldier, he will not
hurt you. Come on, to't.

SIR ANDREW [*drawing his sword*] Pray God he keep his
300 oath.

VIOLA [*drawing his sword*] I do assure you, 'tis against
my will.

---

9. Female warrior (suggesting both ferocity and
feminine appearance).
1. Bout of fencing.
2. The stoccado, a thrust or stab (from the

Italian *stoccata*).
3. He has as horrifying a conception of him.
4. So that he may keep his oath.
5. Possibly a sexual innuendo.

Enter ANTONIO.

ANTONIO [*to* SIR ANDREW]   Put up your sword. If this
    young gentleman
  Have done offense, I take the fault on me.
305 If you offend him, I for him defy you.
SIR TOBY   You, sir? Why, what are you?
ANTONIO [*drawing his sword*]   One, sir, that for his love
    dares yet do more
  Than you have heard him brag to you he will.
SIR TOBY [*drawing his sword*]   Nay, if you be an under-
310 taker,⁶ I am for° you.   *I will fight*
    Enter OFFICERS.
FABIAN   O, good Sir Toby, hold. Here come the officers.
SIR TOBY [*to* ANTONIO]   I'll be with you anon.
VIOLA [*to* SIR ANDREW]   Pray, sir, put your sword up, if
    you please.
315 SIR ANDREW   Marry, will I, sir. And for that° I promised   *that which*
    you, I'll be as good as my word. He° will bear you easily,   *the horse*
    and reins well.   *(Capilet, line 275)*
    [SIR ANDREW *and* VIOLA *put up their swords.*]
FIRST OFFICER   This is the man. Do thy office.
SECOND OFFICER   Antonio, I arrest thee at the suit of
320 Count Orsino.
ANTONIO   You do mistake me, sir.
FIRST OFFICER   No, sir, no jot. I know your favor° well,   *face*
    Though now you have no sea-cap on your head.—
    Take him away. He knows I know him well.
325 ANTONIO   I must obey. [*to* VIOLA] This comes with seeking
    you.
  But there's no remedy. I shall answer° it.   *defend myself*
  What will you do, now my necessity
  Makes me to ask you for my purse? It grieves me
  Much more for what I cannot do for you
330 Than what befalls myself. You stand amazed,
  But be of comfort.
SECOND OFFICER   Come, sir, away.
ANTONIO [*to* VIOLA]   I must entreat of you some of that
    money.
VIOLA   What money, sir?
  For the fair kindness you have showed me here,
335 And part° being prompted by your present trouble,   *partly*
  Out of my lean and low ability
  I'll lend you something. My having is not much.
  I'll make division of my present° with you.   *i.e., what I now have*
  Hold, there's half my coffer.° [*offering him money*]   *funds*
340 ANTONIO   Will you deny me now?
  Is't possible that my deserts to you

_____
6. One who takes up a challenge.

Can lack persuasion?[7] Do not tempt my misery,
Lest that it make me so unsound° a man   *weak*
As to upbraid you with those kindnesses
That I have done for you.
345 VIOLA   I know of none,
Nor know I you by voice or any feature.
I hate ingratitude more in a man
Than lying, vainness, babbling drunkenness,
Or any taint of vice whose strong corruption
Inhabits our frail blood—
350 ANTONIO   O heavens themselves!
SECOND OFFICER   Come, sir, I pray you go.
ANTONIO   Let me speak a little. This youth that you see
here
I snatched one half out of the jaws of death,
Relieved him with such sanctity° of love,   *purity*
355 And to his image,[8] which methought did promise
Most venerable worth,[9] did I devotion.
FIRST OFFICER   What's that to us? The time goes by. Away!
ANTONIO   But O, how vile an idol proves this god!
Thou hast, Sebastian, done good feature shame.°   *shamed physical beauty*
360 In nature there's no blemish but the mind;
None can be called deformed but the unkind.
Virtue is beauty, but the beauteous evil
Are empty trunks o'er-flourished[1] by the devil.
FIRST OFFICER   The man grows mad. Away with him.—
Come, come, sir.
365 ANTONIO   Lead me on.   *Exit [with OFFICERS].*
VIOLA [*aside*]   Methinks his words do from such passion
fly
That he believes himself; so do not I.[2]
Prove true, imagination, O, prove true,
That I, dear brother, be now ta'en for you!
370 SIR TOBY   Come hither, knight; come hither, Fabian. We'll
whisper o'er a couplet or two of most sage saws.°   *sayings*
[SIR TOBY, FABIAN, *and* SIR ANDREW *move aside.*]
VIOLA   He named Sebastian. I my brother know
Yet living in my glass.° Even such and so   *mirror*
In favor° was my brother, and he went   *appearance*
375 Still° in this fashion, color, ornament,   *Always*
For him I imitate. O, if it prove,
Tempests are kind, and salt waves fresh in love!   *Exit.*
SIR TOBY   A very dishonest,° paltry boy, and more a coward   *disgraceful*
than a hare. His dishonesty appears in leaving his
380 friend here in necessity, and denying him; and for his
coward-ship, ask Fabian.

7. Is it possible that my former acts of kindness toward you cannot persuade you?
8. Outward appearance; also, a religious icon.
9. Which appeared to me worthy of veneration.

1. Chests (or bodies) elaborately decorated.
2. That is, I cannot quite dare to believe what
these words suggest to me.

FABIAN   A coward, a most devout coward, religious in it.

SIR ANDREW   'Slid,° I'll after him again and beat him.   *By God's eyelid*

SIR TOBY   Do, cuff him soundly, but never draw thy sword.   *(an oath)*

SIR ANDREW   An° I do not—   [*Exit.*]   *If*

385   FABIAN   Come, let's see the event.°   *outcome*

SIR TOBY   I dare lay any money 'twill be nothing yet.°   *after all*

                                                      Exeunt.

4.1

Enter SEBASTIAN *and* [FESTE, *the*] *clown.*

FESTE   Will you° make me believe that I am not sent for   *Are you attempting to*
   you?

SEBASTIAN   Go to, go to, thou art a foolish fellow.
   Let me be clear° of thee.   *free*

5   FESTE   Well held out,° i' faith. No, I do not know you, nor   *maintained*
   I am not sent to you by my lady to bid you come speak
   with her, nor your name is not Master Cesario, nor
   this is not my nose neither. Nothing that is so is so.

SEBASTIAN   I prithee, vent° thy folly somewhere else.   *air; utter*
10   Thou know'st not me.

FESTE   Vent my folly? He has heard that word of some
   great man and now applies it to a fool. Vent my folly?
   I am afraid this great lubber° the world will prove a cock-   *lout*
   ney.³ I prithee now, ungird thy strangeness⁴ and tell
15   me what I shall vent to my lady. Shall I vent to her
   that thou art coming?

SEBASTIAN   I prithee, foolish Greek,° depart from me.   *buffoon*
   There's money for thee. If you tarry longer,
   I shall give worse payment.

20   FESTE   By my troth, thou hast an open hand. These
   wise men that give fools money get themselves a good
   report—° after fourteen years' purchase.⁵   *reputation*

         Enter SIR ANDREW, SIR TOBY, *and* FABIAN

SIR ANDREW [*to* SEBASTIAN]   Now, sir, have I met you again?
   [*striking him*] There's for you.

25   SEBASTIAN [*returning the blow*]   Why, there's for thee,
   and there, and there.—Are all the people mad?

SIR TOBY   Hold, sir, or I'll throw your dagger o'er the house.

FESTE [*aside*]   This will I tell my lady straight.° I would   *immediately*
   not be in some of your coats for twopence.   [*Exit.*]

30   SIR TOBY [*seizing Sebastian*]   Come on, sir, hold!

SIR ANDREW   Nay, let him alone. I'll go another way to
   work with him. I'll have an action of battery° against   *charges of assault*
   him, if there be any law in Illyria. Though I struck him
   first, yet it's no matter for that.

35   SEBASTIAN [*to* SIR TOBY]   Let go thy hand!

4.1 Location: Somewhere near Olivia's house.
3. A pampered, foppish child.
4. Drop the pretense that you are a stranger.

5. That is, at too high a price (a piece of land
was usually valued at twelve times its annual
rent).

SIR TOBY Come, sir, I will not let you go. Come, my young
    soldier, put up your iron. You are well fleshed.° Come on.   *experienced in combat*
SEBASTIAN I will be free from thee.
    [*He pulls free and draws his sword.*]
                        What wouldst thou now?
    If thou dar'st tempt me further, draw thy sword.
40 SIR TOBY What, what? Nay, then, I must have an ounce
    or two of this malapert° blood from you.   *impudent*
        [*He draws his sword.*]
        Enter OLIVIA.
OLIVIA Hold, Toby! On thy life I charge thee, hold!
SIR TOBY Madam.
OLIVIA Will it be ever thus? Ungracious wretch,
45 Fit for the mountains and the barbarous caves,
    Where manners ne'er were preached! Out of my
    sight!—
    Be not offended, dear Cesario.—
    Rudesby,° be gone!   *Ruffian*
        [*Exeunt* SIR TOBY, SIR ANDREW, *and* FABIAN.]
                    I prithee, gentle friend,
    Let thy fair wisdom, not thy passion, sway
50 In this uncivil and unjust extent°   *attack*
    Against thy peace. Go with me to my house,
    And hear thou there how many fruitless pranks
    This ruffian hath botched up,° that thou thereby   *badly put together*
    Mayst smile at this. Thou shalt not choose but go.
55 Do not deny. Beshrew° his soul for me!   *Curse*
    He started one poor heart of mine, in thee.[6]
SEBASTIAN [*aside*] What relish° is in this? How runs the   *taste; meaning*
    stream?
    Or° I am mad, or else this is a dream.   *Either*
    Let fancy° still my sense in Lethe[7] steep;   *imagination*
60 If it be thus to dream, still° let me sleep!   *always*
OLIVIA Nay, come, I prithee. Would thou'dst be ruled
    by me!
SEBASTIAN Madam, I will.
OLIVIA   O, say so, and so be! *Exeunt.*

4.2

Enter MARIA *and* [FESTE, *the*] *clown.*

MARIA Nay, I prithee, put on this gown and this beard;
    make him believe thou art Sir Topas[8] the curate. Do it
    quickly. I'll call Sir Toby the whilst.°   [*Exit.*]   *in the meantime*

---

6. That is, he has frightened my heart, which
I have given to you. Because "start" (to force
from a hiding place) is also a hunting term,
there may be a pun on "heart" and "hart."
7. The river of forgetfulness in the classical
underworld.

4.2 Location: Olivia's house.
8. Perhaps an allusion to Chaucer's burlesque
knight of the "Rime of Sir Topas" in *The Canterbury Tales.* Also, the semiprecious stone
topaz was thought to cure a variety of ailments, including madness.

FESTE   Well, I'll put it on, and I will dissemble° myself in't,   *disguise*
5   and I would I were the first that ever dissembled° in such   *deceived*
a gown. [*He puts on gown and beard.*] I am not tall°   *stout*
enough to become the function well,[9] nor lean enough
to be thought a good student,° but to be said° an honest   *(of divinity) / known as*
man and a good housekeeper° goes as fairly as[1] to   *household manager*
10   say a careful man and a great scholar. The competi-
tors° enter.   *My partners*

      Enter SIR TOBY [*and* MARIA].

SIR TOBY   Jove bless thee, Master Parson.
FESTE   *Bonos dies*, Sir Toby; for, as the old hermit of
Prague,[2] that never saw pen and ink, very wittily said to
15   a niece of King Gorboduc,[3] "That that is, is," so I,
being Master Parson, am Master Parson; for what is
"that" but "that" and "is" but "is"?
SIR TOBY   To him, Sir Topas.
FESTE [*disguising his voice*]   What ho, I say! Peace in
20   this prison!
SIR TOBY   The knave counterfeits well. A good knave.
[MALVOLIO *within*]
MALVOLIO   Who calls there?
FESTE   Sir Topas the curate, who comes to visit Malvolio the lunatic.
25   MALVOLIO   Sir Topas, Sir Topas, good Sir Topas, go to
my lady—
FESTE   Out, hyperbolical° fiend![4] How vexest thou this   *ranting*
man! Talkest thou nothing but of ladies?
SIR TOBY [*aside*]   Well said, Master Parson.
30   MALVOLIO   Sir Topas, never was man thus wronged.
Good Sir Topas, do not think I am mad. They have laid
me here in hideous darkness—
FESTE   Fie, thou dishonest Satan! I call thee by the most
modest° terms, for I am one of those gentle ones that   *mildest*
35   will use the devil himself with courtesy. Sayst thou
that house° is dark?   *room*
MALVOLIO   As hell, Sir Topas.
FESTE   Why, it hath bay windows transparent as barri-
cadoes,[5] and the clerestories° toward the south-north   *windows in the upper wall*
40   are as lustrous as ebony;[6] and yet complainest thou of
obstruction?
MALVOLIO   I am not mad, Sir Topas. I say to you this
house is dark.

FESTE   Madman, thou errest. I say there is no darkness
45   but ignorance, in which thou art more puzzled than
the Egyptians in their fog.[7]
MALVOLIO   I say this house is as dark as ignorance,
though ignorance were as dark as hell. And I say there
was never man thus abused. I am no more mad than
50   you are. Make the trial of it in any constant question.°   *rational discourse*
FESTE   What is the opinion of Pythagoras[8] concerning
wildfowl?
MALVOLIO   That the soul of our grandam might haply°   *perhaps*
inhabit a bird.
55   FESTE   What thinkest thou of his opinion?
MALVOLIO   I think nobly of the soul, and no way approve
his opinion.
FESTE   Fare thee well. Remain thou still in darkness.
Thou shalt hold th' opinion of Pythagoras ere I will
60   allow of thy wits,° and fear to kill a woodcock[9] lest thou   *certify your sanity*
dispossess the soul of thy grandam. Fare thee well.
MALVOLIO   Sir Topas, Sir Topas!
SIR TOBY   My most exquisite Sir Topas!
FESTE   Nay, I am for all waters.[1]
65   MARIA   Thou mightst have done this without thy beard
and gown. He sees thee not.
SIR TOBY   To him in thine own voice, and bring me word
how thou findest him. I would we were well rid of this
knavery. If he may be conveniently delivered,° I would   *set free*
70   he were, for I am now so far in offense with my niece
that I cannot pursue with any safety this sport to the
upshot.° Come by and by to my chamber.   *conclusion*

[*Exeunt* SIR TOBY *and* MARIA.]

FESTE [*sings*][2]   "Hey, Robin, jolly Robin,
        Tell me how thy lady *does*."
75   MALVOLIO   Fool!
FESTE [*sings*]   "My lady is unkind, perdy."[3]
MALVOLIO   Fool!
FESTE   "Alas, why is she so?"
MALVOLIO   Fool, I say!
FESTE   "She loves another"—
80   Who calls, ha?
MALVOLIO   Good fool, as ever thou wilt deserve well at my
hand, help me to a candle, and pen, ink, and paper. As I
am a gentleman, I will live to be thankful to thee for't.
FESTE   Master Malvolio?

---

7. One of the biblical plagues was a "darkness
over the land of Egypt" (see Exodus 10.21–23).
8. Greek philosopher (6th c. B.C.E.), well-
known for his belief in the transmigration of
souls between living things.
9. A proverbially stupid bird.

1. I can sail any sea (i.e., I am able to handle
all situations).
2. Feste's sung lines are fragments of an old
song.
3. Certainly; indeed (from the French *par-
dieu*, "by God").

85 MALVOLIO Ay, good fool.

FESTE Alas, sir, how fell you besides° your five wits?[4] *out of*

MALVOLIO Fool, there was never man so notoriously° *outrageously*
abused. I am as well in my wits, fool, as thou art.

FESTE But° as well? Then you are mad indeed, if you be *Only*
90 no better in your wits than a fool.

MALVOLIO They have here propertied me,[5] keep me in
darkness, send ministers to me—asses!—and do all
they can to face me[6] out of my wits.

FESTE Advise you° what you say. The minister is here. *Be careful*
95 [*as Sir Topas*] Malvolio, Malvolio, thy wits the heavens
restore. Endeavor thyself to sleep and leave thy vain
bibble-babble.° *idle chatter*

MALVOLIO Sir Topas!

FESTE [*as Sir Topas*] Maintain no words with him, good
100 fellow. [*as fool*] Who, I, sir? Not I, sir. God buy you,° good *God be with you*
Sir Topas. [*as Sir Topas*] Marry, amen. [*as fool*] I will,
sir, I will.

MALVOLIO Fool! Fool! Fool, I say!

FESTE Alas, sir, be patient. What say you, sir? I am shent° *reproved*
105 for speaking to you.

MALVOLIO Good fool, help me to some light and some
paper. I tell thee, I am as well in my wits as any man
in Illyria.

FESTE Welladay° that you were, sir! *Alas*
110 MALVOLIO By this hand, I am. Good fool, some ink,
paper, and light; and convey what I will set down to my
lady. It shall advantage thee more than ever the bearing
of letter did.

FESTE I will help you to't. But tell me true, are you not
115 mad indeed, or do you but counterfeit?

MALVOLIO Believe me, I am not. I tell thee true.

FESTE Nay, I'll ne'er believe a madman till I see his brains.
I will fetch you light and paper and ink.

MALVOLIO Fool, I'll requite it in the highest degree. I
120 prithee, be gone.

FESTE [*sings*]   I am gone, sir,
And anon, sir,
I'll be with you again,
In a trice,
125 Like to the old Vice,[7]
Your need to sustain.
Who with dagger of lath,
In his rage and his wrath,
Cries "aha!" to the devil;
130 Like a mad lad,

---

4. The five wits are common sense, fantasy,
memory, judgment, and imagination.
5. Treated me like a piece of property.

6. Falsely portray me as.
7. A stock comic character in morality plays
and interludes.

"Pare thy nails, dad!
Adieu, goodman[8] devil."   *Exit.*

4.3

Enter SEBASTIAN.

SEBASTIAN   This is the air; that is the glorious sun.
This pearl she gave me, I do feel't and see't.
And though 'tis wonder that enwraps me thus,
Yet 'tis not madness. Where's Antonio, then?
5   I could not find him at the Elephant.
Yet there he was;° and there I found this credit,°   *he had been / report*
That he did range° the town to seek me out.   *wander*
His counsel now might do me golden service.
For though my soul disputes well with my sense[9]
10   That this may be some error, but no madness,
Yet doth this accident and flood of fortune
So far exceed all instance,° all discourse,°   *precedent / reason*
That I am ready to distrust mine eyes
And wrangle with my reason that persuades me
15   To any other trust° but that I am mad—   *conviction*
Or else the lady's mad. Yet if 'twere so,
She could not sway° her house, command her followers,   *rule*
Take and give back affairs and their dispatch[1]
With such a smooth, discreet, and stable bearing
20   As I perceive she does. There's something in't
That is deceivable.° But here the lady comes.   *deceptive*

Enter OLIVIA *and* PRIEST.

OLIVIA   Blame not this haste of mine. If you mean well,
Now go with me and with this holy man
Into the chantry by.° There, before him   *nearby private chapel*
25   And underneath that consecrated roof,
Plight me the full assurance of your faith,[2]
That my most jealous° and too doubtful soul   *anxious*
May live at peace. He shall conceal it
Whiles° you are willing it shall come to note,°   *Until / become public*
30   What° time we will our celebration keep   *At which*
According to my birth.° What do you say?   *social rank*
SEBASTIAN   I'll follow this good man and go with you
And, having sworn truth, ever will be true.
OLIVIA   Then lead the way, good father, and heavens so
shine
35   That they may fairly note° this act of mine.   *Exeunt.*   *look favorably on*

---

8. A vague title of dignity for one of low social
rank, thus an insult to Malvolio.
4.3 Location: Olivia's garden.
9. My reason agrees with my other senses.
1. That is, receive reports on household mat-

ters and issue orders for their management.
2. That is, enter into a betrothal (a binding
contract), to be followed with a marriage ceremony at a later date (lines 30–31).

5.1

Enter [FESTE, *the*] *clown and* FABIAN.

FABIAN   Now, as thou lovest me, let me see his letter.

FESTE   Good Master Fabian, grant me another request.

FABIAN   Anything.

FESTE   Do not desire to see this letter.

5 FABIAN   This is to give a dog and in recompense desire
my dog again.[3]

Enter ORSINO, VIOLA, CURIO, *and lords.*

ORSINO   Belong you to the Lady Olivia, friends?

FESTE   Ay, sir, we are some of her trappings.°   *ornaments; i.e., entourage*

ORSINO   I know thee well. How dost thou, my good fellow?

10 FESTE   Truly, sir, the better for my foes and the worse for
my friends.

ORSINO   Just the contrary: the better for thy friends.

FESTE   No, sir, the worse.

ORSINO   How can that be?

15 FESTE   Marry, sir, they praise me and make an ass of
me.[4] Now my foes tell me plainly I am an ass; so that
by my foes, sir, I profit in the knowledge of myself, and
by my friends I am abused.° So that, conclusions to be   *misled*
as kisses, if your four negatives make your two affirma-

20 tives,[5] why then the worse for my friends and the better
for my foes.

ORSINO   Why, this is excellent.

FESTE   By my troth, sir, no—though it please you to be
one of my friends.

25 ORSINO [*giving a coin*]   Thou shalt not be the worse for
me; there's gold.

FESTE   But° that it would be double-dealing,[6] sir, I would   *Except for the fact*
you could make it another.

ORSINO   O, you give me ill counsel.

30 FESTE   Put your grace in your pocket,[7] sir, for this
once, and let your flesh and blood obey it.

ORSINO   Well, I will be so much a sinner to° be a double-   *as to*
dealer. [*giving a coin*] There's another.

FESTE   *Primo, secundo, tertio*[8] is a good play,° and the old   *game*

35 saying is, the third pays for all.[9] The triplex,° sir, is a   *triple time in music*

5.1 Location: Near Olivia's house.

3. Perhaps a reference to a story about Elizabeth I, related in the diary of John Man-
ningham (ca. 1575–1622): the queen asked
for a dog from a man named Dr. Bullein;
granted a request in return, he asked for the
dog back.
4. That is, they flatter me into thinking better
of myself than I deserve, which makes me
look foolish.
5. That is, because a grammatical double

negative is a positive, a woman who says "no,
no, no, no" in response to a request for kisses
is really saying "yes, yes."
6. Duplicity (because he is asking for a double donation).
7. That is, pocket up your virtue; also, let
your grace (the proper address to a duke)
reach into your purse (to bring out an additional coin).
8. First, second, third (Latin).
9. The third time is the charm.

good tripping measure, or the bells of Saint Bennet,[1]
sir, may put you in mind—one, two, three.

ORSINO You can fool no more money out of me at this
throw.° If you will let your lady know I am here to speak   (of the dice)
40 with her, and bring her along with you, it may awake
my bounty° further.   generosity

FESTE Marry, sir, lullaby to your bounty till I come
again. I go, sir, but I would not have you to think
that my desire of having is the sin of covetousness.
45 But, as you say, sir, let your bounty take a nap. I will
awake it anon.   *Exit.*

        Enter ANTONIO *and* OFFICERS.

VIOLA Here comes the man, sir, that did rescue me.

ORSINO That face of his I do remember well.
Yet when I saw it last, it was besmeared
50 As black as Vulcan[2] in the smoke of war.
A baubling° vessel was he captain of,   paltry
For shallow draft and bulk unprizable,[3]
With which such scatheful° grapple did he make   destructive
With the most noble bottom° of our fleet   ship
55 That very envy and the tongue of loss[4]
Cried fame and honor on him.—What's the matter?

FIRST OFFICER Orsino, this is that Antonio
That took the *Phoenix* and her freight from Candy,°   Candia, capital of Crete
And this is he that did the *Tiger* board
60 When your young nephew Titus lost his leg.
Here in the streets, desperate of shame and state,[5]
In private brabble° did we apprehend him.   brawl

VIOLA He did me kindness, sir, drew on my side,[6]
But in conclusion put strange speech upon° me.   spoke strangely to
65 I know not what 'twas but distraction.°   except madness

ORSINO Notable° pirate, thou salt-water thief,   Notorious
What foolish boldness brought thee to their mercies
Whom thou, in terms so bloody and so dear,°   costly
Hast made thine enemies?

ANTONIO   Orsino, noble sir,
70 Be pleased that I shake off these names you give me.
Antonio never yet was thief or pirate,
Though, I confess, on base° and ground enough,   foundation
Orsino's enemy. A witchcraft drew me hither.
That most ingrateful boy there by your side
75 From the rude sea's enraged and foamy mouth
Did I redeem; a wrack° past hope he was.   castaway

---

1. Perhaps the church of St. Bennet Hithe,
located across the Thames from the Globe
theater.
2. Roman god of fire and metalworking.
3. That is, of no value as a prize because of its
shallow draft (the depth of water required to

float it) and small size.
4. The voices of the losers. *Very envy*: even the
envious, his enemies.
5. That is, without regard for his honor or
safety (as a wanted man).
6. Drew his sword on my behalf.

His life I gave him and did thereto add
My love, without retention° or restraint,   reservation
All his in dedication.° For his sake   dedicated to him
80   Did I expose myself, pure° for his love,   purely
Into the danger of this adverse° town;   hostile
Drew to defend him when he was beset;
Where, being apprehended, his false cunning—
Not meaning to partake with me in danger—
85   Taught him to face me out of his acquaintance[7]
And grew a twenty years' removèd thing
While one would wink;[8] denied me mine own purse,
Which I had recommended° to his use   committed
Not half an hour before.

90 VIOLA   How can this be?

ORSINO [to Antonio]   When came he to this town?

ANTONIO   Today, my lord; and for three months before,
No int'rim, not a minute's vacancy,°   interval
Both day and night did we keep company.

       Enter OLIVIA *and attendants.*

95 ORSINO   Here comes the Countess. Now heaven walks on
     earth!—
But for thee, fellow: fellow, thy words are madness.
Three months this youth hath tended upon me—
But more of that anon. [*to an* OFFICER] Take him aside.

OLIVIA   What would my lord, but that[9] he may not have,
100   Wherein Olivia may seem serviceable?°—   be of service
Cesario, you do not keep promise with me.

VIOLA   Madam?

ORSINO   Gracious Olivia—

OLIVIA   What do you say, Cesario?—Good my lord—

105 VIOLA   My lord would speak; my duty hushes me.

OLIVIA   If it be aught° to the old tune, my lord,   anything
It is as fat and fulsome° to mine ear   gross and repugnant
As howling after music.

ORSINO   Still so cruel?

110 OLIVIA   Still so constant, lord.

ORSINO   What, to perverseness? You, uncivil lady,
To whose ingrate and unauspicious[1] altars
My soul the faithful'st off'rings hath breathed out
That e'er devotion tendered—what shall I do?

115 OLIVIA   Even what it please my lord that shall become°   befit
     him.

ORSINO   Why should I not, had I the heart to do it,
Like to th' Egyptian thief at point of death,
Kill what I love?[2]—a savage jealousy

---

7. To shamelessly deny knowing me.
8. In the time it takes to blink.
9. Except that (my love) which.
1. Ungrateful and unfavorable.
2. In Heliodorus's prose romance *Ethiopica*

(3rd c. C.E.; translated from Greek into English in 1569), an Egyptian robber named Thyamis tries to kill Chariclea (his captive, with whom he has fallen in love) when they are attacked by a larger band of robbers.

That sometime savors nobly.° But hear me this: *has nobility in it*
120 Since you to non-regardance° cast my faith,   *neglect*
And that I partly know the instrument
That screws° me from my true place in your favor,   *forces*
Live you the marble-breasted tyrant still.
But this your minion,° whom I know you love,   *favorite*
125 And whom, by heaven I swear, I tender° dearly,   *regard*
Him will I tear out of that cruel eye
Where he sits crownèd in his master's spite—[3]
Come, boy, with me. My thoughts are ripe in mischief.
I'll sacrifice the lamb that I do love
130 To spite a raven's heart within a dove.
VIOLA And I, most jocund,° apt,° and willingly,   *happily / readily*
To do you rest a thousand deaths would die.
OLIVIA Where goes Cesario?
VIOLA   After him I love
More than I love these eyes, more than my life,
135 More by all mores° than e'er I shall love wife.   *(such) comparisons*
If I do feign, you witnesses above,
Punish my life for tainting of my love.
OLIVIA Ay me, detested!° How am I beguiled!   *rejected*
VIOLA Who does beguile you? Who does do you wrong?
140 OLIVIA Hast thou forgot thyself? Is it so long?
Call forth the holy father.   *[Exit an attendant.]*
ORSINO *[to* VIOLA*]*   Come, away!
OLIVIA Whither, my lord?—Cesario, husband, stay.
ORSINO Husband?
OLIVIA   Ay, husband. Can he that deny?
ORSINO Her husband, sirrah?[4]
VIOLA   No, my lord, not I.
145 OLIVIA Alas, it is the baseness of thy fear
That makes thee strangle thy propriety.[5]
Fear not, Cesario. Take thy fortunes up.
Be that° thou know'st thou art, and then thou art   *that which*
As great as that° thou fear'st.   *he whom (i.e., Orsino)*

Enter PRIEST.

                O, welcome, father.
150 Father, I charge thee by thy reverence
Here to unfold—though lately we intended
To keep in darkness what occasion° now   *necessity*
Reveals before 'tis ripe—what thou dost know
Hath newly° passed between this youth and me.   *recently*
155 PRIEST A contract of eternal bond of love,
Confirmed by mutual joinder° of your hands,   *joining*
Attested by the holy close° of lips,   *meeting*
Strengthened by interchangement of your rings,

---

3. Notwithstanding the opposition of his master.
4. Customary form of address to a male social inferior.
5. That is, kill your own identity (as my husband).

And all the ceremony of this compact
160 Sealed in my function,[6] by my testimony;
Since when, my watch hath told me, toward my grave
I have traveled but two hours.

ORSINO [*to* VIOLA]   O thou dissembling cub! What wilt
thou be
When time hath sowed a grizzle on thy case?[7]
165 Or will not else thy craft° so quickly grow   cunning
That thine own trip shall be thine overthrow?[8]
Farewell, and take her, but direct thy feet
Where thou and I henceforth may never meet.

VIOLA   My lord, I do protest—

OLIVIA   O, do not swear.
170 Hold little° faith, though thou hast too much fear.   Keep a little

Enter SIR ANDREW

SIR ANDREW   For the love of God, a surgeon! Send one
presently° to Sir Toby.   immediately

OLIVIA   What's the matter?

SIR ANDREW   He's broke° my head across, and has given   cut
175 Sir Toby a bloody coxcomb[9] too. For the love of God,
your help! I had rather than forty pound I were at home.

OLIVIA   Who has done this, Sir Andrew?

SIR ANDREW   The Count's gentleman, one Cesario. We took
him for a coward, but he's the very devil incardinate.°   (incarnate)
180 ORSINO   My gentleman Cesario?

SIR ANDREW   'Od's lifelings,[1] here he is!—You broke my
head for nothing, and that that I did, I was set on to
do't by Sir Toby.

VIOLA   Why do you speak to me? I never hurt you.
185 You drew your sword upon me without cause,
But I bespake you fair[2] and hurt you not.

SIR ANDREW   If a bloody coxcomb be a hurt, you have
hurt me. I think you set nothing by° a bloody coxcomb.   think nothing of

Enter SIR TOBY *and* [FESTE, *the*] *clown.*

Here comes Sir Toby halting.° You shall hear more. But   limping
190 if° he had not been in drink, he would have tickled°   if only / chastised
you othergates° than he did.   otherwise

ORSINO   How now, gentleman? How is't with you?

SIR TOBY   That's all one.° He's hurt me, and there's th'   irrelevant
end on't. [*to* FESTE] Sot,° didst see Dick Surgeon,   Fool; drunkard
195 sot?

FESTE   O, he's drunk, Sir Toby, an hour agone. His eyes
were set° at eight i 'th' morning.   closed

---

6. That is, ratified by my priestly authority.
7. Gray hairs on your hide.
8. That your attempt to take down another shall be your own downfall ("trip" is a wrestling term).
9. Head; also, a fool's hat, which resembles the crest of a cock.
1. By God's little lives (an oath).
2. I spoke to you with all courtesy.

SIR TOBY   Then he's a rogue and a passy-measures pavan.[3]
 I hate a drunken rogue.

200 OLIVIA   Away with him! Who hath made this havoc with
 them?

SIR ANDREW   I'll help you, Sir Toby, because we'll be
 dressed[4] together.

SIR TOBY   Will *you* help?—an ass-head, and a coxcomb,°   *fool*
205 and a knave, a thin-faced knave, a gull?°   *dupe*

OLIVIA   Get him to bed, and let his hurt be looked to.

   [*Exeunt* SIR TOBY, SIR ANDREW, FESTE, *and* FABIAN.]

   Enter SEBASTIAN.

SEBASTIAN   I am sorry, madam, I have hurt your kinsman,
 But, had it been the brother of my blood,
 I must have done no less with wit and safety.[5]
210 You throw a strange regard upon me,[6] and by that
 I do perceive it hath offended you.
 Pardon me, sweet one, even for the vows
 We made each other but so late ago.

ORSINO   One face, one voice, one habit, and two persons!
215 A natural perspective,[7] that is and is not!°   *(an illusion)*

SEBASTIAN   Antonio, O, my dear Antonio!
 How have the hours racked and tortured me
 Since I have lost thee!

ANTONIO   Sebastian are you?

220 SEBASTIAN   Fear'st thou that,° Antonio?   *Do you doubt that*

ANTONIO   How have you made division of yourself?
 An apple cleft in two is not more twin
 Than these two creatures. Which is Sebastian?

OLIVIA   Most wonderful!°   *amazing*

225 SEBASTIAN [*looking at* VIOLA]   Do I stand there? I never
 had a brother,
 Nor can there be that deity° in my nature   *divine power*
 Of here and everywhere.° I had a sister,   *omnipresence*
 Whom the blind° waves and surges have devoured.   *indiscriminate*
 Of charity,° what kin are you to me?   *Kindly (tell me)*
230 What countryman? What name? What parentage?

VIOLA   Of Messaline. Sebastian was my father.
 Such a Sebastian was my brother, too.
 So went he suited° to his watery tomb.   *dressed; in appearance*
 If spirits can assume both form and suit,
 You come to fright us.

235 SEBASTIAN   A spirit I am indeed,
 But am in that dimension grossly clad

---

3. A slow, stately dance of Italian origin (*pas-samezzo pavana* [Italian]). Sir Toby may think that its swaying movements resemble the unsteadiness of a drunk.
4. We'll have our wounds tended to.

5. With reasonable prudence for my own safety.
6. That is, you look at me as if I were a stranger.
7. An optical illusion produced by nature (and not by a mirror).

Which from the womb I did participate.[8]
Were you a woman, as the rest goes even,[9]
I should my tears let fall upon your cheek
240 And say "Thrice welcome, drownèd Viola."
VIOLA   My father had a mole upon his brow.
SEBASTIAN   And so had mine.
VIOLA   And died that day when Viola from her birth
Had numbered thirteen years.
245 SEBASTIAN   O, that record is lively[1] in my soul!
He finishèd indeed his mortal act
That day that made my sister thirteen years.
VIOLA   If nothing lets° to make us happy both   *prevents*
But this my masculine usurped attire,
250 Do not embrace me till each circumstance
Of place, time, fortune, do cohere and jump°   *agree*
That I am Viola; which to confirm,
I'll bring you to a captain in this town,
Where lie my maiden weeds;° by whose gentle help   *clothes*
255 I was preserved to serve this noble count.
All the occurrence of my fortune[2] since
Hath been between° this lady and this lord.   *as messenger between*
SEBASTIAN [*to* OLIVIA]   So comes it, lady, you have been
     mistook.
But nature to her bias drew in that.[3]
260 You would have been contracted° to a maid.   *betrothed*
Nor are you therein, by my life, deceived:
You are betrothed both to a maid and man.[4]
ORSINO [*to* OLIVIA]   Be not amazed; right noble is his
     blood.
If this be so, as yet the glass seems true,[5]
265 I shall have share in this most happy wrack.°—   *fortunate shipwreck*
Boy, thou hast said to me a thousand times
Thou never shouldst love woman like to me.°   *as much as (you love) me*
VIOLA   And all those sayings will I overswear°   *swear again*
And all those swearings keep as true in soul
270 As doth that orbèd continent the fire[6]
That severs day from night.
ORSINO   Give me thy hand,
And let me see thee in thy woman's weeds.
VIOLA   The captain that did bring me first on shore
Hath my maid's garments. He, upon some action,°   *legal charge*
275 Is now in durance° at Malvolio's suit,   *prison*
A gentleman and follower of my lady's.

---

8. That is, I am a spirit, yes, but one, like all humans, dressed in flesh from the time I was in the womb.
9. As everything else indicates.
1. The memory of that is vivid.
2. That is, all that has happened to me.
3. That is, but nature caused you to swerve to

me in that matter. (The image is from the game of bowls, played with a weighted ball that curves from a straight path.)
4. That is, a man who is a virgin.
5. That is, the "natural perspective" (of line 215) continues to seem real.
6. That is, as the sun's sphere contains the fire.

OLIVIA   He shall enlarge° him. Fetch Malvolio hither.   *release*
And yet, alas, now I remember me,
They say, poor gentleman, he's much distract.

Enter [FESTE, the] clown with a letter, and FABIAN.

280 A most extracting frenzy° of mine own   *distracting madness*
From my remembrance clearly banished his.°   *his madness*
How does he, sirrah?

FESTE   Truly, madam, he holds Beelzebub at the stave's
end[7] as well as a man in his case may do. He's here writ
285 a letter to you. I should have given't you today morning. But as a madman's epistles are no gospels,[8] so it
skills° not much when they are delivered.   *matters*

OLIVIA   Open't and read it.

FESTE   Look then to be well edified, when the fool deliv-
290 ers° the madman. [*He reads.*] "By the Lord, madam"—   *speaks the words of*

OLIVIA   How now, art thou mad?

FESTE   No, madam, I do but read madness. An° your lady-   *If*
ship will have it as it ought to be, you must allow *vox.*[9]

OLIVIA   Prithee, read i' thy right wits.

295 FESTE   So I do, madonna. But to read his right wits[1] is
to read thus. Therefore, perpend,° my princess, and   *pay attention*
give ear.

OLIVIA   [*giving letter to Fabian*]   Read it you, sirrah.

FABIAN   "By the Lord, madam, you wrong me, and the
300 world shall know it. Though you have put me into
darkness and given your drunken cousin rule over me,
yet have I the benefit of my senses as well as your
Ladyship. I have your own letter that induced me to
the semblance I put on, with the which I doubt not but
305 to do myself much right or you much shame. Think of
me as you please. I leave my duty[2] a little unthought of
and speak out of my injury.

The madly-used Malvolio."

OLIVIA   Did he write this?

310 FESTE   Ay, madam.

ORSINO   This savors not much of distraction.°   *madness*

OLIVIA   See him delivered,° Fabian. Bring him hither.   *released*

[*Exit FABIAN.*]

My lord, so please you, these things further thought on,
To think me as well a sister as a wife,[3]
315 One day shall crown th' alliance on't,[4] so please you,
Here at my house, and at my proper cost.°   *own expense*

ORSINO   Madam, I am most apt° t' embrace your offer.   *ready*

---

7. Keeps the devil at a distance (proverbial).
8. The letters of a madman are not to be taken as gospel truths.
9. The voice (Latin); Feste is using a voice he thinks appropriate for a madman.
1. To read his state of mind correctly.

2. The duty I owe you (as your servant).
3. That is, think of me as favorably as your sister-in-law as you would have had I been your wife.
4. That is, be the occasion of the two marriages that will cement this new relationship.

[*to* VIOLA] Your master quits° you; and for your service   *releases*
   done him,
320 So much against the mettle° of your sex,   *temperament*
   So far beneath your soft and tender breeding,
   And since you called me "master" for so long,
   Here is my hand. You shall from this time be
   Your master's mistress.
OLIVIA [*to* VIOLA]
                A sister! You are she.

Enter MALVOLIO [*and* FABIAN.]

ORSINO   Is this the madman?
OLIVIA   Ay, my lord, this same.—
   How now, Malvolio?
325 MALVOLIO   Madam, you have done me wrong,
   Notorious wrong.
OLIVIA   Have I, Malvolio? No.
MALVOLIA [*handing her a paper*]   Lady, you have. Pray
   you peruse that letter.
   You must not now deny it is your hand.°   *handwriting*
   Write from° it if you can, in hand or phrase,   *differently from*
330 Or say 'tis not your seal, not your invention.°   *composition*
   You can say none of this. Well, grant it then,
   And tell me, in the modesty of honor,⁵
   Why you have given me such clear lights° of favor?   *signs*
   Bade me come smiling and cross-gartered to you,
335 To put on yellow stockings, and to frown
   Upon Sir Toby and the lighter° people?   *lesser*
   And, acting° this in an obedient hope,   *after doing*
   Why have you suffered° me to be imprisoned,   *allowed*
   Kept in a dark house, visited by the priest,
340 And made the most notorious geck° and gull   *fool*
   That e'er invention° played on? Tell me why.   *trickery*
OLIVIA   Alas, Malvolio, this is not my writing,
   Though I confess much like the character.°   *(my) handwriting*
   But out of question, 'tis Maria's hand.
345 And now I do bethink me, it was she
   First told me thou wast mad; then cam'st° in smiling,   *you came*
   And in such forms which here were presupposed°   *previously suggested*
   Upon thee in the letter. Prithee, be content.
   This practice° hath most shrewdly passed° upon thee.   *trick / cleverly played*
350 But when we know the grounds and authors of it,
   Thou shalt be both the plaintiff and the judge
   Of thine own cause.
FABIAN   Good madam, hear me speak,
   And let no quarrel nor no brawl to come
   Taint the condition of this present hour,
355 Which I have wondered at. In hope it shall not,

---

5. As an honorable person would.

Most freely I confess myself and Toby
Set this device against Malvolio here,
Upon some stubborn and uncourteous parts
We had conceived against him.[6] Maria writ
360 The letter, at Sir Toby's great importance,°   *importuning*
In recompense whereof he hath married her.
How with a sportful malice it was followed°   *carried through*
May rather pluck on° laughter than revenge,   *encourage*
If that the injuries be justly weighed
365 That have on both sides passed.
OLIVIA [*to* MALVOLIO]   Alas, poor fool, how have they
        baffled° thee!   *disgraced*
FESTE   Why, "Some are born great, some achieve great-
        ness, and some have greatness thrown upon them." I
        was one, sir, in this interlude,° one Sir Topas, sir, but   *comedy*
370   that's all one. "By the Lord, fool, I am not mad"—
        but, do you remember "Madam, why laugh you at
        such a barren rascal; an° you smile not, he's gagged"?   *if*
        And thus the whirligig° of time brings in his revenges.   *spinning top*
MALVOLIO   I'll be revenged on the whole pack of you!
                                                  [*Exit.*]

375 OLIVIA   He hath been most notoriously abused.
ORSINO   Pursue him and entreat him to a peace.
                                        [*Exit one or more.*]

He hath not told us of the captain yet.
When that is known, and golden time convents,°   *suits*
A solemn combination shall be made
380 Of our dear souls. Meantime, sweet sister,
We will not part from hence.° Cesario, come—   *here (Olivia's house)*
For so you shall be while you are a man.
But when in other habits° you are seen,   *attire*
Orsino's mistress, and his fancy's° queen.   *imagination's; love's*
                            Exeunt [*all but* FESTE].

385 FESTE *sings*   When that I was and a little tiny boy,
                        With hey, ho, the wind and the rain,
                    A foolish thing was but a toy,
                        For the rain it raineth every day.

                    But when I came to man's estate,
390   With hey, ho, the wind and the rain,
                    'Gainst knaves and thieves men shut their gate,
                        For the rain it raineth every day.

                    But when I came, alas, to wive,
                        With hey, ho, the wind and the rain,

---

6. That is, because of some rude and uncivil qualities that we discerned in him and held against him.

395   By swaggering° could I never thrive,   *blustering; bullying*
         For the rain it raineth every day.

         But when I came unto my beds,
           With hey, ho, the wind and the rain,
         With tosspots° still had drunken heads,   *drunkards*
400   For the rain it raineth every day.

         A great while ago the world begun,
           With hey, ho, the wind and the rain,
         But that's all one, our play is done,
           And we'll strive to please you every day.

                                                                 Exit.

BEN JONSON

1572–1637

B EN Jonson, one of the foremost playwrights of the Elizabethan and Jacobean stage, cuts a larger-than-life figure in
the history of English drama. Stepson to
a bricklayer, he killed a fellow actor in a
duel at the age of twenty-six and escaped
hanging only by reading a passage from
the Latin Bible to invoke "benefit of the
clergy"—that is, exemption from the jurisdiction of the secular courts. He was twice
imprisoned for his part in collaborative
works that were deemed seditious or unac-
ceptably satirical and was initially suspected of involvement in the infamous
Gunpowder Plot of 1605, a failed attempt
by a group of English Catholics to kill the
Protestant king James I by blowing up the
Houses of Parliament. His literary career,
which included poetry, epigrams, and
literary criticism as well as plays, court
masques, and other entertainments, was
equally distinctive. A neoclassicist who
scourged his contemporaries for turning
their backs on dramatic harmony, unity,
and restraint, he himself wrote plays incorporating elaborate action and vigorous
idiom, rich in comic incident and dense
with the particularities of urban life. By
the time he was awarded a pension by King
James in 1616, he had established himself
as the court's unofficial poet laureate, and
when he published a number of his earlier
plays as part of *The Works of Benjamin*
Jonson that same year he drew on an
expanding print culture to monumentalize
his achievement as a writer. Jonson's relationship to the theater was at times ambivalent—he referred to it in a prefatory ode
to one of his late plays as "the loathèd
stage"—and his reputation has suffered
over the centuries from the inevitable
comparisons to his contemporary WILLIAM
SHAKESPEARE. Such comparisons, though,
often fail to take into account the very different principles that underlie Shakespearean and Jonsonian comedy and their
divergent dramatic aims. Brilliant in their
theatricality, wit, and biting satire, *VOL-*
PONE and Jonson's other major comedies
are among the finest written in the English
language.

Ben Jonson was born in or near London
in 1572. His father, a minister, died a
month before his birth, and within a few
years his mother remarried a bricklayer living in Westminster. After attending a
nearby private school, the young Jonson
was admitted as a day student to Westminster School, where his teacher was the
great antiquarian and classicist William
Camden. At Westminster Jonson studied
Latin and Greek, imitated the writing style
of such Roman authors as Cicero, Horace,
and the playwright Terence, and developed a respect for classical literary principles that would guide him throughout his

career. He was also introduced to dramatic performance through the school's annual presentations of Latin plays. It is not known how long Jonson attended Westminster; at some point he was taken from school and put to work in his stepfather's trade. Although his time at school was brief and he never received a university education, Jonson continued his studies on his own and acquired, over his lifetime, a prodigious knowledge of classical and contemporary writers.

After brief service as a soldier in the Netherlands—where, he later boasted, he killed an enemy soldier in single combat—Jonson married in 1594 and fathered two children, a son and daughter whose early deaths occasioned two of his best-loved poems. The evidence concerning his early career in the theater is incomplete. By the mid-1590s Jonson was working as an actor and is reported to have acted the role of Hieronimo in a touring production of THOMAS KYD's The Spanish Tragedy. He also wrote and collaborated on a number of plays, most of which have not survived; these early plays include The Isle of Dogs, a satirical collaboration with Thomas Nashe that earned the playwright his first imprisonment. Jonson wrote for a number of acting companies, including the Lord Admiral's Men under Philip Henslowe's management at the Swan Theater; the Lord Chamberlain's Men (subsequently the King's Men), for which Shakespeare worked as actor and playwright; and the company of boy actors known originally as the Children of the Chapel. Jonson's first popular success, Every Man in His Humor (1598), was performed at the Globe theater by the Lord Chamberlain's Men with Shakespeare as one of the actors. Loosely drawing on plot motifs from Roman comedy, Every Man in His Humor was the first of Jonson's surviving plays to employ the humoral model of characterization. In classical and Renaissance medical theory, the "humors" referred to four bodily fluids that were associated with specific physiological and psychological states. Imbalances between these fluids were believed to cause distortions of the personality. The comic possibilities of this theory are evident in Every Man in His Humor's gallery of fools, all of whom are single-mindedly driven by their preoccupations and delusions.

Jonson continued to exploit humoral characterization and comic satire in Every Man Out of His Humor (1599), Cynthia's Revels (1600), and Poetaster (1601). The last of these plays formed part of the so-called Poets' War (or War of the Theaters), a series of public literary attacks between Jonson and the playwrights John Marston and THOMAS DEKKER. In 1603 Jonson turned to tragedy with Sejanus, an austere play about the Roman emperor Tiberius and his favorite, the prefect Sejanus, who unsuccessfully tried to seize imperial power. Like his later Roman tragedy Catiline (1611), Sejanus was a failure with its audience, in part because of the classical formality of its dialogue and its relative lack of dramatic action. It was not the first time that Jonson found himself at odds with theatergoers who failed to meet the high standards he set for them, and it would not be the last. With the accession of James I to the English throne in 1603, however, he discovered another, more appreciative theatrical venue. Jonson wrote masques—formal, occasional entertainments that combined dialogue, music, dance, and elaborate spectacle within a tightly allegorical plot line—to commemorate the arrival and coronation of the new king, and these were so successful that he was commissioned to write others for the court during James's reign and that of his son Charles I. The Masque of Blackness was performed on Twelfth Night in 1605, and Jonson went on to write more than twenty additional masques for this annual holiday and other special occasions.

In Volpone (1606) Jonson demonstrated his developing mastery of comic form. Abandoning the loose dramatic structure of the earlier humors comedies, the play follows a tightly woven intrigue plot driven by the predatory appetites and improvisational maneuvering of its central characters. Jonson followed the success of Volpone with three other comedies that cemented his reputation as one of the foremost writers in this genre: Epicoene, or The Silent Woman (1609–10), The Alchemist (1610), and Bartholomew Fair (1614). These plays display the mixture of classical and native dramatic elements that characterize Jonson's drama, and with their often caustic wit they satirize both the manners and behaviors of London society (the city's Puritans were held up to particular ridicule) and what Jonson considered to be the moral and aesthetic laxness of the contemporary theater. When Jonson included many of his earlier plays in his collected *Works* of 1616 he signaled that his drama, by contrast, fell within a classical literary tradition and was to be evaluated by its standards. It was the first time that a dramatist had included stage plays under the title "works," and Jonson was lampooned by contemporaries for presuming to do so.

After writing *The Devil Is an Ass* (1616) Jonson began a ten-year absence from the theater, devoting his playwriting attention during this time to court masques. He also embarked on a journey by foot to Scotland, where his conversations with the Scottish poet William Drummond were recounted for later publication. Jonson returned to the stage with *The Staple of News* (1626), but this and the other plays of his later years—*The New Inn* (1629), *The Magnetic Lady* (1632), and *A Tale of a Tub* (1633)—were not well received by London audiences. With the accession of Charles I in 1625, Jonson also

found himself out of favor at court. Although he continued to preside at the Apollo Room in London's Devil and St. Dunstan Tavern over a circle of literary admirers who called themselves the "Tribe of Ben," Jonson's final years were not easy ones. Partially paralyzed by a stroke in 1628, he was largely confined to his home, and his finances became so strained that he was forced to ask for money from those who had served as patrons. Ben Jonson died in 1637 and was buried in Westminster Abbey. The inscription on his flagstone marker is simple but eloquent: "O rare Ben Jonson."

Written, as Jonson boasted, in five weeks, *Volpone; or, The Fox* was performed by the King's Men at the Globe theater in early 1606. The play was taken on tour to Oxford and Cambridge, where it was performed in either 1606 or 1607. *Volpone* was published in quarto in 1607 and in the folio *Works* of 1616. To the printed versions of the play Jonson appended a prose epistle "To the Most Noble and Most Equal Sisters, The Two Famous Universities" where *Volpone* had been performed. This, and the play's prologue, argue for the moral responsibilities of dramatic literature and its writers. The epistle declares "the impossibility of any

"The Fox," from Edward Topsell's *Historie of Foure-footed Beastes* (1607).

man's being a good Poet, without first being a good man," while the prologue insists on the classical ideal, proposed by the Roman poet Horace, that art should both teach and instruct: "To mix profit with your pleasure."

The plot of *Volpone* draws on a favorite subject of Roman satirists: legacy hunters who give away their money and possessions in hopes that they will be designated heirs of the wealthy. The play is set in Venice, a city associated by Jonson's contemporaries with material prosperity, cosmopolitanism, political intrigue, decadence, and corruption. The Venetian nobleman Volpone and his parasite (or flatterer) Mosca embody their city's zest for commercial exploitation by attracting the greedy and manipulating their hopes as a way of acquiring ever-increasing riches. In keeping with its central theme of characters preying on each other, the play makes use of the beast fable, made familiar by Aesop's *Fables* and other classical and medieval sources. Volpone's name means "fox" in Italian, and in his cleverness and rapaciousness he resembles Reynard the Fox, a popular trickster character from the Middle Ages. In the play's

network of animal identifications, Mosca is the fly, Voltore the vulture, Corbaccio the raven, and Corvino the crow. Sir Politic Would-be (Sir Pol) and his wife are parrots, and Peregrine is the falcon that pursues them. Jonson's bestiary does not end there, for the play's dialogue teems with animal references: ox, ass, camel, mule, goat, cock, sheep, earwig caterpillar, dog, wildcat, moth, worm, porpoise, sturgeon, lion, spider, bee, whale, chameleon, phoenix, ape, crocodile. These references reflect an inverted world where characters surrender their humanity to debasing appetites and desires and become the moral equivalent of beasts.

A different kind of inversion is evident in the play's opening scene, in which Volpone celebrates his accumulated gold: "Hail the world's soul, and mine!" Through a series of redefinitions, he substitutes material values for spiritual ones and establishes a flattened moral landscape in which the Golden Age is reduced to the precious metal for which it is named. Unmarried and childless, Volpone presides over a household that includes a dwarf, a eunuch, and a hermaphrodite, and his

A 2012 production of *Volpone* staged by the Hans Otto Theater, Potsdam, Germany, featuring (from left to right) Holger Bülow as Mosca, Wolfgang Vogler as Volpone, Franziska Melzer as Celia, and René Schwittay as Corvino.

considerable energies are sterile rather than productive. Even his wealth provides little sustenance; as he confesses to Mosca, "I glory / More in the cunning purchase of my wealth / Than in the glad possession." The fantasies of sexual fulfillment that he expresses during his attempted seduction of Celia involve endless role-playing as he urges that the two of them "in changèd shapes, act Ovid's tales." His inventory of pleasures is revealing, for in this drama of public and private performances—in which references to the popular theater of commedia dell'arte abound—Volpone is a consummate actor. Whether impersonating a dying man, the mountebank (or medical huckster) Scoto of Mantua, or an officer of the court in the play's final act, he finds his greatest fulfillment when pretending to be someone else.

Mosca, too, is an actor, improvising roles, identities, and strategies with the ease of a chameleon; as he boasts in a soliloquy, "I could skip / Out of my skin now like a subtle snake, / I am so limber." Like Volpone, he is also a dramatist, scripting the play's characters within a master plot of his own. Not surprisingly, given the limberness with which he shifts identities, it is Mosca who most fully understands the desires and motivations of others. As he brings the fortune seekers to Volpone's bed, he manipulates their hopes with powerful visions of wealth and fulfillment. The phrase "only you" reverberates throughout Mosca's promises to each of the suitors, and he succeeds in keeping them divided from each other by flattering their inveterate self-centeredness. When Volpone expresses surprise at how easily the suitors have been fooled by Mosca's plots and insinuations, how fully and eagerly they participate in their own gulling—Corvino, for instance, is willing to prostitute his wife and thereby cuckold himself for the sake of his supposed inheritance—Mosca shows his insight into the psychology of delusion:

> Each of 'em
> Is so possessed and stuffed with his own
>   hopes
> That anything unto the contrary,
> Never so true, or never so apparent,
> Never so palpable, they will resist it—

As the audience quickly sees, even Volpone is susceptible to Mosca's flattery, ingratiation, and temptations.

In Jonson's commonplace book (published after his death as part of the collection *Timber, or Discoveries*), the playwright included the following aphorism: "[T]ruth and goodness are plain and open, but imposture is ever ashamed of the light." With its vertiginous action and vivid characterizations, *Volpone* complicates this moral truism. Dissembling, exploitation, and treachery hold the stage in shameless, often spectacular fashion, while those who uphold the values of honesty and faithfulness are, for the most part, ineffectual in combating it. Celia (whose name means "heavenly") and Bonario (whose name means "good") are two-dimensional characters compared to Volpone, Mosca, and their birds of prey, and their invocations of a secure moral order—such as Celia's exclamation in the final act "How ready is heav'n to those that pray!"—come across as mildly fatuous. It is a paradox of satiric writing, perhaps, that goodness is always less interesting than the vices against which it is judged. The play's intricate game of deception and counterdeception collapses not through divine intervention but through its own self-consuming logic. Volpone and Mosca stalk each other— "two rival artists, each trying to end the play on his own terms," in Alexander Leggatt's apt analogy—and the ending is brought about when one of them reveals the masquerade in a suicidal gesture of control. In view of the severe punishments that the guilty receive, there is a harshness in this conclusion of which even Jonson was aware. In his epistle to *Volpone*, Jonson acknowledged that the play's ending violated comic law, that he easily could have changed it, and that he arranged the play's final incident to answer those who claimed that the theater never punished vice.

But despite its dark qualities, *Volpone* is alive with the stage's performative energies. This theatrical exuberance reflects the histrionic energies of Renaissance England, which reveled in public performance and often daring acts of what Stephen Greenblatt has called "self-fashioning." In Volpone's rhapsody to his treasure, the virtuoso catalog of ailments and remedies in his mountebank speech, and the fabulous plenty that Mosca conjures up for his victims, we witness the joy of performance and imaginative creation. As in medieval morality drama, whose vice characters are the funniest and most clever, the theatrical and moral centers of Jonson's play often stand at odds with each other. At no place is this disjunction more evident than in the closing moments of Jonson's play, when Volpone, who has been sentenced to undergo what he terms the "mortifying of a fox," steps forward to solicit the audience's applause.

Jonson further complicates the tone of *Volpone* through the subplot of Sir Politic and Lady Would-be. Travelers from England, Sir Pol and his wife establish a link between the play's Venetian setting and the London of Jonson's audience. While their connections to the main plot are limited—Lady Would-be is one of the suitors for Volpone's inheritance, while Sir Pol

and Peregrine, a fellow traveler, find themselves spectators at Volpone's mountebank performance—their subplot comments on the major action through numerous parallels and counterpoints. Sir Pol, who loves wonders and monstrosities and prides himself on his knowledge of plots, schemes, and gossip, is a more circumscribed version of Volpone, and his punishment at the end of the play mirrors the latter's. Lady Would-be, for her part, parallels the other suitors in her greed while counterpointing Celia in her verbal affectation, artificial appearance, and dubious sexual morality. At the same time, as a number of critics have pointed out, the Would-be subplot is drawn from the lighter, more episodic world of the earlier humors comedies, and its subject is folly rather than the predatory vice that fuels the main plot. When Sir Pol and his wife are finally gulled—driven "out of their humors" in this play of savage exposure—shame and self-knowledge are the worst they merit.   S.G.

Volpone;
or, The Fox

CHARACTERS[1]

VOLPONE, a magnifico°   *Venetian nobleman*
MOSCA, his parasite°   *flatterer; hanger-on*
NANO, a dwarf
ANDROGYNO, a hermaphrodite
CASTRONE, a eunuch
VOLTORE, an advocate°
CORBACCIO, an old gentleman   *lawyer*
BONARIO, a young gentleman [CORBACCIO's son]
CORVINO, a merchant
CELIA, the merchant's wife
Servitore, a SERVANT [to CORVINO]
[Sir] POLITIC Would-be, a knight

---

1. The names of the principal characters are allegorically revealing. *Volpone* is Italian for "fox," *Mosca* for "fly," *Voltore* for "vulture," *Corbaccio* for "raven," and *Corvino* for "crow." *Bonario* means "good," and *Celia* means "heav-

enly." *Politic* means "worldly-wise," with the added insinuation of "scheming" or "artfully contriving"; its abbreviation *Pol* suggests a parrot. *Peregrine* is a kind of falcon, though the word also indicates a "pilgrim" or "traveler."

30 Fine Madame [LADY] WOULD-BE, the knight's wife
    [Two] WOMEN [servants to LADY WOULD-BE]
    PEREGRINE, a gentleman traveler
    AVOCATORI,° four magistrates   *state prosecutors*
    Notario [NOTARY], the register°   *court recorder*
35 COMMENDATORI,° officers   *court deputies*
    [*Other court officials, litter-bearers*]
    Mercatori, three MERCHANTS
    Grege [*members of a* CROWD]

[SCENE: *Venice.*]

The Argument°   *plot outline*

V olpone, childless, rich, feigns sick, despairs,°   *is despaired of*
O ffers his state° to hopes of several heirs,   *estate*
L ies languishing; his parasite receives
P resents of all, assures, deludes, then weaves
O ther cross-plots, which ope° themselves, are told.°   *open / exposed*
N ew tricks for safety are sought; they thrive—when, bold,
E ach tempts th'other again, and all are sold.°   *betrayed*

Prologue

Now, luck yet send us, and a little wit
Will serve to make our play hit
According to the palates° of the season.   *tastes*
Here is rhyme not empty of reason.
5 This we were bid to credit° from our poet,   *believe*
Whose true scope,° if you would know it,   *intention*
In all his poems still hath been this measure,
To mix profit with your pleasure;[2]
And not as some—whose throats their envy failing—
10 Cry hoarsely, "all he writes is railing,"[3]
And when his plays come forth think they can flout them
With saying he was a year about them.
To these there needs no lie but this his creature,
Which was, two months since, no feature;[4]
15 And, though he dares give them° five lives to mend it,   *(his detractors)*
'Tis known five weeks fully penned it
From his own hand, without a coadjutor,°   *coauthor*
Novice, journeyman,° or tutor.   *assistant*
Yet thus much I can give you, as a token
20 Of his play's worth: no eggs are broken,
Nor quaking custards° with fierce teeth affrighted,   *cowards*
Wherewith your rout° are so delighted;   *mob*

2. The Roman poet Horace wrote in his *Art of Poetry* (ca. 10 B.C.E.), influential during the English Renaissance, that the chief purposes of art are to teach and delight.

3. Insulting, abusive language.
4. That is, this play ("his creature") answers their charge, since it wasn't even begun two months ago.

fool / adages

Nor hales he in a gull° old ends° reciting,
To stop gaps in his loose writing,
25 With such a deal of monstrous and forced action
As might make Bethlehem a faction.[5]
Nor made he his play for jests stol'n from each table,
But makes jests to fit his fable,
30 And so presents quick comedy, refined
As best critics have designed.
The laws of time, place, persons[6] he observeth;
From no needful rule he swerveth.
All gall and copperas from his ink he draineth;
35 Only a little salt[7] remaineth
Wherewith he'll rub your cheeks, till, red with laughter,
They shall look fresh a week after.

1.1

[SCENE: VOLPONE's *house.*]

[*Enter* VOLPONE *and* MOSCA.]

VOLPONE   Good morning to the day, and, next, my gold!
Open the shrine that I may see my saint.

[MOSCA *reveals the treasure.*]

Hail the world's soul, and mine! More glad than is
The teeming earth to see the longed-for sun
5 Peep through the horns of the celestial Ram[8]

(the sun's)

Am I to view thy splendor darkening his,°
That, lying here amongst my other hoards,
Show'st like a flame by night, or like the day
Struck out of chaos, when all darkness fled

center of the earth

10 Unto the center.° O thou son of Sol[9]—
But brighter than thy father—let me kiss
With adoration thee and every relic
Of sacred treasure in this blessèd room.
Well did wise poets by thy glorious name
15 Title that age which they would have the best,[1]
Thou being the best of things, and far transcending

kinds

All style° of joy in children, parents, friends,
Or any other waking dream on earth.
Thy looks when they to Venus did ascribe,
20 They should have giv'n her twenty thousand Cupids,[2]

5. That is, make the inhabitants of the Hospital of St. Mary of Bethlehem, a London insane asylum known as "Old Bedlam," into supporters ("a faction").
6. According to the neoclassical rules, which 16th-century critics derived from Aristotle's *Poetics* (ca. 330 B.C.E.), the length of time in a play could not exceed twenty-four hours, the play's action was restricted to a single location, and the comic characters were to be from the lower or middle classes.
7. A traditional metaphor for wit. *Gall and*

copperas: oak gall and ferrous sulphate, corrosive substances used in ink.
8. The sun enters Aries (the Ram) on March 21.
9. Alchemists held gold to be the offspring of the sun ("Sol").
1. The Golden Age, the first and best epoch, according to classical mythology.
2. Venus (the Greek Aphrodite), the Roman goddess of love and mother of Cupid, god of love, was commonly described as "golden."

Such are thy beauties and our loves. Dear saint,
Riches, the dumb god,[3] that giv'st all men tongues,
That canst do naught and yet mak'st men do all things,
The price of souls; even hell, with thee to boot,
25 Is made worth heaven! Thou art virtue, fame,
Honor, and all things else. Who° can get thee,   *Whoever*
He shall be noble, valiant, honest, wise—
MOSCA   And what he will, sir. Riches are in fortune
A greater good than wisdom is in nature.
30 VOLPONE   True, my belovèd Mosca. Yet I glory
More in the cunning purchase° of my wealth   *acquisition*
Than in the glad possession, since I gain
No common way. I use no trade, no venture;°   *risky undertaking*
I wound no earth with plowshares; fat no beasts
35 To feed the shambles;° have no mills for iron,   *slaughterhouse*
Oil, corn, or men, to grind 'em into powder;
I blow no subtle[4] glass; expose no ships
To threat'nings of the furrow-facèd sea;
I turn° no moneys in the public bank,   *exchange*
40 Nor usure° private—   *lend money at interest*
MOSCA   No, sir, nor devour
Soft prodigals.° You shall ha' some will swallow   *spendthrifts*
A melting heir as glibly as your Dutch
Will pills of butter, and ne'er purge for't;[5]
Tear forth the fathers of poor families
45 Out of their beds and coffin them alive
In some kind, clasping prison, where their bones
May be forthcoming° when the flesh is rotten.   *protruding; removed*
But your sweet nature doth abhor these courses;
You loathe the widow's or the orphan's tears
50 Should wash your pavements, or their piteous cries
Ring in your roofs and beat the air for vengeance.
VOLPONE   Right, Mosca, I do loathe it.
MOSCA   And besides, sir,
You are not like the thresher that doth stand
With a huge flail, watching a heap of corn,
55 And, hungry, dares not taste the smallest grain,
But feeds on mallows and such bitter herbs;
Nor like the merchant who hath filled his vaults
With Romagnia and rich Candian wines,[6]
Yet drinks the lees of Lombard's vinegar.[7]
60 You will not lie in straw whilst moths and worms
Feed on your sumptuous hangings° and soft beds.   *draperies*

3. An allusion to the proverb "Silence is golden."
4. Delicate, intricately wrought. Venice was famed for its glass.
5. Take a laxative. The Dutch were known for their love of butter.
6. Wines from the northern Italian region of Romagna and from the Greek island of Crete (Candia).
7. That is, cheap and acidic wine from Lombardy.

You know the use of riches, and dare give now
From that bright heap to me, your poor observer,°   *attendant*
Or to your dwarf, or your hermaphrodite,
65 Your eunuch, or what other household trifle
Your pleasure allows maint'nance°—   *you're pleased to support*
VOLPONE [*giving money*]   Hold thee, Mosca,
Take of my hand; thou strik'st on truth in all,
And they° are envious term thee parasite.   *they who*
Call forth my dwarf, my eunuch, and my fool,
70 And let 'em make me sport.

                                    [*Exit* MOSCA.]
                      What should I do
But cocker up° my genius, and live free   *indulge*
To all delights my fortune calls me to?
I have no wife, no parent, child, ally
To give my substance to, but whom I make°   *whomever I designate*
75 Must be my heir, and this makes men observe me.[8]
This draws new clients° daily to my house,   *followers*
Women and men of every sex and age,
That bring me presents, send me plate,° coin, jewels,   *gold or silver utensils*
With hope that when I die—which they expect
80 Each greedy minute—it shall then return
Tenfold upon them; whilst some, covetous
Above the rest, seek to engross° me whole,   *absorb; monopolize*
And counterwork, the one unto° the other,   *against*
Contend in gifts as they would seem in love;
85 All which I suffer,° playing with their hopes,   *allow; tolerate*
And am content to coin 'em into profit,
And look upon their kindness and take more,
And look on that, still bearing them in hand,°   *leading them on*
Letting the cherry knock against their lips,
90 And draw it by their mouths and back again.[9]—
How now!

1.2

[SCENE: *The scene continues.*]

[*Enter* MOSCA, NANO, ANDROGYNO, *and* CASTRONE.]

NANO Now, room for fresh gamesters° who do will you to know   *merry people*
They do bring you neither play nor university show,[1]
And therefore do entreat you that whatsoever they rehearse
May not fare a whit the worse for the false pace of the verse.[2]
5 If you wonder at this, you will wonder more ere we pass,

8. That is, be obsequious to me.
9. In the game of chop-cherry, a player tries to catch a cherry hung on a string with his or her teeth.
1. University students performed classical

plays or imitations of such plays.
2. The loose, four-stress verse of the skit performed below was common in medieval morality drama.

For know here [*indicating* ANDROGYNO] is enclosed the soul of
    Pythagoras,[3]
That juggler° divine, as hereafter shall follow;   *trickster; magician*
Which soul (fast and loose, sir) came first from Apollo,
And was breathed into Aethalides,[4] Mercurius his° son,   *Mercury's*
10 Where it had the gift to remember all that ever was done.
From thence it fled forth and made quick transmigration
To goldilocked Euphorbus,[5] who was killed in good fashion
At the siege of old Troy, by the cuckold of Sparta.
Hermotimus[6] was next—I find it in my *charta*°—   *written source*
15 To whom it did pass, where no sooner it was missing
But with one Pyrrhus of Delos° it learned to go a-fishing;   *a fisherman*
And thence did it enter the Sophist° of Greece.°   *Sage / (Pythagoras)*
From Pythagore she went into a beautiful piece°   *whore*
Hight° Aspasia the meretrix;[7] and the next toss of her   *Named*
20 Was again of a whore; she became a philosopher,
Crates the Cynic,[8] as itself doth relate it.
Since,° kings, knights, and beggars, knaves, lords, and fools   *Since then*
    gat° it,   *received*
Besides ox and ass, camel, mule, goat, and brock,°   *badger*
In all which it hath spoke as in the cobbler's cock.[9]
25 But I come not here to discourse of that matter,
Or his one, two, or three, or his great oath, "By quater,"[1]
His musics, his trigon, his golden thigh,[2]
Or his telling how elements shift; but I
Would ask how of late thou hast suffered translation,°   *metamorphosis*
30 And shifted thy coat in these days of reformation?[3]
ANDROGYNO   Like one of the reformed,[4] a fool, as you see,
    Counting all old doctrine heresy.
NANO   But not on thine own forbid meats hast thou ventured?
ANDROGYNO   On fish, when first a Carthusian I entered.[5]
35 NANO   Why, then thy dogmatical silence hath left thee?

3. Greek philosopher (6th c. B.C.E.), well
known for his theory of the transmigration of
souls; he is said to have recalled his own previous incarnations. (He also discovered the
mathematical basis of musical intervals; see
3.4.73.) Nano's account of Pythagoras's soul's
journey from Apollo, god of the sun, was
adapted by Jonson from *The Dialogue of the
Cobbler and the Cock* by the Greek satirist
Lucian (2nd c. C.E.).
4. The herald for Jason and the Argonauts; he
gained from his father Mercury (Hermes),
the herald of the gods, the gift of remembering everything.
5. The first Trojan warrior to wound Patro-
clus, according to Homer's *Iliad*. He was
killed by Menelaus, king of Sparta, whose
wife Helen had gone to Troy with Paris.
6. A Greek philosopher (ca. 500 B.C.E.);
according to Lucian and others, his soul
could swiftly journey far from his body.
7. Prostitute. Aspasia (5th c. B.C.E.), famously

learned, was the mistress of the Athenian
statesman Pericles and a friend of the philosopher Socrates.
8. Crates of Thebes (ca. 365–ca. 285 B.C.E.),
student of the founder of Cynic philosophy,
Diogenes.
9. Lucian's *Gallus,* from which Nano's mock-
history of the soul's transmigration is derived,
takes the form of a dialogue between a cobbler and a cock.
1. An equilateral trigon, or triangle, with
sides each four units long.
2. Pythagoras was believed by his followers to
have a golden thigh.
3. The Protestant Reformation of Roman
Catholicism, begun in Germany by Martin
Luther in the 16th century and still in process at the time of this play.
4. Contemporary Puritan reformers.
5. Unlike Pythagoreans, Carthusians (members of a Roman Catholic religious order) ate
fish; they also observed a vow of silence.

ANDROGYNO   Of that an obstreperous lawyer bereft me.[6]
NANO   Oh, wonderful change! When Sir Lawyer forsook thee,
    For Pythagore's sake, what body then took thee?
ANDROGYNO   A good dull mule.
40 NANO   And how, by that means,
    Thou wert brought to allow of the eating of beans?[7]
ANDROGYNO   Yes.
NANO   But from the mule into whom didst thou pass?
ANDROGYNO   Into a very strange beast, by some writers called an ass;
    By others a precise, pure, illuminate brother[8]
45   Of those devour flesh and sometimes one another,
    And will drop you forth a libel[9] or a sanctified lie
    Betwixt every spoonful of a Nativity pie.[1]
NANO   Now quit thee, for heaven, of that profane nation,
    And gently report thy next transmigration.
50 ANDROGYNO   To the same that I am.
NANO   A creature of delight?
    And—what is more than a fool—an hermaphrodite?
    Now pray thee, sweet soul, in all thy variation
    Which body wouldst thou choose to take up thy station?
ANDROGYNO   Troth, this I am in, even here would I tarry.
55 NANO   'Cause here the delight of each sex thou canst vary?
ANDROGYNO   Alas, those pleasures be stale and forsaken.
    No, 'tis your fool wherewith I am so taken,
    The only one creature that I can call blessèd,
    For all other forms I have proved° most distressèd.   *found to be*
60 NANO   Spoke true, as° thou wert in Pythagoras still.   *as if*
    This learnèd opinion we celebrate will,
    Fellow eunuch, as behooves us, with all our wit and art,
    To dignify that° whereof ourselves are so great and special a part.   *(folly)*
VOLPONE [*applauding*]   Now, very, very pretty! Mosca, this
65 Was thy invention?
MOSCA   If it please my patron,
    Not else.
VOLPONE   It doth, good Mosca.
MOSCA   Then it was, sir.

SONG

NANO *and* CASTRONE [*sing*]
    Fools, they are the only nation
    Worth men's envy or admiration,
    Free from care or sorrow-taking,
70   Selves° and others merry making;   *Themselves*
    All they speak or do is sterling.[2]

6. That is, becoming a loud-mouthed lawyer ended his silence.
7. Beans were forbidden to Pythagoreans.
8. That is, a Puritan. Puritans, whom Jonson's plays frequently ridicule, claimed to have visions, or "illuminations," of religious truth.

9. Short treatise; defamatory statement.
1. Puritans avoided the word "Christmas" because it contains a reference to the Catholic Mass.
2. Excellent, of value (literally, in Jonson's day, a silver penny).

Your fool, he is your great man's dearling,°   *darling*
And your lady's sport and pleasure;
Tongue and bauble° are his treasure.   *fool's scepter; penis*
75 E'en his face begetteth laughter,
And he speaks truth free from slaughter.[3]
He's the grace of every feast,
And sometimes the chiefest guest,
Hath his trencher° and his stool,   *platter*
80 When wit waits upon the fool.
  Oh, who would not be
  He, he, he? [*One knocks without.*]

VOLPONE Who's that? Away!

      [*Exeunt*° NANO *and* CASTRONE.] *They exit (Latin)*
     Look, Mosca.

MOSCA   Fool, begone!
        [*Exit* ANDROGYNO.]

'Tis Signor Voltore, the advocate;
85 I know him by his knock.

VOLPONE   Fetch me my gown,
My furs, and nightcaps; say my couch is changing,[4]
And let him entertain himself awhile
Without i'th'gallery.   [*Exit* MOSCA.]
     Now, now, my clients
Begin their visitation! Vulture, kite,
90 Raven, and gorcrow,° all my birds of prey *carrion crow*
That think me turning carcass, now they come.
I am not for 'em[5] yet.
   [*Enter* MOSCA.]
     How now? The news?

MOSCA A piece of plate, sir.

VOLPONE   Of what bigness?

MOSCA   Huge,
Massy, and antique, with your name inscribed
95 And arms° engraven.   *coat of arms*

VOLPONE   Good! And not a fox
Stretched on the earth, with fine delusive sleights° *tricks*
Mocking a gaping crow?[6] Ha, Mosca?

MOSCA [*laughing*]   Sharp, sir.

VOLPONE Give me my furs. Why dost thou laugh so, man?

MOSCA I cannot choose, sir, when I apprehend
100 What thoughts he has, without,° now, as he walks: *outside*
That this might be the last gift he should give;
That this would fetch you; if you died today
And gave him all, what he should be tomorrow;
What large return would come of all his ventures;
105 How he should worshipped be and reverenced;

---

3. That is, without fear of consequences.
4. My bed linens are being changed.
5. Ready for them (i.e., ready to die).

6. In one of Aesop's *Fables*, a fox uses flattery
to trick a crow into dropping her food.

Ride with his furs and footcloths,⁷ waited on
By herds of fools and clients; have clear way
Made for his mule, as lettered° as himself;   *learned*
Be called the great and learnèd advocate;
110 And then concludes there's naught impossible.
VOLPONE   Yes, to be learnèd, Mosca.
MOSCA   Oh, no, rich
Implies it. Hood an ass with reverend purple,
So you can hide his two ambitious° ears,   *towering*
And he shall pass for a cathedral doctor.⁸
115 VOLPONE   My caps, my caps, good Mosca. Fetch him in.
MOSCA   Stay, sir, your ointment for your eyes.
        [MOSCA *helps* VOLPONE *with his disguise.*]
VOLPONE   That's true.
Dispatch,° dispatch! I long to have possession   *Hurry*
Of my new present.
MOSCA   That, and thousands more
I hope to see you lord of.
VOLPONE   Thanks, kind Mosca.
120 MOSCA   And that, when I am lost in blended dust,
And hundred such as I am in succession—
VOLPONE   Nay, that were too much, Mosca.
MOSCA   —you shall live
Still, to delude these Harpies.⁹
VOLPONE   Loving Mosca!
'Tis well. My pillow now, and let him enter.
        [*Exit* MOSCA. VOLPONE *lies down.*]
125 Now, my feigned cough, my phthisic,° and my gout,   *consumption*
My apoplexy, palsy, and catarrhs,°   *mucous discharges*
Help with your forcèd functions this my posture,°   *imposture*
Wherein this three year I have milked their hopes.
He comes, I hear him. [*Coughing*] Uh, uh, uh, uh! Oh—

1.3

[SCENE: *The scene continues.*]

    [*Enter* VOLTORE *with a platter, ushered by* MOSCA.]
MOSCA [*to* VOLTORE]   You still are what you were, sir. Only you,
Of all the rest, are he° commands his love;   *he who*
And you do wisely to preserve it thus
With early visitation and kind notes°   *signs*
5 Of your good meaning to° him, which, I know,   *intention toward*
Cannot but come most grateful. [*Loudly, to* VOLPONE] Patron, sir!   *welcome*
Here's Signor Voltore is come—
VOLPONE [*weakly*]   What say you?

---

7. Large ornamental cloths laid over the back
of a horse.
8. That is, a doctor of divinity, whose academic
hood is purple.

9. In classical mythology, monsters with the
bodies of birds and women's faces who snatched
away people and food.

MOSCA   Sir, Signor Voltore is come this morning
    To visit you.
VOLPONE   I thank him.
MOSCA   And hath brought
10 A piece of antique plate bought of Saint Mark,[1]
    With which he here presents you.
VOLPONE   He is welcome.
    Pray him to come more often.
MOSCA   Yes.
VOLPONE [*straining to hear*]   What says he?
MOSCA   He thanks you, and desires you see him often.
VOLPONE   Mosca.
MOSCA   My patron?
VOLPONE [*groping*]   Bring him near. Where is he?
15 I long to feel his hand.
MOSCA [*guiding* VOLPONE's *hands toward the platter*]   The plate is here, sir.
VOLTORE   How fare you, sir?
VOLPONE   I thank you, Signor Voltore.
    Where is the plate? Mine eyes are bad.
VOLTORE [*relinquishing the platter*]   I'm sorry
    To see you still thus weak.
MOSCA [*aside*]   That he is not weaker.
VOLPONE   You are too munificent.
VOLTORE   No, sir, would to heaven
20 I could as well give health to you as that plate.
VOLPONE   You give, sir, what you can. I thank you. Your love
    Hath taste in° this, and shall not be unanswered.   *Is revealed in*
    I pray you see me often.
VOLTORE   Yes, I shall, sir.
VOLPONE   Be not far from me.
MOSCA [*aside to* VOLTORE]   Do you observe that, sir?
25 VOLPONE   Hearken unto me still. It will concern you.
MOSCA [*aside to* VOLTORE]   You are a happy man, sir. Know your good.
VOLPONE   I cannot now last long—
MOSCA [*aside to* VOLTORE]   You are his heir, sir.
VOLTORE [*aside to* MOSCA]   Am I?
VOLPONE   I feel me going, uh, uh, uh, uh!
    I am sailing to my port, uh, uh, uh, uh!
30 And I am glad I am so near my heaven.
        [*He pretends to lapse into unconsciousness.*]
MOSCA   Alas, kind gentleman! Well, we must all go—
VOLTORE   But Mosca—
MOSCA   Age will conquer.
VOLTORE   Pray thee, hear me.
    Am I inscribed his heir for certain?
MOSCA   Are you?
    I do beseech you, sir, you will vouchsafe°   *kindly grant*
35 To write me i'your family.[2] All my hopes

1. That is, in St. Mark's Square, known for its goldsmiths' shops.   2. To write my name in the list of your household servants (i.e., employ me).

Depend upon Your Worship. I am lost
Except° the rising sun do shine on me.   *Unless*
VOLTORE   It shall both shine and warm thee, Mosca.
MOSCA   Sir,
I am a man that have not done your love
40 All the worst offices:° here I wear your keys,   *services*
See all your coffers and your caskets locked,
Keep the poor inventory of your jewels,
Your plate, and moneys, am your steward, sir,
Husband your goods here.
VOLTORE   But am I sole heir?
45 MOSCA Without a partner, sir, confirmed this morning;
The wax is warm yet, and the ink scarce dry
Upon the parchment.
VOLTORE   Happy, happy me!
By what good chance, sweet Mosca?
MOSCA   Your desert, sir;
I know no second cause.
VOLTORE   Thy modesty
50 Is loath to know it.° Well, we shall requite it.   *acknowledge your role*
MOSCA He ever liked your course, sir; that first took him.
I oft have heard him say how he admired
Men of your large profession, that could speak
To every cause, and things mere contraries,°   *utterly contradictory*
55 Till they were hoarse again, yet all be law;
That with most quick agility could turn
And re-turn, make knots and undo them,
Give forkèd° counsel, take provoking gold   *equivocal*
On either hand, and put it up:³ these men,
60 He knew, would thrive with their humility.
And for his part, he thought he should be blessed
To have his heir of such a suffering spirit,
So wise, so grave, of so perplexed a tongue,
And loud withal,° that would not wag nor scarce   *besides*
65 Lie still without a fee, when every word
Your Worship but lets fall is a *cecchine!*⁴
          [*Another knocks.*]
Who's that? One knocks; I would not have you seen, sir.
And yet—pretend you came and went in haste;
I'll fashion an excuse. And, gentle sir,
70 When you do come to swim in golden lard,
Up to the arms in honey, that your chin
Is born up stiff with fatness of the flood,
Think on your vassal; but° remember me.   *only*
I ha' not been your worst of clients.
VOLTORE   Mosca—

---

3. That is, take court fees from both sides of a   4. That is, a *zecchino*, a Venetian gold coin.
suit and pocket them.

75 MOSCA   When will you have your inventory brought, sir?
    Or see a copy of the will? [*More knocking.*] Anon!°—   *Just a moment*
    I'll bring 'em to you, sir. Away, begone,
    Put business i'your face.[5]

                                        [*Exit* VOLTORE.]

VOLPONE   Excellent, Mosca!
    Come hither, let me kiss thee.
MOSCA   Keep you still, sir.
80   Here is Corbaccio.
VOLPONE   Set the plate away.
    The vulture's gone, and the old raven's come.

1.4

[SCENE: *The scene continues.*]

MOSCA [*to* VOLPONE]   Betake you to your silence and your sleep;
        [*He puts up the plate.*]
    Stand there and multiply.—Now shall we see
    A wretch who is indeed more impotent
    Than this° can feign to be, yet hopes to hop   *(Volpone)*
5   Over his grave.
        [*Enter* CORBACCIO.]
               Signor Corbaccio!
    You're very welcome, sir.
CORBACCIO   How does your patron?
MOSCA   Troth, as he did, sir: no amends.
CORBACCIO   What? Mends he?
MOSCA   No, sir, he is rather worse.
CORBACCIO   That's well. Where is he?
MOSCA   Upon his couch, sir, newly fall'n asleep.
10 CORBACCIO   Does he sleep well?
MOSCA   No wink, sir, all this night,
    Nor yesterday, but slumbers.°   *dozes (now)*
CORBACCIO   Good! He should take
    Some counsel of physicians. I have brought him
    An opiate here, from mine own doctor—
MOSCA   He will not hear of drugs.
CORBACCIO   Why, I myself
15   Stood by while't was made, saw all th'ingredients,
    And know it cannot but most gently work.
    My life for his, 'tis but to make him sleep.
VOLPONE [*aside*]   Ay, his last sleep, if he would take it.
MOSCA   Sir,
    He has no faith in physic.°   *medicine*
CORBACCIO   Say you?° Say you?   *What do you say?*
20 MOSCA He has no faith in physic. He does think
    Most of your doctors[6] are the greater danger
    And worse disease t'escape. I often have

---

5. Look as if you were here on business.   6. That is, doctors as a profession.

    Heard him protest that your physician
    Should never be his heir.
CORBACCIO   Not I his heir?
25 MOSCA   Not your physician, sir.
CORBACCIO   Oh, no, no, no,
    I do not mean it.
MOSCA   No, sir, nor their fees
    He cannot brook.° He says they flay° a man   *tolerate / skin alive*
    Before they kill him.
CORBACCIO   Right, I do conceive° you.   *understand*
MOSCA   And then, they do it by experiment,[7]
30   For which the law not only doth absolve 'em,
    But gives them great reward; and he is loath
    To hire his death so.
CORBACCIO   It is true, they kill
    With as much license as a judge.
MOSCA   Nay, more:
    For he but kills, sir, where the law condemns,
35   And these° can kill him, too.   *(the doctors)*
CORBACCIO   Ay, or me
    Or any man. How does his apoplex?°   *apoplexy, stroke*
    Is that strong on him still?
MOSCA   Most violent.
    His speech is broken and his eyes are set,
    His face drawn longer than 'twas wont°—   *than usual*
CORBACCIO   How? How?
40   Stronger than he was wont?
MOSCA   No, sir: his face
    Drawn longer than 'twas wont.
CORBACCIO   Oh, good.
MOSCA   His mouth
    Is ever gaping, and his eyelids hang.
CORBACCIO   Good.
MOSCA   A freezing numbness stiffens all his joints,
    And makes the color of his flesh like lead.
CORBACCIO   'Tis good.
45 MOSCA   His pulse beats slow and dull.
CORBACCIO   Good symptoms still.
MOSCA   And from his brain—
CORBACCIO   Ha? How? Not from his brain?
MOSCA   Yes, sir, and from his brain—
CORBACCIO   I conceive you, good.
MOSCA   —Flows a cold sweat with a continual rheum
    Forth the resolvèd° corners of his eyes.   *Forth from the watery*
50 CORBACCIO   Is't possible? Yet I am better, ha!
    How does he with the swimming of his head?
MOSCA   Oh, sir, 'tis past the scotomy;[8] he now
    Hath lost his feeling, and hath left to snort,°   *stopped snoring*

---

7. By making trials on the patient.   8. Dimness of vision accompanied by dizziness.

You hardly can perceive him that he breathes.

55 CORBACCIO Excellent, excellent. Sure I shall outlast him!
This makes me young again a score of years.

MOSCA I was a-coming for you, sir,

CORBACCIO   Has he made his will?
What has he giv'n me?

MOSCA   No, sir.

CORBACCIO   Nothing? Ha?

MOSCA He has not made his will, sir.

CORBACCIO   Oh, oh, oh.

60 What then did Voltore, the lawyer, here?

MOSCA He smelt a carcass, sir, when he but heard
My master was about his testament°—   *making his will*
As I did urge him to it, for your good—

CORBACCIO He came unto him, did he? I thought so.

65 MOSCA Yes, and presented him this piece of plate.

CORBACCIO To be his heir?

MOSCA   I do not know, sir.

CORBACCIO   True,
I know it too.

MOSCA [*aside*] By your own scale,[9] sir.

CORBACCIO [*showing a bag of gold*]   Well,
I shall prevent° him yet. See, Mosca, look,   *forestall*
Here I have brought a bag of bright *cecchines*,
Will quite weigh down his plate.

70 MOSCA   Yea, marry, sir!
This is true physic, this your sacred medicine;
No talk of opiates to this great elixir[1]

CORBACCIO 'Tis *aurum palpabile*, if not *potabile*.[2]

MOSCA It shall be ministered to him in his bowl?

75 CORBACCIO Ay, do, do, do.

MOSCA   Most blessed cordial!°   *heart stimulant*
This will recover him.

CORBACCIO   Yes, do, do, do.

MOSCA I think it were not best, sir.

CORBACCIO   What?

MOSCA   To recover him.

CORBACCIO Oh, no, no, no; by no means.

MOSCA   Why, sir, this
Will work some strange effect, if he but feel it.

80 CORBACCIO 'Tis true, therefore forbear, I'll take my venture.°   (*gold at risk*)
Give me 't again.

       [*He snatches for the bag.*]

MOSCA [*keeping it out of his reach*] At no hand.° Pardon me,   *On no account*
You shall not do yourself that wrong, sir. I

---

9. That is, judging by your example.
1. That is, no sedative can be compared to this great elixir. In alchemy, an "elixir" is a preparation believed to prolong life indefi-

nitely or to turn base metals into gold.
2. Gold that can be touched, even if it is not drinkable (Latin). Dissolved gold was drunk as a medicine.

Will so advise you, you shall have it all.
CORBACCIO　How?
MOSCA　　　　　All, sir, 'tis your right, your own; no man
85　Can claim a part. 'Tis yours without a rival,
Decreed by destiny.
CORBACCIO　　　　How? How, good Mosca?
MOSCA　I'll tell you, sir. This fit he shall recover°—　　　　　*recover from*
CORBACCIO　I do conceive you.
MOSCA　　　　　　　—and, on first advantage°　　　　*opportunity*
Of his gained sense, will I re-importune him
90　Unto the making of his testament,
And show him this.
CORBACCIO　　　　Good, good.
MOSCA　　　　　　　　'Tis better yet,
If you will hear, sir.
CORBACCIO　　　　Yes, with all my heart.
MOSCA　Now, would I counsel you, make home with speed;
There frame a will, whereto you shall inscribe
95　My master your sole heir.
CORBACCIO　　　　　　And disinherit
My son?
MOSCA　Oh, sir, the better, for that color°　　　　*appearance; pretense*
Shall make it much more taking.°　　　　*believable*
CORBACCIO　　　　　　Oh, but color?°　　　　*only a pretense*
MOSCA　This will, sir, you shall send it unto me.
Now, when I come to enforce°—as I will do—　　　　*urge*
100　Your cares, your watchings, and your many prayers,
Your more than many gifts, your this day's present,
And last produce your will, where—without thought
Or least regard unto your proper issue,°　　　　*own child*
A son so brave° and highly meriting—　　　　*worthy*
105　The stream of your diverted love hath thrown you
Upon my master, and made him your heir,
He cannot be so stupid or stone dead
But out of conscience and mere gratitude—
CORBACCIO　He must pronounce me his?
MOSCA　　　　　　　　　'Tis true.
CORBACCIO　　　　　　　　　　This plot
110　Did I think on before.
MOSCA　　　　　I do believe it.
CORBACCIO　Do you not believe it?
MOSCA　　　　　　　Yes, sir.
CORBACCIO　　　　　　　　Mine own project.
MOSCA　Which when he hath done, sir—
CORBACCIO　　　　　　　Published me his heir?
MOSCA　And you so certain to survive him—
CORBACCIO　　　　　　　　Ay.
MOSCA　Being so lusty° a man—　　　　*hearty, cheerful*
CORBACCIO　　　　　　'Tis true.
MOSCA　　　　　　　Yes, sir—

115 CORBACCIO I thought on that too. See how he° should be   (*Mosca*)
  The very organ to express my thoughts!
MOSCA You have not only done yourself a good—
CORBACCIO But multiplied it on my son?
MOSCA   'Tis right, sir.
CORBACCIO Still my invention.
MOSCA   'Las, sir, heaven knows,
120 It hath been all my study, all my care,
  (I e'en grow gray withal) how to work things—
CORBACCIO I do conceive, sweet Mosca.
MOSCA   You are he
  For whom I labor here.
CORBACCIO   Ay, do, do, do.
  I'll straight about it. [CORBACCIO *starts to leave.*]
MOSCA   Rook go with you,[3] raven!
125 CORBACCIO I know thee honest.
MOSCA   You do lie, sir—
CORBACCIO   And—
MOSCA Your knowledge is no better than your ears,[4] sir.
CORBACCIO I do not doubt to be a father to thee.
MOSCA Nor I to gull° my brother of his blessing.[5]   *cheat*
CORBACCIO I may ha' my youth restored to me, why not?
130 MOSCA Your Worship is a precious ass—
CORBACCIO   What say'st thou?
MOSCA I do desire Your Worship to make haste, sir.
CORBACCIO 'Tis done, 'tis done, I go.   [*Exit.*]
VOLPONE [*leaping from the bed*]   Oh, I shall burst!
  Let out my sides,° let out my sides—   *Loosen my clothes*
MOSCA   Contain
  Your flux° of laughter, sir. You know this hope   *flood*
135 Is such a bait it covers any hook.
VOLPONE Oh, but thy working and thy placing it!
  I cannot hold;° good rascal, let me kiss thee.   *contain (myself)*
  I never knew thee in so rare a humor.
MOSCA Alas, sir, I but do as I am taught:
140 Follow your grave instructions, give 'em words,
  Pour oil° into their ears, and send them hence.   *i.e., flattery*
VOLPONE 'Tis true, 'tis true. What a rare° punishment   *remarkably fine*
  Is avarice to itself!
MOSCA   Ay, with our help, sir.
VOLPONE So many cares, so many maladies,
145 So many fears attending on old age,
  Yea, death so often called on; as no wish
  Can be more frequent with 'em, their limbs faint,
  Their senses dull, their seeing, hearing, going,°   *ability to walk*
  All dead before them;° yea, their very teeth,   *before they are*

3. May you be cheated (rooked), a play on Corbaccio's name, which is Italian for "raven" (a bird in the crow family, as are rooks).
4. Hearing (i.e., very weak; Corbaccio cannot hear what Mosca is saying).
5. As Jacob tricked Isaac into blessing him instead of his brother Esau (Genesis 27). *My brother*: Corbaccio's son.

150 Their instruments of eating, failing them—
Yet this is reckoned life! Nay, here was one
Is now gone home that wishes to live longer!
Feels not his gout nor palsy, feigns himself
Younger by scores of years, flatters his age

155 With confident belying it,° hopes he may   By confidently denying
With charms, like Aeson,[6] have his youth restored,
And with these thoughts so battens,° as if fate   gluts himself
Would be as easily cheated on as he,
And all turns air   [Another knocks.]
Who's that there, now? A third?

160 MOSCA   Close,° to your couch again. I hear his voice.   Hide (yourself)
It is Corvino, our spruce° merchant.   dapper
VOLPONE [lying down again]   Dead.°   I'll play dead
MOSCA   Another bout, sir, with your eyes.
[He applies ointment.]
Who's there?

1.5

[SCENE: The scene continues.]

[Enter CORVINO.]

Signor Corvino! Come° most wished for! Oh,   You come when you are
How happy were you if you knew it now!
CORVINO   Why? What? Wherein?
MOSCA   The tardy hour is come, sir.
CORVINO   He is not dead?
MOSCA   Not dead, sir, but as good;
5   He knows no man.
CORVINO   How shall I do, then?
MOSCA   Why, sir?
CORVINO   I have brought him here a pearl.
MOSCA   Perhaps he has
So much remembrance left as to know you, sir;
He still calls on you; nothing but your name
Is in his mouth. Is your pearl orient,[7] sir?
10 CORVINO   Venice was never owner of the like.
VOLPONE [weakly]   Signor Corvino—
MOSCA   Hark.
VOLPONE   —Signor Corvino—
MOSCA   He calls you. Step and give it him.—He's here, sir,
And he has brought you a rich pearl.
CORVINO [to VOLPONE]   How do you, sir?
[To MOSCA] Tell him it doubles the twelfth carat.[8]
[He gives VOLPONE the pearl.]

6. In Greek mythology, the father of Jason (captain of the Argonauts); he was restored to youth by the magic of the sorceress Medea, Jason's wife.

7. From the Indian Ocean, the source of particularly brilliant pearls.
8. That is, weighs twenty-four carats (a very large pearl).

MOSCA [*to* CORVINO]   Sir,

15   He cannot understand. His hearing's gone;
      And yet it comforts him to see you—

CORVINO   Say
      I have a diamond for him too.

MOSCA   Best show't, sir.
      Put it into his hand; 'tis only there
      He apprehends; he has his feeling yet.

         [CORVINO *gives* VOLPONE *the diamond.*]

20   See how he grasps it!

CORVINO   'Las, good gentleman!
      How pitiful the sight is!

MOSCA   Tut, forget, sir.
      The weeping of an heir should still° be laughter   *always*
      Under a visor.[9]

CORVINO   Why, am I his heir?

MOSCA   Sir, I am sworn; I may not show the will
25   Till he be dead. But here has been Corbaccio,
      Here has been Voltore, here were others too,
      I cannot number 'em they were so many,
      All gaping here for legacies; but I,
      Taking the vantage° of his naming you—   *opportunity*
30   "Signor Corvino! Signor Corvino!"—took
      Paper and pen and ink, and there I asked him
      Whom he would have his heir? "Corvino." Who
      Should be executor? "Corvino." And
      To any question he was silent to,
35   I still interpreted the nods he made
      Through weakness for consent, and sent home th'others,
      Nothing bequeathed them but to cry and curse.

CORVINO   Oh, my dear Mosca! [*They embrace.*] Does he not perceive us?

MOSCA   No more than a blind harper.[1] He knows no man,
40   No face of friend, nor name of any servant,
      Who 'twas that fed him last or gave him drink;
      Not those he hath begotten or brought up
      Can he remember.

CORVINO   Has he children?

MOSCA   Bastards,
      Some dozen or more, that he begot on beggars,
45   Gypsies and Jews and blackmoors,° when he was drunk.   *black Africans*
      Knew you not that, sir? 'Tis the common fable.°   *report*
      The dwarf, the fool, the eunuch are all his;
      He's the true father of his family
      In all save me, but he has given 'em nothing.

50   CORVINO   That's well, that's well. Art sure he does not hear us?

MOSCA   Sure, sir? Why, look you, credit your own sense.

         [*Shouting at* VOLPONE] The pox° approach and add to your diseases   *syphilis*

9. That is, an heir should feign weeping in   visor).
order to hide his laughter (under a mask, or   1. Proverbial (harpers were often blind).

If it would send you hence the sooner, sir.
For° your incontinence, it hath deserved it   *As for*
55 Throughly° and throughly, and the plague to boot.   *Thoroughly*
    [*To* CORVINO] You may come near, sir. [*Shouting at* VOLPONE *again*]
    Would you would once close
    Those filthy eyes of yours, that flow with slime
    Like two frog-pits,° and those same hanging cheeks,   *stagnant puddles*
    Covered with hide instead of skin—nay, help, sir—
60 That look like frozen dishclouts° set on end!   *dishrags*
    CORVINO [*shouting at* VOLPONE]   Or like an old smoked wall on
        which the rain
    Ran down in streaks!
    MOSCA   Excellent, sir! Speak out;
    You may be louder yet; a culverin°   *musket; cannon*
    Dischargèd in his ear would hardly bore it.
65 CORVINO [*shouting*]   His nose is like a common sewer, still°   *always*
        running.
    MOSCA   'Tis good! And what his mouth?
    CORVINO [*shouting*]   A very draught!°   *cesspool, sewer*
    MOSCA   Oh, stop it up—
    CORVINO   By no means.
    MOSCA   Pray you let me.
    Faith, I could stifle him rarely° with a pillow   *beautifully*
    As well as any woman that should keep° him.   *take care of*
70 CORVINO   Do as you will, but I'll be gone.
    MOSCA   Be so;
    It is your presence makes him last so long.
    CORVINO   I pray you, use no violence.
    MOSCA   No, sir? Why?
    Why should you be thus scrupulous? Pray you, sir.
    CORVINO   Nay, at your discretion.
    MOSCA   Well, good sir, begone.
75 CORVINO   I will not trouble him now to take my pearl?
    MOSCA   Pooh! Nor your diamond. What a needless care
    Is this afflicts you? Is not all here yours?
    Am not I here, whom you have made your creature?
    That owe my being to you?
    CORVINO   Grateful Mosca!
80 Thou art my friend, my fellow, my companion,
    My partner, and shalt share in all my fortunes.
    MOSCA   Excepting one.
    CORVINO   What's that?
    MOSCA   Your gallant° wife, sir.   *fine-looking*
                                      [*Exit* CORVINO.]
    Now is he gone. We had no other means
    To shoot him hence but this.
    VOLPONE   My divine Mosca!
    Thou hast today outgone thyself.   [*Another knocks.*]
85   Who's there?

I will be troubled with no more. Prepare
Me music, dances, banquets, all delights.
The Turk[2] is not more sensual in his pleasures
Than will Volpone.   [*Exit* MOSCA.]
                   Let me see, a pearl?

90 A diamond? Plate? *Cecchines*? Good morning's purchase.°   *haul*
Why, this is better than rob churches, yet,
Or fat° by eating, once a month, a man.[3]   *grow fat*
    [*Enter* MOSCA.]
Who is't?

MOSCA   The beauteous Lady Would-be, sir,
Wife to the English knight, Sir Politic Would-be—
95 This is the style, sir, is directed me[4]—
Hath sent to know how you have slept tonight,°   *last night*
And if you would be visited.

VOLPONE   Not now.
Some three hours hence—

MOSCA   I told the squire° so much.   *messenger*

VOLPONE   When I am high with mirth and wine: then, then.
100 'Fore heaven, I wonder at the desperate° valor   *careless*
Of the bold English, that they dare let loose
Their wives to all encounters![5]

MOSCA   Sir, this knight
Had not his name for nothing. He is politic,°   *canny*
And knows, howe'er his wife affect strange airs,
105 She hath not yet the face[6] to be dishonest.
But had she Signor Corvino's wife's face—

VOLPONE   Has she so rare a face?

MOSCA   Oh, sir, the wonder,
The blazing star° of Italy! A wench   *comet; celestial wonder*
O'the first year![7] A beauty ripe as harvest!
110 Whose skin is whiter than a swan, all over,
Than silver, snow, or lilies! A soft lip,
Would° tempt you to eternity of kissing!   *That would*
And flesh that melteth in the touch to blood°   *in blushes*
Bright as your gold, and lovely as your gold!

115 VOLPONE   Why had not I known this before?

MOSCA   Alas, sir,
Myself but yesterday discovered it.

VOLPONE   How might I see her?

MOSCA   Oh, not possible.
She's kept as warily as is your gold:
Never does come abroad,° never takes air   *out of the house*

---

2. Stereotyped as being highly sensual.
3. That is, by receiving monthly interest payments.
4. That is, this is the mode of address I've been instructed to use.
5. English men were reputed to allow their wives to travel about without accompaniment, a freedom viewed as remarkable.
6. That is, she's not beautiful (or shameless) enough to be unchaste ("dishonest").
7. That is, as unblemished as a baby.

120 But at a window. All her looks are sweet
As the first grapes or cherries, and are watched
As near° as they are.   closely
VOLPONE   I must see her—
MOSCA   Sir,
There is a guard of ten spies thick upon her—
All his whole household—each of which is set
125 Upon his fellow, and have all their charge
When he goes out; when he comes in, examined.[8]
VOLPONE   I will go see her, though but at her window.
MOSCA   In some disguise, then.
VOLPONE   That is true. I must
Maintain mine own shape still the same.[9] We'll think.

[*Exeunt.*]

2.1

[SCENE: *Saint Mark's Square.*]

[*Enter* POLITIC WOULD-BE *and* PEREGRINE.]

POLITIC   Sir, to a wise man all the world's his soil°   country
It is not Italy, nor France, nor Europe
That must bound me if my fates call me forth.
Yet I protest it is no salt° desire   inordinate
5 Of seeing countries, shifting a religion,
Nor any disaffection to the state
Where I was bred—and unto which I owe
My dearest plots°—hath brought me out;° much less   schemes / abroad
That idle, antique, stale, gray-headed project
10 Of knowing men's minds and manners with Ulysses;[1]
But a peculiar humor° of my wife's   whim; passion
Laid for this height° of Venice, to observe,   latitude
To quote,° to learn the language, and so forth.—   make notes
I hope you travel, sir, with license?°   a passport
PEREGRINE   Yes.
15 POLITIC   I dare the safelier converse. How long, sir,
Since you left England?
PEREGRINE   Seven weeks.
POLITIC   So lately!
You ha' not been with my Lord Ambassador?
PEREGRINE   Not yet, sir.
POLITIC   Pray you, what news, sir, vents our climate?[2]
I heard last night a most strange thing reported
20 By some of my lord's° followers, and I long   (the ambassador's)
To hear how't will be seconded°   confirmed
PEREGRINE   What was't, sir?

8. That is, each is questioned about the servant under his charge.
9. That is, I must preserve my appearance as a dying man.
1. In the opening lines of Homer's *Odyssey,*

Odysseus (i.e., Ulysses) is described as a man who was made to wander very far and who "saw the cities and learned the mind of many people."
2. That is, comes from our part of the world.

POLITIC   Marry, sir, of a raven that should build[3]
In a ship royal of the King's.
PEREGRINE [*aside*]   This fellow,
Does he gull me, trow?° Or is gulled?—Your name, sir?   *do you believe*
25 POLITIC   My name is Politic Would-be.
PEREGRINE [*aside*]   Oh, that speaks° him.—   *defines*
A knight, sir?
POLITIC   A poor knight, sir
PEREGRINE   Your lady
Lie° here in Venice for intelligence°   *Stays / news*
Of tires° and fashions and behavior   *attire*
Among the courtesans.[4] The fine Lady Would-be?
30 POLITIC   Yes, sir, the spider and the bee ofttimes
Suck from one flower.
PEREGRINE   Good Sir Politic,
I cry you mercy.° I have heard much of you.   *beg your pardon*
'Tis true, sir, of your raven.
POLITIC   On your knowledge?
PEREGRINE   Yes, and your lion's whelping in the Tower.[5]
35 POLITIC   Another whelp!
PEREGRINE   Another, sir.
POLITIC   Now, heaven!
What prodigies° be these? The fires at Berwick!   *strange omens*
And the new star![6] These things concurring,° strange!   *coinciding*
And full of omen! Saw you those meteors?[7]
PEREGRINE   I did, sir.
POLITIC   Fearful! Pray you sir, confirm me:
40 Were there three porpoises seen above the bridge°   *London Bridge*
As they give out?°   *report*
PEREGRINE   Six, and a sturgeon, sir.
POLITIC   I am astonished!
PEREGRINE   Nay, sir, be not so.
I'll tell you a greater prodigy than these—
POLITIC   What should these things portend!
PEREGRINE   The very day—
45 Let me be sure—that I put forth from London,
There was a whale discovered in the river
As high° as Woolwich,[8] that had waited there—   *far upstream*
Few know how many months—for the subversion
Of the Stode Fleet.[9]

---

3. Reportedly built (a nest). *Raven:* a bird of
ill omen.
4. Venice was famous for the beauty of its
fashionable prostitutes.
5. A lioness kept in the Tower of London gave
birth in 1604 and 1605. Most of the recent
events referred to by Sir Politic and Peregrine
would have been familiar to the play's original
audience.
6. The aurora borealis that appeared in the
skies above Berwick, Northumberland, in

1605, was said to resemble fighting armies,
and the German astronomer Johannes Kepler
documented a supernova in 1604.
7. Believed to be ominous portents.
8. A town in Greenwich on the Thames, east
of London.
9. The ships of the English Merchant Adventurers', which had settled at Stade at the
mouth of the Elbe River in northern
Germany.

POLITIC   Is't possible? Believe it,
50 'Twas either sent from Spain or the Archdukes.
    Spinola's whale, upon my life, my credit![1]
    Will they not leave these projects? Worthy sir,
    Some other news.
PEREGRINE   Faith, Stone[2] the fool is dead;
    And they do lack a tavern-fool extremely.
55 POLITIC Is Mas'[3] Stone dead?
PEREGRINE   He's dead, sir. Why, I hope
    You thought him not immortal? [*Aside*] Oh, this knight,
    Were he well known, would be a precious thing
    To fit our English stage. He that should write
    But such a fellow should be thought to feign°   *indulge in fiction*
60 Extremely, if not maliciously.
POLITIC   Stone dead!
PEREGRINE   Dead. Lord, how deeply, sir, you apprehend° it!   *feel; understand*
    He was no kinsman to you?
POLITIC   That° I know of.   *Not that*
    Well, that same fellow was an unknown fool.[4]
PEREGRINE   And yet you knew him, it seems?
POLITIC   I did so. Sir,
65 I knew him one of the most dangerous heads.
    Living within the state, and so I held him.
PEREGRINE   Indeed, sir?
POLITIC   While he lived, in action,[5]
    He has received weekly intelligence,
    Upon my knowledge, out of the Low Countries,
70 For all parts of the world, in cabbages,[6]
    And those dispensed again to ambassadors
    In oranges, muskmelons, apricots,
    Lemons, pome-citrons,° and suchlike—sometimes   *lemonlike citrus fruit*
    In Colchester oysters, and your Selsey cockles.[7]
75 PEREGRINE   You make me wonder!°   *marvel*
POLITIC   Sir, upon my knowledge.
    Nay, I have observed him at your public ordinary°   *tavern*
    Take his advertisement° from a traveler—   *information*
    A concealed statesman—in a trencher° of meat,   *wooden platter*
    And instantly before the meal was done
80 Convey an answer in a toothpick
PEREGRINE   Strange!
    How could this be, sir?

---

1. Sir Politic suggests that the whale was sent by representatives of Spain, England's maritime enemy. *The Archdukes*: Albert of Austria (1559–1621) and his wife, the Infanta Isabella (1566–1633), who ruled the Spanish Netherlands in the name of King Philip II of Spain. Ambrogio Spinola (1569–1630), general of the Spanish army in the Netherlands.
2. A well-known jester at King James's court.

3. "Master," a term of address for boys and fools.
4. That is, not recognized for what he really was.
5. That is, in his subversive activities.
6. A recent import from the Netherlands.
7. That is, expensive shellfish. Colchester and Selsey are seaports east and south of London, respectively.

POLITIC   Why, the meat was cut
    So like his character,° and so laid as he   *handwriting; code*
    Must easily read the cipher.
PEREGRINE   I have heard
    He could not read, sir.
POLITIC   So 'twas given out,
85   In polity° by those that did employ him.   *As a cover*
    But he could read, and had your languages,
    And to't° as sound a noddle°—   *in addition / head*
PEREGRINE   I have heard, sir,
    That your baboons were spies, and that they were
    A kind of subtle nation near to China.
90 POLITIC   Ay, ay, your *Mamuluchi*.[8] Faith, they had
    Their hand in a French plot or two, but they
    Were so extremely given to women as
    They made discovery of° all. Yet I   *disclosed*
    Had my advices° here, on Wednesday last,   *dispatches*
95   From one of their own coat;° they were returned,   *party, faction*
    Made their relations,° as the fashion is,   *reports*
    And now stand fair° for fresh employment.   *are ready*
PEREGRINE [*aside*]   Heart,°   *By God's heart (an oath)*
    This Sir Pol will be ignorant of nothing.
    [*To* POLITIC] It seems, sir, you know all?
POLITIC   Not all, sir. But
100   I have some general notions; I do love
    To note and to observe. Though I live out,°   *abroad*
    Free from the active torrent, yet I'd mark
    The currents and the passages of things
    For mine own private use, and know the ebbs
    And flows of state.
105 PEREGRINE   Believe it, sir, I hold
    Myself in no small tie unto° my fortunes   *obligation to*
    For casting me thus luckily upon you,
    Whose knowledge—if your bounty equal it—
    May do me great assistance in instruction
110   For my behavior and my bearing, which
    Is yet so rude and raw—
POLITIC   Why, came you forth
    Empty of rules for travel?
PEREGRINE   Faith, I had
    Some common ones from out that vulgar grammar,[9]
    Which he that cried° Italian to me taught me.   *spoke; i.e., taught*
115 POLITIC   Why, this it is that spoils all our brave bloods,°   *wellborn young men*
    Trusting our hopeful° gentry unto pedants,   *promising*
    Fellows of outside and mere bark.[1] You seem

---

8. Mamluks, a class of warriors from Asia Minor who ruled Egypt from 1250 to 1517. They had nothing to do with baboons, China, or French plots.

9. A vernacular language textbook, which sometimes included advice for travelers.

1. That is, superficiality and pretense.

To be a gentleman of ingenuous race°—   *noble family*
I not profess it,° but my fate hath been   *do not brag*
120 To be where I have been consulted with
In this high kind,° touching some great men's sons,   *important matter*
Persons of blood° and honor—   *nobility*
PEREGRINE   Who be these, sir?

2.2

[SCENE: *The scene continues.*]

    [*Enter* MOSCA *and* NANO *disguised as a mountebank's
    assistant.*]

MOSCA   Under that window, there's must be. The same.
    [MOSCA *and* NANO *set up a platform.*]

POLITIC   Fellows to mount a bank![2] Did your instructor
In the dear tongues[3] never discourse to you
Of the Italian mountebanks?
PEREGRINE   Yes, sir.
POLITIC   Why,
5 Here shall you see one.
PEREGRINE   They are quacksalvers,°   *quacks*
Fellows that live by venting° oils and drugs.   *selling*
POLITIC   Was that the character he gave you of them?
PEREGRINE   As I remember.
POLITIC   Pity his ignorance.
They are the only knowing men of Europe!
10 Great general scholars, excellent physicians,
Most admired statesmen, professed favorites
And cabinet counselors° to the greatest princes!   *confidential advisers*
The only languaged° men of all the world!   *most eloquent*
PEREGRINE   And I have heard they are most lewd° impostors,   *ignorant*
15 Made all of terms° and shreds, no less beliers°   *jargon / misrepresenters*
Of great men's favors than their own vile med'cines,
Which they will utter° upon monstrous oaths,   *sell*
Selling that drug for twopence ere they part
Which they have valued at twelve crowns[4] before.
20 POLITIC   Sir, calumnies are answered best with silence.
Yourself shall judge. [*To* MOSCA *and* NANO] Who is it mounts, my friends?
MOSCA   Scoto of Mantua,[5] sir.
POLITIC   Is't he? [*To* PEREGRINE] Nay, then,
I'll proudly promise, sir, you shall behold
Another man than has been fancied to you.[6]
25 I wonder yet that he should mount his bank
Here in this nook, that has been wont t'appear
In face of° the piazza! Here he comes.   *Facing*

---

2. Bench, platform. "Mountebank" derives from the Italian *monta in banco* (mount on bench).
3. That is, in Italian (called *cara lingua*).
4. That is, 360 times as much as two pence

(the crown was a silver coin).
5. An Italian actor, juggler, and magician who performed before Queen Elizabeth I in 1576.
6. Suggested to your imagination.

[*Enter* VOLPONE *disguised as a mountebank, followed by a crowd.*]

VOLPONE [*to* NANO] Mount, zany.[7]

[VOLPONE *and* NANO *climb onto the platform.*]

CROWD Follow, follow, follow, follow, follow!

30 POLITIC See how the people follow him! He's a man
May write ten thousand crowns in bank here. Note,
Mark but his gesture. I do use° to observe   *make it my practice*
The state° he keeps, in getting up.   *stateliness*

PEREGRINE   'Tis worth it, sir.

VOLPONE Most noble gentlemen and my worthy patrons,
35 it may seem strange that I, your Scoto Mantuano, who
was ever wont to fix my bank in face of the public piazza
near the shelter of the portico to the *procuratia*,[8] should
now, after eight months' absence from this illustrious city
of Venice, humbly retire myself into an obscure nook of
40 the piazza.

POLITIC [*to* PEREGRINE] Did not I now object the same?[9]

PEREGRINE   Peace, sir.

VOLPONE Let me tell you: I am not, as your Lombard
proverb saith, cold on my feet,[1] or content to part with my
commodities at a cheaper rate than I accustomed; look
45 not for it. Nor that the calumnious reports of that impudent detractor and shame to our profession (Alessandro
Buttone,[2] I mean) who gave out in public I was condemned
a *'sforzato*° to the galleys for poisoning the Cardinal   *galley slave (Italian)*
Bembo's—cook,[3] hath at all attached,° much less dejected   *stuck to*
50 me. No, no, worthy gentlemen. To tell you true, I cannot
endure to see the rabble of these ground *ciarlitani*,[4] that
spread their cloaks on the pavement as if they meant to do
feats of activity° and then come in lamely with their   *acrobatics*
moldy tales out of Boccaccio, like stale Tabarine,[5] the
55 fabulist: some of them discoursing their travels and of
their tedious captivity in the Turks' galleys, when indeed,
were the truth known, they were the Christians' galleys,
where very temperately they ate bread and drunk water
as a wholesome penance, enjoined them by their confes-
60 sors, for base pilferies.

POLITIC [*to* PEREGRINE] Note but his bearing and contempt of these.

VOLPONE These turdy-facy-nasty-paty-lousy-fartical rogues,

---

7. A clown serving as a mountebank's assistant.

8. The arcade along the north side of the Piazza di San Marco, where the senior government officials (the procurators) resided.

9. Ask the same question (see lines 25–27).

1. That is, forced by poverty to sell my goods cheaply.

2. A fictitious rival mountebank.

3. Apparently a euphemism for mistress.

Pietro Bembo (1470–1547), a Venetian scholar and humanist.

4. Charlatans (Italian) who worked on the ground rather than a platform. All subsequent translations are from Italian, unless otherwise specified.

5. A performer in an Italian comic troupe that performed in France in 1572. Giovanni Boccaccio (1313–1375), Italian writer best known for the *Decameron*, a collection of stories.

with one poor groatsworth° of unprepared antimony[6] finely   *fourpence worth*
65   wrapped up in several *scartoccios*° are able very well to   *paper envelopes*
kill their twenty a week, and play; yet these meager
starved spirits, who have half stopped the organs of their
minds with earthy oppilations;° want° not their favorers   *obstructions / lack*
among your shriveled, salad-eating artisans, who are
70   overjoyed that they may have their ha'p'orth° of physic;   *halfpenny worth*
though it purge 'em into another world, 't makes no matter.
POLITIC   Excellent! Ha' you heard better language, sir?
VOLPONE   Well, let 'em go.° And, gentlemen, honorable   *say no more about them*
gentlemen, know that for this time, our bank, being thus
75   removed from the clamors of the *canaglia*;° shall be the   *rabble*
scene of pleasure and delight. For I have nothing to sell,
little or nothing to sell.
POLITIC   I told you, sir, his end.
PEREGRINE   You did so, sir.
VOLPONE   I protest, I and my six servants are not able to
80   make of this precious liquor so fast as it is fetched away
from my lodging by gentlemen of your city, strangers° of   *foreigners*
the *terra firma*,[7] worshipful° merchants, ay, and senators   *(honorific title)*
too, who ever since my arrival have detained me to their
uses by their splendidous liberalities. And worthily. For
85   what avails your rich man to have his magazines° stuffed   *storehouses*
with *moscadelli*[8] or of° the purest grape, when his cians physi-   *wine of*
cians prescribe him (on pain of death) to drink nothing
but water cocted° with anise seeds? Oh, health, health!   *boiled*
The blessing of the rich! The riches of the poor! Who
90   can buy thee at too dear a rate, since there is no enjoying
this world without thee? Be not then so sparing of your
purses, honorable gentlemen, as to abridge the natural
course of life—
PEREGRINE   You see his end?
POLITIC   Ay, is't not good?
95 VOLPONE   For when a humid flux° or catarrh, by the muta-   *runny discharge*
bility of air, falls from your head into an arm or shoulder
or any other part, take you a ducat° or your *cecchine* of   *a gold coin*
gold and apply to the place affected; see what good effect
it can work. No, no, 'tis this blessed *unguento*,° this rare   *ointment*
100   extraction, that hath only power to disperse all malignant
humors that proceed either of hot, cold, moist, or windy
causes[9]—
PEREGRINE   I would he had put in "dry," too.
POLITIC   Pray you, observe.

---

6. A white metallic substance (native trisul-phide) used in alchemy, in cosmetics, and in medicine (notably, as an emetic); in larger quantities it is poisonous.
7. Solid ground (Latin), here referring to the mainland territories of Venice.
8. Muscatel wine.
9. According to Renaissance medical theory, physical and mental health were determined by the relative balance—or imbalance—of four bodily fluids, or humors, which correspond to the four elements: air (hot and moist), linked to the sanguine temperament; water (cold and moist), to the phlegmatic; fire (hot and dry), to the choleric; and earth (cold and dry), to the melancholic. In listing the qualities that define the humors, Volpone omits "dry," as Peregrine points out.

VOLPONE To fortify the most indigest and crude° stomach, ay, sour

105 were it of one that, through extreme weakness, vomited
blood, applying only a warm napkin to the place after the
unction and fricace,° for the *vertigine°* in the head putting massage / dizziness
but a drop into your nostrils, likewise behind the ears, a
most sovereign° and approved remedy; the *mal caduco,* potent

110 cramps, convulsions, paralyses, epilepsies, *tremor cordia,* retired nerves, ill vapors of the spleen, stoppings of
the liver, the stone, the strangury, *hernia ventosa, iliaca
passio;* stops a *dysenteria* immediately; easeth the torsion
of the small guts; and cures *melancholia hypochondri-*

115 *aca,*[1] being taken and applied according to my printed
receipt.° [*Pointing to his bill and his glass.*] For this is the direction
physician, this the medicine; this counsels, this cures;
this gives the direction, this works the effect; and in sum,
both together may be termed an abstract of the theoric

120 and practic in the Aesculapian[2] art. 'Twill cost you eight
crowns. And, Zan Fritatta,[3] pray thee sing a verse extempore in honor of it.

POLITIC How do you like him, sir?

PEREGRINE Most strangely, I!

POLITIC Is not his language rare?

PEREGRINE But° alchemy Except for

125 I never heard the like, or Broughton's books.[4]

SONG

NANO [*sings*] Had old Hippocrates or Galen[5]
    That to their books put med'cines all in,
    But known this secret, they had never
    (Of which they will be guilty ever)

130   Been murderers of so much paper,
    Or wasted many a hurtless taper,[6]
    No Indian drug had e'er been famed,
    Tobacco, sassafras[7] not named,
    Ne° yet of *guacum*[8] one small stick, sir, Nor

135   Nor Raymond Lully's great elixir.[9]
    Ne had been known the Danish Gonswart
    Or Paracelsus with his long sword.[1]

1. The listed diseases include epilepsy (*mal caduco*), heart palpitations (*tremor cordia;* Latin),
shrunken sinews (retired nerves), kidney stones
(stone), painful urination (stranguary), hernia
filled with gas (*hernia ventosa;* Latin), intestinal
cramps (*iliaca passio;* Latin), and depression
(*melancholia hypochondriaca;* Latin).
2. Medical. Aesculapius was the classical god
of medicine.
3. Jack Pancake (Italian dialect), here referring to Nano the zany.
4. Hugh Broughton (1549–1612), a Puritan
scholar and divine who wrote obscure books
on religious subjects.
5. Two famous Greek physicians; Galen (ca.
130–ca. 200) developed the humoral theory,

possibly building on the ideas of Hippocrates
(ca. 460–ca. 377 B.C.E.).
6. Harmless candle (wasted by their working
at night).
7. New World plants, used medicinally.
8. The resin of the guaiacum tree of the West
Indies, used medicinally.
9. The elixir of life, rumored to have been
discovered by Lully (ca. 1232–1315), a Spanish philosopher, missionary, and astrologer.
1. Paracelsus (1493–1541), a German physician and alchemist (born Phillip von Hohen-
heim), was said to have carried secret
medicines in the pommel of his sword. Scholars have been unable to identify "Gonswart."

PEREGRINE   All this yet will not do; eight crowns is high.
VOLPONE [*to* NANO]   No more.—Gentlemen, if I had but time
140   to discourse to you the miraculous effects of this my oil,
surnamed *oglio del Scoto*,° with the countless catalogue   *oil of Scoto*
of those I have cured of th'aforesaid and many more dis-
eases, the patents and privileges of all the princes and commonwealths of Christendom, or but the depositions of those
145   that appeared on my part before the signory of the *Sanità*[2]
and most learned College of Physicians, where I was
authorized, upon notice taken of the admirable virtues
of my medicaments and mine own excellency in matter
of rare and unknown secrets, not only to disperse them
150   publicly in this famous city but in all the territories that
happily joy under the government of the most pious and
magnificent states of Italy. But may some other gallant
fellow say, "Oh, there be divers that make profession° to   *many that claim*
have as good and as experimented receipts as yours." In-
155   deed, very many have assayed like apes in imitation of
that which is really and essentially in me, to make of this
oil; bestowed great cost in furnaces, stills, alembics, continual fires, and preparation of the ingredients (as indeed
there goes to it six hundred several simples,° besides   *different ingredients*
160   some quantity of human fat for the conglutination,°   *to glue it together*
which we buy of the anatomists); but, when these practi-
tioners come to the last decoction,° blow, blow, puff,   *boiling down*
puff, and all flies *in fumo*.° Ha, ha, ha! Poor wretches!   *up in smoke*
I rather pity their folly and indiscretion° than their loss   *lack of discernment*
165   of time and money; for those may be recovered by indus-
try, but to be a fool born is a disease incurable. For myself, I always from my youth have endeavored to get the
rarest secrets and book° them, either in exchange or for   *record*
money; I spared nor° cost nor labor where anything was   *neither*
170   worthy to be learned. And, gentlemen, honorable gentle-
men, I will undertake, by virtue of chemical art, out of
the honorable hat that covers your head to extract the
four elements—that is to say, the fire, air, water, and
earth—and return you your felt° without burn or stain.   *felt hat*
175   For, whilst others have been at the balloo[3] I have been at
my book, and am now past the craggy paths of study and
come to the flow'ry plains of honor and reputation.
POLITIC   I do assure you, sir, that is his aim.
180   VOLPONE   But to our price.
PEREGRINE   And that withal,° Sir Pol.   *as well*
VOLPONE   You all know, honorable gentlemen, I never valued
this *ampulla*, or vial, at less than eight crowns, but for this
time I am content to be deprived of it for six; six crowns is
the price, and less, in courtesy, I know you cannot offer me.

2. The Venetian board that granted medical   3. Balloon (a Venetian game played with an
licenses.   inflated leather ball).

Take it or leave it howsoever, both it and I am at your ser-
185 vice. I ask you not as the value of the thing, for then I
should demand of you a thousand crowns; so the Cardinals Montalto, Fernese, the great Duke of Tuscany my
gossip,[4] with divers other princes, have given me. But I
despise money. Only to show my affection to you,
190 honorable gentlemen, and your illustrious state here, I
have neglected the messages of these princes, mine own
offices,° framed° my journey hither only to present you   *duties / directed*
with the fruits of my travels. [*To* NANO *and* MOSCA] Tune
your voices once more to the touch of your instruments,
195 and give the honorable assembly some delightful recreation.
PEREGRINE   What monstrous and most painful circum-
    stance°   *beating around the bush*
Is here, to get some three or four *gazets!*°   *small Venetian coins*
Some threepence, i'th'whole, for that 'twill come to.

SONG

[*During the song,* CELIA *appears at her window, above.*]
NANO [*sings*]°   You that would last long, list to my song,   *(accompanied by Mosca)*
200   Make no more coil,° but buy of this oil.   *fuss; noisy disturbance*
             Would you be ever fair and young?
             Stout of teeth and strong of tongue?
             Tart° of palate? Quick of ear?   *Keen*
             Sharp of sight? Of nostril clear?
205   Moist of hand[5] and light of foot?
             Or (I will come nearer to't)
             Would you live free from all diseases,
             Do the act your mistress pleases,
             Yet fright all aches° from your bones?   *i.e., syphilis*
210   Here's a med'cine for the nones.°   *occasion*
VOLPONE   Well, I am in a humor at this time to make a present of the small quantity my coffer contains: to the rich in
courtesy, and to the poor for God's sake. Wherefore, now
mark; I asked you six crowns, and six crowns at other
215 times you have paid me. You shall not give me six crowns,
nor five, nor four, nor three, nor two, nor one, nor half a
ducat, no, nor a *moccenigo*.° Sixpence it will cost you,   *small Venetian coin*
or six hundred pound—expect no lower price, for by the
banner of my front, I will not bate a *bagatine*,[6] that I will
220 have only a pledge of your loves, to carry something from
amongst you to show I am not contemned° by you.   *despised*

---

4. Familiar acquaintance. Cardinal Montalto (1521–1590), born Felice Peretti, became Pope Sixtus V in 1585. *Fernese:* either Alessandro Farnese (1468–1549), who became Pope Paul III in 1543, or his grandson Alessandro Farnese (1520–1589), who was appointed cardinal that same year. *Duke of Tuscany:* a title held by Cosimo de' Medici (1519–1574) after 1569.

5. Believed to be a sign of youth and lustfulness.

6. That is, I won't lower my price by even a small coin. *Banner of my front:* the banner displayed on the front of the mountebank's stand.

Therefore now, toss your handkerchiefs[7] cheerfully,
cheerfully, and be advertised° that the first heroic spirit   *take note*
that deigns to grace me with a handkerchief, I will give it
225   a little remembrance of something beside, shall° please   *which will*
it better than if I had presented it with a double *pistolet*.°   *gold coin*
PEREGRINE   Will you be that heroic spark,° Sir Pol?   *gallant*

[CELIA *at the window throws down her handkerchief*
with a coin tied inside it.]

Oh, see! The window has prevented° you.   *anticipated*
VOLPONE   Lady, I kiss your bounty, and, for this timely
230   grace you have done your poor Scoto of Mantua, I will
return you, over and above my oil, a secret of that high
and inestimable nature shall° make you forever enamored   *that will*
on that minute wherein your eye first descended on
so mean,° yet not altogether to be despised, an object.   *lowly*
235   Here is a powder concealed in this paper of which, if I
should speak to the worth, nine thousand volumes were
but as one page, that page as a line, that line as a word—so
short is this pilgrimage of man, which some call life, to°   *compared to*
the expressing of it. Would I reflect on the price, why,
240   the whole world were but as an empire, that empire as a
province, that province as a bank, that bank as a private
purse, to the purchase of it. I will only tell you it is the
powder that made Venus a goddess, given her by Apollo,[8]
that kept her perpetually young, cleared her wrinkles,
245   firmed her gums, filled her skin, colored her hair; from
her derived to Helen,[9] and at the sack of Troy unfortunately lost; till now in this our age it was as happily° re-   *fortunately*
covered by a studious antiquary out of some ruins of Asia,
who sent a moiety° of it to the court of France (but much   *portion*
250   sophisticated)° wherewith the ladies there now color their   *adulterated*
hair. The rest, at this present, remains with me, extracted
to a quintessence, so that wherever it but touches, in
youth it perpetually preserves, in age restores the complexion; seats your teeth, did° they dance like virginal   *even if*
255   jacks,[1] firm as a wall; makes them white as ivory that were
black as—

2.3

[SCENE: *The scene continues.*]

[*Enter* CORVINO. *He beats away the mountebank, etc.*]
CORVINO   Spite o'the devil, and my shame! Come down here,
Come down! No house but mine to make your scene?°   *stage set*

---

7. That is, with money knotted in their
corners.
8. The classical god of healing, as well as
prophecy and light.
9. Helen of Troy, the most beautiful woman
in the world.

1. The virginal is an instrument in the harpsichord family; its "jacks" are strips of wood to
which are attached the quills that pluck the
strings when its keys are depressed. The term
is sometimes (inaccurately) applied to the
keys themselves.

Signor Flaminio, will you down, sir? Down!
What, is my wife your Franciscina, sir?[2]
5   No windows on the whole piazza here
To make your properties° but mine? But mine?   *stage props; set*
Heart! Ere tomorrow I shall be new christened
And called the *pantalone di besogniosi*[3]
About the town.

        [*Exeunt* VOLPONE, NANO, *and* MOSCA,
        followed by CORVINO *and the crowd.*]

PEREGRINE   What should this mean, Sir Pol?
10 POLITIC   Some trick of state, believe it. I will home.
PEREGRINE   It may be some design on you.
POLITIC   I know not.
I'll stand upon my guard.
PEREGRINE   It is your best,° sir.   *best course of action*
POLITIC   This three weeks, all my advices, all my letters,
They have been intercepted,
PEREGRINE   Indeed, sir?
15 Best have a care.
POLITIC   Nay, so I will.   [*Exit.*]
PEREGRINE   This knight,
I may not lose him,° for my mirth, till night.   [*Exit.*]   *I will not leave him*

2.4

[SCENE: VOLPONE'*s house.*]

[*Enter* VOLPONE *and* MOSCA.]

VOLPONE   Oh, I am wounded!
MOSCA   Where, sir?
VOLPONE   Not without;°   *on the outside*
Those blows were nothing; I could bear them ever,
But angry Cupid, bolting° from her eyes,   *shooting arrows*
Hath shot himself into me like a flame,
5   Where now he flings about his burning heat,
As in a furnace an ambitious° fire   *rising*
Whose vent is stopped. The fight is all within me.
I cannot live except thou help me, Mosca;
My liver[4] melts, and I, without the hope
10 Of some soft air from her refreshing breath,
Am but a heap of cinders.
MOSCA   'Las, good sir!
Would you had never seen her.
VOLPONE   Nay, would thou
Hadst never told me of her.
MOSCA   Sir, 'tis true;

---

2. Conventional names from the Italian commedia dell'arte: Flaminio was the young lover (named after the famous actor Flaminio Scala); Franciscina, the amorous servant girl.
3. Pantalone (here, "from a line of paupers")
was a stock character in the commedia dell'arte, an old man often depicted as a cuckold.
4. Supposed to be the seat of violent passions such as love and hate.

I do confess I was unfortunate,

15 And you unhappy; but I'm bound in conscience
No less than duty to effect my best
To your release of torment, and I will, sir.

VOLPONE   Dear Mosca, shall I hope?

MOSCA   Sir, more than dear,
I will not bid you to despair of aught

20 Within a human compass.°   *That's humanly possible*

VOLPONE   Oh, there spoke
My better angel. Mosca, take my keys.
Gold, plate, and jewels, all's at thy devotion;°   *disposal*
Employ them how thou wilt; nay, coin me° too,   *turn me into coins*
So° thou in this but crown my longings. Mosca?   *Provided that*

25 MOSCA   Use but your patience.

VOLPONE   So I have.

MOSCA   I doubt not
To bring success to your desires.

VOLPONE   Nay, then,
I not° repent me of my late° disguise.   *do not / recent*

MOSCA   If you can horn him,[5] sir, you need not.

VOLPONE   True;
Besides, I never meant him for my heir.

30 Is not the color o'my beard and eyebrows[6]
To make me known?

MOSCA   No jot.

VOLPONE   I did it well.

MOSCA   So well, would I could follow you in mine
With half the happiness.° And yet I would   *aptitude; success*
Escape your epilogue.°   *i.e., the beating*

VOLPONE   But were they gulled°   *fooled*

35 With a belief that I was Scoto?

MOSCA   Sir,
Scoto himself could hardly have distinguished!
I have not time to flatter you now. We'll part,
And, as I prosper, so applaud my art.

                                    [*Exeunt.*]

2.5

[SCENE: CORVINO's *house.*]

        [*Enter* CORVINO *and* CELIA.]

CORVINO   Death of mine honor, with the city's fool?
A juggling, tooth-drawing,[7] prating° mountebank?   *chattering*
And at a public window? Where, whilst he
With his strained action° and his dole of faces[8]   *exaggerated gestures*

5 To his drug lecture draws your itching ears,

---

5. Give him a pair of horns; that is, cuckold
him.
6. Red, the color of foxes.

7. Tooth extraction was practiced by mountebanks and barbers.
8. Small repertoire of facial expressions.

A crew of old, unmarried, noted lechers
Stood leering up like satyrs;[9] and you smile
Most graciously! And fan your favors forth
To give your hot spectators satisfaction!
10 What, was your mountebank their call? Their whistle?[1]
Or were you enamored on his copper rings?
His saffron jewel with the toadstone[2] in't?
Or his embroidered suit with the cope-stitch,°   *large, showy stitch*
Made of a hearse-cloth?° Or his old tilt-feather?[3]   *coffin drapery*
15 Or his starched beard? Well! You shall have him, yes.
He shall come home and minister unto you
The fricace for the mother.[4] Or, let me see,
I think you'd rather mount?[5] Would you not mount?
Why, if you'll mount, you may; yes truly, you may—
20 And so you may be seen down to th'foot.
Get you a cittern, Lady Vanity,[6]
And be a dealer° with the virtuous man.°   *prostitute / virtuoso*
Make one.[7] I'll but protest° myself a cuckold   *proclaim*
And save your dowry.[8] I am a Dutchman, I!
25 For if you thought me an Italian,
You would be damned ere you did this, you whore.[9]
Thou'dst tremble to imagine that the murder
Of father, mother, brother, all thy race,
Should follow as the subject of my justice!
30 CELIA   Good sir, have patience!
CORVINO [*drawing a weapon*]   What couldst thou propose
Less to thyself[1] than, in this heat of wrath
And stung with my dishonor, I should strike
This steel unto thee, with as many stabs
As thou wert gazed upon with goatish° eyes?   *lustful*
35 CELIA   Alas, sir, be appeased! I could not think
My being at the window should more now
Move your impatience than at other times.
CORVINO   No? Not to seek and entertain a parley°   *have a conversation*
With a known knave? Before a multitude?
40 You were an actor with your handkerchief!
Which he most sweetly kissed in the receipt,
And might, no doubt, return it with a letter,
And 'point° the place where you might meet—your sister's,   *appoint*
Your mother's, or your aunt's might serve the turn.°   *do the trick*

---

9. In classical mythology, goat-footed beings connected with the god of the vine, lovers of wine and debauchery.
1. Used (like the "call") to lure game fowl.
2. One of a number of types of stone, believed to be found in the head of a toad and to have therapeutic qualities.
3. A feather from a helmet used in tilting.
4. A massage for the womb, believed to be the source of hysteria (with obvious sexual innuendo).

5. Imitate a mountebank; take the upper sexual position.
6. A character from morality drama.
7. Make a bargain; make a mate.
8. The husband of a proven adulteress could keep her dowry, which otherwise remained in her control.
9. Italians were held to be quick to anger and vengefulness, while the Dutch were viewed as phlegmatic.
1. What less could you expect.

45 CELIA   Why, dear sir, when do I make these excuses?
    Or ever stir abroad° but to the church?   *out of doors*
    And that, so seldom—
    CORVINO   Well, it shall be less;
    And thy restraint before was liberty
    To° what I now decree: and therefore, mark me.   *Compared with*
50 [*Pointing to the window*] First, I will have this bawdy light
    dammed up,°   *shut out*
    And, till't be done, some two or three yards off
    I'll chalk a line, o'er which if thou but chance
    To set thy desp'rate foot, more hell, more horror,
    More wild, remorseless rage shall seize on thee
55 Than on a conjurer that had heedless left
    His circle's safety ere his devil was laid.[2]
    Then here's a lock which I will hang upon thee.
           [*He shows a chastity belt.*]
    And now I think on't, I will keep thee backwards;°   *in the back of the house*
    Thy lodging shall be backwards, thy walks backwards,
60 Thy prospect°—all be backwards; and no pleasure   *view*
    That thou shalt know but backwards. Nay, since you force
    My honest nature, know it is your own
    Being too open makes me use you thus,
    Since you will not contain your subtle° nostrils   *cunning*
65 In a sweet room, but they must snuff the air
    Of rank and sweaty passengers°—   [*Knock within.*]   *passers by*
                 One knocks.
    Away, and be not seen, pain° of thy life!   *on pain*
    Not° look toward the window. If thou dost—   *Do not*
        [CELIA *begins to exit.*]
    Nay stay, hear this—let me not prosper, whore,
70 But I will make thee an anatomy,[3]
    Dissect thee mine own self, and read a lecture
    Upon thee to the city, and in public.
    Away!   [*Exit* CELIA.]
        Who's there?
        [*Enter Servitore, a* SERVANT.]
    SERVANT   'Tis Signor Mosca, sir.

2.6

[SCENE: *The scene continues.*]

CORVINO   Let him come in.   [*Exit* SERVANT.]
                  His master's dead! There's yet
    Some good to help the bad.
        [*Enter* MOSCA.]

---

2. Conjurers were safe within the magic circle they drew until the devils they raised were returned ("laid") to hell.

3. An object of moral analysis, with a suggestion of physical dissection.

My Mosca, welcome!
I guess your news.

MOSCA   I fear you cannot, sir.

CORVINO   Is't not his death?

MOSCA   Rather the contrary.

5 CORVINO   Not his recovery?

MOSCA   Yes, sir.

CORVINO   I am cursed,
I am bewitched! My crosses° meet to vex me!   *misfortunes*
How? How? How? How?

MOSCA   Why, sir, with Scoto's oil.
Corbaccio and Voltore brought of° it   *some of*
Whilst I was busy in an inner room—

10 CORVINO   Death! That damned mountebank! But° for the law,   *Were it not*
Now, I could kill the rascal. 'T cannot be
His oil should have that virtue. Ha' not I
Known him a common rogue, come fiddling in
To th'*osteria*° with a tumbling whore,   *inn*
15 And, when he has done all his forced° tricks, been glad   *contrived*
Of a poor spoonful of dead wine with flies in't?
It cannot be. All his ingredients
Are a sheep's gall, a roasted bitch's marrow,
Some few sod° earwigs, pounded caterpillars,   *boiled*
20 A little capon's grease, and fasting spittle:°   *saliva of a fasting man*
I know 'em to a dram.°   *i.e., a tiny amount*

MOSCA   I know not, sir,
But some on't there they poured into his ears,
Some in his nostrils, and recovered him,
Applying but the fricace.°   *massage*

CORVINO   Pox o'that fricace!

25 MOSCA   And since, to seem the more officious°   *dutiful*
And flatt'ring of his health, there they have had—
At extreme fees—the College of Physicians
Consulting on him how they might restore him;
Where one would have a cataplasm° of spices,   *poultice*
30 Another a flayed ape clapped to his breast,
A third would ha' it a dog, a fourth an oil
With wildcats' skins. At last, they all resolved
That to preserve him was no other means
But some young woman must be straight sought out,
35 Lusty and full of juice, to sleep by him;
And to this service—most unhappily
And most unwillingly—am I now employed,
Which here I thought to preacquaint you with,
For your advice, since it concerns you most,
40 Because I would not do that thing might cross°   *frustrate*
Your ends,° on whom I have my whole dependence, sir. *aims*
Yet if I do it not, they may delate°   *report*
My slackness to my patron, work me out
Of his opinion,° and there all your hopes,   *favor*

45   Ventures, or whatsoever, are all frustrate.
      I do but tell you, sir. Besides, they are all
      Now striving who shall first present him.° Therefore,   *(with a young woman)*
      I could entreat you briefly,° conclude somewhat;[4]   *quickly*
      Prevent 'em° if you can.   *Beat them to it*
    CORVINO   Death to my hopes!
50   This is my villainous fortune! Best to hire
      Some common courtesan.
    MOSCO   Ay, I thought on that, sir.
      But they are all so subtle,° full of art,°   *cunning / wiles*
      And age again[5] doting and flexible,°   *easily led*
      So as—I cannot tell—we may perchance
55   Light on a quean° may cheat us all.   *whore who*
    CORVINO   'Tis true.
    MOSCA   No, no; it must be one that has no tricks, sir,
      Some simple thing, a creature made unto it;[6]
      Some wench you may command. Ha' you no kinswoman?
      Godso°—think, think, think, think, think, think, think, sir.   *(an oath)*
60   One o'the doctors offered there his daughter.
    CORVINO   How!
    MOSCA   Yes, Signor Lupo,° the physician.   *wolf*
    CORVINO   His daughter?
    MOSCA   And a virgin, sir. Why, alas,
      He knows the state of's° body, what it is,   *(of Volpone's)*
      That naught can warm his blood, sir, but a fever,
65   Nor any incantation raise his spirit.°   *vigor; semen*
      A long forgetfulness hath seized that part.°   *i.e., his penis*
      Besides, sir, who shall know it? Some one or two—
    CORVINO   I pray thee give me leave.° [*He walks apart.*] If any   *excuse me*
      man
      But I had had this luck—The thing in 'tself,
70   I know, is nothing.—Wherefore should not I
      As well command my blood and my affections
      As this dull doctor? In the point of honor
      The cases are all one, of wife and daughter.
    MOSCA [*aside*]   I hear him coming.°   *coming around*
    CORVINO [*aside*]   She shall do't. 'Tis done.
75   'Slight,° if this doctor, who is not engaged,   *By God's light (an oath)*
      Unless 't be for his counsel (which is nothing),[7]
      Offer his daughter, what should I, that am
      So deeply in? I will prevent him. Wretch!
      Covetous wretch!—Mosca, I have determined.
80   MOSCA   How, sir?
    CORVINO   We'll make all sure. The party you wot° of   *know*
      Shall be mine own wife, Mosca.
    MOSCA   Sir, the thing°   *the very thing*

---

4. Decide something.
5. And old age, on the other hand.
6. Made for the part; forced into the part.

7. Who is not involved, except through his medical advice, which earns him nothing.

(But that I would not seem to counsel you)
I should have motioned° to you at the first.   *proposed*
And, make your count,° you have cut all their throats.   *count on it*
85   Why, 'tis directly taking a possession!⁸
And in his next fit we may let him go.
'Tis but to pull the pillow from his head
And he is throttled; 't had been done before,
But for your scrupulous doubts,
CORVINO   Ay, a plague on't!
90   My conscience fools my wit.° Well, I'll be brief,   *common sense*
And so be thou, lest they should be before us.
Go home, prepare him, tell him with what zeal
And willingness I do it; swear it was
On the first hearing (as thou mayst do, truly)
95   Mine own free motion.°   *unprompted proposal*
MOSCA   Sir, I warrant you,
I'll so possess him with it° that the rest   *influence his opinion*
Of his starved clients shall be banished all,
And only you received. But come not, sir,
Until I send, for I have something else
100 To ripen for your good; you must not know't.
CORVINO   But do not you forget to send, now.
MOSCO   Fear not.
                                                            [*Exit.*]

2.7

[SCENE: *The scene continues.*]

CORVINO   Where are you, wife? My Celia? Wife?
          [*Enter* CELIA *weeping*].
                                                What, blubbering?
Come, dry those tears. I think thou thought'st me in earnest?
Ha! By this light, I talked so but to try° thee.   *test*
Methinks the lightness° of the occasion   *triviality*
5   Should ha' confirmed° thee. Come, I am not jealous.   *reassured*
CELIA   No?
CORVINO   Faith, I am not, I, nor never was;
It is a poor, unprofitable humor.°   *mood*
Do not I know if women have a will
They'll do 'gainst° all the watches⁹ o'the world?   *despite*
10   And that the fiercest spies are tamed° with gold?   *bribed*
Tut, I am confident in thee, thou shalt see't;
And see, I'll give thee cause too, to believe it.
Come, kiss me. Go and make thee ready straight
In all thy best attire, thy choicest jewels;
15   Put 'em all on, and, with 'em thy best looks.

___

8. That is, taking possession of your inherited   9. Watchmen; precautions.
property.

We are invited to a solemn feast°   *formal banquet*
At old Volpone's, where it shall appear
How far I am free from jealousy or fear.

[Exeunt.]

3.1

[SCENE: *The piazza.*]

[*Enter* MOSCA.]

MOSCA   I fear I shall begin to grow in love
With my dear self and my most prosp'rous parts,°   *talents*
They do so spring and burgeon. I can feel
A whimsy° i'my blood. I know not how,   *giddiness*
5   Success hath made me wanton.° I could skip   *playful; reckless*
Out of my skin now like a subtle snake,
I am so limber. Oh, your parasite
Is a most precious thing, dropped from above,
Not bred 'mongst clods and clodpolls° here on earth.   *blockheads*
10   I muse the mystery was not made a science,[1]
It is so liberally professed!° Almost   *freely practiced*
All the wise world is little else in nature
But parasites or subparasites. And yet
I mean not those that have your bare town-art,[2]
15   To know who's fit to feed 'em; have no house,
No family, no care, and therefore mold
Tales[3] for men's ears, to bait that sense; or get
Kitchen-invention, and some stale receipts°   *recipes*
To please the belly and the groin; nor those,
20   With their court-dog tricks, that can fawn and fleer,°   *smile flatteringly*
Make their revenue out of legs and faces,[4]
Echo my lord, and lick away a moth;[5]
But your fine, elegant rascal, that can rise
And stoop almost together, like an arrow,
25   Shoot through the air as nimbly as a star,°   *meteor*
Turn short as doth a swallow, and be here
And there and here and yonder all at once,
Present to any humor, all occasion,[6]
And change a visor° swifter than a thought!   *mask; appearance*
30   This is the creature had° the art born with him,   *who had*
Toils not to learn it, but doth practice it
Out of most excellent nature,° and such sparks   *innate ability*
Are the true parasites, others but their zanies.°   *clownish assistants*

---

1. That is, I wonder that the craft was not made a branch of formal knowledge.
2. The crude skills of a street parasite.
3. Invent rumors or scandals.
4. Make their living by bowing and making servile faces.
5. That is, fuss obsequiously over a lord (literally, lick the vermin off his clothing).
6. That is, ready to respond to any mood or situation.

3.2

[SCENE: *The scene continues.*]

[*Enter* BONARIO.]

[*Aside*] Who's this? Bonario? Old Corbaccio's son?
The person I was bound° to seek.—Fair sir,   *on my way*
You are happ'ly met.

BONARIO   That cannot be by thee.

MOSCA Why, sir?

BONARIO   Nay, pray thee know thy way and leave me.
5   I would be loath to interchange discourse
With such a mate° as thou art.   *low fellow*

MOSCA   Courteous sir,
Scorn not my poverty.

BONARIO   Not I, by heaven,
But thou shalt give me leave to hate thy baseness.

MOSCA Baseness?

BONARIO   Ay. Answer me, is not thy sloth
10   Sufficient argument? Thy flattery?
Thy means of feeding?

MOSCA   Heaven, be good to me!
These imputations are too common, sir,
And eas'ly stuck on virtue when she's poor.
You are unequal[7] to me, and howe'er
15   Your sentence may be righteous, yet you are not,
That, ere you know me, thus proceed in censure.
Saint Mark° bear witness 'gainst you, 'tis inhuman.   *patron saint of Venice*
[*He weeps.*]

BONARIO [*aside*] What? Does he weep? The sign is soft and good.
I do repent me that I was so harsh.

20   MOSCA 'Tis true that, swayed by strong necessity,
I am enforced to eat my careful° bread   *hard-won*
With too much obsequy;° 'tis true, beside,   *deferential service*
That I am fair° to spin mine own poor raiment   *obliged*
Out of my mere observance,[8] being not born
25   To a free fortune. But that I have done
Base offices in rending friends asunder,
Dividing families, betraying counsels,
Whispering false lies, or mining° men with praises,   *undermining*
Trained° their credulity with perjuries,   *Led on*
30   Corrupted chastity, or am in love
With mine own tender ease, but would not rather
Prove° the most rugged and laborious course   *Undergo*
That might redeem my present estimation,°   *reputation*
Let me here perish in all hope of goodness.

35   BONARIO [*aside*] This cannot be a personated° passion!—   *feigned*
I was to blame, so to mistake thy nature;

---

7. Unjust; superior in station.   8. From dutiful service alone.

Pray thee forgive me, and speak out thy business.

MOSCA   Sir, it concerns you; and though I may seem

At first to make a main° offense in manners   *great*

40   And in my gratitude unto my master,

Yet for the pure love which I bear all right

And hatred of the wrong, I must reveal it.

This very hour your father is in purpose

To disinherit you—

BONARIO   How!

MOSCA   And thrust you forth

45   As a mere° stranger to his blood. 'Tis true, sir.   *absolute*

The work no way engageth me but° as   *except*

I claim an interest in the general state

Of goodness and true virtue, which I hear

T'abound in you, and for which mere respect,°   *for which reason alone*

50   Without a second aim° sir, I have done it.   *ulterior motive*

BONARIO   This tale hath lost thee much of the late° trust   *recent*

Thou hadst with me. It is impossible.

I know not how to lend it any thought°   *how to conceive that*

My father should be so unnatural.

55 MOSCA   It is a confidence that well becomes

Your piety;° and formed, no doubt, it is   *filial love*

From your own simple innocence, which makes

Your wrong[9] more monstrous and abhorred. But sir,

I now will tell you more. This very minute

60   It is or will be doing; and if you

Shall be but pleased to go with me, I'll bring you,

I dare not say where you shall see, but where

Your ear shall be a witness of the deed:

Hear yourself written bastard, and professed

65   The common issue of the earth°   *i.e., a bastard*

BONARIO   I'm mazed!

MOSCA   Sir, if I do it not, draw your just sword

And score your vengeance on my front° and face;   *forehead*

Mark me your villain. You have° too much wrong,   *have suffered*

And I do suffer for you, sir. My heart

70   Weeps blood in anguish—

BONARIO   Lead. I follow thee.

[Exeunt.]

3.3

[SCENE: VOLPONE's *house.*]

[*Enter* VOLPONE, NANO, ANDROGYNO, *and* CASTRONE.]

VOLPONE   Mosca stays long, methinks. Bring forth your sports

And help to make the wretched time more sweet.

NANO   Dwarf, fool, and eunuch, well met here we be.

A question it were now, whethere° of us three,   *which*

5   Being all the known delicates° of a rich man,   *acknowledged playthings*

---

9. That is, the wrong that has been done to you.

In pleasing him, claim the precedency can?

CASTRONE   I claim for myself.

ANDROGYNO   And so doth the fool.

NANO   'Tis foolish indeed; let me set you both to school.

First, for° your dwarf: he's little and witty,   *as for*

10 And everything, as° it is little, is pretty;   *insofar as*

Else why do men say to a creature of my shape,

So soon as they see him, "It's a pretty little ape"?

And why a pretty ape? But for pleasing imitation

Of greater men's action in a ridiculous fashion.

15 Beside, this feat° body of mine doth not crave   *elegant; trim*

Half the meat, drink, and cloth one of your bulks will have.

Admit your fool's face be the mother of laughter,

Yet for his brain, it must always come after;°   *come second*

And though that¹ do feed him, it's a pitiful case,

20 His body is beholding° to such a bad face.   *beholden*

> [*One knocks.*]

VOLPONE   Who's there? My couch. [*He lies down.*] Away, look,

Nano, see!

Give me my caps, first—go, inquire.

> [*Exeunt* NANO, ANDROGYNO, *and* CASTRONE.]

                              Now, Cupid

Send° it be Mosca, and with fair return!°   *Grant / profit*

> [*Enter* NANO.]

NANO   It is the beauteous Madam—

VOLPONE   Would-be—is it?

25 NANO   The same.

VOLPONE   Now, torment on me! Squire her in,

For she will enter or dwell here forever.

Nay, quickly, that my fit were past!   [*Exit* NANO.]

                                    I fear

A second hell, too, that my loathing this

Will quite expel my appetite to° the other.°   *for / (Celia)*

30 Would she were taking, now, her tedious leave.

Lord, how it threats me what I am to suffer!

3.4

[SCENE: *The scene continues.*]

> [*Enter* LADY WOULD-BE *and* NANO.]

LADY WOULD-BE [*to* NANO]   I thank you, good sir. Pray you signify

Unto your patron I am here.   [*Regarding herself in a mirror*]

This band°   *ruff, collar*

Shows not my neck enough. I trouble you, sir.

Let me request you, bid one of my women

5 Come hither to me.   [*Exit* NANO.]

                    In good faith, I am dressed

Most favorably today!° It is no matter;   (*spoken sarcastically*)

---

1. That is, the face, the mouth.

'Tis well enough.

    [*Enter* NANO *and* FIRST WOMAN.]

                Look, see, these petulant things!
How they have done this!

VOLPONE [*aside*]   I do feel the fever
Ent'ring in at mine ears. Oh, for a charm
To fright it hence!

LADY WOULD-BE [*to* FIRST WOMAN]   Come nearer. Is this curl

10   In his° right place? Or this? Why is this higher   *its*
Than all the rest? You ha' not washed your eyes yet?
Or do they not stand even° i'your head?   *level*
Where's your fellow? Call her.   [*Exit* FIRST WOMAN.]

NANO [*aside*]   Now Saint Mark
Deliver us! Anon she'll beat her women

15   Because her nose is red.

        [*Enter* FIRST *and* SECOND WOMEN.]

LADY WOULD-BE   I pray you, view
This tire,° forsooth. Are all things apt or no?   *headdress*

SECOND WOMAN   One hair a little here sticks out, forsooth.

LADY WOULD-BE   Does't so, forsooth? [*To* FIRST WOMAN] And
    where was your dear sight
When it did so, forsooth? What now? Bird-eyed?°   *Startled*

20   [*To* SECOND WOMAN]

And you, too? Pray you both approach and mend it.
        [*They tend to her.*]
Now, by that light, I muse° you're not ashamed!   *wonder that*
I, that have preached these things so oft unto you,
Read you the principles, argued all the grounds,
Disputed every fitness, every grace,

25   Called you to counsel of so frequent dressings—

NANO [*aside*]   More carefully than of your fame° or honor.   *reputation*

LADY WOULD-BE   Made you acquainted what an ample dowry
The knowledge of these things would be unto you,
Able alone to get your noble husbands

30   At your return,° and you thus to neglect it?   (*to England*)
Besides, you seeing what a curious° nation   *fastidious*
Th'Italians are, what will they say of me?
"The English lady cannot dress herself."
Here's a fine imputation to our country!

35   Well, go your ways, and stay i'the next room.
This fucus° was too coarse, too; it's no matter.   *skin cosmetic*
[*To* NANO] Good sir, you'll give 'em entertainment?°   *look after them*
               [*Exeunt* NANO *and* WOMEN.]

VOLPONE [*aside*]   The storm comes toward me.

LADY WOULD-BE [*approaching the bed*]   How does my Volp?

VOLPONE   Troubled with noise. I cannot sleep; I dreamt

40   That a strange Fury[2] entered now my house,

---

2. In Greek mythology, one of the Eumenides, monstrous female personifications of vengeance.

And with the dreadful tempest of her breath
Did cleave my roof asunder

LADY WOULD-BE   Believe me, and I
Had the most fearful dream, could I remember't—

VOLPONE [*aside*]   Out on° my fate! I ha' giv'n her the occasion   *Curses on*
45   How to torment me: she will tell me hers.

LADY WOULD-BE   Methought the golden mediocrity,[3]
Polite and delicate—

VOLPONE   Oh, if you do love me,
No more! I sweat and suffer at the mention
50   Of any dream. Feel how I tremble yet.

LADY WOULD-BE   Alas, good soul! The passion of the heart.°   *heartburn*
Seed pearl were good now, boiled with syrup of apples,
Tincture of gold and coral, citron pills,
Your elecampane root, myrobalans[4]

55 VOLPONE [*aside*]   Ay me, I have ta'en a grasshopper by the wing![5]

LADY WOULD-BE   Burnt silk and amber; you have muscadel
Good i'the house—

VOLPONE   You will not drink and part?

LADY WOULD-BE   No, fear not that. I doubt° we shall not get   *fear*
Some English saffron—half a dram would serve—
60   Your sixteen cloves, a little musk, dried mints,
Bugloss,[6] and barley-meal—

VOLPONE [*aside*]   She's in again.
Before I feigned diseases; now I have one.

LADY WOULD-BE   And these applied with a right scarlet cloth—

VOLPONE [*aside*]   Another flood of words! A very torrent!

65 LADY WOULD-BE   Shall I, sir, make you a poultice?

VOLPONE   No, no, no.
I'm very well; you need prescribe no more.

LADY WOULD-BE   I have a little studied physic, but now
I'm all for music, save i'the forenoons
An hour or two for painting. I would have
70   A lady indeed t' have all letters and arts,
Be able to discourse, to write, to paint,
But principal, as Plato[7] holds, your music
(And so does wise Pythagoras, I take it)
Is your true rapture, when there is concent°   *harmony*
75   In face, in voice, and clothes, and is indeed
Our sex's chiefest ornament.

VOLPONE   The poet[8]
As old in time as Plato, and as knowing,
Says that your highest female grace is silence.

---

3. Lady Would-be's error for "golden mean."
4. An astringent tropical fruit long used in the treatment of many illnesses. *Elecampane*: a perennial herb used as a stimulant.
5. That is, she is ceaselessly making noise.
6. An herb used in the treatment of melancholy and inflammation.

7. Greek philosopher (ca. 427–ca. 347 B.C.E.). In Plato's *Republic* (ca. 375 B.C.E.), Socrates describes music as the primary means of educating the soul.
8. The tragedian Sophocles (ca. 496–406 B.C.E.); the reference is to *Ajax* (ca. 450 B.C.E.).

LADY WOULD-BE   Which o' your poets? Petrarch? Or Tasso? Or Dante?
80   Guarini? Ariosto? Aretine?
    Cieco di Hadria?[9] I have read them all.
VOLPONE [aside]   Is everything a cause to my destruction?
LADY WOULD-BE [searching her garments]   I think I ha' two or three of 'em
    about me.
VOLPONE [aside]   The sun, the sea will sooner both stand still
85   Than her eternal tongue! Nothing can scape it.
LADY WOULD-BE   Here's Pastor Fide[1]—
VOLPONE [aside]   Profess obstinate silence,
    That's now my safest.
LADY WOULD-BE   All our English writers,
    I mean such as are happy° in th'Italian,   °fluent
    Will deign to steal out of this author mainly,
90   Almost as much as from Montaignié;[2]
    He has so modern and facile° a vein,   °graceful
    Fitting the time, and catching the court ear.
    Your Petrarch is more passionate, yet he,
    In days of sonneting, trusted 'em with much.[3]
95   Dante is hard, and few can understand him.
    But for a desperate° wit, there's Aretine!   °outrageous
    Only his pictures are a little obscene—
    You mark me not?
VOLPONE   Alas, my mind's perturbed.
LADY WOULD-BE   Why, in such cases we must cure ourselves,
100   Make use of our philosophy—
VOLPONE   Ay me!
LADY WOULD-BE   And, as we find our passions do rebel,
    Encounter° 'em with reason, or divert 'em   °Oppose
    By giving scope unto some other humor
    Of lesser danger—as in politic bodies°   °kingdoms; states
105   There's nothing more doth overwhelm the judgment
    And clouds the understanding than too much
    Settling and fixing and (as 'twere) subsiding[4]
    Upon one object. For the incorporating
    Of these same outward things into that part
110   Which we call mental leaves some certain feces°   °dregs
    That stop the organs and, as Plato says,

---

9. Lady Would-be mentions a number of famous Italian writers: Francesco Petrarca, or Petrarch (1304–1374), known for his love sonnets; Torquato Tasso (1544–1595), author of the epic poem *Jerusalem Delivered* (1581); Dante Alighieri (1265–1321), author of *The Divine Comedy* (1321); Giovanni Battista Guarini (1538–1612), poet, dramatist, and diplomat; Ludovico Ariosto (1474–1533), who wrote the epic poem *Orlando Furioso* (1516); and Pietro Aretino (1492–1556), satirist and poet best known to Jonson's contemporaries for the libertine poems he wrote to accompany a series of pornographic drawings by Giulio Romano (see line 97, below). Luigi Groto (1541–1585), known as Cieco di Hadria ("the blind man of Adria"), was a minor poet and playwright.
1. A pastoral play by Guarini (1590), published in English as *The Faithful Shepherd* (1647).
2. Michel de Montaigne (1533–1592), celebrated French essayist.
3. That is, entrusted later poets with much that they could borrow. Petrarch's sonnets were widely imitated by English poets in the 16th century.
4. These three verbs (like "incorporating," in the next line) are jargon from alchemy.

Assassinates our knowledge.

VOLPONE [*aside*]   Now, the spirit
Of patience help me!

LADY WOULD-BE   Come, in faith, I must
Visit you more o'days and make you well.

115   Laugh and be lusty.°   *merry*

VOLPONE [*aside*]   My good angel save me!

LADY WOULD-BE   There was but one sole man in all the world
With whom I e'er could sympathize, and he
Would lie you° often three, four hours together   *lie*
To hear me speak, and be sometime so rapt

120   As he would answer me quite from the purpose,
Like you—and you are like him, just. I'll discourse—
An't° be but only, sir, to bring you asleep—   *If it*
How we did spend our time and loves together
For some six years.

VOLPONE   Oh, oh, oh, oh, oh, oh!

125   LADY WOULD-BE   For we were *coaetani*° and brought up—   *the same age (Latin)*

VOLPONE [*aside*]   Some power, some fate, some fortune rescue me!

3.5

[SCENE: *The scene continues.*]

[*Enter* MOSCA.]

MOSCA   God save you, madam.

LADY WOULD-BE   Good sir.

VOLPONE [*aside to* MOSCA]   Mosca? Welcome,
Welcome to my redemption.

MOSCA [*to* VOLPONE]   Why, sir?

VOLPONE [*aside to* MOSCA]   Oh,
Rid me of this my torture quickly, there,
My madam with the everlasting voice!

5   The bells in time of pestilence ne'er made
Like noise, or were in that perpetual motion,[5]
The cockpit° comes not near it. All my house   *cockfighting arena*
But now steamed like a bath with her thick breath.
A lawyer could not have been heard, nor scarce

10   Another woman, such a hail of words
She has let fall. For hell's sake, rid her hence.

MOSCA [*aside to* VOLPONE]   Has she presented?°   *given a present*

VOLPONE [*aside to* MOSCA]   Oh, I do not care.
I'll take her absence upon any price,
With any loss.

MOSCA   Madam—

LADY WOULD-BE   I ha' brought your patron

15   A toy,° a cap here, of mine own work—   *trifle*

MOSCA [*taking it from her*]   'Tis well.

5. Because church bells rang to mark the death of parishioners, they sounded almost continuously in London during times of plague ("pestilence").

      I had forgot to tell you, I saw your knight
      Where you'd little think it—
LADY WOULD-BE   Where?
MOSCA   Marry,
      Where yet, if you make haste, you may apprehend him,
      Rowing upon the water in a gondole°   *gondola*
20   With the most cunning courtesan of Venice.
LADY WOULD-BE Is't true?
MOSCA   Pursue 'em, and believe your eyes.
      Leave me to make your gift.   [*Exit* LADY WOULD-BE.]
                    I knew 'twould take.°   *be effective*
      For lightly,° they that use themselves most license   *commonly*
      Are still° most jealous.   *always*
VOLPONE   Mosca, hearty thanks
25   For thy quick fiction and delivery of me.
      Now, to my hopes, what say'st thou?
          [*Enter* LADY WOULD-BE.]
LADY WOULD-BE   But do you hear, sir?
VOLPONE [*aside*] Again! I fear a paroxysm.°   *worsening of symptoms*
LADY WOULD-BE   Which way
      Rowed they together?
MOSCA   Toward the Rialto.[6]
LADY WOULD-BE I pray you, lend me your dwarf.
MOSCA   I pray you, take him.
          [*Exit* LADY WOULD-BE.]
30   Your hopes, sir, are like happy blossoms: fair,
      And promise timely fruit if you will stay°   *await*
      But the maturing. Keep you at your couch.
      Corbaccio will arrive straight with the will;
      When he is gone I'll tell you more.   [*Exit.*]
VOLPONE   My blood,
35   My spirits are returned. I am alive;
      And like your wanton gamester° at primero,[7]   *reckless gambler*
      Whose thought had whispered to him, not go less,
      Methinks I lie, and draw—for an encounter.[8]
         [*He gets into bed and closes the bed curtains.*]

3.6

[SCENE: *The scene continues.*]

         [*Enter* MOSCA *and* BONARIO. MOSCA *shows* BONARIO *to a
         hiding place.*]

MOSCA   Sir, here concealed you may hear all. But pray you
      Have patience, sir. [*One knocks.*] The same's your father knocks.
      I am compelled to leave you.

---

6. The commercial district of Venice.   from primero; "encounter" also has a sexual
7. A popular card game.   connotation.
8. Like "go less" and "draw," a technical term

BONARIO   Do so. Yet
   Cannot my thought imagine this a truth.
       [*He conceals himself.*]

3.7

      [*Enter* CORVINO *and* CELIA. MOSCA *crosses the stage to intercept
      them.*]

MOSCA   Death on me! You are come too soon. What meant you?
   Did not I say I would send?
CORVINO   Yes, but I feared
   You might forget it, and then they prevent° us.   *act before*
MOSCA [*aside*]   Prevent? Did e'er man haste so for his horns?°   *cuckold's horns*
5   A courtier would not ply it so for a place.[9]
     [*To* CORVINO] Well, now there's no helping it, stay here;
   I'll presently return.
       [*He crosses the stage to* BONARIO.]
CORVINO   Where are you, Celia?
   You know now wherefore I have brought you hither?
CELIA   Not well, except° you told me.   *except what*
CORVINO   Now I will.
10   Hark hither.   [CORVINO *and* CELIA *talk apart.*]
MOSCA [*to* BONARIO]   Sir, your father hath sent word
   It will be half an hour ere he come;
   And therefore, if you please to walk the while
   Into that gallery, at the upper end
   There are some books to entertain the time;
15   And I'll take care no man shall come unto you, sir.
BONARIO   Yes, I will stay there. [*aside*] I do doubt this fellow.
       [*He retires.*]
MOSCA   There, he is far enough; he can hear nothing.
   And for° his father, I can keep him off.   *as for*
       [MOSCA *joins* VOLPONE *and opens his bed curtains.*]
CORVINO [*to* CELIA]   Nay, now, there is no starting back, and therefore
20   Resolve upon it; I have so decreed.
   It must be done. Nor would I move't° afore,   *suggest it*
   Because I would avoid all shifts° and tricks   *evasions*
   That might deny me.
CELIA   Sir, let me beseech you,
   Affect not ° these strange trials. If you doubt   *Do not pretend to make*
25   My chastity, why, lock me up forever;
   Make me the heir of darkness. Let me live
   Where I may please° your fears, if not your trust.   *appease*
CORVINO   Believe it, I have no such humor, I.
   All that I speak, I mean; yet I am not mad,

---

9. That is, work so hard for a position at court.

30   Not horn-mad,[1] see you? Go to, show yourself
       Obedient, and a wife.

CELIA   O heaven!

CORVINO   I say it,
       Do so.

CELIA   Was this the train?°   *trap; stratagem*

CORVINO   I have told you reasons:
       What the physicians have set down; how much
       It may concern me; what my engagements are;
35   My means, and the necessity of those means
       For my recovery. Wherefore, if you be
       Loyal and mine, be won, respect my venture.°   *undertaking*

CELIA   Before your honor?

CORVINO   Honor? Tut, a breath.
       There's no such thing in nature; a mere term
40   Invented to awe fools. What is my gold
       The worse for touching? Clothes for being looked on?
       Why, this's no more. An old, decrepit wretch,
       That has no sense,° no sinew; takes his meat   *sensory awareness*
       With others' fingers; only knows to gape
45   When you do scald his gums; a voice, a shadow.
       And what can this man hurt you?

CELIA   Lord! What spirit
       Is this hath entered him?

CORVINO   And for° your fame,°   *as for / reputation*
       That's such a jig;° as if I would go tell it,   *trifle; joke*
       Cry it on the piazza! Who shall know it
50   But he that cannot speak it,° and this fellow°   *(Volpone) / (Mosca)*
       Whose lips are i'my pocket, save° yourself?   *except for*
       If you'll proclaim't, you may. I know no other
       Should come to know it.

CELIA   Are heaven and saints then nothing?
       Will they be blind or stupid?

CORVINO   How?

CELIA   Good sir,
55   Be jealous still, emulate them, and think
       What hate they burn with toward every sin.

CORVINO   I grant you, if I thought it were a sin
       I would not urge you. Should I offer this
       To some young Frenchman, or hot Tuscan blood
60   That had read Aretine, conned° all his prints,[2]   *learned by heart*
       Knew every quirk within lust's labyrinth,
       And were professed critic° in lechery,   *a qualified expert*
       And° I would look upon him and applaud him,   *If*
       This were a sin. But here 'tis contrary,
65   A pious work, mere charity, for physic,
       And honest polity° to assure mine own.[3]   *prudence*

---

1. That is, mad with the prospect of being a cuckold.
2. See 3.4.97, with note to 3.4.81.
3. That is, the inheritance.

PLAYS IN PERFORMANCE

OEDIPUS THE KING

Gerard Murphy (Oedipus), Joanne Pearce (Antigone) with Chorus at the Royal Shakespeare Company production of Sophocles' *Oedipus at Colonus* (part of the so-called Theban cycle, of which *Oedipus the King* is also a part) at the Swan Theatre, Stratford-upon-Avon, England (October 25, 1991). Members of the Chorus in this production wear masks, mimicking the conventions of classical productions. © Donald Cooper / Photostage

Oedipus the King is one of the most important plays in Western drama, and it continues to inspire directors, playwrights, and audiences around the world. At the same time, it is a Greek tragedy that was written for a theater that is very different from ours. No matter whether directors modernize the play or hark back to the very origins of theater, they must first study the particular type of Greek theater for which this play was originally written.

Classical Greek tragedy was performed in massive outdoor theaters (there were up to 20,000 seats at the theater at Epidaurus, for example) during annual civic festivals. The scale of the theaters required a highly stylized form of acting that in no way resembles modern realistic performance. Three performers played all the speaking parts, a feat achieved by having actors play multiple roles distinguished by the use of large masks. While the episodes composed of dialogue, such as Oedipus's confrontations with Tiresias and Creon, may resemble contemporary drama, modern audiences often have difficulty appreciating the Greek chorus. Perhaps that barrier becomes more manageable if one recognizes that the classical chorus has many similarities with a modern musical theater chorus: both provide background information that clarifies past events and relationships; both comment on the actions of the principal characters; and both move rhythmically around the stage.

Greek audiences also knew the myths and legends dramatized by the playwrights. In addition to participating in a civic and religious occasion, audiences could also appreciate a particular playwright's variation or take on an old story, noticing nuances and new emphases.

Tragedies like *Oedipus the King* confront many of the most basic questions of human existence: Why does the universe seem so cruel and indifferent to human suffering? What is our responsibility in this unfolding drama of life? The audience's identification with these universal dilemmas evokes a primal sense of pity and fear.

To assess modern productions, one can ask if those primal emotions are evoked and how that is accomplished. In 1954, director Tyrone Guthrie, founder of the Stratford Shakespeare Festival in Ontario, Canada, chose to create a highly stylized version of *Oedipus the King* in order to re-create the solemn, religious nature of the drama. He got the audience's attention at the beginning of the production by having a violent explosion shake the theater. The stage filled with smoke and

The National Theatre of Greece's 2000 production of *Oedipus the King.*
© Alberto Pizzoli / Sygma / Corbis

Ralph Fiennes (as Oedipus, standing) and Alan Howard (as Tiresias, lying on table) perform with artists of the company (as the Chorus) in the National Theatre of London's
2008 production. © Robbie Jack / Corbis

incense, and eventually the chorus emerged from this cloud. Dressed in earth-
toned rags, their faces were covered with gray, skeletal masks that one reviewer
compared to Edvard Munch's painting *The Scream*.[1] The principal characters all
wore heavily padded and draped costumes, gloves, masks, and elevated boots
(*kothurni*), making them appear larger than life. In place of possessing individual qualities, each character became an abstraction: King, Queen, Prophet.

Guthrie's interpretation of the play as a primitive, tribal ritual was, by all
accounts, highly effective. Oedipus's transition from the golden, powerful king to
a blood-stained exile led away by his daughters at the play's end managed to evoke
pity and terror in audiences.

The National Theatre of Greece's 2000 production of *Oedipus the King* used
the physical immensity of the Roman Colosseum as its backdrop. This production,
marking the reopening of that formidable space after a partial restoration, was the
first drama to be performed in the colosseum in fifteen hundred years. After its
world premiere in Rome, the production then toured to other sites, including the
ancient theater at Epidaurus and New York's City Center.

In contrast to Guthrie's ritualized production with its emphasis on the Chorus,
the National Theatre's production focused on the figure of Oedipus himself. Through
staging and costume choices, Oedipus was entirely separated from those around
him: As king he is distinct from the chorus, and as outcast he is isolated from
both family and society. It was this existential isolation that evoked pity and fear
in audiences.

1. Laurel Bowman, "Sophocles' Oedipus Rex," *Didaskalia* 4.1 (Spring 1997), www.didaskalia.net/
issues/vol4no1/bowmana.html, (accessed 4/16/13).

After more than twenty-four hundred years, *Oedipus the King* remains the ultimate detective story capable of stirring strong emotions in modern audiences. Whether the director chooses to focus on religious ceremony or on individual isolation as a strategy for seeking answers to Oedipus's mystery, Sophocles' masterpiece still resonates with modern audiences searching for their own place in the world.

M.P.

EVERYMAN

The Royal Shakespeare Company's 1996 production of *Everyman*, directed by Kathryn Hunter and Marcello Magni, featuring Joseph Mydell (center, holding staff) as the eponymous central character. © Donald Cooper Photostage

Everyman, a staple of university, community, and professional productions, has established itself as the most popular medieval play in the modern theatrical repertoire. After a period of several centuries during which *Everyman* was not produced, twentieth-century audiences were reintroduced to the play in 1901, when William Poel, founder of the English Stage Company, presented an outdoor production of *Everyman* in the courtyard of the Charterhouse, a former Carthusian monastery in London. The production, which was taken on tour under different directors in Britain and the United States between 1901 and the 1930s, was enormously successful, although some audience members were scandalized by the representation of God onstage, which many considered sacrilegious.

Originating in the medieval morality play tradition, *Everyman* presents unique challenges to modern directors, actors, and audiences. With characters named "Everyman," "Fellowship," and "Good Deeds," the play employs an allegorical structure largely at odds with the realism that dominates modern characterization, plot, and setting. Its action lacks the stage diversions that characterize other English morality plays, and the theological doctrine it advances reflects a late medieval, rather than a contemporary, belief system. The task of modern productions, therefore, is to bring *Everyman* to life for contemporary spectators.

Some productions, such as a 1981 student version staged with minimal scenery in the Princeton University Chapel, have allowed the play's simplicity to address the longing for spiritual values in a materialist world. As a way of highlighting this simplicity and underscoring the play's allegorical meanings, director Peter D. Arnott staged *Everyman* entirely with puppets in the 1960s. Other productions have sought to embed the play more specifically in the world of its audience. A 1992 production at St. Martin's College in Olympia, Washington, staged the play processionally at a series of locations across campus. Ending in a graveyard, this production made the play's concern with mortality palpably real. Some directors have adapted *Everyman* more radically to the modern world. In 1994, the Cornerstone Theatre Company, a Los Angeles-based company, staged a contemporary adaptation of the play entitled *Everyman at the Mall*. This production, which altered the text to suit its setting, was staged in service corridors and main mall locations in the Santa Monica Place Mall. Everyman was played by different actors in different guises—a well-dressed male executive, a suburban woman—and other characters were presented in contemporary incarnations: Goods was a mannequin in a store window, and Good Deeds was introduced as a hospital patient hooked up to an IV. Using the mall itself as part of its symbolic meaning—Everyman met Fellowship outside a jewelry story—*Everyman at the Mall* provided powerful commentary on the values of American consumer culture.

Two productions from well-respected professional companies in the 1990s also sought contemporary relevance in the 500-year-old text. In 1995, a production by Chicago's Steppenwolf Theatre Company gave the play an urban, industrial setting. With the back wall of the warehouse-like theater providing visual backdrop, the production's bare set was dominated by an industrial elevator that carried God to and from heaven. The actors wore T-shirts and sneakers that made them look, in the words of reviewer Ann James, "like they could have stepped off the streets of Chicago's trendy North Side."[2] Fellowship joined Everyman from a pickup basketball game. As a way of emphasizing Death's unpredictability and universal reach, director Frank Galati had a lottery before each performance to determine which of four ethnically diverse actors (black, East Indian, white, and Hispanic) would

2. Ann James, rev. of the Steppenwolf Theatre Company production of *Everyman, Christian Century,* Feb. 7, 1996.

Death selects Everyman in an erotically charged dance sequence in the 1995 production staged by Chicago's Steppenwolf Theatre Company and directed by Frank Galati. Photo © Michael Brosilow / Steppenwolf Theatre

play Everyman that night. God, for his part, was played by three actors representing the persons of the Trinity. Death, who was played by a woman, found Everyman in a dance club, where he was participating in an energetic, sexually suggestive dance scene. As if to underscore the allusion to a sexual landscape darkened by the arrival of AIDS, the Windy City Gay Men's Chorus provided music for the production from either side of the stage. In the play's concluding scene, Everyman descended into the grave with his shadow lengthening on the back wall; his release

Death looks on as Everyman begins his descent into the grave in the 1995 production directed by Frank Galati. © Michael Brosilow

into salvation was indicated by a white dove that flew over the audience into the back of the theater.

The following year, the Royal Shakespeare Company staged its own updated version of *Everyman*. This production, which opened in Stratford-upon-Avon, subsequently toured in England and was brought to New York, where it played at the Brooklyn Academy of Music in 1998. The production's two directors, Kathryn Hunter and Marcello Magni, staged *Everyman* in a stripped-down landscape of scorched earth strewn with rocks. In Robert Potter's words, these directors "devised an *Everyman* rooted in timeless everyday realities and unexpected stage traditions."[3] Everyman, played by African American actor Joseph Mydell, was introduced lying languidly in a tin bathtub, and when Death (played by a woman) later made her appearance he was dancing as part of a wedding scene. As part of the production's contemporary and occasionally carnivalesque style, Beauty wore one red high heel, the Five Wits arrived on a motorbike with sidecar, and the back-slapping Fellowship was followed by a two-piece band. Good Deeds was depicted as a Scottish peasant stuck in the ground until the moment Everyman confessed his sins. To stage Everyman's death, the directors had the actor return to the tin bathtub and slowly sink beneath the water. In the play's concluding sequence, Everyman rose from the tub and climbed the ladder to heaven, where he was welcomed to eternity in the arms of an angel.

S.G.

3. Robert Potter, "*Everyman* at the Millennium," unpublished paper read at the International Colloquium of the Société internationale pour l'étude du Théâtre Médiéval at Groningen, The Netherlands, July 2001, www.sitm.info/history/Groningen/potter.htm (accessed 5/9/13).

Gugu Mbatha-Raw as Ophelia and Jude Law as Hamlet in the 2009 Donmar Warehouse production of *Hamlet*. © Johan Persson / ArenaPAL

No play looms larger in the history of the stage than *Hamlet*. One of Shakespeare's most popular plays during his lifetime, *Hamlet* has an extensive production history in England and abroad. On September 5, 1607—only six or seven years after its first performance, in London—the play was staged on a merchant ship off the coast of Sierra Leone for an audience that included four native Africans, and nineteen years later it was produced in Germany by a touring company of English actors. In the centuries since, *Hamlet* has been performed in Bengali, Serbian, Japanese, and countless other languages. These productions have often reflected the political, intellectual, and psychological preoccupations of the eras and societies in which they arose. In Japan during the 1880s, the play was adapted to reflect the tenets of Confucian morality, while Laurence Olivier's athletic 1937 London performance was shaped by Sigmund Freud's theory of the "Oedipus complex," in which sons supposedly vie with their fathers for sexual possession of their mothers. In contexts as diverse as Tsarist Russia, apartheid South Africa, and the pre-Arab Spring Middle East, productions of *Hamlet* have been given explicitly political meanings, with Hamlet clearly the dissident in Claudius's repressive court.

The character of Hamlet, of course, is one of the greatest roles in the Western dramatic canon. A figure of mercurial temperament who alternates between self-scrutiny and precipitous bursts of action and who delivers some of the most famous lines ever written, Shakespeare's melancholy Dane has been played by many of the world's leading actors. In the English-speaking world, the legacy of great Hamlets began with Richard Burbage, the leading tragic actor in Shakespeare's company, and continued over the centuries with actors such as Thomas Betterton, David Garrick, John Philip Kemble, Edmund Kean, John Gielgud, and Richard Burton. The description in playwright Hannah More's memoir of Garrick's 1776 portrayal suggests the multifaceted possibilities of this complex role: "Whether in the simulation of madness, in the sinkings of despair, in the familiarity of friendship, in the whirlwind of passion, or in the meltings of tenderness, he never once forgot he was a prince; and in every variety of situation, and transition of feeling, you discovered the highest polish of fine breeding and courtly manners."[4] The list of great Hamlet performers also includes such women actors as Sarah Bernhardt, Eva Le Gallienne, and German actress Angela Winkler, who played the role in Berlin in 2000.

Taking their place in this rich theatrical tradition, contemporary productions have sought to bring *Hamlet* to life for present-day audiences. In the 1960s, a decade that saw the increasing disaffection of young people from the society around them, David Warner's Hamlet was a bored, angry college student decked out in a long red scarf. In Franco Zeffirelli's 1990 film, by contrast, *Lethal Weapon* actor Mel Gibson complicated his action hero to portray what critic Caryn James called "a visceral Hamlet, tortured by his own thoughts and passions, confused by his recognition of evil."[5]

The choice of Gibson for this role reflects a recent trend toward casting well-known film actors in stage and film productions of *Hamlet*. Two recent productions of *Hamlet* brought actors better known for screen performances to the stage. David Tennant, best known for his role in the popular British television series *Doctor Who*, played Shakespeare's prince in a 2008 Royal Shakespeare Company production directed by Gregory Doran. In the production's modern setting, Claudius's court was lavishly formal, with chandeliers, mirrored walls, and characters dressed in formal attire. Claudius himself was played by Patrick Stewart as a figure

4. William Roberts, *Memoires of the Life and Correspondence of Mrs. Hannah More* (New York: Harper and Brothers, 1834).

5. Caryn James, rev. of director Franco Zeffirelli's film *Hamlet, New York Times,* Dec. 19, 1990.

David Tennant addresses Yorick's skull in the 2008 Royal Shakespeare Company production of *Hamlet*. © Alastair Muir

of menacing calm. In contrast to the courtly world around him, Tennant's Hamlet was characterized by emotional intensity, volatility, and irreverence. Delivering his soliloquies with close attention to their emotional shifts and contradictions, Tennant also displayed a frenetic playfulness, imitating those around him and wearing Claudius's crown at a rakish angle. Although critic Michael Billington felt that the character's philosophical nature was underplayed in this production, he considered Tennant's performance original and powerful: "This is a Hamlet of quicksilver intelligence, mimetic vigor and wild humor: one of the funniest I've ever seen."[6] While Charles Spencer, too, praised Tennant's comic touches, he noted the emotional depth that lay behind them: "Tennant also communicates a deeply touching sense of grief and loneliness, as he battles against depression and the need to take a revenge for which he is temperamentally unfitted."[7]

In summer 2009, a production starring film actor Jude Law under the direction of Michael Grandage opened on the London West End. Produced by the Donmar Warehouse, one of London's most acclaimed theater companies, the production was designed, in part, to introduce new audiences to Shakespeare's masterpiece. Unlike the polished and gleaming interior of Doran's production, black castle walls loomed over Grandage's stage. The play's gray and black costumes intensified this monochromatic visual austerity. Against this backdrop, Grandage staged familiar scenes in unfamiliar ways: Law delivered Hamlet's "To be or not to be" soliloquy while shivering in a snowfall outside one of the castle doors, and the scene between Hamlet and his mother was staged from Polonius's point of view behind the curtain. Law's prince was marked by anger and brooding vulnerability, and critics were divided on the effectiveness of his portrayal. Henry Hitchings wrote: "He brings a rumpled charisma to the role: his Hamlet is both disgusted and dangerous. The soliloquies, though they offer larger reflections on the human condition, seem in Law's hands vividly personal."[8] On the other hand, Ben Brantley, who saw the play both in London and during its subsequent run in New York, found Law's portrayal lacking in introspection: "Mr. Law approaches his role with the focus, determination and adrenaline level of an Olympic track competitor staring down an endless line of hurdles."[9]

S.G.

6. Michael Billington, rev. of the Royal Shakespeare Company production of Hamlet, Guardian, Aug. 5, 2008.

7. Charles Spencer, rev. of the Royal Shakespeare Company production of Hamlet, Telegraph, Jan. 8, 2009.

8. Henry Hitchings, rev. of the Donmar Warehouse production of Hamlet, London Evening Standard, June 4, 2009.

9. Ben Brantley, rev. of the Donmar Warehouse production of Hamlet, New York Times, Oct, 7, 2009.

TARTUFFE

Kathryn Meisle as Madame Orgon and Henry Goodman in the title role in the 2003 Roundabout Theatre production of *Tartuffe.* © Joan Marcus

Plays that are considered "classics" have long been staples of both professional and collegiate theater repertoires. Such works usually date from the ancient Greek, Renaissance, Baroque, and modern eras and include better-known plays by Sophocles, Shakespeare, Molière, and Chekhov, among others. When contemporary directors are asked to stage these dramas, they face distinct challenges: how to make the classics relevant for audience members who have never seen them before; and how to keep them fresh for audience members who may have seen multiple previous productions.

The eminent critic Robert Brustein has stated that "the most controversial issue in the theater today continues to be the reinterpretation . . . of celebrated classical plays."[1] Some directors feel an obligation to a drama as it was first conceived and seek to offer a production that suggests its original context as closely

1. Robert Brustein, "Reworking the Classics: Homage or Ego Trip?" *New York Times,* Nov. 6, 1988.

as possible. Yet in trying to be historically faithful, directors may offer spectators "museum theater" that no longer seems vibrant. Other directors see scripts from earlier periods as opportunities for creative revisioning, but such "concept" productions may lose sight of a play's core dramaturgical qualities. Thus Brustein wonders, "Is classical reinterpretation a reinforcing or a defiling act?"

Today's directors of *Tartuffe* face exactly this conundrum. Joe Dowling, currently the artistic director of the Guthrie Theater in Minnesota, is known internationally for his stagings of classic works. In 2003, Dowling cast the respected British actors Brian Bedford (Orgon) and Henry Goodman (Tartuffe) in the Roundabout Theatre Company production on Broadway; Bedford received a Tony Award nomination for his portrayal. Dowling chose to retain the seventeenth-century setting of Molière's time for this production, which Ben Brantley of the *New York Times* claimed was given "ravishingly detailed physical life."[2] John Lee Beatty's scenic design rendered "Orgon's Paris town house as a wood-paneled, ormolu-accented temple to haute bourgeois affluence." Brian MacDevitt's lighting gave the sets the look of Old Master paintings, and Jane Greenwood executed what Charles Isherwood described in *Variety* as "painstakingly accurate period costumes."[3]

But for Brantley, what made the production "more than just another attractively upholstered revival" was the "psychological credibility" that Dowling emphasized with his actors. Especially for American audiences steeped in the psychological complexity of the twentieth-century stage, this directorial decision provided notable depth of character. Isherwood credited Bedford's performance in particular, observing that the actor "understands that it is by penetrating to the eternal psychological truth of Molière's characters that his plays can be made to thrive on stage today." The actors' ability to represent this characterological richness also reinforced the cogency of the play's themes. In this regard, critics pointed to then-current exposés of Washingtonian political hypocrisy, referencing public apologies by Senator Trent Lott and legally questionable directives by Attorney General John Ashcroft to exemplify the relevance of Molière's drama. Thus for this New York production, Dowling navigated between past and present, evoking tradition through design, while gesturing toward contemporaneity with current events and through the psychological truthfulness of character.

The recognition of parallels between the plot or theme of a classic play and events of some other era often prompts directors to set their entire productions in that other time, executing what Robert Brustein calls "simile" stagings—reinterpretations that foreground how the original moment of the drama is like another. This kind of concept is perhaps most frequently used for Shakespeare, but can be applied to any number of classic texts. The other form of reinterpretation Brustein often sees is the "metaphor" production, wherein directors "develop

2. Ben Brantley, "When an Apple Loves a Worm," *New York Times*, Jan. 10, 2003.
3. Charles Isherwood, "Kinder, Gentler Molière," *Variety*, Jan. 13–19, 2003.

The 2003 production of *Tartuffe* by New York's Roundabout Theatre Company, featuring Brian Bedford (standing) as Orgon and Henry Goodman as Tartuffe. Photo © Joan Marcus

provocative theatrical images" to reveal the script's "spiritual core." These stagings are arguably even more risky and may be seen as either brilliant reimaginings or self-indulgent excesses.

Interestingly, while directors of *Tartuffe* are increasingly gravitating toward "simile" or "metaphor" high-concept productions, critics appear to favor more traditional interpretations, or at least ones that, like Dowling's, retain many traditional elements. For the 2007 Yale Repertory Theatre production, director Daniel Fish developed what *New York Times* critic Sylviane Gold called a "time-travel conceit," set in "a contemporary space hung with two large video screens."[4] Noting the given that, regardless of setting, the audience is always in "today," Gold viewed the Fish interpretation as "too emphatically" insisting "on the primacy of this theatrical fact of life." The 1996 production at the American Repertory Theater featured a modernized adaptation of the text by Robert Auletta, which, together with the direction of François Rochaix, ran "a Magic Marker all over the work," according to Ed Siegel of the *Boston Globe*.[5] For this critic, "updating a play . . . is a double-edged sword. In order for it to resonate, more things have to work than not work." In Siegel's view, the production, set in "the world of music videos and recovered memories," not only "knocked the audience off its figurative feet," but also, "by mixing Molière's classicism with contemporary references," knocked "most of the actors off their feet as well."

For Australia's Malthouse Theatre, director Matthew Lutton worked with text adapter Louise Fox to set their 2008 production in twenty-first-century Melbourne. Featuring what critics agreed was a "gorgeous" set and all-white "fashionista" costumes designed by Anna Tregloan, their *Tartuffe* used a transverse playing space, with the audience seated in raked rows across from each other. The stage was dominated by a swimming pool "framed by sumptuous wrought-iron gates." Visually stunning as this may have been, critic Michael Connor felt that "Lutton's direction had more to do with the swimming pool than with hypocrisy or vice."[6] Moreover, Connor asserts, "when a play stars a swimming pool it will be swum in, fallen into, walked on and peed into." And for critic Martin Ball, the updated script, combined with the overpowering scenic environment, forced the actors into "overdrive, histrionically playing up their stereotypes and bellowing at the audience in righteous indignation," lending the production the overall feel of a "burlesque."[7]

Rejecting the notion of a definitive production of any classic work, Robert Brustein argues that "[t]exts develop fullness of being only through the continuing intervention of collective minds. . . . It is the proper role of theater to let us look at plays through a variety of perspectives rather than in a single authorized form."

4. Sylviane Gold, "Today, Would Tartuffe Have His Own Show?" *New York Times*, Dec. 16, 2007.

5. Ed Siegel, "Contemporary Spin Doesn't Help *Tartuffe*," *Boston Globe*, Feb. 16, 1996.

6. Michael Connor, "*Tartuffe* at the Malthouse," *Quadrant*, May 2008.

7. Martin Ball, "*Tartuffe* Is a Timeless Play Because Its Central Theme, Hypocrisy, Is Perennially Relevant," *The Age*, Feb. 22, 2008.

This modern-dress production of *Tartuffe* from Australia's Malthouse Theatre also features a sleek, contemporary scenic design by Anna Tregloan. © Jeff Busby

Whether a director chooses a traditional, a comparative, or a metaphorical approach, the staging of classic works presents infinite possibilities for creative exploration.

J.E.G.

CELIA   O heaven! Canst thou suffer such a change?
VOLPONE [*aside to* MOSCA]   Thou art mine honor, Mosca, and my pride,
  My joy, my tickling,° my delight! Go, bring 'em.   *amusement*
70 MOSCA [*to* CORVINO]   Please you draw near, sir.
  CORVINO [*dragging* CELIA *toward* VOLPONE]   Come on, what—
  You will not be rebellious? By that light—
  MOSCA [*to* VOLPONO]   Sir, Signor Corvino here is come to see you.
  VOLPONE   Oh!
  MOSCA   And, hearing of the consultation had
  So lately for your health, is come to offer,
75 Or rather, sir, to prostitute[4]—
  CORVINO   Thanks, sweet Mosca.
  MOSCA   Freely, unasked or unentreated—
  CORVINO   Well.
  MOSCA   As the true, fervent instance of his love,
  His own most fair and proper wife, the beauty
  Only of price° in Venice—   *Beyond compare*
  CORVINO   'Tis well urged.
80 MOSCA   To be your comfortress and to preserve you.
  VOLPONE   Alas, I am past already! Pray you, thank him
  For his good care and promptness. But for° that,   *as for*
  'Tis a vain labor e'en to fight 'gainst heaven,
  Applying fire to a stone (uh! uh! uh! uh!),
85 Making a dead leaf grow again. I take
  His wishes gently, though; and you may tell him
  What I have done for him. Marry,[5] my state is hopeless!
  Will° him to pray for me, and t' use his fortune   *Ask*
  With reverence when he comes to't.
  MOSCA [*to* CORVINO]   Do you hear, sir?
90 Go to him with your wife.
  CORVINO [*to* CELIA]   Heart of my father!°   *(an oath)*
  Wilt thou persist thus? Come, I pray thee, come.
  Thou see'st 'tis nothing. [*He threatens to strike her.*] Celia! By this hand,
  I shall grow violent. Come, do't, I say.
  CELIA   Sir, kill me, rather. I will take down poison,
95 Eat burning coals, do anything—
  CORVINO   Be damned!
  Heart! I will drag thee hence, home, by the hair,
  Cry thee a strumpet through the streets, rip up
  Thy mouth unto thine ears, and slit thy nose
  Like a raw rochet!°—Do not tempt me. Come,   *red gurnard (a fish)*
100 Yield! I am loath—Death!° I will buy some slave   *God's death (an oath)*
  Whom I will kill,[6] and bind thee to him alive,
  And at my window hang you forth, devising
  Some monstrous crime, which I in capital letters

---

4. With the usual sense of "prostitute" clearly
in mind, Mosca pretends to employ a less
common and now obsolete meaning, "offer
with complete and selfless devotion."
5. By the Virgin Mary (a mild oath).

6. In this passage, Corvino echoes the threats
made by Tarquinius Sextus, son of the last
king of Rome, before he raped Lucretia, the
virtuous wife of his cousin.

Will eat into thy flesh with *aquafortis*[7]
105 And burning cor'sives° on this stubborn breast.   *corrosives*
Now, by the blood thou hast incensed, I'll do't.
CELIA   Sir, what you please, you may; I am your martyr.
CORVINO   Be not thus obstinate. I ha' not deserved it.
Think who it is entreats you. Pray thee, sweet!
110 Good faith, thou shalt have jewels, gowns, attires,
What° thou wilt think and ask. Do but go kiss him.   *Whatever*
Or touch him but. For my sake. At my suit.
This once. No? Not? I shall remember this.
Will you disgrace me thus? Do you thirst my undoing?
115 MOSCA   Nay, gentle lady, be advised.
CORVINO   No, no.
She has watched her time, God's precious,[8] this is scurvy;°   *shabby,*
'Tis very scurvy, and you are—   *contemptible*
MOSCA   Nay, good, sir.
CORVINO   An arrant locust,° by heaven, a locust. Whore,   *destructive creature*
Crocodile,[9] that hast thy tears prepared,
120 Expecting° how thou'lt bid 'em flow!   *Anticipating*
MOSCA   Nay, pray you, sir,
She will consider.
CELIA   Would my life would serve
To satisfy—
CORVINO   'Sdeath, if she would but speak to him
And save my reputation, 'twere somewhat—
But spitefully to effect my utter ruin!
125 MOSCA   Ay, now you've put your fortune in her hands.
Why, i'faith, it is her modesty; I must quit° her.   *absolve*
If you were absent she would be more coming,°   *complaisant*
I know it, and dare undertake for her.
What woman can before her husband? Pray you,
130 Let us depart and leave her here.
CORVINO   Sweet Celia,
Thou mayst redeem all yet; I'll say no more.
If not, esteem yourself as lost.—Nay, stay there.
                [*Exeunt* CORVINO *and* MOSCA.]
CELIA   O God and his good angels! Whither, whither
Is shame fled human breasts, that with such ease
135 Men dare put off your° honors and their own?   *(God's and his angels')*
Is that which ever was a cause of life
Now placed beneath the basest circumstance,
And modesty an exile made for money?
           [VOLPONE *leaps off from his couch.*]
VOLPONE   Ay, in Corvino, and such earth-fed minds
140 That never tasted the true heav'n of love.

---

7. Nitric acid (literally, "strong water"; Latin).
8. God's precious blood (an oath). *Watched her time:* waited for her moment (to ruin me).
9. Said to weep, either to lure its victims (as here) or after eating them.

Assure thee, Celia, he that would sell thee
Only for hope of gain, and that uncertain,
He would have sold his part of paradise
For ready money, had he met a copeman.°   *merchant, dealer*
145   Why art thou mazed to see me thus revived?
Rather applaud thy beauty's miracle;
'Tis thy great work, that hath, not now alone
But sundry times raised me in several shapes,
And but this morning like a mountebank
150   To see thee at thy window. Ay, before
I would have left my practice° for thy love,   *scheming*
In varying figures° I would have contended   *shapes; disguises*
With the blue Proteus or the hornèd flood.[1]
Now art thou welcome.

CELIA   Sir!

VOLPONE   Nay, fly me not,
155   Nor let thy false imagination
That I was bedrid make thee think I am so.
Thou shalt not find it. I am now as fresh,
As hot, as high, and in as jovial plight°   *joyful condition*
As when—in that so celebrated scene,
160   At recitation of our comedy
For entertainment of the great Valois[2]
I acted young Antinoüs,[3] and attracted
The eyes and ears of all the ladies present,
T'admire each graceful gesture, note, and footing°   *step*

SONG

165   [*He sings.*]   Come, my Celia, let us prove,°   *put to the test*
While we can, the sports of love.
Time will not be ours forever;
He at length our good will sever.
Spend not then his gifts in vain.
170   Suns that set may rise again,
But if once we lose this light
'Tis with us perpetual night.
Why should we defer our joys?
Fame and rumor are but toys.
175   Cannot we delude the eyes
Of a few poor household spies?
Or his° easier ears beguile,   *(Corvino's)*
Thus removèd by our wile?
'Tis no sin love's fruits to steal,

1. That is, Achelous, a river god who wrestled with Heracles for the hand of Deianira; he was defeated in the form of a bull, and one of his horns broken off. *Proteus:* a sea god who had the power to assume any shape; one who held him fast could compel him to prophesy the future.

2. Henry of Valois (1551–1589), later King Henry III of France, was lavishly entertained on a visit to Venice in 1574.
3. The favorite of the Roman emperor Hadrian (r. 117–138 C.E.), celebrated for his physical beauty.

180 But the sweet thefts to reveal.
To be taken, to be seen,
These have crimes accounted been.

CELIA   Some serene° blast me, or dire lightning strike   *poisonous mist*
This my offending face!

VOLPONE   Why droops my Celia?

185 Thou hast in place of a base husband found
A worthy lover. Use thy fortune well,
With secrecy and pleasure. See, behold
What thou art queen of, not in expectation,
As I feed others, but possessed and crowned.

[*He reveals his treasures.*]

190 See here a rope of pearl, and each more orient°   *brilliant, precious*
Than that the brave° Egyptian queen caroused;[4]   *splendid*
Dissolve and drink 'em. See a carbuncle[5]
May put out both the eyes of our Saint Mark,
A diamond would° have bought Lollia Paulina[6]   *that would*
195 When she came in like starlight, hid with jewels
That were the spoils of provinces. Take these,
And wear, and lose 'em; yet remains an earring
To purchase them again, and this whole state.
A gem but° worth a private patrimony   *merely*
200 Is nothing; we will eat such at a meal.
The heads of parrots, tongues of nightingales,
The brains of peacocks and of ostriches
Shall be our food, and, could we° get the phoenix,[7]   *if only we could*
Though nature lost her kind,° she were our dish.   *i.e., it became extinct*

205 CELIA   Good sir, these things might move a mind affected
With such delights; but I, whose innocence
Is all I can think wealthy° or worth th'enjoying,   *valuable*
And which once lost, I have naught to lose beyond it,
Cannot be taken with these sensual baits.
210 If you have conscience—

VOLPONE   'Tis the beggar's virtue.
If thou hast wisdom, hear me, Celia.
Thy baths shall be the juice of July flowers,°   *carnations*
Spirit° of roses, and of violets,   *Essence*
The milk of unicorns, and panthers' breath[8]
215 Gathered in bags, and mixed with Cretan wines.
Our drink shall be preparèd gold and amber,
Which we will take° until my roof whirl round   *drink*

---

4. According to a story told in the 1st century
C.E. by the Roman scholar Pliny, Cleopatra (r.
51–30 B.C.E.) dissolved an enormous pearl in
vinegar and drank it during a banquet with
her lover, Mark Antony.
5. A red gemstone, believed able to emit light.
6. The third wife of the Roman emperor Caligula (r. 37–41 C.E.); a wealthy heiress, she
once arrived at a wedding dinner covered in
emeralds and pearls that had been gained by

the "spoil of provinces" (Pliny, *Natural History* 9.63).
7. A mythical bird, only one of which exists at
any time; every 500 years, it builds its own
funeral pyre, burns to death, and is reborn
from its own ashes.
8. Writers of medieval and Renaissance besti-
aries described panthers as having sweet-
smelling breath that attracted their prey.

With the vertigo; and my dwarf shall dance,
My eunuch sing, my fool make up the antic,°   *caper*
220 Whilst we, in changèd shapes, act Ovid's tales:[9]
Thou like Europa now and I like Jove,
Then I like Mars and thou like Erycine,[1]
So of the rest, till we have quite run through
And wearied all the fables of the gods.
225 Then will I have thee in more modern forms,
Attirèd like some sprightly dame of France,
Brave Tuscan lady, or proud Spanish beauty;
Sometimes unto the Persian Sophy's° wife,   *Shah's*
Or the Grand Signor's° mistress; and for change,   *Sultan of Turkey's*
230 To one of our most artful courtesans,
Or some quick° Negro, or cold Russian.   *lively*
And I will meet thee in as many shapes,
Where we may so transfuse° our wand'ring souls   *pour into each other*
Out at our lips, and score up sums of pleasures,
235 [*He sings.*]   That the curious shall not know
         How to tell° them as they flow;   *count*
         And the envious, when they find
         What their number is, be pined.°   *tormented*
CELIA   If you have ears that will be pierced, or eyes
240 That can be opened, a heart may be touched,
Or any part that yet sounds man[2] about you;
If you have touch of holy saints or heaven,
Do me the grace to let me scape. If not,
Be bountiful and kill me. You do know
245 I am a creature hither ill betrayed
By one whose shame I would forget it were.
If you will deign me neither of these graces,
Yet feed your wrath, sir, rather than your lust—
It is a vice comes nearer manliness—
250 And punish that unhappy crime of nature
Which you miscall my beauty. Flay my face
Or poison it with ointments for seducing
Your blood to this rebellion.[3] Rub these hands
With what may cause an eating leprosy
255 E'en to my bones and marrow—anything
That may disfavor me,° save in my honor—   *disfigure*
And I will kneel to you, pray for you, pay down
A thousand hourly vows, sir, for your health,
Report and think you virtuous—
VOLPONE   Think me cold,
260 Frozen, and impotent, and so report me?

9. From the *Metamorphosis* (ca. 10 C.E.) by the Roman poet Ovid (63 B.C.E.–17 C.E.), an epic poem that collects tales of transformations.
1. Jove or Jupiter, king of the gods, took the form of a bull to carry off Europa; Mars, god of war, and Venus, goddess of love (called

"Erycina" from her temple on Sicily's Mount Eryx), were lovers.
2. That proclaims you to be a man (instead of a beast).
3. That is, rebellion against reason and virtue.

That I had Nestor's hernia,[4] thou wouldst think.
I do degenerate, and abuse my nation[5]
To play with opportunity thus long.
I should have done the act and then have parleyed.
265 Yield, or I'll force thee.

CELIA   O just God!

VOLPONE [*seizing* CELIA]   In vain—

[BONARIO *leaps out from where* MOSCA *had placed him.*]

BONARIO   Forbear, foul ravisher, libidinous swine!
Free the forced lady or thou diest, impostor.
But° that I am loath to snatch thy punishment   *Were it not*
Out of the hand of justice, thou shouldst yet
270 Be made the timely sacrifice of vengeance
Before this altar and this dross,° thy idol.—   *(Volpone's treasure)*
Lady, let's quit the place. It is the den
Of villainy. Fear naught; you have a guard;
And he° ere long shall meet his just reward.   *(Volpone)*

[*Exeunt* BONARIO *and* CELIA.]

275 VOLPONE   Fall on me, roof, and bury me in ruin!
Become my grave, that wert my shelter! Oh!
I am unmasked, unspirited, undone,
Betrayed to beggary, to infamy—

3.8

[SCENE: *The scene continues.*]

[*Enter* MOSCA *bloody.*]

MOSCA   Where shall I run, most wretched shame of men,
To beat out my unlucky brains?

VOLPONE   Here, here.
What! Dost thou bleed?

MOSCA   Oh, that his well-driv'n sword
Had been so courteous to have cleft me down
5 Unto the navel, ere I lived to see
My life, my hopes, my spirits, my patron, all
Thus desperately engagèd° by my error!   *placed at risk*

VOLPONE   Woe on thy fortune!

MOSCA   And my follies, sir.

VOLPONE   Th'hast made me miserable.

MOSCA   And myself, sir.
10 Who would have thought he would have hearkened° so?   *eavesdropped*

VOLPONE   What shall we do?

MOSCA   I know not. If my heart
Could expiate the mischance, I'd pluck it out.
Will you be pleased to hang me, or cut my throat?
And I'll requite you, sir. Let's die like Romans,

---

4. A suggestion of sexual impotence. Nestor was the oldest of the Greek leaders in the Trojan War.

5. That is, I fall away from my ancestral virtue and violate the Italian reputation for virility.

15 Since we have lived like Grecians.[6]   [*They knock without.*]

VOLPONE   Hark, who's there?

I hear some footing: officers, the *Saffi*,°   *bailiffs*
Come to apprehend us! I do feel the brand
Hissing already at my forehead; now
Mine ears are boring.[7]

MOSCA   To your couch, sir; you
20 Make that place good, however.[8]   [VOLPONE *gets into bed.*]
                                         Guilty men
Suspect[9] what they deserve still.°   [*He opens the door.*]   *always*
                                         Signor Corbaccio!

3.9

[SCENE: *The scene continues.*]

> [*Enter* CORBACCIO *and converses with* MOSCA; VOLTORE *enters
> unnoticed by them.*]

CORBACCIO   Why, how now, Mosca!

MOSCA   Oh, undone, amazed,° sir   *confused*
Your son—I know not by what accident—
Acquainted with your purpose to my patron
Touching your will and making him your heir,
5 Entered our house with violence, his sword drawn,
Sought for you, called you wretch, unnatural,
Vowed he would kill you.

CORBACCIO   Me?

MOSCA   Yes, and my patron.

CORBACCIO   This act shall disinherit him indeed.
Here is the will.

MOSCA [*taking it from him*]   'Tis well, sir.

CORBACCIO   Right and well.
10 Be you as careful now for me.

MOSCA   My life, sir,
Is not more tendered;° I am only yours.   *dearer to me*

CORBACCIO   How does he? Will he die shortly, think'st thou?

MOSCA   I fear
He'll outlast May.

CORBACCIO   Today?

MOSCA   No, last out May, sir.

CORBACCIO   Couldst thou not gi' him a dram?°   *dose (of poison)*
15 MOSCA   Oh, by no means, sir.

CORBACCIO   Nay, I'll not bid you.

VOLTORE [*aside*]   This is a knave, I see.

> [VOLTORE *comes forward to speak privately with* MOSCA.]

---

6. Greeks had a reputation for dissolute living, Romans for committing suicide when
disgraced.
7. Branding the forehead and boring holes in
the ears were common punishments for

criminals.
8. Defend that place in any way possible;
that is, keep up your invalid role whatever
happens.
9. Expect with dread.

MOSCA [*aside*]   How, Signor Voltore! Did he hear me?

VOLTORE   Parasite!

MOSCA   Who's that? Oh, sir, most timely welcome—

VOLTORE   Scarce°   *Just in time*

To the discovery of your tricks, I fear.
You are his only? And mine also? Are you not?

20 MOSCA   Who, I, sir?   [*They speak out of* CORBACCIO'*s hearing.*]

VOLTORE   You, sir. What device° is this   *scheme*

About a will?

MOSCA   A plot for you, sir.

VOLTORE   Come,

Put not your foists° upon me. I shall scent 'em.   *tricks; fusty smells*

MOSCA   Did you not hear it?

VOLTORE   Yes, I hear Corbaccio

Hath made your patron there his heir.

MOSCA   'Tis true,

25 By my device, drawn to it by my plot,
With hope—

VOLTORE   Your patron should reciprocate?

And you have promised?

MOSCA   For your good I did, sir.

Nay, more, I told his son, brought, hid him here
Where he might hear his father pass the deed,

30 Being persuaded to it by this thought, sir,
That the unnaturalness, first, of the act,
And then, his father's oft disclaiming in° him   *disowning*
(Which I did mean t' help on) would sure enrage him
To do some violence upon his parent,

35 On which the law should take sufficient hold,
And you be stated° in a double hope.   *instated*
Truth be my comfort and my conscience,
My only aim was to dig you a fortune
Out of these two old rotten sepulchres—

40 VOLTORE   I cry thee mercy, Mosca.

MOSCA   Worth your patience

And your great merit, sir. And see the change!

VOLTORE   Why? What success?°   *result*

MOSCA   Most hapless!° You must help, sir.   *unfortunate*

Whilst we expected th'old raven, in comes
Corvino's wife, sent hither by her husband—

45 VOLTORE   What, with a present?

MOSCA   No, sir, on visitation—

I'll tell you how, anon—and, staying long,
The youth, he grows impatient, rushes forth,
Seizeth the lady, wounds me, makes her swear—
Or he would murder her, that was his vow—

50 T'affirm my patron to have done her rape,
Which how unlike° it is, you see! And hence,   *unlikely*
With that pretext, he's gone t'accuse his father,
Defame my patron, defeat you—

VOLTORE   Where's her husband?
Let him be sent for straight.
MOSCA   Sir, I'll go fetch him.
55   VOLTORE   Bring him to the *Scrutineo.*°   *Venetian law court*
MOSCA   Sir, I will.
VOLTORE   This must be stopped.
MOSCA   Oh, you do nobly, sir.
Alas, 'twas labored all, sir, for your good;
Nor was there want of counsel° in the plot.   *lack of prudence*
But fortune can at any time o'erthrow
60   The projects of a hundred learnèd clerks,° sir.   *scholars*
CORBACCIO [*striving to hear*]   What's that?
VOLTORE [*to* CORBACCIO]   Will't please you, sir, to go along?
            [*Exeunt* CORBACCIO *and* VOLTORE.]

MOSCA   Patron, go in and pray for our success.
VOLPONE [*rising*]   Need makes devotion. Heaven your labor bless!

4.1

[SCENE: *The piazza.*]

[*Enter* POLITIC *and* PEREGRINE.]

POLITIC   I told you, sir, it° was a plot. You see   *(the mountebank episode)*
What observation is! You mentioned° me   *asked*
For some instructions; I will tell you, sir,
Since we are met here, in this height° of Venice,   *latitude*
5   Some few particulars I have set down
Only for this meridian, fit to be known
Of your crude° traveler, and they are these.   *inexperienced*
I will not touch, sir, at your phrase or clothes,
For they are old.[1]
PEREGRINE   Sir, I have better.
POLITIC   Pardon,
10   I meant as they are themes.°   *topics*
PEREGRINE   Oh, sir, proceed.
I'll slander° you no more of wit, good sir.   *accuse*
POLITIC   First, for your garb° it must be grave and serious,   *outward bearing*
Very reserved and locked;° not° tell a secret   *guarded / do not*
On any terms, not to your father; scarce
15   A fable° but with caution. Make sure choice   *story*
Both of your company and discourse. Beware
You never speak a truth—
PEREGRINE   How!
POLITIC   Not to strangers,
For those be they you must converse with most;
Others I would not know,° sir, but at distance,   *acknowledge*
20   So as I still might be a saver[2] in 'em.

---

1. Familiar topics. Sir Politic is using "your" impersonally, but Peregrine pretends to misunderstand him in the following line.

2. Escape loss (a gambling term); that is, not be taken advantage of (by them).

You shall have tricks else passed upon you hourly.
And then, for° your religion, profess none,   *as for*
But wonder at the diversity of all,
And, for your part, protest, were there no other
25   But simply the laws o'th'land, you could content you.
Nick Machiavel and Monsieur Bodin both
Were of this mind.³ Then must you learn the use
And handling of your silver fork at meals,⁴
The metal° of your glass—these are main matters   *material*
30   With your Italian—and to know the hour
When you must eat your melons and your figs.
    PEREGRINE   Is that a point of state,° too?   *related to politics*
    POLITIC   Here it is.
For your Venetian, if he see a man
Preposterous in the least, he has him straight;⁵
35   He has, he strips him.° I'll acquaint you, sir.   *plunders*
I now have lived here—'tis some fourteen months;
Within the first week of my landing here,
All took me for a citizen of Venice,
I knew the forms so well—
    PEREGRINE [*aside*]   And nothing else.
40   POLITIC   I had read Contarine,⁶ took me a house,
Dealt with my Jews⁷ to furnish it with movable°—   *personal property*
Well, if I could but find one man, one man
To mine own heart, whom I durst trust, I would—
    PEREGRINE What? What, sir?
    POLITIC   Make him rich, make him a fortune.
45   He should not think again. I would command it.
    PEREGRINE As how?
    POLITIC   With certain projects° that I have—   *money-making schemes*
Which I may not discover.°   *reveal*
    PEREGRINE [*aside*]   If I had
But one° to wager with, I would lay odds, now,   *someone*
He tells me instantly.
    POLITIC   One is—and that
50   I care not greatly who knows—to serve° the state   *supply*
Of Venice with red herrings for three years.
And at a certain rate, from Rotterdam,
Where I have correspondence. [*He shows* PEREGRINE *a paper.*]
    There's a letter
Sent me from one o'th'States,⁸ and to that purpose;
55   He cannot write his name, but that's his mark.

---

3. The Italian and French political philosophers Niccolò Machiavelli (1469–1527) and Jean Bodin (1530–1596) viewed religious disputation as divisive and harmful to the state.
4. Common in Italy in the 16th century, but ridiculed by the English as an affectation.
5. Grasps his nature immediately; *Preposterous*: out of order; foolish.

6. Cardinal Gasparo Contarini (1483–1542); his book *The Commonwealth and Government of Venice* was translated into English in 1599.
7. In Venice Jews served as moneylenders and pawnbrokers.
8. That is, a member of the Dutch parliament, the States-General.

PEREGRINE [*examining the paper*] He is a chandler.⁹

POLITIC   No, a cheesemonger.

There are some other° too, with whom I treat°   *others / deal*

About the same negotiation;

And I will undertake it, for 'tis thus

60   I'll do't with ease; I've cast° it all. Your hoy¹   *figured out*

Carries but three men in her and a boy,

And she shall make me three returns° a year.   *round trips*

So if there come but one of three, I save;°   *break even*

If two, I can defalk.° But this is, now,   *reduce my account*

65   If my main project fail.

PEREGRINE   Then you have others?

POLITIC   I should be loath to draw the subtle air

Of such a place without my thousand aims.

I'll not dissemble, sir: where'er I come,

I love to be considerative,° and 'tis true   *deliberative; careful*

70   I have at my free hours thought upon

Some certain goods unto the state of Venice,

Which I do call my cautions,° and, sir, which   *precautions*

I mean, in hope of pension,° to propound   *a state pension*

To the Great Council, then unto the Forty,

75   So to the Ten.² My means° are made already—   *contacts*

PEREGRINE   By whom?

POLITIC   Sir, one that though his place b'obscure,

Yet he can sway and they will hear him. He's

A *commendatore*.

PEREGRINE   What, a common sergeant?

POLITIC   Sir, such as they are put it in their mouths

80   What they should say, sometimes, as well as greater.³

I think I have my notes to show you—

[*He searches in his garments.*]

PEREGRINE   Good, sir.

POLITIC   But you shall swear unto me on your gentry°   *honor as a gentleman*

Not to anticipate—

PEREGRINE   I, sir?

POLITIC   Nor reveal

A circumstance—My paper is not with me.

85   PEREGRINE   Oh, but you can remember, sir.

POLITIC   My first is

Concerning tinderboxes.° You must know   *(for starting fires)*

No family is here without its box.

Now, sir, it being so portable a thing,

Put case° that you or I were ill affected°   *Suppose / disposed*

90   Unto the state; sir, with it in our pockets

Might not I go into the Arsenale?⁴

---

9. Candle maker (perhaps an inference from grease stains on the paper).

1. A small coastal vessel, used for short hauls.

2. Venice's administrative bodies, in rising order of importance.

3. That is, common sergeants as well as those who are more important sometimes make suggestions to those in power.

4. The dock where Venice's ships were constructed and repaired.

Of you? Come out again? And none the wiser?

PEREGRINE Except yourself, sir.

POLITIC   Go to,[5] then. I therefore

Advertise° to the state how fit it were   *Make known*

95 That none but such as were known patriots,

Sound lovers of their country, should be suffered°   *allowed*

T'enjoy them° in their houses, and even those   *(tinderboxes)*

Sealed[6] at some office, and at such a bigness

As might not lurk in pockets.

PEREGRINE   Admirable!

100 POLITIC My next is, how t'inquire and be resolved°   *convinced*

By present° demonstration whether a ship   *immediate*

Newly arrived from Syria, or from

Any suspected part of all the Levant,°   *eastern Mediterranean*

Be guilty of° the plague. And where they use[7]   *infected with*

105 To lie out forty, fifty days sometimes

About the Lazaretto,° for their trial,   *quarantine station*

I'll save that charge and loss unto the merchant,

And in an hour clear the doubt.

PEREGRINE   Indeed, sir?

POLITIC Or—I will lose my labor.

PEREGRINE   My faith, that's much.

110 POLITIC Nay, sir, conceive° me. 'Twill cost me in onions[8]   *understand*

Some thirty livres°—   *French coins*

PEREGRINE   Which is one pound sterling.

POLITIC Beside my waterworks. For this I do, sir.

First I bring in your ship 'twixt two brick walls—

But those the state shall venture.° On the one   *invest in*

115 I strain° me a fair tarpaulin, and in that   *stretch*

I stick my onions cut in halves; the other

Is full of loopholes out at which I thrust

The noses of my bellows, and those bellows

I keep with° waterworks in perpetual motion—   *by means of*

120 Which is the easiest matter of a hundred.°   *i.e., as easy as can be*

Now, sir, your onion, which doth naturally

Attract th'infection, and your bellows, blowing

The air upon him,° will show instantly   *(the onion)*

By his changed color if there be contagion,

125 Or else remain as fair as at the first.

Now 'tis known, 'tis nothing.°   *there's nothing to it*

PEREGRINE   You are right, sir.

POLITIC I would I had my note.

        [*He searches again in his garments.*]

PEREGRINE   Faith, so would I;

But, you ha' done well for once, sir.

POLITIC   Were I false,°   *traitorous*

Or would be made so, I could show you reasons

---

5. An expression of impatience.   7. Are accustomed.
6. Should be registered under seal.   8. Believed to absorb plague infection.

130   How I could sell this state now to the Turk,[9]

    Spite of their galleys[1] or their—

PEREGRINE   Pray you, Sir Pol.

POLITIC   I have 'em not about me.

PEREGRINE   That I feared.

    They are there, sir? [*He indicates a book* POLITIC *is holding.*]

POLITIC   No, this is my diary,

    Wherein I note my actions of the day.

135 PEREGRINE   Pray you, let's see, sir. What is here? [*Reading*]

      "Notandum,"[2]

    A rat had gnawn my spur leathers,° notwithstanding   *laces*

    I put on new and did go forth, but first

    I threw three beans over the threshold.° *Item,*   *(for good luck)*

    I went and bought two toothpicks, whereof one

140   I burst immediately in a discourse

    With a Dutch merchant, 'bout *ragion' del stato.*[3]

    From him I went, and paid a *moccinigo*°   *small Venetian coin*

    For piecing° my silk stockings; by the way   *mending*

    I cheapened sprats,[4] and at Saint Mark's I urined."

145   Faith, these are politic notes!

POLITIC   Sir, I do slip°   *let pass*

    No action of my life thus but I quote° it.   *without noting*

PEREGRINE   Believe me, it is wise!

POLITIC   Nay, sir, read forth.

4.2

[SCENE: *The scene continues.*]

      [*Enter* LADY WOULD-BE, NANO, *and the two* WOMEN.
      They do not see POLITIC *and* PEREGRINE *at first.*]

LADY WOULD-BE   Where should this loose knight be, trow?°   *do you suppose*

    Sure he's housed.°   *i.e., in a brothel*

NANO   Why, then he's fast°   *secure; quick*

LADY WOULD-BE   Ay, he plays both° with me.   *both fast and loose*

    I pray you, stay. This heat will do more harm

5   To my complexion than his heart is worth.

    I do not care to hinder, but to take° him.   *catch*

      [*She rubs her cheeks.*]

    How it° comes off!   *(the makeup)*

FIRST WOMAN [*pointing*]   My master's yonder.

LADY WOULD-BE   Where?

FIRST WOMAN   With a young gentleman.

LADY WOULD-BE   That same's the party,

    In man's apparel! [*To* NANO] Pray you, sir, jog my knight.

10   I will be tender to his reputation,

    However he demerit.°   *merits blame*

---

9. The Ottoman Turks, Venice's principal rivals in the eastern Mediterranean.
1. In spite of the Venetians' warships.

2. It must be noted (Latin).
3. Reasons and affairs of state.
4. I bargained for some small fish.

POLITIC [*seeing her*]   My lady!

PEREGRINE   Where?

POLITIC   'Tis she indeed, sir; you shall know her. She is,
 Were she not mine,[5] a lady of that merit
 For fashion and behavior; and for beauty

15 I durst compare—

PEREGRINE   It seems you are not jealous,
 That dare commend her.

POLITIC   Nay, and for disclosure—

PEREGRINE   Being your wife, she cannot miss° that.   *lack*

POLITIC [*introducing* PEREGRINE]   Madam,
 Here is a gentleman; pray you use him fairly.
 He seems a youth, but he is—

LADY WOULD-BE   None?

POLITIC   Yes, one

20 Has° put his face as soon[6] into the world—   *Who has*

LADY WOULD-BE   You mean, as early? But° today?   *Only*

POLITIC   How's this!

LADY WOULD-BE   Why, in this habit,° sir; you apprehend° me.   *dress / understand*
 Well, Master Would-be, this doth not become you;
 I had thought the odor, sir, of your good name

25 Had been more precious to you, that you would not
 Have done this dire massacre on your honor—
 One of your gravity and rank besides!
 But knights, I see, care little for the oath
 They make to ladies, chiefly their own ladies.

30 POLITIC   Now, by my spurs—the symbol of my knighthood—

PEREGRINE [*aside*]   Lord, how his brain is humbled[7] for an oath!

POLITIC   —I reach° you not.   *understand*

LADY WOULD-BE   Right, sir, your polity°   *craftiness*
 May bear it through° thus. [*To* PEREGRINE] Sir, a word with you.   *carry it off*
 I would be loath to contest publicly

35 With any gentlewoman, or to seem
 Froward° or violent; as *The Courtier*[8] says,   *Ill-tempered*
 It comes too near rusticity° in a lady,   *ill breeding*
 Which I would shun by all means. And however
 I may deserve from Master Would-be, yet

40 T' have one fair gentlewoman thus be made
 Th'unkind instrument to wrong another,
 And one she knows not, ay, and to persevere,
 In my poor judgment is not warranted
 From being a solecism° in our sex,   *impropriety*

45 If not in manners.

PEREGRINE   How is this?

POLITIC   Sweet madam,
 Come nearer to your aim.[9]

---

5. That is, even were I not, as her husband,
biased in saying so.
6. At so young an age.
7. Brought low (literally, brought down to his

feet, where spurs are worn).
8. Baldassare Castiglione's *The Courtier* (1528),
a famous Renaissance handbook on gentility.
9. Make your point more clearly.

LADY WOULD-BE   Marry, and will, sir.
  Since you provoke me with your impudence
  And laughter of your light land-siren[1] here,
  Your Sporus,[2] your hermaphrodite—
PEREGRINE   What's here?
50 Poetic fury and historic storms.
POLITIC The gentleman, believe it, is of worth,
  And of our nation.
LADY WOULD-BE   Ay, your Whitefriars[3] nation!
  Come, I blush for you, Master Would-be, I,
  And am ashamed you should ha' no more forehead°   *shame*
55 Than thus to be the patron, or Saint George[4]
  To a lewd harlot, a base fricatrice,°   *whore*
  A female devil in a male outside.
POLITIC [*to* PEREGRINE]   Nay,
  An° you be such a one, I must bid adieu   *If*
  To your delights. The case appears too liquid.°   *obvious; transparent*
      [POLITIC *starts to leave.*]
60 LADY WOULD-BE Ay, you may carry't clear, with your state-
      face.°   *solemn expression*
  But for your carnival concupiscence,[5]
  Who here is fled for liberty of conscience[6]
  From furious persecution of the marshal,°   *officer of the court*
  Her will I disc'ple.°   *discipline*
     [*Exit* POLITIC, LADY POLITIC *accosts* PEREGRINE.]
PEREGRINE   This is fine, i'faith!
65 And do you use this° often? Is this part   *act this way*
  Of your wit's exercise, 'gainst you have occasion?[7]
  Madam—
LADY WOULD-BE Go to, sir.
PEREGRINE   Do you hear me, lady?
  Why, if your knight have set you to beg shirts,[8]
  Or to invite me home, you might have done it
70 A nearer° way by far.   *more direct*
LADY WOULD-BE   This cannot work you
  Out of my snare.
PEREGRINE   Why, am I in it, then?
  Indeed, your husband told me you were fair,
  And so you are; only your nose inclines—
  That side that's next the sun—to the queen-apple[9]
75 LADY WOULD-BE This cannot be endured by any patience.

---

1. In classical mythology, beautiful female monsters whose songs lured sailors to destruction on the rocks surrounding their island.
2. A young man whom the Roman emperor Nero (r. 54–68 C.E.) married after having him castrated.
3. A notorious London brothel district.
4. The patron saint of England.

5. Lustful strumpet. "Carnival" may be a malapropism for "carnal."
6. That is, freedom to practice your bawdy trade.
7. In preparation for when you need to use it.
8. Lady Would-be is apparently pulling Peregrine's shirt.
9. That is, your nose is bright red.

4.3

[SCENE: *The scene continues.*]

[*Enter* MOSCA.]

MOSCA   What's the matter, madam?

LADY WOULD-BE   If the Senate
    Right not my quest° in this, I will protest° 'em   *petition / proclaim*
    To all the world no aristocracy.

MOSCA   What is the injury, lady?

LADY WOULD-BE   Why, the callet°   *strumpet*
5   You told me of, here I have ta'en disguised.

MOSCA   Who, this? What means Your Ladyship? The creature
    I mentioned to you is apprehended now
    Before the Senate. You shall see her—

LADY WOULD-BE   Where?

MOSCA   I'll bring you to her. This young gentleman,
10 I saw him land this morning at the port.

LADY WOULD-BE   Is't possible! How has my judgment wandered!
    [*Releasing* PEREGRINE] Sir, I must, blushing, say to you I have erred,
    And plead your pardon.

PEREGRINE   What, more changes yet?

LADY WOULD-BE   I hope you ha' not the malice to remember
15 A gentlewoman's passion. If you stay
    In Venice here, please you to use me,[1] sir—

MOSCA   Will you go, madam?

LADY WOULD-BE   Pray you, sir, use me. In faith,
    The more you see me, the more I shall conceive
    You have forgot our quarrel.

[*Exeunt* MOSCA, LADY WOULD-BE, NANO, *and* WOMEN.]

PEREGRINE   This is rare!
20 Sir Politic Would-be? No, Sir Politic Bawd,
    To bring me thus acquainted with his wife!
    Well, wise Sir Pol, since you have practiced thus
    Upon my freshmanship, I'll try your salt-head,[2]
    What proof° it is against a counterplot.   [*Exit.*]   *How invulnerable*

4.4

[SCENE: *The Scrutineo, or Court of Law, in the Doge's palace.*]

[*Enter* VOLTORE, CORBACCIO, CORVINO, *and* MOSCA.]

VOLTORE   Well, now you know the carriage° of the business,   *management*
    Your constancy is all that is required
    Unto the safety of it.

MOSCA   Is the lie
    Safely conveyed° amongst us? Is that sure?   *agreed on*
5 Knows every man his burden?[3]

---

1. Make use of my services ("use," like "conceive" two lines later, also has a sexual meaning).
2. Experience; lecherousness. *Practiced . . .*

freshmanship: taken advantage of my innocence. Peregrine believes that Sir Politic has set him up for this humiliation.
3. His musical refrain; that is, his part.

CORVINO   Yes.

MOSCA   Then shrink not.

CORVINO [*aside to* MOSCA]   But knows the advocate the truth?

MOSCA [*aside to* CORVINO]   Oh, sir,

By no means. I devised a formal° tale   *elaborate*

That salved° your reputation. But be valiant, sir.   *preserved*

CORVINO   I fear no one but him,° that this his pleading   *(Voltore)*

10   Should make him stand for a co-heir—

MOSCA   Co-halter!⁴

Hang him, we will but use his tongue, his noise,

As we do Croaker's,° here.   *(Corbaccio's)*

CORVINO   Ay, what shall he do?

MOSCA   When we ha' done, you mean?

CORVINO   Yes.

MOSCA   Why, we'll think—

Sell him for *mummia*;⁵ he's half dust already.

15   [*Aside to* VOLTORE] Do not you smile to see this buffalo,⁶

How he doth sport it with his head? [*To himself*] I should,

If all were well and past. [*Aside to* CORBACCIO] Sir, only you

Are he that shall enjoy the crop of all,

And these not know for whom they toil.

CORBACCIO   Ay, peace!

20   MOSCA [*aside to* CORVINO]   But you shall eat it.° [*To himself*]   *(the crop)*

Much!° [*then to* VOLTORE *again*] Worshipful sir,   *Fat chance!*

Mercury⁷ sit upon your thund'ring tongue,

Or the French Hercules, and make your language

As conquering as his club,⁸ to beat along,

25   As with a tempest, flat, our adversaries!

[*Aside to* CORVINO] But much more yours, sir.

VOLTORE   Here they come. Ha' done°   *Shut up*

MOSCA   I have another witness° if you need, sir,   *i.e., Lady Would-be*

I can produce.

VOLTORE   Who is it?

MOSCA   Sir, I have her.

4.5

[SCENE. *The scene continues.*]

[*Enter four* AVOCATORI, BONARIO, CELIA, *Notario* (NOTARY)
COMMENDATORI, *and other court officials.*]

FIRST AVOCATORE   The like of this the Senate never heard of.

SECOND AVOCATORE   'Twill come most strange to them when we report it.

FOURTH AVOCATORE   The gentlewoman has been ever held

Of unreprovèd name.

4. That is, sharer of a hangman's noose.
5. A medicinal substance derived from embalmed human corpses.
6. Corvino, in cuckold's horns.
7. Roman god of heralds, but also of thieves and trickery.

8. The characteristic weapon of the classical hero Hercules (Heracles), who, according to a medieval legend, fathered the Celts in Gaul (or France) as he passed through Europe on his return from his tenth labor.

THIRD AVOCATORE   So, the young man.

5 FOURTH AVOCATORE   The more unnatural part that of his father.

SECOND AVOCATORE   More of the husband.

FIRST AVOCATORE   I not know to give

His act a name, it is so monstrous!

FOURTH AVOCATORE   But the impostor,° he is a thing created   (Volpone)

T'exceed example!°   precedent

FIRST AVOCATORE   And all aftertimes!°   the future

10 SECOND AVOCATORE   I never heard a true voluptuary

Described but him.

THIRD AVOCATORE   Appear yet those were cited?°   summoned

NOTARY   All but the old magnifico, Volpone.

FIRST AVOCATORE   Why is not he here?

MOSCA   Please Your Fatherhoods,°   reverend sirs

Here is his advocate. Himself's so weak,

So feeble—

15 FOURTH AVOCATORE   What are you?

BONARIO   His parasite,

His knave, his pander! I beseech the court

He may be forced to come, that your grave eyes

May bear strong witness of his strange impostures.

VOLTORE   Upon my faith and credit with your virtues,

20 He is not able to endure the air.

SECOND AVOCATORE   Bring him, however.

THIRD AVOCATORE   We will see him.

FOURTH AVOCATORE   Fetch him.

[Exit officers.]

VOLTORE   Your Fatherhoods' fit pleasures be obeyed,

But sure the sight will rather move your pities

Than indignation. May it please the court,

25 In the meantime he may be heard in me.

I know this place most void of prejudice,

And therefore crave it, since we have no reason

To fear our truth should hurt our cause.

THIRD AVOCATORE   Speak free.

VOLTORE   Then know, most honored fathers, I must now

30 Discover° to your strangely abusèd ears   Reveal

The most prodigious and most frontless° piece   shameless

Of solid impudence and treachery

That ever vicious nature yet brought forth

To shame the state of Venice. [Indicating CELIA] This lewd woman,

35 That wants° no artificial looks or tears   Who lacks

To help the visor° she has now put on,   mask

Hath long been known a close° adulteress   secret

To that lascivious youth there [indicating BONARIO]; not suspected,

I say, but known, and taken in the act

40 With him; and by this man, the easy° husband,   indulgent

Pardoned; whose timeless° bounty makes him now   ill-timed; endless

Stand here, the most unhappy, innocent person

That ever man's own goodness made accused.[9]
For these, not knowing how to owe° a gift   *acknowledge*
45 Of that dear grace but° with their shame, being placed   *except*
So above all powers of their gratitude,[1]
Began to hate the benefit, and in place
Of thanks devise t'extirp° the memory   *to eradicate, root out*
Of such an act. Wherein I pray Your Fatherhoods
50 To observe the malice, yea, the rage of creatures
Discovered in their evils, and what heart°   *audacity*
Such take even from their crimes. But that anon
Will more appear. This gentleman, the father,

    [*indicating* CORBACCIO]

Hearing of this foul fact,° with many others   *deed; crime*
55 Which daily struck at his too tender ears,
And grieved in nothing more than that he could not
Preserve himself a parent—his son's ills°   *evil deeds*
Growing to that strange flood—at last decreed
To disinherit him.
FIRST AVOCATORE These be strange turns!
60 SECOND AVOCATORE The young man's fame° was ever fair and   *reputation*
    honest.
VOLTORE So much more full of danger is his vice,
That can beguile so under shade of virtue.
But, as I said, my honored sires, his father
Having this settled purpose, by what means
65 To him° betrayed we know not, and this day   *(Bonario)*
Appointed for the deed, that parricide—
I cannot style him better—by confederacy°   *conspiracy*
Preparing this his paramour to be there,
Entered Volpone's house—who was the man,
70 Your Fatherhoods must understand, designed°   *designated*
For the inheritance—there sought his father.
But with what purpose sought he him, my lords?
I tremble to pronounce it, that a son
Unto a father, and to such a father,
75 Should have so foul, felonious intent:
It was to murder him. When, being prevented
By his more happy° absence, what then did he?   *Corbaccio's fortunate*
Not check° his wicked thoughts; no, now new deeds—   *stop, constrain*
Mischief doth ever end where it begins[2]—
80 An act of horror, fathers! He dragged forth
The agèd gentleman, that had there lain bedrid
Three years and more, out of his innocent couch;
Naked upon the floor there left him; wounded
His servant in the face, and with this strumpet,

9. That is, who ever had his goodness turned
against him.
1. That is, being placed in a position of indebt-

edness so far beyond their powers of
gratitude.
2. Mischief, which begins badly, ends badly.

85 The stale° to his forged practice,° who was glad   *decoy / contrived scheme*
  To be so active—I shall here desire
  Your Fatherhoods to note but° my collections°   *only / conclusions*
  As most remarkable—thought at once to stop
  His father's ends,° discredit his° free choice   *aims / (his father's)*
90 In° the old gentleman,° redeem themselves   *Of / (Volpone)*
  By laying infamy upon this man°   *(Corvino)*
  To whom with blushing they should owe their lives.
FIRST AVOCATORE   What proofs have you of this?
BONARIO   Most honored fathers,
  I humbly crave there be no credit given
95 To this man's mercenary tongue.
SECOND AVOCATORE   Forbear.
BONARIO   His soul moves in his fee.
THIRD AVOCATORE   Oh, sir!
BONARIO   This fellow,
  For six sols° more, would plead against his Maker.   *French coins (sous)*
FIRST AVOCATORE   You do forget yourself.
VOLTORE   Nay, nay, grave fathers,
  Let him have scope. Can any man imagine
100 That he will spare's accuser, that would not
  Have spared his parent?
FIRST AVOCATORE   Well, produce your proofs.
CELIA   I would I could forget I were a creature!°   *living being*
VOLTORE [*calling a witness*]   Signor Corbaccio!
FOURTH AVOCATORE   What is he?
VOLTORE   The father.
SECOND AVOCATORE   Has he had an oath?
NOTARY   Yes.
CORBACCIO   What must I do now?
105 NOTARY   Your testimony's craved.
CORBACCIO [*mis-hearing*]   Speak to the knave?
  I'll ha' my mouth first stopped with earth! My heart
  Abhors his knowledge;[3] I disclaim° in him.   *renounce all part*
FIRST AVOCATORE   But for what cause?
CORBACCIO   The mere portent[4] of nature.
  He is an utter stranger to my loins.
110 BONARIO   Have they made° you to this?   *forced*
CORBACCIO   I will not hear thee,
  Monster of men, swine, goat, wolf, parricide!
  Speak not, thou viper.
BONARIO   Sir, I will sit down,
  And rather wish my innocence should suffer
  Than I resist the authority of a father.
115 VOLTORE [*calling a witness*]   Signor Corvino!
SECOND AVOCATORE   This is strange!
FIRST AVOCATORE   Who's this?

3. Knowledge of him.
4. Complete monster (a deformed child was considered an evil omen).

NOTARY   The husband.

FOURTH AVOCATORE   Is he sworn?

NOTARY   He is.

THIRD AVOCATORE   Speak, then.

CORVINO   This woman, please Your Fatherhoods, is a whore

    Of most hot exercise, more than a partridge,[5]

    Upon record°—   *As the record shows*

FIRST AVOCATORE   No more.

CORVINO   Neighs like a jennet.°   *mare in heat*

120   NOTARY   Preserve the honor of the court.

CORVINO   I shall,

    And modesty of your most reverend ears.

    And yet I hope that I may say these eyes

    Have seen her glued unto that piece of cedar,

    That fine well-timbered° gallant and that here   *well-built*

125   [*Pointing to his forehead*] The letters may be read, thorough° the horn,[6]   *through*

    That make the story perfect.°   *complete*

MOSCA [*aside to* CORVINO]   Excellent, sir!

CORVINO [*aside to* MOSCA]   There is no shame in this, now, is there?

MOSCA [*aside to* CORVINO]   None.

CORVINO [*to the court*]   Or if I said I hoped that she were onward°   *well along*

    To her damnation, if there be a hell

130   Greater than whore and woman—a good Catholic

    May make the doubt°—   *May question*

THIRD AVOCATORE   His grief hath made him frantic.

FIRST AVOCATORE   Remove him hence.   [*She* (CELIA) *swoons.*]

SECOND AVOCATORE   Look to the woman!

CORVINO [*taunting her*]   Rare!

    Prettily feigned! Again!

FOURTH AVOCATORE   Stand from about her.

FIRST AVOCATORE   Give her the air.

THIRD AVOCATORE [*to* MOSCA]   What can you say?

MOSCA   My wound,

135   May't please Your Wisdoms, speaks for me, received

    In aid of my good patron when he° missed   *(Bonario)*

    His sought-for father, when that well-taught dame

    Had her cue given her to cry out a rape.

BONARIO   Oh, most laid° impudence! Fathers—   *carefully designed*

THIRD AVOCATORE   Sir, be silent.

140   You had your hearing free,° so must they theirs.   *without interruption*

SECOND AVOCATORE   I do begin to doubt th'imposture here.

FOURTH AVOCATORE   This woman has too many moods.

VOLTORE   Grave fathers,

    She is a creature of a most professed

    And prostituted lewdness.

---

5. A purportedly lecherous bird. *Most hot exercise:* sexual activity.
6. Both the cuckold's horns and the young student's hornbook, a leaf of paper containing the alphabet and covered with a transparent layer of horn.

CORVINO   Most impetuous!
145 Unsatisfied, grave fathers!
VOLTORE   May her feignings
Not take° Your Wisdoms! But° this day she baited°   *take in / Only / enticed*
A stranger, a grave knight, with her loose eyes
And more lascivious kisses. This man° saw 'em   *(Mosca)*
Together on the water in a gondola.
150 MOSCA   Here is the lady herself that saw 'em too,
Without,° who then had in the open streets   *Waiting outside*
Pursued them, but for saving her knight's honor.
FIRST AVOCATORE   Produce that lady.
SECOND AVOCATORE   Let her come.
                                         [*Exit* MOSCA.]
FOURTH AVOCATORE   These things,
They strike with wonder!
THIRD AVOCATORE   I am turned a stone!

4.6

[SCENE: *The scene continues.*]

          [*Enter* MOSCA *and* LADY WOULD-BE.]
MOSCA   Be resolute, madam.
LADY WOULD-BE   Ay, this same is she.
[*To* CELIA] Out, thou chameleon harlot! Now thine eyes
Vie tears with the hyena.[7] Dar'st thou look
Upon my wrongèd face? [*To the* AVOCATORI] I cry° your pardons.   *beg*
5   I fear I have forgettingly transgressed
Against the dignity of the court—
SECOND AVOCATORE   No, madam.
LADY WOULD-BE   And been exorbitant°—   *excessive*
SECOND AVOCATORE   You have not, lady.
FOURTH AVOCATORE   These proofs are strong.
LADY WOULD-BE   Surely, I had no purpose
To scandalize your honors, or my sex's.
10   THIRD AVOCATORE   We do believe it.
LADY WOULD-BE   Surely, you may believe it.
SECOND AVOCATORE   Madam, we do.
LADY WOULD-BE   Indeed, you may. My breeding
Is not so coarse—
FOURTH AVOCATORE   We know it.
LADY WOULD-BE   —to offend
With pertinacy°—   *stubborn persistence*
THIRD AVOCATORE   Lady—
LADY WOULD-BE   —such a presence;
No, surely.
FIRST AVOCATORE   We well think it.
LADY WOULD-BE   You may think it.

7. Like the chameleon, a symbol of treachery: hyenas were believed able to change their sex and
to imitate the voices of humans.

15 FIRST AVOCATORE [*to the other* AVOCATORI] Let her o'ercome.° *have the last word*

[*To* CELIA *and* BONARIO] What witnesses have you
To make good your report?

BONARIO   Our consciences.

CELIA And heaven, that never fails the innocent.

FOURTH AVOCATORE These are no testimonies.

BONARIO   Not in your courts,
Where multitude and clamor overcomes.

20 FIRST AVOCATORE Nay, then, you do wax insolent.

[VOLPONE *is brought in on a litter, as impotent.*° *physically helpless*
LADY WOULD-BE *embraces him.*]

VOLTORE   Here, here
The testimony comes that will convince
And put to utter dumbness their bold tongues.
See here, grave fathers, here's the ravisher,
The rider on men's wives, the great impostor,

25 The grand voluptuary! Do you not think
These limbs should affect venery.° Or these eyes *be disposed to lust*
Covet a concubine? Pray you, mark these hands:
Are they not fit to stroke a lady's breasts?
Perhaps he doth dissemble?

BONARIO   So he does.

30 VOLTORE Would you ha' him tortured?

BONARIO   I would have him proved.° *put to the test*

VOLTORE Best try him, then, with goads or burning irons;
Put him to the strappado.[8] I have heard
The rack[9] hath cured the gout; faith, give it him
And help° him of a malady; be courteous. *relieve*

35 I'll undertake, before these honored fathers,
He shall have yet as many left° diseases *remaining*
As she has known adulterers, or thou strumpets.
O my most equal° hearers, if these deeds, *just*
Acts of this bold and most exorbitant strain,° *outrageous nature*

40 May pass with sufferance,° what one citizen *May be permitted*
But owes the forfeit of his life, yea, fame
To him that dares traduce him?° Which of you *malign*
Are safe, my honored fathers? I would ask,
With leave of Your grave Fatherhoods, if their plot

45 Have any face or color° like to truth? *appearance*
Or if unto the dullest nostril here
It smell not rank and most abhorrèd slander?
I crave your care of this good gentleman,
Whose life is much endangered by their fable;

50 And as for them, I will conclude with this:
That vicious persons, when they are hot, and fleshed[1]
In impious acts, their constancy° abounds. *determination*

---

8. A form of torture in which the victim was hoisted by the hands, which had been tied behind his or her back, then dropped halfway down.

9. An instrument of torture on which the victim was stretched until joints dislocated.

1. Made eager (like hunting animals incited by the taste of blood).

Damned deeds are done with greatest confidence.

FIRST AVOCATORE   Take 'em to custody, and sever them.[2]

55 SECOND AVOCATORE   'Tis pity two such prodigies° should live.   *freaks; monsters*

[*Exeunt* CELIA *and* BONARIO, *guarded.*]

FIRST AVOCATORE   Let the old gentleman be returned with care.
I'm sorry our credulity wronged him.

[*Exeunt litter-bearers with* VOLPONE.]

FOURTH AVOCATORE   These are two creatures!

THIRD AVOCATORE   I have an earthquake in me!

SECOND AVOCATORE   Their shame, even in their cradles, fled their faces.

60 FOURTH AVOCATORE [*to* VOLTORE]   You've done a worthy service to the
state, sir,
In their discovery.

FIRST AVOCATORE   You shall hear ere night
What punishment the court decrees upon 'em.

VOLTORE   We thank Your Fatherhoods.

[*Exeunt* AVOCATORI, NOTARY, COMMENDATORI.]

[*To* MOSCA]   How like you it?

MOSCA   Rare!
I'd ha' your tongue, sir, tipped with gold for this;

65 I'd ha' you be the heir to the whole city;
The earth I'd have want men ere you want living.°   *lack income*
They're bound to erect your statue in Saint Mark's.—
Signor Corvino, I would have you go
And show yourself, that you have conquered

CORVINO   Yes.

70 MOSCA [*aside to* CORVINO]   It was much better that you should profess
Yourself a cuckold thus, than that the other[3]
Should have been proved.

CORVINO   Nay, I considered that.
Now it is her fault.

MOSCA   Then it had° been yours.   *would have*

CORVINO   True. I do doubt° this advocate still.   *mistrust*

MOSCA   I'faith,

75 You need not; I dare ease you of that care.

CORVINO   I trust thee, Mosca.

MOSCA   As your own soul, sir.

[*Exit* CORVINO.]

CORBACCIO   Mosca!

MOSCA   Now for your business, sir.

CORBACCIO   How? Ha' you business?

MOSCA   Yes, yours, sir.

CORBACCIO   Oh, none else?

MOSCA   None else, not I.

CORBACCIO   Be careful, then.

---

2. Separate them, to face individual trials.
3. That is, his having procured his wife for Volpone.

MOSCA   Rest you with both your eyes,° sir.   *Rest assured*

80 CORBACCIO   Dispatch it.[4]

MOSCA   Instantly.

CORBACCIO   And look that all
Whatever be put in: jewels, plate, moneys,
Household stuff, bedding, curtains.

MOSCA   Curtain rings, sir.
Only the advocate's fee must be deducted.

CORBACCIO   I'll pay him, now; you'll be too prodigal.

85 MOSCA   Sir, I must tender° it.   *give*

CORBACCIO   Two *cecchines* is well?

MOSCA   No, six, sir.

CORBACCIO   'Tis too much.

MOSCA   He talked a great while,
You must consider that, sir.

CORBACCIO [*giving money*]   Well, there's three—

MOSCA   I'll give it him.

CORBACCIO   Do so, and [*he tips* MOSCA] there's for thee.
                        [*Exit* CORBACCIO.]

MOSCA [*aside*]   Bountiful bones! What horrid strange offense

90 Did he commit 'gainst nature in his youth
Worthy this age?[5] [*To* VOLTORE] You see, sir, how I work
Unto your ends; take you no notice.°   *i.e., leave it to me*

VOLTORE   No,
I'll leave you.

MOSCA   All is yours,   [*Exit* VOLTORE.]
              [*aside*] the devil and all,
Good advocate! [*To* LADY WOULD-BE] Madam, I'll bring you home.

95 LADY WOULD-BE   No, I'll go see your patron.

MOSCA   That you shall not.
I'll tell you why. My purpose is to urge
My patron to reform° his will; and, for   *rewrite*
The zeal you've shown today, whereas before
You were but third or fourth, you shall be now

100 Put in the first, which would appear as begged
If you were present. Therefore—

LADY WOULD-BE   You shall sway[6] me.
                   [*Exeunt.*]

5.1

[SCENE: VOLPONE'S *house.*]

[*Enter* VOLPONE *attended.*]

VOLPONE   Well, I am here, and all this brunt° is past.   *crisis*
I ne'er was in dislike with my disguise
Till this fled° moment; here 'twas good, in private,   *past*

---

4. Hurry (to have Volpone's will written).
5. To deserve an old age like this.
6. Rule; command (with possible sexual innuendo).

But, in your public—*cave*° whilst I breathe.   *beware (Latin)*
5   Fore God, my left leg 'gan to have the cramp,
     And I apprehended straight° some power had struck me   *feared immediately that*
     With a dead palsy.° Well, I must be merry   *paralysis*
     And shake it off. A many of these fears
     Would put me into some villainous disease,
10   Should they come thick upon me. I'll prevent 'em.
     Give me a bowl of lusty wine to fright
     This humor° from my heart.—Hum, hum, hum!   [*He drinks.*]   *fearful mood*
     'Tis almost gone already; I shall conquer.°   *i.e., conquer my fears*
     Any device,° now, of rare ingenious knavery,   *scheme*
15   That would possess me with a violent laughter,
     Would make me up° again. So, so, so, so.   [*Drinks again.*]   *restore me*
     This heat is life; 'tis blood by this time. [*Calling*] Mosca!

5.2

[SCENE: *The scene continues.*]

          [*Enter* MOSCA.]

MOSCA   How now, sir? Does the day look clear again?
     Are we recovered and wrought out of error
     Into our way, to see our path before us?
     Is our trade free once more?
VOLPONE   Exquisite Mosca!
5 MOSCA   Was it not carried learnedly?
VOLPONE   And stoutly.°   *bravely; resolutely*
     Good wits are greatest in extremities.
MOSCA   It were° a folly beyond thought to trust   *would be*
     Any grand act unto a cowardly spirit.
     You are not taken with it enough, methinks?
10 VOLPONE   Oh, more than if I had enjoyed the wench!
     The pleasure of all womankind's not like it.
MOSCA   Why, now you speak, sir. We must here be fixed;
     Here we must rest. This is our masterpiece.
     We cannot think to go beyond this.
VOLPONE   True,
15   Th'hast played thy prize, my precious Mosca.
MOSCA   Nay, sir,
     To gull the court—
VOLPONE   And quite divert the torrent
     Upon the innocent.
MOSCA   Yes, and to make
     So rare a music out of discords[7]—
VOLPONE   Right.
     That yet to me's the strangest, how th'ast borne° it!   *managed*
20   That these, being so divided 'mongst themselves,
     Should not scent somewhat,[8] or° in me or thee,   *either*

---

7. That is, out of individuals pursuing their own self-interest.
8. Suspect something.

Or doubt their own side.°   *position*

MOSCA   True, they will not see't.
Too much light blinds 'em, I think. Each of 'em
Is so possessed and stuffed with his own hopes
25 That anything unto the contrary,
Never so true or never so apparent,
Never so palpable, they will resist it—
VOLPONE   Like a temptation of the devil.
MOSCA   Right, sir.
Merchants may talk of trade, and your great signors
30 Of land that yields well; but if Italy
Have any glebe° more fruitful than these fellows,   *soil*
I am deceived. Did not your advocate rare?°   *perform marvelously*
VOLPONE   Oh!—"My most honored fathers, my grave fathers,
Under correction of Your Fatherhoods,
35 What face of truth is here? If these strange deeds
May pass, most honored fathers"—I had much ado
To forbear laughing.
MOSCA   'T seemed to me you sweat,° sir.   *sweated (with fear)*
VOLPONE   In troth, I did a little.
MOSCA   But confess, sir,
Were you not daunted?
VOLPONE   In good faith, I was
40 A little in a mist,° but not dejected,   *uncertain*
Never but still myself.
MOSCA   I think° it, sir.   *believe*
Now, so truth help me, I must needs say this, sir,
And out of conscience for your advocate:
He's taken pains, in faith, sir, and deserved,
45 In my poor judgment—I speak it under favor,°   *with your permission*
Not to contrary° you, sir—very richly—   *contradict*
Well—to be cozened.°   *cheated*
VOLPONE   Troth, and I think so too,
By that I heard him[9] in the latter end.
MOSCA   Oh, but before, sir! Had you heard him first
50 Draw it to certain heads, then aggravate,[1]
Then use his vehement figures[2]—I looked still
When he would shift a shirt;[3] and doing this
Out of pure love, no hope of gain—
VOLPONE   'Tis right.
I cannot answer° him, Mosca, as I would,   *repay*
55 Not yet; but for thy sake, at thy entreaty
I will begin ev'n now to vex 'em all,
This very instant.
MOSCA   Good, sir.
VOLPONE   Call the dwarf
And eunuch forth.

9. Because of what I heard him say.   2. Powerful figures of speech.
1. Gather his material into topics, then   3. Change a shirt, perhaps because he sweated
emphasize.   so heavily during his performance.

MOSCA [*calling*]   Castrone, Nano!
   [*Enter* NANO *and* CASTRONE.]
NANO   Here.
VOLPONE Shall we have a jig, now?
MOSCA   What you please, sir.
VOLPONE [*to* CASTRONE *and* NANO]   Go,

60 Straight give out° about the streets, you two,   *Report at once*
 That I am dead. Do it with constancy,°   *conviction*
 Sadly,° do you hear? Impute it to the grief   *Gravely*
 Of this late slander. [*Exeunt* CASTRONE *and* NANO.]
MOSCA   What do you mean,° sir?   *intend*
VOLPONE   Oh,
 I shall have instantly my vulture, crow,
65 Raven come flying hither on the news
 To peck for carrion, my she-wolf and all,
 Greedy and full of expectation—
MOSCA And then to have it ravished° from their mouths? *torn away*
VOLPONE 'Tis true. I will ha' thee put on a gown
70 And take upon thee as° thou wert mine heir;   *act as though*
 Show 'em a will. Open that chest and reach
 Forth one of those that has the blanks.° I'll straight *blank spaces*
 Put in thy name.
MOSCA [*fetching a blank will*] It will be rare, sir.
VOLPONE   Ay,
 When they e'en gape, and find themselves deluded—
75 MOSCA Yes.
VOLPONE And thou use them scurvily. Dispatch,
 Get on thy gown.
   [VOLPONE *signs the will* MOSCA *has given him.*
   MOSCA *puts on a mourning garment.*]
MOSCA   But, what, sir, if they ask
 After the body?
VOLPONE   Say it was corrupted.
MOSCA I'll say it stunk, sir, and was fain° t'have it *I was obliged*
 Coffined up instantly and sent away.
80 VOLPONE Anything; what thou wilt. Hold, here's my will.
 Get thee a cap, a count-book,° pen and ink,   *account book*
 Papers afore thee; sit as° thou wert taking   *as if*
 An inventory of parcels.[4] I'll get up
 Behind the curtain on a stool, and hearken;
85 Sometime peep over, see how they do look,
 With what degrees their blood doth leave their faces.
 Oh, 'twill afford me a rare meal of laughter!
MOSCA Your advocate will turn stark dull° upon it. *insensible; gloomy*
VOLPONE It will take off his oratory's edge.
90 MOSCA But your *clarissimo,*[5] old round-back, he
 Will crump you° like a hog-louse with the touch. *curl (himself) up*

---

4. Items; that is, his possessions.
5. Venetian of high rank (Corbaccio).

VOLPONE   And what Corvino?

MOSCA   Oh, sir, look for him
Tomorrow morning with a rope and a dagger[6]
To visit all the streets; he must run mad.
95   My lady, too, that came into the court
To bear false witness for Your Worship—

VOLPONE   Yes,
And kissed me 'fore the fathers, when my face
Flowed all with oils.

MOSCA   And sweat, sir. Why, your gold
Is such another° med'cine, it dries up   *such a*
100 All those offensive savors! It transforms
The most deformèd, and restores 'em lovely,
As 'twere the strange poetical girdle.[7] Jove
Could not invent t'himself a shroud more subtle
To pass Acrisius' guards.[8] It is the thing
105 Makes all the world her grace, her youth, her beauty.

VOLPONE   I think she loves me.

MOSCA   Who? The lady, sir?
She's jealous of you.[9]

VOLPONE   Dost thou say so?
                    [*Knocking offstage.*]

MOSCA   Hark,
There's some already.

VOLPONE   Look.

MOSCA [*peeping out the door*]   It is the vulture.
He has the quickest scent.

VOLPONE   I'll to my place,
110 Thou to thy posture.°   *pretense; act*

MOSCA   I am set.

VOLPONE   But, Mosca,
Play the artificer° now; torture 'em rarely.   *craftsman; trickster*
                    [VOLPONE *conceals himself.*]

5.3

[SCENE: *The scene continues.*]

                    [*Enter* VOLTORE.]

VOLTORE   How now, my Mosca?

MOSCA [*pretending not to notice him, and reading from an
    inventory*]   "Turkey carpets,° nine"—   *Oriental rugs*

VOLTORE   Taking an inventory? That is well.

MOSCA   "Two suits of bedding, tissue"[1]

---

6. Traditional stage props of the would-be
suicide.
7. The girdle of Venus, which made its wearer
irresistible.
8. Acrisius, mythical king of Argos, locked his
daughter Danaë in a tower to prevent her
from bearing a son prophesied to kill him; but

Jove (Zeus, king of the gods) came to her in a
shower of gold.
9. Ardently in love with you; also, covetous of
your wealth.
1. Sets of bed covers and hangings, made of
cloth interwoven with gold or silver.

VOLTORE   Where's the will?
  Let me read that the while.°   *while you're occupied*
      [*Enter* CORBACCIO *on a litter.*]
CORBACCIO [*to the litter-bearers*]   So, set me down
5 And get you home.   [*Exeunt litter-bearers.*]
VOLTORE   Is he come now to trouble us?
MOSCA   "Of cloth-of-gold, two more"—
CORBACCIO   Is it done, Mosca?
MOSCA   "Of several velvets,° eight"—   *velvet hangings*
VOLTORE [*aside*]   I like his care.
CORBACCIO [*to* MOSCA]   Dost thou not hear?
      [*Enter* CORVINO.]
CORVINO   Ha! Is the hour come, Mosca?
      [VOLPONE *peeps from behind a traverse.*°]   *curtain*
VOLPONE [*aside*]   Ay, now they muster.°   *assemble; gather*
CORVINO   What does the advocate here?
10 Or this Corbaccio?
CORBACCIO   What do these here?
      [*Enter* LADY WOULD-BE].
LADY WOULD-BE   Mosca,
  Is his thread spun?[2]
MOSCA   "Eight chests of linen"—
VOLPONE [*aside*]   Oh,
  My fine Dame Would-be, too!
CORVINO   Mosca, the will,
  That I may show it these, and rid 'em hence.
MOSCA   "Six chests of diaper, four of damask"[3]—there.
      [*He gives them the will.*]
15 CORBACCIO   Is that the will?
MOSCA   "Down beds and bolsters"—
VOLPONE [*aside*]   Rare!
  Be busy still. Now they begin to flutter;
  They never think of me. Look, see, see, see!
  How their swift eyes run over the long deed
  Unto the name, and to the legacies,
20 What is bequeathed them there—
MOSCA   "Ten suits of hangings"°—   *sets of tapestries*
VOLPONE [*aside*]   Ay, i' their garters,[4] Mosca. Now their hopes
  Are at the gasp.°   *last gasp*
VOLTORE   Mosca the heir!
CORBACCIO   What's that?
VOLPONE [*aside*]   My advocate is dumb. Look to my merchant;
  He has heard of some strange storm, a ship is lost,

2. That is, is he dead? In Greek mythology, the three Fates spun the thread of an individual's life, measured it, and cut it.
3. Fabric woven with designs—linen with a diamond pattern (diaper) and silk with elaborate figures (damask).
4. A play on the derisive phrase "Hang yourself in your own garters."

25 He faints. My lady will swoon. Old glazen-eyes,[5]
  He hath not reached his despair yet.
CORBACCIO   All these
  Are out of hope; I'm sure the man.
CORVINO   But, Mosca—
MOSCA   "Two cabinets"—
CORVINO   Is this in earnest?
MOSCA   "One
  Of ebony"—
CORVINO   Or do you but delude me?
30 MOSCA   "The other, mother-of-pearl"—I am very busy.
  Good faith, it is a fortune thrown upon me—
  "Item, one salt° of agate"—not my seeking.   *saltcellar*
LADY WOULD-BE   Do you hear, sir?
MOSCA   "A perfumed box"—pray you, forbear;
  You see I am troubled°—"made of an onyx"—   *busy*
LADY WOULD-BE   How!
35 MOSCA   Tomorrow or next day I shall be at leisure
  To talk with you all.
CORVINO   Is this my large hope's issue?°   *outcome*
LADY WOULD-BE   Sir, I must have a fairer answer.
MOSCA   Madam!
  Marry, and shall: pray you, fairly° quit my house.   *peaceably*
  Nay, raise no tempest with your looks, but hark you,
40 Remember what Your Ladyship offered me[6]
  To put you in° an heir; go to, think on't,   *write in your name as*
  And what you said e'en your best madams did
  For maintenance,° and why not you? Enough.   *To support themselves*
  Go home and use the poor Sir Pol, your knight, well,
45 For fear I tell some riddles.° Go, be melancholic.   *secrets*
                    [*Exit* LADY WOULD-BE.]
VOLPONE [*aside*]   Oh, my fine devil!
CORVINO   Mosca, pray you a word.
MOSCA   Lord! Will not you take your dispatch hence yet?
  Methinks of all you should have been th'example.[7]
  Why should you stay here? With what thought? What promise?
50 Hear you, do not you know I know you an ass?
  And that you would most fain have been a wittol°   *willing cuckold*
  If fortune would have let you? That you are
  A declared cuckold, on good terms?° This pearl,   *in good standing*
  You'll say, was yours? Right. This diamond?
55 I'll not deny't, but thank you. Much here else?
  It may be so. Why, think that these good works
  May help to hide your bad. I'll not betray you.
  Although you be but extraordinary
  And have it only in title,[8] it sufficeth.

---

5. Corbaccio wears spectacles (see line 63   7. That is, in leading the way out.
below).   8. You are exceptional, being a cuckold in
6. Evidently, sexual favors (see 4.6.101).   name only.

60   Go home. Be melancholic too, or mad.   [*Exit* CORVINO.]
      VOLPONE [*aside*]   Rare, Mosca! How his villainy becomes him!
      VOLTORE [*aside*]   Certain he doth delude all these for me.
      CORBACCIO [*finally making out the will*]   Mosca the heir?
      VOLPONE [*aside*]   Oh, his four eyes have found it!
      CORBACCIO   I'm cozened, cheated by a parasite-slave!
65   Harlot,° th'ast gulled me.   *Knave, villain*
      MOSCA   Yes, sir. Stop your mouth,
      Or I shall draw the only tooth is left.
      Are not you he, that filthy covetous wretch
      With the three legs,[9] that here, in hope of prey,
      Have, any time this three year, snuffed about
70   With your most grov'ling nose, and would have hired
      Me to the pois'ning of my patron? Sir?
      Are not you he that have today in court
      Professed the disinheriting of your son?
      Perjured yourself? Go home, and die, and stink.
75   If you but croak a syllable, all comes out.
      Away and call your porters. Go, go stink! [*Exit* CORBACCIO.]
      VOLPONE [*aside*]   Excellent varlet!°   *rascal; servant*
      VOLTORE   Now, my faithful Mosca,
      I find thy constancy—
      MOSCA   Sir?
      VOLTORE   Sincere.
      MOSCA   "A table
      Of porphyry"—I mar'l° you'll be thus troublesome.   *marvel*
80   VOLTORE   Nay, leave off now, they are gone.
      MOSCA   Why, who are you?
      What? Who did send for you? Oh, cry you mercy,
      Reverend sir! Good faith, I am grieved for you,
      That any chance° of mine should thus defeat   *good fortune*
      Your—I must needs say—most deserving travails.°   *labors, troubles*
85   But I protest, sir, it was cast upon me,
      And I could almost wish to be without it,
      But that the will o'th'dead must be observed.
      Marry, my joy is that you need it not;
      You have a gift, sir—thank your education—
90   Will never let you want, while there are men
      And malice to breed causes.° Would I had   *lawsuits*
      But half the like, for all my fortune, sir!
      If I have any suits—as I do hope,
      Things being so easy and direct,[1] I shall not—
95   I will make bold with your obstreperous° aid,   *vociferous*
      Conceive me, for your fee,[2] sir. In meantime
      You, that have° so much law, I know, ha' the conscience   *know*
      Not to be covetous of what is mine.
      Good sir, I thank you for my plate;[3] 'twill help

9. Corbaccio walks with a cane.   2. I will pay the usual fee, you understand.
1. That is, the will being so simple and   3. Which Voltore earlier presented to Volpone
straightforward.   (see 1.3.1–20).

100　To set up a young man.° Good faith, you look　　　　　　　　*(Mosca himself)*
　　As° you were costive;° best go home and purge, sir.　　　*As if / constipated*
　　　　　　　　　　　　　　　　　　[*Exit* VOLTORE.]

VOLPONE [*coming from behind the traverse*]　Bid him eat
　　lettuce° well. My witty mischief,　　　　　　　　　　　*(a laxative)*
　　Let me embrace thee! [*He hugs* MOSCA.] Oh, that I could now
　　Transform thee to a Venus! Mosca, go,
105　Straight take my habit of *clarissimo*°　　　　　　　　　*aristocrat's robe*
　　And walk the streets; be seen, torment 'em more.
　　We must pursue as well as plot. Who would
　　Have lost° this feast?　　　　　　　　　　　　　　　　　*missed*
MOSCA　　　　　　　　I doubt it will lose them.[4]
VOLPONE　Oh, my recovery shall recover all.
110　That I could now but think on some disguise
　　To meet 'em in, and ask 'em questions.
　　How I would vex 'em still at every turn!
MOSCA　Sir, I can fit you.
VOLPONE　　　　　　　　Canst thou?
MOSCA　　　　　　　　　　　　Yes, I know
　　One o'the *commendatori*,° sir, so like you,　　　　　　　*court deputies*
115　Him will I straight make drunk, and bring you his habit.
VOLPONE　A rare disguise, and answering thy brain!°　　　*suiting your cleverness*
　　Oh, I will be a sharp disease unto 'em.
MOSCA　Sir, you must look for° curses—　　　　　　　　　*expect*
VOLPONE　　　　　　　　　　　　Till they burst!
　　The fox fares ever best when he is curst.°　　[*Exeunt.*]　　*(proverbial)*

5.4

[SCENE: *The* WOULD-BES' *house.*]

[*Enter* PEREGRINE *in disguise, and three* MERCATORI
(MERCHANTS).]

PEREGRINE　Am I enough disguised?
FIRST MERCHANT　　　　　　　I warrant° you.　　　　　　　*assure*
PEREGRINE　All my ambition is to fright him only.
SECOND MERCHANT　If you could ship him away, 'twere excellent.
THIRD MERCHANT　To Zante, or to Aleppo?[5]
PEREGRINE　　　　　　　　　　　　Yes, and ha' his
5　Adventures put i'th'book of voyages,[6]
　　And his gulled story° registered for truth?　　　　　　*the story of his gulling*
　　Well, gentlemen, when I am in awhile,
　　And that you think us warm in our discourse,
　　Know° your approaches.　　　　　　　　　　　　　　　*Make*
FIRST MERCHANT　　　　　　Trust it to our care.

---

4. I fear it will get rid of them (i.e., lose us the
ability to cheat them further of their money
and possessions).
5. A major trading center in Syria. *Zante:* an
island off the coast of Greece, and a Venetian

possession at the time.
6. Accounts such as Richard Hakluyt's *The
Principal Navigations, Voiages, Traffiques and
Discoueries of the English Nation* (1598–1600)
were popular at the time.

[*Exeunt* MERCHANTS.]

[PEREGRINE *knocks. A* WOMAN *servant answers the door.*]

10 PEREGRINE   Save° you, fair lady. Is Sir Pol within?   God save
WOMAN   I do not know, sir.
PEREGRINE   Pray you, say unto him
Here is a merchant upon earnest business
Desires to speak with him.
WOMAN   I will see, sir.
PEREGRINE   Pray you.

[*Exit* WOMAN.]

I see the family° is all female here.   household

[*Enter* WOMAN.]

15 WOMAN   He says, sir, he has weighty affairs of state
That now require him whole,⁷ some other time
You may possess him.°   have his attention
PEREGRINE   Pray you say again,
If those require him whole, these will exact him°   demand his attention
Whereof I bring him tidings.   [*Exit* WOMAN.]
What might be
20 His grave affair of state, now? How to make
Bolognian sausages here in Venice, sparing°   leaving out
One o'th'ingredients?

[*Enter* WOMAN.]

WOMAN   Sir, he says he knows
By your word "tidings" that you are no statesman,⁸
And therefore wills you stay°   wishes you to stay
PEREGRINE   Sweet, pray you return° him   reply to
25 I have not read so many proclamations
And studied them for words as he has done,
But—here he deigns to come.

[*Enter* POLITIC.]

[*Exit* WOMAN.]

POLITIC   Sir, I must crave
Your courteous pardon. There hath chanced today
Unkind disaster 'twixt my lady and me,
30 And I was penning my apology
To give her satisfaction, as you came now.
PEREGRINE   Sir, I am grieved I bring you worse disaster.
The gentleman you met at th'port today,
That told you he was newly arrived—
POLITIC   Ay, was
35 A fugitive punk?°   prostitute
PEREGRINE   No, sir, a spy set on you;
And he has made relation to the Senate

---

7. Require his whole attention.
8. That is, no government agent, who would use the word "intelligence."

That you professed to him to have a plot
To sell the state of Venice to the Turk?°   (see 4.1.128–30)
POLITIC   Oh, me!
PEREGRINE   For which warrants are signed by this time
40   To apprehend you, and to search your study
      For papers—
POLITIC   Alas, sir, I have none but notes
      Drawn out of playbooks°—   *printed plays*
PEREGRINE   All the better, sir.
POLITIC   And some essays. What shall I do?
PEREGRINE   Sir, best
      Convey yourself into a sugar-chest;
45   Or, if you could lie round, a frail were rare,⁹
      And I could send you aboard.
POLITIC   Sir, I but talked so,
      For discourse° sake merely.   [*They knock without.*]   *conversation's*
PEREGRINE   Hark, they are there!
POLITIC   I am a wretch, a wretch!
PEREGRINE   What will you do, sir?
      Ha' you ne'er a currant-butt° to leap into?   *cask for currants*
50   They'll put you to the rack; you must be sudden.°   *quick to act*
POLITIC   Sir, I have an engine°—   *device; contrivance*
THIRD MERCHANT [*without*]   Sir Politic Would-be!
SECOND MERCHANT [*without*]   Where is he?
POLITIC   That I have thought upon beforetime.
PEREGRINE   What is it?
POLITIC   I shall ne'er endure the torture!
      Marry, it is, sir, of a tortoiseshell, [*producing the shell*]
55   Fitted for these extremities. Pray you sir, help me.
      Here I have a place, sir, to put back my legs—
      Please you to lay it on, sir—with this cap
      And my black gloves. I'll lie, sir, like a tortoise
      Till they are gone.
PEREGRINE [*laying the shell on* POLITIC's *back*]   And call you this
      an engine?
60 POLITIC   Mine own device—good sir, bid my wife's women
      To burn my papers.   [*Exit* PEREGRINE.]
              [*The* MERCHANTS *rush in.*]
FIRST MERCHANT   Where's he hid?
THIRD MERCHANT   We must
      And will, sure, find him.
SECOND MERCHANT   Which is his study?
              [*Enter* PEREGRINE.]
FIRST MERCHANT   What
      Are you, sir?
PEREGRINE   I'm a merchant, that came here
      To look upon this tortoise.

9. If you could curl up, a large rush basket (used especially for figs and raisins) would be excellent.

THIRD MERCHANT　　　　　　　How?

FIRST MERCHANT　　　　　　　Saint Mark!

65　What beast is this?

PEREGRINE　　　　　It is a fish.

SECOND MERCHANT [*to* POLITIC]　Come out here!

PEREGRINE　Nay, you may strike him, sir, and tread upon him.
　He'll bear a cart.

FIRST MERCHANT　What, to run over him?

PEREGRINE　　　　　　　　　　　Yes.

THIRD MERCHANT　Let's jump upon him.

SECOND MERCHANT　　　　　　Can he not go?°　　　　　　*walk*

PEREGRINE　　　　　　　　　　He creeps, sir.

FIRST MERCHANT [*poking* POLITIC]　Let's see him creep.

PEREGRINE　　　　　　　　　　No, good sir, you will
　hurt him.

70　SECOND MERCHANT　Heart! I'll see him creep, or prick his guts.

THIRD MERCHANT [*to* POLITIC]　Come out here!

PEREGRINE [*aside to* POLITIC]　　　Pray you, sir, creep a little.
　　　[POLITIC *creeps.*]

FIRST MERCHANT　　　　　　　　　　　　　　Forth!

SECOND MERCHANT　Yet further.

PEREGRINE [*aside to* POLITIC]　Good sir, creep.

SECOND MERCHANT　　　　　　We'll see his legs.
　　[*They pull off the shell and discover*° *him.*]　　*disclose*

THIRD MERCHANT　Godso,° he has garters!　　　　(*interjection*)

FIRST MERCHANT　　　　　　　Ay, and gloves!

SECOND MERCHANT　　　　　　　　　　Is this
　Your fearful tortoise?

PEREGRINE [*revealing himself*]　Now, Sir Pol, we are even.

75　For your next project I shall be prepared.
　I am sorry for the funeral of your notes, sir.

FIRST MERCHANT　'Twere a rare motion[1] to be seen in Fleet Street

SECOND MERCHANT　Ay, i'the term.

FIRST MERCHANT　　　　　　Or Smithfield, in the fair.[2]

THIRD MERCHANT　Methinks 'tis but a melancholic sight!

80　PEREGRINE　Farewell, most politic tortoise.
　　　　[*Exeunt* PEREGRINE *and* MERCHANTS.]
　　　[*Enter* WOMAN.]

POLITIC　　　　　　　　　　　Where's my lady?
　Knows she of this?

WOMAN　　　　　　I know not, sir.

POLITIC　　　　　　　　　　Inquire.
　　　　　　　[*Exit* WOMAN.]

---

1. Puppet show. Such shows were performed on Fleet Street, a busy street in central London near the Inns of Court, the four legal societies in London that control admission to the bar and that were particularly busy when the courts were in session ("i'the term").

2. Bartholomew Fair, four days of trading and entertainment held every year at the end of August in Smithfield, a large open space in northwest London (just outside the city walls).

Oh, I shall be the fable of all feasts,
The freight of the *gazetti*,° ship boys' tale,   *topic of the newspapers*
And, which is worst, even talk for ordinaries°   *taverns*
    [*Enter* WOMAN.]

85 WOMAN My lady's come most melancholic home,
And says, sir, she will straight to sea for physic.°   *for her health*
POLITIC And I, to shun this place and clime forever,
Creeping with house on back, and think it well
To shrink my poor head in my politic shell.   [*Exeunt.*]

5.5

[SCENE: VOLPONE's *house.*]

    [*Enter* VOLPONE *and* MOSCA, *the first in the habit of a*
    commendatore, the other, of a clarissimo.]

VOLPONE Am I then like him?
MOSCA   Oh, sir, you are he.
  No man can sever° you.   *distinguish*
VOLPONE   Good.
MOSCA   But what am I?
VOLPONE 'Fore heav'n, a brave° *clarissimo*; thou becom'st it!   *excellent*
  Pity thou wert not born one.
MOSCA   If I hold
5 My made one,³ 'twill be well.
VOLPONE   I'll go and see
  What news, first, at the court.
MOSCA   Do so.   [*Exit* VOLPONE.]
              My fox
  Is out on° his hole, and ere he shall reenter   *of*
  I'll make him languish in his borrowed case,°   *disguise*
  Except he come to composition⁴ with me.
10 [*Calling*] Androgyno, Castrone, Nano!
    [*Enter* ANDROGYNO, CASTRONE, *and* NANO.]
ALL   Here.
MOSCA Go recreate° yourselves abroad;° go sport.   *amuse / outside*
    [*Exeunt* ANDROGYNO, CASTRONE, *and* NANO.]
  So, now I have the keys, and am possessed.°   *in possession*
  Since he will needs be dead afore his time,
  I'll bury him or gain by him. I am his heir,
15 And so will keep me° till he share at least.   *remain*
  To cozen him of all were but a cheat
  Well placed; no man would construe it a sin.
  Let his sport pay for't.⁵ This is called the Fox Trap.   [*Exit.*]

3. That is, if I keep up (or retain) my assumed   5. That is, let his amusement compensate
identity.   him for his loss.
4. Unless he comes to an agreement.

5.6

[SCENE: *A street in Venice.*]

[*Enter* CORBACCIO *and* CORVINO.]

CORBACCIO They say the court is set.°   *in session*
CORVINO   We must maintain
  Our first tale good, for both our reputations.
CORBACCIO Why, mine's no tale; my son would there have killed me.
CORVINO That's true; I had forgot. [*Aside*] Mine is, I am sure.—
5 But for your will, sir.
CORBACCIO   Ay, I'll come uponhim°   *(Mosca)*
  For that hereafter, now his patron's dead.

[*Enter* VOLPONE *disguised.*]

VOLPONE Signor Corvino! And Corbaccio! Sir,
  Much joy unto you.
CORVINO   Of what?
VOLPONE   The sudden good
  Dropped down upon you—
CORBACCIO   Where?
VOLPONE   And none knows how—
10 From old Volpone, sir.
CORBACCIO   Out, arrant knave!
VOLPONE Let not your too much wealth, sir, make you furious.
CORBACCIO Away, thou varlet!
VOLPONE   Why, sir?
CORBACCIO   Dost thou mock me?
VOLPONE You mock the world, sir.[6] Did you not change° wills?   *exchange*
CORBACCIO Out, harlot!
VOLPONE [*to* CORVINO] Oh, belike° you are the man,   *perhaps*
15 Signor Corvino? Faith, you carry it° well;   *carry it off*
  You grow not mad withal. I love your spirit.
  You are not overleavened° with your fortune.   *puffed up*
  You should ha' some° would swell now like a wine-vat   *some people*
  With such an autumn.° Did he gi' you all, sir?   *harvest*
20 CORVINO Avoid,° you rascal!   *Be gone*
VOLPONE   Troth, your wife has shown
  Herself a very° woman. But you are well;   *true*
  You need not care; you have a good estate
  To bear it out, sir, better by this chance—
  Except° Corbaccio have a share?   *Unless*
CORBACCIO   Hence, varlet!
25 VOLPONE You will not be aknown,° sir; why, 'tis wise.   *acknowledged as heir*
  Thus do all gamesters at all games dissemble.
  No man will seem to win

[*Exeunt* CORBACCIO *and* CORVINO.]

                   Here comes my vulture,
Heaving his beak up i'the air and snuffing.

---

6. That is, by concealing your good fortune.

5.7

[SCENE: *The scene continues.*]

[*Enter* VOLTORE.]

VOLTORE [*to himself*]   Outstripped thus by a parasite? A slave
  Would° run on errands, and make legs[7] for crumbs?   *Who used to*
  Well, what I'll do—
VOLPONE   The court stays° for Your Worship.   *waits*
  I e'en rejoice, sir, at Your Worship's happiness,
5 And that it fell into so learnèd hands
  That understand the fingering[8]—
VOLTORE   What do you mean?
VOLPONE   I mean to be a suitor to Your Worship
  For the small tenement, out of reparations°—   *in need of repair*
  That° at the end of your long row of houses   *The one*
10 By the *piscaria*.° It was in Volpone's time,   *fish market (Latin)*
  Your predecessor, ere he grew diseased,
  A handsome, pretty, customed° bawdy house   *well-patronized*
  As any was in Venice—none dispraised[9]—
  But fell with him; his body and that house
15 Decayed together.
VOLTORE   Come, sir, leave your prating.
VOLPONE   Why, if Your Worship give me but your hand,
  That I may ha' the refusal,° I have done.   *right of first refusal*
  'Tis a mere toy to you, sir, candle-rents,[1]
  As Your learned Worship knows—
VOLTORE   What do I know?
20 VOLPONE   Marry, no end of your wealth, sir, God decrease[2] it.
VOLTORE   Mistaking° knave! What, mock'st thou my misfortune?   *Misunderstanding*
VOLPONE   His blessing on your heart, sir! Would 'twere more.
                                [*Exit* VOLTORE.]

  Now, to my first[3] again, at the next corner.

5.8

[SCENE: *The scene continues.*]

[*Enter* CORBACCIO *and* CORVINO. *Enter* MOSCA, passant° *over*   *passing*
  the stage in clarissimo's attire, and exit.*]

CORBACCIO   See, in our habit! See the impudent varlet!
CORVINO   That° I could shoot mine eyes at him, like gunstones!°   *Would that /*
VOLPONE   But, is this true, sir, of the parasite?   *cannonballs*
CORBACCIO   Again t'afflict us? Monster!
VOLPONE   In good faith, sir,
5 I'm heartily grieved a beard of your grave length[4]
  Should be so overreached. I never brooked°   *could endure*

---

7. Bow and scrape.
8. That is, how to handle money.
9. Not to speak ill of the others.
1. Revenue from deteriorating property; pocket
money for buying candles.
2. A deliberate malapropism for "increase."
3. That is, the first targets of my taunts.
4. That is, a man so old and wise.

That parasite's hair; methought his nose should cozen.°   *he had a cheating nose*
There still° was somewhat in his look did promise   *always*
The bane° of a *clarissimo.*   *ruin*

CORBACCIO   Knave—
VOLPONE [*to* CORVINO]   Methinks
10   Yet you that are so traded° i'the world,   *experienced*
    A witty merchant, the fine bird Corvino,
    That have such moral emblems[5] on your name,
    Should not have sung your shame and dropped your cheese,
    To let the fox laugh at your emptiness
15 CORVINO   Sirrah, you think the privilege of the place,[6]
    And your red saucy cap, that seems to me
    Nailed to your jolt-head with those two *cecchines*,[7]
    Can warrant° your abuses. Come you hither.   *sanction*
    You shall perceive, sir, I dare beat you. Approach!
20 VOLPONE   No haste, sir, I do know your valor well,
    Since you durst publish° what you are,° sir.   *make public / (a cuckold)*
        [VOLPONE *makes as if to leave.*]
CORVINO   Tarry!
    I'd speak with you.
VOLPONE   Sir, sir, another time—
CORVINO   Nay, now.
VOLPONE   Oh, God, sir! I were° a wise man   *would be (ironic)*
    Would stand° the fury of a distracted cuckold.   *To confront*
        [MOSCA *enters and walks by 'em.*]
25 CORBACCIO   What! Come again?
VOLPONE [*aside to* MOSCA]   Upon 'em, Mosca; save me.
CORBACCIO   The air's infected where he breathes.
CORVINO   Let's fly him.
        [*Exeunt* CORVINO *and* CORBACCIO.]
VOLPONE   Excellent basilisk![8] Turn upon the vulture.

5.9

[SCENE: *The scene continues.*]

        [*Enter* VOLTORE.]
VOLTORE [*to Mosca*]   Well, flesh fly,[9] it is summer with you now;
    Your winter will come on.
MOSCA   Good advocate,
    Pray thee not rail, nor threaten out of place thus;
    Thou'lt make a solecism, as madam says.°   *(see 4.2.44)*
5   Get you a biggin more;° your brain breaks loose.   *another lawyer's cap*
VOLTORE   Well, sir.   [*Exit* MOSCA.]

---

5. Drawings or pictures accompanying moral
fables; here, the fable of the fox and the crow
(see 1.2.95–97).
6. Violence was forbidden near the court. *Sirrah*: customary form of address to male social
inferiors; here used contemptuously.

7. A commendatore wore a red cap with gold
buttons similar to coins on its front.
8. A legendary reptile whose glance was fatal.
9. A fly that deposits its eggs in dead flesh;
Mosca in Italian means "fly."

VOLPONE   Would you ha' me beat the insolent slave?
  Throw dirt upon his first good clothes?
VOLTORE   This same°   (*the disguised Volpone*)
  Is doubtless some familiar[1]
VOLPONE   Sir, the court,
  In troth, stays for you. I am mad° a mule   *furious that*
10 That never read Justinian[2] should get up
  And ride an advocate. Had you no quirk°   *trick*
  To avoid gullage,° sir, by such a creature?   *being gulled*
  I hope you do but jest; he has not done't.
  This's but confederacy[3] to blind the rest.
15 You are the heir?
VOLTORE   A strange, officious,
  Troublesome knave! Thou dost torment me.
VOLPONE   I know—
  It cannot be, sir, that you should be cozened;
  'Tis not within the wit of man to do it.
  You are so wise, so prudent, and 'tis fit
20 That wealth and wisdom still should go together.
                                       [*Exeunt.*]

5.10

[SCENE: *The law court.*]

[*Enter four* AVOCATORI, NOTARIO (NOTARY), COMMENDATORI,
BONARIO *and* CELIA *under guard*, CORBACCIO, *and* CORVINO.]

FIRST AVOCATORE   Are all the parties here?
NOTARY   All but the advocate.
SECOND AVOCATORE   And here he comes.
FIRST AVOCATORE   Then bring 'em° forth to sentence.   (*Celia and Bonario*)
  [ENTER VOLTORE, *and* VOLPONE *still disguised as a
  commendatore.*]
VOLTORE   O my most honored fathers, let your mercy
  Once win upon° your justice, to forgive—   *prevail over*
5 I am distracted—
VOLPONE [*aside*]   What will he do now?
VOLTORE   Oh,
  I know not which t'address myself to first,
  Whether Your Fatherhoods or these innocents—
CORVINO [*aside*]   Will he betray himself?
VOLTORE   Whom equally
  I have abused, out of most covetous ends—
10 CORVINO [*aside to* CORBACCIO]   The man is mad!
CORBACCIO   What's that?
CORVINO   He is possessed.

1. Member of the same household; attendant
demon.
2. The Roman emperor (r. 527–565 C.E.),

whose codification of Roman law was the
foundation of European legal codes.
3. A conspiracy (between Voltore and Mosca).

VOLTORE   For which, now struck in conscience, here I prostrate
　　Myself at your offended feet for pardon.
　　　　[*He throws himself down.*]
FIRST AND SECOND AVOCATORI   Arise!
CELIA　　　　　　　　　　　　O heav'n, how just thou art!
VOLPONE [*aside*]　　　　　　　　　　　　　I'm caught
　　I' mine own noose—
CORVINO [*aside to* CORBACCIO]   Be constant, sir; naught now
　　Can help but impudence.°　[VOLTORE *rises.*]　　　　　　　*shamelessness*
15 FIRST AVOCATORE [*to* VOLTORE]   Speak forward.°　　　　　　*Continue*
COMMENDATORI [*to the courtroom*]　　　　Silence!
VOLTORE   It is not passion in me, reverend fathers,
　　But only conscience, conscience, my good sires,
　　That makes me now tell truth. That parasite,
　　That knave hath been the instrument of all.
20 SECOND AVOCATORE   Where is that knave? Fetch him.
VOLPONE [*as commendatore*]　　　　I go.　[*Exit.*]
CORVINO　　　　　　　　　　　　　Grave fathers,
　　This man's distracted; he confessed it now;
　　For, hoping to be old Volpone's heir,
　　Who now is dead—
THIRD AVOCATORE　　How?
SECOND AVOCATORE　　　　Is Volpone dead?
CORVINO   Dead since[4] grave fathers—
BONARIO　　　　　　　　　O sure vengeance!
FIRST AVOCATORE　　　　　　　　　　Stay.
25　Then he was no deceiver?
VOLTORE　　　　　　　Oh, no, none.
　　The parasite, grave fathers.
CORVINO　　　　　　　　He does speak
　　Out of mere envy, 'cause the servant's made
　　The thing he gaped° for. Please Your Fatherhoods,　　　*longed*
　　This is the truth; though I'll not justify
30　The other° but he may be somedeal° faulty.　　　(*Mosca*) / *somewhat*
VOLTORE   Ay, to your hopes as well as mine, Corvino;
　　But I'll use modesty.° Pleaseth Your Wisdoms　　　*restraint*
　　To view these certain notes, and but confer° them.　　　*compare*
　　As I hope favor, they shall speak clear truth.
　　　　[*He gives documents to the* AVOCATORI.]
35 CORVINO   The devil has entered him!
BONARIO　　　　　　　　　Or bides in you.
FOURTH AVOCATORE   We have done ill, by a public officer
　　To send for him, if he be heir.[5]
SECOND AVOCATORE　　　For whom?
FOURTH AVOCATORE   Him that they call the parasite.
THIRD AVOCATORE　　　　　　　　　'Tis true;
　　He is a man of great estate now left.°　　　*bequeathed to him*

---

4. That is, since you last saw him.
5. As the inheritor of a large fortune, Mosca

merits an invitation to the court, not a summons served by a common official.

40 FOURTH AVOCATORE [*to* NOTARY] Go you and learn his name,
and say the court
Entreats his presence here but to the clearing
Of some few doubts.   [*Exit* NOTARY]
SECOND AVOCATORE   This same's a labyrinth!
FIRST AVOCATORE [*to* CORVINO]   Stand you unto° your first report?   *Do you stand by*
CORVINO   My state,°   *estate*
My life, my fame°—   *reputation*
BONARIO   Where is't?
CORVINO   —are at the stake°   *at stake*
45 FIRST AVOCATORE [*to* CORBACCIO]   Is yours so too?
CORBACCIO   The advocate's a knave,
And has a forkèd tongue—
SECOND AVOCATORE   Speak to the point.
CORBACCIO   So is the parasite, too.
FIRST AVOCATORE   This is confusion.
VOLTORE   I do beseech Your Fatherhoods, read but those.
CORVINO   And credit nothing the false spirit hath writ.
50   It cannot be but he is possessed, grave fathers.
[*The* AVOCATORI *examine* VOLTORE'*s papers.*]

5.11

[SCENE: *A street.*]

[*Enter* VOLPONE *on a separate part of the stage.*]

VOLPONE   To make a snare for mine own neck! And run
My head into it willfully! With laughter!
When I had newly scaped, was free and clear!
Out of mere wantonness!° Oh, the dull devil   *caprice; recklessness*
5   Was in this brain of mine when I devised it,
And Mosca gave it second.° He must now   *seconded the idea*
Help to sear up° this vein, or we bleed dead.   *cauterize*
[*Enter* NANO, ANDROGYNO, *and* CASTRONE.]
How now, who let you loose? Whither go you now?
What, to buy gingerbread? Or to drown kitlings?°   *kittens*
10 NANO   Sir, Master Mosca called us out of doors,
And bid us all go play, and took the keys.
ANDROGYNO   Yes.
VOLPONE   Did Master Mosca take the keys? Why, so!
I am farther in.[6] These are my fine conceits!°   *ideas; schemes*
I must be merry, with a mischief to me![7]
15   What a vile wretch was I, that could not bear
My fortune soberly! I must ha' my crotchets°   *perverse fancies*
And my conundrums!° Well, go you and seek him.   *whims*
His meaning may be truer than my fear.[8]

6. Deeper in trouble.   8. That is, his intentions may be more faithful
7. I had to be merry, and this is the mischief   to me than I fear they are.
that resulted for me.

Bid him he straight come to me, to the court.
20 Thither will I, and, if't be possible,
Unscrew⁹ my advocate upon° new hopes.   *by means of*
When I provoked him, then I lost myself.

> [*Exeunt* VOLPONE *and his entourage.*
> *The* AVOCATORI *and parties to the*
> *courtroom proceedings remain onstage.*]

5.12

[SCENE: *The courtroom.*]

FIRST AVOCATORE [*with* VOLTORE'*s notes*]   These things can
   ne'er be reconciled. He here
   Professeth that the gentleman° was wronged,   (*Bonario*)
   And that the gentlewoman was brought thither,
   Forced by her husband, and there left.
VOLTORE   Most true.
5 CELIA   How ready° is heav'n to those that pray!   *responsive*
FIRST AVOCATORE   But that
   Volpone would have ravished her, he holds
   Utterly false, knowing his impotence.
CORVINO   Grave fathers, he is possessed; again I say,
   Possessed. Nay, if there be possession
10 And obsession,¹ he has both.
THIRD AVOCATORE   Here comes our officer.

[*Enter* VOLPONE, *still disguised.*]

VOLPONE   The parasite will straight be here, grave fathers.
FOURTH AVOCATORE   You might invent some other name, sir varlet.
THIRD AVOCATORE   Did not the notary meet him?
VOLPONE   Not that I know.
FOURTH AVOCATORE   His coming will clear all.
SECOND AVOCATORE   Yet° it is misty.   *As yet*
15 VOLTORE   May't please Your Fatherhoods—
VOLPONE [*whispers to the advocate*]   Sir, the parasite
   Willed me to tell you that his master lives,
   That you are still the man, your hopes the same;
   And this was only a jest—
VOLTORE [*aside to* VOLPONE]   How?
VOLPONE [*aside to* VOLTORE]   Sir, to try
   If you were firm, and how you stood affected.°   *how you are inclined*
20 VOLTORE   Art sure he lives?
VOLPONE   Do I live,² sir?
VOLTORE   Oh, me!
   I was too violent.
VOLPONE   Sir, you may redeem it.

---

9. Turn around, change the mind of.
1. "Possession" is control by an evil spirit that has entered one's body; "obsession" is the state of being beset externally by an evil

spirit.
2. Volpone apparently reveals himself to Voltore.

They said you were possessed; fall down, and seem so.
I'll help to make it good.   [VOLTORE *falls.*]
> [*Aloud*] *God bless the man!*

[*Aside to* VOLTORE] Stop your wind[3] hard, and swell. [*Aloud*]
    See, see, see, see!
25 He vomits crooked pins! His eyes are set
Like a dead hare's hung in a poulter's[4] shop!
His mouth's running away!° [*To* CORVINO] Do you see,   *awry; twitching wildly*
  signor?
    Now 'tis in his belly.

CORVINO   Ay, the devil!
VOLPONE   Now in his throat.
CORVINO   Ay, I perceive it plain.
30 VOLPONE   'Twill out, 'twill out! Stand clear. See where it flies,
In shape of a blue toad with a bat's wings!
    [*To* CORBACCIO] Do not you see it, sir?
CORBACCIO   What? I think I do.
CORVINO   'Tis too manifest.
VOLPONE   Look! He comes t' himself!
VOLTORE   Where am I?
VOLPONE   Take good heart; the worst is past, sir.
35 You are dispossessed.
FIRST AVOCATORE   What accident° is this?   *unexpected event*
SECOND AVOCATORE   Sudden, and full of wonder!
THIRD AVOCATORE   If he were
  Possessed, as it appears, all this° is nothing.   *(Voltore's notes)*
CORVINO   He has been often subject to these fits.
FIRST AVOCATORE   Show him that writing. [*To* VOLTORE] Do you
  know it, sir?
40 VOLPONE [*aside to* VOLTORE]   Deny it, sir; forswear it; know it not.
VOLTORE   Yes, I do know it well, it is my hand;°   *handwriting*
But all that it contains is false.
BONARIO   Oh, practice!°   *trickery*
SECOND AVOCATORE   What maze is this!
FIRST AVOCATORE   Is he not guilty, then,
  Whom you there name the parasite?
VOLTORE   Grave fathers,
45 No more than his good patron, old Volpone.
FOURTH AVOCATORE   Why, he is dead!
VOLTORE   Oh, no, my honored fathers.
    He lives—
FIRST AVOCATORE   How! Lives?
VOLTORE   Lives.
SECOND AVOCATORE   This is subtler yet!
THIRD AVOCATORE [*to* VOLTORE]   You said he was dead?
VOLTORE   Never.
THIRD AVOCATORE [*to* CORVINO]   You said so?

---

3. Hold your breath. Voltore's performance includes standard symptoms of possession by and exorcism of a demon.
4. A seller of poultry and small game.

CORVINO   I heard so.

FOURTH AVOCATORE   Here comes the gentleman; make him way.° *make way for him*

[*Enter* MOSCA.]

50 THIRD AVOCATORE   A stool!

FOURTH AVOCATORE [*aside*]   A proper° man! And, were Volpone dead,   *handsome*
    A fit match for my daughter.

THIRD AVOCATORE   Give him way.

VOLPONE [*aside to* MOSCA]   Mosca, I was almost lost; the advocate
    Had betrayed all; but now it is recovered.
    All's o'the hinge° again. Say I am living.   *back in order*

55 MOSCA [*aloud*]   What busy° knave is this? Most reverend fathers,   *meddlesome*
    I sooner had attended your grave pleasures,
    But that my order for the funeral
    Of my dear patron did require me—

VOLPONE [*aside*]   Mosca!

MOSCA   Whom I intend to bury like a gentleman.

VOLPONE [*aside*]   Ay, quick,° and cozen me of all.   *alive*

SECOND AVOCATORE   Still stranger!

60   More intricate!

FIRST AVOCATORE   And come about° again!   *changing course*

FOURTH AVOCATORE [*aside*]   It is a match; my daughter is bestowed.

MOSCA [*aside to* VOLPONE]   Will you gi' me half?

VOLPONE [*aside to* MOSCA]   First, I'll be hanged.

MOSCA [*aside to* VOLPONE]   I know
    Your voice is good. Cry° not so loud.   *Shout*

FIRST AVOCATORE   Demand°   *Ask*
    The advocate. [*To* VOLTORE] Sir, did not you affirm

65   Volpone was alive?

VOLPONE   Yes, and he is;
    This gent'man° told me so. [*Aside to* MOSCA] Thou shalt have half.   *(Mosca)*

MOSCA   Whose drunkard is this same? Speak, some that know him;
    I never saw his face. [*Aside to* VOLPONE] I cannot now
    Afford it° you so cheap.   *Yield it to*

70 VOLPONE [*aside to* MOSCA] No?

FIRST AVOCATORE [*to* VOLTORE]   What say you?

VOLTORE   The officer told me.

VOLPONE   I did, grave fathers,
    And will maintain he lives with mine own life,
    And that this creature told me. [*Aside*] I was born
    With all good stars my enemies.

MOSCA   Most grave fathers,

75   If such an insolence as this must pass°   *be permitted*
    Upon me, I am silent. 'Twas not this
    For which you sent, I hope.

SECOND AVOCATORE [*pointing to* VOLPONE]   Take him away.

VOLPONE [*aside to* MOSCA]   Mosca!

THIRD AVOCATORE   Let him be whipped.

VOLPONE [*aside to* MOSCA]   Wilt thou betray me?
    Cozen me?

THIRD AVOCATORE   And taught to bear himself

80 Toward a person of his° rank.   (Mosca's)
    FOURTH AVOCATORE   Away!
            [*Officers seize* VOLPONE.]
    MOSCA   I humbly thank Your Fatherhoods.
    VOLPONE   Soft, soft. [*Aside*] Whipped?
      And lose all that I have? If I confess,
      It cannot be much more.
    FOURTH AVOCATORE [*to* MOSCA]   Sir, are you married?
    VOLPONE [*aside*]   They'll be allied° anon; I must be resolute.   *linked by marriage*
85   The fox shall here uncase°   [*He puts off his disguise.*]   *reveal himself*
    MOSCA [*aside*]   Patron!
    VOLPONE   Nay, now
      My ruins shall not come alone. Your match
      I'll hinder sure; my substance shall not glue you
      Nor screw you into a family.
    MOSCA [*aside*]   Why, patron!
    VOLPONE   I am Volpone, and [*pointing to* MOSCA] this is my knave;
90   [*Pointing to* VOLTORE] This his own knave; [*pointing to* CORBACCIO]
      this, avarice's fool;
      [*Pointing to* CORVINO] This, a chimera[5] of wittol,° fool, and   *willing cuckold*
      knave;
      And, reverend fathers, since we all can hope
      Naught but a sentence, let's not now despair it.°   *be disappointed*
      You hear me brief.°   *speak briefly*
    CORVINO   May it please Your Fatherhoods—
    COMMENDATORE   Silence!
95 FIRST AVOCATORE   The knot is now undone by miracle!
    SECOND AVOCATORE   Nothing can be more clear.
    THIRD AVOCATORE   Or can more prove
      These innocent.
    FIRST AVOCATORE   Give 'em their liberty.
            [BONARIO *and* CELIA *are released.*]
    BONARIO   Heaven could not long let such gross crimes be hid.
    SECOND AVOCATORE   If this be held the highway to get riches,
      May I be poor!
100 THIRD AVOCATORE   This's not the gain, but torment.
    FIRST AVOCATORE   These possess wealth as sick men possess fevers,
      Which trulier may be said to possess them.
    SECOND AVOCATORE   Disrobe that parasite.
            [MOSCA *is stripped of his clarissimo's robe.*]
    CORVINO [*and*] MOSCA   Most honored fathers!
    FIRST AVOCATORE   Can you plead aught to stay the course of justice?
105   If you can, speak.
    CORVINO [*and*] VOLTORE   We beg favor—
    CELIA   And mercy.

---

5. A monster formed out of different animals (in classical mythology, a fire-breathing creature with a lion's head, a goat's body, and a serpent's tail).

FIRST AVOCATORE [*to* CELIA]   You hurt your innocence, suing° for   *appealing*
the guilty.
[*To the others*] Stand forth; and, first; the parasite. You appear
T'have been the chiefest minister,° if not plotter,   *agent*
In all these lewd impostures° and now, lastly,   *base deceptions*
110 Have with your impudence abused the court
And habit° of a gentleman of Venice,   *garb*
Being a fellow of no birth or blood;
For which our sentence is, first thou be whipped,
Then live perpetual prisoner in our galleys.
115 VOLPONE   I thank you for him.
MOSCA   Bane to° thy wolfish nature!   *A curse on*
FIRST AVOCATORE   Deliver him to the *saffi*° [MOSCA *is placed under*   *bailiffs*
   guard.] Thou, Volpone,
By blood and rank a gentleman, canst not fall
Under like censure, but our judgment on thee
Is that thy substance° all be straight confiscate   *wealth*
120 To the hospital of the *Incurabili*,[6]
And since the most was gotten by imposture,
By feigning lame, gout, palsy, and such diseases,
Thou art to lie in prison, cramped with irons,
Till thou be'st sick and lame indeed.—Remove him.
   [VOLPONE *is placed under guard.*]
125 VOLPONE   This is called mortifying[7] of a fox.
FIRST AVOCATORE   Thou, Voltore, to take away the scandal
Thou hast giv'n all worthy men of thy profession,
Art banished from their fellowship and our state.
   [VOLTORE *is placed under guard.*]
Corbaccio—bring him near.—We here possess
130 Thy son of all thy state,° and confine thee   *estate*
To the monastery of San Spirito,°   *the Holy Spirit*
Where, since thou knew'st not how to live well here,
Thou shalt be learned° to die well.   *taught*
CORBACCIO   Ha! What said he?
COMMENDATORE   You shall know anon,° sir.   *soon enough*
   [CORBACCIO *is placed under guard.*]
FIRST AVOCATORE   Thou, Corvino, shalt
135 Be straight embarked° from thine own house and rowed   *taken by boat*
Bound about Venice, through the Grand Canal,
Wearing a cap with fair° long ass's ears   *fine; clearly visible*
Instead of horns, and so to mount, a paper
Pinned on thy breast, to the *berlino*°   *pillory*
CORVINO   —Yes,
140 And have mine eyes beat out with stinking fish,
Bruised fruit, and rotten eggs—'Tis well. I'm glad

---

6. Venice's Hospital of the Incurables, founded in 1522 to care for those with syphilis.

7. (1) Hanging raw meat, to soften or tenderize it; (2) disciplining the body's appetites and passions; (3) humiliating; (4) killing.

I shall not see my shame yet.

FIRST AVOCATORE   And to expiate
Thy wrongs done to thy wife, thou art to send her
Home to her father with her dowry trebled.

145   And these are all your judgments—

ALL   Honored fathers!

FIRST AVOCATORE   Which may not be revoked. Now you begin,
When crimes are done and past and to be punished,
To think what your crimes are.—Away with them!

> [MOSCA, VOLPONE, VOLTORE, CORBACCIO, *and* CORVINO
> *retire to the back of the stage, guarded.*]

Let all that see these vices thus rewarded

150   Take heart,° and love to study 'em. Mischiefs feed   *Take them to heart*
Like beasts, till they be fat, and then they bleed.

> [*The* AVOCATORI *step back.*]
> [VOLPONE *comes forward.*]

VOLPONE   The seasoning of a play is the applause
Now, though the fox be punished by the laws,
He yet doth hope there is no suff'ring due

155   Nor any fact° which he hath done 'gainst you.   *crime*
If there be, censure him; here he, doubtful,° stands.   *apprehensive*
If not, fare jovially, and clap your hands.

> [*Exeunt.*]

JOHN WEBSTER

1579/80–1630s?

THE settings of the plays for which John Webster is most famous—The White Devil (first performed in 1612) and the duchess of malfi (first performed between 1613 and 1614)—are the courts of Renaissance Italy, which Webster's London audience had already learned to associate with political corruption, violence, and sexual passion. Webster's great dramatic achievement is to tap into the simple, seductive energy of these popular associations in order to fashion complex tragedies that chart the fates of ambitious characters caught in traps of their own and others' designs. None of these fates is more compelling than that of the Duchess, whose finest attributes—her vivacity, her courage, her fierce marital and maternal desires— prove to be the cause of her eventual undoing. But not before she stands up to the murderous intentions of her scheming brothers and their sycophantic spy, Bosola, and eloquently asserts her independence and faithful stoicism, her almost martyrlike willingness to suffer for the choices she has made on behalf of her husband and children. Such a display moved his fellow playwright John Ford to proclaim Webster "a poet, whom nor Rome nor Greece / Transcend, in all theirs, for a masterpiece." This estimation has been shared by later generations, and today Webster is considered second only to shakespeare among Jacobean tragic dramatists.

Unlike Shakespeare, John Webster grew up in the city of London, the hub of English commercial and dramatic life. Born in 1579 or 1580, he was part of a stable, prosperous merchant family headed by his father, also named John, who was a maker and seller of coaches (a relatively new and booming trade at the time). The playwright's father was a member of the Merchant Taylors' Company, a prestigious London guild (or professional society) for those in tailoring and related trades. Webster probably received his primary education at the well-respected Merchant Taylors' School; there he would have studied a rich curriculum of classical and Continental works, allusions to which occur frequently in his plays. In the late 1590s he was admitted to the Middle Temple for legal training, perhaps to prepare for administrative work in his father's business. The Middle Temple, one of the city's Inns of Court— legal societies where lawyers trained and often lived and had their offices—was also

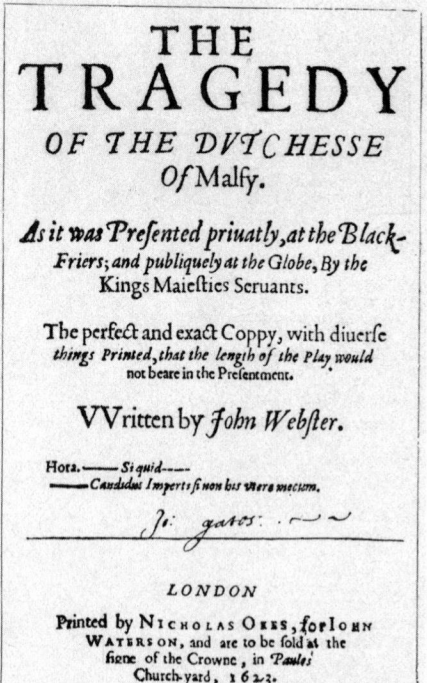

THE
TRAGEDY
OF THE DVTCHESSE
Of Malfy.

As it was Presented priuatly, at the Black-Friers; and publiquely at the Globe, By the Kings Maiesties Seruants.

The perfect and exact Coppy, with diuerse things Printed, that the length of the Play would not beare in the Presentment.

VVritten by John Webster.

Hora.——— Si quid—-
——— Candidus Imperti si non his vtere mecum.

Si: gates: ∽~

LONDON
Printed by NICHOLAS OKES, for JOHN WATERSON, and are to be sold at the signe of the Crowne, in Paules Church-yard, 1623.

Title page of a 1623 printing of The Duchess of Malfi.

a flourishing literary and cultural center, populated by students who were as committed to writing poetry and attending plays as to learning the law. Webster was not the only Inns of Court man to find his way, a few years after embarking on legal studies, to the public theater. As early as 1602 he was being paid for collaborative contributions, offering his services on such lost plays as *Caesar's Fall* as well as popular works such as *Westward Hoe* (performed in 1604) and *Northward Hoe* (performed in 1606). He seems to have disappeared from the theater world between 1606 and 1612, when his *White Devil* was presented before what he later described as an unappreciative audience at one of the city's less prestigious playhouses, the Red Bull, which was occupied by the Queen's Men's company.

A year or two later, *The Duchess of Malfi* was staged by the celebrated King's Men, Shakespeare's acting troupe, at both their outdoor theater, the Globe, and their indoor venue, the Blackfriars. In the subsequent decade, Webster worked on other plays, including the lost *Keep the Widow Waking*, a collaborative effort based on a sordid local murder, and his own *The Devil's Law-Case*. In 1621 he devised the theme and speeches for the annual Lord Mayor's pageant, which celebrated the accession of the new mayor. Webster also wrote poetry and prose for publication: in 1613 his elegy on the death of the beloved young Prince Henry, heir to the throne, was printed, and he contributed essays to the compendium of character sketches grouped under the title *Sir Overbury His Wife*. Webster is believed to have died in the 1630s.

A 1518 portrait of Giovanna d'Aragona, Duchess of Amalfi, attributed to Raphael Sanzio.

Documents from various London archives have allowed scholars to piece together this tenuous outline of Webster's personal and professional life. But the most enduring record of Webster, his fellow dramatists suggest, is his writing itself. As John Ford writes in his commendatory verse, Webster's pen lends memory "a lasting fame, to raise his monument." Ford, while following accepted literary conventions that equated an author's work with his future reputation, has clearly absorbed into his verse *The Duchess of Malfi*'s language of ruins and tombstones. Webster's dramatic characters are haunted by stones and statues, and one of the Duchess's greatest and earliest fears is that others will see her as a "figure cut in alabaster" rather than a woman of real "flesh and blood." But it is impossible to mistake the Duchess or any of the play's other central characters—her doting partner Antonio, her obsequious and conniving servant Bosola, her Machiavellian brother the Cardinal, or her other brother Ferdinand, fixated on the Duchess's sexuality to the point of madness—as anything less than psychologically dynamic human creatures, vital even in their mistakes and sins. This effect is due largely to Webster's dramatic language, as his characters' dialogue, full of metaphysical conceits that work to convey the bestial as well as the transcendent aspects of human life, displays both their unique intentions and their dawning recognition of the precariousness of their situations. The clashes of these characters over basic issues of honor, love, virtue, and wealth combine to offer a multidimensional perspective on the pleasures and dangers of the Renaissance court.

Webster's central source for the story of *The Duchess of Malfi* was a mid-sixteenth-century Italian novella based on the historical figure of Giovanna d'Aragona, who became the duchess of Amalfi when she was married in 1490, at the age of twelve, to the son and heir of the first duke of Amalfi. The novella presents the tale of the widowed duchess's second marriage, to Antonio Bologna, a man of lower station, and the domestic tragedy that followed when she flouted both social convention and the demands of her two brothers. It was published and reshaped in French and English translations in the following decades. Webster most likely used the version of the story in William Painter's *Second Tome of the Palace of Pleasure* (1567), a collection of tales containing "goodlye Histories, Tragicall matters, & other Morall argument," though his depiction of the Duchess is decidedly more positive than Painter's moralizing tone allows.

The Duchess opens with a dialogue between the courtier Antonio, soon to be the Duchess's husband, and his friend Delio. The two men describe an ideal court, an image that will serve as a marked contrast for the events that follow. As a procession of figures fills the Duchess's presence chamber, the room in which select courtiers and officials were received, Antonio and Delio provide vivid character sketches that foreshadow the manipulative conversations about to ensue. Bosola, the envious courtier (or "court gall," as Antonio calls him), has an angry exchange with the duplicitous Cardinal, whom Bosola claims has failed to reward him; then Ferdinand, Duke of Calabria and the Duchess's more possessive brother, hires Bosola to live in his sister's household to observe her, since "[s]he's a young widow; / I would not have her marry again." Ferdinand portrays his interest in controlling the Duchess as a simple matter of maintaining family honor, but his nearly pathological fascination with her erotic life—he will later imagine her "in the shameful act of sin" with a series of commoners—suggests much less rational or socially acceptable motivations. Despite the Cardinal and Ferdinand's injunctions, the first act ends with a triumphant wooing and wedding scene orchestrated by the Duchess, who displays her regal dignity even as she insists on her human desire. "The misery of us that are born great! / We are forced to woo, because none dare woo us," she tells Antonio. "Make not your heart so dead a piece of flesh / To fear more than to love me." But the Duchess's majestic certainty, because it goes against the will of her brothers, remains a source of concern, and her waiting woman and confidante Cariola worries: "Whether the spirit of greatness or of woman / Reign most in her, I know not, but it shows / A fearful madness. I owe her much of pity."

As the following acts provide glimpses into the Duchess and Antonio's affectionate domestic life, they intensify Cariola's sense of impending doom—caused largely by the persistent presence of the "intelligencer" or spy Bosola, who not only watches the Duchess but also, like Ferdinand, wants to plumb the depths of her personal life and uncover the secrets of her body and soul. While still hiding their marriage, the Duchess becomes pregnant and gives birth to a boy (two more children are born in the space between acts 2 and 3, a nonrealistic time frame that Jacobean audiences would have accepted). Ferdinand, horrified by the news, storms into the Duchess's palace and accosts her in her own room. Bosola, who seems to come to her rescue after Ferdinand exits, cannily tricks the Duchess into telling him the identity of her husband, and she and Antonio are forced to fly from their palace to a holy shrine at Loreto. Soon they must separate, as Antonio escapes to Milan and the Duchess is sent to a palace in northern Italy. Here, imprisoned by Ferdinand, the Duchess endures more of her brother's cruel tortures: a waxwork display of her husband and children, designed to convince her that they are dead, and a performance of antic madmen, intended to provoke her own insanity. It is a measure of the Duchess's self-control that these efforts to bring her to despair only strengthen her courage and conviction: "Nothing but noise and folly / Can keep me in my right wits," she tells Cariola, asserting that their foolishness, contrary to the Duke's plan, serves to keep her sane.

Much of act 4 is devoted to the Duchess's preparation for the death she knows is coming for her, and she therefore meets her executioners, sent by Ferdinand and overseen by Bosola, with Christian fortitude: "Pull, and pull strongly," she orders them, "for your able strength / Must pull down heaven upon me." Shortly before their arrival, she had asserted her self-possession with tremendous dignity, declaring. "I am Duchess of Malfi still." While some scholars have maintained that the Duchess, despite her charm, is irresponsible for choosing personal pleasure over the administration of her realm, almost all agree that she becomes a truly tragic figure at her death, when she transcends any

Eve Best in the title role in the 2012 production of *The Duchess of Malfi* staged by the Old Vic Theatre, London.

possible self-absorption or despair to extend her final thoughts to the family she leaves behind.

The repercussions of the devastating murder are worked through in the play's final act, in which the dead Duchess remains a powerful, if ghostly, presence. Antonio, contemplating an encounter with Ferdinand as he wanders through ruins of a Milanese abbey, hears a cautionary echo that seems, as he says, "very like my wife's voice." Ferdinand and Bosola are also haunted by the Duchess. Ferdinand may have had the Duchess killed in order to eradicate her from his life, but her death has only intensified her effect on him: he surrenders to a mental sickness diagnosed as lycanthropia, an imbalance of the humors (the vital fluids Renaissance physicians believed regulated people's health and personality) that makes him see himself as a wolf: he "[s]aid he was a wolf, only the difference / Was, a wolf's skin was hairy on the outside, / His on the inside." In contrast, the suddenly regretful Bosola is converted by the Duchess's final moments of patient acquiescence, and he resolves to exact revenge on both Ferdinand and the Cardinal. Although Bosola was originally willing to become Ferdinand's "creature" in order to improve his worldly fortunes, by the play's close he fully adopts the role of the court's most determined critic. The final scene presents this triangle of men—the Cardinal, Ferdinand, and Bosola—attacking one another to the death for a murder of which they are all guilty.

Guilt is only one of the human emotions that Webster explores in his play. He conveys these emotions with all the resources of the early modern theater, using special props (like the musky apricots that induce the countess's labor) and juxtaposing exits, entrances, and locales (such as the lugubrious ruins of an abbey) to enhance or even trigger his characters' experiences of desire, fear, or melancholy. One of the most suggestive of such scenes involves the Duchess, after an affectionate encounter with Antonio, musing to herself in front of her. The spell of this extraordinarily intimate moment is broken by Ferdinand, who enters thrusting a dagger before the Duchess's face. Characters consciously manipulate each others' feelings: Bosola is an expert at getting information because, like Shakespeare's Iago, he knows which sentiments make the Duchess most vulnerable. Pretending to champion Antonio for his virtue and comeliness, he coaxes from the passionate Duchess a confession of her marriage. Webster's masterly depiction of such delicate emotional exchanges takes a violent turn in the final act, in which inflamed tempers and consciences focus all energies on revenge. Indeed, the bloodbath that concludes the play gives the final act of *The Duchess* the sensibility of an English Renaissance revenge tragedy, a form of drama devoted to a character's single-minded pursuit of vengeance.

Before he succumbs to his wounds in the final scene, Bosola acknowledges that his murderous activity has been "[s]uch a mistake as I have often seen / In a play." Such a theatrically self-conscious remark—a character's comparison of "real-life" experience to the events of a play—provides an occasion to reflect on the complicated relationship between reality and drama, and in particular the relationship between an individual's control over his or her own life and the power of an unseen divinity to direct it, much as a playwright might. *The Duchess of Malfi* repeatedly presents this conundrum, which fascinated Renaissance playwrights and audiences alike, as all of the characters attempt to exert their wills against the demands of family, society, and, finally, a deeper structure of justice that ensures that "[w]hether we fall by ambition, blood, or lust, / Like diamonds, we are cut with our own dust." In Webster's world, ultimately, it is the characters' own desires—whether moral or immoral—that lead to their demise.   HEATHER HIRSCHFELD

The Duchess of Malfi

[Dedication]

*To the Right Honorable George Harding, Baron Berkeley of
Berkeley Castle and Knight of the Order of the Bath to the
Illustrious Prince Charles*[1]

My noble lord,
    That I may present my excuse why, being a stranger
to Your Lordship, I offer this poem° to your patronage, I   *i.e., play*
plead this warrant: men who never saw the sea, yet
desire to behold that regiment° of waters, choose some   *body, group*
eminent river to guide them thither, and make that, as
it were, their conduct° or postilion.° By the like ingen-   *guide / forerunner*
ious means has your fame arrived at my knowledge,
receiving it from some of worth who, both in contem
plation and practice, owe to Your Honor their clearest°   *absolute*
service. I do not altogether look up at° your title, the   *respect you solely for*
ancient'st nobility being but a relic of time past, and
the truest honor indeed being for a man to confer
honor on himself, which your learning strives to prop
agate and shall make you arrive at the dignity of a
great example. I am confident this work is not unworthy Your Honor's perusal; for by such poems as this,
poets have kissed the hands of great princes and
drawn their gentle eyes to look down upon their sheets
of paper when the poets themselves were bound up in
their winding-sheets.° The like courtesy from Your   *shrouds*
Lordship shall make you live in your grave and laurel
spring out of it, when the ignorant scorners of the
Muses[2] (that, like worms in libraries, seem to live
only to destroy learning) shall wither, neglected and
forgotten. This work and myself I humbly present to
your approved censure,° it being the utmost of my   *proven judgment*
wishes to have your honorable self my weighty and

---

1. The thirteenth Baron Berkeley (1601–
1658) was the son and grandson of patrons of
the Lord Chamberlain's Men, the acting
company in which Shakespeare was a shareholder and which became the King's Men in
1603. Harding was known as a friend of the
theater companies, especially the King's Men,
which performed *Duchess*.
2. In Greek mythology, nine daughters of
Memory and Zeus who preside over the arts
and all intellectual pursuits. *Laurel:* associated with poetry (and, more specifically, with
victory in poetry contests) since ancient
Greece.

perspicuous comment;° which grace so done me, shall   *discerning critic*
30   ever be acknowledged.

By Your Lordship's,
in all duty and observance,
John Webster

[Commendatory Verses]³

*In the just worth of that well-deserver, Mr. John
Webster, and upon this masterpiece of tragedy*

In this thou imitat'st one rich and wise
That sees his good deeds done before he dies.
As he by works, thou by this work of fame
Hast well provided for thy living name.
5   To trust to others' honorings is worth's crime;[4]
Thy monument is raised in thy lifetime.
And 'tis most just; for every worthy man
Is his own marble,° and his merit can   *monument*
Cut him to any figure and express
10   More art than Death's cathedral palaces,
Where royal ashes keep their court.[5] Thy note°   *Let your note*
Be ever plainness; 'tis the richest coat.°   *coat of arms*
Thy epitaph only the title be;°   *i.e., the play's title*
Write "Duchess." That will fetch a tear for thee;
15   For whoe'er saw this duchess live and die
That could get off under a bleeding eye?

In Tragediam.
Ut lux ex tenebris ictu percussa tonantis;
Illa, (ruina malis) claris fit vita poetis.
Thomas Middletonus,
*Poeta et Chron: Londinensis*⁶

To his friend Mr. John Webster upon his *Duchess of Malfi*

I never saw thy duchess till the day
That she was lively bodied° in thy play.   *embodied*
Howe'er she answered her low-rated love,
Her brothers' anger did so fatal prove;

---

3. Written by other poets or playwrights in praise of Webster and his play.
4. That is, to expect that other people will honor a deceased person is a fault or crime against one's worthiness.
5. That is, a person's own merit can depict his worth more effectively and more artistically than the elaborate tombs where the remains of royalty are interred.

6. To Tragedy: As light is struck from darkness at the blow of the Thunderer [Jove], may tragedy (the ruin of evil) become life to famous poets.—Thomas Middleton, playwright and chronicler of London (Latin). Middleton (1580–1627), a contemporary of Webster and Jonson, was best known for his city comedies and the tragedies *The Changeling* and *Women Beware Women*.

5 Yet my opinion is, she might speak more,
But never in her life so well before.[7]
William Rowley[8]

To the reader, of° the author and his *Duchess of Malfi*   concerning
Crown him a poet, whom nor° Rome nor Greece   neither
Transcend, in all theirs, for a masterpiece;
In which, whiles words and matter change, and men
5 Act one another,[9] he, from whose clear° pen   illustrious
They all took life, to memory hath lent
A lasting fame, to raise his monument.
John Ford[1]

CHARACTERS

Daniel de BOSOLA, the Duchess's provisor of horse
FERDINAND, Duke of Calabria, brother of the Duchess and the Cardinal
CARDINAL, brother of Ferdinand and the Duchess
ANTONIO, Bologna, steward of the Duchess's household
DELIO, his friend
Forobosco, a nonspeaking minor court official
Count MALATESTE, a courtier
The Marquis of PESCARA, a soldier
SILVIO, a courtier
CASTRUCHIO, an old courtier, husband of Julia
The several MADMEN
The DUCHESS of Malfi, sister of Ferdinand and the Cardinal
JULIA, the Cardinal's mistress (and wife to Castruchio)
The DOCTOR
CARIOLA, the Duchess's waiting woman
Court OFFICERS
Three young children [of the Duchess and Antonio]
Two PILGRIMS
RODERIGO } courtiers at Malfi
GRISOLAN }
An OLD LADY, a midwife
Churchmen
EXECUTIONERS
The ECHO from the Duchess's grave
SERVANTS attending on Ferdinand and the Duchess
    Guards, other servants, attendants, ladies-in-waiting

THE SCENE: *Malfi*[2] *(or Amalfi), Rome, Loreto, the
countryside near Ancona, and Milan.*

7. That is, however eloquently she defended her marriage to a man of a lower station, her brothers' anger led to fatal result; nonetheless, I do not think she could have spoken better in real life (even if she could have spoken more) than she does in your play.
8. An English actor and playwright (ca. 1585–1626), best known for his collabora-tions with Webster, Middleton, and other Jacobean dramatists.
9. That is, as long as literature imitates life and actors portray human beings.
1. English playwright (ca. 1586–ca. 1638), best known for the tragedy *'Tis Pity She's a Whore.*
2. The Elizabethan name for Amalfi, a port city in southern Italy.

1.1

[SCENE: *The* DUCHESS's *palace in Malfi.*]

[*Enter* ANTONIO *and* DELIO.]

DELIO   You are welcome to your country, dear Antonio!
You have been long in France, and you return
A very formal Frenchman in your habit.°   *dress, costume*
How do you like the French court?
ANTONIO   I admire it.
5   In seeking to reduce° both state and people   *bring, lead back*
To a fixed order, their judicious king
Begins at home, quits° first his royal palace   *rids*
Of flatt'ring sycophants, of dissolute
And infamous persons, which° he sweetly terms   *which undertaking*
10   His master's masterpiece, the work of heaven,
Consid'ring duly that a prince's court
Is like a common fountain whence should flow
Pure silver drops in general;° but if't chance   *to everyone; everywhere*
Some cursed example poison't° near the head,   *it (the fountain)*
15   Death and diseases through the whole land spread.
And what is't makes this blessèd government
But a most provident council, who dare freely
Inform him° the corruption of the times?   *Inform the king about*
Though some o'th'court hold° it presumption   *consider*
20   To instruct princes what they ought to do,
It is a noble duty to inform them
What they ought to foresee.

[*Enter* BOSOLA.]

                                   Here comes Bosola,
The only° court gall.° Yet I observe his railing   *preeminent / satirist*
Is not for simple love of piety;
25   Indeed, he rails at those things which he wants,
Would be as lecherous, covetous, or proud,
Bloody, or envious, as any man,
If he had means to be so.

[*Enter* CARDINAL.]

                                   Here's the Cardinal.

[ANTONIO *and* DELIO *stand aside, observing.*]

BOSOLA   [*to the* CARDINAL]   I do haunt you still.
CARDINAL   So.
BOSOLA   I have done you
30   Better service than to be slighted thus.
Miserable age, where only the reward°   *the only reward*
Of doing well is the doing of it!
CARDINAL   You enforce° your merit too much.   *urge*
BOSOLA   I fell into the galleys[3] in your service, where, for
35   two years together, I wore two towels instead of a shirt,
with a knot on the shoulder, after the fashion of a Roman

---

3. That is, into penal servitude.

mantle. Slighted thus? I will thrive some way. Blackbirds
fatten best in hard weather; why not I, in these dog days?[4]

CARDINAL   Would you could become honest!

40 BOSOLA   With all your divinity, do but direct me the way to
it. I have known many travel far for it, and yet return as
arrant knaves as they went forth, because they carried
themselves always along with them.

[*Exit* CARDINAL.]

Are you gone? Some fellows, they say, are possessed with
45   the devil, but this great fellow were° able to possess the   *would be*
greatest devil and make him worse.

ANTONIO [*as he and* DELIO *come forward*]   He hath denied
thee some suit?°   *petition*

BOSOLA   He and his brother are like plum trees that grow
50   crooked over standing° pools; they are rich and   *stagnant*
o'erladen with fruit, but none but crows, pies,° and   *magpies*
caterpillars feed on them. Could I be one of their flat-
t'ring panders, I would hang on their ears like a horse-
leech° till I were full, and then drop off. I pray leave   *a large leech*
55   me. Who would rely upon these miserable dependences° *subordinate positions*
in expectation to be advanced tomorrow? What creature
ever fed worse than hoping Tantalus?[5] Nor ever died any
man more fearfully than he that hoped for a pardon.
There are rewards for hawks and dogs when they have
60   done us service, but for a soldier that hazards his limbs
in a battle, nothing but a kind of geometry is his last sup-
portation.[6]

DELIO   Geometry?

BOSOLA   Ay, to hang in a fair pair of slings,° take his latter   *crutches*
65   swing° in the world upon an honorable pair of crutches,   *last fling*
from hospital to hospital. Fare ye well, sir. And yet do not
you scorn us, for places in the court are but like beds in
the hospital, where this man's head lies at that man's
foot, and so lower and lower.   [*Exit.*]

70 DELIO   I knew this fellow seven years in the galleys
For° a notorious murder, and 'twas thought   *For having committed*
The Cardinal suborned° it. He was released   *secretly procured*
By the French general, Gaston de Foix,[7]
When he recovered° Naples.   *recaptured*

ANTONIO   'Tis great pity
75   He should be thus neglected. I have heard
He's very valiant. This foul melancholy

---

4. The hottest and most unhealthy time of
the summer, when in ancient times Sirius
(the Dog Star) rose around sunrise.
5. In Greek mythology, the punishment of
Tantalus in the underworld was to stand in
water with fruit overhead, both eluding him
whenever he tried to drink or eat.

6. That is, a soldier who risks being crippled
in battle can hope for no support beyond the
crutches that resemble the compass used in
geometry (see lines 140–42 and note).
7. Duc de Nemours (1489–1512), commander
of the French army in Italy.

Will poison all his goodness; for, I'll tell you,
If too immoderate sleep be truly said
To be an inward rust unto the soul,
80   It then doth follow want° of action   *that lack*
Breeds all black malcontents; and their close rearing,
Like moths in cloth, do hurt for want of wearing.[8]

      [*Enter* CASTRUCHIO, SILVIO, RODERIGO, *and* GRISOLAN.
      ANTONIO *and* DELIO *stand aside at first, observing.*]

DELIO   The presence° 'gins to fill. You promised me   *presence chamber*
    To make me the partaker° of the natures   *To inform me*
85   Of some of your great courtiers.
ANTONIO   The Lord Cardinal's
    And other strangers' that are now in court?
    I shall.

      [*Enter* FERDINAND.]

    Here comes the great Calabrian duke.
FERDINAND   Who took the ring oft'nest?[9]
SILVIO   Antonio Bologna, my lord.
90   FERDINAND   Our sister Duchess' great master of her house
    hold? Give him the jewel.° When shall we leave this   *prize*
    sportive action and fall to action indeed?
CASTRUCHIO   Methinks, my lord, you should not desire to
    go to war in person.
95   FERDINAND [*aside to his courtiers*]   Now, for some gravity.—
    Why, my lord?
CASTRUCHIO   It is fitting a soldier arise to be a prince, but
    not necessary a prince descend to be a captain.
FERDINAND   No?
100   CASTRUCHIO   No, my lord. He were° far better do it by a   *would*
    deputy.
FERDINAND   Why should he not as well sleep or eat by a
    deputy? This might take idle, offensive, and base office°   *function*
    from him, whereas the other[1] deprives him of honor.
105   CASTRUCHIO   Believe my experience: that realm is never
    long in quiet where the ruler is a soldier.
FERDINAND   Thou told'st me thy wife could not endure
    fighting.
CASTRUCHIO   True, my lord.
110   FERDINAND   And of a jest she broke° of a captain she met,   *told, cracked*
    full of wounds. I have forgot it.
CASTRUCHIO   She told him, my lord, he was a pitiful fel-
    low, to lie, like the children of Ishmael, all in tents.[2]

---

8. That is, just as moths devour cloth that is
packed tightly away, melancholic malcontents
do more damage when they are confined and
isolated than when they are put to use.
9. That is, who won most often at the tournament sport of carrying off a ring on the point of
one's lance. Ferdinand consciously or uncon-
sciously suggests a bawdy pun on "ring" as a
woman's genitals.

1. That is, having a deputy fight in his stead.
2. "Tents" are surgical dressings as well as
shelters. According to the Bible, Ishmael and
his mother, the servant Hagar, were sent by
Abraham, his father, into the wilderness; his
descendents lived in villages and in tents in
encampments (see Genesis 16–25, especially
25.16). "Ishmael" may be a mistake for "Israel,"
since the Israelites also lived in tents.

FERDINAND Why, there's a wit were° able to undo all the   *that would be*
115 surgeons o'the city, for, although gallants should quarrel
    and had drawn their weapons and were ready to go to it,°   *(with sexual pun)*
    yet her persuasions would make them put up.°   *sheath their swords*

CASTRUCHIO That she would, my lord. How do you like
    my Spanish jennet?°   *small horse*

120 RODERIGO He is all fire.

FERDINAND I am of Pliny's opinion: I think he was begot by
    the wind.[3] He runs as if he were ballasted with quick-
    silver.[4]

SILVIO True, my lord, he reels from the tilt often.[5]

125 RODERIGO [*and*] GRISOLAN Ha, ha, ha!

FERDINAND Why do you laugh? Methinks you that are
    courtiers should be my touchwood:° take fire when I   *tinder*
    give fire, that is, laugh when I laugh, were the subject
    never so witty.

130 CASTRUCHIO True, my lord. I myself have heard a very
    good jest, and have scorned to seem to have so silly° a   *simple*
    wit as to understand it.

FERDINAND But I can laugh at your fool, my lord.

CASTRUCHIO He cannot speak, you know, but he makes
135 faces. My lady cannot abide him.

FERDINAND No?

CASTRUCHIO Nor endure to be in merry company, for she
    says too much laughing and too much company fills her
    too full of the wrinkle.

140 FERDINAND I would then have a mathematical instrument
    made for her face, that she might not laugh out of
    compass.[6]—I shall shortly visit you at Milan, Lord Silvio.

SILVIO Your Grace shall arrive most welcome.

FERDINAND [*turning to* ANTONIO, *who is still standing to one*
    side with DELIO] You are a good horseman, Antonio. You
145 have excellent riders in France. What do you think of good
    horsemanship?

ANTONIO Nobly, my lord. As out of the Grecian horse[7]
    issued many famous princes, so out of brave horse-
    manship arise the first sparks of growing resolution that
150 raise the mind to noble action.

FERDINAND You have bespoke° it worthily.   *spoken of*

[*Enter* CARDINAL, DUCHESS, *and* CARIOLA *with*
attendants.]

---

3. Pliny the Elder (23/24–79 C.E.), the Roman naturalist, reported in his *Natural History* (8.72; 77 C.E.) that Portuguese mares who were impregnated by the west wind gave birth to foals that were swift.
4. Mercury, a heavy but quick-flowing metal that would provide no stability at all. Since mercury was also used in the treatment of syphilis, Ferdinand may be mocking Castru-

chio as well, with an innuendo to which Silvio perhaps responds.
5. He balks often enough at a tournament; possibly also a joke about male impotence.
6. Beyond the bounds of moderation; with a pun on "compass" as the instrument used in geometry.
7. That is, the Trojan horse, filled with Greek warriors who emerged to sack the city of Troy.

SILVIO Your brother, the Lord Cardinal, and sister
  Duchess.
CARDINAL Are the galleys come about?°   *returned to port*
155 GRISOLAN They are, my lord.
FERDINAND Here's the Lord Silvio is come to take his leave.
      [ANTONIO *and* DELIO *talk privately while* FERDINAND,
      the CARDINAL, *and the others confer among them-
      selves.*]

DELIO Now, sir, your promise: what's that Cardinal? I
  mean his temper?° They say he's a brave fellow, will play°   *temperament / gamble*
  his five thousand crowns° at tennis,[8] dance, court ladies,   *gold coins*
160 and one that hath fought single combats.°   *duels*
ANTONIO Some such flashes superficially hang on him for
  form. But observe his inward character: he is a melancholy churchman. The spring in his face is nothing but
  the engend'ring of toads.[9] Where he is jealous of any
165 man, he lays worse plots for them than ever was imposed
  on Hercules,[1] for he strews in his way flatterers, panders, intelligencers,° atheists, and a thousand such   *spies*
  political° monsters. He should have been° pope, but   *scheming / i.e., wished*
  instead of coming to it by the primitive° decency of the   *to be original*
170 church, he did bestow bribes so largely and so impu-   *to be original*
  dently as if he would have carried it away without
  heaven's knowledge. Some good he hath done.
DELIO You have given° too much of him. What's his   *described*
  brother?
ANTONIO The Duke there? A most perverse and turbulent
175 nature.
  What appears in him mirth is merely outside;
  If he laugh heartily, it is to laugh
  All honesty out of fashion.
DELIO   Twins?
ANTONIO   In quality.
  He speaks with others' tongues and hears men's suits
  With others' ears; will seem to sleep o'th'bench°   *(i.e., when a judge)*
180 Only to entrap offenders in their answers;
  Dooms men to death by information,°   *informers' evidence*
  Rewards by hearsay.
DELIO   Then the law to him
  Is like a foul black cobweb to a spider:
  He makes it his dwelling and a prison
185 To entangle those shall feed him.
ANTONIO   Most true.
  He nev'r pays debts unless they be shrewd turns,°   *malicious injuries*
  And those he will confess that he doth owe.
  Last, for° his brother there, the Cardinal: *as for*

---

8. A sport popular among the nobility.
9. That is, what seems attractive is not a healthful spring but a foul pool breeding toads.

1. Hercules (Heracles), the greatest hero of
classical mythology, had to undertake twelve
famously difficult labors.

They that do flatter him most say oracles
190 Hang at his lips; and verily I believe them,
For the devil speaks in them.
But for° their sister, the right noble Duchess   *as for*
You never fixed your eye on three fair medals,
Cast in one figure,° of so different temper.°   *shape / quality*
195 For her discourse, it is so full of rapture
You only will begin then to be sorry
When she doth end her speech, and wish, in wonder,
She held it less vainglory to talk much
Than your penance to hear her.[2] Whilst she speaks,
200 She throws upon a man so sweet a look
That it were able to raise one to a galliard°   *a lively dance*
That lay in a dead palsy,° and to dote   *paralysis*
On that sweet countenance. But in that look
There speaketh so divine a continence°   *(sexual) self-restraint*
205 As cuts off all lascivious and vain hope.
Her days are practiced in such noble virtue
That sure her nights—nay, more, her very sleeps°—   *dreams*
Are more in heaven than other ladies' shrifts.°   *absolutions*
Let all sweet ladies break their flatt'ring glasses°   *mirrors*
210 And dress themselves in her.°   *using her as model*
DELIO   Fie, Antonio,
You play the wire-drawer with her commendations.[3]
ANTONIO   I'll case° the picture up only thus much.   *encase*
All her particular worth grows to this sum:
She stains[4] the time past, lights the time to come.
        [CARIOLA *approaches* ANTONIO *confidentially.*]
215 CARIOLA You must attend my lady in the gallery
Some half an hour hence.
ANTONIO [*privately to* CARIOLA]   I shall.
        [ANTONIO *and* DELIO *withdraw.*]
FERDINAND   Sister, I have a suit to° you.   *petition for*
DUCHESS   To me, sir?
FERDINAND   A gentleman here, Daniel de Bosola,
One that was in the galleys.
DUCHESS   Yes, I know him.
220 FERDINAND A worthy fellow h' is. Pray let me entreat for
The provisorship° of your horse.   *office of manager*
DUCHESS   Your knowledge of him
Commends him and prefers° him.   *advances*
FERDINAND [*to an attendant*]   Call him hither.
           [*Exit attendant.*]
We are now upon parting.° Good Lord Silvio,   *ready to depart*

---

2. You would wonderingly wish that her modesty in speech was less than any pains you might endure in listening to her. (Since such listening causes no pain, this is a wish for her to speak freely.)

3. That is, you draw out her praises excessively, too ingeniously. (Wire is made when metal is drawn through a series of ever-smaller holes.)

4. Eclipses by her excellence.

Do us commend° to all our noble friends   *give our greetings*
225   At the leaguer.°   *military camp*
     SILVIO   Sir, I shall.
     DUCHESS   You are for Milan?
     SILVIO   I am.
     DUCHESS [*to attendants*]   Bring the caroches.° [*To her guests*]   *stately coaches*
230   We'll bring° you down to the haven.   *escort*
          [*Exeunt*° *all except the* CARDINAL *and* FERDINAND.]   *They exit (Latin)*
     CARDINAL   Be sure you entertain° that Bosola   *hire*
     For your intelligence.° I would not be seen in't,   *spying*
     And therefore many times I have slighted him
     When he did court our furtherance,° as this morning.   *seek to win advancement*
     FERDINAND   Antonio, the great master of her household,
235   Had been far fitter.
     CARDINAL   You are deceived in him.
     His nature is too honest for such business.
          [*Enter* BOSOLA.]
     He comes. I'll leave you.   [*Exit.*]
     BOSOLA   I was lured[5] to you.
     FERDINAND   My brother here, the Cardinal, could never
     Abide you.
240 BOSOLA   Never since he was in my debt.
     FERDINAND   Maybe some oblique° character in your face   *perverse*
     Made him suspect you?
     BOSOLA   Doth he study physiognomy?
     There's no more credit to be given to th'face
     Than to a sick man's urine,[6] which some call
245   The physician's whore because she cozens° him.   *deceives*
     He did suspect me wrongfully.
     FERDINAND   For that
     You must give great° men leave to take their times.   *noble*
     Distrust doth cause us seldom be deceived.[7]
     You see, the oft shaking of the cedar tree
250   Fastens it more at root.
     BOSOLA   Yet take heed,
     For to suspect a friend unworthily
     Instructs him the next° way to suspect you,   *most direct*
     And prompts him to deceive you.
     FERDINAND [*giving money*]   There's gold.
     BOSOLA   So,
     What follows? Never rained such showers as these
255   Without thunderbolts i'th'tail of them.[8]
     Whose throat must I cut?

5. Summoned (like a hawk to its handler's lure).
6. Examined to diagnose disease.
7. That is, because we are distrustful, we are seldom deceived.
8. An allusion to the myth of Danaë, locked by her father in a tower to prevent her from bearing the son who was prophesied to kill him; Zeus (Jupiter)—the king of the gods, who wields the thunderbolt—came to her in the form of a shower of gold.

FERDINAND   Your inclination to shed blood rides post°   *with speed*
   Before my occasion to use you. I give you that
   To live i'th'court here and observe the Duchess,
260 To note all the particulars of her havior°—   *behavior*
   What suitors do solicit her for marriage,
   And whom she best affects.° She's a young widow;   *likes*
   I would not have her marry again.
BOSOLA   No, sir?
FERDINAND   Do not you ask the reason, but be satisfied
265 I say I would not.
BOSOLA   It seems you would create me
   One of your familiars.[9]
FERDINAND   Familiar? What's that?
BOSOLA   Why, a very quaint invisible devil, in flesh:
   An intelligencer.
FERDINAND   Such a kind of thriving thing
   I would wish thee; and ere long thou mayst arrive
270 At a higher place by't.
BOSOLA *[offering the money back]*   Take your devils,
   Which hell calls angels!° These cursed gifts would make   *gold coins (with pun)*
   You a corrupter, me an impudent traitor,
   And should I take these, they'd take me to hell.
FERDINAND   Sir, I'll take nothing from you that I have given.
275 There is a place° that I procured for you   *position*
   This morning: the provisorship o'th'horse.
   Have you heard on't?
BOSOLA   No.
FERDINAND   'Tis yours. Is't not worth thanks?
BOSOLA   I would have you curse yourself now, that your bounty,
   Which makes men truly noble, e'er should make
280 Me a villain. Oh, that to avoid ingratitude
   For the good deed you have done me, I must do
   All the ill man can invent! Thus the devil
   Candies° all sins o'er, and what heaven terms vile   *Sugars*
   That names he complemental.°   *expressive of courtesy*
FERDINAND   Be yourself;
285 Keep your old garb° of melancholy; 'twill express   *demeanor*
   You envy those that stand above your reach,
   Yet strive not to come near 'em. This will gain
   Access to private lodgings, where yourself
   May, like a politic° dormouse—   *cunning*
BOSOLA   As I have seen some
290 Feed in a lord's dish,[1] half asleep, not seeming
   To listen to any talk, and yet these rogues
   Have cut his throat in a dream.° What's my place?   *in their fantasies*
   The provisorship o'th'horse? Say then my corruption
   Grew out of horse dung. I am your creature.[2]

---

9. (1) Intimates; (2) attendant evil spirits,
which usually take the form of animals.

1. That is, dine at a lord's table.
2. (1) Your agent; (2) a man you made.

295 FERDINAND   Away!

    BOSOLA   Let good men, for good deeds, covet good fame,
        Since place and riches oft are bribes of shame.
        Sometimes the devil doth preach.   [*Exit* BOSOLA.]

        [*Enter* CARDINAL, DUCHESS, *and* CARIOLA.]

    CARDINAL [*to the* DUCHESS]   We are to part from you, and
        your own discretion
300 Must now be your director.

    FERDINAND   You are a widow;
        You know already what man is. And therefore
        Let not youth, high promotion, eloquence—

    CARDINAL   No, nor anything without the addition,° honor,   *title*
        Sway your high blood.[3]

    FERDINAND   Marry? They are most luxurious°   *lecherous*
305 Will° wed twice.   *Who will*

    CARDINAL   Oh, fie!

    FERDINAND   Their livers[4] are more spotted
        Than Laban's sheep.[5]

    DUCHESS   Diamonds are of most value,
        They say, that have passed through most jewelers' hands.

    FERDINAND   Whores, by that rule, are precious.

    DUCHESS   Will you hear me?
        I'll never marry.

    CARDINAL   So most widows say,
310 But commonly that motion° lasts no longer   *impulse*
        Than the turning of an hourglass; the funeral sermon
        And it end both together.

    FERDINAND   Now hear me:
        You live in a rank pasture here, i'th'court.
        There is a kind of honeydew[6] that's deadly;
315 'Twill poison your fame.° Look to't. Be not cunning,   *reputation*
        For they whose faces do belie their hearts
        Are witches ere they arrive at twenty years—
        Ay, and give the devil suck.[7]

    DUCHESS   This is terrible good counsel.

320 FERDINAND   Hypocrisy is woven of a fine small thread,
        Subtler than Vulcan's engine;[8] yet, believe't,
        Your darkest actions—nay, your privat'st thoughts—
        Will come to light.

    CARDINAL   You may flatter yourself
    And take your own choice, privately be married

---

3. Noble breeding; passionate nature.

4. The liver was believed to be the seat of strong passions.

5. In the Bible, Laban promised Jacob, his nephew and son-in-law, all the spotted and speckled sheep, cattle, and goats in his flock as payment, and Jacob craftily increased their numbers (Genesis 30.25–43).

6. A sweet, sticky substance, excreted onto plants by some aphids and other insects.

7. Witches were believed to suckle both the devil and their familiars.

8. Device, contrivance: that is, the fine, unbreakable net in which Vulcan, the Roman god of fire and metalworking, trapped his wife, the love goddess Venus, in bed with Mars, the god of war.

325   Under the eaves° of night. *i.e., the cover*

FERDINAND   Think 't the best voyage
That e'er you made, like the irregular crab,
Which, though 't goes backward, thinks that it goes right
Because it goes its own way. But observe:
Such weddings may more properly be said
330   To be executed than celebrated.

CARDINAL   The marriage night
Is the entrance into some prison.

FERDINAND   And those joys,
Those lustful pleasures, are like heavy sleeps
Which do forerun man's mischief.

CARDINAL   Fare you well.
Wisdom begins at the end.[9] Remember it.   *[Exit.]*

335 DUCHESS   I think this speech between you both was studied,° *rehearsed*
It came so roundly° off. *thoroughly; fluently*

FERDINAND   You are my sister.
[Showing his dagger] This was my father's poniard. Do you see?
I'd be loath to see't look rusty, 'cause 'twas his.
I would have you to give o'er these chargeable° revels; *expensive*
340   A visor and a mask are whispering rooms[1]
That were nev'r built for goodness. Fare ye well—
And women like that part which, like the lamprey,
Hath nev'r a bone in't.

DUCHESS   Fie, sir!

FERDINAND   Nay,
I mean the tongue. Variety of courtship![2]
345   What cannot a neat° knave with a smooth tale *elegantly dressed*
Make a woman believe? Farewell, lusty widow.   *[Exit.]*

DUCHESS   Shall this move me? If all my royal kindred
Lay in my way unto this marriage,
I'd make them my low footsteps.° And even now, *steps (of a stair)*
350   Even in this hate°—as men in some great battles, *my brothers' hatred*
By apprehending danger, have achieved
Almost impossible actions; I have heard soldiers say so—
So I, through frights and threat'nings, will assay
This dangerous venture. Let old wives report
355   I winked° and chose a husband.—Cariola, *shut my eyes*
To thy known secrecy I have given up
More than my life: my fame.

CARIOLA   Both shall be safe,
For I'll conceal this secret from the world
As warily as those that trade in poison
360   Keep poison from their children.

DUCHESS   Thy protestation

---

9. An allusion to the proverb "Think on the end before you begin."
1. That is, are devices that encourage secrecy

(literally, rooms for private consultations).
2. That is, what a variety of deceptions in courtship!

Is ingenious and hearty.° I believe it.   *candid and heartfelt*
Is Antonio come?
CARIOLA   He attends° you.   *is waiting for*
DUCHESS   Good dear soul,
Leave me; but place thyself behind the arras,°   *wall hanging*
Where thou mayst overhear us. Wish me good speed,°   *success*
365   For I am going into a wilderness
Where I shall find nor path° nor friendly clew[3]   *neither*
To be my guide.   [CARIOLA *withdraws behind the arras.*]
          [*Enter* ANTONIO.]
                    I sent for you. Sit down.
Take pen and ink, and write. Are you ready?
ANTONIO   Yes.
DUCHESS   What did I say?
ANTONIO   That I should write somewhat.
370   DUCHESS   Oh, I remember.
After these triumphs° and this large expense,   *festivities*
It's fit, like thrifty husbands° we inquire   *stewards (with pun)*
What's laid up° for tomorrow.   *stored up*
ANTONIO   So please Your beauteous Excellence.
DUCHESS   Beauteous?
375   Indeed, I thank you. I look young for your sake.
You have ta'en my cares upon you.
ANTONIO   I'll fetch Your Grace
The particulars of your revenue and expense.
DUCHESS   Oh, you are an upright treasurer. But you mistook,
For when I said I meant to make inquiry
380   What's laid up for tomorrow, I did mean
What's laid up yonder for me.
ANTONIO   Where?
DUCHESS   In heaven.
I am making my will, as 'tis fit princes should,
In perfect memory;° and I pray, sir, tell me,   *i.e., sound mind*
Were not one better make it smiling, thus,
385   Than in deep groans and terrible ghastly looks,
As if the gifts we parted with procured°   *caused*
That violent distraction?
ANTONIO   Oh, much better.
DUCHESS   If I had a husband, now, this care were quit.°   *would be removed*
But I intend to make you overseer.
390   What good deed shall we first remember? Say.
ANTONIO   Begin with that first good deed began i'th'world
After man's creation: the sacrament of marriage.
I'd have you first provide for a good husband,
Give him all.
DUCHESS   All?
ANTONIO   Yes, your excellent self.

---

3. A ball of thread used to guide one through a labyrinth or maze.

395	DUCHESS	In a winding-sheet?°	*shroud*
	ANTONIO	In a couple.°	*pair (i.e., marriage)*
	DUCHESS	Saint Winifred,[4] that were a strange will!	
	ANTONIO	'Twere strange if there were no will in you	
		To marry again.	
	DUCHESS	What do you think of marriage?	
	ANTONIO	I take't as those that deny purgatory:	
400		It locally contains or° heaven or hell;	*either*
		There's no third place in't.	
	DUCHESS	How do you affect° it?	*feel about*
	ANTONIO	My banishment, feeding my melancholy,	
		Would often reason thus:—	
	DUCHESS	Pray let's hear it.	
	ANTONIO	Say a man never marry, nor have children,	
405		What takes that from him? Only the bare name	
		Of being a father, or the weak delight	
		To see the little wanton° ride a-cockhorse	*rogue (an endearment)*
		Upon a painted stick, or hear him chatter	
		Like a taught starling.	
	DUCHESS	Fie, fie, what's all this?	
410		One of your eyes is bloodshot. Use my ring to't.	
		[*She gives him a ring.*]	
		They say 'tis very sovereign.° 'Twas my wedding ring,	*potent for healing*
		And I did vow never to part with it	
		But to my second husband.	
	ANTONIO	You have parted with it now.	
415	DUCHESS	Yes, to help your eyesight.	
	ANTONIO	You have made me stark blind.	
	DUCHESS	How?	
	ANTONIO	There is a saucy and ambitious devil	
		Is dancing in this circle.	
	DUCHESS	Remove him.	
	ANTONIO	How?	
420	DUCHESS	There needs small° conjuration when your finger	*is little need for*
		May do it: thus. [*She puts the ring on his finger.*] Is it fit?	
	ANTONIO	What said you? [*He kneels.*]	
	DUCHESS	Sir,	
		This goodly roof of yours is too low built;	
		I cannot stand upright in't, nor discourse,	
		Without° I raise it higher. Raise yourself,	*Unless*
425		Or, if you please, my hand to help you: so.	
		[*She helps him up.*]	
	ANTONIO	Ambition, madam, is a great man's madness,	
		That is not kept in chains and close-pent° rooms,	*tightly locked*
		But in fair, lightsome lodgings, and is girt°	*surrounded*
		With the wild noise of prattling visitants,	

4. A Welsh saint (ca. 600–660), beheaded by a suitor who was enraged at her insistence on becoming a nun. She was restored to life by her uncle, Saint Beuno.

430 Which makes it lunatic beyond all cure.
Conceive not I am so stupid but I aim°   *guess*
Whereto your favors tend; but he's a fool
That, being a-cold, would thrust his hands i'th'fire
To warm them.

DUCHESS   So, now the ground's broke,
435 You may discover what a wealthy mine
I make you lord of.

ANTONIO   Oh, my unworthiness!

DUCHESS You were ill to sell yourself.
This dark'ning of your worth is not like that
Which tradesmen use i'th'city; their false lights
440 Are to rid bad wares off.[5] And I must tell you,
If you will know where breathes a complete° man—   *perfect*
I speak it without flattery—turn your eyes
And progress through[6] yourself.

ANTONIO Were there nor° heaven nor hell,   *neither*
445 I should be honest. I have long served virtue,
And nev'r ta'en wages of her.

DUCHESS   Now she pays it.
The misery of us that are born great!
We are forced to woo, because none dare woo us;
And as a tyrant doubles° with his words,   *acts deceitfully*
450 And fearfully equivocates, so we
Are forced to express our violent passions
In riddles and in dreams, and leave the path
Of simple virtue, which was never made
To seem the thing it is not. Go, go brag
455 You have left me heartless! Mine is in your bosom;
I hope 'twill multiply love there. You do tremble.
Make not your heart so dead a piece of flesh
To fear more than to love me. Sir, be confident.
What is't distracts you? This is flesh and blood, sir;
460 'Tis not the figure cut in alabaster
Kneels° at my husband's tomb. Awake, awake, man!   *That kneels*
I do here put off all vain ceremony,
And only do appear to you a young widow
That claims you for her husband, and, like a widow,[7]
465 I use but half a blush in't.

ANTONIO   Truth speak for me!
I will remain the constant sanctuary
Of your good name.

DUCHESS   I thank you, gentle love,
And, 'cause ° you shall not come to me in debt,   *so that*
Being now my steward, here upon your lips

---

5. That is, they rely on poor lighting to sell defective wares.
6. That is, survey; literally, make a state jour-

ney or official tour through.
7. Widows were stereotyped as lusty (e.g., see line 346 above).

470   I sign your *quietus est.*[8]   [*She kisses him.*]
      This you should have begged now.
      I have seen children oft eat sweetmeats thus,
      As fearful to devour them too soon.
ANTONIO   But for your brothers?
DUCHESS   Do not think of them.
475   All discord, without this circumference,[9]
      Is only to be pitied and not feared.
      Yet, should they know it, time will easily
      Scatter the tempest.
ANTONIO   These words should be mine,
      And all the parts you have spoke, if some part of it
480   Would not have savored flattery.
DUCHESS   Kneel.
        [CARIOLA *comes forth from behind the arras.*]
ANTONIO   Hah?
DUCHESS   Be not amazed. This woman's of my counsel.
      I have heard lawyers say, a contract in a chamber
485   *Per verba de presenti*[1] is absolute marriage.
        [*The* DUCHESS *and* ANTONIO *kneel.*]
      Bless, heaven, this sacred Gordian,[2] which let violence
      Never untwine!
ANTONIO   And may our sweet affections, like the spheres,[3]
      Be still° in motion—   *always*
DUCHESS   Quick'ning, and make
490   The like soft° music—   *Giving life; exciting*
ANTONIO   That we may imitate the loving palms,
      Best emblem of a peaceful marriage,
      That nev'r bore fruit divided[4]—
DUCHESS   What can the church force° more?   *enforce*
495 ANTONIO   That Fortune may not know an accident,
      Either of joy or sorrow, to divide
      Our fixèd wishes!
DUCHESS   How can the church build faster?°   *more securely*
      We now are man and wife, and 'tis the church
      That must but echo this. [*They rise.*] Maid, stand apart.—
500   I now am blind.
ANTONIO   What's your conceit° in this?   *idea; meaning*
DUCHESS   I would have you lead your fortune by the hand

---

8. Literally, "he is quit" (Latin)—a discharge or receipt given when a debt has been fully discharged.
9. Outside of these bounds (i.e., their embrace; the marriage bonds; and perhaps the wedding ring).
1. Through words [spoken] about the present (Latin). Marriage vows, when spoken this way in one another's presence, were legally binding, though the church disapproved.
2. That is, a knot that cannot be undone (the legendary Gordian knot was "untied" by Alex-

ander the Great, with a sword).
3. According to the cosmology of the Greek mathematician and astronomer Ptolemy (active 127–148 C.E.), still dominant in the Renaissance, the planets, sun, moon, and stars all circle the earth in vast crystalline spheres whose movement makes a beautiful music, inaudible to human ears.
4. Because the date palm has separate male and female plants, both are required to bear fruit.

Unto your marriage-bed.
(You speak in me this, for we now are one.)
We'll only lie, and talk together, and plot
505 T'appease my humorous⁵ kindred; and, if you please,
Like the old tale in "Alexander and Lodowick,"
Lay a naked sword between us, keep us chaste.⁶
Oh, let me shroud° my blushes in your bosom,   *veil, hide*
Since 'tis the treasury of all my secrets.

     [*Exit* ANTONIO, *leading the* DUCHESS.]

510 CARIOLA Whether the spirit of greatness or of woman
    Reign most in her, I know not, but it shows
    A fearful madness. I owe her much of pity.   [*Exit.*]

2.1

[SCENE: *The* DUCHESS's *palace in Malfi, about nine months later.*]

    [*Enter* BOSOLA *and* CASTRUCHIO.]

BOSOLA You say you would fain be taken for an eminent
    courtier?°   *member of a law court*
CASTRUCHIO 'Tis the very main° of my ambition.   *chief aim*
BOSOLA Let me see; you have a reasonable good face for't
5   already, and your nightcap° expresses your ears⁷ suffi-   *lawyer's skullcap*
    cient largely. I would have you learn to twirl the strings
    of your band⁸ with a good grace, and in a set speech, at
    th'end of every sentence, to hum three or four times, or
    blow your nose till it smart again, to recover your mem-
10   ory. When you come to be a president° in criminal   *presiding judge*
    causes,° if you smile upon a prisoner, hang him, but if   *cases*
    you frown upon him and threaten him, let him be sure to
    scape the gallows.
CASTRUCHIO I would be a very merry president.
15 BOSOLA Do not sup a-nights; 'twill beget you an admirable wit.
CASTRUCHIO Rather it would make me have a good stom-
    ach° to quarrel, for they say your roaring boys° eat meat   *appetite; disposition /*
    seldom, and that makes them so valiant. But how shall I   *riotous fellows*
    know whether the people take me for an eminent fellow?
20 BOSOLA I will teach a trick to know it. Give out° you lie a   *Announce*
    dying, and if you hear the common people curse you, be
    sure you are taken for one of the prime nightcaps.°   *lawyers*

---

5. Temperamental, emotionally unbalanced: a reference to the humoral theory that dominated early modern accounts of human emotion. Imbalances among the four humors, or bodily fluids, were believed to determine personality. An excess of black bile, a cold, dry substance in the body corresponding to the earth, made people melancholic, while blood and air were associated with the sanguine; yellow bile and fire, with the choleric; and phlegm and water, with the phlegmatic.
6. In the story told by a popular ballad, the friends Alexander and Lodowick were so alike that they could change places without anyone noticing. When Lodowick married the princess of Hungaria in Alexander's name, he placed a sword between the princess and himself in bed each night so that his friend would not be wronged.
7. That is, pushes out your ears like those of a jackass.
8. A pair of strips, hanging down in front from a broad, flat collar, that was part of legal attire.

[*Enter an* OLD LADY.]

You come from painting° now?   *putting on makeup*

OLD LADY   From what?

25 BOSOLA   Why, from your scurvy face physic.° To behold   *medicine*
    thee not painted inclines somewhat near a miracle.
    These in thy face here were deep ruts and foul sloughs°   *ditches*
    the last progress.[9] There was a lady in France that, having
    had the smallpox, flayed the skin off her face to make it
30 more level; and whereas before she looked like a nutmeg-
    grater, after she resembled an abortive hedgehog.

OLD LADY   Do you call this painting?

BOSOLA   No, no, but careening[1] of an old morphewed° lady,   *scabbed*
    to make her disembogue° again. There's roughcast phrase   *go to the open sea*
35 to your plastic.[2]

OLD LADY   It seems you are well acquainted with my closet?°   *private chamber*

BOSOLA   One would suspect it for a shop of witchcraft, to
    find in it the fat of serpents, spawn of snakes, Jews' spit-
    tle, and their young children's ordure°—and all these for   *excrement*
40 the face. I would sooner eat a dead pigeon, taken from the
    soles of the feet of one sick of the plague,[3] than kiss
    one of you fasting. Here are two of you, whose sin of
    your youth° is the very patrimony of the physician,   *i.e., venereal disease*
    makes him renew his footcloth with the spring and
45 change his high-prized courtesan with the fall of the
    leaf.[4] I do wonder you do not loathe yourselves.
    Observe my meditation now:
    What thing is in this outward form of man
    To be beloved? We account it ominous
50 If nature do produce a colt, or lamb,
    A fawn, or goat, in any limb resembling
    A man, and fly from't as a prodigy.°   *monster, freak*
    Man stands amazed to see his deformity
    In any other creature but himself.
55 But in our own flesh, though we bear diseases
    Which have their true names only ta'en from beasts,
    As the most ulcerous wolf and swinish measle,[5]
    Though we are eaten up of lice and worms,
    And though continually we bear about us
60 A rotten and dead body, we delight
    To hide it in rich tissue.° All our fear—   *fabric*
    Nay, all our terror—is, lest our physician

---

9. At the time of the last state journey.
1. Turning a (ship) on its side for cleaning and repairing.
2. That is, there's a blunt (literally, a coarse plaster) answer to your (cosmetic) modeling.
3. Pigeons were believed to be able to draw the poison out of plague sores.
4. That is, what you pay the physician enables

him to buy a new ornamental cloth for his horse ("footcloth") every spring and exchange his old mistress for a new one every fall.
5. Lupus, an ulcerous skin disease, is also the Latin word for wolf; measles is a skin disease in swine as well as a (different) disease in humans.

Should put us in the ground, to be made sweet.
[*To* CASTRUCHIO] Your wife's gone to Rome. You two cou-
65 ple, and get you to the wells at Lucca,[6] to recover your
aches.
        [*Exeunt* CASTRUCHIO *and the* OLD LADY.]
I have other work on foot. I observe our duchess
Is sick a-days. She pukes; her stomach seethes;
The fins° of her eyelids look most teeming blue;[7]   lids
70 She wanes i'th'cheek and waxes fat i'th'flank,
And, contrary to our Italian fashion,
Wears a loose-bodied gown. There's somewhat in't.[8]
I have a trick may chance° discover it,   perchance
A pretty° one: I have bought some apricots,   clever
75 The first our spring yields.
        [*Enter* ANTONIO *and* DELIO *conversing privately.*]
DELIO   And so long since married?
You amaze me.
ANTONIO   Let me seal your lips forever,
For, did I think that anything but th'air
Could carry these words from you, I should wish
You had no breath at all.
80 [*To* BOSOLA] Now, sir, in your contemplation? You are
studying to become a great wise fellow?
BOSOLA Oh, sir, the opinion of° wisdom is a foul tetter[9]   reputation for
that runs all over a man's body. If simplicity direct us to
have° no evil, it directs us to a happy being,° for the subtlest   *i.e., to do /*
85 folly proceeds from the subtlest wisdom. Let me be simply   *makes us happy*
honest.
ANTONIO I do understand your inside.
BOSOLA Do you so?
ANTONIO Because you would not seem to appear to th'-
90 world puffed up with your preferment,° you continue   advancement in status
this out-of-fashion melancholy. Leave it, leave it.
BOSOLA Give me leave to be honest in any phrase, in any
compliment whatsoever. Shall I confess myself to you? I
look no higher than I can reach. They are the gods that
95 must ride on winged horses; a lawyer's mule of a slow
pace will both suit my disposition and business. For
mark me: when a man's mind rides faster than his horse
can gallop, they quickly both tire.
ANTONIO You would look up to heaven, but I think the
100 devil, that rules i'th'air, stands in your light.
BOSOLA Oh, sir, you are lord of the ascendant,[1] chief man

---

6. A famous spa in northern Italy; its warm springs were believed to have healing properties.
7. Taken as a sign of pregnancy.

8. Something inside it; something going on.
9. Skin disease.
1. That is, you are exerting special influence (an astrological term).

with the Duchess; a duke was your cousin-german
removed.[2] Say you were lineally descended from King
Pepin,[3] or he himself: what of this? Search the heads° of   *sources*
105 the greatest rivers in the world, you shall find them but
bubbles of water. Some would think the souls of princes
were brought forth by some more weighty cause than
those of meaner° persons. They are deceived. There's the   *lower in social station*
same hand to them;[4] the like passions sway them. The
110 same reason that makes a vicar go to law for a tithe-pig[5]
and undo his neighbors makes them° spoil° a whole   *(princes) / plunder*
province and batter down goodly cities with the cannon.

       [*Enter the* DUCHESS *attended.*]

DUCHESS   Your arm, Antonio. Do I not grow fat?
    I am exceeding short-winded.—Bosola,
115 would have you, sir, provide for me a litter,[6]
    Such a one as the Duchess of Florence rode in.
BOSOLA   The Duchess used one when she was great with child.
DUCHESS   I think she did. [*To an attendant lady*] Come
    hither; mend my ruff.° [*The lady tends to her.*]   *starched collar*
120 Here. When?[7] Thou art such a tedious lady, and
    Thy breath smells of lemon peels.[8] Would thou hadst done!
    Shall I swoon under thy fingers? I am
    So troubled with the mother![9]
BOSOLA [*aside*]   I fear too much.
DUCHESS [*to* ANTONIO]   I have heard you say that the French
    courtiers
125 Wear their hats on 'fore the King.
ANTONIO   I have seen it.
DUCHESS   In the presence?°   *royal presence*
ANTONIO   Yes.
DUCHESS   Why should not we bring up° that fashion?   *introduce*
    'Tis ceremony, more than duty, that consists
130 In the removing of a piece of felt.
    Be you the example to the rest o'th'court;
    Put on your hat first.
ANTONIO   You must pardon me.
    I have seen, in colder countries than in France,
    Nobles stand bare° to th'prince, and the distinction   *bareheaded*
135 Methought showed reverently.
BOSOLA   I have a present for Your Grace.
DUCHESS   For me, sir?
BOSOLA   Apricots, madam.
DUCHESS   Oh, sir, where are they?

2. First cousin once removed (here, a parent's
first cousin).
3. Frankish king (r. 751–68), the father of
Charlemagne.
4. That is, they were created alike.
5. A pig given as payment of the tithe, the tax
owed to the church.

6. A small couch, shut in by curtains, that
holds a single passenger (usually carried on
men's shoulders).
7. An expression of impatience.
8. Chewed to counteract bad breath.
9. Hysteria; but "mother" is understood by
Bosola in its more common sense.

I have heard of none to-year.°   *this year*

BOSOLA [*aside*]   Good. Her color rises.

DUCHESS [*taking the fruit*]   Indeed, I thank you. They are
    wondrous fair ones.

140   What an unskillful fellow is our gardener!
    We shall have none this month.   [*She eats.*]

BOSOLA   Will not Your Grace pare them?

DUCHESS   No. They taste of musk, methinks. Indeed they do.

BOSOLA   I know not. Yet I wish Your Grace had pared 'em.

145 DUCHESS   Why?

BOSOLA   I forget to tell you the knave gard'ner,
    Only to raise his profit by them the sooner,
    Did ripen them in horse dung.

DUCHESS   Oh, you jest!
    [*To* ANTONIO] You shall judge. Pray, taste one.

ANTONIO   Indeed, madam,

150   I do not love the fruit.

DUCHESS   Sir, you are loath
    To rob us of our dainties. [*To* BOSOLA] 'Tis a delicate fruit;
    They say they are restorative?°   *(of health)*

BOSOLA   'Tis a pretty art, this grafting.

DUCHESS   'Tis so: a bett'ring of nature.

155 BOSOLA   To make a pippin grow upon a crab,
    A damson on a blackthorn.[1] [*Aside*] How greedily she
      eats them!
    A whirlwind strike off these bawd farthingales!°   *hooped petticoats*
    For, but for that and the loose-bodied gown,
    I should have discovered apparently°   *plainly*

160   The young springald cutting a caper° in her belly.   *youngster dancing*

DUCHESS   I thank you, Bosola. They were right good ones,
    If they do not make me sick.

ANTONIO   How now, madam?

DUCHESS   This green fruit and my stomach are not friends.
    How they swell me!

165 BOSOLA [*aside*]   Nay, you are too much swelled already.

DUCHESS   Oh, I am in an extreme cold sweat.

BOSOLA   I am very sorry.

DUCHESS   Lights to my chamber! O good Antonio,
    I fear I am undone.   [*Exit* DUCHESS *attended*].

DELIO   Lights there, lights!
           [*Exeunt all but* ANTONIO *and* DELIO.]

170 ANTONIO   O my most trusty Delio, we are lost!
    I fear she's fall'n in labor, and there's left
    No time for her remove.

DELIO   Have you prepared
    Those ladies to attend her, and procured
    That politic° safe conveyance for the midwife   *shrewd, expedient*

---

1. To make a sweet apple grow upon a crab apple, a sweet plum on a spiny tree.

175   Your duchess plotted?

ANTONIO   I have.

DELIO   Make use then of this forced occasion:
Give out° that Bosola hath poisoned her   *Announce*
With these apricots. That will give some color°   *pretext*
For her keeping close.°   *shut in, secluded*

ANTONIO   Fie, fie! The physicians
180   Will then flock to her.

DELIO   For that you may pretend
She'll use some prepared antidote of her own
Lest the physicians should repoison her.

ANTONIO   I am lost in amazement. I know not what to think on't.

                              [Exeunt.°]   *They exit (Latin)*

2.2

[SCENE: *Scene continues.*]

       [Enter BOSOLA.*]*

BOSOLA   So, so: there's no question but her tetchiness and
most vulturous eating of the apricots are apparent° signs   *obvious*
of breeding.°   *pregnancy*

       [Enter the OLD LADY.*]*

   Now?

5 OLD LADY   I am in haste, sir.   *[He prevents her leaving.]*

BOSOLA   There was a young waiting-woman had° a monstrous   *who had*
desire to see the glasshouse.°   *glass factory*

OLD LADY   Nay, pray let me go.

BOSOLA   And it was only to know what strange instrument it
10   was° should swell up a glass to the fashion of a woman's   *was that*
belly.

OLD LADY   I will hear no more of the glasshouse. You are
still abusing women?

BOSOLA   Who, I? No, only, by the way now and then, men-
15   tion your° frailties. The orange tree bears ripe and green   *(women's)*
fruit and blossoms all together, and some of you give
entertainment for pure love, but more for more precious
reward. The lusty spring smells well, but drooping
autumn tastes well. If we have the same golden showers
20   that rained in the time of Jupiter the Thunderer, you
have the same Danaës still, to hold up their laps to
receive them.[2] Didst thou never study the mathematics?

OLD LADY   What's that, sir?

BOSOLA   Why, to know the trick how to make a many lines
25   meet in one center.[3] Go, go; give your foster daughters
good counsel: tell them that the devil takes delight to hang

---

2. See note to 1.1.254–65. Bosola's point is
that women can always be seduced by men
who present them with gifts.

3. That is, to draw the attention of many
men's attention into a single lap.

at a woman's girdle, like a false, rusty watch, that she cannot discern how the time passes.

[*Exit* OLD LADY.]

[*Enter* ANTONIO, DELIO, RODERIGO, *and* GRISOLAN].

ANTONIO Shut up the court gates.

RODERIGO   Why, sir? What's the danger?

30 ANTONIO Shut up the posterns° presently,° and call   back gates / at once
All the officers° o'th'court.   servants

GRISOLAN   I shall, instantly.   [*Exit.*]

ANTONIO Who keeps the key o'th'park gate?

RODERIGO   Forobosco.°   (*a servant*)

ANTONIO Let him bring't presently.

[RODERIGO *goes to the door.*]

[GRISOLAN *and* RODERIGO *return with* SERVANTS.]

FIRST SERVANT Oh, gentlemen o'th'court, the foulest treason!

35 BOSOLA [*aside*] If that these apricots should be poisoned,
now, without my knowledge!

FIRST SERVANT There was taken even now a Switzer° in   Swiss mercenary
the Duchess' bedchamber.

SECOND SERVANT A Switzer?

40 FIRST SERVANT With a pistol in his great codpiece.[4]

BOSOLA Ha, ha, ha!

FIRST SERVANT The codpiece was the case for't.

SECOND SERVANT There was a cunning traitor. Who would
have searched his codpiece?

45 FIRST SERVANT True, if he had kept out of the ladies' chambers. And all the molds of his buttons were leaden bullets.

SECOND SERVANT Oh, wicked cannibal!° A firelock° in's   savage / i.e., pistol
codpiece?

FIRST SERVANT 'Twas a French plot, upon my life.

50 SECOND SERVANT To see what the devil can do!

ANTONIO All the officers here?

SERVANTS We are.

ANTONIO Gentlemen,
We have lost much plate,° you know; and but this evening   gold or silver utensils

55 Jewels to the value of four thousand ducats°   gold coins
Are missing in° the Duchess' cabinet.°   from / boudoir
Are the gates shut?

FIRST SERVANT Yes.

ANTONIO 'Tis the Duchess' pleasure

60 Each officer be locked into his chamber
Till the sunrising, and to send the keys
Of all their chests and of their outward doors
Into her bedchamber. She is very sick.

RODERIGO At her pleasure.

65 ANTONIO She entreats you take't not ill. The innocent
Shall be the more approved° by it.   esteemed

---

4. A flap or pouch attached at the front of men's breeches.

BOSOLA   Gentleman o'th'woodyard,[5] where's your Switzer
    now?

FIRST SERVANT   By this hand, 'twas credibly reported by one
70   o'th'black guard.°   [*Exeunt all except* ANTONIO *and* DELIO.]   *lowly kitchen servants*

DELIO   How fares it with the Duchess?

ANTONIO   She's exposed
    Unto the worst of torture, pain, and fear.

DELIO   Speak to her all happy comfort.

ANTONIO   How I do play the fool with mine own danger!
75   You are this night, dear friend, to post° to Rome.   *hasten*
    My life lies in° your service.   *depends on*

DELIO   Do not doubt me.

ANTONIO   Oh, 'tis far from me; and yet fear presents me
    Somewhat° that looks like danger.   *Something*

DELIO   Believe it,
    'Tis but the shadow of your fear, no more.
80   How superstitiously we mind° our evils!   *give heed to*
    The throwing down salt, or crossing of a hare,
    Bleeding at nose, the stumbling of a horse,
    Or singing of a cricket are of power
    To daunt whole man in us. Sir, fare you well.
85   I wish you all the joys of a blessed father;
    And, for my faith,° lay this unto your breast: *as for my loyalty*
    Old friends, like old swords, still° are trusted best.   [*Exit.*]   *always*

        [*Enter* CARIOLA.]

CARIOLA   Sir, you are the happy father of a son.
    Your wife commends him to you.

ANTONIO   Blessèd comfort!
90   For heaven sake, tend her well. I'll presently°   *immediately*
    Go set a figure° for 's nativity.   [*Exeunt.*]   *cast a horoscope*

2.3

[SCENE: *Scene continues.*]

        [*Enter* BOSOLA *with a dark° lantern.*]   *shuttered*

BOSOLA   Sure I did hear a woman shriek. List!° Hah?   *Listen!*
    And the sound came, if I received it right,
    From the Duchess' lodgings. There's some stratagem
    In the confining all our courtiers
5   To their several wards.° I must have part of it;   *separate rooms*
    My intelligence° will freeze else. List, again!   *information*
    It may be 'twas the melancholy bird,
    Best friend of silence and of solitariness,
    The owl, that screamed so.

        [*Enter* ANTONIO *with a paper.*]

            Hah? Antonio!

---

5. Mocking address, as if to a common laborer.

10 ANTONIO I heard some noise.—Who's there? What art
     thou? Speak.
   BOSOLA Antonio? Put not your face nor body
     To such a forced expression of fear.
     I am Bosola, your friend.
   ANTONIO   Bosola?
15 [*Aside*] This mole does undermine me. [*Aloud*] Heard you not
     A noise even now?
   BOSOLA   From whence?
   ANTONIO   From the Duchess' lodging.
   BOSOLA Not I. Did you?
   ANTONIO   I did, or else I dreamed.
   BOSOLA Let's walk towards it.
   ANTONIO   No. It may be 'twas
     But the rising of the wind.
   BOSOLA   Very likely.
20   Methinks 'tis very cold, and yet you sweat.
     You look wildly.
   ANTONIO   I have been setting a figure
     For the Duchess' jewels.[6]
   BOSOLA   Ah. And how falls your question?°   *inquiry*
     Do you find it radical?[7]
   ANTONIO   What's that to you?
     'Tis rather to be questioned what design,
25   When all men were commanded to their lodgings,
     Makes you a night walker.
   BOSOLA   In sooth,° I'll tell you: *truth*
     Now all the court's asleep, I thought the devil
     Had least to do here; I came to say my prayers,
     And if it do offend you I do so,
30   You are a fine courtier.°   (*said ironically*)
   ANTONIO [*aside*]   This fellow will undo me.
     [*To him*] You gave the Duchess apricots today.
     Pray heaven they were not poisoned.
   BOSOLA Poisoned? A Spanish fig[8]
     For the imputation!
   ANTONIO   Traitors are ever confident
35   Till they are discovered. There were jewels stol'n too.
     In my conceit,° none are to be suspected   *opinion*
     More than yourself.
   BOSOLA   You are a false steward.
   ANTONIO Saucy slave! I'll pull thee up by the roots.
   BOSOLA Maybe the ruin will crush you to pieces.
40 ANTONIO You are an impudent snake indeed, sir.

---

6. That is, casting a horoscope to investigate
the theft.
7. That is, fit to be judged by astrological
calculation.

8. A contemptuous gesture, made by thrusting the thumb between the first two fingers;
also, a poisoned fig used to commit murder.

Are you scarce warm, and do you show your sting?
[BOSOLA . . . .]⁹
ANTONIO You libel well, sir.
BOSOLA   No, sir. Copy° it out,   *Write*
And I will set my hand to't.°   *sign it*
ANTONIO [*aside*]   My nose bleeds.
45 One that were superstitious would count
This ominous, when it merely comes by chance.
Two letters that are wrought° here for my name   *prepared*
Are drowned in blood! Mere accident.
[*To* BOSOLA] For you, sir, I'll take order.°   *appropriate measures*
50 I'th'morn you shall be safe.° [*Aside*] 'Tis that must color°   *in custody / disguise*
Her lying-in. [*To* BOSOLA] Sir, this door you pass not.
I do not hold it fit that you come near
The Duchess' lodgings till you have quit° yourself.   *acquitted*
[*Aside*] The great are like the base; nay, they are the same,
55 When they seek shameful ways to avoid shame.
        [*Exit having accidentally dropped the horoscope.*]
BOSOLA Antonio hereabout did drop a paper.
Some of your help, false friend.° [*He searches with the help*   *(the dark lantern)*
        of his dark lantern and finds the horoscope.] Oh, here it is.
What's here? A child's nativity calculated?
[*He reads.*] "The Duchess was delivered of a son 'tween the
60 hours twelve and one in the night, *Anno Dom.* 1504"—that's
this year—"*decimo nono Decembris*"¹—that's this night—
"taken according to the meridian of Malfi"—that's our
duchess. Happy discovery! "The Lord of the first
house, being combust° in the ascendant, signifies short   *burned up*
65 life; and Mars being in a human sign, joined to the tail of
the Dragon, in the eighth house, doth threaten a violent
death. *Caetera non scrutantur.*"²
Why now, 'tis most apparent! This precise° fellow   *punctilious*
Is the Duchess' bawd.° I have it to my wish.   *pimp*
70 This is a parcel of intelligency°   *news*
Our courtiers were cased up° for! It needs must follow   *confined*
That I must be committed,° on pretense   *put in prison*
Of poisoning her; which I'll endure, and laugh at.
If one could find the father now! But that
75 Time will discover. Old Castruchio
I'th'morning posts to Rome; by him I'll send
A letter that shall make her brothers' galls°   *bitterness*
O'erflow their livers. This was a thrifty way!
Though Lust do mask in ne'er so strange disguise,
80 She's oft found witty, but is never wise.   [*Exit.*]

9. A line appears to be missing here.   2. The rest is not examined (Latin).
1. December 19, in the year of our Lord 1504
(Latin).

2.4

[SCENE: *The* CARDINAL's *rooms*.]

[*Enter* CARDINAL *and* JULIA.]

CARDINAL   Sit. Thou art my best of wishes. Prithee tell me
    What trick didst thou invent to come to Rome
    Without thy husband.
JULIA   Why, my lord, I told him
    I came to visit an old anchorite°   religious recluse
5   Here, for devotion.
CARDINAL   Thou art a witty false one—
    I mean, to him.
JULIA   You have prevailed with me
    Beyond my strongest thoughts. I would not now
    Find you inconstant.
CARDINAL   Do not put thyself
    To such a voluntary torture, which proceeds
10 Out of your own guilt.
JULIA   How, my lord?
CARDINAL   You fear
    My constancy because you have approved°   experienced
    Those giddy and wild turnings in yourself.
JULIA   Did you e'er find them?
CARDINAL   Sooth, generally for women;[3]
    A man might strive to make glass malleable
15 Ere he should make them fixed.
JULIA   So, my lord.
CARDINAL   We had need go borrow that fantastic glass
    Invented by Galileo the Florentine,[4]
    To view another spacious world i'th'moon,
    And look to find a constant woman there.
20 JULIA [*weeping*]   This is very well, my lord.
CARDINAL   Why do you weep?
    Are tears your justification? The selfsame tears
    Will fall into your husband's bosom, lady,
    With a loud protestation that you love him
    Above the world. Come, I'll love you wisely,
25 That's jealously, since I am very certain
    You cannot make cuckold.
JULIA   I'll go home
    To my husband.
CARDINAL   You may thank me, lady,
    I have taken you off your melancholy perch,
    Bore you upon my fist, and showed you game,
30 And let you fly at it.[5] I pray thee, kiss me.

3. That is, I have generally found women to be
"giddy and wild" (inconstant or unfaithful).
4. An anachronistic reference to the telescope constructed by Galileo (1564–1642) in

1605, a century after the events depicted in
the play.
5. Terms from falconry (with Julia the falcon).

When thou wast with thy husband, thou wast watched°   *guarded*
Like a tame elephant. Still you are to thank me.
Thou hadst only kisses from him, and high feeding,°   *rich food*
But what delight was that? 'Twas just like one
35 That hath a little fing'ring on the lute,
Yet cannot tune° it. Still you are to thank me.   *play upon*

JULIA You told me of a piteous wound i'th'heart,
And a sick liver, when you wooed me first,
And spake like one in physic.[6]
40 CARDINAL [*hearing the approach of someone*] Who's that?
[*To her*] Rest firm.° For° my affection to thee,   *assured / As for*
Lightning moves slow to't.°   *compared to it*
   [*Enter a* SERVANT.]

SERVANT   Madam, a gentleman
That's come post° from Malfi desires to see you.   *in haste*

CARDINAL Let him enter. I'll withdraw.   [*Exit.*]

SERVANT   He says
45 Your husband, old Castruchio, is come to Rome,
Most pitifully tired with riding post.   [*Exit.*]
   [*Enter* DELIO.]

JULIA Signor Delio! [*Aside*] 'Tis one of my old suitors.

DELIO I was bold to come and see you.

JULIA   Sir, you are welcome.

DELIO Do you lie° here? Sure, your own experience   *temporarily lodge*

JULIA
50 Will satisfy you no; our Roman prelates
Do not keep lodging for ladies.

DELIO   Very well.
I have brought you no commendations from your husband,
For I know none by him.

JULIA   I hear he's come to Rome?

DELIO I never knew man and beast, of ° a horse and a knight,   *made up of*
55 So weary of each other; if he had had a good back,
He would have undertook to have borne his horse,
His breech° was so pitifully sore.   *rump*

JULIA   Your laughter
Is my pity.[7]

DELIO   Lady, I know not whether
You want money, but I have brought you some.
60 JULIA From my husband?

DELIO   No, from mine own allowance.

JULIA I must hear the condition ere I be bound to take it.

DELIO [*showing the money*] Look on't, 'tis gold. Hath it
  not a fine color?

JULIA I have a bird more beautiful.

DELIO [*clinking the coins*] Try the sound on't.

JULIA   A lute string far exceeds it.

---

6. Under medical care; that is, sick for love. 7. What you laugh at is what I feel pity for.

65   It hath no smell, like cassia, or civet,[8]
    Nor is it physical,° though some fond° doctors   *medicinal / foolish*
    Persuade us seeth't in cullises.[9] I'll tell you,
    This is a creature bred by—
        [*Enter* SERVANT.]

SERVANT   Your husband's come,
    Hath delivered a letter to the Duke of Calabria

70   That, to my thinking, hath put him° out of his wits.   [*Exit.*]   *(Ferdinand)*

JULIA   Sir, you hear;
    Pray let me know your business and your suit
    As briefly as can be.

DELIO   With good speed. I would wish you,
    At such time as you are nonresident

75   With your husband, my mistress.

JULIA   Sir, I'll go ask my husband if I shall,
    And straight return your answer.   [*Exit.*]

DELIO   Very fine!
    Is this her wit or honesty° that speaks thus?   *chastity, honor*
    I heard one say the Duke was highly moved°   *disturbed; excited*

80   With° a letter sent from Malfi. I do fear   *By*
    Antonio is betrayed. How fearfully
    Shows his ambition now! Unfortunate Fortune!
    They pass through whirlpools, and deep woes do shun,
    Who the event weigh ere the action's done.[1]   [*Exit.*]

2.5

[SCENE: *Rome.* FERDINAND's *private apartments.*]

    [*Enter* CARDINAL, *and* FERDINAND, *with a letter.*]

FERDINAND   I have this night digged up a mandrake.[2]

CARDINAL   Say you?°   *What?*

FERDINAND   And I am grown mad with't.

CARDINAL   What's the prodigy?°   *ominous event; monster*

FERDINAND [*showing him the letter*]   Read there—a sister
    damned! She's loose i'th'hilts,°   *unfaithful in marriage*

5   Grown a notorious strumpet.

CARDINAL   Speak lower.

FERDINAND   Lower?
    Rogues do not whisper't now, but seek to publish't,°   *make it publicly known*
    As servants do the bounty of their lords,
    Aloud, and with a covetous, searching eye
    To mark who note them. Oh, confusion° seize her!   *ruin, perdition*

10   She hath had most cunning bawds to serve her turn,

---

8. A musky-smelling aromatic substance, used in perfumes, obtained from the glands of civet cats. *Cassia:* a spice made from a cinnamon-like bark.
9. To boil gold in broths intended to nourish the sick.

1. Who weigh the outcome before doing the act.
2. The mandrake has a forked root that was thought to resemble a human form and was used to promote conception; when pulled from the ground, it was believed to shriek, causing death or madness in the hearer.

And more secure conveyances for° lust   *safe ways for satisfying*
Than towns of garrison for service.°   *receiving supplies*

CARDINAL   Is't possible?
Can this be certain?

FERDINAND   Rhubarb,° oh, for rhubarb   *(used as a purgative)*
To purge this choler!° Here's the cursèd day   *(see 1.1.505n)*

15 To prompt my memory, and here[3] 't shall stick
Till of her bleeding heart I make a sponge
To wipe it out.

CARDINAL   Why do you make yourself
So wild a tempest?

FERDINAND   Would I could be one,
That I might toss her palace 'bout her ears,

20 Root up her goodly forests, blast her meads,°   *meadows*
And lay her general territory as waste
As she hath done her honors![4]

CARDINAL   Shall our blood,
The royal blood of Aragon and Castile,
Be thus attainted?°   *sullied, corrupted*

FERDINAND   Apply desperate physic.°   *medicine*

25 We must not now use balsamum,° but fire,   *an aromatic balm*
The smarting cupping-glass,[5] for that's the mean°   *means*
To purge infected blood—such blood as hers.
There is a kind of pity in mine eye;
I'll give it to my handkercher; and, now 'tis here,

30 I'll bequeath this to her bastard.

CARDINAL   What to do?

FERDINAND   Why, to make soft lint for his mother's wounds
When I have hewed her to pieces.

CARDINAL   Cursed creature!
Unequal° Nature, to place women's hearts   *Unjust*
So far upon the left° side!   *i.e., the deceitful*

FERDINAND   Foolish men,

35 That e'er will trust their honor in a bark°   *small ship*
Made of so slight, weak bulrush as is woman,
Apt every minute to sink it!

CARDINAL   Thus
Ignorance, when it hath purchased° honor,   *acquired*
It cannot wield it.

FERDINAND   Methinks I see her laughing,

40 Excellent hyena! Talk to me somewhat, quickly,
Or my imagination will carry me
To see her in the shameful act of sin.

CARDINAL   With whom?

FERDINAND   Happily° with some strong-thighed bargeman,   *Perhaps*

---

3. Ferdinand apparently points to his head or heart.
4. That is, her family's honor as well as her personal reputation.

5. A glass used in bleeding patients (the heated glass was placed over a cut made in the skin, and the vacuum formed as it cooled drew blood to the surface).

45   Or one o'th'woodyard, that can quoit the sledge°   *throw the sledgehammer*
     Or toss the bar,[6] or else some lovely squire°   *young man*
     That carries coals up to her privy° lodgings.   *private*

CARDINAL   You fly beyond your reason.

FERDINAND   Go to,° mistress!   *(an expression of anger)*
     'Tis not your whore's milk that shall quench my wildfire,[7]
50   But your whore's blood.

CARDINAL   How idly shows° this rage, which carries you,   *vain appears*
     As men conveyed by witches through the air,
     On violent whirlwinds! This intemperate noise
     Fitly resembles deaf men's shrill discourse,
55   Who talk aloud, thinking all other men
     To have their imperfection.

FERDINAND   Have not you
     My palsy?°   *tremors (from rage)*

CARDINAL   Yes. I can be angry
     Without this rupture.° There is not in nature   *outburst*
60   A thing that makes man so deformed, so beastly,
     As doth intemperate anger. Chide yourself.
     You have divers° men who never yet expressed   *i.e., there are many*
     Their strong desire of rest but by unrest,
     By vexing of themselves. Come, put yourself
65   In tune.

FERDINAND   So. I will only study to seem
     The thing I am not. I could kill her now,
     In you, or in myself, for I do think
     It is some sin in us heaven doth revenge
70   By her.

CARDINAL   Are you stark mad?

FERDINAND   I would have their bodies[8]
     Burnt in a coalpit,[9] with the ventage° stopped,   *airhole*
     That their cursed smoke might not ascend to heaven;
     Or dip the sheets they lie in in pitch or sulfur,
75   Wrap them in't, and then light them like a match;
     Or else to boil their bastard to a cullis,°   *broth*
     And give't his lecherous father, to renew
     The sin of his back.°   *i.e., of his flesh*

CARDINAL   I'll leave you.

FERDINAND   Nay, I have done.
     I am confident, had I been damned in hell
80   And should have heard of this, it would have put me
     Into a cold sweat. In, in. I'll go sleep.
     Till I know who leaps my sister, I'll not stir.

---

6. That is, compete in a trial of strength by throwing a thick rod of wood or metal ("quoit" also suggests a game).
7. (1) A destructive conflagration; (2) a highly flammable and hard-to-extinguish material used in warfare; (3) a skin disease characterized by blisters and inflammation.
8. That is, the bodies of the Duchess and her lover.
9. For making charcoal.

That known, I'll find scorpions[1] to string my whips,
And fix her in a general eclipse.°   [*Exeunt.*]   *total darkness*

3.1

[SCENE: *Malfi. The* DUCHESS' *palace.*]

[*Enter* ANTONIO *and* DELIO.]

ANTONIO   Our noble friend, my most belovèd Delio!
    Oh, you have been a stranger long at court.
    Came you along with the Lord Ferdinand?

DELIO   I did, sir. And how fares your noble duchess?

5 ANTONIO   Right fortunately well. She's an excellent
    Feeder of pedigrees;° since you last saw her,   *Breeder of a lineage*
    She hath had two children more, a son and daughter.

DELIO   Methinks 'twas yesterday. Let me but wink°   *close my eyes*
    And not behold your face, which to mine eye
10   Is somewhat leaner, verily I should dream
    It were within this half hour.

ANTONIO   You have not been in law, friend Delio,
    Nor in prison, nor a suitor at the court,
    Nor begged the reversion° of some great man's place,   *right of succession*
15   Nor troubled with an old wife, which doth make
    Your time so insensibly hasten.°   *pass so unnoticed*

DELIO   Pray, sir, tell me,
    Hath not this news arrived yet to the ear
    Of the Lord Cardinal?

ANTONIO   I fear it hath.
    The Lord Ferdinand, that's newly come to court,
20   Doth bear himself right dangerously.

DELIO   Pray, why?

ANTONIO   He is so quiet that he seems to sleep
    The tempest out, as dormice do in winter.
    Those houses that are haunted are most still
    Till the devil be up.

DELIO   What say the common people?

25 ANTONIO   The common rabble do directly say
    She is a strumpet.

DELIO   And your graver heads,
    Which would be politic, what censure they?°   *what is their judgment*

ANTONIO   They do observe I grow to infinite purchase°   *(stolen) wealth*
    The left-hand way,° and all suppose the Duchess   *i.e., underhandedly*
30   Would amend it if she could; for, say they,
    Great princes, though they grudge their officers
    Should have such large and unconfinèd means
    To get wealth under them, will not complain,
    Lest thereby they should make them odious
35   Unto the people. For other obligation

---

1. Knots or metal spikes to make a whip more painful.

Of love or marriage between her and me
They never dream of.

      [*Enter* FERDINAND *and the* DUCHESS.]

DELIO [*privately to* ANTONIO]   The Lord Ferdinand
Is going to bed. [*He and* ANTONIO *stand aside.*]

FERDINAND [*to the* DUCHESS] I'll instantly to bed,

40   For I am weary. I am to bespeak°   *arrange for*
A husband for you.

DUCHESS   For me, sir? Pray, who is't?

FERDINAND   The great Count Malateste.

DUCHESS   Fie upon him!
A count? He's a mere stick of sugar candy;
You may look quite through him. When I choose

45   A husband, I will marry for your honor.

FERDINAND   You shall do well in't. [*Noticing* ANTONIO]
How is't,° worthy Antonio?   *are you*

DUCHESS   But, sir, I am to have private conference with you
About a scandalous report is° spread   *that is*

50   Touching mine honor.

FERDINAND   Let me be ever deaf to't:
One of Pasquil's paper bullets,[2] court calumny,
A pestilent air which princes' palaces
Are seldom purged of. Yet, say that it were true—
I pour it in your bosom°—my fixed love   *tell you confidentially*

55   Would strongly excuse, extenuate, nay, deny
Faults, were they apparent in you. Go, be safe
In your own innocency.

DUCHESS   Oh, blessed comfort!
This deadly air is purged.   [*Exeunt all but* FERDINAND.]

FERDINAND   Her guilt treads on
Hot burning coulters.[3]

      [*Enter* BOSOLA.]

               Now, Bosola,

60   How thrives our intelligence?

BOSOLA   Sir, uncertainly.
'Tis rumored she hath had three bastards, but
By whom, we may go read i'th'stars.

FERDINAND   Why, some
Hold opinion all things are written there.

BOSOLA Yes, if we could find spectacles to read them.

65   I do suspect there hath been some sorcery
Used on the Duchess.

FERDINAND   Sorcery? To what purpose?

BOSOLA To make her dote on some desertless fellow
She shames to acknowledge.

---

2. Lampoons or pasquinades. Pasquin or Pasquil was the name given to an ancient statue, unearthed and installed on a Roman street corner in 1501; it soon became the custom to attach to its base satirical writings attacking various individuals.
3. Iron blades fixed in front of a plowshare.

FERDINAND   Can your faith give way
　　To think there's power in potions or in charms
70　To make us love, whether we will or no?

BOSOLA　Most certainly.

FERDINAND　Away! These are mere gulleries,° horrid things　　*tricks*
　　Invented by some cheating mountebanks°　　　　　　　　*quacks*
　　To abuse° us. Do you think that herbs or charms　　　*deceive, cheat*
75　Can force the will? Some trials have been made
　　In this foolish practice, but the ingredients
　　Were lenitive° poisons, such as are of force　　　　　*soothing*
　　To make the patient mad; and straight the witch
　　Swears, by equivocation, they are in love.
80　The witchcraft lies in her° rank blood. This night　　*(the Duchess's)*
　　I will force confession from her. You told me
　　You had got, within these two days, a false key°　　　*skeleton key*
　　Into her bedchamber.

BOSOLA   I have.

FERDINAND   As I would wish.

BOSOLA　What do you intend to do?

85 FERDINAND　Can you guess?

BOSOLA   No.

FERDINAND   Do not ask, then.
　　He that can compass° me and know my drifts　　　*fully comprehend*
　　May say he hath put a girdle 'bout° the world　　　*has gone around*
　　And sounded[4] all her quicksands.

BOSOLA   I do not
　　Think so.

FERDINAND　What do you think, then, pray?

BOSOLA   That you are
90　Your own chronicle too much, and grossly
　　Flatter yourself.

FERDINAND   Give me thy hand. I thank thee.
　　I never gave pension° but to flatterers　　　　　　　*payment*
　　Till I entertained° thee. Farewell.　　　　　　　　　*hired*
　　That friend a great man's ruin strongly checks
95　Who rails into his belief all his defects.[5]　　　*[Exeunt.]*

3.2

[SCENE: *Malfi. The* DUCHESS' *bedchamber.*]

[*Enter* DUCHESS, ANTONIO, *and* CARIOLA.]

DUCHESS [*to* CARIOLA]　Bring me the casket° hither, and　　*small box*
　　the glass.°　　　　　　　　　　　　　　　　　　　　*mirror*
　　[*To* ANTONIO] You get no lodging here, tonight, my lord.

ANTONIO　Indeed, I must persuade one.°　　　　*get one by persuasion*

DUCHESS   Very good.
5　I hope in time 'twill grow into a custom,

4. Measured the depth of.

5. That is, the true friend of a great man   helps to prevent the latter's ruin by abusing
　　　　　　　　　　　　　　　　　　　him until he recognizes his flaws.

That noblemen shall come with cap and knee[6]
To purchase a night's lodging of their wives.

ANTONIO   I must lie here.

DUCHESS   Must? You are a Lord of Misrule.[7]

ANTONIO   Indeed, my rule is only in the night.

10 DUCHESS   To what use will you put me?

ANTONIO   We'll sleep together.

DUCHESS   Alas, what pleasure can two lovers find in sleep?

CARIOLA   My Lord, I lie with her often, and I know
She'll much disquiet you.

ANTONIO [to the DUCHESS]   See, you are complained of.

15 CARIOLA   For she's the sprawling'st bedfellow.

ANTONIO   I shall like her the better for that.

CARIOLA   Sir, shall I ask you a question?

ANTONIO   I pray thee, Cariola.

CARIOLA   Wherefore still° when you lie with my lady   *Why invariably*
20 Do you rise so early?

ANTONIO   Laboring men
Count the clock oft'nest, Cariola,
Are glad when their task's ended.

DUCHESS   I'll stop your mouth.

[*She kisses him.*]

ANTONIO   Nay, that's but one. Venus had two soft doves[8]
To draw her chariot; I must have another.   [*He kisses her.*]
25 When wilt thou marry, Cariola?

CARIOLA   Never, my lord.

ANTONIO   Oh, fie upon this single life! Forgo it!
We read how Daphne, for her peevish flight,
Became a fruitless bay tree, Syrinx turned
To the pale empty reed, Anaxarete
30 Was frozen into marble,[9] whereas those
Which married or proved kind unto their friends°   *lovers*
Were, by a gracious influence, transshaped
Into the olive, pomegranate, mulberry;[1]
Became flowers, precious stones, or eminent stars.

6. That is, in a humble posture: with cap in hand and on bended knee.

7. A person of lower rank who presides over festival revels, thereby temporarily reversing the normal social order.

8. Doves are sacred to Venus, the Roman goddess of love.

9. The stories of these transformations of women who spurned their wooers all appear in Ovid's *Metaphorphoses* (ca. 10 C.E.). Daphne fled the god Apollo (book 1); Syrinx, a follower of the virgin goddess Diana (Artemis), prayed to her sister nymphs to transform her so that she might escape Pan (book 1); and Anaxarete,

a princess who mocked the humble Iphis when he confessed his love—a rejection that drove him to suicide—was turned into stone as she gazed at his body, which passed by her house in his funeral procession.

1. Antonio's point is that women who accepted their suitors underwent changes associated with fruitfulness, but of his examples only the mulberry—whose dark purple berries, according to Ovid (*Metamorphoses* 4), take their color from the blood of two lovers, Pyramus and Thisbe—has an origin myth based on transformation.

35   CARIOLA   This is a vain poetry.° But I pray you tell me: *worthless fiction*
      If there were proposed me wisdom, riches, and beauty
      In three several° young men, which should I choose?   *different*
  ANTONIO   'Tis a hard question. This was Paris' case,[2]
      And he was blind° in't, and there was great cause;   *lacked good judgment*
40   For how was't possible he could judge right,
      Having three amorous goddesses in view,
      And they stark naked? 'Twas a motion°   *proposal for deliberation*
      Were° able to benight the apprehension   *That would be*
      Of the severest counselor° of Europe.   *most discerning lawyer*
45   Now° I look on both your faces, so well formed,   *Now that*
      It puts me in mind of a question I would ask.
  CARIOLA   What is't?
  ANTONIO   I do wonder why hard-favored° ladies,   *unattractive*
      For the most part, keep worse-favored waiting-women
50   To attend them, and cannot endure fair ones.
  DUCHESS   Oh, that's soon answered.
      Did you ever in your life know an ill° painter   *bad*
      Desire to have his dwelling next door to the shop
      Of an excellent picture-maker? 'Twould disgrace
55   His face-making, and undo him. I prithee,
      When were we so merry?—My hair tangles.
      [*The* DUCHESS *tends to her toilette.*]
  ANTONIO [*aside to* CARIOLA]   Prithee, Cariola, let's steal forth the room
      And let her talk to herself. I have divers times
      Served her the like, when she hath chafed extremely.
60   I love to see her angry. Softly, Cariola!
      [*Exeunt* ANTONIO *and* CARIOLA.]
  DUCHESS   Doth not the color of my hair 'gin to change?
      When I wax gray, I shall have all the court
      Powder their hair with arras,° to be like me.   *a white powder*
      You have cause to love me; I ent'red you into my heart
65   Before you would vouchsafe to call for the keys.
      [*Enter* FERDINAND *unobserved by her.*]
      We shall one day have my brothers take you napping.
      Methinks his° presence, being now in court,   *(Ferdinand's)*
      Should make you keep your own bed. But, you'll say,
      Love mixed with fear is sweetest. I'll assure you
70   You shall get no more children till my brothers
      Consent to be your gossips.°—Have you lost   *godfathers*
      Your tongue? [*She turns and sees* FERDINAND.] 'Tis welcome;
      For know, whether I am doomed to live or die,

---

2. Paris, a son of King Priam of Troy, was chosen to judge which of three goddesses was the most fair. Each offered a bribe: Athena promised wisdom and great glory in war; Hera (Juno), wealth and rule over Asia; and Aphrodite (Venus), the most beautiful woman in the world as his wife. By choosing a wife he won Helen, the wife of Menelaus, king of Sparta—and his poor judgment caused the Trojan War.

I can do both like a prince.   [FERDINAND *gives her a poniard.*]

FERDINAND   Die then, quickly!

75 Virtue, where art thou hid? What hideous thing
    Is it that doth eclipse thee?

DUCHESS   Pray, sir, hear me.

FERDINAND   Or is it true thou art but a bare name
    And no essential° thing?   *real*

DUCHESS   Sir—

FERDINAND   Do not speak.

DUCHESS   No, sir.

80 I will plant my soul in mine ears to hear you.

FERDINAND   O most imperfect light of human reason,
    That mak'st us so unhappy, to foresee
    What we can least prevent!—Pursue thy wishes,
    And glory in them; there's in shame no comfort

85 But to be past all bounds and sense of shame.

DUCHESS   I pray, sir, hear me: I am married.

FERDINAND   So.

DUCHESS   Haply° not to your liking, but for that,   *Perhaps*
Alas, your shears do come untimely now
To clip the bird's wings that's already flown.

90 Will you see my husband?

FERDINAND   Yes, if I
    Could change eyes with a basilisk.[3]

DUCHESS   Sure,° you came hither   *Surely*
    By his confederacy.°   *collusion*

FERDINAND   The howling of a wolf
    Is music to° thee, screech owl. Prithee, peace!—   *compared with*
    Whate'er thou art, that hast enjoyed my sister

95 (For I am sure thou hear'st me), for thine own sake
    Let me not know thee. I came hither prepared
    To work thy discovery, yet am now persuaded
    It would beget such violent effects
    As would damn us both. I would not for ten millions

100 I had beheld thee; therefore use all means
    I never may have knowledge of thy name.
    Enjoy thy lust still, and a wretched life,
    On that condition.—And for thee, vile woman,
    If thou do wish thy lecher may grow old

105 In thy embracements, I would have thee build
    Such a room for him as our anchorites
    To holier use inhabit. Let not the sun
    Shine on him till he's dead. Let dogs and monkeys
    Only converse with him, and such dumb things

110 To whom Nature denies use to sound° his name.   *ability to speak*
    Do not keep a paraquito,° lest she learn it.   *parrot*

3. A legendary reptile whose glance was fatal.

If thou do love him, cut out thine own tongue
Lest it bewray° him.   *expose, betray*

DUCHESS   Why might not I marry?
I have not gone about, in this, to create
115 Any new world or custom.

FERDINAND   Thou art undone;
And thou hast ta'en that massy sheet of lead
That hid thy husband's bones, and folded it
About my heart.

DUCHESS   Mine bleeds for't.

FERDINAND   Thine? Thy heart?
What should I name't, unless a hollow bullet°   *cannonball*
120 Filled with unquenchable wildfire?°   *(see 2.5.49n)*

DUCHESS   You are, in this,
Too strict, and, were you not my princely brother,
I would say too willful. My reputation
Is safe.

FERDINAND   Dost thou know what reputation is?
125 I'll tell thee, to small purpose, since th'instruction
Comes now too late.
Upon° a time Reputation, Love, and Death   *Once upon*
Would travel o'er the world, and 'twas concluded
That they should part and take three several° ways.   *separate*
130 Death told them they should find him in great battles,
Or cities plagued with plagues. Love gives them counsel
To inquire for him 'mongst unambitious shepherds,
Where dowries were not talked of, and sometimes
'Mongst quiet kindred that had nothing left
135 By their dead parents. "Stay," quoth Reputation,
"Do not forsake me; for it is my nature
If once I part from any man I meet
I am never found again." And so, for you:
You have shook hands with° Reputation,   *bid farewell to*
140 And made him invisible. So, fare you well.
I will never see you more.

DUCHESS   Why should only I,
Of all the other princes of the world,
Be cased up, like a holy relic? I have youth,
145 And a little beauty.

FERDINAND   So you have° some virgins   *there are*
That are witches. I will never see thee more.   [*Exit.*]

        [*Enter* ANTONIO *with a pistol and* CARIOLA.]

DUCHESS   You saw this apparition?

ANTONIO   Yes. We are
Betrayed. How came he hither? [*To* CARIOLA] I should turn
This to thee for that.

        [*He threatens her with the pistol.*]

CARIOLA   Pray, sir, do; and when
150 That you have cleft my heart, you shall read there

Mine innocence.

DUCHESS   That gallery gave him entrance.

ANTONIO   I would this terrible thing° would come again,   *(Ferdinand)*

That, standing on my guard, I might relate

My warrantable° love. [*She shows the poniard.*] Ha!   *justifiable; lawful*

What means this?

155 DUCHESS   He left this with me.

ANTONIO   And, it seems, did wish

You would use it on yourself?

DUCHESS   His action

Seemed to intend so much.

ANTONIO   This hath a handle to't

As well as a point. Turn it towards him

160 And so fasten the keen edge in his rank gall.

[*Knocking within.*]

How now? Who knocks? More earthquakes?

DUCHESS   I stand

As if a mine beneath my feet were ready

To be blown up.

CARIOLA   'Tis Bosola.

DUCHESS   Away!

Oh, misery! Methinks unjust° actions   *dishonest*

165 Should wear these masks and curtains, and not we.

You must instantly part hence; I have fashioned° it already.   *arranged*

[*Exit* ANTONIO.]

[*Enter* BOSOLA.]

BOSOLA   The Duke your brother is ta'en up in a whirlwind,

Hath took horse, and 's rid post° to Rome.   *in haste*

DUCHESS   So late?

BOSOLA   He told me, as he mounted into th'saddle,

170 You were undone.

DUCHESS   Indeed, I am very near it.

BOSOLA   What's the matter?

DUCHESS   Antonio, the master of our household,

Hath dealt so falsely with me in's accounts:

My brother stood engaged with° me for money   *stood as security for*

175 Ta'en up of certain Neapolitan Jews,[4]

And Antonio lets the bonds be forfeit.

BOSOLA   Strange! [*Aside*] This is cunning.

DUCHESS   And hereupon

My brother's bills at Naples are protested

Against.[5] Call up our officers.

BOSOLA   I shall.   [*Exit.*]

[*Enter* ANTONIO.]

4. Because it was illegal for Christians to engage in usury, Jews often became moneylenders, one of the few professions open to them. *Ta'en up of:* borrowed (at interest) from.

5. That is, Neapolitan moneylenders have officially declared that Ferdinand's bills of exchange will not be accepted.

180 DUCHESS [*to* ANTONIO]   The place that you must fly to is Ancona.
Hire a house there. I'll send after you
My treasure and my jewels. Our weak safety
Runs upon enginous° wheels; short syllables   *crafty; deceitful*
Must stand for periods.° I must now accuse you   *full sentences*
185 Of such a feignèd crime as Tasso calls
Magnanima mensogna, a noble lie,[6]
'Cause it must shield our honors. [*Sounds are heard.*]
Hark, they are coming!

> [*Enter* BOSOLA *and* OFFICERS. ANTONIO *and the* DUCHESS
> *speak loudly, so as to be heard by those entering.*]

ANTONIO   Will Your Grace hear me?
190 DUCHESS   I have got well by you! You have yielded me
A million of loss; I am like° to inherit   *likely*
The people's curses for your stewardship.
You had the trick in audit time to be sick,
Till I had signed your quietus,[7] and that cured you
195 Without help of a doctor.—Gentlemen,
I would have this man be an example to you all;
So shall you hold my favor. I pray, let him;°   *let him go*
For he's done that, alas, you would not think of,
And, because I intend to be rid of him,
200 I mean not to publish.° [*To* ANTONIO] Use your fortune   *announce it publicly*
elsewhere.
ANTONIO   I am strongly armed to brook° my overthrow,   *endure*
As commonly men bear with a hard year.°   *i.e., bad harvest*
I will not blame the cause on't, but do think
The necessity of my malevolent star
205 Procures this, not her humor.° Oh, the inconstant   *character; mood*
And rotten ground of service! You may see:
'Tis ev'n like him that in a winter night
Takes a long slumber o'er a dying fire
As loath to part from't, yet parts thence as cold
210 As when he first sat down.
DUCHESS   We do confiscate,
Towards the satisfying of your accounts,
All that you have.
ANTONIO   I am all yours; and 'tis very fit
All mine should be so.
DUCHESS   So, sir; you have your pass.
215 ANTONIO   You may see, gentlemen, what 'tis to serve[8]
A prince with body and soul.   [*Exit.*]
BOSOLA   Here's an example for extortion: what moisture
is drawn out of the sea, when foul weather comes,
pours down and runs into the sea again.

---

6. A phrase from *Jerusalem Delivered* (2.22; 1581), an epic by the Italian poet Torquato Tasso (1544–1595): to save her fellow Christians from slaughter, the virtuous maiden Sophronia falsely confesses to a theft.

7. Discharged your debt (see 1.1.470 and note).

8. With double meaning, as Antonio is both her servant and her husband.

220 DUCHESS   I would know what are your opinions of this
Antonio.

SECOND OFFICER   He could not abide to see a pig's head
gaping.[9] I thought Your Grace would find him a Jew.

THIRD OFFICER   I would you had been his officer,° for your   *steward*
225 own sake.

FOURTH OFFICER   You would have had more money.

FIRST OFFICER   He stopped his ears with black wool, and
to those came° to him for money said he was thick of   *who came*
hearing.

230 SECOND OFFICER   Some said he was an hermaphrodite,
for he could not abide a woman.

FOURTH OFFICER   How scurvy proud he would look when
the treasury was full! Well, let him go.

FIRST OFFICER   Yes, and the chippings of the butt'ry fly
235 after him, to scour his gold chain![1]

DUCHESS   Leave us.   [*Exeunt* OFFICERS.]
What do you think of these?

BOSOLA   That these are rogues, that, in 's prosperity, but
to have waited on his fortune,[2] could have wished his
240 dirty stirrup riveted through their noses, and followed
after 's mule like a bear in a ring; would have prostituted
their daughters to his lust; made their firstborn° intelligen-   *(sons)*
cers;[3] thought none happy but such as were born under
his blessed planet and wore his livery. And do these lice°   *i.e., parasites*
245 drop off now? Well, never look to have the like again.
He hath left a sort° of flatt'ring rogues behind him;   *band*
their doom must follow. Princes pay flatterers in their own
money: flatterers dissemble their vices, and they dissemble their lies;[4] that's justice. Alas, poor gentleman!

250 DUCHESS   Poor? He hath amply filled his coffers.

BOSOLA   Sure he was too honest. Pluto, the god of riches,[5]
when he's sent by Jupiter to any man, he goes limping to
signify that wealth that comes on° God's name comes   *in*
slowly, but when he's sent on the devil's errand, he rides
255 post and comes in by scuttles.° Let me show you what a   *short, hurried runs*
most unvalued[6] jewel you have, in a wanton humor,
thrown away, to bless the man shall° find him. He was an   *who shall*
excellent courtier, and most faithful—a soldier that
thought it as beastly to know his own value too little as
260 devilish to acknowledge it too much. Both his virtue and

---

9. That is, roasted with an apple in its mouth
(an aversion to pork suggests that he is
Jewish).

1. The gold chain of office, which might be
polished with bread crumbs ("chippings")
from the pantry ("butt'ry").

2. Simply to have waited on Antonio when he
was prosperous.

3. Spies for Antonio.

4. That is, flatterers lie about the vices of
princes, and princes lie about (the reward
for) those lies.

5. Pluto, the Roman god of the underworld,
was often confused with Plutus, god of
wealth or riches.

6. (1) Invaluable; (2) viewed as having no
value.

form deserved a far better fortune. His discourse rather
delighted to judge itself than show itself. His breast was
filled with all perfection, and yet it seemed a private
whisp'ring room, it made so little noise of't.

265 DUCHESS   But he was basely descended.

BOSOLA   Will you make yourself a mercenary herald,
rather to examine men's pedigrees than virtues? You
shall want° him. For know° an honest statesman to a   *miss / know that*
prince is like a cedar planted by a spring: the spring

270 bathes the tree's root; the grateful tree rewards it with his
shadow. You have not done so. I would sooner swim to the
Bermoothes° on two politicians'° rotten bladders,[7] tied   *Bermuda islands /*
together with an intelligencer's heartstring, than de-   *schemers'*
pend on so changeable a prince's favor. Fare thee well,

275 Antonio! Since the malice of the world would needs
down with thee,° it cannot be said yet that any ill hap-   *throw you down*
pened unto thee, considering thy fall was accompanied
with virtue.

DUCHESS   Oh, you render me excellent music!

BOSOLA   Say you?

280 DUCHESS   This good one that you speak of is my husband.

BOSOLA   Do I not dream? Can this ambitious age
Have so much goodness in't as to prefer°   *advance in status*
A man merely for worth, without these shadows°   *delusive semblances*
Of wealth and painted° honors? Possible?   *unreal*

285 DUCHESS   I have had three children by him.

BOSOLA   Fortunate lady!
For you have made your private nuptial bed
The humble and fair seminary° of peace.   *seedbed*
No question but many an unbeneficed[8] scholar
Shall pray for you for this deed, and rejoice

290 That some preferment in the world can yet
Arise from merit. The virgins of your land
That have no dowries shall hope your example
Will raise them to rich husbands. Should you want
Soldiers, 'twould make the very Turks and Moors

295 Turn Christians, and serve you for this act.
Last, the neglected poets of your time,
In honor of this trophy of a man,
Raised by that curious engine,° your white hand,   *skillful tool*
Shall thank you in your grave for't,[9] and make that

300 More reverend° than all the cabinets°   *revered / private rooms*
Of living princes. For° Antonio,   *As for*
His fame shall likewise flow from many a pen,
When heralds shall want coats° to sell to men.   *lack coats of arms*

---

7. Bags filled with air.
8. Unpaid; specifically, lacking an ecclesiastical office that gives its holder the revenue

from an endowment.
9. That is, will write praises of you to be read
when you are dead.

DUCHESS As I taste° comfort in this friendly speech,   *experience*
305 So would I find concealment.
BOSOLA Oh, the secret of my prince,
  Which I will wear on th'inside of my heart!
DUCHESS You shall take charge of all my coin and jewels,
  And follow him, for he retires himself
310 To Ancona.
BOSOLA   So.
DUCHESS   Whither, within few days,
  I mean to follow thee.
BOSOLA   Let me think:
  I would wish Your Grace to feign a pilgrimage
  To our Lady of Loreto,¹ scarce seven leagues
  From fair Ancona; so may you depart
315 Your country with more honor, and your flight
  Will seem a princely progress,° retaining   *state journey*
  Your usual train° about you.   *body of attendants*
DUCHESS   Sir, your direction
  Shall lead me by the hand.
CARIOLA   In my opinion,
  She were better progress to the baths
320 At Lucca,° or go visit the Spa   *(see 2.1.65n)*
  In Germany,° for, if you will believe me,   *(modern-day Belgium)*
  I do not like this jesting with religion,
  This feigned pilgrimage.
DUCHESS Thou art a superstitious fool.
325 Prepare us instantly for our departure.—
  Past sorrows, let us moderately lament them;
  For those to come, seek wisely to prevent them.
                              [*Exit with* CARIOLA.]

BOSOLA A politician° is the devil's quilted anvil.   *schemer*
  He fashions all sins on him, and the blows
330 Are never heard; he may work in a lady's chamber,
  As here for proof. What rests° but I reveal   *remains*
  All to my lord? Oh, this base quality°   *occupation*
  Of intelligencer! Why, every quality i'th'world
  Prefers but² gain or commendation.
335 Now, for this act I am certain to be raised,
  And men that paint weeds to the life are praised.   [*Exit.*]

3.3

[SCENE: *Rome. A room in a palace.*]

  [*Enter* CARDINAL, FERDINAND, MALATESTE, PESCARA,
    SILVIO, *and* DELIO.]

CARDINAL Must we turn soldier, then?
MALATESTE   The Emperor,³

---

1. A famous religious shrine in northeast Italy, the house of the Virgin Mary (said to have been carried there by angels).

2. Assists in bringing about.
3. The Holy Roman Emperor Charles V (1500–1558; r. 1519–56).

Hearing your worth that way ere you attained
This reverend garment, joins you in commission
With the right fortunate soldier, the Marquis of Pescara,[4]
5   And the famous Lannoy.[5]
CARDINAL   He that had the honor
Of taking the French king[6] prisoner?
MALATESTE [*producing a document*]   The same.
Here's a plot° drawn for a new fortification   plan
At Naples.   [*He and the* CARDINAL *confer privately.*]
FERDINAND   This great Count Malateste, I perceive,
10 Hath got employment?°   *an official position*
DELIO   No employment, my lord;
A marginal note in the muster book that he is
A voluntary lord.°   *i.e., a volunteer*
FERDINAND   He's no soldier?
DELIO   He has worn gunpowder in 's hollow tooth
For the toothache.
15 SILVIO   He comes to the leaguer° with a full intent   *military camp*
To eat fresh beef and garlic,[7] means to stay
Till the scent be gone, and straight return to court.
DELIO   He hath read all the late service°   *military engagement*
As the city chronicle relates it,
20 And keeps two painters going, only to express°   *represent*
Battles in model.
SILVIO   Then he'll fight by the book.°   *(vs. by experience)*
DELIO   By the almanac, I think,
To choose good° days and shun the critical.[8]   *propitious*
That's his mistress' scarf.[9]
SILVIO   Yes, he protests
25 He would do much for that taffeta.°   *glossy silk*
DELIO   I think he would run away from a battle
To save it from taking° prisoner.   *being taken*
SILVIO   He is horribly afraid
Gunpowder will spoil the perfume on't.
DELIO   I saw a Dutchman break his pate° once   *bruise his head*
30 For calling him potgun;° he made his head   *popgun; braggart*
Have a bore in't, like a musket.
SILVIO   I would he had made a touchhole to't.[1]
DELIO   He is indeed a guarded sumpter cloth
Only for the remove of the court.[2]
[*Enter* BOSOLA. *He confers privately
with the* CARDINAL *and* MALATESTE.]

---

4. A historical figure, the Spanish soldier Fernando Francesco de Ávalos (1490–1525).
5. Charles de Lannoy (1487–1527), viceroy of Naples.
6. Francis I (1494–1547; r. 1515–47), taken prisoner in 1525.
7. To bolster his courage (Greek and Roman soldiers often ate garlic before a battle).
8. Dangerous; crucial.

9. Worn as a favor, or token of love.
1. That is, I wish the Dutchman had made a hole in it for igniting the musket's charge (and blown it up).
2. That is, Malateste is like an ornamented ("guarded") saddlecloth used only for moving the court from one place to another (not for war).

35 PESCARA   Bosola arrived? What should be the business?
  Some falling out amongst the cardinals?
  These factions amongst great men, they are like
  Foxes: when their heads are divided
  They carry fire in their tails, and all the country
40 About them goes to wrack° for't.[3]   *is devastated*
   SILVIO   What's that Bosola?
   DELIO   I knew him in Padua—a fantastical° scholar, like   *fanciful; eccentric*
   such who study to know how many knots was in Her-
   cules' club, of what color Achilles' beard was, or whether
   Hector were not troubled with the toothache.[4] He hath
45 studied himself half blear-eyed to know the true symme-
   try of Caesar's nose by a shoeing-horn;[5] and this he did
   to gain the name of a speculative° man.   *given to speculation*
   PESCARA   Mark Prince Ferdinand:
   A very salamander lives in's eye,
50 To mock the eager violence of fire.[6]
   SILVIO   That Cardinal hath made more bad faces° with his   *made more men suffer*
   oppression than ever Michaelangelo[7] made good ones.
   He lifts up's nose like a foul porpoise before a storm.[8]
   PESCARA   The Lord Ferdinand laughs.
   DELIO   Like a deadly cannon,
55 That lightens° ere it smokes.   *emits flashes*
   PESCARA   These are your true pangs of death,
   The pangs of life, that struggle with° great statesmen.   *within*
   DELIO   In such a deformed silence, witches whisper their
   charms.

        [SILVIO, PESCARA, *and* DELIO *stand aside silently*
        as the focus shifts to BOSOLA, *the* CARDINAL, *and*
        FERDINAND.]

60 CARDINAL   Doth she make religion her riding hood
   To keep her from the sun and tempest?
   FERDINAND   That!
   That damns her. Methinks her fault and beauty,
   Blended together, show like leprosy,
   The whiter the fouler. I make it a question
65 Whether her beggarly brats were ever christened.
   CARDINAL   I will instantly solicit the state of Ancona
   To have them banished.
   FERDINAND   You are for° Loreto?   *heading for*
   I shall not be at your ceremony.° Fare you well.   *(see 3.4)*

                    [*Exit* CARDINAL.]

3. A biblical allusion; after putting 300 foxes
tail to tail, Samson lit their tails with fire-
brands and then set them loose to burn the
Philistines' grain fields, vineyards, and olive
orchards (Judges 15.4–5).
4. All obviously absurd questions about major
figures from classical mythology.
5. That is, whether the nose of the Roman

general and statesman Julius Caesar (100–44
B.C.E.) was as well shaped as a shoehorn.
6. Salamanders were thought to live in fire.
7. Michelangelo (1475–1564), renowned
Italian sculptor and painter.
8. Porpoises were thought to be able to predict storms at sea.

[*To* BOSOLA] Write to the Duke of Malfi, my young nephew
70　She had by her first husband, and acquaint him
　　With 's mother's honesty.°　　　　　　　　　　*(lack of) chastity*
BOSOLA　　　　　　　I will.
FERDINAND　　　　　　　　Antonio!
　　A slave that only smelled of ink and counters,[9]
　　And nev'r in's life looked like a gentleman
　　But in the audit time.—Go, go presently;°　　　*immediately*
75　Draw me out an hundred and fifty of our horse,
　　And meet me at the fort bridge.　　　[*Exeunt.*]

3.4

[SCENE: *The shrine of Our Lady of Loreto, in northeast Italy in
the province of Ancona.*]

　　　　[*Enter two* PILGRIMS *to the shrine of Our Lady of
　　　　Loreto.*]

FIRST PILGRIM　I have not seen a goodlier shrine than this,
　　Yet I have visited many.
SECOND PILGRIM　The Cardinal of Aragon
　　Is this day to resign his cardinal's hat;
5　His sister duchess likewise is arrived
　　To pay her vow of pilgrimage. I expect
　　A noble ceremony.
FIRST PILGRIM　No question.—They come.
　　　　[*Here the ceremony of the* CARDINAL's *installment in
　　　　the habit*° *of a soldier, performed in delivering up his*　　*attire*
　　　　*cross, hat, robes, and ring at the shrine, and investing
　　　　him with sword, helmet, shield, and spurs. Then*
　　　　ANTONIO, *the* DUCHESS, *and their children, having
　　　　presented themselves at the shrine, are (by a form of
　　　　banishment in dumb show*[1] *expressed towards them
　　　　by the* CARDINAL *and the state of Ancona) banished;
　　　　during all which ceremony, this ditty is sung to very
　　　　solemn music by divers churchmen:*]

　　Arms and honors deck thy story,
10　To thy fame's eternal glory!
　　Adverse fortune ever fly thee!
　　No disastrous fate come nigh thee!

　　I alone will sing° thy praises　　　　　　　　*will only sing*
　　Whom to honor virtue raises,
15　And thy study, that divine is,
　　Bent to martial discipline is.
　　Lay aside all those robes lie° by thee;　　　　*that lie*
　　Crown thy arts° with arms; they'll beautify thee.　　*learning*
　　O worthy of worthiest name, adorned in this manner,
20　Lead bravely thy forces on under war's warlike banner!

---

9. Small pieces of metal or other material
used in performing arithmetical operations.

1. Symbolic action without speech.

Oh, mayst thou prove fortunate in all martial courses!°   *encounters*
Guide thou still,° by skill, in arts and forces!°   *always / physical might*
Victory attend thee nigh, whilst Fame sings loud thy powers!
Triumphant conquest crown thy head, and blessings
    pour down showers!

        [*And then exeunt all except the two* PILGRIMS.]

25 FIRST PILGRIM Here's a strange turn of state! Who would
    have thought
  So great a lady would have matched herself
  Unto so mean° a person? Yet the Cardinal   *lowborn*
  Bears himself much too cruel.
SECOND PILGRIM   They are banished.
FIRST PILGRIM But I would ask, what power hath this state
30 Of Ancona to determine of° a free prince?   *render a judgment on*
SECOND PILGRIM They are° a free state, sir, and her   *Ancona is*
    brother showed
  How that the Pope, forehearing of her looseness,
  Hath seized into th'protection of the church
  The dukedom which she held as dowager.[2]
35 FIRST PILGRIM But by what justice?
SECOND PILGRIM   Sure I think by none,
  Only her brother's° instigation.   *(the Cardinal's)*
FIRST PILGRIM What was it with such violence he took
  Off from her finger?
SECOND PILGRIM   'Twas her wedding ring,
  Which he vowed shortly he would sacrifice
40 To his revenge.
FIRST PILGRIM   Alas, Antonio!
  If that a man be thrust into a well,
  No matter who sets hand to't, his own weight
  Will bring him sooner to th'bottom. Come, let's hence.
  Fortune makes this conclusion general:
45 All things do help th'unhappy° man to fall.   [*Exeunt.*]   *unfortunate*

3.5

[SCENE: *Near Loreto.*]

      [*Enter* ANTONIO, DUCHESS, *children,* CARIOLA, *and*
      servants.]

DUCHESS Banished° Ancona!   *Banished from*
ANTONIO   Yes. You see what power
  Lightens° in great men's breath.   *Flashes like lightning*
DUCHESS   Is all our train°   *body of attendants*
  Shrunk to this poor remainder?
ANTONIO   These poor men,
  Which have got little in your service, vow

---

2. As widow of her first husband.

5   To take[3] your fortune; but your wiser buntings,°   *small birds*
    Now they are fledged,° are gone.   *capable of flying*
DUCHESS   They have done wisely.
    This puts me in mind of death; physicians thus,
    With their hands full of money, use to give o'er[4]
    Their patients.
ANTONIO   Right° the fashion of the world!   *Exactly*
10   From decayed fortunes every flatterer shrinks;
    Men cease to build where the foundation sinks.
DUCHESS   I had a very strange dream tonight.°   *last night*
ANTONIO   What was't?
DUCHESS   Methought I wore my coronet of state,
    And on a sudden all the diamonds
15   Were changed to pearls.
ANTONIO   My interpretation
    Is, you'll weep shortly, for to me the pearls
    Do signify your tears.
DUCHESS   The birds that live i'th'field
    On the wild benefit of nature live
20   Happier than we; for they may choose their mates,
    And carol their sweet pleasures to the spring.
        [*Enter* BOSOLA *with a letter.*]
BOSOLA   You are happily° o'erta'en.   *fortunately*
DUCHESS   From my brother?
BOSOLA   Yes, from the Lord Ferdinand, your brother,
    All love and safety.   [*He delivers a letter to her.*]
DUCHESS   Thou dost blanch mischief,°   *whitewash evildoing*
25   Wouldst make it white. See, see! Like to calm weather
    At sea before a tempest, false hearts speak fair
    To those they intend most mischief.
    [*She reads.*] "Send Antonio to me; I want his head in a
      business."
30   A politic° equivocation!   *crafty*
    He doth not want your counsel, but your head;
    That is, he cannot sleep till you be dead.
    And here's another pitfall that's strewed o'er
    With roses: mark it, 'tis a cunning one:
35   [*She reads.*] "I stand engaged for your husband for sev-
    eral debts at Naples.° Let not that trouble him, I had   *(see 3.2.174–79)*
    rather have his heart° than his money."   *his love; his life*
    And I believe so too.
BOSOLA   What do you believe?
DUCHESS   That he so much distrusts my husband's love,
40   He will by no means believe his heart is with him
    Until he see it.° The devil is not cunning enough   *i.e., cuts it out*
    To circumvent us in riddles.
BOSOLA   Will you reject that noble and free league°   *alliance*
    Of amity and love which I present you?

---

3. Adopt as their own.   4. Are accustomed to abandon.

45 DUCHESS   Their league is like that of some politic kings,
　　Only to make themselves of strength and power
　　To be our after-ruin. Tell them so.
　BOSOLA [*to* ANTONIO]   And what from you?
　ANTONIO   Thus tell him: I will not come.
　BOSOLA   And what of this?°   (*the letter*)
　ANTONIO   My brothers° have dispersed   *brothers-in-law*
50 Bloodhounds abroad, which, till I hear are muzzled,
　　No truce, though hatched with ne'er such politic skill,
　　Is safe that hangs upon our enemies' will.
　　I'll not come at° them.   *approach*
　BOSOLA   This proclaims your breeding.
　　Every small thing draws a base mind to fear
55 As the adamant° draws iron. Fare you well, sir.   *magnet*
　　You shall shortly hear from 's.   [*Exit.*]
　DUCHESS   I suspect some ambush.
　　Therefore, by all my love, I do conjure you
　　To take your eldest son and fly towards Milan;
60 Let us not venture all this poor remainder
　　In one unlucky bottom.°   *ship*
　ANTONIO   You counsel safely.
　　Best of my life, farewell! Since we must part,
　　Heaven hath a hand in't, but no otherwise
　　Than as some curious° artist takes in sunder°   *clever / apart*
65 A clock or watch when it is out of frame,°   *out of order*
　　To bring't in better order.
　DUCHESS   I know not which is best,
　　To see you dead, or part with you.—Farewell, boy;
　　Thou art happy that thou hast not understanding
70 To know thy misery, for all our wit
　　And reading brings us to a truer sense
　　Of sorrow.—In the eternal church,° sir,   *i.e., heaven*
　　I do hope we shall not part thus.
　ANTONIO   Oh, be of comfort!
　　Make° patience a noble fortitude,   *Make of*
75 And think not how unkindly we are used.
　　Man, like to cassia,° is proved best, being bruised.   *a cinnamon-like bark*
　DUCHESS   Must I, like to a slave-born Russian,
　　Account it praise° to suffer tyranny?   *Consider it virtue*
　　And yet, O heaven, thy heavy hand is in't.
80 I have seen my little boy oft scourge° his top,   *whip*
　　And compared myself to't. Naught made me e'er
　　Go right but heaven's scourge stick.[5]
　ANTONIO   Do not weep.
　　Heaven fashioned us of nothing, and we strive
　　To bring ourselves to nothing.—Farewell, Cariola,
85 And thy sweet armful!—If I do never see thee more,

5. A whip used with a child's top.

Be a good mother to your little ones,
And save them from the tiger. Fare you well.

[*He and the* DUCHESS *kiss.*]

DUCHESS   Let me look upon you once more, for that speech
Came from a dying father. Your kiss is colder
90 Than that I have seen an holy anchorite
Give to a dead man's skull.

ANTONIO   My heart is turned to a heavy lump of lead,
With which I sound° my danger. Fare you well.   *measure the depths of*

[*Exit with his elder son.*]

DUCHESS   My laurel[6] is all withered.
95 CARIOLA   Look, madam, what a troop of armèd men
Make toward us.

[*Enter* BOSOLA *with a guard, with vizards.*°]   *masks*

DUCHESS   Oh, they are very welcome.
When Fortune's wheel is overcharged° with princes,   *overloaded*
The weight makes it move swift. I would have my ruin
Be sudden.—I am your adventure,° am I not?   *enterprise*
100 BOSOLA   You are. You must see your husband no more.

DUCHESS   What devil art thou, that counterfeits heaven's
thunder?

BOSOLA   Is that terrible? I would have you tell me
Whether is that note worse that frights the silly° birds   *helpless; simple*
Out of the corn,° or that which doth allure them   *grain*
105 To the nets? You have hearkened to the last° too much.[7]   *the latter*

DUCHESS   Oh, misery! Like to a rusty o'erchargèd° cannon,   *(with gunpowder)*
Shall I never fly in pieces? Come, to what prison?

BOSOLA   To none.

DUCHESS   Whither then?

BOSOLA   To your palace.

DUCHESS   I have heard
That Charon's[8] boat serves to convey all o'er
110 The dismal lake, but brings none back again.

BOSOLA   Your brothers mean you safety and pity.

DUCHESS   Pity!
With such a pity men preserve alive
Pheasants and quails when they are not fat enough
To be eaten.

BOSOLA   These are your children?

DUCHESS   Yes.

BOSOLA   Can they prattle?

DUCHESS   No.
115 But I intend, since they were born accurst,°   *doomed*
Curses shall be their first language.

BOSOLA   Fie, madam,

---

6. Usually a symbol of victory.
7. That is, you have paid too much attention
to temptations and too little to warnings.

8. In classical mythology, the ferryman who
takes the dead across the river Styx ("the dismal lake") to the underworld.

Forget this base, low fellow.

DUCHESS   Were I a man,
I'd beat that counterfeit face into thy other.[9]

BOSOLA   One of no birth.

DUCHESS   Say that he was born mean;°   *of low social status*
120   Man is most happy when 's own actions
Be arguments° and examples of his virtue.   *Are proofs*

BOSOLA   A barren, beggarly virtue.

DUCHESS   I prithee, who is greatest, can you tell?
Sad tales befit my woe; I'll tell you one.
125   A salmon, as she swam unto the sea,
Met with a dogfish,° who encounters her   *a small shark*
With this rough language: "Why art thou so bold
To mix thyself with our high state of floods,°   *i.e., the sea*
Being no eminent courtier, but one
130   That for the calmest and fresh time o'th'year
Dost live in shallow rivers, rank'st thyself
With silly° smelts and shrimps? And darest thou   *simple; insignificant*
Pass by our dogship[1] without reverence?"
"Oh," quoth the salmon, "sister, be at peace.
135   Thank Jupiter, we both have passed the net!
Our value never can be truly known
Till in the fisher's basket we be shown;
I'th'market then my price may be the higher,
Even when I am nearest to the cook and fire."
140   So to great men the moral may be stretched:
Men oft are valued high when they're most wretch'd.
But come: whither you please. I am armed 'gainst misery,
Bent to all sways° of the oppressors' will.   *every motion*
There's no deep valley but near some great hill.   [*Exeunt.*]

4.1

[SCENE: *Near Loreto. A prison, or the* DUCHESS' *lodgings serving as a prison.*]

[*Enter* FERDINAND, BOSOLA, *and servants with torches.*]

FERDINAND   How doth our sister duchess bear herself
In her imprisonment?

BOSOLA   Nobly. I'll describe her:
She's sad, as one long used to't, and she seems
Rather to welcome the end of misery
5   Than shun it—a behavior so noble
As gives a majesty to adversity.
You may discern the shape of loveliness
More perfect in her tears than in her smiles;
She will muse four hours together, and her silence,
10   Methinks, expresseth more than if she spake.

---

9. That is, beat Bosola's mask (or his hypoc-   1. That is, the dogfish is the equivalent of
risy) into his real face.   "lordship."

FERDINAND   Her melancholy seems to be fortified
With a strange disdain.

BOSOLA   'Tis so, and this restraint,
Like English mastiffs° that grow fierce with tying,   guard dogs
Makes her too passionately apprehend°   conscious of
15   Those pleasures she's kept from.

FERDINAND   Curse upon her!
I will no longer study in the book
Of another's heart. Inform her what I told you.   [*Exit.*]

        [*Enter* DUCHESS *and* CARIOLA.]

BOSOLA   All comfort to Your Grace!

DUCHESS   I will have none.
Pray thee, why dost thou wrap thy poisoned pills
20   In gold and sugar?

BOSOLA   Your elder brother, the Lord Ferdinand,
Is come to visit you, and sends you word,
'Cause once he rashly made a solemn vow°   (see 3.2.140–41, 146)
Never to see you more, he comes i'th'night,
25   And prays you, gently, neither torch nor taper
Shine in your chamber. He will kiss your hand
And reconcile himself; but, for his vow,
He dares not see you.

DUCHESS   At his pleasure.—
Take hence the lights.   [*Exeunt servants with torches.*]

        [*Enter* FERDINAND.]

                              He's come.

FERDINAND   Where are you?

30   DUCHESS   Here, sir.

FERDINAND   This darkness suits you well.

DUCHESS   I would ask you pardon.

FERDINAND   You have it;
For I account it the honorabl'st revenge,
Where I may kill, to pardon. Where are your cubs?

DUCHESS   Whom?

35   FERDINAND   Call them your children;
For, though our national law distinguish bastards
From true legitimate issue, compassionate nature
Makes them all equal.

DUCHESS   Do you visit me for this?
You violate a sacrament o'th'church°   (*her marriage*)
40   Shall° make you howl in hell for't.   *That shall*

FERDINAND   It had been well
Could you have lived thus always, for indeed
You were too much i'th'light.[2] But no more;
I come to seal my peace with you. Here's a hand,

        [*Gives her a dead man's hand.*]

---

2. (1) Too visible to all; (2) too light (i.e., too wanton).

To which you have vowed much love; the ring upon't
45 You gave.

DUCHESS   I affectionately kiss it.

FERDINAND   Pray do, and bury the print of it in your heart.
I will leave this ring with you for a love token,
And the hand, as sure as the ring; and do not doubt
50 But you shall have the heart too. When you need a friend,
Send it to him that owed° it; you shall see   *owned*
Whether he can aid you.

DUCHESS   You[3] are very cold.
I fear you are not well after your travel.—
Hah? Lights! Oh, horrible!

FERDINAND   Let her have lights enough.
                                        [*Exit.*[4]]

[*Enter servants with torches.*]

55 DUCHESS   What witchcraft doth he practice, that he hath left
A dead man's hand here?

         [*Here is discovered,*° *behind a travers,*° *the artificial*   *revealed / screen*
         figures of ANTONIO *and his children, appearing as if*
         they were dead.]

BOSOLA   Look you, here's the piece from which 'twas ta'en.
He doth present you this sad spectacle
That, now you know directly they are dead,
60 Hereafter you may wisely cease to grieve
For that which cannot be recoverèd.

DUCHESS   There is not between heaven and earth one wish
I stay for after this; it wastes° me more   *destroys; enfeebles*
Than were't my picture, fashioned out of wax,
65 Stuck with a magical needle, and then buried
In some foul dunghill. And yond's an excellent property°   *stage prop*
For a tyrant, which I would account mercy.

BOSOLA   What's that?

DUCHESS   If they would bind me to that lifeless trunk
70 And let me freeze to death.

BOSOLA   Come, you must live.

DUCHESS   That's the greatest torture souls feel in hell,
In hell: that they must live and cannot die.
Portia,[5] I'll new-kindle thy coals again,
And revive the rare and almost dead example
75 Of a loving wife.

BOSOLA   Oh, fie! Despair? Remember

---

3. The Duchess believes she is holding Antonio's hand.
4. Ferdinand may just move to one side, as his later remarks (lines 114–18) suggest he has heard the Duchess's dialogue with Bosola.
5. Portia (d. 43 or 42 B.C.E.), the second wife of Marcus Brutus, one of the conspirators who assassinated Julius Caesar; according to most ancient (but not modern) historians, after the defeat and suicide of Brutus at Philippi in 42 B.C.E., she killed herself by swallowing burning coals.

You are a Christian.[6]

DUCHESS   The church enjoins° fasting;   *commands*
I'll starve myself to death.

BOSOLA   Leave this vain sorrow.
Things being at the worst begin to mend;
The bee, when he hath shot his sting into your hand,
80   May then play with your eyelid.

DUCHESS   Good comfortable fellow,
Persuade a wretch that's broke upon the wheel°   *a device for torture*
To have all his bones new set; entreat him live,
To be executed again. Who must dispatch° me?   *kill*
85   I account this world a tedious theater,
For I do play a part in't 'gainst my will.

BOSOLA   Come, be of comfort. I will save your life.

DUCHESS   Indeed I have not leisure to tend so small a business.

BOSOLA   Now, by my life, I pity you.

DUCHESS   Thou art a fool, then,
90   To waste thy pity on a thing so wretched
As cannot pity it.° I am full of daggers.   *itself*
Puff! Let me blow these vapors from me.

          [*Enter a* SERVANT.]

What are you?

SERVANT   One that wishes you long life.

DUCHESS   I would thou wert hanged for the horrible curse
95   Thou hast given me!   [*Exit* SERVANT.]
                              I shall shortly grow° one   *become*
Of the miracles of pity. I'll go pray. No,
I'll go curse.

BOSOLA   Oh, fie!

DUCHESS   I could curse the stars—

BOSOLA   Oh, fearful!

DUCHESS   And those three smiling seasons of the year°   *(spring, summer, fall)*
100   Into a Russian winter, nay, the world
To its first chaos.

BOSOLA   Look you, the stars shine still.

DUCHESS   Oh, but you must remember,
My curse hath a great way to go.—
105   Plagues, that make lanes through largest families,
Consume them!°   *(her brothers)*

BOSOLA   Fie, lady!

DUCHESS   Let them, like tyrants,
Never be remembered but for the ill they have done!
Let all the zealous prayers of mortified°   *ascetic*
Churchmen forget them!

BOSOLA   Oh, uncharitable!

110 DUCHESS   Let heaven, a little while, cease crowning martyrs,
To punish them!

---

6. That is, forbidden to commit suicide, a mortal sin.

Go, howl them this, and say I long to bleed.
It is some mercy, when men kill with speed.

[*Exit with* CARIOLA.]

[*Enter* FERDINAND.]°   (see 4.1.54 SD and note)

FERDINAND   Excellent; as I would wish; she's plagued in art.°   *by a trick*
115   These presentations are but framed in wax
By the curious° master in that quality°   *expert / profession*
Vincentio Lauriola, and she takes them
For true substantial bodies.

BOSOLA   Why do you do this?

FERDINAND   To bring her to despair.

BOSOLA   Faith,° end here,   *In faith*
120   And go no farther in your cruelty.
Send her a penitential garment to put on
Next to her delicate skin, and furnish her
With beads and prayer books.

FERDINAND   Damn her! That body of hers,
125   While that my blood ran pure in't, was more worth
Than that which thou wouldst comfort, called a soul.
I will send her masques of common courtesans,
Have her meat served up by bawds and ruffians,
And, 'cause she'll needs be mad, I am resolved
130   To remove forth° the common hospital   *out of*
All the mad folk, and place them near her lodging;
There let them practice together, sing, and dance,
And act their gambols° to the full o'th'moon.[7]   *merrymaking*
If she can sleep the better for it, let her.
135   Your work is almost ended.

BOSOLA   Must I see her again?

FERDINAND   Yes.

BOSOLA   Never.

FERDINAND   You must.

140   BOSOLA   Never in mine own shape;
That's forfeited, by my intelligence°   *spying*
And this last cruel lie. When you send me next,
The business shall be comfort.

FERDINAND   Very likely!
Thy pity is nothing of kin° to thee. Antonio   *i.e., is unsuited to*
145   Lurks about Milan; thou shalt shortly thither,
To feed a fire as great as my revenge,
Which nev'r will slack till it have spent his° fuel.   *its*
Intemperate agues° make physicians cruel.   [*Exeunt.*]   *Excessive fevers*

---

7. That is, when their insanity was at its height; "lunacy" was believed to be caused by phases of the moon.

4.2

[SCENE: *The scene continues.*]

[*Enter* DUCHESS *and* CARIOLA. *Noises of Madmen are heard from offstage.*]

DUCHESS   What hideous noise was that?

CARIOLA   'Tis the wild consort°   *company of musicians*
Of madmen, lady, which your tyrant brother
Hath placed about your lodging. This tyranny,
I think, was never practiced till this hour.

5 DUCHESS   Indeed, I thank him. Nothing but noise and folly
Can keep me in my right wits, whereas reason
And silence make me stark mad. Sit down;
Discourse to me some dismal tragedy.

CARIOLA   Oh, 'twill increase your melancholy.

DUCHESS   Thou art deceived;
10 To hear of greater grief would lessen mine.
This is a prison!

CARIOLA   Yes, but you shall live
To shake this durance° off.   *imprisonment*

DUCHESS   Thou art a fool.
The robin redbreast and the nightingale
Never live long in cages.

CARIOLA   Pray dry your eyes.
15 What think you of, madam?

DUCHESS   Of nothing.
When I muse thus, I sleep.

CARIOLA   Like a madman, with your eyes open?

DUCHESS   Dost thou think we shall know one another
In th'other world?

CARIOLA   Yes, out of question.°   *unquestionably*
20 DUCHESS   Oh, that it were possible we might
But hold some two days' conference with the dead!
From them I should learn somewhat, I am sure,
I never shall know here. I'll tell thee a miracle:
I am not mad yet, to my cause of sorrow.
25 Th'heaven o'er my head seems made of molten brass,
The earth of flaming sulfur, yet I am not mad.
I am acquainted° with sad misery   *as familiar*
As the tanned galley-slave is with his oar;
Necessity makes me suffer constantly,
30 And custom makes it easy. Who do I look like now?

CARIOLA   Like to your picture in the gallery,
A deal° of life in show,° but none in practice;   *portion / appearance*
Or rather like some reverend monument
Whose ruins are even pitied.

DUCHESS   Very proper;
35 And Fortune° seems only to have her eyesight   *(often depicted as blind)*
To behold my tragedy. [*A noise is heard.*] How now,
What noise is that?

[*Enter* SERVANT.]

SERVANT   I am come to tell you
    Your brother hath intended you some sport.
    A great physician, when the Pope was sick
40 Of a deep melancholy, presented him
    With several sorts of madmen, which wild object,
    Being full of change and sport° forced him to laugh,   *entertainment*
    And so th'impostume° broke. The selfsame cure   *abscess*
    The Duke intends on you.
DUCHESS   Let them come in.
45 SERVANT   There's a mad lawyer, and a secular° priest,   *nonmonastic*
    A doctor that hath forfeited his wits
    By jealousy; an astrologian,
    That in his works said such a day o'th'month
    Should be the day of doom,° and, failing of't,   *Judgment Day*
50 Ran mad; an English tailor, crazed i'th'brain
    With the study of new fashion; a gentleman-usher[8]
    Quite beside himself with care to keep in mind
    The number of his lady's salutations
    Or "How do you" she employed him in each morning;
55 A farmer, too, an excellent knave in grain,[9]
    Mad 'cause he was hindered transportation.[1]
    And let one broker° that's mad loose to these,   *middleman*
    You'd think the devil were among them.
DUCHESS   Sit, Cariola.—Let them loose when you please,
60 For I am chained to endure all your tyranny.

[*Enter* MADMEN.]

[*Here by a* MADMAN *this song is sung, to a dismal kind of
music.*]

    Oh, let us howl some heavy note,
        Some deadly doggèd howl,
    Sounding as from the threat'ning throat
        Of beasts and fatal fowl,
65 As ravens, screech owls, bulls, and bears!
        We'll bill° and bawl our parts,   *bell (i.e., bellow)*
    Till irksome noise have cloyed your ears
        And corrosived° your hearts.   *vexed; eaten away at*
    At last, whenas our choir wants° breath,   *lacks*
70   Our bodies being blest,
    We'll sing like swans, to welcome death,[2]
        And die in love and rest.

FIRST MADMAN   Doomsday not come yet? I'll draw it
    nearer by a perspective,° or make a glass[3] that shall set   *optical glass*
75 all the world on fire upon an instant. I cannot sleep; my
    pillow is stuffed with a litter of porcupines.

---

8. A gentleman who walks before and introduces a person of higher rank.
9. (1) A person of low social class in the grain
trade; (2) an ingrained rogue.
1. That is, the grain's conveyance to market

was blocked.
2. The mute swan was believed to sing just
once, beautifully, before it died.
3. A lens of concave mirror to focus the sun's
rays.

SECOND MADMAN Hell is a mere glasshouse,° where the   *glass factory*
devils are continually blowing up women's souls on hollow irons, and the fire never goes out.

80 THIRD MADMAN I will lie with every woman in my parish
the tenth night. I will tithe them over,[4] like haycocks.

FOURTH MADMAN Shall my pothecary° outgo° me because   *druggist / outdo*
I am a cuckold? I have found out his roguery: he makes
alum° of his wife's urine and sells it to Puritans that   *a mineral salt*
85 have sore throats with overstraining.[5]

FIRST MADMAN I have skill in heraldry.

SECOND MADMAN Hast?

FIRST MADMAN You do give° for your crest a woodcock's[6]   *display*
head with the brains picked out on't; you are a very
90 ancient gentleman.

THIRD MADMAN Greek is turned Turk; we are only to be
saved by the Helvetian translation.[7]

FIRST MADMAN Come on, sir, I will lay° the law to you.   *expound*

SECOND MADMAN Oh, rather lay a corrosive;[8] the law will
95 eat to the bone.

THIRD MADMAN He that drinks but to satisfy nature° is   *physical need*
damned.

FOURTH MADMAN If I had my glass here, I would show a
sight should make all the women here call me mad
100 doctor.

FIRST MADMAN [*pointing to the* THIRD MADMAN] What's he,
a rope-maker?

SECOND MADMAN No, no, no, a snuffling knave that, while
he shows the tombs, will have his hand in a wench's
105 placket.[9]

THIRD MADMAN Woe to the caroche° that brought home   *luxurious carriage*
my wife from the masque at three o'clock in the morn-
ing! It had a large featherbed in it.

FOURTH MADMAN I have pared the devil's nails forty times,
110 roasted them in ravens' eggs, and cured agues with
them.

THIRD MADMAN Get me three hundred milch-bats to make
possets, to procure sleep.

FOURTH MADMAN All the college may throw their caps
115 at me.[1] I have made a soap-boiler costive;° it was my   *constipated*
masterpiece.

---

4. Collect a tenth from them.
5. That is, throats overstrained (from preaching too much and too loudly). Used as a
medicine.
6. A proverbially stupid bird.
7. The Geneva (and thus Swiss or "Helvetian") Bible, Protestant translation of 1560;
according to the Third Madman, any other
version turns the Greek of the New Testament into heathen matter.
8. Apply a caustic medication.
9. The opening or slit in a skirt or petticoat
(with an obscene sense as well).
1. Pursue me; or, perhaps, show indifference
to me. *College:* society of learned men or
clergy.

[*Here the dance, consisting of eight* MADMEN, *with music answerable° thereunto, after which* BOSOLA *like° an old man, enters.*]   *suitable*
    disguised as

[*Exeunt the* MADMEN.]

DUCHESS   Is he mad too?

SERVANT   Pray question him. I'll leave you.

[*Exit.*]

BOSOLA   I am come to make thy tomb.

DUCHESS   Hah, my tomb?
    Thou speak'st as if I lay upon my deathbed,
120   Gasping for breath. Dost thou perceive me sick?

BOSOLA   Yes, and the more dangerously, since thy sickness
    is insensible.°   *imperceptible*

DUCHESS   Thou art not mad, sure. Dost know me?

BOSOLA   Yes.

125 DUCHESS   Who am I?

BOSOLA   Thou art a box of wormseed, at best but a salva-
    tory of green mummy.[2] What's this flesh? A little crud-
    ded° milk, fantastical puff paste.° Our bodies are weaker   *curdled / pastry*
    than those paper prisons boys use to keep flies in—more
130   contemptible, since ours is to preserve° earthworms.   *keep alive*
    Didst thou ever see a lark in a cage? Such is the soul in
    the body. This world is like her little turf of grass;[3] and
    the heaven o'er our heads, like her looking glass, only
    gives us a miserable knowledge of the small compass of
135   our prison.

DUCHESS   Am not I thy duchess?

BOSOLA   Thou art some great woman, sure, for riot° begins   *i.e., signs of aging*
    to sit on thy forehead, clad in gray hairs, twenty years
    sooner than on a merry milkmaid's. Thou sleep'st worse
140   than if a mouse should be forced to take up her lodging
    in a cat's ear. A little infant that breeds its teeth,° should   *is teething*
    it lie with thee, would cry out as if thou wert the more
    unquiet bedfellow.

DUCHESS   I am Duchess of Malfi still.

145 BOSOLA   That makes thy sleeps so broken.
    Glories, like glowworms, afar off shine bright,
    But, looked to near, have neither heat nor light.

DUCHESS   Thou art very plain.

BOSOLA   My trade is to flatter the dead, not the living. I
150   am a tomb-maker.

DUCHESS   And thou com'st to make my tomb?

BOSOLA   Yes.

DUCHESS   Let me be a little merry. Of what stuff wilt thou
    make it?

155 BOSOLA   Nay, resolve° me first, of what fashion?   *answer*

---

2. An ointment box containing a medicinal
preparation made from mummies ("green"
because the bodies were not completely
mummified).
3. Placed inside the lark's cage (along with a
small mirror).

DUCHESS   Why, do we grow fantastical° in our deathbed?   *fanciful*
    Do we affect° fashion in the grave?   *care about*
BOSOLA   Most ambitiously. Princes' images on their tombs
    do not lie as they were wont, seeming to pray up to
160   heaven, but with their hands under their cheeks as if
    they died of the toothache. They are not carved with
    their eyes fixed upon the stars, but as their minds were
    wholly bent upon the world, the selfsame way they seem
    to turn their faces.
165 DUCHESS   Let me know fully therefore the effect°   *purpose*
    Of this thy dismal preparation,
    This talk fit for a charnel.[4]
BOSOLA   Now I shall.
        [*Enter* EXECUTIONERS *with a coffin, cords, and a bell.*]
    Here is a present from your princely brothers,
    And may it arrive welcome, for it brings
170   Last benefit, last sorrow.
DUCHESS   Let me see it.
    I have so much obedience in my blood,
    I wish it in their veins to do them good.
BOSOLA   This is your last presence-chamber.°   *reception room*
CARIOLA   Oh, my sweet lady!
DUCHESS   Peace, it affrights not me.
175 BOSOLA   I am the common bellman,[5]
    That usually is sent to condemned persons
    The night before they suffer.
DUCHESS   Even now thou said'st
    Thou wast a tomb-maker?
BOSOLA   'Twas to bring you
    By degrees to mortification.[6] Listen:
        [*He sounds the bell and recites this dirge.*]
180   Hark! Now everything is still.
    The screech owl and the whistler° shrill   *any loud bird*
    Call upon our dame° aloud,   *(night)*
    And bid her quickly don her shroud.°   *i.e., darkness*
    Much you had of land and rent;°   *income*
185   Your length in clay's now competent.°   *adequate*
    A long war disturbed your mind;
    Here your perfect peace is signed.
    Of what is't fools make such vain keeping?°   *defending, maintaining*
    Sin their conception, their birth weeping;
190   Their life, a general mist of error,
    Their death, a hideous storm of terror.

---

4. Cemetery; vault in which bones or corpses are piled.
5. The town crier, who tolled a bell to mark a death and who would repeat verses to the condemned in London's Newgate prison the night before their execution to exhort them to repent.
6. (1) Denial of bodily passions; (2) the stupor before death.

Strew your hair with powders sweet;
Don clean linen; bathe your feet;
And, the foul fiend more to check,
195 A crucifix let bless your neck.°   *i.e., wear a crucifix*
'Tis now full tide 'tween night and day;
End your groan, and come away.
CARIOLA   Hence, villains, tyrants, murderers! Alas,
What will you do with my lady?—Call for help.
200 DUCHESS   To whom, to our next neighbors? They are mad folks.
BOSOLA [*to the* EXECUTIONERS]   Remove that noise.
       [*The* EXECUTIONERS *seize* CARIOLA, *who struggles.*]
DUCHESS   Farewell, Cariola.
In my last will I have not much to give;
A many hungry guests have fed upon me.
Thine will be a poor reversion.°   *inheritance*
205 CARIOLA [*to the* EXECUTIONERS]   I will die with her.
DUCHESS [*to* CARIOLA]   I pray thee, look thou giv'st my little
    boy
Some syrup for his cold, and let the girl
Say her prayers ere she sleep.
      [*The* EXECUTIONERS *forcefully remove* CARIOLA *and return.*]
                        Now, what you please.
210 What death?
BOSOLA   Strangling. Here are your executioners.
DUCHESS   I forgive them.
The apoplexy, catarrh,° or cough o'th'lungs   *stroke*
Would do as much as they do.
BOSOLA   Doth not death fright you?
215 DUCHESS   Who would be afraid on't,
Knowing to meet such excellent company
In th'other world?
BOSOLA   Yet methinks
The manner of your death should much afflict you,
220 This cord should terrify you?
DUCHESS   Not a whit.
What would it pleasure me to have my throat cut
With diamonds, or to be smothered
With cassia,° or to be shot to death with pearls?   *cinnamon-like bark*
I know death hath ten thousand several° doors   *different*
225 For men to take their exits, and 'tis found
They go on such strange geometrical hinges,
You may open them both ways.[7] Any way, for heaven sake,
So I were out of your whispering! Tell my brothers
That I perceive death, now I am well awake,
230 Best gift is they can give or I can take.
I would fain put off my last woman's fault:
I'd not be tedious to you.

---

7. That is, you can be pushed through the doors of death, or open them by pulling them toward yourself (by suicide).

EXECUTIONERS   We are ready.
DUCHESS   Dispose my breath how please you, but my body
  Bestow upon my women, will you?
EXECUTIONERS   Yes.
235 DUCHESS   Pull, and pull strongly, for your able strength
  Must pull down heaven upon me.—
  Yet stay.° Heaven gates are not so highly arched   *wait*
  As princes' palaces; they that enter there
  Must go upon their knees. [*She kneels.*] Come, violent
    death,
240 Serve for mandragora,° to make me sleep!—   *mandrake (a sedative)*
  Go tell my brothers, when I am laid out,
  They then may feed in quiet.
      [*They strangle her.*]
BOSOLA   Where's the waiting-woman?
  Fetch her. Some other strangle the children.°   *(done offstage)*
        [*Exeunt* EXECUTIONERS.]
      [*Some return with* CARIOLA.]
245 Look you, there sleeps your mistress.
CARIOLA   Oh, you are damned
  Perpetually for this! My turn is next;
  Is't not so ordered?
BOSOLA   Yes, and I am glad
  You are so well prepared for't.
CARIOLA   You are deceived, sir;
250 I am not prepared for't. I will not die;
  I will first come to my answer,° and know   *reply to the charges*
  How I have offended.
BOSOLA [*to the* EXECUTIONERS]   Come, dispatch her.
  [*To her*] You kept her counsel; now you shall keep ours.
CARIOLA   I will not die! I must not. I am contracted°   *engaged*
255 To a young gentleman.
EXECUTIONER [*showing the cords*] Here's your wedding ring.
CARIOLA   Let me but speak with the Duke. I'll discover°   *reveal*
  Treason to his person.
BOSOLA   Delays!—Throttle her.
EXECUTIONER   She bites, and scratches!
CARIOLA   If you kill me now
  I am damned; I have not been at confession
260 This two years.
BOSOLA   When?[8]
CARIOLA   I am quick° with child.   *pregnant*
BOSOLA   Why, then,
  Your credit's saved.[9]
     [*The* EXECUTIONERS *strangle her.*]
      Bear her into th'next room;

---

8. An exclamation of impatience.
9. Your reputation will be preserved (because

you will die before bearing an illegitimate
child).

Let this° lie still.   [*Exeunt the* EXECUTIONERS, *bearing*   (the Duchess's body)
off the dead CARIOLA.]

[*Enter* FERDINAND.]

FERDINAND   Is she dead?

BOSOLA   She is what
You'd have her. But here begin your pity.
[*Shows the children strangled.*][1]
Alas, how have these offended?

FERDINAND   The death
265   Of young wolves is never to be pitied.

BOSOLA   Fix your eye here.

FERDINAND   Constantly.

BOSOLA   Do you not weep?
Other sins only speak; murder shrieks out.
The element of water moistens the earth,
But blood flies upwards and bedews the heavens.

270   FERDINAND   Cover her face. Mine eyes dazzle; she died young.

BOSOLA   I think not so; her infelicity
Seemed to have years too many.

FERDINAND   She and I were twins;
And, should I die this instant, I had lived
275   Her time to a minute.

BOSOLA   It seems she was born first.[2]
You have bloodily approved° the ancient truth   *proved*
That kindred commonly do worse agree
Than remote strangers.

FERDINAND   Let me see her face again.
280   Why didst not thou pity her? What an excellent
Honest man mightst thou have been
If thou hadst borne her to some sanctuary,
Or, bold in a good cause, opposed thyself
With thy advancèd° sword above thy head   *raised*
285   Between her innocence and my revenge!
I bade thee, when I was distracted of my wits,
Go kill my dearest friend, and thou hast done't.
For let me but examine well the cause:
What was the meanness° of her match to me?   *social inferiority*
290   Only, I must confess, I had a hope,
Had she continued widow, to have gained
An infinite mass of treasure by her death;
And that was the main cause—her marriage,
That drew a stream of gall quite through my heart.
295   For° thee—as we observe in tragedies   *As for*
That a good actor many times is cursed
For playing a villain's part—I hate thee for't,

---

1. The dead bodies are probably revealed as a
curtain is pulled aside.

2. Above, Bosola calls Ferdinand her "elder
brother" (4.1.21).

And for my sake say thou hast done much ill well.

BOSOLA   Let me quicken your memory, for I perceive
300   You are falling into ingratitude. I challenge°   *demand as my right*
The reward due to my service.

FERDINAND   I'll tell thee
What I'll give thee—

BOSOLA   Do.

FERDINAND   I'll give thee a pardon
For this murder.

BOSOLA   Hah?

FERDINAND   Yes, and 'tis
The largest bounty I can study° to do thee.   *endeavor*
305   By what authority didst thou execute
This bloody sentence?

BOSOLA   By yours.

FERDINAND   Mine? Was I her judge?
Did any ceremonial form of law
310   Doom her to not-being? Did a complete jury
Deliver her conviction up i'th'court?
Where shalt thou find this judgment registered
Unless in hell? See, like a bloody fool
Th'hast forfeited thy life, and thou shalt die for't.

315   BOSOLA   The office of justice is perverted quite
When one thief hangs another. Who shall dare
To reveal this?

FERDINAND   Oh, I'll tell thee:
The wolf shall find her grave and scrape it up,
Not to devour the corpse, but to discover
320   The horrid murder.

BOSOLA   You, not I, shall quake for't.

FERDINAND   Leave me.

BOSOLA   I will first receive my pension.°   *fee*

FERDINAND   You are a villain!

BOSOLA   When your ingratitude
Is judge, I am so.

325   FERDINAND   Oh, horror,
That not° the fear of Him° which binds the devils   *not even / (God)*
Can prescribe man obedience!
Never look upon me more.

BOSOLA   Why, fare thee well.
Your brother and yourself are worthy men;
330   You have a pair of hearts are° hollow graves,   *that are*
Rotten, and rotting others; and your vengeance,
Like two chained bullets,³ still goes arm in arm.
You may be brothers, for treason, like the plague,
Doth take much in a blood.⁴ I stand like one

3. Cannonballs linked together so that they   4. Often runs in families.
can do more damage.

335 That long hath ta'en° a sweet and golden dream.   enjoyed
     I am angry with myself, now that I wake.
     FERDINAND   Get thee into some unknown part o'th'world
     That I may never see thee.
     BOSOLA   Let me know
     Wherefore I should be thus neglected. Sir,
340 I served your tyranny, and rather strove
     To satisfy yourself than all the world;
     And, though I loathed the evil, yet I loved
     You that did counsel it, and rather sought
     To appear a true servant than an honest man.
345 FERDINAND   I'll go hunt the badger by owl-light.°   at dusk; at night
     'Tis a deed of darkness.   [Exit.]
     BOSOLA   He's much distracted. Off, my painted° honor!   feigned
     While with vain hopes our faculties we tire,
     We seem to sweat in ice and freeze in fire.
350 What would I do, were this to do again?
     I would not change my peace of conscience
     For all the wealth of Europe. [The DUCHESS shows faint
        signs of life.] She stirs! Here's life!
     Return, fair soul, from darkness, and lead mine
     Out of this sensible° hell!—She's warm, she breathes!—   acutely felt
355 Upon thy pale lips I will melt my heart
     To store° them with fresh color. [Calling] Who's there?   restore
     Some cordial° drink!—Alas! I dare not call.   stimulating
     So pity would destroy pity.⁵—Her eye opes,
     And heaven in it seems to ope, that late was shut,
360 To take me up to mercy.
     DUCHESS   Antonio!
     BOSOLA   Yes, madam, he is living. The dead bodies you saw
     were but feigned statues; he's reconciled to your broth-
     ers. The Pope hath wrought the atonement.°   reconciliation
365 DUCHESS   Mercy!   [She dies.]
     BOSOLA   Oh, she's gone again! There the cords° of life broke.   heartstrings
     Oh, sacred innocence, that sweetly sleeps
     On turtles'° feathers, whilst a guilty conscience   turtledoves'
     Is a black register° wherein is writ   account book
370 All our good deeds and bad, a perspective°   optical glass
     That shows us hell! That we cannot be suffered°   allowed
     To do good when we have a mind to it!
     This is manly sorrow;
     These tears, I am very certain, never grew
375 In my mother's milk. My estate° is sunk   condition
     Below the degree of fear.° Where were   past fear
     These penitent fountains while she was living?
     Oh, they were frozen up. Here is a sight
     As direful to my soul as is the sword

---

5. That is, my calls for help would be fatal to her if Ferdinand heard them.

380 Unto a wretch hath° slain his father. Come,   *who has*
    I'll bear thee hence
    And execute thy last will: that's deliver
    Thy body to the reverend dispose°   *respectful disposal*
    Of some good women. That the cruel tyrant
385 Shall not deny me. Then I'll post° to Milan,   *hasten*
    Where somewhat° I will speedily enact   *something*
    Worth my dejection.[6]   [*Exit with the* DUCHESS' *body.*]

5.1

[SCENE: *Milan. Outdoors, near the palace of* FERDINAND *and the* CARDINAL.]
    [*Enter* ANTONIO *and* DELIO.]

ANTONIO   What think you of my hope of reconcilement
    To the Aragonian brethren?[7]

DELIO   I misdoubt° it,   *have misgivings about*
    For, though they have sent their letters of safe-conduct
    For your repair° to Milan, they appear   *return*
5   But nets to entrap you. The Marquis of Pescara,
    Under whom you hold certain land in cheat,[8]
    Much 'gainst his noble nature hath been moved°   *impelled*
    To seize those lands, and some of his dependents
    Are at this instant making it their suit°   *petitioning*
10 To be invested in your revenues.[9]
    I cannot think they mean well to your life
    That do deprive you of your means of life,
    Your living.

ANTONIO   You are still an heretic°   *unbeliever; skeptic*
    To any safety I can shape myself.
    [*Enter* PESCARA.]

15 DELIO   Here comes the Marquis. I will make myself
    Petitioner for some part of your land,
    To know whither it is flying.

ANTONIO   I pray, do. [*He stands aside.*]

DELIO   Sir, I have a suit to you.

PESCARA   To me?

DELIO   An easy one:
    There is the citadel of Saint Bennet,°   *Benedict*
20 With some demesnes,[1] of late in the possession
    Of Antonio Bologna. Please you bestow them on me?

PESCARA   You are my friend. But this is such a suit
    Nor° fit for me to give nor you to take.   *Neither*

DELIO   No, sir?

PESCARA   I will give you ample reason for't

---

6. Appropriate to (1) my dejected condition;
(2) the lowering of my fortunes.
7. Ferdinand and the Cardinal (see 2.5.22–24).
8. Subject to escheat; that is, liable to revert

to Pescara if Antonio dies without heirs or is
convicted of felony.
9. The income from your lands.
1. Lands attached to the citadel.

25   Soon in private.—Here's the Cardinal's mistress.

       [*Enter* JULIA.]

JULIA   My lord, I am grown your poor petitioner,
        And should be an ill beggar, had I not
        A great man's letter here, the Cardinal's,
        To court you in my favor.   [*She gives* PESCARA *a letter.*]

PESCARA [*after reading*]   He entreats for you
30   The citadel of Saint Bennet, that belonged
        To the banished Bologna.

JULIA   Yes.

PESCARA   I could not have thought of a friend I could
        Rather pleasure with it. 'Tis yours.

35 JULIA   Sir, I thank you;
        And he shall know how doubly I am engaged°   obliged
        Both in your gift and speediness of giving,
        Which makes your grant the greater.   [*Exit.*]

ANTONIO [*aside*]   How they fortify
        Themselves with my ruin!

DELIO   Sir, I am
40   Little bound to you.

PESCARA   Why?

DELIO   Because you denied this suit to me, and gave't
        To such a creature.

PESCARA   Do you know what it was?
        It was Antonio's land, not forfeited
45   By course of law, but ravished from his throat
        By the Cardinal's entreaty. It were not fit
        I should bestow so main a piece of wrong°   ill-gotten land
        Upon my friend; 'tis a gratification
        Only due to a strumpet, for it is injustice.
50   Shall I sprinkle the pure blood of innocents
        To make those followers I call my friends
        Look ruddier[2] upon me? I am glad
        This land, ta'en from the owner by such wrong,
        Returns again unto so foul an use
55   As salary for his° lust. Learn, good Delio,   (the Cardinal's)
        To ask noble things of me, and you shall find
        I'll be a noble giver.

DELIO   You instruct me well.

ANTONIO [*aside*]   Why, here's a man now would fright
            impudence
        From sauciest beggars.[3]

60 PESCARA   Prince Ferdinand's come to Milan,
        Sick, as they give out° of an apoplexy;°   report / stroke
        But some say 'tis a frenzy.° I am going   mental derangement
        To visit him.   [*Exit.*]

---

2. With redder faces (a sign of health).
3. Who would drive even the boldest beggars to meek submission.

ANTONIO [*coming forward*]   'Tis a noble old fellow.

DELIO   What course do you mean to take, Antonio?

65 ANTONIO   This night I mean to venture all my fortune,
Which is no more than a poor ling'ring life,
To the Cardinal's worst of malice. I have got
Private access to his chamber, and intend
To visit him about the mid of night,

70 As once his brother did our noble duchess.
It may be that the sudden apprehension
Of danger—for I'll go in mine own shape—
When he shall see it fraught° with love and duty,   *filled*
May draw the poison out of him and work

75 A friendly reconcilement. If it fail,
Yet it shall rid me of this infamous calling;°   *disgraceful position*
For better fall once than be ever falling.[4]

DELIO   I'll second you in all danger; and, howe'er,°   *whatever happens*
My life keeps rank with° yours.   *stays by the side of*

80 ANTONIO   You are still° my lovèd and best friend.   [*Exeunt.*]   *always*

5.2

[SCENE: *Milan. The palace of the* CARDINAL *and* FERDINAND.]

[*Enter* PESCARA *and a* DOCTOR.]

PESCARA   Now, Doctor, may I visit your patient?

DOCTOR   If't please Your Lordship. But he's instantly°   *in a moment*
To take the air here in the gallery,
By my direction.

PESCARA   Pray thee, what's his disease?

5 DOCTOR   A very pestilent disease, my lord,
They call lycanthropia.

PESCARA   What's that?
I need a dictionary to't.

DOCTOR   I'll tell you.
In those that are possessed with't there o'erflows
Such melancholy humor° they imagine   *(see 1.1.505n)*

10 Themselves to be transformèd into wolves,
Steal forth to churchyards in the dead of night
And dig dead bodies up—as two nights since
One met the Duke 'bout midnight in a lane
Behind Saint Mark's Church, with the leg of a man

15 Upon his shoulder; and he howled fearfully;
Said he was a wolf, only the difference
Was, a wolf's skin was hairy on the outside,
His on the inside; bade them take their swords,
Rip up his flesh, and try.° Straight I was sent for,   *prove it*

20 And, having ministered to him, found His Grace
Very well recovered.

---

4. A sentiment closely paraphrased from Michel de Montaigne's *Essays* 1.32 (1580; trans. 1603).

PESCARA   I am glad on't.

DOCTOR   Yet not without some fear
Of a relapse. If he grow to his fit again,
I'll go a nearer° way to work with him   *more direct*
25   Than ever Paracelsus[5] dreamed of. If
They'll give me leave, I'll buffet his madness out of him.
          [*Enter* FERDINAND, MALATESTE, *and* CARDINAL. BOSOLA
          follows, standing apart and watching.]
Stand aside! He comes.
               [*The* DOCTOR *and* PESCARA *stand aside.*]

FERDINAND   Leave me.
MALATESTE   Why doth Your Lordship love this solitariness?
30   FERDINAND   Eagles commonly fly alone; they are crows,
daws, and starlings that flock together.—Look, what's
that follows me?
MALATESTE   Nothing, my lord.
FERDINAND   Yes!°   *There is something!*
35   MALATESTE   'Tis your shadow.
FERDINAND   Stay° it! Let it not haunt me!   *Stop*
MALATESTE   Impossible, if you move and the sun shine.
FERDINAND   I will throttle it.
               [*He throws himself upon his shadow.*]
MALATESTE   Oh, my lord, you are angry with nothing.
40   FERDINAND   You are a fool.
How is't possible I should catch my shadow
Unless I fall upon't? When I go to hell,
I mean to carry a bribe, for look you,
Good gifts evermore make way for the worst persons.
45   PESCARA   Rise, good my lord.
FERDINAND   I am studying the art of patience.
PESCARA   'Tis a noble virtue.
FERDINAND   To drive six snails before me from this town to
Moscow; neither use goad nor whip to them, but let
50   them take their own time—the patient'st man i'th'world
match me for an experiment!—and I'll crawl after, like a
sheep-biter.°   *a sheep dog*
CARDINAL   Force him up.   [FERDINAND *is lifted to his feet.*]
FERDINAND   Use me well, you were best.°   *you had better*
55   What I have done, I have done. I'll confess nothing.
DOCTOR   Now let me come to him.—Are you mad, my lord?
Are you out of your princely wits?
FERDINAND [*to* PESCARA]   What's he?
PESCARA   Your doctor.
60   FERDINAND   Let me have his beard sawed off and his eye-
brows filed more civil.[6]

---

5. Famous physician and alchemist (1493–   6. Shaped to be more polite or refined.
1541), born in Switzerland.

DOCTOR I must do mad tricks with him, for that's the only
 way on't. [*To* FERDINAND] I have brought Your Grace a sala-
 mander's skin, to keep you from sunburning.
65 FERDINAND I have cruel sore eyes.
DOCTOR The white of a cockatrice's[7] egg is present° remedy.   *an immediate*
FERDINAND Let it be a new-laid one, you were best.—
 Hide me from him! Physicians are like kings;
 They brook° no contradiction.   *tolerate*
70 DOCTOR Now he begins to fear me. Now let me alone with
 him.   [*The* DOCTOR *removes his gown.*]
CARDINAL How now, put off your gown?
DOCTOR Let me have some forty urinals filled with rose-
 water; he and I'll go pelt one another with them. Now he
75 begins to fear me.—Can you fetch a frisk,° sir?—Let him *perform a jig*
 go, let him go, upon my peril.° I find, by his eye, he *on my responsibility*
 stands in awe of me. I'll make him as tame as a dor-
 mouse.
FERDINAND Can you fetch your frisks, sir?—I will stamp° *crush*
80 him into a cullis,° flay off his skin, to cover one of the *broth*
 anatomies[8] this rogue hath set i'th'cold yonder, in
 Barber-Surgeons' Hall.[9]—Hence, hence! You are all of
 you like beasts for sacrifice; there's nothing left of you
 but tongue and belly, flattery and lechery.   [*Exit.*]
85 PESCARA Doctor, he did not fear you throughly.°   *thoroughly*
DOCTOR True, I was somewhat too forward.   [*Exit.*]
BOSOLA [*aside*] Mercy upon me, what a fatal judgment
 Hath fall'n upon this Ferdinand!
PESCARA [*to the* CARDINAL]   Knows Your Grace
 What accident° hath brought unto the prince   *occurrence*
90 This strange distraction?
CARDINAL [*aside*] I must feign somewhat. [*To them*] Thus
  they say it grew:
 You have heard it rumored for these many years,
 None of our family dies but there is seen°   *without first seeing*
 The shape of an old woman, which is given°   *reported*
95 By tradition to us to have been murdered
 By her nephews for her riches. Such a figure
 One night, as the prince sat up late at 's book,
 Appeared to him; when, crying out for help,
 The gentlemen of 's chamber found His Grace
100 All on a cold sweat, altered much in face
 And language. Since which apparition
 He hath grown worse and worse, and I much fear
 He cannot live.

7. A legendary serpent, often identified with a
basilisk (see 3.2.91n).
8. Skeletons, used by medical schools.

9. In London; barbers performed minor surgical procedures.

BOSOLA [*to the* CARDINAL]   Sir, I would speak with you.
105 PESCARA   We'll leave Your Grace,
    Wishing to the sick prince, our noble lord,
    All health of mind and body.
CARDINAL   You are most welcome.
    [*Exeunt all but the* CARDINAL *and* BOSOLA.]
    [*Aside*] Are you come? So. This fellow must not know
    By any means I had intelligence
110 In our duchess' death; for, though I counseled it,
    The full of all th'engagement[1] seemed to grow
    From Ferdinand. [*To* BOSOLA] Now, sir, how fares our sister?
    I do not think but sorrow makes her look
    Like to an oft-dyed garment.° She shall now   *i.e., worn and frayed*
115 Taste comfort from me.—Why do you look so wildly?
    Oh, the fortune of your master here, the prince,
    Dejects you. But be you of happy comfort;
    If you'll do one thing for me I'll entreat,
    Though he had a cold tombstone o'er his bones,[2]
120 I'd make you what you would be.°   *wish*
BOSOLA   Anything;
    Give it me in a breath,° and let me fly to't.   *quickly*
    They that think long small expedition win,°   *accomplish little*
    For, musing much o'th'end, cannot begin.
    [*Enter* JULIA.]
JULIA   Sir, will you come in to supper?
125 CARDINAL   I am busy. Leave me.
JULIA [*aside*]   What an excellent shape hath that fellow!°   (*Bosola*)
                                [*Exit.*]
CARDINAL   'Tis thus: Antonio lurks here in Milan;
    Inquire him out and kill him. While he lives,
    Our sister cannot marry, and I have thought
130 Of an excellent match for her. Do this, and style me
    Thy advancement.°   *name your reward*
BOSOLA   But by what means shall I find him out?
CARDINAL   There is a gentleman called Delio
    Here in the camp° that hath been long approved°   *military camp / proved*
135 His loyal friend. Set eye upon that fellow.
    Follow him to Mass; maybe Antonio,
    Although he do account religion
    But a school name,° for fashion of the world   *mere word*
    May accompany him. Or else go inquire out
140 Delio's confessor, and see if you can bribe
    Him to reveal it. There are a thousand ways
    A man might find to trace him: as,° to know   *such as*
    What fellows haunt the Jews for taking up°   *borrowing*
    Great sums of money, for sure he's in want;

---

1. That is, the entire plan, which involved employing Bosola in the murder.   2. That is, even if Ferdinand were to die.

145   Or else to go to th'picture-makers and learn
       Who brought her° picture lately. Some of these   *(the Duchess')*
       Happily° may take—   *Perhaps*
       BOSOLA   Well, I'll not freeze i'th'business.
       I would see that wretched thing, Antonio,
150   Above all sights i'th'world.
       CARDINAL   Do, and be happy.°   [*Exit.*]   *fortunate*
       BOSOLA   This fellow doth breed basilisks° in's eyes;   *(see 3.2.91n)*
       He's nothing else but murder. Yet he seems
       Not to have notice of the Duchess' death.
       'Tis his cunning. I must follow his example;
155   There cannot be a surer way to trace°   *path to follow*
       Than that of an old fox.
                 [*Enter* JULIA, *pointing a pistol at* BOSOLA.]
       JULIA   So, sir, you are well met.
       BOSOLA   How now?
       JULIA   Nay, the doors are fast° enough.   *tightly shut*
       Now, sir, I will make you confess your treachery.
160 BOSOLA   Treachery?
       JULIA   Yes. Confess to me
       Which of my women 'twas you hired to put
       Love-powder into my drink?
       BOSOLA   Love-powder?
       JULIA   Yes, when I was at Malfi.
165   Why should I fall in love with such a face else?
       I have already suffered for thee so much pain,
       The only remedy to do me good
       Is to kill my longing.
       BOSOLA   Sure your pistol holds
       Nothing but perfumes or kissing-comfits.[3]
170   Excellent lady,
       You have a pretty way on't to discover°   *reveal*
       Your longing. Come, come, I'll disarm you,
       And arm you thus.   [*He embraces her, and takes her pistol.*]
         Yet this is wondrous strange.
175 JULIA   Compare thy form and my eyes together,
       You'll find my love no such great miracle.
       Now you'll say
       I am wanton. This nice° modesty in ladies   *fastidious*
       Is but a troublesome familiar[4]
180   That haunts them.
       BOSOLA   Know you me: I am a blunt soldier.
       JULIA   The better.
       Sure° there wants° fire where there are no lively sparks   *Surely / lacks*
       Of roughness.
185 BOSOLA   And I want compliment.°   *lack polite flattery*
       JULIA   Why, ignorance in courtship cannot make you do amiss,
       If you have a heart to do well.

---

3. Breath-freshening candies.   4. Attendant spirit (see 1.1.266n).

BOSOLA   You are very fair.

JULIA   Nay, if you lay beauty to my charge,
190   I must plead unguilty.

BOSOLA   Your bright eyes
Carry a quiver of darts in them sharper
Than sunbeams.

JULIA   You will mar me with commendation,
Put yourself to the charge° of courting me,   *task*
195   Whereas now I woo you.

BOSOLA [*aside*]   I have it! I will work upon this creature.
[*To her*] Let us grow most amorously familiar.
If the great Cardinal now should see me thus,
Would he not count° me a villain?   *consider*

200 JULIA   No, he might count me a wanton,
Not lay a scruple° of offense on you;   *tiny amount*
For if I see and steal a diamond,
The fault is not i'th'stone but in me the thief
That purloins it. I am sudden with you.
205   We that are great women of pleasure use to cut off[5]
These uncertain wishes and unquiet longings,
And in an instant join the sweet delight
And the pretty excuse together. Had you been
I'th'street, under my chamber window,
210   Even there I should have courted you.

BOSOLA   Oh, you are an excellent lady.

JULIA   Bid me do somewhat for you presently°   *at once*
To express I love you.

BOSOLA   I will, and if you love me,
215   Fail not to effect it.°   *accomplish*
The Cardinal is grown wondrous melancholy.
Demand the cause. Let him not put you off
With feigned excuse; discover the main ground on't.

JULIA   Why would you know this?

BOSOLA   I have depended on him,
220   And I hear that he is fall'n in some disgrace
With the Emperor. If he be, like the mice
That forsake falling houses I would shift
To other dependence.

JULIA   You shall not need follow the wars.
225   I'll be your maintenance.

BOSOLA   And I your loyal servant;
But I cannot leave my calling.

JULIA   Not leave
An ungrateful general for the love
Of a sweet lady? You are like some°   *some who*
Cannot sleep in featherbeds, but must
230   Have blocks for their pillows.

BOSOLA   Will you do this?

5. Are accustomed to cutting off.

JULIA   Cunningly.

BOSOLA   Tomorrow I'll expect th'intelligence.°   *information*

JULIA   Tomorrow? Get you into my cabinet;°   *private room*
    You shall have it with you. Do not delay me,
    No more than I do you. I am like one
235   That is condemned: I have my pardon promised,
    But I would see it sealed.° Go, get you in.   *i.e., signed*
    You shall see me wind my tongue about his heart
    Like a skein of silk.   [BOSOLA *withdraws out of sight.*]

        [*Enter* CARDINAL, *followed by* SERVANTS.]

CARDINAL   Where are you?

SERVANT   Here.

CARDINAL   Let none, upon your lives,
240   Have conference with the Prince Ferdinand
    Unless I know it.   [*Exeunt* SERVANTS.]
             [*Aside*] In this distraction°   *madness*
    He may reveal the murder.
    Yond's my ling'ring consumption.
    I am weary of her, and by any means
245   Would be quit off.°   *rid of her*

JULIA   How now, my lord?
    What ails you?

CARDINAL   Nothing.

JULIA   Oh, you are much altered.
    Come, I must be your secretary,° and remove   *confidante*
    This lead from off your bosom. What's the matter?

CARDINAL   I may not tell you.

250 JULIA   Are you so far in love with sorrow
    You cannot part with part of it? Or think you
    I cannot love Your Grace when you are sad,
    As well as merry? Or do you suspect
    I, that have been a secret to your heart
255   These many winters, cannot be the same
    Unto your tongue?

CARDINAL   Satisfy thy longing.°   *Be satisfied*
    The only way to make thee keep my counsel
    Is not to tell thee.

JULIA   Tell your echo this,
    Or flatterers that like echoes still report
260   What they hear (though most imperfect), and not me.
    For, if that you be true unto yourself,[6]
    I'll know.

CARDINAL   Will you rack° me?   *torture*

JULIA   No. Judgment° shall   *Good sense*
    Draw it from you. It is an equal fault
    To tell one's secrets unto all or none.

265 CARDINAL   The first° argues folly.   *(Telling all)*

JULIA   But the last,° tyranny.   *(telling no one)*

---

6. That is, true to your (other) self, me.

CARDINAL   Very well. Why, imagine I have committed
  Some secret deed which I desire the world
  May never hear of.
JULIA   Therefore may not I know it?
  You have concealed for me as great a sin
270 As adultery. Sir, never was occasion
  For perfect trial of my constancy
  Till now. Sir, I beseech you.
CARDINAL   You'll repent it.
JULIA   Never.
275 CARDINAL   It hurries thee to ruin. I'll not tell thee.
  Be well advised,° and think what danger 'tis   *Reflect carefully*
  To receive a prince's secrets. They that do
  Had need have their breasts hooped with adamant[7]
  To contain them. I pray thee yet be satisfied.
280 Examine thine own frailty; 'tis more easy
  To tie knots than unloose them. 'Tis a secret
  That, like a ling'ring poison, may chance lie
  Spread in thy veins and kill thee seven year hence.
JULIA   Now you dally with me.
285 CARDINAL   No more; thou shalt know it.
  By my appointment, the great Duchess of Malfi
  And two of her young children four nights since
  Were strangled.
JULIA   Oh, heaven! Sir, what have you done?
CARDINAL   How now? How settles° this? Think you your   *sinks in*
    bosom
290 Will be a grave dark and obscure enough
  For such a secret?
JULIA   You have undone yourself, sir.
CARDINAL   Why?
JULIA   It lies not in me° to conceal it.   *in my power*
CARDINAL [*presenting a book of devotion to her*]   No?
  Come, I will swear you to't upon this book.
295 JULIA   Most religiously.
CARDINAL   Kiss it.   [*She kisses the book.*]
  Now you shall never utter it. Thy curiosity
  Hath undone thee. Thou'rt poisoned with that book;
  Because I knew thou couldst not keep my counsel,
300 I have bound thee to't by death.
              [BOSOLA *comes forward from concealment.*]
BOSOLA   For pity sake, hold!
CARDINAL   Ha! Bosola?
JULIA   I forgive you
  This equal° piece of justice you have done,   *fair*
  For I betrayed your counsel to that fellow.
  He overheard it; that was the cause I said
305 It lay not in me to conceal it.

─────────

7. Must encircle their hearts with an impregnable substance.

BOSOLA   Oh, foolish woman!
 Couldst not thou have poisoned him?
JULIA   'Tis weakness
 Too much to think what should have been done.
 I go, I know not whither.   [*She dies.*]
310 CARDINAL [*to* BOSOLA]   Wherefore com'st thou hither?
BOSOLA   That I might find a great man, like yourself,
 Not out of his wits, as the Lord Ferdinand,
 To remember° my service.   *reward*
CARDINAL   I'll have thee hewed in pieces!
BOSOLA   Make not yourself such a promise of that life°   *(my life)*
315 Which is not yours to dispose of.
CARDINAL   Who placed thee here?
BOSOLA   Her lust, as she intended.
CARDINAL   Very well.
 Now you know me for your fellow murderer.
BOSOLA   And wherefore should you lay fair marble colors
 Upon your rotten purposes to me,[8]
320 Unless you imitate some that do plot great treasons,
 And, when they have done, go hide themselves i'th'graves
 Of° those were actors in't?   *i.e., kill*
CARDINAL   No more.
 There is a fortune attends thee.
BOSOLA   Shall I go sue to Fortune any longer?
325 'Tis the fool's pilgrimage.[9]
CARDINAL   I have honors in store for thee.
BOSOLA   There are a many ways that conduct° to seeming   *lead*
 Honor, and some of them very dirty ones.
CARDINAL   Throw to the devil
330 Thy melancholy! The fire burns well;
 What need we keep a-stirring of 't, and make
 A greater smother?° Thou wilt kill Antonio?   *More smoke*
BOSOLA   Yes.
CARDINAL   Take up that body.
BOSOLA   I think I shall
 Shortly grow° the common bier for churchyards!   *Soon become*
335 CARDINAL   I will allow thee some dozen of attendants
 To aid thee in the murder.
BOSOLA   Oh, by no means. Physicians that apply horse
 leeches° to any rank swelling use to[1] cut off their tails,   *large leeches*
 that the blood may run through them the faster. Let me
340 have no train° when I go to shed blood, lest it make me   *attendants*
 have a greater when I ride to the gallows.[2]
CARDINAL   Come to me after midnight, to help to remove
 that body to her own lodging. I'll give out° she died   *report*
 o'th'plague; 'twill breed the less inquiry after her death.

---

8. That is, why would you present your
treacherous designs to me as worthy.
9. That is, only a fool pleads with Fortune.
1. Are accustomed to.

2. That is, lest their numbers (1) make it
more likely that I will be caught and hanged;
(2) make more people die for the performance of the deed.

345 BOSOLA   Where's Castruchio, her husband?

CARDINAL   He's rode to Naples to take possession
   Of Antonio's citadel.

BOSOLA   Believe me, you have done a very happy° turn.   *good*

CARDINAL   [*giving a key*]   Fail not to come. There is the
   master key

350 Of our lodgings; and by that you may conceive
   What trust I plant in you.

BOSOLA   You shall find me ready.

                                             [*Exit* CARDINAL.]

   Oh, poor Antonio! Though nothing be so needful
   To thy estate° as pity, yet I find   *condition*
   Nothing so dangerous. I must look to my footing.

355 In such slippery ice pavements, men had need
   To be frost-nailed³ well; they may break their necks else.
   The precedent's here afore me. How this man
   Bears up in blood,° seems fearless! Why, 'tis well;   *Endures*
   Security° some men call the suburbs of hell,   *Overconfidence*

360 Only a dead° wall between. Well, good Antonio,   *unbroken*
   I'll seek thee out, and all my care shall be
   To put thee into safety from the reach
   Of these most cruel biters,° that have got   *i.e., bloodsuckers*
   Some of thy blood° already. It may be   *(your children)*

365 I'll join with thee in a most just revenge.
   The weakest arm is strong enough that strikes
   With the sword of justice. Still methinks the Duchess
   Haunts me. There, there! 'Tis nothing but my melancholy.
   O Penitence, let me truly taste thy cup,

370 That throws men down only to raise them up!   [*Exit.*]

5.3

[SCENE: *Milan. A courtyard outside the palace of* FERDINAND *and the* CARDINAL.]

[*Enter* ANTONIO *and* DELIO; ECHO *from the* DUCHESS' *grave.*]

DELIO   Yond's the Cardinal's window. This fortification
   Grew from the ruins of an ancient abbey;
   And to yond side o'th'river lies a wall,
   Piece of a cloister, which in my opinion

5 Gives the best echo that you ever heard,
   So hollow and so dismal, and withal°   *besides*
   So plain in the distinction of our words,
   That many have supposed it is a spirit
   That answers.

ANTONIO   I do love these ancient ruins.

10 We never tread upon them but we set
   Our foot upon some reverend° history;   *worthy of reverence*
   And questionless, here in this open court,

---

3. Need to wear shoes with nails driven into them.

Which now lies naked to the injuries
Of stormy weather, some men lie interred
15 Loved° the church so well, and gave so largely to't,   *Who loved*
They thought it should have canopied their bones
Till doomsday. But all things have their end;
Churches and cities, which have diseases like to men,
Must have like death that we have.
20 ECHO   *Like death that we have.*
DELIO   Now the echo hath caught you.
ANTONIO   It groaned, methought, and gave
A very deadly accent.
ECHO   *Deadly accent.*
DELIO   I told you 'twas a pretty one. You may make it
25 A huntsman, or a falconer, a musician,
Or a thing of sorrow.
ECHO   *A thing of sorrow.*
ANTONIO   Ay, sure, that suits it best.
ECHO   *That suits it best.*
ANTONIO   'Tis very like my wife's voice.
ECHO   *Ay, wife's voice.*
DELIO   Come, let us walk farther from't.
30 I would not have you go to th'Cardinal's tonight.
Do not.
ECHO   *Do not.*
DELIO   Wisdom doth not more moderate° wasting sorrow   *more effectively reduce*
Than time. Take time for't;° be mindful of thy safety.   *(to heal sorrow)*
35 ECHO   *Be mindful of thy safety.*
ANTONIO   Necessity compels me.
Make scrutiny throughout the passes⁴
Of your own life; you'll find it impossible
To fly your fate.
ECHO   *Oh, fly your fate!*
40 DELIO   Hark! The dead stones seem to have pity on you
And give you good counsel.
ANTONIO   Echo, I will not talk with thee,
For thou art a dead thing.
ECHO   *Thou art a dead thing.*
ANTONIO   My duchess is asleep now,
45 And her little ones, I hope sweetly. Oh, heaven,
Shall I never see her more?
ECHO   *Never see her more.*
ANTONIO   I marked not one repetition of the echo
But that; and on the sudden, a clear light
Presented me a face folded° in sorrow.   *enveloped*
50 DELIO   Your fancy, merely.
ANTONIO   Come, I'll be out of this ague,°   *fever*
For to live thus is not indeed to live;

4. Closely examine the events.

It is a mockery and abuse of life.
I will not henceforth save myself by halves;
55   Lose all, or nothing.

DELIO   Your own virtue save you!
I'll fetch your eldest son, and second° you.   support
It may be that the sight of his° own blood,°   (the Cardinal's) / kin
Spread° in so sweet a figure, may beget   Displayed
60   The more compassion.

ANTONIO   However,° fare you well.   Whatever happens
Though in our miseries Fortune have a part,
Yet in our noble suff'rings she hath none;
Contempt of pain, that we may call our own.   [*Exeunt.*]

5.4

[SCENE: *Milan. The* CARDINAL's *apartments.*]

[*Enter* CARDINAL, PESCARA, MALATESTE, RODERIGO, *and* GRISOLAN.]

CARDINAL   You shall not watch tonight by the sick prince;
His Grace is very well recoverèd.

MALATESTE   Good my lord, suffer° us.   permit

CARDINAL   Oh, by no means.
The noise, and change of object in his eye,
5   Doth more distract him. I pray, all to bed,
And though you hear him in his violent fit,
Do not rise, I entreat you.

PESCARA   So, sir, we shall not.

CARDINAL   Nay, I must have you promise
10   Upon your honors, for I was enjoined to't
By himself; and he seemed to urge it sensibly.°   clearly

PESCARA   Let our honors bind this trifle.[5]

CARDINAL   Nor any of your followers.

MALATESTE   Neither.

CARDINAL   It may be, to make trial of your promise,
15   When he's asleep, myself will rise and feign
Some of his mad tricks, and cry out for help,
And feign myself in danger.

MALATESTE   If your throat were cutting,°   being cut
I'd not come at you, now I have protested° against it.   solemnly promised
20   CARDINAL   Why, I thank you.

[*As they prepare to leave, the courtiers speak privately
among themselves, out of the* CARDINAL's *hearing.*]

GRISOLAN   'Twas a foul storm tonight.°   last night

RODERIGO   The Lord Ferdinand's chamber shook like an
osier.°   willow tree

MALATESTE   'Twas nothing but pure kindness in the devil
25   To rock his own child.   [*Exeunt all but the* CARDINAL.]

---

5. That is, bind us to fulfill this small request.

CARDINAL   The reason why I would not suffer these
 About my brother is because at midnight
 I may with better privacy convey
 Julia's body to her own lodging. Oh, my conscience!
30 I would pray now, but the devil takes away my heart
 For having any confidence in prayer.
 About this hour I appointed Bosola
 To fetch the body. When he hath served my turn,°   *satisfied my need*
 He dies.   [*Exit.*]
    [*Enter* BOSOLA.]
35 BOSOLA   Hah? 'Twas the Cardinal's voice. I heard him name
 Bosola, and my death.—Listen! I hear one's footing.°   *footsteps*
    [*Enter* FERDINAND.]
FERDINAND   Strangling is a very quiet death.
BOSOLA [*aside*]   Nay, then, I see I must stand upon my guard.
40 FERDINAND   What say° to that? Whisper, softly: Do you agree *do you say*
 to't? So it must be done i'th'dark; the Cardinal would not
 for a thousand pounds the Doctor should see it. [*Exit.*]
BOSOLA   My death is plotted; here's the consequence of
45 murder.
 We value not desert° nor Christian breath   *due reward*
 When we know black deeds must be cured with death.
    [*Enter* ANTONIO *and* SERVANT *unaware of* BOSOLA.]
SERVANT   Here stay, sir, and be confident, I pray.
 I'll fetch you a dark° lantern.   [*Exit.*] *shuttered*
50 ANTONIO [*to himself*]   Could I take him at his prayers,
 There were hope of pardon.
BOSOLA [*attacking* ANTONIO]   Fall right my sword!
 I'll not give thee so much leisure as to pray.
ANTONIO   Oh, I am gone! Thou hast ended a long suit
55 In a minute.
BOSOLA   What art thou?
ANTONIO   A most wretched thing,
 That only have thy benefit in death
 To appear myself.[6]
    [*Enter* SERVANT *with a dark lantern.*]
SERVANT   Where are you, sir?
ANTONIO   Very near my home.°—Bosola?   *i.e., heaven*
SERVANT   Oh, misfortune!
BOSOLA   Smother thy pity; thou art dead else.°—Antonio? *or I'll kill you*
60 The man I would have saved 'bove mine own life!
 We are merely the star's tennis balls, struck and banded° *tossed about*
 Which° way please them. Oh, good Antonio,   *Whichever*
 I'll whisper one thing in thy dying ear
 Shall° make thy heart break quickly: Thy fair duchess *That will*
65 And two sweet children—

---

6. That is, who through your assistance appears in death as myself—a wretched thing, an
unhappy mortal.

ANTONIO   Their very names

 Kindle a little life in me.

BOSOLA   Are murdered!

ANTONIO Some men have wished to die

 At the hearing of sad tidings; I am glad

 That I shall do't in sadness. I would not now

70 Wish my wounds balmed, nor healed, for I have no use

 To put my life to. In all our quest of greatness,

 Like wanton boys, whose pastime is their care,[7]

 We follow after bubbles blown in th'air.

 Pleasure of life, what is't? Only the good hours

75 Of an ague; merely a preparative to rest,

 To endure vexation. I do not ask

 The process° of my death; only commend me   *story*

 To Delio.

BOSOLA Break, heart!

80 ANTONIO And let my son fly the courts of princes. [*He dies.*]

BOSOLA [*to the* SERVANT] Thou seem'st to have loved Antonio?

SERVANT I brought him hither

To have reconciled him to the Cardinal.

BOSOLA I do not ask thee that.

85 Take him up, if thou tender° thine own life,   *care for*

 And bear him where the Lady Julia

 Was wont to lodge.—Oh, my fate moves swift!

 I have this cardinal in the forge already;

 Now I'll bring him to th'hammer. Oh, direful misprision!° *crime; error*

90 I will not imitate things glorious,

 No more than base; I'll be mine own example.[8]—

 On, on; and look thou represent, for silence,

 The thing thou bear'st.[9]

    [*Exeunt with the* SERVANT *carrying* ANTONIO's *body.*]

5.5

[SCENE: *The* CARDINAL's *apartments, near* JULIA's *lodging.*]

   [*Enter the* CARDINAL, *with a book.*]

CARDINAL I am puzzled in a question about hell:

 He says, in hell there's one material fire,

 And yet it shall not burn all men alike.

 Lay him° by. How tedious is a guilty conscience!   (*the book's author*)

5 When I look into the fishponds in my garden,

 Methinks I see a thing armed with a rake

 That seems to strike at me.

   [*Enter* BOSOLA, *and* SERVANT *with* ANTONIO's *body.*]

7. Like unruly boys, whose main concern is
their own amusement.
8. That is, I will make myself the standard of

my own behavior.
9. That is, imitate Antonio, whom you carry,
in your silence.

Now, art thou come? Thou look'st ghastly.
There sits in thy face some great determination,
10   Mixed with some fear.
    BOSOLA   Thus it lightens° into action: *flashes*
    I am come to kill thee.
    CARDINAL   Hah?—Help! Our guard!
    BOSOLA   Thou art deceived.
15   They are out of° thy howling.   *i.e., cannot hear*
    CARDINAL   Hold! And I will faithfully divide
    Revenues with thee.
    BOSOLA   Thy prayers and proffers
    Are both unseasonable.°   *untimely; too late*
    CARDINAL [*calling*]   Raise the watch! We are betrayed!
20   BOSOLA   I have confined your flight.
    I'll suffer your retreat to Julia's chamber,
    But no further.
    CARDINAL   Help! We are betrayed!
        [*Enter above* PESCARA, MALATESTE, RODERIGO, *and*
        GRISOLAN.]
    MALATESTE   Listen!
    CARDINAL   My dukedom for rescue!
25   RODERIGO   Fie upon his counterfeiting!
    MALATESTE   Why, 'tis not the Cardinal.
    RODERIGO   Yes, yes, 'tis he; but I'll see him hanged ere
    I'll go down to him.
    CARDINAL   Here's a plot upon me! I am assaulted! I am
30   lost, unless some rescue!
    GRISOLAN   He doth this pretty well, but it will not serve
    to laugh me out of mine honor.[1]
    CARDINAL   The sword's at my throat!
    RODERIGO   You would not bawl so loud, then.
35   MALATESTE   Come, come, let's go to bed. He told us thus much aforehand.
    PESCARA   He wished you should not come at him: but believe't,
    The accent of the voice sounds not in jest.
    I'll down to him, howsoever, and with engines°   *tools*
    Force ope the doors.   [*Exit above.*]
    RODERIGO   Let's follow him aloof,°   *at a distance*
40   And note how the Cardinal will laugh at him.
                     [*Exeunt those above.*]
    BOSOLA [*to the* SERVANT]   There's for you first, 'cause°   *so that*
    you shall not unbarricade the door to let in rescue.
        [*He kills the* SERVANT.]
    CARDINAL   What cause hast thou to pursue my life?
    BOSOLA [*showing* ANTONIO's *body*]   Look there.
45   CARDINAL   Antonio!
    BOSOLA   Slain by my hand unwittingly.
    Pray, and be sudden. When thou killed'st thy sister,

---

1. Fool me into breaking my oath.

Thou took'st from Justice her most equal balance,
And left her naught but her sword.[2]

50 CARDINAL   Oh, mercy!

BOSOLA   Now it seems thy greatness was only outward, for
thou fall'st faster of thyself° than calamity can drive   *by your own acts*
thee. I'll not waste longer time. There!

[*He stabs the* CARDINAL.]

CARDINAL   Thou hast hurt me!

55 BOSOLA   Again!   [*He stabs again.*]

CARDINAL   Shall I die like a leveret° without any resistance?—   *young hare*
Help, help, help! I am slain!

[*Enter* FERDINAND *and attacks the* CARDINAL.]

FERDINAND   Th'alarum!° Give me a fresh horse!   *Sound the alarm!*
Rally the vaunt-guard,° or the day is lost!   *vanguard*

60 Yield, yield! I give you the honor of arms,[3]
Shake my sword over you. Will you yield?

CARDINAL   Help me! I am your brother.

FERDINAND   The devil!
My brother fight upon the adverse party?

65 There flies your ransom.[4]

[*He wounds the* CARDINAL *and in the scuffle gives*
BOSOLA *his death wound.*]

CARDINAL   Oh, justice!
I suffer now for what hath former been;
Sorrow is held the eldest child of sin.

FERDINAND   Now you're brave fellows. Caesar's fortune was

70 harder than Pompey's; Caesar died in the arms of prosperity, Pompey at the feet of disgrace.[5] You both died in the
field. The pain's nothing; pain many times is taken away
with the apprehension of greater, as the toothache with
the sight of a barber that comes to pull it out. There's

75 philosophy for you.

BOSOLA   Now my revenge is perfect. Sink, thou main cause
Of my undoing!   [*He kills*° FERDINAND.]   *mortally wounds*
                    The last part of my life
Hath done me best service.

FERDINAND   Give me some wet hay. I am broken-winded.[6]

80 I do account this world but a dog kennel.
I will vault credit[7] and affect° high pleasures   *seek to obtain*
Beyond death.

---

2. The figure of Justice is often represented as blindfolded, holding a pair of scales (a "balance") in one hand and a sword in the other.

3. That is, I give you the chance to surrender honorably and retain your arms.

4. That is, your chance to yield and be ransomed is lost, because I will kill you.

5. Caesar was assassinated at the height of his power, after he had become ruler of Rome, but his former ally Pompey the Great (106–48 B.C.E.) was murdered after having been defeated in battle by Caesar.

6. Suffering from broken wind, a respiratory disease of horses; feeding the animal wet hay was a standard treatment.

7. That is, I will surpass my reputation (and thus the expectation that I will burn in hell).

BOSOLA He seems to come to himself,° now he's so near   *recover his wits*
the bottom.

85 FERDINAND My sister, oh, my sister! There's the cause on't.
Whether we fall by ambition, blood, or lust,
Like diamonds, we are cut with our own dust.[8]
    [*He dies.*]

CARDINAL [*to* BOSOLA] Thou hast thy payment too.

BOSOLA Yes, I hold my weary soul in my teeth;[9]
90 'Tis ready to part from me. I do glory
That thou, which stood'st like a huge pyramid
Begun upon a large and ample base,
Shalt end in a little point, a kind of nothing.

    [*Enter* PESCARA, MALATESTE, RODERIGO, *and* GRISOLAN.]

PESCARA How now, my lord?
95 MALATESTE Oh, sad disaster!

RODERIGO How comes this?

BOSOLA Revenge, for the Duchess of Malfi, murdered
By th'Aragonian brethren; for Antonio,
Slain by this hand; for lustful Julia,
100 Poisoned by this man; and lastly for myself,
That was an actor in the main° of all,   *chief part*
Much 'gainst mine own good nature, yet i'th'end
Neglected.

PESCARA [*to the* CARDINAL] How now, my lord?

CARDINAL   Look to my brother.
105 He gave us these large wounds, as we were struggling
Here i'th'rushes.[1] And now, I pray, let me
    Be laid by and never thought of.   [*He dies.*]

PESCARA How fatally, it seems, he did withstand°   *oppose (see lines 5.5.5–20)*
His own rescue!

110 MALATESTE [*to* BOSOLA] Thou wretched thing of blood,
How came Antonio by his death?

BOSOLA In a mist; I know not how,
Such a mistake as I have often seen
In a play. Oh, I am gone!
115 We are only like dead° walls or vaulted graves   *unbroken*
That, ruined, yields no echo. Fare you well.
It may be pain, but no harm to me to die
In so good a quarrel. Oh, this gloomy world!
In what a shadow, or deep pit of darkness,
120 Doth womanish and fearful mankind live!
Let worthy minds ne'er stagger in distrust°   *never waver in fear*
To suffer death or shame for what is just.
Mine is another voyage.   [*He dies.*]

PESCARA The noble Delio, as I came to th'palace,

---

8. That is, just as only pieces of diamond can
cut diamonds, so elements intrinsic to humans
undo us.
9. At death, the soul was believed to leave the
body through the mouth.
1. Green rushes (marsh plants) were commonly used as floor covering.

125   Told me of Antonio's being here, and showed me
    A pretty gentleman, his son and heir.
        [*Enter* DELIO *with* ANTONIO'S *son.*]

MALATESTE   Oh, sir, you come too late.

DELIO   I heard so, and
    Was armed° for't ere I came. Let us make noble use   *prepared*
    Of this great ruin, and join all our force
130   To establish this young hopeful gentleman
    In 's mother's right.° These wretched eminent things°   *inheritance / persons*
    Leave no more fame behind 'em than should one°   *someone who might*
    Fall in a frost and leave his print in snow;
    As soon as the sun shines, it ever melts
135   Both form and matter. I have ever thought
    Nature doth nothing so great for great men
    As when she's pleased to make them lords of truth.
    Integrity of life is fame's best friend,
    Which nobly, beyond death, shall crown the end.   [*Exeunt.*]

Finis.

LOPE DE VEGA CARPIO

1562–1635

DEEMED "the reigning monarch of the stage" by Miguel de Cervantes, his contemporary, Lope de Vega was a national icon—the country's most beloved and revered dramatist during Spain's "Golden Age" (1550–1700)—whose picture hung in homes and whose plays attracted capacity audiences across the land. In an era when theater provided the main form of public entertainment, Lope's writing came to define Spanish dramaturgy. The author of as many as 1,500 plays (of which 470 remain), three novels, four novellas, nine verse epics, about 3,000 sonnets, and countless occasional pieces and poems, Lope remains the most prolific dramatist of Western theater history. He refined the *comedia* (the generic Spanish term for "play" in this era) both stylistically and thematically, moving away from classical dramaturgy and developing narratives that instead reflected Spanish history, folk traditions, religious convictions, and social mores. A professional writer from the middle class, at a time when his fellow playwrights were noblemen and scholars for whom such artistry was primarily an avocation, Lope insisted upon his fealty to and dependence on his audiences.

Lope's *FUENTEOVEJUNA* (sometimes printed as two words, *Fuente Ovejuna*), a folk drama that pits the inhabitants of a small village against an overbearing and cruel Commander (a *comendador*, or "overlord") whom they eventually kill, is a paradigmatic example of the *comedia*. Although unremarked outside Spain for quite some time after its creation, *Fuenteovejuna's* popularity and critical renown have widened since the early nineteenth century, when it began to appear in translation across Europe and, more importantly, began to represent for critics and audiences alike a powerful, even subversive, example of Renaissance political theater. It stands today, along with CALDERÓN's *La vida es sueno* (*Life Is a Dream*), as one of the most studied plays of this culturally rich era.

Lope's biography, like the stage history of many of his plays, remains elusive. Much of the information we have comes from the author's own writings or anecdotes from the period and is of dubious reliability. Born in Madrid, the son of craftspeople, Lope appears to have been a precocious youth who began to compose verse and plays before his adolescence. He was educated by the Jesuits and studied at the University of Alcalá de Henares, and he may also have attended the University of Salamanca. Early in his career, he served as a secretary to the Marqués de las Navas, a Spanish nobleman, who gave Lope time for his own writing. Other comparable posts followed. Lope also served his country in its military campaign against Portugal in the early

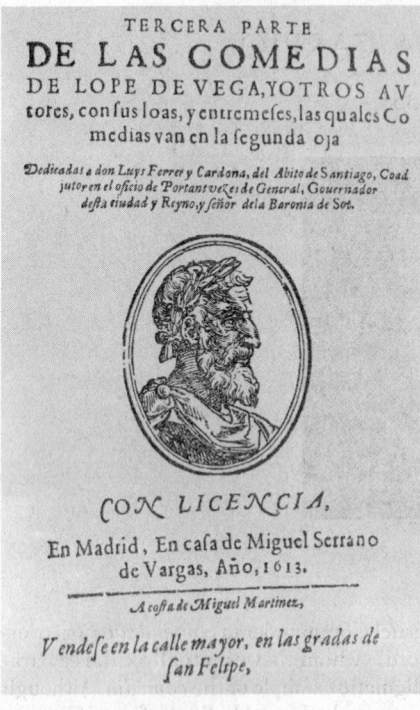

TERCERA PARTE
DE LAS COMEDIAS
DE LOPE DE VEGA, YOTROS AV
tores, con sus loas, y entremeses, las quales Co
medias van en la segunda oja

*Dedicadas a don Luys Ferrer y Cardona, del Abito de Santiago, Coad
jutor en el oficio de Portantveges de General, Gouernador
desta ciudad y Reyno, y señor dela Baronia de Sot.*

CON LICENCIA,
En Madrid, En casa de Miguel Serrano
de Vargas, Año, 1613.

A costa de Miguel Martinez,

*Vendese en la calle mayor, en las gradas de
san Felipe,*

Title page of the third volume of a 1613 printing
of Lope's plays.

1580s, and in 1588 he participated in the
Spanish Armada's ill-fated naval attack on
England.

By 1599 it appears that Lope was working primarily as a dramatist, earning a living solely by his pen. Rather than gaining
financial security from the great success
of a few outstanding works that held the
boards for extended periods, Lope prospered because he was able to generate popular works extremely quickly and regularly,
feeding the public's voracious appetite for
new entertainment. In 1604 the first volume
of his collected plays appeared. Twenty-
four more volumes followed, the last three
of which were published posthumously,
and yet even this extensive collection did
not include all of Lope's writing.

Lope's incredible energy as an author
appears to have been matched by a zest for
sexual intimacy with scores of women. He
is known to have had two wives, three long-
term extramarital relationships with mistresses, and countless short-term affairs. He

fathered at least fourteen children, though
only a few survived to maturity. His amatory adventures also led to formal exile from
both Castile and Madrid for several years
and to a lifelong struggle between the conflicting poles of his libidinous desires and
his devout Catholicism. In 1609, Lope allied
himself with the first of a series of religious
fraternities. In 1613–14, following the death
of his second wife, he sought holy orders.
Yet despite having been ordained and taken
a vow of celibacy, he entered into a lengthy
relationship with another mistress, Marta
de Nevares, which lasted until her death,
in 1632.

Lope's writing, especially his religious
verse, reflects these tensions in his nature.
His recognition of his own spiritual frailties also appears to have cemented his
dedication to presenting in his plays what
he calls—in his treatise *Arte nuevo de hacer
comedias en este tiempo* (*The New Art
of Writing Plays*, 1609)—"the likeness of
truth." Sensitive to his inner conflicts and
the variety of human experience ("[human]
nature gives us good example, for through
[its] variety it is beautiful"), Lope extrapo-
lated from his understanding of his contradictory nature to create characters that
he believed faithfully represented the fascinating complexity of human behavior.
Needless to say, such an approach to characterization was far from the classical ideal.

The stylistic departure from classical
traditions that set Lope apart from other
dramatists went beyond his complex characterizations. While elsewhere in Europe
playwrights upheld the Aristotelian principles of the unities of time, place, and
action—which limited the scope and dura-
tion of, as well as the physical distance
between, dramatic events—Lope believed
that to artificially confine his dramas' plots
either temporally or geographically would
diminish their dramatic truth. He embraced
the unity of action, however, because it led
to concentration on core narratives. He
also encouraged the interweaving of comedy and tragedy because it is true to human
experience, and thus pleasing as well.
Rejecting the traditional five-act form, he
developed a three-act structure for plays
that corresponded to the basic concept of
a narrative's beginning, middle, and end.

In addition, he reminded aspiring play-wrights not to "untie the plot until reaching the last scene" in order to maintain the audience's rapt attention.

In his *New Art,* moreover, he wrote of the importance of matching the form and content of dialogue to character type as well as of keeping dramatic language simple. At the same time, he embraced the classical notion that plays should be a poetic medium, creating a complex and distinctive verse style that may seem quite artificial or non-naturalistic to audiences today, but was highly admired and perceived as truthful in his own time. He espoused the pairing of poetic form to "the subjects being treated," recommending "*tercets* [eleven-syllable lines in terza rima] for grave affairs" and "*redondillas* [eight-syllable quatrains rhyming ABBA] for affairs of love." In *Fuenteovejuna* Lope employed more than a half dozen distinct verse structures to convey the play's variety of moods and plot developments. In a further departure from classical dramaturgy, Lope rendered dialogue spoken by common villagers in *Fuenteovejuna* in poetic forms that were traditionally reserved only for aristocratic characters. These aspects of his writing have proven among the most challenging to capture in translation.

Lope, like his English contemporary WILLIAM SHAKESPEARE, adapted potent narratives from his nation's past to suit his dramaturgical ends. *Fuenteovejuna* is just such an adaptation, based in part on an actual peasant uprising that occurred in April 1476 in the Andalusian village of Fuenteovejuna. The play depicts events that occurred in the midst of a tumultuous period of civil war in Spain, when competing claims to sovereignty arose between the Portuguese rulers, Alfonso and his wife, Juana, and Isabel and Fernando (Ferdinand) of Spain. More generally, struggles for control of the areas now constituting Spain, Portugal, Italy, and southern France raged throughout the late fifteenth century. These regions had not yet coalesced into the nation-states we know today; rather, feudal lords controlled areas under loose monarchical rule, and boundaries and allegiances shifted regularly. Moreover, the tangled relations of blood and marriage linking royal families complicated efforts to establish clear lines of succession and authority. The resulting power plays were often very complex, messy, and bloody.

Even those audiences who know Spanish history may not initially grasp the integral thematic relationship between the scenes in *Fuenteovejuna* at the palace of the Master of Calatrava, the scenes at the Spanish court featuring King Ferdinand and Queen Isabel, and the scenes set in the village. Indeed, some contemporary directors have mistakenly cut the scenes at the palace of Calatrava precisely because they do not understand how the conflicts in the village that dominate the play are connected to the larger political struggles framing this action. The play's opening dialogue between the young nobleman, whose family has long dominated the Almagro region, and the military Commander, who serves under him but tries to influence the young man's political loyalties and thus his martial campaigns, establishes the play's historical context, demonstrating that the struggle for geographical dominance between the rulers of Spain and of Portugal was played out in communities throughout the Iberian peninsula.

Lope's primary historical source for *Fuenteovejuna* appears to be Francisco de Rades y Andrada's *Crónica de las tres órdenes de caballeria de Santiago, Calatrava y Alcántara (A Chronicle of the Three Orders of Chivalry: Santiago, Calatrava, and Alcantara,* 1572). In this account, which details the exploits and endeavors of noblemen, Rades includes the legendary tale of the peasant uprising at Fuenteovejuna. Although other chronicles available to Lope covered the same episode, it is clear that Lope favored Rades's version because it demonized the overlord and idealized the villagers, whereas other renditions vilified the peasants for their collective act of violence.

Lope's fictional account in *Fuenteovejuna* takes liberties with historical chronology and thereby reshapes his audience's sense of how a series of key conflicts resulted in the creation of Spain as a harmonious nation-state. The revisionist history he narrates of the decisive, offstage battles at Ciudad Real and Toro skews his audience's sympathies toward a very specific notion of proper aristocratic action and order. In Lope's (inaccurate) presentation, the events in the military encounter at Ciudad Real appear to anticipate metonymically those at Fuenteovejuna, and then developments in Spain overall, as groups of citizens across the land successively profess loyalty to the crown. The Master of Calatrava forcefully conquers Ciudad Real for Portugal, following the (poor) advice of the Commander, and the Commander overpowers the village, but the citizens of both regions turn to the Spanish monarchs for recourse against their oppressors. Ultimately, members of the feudal aristocracy, who have misapplied (the Master) or abused (the Commander) their power, must suffer the appropriate consequences for their actions at both the local and national levels. We thus may see this manipulation of history as central to Lope's carefully constructed representation of idealized, benevolent, and just leadership.

Audiences of Lope's day may well have perceived the disjunction between his nostalgic representation of monarchs, supporting the causes of the people, and the realities of their own time, when Philip III was demonstrating that he lacked either the vision or the pragmatic skills for leadership that his country desperately needed. Yet Lope also makes sure that a potent image of monarchical control over the populace lingers with his viewers: the formal inquisition and torture scene that follows the villagers' execution of the Commander reminds audiences of what lies in store for those who attempt to usurp central authority.

More immediately, Lope's audiences may have recognized the relevance to their own lives of the play's agricultural theme, epitomized by the villagers' obligatory harvest tributes to the Commander. Written during a period of severe hardship for farmers, *Fuenteovejuna* reflects Spaniards' concerns with a precarious agrarian economy and with such specific issues of the day as problematic grain distribution systems and the feudal abuse of tenant farmers. The play's title, usually translated as "Fountain of the Sheep" or "Sheep's Well," similarly alludes to the importance of the wool trade to the Spanish economy. The metaphorical significance of the sheep—the dehumanized and disempowered villagers—no doubt resonated even more deeply.

The 2008 Stratford Shakespeare Festival production of Lope de Vega's *Fuenteovejuna*, directed by Laurence Boswell.

The Commander's violent exercise of control over the bodies of Fueteovejuna's women has focused contemporary critical attention on gender, sex, and power in both the play and Renaissance Spanish society, but Lope's own views on these matters are not clear. Laurencia, a peasant woman who manages to resist the Commander's sexual advances, might be seen today as a paragon of female strength and agency, but such an interpretation relies on a possibly anachronistic image of women. Her call for the male citizens of Fuenteovejuna to redress the wrongs done to the village's women certainly asks us to consider gender roles in Spanish society, but it tells us little about what those roles can or should be. For example, the women in *Fuenteovejuna* arguably display behavior that Lope's contemporaries would consider an "unnatural" subversion of the "proper" role that women were expected to occupy in patriarchal Renaissance culture. That this behavior is caused by the Commander's brutality, and thus is ultimately his fault, makes it no less likely that Lope's original audience would have seen the actions of the female characters as violating the natural order. From this perspective, instead of delivering a proto-feminist statement, the conflict that arises among the villagers over the rape of its women showcases the masculine code of honor that shaped Spanish society from medieval times forward. The violation of the women of Fuenteovejuna dishonors all the men, husbands, brothers, and fathers alike; thus through this historical narrative Lope makes his audiences confront issues at their culture's core.

Particularly in the nineteenth and twentieth centuries, *Fuenteovejuna* was interpreted ahistorically—as a drama embodying radical ideals of democracy, socialism, and even communism. Subsequent to its 1829 translation into French in the aftermath of the French Revolution, it became popular throughout Europe; it then gained renown in the former Soviet Union, where the play inspired a 1939 adaptation by the Bolshoi Ballet, *Laurencia,* named after the central female character who initiates the villagers' revolt. More recently, the German filmmaker Rainer Werner Fassbinder used *Fuenteovejuna* as the basis for his play on regicide, *Das brennende Dorf* (*The Burning Village,* 1970). Such readings of *Fuenteovejuna* understandably foreground the role of the villagers as a collective, working-class protagonist that avenges its mistreatment by those who abuse their power, but they often ignore the affirmation of monarchy found in the play's stirring conclusion.

The sexual, religious, and political betrayals enacted by the Commander and the Master—violations of the code of honor at all levels of Spanish society—provide the threads that Lope weaves together to make *Fuenteovejuna* a cohesive drama. Today *Fuenteovejuna* stands as a dramatic palimpsest, a play whose accumulated layers of meaning speak not only to its own time and place but also to other pivotal moments in world history. Ultimately, however, the play's timeless narratives of love triumphing over adversity and of individuals' loyalty to their community, as well as its final depiction of a secure and ordered society, give *Fuenteovejuna* its universal appeal and enduring status in the canon of world drama.　　　　　　　　　J.E.G.

Fuenteovejuna[1]

CHARACTERS

Fernán Gómez de Guzmán,
  COMMANDER of the Order of
  Calatrava
FLORES } his retainers
ORTUÑO }
Rodrigo Téllez Girón, MASTER of
  the Order of Calatrava
his retainers
LAURENCIA }
PASCUALA }
JACINTA } villagers
FRONDOSO }
MENGO }
BARRILDO }
ESTEBAN } village magistrates
ALONSO }

CUADRADO, village alderman
JUAN ROJO, village councilman
Queen ISABEL of Castile
King FERDINAND of Aragon
Don MANRIQUE, a courtier
A JUDGE
LEONELO, a University of Salamanca
  graduate
CIMBRANOS, a soldier
A BOY
ALDERMEN from Ciudad Real, soldiers,
  VILLAGERS, MUSICIANS

The action takes place in 1476.

1.1

[SCENE: *Almagro, a town near Ciudad Real, Central Spain. A room in the mansion of Rodrigo Téllez Girón,* MASTER *of the Order of Calatrava.*]

    [*Enter the* COMMANDER, *Fernán Gómez de Guzmán, with his
    retainers* FLORES *and* ORTUÑO.]

COMMANDER   The Master[2] knows I mark my time
  Awaiting him.
FLORES   Indeed, he does.
ORTUÑO   He's more mature, sir, than he was.
COMMANDER   Enough to be aware that I'm
5   Still Fernán Gómez de Guzmán?
FLORES   He's just a boy. Don't take this wrong.
COMMANDER   He has to have known all along
  The title that's conferred upon
  Me is Commander of the Ranks.
10 ORTUÑO   His counselors undoubtedly
  Incline him toward discourtesy.

1. Translated by G. J. Racz.
2. Leader of the Order of Calatrava, a Spanish military and religious order founded by

Cistercian monks in the 12th century to
defend against Moorish attacks.

COMMANDER   This stance will win him little thanks,
　　For courtesy unlocks the gate
　　Behind which man's goodwill resides
15　As surely as offense betides
　　An enmity fomenting hate.

ORTUÑO   If only men so keen to slight
　　Knew how they were abhorred by all—
　　Not least by sycophants who fall
20　To kiss their feet and praise their might—
　　They'd much prefer to die before
　　Insulting anyone again.

FLORES   Mistreatment from unmannered men
　　Is harsh and something to deplore,
25　Yet while discourtesy between
　　Two equals is a foolish game,
　　When men aren't peers, it's not the same
　　But vile, tyrannical, and mean.
　　No sense to take offense, my lord.
30　He's still a boy and ignorant of
　　The need to win his vassals' love.

COMMANDER   The obligation that the sword
　　He girded on when first this Cross
　　Of Calatrava graced his chest
35　Bids courtesy be shown all, lest
　　Our noble Order suffer loss.

FLORES   We'll know soon if his heart's been set
　　Against your person or your cause.

ORTUÑO   Leave now if all this gives you pause.
40　COMMANDER   I'll take the stripling's measure yet.

　　　　　[Enter the MASTER of Calatrava, Rodrigo Téllez Girón,
　　　　　with retinue.]

MASTER   Dear Fernán Gómez de Guzmán!
　　I've just been told that you were come
　　And rue this inattention from
　　My heart's own core.

COMMANDER　　　　　　I looked upon
45　The matter ill, with wounded pride,
　　As I'd thought my affection for
　　You and my standing would ensure
　　More noble treatment by your side,
　　We two of Calatrava, you
50　The Master, I Commander, though
　　Your humble servant, well you know.

MASTER   I only was alerted to
　　Your presence here at this late hour,
　　Fernán, and join you now in fond
55　Embrace.

COMMANDER   You honor well our bond
　　As I've done all that's in my power—
　　Nay, risked my life—to ease affairs

For you, petitioning the pope[3]
To disregard your youth.

MASTER   I hope
60   That, by this holy sign each wears
Upon his chest, as I repay
Your kindness with respect, you'll own
Such honor as my sire had known.

COMMANDER   I'm satisfied with what you say.
65 MASTER   What news have you about the war?

COMMANDER   Attend these words and soon you'll learn
How duty makes this your concern.

MASTER   It's this report I've waited for.

COMMANDER   Rodrigo Téllez Girón, this
70   Illustrious station you've attained
Derives from the profound esteem
Your sire claimed for your family name.[4]
When he relinquished, eight years past,
The rank of Master to his son,
75   Commanders joined with kings to pledge
The cross should pass to one so young
While further confirmation came
From papal bulls that blessed soul
His Holiness Pope Pius wrote,
80   Which Paul[5] did follow with his own.
Your uncle, Juan Pacheco,[6] then
The Master of Santiago, was
Appointed your coadjutor
And, when he died, we placed our trust
85   In your ability to lead
Our Order at your tender age.
Upholding past allegiances
Is vital in the present case
To honor these progenitors,
90   So know your kin, since Henry's[7] death,
Support Alfonso,[8] Portugal's
Good king, who has inherited
Castile, your blood contend, because

3. Pope Pius II (1405–1464), elected to the papacy in 1458. Before his death he issued a papal bull granting Master Pedro Girón's request that he be allowed to relinquish his post and appoint his illegitimate son, Rodrigo, to the position of Master. Pius's successor, Paul II, reaffirmed Pius's decree (see line 80, below) and in 1466 the eight-year-old Rodrigo was appointed Master and his uncle, Don Juan Pacheco, coadjutor (see lines 81–83). In 1474 (not long before the action of the play unfolds), Rodrigo attained his majority and was able to assume full command of the Order of Calatrava.
4. The historical father of Rodrigo Téllez-

Girón, Pedro Girón, relinquished leadership of the Order of Calatrava in order to marry the Infanta Isabel, sister of King Henry IV of Castile, but died before their marriage could take place.
5. Pope Paul II (1417–1471), elected pope in 1464.
6. Marquis of Villena (see line 125), first duke of Escalona and leader of the chivalric Order of Santiago.
7. King Henry IV of Castile (1420–1474; r. 1454–74).
8. King Alfonso V of Portugal (1432–1481; r. 1438–81), who married King Henry IV's daughter Juana in 1475 (see lines 94, 101).

His queen, they vow, was Henry's child.
95 Prince Ferdinand of Aragon[9]
Disputes this claim, and through his wife
And Henry's sister, Isabel,[1]
Asserts his title to the throne
Against your family's cause. In short,
100 They see no treachery imposed
By Juana's[2] just succession here.
Your cousin keeps her under guard
Until the day when she will reign.
I come, then, with this counsel: charge
105 Your Knights of Calatrava in
Almagro here to mount their steeds
And capture Ciudad Real,[3]
Which straddles the frontier between
Castile and Andalusia, thus
110 Strategically commanding both.
You'd hardly need a host of men
To have it fall to your control
As scarcely any gentry guard
The city, only citizens
115 Who'd still defend Queen Isabel
And follow Ferdinand as king.
How grand, Rodrigo, to avail
Yourself of such a siege and prove
Those wrong who think these shoulders far
120 Too slight to bear the cross you do!
Your gallant ancestors, the Counts
Of Urueña,[4] beckon from
Their heights of fame in proud display
Of all the laurels they have won;
125 The Marquis of Villena,[5] too,
And countless other captains bid
You join their noble company
Uplifted on renown's own wings!
Come, bare the whiteness of your sword
130 And stain its blade in fierce assaults
With blood red as our Order's sign

---

9. The future King Ferdinand II of Aragon (1452–1516; r. 1479–1516) and King Ferdinand V of Castile (r. 1474–1516); he claimed the Castilian throne through his marriage to Isabel and was known as "Ferdinand the Catholic."

1. Queen Isabel (sometimes Isabella) of Castile (1451–1504; r. 1474–1504), half sister of King Henry IV. Following her marriage to Ferdinand of Aragon in 1469, Pope Alexander VI named them the "Catholic Monarchs."

2. King Henry IV's only child (1462–1504); because of the alleged infidelity of her mother, Princess Joana of Portugal, Juana was consid-

ered illegitimate by many, and upon her father's death the crown of Castile passed not to Juana but to her aunt, Isabel of Castile, sparking the War of the Castilian Succession (the backdrop of *Fuenteovejuna*).

3. A city in south central Spain whose name means "royal city." *Almagro*: a town near Ciudad Real and the seat of the Order of Calatrava.

4. Among these ancestors was Alfonso Téllez-Girón, the father of Juan Pacheco and grandfather of Rodrigo.

5. That is, Juan Pacheco (see line 81 and note above).

So that you may be rightly called
By all men Master of that Cross
You wear upon your chest! If white
135   It stays, that title stays unearned.
Yes, both the weapon at your side
And that dear cross must shine blood-red.
Thus you, magnificent Girón,
Shall be at last enshrined the first
140   Among your line and most extolled!

MASTER   Fernán Gómez, it's my intent
To side with blood in a dispute
Whose rightness seems beyond refute,
So rest assured of this event.
145   If Ciudad Real, then, must
Be leveled by my hands, I'll burn
Its walls with lightning speed and turn
The city into ash and dust.
The friend or stranger who insists
150   That with my uncle died my youth
Could not be farther from the truth:
The spirit of my years persists.
I'll bare this still-white blade and lead
My forces by its dazzling light
155   Till, like these crosses, it shines bright
With blood the reddened wounded bleed.
Do any soldiers now subsist
Among your village retinue?

COMMANDER   They're loyal servitors, though few,
160   But should you summon them to list
With you, they'll romp like lions, for
In Fuenteovejuna all
The townsfolk heed the humble call
Of agriculture, not of war,
165   And work the fields without a care.

MASTER   You've quarters near?

COMMANDER   It pleased the crown
To grant me land once in that town
So, mid these perils, I dwell there.

MASTER   I'll need a tally of our strength.

170 COMMANDER   No vassal there shall stay behind!

MASTER   This day you'll see me ride, and find
My couching lance atilt full-length!

[*Exit* COMMANDER *and* MASTER.]

1.2

[SCENE: *The town square in Fuenteovejuna, near Ciudad Real.*]

[*Enter the village women* PASCUALA *and* LAURENCIA.]

LAURENCIA   I'd hoped that he was gone for good!

PASCUALA   To tell the truth, I really thought

The news of his return here ought
To have perturbed you . . . and still would!

5 LAURENCIA   I wish to God, I swear to you,
That we had seen the last of him!

PASCUALA   Laurencia, I've known girls as prim
And tough as you—nay, more so—who,
Beneath the guise of harsh facades,

10 Have hearts as soft as cooking lard.

LAURENCIA   You couldn't find an oak as hard
And dry as I am toward these clods!

PASCUALA   Go on, now! You don't mean to say
You'd never drink to quench your thirst?

15 LAURENCIA   I do, though I won't be the first
To have to protest in this way.
Besides, what profit would I see
To have Fernán think he's my beau?
I couldn't marry him, now.

PASCUALA   No.

20 LAURENCIA   I can't abide his infamy!
So many girls were gullible
In trusting the Commander's plights
And now live days that rue those nights.

PASCUALA   Still, it would be a miracle

25 If you don't wind up in his grasp.

LAURENCIA   Pascuala, one full month's gone by
Since you first saw this scapegrace try
In vain to land me in his clasp.
His pander, Flores, and that knave,

30 Ortuño, came by with a hat,
A jerkin, and a choker that
Their master had assumed I'd crave.
They started off regaling me
With vows his lovelorn heart declared,

35 Which left me all a little scared,
Though just as disinclined to see
Myself his latest vanquished maid.

PASCUALA   Where did they speak to you?

LAURENCIA   Down by
The brook six days ago, as I

40 Recall.

PASCUALA   Laurencia, I'm afraid
They'll end up getting what they wish.

LAURENCIA   From me?

PASCUALA   No, from the priest—yes, you!

LAURENCIA   The meat on this young chick's still too
Darn tough to grace his grace's dish.

45 I mean, good lord, Pascuala! Look:
You know how much I'd rather take
A slice of ham when I awake
And place it on the fire to cook;

Then eat it with a hunk of bread
50 I baked and kneaded by myself
With wine pinched off my mother's shelf
From jugs that tightly store her red;
And how much happier I'd be
At noon to watch beef frolicking
55 With heads of cabbage, rollicking
In frothy pots of harmony!
Or, when I come home peeved and tired,
To marry eggplant in full bloom
With bacon—there's no rasher groom!—
60 For just the pick-me-up required.
Then later, for some toothsome snacks
To hold me till our supper's served,
I'd pick grapes off my vines, preserved
By God alone from hail attacks.
65 For dinner, I would eat the lot
Of spicy peppered meat in oil,
Then go to bed content with toil
And give thanks with a "lead us not
Into temptation"[6] of sheer praise.
70 But you know how men are: until
They get their way in love, what skill
They use in finding crafty ways
To make us, in the end, forlorn!
When, worn down, we give up the fight,
75 They take their pleasure in the night
And leave us wretched on the morn.

PASCUALA   You're right, Laurencia! It's no joke!
Once men are sated, they grow rude
And show us more ingratitude
80 Than sparrows do to villagefolk.
In winter, when the weather keeps
Our snowy fields devoid of crops,
These birds swoop down from off the tops
Of houses, all sweet coos and cheeps,
85 But indoors, head straight for the room
Where they can feed upon our crumbs.
Then, once the warm spring weather comes
And sparrows see the fields in bloom,
We hear the last of all their coos.
90 Interrogating us for proof
That we're true Spaniards, from each roof
They chirp accusingly: "Jews? Jews?"[7]
Yes, men are like that, too. As long

6. From the Lord's Prayer: see Mathew 6.13;
Luke 11.4.
7. Intolerance for all non-Christian religions
increased during the Reconquest of territories from Muslim forces, and Jews who did
not convert to Catholicism were expelled
from Spain in 1492.

As they desire us, we're their soul,
95 Their heart, their everything, their whole
Life's being, and can do no wrong,
But once the fire of passion's spent,
They start to treat us worse than Jews
And what were once seductive coos
100 Now chastise us for our consent.

LAURENCIA   You can't trust any of their kind.

PASCUALA   Laurencia, sweetheart, I'm with you!

[*Enter the villagers* MENGO, BARRILDO, *and* FRONDOSO.]

FRONDOSO   Barrildo, argue till you're blue,
You'll never change old Mengo's mind!

105 BARRILDO   Now, here's a person who could bring
An end to this discussion, men.

MENGO   Let's all be in agreement, then,
Before you ask her anything:
If she concurs that I'm correct,
110 You promise that you won't forget
To hand me over what we've bet?

BARRILDO   That's fine with me. I don't object,
But what do we net if you lose?

MENGO   My boxwood rebec,[8] which I hold
115 More precious than a granary's gold,
If I may be allowed to choose.

BARRILDO   That's good enough.

FRONDOSO   Then, let's not wile.
God keep you, lovely ladies both.

LAURENCIA   Frondoso, "ladies"? By my oath!

120 FRONDOSO   Just keeping with the latest style:
These days, a college boy goes by
"Professor," "one-eyed" means you're blind,
The cross-eyed "squint," lame are "inclined,"
And now a spendthrift's a "good guy."
125 The dumbest person is called "bright,"
The none-too-brave are "placable";
No one has thick lips—lips are "full"—
And beady eyes are "piercing," right?
The nitpicker is "thorough," while
130 The meddler is "engaged." In speech,
A windbag is "well-spoken," each
Annoying bore said to "beguile."
Thus, cowards are "dispirited"
And blowhards "full of fight." With twits,
135 The useful catchword "fellows" fits,
While loons are "uninhibited."
The cheerless are alone "discreet";
"Authority" falls to the bald.

---

8. A bowed string instrument of medieval origin, played while held against the arm or under the chin like a violin.

If silliness is "charm," who called
140   "Well-grounded" someone with big feet?
A "chest cold" means the pox in code;
The haughty now are "self-possessed";
The shrewd are "sly," but here's the best:
The humpback "shoulders quite a load"!
145 So maybe now you'll comprehend
Just how you're "ladies," and although
I've more examples, I'll forgo
Reciting all of them on end.
  LAURENCIA   Well, that may pass for courtesy,
150 Frondoso, with the city folk,
But I've heard other people cloak
Their thoughts in language that strikes me
As far more coarse in every phrase
They use and every cutting word.
155 FRONDOSO   Give us a taste of what you've heard.
  LAURENCIA   It's just the opposite of praise:
You're "tiresome" if you're serious
And "brazen" if you look well-heeled.
You're "somber" if you're even-keeled
160 And "spiteful" if you're virtuous.
Give counsel and you "interfere";
You "lavish" when you freely give.
Love justice and you're "punitive,"
Show mercy and be "inaustere."
165 The steadfast now are "dull as sin,"
Politeness is "sheer flattery,"
Sweet charity, "hypocrisy,"
And Christian faith "the sure way in."
"Dumb luck" is hard-won merit's name
170 While truth telling is "recklessness."
Forbearance is deemed "cowardice"
And misadventure now means "blame."
A decent woman's called a "ponce,"
A proper, lovely girl a "freak,"
175 A chaste . . . But I've no need to speak
More. Let this serve as my response.
  MENGO   The devil! That was quite a list!
  BARRILDO   She's not a half-bad orator!
  MENGO   I bet the priest who christened her
180 Laid on the salt, fist after fist![9]
  LAURENCIA   What quarrel is it brings you here,
If I have heard you right, today?
  FRONDOSO   Just listen, on your soul.
  LAURENCIA   Tell, pray.

---

9. Prior to the Second Vatican Council (1962–65), Roman Catholic baptisms often included the placing of a small amount of salt on a baby's lips as a symbol of purification and wisdom.

FRONDOSO   Laurencia, lend me but your ear.
185 LAURENCIA   I'll give it to you out and out,
    A special present, not a loan.
FRONDOSO   I trust your judgment as my own.
LAURENCIA   So, what's this famous bet about?
FRONDOSO   Barrildo casts his lot with me.
190 LAURENCIA   And Mengo?
BARRILDO   He insists upon
    Denying a phenomenon
    That's clearly real.
MENGO   It cannot be;
    Experience refutes its name.
LAURENCIA   Which is . . . ?
BARRILDO   That love does not exist.[1]
195 LAURENCIA   Love's vital and would sure be missed.
BARRILDO   Yes, vital; it's a silly claim.
    This world has a most pressing need
    For love, or life would fade away.
MENGO   Philosophy's not my forte
200 And now I wish that I could read,
    But here goes: if the elements[2]—
    Earth, water, fire, and air—all live
    In endless discord and then give
    Our very bodies sustenance—
205 Their melancholy and, let's see,
    Blood, choler . . . phlegm[3]—I've proved my point.
BARRILDO   This world is nowhere out of joint,
    Dear Mengo; all is harmony[4]
    For harmony is love distilled
210 And love, pure concert from above.
MENGO   I don't dispute that natural love
    Abides on earth, as God has willed.
    Love does exist, but of the sort
    That rules relations in advance—
215 Compulsory ties, not bonds of chance—
    Among all beings these realms support.
    And never once have I denied
    That each man's humor finds some fit

---

1. The following discussion is a comic pastiche of tenets of classical philosophy.
2. That is, the four elements that make up all matter (earth, air, fire, and water); this theory of matter, still current during the Renaissance, was first propounded by the Greek philosopher Empedocles (ca. 493–ca. 433 B.C.E.).
3. According to the humoral theory of psychology and physiology, elaborated by the Greek physician Galen (129–ca. 199 C.E.) and dominant for centuries, imbalances between the four humors, or bodily fluids, determined health and personality. An excess of black bile, a cold, dry substance in the body corresponding to the earth, made people melancholic, while blood and air were associated with the sanguine; yellow bile and fire, with the choleric; and phlegm and water, with the phlegmatic.
4. The harmony produced by a balance in bodily systems; "pure concert from above" (line 210) also suggests the harmony produced by the music of the spheres, a concept generally credited to the Greek mathematician and philosopher Pythagoras (6th c. B.C.E.) but taken up more literally in the Middle Ages.

With love that corresponds to it
220 To keep his being unified.
If someone tries to punch my face,
I block the impact with my arm
And when I'm facing bodily harm,
My feet run to a safer place.
225 My lids and lashes likewise move
To counter danger to my eye
And all from natural love, I vie.

PASCUALA What point is it you seek to prove?

MENGO I mean that we should be agreed
230 That only self-love rules the day.

PASCUALA That's not true, Mengo, if I may,
For isn't there a vital need
A man experiences when
He loves a woman, or a brute
235 Its mate?

MENGO   Yes, but without dispute,
It's self-love and not true love, then.
Now, what is love?

PASCUALA   It's a desire
For beauty.[5]

MENGO   And why does love pursue
Said beauty, in your humble view?

240 PASCUALA For pleasure.

MENGO   Right! May I inquire,
Then, whether this enjoyment might
Serve love itself?

PASCUALA   I'm sure that's so.

MENGO So, selfishness will make love go
And seek what causes it delight?

245 PASCUALA Why, yes.

MENGO   Then, as I'm claiming, there
Can be no love but of the kind
That everybody seeks to find
By courting pleasure everywhere.

BARRILDO I seem to have some memory of
250 A sermon I heard by and by
Regarding Plato,[6] some Greek guy
Who taught humanity to love,
Although the love he felt was aimed
At virtue and his loved one's soul.

255 PASCUALA This line of thought has, on the whole,
Both stumped great intellects and shamed
Top scholars in our 'cademies
Who fry their brains debating it.

---

5. A position drawn from Plato's *Symposium* (ca. 384 B.C.E.). See below, line 251 and note.

6. Greek philosopher (ca. 427–ca. 347 B.C.E.), whose themes were much debated in the 15th century by Neoplatonists.

LAURENCIA   She's right; don't fly into a snit
260   By arguing for such fallacies.
      Go thank your stars for leaving you
      Without love, Mengo, in this sphere.
MENGO   Don't you love?
LAURENCIA   Just my honor here.
FRONDOSO   I hope God makes you jealous, too.
265 BARRILDO   So, who's the winner?
PASCUALA   You can take
      That question to the sacristan.
      If he won't tell you, the priest can
      And that should settle what's at stake.
      As I've not much experience
270   And our Laurencia loves not well,
      I wonder how we'll ever tell?
FRONDOSO   To suffer such indifference!

              [*Enter* FLORES.]

FLORES   God keep you, good folk! As you were.
PASCUALA   So the retainer's sent to talk
275   For the Commander.
LAURENCIA   Chicken hawk!
      What brings you here today, fine sir?
FLORES   You see this uniform, don't you?
LAURENCIA   So then, Fernán is coming back?
FLORES   The battle's won, though our attack
280   Entailed the loss of not a few
      Brave men and blood of good allies.
FRONDOSO   Do tell us how the fighting raged.
FLORES   Who better to, since war was waged
      Before these witnesses, my eyes?
285   To undertake this swift campaign
      Against a city by the name
      Of Ciudad Real, our most
      Courageous, noble Master raised
      An army of two thousand men—
290   All loyal vassals—with whom rode
      Three hundred more of mounted troops
      Comprised of friars and laymen both
      For anyone who wears this Cross
      Must rally to its battle cry,
295   Including priests, especially when
      The foes are Moors,[7] you read me right?
      Thus did the gallant youth ride forth
      Bedecked in an embroidered coat
      Of green with golden monograms.
300   His glistening brassards[8] alone

7. A nomadic Muslim people from North Africa who conquered Spain and Portugal in 711 and ruled for centuries over much of the Iberian Peninsula (see below, line 328 and note).

8. Armor for protecting the arm, usually from elbow to shoulder.

Shone through the openings in his sleeves
Held fast by hooks with golden braids.
A sturdy charger rode he, bred
In our fair South and dapple-gray,
305   Which drank from the Guadalquivir[9]
And grazed upon the fertile spots
Nearby. Its tailpiece was adorned
With buckskin straps, its curled forelock
In pure-white bows resembling cloth
310   That expert weavers deftly wove
To match the patches on its hide,
Or "flies on snow," as they are known.
Your liege lord, Fernán Gómez, rode
Beside him on a honeyed steed
315   That bore some white upon its nose,
Accenting its black mane and feet.
Atop a Turkish coat of mail
His armor breast- and back-plates shone
Both bordered with an orange trim
320   Relucent with pearls set in gold.
And from his burnished helmet waved
A crown of plumes that seemed to stretch
In orange-blossom whiteness down
To meet his orange vestment's edge.
325   A red and white brace held his lance
In readiness, although this bore
More likeness to a huge ash tree
To petrify Granada's[1] Moors.
And so the city took up arms
330   In affirmation of the stance
That it obeyed the rightful crown
And would defend its king and lands.
The Master mounted an attack
And, after fierce resistance there,
335   Decreed that all who'd wagged their tongues
Against his honor be prepared
To die beheaded for their crime,
While those who rallied round the flag
Among the simple city folk
340   Were flogged in public, bound and gagged.
There in the city he abides,
As well loved as he is well feared;
A man who battles, castigates
And crushes foes, still raw in years,
345   The town believes will come to be
The scourge of Africa some day,

---

9. A river that passes through the southern Spanish cities of Cordova and Seville.
1. A city in southern Spain; the site of the Alhambra, the place of the Moorish kings, it was the Moors' last stronghold, from which they were expelled in 1492.

Subjecting blue and crescent moons[2]
To his Red Cross's one true faith.
So many gifts has he bestowed
350   Upon our brave Commander now,
It seems that he's despoiling not
The city, but his manor house.
But listen! Hear the music play?
Come welcome your great hero home,
355   For no wreath suits a victor like
The good will shown him by his own.

[*Enter the* COMMANDER *and* ORTUÑO, MUSICIANS, *Village Magistrates*
ESTEBAN *and* ALONSO, *and Village Councilman* JUAN ROJO.]

MUSICIANS [*Singing*]   *All hail, victorious*
Commander! Thy bold deeds be praised!
For thou hast slain our foes
360   *And left their rebel cities razed!*
Long life to thy Guzmáns
And to our Master's proud Giróns!
In times of peace thy speech
Is couched in calm and measured tones
365   *Though thou wouldst battle Moors*
Courageous as an oak is strong.
From Ciudad Real
To Fuenteovejuna throng
Thy still triumphant troops
370   *And here thy lofty pennants wave!*
Fernán Gómez, God grant
A thousand years to one so brave!

COMMANDER   Kind villagers, I thank you for this true
Outpouring of affection I've been shown.
375 ALONSO   'Tis but a fraction of our love for you
And scarce reflects the sentiments you're known
To merit.

ESTEBAN   Fuenteovejuna deems
Your presence here an honor, and our own
Town council begs you to accept what seems
380   No doubt a paltry offering conveyed
By cart to one the village so esteems
And tendered in goodwill mid poles arrayed
With ribbons, though the gifts themselves be small.
To start, glazed earthenware our potters made.
385   Next, an entire stock of geese—see all
Their heads protruding through the mesh to voice
Praise for your valor with their cackling call!
Ten salted hogs, each specimen more choice,
Jerked beef, rich delicacies, and pork hides
390   Which, more than perfumed gloves, make men rejoice.

2. Islamic insignia.

A hundred capons and plump hens, the brides
Of future widowed roosters of the same
Sort dotting these lush fields, are yours besides.
You'll not fetch arms or horses for your fame,
395 Nor trappings here embroidered with pure gold
Unless you take for gold the love you claim.
And having said "pure," may I be so bold
As to suggest these wineskins hold such wine
That winter soldiers scarce would mind the cold
400 As they patrolled outdoors if they could line
Their stomachs with this, steelier than steel,
For wine can cause the dullest blades to shine.
I'll skip the savories and the cheese you'll feel
Most tempted by, except to say it's right
405 That we should pay you tribute for our weal
And wish your household hearty appetite.
COMMANDER   For this, much thanks, good councilmen.
        You may retire with all my best.
ALONSO   We bid you, sir, enjoy some rest
410 And welcome you back home again.
    This sedge and bulrush at your door,
    A touch of grace our town unfurls,
    Might well have been oriental pearls—
    Though surely you deserve far more—
415 Had we but means to furnish these.
COMMANDER   Kind folk, I doubt not what you say.
        May God be with you.
ESTEBAN   Singers, play
    Our song of triumph once more, please.
MUSICIANS [*Singing.*]   *All hail, victorious*
420 *Commander! Thy bold deeds be praised!*
    For thou hast slain our foes
    And left their rebel cities razed!

        [*Exit* MUSICIANS. *The* COMMANDER *turns toward his residence
        but stops at the entrance to speak with* LAURENCIA *and* PASCUALA.]

COMMANDER   Abide a while, the two of you.
LAURENCIA   What can we do for you, good sir?
425 COMMANDER   Why, just the other day you were
        Aloof toward me, is that not true?
LAURENCIA   I think he's giving you more sass.
PASCUALA   Not me, dear! That's enough of that.
COMMANDER   I'm talking both to you, wildcat,
430 And to this other lovely lass,
    For aren't you mine?
PASCUALA   Good sir, no doubt,
    But hardly in the way you think.
COMMANDER   Then come in, you've no cause to shrink.
        You see my servants are about.
435 LAURENCIA   Well, had the magistrates come, too—

For one's my father, you may know—
It might have seemed correct to go.
COMMANDER   You, Flores!
FLORES   Sir!
COMMANDER   Can it be true
That they refuse what I implore?
440 FLORES   He said, go in!
LAURENCIA   Don't touch us, man!
FLORES   You're being silly.
PASCUALA   While you plan
To lock us in and bolt the door?
FLORES   He only thought you'd like to see
The spoils he gathered in this batch.

   [*The* COMMANDER *turns to enter his dwelling.*]

445 COMMANDER [*Aside to* ORTUÑO.]   If they do enter, draw the latch.
LAURENCIA   I told you, Flores, leave us be!
ORTUÑO   You mean the two of you are not
More booty?
PASCUALA   Let it rest a while
And get out of my way or I'll . . .
450 FLORES   Enough, for now. You see they're hot.
LAURENCIA   How much more tribute would it take
To make him happy with these meats?
ORTUÑO   Your meats would be the sweeter treats.
LAURENCIA   I hope they make his belly ache!

   [*Exit* LAURENCIA *and* PASCUALA.]

455 FLORES   He'll give us both an earful when
We dare return without the girls
And curse us like a pair of churls
While we take his abuse again.
ORTUÑO   Well, masters sometimes grow annoyed.
460 To prosper in the servant class,
You have to let their foul moods pass:
Be patient or be unemployed.

   [*Exit* FLORES *and* ORTUÑO.]

1.3

[SCENE: *A room in the palace of the Catholic kings.*]

   [*Enter King* FERDINAND, *Queen* ISABEL, *the courtier Don* MANRIQUE,
   and retinue.]

ISABEL   You would do well to heed the threat
Alfonso's army now presents.
His Portuguese have pitched their tents
In nearby fields and must be met
5 With troops who'll counter this deceit
By striking ere these foes attack
For if our men don't drive them back
Our side will suffer sure defeat.

FERDINAND   Navarre and Aragon[3] both aid
10   Our righteous cause and shall until
     We steel our forces in Castile
     And see their re-formation made,
     A measure which should guarantee
     Our triumph in an allied thrust.
15 ISABEL   Your Royal Majesty, we must
     Be certain of this victory.
   MANRIQUE   Your Highness, there are aldermen
     From Ciudad Real here who
     Request an audience with you.
20 FERDINAND   Brave Don Manrique, show them in.

     [*Enter two* ALDERMEN *from Ciudad Real.*]

   FIRST ALDERMAN   Great Ferdinand, most Catholic king,
     Whom Heaven's sent with grace to reign
     Through all Castile and Aragon,
     Our noble succor and true aid,
25   On Ciudad Real's behalf
     We've come to sue for royal help
     In true humility before
     Your valiant and all-powerful self.
     We'd held our own selves fortunate
30   To be the subjects of this crown
     Till adverse fortune intervened
     And turned our destinies around.
     Rodrigo Téllez Girón, sire,
     Famed bearer of his family name
35   Whose courage on the battlefield
     And strength belie his tender age,
     Of Calatrava Master, has
     Assailed our city to expand
     The Order's power and estate,
40   His lands erstwhile by royal grant.
     We bravely readied our defense
     In hopes resistance would rebuff
     His forces, but our streams ran red,
     Discolored with the fallen's blood.
45   In short, he took the city but
     He never could have had Fernán
     Gómez withheld his counsel, troops,
     And guidance in this treacherous plot.
     He bides still in our captured town,
50   His vassals and sad subjects we
     Who suffer this loss with regret
     And hope it soon be remedied.

3. Provinces of northern Spain. Following the events depicted in this play, Ferdinand succeeded his father as king of Aragon in 1479; in 1511 he conquered the southern half of the Kingdom of Navarre, uniting it with Spain.

FERDINAND   And where is Fernán Gómez now?

FIRST ALDERMAN   In Fuenteovejuna, sire,

55   A humble village, I believe,
The cruel Commander now retires
To have his way with peasant girls
More freely than we care to state.
He keeps his vassals there as far
60   From happiness as they can stay.

FERDINAND   Have you no captain in your ranks?

SECOND ALDERMAN   It's sure we haven't anymore,
As every nobleman they seized
Was wounded or has faced the sword.

65   ISABEL   This matter begs a quick display
Of strength, for cautious remedy
Would only make this enemy
The bolder given our delay.
Thus Portugal might view this stall
70   A chance occasion fortune yields
To cross Extremadura's[4] fields
And so bring grievous harm to all.

FERDINAND   Manrique, take two companies
Of soldiers to their bivouac
75   And launch a merciless attack
To castigate their tyrannies.
The Count of Cabra, who won fame
For his exploits as Córdoba,[5]
Will ride with you, and never a
80   More valiant soldier could Spain claim.
This seems the most expedient
Proceeding we can now effect.

MANRIQUE   Your judgment, sire, is most correct
And this dispatch most provident.
85   As long as life runs through my veins,
I'll see that youth put in his place.

ISABEL   I'm confident success shall grace
Our cause with such men at the reins.

[*Exit all.*]

1.4

[SCENE: *An open field in Fuenteovejuna.*]

[*Enter* LAURENCIA *and* FRONDOSO.]

LAURENCIA   I had to leave the wash half wet,
Frondoso, just to keep the town
From gossiping. The brook's no place
For men to gallivant around.
5   The villagers are whispering

4. A province of southwest Spain bordering Portugal.

5. Diego Fernández de Córdoba (b. 1438), count of Cabra and marshal of Baena.

About how you persist. They know
I've caught your eye as you have mine
And keep their eyes now on us both.
As you're the type of brazen swain
10   To strut throughout the village clad
In elegant attire that costs
Far more than any other lad's,
There's not a girl or guy about
These woodlands, meadows, groves, and brush
15   Who isn't saying to himself
That we two are already one.
They all await that blessed day
When Juan Chamorro, sacristan,
Will lay down his bassoon just long
20   Enough to carry out our banns,
Though they'd be better off by far
To see their granaries duly stuffed
With heaps of autumn's golden wheat
And have their wine jars filled with must.
25   The rumors that the villagers
Keep spreading here have caused me pique
But aren't so irritating as
To have deprived me of dear sleep.
FRONDOSO   Your harsh disdain so flusters me,
30   Laurencia, that I fear each time
I see your face or hear your voice
I place existence on the line!
For if you know my sole desire
Is that we marry, why repay
35   These good intentions with such scorn?
LAURENCIA   I know but one way to behave.
FRONDOSO   How can it be you feel no pain
To see me in the grip of grief
When, at the merest thought of you,
40   I lose desire for food and sleep?
How can that sweet, angelic face
Bring such hardheartedness with it?
But, Lord, how rabidly I rave!
LAURENCIA   Then you must seek a curative.
45 FRONDOSO   The cure I seek resides in you
So we can be like turtledoves
That perch together rubbing beaks
And coo contentedly in love—
I mean, provided that the church . . .
50 LAURENCIA   Go ask my uncle first and charm
Juan Rojo, for although I feel
No passion yet, I sense a spark.
FRONDOSO   Oh, no! Look over there—it's him!
LAURENCIA   He must be hunting deer nearby.

55   Quick, run and hide within these woods!

FRONDOSO   It's jealousy I need to hide!

      [*Enter the* COMMANDER.]

COMMANDER   I can't say it displeases me
    To set out for a fearsome buck
    And come upon a lovely doe.

60 LAURENCIA   I left my pile of wash half done
    For this brief respite from my chores
    But now, I fear, the brook awaits
    So, by your leave, I'll go now, sir.

COMMANDER   The brusqueness in your cruel disdain,
65   Laurencia, is a sharp affront
    To all the grace and comely looks
    The heavens have bestowed on you
    And makes you seem unnatural.
    You've managed in the past to flee
70   The loving of my arms' embrace
    But now this field, our silent friend,
    Has pledged to keep our secret safe.
    Come, there's no need for diffidence
    Or any reason to avert
75   Your gaze from me, your rightful lord,
    As if I were some peasant churl.
    Did not Pedro Redondo's wife
    Sebastiana gladly yield,
    And young Martín del Pozo's, too,
80   Although the latter's wedding seal
    Had scarcely dried, our happy tryst
    But two days after she was wed?

LAURENCIA   These women, sir, could by that time
    Claim much experience with men
85   As that same road you took to them
    Had been well traveled for some years
    By all the lads with whom they'd lain.
    God keep you as you hunt your deer;
    Were you not costumed with that cross,
90   I'd take you for the devil's spawn
    To hound me so relentlessly.

COMMANDER   What haughty insolence you flaunt!
    I'll lay my crossbow on the ground
    And use these hands to put an end
95   To all your mincing ways.

LAURENCIA   How now?
    You don't mean you'd be capable . . .

      [*Enter* FRONDOSO, *who picks up the crossbow.*]

COMMANDER [*Not noticing* FRONDOSO.]   Don't try to fight me off.

FRONDOSO [*Aside.*]   I pick
    His weapon up, but hope to God
    I'll have no cause for using it.

100 COMMANDER   Relent already!
    LAURENCIA   Heavens, help
      A girl in need!
    COMMANDER   We're all alone.
      There's no need now to be afraid.
    FRONDOSO   Commander, you've a generous soul
      So leave her be or rest assured
105   I'll make a bull's-eye of your chest
      Though, even in my rage, that cross
      Elicits my profound respect.
    COMMANDER   Vile dog!
    FRONDOSO   I see no dogs round here.
      Quick, run, Laurencia!
    LAURENCIA   Careful now,
110   Frondoso!
    FRONDOSO   Off with you, I said!

                    [Exit LAURENCIA.]

    COMMANDER   The fool who'd lay his own sword down
      Deserves the trouble he incurs.
      I feared my prey would hear its clap
      So I pursued the hunt ungirt.
115 FRONDOSO   By God, don't make me loose the catch
      Or you'll be pierced like game, my lord.
    COMMANDER   She's gone! Come, give the crossbow up,
      You thieving, treacherous, peasant rogue!
      Just give it here, I said!
    FRONDOSO   For what,
120   So you could take my life with it?
      Remember, sir, that love is deaf
      And, from that day it reigns supreme,
      Will not be swayed by argument.
    COMMANDER   Am I to turn my back upon
125   A village churl? Shoot! Shoot, you knave,
      But be prepared to stand on guard,
      For as a nobleman I break
      Chivalric code to challenge you.
    FRONDOSO   No need, sir, for I'm satisfied
130   With my low station here on earth,
      But, as I must protect my life,
      I'll take this crossbow as I flee.
    COMMANDER   He plays a rash and perilous game
      But I shall have my vengeance for
135   This crime of standing in my way!
      Why didn't I just attack the clod?
      The heavens see how I've been shamed!

2.1

[SCENE: *The town square in Fuenteovejuna.*]

[*Enter* ESTEBAN *and Village Alderman* CUADRADO.]

ESTEBAN   We've still abundant stocks of wheat reserved
But really mustn't raid our granaries more.
These recent forecasts have us all unnerved
And I believe our strength lies in this store
5   Though some don't see what good these stocks have served.
CUADRADO   I've always been of one mind on this score;
Abundance means there's governance in peace.
ESTEBAN   We'll tell Fernán Gómez, then, this must cease.
These fool astrologers do irritate!
10   Though ignorant of the future, they've a hoard
Of unconvincing prattles that relate
Grave secrets vital only to the Lord.
They think they're theologians and conflate
Before and after into one accord:
15   Ask any one about the present, though,
And you'll soon learn how little any know!
What, do they own the clouds that dot the air
Or the trajectory of the heavens' light?
How can they see what's happening up there
20   To give us all an endless case of fright?
They tell us when to plant our crops and where—
Wheat there, now greens, your barley to the right,
Here mustard, pumpkins, now cucumber beds—
I swear to God that they're the pumpkin heads!
25   First, they predict a herd of cows will die
And die they do—in Transylvania![6]
They forecast that our wine yield won't be high
But see beer flowing in Westphalia.[7]
The cherry frost in Gascony[8] they spy
30   And hordes of tigers in Hyrcania.[9]
Plant what we will, though, blessed by them or cursed,
The year still ends December thirty-first.

[*Enter the university graduate* LEONELO *and* BARRILDO.]

LEONELO   Looks like the gossip corner's doing well;
The tardy pupil can't be teacher's pet!
35 BARRILDO   Was Salamanca[1] grand?
LEONELO   I've much to tell.
BARRILDO   You'll be a second Solomon.[2]
LEONELO   Not yet.
Salami-maker, maybe. But I dwell

---

6. A region of present-day Romania, invoked here as a place remote from Spain.
7. A region in the west of present-day Germany.
8. A region of southwest France.
9. An area of ancient Persia (present-day

northern Iran), associated in classical and later literature with tigers.
1. A city in western Spain where the country's oldest university was founded in 1218.
2. That is, as learned as the proverbially wise king of Israel (10th c. B.C.E.).

Upon what's doctrine for the jurist set.
BARRILDO   I'm sure you studied with the utmost care.
40 LEONELO   I tried to gain important knowledge there.
BARRILDO   So many volumes are in print today
The multitudes imagine they are wise.
LEONELO   Yet they know less, it saddens me to say,
For so much wisdom's hard to summarize
45 And all their vain attempts to find a way
Just make the letters swim before their eyes.
The more a person reads the printed word
The more the letters on the page look blurred.
I don't doubt that the art of print has saved
50 The best cuts from this cloth of rhetoric
By salvaging sage works from Time's depraved
Consignment of all earthly things to quick
Oblivion; this the printing press has staved.
To Gutenberg[3] we owe this curious trick,
55 A German from the town of Mainz whose fame
Is more than any Fame herself can claim.
Some writers who were once deemed erudite,
Though, lost their erudition on the page
While dumber men who never learned to write
60 Have published using names of men more sage.
Still others have penned treatises so trite
That, overcome by jealousy and rage,
They've signed their rivals' names to these poor works
To make their readers think these authors jerks!
65 BARRILDO   They couldn't do such things!
LEONELO   It's natural
For fools to reap revenge on real success.
BARRILDO   Still, Leonelo, print is notable.
LEONELO   We've lived for centuries without the press
And I don't see these modern times more full
70 Of St. Augustines or Jeromes,[4] do you?
BARRILDO   Let's sit a while before you start to stew.

[*Enter* JUAN ROJO *and a* VILLAGER.]

JUAN ROJO   If what we've seen is true, you couldn't raise
A dowry out of what four farms would yield.
Now anyone who'd know the truth can gaze
75 Upon our town's disruption unconcealed.
VILLAGER   Peace, friend. What news of the Commander's days?
JUAN ROJO   He cornered poor Laurencia in a field!
VILLAGER   That lecherous animal! I'd love to see
The villain hanging from that olive tree!

[*Enter the* COMMANDER *with* ORTUÑO *and* FLORES.]

80 COMMANDER   God keep you, townsfolk, in His grace.

---

3. Johannes Gutenberg (ca. 1400–1468), inventor of the movable-type printing press.
4. Two revered church fathers: St. Augustine (354–430), bishop of Hippo and author of many commentaries and the *Confessions*; St. Jerome (ca. 347–419 or 420), author of ecclesiastical histories, exegeses, and a Latin version of the Bible (the Vulgate).

CUADRADO   My lord.

COMMANDER   Good villagers, at ease
Now, as you were.

ESTEBAN   Your lordship, please
Be seated in your wonted place.
We'll stand, as this suits everyone.

85 COMMANDER   I'll order you to sit down, then.

ESTEBAN   You honor us as only men
Of honor can, as men who've none
Can scarcely proffer what they've not.

COMMANDER   Come, sit. I'd like us to confer.

90 ESTEBAN   Have you received the greyhound, sir?

COMMANDER   The dog continues to besot
My valets, magistrate, and stuns
The servants with its noble speed.

ESTEBAN   A fine example of its breed!

95 Good lord, that noble creature runs
As fast as any suspect or
Delinquent that the law pursues.

COMMANDER   Well, given but the choice, I'd choose
To have you point the dog straight for

100 A certain frisky little hare
Too swift for any but this hound.

ESTEBAN   I will, but where might she be found?

COMMANDER   I'm speaking of your daughter there.

ESTEBAN   My daughter?

COMMANDER   Yes.

ESTEBAN   How could she be

105 A consort suitable for you?

COMMANDER   Do give her a good talking to.

ESTEBAN   Why, pray?

COMMANDER   She's set on vexing me.
A lady here in town you'd call
Distinguished noted my designs

110 And, at the first sign of my signs,
Succumbed.

ESTEBAN: Then she disgraced us all.
If you don't mind me saying, sir,
Your language ought to be less free.

COMMANDER   The rustic speaks so loftily!

115 Ah, Flores! Have this villager
Read one of Aristotle's tomes,
The *Politics*.[5]

ESTEBAN   We of the land
Are glad to live by your command
And seek but honor for our homes

120 As Fuenteovejuna, too,
Can boast distinguished residents.

5. A treatise on the city-state by the Greek philosopher (384–322 B.C.E.).

LEONELO [*Aside.*]   To hear that villain's insolence!

COMMANDER   Has what I said offended you
   Or any gathered here today?

125 CUADRADO   Commander, this is most unjust.
   You're wrong to say such things and must
   Not stain our honor in this way.

COMMANDER   Your what? Who do you think you are,
   The Friars of Calatrava, then?

130 CUADRADO   No doubt that Order numbers men
   Who wear the cross with bloodlines far
   Less pure than simple townsfolk own.

COMMANDER   So should our lines mix, theirs would be
   Forever fouled?

CUADRADO   Iniquity
135   Defiles, not cleanses—that's well known.

COMMANDER   Whatever reasoning you seek,
   Your women should be honored so.

ESTEBAN   Such words do shame us all, and no
   One thinks you'd do the deeds you speak.

140 COMMANDER   These peasants can be tiresome!
   In cities they know how to treat
   A man of qualities and meet
   His every wish when he is come.
   There, husbands deem it flattery
145   When other men pursue their wives.

ESTEBAN   You say this so we'll all live lives
   Of equal moral laxity.
   God still inhabits cities, though,
   Where vengeance is more swift and clean.

150 COMMANDER   That's it! Be on your way!

ESTEBAN   You mean
   You wish the two of us to go?

COMMANDER   No, I don't want to see a soul!
   Now clear the square and don't come back!

ESTEBAN   We're leaving then.

COMMANDER   Not in a pack!

155 FLORES   Sir, please, a little self-control.

COMMANDER   They'll plot against me left alone,
   Each boor a co-conspirator.

ORTUÑO   Have patience with these rustics, sir.

COMMANDER   I marvel at how much I've shown.
160   Go severally[6] home now, all of you—
   I won't have anything amiss.

LEONELO [*Aside.*]   Just heavens, will you suffer this?

ESTEBAN   It's time that I returned home, too.

       [*Exit the* VILLAGERS.]

COMMANDER   Men, don't you find these clods absurd?

6. Separately.

165 ORTUÑO   They know you scarcely deign to mask
     Your condescension when they ask
     That their petitioning be heard.
    COMMANDER   So now they think us peers of sorts?
    FLORES   Who equals whom does not pertain.
170 COMMANDER   How does that crossbow thief remain
     At large, unsentenced by our courts?
    FLORES   I thought I'd spied him lingering near
     Laurencia's doorstep late last night,
     Though now I know I wasn't right:
175   I slit some knave's throat ear to ear
     When I mistook his cloak to be
     Frondoso's in the eventide.
    COMMANDER   I can't imagine where he'd hide.
    FLORES   Oh, he'll turn up eventually.
180 COMMANDER   Would anyone who tried to kill
     A man like me remain close by?
    FLORES   The heedless bird will blithely fly
     Into a snare lured by a trill,
     The foolish fish swim toward the hook.
185 COMMANDER   It galls me that a lowborn pest
     Could point a crossbow at the chest
     Of this brave captain, whose sword shook
     Granada and Cordova both.
     It's at an end, this world we knew!
190 FLORES   He acted as love bid him to.
     You're still alive, so by my oath,
     I think you're in the peasant's debt.
    COMMANDER   I swear, Ortuño, had I not
     Disguised my feelings toward this lot,
195   Two hours would not have passed by yet
     And I'd have run the whole town through.
     Until I judge the time is right,
     I'll keep the reins on vengeance tight
     And then do what I need to do.
200   What says Pascuala?
    FLORES   She replied
     That any day now she's to wed.
    COMMANDER   If she'd still care to lend her bed . . .
    FLORES   She's sending you where they'll provide
     Your lordship with such things for cash.
205 COMMANDER   What says Olalla, then?
    ORTUÑO   The girl's
     A lively one.
    COMMANDER   Her quips are pearls.
     To wit?
    ORTUÑO   She and her husband clash
     Of late because, she'd have you know,
     He's jealous of the notes I bring
210   And mad that you'd go visiting

His wife with manservants in tow.
Just wait until he drops his guard
And you'll be first inside again!

COMMANDER　This knight is glad upon it, then.

215　The peasant watches her but hard.

ORTUÑO　It's true, though his attention strays.

COMMANDER　And sweet Inés?

FLORES　　　　　　　　　　　Who?

COMMANDER　　　　　　　　　　　　　　Anton's bit.

FLORES　Her offer stands most definite
And ought to liven up your days.

220　We spoke in the corral outside—
Go round the back and in that door.

COMMANDER　Loose women I've a soft spot for
But less so once I'm satisfied.
Ah, Flores, if they only were

225　Aware of what their charms are worth!

FLORES　As letdowns go, there's none on earth
Like plain capitulation, sir.
A woman's quick surrender blights
The pleasure men anticipate,

230　Though certain girls corroborate
A wise philosopher[7] who writes
That females crave male company
As form desires material shape,
Which shouldn't leave your mouths agape

235　For this is but reality.

COMMANDER　A man whom ardor's heat lays waste
Is glad to have his pleasure sealed
By lady friends who readily yield,
Though he disdain them for this haste.

240　The surest course for love to run
Once all delight has been bestowed
Is down oblivion's well-worn road
Of favors far too easily won.

[Enter CIMBRANOS, a soldier.]

CIMBRANOS　Is the Commander hereabouts?

245　ORTUÑO　What, don't you see him standing there?

CIMBRANOS　Oh, brave Fernán Gómez! Throw off
Your hunter's cap and be prepared
To strap your battle helmet on!
Replace your cloak with armor now!

250　The Master of Santiago and
The Count of Cabra's troops surround
Young Don Rodrigo Girón in
Support of the Castilian queen
At Ciudad Real. Good sir,

___

7. That is, Aristotle, who expresses this idea (in less sexualized terms) in his *Physics* and *On the Generation of Animals*.

255 I'm certain you can plainly see
That all the blood your Order's lost
Will be for naught should they succeed.
Our forces can already glimpse
The figures on their coats of arms:
260 Castile's two castles paired with lions
By Aragon's heraldic bars.[8]
So while the King of Portugal
Would like to honor staunch Girón,
The youth would do well just to reach
265 Almagro and be safely home.
Quick, saddle up your charger, sir;
They'll head back to Castile as soon
As you ride boldly into sight.
COMMANDER   Be still while I think what to do.
270 Ortuño, have the trumpet sound
So all may hear it from the square.
How many soldiers have I here?
ORTUÑO   Some fifty horsemen stand prepared.
COMMANDER   Inform them that we sally forth.
275 CIMBRANOS   If we don't start out now, good sirs,
Then Ciudad Real will fall.
COMMANDER   Fear not, we shan't let this occur.
        [*Exit all.*]

2.2

[SCENE: *An open field in Fuenteovejuna.*]

    [*Enter* MENGO, LAURENCIA, *and* PASCUALA, *fleeing.*]

PASCUALA   Oh, please don't leave us here alone!
MENGO   How can these fields inspire such dread?
LAURENCIA   I think it's best for us to head
To town now, Mengo, on our own—
5 Just women, unaccompanied—
In case we should cross paths with him.
MENGO   He couldn't make our lives more grim
Were he the very demon's seed!
LAURENCIA   He's sure to hound us till we're his.
10 MENGO   Oh, lightning bolts, cast down your fires
And purify these mad desires!
LAURENCIA   A bloody beast is what he is,
Our arsenic and pestilence
In town.
MENGO   Laurencia, I've been told
15 That poor Frondoso grew so bold
In championing your innocence
He aimed at the Commander's chest.

8. The symbols of two formerly autonomous kingdoms joined by the marriage of Isabel of Castile and Ferdinand of Aragon.

LAURENCIA   You know how much I've hated men
        But, Mengo, I confess since then
20   I've realized he's not like the rest.
        How valiant Frondoso was!
        I fear this bravery might mean
        His death.
  MENGO   He never can be seen
        In town, whatever else he does.
25 LAURENCIA   I love the man, although it's plain
        That I, too, know that he must flee.
        Still, he responds to such a plea
        With raging anger and disdain
        While our Commander wastes no breath
30   Affirming he'll hang upside down.
  PASCUALA   Will no one garrotte[9] him in town?
  MENGO   I'd rather see him stoned to death.
        Sweet heavens, if I only knew
        Some way to use my sling, I vouch
35   Just stretching back this leather pouch
        Would good as crack his skull in two!
        You wouldn't find depravity
        Like his in Rome's own Sabalus.[1]
  LAURENCIA   You mean Heliogabalus,[2]
40   Whose reign surpassed indecency.
  MENGO   Sir Gawain's[3] misdeeds were no worse.
        Though history's outside my ken,
        Our own Commander's crueler than
        This legendary rogue of verse.
45   Has nature spawned another man
        The likes of Fernán Gómez?
  PASCUALA   No.
        A savage tiger cannot show
        The fury that this miscreant can.

        [*Enter* JACINTA, *a village woman.*]

  JACINTA   For God's sake, if you hold our oath
50   Of friendship dear, just help me hide!
  LAURENCIA   Jacinta, you look petrified!
  PASCUALA   You may rely upon us both.
  JACINTA   That vile Commander bade his men—
        Armed more with natural infamy
55   Than by their swords' nobility—
        To have me waiting for him when
        He reaches Ciudad Real.

9. A Spanish form of execution or assassination by twisting a chain, metal band, wire, or cord around the victim's neck.
1. A chieftain in North Africa (1st c. C.E.) who unsuccessfully revolted against Roman rule.
2. The Roman emperor Elagabalus (r. 218–222), whose reign was marked by sexual deca-

dence, cruelty, and his devotion to a non-Roman god.
3. One of the legendary knights of the Round Table (and King Arthur's nephew); he is generally presented in English versions of the tales as heroic, courtly, and brave, but in some French works he is cruel and treacherous.

LAURENCIA   Jacinta, God preserve you, but
    If he would fancy you his slut,
60   He'll surely use me as his moll.
           [*Exit* LAURENCIA.]

PASCUALA   A man might help you to escape;
    I can't defend you in distress.
           [*Exit* PASCUALA.]

MENGO   I'll have to act like one, I guess,
    As I'm a man in name and shape.
65   Come by my side and never fear.

JACINTA   But have you arms?

MENGO   The oldest known
    To man.

JACINTA   A sling without a stone?

MENGO   Jacinta, there are stones right here.
           [*Enter* FLORES *and* ORTUÑO.]

FLORES   Thought you could run away, did you?

70 JACINTA   Now I'm as good as dead!

MENGO   Good sirs,
    How can these honest villagers . . .

ORTUÑO   So, mustering up the derring-do
    To champion a lady's cause?

MENGO   I'd first defend her with my pleas,
75   As I'm male kin, but failing these,
    Would look to force and nature's laws.

FLORES   Enough, now. Run the beggar through.

MENGO   Compel me to unsling my sling
    And you will rue the day I fling
80   A volley of these rocks at you.
           [*Enter the* COMMANDER *and* CIMBRANOS.]

COMMANDER   A person of my rank alight
    To settle such a petty case?

FLORES   The rabble in this horrid place,
    Which you could purge by every right
85   For giving you no end of grief,
    Now brandish arms against our own.

MENGO   Good sir, if you cannot condone
    Such conduct, as is my belief,
    Then punish these vile soldiers who'd
90   Abduct this woman in your name.
    Her husband's and her parents' fame
    Bespeaks the highest rectitude.
    Now, by your leave, I'll take the girl
    Back home where all her family wait.

95 COMMANDER   My leave, you want? Retaliate,
    Men, by my leave, against the churl.
    Come, drop the sling.

MENGO   My lord, they bade . . .

COMMANDER   Peace! Flores and Ortuño, bind

His hands. Cimbranos, help in kind.

100 MENGO   You'd act thus, called to virtue's aid?

COMMANDER   What do the townsfolk think of me
In Fuenteovejuna, cur?

MENGO   How has our village or I, sir,
Offended you so grievously?

105 FLORES   Are we to kill him, then?

COMMANDER   Why draw
Your swords to sully steel you'd grace
With honor in a better place?

ORTUÑO   What are your orders?

COMMANDER   Whip him raw.
There, lash the peasant to that oak

110 And, when his back is bared, go seize
Your horse's reins . . .

MENGO   Have mercy, please,
Sir! Mercy! You are gentlefolk.

COMMANDER   . . . And flog this man relentlessly
Until the studs fly off the straps.

115 MENGO   Do heaven's righteous laws collapse
To grant these deeds impunity?

[*Exit* FLORES, ORTUÑO, CIMBRANOS, *and* MENGO.]

COMMANDER   You, girl, what are you running for?
You find a clod that tills the earth
More pleasing than a man of worth?

120 JACINTA   Is this the way you would restore
Lost honor when it was your plan
To have me carried off by force?

COMMANDER   So, I desired you?

JACINTA   Of course,
Because my father is a man

125 Well spoken of, though not your peer
In birth, with manners gentler still
Than any you possess.

COMMANDER   This shrill
Effrontery will not, I fear,
Assuage my wrath or aid your plight.

130 Now, come along at once.

JACINTA   With you?

COMMANDER   Correct.

JACINTA   Pay heed to what you do.

COMMANDER   I'll heed your detriment, all right.
Who needs you? Why should I deprive
The troops of coveted supplies?

135 JACINTA   Not all the force beneath the skies
Could make me suffer this alive!

COMMANDER   Come on now, strumpet, move along.

JACINTA   Have mercy!

COMMANDER   Mercy won't exist.

JACINTA   Then I've no choice but to enlist

140   The heavens to redress this wrong.

          [*The* COMMANDER *exits as soldiers carry* JACINTA *off.*
          Enter LAURENCIA *and* FRONDOSO.]

LAURENCIA   How can you show your face around
    Here unafraid?

FRONDOSO   I thought that some
    Such recklessness would make you come
    To see the troth to which we're bound.
145   I watched the dread Commander part
    While hiding in the hills above
    And, seeing you deserve my love,
    Lost all the fear that plagued my heart.
    I hope he goes far off to thrive!
150   Good riddance, too!

LAURENCIA   Don't waste your breath.
    Besides, the more men wish your death,
    The longer you'll remain alive.

FRONDOSO   If that's so, then long life to him,
    For both sides profit by this quirk:
155   I live while our best wishes work
    Against him in the interim!
    Laurencia, is there any place
    For me in your affections, dear?
    I need to know if my sincere
160   Devotion's found its port of grace.
    I mean, the village speaks as one
    By now, considering us a pair,
    And it astounds the townsfolk there
    To see our coupling left undone.
165   So put aside these harsh extremes
    And tell me if there is or not.

LAURENCIA   I swear to both you and that lot
    That all will soon be as it seems.

FRONDOSO   For this great mercy, let me kiss
170   Your lovely feet, my future wife!
    You've granted me a second life,
    I must confess, in saying this.

LAURENCIA   Enough with blandishments! We mince
    Words when it's evident to us
175   That you have only to discuss
    The matter with my father since
    He comes now with my uncle, see?
    Frondoso, don't lose faith, for I'm
    To be your wedded wife in time—
180   That much is sure.

FRONDOSO   God bolster me!

        [*They hide. Enter* ESTEBAN, ALONSO, *and* JUAN ROJO.]

ALONSO   So, in the end, the townsfolk rose
    In vocal protest on the square,
    And rightly so, for they'll not bear

More crimes from him resembling those.
185 The scale of his intemperance
These days can scarcely fail to stun
While poor Jacinta's now the one
Who suffers his incontinence.

JUAN ROJO   All Spain will soon be governed by
190 The Catholic kings, whose well-earned fame
For piety bestows their name,
Which they do both exemplify.
Soon, too, brave Santiago will
Reach Ciudad Real's razed lands
195 And win it back from Girón's hands
By marshaling his general's skill.
I'm sorry for Jacinta, though,
A stalwart lass in every way.

ALONSO   They whipped old Mengo's hide, you say?
200 JUAN ROJO   No ink or flannel that I know
Of ever looked more black or blue.

ALONSO   Enough! You know my blood begins
To boil just picturing the sins
That make his reputation true.
205 Why should I carry this baton
Of office if it serves no use?

JUAN ROJO   His men inflicted the abuse,
So why should you feel woebegone?

ALONSO   Well, what about the time they found
210 Redondo's wife in this deep glen,
Left raped by the Commander's men,
Among whom she'd been passed around
Detestably when he did cease
To take by force what she'd deny?

215 JUAN ROJO   I hear someone! Who's there?

FRONDOSO   Just I,
Who look for leave to speak my piece.

JUAN ROJO   Frondoso, as my house is yours,
Speak freely if you feel the need.
You owe life to your sire's seed.
220 But I'm owed what your grace ensures.
You're like a son to me; I reared
You with much love.

FRONDOSO   Then, sir, I seek—
Based on this love of which you speak—
A gracious favor volunteered.
225 You know who fathered this proud son.

ESTEBAN   Were you aggrieved by that crazed beast
Fernán Gómez?

FRONDOSO   To say the least.

ESTEBAN   I thought as much—another one.

FRONDOSO   This pledge of love that you confide

230 Now moves me likewise to profess
I love Laurencia and express
My wish here that she be my bride.
This tongue deserves a reprimand
For hastiness, which you'll excuse,
235 As usually another sues
The sire for his daughter's hand.

ESTEBAN   Your swift return here is a boon,
Frondoso, and prolongs my years.
Dispelling what my heart most fears,
240 Your coming is most opportune
And so I thank the skies above
That you've emerged to cleanse my name
And thank your passion just the same
For showing purity in love.
245 It's only right that your good sire
Should learn at once what you've proposed.
For my part, I am well disposed
To help you realize this desire.
I would consider myself blessed
250 If this sweet union came to pass.

JUAN ROJO   Well, first we'd better ask the lass
To verify she's acquiesced.

ESTEBAN   You needn't go through all that fuss;
In this case nothing is untoward:
255 The two were firmly of accord
Before he pled his case to us.
We may as well, then, at our ease,
Discuss the dowry that is due.
The sum I gladly offer you
260 Was saved up in *maravedís*.[4]

FRONDOSO   If I decline, don't feel forlorn;
What I don't need can pass unwept.

JUAN ROJO   You should be thankful he'll accept
The girl as bare as she was born.

265 ESTEBAN   That may be, but in any case,
I'll ask the maid if she approves.

FRONDOSO   Good thinking, as it ill behooves
Your pressing what she won't embrace.

ESTEBAN   Sweet child! Laurencia!

LAURENCIA   Father dear.

270 ESTEBAN   I'm sure she will, though you decide.
You see how promptly she replied?
My child, Laurencia! Only sheer
Love urges me to ask today—
Come closer, girl—would you commend
275 Frondoso marrying your friend,

4. Relatively low-value Spanish coins.

Good Gila? He's some fiancé,
The most upstanding of our men,
Proud Fuenteovejuna's son.
LAURENCIA   What? Gila wed . . . ?
ESTEBAN   If any one
280 Among our maids deserves him, then . . .
LAURENCIA   I do commend their union, yes.
ESTEBAN   Yes—though she's ugly, which makes some
Believe Frondoso should become
Your husband. That we all could bless.
285 LAURENCIA   Oh, father! Still inclined to jest
And gibe at your advanced age, too!
ESTEBAN   You love him, child?
LAURENCIA   He knows I do
And, though his love's likewise professed,
Unpleasant actualities . . .
290 ESTEBAN   Should I inform him you consent?
LAURENCIA   Yes, bring him news of my intent.
ESTEBAN   So then it's I who hold the keys?
Well, said and done! Let's all away
To seek our good friend in the square.
295 JUAN ROJO   Let's go.
ESTEBAN   My lad, as for a fair
Amount in dowry, would you say
Four thousand might work like a charm?
I've that much in *maravedís*.
FRONDOSO   How can you speak of such things? Please,
300 You do my honor grievous harm.
ESTEBAN   Come now, son, you'll feel otherwise
Within a day for, by my word,
A dowry that's left unconferred
Goes wanting in some other guise.

[*All exit except* FRONDOSO *and* LAURENCIA.]

305 LAURENCIA   Frondoso, are you happy, dear?
FRONDOSO   Just happy? I'm so overjoyed,
The state I'm in leaves me devoid
Of all my senses when you're near!
The smiles to which my heart is prone
310 Pour out in gladness from my eyes
To think, Laurencia, my sweet prize,
That I can claim you as my own.

[*Exit* FRONDOSO *and* LAURENCIA. *Enter the* MASTER,
the COMMANDER, FLORES, *and* ORTUÑO.]

COMMANDER   Sir, flee! We can't do more to hold our ground!
MASTER   The weakness of these city walls before
315 Their army's forces brought about our fall.
COMMANDER   The blood it's cost them, and the countless lives!
MASTER   They failed to seize our standard, though, to count
The Calatravan colors mid their spoils,
Though it had brought great honor to their toils.

320 COMMANDER   Your stratagems are at an end, Girón.

MASTER   What can I do if turns of fate from night
To morn appear to be blind Fortune's will?

VOICES [*Within.*]   A victory for the monarchs of Castile!

MASTER   Our foes now crown the battlements with lights,

325 Emblazoning the windows in the towers
Above with standards marking victory.

COMMANDER   And well they might, for all the blood it's cost.

Their joy seems tragic given what they've lost.

MASTER   I'll set back out for Calatrava, then.

330 COMMANDER   And I to Fuenteovejuna while
You ponder whether to support your kin
Or pledge allegiance to the Catholic king.

MASTER   I'll write when I'm resolved of my intent.

COMMANDER   Here Time itself will be your guide.

MASTER   Ah, youth!

335 May your deceptions keep me not from Truth!

2.3

[SCENE: *Fuenteovejuna.* ESTEBAN's *house.*]

> [*The wedding is in progress. Enter* MUSICIANS, MENGO, FRONDOSO,
> LAURENCIA, PASCUALA, BARRILDO, ESTEBAN, ALONSO, *and* JUAN ROJO.]

MUSICIANS   *Oh, many happy years*
To you, sweet bride and groom!
Oh, many happy years!

MENGO   You dashed that off in seconds flat,

5 Now didn't you? It's not much good.

BARRILDO   What? You don't mean to say you could
Compose a better song than that?

FRONDOSO   He's more familiar with the lash
Than with the melodies of verse.

10 MENGO   Don't shrink, but some have suffered worse.
One man that blackguard didn't thrash
Was taken to the vale one day . . .

BARRILDO   Stop, Mengo, please! Be merciful!
That homicidal animal

15 Dishonors all who pass his way.

MENGO   A hundred soldiers—not one less—
Administered my pummeling.
I'd nothing on me but my sling
And never suffered such duress.

20 But, as I was just saying, a
Fine man whose name I won't evoke,
Esteemed by all the village folk,
Was given quite the enema
Of ink and pebbles all in one.

25 Who'd stand for vileness of that sort?

BARRILDO   The savage looked on it as sport.

MENGO   Well, enemas are far from fun

And, while they are salubrious,
I'd rather that my death come fast.

30 FRONDOSO   So, may we hear now at long last
The ditty you've composed for us?

MENGO   *Oh, many happy years to you,*
Dear newlyweds! God's grace decree
That envy and vile jealousy
35 *Should never come between you two!*
And when your years on earth are through,
Depart this life from satiety!
Oh, many happy years!

FRONDOSO   A curse upon the rhyming hack
40 Who dashed off such a poor refrain!

BARRILDO   It did sound hasty.

MENGO   Let me deign
To say a word about this pack:
You know how fritter-makers throw
Their bits of batter in the oil
45 And add more as they watch it boil
Until the kettle's filled with dough?
How some look swollen when they're turned,
Misshapen and a sorry sight,
Some lumpy on the left or right,
50 Some nicely fried but others burned?
That's what I've come to understand
A poet does to draft a strain,
Material sprung from his brain
Like dough he forms with pen in hand.
55 Then, whoosh! He plops the poetry
On sheets—the role the kettle plays—
Assuming that a honey glaze
Will mute the public's mockery.
Though once the audience takes a look,
60 There's scarce a buyer to be found
Because the only one around
Who'll eat that rubbish is the cook!

BARRILDO   I think we've heard enough of this;
It's time the lovers made a speech.

65 LAURENCIA   Give us your hand, sir, we beseech.

JUAN ROJO   Sweet child, my hand you wish to kiss?
First ask your father for this grace
On both yours and Frondoso's part.

ESTEBAN   I pray God sees it in His heart
70 To fold them in His fond embrace
And bless the new life they've begun.

FRONDOSO   May you both bless us all life long.

JUAN ROJO   We shall. Come, lads, let's have a song
For now these two are joined as one!

75 MUSICIANS   *The maid with flowing tresses roamed*
Through Fuenteovejuna's vale

And all the while, unknown to her,
A Knight of Calatrava trailed.
She hid within the leafy wood,
80 *Pretending she had spied him not*
And, by turns bashful and abashed,
Concealed herself amid the copse.
"Why do you steal away, fair lass?"
He asked the maiden in the grove,
85 *"You know full well my lynx-eyed love*
Has penetrated walls of stone."
The knight approached the maiden who,
Abashed and quite disquieted,
Began to fashion jealousies
90 *From boughs entangled overhead.*
But just as anyone who loves
Will think it insignificant
To cross the mountains and the seas,
The knight asked his fair maid again:
95 *"Why do you steal away, fair lass,*
My lovely maiden in the grove?
You know full well my lynx-eyed love
Has penetrated walls of stone."

[*Enter the* COMMANDER, FLORES, ORTUÑO, *and* CIMBRANOS.]

COMMANDER   Don't stop the feast on my account.
100 Calm now, no need to be distraught.
JUAN ROJO   We recognize you're in command,
But this, sir, is no game you halt.
Sit here if you would stay. What cause
Is there for such warlike array?
105 Had you some triumph? But, why ask?
FRONDOSO   Stars, I'm a dead man! Send me aid!
LAURENCIA   Frondoso, flee while you've the chance!
COMMANDER   Not this time. Bind the peasant tight.
JUAN ROJO   Resign yourself to prison, son.
110 FRONDOSO   I'll never leave the place alive!
JUAN ROJO   Why? What is your offense?
COMMANDER   I'm not
The sort to kill without due cause
For, if I were, this cur who stands
Before us would by now have lost
115 His life, run through here by my guard.
Confine him to a prison cell
Until his father should pronounce
The punishment his crime compels.
PASCUALA   Please, sir, not on his wedding day.
120 COMMANDER   Why should these nuptials change my mind?
Are there no other men in town?
PASCUALA   You're able to forgive his crime;
You have that power.
COMMANDER   Were I the one

Aggrieved, Pascuala, then I could.
125 But Master Téllez Girón was
Insulted by this criminal,
His Order and his honor both,
And it's imperative that all
Bear witness to this punishment
130 In case some other foe feels called
To raise a standard versus his.
You may have heard one afternoon
He aimed a crossbow at the chest—
My vassals, such a loyal group!—
135 Of your esteemed commander here.
ESTEBAN   Sir, if a father-in-law may
Defend a deed of his new son,
It isn't hard to contemplate
How someone so in love as he
140 Might well have rankled with chagrin
If it is certain you conspired
To take his wife away from him.
What swain would not have done the same?
COMMANDER   You're talking nonsense, magistrate.
145 ESTEBAN   I speak for your own virtue, sir.
COMMANDER   I'm innocent of all you claim;
She wasn't yet his wife back then.
ESTEBAN   You're guilty, sir. I'll say no more
But rest assured the king and queen
150 Who rule Castile will issue forth
New orders for disorder's end.
They'd be remiss, though now at rest
From war, to suffer that their towns
And far-flung villages let men
155 As powerful and cruel as you
Display a cross so grandiose.
This sign is but for noble breasts
So let it grace the monarch's robes
And not the cloaks of lesser men.
160 COMMANDER   You, there! Relieve him of the staff.
ESTEBAN   Obedient, I surrender it.
COMMANDER [Striking ESTEBAN.]   I'll use it on you as I'd lash
An untamed and unruly horse.
ESTEBAN   As you're my lord, I must submit.
PASCUALA   You'd cudgel an old man like that?
165 LAURENCIA   He thrashes him because he is
My sire. Avenge yourself on me!
COMMANDER   You, take her to the prison grounds
And station ten guards at her cell.
          [The COMMANDER exits with his men.]
ESTEBAN   Sweet heavens, send your justice down!
          [Exit ESTEBAN.]

170 PASCUALA   The wedding has become a wake!

        [*Exit* PASCUALA.]

BARRILDO   Who'll speak? Are there no men around?

MENGO   I took my licks, thanks much! The welts
  Are red as cardinals[5] on my back
  So save yourselves that trip to Rome!

175   Let someone else provoke his wrath.

JUAN ROJO   We'll speak to him as one.

MENGO   Perhaps,
  Though now we'd best let silence reign;
  Don't you recall they whipped my cheeks
  Till they were pink as salmon steaks?

3.1

[SCENE: *The council chamber in Fuenteovejuna.*]

      [*Enter* ESTEBAN, ALONSO, *and* BARRILDO.]

ESTEBAN   What's keeping them?

BARRILDO   They know full well we wait.

ESTEBAN   Assembling here grows riskier by the hour.

BARRILDO   Most everyone's heard why we congregate.

ESTEBAN   With poor Frondoso captive in the tower

5   And my Laurencia under such duress,
  If God does not do all within His power . . .

      [*Enter* JUAN ROJO *and* CUADRADO.]

JUAN ROJO   Why raise your voice, Esteban, when our chief
  Aid must be stealth if we're to have success?

ESTEBAN   My false restraint should bring none here relief.

      [*Enter* MENGO.]

10 MENGO   I'll slip into the meeting hall as well.

ESTEBAN   An old man whose gray hairs are bathed in grief
  Asks you, good villagers, how best the bell
  For our dear town's lost honor might be tolled
  Now that she's been so ravished and abused.

15   And how, if these be honors, can we hold
  Such rites? Is there a single man left here
  Whom that barbarian has not unsoulled?
  Why don't you answer? Is it, as I fear,
  That you've all had your honor basely used?

20   Then, make your firm commiseration clear
  For, if this common loss can't be excused,
  What stays your hand? Or have these blows been slight?

JUAN ROJO   The world knows none more wretched and diffused
  Though news now reaching us appears more bright:

25   The Catholic kings, who brought peace to Castile,
  Will stop soon in Cordova, where we might

---

5. Newly invested cardinals of the Catholic Church are given a scarlet cap, and other scarlet garments also signify their rank.

Dispatch two aldermen who'll sue until
They're pledged redress, bowed at their royal feet.

BARRILDO   Before the monarchs do come, though, we will
30   Still need to find a remedy to meet
This enemy in that our king, who smote
So many foes, has others yet to beat.

CUADRADO   If anyone here asks me for my vote,
I vote that we forsake this baneful town.

35 JUAN ROJO   We haven't time; besides, they might take note.

MENGO   If the Commander hears the noise, he'll frown
So on this council, he might kill us all.

CUADRADO   Our tree of patience has come crashing down,
Our ship of fear floats lost beneath this pall.
40   For such an upright man, who leads this land,
To watch his daughter dragged away in thrall
To brutes, and have the staff of his command
So splintered on his head, I ask of you,
What slave endures more from his master's hand?

45 JUAN ROJO   What is it you would have our village do?

CUADRADO   Die, die or put those tyrants to the sword.
We've many villagers, while they are few.

BARRILDO   Rise up in arms against our rightful lord?

ESTEBAN   The king's our only lord by heaven's laws,
50   Not that barbaric and inhuman horde.
If God assists us in our righteous cause,
What have we all to lose?

MENGO   Take care, good sirs,
Rash actions such as these should give us pause.
I speak for all the simple villagers
55   Who bear the brunt of this vile injury
And fear still more harm from these tormentors.

JUAN ROJO   We suffer this misfortune equally;
Why should we wait until our lives are lost?
They burn our homes and vineyards down with glee;
60   Revenge upon such tyrants bears no cost!

[*Enter* LAURENCIA, *disheveled.*]

LAURENCIA   You let me pass, for I've a right
To enter where the men confer.
A woman may not have a vote
But she can make her voice be heard.
65   Don't you know me?

ESTEBAN   Good God, are you
My daughter?

JUAN ROJO   You don't recognize
Your own Laurencia?

LAURENCIA   I'm afraid
I must appear a dreadful sight
For you to doubt it's I you see.

70 ESTEBAN   My child!

LAURENCIA   Don't dare call me your child
  Again.
ESTEBAN   Why not, my dearest heart,
  Why not?
LAURENCIA   I've reasons of all kinds,
  But let the first among them be
  Allowing tyrants, unavenged,
75 To snatch me from my family's grasp
  Without you seeking due revenge.
  I'm not Frondoso's wife yet, so
  You cannot claim reprisal's weight
  Devolves upon a husband's lot
80 When such revenge is yours to take.
  Until the wedding night has passed,
  Our codes prescribe that you'd assume
  This obligation stands among
  A father's duties, not a groom's.
85 For even if I buy a jewel,
  Until it isn't brought to me,
  It's not my place to fret about
  Who's guarding it or who's a thief.
  You watched Fernán Gómez abduct
90 A maid and didn't lift a hand
  Like coward shepherds who allow
  The wolf to carry off the lamb.
  How many daggers at my heart
  And gallant speeches I endured!
95 How many threats and foul misdeeds
  From one who'd be my paramour
  And yearned to see my chastity
  Surrendered to his appetites!
  Look at my hair for evidence
100 Of how I fought him through the night
  And see the blood spilt by his blows.
  Have you no honor left as men?
  Have I no kinsmen here, no sire?
  How has my sorry plight not left
105 Your likes contorted with the pain
  Of seeing me so cruelly pained?
  You're lambs, the sheep from which our town's
  Old sheep well takes its timid name![6]
  Give me your weapons, then, if you'd
110 Stand useless there like stones, bronze shards
  Or jasper blocks. Brute tigers! No,
  Not tigers. While these creatures are
  Unfeeling, they hunt down and kill
  The beasts that rob them of their cubs.

6. *Fuente ovejuna*, "fount (or well) of sheep" (Spanish).

115   Not even waves can harbor those
     That venture to attack their young.
     You cowards were born craven hares,
     Not Spaniards but barbarians,
     Frail chickens—hens!—whose women are
120   Abandoned to their captors' whims!
     Wear distaffs[7] on your belts, not swords!
     Why even gird those rapiers on?
     By God above, I'll see to it
     That only womenfolk respond
125   To tyrants who'd leave honor stained
     By seeking their perfidious blood!
     They'll just throw stones at you and laugh,
     You spinning women! Powder puffs,
     You're cowardly as little girls!
130   Perhaps, tomorrow you can use
     Our headdresses and petticoats
     Or make your faces up with rouge!
     That cruel Commander, meanwhile, plans
     To hang Frondoso for his crime
135   From high upon a battlement
     In secret and without a trial.
     He'll do the same to all of us,
     You half-men, which I wouldn't spurn
     For, with its women dead, our town
140   Would see its honor cleansed as earth
     Reverted to that Golden Age
     Of Amazons[8] who made men quake.

ESTEBAN   Brave child, I cannot count myself
     Among those you would designate
145   With such dishonorable terms.
     I'll go myself now, even if
     The whole world stands against my cause.

JUAN ROJO   I, too, however daunted with
     The power of this enemy.

150 CUADRADO   We'll die together, then.

BARRILDO   A rag
     Tied to a stick is flag enough.
     Now let those monsters breathe their last!

JUAN ROJO   What order should we recognize?

MENGO   Kill all of them disorderly!
155   The village must be of one mind
     And all the villagers agreed
     The tyrant and his men must die.

ESTEBAN   Then grab your cudgels and your bows,
     Your pikes and swords and lances, too!

---

7. Staffs used in spinning to hold flax or wool, and a traditional symbol of women's work and of women in general.

8. In classical mythology, a fierce race of women warriors.

160 MENGO   Long live the Catholic kings, our sole
　　True lords!
　　ALL　　　　　Long may they live and reign!
　　MENGO   And death to tyrant traitors! Death!
　　ALL　Yes, traitorous tyrants, you must die!
　　　　　[*The men exit.*]
　　LAURENCIA [*To the village women.*]   The heavens echo your behest,
165　So forward, women of the town!
　　March on if you would set about
　　Regaining your lost honor! March!
　　　　　[*Enter* PASCUALA, JACINTA, *and other village women.*]
　　PASCUALA   What's happening? We heard these shouts.
　　LAURENCIA   Girls, can't you see the town is off
170　To kill Fernán Gómez today?
　　The merest boys have joined the men
　　To send that devil to his grave.
　　But why should they alone enjoy
　　The honor stemming from this feat?
175　As women we have suffered most
　　The outrage from his foul misdeeds.
　　JACINTA   What is it you would have us do?
　　LAURENCIA   Let's all of us form ordered ranks
　　And undertake an act so bold
180　We'll leave the wondering world aghast.
　　Jacinta, for your suffering,
　　I name you corporal; you're in charge
　　Of this brave women's squadron here.
　　JACINTA   Yet you've endured much worse by far.
185　LAURENCIA   Pascuala, standard-bearer, right?
　　PASCUALA   I'll look around here for a pole
　　So we can hoist a flag on it.
　　You'll see I'm worthy of the post!
　　LAURENCIA   We haven't time for that right now
190　Since fortune presses us to fight
　　But let us use our headdresses
　　As pennants we can wave on high.
　　PASCUALA   We'll have to name a captain, though.
　　LAURENCIA   Not true.
　　PASCUALA　　　　　　How so?
　　LAURENCIA　　　　　　　　Because who needs
195　El Cid or Rodomonte[9] when
　　It's I who'll lead with gallantry?

---

9. Both great fighters. Rodomonte, a major character in Ludovico Ariosto's Italian epic *Orlando Furioso* (1516, 1532), is a fearsome and boastful leader of the Moors; El Cid ("the Lord"; Arabic) is Rodrigo (or Ruy) Díaz de Vivar (ca. 1043–1099), a Spanish military leader who is the hero of the 12th-century Castilian epic *The Poem of My Cid.*

3.2

[SCENE: *Almagro. A room in the* COMMANDER'*s residence.*]

[*Enter* FRONDOSO *with his hands bound,* FLORES, ORTUÑO, CIMBRANOS, *and the* COMMANDER.]

COMMANDER   Now take the extra rope you used to bind
His hands and hang him so he's punished more.
FRONDOSO   You're leaving a black legacy behind.
COMMANDER   This battlement should serve us on that score.
5   FRONDOSO   But sir, it never even crossed my mind
To seek your death!
FLORES   What's all the ruckus for?
[*Loud noise is heard offstage.*]
COMMANDER   What ruckus?
FLORES   Would the peasants in this town
Obstruct our justice?
ORTUÑO   Sir, the doors are down!
[*The noise grows louder.*]
COMMANDER   How dare they when they know this is the seat
10   Of our command?
FLORES   They to a man rebel!
JUAN ROJO [*Offstage*]   Now burn and raze the place! We'll not retreat!
ORTUÑO   These popular revolts are hard to quell.
COMMANDER   They rise against their lord?
FLORES   The peasants beat
15   Your doors down, sir, from grudges that impel
Their fury on.
COMMANDER   Come, set the prisoner free.
Frondoso, calm the magistrate for me.
FRONDOSO   Yes, sir. It's love that made their passion wake.
[*He exits.*]
MENGO [*Offstage*]   May Ferdinand and Isabel prevail!
20   But death to traitors!
FLORES   Sir, for your own sake
I urge you, flee!
COMMANDER   It's futile to assail
A garrison one cannot hope to take.
They'll soon turn back.
FLORES   Those wronged on such a scale
Aren't likely to retreat until blood flows
25   And they've exacted vengeance on their foes.
COMMANDER   We'll make a stand here at the door and fight,
A false portcullis marking out our cage.[1]
FRONDOSO [*Offstage*]   On, Fuenteovejuna!
COMMANDER   Hey, they've quite
A leader there! I say we meet their rage.
30   FLORES   It's your rage, sir, not theirs that gives me fright.

---

1. That is, their swords will serve as a portcullis, protecting them with metal.

ESTEBAN   The tyrant and accomplices, I wage.
  Fight, Fuenteovejuna! Tyrants, die!
          [*Enter all.*]
COMMANDER   Wait, men!
ALL   Redress cannot sit idly by.
COMMANDER   Then tell me where I've erred. In my renown
  For chivalry, I'll make it up to you.
35 ALL   On, Fuenteovejuna, for the crown!
  Die, wicked Christians and false traitors, too!
COMMANDER   I'm speaking to you and you shout me down?
  I am your rightful lord!
ALL   Our sole true lords
  Remain the Catholic kings!
40 COMMANDER   Men, wait. Stand by!
ALL   On, Fuenteovejuna! Now you die!
          [*The* COMMANDER *and his men flee, pursued by the men of Fuenteovejuna.*
          Enter the village women, armed.]
LAURENCIA   Let's stop a bit and reconnoiter here,
  Not women now but valiant fighting men!
PASCUALA   For vengefulness, a woman has no peer.
  We'll spill his blood right here! If not now, when?
45 JACINTA   Then let's impale his body on a spear.
PASCUALA   We've said we ought to time and time again.
ESTEBAN [*Offstage*]   Now die, Commander traitor!
COMMANDER   Here's my death!
  I beg Your mercy, Lord, with my last breath.
BARRILDO [*Offstage*]   There's Flores!
50 MENGO   That's the rogue so quick to dole
  My lashes out. Lay into him and how!
FRONDOSO [*Offstage*]   I'll be avenged when I tear out his soul!
LAURENCIA   We need no leave to enter.
PASCUALA   Steady now.
  We'll guard the door.
BARRILDO [*Offstage*]   I've lost all self-control
55 So, tears, my lordships, we can disallow.
LAURENCIA   I'm going in, Pascuala, for my sword
  Must stay unsheathed until my name's restored.
          [*She exits.*]
BARRILDO [*Offstage*]   Look, there's Ortuño!
FRONDOSO [*Offstage*]   Slash his ugly face!
          [FLORES *enters, fleeing, with* MENGO *in pursuit.*]
FLORES   Have mercy, Mengo, please! I'm not to blame!
60 MENGO   If being his pimp could not secure our case,
  My flogging would impeach you all the same.
PASCUALA   Come, hand him to us women. Where's the race,
  Man? Stop your pointless running.
MENGO   Sure, I'm game.
  This sounds like punishment enough to me.
65 PASCUALA   You'll be avenged.

MENGO   That's all I want to see.

JACINTA   Die!

FLORES   Being killed by women isn't just.

JACINTA   Seems quite a turn of fate.

PASCUALA   What tears are these?

JACINTA   Perverse procurer for your master's lust!

70 PASCUALA   Oh, die now, traitor!

FLORES   Mercy, ladies, please!

[*Enter* ORTUÑO, *fleeing from* LAURENCIA.]

ORTUÑO   Look here, I'm not . . .

LAURENCIA   I know you well, I trust!
     Come, let the blood of these vile dogs appease
     Your swords!

PASCUALA   Oh, let me meet death slaughtering!

ALL   On, Fuenteovejuna! Thrive, dear king!

[*Exit all.*]

3.3

[SCENE: *A room in the palace of the Catholic kings.*]

[*Enter King* FERDINAND, *Queen* ISABEL, *and Don* MANRIQUE.]

MANRIQUE   Our plan of action worked so well
     That all objectives were attained
     And we were met with no sustained
     Resistance as the city fell.
5   The opposition, sire, was light
     But, had their side presented more
     To counteract our force at war,
     It surely would have proven slight.
     The Count of Cabra stays behind
10   To guard the city from attack
     In case their army doubles back
     To mount a second thrust in kind.

FERDINAND   We deem it wise that he remain
     To muster and command our troops,
15   Ensuring that our force regroups
     And curbing passage through the plain.
     It ought to be impossible
     For any harm to blight us, then,
     Although Alfonso gathers men
20   To join his force in Portugal.
     It's fitting that the city should
     Be left in such reliable hands
     For, where our able Count commands,
     All marvel at his hardihood.
25   In this way, he can turn aside
     The danger threatening our realm,
     A loyal guardian at the helm
     Who'll keep our kingdom fortified.

[*Enter* FLORES, *wounded.*]

FLORES   King Ferdinand, good Catholic sire,
30   To whom the heavens did concede
     The crown of proud Castile in light
     Of all your noble qualities,
     Attend to this account of acts
     Unmatched in cruelty by men
35   Throughout this world, from where the sun
     First rises bright to where it sets.

FERDINAND   Come, steady now, man!

FLORES   Sovereign king,
     The wounds you see would not consent
     To my delaying this report
40   For this life surely nears its end.
     In Fuenteovejuna, sire,
     That farming town from which I've fled,
     The people with inclement breast
     Have put their rightful lord to death.
45   Fernán Gómez lies murdered there,
     A victim of the grievances
     Perfidious vassals claimed to bear,
     For those aggrieved scarce need pretext.
     Thus, dubbing him tyrannical
50   By full consensus, these vile plebs
     Became emboldened over time
     To carry out this treachery.
     They stormed through the Commander's home
     And, though he was a nobleman,
55   Did not provide him with the chance
     To quit these debts and make amends.
     Not only were his pleas ignored
     But, spurred by their impulsiveness,
     The villagers left him with wounds
60   That rent the cross worn on his chest
     Then hurled him out a window down
     Into a furious waiting horde
     Of women, who proceeded to
     Impale him on their pikes and swords.
65   They dragged his body to a house
     And, each displaying greater rage,
     Began to pluck his hair and beard
     While cruelly slicing up his face.
     So outsized did their fury seem
70   And fierce their mounting hate appear,
     The largest pieces left intact
     On the Commander were his ears!
     Expunging, next, his coat of arms,
     They shouted that they wished, instead,
75   To march beneath your own because
     The former caused them great offense.

Then, lastly, they ransacked his home
As if it were some enemy's
And happily among themselves
80   Divided up his property.
All this I saw with my two eyes
For, infelicitously, fate
Would not consent that I should die
While lying in my hiding place,
85   My wounds fresh, waiting out the day
In hope the dark of night would come
So I could steal away unseen
And tell you what the town had done.
You're merciful and just, good sire,
90   So see these wanton criminals
Are punished by your code of law
For acts so reprehensible.
Oh, hear his spilt blood crying out
And make them pay harsh recompense!
95 FERDINAND   Brave fellow, you may rest assured
They won't escape our punishment.
So grievous are these late events
We find ourselves bereft of words
And therefore deem it best a judge
100   Should verify such deeds occurred
To castigate the culpable
And make examples of their breed.
A captain shall escort him hence
To warrant his security.
105   Malfeasance such as this deserves
Exemplary punition soon.
But now, look to this soldier here
And be attentive to his wounds.
                    [*Exit all.*]

3.4

[SCENE: *The town square in Fuenteovejuna.*]
          [*Enter the villagers, with the head of the* COMMANDER,
          Fernán Gómez, on a lance.]
MUSICIANS   *Oh, many happy years*
          To you, good Catholic kings,
          And death to tyrants all!
BARRILDO   Frondoso, let's hear your song now.
5 FRONDOSO   Here goes, however freshly penned.
Let quibblers with my meter mend
The verse the best way they know how.
          Long live our lovely Isabel
          And Ferdinand of Aragon,
10   *Whose union is a paragon*

And who, though two, are one as well!
St. Michael[2] take you both to dwell
In heaven when you hear God's call.
Long life to you, we wish,
15 *But death to tyrants all!*

LAURENCIA   Your turn, Barrildo.

BARRILDO   Here goes mine.
I put a lot of thought in it.

PASCUALA   Recite the poem as you see fit
And it should come out sounding fine.

20 BARRILDO   *Oh, many happy years to you,*
Famed monarchs, fresh from victory!
From this day forward you shall be
Our lords, who bring us luck anew!
May evil dwarves and giants, too,
25 *Succumb before your battle call*
And death to tyrants all!

MUSICIANS   *Oh, many happy years*
To you, good Catholic kings,
And death to tyrants all!

30 LAURENCIA   Now Mengo sing.

FRONDOSO   Let's hear your stuff.

MENGO   I dabble, so I'll take a whack.

PASCUALA   Those hash marks on your belly's back
Are witness you've had whacks enough!

MENGO   *'Twas on a lovely Sunday morn*
35 *When I, on orders of this here,*
Was whipped until my aching rear
Writhed frightfully, its soft skin torn,
I bearing what hence won't be borne.
Long live our Christian monarchers
40 *And death to all these tyranters!*

MUSICIANS   *Oh, many happy years!*

ESTEBAN   Remove his noggin from that lance.

MENGO   His face has all a hanged man's charms.

[*Enter* JUAN ROJO, *bearing an escutcheon with the royal coat of arms.*]

CUADRADO   Look here, the royal coat of arms.

45 ESTEBAN   Let our whole village cast a glance.

JUAN ROJO   Where should its splendidness be hung?

CUADRADO   Right here, upon our own town hall.

ESTEBAN   Shine on, brave shield!

BARRILDO   Bring joy to all!

FRONDOSO   The warm sun rising here among
50 These symbols hails a bright new day.

ESTEBAN   Long live León! Castile, live on,
And prosper, bars of Aragon,[3]

---

2. The archangel who, in Christian tradition, guides the souls of the faithful to heaven.

3. That is, heraldic bars (see 2.1.261 and n). *León:* a province of northwest Spain.

But death to tyrants and their sway!
Dear Fuenteovejuna, heed
55 The sage advice of this old man
For none who've marked my counsel can
Affirm I've ventured to mislead.
It won't be long before the crown
Sends someone to investigate
60 The goings-on round here of late
And, with the king lodged near our town,
We ought devise, while there's still time,
Some pretext no one can dismiss.

FRONDOSO   Your thoughts?

ESTEBAN   Claim unto death that this
65 Was Fuenteovejuna's crime
And not have anyone confess.

FRONDOSO   The murder, all must be agreed,
Was Fuenteovejuna's deed.

ESTEBAN   Is this how we will answer?

ALL   Yes!

70 ESTEBAN   Why don't I act like I've the task
Of the investigator now
So I might best instruct you how
To face the questions he will ask?
Here, let's have Mengo be the first
75 Upon the rack.

MENGO   You couldn't choose
A frailer guy?

ESTEBAN   I'll only use
You to rehearse.

MENGO   Then, do your worst!

ESTEBAN   Who killed the town's Commander, you?

MENGO   All Fuenteovejuna, sir!

80 ESTEBAN   Don't make me torture you, vile cur!

MENGO   Kill me and it would still be true!

ESTEBAN   Confess, thief!

MENGO   I do as I'm told.

ESTEBAN   So?

MENGO   Fuenteovejuna! There!

ESTEBAN   Pull tight.

MENGO   It's nothing I can't bear.

85 ESTEBAN   We'll foul up any trial they hold!

[Enter CUADRADO.]

CUADRADO   What are you doing, dallying here?

FRONDOSO   Cuadrado, what's so troublesome?

CUADRADO   The crown's investigator's come.

ESTEBAN   Hide quickly while the coast is clear!

90 CUADRADO   A captain also guards the man.

ESTEBAN   The Devil watch his back this day!
We all know what we have to say.

CUADRADO   They're seizing everyone they can
        As hardly any soul has hid.
95 ESTEBAN   There's no need fear should make us weak.
        You, who killed the Commander? Speak!
        MENGO   Who? Fuenteovejuna did!
            [*Exit all.*]

3.5

[SCENE: ALMAGRO. *A room in the mansion of the* MASTER *of Calatrava.*]

            [*Enter the* MASTER *of Calatrava and a* SOLDIER.]

MASTER   This murderous deed's left me distraught.
        That such should be his last reward!
        I ought to put you to the sword
        As payment for the news you've brought.
5   SOLDIER   I'm just a message-bearer, sir,
        And never meant to stir your wrath.
    MASTER   Their outrage in the aftermath
        Of insult caused this to occur!
        I'll take five hundred men with me
10   And raze the village to the ground.
        The lawless names of those still found
        There will be struck from memory.
    SOLDIER   You might well calm such fury down
        As they're now subjects of the king
15   And surely not for anything
        Would one wish to enrage the crown.
    MASTER   But they fall under my command
        So whence their fealty to Castile?
    SOLDIER   These grievances our own courts will
20   Consider when the time's at hand.
    MASTER   Now when did any such assize
        Remove possessions from the throne?
        They are our sovereign lords, I own,
        A truth I duly recognize.
25   We're all the monarch's vassals now
        And, given this, I'll check my ire
        Although an audience with my sire
        Might serve my case best and allow
        A youthful aspect to excuse
30   Whatever grave offense I've done.
        My tender age may well be one
        Defense this loyal heart can use.
        I'll go to see the king in shame,
        Compelled by honor to proceed
35   With fortitude in pressing need
        To clear my honorable name.
            [*They exit.*]

3.6

[SCENE: *The town square in Fuenteovejuna.*]

[*Enter* LAURENCIA, *alone.*]

LAURENCIA   True love's concern for its beloved's good
  Becomes thereafter love's appended pain
  For fear harm may befall love is a bane
  That brings concern as all new worries would.
5 Though watchful thought decrease this likelihood,
  The mind, perturbed, will readily show strain
  As love's well-being, stolen, roils the brain,
  A torment nowise easily withstood.
  I do adore my husband and this dire
10 Occasion will condemn me to duress
  Should fortune fail to favor him on high.
  His happiness is all that I desire;
  When he is present, sure is my distress,
  When he is absent, just as sure I die.

[*Enter* FRONDOSO.]

15 FRONDOSO   Laurencia, love!
LAURENCIA   Sweet husband, here?
  This move displays a steely nerve!
FRONDOSO   Does such solicitude deserve
  This cold reception from you, dear?
LAURENCIA   I beg you, darling mine, beware,
20 For here you'll meet a ghastly end.
FRONDOSO   Laurencia, may the skies forfend
  That my well-being should cause you care.
LAURENCIA   Aren't you afraid to view the throes
  Your townsmen face in their ordeal
25 Or the investigator's zeal
  In hastening to inflict their woes?
  Stay out of harm's way while you can
  And flee before they capture you.
FRONDOSO   What? How could you expect me to
30 Do deeds unworthy of a man?
  Would it be proper to betray
  The others in this circumstance
  Or not see you when I've the chance?
  Don't order me to go away.
35 What reason would there be for me
  To save myself, untouched and whole,
  But not acknowledge my own soul
  When facing such calamity?

[*Cries are heard offstage.*]

  If I can trust my ears, it seems
40 The noise I'm hearing are the cries
  Some tortured wretch hurls toward the skies.
  Come listen closely to his screams.

[*The* JUDGE *is heard interrogating villagers offstage.*]

JUDGE   The truth and you'll be freed, kind gent.
FRONDOSO   They torture an old man to make
45   Him speak.
LAURENCIA   He's too strong-willed to break.
ESTEBAN   Pray, loose the ropes a bit.
JUDGE   Relent.
   Now say, who killed Fernán, good man?
ESTEBAN   Give Fuenteovejuna blame.
LAURENCIA   Brave father, may God praise your name!
50 FRONDOSO   What courage!
JUDGE   Grab that boy there. Wretch!
   Lay on! Still tighter, mongrel. I'm
   Convinced you know. Who did this crime?
   No answer? Stretch him, drunkard, stretch!
BOY   Sir, Fuenteovejuna did!
55 JUDGE   Dumb clods, by all the king commands,
   I'll strangle you with my own hands!
   Who murdered the Commander, kid?
FRONDOSO   To think a tender lad could face
   Such torment and resist so long!
60 LAURENCIA   Brave villagers!
FRONDOSO   Yes, brave and strong!
JUDGE   You, seize that woman there and place
   Her body next upon the rack.
   Now it will be the maiden's turn.
LAURENCIA   His anger's causing him to burn.
65 JUDGE   You'll tell me or I'll kill the pack
   Of you right here if he's not caught.
   Which one's the guilty villager?
PASCUALA   It's Fuenteovejuna, sir!
JUDGE   Still tighter!
FRONDOSO   This is all for naught.
70 LAURENCIA   Pascuala hasn't said a thing.
FRONDOSO   The children, either. What's to fear?
JUDGE   Have you bewitched the townsfolk here?
   Pull!
PASCUALA   Heaven ease my suffering!
75 JUDGE   What are you, deaf? I told you, pull!
PASCUALA   Still Fuenteovejuna, yes!
JUDGE   That fat oaf clad in tattered dress
   Is next, the one whose paunch looks full.
LAURENCIA   Poor Mengo! Who else could it be?
80 FRONDOSO   Though no one's broken yet, he might.
MENGO   Ow, ow!
JUDGE   Just slowly stretch him tight.
MENGO   Ow!
JUDGE   This should jog your memory.
MENGO   Ow, ow!
JUDGE   Come, bumpkin, out with it:
   Who laid the town's Commander low?

85 MENGO   Please stop! I'll tell you all I know!
   JUDGE   You, let up on the ropes a bit.
   FRONDOSO   He's breaking.
   JUDGE   Use your back until
   The lever halts.
   MENGO   I'll tell you when
   You stop!
   JUDGE   All right, who slew him, then?
90 MENGO   Old Fuenteovejunaville!
   JUDGE   I've never seen such villainy!
   They make a mockery of pain!
   The one I thought could least refrain
   From talking held up valiantly.
95   I'm weary. Come, let us depart.
   FRONDOSO   Good Mengo, may God keep you near!
   Your courage has dispelled the fear
   I felt for us both in my heart.

             [*Enter* MENGO, BARRILDO, *and* CUADRADO.]

   BARRILDO   Three cheers there, Mengo!
   CUADRADO   Yes, my word!
100 BARRILDO   And one cheer more!
   FRONDOSO   That was some feat!
   MENGO   Ooh!
   BARRILDO   Here, friend, have a bit to eat
   And drink.
   MENGO   What is it?
   BARRILDO   Lemon curd.
   MENGO   Ooh!
   FRONDOSO   There you go, man, drain the cup!
   BARRILDO   I knew you could.
105 FRONDOSO   He's swilling, so it must be good.
   LAURENCIA   More food here while he's drinking up.
   MENGO   Ooh, ooh!
   BARRILDO   This round is my treat, too.
   LAURENCIA   He's stately as he knocks them back.
   FRONDOSO   It's easy once you're off the rack.
110 BARRILDO   More?
   MENGO   Ooh! As long as it's on you . . .
   FRONDOSO   Drink up, old friend. Lord knows you've grounds.
   LAURENCIA   This makes one quaff per turn, all told.
   FRONDOSO   Bring him some clothes, he must be cold.
   BARRILDO   More still?
   MENGO   Uh, maybe three more rounds.
115   Ooh, ooh!
   FRONDOSO   Yooh . . . want the wine you've earned?
   BARRILDO   Yooh dooh? Here's more to slake your thirst.
   Home brew should fill resisters first.
   What's wrong?
   MENGO   I think this wine has turned.
   Let's go before I catch a chill.

120 FRONDOSO   This jug, you'll see, holds better wine,
    But who killed the Commander, swine?
  MENGO   Old Fuenteovejunaville!

    [*Exit all except* FRONDOSO *and* LAURENCIA.]

  FRONDOSO   He's honored by our show of love
    But could you please inform me, wife,
125 Who took the town Commander's life?
  LAURENCIA   Who? Fuenteovejuna, dove.
  FRONDOSO   Who killed him?
  LAURENCIA   Stop, you're scaring me!
    Sure, Fuenteovejuna, churl!
  FRONDOSO   And how did I slay you, sweet girl?
130 LAURENCIA   By loving me so tenderly.

    [*Exit* FRONDOSO *and* LAURENCIA.]

3.7

[SCENE: *Palace of the Catholic kings. The Queen's chamber.*]

    [*Enter* FERDINAND *and* ISABEL.]

  ISABEL   Your presence here is a surprise,
    My lord. Good fortune smiles on me.
  FERDINAND   You are a glorious sight to see,
    My queen, a comfort to these eyes.
5 We make for Portugal and seize
    This chance to stop en route and rest.
  ISABEL   Your Majesty knows when it's best
    To change his course and take his ease.
  FERDINAND   How did you leave our dear Castile?
10 ISABEL   In peace, sire, quiet and serene.
  FERDINAND   We wonder not when such a queen
    Imparts tranquillity at will.

    [*Enter Don* MANRIQUE.]

  MANRIQUE   Sire, Calatrava is now just
    Arrived and seeks an audience
15 With you in humble reverence
    To pledge his troth and ask your trust.
  ISABEL   It's been my hope to meet the lad.
  MANRIQUE   My lady, though he may look young,
    I promise you he ranks among
20 The finest soldiers we have had.

    [*The* MASTER *of Calatrava enters as Don* MANRIQUE *exits.*]

  MASTER   I'm Rodrigo Téllez Girón,
    Your servant, sire, and Master of
    The Calatravan ranks whose love
    Entreats forgiveness from the throne.
25 I here confess I've been deceived
    Into transgressing noble laws
    Established by Castile because
    Of faulty counsel I'd received

From cruel Fernán, who led me down
30 A road of false self-interest, true
But faithless. As you now construe,
I beg forgiveness of the crown
And, should Your Highness grant to me
This mercy, which I scarce deserve,
35 I promise this day forth to serve
The royal cause stoutheartedly
In, say, your long campaign, my lord,
Against Granada, where you ride
And where you will observe with pride
40 The valor latent in my sword
Whose unsheathed steel will bravely vie
With foes who'll suffer crushing loss
So I might drape my Order's cross
O'er Moorish battlements on high.
45 For this, I'll send five hundred men
To fight beside your own troops now
And hereby give my solemn vow,
Sire, never to displease again.

FERDINAND   Rise, Master, off this bended knee,
50 For we two hold your presence dear
And you are always welcome here.

MASTER   These favors are grief's remedy.

ISABEL   Your words are equally as fine
As your brave feats and gallant air.

55 MASTER   You are, dear queen, an Esther fair
And you a Xerxes,[4] sire, divine!

[Enter Don MANRIQUE.]

MANRIQUE   Your Majesty, the judge is back
From Fuenteovejuna, whence
He comes with news of the events
60 There that occasioned the attack.

FERDINAND   You judge the rogues who cut him down.

MASTER   I'd show them, were you not here, sire,
What doom awaits those who conspire
To kill Commanders of the crown.

65 FERDINAND   Their punishment rests with the throne.

ISABEL   I do confess, I'd love to see
My lord wield this authority
Should it please God this power be shown.

[Enter the JUDGE.]

JUDGE   I rode, sire, with due diligence
70 To Fuenteovejuna where,
Attending to my charge with care,
I acted with expedience,

---

4. The Greek name of the king of Persia (r. 486–465 B.C.E.) whom the Bible calls Ahasuerus. The Book of Esther recounts how he made Esther his queen, not knowing that she was Jewish, and how she prevented a massacre of her people.

Investigating how this crime
Was carried out before I'd come
75　But bear no signed confession from
A soul there after all this time.
The townsfolk spoke as one with stout
Conviction for their common good
And when I'd ask, "Who did this?" would
80　Shout "Fuenteovejuna" out!
Three hundred villagers there swore
That they knew nothing through their pain
And I despair we'll ever gain
More information on that score.
85　We even lashed lads ten years old
Upon the rack who held their peace
Despite our promises to cease
And other such things they were told.
In short, I've started so to frown
90　On finding someone to condemn
That either you must pardon them
Or else eradicate the town.
To second what I've said, sire, some
Have journeyed hence to make their case
95　And tell you more of this disgrace.

FERDINAND　Then let them enter if they've come.

[*Enter* ESTEBAN, ALONSO, FRONDOSO, LAURENCIA, *the village
women, and as many other villagers as are needed.*]

LAURENCIA　Are those the monarchs over there?

FRONDOSO　Castile's own might, however far.

LAURENCIA　My God, what handsome beings they are!
100　St. Anthony[5] exalt the pair!

ISABEL　Are these the murderers you mean?

ESTEBAN　Amassed before you at a stroke
Stand Fuenteovejuna's folk
Who humbly wish to serve their queen.
105　It was the tyranny and cursed
Insistence on purveying dread
Of that Commander who's now dead—
But not before he'd done his worst—
That was behind our vengeful role.
110　He had our scant possessions seized
And raped our women when he pleased,
All mercy alien to his soul.

FRONDOSO　So much so that when finally
This lovely lass the heavens sent
115　To make my heart on earth content
And me as happy as can be
Agreed to take me as her spouse,
He acted as if he'd been wived

5. St. Anthony of Padua (1195–1231), a Franciscan missionary who was born in Lisbon.

And, when our wedding night arrived,
120   Had her abducted to his house!
    Were that pure girl not prone to fend
    Off the advances he'd begun,
    I think it's clear to everyone
    Her virtue would have met its end.
125 MENGO   Is it not time I said a word?
    If, by your leave, I may say so,
    You'll all be scandalized to know
    How bruised I was by what occurred
    For rushing straight to the defense
130   Of one of our poor village girls
    As she was being snatched by churls
    To undergo some vile offense.
    My sorry derriere still aches
    From that perverted Nero's[6] lash
135   And darn it if they didn't thrash
    My backside pink as salmon steaks!
    Three men administered the belts
    So utterly unsparingly
    That I'm convinced you still can see
140   The stripes they left beneath the welts.
    All told, the ointment and the salve
    Concocted from the myrtle shrub
    Which I use as a soothing rub
    Are worth more than the farm I have!
145 ESTEBAN   In short, sire, we do gladly serve
    As humble vassals of the crown
    And have long since hung in our town
    Your coat of arms, which all observe.
    We ask, my lord, that you respond
150   With clement mercy in this case.
    To recompense this act of grace,
    We pledge our innocence as bond.
    FERDINAND   As it appears that at no time
    There'll be confessions signed in ink,
155   Though murder is most foul, we think
    To grant forgiveness for this crime.
    It's well the village should repair
    To the protection of Castile
    And may depend on us until
160   We send a new Commander there.
    FRONDOSO   This speech, Your Majesty, commends
    The measure of your providence.
    So with these words, wise audience,
    Here *Fuenteovejuna* ends.

---

6. A Roman emperor (r. 54–68 C.E.) notorious for his cruelty and dissolution.

PEDRO CALDERÓN DE LA BARCA

1600–1681

Pedro Calderón de la Barca's LIFE IS A DREAM (*La vida es sueño*, 1636) has long been revered among Spanish Golden Age dramas as a stage play and literary text of astonishing power. Yet what accounts for its unique popularity and ongoing fascination, hailing as it does from a period that remains comparatively little known outside Spain? At once a mythopoeic narrative of thwarted love and tarnished honor, transcending place and time, and a tale of contested monarchical succession that relies on specific political, cultural, religious, and social contexts of seventeenth-century Spain, *Life Is a Dream* interweaves the universal with the particular in a linguistically rich and theatrically vivid portrait of characters torn between competing desires and obligations. The play, which stands at the apogee of the era's dramaturgical development, remains Calderón's best-known and most-admired work.

Calderón was born in Madrid, to a family in the lower ranks of the nobility. In the expectation that he would enter the priesthood, he received an extensive education. After being taught by Jesuits, renowned for their disciplined approach to writing and critical thinking, he then studied the arts at the University of Alcalá and pursued further training in logic, philosophy, and theology at the University of Salamanca. He delayed taking holy orders, however,

and instead entered the service of the Constable of Castile, which brought him into the court circle of King Philip IV.

Long drawn to poetry and the arts, Calderón began writing plays in the early 1620s; his first play, *Amor, honor y poder* (*Love, Honor, and Power*), was produced in 1623. He appears to have led a rather wild young adulthood, replete with reports of dueling, profanation of a religious sanctuary, and other accusations of blasphemy. Nevertheless, he became a favorite at court and was named court dramatist in 1635. In this capacity, he helped create lavish spectacles that often featured complex stage effects, music, and dance. Meanwhile, he continued to write for the more modestly staged public theater as well, generating works in the forms—cloak and sword, honor and jealousy, nation and religion, and historical—popular with Spanish audiences. Calderón may have entered into a clandestine marriage around 1650; he fathered a child whom he finally acknowledged, and thereby legitimized, only after the mother's death. Just at this time, in 1651, he at last was ordained a priest. He became chaplain to the king, and though he continued to write for another thirty years, he turned his attention to a different form: the *auto sacramental*, or sacred play, which dramatizes Christian themes and narratives. Calderón died in 1681, leaving no immediate heir as a national dramatist. Court and public tastes shifted, first embracing Italian opera and then abandoning it and the religious drama on which he had focused in his latter decades. With Calderón's death, the Spanish Golden Age itself drew to a close.

At the start of Calderón's career, the works of LOPE DE VEGA (1562–1635) dominated the country's popular stage. Lope claimed to have written more than 1,500 plays in his lifetime, almost a third of them still extant. Performed in *corrales*, or open-air theaters originally built in the yards of connected houses, the *comedia*—a generic term for drama of the period—attracted a large, public audience drawn from all classes of Spanish society. Lope revised the established Italian dramatic form into the three-act structure that would become the Spanish national drama. By linking the acts to the basic concept of a narrative's beginning, middle, and end, Lope rejected the neo-Aristotelian ideas of dramaturgy, especially its five-act structure, that held sway elsewhere in Europe during the Renaissance. He similarly eschewed the neoclassical unities that constrained plot and action, favoring complex, lively narratives populated by characters adhering to familiar types. Lope wanted Spanish theater to reflect the country's culture and ethos; hence chivalry, Catholicism, nationalism, and a mixture of popular and erudite traditions all inform the Golden Age drama. Lope also introduced a unique polymetric verse form that signaled tonal shifts within the plays.

Calderón inherited and further reworked the *comedia* of Lope and other Golden Age dramatists. He introduced to his plays the poetic style known as "Gongorism," named for the celebrated Spanish poet Luis de Góngora y Argote (1561–1627) and characterized by the copious ornamentation and elaborate detail associated with the baroque period in the arts (1550–1750). Difficult to capture in translation, such verse incorporates extensive use of mythical allusion and visual imagery as well as highly stylized and calculatedly obscure language. Calderón also honed the double-plot structure of the *comedia* to closely attune his main plot and subplot in theme and action.

Life Is a Dream exemplifies these Calderónian advances in Spanish dramaturgy.

The play's main narrative concerns Prince Segismund of Poland, sequestered and chained in a cave since infancy by order of his father, King Basil, who feared an astrologer's prophecy that Segismund would bring grave harm to the kingdom. Compelled to live like an animal, and denied all comforts, the prince has matured without companionship or society, raised and taught only by the king's nobleman Clotaldo. Calderón gives us an unvarnished portrait of his protagonist; deeply philosophical and highly volatile, Segismund embodies both the great intellect and reason that befit a prince and the extremes of violence and passion associated with base humanity. His story overlaps and intersects with that of Rosaura, a young Russian woman who accidentally discovers the hidden prince. Disguised as a young man and accompanied by her servant Clarion, Rosaura has traveled from her native land to seek her unknown father and the restitution of her honor, lost when her lover Astolf, a prince and cousin to Segismund, abandoned her. The chance meeting irrevocably connects all their lives, initiating a chain of events that alters both personal and political fortunes. Calderón uses this opening to set up a poignant love triangle between Segismund, Astolf, and Rosaura, complicated by the issues of rulership affecting them all. King Basil learns of the unintended meeting shortly after he had decided to gauge the legitimacy of the prophecy by drugging the prince and bringing him to court to observe his behavior. If Segismund fails to pass the king's test, thereby proving himself unfit to be the next king, he will be drugged again and returned to his cave, to be told that what he experienced was only a dream.

The questions of whether one is asleep or awake, and whether what one experiences is life or a dream, underlie the familiar trope of the "Sleeper Awakened," a folktale that was a source for *La vida es sueño*. Calderón may also have drawn on classical literature to develop the narrative of inescapable fate that drives Basil to exile his son. SOPHOCLES' *Oedipus the King* (ca. 428 B.C.E.), which features the famous

Dominic West as Segismundo, prone and chained in his prison cell, in the 2009 Donmar Warehouse (London) production of *Life Is a Dream*.

oracle that a king's son will kill his father and marry his mother, seems a likely influence. Plato's "allegory of the cave," elaborated in book 3 of his *Republic* (ca. 375 B.C.E.), may have given Calderón the idea for his setting; in book 9, Plato notes the bestial desires in every man that are manifest in sleep. The image of Segismund chained to a rock in the opening cave scene also strongly evokes that of the mythical Prometheus, who, in AESCHYLUS's tragedy *Prometheus Bound* (ca. 450 B.C.E.), similarly bewails his isolation and torments himself with his fate. Yet *Life Is a Dream* is far from a derivative work; Calderón judiciously employed these resonant images from other texts to craft his own unique exploration of humanity, power, desire, and social order.

At the same time, Calderón used a specifically Spanish context to complicate and enrich *Life Is a Dream*. One of the critical challenges for readers and audiences today is how to reconcile the seeming contradictions between two aspects of this context that figure prominently in *La vida es sueño*:

the code of honor central to seventeenth-century Spanish culture and the tenets of Catholicism. The conflict between the necessity to avenge violated honor and the Christian commitment to mercy and forgiveness complicates the stories of both Segismund and Rosaura. The play's resolution of the most obvious moral injuries—Basil's dehumanizing treatment of his son and Astolf's cavalier behavior toward Rosaura—has traditionally confounded audiences and analysts alike but is inextricably tied to these core Spanish values.

Life Is a Dream clearly asks us to consider the quality of Basil's kingship, particularly his handling of the question of succession. Did he make the right choice by embracing the astrologer's prediction and exiling his infant son to protect himself and the kingdom, or should he have ignored the prophecy and upheld the rights of his blood? Throughout Renaissance Europe at this time, Niccolò Machiavelli's guidebook for rulers, *The Prince* (1513), was prompting debate on the practices and principles of statecraft. Historians see the Spanish

Golden Age as resistant to Machiavelli's pragmatic, secular, and scientific precepts, viewing Calderón's play in particular as a direct response to this text. *Life Is a Dream* considers, but ultimately rejects, the secularism that was emerging elsewhere in Europe at the time and affirms Spain's ongoing commitment to the divine right of kings and the great chain of being— concepts that structure a world in which God both determines who should rule and establishes the hierarchy that orders and connects all life, from the meanest form up through the divine. *Life Is a Dream* considers what disastrous events can ensue when a leader fails to fulfill his obligations to God's law and to his subjects by interfering with the principle of succession. Basil's ill-advised choices throughout the play reflect Machiavellian precepts; Astolf, who stands ready to rule instead of Segismund, appears to be cut from the same cloth as Basil. Segismund thus learns, in part by observing his father's and his rival's errors, what ideal kingship entails.

Given his concern with Spanish traditions and culture, why did Calderón choose to set *Life Is a Dream* in eastern Europe? Poland's and Spain's shared historical struggles with Moorish occupation may have provided some background connections, but a more reasonable hypothesis is that Calderón, like other Renaissance dramatists close to court circles, found it prudent to distance his work from his immediate milieu. Seen by western Europeans as primitive and untouched by the scientific and cultural advances of the Renaissance, Poland and Russia also provide the ideal location for an allegory of leadership that argues against the rising tide of secular "political science" in other parts of Europe.

Calderón thus builds *Life Is a Dream* around a complex structure of contrasting doubles in plot, setting, and character. The exploration of different notions of leadership on the political level parallels Rosaura's and Segismund's more personal search for their fathers. Moreover, both seek to avenge the wrongs done to them by others, to avoid a pattern in which they would embody the fates of their forebears, and ultimately to assume their rightful places in society. Calderón also doubles his hero and heroine through their repeated changes of costume, each of which brings a new identity and new codes of behavior.

We might also see a resonance between Calderón's choice of a remote setting, which nevertheless stands in for contemporary Spain, and his employment of an equally unlikely character double to throw light on the monarchy: Rosaura's servant Clarion. Briefly and falsely, Clarion answers to the name of prince in the climactic battle scene between Basil's forces and those who desire to place the rightful heir on the throne; soon thereafter he becomes the king's symbolic substitute, attempting to flee from the conflict, offering final revelations from which Basil learns, and dying. Calderón's use of *desengaño* (revelation or epiphany) for each of his major characters by the play's end provides both stylistic continuity and further cohesion between the overlapping narratives.

Perhaps most pointedly, Calderón juxtaposes Segismund and Astolf as suitors for Rosaura. The dramatist's examination of courtly love and the inescapability of the Spanish code of honor lays bare the inherent conflicts between idealized romance and political reality. The revelation that Clotaldo abandoned Rosaura's mother, just as Astolf abandoned the offspring of that relationship, complicates our understanding of the nobleman; Segismund's renunciation of his desire for Rosaura, his recognition that he must contain his impulses, and his commitment to restoring her honor ultimately persuade us of his nobility. The impossible love of Segismund and Rosaura unquestionably lends the drama much of its narrative power and theatrical longevity; indeed, for many audiences and readers, it may overwhelm the play's political and ideological concerns. But the issues of sexuality and paternity that fill out Rosaura's story are inextricable from, and as important as, those of rulership, and they help tie together the play's thematic threads.

Finally, we must not underestimate the audience appeal of the disguised heroine, who tumbles onstage in the play's first action, cross-dressed in form-fitting doublet and hose. Perhaps drawing on a tradition in the Italian novella of young women who cross-dress to avenge their honor, Lope had employed such figures more than a hundred times in his own works; in his playwriting manual he urged other dramatists to follow his lead, because putting Spanish actresses in male disguise had proven to be such a crowd-pleaser. While Calderón chose to use this device more sparingly, he nevertheless explores its full potential in *Life Is a Dream*, where it contributes to Segismund's development. Precisely because Rosaura's presence recurs in different times, places, and guises—first as a young man, then at court as a lady-in-waiting, and finally as herself—the prince finally confronts the assumption that he has dreamed.

Yet the drama's ending has perplexed and frustrated audiences for centuries. The play's first moments suggest that we should anticipate the happy marriage of Segismund and Rosaura, but that does not occur. The Christian spirit of renunciation and forgiveness that finally informs the prince's actions toward Rosaura and his father seems similarly contradicted by his severity toward the soldier who has secured his release and triumph. Both these decisions reflect the need to contain forces that threaten to disrupt the patriarchal social order. The soldier, a representative of the common people, could again imperil the monarchy, while Rosaura's dubious sexual past and personal independence render her doubly unfit to be the king's consort. To be a true leader, Segismund must come to understand and accept his place in the great chain of being and to put divine law and the values of the nation before personal desires. We may long for romantic fulfillment, but like Calderón's protagonist, we must learn to distinguish reality from dreams.   J.E.G.

Life Is a Dream[1]

CHARACTERS

SEGISMUND, the Prince
BASIL, the King
ROSAURA, a Lady
CLOTALDO, an old Nobleman
ASTOLF, a foreign Prince

STELLA, the Infanta
CLARION, a Clown
SERVANTS, SOLDIERS
Guards, Musicians,
Ladies-in-waiting

1.1

[*Enter* ROSAURA, *high on a mountainside in Poland, dressed in a man's traveling clothes. Having been thrown from her horse, she descends while addressing the runaway animal.*]

ROSAURA   Dash off, wild hippogriff![2]
    Why are you charging wind-swift down a cliff
    So barren and strewn with stone
    You'll only tumble headlong all alone
5   Into its tangled maze?

1. Translated by G. J. Racz.
2. A mythical cross between a horse and a

griffin, which gives it the wings and head of an eagle and the claws of a lion.

Dull lightning bolt devoid of fiery rays,
Scaled fish, bird shy of hue,
Where is that horse sense instinct tendered you?
Dwell on these pinnacles
10 And be a Phaëton[3] for the animals,
While I, forlorn and blind,
Oblivious to the path fate has in mind
For me, descend the brow
Of this imposing, sun-burnt mountain now
15 And dodge its tangled hair,
Emerging I could hardly tell you where.
This welcome, Poland, would
Be more hospitable if strangers could
Sign in with ink, not blood.
20 I'm hardly here, but bleed hard on your mud.
Still, fortune foresees all:
Where does one find compassion for a fall?

[*Enter* CLARION, *a clown.*]

CLARION   One? Make that two of us
And count me in when you kick up a fuss!
25 My lady, may I speak?
As two, we left our native land to seek
Adventure in the world,
Both saw strange sights, watched miseries unfurled
Before our very eyes
30 And tumbled down these hills to great surprise.
I've shared all your duress,
So tell me now, what's causing you distress?

ROSAURA   I'd hoped to spare your ear
From my complaining, Clarion, out of fear
35 A servant might be prone
To start bemoaning troubles not his own.
There's so much joy to find
In sorrows, one philosopher opined,
That those who've naught to rue
40 Will seek a share so they can grumble, too.

CLARION   Philosopher? Perhaps
A whiskered drunk! I say a hundred slaps
Would leave the rogue well served,
And then I bet he'd whine they weren't deserved!
45 But what should we do now,
My lady, stranded here, you will allow,
At just the worst of times,
Right when the sun is seeking western climes?

ROSAURA   Who ever tread such singular terrain?
50 If my imagination will refrain
From fooling with my sight,

---

3. In classical mythology, Phaëthon, son of Helios (the sun), drove his father's chariot but lost control of the horses; to save heaven and earth from destruction, Zeus (Jupiter) killed him with a thunderbolt.

I dare say, by this day's faint-hearted light,
I see a structure rise
Amid those peaks.

CLARION   Now, either my heart lies
55   Or hope views what it wills.

ROSAURA   A palace born within these barren hills
So rustic and so crude
The sun is loath to look on frames so rude;
An edifice of rough
60   Construction, fashioned ruggedly enough
That, lying at the base
Of rocky crags that touch the sun's warm face
And bask in brilliant lights,
It looks like some huge stone pitched from the heights.

65 CLARION   Let's wander down a bit
Where we can get a better look at it.
If destiny is kind,
The castle dwellers there might feel inclined
To take us in.

ROSAURA   Its door
70   Stands open like a gaping mouth mid-roar
And night springs from its jowls,
Engendered in the cavern of its bowels.
               [*Chains clank within.*]

CLARION   Good God, do I hear chains?

ROSAURA   I'm frozen stiff, but fire runs through my veins!

75 CLARION   Just dig my early grave!
If that isn't a captive galley slave,
My fear's deceiving me.

1.2

[SEGISMUND, *within.*]

SEGISMUND   Oh, abject wretch! To bear such misery!

ROSAURA   What voice sounds these laments?
Fresh sorrows and new torments wrack my sense!

CLARION   Strange fears besiege my head!

5 ROSAURA   Come, Clarion.

CLARION   Lady mine!

ROSAURA   It's time we fled
From this enchanted tower.

CLARION   I hesitate
To flee our only refuge in this strait.

ROSAURA   Do I glimpse from afar
The weak and pallid gleam as of a star
10   Whose feeble, flickering haze,
The emanation of dull heat and rays,
Diffuses through some room
A light so pale it magnifies the gloom?
Yes, even standing here
15   I spy unlighted hollows that appear

To be dark prison cells,
The rank tomb where some live cadaver dwells.
How wondrous! There within,
A squalid man lies clad in animal skin,
20 Restrained by chains, it seems,
His only company those sickly beams.
Since we've no hope for flight,
Let's listen as he chronicles the plight
Of his lost liberty.

[SEGISMUND *is revealed, chained beneath a faint light*
and dressed in animal pelts.]

25 SEGISMUND   Oh, abject wretch! To bear such misery!
I've struggled, heavens, night and morn
To comprehend what horrid crime
Was perpetrated at the time
When I, offending you, was born.
30 At last I grasp why cosmic scorn
Should be my portion after birth:
Your justice may enlist no dearth
Of reasons to be harsh with me
As being born, I've come to see,
35 Is mankind's greatest sin on earth.
But still I venture, stars, to learn,
If only for some peace of mind,
Discounting my dark birth, what kind
Of crime could warrant in return
40 A punishment as fierce and stern
As this I live, a living hell?
Weren't all the others born as well?
If all came in the world this way,
What sort of privilege had they
45 I'll never savor in this cell?
The bird is born with sumptuous hues
And hatches wielding Beauty's power.
In time, this lovely feathered flower,
A winged bouquet of shades, will choose
50 To soar the sky's blue avenues
As swift as anything flies free,
Forsaking the sure sympathy
And peaceful quiet of its nest.
As I've more soul within my breast,
55 Should I enjoy less liberty?
The beast is born, and on its fur
Fair markings leave their bold design.
In time, this horoscope-like sign
Drawn by the master picturer
60 Will learn, when human cravings stir
In cruel self-interest, not to flee
But act as cruel as man can be,
Like some dread monster in a maze.

As worthier of higher praise,
65 Should I enjoy less liberty?
The fish is born not breathing air,
A freak amid sea slime and grass.
In time, this scaly ship will pass
Unfettered through the waves, aware
70 It's free to swim the hydrosphere[4]
And, measuring the watery
Expanses of the open sea,
Conceive of greater spaces still.
As I possess the freer will,
75 Should I enjoy less liberty?
The stream is born, a snake that wends
Its way where wild flowers bide.
In time, this silvery fresh will glide
Along green banks as it extends
80 A song of gratitude that sends
Its thanks up toward the canopy
For granting it the majesty
Of open fields in which to flow.
As I've more life within me, though,
85 Should I enjoy less liberty?
In suffering that's known no ease,
I smolder like Mount Etna,[5] whose
Release comes only when it spews
Its heart out of its vortices.
90 Which edicts, laws, codes, or decrees
Deny a man who's sepulchered
That sweetest privilege proffered,
The natural prerogative
Just God above would freely give
95 To beast and stream, to fish and bird?
ROSAURA   His words evoke in me a fear
And sympathy that cloud my sense.
SEGISMUND   Who's overheard my soul's laments?
Clotaldo?
CLARION   Answer, "Yes, I'm here!"
100 ROSAURA   Alas, none but this mountaineer
Who, stumbling on your cell, now braves
The melancholy it encaves.
        [He seizes her.]
SEGISMUND   I've no choice but to kill you so
You'll never live to know I know
105 You know how craven I've behaved.
My honor dictates that I stretch
These arms about your neck and wring
The life from you for eavesdropping.

---

4. Bodies of water (literally, both the bodies of water and aqueous vapor surrounding the earth).
5. A volcano in Sicily.

CLARION   I'm hard of hearing, and didn't catch
110   A word you said!
ROSAURA   Were you, poor wretch,
        Born human, I would surely meet
        With mercy, prostrate at your feet.
SEGISMUND   Your voice could cause my heart to melt,
        Your presence challenge all I've felt,
115   Your guise make my disquiet complete.
        Who are you? Pent inside these walls,
        I've known so little of the world—
        My cradle and my grave unfurled
        Before me in this tower's palls—
120   That from my birth my mind recalls—
        If birth it was—no other place
        Than these backwoods of barren space
        Where I endure in wretched strife,
        A living skeleton stripped of life,
125   A dead man only live by grace.
        In all my days, I've spoken to
        One man and one alone. He knows
        The grievous nature of my woes
        And taught me all I hold most true
130   About the earth and heavens. You
        Appear now, shocked that I could be
        The monstrous human rarity
        You spy mid ghosts and wraiths, so feast
        Your eyes: I'm a man of a beast
135   And a beast of a man, you'll see.
        Yet, while I've paid misfortune's price,
        I've versed myself in politics,
        Observing how the wild brutes mix
        And listening to the birds' advice.
140   My measurements have been precise
        When I map starry paths in space.
        But you alone possess the grace
        To cause my anger to subside,
        My eyes to doubt what they've descried,
145   My ears to trust all they embrace.
        And every time I fix my gaze
        On you, I feel fresh wonder soar.
        The more I look at you, the more
        I want to see you all my days.
150   It's dropsy[6] making my eyes glaze
        And brim with water now, I think,
        For knowing it's sure death to drink,
        They drink you in still more like wells.
        Still, seeing that my seeing spells
155   My death, I'll die to let them graze.

_____
6. An excessive accumulation of fluid.

Oh, let me look on you and die!
For all I know, come my last breath,
If seeing you will mean my death,
What will not seeing you imply?
160 Much worse than death would signify—
Dread fury, rage, and wracking pain.
At least in death my teeming brain
Will grasp life's harsh finality:
Why grant life to a wretch like me
165 When happy mortals can be slain?
   ROSAURA   I'm awed by you, yet filled with dread.
Still marveling at your tender speech,
I find it difficult to reach
Conclusions that remain unsaid.
170 I'll only say the heavens led
Me here to this sequestered site
To help console me in my plight,
If by "consoling" what is meant
Is happening on a wretch who's pent
175 And makes one's own distress seem slight.
A learned man down on his luck,
The story goes, became dirt poor
But soon surmised he would endure
By feeding on the herbs he'd pluck.
180 "Who else," he asked, "could be so struck
By worldly cares and yet abide?"
At this, he turned around and spied
His answer straightway, noticing
Another wise man gathering
185 The wild herbs he'd cast aside.
I've sighed my fate could be no worse;
Mere living seemed a daunting task.
So when it came my turn to ask,
"Who else could suffer through the curse
190 Of luck so ill-starred and adverse?"
You answered me with sympathy
Because of which I now can see
How all you've said was but a ploy
To turn my sorrows into joy
195 And thereby ease my pain for me.
So if this sharing of my woes
Can soothe your pain to some extent,
Take all you wish by listening,
I'll still possess no end of them.
200 My name is . . .

1.3

[CLOTALDO, *offstage.*]

   CLOTALDO   Tower guards! Are you
Asleep or simply faint of heart?

Your negligence let travelers
Gain access to the prison yard!

5 ROSAURA   I don't know what to think or feel!

SEGISMUND   My jail keeper Clotaldo's men!
When will my sorrows ever end?

CLOTALDO   Look lively and be vigilant!
They must be seized, alive or dead!

10   Be careful now, they may be armed.

[*The sound of guards offstage.*]

Oh, treason!

CLARION   Tower guards—yes, you
Who've kindly let us come this far—
As long as there's a choice involved,
We're easier to take alive!

[*Enter* CLOTALDO *with a pistol, and* SOLDIERS,
all with their faces hidden.]

15 CLOTALDO   Make sure your faces are concealed
As this precaution's been devised
To keep whoever happens by
From recognizing all of you.

CLARION   I love a jolly masquerade!

20 CLOTALDO   Oh, ignorant, misguided fools!
By trespassing upon a site
Off-limits to all wayfarers,
You violate the king's decree
That stipulates no sojourner
25   Should ever set his curious eyes
Upon the wonder mid these crags.
Surrender and give up your swords
Or else this firearm, an asp
Recast in metal molds, will spew
30   A venom forth that penetrates
Your skin, two bullets with enough
Foul smoke and noise to grieve the air.

SEGISMUND   Say, tyrant master, what you will,
But do these wanderers no harm.
35   I'll hold my bleak existence cheap
And rot here chained among your guards—
Where, by God's name, I'm left no choice
But to dismember this bound flesh
With my own hands or teeth—before
40   I'll stand for their unhappiness
Or end up, mid these lonely crests,
Lamenting more of your abuse.

CLOTALDO   If, Segismund, you know full well
How large your own misfortunes loom,
45   Enough for heaven to have sealed
Your doom before your birth; if you
Know that this prison serves to keep
In check your haughty fits of rage,

A bridle for your furious starts
50　To harness them in lieu of reins,
Why must you go on raving? Guards,
Make fast these prison doors and keep
This man again from sight.

[*They bolt the door.* SEGISMUND's *voice is heard within.*]

SEGISMUND　　　　　　　　How right
You've been, cruel skies, to wrest from me
55　My liberty! I'd only rise
Against you like a giant who,
To smash the crystallinity
The sun displays upon its route,
Would pile jasper mountains high
60　Atop a base of solid stone.[7]

CLOTALDO　Perhaps, preventing such an act
Explains why you must suffer so.

1.4

ROSAURA　As I've observed how arrogance
Offends your grave propriety,
It would be senseless not to beg
You for this life prone at your feet.
5　May you be moved to pity me
And be not unrelenting should
Humility or arrogance
Make sympathy impossible.

CLARION　Humility or Arrogance
10　Should work. As stock protagonists
They move the plots bad playwrights use
In far too many sacred skits.[8]
But if they don't, then mid extremes,
Not overhumble or too proud,
15　I beg you, somewhere in between,
Do what you can to help us out!

CLOTALDO　Guards! Guards!

SOLDIERS　　　　　　　　My lord!

CLOTALDO　　　　　　　　　　　Disarm these two
And blindfold them at once! These men
Must never be allowed to leave
20　These confines or retrace their steps.

ROSAURA　My sword, sir. Duty and respect
Oblige me to surrender this
To you alone, the principal
Among us here, and not permit
25　Its cession to a lesser power.

7. An allusion to the giants of classical mythology, who piled up mountains (Pelion on Ossa) in an unsuccessful effort to overthrow the gods on Mount Olympus.

8. A dismissive reference to *autos sacramentales*—short sacred plays, comparable to morality plays in medieval England, that often feature allegorical characters.

CLARION   My own is such the worse for wear
    That anyone could take it. Here.
ROSAURA   I yield it, should I not be spared,
    To mark the pity I've been shown,
30   A token worthy of regard
    Because of one who wore it girt
    In days gone by. Indulge my charge
    And hold it dear, for I know not
    What muted secret it enfolds,
35   Except to say this gilded sword
    Contains great mysteries untold
    And, having sworn on it a pledge,
    Am come to Poland to avenge
    A grave wrong done me.
CLOTALDO   Stars above!
40   Can this be? All my old suspense
    And sorrow, my remorse and grief
    Conspire to cause me still more pain.
    Who gave you this?
ROSAURA   A woman did.
CLOTALDO   How was the lady called?
ROSAURA   Her name
45   May not be spoken.
CLOTALDO   Is this your
    Assumption or do you avow
    That there's some secret in this sword?
ROSAURA   She who bestowed it said, "Set out
    For Poland, using all the charm
50   And artful cunning you possess
    To make the noblemen you meet
    Bear witness to this testament.
    I'm certain one among them there
    Will show you favor in your quest,"
55   Though she declined to give his name
    In case the man she meant was dead.
CLOTALDO   God help me! What assails my ears?
    Now, how will I contrive to prove
    That what has just transpired here
60   Is no illusion, but the truth?
    This is the sword I left behind
    With fair Viola as a pledge
    That whosoever wore it girt
    Upon his thigh within my ken
65   Would find himself a much-loved son
    And me a sympathetic sire.
    But now, alas, what can I do?
    Chaotic thoughts run through my mind
    For he who brings this sword in grace
70   Brings with it unawares his death,
    Condemned before he ever fell
    On bended knee. This senselessness

Confounds me! What a ruinous fate
And tragic destiny are mine!
75 This is my son; all markers point
To these corroborating signs
Within my heart, now pulsing at
The portals of my breast. Its wings
Still flutter there, incapable
80 Of forcing back the bolts, akin
To one who's locked inside a room
And, hearing noises in the street,
Peers through a window eagerly.
Like him, my heart cannot conceive
85 What's happening and, mid such noise,
Looks through the eyes to catch a view,
As eyes are windows of the soul
Where hearts pour out in teary dews.
What choice have I? God help me now!
90 What choice have I? To lead this man
Before the king—how harsh the blow!—
Would mean his certain death. I can't
Conceal him, though, and thus infringe
Upon my sworn obedience.
95 I'm torn between these deeply felt
Emotions and the duteousness
I owe my liege. Why vacillate?
Pledged loyalty, and not our lives
Or loves, must needs take precedence.
100 Just so, let loyalty abide!
I seem now to recall a claim
He made of having solely come
To right a wrong, yet well I know
How wronged men can be villainous.
105 He's not my son, he's not my son!
He does not share my noble blood!
But if some threat to his good name
Indeed occurred—a plight no one
Escapes, as honor is composed
110 Of such infirm material
The slightest touch can shred its weft
And whispered rumor stain its woof—
What else would any nobleman
Essay for honor's sake, what else
115 But seek the satisfaction owed,
However plenteous the peril?
He is my son! He shares my blood!
We've witnessed his courageous mien
And as I stand here, wracked with doubt,
120 One saving recourse comes to me:
I'll go myself to tell the king
That he's my son, but must be killed.
If honorable piety

Won't stay his hand, then nothing will.
125   Now, should I warrant him his life,
       I'll join his quest to seek amends
       For wrongs endured. But if the king
       Is overly intransigent
       And puts my son to death, he'll die
130   Not ever knowing I'm his sire.
       Come, strangers, we're to journey now,
       But rest assured that I'll provide
       Good company in misery
       For, mired in our present doubts,
135   Unsure which here will live or die,
       Whose wretchedness is paramount?
                    [*Exit all.*]

1.5

[*Enter* ASTOLF, *escorted by Soldiers, and* STELLA,
accompanied by Ladies-in-waiting. Music is playing.]

ASTOLF   Bedazzled by the shimmering rays
       Your eyes shoot forth like comet tails,
       The drums and trumpets fire off praise
       In salvos seldom heard in vales,
5   Where birds and brooks trill other lays.
       This equal musical delight,
       Performed by instruments in thrall
       To one so heavenly a sight,
       Lets feathered clarions sound their call
10   And metal birds put notes to flight.
       Their strains, fair lady, honor you
       Like cannonades salute the queen,
       The birds Aurora's rosy hue,
       The trumpets Pallas the Athene,
15   The flowers Flora damp with dew.[9]
       You've banished black night's sunlessness
       By making light of day, for you're
       Aurora, this earth's happiness,
       Its Flora, peace, its Pallas, war,
20   And my heart's queen in loveliness.
STELLA   Such honeyed discourse flows sincere
       And in accord with how men act,
       But one mistake you make, I fear,
       Is that fine words can't counteract
25   A soldier's garb and martial gear.
       These militate against you while
       My being fights your aspect so
       Intensely I can't reconcile

9. A comparison to three classical goddesses:
Aurora, the Roman goddess of the dawn; Pallas Athena, the Greek goddess of wisdom, the
useful arts, and war; and Flora, the Roman
goddess of flowers and spring.

The flattery I'm hearing flow
30   With all the rigor of your style.
For it is vile and indiscreet,
Unworthy of the basest brute,
The seed of treachery and deceit,
To trade on wiles to win one's suit
35   Or guile to speed a maid's defeat.

ASTOLF   You misconstrue my plain intent
In voicing all this errant doubt
Concerning what these words have meant.
Here, Stella, with your kind consent,
40   Is what this cause has been about:
The death of King Eustorge the Third,[1]
Proud Poland's monarch, left his son
Prince Basil sovereign afterward.
One sister was my mother, one
45   Yours. Not to bore you with absurd
Recitals of each king and queen,
I'll make this brief. Fair Clorilene,
Your mother—and to me, Her Grace,
Who now rules in a better place
50   Beneath the starry damascene[2]—
Was elder, with no progeny
But you. Her younger sister was
Your aunt, but mother unto me,
Fair Recisunda, whom God does
55   Hold likewise dear in memory.
In Moscow, where I came of age,
She'd married. Here, I must forgo
Strict sequence and turn back a page:
King Basil, lady, as you know,
60   Has lost the war all mortals wage
Against Time. Ever with a mind
To study, he was disinclined
To woo. His childless queen now dead,
Our bloodlines stand us in good stead
65   To be the heirs he'll leave behind.
You hold a strong claim to the throne—
His elder sister's daughter would—
But I, a male, the fully grown
Son of his younger sister, should
70   Be favored to ascend alone.
We sought our uncle, then, impelled
To plead the justness of each case.
His reconciling us compelled
The naming of this time and place

1. A fictional Polish monarch; his lineage
includes Basil and his sisters, Clorilene and
Recisunda, below, as well as Basil's deceased
wife, also named Clorilene (see line 1.6.81).

2. That is, the heavens; damascene work is
metal ornamented by having patterns incised
into its surface and then filled in with silver
or gold.

75 So that our meeting could be held.
Such was my aim in setting out
From Moscow's distant, lovely land.
I've come for Poland's crown without
A fight, but found this fight on hand,
80 Though I've declined to press the bout.
Oh, may the people, God of Love,[3]
Precise astrologers they are,
Be wise like you and think well of
Our union! Let them thank the star
85 That designates you queen above,
For you're the queen I choose! Be shown
The honors you deserve! So please
It that our uncle yield his throne,
Your virtue bring you victories
90 And my love make this realm your own.

STELLA   I trust my own heart shares the aim
You've set forth in your dashing speech.
I only wish that I could claim
The throne now sits within my reach
95 So you could rule with lasting fame.
Still, I confess you must convince
Me that your faith will pass the test
Of quelling my suspicions since
The portrait pendant on your chest
100 Belies these fine words from a prince.

ASTOLF   I'd hoped to give you a complete
Account of this, but know not how
As trumpets noisily entreat
Attendance on the king, who now
105 Approaches with his royal suite.

1.6

[Trumpets blare. Enter the aged King BASIL *with retinue.]*

STELLA   Wise Thales!
ASTOLF   Learned Euclid,[4] hail!
STELLA   You rule today . . .
ASTOLF   Today you dwell . . .
STELLA   Mid starry signs . . .
ASTOLF   Mid starry trail . . .
STELLA   And calculate . . .
ASTOLF   And measure well . . .
5 STELLA   Each orbit's path . . .
ASTOLF   Each sphere's true scale.
STELLA   Oh, let me twirl like ivy round . . .
ASTOLF   Oh, let me lie down duty-bound . . .
STELLA   Your trunk, as fitting and discreet.

---

3. Eros, in Greek mythology; Cupid, in Roman.
4. Two Greek thinkers: Thales (6th c. B.C.E.), a philosopher and mathematician, was viewed as the founder of physical science, and Euclid (active ca. 300 B.C.E.) was a mathematician, renowned as the founder of geometry.

ASTOLF   Here prostrate at your royal feet.

10 BASIL   Dear niece and nephew, our[5] profound
　　　　Embrace! As loyal from the start
　　　　To our most sentimental plans,
　　　　You come with such a show of heart
　　　　That we pronounce you, by these banns,
15　　　True equals, each a part to part.
　　　　We ask, though, since our person nears
　　　　Exhaustion from the weight of years,
　　　　That you respectfully refrain
　　　　From speaking, as it will be plain
20　　　Our speech will soon amaze your ears.
　　　　For well you know—now mind our words,
　　　　Beloved nephew, dearest niece,
　　　　Grand nobles of the Polish court,
　　　　Good subjects, kin, friends we esteem—
25　　　For well you know, men have bestowed
　　　　On us the epithet of "wise"
　　　　To honor our enlightenment.
　　　　Against Oblivion and Time,
　　　　Timanthes in his portraits and
30　　　Lysippus[6] in his sculptures grand
　　　　Proclaim us "Basil Rex,[7] the Great"
　　　　And so we're called throughout these lands.
　　　　For well you know, the sciences
　　　　Are what we've loved and cherished most,
35　　　Fine mathematic formulae
　　　　By which we've robbed Time of its role,
　　　　Foreseeing what the future holds,
　　　　The only source of its renown,
　　　　And presaged more events each day.
40　　　For when our charts reveal accounts
　　　　Of incidents set to occur
　　　　In centuries still unbegun,
　　　　The dupe is dull chronology
　　　　As we glimpse first what's yet to come.
45　　　Those circular, snow-colored spheres
　　　　In glassy canopies that move[8]
　　　　Illuminated by the sun
　　　　But rent by cycles of the moon;
　　　　Those gleaming, diamantine orbs
50　　　And planets crystalline in space
　　　　Where incandescent stars shine bright
　　　　And zodiacal creatures graze,
　　　　Remain the major inquiry

5. Here and elsewhere, Basil uses the royal "we."

6. Two Greek artists, Timanthes (late 5th c. B.C.E.), a painter, and Lysippus (active ca. 320 B.C.E.), a sculptor.

7. King (Latin).

8. According to the cosmology of the Greek mathematician and astronomer Ptolemy (active 127–148 C.E.), still dominant in the Renaissance, the planets, sun, moon, and stars all circle the earth in vast crystalline spheres.

Of our declining years, the books
55 In which the heavens list all fates,
Benign or far less merciful,
On paper strewn with diamond dust
In sapphire ledgers finely lined
With patterned bars of glittering gold,
60 Inscribed with multitudes of signs.
We study these celestial tomes
And let our spirit wander free
In fast pursuit of starry trails
Wherever their swift paths should lead.
65 Wise heavens, if you'd only stopped
This active mind before it filled
Their margins with its commentaries
Or indexed every page at will!
If only you'd conceived our life
70 As but the first of casualties
Exacted by their wrath, this might
Have been our only tragedy.
But those who are misfortune-prone
Feel merit slice them like a knife,
75 For whomsoever knowledge harms
Is nothing but a suicide!
Though we be late in voicing this,
Events tell better tales than speech
And so, to leave this congress awed,
80 We ask again that you not speak.
Our late wife, your Queen Clorilene,
Bore us a male child so ill-starred
The wary skies announced his birth
With wonders patently bizarre.
85 Before her womb, that sepulcher
Predating life, gave living light
Unto the boy—for being born
And dying are indeed alike—
His mother had seen countless times,
90 Amid the strange delirium
Of dream, a monstrous form not quite
A human, but resembling one,
Which disemboweled her from within.
Once covered with her body's blood,
95 The brute would kill her, then emerge
Half mortal man, half viper slough.
Now, come the day the child was born,
These omens proved to be correct,
For dire portents never lie
100 And strictly see how things will end.
Spheres inauspiciously aligned
Provoked the scarlet-blooded sun
To challenge the cold moon to duel
And turned the heavens rubicund.

105 With all the earth their battleground,
These two celestial lanterns gleamed
In savage combat perched on high,
Both beaming bright as they could beam.
The longest and most horrible

110 Eclipse that ever did transpire—
Besides the one that dimmed the globe
The day Our Lord was crucified[9]—
Occurred next. As the planet sensed
Itself engulfed in living flames,

115 It must have thought the throes of death
Were making its foundations shake.
Then, suddenly, the skies grew black
And sturdy buildings lurched and spun.
The clouds rained stones upon the land

120 And rivers coursed along like blood.
This fatal confluence of stars
Or planetary pull prevailed
At Segismund's birth, presaging
The foulness of his soul that day.

125 For life, he gave his mother death,
And by such savagery affirmed:
"I am a man who will not cease
To menace all mankind in turn."
Recurring to the sciences

130 For guidance, we divined dire plans
For Segismund. We learned our heir
Would be the most rebellious man
The world could know, the cruelest prince
And even most ungodly king

135 Whose reckless rule would leave the realm
Divided and in open rift,
A fractious School for Treachery
And roiled Academy of Vice.
These signs revealed one so possessed

140 Of furious rage and violent crime
We even saw him set his heels
Upon us as we lay beneath—
This gives us great distress to say—
The brute soles of his conquering feet!

145 The silver hairs that grace this crown
Were but a carpet for his steps.
Who'd not put credence in such doom
Precisely when such doom is read
Secure in one's own study where

150 Self-interest plies its influence?
So, putting credence in the fates
As prophets given to dispense

9. According to Matthew 27.45, Mark 15.33, and Luke 23.44, darkness lasting three hours fell over all the land when Jesus was crucified.

Bleak auguries of promised harm
Through omens and foretokened signs,
155 We ordered that the newborn brute
Be everlastingly confined
To find out whether an old sage
Might thwart the dictates of the stars.
The false news of his stillborn birth
160 Was propagated near and far
While we, forewarned, ordained a tower
Be built between the craggy peaks
Of two remote, secluded hills
Where light could scarcely hope to reach
165 So that these rustic obelisks
Might seal off entry to the place.
The strict laws and harsh penalties
For breaking them were then displayed,
Declaring a forbidden zone
170 Off-limits to all sojourners
Who'd think to pass, the grave result
Of these events we've just referred.
There Segismund, our son, dwells yet,
Imprisoned, wretched, and forlorn,
175 Attended by Clotaldo, still
His only company of sorts,
Who tutored him in sciences
And catechized him in beliefs
Of Christian faith, the only man
180 Who's seen him in captivity.
Three issues guide us here: the first,
As we hold Poland in such high
Esteem, our lasting wish has been
To free her from the heinous plight
185 Of serving tyrant kings. Indeed,
A sovereign who would so imperil
The native soil that is his realm
Cannot be said to govern well.
The second bears upon the charge
190 That, by our actions, we've removed
The right to reign from its true line—
Of which no codex[1] would approve—
Through lack of Christian charity
As no existing law permits
195 A man who'd keep another man
From tyranny and insolence
To take on those same qualities.
For if our son's a tyrant, then
How may we perpetrate vile crimes
200 To keep him from committing them?

1. A compilation of laws.

The third and final point entails
Determining to what extent
A person errs too readily
By trusting in foretold events,
205 For though our heir may be disposed
To outbursts and impetuous acts,
This bent is but a tendency.
The direst fate, we know for fact,
Much like the rashest temperament
210 Or strongest planetary pull,
May boast some influence on free will
But cannot make man bad or good.
Engrossed, then, in these quandaries
And hesitant with self-debate,
215 We hit upon a remedy
That's sure to leave your senses dazed.
Tomorrow, we will have enthroned—
Without him knowing he's our son
Or your next king—the man who bears
220 The fateful name of Segismund.
Beneath our royal canopy
And seated in our august place,
He'll have his chance to reign at last
As all our subjects congregate
225 To pledge their humble fealty.
In doing so, it is our hope
To solve three matters that relate
To questions you have heard us pose.
One, should our heir display a mien
230 Deemed prudent, temperate, and benign
And thus belie what heartless fate
Forebode in all it prophesied,
The realm will see its natural line
Restored, as till this hour the prince
235 Has held court only in those hills,
A neighbor but to woodland things.
Two, should our son reveal himself
Rebellious, reckless, arrogant,
And cruel, inclined to give free rein
240 To vice that typifies his bent,
We will have acted piously,
Complicit with time-honored codes,
And shine like an unvanquished king
When we depose him from our throne,
245 Returning him to prison not
In cruelty, but punishment.
Three, should the heir apparent show
The qualities that we suspect,
Our love for Poland's subjects will
250 Provide you with a king and queen

More worthy of this sceptered crown,
To wit, our nephew and our niece.
The individual right to reign
Comes wedded in these two, conferred
255 By dint of their intended bond,
And both will have what both deserve.
For this is our command as king;
The nation's father bids it so.
We urge it as a learned sage;
260 This wise old man is thus disposed.
If Spanish Seneca[2] believed
The king is but a humble slave
Within his own republic's land,
Then we beseech you as the same.
265 ASTOLF   If, as the man whose future gains
Are most affected by these plans,
I have your leave to answer first,
I'll speak for all the court at hand
And say, let Segismund appear!
270 It's quite sufficient he's your son.
ALL   Restore the royal line! Yes, let
Our long-lost prince rule over us!
BASIL   Good subjects, our sincerest thanks
For this outpouring of support.
275 Escort our kingdom's Atlases[3]
To their respective chamber doors.
You'll have your prince upon the morn.
ALL   Long live our great King Basil! Hail!

[*All exit except* BASIL.]

1.7

[CLOTALDO, ROSAURA, *and* CLARION *enter.*]

CLOTALDO   A word with you, sire?
BASIL   Our good friend
Clotaldo! Welcome here today.
CLOTALDO   I might, indeed, have been most pleased
To come, sire, at some other time,
5 But now it seems a tragic turn
Must for the moment override
The privilege our law confers
And courtesy our ways demand.
BASIL   What's happened?
CLOTALDO   A calamity
10 That in another circumstance
Might not have proved so dire a blow

---

2. Lucius Annaeus Seneca (4 B.C.E.–65 C.E.), a Roman philosopher, statesman, and playwright born in what is now Spain. A constant theme in his writings is that virtue (and thus happiness) lies in the individual, independent of always uncertain fortune.

3. That is, those who support the kingdom, just as in classical mythology the Titan Atlas bears the heavens on his head and hands.

But been a cause for jubilance.

BASIL   Go on.

CLOTALDO   This handsome youth you see,
Through derring-do or recklessness,
15   Gained entrance to the tower grounds
And saw the prince there pent in chains.
He is . . .

BASIL   Clotaldo, have no fear.
Had this occurred some other day,
He would have felt our royal wrath,
20   But as we've just divulged this news,
It matters little that he knows,
As we've today confirmed the truth.
Come see us by and by. We've such
A many wonders to relate
25   And you so much to do for us.
You'll learn soon of the role you'll play
In carrying out the most sublime
Event this world has countenanced.
As for these prisoners—we're loath
30   To punish you for negligence
And thus, with mercy, pardon them.

[Exit BASIL.]

CLOTALDO   Oh, may you rule a thousand years!

1.8

CLOTALDO   The heavens have restored my luck!
I've no need for professing here
That he's my son, as he's been spared.
Strange pilgrims, seek your wonted route,
5   You're free to go.

ROSAURA   I kiss your feet
A thousand times.

CLARION   I'll . . . miss them, too.
So what's one letter more or less
Between friends who have come to terms?

ROSAURA   You've given me my life back, sire;
10   It's thanks to you I walk this earth.
Consider me eternally
Your grateful slave.

CLOTALDO   A life is more
Than I can give you in your plight.
No gentleman that's nobly born
15   Can live as long as he's aggrieved.
For if it's certain that you come,
According to your very words,
To right a wrong that you've been done,
I can't have given your life back;
20   You didn't have one when you came.
A life defamed is not a life.

[*Aside.*] I hope my words leave him inflamed!

ROSAURA   I don't possess one, I confess,
Though I accept what you've bestowed
25   And, after I'm avenged, I'll boast
True honor so pristine and whole
The life I claim as mine that day
Will turn aside all future threats
And seem the gift it is at last.
30 CLOTALDO   Take back this burnished blade you've pledged
To bear. I realize your revenge
Won't be complete until it shines
Bright with your adversary's blood.
Of course, a sword I once called mine—
35   I mean, just as I held it now,
Possessing it to some extent—
Would know how to avenge.
ROSAURA   I wear
It in your name and once again
Do swear on it I'll be avenged
40   Despite my able enemy's
Superior force.
CLOTALDO   Is it so great?
ROSAURA   So great I must forswear my speech
And not because I feel I can't
Confide in you far greater things
45   But so you'll not withdraw from me
The sympathetic ministering
You've shown.
CLOTALDO   I'd sooner join your cause
If you would but disclose his name.
This knowledge also might forestall
50   My rendering him unmindful aid.
[*Aside.*] Who is this mortal enemy?
ROSAURA   Good sir, so you'll not think I hold
Our newfound trust in low esteem,
Know that my honor's bitter foe
55   Is no one less than Astolf, Duke
Of Moscow.
CLOTALDO   [*Aside.*] What a stunning blow
To all these plans! His cause appears
More grave than even I'd supposed.
I'll delve more deeply into this.
60   If you were born a Muscovite,
Then he who is your natural lord
Could hardly be accused of slights.
Return to your ancestral land
And try to quell this ardent zeal
65   That hurls you madly forth.
ROSAURA   The wrong,
My lord, that left me so aggrieved

Was anything but slight.
CLOTALDO   Perhaps,
  A slighting slap that stung too hard,
  Offending, heavens, that dear cheek?
70 ROSAURA   The injury was worse by far.
CLOTALDO   What was it, then? I've seen so much
  Of late it scarce could cause alarm.
ROSAURA   I'll tell you, though I know not how,
  Considering the deep respect
75 And veneration that I feel
  For you and all this represents.
  How can I venture to explain
  The riddle these deceptive clothes
  Conceal? They don't belong to whom
80 You'd guess. Judge wisely what this shows:
  I'm not who I appear to be
  While Astolf's plan has been to come
  Wed Stella. Think, how might I feel
  Insulted? Now I've said too much!

[*Exit* ROSAURA *and* CLARION.]

85 CLOTALDO   Beware! Pay heed! Keep up your guard!
  This is a puzzling labyrinth
  Where even reason toils to find
  The thread laid down to exit it.[4]
  My honor is the one aggrieved,
90 Its foe by all accounts quite strong,
  A vassal I, a woman she.
  May heaven steer my hand from wrongs,
  Though I'm not certain that it can.
  The world is one confused abyss;
95 The skies above portend no good
  And all God's earth seems curious.

2.1

[*Enter* BASIL *and* CLOTALDO.]

CLOTALDO   Your orders have been carried out
  With due dispatch.
BASIL   Then he is come,
  Clotaldo? Tell us what transpired.
CLOTALDO   Sire, this is how the deed was done:
5 I plied him with the calming drink
  You wished distilled, a most superb
  Confection of ingredients
  That blent the might of sundry herbs.
  The tyrant strength of such a mix,
10 Its secret potency concealed,

4. The legendary Greek hero Theseus escaped the first labyrinth, invented by Daedalus to hold the Minotaur (half man, half bull), with the help of string given to him by King Minos's daughter, Ariadne.

Deprives a man outright of sense
And robs him of the power of speech
While rendering him a living corpse.
The violence of its attributes
15 So dulls the mind and saps the force
That those benumbed by it lie mute.
Stale arguments repeatedly
Ask whether this is possible,
But time-honored experience
20 With scientific principles
Has shown this ever to be true.
For nature's secrets find a home
In medicine and there exists
No single creature, plant, or stone
25 That cannot boast of properties
Unique to it. If base intent
First prompted man to catalogue
The thousand poisons causing death,
How little more had he to search
30 When classifying qualities
Of every venom known to kill
To find those that would bring on sleep?
Let's lay aside, then, any doubts
Concerning whether this be true,
35 As reason backed by evidence
Provides us with conclusive proof.
So, bearing that peculiar brew
Of opium and henbane[5] held
Together by the poppy's charms,
40 I slipped down to the narrow cell
Where Segismund dwelt. There, we spoke
Awhile of the philosophies
And disciplines he'd mastered, each
From voiceless nature when she speaks
45 In mute guise of the hills and skies,
For years at so divine a school
Had trained him in the rhetoric
Of every bird and beast he knew.
Attempting, then, to animate
50 His spirit and to sound his mind
Before the task at hand, I turned
The topic to the speedy flight
A mighty eagle flaunted high
Above us, scornful of the wind's
55 Low-lying sphere and soaring like
Some feathery bolt amid the rings
Of fire in the canopy,
A comet blazing on the heights.

5. A narcotic derived from the poisonous plant of the same name.

I praised the creature's lofty sweep
60 By saying, "Now I see how right
You are, grand queen who rules all birds,
To feel that you outshine the rest."
Well, that one reference in my speech
To majesty caused such duress
65 In him, he gave vent to bold thoughts,
His pride and self-conceit stirred up.
The pure blood coursing through his veins
Incites and instigates him thus
To eye great feats, and he exclaimed:
70 "Then even from the raucous realm
Of birds a leader must emerge
To claim the fealty he compels!
My lessons in misfortune should
Console me with the argument
75 That only the superior strength
Of jailors keeps my spirits pent,
For I would never willingly
Submit to any mortal's law."
Thus, seeing him enraged by talk
80 On subjects that recalled the cause
Of so much pain, I offered him
The potent brew. No sooner had
This potion passed from cup to lip
Than all his willful rage collapsed
85 In heavy sleep. An icy sweat
Coursed through his veins and every limb
Perspired to such macabre effect
That had I not been warned that this
Was no true death, I would have thought
90 He'd breathed his last. At just this time,
The men you'd charged to carry out
This bold experiment arrived
And, placing him inside a coach,
Conveyed him to your chambers where
95 Accommodations following
Strict protocol had been prepared
To lodge him with due majesty.
They laid him sleeping in your bed
And, when the potion's numbing force
100 Wears off and his deep slumber ends,
They'll serve him as you've ordered, sire,
As if he were the king himself.
So should my fast obeisance
Incline you to reward me well
105 For all these efforts, lord, my sole
Wish is to learn a puzzling truth.
Pray, pardon me this liberty:
What purpose lies behind this move

Of Segismund unto the court?

110 BASIL   Clotaldo, well might you voice doubts
About our plan, and these we will
Allay if you'll but hear us out:
As Segismund, our only son,
Was born beneath a baleful star
115 That, well you know, predestined him
To sorrows, tragedy, and harm,
We'd hoped to probe the heavens now,
As they're incapable of lies
And never ceased revealing signs
120 Of what that cruelty may be like
Still lodged within his brutal soul.
We'll fathom, then, if stars reprieve
Their harshest edicts or, when moved
By man's restraint and bravery,
125 Reverse dire omens, for we know
Each person rules his stars and fate.
As this is what we wish to probe,
We've had him brought inside these gates
To tell him he's our son and put
130 His inclinations to the test,
For should he prove magnanimous,
He'll reign. But if his temperament
Should rage tyrannical and cruel,
He'll be constrained forthwith by chains.
135 Why is it, you do well to ask,
That this experiment you aid
Could only have been brought to pass
Once deathlike sleep had been induced?
Our sole wish is to satisfy
140 Your every query with the truth.
Should our son learn he's prince today
But on the morrow come to see
His strange existence once again
Subjected to jail's miseries,
145 Mere contemplation of this state
Would doubtless lead him to despair,
For once he's found out who he is,
What could console him in his pain?
It's therefore been our plan to leave
150 The door to pretext open wide
So we may claim that all he saw
Was dreamt, and thereby expedite
Determining two separate things:
His natural condition first,
155 According to which he'll proceed
To bare his soul in deeds and words,
And second, whether such a ruse
Can furnish solace to a wretch

Who, presently obeyed by all,
160 Might soon return to prison depths
To understand that he had dreamt.
This he'd do wisely to believe
Because, Clotaldo, in this world
All think they live who only dream.
165 CLOTALDO   How readily could I present
Sound refutations of this plan!
But these would serve no purpose now
As I am led to understand
The prince has wakened from his sleep
170 And, fully conscious, comes this way.
BASIL   Our thought is to withdraw from sight
While you, as tutor, extricate
Your pupil from what lingering doubt
And puzzlement still plague his mind.
175 The prince will learn the truth at last.
CLOTALDO   Then I have your permission, sire,
To make the plot known?
BASIL   Tell him all.
Thus any danger he may pose
To us while fully cognizant
180 Will be more easily controlled.
            [*Exit* BASIL.]

2.2

            [*Enter* CLARION.]
CLARION   A halberdier[6] whose reddish hair
And whiskers matched his uniform
Just whacked me good and hard four times
As I ran here to stay informed
5 Of court events as they unfold.
What window offers finer views—
Not counting those in front-row seats
That ticket vendors hold for you—
Than man's own eyeballs in his head?
10 For, with or without sense or cent,
Whenever there's a show to see,
He'll sneak a peek with impudence.
CLOTALDO   Ah, faithful Clarion, servant once
To she—sweet heavens!—she indeed
15 Who, trading in misfortune, brought
To Poland my past infamy.
Good Clarion, have you news?
CLARION   Word is,
My lord, that your benevolence
In stating this intent to right

---

6. A soldier armed with a halberd, a weapon common in the 15th century that combined a steel
spike and an axelike blade mounted on a long shaft.

20   Rosaura's wrong has her convinced
        She should again wear ladies' clothes.
  CLOTALDO   It's for the best, lest she be deemed
        Too frivolous.
  CLARION   Word is, she's changed
        Her name to boot and, cleverly
25   Rechristening herself your niece,
        Has watched her reputation surge
        At palace where she now resides,
        Attendant to the singular
        Dame Stella.
  CLOTALDO   Then, I've helped the child
30   Gain part of her lost honor back.
  CLARION   Word is, she's biding time until
        The moment your avenging wrath
        Restores her honored name in full.
  CLOTALDO   No surer thing to bide exists,
35   For only Time as it transpires
        Can put an end to all of this.
  CLARION   And word is, too, that she's regaled
        With treatment fit a queen at court
        By falsely posing as your niece
40   While I, who served her night and morn,
        Am left to die from hunger's want,
        Forgotten and ignored by all,
        Although a Clarion nonetheless.
        For if I ever did sound off
45   To Astolf, Stella, or the king,
        They might be shocked by what they heard.
        Both manservants and clarions toot
        Like trumpets in this noisy world
        And just don't harbor secrets well.
50   The moment that her fingers lift
        This veil of silence from my lips
        The song I sing might well be this:
        No clarion blaring at first light
        Did ever sound more right.
55   CLOTALDO   Your grievance is well taken, man,
        But I can help address this plaint.
        For now, attend me in her stead.
  CLARION   Look! Segismund, and unrestrained!

2.3

[Enter musicians, singing, and SERVANTS *attiring*
    SEGISMUND, *who appears dazed.]*

  SEGISMUND   God save me! What's this I perceive?
        God help me grasp what I've seen here!
        I'm awed and not untouched by fear
        But can't be sure what to believe.

5   Do I stand at the court today
     Mid sumptuous fabrics, lush brocades,
     Lithe footmen and fair chambermaids
     Who serve me in their fine array?
     Did I awake completely free
10   And resting in some stately bed
     Surrounded, like one highly bred,
     With valets to attire me?
     To claim I dream would be a ruse,
     For sleep and waking aren't the same.
15   Still, isn't Segismund my name?
     Fair heavens, won't you disabuse
     My fancy's flight and make it clear
     What wondrous circumstances might
     Have troubled it thus in the night
20   To leave me so convinced I'm here?
     Whatever turns out to be true,
     Who could dispute what I've observed?
     I'll let myself be richly served
     Here, come what may, in this milieu.

25   SECOND SERVANT   Despondence sits upon his cheek.
     FIRST SERVANT   Could anyone who's led a life
     So drear not bear such signs of strife?
     CLARION   Yes, me.
     SECOND SERVANT   Approach the man and speak.
     FIRST SERVANT   Another round of singing?
     SEGISMUND   Why,
30   Not now. I don't care to hear more.
     SECOND SERVANT   You looked so lost and dazed before,
     I thought songs might amuse you.
     SEGISMUND   My
     Ordeal would be as burdensome
     Without these choruses of cheer.
35   I only truly wish to hear
     The martial strains of fife and drum.
     CLOTALDO   Your Royal Highness! Majesty!
     Oh, let me be the first to kiss
     Your hand lest I appear remiss
40   In pledging you my fealty.
     SEGISMUND   Is this Clotaldo, my jail keep,
     Whose torments I could once expect,
     Now treating me with such respect?
     I know not if I wake or sleep!
45   CLOTALDO   The great confusion that you find
     This new condition brings about
     Has raised in you some lingering doubt
     That clouds your reason and your mind.
     I've come to help you be less prone
50   To things that cause undue concern
     Because today my lord will learn

He's heir apparent to the throne
Of Poland. If till now you've dwelt
Sequestered vilely far afield,
55   It's all because your fate was sealed
By cards intemperate fate had dealt,
Portending bane that would allow
Our empire here to come to grief
The moment that the laurel leaf
60   Would come to grace your august brow.[7]
But trusting in your better will
To prove the stars erroneous—
For men who are magnanimous
Find ways to overrule them still—
65   They've brought you to the palace from
The tower where they kept your cell,
Your senses dulled by sleep's deep spell
And all your forces rendered numb.
The king, your sire and my liege lord,
70   Will come soon, Segismund, to call,
At which time he will tell you all.
SEGISMUND   Vile traitor, born to be abhorred!
What could remain for me to know
When knowing my identity
75   From this day forward leaves me free
To flaunt my power and cause men woe?
How could you bring this treasonous act
Against your land, to jail your prince
And strip him of all honors, since
80   No right or reason could retract
A crown, blood-pledged?
CLOTALDO   Is this my plight?
SEGISMUND   You've long betrayed our country's laws,
Fawned on the king to aid your cause
And treated me with cruel delight.
85   For this, the king, the law, and I,
In light of crimes we three condemn,
Now sentence you to die for them
At my own hands.
SECOND SERVANT   My lord!
SEGISMUND   Don't try
To thwart me or impede my plan;
90   I won't be hindered. By the cross,
Dare step between us and I'll toss
You headfirst through that window, man!
FIRST SERVANT   Clotaldo, flee!
CLOTALDO   Oblivious dunce,
To manifest such reckless pride

7. Roman emperors were frequently represented wearing a crown of laurel, symbolic of victory (and specifically, in Rome, of military triumph).

95   Not conscious you've dreamt all you spied!
                [*Exit* CLOTALDO.]
SECOND SERVANT   Be mindful that . . .
SEGISMUND   Leave here at once!
SECOND SERVANT   He looked but to obey his king.
SEGISMUND   When unjust laws are duly weighed,
        The king, too, may be disobeyed.
100   They owed their true prince everything.
SECOND SERVANT   His charge was not to reason why
        The king's will isn't sovereign.
SEGISMUND   You must care little for your skin
        To make me constantly reply.
105 CLARION   Correct, sire! Right the prince is, too!
        It seems like you're the one remiss.
SECOND SERVANT   What gives you leave to speak like this?
CLARION   I took the leave myself, man.
SEGISMUND   Who
        On earth are you?
CLARION   A meddling drone
110   And chief among that nosy group,
        The best example of a snoop
        Our great wide world has ever known.
SEGISMUND   In this strange realm, I've yet to greet
        A man who's pleased me more.
CLARION   Kind lord,
115   I aim to please and am adored
        By every Segismund I meet.

2.4

                [*Enter* ASTOLF.]
ASTOLF   Oh, ever happy dawns the day
        When you, the son of Poland, show
        Your face resplendent and aglow
        In joyfulness and bright array!
5   You tinge the earth's horizons red;
        Your crimson mantle hues the skies,
        For like the morning sun you rise
        Out some secluded mountain bed.
        Ascend, however late! Defer
10   No more the crowning of these slopes
        With laurel leaves the palace hopes
        Shall never fade.
SEGISMUND   God keep you, sir.
ASTOLF   You might have earned a stern rebuke
        For having failed to see in time
15   That rank deserves more reverence.[8] I'm
        The titled Astolf, highborn Duke

8. That is, a duke should not be addressed merely as "sir" (2.4.12).

Of Moscow, cousin to your line.
We're equals, each a noble peer.

SEGISMUND   So, when I say "God keep you" here,

20   What does that greeting undermine?
Prone as you are to boastful rot
About your name and to complaint,
I'll say without the least restraint
When next we meet, "God keep you not."

25 SECOND SERVANT   Such brusqueness, Highness, still occurs
Throughout his speech and can cause chills,
But then, they raised him in the hills.
The noble Astolf far prefers . . .

SEGISMUND   His smug complacency and strut

30   Annoyed me greatly. Then to doff
His hat and fail to keep it off . . .

SECOND SERVANT   He's royal.

SEGISMUND   But a royal what?

SECOND SERVANT   That said, it's fitting there should be
More mutual respect from two

35   Who aren't mere noblemen.

SEGISMUND   Pray, who
Dispatched you here to torment me?

2.5

[*Enter* STELLA.]

STELLA   Your Royal Highness, may the throne
Beneath this canopy extend
A welcome that shall never end
To one it proudly claims its own.

5   And may you reign here free from fears
Of intrigue as our monarch who'll
Augustly and serenely rule
For centuries, not merely years.

SEGISMUND   Oh, tell me, who is that discreet

10   And sovereign beauty standing there?
What human goddess passing fair
At whose divine, celestial feet
The skies cast down their crimson light?
What lovely maid do I admire?

15 CLARION   Your cousin, Lady Stella, sire.

SEGISMUND   Say "sun" and you'd be no less right.
How fine of you to wish me well
With fine-wrought words in this strange place.
Since first I saw that fine-shaped face,

20   Your well-wishing has worked its spell
And as I've come to feel such fine
Remarks unearned, though gladly heard,
I'm grateful for the gracious word.

Sweet Stella, you who rise and shine
25 To light the mornings with your rays
And cheer the radiant orb's bright run,
What function do you leave the sun
By rising at the break of days?
Oh, let me kiss that gorgeous hand,
30 A snow-white chalice where the breeze
Imbibes quintessence at its ease.

STELLA   My lord, be courteous in your stand.

ASTOLF [*Aside.*]   If she succumbs to this, then I
Am lost!

SECOND SERVANT   I sense good Astolf's pain
35 But can I make the prince refrain?
My lord, I'm sure you fathom why
This violates court protocol
With Astolf present . . .

SEGISMUND   Didn't we
Agree you'd stop tormenting me?

40 SECOND SERVANT   I said it's not correct.

SEGISMUND   This all
Has greatly angered me today!
Thwart any outcome I expect
And I will deem that incorrect.

SECOND SERVANT   But sire, I even heard you say
45 That service and obeyance both
Are acts correct beyond compare.

SEGISMUND   I think you also heard me swear
I'd throw a nuisance, on my oath,
From off this balcony to die.

50 SECOND SERVANT   You can't treat men like me with so
Much disregard and scorn.

SEGISMUND   Oh, no?
Why don't I just give this a try?
            [*He grabs the* SECOND SERVANT, *exits followed by all,
            and returns.*]

ASTOLF   I can't believe what I've just seen!

STELLA   Come quickly and help stop this row!
            [*She exits.*]

55 SEGISMUND   He plunged into the sea below
And God let no one intervene!

ASTOLF   I'd look to moderate these sorts
Of reckless acts and rash pursuits;
Men are no further from base brutes
60 Than mountains are from palace courts.

SEGISMUND   Keep talking like some paragon
Of virtue as you lecture me
And, sooner than you think, you'll see
You've naught to place your hat upon.
            [*Exit* ASTOLF.]

2.6

[*Enter* BASIL.]

BASIL   What's going on here?

SEGISMUND   Not a thing.
    I stopped a knave from pestering me
    And tossed him off the balcony.

CLARION   Take care, you're talking to the king.

5   BASIL   Not one day at the palace, yet
    Already human life's been lost.

SEGISMUND   He claimed I couldn't, and it cost
    Him dear. Looks like I won that bet.

BASIL   It grieves us greatly that our late
10   Reunion be so villainized.
    We'd thought that, having been apprised
    Of how the stars have steered your fate,
    You might supplant this rage with tact.
    And yet, to what do you resort
15   On first appearing at the court?
    A savage, homicidal act.
    What kind of fatherly embrace
    Could you expect these arms to give
    When we could only hope to live
20   To breathe the air by God's good grace
    Far from your murderous grasp? Who could
    Behold a naked dagger glow
    Before it struck a mortal blow
    And fail to shrink in fear? Who would
25   Bear witness to the blood-red pall
    That lingered where a man was killed
    And not be moved? The strongest willed
    Among us would heed instinct's call.
    As we perceive the grievous harms
30   That issue from your cruel embrace
    And contemplate this bloodied place,
    We'll keep safe distance from those arms.
    So though we'd planned, our love revealed,
    To fling these arms about your neck,
35   We hold these sentiments in check,
    Fear-stricken by the might you wield.

SEGISMUND   I've lived outside their fold till now
    And don't see what I stand to lose.
    A father who would so abuse
40   Authority to disavow
    His own son's birthright merits scorn.
    Entombed as if I were deceased,
    Raised wild like a savage beast
    And treated like some monster born
45   To forfeit life by your decree,
    I hold that clasp for which you yearn

Of no emotional concern—
You robbed me of humanity.

BASIL   By heaven's just omnipotence,
50   We rue the day we gave you life
To countenance this fiery strife
And tolerate such insolence.

SEGISMUND   Had you not sired me willfully,
I'd have no basis for complaint,
55   But since you did, what need restraint?
You took my life away from me.
And while no act is nobler than
To give, whatever that gift's worth,
No baser act exists on earth
60   Than taking back that gift again.

BASIL   Are these the thanks that lay in store
For turning a foul prisoner
Into a prince?

SEGISMUND   I can't infer
What I've to be so thankful for,
65   You tyrant to my will! Malign,
Decrepit despot! You'll soon breathe
Your last! What gift do you bequeath
But that which rightfully is mine?
Since you're my father and my king,
70   The grandeur and nobility
That nature's law bestowed on me
Were mine for the inheriting.
So in my new exalted state
And in no way obliged to you,
75   I say your day of reckoning's due
For all the years you'd abrogate
My honor, life, and liberty.
You should be thanking me, you know,
For not collecting what you owe,
80   As you, sir, are in debt to me.

BASIL   Impulsive, wild, and barbarous!
All heaven augured has come true.
Look down, skies, on his rage and view
Him utterly contrarious!
85   Although our ultimate behest
Disclosed your true identity
And palace graces guarantee
The prince be prized above the rest,
Attend these words for your soul's sake:
90   Be humble, man, and less extreme,
For all you see might be a dream,
Though you may think you're wide awake.
          [Exit.]

SEGISMUND   What could he mean? I, dreaming, when
All this is patent to my eyes?

95   I touch, I feel and can devise
      What I am now and was back then.
      You may well rue your choices, yet
      You're powerless to change them now.
      I'm noble, and no matter how
100   Intently you may feel regret,
      No man can ever strip away
      The prince and heir apparent's crown.
      Though your first sight of me was down
      In that dank prison where I lay,
105   My fast self-knowledge has increased
      And now that I've seen through the sham
      Of what I was, I know I am
      Some mongrel mix of man and beast.

2.7

[Enter ROSAURA, *dressed as a lady-in-waiting.]*

    ROSAURA   Dame Stella wants me near,
      Though I'm afraid of meeting Astolf here.
      Clotaldo thinks it best
      He neither see me nor divine my quest,
5   As cleansing honor warrants sacrifice.
      I trust his sage advice,
      Indebted as I am to him who came
      And rescued both my life and honored name.
    CLARION   So, which among the host
10   Of things you've seen today has pleased you most?
    SEGISMUND   I wasn't much surprised
      By anything. All was as I'd surmised.
      But since you have inquired,
      The thing on earth that's most to be admired
15   Is woman's beauty. Mind
      Me now: I'd read, while odiously confined,
      That out of all the creatures in His plan,
      God spent most time on that small cosmos, man.
      But this cannot be true,
20   For woman is a slice of heaven, too,
      And lovelier by far,
      As distant from male clay as earth from star,
      Like her I now behold.
    ROSAURA   The prince! I must withdraw and be less bold.
25 SEGISMUND   I beg you, woman, stay.
      Don't make the sun set at the break of day
      By leaving on the run.
      You'll blend the dawn and twilight into one,
      Cold dark with sunbeams bright,
30   And cut too short the shining of the light.
      Wait! What's this I perceive?
    ROSAURA   I can't trust my own eyes, yet must believe.

SEGISMUND   I've seen this loveliness
  Before.
ROSAURA   And I this grandeur, though with less
35 Solemnity back when
  It lay in chains.
SEGISMUND   I've found my life again!
  Speak, woman—yes, I use
  The most endearing term a man can choose—
  Who are you? Have we met?
40 No matter; you owe me allegiance, yet
  Some strange bond links us more.
  I'm certain that I've seen your face before.
  Who are you, woman fair?
ROSAURA [*Aside.*]   I must pretend. A lady wrought with care
45 Who serves in Stella's train.
SEGISMUND   No, say you are the sun, in whose domain
  Of fire the stellar bides,
  For Stella basks in rays your light provides.
  In all the fragrant realm
50 Of flowers, there's but one goddess at the helm,
  The rose, whom others call
  Their empress, being loveliest of all.
  I've seen the finest stones
  Extracted from the earth's profoundest zones
55 Revere the diamond's shine,
  Their emperor as brightest in the mine.
  At lush courts in the sky
  Where stars from teetering republics vie,
  I've seen fair Venus[9] reign
60 As queen of all that vast and starred demesne.
  In those ethereal climes,
  I've seen the sun convene the orbs oftimes
  At court, where he holds sway,
  Presiding as the oracle of day.
65 How could a case arise,
  Then, where the planets, stones, and flowers prize
  Great beauty, yet yours serves
  A lady far less fair? Your charm deserves
  More praise than hers bestows,
70 Oh bright sun, Venus, diamond, star, and rose!

2.8

[*Enter* CLOTALDO.]

CLOTALDO   Restraining Segismund devolves on me,
  As he was once my ward. What's this I see?
ROSAURA   I'm flattered by your praise,
  Though silence plies a lofty turn of phrase,
5 For when a person's judgment seems most blurred,

9. The Roman goddess of love.

The best response is not to say a word.

SEGISMUND   You mustn't go yet. Wait!
   You wouldn't want to leave in such a state,
   Misjudging my desire?

10 ROSAURA   I beg permission, Highness, to retire.

SEGISMUND   Your veiled demands aggrieve;
   You don't so much request as take your leave.

ROSAURA   What choice have I when you won't let me pass?

SEGISMUND   I'm civil now, but might become more crass
15   Soon, for resistance strains
   My patience like a poison in my veins!

ROSAURA   Not even poison laced
   With fury so intensive it effaced
   This patience you declare
20   Could ever stain my honor, nor would dare.

SEGISMUND   You're trying hard, I see,
   To make yourself appear less fair to me.
   You'll always find me game
   To take on the impossible. The claim
25   Some knave made that I couldn't cause his death
   Was breathed with his last breath,
   So if I dared to probe all I could do,
   I'd throw your honor out the window, too!

CLOTALDO   His rage will not relent.
30 What should I do, dear heavens, with him bent
   Upon this lustful crime,
   Imperiling my name a second time?

ROSAURA   The fateful prophecy
   That warned this kingdom of your tyranny
35   Foresaw the crimes you'd bear,
   The scandal, murder, treason, and despair.
   Still, who could stoop to blame
   A human being who's just a man in name,
   Cruel, reckless, inhumane,
40   A barbarous tyrant no one can restrain,
   Reared like some savage beast?

SEGISMUND   I'd thought my wooing at the very least
   Would spare me this display
   And hoped to win your favor in this way.
45   But since my suit occasions such alarm,
   See what you think of me without the charm!
   Leave us, the lot of you, and bolt the door.
   See no one enters here.

      [CLARION exits.]

ROSAURA   I die for sure!
   Wait . . .

SEGISMUND   Fleeing my embrace
50 Will hardly put this tyrant in his place.

CLOTALDO   Again he kindles strife!
   I hope this meddling won't cost me my life.

Desist, sire! Let her be.

SEGISMUND   This is the second time you've angered me,
55   You doddering old dunce.
      Have you no fear you'll pay for these affronts?
      How did you slip in here?

CLOTALDO   I entered, summoned by these tones of fear,
      To urge you to restrain
60   Such impulse if you ever wish to reign.
      You're not king yet, so temper this extreme
      Behavior. All you see may be a dream.

SEGISMUND   You know I grow irate
      When you use fantasy to set me straight.
65   Would it be dream to slay
      You or quite real?

[As SEGISMUND *draws his sword,* CLOTALDO *grabs his arm and kneels before him.*]

CLOTALDO   I know no other way
      To save my life, my lord!

SEGISMUND   How dare you place your hands upon my sword!

CLOTALDO   I won't release this blade
70   Until a body comes to give me aid
      And calm your rage.

ROSAURA   My God!

SEGISMUND   Let go, I said,
      You senile fool, or you're as good as dead!
      If you continue so,   [*They struggle.*]
      I'll crush you in my arms, detested foe!

75 ROSAURA   Who'll help us? Anyone!
      Clotaldo's being killed!

[*She exits.*]

2.9

[ASTOLF *enters,* CLOTALDO *falls at his feet, and* ASTOLF *steps between* CLOTALDO *and* SEGISMUND.]

ASTOLF   What have you done
      To him, good-hearted lord?
      Cold blood should never blight so brave a sword
      With stains of infamy.
5   Resheathe your blade and let the old man be.

SEGISMUND   I will when his depraved
      Blood tinges it bright red.

ASTOLF   His life is saved—
      He's sued for sanctuary at my feet
      And not to spare him, sire, would scarce be meet.

10 SEGISMUND   Allow me, then, to spear your life as well
      So I might have revenge for what befell
      Me earlier at your hands.

ASTOLF   No self-defense
      Could cause judicious majesty offense.

2.10

[*They draw their swords. Enter King* BASIL *and* STELLA.]

CLOTALDO   Don't injure him!

BASIL   What, drawn before the king?

STELLA   It's Astolf, furious and battling!

BASIL   Just what is happening here?

ASTOLF   Sire, not a thing now that Your Grace is near.

[*They sheathe their swords.*]

5   SEGISMUND   A great deal, sire, be you near or not.
     I'd just begun to murder this old sot.

BASIL   Why, was no reverence shown
     For these gray hairs?

CLOTALDO   My liege, they're mine alone
     And little matter.

SEGISMUND   Nothing you could say

10   Would force me to respect that hoary gray
     And all its vile deceit.
     I'll see it some day, too, beneath my feet,
     Which may at last avenge
     My stolen life and bring me sweet revenge.

         [*He exits.*]

15   BASIL   Before you see these things,
     You'll sleep again, and all the happenings
     You'd once believed were real
     Will only prove to be what dreams reveal.

         [*Exit* BASIL *and* CLOTALDO.]

2.11

ASTOLF   The stars above so rarely lie
     When they predict catastrophes.
     They forecast ills with acumen
     But blessings hesitatingly.

5   How famous an astrologer
     Would that man be who only spied
     Disasters for, without a doubt,
     These always manage to transpire!
     My life and Segismund's attest

10   To this contrivance of the stars,
     Which presaged for the two of us
     Divergent fortunes from the start.
     For him, they foresaw misery,
     Misfortune, insolence, and death.

15   As all these have been evident,
     The stars have since been proved correct.
     For me, though, lady, once I'd gazed
     Upon your eyes' unrivalled beams—
     Beside which sunshine looks like shade

20   And light from heaven epicene[1]—
      They seemed to foretell gladdened times
      Of triumph, comfort, and acclaim,
      Which proved to be both true and false
      Because stars only forecast fates
25   With accuracy when they turn
      The joy they bode to wretchedness.
STELLA   I've no doubt that these gallant words
      Are spoken with the best intent
      But you must mean them for the maid
30   Whose painted likeness hung about
      Your neck, good Astolf, first you came
      To visit me and seek the crown.
      As this is so, these sentiments
      Belong to her, and her alone.
35   Go seek sweet recompense from her
      Because, as promissory notes,
      The courtly grace and oaths of faith
      You use as currency to serve
      For other maids and other kings
40   Are worthless in love's constant world.

2.12

      [*Enter* ROSAURA.]
ROSAURA [*Aside.*]   Thank heavens my calamitous
      Adversity has reached its end!
      Whoever's seen what I've seen should
      Have nothing more to fear again!
5 ASTOLF   I'll take her portrait from my chest
      And lovingly hang in its place
      The image of your loveliness.
      For where fair Stella shines, no shade
      Can fall, no lowly star besmirch
10   The sun's bright realm! I'll fetch it now.
      Oh, fair Rosaura, pardon this
      Transgression, but you aren't around.
      When men and women are apart,
      Their troth is worth no more than this.
            [*He exits.*]
15 ROSAURA   Because I feared I might be seen,
      I hid and couldn't hear a thing.
STELLA   Astrea![2]
ROSAURA   Yes, fair lady mine.
STELLA   How very much my heart's consoled
      To find you here of all my train,
20   For I could think to bare my soul

1. That is, delicate, lacking vigor.
2. The name Rosaura has assumed (see

2.14.8), derived from the Greek word for star
(as Stella is from the Latin).

To no one else.

ROSAURA   You honor one
Whose only wish has been to please.

STELLA   Astrea, I can scarcely claim
I know you, yet you hold the key
25   To opening my inmost heart.
Because of all you clearly are,
I'll risk confiding to you what
I've long been keeping in the dark
From my own self.

ROSAURA   I'm here to serve.

30 STELLA   Then, let me keep the story brief.
My cousin Astolf—cousin, sure!
Why say he's so much more to me
When some things are as good as said
In thought, where wishes are fulfilled?—
35   Yes, Astolf and I are to wed
If it should be the heavens' will
To undo countless miseries
By granting us this happiness.
A lady's portrait that he wore
40   About his neck when we first met
So saddened me, I gently pressed
To know the maid's identity.
A gallant man, he loves me well
And has withdrawn now to retrieve
45   The likeness. Modesty forbids
My being here on his return,
So wait for him and, when he comes,
Request he leave the miniature
With you. For now, I'll say no more.
50   Your beauty and discretion show
That you'll soon know what love is, too.

             [*She exits.*]

2.13

ROSAURA   I wish to God I'd never known!
Just heavens, help me now! Is there
A woman anywhere alive
Whose artfulness could find a means
5   To rescue her from such a bind?
Have those inclement skies above
Oppressed a lady so before,
Assailing her with ceaseless grief
Until she's wretched and forlorn?
10   My delicate predicament
Makes it impossible for me
To be consoled by arguments
Or counseled on my miseries,

As ever since that first mischance
15 Befell me, not one incident's
Occurred that hasn't brought me grief.
This sad succession of events,
All heirs apparent of themselves,
Arise like phoenixes from ash
20 As each, newborn, begets the next.[3]
They come to life mid smoldering death,
The cinders of this renaissance
Their sepulcher and birthing bed.
"Our cares are cowards, and poltroons,"[4]
25 A certain sage was wont to say,
"Stalk humans cravenly in packs."
But I declare misfortunes brave
For always forging nobly on
And never beating weak retreats.
30 Whoever has experienced
The strain of care may face life free
Of worries or the nagging fear
That cares will ever leave his side.
I know this far too well from all
35 The woes inflicted on my life
And can't recall a time when cares
Were absent. They'll refuse to rest
Till I succumb, a casualty
Of fate, into the arms of death.
40 What choice would any woman have
If she were in my place?
Disclosing my identity
Might cause Clotaldo great offense,
For he's vouchsafed my refuge, life,
45 And honor under great duress.
By keeping silence, he believes,
I'll see my honored name restored,
But if I don't say who I am
When Astolf spies me here at court,
50 How will I feign not knowing him?
For even if my voice and eyes
Unite to fake their ignorance,
My soul would give them all the lie.
So what am I to do? Why plan
55 Contrivances when it's so plain
To see that, notwithstanding all
The thought I'd given to prepare
For my encountering him again,

3. The phoenix was a mythical bird that immo-
lated itself on a self-built pyre and was reborn
from its own ashes.
4. A Spanish expression akin to "cares come

in threes," with the added suggestion that
misfortunes are too cowardly to bully people
individually.

This heartache will respond the way
60   It pleases? Who among us boasts
Dominion over all his pain?
So with a soul too timorous
To dare determine what my course
Should be, oh, may my heartache end
65   Today, may all the pains I've borne
Desist, and may I leave behind
Both semblances that once deceived
And lingering doubt. But until then,
Sweet heavens, stand guard over me!

2.14

[Enter ASTOLF *with the portrait.*]

ASTOLF   Fair lady, here's the portrait you . . .
My God, what's this?
ROSAURA   My lord appears
Amazed. What causes his surprise?
ASTOLF   Beholding you, Rosaura, here.
5 ROSAURA   Rosaura? Why, Your Lordship is
Confused and certainly mistakes
Me for another maid. I'm called
Astrea, and my humble state
Could scarcely captivate a prince
10   Or bring such rapture to my life.
ASTOLF   Rosaura, let this pretense end.
You know the soul can never lie;
Though I may see Astrea here,
I'll love her like Rosaura yet.
15 ROSAURA   I comprehend you not, my lord,
Hence my replies are hesitant.
I'll only say that I was bid
By Stella, Venus's star here,
To tarry in this place until
20   Such time as you, my lord, appeared
To ask from you on her behalf
The portrait causing her such hurt—
An understandable demand—
Which I would then remit to her.
25   My lady's pleasure wills it so;
However small the pleas she makes,
Though they be to my detriment,
Are Stella's still, and I obey.
ASTOLF   Say what you will, Rosaura, though
30   You're terrible at subterfuge.
Go tell that music in your eyes
To play in concert with the tune
Your voice sings so their melody
Might temper this discordant clash

35 And harmonize their instrument,
   Adjusting measures in the dance
   Of all the falsehoods that you speak
   And that one verity you feel.
 ROSAURA Let me repeat, I wait but for
40 The portrait.
 ASTOLF   Very well. I see
   You won't forsake this pretense, so
   I'll answer, then, with one my own.
   Astrea, given my esteem
   For Stella, let the lady know
45 That my obliging her request
   To fetch this pendant seems a poor
   Example of gentility.
   Hence, as she is so well-adored,
   I send her the original,
50 Which you may bear her in the flesh,
   Revealing the extent to which
   You and the likeness are enmeshed.
 ROSAURA A man who sets out bold and brave
   To bring back something on his word
55 And then returns not with this prize
   But with some thing of greater worth
   Conceded him, still thinks himself
   A slighted fool whose mission failed.
   I'd hoped to take my portrait back
60 Though the original won't pale
   In force beside it. Still, I can't
   Return so slighted. Come, my lord,
   You'll hand the portrait over now—
   Without it I must shun the court.
65 ASTOLF And if I don't relinquish this,
   What will you then?
 ROSAURA   All out assault—
   Let go of it!
 ASTOLF   You strike in vain.
 ROSAURA The portrait mustn't ever fall
   Into another woman's hands.
70 ASTOLF You're spirited!
 ROSAURA   False-hearted cheat!
 ASTOLF That's quite enough, Rosaura mine.
 ROSAURA I yours, you scoundrel? You're deceived!

2.15

 [*Enter* STELLA.]
 STELLA Astrea! Astolf! What's all this?
 ASTOLF Now Lady Stella's come.
 ROSAURA [*Aside.*]   Oh, Love,
   Grant me the prowess to retrieve

My portrait! [*To* STELLA.] Lady, if you want
5   To know why we are quarreling,
I'll tell you.

ASTOLF   What's the point of this?

ROSAURA You bade me, lady, tarry here
For Astolf so he might remit
To me the portrait you desired.
10   Well, once I found myself alone—
The mind can traipse so easily
Through scores of subjects, as you know—
This talk of portraits drifted back
To jog my memory, as it would,
15   Till I recalled my sleeve bore one
Of me, and thought I'd take a look—
For when no one's around, we must
Amuse ourselves with what is near—
But then I dropped the thing just as
20   Duke Astolf presently appeared
To bring the other portrait by.
He picked mine up, but so resists
Complying with the charge he's borne
That now he says he'll harbor it
25   Along with yours. Despite my pleas,
He won't consent to hand mine back.
Your Ladyship came just in time
To see me in the frenzied act
Of repossessing it by force.
30   The portrait dangling in his grasp
Is mine, which you could verify,
My lady, with a simple glance.

STELLA You may return her miniature.

[*She takes it from him.*]

ASTOLF My lady . . .

STELLA   Yes, I must allow
35   It almost does you justice, maid.

ROSAURA You see it's mine, then?

STELLA   I've no doubt.

ROSAURA Now ask him for the other one.

STELLA Please take your portrait and retire.

ROSAURA [*Aside.*] Why should I care what happens next
40   As long as I've reclaimed what's mine?

[*She exits.*]

2.16

STELLA I'd like the portrait that I asked
You for. I'll never lay my eyes
On you or speak to you again.
Still, knowing it remains your prized

5   Possession pains me to no end,
       Not least because I fondly did
       Petition it.

ASTOLF [*Aside.*]   What's there to say
       In such confused predicaments?
       [*To* STELLA.] Fair Stella, I'm your servant still
10   In every possible regard.
       It's just not in my power now
       To grant your wish because . . .

STELLA   You are
       A faithless lover and vile man.
       Forget I asked for it at all;
15   Why should I want her portrait when
       The very sight of it recalls
       My having had to plead for it?
                [*She exits.*]

ASTOLF   Don't go! Please listen! Give me time,
       Rosaura! Dear Lord, grant me strength!
20   Just how, from where, for what and why
       Did you turn up in Poland now
       To seek your ruin as well as mine?

2.17

[SEGISMUND *appears as he did at play's start, wearing
animal pelts and in chains, asleep on the ground. Enter*
CLOTALDO, CLARION, *and two* SERVANTS.]

CLOTALDO   Just leave him drowsing on the ground.
       Today his overweening pride
       Will end where it began.

FIRST SERVANT   I've tried
       To chain him as he'd once been bound.

5 CLARION   Why rush to wake and be decrowned
       When sleeping, Segismund, will save
       Yourself the sight of fortune's knave?
       The glory you've enjoyed is fled
       And you'll endure, alive but dead,
10   A specter from beyond the grave.

CLOTALDO   An orator with this much flair
       Will also need a cloistered space,
       Some quiet, isolated place
       Where he might discourse free of care.
15   Go seize that speechifier there
       And lock him in his tower retreat.

CLARION   Why me?

CLOTALDO   Because it's understood
       That clarions left unmuffled could
       Sound off and noisily repeat
20   Our palace secrets in the street.

CLARION   Do I, perchance, plot endlessly

To murder my own father? No!
Was I the one who dared to throw
That sorry Icarus in the sea?[5]
25   Am I reborn or still just me?
Is this a bad dream? Why this plan
To jail me?

CLOTALDO   Your name's Clarion, man.

CLARION   Then during my imprisonment
I'll be a viler instrument,
30   The cornet, and stay mute a span.

[*The servants take* CLARION *away.*]

2.18

[*Enter King* BASIL, *disguised.*]

BASIL   Clotaldo.

CLOTALDO   Sire! Does this disguise
Befit your Royal Majesty?

BASIL   The foolish curiosity
To view the prince with our own eyes
5   And see the state in which he lies
Has led us to his cell today.

CLOTALDO   Just look at him there, brought to bay
In chains, dejected and forlorn.

BASIL   The star beneath which you were born
10   Determined it would be this way.
Go wake him. So much for our schemes.
The drink you brewed has run its course
And all its herbs have lost their force.

CLOTALDO   His sleep is restless, yet he seems
15   To speak.

BASIL   What manner of strange dreams
Could visit Segismund alone?

SEGISMUND [*In his world of dream.*]   A pious prince is one who's known
For purging tyrants from his lands.
Clotaldo dies by these two hands
20   While Basil, prostrate, yields his throne.

CLOTALDO   My dying makes the plot complete.

BASIL   He joins effrontery with threat.

CLOTALDO   He'll see me foully murdered yet.

BASIL   And vanquish us beneath his feet.

25 SEGISMUND [*Still dreaming.*]   Parade your valor in the street,
The world's great theater, onstage where
Its size will loom beyond compare.
Avenging my base sire's neglect
Will only have the right effect
30   If Segismund's triumphant there. [*He awakens.*]

---

5. In Greek mythology, Icarus and his father, Daedalus, escaped from King Minos's island of Crete by using wings made with wax; but ignoring his father's warning, Daedalus flew too close to the sun, the wax melted, and he plunged to his death in the sea.

What's this about? Where can I be?

BASIL   He's not to learn that we're here, too.
Now do what you've been charged to do
As we retire where we can see.

[*He withdraws from view.*]

35 SEGISMUND   What's happened? Is this really me
In chains again amid this blight,
A horrid and pathetic sight?
And is that you, my living tomb,
Old tower? God help me meet this doom!
40 But, what strange things I dreamt tonight!

CLOTALDO   I'm duty bound to keep this mime
Alive, whatever it may take.
Is it not time for you to wake?

SEGISMUND   Yes, it's well past my waking time.

45 CLOTALDO   Do you intend to spend the prime
Of day asleep? Can it be right
That, ever since we tracked the flight
Of that grand eagle heaven-bound,
You've lain here drowsing on the ground
50 And never once awakened?

SEGISMUND   Quite,
And haven't yet, as I'd conceived.
As far as I can ascertain,
I sleepwalk still through dream's domain
And would not feel at all deceived
55 If everything that I'd believed
Took place would dissipate anew
Or if what I saw now weren't true.
For one in chains, it's no great leap
To understand, though fast asleep,
60 That one can dream while waking, too.

CLOTALDO   What did you dream while so confined?

SEGISMUND   Supposing that it was a dream,
Clotaldo! Here is what I deem
Occurred, and not just in my mind:
65 I wakened yesterday to find
Myself—this taunts me!—lounging in
A bed so bright it might have been
The flowery cot by which the Spring
Adorns the earth with coloring
70 From all the hues contained therein.
A thousand nobles bowed before
My vaunted feet and, once they'd hailed
Me as their prince, I was regaled
With banquets, jewels, robes, and more.
75 You purged what calm my senses bore
By naming me, to my delight,
King Basil's heir by natural right
And though my fortune's fallen since,

I briefly reigned as Poland's prince.

80 CLOTALDO   What great reward had I in sight?

SEGISMUND   Accusing you of treachery,
My heart made bold with power and vice,
I tried disposing of you twice.

CLOTALDO   But why were you so cruel to me?

85 SEGISMUND   I'd thought to rule with tyranny
And match the evil I'd been done.
I loved none but one woman—one—
The only real thing to transcend,
As I believe, my dreaming's end,
90   An endless need that's just begun.

[BASIL exits.]

CLOTALDO [Aside.]   The king was moved by what he heard
And fled affected from the tower.
[To SEGISMUND.] Our talk in your last waking hour
About that eagle must have spurred
95   These dreams of empire afterward.
Still, Segismund, you really ought
To honor one who reared and taught
You, even in the realm of dream.
For doing good is man's supreme
100   Imperative and not for naught.

[He exits.]

2.19

SEGISMUND   How very true! Then let's suppress
The fury of our savage state,
The vile ambition and the hate,
So when we dream we won't transgress.
5   For dream we will, though we possess
No sense of where it is we thrive
And dreaming just means being alive.
The insight life's experience gives
Is that, until man wakes, he lives
10   A life that only dreams contrive.
The king dreams he is king and reigns
Deluded in his full command,
Imposing order in his land.
The borrowed plaudits he obtains
15   Blow scattered through the wind's domains
As death—man's life is so unjust!—
Transmutes them into ash and dust.
Oh, who on earth could wish to wield
Such might when waking means to yield
20   It all to death's dream, as we must?
The rich man dreams his riches great,
Which makes his wealth more burdensome.
The poor man dreams that he'll succumb

To misery in his beggared state.
25 He also dreams who prospers late.
The striver and aspirer do,
The mocker and offender, too.
In fact, all mortal souls on earth
Dream their conditions from their birth,
30 Though no one knows this to be true.
I'm dreaming now that darker days
Await me, chained, in this dark cell
As I'd dreamt I'd been treated well
Of late in some strange coddled phase.
35 What's life? A frenzied, blurry haze.
What's life? Not anything it seems.
A shadow. Fiction filling reams.
All we possess on earth means nil,
For life's a dream, think what you will,
40 And even all our dreams are dreams.

3.1

[*Enter* CLARION.]

CLARION   I lodge in this enchanted tower
A captive, for I know the truth,
But if my knowledge means sure death,
What will my ignorance lead to?
5 That such a hungry, hungry man
Should perish like a living corpse!
I'm feeling sorry for myself,
So go ahead, say, "That's for sure,"
For surely, that's not hard to see.
10 This silence, too, is pretty rough,
But when your name is Clarion, well,
There's just no way to hold your tongue.
My sole companions in this place—
And this would be a wild guess—
15 Are mice and spiders lurking here.
Who needs a goldfinch for a pet?
My teeming brain is still awhirl
With everything I dreamt last night:
The sound of trumpet blares and shawms[6]
20 Came mingled with deceptive sights
Like one of flagellants that marched
In some procession of the cross,
First rising, then descending, then
Succumbing once they saw the lost
25 Blood flowing down their fellows' backs.
These bouts with hunger here of late
May cause the swoons in me as well,

6. Double-reed Renaissance woodwinds, forerunners of the modern oboe.

For, while I'm left to starve by day,
An empty Plato[7] offers no
30 Consolement of philosophy,
While each night I appear before
A Diet of Worms,[8] which isn't meet.
So if this new Church calendar
Considers silence "blessed" now,
35 Let Secret be my patron saint—
I'll fast for him and break no vows.
I haven't breathed a word yet, so
My punishment seems well deserved:
What greater sacrilege is there
40 Than quiet from one hired to serve?

3.2

[The sound of drums and SOLDIERS' *voices offstage.]*

FIRST SOLDIER They're holding him inside this tower.
Here, batter down these bolted doors
And storm the cell!
CLARION Good heavens, have
They come for me? I'm pretty sure,
5 Since they seem pretty sure I'm here.
Whatever could they want?
FIRST SOLDIER Charge in!
SECOND SOLDIER He's here!
CLARION Oh, no he's not!
ALL My lord!
CLARION They must be drunkards on a binge!
SECOND SOLDIER All hail, our prince and rightful liege!
10 To you alone do we submit
Our forces, natural-born heir,
And not to any foreign prince.
To prove our troth, we kiss your feet.
ALL Long live the prince, whom we love well!
15 CLARION Good God, can this be happening?
Is it the custom in this realm
To seize a body every day
And make a prince of him before
He's thrown back in the tower? Must be,
20 Since each day there's a different lord.
Looks like I'll have to play the part.
ALL Give us your feet!
CLARION I can't because
I need to use them for myself

---

7. Greek philosopher (ca. 427–ca. 347 B.C.E.); though here invoked to play on the word "plate," Plato is a particularly appropriate choice, given his concern with the nature of reality.

8. Another food-related pun, on the assembly ("diet") held in 1521 in the German city of Worms to which Martin Luther was summoned to defend his religious beliefs.

And it would be a tragic flaw
25   To govern as a soleless prince.
  SECOND SOLDIER   We've seen your father and declared
    Our will to him: it's you alone
    We recognize as Poland's heir,
    And not the Muscovite.
  CLARION   You told
30   My father? Have you no respect,
    You lousy bunch of so-and-so's?
  FIRST SOLDIER   One can't keep loyal hearts in check.
  CLARION   Well, loyalty I can excuse.
  SECOND SOLDIER   Restore the kingdom to your line.
35   Long live Prince Segismund!
  ALL   Long life!
  CLARION   Ah, they said "Segismund." All right,
    So Segismund's the word they use
    To mean a prince is counterfeit.

3.3

[*Enter* SEGISMUND.]

  SEGISMUND   Is someone calling out my name?
  CLARION   Am I a has-been as a prince?
  SECOND SOLDIER   Who here is Segismund?
  SEGISMUND   I am.
  SECOND SOLDIER   You reckless fool! Impersonate
5   The heir apparent to the throne?
  CLARION   Now that's a game I'd never play.
    Besides, it was the lot of you
    That segismundized me. Ergo,[9]
    The only foolish recklessness
10   Put on display here was your own.
  FIRST SOLDIER   Great prince, brave Segismund! Although
    The standards that we bear are yours,
    It's solemn faith alone compels
    Our number to proclaim you lord.
15   Your father Basil, our great king,
    Has lived in terror of the skies
    Fulfilling their dread prophecy
    That presaged you would see him lie
    Subdued beneath your feet. For this,
20   He'd planned to yield your titled claim
    And highborn right to Astolf, Duke
    Of Moscow, and eclipse your reign.
    King Basil had convened the court
    When Poland learned an heir survived
25   And wished him to succeed the king,
    Reluctant that a foreign line

---

9. Clarion mocks the language of philosophical argumentation.

Should govern them on native soil.
So, holding the inclemency
Of starry fate in noble scorn,
30 They sought your cell to see you freed
From these cruel chains. All live in hope
The rightful heir will leave these grounds
And, buttressed by their arms, reclaim
For them the scepter and the crown
35 Out that usurping tyrant's grip!
Come forth! Amid this barrenness
An army, sizable and strong,
Of bandits and staunch citizens
Acclaims you. Longed-for liberty
40 Awaits you, hear its beckoning call!
  ALL [*Offstage.*] Long live Prince Segismund! All hail!
  SEGISMUND What's this? Must I be held enthralled
Again, cruel skies, to fleeting dreams
Of grandeur Time will surely mock?
45 Must I again be forced to glimpse
Amid the shadows and the fog
The majesty and faded pomp
That waft inconstant on the wind?
Must I again be left to face
50 Life's disillusion or the risks
To which man's limits are exposed
From birth and never truly end?
This cannot be. It cannot be.
Behold me here, a slave again
55 To fortune's whims. As I have learned
That life is really just a dream,
I say to you, false shadows, Go!
My deadened senses know your schemes,
To feign a body and a voice
60 When voice and body both are shams.
I've no desire for majesty
That's phony or for pompous flam,
Illusions of sheer fantasy
That can't withstand the slightest breeze
65 And dissipate entirely like
The blossoms on an almond tree
That bloom too early in the spring
Without a hint to anyone.
The beauty, light, and ornament
70 Reflecting from their rosy buds
Fade all too soon and, wilting fall
When but the gentlest gusts blow by.
I know you all too well, I do,
To fancy you'd act otherwise
75 Toward other souls who likewise sleep.

So let this vain pretending cease;
I'm disabused of all I thought
And know now life is but a dream.

SECOND SOLDIER   We have not come here to deceive.
80   Just cast your eyes upon the lair
Of haughty hills that ring this tower
And see the host of men prepared
To follow and obey you.

SEGISMUND   Once
I saw the same approving crowd
85   Appear before me as distinct
And clear as I perceive things now,
But I was dreaming.

SECOND SOLDIER   Great events
Are oft preceded, good my lord,
By portents, which is what occurred
90   When you did dream these things before.

SEGISMUND   A portent. Yes, you must be right.
If all is truly as you've deemed
And man's life, sadly, is so short,
Then let us dream, my soul, let's dream
95   Again! But this time we will face
Full recognition of the fact
That we may waken from this sleep
At any hour and be brought back.
Still, knowing such things in advance
100   Should temper disappointment's stings;
To put the cure before the harm
Does much to mock the injuring.
In short, as all have been forewarned
That, even when man's sway seems sure,
105   Our power is borrowed on this earth
And harks back always to its source,
What can we lose by venturing?
I thank you, vassals, for this show
Of loyalty. With all my skill
110   And bravery I'll smash this yoke
Of foreign slavery you fear!
Come, sound the call to arms. This sword
Will vouch my courage is no lie.
It's my intent to levy war
115   Against my father, proving thus
That heaven prophesied the truth.
I'll see him prone beneath my feet—
Unless I wake before I do,
In which case it might just be best
120   To say no more about these plans.

ALL   All hail to you, Prince Segismund!

3.4

[*Enter* CLOTALDO.]

CLOTALDO   Good heavens, what's this uproar, man?
SEGISMUND   Clotaldo.
CLOTALDO   Sire. [*Aside.*] He's sure to vent
    His rage upon me now.
CLARION [*Aside.*]   I bet
    He throws the codger off this cliff.
            [*He exits.*]
5   CLOTALDO   I bow to you, though I expect
    To die here at your feet.
SEGISMUND   Pray stand,
    Good father. Rise up from the ground,
    My polestar and sole guiding light!
    You coaxed my better nature out
10   And well I know the debt you're owed
    For rearing me so faithfully.
    Let me embrace you.
CLOTALDO   How is that?
SEGISMUND   I'm dreaming now, but in my dream
    I'm striving to do good. No chance
15   To do kind deeds should be ignored.
CLOTALDO   My lord, since you profess these acts
    Of grace as your new creed, I'm sure
    You'll take no great offense with me
    For likewise cleaving to these views.
20   Wage war against your father? Then
    I simply cannot counsel you
    And aid the downfall of my king.
    So slay me, humbled still upon
    This ground you tread.
SEGISMUND   Oh, traitor! Vile,
25   Ungrateful wretch! Almighty God!
    Some self-command might serve me well
    Until it's certain that I wake.
    I envy your stouthearted show,
    Clotaldo. Thank you for this faith.
30   Go, then, and serve the king you love;
    We'll meet upon the battle lines.
    All others, sound the call to arms!
CLOTALDO   I kiss your feet a thousand times.
SEGISMUND   Come, Fortune! Off we go to reign,
35   So dare not wake me if I sleep
    Nor let me sleep should this be true,
    For whether I now sleep or dream
    It's vital still that man do good
    In dream or sleep for good's own sake,
40   At least to win himself some friends
    For when he ultimately wakes.
            [*All exit as the call to arms sounds.*]

3.5

[*Enter King* BASIL *and* ASTOLF.]

BASIL   Good Astolf, who can stop a bolting horse
And still its rage into serenity?
Or check a surging river's headlong course
Before its waters flow into the sea?
5   Or halt a falling boulder gathering force
While hurtling down a mountain fast and free?
Yet, none of these is harder to arrest
Than masses who feel angered and oppressed.
Divulge by edict any news from court
10   And all at once you'll hear the echoes sound
Throughout the hills, as anguished cries exhort
"Hail Astolf" while "Hail Segismunds" resound.
Our throne room has been turned into a sort
Of second stage where horrid plays abound,
15   A baneful theater where Fate flaunts her will
And only tragedy is on the bill.
ASTOLF   Then, sire, I will assuredly delay this cause
For celebration proffered by your hand
And shun both flattery and loud applause,
20   For Poland, where I'd looked to rule as planned,
Resists my reign today and flouts your laws
So I might prove my worth to lead the land.
Bring me a steed whose spirit knows no like;
You've heard me thunder, now watch lightning strike!
[*He exits.*]
25   BASIL   No one escapes the inescapable
Or any danger omens have in store.
Resisting Fortune is impossible;
Ignoring forecasts just makes them more sure.
In our case, this harsh law looms terrible
30   As fleeing danger brings one to its door.
Base ruin now appears our secret's cost,
For we're alone to blame now Poland's lost.

3.6

[*Enter* STELLA.]

STELLA   If your wise presence, sire, can't stop the spread
Of opposition forces gaining ground
While ever more combative factions head
Throughout our streets and plazas, palace bound,
5   You'll see the realm awash in waves of red,
Your subjects bathing in the blood now found
But in their crimson veins. What tragic gloom
Surrounds our kingdom's decadence and doom!
To sense the downfall of your rule so near
10   Amid the savage violence of this plot
Astounds the eye and terrifies the ear.

The wind grows still, the sun turns to a blot;
Each rock will be a headstone to revere,
Each flower the marker on a fresh grave's spot,
15   Each edifice a lofty house of death,
Each soldier but a skeleton with breath.

3.7

[*Enter* CLOTALDO.]

CLOTALDO   I've made it here alive, for God is kind.
BASIL   Clotaldo, have you news about our son?
CLOTALDO   The masses, sire, a monster rash and blind,
Besieged the tower and, seeing it overrun,
5   Freed Segismund. No sooner did he find
A second time this second honor won
Than out he burst emboldened and uncouth,
Resolved to prove the heavens spoke the truth.
BASIL   Bring us a steed, for as your king we must
10   Defeat this ingrate out of royal pride.
But this time in our crown's defense we'll trust
Cold steel where once our hapless science vied.
[*He exits.*]

STELLA   Bright sun, I'll be Bellona[1] at your side
And join my name to one far more august.
15   On outstretched wings I'll soar above the frays
And rival Pallas in my warlike ways.
[*She exits as the call to arms is sounded.*]

3.8

[*Enter* ROSAURA, *who stops* CLOTALDO.]

ROSAURA   I know the seething valor pent
Within your breast attends the call
To arms, but hear me now, for all
Can see that war is imminent.
5   When I arrived in Poland just
A poor, humiliated maid,
Your valor was my only aid
And you the sole man I could trust
To pity me. Then you procured
10   That I'd reside—oh, heart!—disguised
At palace, where I was advised
To keep my jealousy obscured
And my good self from Astolf's sight.
He spied me, though, and now insists
15   On mocking me with garden trysts
He holds with Stella every night.

1. The Roman goddess of war.

But I hold this, the garden's key,
Which you could use for entering
The place unseen, and thereby bring
20 An end to all my cares for me.
So might my honor be restored
By one who's strong, brave, and resolved
To see this problem duly solved
By winning vengeance with the sword.

25 CLOTALDO   It's true I've been disposed to act
On your behalf since first we met,
Rosaura, and collect that debt—
Your tears bore witness to this fact—
By all the powers I possess.
30 That's why I urged you to acquire
More proper feminine attire
So you'd be clad in seemly dress
When Astolf sighted you at court.
It couldn't, then, occur to him
35 Your clothes were but a flighty whim
To turn lost honor into sport.
At just that time I moved to find
Some way to make the rogue repent
His insult, even if this meant—
40 For honor so engaged my mind!—
Contriving Astolf's death. See where
The ravings of an old man lead?
He's not my king, and thus the deed
Should cause not wonder or despair.
45 I'd plotted murder when the same
Urge struck Prince Segismund, who tried
Dispatching me! Good Astolf spied
This wrong and, self-neglecting, came
To my defense stoutheartedly.
50 His noble showing of largesse
Bore all the marks of recklessness
And far surpassed mere bravery.
Now, as mine is a grateful soul,
How could I ever cause the death
55 Of one whose heart left me with breath
And handed me my life back whole?
My care and my affection stand
Divided now between you two:
As I gave back a life to you
60 But then received one from his hand,
To which of you do I owe more?
Which action claims priority?
Receiving now obliges me
As much as giving did before
65 And so fulfillment of my plan,

Which once seemed certain, now does not.
I'd suffer compassing the plot
And wrongly kill a worthy man.

ROSAURA   It's not my place here, I believe,
70   To sway one so superlative
But, noble as it is to give,
It's just as vile to receive.
So, following this principle,
You owe that man no gratitude,
75   For anyone would now conclude
That, though he made life possible
For you and you for me, it's clear
He basely undermined your fame
And compromised your noble name
80   While I've made you look cavalier.
He, therefore, causes you offense.
I, therefore, merit your first thought
As what you've given me is naught
But what he gave in impudence.
85   You, therefore, ought to strive to save
A reputation thus disgraced
And favor my claim, not his, based
On what you both received and gave.

CLOTALDO   A mark of true nobility
90   Entails this giving with free hands,
But showing gratitude demands
That one receive as graciously.
The reputation that's pursued
My person holds me generous
95   And honored by the populace,
So add to these marks gratitude,
A noble trait I hope to claim
By acting now both liberally
And gratefully, for honesty
100   Is giving and receiving's name.

ROSAURA   You gave this damaged life to me
And I recall well how you pled.
When I accepted it, you said
A life lived with indignity
105   Was no true life and so the thought
That I've received one is absurd.
The life your giving hand conferred
On me was not a life, but naught.
If you'd be liberal before
110   You're grateful, following your fame,
As I have heard you just proclaim,
My hope is that you'll soon restore
The life you thought you'd given. Why,
If giving makes one seem sublime,
115   Be liberal first and you'll have time

For feeling grateful by and by.
CLOTALDO   Then liberal first I'll be, for these
　　　Persuasive arguments declare
　　　Your fitness to be named my heir.
120　　Take my bequest and seek the ease
　　　A convent grants,[2] for in your case
　　　This recourse makes the greatest sense:
　　　Exchange this fleeing from offense
　　　For refuge in a holy place.
125　　The kingdom presently is torn
　　　By factional extremity
　　　And such affliction mustn't be
　　　Made worse by one who's nobly born.
　　　Through this solution, I'll be viewed
130　　Both loyal to my country's fight
　　　And generous to your suffered slight
　　　While showing Astolf gratitude.
　　　This remedy resolves things best;
　　　What else might you have settled for?
135　　God knows I couldn't help you more
　　　Were I your father in this quest.
ROSAURA   Were you my sire out to avenge
　　　This wrong, I'd suffer it as mine.
　　　But as you aren't, I must decline.
140　CLOTALDO   How, then, will you exact revenge?
ROSAURA   I'll kill the duke.
CLOTALDO　　　　　　　　　What's this? The same
　　　Poor maid who grew up fatherless
　　　Displaying such courageousness?
ROSAURA   That's right.
CLOTALDO　　　　　　　What moves you?
ROSAURA　　　　　　　　　　　　My good name.
145　CLOTALDO   Soon Astolf will claim reverence . . .
ROSAURA   He stole all honor from my life.
CLOTALDO   As king, and Stella as his wife.
ROSAURA   An outrage God won't countenance!
CLOTALDO   It's madness, child.
ROSAURA　　　　　　　　　I'm sure you're right.
150　CLOTALDO   Control these urges.
ROSAURA　　　　　　　　　　　So you say.
CLOTALDO   You'll lose your life . . .
ROSAURA　　　　　　　　　　It's true, I may.
CLOTALDO   And honor, too.
ROSAURA　　　　　　　　　How well I might.
CLOTALDO   What will this mean?
ROSAURA　　　　　　　　　My death.
CLOTALDO　　　　　　　　　　　　Don't wage

2. Women were expected to pay a dowry to the religious order when they entered a convent.

War out of spite.
ROSAURA   My honor calls.
155 CLOTALDO   That's folly!
ROSAURA   Valor never palls.
CLOTALDO   Sheer lunacy!
ROSAURA   Or wrath and rage.
CLOTALDO   Can't this blind fury be allayed
    In any other way?
ROSAURA   No, none.
CLOTALDO   But who will second you?
ROSAURA   No one.
160 CLOTALDO   You won't be swayed?
ROSAURA   I won't be swayed.
CLOTALDO   The deed brings with it quite a cost.
ROSAURA   I would be lost at any rate.
CLOTALDO   If that's the case, my child, then wait—
    Together let us both be lost.

            [*They exit.*]

                    3.9

        [*Trumpets blare as Soldiers march onstage with* CLARION
        and SEGISMUND, *who is dressed in animal pelts.*]

SEGISMUND   If proud Rome's Golden Age
    Could view my entrance on this martial stage,
    How loudly would it voice
    Delight at this strange triumph and rejoice
5   Amazed to understand
    A beast had armies under his command!
    With such unbridled might,
    The heavens could be mine without a fight!
    But spirit, help me quell
10 These arrogant displays and not dispel
    This lingering applause;
    I'd grieve to wake without it now because
    To lose what dreams contain
    Would surely bring me pain.
15 The less I hold things dear,
    The less I'll suffer when they disappear.
            [*A clarion sounds offstage.*]
CLARION   Look there! A wingèd horse—
    I'm sorry, but my stories pack more force
    When I hyperbolize—
20 Four elements incarnate in its guise:[3]
    Its body mass the earth,
    Its soul the fire ablaze beneath its girth,

---

3. According to the theory of matter dominant from classical Greece through the Renaissance, all matter is made up of four elements: earth, air, fire, and water.

Its froth the water and its breath the air.
I relish chaos and confusion where
25 The soul, froth, breath, and body all can be
A monster made of fire, wind, land, and sea,
Though dapple-gray of hue
And patchy, straddled by a horseman who
Digs spurs into its side
30 To fly upon his ride.
But, this is a refined
And jaunty dame!

SEGISMUND   Her radiance leaves me blind.

CLARION   Lord, it's Rosaura! See?

        [*He exits.*]

SEGISMUND   The heavens have restored this sight to me.

3.10

        [*Enter* ROSAURA, *dressed in a loose-fitting skirt,*
        with a dagger and sword.]

ROSAURA   Magnanimous Prince Segismund!
Your lordly heroism shines
Upon this day of noble feats
From out the shades of darkest night!
5 For as the brightest-gleaming orb
Among the stars displays its power
In Dawn's embrace, restoring light
To roses and to blooming flowers,
Emerging crowned with fulgent rays
10 Above the mountains and the seas,
Dispersing beams, dispensing glow,
Illuming froth and bathing peaks,
So may you rise atop the world,
Proud Poland's shining sun! Avail
15 A woman fraught with wretchedness
Who, prostrate at your feet today,
A woman first and then a wretch,
Trusts you'll comply—as either one
Of these conditions should suffice—
20 Since each is more than I could want
To obligate a gentleman
Who boasts of gallantry to act.
Three times already have you looked
On me with wonder, blind to facts
25 About my life, as all three times
My clothes displayed a different self:
On the occasion we first met
Inside a cell so dank I held
My grieved existence charmed beside
30 Your own, you took me for a man.
When next you gazed on me you saw

       A woman, as the palace plans
       Suspending you mid dream and pomp
       Turned all to shadows and vain schemes.
35   The third time here, your eyes behold
       This monstrous and unnatural freak
       Attired in female finery
       Yet bravely bearing manly arms.
       As you'll be more disposed to aid
40   My cause once pity moves your heart,
       I'll tell now of the tragic blows
       That fate's compelled me to absorb.
       I was of woman nobly born
       In Moscow at the royal court.
45   My mother had to have been fair,
       For she was not a happy maid.
       A vile deceiver laid his eyes
       On her, a villain who remains
       Both nameless and unknown to me.
50   His valor, though, has given rise
       To mine, and being the result
       Of his desires, I now repine
       Not being born a pagan child
       So I half-madly might feel pleased
55   To think this man was like those gods
       Whose cunning metamorphoses
       Into a swan, gold shower, or bull
       Left Leda ravished, Danaë duped,
       And fair Europa raped.[4] I thought
60   I was digressing, but these lewd
       Accounts of perfidy provide
       An overview to this sad tale.
       My mother, far more lovely still
       Than any woman, fell betrayed
65   By her seducer's gallant words
       And thus, like many, was undone.
       The old trick of a marriage pledge
       Imparted by a honeyed tongue
       Beguiled her so, that to this day
70   Its memory dispels her joys.
       In fact, the tyrant so recalled
       Aeneas[5] in his flight from Troy
       He even left his sword behind.
       We'll leave its blade ensheathed for now
75   But have no doubt I'll draw this steel

---

4. All the transformations listed were of a single Greek god, Zeus (Jupiter), undertaken respectively in sexual pursuit of the women named, and all were retold in the *Metamorphoses* (ca. 10 C.E.), by the Roman poet Ovid.
5. The mythical Trojan hero and progenitor of the Roman people, whose story is told in Virgil's *Aeneid* (19 B.C.E.); as he fled with his family from the Greek sack of Troy, his wife (though not his sword) was left inadvertently behind.

Before I end my sad account.
So, from their bond, a loose-tied knot
That neither ties one down nor binds,
Not quite a marriage or a crime—
80 It's all the same now to my mind—
I issued forth, my mother's twin
And living picture when it came
Not to her comely countenance
But all her sorrows and travails.
85 As heiress to the vast estate
Of love's misfortune she bequeathed,
I hardly feel the need to say
I've come into her destiny.
The most I'll say about myself
90 Is that the thief who dared despoil
The trophy of my honor's claim
And left my maiden virtue soiled
Is Astolf! Heavens, how my heart
Beats quick with rage when I pronounce
95 His name, a natural response
To hearing enemies announced.
Duke Astolf, disremembering
The joys he'd so ungratefully found—
Yes, memories of love gone by
100 Are just that quickly blotted out—
Arrived in Poland, called away
From this great conquest, having come
To claim fair Stella as his bride,
A torch beside my setting sun.
105 Now who would think so stellar-made
A union, sanctioned by the stars,
Could come unraveled just because
Maid Stella came between our hearts?
I, then, dishonored and deceived,
110 Remained forlorn, remained half-crazed,
Remained a corpse, remained myself,
Which is to say, too much remained
Of that infernal turmoil lodged
Within the Babylon[6] of my mind.
115 I swore myself to silence, then,
As there are trials and pains in life
Authentic feeling can convey
Far better than the mouth could hope,
And voiced my grief by keeping mute.
120 One day, though, as I sat alone,

6. Literally, the capital of Babylonia, a powerful state in southern Mesopotamia and in the
Old Testament a place of exile for the Jews in
the 6th century B.C.E.; metaphorically, associated with the confusion of tongues (in the
story of the Tower of Babel, Genesis 11.1–9)
and, in the New Testament's Book of Revelation, the symbol for evil.

My mother, Violante, stormed
The fortress where these miseries lay
And out they poured like prisoners
Colliding all in unleashed haste.
125 I felt no shame confessing them,
For when a person shares her griefs
With one she knows has likewise felt
Her share of them from being weak,
The sorrow starts to dissipate
130 And spreads a balm upon the hurt.
A bad example, after all,
Can be of use. In short, she heard
My plaints with sympathy and tried
Consoling me with her own woes—
135 A judge who's been delinquent finds
Forgiveness easy to bestow!
So, as she'd learned that honor wronged
Could never hope to be set right
By whiling idle hours away
140 Or simply watching time go by,
She set me on a different course.
Her sage advice? That I pursue
And hold my tempter liable for
The loss his blandishments produced,
145 Obliging him with courtly ways.
Now, to ensure this quest would pose
Small risk to me, fate intervened
To outfit me in manly clothes.
My mother took an old sword down,
150 The one I've girded round my waist,
And so the time has come at last,
As I have pledged, to bare its blade.
Convinced this sword would be a sign,
She said, "Set out for Poland's fields
155 And let her grandest noblemen
Be certain to observe the steel
Now gracing you. In one of them
Your luckless fortune may well find
A sympathetic ear, and all
160 Your sorrows solace in due time."
I came, indeed, to Poland, where—
Let's skip a bit, for why repeat
What everyone already knows?—
A bolting brute, half-horse, half-beast,
165 Unsaddled me outside that cave
Where you first spied my loveliness.
Now skip to where Clotaldo takes
A special interest in my quest
And begs the king to spare my life,
170 A favor Basil deigns to grant.

On learning my identity,
He urges me, dressed like man,
To put on lady's clothes and serve
Maid Stella on the palace grounds
175 Where I've used all my craft to thwart
Duke Astolf's love and Stella's vows.
Let's also skip where seeing me
Confounded you that time at court
As I, then wearing female garb,
180 Appeared in yet another form,
And speak of what Clotaldo's done.
Self-servingly, he now ascribes
Great weight to Astolf being king
With Stella reigning as his bride
185 And, to my honor's detriment,
Has bid me suffer this offense.
Brave Segismund, how clear it dawns
On all this day that sweet revenge
Belongs to you! The heavens smile
190 On your felicitous release
From out so crude a prison cell
Where you had grown resigned to be
A rock against all suffering
And beast unmoved by sentiment.
195 Now, as you take up arms to fight
Your native land and sovereign,
I come to pledge my aid, bedecked
In chaste Diana's[7] flowing robes
Atop a suit of Pallas's
200 Own armor. Draped in clashing clothes
Of genteel fabric and cold steel,
I join your forces dually dressed.
To battle, then, bold general!
For it's in both our interests
205 To stop these banns from going forth
And set this royal bond aside:
For me, so that the man I call
My husband takes no other wife;
For you, so that no gain in strength
210 Resulting from their allied states
Will threaten our great victory
Once you've returned as prince to reign.
I come, a woman, urging you
To join the cause to which I'm bound;
215 But as a man, I come to press
This late reclaiming of your crown.
I come, a woman, at your feet

7. The Roman virgin goddess of the hunt and the moon.

To move you to commiserate;
But as a man, I come to serve
220   Beside you in your people's aid.
I come, a woman, so you might
Assuage my sorrows and my pain;
But as a man, I come with sword
And person ready to assail.
225   So, should you find yourself inclined
To woo me as a woman, rest
Assured that, as a man, I'd be
Compelled to kill you in defense
Of honor, honorably, because
230   In this campaign of love you've planned,
I'll play the woman with my plaints,
But fight with honor like a man.

SEGISMUND   Just heavens! If it's really true
I dream, suspend my memory!
235   It isn't possible for all
I've seen to fit into a dream!
If God would but reveal to me
How I might blot these troubles out
And give them not another thought!
240   What mortal ever faced such doubts?
If I had only dreamt I dwelt
Amid such luxury, how could
This woman have recounted what
I saw and seemed so plausible?
245   It was true, then. That was no dream.
If this is so, which by all rights
Should leave me more confused, not less,
Who is it that could call my life
A dream? Do this world's glories so
250   Resemble dreams in what they vaunt
That even the most genuine
Are destined to be reckoned false
As fake ones are considered true?
Have these so little difference
255   That every man must ask himself
Now whether all he relishes
Around him is a lie or truth?
Why must the copy counterfeit
The true original so well
260   That none dare hazard which is which?
If such be life's design, and all
Our splendid pageantry and strength,
Our solemn pomp and majesty,
Must vanish into shadow's depths,
265   Let's seize the time that's given us
And reap what pleasures may be reaped,
For all we now enjoy on earth

Is but what we enjoy in dreams.
I hold Rosaura in my power;
270   Her beauty captivates my soul.
So let me profit from this chance
To let love set aside the codes
Of valor, trust, and chivalry
That she's invoked in her request.
275   As this is but another dream,
Let's all dream happy things on end
And rue them only once we wake!
Be careful or your logic might
Convince you this is fact again!
280   A dream may reach vainglorious heights,
But who'd pass heaven's glories up
For human ones, had he the choice?
What happy turns of fate weren't dreams?
What man has felt tremendous joy
285   And not then asked himself in time,
Once memory had reviewed the scene:
"Weren't all these things I witnessed but
A dream?" If knowledge like this means
Great disappointment—for I've learned
290   That pleasure is a lovely flame
The merest breath of air blows out
So only wafting ash remains—
Let's look toward the eternal, then,
And seek renown that never dies
295   Where joy will not succumb to sleep
Or splendor ever napping lie!
Rosaura's honor lingers lost
And it's incumbent on a prince
To see that honor be restored.
300   I swear by God above I'll win
Her honor back before my crown
And save her name from future harm!
It's best I flee temptation so
Enticing. Sound the call to arms!
305   I'll wage war on my foes this day
Before the night's encroaching shade
Can shroud the sunlight's golden rays
In somber black and dark-green waves.
    ROSAURA Sire, why do you withdraw from me?
310   I would have hoped that soothing words
Were due my sorrows at the least
As balm for salving heartfelt hurt.
How is it possible, then, lord,
That I should go unseen, unheard?
315   Why won't you even look this way?
    SEGISMUND Rosaura, only honor's call
Could prompt this seeming cruelty

In serving kinder mercy's cause.
My voice declines to answer you
320   To let my honor give reply.
I hold my speech so that my deeds
Will speak for me in their own right
And shield my gaze from you because
No man in such dire straits can pledge
325   To aid a woman's honor when
She looks the sight of loveliness.

[*Exit* SEGISMUND *and Soldiers.*]

ROSAURA   Why does he speak in riddles, skies?
He knows my suffering has been great,
So how could he equivocate
330   By giving such abstruse replies?

3.11

[*Enter* CLARION.]

CLARION   My lady, when you've time to spare . . .
ROSAURA   Why, Clarion! Man, where have you been?
CLARION   Just trying to read my fortune in
A deck of cards, confined up there—
5   They slay me . . . no, they slay me not—
A face card would ensure a brush
With death, but trumped, would leave me flush
With life again. That parlous spot
All but convinced me I would bust.
10   ROSAURA   Whatever from?
CLARION   From finding out
The secret of your past. No doubt

[*Drumbeats sound offstage.*]

Clotaldo— What's that sound I just
Heard?
ROSAURA   Beating drums and battle whoops?
CLARION   Armed soldiers sortie from the court
15   To end the palace siege. To thwart
Prince Segismund's unruly troops,
They'll make a stand for all they're worth!
ROSAURA   It's cowardly to be allied
With him and not fight at his side,
20   A scandalous wonder on this earth,
Where cruel acts flourish and survive
In anarchy despite man's laws.

[*She exits.*]

3.12

SOME VOICES [*Offstage.*]   Long live our king's triumphant cause!
OTHER VOICES [*Offstage.*]   Long may our freedom live and thrive!
CLARION   Long live their freedom and their king!

I wish the both of them the best,
5   But nothing leaves me more distressed
Than being forced to choose one thing.
Instead of risking life and limb,
I'll step aside, avoid distress,
And act like Nero[8] through this mess—
10   He never let things get to him!
It's up to me now to decide
What else should worry me but me.
I'll just make sure that I can see
The party rage from where I hide.
15   Ah, this is where I'll catch my breath,
Secluded in this rocky sheer.
No, death will never find me here
And I don't give two figs for death.

         [*He hides.*]

3.13

         [*With the sound of arms clashing, King* BASIL, CLOTALDO,
         and ASTOLF *enter fleeing.*]

BASIL   What king has ever felt defeat
    Or father harassment so dire?
CLOTALDO   Your army has been routed, sire,
    And scatters in confused retreat.
5 ASTOLF   None but the treacherous victors stride
    The field.
BASIL   The battle thus desists
    To make of victors loyalists
    And traitors of the losing side.
    Let's flee our tyrant son and his
10   Inhuman rage, Clotaldo, flee
    His savage wrath and cruelty!
         [*Shots are heard offstage, and* CLARION *falls wounded
         from his hiding place.*]
CLARION   Sweet heavens, help me now!
ASTOLF   Who is
    This soldier of misfortune here
    That wallows at our feet in mud,
15   His body soaked and stained with blood?
CLARION   A hapless piece of man, I fear,
    Who vainly sought to turn his face
    From death, but met it anyhow,
    Whose final dodge did not allow
20   Him final shrift.[9] There's just no place
    To hide from death and not be found,
    From which a man might well assume

8. The notoriously dissolute Roman emperor (r. 54–68 C.E.) who, according to Roman historians, is said to have played his lyre and sung during a fire that devastated Rome in 64.
9. That is, a final confession to a priest.

The more he tries to spurn the tomb,
The sooner he'll lie underground.

25 Go, then, rejoin your vast brigades
And charge into the bloody breach
Where you'll be farthest from harm's reach,
Mid clashing swords and cannonades,
More safe than hiding in the hills,

30 Which offer no security
Against the tide of destiny
Or what inclement fortune wills.
Think you by fleeing you'll be fine
And cheat death in this way again?

35 You'll die precisely where and when
Your deaths fulfill God's grand design.

[*He collapses offstage.*]

BASIL   You'll die precisely where and when
Your deaths fulfill God's grand design!
Almighty heavens, truer words

40 Than these man never spoke before!
They lead us toward a greater truth
Imparted by this talking corpse
Whose wound is but a second mouth
From which that trickling liquid drips

45 Like wisdom off a bloody tongue
To teach how man's initiatives
All come to naught when they presume
To counteract the powers on high.
Our own attempts to rid this land

50 Of treachery and homicide
Have ended in its capture by
The forces we had most opposed.

CLOTALDO   Though it is common knowledge, sire,
That fate's familiar with all roads

55 And hunts down even those who think
Themselves hid mid these stones, it still
Is hardly Christian sentiment
To say one can't escape its ills.
A prudent man might easily

60 Emerge victorious over Fate.
I beg you, sire, if you stand fair
To common wretchedness and pain,
Seek refuge where it might be had.

ASTOLF   Your Majesty, Clotaldo may

65 Advise you as a prudent man
Who's reached a wise, mature old age,
But I'll speak as a daring youth:
You'll find a horse concealed within
The tangled thickets of these hills,

70 A fleet abortion of the wind.
Ride hard until you're safe; I'll guard

The rear to safeguard your escape.
BASIL   If death fulfills God's grand design
    Or otherwise should lie in wait
75 For us today, we'll stand our ground
    And meet it face to face at last.

3.14

[The call to arms sounds, and SEGISMUND *enters with his entire company.]*

SOLDIER   Here! Somewhere mid these bosky hills
    In thickets off the beaten path
    The king is hiding.
SEGISMUND   After him!
    Look under every living plant!
5 I'll see this dusky forest combed
    First trunk by trunk, then branch by branch!
CLOTALDO   Flee, sire!
BASIL   What purpose would it serve?
ASTOLF   Who holds you?
BASIL   Astolf, step aside.
CLOTALDO   Where will you turn, my lord?
BASIL   We've but
10 One recourse left us at this time.
    If it is us you look for, prince,
    Then look no further than your feet
    Where we now lay this carpet wove
    Of white hairs from our snowy peak.
15 Come, tread upon our neck and trounce
    Our crown, humiliate us, drag
    Our dignity and reverence down,
    Take vengeance on our honor fast
    And use us as your captive slave.
20 For what has our precaution served?
    Let fate receive its proper due:
    The heavens stayed true to their word.
SEGISMUND   Proud worthies of the Polish court,
    Attend your true and rightful prince
25 And I'll make sense of what these strange
    Events you've witnessed have evinced.
    What heaven has decreed shall come
    To pass is writ in God's own script
    Upon this drawing board of blue,
30 Where shining print and twinkling signs
    Embellish these celestial sheets
    Like gilded letters hand-inscribed.
    Not once have stars deceived or lied,
    Though one soul does lie and deceive:
35 That man who'd read this coded script
    To hazard wildly what stars mean.
    My father, humbled at my feet,

Believing he could shun the rage
Portended for me, had his son,
40   Born human, made a beast and caged.
His action thus ensured, despite
My natural nobility,
My pure aristocratic blood,
And all my gallant qualities—
45   For I was born a docile soul
And gentle child—that so deprived
An upbringing and inhumane,
Debasing, brutish way of life
Would father in me beastlike ways.
50   Now, how was this confounding fate?
For say some stranger should predict
One day: "An animal shall slay
You by and by." What strategy
For thwarting such a fate would force
55   A man to rouse brutes from their sleep?
Or if that stranger warned, "The sword
You gird upon your thigh shall be
The one to cause your death," how vain
All efforts to eschew this end
60   Should seem if one then bared the blade
And left it pointing at his chest!
Or if he bode, "The silvery spumes
That cap the sea shall someday serve
As gravestones on your watery tomb,"
65   How prudent would it be to brave
The ocean deep precisely as
Its cresting waves and snow-capped peaks
Arose like mountains of clear glass?
To act so heedlessly tempts fate,
70   As he who wakes a sleeping beast
Discovers once he's sensed its threat;
As he who fears a sword's cold steel
Learns while unsheathing it; as he
Who swims in stormy seas construes.
75   For even if—now hear me out—
My fury were a sleeping brute,
My savagery a tempered sword,
And all my raging tranquil seas,
Harsh treatment and blind vengefulness
80   Would not reverse man's destiny,
But hasten that it come to pass.
That mortal who, by hopeful acts,
Would influence the turns of fate
Must seek a more judicious path.
85   Foreseeing future harm does not
Ensure the victim will be spared
Its ravages, for while it's true

That man may save himself some care
Through sheer humility—that's clear—
90 This happens only once the harm
Presents itself, as there is just
No chance that fate will be disarmed.
Let this amazing spectacle,
These strange events, this horror show
95 And wondrous pageant play serve as
A lesson to us all. Who knows
A more exemplary case? Despite
Divining heaven's plans,
A father lies at his son's heels,
100 A king who's forfeited command.
The skies had willed this to occur
And, intrigue as he might to stave
Off fate, he failed. What chance could I
Then hope to have—a man less gray,
105 Less brave, less erudite than he—
To alter fortune's ways? Rise, sire.
Give me your hand. Since heaven has
Exposed the ruses you contrived
As yet more futile ploys to change
110 Their plotted course, I humbly bare
My neck to you, beneath your heels,
So you might settle these affairs.

BASIL   Our noble son, this virtuous
Display has fathered you again
115 In our own heart. You'll reign as prince.
The laurel leaf and palm are meant
For you as victor on this day.
Let gallant actions be your crown.

ALL   Long live Prince Segismund! All hail!

120 SEGISMUND   Now that it seems my valor's bound
To win me yet more victories,
I'll start with my most dogged foe
And quell myself. Come, Astolf, take
Rosaura's hand and be betrothed.
125 Thus will your debt of honor be
Repaid, and I'll vouchsafe for this.

ASTOLF   Correct though you may be about
Such satisfaction, lord, admit
The lady cannot claim descent
130 And that I'd stain my family name
By marrying a woman who . . .

CLOTALDO   Before you say more, Astolf, wait.
Rosaura's blood is noble as
Your own, and gladly would I duel
135 The man who'd gainsay this, for she's
My child. That should suffice for you.

ASTOLF   How's that?

CLOTALDO   I thought it best to keep
  The secret hid till she could be
  Both honorably and nobly wed.
140 The story is quite long, indeed,
  But in the end, she is my child.
ASTOLF If this is true, I will uphold
  My pledge.
SEGISMUND We've only Stella now
  To turn our thoughts to and console.
145 Considering her sudden loss
  Of so renowned and brave a prince,
  I place in my own hands the charge
  Of finding one who rivals him,
  If not superior in worth
150 And riches, then at least his peer.
  Fair Stella, take my hand.
STELLA   I've no
  Right to the happiness I feel.
SEGISMUND Clotaldo, loyal servitor
  Of my good sire, these arms now stretch
155 Forth to embrace you, promising
  To render all you may request.
FIRST SOLDIER This man has never served your cause
  And yet is honored so? What lies
  Ahead for me, then, as the font
160 Of all this turmoil and the might
  That freed you from your tower jail?
SEGISMUND That selfsame tower. And to ensure
  You'll not set foot from there alive,
  We'll station guards at all the doors.
165 Of what use is the traitor once
  The treason has been carried out?
BASIL Your wisdom awes this gathering.
ASTOLF He seems a different person now.
ROSAURA A prudent and judicious prince!
170 SEGISMUND But why should you feel awe or fear?
  The dream that was my schoolmaster
  Will grieve me if it reappears
  And I awake to find myself
  Imprisoned once again, locked up
175 In my rank cell. But should it not,
  To dream this would be quite enough!
  For on this earth, I've come to see
  That all of human happiness
  Must reach an end, just like a dream.
180 So in what little time is left,
  I'll seize this opportunity
  To ask forgiveness for our flaws,
  As noble souls like yours are wont
  To pardon others for their faults.

MOLIÈRE (JEAN-BAPTISTE POQUELIN)

1621?–1673

FRANCE'S greatest comic dramatist, Molière (born Jean-Baptiste Poquelin) has remained, since the seventeenth century, among the world's most frequently produced and widely studied playwrights. An actor, a director, and a manager as well, Molière was a consummate man of the theater, completely dedicated to art; his thirty-year career coincided with, and significantly contributed to, the flowering of French dramaturgy. A contemporary of the renowned tragic dramatists Pierre Corneille (1606–1684) and JEAN RACINE (1639–1699), Molière joined his colleagues in catapulting the French theater to European prominence. Under the leadership of Louis XIV (r. 1643–1715), whose appreciation for and support of the arts defined his reign, France emerged at the cultural vanguard in the baroque era, setting standards for dramatic composition and production that lasted until the advent of modernism.

Born into a family of bourgeois artisan merchants, Jean-Baptiste was baptized on January 15, 1622. His father, Jean Poquelin, and mother, Marie Cressé, worked in the bedding trade, and in 1631 Jean was named *tapissier ordinaire du roi*, a royal appointment that involved caring for the king's furniture. Their gain in economic security and prestige enabled them to send their son to the Collège de Clermont, the most fashionable school in Paris at the

time. This Jesuit institution introduced Jean-Baptiste to a study of the humanities, which included classical languages and literatures, rhetoric, theology, and philosophy. Very probably he acted in Latin comedies and tragedies as part of his education; the works of the Roman comic dramatists PLAUTUS and Terence, replete with narratives of frustrated young lovers, overbearing parents, and cunning slaves, clearly informed his development as a writer. He likely also saw the popular folk theater of the day.

When Jean-Baptiste reached age fifteen, Jean Poquelin conveyed his royal appointment to his son, securing for the youth a solid future in the family trade. Though the young man may have accompanied the king in this capacity on a military campaign in 1642, he apparently continued his studies, including a new focus in law. In any case, in 1643 Jean-Baptiste's career took a novel and decisive turn. In exchange for 630 livres from his father, he gave up his royal office and with a small group of colleagues formed the Illustre Théâtre. The creation of the company benefited the actors in a number of ways: they gained control of their employment, the profits, and the kinds of work produced, as they moved away from older dramatic traditions. About a year later, Jean-Baptiste assumed the stage name Molière.

It was a challenging time to embark on a theatrical career. Elsewhere in Europe, dramatic writing had already blossomed in the Renaissance, but France lagged behind. Theatrical activity there in the early decades of the seventeenth century consisted mainly of productions of scripts from other countries as well as the lively Italian farces performed in the streets of Paris and in the provinces. A native variant of this latter tradition had also developed after liturgical drama was secularized in the late medieval period. Equally popular were the traveling companies specializing in the Italian commedia dell'arte, with its repertoire of stock characters, familiar plots, and improvised comic business called *lazzi* that surmounted the language barrier. We can trace the direct impact of all these traditions on a play like TARTUFFE (1664–69), one of Molière's greatest and most controversial comedies.

Just a decade before the founding of the Illustre Théâtre, the shape of French literature had been transformed by the establishment of the French Academy (*Académie Française*), under the sponsorship of the influential minister Cardinal Richelieu. The Academy created rules for the composition of French literature and national standards for literary taste. Drawing on Aristotle's *Poetics,* the Academy emphasized the importance of adhering to the unities of time, place, and action for the drama and stressed that tragedy should depict the lives of kings and the aristocracy, while comedy should portray those of lower social status. Under the Academy's direction, verse drama prevailed. The twelve-syllable line called the *alexandrine* dominated French dramaturgy, and Molière frequently utilized the rhyming couplets that were standard for his era. (The translation of *Tartuffe* included here renders the couplets in the pentameter line more natural in English.) The Academy also established that plausibility (*vraisemblance*) and propriety (*bienséance*) should inform all dramatic writing. Many of Molière's works display the tension between his efforts to conform to these rules and his appreciation of the bawdier farce traditions that had proven so popular with the audiences he now sought to attract. He also recognized that his plays had to somehow acknowledge and win the king's invaluable ongoing patronage.

Before he could pen the masterpieces that define his theatrical legacy, Molière and his colleagues struggled for more than a decade just to make ends meet. Finding it impossible to pay its bills in Paris, the Illustre Théâtre survived for almost fifteen years by touring the provinces. During this period, the company members honed their skills as actors, and Molière began to compose some short, comic plays for the group to perform before their main productions—for the most part, tragic dramas from the emerging French repertoire. His first full-length work, *L'Étourdi* (*The Blockhead*), based on a commedia scenario, dates from about 1655. The troupe returned to Paris in 1658, under the patronage of the king's brother; the successful production of Molière's *Les Précieuses ridicules* (*The Affected Young Ladies*) the following year secured their standing both at court and with the Parisian public. In 1660 the king granted them the right to perform at the Palais Royal theater. New challenges soon arose, however. Beginning with his companion pieces *L'École des maris* and *L'École des femmes* (*The School for Husbands* and *The School for Wives,* 1661–62), Molière repeatedly found himself embroiled in public controversy, as his comedies assailed the mores and exposed the foibles of Parisian society. Yet these disputes pale in comparison to the religious furor that erupted over *Tartuffe.*

The Protestant reform movement that had swept over much of Europe during the sixteenth century had little effect on France owing mainly to the Catholic Church's brutal suppression of the Protestant Huguenots, which began with the St. Bartholomew's Day Massacre in 1572. Henry IV's Edict of Nantes, issued in 1598, officially ended France's half century of religious wars and placed the country firmly within the control of a moderate but decidedly Catholic monarchy. Although Catholic rule by Molière's time was more tolerant than the bloody repression that had preceded it, the church's oversight of many aspects of French life remained largely unchecked throughout the seventeenth century. At the same time, a wide range of ideological positions existed within French Catholicism, from the strict asceticism of the Jansenists to the more worldly open-mindedness of the Christian humanists to the scholastics' focus on doctrine. Adding to this sometimes fractious mix were religious organizations such as the Compagnie du Saint-Sacrement (Society of the Blessed Sacrament), whose members—many powerful laypeople among them—combined charitable work with efforts to enforce a strict moral code. Such internal frictions did not affect the church's hostility to the theater, especially the profession of acting; its opposition had been strong since the late Middle Ages. Because the church viewed theatrical representation, or pretense to another identity, as inherently sinful, actors lived under the constant threat of excommunication. Indeed, because Molière died suddenly—within hours after coughing up blood while performing in his *Le Malade imaginaire* (*The Imaginary Invalid*, 1673)—as an unrepentant actor he was denied a full Christian burial.

Even Louis XIV had to approach such matters carefully. Far from devout, he nevertheless recognized the enormous political power of the clergy in his country. Within his own household, he had to deal with the exacting religious strictures of his mother, the Dowager Queen Anne d'Autriche—a model, scholars believe, for Mme Pernelle, *Tartuffe*'s overbearing mother figure. Yet the king, like Molière, well understood that some individuals used declarations of faith for personal gain; with royal acquiescence or perhaps even encouragement, Molière could expose their hypocrisy and turn the tables on those who defamed his profession. In *Tartuffe*, the vices long attributed to the theater are ascribed to the character who would have been among the theater's most vocal opponents: Tartuffe himself.

Molière quickly establishes the conflict that will dominate the play's action. The well-to-do but gullible Monsieur Orgon and his domineering mother have fallen under the influence of Monsieur Tartuffe, a man who pretends to great humility, self-sacrifice, and religious devotion. Orgon takes Tartuffe into his home and begins to treat him as his most valued relation. Although Orgon's wife and children see through Tartuffe, they cannot convince Orgon or his mother of the pretense. Events take a more serious turn when Orgon

decides to marry his daughter to the hypocrite rather than the man to whom she is betrothed, Valère. This decision in turn threatens the happiness of his son, Damis, who is engaged to Valère's sister. Indeed, Orgon endangers the well-being of his entire family by entrusting Tartuffe with secret information and even his property. Ultimately, through the efforts of his resourceful wife, Elmire, and the intervention of the king, Tartuffe's true nature is revealed, and the family is saved from disaster.

Molièristes have long argued inconclusively about whether the playwright based the figure of Tartuffe on any particular individual or on features of any specific Catholic faction. Just as plausibly, Tartuffe may be a composite portrait drawn from Molière's keen observations of false devotion. Realistic yet indeterminate, the characterization incensed a number of religious leaders, precisely because its subtle inclusion of elements of many different groups' ideologies enabled it to be interpreted as an attack on widely disparate religious individuals and their affiliations. As Molière noted in a letter to the king in 1667,

> The men whom I depict in my comedy [*Tartuffe*] . . . know how to display all of their aims in the most favorable light; yet, no matter how pious they may seem, it is surely not the interests of God which stir them; they have proven this often enough in the comedies they have allowed to be performed hundreds of times without making the least objection. Those plays attacked only piety and religion, for which they care very little; but this play attacks and makes fun of them, and that is what they cannot bear.

Already in 1664, after the king—clearly under pressure from religious leaders or powerful members of the Compagnie du Saint-Sacrement—had banned the play following its initial performance, Molière was warning Louis XIV that "the Tartuffes have skillfully gained Your Majesty's favor, and the models [i.e., the religious hypocrites] have succeeded in eliminating the copy [i.e., the play]." In both letters, Molière tried to alert the king to the connections between what was represented in the play itself and what was going on at court and in

Frontispiece of a 1682 printing of *Tartuffe ou L'Imposteur.*

Parisian society, and to persuade him to allow the play to be staged once again.

Complicating our understanding of these issues and the elements of the play that initially spawned the controversy is the script's history: only the last of its three different versions still exists. On May 12, 1664, at the request of Louis XIV, Molière presented at Versailles a new three-act play titled *Tar-*

tuffe, ou L'Hypocrite. While we will never know how closely the final play corresponds to this first performance, many scholars believe that it contained what in our text are acts 1, 3, and 4—those scenes focusing on Tartuffe and his increasing dominance in Orgon's household. Over the next five years, Molière would make numerous attempts to have the ban on *Tartuffe* lifted;

to appease his opponents, he also significantly revised and expanded the play. Molière hints in his second letter to the king that Tartuffe was originally costumed as a cleric, but that he was attired later as a lay figure, with long hair and lace on his clothing. In the second version Molière also changed the character's name to Panulphe, making him a sword-carrying man of the world. But these alterations satisfied no one, and Molière subsequently dropped them. In his preface to the final version, Molière explains that in revising the play, he had

> used all the art and skill that I could to distinguish clearly the character of the hypocrite from that of the truly devout man. For that purpose I used two whole acts to prepare the appearance of my scoundrel. Never is there a moment's doubt about his character; he is known at once from the qualities I have given him; and from one end of the play to the other, he does not say a word, he does not perform an action which does not depict to the audience the character of a wicked man.

Finally, in February 1669, the king acceded to the playwright's requests, allowing the work now titled *Tartuffe, ou L'Imposteur* to be performed in public. The reason for his change of heart remains a mystery, but scholars believe that the death of the dowager queen may have removed one major obstacle; other likely factors were Molière's revisions and his persuasive arguments that by exposing and ridiculing hypocrisy, the comedy could benefit the public. Audiences responded with wild enthusiasm; *Tartuffe* became the most popular play of its era and beyond, with more than 2,000 performances at the Comédie Française, the French national theater, between 1680 and 1900.

One of the keys to the work's success is its timelessness: the bourgeois family narrative of generational conflict and endangered love relationships transcends the play's origins in the specific religious and political context of the 1660s. *Tartuffe* weaves together time-honored characters and plot elements, popular since the heyday of Roman comedy, with enduring concerns about the law, justice, leadership, and the relationship between the family and the state.

To be sure, the second act, with its extended quarrel between Mariane and her lover Valère over their true feelings for each other, and the fifth act, with its whirlwind of events leading up to the ultimately happy ending, may at first strike some as tacked on and having little relation to the play's central concern—Tartuffe and his duplicitous

Brian Bedford (left) as Orgon and Henry Goodman (right) in the title role of the 2003 Roundabout Theater Company (New York) production of *Tartuffe*.

nature. Yet a common theme of illusion versus reality ties the marriage plot to the revelation of Tartuffe's deceptions. Just as the lovers must work through their false assumptions to rediscover the truth of their mutual devotion, so Orgon and his mother must be made to see Tartuffe for who he really is. In addition, Mariane's understanding of her father's control of her marital destiny resonates with other questions of power and appropriate social behavior in the play. Orgon rules the home as the king rules the state; Orgon must learn from his monarch how to exercise that authority wisely. Tartuffe thus emerges as a threat not only to the family of Orgon but also to the entire kingdom.

Molière builds his resolution around the political trope "*L'état, c'est moi*" (I am the state), which equates monarch and realm. The somewhat fantastical denouement—which some scholars have called a "rex ex machina" on the model of the classical deus ex machina—certainly stretches the limits of verisimilitude, or *vraisemblance*. But as an extended tribute to Louis XIV, the ending did realize the Academy's principle of propriety (*bienséance*) and appears to have contributed to the work's ultimate success. Molière, here as in many of his plays, walks a fine line between following the dictates of the French Academy and realizing his own dramatic goals. His calculated decision to acknowledge the king's beneficence within *Tartuffe*, as well as to represent an idealized monarchy, provides a space that also enables him to remind Louis XIV of how to best deploy royal power to the benefit of all France.

Molière continued to explore the issues of hypocrisy, authority, and benevolence in many of his later works, including *Dom Juan, ou le Festin de pierre* (*Dom Juan, or the Feast with the Statue*, 1665), *Le Misanthrope* (1666), and *Le Bourgeois gentilhomme* (*The Bourgeois Gentleman*, 1670). Written for actors by an actor, the plays have sparked some of the theater's most legendary performances and productions. And because the timelessness of his themes ensures their timeliness across the ages, Molière's comedies have continued to serve as vehicles for social commentary. Since the seventeenth century, directors have repeatedly found these works able to critique the present moment and to reveal the vagaries and varieties of human behavior. To learn more about the staging of *Tartuffe* and to view photographs from select performances of the play, see the "Plays in Performance" color insert near the center of this volume.   J.E.G.

Tartuffe[1]

CHARACTERS

MADAME PERNELLE, mother of Orgon
ORGON, husband of Elmire
ELMIRE, wife of Orgon
DAMIS, son of Orgon
MARIANE, daughter of Orgon
VALÈRE, fiancé of Mariane
CLÉANTE, brother-in-law of Orgon

TARTUFFE,[2] a religious hypocrite
DORINE, lady's maid to Mariane
MONSIEUR LOYAL, a bailiff
THE EXEMPT, an officer of the king
FLIPOTE, lady's maid to Madame Pernelle
LAURENT, a servant of Tartuffe

1. Versification by Constance Congdon, from a translation by Virginia Scott.
2. The name Tartuffe is similar both to the Italian word *tartufo*, meaning "truffle," and to the French word for truffle, *truffe*, from which is derived the French verb *truffer*—one meaning of which in Molière's day was "to deceive or cheat."

The scene is Paris, in ORGON's *house.*

1.1

[MADAME PERNELLE, FLIPOTE, ELMIRE, MARIANE,
DORINE, DAMIS, CLÉANTE]

MADAME PERNELLE[3]   Flipote, come on! My visit here is through!

ELMIRE   You walk so fast I can't keep up with you!

MADAME PERNELLE   Then stop! That's your last step! Don't take another.
After all, I'm just your husband's mother.

5 ELMIRE   And, as his wife, I have to see you out—
Agreed? Now, what is this about?

MADAME PERNELLE   I cannot bear the way this house is run—
As if I don't know how things should be done!
No one even thinks about my pleasure,

10 And, if I ask, I'm served at someone's leisure.
It's obvious—the values here aren't good
Or everyone would treat me as they should.
The Lord of Misrule here has his dominion—

DORINE   But—

MADAME PERNELLE   See? A servant with an opinion.

15 You're the former nanny, nothing more.
Were I in charge here, you'd be out the door.

DAMIS   If—

MADAME PERNELLE   —You—be quiet. Now let Grandma spell
Her special word for you: "F-O-O-L."
Oh yes! Your dear grandmother tells you that,

20 Just as I told my son, "Your son's a brat.
He won't become a drunkard or a thief,
And yet, he'll be a lifetime full of grief."

MARIANE   I think—

MADAME PERNELLE   —Oh, don't do that, my dear grandchild.
You'll hurt your brain. You think that we're beguiled

25 By your quietude, you fragile flower,
But as they say, still waters do run sour.

ELMIRE   But Mother—

MADAME PERNELLE   —Daughter-in-law, please take this well—
Behavior such as yours leads straight to hell.
You spend money like it grows on trees

30 Then wear it on your back in clothes like these.
Are you a princess? No? You're dressed like one!
One wonders whom you dress for—not my son.
Look to these children whom you have corrupted
When their mama's life was interrupted.

35 She spun in her grave when you were wed;
She's still a better mother, even dead.

CLÉANTE   Madame, I do insist—

MADAME PERNELLE   —You do? On what?

---

3. The role of Madame Pernelle was originally played by a male actor, a practice that was already
a comic convention in Molière's time.

That we live life as you do, caring not
For morals? I hear each time you give that speech
40 Your sister memorizing what you teach.
I'd slam the door on you. Forgive my frankness.
That is how I am! And it is thankless.

DAMIS   Tartuffe would, from the bottom of his heart,
If he had one, thank you.

MADAME PERNELLE   Oh, now you start.
45 Grandson, it's "Monsieur Tartuffe" to you.
And he's a man who should be listened to.
If you provoke him with ungodly chat,
I will not tolerate it, and that's that.

DAMIS   Yet I should tolerate this trickster who
50 Has become the voice we answer to.
And I'm to be as quiet as a mouse
About this tyrant's power in our house?
All the fun things lately we have planned,
We couldn't do. And why? Because they're banned—

55 DORINE   By him! Anything we take pleasure in
Suddenly becomes a mortal sin.

MADAME PERNELLE   Then "he's here just in time" is what I say!
Don't you see? He's showing you the way
To heaven! Yes! So follow where he leads!
60 My son knows he is just what this house needs.

DAMIS   Now Grandmother, listen. Not Father, not you,
No one can make me follow this man who
Rules this house, yet came here as a peasant.
I'll put him in his place. It won't be pleasant.

65 DORINE   When he came here he wasn't wearing shoes.
But he's no village saint—it's all a ruse.
There was no vow of poverty—he's poor!
And he was just some beggar at the door
Whom we should have tossed. He's a disaster!
70 To think this street bum now plays the master.

MADAME PERNELLE   May God have mercy on me. You're all blind.
A nobler, kinder man you'll never find.

DORINE   So you think he's a saint. That's what he wants.
But he's a hypocrite and merely flaunts
75 This so-called godliness.

MADAME PERNELLE   Will you be quiet!?

DORINE   And that man of his—I just don't buy it—
He's supposed to be his servant? No.
They're in cahoots, I bet.

MADAME PERNELLE   How would you know?
When, clearly, you don't understand, in fact,
80 How a servant is supposed to act?
This holy man you think of as uncouth,
Tries to help by telling you the truth
About yourself. But you can't hear it.
He knows what heaven wants and that you fear it.

85 DORINE   So "heaven" hates these visits by our friends?
        I see! And that's why Tartuffe's gone to any ends
        To ruin our fun? But it is he who's zealous
        About "privacy"—and why? He's jealous.
        You can't miss it, whenever men come near—
90   He's lusting for our own Madame Elmire.
    MADAME PERNELLE   Since you, Dorine, have never understood
        Your place, or the concepts of "should"
        And "should not," one can't expect you to see
        Tartuffe's awareness of propriety.
95   When these men visit, they bring noise and more—
        Valets and servants planted at the door,
        Carriages and horses, constant chatter.
        What must the neighbors think? These things matter.
        Is something going on? Well, I hope not.
100   You know you're being talked about a lot.
    CLÉANTE   Really, Madame, you think you can prevent
        Gossip? When most human beings are bent
        On rumormongering and defamation,
        And gathering or faking information
105   To make us all look bad—what can we do?
        The fools who gossip don't care what is true.
        You would force the whole world to be quiet?
        Impossible! And each new lie—deny it?
        Who in the world would want to live that way?
110   Let's live our lives. Let gossips have their say.
    DORINE   It's our neighbor, Daphne. I just know it.
        They don't like us. It's obvious—they show it
        In the way they watch us—she and her mate.
        I've seen them squinting at us, through their gate.
115   It's true—those whose private conduct is the worst
        Will mow each other down to be the first
        To weave some tale of lust, so hearts are broken
        Out of a simple kiss that's just a token
        Between friends—just friends and nothing more.
120   See—those whose trysts are kept behind a door
        Yet everyone finds out? Well, then, they need
        New stories for the gossip mill to feed
        To all who'll listen. So they must repaint
        The deeds of others, hoping that a taint
125   Will color others' lives in darker tone
        And, by this process, lighten up their own.
    MADAME PERNELLE   Daphne and her mate are not the point.
        But when Orante says things are out of joint,
        There's a problem. She's a person who
130   Prays every day and should be listened to.
        She condemns the mob that visits here.
    DORINE   This good woman shouldn't live so near
        Those, like us, who run a bawdy house.
        I hear she lives as quiet as a mouse—

135　　Devout, though. Everyone applauds her zeal.
　　　　She needed that when age stole her appeal.
　　　　Her passion is policing—it's her duty
　　　　And compensation for her loss of beauty.
　　　　She's a reluctant prude. And now, her art,
140　　Once used so well to win a lover's heart,
　　　　Is gone. Her eyes, that used to flash with lust,
　　　　Are steely from her piety. She must
　　　　Have seen that it's too late to be a wife,
　　　　And so she lives a plain and pious life.
145　　This is a strategy of old coquettes.
　　　　It's how they manage once the world forgets
　　　　Them. First, they wallow in a dark depression,
　　　　Then see no recourse but in the profession
　　　　Of a prude. They criticize the lives of everyone.
150　　They censure everything, and pardon none.
　　　　It's envy. Pleasures that they are denied
　　　　By time and age, now, they just can't abide.

MADAME PERNELLE　You do go on and on. [*To* ELMIRE] My dear Elmire,
　　　　This is all your doing. It's so clear
155　　Because you let a servant give advice.
　　　　Just be aware—I'm tired of being nice.
　　　　It's obvious to anyone with eyes
　　　　That what my son has done is more than wise
　　　　In welcoming this man who's so devout;
160　　His very presence casts the devils out.
　　　　Or most of them—that's why I hope you hear him.
　　　　And I advise all of you to stay near him.
　　　　You need his protection and advice.
　　　　Your casual attention won't suffice.
165　　It's heaven sent him here to fill a need,
　　　　To save you from yourselves—oh yes, indeed.
　　　　These visits from your friends you seem to want—
　　　　Listen to yourselves! So nonchalant!
　　　　As if no evil lurks in these events.
170　　As if you're blind to what Satan invents.
　　　　And dances! What are those but food for slander!
　　　　It's to the worst desires these parties pander.
　　　　I ask you now, what purpose do they serve?
　　　　Where gossip's passed around like an hors-d'oeuvre.
175　　A thousand cackling hens, busy with what?
　　　　It takes a lot of noise to cover smut.
　　　　It truly is the tower of Babylon,[4]
　　　　Where people babble on and on and on.
　　　　Ah! Case in point—there stands Monsieur Cléante,

4. That is, the biblical Tower of Babel (the Hebrew equivalent of the Akkadian Bab-ilu, or Babylon—a name explained by the similar sounding but unrelated Hebrew verb *balal*, "confuse"), described in Genesis 11.1–9; to prevent it from being constructed and reaching heaven, God scattered all the people and confused their language, creating many tongues where there had been only one.

180   Sniggering and eyeing me askant,
      As if this has nothing to do with him,
      And nothing that he does would God condemn.
      And so, Elmire, my dear, I say farewell.
      Till when? When it is a fine day in hell.
185   Farewell, all of you. When I pass through that door,
      You won't have me to laugh at anymore.
      Flipote! Wake up! Have you heard nothing I have said?
      I'll march you home and beat you till you're dead.
      March, slut, march.

1.2[5]

[DORINE, CLÉANTE]

CLÉANTE   I'm staying here. She's scary,
    That old lady—
DORINE   I know why you're wary.
    Shall I call her back to hear you say,
    "That *old* lady"? That would make her day.
5 CLÉANTE   She's lost her mind, she's—now we have the proof—
    Head over heels in love with whom? Tartuffe.
DORINE   So here's what's worse and weird—so is her son.
    What's more—it's obvious to everyone.
    Before Tartuffe and he became entwined,
10   Orgon once ruled this house in his right mind.
    In the troubled times,[6] he backed the prince,
    And that took courage. We haven't seen it since.
    He is intoxicated with Tartuffe—
    A potion that exceeds a hundred proof.
15   It's put him in a trance, this devil's brew.
    And so he worships this imposter who
    He calls "brother" and loves more than one—
    This charlatan—more than daughter, wife, son.
    This charlatan hears all our master's dreams,
20   And all his secrets. Every thought, it seems,
    Is poured out to Tartuffe, like he's his priest!
    You'd think they'd see the heresy, at least.
    Orgon caresses him, embraces him, and shows
    More love for him than any mistress knows.
25   Come for a meal and who has the best seat?
    Whose preferences determine what we eat?
    Tartuffe consumes enough for six, is praised,
    And to his health is every goblet raised,
    While on his plate are piled the choicest bites.

---

5. In classical French drama, a new scene begins whenever a character enters or leaves the stage, even if the action continues without interruption; this convention has become known as "French scenes." Characters remaining onstage are listed; others from the previous scene can be assumed to have exited.

6. That is, during the Fronde (literally, "sling"; 1648–53), a civil war that took place while France was being ruled by a regent for Louis XIV—"the prince" whom Orgon supported—as various factions of the nobility sought to limit the growing authority of the monarchy.

30   Then when he belches, our master delights
     In that and shouts, "God bless you!" to the beast,
     As if Tartuffe's the reason for the feast.
     Did I mention the quoting of each word,
     As if it's the most brilliant thing we've heard?
35   And, oh, the miracles Tartuffe creates!
     The prophecies! We write while he dictates.
     All that's ridiculous. But what's evil
     Is seeing the deception and upheaval
     Of the master and everything he owns.
40   He hands him money. They're not even loans—
     He's giving it away. It's gone too far.
     To watch Tartuffe play him like a guitar!
     And this Laurent, his man, found some lace.
     Shredded it and threw it in my face.
45   He'd found it pressed inside *The Lives of Saints*,[7]
     I thought we'd have to put him in restraints.
     "To put the devil's finery beside
     The words and lives of saintly souls who died—
     Is action of satanical transgression!"
50   And so, of course, I hurried to confession.

1.3

[ELMIRE, MARIANE, DAMIS, CLÉANTE, DORINE]

ELMIRE [*to* CLÉANTE]   Lucky you, you stayed. Yes, there was more,
     And more preaching from Grandma, at the door.
     My husband's coming! I didn't catch his eye.
     I'll wait for him upstairs. Cléante, good-bye.
5 CLÉANTE   I'll see you soon. I'll wait here below,
     Take just a second for a brief hello.
DAMIS   While you have him, say something for me?
     My sister needs for Father to agree
     To her marriage with Valère, as planned.
10   Tartuffe opposes it and will demand
     That Father break his word, and that's not fair;
     Then I can't wed the sister of Valère.
     Listening only to Tartuffe's voice,
     He'd break four hearts at once—
DORINE   He's here.

1.4

[ORGON, CLÉANTE, DORINE]

ORGON   Rejoice!
     I'm back.
CLÉANTE   I'm glad to see you, but I'm on my way.
     Just stayed to say hello.
ORGON   No more to say?
     Dorine! Come back! And Cléante, why the hurry?

---

7. A text (*Flos Sanctorum*, 1599–1601) by the Spanish Jesuit Pedro de Ribadeneyra, available in French translation by 1646.

5 Indulge me for a moment. You know I worry.
  I've been gone two days! There's news to tell.
  Now don't hold back. Has everyone been well?

DORINE Not quite. There was that headache Madame had
  The day you left. Well, it got really bad.
10 She had a fever—

ORGON   And Tartuffe?

DORINE   He's fine—
  Rosy-nosed and red-cheeked, drinking your wine.

ORGON Poor man!

DORINE   And then, Madame became unable
  To eat a single morsel at the table.

ORGON Ah, and Tartuffe?

DORINE   He sat within her sight,
15 Not holding back, he ate with great delight,
  A brace of partridge, and a leg of mutton.
  In fact, he ate so much, he popped a button.

ORGON Poor man!

DORINE   That night until the next sunrise,
  Your poor wife couldn't even close her eyes.
20 What a fever! Oh, how she did suffer!
  I don't see how that night could have been rougher.
  We watched her all night long, worried and weepy.

ORGON Ah, and Tartuffe?

DORINE   At dinner he grew sleepy.
  After such a meal, it's not surprising.
25 He slept through the night, not once arising.

ORGON Poor man!

DORINE   At last won over by our pleading,
  Madame agreed to undergo a bleeding.[8]
  And this, we think, has saved her from the grave.

ORGON Ah, and Tartuffe?

DORINE   Oh, he was very brave.
30 To make up for the blood Madame had lost
  Tartuffe slurped down red wine, all at your cost.

ORGON Poor man!

DORINE   Since then, they've both been fine, although
  Madame needs me. I'll go and let her know
  How anxious you have been about her health,
35 And that you prize it more than all your wealth.

1.5

[ORGON, CLÉANTE]

CLÉANTE You know that girl was laughing in your face.
  I fear I'll make you angry, but in case
  There is a chance you'll listen, I will try
  To say that you are laughable and why.
5 I've never known of something so capricious

---

8. Bloodletting (whether by leeches or other means), for centuries a standard medical treatment for a wide range of diseases.

As letting this man do just as he wishes
In your home and to your family.
You brought him here, relieved his poverty,
And, in return—

ORGON   Now you listen to me!

10   You're just my brother-in-law, Cléante. Quite!
You don't know this man. And don't deny it!

CLÉANTE   I don't know him, yes, that may be so,
But men like him are not so rare, you know.

ORGON   If you only could know him as I do,

15   You would be his true disciple, too.
The universe, your ecstasy would span.
This is a man . . . who . . . ha! . . . well, such a man.
Behold him. Let him teach you profound peace.
When first we met, I felt my troubles cease.

20   Yes, I was changed after I talked with him.
I saw my wants and needs as just a whim!
Everything that's written, all that's sung,
The world, and you and me, well, it's all dung!
Yes, it's crap! And isn't that a wonder!

25   The real world—it's just some spell we're under!
He's taught me to love nothing and no one!
Mother, father, wife, daughter, son—
They could die right now, I'd feel no pain.

CLÉANTE   What feelings you've developed, how humane.

30 ORGON   You just don't see him in the way I do,
But if you did, you'd feel what I feel, too.
Every day he came to church and knelt,
And from his groans, I knew just what he felt.
Those sounds he made from deep inside his soul,

35   Were fed by piety he could not control.
Of the congregation, who could ignore
The way he humbly bowed and kissed the floor?
And when they tried to turn away their eyes,
His fervent prayers to heaven and deep sighs

40   Made them witness his deep spiritual pain.
Then something happened I can't quite explain.
I rose to leave—he quickly went before
To give me holy water at the door.
He knew what I needed, so he blessed me.

45   I found his acolyte, he'd so impressed me,
To ask who he was and there I learned
About his poverty and how he spurned
The riches of this world. And when I tried
To give him gifts, in modesty, he cried,

50   "That is too much," he'd say, "A half would do."
Then gave a portion back, with much ado.
"I am not worthy. I do not deserve
Your gifts or pity. I am here to serve
The will of heaven, that and nothing more."

55 Then takes the gift and shares it with the poor.
So heaven spoke to me inside my head.
"Just bring him home with you" is what it said
And so I did. And ever since he came,
My home's a happy one. I also claim
60 A moral home, a house that's free of sin,
Tartuffe's on watch—he won't let any in.
His interest in my wife is reassuring,
She's innocent of course, but so alluring,
He tells me whom she sees and what she does.
65 He's more jealous than I ever was.
It's for my honor that he's so concerned.
His righteous anger's all for me, I've learned,
To the point that just the other day,
A flea annoyed him as he tried to pray,
70 Then he rebuked himself, as if he'd willed it—
His excessive anger when he killed it.

CLÉANTE Orgon, listen. You're out of your mind.
Or you're mocking me. Or both combined.
How can you speak such nonsense without blinking?

75 ORGON I smell an atheist! It's that freethinking!
Such nonsense is the bane of your existence.
And that explains your damnable resistance.
Ten times over, I've tried to save your soul
From your corrupted mind. That's still my goal.

80 CLÉANTE You have been corrupted by your friends,
You know of whom I speak. Your thought depends
On people who are blind and want to spread it
Like some horrid flu, and, yes, I dread it.
I'm no atheist. I see things clearly.
85 And what I see is loud lip service, merely,
To make exhibitionists seem devout.
Forgive me, but a prayer is not a shout.
Yet those who don't adore these charlatans
Are seen as faithless heathens by your friends.
90 It's as if you think you'd never find
Reason and the sacred intertwined.
You think I'm afraid of retribution?
Heaven sees my heart and their pollution.
So we should be the slaves of sanctimony?
95 Monkey see, monkey do, monkey phony.
The true believers we should emulate
Are not the ones who groan and lay prostrate.
And yet you see no problem in the notion
Of hypocrisy as deep devotion.
100 You see as one the genuine and the spurious.
You'd extend this to your money? I'm just curious.
In your business dealings, I'd submit,
You'd not confuse the gold with counterfeit.
Men are strangely made, I'd have to say.

105   They're burdened with their reason, till one day,
       They free themselves with such force that they spoil
       The noblest of things for which they toil.
       Because they must go to extremes. It's a flaw.
       Just a word in passing, Brother-in-law.

110 ORGON   Oh, you are the wisest man alive, so
       You know everything there is to know.
       You are the one enlightened man, the sage.
       You are Cato the Elder[9] of our age.
       Next to you, all men are dumb as cows.

115 CLÉANTE   I'm not the wisest man, as you espouse,
       Nor do I know—what—all there is to know?
       But I do know, Orgon, that quid pro quo
       Does not apply at all to "false" and "true,"
       And I would never trust a person who

120   Cannot tell them apart. See, I revere
       Everyone whose worship is sincere.
       Nothing is more noble or more beautiful
       Than fervor that is holy, not just dutiful.
       So nothing is more odious to me

125   Than the display of specious piety
       Which I see in every charlatan
       Who tries to pass for a true holy man.
       Religious passion worn as a facade
       Abuses what's sacred and mocks God.

130   These men who take what's sacred and most holy
       And use it as their trade, for money, solely,
       With downcast looks and great affected cries,
       Who suck in true believers with their lies,
       Who ceaselessly will preach and then demand

135   "Give up the world!" and then, by sleight of hand,
       End up sitting pretty at the court,
       The best in lodging and new clothes to sport.
       If you're their enemy, then heaven hates you.
       That's their claim when one of them berates you.

140   They'll say you've sinned. You'll find yourself removed
       And wondering if you'll be approved
       For anything, at all, ever again.
       Because so heinous was this fictional "sin."
       When these men are angry, they're the worst,

145   There's no place to hide, you're really cursed.
       They use what we call righteous as their sword,
       To coldly murder in the name of the Lord.
       But next to these imposters faking belief,
       The devotion of the true is a relief.

150   Our century has put before our eyes
       Glorious examples we can prize.

---

9. Roman statesman and author (234–149 B.C.E.), famous as a stern moralist devoted to traditional Roman ideals of honor, courage, and simplicity.

Look at Ariston, and look at Periandre,
Oronte, Alcidamas, Polydore, Clitandre:[1]
Not one points out his own morality,
155 Instead they speak of their mortality.
They don't form cabals,[2] they don't have factions,
They don't censure other people's actions.
They see the flagrant pride in such correction
And know that humans can't achieve perfection.
160 They know this of themselves and yet their lives
Good faith, good works, all good, epitomize.
They don't exhibit zeal that's more intense
Than heaven shows us in its own defense.
They'd never claim a knowledge that's divine
165 And yet they live in virtue's own design.
They concentrate their hatred on the sin,
And when the sinner grieves, invite him in.
They leave to others the arrogance of speech.
Instead they practice what others only preach.
170 These are the men who show us how to live.
Their lives, the best example I can give.
These are my men, the ones whom I would follow.
Your man and his life, honestly, are hollow.
I believe you praise him quite sincerely,
175 I also think you'll pay for this quite dearly.
He's a fraud, this man whom you adore.
ORGON   Oh, you've stopped talking. Is there any more?
CLEANTE   No.
ORGON   I am your servant, sir.
CLÉANTE   No! wait!
There's one more thing—no more debate—
180 I want to change the subject, if I might.
I heard that you said the other night,
To Valère, he'd be your son-in-law.
ORGON   I did.
CLÉANTE   And set the date?
ORGON   Yes.
CLÉANTE   Did you withdraw?
ORGON   I did.
CLÉANTE   You're putting off the wedding? Why?
185 ORGON   Don't know.
CLÉANTE   There's more?
ORGON   Perhaps.
CLÉANTE   Again I'll try:
You would break your word?
ORGON   I couldn't say.
CLÉANTE   Then, Orgon, why did you change the day?

---

1. Made-up names.
2. A possible allusion to the Compagnie de Saint-Sacrement, a tightly knit group of

prominent French citizens known for public works as well as strict morality; they were pejoratively referred to as the *cabale*.

ORGON   Who knows?

CLÉANTE   But we need to know, don't we now?
Is there a reason you would break your vow?

190 ORGON   That depends.

CLÉANTE   On what? Orgon, what is it?
Valère was the reason for my visit.

ORGON   Who knows? Who knows?

CLÉANTE   So there's some mystery there?

ORGON   Heaven knows.

CLÉANTE   It does? And now, Valère—
May he know, too?

ORGON   Can't say.

CLÉANTE   But, dear Orgon,

195 We have no information to go on.
We need to know—

ORGON   What heaven wants, I'll do.

CLÉANTE   Is that your final answer? Then I'm through.
But your pledge to Valère? You'll stand by it?

ORGON   Good-bye.

                            [ORGON *exits.*]

CLÉANTE   More patience, yes, I should try it.

200 I let him get to me. Now I confess
I fear the worst for Valère's happiness.

2.1

[ORGON, MARIANE]

ORGON   Mariane.

MARIANE   Father.

ORGON   Come. Now. Talk with me.

MARIANE   Why are you looking everywhere?

ORGON   To see
If everyone is minding their own business.
So. Child, I've always loved your gentleness.

5 MARIANE   And for your love, I'm grateful, Father dear.

ORGON   Well said. And so to prove that you're sincere,
And worthy of my love, you have the task
Of doing for me anything I ask.

MARIANE   Then my obedience will be my proof.

10 ORGON   Good. What do you think of our guest, Tartuffe?

MARIANE   Who, me?

ORGON   Yes, you. Watch what you say right now.

MARIANE   Then, Father, I will say what you allow.

ORGON   Wise words, Daughter. So this is what you say:
"He is a perfect man in every way;

15 In body and soul, I find him divine."
And then you say, "Please Father, make him mine."
Huh?

MARIANE   Huh?

ORGON   Yes?

MARIANE   I heard . . .

ORGON   Yes.

MARIANE   What did you say?
     Who is this perfect man in every way,
     Whom in body and soul I find divine
20   And ask of you, "Please, Father, make him mine?"

ORGON   Tartuffe.

MARIANE   All that I've said, I now amend
     Because you wouldn't want me to pretend.

ORGON   Absolutely not—that's so misguided.
     Have it be the truth, then. It's decided.

25 MARIANE   What?! Father, you want—

ORGON   Yes, my dear, I do—
     To join in marriage my Tartuffe and you.
     And since I have—

2.2

[DORINE, ORGON, MARIANE]

ORGON   Dorine, I know you're there!
     Any secrets in this house you don't share?

DORINE   "Marriage"—I think, yes, I heard a rumor,
     Someone's failed attempt at grotesque humor,
5   So when I heard the story, I said, "No!
     Preposterous! Absurd! It can't be so."

ORGON   Oh, you find it preposterous? And why?

DORINE   It's so outrageous, it must be a lie.

ORGON   Yet it's the truth and you will believe it.

10 DORINE   Yet as a joke is how I must receive it.

ORGON   But it's a story that will soon come true.

DORINE   A fantasy!

ORGON   I'm getting tired of you.
     Mariane, it's not a joke—

DORINE   Says he,
     Laughing up his sleeve for all to see.

15 ORGON   I'm telling you—

DORINE   —more make-believe for fun.
     It's very good—you're fooling everyone.

ORGON   You have made me really angry now.

DORINE   I see the awful truth across your brow.
     How can a man who looks as wise as you
20   Be such a fool to want—

ORGON   What can I do
     About a servant with a mouth like that?
     The liberties you take! Decorum you laugh at!
     I'm not happy with you—

DORINE   Oh sir, don't frown.
     A smile is just a frown turned upside down.
25   Be happy, sir, because you've shared your scheme,
     Even though it's just a crazy dream.
     Because, dear sir, your daughter is not meant
     For this zealot—she's too innocent.

She'd be alarmed by his robust desire
30 And question heaven's sanction of this fire
    And then the gossip! Your friends will talk a lot,
    Because you're a man of wealth and he is not.
    Could it be your reasoning has a flaw—
    Choosing a beggar for a son-in-law?
35 ORGON You, shut up! If he has nothing now
    Admire that, as if it were his vow,
    This poverty. His property was lost
    Because he would not pay the deadly cost
    Of daily duties nibbling life away,
40 Leaving him with hardly time to pray.
    The grandeur in his life comes from devotion
    To the eternal, thus his great emotion.
    And at those moments, I can plainly see
    What my special task has come to be:
45 To end the embarrassment he feels
    And the sorrow he so nobly conceals
    Of the loss of his ancestral domain.
    With my money, I can end his pain.
    I'll raise him up to be, because I can,
50 With my help, again, a gentleman.
    DORINE So he's a gentleman. Does that seem vain?
    Then what about this piety and pain?
    Those with "domains" are those of noble birth.
    A holy man's domain is not on earth.
55 It seems to me a holy man of merit
    Wouldn't brag of what he might inherit—
    Even gifts in heaven, he won't mention.
    To live a humble life is his intention.
    Yet he wants something back? That's just ambition
60 To feed his pride. Is that a holy mission?
    You seem upset. Is it something I said?
    I'll shut up. We'll talk of her instead.
    Look at this girl, your daughter, your own blood.
    How will her honor fare covered with mud?
65 Think of his age. So from the night they're wed,
    Bliss, if there is any, leaves the marriage bed,
    And she'll be tied unto this elderly person.
    Her dedication to fidelity will worsen
    And soon he will sprout horns,[3] your holy man,
70 And no one will be happy. If I can
    Have another word, I'd like to say
    Old men and young girls are married every day,
    And the young girls stray, but who's to blame
    For the loss of honor and good name?
75 The father, who proceeds to pick a mate,
    Blindly, though it's someone she may hate,

---

3. The traditional sign of the cuckold.

Bears the sins the daughter may commit,
Imperiling his soul because of it.
If you do this, I vow you'll hear the bell,
80 As you die, summoning you to hell.
ORGON   You think that you can teach me how to live.
DORINE   If you'd just heed the lessons that I give.
ORGON   Can heaven tell me why I still endure
This woman's ramblings? Yet, of this I'm sure,
85 I know what's best for you—I'm your father.
I gave you to Valère, without a bother.
But I hear he gambles and what's more,
He thinks things that a Christian would abhor.
It's from free thinking that all evils stem.
90 No wonder, then, at church, I don't see him.
DORINE   Should he race there, if he only knew
Which Mass you might attend, and be on view?
He could wait at the door with holy water.
ORGON   Go away. I'm talking to my daughter.
95 Think, my child, he is heaven's favorite!
And age in marriage? It can flavor it,
A sweet comfit suffused with deep, deep pleasure.
You will be loving, faithful, and will treasure
Every single moment—two turtledoves—
100 Next to heaven, the only thing he loves.
And he will be the only one for you.
No arguments or quarrels. You'll be true.
Like two innocent children, you will thrive,
In heaven's light, thrilled to be alive.
105 And as a woman, surely you must know
Wives mold husbands, like making pies from dough.
DORINE   Four and twenty cuckolds baked in a pie.
ORGON   Ugh! What a thing to say!
DORINE   Oh, really, why?
He's destined to be cheated on, it's true.
110 You know he'd always question her virtue.
ORGON   Quiet! Just be quiet. I command it!
DORINE   I'll do just that, because you do demand it!
But your best interests—I will protect them.
ORGON   Too kind of you. Be quiet and neglect them.
115 DORINE   If I weren't fond of you—
ORGON   —Don't want you to
DORINE   I will be fond of you in spite of you.
ORGON   Don't!
DORINE   But your honor is so dear to me,
How can you expose yourself to mockery?
ORGON   Will you never be quiet!
DORINE   Oh, dear sir,
120 I can't let you do this thing to her,
It's against my conscience—
ORGON   You vicious asp!

DORINE   Sometimes the things you call me make me gasp.
    And anger, sir, is not a pious trait.
ORGON   It's your fault, girl! You make me irate!
125   I am livid! Why won't you be quiet!
DORINE   I will. For you, I'm going to try it.
    But I'll be thinking.
ORGON   Fine. Now, Mariane,
    You have to trust—your father's a wise man.
    I have thought a lot about this mating.
130   I've weighed the options—
DORINE   It's infuriating
    Not to be able to speak.
ORGON   And so
    I'll say this. Of up and coming men I know,
    He's not one of them, no money in the bank,
    Not handsome.
DORINE   That's the truth. Arf! Arf! Be frank.
135   He's a dog!
ORGON   He has manly traits.
    And other gifts.
DORINE   And who will blame the fates
    For failure of this marriage made in hell?
    And whose fault will it be? Not hard to tell.
    Since everyone you know will see the truth:
140   You gave away your daughter to Tartuffe.
    If I were in her place, I'd guarantee
    No man would live the night who dared force me
    Into a marriage that I didn't want.
    There would be war with no hope of détente.
145 ORGON   I asked for silence. This is what I get?
DORINE   You said not to talk to *you*. Did you forget?
ORGON   What do you call what you are doing now?
DORINE   Talking to myself.
ORGON   You insolent cow!
    I'll wait for you to say just one more word.
150   I'm waiting . . .
            [ORGON *prepares to give* DORINE *a smack but each time he
            looks over at her, she stands silent and still.*]
                    Just ignore her. Look at me.
    I've chosen you a husband who would be,
    If rated, placed among the highest ranks.
    [*To* DORINE]   Why don't you talk?
DORINE   Don't feel like it, thanks.
ORGON   I'm watching you.
DORINE   Do you think I'm a fool?
155 ORGON   I realize that you may think me cruel.
    But here's the thing, child, I will be obeyed,
    And this marriage, child, will not be delayed.
DORINE [*running from* ORGON, DORINE *throws a line to* MARIANE]
    You'll be a joke with Tartuffe as a spouse.

[ORGON *tries to slap her but misses.*]

ORGON   What we have is a plague in our own house!
160   It's her fault that I'm in the state I'm in,
        So furious, I might commit a sin.
        She'll drive me to murder. Or to curse.
        I need fresh air before my mood gets worse.   [ORGON *exits.*]

2.3

[DORINE, MARIANE]

DORINE   Tell me, have you lost the power of speech?
        I'm forced to play your role and it's a reach.
        How can you sit there with nothing to say
        Watching him tossing your whole life away?
5   MARIANE   Against my father, what am I to do?
    DORINE   You want out of this marriage scheme, don't you?
    MARIANE   Yes.
    DORINE   Tell him no one can command a heart.
        That when you marry, you will have no part
        Of anyone unless he pleases you.
10   And tell your father, with no more ado,
        That you will marry for yourself, not him,
        And that you won't obey his iron whim.
        Since he finds Tartuffe to be such a catch,
        He can marry him himself. There's a match.
15 MARIANE   You know that fathers have such sway
        Over our lives that I've nothing to say.
        I've never had the strength.
    DORINE   Let's think. All right?
        Didn't Valère propose the other night?
        Do you or don't you love Valère?
20 MARIANE   You know the answer, Dorine—that's unfair.
        Just talking about it tears me apart.
        I've said a hundred times, he has my heart.
        I'm wild about him. I know. And I've told you.
    DORINE   But how am I to know, for sure, that's true?
25 MARIANE   Because I told you. And yet you doubt it?
        See me blushing when I speak about it?
    DORINE   So you do love him?
    MARIANE   Yes, with all my might.
    DORINE   He loves you just as much?
    MARIANE   I think that's right.
    DORINE   And it's to the altar you're both heading?
30 MARIANE   Yes.
    DORINE   So what about this other wedding?
    MARIANE   I'll kill myself. That's what I've decided.
    DORINE   What a great solution you've provided!
        To get out of trouble, you plan to die!
        Immediately? Or sometime, by and by?
35 MARIANE   Oh, really, Dorine, you're not my friend.
        Unsympathetic—

DORINE   I'm at my wit's end,
  Talking to you whose answer is dying,
  Who, in a crisis, just gives up trying.
MARIANE   What do you want of me, then?
DORINE   Come alive!
40 Love needs a resolute heart to survive.
MARIANE   In my love for Valère, I'm resolute.
  But the next step is his.
DORINE   And so, you're mute?
MARIANE   What can I say? It's the job of Valère,
  His duty, before I go anywhere,
45 To deal with my father—
DORINE   —Then, you'll stay.
  "Orgon was born bizarre" is what some say.
  It there were doubts before, we have this proof—
  He is head over heels for his Tartuffe,
  And breaks off a marriage that he arranged.
50 Valère's at fault if your father's deranged?
MARIANE   But my refusal will be seen as pride
  And, worse, contempt. And I have to hide
  My feelings for Valère, I must not show
  That I'm in love at all. If people know,
55 Then all the modesty my sex is heir to
  Will be gone. There's more: how can I bear to
  Not be a proper daughter to my father?
DORINE   No, no, of course not. God forbid we bother
  The way the world sees you. What people see,
60 What other people think of us, should be
  Our first concern. Besides, I see the truth:
  You really want to be Madame Tartuffe.
  What was I thinking, urging opposition
  To Monsieur Tartuffe! This proposition,
65 To merge with him—he's such a catch!
  In fact, for you, he's just the perfect match.
  He's much respected, everywhere he goes.
  And his ruddy complexion nearly glows.
  And as his wife, imagine the delight
70 Of being near him, every day and night.
  And vital? Oh, my dear, you won't want more.
MARIANE   Oh, heaven help me!
DORINE   How your soul will soar,
  Savoring this marriage down to the last drop,
  With such a handsome—
MARIANE   All right! You can stop!
75 Just help me. Please. And tell me there's a way
  To save me. I'll do whatever you say.
DORINE   Each daughter must choose always to say yes
  To what her father wants, no more and no less.
  If he wants to give her an ape to marry,
80 Then she must do it, without a query.

But it's a happy fate! What is this frown?
You'll go by wagon to his little town,
Eager cousins, uncles, aunts will greet you
And will call you "sister" when they meet you,
85 Because you're family now. Don't look so grim.
You will so adore chatting with them.
Welcomed by the local high society,
You'll be expected to maintain propriety
And sit straight, or try to, in the folding chair
90 They offer you, and never, ever stare
At the wardrobe of the bailiff's wife
Because you'll see her every day for life.[4]
Let's not forget the village carnival!
Where you'll be dancing at a lavish ball
95 To a bagpipe orchestra of locals,
An organ grinder's monkey doing vocals—
And your husband—

MARIANE   —Dorine, I beg you, please,
Help me. Should I get down here on my knees?

DORINE   Can't help you.

MARIANE   Please, Dorine, I'm begging you!

100 DORINE   And you deserve this man.

MARIANE   That just not true!

DORINE   Oh yes? What changed?

MARIANE   My darling Dorine . . .

DORINE   No.

MARIANE   You can't be this mean.
I love Valère. I told you and it's true.

DORINE   Who's that? Oh. No, Tartuffe's the one for you.

105 MARIANE   You've always been completely on my side.

DORINE   No more. I sentence you to be Tartuffified!

MARIANE   It seems my fate has not the power to move you,
So I'll seek my solace and remove to
A private place for me in my despair.
110 To end the misery that brought me here.

          [MARIANE *starts to exit.*]

DORINE   Wait! Wait! Come back! Please don't go out that door.
I'll help you. I'm not angry anymore.

MARIANE   If I am forced into this martyrdom,
You see, I'll have to die, Dorine.

DORINE   Oh come,
115 Give up this torment. Look at me—I swear.
We'll find a way. Look, here's your love, Valère.

          [DORINE *moves to the side of the stage.*]

---

4. Dorine's description reflects the stereotypes associated with rural pretensions to culture.

2.4

[VALÈRE, MARIANE, DORINE]

VALÈRE   So I've just heard some news that's news to me,
And very fine news it is, do you agree?
MARIANE   What?
VALÈRE   You have plans for marriage I didn't know.
You're going to marry Tartuffe. Is this so?
5 MARIANE   My father has that notion, it is true.
VALÈRE   Madame, your father promised—
MARIANE   —me to you?
He changed his mind, announced this change to me,
Just minutes ago . . .
VALÈRE   Quite seriously?
MARIANE   It's his wish that I should marry this man.
10 VALÈRE   And what do you think of your father's plan?
MARIANE   I don't know.
VALÈRE   Honest words—better than lies.
You don't know?
MARIANE   No.
VALÈRE   No?
MARIANE   What do you advise?
VALÈRE   I advise you to . . . marry Tartuffe. Tonight.
MARIANE   You advise me to . . .
VALÈRE   Yes.
MARIANE   Really?
VALÈRE   That's right.
15 Consider it. It's an obvious choice.
MARIANE   I'll follow your suggestion and rejoice.
VALÈRE   I'm sure that you can follow it with ease.
MARIANE   Just as you gave it. It will be a breeze.
VALÈRE   Just to please you was my sole intent.
20 MARIANE   To please you, I'll do it and be content.
DORINE   I can't wait to see what happens next.
VALÈRE   And this is love to you? I am perplexed.
Was it a sham when you—
MARIANE   That's in the past
Because you said so honestly and fast
25 That I should take the one bestowed on me.
I'm nothing but obedient, you see,
So, yes, I'll take him. That's my declaration,
Since that's your advice and expectation.
VALÈRE   I see, you're using me as an excuse,
30 Any pretext, so you can cut me loose.
You didn't think I'd notice—I'd be blind
To the fact that you'd made up your mind?
MARINE   How true. Well said.
VALÈRE   And so it's plain to see,
Your heart never felt a true love for me.

35 MARIANE   If you want to, you may think that is true.
It's clear this thought has great appeal for you.
VALÈRE   If I want? I will, but I'm offended
To my very soul. But your turn's ended,
And I can win this game we're playing at:
40 I've someone else in mind.
MARIANE   I don't doubt that.
Your good points—
VALÈRE   Oh, let's leave them out of this.
I've very few—in fact, I am remiss.
I must be. Right? You've made that clear to me.
But I know someone, hearing that I'm free,
45 To make up for my loss, will eagerly consent.
MARIANE   The loss is not that bad. You'll be content
With your new choice, replacement, if you will.
VALÈRE   I will. And I'll remain contented still,
In knowing you're as happy as I am.
50 A woman tells a man her love's a sham.
The man's been fooled and his honor blighted.
He can't deny his love is unrequited,
Then he forgets this woman totally,
And if he can't, pretends, because, you see,
55 It is ignoble conduct and weak, too,
Loving someone who does not love you.
MARIANE   What a fine, noble sentiment to heed.
VALÈRE   And every man upholds it as his creed.
What? You expect me to keep on forever
60 Loving you after you blithely sever
The bond between us, watching as you go
Into another's arms and not bestow
This heart you've cast away upon someone
Who might welcome—
MARIANE   I wish it were done.
65 That's exactly what I want, you see.
VALÈRE   That's what you want?
MARIANE   Yes.
VALÈRE   Then let it be.
I'll grant your wish.
MARIANE   Please do.
VALÈRE   Just don't forget,
Whose fault it was when you, filled with regret,
Realize that you forced me out the door.
70 MARIANE   True.
VALÈRE   You've set the example and what's more,
I'll match you with my own hardness of heart.
You won't see me again, if I depart.
MARIANE   That's good!
        [VALÈRE *goes to exit, but when he gets to the door, he*
        returns.]

VALÈRE	What?
MARIANE	What?
VALÈRE	You said . . . ?
MARIANE	Nothing at all.

VALÈRE Well, I'll be on my way, then.

[*He goes, stops.*]

Did you call?

75 MARIANE Me? You must be dreaming.

VALÈRE I'll go away.
Good-bye, then.

MARIANE Good-bye.

DORINE I am here to say,
You both are idiots! What's this about?
I left you two alone to fight it out,
To see how far you'd go. You're quite a pair
80 In matching tit for tat— Hold on, Valère!
Where are you going?

VALÈRE What, Dorine? You spoke?

DORINE Come here.

VALÈRE I'm upset and will not provoke
This lady. Do not try to change my mind.
I'm doing what she wants.

DORINE You are so blind.
85 Just stop.

VALÈRE No. It's settled.

DORINE Oh, is that so?

MARIANE He can't stand to look at me, I know.
He wants to go away, so please let him.
No, I shall leave so I can forget him.

DORINE Where are you going?

MARIANE Leave me alone.

90 DORINE Come back here at once.

MARIANE No. Even that tone
Won't bring me. I'm not a child, you see.

VALÈRE She's tortured by the very sight of me.
It's better that I free her from her pain.

DORINE What more proof do you need? You are insane!
95 Now stop this nonsense! Come here both of you.

VALÈRE To what purpose?

MARIANE What are you trying to do?

DORINE Bring you two together! And end this fight.
It's so stupid! Yes?

VALÈRE No. It wasn't right
The way she spoke to me. Didn't you hear?

100 DORINE Your voices are still ringing in my ear.

MARIANE The way he treated me—you didn't see?

DORINE Saw and heard it all. Now listen to me.
The only thing she wants, Valère, is you.
I can attest to that right now. It's true.

105 And Mariane, he wants you for his wife,
And only you. On that I'll stake my life.
MARIANE   He told me to be someone else's bride!
VALÈRE   She asked for my advice and I replied!
DORINE   You're both impossible. What can I do?
110 Give your hand—
VALÈRE   What for?
DORINE   Come on, you.
Now yours, Mariane—don't make me shout.
Come on!
MARIANE   All right. But what is this about?
DORINE   Here. Take each other's hand and make a link.
You love each other better than you think.
115 VALÈRE   Mademoiselle, this is your hand I took,
You think you could give me a friendly look?

[MARIANE *peeks at* VALÈRE *and smiles.*]

DORINE   It's true. Lovers are not completely sane.
VALÈRE   Mariane, haven't I good reason to complain?
Be honest. Wasn't it a wicked ploy?
120 To say—
MARIANE   You think I told you that with joy?
And you confronted me.
DORINE   Another time.
This marriage to Tartuffe would be a crime,
We have to stop it.
MARIANE   So, what can we do?
Tell us.
125 DORINE   All sorts of things involving you.
It's all nonsense and your father's joking.
But if you play along, say, without choking,
And give your consent, for the time being,
He'll take the pressure off, thereby freeing
130 All of us to find a workable plan
To keep you from a marriage with this man.
Then you can find a reason every day
To postpone the wedding, in this way:
One day you're sick and that can take a week.
135 Another day you're better but can't speak,
And we all know you have to say "I do,"
Or the marriage isn't legal. And that's true.
Now bad omens—would he have his daughter
Married when she's dreamt of stagnant water,
140 Or broken a mirror or seen the dead?
He may not care and say it's in your head,
But you will be distraught in your delusion,
And require bed rest and seclusion.
I do know this—if we want to succeed,
145 You can't be seen together. [*To* VALÈRE] With all speed,
Go, and gather all your friends right now,
Have them insist that Orgon keep his vow.

Social pressure helps. Then to her brother.
All of us will work on her stepmother.
150 Let's go.

VALÈRE   Whatever happens, can you see?
My greatest hope is in your love for me.

MARIANE   Though I don't know just what Father will do,
I do know I belong only to you.

VALÈRE   You put my heart at ease! I swear I will . . .

155 DORINE   It seems that lovers' tongues are never still.
Out, I tell you.

VALÈRE [taking a step and returning]   One last—

DORINE   No more chat!
You go out this way, yes, and you go that.

3.1

[DAMIS, DORINE]

DAMIS   May lightning strike me dead, right here and now,
Call me a villain, if I break this vow:
Forces of heaven or earth won't make me sway
From this my—

DORINE   Let's not get carried away.
5 Your father only said what he intends
To happen. The real event depends
On many things and something's bound to slip,
Between this horrid cup and his tight lip.

DAMIS   That this conceited fool Father brought here
10 Has plans? Well, they'll be ended—do not fear.

DORINE   Now stop that! Forget him. Leave him alone.
Leave him to your stepmother. He is prone,
This Tartuffe, to indulge her every whim.
So let her use her power over him.
15 It does seem pretty clear he's soft on her,
Pray God that's true. And if he will concur
That this wedding your father wants is bad,
That's good. But he might want it, too, the cad.
She's sent for him so she can sound him out
20 On this marriage you're furious about,
Discover what he feels and tell him clearly
If he persists that it will cost him dearly.
It seems he can't be seen while he's at prayers,
So I have my own vigil by the stairs
25 Where his valet says he will soon appear.
Do leave right now, and I'll wait for him here.

DAMIS   I'll stay to vouch for what was seen and heard.

DORINE   They must be alone.

DAMIS   I won't say a word.

DORINE   Oh, right. I know what you are like. Just go.
30 You'll spoil everything, believe me, I know.
Out!

DAMIS   I promise I won't get upset.

> [DORINE *pinches* DAMIS *as she used to do when he was a child.*]

                                    Ow!

DORINE   Do as I say. Get out of here right *now!*

3.2

[TARTUFFE, LAURENT, DORINE]

TARTUFFE [*noticing* DORINE]   Laurent, lock up my scourge and hair shirt,[5] too.
   And pray that our Lord's grace will shine on you.
   If anyone wants me, I've gone to share
   My alms at prison with the inmates there.
5 DORINE   What a fake! What an imposter! What a sleaze!
TARTUFFE   What do you want?
DORINE   To say—
TARTUFFE [*taking a handkerchief from his pocket*]   Good heavens, please,
   Do take this handkerchief before you speak.
DORINE   What for?
TARTUFFE   Cover your bust. The flesh is weak.
   Souls are forever damaged by such sights,
10   When sinful thoughts begin their evil flights.
DORINE   It seems temptation makes a meal of you—
   To turn you on, a glimpse of flesh will do.
   Inside your heart, a furnace must be housed.
   For me, I'm not so easily aroused.
15   I could see you naked, head to toe—
   Never be tempted once, and this I know.
TARTUFFE   Please! Stop! And if you're planning to resume
   This kind of talk, I'll leave the room.
DORINE   If someone is to go, let it be me.
20   Yes, I can't wait to leave your company.
   Madame is coming down from her salon,
   And wants to talk to you, if you'll hang on.
TARTUFFE   Of course. Most willingly.
DORINE [*aside*]   Look at him melt.
   I'm right. I always knew that's how he felt.
25 TARTUFFE   Is she coming soon?
DORINE   You want me to leave?
   Yes, here she is in person, I believe.

3.3

[ELMIRE, TARTUFFE]

TARTUFFE   Ah, may heaven in all its goodness give
   Eternal health to you each day you live,
   Bless your soul and body, and may it grant
   The prayerful wishes of this supplicant.

---

5. Implements to mortify his flesh (penitential practices of religious ascetics).

5 ELMIRE   Yes. Thank you for that godly wish, and please,
 Let's sit down so we can talk with ease.
 TARTUFFE   Are you recovered from your illness now?
 ELMIRE   My fever disappeared, I don't know how.
 TARTUFFE   My small prayers, I'm sure, had not the power,
10 Though I was on my knees many an hour.
 Each fervent prayer wrenched from my simple soul
 Was made with your recovery as its goal.
 ELMIRE   I find your zeal a little disconcerting.
 TARTUFFE   I can't enjoy my health if you are hurting.
15 Your health's true worth, I can't begin to tell.
 I'd give mine up, in fact, to make you well.
 ELMIRE   Though you stretch Christian charity too far,
 Your thoughts are kind, however strange they are.
 TARTUFFE   You merit more, that's in my humble view.
20 ELMIRE   I need a private space to talk to you.
 I think that this will do—what do you say?
 TARTUFFE   Excellent choice. And this is a sweet day,
 To find myself here tête-à-tête with you,
 That I've begged heaven for this, yes, is true,
25 And now it's granted to my great relief.
 ELMIRE   Although our conversation will be brief,
 Please open up your heart and tell me all.
 You must hide nothing now, however small.
 TARTUFFE   I long to show you my entire soul,
30 My need for truth I can barely control.
 I'll take this time, also, to clear the air—
 The criticisms I have brought to bear
 Around the visits that your charms attract,
 Were never aimed at you or how you act,
35 But rather were my own transports of zeal,
 Which carried me away with how I feel,
 Consumed by impulses, though always pure,
 Nevertheless, intense in how—
 ELMIRE   I'm sure
 That my salvation is your only care.
40 TARTUFFE [grasping her fingertips] Yes, you're right, and so my fervor there—
 ELMIRE   Ouch! You're squeezing too hard.
 TARTUFFE   —comes from this zeal . . .
 I didn't mean to squeeze. How does this feel?
   [He puts his hand on ELMIRE's knee.]
 ELMIRE   Your hand—what is it doing . . . ?
 TARTUFFE   So tender,
 The fabric of your dress, a sweet surrender
45 Under my hand—
 ELMIRE   I'm quite ticklish. Please, don't.
   [She moves her chair back, and TARTUFFE moves his forward.]
 TARTUFFE   I want to touch this lace—don't fret, I won't.
 It's marvelous! I so admire the trade
 Of making lace. Don't tell me you're afraid.

ELMIRE   What? No. But getting back to business now,
50   It seems my husband plans to break a vow
      And offer you his daughter. Is this true?

TARTUFFE   He mentioned it, but I must say to you,
      The wondrous gifts that catch my zealous eye,
      I see quite near in bounteous supply.

55 ELMIRE   Not earthly things for which you would atone.

TARTUFFE   My chest does not contain a heart of stone.

ELMIRE   Well, I believe your eyes follow your soul,
      And your desires have heaven as their goal.

TARTUFFE   The love that to eternal beauty binds us
60   Doesn't stint when temporal beauty finds us.
      Our senses can as easily be charmed
      When by an earthly work we are disarmed.
      You are a rare beauty, without a flaw,
      And in your presence, I'm aroused with awe,
65   But for the Author of All Nature, so,
      My heart has ardent feelings, even though
      I feared them at first, questioning their source.
      Had I been ambushed by some evil force?
      I felt that I must hide from this temptation:
70   You. My feelings threatened my salvation.
      Yes, I found this sinful and distressing,
      Until I saw your beauty as a blessing!
      So now my passion never can be wrong,
      And, thus, my virtue stays intact and strong.
75   That is how I'm here in supplication,
      Offering my heart in celebration
      Of the audacious truth that I love you,
      That only you can make this wish come true,
      That through your grace, my offering's received,
80   And accepted, and that I have achieved
      Salvation of a sort, and by your grace,
      I could be content in this low place.
      It all depends on you, at your behest—
      Am I to be tormented or be blest?
85   You are my welfare, solace, and my hope,
      But, whatever your decision, I will cope.
      Will I be happy? I'll rely on you.
      If you want me to be wretched, that's fine, too.

ELMIRE   Well, what a declaration! How gallant!
90   But I'm surprised you want the things you want.
      It seems your heart could use a talking to—
      It's living in the chest of someone who
      Proclaims to be pious—

TARTUFFE   —And so I am.
      My piety's a true thing—not a sham,
95   But I'm no less a man, so when I find
      Myself with you, I quickly lose my mind.
      My heart is captured and, with it, my thought.

Yet since I know the cause, I'm not distraught.
Words like these from me must be alarming,
100 But it is your beauty that's so charming,
I cannot help myself, I am undone.
And I'm no angel, nor could I be one.
If my confession earns your condemnation,
Then blame your glance for the annihilation
105 Of my command of this: my inmost being.
A surrender of my soul is what you're seeing.
Your eyes blaze with more than human splendor,
And that first look had the effect to render
Powerless the bastions of my heart.
110 No fasting, tears or prayers, no pious art
Could shield my soul from your celestial gaze
Which I will worship till the End of Days.[6]
A thousand times my eyes, my sighs have told
The truth that's in my heart. Now I am bold,
115 Encouraged by your presence, so I say,
With my true voice, will this be the day
You condescend to my poor supplication,
Offered up with devout admiration,
And save my soul by granting this request:
120 Accept this love I've lovingly confessed?
Your honor has, of course, all my protection,
And you can trust my absolute discretion.
For those men that all the women die for,
Love's a game whose object is a high score.
125 Although they promise not to talk, they will.
They need to boast of their superior skill,
Receive no favors not as soon revealed,
Exposing what they vowed would be concealed.
And in the end, this love is overpriced,
130 When a woman's honor's sacrificed.
But men like me burn with a silent flame,
Our secrets safe, our loves we never name,
Because our reputations are our wealth.
When we transgress, it's with the utmost stealth.
135 Your honor's safe as my hand in a glove,
So I can offer, free from scandal, love,
And pleasure without fear of intervention.
ELMIRE Your sophistry does not hide your intention.
In fact, you know, it makes it all too clear.
140 What if, through me, my husband were to hear
About this love for me you now confess
Which shatters the ideals you profess?
How would your friendship fare, then, I wonder?
TARTUFFE It's your beauty cast this spell I suffer under.
145 I'm made of flesh, like you, like all mankind.

6. That is, the final days before human history ends and the Kingdom of God is established.

And since your soul is pure, you will be kind,
And not judge me harshly for my brashness
In speaking of my love in all its rashness.
I beg you to forgive me my offense,
150　I plead your perfect face as my defense.
　　ELMIRE　Some might take offense at your confession,
　　But I will show a definite discretion,
　　And keep my husband in the dark about
　　These sinful feelings for me that you spout.
155　But I want something from you in return:
　　There's a promised marriage, you will learn,
　　That supersedes my husband's recent plan—
　　The marriage of Valère and Mariane.
　　This marriage you will openly support,
160　Without a single quibble, and, in short,
　　Renounce the unjust power of a man
　　Who'd give his own daughter, Mariane,
　　To another when she's promised to Valère.
　　In return, my silence—

3.4

[ELMIRE, DAMIS, TARTUFFE]

DAMIS [jumping out from where he had been hiding]
　　　　　　　—Hold it right there!
　　No, no! You're done. All this will be revealed.
　　I heard each word. And as I was concealed,
　　Something besides your infamy came clear:
5　Heaven in its great wisdom brought me here,
　　To witness and then give my father proof
　　Of the hypocrisy of his Tartuffe,
　　This so-called saint anointed from above.
　　Speaking to my father's wife of love!
10　ELMIRE　Damis, there is a lesson to be learned,
　　And there is my forgiveness to be earned.
　　I promised him. Don't make me take it back.
　　It's not my nature to see as an attack
　　Such foolishness as this, or see the need
15　To tell my husband of the trivial deed.
　　DAMIS　So, you have your reasons, but I have mine.
　　To grant this fool forgiveness? I decline.
　　To want to spare him is a mockery,
　　Because he's more than foolish, can't you see?
20　This fanatic in his insolent pride,
　　Brought chaos to my house, and would divide
　　Me and my father—unforgivable!
　　What's more, he's made my life unlivable,
　　As he undermines two true love affairs,
25　Mine and Valère's sister, my sister and Valère's!
　　Father must hear the truth about this man.
　　Heaven helped me—I must do what I can

To use this chance. I'd deserve to lose it,
If I dropped it now and didn't use it.
30 ELMIRE   Damis—
DAMIS   No, please, I have to follow through.
I've never felt as happy as I do
Right now. And don't try to dissuade me—
I'll have my revenge. If you forbade me,
I'd still do it, so you don't have to bother.
35 I'll finish this for good. Here comes my father.

3.5

[ORGON, DAMIS, TARTUFFE, ELMIRE]

DAMIS   Father! You have arrived. Let's celebrate!
I have a tale that I'd like to relate.
It happened here and right before my eyes,
I offer it to you—as a surprise!
5 For all your love, you have been repaid
With duplicity. You have been betrayed
By your dear friend here, whom I just surprised
Making verbal love, I quickly surmised,
To your wife. Yes, this is how he shows you
10 How he honors you—he thinks he knows you.
But as your son, I know you much better—
You demand respect down to the letter.
Madame, unflappable and so discreet,
Would keep this secret, never to repeat.
15 But, as your son, my feelings are too strong,
And to be silent is to do you wrong.
ELMIRE   One learns to spurn without being unkind,
And how to spare a husband's peace of mind.
Although I understood just what he meant,
20 My honor wasn't touched by this event.
That's how I feel. And you would have, Damis,
Said nothing, if you had listened to me.

3.6

[ORGON, DAMIS, TARTUFFE]

ORGON   Good heavens! What he said? Can it be true?
TARTUFFE   Yes, my brother, I'm wicked through and through.
The most miserable of sinners, I.
Filled with iniquity, I should just die.
5 Each moment of my life's so dirty, soiled,
Whatever I come near is quickly spoiled.
I'm nothing but a heap of filth and crime.
I'd name my sins, but we don't have the time.
And I see that heaven, to punish me,
10 Has mortified my soul quite publicly.
What punishment I get, however great,
I well deserve so I'll accept my fate.
Defend myself? I'd face my own contempt,

If I thought that were something I'd attempt.
15 What you've heard here, surely, you abhor,
So chase me like a criminal from your door.
Don't hold back your rage, please, let it flame,
For I deserve to burn, in my great shame.

ORGON [*to* DAMIS]   Traitor! And how dare you even try
20 To tarnish this man's virtue with a lie?

DAMIS   What? This hypocrite pretends to be contrite
And you believe him over me?

ORGON   That's spite!
And shut your mouth!

TARTUFFE   No, let him have his say.
And don't accuse him. Don't send him away.
25 Believe his story—why be on my side?
You don't know what motives I may hide.
Why give me so much loyalty and love?
Do you know what I am capable of?
My brother, you have total trust in me,
30 And think I'm good because of what you see?
No, no, by my appearance you're deceived,
And what I say you think must be believed.
Well, believe this—I have no worth at all.
The world sees me as worthy, yet I fall
35 Far below. Sin is so insidious.
[*To* DAMIS] Dear son, do treat me as perfidious,
Infamous, lost, a murderer, a thief.
Speak on, because my sins, beyond belief,
Can bring this shameful sinner to his knees,
40 In humble, paltry effort to appease.

ORGON [*to* TARTUFFE]   Brother, there is no need . . .
                                    [*To* DAMIS] Will you relent?

DAMIS   He has seduced you!

ORGON   Can't you take a hint?
Be quiet! [*To* TARTUFFE] Brother, please get up. [*To* DAMIS] Ingrate!

DAMIS   But father, this man

ORGON   —whom you denigrate.

45 DAMIS   But you should—

ORGON   Quiet!

DAMIS   But I saw and heard—

ORGON   I'll slap you if you say another word.

TARTUFFE   In the name of God, don't be that way.
Brother, I'd rather suffer, come what may,
Than have this boy receive what's meant for me.

50 ORGON [*to* DAMIS]   Heathen!

TARTUFFE   Please! I beg of you on bended knee.

ORGON [*to* DAMIS]   Wretch! See his goodness?!

DAMIS   But—

ORGON   No!

DAMIS   But—

ORGON   Be still!
And not another word from you until

You admit the truth. It's plain to see
Although you thought that I would never be
55   Aware and know your motives, yet I do.
You all hate him. And I saw today, you,
Wife, servants—everyone beneath my roof—
Are trying everything to force Tartuffe
Out of my house—this holy man, my friend.
60   The more you try to banish him and end
Our sacred brotherhood, the more secure
His place is. I have never been more sure
Of anyone. I give him as his bride
My daughter. If that hurts the family pride,
65   Then good. It needs humbling. You understand?
DAMIS   You're going to force her to accept his hand?
ORGON   Yes, traitor, and this evening. You know why?
To infuriate you. Yes, I defy
You all. I am master and you'll obey.
70   And you, you ingrate, now I'll make you pay
For your abuse of him—kneel on the floor,
And beg his pardon, or go out the door.
DAMIS   Me? Kneel and ask the pardon of this fraud?
ORGON   What? You refuse? Someone get me a rod!
75   A stick! Something! [*To* TARTUFFE] Don't hold me.
      [*To* DAMIS] Here's your whack!
Out of my house and don't ever come back!
DAMIS   Yes, I'll leave, but—
ORGON   Get out of my sight!
I disinherit you, you traitor, you're a blight
On this house. And you'll get nothing now
80   From me, except my curse!

3.7

[ORGON, TARTUFFE]

ORGON   You have my vow,
He'll never more question your honesty.
TARTUFFE [*to heaven*]   Forgive him for the pain he's given me.
    [*To* ORGON] How I suffer. If you could only see
5   What I go through when they disparage me.
ORGON   Oh no!
TARTUFFE   The ingratitude, even in thought,
Tortures my soul so much, it leaves me fraught
With inner pain. My heart's stopped. I'm near death,
I can barely speak now. Where is my breath?
ORGON [*running in tears to the door through which he chased* DAMIS]
10   You demon! I held back, you little snot
I should have struck you dead right on the spot!
    [*To* TARTUFFE] Get up, Brother. Don't worry anymore.
TARTUFFE   Let us end these troubles, Brother, I implore.
For the discord I have caused, I deeply grieve,
15   So for the good of all, I'll take my leave.

ORGON   What? Are you joking? No!

TARTUFFE   They hate me here.

It pains me when I see them fill your ear
With suspicions.

ORGON   But that doesn't matter.

I don't listen.

TARTUFFE   That persistent chatter

20   You now ignore, one day you'll listen to.
Repetition of a lie can make it true.

ORGON   No, my brother. Never.

TARTUFFE   A man's wife

Can so mislead his soul and ruin his life.

ORGON   No, no.

TARTUFFE   Brother, let me, by leaving here,

25   Remove any cause for doubt or fear.

ORGON   No, no. You will stay. My soul is at stake.

TARTUFFE   Well, then, a hefty penance I must make.

I'll mortify myself, unless . . .

ORGON   No need!

TARTUFFE   Then we will never speak of it, agreed?

30   But the question of your honor still remains,
And with that I'll take particular pains
To prevent rumors. My absence, my defense—
I'll never see your wife again, and hence—

ORGON   No. You spend every hour with her you want,

35   And be seen with her. I want you to flaunt,
In front of them, this friendship with my wife.
And I know how to really turn the knife
I'll make you my heir, my only one,
Yes, you will be my son-in-law and son.[7]

40   A good and faithful friend means more to me
Than any member of my family.
Will you accept this gift that I propose?

TARTUFFE   Whatever heaven wants I can't oppose.

ORGON   Poor man! A contract's what we need to write.

45   And let all the envious burst with spite.

4.1

[CLÉANTE, TARTUFFE]

CLÉANTE   Yes, everyone is talking and each word
Diminishes your glory, rest assured.
Though your name's tainted with scandal and shame,
I'm glad I ran across you, all the same,

5   Because I need to share with you my view
On this disaster clearly caused by you.
Damis, let's say for now, was so misguided,
He spoke before he thought. But you decided

---

7. In fact, French laws governing inheritance would have made such a change extremely difficult
to accomplish.

To just sit back and watch him be exiled
10   From his own father's house. Were he a child,
Then, really, would you dare to treat him so?
Shouldn't you forgive him, not make him go?
However, if there's vengeance in your heart,
And you act on it, tell me what's the part
15   That's Christian in that? And are you so base,
You'd let a son fall from his father's grace?
Give God your anger as an offering,
Bring peace and forgive all for everything.

   TARTUFFE   I'd do just that, if it were up to me.
20   I blame him for nothing, don't you see?
I've pardoned him already. That's my way.
And I'm not bitter, but have this to say:
Heaven's best interests will have been served,
When wrongdoers have got what they deserved.
25   In fact, if he returns here, I would leave,
Because God knows what people might believe.
Faking forgiveness to manipulate
My accuser, silencing the hate
He has for me could be seen as my goal.
30   When I would only wish to save his soul.
What he said to me, though unforgivable,
I give unto God to make life livable.

   CLÉANTE   To this conclusion, sir, I have arrived:
Your excuses could not be more contrived.
35   Just how did you come by the opinion
Heaven's business is in your dominion,
Judging who is guilty and who is not?
Taking revenge is heaven's task, I thought.
And if you're under heaven's sovereignty,
40   What human verdict would you ever be
The least bit moved by. No, you wouldn't care—
Judging other's lives is so unfair.
Heaven seems to say "live and let live,"
And our task, I believe, is to forgive.

45 TARTUFFE   I said I've pardoned him. I take such pains
To do exactly what heaven ordains.
But after his attack on me, it's clear,
Heaven does not ordain that he live here.

   CLÉANTE   Does it ordain, sir, that you nod and smile,
50   When taking what is not yours, all the while?
On this inheritance you have no claim
And yet you think it's yours. Have you no shame?

   TARTUFFE   That this gift was, in any way, received
Out of self-interest, would not be believed
55   By anyone who knows me well. They'd say,
"The world's wealth, to him, holds no sway."
I am not dazzled by gold nor its glitter,
So lack of wealth has never made me bitter.

If I take this present from the father,
60 The source of all this folderol and bother,
I am saving, so everyone understands,
This wealth from falling into the wrong hands.
Waste of wealth and property's a crime,
And that is what would happen at this time.
65 But I would use it as part of my plan:
For glory of heaven, and the good of man.

CLÉANTE   Well, sir, I think these small fears that plague you,
In fact, may cause the rightful heir to sue.
Why trouble yourself, sir—couldn't you just
70 Let him own his property, if he must?
Let others say his property's misused
By him, rather than have yourself accused
Of taking it from its rightful owner.
Wouldn't a pious man be a donor
75 Of property? Unless there is a verse
Or proverb about how you fill your purse
With what's not yours, at all, in any part.
And if heaven has put into your heart
This obstacle to living with Damis,
80 The honorable thing, you must agree,
As well as, certainly, the most discreet,
Is pack your bags and, quickly, just retreat.
To have the son of the house chased away,
Because a guest objects, is a sad day.
85 Leaving now would show your decency,
Sir . . .

TARTUFFE   Yes. Well, it is half after three;
Pious duties consume this time of day,
You will excuse my hurrying away.

CLÉANTE   Ah!

4.2

[ELMIRE, MARIANE, DORINE, CLÉANTE]

DORINE   Please, come to the aid of Mariane.
She's suffering because her father's plan
To force this marriage, impossible to bear,
Has pushed her from distress into despair.
5 Her father's on his way here. Do your best,
Turn him around. Use subtlety, protest,
Whatever way will work to change his mind.

4.3

[ORGON, ELMIRE, MARIANE, CLÉANTE, DORINE]

ORGON   Ah! Here's everyone I wanted to find!
[To MARIANE] This document I have here in my hand
Will make you very happy, understand?

MARIANE   Father, in the name of heaven, I plead

5   To all that's good and kind in you, concede
      Paternal power, just in this sense:
      Free me from my vows of obedience.
      Enforcing that inflexible law today
      Will force me to confess each time I pray
10   My deep resentment of my obligation.
      I know, father, that I am your creation,
      That you're the one who's given life to me.
      Why would you now fill it with misery?
      If you destroy my hopes for the one man
15   I've dared to love by trying now to ban
      Our union, then I'm kneeling to implore,
      Don't give me to a man whom I abhor.
      To you, Father, I make this supplication.
      Don't drive me to some act of desperation,
20   By ruling me simply because you can.
      ORGON [*feeling himself touched*]   Be strong! Human weakness shames a man!
      MARIANE   Your affection for him doesn't bother me—
      Let it erupt, give him your property,
      And if that's not enough, then give him mine.
25   Any claim on it, I do now decline.
      But in this gifting, don't give him my life.
      If I must wed, then I will be God's wife,
      In a convent, until my days are done.
      ORGON   Ah! So you will be a holy, cloistered nun,
30   Because your father thwarts your love affair.
      Get up! The more disgust you have to bear,
      The more of heaven's treasure you will earn.
      And the heaven will bless you in return.
      Through this marriage, you'll mortify your senses.
35   Don't bother me with any more pretenses.
      DORINE   But . . . !
      ORGON   Quiet, you! I see you standing there.
      Don't speak a single world! don't even dare!
      CLÉANTE   If you permit, I'd like to say a word . . .
      ORGON   Brother, the best advice the world has heard
40   Is yours—its reasoning, hard to ignore.
      But I refuse to hear it anymore.
      ELMIRE [*to* ORGON]   And now, I wonder, have you lost your mind?
      Your love for this one man has made you blind.
      Can you stand there and say you don't believe
45   A word we've said? That we're here to deceive?
      ORGON   Excuse me—I believe in what I see.
      You, indulging my bad son, agree
      To back him up in this terrible prank,
      Accusing my dear friend of something rank.
50   You should be livid if what you claim took place,
      And yet this look of calm is on your face.
      ELMIRE   Because a man says he's in love with me,
      I'm to respond with heavy artillery?

I laugh at these unwanted propositions.
55   Mirth will quell most ardent ambitions.
Why make a fuss over an indiscretion?
My honor's safe and in my possession.
You say I'm calm? Well, that's my constancy—
It won't need a defense, or clemency.
60   I know I'll never be a vicious prude
Who always seems to hear men being rude,
And then defends her honor tooth and claw,
Still snarling, even as the men withdraw.
From honor like that heaven preserve me,
65   If that's what you want, you don't deserve me.
Besides, you're the one who has been betrayed.

ORGON   I see through this trick that's being played.

ELMIRE   How can you be so dim? I am amazed
How you can hear these sins and stay unfazed.
70   But what if I could show you what he does?

ORGON   Show?

ELMIRE   Yes.

ORGON   A fiction!

ELMIRE   No, the truth because
I am quite certain I can find a way
To show you in the fullest light of day . . .

ORGON   Fairy tales!

ELMIRE   Come on, at least answer me.
75   I've given up expecting you to be
My advocate. What have you got to lose,
By hiding somewhere, anyplace you choose,
And see for yourself. And then we can
Hear what you say about your holy man.

80   ORGON   Then I'll say nothing because it cannot be.

ELMIRE   Enough. I'm tired. You'll see what you see.
I'm not a liar, though I've been accused.
The time is now and I won't be refused.
You'll be a witness. And we can stop our rants.

85   ORGON   All right! I call your bluff, Miss Smarty Pants.

ELMIRE [to DORINE]   Tell Tartuffe to come.

DORINE   Watch out. He's clever.
Men like him are caught, well, almost never.

ELMIRE   Narcissism is a great deceiver,
And he has lots of that. He's a believer
90   In his charisma. [To CLÉANTE and MARIANE] Leave us for a bit.

4.4

[ELMIRE, ORGON]

ELMIRE   See this table? Good. Get under it.

ORGON   What!

ELMIRE   You are hiding. Get under there and stay.

ORGON   Under the table?

ELMIRE: Just do as I say.

5   I have a plan, but for it to succeed,
      You must be hidden. So are we agreed?
      You want to know? I'm ready to divulge it.
    ORGON   This fantasy of yours—I'll indulge it.
      But then I want to lay this thing to rest.
10   ELMIRE   Oh, that'll happen. Because he'll fail the test.
      You see, I'm going to have a conversation
      I'd never have—just as an illustration
      Of how this hypocrite behaved with me.
      So don't be scandalized. I must be free
15   To flirt. Clearly, that's what it's going to take
      To prove to you your holy man's a fake.
      I'm going to lead him on, to lift his mask,
      Seem to agree to anything he'll ask,
      Pretend to respond to his advances.
      It's for you I'm taking all these chances.
20   I'll stop as soon as you have seen enough;
      I hope that comes before he calls my bluff.
      His plans for me must be circumvented,
      His passion's strong enough to be demented,
      So the moment you're convinced, you let me know
25   That I've revealed the fraud I said I'd show.
      Stop him so I won't have a minute more
      Exposure to your friend, this lecherous boor.
      You're in control. I'm sure I'll be all right.
      And . . . here he comes—so hush, stay out of sight.

4.5

[TARTUFFE, ELMIRE, ORGON *(under the table)*]

    TARTUFFE   I'm told you want to have a word with me.
    ELMIRE   Yes. I have a secret but I'm not free
      To speak. Close that door, have a look around,
      We certainly do not want to be found
5   The way we were just as Damis appeared.
      I was terrified for you and as I feared,
      He was irate. You saw how hard I tried
      To calm him down and keep him pacified.
      I was so upset; I never had the thought
10   "Deny it all," which might have helped a lot,
      But as it turns out, we've nothing to fear.
      My husband's not upset, it would appear.
      Things are good, to heaven I defer,
      Because they're even better than they were.
15   I have to say I'm quite amazed, in fact,
      His good opinion of you is intact.
      To clear the air and quiet every tongue,
      And to kill any gossip that's begun—
      You could've pushed me over with a feather—
20   He wants us to spend all our time together!
      That's why, with no fear of a critical stare,

I can be here with you or anywhere.
Most important, I am completely free
To show my ardor for you, finally.
25 TARTUFFE   Ardor? This is a sudden change of tone
From the last time we found ourselves alone.
ELMIRE   If thinking I was turning you away
Has made you angry, all that I can say
Is that you do not know a woman's heart!
30 Protecting our virtue keeps us apart,
And makes us seem aloof, and even cold.
But cooler outside, inside the more bold.
When love overcomes us, we are ashamed,
Because we fear that we might be defamed.
35 We must protect our honor—not allow
Our love to show. I fear that even now,
In this confession, you'll think ill of me.
But now I've spoken, and I hope you see
My ardor that is there. Why would I sit
40 And listen to you? Why would I permit
Your talk of love, unless I had a notion
Just like yours, and with the same emotion?
And when Damis found us, didn't I try
To quiet him? And did you wonder why,
45 In speaking of Mariane's marriage deal,
I not only asked you, I made an appeal
That you turn it down? What was I doing?
Making sure I'd be the one you'd be wooing.
TARTUFFE   It is extremely sweet, without a doubt,
50 To watch your lips as loving words spill out.
Abundant honey there for me to drink,
But I have doubts. I cannot help but think,
"Does she tell the truth, or does she lie,
To get me to break off this marriage tie?
55 Is all this ardor something she could fake,
And just an act for her stepdaughter's sake?"
So many questions, yet I want to trust.
But need to know the truth, in fact, I must.
Pleasing you, Elmire, is my main task,
60 And happiness, and so I have to ask
To sample this deep ardor felt for me
Right here and now, in blissful ecstasy.
ELMIRE [coughing to alert ORGON]
You want to spend this passion instantly?
I've been opening my heart consistently,
65 But for you, it's not enough, this sharing.
Yet for a woman, it is very daring.
So why can't you be happy with a taste,
Instead of the whole meal consumed in haste?
TARTUFFE   We dare not hope, all those of us who don't
70 Deserve a thing. And so it is I won't

Be satisfied with words. I'll always doubt,
Assume my fortune's taken the wrong route
On its way to me. And that is why
I don't believe in anything till I
75 Have touched, partaken until satisfied.
    ELMIRE   So suddenly, your love can't be denied.
It wants complete dominion over me,
And what it wants, it wants violently.
I know I'm flustered, I know I'm out of breath—
80 Your power over me could be the death
Of my reason. Does this seem right to you?
To use my weakness against me, just to
Conquer? No one's gallant anymore.
I invite you in. You break down the door.
85 TARTUFFE   If your passion for me isn't a pretense,
Then why deny me its best evidence?
    ELMIRE   But, heaven, sir, that place that you address
So often, would judge us both if we transgress.
    TARTUFFE   That's all that's in the way of my desires?
90 These judgments heaven makes of what transpires?
All you fear is heaven's bad opinion.
    ELMIRE   But I am made to fear its dominion.
    TARTUFFE   And I know how to exorcise these fears.
To sin is not as bad as it appears
95 If, and stay with me on this, one can think
That in some cases, heaven gives a wink

      [It is a scoundrel speaking.][8]

When it comes to certain needs of men
Who can remain upright but only when
There is a pure intention. So you see,
100 If you just let yourself be led by me,
You'll have no worries, and I can enjoy
You. And you, me. Because we will employ
This way of thinking—a real science
And a secret, thus, with your compliance,
105 Fulfilling my desires without fear,
Is easy now, so let it happen here.

      [ELMIRE coughs.]

That cough, Madame, is bad.
    ELMIRE   I'm in such pain.
    TARTUFFE   A piece of licorice might ease the strain.
    ELMIRE [directed to ORGON]   This cold I have is very obstinate.
110 It stubbornly holds on. I can't shake it.
    TARTUFFE   That's most annoying.
    ELMIRE   More than I can say.
    TARTUFFE   Let's get back to finding you a way,
Finally, to get around your scruples:

---

8. This stage direction, inserted by Molière himself, supports the playwright's assertion that he took pains to demonstrate Tartuffe's true nature.

Secrecy—I'm one of its best pupils
115 And practitioners. Responsibility
For any evil—you can put on me.
I will answer up to heaven if I must,
And give a good accounting you can trust.
There'll be no sins for which we must atone,
120 'Cause evil exists only when it's known.
Adam and Eve were public in their fall.
To sin in private is not to sin at all.

ELMIRE [*after coughing again*]   Obviously, I must give in to you,
Because, it seems, you are a person who
125 Refuses to believe anything I say.
Live testimony only can convey
The truth of passion here, no more, no less.
That it should go that far, I must confess,
Is such a pity. But I'll cross the line,
130 And give myself to you. I won't decline
Your offer, sir, to vanquish me right here.
But let me make one point extremely clear:
If there's a moral judgment to be made,
If anyone here feels the least betrayed,
135 Then none of that will be my fault. Instead,
The sin weighs twice as heavy on your head.
You forced me to this brash extremity.

TARTUFFE   Yes, yes, I will take all the sin on me.

ELMIRE   Open the door and check because I fear
140 My husband—just look—might be somewhere near.

TARTUFFE   What does it matter if he comes or goes?
The secret is, I lead him by the nose.
He's urged me to spend all my time with you.
So let him see—he won't believe it's true.

145 ELMIRE   Go out and look around. Indulge my whim.
Look everywhere and carefully for him.

4.6

[ORGON, ELMIRE]

ORGON [*coming out from under the table*]
I swear that is the most abominable man!
How will I bear this? I don't think I can.
I'm stupefied!

ELMIRE   What? Out so soon? No, no.
You can't be serious. There's more to go.
5 Get back under there. You can't be too sure.
It's never good relying on conjecture.

ORGON   That kind of wickedness comes straight from hell.

ELMIRE   You've turned against this man you know so well?
Good lord, be sure the evidence is strong
10 Before you are convinced. You might be wrong.

[*She steps in front of* ORGON.]

4.7

[TARTUFFE, ELMIRE, ORGON]

TARTUFFE   Yes, all is well; there's no one to be found,
　　And I was thorough when I looked around.
　　To my delight, my rapture, at last . . .
ORGON [*stopping him*]   Just stop a minute there! You move too fast!
5　　Delight and rapture? Fulfilling desire?
　　Ah! Ah! You are a traitor and a liar!
　　Some holy man you are, to wreck my life,
　　Marry my daughter? Lust after my wife?
　　I've had my doubts about you, but kept quiet,
10　　Waiting for you to slip and then deny it.
　　Well, now it's happened and I'm so relieved,
　　To stop pretending that I am deceived.
ELMIRE [*to* TARTUFFE]   I don't approve of what I've done today,
　　But I needed to do it, anyway.
15 TARTUFFE   What? You can't think . . .
ORGON　　　　　　　　　　　　　No more words from you.
　　Get out of here, you. . . . You and I are through.
TARTUFFE   But my intentions . . .
ORGON　　　　　　　　　　　　You still think I'm a dunce?
　　You shut your mouth and leave this house at once!
TARTUFFE   You're the one to leave, you, acting like the master.
20　　Now I'll make it known, the full disaster:
　　This house belongs to me, yes, all of it,
　　And I'll decide what's true, as I see fit.
　　You can't entrap me with demeaning tricks,
　　Yes, here's a situation you can't fix.
25　　Here nothing happens without my consent.
　　You've offended heaven. You must repent.
　　But I know how to really punish you.
　　Those who harm me, they know not what they do.

4.8

[ELMIRE, ORGON]

ELMIRE   What was that about? I mean, the latter.
ORGON   I'm not sure, but it's no laughing matter.
ELMIRE   Why?
ORGON　　　　I've made a mistake I now can see,
　　The deed I gave him is what troubles me.
5 ELMIRE   The deed?
ORGON　　　　　　　And something else. I am undone.
　　I think my troubles may have just begun.
ELMIRE   What else?
ORGON　　　　　　　You'll know it all. I have to race,
　　To see if a strongbox is in its place.

5.1

[ORGON, CLÉANTE]

CLÉANTE   Where are you running to?

ORGON   Who knows.

CLÉANTE   Then wait.

It seems to me we should deliberate,
Meet, plan, and have some family talks.

ORGON   I can't stop thinking about the damned box
5   More than anything, that's the loss I fear.

CLÉANTE   What about this box makes it so dear?

ORGON   I have a friend whom I felt sorry for,
Because he chose the wrong side in the war;[9]
Before he fled, he brought it to me,
10   This locked box. He didn't leave a key.
He told me it has papers, this doomed friend,
On which his life and property depend.

CLÉANTE   Are you saying you gave the box away?

ORGON   Yes, that's true, that's what I'm trying to say.
15   I was afraid that I would have to lie,
If I were confronted. That is why
I went to my betrayer and confessed
And he, in turn, told me it would be best
If I gave him the box, to keep, in case
20   Someone were to ask me to my face
About it all, and I might lie and then,
In doing so, commit a venial sin.[1]

CLÉANTE   As far as I can see, this is a mess,
And with a lot of damage to assess.
25   This secret that you told, this deed you gave,
Make the situation hard to save.
He's holding all the cards, your holy man,
Because you gave them to him. If you can,
Restrain yourself a bit and stay away.
30   That would be best. And do watch what you say.

ORGON   What? With his wicked heart and corrupt soul,
Yet I'm to keep my rage under control?
Yes, me who took him in, right off the street?
Damn all holy men! They're filled with deceit!
35   I now renounce them all, down to the man,
And I'll treat them worse than Satan can.

CLÉANTE   Listen to yourself! You're over the top,
Getting carried away again. Just stop.
"Moderation." Is that a word you know?
40   I think you've learned it, but then off you go,

---

9. That is, he opposed Louis in the Fronde (see 1.2.11 and note). Although Orgon supported the king, this act left him open to the charge of being a traitor to the throne—a capital offense.

1. Because Tartuffe had possession of the box, Orgon could deny that he had it without lying. A venial (or "pardonable") sin is relatively minor.

Always ignoring the strength in reason,
Flinging yourself from loyalty to treason.
Why can't you just admit that you were swayed
By the fake piety that man displayed?
45 But no. Rather than change your ways, you turned
Like that. [Snaps fingers] Attacking holy men who've earned
The right to stand among the true believers.
So now all holy men are base deceivers?
Instead of just admitting your delusion,
50 "They're all like that!" you say—brilliant conclusion.
Why trust reason, when you have emotion?
You've implied there is no true devotion.
Freethinkers are the ones who hold that view,
And yet, you don't agree with them, do you?
55 You judge a man as good without real proof.
Appearances can lie—witness: Tartuffe.
If your respect is something to be prized,
Don't toss it away to those disguised
In a cloak of piety and virtue.
60 Don't you see how deeply they can hurt you?
Look for simple goodness—it does exist.
And just watch for imposters in our midst,
With this in mind, try not to be unjust
To true believers, sin on the side of trust.

5.2

[DAMIS, ORGON, CLÉANTE]

DAMIS   Father, what? I can't believe it's true,
That scoundrel has the gall to threaten you?
And use the things you gave him in his case
'Gainst you? To throw you out? I'll break his face.
5 ORGON   My son, I'm in more pain than you can see.
DAMIS   I'll break both his legs. Leave it to me.
We must not bend under his insolence.
I'll finish this business, punish his offense.
I'll murder him and do it with such joy.
10 CLÉANTE   Damis, you're talking like a little boy,
Tantrums head the list of your main flaws.
We live in modern times, with things called "laws."
Murder is illegal. At least for us.

5.3

[MADAME PERNELLE, MARIANE, ELMIRE, DORINE,
DAMIS, ORGON, CLÉANTE]

MADAME PERNELLE   It's unbelievable! Preposterous!
ORGON   Believe it. I've seen it with my own eyes.
He returned kindness with deceit and lies.
I took in a man, miserable and poor,
5 Brought him home, gave him the key to my door,

I loaded him with favors every day,
To him, my daughter, I just gave away,
My house, my wealth, a locked box from a friend.
But to what depths this devil would descend.
10 This betrayer, this abomination,
Who had the gall to preach about temptation,
And know in his black heart he'd woo my wife,
Seduce her! Yes! And then to steal my life,
Using my property, which I transferred to him,
15 I know, I know—it was a stupid whim.
He wants to ruin me, chase me from my door,
He wants me as he was, abject and poor.

DORINE   Poor man!

MADAME PERNELLE   I don't believe a word, my son,
This isn't something that he could have done.

20 ORGON   What?

MADAME PERNELLE   Holy men always arouse envy.

ORGON   Mother, what are you trying to say to me?

MADAME PERNELLE   That you live rather strangely in this house;
He's hated here, especially by your spouse.

ORGON   What has this got to do with what I said?

25 MADAME PERNELLE   Heaven knows, I've beat into your head:
"In this world, virtue is mocked forever;
Envious men may die, but envy never."

ORGON   How does that apply to what's happened here?

MADAME PERNELLE   Someone made up some lies; it's all too clear.

30 ORGON   But I saw it myself, you understand.

MADAME PERNELLE   "Whoever spreads slander has a soiled hand."

ORGON   You'll make me, Mother, say something not nice.
I saw it for myself; I've told you twice.

MADAME PERNELLE   "No one can trust what gossips have to say,
35 Yet they'll be with us until Judgment Day."

ORGON   You're talking total nonsense, Mother!
I said I saw him, this man I called Brother!
I saw him with my wife, with these two eyes.
The word is "saw," past tense of "see." These "lies"
40 That you misnamed are just the truth.
I saw my wife almost beneath Tartuffe.

MADAME PERNELLE   Oh, is that all? Appearances deceive.
What we think we see, we then believe.

ORGON   I'm getting angry.

MADAME PERNELLE   False suspicions, see?
45 We are subject to them, occasionally,
Good deeds can be seen as something other.

ORGON   So I'm to see this as a good thing, Mother,
A man trying to kiss my wife?

MADAME PERNELLE   You must.
Because, to be quite certain you are just,
50 You should wait until you're very, very sure
And not rely on faulty conjecture.

ORGON   Goddammit! You would have me wait until . . . ?
    And just be quiet while he has his fill,
    Right before my very eyes, Mother, he'd—
55 MADAME PERNELLE   I can't believe that he would do this "deed"
    Of which he's been accused. There is no way.
    His soul is pure.
ORGON   I don't know what to say!
    Mother!
DORINE   Just deserts, for what you put us through.
    You thought we lied, now she thinks that of you.
60 CLÉANTE   Why are we wasting time with all of this?
    We're standing on the edge of the abyss.
    This man is dangerous! He has a plan!
DAMIS   How could he hurt us? I don't think he can.
ELMIRE   He won't get far, complaining to the law—
65   You'll tell the truth, and he'll have to withdraw.
CLÉANTE   Don't count on it; trust me, he'll find a way
    To use these weapons you gave him today.
    He has legal documents, and the deed.
    To kick us out, just what else does he need?
70   And if he's doubted, there are many ways
    To trap you in a wicked legal maze.
    You give a snake his venom, nice and quick,
    And after that you poke him with a stick?
ORGON   I know. But what was I supposed to do?
75   Emotions got the best of me, it's true.
CLÉANTE   If we could placate him, just for a while,
    And somehow get the deed back with a smile.
ELMIRE   Had I known we had all this to lose,
    I never would have gone through with my ruse.
80   I would've—
          [A knock on the door.]
ORGON   What does that man want? You go find out.
    But I don't want to know what it's about.

5.4

[MONSIEUR LOYAL, MADAME PERNELLE, ORGON,
DAMIS, MARIANE, DORINE, ELMIRE, CLÉANTE]

MONSIEUR LOYAL [to DORINE]   Dear sister, hello. Please, I beg of you,
    Your master is the one I must speak to.
DORINE   He's not receiving visitors today.
MONSIEUR LOYAL   I bring good news so don't send me away.
5   My goal in coming is not to displease;
    I'm here to put your master's mind at ease.
DORINE   And you are . . . who?
MONSIEUR LOYAL   Just say that I have come
    For his own good and with a message from
    Monsieur Tartuffe.
DORINE [to ORGON]   It's a soft-spoken man,

10   Who says he's here to do just what he can
     To ease your mind. Tartuffe sent him.

CLÉANTE   Let's see
     What he might want.

ORGON   Oh, what's my strategy?
     He's come to reconcile us, I just know.

CLÉANTE   Your strategy? Don't let your anger show,
15   For heaven's sake. And listen for a truce.

MONSIEUR LOYAL   My greetings, sir. I'm here to be of use.

ORGON   Just what I thought. His language is benign.
     For the prospect of peace, a hopeful sign.

MONSIEUR LOYAL   Your family's dear to me, I hope you know.
20   I served your father many years ago.

ORGON   I humbly beg your pardon, to my shame,
     I don't know you, nor do I know your name.

MONSIEUR LOYAL   My name's Loyal. I'm Norman by descent.
     My job of bailiff is what pays my rent.
25   Thanks be to heaven, it's been forty years
     I've done my duty free of doubts or fear.
     That you invited me in, I can report,
     When I serve you with this writ from the court.

ORGON   What? You're here . . .

MONSIEUR LOYAL   No upsetting outbursts, please.
30   It's just a warrant saying we can seize,
     Not me, of course, but this Monsieur Tartuffe—
     Your house and land as his. Here is the proof.
     I have the contract here. You must vacate
     These premises. Please, now, don't be irate.
35   Just gather up your things now, and make way
     For this man, without hindrance or delay.

ORGON   Me? Leave my house?

MONSIEUR LOYAL   That's right, sir, out the door.
     This house, at present, as I've said before,
     Belongs to good Monsieur Tartuffe, you see,
40   He's lord and master of this property
     By virtue of this contract I hold right here.
     Is that not your signature? It's quite clear.

DAMIS   He's so rude, I do almost admire him.

MONSIEUR LOYAL   Excuse me. Is it possible to fire him?
45   My business is with you, a man of reason,
     Who knows resisting would be seen as treason.
     You understand that I must be permitted
     To execute the orders as committed.

DAMIS   I'll execute him, Father, to be sure.
50   His long black nightgown won't make him secure.

MONSIEUR LOYAL   He's your son! I thought he was a servant.
     Control the boy. His attitude's too fervent,
     His anger is a bone of contention—
     Throw him out, or I will have to mention
55   His name in this, my official report.

DORINE   "Loyal" is loyal only to the court.

MONSIEUR LOYAL   I have respect for all God-fearing men,
So instantly I knew I'd come here when
I heard your name attached to this assignment.

60   I knew you'd want a bailiff with refinement.
I'm here for you, just to accommodate,
To make removal something you won't hate.
Now, if I hadn't come, then you would find
You got a bailiff who would be less kind.

65   ORGON   I'm sorry, I don't see the kindness in
An eviction order.

MONSIEUR LOYAL   Let me begin:
I'm giving you time. I won't carry out
This order you are so upset about.
I've come only to spend the night with you,

70   With my men, who will be coming through.
All ten of them, as quiet as a mouse.
Oh, you must give me the keys to the house.
We won't disturb you. You will have your rest—
You need a full night's sleep—that's always best.

75   There'll be no scandal, secrets won't be bared;
Tomorrow morning you must be prepared,
To pack your things, down to the smallest plate,
And cup, and then these premises vacate.
You'll have helpers; the men I chose are strong,

80   And they'll have this house empty before long.
I can't think of who would treat you better
And still enforce the law down to the letter,
Just later with the letter is my gift.
So, no resistance. And there'll be no rift.

85   ORGON   From that which I still have, I'd give this hour,
One hundred coins of gold to have the power
To sock this bailiff with a punch as great
As any man in this world could create.

CLÉANTE   That's enough. Let's not make it worse.

DAMIS   The nerve

90   Of him. Let's see what my right fist can serve.

DORINE   Mister Loyal, you have a fine, broad back,
And if I had a stick, you'd hear it crack.

MONSIEUR LOYAL   Words like that are punishable, my love—
Be careful when a push becomes a shove.

95   CLÉANTE   Oh, come on, there's no reason to postpone,
Just serve your writ and then leave us alone.

MONSIEUR LOYAL   May heaven keep you, till we meet again!

ORGON   And strangle you, and him who sent you in!

5.5

[ORGON, CLÉANTE, MARIANE, ELMIRE, MADAME
PERNELLE, DORINE, DAMIS]

ORGON   Well, Mother, look at this writ. Here is proof
Of treachery supreme by your Tartuffe.
Don't jump to judgment—that's what you admonished.
MADAME PERNELLE   I'm overwhelmed, I'm utterly astonished.
5 DORINE   I hear you blaming him and that's just wrong.
You'll see his good intentions before long.
"Just love thy neighbor" is here on this writ,
Between the lines, you see him saying it.
Because men are corrupted by their wealth.
10 Out of concern for your spiritual health,
He's taking, with a pure motivation,
Everything that keeps you from salvation.
ORGON   Aren't you sick of hearing "Quiet!" from me?
CLÉANTE   Thoughts of what to do now? And quickly?
15 ELMIRE   Once we show the plans of that ingrate,
His trickery can't get him this estate.
As soon as they see his disloyalty,
He'll be denied, I hope, this property.

5.6

[VALÈRE, ORGON, CLÉANTE, ELMIRE, MARIANE, *etc.*]

VALÈRE   I hate to ruin your day—I have bad news.
Danger's coming. There's no time to lose.
A good friend, quite good, as it turns out,
Discovered something you must know about,
5 Something at the court that's happening now.
That swindler—sorry, if you will allow,
That holy faker—has gone to the king,
Accusing you of almost everything.
But here's the worst: he says that you have failed
10 Your duty as a subject, which entailed
The keeping of a strongbox so well hidden,
That you could deny knowledge, if bidden,
Of a traitor's whereabouts. What's more,
That holy fraud will come right through that door,
15 Accusing you. You can't do anything.
He had this box and gave it to the king.
So there's an order out for your arrest!
And evidently, it's the king's behest,
That Tartuffe come, so justice can be done.
20 CLÉANTE   Well, there it is, at last, the smoking gun.
He can claim this house, at the very least.
ORGON   The man is nothing but a vicious beast.
VALÈRE   You must leave now, and I will help you hide.
Here's ten thousand in gold. My carriage is outside.
25 When a storm is bearing down on you

Running is the best thing one can do.
I have a place where both of us can stay.
ORGON   My boy, I owe you more than I can say.
I pray to heaven that, before too long,
30   I can pay you back and right the wrong
I've done to you. [*To* ELMIRE] Good-bye. Take care, my dear.
CLÉANTE   We'll plan. You go while the way is still clear.

5.7

[THE EXEMPT, TARTUFFE, VALÈRE, ORGON, ELMIRE,
MARIANE, DORINE, *etc.*[2]]

TARTUFFE   Easy, just a minute, you move too fast.
Your cowardice, dear sir, is unsurpassed.
What I have to say is uncontested.
Simply put, I'm having you arrested.
5   ORGON   You villain, you traitor, your lechery
Is second only to your treachery.
And you arrest me—that's the crowning blow.
TARTUFFE   Suffering for heaven is all I know,
So revile me. It's all for heaven's sake.
10   CLÉANTE   Why does he persist when we know it's fake?
DAMIS   He's mocking heaven. What a loathsome beast.
TARTUFFE   Get mad—I'm not bothered in the least.
It is my duty, what I'm doing here.
MARIANE   You really think that if you persevere
15   In this lie, you'll keep your reputation?
TARTUFFE   My honor is safeguarded by my station,
As I am on a mission from the king.
ORGON   You dog, have you forgotten everything?
Who picked you up from total poverty?
20   TARTUFFE   I know that there were things you did for me.
My duty to our monarch is what stifles
Memory, so your past gifts are trifles.
My obligations to him are so rife,
That I would give up family, friends, and life.
25   ELMIRE   Fraud!
DORINE   Now there's a lie that beats everything,
His pretended reverence for our king!
CLÉANTE   This "duty to our monarch," as you say,
Why didn't it come up before today?
You had the box, you lived here for some time,
30   To say the least, and yet this crime
That you reported—why then did you wait?
Orgon caught you about to desecrate
The holy bonds of marriage with his wife.
Suddenly, your obligations are so "rife"
35   To our dear king, that you're here to turn in

---

2. Molière himself added "etc." to the list of speaking characters. Thus Laurent and Flipote may
return to the stage for this final scene.

Your former friend and "brother" and begin
To move into his house, a gift, but look,
Why would you accept gifts from a crook?
TARTUFFE [*to* THE EXEMPT]   Save me from this whining! I have had my fill!
40   Do execute your orders, if you will.
THE EXEMPT   I will. I've waited much too long for that.
I had to let you have your little chat.
It confirmed the facts our monarch knew,
That's why, Tartuffe, I am arresting you.[3]
45   TARTUFFE   Who, me?
THE EXEMPT   Yes, you.
TARTUFFE   You're putting me in jail?
THE EXEMPT   Immediately. And there will be no bail.
[*To* ORGON] You may compose yourself now, sir, because
We're fortunate in leadership and laws.
We have a king who sees into men's hearts,
50   And cannot be deceived, so he imparts
Great wisdom, and a talent for discernment.
Thus frauds are guaranteed a quick internment.
Our Prince of Reason sees things as they are,
So hypocrites do not get very far.
55   But saintly men and the truly devout,
He cherishes and has no doubts about.
This man could not begin to fool the king
Who can defend himself against the sting
Of much more subtle predators. And thus,
60   When this craven pretender came to us,
Demanding justice and accusing you,
He betrayed himself. Our king could view
The baseness lurking in his coward's heart.
Evil like that can set a man apart.
65   And so divine justice nodded her head,
The king did not believe a word he said.
It was soon confirmed, he has a crime
For every sin, but why squander the time
To list them or the aliases he used.
70   For the king, it's enough that he abused
Your friendship and your faith. And though we knew
Each accusation of his was untrue,
Our monarch himself, wanting to know
Just how far this imposter planned to go,
75   Had me wait to find this out, then pounce,
Arrest this criminal, quickly denounce
The man and all his lies. And now, the king
Orders delivered to you, everything
This scoundrel took, the deed, all documents,
80   This locked box of yours and all its contents,

3. In his capacity as officer of the king, The Exempt becomes both Louis's representative and his surrogate.

And nullifies the contract giving away
Your property, effective today.
And finally, our monarch wants to end
Your worries about aiding your old friend
85 Before he went into exile because,
In that same way, and in spite of the laws,
You openly defended our king's right
To his throne. And you were prepared to fight.
From his heart, and because it makes good sense
90 That a good deed deserves a recompense,
He pardons you. And wanted me to add:
He remembers good longer than the bad.

DORINE May heaven be praised!

MADAME PERNELLE   I am so relieved.

ELMIRE A happy ending!

MARIANE   Can it be believed?

95 ORGON [to TARTUFFE] Now then, you traitor . . .

CLÉANTE   Stop that, Brother, please.
You're sinking to his level. Don't appease
His expectations of mankind. His fate
Is misery. But it's never too late
To take another path, and feel remorse.
100 So let's wish, rather, he will change his course,
And turn his back upon his life of vice,
Embrace the good and know it will suffice.
We've all seen the wisdom of this great king,
Whom we should go and thank for everything.

105 ORGON Yes, and well said. So come along with me,
To thank him for his generosity.
And then once that glorious task is done,
We'll come back here for yet another one—
I mean a wedding for which we'll prepare,
110 To give my daughter to the good Valère.

WILLIAM WYCHERLEY

1641-1715

THE dramatic form called Restoration comedy carries into our present day a reputation for risque sexuality, highly mannered behavior, exaggerated concerns about physical appearance and social comportment, and striking linguistic complexity. But on an even more fundamental level, the phrase "Restoration comedy" reveals the conjunction of political and cultural events central to this historic moment: the return of Charles II to the throne of England and the reopening of the theaters as one of his first formal acts of office in 1660. Charles's love of entertainment, combined with his significant influence on London society and fashion of the late seventeenth century, resulted in a period of remarkable theatrical creativity, epitomized by the comedies that are assumed to reflect the ethos of that giddy era—perhaps none more fully than William Wycherley's THE COUNTRY WIFE (1675).

When the Puritans seized control of the English government, propelling the nation into the English Civil War in 1642, they closed London's theaters and thereby brought to an end a period of sustained dramatic innovation that stretched as far back as the medieval pageant cycles and carried on through the heydays of CHRISTOPHER MARLOWE, WILLIAM SHAKESPEARE, and BEN JONSON. Eighteen years later, managers of the reopened theaters quickly turned to the earlier drama to fill their repertoires, introducing audiences and young artists to this older work while waiting for a new cadre of playwrights to meet the demand for original productions. We can see in the new Restoration plays, including *The Country Wife,* the influence of the previous generation's dramaturgy: vestiges of the humors comedy of Jonson, for example, as well as the turn toward witty repartee and social maneuverings evident in a work such as James Shirley's *Hyde Park* (1632).

Other traditions also shaped Restoration comedy. During the Interregnum (1649–60), when Prince Charles and many of his followers were exiled abroad, members of the English aristocracy developed a keen taste for the French and Spanish culture of the late Renaissance. Once restored to power, Charles brought these Continental predilections back with him, and his preferences soon enriched the new work on the British stage. Elements from the dramas of MOLIÈRE and CALDERÓN proved particularly amenable to adaptation. The era's preeminent comic dramatists—notably John Dryden, George Etherege, APHRA BEHN, Wycherley, and William Congreve—each embraced this multiplicity of creative options and influences in crafting plays suited to the changed theatrical, political, and social circumstances of Carolean London.

A reconstruction of the view from the mezzanine of the Theatre Royal, Drury Lane, ca. 1674.

Although we speak of the theaters "reopening" in 1660, by the time Charles was restored to power London's former theatrical venues had fallen into irreversible disrepair. Thus the first task of the two managers who received royal patents in 1660 to stage plays was to identify workable performance spaces. The patentees, Thomas Killigrew and Sir William Davenant, apparently gave no consideration to outdoor sites and quickly rejected the remaining indoor theaters. They instead renovated small, enclosed tennis courts to suit their needs, following Continental practices. But competition soon led them to construct purpose-built theaters; in 1671 Davenant opened the Duke's Theatre in Dorset Garden, which could accommodate greater flexibility in stage sets and a larger audience, and in 1674 Killigrew followed with the Theatre Royal in Drury Lane, where *The Country Wife* premiered.

While earlier theaters had been limited to depicting a generic locale (e.g., a palace or a town square) by using a single fixed set, these new theaters could represent multiple scenic locations through a system of sliding upstage shutters and side wings, with changeable hanging borders. This signal technical advance not only attracted ticket buyers eager to see the rapid scenic transformations but also prompted the development of new techniques in playwriting. Dramatists could now rely on sets, rather than primarily on dramatic language, to suggest location; in *The Country Wife*, Wycherley switches his action between the residences of his male antagonists Horner and Pinchwife as well as between a private bedchamber and more public locales; these repeated shifts lend the comedy a visual dynamism underscored by the characters' fast-paced repartee.

The other major development in the Restoration theater was of course the introduction of English actresses to the professional stage (although we have evidence of women's involvement in performance activities from earlier periods). The well-established tradition and success of women performing abroad, coupled with their visual attractions, no doubt contributed to Charles's enthusiastic support of this change. Moreover, the court theatricals of his father, Charles I (r. 1625–49), had already featured female participants, and the appearance of women in other theatrical venues supported by the Crown seemed a logical extension of this tradition. Equally important were practical considerations: because of the Puritan suppression of the theater, the boy actors from the late Renaissance who had formerly played women's roles had grown to maturity without any replacements having been trained. In addition, the new king's consciousness of the Puritans' distaste for transvestism made his giving permission for women to appear onstage seem a conciliatory gesture, though ironically the Puritans' opposition to what they perceived as the sexual licentiousness of the Restoration theater only grew once women began to perform.

William Wycherley was just an infant when the Puritans succeeded in eliminating all public theaters, and thus he came of age in an era devoid of stage artistry. Born in the spring of 1641, Wycherley spent his childhood on the estate of the marquess of Winchester, where his father served as the chief steward and his mother had formerly worked as an attendant to the marchioness. William seems to have received an excellent early education in Shrewsbury, studying classical languages and literatures privately with his father as well as at the Royal Free School of King Edward VI. Royalist supporters of Charles I, as were their employers, Daniel and Bethia Wycherley determined to send their teenage son to France for his training as a gentleman, and William arrived in 1656 in the southern region of Angoulême. There he learned French, encountered the works of Molière, and perhaps more importantly, entered the circle of Madame de Montausier, whose salon was modeled after those of the famous Parisian *précieux* and reflected their cultivated sense of taste, their wit, and their courtly manners.

When Daniel discerned that the end of the Puritan regime was near, he recalled his son from the Continent. In 1659 Wycherley traveled back to England, where he first pursued a law career at the Inner Temple of the Inns of Court; he then moved very briefly to Queen's College, Oxford, before returning to London to take up a more fashionable life as a gentleman and aspiring courtier. He apparently entered the army and then naval service; he probably participated in England's wars with the Dutch and later was appointed a captain in the duke of Buckingham's regiment. There is also some evidence that he was part of a diplomatic mission to Spain in 1664, serving as an attaché of the English ambassador. It may have been at this time that he gained familiarity with Spanish drama, particularly the works of Calderón.

Wycherley's literary career began with the anonymous publication in 1669 of his comic poem *Hero and Leander, in Burlesque.* Two years later his first play, *Love in a Wood,* was produced, quickly establishing him as a new dramatist of note. The comedy provided his entrée into court circles, and he soon became a favorite of Charles II. *The Gentleman Dancing Master,* which followed the next year, was less successful but seems not to have damaged his standing as a leading wit at court. Wycherley's even more biting comedies, *The Country Wife* and *The Plain Dealer* (1676), elevated him to the status of England's leading dramatic satirist. On these four plays alone hangs his artistic reputation: though he published some miscellaneous verse many years later, he wrote no more for the theater. Wycherley suffered a serious illness in 1678 that appears to have affected his memory and creative abilities, and in 1679 he made a disastrous marriage that cost him the support of the king. The last thirty-five years of his life were marked by financial hardship, legal difficulties, and the vagaries of English politics, as he regained favor at court under James II (r. 1685–88) but then lost it again under William III (r. 1689–1702). The bright spot in his later years seems to have been his friendship with the young Alexander Pope (1688–1744), who would soon become England's leading satiric poet. Wycherley died on New Year's Eve, 1715, and was buried at St. Paul's, in Covent Garden.

Although Wycherley's career as a dramatist was remarkably short, the legacy of his drama has been rich. *The Country Wife* continued to be a staple of the repertoire until the 1750s, when the rise of stricter moral codes prompted a shift in theatrical styles. In the eighteenth century, the actor-manager David Garrick adapted the play (renaming it *The Country Girl*) and secured its renewed popularity. In 1924 *The Country Wife* was revived in its original form, and it has since remained, with Congreve's *The Way of the World* (1700), the most regularly produced work from the Restoration. Yet despite—or perhaps because of—this ongoing popularity, *The Country Wife* also remains the most controversial play of its era.

Right from the comedy's beginning, we find ourselves in a world of deception and the thrall to pleasure. In the opening scene, the protagonist Horner convinces his physician Quack to help spread a rumor that Horner has been rendered sexually impotent by a surgical mishap. Through this device, Horner believes he will have ready access to women of his choosing for sexual liaisons without raising the suspicions of their husbands. Sir Jasper Fidget, too busy with his own financial interests to pay attention to his wife, is happy to have Horner attend to her, and Lady Fidget and her circle are soon enjoying Horner's companionship. But Horner is particularly captivated by a woman he sees at the theater, Margery Pinchwife, whom the former libertine Jack Pinchwife has recently brought to London for his sister Alithea's wedding to Sparkish. Pinchwife aggressively tries to safeguard his "country wife" from exposure to the licentious ways of the town, but of course to no avail. Sparkish, meanwhile, develops a rival in Horner's circle of men-about-town, Harcourt, who tries to convince Alithea of his deeper and worthier affection for her. Deceptions and complications ensue as the comedy reaches a fever pitch of titillation, innuendo, and chicanery.

Each and every element of *The Country Wife*—characters, themes, values—has, since its premiere, incited critical debate. Is Horner a shameful debaucher of women or an appealing rake celebrating sexual pleasure? Does Wycherley condemn libertinism or does he applaud it? Are Alithea

Toby Stephens (center) is Mr. Horner in the 2007 Theatre Royal (London) production of *The Country Wife*, directed by Jonathan Kent. Surrounding Stephens are, left to right, Lucy Treager as Mrs. Dainty Fidget, Patricia Hodge as My Lady Fidget, and Liz Crowther as Mrs. Squeamish.

and Harcourt the moral and dramatic centers of the play or do their characters simply reflect a rather tired continuation of love plot traditions? In considering such questions, we must never forget that the text is, first and foremost, a script intended to ground a theatrical production. Some interpretations may thus be rendered insupportable by the realities of performance, no matter how cogent they seem when the printed text alone is analyzed. For example, audiences will not perceive Alithea and Harcourt as the play's central figures, whatever their morality or propriety, for the simple reason that they appear in fewer scenes than and are overshadowed onstage by other, more vivid characters. Conversely, casting and directorial choices may impart widely varied interpretations of the play, all theatrically viable; audiences may come to very different understandings of the play simply through the different portrayals of Horner, Pinchwife, or Lady Fidget.

All such options rest on the foundational elements with which Wycherley crafts his comedy. He weaves together three plotlines that reflect the era's prevailing attitudes toward "the town," "the city," and "the country." Horner and his friends Dorilant, Harcourt, and Sparkish inhabit the town—the fashionable world of aristocratic London, defined by its concern with wit, marriage (and the income to support it), and social standing (reflected in the play's repeated references to "quality" and "honor"). Sir Jasper Fidget and his entourage anchor the city plot—"the city" being the term used to designate the business and financial section of London and its attendant issues of power. The Pinchwifes represent the country, which, in the Restoration comic milieu, is always set in opposition to the town—the antithesis of London's sophistication, culture, and social activity.

The dramatic sources from which Wycherley draws to produce his intertwined narratives of love and sexual intrigue are likewise three. From the classical Roman comic playwright Terence, Wycherley borrows the device of the (feigned) eunuch—developed in Terence's play *Eunuchus* (161 B.C.E.), as in Wycherley's, to facilitate illicit sexual relations.

Molière's *L'École des maris* (*The School for Husbands,* 1661) and *L'École des femmes* (*The School for Wives,* 1662) provide many elements of the Pinchwife plot, most notably the latter's story of a middle-aged man who plans to marry an innocent girl to avoid being cuckolded. Horner's exploits resemble those of Molière's Tartuffe (*Tartuffe,* 1664), who deceives his friend Orgon in order to gain access to Orgon's wife and property. In addition, in the role of the clever servants we can see a line of influence stretching from the classical Roman comic tradition through Dorine in Molière's *Tartuffe* to Lucy in *The Country Wife.* A number of these elements also appear in Jonson's *Volpone* (1612)—a calculating protagonist who feigns illness, an overbearing and threatening husband, a sheltered but inquisitive wife. Jonson's comedies are rife with deceit, social pretensions, and complex wordplay—qualities that translated directly onto the Restoration stage.

The density of Jonsonian language is matched by Wycherley's deft layerings and slipperiness of meaning. Famous for its sexual double entendres, *The Country Wife* also demonstrates how the sense of words like "honor" can be in constant flux, dependent on context, intonation, and intent. The "china scene" in act 4 has long been recognized not only as among the most bawdy in Restoration comedy but also as epitomizing its wit and verbal dexterity: Sir Jasper's understanding of china as a domestic commodity provides the literal underpinning for other characters' shift of the word into a very different, highly charged sexual arena. Yet Wycherley's metaphorical sensibility pervades the entire drama, operating along many tonal registers. His use of figurative language is one of the hallmarks of the play, and the characters' ability to deploy and understand such language marks them as either genuine wits or mere pretenders.

There is a direct relationship, moreover, between Wycherley's metaphors and the play's core concerns. The equation of women with their financial value, as in Sparkish's comment about marrying Alithea's "portion" (5.3), exemplifies the ongoing public dialogue during the seventeenth and eighteenth centuries on different forms of marriage, especially the relative merits of marriage for love versus marriage for money. The accompanying question of the "proper" relation of the sexes in marriage reflects the equally contested terrain of gender roles and the dynamics and balance of power between men and women in society. We might also see in the play a representation of the era's crisis of masculinity; concerns with impotence and the sexual satisfaction of women, depicted here through Horner's identity as both the eunuch and the rake, mirror larger questions about male power and efficacy after the English Civil War. Fops such as Sparkish, who conveys both Continental fashion and male effeminacy, also appeared regularly onstage in Restoration dramas, often in conjunction with misogynist figures like Pinchwife—another characterological pairing that reflects anxiety about women's and men's changing roles in the new social order.

Although the concerns that The Country Wife and other Restoration comedies raise are genuine, we should not assume that these works realistically portray the attitudes, issues, and events of their day. Like William Hogarth's drawings from the eighteenth century, The Country Wife captures the spirit of the time in a mode closer to caricature—it presents a picture that derives from the structures and customs of its era but is slightly skewed. The result is recognizable but not necessarily realistic.

J.E.G.

The Country Wife

Indignor quicquam reprehendi, non quia crasse
Compositum illepideve putetur, sed quia nuper:
Nec veniam antiquis, sed honorem et praemia posci.[1]

Prologue
Spoken by Mr. Hart[2]

Poets, like cudgel'd bullies, never do
At first or second blow submit to you;
But will provoke you still, and ne'er have done,
Till you are weary first with laying on.
5 The late so baffled scribbler[3] of this day,
Though he stands trembling, bids me boldly say,
What we before most plays are us'd to do,
For poets out of fear first draw on you;
In a fierce prologue the still pit[4] defy,
10 And ere you speak, like Castril[5] give the lie.

---

1. Horace, *Epistles* 2.1.76–78 (ca. 15 B.C.E.). It makes me annoyed that a thing should be faulted, not for being / crudely or clumsily made but simply for being recent, / and that praise and prizes should be asked for the old, instead of forbearance (Latin). Translated by Niall Rudd (1973).
2. Charles Hart (ca. 1625–1683), the first actor to play the role of Horner.
3. Possibly a reference to Wycherley himself, whose previous play, *The Gentleman Dancing Master* (1672), had not been a success.
4. The section of the theater at ground level, close to the stage.
5. A quarrelsome character in Ben Jonson's comedy *The Alchemist* (1610).

But though our Bayes's[6] battles oft I've fought,
And with bruis'd knuckles their dear conquests bought;
Nay, never yet fear'd odds upon the stage,
In prologue dare not hector with the age,
15 But would take quarter from your saving hands,
Though Bayes within° all yielding countermands,   *backstage*
Says you confed'rate wits no quarter give,
Therefore his play shan't ask your leave to live.
Well, let the vain rash fop, by huffing so,
20 Think to obtain the better terms of you;
But we, the actors, humbly will submit,
Now, and at any time, to a full pit;
Nay, often we anticipate your rage,
And murder poets for you on our stage.
25 We set no guards upon our tiring-room,°   *dressing room*
But when with flying colors there you come,
We patiently, you see, give up to you
Our poets, virgins, nay, our matrons too.

THE PERSONS

MR. HORNER	MY LADY FIDGET
MR. HARCOURT	MRS. DAINTY FIDGET
MR. DORILANT	MRS. SQUEAMISH
MR. PINCHWIFE	OLD LADY SQUEAMISH
MR. SPARKISH	Waiters, servants, and attendants
SIR JASPER FIDGET	A BOY
MRS. MARGERY PINCHWIFE	A QUACK
Mrs. ALITHEA	LUCY, Alithea's maid

The scene: *London*

1.1

[SCENE: HORNER's *lodging.*]

> [*Enter* HORNER, *and* QUACK *following him at a distance.*]

HORNER [*aside*]   A quack is as fit for a pimp as a midwife for
a bawd;° they are still but in their way both helpers   *procuress*
of nature. —Well, my dear doctor, hast thou done what I
desired?

5 QUACK   I have undone you forever with the women, and
reported you throughout the whole town as bad as a
eunuch, with as much trouble as if I had made you one
in earnest.

---

6. The poet-hero of *The Rehearsal* (1671), a
satire by the duke of Buckingham; the character is based on John Dryden (1631–1700),
the dominant literary figure of Restoration
England.

HORNER   But have you told all the midwives you know, the
orange-wenches at the playhouses, the city husbands,
and old fumbling keepers of this end of the town? for
they'll be the readiest to report it.

QUACK   I have told all the chambermaids, waiting-
women, tire-women,[7] and old women of my acquaintance; nay, and whispered it as a secret to 'em, and to
the whisperers of Whitehall;[8] so that you need not
doubt 'twill spread, and you will be as odious to the
handsome young women as—

HORNER   As the smallpox. Well—

QUACK   And to the married women of this end of the
town as—

HORNER   As the great ones;° nay, as their own husbands.   *syphilis (the great pox)*

QUACK   And to the city dames as aniseed Robin[9] of filthy
and contemptible memory; and they will frighten their
children with your name, especially their females.

HORNER   And cry, "Horner's coming to carry you away." I
am only afraid 'twill not be believed. You told 'em 'twas
by an English-French disaster,[1] and an English-French
surgeon, who has given me at once not only a cure but
an antidote for the future against that damned malady,
and that worse distemper, love, and all other women's
evils?

QUACK   Your late journey into France has made it the more
credible, and your being here a fortnight before you appeared in public looks as if you apprehended the shame,
which I wonder you do not. Well, I have been hired by
young gallants to belie 'em t'other way; but you are the
first would be thought a man unfit for women.

HORNER   Dear Mr. Doctor, let vain rogues be contented
only to be thought abler men than they are, generally 'tis
all the pleasure they have; but mine lies another way.

QUACK   You take, methinks, a very preposterous way to it,
and as ridiculous as if we operators in physic° should put   *doctors*
forth bills° to disparage our medicaments, with hopes to   *advertisements*
gain customers.

HORNER   Doctor, there are quacks in love as well as
physic,° who get but the fewer and worse patients for   *medicine*
their boasting; a good name is seldom got by giving it
oneself, and women no more than honor are com
passed by bragging. Come, come, doctor, the wisest
lawyer never discovers° the merits of his cause till the   *reveals*
trial; the wealthiest man conceals his riches, and the

7. Ladies' maids; sellers of women's
accessories.
8. The royal palace of Charles II in London—a center of gossip, intrigue, and political maneuverings.
9. A well-known seller of anise seed–flavored

gin, widely believed to be a hermaphrodite.
1. Venereal disease was associated with
France; Quack's story is that the doctor who
attempted to cure Horner has rendered him
impotent.

cunning gamester his play. Shy husbands and keepers, like old rooks,° are not to be cheated but by a new

55 unpracticed trick; false friendship will pass now no more than false dice upon 'em; no, not in the city.

[Enter BOY.]

BOY There are two ladies and a gentleman coming up.

[Exit.]

HORNER A pox! some unbelieving sisters° of my former acquaintance, who, I am afraid, expect their sense should

60 be satisfied of the falsity of the report. No—this formal° fool and women!

[Enter SIR JASPER FIDGET, LADY FIDGET, *and* MRS. DAINTY FIDGET.]

QUACK His wife and sister.

SIR JASPER FIDGET My coach breaking° just now before your door, sir, I look upon as an occasional° reprimand

65 to me, sir, for not kissing your hands, sir, since your coming out of France, sir; and so my disaster, sir, has been my good fortune, sir; and this is my wife and sister, sir.

HORNER What then, sir?

SIR JASPER FIDGET My lady, and sister, sir.—Wife, this is

70 Master Horner.

LADY FIDGET Master Horner, husband!

SIR JASPER FIDGET My lady, my Lady Fidget, sir.

HORNER So, sir.

SIR JASPER FIDGET Won't you be acquainted with her

75 sir?—*[Aside.]* So, the report is true, I find, by his coldness or aversion to the sex; but I'll play the wag° with him.—Pray salute my wife, my lady, sir.

HORNER I will kiss no man's wife, sir, for him, sir; I have taken my eternal leave, sir, of the sex already, sir.

80 SIR JASPER FIDGET *[aside]* Ha, ha, ha! I'll plague him yet.—Not know my wife, sir?

HORNER I do know your wife, sir; she's a woman, sir, and consequently a monster, sir, a greater monster than a husband, sir.

85 SIR JASPER FIDGET A husband! how, sir?

HORNER So, sir; but I make no more cuckolds,[2] sir.

[Makes horns.[3]]

SIR JASPER FIDGET Ha, ha, ha! Mercury, Mercury![4]

LADY FIDGET Pray, Sir Jasper, let us be gone from this rude fellow.

90 MRS. DAINTY FIDGET Who, by his breeding, would think he had ever been in France?

----

swindlers

whores

ceremonious

breaking down
opportune

play the joker

----

2. A "horner" is a cuckold maker.
3. That is, he makes the sign of the cuckold by holding his fists to his temples, with his index fingers pointing up; an unfaithful wife is said to "put the horns" on her husband.

4. Substance used to treat venereal disease; also, the Roman herald of the gods, the patron of tricksters and thieves, who wore a winged hat.

LADY FIDGET   Foh! he's but too much a French fellow,°   *i.e., a fop*
   such as hate women of quality and virtue for their love to
   their husbands, Sir Jasper; a woman is hated by 'em as
95   much for loving her husband as for loving their money.
   But pray let's be gone.
HORNER   You do well, madam, for I have nothing that you
   came for. I have brought over not so much as a bawdy
   picture, new postures, nor the second part of the *École*
100 *des Filles*,[5] nor—
QUACK [*apart to* HORNER]   Hold, for shame, sir! What d'ye
   mean? You'll ruin yourself forever with the sex—
SIR JASPER FIDGET   Ha, ha, ha! He hates women perfectly,
   I find.
105 MRS. DAINTY FIDGET   What pity 'tis he should.
LADY FIDGET   Ay, he's a base, rude fellow for't; but affectation makes not a woman more odious to them than
   virtue.
HORNER   Because your virtue is your greatest affectation,
110 madam.
LADY FIDGET   How, you saucy fellow! Would you wrong
   my honor?
HORNER   If I could.
LADY FIDGET   How d'ye mean, sir?
115 SIR JASPER FIDGET   Ha, ha, ha! No, he can't wrong your
   ladyship's honor, upon my honor; he, poor man—hark
   you in your ear—a mere eunuch.
LADY FIDGET   O filthy° French beast! foh, foh! Why do we   *obscene*
   stay? Let's be gone; I can't endure the sight of him.
120 SIR JASPER FIDGET   Stay but till the chairs° come; they'll   *sedan chairs*
   be here presently.°   *quickly*
LADY FIDGET   No, no.
SIR JASPER FIDGET   Nor can I stay longer. 'Tis—let me see,
   a quarter and a half quarter of a minute past eleven; the
125 council[6] will be sat, I must away. Business must be preferred always before love and ceremony with the wise,
   Mr. Horner.
HORNER   And the impotent, Sir Jasper.
SIR JASPER FIDGET   Ay, ay, the impotent, Master Horner,
130 ha, ha, ha!
LADY FIDGET   What, leave us with a filthy man alone in his
   lodgings?
SIR JASPER FIDGET   He's an innocent man now, you know.
   Pray stay, I'll hasten the chairs to you.—Mr. Horner,
135 your servant; I should be glad to see you at my house.
   Pray come and dine with me, and play at cards with my
   wife after dinner; you are fit for women at that game
   yet, ha, ha!—[*Aside*] 'Tis as much a husband's prudence to provide innocent diversion for a wife as to

---

5. *Girls' School* (French), an erotic book
(1655) by Michel Millot. *Postures*: pornographic engravings.
6. The Privy Council, which advised the king.

140   hinder her unlawful pleasures, and he had better employ
       her than let her employ herself.—Farewell.

HORNER   Your servant,° Sir Jasper.   *(a polite leave-taking)*

[*Exit* SIR JASPER.]

LADY FIDGET   I will not stay with him, foh!

HORNER   Nay, madam, I beseech you stay, if it be but to
145   see I can be as civil to ladies yet as they would desire.

LADY FIDGET   No, no, foh! You cannot be civil to ladies.

MRS. DAINTY FIDGET   You as civil as ladies would desire?

LADY FIDGET   No, no, no! foh, foh, foh!

[*Exeunt* LADY FIDGET *and* MRS. DAINTY.]

QUACK   Now, I think, I, or you yourself rather, have done
150   your business with the women.

HORNER   Thou art an ass. Don't you see already, upon the
       report and my carriage, this grave man of business
       leaves his wife in my lodgings, invites me to his house
       and wife, who before would not be acquainted with me
155   out of jealousy?

QUACK   Nay, by this means you may be the more acquainted
       with the husbands, but the less with the wives.

HORNER   Let me alone; if I can but abuse the husbands,
160   I'll soon disabuse the wives. Stay°—I'll reckon you   *Wait*
       up the advantages I am like to have by my stratagem:
       First, I shall be rid of all my old acquaintances, the most
       insatiable sorts of duns,[7] that invade our lodgings in a
       morning. And next to the pleasure of making a new mis-
165   tress is that of being rid of an old one, and of all old
       debts; love, when it comes to be so, is paid the most
       unwillingly.

QUACK   Well, you may be so rid of your old acquaintances;
       but how will you get any new ones?

170 HORNER   Doctor, thou wilt never make a good chemist,
       thou art so incredulous and impatient. Ask but all the
       young fellows of the town if they do not lose more
       time, like huntsmen, in starting the game[8] than in
       running it down; one knows not where to find 'em,
175   who will or will not. Women of quality are so civil you
       can hardly distinguish love from good breeding, and a
       man is often mistaken; but now I can be sure she that
       shows an aversion to me loves the sport, as those
       women that are gone, whom I warrant to be right.°   *suitable*
180   And then the next thing is, your women of honor, as you
       call 'em, are only chary of their reputations, not their
       persons, and 'tis scandal they would avoid, not men.
       Now may I have, by the reputation of a eunuch, the
       privileges of one; and be seen in a lady's chamber in a

---

7. Bill collectors; here, those making demands   8. Forcing the hunted animal to leave its lair
more generally.   or hiding place.

185   morning as early as her husband; kiss virgins before
their parents or lovers; and may be, in short, the *passe
partout*[9] of the town. Now, doctor.

QUACK   Nay, now you shall be the doctor; and your process is so new that we do not know but it may succeed.

190 HORNER   Not so new neither; *probatum est*,[1] doctor.

QUACK   Well, I wish you luck and many patients whilst I
go to mine.   [*Exit* QUACK.]

[*Enter* HARCOURT *and* DORILANT *to* HORNER.]

HARCOURT   Come, your appearance at the play yesterday
has, I hope, hardened you for the future against the
195   women's contempt and the men's raillery; and now you'll
abroad° as you were wont.   *go out*

HORNER   Did I not bear it bravely?

DORILANT   With a most theatrical impudence; nay, more
than the orange-wenches show there, or a drunken
200   vizard-mask,[2] or a great-bellied actress; nay, or the most
impudent of creatures, an ill poet; or what is yet more
impudent, a secondhand critic.

HORNER   But what say the ladies? Have they no pity?

HARCOURT   What ladies? The vizard-masks, you know,
205   never pity a man when all's gone, though in their
service.

DORILANT   And for the women in the boxes,[3] you'd never
pity them when 'twas in your power.

HARCOURT   They say, 'tis pity but all that deal with com-
210   mon women should be served so.

DORILANT   Nay, I dare swear, they won't admit you to play at
cards with them, go to plays with 'em, or do the little duties which other shadows of men are wont to do for 'em.

HORNER   Who do you call shadows of men?

215 DORILANT   Half-men.

HORNER   What, boys?

DORILANT   Ay, your old boys, old *beaux garçons*,[4] who,
like superannuated stallions, are suffered to run, feed,
and whinny with the mares as long as they live, though
220   they can do nothing else.

HORNER   Well, a pox on love and wenching! Women
serve but to keep a man from better company; though I
can't en-joy them, I shall you the more. Good fellowship and friendship are lasting, rational, and manly
pleasures.

225 HARCOURT   For all that, give me some of those pleasures
you call effeminate too; they help to relish one another.

---

9. Master key (French); literally, something
that permits one to go everywhere.
1. It has been tested (Latin); perhaps an allusion to a similar ruse in *The Eunuch* (161
B.C.E.), a comedy by the Roman playwright
Terence.

2. A whore; prostitutes often wore masks in
such public venues as theaters.
3. The most expensive section of the theater,
frequented by those of the highest social
rank.
4. Fops (literally, "pretty boys"; French).

HORNER   They disturb one another.

HARCOURT   No, mistresses are like books. If you pore upon
them too much, they doze° you and make you unfit for   *stupefy; confuse*
230   company; but if used discreetly, you are the fitter for
conversation by 'em.

DORILANT   A mistress should be like a little country retreat
near the town, not to dwell in constantly, but only for a
night and away, to taste the town the better when a man
235   returns.

HORNER   I tell you, 'tis as hard to be a good fellow, a good
friend, and a lover of women, as 'tis to be a good fellow,
a good friend, and a lover of money. You cannot follow
both, then choose your side. Wine gives you liberty, love
240   takes it away.

DORILANT   Gad, he's in the right on't.

HORNER   Wine gives you joy; love, grief and tortures, besides the surgeon's. Wine makes us witty; love, only sots.
Wine makes us sleep; love breaks it.

245   DORILANT   By the world, he has reason, Harcourt.

HORNER   Wine makes—

DORILANT   Ay, wine makes us—makes us princes; love
makes us beggars, poor rogues, egad—and wine—

HORNER   So, there's one converted.—No, no, love and
250   wine, oil and vinegar.

HARCOURT   I grant it; love will still be uppermost.[5]

HORNER   Come, for my part I will have only those glorious,
manly pleasures of being very drunk and very slovenly.

    [*Enter* BOY.]

BOY   Mr. Sparkish is below, sir.   [*Exit.*]

255   HARCOURT   What, my dear friend! a rogue that is fond of
me only, I think, for abusing him.

DORILANT   No, he can no more think the men laugh at
him than that women jilt him, his opinion of himself is
so good.

260   HORNER   Well, there's another pleasure by drinking I
thought not of; I shall lose his acquaintance, because he
cannot drink; and you know 'tis a very hard thing to be rid
of him, for he's one of those nauseous offerers at wit, who,
265   like the worst fiddlers, run themselves into all companies.

HARCOURT   One that, by being in the company of men of
sense, would pass for one.

HORNER   And may so to the shortsighted world, as a false
jewel amongst true ones is not discerned at a distance.
270   His company is as troublesome to us as a cuckold's when
you have a mind to his wife's.

HARCOURT   No, the rogue will not let us enjoy one another,
but ravishes° our conversation, though he signifies no   *spoils*
more to't than Sir Martin Mar-all's gaping, and awkward

---

5. That is, as oil will rise above vinegar when the two are poured together.

275 thrumming upon the lute, does to his man's voice and
music.[6]

DORILANT   And to pass for a wit in town shows himself a
fool every night to us, that are guilty of the plot.

HORNER   Such wits as he are, to a company of reasonable

280 men, like rooks° to the gamesters, who only fill a   *gulls, dupes*
room at the table, but are so far from contributing to
the play that they only serve to spoil the fancy° of those   *pleasure*
that do.

DORILANT   Nay, they are used like rooks too, snubbed,

285 checked, and abused; yet the rogues will hang on.

HORNER   A pox on 'em, and all that force nature, and
would be still what she forbids 'em! Affectation is her
greatest monster.

HARCOURT   Most men are the contraries to that they

290 would seem. Your bully, you see, is a coward with a long
sword; the little, humbly fawning physician, with his
ebony cane, is he that destroys men.

DORILANT   The usurer, a poor rogue possessed of moldy
bonds and mortgages; and we they call spendthrifts are

295 only wealthy who lay out his money upon daily new purchases of pleasure.

HORNER   Ay, your arrantest cheat is your trustee, or execu-
tor; your jealous man, the greatest cuckold; your churchman, the greatest atheist; and your noisy, pert rogue of a

300 wit, the greatest fop, dullest ass, and worst company, as
you shall see. For here he comes.

[*Enter* SPARKISH *to them.*]

SPARKISH   How is't, sparks,° how is't? Well, faith, Harry,   *young fops*
I must rally thee a little, ha, ha, ha! upon the report in
town of thee, ha, ha, ha! I can't hold i' faith; shall I
speak?

305 HORNER   Yes, but you'll be so bitter then.

SPARKISH   Honest Dick and Frank here shall answer for
me, I will not be extreme bitter, by the universe.

HARCOURT   We will be bound in ten thousand pound
bond, he shall not be bitter at all.

310 DORILANT   Nor° sharp, nor sweet.   *Neither*

HORNER   What, not downright insipid?

SPARKISH   Nay then, since you are so brisk° and provoke   *sharp-witted*
me, take what follows. You must know, I was discoursing
and rallying° with some ladies yesterday, and they   *bantering*

315 happened to talk of the fine new signs° in town.   *i.e., shop signs*

HORNER   Very fine ladies, I believe.

SPARKISH   Said I, "I know where the best new sign is."
"Where?" says one of the ladies. "In Covent Garden," I

---

6. In Dryden's play *Sir Martin Mar-All*
(1667), the title character pretends to sere-
nade his mistress while his concealed servant
actually plays the lute and sings.

replied. Said another, "In what street?" "In Russell
Street," answered I.[7] "Lord," says another, "I'm sure there
320 was ne'er a fine new sign there yesterday." "Yes, but there
was," said I again, "and it came out of France, and has
been there a fortnight."

DORILANT A pox! I can hear no more, prithee.

325 HORNER No, hear him out; let him tune his crowd° a   *fiddle*
while.

HARCOURT The worst music, the greatest preparation.

SPARKISH Nay, faith, I'll make you laugh. "It cannot be,"
says a third lady. "Yes, yes," quoth I again. Says a fourth
330 lady—

HORNER Look to't, we'll have no more ladies.

SPARKISH No—then mark, mark, now. Said I to the
fourth, "Did you never see Mr. Horner? He lodges in
Russell Street, and he's a sign° of a man, you know,   *a mere semblance*
335 since he came out of France." He, ha, he!

HORNER But the devil take me, if thine be the sign of a
jest.

SPARKISH With that they all fell a-laughing, till they
bepissed themselves! What, but it does not move you,
340 methinks? Well, I see one had as good go to law°   *court*
without a witness, as break a jest without a laugher
on one's side. Come, come, sparks, but where do
we dine? I have left at Whitehall an earl to dine with
you.

345 DORILANT Why, I thought thou hadst loved a man with a
title better than a suit with a French trimming to't.

HARCOURT Go to him again.

SPARKISH No, sir, a wit to me is the greatest title in the
world.

350 HORNER But go dine with your earl, sir; he may be excep-
tious.° We are your friends, and will not take it ill   *peeved*
to be left, I do assure you.

HARCOURT Nay, faith, he shall go to him.

SPARKISH Nay, pray, gentlemen.

355 DORILANT We'll thrust you out, if you wo'not.° What,   *will not*
disappoint anybody for us?

SPARKISH Nay, dear gentlemen, hear me.

HORNER No, no, sir, by no means; pray go, sir.

SPARKISH Why, dear rogues—

360 DORILANT No, no.

[*They all thrust him out of the room.*]

ALL Ha, ha, ha!

[SPARKISH *returns.*]

SPARKISH But, sparks, pray hear me. What, d'ye think I'll
eat then with gay, shallow fops and silent coxcombs?° I   *fools*
think wit as necessary at dinner as a glass of good wine,

7. Two fashionable areas of London.

365   and that's the reason I never have any stomach when I
        eat alone.—Come, but where do we dine?

HORNER   Even where you will.

SPARKISH   At Chateline's?

DORILANT   Yes, if you will.

370 SPARKISH   Or at the Cock?

DORILANT   Yes, if you please.

SPARKISH   Or at the Dog and Partridge?[8]

HORNER   Ay, if you have mind to't, for we shall dine at
        neither.

375 SPARKISH   Pshaw! with your fooling we shall lose the new
        play; and I would no more miss seeing a new play the
        first day than I would miss sitting in the wits' row. There-
        fore I'll go fetch my mistress and away.   [*Exit* SPARKISH.]

        [*Manent*° HORNER, HARCOURT, DORILANT. *Enter to*   *They remain (Latin)*
        them MR. PINCHWIFE.]

HORNER   Who have we here? Pinchwife?

380 PINCHWIFE   Gentlemen, your humble servant.

HORNER   Well, Jack, by thy long absence from the town, the
        grumness° of thy countenance, and the slovenliness of of   *gloominess*
        thy habit, I should give thee joy, should I not, of marriage?

PINCHWIFE   [*aside*]   Death! does he know I'm married

385   too? I thought to have concealed it from him at
        least.—My long stay in the country will excuse my dress,
        and I have a suit of law, that brings me up to town, that
        puts me out of hu-mour; besides, I must give Sparkish
        tomorrow five thousand pound to lie with my sister.[9]

390 HORNER   Nay, you country gentlemen, rather than not
        purchase, will buy anything; and he is a cracked title,[1]
        if we may quibble. Well, but am I to give thee joy? I
        heard thou wert married.

PINCHWIFE   What then?

395 HORNER   Why, the next thing that is to be heard is,
        thou'rt a cuckold.

PINCHWIFE   [*aside*]   Insupportable name!

HORNER   But I did not expect marriage from such a
        whoremaster as you, one that knew the town so much,

400   and women so well.

PINCHWIFE   Why, I have married no London wife.

HORNER   Pshaw! that's all one;° that grave circumspection   *all the same*
        in marrying a country wife is like refusing a deceitful,
        pampered Smithfield jade[2] to go and be cheated by a

405   friend in the country.

PINCHWIFE   [*aside*]   A pox on him and his simile!—At

---

8. All taverns near Covent Garden.
9. That is, to provide a (large) dowry.
1. He has a flawed right of ownership.

2. An inferior horse (or disreputable woman)
bought at London's Smithfield market.

least we are a little surer of the breed there, know what
her keeping has been, whether foiled[3] or unsound.

HORNER Come, come, I have known a clap° gotten in   *gonorrhea*
410 Wales;[4] and there are cousins, justices' clerks, and chaplains in the country, I won't say coachmen. But she's
handsome and young?

PINCHWIFE [*aside*] I'll answer as I should do.—No, no,
she has no beauty but her youth; no attraction but
415 her modesty; wholesome, homely, and housewifely;
that's all.

DORILANT He talks as like a grazier[5] as he looks.

PINCHWIFE She's too awkward, ill-favored, and silly° to   *unsophisticated*
bring to town.

420 HARCOURT Then methinks you should bring her, to be
taught breeding.

PINCHWIFE To be taught! no, sir, I thank you. Good
wives and private soldiers should be ignorant.—
[*Aside*] I'll keep her from your instructions, I warrant
425 you.

HARCOURT [*aside*] The rogue is as jealous as if his wife
were not ignorant.

HORNER Why, if she be ill-favored, there will be less
danger here for you than by leaving her in the country;
430 we have such variety of dainties that we are seldom
hungry.

DORILANT But they have always coarse, constant, swinge-
ing stomachs° in the country.   *huge appetites*

HARCOURT Foul feeders indeed.

435 DORILANT And your hospitality is great there.

HARCOURT Open house, every man's welcome.

PINCHWIFE So, so, gentlemen.

HORNER But, prithee, why wouldst thou marry her? If she
be ugly, ill-bred, and silly, she must be rich then.

440 PINCHWIFE As rich as if she brought me twenty thousand pound out of this town; for she'll be as sure not
to spend her moderate portion as a London baggage°   *strumpet*
would be to spend hers, let it be what it would; so 'tis all
one. Then, because she's ugly, she's the likelier to be my
445 own; and being ill-bred, she'll hate conversation;[6] and
since silly and innocent, will not know the difference
betwixt a man of one-and-twenty and one of forty.

HORNER Nine—to my knowledge; but if she be silly,
she'll expect as much from a man of forty-nine as from
450 him of one-and-twenty. But methinks wit is more necessary than beauty, and I think no young woman ugly
that has it, and no handsome woman agreeable without it.

3. Injured (of horses); deflowered, defiled (of
women).
4. That is, far from London, in the sticks.

5. One who fattens cattle for market.
6. Social intercourse; sexual intercourse.

PINCHWIFE 'Tis my maxim, he's a fool that marries, but
455   he's a greater that does not marry a fool. What is wit in
  a wife good for, but to make a man cuckold?

HORNER   Yes, to keep it from his knowledge.

PINCHWIFE   A fool cannot contrive to make her husband
  a cuckold.

460 HORNER   No, but she'll club° with a man that can; and   *associate*
  what is worse, if she cannot make her husband a cuck-
  old, she'll make him jealous, and pass for one, and
  then 'tis all one.

PINCHWIFE   Well, well, I'll take care for one, my wife shall
465   make me no cuckold, though she had your help, Mr.
  Horner; I understand the town, sir.

DORILANT [*aside*]   His help!

HARCOURT [*aside*]   He's come newly to town, it seems, and
  has not heard how things are with him.

470 HORNER   But tell me, has marriage cured thee of whoring,
  which it seldom does?

HARCOURT   'Tis more than age can do.

HORNER   No, the word is, I'll marry and live honest;° but a   *honorably*
  marriage vow is like a penitent gamester's oath, and en-
475   tering into bonds and penalties to stint himself to such
  a particular small sum at play for the future, which
  makes him but the more eager, and not being able to
  hold out, loses his money again, and his forfeit to boot.

DORILANT   Ay, ay, a gamester will be a gamester whilst
480   his money lasts, and a whoremaster whilst his vigor.

HARCOURT   Nay, I have known 'em, when they are broke
  and can lose no more, keep a-fumbling with the box[7]
  in their hands to fool with only, and hinder other
  gamesters.

DORILANT   That had wherewithal to make lusty stakes.

485 PINCHWIFE   Well, gentlemen, you may laugh at me, but
  you shall never lie with my wife; I know the town.

HORNER   But prithee, was not the way you were in better? Is not keeping better than marriage?

PINCHWIFE   A pox on't! The jades would jilt me; I could
490   never keep a whore to myself.

HORNER   So, then you only married to keep a whore to
  yourself. Well, but let me tell you, women, as you say,
  are like soldiers, made constant and loyal by good pay
  rather than by oaths and covenants. Therefore I'd
495   advise my friends to keep rather than marry, since too I
  find, by your example, it does not serve one's turn; for
  I saw you yesterday in the eighteen-penny place[8] with
  a pretty country wench.

---

7. Box in which dice are shaken; also, vagina.
8. The middle gallery, which was the section of the theater most frequented by prostitutes.

PINCHWIFE [*aside*]   How the devil! Did he see my wife
500   then? I sat there that she might not be seen. But she
shall never go to a play again.

HORNER   What, dost thou blush at nine-and-forty, for having been seen with a wench?

DORILANT   No, faith, I warrant 'twas his wife, which he
505   seated there out of sight, for he's a cunning rogue and
understands the town.

HARCOURT   He blushes. Then 'twas his wife, for men are
now more ashamed to be seen with them in public than
with a wench.

510   PINCHWIFE [*aside*]   Hell and damnation! I'm undone,
since Horner has seen her, and they know 'twas she.

HORNER   But prithee, was it thy wife? She was exceedingly
pretty; I was in love with her at that distance.

PINCHWIFE   You are like never to be nearer to her. Your
515   servant, gentlemen. [*Offers° to go.*]   *Attempts*

HORNER   Nay, prithee stay.

PINCHWIFE   I cannot, I will not.

HORNER   Come, you shall dine with us.

PINCHWIFE   I have dined already.

520   HORNER   Come, I know thou hast not. I'll treat thee, dear
rogue; thou shalt spend none of thy Hampshire[9] money
today.

PINCHWIFE [*aside*]   Treat me! So, he uses me already like
his cuckold.

525   HORNER   Nay, you shall not go.

PINCHWIFE   I must, I have business at home.

[*Exit* PINCHWIFE.]

HARCOURT   To beat his wife; he's as jealous of her as a
Cheapside husband of a Covent Garden wife.[1]

HORNER   Why, 'tis as hard to find an old whoremaster
530   without jealousy and the gout, as a young one without
fear or the pox.

> As gout in age from pox in youth proceeds,
> So wenching past, then jealousy succeeds,
> The worst disease that love and wenching breeds.

[*Exeunt.*]

2.1

[SCENE: PINCHWIFE's *house*.]

[MRS. MARGERY PINCHWIFE *and* ALITHEA.]

[MR. PINCHWIFE *peeping behind at the door.*]

MRS. PINCHWIFE   Pray, sister, where are the best fields and
woods to walk in, in London?

---

9. A largely rural county in south England.
1. That is, a merchant husband and a fashionable wife (Cheapside was a commercial
street in the City of London).

ALITHEA A pretty question! Why, sister, Mulberry Garden
and St. James's Park,° and for close walks, the New   *(fashionable parks)*
5 Exchange.[2]

MRS. PINCHWIFE Pray, sister, tell me why my husband
looks so grum° here in town, and keeps me up so close,   *glum*
and will not let me go a-walking, nor let me wear my best
gown yesterday.

10 ALITHEA Oh, he's jealous, sister.

MRS. PINCHWIFE Jealous? What's that?

ALITHEA He's afraid you should love another man.

MRS. PINCHWIFE How should he be afraid of my loving
another man, when he will not let me see any but
15 himself?

ALITHEA Did he not carry you yesterday to a play?

MRS. PINCHWIFE Ay, but we sat amongst ugly people; he
would not let me come near the gentry, who sat under
us, so that I could not see 'em. He told me none but
20 naughty women sat there, whom they toused and
moused.° But I would have ventured for all that.   *fondled sexually*

ALITHEA But how did you like the play?

MRS. PINCHWIFE Indeed, I was a-weary of the play, but I
liked hugeously the actors; they are the goodliest, pro-
25 perest° men, sister!   *most handsome*

ALITHEA Oh, but you must not like the actors, sister.

MRS. PINCHWIFE Ay, how should I help it, sister? Pray,
sister, when my husband comes in, will you ask leave
for me to go a-walking?

30 ALITHEA [*aside*] A-walking! Ha, ha! Lord, a country gentlewoman's leisure is the drudgery of a foot-post,° and   *messenger on foot*
she requires as much airing as her husband's horses.

[*Enter* MR. PINCHWIFE *to them.*]

But here comes your husband; I'll ask, though I'm sure
he'll not grant it.

35 MRS. PINCHWIFE He says he won't let me go abroad for
fear of catching the pox.

ALITHEA Fie! "the smallpox" you should say.

MRS. PINCHWIFE O my dear, dear bud,° welcome home!   *(endearment)*
Why dost thou look so froppish? Who has nangered[3]
40 thee?

PINCHWIFE You're a fool.

[MRS. PINCHWIFE *goes aside and cries.*]

ALITHEA Faith, so she is, for crying for no fault, poor tender creature!

PINCHWIFE What, you would have her as impudent as
45 yourself, as arrant a jill-flirt, a gadder,° a magpie,° and to   *gadabout / chatterer*
say all, a mere, notorious town-woman?

---

2. A shopping arcade on the strand; its lower
level was associated with sexual intrigue.
3. Angered; like "froppish" (peevish), an

archaism that underscores Mrs. Pinchwife's
lack of sophistication.

ALITHEA   Brother, you are my only censurer; and the honor
of your family shall sooner suffer in your wife there than in
me, though I take the innocent liberty of the town.

50 PINCHWIFE   Hark you, mistress, do not talk so before my
wife. The innocent liberty of the town!

ALITHEA   Why, pray, who boasts of any intrigue with me?
What lampoon has made my name notorious? What ill
women frequent my lodgings? I keep no company with

55 any women of scandalous reputations.

PINCHWIFE   No, you keep the men of scandalous reputations company.

ALITHEA   Where? Would you not have me civil? answer
'em in a box at the plays, in the drawing room at White-

60 hall, in St. James's Park, Mulberry Garden, or—

PINCHWIFE   Hold, hold! Do not teach my wife where the
men are to be found! I believe she's the worse for your
town documents° already. I bid you keep her in igno-   *lessons*
rance, as I do.

65 MRS. PINCHWIFE   Indeed, be not angry with her, bud; she
will tell me nothing of the town, though I ask her a thousand times a day.

PINCHWIFE   Then you are very inquisitive to know, I find!

MRS. PINCHWIFE   Not I, indeed, dear; I hate London. Our
70 place-house° in the country is worth a thousand of 't;   *manor house*
would I were there again!

PINCHWIFE   So you shall, I warrant. But were you not talking of plays and players when I came in?—[*To* ALITHEA]
You are her encourager in such discourses.

75 MRS. PINCHWIFE   No, indeed, dear; she chid me just now
for liking the playermen.

PINCHWIFE [*aside*]   Nay, if she be so innocent as to own to
me her liking them, there is no hurt in't.—Come, my
poor rogue, but thou lik'st none better than me?

80 MRS. PINCHWIFE   Yes, indeed, but I do; the playermen are
finer folks.

PINCHWIFE   But you love none better than me?

MRS. PINCHWIFE   You are mine own dear bud, and I know
you; I hate a stranger.

85 PINCHWIFE   Ay, my dear, you must love me only, and not be
like the naughty town-women, who only hate their husbands and love every man else, love plays, visits, fine
coaches, fine clothes, fiddles, balls, treats, and so lead a
wicked town-life.

90 MRS. PINCHWIFE   Nay, if to enjoy all these things be a
town-life, London is not so bad a place, dear.

PINCHWIFE   How! If you love me, you must hate London.

ALITHEA [*aside*]   The fool has forbid me discovering° to   *revealing*
her the pleasures of the town, and he is now setting her

95 agog upon them himself.

MRS. PINCHWIFE   But, husband, do the town-women love
the playermen too?

PINCHWIFE   Yes, I warrant you.

MRS. PINCHWIFE   Ay, I warrant you.

100 PINCHWIFE   Why, you do not, I hope?

MRS. PINCHWIFE   No, no, bud; but why have we no player-men in the country?

PINCHWIFE   Ha!—Mrs. Minx,° ask me no more to go to a play.   *hussy*

105 MRS. PINCHWIFE   Nay, why, love? I did not care for going; but when you forbid me, you make me, as 'twere, desire it.

ALITHEA [*aside*]   So t'will be in other things, I warrant.

MRS. PINCHWIFE   Pray let me go to a play, dear.

110 PINCHWIFE   Hold your peace, I wo'not.

MRS. PINCHWIFE   Why, love?

PINCHWIFE   Why, I'll tell you.

ALITHEA [*aside*]   Nay, if he tell her, she'll give him more cause to forbid her that place.

115 MRS. PINCHWIFE   Pray, why, dear?

PINCHWIFE   First, you like the actors, and the gallants may like you.

MRS. PINCHWIFE   What, a homely country girl? No, bud, nobody will like me.

120 PINCHWIFE   I tell you, yes, they may.

MRS. PINCHWIFE   No, no, you jest—I won't believe you, I will go.

PINCHWIFE   I tell you then that one of the lewdest fellows in town, who saw you there, told me he was in
125 love with you.

MRS. PINCHWIFE   Indeed! Who, who, pray who was't?

PINCHWIFE [*aside*]   I've gone too far, and slipped before I was aware. How overjoyed she is!

MRS. PINCHWIFE   Was it any Hampshire gallant, any of
130 our neighbors? I promise you, I am beholding° to him.   *beholden*

PINCHWIFE   I promise you, you lie; for he would but ruin you, as he has done hundreds. He has no other love for women but that; such as he look upon women, like basilisks,[4] but to destroy 'em.

135 MRS. PINCHWIFE   Ay, but if he loves me, why should he ruin me? Answer me to that. Methinks he should not; I would do him no harm.

ALITHEA   Ha, ha, ha!

PINCHWIFE   'Tis very well; but I'll keep him from doing
140 you any harm, or me either.

[*Enter* SPARKISH *and* HARCOURT.]

But here comes company; get you in, get you in.

MRS. PINCHWIFE   But pray, husband, is he a pretty gentleman that loves me?

PINCHWIFE   In, baggage, in. [*Thrusts her in; shuts the*

4. Mythical serpents whose glance was deadly.

145   *door.*]—[*Aside*] What, all the lewd libertines of the town
    brought to my lodging by this easy coxcomb! 'Sdeath,°   *God's death (an oath)*
    I'll not suffer it.

    SPARKISH   Here, Harcourt, do you approve my choice?—
    [*To* ALITHEA] Dear little rogue, I told you I'd bring you
150   acquainted with all my friends, the wits, and—

                          [HARCOURT *salutes*[5] *her.*]

    PINCHWIFE [*aside*]   Ay, they shall know her, as well as you
    yourself will, I warrant you.

    SPARKISH   This is one of those, my pretty rogue, that are to
    dance at your wedding tomorrow; and him you must bid
155   welcome ever to what you and I have.

    PINCHWIFE [*aside*]   Monstrous!

    SPARKISH   Harcourt, how dost thou like her, faith?—Nay,
    dear, do not look down; I should hate to have a wife of
    mine out of countenance at anything.

160   PINCHWIFE [*aside*]   Wonderful!°   *Amazing*

    SPARKISH   Tell me, I say, Harcourt, how dost thou like her?
    Thou hast stared upon her enough to resolve° me.   *answer*

    HARCOURT   So infinitely well that I could wish I had a mis-
    tress too, that might differ from her in nothing but her
165   love and engagement to you.

    ALITHEA   Sir, Master Sparkish has often told me that his
    acquaintance were all wits and railleurs,° and now I   *banterers*
    find it.

    SPARKISH   No, by the universe, madam, he does not rally
170   now; you may believe him. I do assure you, he is the hon-
    estest, worthiest, true-hearted gentleman—a man of such
    perfect honor, he would say nothing to a lady he does
    not mean.

    PINCHWIFE [*aside*]   Praising another man to his mistress!

175   HARCOURT   Sir, you are so beyond expectation obliging that—

    SPARKISH   Nay, egad, I am sure you do admire her ex-
    tremely; I see't in your eyes.—He does admire you,
    madam.—By the world, don't you?

180   HARCOURT   Yes, above the world, or the most glorious part
    of it, her whole sex; and till now I never thought I should
    have envied you, or any man about to marry, but you
    have the best excuse for marriage I ever knew.

    ALITHEA   Nay, now, sir, I'm satisfied you are of the soci-
185   ety of the wits and railleurs, since you cannot spare
    your friend, even when he is but too civil to you; but
    the surest sign is, since you are an enemy to marriage,
    for that, I hear, you hate as much as business or bad
    wine.

190   HARCOURT   Truly, madam, I never was an enemy to mar-
    riage till now, because marriage was never an enemy to
    me before.

---

5. Makes a gesture of greeting; greets with a kiss.

ALITHEA   But why, sir, is marriage an enemy to you now?
Because it robs you of your friend here? For you look
upon a friend married as one gone into a monastery,
that is, dead to the world.

HARCOURT   'Tis indeed because you marry him; I see,
madam, you can guess my meaning. I do confess heartily and openly, I wish it were in my power to break the
match; by heavens I would.

SPARKISH   Poor Frank!

ALITHEA   Would you be so unkind to me?

HARCOURT   No, no, 'tis not because I would be unkind to
you.

SPARKISH   Poor Frank! No, gad, 'tis only his kindness to me.

PINCHWIFE [aside]   Great kindness to you indeed! Insensible fop, let a man make love to his wife to his face!

SPARKISH   Come, dear Frank, for all my wife there that
shall be, thou shalt enjoy me sometimes, dear rogue.
By my honor, we men of wit condole for our deceased
brother in marriage as much as for one dead in earnest. I think that was prettily said of me, ha, Harcourt?
But come, Frank, be not melancholy for me.

HARCOURT   No, I assure you I am not melancholy for you.

SPARKISH   Prithee, Frank, dost think my wife that shall
be there a fine person?

HARCOURT   I could gaze upon her till I became as blind
as you are.

SPARKISH   How, as I am? How?

HARCOURT   Because you are a lover, and true lovers are
blind, stock blind.

SPARKISH   True, true; but by the world, she has wit too,
as well as beauty. Go, go with her into a corner, and try
if she has wit; talk to her anything; she's bashful before
me.

HARCOURT   Indeed, if a woman wants° wit in a corner, she   *lacks*
has it nowhere.

ALITHEA [aside to SPARKISH]   Sir, you dispose of me a little
before your time—

SPARKISH   Nay, nay, madam, let me have an earnest of
your obedience, or—go, go, madam—

[HARCOURT *courts* ALITHEA *aside*.]

PINCHWIFE   How, sir! If you are not concerned for the
honor of a wife, I am for that of a sister; he shall not debauch her. Be a pander to your own wife, bring men to
her, let 'em make love before your face, thrust 'em into a
corner together, then leave 'em in private! Is this your
own town wit and conduct?

SPARKISH   Ha, ha, ha! A silly wise rogue would make one
laugh more than a stark fool, ha, ha! I shall burst. Nay,
you shall not disturb 'em; I'll vex thee, by the world.

[*Struggles with* PINCHWIFE *to keep him from*
HARCOURT *and* ALITHEA]

ALITHEA   The writings are drawn, sir, settlements[6] made;
'tis too late, sir, and past all revocation.

HARCOURT   Then so is my death.

ALITHEA   I would not be unjust to him.

245   HARCOURT   Then why to me so?

ALITHEA   I have no obligation to you.

HARCOURT   My love.

ALITHEA   I had his before.

HARCOURT   You never had it; he wants, you see, jealousy,
250   the only infallible sign of it.

ALITHEA   Love proceeds from esteem; he cannot distrust
my virtue; besides, he loves me, or he would not marry
me.

HARCOURT   Marrying you is no more sign of his love than
255   bribing your woman,° that he may marry you, is a sign   servant
of his generosity. Marriage is rather a sign of interest
than love; and he that marries a fortune covets a mistress, not loves her. But if you take marriage for a sign of
love, take it from me immediately.

260   ALITHEA   No, now you have put a scruple in my head; but,
in short, sir, to end our dispute, I must marry him, my
reputation would suffer in the world else.

HARCOURT   No, if you do marry him, with your pardon,
madam, your reputation suffers in the world, and you
265   would be thought in necessity for a cloak.[7]

ALITHEA   Nay, now you are rude, sir.—Mr. Sparkish, pray
come hither, your friend here is very troublesome, and
very loving.

HARCOURT   [*aside to* ALITHEA]   Hold, hold!—

270   PINCHWIFE   D'ye hear that?

SPARKISH   Why, d'ye think I'll seem to be jealous, like a
country bumpkin?

PINCHWIFE   No, rather be a cuckold, like a credulous cit.[8]

HARCOURT   Madam, you would not have been so little
275   generous as to have told him.

ALITHEA   Yes, since you could be so little generous as to
wrong him.

HARCOURT   Wrong him! No man can do't, he's beneath an
injury; a bubble,° a coward, a senseless idiot, a wretch   dupe
280   so contemptible to all the world but you that—

ALITHEA   Hold, do not rail at him, for since he is like to be
my husband, I am resolved to like him. Nay, I think I am
obliged to tell him you are not his friend.—Master
Sparkish, Master Sparkish!

6. Income or property bestowed on a future
wife.
7. In need of a cloak for traveling, disguised,
to assignations.

8. A citizen, or merchant of the city, as opposed
to a man of the town (see introduction).

285 SPARKISH What, what?—Now, dear rogue, has not she wit?

HARCOURT [*speaks surlily*] Not so much as I thought,
and hoped she had.

ALITHEA Mr. Sparkish, do you bring people to rail at you?

HARCOURT Madam—

290 SPARKISH How! No, but if he does rail at me, 'tis but in
jest, I warrant; what we wits do for one another, and
never take any notice of it.

ALITHEA He spoke so scurrilously of you, I had no patience
to hear him; besides, he has been making love to me.

295 HARCOURT [*aside*] True, damned, telltale woman!

SPARKISH Pshaw! to show° his parts°—we wits rail and   *show off / qualities*
make love often but to show our parts; as we have no
affections, so we have no malice; we—

ALITHEA He said you were a wretch, below an injury.

300 SPARKISH Pshaw!

HARCOURT [*aside*] Damned, senseless, impudent, virtuous jade! well, since she won't let me have her, she'll
do as good, she'll make me hate her.

ALITHEA A common bubble.

305 SPARKISH Pshaw!

ALITHEA A coward.

SPARKISH Pshaw, pshaw!

ALITHEA A senseless, driveling idiot.

SPARKISH How! Did he disparage my parts? Nay, then my
310 honor's concerned; I can't put up that, sir, by the world.
Brother, help me to kill him.—[*Aside*] I may draw° now,   *draw a sword*
since we have the odds of him.⁹ 'Tis a good occasion,
too, before my mistress—[*Offers to draw.*]

ALITHEA Hold, hold!

315 SPARKISH What, what?

ALITHEA [*aside*] I must not let 'em kill the gentleman neither, for his kindness to me; I am so far from hating him
that I wish my gallant had his person and understanding.
Nay, if my honor—

320 SPARKISH I'll be thy death.

ALITHEA Hold, hold! Indeed, to tell the truth, the gentleman said after all that what he spoke was but out of
friendship to you.

SPARKISH How! say I am—I am a fool, that is, no wit, out
325 of friendship to me?

ALITHEA Yes, to try whether I was concerned enough for
you, and made love to me only to be satisfied of my
virtue, for your sake.

HARCOURT [*aside*] Kind, however—

9. That is, we have him outnumbered.

330 SPARKISH   Nay, if it were so, my dear rogue, I ask thee pardon; but why would not you tell me so, faith?

HARCOURT   Because I did not think on't, faith.

SPARKISH   Come, Horner does not come; Harcourt, let's be gone to the new play.—Come, madam.

335 ALITHEA   I will not go if you intend to leave me alone in the box and run into the pit, as you use° to do.   *are accustomed*

SPARKISH   Pshaw! I'll leave Harcourt with you in the box to entertain you, and that's as good; if I sat in the box, I should be thought no judge, but of trimmings.°—Come, away   *(on women's clothes)*
340 away, Harcourt, lead her down.

> [*Exeunt* SPARKISH, HARCOURT, *and* ALITHEA.]

PINCHWIFE   Well, go thy ways, for the flower of the true town fops, such as spend their estates before they come to 'em, and are cuckolds before they're married. But let me go look to my own freehold.[1] How!—

> [*Enter* MY LADY FIDGET, MRS. DAINTY FIDGET, *and* MRS. SQUEAMISH.]

345 LADY FIDGET   Your servant, sir; where is your lady? We are come to wait upon° her to the new play.   *accompany*

PINCHWIFE   New play!

LADY FIDGET   And my husband will wait upon you presently.

350 PINCHWIFE [*aside*]   Damn your civility.—Madam, by no means; I will not see Sir Jasper here till I have waited upon[2] him at home; nor shall my wife see you till she has waited upon your ladyship at your lodgings.

LADY FIDGET   Now we are here, sir—

355 PINCHWIFE   No, madam.

MRS. DAINTY FIDGET   Pray, let us see her.

MRS. SQUEAMISH   We will not stir till we see her.

PINCHWIFE [*aside*]   A pox on you all! [*Goes to the door, and returns.*]—She has locked the door, and is gone abroad.°   *out of the house*
360 LADY FIDGET   No, you have locked the door, and she's within.

MRS. DAINTY FIDGET   They told us below she was here.

PINCHWIFE [*aside*]   Will nothing do?—Well, it must out then. To tell you the truth, ladies, which I was afraid to
365 let you know before, lest it might endanger your lives, my wife has just now the smallpox come out upon her. Do not be frightened; but pray, be gone, ladies; you shall not stay here in danger of your lives; pray get you gone, ladies.

370 LADY FIDGET   No, no, we have all had 'em.

MRS. SQUEAMISH   Alack, alack!

MRS. DAINTY FIDGET   Come, come, we must see how it goes with her; I understand the disease.

---

1. That is, his wife (literally, an estate owned absolutely by its possessor).   2. Paid a respectful visit to.

LADY FIDGET   Come.

375   PINCHWIFE [*aside*]   Well, there is no being too hard for women at their own weapon, lying; therefore I'll quit the field.   [*Exit* PINCHWIFE.]

MRS. SQUEAMISH   Here's an example of jealousy.

LADY FIDGET   Indeed, as the world goes, I wonder there
380   are no more jealous, since wives are so neglected.

MRS. DAINTY FIDGET   Pshaw! as the world goes, to what end should they be jealous?

LADY FIDGET   Foh! 'tis a nasty world.

MRS. SQUEAMISH   That men of parts, great acquaintance,
385   and quality should take up with and spend themselves and fortunes in keeping little playhouse creatures, foh!

LADY FIDGET   Nay, that women of understanding, great acquaintance, and good quality should fall a-keeping too of little creatures, foh!

390   MRS. SQUEAMISH   Why, 'tis the men of quality's fault; they never visit women of honor and reputation, as they used to do; and have not so much as common civility for ladies of our rank, but use us with the same indifferency and ill-breeding as if we were all married to 'em.

395   LADY FIDGET   She says true; 'tis an arrant shame women of quality should be so slighted. Methinks birth—birth should go for something; I have known men admired, courted, and followed for their titles only.

MRS. SQUEAMISH   Ay, one would think men of honor
400   should not love, no more than marry, out of their own rank.

MRS. DAINTY FIDGET   Fie, fie upon 'em! They are come to think cross-breeding for themselves best, as well as for their dogs and horses.

405   LADY FIDGET   They are dogs and horses for't.

MRS. SQUEAMISH   One would think, if not for love, for vanity a little.

MRS. DAINTY FIDGET   Nay, they do satisfy their vanity upon us sometimes; and are kind to us in their report, tell all
410   the world they lie with us.

LADY FIDGET   Damned rascals! That we should be only wronged by 'em; to report a man has had a person, when he has not had a person, is the greatest wrong in the whole world that can be done to a person.

415   MRS. SQUEAMISH   Well, 'tis an arrant shame noble persons should be so wronged and neglected.

LADY FIDGET   But still 'tis an arranter shame for a noble person to neglect her own honor, and defame her own noble person with little inconsiderable fellows, foh!

420   MRS. DAINTY FIDGET   I suppose the crime against our honor is the same with a man of quality as with another.

LADY FIDGET   How! No, sure, the man of quality is likest one's husband, and therefore the fault should be the less.

MRS. DAINTY FIDGET But then the pleasure should be the
425 less.

LADY FIDGET Fie, fie, fie, for shame, sister! Whither shall
we ramble? Be continent° in your discourse, or I shall   *chaste*
hate you.

MRS. DAINTY FIDGET Besides, an intrigue is so much the
430 more notorious for the man's quality.

MRS. SQUEAMISH 'Tis true, nobody takes notice of a private man, and therefore with him 'tis more secret, and
the crime's the less when 'tis not known.

LADY FIDGET You say true; i'faith, I think you are in the
435 right on't. 'Tis not an injury to a husband till it be an
injury to our honors; so that a woman of honor loses no
honor with a private person; and to say truth—

MRS. DAINTY FIDGET [*apart to* MRS. SQUEAMISH] So, the little fellow is grown a private person—with her—

440 LADY FIDGET But still my dear, dear honor.

[*Enter* SIR JASPER, HORNER, DORILANT.]

SIR JASPER FIDGET Ay, my dear, dear of honor, thou hast
still so much honor in thy mouth—

HORNER [*aside*] That she has none elsewhere.

LADY FIDGET Oh, what d'ye mean to bring in these upon us?

445 MRS. DAINTY FIDGET Foh! these are as bad as wits.

MRS. SQUEAMISH Foh!

LADY FIDGET Let us leave the room.

SIR JASPER FIDGET Stay, stay; faith, to tell you the naked
truth—

450 LADY FIDGET Fie, Sir Jasper! Do not use that word
"naked."

SIR JASPER FIDGET Well, well, in short, I have business at
Whitehall, and cannot go to the play with you, therefore
would have you go—

455 LADY FIDGET With those two to a play?

SIR JASPER FIDGET No, not with t'other, but with Mr.
Horner; there can be no more scandal to go with him
than with Mr. Tattle, or Master Limberham.³

LADY FIDGET With that nasty fellow! No—no!

460 SIR JASPER FIDGET Nay, prithee, dear, hear me.

[*Whispers to* LADY FIDGET.]

HORNER Ladies—

[HORNER, DORILANT *drawing near* MRS. SQUEAMISH
and MRS. DAINTY.]

MRS. DAINTY FIDGET Stand off.

MRS. SQUEAMISH Do not approach us.

MRS. DAINTY FIDGET You herd with the wits, you are ob-
465 scenity all over.

MRS. SQUEAMISH And I would as soon look upon a picture
of Adam and Eve, without fig leaves, as any of you, if I

---

3. Stock names for fops in Restoration comedies.

could help it; therefore keep off, and do not make us sick.

470 DORILANT   What a devil are these?

HORNER   Why, these are pretenders to honor, as critics to wit, only by censuring others; and as every raw, peevish, out-of-humored, affected, dull, tea-drinking, arithmetical fop sets up for a wit by railing at men of

475 sense, so these for honor by railing at the Court, and ladies of as great honor as quality.

SIR JASPER FIDGET   Come, Mr. Horner, I must desire you to go with these ladies to the play, sir.

HORNER   I, sir!

480 SIR JASPER FIDGET   Ay, ay, come, sir.

HORNER   I must beg your pardon, sir, and theirs; I will not be seen in women's company in public again for the world.

SIR JASPER FIDGET   Ha, ha! strange aversion!

485 MRS. SQUEAMISH   No, he's for women's company in private.

SIR JASPER FIDGET   He—poor man—he! Ha, ha, ha!

MRS. DAINTY FIDGET   'Tis a greater shame amongst lewd fellows to be seen in virtuous women's company than for

490 the women to be seen with them.

HORNER   Indeed, madam, the time was I only hated virtuous women, but now I hate the other too; I beg your pardon, ladies.

LADY FIDGET   You are very obliging, sir, because we would

495 not be troubled with you.

SIR JASPER FIDGET   In sober sadness,° he shall go.   *In all seriousness*

DORILANT   Nay, if he wo'not, I am ready to wait upon the ladies; and I think I am the fitter man.

SIR JASPER FIDGET   You, sir, no, I thank you for that—

500 Master Horner is a privileged man amongst the virtuous ladies; 'twill be a great while before you are so, he, he, he! He's my wife's gallant, he, he, he! No, pray withdraw, sir, for as I take it, the virtuous ladies have no business with you.

505 DORILANT   And I am sure he can have none with them. 'Tis strange a man can't come amongst virtuous women now but upon the same terms as men are admitted into the Great Turk's° seraglio; but heavens keep me from   *Ottoman Sultan's* being an ombre⁴ player with 'em! But where is Pinch-

510 wife?   [*Exit* DORILANT.]

SIR JASPER FIDGET   Come, come, man; what, avoid the sweet society of womankind? that sweet, soft, gentle, tame, noble creature, woman, made for man's companion—

HORNER   So is that soft, gentle, tame and more noble

515 creature a spaniel, and has all their tricks—can fawn, lie

---

4. A fashionable card game, with a pun on *hombre*, or "man" (Spanish).

down, suffer beating, and fawn the more; barks at your
friends when they come to see you; makes your bed
hard; gives you fleas, and the mange sometimes. And all
the difference is, the spaniel's the more faithful animal,
520 and fawns but upon one master.

SIR JASPER FIDGET He, he, he!

MRS. SQUEAMISH Oh, the rude beast!

MRS. DAINTY FIDGET Insolent brute!

LADY FIDGET Brute! Stinking, mortified, rotten French
525 wether,° to dare—

SIR JASPER FIDGET Hold, an't please your ladyship.—For
shame, Master Horner, your mother was a woman.—
[*Aside*] Now shall I never reconcile 'em.—[*Aside to*
LADY FIDGET] Hark you, madam, take my advice in your
530 anger. You know you often want one to make up your
drolling° pack of ombre players; and you may
cheat him easily, for he's an ill gamester, and consequently loves play. Besides, you know, you have but two
old civil gentlemen, with stinking breaths too, to wait
535 upon you abroad; take in the third into your service.
The other are but crazy,° and a lady should have a
supernumerary gentleman-usher, as a supernumerary
coach-horse, lest sometimes you should be forced to stay
at home.

540 LADY FIDGET But are you sure he loves play, and has
money?

SIR JASPER FIDGET He loves play as much as you, and has
money as much as I.

LADY FIDGET Then I am contented to make him pay for
545 his scurrility; money makes up in a measure all other
wants in men.—[*aside*] Those whom we cannot make
hold for gallants, we make fine.°

SIR JASPER FIDGET [*aside*] So, so; now to mollify, to wheedle him.—Master Horner, will you never keep civil com-
550 pany? Methinks 'tis time now, since you are only fit for
them. Come, come, man, you must e'en fall to visiting
our wives, eating at our tables, drinking tea with our virtuous relations after dinner, dealing cards to 'em, reading plays and gazettes to 'em, picking fleas out of their
555 shocks° for 'em, collecting receipts,° new songs, women,
pages and footmen for 'em.

HORNER I hope they'll afford me better employment, sir.

SIR JASPER FIDGET He, he, he! 'Tis fit you know your
work before you come into your place; and since
560 you are unprovided of a lady to flatter and a good
house to eat at, pray frequent mine, and call my wife
mistress, and she shall call you gallant, according to the
custom.

HORNER Who, I?

565 SIR JASPER FIDGET Faith, thou shalt for my sake; come, for
my sake only.

---

525 *astrated ram*

531 *jesting*

536 *sickly; frail*

547 *pay the penalty*

555 *poodles / recipes*

HORNER For your sake—

SIR JASPER FIDGET [*to* LADY FIDGET] Come, come here's a
gamester for you; let him be a little familiar sometimes;
570 nay, what if a little rude? Gamesters may be rude with
ladies, you know.

LADY FIDGET Yes, losing gamesters have a privilege with
women.

HORNER I always thought the contrary, that the winning
575 gamester had most privilege with women; for when you
have lost your money to a man, you'll lose anything you
have, all you have, they say, and he may use you as he
pleases.

SIR JASPER FIDGET He, he, he! Well, win or lose, you shall
580 have your liberty with her.

LADY FIDGET As he behaves himself; and for your sake I'll
give him admittance and freedom.

HORNER All sorts of freedom, madam?

SIR JASPER FIDGET Ay, ay, ay, all sorts of freedom thou
585 canst take and so go to her, begin thy new employment;
wheedle her, jest with her, and be better acquainted one
with another.

HORNER [*aside*] I think I know her already, therefore
may venture with her, my secret for hers.

[HORNER *and* LADY FIDGET *whisper.*]

590 SIR JASPER FIDGET Sister, cuz, I have provided an innocent
playfellow for you there.

MRS. DAINTY FIDGET Who, he!

MRS. SQUEAMISH There's a playfellow indeed!

SIR JASPER FIDGET Yes, sure; what, he is good enough to
595 play at cards, blindman's buff, or the fool with sometimes.

MRS. SQUEAMISH Foh! we'll have no such playfellows.

MRS. DAINTY FIDGET No, sir, you shan't choose playfellows
for us, we thank you.

600 SIR JASPER FIDGET Nay, pray hear me.

[*Whispering to them.*]

LADY FIDGET [*aside to* HORNER] But, poor gentleman, could
you be so generous, so truly a man of honor, as for the
sakes of us women of honor, to cause yourself to be reported no man? No man! And to suffer yourself the great-
605 est shame that could fall upon a man, that none might
fall upon us women by your conversation? But indeed,
sir, as perfectly, perfectly, the same man as before your
going into France, sir? as perfectly, perfectly, sir?

HORNER As perfectly, perfectly, madam. Nay, I scorn you
610 should take my word; I desire to be tried only, madam.

LADY FIDGET Well, that's spoken again like a man of
honor; all men of honor desire to come to the test.
But, indeed, generally you men report such things of

yourselves, one does not know how or whom to believe;
615 and it is come to that pass we dare not take your words,
no more than your tailor's, without some staid servant of
yours be bound with you. But I have so strong a faith in
your honor, dear, dear, noble sir, that I'd forfeit mine for
yours at any time, dear sir.

620 HORNER   No, madam, you should not need to forfeit it for
me; I have given you security already to save you harmless, my late reputation being so well known in the world,
madam.

LADY FIDGET   But if upon any future falling out, or upon a
625 suspicion of my taking the trust out of your hands, to
employ some other, you yourself should betray your
trust, dear sir? I mean, if you'll give me leave to speak
obscenely, you might tell, dear sir.

HORNER   If I did, nobody would believe me; the reputation
630 of impotency is as hardly recovered again in the world as
that of cowardice, dear madam.

LADY FIDGET   Nay then, as one may say, you may do your
worst, dear, dear sir.

SIR JASPER FIDGET   Come, is your ladyship reconciled to
635 him yet? Have you agreed on matters? For I must be
gone to Whitehall.

LADY FIDGET   Why, indeed, Sir Jasper, Master Horner is a
thousand, thousand times a better man than I thought
him. Cousin Squeamish, Sister Dainty, I can name him
640 now; truly, not long ago, you know, I thought his very
name obscenity, and I would as soon have lain with him
as have named him.

SIR JASPER FIDGET   Very likely, poor madam.

MRS. DAINTY FIDGET   I believe it.

645 MRS. SQUEAMISH   No doubt on't.

SIR JASPER FIDGET   Well, well—that your ladyship is as virtuous as any she, I know, and him all the town knows—
he, he, he! Therefore, now you like him, get you gone to
your business together; go, go to your business, I say, plea-
650 sure, whilst I go to my pleasure, business.

LADY FIDGET   Come, then, dear gallant.

HORNER   Come away, my dearest mistress.

SIR JASPER FIDGET   So, so; why, 'tis as I'd have it.

[Exit SIR JASPER.]

HORNER   And as I'd have it.
655 LADY FIDGET

> *Who for his business from his wife will run,*
> *Takes the best care to have her business done.*

[*Exeunt* OMNES.°]   *They exit (Latin)*

3.1

[SCENE: PINCHWIFE's *house*.]

[ALITHEA *and* MRS. PINCHWIFE.]

ALITHEA Sister, what ails you? You are grown melancholy.

MRS. PINCHWIFE Would it not make anyone melancholy, to see you go every day fluttering about abroad, whilst I must stay at home like a poor, lonely, sullen bird in a
5 cage?

ALITHEA Ay, sister, but you came young and just from the nest to your cage, so that I thought you liked it, and could be as cheerful in't as others that took their flight themselves early, and are hopping abroad in the open air.

10 MRS. PINCHWIFE Nay, I confess I was quiet enough till my husband told me what pure° lives the London ladies live abroad, with their dancing, meetings, and junketings, and dressed every day in their best gowns; and I warrant you, play at ninepins⁵ every day of the week, so they do.

fine, splendid

[*Enter* MR. PINCHWIFE.]

15 PINCHWIFE Come, what's here to do? You are putting the town pleasures in her head, and setting her a-longing.

ALITHEA Yes, after ninepins; you suffer none to give her those longings, you mean, but yourself.

PINCHWIFE I tell her of the vanities of the town like a
20 confessor.

ALITHEA A confessor! Just such a confessor as he that, by forbidding a silly° ostler to grease the horse's teeth,⁶ taught him to do't.

ignorant

PINCHWIFE Come, Mistress Flippant, good precepts are
25 lost when bad examples are still before us; the liberty you take abroad makes her hanker after it, and out of hu-mour at home. Poor wretch! she desired not to come to London; I would bring her.

ALITHEA Very well.

30 PINCHWIFE She has been this week in town, and never desired, till this afternoon, to go abroad.

ALITHEA Was she not at a play yesterday?

PINCHWIFE Yes, but she ne'er asked me; I was myself the cause of her going.

35 ALITHEA Then, if she ask you again, you are the cause of her asking, and not my example.

PINCHWIFE Well, tomorrow night I shall be rid of you; and the next day, before 'tis light, she and I'll be rid of the town, and my dreadful apprehensions.—[*To* MRS.
40 PINCHWIFE] Come, be not melancholy, for thou shalt go into the country after tomorrow, dearest.

ALITHEA Great comfort!

---

5. A bowling game considered unfashionable.
6. An innkeeper's trick to keep a horse from eating (thereby saving money).

MRS. PINCHWIFE   Pish! what d'ye tell me of the country for?

PINCHWIFE   How's this! What, pish at the country?

45   MRS. PINCHWIFE   Let me alone, I am not well.

PINCHWIFE   Oh, if that be all—what ails my dearest?

MRS. PINCHWIFE   Truly I don't know; but I have not been well since you told me there was a gallant at the play in love with me.

50   PINCHWIFE   Ha!—

ALITHEA   That's by my example too!

PINCHWIFE   Nay, if you are not well, but are so concerned because a lewd fellow chanced to lie, and say he liked you, you'll make me sick too.

55   MRS. PINCHWIFE   Of what sickness?

PINCHWIFE   Oh, of that which is worse than the plague, jealousy.

MRS. PINCHWIFE   Pish, you jeer! I'm sure there's no such disease in our receipt-book at home.

60   PINCHWIFE   No, thou never met'st with it, poor innocent.—[Aside] Well, if thou cuckold me, 'twill be my own fault—for cuckolds and bastards are generally makers of their own fortune.

MRS. PINCHWIFE   Well, but pray, bud, let's go to a play
65   tonight.

PINCHWIFE   'Tis just done, she comes from it. But why are you so eager to see a play?

MRS. PINCHWIFE   Faith, dear, not that I care one pin for their talk there; but I like to look upon the playermen,
70   and would see, if I could, the gallant you say loves me; that's all, dear bud.

PINCHWIFE   Is that all, dear bud?

ALITHEA   This proceeds from my example.

MRS. PINCHWIFE   But if the play be done, let's go abroad,
75   however dear bud.

PINCHWIFE   Come, have a little patience, and thou shalt go into the country on Friday.

MRS. PINCHWIFE   Therefore I would see first some sights, to tell me neighbors of. Nay, I will go abroad, that's
80   once.

ALITHEA   I'm the cause of this desire too.

PINCHWIFE   But now I think on't, who was the cause of Horner's coming to my lodging today? That was you.

85   ALITHEA   No, you, because you would not let him see your handsome wife out of your lodging.

MRS. PINCHWIFE   Why, O Lord! did the gentleman come hither to see me indeed?

PINCHWIFE   No, no.—You are not cause of that damned
90   question too, Mistress Alithea?—[Aside] Well, she's in the right in it. He is in love with my wife—and comes after her—'tis so—but I'll nip his love in the bud; lest he should follow us into the country, and break his chariot-wheel near our house on purpose for an excuse to come
95   to't. But I think I know the town.

MRS. PINCHWIFE Come, pray, bud, let's go abroad before 'tis late; for I will go, that's flat and plain.

PINCHWIFE [*aside*] So! the obstinacy already of a town-wife, and I must, whilst she's here, humour her like one.
100 —Sister, how shall we do, that she may not be seen or known?

ALITHEA Let her put on her mask.

PINCHWIFE Pshaw! A mask makes people but the more inquisitive, and is as ridiculous a disguise as a stage-beard;
105 her shape, stature, habit will be known. And if we should meet with Horner, he would be sure to take acquaintance with us, must wish her joy, kiss her, talk to her, leer upon her, and the devil and all. No, I'll not use her to a mask, 'tis dangerous; for masks have made more cuckolds than the
110 best faces that ever were known.

ALITHEA How will you do then?

MRS. PINCHWIFE Nay, shall we go? The Exchange[7] will be shut, and I have a mind to see that.

PINCHWIFE So—I have it—I'll dress her up in the suit
115 we are to carry down to her brother, little sir James; nay, I understand the town tricks. Come, let's go dress her. A mask! No—a woman masked, like a covered dish, gives a man curiosity and appetite, when, it may be, uncovered, 'twould turn his stomach; no, no.

120 ALITHEA Indeed your comparison is something a greasy° one. But I had a gentle gallant used to say, "A beauty masked, like the sun in eclipse, gathers together more gazers than if it shined out."

low, obscene

[*Exeunt.*]

3.2

[SCENE: *The scene changes to the New Exchange.*]

[*Enter* HORNER, HARCOURT, DORILANT.]

DORILANT Engaged to women, and not sup with us?

HORNER Ay, a pox on 'em all!

HARCOURT You were much a more reasonable man in the morning, and had as noble resolutions against 'em
5 as a widower of a week's liberty.

DORILANT Did I ever think to see you keep company with women in vain?

HORNER In vain! No—'tis, since I can't love 'em, to be revenged on 'em.

10 HARCOURT Now your sting is gone, you looked in the box, amongst all those women, like a drone in the hive, all upon you; shoved and ill-used by 'em all, and thrust from one side to t'other.

7. The New Exchange (see 2.1, first note 2).

DORILANT Yet he must be buzzing amongst 'em still, like
15   other old beetle-headed,° liquorish° drones. Avoid 'em,   *stupid / fond of liquor*
  and hate 'em as they hate you.

HORNER Because I do hate 'em, and would hate 'em yet
  more, I'll frequent 'em; you may see by marriage, nothing
  makes a man hate a woman more than her constant con
20   versation. In short, I converse with 'em, as you do with rich
  fools, to laugh at 'em and use 'em ill.

DORILANT But I would no more sup with women, unless
  I could lie with 'em, than sup with a rich coxcomb,
  unless I could cheat him.

25 HORNER Yes, I have known thee sup with a fool for his
  drinking; if he could set out your hand° that way only,   *serve your purpose*
  you were satisfied, and if he were a wine-swallowing
  mouth 'twas enough.

HARCOURT Yes, a man drinks often with a fool, as he tosses
30   with a marker,[8] only to keep his hand in ure.° But   *practice*
  do the ladies drink?

HORNER Yes, sir, and I shall have the pleasure at least of
  laying 'em flat with a bottle, and bring as much scandal
  that way upon 'em as formerly t'other.

35 HARCOURT Perhaps you may prove as weak a brother
  amongst 'em that way as t'other.

DORILANT Foh! drinking with women is as unnatural as
  scolding with 'em; but 'tis a pleasure of decayed fornica-
  tors, and the basest way of quenching love.

40 HARCOURT Nay, 'tis drowning love instead of quenching
  it. But leave us for civil women too!

DORILANT Ay, when he can't be the better for 'em. We
  hardly pardon a man that leaves his friend for a wench,
  and that's a pretty lawful call.

45 HORNER Faith, I would not leave you for 'em, if they
  would not drink.

DORILANT Who would disappoint his company at Lewis's[9]
  for a gossiping?

HARCOURT Foh! Wine and women, good apart, together
50   as nauseous as sack[1] and sugar. But hark you, sir,
  before you go, a little of your advice; an old maimed
  general, when unfit for action, is fittest for counsel.
  I have other designs upon women than eating and
  drinking with them. I am in love with Sparkish's mis-
55   tress, whom he is to marry tomorrow. Now how shall
  I get her?

        [*Enter* SPARKISH, *looking about.*]

HORNER Why, here comes one will help you to her.

HARCOURT He! He, I tell you, is my rival, and will hinder
  my love.

---

8. Plays dice with the scorekeeper.
9. A fashionable tavern.

1. Spanish white wine, often drunk with sugar.

60 HORNER   No, a foolish rival and a jealous husband assist
their rival's designs; for they are sure to make their
women hate them, which is the first step to their love for
another man.

HARCOURT   But I cannot come near his mistress but in his
65 company.

HORNER   Still the better for you, for fools are most easily
cheated when they themselves are accessories; and he
is to be bubbled° of his mistress, as of his money, the   *cheated*
common mistress, by keeping him company.

70 SPARKISH   Who is that, that is to be bubbled? Faith, let me
snack,° I han't met with a bubble since Christmas. Gad,   *share*
I think bubbles are like their brother woodcocks,[2]
go out with cold weather.

HARCOURT [*apart to* HORNER]   A pox! he did not hear all,
75 I hope.

SPARKISH   Come, you bubbling rogues you, where do
we sup?—Oh, Harcourt, my mistress tells me you
have been making fierce love to her all the play long,
ha, ha! But I—

80 HARCOURT   I make love to her?

SPARKISH   Nay, I forgive thee; for I think I know thee,
and I know her, but I am sure I know myself.

HARCOURT   Did she tell you so? I see all women are like
these of the Exchange, who, to enhance the price of
85 their commodities, report to their fond customers
offers which were never made 'em.

HORNER   Ay, women are as apt to tell before the intrigue
as men after it, and so show themselves the vainer sex.
But hast thou a mistress, Sparkish? 'Tis as hard for me
90 to believe it as that thou ever hadst a bubble, as you
bragged just now.

SPARKISH   Oh, your servant, sir; are you at your raillery,
sir? But we were some of us beforehand with you today
at the play. The wits were something bold with you, sir;
95 did you not hear us laugh?

HORNER   Yes, but I thought you had gone to plays to
laugh at the poet's wit, not at your own.

SPARKISH   Your servant, sir; no, I thank you. Gad, I go to
a play as to a country treat; I carry my own wine to one,
100 and my own wit to t'other, or else I'm sure I should not
be merry at either. And the reason why we are so often
louder than the players is because we think we speak
more wit, and so become the poet's rivals in his audience. For to tell you the truth, we hate the silly rogues;
105 nay, so much that we find fault even with their bawdy°   *lewdness*
upon the stage, whilst we talk nothing else in the pit as
loud.

2. Proverbially stupid birds, easily snared.

HORNER　But why shouldst thou hate the silly poets? Thou
hast too much wit to be one, and they, like whores, are
110　only hated by each other; and thou dost scorn writing, I'm
sure.

SPARKISH　Yes, I'd have you to know I scorn writing; but
women, women, that make men do all foolish things,
make 'em write songs too; everybody does it. 'Tis even as
115　common with lovers as playing with fans; and you can no
more help rhyming to your Phyllis than drinking to your
Phyllis.[3]

HARCOURT　Nay, poetry in love is no more to be avoided
than jealousy.

120　DORILANT　But the poets damned your songs, did they?

SPARKISH　Damn the poets! They turned 'em into burlesque, as they call it. That burlesque is a hocus-pocus
trick they have got, which, by the virtue of *hictius doc-
tius*,[4] *topsy-turvy*, they make a wise and witty man in the
125　world a fool upon the stage, you know not how; and 'tis
therefore I hate 'em too, for I know not but it may be my
own case; for they'll put a man into a play for looking
asquint. Their predecessors were contented to make
serving-men only their stage-fools, but these rogues must
130　have gentlemen, with a pox to 'em, nay, knights. And,
indeed, you shall hardly see a fool upon the stage but he's
a knight; and to tell you the truth, they have kept me these
six years from being a knight in earnest, for fear of being
knighted in a play, and dubbed a fool.

135　DORILANT　Blame 'em not; they must follow their copy, the
age.

HARCOURT　But why shouldst thou be afraid of being in a
play, who expose yourself every day in the playhouses,
and at public places?

140　HORNER　'Tis but being on the stage, instead of standing
on a bench in the pit.

DORILANT　Don't you give money to painters to draw you
like?° And are you afraid of your pictures at length in a　　*your likeness*
playhouse, where all your mistresses may see you?

145　SPARKISH　A pox! Painters don't draw the smallpox or pim-
ples in one's face. Come, damn all your silly authors
whatever, all books and booksellers, by the world, and all
readers, courteous or uncourteous.

HARCOURT　But who comes here, Sparkish?

> [*Enter* MR. PINCHWIFE, *and his wife in man's
> clothes,* ALITHEA, LUCY *her maid.*]

150　SPARKISH　Oh, hide me! There's my mistress too.

> [SPARKISH *hides himself behind* HARCOURT.]

HARCOURT　She sees you.

---

3. Conventional name of the shepherd's
beloved in pastoral verse.

4. Pseudo-Latin phrase used by jugglers and
street magicians.

SPARKISH But I will not see her. 'Tis time to go to Whitehall, and I must not fail the drawing room.

HARCOURT Pray, first carry me, and reconcile me to her.

155 SPARKISH Another time; faith, the king will have supped.

HARCOURT Not with the worse stomach for thy absence; thou art one of those fools that think their attendance at the king's meals[5] as necessary as his physicians', when you are more troublesome to him than his doc-

160 tors, or his dogs.

SPARKISH Pshaw! I know my interest, sir; prithee, hide me.

HORNER Your servant, Pinchwife.—What, he knows us not!

PINCHWIFE [to his wife aside] Come along.

165 MRS. PINCHWIFE Pray, have you any ballads? Give me sixpenny worth.

CLASP[6] We have no ballads.

MRS. PINCHWIFE Then give me *Covent Garden Drollery*, and a play or two—Oh, here's *Tarugo's Wiles*, and *The*

170 *Slighted Maiden*,[7] I'll have them.

PINCHWIFE [apart to her] No, plays are not for your reading. Come along; will you discover° yourself?   reveal

HORNER Who is that pretty youth with him, Sparkish?

SPARKISH I believe his wife's brother, because he's

175 something like her; but I never saw her but once.

HORNER Extremely handsome; I have seen a face like it too. Let us follow 'em.

[*Exeunt* PINCHWIFE, MRS. PINCHWIFE, ALITHEA,
LUCY, HORNER, DORILANT *following them.*]

HARCOURT Come, Sparkish, your mistress saw you, and will be angry you go not to her. Besides, I would

180 fain° be reconciled to her, which none but you can   prefer to
do, dear friend.

SPARKISH Well, that's a better reason, dear friend. I would not go near her now, for hers or my own sake, but I can deny you nothing; for though I have known

185 thee a great while, never go, if I do not love thee as well as a new acquaintance.

HARCOURT I am obliged to you indeed, dear friend. I would be well with her, only to be well with thee still; for these ties to wives usually dissolve all ties to friends.

190 I would be contented she should enjoy you a-night, but I would have you to myself a-days, as I have had, dear friend.

SPARKISH And thou shalt enjoy me a-days, dear, dear

friend, never stir; and I'll be divorced from her sooner
195 than from thee. Come along.

HARCOURT [*aside*]   So, we are hard put to't when we make
our rival our procurer; but neither she nor her brother
would let me come near her now. When all's done, a ri-val
is the best cloak to steal to a mistress under, without
200 suspicion; and when we have once got to her as we desire, we throw him off like other cloaks.

[*Exit* SPARKISH, *and* HARCOURT *following him.*]

[*Re-enter* MR. PINCHWIFE, MRS. PINCHWIFE *in man's
clothes.*]

PINCHWIFE [*to* ALITHEA *offstage*]   Sister, if you will not go,
we must leave you.—[*Aside.*] The fool her gallant and
she will muster up all the young saunterers of this
205 place, and they will leave their dear seamstress to follow us. What a swarm of cuckolds, and cuckold-
makers, are here!—Come, let's be gone, Mistress
Margery.

MRS. PINCHWIFE   Don't you believe that, I han't half my
210 bellyfull of sights yet.

PINCHWIFE   Then walk this way.

MRS. PINCHWIFE   Lord, what a power° of brave° signs   great deal / grand
are here! Stay—the Bull's-Head, the Ram's-Head, and the
Stag's-Head, dear—

215 PINCHWIFE   Nay, if every husband's proper sign° here   i.e., cuckold's horn
were visible, they would be all alike.

MRS. PINCHWIFE   What d'ye mean by that, bud?

PINCHWIFE   'Tis no matter—no matter, bud.

MRS. PINCHWIFE   Pray tell me; nay, I will know.

220 PINCHWIFE   They would be all bulls', stags', and rams'
heads.

[*Exeunt* MR. PINCHWIFE, MRS. PINCHWIFE.]

[*Re-enter* SPARKISH, HARCOURT, ALITHEA, LUCY,
at t'other door.]

SPARKISH   Come, dear madam, for my sake you shall be
reconciled to him.

ALITHEA   For your sake I hate him.

225 HARCOURT   That's something too cruel, madam, to hate
me for his sake.

SPARKISH   Ay indeed, madam, too, too cruel to me, to hate
my friend for my sake.

ALITHEA   I hate him because he is your enemy; and you
230 ought to hate him too, for making love to me, if you
love me.

SPARKISH   That's a good one; I hate a man for loving
you! If he did love you, 'tis but what he can't help;
and 'tis your fault, not his, if he admires you. I hate a man
235 for being of my opinion! I'll ne'er do't, by the world.

ALITHEA   Is it for your honor or mine, to suffer a man to
make love to me, who am to marry you tomorrow?

SPARKISH It is for your honor or mine, to have me jeal-
240 ous? That he makes love to you is a sign you are handsome; and that I am not jealous is a sign you are
virtuous. That, I think, is for your honor.

ALITHEA But 'tis your honor too I am concerned for.

HARCOURT But why, dearest madam, will you be more
245 concerned for his honor than he is himself? Let his
honor alone, for my sake and his. He, he has no honor—

SPARKISH How's that?

HARCOURT But what my dear friend can guard himself.

SPARKISH O ho—that's right again.

250 HARCOURT Your care of his honor argues his neglect of it,
which is no honor to my dear friend here; therefore once
more, let his honor go which way it will, dear madam.

SPARKISH Ay, ay, were it for my honor to marry a woman
whose virtue I suspected, and could not trust her in a
255 friend's hands?

ALITHEA Are you not afraid to lose me?

HARCOURT He afraid to lose you, madam! No, no—you may
see how the most estimable and most glorious creature in
the world is valued by him. Will you not see it?

260 SPARKISH Right, honest Frank, I have that noble value
for her that I cannot be jealous of her.

ALITHEA You mistake him, he means you care not for
me, nor who has me.

SPARKISH Lord, madam, I see you are jealous.° Will you   *furious*
265 wrest a poor man's meaning from his words?

ALITHEA You astonish me, sir, with your want of jealousy.

SPARKISH And you make me giddy, madam, with your
jealousy and fears, and virtue and honor. Gad, I see
virtue makes a woman as troublesome as a little read-
270 ing or learning.

ALITHEA Monstrous!

LUCY [*behind*] Well, to see what easy husbands these
women of quality can meet with; a poor chambermaid can
never have such lady-like luck. Besides, he's thrown away
275 upon her; she'll make no use of her fortune, her blessing;
none to° a gentleman for a pure cuckold, for it requires   *there is no one like*
good breeding to be a cuckold.

ALITHEA I tell you then plainly, he pursues me to marry me.

SPARKISH Pshaw!

280 HARCOURT Come, madam, you see you strive in vain to
make him jealous of me; my dear friend is the kindest
creature in the world to me.

SPARKISH Poor fellow.

HARCOURT But his kindness only is not enough for me,
285 without your favor; your good opinion, dear madam, 'tis
that must perfect my happiness. Good gentleman, he
believes all I say; would you would do so. Jealous of me!
I would not wrong him nor you for the world.

SPARKISH   Look you there; hear him, hear him, and do not
290   walk away so.

[ALITHEA *walks carelessly to and fro.*]

HARCOURT   I love you, madam, so—

SPARKISH   How's that! Nay—now you begin to go too far
indeed.

HARCOURT   So much, I confess, I say I love you, that I
295   would not have you miserable, and cast yourself away
upon so unworthy and inconsiderable a thing as what
you see here.

[*Clapping his hand on his breast, points at* SPARKISH.]

SPARKISH   No, faith, I believe thou wouldst not; now his
meaning is plain. But I knew before thou wouldst not
300   wrong me nor her.

HARCOURT   No, no, heavens forbid the glory of her sex
should fall so low as into the embraces of such a contemptible wretch, the last of mankind—my dear friend
here—I injure him! [*Embracing* SPARKISH.]

305 ALITHEA   Very well.

SPARKISH   No, no, dear friend, I knew it.—Madam, you
see he will rather wrong himself than me, in giving himself
such names.

ALITHEA   Do not you understand him yet?

310 SPARKISH   Yes, how modestly he speaks of himself, poor
fellow.

ALITHEA   Methinks he speaks imprudently of yourself,
since—before yourself too; insomuch that I can no longer suffer his scurrilous abusiveness to you, no more
315   than his love to me. [*Offers to go.*]

SPARKISH   Nay, nay, madam, pray stay—his love to you!
Lord, madam, has he not spoke yet plain enough?

ALITHEA   Yes, indeed, I should think so.

SPARKISH   Well then, by the world, a man can't speak
320   civilly to a woman now but presently° she says he   *immediately*
makes love to her. Nay, madam, you shall stay, with
your pardon, since you have not yet understood him,
till he has made an *éclaircissement*° of his love to you,   *explanation (French)*
that is, what kind of love it is.—[*To* HARCOURT] Answer
325   to thy catechism. Friend, do you love my mistress
here?

HARCOURT   Yes, I wish she would not doubt it.

SPARKISH   But how do you love her?

HARCOURT   With all my soul.

330 ALITHEA   I thank him; methinks he speaks plain enough
now.

SPARKISH [*to* ALITHEA]   You are out° still.—But with what   *mistaken*
kind of love, Harcourt?

HARCOURT   With the best and truest love in the world.

335 SPARKISH   Look you there then, that is with no matrimonial love, I'm sure.

ALITHEA How's that? Do you say matrimonial love is not best?

SPARKISH Gad, I went too far ere I was aware. But speak
340   for thyself, Harcourt; you said you would not wrong me nor her.

HARCOURT No, no, madam, e'en take him for heaven's sake—

SPARKISH Look you there, madam.

345 HARCOURT Who should in all justice be yours, he that loves you most. [*Claps his hand on his breast.*]

ALITHEA Look you there, Mr. Sparkish, who's that?

SPARKISH Who should it be?—Go on, Harcourt.

HARCOURT Who loves you more than women titles, or
350   fortune fools. [*Points at* SPARKISH.]

SPARKISH Look you there, he means me still, for he points at me.

ALITHEA Ridiculous!

HARCOURT Who can only match your faith and con-
355   stancy in love.

SPARKISH Ay.

HARCOURT Who knows, if it be possible, how to value so much beauty and virtue.

SPARKISH Ay.

360 HARCOURT Whose love can no more be equaled in the world than that heavenly form of yours.

SPARKISH No.

HARCOURT Who could no more suffer a rival than your absence, and yet could no more suspect your virtue than
365   his own constancy in his love to you.

SPARKISH No.

HARCOURT Who, in fine,° loves you better than his eyes,   *in conclusion*
  that first made him love you.

SPARKISH Ay—nay, madam, faith, you shan't go till—

370 ALITHEA Have a care, lest you make me stay too long—

SPARKISH But till he has saluted you; that I· may be assured you are friends, after his honest advice and declaration. Come, pray, madam, be friends with him.

     [*Enter* MR. PINCHWIFE, MRS. PINCHWIFE.]

375 ALITHEA You must pardon me, sir, that I am not yet so obedient to you.

PINCHWIFE What, invite your wife to kiss men? Monstrous! Are you not ashamed? I will never forgive you.

SPARKISH Are you not ashamed that I should have more confidence in the chastity of your family than you
380   have? You must not teach me; I am a man of honor, sir,   *unrestricted / candid*
  though I am frank and free;° I am frank,° sir—   *generous*

PINCHWIFE Very frank,° sir, to share your wife with your friends.

SPARKISH He is an humble, menial friend, such as recon-
385   ciles the differences of the marriage bed. You know man

and wife do not always agree; I design him for that use, therefore would have him well with my wife.

PINCHWIFE A menial friend! you will get a great many menial friends by showing your wife as you do.

390 SPARKISH What then? It may be I have a pleasure in't, as I have to show fine clothes at a playhouse the first day, and count money before poor rogues.

PINCHWIFE He that shows his wife or money will be in danger of having them borrowed sometimes.

395 SPARKISH I love to be envied, and would not marry a wife that I alone could love; loving alone is as dull as eating alone. Is it not a frank age? and I am a frank person. And to tell you the truth, it may be I love to have rivals in a wife, they make her seem to a man still but as a

400 kept mistress; and so good night, for I must to Whitehall.—Madam, I hope you are now reconciled to my friend; and so I wish you a good night, madam, and sleep if you can, for tomorrow you know I must visit you early with a canonical gentleman.[8] Good night, dear

405 Harcourt.   [*Exit* SPARKISH.]

HARCOURT Madam, I hope you will not refuse my visit tomorrow, if it should be earlier, with a canonical gentleman, than Mr. Sparkish's.

PINCHWIFE This gentlewoman is yet under my care;

410 therefore you must yet forbear your freedom with her, sir. [*Coming between* ALITHEA *and* HARCOURT.]

HARCOURT Must, sir!—

PINCHWIFE Yes, sir, she is my sister.

HARCOURT 'Tis well she is, sir—for I must be her servant,

415 sir.—Madam—

PINCHWIFE Come away, sister; we had been gone, if it had not been for you, and so avoided these lewd rakehells,° *vile rakes* who seem to haunt us.

[*Enter* HORNER, DORILANT *to them.*]

HORNER How now, Pinchwife!

420 PINCHWIFE Your servant.

HORNER What! I see a little time in the country makes a man turn wild and unsociable, and only fit to converse with his horses, dogs, and his herds.

PINCHWIFE I have business, sir, and must mind it; your

425 business is pleasure; therefore you and I must go different ways.

HORNER Well, you may go on, but this pretty young gentleman—[*Takes hold of* MRS. PINCHWIFE.]

HARCOURT The lady—

430 DORILANT And the maid—

HORNER Shall stay with us, for I suppose their business is the same with ours, pleasure.

8. That is, a minister (to marry them).

PINCHWIFE [*aside*] 'Sdeath, he knows her, she carries it
    so sillily!° Yet if he does not, I should be more silly to   *badly; foolishly*
435 discover° it first.   *reveal*
ALITHEA Pray, let us go, sir.
PINCHWIFE Come, come—
HORNER [*to* MRS. PINCHWIFE] Had you not rather stay
    with us? —Prithee, Pinchwife, who is this pretty young
440 gentleman?
PINCHWIFE One to whom I'm a guardian. —[*Aside*] I wish
    I could keep her out of your hands.
HORNER Who is he? I never saw anything so pretty in all
    my life.
445 PINCHWIFE Pshaw! do not look upon him so much; he's a
    poor bashful youth, you'll put him out of countenance.
    —Come away, brother. [*Offers to take her away.*]
HORNER Oh, your brother.
PINCHWIFE Yes, my wife's brother. —Come, come, she'll
450 stay supper for us.
HORNER I thought so, for he is very like her I saw you at
    the play with, whom I told you I was in love with.
MRS. PINCHWIFE [*aside*] O jeminy! Is this he that was in
    love with me? I am glad on it, I vow, for he's a curious°   *excellent*
455 fine gentleman, and I love him already too. —[*To* MR.
    PINCHWIFE] Is this he, bud?
PINCHWIFE [*to his wife*] Come away, come away.
HORNER Why, what haste are you in? Why won't you let
    me talk with him?
460 PINCHWIFE Because you'll debauch him; he's yet young
    and innocent, and I would not have him debauched for
    anything in the world. —[*Aside.*] How she gazes on him!
    the devil!
HORNER Harcourt, Dorilant, look you here; this is the
465 likeness of that dowdy° he told us of, his wife. Did you   *unattractive woman*
    ever see a lovelier creature? The rogue has reason to be
    jealous of his wife, since she is like him, for she would
    make all that see her in love with her.
HARCOURT And as I remember now, she is as like him
470 here as can be.
DORILANT She is indeed very pretty, if she be like him.
HORNER Very pretty? A very pretty commendation! —She
    is a glorious creature, beautiful beyond all things I ever
    beheld.
475 PINCHWIFE So, so.
HARCOURT More beautiful than a poet's first mistress of
    imagination.
HORNER Or another man's last mistress of flesh and
    blood.
480 MRS. PINCHWIFE Nay, now you jeer, sir; pray don't jeer me.
PINCHWIFE Come, come. —[*Aside*] By heavens, she'll
    discover herself!

HORNER   I speak of your sister, sir.

PINCHWIFE   Ay, but saying she was handsome, if like him,
485   made him blush. —[*Aside*] I am upon a rack!

HORNER   Methinks he is so handsome he should not be a
man.

PINCHWIFE [*aside*]   Oh, there 'tis out! He has discovered
her! I am not able to suffer any longer. —[*To his wife*]
490   Come, come away, I say.

HORNER   Nay, by your leave, sir, he shall not go yet. —[*To
them*] Harcourt, Dorilant, let us torment this jealous
rogue a little.

HARCOURT, DORILANT   How?

495   HORNER   I'll show you.

PINCHWIFE   Come, pray let him go, I cannot stay fooling
any longer; I tell you his sister stays supper for us.

HORNER   Does she? Come then, we'll all go sup with her
and thee.

500   PINCHWIFE   No, now I think on't, having stayed so long for
us, I warrant she's gone to bed. —[*Aside*] I wish she and
I were well out of their hands. —Come, I must rise early
tomorrow, come.

HORNER   Well, then, if she be gone to bed, I wish her and
505   you a good night. But pray, young gentlemen, present my
humble service to her.

MRS. PINCHWIFE   Thank you heartily, sir.

PINCHWIFE [*aside*]   'Sdeath! she will discover herself yet in
spite of me. —He is something more civil to you, for
510   your kindness to his sister, than I am, it seems.

HORNER   Tell her, dear sweet little gentleman, for all your
brother there, that you revived the love I had for her at
first sight in the playhouse.

MRS. PINCHWIFE   But did you love her indeed, and indeed?

515   PINCHWIFE [*aside*]   So, so. —Away, I say.

HORNER   Nay, stay. Yes, indeed, and indeed, pray do you
tell her so, and give her this kiss from me. [*Kisses her.*]

PINCHWIFE [*aside*]   O heavens! what do I suffer! Now 'tis
too plain he knows her, and yet—

520   HORNER   And this, and this—[*Kisses her again.*]

MRS. PINCHWIFE   What do you kiss me for? I am no woman.

PINCHWIFE [*aside*]   So—there, 'tis out. —Come, I cannot,
nor will stay any longer.

HORNER   Nay, they shall send your lady a kiss too. Here,
525   Harcourt, Dorilant, will you not?

[*They kiss her.*]

PINCHWIFE [*aside*]   How! do I suffer this? Was I not accusing another just now for this rascally patience, in permitting his wife to be kissed before his face? Ten thousand
ulcers gnaw away their lips! —Come, come.

530   HORNER   Good night, dear little gentleman; madam, good
night; farewell, Pinchwife. —[*Apart to* HARCOURT *and*

DORILANT] Did not I tell you I would raise his jealous
gall?

[*Exeunt* HORNER, HARCOURT, *and* DORILANT.]

PINCHWIFE   So, they are gone at last; stay, let me see first
535   if the coach be at this door.   [*Exit.*]

[HORNER, HARCOURT, DORILANT *return.*]

HORNER   What, not gone yet? Will you be sure to do as I
desired you, sweet sir?

MRS. PINCHWIFE   Sweet sir, but what will you give me
then?

540   HORNER   Anything. Come away into the next walk.

[*Exit* HORNER, *hauling away* MRS. PINCHWIFE.]

ALITHEA   Hold, hold! What d'ye do?

LUCY   Stay, stay, hold—

HARCOURT   Hold, madam, hold! let him present° him, he'll   *give a present to*
come presently; nay, I will never let you go till you
545   answer my question.

LUCY   For God's sake, sir, I must follow 'em.

DORILANT   No, I have something to present you with too;
you shan't follow them.

[ALITHEA, LUCY *struggling with* HARCOURT *and*
DORILANT. PINCHWIFE *returns.*]

PINCHWIFE   Where?—how?—what's become of—gone!—
550   whither?

LUCY   He's only gone with the gentleman, who will give
him something, an't please your worship.

PINCHWIFE   Something—give him something, with a pox!—
where are they?

555   ALITHEA   In the next walk only, brother.

PINCHWIFE   Only, only! Where, where?

[*Exit* PINCHWIFE, *and returns presently,*
then goes out again.]

HARCOURT   What's the matter with him? Why so much
concerned? But dearest madam—

ALITHEA   Pray let me go, sir; I have said and suffered
560   enough already.

HARCOURT   Then you will not look upon, nor pity, my
sufferings?

ALITHEA   To look upon 'em, when I cannot help 'em,
were cruelty, not pity; therefore I will never see you
565   more.

HARCOURT   Let me then, madam, have my privilege of a
banished lover, complaining or railing, and giving you
but a farewell reason why, if you cannot condescend to
marry me, you should not take that wretch, my rival.

570   ALITHEA   He only, not you, since my honor is engaged so
far to him, can give me a reason why I should not
marry him; but if he be true, and what I think him to
me, I must be so to him. Your servant, sir.

HARCOURT Have women only constancy when 'tis a vice,
575 and, like fortune, only true to fools?

DORILANT [to LUCY, who struggles to get from him] Thou
shalt not stir, thou robust creature; you see I can deal
with you, therefore you should stay the rather, and be
kind.

[Enter PINCHWIFE.]

580 PINCHWIFE Gone, gone, not to be found! quite gone!
Ten thousand plagues go with 'em! Which way went
they?

ALITHEA But into t'other walk, brother.

LUCY Their business will be done presently sure, an't please
585 your worship; it can't be long in doing, I'm sure on't.

ALITHEA Are they not there?

PINCHWIFE No; you know where they are, you infamous
wretch, eternal shame of your family, which you do not
dishonor enough yourself, you think, but you must help
590 her to do it too, thou legion of bawds!

ALITHEA Good brother—

PINCHWIFE Damned, damned sister!

ALITHEA Look you here, she's coming.

[Enter MRS. PINCHWIFE in man's clothes, running,
with her hat under her arm, full of oranges and
dried fruit; HORNER following.]

MRS. PINCHWIFE O dear bud, look you here what I have
595 got, see!

PINCHWIFE [aside, rubbing his forehead] And what I have
got here too, which you can't see.

MRS. PINCHWIFE The fine gentleman has given me better
things yet.

600 PINCHWIFE Has he so? —[Aside] Out of breath and colored! I must hold yet.

HORNER I have only given your little brother an orange, sir.

PINCHWIFE [to HORNER] Thank you, sir. —[Aside] You
have only squeezed my orange, I suppose, and given it
605 me again; yet I must have a city patience.[9]—[To his wife]
Come, come away.

MRS. PINCHWIFE Stay, till I have put up my fine things, bud.

[Enter SIR JASPER FIDGET.]

SIR JASPER FIDGET Master Horner, come, come, the ladies
stay for you; your mistress, my wife, wonders you make
610 not more haste to her.

HORNER I have stayed this half hour for you here, and 'tis
your fault I am not now with your wife.

SIR JASPER FIDGET But pray, don't let her know so much;
the truth on't is, I was advancing a certain project to his
615 Majesty about—I'll tell you.

9. The patience of a city husband—that is, one who has been cuckolded.

HORNER No, let's go, and hear it at your house. —Good
night, sweet little gentleman. One kiss more; you'll remember me now, I hope. [*Kisses her.*]

DORILANT What, Sir Jasper, will you separate friends? He
620 promised to sup with us; and if you take him to your
house, you'll be in danger of our company too.

SIR JASPER FIDGET Alas, gentlemen, my house is not fit for
you; there are none but civil women there, which are not
for your turn. He, you know, can bear with the society of
625 civil women now, ha, ha, ha! Besides, he's one of my
family—he's—he, he, he!

DORILANT What is he?

SIR JASPER FIDGET Faith, my eunuch, since you'll have
it, he, he, he!

[*Exeunt* SIR JASPER FIDGET, *and* HORNER.]

630 DORILANT I rather wish thou wert his, or my cuckold.
Harcourt, what a good cuckold is lost there for want of a
man to make him one! Thee and I cannot have Horner's
privilege, who can make use of it.

HARCOURT Ay, to poor Horner 'tis like coming to an
635 estate at threescore,° when a man can't be the better   age 60
for't.

PINCHWIFE Come.

MRS. PINCHWIFE Presently, bud.

DORILANT Come, let us go too. —[*To* ALITHEA] Madam,
640 your servant.—[*To* LUCY] Good night, strapper.[1]

HARCOURT Madam, though you will not let me have a
good day or night, I wish you one; but dare not name
the other half of my wish.

ALITHEA Good night, sir, forever.

645 MRS. PINCHWIFE I don't know where to put this here,
dear bud, you shall eat it; nay, you shall have part of
the fine gentleman's good things, or treat as you call it,
when we come home.

PINCHWIFE Indeed, I deserve it, since I furnished the
650 best part of it. [*Strikes away the orange.*]

> The gallant treats, presents, and gives the ball;
> But 'tis the absent cuckold pays for all.

[*Exeunt.*]

4.1

[SCENE: *In* PINCHWIFE's *house in the morning.*]

[LUCY, ALITHEA *dressed in new clothes.*]

LUCY Well—madam, now have I dressed you, and set
you out with so many ornaments, and spent upon you
ounces of essence and pulvilio;° and all this for no   *fine scented powder*
other purpose but as people adorn and perfume a corpse

---

1. A tall and robust ("strapping") woman.

5   for a stinking secondhand grave; such or as bad I think
Master Sparkish's bed.

ALITHEA Hold your peace.

LUCY Nay, madam, I will ask you the reason why you
would banish poor Master Harcourt forever from your
10   sight. How could you be so hardhearted?

ALITHEA 'Twas because I was not hardhearted.

LUCY No, no; 'twas stark love and kindness, I warrant.

ALITHEA It was so; I would see him no more because I
love him.

15 LUCY Hey-day, a very pretty reason!

ALITHEA You do not understand me.

LUCY I wish you may yourself.

ALITHEA I was engaged to marry, you see, another man,
whom my justice will not suffer me to deceive or
20   injure.

LUCY Can there be a greater cheat or wrong done to a
man than to give him your person without your heart? I
should make a conscience of it.

ALITHEA I'll retrieve it for him after I am married a
25   while.

LUCY The woman that marries to love better will be as
much mistaken as the wencher[2] that marries to live better. No, madam, marrying to increase love is like gaming
to become rich; alas, you only lose what little stock you
30   had before.

ALITHEA I find by your rhetoric you have been bribed to
betray me.

LUCY Only by his merit, that has bribed your heart, you
see, against your word and rigid honor. But what a devil is
35   this honor! 'Tis sure a disease in the head, like the
megrim,° or falling sickness,° that always hurries people   *migraine / epilepsy*
away to do themselves mischief. Men lose their lives by it;
women what's dearer to 'em, their love, the life of life.

ALITHEA Come, pray talk you no more of honor, nor Master
40   Harcourt. I wish the other would come to secure my fidelity to him and his right in me.

LUCY You will marry him then?

ALITHEA Certainly; I have given him already my word, and
will my hand too, to make it good when he comes.

45 LUCY Well, I wish I may never stick pin more if he be not
an arrant natural° to t'other fine gentleman.   *half-wit, fool*

ALITHEA I own he wants° the wit of Harcourt, which I will   *lacks*
dispense withal° for another want he has, which is want   *disregard*
of jealousy, which men of wit seldom want.

50 LUCY Lord, madam, what should you do with a fool to your
husband? You intend to be honest, don't you? Then that
husbandly virtue, credulity, is thrown away upon you.

2. One who consorts with prostitutes.

ALITHEA He only that could suspect my virtue should
have cause to do it; 'tis Sparkish's confidence in my truth
55 that obliges me to be so faithful to him.

LUCY You are not sure his opinion may last.

ALITHEA I am satisfied 'tis impossible for him to be jealous
after the proofs I have had of him. Jealousy in a
husband—Heaven defend me from it! It begets a thou-
60 sand plagues to a poor woman, the loss of her honor, her
quiet, and her—

LUCY And her pleasure.

ALITHEA What d'ye mean, impertinent?

LUCY Liberty is a great pleasure, madam.

65 ALITHEA I say, loss of her honor, her quiet, nay, her life
sometimes; and what's as bad almost, the loss of this
town; that is, she is sent into the country, which is the
last ill usage of a husband to a wife, I think.

LUCY [aside] Oh, does the wind lie there?[3]—Then, of
70 necessity, madam, you think a man must carry his wife
into the country, if he be wise. The country is as terrible, I find, to our young English ladies as a monastery
to those abroad; and on my virginity, I think they would
rather marry a London jailer than a high sheriff of a
75 county, since neither can stir from his employment. Formerly women of wit married fools for a great estate, a
fine seat, or the like; but now 'tis for a pretty seat only in
Lincoln's Inn Fields, St. James's Fields, or the Pall Mall.[4]

[Enter to them SPARKISH, and HARCOURT dressed
like a parson.]

SPARKISH Madam, your humble servant, a happy day to
80 you, and to us all.

HARCOURT Amen.

ALITHEA Who have we here?

SPARKISH My chaplain, faith. O madam, poor Harcourt
remembers his humble service to you; and in obedience
85 to your last commands, refrains coming into your sight.

ALITHEA Is not that he?

SPARKISH No, fie, no; but to show that he ne'er intended
to hinder our match, has sent his brother here to join
our hands. When I get me a wife, I must get her a
90 chaplain, according to the custom; this is his brother,
and my chaplain.

ALITHEA His brother?

LUCY [aside] And your chaplain, to preach in your pulpit
then.

95 ALITHEA His brother!

SPARKISH Nay, I knew you would not believe it.—I told
you, sir, she would take you for your brother Frank.

3. Is that the way the wind is blowing?   4. All fashionable places in London.

ALITHEA Believe it!

LUCY [aside] His brother! ha, ha, he! He has a trick left
100 still, it seems.

SPARKISH Come, my dearest, pray let us go to church before the canonical hour[5] is past.

ALITHEA For shame, you are abused° still.   deceived

SPARKISH By the world, 'tis strange now you are so incred-
105 ulous.

ALITHEA 'Tis strange you are so credulous.

SPARKISH Dearest of my life, hear me. I tell you this is
Ned Harcourt of Cambridge, by the world; you see he
has a sneaking college look. 'Tis true he's something like
110 his brother Frank, and they differ from each other no
more than in their age, for they were twins.

LUCY Ha, ha, he!

ALITHEA Your servant, sir; I cannot be so deceived, though
you are. But come, let's hear, how do you know what you
115 affirm so confidently?

SPARKISH Why, I'll tell you all. Frank Harcourt coming
to me this morning, to wish me joy and present his service to you, I asked him if he could help me to a parson; whereupon he told me he had a brother in town
120 who was in orders,° and he went straight away   an ordained minister
and sent him you see there to me.

ALITHEA Yes, Frank goes and puts on a black coat, then
tells you he is Ned; that's all you have for't.

SPARKISH Pshaw, pshaw! I tell you by the same token, the
125 midwife put her garter about Frank's neck to know 'em as
under, they were so like.

ALITHEA Frank tells you this too.

SPARKISH Ay, and Ned there too; nay, they are both in a
story.

130 ALITHEA So, so; very foolish!

SPARKISH Lord, if you won't believe one, you had best try
him by your chambermaid there; for chambermaids must
needs know chaplains from other men, they are so used to
'em.

135 LUCY Let's see; nay, I'll be sworn he has the canonical
smirk, and the filthy, clammy palm of a chaplain.

ALITHEA Well, most reverend doctor, pray let us make an
end of this fooling.

HARCOURT With all my soul, divine, heavenly creature,
140 when you please.

ALITHEA He speaks like a chaplain indeed.

SPARKISH Why, was there not "soul," "divine," "heavenly,"
in what he said?

<hr>

5. During this era, the church deemed the morning hours between eight and noon proper for
marriage ceremonies.

ALITHEA   Once more, most impertinent black coat, cease
145   your persecution, and let us have a conclusion of this
ridiculous love.

HARCOURT [*aside*]   I had forgot; I must suit my style to my
coat, or I wear it in vain.

ALITHEA   I have no more patience left; let us make once an
150   end of this troublesome love, I say.

HARCOURT   So be it, seraphic lady, when your honor
shall think it meet and convenient so to do.

SPARKISH   Gad, I'm sure none but a chaplain could
speak so, I think.

155   ALITHEA   Let me tell you, sir, this dull trick will not serve
your turn; though you delay our marriage, you shall
not hinder it.

HARCOURT   Far be it from me, munificent patroness, to
delay your marriage. I desire nothing more than to marry
160   you presently,° which I might do, if you yourself would;   immediately
for my noble, good-natured, and thrice generous patron
here would not hinder it.

SPARKISH   No, poor man, not I, faith.

HARCOURT   And now, madam, let me tell you plainly, no-
165   body else shall marry you; by heavens, I'll die first, for
I'm sure I should die after it.⁶

LUCY [*aside*]   How his love has made him forget his
function, as I have seen it in real parsons!

ALITHEA   That was spoken like a chaplain too! Now you
170   understand him, I hope.

SPARKISH   Poor man, he takes it heinously° to be refused; I   *is grievously offended*
can't blame him, 'tis putting an indignity upon him not
to be suffered. But you'll pardon me, madam, it shan't
be, he shall marry us; come away, pray, madam.

175   LUCY   Ha, ha, he! More ado! 'Tis late.

ALITHEA   Invincible stupidity! I tell you he would marry
me as your rival, not as your chaplain.

SPARKISH   Come, come, madam. [*Pulling her away.*]

LUCY   I pray, madam, do not refuse this reverend divine
180   the honor and satisfaction of marrying you; for I dare
say he has set his heart upon't, good doctor.

ALITHEA   What can you hope, or design by this?

HARCOURT [*aside*]   I could answer her, a reprieve for a
day only often revokes a hasty doom; at worst, if she
185   will not take mercy on me and let me marry her, I have
at least the lover's second pleasure, hindering my rival's
enjoyment, though but for a time.

SPARKISH   Come, madam, 'tis e'en twelve o'clock, and
my mother charged me never to be married out of the
190   canonical hours. Come, come; Lord, here's such a deal
of modesty, I warrant, the first day.

6. Harcourt puns on "die," which can mean "experience orgasm."

LUCY   Yes, an't please your worship, married women show
all their modesty the first day, because married men
show all their love the first day.

[*Exeunt* SPARKISH, ALITHEA, HARCOURT, *and* LUCY.]

4.2

[SCENE: *The scene changes to a bedchamber, where appear*
PINCHWIFE, MRS. PINCHWIFE.]

PINCHWIFE   Come, tell me, I say.

MRS. PINCHWIFE   Lord! han't I told it an hundred times over?

PINCHWIFE [*aside*]   I would try if, in the repetition of the
ungrateful° tale, I could find her altering it in the least   *unpleasant*
5   circumstance; for if her story be false, she is so too. —
Come, how was't, baggage?

MRS. PINCHWIFE   Lord, what pleasure you take to hear it,
sure!

PINCHWIFE   No, you take more in telling it, I find; but
10   speak, how was't?

MRS. PINCHWIFE   He carried me up into the house next
to the Exchange.

PINCHWIFE   So; and you two were only in the room.

MRS. PINCHWIFE   Yes, for he sent away a youth that was
15   there, for some dried fruit and China oranges.

PINCHWIFE   Did he so? Damn him for it—and for—

MRS. PINCHWIFE   But presently came up the gentlewoman
of the house.

PINCHWIFE   Oh, 'twas well she did; but what did he do
20   whilst the fruit came?

MRS. PINCHWIFE   He kissed me an hundred times, and told
me he fancied he kissed my fine sister, meaning me, you
know, whom he said he loved with all his soul, and bid me
be sure to tell her so, and to desire her to be at her
25   window by eleven of the clock this morning, and he
would walk under it at that time.

PINCHWIFE [*aside*]   And he was as good as his word, very
punctual; a pox reward him for't.

MRS. PINCHWIFE   Well, and he said if you were not within,
30   he would come up to her, meaning me, you know, bud,
still.

PINCHWIFE [*aside*]   So—he knew her certainly; but for this
confession, I am obliged to her simplicity. —But what, you
stood very still when he kissed you?

35   MRS. PINCHWIFE   Yes, I warrant you; would you have had
me discovered myself?

PINCHWIFE   But you told me he did some beastliness to
you, as you called it; what was't?

MRS. PINCHWIFE   Why, he put—

40   PINCHWIFE   What?

MRS. PINCHWIFE Why, he put the tip of his tongue between
    my lips, and so mousled° me—and I said, I'd bite it.   *pulled about roughly*
PINCHWIFE An eternal canker seize it, for a dog!
MRS. PINCHWIFE Nay, you need not be so angry with
45   him neither, for to say truth, he has the sweetest breath
    I ever knew.
PINCHWIFE The devil!—you were satisfied with it then,
    and would do it again.
MRS. PINCHWIFE Not unless he should force me.
50 PINCHWIFE Force you, changeling!° I tell you no woman   *idiot*
    can be forced.
MRS. PINCHWIFE Yes, but she may sure by such as he,
    for he's a proper, goodly strong man; 'tis hard, let me
    tell you, to resist him.
55 PINCHWIFE [*aside*] So, 'tis plain she loves him, yet she has
    not love enough to make her conceal it from me; but the
    sight of him will increase her aversion for me and love for
    him, and that love instruct her how to deceive me and sat-
    isfy him, all idiot as she is. Love! 'Twas he gave women
60   first their craft, their art of deluding; out of nature's hands
    they came plain, open, silly, and fit for slaves, as she and
    Heaven intended 'em; but damned love—well—I must
    strangle that little monster[7] whilst I can deal with him. —
    Go fetch pen, ink, and paper out of the next room.
65 MRS. PINCHWIFE Yes, bud.   [*Exit* MRS. PINCHWIFE.]
PINCHWIFE [*aside*] Why should women have more inven-
    tion in love than men? It can only be because they have
    more desires, more soliciting passions, more lust, and
    more of the devil.
            [MRS. PINCHWIFE *returns.*]
70   Come, minx, sit down and write.
MRS. PINCHWIFE Ay, dear bud, but I can't do't very well.
PINCHWIFE I wish you could not at all.
MRS. PINCHWIFE But what should I write for?
PINCHWIFE I'll have you write a letter to your lover.
75 MRS. PINCHWIFE O Lord, to the fine gentleman a letter!
PINCHWIFE Yes, to the fine gentleman.
MRS. PINCHWIFE Lord, you do but jeer; sure you jest.
PINCHWIFE I am not so merry; come, write as I bid you.
MRS. PINCHWIFE What, do you think I am a fool?
80 PINCHWIFE [*aside*] She's afraid I would not dictate any
    love to him, therefore she's unwilling. —But you had
    best begin.
MRS. PINCHWIFE Indeed, and indeed, but I won't, so I won't!
PINCHWIFE Why?
85 MRS. PINCHWIFE Because he's in town; you may send for
    him if you will.

---

7. Eros ("love," in Greek) or Cupid, the god of love.

PINCHWIFE   Very well, you would have him brought to you; is it come to this? I say, take the pen and write, or you'll provoke me.

90 MRS. PINCHWIFE   Lord, what d'ye make a fool of me for? Don't I know that letters are never writ but from the country to London, and from London into the country? Now he's in town, and I am in town too; therefore I can't write to him, you know.

95 PINCHWIFE [*aside*]   So, I am glad it is no worse; she is innocent enough yet. —Yes, you may, when your husband bids you, write letters to people that are in town.

MRS. PINCHWIFE   Oh, may I so? Then I'm satisfied.

PINCHWIFE   Come, begin. —[*Dictates.*] "Sir"—

100 MRS. PINCHWIFE   Shan't I say, "Dear Sir"? You know one says always something more than bare "Sir."

PINCHWIFE   Write as I bid you, or I will write "whore" with this penknife in your face.

MRS. PINCHWIFE   Nay, good bud—[*She writes.*] "Sir"—

105 PINCHWIFE   "Though I suffered last night your nauseous, loathed kisses and embraces"—Write.

MRS. PINCHWIFE   Nay, why should I say so? You know I told you he had a sweet breath.

PINCHWIFE   Write!

110 MRS. PINCHWIFE   Let me but put out "loathed."

PINCHWIFE   Write, I say!

MRS. PINCHWIFE   Well then. [*Writes.*]

PINCHWIFE   Let's see, what have you writ?—[*Takes the paper, and reads.*] "Though I suffered last night your kisses

115 and embraces"—Thou impudent creature! Where is "nauseous" and "loathed"?

MRS. PINCHWIFE   I can't abide to write such filthy words.

PINCHWIFE   Once more write as I'd have you, and question it not, or I will spoil thy writing with this. [*Holds up

120 the penknife.*] I will stab out those eyes that cause my mischief.

MRS. PINCHWIFE   O Lord, I will!

PINCHWIFE   So—so—let's see now! —[*Reads.*] "Though I suffered last night your nauseous, loathed kisses and

125 embraces" —go on—"Yet I would not have you presume that you shall ever repeat them."—So.

[*She writes.*]

MRS. PINCHWIFE   I have writ it.

PINCHWIFE   On then. —"I then concealed myself from your knowledge, to avoid your insolencies"—

[*She writes.*]

130 MRS. PINCHWIFE   So—

PINCHWIFE   "The same reason, now I am out of your hands"—

[*She writes.*]

MRS. PINCHWIFE   So—

PINCHWIFE   "Makes me own to you my unfortunate,
135   though innocent frolic, of being in man's clothes"—
        [*She writes.*]

MRS. PINCHWIFE   So—

PINCHWIFE   "That you may forevermore cease to pursue
her, who hates and detests you"—
        [*She writes on.*]

MRS. PINCHWIFE   So-h—[*Sighs.*]

140   PINCHWIFE   What, do you sigh?—"detests you—as much
as she loves her husband and her honor."

MRS. PINCHWIFE   I vow, husband, he'll ne'er believe I
should write such a letter.

PINCHWIFE   What, he'd expect a kinder from you? Come,
145   now your name only.

MRS. PINCHWIFE   What, shan't I say, "Your most faithful,
humble servant till death"?

PINCHWIFE   No, tormenting fiend! —[*Aside*] Her style, I
find, would be very soft. —Come, wrap it up now,
150   whilst I go fetch wax and a candle; and write on the
backside, "For Mr. Horner."   [*Exit* PINCHWIFE.]

MRS. PINCHWIFE   "For Mr. Horner." —So, I am glad he
has told me his name. Dear Mr. Horner! But why
should I send thee such a letter that will vex thee,
155   and make thee angry with me?—Well, I will not send
it—Ay, but then my husband will kill me—for I see
plainly he won't let me love Mr. Horner—but what
care I for my husband? —I won't, so I won't send poor
Mr. Horner such a letter—But then my husband—But
160   oh, what if I writ at bottom, my husband made me
write it?—Ay, but then my husband would see't—Can
one have no shift?° Ah, a London woman would have   *stratagem; expedient*
had a hundred presently. Stay—what if I should write a
letter, and wrap it up like this, and write upon't too? Ay,
165   but then my hus-band would see't—I don't know what
to do—But yet y'-vads° I'll try, so I will—for I will not send   *in faith*
this letter to poor Mr. Horner, come what will on't.
       [*She writes, and repeats what she hath writ.*]

"Dear, sweet Mr. Horner"—so—"my husband would have
me send you a base, rude, unmannerly letter—but I
170   won't"—so—"and would have me forbid you loving me—
but I won't"—so—"and would have me say to you, I hate
you, poor Mr. Horner—but I won't tell a lie for him"—
there—"for I'm sure if you and I were in the country at
cards together"—so—"I could not help treading on your
175   toe under the table"—so—"or rubbing knees with you, and
staring in your face till you saw me"—very well—"and then
looking down, and blushing for an hour together"—so—
"but I must make haste before my husband come; and now

he has taught me to write letters, you shall have longer
180   ones from me, who am, dear, dear, poor, dear Mr. Horner,
your most humble friend, and servant to command till
death, Margery Pinchwife."
    Stay, I must give him a hint at bottom—so—now wrap it
up just like t'other—so—now write, "For Mr. Horner"—
185   But, oh now, what shall I do with it? for here comes my
husband.

        [*Enter* PINCHWIFE.]

  PINCHWIFE [*aside*]   I have been detained by a sparkish coxcomb, who pretended a visit to me; but I fear 'twas to my
  wife.—What, have you done?°   *finished*
190 MRS. PINCHWIFE   Ay, ay, bud, just now.
  PINCHWIFE   Let's see't; what d'ye tremble for? What, you
  would not have it go?
  MRS. PINCHWIFE   Here. —[*Aside*] No, I must not give him
  that; so I had been served if I had given him this.
195 PINCHWIFE [*he opens, and reads the first letter*]   Come,
  where's the wax and seal?
  MRS. PINCHWIFE [*aside*]   Lord, what shall I do now? Nay,
  then, I have it. —Pray let me see't. Lord, you think me so
  arrant a fool I cannot seal a letter; I will do't, so I will.

        [*Snatches the letter from him, changes it for the
        other, seals it, and delivers it to him.*]

200 PINCHWIFE   Nay, I believe you will learn that, and other
  things too, which I would not have you.
  MRS. PINCHWIFE   So, han't I done it curiously?° —[*Aside*] I   *cunningly; carefully*
  think I have; there's my letter going to Mr. Horner, since
  he'll needs have me send letters to folks.
205 PINCHWIFE   'Tis very well; but I warrant you would not
  have it go now?
  MRS. PINCHWIFE   Yes, indeed, but I would, bud, now.
  PINCHWIFE   Well, you are a good girl then. Come, let me
  lock you up in your chamber till I come back; and be
210   sure you come not within three strides of the window
when I am gone, for I have a spy in the street.

                           [*Exit* MRS. PINCHWIFE.]

[PINCHWIFE *locks the door.*] At least, 'tis fit she think so. If
we do not cheat women, they'll cheat us; and fraud may
be justly used with secret enemies, of which a wife is the
215   most dangerous; and he that has a handsome one to keep,
and a frontier town,[8] must provide against treachery
rather than open force. Now I have secured all within, I'll
deal with the foe without with false intelligence.

       [*Holds up the letter.*]   [*Exit* PINCHWIFE.]

---

8. That is, London is on the front lines of the war between husbands and the wives who would
cheat on them.

4.3

[SCENE: *The scene changes to* HORNER's *lodging.*]

[QUACK *and* HORNER.]

QUACK   Well, sir, how fadges° the new design? Have you   *succeeds*
  not the luck of all your brother projectors,° to deceive   *schemers*
  only yourself at last?

HORNER   No, good domine° doctor, I deceive you, it seems,   *master (Latin)*
5   and others too; for the grave matrons and old, rigid
  husbands think me as unfit for love as they are; but
  their wives, sisters, and daughters know some of 'em
  better things already.

QUACK   Already!

10 HORNER   Already, I say. Last night I was drunk with half
  a dozen of your civil persons, as you call 'em, and people
  of honor, and so was made free of their society and
  dressing rooms forever hereafter; and am already come
  to the privileges of sleeping upon their pallets, warm-
15   ing smocks, tying shoes and garters, and the like, doctor, already, already, doctor.

QUACK   You have made use of your time, sir.

HORNER   I tell thee, I am now no more interruption to 'em
  when they sing or talk bawdy than a little squab° French   *short and stout*
20   page who speaks no English.

QUACK   But do civil persons and women of honor drink,
  and sing bawdy songs?

HORNER   Oh, amongst friends, amongst friends. For
  your bigots in honor are just like those in religion; they
25   fear the eye of the world more than the eye of Heaven,
  and think there is no virtue but railing at vice, and no
  sin but giving scandal. They rail at a poor, little, kept
  player, and keep themselves some young, modest pulpit
  comedian to be privy to their sins in their closets,°   *private chambers*
30   not to tell 'em of them in their chapels.

QUACK   Nay, the truth on't is, priests amongst the women
  now have quite got the better of us lay confessors,
  physicians.

HORNER   And they are rather their patients, but—

  [*Enter* MY LADY FIDGET, *looking about her.*]

35   Now we talk of women of honor, here comes one. Step
  behind the screen there, and but observe if I have not
  particular privileges with the women of reputation
  already, doctor, already.

  [QUACK *steps behind screen.*]

LADY FIDGET   Well, Horner, am not I a woman of honor?
40   You see I'm as good as my word.

HORNER   And you shall see, madam, I'll not be behind-
  hand with you in honor; and I'll be as good as my word
  too, if you please but to withdraw into the next room.

LADY FIDGET   But first, my dear sir, you must promise to
45 have a care of my dear honor.

HORNER   If you talk a word of your honor, you'll make me
incapable to wrong it. To talk of honor in the mysteries of
love is like talking of Heaven or the Deity in an operation
of witchcraft, just when you are employing the devil; it
50 makes the charm impotent.

LADY FIDGET   Nay, fie! let us not be smutty. But you talk of
mysteries and bewitching to me; I don't understand you.

HORNER   I tell you, madam, the word "money" in a mis-
tress's mouth, at such a nick of time,° is not a more dis-   *critical time*
55 heartening sound to a younger brother⁹ than that of
"honor" to an eager lover like myself.

LADY FIDGET   But you can't blame a lady of my reputation
to be chary.

HORNER   Chary! I have been chary of it already, by the
60 report I have caused of myself.

LADY FIDGET   Ay, but if you should ever let other women
know that dear secret, it would come out. Nay, you must
have a great care of your conduct; for my acquaintance
are so censorious (oh, 'tis a wicked, censorious world,
65 Mr. Horner!), I say, are so censorious and detracting that
perhaps they'll talk, to the prejudice of my honor, though
you should not let them know the dear secret.

HORNER   Nay, madam, rather than they shall prejudice
your honor, I'll prejudice theirs; and to serve you, I'll lie
70 with 'em all, make the secret their own, and then they'll
keep it. I am a Machiavel¹ in love, madam.

LADY FIDGET   Oh, no, sir, not that way.

HORNER   Nay, the devil take me if censorious women are
to be silenced any other way.

75 LADY FIDGET   A secret is better kept, I hope, by a single
person than a multitude; therefore pray do not trust anybody else with it, dear, dear Mr. Horner. [*Embracing him.*]

[*Enter* SIR JASPER FIDGET.]

SIR JASPER FIDGET   How now!

LADY FIDGET [*aside*]   Oh, my husband!—prevented—and
80 what's almost as bad, found with my arms about another
man—that will appear too much—what shall I say?
     Sir Jasper, come hither. I am trying if Mr. Horner were
ticklish, and he's as ticklish as can be; I love to torment
the confounded toad; let you and I tickle him.

85 SIR JASPER FIDGET   No, your ladyship will tickle him better
without me, I suppose. But is this your buying china? I
thought you had been at the china house.

HORNER [*aside*]   China house! That's my cue, I must
take it.—A pox! can't you keep your impertinent wives

---

9. That is, who inherits little or nothing.
1. That is, an unprincipled schemer—the

reputation of Niccolò Machiavelli (1469–
1527), author of *The Prince* (1513).

90 at home? Some men are troubled with the husbands,
    but I with the wives. But I'd have you to know, since I
    cannot be your journeyman by night, I will not be your
    drudge by day, to squire your wife about and be your
    man of straw, or scarecrow, only to pies and jays,° that   *idle chatterers*
95 would be nibbling at your forbidden fruit; I shall be
    shortly the hackney° gentleman-usher of the town.   *hired*
    SIR JASPER FIDGET [*aside*] He, he, he! Poor fellow, he's in
    the right on't, faith; to squire women about for other
    folks is as ungrateful an employment as to tell° money   *count*
100 for other folks.—He, he, he! Ben't° angry, Horner.   *Be not*
    LADY FIDGET No, 'tis I have more reason to be angry,
    who am left by you to go abroad indecently alone; or,
    what is more indecent to pin myself upon such ill-bred
    people of your acquaintance as this is.
105 SIR JASPER FIDGET Nay, prithee what has he done?
    LADY FIDGET Nay, he has done nothing.
    SIR JASPER FIDGET But what d'ye take ill, if he has done
    nothing?
    LADY FIDGET Ha, ha, ha! Faith, I can't but laugh, how
110 ever; why, d'ye think the unmannerly toad would come
    down to me to the coach? I was fain to come up to fetch
    him, or go without him, which I was resolved not to do;
    for he knows china very well, and has himself very good,
    but will not let me see it lest I should beg some. But I
115 will find it out, and have what I came for yet.

            [*Exit* LADY FIDGET, *and locks the door, followed by*
                                    HORNER *to the door.*]

    HORNER [*apart to* LADY FIDGET] Lock the door, madam.—
    So, she has got into my chamber, and locked me out.
    Oh, the impertinency of womankind! Well, Sir Jasper,
    plain dealing is a jewel; if ever you suffer your wife to
120 trouble me again here, she shall carry you home a pair of
    horns, by my Lord Mayor she shall; though I cannot fur-
    nish you myself, you are sure, yet I'll find a way.
    SIR JASPER FIDGET [*aside*] Ha, ha, he! At my first coming
    in and finding her arms about him, tickling him it seems,
125 I was half jealous, but now I see my folly. —He, he, he!
    Poor Horner.
    HORNER Nay, though you laugh now, 'twill be my turn ere
    long. Oh, women, more impertinent, more cunning, and
    more mischievous than their monkeys, and to me almost
130 as ugly! Now is she throwing my things about and rifling
    all I have, but I'll get in to her the back way, and so rifle
    her for it.
    SIR JASPER FIDGET Ha, ha, ha! Poor angry Horner.
    HORNER Stay here a little; I'll ferret her out to you
135 presently, I warrant.

                        [*Exit* HORNER *at t'other door.*]

    SIR JASPER FIDGET Wife! My Lady Fidget! Wife! He is
    coming in to you the back way.

[SIR JASPER *calls through the door to his wife; she answers from within.*]

LADY FIDGET   Let him come, and welcome, which way he will.

SIR JASPER FIDGET   He'll catch you, and use you roughly,
140   and be too strong for you.

LADY FIDGET   Don't you trouble yourself, let him if he can.

QUACK [*behind*]   This indeed I could not have believed from him, nor any but my own eyes.

[*Enter* MRS. SQUEAMISH.]

MRS. SQUEAMISH   Where's this woman-hater, this toad, this
145   ugly, greasy, dirty sloven?

SIR JASPER FIDGET [*aside*]   So, the women all will have him ugly; methinks he is a comely person, but his wants° make   *lacks*
his form contemptible to 'em; and 'tis e'en as my wife said yesterday, talking of him, that a proper handsome eunuch
150   was as ridiculous a thing as a gigantic coward.

MRS. SQUEAMISH   Sir Jasper, your servant. Where is the odious beast?

SIR JASPER FIDGET   He's within in his chamber, with my wife; she's playing the wag² with him.

155   MRS. SQUEAMISH   Is she so? And he's a clownish beast, he'll give her no quarter, he'll play the wag with her again, let me tell you. Come, let's go help her.—What, the door's locked?

SIR JASPER FIDGET   Ay, my wife locked it.

160   MRS. SQUEAMISH   Did she so? Let us break it open then.

SIR JASPER FIDGET   No, no, he'll do her no hurt.

MRS. SQUEAMISH   No. [*Aside.*] But is there no other way to get in to 'em? Whither goes this? I will disturb 'em.

[*Exit* MRS. SQUEAMISH *at another door.*]

[*Enter* OLD LADY SQUEAMISH.]

OLD LADY SQUEAMISH   Where is this harlotry, this impudent
165   baggage,° this rambling tomrig?° O Sir Jasper, I'm glad to   *prostitute / strumpet*
see you here, did you not see my vile grandchild come in hither just now?

SIR JASPER FIDGET   Yes.

OLD LADY SQUEAMISH   Ay, but where is she then? where is
170   she? Lord, Sir Jasper, I have e'en rattled myself to pieces in pursuit of her. But can you tell what she makes° here?   *what she is doing*
They say below, no woman lodges here.

SIR JASPER FIDGET   No.

OLD LADY SQUEAMISH   No! What does she here then? Say,
175   if it be not a woman's lodging, what makes she here? But are you sure no woman lodges here?

SIR JASPER FIDGET   No, nor no man neither; this is Mr. Horner's lodging.

---

2. Playing the joker, making mischief (but there is a sexual meaning) in Mrs. Squeamish's repetition of the phrase.

OLD LADY SQUEAMISH   Is it so, are you sure?

180 SIR JASPER FIDGET   Yes, yes.

OLD LADY SQUEAMISH   So; then there's no hurt in't, I hope.
But where is he?

SIR JASPER FIDGET   He's in the next room with my wife.

OLD LADY SQUEAMISH   Nay, if you trust him with your wife,
185 I may with my Biddy. They say he's a merry harmless man
now, e'en as harmless a man as ever came out of Italy
with a good voice,[3] and as pretty harmless company for a
lady as a snake without his teeth.

SIR JASPER FIDGET   Ay, ay, poor man.

[*Enter* MRS. SQUEAMISH.]

190 MRS. SQUEAMISH   I can't find 'em. —Oh, are you here,
Grandmother? I followed, you must know, my Lady
Fidget hither; 'tis the prettiest lodging, and I have been
staring on the prettiest pictures.

[*Enter* LADY FIDGET *with a piece of china in her
hand, and* HORNER *following.*]

LADY FIDGET   And I have been toiling and moiling° for the   drudging
195 prettiest piece of china, my dear.

HORNER   Nay, she has been too hard for me, do what I
could.

MRS. SQUEAMISH   O Lord, I'll have some china too. Good
Mr. Horner, don't think to give other people china, and
200 me none; come in with me too.

HORNER   Upon my honor, I have none left now.

MRS. SQUEAMISH   Nay, Nay, I have known you deny your
china before now, but you shan't put me off so. Come.

HORNER   This lady had the last there.

205 LADY FIDGET   Yes, indeed, madam, to my certain knowledge he has no more left.

MRS. SQUEAMISH   Oh, but it may be he may have some
you could not find.

LADY FIDGET   What, d'ye think if he had had any left, I
210 would not have had it too? For we women of quality
never think we have china enough.

HORNER   Do not take it ill, I cannot make china for you all,
but I will have a rol-waggon[4] for you too, another time.

MRS. SQUEAMISH   Thank you, dear toad.

215 LADY FIDGET [*to* HORNER, *aside*]   What do you mean by
that promise?

HORNER [*apart to* LADY FIDGET]   Alas, she has an innocent,
literal understanding.

OLD LADY SQUEAMISH   Poor Mr. Horner! He has enough to
220 do to please you all, I see.

HORNER   Ay, madam, you see how they use me.

---

3. That is, as a castrato singer.
4. A cylindrical china vase; a low-wheeled vehicle for carrying goods.

OLD LADY SQUEAMISH   Poor gentleman, I pity you.

HORNER   I thank you, madam. I could never find pity but
from such reverend ladies as you are; the young ones will
25   never spare a man.

MRS. SQUEAMISH   Come, come, beast, and go dine with us,
for we shall want a man at ombre after dinner.

HORNER   That's all their use of me, madam, you see.

MRS. SQUEAMISH   Come, sloven, I'll lead you, to be sure of
230   you. [Pulls him by the cravat.]

OLD LADY SQUEAMISH   Alas, poor man, how she tugs him!
Kiss, kiss her; that's the way to make such nice° women   fastidious
quiet.

HORNER   No, madam, that remedy is worse than the tor-
235   ment; they know I dare suffer anything rather than
do it.

OLD LADY SQUEAMISH   Prithee kiss her, and I'll give you her
picture in little, that you admired so last night; prithee do.

HORNER   Well, nothing but that could bribe me; I love a
240   woman only in effigy and good painting, as much as I hate
them. I'll do't, for I could adore the devil well painted.

[Kisses MRS. SQUEAMISH.]

MRS. SQUEAMISH   Foh, you filthy toad! Nay, now I've done
jesting.

OLD LADY SQUEAMISH   Ha, ha, ha! I told you so.

245   MRS. SQUEAMISH   Foh! a kiss of his—

SIR JASPER FIDGET   Has no more hurt in't than one of my
spaniel's.

MRS. SQUEAMISH   Nor no more good neither.

QUACK [behind]   I will now believe anything he tells me.

[Enter MR. PINCHWIFE.]

250   LADY FIDGET   O Lord, here's a man! Sir Jasper, my mask,
my mask! I would not be seen here for the world.

SIR JASPER FIDGET   What, not when I am with you?

LADY FIDGET   No, no, my honor—let's be gone.

MRS. SQUEAMISH   Oh, grandmother, let us be gone; make
255   haste, make haste, I know not how he may censure us.

LADY FIDGET   Be found in the lodging of anything like a
man! Away!

[Exeunt SIR JASPER, LADY FIDGET,
OLD LADY SQUEAMISH, MRS. SQUEAMISH.]

QUACK [behind]   What's here? another cuckold? He looks
like one, and none else sure have any business with him.

260   HORNER   Well, what brings my dear friend hither?

PINCHWIFE   Your impertinency.

HORNER   My impertinency! —Why, you gentlemen that
have got handsome wives think you have a privilege of
saying anything to your friends, and are as brutish as if
265   you were our creditors.

PINCHWIFE   No, sir, I'll ne'er trust you any way.

HORNER But why not, dear Jack? Why diffide in° me thou   *distrust*
know'st so well?

PINCHWIFE Because I do know you so well.

270 HORNER Han't I been always thy friend, honest Jack, always ready to serve thee, in love or battle, before thou
wert married, and am so still?

PINCHWIFE I believe so; you would be my second° now   *supporter*
indeed.

275 HORNER Well then, dear Jack, why so unkind, so grum,
so strange to me? Come, prithee kiss me, dear rogue.
Gad, I was always, I say, and am still as much thy servant as—

PINCHWIFE As I am yours, sir. What, you send a kiss to my
280 wife, is that it?

HORNER So, there 'tis—a man can't show his friendship to
a married man, but presently he talks of his wife to you.
Prithee, let thy wife alone, and let thee and I be all one,
as we were wont. What, thou art as shy of my kindness
285 as a Lombard Street alderman of a courtier's civility at
Locket's.[5]

PINCHWIFE But you are overkind to me, as kind as if I
were your cuckold already; yet I must confess you
ought to be kind and civil to me, since I am so kind, so
290 civil to you, as to bring you this. Look you there sir.

[*Delivers him a letter.*]

HORNER What is't?

PINCHWIFE Only a love letter, sir.

HORNER From whom?—how! this is from your wife!—
hum—and hum—

295 PINCHWIFE Even from my wife, sir. Am I not wondrous
kind and civil to you now too? —[*Aside*] But you'll not
think her so.

HORNER [*aside*] Ha! Is this a trick of his or hers?

PINCHWIFE The gentleman's surprised, I find. What, you
300 expected a kinder letter?

HORNER No, faith, not I, how could I?

PINCHWIFE Yes, yes, I'm sure you did; a man so well
made as you are must needs be disappointed if the
women declare not their passion at first sight or
opportunity.

305 HORNER [*aside*] But what should this mean? Stay, the
postscript. —[*Reads aside.*] "Be sure you love me whatsoever my husband says to the contrary, and let him
not see this, lest he should come home and pinch me,
or kill my squirrel."[6]—[*Aside*] It seems he knows not
310 what the letter contains.

---

5. That is, as wary as a financier ("Lombard
Street alderman") would be if a courtier came
smiling to him in a tavern (Locket's).

6. Possibly an allusion to the fashionable
practice of keeping squirrels as pets.

PINCHWIFE   Come, ne'er wonder at it so much.

HORNER   Faith, I can't help it.

PINCHWIFE   Now, I think, I have deserved your infinite friendship and kindness, and have showed myself suffi-
315   ciently an obliging kind friend and husband; am I not so, to bring a letter from my wife to her gallant?

HORNER   Ay, the devil take me, art thou the most obliging, kind friend and husband in the world, ha, ha!

PINCHWIFE   Well, you may be merry, sir; but in short I
320   must tell you, sir, my honor will suffer no jesting.

HORNER   What dost thou mean?

PINCHWIFE   Does the letter want a comment? Then know, sir, though I have been so civil a husband as to bring you a letter from my wife, to let you kiss and court her to my
325   face, I will not be a cuckold, sir, I will not.

HORNER   Thou art mad with jealousy. I never saw thy wife in my life but at the play yesterday, and I know not if it were she or no. I court her, kiss her!

PINCHWIFE   I will not be a cuckold, I say; there will be
330   danger in making me a cuckold.

HORNER   Why, wert thou not well cured of thy last clap?°   *bout of gonorrhea*

PINCHWIFE   I wear a sword.

HORNER   It should be taken from thee lest thou shouldst do thyself a mischief with it; thou art mad, man.

335   PINCHWIFE   As mad as I am, and as merry as you are, I must have more reason from you ere we part. I say again, though you kissed and courted last night my wife in man's clothes, as she confesses in her letter—

HORNER [*aside*]   Ha!

340   PINCHWIFE   Both she and I say, you must not design it again, for you have mistaken your woman, as you have done your man.

HORNER [*aside*]   Oh—I understand something now. —Was that thy wife? Why wouldst thou not tell me
345   'twas she? Faith, my freedom with her was your fault, not mine.

PINCHWIFE [*aside*]   Faith, so 'twas.

HORNER   Fie! I'd never do't to a woman before her hus-band's face, sure.

350   PINCHWIFE   But I had rather you should do't to my wife before my face than behind my back, and that you shall never do.

HORNER   No—you will hinder me.

PINCHWIFE   If I would not hinder you, you see by her letter,
355   she would.

HORNER   Well, I must e'en acquiesce then, and be con-tented with what she writes.

PINCHWIFE   I'll assure you 'twas voluntarily writ; I had no hand in't, you may believe me.

360   HORNER   I do believe thee, faith.

PINCHWIFE   And believe her too, for she's an innocent creature, has no dissembling in her; and so fare you well, sir.

HORNER   Pray, however, present my humble service to her,
365   and tell her I will obey her letter to a tittle, and fulfill her desires, be what they will, or with what difficulty soever I do't, and you shall be no more jealous of me, I warrant her and you.

PINCHWIFE   Well, then, fare you well, and play with any
370   man's honor but mine, kiss any man's wife but mine, and welcome.   [*Exit* MR. PINCHWIFE.]

HORNER   Ha, ha, ha! doctor.

QUACK   It seems he has not heard the report of you, or does not believe it.

375   HORNER   Ha, ha! Now, doctor, what think you?

QUACK   Pray let's see the letter—hum—[*Reads the letter.*] "for—dear—love you"—

HORNER   I wonder how she could contrive it! What say's thou to't? 'Tis an original.

380   QUACK   So are your cuckolds, too, originals, for they are like no other common cuckolds, and I will henceforth believe it not impossible for you to cuckold the Grand Signior° amidst his guards of eunuchs, that I say.   *Ottoman sultan*

HORNER   And I say for the letter, 'tis the first love letter
385   that ever was without flames, darts, fates, destinies, lying and dissembling in't.

[*Enter* SPARKISH, *pulling in* MR. PINCHWIFE.]

SPARKISH   Come back, you are a pretty brother-in-law, neither go to church, nor to dinner with your sister bride!

PINCHWIFE   My sister denies her marriage, and you see
390   is gone away from you dissatisfied.

SPARKISH   Pshaw! upon a foolish scruple, that our parson was not in lawful orders, and did not say all the Common Prayer; but 'tis her modesty only, I believe. But let women be never so modest the first day, they'll be sure to
395   come to themselves by night, and I shall have enough of her then. In the meantime, Harry Horner, you must dine with me; I keep my wedding at my aunt's in the Piazza.[7]

HORNER   Thy wedding! What stale° maid has lived to despair   *past her prime*
of a husband, or what young one of a gallant?

400   SPARKISH   Oh, your servant, sir—this gentleman's sister then—no stale maid.

HORNER   I'm sorry for't.

PINCHWIFE [*aside*]   How comes he so concerned for her?

SPARKISH   You sorry for't? Why, do you know any ill by her?

---

7. An open-air arcade in Covent Garden.

405 HORNER   No, I know none but by thee; 'tis for her sake, not
yours, and another man's sake that might have hoped, I
thought.

SPARKISH   Another man! another man! What is his name?

HORNER   Nay, since 'tis past he shall be nameless. —

410   [*Aside.*] Poor Harcourt! I am sorry thou hast missed her.

PINCHWIFE [*aside*]   He seems to be much troubled at the
match.

SPARKISH   Prithee tell me—nay, you shan't go, brother.

PINCHWIFE   I must of necessity, but I'll come to you to

415   dinner.   [*Exit* PINCHWIFE.]

SPARKISH   But, Harry, what, have I a rival in my wife
already? But with all my heart, for he may be of use to me
hereafter; for though my hunger is now my sauce, and I
can fall on° heartily without,° but the time will come   *eat / (sauce)*

420   when a rival will be as good sauce for a married man to a
wife as an orange to veal.

HORNER   O thou damned rogue! Thou has set my teeth on
edge with thy orange.

SPARKISH   Then let's to dinner—there I was with you

425   again. Come.

HORNER   But who dines with thee?

SPARKISH   My friends and relations, my brother Pinchwife, you see, of your acquaintance.

HORNER   And his wife?

430 SPARKISH   No, gad, he'll ne'er let her come amongst us good
fellows. Your stingy country coxcomb keeps his wife from his
friends, as he does his little firkin° of ale for his own   *small cask*
drinking, and a gentleman can't get a smack on't;°   *mere taste of*
but his servants, when his back is turned, broach it at

435   their pleasures, and dust it away,° ha, ha, ha! Gad, I am   *drink it quickly*
witty, I think, considering I was married today, by the
world; but come—

HORNER   No, I will not dine with you, unless you can
fetch her too.

440 SPARKISH   Pshaw! what pleasure canst thou have with
women now, Harry?

HORNER   My eyes are not gone; I love a good prospect yet,
and will not dine with you unless she does too. Go fetch

445   her, therefore, but do not tell her husband 'tis for my sake.

SPARKISH   Well, I'll go try what I can do; in the meantime
come away to my aunt's lodging, 'tis in the way to
Pinchwife's.

HORNER   The poor woman has called for aid, and stretched

450   forth her hand, doctor; I cannot but help her over the
pale° out of the briars.   *fence*

[*Exeunt* SPARKISH, HORNER, QUACK.]

4.4

[SCENE: *The scene changes to* PINCHWIFE's *house.*]

> [MRS. PINCHWIFE *alone, leaning on her elbow.*
> *A table, pen, ink, and paper.*]

MRS. PINCHWIFE   Well, 'tis e'en so, I have got the London
disease they call love; I am sick of my husband, and for
my gallant. I have heard this distemper called a fever,
but methinks 'tis liker an ague, for when I think of my
5   husband, I tremble and am in a cold sweat and have
inclinations to vomit; but when I think of my gallant,
dear Mr. Horner, my hot fit comes and I am all in a
fever, indeed, and as in other fevers my own chamber is
tedious to me, and I would fain be removed to his, and
10   then methinks I should be well. Ah, poor Mr. Horner!
Well, I cannot, will not stay here; therefore I'll make an
end of my letter to him, which shall be a finer letter
than my last, because I have studied it like anything.
Oh, sick, sick! [*Takes the pen and writes.*]

> [*Enter* MR. PINCHWIFE, *who seeing her writing*
> *steals softly behind her, and looking over her*
> *shoulder, snatches the paper from her.*]

15   PINCHWIFE   What, writing more letters?
MRS. PINCHWIFE   O Lord, bud! why d'ye fright me so?

> [*She offers to run out; he stops her, and reads.*]

PINCHWIFE   How's this! Nay, you shall not stir, madam.
"Dear, dear, dear Mr. Horner"—very well—I have taught
you to write letters to good purpose—but let's see't.
20   "First, I am to beg your pardon for my boldness in writing to you, which I'd have you to know I would not have
done had not you said first you loved me so extremely,
which if you do, you will never suffer me to lie in the
arms of another man, whom I loathe, nauseate, and
25   detest."—Now you can write these filthy words. But what
follows? —"Therefore I hope you will speedily find some
way to free me from this unfortunate match, which was
never, I assure you, of my choice, but I'm afraid 'tis
already too far gone. However, if you love me, as I do you,
30   you will try what you can do, but you must help me away
before tomorrow, or else, alas, I shall be forever out of
your reach, for I can defer no longer our—our" [*The letter*
concludes.]—What is to follow "our"?—Speak, what?
Our journey into the country, I suppose—Oh, woman,
35   damned woman! and love, damned love, their old tempter!
for this is one of his miracles; in a moment he can make
those blind that could see, and those see that were blind,
those dumb that could speak, and those prattle who were
dumb before; nay, what is more than all, make these
40   dough-baked,° senseless, indocile° animals, women, too   *half-baked / intractable*

hard for us, their politic° lords and rulers, in a moment.   *prudent*
But make an end of your letter, and then I'll make an end
of you thus, and all my plagues together. [*Draws his sword.*]

MRS. PINCHWIFE O Lord, O Lord, you are such a passionate
45 man, bud!

       [*Enter* SPARKISH.]

SPARKISH How now, what's here to do?

PINCHWIFE This fool here now!

SPARKISH What, drawn upon your wife? You should never
do that but at night in the dark, when you can't hurt her.
50 This is my sister-in-law, is it not? [*Pulls aside her handkerchief.*] Ay, faith, e'en our country Margery; one may
know her. Come, she and you must go dine with me;
dinner's ready, come. But where's my wife? Is she not
come home yet? Where is she?

55 PINCHWIFE Making you a cuckold; 'tis that they all do, as
soon as they can.

SPARKISH What, the wedding day? No, a wife that designs
to make a cully° of her husband will be sure to let him   *dupe*
win the first stake of love, by the world. But come, they
60 stay dinner for us; come, I'll lead down our Margery.

MRS. PINCHWIFE No—so, go, we'll follow you.

SPARKISH I will not wag° without you.   *move*

PINCHWIFE [*aside*] This coxcomb is a sensible° torment to   *acutely felt*
me amidst the greatest in the world.

65 SPARKISH Come, come, Madam Margery.

PINCHWIFE No, I'll lead her my own way. What, would you
treat your friends with mine, for want of your own wife?
[*Leads her to t'other door, and locks her in, and returns.*]
—[*Aside*] I am contented my rage should take breath.

SPARKISH [*aside*] I told Horner this.

70 PINCHWIFE Come now.

SPARKISH Lord, how shy° you are of your wife! But let me   *suspicious*
tell you, brother, we men of wit have amongst us a saying
that cuckolding, like the smallpox, comes with a fear, and
you may keep your wife as much as you will out of danger
75 of infection, but if her constitution incline her to't, she'll
have it sooner or later, by the world, say they.

PINCHWIFE [*aside*] What a thing is a cuckold, that every
fool can make him ridiculous!—Well, sir—but let me
advise you, now you are come to be concerned, because
80 you suspect the danger, not to neglect the means to prevent it, especially when the greatest share of the malady
will light upon your own head,[8] for

      Hows'e'er the kind wife's belly comes to swell,
      The husband breeds for her, and first is ill.

       [*Exeunt* PINCHWIFE *and* SPARKISH.]

8. In the form of cuckold's horns that the husband "breeds."

5.1

[SCENE: MR. PINCHWIFE'S *house.*]

[*Enter* MR. PINCHWIFE *and* MRS. PINCHWIFE.
A table and candle.]

PINCHWIFE   Come, take the pen and make an end of the
letter, just as you intended; if you are false in a tittle, I
shall soon perceive it, and punish you with this as you
deserve. [*Lays his hand on his sword.*] Write what was to
5   follow—let's see—"You must make haste and help me
away before tomorrow, or else I shall be forever out of
your reach, for I can defer no longer our"—What follows "our"?

MRS. PINCHWIFE   Must all out then, bud? [MRS. PINCH-
10   WIFE *takes the pen and writes.*] Look you there then.

PINCHWIFE   Let's see—"For I can defer no longer our—
wedding—Your slighted Alithea."—What's the meaning of this? My sister's name to't. Speak, unriddle!

MRS. PINCHWIFE   Yes, indeed, bud.

15   PINCHWIFE   But why her name to't? Speak—speak, I say!

MRS. PINCHWIFE   Ay, but you'll tell her then again; if you
would not tell her again—

PINCHWIFE   I will not—I am stunned, my head turns
around. Speak.

20   MRS. PINCHWIFE   Won't you tell her indeed, and indeed?

PINCHWIFE   No, speak, I say.

MRS. PINCHWIFE   She'll be angry with me, but I had
rather she should be angry with me than you, bud; and
to tell you the truth, 'twas she made me write the let-
25   ter, and taught me what I should write.

PINCHWIFE   [*aside*] Ha! I thought the style was somewhat better than her own.—But how could she come
to you to teach you, since I had locked you up alone?

MRS. PINCHWIFE   Oh, through the keyhole, bud.

30   PINCHWIFE   But why should she make you write a letter
for her to him, since she can write herself?

MRS. PINCHWIFE   Why, she said because—for I was
unwilling to do it.

PINCHWIFE   Because what—because?

35   MRS. PINCHWIFE   Because, lest Mr. Horner should be
cruel, and refuse her; or vain afterwards, and show the
letter, she might disown it, the hand° not being hers.

hand° · *handwriting*

PINCHWIFE   [*aside*] How's this? Ha! —then I think I shall
come to myself again. This changeling could not invent
40   this lie; but if she could, why should she? She might
think I should soon discover it—stay—now I think on't
too, Horner said he was sorry she had married Sparkish,
and her disowning her marriage to me makes me think
she has evaded it for Horner's sake. Yet why should she
45   take this course? But men in love are fools; women may

well be so. —But hark you, madam, your sister went out
in the morning, and I have not seen her within since.

MRS. PINCHWIFE Alackaday, she has been crying all day
above, it seems, in a corner.

50 PINCHWIFE Where is she? Let me speak with her.

MRS. PINCHWIFE [*aside*] O Lord, then he'll discover all!
—Pray hold, bud; what, d'ye mean to discover me? She'll
know I have told you then. Pray, bud, let me talk with her
first.

55 PINCHWIFE I must speak with her, to know whether
Horner ever made her any promise, and whether she be
married to Sparkish or no.

MRS. PINCHWIFE Pray, dear bud, don't, till I have spoken
with her and told her that I have told you all, for she'll
60 kill me else.

PINCHWIFE Go then, and bid her come out to me.

MRS. PINCHWIFE Yes, yes, bud.

PINCHWIFE Let me see—

MRS. PINCHWIFE [*aside*] I'll go, but she is not within to
65 come to him. I have just got time to know of Lucy her
maid, who first set me on work, what lie I shall tell next,
for I am e'en at my wit's end.   [*Exit* MRS. PINCHWIFE.]

PINCHWIFE Well, I resolve it; Horner shall have her. I'd
rather give him my sister than lend him my wife, and
70 such an alliance will prevent his pretensions to my wife,
sure. I'll make him of kin to her, and then he won't care
for her.

          [MRS. PINCHWIFE *returns.*]

MRS. PINCHWIFE O Lord, bud! I told you what anger you
would make me with my sister.

75 PINCHWIFE Won't she come hither?

MRS. PINCHWIFE No, no, alackaday, she's ashamed to look
you in the face, and she says, if you go in to her, she'll run
away downstairs, and shamefully go herself to Mr. Horner,
who has promised her marriage, she says, and she will
80 have no other, so she won't.

PINCHWIFE Did he so—promise her marriage?—then she
shall have no other. Go tell her so, and if she will come
and discourse with me a little concerning the means, I
will about it immediately. Go.

          [*Exit* MRS. PINCHWIFE.]

85 His estate is equal to Sparkish's, and his extraction° as   *lineage*
much better than his as his parts are; but my chief reason
is, I'd rather be of kin to him by the name of brother-in-
law than that of cuckold.

          [*Enter* MRS. PINCHWIFE.]

Well, what says she now?

90 MRS. PINCHWIFE Why, she says she would only have you
lead her to Horner's lodging—with whom she first will

discourse the matter before she talk with you, which yet
she cannot do; for alack, poor creature, she says she can't
so much as look you in the face, therefore she'll come to
95   you in a mask; and you must excuse her if she make you
no answer to any question of yours, till you have brought
her to Mr. Horner; and if you will not chide her, nor question her, she'll come out to you immediately.

PINCHWIFE   Let her come; I will not speak a word to her,
100   nor require a word from her.

MRS. PINCHWIFE   Oh, I forgot; besides, she says she cannot look you in the face though through a mask, therefore would desire you to put out the candle.

PINCHWIFE   I agree to all; let her make haste—there, 'tis
105   out. [*Puts out the candle.*]   [*Exit* MRS. PINCHWIFE.]
—My case is something better. I'd rather fight with
Horner for not lying with my sister than for lying with
my wife, and of the two I had rather find my sister too
forward than my wife; I expected no other from her free°   (overly) liberal
110   education, as she calls it, and her passion for the
town. Well—wife and sister are names which make us
expect love and duty, pleasure and comfort, but we find
'em plagues and torments, and are equally, though
differently, troublesome to their keeper; for we have as
115   much ado to get people to lie with our sisters as to
keep 'em from lying with our wives.

> [*Enter* MRS. PINCHWIFE *masked, and in hoods and
> scarves and a nightgown° and petticoat of*   dressing gown
> ALITHEA's, *in the dark.*]

What, are you come, sister? Let us go then—but first
let me lock up my wife.—Mrs. Margery, where are you?

MRS. PINCHWIFE   Here, bud.

120   PINCHWIFE   Come hither, that I may lock you up; get you
in. [*Locks the door.*]—Come, sister, where are you now?

> [MRS. PINCHWIFE *gives him her hand, but when he
> lets her go, she steals softly on t'other side of him,
> and is led away by him for his sister* ALITHEA.]

5.2

[SCENE: *The scene changes to* HORNER's *lodging.*]

> [QUACK, HORNER.]

QUACK   What, all alone? Not so much as one of your cuckolds here, nor one of their wives! They use to take their
turns with you, as if they were to watch you.

HORNER   Yes, it often happens that a cuckold is but his
5   wife's spy, and is more upon family duty when he is with
her gallant abroad, hindering his pleasure, than when he
is at home with her, playing the gallant. But the hardest
duty a married woman imposes upon a lover is keeping
her husband company always.

10   QUACK   And his fondness wearies you almost as soon as hers.

HORNER   A pox! keeping a cuckold company, after you
have had his wife, is as tiresome as the company of a
country squire to a witty fellow of the town, when he has
got all his money.

15 QUACK   And as at first a man makes a friend of the husband to get the wife, so at last you are fain to fall out
with the wife to be rid of the husband.

HORNER   Ay, most cuckold-makers are true courtiers; when
once a poor man has cracked° his credit for 'em, they can't   ruined
20 abide to come near him.

QUACK   But at first, to draw him in, are so sweet, so kind, so
dear, just you are to Pinchwife. But what becomes of that
intrigue with his wife?

HORNER   A pox! he's as surly as an alderman that has been
25 bit, and since he's so coy, his wife's kindness is in vain, for
she's a silly innocent.

QUACK   Did she not send you a letter by him?

HORNER   Yes, but that's a riddle I have not yet solved. Allow
the poor creature to be willing, she is silly too, and he
30 keeps her up so close—

QUACK   Yes, so close that he makes her but the more willing, and adds but revenge to her love, which two, when
met, seldom fail of satisfying each other one way or
other.

35 HORNER   What! here's the man we are talking of, I think.

> [Enter MR. PINCHWIFE, leading in his wife masked,
> muffled, and in her sister's gown.]

Pshaw!

QUACK   Bringing his wife to you is the next thing to bringing
a love letter from her.

HORNER   What means this?

40 PINCHWIFE   The last time, you know, sir, I brought you a
love letter; now, you see, a mistress. I think you'll say I
am a civil man to you.

HORNER   Ay, the devil take me, will I say thou art the
civilest man I ever met with, and I have known some. I
45 fancy I understand thee now better than I did the letter;
but hark thee, in thy ear—

PINCHWIFE   What?

HORNER   Nothing but the usual question, man: is she
sound,⁹ on thy word?

50 PINCHWIFE   What, you take her for a wench, and me for a
pimp?

HORNER   Pshaw! wench and pimp, paw° words. I know   nasty, obscene
thou art an honest fellow, and hast a great acquaintance
among the ladies, and perhaps hast made love for me
55 rather than let me make love to thy wife.

PINCHWIFE   Come, sir, in short, I am for no fooling.

---

9. Free of (venereal) disease.

HORNER Nor I neither; therefore prithee let's see her face presently.° Make her show, man; art thou sure I don't know her?

immediately

60 PINCHWIFE I am sure you do know her.

HORNER A pox! why dost thou bring her to me then?

PINCHWIFE Because she's a relation of mine—

HORNER Is she, faith, man? Then thou are still more civil and obliging, dear rogue.

65 PINCHWIFE Who desired me to bring her to you.

HORNER Then she is obliging, dear rogue.

PINCHWIFE You'll make her welcome for my sake, I hope.

HORNER I hope she is handsome enough to make herself welcome. Prithee, let her unmask.

70 PINCHWIFE Do you speak to her; she would never be ruled by me.

HORNER Madam—[MRS. PINCHWIFE *whispers to* HORNER.] —She says she must speak with me in private. Withdraw, prithee.

75 PINCHWIFE [*aside*] She's unwilling, it seems, I should know all her undecent conduct in this business. — Well then, I'll leave you together, and hope when I am gone you'll agree; if not, you and I shan't agree, sir.

HORNER [*aside*] What means the fool? —If she and I

80 agree, 'tis no matter what you and I do.

[*Whispers to* MRS. PINCHWIFE, *who makes signs with her hand for* PINCHWIFE *to be gone.*]

PINCHWIFE In the meantime, I'll fetch a parson, and find out Sparkish and disabuse him. You would have me fetch a parson, would you not? Well then—now I think I am rid of her, and shall have no more trouble with her. Our

85 sisters and daughters, like usurers' money, are safest when put out; but our wives, like their writings,[1] never safe but in our closets under lock and key.

[*Exit* MR. PINCHWIFE.]

[*Enter* BOY.]

BOY Sir Jasper Fidget, sir, is coming up. [*Exit.*]

HORNER Here's the trouble of a cuckold, now, we are talk-

90 ing of. A pox on him! Has he not enough to do to hinder his wife's sport, but he must other women's too? —Step in here, madam.

[*Exit* MRS. PINCHWIFE.]

[*Enter* SIR JASPER.]

SIR JASPER FIDGET My best and dearest friend.

HORNER [*aside to* QUACK] The old style, doctor. —Well, be

95 short, for I am busy. What would your impertinent wife have now?

SIR JASPER FIDGET Well guessed, i'faith, for I do come from her.

---

1. Marriage settlements and other legal documents.

HORNER   To invite me to supper. Tell her I can't come; go.

100 SIR JASPER FIDGET   Nay, now you are out,° faith; for my lady   *mistaken*
and the whole knot of the virtuous gang, as they call
themselves, are resolved upon a frolic of coming to you
tonight in a masquerade, and are all dressed already.

HORNER   I shan't be at home.

105 SIR JASPER FIDGET [*aside*]   Lord, how churlish he is to women!
—Nay, prithee don't disappoint 'em; they'll think 'tis my
fault; prithee don't. I'll send in the banquet and the fiddles.
But make no noise on't, for the poor virtuous rogues would
not have it known for the world that they go a-masquerad-
110 ing, and they would come to no man's ball but yours.

HORNER   Well, well—get you gone, and tell 'em, if they
come, 'twill be at the peril of their honor and yours.

SIR JASPER FIDGET   He, he, he!—we'll trust you for that; farewell.

[*Exit* SIR JASPER.]

HORNER

115   Doctor, anon you too shall be my guest,
         But now I'm going to a private feast.

[*Exeunt.*]

5.3

[SCENE: *The scene changes to the Piazza of Covent Garden.*]

[SPARKISH, PINCHWIFE.]

SPARKISH [*with the letter in his hand*]   But who would have
thought a woman could have been false to me? By the
world, I could not have thought it.

PINCHWIFE   You were for giving and taking liberty; she has
5 taken it only, sir, now you find in that letter. You are a
frank person, and so is she, you see there.

SPARKISH   Nay, if this be her hand—for I never saw it.

PINCHWIFE   'Tis no matter whether that be her hand or
no; I am sure this hand, at her desire, led her to Mr.
10 Horner, with whom I left her just now, to go fetch a parson to 'em, at their desire too, to deprive you of her
forever, for it seems yours was but a mock marriage.

SPARKISH   Indeed, she would needs have it that 'twas Harcourt himself in a parson's habit that married us, but I'm
15 sure he told me 'twas his brother Ned.

PINCHWIFE   Oh, there 'tis out, and you were deceived, not
she, for you are such a frank person—but I must be
gone. You'll find her at Mr. Horner's; go and believe your
eyes.   [*Exit* MR. PINCHWIFE.]

20 SPARKISH   Nay, I'll to her, and call her as many crocodiles,
sirens, harpies,[2] and other heathenish names as a poet
would do a mistress who had refused to hear his suit,

2. Creatures that in legend and myth destroyed men (after first enticing them, in the case of
crocodiles and sirens).

nay more, his verses on her. —But stay, is not that she
following a torch at t'other end of the Piazza? And
25   from Horner's certainly—'tis so.

> [*Enter* ALITHEA, *following a torch, and* LUCY *behind.*]

You are well met, madam, though you don't think so.
What, you have made a short visit to Mr. Horner, but I
suppose you'll return to him presently; by that time the
parson can be with him.

30 ALITHEA   Mr. Horner, and the parson, sir!

SPARKISH   Come, madam, no more dissembling, no
more jilting, for I am no more a frank person.

ALITHEA   How's this?

LUCY [*aside*]   So, 'twill work, I see.

35 SPARKISH   Could you find out no easy country fool to
abuse? none but me, a gentleman of wit and pleasure
about the town? But it was your pride to be too hard
for a man of parts, unworthy false woman! false as a
friend that lends a man money to lose; false as dice,
40   who undo those that trust all they have to 'em.

LUCY [*aside*]   He has been a great bubble° by his similes, as   *dupe*
they say.

ALITHEA   You have been too merry,[3] sir, at your wedding
dinner, sure.

45 SPARKISH   What, d'ye mock me too?

ALITHEA   Or you have been deluded.

SPARKISH   By you.

ALITHEA   Let me understand you.

SPARKISH   Have you the confidence—I should call it
50   something else, since you know your guilt—to stand my
just reproaches? You did not write an impudent letter to
Mr. Horner! who I find now has clubbed° with you in   *combined*
deluding me with his aversion for women, that I might
not, forsooth, suspect him for my rival.

55 LUCY [*aside*]   D'ye think the gentleman can be jealous
now, madam?

ALITHEA   I write a letter to Mr. Horner!

SPARKISH   Nay, madam, do not deny it; your brother
showed it me just now, and told me likewise he left you
60   at Horner's lodging to fetch a parson to marry you to
him, and I wish you joy, madam, joy, joy! and to him, too,
much joy, and to myself more joy for not marrying you.

ALITHEA [*aside*]   So, I find my brother would break off the
match, and I can consent to't, since I see this gentleman
65   can be made jealous. —O Lucy, by his rude usage and
jealousy, he makes me almost afraid I am married to
him. Art thou sure 'twas Harcourt himself and no parson
that married us?

3. That is, had too much to drink.

SPARKISH   No, madam, I thank you. I suppose that was a
70   contrivance too of Mr. Horner's and yours, to make Harcourt play the parson; but I would as little as you have
him one now, no, not for the world, for shall I tell you
another truth? I never had any passion for you till now,
for now I hate you. 'Tis true I might have married your
75   portion,° as other men of parts of the town do sometimes,   *dowry*
and so your servant; and to show my unconcernedness,
I'll come to your wedding, and resign you with as much
joy as I would a stale wench to a new cully; nay, with as
much joy as I would after the first night, if I had been
80   married to you. There's for you, and so your servant,
servant.   [*Exit* SPARKISH.]

ALITHEA   How was I deceived in a man!

LUCY   You'll believe, then, a fool may be made jealous
now? For that easiness in him that suffers him to be led
85   by a wife will likewise permit him to be persuaded
against her by others.

ALITHEA   But marry Mr. Horner! My brother does not
intend it, sure; if I thought he did, I would take thy
advice, and Mr. Harcourt for my husband. And now I
90   wish that if there be any overwise woman of the town,
who, like me, would marry a fool for fortune, liberty, or
title, first, that her husband may love play, and be a cully
to all the town but her, and suffer none but fortune to be
mistress of his purse; then, if for liberty, that he may
95   send her into the country under the conduct of some
housewifely mother-in-law; and if for title, may the
world give 'em none but that of cuckold.

LUCY   And for her greater curse, madam, may he not
deserve it.

100 ALITHEA   Away, impertinent! —Is not this my old Lady
Lanterlu's?[4]

LUCY   Yes, madam. —[*Aside*] And here I hope we shall find
Mr. Harcourt.

[*Exeunt* ALITHEA, LUCY.]

5.4

[SCENE: *The scene changes again to* HORNER's *lodging.*]

[HORNER, LADY FIDGET, MRS. DAINTY FIDGET,
MRS. SQUEAMISH. *A table, banquet, and bottles.*]

HORNER [*aside*]   A pox! they are come too soon—before I
have sent back my new mistress. All I have now to do is
to lock her in, that they may not see her.

LADY FIDGET   That we may be sure of our welcome, we
5   have brought our entertainment with us, and are resolved
to treat thee, dear toad.

4. Lanterloo was a popular card game, often called "loo."

MRS. DAINTY FIDGET   And that we may be merry to purpose, have left Sir Jasper and my old Lady Squeamish quarreling at home at backgammon.

10 MRS. SQUEAMISH   Therefore let us make use of our time, lest they should chance to interrupt us.

LADY FIDGET   Let us sit then.

HORNER   First, that you may be private, let me lock this door and that, and I'll wait upon you presently.

15 LADY FIDGET   No, sir, shut 'em only and your lips forever, for we must trust you as much as our women.

HORNER   You know all vanity's killed in me; I have no occasion for talking.

LADY FIDGET   Now, ladies, supposing we had drank each of 20 us our two bottles, let us speak the truth of our hearts.

MRS. DAINTY FIDGET *and* MRS. SQUEAMISH   Agreed.

LADY FIDGET   By this brimmer,° for truth is nowhere else to be found. —[*Aside to* HORNER] Not in thy heart, false man!   *brimming cup*

25 HORNER [*aside to* LADY FIDGET]   You have found me a true man, I'm sure.

LADY FIDGET [*aside to* HORNER]   Not every way. —But let us sit and be merry.

[LADY FIDGET *sings.*]

I

Why should our damn'd tyrants oblige us to live
30   On the pittance of pleasure which they only give?
                We must not rejoice,
                With wine and with noise.
      In vain we must wake in a dull bed alone,
      Whilst to our warm rival, the bottle, they're gone.
35   Then lay aside charms,
                And take up these arms.°   *i.e., these glasses*

2

'Tis wine only gives 'em their courage and wit;
Because we live sober, to men we submit.
                If for beauties you'd pass,
40   Take a lick of the glass,
      'Twill mend your complexions, and when they are gone,
      The best red we have is the red of the grape.
                Then, sisters, lay't on,
                And damn a good shape.

45 MRS. DAINTY FIDGET   Dear brimmer! Well, in token of our openness and plain-dealing, let us throw our masks over our heads.

HORNER   So, 'twill come to the glasses anon.

MRS. SQUEAMISH   Lovely brimmer! Let me enjoy him first.

50 LADY FIDGET   No, I never part with a gallant till I've tried
   him. Dear brimmer, that mak'st our husbands shortsighted.

MRS. DAINTY FIDGET   And our bashfull gallants bold.

MRS. SQUEAMISH   And for want of a gallant, the butler
55   lovely in our eyes. —Drink, eunuch.

LADY FIDGET   Drink, thou representative of a husband.
   Damn a husband!

MRS. DAINTY FIDGET   And, as it were a husband, an old
   keeper.

60 MRS. SQUEAMISH   And an old grandmother.

HORNER   And an English bawd, and a French surgeon.[5]

LADY FIDGET   Ay, we have all reason to curse 'em.

HORNER   For my sake, ladies?

LADY FIDGET   No, for our own, for the first spoils all young
65   gallants' industry.

MRS. DAINTY FIDGET   And the other's art makes 'em bold
   only with common women.

MRS. SQUEAMISH   And rather run the hazard of the vile
   distemper amongst them than of a denial amongst us.

70 MRS. DAINTY FIDGET   The filthy toads choose mistresses
   now as they do stuffs,° for having been fancied and worn   *fabrics; clothes*
   by others.

MRS. SQUEAMISH   For being common and cheap.

LADY FIDGET   Whilst women of quality, like the richest
75   stuffs, lie untumbled and unasked for.

HORNER   Ay, neat, and cheap, and new, often they think
   best.

MRS. DAINTY FIDGET   No, sir, the beasts will be known by a
   mistress longer than by a suit.

80 MRS. SQUEAMISH   And 'tis not for cheapness neither.

LADY FIDGET   No, for the vain fops will take up druggets°   *coarse woolen material*
   and embroider 'em. But I wonder at the depraved appe-
   tites of witty men; they use to be out of the common
   road, and hate imitation. Pray tell me, beast, when
85   you were a man, why you rather chose to club° with a   *join*
   multitude in a common house° for an entertainment than   *eating house; brothel*
   to be the only guest at a good table.

HORNER   Why, faith, ceremony and expectation are unsuf-
   ferable to those that are sharp bent;° people always eat   *hungry*
90   with the best stomach at an ordinary,° where every man   *tavern*
   is snatching for the best bit.

LADY FIDGET   Though he get a cut over the fingers. —But
   I have heard people eat most heartily of another man's
   meat, that is, what they do not pay for.

95 HORNER   When they are sure of their welcome and freedom, for ceremony in love and eating is as ridiculous as

5. A doctor to treat syphilis (known to the English as the "French disease"); perhaps, specifically,
the doctor supposedly responsible for Horner's impotence.

in fighting; falling on briskly is all should be done in
those occasions.

LADY FIDGET   Well, then, let me tell you, sir, there is
100   nowhere more freedom than in our houses, and we
take freedom from° a young person as a sign of good   *in*
breeding, and a person may be as free as he pleases with
us, as frolic, as gamesome, as wild as he will.

HORNER   Han't I heard you all declaim against wild men?

105   LADY FIDGET   Yes, but for all that, we think wildness in a
man as desirable a quality as in a duck or rabbit; a
tame man, foh!

HORNER   I know not, but your reputations frightened
me, as much as your faces invited me.

110   LADY FIDGET   Our reputation! Lord, why should you not
think that we women make use of our reputation, as you
men of yours, only to deceive the world with less suspicion? Our virtue is like the statesman's religion, the
Quaker's word, the gamester's oath, and the great man's
115   honor—but to cheat those that trust us.

MRS. SQUEAMISH   And that demureness, coyness, and modesty that you see in our faces in the boxes at plays, is as
much a sign of a kind woman as a vizard-mask in the pit.

MRS. DAINTY FIDGET   For, I assure you, women are least
120   masked when they have the velvet vizard on.

LADY FIDGET   You would have found us modest women in
our denials only.

MRS. SQUEAMISH   Our bashfulness is only the reflection
of the men's.

125   MRS. DAINTY FIDGET   We blush when they are shamefaced.

HORNER   I beg your pardon, ladies; I was deceived in you
devilishly. But why that mighty pretense to honor?

LADY FIDGET   We have told you. But sometimes 'twas for
the same reason you men pretend business often, to
130   avoid ill company, to enjoy the better and more privately those you love.

HORNER   But why would you ne'er give a friend a wink
then?

LADY FIDGET   Faith, your reputation frightened us as
135   much as ours did you, you were so notoriously lewd.

HORNER   And you so seemingly honest.°   *chaste*

LADY FIDGET   Was that all that deterred you?

HORNER   And so expensive—you allow freedom, you say—

LADY FIDGET   Ay, ay.

140   HORNER   That I was afraid of losing my little money, as
well as my little time, both which my other pleasures
required.

LADY FIDGET   Money, foh! You talk like a little fellow
now; do such as we expect money?

145   HORNER   I beg your pardon, madam; I must confess, I have
heard that great ladies, like great merchants, set but

the higher prices upon what they have, because they are not in necessity of taking the first offer.

MRS. DAINTY FIDGET   Such as we make sale of our hearts?

150 MRS. SQUEAMISH   We bribed for our love? Foh!

HORNER   With your pardon, ladies, I know, like great men in offices, you seem to exact flattery and attendance only from your followers; but you have receivers[6] about you, and such fees to pay, a man is afraid to pass your grants.°   accept your favors

155 Besides, we must let you win at cards, or we lose your hearts; and if you make an assignation, 'tis at a goldsmith's, jeweler's, or china house, where, for your honor you deposit to him, he must pawn his to the punctual cit,°   shopkeeper and so paying for what you take up, pays for what he

160 takes up.

MRS. DAINTY FIDGET   Would you not have us assured of our gallant's love?

MRS. SQUEAMISH   For love is better known by liberality than by jealousy.

165 LADY FIDGET   For one may be dissembled, the other not. —[Aside.] But my jealousy can be no longer dissembled, and they are telling ripe. —Come, here's to our gallants in waiting, whom we must name, and I'll begin. This is my false rogue. [Claps him on the back.]

170 MRS. SQUEAMISH   How!

HORNER [aside]   So, all will out now.

MRS. SQUEAMISH [aside to HORNER]   Did you not tell me, 'twas for my sake only you reported yourself no man?

MRS. DAINTY FIDGET [aside to HORNER]   Oh, wretch! Did

175 you not swear to me, 'twas for my love and honor you passed for that thing you do?

HORNER   So, so.

LADY FIDGET   Come, speak, ladies; this is my false villain.

180 MRS. SQUEAMISH   And mine too.

MRS. DAINTY FIDGET   And mine.

HORNER   Well then, you are all three my false rogues too, and there's an end on't.

LADY FIDGET   Well then, there's no remedy; sister sharers, let us not fall out, but have a care of our honor. Though

185 we get no presents, no jewels of him, we are savers of our honor, the jewel of most value and use, which shines yet to the world unsuspected, though it be counterfeit.

HORNER   Nay, and is e'en as good as if it were true, provided the world think so; for honor, like beauty now, only depends

190 on the opinion of others.

LADY FIDGET   Well, Harry Common,[7] I hope you can be true to three. Swear—but 'tis no purpose to require your oath, for you are as often forsworn as you swear to new women.

6. That is, servants to be bribed.
7. (1) Harry shared by all; (2) Harry the prostitute (one meaning of "commoner" or "common [woman]").

HORNER   Come, faith, madam, let us e'en pardon one an-
195   other, for all the difference I find betwixt we men and
you women, we forswear ourselves at the beginning of
an amour, you as long as it lasts.

[*Enter* SIR JASPER FIDGET, *and* OLD LADY SQUEAMISH.]

SIR JASPER FIDGET   Oh, my Lady Fidget, was this your cunning, to come to Mr. Horner without me? But you have
200   been nowhere else, I hope.

LADY FIDGET   No, Sir Jasper.

OLD LADY SQUEAMISH   And you came straight hither,
Biddy?

MRS. SQUEAMISH   Yes, indeed, Lady Grandmother.

205   SIR JASPER FIDGET   'Tis well, 'tis well; I knew when once they
were thoroughly acquainted with poor Horner, they'd
ne'er be from him. You may let her masquerade it with my
wife and Horner, and I warrant her reputation safe.

[*Enter* BOY.]

BOY   Oh, sir, here's the gentleman come whom you bid me
210   not suffer to come up without giving you notice, with a
lady too, and other gentlemen.

HORNER   Do you all go in there, whilst I send 'em away,
and, boy, do you desire 'em to stay below till I come,
which shall be immediately.

[*Exeunt* SIR JASPER, OLD LADY SQUEAMISH,
LADY FIDGET, MRS. DAINTY, MRS. SQUEAMISH.]

215   BOY   Yes, sir.   [*Exit.*]

[*Exit* HORNER *at t'other door, and
returns with* MRS. PINCHWIFE.]

HORNER   You would not take my advice to be gone home
before your husband came back; he'll now discover all. Yet
pray, my dearest, be persuaded to go home, and leave the
rest to my management; I'll let you down the back way.

220   MRS. PINCHWIFE   I don't know the way home, so I don't.

HORNER   My man shall wait upon you.

MRS. PINCHWIFE   No, don't you believe that I'll go at all;
what, are you weary of me already?

HORNER   No, my life, 'tis that I may love you long, 'tis to
225   secure my love, and your reputation with your husband; he'll never receive you again else.

MRS. PINCHWIFE   What care I? D'ye think to frighten me
with that? I don't intend to go to him again; you shall
be my husband now.

230   HORNER   I cannot be your husband, dearest, since you
are married to him.

MRS. PINCHWIFE   Oh, would you make me believe that?
Don't I see every day, at London here, women leave their
first husbands, and go and live with other men as
235   their wives? Pish, pshaw! you'd make me angry, but
that I love you so mainly.°

                                                                    strongly

HORNER   So, they are coming up—in again, in, I hear 'em.

[*Exit* MRS. PINCHWIFE.]

Well, a silly mistress is like a weak place, soon got, soon
lost, a man has scarce time for plunder; she betrays her
240   husband first to her gallant, and then her gallant to her
husband.

[*Enter* PINCHWIFE, ALITHEA, HARCOURT, SPARKISH,
LUCY, *and a* PARSON.]

PINCHWIFE   Come, madam, 'tis not the sudden change of
your dress, the confidence of your asseverations, and
your false witness there, shall persuade me I did not
245   bring you hither just now; here's my witness, who cannot
deny it, since you must be confronted. —Mr. Horner, did
not I bring this lady to you just now?

HORNER [*aside*]   Now must I wrong one woman for
another's sake, but that's no new thing with me; for in
250   these cases I am still on the criminal's side, against the
innocent.

ALITHEA   Pray, speak, sir.

HORNER [*aside*]   It must be so—I must be impudent,
and try my luck; impudence uses to be too hard for
255   truth.

PINCHWIFE   What, you are studying an evasion or excuse
for her. Speak, sir.

HORNER   No, faith, I am something backward only to
speak in women's affairs or disputes.

260   PINCHWIFE   She bids you speak.

ALITHEA   Ay, pray, sir, do; pray satisfy him.

HORNER   Then truly, you did bring that lady to me just
now.

PINCHWIFE   O ho!

265   ALITHEA   How, sir!

HARCOURT   How, Horner!

ALITHEA   What mean you, sir? I always took you for a man
of honor.

HORNER [*aside*]   Ay, so much a man of honor that I must
270   save my mistress, I thank you, come what will on't.

SPARKISH   So, if I had had her, she'd have made me believe
the moon had been made of a Christmas pie.

LUCY [*aside*]   Now could I speak, if I durst, and solve the
riddle, who am the author of it.

275   ALITHEA   O unfortunate woman! A combination° against   *conspiracy*
my honor, which most concerns me now, because you
share in my disgrace, sir, and it is your censure, which I
must now suffer, that troubles me, not theirs.

HARCOURT   Madam, then have no trouble, you shall
280   now see 'tis possible for me to love too, without being
jealous; I will not only believe your innocence
myself, but make all the world believe it.—[*Apart to*

HORNER]. Horner, I must now be concerned for this lady's
    honor.
285 HORNER   And I must be concerned for a lady's honor too.
HARCOURT   This lady has her honor, and I will protect it.
HORNER   My lady has not her honor, but has given it me to
    keep, and I will preserve it.
HARCOURT   I understand you not.
290 HORNER   I would not have you.
MRS. PINCHWIFE [*peeping in behind*]   What's the matter
    with 'em all?
PINCHWIFE   Come, come, Mr. Horner, no more disput-
    ing; here's the parson. I brought him not in vain.
295 HARCOURT   No, sir, I'll employ him, if this lady please.
PINCHWIFE   How! what d'ye mean?
SPARKISH   Ay, what does he mean?
HORNER   Why, I have resigned your sister to him; he has
    my consent.
300 PINCHWIFE   But he has not mine, sir; a woman's injured
    honor, no more than a man's, can be repaired or satis-
    fied by any but him that first wronged it; and you shall
    marry her presently,° or—[*Lays his hand on his sword.*]   *at once*
        [*Enter to them* MRS. PINCHWIFE.]

MRS. PINCHWIFE [*aside*]   O Lord, they'll kill poor Mr.
305   Horner! Besides, he shan't marry her whilst I stand by
    and look on; I'll not lose my second husband so.
PINCHWIFE   What do I see?
ALITHEA   My sister in my clothes!
SPARKISH   Ha!
310 MRS. PINCHWIFE [*to* MR. PINCHWIFE]   Nay, pray now don't
    quarrel about finding work for the parson; he shall
    marry me to Mr. Horner; for now, I believe, you have
    enough of me.
HORNER [*aside*]   Damned, damned, loving changeling!°   *idiot*
315 MRS. PINCHWIFE   Pray, sister, pardon me for telling so
    many lies of you.
HARCOURT   I suppose the riddle is plain now.
LUCY   No, that must be my work. Good sir, hear me.
        [*Kneels to* MR. PINCHWIFE, *who stands doggedly,*
        with his hat over his eyes.]
PINCHWIFE   I will never hear woman again, but make
320   'em all silent, thus—[*Offers to draw upon his wife.*]
HORNER   No, that must not be.
PINCHWIFE   You then shall go first, 'tis all one to me.
        [*Offers to draw on* HORNER; *stopped by* HARCOURT.]
HARCOURT   Hold!
        [*Enter* SIR JASPER FIDGET, LADY FIDGET, OLD LADY
        SQUEAMISH, MRS. DAINTY FIDGET, MRS. SQUEAMISH.]
SIR JASPER FIDGET   What's the matter? what's the matter?
325   pray, what's the matter, sir? I beseech you communicate, sir.

PINCHWIFE Why, my wife has communicated,° sir, as your   *had (sexual) intercourse*
wife may have done too, sir, if she knows him, sir.

SIR JASPER FIDGET Pshaw! with him! Ha, ha, he!

PINCHWIFE D'ye mock me, sir? A cuckold is a kind of a
330   wild beast; have a care, sir.

SIR JASPER FIDGET No, sure, you mock me, sir—he cuckold you! It can't be, ha, ha, he! Why, I'll tell you, sir—

      [*Offers to whisper.*]

PINCHWIFE I tell you again, he has whored my wife, and
yours too, if he knows her, and all the women he comes
335   near; 'tis not his dissembling, his hypocrisy, can wheedle
me.

SIR JASPER FIDGET How! does he dissemble? Is he a hypocrite? Nay, then—how—wife—sister, is he an hypocrite?

OLD LADY SQUEAMISH An hypocrite! a dissembler! Speak,
340   young harlotry, speak, how?

SIR JASPER FIDGET Nay, then—oh, my head too!—O thou
libidinous lady!

OLD LADY SQUEAMISH O thou harloting harlotry! Hast
thou done't then?

345 SIR JASPER FIDGET Speak, good Horner, art thou a dissembler, a rogue? Hast thou—

HORNER Soh!

LUCY [*apart to* HORNER] I'll fetch you off,° and her too, if   *rescue you*
she will but hold her tongue.

350 HORNER [*apart to* LUCY] Canst thou? I'll give thee—

LUCY [*to* MR. PINCHWIFE] Pray have but patience to hear
me, sir, who am the unfortunate cause of all this confusion. Your wife is innocent, I only culpable; for I put her
upon telling you all these lies concerning my mistress, in
355   order to the breaking off the match between Mr. Sparkish
and her, to make way for Mr. Harcourt.

SPARKISH Did you so, eternal rotten tooth? Then, it
seems, my mistress was not false to me, I was only
deceived by you.—Brother that should have been, now,
360   man of conduct,[8] who is a frank person now? to bring
your wife to her lover—ha!

LUCY I assure you, sir, she came not to Mr. Horner out of
love, for she loves him no more—

MRS. PINCHWIFE Hold, I told lies for you, but you shall
365   tell none for me, for I do love Mr. Horner with all my
soul, and nobody shall say me nay; pray, don't you go to
make poor Mr. Horner believe to the contrary, 'tis spitefully done of you, I'm sure.

HORNER [*aside to* MRS. PINCHWIFE] Peace, dear idiot.

370 MRS. PINCHWIFE Nay, I will not peace.

PINCHWIFE Not till I make you.

      [*Enter* DORILANT, QUACK.]

---

8. Skill in managing affairs; discretion.

DORILANT   Horner, your servant; I am the doctor's guest, he must excuse our intrusion.

QUACK   But what's the matter, gentlemen? For heaven's
375   sake, what's the matter?

HORNER   Oh, 'tis well you are come. 'Tis a censorious world we live in; you may have brought me a reprieve, or else I had died for a crime I never committed, and these innocent ladies had suffered with me; therefore
380   pray satisfy these worthy, honorable, jealous gentlemen— that—[Whispers.]

QUACK   Oh, I understand you; is that all? —[Whispers to SIR JASPER.] Sir Jasper, by heavens and upon the word of a physician, sir—

385   SIR JASPER FIDGET   Nay, I do believe you truly. —Pardon me, my virtuous lady, and dear of honor.

OLD LADY SQUEAMISH   What, then all's right again?

SIR JASPER FIDGET   Ay, ay, and now let us satisfy him too.

[They whisper with MR. PINCHWIFE.]

PINCHWIFE   An eunuch! Pray, no fooling with me.
390   QUACK   I'll bring half the surgeons in town to swear it.

PINCHWIFE   They!—they'll swear a man bled to death through his wounds died of an apoplexy.[9]

QUACK   Pray hear me, sir—why, all the town has heard the report of him.
395   PINCHWIFE   But does all the town believe it?

QUACK   Pray inquire a little, and first of all these.

PINCHWIFE   I'm sure when I left the town he was the lewdest fellow in't.

QUACK   I tell you, sir, he has been in France since; pray
400   ask but these ladies and gentlemen, your friend Mr. Dorilant. —Gentlemen and ladies han't you all heard the late sad report of poor Mr. Horner?

ALL THE LADIES   Ay, ay, ay.

DORILANT   Why, thou jealous fool, dost thou doubt it?
405   He's an arrant French capon.[1]

MRS. PINCHWIFE   'Tis false, sir, you shall not disparage poor Mr. Horner, for to my certain knowledge—

LUCY   Oh, hold!

MRS. SQUEAMISH [aside to LUCY]   Stop her mouth!
410   LADY FIDGET [to PINCHWIFE]   Upon my honor, sir, 'tis as true—

MRS. DAINTY FIDGET   D'ye think we would have been seen in his company?

MRS. SQUEAMISH   Trust our unspotted reputations with him!
415   LADY FIDGET [aside to HORNER]   This you get, and we too, by trusting your secret to a fool.

---

9. That is, the local surgeons will swear that a man killed in an illegal duel died of a stroke.

1. Castrated cock; eunuch.

HORNER Peace, madam.—[*Aside to* QUACK] Well, doctor, is not this a good design, that carries a man on unsuspected, and brings him off safe?

420 PINCHWIFE [*aside*] Well, if this were true, but my wife—

[DORILANT *whispers with* MRS. PINCHWIFE.]

ALITHEA Come, brother, your wife is yet innocent, you see; but have a care of too strong an imagination, lest like an overconcerned, timorous gamester, by fancying an unlucky cast, it should come. Women and fortune are 425 truest still to those that trust 'em.

LUCY And any wild thing grows but the more fierce and hungry for being kept up,° and more dangerous to the keeper. | *confined*

ALITHEA There's doctrine for all husbands, Mr. Harcourt.

430 HARCOURT I edify, madam, so much that I am impatient till I am one.

DORILANT And I edify so much by example I will never be one.

SPARKISH And because I will not disparage my parts I'll 435 ne'er be one.

HORNER And I, alas, can't be one.

PINCHWIFE But I must be one—against my will, to a country wife, with a country murrain° to me. | *rural pestilence*

MRS. PINCHWIFE [*aside*] And I must be a country wife still 440 too, I find, for I can't, like a city one, be rid of my musty husband and do what I list.° | *wish, like*

HORNER Now, sir, I must pronounce your wife innocent, though I blush whilst I do it, and I am the only man by her now exposed to shame, which I will straight drown in 445 wine, as you shall your suspicion, and the ladies' troubles we'll divert with a ballet.—Doctor, where are your maskers?

LUCY Indeed, she's innocent, sir, I am her witness; and her end of coming out was but to see her sister's wed- 450 ding, and what she has said to your face of her love to Mr. Horner was but the usual innocent revenge on a husband's jealousy—was it not, madam? Speak.

MRS. PINCHWIFE [*aside to* LUCY *and* HORNER] Since you'll have me tell more lies—Yes, indeed, bud.

PINCHWIFE

455   *For my own sake fain I would all believe;*
       Cuckolds, like lovers, should themselves deceive.
       But—[Sighs.]
       His honor is least safe, too late I find,
       Who trusts it with a foolish wife or friend.

       [*A dance of cuckolds.*]

HORNER

460   *Vain fops but court, and dress, and keep a pother,*

> To pass for women's men with one another;
> But he who aims by women to be priz'd,
> First by the men, you see, must be despis'd.

FINIS

Epilogue

Spoken by Mrs. Knep.[2]

Now, you the vigorous, who daily here
O'er vizard-mask in public domineer,
And what you'd do to her if in place where; }
Nay, have the confidence to cry, "Come out!"
5 Yet when she says, "Lead on," you are not stout;°   *courageous*
But to your well-dress'd brother straight turn round
And cry, "Pox on her, Ned, she can't be sound!"
Then slink away, a fresh one to engage, }
With so much seeming heat and loving rage, }
10 You'd frighten listening actress on the stage; }
Till she at last has seen you huffing come, }
And talk of keeping in the tiring-room, }
Yet cannot be provok'd to lead her home. }
Next, you Falstaffs of fifty, who beset
15 Your buckram maidenheads,[3] which your friends get;
And whilst to them you of achievements boast,
They share the booty, and laugh at your cost.
In fine, you essenc'd boys, both old and young, }
Who would be thought so eager, brisk, and strong, }
20 Yet do the ladies, not their husbands, wrong;
Whose purses for your manhood make excuse,
And keep your Flanders mares[4] for show, not use;
Encourag'd by our woman's man today,
A Horner's part may vainly think to play;
25 And may intrigues so bashfully disown
That they may doubted be by few or none;
May kiss the cards at picquet, ombre, loo, }
And so be thought to kiss the lady too; }
But, gallants, have a care, faith, what you do. }
30 The world, which to no man his due will give,
You by experience know you can deceive,
And men may still believe you vigorous,
But then we women—there's no coz'ning° us.   *deceiving*

FINIS.

---

2. Elizabeth Knepp (d. 1681), the first to play the role of Lady Fidget.
3. An allusion to Shakespeare's *1 Henry IV* (2.5.176–202), in which Falstaff lies about his triumphs over "buckram suits"; buckram is a stiff fabric.
4. Horses that should be used for breeding; here, mistresses.

APHRA BEHN

1640?–1689

I n her famous essay on women's writing, *A Room of One's Own* (1929), Virginia Woolf opines, "All women together ought to let flowers fall upon the tomb of Aphra Behn . . . , for it was she who earned them the right to speak their minds." As one of the first professional woman writers, Behn personifies for Woolf the struggles and triumphs attendant on living solely by one's pen. Yet the phenomenon of Behn as a professional writer, and the discovery of the circumstances that spawned her theatrical and literary career, initially drew more attention than her prodigious output itself. Indeed, even for Woolf, Behn's financial achievement "outweighs anything that she actually wrote." Ironically, Behn's unique professional status long allowed critics to dismiss her work as that of a hack and, more pointedly, of an immodest woman. Alexander Pope's notorious observation that Behn "fairly puts all characters to bed" reinforced the presumption that her dramas reflected personal licentiousness. Only in recent decades has her writing received a thorough analysis. That thoughtful reconsideration has established her importance as a Restoration dramatist and theater theorist, as a poet, and as a progenitor of the English novel.

Indisputably, the scarcity of concrete facts about her life combined with persistent insinuations of "irregular" behavior, including stories of her having spied for the English Crown, continues to tantalize us about Behn. No records exist to confirm her birth, but most biographers believe she was born in 1640, in the vicinity of Canterbury, to parents (possibly named Johnson) of uncertain social position. The biographer Angeline Goreau argues that the sophistication of Behn's writing, even in her earliest works, suggests a level of education available only to women of the gentry and higher social orders. Perhaps more significantly, we can see clear textual evidence in THE ROVER (1677) and elsewhere of Behn's keen understanding of class positions and their pervasive social impact. Moreover, as a child of a Royalist family, growing up in the periods of the English Civil War (1642–49) and the Commonwealth (1649–60), she developed an acute sensitivity to her country's shifting tides of power. Political concerns, and a sense of political commitment, underlie much of her dramaturgy.

It appears that in 1663 Aphra and her family embarked on a voyage to the then British colony of Surinam, where her father may have been assigned to a government post or may have hoped to profit as a planter. He died during the journey, however, and the surviving family members left Surinam in early 1664. Yet the brief stay made a strong impression; Aphra's observations of plantation life and the practices of slavery inform her best-known novel, *Oroonoko* (1688). Upon her return to England, she apparently married one Mr. Behn, who may have been a merchant. Some biographers conjecture that he soon died in the plague that swept London in 1664 to 1666, leaving her without financial support; others believe that the marriage was fictitious, created by Behn to provide herself social legitimacy.

During her time in Surinam, Aphra had met William Scot, whose father, Thomas Scot, had been executed for his role in the regicide of Charles I. Although the nature of their relationship is unknown, it seems likely that William introduced Aphra to the world of political intrigue, which would soon involve her directly. In 1666, Behn probably became a spy for the restored Charles II, traveling to Antwerp to reconnect with William Scot, who was living there in exile and was probably an informant in the Anglo-Dutch War. Behn, like many in government service at the time, quickly fell into financial distress when promised payments failed to materialize. When she returned to England in 1667, she was seriously in debt and was briefly held in debtor's prison. This experience of privation marked her indelibly, and the precarious financial status of women in Restoration society became one of her dominant concerns. Yet her time in Antwerp had also persuaded her of her self-sufficiency, even in dangerous and male-dominated arenas. In the preface to her late play *The Lucky Chance* (1687), she openly connected her creativity to her understanding of the masculine sphere in which she worked, claiming privilege "for my Masculine Part the Poet in me."

After her release from jail, Behn decided to embark on a career as a professional playwright. In September 1670, her first piece, *The Forced Marriage,* premiered at Lincoln's Inn Fields and ran for six nights—a solid performance record for the period. Behn followed with *The Amorous Prince* (1671), *The Dutch Lover* (1673), *Abdelazer* (1676), *The Town Fop* (1676), *The Debauchee* (later attributed to her, 1677), and in March 1677, the first part of *The Rover.*

Over the next twelve years, Behn's output included approximately a dozen more plays (attributions remain conjectural for some, produced anonymously), including the second part of *The Rover* (1681), numerous translations, several volumes of verse, the protonovelistic *Love Letters between a Nobleman and His Sister,* and the fictional prose works *Oroonoko* and *The Fair Jilt.* Two other plays and several other fictional works appeared posthumously. Behn died in April 1689, shortly after the coronation of William and Mary, and is buried in Westminster Abbey.

That Behn could maintain even a meager livelihood in the professional theater for more than twenty years clearly indicates that she was a popular dramatist. The reasons aren't hard to imagine. What is true of mass culture today was equally valid for the Restoration: though some degree of novelty may be welcome, the public enjoys entertainment forms that it already knows well. Behn had a quick wit and a ready hand at adaptation and translation, and she used these skills to create new plays that incorporated themes, dramatic structures, character types, and plot devices that had already proven their stageworthiness.

The closure of the theaters from 1642 to 1660 by the Puritan government had severely impeded but could not altogether quash the ongoing development of the English drama, which had flourished in the Renaissance. When Thomas Killigrew and Sir William Davenant received patents from Charles II to operate London's two licensed theaters, they looked to published drama, especially by WILLIAM SHAKESPEARE, BEN JONSON, and Francis Beaumont and John Fletcher, to remount. These revivals, as well as adaptations of established works and of closet dramas written during the interregnum (the time between the beheading of Charles I in 1649 and the restoration of the monarchy in 1660), constituted most of the early Restoration stage repertoire. The new dramas that had immediately preceded the Commonwealth period, such as the comedies of James Shirley, provided further inspiration for aspiring Restoration dramatists.

The Rover may be best understood within these complex political and theatrical contexts. Following common dramatic practice, Behn decided to adapt a lengthy unproduced work by Killigrew, written in 1654 and published a decade later, titled *Thomaso, or, The Wanderer*. By refashioning characters, streamlining action, and highlighting plot elements from *Thomaso* that she suspected would please her audience, Behn created in *The Rover* a play that could also carry her distinctive themes. Her subtle revisions of well-established patterns of stage dialogue and character types, which had been codified over the preceding decade through the dramas of Sir George Etherege, John Dryden, and WILLIAM WYCHERLEY, among others, enabled her both to develop these themes and to build upon her growing theatrical reputation.

Behn's first strategic choice in adapting *Thomaso* was to change its setting. She moves the action from the time of the Spanish Inquisition to the more recent past—the period of Royalist exile—and places her characters in Naples during the carnival season of revelry that precedes Lent. After the murder of Charles I, his son Prince Charles fled England, as did a good number of his supporters, who feared persecution under the Puritan regime. That Cromwell then confiscated many of the Royalists' estates may account for the impecunious state of characters like the "rover" Willmore, whose seaboard travels also associate him with the Prince. As the Royalists' friend Blunt avows, "I thank my stars I had more grace than to forfeit my estate by cavaliering." But he also admits that supporting his friends "is a greater crime to my conscience, gentlemen, than to the commonwealth."

Behn depicts the adventures of a band of these traveling Englishmen (her subtitle is "The Banished Cavaliers"), led by the rakish Willmore and his more earnest friend Belvile. They encounter the local women "of quality," Hellena, Florinda, and Valeria, as well as prostitutes, especially the courtesan Angellica. Although the setting is foreign and somewhat exotic, the narrative arc is traditional, centering on which of the characters will marry and how those relationships will be solidified. Behn thus brings together conventions from both the drama of intrigue and romantic comedy. She retains the swashbuckling flavor of Killigrew's Spanish setting and peppers her action with lively swordplay between rivals for the favors of

"Venetian" masquerades, such as the one pictured here that was held in Ranelagh Gardens, London, in April of 1749, were quite popular in England during the late seventeenth and early eighteenth centuries.

Angellica and protectors of the honor of the chaste Florinda. By removing the drama from a court setting, moreover, she participates in the Restoration theater's shift of focus away from the aristocracy and toward those in the growing middle ranks of society. By interweaving dramatic forms and broadening the range of characters, Behn can explore issues of class and gender frankly while simultaneously confirming her loyalty to the returned monarch and his supporters.

From the medieval era forward, Western literature has depicted the carnival season preceding Lent as a time of culturally sanctioned upheaval, when rigid social structures are briefly relaxed. Behn dramatizes just such a moment in *The Rover*, as the aristocratic young women of Naples disguise themselves and escape their sequestered home environment to join the revelry, where they meet the English cavaliers. Behn must have seen a direct link between her carnival setting and Restoration culture writ large, given their shared predilections for masking, posturing, and sexual license; we may assume that audiences for *The Rover* grasped these connections through such devices as the thinly disguised characterization of the libertine John Wilmot, earl of Rochester, as her libertine Willmore. At the same time, however, Behn demonstrates that even within the freedoms offered by masquerade, women remained subject to male power and assumed sexual privilege. Behn's viewers may also have perceived the metatheatrical quality of the play, as she repeatedly calls our attention to the donning of a series of costumes by Hellena, Florinda, and Valeria as well as to the highly staged yet ignominious duping of Blunt by the conniving Lucetta.

Behn signals her focus on the female characters from her opening scene, which introduces us to Florinda and her sister Hellena. We are privy to the sisters' exchanges about Florinda's multiple suitors and Hellena's desire to find a man and to avoid having to become a nun: "I'm resolved to provide myself this Carnival, if there be e'er a handsome proper fellow of my humour above ground, though I ask first." Behn contrasts the sisters through their attitudes toward sexuality. While Hellena is willing to transcend traditional feminine passivity by "ask[ing] first," Florinda is the more conventional romantic heroine. We learn that Florinda has previously been rescued in Pamplona from the "licensed lust of common soldiers" by her admirer, Captain Belvile, but she will face three more threats of sexual assault before she is safely united with him. She must also outwit her brother Pedro and her father, each of whom has arranged for her marriage to an eligible, but undesired, suitor. The feistier Hellena soon develops an attraction for the rake Willmore, but finds she must plot to secure his complete attention and fidelity.

Through the play's opening dialogue, Behn establishes the competing tensions that will shape her comedy: between women's desire to make their own matrimonial choices and men's assumption of that privilege, between women's interest in reciprocal enjoyment of sex and men's single-minded lust, between women's financial dependence on men and their wish to gain some control over their economic future. Behn deploys the familiar trope of marriage and money central to Restoration comedy but refocuses it by realistically depicting the social and financial constraints affecting the female characters. The introduction of the courtesan Angellica Bianca and the "jilting wench" Lucetta, who play important roles in the play's examination of women's economic status, also enables Behn to explore the traditional depiction of women as either virgins or whores and to question the relationship of these opposing roles to the exchange economy she portrays.

Restoration comedy frequently critiqued marriages based solely on economic convenience, but Behn portrays the emotional and personal costs of such arrangements to women with real poignancy. Women of the era were legally considered the property of their fathers until, through the dowry system, they became the property of their husbands, who thereby gained complete control of their wealth and their person. Arranged marriages thus served to protect and enhance family fortunes. As Behn's contemporary Margaret Cavendish, duchess of Newcastle, once remarked, "Daughters are to be accounted but as Movable Goods or Furniture that wear out." In the opening scene of *The Rover,* Florinda implores her brother not to "follow the ill customs of our country and make a slave of his sister" by marrying her to a man she hates.

Where Behn departs from Restoration dramatic convention is in overtly connecting the financial networks of marriage and prostitution—especially in the absence of true affection. When Willmore tries to convince Angellica to favor him sexually for the sake of desire alone, chastising her, "Poor as I am I would not sell myself, / No, not to gain your charming high-prized person," Angellica exposes his hypocrisy:

> Pray tell me, sir, are not you guilty of the same mercenary crime? When a lady is proposed to you for a wife, you never ask how fair, discreet, or virtuous she is, but what's her fortune; which, if but

small, you cry "She will not do my business," and basely leave her, though she languish for you. Say, is not this as poor?

That Hellena and Florinda both possess fortunes, enhancing their suitability for marriage to the impecunious but noble cavaliers, underscores this irony. Behn does not attempt to overcome the power of dramatic (and moral) convention by disrupting the inevitable union of the "gay couple" Hellena and Willmore with a serious relationship between Willmore and Angellica. But she does, through the amorous triangulation of these three characters, resist typical structures of jealousy and opposition between women. Indeed, throughout the play, Behn provides multiple instances of women joining forces to achieve their economic and amatory goals.

However, a darker corollary to these associations among the play's women emerges from the male characters' repeated inability to distinguish between prostitutes

Jeremy Irons as Willmore ("the Rover") in the 1986 production of *The Rover* by the Royal Shakespeare Company.

and women "of quality." Blunt, after being tricked out of his belongings by Lucetta, whom he erroneously assumed was a lady of elevated social standing, displays open hostility to the female sex as a whole. For Blunt, virgins and whores are "as much one as t'other," and his plan to rape Florinda blatantly displays male sexuality as the exercise of power over women: "Cruel? Yes, I will kiss and beat thee all over, kiss and see thee all over; thou shalt lie with me, too, not that I care for the enjoyment, but to let thee see I have ta'en deliberated malice to thee, and will be revenged on one whore for the sins of another." Behn makes clear that no woman is immune to the potential for sexual violation in the carnivalesque culture she depicts.

In his rage, Blunt calls attention to the pretense he associates with prostitution, designating all whores "dissembling witches." He describes Florinda's tale of persecution by a group of unknown men she encounters while trying to flee to Belvile as if it were a performance—a calculated impersonation of the damsel in distress designed to fool him yet again. Such gestures point toward Behn's understanding of the increasingly complex interplay of women and theatricality in the Restoration. Behn's own entry into the theater as a playwright coincided with the appearance of the first professional English actresses. The display of women onstage quickly became associated with prostitution, a linkage made notorious by the actress Nell Gwynn, who was Charles II's mistress. But Behn realized that her own self-promotion, required of her as a playwright, drew a similar judgment; she very possibly retained the name Angellica Bianca from Killigrew and treated the character more sympathetically because she perceived that the courtesan character and she had much in common.

By deftly balancing sympathetic portraits of female characters with their frank display—particularly of Hellena, costumed in the breeches that allowed for more of the actress's body to be revealed—Behn calculatedly negotiated her position in the Restoration playhouse. She recognized that she could interject her own perspectives on women's lives as long as she also worked within established theatrical practices that appealed to the male patrons of the stage. Her combination of comic action, witty dialogue, bravado, romantic suspense, and titillation succeeded theatrically well into the eighteenth century. *The Rover* remained a regular part of the repertoire throughout the first half of that century and returned to popularity late in the twentieth, demonstrating its worth not only as an exemplar of Restoration drama but also as successful and timeless stage comedy.   J.E.G.

The Rover;
or, *The Banished Cavaliers*[1]

Prologue

Wits, like physicians, never can agree,
When of a different society.
And Rabel's drops[2] were never more cried down
By all the learned doctors of the town,
5   Than a new play whose author is unknown.[3]
Nor can those doctors with more malice sue
(And powerful purses) the dissenting few,
Than those, with an insulting pride, do rail
At all who are not of their own cabal.°   *clique*
10   If a young poet hit your humour° right,   *mood*
You judge him then out of revenge and spite.
So amongst men there are ridiculous elves,
Who monkeys hate for being too like themselves.
So that the reason of the grand debate
15 Why wit so oft is damned when good plays take,
Is that you censure as you love, or hate.
   Thus like a learned conclave poets sit,
Catholic° judges both of sense and wit,   *Universal*
And damn or save as they themselves think fit.
20 Yet those who to others' faults are so severe,
Are not so perfect but themselves may err.
Some write correct, indeed, but then the whole
(Bating° their own dull stuff i'th' play) is stole: *Excepting*
As bees do suck from flowers their honeydew,
25 So they rob others striving to please you.
   Some write their characters genteel and fine,
But then they do so toil for every line,
That what to you does easy seem, and plain,
Is the hard issue of their laboring brain.
30 And some th'effects of all their pains, we see,
Is but to mimic good extempore.°   *improvisation*
Others, by long converse about the town,
Have wit enough to write a lewd lampoon,
But their chief skill lies in a bawdy song.
35 In short, the only wit that's now in fashion,
Is but the gleanings of good conversation.
As for the author of this coming play,

---

1. The Royalist supporters of Charles I; as many went into exile during the English Civil War and interregnum of 1642–60, often their estates were confiscated by Oliver Cromwell.

2. A well-known patent medicine.
3. *The Rover* was initially produced and published anonymously.

I asked him[4] what he thought fit I should say
In thanks for your good company today:
He called me fool, and said it was well known
You came not here for our sakes, but your own.
New plays are stuffed with wits and with deboches,°   *debauchees*
That crowd and sweat like cits in May-Day coaches.[5]

WRITTEN BY A PERSON OF QUALITY

40

CHARACTERS

DON ANTONIO, the Viceroy's son
DON PEDRO, a noble Spaniard, his friend
BELVILE, an English colonel in love with Florinda
WILLMORE, the Rover
FREDERICK, an English gentleman, and friend to Belvile and Blunt
BLUNT, an English country gentleman
STEPHANO, servant to Don Pedro
PHILIPPO, Lucetta's gallant
SANCHO, pimp to Lucetta
BISKEY and SEBASTIAN, two bravos° to Angellica   *hired ruffians, henchmen*
OFFICER and SOLDIERS
DIEGO, Page to Don Antonio
FLORINDA, sister to Don Pedro
HELLENA, a gay young woman designed for[6] a nun, and sister to Florinda
VALERIA, a kinswoman to Florinda
ANGELLICA BIANCA, a famous courtesan
MORETTA, her woman
CALLIS, governess to Florinda and Hellena
LUCETTA, a jilting wench
SERVANTS, OTHER MASQUERADERS, MEN AND WOMEN

THE SCENE: *Naples, in Carnival time.*[7]

1.1

[SCENE: *A chamber.*]

[*Enter* FLORINDA *and* HELLENA.]

FLORINDA   What an impertinent thing is a young girl bred
in a nunnery! How full of questions! Prithee no more,
Hellena; I have told thee more than thou understand'st
already.

5 HELLENA   The more's my grief. I would fain° know as much   *gladly*
as you, which makes me so inquisitive; nor is't enough
I know you're a lover, unless you tell me too who 'tis
you sigh for.

---

4. Behn used the masculine pronoun so that
playgoers would not dismiss this work as written by a woman.
5. It was customary to ride around Hyde Park
in coaches on May Day. *Cits*: urban males,
but not gentlemen (slang).

6. That is, designated (by her family) to
become.
7. The period of festival before the fasting
and prayer of Lent, commonly celebrated in
Roman Catholic countries.

FLORINDA   When you're a lover I'll think you fit for a
10   secret of that nature.

HELLENA   'Tis true, I never was a lover yet, but I begin to
have a shrewd guess what 'tis to be so, and fancy it very
pretty to sigh, and sing, and blush, and wish, and dream
and wish, and long and wish to see the man, and when I
15   do, look pale and tremble, just as you did when my
brother brought home the fine English colonel to see
you. What do you call him? Don Belvile?

FLORINDA   Fie, Hellena.

HELLENA   That blush betrays you. I am sure 'tis so. Or is it
20   Don Antonio the Viceroy's son? Or perhaps the rich old
Don Vincentio, whom my father designs you for a husband? Why do you blush again?

FLORINDA   With indignation; and how near soever my
father thinks I am to marrying that hated object, I shall let
25   him see I understand better what's due to my beauty,
birth, and fortune, and more to my soul, than to obey
those unjust commands.

HELLENA   Now hang me, if I don't love thee for that dear
disobedience. I love mischief strangely, as most of our
30   sex do who are come to love nothing else. But tell me,
dear Florinda, don't you love that fine *Anglese*?° For I   *Englishman (Italian)*
vow, next to loving him myself, 'twill please me most
that you do so, for he is so gay and so handsome.

FLORINDA   Hellena, a maid designed for a nun ought not
35   to be so curious in a discourse of love.

HELLENA   And dost thou think that ever I'll be a nun? Or
at least till° I'm so old I'm fit for nothing else? Faith no,   *before*
sister; and that which makes me long to know whether
you love Belvile, is because I hope he has some mad
40   companion or other that will spoil my devotion. Nay, I'm
resolved to provide myself this Carnival, if there be e'er a
handsome proper fellow of my humour above ground,
though I ask first.

FLORINDA   Prithee be not so wild.

45   HELLENA   Now you have provided yourself of a man you
take no care of poor me. Prithee tell me, what dost thou
see about me that is unfit for love? Have I not a world of
youth? A humour gay? A beauty passable? A vigor desirable? Well shaped? Clean limbed? Sweet breathed? And
50   sense enough to know how all these ought to be employed to the best advantage? Yes, I do and will; therefore
lay aside your hopes of my fortune by my being a devote,°   *nun*
and tell me how you came acquainted with this Belvile.
For I perceive you knew him before he came to Naples.

55   FLORINDA   Yes, I knew him at the siege of Pamplona;[8]
he was then a colonel of French horse, who when the

8. The capital of the Spanish province of Navarre, which was several times attacked by the
French during the Thirty Years War (1618–48) waged throughout Europe.

town was ransacked, nobly treated my brother and myself, preserving us from all insolences. And I must own,
besides great obligations, I have I know not what that
60   pleads kindly for him about my heart, and will suffer no
other to enter. But see, my brother.

        [*Enter* DON PEDRO, STEPHANO *with a masking habit,*°   *masquerade costume*
        and CALLIS.]

PEDRO   Good morrow, sister. Pray when saw you your
      lover Don Vincentio?

FLORINDA   I know not, sir. Callis, when was he here? For I
65   consider it so little I know not when it was.

PEDRO   I have a command from my father here to tell you
      you ought not to despise him, a man of so vast a fortune,
      and such a passion for you. —Stephano, my things.

        [*Puts on his masking habit.*]

FLORINDA   A passion for me? 'Tis more than e'er I saw, or he
70   had a desire should be known. I hate Vincentio, sir, and I
      would not have a man so dear to me as my brother follow
      the ill customs of our country and make a slave of his sis-
      ter. And, sir, my father's will I'm sure you may divert.

PEDRO   I know not how dear I am to you, but I wish only
75   to be ranked in your esteem equal with the English colo-
      nel Belvile. Why do you frown and blush? Is there any
      guilt belongs to the name of that cavalier?

FLORINDA   I'll not deny I value Belvile. When I was exposed
      to such dangers as the licensed lust of common soldiers
80   threatened, when rage and conquest flew through the city,
      then Belvile, this criminal for my sake, threw himself into
      all dangers to save my honor. And will you not allow him
      my esteem?

PEDRO   Yes, pay him what you will in honor, but you
85   must consider Don Vincentio's fortune, and the join-
      ture[9] he'll make you.

FLORINDA   Let him consider my youth, beauty, and for-
      tune, which ought not to be thrown away on his age and
      jointure.

90 PEDRO   'Tis true, he's not so young and fine a gentleman
      as that Belvile. But what jewels will that cavalier present
      you with. Those of his eyes and heart?

HELLENA   And are not those better than any Don Vin-
      centio has brought from the Indies?

95 PEDRO   Why, how now! Has your nunnery breeding taught
      you to understand the value of hearts and eyes?

HELLENA   Better than to believe Vincentio's deserve value
      from any woman. He may perhaps increase her bags,°   *wealth*
      but not her family.

100 PEDRO   This is fine! Go! Up to your devotion! You are not
      designed for the conversation of lovers.

---

9. The property promised to a wife at marriage in the event of her husband's death.

HELLENA [*aside*]   Nor saints yet a while, I hope. —Is't not
enough you make a nun of me, but you must cast my
sister away too, exposing her to a worse confinement than
105   a religious life?

PEDRO   The girl's mad! It is a confinement to be carried
into the country to an ancient villa belonging to the family of the Vincentios these five hundred years, and have
no other prospect° than that pleasing one of seeing all   *view*
110   her own that meets her eyes: a fine air, large fields, and
gardens where she may walk and gather flowers?

HELLENA   When, by moonlight? For I am sure she dares
not encounter with the heat of the sun; that were a task
only for Don Vincentio and his Indian breeding, who
115   loves it in the dog days.[1] And if these be her daily divertissements,° what are those of the night? To lie in a wide   *amusements*
moth-eaten bedchamber with furniture in fashion in the
reign of King Sancho the First;[2] the bed, that which his
forefathers lived and died in.

120   PEDRO   Very well.

HELLENA   This apartment, new furbished and fitted out
for the young wife, he out of freedom makes his dressing
room; and being a frugal and a jealous coxcomb,° instead   *fool*
of a valet to uncase° his feeble carcass, he desires you to   *undress*
125   do that office. Signs of favor, I'll assure you, and such as
you must not hope for unless your woman be out of the
way.

PEDRO   Have you done yet?

HELLENA   That honor being past, the giant stretches itself,
130   yawns and sighs a belch or two loud as a musket, throws
himself into bed, and expects° you in his foul sheets; and   *waits for*
ere you can get yourself undressed, calls you with a
snore or two. And are not these fine blessings to a young
lady?

135   PEDRO   Have you done yet?

HELLENA   And this man you must kiss, nay you must kiss
none but him too, and nuzzle through his beard to find
his lips. And this you must submit to for threescore
years, and all for a jointure.

140   PEDRO   For all your character of Don Vincentio, she is as
like to marry him as she was before.

HELLENA   Marry Don Vincentio! Hang me, such a wedlock
would be worse than adultery with another man. I had
rather see her in the *Hostel de Dieu*,[3] to waste her youth
145   there in vows, and be a handmaid to lazars° and cripples,   *lepers*
than to lose it in such a marriage.

PEDRO   You have considered, sister, that Belvile has no

1. The hottest part of summer, when Sirius
(the Dog Star) rises. *Indian breeding*: birth in
the West Indies.
2. King of Pamplona (Navarre) in the 10th
century.
3. A charitable hospital operated by a religious order.

fortune to bring you to; banished his country, despised at
home, and pitied abroad.

150 HELLENA What then? The Viceroy's son is better than
that old Sir Fifty. Don Vincentio! Don Indian! He thinks
he's trading to Gambo[4] still, and would barter himself—
that bell and bauble—for your youth and fortune.

PEDRO Callis, take her hence and lock her up all this Car-
155 nival, and at Lent she shall begin her everlasting penance in a monastery.

HELLENA I care not; I had rather be a nun than be obliged
to marry as you would have me if I were designed for't.

PEDRO Do not fear the blessing of that choice. You shall be
160 a nun.

HELLENA [aside] Shall I so? You may chance to be mistaken in my way of devotion. A nun! Yes, I am like to
make a fine nun! I have an excellent humour for a grate![5]
No, I'll have a saint of my own to pray to shortly, if I like
165 any that dares venture on me.

PEDRO Callis, make it your business to watch this wildcat.
—As for you, Florinda, I've only tried° you all this while   *tested*
and urged my father's will; but mine is that you would
love Antonio: he is brave and young, and all that can
170 complete the happiness of a gallant maid. This absence
of my father will give us opportunity to free you from Vincentio by marrying here, which you must do tomorrow.

FLORINDA Tomorrow!

PEDRO Tomorrow, or 'twill be too late. 'Tis not my friendship
175 to Antonio which makes me urge this, but love to thee and
hatred to Vincentio; therefore resolve upon tomorrow.

FLORINDA Sir, I shall strive to do as shall become your sister.

PEDRO I'll both believe and trust you. Adieu.

[*Exeunt*° PEDRO *and* STEPHANO.]   *They exit (Latin)*

HELLENA As becomes his sister! That is to be as resolved
180 your way as he is his.

[HELLENA *goes to* CALLIS.]

FLORINDA I ne'er till now perceived my ruin near.
I've no defence against Antonio's love,
For he has all the advantages of nature,
The moving arguments of youth and fortune.

185 HELLENA But hark you, Callis, you will not be so cruel to
lock me up indeed, will you?

CALLIS I must obey the commands I have. Besides, do
you consider what a life you are going to lead?

HELLENA Yes, Callis, that of a nun; and till then I'll be in-
190 debted a world of prayers to you if you'll let me now see
what I never did, the divertissements of a Carnival.

---

4. The British colony of Gambia in West
Africa, a center of the slave trade.
5. The framework of bars on a convent's

doors and windows, separating nuns from the
secular world.

CALLIS   What, go in masquerade? 'Twill be a fine farewell
    to the world, I take it. Pray what would you do there?

HELLENA   That which all the world does, as I am told: be as
195   mad as the rest and take all innocent freedoms. Sister,
    you'll go too, will you not? Come, prithee be not sad.
    We'll outwit twenty brothers if you'll be ruled by me.
    Come, put off this dull humour with your clothes, and
    assume one as gay and as fantastic as the dress my cousin
200   Valeria and I have provided, and let's ramble.

FLORINDA   Callis, will you give us leave to go?

CALLIS [aside]   I have a youthful itch of going myself. —
    Madam, if I thought your brother might not know it, and
    I might wait on you; for by my troth I'll not trust young
205   girls alone.

FLORINDA   Thou seest my brother's gone already, and thou
    shalt attend and watch us.

        [Enter STEPHANO.]

STEPHANO   Madam, the habits° are come, and your cousin   *costumes*
    Valeria is dressed and stays for you.

210 FLORINDA [aside]   'Tis well. I'll write a note, and if I
    chance to see Belvile and want an opportunity to speak
    to him, that shall let him know what I've resolved in favor
    of him.

HELLENA   Come, let's in and dress us.

                    [Exeunt.]

1.2

[SCENE: *A long street.*]

    [Enter BELVILE, *melancholy;* BLUNT *and* FREDERICK.]

FREDERICK   Why, what the devil ails the colonel, in a time
    when all the world is gay, to look like mere° Lent thus?   *pure*
    Hadst thou been long enough in Naples to have been in
    love, I should have sworn some such judgment had be-
5   fallen thee.

BELVILE   No, I have made no new amours since I came to
    Naples.

FREDERICK   You have left none behind you in Paris?

BELVILE   Neither.

10 FREDERICK   I cannot divine the cause then, unless the old
    cause, the want of money.

BLUNT   And another old cause, the want of a wench.
    Would not that revive you?

BELVILE   You are mistaken, Ned.

15 BLUNT   Nay, 'adsheartlikins,° then thou'rt past cure.   *God's little heart (oath)*

FREDERICK   I have found it out: thou hast renewed thy ac-
    quaintance with the lady that cost thee so many sighs at
    the siege of Pamplona—pox on't,° what d'ye call her—her   *(an oath)*
    brother's a noble Spaniard, nephew to the dead general.

20   Florinda. Ay, Florinda. And will nothing serve thy turn
       but that damned virtuous woman, whom on my con-
       science thou lov'st in spite too, because thou seest little
       or no possibility of gaining her.

    BELVILE   Thou art mistaken; I have int'rest enough in that
25   lovely virgin's heart to make me proud and vain, were it
       not abated by the severity of a brother, who, perceiving
       my happiness—

    FREDERICK   Has civilly forbid thee the house?

    BELVILE   'Tis so, to make way for a powerful rival, the
30   Viceroy's son, who has the advantage of me in being a
       man of fortune, a Spaniard, and her brother's friend;
       which gives him liberty to make his court, whilst I have
       recourse only to letters and distant looks from her win-
       dow, which are as soft and kind as those which heaven
35   sends down on penitents.

    BLUNT   Heyday! 'Adsheartlikins, simile! By this light the
       man is quite spoiled. Fred, what the devil are we made of
       that we cannot be thus concerned for a wench? 'Ads-
       heartlikins, our Cupids[6] are like the cooks of the camp:
40   they can roast or boil a woman, but they have none of the
       fine tricks to set 'em off; no hogoes° to make the sauce   *savory relishes*
       pleasant and the stomach sharp.

    FREDERICK   I dare swear I have had a hundred as young,
       kind, and handsome as this Florinda; and dogs eat me if
45   they were not as troublesome to me i'th' morning as they
       were welcome o'er night.

    BLUNT   And yet I warrant he would not touch another
       woman if he might have her for nothing.

    BELVILE   That's thy joy, a cheap whore.

50   BLUNT   Why, 'adsheartlikins, I love a frank soul. When did
       you ever hear of an honest woman that took a man's
       money? I warrant 'em good ones. But gentlemen, you
       may be free; you have been kept so poor with parlia-
       ments and protectors that the little stock you have is not
55   worth preserving. But I thank my stars I had more grace
       than to forfeit my estate by cavaliering.[7]

    BELVILE   Methinks only following the court should be suf-
       ficient to entitle 'em to that.

    BLUNT   'Adsheartlikins, they know I follow it to do it no
60   good, unless they pick a hole in my coat for lending you
       money now and then, which is a greater crime to my
       conscience, gentlemen, than to the commonwealth.

          [*Enter* WILLMORE.]

---

6. Cupid is the Roman god of love, often depicted as winged; his arrows cause their target to fall in love.
7. The estates of many Royalists (i.e., Cavaliers) were confiscated by Oliver Cromwell's government following the Parliamentarian victory in the English Civil War. The official title of the country's leader during that period was Lord Protector of the Commonwealth.

WILLMORE   Ha! Dear Belvile! Noble colonel!

BELVILE   Willmore! Welcome ashore, my dear rover! What
65   happy wind blew us this good fortune?

WILLMORE   Let me salute my dear Fred, and then command me. —How is't, honest lad?

FREDERICK   Faith, sir, the old compliment, infinitely the
better to see my dear mad Willmore again. Prithee, why
70   camest thou ashore? And where's the Prince?[8]

WILLMORE   He's well, and reigns still lord of the wat'ry element. I must aboard again within a day or two, and my
business ashore was only to enjoy myself a little this Carnival.

75   BELVILE   Pray know our new friend, sir; he's but bashful, a
raw traveler, but honest, stout, and one of us.

[*Embraces* BLUNT.]

WILLMORE   That you esteem him gives him an int'rest here.

BLUNT   Your servant, sir.

WILLMORE   But well, faith, I'm glad to meet you again in a
80   warm climate, where the kind sun has its godlike power
still over the wine and women. Love and mirth are my
business in Naples, and if I mistake not the place, here's
an excellent market for chapmen° of my humour.   merchants

BELVILE   See, here be those kind merchants of love you
85   look for.

[*Enter several men in masking habits, some playing on
music, others dancing after; women dressed like courtesans, with papers pinned on their breasts, and baskets
of flowers in their hands.*]

BLUNT   'Adsheartlikins, what have we here?

FREDERICK   Now the game begins.

WILLMORE   Fine pretty creatures! May a stranger have
leave to look and love? What's here? "Roses for every
90   month"?   [*Reads the papers.*]

BLUNT   Roses for every month? What means that?

BELVILE   They are, or would have you think they're courtesans, who here in Naples are to be hired by the month.

WILLMORE   Kind and obliging to inform us, pray where do
95   these roses grow? I would fain plant some of 'em in a bed
of mine.

WOMAN   Beware such roses, sir.

WILLMORE   A pox of fear: I'll be baked with thee between a
pair of sheets, and that's thy proper still;[9] so I might but
100   strew such roses over me and under me. Fair one, would
you would give me leave to gather at your bush this idle
month; I would go near to make somebody smell of it all
the year after.

---

8. The exiled son of Charles I, soon to be
crowned Charles II (1630–1685; r. 1660–85).

9. That is, apparatus for distilling rose petals
to make perfume.

BELVILE And thou hast need of such a remedy, for thou
105   stink'st of tar and ropes' ends like a dock or pesthouse.[1]

> [*The* WOMAN *puts herself into the hands of a man
> and exeunt.*]

WILLMORE Nay, nay, you shall not leave me so.

BELVILE By all means use no violence here.

WILLMORE Death!° Just as I was going to be damnably in   God's death (an oath)
love, to have her led off! I could pluck that rose out of
110   his hand, and even kiss the bed the bush grew in.

FREDERICK No friend to love like a long voyage at sea.

BLUNT Except a nunnery,° Fred.   convent; brothel

WILLMORE Death! But will they not be kind? Quickly be
kind? Thou know'st I'm no tame sigher, but a rampant
115   lion of the forest.

> [*Advances from the farther end of the scenes two men
> dressed all over with horns*[2] *of several sorts, making
> grimaces at one another, with papers pinned on their
> backs.*]

BELVILE Oh the fantastical rogues, how they're dressed!
'Tis a satire against the whole sex.

WILLMORE Is this a fruit that grows in this warm country?

BELVILE Yes, 'tis pretty to see these Italians start, swell,
120   and stab at the word *cuckold*, and yet stumble at horns
on every threshold.

WILLMORE See what's on their back. [*Reads.*] "Flowers of
every night." Ah, rogue! And more sweet than roses of
every month! This is a gardener of Adam's own breeding.[3]

> [*They dance.*]

125 BELVILE What think you of these grave people? Is a wake
in Essex[4] half so mad or extravagant?

WILLMORE I like their sober grave way; 'tis a kind of legal
authorized fornication, where the men are not chid for't,
nor the women despised, as amongst our dull English.
130   Even the monsieurs want that part of good manners.

BELVILE But here in Italy, a monsieur is the humblest
best-bred gentleman: duels are so baffled by bravos° that   hired ruffians
an age shows not one but between a Frenchman and a
hangman, who is as much too hard for him on the Piazza
135   as they are for a Dutchman on the New Bridge.[5] But see,
another crew.

> [*Enter* FLORINDA, HELLENA, *and* VALERIA, *dressed like
> gipsies;* CALLIS *and* STEPHANO, LUCETTA, PHILIPPO
> *and* SANCHO *in masquerade.*]

---

1. A hospital for victims of the plague.
2. The symbol of a cuckold.
3. An allusion to the Garden of Eden.
4. The location of Blunt's home in rural
southeastern England (see also 2.1).

5. Nieuwerbrug (New Bridge), in southern
Holland, was attacked by the French in the
Third Anglo-Dutch War (1672–74)—an
anachronistic reference, as the play is set
before 1660.

HELLENA   Sister, there's your Englishman, and with him a
handsome proper fellow. I'll to him, and instead of telling him his fortune, try my own.

140 WILLMORE   Gipsies, on my life. Sure these will prattle if a
man cross their hands. [*Goes to* HELLENA.] —Dear,
pretty, and, I hope, young devil, will you tell an amorous
stranger what luck he's like to have?

HELLENA   Have a care how you venture with me, sir, lest I
145 pick your pocket, which will more vex your English
humor than an Italian fortune will please you.

WILLMORE   How the devil cam'st thou to know my country
and humor?

HELLENA   The first I guess by a certain forward impu-
150 dence, which does not displease me at this time; and the
loss of your money will vex you because I hope you have
but very little to lose.

WILLMORE   Egad, child, thou'rt i'th' right; it is so little I
dare not offer it thee for a kindness. But cannot you di-
155 vine what other things of more value I have about me
that I would more willingly part with?

HELLENA   Indeed no, that's the business of a witch, and I
am but a gipsy yet. Yet without looking in your hand, I
have a parlous guess 'tis some foolish heart you mean, an
160 inconstant English heart, as little worth stealing as your
purse.

WILLMORE   Nay, then thou dost deal with the devil, that's
certain. Thou hast guessed as right as if thou hadst been
one of that number it has languished for. I find you'll be
165 better acquainted with it, nor can you take it in a better
time; for I am come from sea, child, and Venus not being
propitious to me in her own element,[6] I have a world of
love in store. Would you would be good-natured and take
some on't off my hands.

170 HELLENA   Why, I could be inclined that way, but for a foolish vow I am going to make to die a maid.

WILLMORE   Then thou art damned without redemption,
and as I am a good Christian, I ought in charity to divert
so wicked a design. Therefore prithee, dear creature, let
175 me know quickly when and where I shall begin to set a
helping hand to so good a work.

HELLENA   If you should prevail with my tender heart, as I
begin to fear you will, for you have horrible loving eyes,
there will be difficulty in't that you'll hardly° undergo for   *with hardship*
180 my sake.

WILLMORE   Faith, child, I have been bred in dangers, and
wear a sword that has been employed in a worse cause
than for a handsome kind woman. Name the danger; let
it be anything but a long siege, and I'll undertake it.

6. Venus, the Roman goddess of love, was born from the sea foam off the island of Cythera.

185   HELLENA   Can you storm?

     WILLMORE   Oh, most furiously.

     HELLENA   What think you of a nunnery wall? For he that
wins me must gain that first.

     WILLMORE   A nun! Oh, now I love thee for't! There's no sin-
190   ner like a young saint. Nay, now there's no denying me;
the old law had no curse to a woman like dying a maid:
witness Jeptha's daughter.[7]

     HELLENA   A very good text this, if well handled; and I per-
ceive, Father Captain, you would impose no severe
195   penance on her who were inclined to console herself
before she took orders.°   *became a nun*

     WILLMORE   If she be young and handsome.

     HELLENA   Ay, there's it. But if she be not—

     WILLMORE   By this hand, child, I have an implicit faith,
200   and dare venture on° thee with all faults. Besides, 'tis more   *dare to approach*
meritorious to leave the world when thou hast tasted and
proved the pleasure on't. Then 'twill be a virtue in thee,
which now will be pure ignorance.

     HELLENA   I perceive, good Father Captain, you design
205   only to make me fit for heaven. But if, on the contrary,
you should quite divert me from it, and bring me back to
the world again, I should have a new man to seek, I find.
And what a grief that will be; for when I begin, I fancy I
shall love like anything; I never tried yet.

210   WILLMORE   Egad, and that's kind! Prithee, dear creature,
give me credit for a heart, for faith, I'm a very honest fellow. Oh, I long to come first to the banquet of love! And
such a swinging° appetite I bring. Oh, I'm impatient. Thy   *hearty*
lodging, sweetheart, thy lodging, or I'm a dead man!

215   HELLENA   Why must we be either guilty of fornication or
murder if we converse with you men? And is there no difference between leave to love me, and leave to lie with me?

     WILLMORE   Faith, child, they were made to go together.

     LUCETTA   [*pointing to* BLUNT]   Are you sure this is the
220   man?

     SANCHO   When did I mistake your game?

     LUCETTA   This is a stranger, I know by his gazing; if he be
brisk he'll venture to follow me, and then, if I understand
my trade, he's mine. He's English, too, and they say that's
225   a sort of good-natured loving people, and have generally
so kind an opinion of themselves that a woman with any
wit may flatter 'em into any sort of fool she pleases.

        [*She often passes by* BLUNT *and gazes on him; he
        struts and cocks, and walks and gazes on her.*]

     BLUNT   'Tis so, she is taken; I have beauties which my
false glass° at home did not discover.°   *mirror / reveal*

---

7. Sacrificed by Jephthah to fulfill his vow to God, after she was allowed two months to "bewail
[her] virginity" (see Judges 11.30–39).

230 FLORINDA [*aside*]   This woman watches me so, I shall get
no opportunity to discover myself to him, and so miss
the intent of my coming. —[*To* BELVILE.] But as I was
saying, sir, by this line you should be a lover.

    [*Looking in his hand.*]

BELVILE   I thought how right you guessed: all men are in
235 love, or pretend to be so. Come, let me go; I'm weary of
this fooling.

    [*Walks away.*]

FLORINDA   I will not, sir, till you have confessed whether
the passion that you have vowed Florinda be true or false.

    [*She holds him; he strives to get from her.*]

BELVILE   Florinda!

    [*Turns quick towards her.*]

240 FLORINDA   Softly.

BELVILE   Thou hast nam'd one will fix me here forever.

FLORINDA   She'll be disappointed then, who expects you this
night at the garden gate. And if you fail not, as— [*Looks on*
CALLIS, *who observes 'em.*] Let me see the other hand—you
245 will go near to do, she vows to die or make you happy.

BELVILE   What canst thou mean?

FLORINDA   That which I say. Farewell.

    [*Offers° to go.*]   *Attempts*

BELVILE   Oh charming sibil,° stay; complete that joy which   *prophetess*
as it is will turn into distraction! Where must I be? At
250 the garden gate? I know it. At night, you say? I'll sooner
forfeit heaven than disobey.

    [*Enter* DON PEDRO *and other maskers, and pass over
the stage.*]

CALLIS   Madam, your brother's here.

FLORINDA   Take this to instruct you farther.

                  [*Gives him a letter, and goes off.*]

FREDERICK   Have a care, sir, what you promise; this may
255 be a trap laid by her brother to ruin you.

BELVILE   Do not disturb my happiness with doubts.

    [*Opens the letter.*]

WILLMORE   My dear pretty creature, a thousand blessings
on thee! Still in this habit, you say? And after dinner at
this place?

260 HELLENA   Yes, if you will swear to keep your heart and not
bestow it between this and that.

WILLMORE   By all the little gods of love, I swear; I'll leave
it with you, and if you run away with it, those deities of
justice will revenge me.

        [*Exeunt all the women except* LUCETTA.]

265 FREDERICK   Do you know the hand?°   *handwriting*

BELVILE   'Tis Florinda's. All blessings fall upon the virtuous
maid.

FREDERICK   Nay, no idolatry; a sober sacrifice I'll allow you.

BELVILE   Oh friends, the welcom'st news! The softest° letter!   most tender

270 Nay, you shall all see it! And could you now be serious, I
might be made the happiest man the sun shines on!

WILLMORE   The reason of this mighty joy?

BELVILE   See how kindly she invites me to deliver her from
the threatened violence of her brother. Will you not
275 assist me?

WILLMORE   I know not what thou mean'st, but I'll make
one at any mischief where a woman's concerned. But
she'll be grateful to us for the favor, will she not?

BELVILE   How mean you?

280 WILLMORE   How should I mean? Thou know'st there's but
one way for a woman to oblige me.

BELVILE   Do not profane; the maid is nicely virtuous.

WILLMORE   Who, pox, then she's fit for nothing but a husband. Let her e'en go, colonel.

285 FREDERICK   Peace, she's the colonel's mistress, sir.

WILLMORE   Let her be the devil; if she be thy mistress, I'll
serve her. Name the way.

BELVILE   Read here this postscript.

[Gives him a letter.]

WILLMORE [reads]   "At ten at night, at the garden gate, of
290 which, if I cannot get the key, I will contrive a way over
the wall. Come attended with a friend or two." —Kind
heart, if we three cannot weave a string to let her down a
garden wall, 'twere pity but the hangman wove one for
us all.

295 FREDERICK   Let her alone for that; your woman's wit, your
fair kind woman, will out-trick a broker or a Jew, and
contrive like a Jesuit in chains.[8] But see, Ned Blunt is
stolen out after the lure of a damsel.

[Exeunt BLUNT and LUCETTA.]

BELVILE   So, he'll scarce find his way home again unless
300 we get him cried by the bellman° in the market place.   town crier
And 'twould sound prettily: "A lost English boy of thirty."

FREDERICK   I hope 'tis some common crafty sinner, one that
will fit him. It may be she'll sell him for Peru:[9] the rogue's
sturdy, and would work well in a mine. At least I hope
305 she'll dress him for our mirth, cheat him of all, then have
him well-favoredly banged,° and turned out at midnight.   beaten

WILLMORE   Prithee what humor is he of, that you wish
him so well?

BELVILE   Why, of an English elder brother's humour: edu-
310 cated in a nursery, with a maid to tend him till fifteen,
and lies with his grandmother till he's of age; one that

---

8. A description that rests on stereotypes of
Jews as cheating bargainers and Jesuits as
equivocal and deceptive in argument.

9. That is, sell him for slave labor in the
mines of Peru, then a Spanish colony.

knows no pleasure beyond riding to the next fair, or
going up to London with his right worshipful father in parliament time, wearing gay clothes, or making honorable
315 love to his lady mother's laundry maid; gets drunk at a
hunting match, and ten to one then gives some proofs of
his prowess. A pox upon him, he's our banker, and has all
our cash about him; and if he fail, we are all broke.

FREDERICK   Oh, let him alone for that matter; he's of a
320 damned stingy quality that will secure our stock. I know
not in what danger it were indeed if the jilt should pretend
she's in love with him, for 'tis a kind believing coxcomb;
otherwise, if he part with more than a piece of eight,° geld   *Spanish dollar*
him—for which offer he may chance to be beaten if she
325 be a whore of the first rank.

BELVILE   Nay, the rogue will not be easily beaten; he's stout
enough. Perhaps if they talk beyond his capacity he may
chance to exercise his courage upon some of them, else
I'm sure they'll find it as difficult to beat as to please him.

330 WILLMORE   'Tis a lucky devil to light upon so kind a wench!

FREDERICK   Thou hadst a great deal of talk with thy little
gipsy; couldst thou do no good upon her? For mine was
hardhearted.

WILLMORE   Hang her, she was some damned honest person
335 of quality, I'm sure, she was so very free and witty. If her
face be but answerable to her wit and humor, I would be
bound to constancy this month to gain her. In the meantime, have you made no kind acquaintance since you came
to town? You do not use to be honest so long, gentlemen.

340 FREDERICK   Faith, love has kept us honest: we have been
all fir'd with a beauty newly come to town, the famous
Paduana° Angellica Bianca.   *woman from Padua*

WILLMORE   What, the mistress of the dead Spanish general?

BELVILE   Yes, she's now the only ador'd beauty of all the
345 youth in Naples, who put on all their charms to appear
lovely in her sight: their coaches, liveries, and themselves all gay as on a monarch's birthday to attract the
eyes of this fair charmer, while she has the pleasure to
behold all languish for her that see her.

350 FREDERICK   'Tis pretty to see with how much love the men
regard her, and how much envy the women.

WILLMORE   What gallant has she?

BELVILE   None; she's exposed to sale, and four days in the
week she's yours, for so much a month.

355 WILLMORE   The very thought of it quenches all manner of
fire in me. Yet prithee, let's see her.

BELVILE   Let's first to dinner, and after that we'll pass the day
as you please. But at night ye must all be at my devotion.

360 WILLMORE   I will not fail you.

[*Exeunt.*]

2.1

[SCENE: *The long street.*]

[*Enter* BELVILE *and* FREDERICK *in masking habits, and* WILLMORE *in his own clothes, with a vizard° in his hand.*]   mask

WILLMORE   But why thus disguised and muzzled?

BELVILE   Because whatever extravagances we commit in these faces, our own may not be obliged to answer 'em.

WILLMORE   I should have changed my eternal buff,° too; but   *habitual*
5   no matter, my little gipsy would not have found me out   *military jacket*
then. For if she should change hers, it is impossible I should know her unless I should hear her prattle. A pox on't, I cannot get her out of my head. Pray heaven, if ever I do see her again, she prove damnably ugly, that I
10   may fortify myself against her tongue.

BELVILE   Have a care of love, for o' my conscience she was not of a quality to give thee any hopes.

WILLMORE   Pox on 'em, why do they draw a man in then? She has played with my heart so, that 'twill never lie still
15   till I have met with some kind wench that will play the game out with me. Oh, for my arms full of soft, white, kind woman—such as I fancy Angellica.

BELVILE   This is her house, if you were but in stock° to get   *possessed of capital*
admittance. They have not dined yet; I perceive the pic-
20   ture is not out.

[*Enter* BLUNT.]

WILLMORE   I long to see the shadow of the fair substance; a man may gaze on that for nothing.

BLUNT   Colonel, thy hand. And thine, Fred. I have been an ass, a deluded fool, a very coxcomb from my birth till this
25   hour, and heartily repent my little faith.

BELVILE   What the devil's the matter with thee, Ned?

BLUNT   Oh, such a mistress, Fred! Such a girl!

WILLMORE   Ha! Where?

FREDERICK   Ay, where?

30   BLUNT   So fond, so amorous, so toying,° and so fine! And   *flirting*
all for sheer love, ye rogue! Oh, how she looked and kissed! And soothed my heart from my bosom! I cannot think I was awake, and yet methinks I see and feel her charms still. Fred, try if she have not left the taste of her
35   balmy kisses upon my lips.

[*Kisses him.*]

BELVILE   Ha! Ha! Ha!

WILLMORE   Death, man, where is she?

BLUNT   What a dog was I to stay in dull England so long! How have I laughed at the colonel when he sighed for
40   love! But now the little archer° has revenged him! And by   *i.e., Cupid*
this one dart I can guess at all his joys, which then I took

for fancies, mere dreams and fables. Well, I'm resolved
to sell all in Essex and plant here forever.

BELVILE   What a blessing 'tis, thou hast a mistress thou
45   dar'st boast of; for I know thy humour is rather to have a
proclaimed clap° than a secret amour.   *gonorrhea*

WILLMORE   Dost know her name?

BLUNT   Her name? No, 'adsheartlikins. What care I for
names? She's fair, young, brisk and kind, even to ravish-
50   ment! And what a pox care I for knowing her by any
other title?

WILLMORE   Didst give her anything?

BLUNT   Give her? Ha! Ha! Ha! Why, she's a person of quality. That's a good one! Give her? 'Adsheartlikins, dost
55   think such creatures are to be bought? Or are we provided for such a purchase? Give her, quoth ye? Why, she
presented me with this bracelet for the toy of a diamond
I used to wear. No, gentlemen, Ned Blunt is not everybody. She expects me again tonight.

60 WILLMORE   Egad, that's well; we'll all go.

BLUNT   Not a soul! No, gentlemen, you are wits; I am a
dull country rogue, I.

FREDERICK   Well, sir, for all your person of quality, I shall
be very glad to understand your purse be secure; 'tis our
65   whole estate at present, which we are loath to hazard in
one bottom.[1] Come sir, unlade.°   *unload*

BLUNT   Take the necessary trifle useless now to me, that
am beloved by such a gentlewoman. 'Adsheartlikins,
money! Here, take mine too.

70 FREDERICK   No, keep that to be cozened,° that we may laugh.   *tricked, cheated*

WILLMORE   Cozened? Death! Would I could meet with one
that would cozen me of all the love I could spare tonight.

FREDERICK   Pox, 'tis some common whore, upon my life.

BLUNT   A whore? Yes, with such clothes, such jewels, such
75   a house, such furniture, and so attended! A whore!

BELVILE   Why yes, sir, they are whores, though they'll neither entertain you with drinking, swearing, or bawdry;
are whores in all those gay clothes and right jewels; are
whores with those great houses richly furnished with
80   velvet beds, store of plate,° handsome attendance, and fine   *silver or gold utensils*
coaches; are whores, and arrant°ones.   *thorough; notorious*

WILLMORE   Pox on't, where do these fine whores live?

BELVILE   Where no rogues in office, ycleped° constables, dare   *called*
give 'em laws, nor the wine-inspired bullies of the town
85   break their windows; yet they are whores though this Essex
calf° believe 'em persons of quality.   *fool*

BLUNT   'Adsheartlikins, y'are all fools. There are things
about this Essex calf that shall take with the ladies, beyond
all your wit and parts. This shape and size, gentlemen, are

---

1. In the hold of one ship; that is, in a single location.

90   not to be despised; my waist, too, tolerably long, with
other inviting signs that shall be nameless.

WILLMORE   Egad, I believe he may have met with some
person of quality that may be kind to him.

BELVILE   Dost thou perceive any such tempting things
95   about him that should make a fine woman, and of quality, pick him out from all mankind to throw away her
youth and beauty upon; nay, and her dear heart, too? No,
no, Angellica has raised the price too high.

WILLMORE   May she languish for mankind till she die, and
100   be damned for that one sin alone.

> [*Enter two* BRAVOS *and hang up a great picture of*
> ANGELLICA'S *against the balcony, and two little ones
> at each side of the door.*]

BELVILE   See there the fair sign to the inn where a man
may lodge that's fool enough to give her price.

> [WILLMORE *gazes on the picture.*]

BLUNT   'Adsheartlikins, gentlemen, what's this?

BELVILE   A famous courtesan, that's to be sold.

105 BLUNT   How? To be sold? Nay, then I have nothing to say
to her. Sold? What impudence is practiced in this country; with what order and decency whoring's established
here by virtue of the Inquisition![2] Come, let's be gone;
I'm sure we're no chapmen for this commodity.

110 FREDERICK   Thou art none, I'm sure, unless thou couldst
have her in thy bed at a price of a coach in the street.

WILLMORE   How wondrous fair she is! A thousand crowns
a month? By heaven, as many kingdoms were too little! A
plague of this poverty, of which I ne'er complain but
115   when it hinders my approach to beauty which virtue
ne'er could purchase.

> [*Turns from the picture.*]

BLUNT   What's this? [*Reads.*] "A thousand crowns a
month"! 'Adsheartlikins, here's a sum! Sure 'tis a mistake. —[*To one of the* BRAVOS.] Hark you, friend, does
120   she take or give so much by the month?

FREDERICK   A thousand crowns! Why, 'tis a portion° for the   *dowry*
Infanta![3]

BLUNT   Hark ye, friends, won't she trust?

BRAVO   This is a trade, sir, that cannot live by credit.

> [*Enter* DON PEDRO *in masquerade, followed by*
> STEPHANO.]

125 BELVILE   See, here's more company; let's walk off a while.

> [*Exeunt English;* PEDRO *reads.*]

PEDRO   Fetch me a thousand crowns; I never wished to
buy this beauty at an easier rate.   [*Passes off.*°]   *Departs*

---

2. A Roman Catholic tribunal set up to com-   3. The daughter of the king of Spain.
bat heresy.

[*Enter* ANGELLICA *and* MORETTA *in the balcony, and draw a silk curtain.*]

ANGELLICA Prithee, what said those fellows to thee?

BRAVO Madam, the first were admirers of beauty only, but
130 no purchasers; they were merry with your price and picture, laughed at the sum, and so passed off.

ANGELLICA No matter, I'm not displeased with their rally-
ing; their wonder feeds my vanity, and he that wishes but°   *only wishes*
to buy gives me more pride than he that gives my price
135 can make my pleasure.

BRAVO Madam, the last I knew through all his disguises
to be Don Pedro, nephew to the general, and who was
with him in Pamplona.

ANGELLICA Don Pedro? My old gallant's nephew? When
140 his uncle died he left him a vast sum of money; it is he
who was so in love with me at Padua, and who used to
make the general so jealous.

MORETTA Is this he that used to prance before our window,
and take such care to show himself an amorous ass? If I
145 am not mistaken, he is the likeliest man to give your price.

ANGELLICA The man is brave and generous, but of a
humour so uneasy and inconstant that the victory over his
heart is as soon lost as won; a slave that can add little to
the triumph of the conqueror. But inconstancy's the sin
150 of all mankind, therefore I'm resolved that nothing but
gold shall charm my heart.

MORETTA I'm glad on't; 'tis only interest that women of
our profession ought to consider, though I wonder what
has kept you from that general disease of our sex so long;
155 I mean, that of being in love.

ANGELLICA A kind but sullen star under which I had the
happiness to be born. Yet I have had no time for love; the
bravest and noblest of mankind have purchased my favors at so dear a rate, as if no coin but gold were current
160 with our trade. But here's Don Pedro again; fetch me my
lute, for 'tis for him or Don Antonio the Viceroy's son
that I have spread my nets.

[*Enter at one door* DON PEDRO, STEPHANO; DON ANTO-
NIO *and* DIEGO (*his page*) *at the other door, with
people following him in masquerade, anticly*° *attired,*   *bizarrely*
some with music. They both go up to the picture.]

ANTONIO A thousand crowns! Had not the painter flattered her, I should not think it dear.

165 PEDRO Flattered her? By heaven, he cannot. I have seen
the original, nor is there one charm here more than
adorns her face and eyes; all this soft and sweet, with a
certain languishing air that no artist can represent.

ANTONIO What I heard of her beauty before had fired my
170 soul, but this confirmation of it has blown it to a flame.

PEDRO Ha!

DIEGO   Sir, I have known you throw away a thousand
crowns on a worse face, and though y'are near your marriage, you may venture a little love here; Florinda will
175   not miss it.
PEDRO [aside]   Ha! Florinda! Sure 'tis Antonio.
ANTONIO   Florinda! Name not those distant joys; there's
not one thought of her will check my passion here.
PEDRO [aside]   Florinda scorned! [A noise of a lute above.]
180   And all my hopes defeated of the possession of Angellica! [ANTONIO gazes up.] Her injuries, by heaven, he
shall not boast of!

> [Song to a lute above.]

SONG

I

When Damon first began to love
He languished in a soft desire,
185   And knew not how the gods to move,
To lessen or increase his fire.
For Caelia in her charming eyes
Wore all love's sweets, and all his cruelties.

II

But as beneath a shade he lay,
190   Weaving of flowers for Caelia's hair,
She chanced to lead her flock that way,
And saw the am'rous shepherd there.
She gazed around upon the place,
And saw the grove, resembling night,
195   To all the joys of love invite,
Whilst guilty smiles and blushes dressed her face.
At this the bashful youth all transport grew,
And with kind force he taught the virgin how
To yield what all his sighs could never do.

> [ANGELLICA throws open the curtains and bows to
> ANTONIO, who pulls off his vizard and bows and blows
> up kisses. PEDRO, unseen, looks in's face.]

200   ANTONIO   By heaven, she's charming fair!
PEDRO [aside]   'Tis he, the false Antonio!
ANTONIO [to a bravo]   Friend, where must I pay my off'ring
of love?
My thousand crowns I mean.
PEDRO   That off'ring I have designed to make,
205   And yours will come too late.
ANTONIO   Prithee begone; I shall grow angry else,
And then thou art not safe.
PEDRO   My anger may be fatal, sir, as yours,
And he that enters here may prove this truth.

210 ANTONIO   I know not who thou art, but I am sure thou'rt
    worth my killing, for aiming at Angellica.

    [They draw and fight.]

    [Enter WILLMORE *and* BLUNT, *who draw and part'em.]*

BLUNT   'Adsheartlikins, here's fine doings.

WILLMORE   Tilting for the wench, I'm sure. Nay, gad, if that
    would win her I have as good a sword as the best of ye.

215 Put up,° put up, and take another time and place, for this   *Sheathe (your swords)*
    is designed for lovers only.

    [They all put up.]

PEDRO   We are prevented; dare you meet me tomorrow on the Molo?°   *pier*
    For I've a title to a better quarrel,
    That of Florinda, in whose credulous heart
220 Thou'st made an int'rest, and destroyed my hopes.

ANTONIO   Dare! I'll meet thee there as early as the day.

PEDRO   We will come thus disguised, that whosoever
    chance to get the better, he may escape unknown.

ANTONIO   It shall be so.

    [Exeunt PEDRO *and* STEPHANO.]

225 —Who should this rival be? Unless the English colonel,
    of whom I've often heard Don Pedro speak. It must be
    he, and time he were removed who lays a claim to all my
    happiness.

    *[*WILLMORE, *having gazed all this while on the
    picture, pulls down a little one.]*

WILLMORE   This posture's loose and negligent;
230 The sight on't would beget a warm desire
    In souls whom impotence and age had chilled.
    This must along with me.

BRAVO   What means this rudeness, sir? Restore the picture.

ANTONIO   Ha! Rudeness committed to the fair Angellica!
235 —Restore the picture, sir.

WILLMORE   Indeed I will not, sir.

ANTONIO   By heaven, but you shall.

WILLMORE   Nay, do not show your sword; if you do, by this
    dear beauty, I will show mine too.

240 ANTONIO   What right can you pretend to't?

WILLMORE   That of possession, which I will maintain. You,
    perhaps, have a thousand crowns to give for the original.

ANTONIO   No matter, sir, you shall restore the picture.

ANGELLICA   Oh, Moretta, what's the matter?

    *[*ANGELLICA *and* MORETTA *above.]*

245 ANTONIO   Or leave your life behind.

WILLMORE   Death! You lie; I will do neither.

    [They fight. The Spaniards join with ANTONIO, BLUNT
    laying on° like mad.]*   *vigorously attacking*

ANGELLICA   Hold, I command you, if for me you fight.

    [They leave off and bow.]

WILLMORE [*aside*]   How heavenly fair she is! Ah, plague of
her price!

250 ANGELLICA   You sir, in buff, you that appear a soldier, that
first began this insolence—

WILLMORE   'Tis true, I did so, if you call it insolence for a
man to preserve himself. I saw your charming picture
and was wounded; quite through my soul each pointed
255 beauty ran; and wanting a thousand crowns to procure
my remedy, I laid this little picture to my bosom, which,
if you cannot allow me, I'll resign.

ANGELLICA   No, you may keep the trifle.

ANTONIO   You shall first ask me leave, and this.

> [*Fight again as before.*]
> [*Enter* BELVILE *and* FREDERICK, *who join with the
> English.*]

260 ANGELLICA   Hold! Will you ruin me? —Biskey! Sebastian!
Part 'em!

> [*The Spaniards are beaten off.*]

MORETTA   Oh, madam, we're undone. A pox upon that
rude fellow; he's set on to ruin us. We shall never see
good days again till all these fighting poor rogues are
265 sent to the galleys.

> [*Enter* BELVILE, BLUNT, FREDERICK, *and* WILLMORE
> *with's shirt bloody.*]

BLUNT   'Adsheartlikins, beat me at this sport and I'll ne'er
wear sword more.

BELVILE [*to* WILLMORE]   The devil's in thee for a mad fellow; thou art always one at an unlucky adventure. Come,
270 let's be gone whilst we're safe, and remember these are
Spaniards, a sort of people that know how to revenge an
affront.

FREDERICK   You bleed! I hope you are not wounded.

WILLMORE   Not much. A plague on your dons;° if they fight   *Spaniards*
275 no better they'll ne'er recover Flanders.[4] What the devil
was't to them that I took down the picture?

BLUNT   Took it! 'Adsheartlikins, we'll have the great one
too; 'tis ours by conquest. Prithee help me up and I'll
pull it down.

280 ANGELLICA [*to* WILLMORE]   Stay, sir, and ere you affront
me farther let me know how you durst commit this outrage. To you I speak, sir, for you appear a gentleman.

WILLMORE   To me, madam? —Gentlemen, your servant.[5]

> [BELVILE *stays him.*]

BELVILE   Is the devil in thee? Dost know the danger of
285 ent'ring the house of an incensed courtesan?

WILLMORE   I thank you for your care, but there are other

---

4. The Low Countries, which largely revolted
from Spanish rule in the 16th century.

5. That is, "I am your servant," a polite
leave-taking.

matters in hand, there are, though we have no great
temptation. Death! Let me go!

FREDERICK   Yes, to your lodging if you will, but not in here.

290   Damn these gay harlots; by this hand I'll have as sound
and handsome a whore for a patacoon.[6] Death, man,
she'll murder thee!

WILLMORE   Oh, fear me not. Shall I not venture where a
beauty calls? A lovely charming beauty! For fear of dan-
295   ger? When, by heaven, there's none so great as to long
for her whilst I want money to purchase her.

FREDERICK   Therefore 'tis loss of time unless you had the
thousand crowns to pay.

WILLMORE   It may be she may give a favor; at least I shall
300   have the pleasure of saluting° her when I enter and when   *kissing*
I depart.

BELVILE   Pox, she'll as soon lie with thee as kiss thee, and
sooner stab than do either. You shall not go.

ANGELLICA   Fear not, sir, all I have to wound with is my eyes.

305   BLUNT   Let him go. 'Adsheartlikins, I believe the gentlewoman means well.

BELVILE   Well, take thy fortune; we'll expect you in the
next street. Farewell, fool, farewell.

WILLMORE   'Bye, colonel.   [*Goes in.*]

310   FREDERICK   The rogue's stark mad for a wench.

[*Exeunt.*]

2.2

[SCENE: *A fine chamber.*]

[*Enter* WILLMORE, ANGELLICA, *and* MORETTA.]

ANGELLICA   Insolent sir, how durst you pull down my picture?

WILLMORE   Rather, how durst you set it up to tempt poor
am'rous mortals with so much excellence, which I find
you have but too well consulted by the unmerciful price
5   you set upon't. Is all this heaven of beauty shown to
move despair in those that cannot buy? And can you
think th'effects of that despair should be less extravagant
than I have shown?

ANGELLICA   I sent for you to ask my pardon, sir, not to ag-
10   gravate your crime. I thought I should have seen you at
my feet imploring it.

WILLMORE   You are deceived. I came to rail at you, and rail
such truths too, as shall let you see the vanity of that
pride which taught you how to set such price on sin.
15   For such it is whilst that which is love's due is meanly
bartered for.

ANGELLICA   Ha! Ha! Ha! Alas, good captain, what pity 'tis
your edifying doctrine will do no good upon me.

6. A Portuguese and Spanish coin of relatively little value.

Moretta, fetch the gentleman a glass, and let him survey
20 himself to see what charms he has. —[*Aside, in a soft
tone.*] And guess my business.

MORETTA He knows himself of old: I believe those
breeches and he have been acquainted ever since he was
beaten at Worcester.[7]

25 ANGELLICA Nay, do not abuse the poor creature.

MORETTA Good weatherbeaten corporal, will you march
off? We have no need of your doctrine, though you have of
our charity. But at present we have no scraps; we can afford
no kindness for God's sake. In fine,° sirrah,[8] the price   *In conclusion*
30 is too high i'th' mouth for you, therefore troop,° I say.   *be off*

WILLMORE Here, good forewoman of the shop, serve me
and I'll be gone.

[*Offers money.*]

MORETTA Keep it to pay your laundress; your linen stinks
of the gun room. For here's no selling by retail.

35 WILLMORE Thou hast sold plenty of thy stale ware at a
cheap rate.

MORETTA Ay, the more silly kind heart I, but this is an age
wherein beauty is at higher rates. In fine, you know the
price of this.

40 WILLMORE I grant you 'tis here set down, a thousand
crowns a month. Pray, how much may come to my share
for a pistole?° Bawd, take your black lead and sum it   *a gold coin*
up, that I may have a pistole's worth of this vain gay
thing, and I'll trouble you no more.

45 MORETTA Pox on him, he'll fret me to death! Abominable
fellow, I tell thee we only sell by the whole piece.

WILLMORE 'Tis very hard, the whole cargo or nothing.
Faith, madam, my stock will not reach it; I cannot be
your chapman. Yet I have countrymen in town, mer-
50 chants of love like me; I'll see if they'll put in for a share.
We cannot lose much by it, and what we have no use for,
we'll sell upon the Friday's mart at "Who gives more?"—
I am studying, madam, how to purchase you, though at
present I am unprovided of money.

55 ANGELLICA [*aside*] Sure this from any other man would
anger me; nor shall he know the conquest he has made.
—Poor angry man, how I despise this railing.

WILLMORE Yes, I am poor. But I'm a gentleman,
And one that scorns this baseness which you practice.
60 Poor as I am I would not sell myself,
No, not to gain your charming high-prized person.
Though I admire you strangely for your beauty,

---

7. The site of Cromwell's 1651 defeat of   8. A form of address to male social inferiors,
Prince Charles in the final battle of the   and thus here indicating contempt.
English Civil War.

Yet I contemn° your mind.   *scorn, despise*
And yet I would at any rate enjoy you;
65   At your own rate; but cannot. See here
The only sum I can command on earth:
I know not where to eat when this is gone.
Yet such a slave I am to love and beauty
This last reserve I'll sacrifice to enjoy you.
70   Nay, do not frown, I know you're to be bought,
And would be bought by me. By me,
For a meaning trifling sum, if I could pay it down.
Which happy knowledge I will still repeat,
And lay it to my heart: it has a virtue in't,
75   And soon will cure those wounds your eyes have made.
And yet, there's something so divinely powerful there—
Nay, I will gaze, to let you see my strength.
       [*Holds her, looks on her, and pauses and sighs.*]
By heav'n, bright creature, I would not for the world
Thy fame° were half so fair as is thy face.   *reputation*
       [*Turns her away from him.*]
80   ANGELLICA [*aside*]   His words go through me to the very soul.—
If you have nothing else to say to me—
WILLMORE   Yes, you shall hear how infamous you are—
For which I do not hate thee—
But that secures my heart, and all the flames it feels
85   Are but so many lusts:
I know it by their sudden bold intrusion.
The fire's impatient and betrays; 'tis false.
For had it been the purer flame of love,
I should have pined and languished at your feet,
90   Ere found the impudence to have discovered it.
I now dare stand your scorn and your denial.
MORETTA [*aside*]   Sure she's bewitched, that she can stand
thus tamely and hear his saucy railing. —Sirrah, will you
be gone?
95   ANGELLICA [*to* MORETTA]   How dare you take this liberty!
Withdraw! —Pray tell me, sir, are not you guilty of the
same mercenary crime? When a lady is proposed to you
for a wife, you never ask how fair, discreet, or virtuous
she is, but what's her fortune; which, if but small, you cry
100 "She will not do my business," and basely leave her,
though she languish for you. Say, is not this as poor?
WILLMORE   It is a barbarous custom, which I will scorn to
defend in our sex, and do despise in yours.
ANGELLICA   Thou'rt a brave° fellow! Put up thy gold, and know,   *fine, handsome*
105 That were thy fortune as large as is thy soul,
Thou shouldst not buy my love.
Couldst thou forget those mean effects of vanity
Which set me out to sale,

And as a lover prize my yielding joys.

110 Canst thou believe they'll be entirely thine,
Without considering they were mercenary?

WILLMORE   I cannot tell, I must bethink me first.
[*Aside.*] Ha! Death, I'm going to believe her.

ANGELLICA   Prithee confirm that faith, or if thou canst not,

115 Flatter me a little: 'twill please me from thy mouth.

WILLMORE [*aside*]   Curse on thy charming tongue! Dost thou return
My feigned contempt with so much subtlety?—
Thou'st found the easiest way into my heart,
Though I yet know that all thou say'st is false.

[*Turning from her in rage.*]

120 ANGELLICA   By all that's good, 'tis real;
I never loved before, though oft a mistress.
Shall my first vows be slighted?

WILLMORE [*aside*]   What can she mean?

ANGELLICA [*in an angry tone*]   I find you cannot credit me.

125 WILLMORE   I know you take me for an errant ass,
An ass that may be soothed into belief,
And then be used at pleasure;
But, madam, I have been so often cheated
By perjured, soft, deluding hypocrites,

130 That I've no faith left for the cozening sex,
Especially for women of your trade.

ANGELLICA   The low esteem you have of me perhaps
May bring my heart again:
For I have pride that yet surmounts my love.

[*She turns with pride; he holds her.*]

135 WILLMORE   Throw off this pride, this enemy to bliss,
And show the power of love: 'tis with those arms
I can be only vanquished, made a slave.

ANGELLICA   Is all my mighty expectation vanished?
No, I will not hear thee talk; thou hast a charm

140 In every word that draws my heart away,
And all the thousand trophies I designed
Thou hast undone. Why art thou soft?
Thy looks are bravely rough, and meant for war.
Couldst thou not storm on still?

145 I then perhaps had been as free as thou.

WILLMORE [*aside*]   Death, how she throws her fire about my soul!—
Take heed, fair creature, how you raise my hopes,
Which once assumed pretends to all dominion:
There's not a joy thou hast in store

150 I shall not then command.
For which I'll pay you back my soul, my life!
Come, let's begin th'account this happy minute!

ANGELLICA   And will you pay me then the price I ask?

WILLMORE   Oh, why dost thou draw me from an awful° worship,   awe-filled

155 By showing thou art no divinity.

Conceal the fiend, and show me all the angel!
Keep me but ignorant, and I'll be devout
And pay my vows forever at this shrine.

[*Kneels and kisses her hand.*]

ANGELLICA The pay I mean is but thy love for mine.
160 Can you give that?

WILLMORE Entirely. Come, let's withdraw where I'll renew
my vows, and breathe 'em with such ardor thou shalt not
doubt my zeal.

ANGELLICA Thou hast a power too strong to be resisted.

[*Exeunt* WILLMORE *and* ANGELLICA.]

165 MORETTA Now my curse go with you! Is all our project fallen
to this? To love the only enemy to our trade? Nay, to love
such a shameroon,° a very beggar; nay, a pirate beggar,   phony, deceiver
whose business is to rifle and be gone; a no-purchase,
no-pay tatterdemalion, and English picaroon;° a rogue   rogue; pirate
170 that fights for daily drink, and takes a pride in being loy-
ally lousy? Oh, I could curse now, if I durst. This is the
fate of most whores.

Trophies, which from believing fops we win,
Are spoils to those who cozen us again.   [*Exit.*]

3.1

[SCENE: *A street.*]

[*Enter* FLORINDA, VALERIA, HELLENA, *in antic different dresses from what they were in before;* CALLIS
attending.]

FLORINDA I wonder what should make my brother in so ill
a humor? I hope he has not found out our ramble this
morning.

HELLENA No, if he had, we should have heard on't at both
5 ears, and have been mewed up° this afternoon, which I   pent up,
would not for the world should have happened. Hey ho,   confined
I'm as sad as a lover's lute.

VALERIA Well, methinks we have learnt this trade of gipsies as readily as if we had been bred upon the road to
10 Loretto;[9] and yet I did so fumble when I told the stranger
his fortune that I was afraid I should have told my own
and yours by mistake. But methinks Hellena has been
very serious ever since.

FLORINDA I would give my garters she were in love, to
15 be revenged upon her for abusing me. How is't,
Hellena?

HELLENA Ah, would I had never seen my mad monsieur.
And yet, for all your laughing, I am not in love. And yet

---

9. An Italian town near the Adriatic coast; it is the site of a shrine of the Virgin Mary visited by
many pilgrims.

this small acquaintance, o' my conscience, will never out
20 of my head.
VALERIA   Ha! Ha! Ha! I laugh to think how thou art fitted
with a lover, a fellow that I warrant loves every new face
he sees.
HELLENA   Hum, he has not kept his word with me here,
25 and may be taken up. That thought is not very pleasant
to me. What the deuce should this be now that I feel?
VALERIA   What is't like?
HELLENA   Nay, the Lord knows, but if I should be hanged
I cannot choose but be angry and afraid when I think that
30 mad fellow should be in love with anybody but me. What
to think of myself I know not: would I could meet with
some true damned gipsy, that I might know my fortune.
VALERIA   Know it! Why there's nothing so easy: thou wilt
love this wand'ring inconstant till thou find'st thyself
35 hanged about his neck, and then be as mad to get free
again.
FLORINDA   Yes, Valeria, we shall see her bestride his baggage horse and follow him to the campaign.
HELLENA   So, so, now you are provided for there's no care
40 taken of poor me. But since you have set my heart
a-wishing, I am resolved to know for what; I will not die
of the pip,[1] so I will not.
FLORINDA   Art thou mad to talk so? Who will like thee well
enough to have thee, that hears what a mad wench thou
45 art?
HELLENA   Like me? I don't intend every he that likes me
shall have me, but he that I like. I should have stayed in
the nunnery still if I had liked my lady abbess as well as
she liked me. No, I came thence not, as my wise brother
50 imagines, to take an eternal farewell of the world, but to
love and to be beloved; and I will be beloved, or I'll get
one of your men, so I will.
VALERIA   Am I put into the number of lovers?
HELLENA   You? Why, coz,[2] I know thou'rt too good-natured
55 to leave us in any design; thou wouldst venture a cast°   *i.e., roll the dice*
though thou comest off a loser, especially with such a
gamester. I observe your man, and your willing ear
incline that way; and if you are not a lover, 'tis an art
soon learnt—that I find.   [*Sighs.*]
60 FLORINDA   I wonder how you learnt to love so easily. I had
a thousand charms to meet my eyes and ears ere I could
yield, and 'twas the knowledge of Belvile's merit, not the
surprising person, took my soul. Thou art too rash, to
give a heart at first sight.
65 HELLENA   Hang your considering lover! I never thought

---

1. A vague, catchall term for human diseases;
here, heartache or depression.

2. Cousin, an affectionate term for any relative outside the speaker's immediate family.

beyond the fancy that 'twas a very pretty, idle, silly kind of
pleasure to pass one's time with: to write little soft nonsensical billets,° and with great difficulty and danger   *brief notes*
receive answers in which I shall have my beauty praised,
70   my wit admired, though little or none, and have the vanity
and power to know I am desirable. Then I have the more
inclination that way because I am to be a nun, and so
shall not be suspected to have any such earthly thoughts
about me; but when I walk thus—and sigh thus—they'll
75   think my mind's upon my monastery, and cry, "How happy
'tis she's so resolved." But not a word of man.

FLORINDA   What a mad creature's this!

HELLENA   I'll warrant, if my brother hears either of you
sigh, he cries gravely, "I fear you have the indiscretion to
80   be in love, but take heed of the honor of our house, and
your own unspotted fame"; and so he conjures on till he
has laid the soft-winged god in your hearts, or broke the
bird's nest. But see, here comes your lover, but where's my
inconstant? Let's step aside, and we may learn something.

                         [*Go aside.*]

       [*Enter* BELVILE, FREDERICK, *and* BLUNT.]

85 BELVILE   What means this! The picture's taken in.

BLUNT   It may be the wench is good-natured, and will be
kind gratis. Your friend's a proper handsome fellow.

BELVILE   I rather think she has cut his throat and is fled; I
am mad he should throw himself into dangers. Pox on't, I
90   shall want him, too, at night. Let's knock and ask for him.

HELLENA   My heart goes a-pit, a-pat, for fear 'tis my man
they talk of.

              [*Knock;* MORETTA *above.*]

MORETTA   What would you have?

BELVILE   Tell the stranger that entered here about two
95   hours ago that his friends stay here for him.

MORETTA   A curse upon him for Moretta: would he were
at the devil!
But he's coming to you.

            [*Enter* WILLMORE.]

HELLENA   Ay, ay 'tis he. Oh, how this vexes me!

100 BELVILE   And how and how, dear lad, has fortune smiled?
Are we to break her windows, or raise up altars to her, hah?

WILLMORE   Does not my fortune sit triumphant on my
brow? Dost not see the little wanton god there all gay and
smiling? Have I not an air about my face and eyes that
105   distinguish me from the crowd of common lovers? By
heaven, Cupid's quiver has not half so many darts as her
eyes! Oh, such a *bona roba*!³ To sleep in her arms is lying
in fresco,° all perfumed air about me.   *in fresh air (Italian)*

---

3. Courtesan; literally, "good stuff" (*buonaroba*, Italian).

HELLENA [*aside*] Here's fine encouragement for me to fool
110 on!

WILLMORE Hark'ee, where didst thou purchase that rich
Canary[4] we drank today? Tell me, that I may adore the
spigot and sacrifice to the butt. The juice was divine; into
which I must dip my rosary, and then bless all things that
115 I would have bold or fortunate.

BELVILE Well, sir, let's go take a bottle and hear the story
of your success.

FREDERICK Would not French wine do better?

WILLMORE Damn the hungry balderdash! Cheerful sack[5]
120 has a generous virtue in't inspiring a successful confidence, gives eloquence to the tongue and vigor to the
soul, and has in a few hours completed all my hopes and
wishes! There's nothing left to raise a new desire in me.
Come, let's be gay and wanton. And, gentlemen, study;
125 study what you want, for here are friends that will supply
gentlemen. [*Jingles gold.*] Hark what a charming sound
they make! 'Tis the he and the she gold whilst here, and
shall beget new pleasures every moment.

BLUNT But hark'ee, sir, you are not married, are you?

130 WILLMORE All the honey of matrimony but none of the
sting, friend.

BLUNT 'Adsheartlikins, thou'rt a fortunate rogue!

WILLMORE I am so, sir: let these inform you! Ha, how
sweetly they chime! Pox of poverty: it makes a man a
135 slave, makes wit and honor sneak. My soul grew lean
and rusty for want of credit.

BLUNT 'Adsheartlikins, this I like well; it looks like my
lucky bargain! Oh, how I long for the approach of my
squire, that is to conduct me to her house again. Why,
140 here's two provided for!

FREDERICK By this light, y'are happy men.

BLUNT Fortune is pleased to smile on us, gentlemen, to
smile on us.

[*Enter* SANCHO *and pulls down* BLUNT *by the sleeve;
they go aside.*]

SANCHO Sir, my lady expects you. She has removed all
145 that might oppose your will and pleasure, and is impatient till you come.

BLUNT Sir, I'll attend you. —Oh the happiest rogue! I'll
take no leave, lest they either dog me or stay me.

[*Exit with* SANCHO.]

BELVILE But then the little gipsy is forgot?

150 WILLMORE A mischief on thee for putting her into my

---

4. A sweet wine from the Canary Islands.
5. A dry white wine from Spain and the Canary Islands.

thoughts! I had quite forgot her else, and this night's debauch had drunk her quite down.

HELLENA   Had it so, good captain!   [*Claps him on the back.*]

WILLMORE [*aside*]   Ha! I hope she did not hear me!

155 HELLENA   What, afraid of such a champion?

WILLMORE   Oh, you're a fine lady of your word, are you
not? To make a man languish a whole day—

HELLENA   In tedious search of me.

WILLMORE   Egad, child, thou'rt in the right. Hadst thou
160 seen what a melancholy dog I have been ever since I was
a lover, how I have walked the streets like a Capuchin,°   Franciscan monk
with my hands in my sleeves—faith, sweetheart, thou
wouldst pity me.

HELLENA [*aside*]   Now if I should be hanged I can't be
165 angry with him, he dissembles so heartily. —Alas, good
captain, what pains you have taken; now were I ungrateful not to reward so true a servant.

WILLMORE   Poor soul, that's kindly said; I see thou barest
a conscience. Come then, for a beginning show me thy
170 dear face.

HELLENA   I'm afraid, my small acquaintance, you have
been staying that swinging stomach you boasted of this
morning. I then remember my little collation° would   light meal
have gone down with you without the sauce of a hand-
175 some face. Is your stomach so queasy now?

WILLMORE   Faith, long fasting, child, spoils a man's appetite.
Yet if you durst treat, I could so lay about me° still—   i.e., eat heartily

HELLENA   And would you fall to before a priest says grace?

WILLMORE   Oh fie, fie, what an old out-of-fashioned thing
180 hast thou named? Thou couldst not dash me more out of
countenance shouldst thou show me an ugly face.

> [*Whilst he is seemingly courting* HELLENA, *enter* AN-
> GELLICA, MORETTA, BISKEY, *and* SEBASTIAN, *all in
> masquerade.* ANGELLICA *sees* WILLMORE *and stares.*]

ANGELLICA   Heavens, 'tis he! And passionately fond to see
another woman!

MORETTA   What could you less expect from such a swag-
185 gerer?

ANGELLICA   Expect? As much as I paid him: a heart entire,
Which I had pride enough to think when'er I gave,
It would have raised the man above the vulgar,
Made him all soul, and that all soft and constant.

190 HELLENA   You see, captain, how willing I am to be friends
with you, till time and ill luck make us lovers; and ask
you the question first rather than put your modesty to
the blush by asking me. For alas, I know you captains
are such strict men, and such severe observers of your
195 vows to chastity, that 'twill be hard to prevail with your
tender conscience to marry a young willing maid.

WILLMORE   Do not abuse me, for fear I should take thee at thy word and marry thee indeed, which I'm sure will be revenge sufficient.

200   HELLENA   O' my conscience, that will be our destiny, because we are both of one humor: I am as inconstant as you, for I have considered, captain, that a handsome woman has a great deal to do whilst her face is good. For then is our harvesttime to gather friends, and should I in

205   these days of my youth catch a fit of foolish constancy, I were undone: 'tis loitering by daylight in our great journey. Therefore, I declare I'll allow but one year for love, one year for indifference, and one year for hate; and then go hang yourself, for I profess myself the gay, the kind, and

210   the inconstant. The devil's in't if this won't please you!

WILLMORE   Oh, most damnably. I have a heart with a hole quite through it too; no prison mine, to keep a mistress in.

ANGELLICA [aside]   Perjured man! How I believe thee now!

HELLENA   Well, I see our business as well as humors are

215   alike: yours to cozen as many maids as will trust you, and I as many men as have faith. See if I have not as desperate a lying look as you can have for the heart of you. [Pulls off her vizard; he starts.] How do you like it, captain?

WILLMORE   Like it! By heaven, I never saw so much

220   beauty! Oh, the charms of those sprightly black eyes! That strangely fair face, full of smiles and dimples! Those soft round melting cherry lips and small even white teeth! Not to be expressed, but silently adored! [She replaces her mask.] Oh, one look more, and strike

225   me dumb, or I shall repeat nothing else till I'm mad.

> [He seems to court her to pull off her vizard; she refuses.]

ANGELLICA   I can endure no more. Nor is it fit to interrupt him, for if I do, my jealousy has so destroyed my reason I shall undo° him. Therefore I'll retire, and you, Sebastian [to one of her bravos], follow that woman and learn who

230   'tis; while you [to the other bravo] tell the fugitive I would speak to him instantly.   [Exit.]

       °destroy

> [This while FLORINDA is talking to BELVILE, who stands sullenly; FREDERICK courting VALERIA.]

VALERIA [to BELVILE]   Prithee, dear stranger, be not so sullen, for though you have lost your love you see my friend frankly offers you hers to play with in the meantime.

235   BELVILE   Faith, madam, I am sorry I can't play at her game.

FREDERICK [to VALERIA]   Pray leave your intercession and mind your own affair. They'll better agree apart: he's a modest sigher in company, but alone no woman 'scapes him.

240   FLORINDA [aside]   Sure he does but rally.° Yet, if it should be true? I'll tempt him farther. —Believe me, noble stranger, I'm no common mistress. And for a little proof

      °banter

on't, wear this jewel. Nay, take it, sir, 'tis right, and bills
of exchange may sometimes miscarry.

245 BELVILE   Madam, why am I chose out of all mankind to be
the object of your bounty?

VALERIA   There's another civil question asked.

FREDERICK [aside]   Pox of's modesty; it spoils his own mar-
kets and hinders mine.

250 FLORINDA   Sir, from my window I have often seen you, and
women of my quality have so few opportunities for love
that we ought to lose none.

FREDERICK [to VALERIA]   Ay, this is something! Here's a
woman! When shall I be blest with so much kindness
255 from your fair mouth? —[Aside to BELVILE.] Take the
jewel, fool!

BELVILE   You tempt me strangely, madam, every way—

FLORINDA [aside]   So, if I find him false, my whole repose
is gone.

260 BELVILE   And but for a vow I've made to a very fair lady,
this goodness had subdued me.

FREDERICK [aside to BELVILE]   Pox on't, be kind, in pity to me
be kind. For I am to thrive here but as you treat her friend.

HELLENA   Tell me what you did in yonder house, and I'll
265 unmask.

WILLMORE   Yonder house? Oh, I went to a—to—why,
there's a friend of mine lives there.

HELLENA   What, a she or a he friend?

WILLMORE   A man, upon honor, a man. A she friend? No,
270 no, madam, you have done my business, I thank you.

HELLENA   And was't your man friend that had more darts
in's eyes than Cupid carries in's whole budget° of arrows?   quiver

WILLMORE   So—

HELLENA   "Ah, such a *bona roba*! To be in her arms is lying
275 *in fresco*, all perfumed air about me." Was this your man
friend too?

WILLMORE   So—

HELLENA   That gave you the he and the she gold, that
begets young pleasures?

280 WILLMORE   Well, well, madam, then you can see there are
ladies in the world that will not be cruel. There are,
madam, there are.

HELLENA   And there be men, too, as fine, wild, inconstant
fellows as yourself. There be, captain, there be, if you go
285 to that now. Therefore, I'm resolved—

WILLMORE   Oh!

HELLENA   To see your face no more—

WILLMORE   Oh!

HELLENA   Till tomorrow.

290 WILLMORE   Egad, you frighted me.

HELLENA   Nor then neither, unless you'll swear never to
see that lady more.

WILLMORE   See her! Why, never to think of womankind again.

HELLENA   Kneel, and swear.

[*Kneels; she gives him her hand.*]

295 WILLMORE   I do, never to think, to see, to love, nor lie,
with any but thyself.

HELLENA   Kiss the book.

WILLMORE   Oh, most religiously. [*Kisses her hand.*]

HELLENA   Now what a wicked creature am I, to damn a
300 proper fellow.

CALLIS [*to* FLORINDA]   Madam, I'll stay no longer: 'tis e'en
dark.

FLORINDA [*to* BELVILE]   However, sir, I'll leave this with
you, that when I'm gone you may repent the opportunity
305 you have lost by your modesty.

[*Gives him the jewel, which is her picture, and exit.
He gazes after her.*]

WILLMORE [*to* HELLENA]   'Twill be an age till tomorrow,
and till then I will most impatiently expect you. Adieu,
my dear pretty angel.

[*Exeunt all the women.*]

BELVILE   Ha! Florinda's picture! 'Twas she herself. What a
310 dull dog was I! I would have given the world for one minute's discourse with her.

FREDERICK   This comes of your modesty. Ah, pox o' your
vow; 'twas ten to one but we had lost the jewel by't.

BELVILE   Willmore, the blessed'st opportunity lost! Florinda,
315 friends, Florinda!

WILLMORE   Ah, rogue! Such black eyes! Such a face! Such
a mouth! Such teeth! And so much wit!

BELVILE   All, all, and a thousand charms besides.

WILLMORE   Why, dost thou know her?

320 BEVILE   Know her! Ay, ay, and a pox take me with all my
heart for being so modest.

WILLMORE   But hark'ee, friend of mine, are you my rival?
And have I been only beating the bush all this while?

BELVILE   I understand thee not. I'm mad! See here—

[*Shows the picture.*]

325 WILLMORE   Ha! Whose picture's this? 'Tis a fine wench!

FREDERICK   The colonel's mistress, sir.

WILLMORE   Oh, oh, here. [*Gives the picture back.*] I
thought't had been another prize. Come, come, a bottle
will set thee right again.

330 BELVILE   I am content to try, and by that time 'twill be late
enough for our design.

WILLMORE   Agreed.

Love does all day the soul's great empire keep,
But wine at night lulls the soft god asleep.

[*Exeunt.*]

3.2

[SCENE: LUCETTA'S *house*.]

[*Enter* BLUNT *and* LUCETTA *with a light*.]

LUCETTA   Now we are safe and free: no fears of the coming home of my old jealous husband, which made me a
little thoughtful° when you came in first. But now love is   *preoccupied*
all the business of my soul.

5 BLUNT   I am transported!—[*Aside*.] Pox on't, that I had but
some fine things to say to her, such as lovers use. I was a
fool not to learn of° Fred a little by heart before I came.   *from*
Something I must say. —'Adsheartlikins, sweet soul, I
am not used to compliment, but I'm an honest gentle
10 man, and thy humble servant.

LUCETTA   I have nothing to pay for so great a favor, but
such a love as cannot but be great, since at first sight of
that sweet face and shape it made me your absolute
captive.

15 BLUNT [*aside*]   Kind heart, how prettily she talks! Egad, I'll
show her husband a Spanish trick: send him out of the
world and marry her; she's damnably in love with me,
and will ne'er mind settlements,[6] and so there's that
saved.

20 LUCETTA   Well, sir, I'll go and undress me, and be with you
instantly.

BLUNT   Make haste then, for 'adsheartlikins, dear soul,
thou canst not guess at the pain of a longing lover
when his joys are drawn within the compass of a few
25 minutes.

LUCETTA   You speak my sense, and I'll make haste to prove it.
[*Exit*.]

BLUNT   'Tis a rare girl, and this one night's enjoyment with
her will be worth all the days I ever passed in Essex.
Would she would go with me into England, though to
30 say truth, there's plenty of whores already. But a pox on
'em, they are such mercenary prodigal whores that they
want such a one as this, that's free and generous, to give
'em good examples. Why, what a house she has, how rich
and fine!

[*Enter* SANCHO.]

35 SANCHO   Sir, my lady has sent me to conduct you to her
chamber.

BLUNT   Sir, I shall be proud to follow.—[*Aside*.] Here's one
of her servants too; 'adsheartlikins, by this garb and gravity he might be a justice of peace in Essex, and is but a
40 pimp here.

[*Exeunt*.]

6. Property secured for a wife at marriage.

3.3

[SCENE: *The scene changes to a chamber with an alcove bed in't, a table, etc.*; LUCETTA *in bed.*]

    [*Enter* SANCHO *and* BLUNT, *who takes the candle of* SANCHO *at the door.*]

SANCHO   Sir, my commission reaches no farther.

BLUNT   Sir, I'll excuse your compliment.

                         [*Exit* SANCHO.]

    —What, in bed, my sweet mistress?

LUCETTA   You see, I still outdo you in kindness.

5 BLUNT   And thou shalt see what haste I'll make to quit scores. Oh, the luckiest rogue!

        [*He undresses himself.*]

LUCETTA   Should you be false or cruel now—

BLUNT   False! 'Adsheartlikins, what dost thou take me for, a Jew? An insensible heathen? A pox of thy old jealous

10   husband: an° he were dead, egad, sweet soul, it should   *if* be none of my fault if I did not marry thee.

LUCETTA   It never should be mine.

BLUNT   Good soul! I'm the fortunatest dog!

LUCETTA   Are you not undressed yet?

15 BLUNT   As much as my impatience will permit.

        [*Goes toward the bed in his shirt, drawers, etc.*]

LUCETTA   Hold, sir, put out the light; it may betray us else.

BLUNT   Anything; I need no other light but that of thine eyes.—[*Aside.*] 'Adsheartlikins, there I think I had it.

        [*Puts out the candle; the bed descends; he gropes about to find it.*]

    Why, why, where am I got? What, not yet? Where are

20   you, sweetest? —Ah, the rogue's silent now. A pretty love-trick this; how she'll laugh at me anon! —You need not, my dear rogue, you need not! I'm all on fire already; come, come, now call me, in pity.—Sure I'm enchanted! I have been round the chamber, and can find neither

25   woman nor bed. I locked the door; I'm sure she cannot go that way, or if she could, the bed could not. — Enough, enough, my pretty wanton; do not carry the jest too far! [*Lights on a trap, and is let down.*] —Ha! Betrayed! Dogs! Rogues! Pimps! Help! Help!

        [*Enter* LUCETTA, PHILLIPO, *and* SANCHO *with a light.*]

30 PHILLIPO   Ha! Ha! Ha! He's dispatched finely.

LUCETTA   Now, sir, had I been coy, we had missed of this booty.

PHILLIPO   Nay, when I saw 'twas a substantial fool, I was mollified. But when you dote upon a serenading coxcomb, upon a face, fine clothes, and a lute, it makes me rage.

35 LUCETTA   You know I was never guilty of that folly, my dear Phillipo, but with yourself. But come, let's see what we have got by this.

PHILLIPO   A rich coat; sword and hat; these breeches, too,
are well lined! See here, a gold watch! A purse—Ha!
40   Gold! At least two hundred pistoles! A bunch of diamond
rings, and one with the family arms! A gold box, with a
medal of his king, and his lady mother's picture! These
were sacred relics, believe me. See, the waistband of his
breeches have a mine of gold—old queen Bess's![7] We
45   have a quarrel to her ever since eighty-eight,[8] and may
therefore justify the theft: the Inquisition might have
committed it.
LUCETTA   See, a bracelet of bowed gold! These his sisters
tied about his arm at parting. But well, for all this, I fear
50   his being a stranger may make a noise and hinder our
trade with them hereafter.
PHILLIPO   That's our security: he is not only a stranger to
us, but to the country too. The common shore° into,   *sewer*
which he is descended thou know'st, conducts him into
55   another street, which this light will hinder him from ever
finding again. He knows neither your name, nor that of
the street where your house is; nay, nor the way to his
own lodgings.
LUCETTA   And art thou not an unmerciful rogue, not to af-
60   ford him one night for all this? I should not have been
such a Jew.
PHILLIPO   Blame me not, Lucetta, to keep as much of thee
as I can to myself. Come, that thought makes me wanton; let's to bed. —Sancho, lock up these.
65   This is the fleece which fools do bear,
                         Designed for witty men to shear.
                                                        [*Exeunt.*]

3.4

[SCENE: *The scene changes, and discovers* BLUNT *creeping out of
a common shore; his face, etc., all dirty.*]

BLUNT [*climbing up*]   Oh, Lord, I am got out at last, and,
which is a miracle, without a clue.[9] And now to damning
and cursing! But if that would ease me, where shall I
begin? With my fortune, myself, or the quean° that coz-   *whore*
5   ened me? What a dog was I to believe in woman! Oh, cox-
comb! Ignorant conceited coxcomb! To fancy she could
be enamored with my person! At first sight enamored!
Oh, I'm a cursed puppy! 'Tis plain, fool was writ upon my
forehead! She perceived it; saw the Essex calf there. For
10   what allurements could there be in this countenance,
which I can endure because I'm acquainted with it.
Oh dull, silly dog, to be thus soothed into a cozening! Had

7. Queen Elizabeth I of England (r.
1558–1603).
8. That is, 1588, when the Spanish Armada

was defeated by the English navy.
9. A ball of thread used to guide one's way out
of a maze.

I been drunk, I might fondly have credited the young
quean; but as I was in my right wits to be thus cheated, con-
15   firms it: I am a dull believing English country fop. But my
comrades! Death and the devil, there's the worst of all! Then
a ballad will be sung tomorrow on the Prado,° to a lousy   *fashionable*
tune of the enchanted squire and the annihilated damsel.   *promenade*
But Fred—that rogue—and the colonel will abuse me be-
20   yond all Christian patience. Had she left me my clothes,
I have a bill of exchange at home would have saved my
credit. But now all hope is taken from me. Well, I'll
home, if I can find the way, with this consolation: that I
am not the first kind believing coxcomb; but there are,
25   gallants, many such good natures amongst ye.
     And though you've better arts to hide your follies,
     'Adsheartlikins, y'are all as arrant cullies.°   [*Exit.*]   *dupes*

3.5

[SCENE: *The garden in the night.*]

> [*Enter* FLORINDA *in an undress, with a key and a
> little box.*]

FLORINDA   Well, thus far I'm in my way to happiness. I
have got myself free from Callis; my brother too, I find
by yonder light, is got into his cabinet,° and thinks not of   *small private room*
me; I have by good fortune got the key of the garden back
5   door. I'll open it to prevent Belvile's knocking: a little
noise will now alarm my brother. Now am I as fearful as
a young thief. [*Unlocks the door.*] Hark! What noise is
that? Oh, 'twas the wind that played amongst the boughs.
Belvile stays long, methinks; it's time. Stay, for fear of a
10   surprise,° I'll hide these jewels in yonder jasmine.   *sudden attack*

> [*She goes to lay down the box.*]
> [*Enter* WILLMORE, *drunk.*]

WILLMORE   What the devil is become of these fellows
Belvile and Frederick? They promised to stay at the next
corner for me, but who the devil knows the corner of a
full moon? Now, whereabouts am I? Ha, what have we
15   here? A garden! A very convenient place to sleep in. Ha!
What has God sent us here? A female! By this light, a
woman! I'm a dog if it be not a very wench!

FLORINDA   He's come! Ha! Who's there?

WILLMORE   Sweet soul, let me salute thy shoestring.

20   FLORINDA [*aside*]   'Tis not my Belvile. Good heavens, I know
him not!—Who are you, and from whence come you?

WILLMORE   Prithee, prithee, child, not so many hard questions! Let it suffice I am here, child. Come, come kiss
me.

25 FLORINDA   Good gods! What luck is mine?

WILLMORE   Only good luck, child, parlous° good luck. Come   *extremely*
hither. —[*Aside.*] 'Tis a delicate shining wench. By this
hand, she's perfumed, and smells like any nosegay. —[*To*
FLORINDA.] Prithee, dear soul, let's not play the fool and
30 lose time—precious time. For as Gad shall save me, I'm as
honest a fellow as breathes, though I'm a little disguised°   *drunk*
at present. Come, I say. Why, thou mayst be free with me:
I'll be very secret. I'll not boast who 'twas obliged me, not
I; for hang me if I know thy name.

35 FLORINDA   Heavens! What a filthy beast is this!

WILLMORE   I am so, and thou ought'st the sooner to lie
with me for that reason. For look you, child, there will be
no sin in't, because 'twas neither designed nor premeditated: 'tis pure accident on both sides. That's a certain
40 thing now. Indeed, should I make love to you, and you
vow fidelity, and swear and lie till you believed and
yielded—that were to make it wilful fornication, the crying sin of the nation. Thou art, therefore, as thou art a
good Christian, obliged in conscience to deny me noth-
45 ing. Now, come be kind without any more idle prating.

[*He seizes her by the arm.*]

FLORINDA   Oh, I am ruined! Wicked man, unhand me!

WILLMORE   Wicked? Egad, child, a judge, were he young and
vigorous, and saw those eyes of thine, would know 'twas
they gave the first blow, the first provocation. Come, prithee
50 let's lose no time, I say. This is a fine convenient place.

FLORINDA   Sir, let me go, I conjure° you, or I'll call out.   *beseech*

WILLMORE   Ay, ay, you were best to call witness to see how
finely you treat me. Do!

FLORINDA   I'll cry murder, rape, or anything, if you do not
55 instantly let me go!

WILLMORE   A rape! Come, come, you lie, you baggage,° you   *whore*
lie. What! I'll warrant you would fain° have the world be-   *gladly*
lieve now that you are not so forward as I. No, not you.
Why at this time of night was your cobweb door set open,
60 dear spider, but to catch flies? Ha! Come, or I shall be
damnably angry. Why, what a coil° is here!   *fuss*

FLORINDA   Sir, can you think—

WILLMORE   That you would do't for nothing? Oh, oh, I
find what you would be at. Look here, here's a pistole for
65 you. Here's a work indeed! Here, take it, I say!

FLORINDA   For heaven's sake, sir, as you're a gentleman—

WILLMORE   So now, now, she would be wheedling me for
more! What, you will not take it then? You are resolved
you will not? Come, come, take it or I'll put it up again,
70 for look ye, I never give more. Why, how now, mistress,
are you so high i'th' mouth a pistole won't down with
you? Ha! Why, what a work's here! In good time! Come,

no struggling to be gone. But an° y'are good at a dumb   *if*
wrestle, I'm for ye. Look ye, I'm for ye.

[*She struggles with him.*]

[*Enter* BELVILE *and* FREDERICK.]

75 BELVILE   The door is open. A pox of this mad fellow! I'm
angry that we've lost him; I durst have sworn he had followed us.

FREDERICK   But you were so hasty, colonel, to be gone.

FLORINDA   Help! Help! Murder! Help! Oh, I am ruined!

80 BELVILE   Ha! Sure that's Florinda's voice! [*Comes up to
them.*] A man! —Villain, let go that lady!

[*A noise;* WILLMORE *turns and draws;* FREDERICK
interposes.]

FLORINDA   Belvile! Heavens! My brother too is coming,
and 'twill be impossible to escape. Belvile, I conjure you
to walk under my chamber window, from whence I'll give
85   you some instructions what to do. This rude man has
undone us.   [*Exit.*]

WILLMORE   Belvile!

[*Enter* PEDRO, STEPHANO, *and other servants, with lights.*]

PEDRO   I'm betrayed! Run, Stephano, and see if Florinda
be safe.

                       [*Exit* STEPHANO.]

[*They fight, and* PEDRO'S *party beats 'em out.*]

90   —So, whoe'er they be, all is not well. I'll to Florinda's chamber.

[*Going out, meets* STEPHANO.]

STEPHANO   You need not, sir: the poor lady's fast asleep,
and thinks no harm. I would not awake her, sir, for fear
of frighting her with your danger.

PEDRO   I'm glad she's there. —Rascals, how came the gar-
95   den door open?

STEPHANO   That question comes too late, sir. Some of my
fellow servants masquerading, I'll warrant.

PEDRO   Masquerading! A lewd custom to debauch our
youth! There's something more in this than I imagine.

                       [*Exeunt.*]

3.6

[SCENE: *Scene changes to the street.*]

[*Enter* BELVILE *in rage,* FREDERICK *holding him,*
WILLMORE *melancholy.*]

WILLMORE   Why, how the devil should I know Florinda?

BELVILE   Ah, plague of your ignorance! If it had not been
Florinda, must you be a beast? A brute? A senseless swine?

WILLMORE   Well, sir, you see I am endued with patience: I
5   can bear. Though egad, y'are very free with me, methinks.
I was in good hopes the quarrel would have been on my
side, for so uncivilly interrupting me.

BELVILE Peace, brute, whilst thou'rt safe. Oh, I'm distracted!

WILLMORE Nay, nay, I'm an unlucky dog, that's certain.

10 BELVILE Ah, curse upon the star that ruled my birth, or whatsoever other influence that makes me still so wretched.

WILLMORE Thou break'st my heart with these complaints. There is no star in fault, no influence but sack, the 15 cursed sack I drunk.

FREDERICK Why, how the devil came you so drunk?

WILLMORE Why, how the devil came you so sober?

BELVILE A curse upon his thin skull, he was always beforehand that way.

20 FREDERICK Prithee, dear colonel, forgive him; he's sorry for his fault.

BELVILE He's always so after he has done a mischief. A plague on all such brutes!

WILLMORE By this light, I took her for an errant harlot.

25 BELVILE Damn your debauched opinion! Tell me, sot, hadst thou so much sense and light about thee to distinguish her woman, and couldst not see something about her face and person to strike an awful reverence into thy soul?

WILLMORE Faith no, I considered her as mere a woman as 30 I could wish.

BELVILE 'Sdeath, I have no patience. Draw, or I'll kill you!

WILLMORE Let that alone till tomorrow, and if I set not all right again, use your pleasure.

BELVILE Tomorrow! Damn it,
35 The spiteful light will lead me to no happiness.
Tomorrow is Antonio's, and perhaps
Guides him to my undoing. Oh, that I could meet
This rival, this powerful fortunate!

WILLMORE What then?

40 BELVILE Let thy own reason, or my rage, instruct thee.

WILLMORE I shall be finely informed then, no doubt. Hear me, colonel, hear me; show me the man and I'll do his business.

BELVILE I know him no more than thou, or if I did I 45 should not need thy aid.

WILLMORE This you say is Angellica's house; I promised the kind baggage to lie with her tonight.

> [*Offers to go in.*]
> [*Enter* ANTONIO *and* DIEGO. ANTONIO *knocks on the hilt of's sword.*]

ANTONIO You paid the thousand crowns I directed?

DIEGO To the lady's old woman, sir, I did.

50 WILLMORE Who the devil have we here?

BELVILE I'll now plant myself under Florinda's window, and if I find no comfort there, I'll die.

> [*Exeunt* BELVILE *and* FREDERICK.]
> [*Enter* MORETTA.]

MORETTA   Page?

DIEGO   Here's my lord.

55 WILLMORE   How is this? A picaroon° going to board my   *pirate*
      frigate?— Here's one chase gun[1] for you!

          [*Drawing his sword, justles* ANTONIO, *who turns and
          draws. They fight;* ANTONIO *falls.*]

MORETTA   Oh, bless us! We're all undone!

          [*Runs in and shuts the door.*]

DIEGO   Help! Murder!

          [BELVILE *returns at the noise of fighting.*]

BELVILE   Ha! The mad rogue's engaged in some unlucky
60   adventure again.

          [*Enter two or three* MASQUERADERS.]

MASQUERADER   Ha! A man killed!

WILLMORE   How, a man killed? Then I'll go home to sleep.

          [*Puts up° and reels out. Exeunt* MASQUERADERS   *Sheathes his sword*
          another way.]

BELVILE   Who should it be? Pray heaven the rogue is safe,
      for all my quarrel to him.

          [*As* BELVILE *is groping about, enter an* OFFICER *and
          six* SOLDIERS.]

65 SOLDIER   Who's there?

OFFICER   So, here's one dispatched. Secure the murderer.

BELVILE   Do not mistake my charity for murder! I came to
      his assistance!

          [*Soldiers seize on* BELVILE.]

OFFICER   That shall be tried, sir. St. Jago![2] Swords drawn
70   in the Carnival time!

          [*Goes to* ANTONIO.]

ANTONIO   Thy hand, prithee.

OFFICER   Ha! Don Antonio! Look well to the villain there.
      —How is it, sir?

ANTONIO   I'm hurt.

75 BELVILE   Has my humanity made me a criminal?

OFFICER   Away with him!

BELVILE   What a curst chance is this!

                          [*Exeunt soldiers with* BELVILE.]

ANTONIO [*aside*]   This is the man that has set upon me
      twice. —[*To the officer.*] Carry him to my apartment till
80   you have farther orders from me.

                          [*Exit* ANTONIO, *led.*]

---

1. A cannon mounted at a port in the bow or stern of a ship.

2. St. James, revered in Spain (where, according to tradition, he preached and his body was brought).

4.1

[SCENE: *A fine room.*]

[*Discovers* BELVILE *as by dark alone.*]

BELVILE When shall I be weary of railing on fortune, who
is resolved never to turn with smiles upon me? Two such
defeats in one night none but the devil and that mad
rogue could have contrived to have plagued me with. I
5 am here a prisoner. But where, heaven knows. And if
there be murder done, I can soon decide the fate of a
stranger in a nation without mercy. Yet this is nothing to
the torture my soul bows with when I think of losing my
fair, my dear Florinda. Hark, my door opens. A light! A
10 man, and seems of quality. Armed, too! Now shall I die
like a dog, without defense.

> [*Enter* ANTONIO *in a nightgown, with a light; his arm
> in a scarf, and a sword under his arm. He sets the
> candle on the table.*]

ANTONIO Sir, I come to know what injuries I have done
you, that could provoke you to so mean an action as to
attack me basely without allowing time for my defense?
15 BELVILE Sir, for a man in my circumstances to plead
innocence would look like fear. But view me well, and
you will find no marks of coward on me, nor anything
that betrays that brutality you accuse me with.

ANTONIO In vain, sir, you impose upon my sense. You are
20 not only he who drew on me last night, but yesterday
before the same house, that of Angellica. Yet there is something in your face and mien that makes me wish I were
mistaken.

BELVILE I own I fought today in the defense of a friend of
25 mine with whom you, if you're the same, and your party
were first engaged. Perhaps you think this crime enough
to kill me, but if you do, I cannot fear you'll do it basely.

ANTONIO No sir, I'll make you fit for a defense with this.

> [*Gives him the sword.*]

BELVILE This gallantry surprises me, nor know I how to
30 use this present, sir, against a man so brave.

ANTONIO You shall not need. For know, I come to snatch
you from a danger that is decreed against you: perhaps
your life, or long imprisonment. And 'twas with so much
courage you offended, I cannot see you punished.

35 BELVILE How shall I pay this generosity?

ANTONIO It had been safer to have killed another than
have attempted me. To show your danger, sir, I'll let you
know my quality: and 'tis the Viceroy's son whom you
have wounded.

40 BELVILE The Viceroy's son! —[*Aside.*] Death and confusion!
Was this plague reserved to complete all the rest? Obliged
by him, the man of all the world I would destroy!

ANTONIO   You seem disordered, sir.

BELVILE   Yes, trust me, I am, and 'tis with pain that man
45   receives such bounties who wants° the power to pay 'em   *lacks*
     back again.

ANTONIO   To gallant spirits 'tis indeed uneasy, but you may
     quickly overpay me, sir.

BELVILE [*aside*]   Then I am well. Kind heaven, but set us
50   even, that I may fight with him and keep my honor safe.
     —Oh, I'm impatient, sir, to be discounting° the mighty   *reducing*
     debt I owe you. Command me quickly.

ANTONIO   I have a quarrel with a rival, sir, about the maid
     we love.

55 BELVILE [*aside*]   Death, 'tis Florinda he means! That
     thought destroys my reason, and I shall kill him.

ANTONIO   My rival, sir, is one has all the virtues man can
     boast of—

BELVILE [*aside*]   Death, who should this be?

60 ANTONIO   He challenged me to meet him on the Molo as
     soon as day appeared, but last night's quarrel has made
     my arm unfit to guide a sword.

BELVILE   I apprehend you, sir. You'd have me kill the man
     that lays a claim to the maid you speak of. I'll do't. I'll fly
65   to do't!

ANTONIO   Sir, do you know her?

BELVILE   No, sir, but 'tis enough she is admired by you.

ANTONIO   Sir, I shall rob you of the glory on't, for you must
     fight under my name and dress.

70 BELVILE   That opinion must be strangely obliging that
     makes you think I can personate the brave Antonio,
     whom I can but strive to imitate.

ANTONIO   You say too much to my advantage. Come, sir,
     the day appears that calls you forth. Within, sir, is the
75   habit.   [*Exit* ANTONIO.]

BELVILE   Fantastic fortune, thou deceitful light,
     That cheats the wearied traveler by night,
     Though on a precipice each step you tread,
     I am resolved to follow where you lead.   [*Exit.*]

4.2

[SCENE: *The Molo.*]

     [*Enter* FLORINDA *and* CALLIS *in masks, with*
     STEPHANO.]

FLORINDA [*aside*]   I'm dying with my fears: Belvile's not
     coming as I expected under my window makes me
     believe that all those fears are true.—Canst thou not tell
     with whom my brother fights?

5 STEPHANO   No, madam, they were both in masquerade. I
     was by when they challenged one another, and they
     had decided the quarrel then, but were prevented by

some cavaliers; which made 'em put it off till now. But I
am sure 'tis about you they fight.

10 FLORINDA [*aside*] Nay, then, 'tis with Belvile, for what
other lover have I that dares fight for me except Antonio,
and he is too much in favor with my brother. If it be he,
for whom shall I direct my prayers to heaven?

STEPHANO Madam, I must leave you, for if my master see
15 me, I shall be hanged for being your conductor. I escaped narrowly for the excuse I made for you last night
i'th' garden.

FLORINDA And I'll reward thee for't. Prithee, no more.

[*Exit* STEPHANO.]

[*Enter* DON PEDRO *in his masking habit.*]

PEDRO Antonio's late today; the place will fill, and we may
20 be prevented.

[*Walks about.*]

FLORINDA [*aside*] Antonio? Sure I heard amiss.

PEDRO But who will not excuse a happy lover
When soft fair arms confine the yielding neck,
And the kind whisper languishingly breathes
25 "Must you be gone so soon?"
Sure I had dwelt forever on her bosom—
But stay, he's here.

[*Enter* BELVILE *dressed in Antonio's clothes.*]

FLORINDA [*aside*] 'Tis not Belvile; half my fears are vanished.

30 PEDRO Antonio!

BELVILE [*aside*] This must be he.—You're early, sir; I do
not use° to be outdone this way.   *am not accustomed*

PEDRO The wretched, sir, are watchful, and 'tis enough
you've the advantage of me in Angellica.

35 BELVILE [*aside*] Angellica! Or° I've mistook my man, or   *Either*
else Antonio! Can he forget his interest in Florinda and
fight for common prize?

PEDRO Come, sir, you know our terms.

BELVILE [*aside*] By heaven, not I. —No talking; I am
40 ready, sir.

[*Offers to fight;* FLORINDA *runs in.*]

FLORINDA [*to* BELVILE] Oh, hold! Whoe'er you be, I do
conjure you hold! If you strike here, I die!

PEDRO Florinda!

BELVILE Florinda imploring for my rival!

45 PEDRO Away; this kindness is unseasonable.

[*Puts her by; they fight; she runs in just as* BELVILE
disarms PEDRO.]

FLORINDA Who are you, sir, that dares deny my prayers?

BELVILE Thy prayers destroy him; if thou wouldst preserve
him, do that thou'rt unacquainted with, and curse him.

[*She holds him.*]

FLORINDA By all you hold most dear, by her you love,
50 I do conjure you, touch him not.

BELVILE By her I love?
See, I obey, and at your feet resign
The useless trophy of my victory.
[*Lays his sword at her feet.*]

PEDRO Antonio, you've done enough to prove you love
55 Florinda.

BELVILE Love Florinda! Does heaven love adoration, prayer,
or penitence? Love her? Here, sir, your sword again.
[*Snatches up the sword and gives it to him.*]
Upon this truth I'll fight my life away.

PEDRO No, you've redeemed my sister, and my friend-
60 ship.
[*He gives him* FLORINDA, *and pulls off his vizard to
show his face, and puts it on again.*]

BELVILE Don Pedro!

PEDRO Can you resign your claims to other women, and
give your heart entirely to Florinda?

BELVILE Entire, as dying saints' confessions are!
65 I can delay my happiness no longer:
This minute let me make Florinda mine.

PEDRO This minute let it be. No time so proper: this night
my father will arrive from Rome, and possibly may hinder what we purpose.

70 FLORINDA Oh, heavens! This minute?
[*Enter masqueraders and pass over.*]

BELVILE Oh, do not ruin me!

PEDRO The place begins to fill, and that we may not be
observed, do you walk off to St. Peter's church, where I
will meet you and conclude your happiness.

75 BELVILE I'll meet you there. —[*Aside.*] If there be no more
saints' churches in Naples.

FLORINDA Oh, stay, sir, and recall your hasty doom!
Alas, I have not yet prepared my heart
To entertain so strange a guest.

80 PEDRO Away; this silly modesty is assumed too late.

BELVILE Heaven, madam, what do you do?

FLORINDA Do? Despise the man that lays a tyrant's claim
To what he ought to conquer by submission.

BELVILE You do not know me. Move a little this way.
[*Draws her aside.*]

85 FLORINDA Yes, you may force me even to the altar,
But not the holy man that offers° there   *worships*
Shall force me to be thine.
[PEDRO *talks to* CALLIS *this while.*]

BELVILE Oh, do not lose so blest an opportunity!
[*Pulls off his vizard.*]

See, 'tis your Belvile, not Antonio,
90   Whom your mistaken scorn and anger ruins.
FLORINDA   Belvile!
Where was my soul it could not meet thy voice,
And take this knowledge in.

> [*As they are talking, enter* WILLMORE, *finely dressed,*
> *and* FREDERICK.]

WILLMORE   No intelligence? No news of Belvile yet? Well, I
95   am the most unlucky rascal in nature. Ha! Am I deceived,
or is it he? Look, Fred! 'Tis he, my dear Belvile!

> [*Runs and embraces him;* BELVILE's *vizard falls out*
> *on's hand.*]

BELVILE   Hell and confusion seize thee!
PEDRO   Ha! Belvile! I beg your pardon, sir.

> [*Takes* FLORINDA *from him.*]

BELVILE   Nay, touch her not. She's mine by conquest, sir;
100   I won her by my sword.
WILLMORE   Didst thou so? And egad, child, we'll keep her
by the sword.

> [*Draws on* PEDRO; BELVILE *goes between.*]

BELVILE   Stand off!
Thou'rt so profanely lewd, so curst by heaven,
105   All quarrels thou espousest must be fatal.
WILLMORE   Nay, an° you be so hot, my valor's coy,   *if*
And shall be courted when you want it next.

> [*Puts up his sword.*]

BELVILE [*to* PEDRO]   You know I ought to claim a victor's right,
But you're the brother to divine Florinda,
110   To whom I'm such a slave. To purchase her
I durst not hurt the man she holds so dear.
PEDRO   'Twas by Antonio's, not by Belvile's sword
This question should have been decided, sir.
I must confess much to your bravery's due,
115   Both now and when I met you last in arms;
But I am nicely punctual° in my word,   *punctilious*
As men of honor ought, and beg your pardon:
For this mistake another time shall clear.

> [*Aside to* FLORINDA *as they are going out*]

—This was some plot between you and Belvile,
120   But I'll prevent you.

> [*Exeunt* PEDRO *and* FLORINDA.]

> [BELVILE *looks after her and begins to walk up and*
> *down in rage.*]

WILLMORE   Do not be modest now and lose the woman.
But if we shall fetch her back so—
BELVILE   Do not speak to me!
WILLMORE   Not speak to you? Egad, I'll speak to you, and
125   will be answered, too.

BELVILE Will you, sir?

WILLMORE I know I've done some mischief, but I'm so
dull a puppy that I'm the son of a whore if I know how or
where. Prithee inform my understanding.

130 BELVILE Leave me, I say, and leave me instantly!

WILLMORE I will not leave you in this humor, nor till I
know my crime.

BELVILE Death, I'll tell you, sir—

[*Draws and runs at* WILLMORE; *he runs out,* BELVILE
after him, FREDERICK *interposes.*]

[*Enter* ANGELLICA, MORETTA, *and* SEBASTIAN.]

ANGELLICA Ha! Sebastian, is that not Willmore? Haste!
135 haste and bring him back.

[*Exit* SEBASTIAN.]

FREDERICK [*aside*] The colonel's mad: I never saw him
thus before. I'll after 'em lest he do some mischief, for I
am sure Willmore will not draw on him.   [*Exit.*]

ANGELLICA I am all rage! My first desires defeated!
140 For one for aught he knows that has no
Other merit than her quality,
Her being Don Pedro's sister. He loves her!
I know 'tis so. Dull, dull, insensible,
He will not see me now, though oft invited,
145 And broke his word last night. False perjured man!
He that but yesterday fought for my favors,
And would have made his life a sacrifice
To've gained one night with me,
Must now be hired and courted to my arms.

150 MORETTA I told you what would come on't, but Moretta's
an old doting fool. Why did you give him five hundred
crowns, but to set himself out for other lovers? You should
have kept him poor if you had meant to have had any
good from him.

155 ANGELLICA Oh, name not such mean trifles! Had I given
him all
My youth has earned from sin,
I had not lost a thought nor sigh upon't.
But I have given him my eternal rest,
160 My whole repose, my future joys, my heart!
My virgin heart, Moretta! Oh, 'tis gone!

MORETTA Curse on him, here he comes. How fine she has
made him, too.

[*Enter* WILLMORE *and* SEBASTIAN; ANGELLICA *turns
and walks away.*]

WILLMORE How now, turned shadow?
165 Fly when I pursue, and follow when I fly?

[*Sings.*]

Stay, gentle shadow of my dove,
And tell me ere I go,

Whether the substance may not prove
A fleeting thing like you.

[*As she turns she looks on him.*]

170 There's a soft kind look remaining yet.

ANGELLICA Well, sir, you may be gay: all happiness, all
joys pursue you still. Fortune's your slave, and gives you
every hour choice of new hearts and beauties, till you are
cloyed with the repeated bliss which others vainly lan-
175 guish for. But know, false man, that I shall be revenged.

[*Turns away in rage.*]

WILLMORE So, gad, there are of those faint-hearted lovers,
whom such a sharp lesson next their hearts would make as
impotent as fourscore.° Pox o' this whining; my business   *as an 80-year-old man*
is to laugh and love. A pox on't, I hate your sullen lover:
180 a man shall lose as much time to put you in humor now
as would serve to gain a new woman.

ANGELLICA I scorn to cool that fire I cannot raise,
Or do the drudgery of your virtuous mistress.

WILLMORE A virtuous mistress? Death, what a thing thou
185 hast found out for me! Why, what the devil should I do
with a virtuous woman, a sort of ill-natured creatures that
take a pride to torment a lover. Virtue is but an infirmity in
woman, a disease that renders even the handsome ungrateful; whilst the ill-favored, for want of solicitations and ad-
190 dress, only fancy themselves so. I have lain with a woman
of quality who has all the while been railing at whores.

ANGELLICA I will not answer for your mistress's virtue,
Though she be young enough to know no guilt;
And I could wish you would persuade my heart
195 'Twas the two hundred thousand crowns you courted.

WILLMORE Two hundred thousand crowns! What story's
this? What trick? What woman, ha?

ANGELLICA How strange you make it. Have you forgot the
creature you entertained on the Piazzo last night?

200 WILLMORE [*aside*] Ha! My gipsy worth two hundred thousand crowns! Oh, how I long to be with her! Pox, I knew
she was of quality.

ANGELLICA False man! I see my ruin in thy face.
How many vows you breathed upon my bosom
205 Never to be unjust. Have you forgot so soon?

WILLMORE Faith, no; I was just coming to repeat 'em. But
here's a humor indeed would make a man a saint. —
[*Aside.*] Would she would be angry enough to leave me,
and command me not to wait on her.

[*Enter* HELLENA *dressed in man's clothes.*]

210 HELLENA This must be Angellica: I know it by her mump-
ing° matron here. Ay, ay, 'tis she. My mad captain's with   *grimacing*
her, too, for all his swearing. How this unconstant humor
makes me love him! —Pray, good grave gentlewoman, is
not this Angellica?

215 MORETTA My too young sir, it is. —[*Aside.*] I hope 'tis one
from Don Antonio.

[*Goes to* ANGELLICA.]

HELLENA [*aside*] Well, something I'll do to vex him for this.

ANGELLICA I will not speak with him. Am I in humor to
receive a lover?

220 WILLMORE Not speak with him? Why, I'll be gone, and
wait your idler minutes. Can I show less obedience to
the thing I love so fondly?

[*Offers to go.*]

ANGELLICA A fine excuse this! Stay—

WILLMORE And hinder your advantage? Should I repay
225 your bounties so ungratefully?

ANGELLICA [*to* HELLENA] Come hither, boy. —[*To* WILLMORE.]
That I may let you see
How much above the advantages you name
I prize one minute's joy with you.

WILLMORE [*impatient to be gone*] Oh, you destroy me
230 with this endearment.—[*Aside.*] Death, how shall I get
away?—Madam, 'twill not be fit I should be seen with
you. Besides, it will not be convenient. And I've a friend—
that's dangerously sick.

ANGELLICA I see you're impatient. Yet you shall stay.

235 WILLMORE [*aside*] And miss my assignation with my
gipsy.

[*Walks about impatiently;* MORETTA *brings* HELLENA,
who addresses herself to ANGELLICA.]

HELLENA Madam,
You'll hardly pardon my intrusion
When you shall know my business;
And I'm too young to tell my tale with art;
240 But there must be a wondrous store of goodness
Where so much beauty dwells.

ANGELLICA A pretty advocate, whoever sent thee.
Prithee proceed.

[*To* WILLMORE, *who is stealing off.*]

—Nay, sir, you shall not go.

245 WILLMORE [*aside*] Then I shall lose my dear gipsy forever.
Pox on't, she stays me out of spite.

HELLENA I am related to a lady, madam,
Young, rich, and nobly born, but has the fate
To be in love with a young English gentleman.
250 Strangely she loves him, at first sight she loved him,
But did adore him when she heard him speak;
For he, she said, had charms in every word
That failed not to surprise, to wound and conquer.

WILLMORE [*aside*] Ha! Egad, I hope this concerns me.

255 ANGELLICA [*aside*] 'Tis my false man he means. Would he were gone:
This praise will raise his pride, and ruin me.

[*To* WILLMORE.] —Well,
Since you are so impatient to be gone,
I will release you, sir.

WILLMORE [*aside*] Nay, then I'm sure 'twas me he spoke
260 of: this cannot be the effects of kindness in her. —No,
Madam, I've considered better on't, and will not give you
cause of jealousy.

ANGELLICA But sir, I've business that—

WILLMORE This shall not do; I know 'tis but to try me.

265 ANGELLICA Well, to your story, boy. —[*Aside*]. Though
'twill undo me.

HELLENA With this addition to his other beauties,
He won her unresisting tender heart.
He vowed, and sighed, and swore he loved her dearly;
270 And she believed the cunning flatterer,
And thought herself the happiest maid alive.
Today was the appointed time by both
To consummate their bliss:
The virgin, altar, and the priest were dressed;
275 And whilst she languished for th'expected bridegroom,
She heard he paid his broken vows to you.

WILLMORE [*aside*] So, this is some dear rogue that's in
love with me, and this way lets me know it. Or, if it be
not me, she means someone whose place I may
280 supply.

ANGELLICA Now I perceive
The cause of thy impatience to be gone,
And all the business of this glorious dress.

WILLMORE Damn the young prater; I know not what he
285 means.

HELLENA Madam,
In your fair eyes I read too much concern
To tell my farther business.

ANGELLICA Prithee, sweet youth, talk on: thou mayst perhaps
290 Raise here a storm that may undo my passion,
And then I'll grant thee anything.

HELLENA Madam, 'tis to entreat you (oh unreasonable)
You would not see this stranger.
For if you do, she vows you are undone;
295 Though nature never made a man so excellent,
And sure he 'ad been a god, but for inconstancy.

WILLMORE [*aside*] Ah, rogue, how finely he's instructed!
'Tis plain, some woman that has seen me *en passant.*°   *in passing (French)*

ANGELLICA Oh, I shall burst with jealousy! Do you know
300 the man you speak of?

HELLENA Yes, madam, he used to be in buff and scarlet.

ANGELLICA [*to* WILLMORE] Thou false as hell, what canst
thou say to this?

WILLMORE By heaven—

305 ANGELLICA Hold, do not damn thyself—

HELLENA   Nor hope to be believed.

[*He walks about; they follow.*]

ANGELLICA   Oh perjured man!
Is't thus you pay my generous passion back?

HELLENA   Why would you, sir, abuse my lady's faith?

310 ANGELLICA   And use me so unhumanely.

HELLENA   A maid so young, so innocent—

WILLMORE   Ah, young devil!

ANGELLICA   Dost thou not know thy life is in my power?

HELLENA   Or think my lady cannot be revenged?

315 WILLMORE [*aside*]   So, so, the storm comes finely on.

ANGELLICA   Now thou art silent: guilt has struck thee dumb.
Oh, hadst thou still been so, I'd lived in safety.

[*She turns away and weeps.*]

WILLMORE [*aside to* HELLENA]   Sweetheart, the lady's name
and house—quickly! I'm impatient to be with her.

[*Looks toward* ANGELLICA *to watch her turning, and
as she comes towards them he meets her.*]

320 HELLENA [*aside*]   So, now is he for another woman.

WILLMORE   The impudent'st young thing in nature: I cannot persuade him out of his error, madam.

ANGELLICA   I know he's in the right; yet thou'st a tongue
That would persuade him to deny his faith.

[*In rage walks away.*]

325 WILLMORE [*said softly to* HELLENA]   Her name, her name,
dear boy!

HELLENA   Have you forgot it, sir?

WILLMORE [*aside*]   Oh, I perceive he's not to know I am a
stranger to his lady. —Yes, yes, I do know, but I have forgot

330 the—[ANGELLICA *turns.*] —By heaven, such early confidence I never saw.

ANGELLICA   Did I not charge you with this mistress, sir?
Which you denied, though I beheld your perjury.
This little generosity of thine has rendered back my

335 heart.   [*Walks away.*]

WILLMORE [*to* HELLENA]   So, you have made sweet work
here, my little mischief. Look your lady be kind and
good-natured now, or I shall have but a cursed bargain
on't. [ANGELLICA *turns toward them.*] — The rogue's bred

340 up to mischief; art thou so great a fool to credit him?

ANGELLICA   Yes, I do, and you in vain impose upon me.
Come hither, boy. Is not this he you spake of?

HELLENA   I think it is. I cannot swear, but I vow he has
just such another lying lover's look.

[HELLENA *looks in his face; he gazes on her.*]

345 WILLMORE [*aside*]   Ha! Do I not know that face? By
heaven, my little gipsy! What a dull dog was I: had I but
looked that way I'd known her. Are all my hopes of a new

woman banished?—Egad, if I do not fit° thee for this,   *punish*
hang me. —[*To* ANGELLICA.] Madam, I have found out
350   the plot.

HELLENA [*aside*] Oh lord, what does he say? Am I discovered now?

WILLMORE Do you see this young spark here?

HELLENA [*aside*] He'll tell her who I am.

355 WILLMORE Who do you think this is?

HELLENA [*aside*] Ay, ay, he does know me. —Nay, dear
captain, I am undone if you discover me.

WILLMORE Nay, nay, no cogging°; she shall know what a   *deceit; wheedling*
precious mistress I have.

360 HELLENA Will you be such a devil?

WILLMORE Nay, nay, I'll teach you to spoil sport you will
not make. — This small ambassador comes not from a
person of quality, as you imagine and he says, but from a
very errant° gipsy: the talking'st, prating'st, canting'st   *good-for-nothing*
365   little animal thou ever saw'st.

ANGELLICA What news you tell me, that's the thing I
mean.

HELLENA [*aside*] Would I were well off the place! If ever I
go a-captain-hunting again—

370 WILLMORE Mean that thing? That gipsy thing? Thou
mayst as well be jealous of thy monkey or parrot as of
her. A German motion° were worth a dozen of her, and   *puppet*
a dream were a better enjoyment—a creature of a constitution fitter for heaven than man.

375 HELLENA [*aside*] Though I'm sure he lies, yet this vexes me.

ANGELLICA You are mistaken: she's a Spanish woman
made up of no such dull materials.

WILLMORE Materials? Egad, an she be made of any that
will either dispense or admit of love, I'll be bound to con-
380   tinence.

HELLENA [*aside to him*] Unreasonable man, do you
think so?

WILLMORE You may return, my little brazen head, and tell
your lady, that till she be handsome enough to be
385   beloved, or I dull enough to be religious, there will be
small hopes of me.

ANGELLICA Did you not promise, then, to marry her?

WILLMORE Not I, by heaven.

ANGELLICA You cannot undeceive my fears and torments,
390   till you have vowed you will not marry her.

HELLENA [*aside*] If he swears that, he'll be revenged on
me indeed for all my rogueries.

ANGELLICA I know what arguments you'll bring against
me: fortune and honor.

395 WILLMORE Honor! I tell you, I hate it in your sex; and those
that fancy themselves possessed of that foppery are
the most impertinently troublesome of all womankind,

and will transgress nine commandments to keep one.[3]
And to satisfy your jealousy, I swear—

400 HELLENA [*aside to him*]   Oh, no swearing, dear captain.

WILLMORE   If it were possible I should ever be inclined to
marry, it should be some kind young sinner: one that has
generosity enough to give a favor handsomely to one that
can ask it discreetly, one that has wit enough to manage

405 an intrigue of love. Oh, how civil such a wench is to a
man that does her the honor to marry her.

ANGELICA   By heaven, there's no faith in anything he says.

[*Enter* SEBASTIAN.]

SEBASTIAN   Madam, Don Antonio—

ANGELICA   Come hither.

410 HELLENA [*aside*]   Ha! Antonio! He may be coming hither,
and he'll certainly discover me. I'll therefore retire without a ceremony.   [*Exit* HELLENA.]

ANGELICA   I'll see him. Get my coach ready.

SEBASTIAN   It waits you, madam.

415 WILLMORE [*aside*]   This is lucky. —What, madam, now
I may be gone and leave you to the enjoyment of my
rival?

ANGELICA   Dull man, that canst not see how ill, how poor,
That false dissimulation looks. Be gone,

420 And never let me see thy cozening face again,
Lest I relapse and kill thee.

WILLMORE   Yes, you can spare me now. Farewell, till you're
in better humor. —[*Aside.*] I'm glad of this release. Now
for my gipsy:

425 For though to worse we change, yet still we find
New joys, new charms, in a new miss that's kind.

[*Exit* WILLMORE.]

ANGELICA   He's gone, and in this ague of my soul
The shivering fit returns.
Oh, with what willing haste he took his leave,

430 As if the longed-for minute were arrived
Of some blest assignation.
In vain I have consulted all my charms,
In vain this beauty prized, in vain believed
My eyes could kindle any lasting fires;

435 I had forgot my name, my infamy,
And the reproach that honor lays on those
That dare pretend a sober passion here.
Nice° reputation, though it leave behind   *Strict in conduct*
More virtues than inhabit where that dwells,

440 Yet that once gone, those virtues shine no more,
Then since I am not fit to be beloved,

---

3. That is, the commandment forbidding adultery (Exodus 20.14; Deuteronomy 5.18).

I am resolved to think on a revenge
On him that soothed° me thus to my undoing.   *flattered*

[*Exeunt.*]

4.3

[SCENE: *A street.*]

[*Enter* FLORINDA *and* VALERIA *in habits different from what they have been seen in.*]

FLORINDA   We're happily escaped, and yet I tremble still.

VALERIA   A lover, and fear? Why, I am but half an one, and yet I have courage for any attempt. Would Hellena were here: I would fain have had her as deep in this mischief
5   as we; she'll fare but ill else, I doubt.

FLORINDA   She pretended a visit to the Augustine nuns; but I believe some other design carried her out; pray heaven we light on her. Prithee, what didst do with Callis?

VALERIA   When I saw no reason would do good on her, I
10   followed her into the wardrobe,° and as she was looking   *dressing room*
for something in a great chest, I toppled her in by the heels, snatched the key of the apartment where you were confined, locked her in, and left her bawling for help.

FLORINDA   'Tis well you resolve to follow my fortunes, for
15   thou darest never appear at home again after such an action.

VALERIA   That's according as the young stranger and I shall agree. But to our business. I delivered your note to Belvile when I got out under pretense of going to Mass. I
20   found him at his lodging, and believe me it came seasonably, for never was man in so desperate a condition. I told him of your resolution of making your escape today if your brother would be absent long enough to permit you; if not, to die rather than be Antonio's.

25   FLORINDA   Thou should'st have told him I was confined to my chamber upon my brother's suspicion that the business on the Molo was a plot laid between him and I.

VALERIA   I said all this, and told him your brother was now gone to his devotion; and he resolves to visit every
30   church till he find him, and not only undeceive him in that, but caress him so as shall delay his return home.

FLORINDA   Oh heavens! He's here, and Belvile with him, too.

[*They put on their vizards.*]

[*Enter* DON PEDRO, BELVILE, WILLMORE; BELVILE *and* DON PEDRO *seeming in serious discourse.*]

VALERIA   Walk boldly by them, and I'll come at a distance,
35   lest he suspect us.

[*She walks by them and looks back on them.*]

WILLMORE   Ha! A woman, and of excellent mien!

PEDRO   She throws a kind look back on you.

WILLMORE   Death, 'tis a likely wench, and that kind look
shall not be cast away. I'll follow her.

40   BELVILE   Prithee do not.

WILLMORE   Do not? By heavens, to the antipodies,[4] with
such an invitation.

[*She goes out, and* WILLMORE *follows her.*]

BELVILE   'Tis a mad fellow for a wench.

[*Enter* FREDERICK.]

FREDERICK   Oh, colonel, such news!

45   BELVILE   Prithee what?

FREDERICK   News that will make you laugh in spite of
fortune.

BELVILE   What, Blunt has had some damned trick put
upon him? Cheated, banged, or clapped?[5]

50   FREDERICK   Cheated, sir, rarely° cheated of all but his shirt   *superbly*
and drawers; the unconscionable whore too turned him
out before consummation, so that, traversing the streets
at midnight, the watch found him in this *fresco* and conducted him home. By heaven, 'tis such a sight, and yet I
55   durst as well been hanged as laughed at him or pity him:
he beats all that do but ask him a question, and is in
such an humour.

PEDRO   Who is't has met with this ill usage, sir?

BELVILE   A friend of ours whom you must see for mirth's
60   sake. — [*Aside.*] I'll employ him to give Florinda time for
an escape.

PEDRO   What is he?

BELVILE   A young countryman of ours, one that has been
educated at so plentiful a rate he yet ne'er knew the
65   want of money; and 'twill be a great jest to see how simply
he'll look without it. For my part, I'll lend him none: and
the rogue know not how to put on a borrowing face and
ask first, I'll let him see how good 'tis to play our parts
whilst I play his. Prithee, Fred, do you go home and keep
70   him in that posture till we come.

[*Exeunt.*]

[*Enter* FLORINDA *from the farther end of the scene,
looking behind her.*]

FLORINDA   I am followed still. Ha! My brother too
advancing this way! Good heavens defend me from
being seen by him!   [*She goes off.*]

[*Enter* WILLMORE, *and after him* VALERIA, *at a little
distance.*]

WILLMORE   Ah, there she sails! She looks back as she were
75   willing to be boarded; I'll warrant her prize.°   *a ship legally captured*

[*He goes out,* VALERIA *following.*]

[*Enter* HELLENA, *just as he goes out, with a page.*]

HELLENA   Ha, is not that my captain that has a woman in
chase? 'Tis not Angellica.—Boy, follow those people at a
distance, and bring me an account where they go in.

[*Exit page.*]

—I'll find his haunts, and plague him everywhere. Ha!
80   My brother!

[BELVILE, WILLMORE, PEDRO *cross the stage;* HELLENA
runs off.]

4.4

[SCENE: *Scene changes to another street.*]

[*Enter* FLORINDA.]

FLORINDA   What shall I do? My brother now pursues me.
Will no kind power protect me from his tyranny? Ha!
Here's a door open; I'll venture in, since nothing can be
worse than to fall into his hands. My life and honor are
5   at stake, and my necessity has no choice.   [*She goes in.*]

[*Enter* VALERIA, *and* HELLENA'S PAGE *peeping after*
FLORINDA.]

PAGE   Here she went in; I shall remember this house.

[*Exit boy.*]

VALERIA   This is Belvile's lodging; she's gone in as readily
as if she knew it. Ha! Here's that mad fellow again; I
dare not venture in. I'll watch my opportunity.

[*Goes aside.*]

[*Enter* WILLMORE, *gazing about him.*]

10   WILLMORE   I have lost her hereabouts. Pox on't, she must
not 'scape me so.   [*Goes out.*]

4.5

[SCENE: *Scene changes to* BLUNT'S *chamber, discovers him sitting on a couch in his shirt and drawers, reading.*]

BLUNT   So, now my mind's a little at peace, since I have
resolved revenge. A pox on this tailor, though, for not
bringing home the clothes I bespoke.° And a pox of all   *ordered*
poor cavaliers: a man can never keep a spare suit for 'em,
5   and I shall have these rogues come in and find me naked,
and then I'm undone. But I'm resolved to arm myself: the
rascals shall not insult over me too much. [*Puts on an old
rusty sword and buff belt.*] Now, how like a morris dancer[6]
I am equipped! A fine ladylike whore to cheat me thus
10   without affording me a kindness for my money! A pox
light on her, I shall never be reconciled to the sex more;

6. That is, costumed in white, like an English folk dancer.

she has made me as faithless as a physician, as uncharitable as a churchman, and as ill-natured as a poet. Oh,
how I'll use all womankind hereafter! What would I give
15 to have one of 'em within my reach now! Any mortal
thing in petticoats, kind fortune, send me, and I'll forgive
thy last night's malice. —Here's a cursed book, too—a
warning to all young travelers—that can instruct me how
to prevent such mischiefs now 'tis too late. Well, 'tis a
20 rare convenient thing to read a little now and then, as
well as hawk and hunt.

[*Sits down again and reads.*]

[*Enter to him* FLORINDA.]

FLORINDA This house is haunted, sure: 'tis well furnished,
and no living thing inhabits it. Ha! A man! Heavens,
how he's attired! Sure 'tis some rope dancer,° or fencing   tightrope walker
25 master. I tremble now for fear, and yet I must venture
now to speak to him. —Sir, if I may not interrupt your
meditations—

[*He starts up and gazes.*]

BLUNT Ha, what's here? Are my wishes granted? And is
not that a she creature? 'Adsheartlikins, 'tis. —What
30 wretched thing art thou, ha?

FLORINDA Charitable sir, you've told yourself already what
I am: a very wretched maid, forced by a strange unlucky
accident to seek a safety here, and must be ruined if you
do not grant it.

35 BLUNT Ruined! Is there any ruin so inevitable as that
which now threatens thee? Dost thou know, miserable
woman, into what den of mischiefs thou art fallen; what
abyss of confusion, ha? Dost not see something in my
looks that frights thy guilty soul, and makes thee wish to
40 change that shape of woman for any humble animal, or
devil? For those were safer for thee, and less mischievous.

FLORINDA Alas, what mean you, sir? I must confess, your
looks have something in 'em makes me fear, but I
beseech you, as you seem a gentleman, pity a harmless
45 virgin that takes your house for sanctuary.

BLUNT Talk on, talk on; and weep, too, till my faith return. Do, flatter me out of my senses again. A harmless
virgin with a pox; as much one as t'other, 'adsheartlikins. Why, what the devil, can I not be safe in my
50 house for you, not in my chamber? Nay, not even being
naked too cannot secure me? This is an impudence
greater than has invaded me yet. Come, no resistance.

[*Pulls her rudely.*]

FLORINDA Dare you be so cruel?

BLUNT Cruel? 'Adsheartlikins, as a galley slave, or a Span-
55 ish whore. Cruel? Yes, I will kiss and beat thee all over,

kiss and see thee all over; thou shalt lie with me too, not
that I care for the enjoyment, but to let thee see I have
ta'en deliberated malice to thee, and will be revenged on
one whore for the sins of another. I will smile and deceive
60 thee; flatter thee, and beat thee; embrace thee and rob
thee, as she did me; fawn on thee, and strip thee stark
naked; then hang thee out at my window by the heels,
with a paper of scurvy verses fastened to thy breast in
praise of damnable women. Come, come, along.

65 FLORINDA Alas, sir, must I be sacrificed for the crimes of
the most infamous of my sex? I never understood the
sins you name.

BLUNT Do, persuade the fool you love him, or that one of you
can be just or honest; tell me I was not an easy coxcomb, or
70 any strange impossible tale: it will be believed sooner than
thy false showers or protestations. A generation of damned
hypocrites! To flatter my very clothes from my back! Dissembling witches! Are these the returns you make an honest
gentleman that trusts, believes, and loves you? But if I be
75 not even with you—Come along, or I shall—

[*Pulls her again.*]

[*Enter* FREDERICK.]

FREDERICK Ha, what's here to do?

BLUNT 'Adsheartlikins, Fred, I am glad thou art come, to
be a witness of my dire revenge.

FREDERICK What's this, a person of quality too, who is
80 upon the ramble to supply the defects of some grave impotent husband?

BLUNT No, this has another pretense: some very unfortunate accident brought her hither, to save a life pursued by
I know not who or why, and forced to take sanctuary here
85 at fool's haven. 'Adsheartlikins, to me of all mankind for
protection? Is the ass to be cajoled again, think ye? No,
young one, no prayers or tears shall mitigate my rage;
therefore prepare for both my pleasures of enjoyment
and revenge. For I am resolved to make up my loss here
90 on thy body: I'll take it out in kindness and in beating.

FREDERICK Now, mistress of mine, what do you think of
this?

FLORINDA I think he will not, dares not be so barbarous.

FREDERICK Have a care, Blunt, she fetched a deep sigh;
95 she is enamoured with thy shirt and drawers. She'll strip
thee even of that; there are of her calling such unconscionable baggages and such dexterous thieves, they'll
flay a man and he shall ne'er miss his skin till he feels
the cold. There was a countryman of ours robbed of a
100 row of teeth whilst he was a-sleeping, which the jilt
made him buy again when he waked. You see, lady, how
little reason we have to trust you.

BLUNT 'Adsheartlikins, why this is most abominable!

FLORINDA Some such devils there may be, but by all
that's holy, I am none such. I entered here to save a life
in danger.

BLUNT For no goodness, I'll warrant her.

FREDERICK Faith, damsel, you had e'en confessed the
plain truth, for we are fellows not to be caught twice in
the same trap. Look on that wreck: a tight vessel when
he set out of haven, well trimmed and laden. And see
how a female picaroon of this island of rogues has shattered him, and canst thou hope for any mercy?

BLUNT No, no, gentlewoman, come along; 'adsheartlikins,
we must be better acquainted.—We'll both lie with her,
and then let me alone to bang° her.   *beat*

FREDERICK I'm ready to serve you in matters of revenge
that has a double pleasure in't.

BLUNT Well said.—You hear, little one, how you are condemned by public vote to the bed within; there's no
resisting your destiny, sweetheart.

        [*Pulls her.*]

FLORINDA Stay, sir. I have seen you with Belvile, an English
cavalier. For his sake, use me kindly. You know him, sir.

BLUNT Belvile? Why yes, sweeting, we do know Belvile, and
wish he were with us now. He's a cormorant[7] at whore and
bacon: he'd have a limb or two of thee, my virgin pullet.
But 'tis no matter; we'll leave him the bones to pick.

FLORINDA Sir, if you have any esteem for that Belvile, I
conjure you to treat me with more gentleness; he'll
thank you for the justice.

FREDERICK Hark'ee, Blunt, I doubt° we are mistaken in   *fear*
this matter.

FLORINDA Sir, if you find me not worth Belvile's care, use
me as you please. And that you may think I merit better
treatment than you threaten, pray take this present.

        [*Gives him a ring; he looks on it.*]

BLUNT Hum, a diamond! Why, 'tis a wonderful virtue now
that lies in this ring, a mollifying virtue. 'Adsheartlikins,
there's more persuasive rhetoric in't than all her sex can
utter.

FREDERICK I begin to suspect something, and 'twould
anger us vilely to be trussed up for a rape upon a maid of
quality, when we only believe we ruffle[8] a harlot.

BLUNT Thou art a credulous fellow, but 'adsheartlikins, I
have no faith yet. Why, my saint prattled as parlously° as   *excessively*
this does; she gave me a bracelet, too, a devil on her! But
I sent my man to sell it today for necessaries, and it
proved as counterfeit as her vows of love.

---

7. That is, he is insatiably greedy; cormorants   8. Handle with rude familiarity.
are voracious seabirds.

FREDERICK   However, let it reprieve her till we see Belvile.

BLUNT   That's hard, yet I will grant it.

[Enter a SERVANT.*]*

150 SERVANT   Oh, sir, the colonel is just come in with his new
friend and a Spaniard of quality, and talks of having you
to dinner with 'em.

BLUNT   'Adsheartlikins, I'm undone! I would not see 'em
for the world. Hark'ee, Fred, lock up the wench in your
155 chamber.

FREDERICK   Fear nothing, madam: whate'er he threatens,
you are safe whilst in my hands.

[Exeunt FREDERICK *and* FLORINDA.*]*

BLUNT   And sirrah, upon your life, say I am not at home, or
that I'm asleep, or—or—anything. Away; I'll prevent their
160 coming this way.

[Locks the door, and exeunt.]

5.1

[SCENE: BLUNT's *chamber.*]

[After a great knocking as at his chamber door, enter
BLUNT *softly crossing the stage, in his shirt and drawers as before.]*

VOICES [*call within*]   Ned! Ned Blunt! Ned Blunt!

BLUNT   The rogues are up in arms. 'Adsheartlikins, this
villainous Frederick has betrayed me: they have heard of
my blessed fortune.

5 VOICES [*and knocking within*]   Ned Blunt! Ned! Ned!

BELVILE [*within*]   Why, he's dead, sir, without dispute
dead; he has not been seen today. Let's break open the
door. Here, boy—

BLUNT   Ha, break open the door? 'Adsheartlikins, that
10 mad fellow will be as good as his word.

BELVILE [*within*]   Boy, bring something to force the door.

[A great noise within, at the door again.]

BLUNT   So, now must I speak in my own defense; I'll try
what rhetoric will do.—Hold, hold! What do you mean,
gentlemen, what do you mean?

15 BELVILE [*within*]   Oh, rogue, art alive? Prithee open the
door and convince us.

BLUNT   Yes, I am alive, gentlemen, but at present a little busy.

BELVILE [*within*]   How, Blunt grown a man of business?
Come, come, open and let's see this miracle.

20 BLUNT   No, no, no, no, gentlemen, 'tis no great business.
But—I am—at—my devotion. 'Adsheartlikins, will you
not allow a man time to pray?

BELVILE [*within*]   Turned religious? A greater wonder than
the first! Therefore open quickly, or we shall unhinge, we
25 shall.

BLUNT [*aside*] This won't do.—Why hark'ee, colonel, to tell you the truth, I am about a necessary affair of life: I have a wench with me. You apprehend me?—The devil's in't if they be so uncivil as to disturb me now.

30 WILLMORE [*within*] How, a wench? Nay then, we must enter and partake. No resistance. Unless it be your lady of quality, and then we'll keep our distance.

BLUNT So, the business is out.

WILLMORE [*within*] Come, come, lend's more hands to the door. Now heave, all together. [*Breaks open the door.*] So, well done, my boys.

> [*Enter* BELVILE *and his* PAGE, WILLMORE, FREDERICK, *and* PEDRO. BLUNT *looks simply,°* they all laugh at   foolish
> *him; he lays his hand on his sword, and comes up to*
> WILLMORE.]

BLUNT Hark'ee, sir, laugh out your laugh quickly, d'ye hear, and be gone. I shall spoil your sport else, 'adsheartlikins, sir, I shall. The jest has been carried on too

40 long.—[*Aside.*] A plague upon my tailor!

WILLMORE 'Sdeath, how the whore has dressed him! Faith, sir, I'm sorry.

BLUNT Are you so, sir? Keep't to yourself then, sir, I advise you, d'ye hear, for I can as little endure your pity as his

45 mirth.

> [*Lays his hand on's sword.*]

BELVILE Indeed, Willmore, thou wert a little too rough with Ned Blunt's mistress. Call a person of quality whore, and one so young, so handsome, and so eloquent? Ha, ha, he.

50 BLUNT Hark'ee, sir, you know me, and know I can be angry. Have a care, for 'adsheartlikins, I can fight, too, I can, sir. Do you mark me? No more.

BELVILE Why so peevish, good Ned? Some disappointments, I'll warrant. What, did the jealous count, her

55 husband, return just in the nick?

BLUNT Or the devil, sir. [*They laugh.*] D'ye laugh? Look ye settle me a good sober countenance, and that quickly, too, or you shall know Ned Blunt is not—

BELVILE Not everybody, we know that.

60 BLUNT Not an ass to be laughed at, sir.

WILLMORE Unconscionable sinner! To bring a lover so near his happiness—a vigorous passionate lover—and then not only cheat him of his movables,° but his very   *personal property*
desires, too.

65 BELVILE Ah, sir, a mistress is a trifle with Blunt; he'll have a dozen the next time he looks abroad. His eyes have charms not to be resisted; there needs no more than to expose that taking person to the view of the fair, and he leads 'em all in triumph.

70 PEDRO   Sir, though I'm a stranger to you, I am ashamed at
the rudeness of my nation; and could you learn who did
it, would assist you to make an example of 'em.

BLUNT   Why ay, there's one speaks sense now, and handsomely. And let me tell you, gentlemen, I should not have
75 showed myself like a jack pudding° thus to have made you   *clown, buffoon*
mirth, but that I have revenge within my power. For
know, I have got into my possession a female, who had
better have fallen under any curse than the ruin I design
her. 'Adsheartlikins, she assaulted me here in my own
80 lodgings, and had doubtless committed a rape upon me,
had not this sword defended me.

FREDERICK   I know not that, but o' my conscience thou had
ravished her, had she not redeemed herself with a ring.
Let's see't, Blunt.

   [*Blunt shows the ring.*]

85 BELVILE   [*aside*] Ha! The ring I gave Florinda when we
exchanged our vows!—Hark'ee, Blunt—

   [*Goes to whisper to him.*]

WILLMORE   No whispering, good colonel, there's a woman
in the case. No whispering.

BELVILE   [*aside to* BLUNT] Hark'ee, fool, be advised, and
90 conceal both the ring and the story for your reputation's
sake. Do not let people know what despised cullies we
English are; to be cheated and abused by one whore, and
another rather bribe thee than be kind to thee, is an infamy to our nation.

95 WILLMORE   Come, come, where's the wench? We'll see
her; let her be what she will, we'll see her.

PEDRO   Ay, ay, let us see her. I can soon discover whether
she be of quality, or for your diversion.

BLUNT   She's in Fred's custody.

100 WILLMORE   Come, come, the key—

   [*To* FREDERICK, *who gives him the key; they are going.*]

BELVILE [*aside*]   Death, what shall I do?—Stay, gentlemen.—
[*Aside.*] Yet if I hinder 'em, I shall discover all.—Hold, let's
go one at once. Give me the key.

WILLMORE   Nay, hold there, colonel, I'll go first.

105 FREDERICK   Nay, no dispute, Ned and I have the propriety°   *right of possession*
of her.

WILLMORE   Damn propriety! Then we'll draw cuts.°   *draw lots*
[BELVILE *goes to whisper* WILLMORE.] Nay, no corruption,
good colonel. Come, the longest sword carries her.

   [*They all draw, forgetting* DON PEDRO, *being a Spaniard, had the longest.*[9]]

110 BLUNT   I yield up my interest to you, gentlemen, and that
will be revenge sufficient.

9. The English commonly fought with a shorter sword than the Spanish.

WILLMORE [*to* PEDRO]   The wench is yours. —[*Aside.*] Pox
of his Toledo,[1] I had forgot that.

FREDERICK   Come, sir, I'll conduct you to the lady.

[*Exeunt* FREDERICK *and* PEDRO.]

115 BELVILE [*aside*]   To hinder him will certainly discover her.
—Dost know, dull beast, what mischief thou hast done?

[WILLMORE *walking up and down, out of humor.*]

WILLMORE   Ay, ay, to trust our fortune to lots! A devil on't,
'twas madness, that's the truth on't.

BELVILE   Oh, intolerable sot—

[*Enter* FLORINDA *running, masked,* PEDRO *after her;*
WILLMORE *gazing round her.*]

120 FLORINDA [*aside*]   Good heaven defend me from discovery!

PEDRO   'Tis but in vain to fly me; you're fallen to my lot.

BELVILE [*aside*]   Sure she's undiscovered yet, but now I
fear there is no way to bring her off.°   rescue her

WILLMORE [*aside*]   Why, what a pox, is not this my woman,
125 the same I followed but now?

[PEDRO *talking to* FLORINDA, *who walks up and down.*]

PEDRO   As if I did not know ye, and your business here.

FLORINDA [*aside*]   Good heaven, I fear he does indeed!

PEDRO   Come, pray be kind; I know you meant to be so
when you entered here, for these are proper gentlemen.

130 WILLMORE   But sir, perhaps the lady will not be imposed
upon: she'll choose her man.

PEDRO   I am better bred than not to leave her choice free.

[*Enter* VALERIA, *and is surprised at sight of* DON PEDRO.]

VALERIA [*aside*]   Don Pedro here! There's no avoiding him.

FLORINDA [*aside*]   Valeria! Then I'm undone.

135 VALERIA [*to* PEDRO, *running to him*]   Oh, I have found you,
sir! The strangest accident—if I had breath—to tell it.

PEDRO   Speak! Is Florinda safe? Hellena well?

VALERIA   Ay, ay, sir. Florinda is safe. —[*Aside.*] From any
fears of you.

140 PEDRO   Why, where's Florinda? Speak!

VALERIA   Ay, where indeed, sir; I wish I could inform you.
But to hold you no longer in doubt—

FLORINDA [*aside*]   Oh, what will she say?

VALERIA   She's fled away in the habit—of one of her pages,
145 sir. But Callis thinks you may retrieve her yet, if you
make haste away. She'll tell you, sir, the rest. —[*Aside.*]
If you can find her out.

PEDRO   Dishonorable girl, she has undone my aim. —[*To*
BELVILE.] Sir, you see my necessity of leaving you, and I
150 hope you'll pardon it. My sister, I know, will make her
flight to you; and if she do, I shall expect she should be
rendered back.

---

1. A sword made in Toledo, a city in Spain famous for the quality of its steel blades.

BELVILE   I shall consult my love and honor, sir.

[*Exit* PEDRO.]

FLORINDA [*to* VALERIA]   My dear preserver, let me embrace
155   thee.

WILLMORE   What the devil's all this?

BLUNT   Mystery, by this light.

VALERIA   Come, come, make haste and get yourselves
    married quickly, for your brother will return again.

160 BELVILE   I'm so surprised with fears and joys, so amazed to
    find you here in safety, I can scarce persuade my heart
    into a faith of what I see.

WILLMORE   Hark'ee, colonel, is this that mistress who has
    cost you so many sighs, and me so many quarrels with
165   you?

BELVILE   It is. —[*To* FLORINDA.] Pray give him the honor of
    your hand.

WILLMORE   Thus it must be received, then. [*Kneels and
    kisses her hand*.] And with it give your pardon, too.

170 FLORINDA   The friend to Belvile may command me
    anything.

WILLMORE [*aside*]   Death, would I might; 'tis a surprising
    beauty.

BELVILE   Boy, run and fetch a father° instantly.   *priest*

[*Exit* BOY.]

175 FREDERICK   So, now do I stand like a dog, and have not a
    syllable to plead my own cause with. By this hand,
    madam, I was never thoroughly confounded before, nor
    shall I ever more dare look up with confidence, till you
    are pleased to pardon me.

180 FLORINDA   Sir, I'll be reconciled to you on one condition:
    that you'll follow the example of your friend in marrying
    a maid that does not hate you, and whose fortune, I be-
    lieve, will not be unwelcome to you.

FREDERICK   Madam, had I° no inclinations that way, I   *even if I had*
185   should obey your kind commands.

BELVILE   Who, Fred marry? He has so few inclinations for
    womankind that had he been possessed of paradise he
    might have continued there to this day, if no crime but
    love could have disinherited him.

190 FREDERICK   Oh, I do not use to boast of my intrigues.

BELVILE   Boast! Why, thou dost nothing but boast. And I
    dare swear, wert thou as innocent from the sin of the
    grape as thou art from the apple,[2] thou might'st yet claim
    that right in Eden which our first parents lost by too
195   much loving.

FREDERICK   I wish this lady would think me so modest a
    man.

2. That is, the fruit of the tree of knowledge; the disobedience of Adam and Eve in eating it (not
"too much loving") led to their expulsion from Eden (Genesis 2.15–17, 3.1–24).

VALERIA She would be sorry then, and not like you half so
well. And I should be loath to break my word with you,
200 which was, that if your friend and mine agreed, it should
be a match between you and I.

[*She gives him her hand.*]

FREDERICK Bear witness, colonel, 'tis a bargain.

[*Kisses her hand.*]

BLUNT [*to* FLORINDA] I have a pardon to beg, too; but 'adsheartlikins, I am so out of countenance° that I'm a dog   *abashed*
205 if I can say anything to purpose.

FLORINDA Sir, I heartily forgive you all.

BLUNT That's nobly said, sweet lady.—Belvile, prithee
present her her ring again, for I find I have not courage
to approach her myself.

[*Gives him the ring; he gives it to* FLORINDA.]
[*Enter* BOY.]

210 BOY Sir, I have brought the father that you sent for.

[*Exit* BOY.]

BELVILE 'Tis well. And now, my dear Florinda, let's fly to
complete that mighty joy we have so long wished and
sighed for.—Come, Fred, you'll follow?

FREDERICK Your example, sir, 'twas ever my ambition in
215 war, and must be so in love.

WILLMORE And must not I see this juggling° knot tied?   *cheating, deceptive*

BELVILE No, thou shalt do us better service and be our
guard, lest Don Pedro's sudden return interrupt the ceremony.

220 WILLMORE Content; I'll secure this pass.

[*Exeunt* BELVILE, FLORINDA, FREDERICK, *and* VALERIA.]
[*Enter* BOY.]

BOY [*to* WILLMORE] Sir, there's a lady without would speak
to you.

WILLMORE Conduct her in; I dare not quit my post.

BOY [*to* BLUNT] And sir, your tailor waits you in your
225 chamber.

BLUNT Some comfort yet: I shall not dance naked at the
wedding.

[*Exeunt* BLUNT *and* BOY.]

[*Enter again the* BOY, *conducting in* ANGELLICA *in a
masking habit and a vizard.* WILLMORE *runs to her.*]

WILLMORE [*aside*] This can be none but my pretty gipsy.—
Oh, I see you can follow as well as fly. Come, confess
230 thyself the most malicious devil in nature; you think you
have done my business with Angellica—

ANGELLICA Stand off, base villain!

[*She draws a pistol and holds it to his breast.*]

WILLMORE Ha, 'tis not she! Who art thou, and what's
thy business?

235 ANGELLICA One thou hast injured, and who comes to kill
thee for't.

WILLMORE What the devil canst thou mean?

ANGELLICA By all my hopes to kill thee—

[*Holds still the pistol to his breast; he going back, she
following still.*]

WILLMORE Prithee, on what acquaintance? For I know
240 thee not.

ANGELLICA Behold this face so lost to thy remembrance,

[*Pulls off her vizard.*]

And then call all thy sins about thy soul,
And let 'em die with thee.

WILLMORE Angellica!

245 ANGELLICA Yes, traitor! Does not thy guilty blood run
shivering through thy veins? Hast thou no horror at this
sight, that tells thee thou hast not long to boast thy
shameful conquest?

WILLMORE Faith, no, child. My blood keeps its old ebbs
250 and flows still, and that usual heat too, that could oblige
thee with a kindness, had I but opportunity.

ANGELLICA Devil! Dost wanton with my pain? Have at thy
heart!

WILLMORE Hold, dear virago!° Hold thy hand a little; I am   *warrior woman*
255 not now at leisure to be killed. Hold and hear me. —
[*Aside.*] Death, I think she's in earnest.

ANGELLICA [*aside, turning from him*] Oh, if I take not
heed, my coward heart will leave me to his mercy. —
What have you, sir, to say? —But should I hear thee,
260 thoud'st talk away all that is brave about me, and I have
vowed thy death by all that's sacred.

[*Follows him with the pistol to his breast.*]

WILLMORE Why then, there's an end of a proper handsome fellow, that might 'a lived to have done good service
yet. That's all I can say to't.

265 ANGELLICA [*pausingly*] Yet—I would give thee time
for—penitence.

WILLMORE Faith, child, I thank God I have ever took care
to lead a good, sober, hopeful life, and am of a religion
that teaches me to believe I shall depart in peace.

270 ANGELLICA So will the devil! Tell me,
How many poor believing fools thou hast undone?
How many hearts thou hast betrayed to ruin?
Yet these are little mischiefs to the ills
Thou'st taught mine to commit: thou'st taught it love.

275 WILLMORE Egad, 'twas shrewdly hurt the while.

ANGELLICA Love, that has robbed it of its unconcern,
Of all that pride that taught me how to value it.
And in its room
A mean submissive passion was conveyed,

280   That made me humbly bow, which I ne'er did
    To anything but heaven.
    Thou, perjured man, didst this; and with thy oaths,
    Which on thy knees thou didst devoutly make,
    Softened my yielding heart, and then I was a slave.
285   Yet still had been content to've worn my chains,
    Worn 'em with vanity and joy forever,
    Hadst thou not broke those vows that put them on.
    'Twas then I was undone.
        [*All this while follows him with the pistol to his breast.*]

WILLMORE   Broke my vows? Why, where hast thou lived?
290   Amongst the gods? For I never heard of mortal man that
has not broke a thousand vows.

ANGELLICA   Oh, impudence!

WILLMORE   Angellica, that beauty has been too long tempting, not to have made a thousand lovers languish; who, in
295   the amorous fever, no doubt have sworn like me. Did they
all die in that faith, still adoring? I do not think they did.

ANGELLICA   No, faithless man; had I repaid their vows, as
I did thine, I would have killed the ingrateful that had
abandoned me.

300 WILLMORE   This old general has quite spoiled thee: nothing makes a woman so vain as being flattered. Your old
lover ever supplies the defects of age with intolerable
dotage, vast charge, and that which you call constancy;
and attributing all this to your own merits, you domineer,
305   and throw your favors in's teeth, upbraiding him still with
the defects of age, and cuckold him as often as he deceives your expectations. But the gay, young, brisk lover,
that brings his equal fires, and can give you dart for dart,
he'll be as nice° as you sometimes.   *wanton*

310 ANGELLICA   All this thou'st made me know, for which I
    hate thee.
    Had I remained in innocent security,
    I should have thought all men were born my slaves,
    And worn my power like lightning in my eyes,
315   To have destroyed at pleasure when offended.
    But when love held the mirror, the undeceiving glass
    Reflected all the weakness of my soul, and made me know
    My richest treasure being lost, my honor,
    All the remaining spoil could not be worth
320   The conqueror's care or value.
    Oh, how I fell, like a long-worshiped idol,
    Discovering all the cheat.
    Would not the incense and rich sacrifice
    Which blind devotion offered at my altars
325   Have fallen to thee?
    Why wouldst thou then destroy my fancied power?

WILLMORE   By heaven, thou'rt brave, and I admire thee
    strangely.°   *to an exceptional degree*

I wish I were that dull, that constant thing
330 Which thou wouldst have, and nature never meant me.
I must, like cheerful birds, sing in all groves,
And perch on every bough,
Billing the next kind she that flies to meet me;
Yet, after all, could build my nest with thee,
335 Thither repairing when I'd loved my round,
And still reserve a tributary flame.
To gain your credit, I'll pay you back your charity,
And be obliged for nothing but for love.

    [*Offers her a purse of gold.*]

ANGELLICA Oh, that thou wert in earnest!
340 So mean a thought of me
Would turn my rage to scorn, and I should pity thee,
And give thee leave to live;
Which for the public safety of our sex,
And my own private injuries, I dare not do.
345 Prepare— [*Follows still, as before.*]
I will no more be tempted with replies.

WILLMORE Sure—

ANGELLICA Another word will damn thee! I've heard thee
talk too long.

    [*She follows him with the pistol ready to shoot; he*
    retires, still amazed. Enter DON ANTONIO, *his arm in a*
    scarf, and lays hold on the pistol.]

350 ANTONIO Ha! Angellica!

ANGELLICA Antonio! What devil brought thee hither?

ANTONIO Love and curiosity, seeing your coach at door.
Let me disarm you of this unbecoming instrument of
death. [*Takes away the pistol.*] Amongst the number of
355 your slaves was there not one worthy the honor to have
fought your quarrel? —[*To* WILLMORE.] Who are you, sir,
that are so very wretched to merit death from her?

WILLMORE One, sir, that could have made a better end of
an amorous quarrel without you, than with you.

360 ANTONIO Sure 'tis some rival. Ha! The very man took
down her picture yesterday; the very same that set on me
last night! Blessed opportunity—

    [*Offers to shoot him.*]

ANGELLICA Hold, you're mistaken, sir.

ANTONIO By heavens, the very same!—Sir, what preten-
365 sions have you to this lady?

WILLMORE Sir, I do not use° to be examined, and am ill at   *am not accustomed*
all disputes but this—

    [*Draws;* ANTONIO *offers to shoot.*]

ANGELLICA [*to* WILLMORE] Oh, hold! You see he's armed
with certain death.

370 —And you, Antonio, I command you hold,

By all the passion you've so lately vowed me.

[*Enter* DON PEDRO, *sees* ANTONIO, *and stays.*]

PEDRO [*aside*]   Ha! Antonio! And Angellica!

ANTONIO   When I refuse obedience to your will,
May you destroy me with your mortal hate.
375   By all that's holy, I adore you so,
That even my rival, who has charms enough
To make him fall a victim to my jealousy,
Shall live; nay, and have leave to love on still.

PEDRO [*aside*]   What's this I hear?

380   ANGELLICA [*pointing to* WILLMORE]   Ah thus, 'twas thus he
        talked, and I believed.
Antonio, yesterday
I'd not have sold my interest in his heart
For all the sword has won and lost in battle.
385   —But now, to show my utmost of contempt,
I give thee life; which, if thou wouldst preserve,
Live where my eyes may never see thee more.
Live to undo someone whose soul may prove
So bravely constant to revenge my love.

[*Goes out.* ANTONIO *follows, but* PEDRO *pulls him back.*]

390   PEDRO   Antonio, stay.

ANTONIO   Don Pedro!

PEDRO   What coward fear was that prevented thee from
meeting me this morning on the Molo?

ANTONIO   Meet thee?

395   PEDRO   Yes, me; I was the man that dared thee to't.

ANTONIO   Hast thou so often seen me fight in war, to find
no better cause to excuse my absence? I sent my sword
and one to do thee right, finding myself uncapable to use
a sword.

400   PEDRO   But 'twas Florinda's quarrel that we fought, and
you, to show how little you esteemed her, sent me your
rival, giving him your interest. But I have found the cause
of this affront, and when I meet you fit for the dispute,
I'll tell you my resentment.

405   ANTONIO   I shall be ready, sir, ere long, to do you
reason.   [*Exit* ANTONIO.]

PEDRO   If I could find Florinda, now whilst my anger's
high, I think I should be kind, and give her to Belvile in
revenge.

410   WILLMORE   Faith, sir, I know not what you would do, but I
believe the priest within has been so kind.

PEDRO   How? My sister married?

WILLMORE   I hope by this time he is, and bedded too, or
he has not my longings about him.

415   PEDRO   Dares he do this? Does he not fear my power?

WILLMORE   Faith, not at all; if you will go in and thank
him for the favor he has done your sister, so; if not, sir,

my power's greater in this house than yours: I have a
damned surly crew here that will keep you till the next
420 tide, and then clap you on board for prize.° My ship lies   *as a captive of*
but a league off the Molo, and we shall show your don-
ship a damned Tramontana³ rover's trick.

           [*Enter* BELVILE.]

BELVILE   This rogue's in some new mischief. Ha! Pedro
      returned!
425 PEDRO   Colonel Belvile, I hear you have married my sister.

BELVILE   You have heard truth then, sir.

PEDRO   Have I so? Then, sir, I wish you joy.

BELVILE   How?

PEDRO   By this embrace I do, and I am glad on't.

430 BELVILE   Are you in earnest?

PEDRO   By our long friendship and my obligations to thee,
      I am; the sudden change I'll give you reasons for anon.
      Come, lead me to my sister, that she may know I now
      approve her choice.

              [*Exit* BELVILE *with* PEDRO.]

      [WILLMORE *goes to follow them. Enter* HELLENA, *as
      before in boy's clothes, and pulls him back.*]

435 WILLMORE   Ha! My gipsy! Now a thousand blessings on
      thee for this kindness. Egad, child, I was e'en in despair
      of ever seeing thee again; my friends are all provided for
      within, each man his kind woman.

HELLENA   Ha! I thought they had served me some such
440   trick!

WILLMORE   And I was e'en resolved to go aboard, and con-
      demn myself to my lone cabin, and the thoughts of thee.

HELLENA   And could you have left me behind? Would you
      have been so ill natured?

445 WILLMORE   Why, 'twould have broke my heart, child. But
      since we are met again, I defy foul weather to part us.

HELLENA   And would you be a faithful friend now, if a
      maid should trust you?

WILLMORE   For a friend I cannot promise: thou art of a
450   form so excellent, a face and humour too good for cold
      dull friendship. I am parlously afraid of being in love,
      child; and you have not forgotten how severely you have
      used me?

HELLENA   That's all one; such usage you must still look
455   for: to find out all your haunts, to rail at you to all that
      love you, till I have made you love only me in your own
      defense, because nobody else will love you.

WILLMORE   But hast thou no better quality to recommend
      thyself by?

3. Barbarous (literally, "north wind" in Italian—i.e., across the mountains).

460 HELLENA Faith, none, captain. Why, 'twill be the greater
charity to take me for thy mistress. I am a lone child, a
kind of orphan lover; and why I should die a maid, and in
a captain's hands too, I do not understand.

WILLMORE Egad, I was never clawed away with broad
465 sides from any female before. Thou hast one virtue I
adore—good nature. I hate a coy demure mistress, she's
as troublesome as a colt; I'll break none. No, give me a
mad mistress when mewed,° and in flying, one I dare   *confined (as a hawk)*
trust upon the wing, that whilst she's kind will come to
470 the lure.

HELLENA Nay, as kind as you will, good captain, whilst it
lasts. But let's lose no time.

WILLMORE My time's as precious to me as thine can be.
Therefore, dear creature, since we are so well agreed,
475 let's retire to my chamber; and if ever thou wert treated
with such savory love! Come, my bed's prepared for such
a guest all clean and sweet as thy fair self. I love to steal
a dish and a bottle with a friend, and hate long graces.
Come, let's retire and fall to.

480 HELLENA 'Tis but getting my consent, and the business is
soon done. Let but old gaffer Hymen[4] and his priest say
amen to't, and I dare lay my mother's daughter by as proper
a fellow as your father's son, without fear or blushing.

WILLMORE Hold, hold, no bug° words, child. Priest and   *terrifying*
485 Hymen? Prithee add a hangman to 'em to make up the
consort. No, no, we'll have no vows but love, child, nor
witness but the lover: the kind deity enjoins naught but
love and enjoy. Hymen and priest wait still upon portion
and jointure; love and beauty have their own cere-
490 monies. Marriage is as certain a bane to love as lending
money is to friendship. I'll neither ask nor give a vow,
though I could be content to turn gipsy and become a
left-handed bridegroom[5] to have the pleasure of working
that great miracle of making a maid a mother, if you
495 durst venture. 'Tis upse° gipsy that, and if I miss I'll lose   *in the manner of*
my labor.

HELLENA And if you do not lose, what shall I get? A cradle
full of noise and mischief, with a pack of repentance at
my back? Can you teach me to weave incle° to pass my   *linen thread*
500 time with? 'Tis upse gipsy that, too.

WILLMORE I can teach thee to weave a true love's knot
better.

HELLENA So can my dog.

WILLMORE Well, I see we are both upon our guards, and I
505 see there's no way to conquer good nature but by yielding.
Here, give me thy hand: one kiss, and I am thine.

---

4. The classical god of marriage, usually represented not as an old man ("gaffer") but as
youthful.

5. That is, a "bridegroom" in a wedding not
properly solemnized and thus not fully legal.

HELLENA   One kiss! How like my page he speaks! I am resolved you shall have none, for asking such a sneaking sum.
He that will be satisfied with one kiss will never die of that
510   longing. Good friend single-kiss, is all your talking come to
this? A kiss, a caudle!⁶ Farewell, captain single-kiss.

[*Going out; he stays her.*]

WILLMORE   Nay, if we part so, let me die like a bird upon a
bough, at the sheriff's charge. By heaven, both the Indies shall not buy thee from me. I adore thy humour and
515   will marry thee, and we are so of one humour it must be
a bargain. Give me thy hand. [*Kisses her hand.*] And now
let the blind ones, love and fortune, do their worst.

HELLENA   Why, god-a-mercy, captain!

WILLMORE   But hark'ee: the bargain is now made, but is it
520   not fit we should know each other's names, that when we
have reason to curse one another hereafter, and people
ask me who 'tis I give to the devil, I may at least be able to
tell what family you came of?

HELLENA   Good reason, captain; and where I have cause, as
525   I doubt not but I shall have plentiful, that I may know at
whom to throw my—blessings, I beseech ye your name.

WILLMORE   I am called Robert the Constant.

HELLENA   A very fine name! Pray was it your faulkner° or   hawk keeper
butler that christened you? Do they not use to whistle
530   when they call you?

WILLMORE   I hope you have a better, that a man may name
without crossing himself—you are so merry with mine.

HELLENA   I am called Hellena the Inconstant.

[*Enter* PEDRO, BELVILE, FLORINDA, FREDERICK, VALERIA.]

PEDRO   Ha! Hellena!

535   FLORINDA   Hellena!

HELLENA   The very same. Ha! My brother! Now, captain,
show your love and courage; stand to your arms and
defend me bravely, or I am lost forever.

PEDRO   What's this I hear? False girl, how came you hither,
540   and what's your business? Speak!

[*Goes roughly to her.*]

WILLMORE   Hold off, sir; you have leave to parley° only.   speak; negotiate

[*Puts himself between.*]

HELLENA   I had e'en as good tell it, as you guess it. Faith,
brother, my business is the same with all living creatures
of my age: to love and be beloved—and here's the man.

545   PEDRO   Perfidious maid, hast thou deceived me too;
deceived thyself and heaven?

HELLENA   'Tis time enough to make my peace with that.
Be you but kind, let me alone with heaven.

---

6. A warm drink (of thin gruel mixed with ale or wine) for an invalid, given especially to women
after childbirth.

PEDRO   Belvile, I did not expect this false play from you.
550   Was't not enough you'd gain Florinda, which I pardoned,
      but your lewd friends too must be enriched with the
      spoils of a noble family?
BELVILE   Faith, sir, I am as much surprised at this as you
      can be. Yet, sir, my friends are gentlemen, and ought to
555   be esteemed for their misfortunes, since they have the
      glory to suffer with the best of men and kings. 'Tis true,
      he's a rover of fortune, yet a prince aboard his little
      wooden world.
PEDRO   What's this to the maintenance of a woman of her
560   birth and quality?
WILLMORE   Faith, sir, I can boast of nothing but a sword
      which does me right where'er I come, and has defended a
      worse cause than a woman's; and since I loved her before
      I either knew her birth or name, I must pursue my reso-
565   lution and marry her.
PEDRO   And is all your holy intent of becoming a nun
      debauched into a desire of man?
HELLENA   Why, I have considered the matter, brother, and
      find the three hundred thousand crowns my uncle left me,
570   and you cannot keep from me, will be better laid out in
      love than in religion, and turn to as good an account. Let
      most voices carry it: for heaven or the captain?
ALL CRY   A captain! A captain!
HELLENA   Look ye, sir, 'tis a clear case.
575   PEDRO   Oh, I am mad! —[Aside.] If I refuse, my life's in
      danger. —Come, there's one motive induces me. Take her;
      I shall now be free from fears of her honor. Guard it you
      now, if you can; I have been a slave to't long enough.
            [Gives her to him.]
WILLMORE   Faith, sir, I am of a nation that are of opinion
580   a woman's honor is not worth guarding when she has a
      mind to part with it.
HELLENA   Well said, captain.
PEDRO [to VALERIA]   This was your plot, mistress, but I
      hope you have married one that will revenge my quar-
585   rel to you.
VALERIA   There's no altering destiny, sir.
PEDRO   Sooner than a woman's will; therefore I forgive
      you all, and wish you may get my father's pardon as eas-
      ily, which I fear.
            [Enter BLUNT dressed in a Spanish habit, looking
            very ridiculously; his MAN adjusting his band.°]
                                                          collar
590   MAN   'Tis very well, sir.
BLUNT   Well, sir! 'Adsheartlikins, I tell you 'tis damnable
      ill, sir. A Spanish habit! Good Lord! Could the devil and
      my tailor devise no other punishment for me but the
      mode of a nation I abominate?
595   BELVILE   What's the matter, Ned?

BLUNT   Pray view me round, and judge.

> [*Turns round.*]

BELVILE   I must confess thou art a kind of an odd figure.

BLUNT   In a Spanish habit with a vengeance! I had rather
be in the Inquisition for Judaism than in this doublet
600   and breeches; a pillory were an easy collar to this, three
handfuls high; and these shoes, too, are worse than the
stocks, with the sole an inch shorter than my foot. In
fine, gentlemen, methinks I look like a bag of bays[7]
stuffed full of fool's flesh.

605   BELVILE   Methinks 'tis well, and makes thee look e'en
cavalier. Come, sir, settle your face and salute our
friends. Lady—

BLUNT [*to* HELLENA]   Ha! Sayst thou so, my little rover?
Lady, if you be one, give me leave to kiss your hand, and
610   tell you, 'adsheartlikins, for all I look so, I am your humble servant. A pox of my Spanish habit!

> [*Music is heard to play.*]

WILLMORE   Hark! What's this?

> [*Enter* BOY.]

BOY   Sir, as the custom is, the gay people in masquerade,
who make every man's house their own, are coming up.

> [*Enter several men and women in masking habits,
> with music; they put themselves in order and dance.*]

615   BLUNT   'Adsheartlikins, would 'twere lawful to pull off
their false faces, that I might see if my doxy° were not   prostitute
amongst 'em.

BELVILE [*to the maskers*]   Ladies and gentlemen, since you
are come so *a propos*,° you must take a small collation   opportunely (French)
620   with us.

WILLMORE [*to* HELLENA]   Whilst we'll to the good man
within, who stays to give us a cast of his office.[8] Have
you no trembling at the near approach?

HELLENA   No more than you have in an engagement or a
625   tempest.

WILLMORE   Egad, thou'rt a brave girl, and I admire thy
love and courage.

> Lead on; no other dangers they can dread,
> Who venture in the storms o'th' marriage bed.

> > [*Exeunt.*]

> ### The End

---

7. Perhaps "baize," a thick cloth; or perhaps a bag containing bay leaves, used in cooking.
8. A taste of his customary function.

Epilogue

The banished cavaliers! A roving blade!
A popish carnival! A masquerade!
The devil's in't if this will please the nation
In these our blessed times of reformation,
5   When conventickling[9] is so much in fashion.
And yet—
That mutinous tribe less factions do beget,
Than your continual differing in wit.
Your judgment's, as your passion's, a disease:
10   Nor° muse nor miss your appetite can please;   *Neither*
You're grown as nice° as queasy consciences,   *fastidious*
Whose each convulsion, when the spirit moves,
Damns everything that maggot° disapproves.   *capricious person*
    With canting rule you would the stage refine,
15   And to dull method all our sense confine.
With th'insolence of commonwealths you rule,
Where each gay fop and politic grave fool
On monarch wit impose, without control.
As for the last, who seldom sees a play,
20   Unless it be the old Blackfriars[1] way;
Shaking his empty noddle o'er bamboo,°   *cane*
He cries, "Good faith, these plays will never do!
Ah, sir, in my young days, what lofty wit,
What high-strained scenes of fighting there were writ.
25   These are slight airy toys. But tell me, pray,
What has the House of Commons done today?"
Then shows his politics, to let you see
Of state affairs he'll judge as notably
As he can do of wit and poetry.
30   The younger sparks, who hither do resort,
Cry,
"Pox o' your genteel things! Give us more sport!
Damn me, I'm sure 'twill never please the court."
    Such fops are never pleased, unless the play
35   Be stuffed with fools as brisk° and dull as they.   *pert*
Such might the half-crown spare, and in a glass°   *mirror*
At home behold a more accomplished ass.
Where they may set their cravats, wigs, and faces,
And practice all their buffoonry grimaces:
40   See how this huff becomes, this damny,° stare,   *damn me!*
Which they at home may act because they dare,
But must with prudent caution do elsewhere.
Oh that our Nokes, or Tony Lee,[2] could show
A fop but half so much to th' life as you.

---

9. Holding meetings of religious noncon-
formists.
1. A London theater that closed in 1642, at
the onset of the English Civil War.

2. James Nokes (1642–1696) and Anthony
Leigh (d. 1692), popular comic actors of the
1670s who often appeared together.

Postscript

This play had been sooner in print, but for a report about the town (made by some either very malicious or very ignorant) that 'twas *Thomaso*[3] altered; which made the booksellers fear some trouble from the proprietor of that admirable play, which indeed has wit enough to stock a poet, and is not to be pieced or mended by any but the excellent author himself. That I have stolen some hints from it, may be a proof that I valued it more than to pretend to alter it, had I the dexterity of some poets, who are not more expert in stealing than in the art of concealing, and who even that way outdo the Spartan boys.[4] I might have appropriated all to myself; but I, vainly proud of my judgment, hang out the sign of Angellica (the only stolen object) to give notice where a great part of the wit dwelt; though if the *Play of the Novella*[5] were as well worth remembering as *Thomaso*, they might (bating the name) have as well said I took it from thence. I will only say the plot and business (not to boast on't) is my own; as for the words and characters, I leave the reader to judge and compare 'em with *Thomaso*, to whom I recommend the great entertainment of reading it. Though had this succeeded ill, I should have had no need of imploring that justice from the critics, who are naturally so kind to any that pretend to usurp their dominion, especially of our sex:[6] they would doubtless have given me the whole honor on't. Therefore I will only say in English what the famous Virgil[7] does in Latin: I make verses, and others have the fame.

Finis

3. The 1654 play by Thomas Killigrew on which *The Rover* is largely based.
4. In ancient Sparta, boys were deliberately underfed so that they would learn to steal food; but if caught, they were disgraced.
5. The 1632 play by Richard Brome that inspired some elements of *The Rover*.
6. This acknowledgment of female author-

ship did not appear in the first issue of the first quarto or in some copies of the second issue.
7. Roman poet (70–19 B.C.E.), author of the *Aeneid*; according to the Roman grammarian Donatus (4th c. C.E.), a couplet he wrote anonymously in praise of the emperor Augustus was claimed by another.

JEAN RACINE

1639–1699

Like his contemporary and rival Pierre Corneille (1606–1684), Jean Racine was one of the masters of French neoclassical drama. Unlike Corneille, however, he has achieved an undisputed place in the world repertoire. To the eighteenth-century writer and philosopher Voltaire, he was the best of France's tragedians: "It is he alone who spoke to the heart and the reasoning mind, who alone was truly sublime without being bombastic, and who brought to poetic diction a charm unknown before him." To the twentieth-century actor and director Jean-Louis Barrault, he was "perhaps the greatest and certainly the most musical of all our French poets." This most French of playwrights in terms of dramatic language and dramatic structure—whose plays are inseparable from seventeenth-century notions of dramatic form and subject matter—wrote a body of drama that transcended nationality and historical conventions.

During the reign (1643–1715) of Louis XIV, the "Sun King," France established itself as Europe's leading power, and through the splendor and the patronage system of the court at Versailles it achieved cultural predominance as well. But though this period was defined by unprecedented social order and cohesiveness, mid- and late seventeenth-century France was not without its conflicts, latent and otherwise. The religious wars that had torn apart Europe earlier in the century had ended, but the aftertremors of the Reformation and Counter-Reformation continued to affect Catholic France, taking the form of intermittent religious persecution (Louis outlawed the public practice of any religion other than Roman Catholicism in 1685), polemical debates over questions of doctrine, and wars with France's Protestant neighbors. Moreover, even as Louis presided over an aristocratic court, the social changes taking place in the country—including the steady growth of a bourgeois, mercantile class—began to destabilize French society, a process that accelerated during the eighteenth century and contributed to the overthrow of the monarchy in the revolution of 1789–99. Late seventeenth-century France was an age of absolute monarchy, when Louis ruled by the "divine right of kings," but it was also a period of increasing economic and social mobility.

Racine's career unfolded against this political, social, and religious backdrop, and it reflects the opportunities available in the French court to a person of literary abilities. He was born to a bourgeois family in a small village in the Valois region of France, where he was baptized on December 22, 1639. His parents died before he was five, and until 1649 he lived with his paternal grandparents; he spent much of the next nine years studying in a school associated with the monastery of Port-Royal des Champs near Paris. Port-Royal was the spiritual center for Jansenism, an austere branch of Roman Catholicism that adhered to strict principles of piety and morality. The education provided there centered on the study of rhetoric, and as part of his studies Racine read deeply in the Greek and Roman masters. In 1658, at the age of eighteen, he was sent by the Jansenists to study law at the College of Harcourt in Paris.

Racine adapted easily to the political and social world of midcentury Paris. Aware that social advancement could be won by literary means, he wrote verses commemorating the marriage of Louis XIV and Marie-Thérèse and lauding Cardinal Mazarin, the minister of France. He also wrote two early tragedies, now lost, that were never produced. In 1663, after living for two years with his uncle, who was vicar general of the diocese of Uzès in the south of France, Racine finally produced two odes—one of which commemorated the king's recovery from measles—that earned him the patronage of the future duke of Saint-Aignan and an annual pension from the royal court.

During this time Racine made the acquaintance of MOLIÈRE (Jean-Baptiste Poquelin), who had established himself as France's leading comic playwright. Impressed by the younger writer, Molière agreed to produce a play of Racine's at the Theater of the Palais Royal, where his acting company was in residence. The Thebiad, a tragedy based on Greek sources, premiered on June 20, 1664, and following its modest success Molière produced Racine's second tragedy, Alexander the Great, on December 4, 1665. Though the play was widely acclaimed, the match between a company that specialized in comedy and a writer of classically influenced tragedy was not ideal. Racine immediately began negotiating with the company at the Hôtel de Bourgogne, a rival group that more often produced tragedies, and it mounted a second premiere of Alexander ten days later. This apparent lack of compunction in abandoning the dramatist and theater manager who had first brought his plays to public attention supports the argument, made by several recent biographers, that Racine was a careerist, remarkably adept at advancing himself socially and economically both within the literary marketplace and at court. In 1665 he also received from Louis XIV the first of many financial gifts, which continued until the playwright's death in April 1699. The patronage of Louis and other members of the French nobility enabled Racine to become a successful and prosperous member of the court. In 1677 he married Catherine de Romanet, who came from a prominent bourgeois family and who bore him seven children.

During the years 1667–77 Racine wrote his best-known plays, all of which were produced at the Hôtel de Bourgogne and all but one of which were tragedies: Andromache (1667); The Litigants (1668), his only comedy; Britannicus (1669); Berenice (1671); Bajazet (1672); Mithridates (1673); Iphigenia (1674); and PHÈDRE (1677). During these years he was also embroiled in literary battles with the supporters of Corneille, his chief rival in the writing of neoclassical French tragedy. As the controversy that greeted Corneille's heroic play The Cid (1637) indicates, the literary authorities of seventeenth-century France argued bitterly over the nature of tragedy, the precepts of neoclassical theory, and the relation of theater to its audience. Racine's plays were often attacked by the Corneille camp, and Racine responded with polemical counterarguments in the prefaces he wrote when the works were published. Though Racine's dramas eventually eclipsed Corneille's in popularity, the debates over the relative merits of the two playwrights would continue into the eighteenth century.

Iphigenia and Phèdre were high-water marks in Racine's career: the former played for three months in Paris to wide acclaim, while the latter was performed a number of times at court and was chosen for the inaugural performance of the Comédie Française, which was formed when Theater of the Palais Royal and the Hôtel de Bourgogne merged in 1680. Indeed, after Phèdre Racine wrote no more plays for the theater for twelve years. The question of why he gave up playwriting has preoccupied biographers and theater historians for more than three hundred years. One factor no doubt was that in the fall of 1677 Racine—along with Nicolas Boileau, author of the influential critical treatise *The Art of Poetry* (1674)—was named royal historiographer to the king. Having received this high honor (a surprising elevation for a commoner), Racine may have thought it prudent to abandon a less socially desirable career. Though his earlier works continued to be performed, and he continued to produce some occasional verse and librettos for operas, Racine's only original work for the theater after 1677 consisted of two religious plays he was asked to write for the moral instruction of the girls at the convent of Saint-Cyr: *Esther* (1689) and *Athaliah* (1691).

Phèdre is Racine's crowning achievement as a dramatist. Its characters, background, and story, found in a number of classical sources, were widely familiar to his audience. Theseus, king of Athens, has married Phèdre, the daughter of Minos, king of Crete, and the sister of Ariadne, who had helped Theseus in his quest to slay the Cretan Minotaur (Theseus subsequently abandoned Ariadne on the island of Naxos). Before embarking on a journey, Theseus leaves Phèdre in the city of Troezen with Hippolytus, his son by the Amazon Antiope. When she had first encountered the young man, a hunter famous for disdaining the affairs of the heart, Phèdre was seized by a strong passion, which she has hidden by feigning a public antagonism toward him. The play begins with a discussion of Theseus's long absence; when word arrives that he is dead, Phèdre confesses her love to Hippolytus, who rejects her advances. But Theseus is not dead, and when he returns Phèdre, through her nurse, accuses Hippolytus of attempted rape. Blinded by rage, Theseus calls on the god Neptune to exact vengeance on the son he believes has betrayed him, and it comes swiftly. As Hippolytus is driving his chariot by the shore, a sea monster rises from the deep; he fights it but is dragged to his death by his terrified horses. Learning of his son's death, Theseus is stricken with remorse. Phèdre, for her part, confesses her deception and takes her own life.

Marie Champmesle (1642–1698), the first actress to perform the role of Phaedra, pictured here in the role.

This tragic tale of quasi-incestuous love, rejection, and misplaced retribution had a venerable stage history—from EURIPIDES (*Hippolytus*) and the Roman SENECA (*Phèdre*) to Matthieu Bidar, whose *Hippolytus* was produced in 1675. Its classical lineage naturally helped make the story attractive to Racine, who followed the aesthetic precepts of neoclassical theory that dominated mid- and late seventeenth-century France. This theory, drawn from the practice of Greek and Roman drama and the writings of Aristotle (as interpreted by sixteenth- and seventeenth-century commentators), offered principles and rules to govern dramatic representation. Chief among these were the notions of verisimilitude (*vraisemblance*) and decorum (*bienséance*). According to the principle of verisimilitude, characters and events onstage must not strain the spectators' credulity by venturing into the fantastic or improbable. To satisfy the principle of decorum, dramatic action must not exceed the bounds of propriety: characters must speak and act in ways appropriate to their standing and situation, without violating the audience's expectations or disturbing its sensibilities. As in the plays of the great Greek tragedians, violence should take place offstage.

From these central principles follow others. According to the unities of time, place, and action, dramatic events should occupy a time frame proportionate to the time of performance, the stage should represent a single place, and extraneous characters and plot lines should not detract from a single, focused action. In order to support the seamlessness of all three unities, the stage must never be left empty during an act; instead, character entrances and exits are designed to provide continuity between scenes. Finally, as Aristotle suggested, tragedy must deal with the fate of noble characters, who were viewed as alone capable of exalted emotion. In keeping with this dramatic elevation, the characters of Racine speak in the formal pattern of rhymed alexandrines, which are iambic hexameter (twelve-syllable) lines.

More familiar with the drama of SHAKESPEARE and other playwrights who flout the dramatic unities, mix genres, and are far more flexible in their approach to characterization, plot, and style, modern readers and audiences may initially find the tenets of neoclassicism constraining and artificial. Yet the theory effectively supported its aim of creating a particular audience experience. Through the principles of verisimilitude and decorum seventeenth-century dramatists sought to give the dramatic world compression, coherence, and logic. At its finest, neoclassical tragedy offers an intensified dramatic experience in which the operations of character and fate are revealed within a theatrically distilled, internally coherent moment of time.

Racine's drama also illustrates the richness that can result from the tension between the localized and the universal. In *Phèdre*, the action unfolds over a period of a few hours, and its setting—within or just outside the palace of Troezen—remains the same throughout the play. As Martin Turnell notes, there is "something of the prison" about Racine's palace settings, and this singular locale enforces a sense of confinement. But counterpointing its temporal and geographical concentration is an expansive awareness of time and space. Through the references and descriptions in Racine's dramatic poetry, the staged action is illuminated by the backdrop of the ancient Mediterranean—with its exotic regions above and the underworld below—and its stories, both human and divine, from history and myth. The rocky shore of Troezen where Hippolytus meets his fate, like the distant lands of Theseus's journeys, opens a space beyond *Phèdre*'s claustrophobic setting in which the characters' fates are decided.

While the tragedies of Corneille dealt with larger-than-life characters in heroic situations, it was Racine's genius to trace the psychological conflicts of his characters as revealed in states of passion. Despite their historical remoteness and elevated station, Racine's characters are recognizably human and even seem to display their intimate feelings. The figure of Hippolytus is a case in point. In Euripides, Hippolytus is true to the blood of his Amazon mother: a devotee of the goddess Artemis (Diana to the Romans), he lives a self-sufficient life as a hunter, roaming the forests and scorning erotic passion. In Seneca, his dislike of women rises to the level of misogyny. Racine's Hippolytus, by contrast, is no stranger to desire. Seeking to modulate the audience's sympathies and to balance the emotions of pity and fear (seen by Aristotle as essential to tragedy), Racine introduced the character of Aricia, the only surviving member of a lineage that had challenged Theseus's right to the Athenian throne, to provide the longtime scorner of women with his own undeclared love. In so doing, he laid the foundation for a Hippolytus of greater psychological complexity. Son of one of the classical world's greatest adventurers, he longs to emulate his father's glorious exploits while distancing himself from Theseus's notorious womanizing. Preparing, in the play's opening scene, to embark in search of the missing king, he harbors—like Phèdre—a secret love that familial obligations would forbid.

By thus paralleling the situations of Phèdre and her son-in-law, Racine heightens the play's preoccupation with desire and retribution. In fact, the play was titled *Phèdre and Hippolyte* until its publication in the 1687 edition of the playwright's *Complete Works*. But though Racine took pains to underscore the similarities between the two characters, the dominant figure in the play is clearly Phèdre. Racine himself considered her "perhaps the most compelling character I have put upon the stage," and this verdict has been shared by generations of actresses who have made the role one of the most revered and frequently interpreted on the French stage. Here, too, Racine's power as a dramatist is evident in the way he reworked his classical sources. Cursed at the end of Seneca's play as an "unnatural being" for her unchaste passion and her duplicity, Phèdre is transformed by Racine into a character truly deserving of pity and fear. As elsewhere in Racine's works, where desire is often described in the language of disease and affliction, the passion she conceives for her stepson is overwhelming in its intensity—"My eyes no longer saw, my lips were dumb; / My body burned, and yet was cold and numb." Yet strong as this desire certainly is, it is more than matched by the force of Phèdre's self-condemnation. Racine's tragic protagonist is harsher than any external judge would be on her misdirected emotions: "[a] dying woman who desires to die" as the play opens, she loathes her life and now seeks to escape it. In a play in which the word *monster* occurs eighteen times and the image of the Minotaur looms over the play's action, she becomes a monster to herself, wandering in a labyrinth of guilt and desire.

Is Phèdre's self-contempt fully merited? As Racine's play suggests, her love for Hippolytus was brought upon her by the goddess Venus, who had visited the curses of unnatural and fatal desire on other members of her family (her mother Pasiphaë fell in love with a bull, a union that produced the half-man, half-bull Minotaur; her sister Ariadne was abandoned by Theseus after leaving Crete with him). But Theseus's queen is also the daughter of Minos, the king of Crete who, upon his death, became a judge in Hades and whose father was Zeus (Jupiter), king of the gods.

Helen Mirren (right) in the title role and Dominic Cooper (left) as Hippolytus in the 2009 National Theatre (London) production of *Phèdre*.

Moreover, through her mother, she is the granddaughter of the Sun (Helios in Greek, Sol in Latin), whose eye sees everything. As is so often the case in classical Greek tragedy, which depicts behaviors and conflicts persisting over generations, genealogy is destiny. Because of her lineage, Phèdre is unhappily destined to be both victim of "implacable Venus" and judge of her own inordinate desire.

Marked by passion and self-loathing, which becomes a kind of passion in its own right, Phèdre's tragedy is that of a psyche polarized by tempestuous inner forces. But while "[d]isorder rules within her heart and head," Phèdre never loses her fundamental moral stature. Throughout the play, she retains a clear awareness of the moral and social orders that her emotions, and then her actions, violate. Her scrupulous moral sense is reflected in the imagery of light and darkness, day and night, vision and blindness, that recurs throughout her lines and the play as a whole. Described before her first appearance onstage as a woman who "longs to see the light" but "is unwilling to be seen," she both desires and fears the light of truth embodied by her celestial grandfather. Her flight from daylight manifests a fear both of exposure and of befoul-

ing light's inherent innocence. From this perspective, her suicide at play's end is an affirmation of meaning, justice, and moral vision: "Death dims my eyes, which soiled what they could see, / Restoring to the light its purity."

Racine, it is widely acknowledged, is one of the most difficult writers to render in English. As Patrick Swinden observes in his article "Translating Racine," Racine's language is "formal, exact, syntactically tightly sprung, and rhythmically mesmeric," and its speed, pace, sound, and grammatical arrangement—to say nothing of its hexameter lines—are notoriously resistant to translation. In the translation of *Phèdre* that follows, the poet Ted Hughes employs a taut free verse that captures the formal restraint and emotional volatility of Racine's play. Words follow each other with precipitous urgency, and they track the searing disclosures that make *Phèdre* one of the richest, most intense tragedies in the western canon. As the highly acclaimed 2009 London production with Helen Mirren in the role of Phèdre illustrated, Hughes's version succeeds brilliantly in bringing the power of Racine's dramatic vision to the modern stage.   S.G.

Phèdre[1]

DRAMATIS PERSONAE

PHÈDRE, Queen of Athens
THESEUS, King of Athens, Phèdre's
   husband
HIPPOLYTUS, son of Theseus and Antiope,
   an Amazon
ARICIA, granddaughter of Erechtheus,
   once the King of Athens

OENONE, Phèdre's nurse and retainer
THÉRAMÈNE, Hippolytus's friend and
   counsellor
ISMÈNE, Aricia's attendant
PANOPE, citizen of Troezen

---

1. Translated by Ted Hughes.

Act I

[HIPPOLYTUS, THÉRAMÈNE.]

HIPPOLYTUS   I have made my decision.
It is six months now
And there hasn't been one word of my father.
Somebody somewhere knows what's happened to him.

5   Life here in Troezen[2] is extremely pleasant
But I can't hang around doing nothing
With this uncertainty. My idleness makes me sweat.
I must find my father.

THÉRAMÈNE   But where, my lord, would you begin to look?
10   We have done all we can to find him.
Our ships have searched both seas,[3] they have gone
As far as the Acheron[4]
Where it dives to the underworld, and nowhere
Can Theseus be found.
15   We have searched Elis, and on past Tenaros,[5]
As far as the ocean
That drowned Icarus when he fell out of heaven.[6]
We have searched every coast within reach
For news of the King and found nothing.
20   Do you think you'll fare better?
What unsearched patch of the earth do you think might hold him?
In any case, who knows—
He might have chosen to vanish.
He might be lying low for his own good reasons.
25   Perhaps while we rack ourselves
Imagining his death,
He is lolling at ease, tucked away
With some beauty—soon to be deserted.

HIPPOLYTUS   Théramène, Theseus is our King.
30   He is also my father.
His youthful follies are over.
Phèdre need no longer fear a rival.
Nothing of that kind can have detained him.
But this is now my duty: to find him.

2. The large peninsula that makes up the south of mainland Greece. Troezen is a small town on its northeast coast, across the Saronic Gulf from Athens.
3. Corinth, on the southern base of the isthmus linking the Peloponnesus with northern Greece, lies between the Gulf of Corinth and the Saronic Gulf.
4. This river of Hades, the underworld, was believed to come to the surface at the Acherusian Cape in Asia Minor, on the southwestern coast of the Black Sea. Another Acheron was located in northwestern Greece (see note to 3.54).

5. The middle of the three southern points of the Peloponnesus (thought to be the location of one of the mouths of descent into Hades). *Elis:* a northwestern district of the Peloponnesus.
6. The Icarian Sea (the Aegean between the islands of Patmos and Leros and the coast of Asia Minor). According to legend, Icarus and his father, the great inventor Daedalus, used wings made of wax and feathers to escape from Crete, but because Icarus flew too close to the sun, the wax melted, and he fell into the sea.

35   I cannot stay here. Anyway, I dare not.
    THÉRAMÈNE   Dare not?
    Stay here—in your childhood sanctuary?
    As long as I have known you
    You have preferred this house,
40   These gardens and woods and these hills,
    To the pompous tedium of the court
    And the din of Athens.
    What can have occurred in this household
    To make you fear it?
45 HIPPOLYTUS   Everything has changed since the gods
    Decided to grace this palace
    With the daughter of Minos and Pasiphae.[7]
    THÉRAMÈNE   I understand. The world is not blind.
    Your problem is real. It is Phèdre.
50   She persecutes you and she spoils your life.
    Your stepmother!
    Yes, a diabolical woman!
    She had hardly set eyes on you
    When she had you removed—right out of the country.
55   But is her hatred still so virulent?
    Is it what it was?
    Besides—what could you fear from her?
    A dying woman, wanting only to die,
    Sick with some sickness of which she will say nothing,
60   Tired of herself, tired of the very daylight!
    How could she plot anything against you?
    HIPPOLYTUS   Phèdre's futile hatred of me
    Is something I never feared. Théramène,
    What drives me away from this house
65   Is a peril of another order.
    The girl Aricia! The surviving daughter
    Of that family sworn to eliminate ours.
    I have to get away from Aricia!
    THÉRAMÈNE   What?
70   You can think that girl your enemy?
    What if she does belong
    To the venomous lineage of Pallas—
    She never shared their guilt,[8] not one spot of it.
    She is utterly innocent. And such a beauty!
75   How can you hate her?
    HIPPOLYTUS   If hate were what I felt, would I run from her?
    THÉRAMÈNE   My lord—
    How am I to understand you?
    Is this the man I know?
80   Is this Hippolytus?

---

7. That is, Phèdre; her father, Minos, was king of Crete, and her mother, Pasiphae, was a daughter of Helios (the sun).
8. After Theseus killed Pallas—his uncle, who challenged his claim to be king of Athens—the sons of Pallas rose up against him, and he killed them all.

Our Prince of Scorn, who laughed at love and lovers?
Who mocked the yoke that time and again
Bent your father's neck and brought him down
On all fours, like any common man?
85   Maybe Venus[9]
Has suffered your taunts
A day too long?
Maybe she now vindicates your father.
Has she forced you,
90   Even you,
To kneel at her altar
Bending your neck—
Hapless, her sacrificial victim?
Is she bringing the groans out of you?
95   Are you in love?
HIPPOLYTUS   My dear old friend,
From the first breath I drew you have known me.
You know my pride. It is inborn.
Do you think I could renounce it?
100   It is no small thing.
I drank this spirit in with my milk
From the breast of an Amazon.[1]
And when I grew up
I exulted to find it in me, like a strength.
105   You remember, in my boyhood,
When you told me stories about my father,
How I devoured your voice.
My whole body blazed when you described him
Filling the empty place of Hercules.[2]
110   Monsters slaughtered, bandits rooted out,
Procrustes, Cercyon, Sciron, Sinis,
The giant's bones littered through Epidaurus,
Crete reeking with the blood of the Minotaur.[3]
But when you came to his lighter conquests—remember
115   How little I liked it?

---

9. The Roman goddess of love. In some accounts, including Euripides' *Hippolytus* (428 B.C.E.), Hippolytus has rejected Aphrodite (Venus) to worship Artemis (called Diana by the Romans), the virgin goddess of the hunt.

1. Antiope (or, in some versions, Hippolyte). The Amazons were warrior women who, according to most ancient authorities, lived in Asia Minor, on the southeastern shore of the Black Sea.

2. The greatest hero of classical mythology.

3. Theseus grew up in Troezen with no idea as to his father's identity—a matter of dispute in any case, since his mother lay with Aegeus, king of Athens, and Poseidon, god of the sea, on the same night. On his journey to Athens

as a young man, he killed a series of murderous robbers, in each case making them suffer the ends they had inflicted on others: Procrustes, who forced travelers to fit his bed; Cercyon, who made passersby wrestle him; Sciron, who kicked passersby into the sea; Sinis, who fastened victims to bent-over trees, which tossed them to their death; and Periphates (the "giant"), who killed with an iron club. The Minotaur was the monstrous offspring of Pasiphae and the bull with which she fell in love; Theseus killed it with the help of Phèdre's sister, Ariadne (whom Theseus deserted on the island of Naxos; see line 120).

All those false vows given, and all swallowed!
Periboea's tears at Salamis,[4]
Helen stolen out of her bed in Sparta[5]—
So many, he has forgotten their names.
120 Ariadne[6] wailing under a cliff,
Phèdre kidnapped—though she became his wife.
Recall how I begged you to be brief?
I would have been happy
To see rased from the memory of mankind
125 That half of his record.
And now you think I could follow him
Into that kind of dishonour?
You think the gods
Could do that to me?
130 If I went that way
My sighs would be more than pathetic,
They would be contemptible.
Theseus
Has amassed huge wealth
135 In superhuman feats and trophies and triumphs
To excuse his occasional foible.
My story contains not one monster.
My only wealth is my pride,
Which leaves me no leeway for folly.
140 But even if I had to succumb
Would I have picked Aricia?
Do you think I am unaware
Of the gulf between that girl and me?
My father has condemned her never to marry.
145 He fears a shoot from that unruly stock.
He will bury their lineage with their sister,
Keeping it under guard until she dies.
Do you think I am mad enough
To take this girl's part against my father?
150 Defy such a man as my father?
Make my name
A synonym for—imbecility?
To launch my life with that doomed enterprise?
THÉRAMÈNE   My lord, once love has picked its man
155 The gods cancel all his protestations.
Theseus, trying to seal Aricia
From the eyes of every man,
Opened yours.
Theseus' hatred for Aricia

---

4. Mother of the Greek hero Ajax, son of Telamon.
5. Helen, the daughter of Zeus and Leda, queen of Sparta, was abducted as a child by Theseus and his friend Pirithoüs (in ancient accounts, this occurs after the death of Phèdre). Later Helen married Menelaus, king of Sparta; when the Trojan prince Paris took her away, he precipitated the Trojan War.
6. Phèdre's sister (see note to line 113).

160 Surprised in you the opposite emotion.
    Aricia
    Has become irresistible—to you.
    But why shy from this passion?
    If you feel it—embrace it.
165 Why forever tangle yourself, my lord,
    In these timid scruples?
    Hercules never hesitated.
    No heart ever begrudged the touch of Venus.
    You reject love
170 But where would Hippolytus be
    If Antiope, your indomitable mother,
    Had not nursed that flame for your father?
    In any case,
    This pride which has given you such a name,
175 What does it amount to?
    Admit it, things have changed.
    You are not seen much lately, my lord,
    Unperturbed, untouched, untouchable,
    Hurtling along the sands in your chariot.
180 Or imitating the god of the ocean
    Breaking a wild horse to amuse yourself.[7]
    And why are you heard so rarely these days
    Scouring the woods with your hounds?
    In your eye there's a new kind of fire—
185 Secretive, heavy, like an ailment.
    You try to hide it. But it is killing you.
    There is no hiding it. You are in love.
    Is this Aricia?
    HIPPOLYTUS I am going. The King must be found.
190 THÉRAMÈNE Will you see Phèdre before you leave?
    HIPPOLYTUS Since it is my duty I cannot avoid it.
    But here comes Oenone. Something has happened.

                [*Enter* OENONE.]

    OENONE My lord, I can't think how I can bear it.
    The Queen is slipping away. She cannot last.
195 Day and night I watch her, but it's no use,
    She is dying of some disease she hides from me.
    Her soul is in turmoil. Her entire body
    Is convulsed with anguish. She flings out of her bed
    Desperate to see the day
200 At the same time she orders me
    To shut the whole world from her sight.
    Her suffering frightens me. She is coming.
    HIPPOLYTUS And I am going. At the very least
    I will spare her the sight of a face she hates.

            [*Exeunt* HIPPOLYTUS *and* THÉRAMÈNE. *Enter* PHÈDRE.]

---

7. Neptune (the Greek Poseidon), god of the sea, was also the first to tame horses, and he drove
a chariot over the waves.

205 PHÈDRE   No further, Oenone. I stop here.
　　　That last scrap of strength has left me suddenly.
　　　The sun's light is too painful.
　　　My wretched, trembling legs cannot support me.
　　OENONE   O you gods, look at her tears!
210 PHÈDRE   What a useless weight, all these jewels!
　　　And these veils! Whose interfering fingers
　　　Twisted up my hair in these knots?
　　　Everything conspires to torment me.
　　OENONE   No matter what you say, you contradict it.
215 　　One minute ago you ordered us
　　　To braid and set those coils exactly so.
　　　And it was you, madam,
　　　Gathering all your strength, made the decision
　　　To face this splendid sun and the world.
220 　　And now at your first glimpse of it you recoil.
　　　How can you fear the sun you longed to feel?
　　PHÈDRE   You brilliant founder of a benighted family[8],
　　　You whom my mother dared to call her father,
　　　Maybe you blush to see me like this.
225 　　You god of the sun—look at me for the last time.
　　OENONE   This longing for death is going to kill us both.
　　　I exhaust myself to keep you alive
　　　When all you are doing is trying to die.
　　PHÈDRE   I want to be hidden in a dark wood.
230 　　I want to see the chariot go bounding past
　　　In a fearless cloud of dust.
　　OENONE   What do you mean?
　　PHÈDRE   Where am I? What am I saying?
　　　Where did those words come from? My mind is strange.
235 　　Some god has taken my senses.
　　　My face feels to be coming apart
　　　With all the turmoil. Oenone!
　　　I can't hide it—everybody
　　　Stares into my shame and its secret.
240 　　I can't control this weeping.
　　OENONE   If you have to weep—then weep
　　　For the way you are stifling what you suffer
　　　Which makes it all the more violent.
　　　You reject our care, our advice.
245 　　Do you intend to die in this fashion?
　　　What kind of perversity
　　　Cuts off your days halfway? Is it witchcraft
　　　Shrivelling the springs of life? Is it poison?
　　　Three whole days and three whole nights
250 　　You have not slept or broken your fast.
　　　What right have you to throw away your life?
　　　You insult the gods who gave it to you.

8. Helios, the sun god—Phèdre's grandfather.

And you betray the oath you gave your husband.
Also remember your children.
255 What will your death mean for their future?
The day their mother dies—
The same day brings new hope
To the son of the foreign woman.
That born enemy of your blood.
260 That boy from the womb of an Amazon—
Hippolytus.

PHÈDRE Aaagh!

OENONE Now I have touched you.

PHÈDRE The name! You spoke that name!

265 OENONE Yes, let your rage blaze out. Curse that name!
I am glad to see you shudder at it.
Live. Renew yourself
With love, with duty. Live—
If only to prevent this sprig of a Scythian[9]
270 From crushing your sons and all the noble blood
Of Greece, and the gods, under his arrogant throne.

Hurry!
Every moment takes a little life.
You have damaged your strength. You can repair it.
275 Your flame has burned low, but it burns.
It will grow if you will nourish it.

PHÈDRE I have lived too guilty for too long.

OENONE Guilty of what? What is all this remorse?
What crime could be so awful?
280 You never stained your hands in innocent blood.

PHÈDRE I thank heaven, my hands are clean enough.
I wish to God my heart resembled them.

OENONE I think you have plotted something dreadful—
Something so evil you have frightened yourself.
285 What is it?

PHÈDRE I have said too much. Let us leave it.
Let me die before I do something worse.

OENONE Then die—and take your monstrous secret with you.
But find somebody else to close your eyes.
290 Your flame may have shrunk to next to nothing
But mine will be out before it.
Among the thousand roads to the land of the dead
Mine will be the shortest and the quickest.
Madam, when did I ever betray your trust?
295 When you dropped from the womb my arms caught you.
You know I gave up everything for you—
Country, children, everything. And now
You repay my loyalty with this.

---

9. That is, Hippolytus, son of the Amazon
Antiope (to classical authors, Scythia was a
vaguely defined, barbarous region, north and
east of the Black Sea).

PHÈDRE   What do you hope to gain by such anger?

300   If I were to say what I could say
    You would be struck dumb.

OENONE   What could be worse than standing here
    Helpless—watching you kill yourself.

PHÈDRE   When you know my crime, when you know

305   The fate that has broken me,
    My death will be no lighter. But my guilt
    Will be by that much heavier.

OENONE   Madam,
    By all the tears I have shed throughout your life,

310   For your sake, let me know. What is it?

PHÈDRE   Very well.

OENONE   Open your heart. Let me hear it.

PHÈDRE   What can I tell her? Where can I begin?

OENONE   These vague terrors mangle me. Be clear.

315 PHÈDRE   The curse of Venus is fatal.
    What a crazed, pitiful thing
    She made of my mother![1]

OENONE   Madam, forget that. Let the future too
    Utterly forget it.

320 PHÈDRE   Remember Ariadne, my sister.
    Her love was like some hideous injury
    That killed her on the beach where she lay abandoned.[2]

OENONE   What is it? Why bring all this up?
    Your family had bad luck in love.

325   Why mourn them again?

PHÈDRE   Because Venus demands it. And because
    In our whole unfortunate succession
    I die last and the most miserable.

OENONE   You are in love?

330 PHÈDRE   I am in love, yes, I am in love.

OENONE   Who is it?

PHÈDRE   I cannot think of the name steadily.
    It fills me with fear to whisper it.
    I love—the very name will kill me, I think.

335   I tremble at it, I shiver—

OENONE   Who?

PHÈDRE   You know him.
    That son of the Amazon. That noble prince
    I persecuted since the day we met.

340 OENONE   Hippolytus!

PHÈDRE   You named him.

OENONE   God in heaven!
    Ah, my whole body's gone to ice.
    What an inheritance!

345   Yes, your family is pitiable.

---

1. See note to line 113.
2. The island of Naxos (see line 120 and note to line 113).

Why did we come to this accursèd country?
PHÈDRE   My sickness began much earlier.
That day I married Theseus in Athens,
The moment the ceremony was over,
350 That moment of the surest happiness
I had ever felt in my life—
Suddenly he was there
Standing in front of me,
He had simply appeared—
355 Staring at me,
The man created
To destroy me.
Before I could grasp what I'd seen
I felt my face flame crimson—then go numb.
360 My whole body scorched—then icy sweat.
My eyes went dark.
I could not speak. I could hardly stand.
I knew then the goddess had found me—
The latest in the lineage that she loathes.
365 I had fallen
Into her furnace—
And I was trapped.
I tried to appease her.
My prayers were incessant.
370 I built her a shrine.
I spent half my wealth to decorate it.
From dawn to dusk I sacrificed beasts,
Searching their bodies[3] for my sanity.
Futile placebo for a fatal illness!
375 And the incense I burned—equally futile!
All useless. Whenever I prayed
And bowed down to her image
I saw only his—
I adored only his.
380 Though I made the air shake with her titles
My whole heart and soul, my whole body
Worshipped only him—Hippolytus!
Then I began to avoid him.
But that was useless too.
385 I met him everywhere
In the face of his father—
Everywhere I saw him staring at me
Through his father's features.
So then I turned against him.
390 I turned against myself—to defend myself.
I forced myself
To make his life a misery. At last
I went the whole way—and drove him into exile.

3. Examining the internal organs of animals was a common method of divination in the ancient world.

Yes, I played the stepmother.
395   I pretended to hate him as my stepson.
As if his very presence poisoned me.
Night and day, Theseus had to hear that.
And finally he relented.
So—his own father forced him to go.
400   Then I could breathe again, Oenone.
Once he'd gone the days flowed past me calmly.

I could conceal my anguish. I could be faithful.
I could even bear children.
But then, of a sudden,
405   All my precautions came to nothing.
Fate is inescapable.
Theseus brought me to Troezen.
And here, in Troezen,
I had to confront the one I had banished.
410   The first sight of him ripped my wounds wide open.
No longer a fever in my veins,
Venus has fastened on me like a tiger.
I know my guilt, and it terrifies me.
My own craving fills me with horror.
415   I detest my life.
I would have preferred to die
With what ought to be hidden cleanly hidden,
And my name intact,
But now you know everything
420   I will not regret it.
If only you will let me die quietly
And stop lashing me with these pointless reproaches,
And stop making such efforts to keep me alive.
          [*Enter* PANOPE.]
PANOPE   Madam, against my will I bring bad news.
425   And you will have to hear it. Forgive me.
Death has taken your husband, Theseus.
The whole world knows of it. Except you.
OENONE   What did you say?
PANOPE   The Queen must now accept that her prayers
430   For the King's safe return are unavailing.
His son, Prince Hippolytus, has learned
From ships just docked in port: the King is dead.
PHÈDRE   Oh God!
PANOPE   Now the question is: who rules Athens?
435   The city is divided. Madam,
One side gives its voice to your son.
But the other, ignoring ancient law,
Gives its voice to the son of the foreign woman—
To Hippolytus.
440   And rumour has it that a turbulent faction
Is determined to crown Aricia,

Heiress to the blood of the Pallantes.[4]
I thought it right to warn you.
Hippolytus is almost aboard.
445   Once he sets foot among the Athenians
In this broil, with everything so doubtful,
That giddy population will be his.
You would be right to fear it.
OENONE   You have said all that is needed, Panope.
450   The Queen, you can be sure,
Will not be blind to its significance.

[*Exit* PANOPE.]

Madam, I had given up all hope.
I meant to go with you
Into the grave. I had not a word left
455   To restrain you one more hour.
But this news demands a different spirit.
Fortunes have changed and yours is smiling at you.
The King is dead.
Who takes his place?
460   Your son is the heir.
The King's death leaves you to enforce his claim.
Die—and he's a slave.
Live—and he is a king.
If you die who will support him, or guide him,
465   Or console him?
You will have betrayed him.
His bitterness
Will be heard in heaven, the gods will hear it.
He has forebears among them
470   And they will not forgive you.
Live—live! You have nothing to be ashamed of.
Your love is as guiltless as love can be.
Theseus' death has liberated it.
It is no longer criminal and condemned.
475   Hippolytus becomes accessible—
No longer a man to be feared.
You can meet him freely as you please.
But you must move quickly.
Most likely,
480   Convinced as he is of your antipathy,
He will mount this coup—to seize Athens.
Madam, undeceive him.
Confuse his decision.
He knows too well that ancient law debars him
485   From the throne of Athens. Ancient law
Gives that throne to your son[5] and to no other.
Hippolytus inherits

4. Sons of Pallas (see note to line 73).
5. Demophon, the son of Phèdre and The-

seus; his younger brother was Acamas.

Only the crown of Troezen.
This is his lawful share of Theseus' realm.
490   Let him have this.
Then you can join with him, madam,
Against the common enemy: you and he
Combine your forces against Aricia.

PHÈDRE   Yes, yes, yes, your words are only too clear.
495   Now let me live—if that be possible.
Let my love for my son be strong enough
To revive what's left of my spirit.

Act II

[ARICIA, ISMÈNE.]

ARICIA   You say Hippolytus has asked to see me?
It can't be true. You must be mistaken.
You say he's looking for me?

ISMÈNE   To say farewell.
5   This is the first effect of the King's death.
Prepare yourself.
The hearts that Theseus diverted from you
Will now come flocking back. Aricia
Is queen of her own destiny—at last.
10   Soon the whole of Greece will be at your feet.

ARICIA   You are sure this isn't a rumour, Ismène?
Am I free? Is my jailer dead?

ISMÈNE   The gods are no longer against you.
The ghost of Theseus has joined your brothers.

15 ARICIA   How did he die?

ISMÈNE   Accounts conflict.
Mostly incredible. They say
This faithless husband drowned
In some escapade with a woman.
20   Others go further. They say
He went with his friend Pirithous[6]
Down into the underworld.
If it can be believed
He strolled along the banks of Hell's river
25   Letting the dead gaze at his living body.
Then found himself trapped in that black land
From which nothing emerges.
All Greece is buzzing with it.

ARICIA   Can you believe that a man before his death
30   Would visit the land of the dead? Why should he?
What could be the attraction?

---

6. A hero (in some accounts, a son of Zeus, king of the gods) who was a friend of Theseus and his partner in several famous exploits. The two men descended into the underworld because Pirithous wished to carry off Persephone, the consort of its lord, Hades, who trapped them there. Hercules found them when he came to fetch Hades' three-headed dog, Cerberus (his twelfth labor); in some versions of the story he rescued both, in others only Theseus.

ISMÈNE   The King is dead. Nobody doubts that.
　　　　 Except you. Athens is in mourning.
　　　　 Troezen confirms his death
35 　　　 By crowning Hippolytus.
　　　　 Phèdre is frightened for her son.
　　　　 She has summoned her anxious friends to advise her.
ARICIA   You think Hippolytus will treat me kindlier
　　　　 Than his father did? A longer chain?
40 　　　 Will he pity me, do you think?
ISMÈNE   Madam, he will.
ARICIA   Haven't you heard? Hippolytus is bronze—
　　　　 Dangerous and hard, without feeling.
　　　　 To think he will pity me
45 　　　 And exempt me alone
　　　　 From the revulsion he feels for all our sex
　　　　 Ignores the reality. Have you not noticed
　　　　 The lengths he goes to—simply to avoid me?
　　　　 How carefully he limits all his movements
50 　　　 To my absence?
ISMÈNE   Of course I know what others say about him,
　　　　 But I have also watched him in your presence.
　　　　 That awesome, inflexible hauteur,
　　　　 The very fame of it, as I observed him,
55 　　　 Doubled my curiosity. Madam,
　　　　 What I had heard of him and what I saw
　　　　 Were nothing like each other. Your first glance
　　　　 Reduced him to total confusion.
　　　　 I saw he could not take his eyes off you—
60 　　　 He tried to, but he could not. Those eyes, madam,
　　　　 Were painful with longing—helpless longing.
　　　　 The name of lover, perhaps, hurts his pride.
　　　　 His words, maybe, protect his reputation.
　　　　 But those eyes told everything.
65 ARICIA   Ismène,
　　　　 What you say you might have imagined
　　　　 But I am famished for it, I devour it.
　　　　 You know my life—
　　　　 You know how Fate has used me,
70 　　　 Like the toy of a cruel child.
　　　　 Whatever feeling I had
　　　　 Was what could survive on grief,
　　　　 Nourished only by tears.
　　　　 What can I know about love?
75 　　　 What can I know about the follies,
　　　　 The luxury, the anguish?
　　　　 How could I possibly know it?
　　　　 Among all Erechtheus' descendants
　　　　 I am the last.
80 　　　 Of all my family, war spared only me.
　　　　 The sword cut off our name.

It cut off all my brothers.
The earth[7] could hardly stomach so much blood.
You know, too, when Theseus murdered them
85 He made a law
That no Greek should ever marry me.
Afraid my brothers' ashes might somehow
Blaze into life—out of their sister's womb.
But you know what contempt I felt
90 For this conqueror's petty vigilance.
Love had never interested me.
My whole life I despised it.
So I could almost thank him for his fears.
He merely officialised my chosen life.
95 But that—that was before I saw his son.

The whole world admires Hippolytus,
For grace, for beauty.
They are his natural gifts—the more dazzling
For seeming so unconscious.
100 I was dazzled.
I was even more dazzled
By something richer:
His father's strengths—without the weaknesses.
But what dazzled me most, and I admit it,
105 Was that pride—that flawless disdain
No woman has ever touched.
The dubious kisses of Theseus
May be the glory of Phèdre.
I set a higher value on myself.
110 I would be ashamed to cling to favours
Debased and distributed among hundreds.
To be locked up in a heart open to any.
No. But think—
To bring that obdurate spirit to its knees!
115 To render that unfeeling arrogant soul
Sick with desire.
To see him bound
In bonds he cannot break—
Bonds he only prays to be tighter.
120 This thrills me. This is what I want.
Hercules was overpowered
Far too easily to bring much credit
To the various women who won him.
Perhaps I am prattling foolishly.
125 You may hear me regret these words.
More likely he will resist me, or ignore me,
And stay impenetrable.
This hard pride of his that fascinates me

7. According to Homer, Erechtheus, a king of Athens and the great-great-grandfather of Aricia,
was a son of Gaia (Earth).

Might yet break me. Hippolytus in love!
130   What freakish reversal of my fortunes
Could begin to sway—

ISMÈNE   Hear for yourself. He's coming.

[*Enter* HIPPOLYTUS.]

HIPPOLYTUS   Princess, before I leave I should inform you
What has been decided for you.
135   My father is dead. My fears were not misplaced.
Nothing but death could have imposed on Theseus
Such a protracted silence.
The gods have finally
Given to the fatal three sisters
140   Hercules' friend, and heir,[8] and sole equal.
You hated him, I know.
And yet I think you will grant him those honours,
And acknowledge his achievements.
I must mourn for my father.
145   But one thing lightens my grief:
You live a prisoner: I can free you.
I free you: from a law
That has always seemed to me barbarous.
Your life and your heart are now your own.
150   Do with them as you please.
Troezen has descended to me
Direct from my grandsire Pittheus.[9]
By a unanimous voice, I am now King.
In this kingdom of mine
155   You are as free, madam, as I am myself.
Or rather, much freer.

ARICIA   Your generosity is too great—too sudden.
More than you can know,
Bestowing so much on my misfortune
160   You bind me
To the same austere law from which you have freed me.

HIPPOLYTUS   The Athenians cannot decide who shall rule them.
They have named the son of Phèdre. And me. And you.

ARICIA   Me?

165 HIPPOLYTUS   For myself I have no illusions.
A Greek law discriminates against me
Because my mother was a foreigner.
Even so, if my only rival
Were the son of Phèdre, my half-brother,
170   My claim is strong enough. And I could assert it
To push aside that scruple of the law.
But, Princess,
An even stronger claim reins me back
From entering this race. I mean—your claim.

8. As doer of heroic deeds.
9. King of Troezen, the grandfather and former guardian of Theseus.

175 I pass to you, or rather I restore it,
   The throne of Athens, which is yours by right—
   Descending directly to you
   From Erechtheus, the great son of Earth.
   Aegeus came to it by adoption.[1]
180 Athens then confirmed the succession
   To Theseus, his son, for his tireless service
   Enlarging and defending the city.
   Your brothers' claim
   Was meanwhile passed over and forgotten.
185 Now Athens wants you back.
   She is sick of this everlasting quarrel.
   Too much of your family's blood, for too long,
   Has gone smoking into the very soil
   That bore your progenitor.
190 Troezen is mine. Crete and its territories
   Are kingdoms rich enough for Phèdre's child.
   And Greece is yours. What I shall do now
   Is reunite the votes scattered among us
   Behind your single name.
195 ARICIA   Everything you say is astonishing.
   It is too like a dream. Is it a dream?
   Am I awake? Who could believe this?
   Some god has possessed you to think such thoughts.
   I see now why the whole world honours you,
200 And how far you surpass their admiration.
   To crown me you will depose yourself!
   It was enough simply not to hate me.
   Simply to have withheld yourself so long
   From that hostility—
205 HIPPOLYTUS   Me hate you?
   My pride, I know, is given hard names
   But do you think I came from the womb of a monster?
   There is no human temperament so brutal,
   No hatred so ossified with habit
210 That could look at you and not soften,
   Not be enchanted, not be captivated.
   Could I be the exception?
   ARICIA   My lord!
   HIPPOLYTUS   No!
215 Now let me tell you. Now I have begun.
   When passion boils, reason evaporates.
   I mean—when the heart boils, when love moves.
   My secret has become unbearable.
   I cannot hold it in any longer.
220 Am I Hippolytus the arrogant?
   Am I a prince? Or a king?
   No, I am a beggar—to be pitied.

---

1. In some accounts, Aegeus was adopted by Pandion, the father of Pallas; in others, he was the older brother of Pallas.

Not so much the exemplar of pride
As of the stupidity of pride.
225 I set this lofty pride against love.
I mocked her captives in their ridiculous chains,
I saw her clowns shipwrecked and I laughed
To watch their storms while I sat safe ashore.
But now you see me,
230 Flotsam in that tide of the common law.
A single surge has swept me far from myself.
A single wave, and it has overwhelmed me.
It happened in a moment.
Now this famous pride is crying for help.
235 Desperate, humiliated,
With the arrow in me,
Six months of mortification,
Fighting you, fighting myself.
I search your absence for you like a madman,
240 And yet I run from your presence.
Everywhere in the woods your image hunts me.
I try to escape you
But every shaft of sunlight,
Every night shadow
245 Sets you in front of me, surrounds me with you.
Everything competes to fling
The obstinate fool Hippolytus
Helpless at your feet.
All my studied care to preserve myself
250 Has brought me to this—I have lost myself,
I search—but I cannot find myself,
My bow, my spears, my chariot,
They beckon to me, I ignore them.
The breaking and taming of wild horses,
255 Everything the god of the sea taught me,
It is beyond me—I have forgotten it.
My own horses run wild—
They have forgotten my voice.
Nothing hears my voice but the forest—
260 The black echoing depth of the forest.
Yes, my love is a savage.
What raving words these are!
Maybe you blush to hear them.
All I had meant to do was declare my love.
265 Your delicate snare has caught a strange creature.
Princess, grant my words
Perhaps a little more than their face value.
You know this is a language alien to me.
My love speaks crudely, but do not reject it.
270 Without you, I never could have known it.

[*Enter* THÉRAMÈNE.]

THÉRAMÈNE   My lord, the Queen is coming.

She's looking for you.

HIPPOLYTUS   For me? Why?

THÉRAMÈNE   She instructed me

275   That she must speak with you before you go.
        I know no more than that.

HIPPOLYTUS   Phèdre! What can I say?
        What is she expecting me to say?

ARICIA   My lord, you cannot well refuse to hear her.

280   As your enemy, it is true,
        She is implacable.
        But in her state show her a little pity.

HIPPOLYTUS   You must go now. And I shall leave
        Uncertain how far I have offended

285   This beauty I adore,
        Or whether the heart I have given you—

ARICIA   Prince, do not delay!
        Follow your noble plan and complete it.
        Persuade Athens to acknowledge me.

290   Everything that you have given me—
        I accept it. But the throne of Athens,
        Glorious and great as it is,
        To me is the least precious of your gifts.

        [*Exeunt* ARICIA *and* ISMÈNE.]

HIPPOLYTUS   Old friend, are we all set? Here comes the Queen.

295   Go, make sure every man is ready
        For immediate departure. That done,
        Hurry back here and extract me
        From a conversation I do not relish.

        [*Exit* THÉRAMÈNE. *Enter* PHÈDRE *and* OENONE.]

PHÈDRE   He is there.

300   My heart labours. My legs tremble.
        I had my words prepared but where are they?

OENONE   Only remember—
        You are your son's sole hope.

PHÈDRE   My lord, we hear this sudden emergency

305   Is removing you from us. I had hoped
        We might mourn a little together.
        Also, dare I mention it,
        I am anxious for my son. He is fatherless
        And soon, very soon, he will be bowed

310   At the grave of his mother.
        The boy has few friends,
        But, of a sudden, many enemies—
        Already moving
        To take advantage

315   Of this moment. My lord,
        You are the one man who can defend him.
        But you know my fear:
        It may be I have turned you against him.
        I am afraid

320   A hatred created by his difficult mother
        Will make him its object.
     HIPPOLYTUS   Madam,
        The very thought of that—I find repugnant.
     PHÈDRE   I understand your distaste for me.
325   It is logical. Inevitable.
        You have seen me relentless to hurt you.
        But you never looked any deeper.
        Yes, I did all I could to provoke in you
        A fury of revulsion for me.
330   I drove you away from wherever I came.
        Public or private
        In all I said
        I was against you.
        I set a whole ocean between us.
335   I made a law that even your name
        Should never be pronounced in my presence.
        But if the measured penalty for all this
        Were truly to match the motive, if your hatred
        Answered my hatred and nothing but my hatred,
340   No woman ever earned more pity
        Or less enmity from you than I have.
     HIPPOLYTUS   I know that a mother, jealous for her son,
        Rarely tolerates the rivalry
        Of a half-brother, the son of some other woman.
345   Seizures of resentment and suspicion
        Are expected of a stepmother.
        No matter who my father had married
        I would have faced the same, and perhaps worse.
     PHÈDRE   My lord, God knows, I can swear
350   Heaven has exonerated me
        From that common failing.
        A far different passion
        Oppresses me, devours me.
     HIPPOLYTUS   Madam, our time to mourn has not yet come.
355   Your husband may be alive.
        We weep, but the world might still produce him.
        The god of the sea loves him. That great god
        Will not have been deaf to his prayers.
     PHÈDRE   Nobody goes twice to the underworld.
360   Once he strayed that far,
        If you think some god can extricate him
        You are deluded.
        Hell never surrenders its prey.
        But what am I saying? No—
365   You are right: he is not dead. I see him.
        Theseus is alive. He lives in you.
        I look at you and I see him.
        My husband's face is this face.
        And my love, my need, yes, in spite of myself,

370 My deprivation, my starvation, my fever—
I can't hide it. He has to know it.
It has to come out.

HIPPOLYTUS   Madam, the abnormal hunger of your love
Projects his image onto other faces.
375 Though he is dead, his love possesses you.

PHÈDRE   Prince, you are right. I am possessed.
I sicken for Theseus.
But not as the underworld saw him—
The laughing ravisher of a thousand women,
380 Ready to cuckold even the god of the dead.[2]
Not like that, but loyal and proud,
Even a little diffident perhaps,
Young, and bewitching everybody
With an aura, a magic—
385 Just as they portray the gods.
Or just as I see you. Yes—
The Theseus I see
Has your bearing, exactly,
Your eyes, your lips,
390 The very pitch of your voice,
This noble modesty
Gives his cheeks just that flush of colour.
When he came over the sea, to my home in Crete,
The daughters of Minos[3] were besotted—
395 For a good reason.
Where were you then?
How could he have gathered the flower of Athens
To pay the tribute without Hippolytus?
You were too young! Even so
400 You could have come with him, on that voyage.
Why didn't you come with him?
To our shores, in that ship?
In spite of all the labyrinth's knots and tangles[4]
You would have slaughtered the Minotaur.
405 My sister Ariadne
Would have given the thread to you, not to Theseus,
To lead you back to the light
Out of the heart of the monster's riddle.
No, she would not—no, no, she would not—
410 I would have been there before her
With the plan, and the spool of thread,
To unravel that snarl of dark tunnels
And bring you out of the maze.
Ah, what care and love I could have lavished
415 On this darling head! Phèdre
Would have come into the labyrinth with you.

2. By helping Pirithous in his attempt to
abduct Persephone (see note to line 21).
3. Phèdre and Ariadne.

4. The Minotaur, slain by Theseus, was shut
up in a labyrinth designed by Daedalus.

She would have come the whole way beside you
To guide you back. Or be killed in there beside you.

HIPPOLYTUS   You gods, what am I hearing?
420   Have you forgotten that King Theseus
Is my father, and that you are his wife?

PHÈDRE   Can you believe I have lost my memory?
Could I be so reckless with my title?

HIPPOLYTUS   Forgive me, madam. I misinterpreted
425   Your words about my father.
They confused me. You see, I am blushing.
I am ashamed even to look at you:
I must go—

PHÈDRE   Now you torture me worse!
430   Prince, you have understood me perfectly.
I said enough to show you the truth.
Look at me—see a woman in frenzy.
I am in love.
But do not suppose for a second
435   I think myself guiltless
For loving you as I love you.
I have not
Indulged myself out of empty boredom.
I have not drunk this strychnine day after day
440   As an idle refreshment.
Wretched victim of a divine vengeance!
I detest myself
More than you can ever detest me.
You are right, the gods are watching me.
445   Yes, the same gods
Who have filled me with these horrible flames
That are killing me—as they have killed
All the women in my family.
Those sadistic gods
450   Who amuse themselves, and make their names,
Playing with human hearts.
You know too well how I have treated you.
I not only shunned you.
I acted like a tyrant, I had you banished.
455   I wanted you to hate me. I wanted you
To regard me as loathsome, inhuman—
Simply to help me to resist you.
All that agony—to no purpose!
Yes, you hated me more. And more and more—
460   But my love never lessened.
Your sufferings made your beauty more painful.
I writhed, I was consumed
In burnings and tears—
You only had to look at me to see it.
465   If you could force yourself to look at me.
What am I saying? Oh this is shameful.

Shameful confession! Shameful!
It's you—I have to speak.
You are crushing it out of me.
470 I came here with a simple small request:
Fearful for my son who depends on me,
I meant to beg you, Prince, not to hate him.
But see how I flung it aside!
My mania burst out, I cannot stop it!
475 O Prince, I cannot speak to you
Of anything but you. Avenge yourself.
I am depraved. Act. Punish me.
Prove yourself the son of your father—
Rid the world of a monster!
480 The widow of King Theseus has dared
To fall in love with his son, Hippolytus.
This disgusting pest should be killed.
Look—my heart. Here.
Bury your sword here.
485 This heart is utterly corrupt.
It cannot wait to expiate its evil.
I feel it lifting to meet your stroke. Strike!
Or am I beneath your contempt?
Maybe my death seems too light a sentence.
490 Or are you apprehensive
That my polluted blood might foul your hand?
If your hands are reluctant, give me your sword.
Give me that sword!

OENONE   What are you doing, madam! Holy God!
495 Somebody's coming. Don't let them find you here.
Come, quickly, before they see too much.

[*Exeunt* PHÈDRE *and* OENONE. *Enter* THÉRAMÈNE.]

THÉRAMÈNE   Was that the Queen? What has happened?
Is there more bad news? My lord,
You look half-crazed. Where is your sword?
500 HIPPOLYTUS   Théramène, we must leave and leave quickly.
I cannot think of myself without horror.
Phèdre—O you mighty gods in heaven,
If there is a hole in your creation
Drop this secret through it.
505 THÉRAMÈNE   The ship is rigged and ready. But I must tell you
Athens has announced her decision.
Her chieftains and their tribes have given the crown
To your half-brother. Phèdre has triumphed.

HIPPOLYTUS   Phèdre!
510 THÉRAMÈNE   A delegation from Athens is here.
Waiting to hand the reins of government
Over to Phèdre. Her son will be King.

HIPPOLYTUS   You gods who know her—is this how you reward her?

THÉRAMÈNE   Meanwhile, my lord, there are murmurs
515 That Theseus is alive. In Epirus—

So it is said. But we have searched for him
In that very place and we—

HIPPOLYTUS   No matter.

Question everybody. Neglect nothing.
520   Investigate this rumour. Follow it right back
To its source in Epirus.[5] If it is false
Then it cannot hinder me. Come,
Whatever the cost, I am going to set this crown
On the head it belongs to.

Act III

[PHÈDRE, OENONE.]

PHÈDRE   Can't I be free of all this regalia?
How can I parade myself now?
Stop insisting.
And stop trying to console me.
5   You would be better to conceal me.
I have said too much.
This uncontainable obsession
Has stooped to reveal itself.
I have said what nobody alive
10   Should ever have heard.
Did you see him?
How he stared as I spoke?
Oh God—how he twisted about
Pretending to misunderstand me.
15   How he strained to be gone?
And that blushing of his—
The humiliation!
Why did you prevent me
When I had the solution there in my grasp?
20   That sword has a point like a needle.
When I rested it here, just touching my skin,
Here under my breast—
Did he go pale? For me?
Did he snatch the blade out of my hand?
25   It needed only a push, one little push—
But the mere fact that I'd touched it
Made his own sword horrifying to him.
He was afraid
That what I'd handled
30   Might profane
His sacred skin.

OENONE   Madam, enough of this. You must stop
Raking your miseries over.
You are feeding a fire that you should quench.
35   You are the daughter of Minos—
The grand-daughter of Zeus—

5. A region in northwest Greece on the Ionian Sea.

Far more fitting now to turn your mind
To practical matters.
And far wiser too, to forget this boy
40 Who has proved so unresponsive.
Take up your proper task, and rule your kingdom.

PHÈDRE Me? Rule? Me take control
Of a state flying to pieces
When I cannot control myself?
45 When I have abdicated
The throne of my own being?
When I am occupied by an enemy
That hardly lets me breathe?
When I am all but dead?

50 OENONE Get right away.

PHÈDRE Ah!
I cannot remove myself from him.

OENONE You dared to banish him. Dare to banish yourself.

PHÈDRE Too late. He knows my whole madness.
55 Prudence and restraint are out of date.
Like weak prey torn open
I have bared my innermost, hidden pulse
To my killer. And I cannot help it—
In spite of myself, I still cling to a hope.
60 When my strength failed before
You brought me back to life.
When my soul was shivering at my lips
You restored it, you flattered its misery.
You gave it hope.
65 You made me think this love was possible.

OENONE Whether I am guilty or innocent
I cannot tell. Could I have let you die?
But if my intervention vexes you
What about that spoiled brat's contempt?
70 Can you forget that face? That baleful blank.
That stone, hewn block. He hardly saw you
While you writhed at his feet.
His ferocious pride makes him repellent.
If only Phèdre had my eyes to see him.

75 PHÈDRE Oenone, he might not be what we think.
The forests that bred him kept him wild.
Hunting has made him violent and harsh.
He never heard love speak until today.
He was silent because he was stunned.
80 It could be we have misunderstood him.

OENONE Remember, an Amazon bore him.

PHÈDRE Barbaric, maybe, but she must have loved.

OENONE His hatred for all women is absolute.

PHÈDRE In that case I need never fear a rival.
85 It is too late for this kind of discussion.
Serve my madness now, not my reason.

If his heart is walled up against me
We must find some other unguarded spot.
I noticed how the charms of kingship touched him.
90   Athens excited him. He could not hide it.
His ships were on the leash—ready to dash
Across the seas to pluck the Athenian crown.
Oenone, go now, work on him cleverly.
Dangle the crown until it dazzles him.
95   Let him understand—it can be his.
And tell him, Phèdre asks no other favour
Than to set that royal jewel on him.
I cede him all my power. I cannot defend it.
And he can teach my son how to command.
100 Perhaps be like a father to the boy.
I put both mother and son under his ward.
Go to any limit to persuade him.
Words from you will enter where mine cannot.
Be shameless, weep, groan, anything. Describe me
105 Close to death. Prostrate yourself. Implore him.
I grant you total licence. Oenone, quickly,
You are my only hope. I shall wait
Here till you return with my fate.

[*Exit* OENONE.]

You great goddess Venus, are you watching?
110 Are you happy
To see just how far I have fallen?
It is impossible
To humiliate me any further.
Your victory is complete. Your every stroke
115 Has gone home.
Goddess of pure remorseless cruelty,
If you still seek for fame
Choose a harder target.
Hippolytus mocks you. He laughs at your furies.
120 He never uttered one prayer at your altar.
Your very name offends him.
He waves it aside like some polluted fly.
Why not choose him?
He pours the same derision
125 On you as on me. Avenge yourself.
Make him love.

[*Enter* OENONE.]

Oenone, why are you back so quickly?
Wouldn't he listen? Is he still adamant?
OENONE.   Madam,
130 Now you need your former fortitude.
Forget your great love: you can bury it.
PHÈDRE   What did he say?
OENONE   I could not find Hippolytus. Madam,

All those rumours, that seemed so certain,
135 That convinced everybody, have betrayed us.
Do you hear the roar of the people?
They are welcoming their King.
Theseus is coming from the harbour.

PHÈDRE   Theseus is alive?

140 OENONE   Any moment
He will be here.

PHÈDRE   Oenone, it's finished.
I have confessed
An appetite that is unspeakable.
145 With a few greedy words
I have stripped my husband of all honour.
He is alive? Let me hear nothing else.

OENONE   Madam—

PHÈDRE   I foresaw all this.
150 But you—you were blind.
My guilt was unrelenting—
I only wanted to die.
Then your tears came like anaesthesia.
Even this morning
155 I could have died with honour.
But then I drank your advice.
However I die now, I die in shame.

OENONE   Die? Why must you always talk of dying?

PHÈDRE   What have I done, O God?
160 My husband is coming. And his son
Hippolytus—still dazed by my outburst.
I shall have to face my enemy.
I shall have to feel his eyes on me—
Observing just what face I show his father.
165 Noting my loving words—which he spurned.
And my tears—which meant so little to him.
What do you think?
Is he so sensitive to his father's honour
That he will keep hidden at all costs
170 What I revealed?
How could he do that? How could he stay silent?
How could he rather connive
At the betrayal of his sire and monarch
Than spit out his loathing for me?
175 In any case
There's no point in him hiding it.
I am not one of those women
Who manage their infidelity
With a polished smile and a stone heart.
180 I have not forgotten my ravings.
Every gasp is still alive in me.
Even these walls remember them,
These ceilings are saturated with them,

Every room and passage in this palace
185   Is bursting to shout my secret
And accuse me. The air is quivering with it.
The moment he steps through the door
He will hear it.
Let me die. My one escape
190   From all this
Is annihilation.
Is it so dreadful to be nothing?
Despair can find death friendly.
But what a bequest for my children!
195   Descent from Jupiter[6] is their confidence.
How will they lift their heads
Under my degradation?
Under my folly,
My self-immolation?
200   Ah!
How will their poor minds endure
The revelations about me, all too true?
The tales that every gossip will barb
And stick into them?
205   I dare not think
How they will live, buried in their mother's shame.
    OENONE   They will not escape. I pity both.
No mother's fears were ever more prophetic.
But why create such a catastrophe?
210   Why mount this great case against yourself:
If you kill yourself, the whole world
Will be certain you did it because you were guilty,
And could not face the man you had deceived.
Who will be happier than Hippolytus
215   To have your suicide
Validate the story he will tell?
And what will my version of events
Amount to then? My voice will be wafted aside,
Like a feather. I shall have to listen
220   To his conceited triumphant sneer
While he regales the court with your behaviour.
Better a thunderbolt wipe me off the earth.
But, madam, has your feeling for him changed?
What do you feel? How do you see him now?
225 PHÈDRE   A monster! He terrifies me.
    OENONE   Then why grant him so easy a victory?
You dread what he might say—that is your terror.
Madam—strike first.
Any moment now he can accuse you.
230   Accuse him first—of the same crime.
Who could contradict you? Everything

---

6. Phèdre's father, Minos, was the son of Zeus (the Roman Jupiter or Jove), king of the gods.

Is evidence against him. His own sword—
Which he left in your hand so luckily.
Your present agitation. Your past distress.
235 Your perpetual grievance—so emphatic
It turned even his own father against him.
The fact you went so far as to have him banished.
PHÈDRE   Me attack him? Perjure myself
To convict a man who is innocent?
240 OENONE   Say nothing.
All my plan requires is your silence.
I too have to smother a conscience.
I would rather confront death
A thousand times, than perform this.
245 But since without precarious surgery
Your death is inevitable, to my mind
The cost is meaningless.
Leave it to me to speak to Theseus.
He will go mad, for a while.
250 But in the end, like a wise horseman,
He'll halt the runaway furies.
He will punish his son, you can be sure,
With nothing more than exile, as before.
When a father judges his own son
255 He remains a daddy. For all that,
Innocent blood might still have to be spilt
If it threatens your name. They are coming,
I see Theseus.
PHÈDRE   Aye! And Hippolytus!
260 That arrogant gaze, plain as speech,
Tells me just how hopeless my case is.
Do what you want, Oenone.
I leave everything to your discretion.
I cannot make one move to help myself.

    [*Enter* THESEUS, HIPPOLYTUS *and* THÉRAMÈNE.]

265 THESEUS   After my long ordeal, at last
Fate has let me through
To my Queen's arms—
PHÈDRE   Stop, Theseus.
Do not profane a greeting of such sweetness.
270 Phèdre is no longer fit to hear it.
The gods, you should know, are jealous of you.
In your long absence they have not spared your wife.
I cannot delight you. I am no longer worthy
Even to approach you.
275 Your honour, my lord, has been violated.
Nothing is left to me but to hide myself.

    [*Exeunt* PHÈDRE *and* OENONE.]

THESEUS   Hippolytus,
This is a strange welcome for your father.

HIPPOLYTUS   Nobody but Phèdre can explain it.
280   For my part, sir,
       I want nothing more to do with her.
       And I beg your permission to leave.
       You see how this disturbs me. Let me go.
       I cannot exist in her proximity.
285   Let me simply vanish.
    THESEUS   You, my son, leave me?
    HIPPOLYTUS   I never wanted her. I never sought her.
       She was yours. You brought her into this country,
       Into Troezen, with Aricia.
290   Before you left
       You charged me, you remember, to protect them.
       That duty is now redundant.
       And I have squandered enough life in these forests,
       Accumulating boars' tusks and antlers.
295   I cannot believe you would not prefer me
       To be out of this nursery,
       Facing something more formidable.
       Before you were my age
       You were the hero of your own epic,
300   You had emptied the known world
       Of monsters and tyrants.
       For every pirate of the two seas
       You were Nemesis itself.
       Wherever you turned, they simply ceased to exist.
305   To this day
       Travellers are safe.
       Hercules could rest on your laurels
       And leave his work to you, confidently.
       While I decayed here—
310   The unheard-of child of a prodigious father.
       Unmentioned in the hymns of adulation
       Sung to my heroic mother.
       Let me find employment for my strength.
       Let me take up your work.
315   Or let me at least die the kind of death
       That will be remembered
       And prove to the world that I was your son.
    THESEUS   What is happening?
       What is it about me
320   Sends my family reeling from me?
       Has that hellish pit done something to me?
       Has it made me a pariah?
       If it has
       You gods that helped me out of it
325   Should have left me rotting inside it.
       My friend Pirithous was responsible.
       He let his idiot lust
       Get the upper hand of his judgement.

He tried to ravish the consort
330 Of the tyrant of Epirus.[7]
Witless, rampant, suicidal folly!
And I—out of pure loyalty—
Was rash enough to aid and abet.
Fate was rightly angered—she made us stupid.
335 The tyrant surprised us—weaponless.
Then I was forced to watch as he flung
My lecherous companion Pirithous
To horrible reptiles, monsters of the swamp,
Which he kept as pets and fed on men.
340 For me he had a pit, a steep cavern,
Foetid with stench from the underworld.
I lay under the showering dung of bats.
It was a long time
Before the gods remembered me there.
345 But they did. They let me outwit my guards.
I paused only to pick up a sword
And butcher that King for his scavengers.
Then came hurrying home. And what meets me?
Just when I think I can be happy
350 With my family,
Just when I feel my soul
Is coming back to itself—
And only wants to feast and sate itself
In gazing at my family, my beloved,
355 My children—
I see them staring at me horrified.
I see them shuddering as I approach them.
They squirm from my embraces, they back off,
They cannot get away from me fast enough.
360 I see such fear in their faces
It fills me with horror—at myself.
I would be happier back in that cavern.
What did my wife mean by what she said?
My honour violated? How? Who did it?
365 If it's true, why am I unavenged?
Greece looked to me to defend it—
Has it given asylum to the culprit?
You say nothing. Can't you say something?
Am I to assume my own son
370 Is in collusion with an enemy?
Where is Phèdre?
She swamps me with suspicions
Then disappears. Come.
No man on earth could endure this.

7. According to the Greek geographer Pausa-nias, Theseus and Pirithous invaded Thespro-tia (the district south of Epirus, in northwestern Greece) to carry off the wife of the king; they were captured and imprisoned at Cichyrus, near rivers whose names (Acheron and Cocy-tus) linked the place with the underworld.

375   And only Phèdre can unravel it.

        [*Exit* THESEUS.]

  HIPPOLYTUS   My father's words are more than ominous.
    I have seen how far the Queen's derangement
    Is beyond her control.
    When he challenges her what will she do:
380   Denounce and destroy herself?
    God in heaven, what will he make of it?
    Love has unbalanced his entire family.
    He thinks I am what I was.
    But even I hide a passion
385   That subverts his law.
    I am full of sickening premonitions.
    Yet innocence has nothing to fear.
    Maybe I can soften him a little,
    Find the right words to bring him round,
390   Persuade him to forbearance
    For a love he may not like, but cannot change.

Act IV

    [THESEUS, OENONE.]

  THESEUS   What? What? This is like vandalism.
    Such malignity! So light-minded!
    The whole thing so carefully designed
    To desecrate his own father's honour.
5   To deface my name? Defile me?
    Nothing could do me worse damage.
    Shall I never get out of the labyrinth?
    Where am I? Which way can I turn?
    That he could think it, is inconceivable!
10   The brutalised audacity of it!
    This is how he repays my paternal care.
    And to drive the atrocity home
    This thug did not reject the use of force.
    I recognise that sword.
15   I gave it to him—for a different purpose.
    The bonds of his own blood could not restrain him.
    Phèdre has been at fault. Phèdre
    Bears some blame. She deferred his exposure
    For too long. Too loath to see him punished,
20   Phèdre's silence has protected him.

  OENONE   Phèdre protected a pitiable father.
    She was so distraught to meet the lust
    Aroused in Hippolytus by her beauty,
    So shamed by his shamelessness, his importunate grossness—
25   My lord, Phèdre was dying. I watched her own fingers
    Guide that point to a softness between her ribs.
    I saw her resolution. Had I not wrenched
    The sword out of her hands nothing could have saved her.

It is my pity for her and for you
30　Prompts me now to tell you what I know.
　　THESEUS　I saw it! He went white when I met him.
　　And when I approached him—
　　I recognise fear.
　　To see his face so drawn—that made me wonder.
35　And his embrace—
　　It was so stiff and cold it froze mine.
　　How long has he been possessed by this?
　　Was it there earlier—in Athens?
　　OENONE　My lord, recall how Phèdre avoided him.
40　His prurient attentions drove her mad.
　　THESEUS　He started it again—here in Troezen?
　　OENONE　My lord, I have described what I saw.
　　You must excuse me. I have left the Queen
　　Alone too long with her dangerous thoughts.
45　Allow me to withdraw to be near her.
　　　　　　[Exit OENONE. Enter HIPPOLYTUS.]
　　THESEUS　Ha! Here he comes. You gods in heaven,
　　How nobly he carries himself!
　　Who would not be deceived—
　　As I have been?
50　But isn't it natural—?
　　The adulterer's gaze has to inveigle us
　　With that seamless mask of probity.
　　If only there were a window
　　Fixed in the face of every blackguard
55　To show us the heart behind it!
　　HIPPOLYTUS　My lord, may I ask
　　What is weighing on you. I am aware
　　A dark cloud of some sort sits on you.
　　You know you can trust my discretion.
60　THESEUS　Trust you? How dare you
　　Show your impudent face in front of me?
　　The thunderbolt has spared you too long.
　　Last of the vermin to be exterminated!
　　After your ravenous lust
65　Has sated itself in your father's bed
　　You dare to confront him?
　　To bare that despicable face of yours
　　Within the reach of my weapon?
　　In this very palace you have despoiled?
70　You should be away. That would be wise.
　　You should be under some other heaven.
　　In some land ignorant of my name
　　Where nobody knows or could guess
　　How rabid you are.
75　Get out. Don't brave me with your lies.
　　Do not tempt me to the act
　　That I am reining back with difficulty.

I have enough—
The everlasting shame of such a son

80 Is enough
Without the last ignominy
Of having put an end to him myself.
That might soil the glory of all I have done.
Get out. Unless you want to die

85 Among the trash I have swept into ditches.
And make sure that the sun, the blessed sun,
Never again casts your accursèd shadow
On the threshold of this house
Or on the roads to it,

90 Or anywhere within my territories.
Get out. Now. Get out.

Neptune, O great God of the Oceans,
Remember how I scoured your shores clean
Of every ruffian.

95 Remember how you swore to reward me.
You promised me one wish. A single wish.
When I lay festering in that putrid dungeon
I didn't trouble you with it. I saved it.
I kept it for my moment of true need.

100 That moment has come. Grant me my wish.
Now! Avenge a heart-broken father.
Break your wrath on the head of this traitor.
Smash the bones of his effrontery.
Show how a great god can demolish a man.

105 Let me see the infinite of your favour
In how utterly you annihilate him.

HIPPOLYTUS   Am I to understand—the Queen has accused me?
I cannot speak for horror.
What you are saying is unthinkable.

110 The horror of it paralyses me.

THESEUS   You assumed that Phèdre, for shame,
Would hide her defilement,
So your assault on her fidelity
Would stay hidden with it.

115 You made a mistake. Have you forgotten?
You dropped your sword.
In her hand it convicts you.
You made another mistake. You omitted
To kill her—and cut off her voice.

120 HIPPOLYTUS   Sir, anger forces me to speak.
To stand accused by you, of such an outrage,
Should force me to give you the whole truth.
Yes, I know the truth. But I suppress it.
It touches you too close. My lord,

125 Consider a son's solicitude
For the father he loves.

That keeps my mouth sealed.
Unless you wish to open an abyss
Under the gulf that is already gaping.
130 Recall how I have lived, and what I am.
The first steps towards a great crime
Are trivial misdemeanours.
There is a stairway of degrees
To crime, just as to virtue.
135 Innocence is demure. A single day
Cannot transform a man of loyal conscience
To an incestuous lecher, a hardened killer.
My mother's chastity was her fame.
There's not a drop of dissolute blood in me.
140 She formed me. Then Pittheus was my teacher.
The wisest, noblest, best man of his day.
I do not wish to boast but, my lord,
Above all other virtues, the one virtue
That I was born to, and have been bred up to,
145 Is hatred of this crime you charge me with.
My aversion to it is a legend.
Throughout Greece I am famed for just this.
Some say my rigour is so stubborn,
So severe, so blunt, they think it ugly,
150 Yet God knows the depth of my heart
Is pure as the blue sky! And still I hear you
Call me a hypocrite—
THESEUS   And I repeat it.
I see through your chastity—plain as day.
155 That frigid pride of yours is precisely
What betrays you.
Your lascivious eyes are locked on Phèdre.
Indifferent to every other woman
You have no trouble ignoring their attractions.
160 HIPPOLYTUS   Father, it is not so. You compel me
To tell you what I must withhold no longer.
I am in love.
This will anger you, but I must confess it.
I have done one thing you have forbidden.
165 Your son has submitted his whole being
To the daughter of the Pallantes—Aricia.
I worship Aricia.
Father, I adore her. My inmost soul
Belongs only to Aricia.
170 THESEUS   You love Aricia? Heaven sees what this is
As clearly as I do. A fairy tale for fools!
You concoct one crime to hide the other.
HIPPOLYTUS   Father, six months, against my will, I have loved her.
I came here to inform you. It is not easy.
175 What can I say to make you see the truth?
What heaven-shaking oaths do I have to swear

To make you understand you are mistaken?
I swear on the earth, the heavens, on all nature—
THESEUS   Blasphemy is child's play to a liar.
180   Stop! Spare me the babbling. You insult me.
Your posturing virtue is incredible.
HIPPOLYTUS   Only to you while you believe the lie.
Phèdre knows the truth. I am not guilty.
THESEUS   Ah! Your insolence is intolerable.
185   HIPPOLYTUS   If I am to be banished—where and when?
THESEUS   Beyond Atlas,[8] far out in the Atlantic—
You would still be much too close to me.
HIPPOLYTUS   Once you have branded my name as a felon
Who in the world will befriend me? If Theseus
190   Casts me out, who dare take me in?
THESEUS   Find friends among men debauched enough
To approve adultery and relish incest.
Thankless, treacherous men, without laws or honour.
The kind who will welcome such as you.
195   HIPPOLYTUS   Adultery and incest! You are obsessed
With adultery and incest. Shall I say it?
Phèdre had a mother.
Remember Phèdre's mother.
Phèdre bears the blood of a lineage
200   Far more heavily charged with such crimes
Than mine ever was and you know it.
THESEUS   What? You are mad!
Get out. For the last time—get out.
Must you wait till I'm speechless?
205   Do you have to be flung out bodily?
          [Exit HIPPOLYTUS.]
Yes, go, you filth. You will not escape.
Destruction is hurrying towards you.
The god of the oceans
Swore on that river in Hell[9]
210   To give me satisfaction.
A god of vengeance out of the seas pursues you.
And yet in spite of your nature,
So strangely diseased,
I loved you. My bowels are twisting
215   With a horrible foreboding.
You forced me to curse you.
How many fathers have known this?
You gods, you see what I suffer.
How did I sire this deformity?
          [Enter PHÈDRE.]
220   PHÈDRE   My lord, your voice rings through the palace.

---

8. That is, the Atlas Mountains, which rise on the Atlantic coast of northern Africa and therefore marked the western boundary of the classical world.
9. The river Styx in Hades, by which the gods swore their greatest and most solemn oaths.

I could not help but hear it.
I am terrified. O my lord,
What if your prayers are answered?
Is it too late to save him?
225   He is your own blood—rescue him!
Your own sacred blood—cherish it
Before it is too late. I beg you
Save me, Theseus,
From having to hear his screams.
230   Save me from a life
Haunted by the screams of Hippolytus.
Save me
From the everlasting horror
Of having prompted his own father's hand
235   To destroy him.

THESEUS   No, Phèdre, I have refrained, not easily,
From dipping my hand in my own blood.
Nevertheless, this rapist is doomed.
Immortal hands are already at it.
240   Neptune's debt to me will avenge you.

PHÈDRE   Neptune's debt? What?
You call on—

THESEUS   Would you prefer the god to ignore me
Like some ordinary creditor?
245   My plea to him is holy—you should join me.
Recount my son's crime. In all its detail.
Let me hear the full enormity of it.
Shake up my sluggish spirits.
My blood is too torpid.
250   You do not know one half his perfidy.
He reviles you in particular—
Nothing but lies, he says, comes from your mouth.
He was almost incoherent.
Finally, as a last insult to me,
255   He dares to pretend
That he has fallen in love with Aricia.
He swears he has given his soul to Aricia.

PHÈDRE   Given his soul?

THESEUS   Another of his lies.
260   Everything he says is counterfeit.
He lies as he breathes—
To keep himself alive.
But Neptune, our great green god of the ocean,
His judgement will be swift.
265   And now I am going
To add my prayers to it.
                    [Exit THESEUS.]

PHÈDRE   Can I believe this?
Am I sick? A smouldering
Here, under my ribs—

270 Trying to burst into hard flames.
This cannot be true.
I rushed here to save his son.
Oenone tried to stop me.
But her arms were powerless
275 To hold back the guilt that lashed me,
The remorse that dragged me—
I was out of my mind.
How far would I have let myself go?
Maybe, if what Theseus told me
280 Had not choked me
I would have gone on. I would have confessed.
The truth would have come vomiting out of my mouth.
But now—
Now I know Hippolytus can feel.
285 Only—he feels nothing for me.
He loves Aricia!
His heart, his soul, everything
Sworn to Aricia!
Oh God, when I howled at his feet—
290 When he stared at me
With that statue's face
I thought he was impenetrable, proof,
A bronze burnished visor, deflecting
The whole female sex—
295 Like his reputation. I was wrong.
It was all a front.
The right woman's touch undid his armour.
I thought his eyes were stone—she found tears in them.
Perhaps he is too susceptible to women.
300 I am the only one he cannot stand!
And I came rushing here to defend him!

                    [*Enter* OENONE.]

Oenone, I have learned something.
OENONE   Madam, when you ran out I almost fainted.
You were in such a state.
305 I feared it might be the end of you.
PHÈDRE   Would you believe it? I have a rival.
OENONE   What?
PHÈDRE   Hippolytus is in love.
Beyond any doubt.
310 This enemy of mine, so wild and shy,
So alien to subjection,
Who found my entreaty so appalling,
My tears so irritating,
This tiger
315 That I could never approach without trembling—
He has been tamed. He is humbled.
And now he announces his love.
Aricia has taken possession.

OENONE   Aricia!

320 PHÈDRE   What now, Oenone?
     What new constellations of torment,
     Reserved for this moment,
     Of a magnitude I never imagined,
     Rise for me now?
325 All I have suffered before this—
     The terror, the delirium,
     The agonies of craving, the impossible pain
     Of that brutal rebuff, the horror of my guilt,
     The bottomless degradation,
330 The loathing of myself, the despair—
     All that was no more than the overture
     For what is taking hold of me now.
     They love each other!
     What sort of witchcraft did they use
335 To delude me?
     How long have they loved each other?
     Where have they been meeting? How often?
     You knew! You knew it! Oenone,
     Why did you let me be fooled?
340 Couldn't you breathe one whisper of their secret?
     Wasn't it plain?
     Weren't they forever
     Running around looking for each other?
     Heads together in corners, thinking themselves unnoticed
345 In plain view of everybody?
     Or did they hide it all in the forest?
     Ah! They were free!
     Heaven was pleased with their innocent affection.
     Wherever their love led, they went light-hearted.
350 For them the days dawned calm.
     But for me, rejected by nature,
     I dreaded every sunbeam.
     I buried myself.
     Daylight was a horror to me.
355 Death was the only god I prayed to.
     I waited only for death.
     Nothing but gall sustained me, and tears.
     Surrounded by spies
     I did not even dare
360 To unburden myself of my grief.
     I concealed it.
     I sank
     Into the horrible secret luxury of it.
     My sobbing was soundless.
365 My weeping was dry.
     I trembled with calm.

OENONE   Their love is futureless. It has come to nothing.
     They will never meet again.

PHÈDRE   Yes, but their love exists.
370   It exists. And it will last.
I cannot bear to imagine it.
Even this moment, as I speak,
They have not a thought for me,
They are heedless
375   Of the fury of my love—
It is meaningless to them.
But I have to endure it—
I have to burn in it.
Banishment may separate them
380   But it cannot injure their love,
Only intensify their million vows
To love each other for ever.
No, it's their happiness—it's their hope
That torments me.
385   Oenone, I am going mad with jealousy.
Aricia must die.
Theseus must be made to kill her.
No punishment is enough.
She has outdone her criminal brothers.
390   I'll use every bit of rage in my body
To persuade him to kill her.
Oh God, what am I doing? What am I saying?
I think I'm losing my senses.
Me jealous? Me beg Theseus
395   To avenge my jealousy? Implore my husband
To remove my rival
From my monstrous passion for his son?
Everything I say makes my hair stand up.
My life is so bloated with my crimes
400   There's no room for another. I stink
Of incest and deceit. And worse—
My own hands are twitching
To squeeze the life out of that woman,
To empty that innocent blood out of her carcase
405   And smash her to nothing.
Yet I stand here facing the sun.
The light of heaven, my greatest ancestor,
Is the father and ruler of the gods.
The whole universe is full of my forebears.
410   Where can I hide?
I cannot hide even in Hell—
My father, Minos, is the judge of the dead.[1]
There, the judgement favours nobody.
He will be stupefied
415   When I appear before him. His own daughter!

---

1. After his death, Minos was made one of three judges in Hades who determined whether individual souls were to be sent to Tartarus for punishment or to Elysium, the fields of the blessed.

Forced to confess to such crimes,
So different and so many,
Some of them perhaps
Unknown even in Hell.
420 Father, how will you judge my life?
I see your hand fall from the dark urn
That contains the lots for the common dead.
I see you groping, aghast,
For the just sentence
425 That you must execute on your own daughter.
O Father, you have to forgive me.
The pitiless goddess
Would not loosen her grip on your family.
I am one more trophy of her vengeance.
430 My crimes were execrable.
Their shame walks with me like my shadow.
But they brought me no profit—
Not one flicker of gratification.
No, my every step
435 Carried me deeper into evil fortune.
My whole life has been wretched and ends in torment.
OENONE Ah, madam, get rid of these thoughts.
You made mistakes, but view them in a new light.
You are in love: that's fate, it cannot be altered.
440 Destiny cast the spell that leads you spellbound.
Is that such a novelty?
Mankind is frail by nature.
Submit to being mortal. You are mortal.
The creation has laws.
445 Even the gods, the high Olympian gods,
Who come down so hard on our weakness,
They find passion uncontrollable.
PHÈDRE What am I hearing?
How dare you go on mixing these drugs?
450 Will you try to poison me to the last?
Witch. This is how you have destroyed me.
When I tried to crawl out of my life
You won me to stay.
Your reasoning blinded me to my duty.
455 I shunned Hippolytus. You made me see him.
Can't you see what you've done?
Your evil incriminating mouth
Has ruined his name
And blasted his life.
460 It will have killed him
If the god fulfils the inhuman prayer
Of a father you have driven mad.
Get away from me.
Leave me to mourn what you have made of me.
465 And may the heavens

Pay you exactly
What you have earned.
And your punishment
Terrify
470 Everybody like you.
All those who do as you have done.
Bending their supple speeches to the failings
Of erratic monarchs.
Giving a little push to their inclinations,
475 Easing their descent into crime.
Vile whisperers!
Sycophants,
The most
Pernicious of the gifts an angered god
480 Can give to the wearer of the crown.
OENONE   Ah God, I have spent my life to save her.
Have I now been paid as I deserved?

Act V

[HIPPOLYTUS, ARICIA, ISMÈNE.]

ARICIA   You have to speak out.
The danger you are in numbs my mind.
Your father loves you.
You cannot let misapprehension craze him
5 Against you.
Speak, and save yourself from it. Save us.
You are forgetting us.
Are my tears meaningless? Can you accept
Our separation for ever
10 Without a word? Then go. Leave me hopeless.
But at least, if you must go, save your life.
Save your name, your fame
From this scandal and this preposterous lie.
Though the truth is vile, force him to face it.
15 Make him reverse the curse. There is still time.
What nicety of honour
Creeps off speechless leaving all the credit
With an unscrupulous liar? Tell your father,
Tell him everything.
20 HIPPOLYTUS   Ah God, what haven't I said?
You want me to disclose
The shame of his bedchamber
For the mere relief of feeling truthful?
Can I humiliate my own father
25 And make him laughable? Nobody
Has looked into this secret
Except you and the gods.
See now how I love you. I have shown you
What I tried to hide even from myself.

30   Aricia, forget you ever heard it.
     I opened this to you in confidence.
     Never mention it. It's too filthy a business.
     It would contaminate your mouth.
     But if the gods can be trusted,
35   If they want justice, they must favour me.
     The situation can be left to them,
     And I need fear nothing.
     Sooner or later Phèdre and her great lie
     Must meet their judgement, which is immovable.
40   Only for this I beg you to be patient.
     But for everything else—I have done with patience.

     Aricia, your prison
     Need no longer hold you. Come with me.
     Gather your courage. We can leave together.
45   Everything about this place is abhorrent.
     The very air corrodes honesty.
     Your disappearance now will pass unnoticed.
     My sudden disgrace and banishment
     Has turned the whole palace upside down.
50   We can use the confusion.
     All that you require, I can give you.
     Your guards are my men.
     Across the sea our allies are powerful.
     Argos calls us. Sparta[2] welcomes us.
55   Our interests are theirs.
     Phèdre shall never dethrone you or me.
     She shall never build her empire
     Out of our absence,
     Or give what is ours to her son.
60   What now? You hold back?
     This is the moment and we have to seize it.
     Are you wavering?
     Aricia! I am resolved.
     If I seem to be moving too fast
65   It is for your sake.
     Do you hesitate
     To share your escape with a banished man?
  ARICIA   I want no other freedom.
     To share your fate is the only
70   Happiness I can imagine.
     But if I come
     There is one thing lacking between us
     Not only to complete my happiness
     But also preserve my honour.
75   If I can escape
     From one who has dealt with me

2. Argos is a city-state on the Peloponnesus, northwest of Troezen; Sparta is in the southern part of the peninsula.

As cruelly as your father has,
I break no code of honour.
Flight from a tyrant is acceptable.
80 And neither home nor kindred holds me here.
But, my lord, you love me, and my good name—
HIPPOLYTUS   Aricia, your good name is my first care.
Now hear my plan.
Desert your enemies and marry me.
85 Misfortune has freed us to do what the gods ordain.
We need no one's presence or permission,
No torches or procession.
Outside the gates of the city,
Among the tombs where my family are interred
90 There stands an ancient shrine.
That place is so holy
No perjurer dare come near it.
Whoever makes an oath in those precincts
And breaks it is instantly punished,
95 Their death follows quickly.
In that shrine, Aricia, if you will trust me,
We will consecrate together
An everlasting love. Our one witness
Will be the god of the place.
100 That god can perform
The role of priest and father to us both.
Then I will beseech Diana,[3]
Goddess of chastity, brightest of all the gods,
To sanctify my vows, and to bless us.
105 ARICIA   Here's the King. Oh go. Oh God,
Go, go. I will stay here to cover you,
And allay his suspicions. Quickly, quickly.
But leave somebody who can guide me
To the place.
           [*Exit* HIPPOLYTUS. *Enter* THESEUS.]
110 THESEUS   You gods, permit me one ray of light.
Let me catch one glimmer of the truth I search for.
ARICIA   Ismène,
Have everything prepared. And be ready.
           [*Exit* ISMÈNE.]
THESEUS   Madam, you change colour. You seem startled.
115 What was Hippolytus doing here?
ARICIA   Giving me his last goodbye, my lord.
THESEUS   Those eyes of yours have humbled that arrogant stare.
His first sighs of passion—are all your work.
ARICIA   If that is true I shall not deny it.
120 One thing he has not inherited from you
Is your hatred for me.
He never saw me as a threat to the state.

---

3. Diana (Artemis) is the virgin goddess of the hunt.

THESEUS   Of course not. He was too busy
    Swearing eternal love.
125   Do not depend, girl, on that facile mouth.
    He has sworn the same to others.
ARICIA   He has?
THESEUS   You should have restrained him.
    How can you entertain such a pretender?
130 ARICIA   And how can you let that rotten libel
    Pollute his life—a current like sunlight!
    Do you know your own son's heart so little?
    Can't you distinguish between good and evil?
    The whole world can see what he is.
135   Must you—his father—be the only one
    Blundering about in the dark?
    I can't leave him and his name
    To the tongues and fangs of vipers.
    Stop now: halt your homicidal curse
140   And beg the gods to forgive you for it.
    Has it occurred to you
    They may hate you enough to grant it?
    Sometimes the gods accept our prayers
    Just for the opportunity it gives them
145   To punish us in full, at our own request.
THESEUS   Enough. You have scolded enough.
    You cannot change the nature of his crime.
    Love has blinded you to his ugliness.
    I have witnesses—impeccable.
150   I have seen tears that were incorruptible.
    And I believe them.
ARICIA   Be careful, my lord. Your hands
    May have eradicated many monsters
    And never once failed. But let me say:
155   Not every monster has been accounted for.
    There is one monster you have not recognised—
    Your son, my lord, forbids me to say more.
    He is concerned for you.
    And his concern for you must also be mine.
160   If I told all I know—he too would be injured.
    My lord, let me share his reticence.
    And rather than be forced by you to break it
    Allow me to withdraw.
        [*Exit* ARICIA.]
THESEUS   What's in her mind? What is this woman hiding?
165   She seems to be trying to tell me
    Something she dare not tell me. Starting and stopping.
    Going straight at it—then dodging past it.
    Maybe the pair have put their heads together
    To trick me, and lead me by the nose
170   Into some fresh maze of new clues—
    And new darkness. At the same time,

In spite of my determination,
And in spite of my anger,
A voice—
175 Somewhere, beneath all this, a voice,
A pleading voice, inexplicable:
Pity—surprising and painful.
Oenone has to be questioned again—more thoroughly.
I need to know more about what happened.
180 Guards, bring Oenone. Here, alone.

[*Enter* PANOPE.]

PANOPE I dare not guess what is in Queen Phèdre's mind
But her agitation, my lord,
Puts her life in danger.
If despair can be fatal
185 And if we can recognise its signs,
I see it in her face. She is white as death.
As for Oenone—everything is too late.
She abandoned Phèdre and ran from the palace.
My lord, she leapt from the cliff-head—
190 And if that drop to the sea did not kill her
The sea did. Whatever her reasons
The waves that are now pounding her body on the rocks
Have washed them away, beyond recovery.
THESEUS What?
195 PANOPE This death has not quieted the Queen.
Only made her worse—if anything could.
She rushes to her children, like a mother
Seeking her own consolation,
Embracing them and sobbing over them,
200 But then she thrusts them away, with shrieks of horror,
As if maternal love were some contagion,
And staggers about the palace,
Falling on the stairs, colliding with walls
Like a blind madwoman.
205 She stares at everybody and sees nobody.
Three times she started a letter—
Each time changed her mind and tore it up.
You must see her, my lord. And perhaps help her.
THESEUS Oh God—Oenone dead?
210 And Phèdre wanting to die?
Call my son back.
Let me hear my son defend himself.
Let him tell me all he has to tell me.
I will listen. Tell him I will listen.

[*Exit* PANOPE.]

215 O Neptune,
If you heard my prayer, if you heard my curse,
Hear me. Withhold your favour to me.
Perhaps I believed the wrong story,

Perhaps I based my judgement on lies—
220 Too credulous and too precipitous.
Perhaps my berserk rage, that called on you
To destroy my son, was mistaken!
Oh God, God, if I am too late—

[*Enter* THÉRAMÈNE.]

Where is Hippolytus? What have you done with him?
225 I gave him into your care, Théramène,
When he was only a child.
Where is my son?

THÉRAMÈNE   Ah—so much concern
Coming so late and so superfluously.
230 Such paternal love. And all so useless.
Hippolytus is dead.

THESEUS   Aaah!

THÉRAMÈNE   I have seen
The death of the most lovable of men.
235 And the most innocent, my lord.

THESEUS   My son dead? Ah! Only now
When I stretch my arms wide open to him
The gods rip him away.
What happened to him? How did they do it?

240 THÉRAMÈNE   We were hardly clear of the city gates
And onto the beach road, towards Mycenae.[4]
Hippolytus was leading, in his chariot.
His bodyguards close round him. A sombre troop.
The prince was taciturn.
245 His mood made the mood of every man.
We all shared one dark thought and were silent.
No sound but the click of hooves and jingle of harness.
Those horses of his were strange.
Usually so bursting with spirits—
250 So headstrong, so eager to be off,
They need the constant touch of his voice and the reins
To hold them in—today they were listless.
He left the pace to them,
Letting the reins lie loose over their backs.
255 They hung their heads, they seemed preoccupied,
As if they were helping him, with their hanging heads,
To think what he was thinking.
I noticed it. It seemed very strange.
As I was watching that,
260 A sudden skull-splitting roar,
An indescribable, terrible, tearing voice,
Like lightning flash and thunderclap together,
Made us all duck and cower.
It came out of the sea, as if the whole sea
265 Had bellowed.

4. A city-state on the Peloponnesus northwest of Troezen.

And then, like an echo to it,
Another roaring groan, subterranean,
As if something that groaned were trying to scream,
Rolled through the earth under our feet.
270 The ground was bulging, jumping beneath us.
We were petrified and bewildered.
The horses' manes and tails flared on end.
And now I saw out at sea
A mountain of water boiling up,
275 Heaping higher,
Irrupting from under the horizon
And racing towards us.
Till it towered above us, seeming to hang.
And there, in slow motion,
280 It collapsed, a solid fall of thunder.
Quaking the bedrock. And out of it,
The foam cascading from a colossal body,
Came a beast—
Up the sand, with the fury
285 Of a supernatural existence.
Its head was one huge monster all to itself,
Like a bull's head, with bull's horns.
But from the shoulders backwards
The whole body was plated,
290 Humped and plated, the scales greeny yellow,
A nauseating colour, that sickened the eye.
And beyond the humped bulk of the body
Came scaled and lashing coils. Half bull, half dragon—
Mouth hanging open,
295 And bellowing, like a heavy surf
Exploding in a cavern.
The earth trembled, the air was thick with horror.
We breathed a mist of horror.
Weapons or courage were out of the question.
300 Everybody fled. We all took cover
In that small temple among the tombs.
Then I looked back and saw Hippolytus—
He was lashing his horses and making a run
Straight at the monster—at the last moment
305 I saw him swerve
Tight past its jaws and bury a javelin
All but for a span length of the shaft
Behind that thing's shoulder, right where the heart is
In creatures that have hearts.
310 I never saw anything so fearless.
But whether the javelin blade found a heart,
Or the beast was convulsed
With fury at his daring—the whole mass of it
Rose and collapsed on to Hippolytus,
315 Like another mountain of ocean,

Or like a giant octopus of water.
I saw horses and chariot
Tossing among foam and tentacles
That dragged back down towards the sea.
320 But then, a miracle.
The horses were clambering free,
Like a team scrambling across an avalanche.
And I saw Hippolytus braced in the chariot—
Fists bunched and legs wide,
325 I thought he was getting clear. But a god was watching.
In a surf of churning sand,
A last scything swipe of the monster's tail
Came round under their hooves,
Toppled the horses and smashed the wheels of the chariot.
330 Then the horses went mad—
I heard Hippolytus shouting among the screams
Of the horses, and the blasts of that beast.
The wonderful strength of Hippolytus was helpless.
Some of the others saw something
335 I can hardly credit, I did not see it.
They saw the glowing figure of a naked god
Astride the shoulders of the demented horses—
Goading and urging them
Among the rocks of the foreshore
340 With the chariot, stripped of its wheels,
Bounding like a bucket behind them.
Hippolytus had wound his arms in the reins.
He tore the horses' mouths but they felt nothing.
And the voice they had grown up with
345 Became a scream that added to their terror
As the chariot disintegrated beneath him.
Then it was two mad horses dragging a man.
Oh my lord, forgive me! The sight of it
Is like a great wound through my body,
350 It's never going to heal.
The horses galloped away with their weightless bundle
That had fed them, and that was your son.
We followed—all of us crying openly
Like forsaken children.
355 The trail was easy—he had signed every stone,
Left us a rag of flesh on every thorn.
The horses careered in a wide circle—
Till they were exhausted.
They came to a halt, as it happened,
360 Among the royal tombs. There we found them,
Streaming with lather and shuddering,
The eyes crazed in their heads. And there he lay.
It is part of the marvel of his strength
That he was still alive. When I clasped his hand
365 And called to him, his fingers squeezed my fingers.

His eyes opened—they stared past me awhile
At something he tried to recognise.
Then closed slowly. They did not open again.
He was trying to speak. I bent close.
370 'The gods have taken my life,' he whispered,
'Though it was innocent. Dear old friend,' he said,
'After my death protect Aricia.
And if my father ever frees himself
From his delusion, and feels any remorse
375 For that false charge which has destroyed his son,
Ask him to treat Aricia kindly.
Ask him to give back to her—' My lord,
With those words
His voice and his life failed together.
380 And I was left embracing the latest prize
Of the triumphant gods—an object
Hardly recognisable as a man.
I think his own father would not know him.
THESEUS   My son! I did it to myself—
385 Killed my only hope. Inexorable—
That is the word for the gods.
They kept their word too well.
Nothing is left to me now, but to mourn.
THÉRAMÈNE   There is a little more to tell you.
390 Aricia came running towards us.
My lord, she was running away from you,
And hurrying to meet Hippolytus
At that very temple, there, among the tombs,
Where they had planned a marriage solemnised
395 Only by the god. As she came near
She saw the horses steaming and shivering
In their broken traces. Then she saw
What we stood around and looked down at.
The drained rag of Hippolytus' body.
400 For a moment she could not recognise
That this was all that remained of her happiness.
Her eyes refused to understand it.
She stared at the corpse and asked for Hippolytus.
But then it sank in.
405 And she let it happen.
She cried out just once, then dropped, silent,
Like somebody jabbed through the heart.
Ismène was with her.
She managed to bring her round. Aricia
410 Returned to what was waiting for her—
Daylight, that mangled shape, her future.
And I have come, my lord,
Hating what I have to reveal
And to discharge the task allotted to me
415 By the dying breath of Hippolytus.

I pass his last wishes to you.
And here comes the cause of everything—

[*Enter* PHÈDRE.]

THESEUS   Now you can be happy. My son is dead.
I cannot help it, these vile fantasies
420   Overwhelm me—though I lack evidence.
I have only one fact—my son is dead.
Madam, he is your victim, rejoice.
Whether guilty or innocent
He can no longer aggrieve you. Accept it.
425   I am ready to look no deeper.
If you accuse him, let me live with that.
I will think him a criminal and a traitor.
His death alone is suffering enough
Without me searching for scraps and broken bits
430   Of information that could drive me mad
But never bring him back.
Let me get away from this land
That holds you
And the dismembered body of my boy.
435   Even if I found another universe
This memory would be with me.
Everything proclaims what I have done.
My very fame blazes with my shame.
If I were unknown I could hide.
440   The favour of the gods terrifies me—
I dare not ever again pray to them.
Their answers to my prayers have finished me.
However much they have helped me in the past
They have taken everything back, they have taken my son—
445   My son, my hope, my life.
PHÈDRE   No, Theseus. Now hear me speak.
Let me restore your son's lost innocence.
Hippolytus was not guilty.
THESEUS   My son was not guilty? So simple.
450   And it was on your word that I cursed him?
You are Hell itself.
You think this can be forgiven?
PHÈDRE   Listen to me carefully, Theseus.
Every moment now is precious to me.
455   Hippolytus was chaste. And loyal to you.
I was the monster in this riddle.
I was insane with an incestuous passion,
To amuse some malevolent deity.
That viper Oenone plotted the rest.
460   Once I had bared my affliction to your son
Oenone feared he might in time inform you
Of my shameless obsession, my shameless attempt
To force my lust on him. While I was helpless
That infernal woman slithered to you

465   And fixed the guilt on the prince
       As if she had witnessed it. So you were poisoned.
       She has been punished. She escaped my rage,
       And found a gentler executioner
       Where the sea breaks under the cliff.
470   The sword would have been my own choice, before this,
       But that would have left the prince's innocence
       To the play of suspicion and conjecture.
       I have chosen a slower conveyance
       To the land of the dead. This has allowed me
475   Time to show you, Theseus, my remorse.
       Now I am drunk on an infallible poison
       That my sister Medea[5] brought to Athens.
       I feel my pulses pushing it icily
       Into my feet, hands and the roots of my hair.
480   I see the sun's ball through a mist,
       And you, whom my very presence sickens,
       I see you in a mist, darkening.
       My eyes go dark. Now the light of the sun
       Can resume its purity unspoiled.
485 PANOPE   My lord, she is dying.
    THESEUS   If only
       The results of her evil could die with her.
       Come. Now my error of judgement
       Is so monumental and plain
490   Let us go weep at my son's body.
       Let us embrace the little of him that's left
       And expiate the madness of my prayer.
       We shall give him the honours he has earned.
       And to appease his shade,
495   And in spite of the old crime of your brothers,
       Aricia, from today you are my daughter.

5. A powerful sorceress from Colchis and the granddaughter of Helios (the sun); Jason brought her back to Greece after she helped him obtain the Golden Fleece. Later she killed their sons, because Jason planned to marry the daughter of the king of Corinth; Aegeus, The-seus's father, offered her sanctuary in Athens, and she married him. She left Greece after her unsuccessful attempt to poison Theseus, whom she saw as a threat to the son she had borne to Aegeus.

SOR JUANA INÉS DE LA CRUZ
1648–1695

CONSIDERED the last great writer of the Spanish Golden Age, Sor Juana Inés de la Cruz was also deemed the first feminist in the New World by early twentieth-century critics who had rediscovered her work. This remarkable seventeenth-century Mexican author penned hundreds of poems, more than a dozen carol sequences for use in church services, and twenty-seven plays, including religious dramas (*autos sacramentales*), comedies, farces, and *loas*—short dramatic pieces that either preceded full-length works or were performed on their own at religious or court celebrations. Although Sor Juana may be best known for the controversial theological essay *Carta atenagórica* (*Letter Worthy of Athena*) and its defense, *La Respuesta* (*The Answer*), written toward the end of her career, her critical reputation rests on other works as well. These include *Primero sueño* (*First Dream*), a 975-stanza poem considered the most important philosophical verse of the Golden Age, and *EL DIVÍNO NARCISO* (*THE DIVINE NARCISSUS*), an *auto sacramental* that reflects Sor Juana's deep engagements with baroque dramaturgy, Ovidian mythology, and Christian allegory. The *loa* to this drama reveals with great clarity both Sor Juana's sophisticated understanding of gender roles within a highly structured Catholic culture and her prescient sensitivity to the

impact of Spanish colonialism in the New World.

Juana Inés de Asbaje y Ramírez de Santillana was born in Nepantla, near Mexico City. Her father, Pedro Manuel de Asbaje y Vargas Machuca, was a Basque military officer, and her mother, Isabel Ramírez, helped manage the family's lands while raising six children. Juana spent her childhood years in the home of her maternal grandfather, whose extensive library provided her initial education. She states that she learned to read at age three, and she supposedly wrote her first *loa* at age eight. She claims that she unsuccessfully pleaded with her mother to allow her to dress as a boy so that she could attend school in Mexico City, but she was soon sent there to live with her aunt and uncle—a move that enabled her to learn Latin and, more importantly, to come to the attention of the Spanish viceroy and his wife, who in short order brought her to live at court. A great favorite of the vicereine, Juana composed much of her early verse in honor of her benefactor. At the request of the viceroy, who was eager to showcase the prodigy, Juana agreed to be examined by forty scholars, representing all branches of learning. According to an early biography by Father Diego Calleja, a Jesuit priest, Juana triumphed during this examination: "in the manner that a royal galleon might fend off the attacks of small canoes, so did Juana extricate herself from the questions, arguments, and objections these many men, each in his speciality, directed to her."

Juana spent five years as a lady-in-waiting at court and then decided to enter the convent of Santa Paula in 1668. She made this choice, she explained later, because of her unwillingness to marry, the only other suitable option for a woman of her class at that time. Juana understood that as a married woman she would have little say in her day-to-day activities and most probably would have to devote herself exclusively to her family. Though convent life was highly structured and restricted in some ways, it also afforded her time and space to continue her studies and writing. In 1690 Sor Juana drafted a critique of a well-known sermon by the Jesuit Antonio Vieyra on Christ's greatest gift to humanity. The document came to the attention of Don Manuel Fernández de Santa Cruz, bishop of Puebla, and without her knowledge he had the essay published under the title *Carta atenagórica*. He sent her a copy but appended a strong rejoinder, under the pseudonym Sor Filotea de la Cruz, that criticized her entrance into the arena of theological discourse and urged her to focus on forms of devotion more appropriate for a woman. In response, she wrote her famous *La Respuesta*. This essay, although unpublished in her lifetime, provides much of the biographical information we have on Sor Juana. It also serves more broadly as a defense of women's right to education, culture, and independence of thought that was unprecedented for its time.

The Answer proved to be Sor Juana's last major work. In 1695, while nursing others at the convent, she contracted the plague that had swept through their community; she died on April 17. Aware of the controversies surrounding her writing, critics have subsequently combed her verse, plays, and essays in an attempt to gain a fuller understanding of Sor Juana both as an individual and as a seventeenth-century woman attempting to find self-fulfillment and self-expression under Spanish colonial and ecclesiastical rule. Her literary works in particular have been scrutinized for the light they might shed on her theological beliefs and

her discomfort—veiled though it was—with the rigid structures that shaped her life.

In *The Divine Narcissus,* for example, we find some of the same themes that Sor Juana later incorporated in the more personal *Answer*—in particular, the significance of secular writing to an understanding of scripture. Yet to employ her dramas and verse only as a lens through which to read her essays or understand her as an individual would be to undervalue and misrepresent these works' importance to the Golden Age and to Hispanic culture. Indeed, a focus on the plays themselves reveals her remarkable sensitivity to and skill in deploying the range of dramaturgical styles and conventions that flourished in the era. Sor Juana's dramatic works delighted audiences at court as well as at public festivals and display equal ease in engaging with religious and with secular themes.

The sheer volume of her writing in one form, the *loa,* suggests Sor Juana's special affinity for this kind of drama; the eighteen *loas* she composed during her career represent two-thirds of her total dramatic output. *Loa,* like the English word *laud,* is derived from the Latin *laus* (praise), and the form arose in a context of praise for audience or locale. Originally a monologue that served as a prelude to a comedy, the *loa* evolved during the sixteenth century into a short, highly stylized drama with multiple characters, frequently on allegorical themes. In keeping with baroque conventions, *loas* reflect considerable metric variety and elaborate wordplay (often difficult to capture in translation), as well as vivid imagery. All the leading Golden Age playwrights wrote *loas,* and it is reasonable to hypothesize that Sor Juana's pieces were influenced by their published works, especially those of PEDRO CALDERÓN DE LA BARCA (1600–1681), whose style of intellectual allegory she appears to have embraced. The *loas* that accompanied the *autos sacramentales* also bolstered Spain's efforts in the Counter-Reformation. Because these short plays emphasized traditional religious values and teachings, they helped oppose the tide of religious and political reform sweeping across other parts of Europe. The insularity of Spain during this period shielded its artistry from the influence of other cultures, and religious drama in particular survived longer in the Spanish empire than in other regions where supporters of the Reformation strongly opposed such practices.

We can trace the lineage of the *autos* themselves back to medieval liturgical drama. In Spain the springtime celebration of the feast of Corpus Christi had, since the thirteenth century, included such theatrical elements as processions and performances on *carros*—that is, traveling stages on which actors sang, danced, and recited. In reaction to the Reformation, the Catholic Church urged that this celebration be refined and returned to its religious roots. In New Spain (as Spain's imperial holdings in Latin America were then called) such celebrations date to the 1530s. Records note that a Calderónian *auto* was translated into Nahuatl, one of the native Indian languages spoken in the Mexico City area, and that Mexican

A human sacrifice in honor of the Aztec god Huitzilopoxtli, as depicted in the early seventeenth-century *Codex Magliabecchi*.

colonial authors' *autos* were produced in other native Indian languages and in Spanish. Documentation from the era is incomplete, however, and it is unclear whether Sor Juana's *autos* were performed in Mexico. Historians speculate that she was encouraged to begin writing more regularly in the form in 1687 when the vicereine learned that pieces by dramatists other than Calderón might be produced in Madrid. The *loa* to *The Divine Narcissus* supports this theory, as it ends by briefly noting that the piece is suitable for audiences in Madrid as well as in New Spain. It may indeed have been performed in Madrid in 1689, after the vicereine's return to Spain, but we know with certainty only that the play was published there in 1690.

In keeping with the festival theme, *autos sacramentales* all consider in some way humanity's redemption through the Eucharist—the body and blood of Christ. *The Divine Narcissus* focuses on Christ's death as the foundation for this sacrament, using an Ovidian myth of transformation as an allegory of Jesus's crucifixion and resurrection. As the translator Patricia Peters observes, this *auto* is "a lovely pastoral drama of redemption, framed by a remarkable reflection on the plight of the Aztecs under the scourge of Spanish colonization."

Its colonial frame provides, within the eucharistic context, the core thematic link between *loa* and *auto* in *The Divine Narcissus*: the *loa* explicitly pits the native Indian rulers, Occident and his consort America, as well as their Aztec traditions, against the Spanish conqueror Zeal and lady Religion in a battle for both political and religious dominance. Yet labels as critical or direct as Peters's "plight" or "scourge" are found nowhere in the *loa* itself. As a nun writing during the Inquisition, Sor Juana would have been acutely aware that heresy or opposition to the Catholic Church could not be overtly expressed. Moreover, her loyalty to the vicereine would have made inconceivable any blatant critique of the Spanish government or Spain's imperial mission, which was inextricable from Counter-Reformation ideology. But as a *criolla*—a Mexican-born woman of Spanish ancestry—Sor Juana may have felt considerable ambivalence about Spain's treatment of the native peoples among whom she lived. Sor Juana thus may have written her *loas* in part to assist Spanish audiences in understanding the Indians and their beliefs, even as she appears to embrace the necessity of the Aztec conversion to Catholicism that provides the arc of the drama. From her poems, we know that Sor Juana understood and used Nahuatl and other native dialects; and the language and tone of the speeches of the Aztecs in the *loa* imbue these characters with a dignity not found in the conquistador Zeal. Her knowledge of and respect for native culture emerge through her use of an Aztec song and dance, the *tocotín,* in the *loa*'s opening scene, as well as through her engagement with the Indian myths and religious practices that ultimately provide the grounds for intercultural communication. Sor Juana invokes as a bridging figure the "great God of the Seeds," Huitzilopoxtli, who was also the Aztec god of war and of the sun and who required the blood of sacrificial victims to protect his people. The Aztecs were said to mix seeds and grain with the victims' blood to form a life-size statue of the god, which was then shot with arrows until it toppled, at which time participants in the ritual broke up and ate small bits of the figure. The rite was called "God is eaten." In highlighting the similarity of this ceremony to the Eucharist, Sor Juana demonstrates why this myth suits the *auto sacramental* so perfectly.

Yet the violence endemic to both Aztec ritual and Spanish colonialism lends the play a dark center. Historians believe that Sor Juana accepted the concept of the "just war," as articulated by Thomas Aquinas, which rationalized Christian crusaders' attacks on "sinful" non-Christians' bloody practices. The play, however, clearly endorses only female Religion's verbal, intellectual means of conversion, rejecting the violent methods of Zeal and his soldiers. The *loa*'s final lines, in which all characters acknowledge and worship "the great God of Seeds," are ambiguous, as they might be seen as a subversive endorsement of the native beliefs that Occident and America both insist cannot be shaken.

Like her medieval predecessor HROTSVIT, the "strong voice" of Gandersheim, Sor Juana was a remarkable and singular strong voice for her time. Frequently labeled "the Tenth Muse," in the poetic tradition of Sappho and of her American contemporary Anne Bradstreet, Sor Juana has become a cultural icon in Mexico, memorialized on both the 1,000 peso coin and the 200 peso bill. A model for women writers and a critical link in the creation of Western female literary and theatrical traditions, Sor Juana nevertheless emerges as exceptional within her culture and her time, a figure who throws into relief the multiple forces against which she struggled to achieve her unique place in history.   J.E.G.

The Loa for the Auto Sacramental of the Divine Narcissus
An Allegory[1]

CHARACTERS

OCCIDENT	RELIGION
AMERICA	MUSIC[2]
ZEAL	MUSICIANS
	SOLDIERS

Scene 1

[*Enter* OCCIDENT, *a gallant-looking Aztec, wearing a crown. By his side is* AMERICA, *an Aztec woman of poised self-possession. They are dressed in the mantas and huipiles worn for singing a tocotin.[3] They seat themselves on two chairs. On each side, Aztec men and women dance with feathers and rattles in their hands, as is customary for those doing this dance. While they dance,* MUSIC *sings.*]

MUSIC   O, Noble Mexicans,
  whose ancient ancestry
  comes forth from the clear light
  and brilliance of the Sun,
5 since this, of all the year,
  is your most happy feast
  in which you venerate

1. Translated by Patricia A. Peters and Reneé Domeier, O.S.B.
2. Probably an unintentional omission in the cast list by Sor Juana. The copy text of 1725, which Alfonso Méndez Plancarte used as the basis for his definitive edition, does not distinguish between Music as a character and the Musicians who perform during the play.
3. An Aztec song and dance. *Mantas:* men's garments similar to ponchos. *Huipiles:* women's garments similar to ponchos, but not open on the sides.

your greatest deity,
come and adorn yourselves
10   with vestments of your rank;
let your holy fervor be
made one with jubilation;
and celebrate in festive pomp
the great God of the Seeds![4]

15   Since the abundance of
our native fields and farms
is owed to him alone
who gives fertility,
then offer him your thanks,
20   for it is right and just
to give from what has grown,
the first of the new fruits.
From your own veins, draw out
and give, without reserve,
25   the best blood, mixed with seed,
so that his cult be served,
and celebrate in festive pomp,
the great God of the Seeds!

[OCCIDENT *and* AMERICA *rise, and* MUSIC *ceases singing.*]

OCCIDENT   Of all the deities to whom
30   our rites demand I bend my knee—
among two thousand gods or more
who dwell within this royal city
and who require the sacrifice
of human victims still entreating
35   for life until their blood is drawn
and gushes forth from hearts still beating
and bowels still pulsing—I declare,
among all these, (it bears repeating),
whose ceremonies we observe,
40   the greatest is, surpassing all
this pantheon's immensity,
the great God of the Seeds.

AMERICA   And you are right, since he alone
daily sustains our monarchy
45   because our lives depend on his
providing crops abundantly;
and since he gives us graciously
the gift from which all gifts proceed,
our fields rich with golden maize,
50   the source of life through daily bread,
we render him our highest praise.
Then how will it improve our lives
if rich America abounds

4. Huitzilopoxtli, the Aztec god of war and the sun.

in gold from mines whose smoke deprives
55   the fields of their fertility
and with their clouds of filthy soot
will not allow the crops to grow
which blossom now so fruitfully
from seeded earth? Moreover, his
60   protection of our people far
exceeds our daily food and drink,
the body's sustenance. Indeed,
he feeds us with his very flesh
(first purified of every stain).
65   We eat his body, drink his blood,
and by this sacred meal are freed
and cleansed from all that is profane,
and thus, he purifies our soul.
And now, attentive to his rites,
70   together let us all proclaim:

[*They* (OCCIDENT, AMERICA, *Dancers, and* MUSIC) *sing.*]

we celebrate in festive pomp, the great God of the Seeds!

[*They exit dancing.*]

Scene 2

[*Enter Christian* RELIGION *as a Spanish lady,* ZEAL *as a
Captain General in armor, and Spanish soldiers.*]

RELIGION   How, being Zeal, can you suppress
the flames of righteous Christian wrath
when here before your very eyes
idolatry, so blind with pride,
5   adores, with superstitious rites,
an idol, leaving your own bride,
the holy faith of Christ, disgraced?

ZEAL   Religion, trouble not your mind
or grieve my failure to attack,
10   complaining that my love is slack,
for now the sword I wear is bared,
its hilt in hand, clasped ready and
my arm raised high to take revenge.
Please stand aside and deign to wait
15   till I requite your grievances.

[*Enter* OCCIDENT *and* AMERICA *dancing, and accompanied
by* MUSIC, *who enters from the other side.*]

MUSIC   And celebrate in festive pomp,
the great God of the Seeds!

ZEAL   Here they come! I will confront them.

RELIGION   And I, in peace, will also go
20   (before your fury lays them low)
for justice must with mercy kiss;
I shall invite them to arise
from superstitious depths to faith.

ZEAL   Let us approach while they are still
25   absorbed in their lewd rituals.

MUSIC   And celebrate in festive pomp,
    the great God of the Seeds!

[ZEAL *and* RELIGION *cross the stage.*]

RELIGION   Great Occident, most powerful;
    America, so beautiful
30   and rich; you live in poverty
    amid the treasures of your land.
    Abandon this irreverent cult
    with which the demon has waylaid you.
    Open your eyes! Follow the path
35   that leads straightforwardly to truth,
    to which my love yearns to persuade you.

OCCIDENT   Who are these unknown people, so
    intrusive in my sight, who dare
    to stop us in our ecstasy?
40   Heaven forbid such infamy!

AMERICA   Who are these nations, never seen,
    that wish, by force, to pit themselves
    against my ancient power supreme?

OCCIDENT   Oh, you alien beauty fair;
45   oh, pilgrim woman from afar,
    who comes to interrupt my prayer,
    please speak and tell me who you are.

RELIGION   Christian Religion is my name,
    and I intend that all this realm
50   will make obeisance unto me.

OCCIDENT   An impossible concession!

AMERICA   Yours is but a mad obsession!

OCCIDENT   You will meet with swift repression!

AMERICA   Pay no attention; she is mad!
55   Let us go on with our procession.

MUSIC *and all* [Aztecs on stage]   And celebrate in festive pomp,
    the great God of the Seeds!

ZEAL   How is this, barbarous Occident?
    Can it be, sightless Idolatry,
60   that you insult Religion,
    the spouse I cherish tenderly?
    Abomination fills your cup
    and overruns the brim, but see
    that God will not permit you to
65   continue drinking down delight,
    and I am sent to deal your doom.

OCCIDENT   And who are you who frightens all
    who only look upon your face?

ZEAL   I am Zeal. Does that surprise you?
70   Take heed! For when your excesses
    bring disgrace to fair Religion,

then will Zeal arise to vengeance;
for insolence I will chastise you.
I am the minister of God,
75 Who, growing weary with the sight
of overreaching tyrannies
so sinful that they reach the height
of error, practiced many years,
has sent me forth to penalize you.
80 And thus, these military hosts,
with flashing thunderbolts of steel,
the ministers of His great wrath,
are sent, His anger to reveal.

OCCIDENT   What god? What sin? What tyranny?
85 What punishment do you foresee?
Your reasons make no sense to me,
nor can I make the slightest guess
who you might be with your insistence
on tolerating no resistance,
90 impeding us with rash persistence
from lawful worship as we sing.

MUSIC   And celebrate with festive pomp,
the great God of the Seeds!

AMERICA   Madman, blind, and barbarous,
95 with mystifying messages
you try to mar our calm and peace,
destroying the tranquility
that we enjoy. Your plots must cease,
unless, of course, you wish to be
100 reduced to ashes, whose existence
even the winds will never sense.
[To OCCIDENT]   And you, my spouse, and your cohort,
close off your hearing and your sight
to all their words; refuse to heed
105 their fantasies of zealous might;
proceed to carry out your rite.
Do not concede to insolence
from foreigners intent to dull
our ritual's magnificence.

110 MUSIC   And celebrate with festive pomp,
the great God of the Seeds!

ZEAL   Since our initial offering
of peaceful terms you held so cheap,
the dire alternative of war,
115 I guarantee, you'll count more dear.
Take up your arms! To war! To war!
          [Drums and trumpets sound.]

OCCIDENT   What miscarriages of justice
has heaven sent against me?
What are these weapons, blazing fire,

120   before my unbelieving eyes?
        Get ready, guards! Aim well, my troops,
        Your arrows at this enemy!
    AMERICA   What lightning bolts does heaven send
        to lay me low? What molten balls
125   of burning lead so fiercely rain?
        What centaurs[5] crush with monstrous force
        and cause my people such great pain?
            [*Within*]
    To arms! To arms! War! War!
            [*Drums and trumpets sound.*]
    Long life to Spain! Long live her king!
            [*The battle begins. Indians enter through one door and flee
            through another with the Spanish pursuing at their heels.
            From backstage,* OCCIDENT *backs away from* RELIGION *and*
            AMERICA *retreats before* ZEAL's *onslaught.*]

Scene 3

RELIGION   Give up, arrogant Occident!
OCCIDENT   I must bow to your aggression,
    but not before your arguments.
ZEAL   Die, impudent America!
5 RELIGION   Desist! Do not give her to Death;
    her life is of some worth to us.
ZEAL   How can you now defend this maid
    who has so much offended you?
RELIGION   America has been subdued
10   because your valor won the strife,
    but now my mercy intervenes
    in order to preserve her life.
    It was your part to conquer her
    by force with military might;
15   mine is to gently make her yield,
    persuading her by reason's light.
ZEAL   But you have seen the stubbornness
    with which these blind ones still abhor
    your creed; is it not better far
20   that they all die?
RELIGION   Good Zeal, restrain
    your justice, and do not kill them.
    My gentle disposition deigns
    to forbear vengeance and forgive.
    I want them to convert and live.
25 AMERICA   If your petition for my life
    and show of Christian charity

---

5. That is, mounted troops, who—to the people of the New World, who had not seen horses before—might well seem to resemble the half human, half horse creatures of Greek mythology.

are motivated by the hope
that you, at last, will conquer me,
defeating my integrity
30   with verbal steel where bullets failed,
then you are sadly self-deceived.
A weeping captive, I may mourn
for liberty, yet my will grows
beyond these bonds; my heart is free,
35   and I will worship my own gods!
  OCCIDENT   Forced to surrender to your power,
I have admitted my defeat,
but still it must be clearly said
that violence cannot devour
40   my will, nor force constrain its right.
Although in grief, I now lament,
a prisoner, your cruel might
has limits. You cannot prevent
my saying here within my heart
45   I worship the great God of Seeds!

Scene 4

  RELIGION   Wait! What you perceive as force
is not coercion, but affection.
What god is this that you adore?
  OCCIDENT   The great God of the Seeds
5   who causes fields to bring forth fruit.
To him the lofty heavens bow;
to him the rains obedience give;
and when, at last, he cleanses us
from stains of sin, then he invites
10   us to the meal that he prepares.
Consider whether you could find
a god more generous and good
who blesses more abundantly
than he whom I describe to you.
15 RELIGION [aside] O God, help me! What images,
what dark designs, what shadowings
of truths most sacred to our Faith
do these lies seek to imitate?
O false, sly, and deceitful snake!
20   O asp, with sting so venomous!
O hydra,[6] that from seven mouths
pours noxious poisons, every one
a passage to oblivion!
To what extent, with this façade,
25   do you intend maliciously
to mock the mysteries of God?

---

6. In Greek mythology, a monstrous water snake that lived in a swamp; it had many heads, which
grew back as quickly as they were cut off, and its breath was poisonous.

Mock on! For with your own deceit,
if God empowers my mind and tongue,
I'll argue and impose defeat.

30 AMERICA   Why do you find yourself perplexed?
Do you not see there is no god
other than ours who verifies
with countless blessings his great works?

RELIGION   In doctrinal disputes, I hold
35   with the apostle Paul, for when
he preached to the Athenians
and found they had a harsh decree
imposing death on anyone
who tried to introduce new gods,
40   since he had noticed they were free
to worship at a certain shrine,
an altar to "the Unknown God,"
he said to them, "This Lord of mine
is no new god, but one unknown
45   that you have worshipped in this place,
and it is He my voice proclaims."[7]
And thus I—

            [OCCIDENT *and* AMERICA *whisper to each other.*]
            Listen, Occident!
and hear me, blind Idolatry!
For all your happiness depends
50   on listening attentively.
        These miracles that you recount,
these prodigies that you suggest,
these apparitions and these rays
of light in superstition dressed
55   are glimpsed but darkly through a veil.
These portents you exaggerate,
attributing to your false gods
effects that you insinuate,
but wrongly so, for all these works
60   proceed from our true God alone,
and of His Wisdom come to birth.
Then if the soil richly yields,
and if the fields bud and bloom,
if fruits increase and multiply,
65   if seeds mature in earth's dark womb,
if rains pour forth from leaden sky,
all is the work of His right hand;
for neither the arm that tills the soil
nor rains that fertilize the land
70   nor warmth that calls life from the tomb
of winter's death can make plants grow;
for they lack reproductive power

7. See Acts 17.22–31.

if Providence does not concur,
by breathing into each of them
75   a vegetative soul.
AMERICA   That might be so;
then tell me, is this God so kind—
this deity whom you describe—
that I might touch Him with my hands,
these very hands that carefully
80   create the idol, here before you,
an image made from seeds of earth
and innocent, pure human blood
shed only for this sacred rite?
RELIGION   Although the Essence of Divinity
85   is boundless and invisible,
because already It has been
eternally united with
our nature, He resembles us
so much in our humanity
90   that He permits unworthy priests
to take Him in their humble hands.[8]
AMERICA   In this, at least, we are agreed,
for to my God no human hands
are so unstained that they deserve
95   to touch Him; nonetheless, He gives
this honor graciously to those
who serve Him with their priestly lives.
No others dare to touch the God,
nor in the sanctuary stand.
100 ZEAL   A reverence most worthily
directed to the one true God!
OCCIDENT   Whatever else you claim, now tell
me this: Is yours a God composed
of human blood, an offering
105 of sacrifice, and in Himself
does He combine with bloody death
the life-sustaining seeds of earth?
RELIGION   As I have said, His boundless
Majesty is insubstantial,
110 but in the Holy Sacrifice
of Mass, His blessed humanity
is placed unbloody under the
appearances of bread, which comes
from seeds of wheat and is transformed
115 into His Body and His Blood;[9]
and this most holy Blood of Christ,
contained within a sacred cup,

8. That is, holding the bread and wine while delivering Holy Communion.
9. In the Eucharist.

is verily the offering
most innocent, unstained, and pure
120 that on the altar of the cross
was the redemption of the world.
AMERICA Such miracles, unknown to us,
make me desire to believe;
but would the God that you reveal
125 offer Himself so lovingly
transformed for me into a meal
as does the god that I adore?
RELIGION In truth, He does. For this alone
His Wisdom came upon the earth
130 to dwell among all humankind.
AMERICA And so that I can be convinced,
may I not see this Deity?
OCCIDENT And so that I can be made free
of old beliefs that shackle me?
135 RELIGION Yes, you will see when you are bathed
in crystal waters from the font
of baptism.
OCCIDENT And well I know,
in preparation to attend
a banquet, I must bathe, or else
140 our ancient custom I offend.
ZEAL Your vain ablutions will not do
the cleansing that your stains require.
OCCIDENT Then what?
RELIGION There is a sacrament
of living waters, which can cleanse
145 and purify you of your sins.
AMERICA Because you deluge my poor mind
with concepts of theology,
I've just begun to understand;
there is much more I want to see,
150 and my desire to know is now
by holy inspiration led.
OCCIDENT And I desire more keenly still
to know about the life and death
of the God you say is in the bread.
155 RELIGION Then come along with me, and I
shall make for you a metaphor,
a concept clothed in rhetoric
so colorful that what I show
to you, your eyes will clearly see;
160 for now I know that you require
objects of sight instead of words,
by which faith whispers in your ears
too deaf to hear. I understand,
for you necessity demands

165 that through the eyes faith find her way
to her reception in your hearts.
OCCIDENT Exactly so. I do prefer
to see the things you would impart.

Scene 5

RELIGION Then come.
ZEAL   Religion, answer me:
what metaphor will you employ
to represent these mysteries?
RELIGION An *auto*[1] will make visible
5 through allegory images
of what America must learn
and Occident implores to know
about the questions that now burn
within him so.
ZEAL   What will you call
10 this play in allegory cast?
RELIGION *Divine Narcissus*,[2] let it be,
because if that unhappy maid
adored an idol which disguised
in such strange symbols the attempt
15 the demon made to counterfeit
the great and lofty mystery
of the most Blessed Eucharist,
then there were also, I surmise,
among more ancient pagans hints
20 of such high marvels symbolized.
ZEAL Where will your drama be performed?
RELIGION In the crown city of Madrid,
which is the center of the Faith,
the seat of Catholic majesty,[3]
25 to whom the Indies owe their best
beneficence, the blessed gift
of Holy Writ, the Gospel light
illuminating all the West.
ZEAL That you should write in Mexico
30 for royal patrons don't you see
to be an impropriety?

1. A short play on a spiritual or religious subject, popular in Spain from medieval times up to the middle of the 18th century.
2. In Greek mythology, a beautiful youth who loved none who became enamored of him. As Ovid told the story (*Metamorphoses* 3.344–510; ca. 10 B.C.E.), the nymph Echo faded to nothing but a voice because he rejected her; after another whom he scorned prayed for vengeance, Narcissus fell in love

with his own image, wasted away, and after death was turned into the flower that bears his name.
3. At the time during which this *loa* is set, Madrid was both home to the Spanish court and the seat of the Holy Roman Empire; Charles I, king of Spain (1500–1558; r. 1516–56) was also Holy Roman Emperor (as Charles V; r. 1519–56).

RELIGION   Is it beyond imagination
that something made in one location
can in another be of use?

35 Furthermore, my writing it
comes, not of whimsical caprice,
but from my vowed obedience
to do what seems beyond my reach.
Well, then, this work, however rough
40 and little polished it might be,
results from my obedience,
and not from any arrogance.

ZEAL   Then answer me, Religion, how
(before you leave the matter now)
45 will you respond when you are chid
for loading the whole Indies on
a stage to transport to Madrid?

RELIGION   The purpose of my play can be
none other than to glorify
50 the Eucharistic Mystery;
and since the cast of characters
are no more than abstractions which
depict the theme with clarity,
then surely no one should object
55 if they are taken to Madrid;
distance can never hinder thought
with persons of intelligence,
nor seas impede exchange of sense.

ZEAL   Then, prostrate at his royal feet,
60 beneath whose strength two worlds are joined,
we beg for pardon of the King;

RELIGION   and from her eminence, the Queen;[4]

AMERICA   whose sovereign and anointed feet
the humble Indies bow to kiss;

65 ZEAL   and from the Royal High Council;

RELIGION   and from the ladies, who bring light
into their hemisphere;

AMERICA   and from
their poets, I most humbly beg
forgiveness for my crude attempt,
70 desiring with these awkward lines
to represent the Mystery.

OCCIDENT   Let's go, for anxiously I long to see
exactly how this God of yours
will give Himself as food to me.

[AMERICA, OCCIDENT, *and* ZEAL *sing:*]

75 The Indies know
and do concede
who is the true

---

4. Isabella of Portugal (1503–1539), who married Charles I (see note 3, above) in 1526.

God of the Seeds.
In loving tears
80 which joy prolongs
we gladly sing
our happy songs.
ALL   Blest be the day
when I could see
85 and worship the
great God of Seeds.
     [*They all exit, dancing and singing.*]

GEORGE LILLO

1693–1739

GEORGE Lillo, the author of eight plays between 1730 and his death in 1739, achieved an importance in eighteenth-century drama that little in his early life seemed to anticipate. A goldsmith-jeweler by trade and a Dissenter (or radical Protestant) by faith, he was born in London in 1693 (or 1691, as baptismal records may suggest) to Dutch and English parents. Those who knew him spoke of his modesty, observance of moral principles, and good sense. To the novelist Henry Fielding, who produced his play *Fatal Curiosity* at the

Title page of the 1731 first edition of *The London Merchant*.

Haymarket Theatre in 1736, Lillo was "one of the best of Men." His first foray into the theater came in 1730 with a ballad opera titled *Silvia, or The Country Burial*. Written in an attempt to replicate the phenomenal success of John Gay's *The Beggar's Opera* (1728), this play drew a mixed response and played only three nights. The following year, Lillo wrote what would become one of the most popular and widely produced plays of the century: THE LONDON MERCHANT; OR, THE HISTORY OF GEORGE BARNWELL. This tragedy of an apprentice's moral downfall represented an important innovation in the development of its genre. By redefining the subject of dramatic tragedy and demonstrating to its increasingly middle-class audience that common individuals were worthy of tragic treatment, *The London Merchant* represents, in the opinion of many, the first modern tragedy.

The source for Lillo's play is a seventeenth-century ballad about a murder in Shropshire. In this ballad, an apprentice named George Barnwell falls into a sexual relationship with Sarah Millwood, a "gallant dainty dame," or woman of pleasure. After stealing money from his master to fund his dalliances with Sarah, Barnwell robs and murders his uncle. In the end, both he and Millwood are arrested and executed, and Barnwell's story becomes a cautionary tale for other youths:

> Take heed of harlots then,
> And their enticing trains,
> For by that means I have been brought
> To hang alive in chains.

Lillo was drawn to this story for its moral dimension and its concern with characters from the nonaristocratic spheres of life. "[T]he more extensively useful the moral of any tragedy is," Lillo wrote in the play's dedicatory epistle (addressed, fittingly, to Sir John Eyles, a prominent member of London's merchant class), "the more excellent that piece must be of its kind." The purpose of tragedy, according to Lillo, is to excite the passions in such a way that those tending toward vice are identified and corrected. To this end, tragic playwrights must no longer restrict themselves to the fortunes of princes and other nobility. "[T]ragedy is so far from losing its dignity by being accommodated to the circumstances of the generality of mankind," Lillo declared, "that it is more truly august in proportion to the extent of its influence and the numbers that are properly affected by it, as it is more truly great to be the instrument of good to many who stand in need of our assistance than to a very small part of that number."

Lillo was not the first dramatist to make common characters and private concerns the subjects of dramatic tragedy. Domestic tragedies such as Thomas Heywood's *A Woman Killed with Kindness* (1603) and the anonymous plays *Arden of Feversham* and *A Yorkshire Tragedy* were popular in the Elizabethan and Jacobean theater. Lillo, who wrote a version of *Arden of Feversham* (staged posthumously in 1759), was certainly aware of this tradition. Nor was Lillo the first to advocate the moral use of theater through exemplary representations of virtue and vice. In the prologue to his play *The Conscious Lovers* (1722), for example, Richard Steele called on playwrights and audiences "to refine the age, / To chasten wit, and moralize the stage." What distinguishes *The London Merchant* from other "plays founded on moral tales in private life" (in Lillo's words) was the extent to which it represented the economic values and mercantilist ideology of a theater audience whose identity, since the Restoration, had grown ever more middle class.

With the expansion of British trade in the late seventeenth and early eighteenth centuries, the merchant class had achieved increasing prominence in British society. Daniel Defoe (author of *Robinson Crusoe* [1719]) called the mercantile profession "certainly the most Noble, most instructive and Improving of any way of Life." In Lillo's play, which is set in Elizabethan England before the attempted invasion of the Spanish Armada in 1588, this belief in the nobil-

ity of mercantilism is articulated by Thorowgood, the London merchant for whom the play is named. In the opening scene, Thorowgood instructs Trueman, one of two apprentices under his supervision, concerning the dignity of his profession. Citing the successful efforts of London's merchants to delay the Spanish invasion by persuading the Bank of Genoa to revoke a loan to the king of Spain, Thorowgood argues that merchants "may sometimes contribute to the safety of their country as they do at all times to its happiness." At the start of act 3, he urges Trueman to study mercantilism as a science "founded in reason and the nature of things." Merchants, who institute commerce between nations remote from each other in geography and customs, promote "arts, industry, peace, and plenty; by mutual benefits diffusing mutual love from pole to pole." The merchant's pursuit of wealth, like Britain's exploitation of foreign resources for its economic advantage, is subsumed within a broader pursuit of the collective good.

By arguing for the virtue of economic activity, Thorowgood reinforces a connection between public activity and personal morality. As initiates into the merchant class, apprentices should take care to avoid "any action that has the appearance of vice or meanness in it." Like his virtuous daughter Maria, Thorowgood himself embodies the ideals that should govern personal and public conduct in the play's ethical universe: moral sensibility, benevolence, modesty, forgiveness, faith in a higher power.

In George Barnwell, the play's protagonist, Lillo explores the temptations that threaten such moral security and the consequences that ensue when virtue is abandoned. Born and raised well (as his name suggests), Barnwell is praised, by those who know him, for his moral rectitude and delicacy of soul. "Never had youth a higher sense of virtue," says Trueman, his friend and moral confidant. Inexperienced in the ways of vice, of course, and therefore initially unable to recognize moral behavior so unlike his own, this innocence is fatally naive. Yet Barnwell's transgressions never obscure his essential goodness. In a departure from the play's source ballad, he accepts Millwood's request to meet her at his house out of courtesy rather than sexual desire, and he continues on the path of moral downfall in part out of a sense of responsibility toward her dissembled protestations of love. While his namesake in the ballad conceives the idea of murdering his uncle in collaboration with Millwood, Lillo's Barnwell, who immediately reacts to the idea with moral horror, must be convinced of its necessity. The actual murder, as Lillo portrays it, happens almost in self-defense: when the hidden Barnwell drops his pistol, his uncle draws his sword, and Barnwell stabs him in return. Finally, of the decisions and actions that lead him deeper into crime nobody is more severely judgmental than Barnwell himself.

By maintaining Barnwell's Christian values throughout his fall, Lillo makes possible his reintegration into the company of the virtuous at the play's end. Having prepared himself for death by reading scriptural assurances of divine forgiveness, Barnwell attains the joy of promised salvation, and the visitors who in turn share his final moments—Thorowgood, Trueman, Maria—reconfirm the bonds of virtuous mentorship, friendship, and love. Barnwell meets his death with spiritual serenity, and

the moral understanding he has achieved transforms his life into a cautionary tale for those who might be confronted with similar temptation. Trueman underscores this lesson in the play's closing lines:

> *In vain*
> *With bleeding hearts and weeping eyes*
>   *we show*
> *A human gen'rous sense of others' woe,*
> *Unless we mark what drew their ruin on,*
> *And, by avoiding that, prevent our own.*

Caught between the tenets of virtue and the allure of vice, Barnwell bears more than passing resemblance to the protagonists of medieval morality drama. Like Everyman, he chooses the path of reclamation and dissociates himself from past temptation. But though the moral, religious, and economic values represented by Thorowgood triumph at the end of *The London Merchant*, Lillo's Millwood acquires a formidable presence within the play's moral landscape. "[S]candal to her own sex, and curse of ours" (in the words of Thorowgood), she acts with duplicity, covetousness, and cruelty toward the innocent Barnwell. At the same time,

The Idle 'Prentice betray'd by his Whore & taken in a Night Cellar with his Accomplice. From William Hogarth's engraving series *Industry and Idleness* (1747).

her character is more complex than Thorowgood's judgment implies. Accompanied by Lucy, her servant and confidante, she recalls the aristocratic women in Restoration comedy in her ingenuity and verbal skill. She is a shrewd and effective economic agent, seeking advantage in a world where sexuality, money, and power are, for women, inescapably intertwined. While Thorowgood stands for the rationality of commerce understood as an instrument of the common good, Millwood views human interaction, economic and otherwise, through the lens of ruthless self-interest. To acquire the wealth she needs in order to secure her place in society, she preys on the innocent, and her success in doing so demonstrates how adept she is at social performance and the game of power. "All actions are alike natural and indifferent to man and beast who devour or are devoured as they meet with others weaker or stronger than themselves," she proclaims. Echoing the philosophy of Thomas Hobbes, who viewed natural human society as a state of perpetual struggle, Millwood represents a less benevolent face of the capitalist society that Thorowgood seeks to moralize.

Millwood's actions clearly make her morally culpable, but her articulate self-defense complicates too easy a view of her as the play's villain. Her vengeful pursuit of men derives from her own exploitation at their hands. "It's a general maxim among the knowing part of mankind," she says, "that a woman without virtue, like a man without honor or honesty, is capable of any action, though never so vile. And yet, what pains will they not take, what arts not use to seduce us from our innocence and make us contemptible and wicked, even in their own opinions?" When Thorowgood and Trueman confront her with her villainy in act 4, she responds with an eloquent condemnation of male society's hypocrisy toward women and its abuse of female innocence. So persuasive is her account that even Thorowgood must acknowledge its validity: "Truth is truth, though from an enemy and spoke in malice." In the eyes of a modern audience, in particular, her unapologetic self-defense gives her a certain stature. Though she meets her death in anguish and despair, it is reported, her refusal to submit to the judgment of others is marked by defiant self-possession: "I know you, and expect no mercy—nay, I ask for none. I have done nothing that I am sorry for." That Lillo would give her voice such force in a play otherwise steeped in Christian self-renunciation has led some modern critics to see her as a tragic figure in her own right.

The social standing of The London Merchant's tragic protagonist and the uneven response to Lillo's first theatrical effort led the author and the producer—Theophilus Cibber, who also played the role of George Barnwell—to schedule its opening at Drury Lane Theater on June 22, 1731, during the theater's off-season, rather than risk an unfavorable response by winter critics. This precaution proved unnecessary. The London Merchant was given seventeen performances that summer and eleven during the regular season that followed, an impressive run by eighteenth-century standards. Of the play's ending, one review noted that "there was hardly a Spectator that did not witness his Approbation by his Tears," while Lady Mary Wortley Montagu declared that whoever did not cry at The London Merchant "must deserve to be hanged." Although Lillo's play was understandably popular with middle-class audiences, its appeal was not restricted to this class; Queen Caroline, for one, requested a copy of the manuscript. Between 1731 and 1747, the play—popularly referred to as "The History (or Tragedy) of George Barnwell"—was staged ninety-six times, and it was performed later in the century on London and provincial stages as well as on the American theater circuit. Because of The London Merchant's salutary moral and economic lessons, the play was a regular holiday offering for audiences of apprentices in productions subsidized by prominent merchants. Stories circulated of apprentices who had been dissuaded from a life of crime by the example of Lillo's protagonist.

The London Merchant was equally admired by writers throughout the eighteenth century. Translated into French, German, and other European languages, the play was praised by Voltaire, Jean-Jacques Rousseau, Friedrich von Schiller, and JOHANN WOLFGANG VON GOETHE. The encyclopedist and philosopher Denis Diderot compared Lillo's play to the tragedies of SOPHOCLES and EURIPIDES. But as tastes changed the play eventually fell out of favor, particularly in Britain. By the last decades of the eighteenth century *The London Merchant* was often performed without its most didactic speeches; and while the play continued to be staged into the early nineteenth century, it was increasingly seen as melodramatic and artificial. Charles Lamb called *The London Merchant* "a nauseous sermon," and Charles Dickens subjected his character Pip to a tedious reading of it in *Great Expectations* (1860–61). This opinion of the play prevailed for much of the twentieth century; thus, although the importance of *The London Merchant* as precursor to the drama of HENRIK IBSEN and ARTHUR MILLER has been widely acknowledged, as recently as 1963 a scholar could pronounce it "a long and dull

play." Since the 1980s, however, a critical reappraisal of Lillo's play has occurred. Approaching *The London Merchant* through new theoretical lenses, recent scholars have explored its mercantilist ideology, its relationship to the institution of apprenticeship, its gender politics, its place within the discourses of nationhood and imperialism, and the history of audience response. Such critical readings have opened up previously unrecognized aspects of *The London Merchant*, revealing fascinating contradictions and new sources of historical and theatrical power. Lillo's play, from this perspective, reflects a moment in the emergence of the modern world when a newly dominant capitalism sought to contain the conflicts and wayward energies out of which it emerged. 　　　　S.G.

The London Merchant;
or, *The History of George Barnwell*

To Sir John Eyles,[1] Baronet, Member of Parliament for, and Alderman of the City of London, and Sub-Governor of the South Sea Company.

Sir,

If tragic poetry be, as Mr. Dryden[2] has somewhere said, the most excellent and most useful kind of writing, the more extensively useful the moral of any tragedy is, the more excellent that piece must be of its kind.

I hope I shall not be thought to insinuate that this, to which I have presumed to prefix your name, is such. That depends on its fitness to answer the end of tragedy: the exciting of the passions in order to the correcting such of them as are criminal, either in their nature or through their excess. Whether the following scenes do this in any tolerable degree is, with the deference that becomes one who would not be thought vain, submitted to your candid and impartial judgment.

What I would infer is this, I think, evident truth: that tragedy is so far from losing its dignity by being accommodated to the circumstances of the generality of mankind that it is more truly august in proportion to the extent of its influence and the numbers that are properly affected by it, as it is more truly

1. A highly respected merchant, Sir John Eyles (1683–1745) served as a member of Parliament (1713–34) and was elected Lord Mayor of London in 1726.
2. John Dryden (1631–1700), dramatist and author of *An Essay of Dramatic Poesy* (1668).

Lillo's reference here is uncertain; however, in his "Discourse concerning the Original and Progress of Satire" (1693) Dryden attributes to Aristotle the claim that "the most perfect work of Poetry is Tragedy."

great to be the instrument of good to many who stand in need of our assistance than to a very small part of that number.

If princes, &c., were alone liable to misfortunes arising from vice or weakness in themselves or others, there would be good reason for confining the characters in tragedy to those of superior rank; but, since the contrary is evident, nothing can be more reasonable than to proportion the remedy to the disease.

I am far from denying that tragedies founded on any instructive and extraordinary events in history, or a well-invented fable where the persons introduced are of the highest rank, are without their use, even to the bulk of the audience. The strong contrast between a Tamerlane and a Bajazet[3] may have its weight with an unsteady people and contribute to the fixing of them in the interest of a prince of the character of the former, when, through their own levity or the arts of designing men, they are rendered factious and uneasy, though they have the highest reason to be satisfied. The sentiments and example of a Cato[4] may inspire his spectators with a just sense of the value of liberty, when they see that honest patriot prefer death to an obligation from a tyrant who would sacrifice the constitution of his country and the liberties of mankind to his ambition or revenge. I have attempted, indeed, to enlarge the province of the graver kind of poetry, and should be glad to see it carried on by some abler hand. Plays founded on moral tales in private life may be of admirable use by carrying conviction to the mind with such irresistible force as to engage all the faculties and powers of the soul in the case of virtue by stifling vice in its first principles. They who imagine this to be too much to be attributed to tragedy must be strangers to the energy of that noble species of poetry. Shakespeare, who has given such amazing proofs of his genius in that as well as in comedy, in his *Hamlet* has the following lines:[5]

> Had he the motive and the cause for passion
> That I have, he would drown the stage with tears
> And cleave the general ear with horrid speech,
> Make mad the guilty, and appall the free,
> Confound the ignorant, and amaze indeed
> The very faculty of eyes and ears.

And farther, in the same speech:

> I've heard that guilty creatures at a play
> Have, by the very cunning of the scene,
> Been so struck to the soul that presently
> They have proclaimed their malefactions.

Prodigious! yet strictly just. But I shan't take up your valuable time with my remarks. Only give me leave just to observe that he seems so firmly persuaded of the power of a well-wrote piece to produce the effect here ascribed to it as to make Hamlet venture his soul on the event and rather trust that than a

3. Characters in Nicholas Rowe's heroic drama *Tamerlane* (1702), based on the actual Timur Lenk (1336–1405), the Turco-Mongol conqueror of much of Asia, and Bayezid I, sultan of the Ottoman Empire (r. 1389–1402). In Rowe's play Tamerlane was understood to represent the British king William III (r. 1689–1702), and the defeated Bajazet was the French monarch Louis XIV (r. 1643–1715).

4. The protagonist of Joseph Addison's *Cato* (1713), a drama based on the last days of Cato the Younger (95–46 B.C.E.), Roman politician who was a constitutionalist and Stoic.

5. Lillo quotes (closely but not exactly) *Hamlet* (1600–01) 2.2.538–43, 566–69, and 580–82.

messenger from the other world, though it assumed, as he expresses it, his noble father's form and assured him that it was his spirit. "I'll have," says Hamlet, "grounds more relative.

> . . . The play's the thing,
>   Wherein I'll catch the conscience of the king."

Such plays are the best answers to them who deny the lawfulness of the stage.[6]

Considering the novelty of this attempt, I thought it would be expected from me to say something in its excuse; and I was unwilling to lose the opportunity of saying something of the usefulness of tragedy in general, and what may be reasonably expected from the farther improvement of this excellent kind of poetry.

Sir, I hope you will not think I have said too much of an art, a mean specimen of which I am ambitious enough to recommend to your favor and protection. A mind conscious of superior worth as much despises flattery as it is above it. Had I found in myself an inclination to so contemptible a vice, I should not have chose Sir John Eyles for my patron. And, indeed, the best-writ panegyric, though strictly true, must place you in a light much inferior to that in which you have long been fixed by the love and esteem of your fellow citizens, whose choice of you for one of their representatives in Parliament has sufficiently declared their sense of your merit. Nor hath the knowledge of your worth been confined to the City.[7] The proprietors in the South Sea Company, in which are included numbers of persons as considerable for their rank, fortune, and understanding as any in the kingdom, gave the greatest proof of their confidence in your capacity and probity when they chose you Sub-Governor of their company at a time when their affairs were in the utmost confusion and their properties in the greatest danger.[8] Nor is the Court insensible of your importance. I shall not therefore attempt your character, nor pretend to add anything to a reputation so well established.

Whatever others may think of a dedication wherein there is so much said of other things and so little of the person to whom it is addressed, I have reason to believe that you will the more easily pardon it on that very account. I am, sir,

> Your most obedient
> Humble servant,
> GEORGE LILLO.

---

6. The "lawfulness" of drama had long been a contentious matter in England. The Puritans condemned drama as immoral and politically dangerous; when they won control of Parliament in 1642 they ordered all theaters closed, a ban that lasted until the restoration of the monarchy in 1660. Restoration drama delighted in being licentious, pleasing the tastes of Charles II and his court, but by the 18th century plays had grown more conservative and moralistic.

7. That is, the City of London, that part of the metropolis situated within its original walls, which by Lillo's time was the country's financial and commercial center.

8. The South Sea Company, which held a monopoly on British trade with most of Asia and South America, was given responsibility for the national debt in 1720; speculative overinvestment in the company resulted in falling stock prices and the panic known as the "South Sea Bubble." Sir John Eyles was appointed subgovernor in 1721.

CHARACTERS

MEN	WOMEN

THOROWGOOD, a London merchant

GEORGE BARNWELL, apprentice to
    Thorowgood

TRUEMAN, apprentice to Thorowgood

BLUNT, servant of Millwood

BARNWELL, uncle of George Barnwell

MARIA, daughter of Thorowgood

MILLWOOD, a lady of pleasure

LUCY, servant of Millwood

Officers with their attendants

KEEPER of the prison

Executioner

FOOTMEN

[SCENE: *London and an adjacent village.*]

Prologue

Spoke by Mr. Cibber, *Jun.*[9]

The Tragic Muse, sublime, delights to show
Princes distrest, and scenes of royal woe;
In awful pomp, majestic, to relate
The fall of nations, or some hero's fate,
5   That scepter'd chiefs may by example know
The strange vicissitude of things below;
What dangers on security attend;
How pride and cruelty in ruin end;
Hence Providence supreme to know, and own°   acknowledge
10   Humanity adds glory to a throne.
    In ev'ry former age, and foreign tongue,
With native grandeur thus the goddess sung.
Upon our stage, indeed, with wish'd success,
You've sometimes seen her in a humbler dress,
15   Great only in distress. When she complains
In Southerne's, Rowe's, or Otway's[1] moving strains,
The brillant drops that fall from each bright eye
The absent pomp, with brighter gems, supply.
Forgive us then, if we attempt to show,
20   In artless strains, a tale of private woe.
A London 'prentice ruin'd is our theme,
Drawn from the fam'd old song[2] that bears his name.
We hope your taste is not so high to scorn
A moral tale, esteem'd ere you were born,
25   Which for a century of rolling years
Has fill'd a thousand thousand eyes with tears.
If thoughtless youth to warn, and shame the age

---

9. As acting manager of Drury Lane Theater, Theophilus Cibber (1703–1758) produced *The London Merchant* and performed the role of George Barnwell. He is "junior" because his father, Colley Cibber, was one of the leading actors of his day (see note 8 to epilogue heading, below).

1. Thomas Southerne (1660–1746), Nicholas Rowe (1674–1718), and Thomas Otway (1652–1685), popular Restoration and early 18th century dramatists whose plays included domestic tragedies.
2. A popular ballad on the life of George Barnwell, published in the 17th century.

From vice destructive, well becomes the stage;
If this example innocence secure,
30 Prevent our guilt, or by reflection cure;
If Millwood's dreadful guilt and sad despair
Commend the virtue of the good and fair,
Though art be wanting, and our numbers fail,
Indulge th'attempt, in justice to the tale.

1.1

[SCENE: *A room in* THOROWGOOD'S *house.*]

[*Enter* THOROWGOOD *and* TRUEMAN.]

TRUEMAN   Sir, the packet[3] from Genoa is arrived.
[*Gives letters.*]

THOROWGOOD   Heaven be praised! The storm that threatened our royal mistress, pure religion, liberty, and laws,
is for a time diverted. The haughty and revengeful
5   Spaniard,[4] disappointed of the loan on which he depended from Genoa, must now attend the slow return of
wealth from his New World to supply his empty coffers
ere he can execute his purposed invasion of our happy
island; by which means time is gained to make such prepa-
10 rations on our part as may, Heaven concurring, prevent
his malice or turn the meditated mischief on himself.

TRUEMAN   He must be insensible, indeed, who is not
affected when the safety of his country is concerned. Sir,
may I know by what means—if I am too bold—

15 THOROWGOOD   Your curiosity is laudable, and I gratify it with
the greater pleasure because from thence you may learn
how honest merchants, as such, may sometimes contribute to the safety of their country as they do at all times to
its happiness; that if hereafter you should be tempted to
20 any action that has the appearance of vice or meanness in
it, upon reflecting on the dignity of our profession, you
may with honest scorn reject whatever is unworthy of it.

TRUEMAN   Should Barnwell, or I, who have the benefit of
your example, by our ill conduct bring any imputation on
25 that honorable name, we must be left without excuse.

THOROWGOOD   You compliment, young man. [TRUEMAN *bows
respectfully.*] Nay, I'm not offended. As the name of merchant never degrades the gentleman, so by no means does
it exclude him. Only take heed not to purchase the charac-
30 ter of complaisant[5] at the expense of your sincerity. But to
answer your question. The bank of Genoa had agreed, at
excessive interest and on good security, to advance the
King of Spain a sum of money sufficient to equip his vast
Armado.[6] Of which, our peerless Elizabeth (more than in

3. That is, packet boat, a vessel carrying passengers and mail on a regular schedule.
4. Philip II of Spain (r. 1556–98). This reference sets the play's action before 1588, when

Philip dispatched the Spanish Armada in an
unsuccessful attempt to invade England.
5. Being amiable (here with a sense of flattery).
6. An obsolete spelling of *armada*.

35   name the mother of her people) being well informed,
sent Walsingham,[7] her wise and faithful secretary, to consult the merchants of this loyal city, who all agreed to
direct their several agents to influence, if possible, the
Genoese to break their contract with the Spanish court.
40   'Tis done. The state and bank of Genoa, having mat-
urely weighed and rightly judged of their true interest,
prefer the friendship of the merchants of London to that
of a monarch who proudly styles himself King of both
Indies.[8]

45 TRUEMAN Happy success of prudent councils! What an
expense of blood and treasure is here saved! Excellent
queen! Oh, how unlike to former princes who made the
danger of foreign enemies a pretense to oppress their
subjects by taxes great and grievous to be borne.

50 THOROWGOOD Not so our gracious Queen, whose richest
exchequer° is her people's love, as their happiness her   *treasury*
greatest glory.

TRUEMAN On these terms to defend us is to make our protection a benefit worthy her who confers it and well
55   worth our acceptance.—Sir, have you any commands for
me at this time?

THOROWGOOD Only to look carefully over the files to see
whether there are any tradesmen's bills unpaid and, if
there are, to send and discharge 'em. We must not let arti-
60   ficers° lose their time, so useful to the public and their   *manufacturers*
families, in unnecessary attendance.

[*Exit* TRUEMAN.]

1.2[9]

[*Enter* MARIA.]

THOROWGOOD Well, Maria, have you given orders for the
entertainment? I would have it in some measure worthy
the guests. Let there be plenty and of the best, that the
courtiers, though they should deny us citizens polite-
5   ness,[1] may at least commend our hospitality.

MARIA Sir, I have endeavored not to wrong your well-
known generosity by an ill-timed parsimony.

THOROWGOOD Nay, 'twas a needless caution. I have no
cause to doubt your prudence.

10 MARIA Sir, I find myself unfit for conversation at present.
I should but increase the number of the company without adding to their satisfaction.

THOROWGOOD Nay, my child, this melancholy must not be
indulged.

7. Sir Francis Walsingham (ca. 1532–1590),
secretary of state under Elizabeth I (1533–
1603; r. 1558–1603).
8. That is, the East Indies in the Pacific and Indian oceans and the West Indies in the Atlantic.

9. *The London Merchant* employs "French
scenes"—that is, a new scene begins whenever characters enter or exit the stage.
1. That is, even if they refuse to acknowledge
in us any refinement.

15   MARIA   Company will but increase it. I wish you would dispense with° my absence; solitude best suits my present   *allow, pardon*
temper.

  THOROWGOOD   You are not insensible that it is chiefly on
your account these noble lords do me the honor so fre-
20   quently to grace my board. Should you be absent, the
disappointment may make them repent their condescen-
sion[2] and think their labor lost.

  MARIA   He that shall think his time or honor lost in visiting you can set no real value on your daughter's com-
25   pany, whose only merit is that she is yours. The man of
quality, who chooses to converse with a gentleman and
merchant of your worth and character, may confer honor
by so doing, but he loses none.

  THOROWGOOD   Come, come, Maria, I need not tell you that
30   a young gentleman may prefer your conversation to mine,
yet intend me no disrespect at all, for, though he may lose
no honor in my company, 'tis very natural for him to
expect more pleasure in yours. I remember the time when
the company of the greatest and wisest man in the king-
35   dom would have been insipid and tiresome to me if it had
deprived me of an opportunity of enjoying your mother's.

  MARIA   Yours no doubt was as agreeable to her, for generous
minds know no pleasure in society but where 'tis mutual.

  THOROWGOOD   Thou[3] know'st I have no heir, no child but
40   thee; the fruits of many years' successful industry must
all be thine. Now it would give me pleasure great as my
love to see on whom you would bestow it. I am daily solicited by men of the greatest rank and merit for leave to
address you, but I have hitherto declined it in hopes
45   that, by observation, I should learn which way your inclination tends, for, as I know love to be essential to happiness in the marriage state, I had rather my approbation
should confirm your choice than direct it.

  MARIA   What can I say? How shall I answer as I ought this
50   tenderness so uncommon even in the best of parents?
But you are without example. Yet, had you been less
indulgent, I had been most wretched. That I look on the
crowd of courtiers that visit here with equal esteem but
equal indifference you have observed, and I must needs
55   confess. Yet, had you asserted your authority and insisted
on a parent's right to be obeyed, I had submitted and to
my duty sacrificed my peace.

  THOROWGOOD   From your perfect obedience in every other
instance I feared as much, and therefore would leave
60   you without a bias in an affair wherein your happiness is
so immediately concerned.

  MARIA   Whether from a want of that just ambition that

---

2. Affability toward social inferiors (without the negative implication of today's usage).

3. "Thou" and "thee" are the more familiar forms of the second-person pronoun.

would become your daughter, or from some other cause,
I know not, but I find high birth and titles don't recom-
65 mend the man who owns them to my affections.

THOROWGOOD   I would not that they should, unless his
merit recommends him more. A noble birth and fortune,
though they make not a bad man good, yet they are a
real advantage to a worthy one and place his virtues in
70 the fairest light.

MARIA   I cannot answer for my inclinations, but they shall
ever be submitted to your wisdom and authority; and, as
you will not compel me to marry where I cannot love, so
love shall never make me act contrary to my duty. Sir,
75 have I your permission to retire?

THOROWGOOD.   I'll see you to your chamber.

[*Exeunt.*°]   *They exit (Latin)*

1.3

[SCENE: *A room in* MILLWOOD's *house.*]

[MILLWOOD. LUCY, *waiting.*⁴]

MILLWOOD   How do I look today, Lucy?

LUCY   Oh, killingly, madam! A little more red, and you'll be
irresistible! But why this more than ordinary care of your
dress and complexion? What new conquest are you aim-
5 ing at?

MILLWOOD   A conquest would be new indeed!

LUCY   Not to you, who make 'em every day—but to me—
well, 'tis what I'm never to expect, unfortunate as I am.
But your wit and beauty—

10 MILLWOOD   First made me a wretch, and still continue me
so. Men, however generous or sincere to one another,
are all selfish hypocrites in their affairs with us. We are
no otherwise esteemed or regarded by them but as we
contribute to their satisfaction.

15 LUCY   You are certainly, madam, on the wrong side in this
argument. Is not the expense all theirs? And I am sure it
is our own fault if we haven't our share of the pleasure.

MILLWOOD   We are but slaves to men.

LUCY   Nay, 'tis they that are slaves most certainly, for we
20 lay them under contribution.⁵

MILLWOOD   Slaves have no property—no, not even in themselves. All is the victor's.

LUCY   You are strangely arbitrary in your principles, madam.

MILLWOOD   I would have my conquests complete, like those
25 of the Spaniards in the New World, who first plundered
the natives of all the wealth they had and then condemned
the wretches to the mines for life to work for more.

LUCY   Well, I shall never approve of your scheme of
government. I should think it much more politic, as
30 well as just, to find my subjects an easier employment.

---

4. That is, in attendance, as a servant.   5. That is, exact contributions from them.

MILLWOOD   It's a general maxim among the knowing part of
   mankind that a woman without virtue, like a man without
   honor or honesty, is capable of any action, though never
   so vile. And yet, what pains will they not take, what arts
35   not use, to seduce us from our innocence and make us
   contemptible and wicked, even in their own opinions?
   Then, is it not just the villains, to their cost, should find us
   so? But guilt makes them suspicious and keeps them on
   their guard. Therefore we can take advantage only of the
40   young and innocent part of the sex who, having never
   injured women, apprehend no injury from them.
LUCY   Aye, they must be young indeed.
MILLWOOD   Such a one, I think, I have found. As I've passed
   through the City, I have often observed him receiving and
45   paying considerable sums of money; from thence I conclude he is employed in affairs of consequence.
LUCY   Is he handsome?
MILLWOOD   Aye, aye, the stripling is well made.
LUCY   About—
50 MILLWOOD   Eighteen.
LUCY   Innocent, handsome, and about eighteen! You'll be
   vastly happy. Why, if you manage well, you may keep him
   to yourself these two or three years.
MILLWOOD   If I manage well, I shall have done with him
55   much sooner. Having long had a design on him, and
   meeting him yesterday, I made a full stop and, gazing
   wishfully on his face, asked him his name. He blushed
   and, bowing very low, answered, "George Barnwell." I
   begged his pardon for the freedom I had taken and told
60   him that he was the person I had long wished to see and
   to whom I had an affair of importance to communicate, at
   a proper time and place. He named a tavern; I talked of
   honor and reputation, and invited him to my house. He
   swallowed the bait, promised to come, and this is the time
65   I expect him. [*Knocking at the door.*] Somebody knocks.
   D'ye hear, I am at home to nobody today but him.

                              [*Exit* LUCY.]

1.4

MILLWOOD   Less° affairs must give way to those of more   *Lesser*
   consequence, and I am strangely mistaken if this does not
   prove of great importance to me and him too, before I have
   done with him. Now, after what manner shall I receive
5   him? Let me consider. What manner of person am I to receive? He is young, innocent, and bashful. Therefore I must
   take care not to shock him at first. But then, if I have any
   skill in physiognomy,[6] he is amorous and, with a little assistance, will soon get the better of his modesty. I'll trust to
10   nature, who does wonders in these matters. If to seem

---

6. The art of judging character and temperament from facial features.

what one is not in order to be the better liked for what one really is, if to speak one thing and mean the direct contrary, be art in a woman, I know nothing of nature.

1.5

[*To her,* BARNWELL, *bowing very low.* LUCY *at a distance.*]

MILLWOOD   Sir, the surprise and joy!

BARNWELL   Madam—

MILLWOOD   This is such a favor—[*Advancing*]

BARNWELL   Pardon me, madam.

5 MILLWOOD   So unhoped for—[*Still advances.*]

[BARNWELL *salutes[7] her, and retires in confusion.*]

MILLWOOD   To see you here! Excuse the confusion—

BARNWELL   I fear I am too bold—

MILLWOOD   Alas, sir, all my apprehensions proceed from my fears of your thinking me so. Please, sir, to sit. I am as
10 much at a loss how to receive this honor as I ought as I am surprised at your goodness in conferring it.

BARNWELL   I thought you had expected me. I promised to come.

MILLWOOD   That is the more surprising. Few men are such
15 religious observers of their word.

BARNWELL   All who are honest are.

MILLWOOD   To one another. But we silly women are seldom thought of consequence enough to gain a place in your remembrance. [*Laying her hand on his, as by accident.*]

20 BARNWELL [*aside*]   Her disorder is so great she don't perceive she has laid her hand on mine. Heaven! How she trembles! What can this mean?

MILLWOOD   The interest I have in all that relates to you (the reason of which you shall know hereafter) excites
25 my curiosity and, were I sure you would pardon my presumption, I should desire to know your real sentiments on a very particular affair.

BARNWELL   Madam, you may command my poor thoughts on any subject. I have none that I would conceal.

30 MILLWOOD   You'll think me bold.

BARNWELL   No, indeed.

MILLWOOD   What, then, are your thoughts of love?

BARNWELL   If you mean the love of women, I have not thought of it all. My youth and circumstances make
35 such thoughts improper in me yet. But if you mean the general love we owe to mankind, I think no one has more of it in his temper than myself. I don't know that person in the world whose happiness I don't wish and wouldn't promote, were it in my power. In an especial
40 manner I love my uncle, and my master, but, above all, my friend.

7. Makes a gesture of greeting.

MILLWOOD   You have a friend, then, whom you love?

BARNWELL   As he does me, sincerely.

MILLWOOD   He is, no doubt, often blessed with your com-
45   pany and conversation.

BARNWELL   We live in one house together, and both serve
the same worthy merchant.

MILLWOOD   Happy, happy youth! Whoe'er thou art, I envy
thee, and so must all who see and know this youth.
50   What have I lost by being formed a woman! I hate my
sex, myself! Had I been a man, I might, perhaps, have
been as happy in your friendship as he who now enjoys
it. But, as it is—oh!

BARNWELL   [aside]   I never observed women before, or this
55   is sure the most beautiful of her sex! —You seem disordered, madam. May I know the cause?

MILLWOOD   Do not ask me. I can never speak it, whatever
is the cause. I wish for things impossible. I would be a
servant, bound to the same master as you are, to live in
60   one house with you.

BARNWELL   [aside]   How strange, and yet how kind, her
words and actions are! And the effect they have on me is
as strange. I feel desires I never knew before. I must be
gone, while I have power to go. —Madam, I humbly take
65   my leave.

MILLWOOD   You will not, sure, leave me so soon!

BARNWELL   Indeed, I must.

MILLWOOD   You cannot be so cruel! I have prepared a poor
supper at which I promised myself your company.

70   BARNWELL   I am sorry I must refuse the honor that you
designed me, but my duty to my master calls me hence.
I never yet neglected his service. He is so gentle and so
good a master that should I wrong him, though he might
forgive me, I never should forgive myself.

75   MILLWOOD   Am I refused, by the first man, the second favor I ever stopped to ask? Go then, thou proud hardhearted youth! But know you are the only man that could
be found who would let me sue twice for greater favors.

BARNWELL   [aside]   What shall I do? How shall I go or stay?

80   MILLWOOD   Yet do not, do not leave me! I wish my sex's
pride would meet your scorn, but when I look upon you,
when I behold those eyes—oh, spare my tongue, and let
my blushes speak! This flood of tears to that will force
their way and declare what woman's modesty should
85   hide.

BARNWELL   [aside]   Oh, Heavens! She loves me, worthless
as I am. Her looks, her words, her flowing tears confess
it. And can I leave her then? Oh, never, never! —Madam,
dry up those tears. You shall command me always. I will
90   stay here forever, if you'd have me.

LUCY   [aside]   So! She has wheedled him out of his virtue
of obedience already and will strip him of all the rest, one

after another, till she has left him as few as her ladyship
or myself.

95 MILLWOOD   Now you are kind indeed, but I mean not to
detain you always. I would have you shake off all slavish
obedience to your master, but you may serve him still.

LUCY [*aside*]   Serve him still! Aye, or he'll have no opportunity of fingering his cash, and then he'll not serve your
100   end, I'll be sworn.

1.6

[*To them*, BLUNT.]

BLUNT   Madam, supper's on the table.

MILLWOOD   Come, sir, you'll excuse all defects. My
thoughts were too much employed on my guest to
observe the entertainment.°   *elegant meal*

[*Exeunt* BARNWELL *and* MILLWOOD.]

1.7

BLUNT   What is all this preparation, this elegant supper,
variety of wines, and music? For the entertainment of
that young fellow?

LUCY   So it seems.

5 BLUNT   What! Is our mistress turned fool at last? She's in
love with him, I suppose.

LUCY   I suppose not. But she designs to make him in love
with her if she can.

BLUNT   What will she get by that? He seems under age
10   and can't be supposed to have much money.

LUCY   But his master has, and that's the same thing, as
she'll manage it.

BLUNT   I don't like this fooling with a handsome young fellow. While she's endeavoring to ensnare him, she may be
15   caught herself.

LUCY   Nay, were she like me that would certainly be the
consequence, for I confess there is something in youth
and innocence that moves me mightily.

BLUNT   Yes, so does the smoothness and plumpness of a
20   partridge move a mighty desire in the hawk to be the destruction of it.

LUCY   Why, birds are their prey as men are ours, though,
as you observed, we are sometimes caught ourselves. But
that, I dare say, will never be the case with our mistress.

25 BLUNT   I wish it may prove so, for you know we all depend
upon her. Should she trifle away her time with a young
fellow that there's nothing to be got by, we must all starve.

LUCY   There's no danger of that, for I am sure she has no
view in this affair but interest.°   *i.e., self-interest*

30 BLUNT   Well, and what hopes are there of success in that?

LUCY   The most promising that can be. 'Tis true, the lad

has his scruples, but she'll soon teach him to answer them by stifling his conscience. Oh, the lad is in a hopeful way, depend upon't.

[*Exeunt.*]

1.8

[BARNWELL *and* MILLWOOD *at an entertainment.*]

BARNWELL   What can I answer? All that I know is that you are fair and I am miserable.

MILLWOOD   We are both so, and yet the fault is in ourselves.

BARNWELL   To ease our present anguish by plunging into
5   guilt is to buy a moment's pleasure with an age of pain.

MILLWOOD   I should have thought the joys of love as lasting as they are great. If ours prove otherwise, 'tis your inconstancy must make them so.

BARNWELL   The law of Heaven will not be reversed, and
10   that requires us to govern our passions.

MILLWOOD   To give us sense of beauty and desires, and yet forbid us to taste and be happy, is cruelty to nature. Have we passions only to torment us?

BARNWELL   To hear you talk, though in the cause of vice,
15   to gaze upon your beauty, press your hand, and see your snow-white bosom heave and fall, enflames my wishes. My pulse beats high. My senses all are in a hurry, and I am on the rack of wild desire. Yet, for a moment's guilty pleasure, shall I lose my innocence, my peace of mind,
20   and hopes of solid happiness?

MILLWOOD   Chimeras[8] all!
                                    Come on with me and prove
            No joy's like woman kind, nor Heav'n like love.

BARNWELL   I would not—yet I must on.
            Reluctant thus, the merchant quits his ease
25   And trusts to rocks and sands and stormy seas;
            In hopes some unknown golden coast to find,
            Commits himself, though doubtful, to the wind; ⎫
            Longs much for joys to come, yet mourns those left behind. ⎬

[*Exeunt.*]

The End of the First Act

2.1

[SCENE: *A room in* THOROWGOOD'S *house.*]

[*Enter* BARNWELL.]

BARNWELL   How strange are all things round me! Like some thief who treads forbidden ground, fearful I enter each apartment of this well-known house. To guilty love, as if that was too little, already have I added breach of trust.[9]

8. Unreal creations of the mind.
9. Barnwell apparently has given Millwood   the money that he had been carrying for his
                                            master.

5   A thief! Can I know myself that wretched thing and look
       my honest friend and injured master in the face? Though
       hypocrisy may a while conceal my guilt, at length it will be
       known, and public shame and ruin must ensue. In the
10   meantime, what must be my life? Ever to speak a lan-
       guage foreign to my heart, hourly to add to the number of
       my crimes to conceal 'em. Sure, such was the condition of
       the grand apostate[1] when first he lost his purity. Like me,
       disconsolate he wandered, and, while yet in Heaven, bore
15   all his future Hell about him.

2.2

[*Enter* TRUEMAN.]

TRUEMAN   Barnwell! Oh, how I rejoice to see you safe! So
       will our master and his gentle daughter, who during your
       absence often inquired after you.

BARNWELL [*aside*] Would he were gone! His officious°   attentive
5   love will pry into the secrets of my soul.

TRUEMAN   Unless you knew the pain the whole family has
       felt on your account, you can't conceive how much you
       are beloved. But why thus cold and silent? When my
       heart is full of joy for your return, why do you turn away?
10   Why thus avoid me? What have I done? How am I al-
       tered since you saw me last? Or rather, what have you
       done? And why are you thus changed, for I am still the
       same.

BARNWELL [*aside*] What have I done, indeed!

15 TRUEMAN   Not speak, nor look upon me?

BARNWELL [*aside*] By my face he will discover all I would
       conceal. Methinks already I begin to hate him.

TRUEMAN   I cannot bear this usage from a friend, one
       whom till now I ever found so loving, whom yet I love,
20   though this unkindness strikes at the root of friendship
       and might destroy it in any breast but mine.

BARNWELL [*turning to him*] I am not well. Sleep has
       been a stranger to these eyes since you beheld them
       last.

25 TRUEMAN   Heavy they look, indeed, and swoll'n with tears.
       Now they overflow. Rightly did my sympathizing heart
       forebode last night, when thou wast absent, something
       fatal to our peace.

BARNWELL   Your friendship engages you too far. My trou-
30   bles, whate'er they are, are mine alone. You have no
       interest in them, nor ought your concern for me give you
       a moment's pain.

TRUEMAN   You speak as if you knew of friendship noth-
       ing but the name. Before I saw your grief I felt it. Since

1. That is, the renegade fallen angel, Lucifer.

35   we parted last I have slept no more than you, but pen-
      sive in my chamber sat alone and spent the tedious night
      in wishes for your safety and return. E'en now, though
      ignorant of the cause, your sorrow wounds me to the
      heart.

40 BARNWELL   'Twill not be always thus. Friendship and all
      engagements cease as circumstances and occasions vary,
      and, since you once may hate me, perhaps it might be
      better for us both that now you loved me less.

   TRUEMAN   Sure I but dream! Without a cause would Barn-
45   well use me thus? Ungenerous and ungrateful youth,
      farewell! I shall endeavor to follow your advice. [Going]
      [Aside] Yet, stay. Perhaps I am too rash and angry when
      the cause demands compassion. Some unforeseen
      calamity may have befallen him too great to bear.

50 BARNWELL [aside]   What part am I reduced to act! 'Tis vile
      and base to move his temper thus, the best of friends
      and men.

   TRUEMAN   I am to blame. Prithee, forgive me, Barnwell.
      Try to compose your ruffled mind and let me know the
55   cause that thus transports you from yourself. My friendly
      counsel may restore your peace.

   BARNWELL   All that is possible for man to do for man your
      generous friendship may effect but, here, even that's in
      vain.

60 TRUEMAN   Something dreadful is laboring in your breast.
      Oh, give it vent and let me share your grief! 'Twill ease
      your pain, should it admit no cure, and make it lighter by
      the part I bear.

   BARNWELL   Vain supposition! My woes increase by being
65   observed. Should the cause be known, they would exceed
      all bounds.

   TRUEMAN   So well I know thy honest heart, guilt cannot
      harbor there.

   BARNWELL [aside]   Oh, torture insupportable!

70 TRUEMAN   Then why am I excluded? Have I a thought I
      would conceal from you?

   BARNWELL   If still you urge me on this hated subject, I'll
      never enter more beneath this roof nor see your face
      again.

75 TRUEMAN   'Tis strange. But I have done. Say but you hate
      me not.

   BARNWELL   Hate you? I am not that monster yet.

   TRUEMAN   Shall our friendship still continue?

   BARNWELL   It's a blessing I never was worthy of, yet now
80   must stand on terms,[2] and but upon conditions can con-
      firm it.

   TRUEMAN   What are they?

2. Insist on specified conditions.

BARNWELL   Never hereafter, though you should wonder
   at my conduct, desire to know more than I am willing
85 to reveal.

TRUEMAN   'Tis hard but, upon any conditions, I must be
   your friend.

BARNWELL   Then, as much as one lost to himself can be
   another's, I am yours.

   [*Embracing.*]

90 TRUEMAN   Be ever so, and may Heaven restore your peace.

BARNWELL   Will yesterday return? We have heard the glorious sun, that till then incessant rolled, once stopped
   his rapid course, and once went back. The dead have
   risen, and parched rocks poured forth a liquid stream to
95 quench a people's thirst; the sea divided and formed
   walls of water, while a whole nation passed in safety
   through its sandy bosom. Hungry lions have refused
   their prey; and men, unhurt, have walked amidst consuming flames.[3] But never yet did time, once past, re-
100 turn.

TRUEMAN   Though the continued chain of time has never
   once been broke, nor ever will, but uninterrupted must
   keep on its course till, lost in eternity, it ends there
   where it first begun, yet, as Heaven can repair whatever
105 evils time can bring upon us, he who trusts Heaven
   ought never to despair.—But business requires our
   attendance—business, the youth's best preservative
   from ill, as idleness his worst of snares. Will you go with
   me?

110 BARNWELL   I'll take a little time to reflect on what has
   passed and follow you.

   [*Exit* TRUEMAN.]

2.3

BARNWELL   I might have trusted Trueman to have applied
   to my uncle to have repaired the wrong I have done my
   master. But what of Millwood? Must I expose her too?
   Ungenerous and base! Then Heaven requires it not. But
5 Heaven requires that I forsake her. What! Never see her
   more? Does Heaven require that? I hope I may see her,
   and Heaven not be offended. Presumptuous hope!
   Dearly already have I proved my frailty. Should I once
   more tempt Heaven, I may be left to fall never to rise
10 again. Yet shall I leave her, forever leave her, and not let
   her know the cause? She who loves me with such a
   boundless passion! Can cruelty be duty? I judge of what
   she then must feel by what I now endure. The love of life

---

3. For the biblical wonders to which Barnwell refers, see Joshua 10.13, John 11.38–44, Numbers 20.8–11, Exodus 14.21–22, Daniel 6.16–23, and Daniel 3.19–27.

and fear of shame, opposed by inclination strong as
15   death or shame, like wind and tide in raging conflict met
     when neither can prevail, keep me in doubt. How then
     can I determine?

2.4

[*Enter* THOROWGOOD.]

THOROWGOOD   Without a cause assigned or notice given,
     to absent yourself last night was a fault, young man, and
     I came to chide you for it but hope I am prevented.[4] That
     modest blush, the confusion so visible in your face,
5   speak grief and shame. When we have offended Heaven,
     it requires no more. And shall man, who needs himself
     to be forgiven, be harder to appease? If my pardon or love
     be of moment to° your peace, look up, secure of both.   *important to*
BARNWELL [*aside*]   This goodness has o'ercome me. —Oh,
10   sir, you know not the nature and extent of my offense,
     and I should abuse your mistaken bounty to receive 'em.
     Though I had rather die than speak my shame, though
     racks could not have forced the guilty secret from my
     breast, your kindness has.
15 THOROWGOOD   Enough, enough! Whate'er it be, this con-
     cern shows you're convinced, and I am satisfied. [*Aside.*]
     How painful is the sense of guilt to an ingenuous mind!
     Some youthful folly which it were prudent not to inquire
     into. When we consider the frail condition of humanity'
20   it may raise our pity, not our wonder, that youth should
     go astray when reason, weak at the best when opposed to
     inclination, scarce formed and wholly unassisted by ex-
     perience, faintly contends or willingly becomes the slave
     of sense. The state of youth is much to be deplored, and
25   the more so because they see it not, they being then to
     danger most exposed when they are least prepared for
     their defense.
BARNWELL   It will be known, and you recall your pardon
     and abhor me.
30 THOROWGOOD   I never will, so Heaven confirm to me the
     pardon of my offenses. Yet, be upon your guard in this
     gay thoughtless season of your life. Now, when the sense
     of pleasure's quick and passion high, the voluptuous
     appetites, raging and fierce, demand the strongest curb.
35   Take heed of a relapse. When vice becomes habitual, the
     very power of leaving it is lost.
BARNWELL   Hear me, then, on my knees confess.
THOROWGOOD   I will not hear a syllable more upon this
     subject. It were not mercy, but cruelty, to hear what
40   must give you such torment to reveal.

---

4. That is, my rebuke is anticipated (by your own self-reproach).

BARNWELL   This generosity amazes and distracts me.

THOROWGOOD   This remorse makes thee dearer to me than
if thou hadst never offended. Whatever is your fault, of
this I'm certain: 'twas harder for you to offend than me
45   to pardon.   [*Exit* THOROWGOOD.]

2.5

BARNWELL   Villain, villain, villain! Basely to wrong so
excellent a man! Should I again return to folly—detested
thought! But what of Millwood, then? Why, I renounce
her. I give her up! The struggle's over and virtue has pre-
5   vailed. Reason may convince, but gratitude compels.
This unlooked-for generosity has saved me from destruction. [*Going*]

2.6

[*To him, a* FOOTMAN.]

FOOTMAN   Sir, two ladies from your uncle in the country
desire to see you.

BARNWELL [*aside*]   Who should they be?—Tell them I'll
wait upon 'em.

[*Exit* FOOTMAN.]

2.7

BARNWELL   Methinks I dread to see 'em. Guilt, what a
coward hast thou made me! Now everything alarms me.

[*Exit.*]

2.8

[SCENE: *Another room in* THOROWGOOD's *house.*]

[MILLWOOD *and* LUCY, *and to them, a* FOOTMAN.]

FOOTMAN   Ladies, he'll wait upon you immediately.

MILLWOOD   'Tis very well. I thank you.

[*Exit* FOOTMAN.]

2.9

[*Enter* BARNWELL.]

BARNWELL   Confusion!° Millwood!   (*an exclamation*)

MILLWOOD   That angry look tells me that here I'm an un-
welcome guest. I feared as much. The unhappy are so
everywhere.

5   BARNWELL   Will nothing but my utter ruin content you?

MILLWOOD   Unkind and cruel! Lost myself, your happiness is now my only care.

BARNWELL   How did you gain admission?

MILLWOOD   Saying we were desired by your uncle to visit
10   and deliver a message to you, we were received by the

family without suspicion and with much respect directed
here.

BARNWELL   Why did you come at all?

MILLWOOD   I never shall trouble you more. I'm come to
15   take my leave forever. Such is the malice of my fate. I go
hopeless, despairing ever to return. This hour is all I
have left me. One short hour is all I have to bestow on
love and you, for whom I thought the longest life too
short.

20   BARNWELL   Then we are met to part forever?

MILLWOOD   It must be so. Yet think not that time or absence ever shall put a period to my grief or make me love
you less. Though I must leave you, yet condemn me not.

BARNWELL   Condemn you? No, I approve your resolution,
25   and rejoice to hear it. 'Tis just; 'tis necessary. I have well
weighed and found it so.

LUCY [aside]   I'm afraid the young man has more sense
than she thought he had.

BARNWELL   Before you came I had determined never to
30   see you more.

MILLWOOD [aside]   Confusion!

LUCY [aside]   Aye, we are all out! This is a turn so unexpected that I shall make nothing of my part. They must
e'en play the scene betwixt themselves.

35   MILLWOOD   'Twas some relief to think, though absent, you
would love me still. But to find, though Fortune had
been kind, that you, more cruel and inconstant, had resolved to cast me off—this, as I never could expect,
I have not learnt to bear!

40   BARNWELL   I am sorry to hear you blame in me a resolution that so well becomes us both.

MILLWOOD   I have reason for what I do, but you have
none.

BARNWELL   Can we want a reason for parting, who have so
45   many to wish we never had met?

MILLWOOD   Look on me, Barnwell! Am I deformed or old,
that satiety so soon succeeds enjoyment? Nay, look
again! Am I not she whom yesterday you thought the
fairest and the kindest of her sex? Whose hand, trem-
50   bling with ecstasy, you pressed and molded thus, while
on my eyes you gazed with such delight as if desire increased by being fed?

BARNWELL   No more! Let me repent my former follies, if
possible, without remembering what they were.

55   MILLWOOD   Why?

BARNWELL   Such is my frailty that 'tis dangerous.

MILLWOOD   Where is the danger, since we are to part?

BARNWELL   The thought of that already is too painful.

MILLWOOD   If it be painful to part, then I may hope at
60   least you do not hate me?

BARNWELL   No, no, I never said I did! [*Aside*] Oh, my
heart!

MILLWOOD   Perhaps you pity me?

BARNWELL   I do, I do. Indeed, I do!

65 MILLWOOD   You'll think upon me?

BARNWELL   Doubt it not, while I can think at all.

MILLWOOD   You may judge an embrace at parting too great
a favor, though it would be the last? [*He draws back.*] A
look shall then suffice. Farewell, forever!

[*Exeunt* MILLWOOD *and* LUCY.]

2.10

BARNWELL   If to resolve to suffer be to conquer, I have
conquered. Painful victory!

2.11

[*Re-enter* MILLWOOD *and* LUCY.]

MILLWOOD   One thing I had forgot: I never must return to
my own house again. This I thought proper to let you
know, lest your mind should change and you should seek
in vain to find me there. Forgive this second intrusion. I
5   only came to give you this caution, and that, perhaps,
was needless.

BARNWELL   I hope it was. Yet, it is kind, and I must thank
you for it.

MILLWOOD   [*to* LUCY]   My friend, your arm. —Now I am
10   gone forever. [*Going*]

BARNWELL   One thing more. Sure, there's no danger in my
knowing where you go? If you think otherwise—

MILLWOOD   [*weeping*]   Alas!

LUCY   [*aside*]   We are right, I find. That's my cue. —Ah,
15   dear sir, she's going she knows not whither, but go she
must.

BARNWELL   Humanity obliges me to wish you well. Why
will you thus expose yourself to needless troubles?

LUCY   Nay, there's no help for it. She must quit the town
20   immediately, and the kingdom as soon as possible. It was
no small matter, you may be sure, that could make her
resolve to leave you.

MILLWOOD   No more, my friend, since he for whose dear
sake alone I suffer, and am content to suffer, is kind and
25   pities me. Where'er I wander through wilds and deserts,
benighted and forlorn, that thought shall give me comfort.

BARNWELL   For my sake! Oh, tell me how! Which way am
I so cursed as to bring such ruin on thee?

30 MILLWOOD   No matter; I am contented with my lot.

BARNWELL   Leave me not in this uncertainty.

MILLWOOD   I have said too much.

BARNWELL   How, how am I the cause of your undoing?

MILLWOOD   'Twill but increase your troubles.

35   BARNWELL   My troubles can't be greater than they are.

LUCY   Well, well, sir, if she won't satisfy you, I will.

BARNWELL   I am bound to you beyond expression.

MILLWOOD   Remember, sir, that I desired you not to hear it.

40   BARNWELL   Begin, and ease my racking expectation.

LUCY   Why, you must know my lady here was an only child, but her parents, dying while she was young, left her and her fortune (no inconsiderable one, I assure you) to the care of a gentleman who has a good estate of
45   his own.

MILLWOOD   Aye, aye, the barbarous man is rich enough, but what are riches when compared to love?

LUCY   For a while he performed the office of a faithful guardian, settled her in a house, hired her servants—but
50   you've seen in what manner she lived, so I need say no more of that.

MILLWOOD   How I shall live hereafter, Heaven knows!

LUCY   All things went on as one could wish till, some time ago, his wife dying, he fell violently in love with his
55   charge and would fain have married her. Now, the man is neither old nor ugly, but a good personable sort of a man. But, I don't know how it was, she could never endure him. In short, her ill usage so provoked him that he brought in an account of his executorship, wherein
60   he makes her debtor to him.

MILLWOOD   A trifle in itself, but more than enough to ruin me, whom, by this unjust account, he had stripped of all before.

LUCY   Now she having neither money nor friend, except
65   me who am as unfortunate as herself, he compelled her to pass his account and give bond for the sum he demanded,[5] but still provided handsomely for her and continued his courtship, till being informed by his spies (truly, I suspect some in her own family) that you were
70   entertained at her house and stayed with her all night, he came this morning raving and storming like a madman, talks no more of marriage (so there's no hopes of making up matters that way), but vows her ruin, unless she'll allow him the same favor that he supposes she
75   granted you.

---

5. Lucy seems to be suggesting here that Millwood's (fictitious) guardian forced her to approve withdrawals from her inheritance, which he used for his own ends, and then to provide an I.O.U. for the amount he demanded—in effect, robbing her twice. Both actions would have violated legal statutes governing the guardian-ward relationship.

BARNWELL   Must she be ruined, or find her refuge in
   another's arms?

MILLWOOD   He gave me but an hour to resolve in. That's
   happily spent with you. And now I go.

80 BARNWELL   To be exposed to all the rigors of the various
   seasons, the summer's parching heat and winter's cold,
   unhoused to wander friendless through the unhospitable
   world in misery and want, attended with fear and danger,
   and pursued by malice and revenge. Would'st thou en-
85 dure all this for me, and can I do nothing, nothing to
   prevent it?

LUCY   'Tis really a pity there can be no way found out.

BARNWELL [aside]   Oh, where are all my resolutions now?
   Like early vapors, or the morning dew, chased by the
90 sun's warm beams, they're vanished and lost, as though
   they had never been.

LUCY   Now, I advised her, sir, to comply with the gentleman. That would not only put an end to her troubles but
   make her fortune at once.

95 BARNWELL   Tormenting fiend, away! I had rather perish—
   nay, see her perish—than have her saved by him. I will
   myself prevent her ruin, though with my own. A moment's patience; I'll return immediately.

[Exit BARNWELL.]

2.12

LUCY   'Twas well you came or, by what I can perceive, you
   had lost him.

MILLWOOD   That, I must confess, was a danger I did not
   foresee. I was only afraid he should have come without
5   money. You know a house of entertainment, like mine, is
   not kept with nothing.

LUCY   That's very true. But, then, you should be reasonable in your demands. 'Tis pity to discourage a young
   man.

2.13

[Re-enter BARNWELL.]

BARNWELL [aside]   What am I about to do? Now you
   who boast your reason all-sufficient, suppose yourselves in my condition and determine for me whether
   it's right to let her suffer for my faults or, by this small
5   addition to my guilt, prevent the ill effects of what is
   past.

LUCY [aside]   These young sinners think everything in the
   ways of wickedness so strange. But I could tell him that
   this is nothing but what's very common, for one vice as
10   naturally begets another as a father a son. But he'll
   find out that himself, if he lives long enough.

BARNWELL   Here, take this and with it purchase your deliverance. Return to your house and live in peace and safety.

MILLWOOD   So I may hope to see you there again.

15 BARNWELL   Answer me not but fly, lest in the agonies of
my remorse I take again what is not mine to give and
abandon thee to want and misery.

MILLWOOD   Say but you'll come!

BARNWELL   You are my fate, my Heaven or my Hell. Only
20   leave me now; dispose of me hereafter as you please.

                           [*Exeunt* MILLWOOD *and* LUCY.]

2.14

BARNWELL   What have I done! Were my resolutions
founded on reason and sincerely made? Why, then, has
Heaven suffered me to fall? I sought not the occasion
and, if my heart deceives me not, compassion and gen-
5 erosity were my motives. Is virtue inconsistent with itself? Or are vice and virtue only empty names? Or do
they depend on accidents beyond our power to produce or to prevent, wherein we have no part and yet
must be determined by the event?—But why should I
10 attempt to reason? All is confusion, horror, and remorse. I find I am lost, cast down from all my late-
erected hopes, and plunged again in guilt, yet scarce
know how or why.

        Such undistinguish'd horrors make my brain,
15   Like Hell, the seat of darkness and of pain.

                                [*Exit.*]

           The End of the Second Act

3.1

[SCENE: *A room in* THOROWGOOD's *house.*]

THOROWGOOD   Methinks I would not have you only learn
the method of merchandise and practice it hereafter
merely as a means of getting wealth. 'Twill be well worth
your pains to study it as a science, see how it is founded
5 in reason and the nature of things, how it has promoted
humanity as it has opened and yet keeps up an intercourse between nations far remote from one another in
situation, customs, and religion; promoting arts, industry, peace, and plenty; by mutual benefits diffusing
10 mutual love from pole to pole.

TRUEMAN   Something of this I have considered, and hope,
by your assistance, to extend my thoughts much farther.
I have observed those countries where trade is promoted
and encouraged do not make discoveries to destroy but

15   to improve mankind—by love and friendship to tame the
      fierce and polish the most savage; to teach them the
      advantages of honest traffic by taking from them, with
      their own consent, their useless superfluities, and giving
      them in return what, from their ignorance in manual
20   arts, their situation, or some other accident, they stand
      in need of.

THOROWGOOD   'Tis justly observed. The populous East,
      luxuriant, abounds with glittering gems, bright pearls,
      aromatic spices, and health-restoring drugs. The late-
25   found western world glows with unnumbered veins of
      gold and silver ore. On every climate and on every coun-
      try Heaven has bestowed some good peculiar to itself. It
      is the industrious merchant's business to collect the vari-
      ous blessings of each soil and climate and, with the
30   product of the whole, to enrich his native country. —
      Well! I have examined your accounts. They are not only
      just, as I have always found them, but regularly kept and
      fairly entered. I commend your diligence. Method in
      business is the surest guide. He who neglects it fre-
35   quently stumbles and always wanders perplexed, uncer-
      tain, and in danger. Are Barnwell's accounts ready for my
      inspection? He does not use° to be the last on these   is not accustomed
      occasions.

TRUEMAN   Upon receiving your orders he retired,
40   I thought, in some confusion. If you please, I'll go and
      hasten him. I hope he hasn't been guilty of any
      neglect.

THOROWGOOD   I'm now going to the Exchange.[6] Let him
      know, at my return, I expect to find him ready.

                                        [*Exeunt.*]

3.2

[MARIA, *with a book; sits and reads.*]

MARIA   How forcible is truth! The weakest mind, inspired
      with love of that, fixed and collected in itself, with indif-
      ference beholds the united force of earth and Hell oppos-
      ing. Such souls are raised above the sense of pain or so
5   supported that they regard it not. The martyr cheaply
      purchases his Heaven. Small are his sufferings, great is
      his reward. Not so the wretch who combats love with
      duty when the mind, weakened and dissolved by the soft
      passion, feeble and hopeless, opposes its own desires.
10   What is an hour, a day, a year of pain to a whole life of
      tortures such as these?

---

6. That is, the Royal Exchange, a building where the merchants of London gathered to conduct
business.

3.3

[Enter TRUEMAN.*]*

TRUEMAN   Oh, Barnwell! Oh, my friend, how art thou fallen!

MARIA   Ha! Barnwell? What of him? Speak! Say, what of Barnwell?

5   TRUEMAN   'Tis not to be concealed. I've news to tell of him that will afflict your generous father, yourself, and all who knew him.

MARIA   Defend us, Heaven!

TRUEMAN   I cannot speak it. See there.

[Gives a letter. MARIA *reads.]*

10   MARIA   "Trueman,
I know my absence will surprise my honored master and yourself, and the more when you shall understand that the reason of my withdrawing is my having embezzled part of the cash with which I was entrusted. After this,
15   'tis needless to inform you that I intend never to return again. Though this might have been known by examining my accounts, yet, to prevent that unnecessary trouble and to cut off all fruitless expectations of my return, I have left this from the lost
20   George Barnwell."

TRUEMAN   Lost, indeed! Yet how he should be guilty of what he there charges himself withal° raises my wonder equal   *with*
to my grief. Never had youth a higher sense of virtue. Justly he thought and, as he thought, he practiced. Never
25   was life more regular than his—an understanding uncommon at his years; an open, generous manliness of temper; his manners easy, unaffected, and engaging.

MARIA   This and much more you might have said with truth. He was the delight of every eye and joy of every
30   heart that knew him.

TRUEMAN   Since such he was, and was my friend, can I support his loss? See, the fairest and happiest maid this wealthy city boasts kindly condescends to weep for thy unhappy fate, poor, ruined Barnwell.

35   MARIA   Trueman, do you think a soul so delicate as his, so sensible of shame, can e'er submit to live a slave to vice?

TRUEMAN   Never, never! So well I know him, I'm sure this act of his, so contrary to his nature, must have been caused by some unavoidable necessity.

40   MARIA   Is there no means yet to preserve him?

TRUEMAN   Oh, that there were! But few men recover reputation lost; a merchant, never. Nor would he, I fear, though I should find him, ever be brought to look his injured master in the face.

45   MARIA   I fear as much, and therefore would never have my father know it.

TRUEMAN   That's impossible.

MARIA   What's the sum?

TRUEMAN   'Tis considerable. I've marked it here, to show
50   it, with the letter, to your father at his return.

MARIA   If I should supply the money, could you so dispose
of that and the account as to conceal this unhappy mis-
management from my father?

TRUEMAN   Nothing more easy. But can you intend it?
55   Will you save a helpless wretch from ruin? Oh, 'twere
an act worthy such exalted virtue as Maria's! Sure,
Heaven in mercy to my friend inspired the generous
thought.

MARIA   Doubt not but I would purchase so great a happi-
60   ness at a much dearer price. But how shall he be
found?

TRUEMAN   Trust to my diligence for that. In the meantime, I'll conceal his absence from your father, or find
such excuses for it that the real cause shall never be
65   suspected.

MARIA   In attempting to save from shame one whom we
hope may yet return to virtue, to Heaven and you, the
judges of this action, I appeal whether I have done anything misbecoming my sex and character.

70 TRUEMAN   Earth must approve the deed, and Heaven, I
doubt not, will reward it.

MARIA   If Heaven succeed it,[7] I am well rewarded. A virgin's fame is sullied by suspicion's slightest breath; and,
therefore, as this must be a secret from my father and
75   the world for Barnwell's sake, for mine let it be so to
him.

[*Exeunt.*]

3.4

[SCENE: *A room in* MILLWOOD's *house.*]

[*Enter* LUCY *and* BLUNT.]

LUCY   Well, what do you think of Millwood's conduct
now?

BLUNT   I own it is surprising. I don't know which to admire
most—her feigned, or his real passion—though I have
5   sometimes been afraid that her avarice would discover°   *reveal; betray*
her. But his youth and want of experience make it the
easier to impose on° him.   *deceive*

LUCY   No, it is his love. To do him justice, notwithstanding
his youth, he don't want° understanding; but you men   *doesn't lack*
10   are much easier imposed on in these affairs than your
vanity will allow you to believe. Let me see the wisest of

7. That is, cause it to succeed.

you all as much in love with me as Barnwell is with Millwood, and I'll engage to make as great a fool of him.

BLUNT   And, all circumstances considered, to make as
15   much money of him, too?

LUCY   I can't answer for that. Her artifice in making him
rob his master at first, and the various stratagems by
which she has obliged him to continue in that course,
astonish even me who know her so well.

20   BLUNT   But then you are to consider that the money was
his master's.

LUCY   There was the difficulty of it. Had it been his own,
it had been nothing. Were the world his, she might have
it for a smile. But those golden days are done. He's
25   ruined, and Millwood's hopes of farther profits there are
at an end.

BLUNT   That's no more than we all expected.

LUCY   Being called by his master to make up his accounts,
he was forced to quit his house and service, and wisely
30   flies to Millwood for relief and entertainment.

BLUNT   I have not heard of this before! How did she receive him?

LUCY   As you would expect. She wondered what he
meant, was astonished at his impudence, and, with an
35   air of modesty peculiar to herself, swore so heartily that
she never saw him before that she put me out of countenance.

BLUNT   That's much, indeed! But how did Barnwell
behave?

40   LUCY   He grieved and, at length, enraged at this barbarous
treatment, was preparing to be gone and, making toward
the door, showed a bag of money which he had stolen
from his master—the last he's ever like to have from
thence.

45   BLUNT   But then, Millwood?

LUCY   Aye, she, with her usual address,° returned to her   *adroitness*
old arts of lying, swearing, and dissembling; hung on his
neck and wept and swore 'twas meant in jest till the easy
fool, melted into tears, threw the money into her lap and
50   swore he had rather die than think her false.

BLUNT   Strange infatuation!

LUCY   But what followed was stranger still! As doubts and
fears followed by reconcilement ever increase love, where
the passion is sincere, so in him it caused so wild a trans-
55   port of excessive fondness—such joy, such grief, such
pleasure, and such anguish—that nature in him seemed
sinking with the weight and the charmed soul disposed
to quit his breast for hers. Just then, when every passion
with lawless anarchy prevailed and reason was in the
60   raging tempest lost, the cruel, artful Millwood prevailed

upon the wretched youth to promise what I tremble but
to think on.

BLUNT   I am amazed! What can it be?

LUCY   You will be more so to hear it is to attempt the life of
65   his nearest relation and best benefactor.

BLUNT   His uncle, whom we have often heard him speak
of as a gentleman of a large estate and fair character in
the country where he lives?

LUCY   The same! She was no sooner possessed of the last
70   dear purchase of his ruin but her avarice, insatiate as the
grave, demands this horrid sacrifice. Barnwell's near relation and unsuspected virtue must give too easy means
to seize the good man's treasure, whose blood must seal
the dreadful secret and prevent the terrors of her guilty
75   fears.

BLUNT   Is it possible she could persuade him to do an act
like that? He is by nature honest, grateful, compassionate, and generous; and though his love and her artful
persuasions have wrought him to practice what he most
80   abhors, yet we all can witness for him with what reluc-
tance he has still complied. So many tears he shed o'er
each offense as might, if possible, sanctify theft and
make a merit of a crime.

LUCY   'Tis true, at the naming of the murder of his uncle,
85   he started into rage and, breaking from her arms, where
she till then had held him with well-dissembled love and
false endearments, called her "cruel, monster, devil,"
and told her she was born for his destruction. She
thought it not for her purpose to meet his rage with rage
90   but affected a most passionate fit of grief, railed at her
fate, and cursed her wayward stars that still her wants
should force her to press him to act such deeds as she
must needs abhor as well as he, but told him necessity
had no law and love no bounds, that therefore he never
95   truly loved but meant, in her necessity, to forsake her;
then kneeled and swore that since by his refusal he had
given her cause to doubt his love, she never would see
him more unless, to prove it true, he robbed his uncle to
supply her wants and murdered him to keep it from dis-
100   covery.

BLUNT   I am astonished! What said he?

LUCY   Speechless he stood, but in his face you might have
read that various passions tore his very soul. Oft he in
anguish threw his eyes towards Heaven, and then as of-
105   ten bent their beams on her, then wept and groaned and
beat his breast. At length, with horror not to be expressed, he cried, "Thou cursed fair, have I not given
dreadful proofs of love? What drew me from my youthful
innocence to stain my then-unspotted soul, but cursed
110   love? What caused me to rob my gentle master, but love?

What makes me now a fugitive from his service, loathed
by myself and scorned by all the world, but love? What
fills my eyes with tears, my soul with torture never felt
on this side death before? Why, love, love, love! And why,
115   above all, do I resolve (for, tearing his hair, he cried, 'I do
resolve') to kill my uncle?"

BLUNT   Was she not moved? It makes me weep to hear the
sad relation.

LUCY   Yes, with joy that she had gained her point. She gave
120   him no time to cool but urged him to attempt it instantly. He's now gone. If he performs it and escapes,
there's more money for her; if not, he'll ne'er return, and
then she's fairly rid of him.

BLUNT   'Tis time the world was rid of such a monster.

125 LUCY   If we don't do our endeavors to prevent this murder,
we are as bad as she.

BLUNT   I'm afraid it is too late.

LUCY   Perhaps not. Her barbarity to Barnwell makes me
hate her. We've run too great a length with her already. I
130   did not think her or myself so wicked as I find, upon reflection, we are.

BLUNT   'Tis true we have all been too much so. But there
is something so horrid in murder that all other crimes
seem nothing when compared to that. I would not be in-
135   volved in the guilt of that for all the world.

LUCY   Nor I, Heaven knows. Therefore, let us clear ourselves by doing all that is in our power to prevent it. I
have just thought of a way that to me seems probable.
Will you join with me to detect this cursed design?

140 BLUNT   With all my heart. How else shall I clear myself?
He who knows of a murder intended to be committed
and does not discover it, in the eye of the law and reason, is a murderer.

LUCY   Let us lose no time. I'll acquaint you with the par-
145   ticulars as we go.

[*Exeunt.*]

3.5

[SCENE: *A walk at some distance from a country seat.*°]   residence
[*Enter* BARNWELL.]

BARNWELL   A dismal gloom obscures the face of day. Either the sun has slipped behind a cloud, or journeys
down the west of Heaven with more than common
speed, to avoid the sight of what I'm doomed to act.
5   Since I set forth on this accursed design, where'er I tread,
methinks, the solid earth trembles beneath my feet. Yonder limpid stream, whose hoary fall has made a natural
cascade, as I passed by, in doleful accents, seemed to
murmur, "Murder." The earth, the air, and water seem

10   concerned, but that's not strange. The world is punished
      and nature feels the shock when Providence permits a
      good man's fall. Just Heaven, then what should I be! For
      him that was my father's only brother, and since his
      death has been to me a father; who took me up an infant
15   and an orphan, reared me with tenderest care, and still
      indulged me with most paternal fondness. Yet here I
      stand avowed his destined murderer. I stiffen with hor-
      ror at my own impiety! 'Tis yet unperformed. What if I
      quit my bloody purpose and fly the place? [*Going, then*
20   *stops.*] But whither, oh, whither shall I fly? My master's
      once-friendly doors are ever shut against me; and, with-
      out money, Millwood will never see me more, and life
      is not to be endured without her. She's got such firm
      possession of my heart and governs there with such
25   despotic sway—aye, there's the cause of all my sin and
      sorrow. 'Tis more than love; 'tis the fever of the soul and
      madness of desire. In vain does nature, reason, con-
      science, all oppose it. The impetuous passion bears
      down all before it and drives me on to lust, to theft, and
30   murder. Oh, conscience, feeble guide to virtue, who only
      shows us when we go astray but wants the power to
      stop us in our course!—Ha! In yonder shady walk I see
      my uncle. He's alone. Now for my disguise. [*Plucks out
      a vizor.°*] This is his hour of private meditation. Thus   mask
35   daily he prepares his soul for Heaven, whilst I—but
      what have I to do with Heaven? Ha! No struggles,
      conscience!
         Hence, hence, remorse, and every thought that's good!
         The storm that lust began must end in blood.
                    [*Puts on the vizor, and draws a pistol. Exit.*]

3.6

[SCENE: *A close walk in the wood.*]
                 [*Enter* UNCLE.]

UNCLE   If I was superstitious, I should fear some danger
         lurked unseen, or death were nigh. A heavy melancholy
         clouds my spirits. My imagination is filled with gashly°   ghastly
         forms of dreary graves and bodies changed by death,
5   when the pale lengthened visage attracts each weeping
         eye and fills the musing soul at once with grief and hor-
         ror, pity and aversion. I will indulge the thought. The
         wise man prepares himself for death by making it fa-
         miliar to his mind. When strong reflections hold the
10   mirror near, and the living in the dead behold their
         future selves, how does each inordinate passion and
         desire cease or sicken at the view! The mind scarce
         moves; the blood, curdling and chilled, creeps slowly
         through the veins; fixed, still, and motionless, like the

15 solemn object of our thoughts, we are almost, at present, what we must be hereafter, till curiosity awakes the soul and sets it on inquiry.

3.7

[*Enter* BARNWELL, *at a distance.*]

UNCLE O Death, thou strange mysterious power, seen every day yet never understood but by the incommunicative dead, what art thou? The extensive mind of man that, with a thought, circles the earth's vast globe, sinks
5 to the center, or ascends above the stars, that worlds exotic finds or thinks it finds, thy thick clouds attempts to pass in vain. Lost and bewildered in the horrid gloom, defeated she returns more doubtful than before, of nothing certain but of labor lost.

[*During this speech,* BARNWELL *sometimes presents°*   aims
the pistol, and draws it back again. At last he drops it,
at which his uncle starts and draws his sword.]

10 BARNWELL Oh, 'tis impossible!
UNCLE A man so near me, armed and masked!
BARNWELL Nay then, there's no retreat!

[*Plucks a poniard from his bosom and stabs him.*]

UNCLE Oh, I am slain! All-gracious Heaven, regard the prayer of thy dying servant! Bless with thy choicest bless-
15 ings my dearest nephew, forgive my murderer, and take my fleeting soul to endless mercy!

[BARNWELL *throws off his mask, runs to him, and,*
kneeling by him, raises and chafes him.]

BARNWELL Expiring saint! Oh, murdered, martyred uncle! Lift up your dying eyes and view your nephew in your murderer. Oh, do not look so tenderly upon me. Let
20 indignation lighten from your eyes and blast me ere you die. By Heaven, he weeps in pity of my woes. Tears, tears, for blood! The murdered in the agonies of death weeps for his murderer! Oh, speak your pious purpose. Pronounce my pardon then, and take me with you! He
25 would, but cannot. Oh, why with such fond affection do you press my murdering hand? What! Will you kiss me?

[*Kisses him.*]

UNCLE [*Groans and dies.*]

BARNWELL He's gone forever, and, oh, I follow! [*Swoons away upon his uncle's dead body.*] Do I still live to press
30 the suffering bosom of the earth? Do I still breathe and taint with my infectious breath the wholesome air? Let Heaven from its high throne, in justice or in mercy, now look down on that dear murdered saint and me, the murderer. And if His vengeance spares, let pity strike and
35 end my wretched being. Murder the worst of crimes, and parricide the worst of murders, and this the worst of

parricides. Cain, who stands on record from the birth of time and must to its final period as accursed, slew a brother favored above him. Detested Nero, by another's
40 hand, dispatched a mother that he feared and hated.[8] But I, with my own hand, have murdered a brother, mother, father, and a friend most loving and beloved. This execrable act of mine's without a parallel. Oh, may it ever stand alone—the last of murders, as it is the worst.

45 The rich man thus, in torment and despair,
Preferr'd° his vain but charitable prayer.   *Proffered*
The fool, his own soul lost, would fain be wise
For other's good, but Heaven his suit denies.[9]
By laws and means well known we stand or fall,
50 And one eternal rule remains for all.

The End of the Third Act

4.1

[SCENE: *A room in* THOROWGOOD's *house.*]

[*Enter* MARIA.]

MARIA   How falsely do they judge who censure or applaud as we're afflicted or rewarded here. I know I am unhappy, yet cannot charge myself with any crime, more than the common frailties of our kind, that should provoke just
5 Heaven to mark me out for sufferings so uncommon and severe. Falsely to accuse ourselves, Heaven must abhor. Then it is just and right that innocence should suffer, for Heaven must be just in all its ways. Perhaps by that they are kept from moral evils much worse than penal, or
10 more improved in virtue. Or may not the lesser ills that they sustain be the means of greater good to others? Might all the joyless days and sleepless nights that I have passed but purchase peace for thee,

Thou dear, dear cause of all my grief and pain,
15 Small were the loss, and infinite the gain;
Though to the grave in secret love I pine,
So life and fame and happiness were thine.

4.2

[*Enter* TRUEMAN.]

MARIA   What news of Barnwell?

TRUEMAN   None. I have sought him with the greatest diligence, but all in vain.

---

8. Julia Agrippina (15–59 C.E.), who was murdered by a freedman on the orders of her son, the Roman emperor Nero (r. 54–68). For the killing of Abel by Cain—the first murder ever committed, according to the Bible—see Genesis 4.8–16.

9. An allusion to the New Testament story of the rich man (conventionally called Dives) who ignored the beggar Lazarus and after death suffered the torments of hell (Luke 16.19–31). His plea that his brothers be warned to save them from sharing his fate was denied.

MARIA Doth my father yet suspect the cause of his absent-
5 ing himself?

TRUEMAN All appeared so just and fair to him, it is not possible he ever should; but his absence will no longer be
concealed. Your father's wise, and though he seems to
harken° to the friendly excuses I would make for Barn- *listen with sympathy*
10 well, yet I am afraid he regards them only as such, without
suffering them to influence his judgment.

MARIA How does the unhappy youth defeat all our designs to serve him! Yet I can never repent what we have
done. Should he return, 'twill make his reconciliation
15 with my father easier and preserve him from future reproach from a malicious, unforgiving world.

4.3

[*Enter to them,* THOROWGOOD *and* LUCY.]

THOROWGOOD This woman here has given me a sad and
(bating° some circumstances) too-probable account of *excluding*
Barnwell's defection.

LUCY I am sorry, sir, that my frank confession of my for-
5 mer unhappy course of life should cause you to suspect
my truth on this occasion.

THOROWGOOD It is not that; your confession has in it all
the appearance of truth. [*To them*] Among many other
particulars, she informs me that Barnwell has been in-
10 fluenced to break his trust and wrong° me, at several *defraud*
times, of considerable sums of money. Now, as I know
this to be false, I would fain doubt the whole of her relation, too dreadful to be willingly believed.

MARIA Sir, your pardon. I find myself on a sudden so
15 indisposed that I must retire. [*Aside*] Providence opposes
all attempts to save him. Poor, ruined Barnwell!
Wretched, lost Maria! [*Exit.*]

4.4

THOROWGOOD How am I distressed on every side! Pity for
that unhappy youth, fear for the life of a much-valued
friend, and then my child, the only joy and hope of my
declining life! Her melancholy increases hourly and
5 gives me painful apprehensions of her loss. Oh, Trueman, this person informs me that your friend, at the
instigation of an impious woman, is gone to rob and
murder his venerable uncle.

TRUEMAN Oh, execrable deed! I am blasted with the hor-
10 ror of the thought!

LUCY This delay may ruin all.

THOROWGOOD What to do or think I know not. That he
ever wronged me, I know is false. The rest may be so,
too. There's all my hope.

15 TRUEMAN Trust not to that; rather suppose all true than
lose a moment's time. Even now the horrid deed may be
a-doing—dreadful imagination!—or it may be done, and
we are vainly debating on the means to prevent what is
already past.

20 THOROWGOOD [*aside*] This earnestness convinces me that
he knows more than he has yet discovered.°—What ho!   *revealed*
Without there! Who waits?

4.5

[*Enter to them, a servant.*]

THOROWGOOD Order the groom to saddle the swiftest
horse and prepare himself to set out with speed! An affair of life and death demands his diligence.

[*Exit servant.*]

4.6

THOROWGOOD [*to* LUCY] For you, whose behavior on this
occasion I have no time to commend as it deserves, I
must engage your further assistance. Return and observe
this Millwood till I come. I have your directions and will
5 follow you as soon as possible.

[*Exit* LUCY.]

4.7

THOROWGOOD Trueman, you, I am sure, would not be idle
on this occasion.   [*Exit* THOROWGOOD.]

4.8

TRUEMAN He only, who is a friend, can judge of my distress.
[*Exit.*]

4.9

[SCENE: MILLWOOD's *house.*]

[*Enter* MILLWOOD.]

MILLWOOD I wish I knew the event° of his design. The at-   *outcome*
tempt without success would ruin him. Well, what have
I to apprehend from that? I fear too much. —The mischief being only intended, his friends, in pity of his
5 youth, turn all their rage on me? I should have thought
of that before.—Suppose the deed done. Then, and then
only, I shall be secure. Or what if he returns without attempting it at all?

4.10

[*Enter* BARNWELL, *bloody.*]

MILLWOOD [*aside*] But he is here, and I have done him
wrong. His bloody hands show he has done the deed, but
show he wants° the prudence to conceal it.   lacks

BARNWELL Where shall I hide me? Whither shall I fly to
5   avoid the swift, unerring hand of justice?

MILLWOOD Dismiss those fears! Though thousands had
pursued you to the door, yet being entered here you are
safe as innocence. I have such a cavern, by art so cunningly contrived, that the piercing eyes of jealousy and
10   revenge may search in vain, nor find the entrance to the
safe retreat. There will I hide you if any danger's near.

BARNWELL Oh, hide me from myself, if it be possible! For,
while I bear my conscience in my bosom, though I were
hid where man's eye never saw nor light e'er dawned,
15   'twere all in vain. For that inmate, that impartial judge,
will try, convict, and sentence me for murder, and execute me with never-ending torments. Behold these
hands all crimsoned o'er with my dear uncle's blood!
Here's a sight to make a statue start with horror, or turn
20   a living man into a statue.

MILLWOOD Ridiculous! Then it seems you are afraid of
your own shadow or what's less than a shadow, your conscience.

BARNWELL Though to man unknown I did the accursed
25   act, what can we hide from Heaven's omniscient eye?

MILLWOOD No more of this stuff! What advantage have
you made of his death? Or what advantage may yet be
made of it? Did you secure the keys of his treasure?
Those, no doubt, were about him. What gold, what jew-
30   els, or what else of value have you brought me?

BARNWELL Think you I added sacrilege to murder? Oh,
had you seen him as his life flowed from him in a crimson flood, and heard him praying for me by the double
name of nephew and of murderer (alas, alas, he knew
35   not then that his nephew was his murderer), how would
you have wished, as I did, though you had a thousand
years of life to come, to have given them all to have
lengthened his one hour. But being dead, I fled the sight
of what my hands had done, nor could I, to have gained
40   the empire of the world, have violated his sacred corpse.

MILLWOOD Whining, preposterous, canting villain! To
murder your uncle, rob him of life—nature's first, last
dear prerogative, after which there's no injury—then
fear to take what he no longer wanted, and bring to me
45   your penury and guilt! Do you think I'll hazard my
reputation—nay, my life—to entertain you?

BARNWELL   Oh, Millwood! This from thee? But I have
done. If you hate me, if you wish me dead, then are you
happy, for, oh, 'tis sure my grief will quickly end me.

50 MILLWOOD [*aside*]   In his madness he will discover° all and   *reveal*
involve me in his ruin. We are on a precipice from whence
there's no retreat for both. Then, to preserve myself.
[*Pauses.*] There is no other way. 'Tis dreadful, but reflection comes too late when danger's pressing, and there's no
55 room for choice. It must be done. [*Stamps.*]

4.11

[*Enter to them, a servant.*]

MILLWOOD   Fetch me an officer and seize this villain! He
has confessed himself a murderer. Should I let him
escape, I justly might be thought as bad as he.

[*Exit servant.*]

4.12

BARNWELL   Oh, Millwood, sure thou dost not, cannot
mean it! Stop the messenger! Upon my knees I beg you
call him back! 'Tis fit I die, indeed, but not by you. I will
this instant deliver myself into the hands of justice; in-
5 deed I will, for death is all I wish. But thy ingratitude so
tears my wounded soul, 'tis worse ten thousand times
than death with torture.

MILLWOOD   Call it what you will. I am willing to live, and
live secure, which nothing but your death can warrant.

10 BARNWELL   If there be a pitch° of wickedness that seats   *height*
the author beyond the reach of vengeance, you must be
secure. But what remains for me but a dismal dungeon,
hard-galling fetters, an awful trial, and ignominious
death—justly to fall, unpitied and abhorred! After death,
15 to be suspended between Heaven and earth, a dreadful
spectacle, the warning and horror of a gaping crowd!
This I could bear—nay, wish not to avoid—had it but
come from any hand but thine.

4.13

[*Enter BLUNT, officer, and attendants.*]

MILLWOOD   Heaven defend me! Conceal a murderer? [*To
officer*] Here, sir, take this youth into your custody! I
accuse him of murder and will appear[1] to make good my
charge.

[*They seize him.*]

5 BARNWELL   To whom, of what, or how shall I complain?
I'll not accuse her. The hand of Heaven is in it, and this
the punishment of lust and parricide. Yet Heaven, that

---

1. That is, appear before a magistrate (to testify against Barnwell).

justly cuts me off, still suffers her to live, perhaps to punish
others. Tremendous mercy! So fiends are cursed with im-
10 mortality to be the executioners of Heaven.

Be warn'd, ye youths, who see my sad despair,
Avoid lewd women, false as they are fair;
By reason guided, honest joys pursue;
The fair, to honor and to virtue true,
15 Just to herself, will ne'er be false to you.
By my example learn to shun my fate;
(How wretched is the man who's wise too late!)
Ere innocence and fame and life be lost,
Here purchase wisdom cheaply, at my cost.

[*Exeunt* BARNWELL, *officer, and attendants.*]

4.14

MILLWOOD [*to* BLUNT] Where's Lucy? Why is she absent
at such a time?
BLUNT Would I had been so too, thou devil!
MILLWOOD Insolent! This, to me?
5 BLUNT The worst that we know of the Devil is that he first
seduces to sin and then betrays to punishment.

[*Exit* BLUNT.]

4.15

MILLWOOD They disapprove of my conduct and mean to
take this opportunity to set up for themselves. My ruin is
resolved.° I see my danger, but scorn both it and them. I   settled, assured
was not born to fall by such weak instruments. [*Going*]

4.16

[*Enter* THOROWGOOD.]

THOROWGOOD Where is this scandal to her own sex, and
curse of ours?
MILLWOOD What means this insolence? Whom do you seek?
THOROWGOOD Millwood.
5 MILLWOOD Well, you have found her then. I am Millwood.
THOROWGOOD Then you are the most impious wretch that
e'er the sun beheld.
MILLWOOD From your appearance I should have expected
wisdom and moderation, but your manners belie your
10 aspect. What is your business here? I know you not.
THOROWGOOD Hereafter you may know me better. I am
Barnwell's master.
MILLWOOD Then you are master to a villain, which, I think,
is not much to your credit.
15 THOROWGOOD Had he been as much above thy arts as my
credit is superior to thy malice, I need not blush to own°   acknowledge
him.

MILLWOOD   My arts? I don't understand you, sir. If he has
done amiss, what's that to me? Was he my servant, or
20   yours? You should have taught him better.

THOROWGOOD   Why should I wonder to find such uncommon impudence in one arrived to such a height of wickedness? When innocence is banished, modesty soon
follows. Know, sorceress, I'm not ignorant of any of your
25   arts by which you first deceived the unwary youth. I
know how, step by step, you've led him on, reluctant and
unwilling, from crime to crime, to this last horrid act
which you contrived and, by your cursed wiles, even
forced him to commit, and then betrayed him.

30 MILLWOOD [*aside*]   Ha! Lucy has got the advantage of me
and accused me first. Unless I can turn the accusation
and fix it upon her and Blunt, I am lost.

THOROWGOOD   Had I known your cruel design sooner, it
had been prevented. To see you punished as the law
35   directs is all that now remains. Poor satisfaction, for he,
innocent as he is compared to you, must suffer too. But
Heaven, who knows our frame and graciously distinguishes between frailty and presumption, will make a
difference, though man cannot, who sees not the heart
40   but only judges by the outward action.

MILLWOOD   I find, sir, we are both unhappy in our servants.
I was surprised at such ill treatment, from a gentleman of
your appearance, without cause, and therefore too hastily
returned it, for which I ask your pardon. I now perceive
45   you have been so far imposed on° as to think me engaged   *deceived*
in a former correspondence° with your servant and, some   *illicit affair*
way or other, accessory to his undoing.

THOROWGOOD   I charge you as the cause, the sole cause of
all his guilt and all his suffering, of all he now endures
50   and must endure till a violent and shameful death shall
put a dreadful period to his life and miseries together.

MILLWOOD   'Tis very strange! But who's secure from scandal and detraction? So far from contributing to his ruin,
I never spoke to him till since° that fatal accident, which   *until after*
55   I lament as much as you. 'Tis true, I have a servant on
whose account he has of late frequented my house. If
she has abused my good opinion of her, am I to blame?
Hasn't Barnwell done the same by you?

THOROWGOOD   I hear you. Pray go on.

60 MILLWOOD   I have been informed he had a violent passion
for her, and she for him, but I always thought it innocent. I know her poor and given to expensive pleasures.
Now, who can tell but she may have influenced the
amorous youth to commit this murder to supply her
65   extravagancies? It must be so! I now recollect a thousand circumstances that confirm it. I'll have her and a
manservant, that I suspect as an accomplice, secured

immediately. I hope, sir, you will lay aside your
ill-grounded suspicions of me and join to punish the real
70 contrivers of this bloody deed. [*Offers° to go.*] *Tries*

THOROWGOOD Madam, you pass not this way. I see your
design, but shall protect them from your malice.

MILLWOOD I hope you will not use your influence and the
credit of your name to screen such guilty wretches! Con-
75 sider, sir, the wickedness of persuading a thoughtless
youth to such a crime!

THOROWGOOD I do. And of betraying him when it was done.

MILLWOOD That which you call betraying him may convince you of my innocence. She who loves him, though
80 she contrived the murder, would never have delivered
him into the hands of justice as I, struck with the horror
of his crimes, have done.

THOROWGOOD [*aside*] How should an unexperienced
youth escape her snares? The powerful magic of her wit
85 and form might betray the wisest to simple dotage, and
fire the blood that age had froze long since. Even I, that
with just prejudice[2] came prepared, had by her artful
story been deceived but that my strong conviction of her
guilt makes even a doubt impossible. —Those whom
90 subtly you would accuse, you know are your accusers.
And what proves unanswerably their innocence and your
guilt, they accused you before the deed was done, and
did all that was in their power to have prevented it.

MILLWOOD Sir, you are very hard to be convinced, but I
95 have such a proof which, when produced, will silence all
objections. [*Exit* MILLWOOD.]

4.17

[*Enter* LUCY, TRUEMAN, BLUNT, *officers, &c.*]

LUCY Gentlemen, pray place yourselves some on one side
of that door and some on the other. Watch her entrance
and act as your prudence shall direct you. [*To* THOROW-
GOOD] This way, and note her behavior. I have observed
5 her. She's driven to the last extremity and is forming
some desperate resolution. I guess at her design.

4.18

[*Enter to them,* MILLWOOD *with a pistol.* TRUEMAN
secures her.]

TRUEMAN Here thy power of doing mischief ends, deceitful, cruel, bloody woman!

MILLWOOD Fool, hypocrite, villain—man! Thou canst not
call me that!

---

2. Justly preconceived conviction (of Millwood's guilt).

5 TRUEMAN To call thee woman were to wrong the sex, thou
devil!

MILLWOOD That imaginary being is an emblem of thy
cursed sex collected, a mirror wherein each particular
man may see his own likeness and that of all mankind!

10 TRUEMAN Think not by aggravating the fault of others to
extenuate thy own, of which the abuse of such uncommon perfections of mind and body is not the least.

MILLWOOD If such I had, well may I curse your barbarous
sex who robbed me of 'em, ere I knew their worth, then

15 left me, too late, to count their value by their loss. Another and another spoiler came, and all my gain was
poverty and reproach. My soul disdained, and yet dis-
dains, dependence and contempt. Riches, no matter by
what means obtained, I saw secured the worst of men

20 from both. I found it, therefore, necessary to be rich and
to that end I summoned all my arts. You call 'em wicked;
be it so! They were such as my conversation[3] with your
sex had furnished me withal.°   *with*

THOROWGOOD Sure, none but the worst of men conversed

25 with thee!

MILLWOOD Men of all degrees and all professions I have
known, yet found no difference but in their several° ca-   *various*
pacities. All were alike wicked to the utmost of their
power. In pride, contention, avarice, cruelty, and revenge

30 the reverend priesthood were my unerring guides. From
suburb-magistrates, who live by ruined reputations, as
the unhospitable natives of Cornwall do by shipwrecks,[4]
I learned that to charge my innocent neighbors with my
crimes was to merit their protection, for to screen the

35 guilty is the less scandalous when many are suspected,
and detraction, like darkness and death, blackens all objects and levels all distinction. Such are your venal magistrates who favor none but such as, by their office, they
are sworn to punish. With them, not to be guilty is the

40 worst of crimes and large fees, privately paid, is every
needful virtue.

THOROWGOOD Your practice has sufficiently discovered
your contempt of laws, both human and divine. No wonder, then, that you should hate the officers of both.

45 MILLWOOD I hate you all! I know you, and expect no
mercy—nay, I ask for none. I have done nothing that I
am sorry for. I followed my inclinations, and that the
best of you does every day. All actions are alike natural

---

3. Dealings; sexual intercourse.
4. Cornwall, the peninsula at the extreme
southwest of England, has a dangerous coast;
its inhabitants were known for plundering the
cargo of shipwrecks (and were widely believed

to light beacons to lure ships onto the rocks).
Suburb-magistrates: magistrates outside the
City of London, who collected fees for admin-
istering the law and hence were widely seen
as profiting from vice.

and indifferent to man and beast who devour or are de-
50   voured as they meet with others weaker or stronger than
     themselves.

   THOROWGOOD   What pity it is, a mind so comprehensive,
     daring, and inquisitive should be a stranger to religion's
     sweet but powerful charms.

55 MILLWOOD   I am not fool enough to be an atheist, though
     I have known enough of men's hypocrisy to make a thou-
     sand simple women so. Whatever religion is in itself, as
     practiced by mankind it has caused the evils you say it
     was designed to cure. War, plague, and famine have not
60   destroyed so many of the human race as this pretended
     piety has done, and with such barbarous cruelty as if the
     only way to honor Heaven were to turn the present
     world into Hell.

   THOROWGOOD   Truth is truth, though from an enemy and
65   spoke in malice. You bloody, blind, and superstitious big-
     ots, how will you answer this?

   MILLWOOD   What are your laws, of which you make your
     boast, but the fool's wisdom and the coward's valor, the
     instrument and screen of all your villainies by which you
70   punish in others what you act yourselves or would have
     acted, had you been in their circumstances? The judge
     who condemns the poor man for being a thief had° been   *would have*
     a thief himself, had he been poor. Thus, you go on de-
     ceiving and being deceived, harassing, plaguing, and de-
75   stroying one another, but women are your universal prey.
     Women, by whom you are, the source of joy,

     With cruel arts you labor to destroy.
     A thousand ways our ruin you pursue,
     Yet blame in us those arts first taught by you.
80   Oh, may, from hence, each violated maid,
     By flatt'ring, faithless, barb'rous man betray'd,
     When robb'd of innocence and virgin fame,
     From your destruction raise a nobler name:
     To right their sex's wrongs devote their mind,
85   And future Millwoods prove, to plague mankind!
                                          [*Exeunt.*]
                    The End of the Fourth Act

                         5.1

[SCENE: *A room in a prison.*]

     [*Enter* THOROWGOOD, BLUNT, *and* LUCY.]

   THOROWGOOD   I have recommended to Barnwell a rev-
     erend divine whose judgment and integrity I am well ac-
     quainted with. Nor has Millwood been neglected but
     she, unhappy woman, still obstinate, refuses his assis-
5   tance.

LUCY This pious charity to the afflicted well becomes
your character. Yet pardon me, sir, if I wonder° you were *am surprised that*
not at their trial.

THOROWGOOD I knew it was impossible to save him, and I
10 and my family bear so great a part in his distress that to
have been present would have aggravated our sorrows
without relieving his.

BLUNT It was mournful, indeed. Barnwell's youth and
modest deportment as he passed drew tears from every
15 eye. When placed at the bar and arraigned before the reverend judges, with many tears and interrupting sobs he
confessed and aggravated° his offenses, without accusing *made more heinous*
or once reflecting on Millwood, the shameless author
of his ruin, who, dauntless and unconcerned, stood by
20 his side, viewing with visible pride and contempt the
vast assembly who all, with sympathizing sorrow, wept
for the wretched youth. Millwood, when called upon
to answer, loudly insisted upon her innocence and
made an artful and a bold defense but finding all in
25 vain (the impartial jury and the learned bench concurring to find her guilty), how did she curse herself, poor
Barnwell, us, her judges, all mankind! But what could
that avail? She was condemned and is this day to suffer with him.

30 THOROWGOOD The time draws on. I am going to visit
Barnwell, as you are Millwood.

LUCY We have not wronged her, yet I dread this interview.
She's proud, impatient, wrathful, and unforgiving. To be
the branded instruments of vengeance, to suffer in her
35 shame, and sympathize with her in all she suffers, is the
tribute we must pay for our former ill-spent lives and
long confederacy with her wickedness.

THOROWGOOD Happy for you it ended when it did. What
you have done against Millwood I know proceeded from
40 a just abhorrence of her crimes, free from interest,° mal- *self-interest*
ice, or revenge. Proselytes to virtue should be encour-
aged. Pursue your proposed reformation, and know me
hereafter for your friend.

LUCY This is a blessing as unhoped-for as unmerited, but
45 Heaven that snatched us from impending ruin sure
intends you as its instrument to secure us from
apostasy.

THOROWGOOD With gratitude to impute your deliverance to
Heaven is just. Many, less virtuously disposed than Barn-
50 well was, have never fallen in the manner he has done. May
not such owe their safety rather to Providence than to themselves? With pity and compassion let us judge him. Great
were his faults, but strong was the temptation. Let his
ruin learn us diffidence,° humanity, and circumspection, *teach us modesty*

55   for we who wonder at his fate—perhaps had we like him
      been tried, like him we had fallen too.

                                                      [*Exeunt.*]

                            5.2

[SCENE: *A dungeon. A table and lamp.*]

      [*Enter* THOROWGOOD. BARNWELL *reading.*]

THOROWGOOD [*aside*]   See there the bitter fruits of pas-
      sion's detested reign and sensual appetites indulged—
      severe reflections, penitence, and tears.

BARNWELL   My honored, injured master, whose goodness
5   has covered me a thousand times with shame, forgive
      this last unwilling disrespect! Indeed, I saw you not.

THOROWGOOD   'Tis well. I hope you were better employed
      in viewing of yourself. Your journey's long, your time for
      preparation almost spent. I sent a reverend divine to
10   teach you to improve it and should be glad to hear of his
      success.

BARNWELL   The word of truth which he recommended for
      my constant companion in this my sad retirement has at
      length removed the doubts I labored under. From thence
15   I've learned the infinite extent of heavenly mercy—that
      my offenses, though great, are not unpardonable and
      that 'tis not my interest only but my duty to believe and
      to rejoice in that hope. So shall Heaven receive the glory,
      and future penitents the profit of my example.

20 THOROWGOOD   Go on. How happy am I who live to see this!

BARNWELL   'Tis wonderful that words should charm de-
      spair, speak peace and pardon to a murderer's con-
      science, but truth and mercy flow in every sentence
      attended with force and energy divine. How shall I de-
25   scribe my present state of mind? I hope in doubt, and
      trembling I rejoice. I feel my grief increase, even as my
      fears give way. Joy and gratitude now supply more tears
      than the horror and anguish of despair before.

THOROWGOOD   These are the genuine signs of true repen-
30   tance, the only preparatory, certain way to everlasting
      peace. Oh, the joy it gives to see a soul formed and prepa-
      red for Heaven! For this the faithful minister devotes him-
      self to meditation, abstinence, and prayer, shunning the
      vain delights of sensual joys, and daily dies that others may
35   live forever. For this he turns the sacred volumes o'er, and
      spends his life in painful search of truth. The love of riches
      and the lust of power he looks on with just contempt and
      detestation, who only counts for wealth the souls he wins
      and whose highest ambition is to serve mankind. If the re-
40   ward of all his pains be to preserve one soul from wander-
      ing or turn one from the error of his ways, how does he
      then rejoice and own his little labors overpaid!

BARNWELL   What do I owe you for all your generous kindness? But, though I cannot, Heaven can and will reward
45   you.

THOROWGOOD   To see thee thus is joy too great for words.
Farewell! Heaven strengthen thee! Farewell!

BARNWELL   Oh, sir! There's something I could say, if my
sad swelling heart would give me leave.

50   THOROWGOOD   Give it vent a while and try.

BARNWELL   I had a friend. 'Tis true I am unworthy, yet methinks your generous example might persuade—could I
not see him once before I go from whence there's no return?

55   THOROWGOOD   He's coming, and as much thy friend as
ever. [Aside] But I'll not anticipate his sorrow.[5] Too
soon he'll see the sad effects of his contagious ruin.
This torrent of domestic misery bears too hard upon
me. I must retire to indulge a weakness I find impos-
60   sible to overcome. —Much loved, and much lamented
youth, farewell. Heaven strengthen thee! Eternally farewell!

BARNWELL   The best of masters and of men, farewell!
While I live, let me not want your prayers.

65   THOROWGOOD   Thou shalt not. Thy peace being made with
Heaven, death's already vanquished. Bear a little longer
the pains that attend this transitory life, and cease from
pain forever.   [Exit THOROWGOOD.]

5.3

BARNWELL   I find a power within that bears my soul above
the fears of death and, spite of° conscious shame and guilt,   *despite*
gives me a taste of pleasure more than mortal.

5.4

[Enter to him, TRUEMAN and KEEPER.]

KEEPER   Sir, there's the prisoner.   [Exit KEEPER.]

5.5

BARNWELL [aside]   Trueman! My friend whom I so wished
to see! Yet now he's here I dare not look upon him. [Weeps.]

TRUEMAN   Oh, Barnwell! Barnwell!

BARNWELL   Mercy, mercy, gracious Heaven! For death, but
5   not for this, was I prepared.

TRUEMAN   What have I suffered since I saw you last! What
pain has absence given me! But, oh, to see thee thus!

5. That is, make him suffer sorrow before he inevitably must.

BARNWELL   I know it is dreadful. I feel the anguish of thy generous soul—but I was born to murder all who love me.

[*Both weep.*]

10 TRUEMAN   I came not to reproach you. I thought to bring you comfort but I'm deceived, for I have none to give. I came to share thy sorrow, but cannot bear my own.

BARNWELL   My sense of guilt, indeed, you cannot know. 'Tis what the good and innocent like you can ne'er
15 conceive. But other griefs at present I have none but what I feel for you. In your sorrow I read you love me still. But, yet, methinks 'tis strange, when I consider what I am.

TRUEMAN   No more of that. I can remember nothing but
20 thy virtues, thy honest, tender friendship, our former happy state and present misery. Oh, had you trusted me when first the fair seducer tempted you, all might have been prevented.

BARNWELL   Alas, thou knowest not what a wretch I've
25 been! Breach of friendship was my first and least offense. So far was I lost to goodness, so devoted to the author of my ruin, that had she insisted on my murdering thee, I think I should have done it.

TRUEMAN   Prithee, aggravate thy faults no more.

30 BARNWELL   I think I should! Thus good and generous as you are, I should have murdered you!

TRUEMAN   We have not yet embraced, and may be interrupted. Come to my arms!

BARNWELL   Never, never will I taste such joys on earth;
35 never will I so soothe my just remorse. Are those honest arms and faithful bosom fit to embrace and to support a murderer? These iron fetters only shall clasp, and flinty pavements bear me. [*Throwing himself on the ground.*] Even these too good for such a bloody monster!

40 TRUEMAN   Shall fortune sever those whom friendship joined? Thy miseries cannot lay thee so low but love will find thee. [*Lies down by him.*] Upon this rugged couch then let us lie, for well it suits our most deplorable condition. Here will we offer to stern calamity, this earth the
45 altar and ourselves the sacrifice. Our mutual groans shall echo to each other through the dreary vault. Our sighs shall number the moments as they pass, and mingling tears communicate such anguish as words were never made to express.

50 BARNWELL   Then be it so! [*Rising*] Since you propose an intercourse of woe, pour all your griefs into my breast, and in exchange take mine. [*Embracing*] Where's now the anguish that you promised? You've taken mine and make me no return. Sure, peace and comfort dwell
55 within these arms, and sorrow can't approach me while

I'm here. This, too, is the work of Heaven who, having
before spoke peace and pardon to me, now sends thee to
confirm it. Oh, take, take some of the joy that overflows
my breast!

60 TRUEMAN   I do, I do! Almighty Power, how have you made
us capable to bear, at once, the extremes of pleasure and
of pain.

5.6

[*Enter to them*, KEEPER.]

KEEPER   Sir!

TRUEMAN   I come.

[*Exit* KEEPER.]

5.7

BARNWELL   Must you leave me? Death would soon have
parted us forever.

TRUEMAN   Oh, my Barnwell, there's yet another task behind. Again your heart must bleed for others' woes.

5 BARNWELL   To meet and part with you I thought was all I
had to do on earth. What is there more for me to do or
suffer?

TRUEMAN   I dread to tell thee, yet it must be known.
Maria—

10 BARNWELL   Our master's fair and virtuous daughter?

TRUEMAN   The same.

BARNWELL   No misfortune, I hope, has reached that lovely
maid! Preserve her, Heaven, from every ill to show mankind that goodness is your care.

15 TRUEMAN   Thy, thy misfortunes, my unhappy friend, have
reached her. Whatever you and I have felt and more, if
more be possible, she feels for you.

BARNWELL [*aside*]   I know he doth abhor a lie and would
not trifle with his dying friend. This is, indeed, the bit-

20 terness of death.

TRUEMAN   You must remember, for we all observed it, for
some time past a heavy melancholy weighed her down.
Disconsolate she seemed, and pined and languished
from a cause unknown, till, hearing of your dreadful

25 fate, the long-stifled flame blazed out. She wept, she
wrung her hands and tore her hair, and in the transport
of her grief discovered° her own lost state, whilst she   *revealed*
lamented yours.

BARNWELL   Will all the pain I feel restore thy ease, lovely,

30 unhappy maid? [*Weeping*] Why didn't you let me die and
never know it?

TRUEMAN   It was impossible. She makes no secret of her
passion for you and is determined to see you ere you die.
She waits for me to introduce her.°   [*Exit* TRUEMAN.]   *lead her in*

5.8

BARNWELL   Vain, busy thoughts, be still! What avails it to think on what I might have been? I now am—what I've made myself.

5.9

[*Enter to him,* TRUEMAN *and* MARIA.]

TRUEMAN   Madam, reluctant I lead you to this dismal scene. This is the seat of misery and guilt. Here awful° justice reserves her public victims. This is the entrance to shameful death.

° awe-inspiring

5 MARIA   To this sad place, then, no improper guest, the abandoned, lost Maria brings despair. And see the subject and the cause of all this world of woe! Silent and motionless he stands, as if his soul had quitted her abode, and the lifeless form alone was left behind—yet
10 that so perfect that beauty and death, ever at enmity, now seem united there.

BARNWELL [*aside*]   I groan but murmur not. Just Heaven, I am your own! Do with me what you please.

MARIA   Why are your streaming eyes still fixed below, as
15 though thou'dst give the greedy earth thy sorrows and rob me of my due. Were happiness within your power, you should bestow it where you pleased, but in your misery I must and will partake.

BARNWELL   Oh, say not so, but fly, abhor, and leave me to
20 my fate! Consider what you are—how vast your fortune and how bright your fame. Have pity on your youth, your beauty, and unequaled virtue, for which so many noble peers have sighed in vain! Bless with your charms some honorable lord! Adorn with your beauty, and by your ex-
25 ample improve, the English court that justly claims such merit! So shall I quickly be to you as though I had never been.

MARIA   When I forget you, I must be so, indeed. Reason, choice, virtue all forbid it. Let women like Millwood, if
30 there be more such women, smile in prosperity and in adversity forsake. Be it the pride of virtue to repair or to partake the ruin such have made!

TRUEMAN   Lovely, ill-fated maid! Was there ever such generous distress before? How must this pierce his grateful
35 heart and aggravate his woes!

BARNWELL   Ere I knew guilt or shame, when fortune smiled, and when my youthful hopes were at the highest—if then to have raised my thoughts to you had been presumption in me never to have been pardoned, think how much be-
40 neath yourself to condescend to regard me now!

MARIA   Let her blush who, professing love, invades the freedom of your sex's choice and meanly sues in hopes of a

return. Your inevitable fate hath rendered hope impossible
as vain. Then, why should I fear to avow a passion so
45   just and so disinterested?

TRUEMAN   If any should take occasion from Millwood's
crimes to libel the best and fairest part of the creation,
here let them see their error. The most distant hopes of
such a tender passion from so bright a maid might add to
50   the happiness of the most happy and make the greatest
proud. Yet here 'tis lavished in vain. Though by the rich
present the generous donor is undone, he on whom it is
bestowed receives no benefit.

BARNWELL   So the aromatic spices of the East, which all
55   the living covet and esteem, are with unavailing kindness
wasted on the dead.

MARIA   Yes, fruitless is my love, and unavailing all my sighs
and tears. Can they save thee from approaching death?
From such a death? Oh, terrible idea! What is her misery
60   and distress who sees the first, last object of her love, for
whom alone she'd live—for whom she'd die a thousand,
thousand deaths if it were possible—expiring in her
arms? Yet she is happy when compared to me. Were mil-
lions of worlds mine, I'd gladly give them in exchange for
65   her condition. The most consummate woe is light to
mine. The last of curses to other miserable maids is all I
ask, and that's denied me.

TRUEMAN   Time and reflection cure all ills.

MARIA   All but this; this dreadful catastrophe virtue herself
70   abhors. To give a holiday to suburb slaves and, passing,[6]
entertain the savage herd who, elbowing each other for a
sight, pursue and press upon him like his fate. A mind
with piety and resolution armed may smile on death. But
public ignominy, everlasting shame (shame, the death of
75   souls, to die a thousand times and yet survive even death
itself in never-dying infamy), is this to be endured? Can
I, who live in him and must each hour of my devoted life
feel all these woes renewed, can I endure this?

TRUEMAN   Grief has impaired her spirits. She pants as in
80   the agonies of death.

BARNWELL   Preserve her, Heaven, and restore her peace,
nor let her death be added to my crimes! [*Bell tolls.*] I am
summoned to my fate.

5.10

[*Enter to them,* KEEPER.]

KEEPER   The officers attend° you, sir. Mrs.[7] Millwood is   *wait for*
already summoned.

6. That is, to give the morally coarse inhabitants of the London suburbs an opportunity to
gawk at the passing executioner's cart.

7. A courtesy title for any adult woman in the
18th century.

BARNWELL Tell 'em I'm ready. —And now, my friend,
farewell! [*Embracing*] Support and comfort the best you
5   can this mourning fair. No more! Forget not to pray for
me! [*Turning to* MARIA] Would you, bright excellence,
permit me the honor of a chaste embrace, the last happiness this world could give were mine.

[*She inclines toward him; they embrace.*]

Exalted goodness! Oh, turn your eyes from earth and me
10   to Heaven, where virtue like yours is ever heard. Pray for
the peace of my departing soul! —Early my race of
wickedness began and soon has reached the summit.
Ere nature has finished her work and stamped me man,
just at the time that others begin to stray, my course is
15   finished. Though short my span of life and few my days,
yet count my crimes for years and I have lived whole
ages. Justice and mercy are in Heaven the same; its utmost severity is mercy to the whole, thereby to cure
man's folly and presumption which else would render
20   even infinite mercy vain and ineffectual. Thus justice,
in compassion to mankind, cuts off a wretch like me, by
one such example to secure thousands from future ruin.

If any youth, like you, in future times
Shall mourn my fate, though he abhors my crimes,
25   Or tender maid, like you, my tale shall hear
And to my sorrows give a pitying tear,
To each such melting eye and throbbing heart,
Would gracious Heaven this benefit impart:
Never to know my guilt, nor feel my pain. ⎫
30   Then must you own you ought not to complain, ⎬
Since you nor weep, nor shall I die in vain. ⎭

[*Exeunt.*]

5.11

[*Enter* TRUEMAN, BLUNT, *and* LUCY.]

LUCY Heart-breaking sight! Oh, wretched, wretched Millwood!

TRUEMAN You came from her then. How is she disposed
to meet her fate?

5   BLUNT Who can describe unalterable woe?

LUCY She goes to death encompassed with horror,
loathing life and yet afraid to die. No tongue can tell her
anguish and despair.

TRUEMAN Heaven be better to her than her fears! May
10   she prove a warning to others, a monument of mercy in
herself.

LUCY Oh, sorrow insupportable! Break, break, my heart!

TRUEMAN   In vain

With bleeding hearts and weeping eyes we show
15   A human gen'rous sense of others' woe,
Unless we mark what drew their ruin on,
And, by avoiding that, prevent our own.

Finis

Epilogue

Written by Colley Cibber, Esq.,[8]

and spoke by Mrs. Cibber[9]

Since fate has robb'd me of the hapless youth
For whom my heart had hoarded up its truth,
By all the laws of love and honor, now
I'm free again to choose—and one of you.

5   But, soft—with caution first I'll round me peep;
Maids, in my case, should look before they leap.
Here's choice enough, of various sorts and hue, ⎤
The cit, the wit, the rake cock'd up in cue,[1] ⎬
The fair spruce mercer,° and the tawny Jew. ⎦   *dealer in fabric*

10   Suppose I search the sober gallery? No, ⎤
There's none but 'prentices—and cuckolds all a-row, ⎬
And these, I doubt,° are those that make 'em so. ⎦   *do not doubt*
[*Pointing to the boxes.*]

  'Tis very well, enjoy the jest! But you, ⎤
Fine powder'd sparks[2]—nay, I'm told 'tis true, ⎬
15 Your happy spouses—can make cuckolds, too. ⎦
'Twixt you and them, the diff'rence this, perhaps:
The cit's asham'd whene'er his duck he traps,
But you, when Madam's tripping, let her fall,
Cock up your hats, and take no shame at all.

20   What if some favor'd poet I could meet,
Whose love would lay his laurels at my feet?
No! Painted passion real love abhors;
His flame would prove the suit of creditors.[3]
  Not to detain you then with longer pause, ⎤
25 In short, my heart to this conclusion draws: ⎬
I yield it to the hand that's loudest in applause. ⎦

8. Playwright and actor (1671–1757), named
poet laureate in 1730.
9. Susannah Maria Cibber (1714–1766), the
wife of Theophilus Cibber, performed the
role of Maria.
1. That is, with his hair done up ("cock'd up")
in a fashionable queue or pigtail. *Cit*: com-

mon citizen.
2. Young men with elegant or foppish dress
and manners.
3. That is, his pursuit of her would resemble
the self-interested chase undertaken by
creditors.

RICHARD BRINSLEY SHERIDAN

1751–1816

THE career of Richard Brinsley Sheridan crosses the fields of literature, theater, and politics. The son of an actor and elocutionist, he became, at the age of twenty-four, co-owner and manager of Drury Lane Theatre. Elected to Parliament at the age of twenty-nine, he served thirty-two years in the House of Commons and was one of the most acclaimed orators of his time. But it is as a playwright that Sheridan earned his most lasting fame. Within a span of five years he wrote four of the most popular plays of his age: *The Rivals* (1775), *The Duenna* (1775), THE SCHOOL FOR SCANDAL (1777), and *The Critic* (1779). Two of these—*The Rivals* and *The School for Scandal*—have assumed a lasting place in the dramatic repertoire, and the latter has been called the greatest comedy of manners written in English. Celebrated for his wit and craft, Richard Brinsley Sheridan is considered the foremost writer of English comedy during the two hundred years that separate the drama of William Congreve from that of OSCAR WILDE.

Sheridan was born in Dublin in September or October 1751. His father, Thomas Sheridan, was an actor and theatrical manager whose love of elocution made him a respected educational reformer of his day, while his mother, Frances Sheridan, was a respected writer

of prose fiction and drama. After moving with his family to London, Richard was educated for six years at Harrow School, where he was taunted by his classmates as a "poor player's son." He continued his studies in London under his father's guidance, and at the age of nineteen he moved to Bath, the Midlands spa where the middle and upper reaches of Georgian society went to enjoy the town's medicinal waters and the pleasures of fashionable society. His father founded a short-lived "academy of oratory" in Bath, and as a way of publicizing this venture the elder Sheridan conducted "Attic Entertainments" that featured lectures on oratory and musical performances. At these entertainments Richard met the sixteen-year-old Elizabeth Ann Linley, a renowned singer and great beauty, and the two eloped to France in 1772. Upon their return Sheridan fought two duels with Captain Thomas Matthews, an indignant admirer of Elizabeth, to defend his honor in the matter, and the two lovers also had to deal with the disapproval of their two families. Reconciled with Elizabeth's father (though not with Sheridan's), the two were officially married in 1773 and shortly thereafter took up residence in London.

Sheridan showed a hand for writing at an early age. At Harrow he attempted to dramatize Oliver Goldsmith's novel *The*

Vicar of Wakefield (1766), and in subsequent years he embarked on a number of other literary projects. Most of this early work was unpublished, though, and there was certainly little to indicate the success he would subsequently win as a dramatist. When he found himself living in London with little money and a family to support (his son Thomas would be born in 1775), Sheridan wrote *The Rivals* in 1774 and submitted it to the Covent Garden Theatre, one of two "patent" playhouses in London that were allowed to produce spoken-word drama under the Theatrical Licensing Act of 1737. As *The Rivals* progressed through rehearsals, expectations for Sheridan's first comedy were high, but its premier performance on January 17, 1775, proved a disappointment with critics and audience. The Covent Garden management withdrew the play, Sheridan revised the text, and when *The Rivals* reopened on January 28 it was greeted with widespread acclaim. Drawn with a skillful sense of comic exaggeration and an eye for social observation, the dramatic ensemble of Sir Anthony Absolute and his son Captain Jack, Lydia Languish, Julia and her self-tormenting lover Faulkand, Bob Acres, Sir Lucius O'Trigger, and the inimitable Mrs. Malaprop established Sheridan as a dramatist to watch.

Sheridan provided Covent Garden with two additional plays during 1775: a farce titled *St. Patrick's Day* and a comic opera, *The Duenna*. The latter, which falls in the tradition of John Gay's celebrated play *The Beggar's Opera* (1728), proved extremely popular and would continue to be performed across England through the eighteenth century and the first half of the nineteenth. When Sheridan was elected two years later to London's exclusive Literary Club, the great Samuel Johnson commented, "He who has written the two best comedies of his age is surely a considerable man." By this time he had added the title of theater manager to that of playwright, replacing David Garrick as co-owner and manager of Drury Lane, London's other patent theater. While Sheridan's tenure in this position during the years 1776–1811 were not, on the whole, illustrious—those who worked with him complained of fiscal improvidence and negligence—his early years as playwright/manager were certainly promising. In February 1777 Sheridan staged *A Trip to Scarborough*, his adaptation of Sir John Vanbrugh's 1696 Restoration comedy *The Relapse*. And three months later he produced *The School for Scandal*, which opened on May 8, 1777, and became an immediate sensation; it was performed

A contemporary print of the "scene" from *The School for Scandal*.

more often than any other play during the final quarter of the eighteenth century.

Sheridan scored another theatrical success two years later with *The Critic*, which opened on October 30, 1779. A dramatic afterpiece of the kind that typically followed full-length plays in eighteenth-century theater programs, *The Critic* is a burlesque on the contemporary theater staged in the form of a rehearsal. Parodying contemporary conventions and popular tastes, it proved a popular successor to the Duke of Buckingham's *The Rehearsal*, which had been a favorite on the stage since 1672. But other than a melodramatic tragedy titled *Pizarro* (1799), *The Critic* was the last of Sheridan's original contributions to the theater. In 1780 Sheridan was elected to the House of Commons as a supporter of Charles James Fox's reformist Whig Party. As a member of Parliament, this son of Thomas Sheridan earned considerable praise as an orator. One of his two major speeches during the impeachment and trial of Warren Hastings, governor-general of the East India Company, was called by Edmund Burke "the most astonishing effort of eloquence, argument and wit united, of which there is any record or tradition." Sheridan briefly held several minor governmental offices, but his political career was spent mostly in opposition, and he never held the positions of power that his abilities and reputation may have led him to expect. When he lost a bid for reelection to the House of Commons in 1812, his finances were in disarray; he spent his final years pursued by the debtors from whom he had been immune while a member of Parliament. He died on July 7, 1816, and after a public funeral attended by nobility, was buried in Westminster Abbey's Poets' Corner.

The School for Scandal, which evolved from notebook jottings and a number of dramatic fragments that Sheridan had written several years earlier, appeared at an important juncture in the history of British eighteenth-century comedy. With its humorous characters, clever lines, and skillful structure of concealment and surprise, it championed "laughing comedy" over the sentimental drama popular during the early and middle years of the century. Sentimental comedy, which emerged in England around the same time that Jeremy Collier published his attack on the immorality of Restoration comedy (*A Short View of the Immorality and Profaneness of the English Stage* [1698]) and won over the public in such plays as Richard Steele's *The Conscious Lovers* (1722), rejected the bawdiness and satire of traditional comedy in favor of noble feeling, refined sensibility, and moral elevation. The audience of such drama, in which character foibles matter less than a good heart, is to be brought through tears and benevolent laughter to what Steele termed "a joy too exquisite for words." In recent decades theatrical historians have challenged the notion that sentimental drama dominated the mid-eighteenth-century stage, arguing that audiences were in fact provided with a variety of theatrical fare, including traditional and contemporary comedies. But there is no doubt that such comedies, which formed part of a wider culture of sensibility that found expression in poetry and such novels as Henry Mackenzie's *The Man of Feeling* (1771), maintained a considerable following during midcentury.

After the genre enjoyed a particular vogue in the 1760s, the 1770s witnessed a reaction against it. Oliver Goldsmith, author of the comedy *She Stoops to Conquer* (1773), claimed in "An Essay on the Theatre" (1773) that "Humor at present seems to be departing from the stage, and it will soon happen that our comic players will have nothing left for it but a fine coat and a song." Sheridan joined Goldsmith's call for a revival of laughing comedy. In the opening months of his first season as manager of Drury Lane he revived three comedies by Congreve, and in his second prologue to *The Rivals* he contrasted the comic with the sentimental muse, "too chaste to look like flesh and blood." *The School for Scandal* carried this banner further. As the *London Evening Post* wrote in its review of the opening performance, "Under this *poetical St. George,* we may expect to see the *Dragon of mere sentimental drama* entirely subdued, and the standard of *real comedy* once more unfurled."

In reality, Sheridan's attitude toward benevolence and morality in *The School for Scandal* is more complex than this heroic analogy indicates. The play's credentials as a "real comedy" are, of course, undeniable. The idea of a School for Scandal allowed Sheridan to indulge the witty and often malicious verbal play so popular in Restoration comedy while satirizing the excesses to which this wit could easily be taken. Scandal, which flourished both in the gatherings of fashionable society and in popular journalism (such publications as *Town and Country Magazine,* to which Snake refers in the play's opening exchange), becomes, in Sheridan's play, an art with its own rules and refinement. Lady Sneerwell is a virtuoso of this art, and the pleasure that she and her scandal companions take in their witty exchanges is inseparable from its ability to victimize. "The malice of a good thing," she asserts, "is the barb that makes it stick." Brilliantly inventive though this scandalous wit may be, however—the scenes with Lady Sneerwell and her circle are among the play's funniest—it represents, for Sheridan, a threat to civil society. Replacing truth with rumor and innuendo, scandal undermines the relationship between language and the world it refers to.

This concern with the misuses of language can be seen in the character of Joseph Surface, who carries much of the play's satire on the culture of sentimentality. Joseph is known as a "man of sentiment" because he professes moral views in the form of sentiments, or edifying moral statements. "There is nothing *in the world so noble as a man of sentiment!*" Sir Peter Teazle says of him, and the elder Surface glides his way through the play making sermonlike pronouncements on such subjects as charity and compassion. As his surname implies, though, Joseph's profession of moral feeling is hypocritical; it masks his opportunism and lack of moral principles. In this regard Joseph contrasts markedly with his younger brother Charles, for whom surface and inner reality hold a different relationship. To all appearances Charles is a "libertine," a title that evokes the hedonism and profligacy that flourished in the Restoration court of his namesake, Charles II. He dispenses with the rituals, pretensions, and niceties of established society, selling his family possessions to finance his appetite

for the good life. But unlike the rakes featured in the plays of WILLIAM WYCHERLEY, George Etherege, and Congreve—and most decidedly unlike his brother—his heart is fundamentally good. He gives money to a poor relation and cannot bear to sell the portrait of his uncle and benefactor Oliver Surface. A plain dealer in his relationships with others, he says what he means, and this endears him to his uncle, who has undertaken a character test of his two nephews. As is true of the youthful protagonist of Henry Fielding's *Tom Jones* (1749), the faults and indiscretions that result from Charles's youthful spirits only highlight his intrinsic honesty and charity of temperament. Unlike its comic predecessors, in short, *The School for Scandal* portrays a world where benevolence, generosity of spirit, and natural feeling are rewarded. In so doing, it underscores Sir Peter's claim (to Lady Sneerwell) that "true wit is more nearly allied to good nature than your ladyship is aware of."

The characters of Sir Peter and Lady Teazle offer further insight into Sheridan's simultaneously comic and deeply moral universe. The December-May relationship of an older husband and a younger wife has a long literary and theatrical pedigree, and it provides endless opportunities for dramatizing marital discord and infidelity (or cuckoldry). As a woman "bred wholly in the country," Lady Teazle recalls Margery Pinchwife in Wycherley's play *The Country Wife* (1675), who is brought to London by a jealous husband but finds herself a willing object of sexual interest for the rake Horner. In keeping with her prototype, Lady Teazle bickers with her husband of seven months (a "teazle" is a plant with prickly leaves) and, as part of her determination to be a "woman of fashion," becomes an initiate in Lady Sneerwell's scandal club. But her motives and nature are fundamentally different from those of her fellow scandal connoisseurs. "I have no malice against the people I abuse," she says to Sir Peter. "When I say an ill-natured thing, 'tis out of pure good humour—and I take it for granted they deal exactly in the same manner with me." When Joseph invites her to be unfaithful to her husband, she agrees to admit him

Zoe Rainey (left) as Maria, Grant Gillespie (center) as Sir Benjamin Backbite, and Maggie Steed (right) as Mrs. Candour in the 2012 production of *The School for Scandal* at the Theatre Royal, Bath (England).

as her lover "no further than *fashion* requires." She knows, she says, the integrity of her own heart, and her only real fault in the play may be her naiveté or carelessness in misreading the moral barometer of those around her. In the end, she chooses truth over falsehood, and acknowledgment of her husband's generosity over the sparring dissonance that has characterized their relationship until that point. Like Charles, she affirms a value system rooted in moral discernment and natural sentiment.

Modern critics of *The School for Scandal* have often taken the play to task for what they see as its clear moral dichotomies and essentially conservative moral vision. According to Louis Kronenberger, the play "clicks its heels before conventional morality." Though Sheridan may be "delightfully impudent," Kronenberger writes, he is "*never* challenging or subversive." John Loftis characterizes Sheridan's plays as "benign comedies with a satirical bite that reaches only to fatuous and malicious individuals." But if *The School for Scandal* lacks the ambiguities, moral complexity, and undercurrents that mark the comedies of SHAKESPEARE, JONSON, and Congreve, its genial vision of human nature has a resonance of its own. And as a display of dramatic and theatrical skill, Sheridan's comedy with a heart has few equals.   S.G.

The School for Scandal

Prologue

Spoken by Mr. King[1]
Written by D. Garrick, Esq.[2]

A School for Scandal! tell me, I beseech you,
Needs there a school this modish art to teach you?
No need of lessons now, the knowing think—
We might as well be taught to eat and drink.
5 Caused by a dearth of scandal, should the vapors[3]
Distress our fair ones—let 'em read the papers;
Their pow'rful mixtures such disorders hit;
Crave what they will, there's *quantum sufficit.*[4]
　　"Lord!" cries my Lady Wormwood (who loves tattle,
10 And puts much salt and pepper in her prattle),
Just ris'n at noon, all night at cards when threshing
Strong tea and scandal—"Bless me, how refreshing!
Give me the papers, Lisp—how bold and free! (*Sips.*)
Last night Lord L—— (sips) was caught with Lady D——
15 For aching heads what charming sal volatile![5] (*Sips.*)
If Mrs. B.——will still continue flirting,
We hope she'll DRAW, *or we'll* UNDRAW *the curtain.*
Fine satire, poz°—in public all abuse it,　　　　　　positively (slang)
But, by ourselves (*sips*), our praise we can't refuse it.
20 Now, Lisp, *read you*—there, at that dash and star."[6]
　　"Yes, ma'am.—*A certain Lord had best beware,*
Who lives not twenty miles from Grosv'nor Square;[7]
For should he Lady W—— find willing,
WORMWOOD *is bitter*"—"Oh! that's me! the villain!
25 Throw it behind the fire, and never more
Let that vile paper come within my door."—
　　Thus at our friends we laugh, who feel the dart;
　　To reach our feelings, we ourselves must smart.
　　Is our young bard so young,[8] to think that he

---

1. Thomas King (1730–1805), the actor who played Sir Peter Teazle in the original London production of 1777.
2. David Garrick (1717–1779), the manager of Drury Lane Theatre before Sheridan and the most celebrated actor of his age.
3. An 18th-century term for depression, hypochondria, or other nervous disorder.
4. As much as suffices (Latin); that is, plenty.

5. Ammonium carbonate, or smelling salts (a stimulant and restorative).
6. Newspapers replaced letters in names with dashes and stars to disguise—and, at the same time, hint at—the identities of those involved in intrigues.
7. A fashionable neighborhood in London.
8. Sheridan was 26 when *The School for Scandal* premiered.

30   Can stop the full spring-tide of calumny?
   Knows he the world so little, and its trade?
   Alas! the devil is sooner raised than laid.
   So strong, so swift, the monster there's no gagging:
   Cut Scandal's head off—still the tongue is wagging.
35   Proud of your smiles once lavishly bestow'd,
   Again your young Don Quixote[9] takes the road:
   To show his gratitude, he draws his pen,
   And seeks this hydra,[1] Scandal, in his den.
   For your applause all perils he would through—
40   He'll fight—that's *write*—a cavalliero° true,   *knight (Spanish)*
   Till every drop of blood—that's *ink*—is spilt for you.

CHARACTERS

SIR PETER TEAZLE	CARELESS
SIR OLIVER SURFACE	and other Companions
JOSEPH SURFACE	to CHARLES [SURFACE],
CHARLES SURFACE	Servants, etc.
CRABTREE	
SIR BENJAMIN BACKBITE	LADY TEAZLE
ROWLEY	MARIA
TRIP	LADY SNEERWELL
MOSES	MRS. CANDOUR
SNAKE	

1.1

[SCENE: LADY SNEERWELL's *house*.]

> [LADY SNEERWELL *at the dressing-table*—SNAKE
> *drinking chocolate.*[2]]

LADY SNEERWELL   The paragraphs, you say, Mr. Snake,
were all inserted?

SNAKE   They were, madam, and as I copied them myself in
a feigned hand, there can be no suspicion whence they
5   came.

LADY SNEERWELL   Did you circulate the reports of Lady
Brittle's intrigue with Captain *Boastall*?

SNAKE   That is in as fine a train° as your ladyship could   *in as good order*
wish,—in the common sense of things, I think it must
10   reach Mrs. *Clackit's* ears within four-and-twenty hours;
and then, you know, the business is as good as done.

LADY SNEERWELL   Why, truly, Mrs. *Clackit* has a very pretty
talent, and a great deal of industry.

---

9. The eponymous hero of Miguel de Cervantes's novel (1605, 1615), who wandered in search of monsters to slay.
1. In Greek mythology, a monstrous water snake that lived in a swamp; it had many heads, which grew back as quickly as they were cut off, and its breath was poisonous.
2. Chocolate was introduced to Europe as a beverage in the 17th century, and it remained a fashionable drink through the 18th century.

SNAKE   True, madam, and has been tolerably successful
15   in her day: —to my knowledge, she has been the cause
of six matches being broken off, and three sons being
disinherited, of four forced elopements, as many close
confinements,° nine separate maintenances,[3] and two   *secret pregnancies*
divorces;—nay, I have more than once traced her caus-
20   ing a *Tête-à-Tête* in the *Town and Country Magazine*,[4]
when the parties perhaps had never seen each other's
faces before in the course of their lives.
LADY SNEERWELL   She certainly has talents, but her man-
ner is gross.°   *coarse*
25   SNAKE   'Tis very true,—she generally designs well, has a
free tongue, and a bold invention; but her coloring is too
dark, and her outline often extravagant. She wants° that   *lacks*
delicacy of *hint,* and *mellowness* of *sneer,* which distinguish your ladyship's scandal.
30   LADY SNEERWELL   Ah! you are partial, Snake.
SNAKE   Not in the least; everybody allows that Lady *Sneerwell* can do more with a *word* or a *look* than many can
with the most labored detail, even when they happen to
have a little truth on their side to support it.
35   LADY SNEERWELL   Yes, my dear Snake; and I am no hypocrite to deny the satisfaction I reap from the success of
my efforts. Wounded myself, in the early part of my life,
by the envenomed tongue of slander, I confess I have
since known no pleasure equal to the reducing others to
40   the level of my own injured reputation.
SNAKE   Nothing can be more natural. But, Lady Sneerwell,
there is one affair in which you have lately employed me,
wherein, I confess, I am at a loss to guess your motives.
LADY SNEERWELL   I conceive you mean with respect to my
45   neighbor, Sir Peter Teazle, and his family?
SNAKE   I do; here are two young men, to whom Sir Peter
has acted as a kind of guardian since their father's death;
the elder possessing the most amiable character, and
universally well spoken of; the youngest, the most dissi-
50   pated and extravagant young fellow in the kingdom,
without friends or character,—the former an avowed
admirer of your ladyship, and apparently your favorite; the
latter attached to Maria, Sir Peter's ward, and confess-
edly beloved by her. Now, on the face of these circum-
55   stances, it is utterly unaccountable to me, why you, the
widow of a city knight, with a good jointure,[5] should not

3. Instances of financial support provided by
a husband to his wife when the two were formally separated.
4. A monthly magazine; its section devoted to
sexual scandals was titled "Tête-à-Tête"
(French for "head-to-head").

5. Property settled upon a woman at marriage
as a means of providing for her on the death
of her husband. *City knight:* one who has
been knighted in recognition of commercial
or social rather than military achievements.

close with the passion of a man of such character and
expectations as Mr. *Surface*; and more so why you should
be so uncommonly earnest to destroy the mutual attach-
60   ment subsisting between his brother *Charles* and *Maria.*
LADY SNEERWELL   Then, at once to unravel this mystery, I
must inform you that love has no share whatever in the
intercourse between Mr. *Surface* and me.
SNAKE   No!
65 LADY SNEERWELL   His real attachment is to *Maria,* or her
fortune; but, finding in his brother a favored rival, he has
been obliged to mask his pretensions, and profit by my
assistance.
SNAKE   Yet still I am more puzzled why you should interest
70   yourself in his success.
LADY SNEERWELL   Heav'ns! how dull you are! Cannot you
surmise the weakness which I hitherto, through shame,
have concealed even from *you?* Must I confess that
Charles—that libertine, that extravagant, that bankrupt
75   fortune and reputation—that he it is for whom I am thus
anxious and malicious, and to gain whom I would sacrifice everything?
SNAKE   Now, indeed, your conduct appears consistent; but
how came you and Mr. *Surface* so confidential?
80 LADY SNEERWELL   For our mutual interest. I have found
him out a long time since—I know him to be artful, selfish, and malicious—in short, a sentimental[6] knave.
SNAKE   Yet, Sir Peter vows he has not his equal in
England—and, above all, he praises him as a man of sen-
85   timent.
LADY SNEERWELL   True; and with the assistance of his sentiment and hypocrisy he has brought him° entirely into   *(Sir Peter)*
his interest[7] with regard to *Maria.*

       [*Enter* SERVANT.]

SERVANT   Mr. Surface.
90 LADY SNEERWELL   Show him up.

                                 [*Exit* SERVANT.]

He generally calls about this time. I don't wonder at
people's giving him to me for a lover.

       [*Enter* JOSEPH SURFACE.]

JOSEPH SURFACE   My dear Lady Sneerwell, how do you do
to-day? Mr. Snake, your most obedient.[8]
95 LADY SNEERWELL   Snake has just been arraigning me on
our mutual attachment, but I have informed him of our
real views; you know how useful he has been to us; and,
believe me, the confidence is not ill placed.

---

6. Exhibiting elevated and refined feeling; apt
to deliver sentiments (moral pronouncements).
7. That is, into supporting his designs.

8. That is, "I am your most obedient servant"—
an abbreviated and thus perfunctory form of a
standard greeting.

JOSEPH SURFACE   Madam, it is impossible for me to sus-
100   pect a man of Mr. *Snake's* sensibility and discernment.

LADY SNEERWELL   Well, well, no compliments now;—but
   tell me when you saw your mistress, *Maria*—or, what is
   more material to me, your brother.

JOSEPH SURFACE   I have not seen either since I left you;
105   but I can inform you that they never meet. Some of your
   stories have taken a good effect on Maria.

LADY SNEERWELL   Ah, my dear Snake! the merit of this
   belongs to you. But do your brother's distresses increase?

JOSEPH SURFACE   Every hour;—I am told he has had another
110   execution[9] in the house yesterday; in short, his dissipation
   and extravagance exceed any thing I ever heard of.

LADY SNEERWELL   Poor Charles!

JOSEPH SURFACE   True, madam;—notwithstanding his vices,
   one can't help feeling for him.—Aye, poor Charles! I'm
115   sure I wish it was in *my* power to be of any essential service to him.—For the man who does not share in the distress of a brother, even though merited by his own
   misconduct, deserves——

LADY SNEERWELL   O lud! you are going to be moral,° and   *indulge in moralizing*
120   forget that you are among friends.

JOSEPH SURFACE   Egad, that's true!—I'll keep that sentiment till I see Sir Peter. However, it is certainly a charity
   to rescue Maria from such a libertine, who, if he is to be
   reclaimed, can be so only by a person of your ladyship's
125   superior accomplishments and understanding.

SNAKE   I believe, Lady Sneerwell, here's company
   coming,—I'll go and copy the letter I mentioned to
   you.—Mr. Surface, your most obedient.   [*Exit* SNAKE.]

JOSEPH SURFACE   Sir, your very devoted.—Lady Sneerwell,
130   I am very sorry you have put any further confidence in
   that fellow.

LADY SNEERWELL   Why so?

JOSEPH SURFACE   I have lately detected him in frequent
   conference with old *Rowley,* who was formerly my
135   father's steward, and has never, you know, been a friend
   of mine.

LADY SNEERWELL   And do you think he would betray us?

JOSEPH SURFACE   Nothing more likely: take my word for't,
   Lady Sneerwell, that fellow hasn't virtue enough to be
140   faithful even to his own villainy.—Hah! Maria!
          [*Enter* MARIA.]

LADY SNEERWELL   Maria, my dear, how do you do?—What's
   the matter?

---

9. Seizure of a debtor's goods for failure to pay.

MARIA   Oh! there is that disagreeable lover of mine, Sir *Benjamin Backbite*, has just called at my guardian's, with
145   his odious uncle, *Crabtree*, so I slipped out, and ran hither to avoid them.

LADY SNEERWELL   Is that all?

JOSEPH SURFACE   If my brother *Charles* had been of the party, ma'am, perhaps you would not have been so much
150   alarmed.

LADY SNEERWELL   Nay, now you are severe; for I dare swear the truth of the matter is, Maria heard *you* were here;—but, my dear, what has Sir Benjamin done, that you should avoid him so?

155   MARIA   Oh, he has done nothing—but 'tis for what he has said,—his conversation is a perpetual libel on all his acquaintance.

JOSEPH SURFACE   Aye, and the worst of it is, there is no advantage in not knowing him; for he'll abuse a stranger
160   just as soon as his best friend—and his uncle's as bad.

LADY SNEERWELL   Nay, but we should make allowance; Sir Benjamin is a wit and a poet.

MARIA   For my part, I own, madam, wit loses its respect with me, when I see it in company with malice.—What
165   do you think, Mr. Surface?

JOSEPH SURFACE   Certainly, madam; to smile at the jest which plants a thorn in another's breast is to become a principal in the mischief.

LADY SNEERWELL   Pshaw! there's no possibility of being
170   witty without a little ill nature: the malice of a good thing is the barb that makes it stick.—What's your opinion, Mr. Surface?

JOSEPH SURFACE   To be sure, madam, that conversation, where the spirit of raillery is suppressed, will ever appear
175   tedious and insipid.

MARIA   Well, I'll not debate how far scandal may be allowable; but in a man, I am sure, it is always contemptible.— We have pride, envy, rivalship, and a thousand motives to depreciate each other; but the male slanderer must have
180   the cowardice of a woman before he can traduce° one.   *slander*

[*Enter* SERVANT.]

SERVANT   Madam, Mrs. Candour is below, and, if your ladyship's at leisure, will leave her carriage.

LADY SNEERWELL   Beg her to walk in.

[*Exit* SERVANT.]

Now Maria, however, here is a character to your taste; for
185   though Mrs. Candour is a little talkative, everybody allows her to be the best-natured and best sort of woman.

MARIA   Yes, with a very gross affectation of good nature and benevolence, she does more mischief than the direct malice of old Crabtree.

190 JOSEPH SURFACE I'faith 'tis very true, Lady Sneerwell; whenever I hear the current running against the characters of my friends, I never think them in such danger as when Candour undertakes their defence.

LADY SNEERWELL Hush!—here she is!

[*Enter* MRS. CANDOUR.]

195 MRS. CANDOUR My dear Lady Sneerwell, how have you been this century?—Mr. Surface, what news do you hear?—though indeed it is no matter, for I think one hears nothing else but scandal.

JOSEPH SURFACE Just so, indeed, madam.

200 MRS. CANDOUR Ah, Maria! child,—what, is the whole affair off between you and Charles? His extravagance, I presume—the town talks of nothing else.

MARIA I am very sorry, ma'am, the town has so little to do.

MRS. CANDOUR True, true, child: but there is no stopping
205 people's tongues.—I own I was hurt to hear it, as indeed I was to learn, from the same quarter, that your guardian, Sir Peter, and Lady Teazle have not agreed lately so well as could be wished.

MARIA 'Tis strangely impertinent for people to busy them-
210 selves so.

MRS. CANDOUR Very true, child, but what's to be done? People will talk—there's no preventing it.—Why, it was but yesterday I was told that Miss Gadabout had eloped with Sir Filigree Flirt.—But, Lord! there's no minding
215 what one hears—though, to be sure, I had this from very good authority.

MARIA Such reports are highly scandalous.

MRS. CANDOUR So they are, child—shameful, shameful! But the world is so censorious, no character escapes.—
220 Lord, now who would have suspected your friend, Miss Prim, of an indiscretion? Yet such is the ill-nature of people, that they say her uncle stopped her last week, just as she was stepping into the York Diligence[1] with her dancing-master.

225 MARIA I'll answer for't there are no grounds for the report.

MRS. CANDOUR Oh, no foundation in the world, I dare swear; no more, probably, than for the story circulated last month, of Mrs. Festino's affair with Colonel Cassino;—though; to be sure, that matter was never
230 rightly cleared up.

JOSEPH SURFACE The license of invention some people take is monstrous indeed.

MARIA 'Tis so.—But, in my opinion, those who report such things are equally culpable.

---

1. The public stagecoach to the city of York.

235 MRS. CANDOUR   To be sure they are; tale-bearers are as bad
as the tale-makers—'tis an old observation, and a very true
one—but what's to be done, as I said before? how will you
prevent people from talking?—To-day, Mrs. Clackit
assured me Mr. and Mrs. Honeymoon were at last become
240 mere man and wife, like the rest of their acquaintances.—
She likewise hinted that a certain widow, in the next
street, had got rid of her dropsy[2] and recovered her shape
in a most surprising manner. And at the same time Miss
Tattle, who was by, affirmed that Lord Buffalo had discov-
245 ered his lady at a house of no extraordinary fame—and
that Sir Harry Bouquet and Tom Saunter were to measure
swords° on a similar provocation. But, Lord, do you think   *i.e., to duel*
I would report these things! No, no! tale-bearers, as I said
before, are just as bad as tale-makers.
250 JOSEPH SURFACE   Ah! Mrs. Candour, if everybody had your
forbearance and good nature!
MRS. CANDOUR   I confess, Mr. Surface, I cannot bear to
hear people attacked behind their backs, and when ugly
circumstances come out against one's acquaintance I
255 own I always love to think the best.—By the bye, I hope
it is not true that your brother is absolutely ruined?
JOSEPH SURFACE   I am afraid his circumstances are very
bad indeed, ma'am.
MRS. CANDOUR   Ah!—I heard so—but you must tell him to
260 keep up his spirits—everybody almost is in the same
way! Lord Spindle, Sir Thomas Splint, Captain Quinze,
and Mr. Nickit—all up,° I hear, within this week; so, if   *bankrupt*
Charles is undone, he'll find half his acquaintances
ruined too—and that, you know, is a consolation.
265 JOSEPH SURFACE   Doubtless, ma'am—a very great one.

[*Enter* SERVANT.]

SERVANT   Mr. Crabtree and Sir Benjamin Backbite.
LADY SNEERWELL   So, Maria, you see your lover pursues
you; positively you shan't escape.

[*Enter* CRABTREE *and* SIR BENJAMIN BACKBITE.]

CRABTREE   Lady Sneerwell, I kiss your hands. Mrs. Can-
270 dour, I don't believe you are acquainted with my nephew,
Sir Benjamin Backbite? Egad, ma'am, he has a pretty
wit, and is a pretty poet too; isn't he, Lady Sneerwell?
SIR BENJAMIN   O fie, uncle!
CRABTREE   Nay, egad it's true—I'll back him at a rebus or a
275 charade[3] against the best rhymer in the kingdom. Has
your ladyship heard the epigram he wrote last week on
Lady Frizzle's feather catching fire?—Do, Benjamin,
repeat it—or the charade you made last night extempore at

2. A swelling of the body due to excess fluids;
here, an allusion to pregnancy.
3. A riddle game in which words are guessed
by syllable; in the 18th century, the clues

were given by enigmatic description. *Rebus:*
a riddle game in which pictures or symbols
represent the syllables of the word to be
guessed.

Mrs. Drowzie's conversazione.[4]— Come now; your *first*
280 is the name of a fish, your *second* a great naval commander,
and——

SIR BENJAMIN Uncle, now—prithee——

CRABTREE I'faith, ma'am, 'twould surprise you to hear
how ready he is at these things.

285 LADY SNEERWELL I wonder, Sir Benjamin, you never publish anything.

SIR BENJAMIN To say truth, ma'am, 'tis very vulgar to print;
and as my little productions are mostly satires and lampoons on particular people, I find they circulate more by
290 giving copies in confidence to the friends of the parties—
however, I have some love elegies, which, when favored
with this lady's smiles, I mean to give to the public.

CRABTREE 'Fore heav'n, ma'am, they'll immortalize you!—
you'll be handed down to posterity like Petrarch's Laura,
295 or Waller's Sacharissa.[5]

SIR BENJAMIN Yes, madam, I think you will like them,
when you shall see them on a beautiful quarto[6] page,
where a neat rivulet of text shall murmur through a
meadow of margin. 'Fore gad, they will be the most ele-
300 gant things of their kind!

CRABTREE But, ladies, that's true—have you heard the
news?

MRS. CANDOUR What, sir, do you mean the report of—

CRABTREE No, ma'am, that's not it.—Miss Nicely is going
305 to be married to her own footman.

MRS. CANDOUR Impossible!

CRABTREE Ask Sir Benjamin.

SIR BENJAMIN 'Tis very true, ma'am—everything is fixed,
and the wedding liveries bespoke.°   *clothes ordered*

310 CRABTREE Yes—and they *do* say there were pressing reasons for it.

LADY SNEERWELL Why, I *have* heard something of this
before.

MRS. CANDOUR It can't be—and I wonder any one should
315 believe such a story of so prudent a lady as Miss Nicely.

SIR BENJAMIN O lud! ma'am, that's the very reason 'twas
believed at once. She has always been so *cautious* and so
reserved, that everybody was sure there was some reason
for it at bottom.

320 MRS. CANDOUR Why, to be sure, a tale of scandal is as fatal
to the credit of a prudent lady of her stamp as a fever is
generally to those of the strongest constitutions; but

---

4. A fashionable social gathering that
included discussion of arts and literature
(Italian).

5. The names given to women addressed in
the love poetry of Francesco Petrarca (1304–
1374) and Edmund Waller (1606–1687),

respectively. Laura has never been identified;
Sacharissa ("most sweet") was Lady Dorothy
Sidney (1617–1684).

6. A standard book size (made by folding a
sheet of paper twice, into quarters).

there is a sort of puny, sickly reputation that is always ailing, yet will outlive the robuster characters of a hundred
325 prudes.

SIR BENJAMIN True, madam, there are valetudinarians in
reputation as well as constitution, who, being conscious
of their weak part, avoid the least breath of air, and supply their want of stamina by care and circumspection.

330 MRS. CANDOUR Well, but this may be all a mistake. You
know, Sir Benjamin, very trifling circumstances often
give rise to the most injurious tales.

CRABTREE That they do, I'll be sworn, ma'am. Did you
ever hear how Miss Piper came to lose her lover and her
335 character last summer at Tunbridge?[7]—Sir Benjamin, you
remember it?

SIR BENJAMIN Oh, to be sure!—the most whimsical circumstance—

LADY SNEERWELL How was it, pray?

340 CRABTREE Why, one evening, at Mrs. Ponto's assembly,
the conversation happened to turn on the difficulty of
breeding Nova Scotia sheep in this country. Says a young
lady in company, "I have known instances of it; for Miss
Letitia Piper, a first cousin of mine, had a Nova Scotia
345 sheep that produced her twins." "What!" cries the old
Dowager[8] Lady Dundizzy (who you know is as deaf as a
post), "has Miss Piper had twins?" This mistake, as you
may imagine, threw the whole company into a fit of
laughing. However, 'twas the next morning everywhere
350 reported, and in a few days believed by the whole town,
that Miss Letitia Piper had actually been brought to bed
of a fine boy and a girl—and in less than a week there
were people who could name the father, and the farm-
house where the babies were put out to nurse!

355 LADY SNEERWELL Strange, indeed!

CRABTREE Matter of fact, I assure you.—O lud! Mr. Surface, pray is it true that your uncle, Sir Oliver, is coming
home?

JOSEPH SURFACE Not that I know of, indeed, sir.

360 CRABTREE He has been in the East Indias a long time. You
can scarcely remember him, I believe.—Sad comfort,
whenever he returns, to hear how your brother has gone
on!

JOSEPH SURFACE Charles has been imprudent, sir, to be
365 sure; but I hope no busy people have already prejudiced
Sir Oliver against him,—he may reform.

SIR BENJAMIN To be sure he may—for my part I never
believed him to be so utterly void of principle as people

---

7. Tunbridge Wells, a fashionable resort in
Kent (about 30 miles southeast of London).

8. Widow whose title comes from her
deceased husband.

say—and though he has lost all his friends, I am told
370   nobody is better spoken of by the Jews.[9]

CRABTREE   That's true, egad, nephew. If the old Jewry[1]
were a ward, I believe Charles would be an alderman; no
man more popular there, 'fore gad! I hear he pays as
many annuities as the Irish tontine;[2] and that, whenever
375   he's sick, they have prayers for the recovery of his health
in the Synagogue.

SIR BENJAMIN   Yet no man lives in greater splendor.—They
tell me, when he entertains his friends, he can sit down
to dinner with a dozen of his own securities;[3] have a
380   score [of] tradesmen waiting in the antechamber; and
an officer behind every guest's chair.

JOSEPH SURFACE   This may be entertainment to you, gentlemen, but you pay very little regard to the feelings of a
brother.

385   MARIA [aside]   Their malice is intolerable!—Lady Sneerwell,
I must wish you a good morning—I'm not very well.

                                            [Exit MARIA.]

MRS. CANDOUR   O dear! She changes color very much!

LADY SNEERWELL   Do, Mrs. Candour, follow her—she may
want assistance.

390   MRS. CANDOUR   That I will, with all my soul, ma'am.—Poor
dear girl! who knows what her situation may be!

                                            [Exit MRS. CANDOUR.]

LADY SNEERWELL   'Twas nothing but that she could not
bear to hear Charles reflected on, notwithstanding their
difference.

395   SIR BENJAMIN   The young lady's *penchant*° is obvious.   inclination (French)

CRABTREE   But, Benjamin, you mustn't give up the pursuit
for that; follow her, and put her into good humour.
Repeat her some of your own verses.—Come, I'll assist
you.

400   SIR BENJAMIN   Mr. Surface, I did not mean to hurt you; but
depend upon't your brother is utterly undone. [Going]

CRABTREE   O, lud, aye! undone as ever man was—can't
raise a guinea.[4] [Going]

SIR BENJAMIN   And everything sold, I'm told, that was mov-
405   able. [Going]

CRABTREE   I have seen one that was at his house—not a
thing left but some empty bottles that were overlooked,
and the family pictures, which I believe are framed in
the wainscot.° [Going]   wooden wall paneling

9. That is, Jewish moneylenders in London.
1. The Jewish quarter of 13th-century London, near the Bank of England.
2. A form of life annuity plan used mainly by
governments to raise funds; though poorly
subscribed in England when introduced, they
were successful in Ireland in the 1770s.

3. That is, friends who have pledged themselves to cover his loans.
4. A gold coin worth 21 shillings (i.e., 1 shilling more than a pound), with aristocratic
associations; professional fees and the prices
of artworks, horses, and land were often calculated in guineas.

410 SIR BENJAMIN And I am very sorry to hear also some bad
stories against him. [*Going*]

CRABTREE Oh, he has done many mean things, that's certain. [*Going*]

SIR BENJAMIN But, however, as he's your brother—[*Going*]

415 CRABTREE We'll tell you all, another opportunity.

[*Exeunt*° CRABTREE *and* SIR BENJAMIN.]   *They exit (Latin)*

LADY SNEERWELL Ha, ha! ha! 'tis very hard for them to
leave a subject they have not quite run down.

JOSEPH SURFACE And I believe the abuse was no more
acceptable to your ladyship than to Maria.

420 LADY SNEERWELL I doubt° her affections are farther   *fear*
engaged than we imagined; but the family are to be here
this evening, so you may as well dine where you are, and
we shall have an opportunity of observing farther;—in
the meantime, I'll go and plot mischief, and you shall

425 study sentiments.

[*Exeunt.*]

1.2

[SCENE: SIR PETER TEAZLE'*s house.*]

[*Enter* SIR PETER.]

SIR PETER When an old bachelor takes a young wife, what
is he to expect?—'Tis now six months since Lady Teazle
made me the happiest of men—and I have been the miserablest dog ever since that ever committed wedlock! We

5 tift a little[5] going to church, and came to a quarrel before
the bells were done ringing. I was more than once nearly
choked with gall° during the honeymoon, and had lost all   *rancor*
comfort in life before my friends had done wishing me
joy! Yet I chose with caution—a girl bred wholly in the

10 country, who never knew luxury beyond one silk gown,
nor dissipation above the annual gala of a race ball. Yet
now she plays her part in all the extravagant fopperies of
the fashion and the town, with as ready a grace as if she
had never seen a bush nor a grassplat° out of Grosvenor   *patch of grass*

15 Square! I am sneered at by my old acquaintance—
paragraphed in the newspapers. She dissipates my fortune, and contradicts all my humors;° yet the worst of   *moods*
it is, I doubt° I love her, or I should never bear all this.   *fear*
However, I'll never be weak enough to own it.

[*Enter* ROWLEY.]

20 ROWLEY Oh! Sir Peter, your servant,—how is it with you, sir?

SIR PETER Very bad, Master Rowley, very bad;—I meet
with nothing but crosses and vexations.

5. Had a small tiff or spat.

ROWLEY What can have happened to trouble you since yesterday?

25 SIR PETER A good question to a married man!

ROWLEY Nay, I'm sure your lady, Sir Peter, can't be the cause of your uneasiness.

SIR PETER Why, has anyone told you she was dead?

ROWLEY Come, come, Sir Peter, you love her, notwith-
30 standing your tempers don't exactly agree.

SIR PETER But the fault is entirely hers, Master Rowley. I am, myself, the sweetest-tempered man alive, and hate a teasing temper—and so I tell her a hundred times a day.

ROWLEY Indeed!

35 SIR PETER Aye; and what is very extraordinary, in all our disputes she is always in the wrong! But Lady Sneerwell, and the set she meets at her house, encourage the perverseness of her disposition. Then, to complete my vexations, Maria, my ward, whom I ought to have the power
40 of a father over, is determined to turn rebel too, and absolutely refuses the man whom I have long resolved on for her husband;—meaning, I suppose, to bestow herself on his profligate brother.

ROWLEY You know, Sir Peter, I have always taken the lib-
45 erty to differ with you on the subject of these two young gentlemen. I only wish you may not be deceived in your opinion of the elder. For Charles, my life on't! he will retrieve his errors yet. Their worthy father, once my honored master, was, at his years, nearly as wild a spark; yet,
50 when he died, he did not leave a more benevolent heart to lament his loss.

SIR PETER You are wrong, Master Rowley. On their father's death, you know, I acted as a kind of guardian to them both, till their uncle Sir Oliver's Eastern liberality
55 gave them an early independence; of course, no person could have more opportunities of judging of their hearts, and I was never mistaken in my life. Joseph is indeed a model for the young men of the age. He is a man of sentiment, and acts up to the sentiments he professes; but,
60 for the other, take my word for't, if he had any grains of virtue by descent, he has dissipated them with the rest of his inheritance. Ah! my old friend, Sir Oliver, will be deeply mortified when he finds how part of his bounty has been misapplied.

65 ROWLEY I am sorry to find you so violent against the young man, because this may be the most critical period of his fortune. I came hither with news that will surprise you.

SIR PETER What! let me hear.

70 ROWLEY Sir Oliver *is* arrived, and at this moment in town.

SIR PETER How! you astonish me! I thought you did not expect him this month.

ROWLEY   I did not; but his passage has been remarkably quick.

75 SIR PETER   Egad, I shall rejoice to see my old friend,—'tis sixteen years since we met—we have had many a day together; but does he still enjoin us not to inform his nephews of his arrival?

ROWLEY   Most strictly. He means, before it is known, to 80 make some trial of their dispositions.

SIR PETER   Ah! There needs no art to discover their merits—however, he shall have his way; but, pray, does he know I am married?

ROWLEY   Yes, and will soon wish you joy.

85 SIR PETER   What, as we drink health of a friend in a consumption![6] Ah, Oliver will laugh at me—we used to rail at matrimony together—but he has been steady to his text.°   *maxim* Well, he must be at my house, though—I'll instantly give orders for his reception. But, Master Rowley, don't drop a 90 word that Lady Teazle and I ever disagree.

ROWLEY   By no means.

SIR PETER   For I should never be able to stand Noll's° jokes;   *Oliver's (nickname)* so I'd have him think, Lord forgive me! that we are a very happy couple.

95 ROWLEY   I understand you—but then you must be very careful not to differ while he's in the house with you.

SIR PETER   Egad, and so we must—and that's impossible. Ah! Master Rowley, when an old bachelor marries a young wife, he deserves—no—the crime carries the pun-100 ishment along with it.

                                        [Exeunt.]

2.1

[SCENE: SIR PETER TEAZLE'S *house.*]

[*Enter* SIR PETER *and* LADY TEAZLE.]

SIR PETER   Lady Teazle, Lady Teazle, I'll not bear it!

LADY TEAZLE   Sir Peter, Sir Peter, you may bear it or not, as you please; but I ought to have my own way in everything, and what's more, I *will* too.—What! though I was 5 educated in the country, I know very well that women of fashion in London are accountable to nobody after they are married.

SIR PETER   Very well, ma'am, very well,—so a husband is to have no influence, no authority?

10 LADY TEAZLE   Authority! No, to be sure—if you wanted authority over me, you should have adopted me, and not married me; I am sure you were old enough.

SIR PETER   Old enough!—aye, there it is!—Well, well, Lady

6. Suffering from a wasting disease (especially tuberculosis of the lungs).

Teazle, though my life may be made unhappy by your tem-
15 per, I'll not be ruined by your extravagance.

LADY TEAZLE My extravagance! I'm sure I'm not more
extravagant than a woman of fashion ought to be.

SIR PETER No, no, madam, you shall throw away no more
sums on such unmeaning luxury. 'Slife!° to spend as much   By God's life! (oath)
20 to furnish your dressing room with flowers in a winter as
would suffice to turn the Pantheon into a greenhouse,
and give a *fête champêtre*[7] at Christmas!

LADY TEAZLE Lord, Sir Peter, am I to blame because flowers are dear in cold weather? You should find fault with
25 the climate, and not with me. For my part, I am sure I
wish it was spring all the year round, and that roses grew
under one's feet!

SIR PETER Oons![8] madam—if you had been born to this, I
shouldn't wonder at your talking thus.—But you forget
30 what your situation was when I married you.

LADY TEAZLE No, no, I don't; 'twas a very disagreeable
one, or I should never have married *you*.

SIR PETER Yes, yes, madam, you were then in somewhat
an humbler style—the daughter of a plain country squire.
35 Recollect, Lady Teazle, when I saw you first, sitting at
your tambour in a pretty figured linen gown, with a
bunch of keys by your side, your hair combed smooth
over a roll,[9] and your apartment hung round with fruits
in worsted, of your own working.

40 LADY TEAZLE O, yes! I remember it very well, and a curious[1] life I led—my daily occupation to inspect the dairy,
superintend the poultry, make extracts from the family
receipt-book,° and comb my aunt Deborah's lapdog.   book of recipes

SIR PETER Yes, yes, ma'am, 'twas so indeed.

45 LADY TEAZLE And then, you know, my evening amusements! To draw patterns for ruffles, which I had not the
materials to make; to play Pope Joan with the curate; to
read a novel to my aunt; or to be stuck down to an old
spinet[2] to strum my father to sleep after a fox-chase.

50 SIR PETER I am glad you have so good a memory. Yes,
madam, these were the recreations I took you from; but
now you must have your coach—*vis-à-vis*[3]—and three
powdered footmen before your chair° and, in summer, a   sedan chair
pair of white cats° to draw you to Kensington Gardens.[4]—   ponies

---

7. Outdoor entertainment (French). *Pantheon:*
a large hall in London, opened in 1772 as a
fashionable place of public entertainment.
8. By God's wounds (euphemistic contraction).
9. A round cushion or pad used in styling a
woman's hair. *Tambour:* embroidery frame.
Figured: ornamented with patterns or designs.
1. Careful, attentive to details; odd.

2. A type of small harpsichord, typically found
in homes. *Pope Joan:* a card game.
3. A light two-person carriage in which passengers sit face-to-face (the literal meaning of
the French *vis-à-vis*).
4. A fashionable gathering place attached to
Kensington Palace.

55 No recollection, I suppose, when you were content to ride
double, behind the butler, on a docked° coach-horse?   *cropped tail*

LADY TEAZLE   No—I swear I never did that—I deny the
butler and the coach-horse.

SIR PETER   This, madam, was your situation—and what
60 have I not done for you? I have made you a woman of
fashion, of fortune, of rank—in short, I have made you
my wife.

LADY TEAZLE   Well, then, and there is but one thing more
you can make me to add to the obligation—and that is—

65 SIR PETER   My widow, I suppose?

LADY TEAZLE   Hem! hem!

SIR PETER   Thank you, madam—but don't flatter yourself;
for though your ill-conduct may disturb my peace, it
shall never break my heart, I promise you: however, I am
70 equally obliged to you for the hint.

LADY TEAZLE   Then why will you endeavor to make yourself so disagreeable to me, and thwart me in every little
elegant expense?

SIR PETER   'Slife, madam, I say, had you any of these ele-
75 gant expenses when you married me?

LADY TEAZLE   Lud, Sir Peter! would you have me be out of
the fashion?

SIR PETER   The fashion, indeed! what had you to do with
the fashion before you married me?

80 LADY TEAZLE   For my part, I should think you would like to
have your wife thought a woman of taste.

SIR PETER   Aye—there again—taste! Zounds!° madam, you   *God's wounds!*
had no taste when you married *me!*

LADY TEAZLE   That's very true, indeed, Sir Peter! and *after*
85 having married you, I am sure I should never pretend to
taste again! But now, Sir Peter, if we have finished our
daily jangle,° I presume I may go to my engagement of   *quarrel*
Lady Sneerwell's?

SIR PETER   Aye—there's another precious circumstance!—
90 a charming set of acquaintance you have made there!

LADY TEAZLE   Nay, Sir Peter, they are people of rank and
fortune, and remarkably tenacious of reputation.

SIR PETER   Yes, egad, they are tenacious of reputation with
a vengeance; for they don't choose anybody should have
95 a character but themselves! Such a crew! Ah! many a
wretch has rid on a hurdle who has done less mischief
than those utterers of forged tales, coiners° of scandal,—   *counterfeiters*
and clippers[5] of reputation.

LADY TEAZLE   What! would you restrain the freedom of
100 speech?

5. Those who clip off and sell the edges of coins. *Hurdle:* a sledge or frame on which traitors
were drawn through the streets to execution.

SIR PETER   Oh! they have made you just as bad as any one
   of the society.
LADY TEAZLE   Why, I believe I do bear a part with a tolerable grace. But I vow I have no malice against the people
105   I abuse; when I say an ill-natured thing, 'tis out of pure
   good humor—and I take it for granted they deal exactly
   in the same manner with me. But, Sir Peter, you know
   you promised to come to Lady Sneerwell's too.
SIR PETER   Well, well, I'll call in just to look after my own
110   character.
LADY TEAZLE   Then, indeed, you must make haste after me
   or you'll be too late.—So good-bye to ye.

                              [*Exit* LADY TEAZLE.]

SIR PETER   So—I have gained much by my intended expos-
   tulations! Yet with what a charming air she contradicts
115   everything I say, and how pleasingly she shows her contempt of my authority. Well, though I can't make her
   love me, there is a great satisfaction in quarreling with
   her; and I think she never appears to such advantage as
   when she's doing everything in her power to plague me.

                              [*Exit.*]

2.2

[SCENE: LADY SNEERWELL'S.]

   [LADY SNEERWELL, MRS. CANDOUR, CRABTREE, SIR
   BENJAMIN BACKBITE, *and* JOSEPH SURFACE.]

LADY SNEERWELL   Nay, positively, we will hear it.
JOSEPH SURFACE   Yes, yes, the epigram, by all means.
SIR BENJAMIN   Plague on't, uncle! 'tis mere nonsense.
CRABTREE   No, no; 'fore gad, very clever for an extempore![6]
5 SIR BENJAMIN   But, ladies, you should be acquainted with
   the circumstance,—you must know, that one day last
   week, as Lady Betty Curricle was taking the dust in
   Hyde Park in a sort of duodecimo phaëton,[7] she desired
   me to write some verses on her ponies; upon which, I
10   took out my pocket-book, and in one moment produced
   the following:

        Sure never were seen two such beautiful ponies!
        Other horses are clowns,° and these macaronies![8]   *rustics*
        Nay, to give 'em this title I'm sure isn't wrong—
15   Their legs are so slim, and their tails so long.

CRABTREE   There, ladies—done in the smack of a whip,
   and on horseback too!

---

6. An extemporaneous composition.
7. A very small horse-drawn open carriage.
Hyde Park: fashionable London park.
8. Dandies who affect a preference for Continental (in particular, Italian) fashion. The following lines play on *macarons* as long tubes of
pasta.

JOSEPH SURFACE   A very Phoebus,[9] mounted—indeed, Sir
Benjamin.
20 SIR BENJAMIN   O dear sir—trifles—trifles.

[*Enter* LADY TEAZLE *and* MARIA.]

MRS. CANDOUR   I must have a copy.
LADY SNEERWELL   Lady Teazle, I hope we shall see Sir Peter.
LADY TEAZLE   I believe he'll wait on[1] your ladyship presently.
LADY SNEERWELL   Maria, my love, you look grave. Come,
25 you shall sit down to cards with Mr. Surface.
MARIA   I take very little pleasure in cards—however, I'll do
as your ladyship pleases.
LADY TEAZLE [*aside*]   I am surprised Mr. Surface should sit
down with *her.*—I thought he would have embraced this
30 opportunity of speaking to me before Sir Peter came.
MRS. CANDOUR [*coming forward*]   Now, I'll die but you are
so scandalous, I'll forswear your society.
LADY TEAZLE   What's the matter, Mrs. Candour?
MRS. CANDOUR   They'll not allow° our friend Miss Vermilion   *acknowledge*
35 to be handsome.
LADY SNEERWELL   Oh, surely, she's a pretty woman.
CRABTREE   I am very glad you think so, ma'am.
MRS. CANDOUR   She has a charming fresh color.
LADY TEAZLE   Yes, when it is fresh put on.
40 MRS. CANDOUR   O fie! I'll swear her color is natural—I
have seen it come and go.
LADY TEAZLE   I dare swear you have, ma'am—it goes of a
night, and comes again in the morning.
MRS. CANDOUR   Ha! ha! ha! how I hate to hear you talk so!
45 But surely, now, her sister *is,* or *was,* very handsome.
CRABTREE   Who? Mrs. Evergreen?—O Lord! she's six-and-
fifty if she's an hour!
MRS. CANDOUR   Now positively you wrong her; fifty-two or
fifty-three is the utmost—and I don't think she looks
50 more.
SIR BENJAMIN   Ah! there is no judging by her looks, unless
one could see her face.
LADY SNEERWELL   Well, well, if Mrs. Evergreen *does* take
some pains to repair the ravages of time, you must allow
55 she effects it with great ingenuity; and surely that's better than the careless manner in which the widow Ochre
caulks her wrinkles.
SIR BENJAMIN   Nay, now, Lady Sneerwell, you are severe
upon the widow. Come, come, it is not that she paints so
60 ill—but, when she has finished her face, she joins it on
so badly to her neck, that she looks like a mended statue,
in which the connoisseur sees at once that the head's
modern, though the trunk's antique!

9. Apollo, in classical mythology the god of   1. Pay a respectful visit to.
poetry and music.

65 CRABTREE   Ha! ha! ha! Well said, nephew!

MRS. CANDOUR   Ha! ha! ha! Well, you make me laugh, but I
vow I hate you for't.—What do you think of Miss Simper?

SIR BENJAMIN   Why, she has very pretty teeth.

LADY TEAZLE   Yes; and on that account, when she is neither speaking nor laughing (which very seldom hap-
70   pens), she never absolutely shuts her mouth, but leaves
it always on a jar,° as it were.   *ajar*

MRS. CANDOUR   How can you be so ill-natured?

LADY TEAZLE   Nay, I allow even that's better than the pains
Mrs. Prim takes to conceal her losses in front. She draws
75   her mouth till it positively resembles the aperture of a
poor's-box,[2] and all her words appear to slide out edge-
ways.

LADY SNEERWELL   Very well, Lady Teazle, I see you can be
a little severe.

80 LADY TEAZLE   In defence of a friend it is but justice;—but
here comes Sir Peter to spoil our pleasantry.

[*Enter* SIR PETER TEAZLE.]

SIR PETER   Ladies, your most obedient—[*Aside*] Mercy on
me, here is the whole set! a character dead at every
word, I suppose.

85 MRS. CANDOUR   I am rejoiced you are come, Sir Peter.
They have been *so* censorious. They will allow good qual-
ities to nobody—not even good nature to our friend Mrs.
Pursy.

LADY TEAZLE   What, the fat dowager who was at Mrs.
90   Codille's last night?

MRS. CANDOUR   Nay, her bulk is her misfortune; and, when
she takes such pains to get rid of it, you ought not to
reflect° on her.   *cast blame*

LADY SNEERWELL   That's very true, indeed.

95 LADY TEAZLE   Yes, I know she almost lives on acids and
small whey;[3] laces herself by pulleys; and often, in the
hottest noon of summer, you may see her on a little
squat pony, with her hair platted up behind like a drummer's, and puffing round the Ring[4] on a full trot.

100 MRS. CANDOUR   I thank you, Lady Teazle, for defending
her.

SIR PETER   Yes, a good defense, truly.

MRS. CANDOUR   But Sir Benjamin is as censorious as Miss
Sallow.

105 CRABTREE   Yes, and she is a curious being to pretend to be
censorious!—an awkward gawky, without any one good
point under heaven.

2. A money box, usually in a church, for dona-
tions to the poor.
3. Vinegar and the watery part of milk left
behind in the manufacture of cheese.

4. A circular road in Hyde Park where fashionable Londoners would drive in order to see
and be seen.

MRS. CANDOUR   Positively you shall not be so very severe.
Miss Sallow is a relation of mine by marriage, and, as for
110   her person, great allowance is to be made; for, let me tell
you, a woman labors under many disadvantages who
tries to pass for a girl at six-and-thirty.

LADY SNEERWELL   Though, surely, she is handsome still—
and for the weakness in her eyes, considering how much
115   she reads by candlelight, it is not to be wondered at.

MRS. CANDOUR   True; and then as to her manner, upon my
word I think it is particularly graceful, considering she
never had the least education; for you know her mother
was a Welch milliner, and her father a sugar-baker° at   *sugar refiner*
120   Bristol.

SIR BENJAMIN   Ah! you are both of you too good-natured!

SIR PETER   [*aside*] Yes, damned good-natured! This their
own relation! mercy on me!

SIR BENJAMIN   And Mrs. Candour is of so moral a turn she
125   can sit for an hour to hear Lady Stucco talk sentiment.

LADY TEAZLE   Nay, I vow Lady Stucco is very well with the
dessert after dinner; for she's just like the French fruit[5]
one cracks for mottoes—made up of paint and proverb.

MRS. CANDOUR   Well, I never will join in ridiculing a
130   friend; and so I constantly tell my cousin Ogle, and you
all know what pretensions she has to be critical in beauty.

CRABTREE   Oh, to be sure! she has herself the oddest
countenance that ever was seen; 'tis a collection of features from all the different countries of the globe.

135   SIR BENJAMIN   So she has, indeed—an Irish front!

CRABTREE   Caledonian locks!

SIR BENJAMIN   Dutch nose!

CRABTREE   Austrian lip!

SIR BENJAMIN   Complexion of a Spaniard!

140   CRABTREE   And teeth *à la Chinoise!*[6]

SIR BENJAMIN   In short, her face resembles a *table d'hôte* at
Spa[7]—where no two guests are of a nation—

CRABTREE   Or a congress at the close of a general war—
wherein all the members, even to her eyes, appear to
145   have a different interest, and her nose and chin are the
only parties likely to join issue.°   *i.e., unite*

MRS. CANDOUR   Ha! ha! ha!

SIR PETER   [*aside*] Mercy on my life!—a person they dine
with twice a week!

150   MRS. CANDOUR   Nay, but I vow you shall not carry the
laugh off so—for give me leave to say, that Mrs. Ogle—

---

5. Sugar candies that contain sayings on slips
of paper.
6. Chinese (French). "Caledonian locks"
were long and shaggy, like a Scottish High-
lander's; a "Dutch nose" was flat; "Austrian
lips" were characterized by a protruding lower

lip; a "Spanish complexion" was dark; and
Chinese teeth were allegedly stained black. It
is not clear what Sheridan meant by an "Irish
front" (or forehead).
7. A dining table (French) for guests at Spa, a
popular resort in Belgium.

SIR PETER Madam, madam, I beg your pardon—there's no
stopping these good gentlemen's tongues. But when I tell
you, Mrs. Candour, that the lady they are abusing is a
155 particular friend of mine—I hope you'll not take her part.

LADY SNEERWELL Well said, Sir Peter! but you are a cruel
creature—too phlegmatic yourself for a jest, and too
peevish to allow wit on others.

SIR PETER Ah, madam, true wit is more nearly allied to
160 good nature than your ladyship is aware of.

LADY TEAZLE True, Sir Peter; I believe they are so near
akin that they can never be united.

SIR BENJAMIN Or rather, madam, suppose them man and
wife, because one so seldom sees them together.

165 LADY TEAZLE But Sir Peter is such an enemy to scandal, I
believe he would have it put down by parliament.

SIR PETER 'Fore heaven, madam, if they were to consider
the sporting with reputation of as much importance as
poaching on manors,[8] and pass *An Act for the Preservation
170 of Fame,*° I believe many would thank them for the bill. °reputation

LADY SNEERWELL O lud! Sir Peter; would you deprive us
of our privileges?

SIR PETER Aye, madam; and then no person should be
permitted to kill characters or run down reputations, but
175 qualified old maids and disappointed widows.

LADY SNEERWELL Go, you monster!

MRS. CANDOUR But sure you would not be quite so severe
on those who only report what they hear.

SIR PETER Yes, madam, I would have law merchant[9] for
180 them too; and in all cases of slander currency, whenever
the drawer of the lie was not to be found, the injured parties should have a right to come on any of the endorsers.[1]

CRABTREE Well, for my part, I believe there never was a
scandalous tale without some foundation.

185 LADY SNEERWELL Come, ladies, shall we sit down to cards
in the next room?

[*Enter* SERVANT *and whispers to* SIR PETER.]

SIR PETER I'll be with them directly—.

[*Exit* SERVANT.]

[*Aside*] I'll get away unperceived.

LADY SNEERWELL Sir Peter, you are not leaving us?

190 SIR PETER Your ladyship must excuse me; I'm called away by
particular business—but I leave my character behind me.

[*Exit* SIR PETER.]

---

8. Illegal hunting on rural estates.
9. Rules governing commerce.
1. Those who endorse a loan. In Sir Peter's
metaphor, originators of slander are like
those who enter into debt: when they default

on their loans, those who endorse the note
to guarantee that it will be repaid (i.e., those
who repeat scandal) must also be held
accountable.

SIR BENJAMIN Well certainly, Lady Teazle, that lord of yours is a strange being; I could tell you some stories of him would make you laugh heartily, if he wasn't your husband.

195 LADY TEAZLE O pray don't mind that—come, do let's hear them.

[They join the rest of the company, all talking as they are going into the next room.]

JOSEPH SURFACE *[rising with* MARIA*]* Maria, I see you have no satisfaction in this society.

MARIA How is it possible I should? If to raise malicious
200 smiles at the infirmities and misfortunes of those who have never injured us be the province of wit or humour, heaven grant me a double portion of dulness!

JOSEPH SURFACE Yet they appear more ill-natured than they are; they have no malice at heart.

205 MARIA Then is their conduct still more contemptible; for, in my opinion, nothing could excuse the intemperance of their tongues but a natural and ungovernable bitterness of mind.

JOSEPH SURFACE But can you, Maria, feel thus for others,
210 and be unkind to me alone? Is hope to be denied the tenderest passion?

MARIA Why will you distress me by renewing this subject?

JOSEPH SURFACE Ah, Maria! you would not treat me thus, and oppose your guardian, Sir Peter's will, but that I see
215 that profligate *Charles* is still a favored rival.

MARIA Ungenerously urged! But, whatever my sentiments of that unfortunate young man are, be assured I shall not feel more bound to give him up, because his distresses have lost him the regard even of a brother.

[LADY TEAZLE returns.]

220 JOSEPH SURFACE Nay, but, Maria, do not leave me with a frown—by all that's honest, I swear—*[Aside]* Gad's life, here's Lady Teazle. —You must not—no, you shall not— for, though I have the greatest regard for Lady Teazle——

MARIA Lady Teazle!

225 JOSEPH SURFACE Yet were Sir Peter to suspect——

LADY TEAZLE *[coming forward]* What's this, pray? Do you take her for me?—Child, you are wanted in the next room.——

[Exit MARIA.]

What is all this, pray?

230 JOSEPH SURFACE Oh, the most unlucky circumstance in nature! Maria has somehow suspected the tender concern I have for your happiness, and threatened to acquaint Sir Peter with her suspicions, and I was just endeavoring to reason with her when you came.

235 LADY TEAZLE Indeed! but you seemed to adopt a very tender mode of reasoning—do you *usually* argue on your knees?

JOSEPH SURFACE   Oh, she's a child—and I thought a little
  bombast°—but, Lady Teazle, when are you to give me   *pompous*
  your judgment on my library, as you promised?
240 LADY TEAZLE   No, no,—I begin to think it would be imprudent, and you know I admit you as a lover no further
  than *fashion* requires.
JOSEPH SURFACE   True—a mere Platonic cicisbeo,[2] what
  every London wife is *entitled* to.
245 LADY TEAZLE   Certainly, one must not be out of the fashion; however, I have so much of my country prejudices
  left, that, though Sir Peter's ill humour may vex me ever
  so, it never shall provoke me to——
JOSEPH SURFACE   The only revenge in your power. Well, I
250 applaud your moderation.
LADY TEAZLE   Go—you are an insinuating wretch! But we
  shall be missed—let us join the company.
JOSEPH SURFACE   But we had best not return together.
LADY TEAZLE   Well, don't stay—for Maria shan't come to
255 hear any more of your *reasoning*, I promise you.
                                        [*Exit* LADY TEAZLE.]
JOSEPH SURFACE   A curious dilemma, truly, my politics°   *schemes*
  have run me into! I wanted, at first, only to ingratiate
  myself with Lady Teazle, that she might not be my enemy
  with Maria; and I have, I don't know how, become her
260 serious lover. Sincerely I begin to wish I had never made
  such a point of gaining so *very good* a character, for it has
  led me into so many cursed rogueries that I doubt° I shall   *fear*
  be exposed at last.   [*Exit.*]

2.3

[SCENE: SIR PETER'S.]

[*Enter* SIR OLIVER SURFACE *and* ROWLEY.]

SIR OLIVER   Ha! ha! ha! and so my old friend is married,
  hey?—a young wife out of the country.—Ha! ha! ha!—
  that he should have stood bluff to° old bachelor so long,   *stood firm as an*
  and sink into a husband at last!
5 ROWLEY   But you must not rally him on the subject, Sir
  Oliver; 'tis a tender point, I assure you, though he has
  been married only seven months.
SIR OLIVER   Then he has been just half a year on the stool
  of repentance![3] Poor Peter! But you say he has entirely
10 given up Charles—never sees him, hey?

---

2. A recognized gallant or escort (Italian);
that is, a man who devotes himself to, but is
not the lover of, a married woman.

3. In churches, a stool on which offenders
(especially against chastity) stood to publicly
repent.

ROWLEY His prejudice against him is astonishing, and I
am sure greatly increased by a jealousy of him with Lady
Teazle, which he has been industriously led into by a
scandalous society in the neighborhood, who have con-
15 tributed not a little to Charles's ill name; whereas the
truth is, I believe, if the lady is partial to either of them,
his brother is the favorite.

SIR OLIVER Aye,—I know there are a set of malicious,
prating, prudent gossips, both male and female, who
20 murder characters to kill time, and will rob a young fellow of his good name before he has years to know the
value of it,—but I am not to be prejudiced against my
nephew by such, I promise you! No, no;—if Charles has
done nothing false or mean, I shall compound for his
25 extravagance.°   *i.e., pay his debts*

ROWLEY Then, my life on't, you will reclaim° him.—Ah,   *reform*
sir, it gives me new life to find that *your* heart is not
turned against him, and that the son of my good old
master has one friend, however, left.

30 SIR OLIVER What! shall I forget, Master Rowley, when I
was at his years myself? Egad, my brother and I were
neither of us very *prudent* youths—and yet, I believe,
you have not seen many better men than your old master
was?

35 ROWLEY Sir, 'tis this reflection gives me assurance that
Charles may yet be a credit to his family.—But here
comes Sir Peter.

SIR OLIVER Egad, so he does!—Mercy on me, he's greatly
altered, and seems to have a settled married look! One
40 may read husband in his face at this distance!

[*Enter* SIR PETER TEAZLE.]

SIR PETER Hah! Sir Oliver—my old friend! Welcome to
England a thousand times!

SIR OLIVER Thank you, thank you, Sir Peter! and i'faith I
am glad to find you well, believe me!

45 SIR PETER Ah! 'tis a long time since we met—sixteen years,
I doubt, Sir Oliver, and many a cross accident° in the   *adverse occurrence*
time.

SIR OLIVER Aye, I have had my share—but, what! I find
you are married, hey, my old boy?—Well, well, it can't be
50 helped—and so I wish you joy with all my heart!

SIR PETER Thank you, thank you, Sir Oliver.—Yes, I have
entered into the happy state—but we'll not talk of that
now.

SIR OLIVER True, true, Sir Peter; old friends should not
55 begin on grievances at first meeting. No, no, no.

ROWLEY [*to* SIR OLIVER] Take care, pray, sir.

SIR OLIVER Well, so one of my nephews is a wild rogue,
hey?

SIR PETER   Wild! Ah! my old friend, I grieve for your disap-
60   pointment there—he's a lost young man, indeed; however, his brother will make you amends; *Joseph* is,
indeed, what a youth should be—everybody in the world
speaks well of him.

SIR OLIVER   I am sorry to hear it—he has too good a char-
65   acter to be an honest fellow.—Everybody speaks well of
him! Psha! then he has bowed as low to knaves and fools
as to the honest dignity of genius or virtue.

SIR PETER   What, Sir Oliver! do you blame him for not
making enemies?

70   SIR OLIVER   Yes, if he has merit enough to deserve them.

SIR PETER   Well, well—you'll be convinced when you
know him. 'Tis edification to hear him converse—he professes the noblest sentiments.

SIR OLIVER   Ah, plague of his sentiments! If he salutes me
75   with a scrap of morality in his mouth, I shall be sick
directly. But, however, don't mistake me, Sir Peter; I
don't mean to defend Charles's errors—but, before I
form my judgment of either of them, I intend to make a
trial of their hearts—and my friend Rowley and I have
80   planned something for the purpose.

ROWLEY   And Sir Peter shall own for once he has been
mistaken.

SIR PETER   Oh, my life on Joseph's honor!

SIR OLIVER   Well, come, give us a bottle of good wine, and
85   we'll drink the lad's health, and tell you our scheme.

SIR PETER   *Allons,*° then!   *Let's go (French)*

SIR OLIVER   And don't, Sir Peter, be so severe against your
old friend's son. Odds my life! I am not sorry that he has
run out of the course a little; for my part, I hate to see
90   prudence clinging to the green succors° of youth; 'tis like   *suckers, shoots*
ivy round a sapling, and spoils the growth of the tree.

                                                                  [*Exeunt.*]

3.1

[SCENE: SIR PETER'S.]

[SIR PETER TEAZLE, SIR OLIVER SURFACE, *and*
ROWLEY.]

SIR PETER   Well, then—we will see this fellow first, and
have our wine afterwards. But how is this, Master Row-
ley? I don't see the jet° of your scheme.   *gist; real point*

ROWLEY   Why, sir, this Mr. Stanley, whom I was speaking of,
5   is nearly° related to them, by their mother; he was once a   *closely*
merchant in Dublin, but has been ruined by a series of
undeserved misfortunes. He has applied, by letter, since
his confinement° both to Mr. Surface and Charles—from   *imprisonment (for debt)*
the former he has received nothing but evasive promises

10　of future service, while Charles has done all that his
　　extravagance has left him power to do; and he is, at this
　　time, endeavoring to raise a sum of money, part of which,
　　in the midst of his own distresses, I know he intends for
　　the service of poor Stanley.
15 SIR OLIVER　Ah! he is my brother's son.
　　SIR PETER　Well, but how is Sir Oliver personally to——
　　ROWLEY　Why, sir, I will inform Charles and his brother that
　　Stanley has obtained permission to apply in person to his
　　friends, and, as they have neither of them ever seen him,
20　let Sir Oliver assume his character, and he will have a fair
　　opportunity of judging at least of the benevolence of their
　　dispositions; and believe me, sir, you will find in the youn-
　　gest brother one who, in the midst of folly and dissipation,
　　has still, as our immortal bard[4] expresses it,——

25　　　　　　　　a tear for pity, and a hand
　　　　　　　Open as day, for melting charity.

　　SIR PETER　Psha! What signifies his having an open hand
　　or purse either, when he has nothing left to give? Well,
　　well, make the trial, if you please; but where is the fellow
30　whom you brought for Sir Oliver to examine, relative to
　　Charles's affairs?
　　ROWLEY　Below, waiting his commands, and no one can
　　give him better intelligence.—This, Sir Oliver, is a
　　friendly Jew, who, to do him justice, has done everything
35　in his power to bring your nephew to a proper sense of
　　his extravagance.
　　SIR PETER　Pray let us have him in.
　　ROWLEY　Desire Mr. Moses to walk upstairs.
　　SIR PETER　But why should you suppose he will speak the
40　truth?
　　ROWLEY　Oh, I have convinced him that he has no chance
　　of recovering certain sums advanced to Charles but
　　through the bounty of Sir Oliver, who he knows is
　　arrived; so that you may depend on his fidelity to his
45　interest. I have also another evidence° in my power, one　　　　　*witness*
　　Snake, whom I have detected in a matter little short of
　　forgery, and shall shortly produce to remove some of
　　your prejudices, Sir Peter, relative to Charles and Lady
　　Teazle.
50 SIR PETER　I have heard too much on that subject.
　　ROWLEY　Here comes the honest Israelite.
　　　　　　[*Enter* MOSES.]
　　—This is Sir Oliver.
　　SIR OLIVER　Sir, I understand you have lately had great
　　dealings with my nephew Charles.

---

4. That is, William Shakespeare (1546–1616); the quotation is from *2 Henry IV* (1599),
4.3.31–32.

55 MOSES   Yes, Sir Oliver—I have done all I could for him,
but he was ruined before he came to me for assistance.

SIR OLIVER   That was unlucky, truly—for you have had no
opportunity of showing your talents.

MOSES   None at all—I hadn't the pleasure of knowing his
60 distresses—till he was some thousands worse than
nothing.°   *i.e., in debt*

SIR OLIVER   Unfortunate, indeed! But I suppose you have
done all in your power for him, honest Moses?

MOSES   Yes, he knows that. This very evening I was to have
65 brought him a gentleman from the city, who doesn't
know him, and will, I believe, advance him some money.

SIR PETER   What, one Charles has never had money from
before?

MOSES   Yes; Mr. Premium, of Crutched Friars[5]—formerly
70 a broker.

SIR PETER   Egad, Sir Oliver, a thought strikes me!—
Charles, you say, doesn't know Mr. Premium?

MOSES   Not at all.

SIR PETER   Now then, Sir Oliver, you may have a better
75 opportunity of satisfying yourself than by an old romanc-
ing tale of a poor relation;—go with my friend Moses,
and represent Mr. *Premium*, and then, I'll answer for't,
you will see your nephew in all his glory.

SIR OLIVER   Egad, I like this idea better than the other,
80 and I may visit *Joseph* afterwards, as old *Stanley*.

SIR PETER   True—so you may.

ROWLEY   Well, this is taking Charles rather at a disadvan-
tage, to be sure. However, Moses—you understand Sir
Peter, and will be faithful?

85 MOSES   You may depend upon me,—this is near the time I
was to have gone.

SIR OLIVER   I'll accompany you as soon as you please,
Moses; but hold! I have forgot one thing—how the
plague shall I be able to pass for a Jew?

90 MOSES   There's no need—the principal° is Christian.   *head of the business*

SIR OLIVER   Is he?—I'm sorry to hear it—but, then again,
an't I rather too smartly dressed to look like a moneylender?

SIR PETER   Not at all; 'twould not be out of character, if
95 you went in your own carriage—would it, Moses?

MOSES   Not in the least.

SIR OLIVER   Well, but how must I talk? there's certainly
some cant° of usury, and mode of treating,° that I ought   *jargon / negotiating*
to know.

100 SIR PETER   Oh, there's not much to learn—the great point,
as I take it, is to be exorbitant enough in your demands—
hey, Moses?

5. A small street in the commercial center of London.

MOSES Yes, that's a very great point.

SIR OLIVER I'll answer for't I'll not be wanting in that. I'll
105 ask him eight or ten per cent on the loan, at least.

MOSES If you ask him no more than that, you'll be discov-
ered° immediately.   found out

SIR OLIVER Hey! what the plague! how much then?

MOSES That depends upon the circumstances. If he
110 appears not very anxious for the supply, you should
require only forty or fifty per cent, but if you find him in
great distress, and want the moneys very bad—you may
ask double.

SIR PETER A good honest trade you're learning, Sir Oliver!

115 SIR OLIVER Truly I think so—and not unprofitable.

MOSES Then, you know, you haven't the moneys yourself,
but are forced to borrow them for him of a friend.

SIR OLIVER Oh! I borrow it of a friend, do I?

MOSES Yes, and your friend is an unconscionable dog, but
120 you can't help it.

SIR OLIVER My friend is an unconscionable dog, is he?

MOSES Yes, and he himself has not the moneys by him—
but is forced to sell stock at a great loss.

SIR OLIVER He is forced to sell stock, is he, at a great loss,
125 is he? Well, that's very kind of him.

SIR PETER I'faith, Sir Oliver—Mr. Premium, I mean—
you'll soon be master of the trade. But, Moses! wouldn't
you have him run out° a little against the Annuity Bill?[6]   expound
That would be in character, I should think.

130 MOSES Very much.

ROWLEY And lament that a young man now must be at
years of discretion before he is suffered to ruin himself?

MOSES Aye, great pity!

SIR PETER And abuse the public for allowing merit to an
135 act whose only object is to snatch misfortune and imprudence from the rapacious relief of usury, and give the
minor a chance of inheriting his estate without being
undone by coming into possession.

SIR OLIVER So, so—Moses shall give me further instruc-
140 tions as we go together.

SIR PETER You will not have much time, for your nephew
lives hard by.°   nearby

SIR OLIVER Oh, never fear! my tutor appears so able, that
though Charles lived in the next street, it must be my own
145 fault if I am not a complete rogue before I turn the corner.

[Exeunt SIR OLIVER and MOSES.]

SIR PETER So now I think Sir Oliver will be convinced;—
you are partial, Rowley, and would have prepared Charles
for the other plot.

6. A bill protecting the property of minors; it became law in May 1777, the same month that *The
School for Scandal* opened.

ROWLEY   No, upon my word, Sir Peter.

150 SIR PETER   Well, go bring me this Snake, and I'll hear what
he has to say presently.—I see Maria, and want to speak
with her.—

[*Exit* ROWLEY.]

I should be glad to be convinced my suspicions of Lady
Teazle and Charles were unjust. I have never yet
155 opened my mind on this subject to my friend *Joseph*—
I'm determined I will do it—*he* will give me his opinion
sincerely.

[*Enter* MARIA.]

So, child, has Mr. Surface returned with you?

MARIA   No, sir—he was engaged.

160 SIR PETER   Well, Maria, do you not reflect, the more you
converse with that amiable young man, what return his
partiality for you deserves?

MARIA   Indeed, Sir Peter, your frequent importunity on this
subject distresses me extremely—you compel me to
165 declare, that I know no man who has ever paid me a particular attention whom I would not prefer to Mr. Surface.

SIR PETER   So—here's perverseness! No, no, Maria, 'tis
Charles only whom you would prefer—'tis evident his
vices and follies have won your heart.

170 MARIA   This is unkind, sir—you know I have obeyed you in
neither seeing nor corresponding with him; I have heard
enough to convince me that he is unworthy my regard.
Yet I cannot think it culpable, if, while my understanding
severely condemns his vices, my heart suggests some
175 pity for his distresses.

SIR PETER   Well, well, pity him as much as you please, but
give your heart and hand to a worthier object.

MARIA   Never to his brother!

SIR PETER   Go, perverse and obstinate! But take care,
180 madam; you have never yet known what the authority of
a guardian is—don't compel me to inform you of it.

MARIA   I can only say, you shall not have *just* reason. 'Tis
true, by my father's will, I am for a short period bound to
regard you as his substitute, but must cease to think you
185 so, when you compel me to be miserable.   [*Exit* MARIA.]

SIR PETER   Was ever man so crossed as I am! everything
conspiring to fret me!—I had not been involved in matrimony a fortnight, before her father, a hale and hearty
man, died—on purpose, I believe, for the pleasure of
190 plaguing me with the care of his daughter. But here
comes my helpmate! She appears in great good humour.
How happy I should be if I could tease her into loving
me, though but a little!

[*Enter* LADY TEAZLE.]

LADY TEAZLE   Lud! Sir Peter, I hope you haven't been quar-
195   reling with Maria—it isn't using me well to be ill
humored when I am not by.
SIR PETER   Ah, Lady Teazle, you might have the power to
make me good humoured at all times.
LADY TEAZLE   I am sure I wish I had—for I want you to be
200   in charming sweet temper at this moment. Do be good
humored now, and let me have two hundred pounds,
will you?
SIR PETER   Two hundred pounds! what, an't I to be in a
good humor without paying for it! But speak to me thus,
205   and i'faith there's nothing I could refuse you. You shall
have it; but seal° me a bond for the repayment.   *i.e., sign*
LADY TEAZLE   O, no—there—my note of hand will do as well.
SIR PETER [*kissing her hand*]   And you shall no longer
reproach me with not giving you an independent
210   settlement,—I mean shortly to surprise you; shall we
always live thus, hey?
LADY TEAZLE   If you please. I'm sure I don't care how soon
we leave off quarreling, provided you'll own *you* were
tired first.
215   SIR PETER   Well—then let our future contest be, who shall
be most obliging.
LADY TEAZLE   I assure you, Sir Peter, good nature becomes
you. You look now as you did before we were married!—
when you used to walk with me under the elms, and tell
220   me stories of what a gallant you were in your youth, and
chuck me under the chin, you would, and ask me if I
thought I could love an old fellow, who would deny me
nothing—didn't you?
SIR PETER   Yes, yes, and you were as kind and attentive.
225   LADY TEAZLE   Aye, so I was, and would always take your
part, when my acquaintance used to abuse you, and turn
you into ridicule.
SIR PETER   Indeed!
LADY TEAZLE   Aye, and when my cousin Sophy has called
230   you a stiff, peevish old bachelor, and laughed at me for
thinking of marrying one who might be my father, I have
always defended you—and said, I didn't think you so
ugly by any means, and that I dared say you'd make a
very good sort of a husband.
235   SIR PETER   And you prophesied right—and we shall certainly now be the happiest couple——
LADY TEAZLE   And never differ again!
SIR PETER   No, never!—though at the same time, indeed,
my dear Lady Teazle, you must watch your temper very
240   narrowly; for in all our little quarrels, my dear, if you recollect, my love, you always began first.
LADY TEAZLE   I beg your pardon, my dear Sir Peter: indeed,
you always gave the provocation.

SIR PETER   Now, see, my angel! take care—*contradicting*
245   isn't the way to keep friends.
LADY TEAZLE   Then, don't *you* begin it, my love!
SIR PETER   There, now! you—you are going on—you don't
perceive, my life, that you are just doing the very thing
which you know always makes me angry.
250   LADY TEAZLE   Nay, you know if you will be angry without
any reason—
SIR PETER   There now! you want to quarrel again.
LADY TEAZLE   No, I am sure I don't—but, if you will be so
peevish—
255   SIR PETER   There now! who begins first?
LADY TEAZLE   Why, you, to be sure. I said nothing—but
there's no bearing your temper.
SIR PETER   No, no, madam, the fault's in your own temper.
LADY TEAZLE   Aye, you are just what my cousin Sophy said
260   you would be.
SIR PETER   Your cousin Sophy is a forward, impertinent
gipsy.
LADY TEAZLE   You are a great bear, I'm sure, to abuse my
relations.
265   SIR PETER   Now may all the plagues of marriage be doubled on me, if ever I try to be friends with you any more!
LADY TEAZLE   So much the better.
SIR PETER   No, no, madam; 'tis evident you never cared a
pin for me, and I was a madman to marry you—a pert,
270   rural coquette, that had refused half the honest squires
in the neighborhood!
LADY TEAZLE   And I am sure, I was a fool to marry you—an
old dangling bachelor,[7] who was single at fifty, only
because he never could meet with any one who would
275   have him.
SIR PETER   Aye, aye, madam; but you were pleased enough
to listen to me—*you* never had such an offer before.
LADY TEAZLE   No! didn't I refuse Sir Twivy Tarrier, who
everybody said would have been a better match—for his
280   estate is just as good as yours—and he has broke his
neck since we have been married.
SIR PETER   I have done with you, madam! You are an
unfeeling, ungrateful—but there's an end of everything.
I believe you capable of anything that's bad. Yes, madam,
285   I now believe the reports relative to you and Charles,
madam—yes, madam, you and Charles—are not without
grounds——
LADY TEAZLE   Take care, Sir Peter! you had better not
insinuate any such thing! I'll not be suspected with*out*
290   *cause*, I promise you.

7. A "dangler" is a man who hangs around women.

SIR PETER   Very well, madam! very well! a separate maintenance as soon as you please. Yes, madam, or a divorce!
I'll make an example of myself for the benefit of all old
bachelors. Let us separate, madam.

295   LADY TEAZLE   Agreed! agreed! And now, my dear Sir Peter,
we are of a mind once more, we may be the *happiest
couple*, and *never differ again*, you know: ha! ha! Well, you
are going to be in a passion, I see, and I shall only interrupt you—so, bye! bye!   [*Exit.*]

300   SIR PETER   Plagues and tortures! can't I make her angry
neither? Oh, I am the miserablest fellow! But I'll not
bear her presuming to keep her temper—no! she may
break my heart, but she shan't keep her temper.   [*Exit.*]

3.2

[SCENE: CHARLES'*s house.*]

[*Enter* TRIP, MOSES, *and* SIR OLIVER SURFACE.]

TRIP   Here, Master Moses! if you'll stay a moment, I'll try
whether—what's the gentleman's name?

SIR OLIVER   Mr. —[*aside*] Moses, what *is* my name?

MOSES   Mr. Premium.

5   TRIP   Premium—very well.   [*Exit* TRIP, *taking snuff.*]

SIR OLIVER   To judge by the servants one wouldn't believe
the master was ruined. But what!—sure, this was my
brother's house?

MOSES   Yes, sir; Mr. Charles bought it of Mr. Joseph, with

10   the furniture, pictures, &c., just as the old gentleman
left it—Sir Peter thought it a great piece of extravagance
in him.

SIR OLIVER   In my mind, the other's economy in *selling* it
to him was more reprehensible by half.

[*Re-enter* TRIP.]

15   TRIP   My master says you must wait, gentlemen; he has
company, and can't speak with you yet.

SIR OLIVER   If he knew *who* it was wanted to see him, perhaps he wouldn't have sent such a message?

TRIP   Yes, yes, sir; he knows *you* are here—I didn't forget

20   little Premium—no, no, no.

SIR OLIVER   Very well—and I pray, sir, what may be your
name?

TRIP   Trip, sir—my name is Trip, at your service.

SIR OLIVER   Well, then, Mr. Trip, you have a pleasant sort

25   of a place° here, I guess.   *employment*

TRIP   Why, yes—here are three or four of us pass our time
agreeably enough; but then our wages are sometimes a
little in arrear—and not very great either—but fifty
pounds a year, and find our own bags and bouquets.[8]

8. That is, supply our own fashionable accessories. *Bags:* small silken pouches to hold the back
hair of a wig.

30 SIR OLIVER [aside] Bags and bouquets! halters and basti-
nadoes!°   *nooses and cudgels*

TRIP But à propos,[9] Moses, have you been able to get me
that little bill discounted?

SIR OLIVER [aside] Wants to raise money, too!—mercy on
35 me! Has his distresses, I warrant, like a lord,—and
affects° creditors and duns.   *presumes to deal with*

MOSES 'Twas not to be done, indeed, Mr. Trip.
[*Gives the note.*]

TRIP Good lack, you surprise me! My friend *Brush* has
endorsed it, and I thought when he put his mark on the
40 back of a bill 'twas as good as cash.

MOSES No, 'twouldn't do.

TRIP A small sum—but twenty pounds. Hark'ee, Moses,
do you think you couldn't get it me by way of annuity?[1]

SIR OLIVER [aside] An annuity! ha! ha! a footman raise
45 money by way of annuity! Well done, luxury, egad!

MOSES But you must insure your place.

TRIP Oh, with all my heart! I'll insure my place, and my
life too, if you please.

SIR OLIVER [aside] It's more than I would your neck.

50 TRIP But then, Moses, it must be done before this d——d
register[2] takes place—one wouldn't like to have one's
name made public, you know.

MOSES No, certainly. But is there nothing you could deposit?

TRIP Why, nothing capital of my master's wardrobe has
55 dropped lately; but I could give you a mortgage on some
of his winter clothes, with equity of redemption before
November[3]—or you shall have the reversion of the
French velvet, or a post-obit[4] on the blue and silver;—
these, I should think, Moses, with a few pair of point
60 ruffles, as a collateral security—hey, my little fellow?

MOSES Well, well.
[*Bell rings.*]

TRIP Gad, I heard the bell! I believe, gentlemen, I can
now introduce you. Don't forget the annuity, little
Moses! This way, gentlemen, insure my place, you know.

65 SIR OLIVER [aside] If the man be a shadow of his master,
this is the temple of dissipation indeed!

[*Exeunt.*]

---

9. On that subject (French).
1. A loan that is repaid through a series of annual payments.
2. The Annuity Bill of 1777 required that such annuities be registered.
3. That is, the option of buying back the mortgaged clothes by paying back the loan

and interest before November, when they will be needed.
4. A bond given by a borrower to be repaid after the death of a specific individual from whom the borrower expects to inherit. *Reversion*: anticipated inheritance (servants often received cast-off clothing from their masters).

3.3

[SCENE: *Another room in* CHARLES's *house*.]

[CHARLES SURFACE, CARELESS, &c., &c. *at a table with wine, &c.*]

CHARLES 'Fore heaven, 'tis true!—there's the great degeneracy of the age. Many of our acquaintance have taste, spirit, and politeness; but, plague on't, they won't drink.

CARELESS It is so, indeed, Charles! they give in to all the
5   substantial luxuries of the table, and abstain from nothing but wine and wit.

CHARLES Oh, certainly society suffers by it intolerably! for now, instead of the social spirit of raillery that used to mantle over° a glass of bright Burgundy, their conversation   *form a froth on*
10   is become just like the Spa-water they drink, which has all the pertness[5] and flatulence° of champagne, without its   *i.e., bubbles* spirit or flavor.

1 GENT But what are *they* to do who love play° better than   *gambling* wine?

15 CARELESS True! there's Harry diets himself for gaming, and is now under a hazard° regimen.   *a dice game*

CHARLES Then he'll have the worst of it. What! you wouldn't train a horse for the course by keeping him from corn!° For my part, egad, I am now never so successful as   *grain*
20   when I am a little merry—let me throw on a bottle of champagne, and I never lose—at least I never feel my losses, which is exactly the same thing.

2 GENT Aye, that I believe.

CHARLES And, then, what man can pretend to be a
25   believer in love, who is an abjurer of wine? 'Tis the test by which the lover knows his own heart. Fill a dozen bumpers[6] to a dozen beauties, and she that floats at top is the maid that has bewitched you.

CARELESS Now then, Charles, be honest, and give us your
30   real favorite.

CHARLES Why, I have withheld her only in compassion to you. If I toast her, you must give a round of her peers— which is impossible—on earth.

CARELESS Oh, then we'll find some canonised vestals[7] or
35   heathen goddesses that will do, I warrant!

CHARLES Here then, bumpers, you rogues! bumpers! Maria! Maria—

[*Drink*.]

1 GENT Maria who?

CHARLES O, damn the surname!—'tis too formal to be
40   registered in Love's calendar—but now, Sir Toby Bumper, beware—we must have beauty superlative.

---

5. Pungency of taste.
6. Glasses filled to the brim, especially for toasting.

7. Vestal virgins, the priestesses at the temple in Rome of Vesta, goddess of the hearth.

CARELESS   Nay, never study,° Sir Toby: we'll stand to the   *think intently*
toast, though your mistress should want an eye—and
you know you have a song will excuse you.

45 SIR TOBY   Egad, so I have! and I'll give him the song
instead of the lady.

SONG AND CHORUS

Here's to the maiden of bashful fifteen;
  Here's to the widow of fifty;
Here's to the flaunting extravagant quean,°   *hussy, whore*
50   And here's to the housewife that's thrifty.
Chorus.   Let the toast pass—
      Drink to the lass—
I'll warrant she'll prove an excuse for the glass.

Here's to the charmer whose dimples we prize;
55   Now to the maid who has none, sir;
Here's to the girl with a pair of blue eyes,
  And here's to the nymph with but one, sir.
Chorus.   Let the toast pass, &c.

Here's to the maid with a bosom of snow:
60   Now to *her* that's as brown as a berry:
Here's to the wife with a face full of woe,
  And now for the damsel that's merry.
Chorus.   Let the toast pass, &c.

For let 'em be clumsy, or let 'em be slim,
65   Young or ancient, I care not a feather:
So fill a pint bumper quite up to the brim,
  —And let us e'en toast 'em together.
Chorus.   Let the toast pass, &c.

ALL   Bravo! Bravo!
      [*Enter* TRIP, *and whispers to* CHARLES SURFACE.]

70 CHARLES   Gentlemen, you must excuse me a little.—
Careless, take the chair, will you?

CARELESS   Nay, prithee, Charles, what now? This is one of
your peerless beauties, I suppose, has dropped in by
chance?

75 CHARLES   No, faith! To tell you the truth, 'tis a Jew and a
broker, who are come by appointment.

CARELESS   Oh, damn it! let's have the Jew in—

I GENT   Aye, and the broker too, by all means.

2 GENT   Yes, yes, the Jew and the broker.

80 CHARLES   Egad, with all my heart!—Trip bid the gentlemen walk in.—

[*Exit* TRIP.]

Though there's one of them a stranger, I can tell you.

CARELESS   Charles, let us give them some generous Bur-
gundy, and perhaps they'll grow conscientious.°   *gain a conscience*

85 CHARLES   Oh, hang 'em, no! wine does but draw forth a
man's *natural* qualities; and to make *them* drink would
only be to whet their knavery.

[*Enter* TRIP, SIR OLIVER SURFACE, *and* MOSES.]

CHARLES   So, honest Moses; walk in, pray, Mr. Premium—
that's the gentleman's name, isn't it, Moses?

90 MOSES   Yes, sir.

CHARLES   Set chairs, Trip.—Sit down, Mr. Premium.—
Glasses, Trip.—Sit down, Moses.—Come, Mr. Premium,
I'll give you a sentiment;° here's "Success to usury!"—   *pithy wish*
Moses, fill the gentleman a bumper.

95 MOSES   Success to usury!

CARELESS   Right, Moses—usury is prudence and industry,
and deserves to succeed.

SIR OLIVER   Then here's—All the success it deserves!

CARELESS   No, no, that won't do! Mr. Premium, you
100 have demurred to° the toast, and must drink it in a   *taken exception to*
pint bumper.

1 GENT   A pint bumper, at least.

MOSES   Oh, pray, sir, consider—Mr. Premium's a gentleman.

105 CARELESS   And therefore loves good wine.

2 GENT   Give Moses a quart glass—this is mutiny, and a
high contempt of the chair.

CARELESS   Here, now for't! I'll see justice done, to the last
drop of my bottle.

110 SIR OLIVER   Nay, pray, gentlemen—I did not expect this
usage.

CHARLES   No hang it, Careless, you shan't; Mr. Premium's
a stranger.

SIR OLIVER   [*aside*]   Odd! I wish I was well out of this
115 company.

CARELESS   Plague on 'em then! if they won't drink, we'll
not sit down with 'em. Come, Harry, the dice are in the
next room.—Charles, you'll join us—when you have finished your business with these gentlemen?

120 CHARLES   I will! I will!—
Careless!

[*Exeunt* GENTLEMEN.]

CARELESS   Well!

CHARLES   Perhaps I may want *you.*

CARELESS   Oh, you know I am always ready—word, note,
125 or bond, 'tis all the same to me.   [*Exit.*]

MOSES   Sir, this is Mr. Premium, a gentleman of the strict-
est honor and secrecy; and always performs what
he undertakes. Mr. Premium, this is—

CHARLES   Pshaw! have done! Sir, my friend Moses is a very
honest fellow, but a little slow at expression; he'll be an
hour giving us our titles. Mr. Premium, the plain state of
the matter is this—I am an extravagant young fellow who
wants money to borrow; you I take to be a prudent old fellow, who has got money to lend. I am blockhead enough
to give fifty per cent sooner than not have it; and you, I
presume, are rogue enough to take a hundred if you could
get it. Now, sir, you see we are acquainted at once, and
may proceed to business without farther ceremony.

SIR OLIVER   Exceeding frank, upon my word. I see, sir, you
are not a man of many compliments.

CHARLES   Oh, no, sir! plain dealing in business I always
think best.

SIR OLIVER   Sir, I like you the better for't. However, you
are mistaken in one thing—I have no money to lend, but
I believe I could procure some of a friend; but then he's
an unconscionable dog—isn't he, Moses? And must sell
stock to accommodate you—mustn't he, Moses?

MOSES   Yes, indeed! You know I always speak the truth,
and scorn to tell a lie!

CHARLES   Right! People that expect truth generally do.
But these are trifles, Mr. Premium. What! I know money
isn't to be bought without paying for't!

SIR OLIVER   Well, but what security could you give? You
have no land, I suppose?

CHARLES   Not a mole-hill, nor a twig, but what's in beau-
pots[8] out at the window!

OLIVER   Nor any stock, I presume?

CHARLES   Nothing but live stock—and that's only a few
pointers and ponies. But pray, Mr. Premium, are you
acquainted at all with any of my connections?

SIR OLIVER   Why, to say truth, I am.

CHARLES   Then you must know that I have a devilish rich
uncle in the East Indies, Sir *Oliver Surface*, from whom
I have the greatest expectations.

SIR OLIVER   That you have a wealthy uncle, I have heard—
but how your expectations will turn out is more, I believe,
than you can tell.

CHARLES   Oh, no!—there can be no doubt—they tell me
I'm a prodigious favorite—and that he talks of leaving
me everything.

SIR OLIVER   Indeed! this is the first I've heard on't.

CHARLES   Yes, yes, 'tis just so.—Moses knows 'tis true;
don't you, Moses?

MOSES   Oh, yes! I'll swear to't.

SIR OLIVER [*aside*]   Egad, they'll persuade me presently I'm
at Bengal.

8. Large ornamental vases for flowers.

CHARLES   Now I propose, Mr. Premium, if it's agreeable to
you, a post-obit on Sir Oliver's life; though at the same
time the old fellow has been so liberal to me that I give
180   you my word I should be very sorry to hear anything had
happened to him.

SIR OLIVER   Not more than *I* should, I assure you. But the
bond you mention happens to be just the worst security
you could offer me—for I might live to a hundred and
185   never recover the principal.

CHARLES   Oh, yes, you would!—the moment Sir Oliver
dies, you know, you'd come on me for the money.

SIR OLIVER   Then I believe I should be the most unwel-
come dun you ever had in your life.

190   CHARLES   What! I suppose you are afraid now that Sir
Oliver is too good a life?[9]

SIR OLIVER   No, indeed I am not—though I have heard he
is as hale and healthy as any man of his years in Christendom.

195   CHARLES   There again you are misinformed. No, no, the
climate has hurt him considerably, poor uncle Oliver.
Yes, he breaks apace[1] I'm told—and so much altered
lately that his nearest relations don't know him.

SIR OLIVER   No! Ha! ha! ha! so much altered lately that his
200   relations don't know him! Ha! ha! ha! that's droll,
egad—ha! ha! ha!

CHARLES   Ha! ha!—you're glad to hear that, little Premium.

SIR OLIVER   No, no, I'm not.

CHARLES   Yes, yes, you are—ha! ha! ha!—you know that
205   mends° your chance.°   betters / (of repayment)

SIR OLIVER   But I'm told Sir Oliver is coming over—nay,
some say he is actually arrived.

CHARLES   Pshaw! sure I must know better than you
whether he's come or not. No, no, rely on't, he is at this
210   moment at Calcutta, isn't he, Moses?

MOSES   Oh, yes, certainly.

SIR OLIVER   Very true, as you say, you must know better
than I, though I have it from pretty good authority—
haven't I, Moses?

215   MOSES   Yes, most undoubted!

SIR OLIVER   But, sir, as I understand you want a few hundreds immediately, is there nothing you would dispose of?

CHARLES   How do you mean?

SIR OLIVER   For instance, now—I have heard—that your
220   father left behind him a great quantity of massy old plate.[2]

CHARLES   O lud! that's gone long ago—Moses can tell you
how better than I can.

---

9. That is, is likely to live too long.   2. Heavy (probably silver) utensils and dishes.
1. Fails in health quickly.

SIR OLIVER [aside] Good lack! all the family race-cups and
corporation-bowls![3] —Then it was also supposed that his
225 library was one of the most valuable and complete.

CHARLES Yes, yes, so it was—vastly too much so for a private gentleman—for my part, I was always of a commu-
nicative disposition, so I thought it a shame to keep so
much knowledge to myself.

230 SIR OLIVER [aside] Mercy on me! learning that had run in
the family like an heirloom!—[Aloud] Pray, what are
become of the books?

CHARLES You must inquire of the auctioneer, Master Premium, for I don't believe even Moses can direct you
there.

235 MOSES I never meddle with books.

SIR OLIVER So, so, nothing of the family property left, I
suppose?

CHARLES Not much, indeed; unless you have a mind to
the family pictures. I have got a room full of ancestors
240 above—and if you have a taste for old paintings, egad,
you shall have 'em a bargain!

SIR OLIVER Hey! and the devil! sure, you wouldn't sell your
forefathers, would you?

CHARLES Every man of 'em, to the best bidder.

245 SIR OLIVER What! your great-uncles and aunts?

CHARLES Aye, and my great-grandfathers and grandmoth-
ers too.

SIR OLIVER [aside] Now I give him up!—What the plague,
have you no bowels° for your own kindred? Odd's life!   feelings
250 do you take me for Shylock in the play,[4] that you would
raise money of me on your own flesh and blood?

CHARLES Nay, my little broker, don't be angry: what need
you care, if you have your money's worth?

SIR OLIVER Well, I'll be the purchaser—I think I can dis-
255 pose of the family.—[Aside] Oh, I'll never forgive him
this! never!

[Enter CARELESS.]

CARELESS Come, Charles, what keeps you?

CHARLES I can't come yet. I'faith! we are going to have a
sale above—here's little Premium will buy all my ances-
260 tors!

CARELESS Oh, burn your ancestors!

CHARLES No, he may do that afterwards, if he pleases. Stay,
Careless, we want you; egad, you shall be auctioneer—so
come along with us.

265 CARELESS Oh, have with you, if that's the case.—I can
handle a hammer as well as a dice box!

SIR OLIVER [aside] Oh, the profligates!

3. Cups won at horse races and honorary
bowls bestowed by civic authorities.
4. The Jewish moneylender in Shakespeare's

The Merchant of Venice (1596–97), who
demands a pound of flesh as security for a
loan.

CHARLES Come, Moses, you shall be appraiser, if we want
one.—Gad's life, little Premium, you don't seem to like
270 the business.
SIR OLIVER Oh, yes, I do, vastly! Ha! ha! yes, yes, I think it
a rare joke to sell one's family by auction—ha! ha!—
[Aside] Oh, the prodigal!
CHARLES To be sure! when a man wants money, where the
275 plague should he get assistance, if he can't make free
with his own relations?

4.1

[SCENE: *Picture-room at* CHARLES's.]

[*Enter* CHARLES SURFACE, SIR OLIVER SURFACE,
MOSES, *and* CARELESS.]

CHARLES Walk in, gentlemen, pray walk in!—here they
are, the family of the Surfaces, up to the Conquest.[5]
SIR OLIVER And, in my opinion, a goodly collection.
CHARLES Aye, aye, these are done in true spirit of portrait-
5 painting—no volunteer° grace or expression—not like   *spontaneous*
the works of your modern Raphael,[6] who gives you the
strongest resemblance, yet contrives to make your own
portrait independent of you; so that you may sink the
original and not hurt the picture. No, no; the merit of
10 these is the inveterate likeness—all stiff and awkward as
the originals, and like nothing in human nature beside!
SIR OLIVER Ah! we shall never see such figures of men
again.
CHARLES I hope not. Well, you see, Master Premium,
15 what a domestic character I am—here I sit of an evening
surrounded by my family. But come, get to your pulpit,
Mr. Auctioneer—here's an old gouty chair[7] of my grandfather's will answer the purpose.
CARELESS Aye, aye, this will do. But, Charles, I have ne'er
20 a hammer; and what's an auctioneer without his hammer?
CHARLES Egad, that's true. What parchment have we
here? [*Takes down a roll.*] "Richard, heir to Thomas"—
our genealogy in full. Here, Careless, you shall have no
common bit of mahogany—here's the family tree for
25 you, you rogue—this shall be your hammer, and now you
may knock down[8] my ancestors with their own pedigree.
SIR OLIVER [*aside*] What an unnatural rogue!—an *ex post
facto*[9] parricide!

---

5. Back to the Norman conquest of England
(1066).
6. That is, Sir Joshua Reynolds (1723–1792),
the foremost portrait painter in England in
the 18th century; Raphael (Raffaello Sanzio,
1483–1520) was a leading painter of the Italian Renaissance.

7. A chair that raises the feet of someone suffering from gout, which causes painful swelling of the small joints (often in the big toe).
8. Dispose of (an item) to a bidder at an auction sale.
9. After the fact (Latin).

CARELESS   Yes, yes, here's a list of your generation indeed;—
30   faith, Charles, this is the most convenient thing you
could have found for the business, for 'twill serve not
only as a hammer, but a catalogue into the bargain.—But
come, begin—A-going, a-going, a-going!

CHARLES   Bravo, Careless! Well, here's my great uncle, Sir
35   Richard Raviline, a marvelous good general in his day, I
assure you. He served in all the Duke of Marlborough's
wars, and got that cut over his eye at the battle of
Malplaquet.[1] What say you, Mr. Premium? look at
him—there's a hero for you! not cut out of his feathers,
40   as your modern clipped captains are, but enveloped in
wig and regimentals, as a general should be. What do
you bid?

MOSES   Mr. Premium would have you speak.

CHARLES   Why, then, he shall have him for ten pounds,
45   and I am sure that's not dear for a staff officer.

SIR OLIVER   [aside] Heaven deliver me! his famous uncle
Richard for ten pounds!—Very well, sir, I take him at
that.

CHARLES   Careless, knock down my uncle Richard.—
50   Here, now, is a maiden sister of his, my great-aunt Deborah, done by Kneller,[2] thought to be in his best manner,
and a very formidable likeness. There she is, you see, a
shepherdess feeding her flock. You shall have her for five
pounds ten—the sheep are worth the money.

55   SIR OLIVER   [aside] Ah! poor Deborah! a woman who set
such a value on herself!—Five pound ten—she's mine.

CHARLES   Knock down my aunt Deborah! Here, now, are
two that were a sort of cousins of theirs.—You see, Moses,
these pictures were done some time ago, when beaux
60   wore wigs, and the ladies wore their own hair.

SIR OLIVER   Yes, truly, head-dresses appear to have been a
little lower in those days.

CHARLES   Well, take that couple for the same.

MOSES   'Tis a good bargain.

65   CHARLES   Careless!—This, now, is a grandfather of my
mother's, a learned judge, well known on the western
circuit.[3]—What do you rate him at, Moses?

MOSES   Four guineas.

CHARLES   Four guineas! Gad's life, you don't bid me the
70   price of his wig.—Mr. Premium, *you* have more respect

1. John Churchill, 1st duke of Marlborough
(1650–1722), successfully commanded the
allied (British, Dutch, and Austrian) forces
against the French in the War of the Spanish
Succession (1701–14). The indecisive battle
fought in the French village of Malplaquet in
September 1709 was the bloodiest of the 18th
century.

2. Sir Godfrey Kneller (1646–1723), German-
born portrait painter.
3. One of the routes traveled by justices to
hold court or perform other official duties at
designated locations.

for the woolsack;[4] do let us knock his lordship down at fifteen.

SIR OLIVER   By all means.

CARELESS   Gone!

75   CHARLES   And there are two brothers of his, William and Walter Blunt, Esquires, both members of Parliament, and noted speakers; and, what's very extraordinary, I believe this is the first time they were ever bought and sold.

80   SIR OLIVER   That's very extraordinary, indeed! I'll take them at your own price, for the honor of Parliament.

CARELESS   Well said, little Premium! I'll knock 'em down at forty.

CHARLES   Here's a jolly fellow—I don't know what rela-
85   tion, but he was mayor of Manchester; take him at eight pounds.

SIR OLIVER   No, no—six will do for the mayor.

CHARLES   Come, make it guineas, and I'll throw you the two aldermen there into the bargain.

90   SIR OLIVER   They're mine.

CHARLES   Careless, knock down the mayor and aldermen. But, plague on't! we shall be all day retailing in this manner; do let us deal wholesale—what say you, little Premium? Give me three hundred pounds for the rest of the
95   family in the lump.

CARELESS   Aye, aye, that will be the best way.

SIR OLIVER   Well, well, anything to accommodate you; they are mine. But there is one portrait which you have always passed over.

100   CARELESS   What, that ill-looking little fellow over the settee?

SIR OLIVER   Yes, sir, I mean that; though I don't think him so ill-looking a little fellow, by any means.

CHARLES   What, that? Oh, that's my uncle Oliver! 'Twas done before he went to India.

105   CARELESS   Your uncle Oliver! Gad, then you'll never be friends, Charles. That, now, to me, is as stern a looking rogue as ever I saw—an unforgiving eye, and a damned disinheriting countenance! an inveterate knave, depend on't. Don't you think so, little Premium?

110   SIR OLIVER   Upon my soul, sir, I do not; I think it is as honest a looking face as any in the room, dead or alive. But I suppose your uncle Oliver goes with the rest of the lumber?

CHARLES   No, hang it! I'll not part with poor Noll. The old fellow has been very good to me, and, egad, I'll keep his
115   picture while I've a room to put it in.

---

4. A seat made of a large bag of wool, covered by cloth and lacking back or arms, traditionally used by the Lord Chancellor when presiding over the House of Lords; figuratively, judges in general.

SIR OLIVER [aside]   The rogue's my nephew after all!—But,
    sir, I have somehow taken a fancy to that picture.
CHARLES   I'm sorry for't, for you certainly will not have it.
    Oons! haven't you got enough of 'em?
120 SIR OLIVER [aside]   I forgive him everything!—But, sir, when
    I take a whim in my head, I don't value money. I'll give you
    as much for that as for all the rest.
CHARLES   Don't tease me, master broker; I tell you I'll not
    part with it, and there's an end on't.
125 SIR OLIVER [aside]   How like his father the dog is!—[Aloud]
    Well, well, I have done.—I did not perceive it before, but
    I think I never saw such a resemblance.—Well, sir—here
    is a draught[5] for your sum.
CHARLES   Why, 'tis for eight hundred pounds!
130 SIR OLIVER   You will not let Sir Oliver go?
CHARLES   Zounds! no! I tell you, once more.
SIR OLIVER   Then never mind the difference; we'll balance
    another time. But give me your hand on the bargain; you
    are an honest fellow, Charles—I beg pardon, sir, for
135 being so free.—Come, Moses.
CHARLES   Egad, this is a whimsical old fellow!—but
    hark'ee, Premium, you'll prepare lodgings for these gen-
    tlemen.
SIR OLIVER   Yes, yes, I'll send for them in a day or two.
140 CHARLES   But hold—do now—send a genteel conveyance
    for them, for, I assure you, they were most of them used
    to ride in their own carriages.
SIR OLIVER   I will, I will, for all but—Oliver.
CHARLES   Aye, all but the little honest nabob.[6]
145 SIR OLIVER   You're fixed on that?
CHARLES   Peremptorily.°   Absolutely
SIR OLIVER   A dear extravagant rogue!—Good day!—
    Come, Moses,—Let me hear now who dares call him
    profligate!

                            [Exeunt SIR OLIVER and MOSES.]

150 CARELESS   Why, this is the oddest genius of the sort[7] I ever
    saw!
CHARLES   Egad, he's the prince of brokers, I think. I won-
    der how the devil Moses got acquainted with so honest a
    fellow.—Ha! here's Rowley.—Do, Careless, say I'll join
155 the company in a moment.
CARELESS   I will—but don't let that old blockhead per-
    suade you to squander any of that money on old musty
    debts, or any such nonsense; for tradesmen, Charles, are
    the most exorbitant fellows!

5. A written order for the payment of funds
drawn on the writer's bank account; a check.
6. An Englishman who made a fortune in
India during the period of British rule; liter-

ally, "governor" (from a similar word in Hindi
and Urdu).
7. That is, embodiment of his profession.

160 CHARLES Very true, and paying them is only encouraging
them.

CARELESS Nothing else.   [*Exit* CARELESS.]

CHARLES Aye, aye, never fear.

So! this was an odd fellow, indeed! Let me see, two-thirds
165 of this is mine by right—five hundred and thirty pounds.
'Fore heaven! I find one's ancestors are more valuable
relations than I took 'em for!—Ladies and gentlemen,
your most obedient and very grateful humble servant.

[*Enter* ROWLEY.]

Ha! old Rowley! egad, you are just come in time to take
170 leave of your old acquaintance.

ROWLEY Yes, I heard they were going. But I wonder you
can have such spirits under so many distresses.

CHARLES Why, there's the point—my distresses are so
many, that I can't afford to part with my spirits; but I shall
175 be rich and splenetic,° all in good time. However, I suppose   ill-humored
you are surprised that I am not more sorrowful at parting
with so many near relations; to be sure, 'tis very affecting;
but, rot 'em, you see they never move a muscle, so why
should I?

180 ROWLEY There's no making you serious a moment.

CHARLES Yes, faith: I am so now. Here, my honest Rowley,
here, get me this changed, and take a hundred pounds of
it immediately to old Stanley.

ROWLEY A hundred pounds! Consider only—

185 CHARLES Gad's life, don't talk about it! poor Stanley's
wants are pressing, and, if you don't make haste, we shall
have some one call that has a better right to the money.

ROWLEY Ah! there's the point! I never will cease dunning
you with the old proverb—

190 CHARLES "Be *just* before you're *generous*," hey!—Why so I
would if I could; but Justice is an old lame hobbling bel-
dame,° and I can't get her to keep pace with Generosity,   old woman; hag
for the soul of me.

ROWLEY Yet, Charles, believe me, one hour's reflection——

195 CHARLES Aye, aye, it's all very true; but hark'ee, Rowley,
while I have, by heaven I'll give—so, damn your economy! and now for hazard.

[*Exeunt.*]

4.2

[SCENE: *The parlor.*]

[*Enter* SIR OLIVER SURFACE *and* MOSES.]

MOSES Well, sir, I think, as Sir Peter said, you have seen Mr.
Charles in high glory; 'tis great pity he's so extravagant.

SIR OLIVER True, but he wouldn't sell my picture.

MOSES And loves wine and women so much.

5 SIR OLIVER   But he wouldn't sell my picture!

MOSES   And games so deep.°   *heavily*

SIR OLIVER   But he wouldn't sell my picture. Oh, here's
Rowley.

[*Enter* ROWLEY.]

ROWLEY   So, Sir Oliver, I find you have made a purchase——

10 SIR OLIVER   Yes, yes, our young rake has parted with his
ancestors like old tapestry.

ROWLEY   And here has he commissioned me to redeliver
you part of the purchase-money—I mean, though, in
your necessitous character of old *Stanley.*

15 MOSES   Ah! there is the pity of all: he is so damned charitable.

ROWLEY   And I left a hosier and two tailors in the hall,
who, I'm sure, won't be paid, and this hundred would
satisfy 'em.

SIR OLIVER   Well, well, I'll pay his debts—and his benevo-
20 lence too; but now I am no more a broker, and you shall
introduce me to the elder brother as old Stanley.

ROWLEY   Not yet awhile; Sir Peter, I know, means to call
there about this time.

[*Enter* TRIP.]

TRIP   O gentlemen, I beg pardon for not showing you out;
25 this way—Moses, a word.

[*Exeunt* TRIP *and* MOSES.]

SIR OLIVER   There's a fellow for you! Would you believe it,
that puppy intercepted the Jew on our coming, and
wanted to raise money before he got to his master!

ROWLEY   Indeed!

30 SIR OLIVER   Yes, they are now planning an annuity business. Ah, Master Rowley, in my days, servants were content with the follies of their masters, when they were
worn a little threadbare—but now they have their vices,
like their birthday clothes,[8] with the gloss on.

[*Exeunt.*]

4.3

[SCENE: *A library in* JOSEPH SURFACE's *house.*]

[JOSEPH SURFACE *and* SERVANT.]

JOSEPH SURFACE   No letter from Lady Teazle?

SERVANT   No, sir.

JOSEPH SURFACE [*aside*]   I am surprised she hasn't sent, if
she is prevented from coming. Sir Peter certainly does
5 not suspect me. Yet I wish I may not lose the heiress,
through the scrape I have drawn myself in with the wife;

8. Lavish clothes worn in honor of the king's birthday.

however, Charles's imprudence and bad character are great points in my favor.

[*Knocking.*]

SERVANT   Sir, I believe that must be Lady Teazle.

10 JOSEPH SURFACE   Hold! See whether it is or not, before you go to the door—I have a particular message for you, if it should be my brother.

SERVANT   'Tis her ladyship, sir; she always leaves her chair at the milliner's in the next street.

15 JOSEPH SURFACE   Stay, stay—draw that screen before the window—that will do;—my opposite neighbor is a maiden lady of so curious a temper.——

[SERVANT *draws the screen, and exit.*]

I have a difficult hand to play in this affair. Lady Teazle has lately suspected my views on Maria; but she must by
20   no means be let into that secret,—at least, not till I have her more in my power.

[*Enter* LADY TEAZLE.]

LADY TEAZLE   What, sentiment in soliloquy! Have you been very impatient now? O lud! don't pretend to look grave. I vow I couldn't come before.

25 JOSEPH SURFACE   O madam, punctuality is a species of constancy, a very unfashionable quality in a lady.

LADY TEAZLE   Upon my word, you ought to pity me. Do you know that Sir Peter is grown so ill-tempered to me of late, and so jealous of *Charles* too—that's the best of the
30   story, isn't it?

JOSEPH SURFACE   [*aside*]   I am glad my scandalous friends keep that up.

LADY TEAZLE   I am sure I wish he would let Maria marry him, and then perhaps he would be convinced; don't
35   you, Mr. Surface?

JOSEPH SURFACE   [*aside*]   Indeed I do not.—Oh, certainly I do! for then my dear Lady Teazle would also be convinced how wrong her suspicions were of my having any design on the silly girl.

[*Sit.*]

40 LADY TEAZLE   Well, well I'm inclined to believe you. But isn't it provoking, to have the most ill-natured things said to one? And there's my friend Lady Sneerwell has circulated I don't know how many scandalous tales of me! and all without any foundation, too—that's what vexes me.

45 JOSEPH SURFACE   Aye, madam, to be sure, that *is* the provoking circumstance—without foundation! yes, yes, there's the mortification, indeed; for, when a scandalous story is believed against one, there certainly is no comfort like the consciousness of having deserved it.

50 LADY TEAZLE   No, to be sure—then I'd forgive their malice; but to attack me, who am really so innocent, and who

never say an ill-natured thing of anybody—that is, of any
friend—and then Sir Peter, too, to have him so peevish,
and so suspicious, when I know the integrity of my own
55 heart—indeed 'tis monstrous!

JOSEPH SURFACE   But, my dear Lady Teazle, 'tis your own
fault if you suffer it. When a husband entertains a
groundless suspicion of his wife, and withdraws his confidence from her, the original compact is broke, and she
60 owes it to the honor of her sex to endeavor to outwit him.

LADY TEAZLE   Indeed! So that, if he suspects me without
cause, it follows that the best way of curing his jealousy
is to give him reason for't?

JOSEPH SURFACE   Undoubtedly—for your husband should
65 never be deceived in you: and in that case it becomes *you*
to be frail in compliment to *his* discernment.

LADY TEAZLE   To be sure, what you say is very reasonable,
and when the consciousness of my own innocence—

JOSEPH SURFACE   Ah, my dear madam, there is the great
70 mistake; 'tis this very conscious innocence that is of the
greatest prejudice to you. What is it makes you negligent
of forms, and careless of the world's opinion? why, the
consciousness of your innocence. What makes you
thoughtless in your conduct, and apt to run into a thou-
75 sand little imprudences? why, the *consciousness* of your
innocence. What makes you impatient of Sir Peter's
temper and outrageous at his suspicions? why, the *consciousness* of your own innocence!

LADY TEAZLE   'Tis very true!

80 JOSEPH SURFACE   Now, my dear Lady Teazle, if you would
but once make a trifling *faux pas*,[9] you can't conceive
how cautious you would grow—and how ready to
humour and agree with your husband.

LADY TEAZLE   Do you think so?

85 JOSEPH SURFACE   Oh, I'm sure on't; and then you would
find all scandal would cease at once, for—in short, your
character at present is like a person in a plethora,[1]
absolutely dying of too much health.

LADY TEAZLE   So, so; then I perceive your prescription is,
90 that I must sin in my own defence, and part with my
virtue to preserve my reputation?

JOSEPH SURFACE   Exactly so, upon my credit, ma'am.

LADY TEAZLE   Well, certainly that is the oddest doctrine,
and the newest receipt for avoiding calumny?

95 JOSEPH SURFACE   An infallible one, believe me. *Prudence*,
like *experience*, must be paid for.

LADY TEAZLE   Why, if my understanding were once
convinced——

9. Literally, "false step" (French); here, an
indiscreet act (with sexual overtones).

1. A medical disorder characterized by an
excess of blood.

JOSEPH SURFACE   Oh, certainly, madam, your understand-
100   ing *should* be convinced. Yes, yes—heaven forbid I
should persuade you to do anything you *thought* wrong.
No, no, I have too much honor to desire it.

LADY TEAZLE   Don't you think we may as well leave honor
out of the argument?

105   JOSEPH SURFACE   Ah, the ill effects of your country education, I see, still remain with you.

LADY TEAZLE   I doubt° they do, indeed; and I will fairly own   *fear*
to you, that if I could be persuaded to do wrong, it would
be by Sir Peter's ill-usage sooner than your honorable
110   logic, after all.

JOSEPH SURFACE   Then, by this hand, which he is unworthy of—— [*Taking her hand*]

   [*Re-enter* SERVANT.]

'Sdeath° you blockhead—what do you want?   *God's death (oath)*

SERVANT   I beg pardon, sir, but I thought you wouldn't
115   choose Sir Peter to come up without announcing him.

JOSEPH SURFACE   Sir Peter!—Oons—the devil!

LADY TEAZLE   Sir Peter! O lud! I'm ruined! I'm ruined!

SERVANT   Sir, 'twasn't I let him in.

LADY TEAZLE   Oh! I'm undone! What will become of me,
120   now, Mr. Logic?—Oh! mercy, he's on the stairs—I'll get
behind here—and if ever I'm so imprudent again——

   [*Goes behind the screen.*]

JOSEPH SURFACE   Give me that book.

   [*Sits down.* SERVANT *pretends to adjust his hair.*]

   [*Enter* SIR PETER TEAZLE.]

SIR PETER   Aye, ever improving himself!—Mr. Surface,
Mr. Surface——

125   JOSEPH SURFACE   Oh, my dear Sir Peter, I beg your pardon.
[*Gaping,° and throws away the book.*] I have been dozing   *Yawning*
over a stupid book. Well, I am much obliged to you for
this call. You haven't been here, I believe, since I fitted
up this room. Books, you know, are the only things I am
130   a coxcomb in.°   *vain about*

SIR PETER   'Tis very neat indeed. Well, well, that's proper;
and you make even your screen a source of knowledge—
hung, I perceive, with maps.

JOSEPH SURFACE   Oh, yes, I find great use in that screen.

135   SIR PETER   I dare say you must—certainly—when you
want to find anything in a hurry.

JOSEPH SURFACE   [*aside*] Aye, or to hide anything in a
hurry either.

SIR PETER   Well, I have a little private business——

140   JOSEPH SURFACE   [*to* SERVANT] You needn't stay.

SERVANT   No, sir.   [*Exit.*]

JOSEPH SURFACE   Here's a chair, Sir Peter—I beg——

SIR PETER Well, now we are alone, there is a subject, my
dear friend, on which I wish to unburden my mind to
145 you—a point of the greatest moment to my peace: in
short, my good friend, Lady Teazle's conduct of late has
made me extremely unhappy.

JOSEPH SURFACE Indeed! I am very sorry to hear it.

SIR PETER Yes, 'tis but too plain she has not the least
150 regard for me; but, what's worse, I have pretty good
authority to suspect she must have formed an attachment to another.

JOSEPH SURFACE You astonish me!

SIR PETER Yes! and, between ourselves, I think I have dis-
155 covered the person.

JOSEPH SURFACE How! you alarm me exceedingly.

SIR PETER Aye, my dear friend, I knew you would sympathize with me!

JOSEPH SURFACE Yes, believe me, Sir Peter, such a discov-
160 ery would hurt me just as much as it would you.

SIR PETER I am convinced of it.—Ah! it is a happiness to
have a friend whom one can trust even with one's family
secrets. But have you no guess who I mean?

JOSEPH SURFACE I haven't the most distant idea. It can't
165 be Sir Benjamin Backbite!

SIR PETER O, no! What say you to Charles?

JOSEPH SURFACE My brother! impossible!

SIR PETER Ah, my dear friend, the goodness of your own
heart misleads you—you judge of others by yourself.

170 JOSEPH SURFACE Certainly, Sir Peter, the heart that is conscious of its own integrity is ever slow to credit another's
treachery.

SIR PETER True; but your brother has no sentiment—you
never hear him talk so.

175 JOSEPH SURFACE Yet I can't but think Lady Teazle herself
has too much principle—

SIR PETER Aye; but what's her principle against the flattery of a handsome, lively young fellow?

JOSEPH SURFACE That's very true.

180 SIR PETER And then, you know, the difference of our ages
makes it very improbable that she should have any great
affection for me; and if she were to be frail, and I were to
make it public, why the town would only laugh at me,
the foolish old bachelor who had married a girl.

185 JOSEPH SURFACE That's true, to be sure—they *would*
laugh.

SIR PETER Laugh! aye, and make ballads, and paragraphs,[2]
and the devil knows what of me.

JOSEPH SURFACE No, you must never make it public.

2. Short notices in a journal or newspaper.

190 SIR PETER But then again—that the nephew of my old
friend, Sir Oliver, should be the person to attempt such a
wrong, hurts me more nearly.

JOSEPH SURFACE Aye, there's the point. When ingratitude
barbs the dart of injury, the wound has double danger
195 in it.

SIR PETER Aye—I, that was, in a manner, left his guardian—
in whose house he had been so often entertained—who
never in my life denied him—my advice!

JOSEPH SURFACE Oh, 'tis not to be credited! There *may* be
200 a man capable of such baseness, to be sure; but, for my
part, till you can give me positive proofs, I cannot but
doubt it. However, if it should be proved on him, he is no
longer a brother of mine! I disclaim kindred with him—
for the man who can break through the laws of hospital-
205 ity, and attempt the wife of his friend, deserves to be
branded as the pest of society.

SIR PETER What a difference there is between you! What
noble sentiments!

JOSEPH SURFACE Yet I cannot suspect Lady Teazle's honor.

210 SIR PETER I am sure I wish to think well of her, and to
remove all ground of quarrel between us. She has lately
reproached me more than once with having made no
settlement on her; and, in our last quarrel, she almost
hinted that she should not break her heart if I was
215 dead. Now, as we seem to differ in our ideas of expense,
I have resolved she shall be her own mistress in that
respect for the future; and if I *were* to die, she shall find
that I have not been inattentive to her interest while
living. Here, my friend, are the drafts of two deeds,
220 which I wish to have your opinion on. By one, she will
enjoy eight hundred a year independent while I live;
and, by the other, the bulk of my fortune after my
death.

JOSEPH SURFACE This conduct, Sir Peter, is indeed truly
225 generous.—[*Aside*] I wish it may not corrupt my pupil.

SIR PETER Yes, I am determined she shall have no cause to
complain, though I would not have her acquainted with
the latter instance of my affection yet awhile.

JOSEPH SURFACE [*aside*] Nor I, if I could help it.

230 SIR PETER And now, my dear friend, if you please, we will
talk over the situation of your hopes with *Maria.*

JOSEPH SURFACE [*softly*] No, no, Sir Peter; another time, if
you please.

SIR PETER I am sensibly° chagrined at the little progress   acutely
235 you seem to make in her affection.

JOSEPH SURFACE [*softly*] I beg you will not mention it.
What are my disappointments when your happiness is in
debate! [*Aside*] 'Sdeath, I shall be ruined every way!

SIR PETER   And though you are so averse to my acquaint-
ing Lady Teazle with your passion, I am sure she's not
your enemy in the affair.

JOSEPH SURFACE   Pray, Sir Peter, now oblige me. I am
really too much affected by the subject we have been
speaking on to bestow a thought on my own concerns.
The man who is entrusted with his friend's distresses
can never——

[*Enter* SERVANT.]

Well, sir?

SERVANT   Your brother, sir, is speaking to a gentleman in
the street, and says he knows you are within.

JOSEPH SURFACE   'Sdeath, blockhead—I'm not within—
I'm out for the day.

SIR PETER   Stay—hold—a thought has struck me—you
shall be at home.

JOSEPH SURFACE   Well, well, let him up.

[*Exit* SERVANT.]

He'll interrupt, Sir Peter—however—

SIR PETER   Now, my good friend, oblige me, I entreat you.
Before Charles comes, let me conceal myself some-
where; then do you tax° him on the point we have been   *challenge*
talking on, and his answers may satisfy me at once.

JOSEPH SURFACE   O, fie, Sir Peter! would you have me join
in so mean a trick?—to trepan° my brother too?   *entrap*

SIR PETER   Nay, you tell me you are *sure* he is innocent; if
so, you do him the greatest service by giving him an
opportunity to clear himself, and you will set my heart at
rest. Come, you shall not refuse me; here, behind the
screen will be [*Goes to the screen.*]—Hey! what the devil!
there seems to be *one* listener here already—I'll swear I
saw a petticoat!

JOSEPH SURFACE   Ha! ha! ha! Well, this is ridiculous
enough. I'll tell you, Sir Peter, though I hold a man of
intrigue to be a most despicable character, yet you know,
it doesn't follow that one is to be an absolute Joseph[3]
either! Hark'ee! 'tis a little French milliner, a silly rogue
that plagues me—and having some character—on your
coming, she ran behind the screen.

SIR PETER   Ah, you rogue!—But, egad, she has overheard
all I have been saying of my wife.

JOSEPH SURFACE   Oh, 'twill never go any further, you may
depend on't!

SIR PETER   No! then, i'faith, let her hear it out.— Here's a
closet° will do as well.   *small room*

JOSEPH SURFACE   Well, go in then.

---

3. That is, imitate the biblical Joseph, who refused the sexual invitations of Potiphar's wife (Genesis 39.7–12).

SIR PETER   Sly rogue! sly rogue! [*Goes into the closet.*]

JOSEPH SURFACE   A very narrow escape, indeed! and a curi-
285   ous situation I'm in, to part man and wife in this manner.

LADY TEAZLE [*peeping from the screen*]   Couldn't I steal
off?

JOSEPH SURFACE   Keep close,° my angel!   *hidden*

SIR PETER [*peeping out*]   Joseph, tax him home.

290   JOSEPH SURFACE   Back, my dear friend!

LADY TEAZLE [*peeping*]   Couldn't you lock Sir Peter in?

JOSEPH SURFACE   Be still, my life!

SIR PETER [*peeping*]   You're sure the little milliner won't
blab?

295   JOSEPH SURFACE   In, in, my dear Sir Peter!—'Fore gad, I
wish I had a key to the door.

[*Enter* CHARLES SURFACE.]

CHARLES   Hollo! brother, what has been the matter? Your
fellow would not let me up at first. What! have you had a
Jew or a wench with you?

300   JOSEPH SURFACE   Neither, brother, I assure you.

CHARLES   But what has made Sir Peter steal off? I thought
he had been with you.

JOSEPH SURFACE   He was, brother; but, hearing *you* were
coming, he did not choose to stay.

305   CHARLES   What! was the old gentleman afraid I wanted to
borrow money of him!

JOSEPH SURFACE   No, sir, but I am sorry to find, Charles,
that you have lately given that worthy man grounds for
great uneasiness.

310   CHARLES   Yes, they tell me I do that to a great many worthy men. But how so, pray?

JOSEPH SURFACE   To be plain with you, brother, he thinks
you are endeavoring to gain Lady Teazle's affections
from him.

315   CHARLES   Who, I? O lud! not I, upon my word. —Ha! ha!
ha! so the old fellow has found out that he has got a
young wife, has he?—or, what's worse, has her ladyship
discovered that she has an old husband?

JOSEPH SURFACE   This is no subject to jest on, brother.—
320   He who can laugh——

CHARLES   True, true, as you were going to say—then, seriously, I never had the least idea of what you charge me
with, upon my honor.

JOSEPH SURFACE [*aloud*]   Well, it will give Sir Peter great
325   satisfaction to hear this.

CHARLES   To be sure, I once thought the lady seemed to
have taken a fancy to me; but, upon my soul, I never
gave her the least encouragement. Besides, you know my
attachment to Maria.

330 JOSEPH SURFACE　But sure, brother, even if Lady Teazle
　　had betrayed the fondest partiality for you——

　　CHARLES　Why, look'ee, Joseph, I hope I shall never delib-
　　erately do a dishonorable action—but if a pretty woman
　　were purposely to throw herself in my way—and that
335　pretty woman married to a man old enough to be her
　　father——

　　JOSEPH SURFACE　Well!

　　CHARLES　Why, I believe I should be obliged to borrow a
　　little of your morality, that's all.—But, brother, do you
340　know now that you surprise me exceedingly, by naming
　　me with Lady Teazle; for, faith, I always understood *you*
　　were her favorite.

　　JOSEPH SURFACE　Oh, for shame, Charles! This retort is
　　foolish.

345 CHARLES　Nay, I swear I have seen you exchange such sig-
　　nificant glances——

　　JOSEPH SURFACE　Nay, nay, sir, this is no jest——

　　CHARLES　Egad, I'm serious! Don't you remember—one
　　day, when I called here——

350 JOSEPH SURFACE　Nay, prithee, Charles——

　　CHARLES　And found you together——

　　JOSEPH SURFACE　Zounds, sir, I insist——

　　CHARLES　And another time, when your servant——

　　JOSEPH SURFACE　Brother, brother, a word with you!—
355　[*Aside*] Gad, I must stop him.

　　CHARLES　Informed me, I say, that——

　　JOSEPH SURFACE　Hush! I beg your pardon, but Sir Peter
　　has overheard all we have been saying—I knew you
　　would clear yourself, or I should not have consented.

360 CHARLES　How, Sir Peter! Where is he?

　　JOSEPH SURFACE　Softly, there! [*Points to the closet.*]

　　CHARLES　Oh, 'fore heaven, I'll have him out.—Sir Peter,
　　come forth!

　　JOSEPH SURFACE　No, no——

365 CHARLES　I say, Sir Peter, come into court.—[*Pulls in* SIR
　　PETER.] What! my old guardian!—What—turn inquisitor,
　　and take evidence, incog.?°　　　　　　　　　　　　　　incognito; concealed

　　SIR PETER　Give me your hand, Charles—I believe I have
　　suspected you wrongfully—but you mustn't be angry
370　with Joseph—'twas my plan!

　　CHARLES　Indeed!

　　SIR PETER　But I acquit you. I promise you I don't think
　　near so ill of you as I did. What I have heard has given
　　me great satisfaction.

375 CHARLES　Egad, then, 'twas lucky you didn't hear any
　　more. [*Half aside*] Wasn't it, Joseph?

　　SIR PETER　Ah! you would have retorted on him.

　　CHARLES　Aye, aye, that was a joke.

　　SIR PETER　Yes, yes, I know his honor too well.

380 CHARLES   But you might as well have suspected him as me in this matter, for all that. Mightn't he, Joseph? [*Half aside*]

SIR PETER   Well, well, I believe you.

JOSEPH SURFACE [*aside*]   Would they were both out of the room!

385 SIR PETER   And in future, perhaps, we may not be such strangers.

[*Enter* SERVANT *who whispers to* JOSEPH SURFACE.]

JOSEPH SURFACE   Lady Sneerwell!—stop her by all means—

[*Exit* SERVANT.]

Gentlemen—I beg pardon—I must wait on you downstairs—here's a person come on particular business.

390 CHARLES   Well, you can see him in another room. Sir Peter and I haven't met a long time, and I have something to say to him.

JOSEPH SURFACE [*aside*]   They must not be left together.— I'll send Lady Sneerwell away, and return directly.—Sir
395 Peter, not a word of the French milliner.

[*Exit* JOSEPH SURFACE.]

SIR PETER   Oh! not for the world!—Ah, Charles, if you associated more with your brother, one might indeed hope for your reformation. He is a man of sentiment.—Well, there is nothing in the world so noble as a man of sentiment!

400 CHARLES   Pshaw! he is too moral by half, and so apprehensive of his good name, as he calls it, that I suppose he would as soon let a priest into his house as a girl.

SIR PETER   No, no,—come, come,—you wrong him. No, no, Joseph is no rake, but he is not such a saint in that
405 respect either,—[*Aside*] I have a great mind to tell him— we should have a laugh!

CHARLES   Oh, hang him! he's a very anchorite,° a young   *pious recluse*
hermit!

SIR PETER   Hark'ee—you must not abuse him; he may
410 chance to hear of it again, I promise you.

CHARLES   Why, you won't tell him?

SIR PETER   No—but—this way.—[*Aside*] Egad, I'll tell him.—Hark'ee, have you a mind to have a good laugh at Joseph?

415 CHARLES   I should like it of all things.

SIR PETER   Then, i'faith, we will!—[*Aside*] I'll be quit with him for discovering me.[4] —He had a girl with him when I called.

CHARLES   What! Joseph? you jest.

420 SIR PETER   Hush!—a little—French milliner—[*whispers*] and the best of the jest is—she's in the room now.

4. I'll get even with him for revealing me.

CHARLES The devil she is!

SIR PETER Hush! I tell you. [*Points to the screen.*]

CHARLES Behind the screen! 'Slife, let's unveil her!

425 SIR PETER No, no, he's coming:—you shan't, indeed!

CHARLES Oh, egad, we'll have a peep at the little milliner!

SIR PETER Not for the world!—Joseph will never forgive me.

CHARLES I'll stand by you——

SIR PETER [*struggling with* CHARLES] Odds, here he is!

[JOSEPH SURFACE *enters just as* CHARLES *throws
        down the screen.*]

430 CHARLES Lady Teazle, by all that's wonderful!

SIR PETER Lady Teazle, by all that's horrible!

CHARLES Sir Peter, this is one of the smartest° French   *most elegant*
        milliners I ever saw. Egad, you seem all to have been
        diverting yourselves here at hide and seek—and I don't
435   see who is out of the secret. Shall I beg your ladyship to
        inform me?—Not a word!—Brother, will you please to
        explain this matter? What! Morality dumb too!—Sir
        Peter, though I *found* you in the dark, perhaps you are
        not so now! All mute! Well—though *I* can make nothing
440   of the affair, I suppose you perfectly understand one
        another; so I'll leave you to yourselves.—[*Going*]
        Brother, I'm sorry to find you *have given that worthy man
        so much uneasiness,*—Sir Peter! there's nothing *in the
        world so noble as a man of sentiment!*   [*Exit* CHARLES.]
        [*They stand for some time looking at each other.*]

445 JOSEPH SURFACE Sir Peter—notwithstanding I confess
        that appearances are against me—if you will afford me
        your patience—I make no doubt but I shall explain
        everything to your satisfaction.

SIR PETER If you please—

450 JOSEPH SURFACE The fact is, sir, Lady Teazle, knowing my
        pretensions° to your ward Maria—I say, sir, Lady Teazle,   *aspirations*
        being apprehensive of the jealousy of your temper—and
        knowing my friendship to the family—she, sir, I say—called
        here—in order that—I might explain those pretensions—
455   but on your coming—being apprehensive—as I said—of
        your jealousy—she withdrew—and this, you may depend
        on't is the whole truth of the matter.

SIR PETER A very clear account, upon my word; and I dare
        swear the lady will vouch for every article of it.

460 LADY TEAZLE [*coming forward*] For not one word of it, Sir
        Peter!

SIR PETER How! don't you think it worth while to agree in
        the lie?

LADY TEAZLE There is not one syllable of truth in what the
465   gentleman has told you.

SIR PETER I believe you, upon my soul, ma'am!

JOSEPH SURFACE [*aside*] 'Sdeath, madam, will you betray
        me?

LADY TEAZLE   Good Mr. Hypocrite, by your leave, I will
470   speak for myself.

SIR PETER   Aye, let her alone, sir; you'll find she'll make
out a better story than *you*, without prompting.

LADY TEAZLE   Hear me, Sir Peter!—I came here on no matter relating to your ward, and even ignorant of this gentle-
475   man's pretensions to her—but I came, seduced by his
insidious arguments, at least to listen to his pretended
passion, if not to sacrifice *your* honor to his baseness.

SIR PETER   Now, I believe, the truth *is* coming, indeed!

JOSEPH SURFACE   The woman's mad!

480   LADY TEAZLE   No sir; she has recovered her senses, and
your own arts have furnished her with the means.—Sir
Peter, I do not expect you to credit me—but the tenderness you expressed for me, when I am sure you could not
think I was a witness to it, has penetrated to my heart,
485   and had I left the place without the shame of this discovery, my future life should have spoken the sincerity of
my gratitude. As for that smooth-tongue hypocrite, who
would have seduced the wife of his too-credulous friend,
while he affected honorable addresses to his ward—I
490   behold him now in a light so truly despicable, that I shall
never again respect myself for having listened to him.

[*Exit.*]

JOSEPH SURFACE   Notwithstanding all this, Sir Peter, heaven
knows——

SIR PETER   That you are a villain!—and so I leave you to
495   your conscience.

JOSEPH SURFACE   You are too rash, Sir Peter; you shall
hear me. The man who shuts out conviction by refusing
to——

SIR PETER   Oh!—

[*Exeunt,* JOSEPH SURFACE *following and speaking.*]

5.1

[SCENE: *The library in* JOSEPH SURFACE's *house.*]

[*Enter* JOSEPH SURFACE *and* SERVANT.]

JOSEPH SURFACE   Mr. Stanley! why should you think I
would see him? you *must* know he comes to ask something.

SERVANT   Sir, I should not have let him in, but that Mr.
5   Rowley came to the door with him.

JOSEPH SURFACE   Pshaw! blockhead! to suppose that I
should *now* be in a temper to receive visits from poor
relations!—Well, why don't you show the fellow up?

SERVANT   I will, sir.—Why, sir, it was not my fault that Sir
10   Peter discovered my lady——

JOSEPH SURFACE   Go, fool!

[*Exit* SERVANT.]

Sure, Fortune never played a man of my policy° such a trick   *shrewdness; cunning*
before! My character with Sir Peter, my hopes with Maria,
destroyed in a moment! I'm in a rare humour to listen to
15   other people's distresses! I shan't be able to bestow even a
benevolent sentiment on Stanley.—So! here he comes,
and Rowley with him. I must try to recover myself—and
put a little charity into my face, however.   *[Exit.]*

        [Enter SIR OLIVER SURFACE *and* ROWLEY.*]*

SIR OLIVER   What! does he avoid us? That was he, was it not?
20 ROWLEY   It was, sir—but I doubt° you are come a little too   *fear*
abruptly—his nerves are so weak, that the sight of a poor
relation may be too much for him.—I should have gone
first to break you° to him.   *make you known*
SIR OLIVER   A plague of his nerves!—Yet this is he whom
25   Sir Peter extols as a man of the most benevolent way of
thinking!
ROWLEY   As to his way of thinking, I cannot pretend to
decide; for, to do him justice, he appears to have as much
speculative° benevolence as any private gentleman in the   *theoretical*
30   kingdom, though he is seldom so sensual as to indulge
himself in the exercise of it.
SIR OLIVER   Yet has a string of charitable sentiments, I
suppose, at his fingers' ends!
ROWLEY   Or, rather, at his tongue's end, Sir Oliver; for I
35   believe there is no sentiment he has more faith in than
that "Charity begins at home."
SIR OLIVER   And his, I presume, is of that domestic sort
which never stirs abroad at all.
ROWLEY   I doubt you'll find it so;—but he's coming—I
40   mustn't seem to interrupt you; and you know, immediately as you leave him, I come in to announce your
arrival in your real character.
SIR OLIVER   True; and afterwards you'll meet me at Sir
Peter's.
45 ROWLEY   Without losing a moment.   *[Exit* ROWLEY.*]*
SIR OLIVER   So! I don't like the complaisance° of his features.   *obligingness*

        [Re-enter JOSEPH SURFACE.*]*

JOSEPH SURFACE   Sir, I beg you ten thousand pardons for
keeping you a moment waiting—Mr. Stanley, I presume.
SIR OLIVER   At your service.
50 JOSEPH SURFACE   Sir, I beg you will do me the honor to sit
down—I entreat you, sir.
SIR OLIVER   Dear sir—there's no occasion.—*[Aside]* Too
civil by half!
JOSEPH SURFACE   I have not the pleasure of knowing you,
55   Mr. Stanley; but I am extremely happy to see you look so
well. You were nearly related to my mother, I think, Mr.
Stanley?

SIR OLIVER   I was, sir—so nearly that my present poverty, I
fear, may do discredit to her wealthy children—else I
60   should not have presumed to trouble you.

JOSEPH SURFACE   Dear sir, there needs no apology: he that
is in distress, though a stranger, has a right to claim kindred with the wealthy;—I am sure I wish *I* was one of that
class, and had it in my power to offer you even a small
relief.

65   SIR OLIVER   If your uncle, Sir Oliver, were here, I should
have a friend.

JOSEPH SURFACE   I wish he were, sir, with all my heart: you
should not want° an advocate with him, believe me, sir.   *lack*

SIR OLIVER   I should not *need* one—my distresses would
70   recommend me; but I imagined his bounty had enabled
you to become the agent of his charity.

JOSEPH SURFACE   My dear sir, you were strangely misinformed. Sir Oliver is a worthy man, a very worthy sort of
man; but—avarice, Mr. Stanley, is the vice of age. I will
75   tell you, my good sir, in confidence, what he has done for
me has been a mere nothing; though people, I know,
have thought otherwise, and, for my part, I never chose
to contradict the report.

SIR OLIVER   What! has he never transmitted you bullion!
80   rupees! pagodas!⁵

JOSEPH SURFACE   O dear sir, nothing of the kind! No, no; a
few presents now and then—china—shawls—Congo
tea—avadavats⁶ and India crackers°—little more, believe   *firecrackers*
me.

85   SIR OLIVER [*aside*]   Here's gratitude for twelve thousand
pounds! —Avadavats and Indian crackers!

JOSEPH SURFACE   Then, my dear sir, you have heard, I
doubt not, of the extravagance of my brother; there are
very few would credit what I have done for that unfortu-
90   nate young man.

SIR OLIVER [*aside*]   Not I, for one!

JOSEPH SURFACE   The sums I have lent him! Indeed I have
been exceedingly to blame—it was an amiable weakness:
however, I don't pretend to defend it—and now I feel it
95   doubly culpable, since it has deprived me of the pleasure
of serving *you*, Mr. Stanley, as my heart dictates.

SIR OLIVER [*aside*]   Dissembler!—Then, sir, you cannot
assist me?

JOSEPH SURFACE   At present, it grieves me to say, I cannot;
but, whenever I have the ability, you may depend upon
100   hearing from me.

---

5. Rupees and pagodas are Indian coins.
6. Avadavats or amadavats: small songbirds from India (a waxbill).

SIR OLIVER   I am extremely sorry——

JOSEPH SURFACE   Not more than I am, believe me; to pity, without the power to relieve, is still more painful than to ask and be denied.

105 SIR OLIVER   Kind sir, your most obedient humble servant.

JOSEPH SURFACE   You leave me deeply affected, Mr. Stanley.—William, be ready to open the door.

SIR OLIVER   O dear sir, no ceremony.

JOSEPH SURFACE   Your very obedient.

110 SIR OLIVER   Sir, your most obsequious.

JOSEPH SURFACE   You may depend upon hearing from me, whenever I can be of service.

SIR OLIVER   Sweet sir, you are too good.

JOSEPH SURFACE   In the meantime I wish you health and
115 spirits.

SIR OLIVER   Your ever grateful and perpetual humble servant.

JOSEPH SURFACE   Sir, yours as sincerely.

SIR OLIVER   Now I am satisfied!   [*Exit.*]

120 JOSEPH SURFACE [*solus*°]   This is one bad effect of a good   *alone (Latin)*
character; it invites applications from the unfortunate,
and there needs no small degree of address° to gain the   *skill*
reputation of benevolence without incurring the
expense. The silver one of pure charity is an expensive
125 article in the catalogue of a man's good qualities;
whereas the sentimental French plate[7] I use instead of it
makes just as good a show, and pays no tax.

[*Enter* ROWLEY.]

ROWLEY   Mr. Surface, your servant—I was apprehensive of
interrupting you—though my business demands imme-
130 diate attention—as this note will inform you.

JOSEPH SURFACE   Always happy to see Mr. Rowley.—
[*Reads.*] How! *"Oliver—Surface"*—My uncle arrived!

ROWLEY   He is, indeed—we have just parted—quite well,
after a speedy voyage, and impatient to embrace his wor-
135 thy nephew.

JOSEPH SURFACE   I am astonished!—William! stop Mr. Stanley, if he's not gone.

ROWLEY   Oh! he's out of reach, I believe.

JOSEPH SURFACE   Why didn't you let me know this when
140 you came in together?

ROWLEY   I thought you had particular business. But I
must be gone to inform your brother, and appoint him
here to meet his uncle. He will be with you in a quarter
of an hour.

7. That is, cheap imported plate.

145 JOSEPH SURFACE   So he says. Well, I am strangely overjoyed at his coming.—[*Aside*] Never, to be sure, was anything so damned unlucky!

ROWLEY   You will be delighted to see how well he looks.

JOSEPH SURFACE   Oh! I'm rejoiced to hear it.—[*Aside*] Just
150   at this time!

ROWLEY   I'll tell him how impatiently you expect him.

JOSEPH SURFACE   Do, do; pray give my best duty and affection. Indeed, I cannot express the sensations I feel at the
thought of seeing him.—

[*Exit* ROWLEY.]

155   Certainly his coming just at this time is the cruellest
piece of ill fortune.   [*Exit.*]

5.2

[SCENE: *At* SIR PETER'S.]

[*Enter* MRS. CANDOUR *and* MAID.]

MAID   Indeed, ma'am, my lady will see nobody at present.

MRS. CANDOUR   Did you tell her it was her friend Mrs.
Candour?

MAID   Yes, madam; but she begs you will excuse her.

5 MRS. CANDOUR   Do go again; I shall be glad to see her, if it
be only for a moment, for I am sure she must be in great
distress.—

[*Exit* MAID.]

Dear heart, how provoking; I'm not mistress of half the
circumstances! We shall have the whole affair in the
10   newspapers, with the names of the parties at length,
before I have dropped the story at a dozen houses.

[*Enter* SIR BENJAMIN BACKBITE.]

O dear Sir Benjamin! you have heard, I suppose——

SIR BENJAMIN   Of Lady Teazle and Mr. Surface——

MRS. CANDOUR   And Sir Peter's discovery——

15 SIR BENJAMIN   Oh, the strangest piece of business, to be
sure!

MRS. CANDOUR   Well, I never was so surprised in my life. I
am so sorry for all parties, indeed I am.

SIR BENJAMIN   Now, I don't pity Sir Peter at all—he was so
20   extravagantly partial to Mr. Surface.

MRS. CANDOUR   Mr. Surface! Why, 'twas with Charles
Lady Teazle was detected.

SIR BENJAMIN   No such thing—Mr. Surface is the gallant.

MRS. CANDOUR   No, no—Charles is the man. 'Twas Mr.
25   Surface brought Sir Peter on purpose to discover them.

SIR BENJAMIN   I tell you I have it from one——

MRS. CANDOUR   And I have it from one——

SIR BENJAMIN   Who had it from one, who had it——

MRS. CANDOUR   From one immediately—— But here's
30   Lady Sneerwell; perhaps she knows the whole affair.

[*Enter* LADY SNEERWELL.]

LADY SNEERWELL   So, my dear Mrs. Candour, here's a sad
   affair of our friend Lady Teazle!

MRS. CANDOUR   Aye, my dear friend, who could have
   thought it——

35   LADY SNEERWELL   Well, there's no trusting appearances;
   though, indeed, she was always too lively for me.

MRS. CANDOUR   To be sure, her manners were a little too
   free—but she was very young!

LADY SNEERWELL   And had, indeed, some good qualities.

40   MRS. CANDOUR   So she had, indeed. But have you heard
   the particulars?

LADY SNEERWELL   No; but everybody says that Mr.
   Surface——

SIR BENJAMIN   Aye, there, I told you—Mr. Surface was the man.

45   MRS. CANDOUR   No, no, indeed—the assignation was with
   Charles.

LADY SNEERWELL   With Charles! You alarm me, Mrs.
   Candour.

MRS. CANDOUR   Yes, yes, he was the lover. Mr. Surface—do
50   him justice—was only the informer.

SIR BENJAMIN   Well, I'll not dispute with you, Mrs. Candour; but, be it which it may, I hope that Sir Peter's
   wound will not——

MRS. CANDOUR   Sir Peter's wound! Oh, mercy! I didn't hear
55   a word of their fighting.

LADY SNEERWELL   Nor I, a syllable.

SIR BENJAMIN   No! what, no mention of the duel?

MRS. CANDOUR   Not a word.

SIR BENJAMIN   O Lord—yes, yes—they fought before they
60   left the room.

LADY SNEERWELL   Pray let us hear.

MRS. CANDOUR   Aye, do oblige us with the duel.

SIR BENJAMIN   "Sir," says Sir Peter—immediately after the
   discovery—"you are a most ungrateful fellow."

65   MRS. CANDOUR   Aye, to Charles——

SIR BENJAMIN   No, no—to Mr. Surface—"a most ungrateful fellow; and old as I am, sir," says he, "I insist on
   immediate satisfaction."

MRS. CANDOUR   Aye, that must have been to Charles; for 'tis
70   very unlikely Mr. Surface should go to fight in his house.

SIR BENJAMIN   'Gad's life, ma'am, not at all—"giving me
   immediate satisfaction."—On this, madam, Lady Teazle,
   seeing Sir Peter in such danger, ran out of the room in
   strong hysterics, and Charles after her, calling out for
75   hartshorn° and water! Then, madam, they began to fight   *smelling salts*
   with swords——

[*Enter* CRABTREE.]

CRABTREE   With pistols, nephew—I have it from undoubted authority.

MRS. CANDOUR   O Mr. Crabtree, then it is all true!

80 CRABTREE   Too true, indeed, ma'am, and Sir Peter's dangerously wounded——

SIR BENJAMIN   By a thrust of *in seconde*[8] quite through his left side——

CRABTREE   By a bullet lodged in the thorax.

85 MRS. CANDOUR   Mercy on me! Poor Sir Peter!

CRABTREE   Yes, ma'am—though Charles would have avoided the matter, if he could.

MRS. CANDOUR   I knew Charles was the person.

SIR BENJAMIN   Oh, my uncle, I see, knows nothing of the
90 matter.

CRABTREE   But Sir Peter taxed him with the basest ingratitude——

SIR BENJAMIN   That I told you, you know.

CRABTREE   Do, nephew, let me speak!—and insisted on an
95 immediate——

SIR BENJAMIN   Just as I said.

CRABTREE   Odds life, nephew, allow others to know something too! A pair of pistols lay on the bureau (for Mr. Surface, it seems, had come the night before late from
100 Salt-Hill, where he had been to see the Montem with a friend, who has a son at Eton),[9] so, unluckily, the pistols were left charged.

SIR BENJAMIN   I heard nothing of this.

CRABTREE   Sir Peter forced Charles to take one, and they
105 fired, it seems, pretty nearly together. Charles's shot took place,° as I told you, and Sir Peter's missed; but, what is very extraordinary, the ball struck against a little bronze Pliny[1] that stood over the chimney-piece, grazed out of the window at a right angle, and wounded the postman,
110 who was just coming to the door with a double letter[2] from Northamptonshire.

                     succeeded

SIR BENJAMIN   My uncle's account is more circumstantial, I must confess; but I believe mine is the true one, for all that.

115 LADY SNEERWELL [*aside*]   I am more interested in this affair than they imagine, and must have better information.

             [*Exit* LADY SNEERWELL.]

SIR BENJAMIN [*after a pause looking at each other*]   Ah! Lady Sneerwell's alarm is very easily accounted for.

CRABTREE   Yes, yes, they certainly *do* say—but that's nei-
120 ther here nor there.

---

8. That is, with one of the standard fencing parries (French).
9. During the annual festival of Montem, students at Eton College (a secondary school) made a formal procession to a mound named Salt Hill.
1. A statue of Pliny the Elder (23–79 C.E.), Roman naturalist and statesman.
2. A letter written on two sheets of paper and thus charged double postage.

MRS. CANDOUR   But, pray, where is Sir Peter at present?

CRABTREE   Oh! they brought him home, and he is now in
the house, though the servants are ordered to deny it.

MRS. CANDOUR   I believe so, and Lady Teazle, I suppose,
125   attending him.

CRABTREE   Yes, yes; I saw one of the faculty° enter just   *i.e., a doctor*
before me.

SIR BENJAMIN   Hey! who comes here?

CRABTREE   Oh, this is he—the physician, depend on't.

130   MRS. CANDOUR   Oh, certainly! it must be the physician;
and now we shall know.

[*Enter* SIR OLIVER SURFACE.]

CRABTREE   Well, doctor, what hopes?

MRS. CANDOUR   Aye, doctor, how's your patient?

SIR BENJAMIN   Now, doctor, isn't it a wound with a small-
135   sword?

CRABTREE   A bullet lodged in the thorax, for a hundred![3]

SIR OLIVER   Doctor! a wound with a small-sword! and a
bullet in the thorax?—Oons! are you mad, good people?

SIR BENJAMIN   Perhaps, sir, you are not a doctor?

140   SIR OLIVER   Truly, I am to thank you for my degree, if I am.

CRABTREE   Only a friend of Sir Peter's, then, I presume.
But, sir, you must have heard of this accident?

SIR OLIVER   Not a word!

CRABTREE   Not of his being dangerously wounded?

145   SIR OLIVER   The devil he is!

SIR BENJAMIN   Run through the body——

CRABTREE   Shot in the breast——

SIR BENJAMIN   By one Mr. Surface——

CRABTREE   Aye, the younger.

150   SIR OLIVER   Hey! what the plague! you seem to differ
strangely in your accounts—however, you agree that Sir
Peter is dangerously wounded.

SIR BENJAMIN   Oh, yes, we agree there.

CRABTREE   Yes, yes, I believe there can be no doubt of
155   that.

SIR OLIVER   Then, upon my word, for a person in that situation, he is the most imprudent man alive—for here he
comes, walking as if nothing at all were the matter.

[*Enter* SIR PETER TEAZLE.]

Odds heart, Sir Peter! you are come in good time, I
160   promise you; for we had just *given you over*.[4]

SIR BENJAMIN   Egad, uncle, this is the most sudden recovery!

SIR OLIVER   Why, man! what do you do out of bed with a
small-sword through your body, and a bullet lodged in
your thorax?

---

3. For a wager of 100 pounds.
4. That is, given you over for dead; given up on you.

165   SIR PETER   A small-sword and a bullet?

    SIR OLIVER   Aye; these gentlemen would have killed you
    without law or physic,° and wanted to dub me a doctor—   *medicine*
    to make me an accomplice.

    SIR PETER   Why, what is all this?

170   SIR BENJAMIN   We rejoice, Sir Peter, that the story of the
    duel is not true, and are sincerely sorry for your other
    misfortunes.

    SIR PETER   [*aside*]   So, so; all over the town already.

    CRABTREE   Though, Sir Peter, you were certainly vastly to
175   blame to marry at all, at your years.

    SIR PETER   Sir, what business is that of yours?

    MRS. CANDOUR   Though, indeed, as Sir Peter made so
    good a husband, he's very much to be pitied.

    SIR PETER   Plague on your pity, ma'am! I desire none of it.

180   SIR BENJAMIN   However, Sir Peter, you must not mind the
    laughing and jests you will meet with on this occasion.

    SIR PETER   Sir, I desire to be master in my own house.

    CRABTREE   'Tis no uncommon case, that's one comfort.

    SIR PETER   I insist on being left to myself: without cere-
185   mony, I insist on your leaving my house directly!

    MRS. CANDOUR   Well, well, we are going; and depend on't,
    we'll make the best report of you we can.

    SIR PETER   Leave my house!

    CRABTREE   And tell how hardly you have been treated.

190   SIR PETER   Leave my house!

    SIR BENJAMIN   And how patiently you bear it.

    SIR PETER   Fiends! vipers! furies![5] Oh! that their own
    venom would choke them!

        [*Exeunt* MRS. CANDOUR, SIR BENJAMIN BACKBITE,
        CRABTREE, &c.]

    SIR OLIVER   They are very provoking indeed, Sir Peter.

        [*Enter* ROWLEY.]

195   ROWLEY   I heard high words—what has ruffled you, Sir
    Peter?

    SIR PETER   Pshaw! what signifies asking? Do I ever pass a
    day without my vexations?

    SIR OLIVER   Well, I'm not inquisitive—I come only to tell
200   you that I have seen both my nephews in the manner we
    proposed.

    SIR PETER   A precious couple they are!

    ROWLEY   Yes, and Sir Oliver is convinced that your judg-
    ment was right, Sir Peter.

205   SIR OLIVER   Yes, I find *Joseph* is indeed the man, after all.

    ROWLEY   Yes, as Sir Peter says, he's a man of sentiment.

    SIR OLIVER   And acts up to the sentiments he professes.

    ROWLEY   It certainly is edification to hear him talk.

---

5. In classical mythology, monstrous female personifications of vengeance.

SIR OLIVER   Oh, he's a model for the young men of the
210   age! But how's this, Sir Peter? you don't join in your
friend Joseph's praise, as I expected.
SIR PETER   Sir Oliver, we live in a damned wicked world,
and the fewer we praise the better.
ROWLEY   What! do *you* say so, Sir Peter, who were never
215   mistaken in your life?
SIR PETER   Pshaw! plague on you both! I see by your
sneering you have heard the whole affair. I shall go mad
among you!
ROWLEY   Then, to fret you no longer, Sir Peter, we are
220   indeed acquainted with it all. I met Lady Teazle coming
from Mr. Surface's, so humbled that she deigned to
request me to be her advocate with you.
SIR PETER   And does Sir Oliver know all too?
SIR OLIVER   Every circumstance.
225   SIR PETER   What, of the closet—and the screen, hey?
SIR OLIVER   Yes, yes, and the little French milliner. Oh, I
have been vastly diverted with the story! ha! ha!
SIR PETER   'Twas very pleasant.
SIR OLIVER   I never laughed more in my life, I assure you:
230   ha! ha!
SIR PETER   O, vastly diverting! ha! ha!
ROWLEY   To be sure, Joseph with his sentiments! ha! ha!
SIR PETER   Yes, yes, his sentiments! ha! ha! A hypocritical
villain!
235   SIR OLIVER   Aye, and that rogue Charles to pull Sir Peter
out of the closet: ha! ha!
SIR PETER   Ha! ha! 'twas devilish entertaining, to be sure!
SIR OLIVER   Ha! ha! Egad, Sir Peter, I should like to have
seen your face when the screen was thrown down: ha!
240   ha!
SIR PETER   Yes, yes, my face when the screen was thrown
down: ha! ha! Oh, I must never show my head again!
SIR OLIVER   But come, come, it isn't fair to laugh at you
neither, my old friend—though, upon my soul, I can't
245   help it.
SIR PETER   Oh, pray don't restrain your mirth on my
account—it does not hurt me at all! I laugh at the
whole affair myself. Yes, yes, I think being a standing
jest for all one's acquaintances a very happy situation. O
250   yes, and then of a morning to read the paragraphs about
Mr. S——, Lady T——, and Sir P——, will be so entertaining!
ROWLEY   Without affection,° Sir Peter, you may despise   *i.e., Seriously*
the ridicule of fools. But I see Lady Teazle going towards
255   the next room; I am sure you must desire a reconciliation
as earnestly as she does.
SIR OLIVER   Perhaps my being here prevents her coming to
you. Well, I'll leave honest Rowley to mediate between

you; but he must bring you all presently to Mr. Surface's,
260 where I am now returning, if not to reclaim a libertine,
at least to expose hypocrisy.
  SIR PETER Ah! I'll be present at your discovering° yourself   *revealing*
there with all my heart—though 'tis a vile unlucky place
for discoveries!
265 ROWLEY We'll follow.

[Exit SIR OLIVER SURFACE.]

  SIR PETER She is not coming here, you see, Rowley.
  ROWLEY No, but she has left the door of that room open,
you perceive. See, she is in tears!
  SIR PETER Certainly a little mortification appears very
270 becoming in a wife! Don't you think it will do her good to
let her pine a little?
  ROWLEY Oh, this is ungenerous in you!
  SIR PETER Well, I know not what to think. You remember,
Rowley, the letter I found of hers, evidently intended for
275 Charles!
  ROWLEY A mere forgery, Sir Peter! laid in your way on
purpose. This is one of the points which I intend *Snake*
shall give you conviction on.
  SIR PETER I wish I were once satisfied of that. She looks
280 this way. What a remarkably elegant turn of the head she
has! Rowley, I'll go to her.
  ROWLEY Certainly.
  SIR PETER Though, when it is known that we are reconciled, people will laugh at me ten times more!
285 ROWLEY Let them laugh, and retort their malice only by
showing them you are happy in spite of it.
  SIR PETER I'faith, so I will! and, if I'm not mistaken, we
may yet be the happiest couple in the country.
  ROWLEY Nay, Sir Peter—he who once lays aside suspi-
290 cion——
  SIR PETER Hold, my dear Rowley! if you have any regard
for me, never let me hear you utter anything like a sentiment—I have had enough of them to serve me the rest
of my life.

[Exeunt.]

5.3

[SCENE: *The library in* JOSEPH SURFACE's *house.*]

[JOSEPH SURFACE *and* LADY SNEERWELL.]

  LADY SNEERWELL Impossible! Will not Sir Peter immediately be reconciled to Charles, and of consequence no
longer oppose his union with Maria? The thought is distraction to me!
5 JOSEPH SURFACE Can passion furnish a remedy?
  LADY SNEERWELL No, nor cunning either. Oh, I was a
fool, an idiot, to league with such a blunderer!

JOSEPH SURFACE   Sure, Lady Sneerwell, *I* am the greatest
sufferer; yet you see I bear the accident with calmness.

10 LADY SNEERWELL   Because the disappointment doesn't
reach your *heart;* your *interest* only attached you to
Maria. Had you felt for *her* what *I* have for that ungrateful libertine, neither your temper nor hypocrisy could
prevent your showing the sharpness of your vexation.

15 JOSEPH SURFACE   But why should your reproaches fall on
me for this disappointment?

LADY SNEERWELL   Are you not the cause of it? What had
you to do to bate° in your pursuit of Maria to pervert   *slow down*
Lady Teazle by the way? Had you not a sufficient field for

20   your roguery in blinding Sir Peter, and supplanting your
brother? I hate such an avarice of crimes; 'tis an unfair
monopoly, and never prospers.

JOSEPH SURFACE   Well, I admit I have been to blame. I
confess I deviated from the direct road of wrong, but I

25   don't think we're so totally defeated neither.

LADY SNEERWELL   No!

JOSEPH SURFACE   You tell me you have made a trial of
Snake since we met, and that you still believe him faithful to us—

30 LADY SNEERWELL   I do believe so.

JOSEPH SURFACE   And that he has undertaken, should it be
necessary, to swear and prove that Charles is at this time
contracted by vows and honor to your ladyship—which
some of his former letters to you will serve to support?

35 LADY SNEERWELL   This, indeed, might have assisted.

JOSEPH SURFACE   Come, come; it is not too late yet.—
[*Knocking at the door.*] But hark! this is probably my
uncle, Sir Oliver: retire to that room; we'll consult farther when he's gone.

40 LADY SNEERWELL   Well! but if *he* should find you out too—

JOSEPH SURFACE   Oh, I have no fear of that. Sir Peter will
hold his tongue for his own credit's sake—and you may
depend on't I shall soon discover Sir Oliver's weak side!

LADY SNEERWELL   I have no diffidence° of your abilities—   *doubt*
45   only be constant to one roguery at a time.   [*Exit.*]

JOSEPH SURFACE   I will, I will! So! 'tis confounded hard, after
such bad fortune, to be baited° by one's confederate in   *harassed*
evil. Well, at all events, my character° is so much better   *reputation*
than Charles's, that I certainly—hey!—what!—this is not

50   *Sir Oliver,* but old *Stanley* again! Plague on't! that he
should return to tease me just now! We shall have Sir
Oliver come and find him here—and——

[*Enter* SIR OLIVER SURFACE.]

Gad's life, Mr. Stanley, why have you come back to
plague me just at this time? You must not stay now, upon

55   my word.

SIR OLIVER   Sir, I hear your uncle Oliver is expected here,
and though he has been so penurious° to *you*, I'll try   *stingy*
what he'll do for *me*.

JOSEPH SURFACE   Sir, 'tis impossible for you to stay now, so
60   I must beg——Come any other time, and I promise you
you shall be assisted.

SIR OLIVER   No: Sir Oliver and I must be acquainted.

JOSEPH SURFACE   Zounds, sir! then I insist on your quitting
the room directly.

65 SIR OLIVER   Nay, sir!

JOSEPH SURFACE   Sir, I insist on't—Here, William! show this
gentleman out. Since you compel me, sir—not one
moment—this is such insolence! [*Going to push him out.*]

> [*Enter* CHARLES SURFACE.]

CHARLES   Heyday! what's the matter now? What the devil,
70   have you got hold of my little broker here? Zounds,
brother, don't hurt little Premium. What's the matter, my
little fellow?

JOSEPH SURFACE   So! he has been with you, too, has he?

CHARLES   To be sure he has! Why, 'tis as honest a little——
75   But sure, Joseph, you have not been borrowing money
too, have you?

JOSEPH SURFACE   Borrowing! no! But, brother, you know
here we expect Sir Oliver every——

CHARLES   O gad, that's true! Noll mustn't find the little
80   broker here to be sure.

JOSEPH SURFACE   Yet, Mr. *Stanley* insists——

CHARLES   Stanley! why his name is *Premium*.

JOSEPH SURFACE   No, no, *Stanley*.

CHARLES   No, no, *Premium*.

85 JOSEPH SURFACE   Well, no matter which—but—

CHARLES   Aye, aye, Stanley or Premium, 'tis the same
thing, as you say; for I suppose he goes by half [a] hundred names, besides A.B.'s at the coffee-houses.[6]

JOSEPH SURFACE   Death! here's Sir Oliver at the door.

90   [*Knocking again.*] Now I beg, Mr. Stanley——

CHARLES   Aye, and I beg, Mr. Premium——

SIR OLIVER   Gentlemen——

JOSEPH SURFACE   Sir, by heaven you shall go!

CHARLES   Aye, out with him, certainly.

95 SIR OLIVER   This violence——

JOSEPH SURFACE   'Tis your own fault.

CHARLES   Out with him, to be sure.

> [*Both forcing* SIR OLIVER *out.*]
>
> [*Enter* SIR PETER *and* LADY TEAZLE, MARIA, *and*
> ROWLEY.]

---

6. Moneylenders often met their clients at coffeehouses under assumed or intentionally concealed names.

SIR PETER   My old friend, Sir Oliver—hey! What in the
name of wonder!—Here are dutiful nephews!—assault
100   their uncle at the first visit!

LADY TEAZLE   Indeed, Sir Oliver, 'twas well we came in to
rescue you.

ROWLEY   Truly it was; for I perceive, Sir Oliver, the character of old Stanley was no protection to you.

105   SIR OLIVER   Nor of Premium either: the necessities of the
former could not extort a shilling from *that* benevolent
gentleman; and now, egad, I stood a chance of faring
worse than my ancestors, and being knocked down without being bid for.

[*After a pause,* JOSEPH *and* CHARLES *turning to each
other.*]

110   JOSEPH SURFACE [*aside*] Charles!

CHARLES   Joseph!

JOSEPH SURFACE   'Tis now complete!

CHARLES   Very!

SIR OLIVER   Sir Peter, my friend, and Rowley too—look on
115   that elder nephew of mine. You know what he has
already received from my bounty; and you know also
how gladly I would have regarded half my fortune as
held in trust for him—judge, then, my disappointment
in discovering him to be destitute of truth—charity—
120   and gratitude!

SIR PETER   Sir Oliver, I should be more surprised at this
declaration, if I had not myself found him selfish, treacherous, and hypocritical!

LADY TEAZLE   And if the gentleman pleads not guilty to
125   these, pray let him call *me* to his character.

SIR PETER   Then, I believe, we need add no more.—If he
knows himself, he will consider it as the most perfect
punishment that he is known to the world.

CHARLES [*aside*]   If they talk this way to *Honesty,* what will
130   they say to *me,* by and by?

[SIR PETER, LADY TEAZLE, *and* MARIA *retire.*]

SIR OLIVER   As for that prodigal, his brother, there—

CHARLES [*aside*]   Aye, now comes my turn: the damned
family pictures will ruin me!

JOSEPH SURFACE   Sir Oliver!—uncle!—will you honor me
135   with a hearing?

CHARLES [*aside*]   Now if Joseph would make one of his
long speeches, I might recollect myself a little.

SIR OLIVER [*to* JOSEPH SURFACE]   I suppose you would
undertake to justify yourself entirely?

140   JOSEPH SURFACE   I trust I could.

SIR OLIVER   Pshaw!—Well, sir! and *you* [*To* CHARLES]
could justify yourself too, I suppose?

CHARLES   Not that I know of, Sir Oliver.

SIR OLIVER   What!—Little Premium has been let too
145   much into the secret, I presume?

CHARLES   True, sir; but they were family secrets, and
should never be mentioned again, you know.

ROWLEY   Come, Sir Oliver, I know you cannot speak of
Charles's follies with anger.

150   SIR OLIVER   Odd's heart, no more I can—nor with gravity
either. Sir Peter, do you know the rogue bargained with
me for all his ancestors—sold me judges and generals
by the foot—and maiden aunts as cheap as broken
china.

155   CHARLES   To be sure, Sir Oliver, I did make a little free
with the family canvas, that's the truth on't. My ancestors may certainly rise in evidence against me, there's no
denying it; but believe me sincere when I tell you—and
upon my soul I would not say it if I was not—that if I do
160   not appear mortified at the exposure of my follies, it is
because I feel at this moment the warmest satisfaction
in seeing you, my liberal benefactor.

SIR OLIVER   Charles, I believe you. Give me your hand
again; the ill-looking little fellow over the settee has
165   made your peace.

CHARLES   Then, sir, my gratitude to the original is still
increased.

LADY TEAZLE   [*pointing to* MARIA]   Yet, I believe, Sir Oliver,
here is one whom Charles is still more anxious to be rec-
170   onciled to.

SIR OLIVER   Oh, I have heard of his attachment there; and,
with the young lady's pardon, if I construe right—that
blush——

SIR PETER   Well, child, speak your sentiments.

175   MARIA   Sir, I have little to say, but that I shall rejoice to hear
that he is happy; for me, whatever claim I had to his affection, I willingly resign it to one who has a better title.

CHARLES   How, Maria!

SIR PETER   Heyday! what's the mystery now? While he
180   appeared an incorrigible rake, you would give your hand
to no one else; and now that he is likely to reform, I warrant you won't have him.

MARIA   His own heart—and Lady Sneerwell know the
cause.

185   CHARLES   Lady Sneerwell!

JOSEPH SURFACE   Brother, it is with great concern I am
obliged to speak on this point, but my regard to justice
compels me, and Lady Sneerwell's injuries can no longer
be concealed. [*Goes to the door.*]

[*Enter* LADY SNEERWELL.]

190   SIR PETER   So! another French milliner!—Egad, he has
one in every room in the house, I suppose!

LADY SNEERWELL   Ungrateful Charles! Well may you be
surprised, and feel for the indelicate situation which
your perfidy has forced me into.
195 CHARLES   Pray, uncle, is this another plot of yours? For, as
I have life, I don't understand it.
JOSEPH SURFACE   I believe, sir, there is but the evidence of
one person more necessary to make it extremely clear.
SIR PETER   And that person, I imagine, is Mr. Snake.—
200 Rowley, you were perfectly right to bring him with us,
and pray let him appear.
ROWLEY   Walk in, Mr. Snake.

> [*Enter* SNAKE.]

I thought his testimony might be wanted; however, it
happens unluckily, that he comes to confront Lady
205 Sneerwell, and not to support her.
LADY SNEERWELL   Villain! Treacherous to me at last!
[*Aside*]—Speak, fellow, have *you* too conspired against me?
SNAKE   I beg your ladyship ten thousand pardons: you
paid me extremely liberally for the lie in question; but I
210 have unfortunately been offered double to speak the
truth.
SIR PETER   Plot and counterplot, egad—I wish your ladyship joy of the success of your negotiation.
LADY SNEERWELL   The torments of shame and disappoint-
215 ment on you all!
LADY TEAZLE   Hold, Lady Sneerwell—before you go, let
me thank you for the trouble you and that gentleman
have taken, in writing letters to me from Charles, and
answering them yourself; and let me also request you to
220 make my respects to the Scandalous College, of which
you are president, and inform them, that Lady Teazle,
licentiate,[7] begs leave to return the diploma they granted
her, as she leaves off practice, and kills characters no
longer.
225 LADY SNEERWELL   You too, madam!—provoking—insolent!
May your husband live these fifty years!   [*Exit.*]
SIR PETER   Oons! what a fury!
LADY TEAZLE   A malicious creature, indeed!
SIR PETER   Hey! not for her last wish?
230 LADY TEAZLE   Oh, no!
SIR OLIVER   Well, sir, and what have you to say now?
JOSEPH SURFACE   Sir, I am so confounded, to find that Lady
Sneerwell could be guilty of suborning° Mr. *Snake* in this   *bribing*
manner, to impose on us all, that I know not what to say;
235 however, lest her revengeful spirit should prompt her to
injure my brother, I had certainly better follow her directly.
                                                    [*Exit.*]

---

7. Holder of a professional license or diploma.

SIR PETER Moral to the last drop!

SIR OLIVER Aye, and marry her, Joseph, if you can.—Oil and vinegar, egad! you'll do very well together.

240 ROWLEY I believe we have no more occasion for Mr. Snake at present.

SNAKE Before I go, I beg pardon once for all, for whatever uneasiness I have been the humble instrument of caus- ing to the parties present.

245 SIR PETER Well, well, you have made atonement by a good deed at last.

SNAKE But I must request of the company, that it shall never be known.

SIR PETER Hey! what the plague! are you ashamed of hav-
250 ing done a right thing once in your life?

SNAKE Ah, sir,—consider I live by the badness of my char- acter—I have nothing but my infamy to depend on! and, if it were once known that I had been betrayed into an honest action, I should lose every friend I have in the
255 world.

SIR OLIVER Well, well—we'll not traduce° you by saying   *defame*
anything in your praise, never fear.

[*Exit* SNAKE.]

SIR PETER There's a precious rogue! yet that fellow is a writer and a critic!

260 LADY TEAZLE See, Sir Oliver, there needs no persuasion now to reconcile your nephew and Maria.

[CHARLES *and* MARIA *apart.*]

SIR OLIVER Aye, aye, that's as it should be, and, egad, we'll have the wedding to-morrow morning.

CHARLES Thank you, my dear uncle.

265 SIR PETER What, you rogue! don't you ask the girl's con- sent first?

CHARLES Oh, I have done that a long time—above a minute ago—and she has looked yes.

MARIA For shame, Charles!—I protest, Sir Peter, there
270 has not been a word——

SIR OLIVER Well, then, the fewer the better—may your love for each other never know abatement.

SIR PETER And may you live as happily together as Lady Teazle and I—intend to do!

275 CHARLES Rowley, my old friend, I am sure you congratu- late me; and I suspect that I owe you much.

SIR OLIVER You do, indeed, Charles.

ROWLEY If my efforts to serve you had not succeeded you would have been in my debt for the attempt—but deserve
280 to be happy—and you overpay me.

SIR PETER Aye, honest Rowley always said you would reform.

CHARLES   Why as to reforming, Sir Peter, I'll make no promises, and that I take to be a proof that I intend to set about
285   it.—But here shall be my monitor—my gentle guide.—Ah!
can I leave the virtuous path those eyes illumine?

> Though thou, dear maid, shouldst waive thy *beauty's* sway,[8]
> Thou still must rule, because I *will* obey:
> An humbled fugitive from Folly view,
> 290   No sanctuary near but *Love* and—You;
>
> [*To the audience.*]
>
> *You* can, indeed, each anxious fear remove,
> For even *Scandal* dies, if *you* approve.

Finis

Epilogue

Written by G. Colman, Esq.[9]
Spoken by Mrs. Abington[1]

I, who was late so volatile and gay,
Like a trade-wind must now blow all one way,
Bend all my cares, my studies, and my vows,
To one old rusty weathercock—my spouse!
5   So wills our virtuous bard—the motley Bayes[2]
Of crying epilogues[3] and laughing plays!
   Old bachelors, who marry smart young wives,
Learn from our play to regulate your lives:
Each bring his dear to town, all faults upon her—
10   London will prove the very source of honor.
Plunged fairly in, like a cold bath it serves,
When principles relax, to brace the nerves.
   Such is my case;—and yet I might deplore
That the gay dream of dissipation's o'er;
15   And say, ye fair, was ever lively wife,
Born with a genius for the highest life,
Like me untimely blasted in her bloom,
Like me condemned to such a dismal doom?
Save money—when I just knew how to waste it!
20   Leave London—just as I began to taste it!
Must I then watch the early crowing cock,
The melancholy ticking of a clock;
In the lone rustic hall for ever pounded,
With dogs, cats, rats, and squalling brats surrounded?
25   With humble curates can I now retire,
(While good Sir Peter boozes with the squire,)

---

8. That is, relinquish the power that your
beauty holds over me.
9. George Colman (1732–1794), playwright
and manager of the Haymarket Theatre.
1. Frances Abington (1737–1815), celebrated
comic actress who played Lady Teazle.

2. The poet who is the protagonist ridiculed
in the Duke of Buckingham's satiric play *The
Rehearsal* (1671).
3. Sheridan wrote the epilogue to George
Ayscough's tragedy *Semiramis* (1776).

And at backgammon mortify my soul,
That pants for loo,° or flutters at a vole?[4]   *a card game*
Seven's the main![5] Dear sound!—that must expire,
30   Lost at hot cockles,[6] round a Christmas fire!
The transient hour of fashion too soon spent,
Farewell the tranquil mind, farewell content![7]
Farewell the plumèd head, the cushioned *tête*,[8]
That takes the cushion from its proper seat!
35   That spirit-stirring drum!—card drums° I mean,   *card parties*
Spadille—odd trick—pam—basto[9]—king and queen!
And you, ye knockers,° that, with brazen throat,   *door knockers*
The welcome visitors approach denote;
Farewell! all quality of high renown,
40   Pride, pomp, and circumstance of glorious town!
Farewell! your revels I partake no more,
And Lady Teazle's occupation's o'er!
All this I told our bard—he smiled, and said 'twas clear,
I ought to play deep tragedy next year.
45   Meanwhile he drew wise morals from his play,
And in these solemn periods° stalked away:—   *sentences*
"Blest were the fair like you; her faults who stopped,
And closed her follies when the curtain dropped!
No more in vice or error to engage,
50   Or play the fool at large on life's great stage."

4. The winning of all the tricks (a term used in several card games).
5. A call in the dice game hazard.
6. A rural game in which a blindfolded player tried to guess which other player struck him or her on the back.
7. This and the following ten lines parody Shakespeare's *Othello* (1604), 3.3.353–62.

8. An elaborately ornamented tall wig, worn by fashionable women in the second half of the 18th century (literally, "head"; French).
9. Names for various playing cards: *spadille:* the ace of spades, in quadrille and ombre; *pam:* the knave of clubs, in loo; *basto:* the ace of clubs, in quadrille and ombre.

JOHANN WOLFGANG VON GOETHE
1749–1832

Even during his lifetime, Goethe achieved such renown throughout Europe that the late eighteenth and early nineteenth centuries are sometimes called the Age of Goethe. Goethe was perhaps the last European to live up to the Renaissance ideal of the universal man, making distinguished contributions not only in all major literary genres but also in art criticism and the study of classical culture. In addition, he worked extensively in the fields of botany, mineralogy, comparative anatomy, and optics. He held many administrative and political positions at the court of Weimar, where he was responsible, in his function as privy councillor, for finance, the military, and mining, as well as for the Weimar Court Theater, which he turned from an amateur theater to a professional troupe that premiered many of his own plays. Distrusting both the French Revolution, whose effects he witnessed at close hand, and the growing nationalism of the nineteenth century in Germany and elsewhere, Goethe considered himself not a German but a European, and he coined the visionary notion of "world literature" (*Weltliteratur*) to open Europe to the intellectual and artistic production of the non-European world.

Goethe was born into a bourgeois family in Frankfurt. As he recounts in his autobiography, *From My Life: Poetry and Truth* (1811–13), he was introduced to the arts at an early age by playing extensively with the family's puppet theater. Despite his early interest in the arts and the theater, Goethe followed his father's wish and studied law. But his artistic ambitions could not be held back for long, and he soon started to publish various kinds of literary works. Goethe's first significant play, *Götz of Berlechingen* (1773), was shaped by his discovery of WILLIAM SHAKESPEARE. Goethe was particularly taken with Shakespeare's willingness to violate the strict rules of drama and tried to instill a similar spirit of imagination in his own play. The most important work of this early period was a novel, *The Sorrows of Young Werther* (1774); it turned Goethe into the representative of a literary movement called Sturm und Drang (storm and stress), which emphasized the expression of feelings over the strictures of literary form. Centered on subjective impressions, extreme emotions, and literary outbursts, the novel follows its tragic protagonist, who is caught in a love triangle with a married woman, to his eventual suicide. *The Sorrows of Young Werther* inspired a veritable mass hysteria, also called the "Werther fever," that allegedly led to a rash of copycat suicides as well as to the marketing of Werther paraphernalia. Goethe had become famous almost overnight.

One year later, Duke Karl August of Weimar called Goethe to his elegant but provincial court. Goethe first served as educator, but he soon fulfilled more important functions and was ultimately elevated to the aristocracy, thereby acquiring the title "von Goethe." It was here, amid his far-flung duties, that Goethe began his mature and more classical works: for example, his influential novel *Wilhelm Meister's Apprenticeship* (1795–96), as well as the plays *Egmont* (1787), *Iphigenia on Tauris* (1787), *Torquato Tasso* (1790), and *Faust: A Fragment* (1790). Most of these works were begun shortly after Goethe arrived at Weimar, but they all went through innumerable revisions, during which Goethe slowly forged a new, less unruly and more measured style, thus leaving the earlier Sturm und Drang behind. *Torquato Tasso* also shows Goethe's increasing fascination with the Italian Renaissance. The source of inspiration for this and other works was Goethe's extended voyage to Italy (1786–88), which reflected the revival of interest in classical forms and ideas in Germany and Europe more generally, a revival of which Goethe became the chief representative. His travel book, *Italian Journeys* (published 1816–17), and the acclaimed cycle of poetry *Roman Elegies* (1795) were some of the immediate fruits of this voyage, which also led him to revise *Faust* and other works in accordance with the classicist style. At the same time, Goethe wrote a large number of occasional and minor dramatic works for the court, including masques, curtain-raisers, operas, operetta libretti, and a draft of a sequel to Mozart's *The Magic Flute* (1791).

Beginning in 1794, Goethe began an intense collaboration and friendship with the poet and dramatist Friedrich Schiller. This collaboration inaugurated what is now known as the era of Weimar Classicism. The two writers exchanged works and thoughts; their correspondence on the epic and drama laid the foundation for a new theory of drama; and they turned Weimar into a center for new theater production. All these activities were in the service of reviving classical models of art and literature. To that end, Goethe collected classical sculpture (he contented himself with copies) and adapted classical stories, poetry, and drama. But the theater stood at the center of the classical revival. Goethe had promoted the amateur theater at the court soon after arriving in Weimar and subsequently oversaw the construction of a proper theater, with five sets of wings, traps, and other elements of late eighteenth-century stage machinery. However, it was not until the early nineties that a properly funded and equipped Weimar Court Theater was established, with Goethe as its director. Goethe worried about the training of actors, developing guidelines later published as *Rules for Actors* (1803), and intervened in all other aspects of theater production. The Weimar Court Theater performed many of the important plays of Schiller and Goethe, but Goethe also insisted on introducing his provincial audience to international playwrights, including Shakespeare, PEDRO CALDERÓN DE LA BARCA, and Carlo Goldoni. Even though Goethe used the Weimar Court Theater as a vehicle for his revival of classical drama, he also opened it to a variety of dramatic styles.

In the first decades of the nineteenth century, Goethe finally completed the long-awaited first part of *FAUST* (1806) as well as two important novels: *Elective Affinities* (1809), regarded by many as his most accomplished novel, and the second part of *Wilhelm Meister* (1821). Goethe was now so famous that he was in contact with a large number of personalities and attracted Europe-wide attention, including and especially in England, where Lord Byron, Thomas Carlyle, and, later, George Eliot were among his most avid supporters. Drawn by the illustrious man's fame, Johann Eckermann began recording his conversations with Goethe in 1823; published between 1837 and 1848, they provide us with a fascinating record of Goethe's final years as a cultural institution.

Among Goethe's wide-ranging activities and works, many of them paradigmatic in their respective genres, the two parts of *Faust* stand out as his masterpiece. His tendency to revise his writing substantially is nowhere demonstrated more clearly than in this work, which he began in his early twenties and worked on until a few months before his death. It underwent significant changes, from the first drafts in the 1770s, the so-called *Urfaust,* to the publication of a first fragment in 1790, through the appearance in print of the first part in 1808 and then to the final version of the second part, completed just before his last birthday in 1832. Goethe probably never read CHRISTOPHER MAR-LOWE's play *Dr. Faustus* (ca. 1588), but he relied on the same medieval folk legend, *Historia of D. Johann Faustus* (1578), that Marlowe used, and he had encountered adaptations of Marlowe's versions as a child. The original Faust story is a quint-essential medieval morality tale, in which the arrogant doctor gives in to the tempta-tions of the devil, in particular to black magic, makes the famous pact, and finally suffers for his sins in hell. In the course of

his many revisions, Goethe transformed this simple material into a text that cap-tured the spirit and desires of the modern world. While preserving key set pieces, such as the pact with the devil, he empha-sized the relation between abstract learn-ing and sensuous experience and, even more importantly, the nature of human striving and industry, the transformative energies unleashed by modernity. Though this modernity is expressed much more directly in *Faust II,* where the doctor builds dams, prints money, and creates new political institutions, the principle of human striving is a prominent theme in the first part as well. It is also the quality that will finally save Faust's soul. For whereas Faust's earlier counterparts were lost to the devil, Goethe has him escape

Mephistopheles appears before Faust in his study. Engraving by the French artist Eugène Delacroix (c. 1828).

Mephistopheles' clutches at the end of *Faust* II.

The decision to save Faust represents an important change in the legend, which after all had started as a morality play intended to illustrate the punishment of its blaspheming protagonist. Christopher Marlowe moved the morality play to the cusp of Renaissance drama by introducing vividly drawn characters, internal conflicts, and complex motivation. Goethe, however, altered the legend's entire moral structure. His justification was the value placed on human striving, on Faust's tireless desire to know and to act. Whereas the older versions had condemned Faust for overstepping the bounds of religious belief, for Goethe the limitless thirst for knowledge becomes a value that deserves special consideration. He still depicts Faust as a sinner, as the earlier versions had done. But now Faust's sinning has to be balanced against his thirst for knowledge, which—though irreverent—is presented very much as a good thing. Goethe's Faust is a puzzle: the very quality that drives him to his pact with the devil will also lead him to salvation.

This major shift is indicated in "Prologue in Heaven," one of three pieces that frame the play before its proper action begins. Borrowed from the opening of the biblical book of Job, the prologue depicts a debate between God and Mephistopheles that ends in a wager. Mephistopheles has leave to tempt Faust, since God is certain that Faust's restless striving, his search for true knowledge, will eventually guide him back to the right path. Goethe opens with a dedication, in which he evokes the youthful world in which he began this work some thirty years earlier. Between the two is a kind of curtain-raiser, "Prelude in the Theater," in which a Manager, a Poet, and a Clown argue for their respective visions of a theater poised between popular entertainment and high art, a debate undoubtedly grounded in Goethe's experience as a dramatist and theater director.

The main drama of *Faust* I can be divided into two parts. The first part introduces us to Faust, who has mastered all the higher disciplines of the medieval university—philosophy, law, medicine, and theology—but who still has not learned

Faust seduces Gretchen. Engraving attributed to Ary Scheffer (c. 1820).

the inner essence of the world. Dissatisfied with his lack of knowledge, he daringly turns to magic and alchemy, and it is this daring that is, for Goethe, Faust's most modern attribute. Shunning inherited pieties and religious prejudices, Faust is ready to sacrifice everything to gain knowledge. Yet this thirst is only one part of Faust's constitution: equally important is his desire to experience life to the full. While the first leads him to magic, the second makes him even more susceptible to Mephistopheles, who offers him precisely such experiences—which include the sensual.

Faust's experiences compose the second section of *Faust* I, in which Mephistopheles tries to satisfy his demands and desires. Although Faust often dismisses Mephistopheles' efforts at satisfaction as "mere spectacle," he nevertheless tries them all, culminating in the famous orgiastic "Walpurgis Night" scene, a delirious meeting of all creatures of the night. None of these sensuous pleasures, however, can give Faust the kind of satisfaction he derives from what is the culminating event of the play: the seduction of Gretchen. It is this episode that earns *Faust* its subtitle, "A Tragedy." Gretchen is different from the other pleasures provided by Mephistopheles. Faust genuinely falls in love with her and eloquently praises her innocence and simple-minded religiosity. At the same time, he alternates between neglecting her and showering her with presents as he pursues and finally achieves his physical satisfaction, which sets off a string of tragic events. So the first part of *Faust* ends. These tragic events are blissfully forgotten in *Faust* II, which takes Faust and Mephistopheles on a wild tour through politics, science, and learning.

Goethe's most obvious change to the legend is Faust's ultimate rescue from damnation, but another, possibly more radical, revision is evident from the beginning. For the real protagonist of the first part is not Faust, who is by turn pompous, idealistic, and fatuous, who does not know himself, and who manages to bring everything, including poor Gretchen, to ruin, but the witty, realistic, and caustic Mephistopheles. It is Mephistopheles who criticizes the medieval world of Faust and who deflates his grandiose speeches, including his self-serving declarations of love for Gretchen. This devil is the spirit of negation, as he says of himself, but it is a negation that serves to test the validity of authority. Mephistopheles thus embodies the principle of critique, of closely scrutinizing all kinds of inherited religious belief and orthodoxies. Because this critical spirit is central to modernity, Mephistopheles becomes the truly modern character in the play. Goethe's intent to clandestinely turn Mephistopheles into the main protagonist of the play is borne out on stage. Mephistopheles is by far the most attractive role in the entire play. He has all the pithiest and also all the wittiest lines. Mephistopheles simply steals the show.

This tension between a modernized Faust and an even more modern Mephistopheles is one reason for the influence of Goethe's *Faust*; another is the play's daring structure and form. Goethe refused to submit to the narrow neo-Aristotelian rules of drama, presenting instead a play of epic length that is composed of loosely connected scenes. *Faust* contains passages in different meters and rhymes as well as in prose. It includes interludes, an allegorical dream, a satire of the university, erotic songs, and an orgy. As a play that tries to encompass the entirety of the modern world, a hybrid genre that aspires to a rare totality approached a number of different ways: as a total work of art, as a modern epic, and as a new type of dramatic text.

Because of its ambitious scope, Goethe never sought to mount even the more manageable first part of *Faust* in his Weimar Court Theater and did not consider it fit for the stage. A few years before his death, another theater—undoubtedly seeking to take advantage of his unrivaled fame—did perform it, but he showed little interest in the production. The allegorical second part has been staged even less often, and the length of both parts taken together ensures that a performance of Goethe's *Faust* in its entirety is almost never undertaken. In the course of the twentieth century, however, the first part attracted some of the world's most renowned theater directors and actors, including, in Germany, Friedrich Dorn and Peter Stein (the latter presented an acclaimed production of both parts in 2000), and the French director Patrice Chéreau. Many other artists have responded to *Faust* as well. Hector Berlioz sent Goethe a composition titled *Eight Scenes from Faust* (1829), later incorporated into his *Damnation of Faust,* and Charles Gounod's *Faust* (1859) has remained part of the opera repertory. In the twentieth century, Gertrude Stein's play *Doctor Faustus Lights the Lights* (1938) is among the most typically modernist of responses to Goethe's text, and the expressionist film director F. Murnau was among the first to transpose *Faust* into the medium of film (1926). Goethe's *Faust* has thus remained an important touchstone for contemporary art, a testament to Goethe's ability to turn a simple medieval morality tale into an allegory of modernity.   M.P.

Faust, a Tragedy
Part One[1]

CHARACTERS

Heinrich FAUST, a scholar
MEPHISTOPHELES, a devil
GRETCHEN (or MARGARETE, for which
   "Gretchen" is a diminutive),
   a maiden

MARTHE, Gretchen's neighbor
VALENTINE, Gretchen's brother
WAGNER, Faust's *famulus* (attendant)

and dozens of minor characters

Dedication

Come back again, you figures shifting, spectral,
Whom I first dimly glimpsed when I was young?[2]
Try, shall I, this time, to hold on to you all?
Those phantom forms, their pull is still as strong?
5   Closer and closer, out of mist and vapor,
You rise up round me—all right, I surrender!
The magic breezes blowing round your shapes
Wakes youthful throbbings in me, youthful hopes.

What lively scenes you bring back, days how happy,
10   What once-loved shadows come again to life!,
First love, first friendships, like some old, old story
All but forgotten, come back with then, and grief
Comes back, and sighing I retrace life's labyrinthine,
Wandering course, naming the dear ones ill fortune
15   Cheated of golden hours and hurried away
Into the darkness before me, out of the day.

They will not hear it, what's about to follow,
Those hearts who were the first to hear me sing,
All that brave company are scattered now,
20   That first applause has long ceased echoing;
My song is poured out to the anonymous crowd,
Whose very praises fill me with misgiving.
Among those my verses once gave such delight,
If any live, they've long been lost to sight.

25   And a yearning, unfelt, unroused for so long,
For that solemn spirit world seizes me,

---

1. Translated by Martin Greenberg.
2. A reference to the earlier versions of *Faust* and to Goethe's younger self.

Like an Aeolian harp[3] my renewed song
Trembles into sound uncertainly,
A shudder shakes my frame, my eyes brim over till
30   My too strict heart, relenting, is turned gentle;
What's all around me, mine, looks leagues away,
And a vanished world is my reality.

Prelude in the Theater

[MANAGER, POET, CLOWN]

MANAGER   You two who've always stood by me
When times were hard and the playhouse empty,
35   What do you think we can expect
From this tour of ours through German country?
I'd like so much to please the crowd,
For they're really so easygoing, so patient;
The posts are up, the floorboards laid,
40   And all looking forward to the entertainment.
They sit there staring round, at ease,
In hopes of a real surprise, every one,
I know with this audience how to please,
But I've never been in a fix like this one.
45   It's true what they're used to is pretty bad,
But Lord, what a terrible lot they've read.
So how surprise them with something lively and new,
A piece with some meaning that amuses them too?
I don't deny what please me most
50   Are droves of people, a great host,
Trying with all their might to squeeze
Through the strait gate to our paradise,
When it's daylight still, not even four,
Using elbow and fist to get to the ticket seller,
55   Like starving men rushing the baker's door—
For the sake of a seat prepared to commit murder.
Who works such a wonder on such a mixture
Of people? Why, of course it's the poet,
So fall to, then, dear colleague, and let's see you do it!
60 POET   Don't talk to me about that crowd of yours—
One look at them and all my wits desert me!
Oh, shield me from those struggling, screaming hordes
Which swallow you up, against your will, completely!
No, lead me to some dear, secluded place,
65   Only there is where a poet is happy,
There love and friendship, godlike, inspire and nurse
The precious gift that is the power of verse.
   Oh dear, what struggles up from deep inside us,
Syllables our lips shape slowly, haltingly,
70   Into scenes ineffective now, and now effective,

---

3. A stringed instrument popular during the Romantic era; because it is "played" by the wind, its sounds are unpredictable.

Is drowned out in the present's hurlyburly;[4]
Years must pass till, seen in time's perspective,
Its shape and soul shine forth as they are truly.
What's all flash and glitter lives a day,
75 The real thing's treasured by posterity.
CLOWN Posterity! oh that word—don't let's start a row!
If all *I* ever thought of was the hereafter,
Who'd set the audience laughing in the here and now?
To be amused, that's their hearts' desire.
80 Having a clown on the stage who knows what his business is
Is not to be sneezed at—it matters to know how to please.
When yours is the stuff to delight and enchant a whole theaterful,
You don't sourly mutter the public's a mob and it's fickle.
What you want's a full house, the sign out saying Standing Room Only,
85 For the bigger the house, the better the response you can count on,
So be a good fellow and show us what drama should be—
Your imagination, let it pour out like a fountain,
Its wonders matched by wisdom, good sense, feeling,
By passion too—but mind you, show us some fooling!
90 MANAGER But what's the first requirement? Plenty of action!
They're spectators, so what they want to see is things happen.
If you've got business going on every minute
That catches people's attention, that makes them all sit up,
Then you don't have to worry, they're yours, they're won over,
95 When the curtain comes down they'll shout "Author! Author!"
With a public so large you need an abundance to please them all,
Something for everyone, that's how to seize them all,
The last thing you want is to be classically economical!
In the theater today only scenes and set pieces do,
100 The way to succeed is to serve up a stew,
You can cook it up fast, dish it out easy too.
Now tell me, what good is your artistic unity—
The public will only make hash of it anyway.
POET But you don't understand—all that's just hackwork!
105 You don't stoop to such things if you're a true artist!
Those butchers you're fond of, those experts at patchwork,
Are your measure, I see, of what is a dramatist.
MANAGER Go ahead, scold me, I don't mind your censure,
To do a job right you use the tools that are called for.
110 Remember it's soft wood you've got to split,
Consider the people for whom you write!
One's here because he's bored, another
Comes stuffed from eating a seven-course dinner,
But worst by far are the ones who come to us
115 Straight from reading the latest newspapers.
The crowd arrives here distracted, distrait,
Thinking of this and that, not of a play,
The reason they come is mere curiosity,

4. Uproar.

The ladies exhibit their shoulders and finery,
120 Put on a great show without asking a salary.
Oh, the dreams poets dream in their ivory tower!
Flattered, are you, to see the house full?
Well, take a good look at our clientele,
The half vulgar and loud, half unmoved and sour;
125 One's mind's on his card game after the play,
Another's on tumbling a girl in the hay.
It's for people like that you fools torture the Muses?[5]
Listen to me: You'll never go wrong
If you pile it on, pile it on, and still pile it on.
130 Bewilder, confound them with all your variety,
The public's the public, they're a hard lot to satisfy.
But goodness, you seem so worked up to me!
What's wrong? I can't tell if it's anguish or ecstasy.
POET   Go out and find yourself some other lackey!
135 You expect the poet, do you, frivolously
For the sake of your blue eyes to debase
Nature's dearest gift to the human race?
How does he teach humankind feeling,
Master the elements, every one?
140 I'll tell you, by the music pealing
Forth from his breast orphically,[6]
Which then by reflux back on him returning
Reverberates as Nature's deep-voiced harmony.
When Nature winds life's endless thread
145 Indifferently on the bobbin, when
The noisy cries of her countless creatures
No music makes, uproar instead,
Who melodizes the monotonous din
And makes all move in living measures?
150 Who calls each mute particular
To sing its part in the general chorus
In a glorious concord of myriad voices?
Who links our passions to wild tempests,
Our solemn moods to fading sunsets?
155 Unrolls before the feet of lovers
A lovely carpet of spring flowers?
Twines green leaves, ordinary, meaningless,
Into a wreath to honor the meritorious?
Assures us there's an Olympus,[7] gives order to its gods—
160 That revelation of man's powers, the poet, does!
CLOWN   Then go on and use them, your marvelous powers!
Go at your business of making verses
The way you go at a love adventure:

5. In classical mythology, goddesses who preside over the arts and all intellectual pursuits.
6. Musically, mystically; Orpheus, the greatest poet and singer of classical mythology, was
also credited with founding mystery religions
and was celebrated in cult worship.
7. A mountain in northern Greece where the
classical gods were believed to live.

A chance encounter, you're attracted, linger,
165   And little by little you find you're caught;
You're so happy, later you're not,
First you're enraptured, then it's pure misery,
And before you know it it's a whole history.
That's how to do it, write the play we want that way.
170   Jump right into life's richness and riot,
All of us live life, few have an idea about it,
And my, how it interests wherever you scratch it!
Color, confusion, a wild hurlyburly,
With a glimmer of truth amid errors' obscurity,
175   And there you have it, exactly the right brew
To refresh everyone, make them think a bit too.
Then the best of our youth will flock here to listen,
Gripping their seats in anticipation;
The sensitive soul will find in your play
180   Food to feed his melancholy;
One thing touches one man, another another,
The end result is, all discover
What's in their hearts. The young are still ready
To laugh at a good thrust, let their tears flow in pity,
185   Warmly respond to high aspirations,
Cherishing still their bright dreams and illusions.
You'll never please people who find everything
Is an old story, nothing more's to be done;
But the youth, still growing, still developing,
190   How they will thank you, every one!
POET   Then give me back *my* youth again,
When all was growing, changing with me,
When song after song gushed from my lips
Like a fountain flowing uninterruptedly,
195   When a morning mist still veiled the world
And a bud was a promised miracle,
When I plucked the thousand flowers that filled
The vales with their rich spectacle.
The nothing I owned was more than enough,
200   I hungered for truth, rejoiced in illusion.
O days of anguished happiness,
Of unsubdued, of purest passion,
Of burning hatred and burning love—
Oh, give me back my youth again!
205   CLOWN   Youth, my dear colleague, you need in the following cases:
When the enemy's crowding you hard in the fight,
When pretty girls in summer dresses
Kiss and squeeze you with all their might,
When running hard, you glimpse in the distance
210   The wreath[8] that rewards the fleetest foot,
When after the madly whirling dances

8. The laurel wreath, given to the victors in Greek athletic games.

You wear the night out draining your cup.
But to sweep the old familiar harp strings
Boldly, yet with some grace too,
215 To make by pleasing indirections
For the end your drama has in view—
That's a job for you old fellows
And we respect you for your skill;
Age doesn't make us childish, God knows,
220 Just finds us the same old children still.

MANAGER We've talked enough, now let me see,
You get to work, produce results.
Our business is to stage a play,
Not pass the time in compliments.
225 And please—don't tell me you're not in the mood,
It never arrives if you hesitate timidly.
You claim you're a poet, then go ahead,
Bid your muse pour out her grandest poetry.
You know what's wanted: good strong stuff,
230 Come on, come on, stop fussing about it.
What's put off today still tomorrow's put off;
Don't, do you hear me, lose even a minute.
Resolution's a spirit that bravely
Seizes occasion by the short hairs,
235 It won't let go but hangs on grimly;
Once committed, it perseveres.

You know how on our German stage
We're free to try whatever we please,
So don't imagine I want you to save
240 Me money on paint and properties.
Hang out heaven's big and little lamps,
Scatter stars over the canvas sky,
Let's have fire and flood and dizzying steeps,
All sorts of birds and beasts—do the thing liberally.
245 And thus on a narrow platform you're able
To go all the way round Creation's great circle
At a brisk enough pace, yet deliberately as well,
From Heaven, through this our world, down to Hell.

Prologue in Heaven

[THE LORD. THE HEAVENLY HOST. *Then* MEPHISTOPHELES.
The three ARCHANGELS *advance to front.*]

RAPHAEL The sun sounds out his ancient measure
In contest with each brother sphere,[9]
Marching around and around, with steps of thunder,

9. According to the cosmology of the Greek mathematician and astronomer Ptolemy (active 127–148 C.E.), still dominant in the Middle Ages and Renaissance, the planets, sun, moon, and stars all circle the earth in vast crystalline spheres whose movement makes a beautiful music, inaudible to human ears.

His appointed circuit, year after year.
5   To see him lends us angels strength,
But what he *is*, oh who can say?
The inconceivably great works are great
As on the first creating day.

GABRIEL   And swift, past all conception swift,
10   The jeweled globe spins on its axletree,
Celestial brightness alternating
With shuddering night's obscurity.
Against earth's deep-based precipices
The broad-running ocean tides are hurled,
15   And rock and sea together hurtle
With the eternally turning world.

MICHAEL   And hurricanes, contending, roar
From sea to land, from land to sea,
Linking in tremendous circuit
20   A chain of blazing energy.
The lightning bolt makes ready for
The thunderclap a ruinous way—
Yet Lord, your servants reverence
The stiller motions of your day.

25   ALL THREE   From seeing this we draw our strength,
But what You *are*, oh who can say?
And all your great works are as great
As on the first creating day.

MEPHISTOPHELES   Lord, since you've stopped by here again, liking to know
30   How all of us are doing, for which we're grateful,
And since you've never made me feel *de trop*,[1]
Well, here I am too with your other people.
Excuse, I hope, my lack of eloquence,
Though this whole host, I'm sure, will think I'm stupid;
35   Coming from me, high-sounding sentiments
Would only make you laugh—that is, provided
Laughing was a thing Your Worship still did.
About suns and worlds I don't know beans, I only see
How mortals find their lives pure misery.
40   Earth's little god's shaped out of the same old clay,
He's the same queer fish he was on the first day.
He'd be much better off, in my opinion, without
The bit of heavenly light you dealt him out.
He calls it Reason and the use he puts it to?
45   To act more beastly than beasts ever do.
To me he seems, if you'll pardon my saying so,
Like a long-legged grasshopper all of whose leaping
Only lands him back in the grass again chirping
The tune he's always chirped. And if only he'd
50   Stay put in the grass! But no! It's an absolute need
With him to creep and crawl and strain and sweat

1. Too much; superfluous; unwanted (French).

And stick his nose in every pile of dirt.

THE LORD   Is that all you have got to say to me?
Is that all you can do, accuse eternally?
55   Is nothing ever right for you down there, sir?

MEPHISTOPHELES   No, nothing, Lord—all's just as bad as ever.
I really pity humanity's myriad miseries,
I swear I hate tormenting the poor ninnies.

THE LORD   Do you know Faust?

MEPHISTOPHELES   The Doctor?

THE LORD   My good servant!

60   MEPHISTOPHELES   You don't say! Well, he serves you in a funny way,
Finds meat and drink, the fool, in nothing earthly,
Drives madly on, there's in him such a torment,
He himself is half aware he's crazy;
From Heaven he must have the brightest stars,
65   From earth the most ecstatic raptures,
And all that's near at hand or far and wide
Leaves your good servant quite unsatisfied.

THE LORD   If today his service shows confused, disordered,
With my help he'll see his way clearly forward.
70   When the sapling greens, the gardener can feel certain
Flower and fruit will follow in due season.

MEPHISTOPHELES   Would you care to bet on that? You'll lose, I tell you,
If you'll just give me leave to lead the fellow
Gently down my broad, my primrose path.

75   THE LORD   As long as Faustus walks the earth
I shan't, I promise, interfere.
Still as man strives, still he must err.

MEPHISTOPHELES   Well thanks, Lord, for it's not the dead and gone
I like dealing with. By far what I prefer
80   Are round and rosy cheeks. When corpses come
A-knocking, sorry, Master's left the house;
My way of working's the cat's way with a mouse.

THE LORD   So it's agreed, you have my full consent.
Divert the soul of Faust from its true source
85   And if you're able, lead him along, Hell bent
With you, upon the downward course—
Then blush for shame when you find you must admit:
Stumbling along as he must, through darkness and confusion,
A good man still knows which road is the right one.

90   MEPHISTOPHELES   Of course, of course! Yet I'll seduce him from it
Soon enough. I'm not afraid I'll lose my bet.
And after I have won it,
You won't, I trust, begrudge me
My whoops of triumph, shouts of victory.
95   Dust he'll eat
And find that he enjoys it, exactly like
That old aunt of mine, the famous snake.[2]

2. That is, the serpent in the garden of Eden, in the story told in Genesis; for its role in the fall
of Adam and Eve, God condemned it to eat dust (3.14).

THE LORD   There too feel free, you have carte blanche.
    I've never hated your likes much;
100 I find, of all the spirits of denial,
    You jeerers not my hardest trial.
    Man's very quick to slacken in his effort,
    What he likes best is Sunday peace and quiet;
    So I'm glad to give him a devil—for his own good,
105 To prod and poke and incite him as a devil should.
    [To the ANGELS] But you who are God's true and faithful children—
    Delight in the world's wealth of living beauty!
    May that which moves the great work of creation,
    That makes all things to grow, evolve eternally,
110 Bound you about with smiling love, fraternally,
    And the fitfulness, the flux of all appearance—
    By enduring thoughts give enduring forms to its transience.
        [The Heavens close, the ARCHANGELS withdraw.]

MEPHISTOPHELES   I like to see the Old Man now and then,
    And take good care I don't fall out with him.
    How very decent of a Lord Celestial
115 To talk man to man with the Devil of all people.

PART I

Night

*[In a narrow, high-vaulted Gothic room, FAUST, seated restlessly
in an armchair at his desk.]*

FAUST   I've studied, alas, philosophy,
    Law and medicine, recto and verso,[3]
    And how I regret it, theology also,
    Oh God, how hard I've slaved away,
120 With what result? Poor foolish old man,
    I'm no whit wiser than when I began!
    I've got a Master of Arts degree,
    On top of that a Ph.D.,
    For ten long years, around and about,
125 Upstairs, downstairs, in and out,
    I've led my students by the nose
    To what conclusion?—that nobody knows,
    Or ever can know, the tiniest crumb!
    Which is why I feel completely undone.
130   Of course I'm cleverer than these stuffed shirts,
    These Doctors, Masters, Clerics, Priests,
    I'm not bothered by a doubt or a scruple,
    I'm not afraid of Hell or the Devil—
    But the consequence is, my mirth's all gone;
135 No longer can I fool myself
    I'm able to teach anyone
    How to be better, love true worth;

3. The two sides of a page in a book (literally, "on the right [page]," "on the turned [page]"; Latin).

I've got no money or property,
Worldly honors or celebrity;
140 A dog wouldn't put up with this life!
Which is why I've turned to magic,
Seeking to know, by ways occult,
From ghostly mouths, many a secret;
So I no longer need to sweat
145 Painfully explaining what
I don't know anything about;
So I may penetrate the power
That holds the universe together,
Its founts of energy, living seeds,
150 And deal no more in words, words, words.

O full moon, melancholy-bright,
Friend I've watched for, many a night,
Till your quiet-shining circle
Appeared above my high-piled table,
155 If only you might never again
Look below down on my pain,
If only I might stray at will
In your mild light, high on the hill,
Haunt with spirits upland hollows,
160 Fade with you in dim-lit meadows,
And soul no longer gasping in
The stink of learning's midnight oil,
Bathe in your dews till well again!

Oh misery! Oh am I still
165 Stuck here in this dismal prison,
A musty goddamned hole in the wall
Where even the golden light of heaven
Can only weakly make its way through
The painted panes of the gothic window;
170 Where all about me shelves of books
Rise up to the vault in stacks,
Books gray with dust, worm-eaten, rotten,
With soot-stained paper for a curtain;
Where instruments, retorts and glasses[4]
175 Are crammed in everywhere a space is;
And stuck in somehow with these things
My family's ancient furnishings
Make complete the sad confusion—
Call this a world, this world you live in?

180 Can you still wonder why your heart
Should clench in your breast so anxiously?
Why your every impulse is stopped short

4. Apparatus used in alchemy.

By an inexplicable misery?
Instead of Nature's flourishing garden
185 God created and man to dwell there,
Rubbish, dirt are everywhere
Your gaze turns, old bones, a skeleton.

Off, off, to the open countryside!
And this mysterious book, inscribed
190 By Nostradamus'[5] own hand—
What better help to master the secrets
Of how the stars turn in their orbits,
From Nature learn to understand
The spirits' power to speak to spirits;
195 Sitting here and racking your brains
To puzzle out the sacred signs—
What a sterile, futile business!
Spirits, I feel your presence around me:
Announce yourselves if you hear me!

 [He opens the book and his eye encounters the sign of the Macrocosm.[6]]
200 The pure bliss flooding all my senses
Seeing this! Through every nerve and vein
I feel youth's fiery, fresh spirit race again.
Was it a god marked out these signs
By which my agitated bosom's stilled,
205 By which my bleak heart's filled with joy,
By whose mysterious agency
The powers of Nature all around me stand revealed?
Am I a god? All's bright as day!
By these pure tracings I can see,
210 At my soul's feet, great Nature unconcealed.
And the sage's words—I understand them, finally:
"The spirit world is not barred shut,
It's your closed mind, your dead heart!
Stand up unappalled, my scholar,
215 And bathe your breast in the rose of Aurora!"[7]
 [He contemplates the sign.]
How all is woven one, uniting,
Each in the other living, working!
How Heavenly Powers rise, descend,
Passing gold vessels from hand to hand!
220 On wings that scatter sweet-smelling blessings,
Everywhere they post in earth
And make a universal harmony sound forth!
Oh, what a sight! But a sight, and no more!
How, infinite Nature, lay hold of you, where?

---

5. Michel de Notredame (1503–1566), French physician, astrologer, and author of a famous book of prophecies.
6. A six-pointed star (also known as the Seal of Solomon) believed to possess the magical power to compel spirits.
7. That is, the sunrise (Aurora is the Roman goddess of dawn).

225 Where find your all-life-giving fountains?—breasts that sustain
The earth and the heavens, which my shrunken breast
Yearns for with a feverish thirst—
You flow, overflow, must I keep on thirsting in vain?

[*Morosely, he turns the pages of the book and comes on the sign of the Spirit of Earth.*]

What a different effect this sign has on me!
230 Spirit of Earth, how nearer you are to me!
Already fresh lifeblood pours through every vein,
Already I'm aglow as if with new wine—
Now I have the courage to dare
To venture out into the world and bear
235 The ill and well of life, to battle
Storms, when the ship splits, not to tremble.

The air grows dark overhead—
The moon's put out her light,
The oil lamp looks like dying.
240 Vapors rise, red flashes dart
Around my head—fright,
Shuddering down from the vault,
Seizes me by the throat!
Spirit I have invoked, hovering near:
245 Reveal yourself!
Ha! How my heart beats! All of my being's
Fumbling and groping amid never felt feelings!
Spirit, I feel I am yours, body and breath!
Appear! Oh, you must! Though it costs me my life!

[*He seizes the book and pronounces the* SPIRIT's *mystic spell. A red flame flashes, in the midst of which the* SPIRIT *appears.*]

250 SPIRIT Who's calling?
FAUST [*Averting his face*] Overpowering! Dreadful!
SPIRIT Potently you've drawn me here,
A parched mouth sucking at my sphere.
And now—?
FAUST   Oh, you're unbearable!
255 SPIRIT You're breathless from your implorations
To see my face, to hear me speak,
I've yielded to your supplications
And here I am.—Well, in a funk
I find the superman! I come at your bidding
260 And you're struck dumb! Is this the mind
That builds a whole interior world, doting
On its own creation, puffed to find
Itself quite on a par, the equal,
Of us spirits? Wherever is that Faust
265 Who urged himself just now with all
His strength on me, made such a fuss?
You're Faust? The one who at my breath's
Least touch, shudders to his depths,

A worm that wriggles off scared, a mouse!

270 FAUST   *I shrink back from you, an airy flame?*
I'm him, yes Faust, your equal, the same.

SPIRIT   I surge up and down
In the tides of being,
Drive forward and back
275 In the shocks of men's striving!
I am birth and the grave,
An eternal ocean,
A web changing momently,
A life burning fervently.
280 Thus seated at time's whirring loom
I weave the Godhead's living gown.

FAUST   We're equals, I know! I feel so close to you, near,
You busy spirit ranging everywhere!

SPIRIT   You equal the spirit you think I am,
285 Not me! [*Vanishes*]

FAUST [*Deflated*]   Not you?
Then who?
Me, made in God's own image,
Not even equal to you?

[*A knocking*]

290 Death! My famulus[8]—I know that knock.
Finis[9] my supremest moment—worse luck!
That visions richer than I could have guessed
Should be scattered by a shuffling Dryasdust!

[WAGNER *in dressing gown and nightcap, carrying a lamp.*
FAUST *turns around impatiently.*]

WAGNER   Excuse me, sir, but wasn't that
295 Your voice I heard declaiming? A Greek tragedy,
I'm sure. Well, that's an art that comes in handy
Nowadays. I'd love to master it.
People say, how often I have heard it,
Actors could really give lessons to the clergy.

300 FAUST   Yes, so parsons can make a stage out of the pulpit—
Something I've seen done in more than one case.

WAGNER   Oh dear, to be so cooped up in one's study all day,
Seeing the world only now and then, on holiday,
Seeing people from far off, as if through a spyglass—
305 How can you persuade and direct them that way?

FAUST   You can't—unless you speak with feeling's own
True voice, unless your words are from
The soul and by their spontaneous power,
Seize with delight the soul of your hearer.
310 But no! Stick in your seats, you scholars!
Paste bits and pieces together, cook up
A beggar's stew from others' leftovers,

8. Assistant (Latin); that is, Wagner.   9. An end (Latin).

Over a flame you've sweated to coax up
From your own little heap of smoldering ashes,
315 Filling with wonder all the jackasses,
If that's the kind of stuff your taste favors—
But you'll never get heart to cleave to heart
Unless your words spring from the heart.

WAGNER   Still and all, a good delivery is what
320 Makes the orator. I'm far behind in that art.

FAUST   Advance yourself in an honest way!
Don't play the fool in cap and bells!
Good sense, good understanding, they
Are art enough, speak for themselves.
325 When you have something serious to say
What need is there for hunting up
Fancy words, high-sounding phrases?
Your brilliant speeches, polished up
With bits and pieces collected out
330 Of a miscellany of commonplaces
From all the languages spoken by all the races,
Are about as bracing as the foggy autumnal breeze
Swaying the last leaves on the trees.

WAGNER   Dear God, but art is long
335 And our life—lots shorter.[1]
Often in the middle of my labor
My confidence and courage falter.
How hard it is to master all the stuff
For dealing with each and every source,
340 And before you've traveled half the course,
Poor devil, you have gone and left this life.

FAUST   Parchment, tell me—that's the sacred fount
You drink out of, to slake your eternal thirst?
The only true refreshment that exists
345 You get from where? Yourself—where all things start.

WAGNER   But sir, it's such a pleasure, isn't it,
To enter into another age's spirit,
To see what the sages before us thought
And measure how far since then we've got.

350 FAUST   As far as to the stars, no doubt!
Your history, why, it's a joke;
Bygone times are a seven-sealed book.[2]
What you call an age's spirit
Is nothing more than your own spirit
355 With the age reflected as you see it.
And it's pathetic, what's to be seen in your mirror!
One look and off I head for the exit:

---

1. A play on the aphorism "life is short, art long," attributed to the Greek physician Hippocrates (ca. 460–ca. 377 B.C.E.).
2. An allusion to the book "sealed with seven seals" (Revelation 5.1), which, according to the apocalyptic narrative of the New Testament, is to be opened on the Day of Judgment.

A trash can, strewn attic, junk-filled cellar,
At best a blood-and-thunder thriller
360 Improved with the most high-minded sentiments
Exactly suited for mouthing by marionettes.
WAGNER   But this great world, the human mind and heart,
They are things everyone wants to know about.
FAUST   Yes, know as the world knows knowing!
365 Who wants to know the real truth, tell me?
Those few who had true understanding,
Who failed to stand guard, most unwisely,
Over their tongues, speaking their minds and hearts
For the mob to hear—you know what's been their fate:
370 They were crucified, burnt, torn to bits.
But we must break off, friend, it's getting late.
WAGNER   I love such serious conversation, I do!
I'd stay up all night gladly talking to you.
But, sir, it's Easter Sunday in the morning
375 And perhaps I may ask you a question or two then, if you're willing?
I've studied hard, with unrelaxing zeal,
I know a lot, but I want, sir, to know all.   [Exit]
FAUST [Alone]   How such fellows keep their hopes up is a wonder!
Their attention forever occupied with trivialities,
380 Digging greedily in the ground for treasure,
And when they've turned a worm up—what ecstacies!
That banal, commonplace human accents
Should fill air just now filled with spirits' voices!
Still, this one time you've earned my thanks,
385 Oh sorriest, oh shallowest of wretches!
You snatched me from the grip of a dejection
So profound I was nearly driven off
My head. So gigantic was the apparition
It made me feel no bigger than a dwarf—

390 Me, the image of God, absolutely sure in the belief
Soon, soon I'd behold the eternal mirror of truth
Whose near presence I felt; already basking in
Heaven's clear ether, mortal clothing stripped off;
Me, higher placed than the angels, presuming wildly
395 My strength was already streaming freely,
Creative as the gods, through Nature's live body—
Well, it had to be paid for: one word
Thundered out and I am knocked flat, all self-conceit curbed.
No, I can't claim we are equals, presumptuously!
400 Though I was strong enough to draw you down to me,
Holding on to you was another matter entirely.
In that exalted-humbling moment of pure delight
I felt myself at once both small and great.
And then you thrust me remorselessly back
405 Into uncertainty, which is all of humanity's fate.
Who'll tell me what to do? What not to do?

Still seek out the spirits to learn what they know?
Oh what we do, as much as what's done to us,
Hinders and frustrates our entire life's progress.

410   The noblest thoughts our minds are able to entertain
Are undermined by a corrupting grossness;
When we gain a bit of the good of the world as our prize,
Then the better's dismissed as delusion and lies;
Those radiant sentiments, once our breath of life,

415   Weaken and fade in the madding crowd's strife.
There was that hope and brave imagination
Boldly reached as far as to infinity,
But now misfortune piling on misfortune,
A little, confined space will satisfy.

420   It's then, heart-deep, Care builds her nest,
Dithering nervously, killing joy, ruining rest,
Masking herself as this, as that concern
For house and home, for wife and children,
Fearing fire and flood, daggers and poison;

425   You shrink back in terror from imagined blows
And cry over losing what you never in fact lose.

Oh no, I'm no god, only too well do I know it!
A worm's what I am, wriggling through the dirt
And finding his nourishment in it,

430   Whom the passerby treads underfoot.

These high walls, every shelf crammed, every niche,
Dust is what shrinks them to a stifling cell,
This moth-eaten world with its oddments and trash,
It's the reason I feel shut up in jail.

435   And here I'll discover what it is that I lack?
Devour thousands of books so as to learn, shall I,
Mankind has always been stretched on the rack,
With now and then somebody, somewhere, who's been happy?
You, empty skull there, smirking so, I know why—

440   What does it tell me if not that your brain,
Whirling like mine, sought the bright sun of truth,
Only to wander, night-bewildered, in vain.
And all that apparatus, you mock me, you laugh
With your every wheel, cylinder, cog and ratchet;

445   I stood at the door, sure you provided the key,
Yet for all the bit's cunning design you couldn't unlatch it.
Great Nature, so mysterious even in broad day,
Still hides her face, do what you may;
All those screws and levers can't make her reveal

450   The mystery hidden behind her veil.
You, ancient stuff I've left lying about,
You're here, and why?—my father found you useful.
And you, old scrolls, have gathered soot

For as long as the lamp's smoked on this table.
455   Much better to have squandered the little I got
Than find myself sweating under the lot.
It's from our fathers, what we inherit,
To possess it really we have to earn it.
What's never used is a dead weight,
460   What's useful is what you spontaneously create.

But why do I find I must stare in that corner,
Is that bottle a magnet enchanting my sight?
Why is everything all at once brighter, clearer,
Like woods when the moon's up and floods them with light?

465   Vial, I salute you, exeptional, rare thing,
And reverently bring you down from the shelf,
Honoring in you man's craft and cunning;
Quintessence of easeful sleeping potions,
Pure distillation of subtle poisons,
470   Do your master the kindness that lies in your power!
One look at you and my agony lessens,
One touch and my feverish straining grows calmer
And my tight-stretched spirit bit by bit slackens.
The spirit's flood tide runs more and more out,
475   My way is clear, into death's immense sea;
The bright waters glitter before my feet,
A new day is dawning, new shores calling to me.

A fiery chariot, bird-winged, swoops down on me,
I am ready to follow new paths and higher,
480   Aloft into new spheres of purest activity.
An existence so exalted, so godlike a rapture,
Does the worm of a minute ago deserve it?
No matter. Never falter! Turn your back bravely
On the sunlight, sweet sunlight, of our earth forever!
485   Tear wide open those dark gates boldly
Which the whole world skulks past with averted heads!
The time has come to disprove by deeds,
Because the gods are great, man's a derision,
To cringe back no more from that black pit
490   Whose unspeakable tortures are your own invention,
To struggle toward that narrow gate
Around which Hell fires flame in eternal eruption,
To do it calmly, without regret,
Even at the risk of utter extinction.
495   And now let me take this long forgotten
Crystal wine cup down out of its chest.
You used to shine bright at the family feast,
Making the solemn guests' faces lighten
When you went round with each lively toast.
500   The figures artfully cut in the crystal,

Which it was the duty of all at the table,
In turn, to make up rhymes about,
Then drain the cup at a single draught—
How they recall the nights of my youth!
505 But now there's no passing you on to my neighbor,
Or thinking up rhymes to parade my quick wit;
Here is a juice that is quick too—to intoxicate,
A brownish liquid, see, filling the beaker,
Chosen by me, by me mixed together,
510 My last drink! Which now I lift up in festal greeting
To the bright new day I can see dawning!

[*He raises the cup to his lips. Bells peal, a choir bursts into song.*]

CHORUS OF ANGELS   Christ is arisen!
Joy to poor mortals
By their own baleful,
515   Inherited, subtle
Failings imprisoned.

FAUST   What deep-sounding burden, what tremelo strain
Arrest the glass before I can drink?
Does that solemn ringing already proclaim
520 The glorious advent of Holy Week?
Already, choirs, are you intoning
What angels' lips sang once, a comforting chant,
Above the sepulcher's darkness sounding,
Certain assurance of a new covenant?

CHORUS OF WOMEN
525   With balm and with spices
We anointed the man,
We, his true, faithful ones,
Laid him out in the tomb;
In linen we wound him
530   And bound up his hair—
Oh, what do we find now?
Christ is not here.

CHORUS OF ANGELS   Christ is arisen!
Blest is the man of love,
535   He who in triumph passed
The hard, the bitter test,
Bringing salvation.

FAUST   But why do you seek me out in the dust,
You music of Heaven, mild and magnificent?
540 Ring out where men and women are simple,
I hear your message but lack all belief in it,
And where belief's lacking, no miracle's possible.
The spheres whence those glad tidings come
Are not for me to try and enter—
545 Yet all's familiar from when I was young
And back to life I feel myself sent for.

Years ago the Heavenly Love
Flew down to me in the Sabbath hush
And caught me in His strong embrace;
550 Oh, with what meaning the deep bells sounded,
Praying to Jesus, oh what bliss!
A yearning so sweet it was not to be fathomed
Drove me out to the woods and the fields.
Inside my soul a new world opened
555 And my cheeks were streaming with scalding tears.
Your song gave the signal for the games we rejoiced in
When the springtime arrived with its gay festival,
Innocent childhood's remembered feelings
Hold me back from the last step of all.
560 O sound away, sound away, sweet songs of Heaven,
Tears fill my eyes, the earth claims me again!

CHORUS OF DISCIPLES

He but now buried
Already's ascended,
Who while he dwelt below
565 Lived most sublimely,
Then rose up in glory
So he might share in
The bliss of creation.
But here on earth
570 We huddle afflicted—
He has left us, his children,
To wish for him, wait.
Master, we pity your bitter fate!

CHORUS OF ANGELS

Christ is arisen
575 From the womb of decay,
Strike off your fetters
And shout for joy!
Praise him by sweetest charity,
Loving-kindness, fraternity,
580 Relieving the least of all,
Preaching him east and west to all,
Promising Heaven's bliss to all.
You have the Master near,
You have him here, right here!

Outside the City Gate

[*All sorts of people out walking.*]

585 SOME APPRENTICES   Where are you fellows off to?
OTHERS   To the hunters' lodge—over that way.
FIRST BUNCH   Well, we're on our way to the old mill.
ONE APPRENTICE   The river inn—that's what I say.
SECOND APPRENTICE   But the walk there's not pleasant, I feel.
590 SECOND BUNCH   And what about you?
THIRD APPRENTICE   I'll stick with the rest of us here.

FOURTH APPRENTICE   Let's go up to the village. There, I can promise you
    The best-looking girls, the best-tasting beer,
    And some very good roughhousing too.

FIFTH APPRENTICE   My, but aren't you greedy!
595 A third bloody nose—don't you care?
    I'll never go there, it's too scary.

SERVANT GIRL   No, no, I'm turning back, now let me be.

ANOTHER   We're sure to find him at those poplar trees.

FIRST GIRL   Is that supposed to make me jump for joy?
600 It's you he wants to walk with, wants to please,
    And you're the one he'll dance with. Fine
    For you. But what's it to me, your good time?

THE OTHER   He's not alone, I know, today. He said
    He'd bring his friend—you know, that curlyhead.

605 A STUDENT   Those fast-stepping girls there, look at the heft of them!
    Into action, old fellow, we're taking out after them.
    Beer with body, tobacco with a good sharp taste
    And red-cheeked housemaids in their Sunday best
    Are just the things to make your Hermann happiest.

610 A BURGHER'S DAUGHTER   Oh look over there, such fine-looking boys!
    Really, I think they are so outrageous,
    They have their pick of the nicest girls,
    Instead they run after overweight wenches.

SECOND STUDENT [To the first]   Hold up, go slow! I see two more,
615 And the pair of them dressed so pretty, so proper.
    But I know that one! She lives next door,
    And she, I can tell you, I think I could go for.
    They loiter along, eyes lowered decorously,
    But after saying no twice, they'll jump at our company.

620 FIRST STUDENT   No, no—all that bowing and scraping, it makes me
      feel ill at ease,
    If we don't get a move on we'll lose our two birds in the bushes!
    The work-reddened hand that swings the broom Saturdays
    On Sundays knows how to give the softest caresses.

A BURGHER   No, you can have him, our new Mayor,
625 Since he took office he's been a dictator,
    All he's done is make the town poorer,
    Every day I get madder and madder,
    When he says a thing's so, not a peep, not a murmur,
    Dare we express—and the taxes climb higher.

A BEGGAR [Singing]
630   Good sirs and all you lovely ladies,
    Healthy in body and handsome in dress,
    Turn, oh turn your eyes on me, please,
    And pity the beggarman's distress!
    Must I grind the organ fruitlessly,
635   Only the charitable know true joy.
    This day when all the world make merry,
    Oh make it for me a harvest day.

ANOTHER BURGHER   On a Sunday or holiday nothing in all my experience

Beats talking about war and rumors of war,
640 When leagues away, in Turkey, for instance,
Armies are wading knee deep in gore.
You stand at the window, take long pulls at your schooner,[3]
And watch the gaily colored boats glide past,
And then at sunset go home in the best of humor
645 And praise God for the peace by which we're blest.
THIRD BURGHER Yes, neighbor, yes, exactly my opinion.
Let them go and beat each other's brains in,
Let them turn the whole world upside down,
As long as things are just as always here at home.
650 OLD CRONE [To the BURGHERS' DAUGHTERS] Well, aren't we the smart ones!
    And so pretty and young!
I'd like to see the man who could resist you.
But not so proud, my dears! And never fear—I'm mum.
Oh, I know how to get what you want for you.
BURGHER'S DAUGHTER Agatha, come, we've got to leave!
655 I'm afraid of being seen with that witchwoman.
Oh dear, and only last St. Andrew's Eve[4]
She showed me in a glass my very own one.
HER FRIEND And mine she showed me in a crystal sphere
Looking a soldier, with swaggering friends around him,
660 And though I watch out everywhere,
I have no luck, I never seem to find him.
SOLDIERS
    Castles have ramparts,
    Great walls and towers,
    Girls turn their noses up
665   At soldier-boy lovers—
    We'll make both ours!
    Boldly adventure
    And rake in the pay!

    Hear the shrill bugle
670   Summon to battle,
    Forward to rapture
    Or forward to ruin!
    Oh what a struggle!
    Our life—oh how stirring!
675   Haughty girls, high-walled castles,
    We'll make them surrender!
    Boldly adventure
    And rake in the pay!
    —And after, the soldiers
680   Go marching away.

3. A tall glass used for beer.
4. November 29, a time associated in central European folklore with fortune-telling (and when, in Germany, it was believed that girls could cause their future husbands to appear to them in a dream).

[FAUST *and* WAGNER]

FAUST The streams put off their icy mantle
Under the springtime's kindly smile;
Hope's green banner flies in the valley;
White-bearded winter, old and frail,
685 Retreats back up into the mountains,
And still retreating, down he sends
Feeble volleys of sleet showers,
Whitening in patches the green plains.
But the sun can bear with white no longer,
690 When life stirs, shaping all anew,
He wants a scene that has some color,
And since there's nowhere yet one flower,
Holiday crowds have got to do.

Now face about, and looking down
695 From the hilltop back to town,
See the brightly colored crowd
Pouring like a spring flood
Through the gaping, gloomy arch
To bask in the sun all love so much.
700 They celebrate the Savior's Rising,
For they themselves are risen:
From airless rooms in huddled houses,
From drudgery at counters and benches,
From under cumbrous roofs and gables,
705 From crowded, suffocating alleys,
From the mouldering dimness of the churches,
All are brought forth into brightness.
And look there, how the eager crowd
Scatters through the fields and gardens.
710 How over the river's length and breadth
Skiffs and sculls are busily darting,
And that last boat, packed near to sinking,
Already's pulled a good ways off.
Even from distant mountain slopes
715 Bright colored clothes wink back at us.
Now I can hear it, the village commotion,
Out here, you can tell, is the people's true heaven,
Young and old crying exultingly:
Here I am human, here I can be free.
720 WAGNER To go for a walk with you, dear Doctor,
Is a treat for my mind as well as honoring me;
But by myself I'd never come near here,
For I can't abide the least vulgarity.
The fiddling, the shrieking, the clashing bowls
725 For me are all an unbearable uproar,
All scream and shout like possessed souls
And call it music, call it pleasure.

PEASANTS [*Singing and dancing under the linden tree*]

   The shepherd dressed up in his best,
   Pantaloons and flowered vest,
730   Oh my, how brave and handsome!
   Within the broad-leaved linden's shade
   Madly spun both man and maid,
    Hooray, hooray,
    Hurrah, hurrah, hooray!
735   The fiddle bow flew, and then some.
   He flung himself into their midst
   And seized a young thing round the waist,
    While saying, "Care to dance, ma'am?"
   The snippy miss she tossed her head,
740   "You boorish shepherd boy!" she said,
    Hooray, hooray,
    Hurrah, hurrah, hooray!
   "Observe, do, some decorum!"

   But round the circle swiftly wheeled,
745   To right and left the dancers whirled,
    Till all the breath flew from them.
   They got so red, they got so warm,
   They rested, panting, arm in arm,
    Hooray, hooray,
750   Hurrah, hurrah, hooray!
   And breast to breast—a twosome.

   "I'll thank you not to make so free!
   We girls know well how men betray,
    What snakes lurk in your bosom!"
755   But still he wheedled her away—
   Far off they heard the fiddles play,
    Hooray, hooray,
    Hurrah, hurrah, hooray!
   The shouting, uproar, bedlam.

760 OLD PEASANT Professor, it's so good of you
  To join us common folk today,
  Though such a wise and learned man,
  Not to scorn our holiday.
  So please accept our best cup, sir,
765 Brimful with the freshest beer;
  We hope that it will quench your thirst,
  But more than that, we pray and hope
  Your sum of days may be increased
  By as many drops as fill the cup!
770 FAUST Friends, thanks for this refreshment, I
  In turn wish you all health and joy.

   [*The people make a circle around him.*]

  OLD PEASANT Indeed it's only right that you
  Should be with us this happy day,

Who when our times were bitter, proved
775   Himself our friend in every way.
Many a one stands in his boots here
Whom your good father, the last minute,
Snatched from the hot grip of the fever,
That time he quelled the epidemic.
780   And you yourself, a youngster then,
Never shrank back; every house
The pest went in, you did too.
Out they carried many a corpse,
But never yours. Much you went through;
785   Us you saved, and God saved you.
ALL   Health to our tried and trusty friend,
And may he help us yet again.
FAUST   Bow down to him who dwells above,
Whose love shows us how we should love.
          [*He continues on with* WAGNER.]
790 WAGNER   The gratification you must get from all of this,
From knowing the reverence these people hold you in!
The man whose gifts can gain him such advantages,
Oh, he's a lucky one in my opinion.
Who is it, each one asks as he runs to see,
795   Fathers point you out to their boys,
The fiddle stops, the dancers pause,
And as you pass between the rows
Of people, caps fly in the air, why,
Next you know they'll all be on their knees
800   As if the Host itself were passing by.
FAUST   A few steps more to that rock where we'll rest
A bit, shall we, from our walk. How often
I would sit alone here thinking, thinking,
And torture myself with praying hard and fasting.
805   So much hope I had then, such great trust—
I'd wring my hands, I'd weep, fall on my knees,
Believing in this way the Lord being forced
To look below, would cry halt to the disease.
But now these people's generous praises are
810   A mockery to me. If only you could peer
Into my heart, you'd realize
How little worthy father and son were really.
      My father was an upright man, a lonely,
Brooding soul who searched great Nature's processes
815   With a head crammed full of the most bizarre hypotheses.
Shutting himself with fellow masters up in
The vaulted confines of their vaporous Black Kitchen,
He mixed together opposites according
To innumerable recipes. A bold Red Lion,
820   Handsome suitor he, took for wedding
Partner a pure White Lily, the two uniting
In a tepid bath; then being tested by fire,

    The pair precipitately fled
    From one bridal chamber to another,
825 Till there appeared within the glass
    The young Queen, dazzlingly dressed
    In every color of the spectrum:
    The Sovereign Remedy—a futile nostrum.[5]
    The patients died; none stopped to inquire
830 How many there were who'd got better.
       So with our infernal electuary
    We killed our way across the country.
    I poisoned, myself, by prescription, thousands,
    They sickened and faded; yet I must live to see
835 On every side the murderers' fame emblazoned.
  WAGNER But why be so distressed, there is no reason.
    If an honest man with conscientious devotion
    Practises the arts his forebears practised,
    It's understandable, it's what's to be expected.
840 A youth who is respectful of his father
    Listens and soaks up all he has to teach;
    If the grown man's able to lengthen science's reach,
    His son in turn can reach goals even farther.
  FAUST Oh, he's a happy man who hopes
845 To keep from drowning in these seas of error!
    What we know least about, we need the most,
    And what we do know, is no use whatever.
       But we mustn't poison with our gloomy thoughts
    The sweetness of the present hour!
850 Look how the sunset's level rays
    Gild those cottages in their green bower,
    The day fades quietly, the sun departs,
    Hurrying off to kindle new life elsewhere—
    If only I had wings to bear me up
855 Into the air and follow after!
    Then I would see the whole world at my feet.
    Quietly shining in the eternal sunset,
    The peaks ablaze, the valleys gone to sleep,
    And every silver stream a golden current.
860 The savage mountain with its plunging cliffs
    Should never balk my godlike soaring,
    And there's the ocean, see, already swelling
    Before my wondering gaze, with its sun-warmed gulfs.
    But finally the bright god looks like sinking,
865 Whereupon a renewed urgency
    Drives me on to drink his eternal light,
    The day always before, behind the night,
    The heavens overhead, below the heaving sea . . .

5. That is, the desired medicine having general curative powers, a colorful chemical sublimate (the "young Queen") obtained by combining red mercury ("Red Lion") with tincture of antimony ("White Lily").

A lovely dream!—and meanwhile it grows dark.
870   Oh dear, oh dear, that our frames should lack
      Wings with which to match the spirit's soaring.
      Still our nature's such that all of us
      Know feelings that strive upwards, always straining,
      When high above, lost in the azure emptiness,
875   The skylark pours out his shrill rhapsody,
      When over fir-clad mountain peaks
      The eagle on his broad wings gyres silently,
      And passing over prairies, over lakes,
      The homeward-bound crane labors steadily.
880 WAGNER   Well, I've had more than one odd moment, I have,
      But I have never felt those impulses you have.
      Soon enough you get your fill of woods and things,
      I don't really envy birds their wings.
      How different are the pleasures of the intellect,
885   Sustaining one from page to page, from book to book,
      And warming winter nights with dear employment
      And with the consciousness your life's so lucky.
      And goodness, when you spread out an old parchment,
      Heaven's fetched straight down into your study.
890 FAUST   You know the one great driving force,
      May you never know the other!
      Two souls live in me, alas,
      Forever warring with each other.
      One, amorous of the world, with all its might
895   Grapples it close, greedy of all its pleasures;
      The other fights to rise out of the dirt,
      Up, up into the heaven of our great forebears.

      You beings of the air, if such exist,
      Holding sway between the skies and earth,
900   Come down to me out of the golden mist
      And translate me to a new, a vivid life!
      Oh, if I only had a magic mantle
      To bear me off to unknown lands,
      I'd never trade it for the costliest gowns,
905   Or for a cloak however rich and royal.
      WAGNER   Never call them down, the dreadful swarm
      That swoops and hovers through the atmosphere,
      Bringing mankind every kind of harm
      From every corner of the terrestrial sphere.
910   From the North they bare their razor teeth
      And prick you with their arrow-pointed tongues,
      From the East, sighing with parched breath,
      They eat away your dessicated lungs;
      And when from Southern wastes they gust and sough,
915   Fire on fire on your sunk head heaping,
      From the West they send for your relief
      Cooling winds—then drown fields just prepared for reaping.

Their ears are cocked, on trickery intent,
Seem dutiful while scheming to defeat us,
920   Their pretense is that they are heaven-sent
And lisp like angels even as they cheat us.
    However, come, let's go, the world's turned gray
And chilly, evening mists are rising!
At nightfall it's indoors you want to be.
925   But why should you stand still, astonished, staring?
What can you see in the dusk to find upsetting?

FAUST   Don't you see that black dog in the stubble,
Coursing back and forth?

WAGNER   I do. I noticed him.
A while back. What about him?

FAUST   Look again.
930   What kind of creature is it?

WAGNER   Kind? A poodle—
Worried where his master is, and always
Sniffing about to find his scent.

FAUST   Look, he's
Circling around us, coming nearer and nearer.
Unless I'm much mistaken, a wake of fire
935   Is streaming after him.

WAGNER   I see nothing
But a black-haired poodle. Your eyes are playing
Tricks on you, perhaps.

FAUST   I think I see
Him winding a magic snare, quietly,
Around our feet, a noose which he'll pull tight
940   In the future, when the time is right.

WAGNER   He's circling us because he's timid and uncertain;
He's missed his master, come on men unknown to him.

FAUST   The circle's getting tighter, he's much closer!

WAGNER   You see!—a dog, it's no ghost, sir.
945   He growls suspiciously, he hesitates,
He wags his tail, lies down and waits.
Never fear, it's all just dog behavior.

FAUST   Come here, doggie, here, to us!

WAGNER   A silly poodle, a poor creature,
950   When you stop, he stops too at once,
Speak to him, he'll leap and bark,
Throw something and he'll fetch it back,
Go after your stick right into the river.

FAUST   I guess you're right, it's just what he's been taught;
955   I see no sign of anything occult.

WAGNER   A dog so good, so well-behaved by nature—
Why, even a philosopher would like him.
Some students trained him, found him an apt scholar—
Sir, he deserves you should adopt him.

      [*They enter at the City Gate.*]

Faust's Study [I]

FAUST [*Entering with the poodle*]

960 Behind me lie the fields and meadows
Shrouded in the lowering dark,
In dread of what waits in the shadows
Our better soul now starts awake.
Our worser one, unruly, reckless,
965 Quietens and starts to nod;
In me the love of my own fellows
Begins to stir, and the love of God.

Poodle, stop! How you race round! A dozen
Dogs you seem. Why all that sniffing at the door?
970 Here's my best cushion, it's yours to doze on,
Behind the stove, there on the floor.
Just now when we came down the hillside
We found you a charming, playful beast.
I'm glad to welcome you in here, provide
975 Your keep—as long as you're a silent guest.

When once again the lamp light brightens
With its soft glow your narrow cell,
Oh then it lightens in your bosom,
And deeper in your heart as well.
980 Again you hear the voice of reason,
And hope revives, it breathes afresh,
You long to drink the living waters,
Mount upwards to our being's source.

You're growling, poodle! Animal squealings
985 Hardly suit the exalted feelings
Filling my soul to overflowing.
We're used to people ridiculing
What they hardly understand,
Grumbling at the good and beautiful—
990 It makes them so uncomfortable!
Do dogs now emulate mankind?
   Yet even with the best of will
I feel my new contentment fail.
Why must the waters cease so soon
995 And leave us thirsting once again?
Oh, this has happened much too often!
But there's an answer to it all:
I mean the supernatural,
I mean our hope of revelation,
1000 Which nowhere shines so radiant
As here in the New Testament.
I'll look right now at the original
And see if it is possible
For me to make a true translation

1005   Into my beloved German.

    [*He opens the volume and begins.*]

"In the beginning was the Word"[6]—so goes
The text. And right off I am given pause!
A little help, please, someone, I'm unable
To see the *word* as first, most fundamental.
1010   If I am filled with the true spirit
I'll find a better way to say it.
So: "In the beginning *mind* was"—right?
Give plenty of thought to what you write,
Lest your pen prove too impetuous:
1015   Is it mind that makes and moves the universe?
Shouldn't it be: "In the beginning
Power was," before it nothing?
Yet even as I write this down on paper
Something tells me don't stop there, go further.
1020   The Spirit's prompt in aid; now, now, indeed
I know for sure: "In the beginning was the *deed*!"

If this cell's one that we'll be sharing,
Poodle, stop that barking, yelping!
You're giving me a splitting headache,
1025   I can't put up with such a roommate.
I'm sorry to say that one of us
Has got to quit the premises.
It goes against the grain with me
To renege on hospitality,
1030   But there's the door, dog, leave, goodbye.

But what the devil's happening?
What I see's beyond belief!
Is it real, that monstrous thing?
My poodle's swelled up bigger than life!
1035   Now he's heaving up his bulk—
That's no dog, that great hulk!
What a dreadful spook I've brought
Into my house without a thought.
He looks, with his fierce eyes and jaws,
1040   Just like a hippopotamus—
But I have got you in my power!
With a demi-imp of Hell, as you are,
Solomon's Key[7] is what is called for.

SPIRITS [*Outside the door*]

    Someone is locked in there!
1045   No one's allowed in there!
    Like a fox hunters snared,
    Old Scratch, he shivers, scared.

6. The first words of the Gospel according to
John.

7. A book containing magical spells.

Be careful, watch out!
Hover this way, now that,
1050   About and again about,
You'll soon find he's got out.
If you can help him,
Don't let him sit there,
All of us owe him
1055   For many a favor.

FAUST   Against such a creature, my first defense:
The Spell of the Four Elements.[8]

Salamander glow hot,
Undine, undulate,
1060   Sylph, melt away quick,
Kobold, off to work.

Ignorance
Of the elements,
Their powers and properties,
1065   Denies you all mastery
Over the demonry.

Vanish in flames,
Salamander!
Undine, make babbling streams
1070   All flow together!

Glitter meteor-beauteous,
Aërial Sylph!
Give household help to us,
Incubus! Incubus!
1075   Come out, come out, enough's enough.

None of the four
Is in the cur.
Calmly he lies there, grinning at me,
My spells glance off him harmlessly.
1080   Now hear me conjure
With something stronger.

Are you, grim fellow,
Escaped here from Hell below?
Then look at this symbol[9]
1085   Before which the legions
Of devils and demons
Fearfully bow.

How his hair bristles, how he swells up now!

---

8. That is, fire, water, air, and earth, which correspond to the four creatures Salamander,
Undine, Sylph, and Hobgoblin.
9. The sign of the cross.

Creature cast into darkness,
1090 Can you make out its meaning?
The never-begotten One.
Wholly ineffable One,
Cruelly pierced in the side One,
Whose blood in the heavens
1095 Is everywhere streaming?[1]

Behind the stove, captive, the miscreant
Puffs himself up big as an elephant,
Filling the whole chamber
Disappearing into vapor.
1100 —Now don't you try going through the ceiling!
Down at my feet, do your master's bidding!
You see, my threats are scarcely idle—
With fire I'll rout you out, yes I will!
Wait if you wish,
1105 For my triune[2] light's hot flash,
Wait till you force me
To employ my most potent sorcery.

[*The smoke clears, and* MEPHISTOPHELES, *dressed as an itinerant
student, emerges from behind the stove.*]

MEPHISTO   Why all the racket? What's your wish, sir?
FAUST   So it's you who was the poodle!
1110 I have to laugh—a wandering scholar!
MEPHISTO   My greetings to you, learned doctor,
You really had me sweating hard there.
FAUST   And what's your name?
MEPHISTO   Your question's trivial
From one who finds words superficial,
1115 Who strives to pass beyond mere seeming
And penetrate the heart of being.
FAUST   With gentry like yourself, it's common
To find the name declares what you are
Very plainly. I'll just mention
1120 Lord of the Flies,[3] Destroyer, Liar.
So say who are you, if you would.
MEPHISTO   A humble part of that great power
Which always means evil, always does good.
FAUST   Those ridding words mean what, I'd like to know.
1125 MEPHISTO   I am the spirit that says no,
No always![4] And how right I am! For surely
It's only fitting everything that comes to be

1. Invocations of Jesus on the cross were
believed to contain power against demons.
2. Pertaining to the Trinity, the Christian doctrine that holds that God exists simultaneously in three persons (the Father, the Son,
and the Holy Spirit).
3. The literal meaning of the Hebrew Baal-

zebub (2 Kings 1.2), a name that later became
synonymous with Satan and that was rendered Beelzebub in the Vulgate (the 5th-
century Latin translation by St. Jerome).
4. The name Satan in Hebrew literally means
"Adversary."

Should cease to be. And so they do.
Still better yet that nothing ever was. Hence sin,
1130   Destruction, ruin—all you call evil, in sum—
For me's the element that I swim in.

FAUST   A part, you say? You look like the whole works to me.

MEPHISTO   I say what's so, it isn't modesty—
Man in his world of self's a fool,
1135   He likes to think he's all in all.
I'm part of the part which was all at first,
A part of the dark from which light burst forth,[5]
Arrogant light which now usurps the air
And seeks to thrust Night from her ancient chair,
1140   To no avail. Since light is one with all
Things bodily, making them beautiful,
Streams from them, from them is reflected,
Since light by matter's manifested—
When by degrees all matter's burnt up and no more,
1145   Why, then light shall not matter any more.

FAUST   Oh, now I understand your office:
Since you can't wreck Creation wholesale,
You're going at it bit by bit, retail.

MEPHISTO   And making little headway, I confess.
1150   The opposite of nothing-at-all,
The *something*, this great shambling world,
In spite of how I exert myself against it,
Phlegmatically endures my every onset
By earthquake, fire, tidal wave and storm:
1155   Next day the land and sea again are calm.
And all that *stuff*, those animal and human species—
I can hardly make a dent in them.
The numbers I've already buried, armies!
Yet fresh troops keep on marching up again.
1160   That's how it is, it's enough to drive you crazy!
From air, from water, from the earth
Seeds innumerable sprout forth
In dry and wet and cold and warm!
If I hadn't kept back fire for myself,
1165   What the devil could I call my own?

FAUST   So against the good, the never-resting,
All-powerful creative force
In impotent spite you raise your fist and
Try to arrest life's onward course?
1170   Look around for work that's more rewarding,
You singular son of old Chaos![6]

MEPHISTO   Well, it's a subject for discussion—
At our next meeting. Now I wish

5. That is, before Lucifer and his followers
were banished from God's presence.
6. In ancient Greek cosmology, the earliest
state of the universe (Chaos) from which
emerged all that exists.

To go. That is, with your permission.

1175 FAUST   But why should *you* ask *me* for leave?
We've struck up an acquaintance, we two,
Drop in on me whenever you please.
There's the door and there's the window,
And ever reliable, there's the chimney.

1180 MEPHISTO   Well . . . you see . . . an obstacle
Keeps me from dropping *out*—so sorry!
That witch's foot chalked on your doorsill.

FAUST   The pentagram's[7] the difficulty?
But if it's that that has you stopped,

1185 How did you ever manage an entry?
And how should a devil like you get trapped?

MEPHISTO   Well, look close and you'll see that
A corner's open: the outward pointing
Angle's lines don't quite meet.

1190 FAUST   What a stroke of luck! I'm thinking
Now you are my prisoner.
Pure chance has put you in my power!

MEPHISTO   The poodle dashed right in, saw nothing;
But now the case is the reverse:

1195 The Devil can't get out of the house!

FAUST   There's the window, why don't you use it?

MEPHISTO   It's an iron law we devils can't flout,
The way we come in, we've got to go out,
We're free as to entrée, but not as to exit.

1200 FAUST   So even in Hell there's law and order!
I'm glad, for then a man might sign
A contract with you gentlemen.

MEPHISTO   Whatever we promise, you get, full measure,
There's no cutting corners, no skulduggery—

1205 But it's not a thing to be done in a hurry;
Let's save the subject for our next get-together.
And as for now, I beg you earnestly,
Release me from the spell that binds me!

FAUST   Why rush off, stay a while, do.

1210 I'd love to hear some more from you.

MEPHISTO   Let me go now. I swear I'll come back,
Then you can ask me whatever you like.

FAUST   Don't blame me because you're caught;
You trapped yourself, it's your own fault.

1215 Who's nabbed the Devil must keep a tight grip,
You don't grab him again once he gives you the slip.

MEPHISTO   Oh, all right! To please you I
Will stay and keep you company;
Provided with my arts you let me

1220 Entertain you in my own way.

FAUST   Delighted, go ahead. But please

---

7. The pentagram (five-pointed star), used as a magical sign to compel demons.

Make sure those arts of yours amuse!

MEPHISTO   You'll find, my friend, your senses, in one hour,
More teased and roused than all the long dull year.

1225   The songs the fluttering spirits murmur in your ear,
The visions they unfold of sweet desire,
Oh they are more than just tricks meant to fool.
By Arabian scents you'll be delighted,
Your palate tickled, never sated,

1230   The ravishing sensations you will feel!
No preparation's needed, none.
Here we are. Let the show begin!

SPIRITS   Open, you gloomy
Vaulted ceiling above him,

1235   Let the blue ether
Look benignly in on him,
And dark cloudbanks scatter
So that all is fair for him!
Starlets are glittering,

1240   Milder suns glowing,
Angelic troops shining
In celestial beauty
Hover past smiling,
Swaying and stooping.

1245   Ardent desire
Follows them yearning;
And their robes streaming ribbons
Veil the fields, veil the meadows,
Veil the arbors where lovers

1250   In pensive surrender
Give themselves to each other
For ever and ever.
Arbor on arbor!
Vines clambering and twining!

1255   Their heavy clusters,
Poured into presses,
Pour out purple wines
Which descend in dark streams
Over beds of bright stones

1260   Down the vineyards' steep slopes
To broaden to lakes
At the foot of green hills.
Birds blissfully drink there,
With beating wings sunwards soar,

1265   Soar towards the golden isles
Shimmering hazily
On the horizon;
Where we hear voices
Chorusing jubilantly,

1270   Where we see dancers
Whirling exuberantly

Over the meadows,
Here, there and everywhere.
Some climb the heights,
1275   Some swim in the lakes,
Others float in the air—
Joying in life, all,
Beneath the paradisal
Stars glowing with love
1280   Afar in the distance.

MEPHISTO   Asleep! Oh bravely done, my airy younglings!
How duly to his slumbers you have sung him!
I am in your debt for this performance.
—As for you, sir, you were never born
1285   To keep the Prince of Darkness down!
Weave a net of sweet dreams all about him,
Drown him in a deep sea of delusion.
But to break the spell that holds me here,
A rat's tooth is what I require.
1290   No need for conjuring long-windedly—
Listen! I hear a rat rustling already.

The lord of flies and rats and mice,
Of frogs and bedbugs, worms and lice,
Commands you forth from your dark hole
1295   To gnaw, beast, for me that doorsill
Whereon I dab this drop of oil!
—And there you are! Begin, begin!
The corner that is pointing in,
That's the one that shuts me in;
1300   One last crunch to clear my way:
Now Faustus, till we meet next—dream away!

FAUST [*Awakening*]   Deceived again, am I, by tricks,
Those vanished spirits just a hoax,
A dream the Devil, nothing more,
1305   The dog I took home just a cur?

Faust's Study [II]

[FAUST, MEPHISTOPHELES.]

FAUST   A knock, was that? Come in! Who is it this time?
MEPHISTO   Me.
FAUST   Come in!
MEPHISTO   You have to say it still a third time.
FAUST   All right, all right—come in!
MEPHISTO   Good, very good!
We two will get along, I see, just as we should.
1310   I've come here dressed up as a grandee. Why?
To help you drive your blues away!
In a scarlet suit, all over gold braid,
Across my shoulders a stiff silk cape,

A gay cock's feather in my cap,
1315   At my side a gallant's long blade—
And bringing you advice that's short and sweet:
Put fine clothes on like me, cut loose a bit,
Be free and easy, man, throw off your yoke
And find out what real life is like.
1320   FAUST   In any clothes, I'd feel the misery
Of this cramped, suffocating life on earth.
I'm too old to live for amusement only,
Too young to live without desire or wish.
The world—what has it got to say to me?
1325   Renounce all that you long for, all—renounce!
That's the everlasting song-and-dance
You are greeted by on every side,
The croak you hear year in, year out;
You can't have what you want, you can't!
1330   I awake each morning, how? Horrified,
On the verge of tears, to confront a day
Which at its close will not have satisfied
One smallest wish of mine, not one. Why,
Even the hope of a bit of pleasure, some pleasantness,
1335   Withers in the atmosphere of mean-spirited fault-finding;
My nature's active inventiveness
Is thwarted daily by endless interfering.
And when the night draws on and all is hushed,
I go to bed not soothed at last but apprehensively,
1340   Well knowing what awaits me is not rest,
But wild and whirling dreams that terrify me.
The god who thrones inside my bosom,
Able to shake me to the depths, so powerfully,
The lord and master of all my energies,
1345   Is impotent to effect a single thing outside me;
And so I find existence burdensome, wretched,
Death eagerly desired, my life hated.
MEPHISTO   Yet the welcome men give death is never wholehearted.
FAUST   Happy the man, even as he conquers gloriously,
1350   Upon whose brow death sets the blood-stained laurel!
Happy the man, after dancing the night through furiously,
Whom it finds out in the white arms of a girl!
If only, overwhelmed by the Spirit's power,
In raptures, I had died right then and there!
1355   MEPHISTO   And yet that very night, I seem to remember,
A fellow didn't down a drink he'd prepared.[8]
FAUST   Spying around, I see, is what you like to do.
MEPHISTO   I don't know everything, but I know a thing or two.
FAUST   If a sweet, familiar strain of music,
1360   When I was staggering, steadied me,

---

8. A reference to Faust's aborted suicide attempt (see lines 461–511).

Beguiled what's left of childhood feeling
With echoes of a happier day—
Well, never again! I pronounce a curse on
All tales that snare and cheat the soul,
1365   All false and flattering persuasion
That ties it to this *corpus vile*.[9]
First I curse man's mind, for thinking
Much too well of itself; I curse
The show of things, so dazzling, glittering,
1370   That assails us through our every sense;
Our dreams of fame, of our name's enduring,
Oh what a sham, I curse them too;
I curse as hollow all our having,
Curse wife and child, peasant and plow;
1375   I curse Mammon[1] when he incites us
With dreams of treasure to reckless deeds,
Or plumps the cushions for our pleasure
As we lie lazily at ease;
Curse comfort sucked out of the grape,
1380   Curse love on its pinnacle of bliss,
Curse faith, so false, curse all vain hope,
And patience most of all I curse!

SPIRIT CHORUS [*Invisible*]
            Oh, what a pity,
            Now you've destroyed it!
1385   The world once so lovely,
            How you have wrecked it!
            Down it goes, smashed
            By a demigod's fist!
            Out of existence
1390   We sweep its poor remnants,
            Sorrowing over
            Beauty now lost forever.
            —Then build again, better,
            Potent son of the earth,
1395   Build a new world, a fairer,
            Inside your own self,
            Within your own heart!
            With a mind clear and strong,
            On your lips a new song,
1400   Come, make a fresh start!

MEPHISTO   Do you hear them, my angels,
            My dear little wise ones,
            Sagely advising you
            To do things, be cheerful?
1405   Their wish is to draw you
            Out of the shell you're shut up in,

---

9. Worthless body (Latin).
1. Riches (Aramaic), a personification derived

from the word's appearance in the New Testament (Matthew 6.24; Luke 16.13).

Out of your torpid stagnation
Into the wide world before you.

Stop making love to your misery,
1410 It gnaws away at you like a vulture;
Even in the meanest company
You'd feel yourself a man like any other.
Not that I'm advising you
To mingle with the hoi poloi;
1415 Among demons I am not a V.I.P.,
But still, if you'll throw in with me,
I'll walk beside you life's long route,
Your good companion. If I suit,
I'm ready to serve you hand and foot.
1420 FAUST   And in return what must I do?
MEPHISTO   There's plenty of time for that, forget it.
FAUST   No, no, the Devil must have his due,
He doesn't do things for the hell of it,
Just to see another fellow through.
1425 So let's hear the terms, what the fine print is;
Having you for a servant's a tricky business.
MEPHISTO   I promise I will serve your wishes—here,
A slave who'll do your bidding faithfully;
But if we meet each other—there,
1430 Why, you must do the same for me.
FAUST   That "there" of yours—it doesn't scare me off;
If you pull this world down about my ears,
Let the other one come on, who cares?
My joys are part and parcel of this earth,
1435 It's under this sun that I suffer,
And once it's goodbye and I've left them
Then let whatever happens happen,
And that is that. About the hereafter
We have had enough palaver,
1440 More than I want to hear, by far:
If still we love and hate each other,
If some stand high and some stand lower,
Et cetera, et cetera.
MEPHISTO   In that case an agreement's easy.
1445 Come, dare it! Come, your signature!
Oh, how my tricks will tickle your fancy!
I'll show you things no man has seen before.
FAUST   You poor devil, really, what have you got to offer?
The mind of man in its sublime endeavor,
1450 Tell me, have you ever understood it?
Oh yes indeed, you've bread, and when I eat it
I'm hungry still; you've yellow gold, like yellow sand
It runs away fast through the hand;
Games of chance no man can win at ever;
1455 Girls who wind me in their arms, their lover,

While eyeing up a fresh one over my shoulder;
There's fame, last failing of a noble nature;
It shoots across the sky a second, then it's over—
Oh yes, do show me fruit that rots as you try
1460 To pick it, trees whose leaves bud daily, daily die!
   MEPHISTO   Marvels like that? For a devil, not so daunting.
I'm good for whatever you have in mind.
—But friend, the day comes when you find
A share of your own in life's good things,
1465 And peace and quiet, are what you're wanting.
   FAUST   If ever you see me loll at ease,
Then it's all yours, you can have it, my life!
If ever you fool me with flatteries
Into feeling satisfied with myself,
1470 Or tempt me with visions of luxuries,
That day's the last my voice on earth is heard,
I'll bet you!
   MEPHISTO   Done! A bet!
   FAUST   A bet—agreed!
If ever I plead with the passing moment,
"Linger awhile, you are so fair!"
1475 Then shut me up in close confinement,
I'll gladly breathe the air no more!
Then let the death bell toll my finis,
Then you are free of all your service,
The clock may stop, hands break, fall off,
1480 And time for me be over with.
   MEPHISTO   Think twice. Forgetting's not a thing we do.
   FAUST   Of course, quite right—a bet's a bet.
This isn't anything I'm rushing into.
But if I stagnate, fall into a rut,
1485 I'm a slave, it doesn't matter who to,
To this one, that one, or to you.
   MEPHISTO   My service starts now—no procrastinating!—
At the dinner tonight for the just-made Ph.D.s.
But there's one thing: you know, for emergencies,
1490 I'd like to have our arrangement down in writing.
   FAUST   In black and white you want it! Oh, what pedantry!
You've never learnt a *man's* word's your best guarantee?
It's not enough for you that I'm committed
By what I promise till the end of days?
1495 —Yet the world's a flood sweeps all along before it,
And why should I feel my word must hold always?
A strange idea, but that's the way we are,
And who would want it otherwise?
That man's blessed who keeps his conscience clear,
1500 He'll regret no sacrifice.
But parchment signed and stamped and sealed,
Is a bogey all recoil from, scared.
The pen does in the living word,

Only sealing wax and vellum count, honor must yield.
1505 Base spirit, say what you require!
Brass or marble, parchment or paper?
Shall I write with quill, with stylus, chisel,
I leave it up to you, you devil!
MEPHISTO   Why get so hot, make extravagant speeches?
1510 Ranting away does no good.
A scrap of paper takes care of the business.
And sign it with a drop of blood.
FAUST   Oh, all right. If that's what makes you happy,
I'll go along with the useless comedy.
1515 MEPHISTO   Blood's a very special ink, you know.
FAUST   Are you afraid that I won't keep our bargain?
Till doomsday I will strive, I'll never slacken!
So I've promised, that's what I will do.
I had ideas too big for me,
1520 Your level's mine, that's all I'm good for.
The Spirit laughed derisively,
Nature won't allow me near her.
With thinking, speculating, I'm through,
Learning and knowledge have sickened me.
1525 —Then let's unloose our passions, dive into
The depths of sensuality!
Bring on your miracles, each one,
Worked by inscrutable sorcery!
We'll plunge into time's racing current,
1530 The vortex of activity,
Where pleasure and distress,
Setbacks and success,
May come as they come, by turn-about, however;
To be always up and doing is man's nature.
1535 MEPHISTO   Try this, sample that, you're free, man, we impose no limitations,
Whatever you like, snatch it up on the run,
And may they agree with you, all your pleasant diversions!
Only don't be bashful, wade right in.
FAUST   I told you, I'm not out to enjoy myself, have fun,
1540 I want frenzied excitements, gratifications that are painful,
Love and hatred violently mixed,
Anguish that enlivens, inspiriting trouble.
Cured of my thirst to know at last,
I'll never again shun anything distressful;
1545 From now on my wish is to undergo
All that men everywhere undergo, their whole portion,
Make mine their heights and depths, their weal and woe,
Everything human embrace in my single person,
And so enlarge my soul to encompass all humanity,
1550 And shipwreck with them when all shipwreck finally.
MEPHISTO   Believe me, I have chewed away in vain
At that tough meat, mankind, since long ago,
From birth to death's by far too short a time

For any man to digest such a lump of sourdough!
1555   Only a God can take in all of them,
       The whole lot. For He dwells in eternal light,
       While we poor devils are stuck down below
       In darkness and gloom, lacking even candlelight,
       And all *you* qualify for is, half day, half night.
1560 FAUST   Nevertheless I will!
       MEPHISTO   Bravely proclaimed!
       Still, there's one thing worries me.
       The time allotted you is very short,
       But art has always been around and shall be,
       So listen, hear what is my thought:
1565   Hire a poet, learn by his instruction.
       Let the good gentleman rove through
       All the realm of imagination,
       And every noble attribute and virtue
       He discovers, heap on you, his inspired creation:
1570   The lion's fierceness,
            Mild hart's swiftness,
            Italian fieriness,
            Northern steadiness.
       Let your poet solve that old conundrum,
1575   How to be generous and also cunning;
       How, driven by youthful impulsiveness, unrestrained,
       To fall in love as beforehand planned.
       Such a creature—my, I'd love to know him!—
       I'd call him Mr. Microcosm.
1580 FAUST   What am I, then, if it can never be:
       The realization of all human possibility,
       That crown my soul so avidly reaches for?
       MEPHISTO   In the end you are—just what you are.
       Wear wigs high-piled with curls, oh thousands,
1585   Stick your legs in yard-high hessians,[2]
       You're still you, the one you always were.
       FAUST   I feel it now, how pointless my long grind
       To make mine all the treasures of man's mind;
       When I sit back and interrogate my soul,
1590   No new powers answer to my call;
       I'm not a hair's breadth more in height,
       A step nearer to the infinite.
       MEPHISTO   Your understanding, my dear Faust,
       Is commonplace, I must say vulgar,
1595   We've got to understand things better
       Or lose our seat at life's rich feast.
       Hell, man, you have hands and feet,
       A headpiece and a pair of balls;
       And pleasures freshly savored, don't

---

2. High boots, a style originally worn by troops from Hesse, Germany, that became fashionable
in the early 19th century.

1600   You have them too? They're no less yours.
        If I can keep six spanking stallions,
        That horsepower's mine, my property,
        My coach bowls on, ain't I the fellow,
        Two dozen legs I've got for me!
1605   Sir, come on, quit all that thinking,
        Into the world, the pair of us!
        The man who lives in his head only's
        Like a donkey in the rough
        Led round and round by the bad fairies,
1610   While green grass grows a stone's throw off.
        FAUST   And how do we begin?
        MEPHISTO   By clearing out—just leaving.
        A torture chamber, that's what this place is!
        You call it living, to be boring
        Yourself and your young men to death?
1615   Leave that to Dr. Bacon Fat next door!
        Why toil and moil at threshing heaps of straw?
        Anyhow, the deepest knowledge you possess
        You daren't let on to before your class.
        —Oh now I hear one in the passageway!
1620   FAUST   I can't see him—tell him to go away.
        MEPHISTO   The poor boy's been so patient, don't be cross;
        We mustn't let him leave here *désolé*.[3]
        Let's have your cap and gown, Herr[4] Doctor.
        Won't I look the fine professor!
                    [*Changes clothes*]
1625   Count on me to know just what to say!
        Fifteen minutes's all I need for it—
        Meanwhile get ready for our little junket!
                                        [*Exit* FAUST]

        MEPHISTO [*Wearing* FAUST's *gown*]
        Despise learning, heap contempt on reason,
        The human race's best possession,
1630   Only let the lying spirit draw you
        Over into mumbo-jumbo,
        Make-believe and pure illusion—
        And then you're mine for sure, I have you,
        No matter what we just agreed to.
1635   Fate's given him a spirit knows no measure,
        On and on it strives relentlessly,
        It soars away disdaining every pleasure,
        Yet I will lead him deep into debauchery
        Where all proves shallow, meaningless,
1640   Till he is limed[5] and thrashes wildly, stuck;
        Before his greedy insatiableness
        I'll dangle food and drink; he'll shriek

---

3. Desolate, saddened (French).   5. Snared; literally, caught with birdlime, a
4. Mr. (German).   sticky substance spread on twigs to trap birds.

In vain for relief from his torturing dryness!
And even if he weren't the Devil's already,
1645 He'd still be sure to perish miserably.

[*Enter a* STUDENT]

STUDENT Allow me, sir, but I am a beginner
And come in quest of an adviser,
One whom all the people here
Greatly esteem, indeed revere.
1650 MEPHISTO I thank you for your courtesy.
But I'm a man, as you can see,
Like any other. Perhaps you should look further.
STUDENT It's you, sir, you, I want for adviser!
I came here full of youthful zeal,
1655 Eager to learn everything worthwhile.
Mother cried to see me go;
I've got an allowance, not much, but it'll do.
MEPHISTO You've come to the right place, my son.
STUDENT But I'm ready to turn right around and run!
1660 It seems so sad inside these walls,
My heart misgives me; I find all's
Confined, shut in; there's nothing green,
Not even a single tree to be seen.
I can't, on the beach in the lecture hall,
1665 Hear or see or think at all!
MEPHISTO It's a matter of getting used to things first.
At infant starts out fighting the breast,
But soon it's feeding lustily.
Just so your appetite will sharpen day by day
1670 The more you nurse at Wisdom's bosom.
STUDENT I'll cling tight to her bosom, happily,
But where do I find her, by what way?
MEPHISTO First of all, then—have you chosen
A faculty?[6]
STUDENT Well, you see,
1675 I'd like to be a learned man.
The earth below, the heavens on high—
All those things I long to understand,
All the sciences; all nature.
MEPHISTO You've got the right idea; however,
1680 It demands close application.
STUDENT Oh never fear, I'm in this heart and soul;
But still, a fellow gets so dull
Without time off for recreation,
In the long and lovely days of summer.
1685 MEPHISTO Time slips away so fast you need to use it
Rationally, and not abuse it.
And for that reason I advise you:

6. That is, a specific course of study, a discipline.

The Principles of Logic *primo*![7]
We will drill your mind by rote,
1690   Strap it in the Spanish boot[8]
So it never shall forget
The road that's been marked out for it
And stray about incautiously,
A will-o'-the-wisp, this way, that way.
1695   Day after day you'll be taught
All you once did just like that,
Like eating and drinking, thoughtlessly,
Now needs a methodology—
Order and system: *A, B, C!*
1700   Our thinking instrument behaves
Like a loom: every thread
At a step on the treadle's set in motion,
Back and forth the shuttle's sped,
The strands flow too fast for the eye,
1705   A blow of the batten and there's cloth, woven!
Now enter your philosopher, he
Proves all is just as it should be:
A being thus and *B* also,
Then *C* and *D* inevitably follow;
1710   And if there were no *A* and *B*,
There'd never be a *C* and *D*.
They're struck all of a heap, his admiring hearers,
But still, it doesn't make them weavers.
How do you study something living?
1715   Drive out the spirit, deny it being,
So there're just parts with which to deal,
Gone is what binds it all, the soul.
With lifeless pieces as the only things real,
The wonder's where's the life of the whole—
1720   *Encheiresis naturae*,[9] the chemists then call it,
Make fools of themselves and never know it.
STUDENT   I have trouble following what you say.
MEPHISTO   You'll get the hang of it by and by,
When you learn to distinguish and classify.
1725   STUDENT   How stupid all this makes me feel;
It spins around in my head like a wheel.
MEPHISTO   Next[1] metaphysics—a vital part
Of scholarship, its very heart.
Exert your faculties to venture
1730   Beyond the boundaries of our nature,
Gain intelligence the brain
Has difficulty taking in,
And whether it goes in or not,

7. First (Italian).
8. A torture implement designed to crush the
leg or foot and leg.
9. Literally, "making an attempt on" or "laying hands on, nature" (Greek and Latin,
respectively).
1. That is.

There's always a big word for it.
1735 Be very sure, your first semester,
To do things right, attend each lecture.
Five of them you'll have daily;
Be in your seat when the bell peals shrilly.
Come to class with your homework done,
1740 The sections memorized, each one,
So you are sure there's no mistake
And no word's said not in the book.
Still, all you hear set down in your notes
As if it came from the Holy Ghost.
1745 STUDENT   No need to say that to me twice,
I realize notes help a lot;
What you've got down in black and white
Goes home with you to a safe place.
MEPHISTO   But your faculty—you've still not told me!
1750 STUDENT   Well, I think the law wouldn't suit me.
MEPHISTO   I can't blame you for disliking it,
Jurisprudence's in a dreadful state,
Laws are like a disease we inherit,
Passed down through generations, spread about
1755 From people to people, region to region;
What once made sense in time becomes nonsensical,
What first was beneficial's lost all reason.
O grandsons coming after, how I wince for you all!
As for the rights we have from Nature as her heir—
1760 Never a word about *them* will you hear!
STUDENT   I hate the stuff now more than ever!
How lucky I am to have you for adviser.
Perhaps I'll take theology.
MEPHISTO   I shouldn't want to lead you astray,
1765 But it's a science, if you'll allow me to say it,
Where it's easy to lose your way.
There's so much poison hidden in it,
It's very nearly impossible
To tell what's toxic from what's medicinal.
1770 Here again it's safer to choose
One single master and echo his words dutifully—
As a general rule, put your trust in *words*,
They'll guide you safely past doubt and dubiety
Into the Temple of Absolute Certainty.
1775 STUDENT   But shouldn't words convey ideas, a meaning?
MEPHISTO   Of course they should! But why overdo it?
It's exactly when ideas are lacking
Words come in so handy as a substitute.
With words we argue pro and con,
1780 With words invent a whole system.
Believe in words! Have faith in them!
No jot or tittle shall pass from them.

STUDENT   Sorry to keep you; I've another query,
          My last one and then I'll go.
1785   Medicine, sir—what might you care to tell me
          About that study I should know?
          Three years, my God, why, they're just minutes
          For a field so vast—oh, it defeats me.
          One or two professional shrewd hints
1790   Could help one along wonderfully.
     MEPHISTO [Aside]   Enough of all this academic chatter.
          Back again to deviltry!
          [Aloud] Medicine's an easy art to master.
          You study, study, man in himself and man abroad,
1795   Only at last to see what happens happens at the pleasure
          Of the Lord.
          Plough your way through all the sciences you please,
          Each learns only what he can;
          But the man who understands his opportunities,
1800   Him I call a man.
          You seem a pretty strapping fellow,
          Not one to hang back bashfully;
          If you don't doubt yourself, I know,
          Nobody else will doubt you, nobody.
1805   Above all learn your way with women;
          With their eternal sighs and groans.
          Their never-ending aches and pains,
          There's one way only, one, to treat them,
          And if your manners are half decent,
1810   You'll have them all just where you want them.
          With an M.D. you enjoy great credit,
          Your art, they're sure, beats others' arts;
          The doctor, when he pays a visit,
          For greeting reaches for those parts
1815   It takes a layman years to get at;
          You feel her pulse with extra emphasis,
          And your arm slipping, with sly, burning glances,
          Around her slender waist,
          See if it's because she's so tight-laced.
1820 STUDENT   Oh, that's much better—practical, down to earth!
     MEPHISTO   All theory, my dear boy, is gray,
          And green the golden tree of life.
     STUDENT   I swear it seems a dream to me!
          Would you permit me, sir, to impose on
1825   Your generous kindness another day
          And drink still more draughts of your wisdom?
     MEPHISTO   I'm glad to help you in any way.
     STUDENT   I mustn't leave without presenting
          You my album. Do write something
1830   In it for me, would you?
     MEPHISTO   Happily.

[*Writes and hands back the album*]

STUDENT [*Reading*]   *Eritis sicut Deus, scientes bonum et malum.*[2]

[*Closes the book reverently and exits*]

MEPHISTO   Faithfully follow that good old verse,
That favorite line of my aunt's, the snake,
And for all your precious godlikeness,
1835   You'll end up how? A nervous wreck.

[*Enter* FAUST]

FAUST   And now where to?

MEPHISTO   Wherever you like.
First we'll mix with little people, then with great.
The pleasure and the profit you will get
From our course—and never pay tuition for it!

1840   FAUST   But me and my long beard—we're hardly suited
For the fast life. I feel myself defeated
Even before we start. I've never been
A fellow to fit in. Among other men
I feel so small, so mortified—I freeze.
1845   Oh, in the world I'm always ill at ease!

MEPHISTO   My friend, that's all soon changed, it doesn't matter;
With confidence comes *savoir-vivre.*[3]

FAUST   But how do we get out of here?
Where are your horses, groom and carriage?

1850   MEPHISTO   By air's how we make our departure,
On my cloak—you'll enjoy the voyage.
But take care, on so bold a venture,
You're sparing in the matter of luggage.
I'll heat some gas,[4] that way we'll lift
1855   Quickly off the face of earth;
If we're light enough we'll rise right up—
I offer my congratulations, sir, on your new life!

Auerbach's Cellar in Leipzig

[*Drinkers carousing.*]

FROSCH   Faces glum and glasses empty?
I don't call this much of a party.
1860   You fellows seem wet straw tonight,
Who always used to blaze so bright.

BRANDER   It's your fault—he just sits there, hardly speaks!
Where's the horseplay, where the dirty jokes?

FROSCH [*Emptying a glass of wine on his head*]
There! Both at once!

BRANDER   O horse and swine!

1865   FROSCH   You asked for it, so don't complain.

SIEBEL   Out in the street if you want to punch noses!

---

2. "You will be like God, knowing good and evil," almost exactly quoting Genesis 3.5, from the Vulgate (spoken by the serpent to Eve).

3. Knowing how to live (French).
4. That is, for a hot-air balloon, a new technology in Goethe's era.

—Now take a deep breath and roar out a chorus
In praise of the grape and the jolly god Bacchus.[5]
Come, all together with a rollicking round-o!

1870 ALTMAYER   Stop, stop, man, I'm wounded, someone fetch me some cotton,
The terrible fellow has burst me an eardrum!

SIEBEL   Hear the sound rumble above in the vault?
That tells you you're hearing the true bass note.

FROSCH   That's right! Out the door, whoever don't like it!
1875 With a do-re-mi,

ALTMAYER   And a la-ti-do,

FROSCH   We will have us a concert!
    [Sings]
    Our dear Holy Roman Empire,[6]
    How does the damn thing hold together?

1880 BRANDER   Oh, but that's dreadful, and dreadfully sung,
A dreary, disgusting *political* song!
Thank the Lord when you wake each morning
You're not the one must keep the Empire going.
It's a blessing I'm grateful for
1885 To be neither Kaiser[7] nor Chancellor.
But we, too, need a chief for our group,
So let's elect ourselves a pope.
To all of us here I'm sure it's well known
What a man must do to sit on that throne.

FROSCH [Singing]
1890   Nightingale, fly away, o'er lawn, o'er bower,
    Tell her I love her ten thousand times over.

SIEBEL   Enough of that love stuff, it turns my stomach.

FROSCH   Ten thousand times, though it drives you frantic!
    [Sings]
    Unbar the door, the night is dark!
1895   Unbar the door, my love, awake!
    Bar up the door now it's daybreak.

SIEBEL   Go on, then, boast about her charms, her favor,
But I will have the latest laugh of all.
She played me false—just wait, she'll play you falser.
1900 A horned imp's what I wish her, straight from Hell,
To dawdle with her in the dust of crossroads;
And may an old goat stinking from the Brocken[8]
Bleat "Goodnight, dearie," to her, galloping homewards.
A fellow made of honest flesh and blood
1905 For a slut like that is much too good.
What love note would I send that scarecrow?—

5. The Roman god of wine (equivalent to the Greek god Dionysus).
6. First created by Charlemagne (800 C.E.), the Holy Roman Empire had, by the 18th century, long since disintegrated into a loose federation of autonomous states, many of which were later consolidated into modern Germany.

7. Emperor (German), whose chief minister was his chancellor.
8. Also known as the Blocksberg, the highest peak in the Harz Mountains of central Germany. Popular legend has long associated the Brocken with witches and devils.

A beribboned rock through her kitchen window.
BRANDER [*Banging on the table*]
    Good fellows, your attention! None here will deny
    I know what should be done and shouldn't at all.
1910   Now we have lovers in our company
    Whom we must treat in manner suitable
    To their condition, our jollity,
    With a song just lately written. So mind the air
    And come in on the chorus loud and clear!
        [*He sings.*]
1915   A rat lived downstairs in the cellar,
        Dined every day on cheese and butter,
        His paunch grew round as any burgher's,
        As round as Dr. Martin Luther's.[9]
        The cook put poison down for it,
1920   Oh, how it groaned, the pangs it felt,
            As if by Cupid[1] smitten.
CHORUS [*Loud and clear*]
            As if by Cupid smitten!
BRANDER
        It rushed upstairs, it raced outdoors
        And drank from every gutter,
1925   It gnawed the woodwork, scratched the floors,
        Its fever burned still hotter,
        In agony it hopped and leaped,
        Oh, piteously the creature squeaked,
            As if by Cupid smitten.
CHORUS
1930   As if by Cupid smitten!
BRANDER
        Its torment drove it, in broad day,
        Out into the kitchen;
        Collapsing on the hearth, it lay
        Panting hard and twitching.
1935   But that cruel Borgia[2] smiled with pleasure,
        That's it, that's that beast's final seizure.
            As if by Cupid smitten.
CHORUS
            As if by Cupid smitten!
SIEBEL   You find it funny, you coarse louts,
1940   Oh, quite a stunt, so very cunning,
    To put down poison for poor rats!
BRANDER   You like rats, do you, find them charming?
ALTMAYER   O big of gut and bald of pate!

9. German monk, priest, and theologian (1483–1546); his attempts to reform the Roman Catholic Church led to the founding of Protestantism.
1. The Roman god of love, traditionally depicted with wings (see line 2226, below).

2. A reference to Lucrezia Borgia (1480–1519), to Cesare Borgia (ca. 1475–1507), or to their father, Rodrigo Borgia (Pope Alexander VI, 1431–1503), members of a powerful Italian family who were widely believed to have killed their enemies with poison.

Losing out's subdued the oaf;
1945 What he sees in the bloated rat
'S the spitting image of himself.

[FAUST *and* MEPHISTOPHELES *enter.*]

MEPHISTO   What your case calls for, Doctor, first,
Is some diverting company,
To teach you life affords some gaiety.
1950 For these men every night's a feast
And every day a holiday;
With little wit but lots of zest
All spin inside their little orbit
Like young cats chasing their own tails.
1955 As long as the landlord grants them credit
And they are spared a splitting headache,
They find life good, unburdened by travails.
BRANDER   They're travelers is what your Brander says,
You can tell it by their foreign ways,
1960 They've not been here, I'll bet, an hour.
FROSCH   Right, right! My Leipzig's an attraction, how I love her,
A little Paris spreading light and culture![3]
SIEBEL   Who might they be? What's your guess?
FROSCH   Leave it to me. I'll fill their glass,
1965 Gently extract, as you do a baby's tooth,
All there is to know about them, the whole truth.
I'd say we're dealing with nobility,
They look so proud, so dissatisfied, to me.
BRANDER   They're pitchmen at the Fair, is what I think.
1970 ALTMAYER   Maybe so.
FROSCH   Now watch me go to work.
MEPHISTO [*To* FAUST]
These dolts can't ever recognize Old Nick
Even when he's got them by the neck.
FAUST   Gentlemen, good day.
SIEBEL   Thank you, the same.
[*Aside, obliquely studying* MEPHISTOPHELES]
What the hell, the fellow limps, he's lame!
1975 MEPHISTO   We'd like to join you, sirs, if you'll allow it.
Our landlord's wine looks so-so, I am thinking,
So the company shall make up for it.
ALTMAYER   Particular, you are, about your drinking.
FROSCH   Fresh from Dogpatch, right? From supper
1980 On cabbage soup with Goodman Clodhopper?
MEPHISTO   We couldn't stop on this trip, more's the pity!
But last time he went on so tenderly
About his Leipzig kith and kin,
And sent his very best to you, each one.
[*Bowing to* FROSCH]

3. Leipzig was a cultural center of Europe in the 17th and 18th centuries.

ALTMAYER [*Aside to* FROSCH]
1985   Score one for him. He's got some wit.
SIEBEL   A sly one, he is.
FROSCH   Wait, I'll fix him yet!
MEPHISTO   Unless I err, weren't we just now hearing
        Some well-schooled voices joined in choral singing?
        Voices, I am sure, must resonate
1990   Inside this vault to very fine effect.
FROSCH   You know music professionally, I think.
MEPHISTO   Oh no—the spirit's eager, but the voice is weak.[4]
ALTMAYER   Give us a song!
MEPHISTO   Whatever you'd like to hear.
SIEBEL   The latest, nothing we've heard before.
1995   MEPHISTO   Easily done. We've just come back from Spain,
        Land where the air breathes song, the rivers run wine.
                [*Sings*]
            Once upon a time a King
                Had a flea, a big one—
FROSCH   Did you hear that? A flea, goddamn!
2000   I'm all for fleas, myself, I am.
MEPHISTO [*Sings*]
            Once upon a time a King
                Had a flea, a big one,
            Doted fondly on the thing
                With fatherly affection.
2005   Calling his tailor in, he said,
                Fetch needles, thread and scissors,
            Measure the Baron up for shirts,
                Measure him, too, for trousers.
BRANDER   And make it perfectly clear to the tailor
2010   He must measure exactly, sew perfect stitches,
        If he's fond of his head, not the least little error,
        Not a wrinkle, you hear, not one, in those breeches!
MEPHISTO
            Glowing satins, gleaming silks
                Now were the flea's attire,
2015   Upon his chest red ribbons crossed
                And a great star shone like fire,
            In sign of his exalted post
                As the King's First Minister.
            His sisters, cousins, uncles, aunts
2020   Enjoyed great influence too—
            The bitter torments that that Court's
                Nobility went through!
            And the Queen as well, and her lady's maid,
                Though bitten till delirious,
2025   Forbore to squash the fleas, afraid

---

4. A play on "the spirit indeed is willing, but the flesh is weak," a saying attributed to Jesus (Matthew 26.41).

       To incur the royal animus.

       But we free souls, we squash all fleas

       The instant they light on us!

CHORUS [*Loud and clear*]

       But we free souls, we squash all fleas

2030   *The instant they light on us!*

FROSCH   Bravo, bravo! That was fine!

SIEBEL   May every flea's fate be the same!

BRANDER   Between finger and nail, then crack! and they're done for.

ALTMAYER   Long live freedom, long live wine!

2035 MEPHISTO   I'd gladly drink a glass in freedom's honor,

       If only your wine was a little better.

SIEBEL   Again! You try, sir, our good humor!

MEPHISTO   I'm sure our landlord wouldn't take it kindly,

       For otherwise I'd treat this company

2040   To wine that's wine—straight out of our own cellar.

SIEBEL   Go on, go on, let the landlord be my worry.

FROSCH   You're princes, you are, if you're able

       To put good wine upon the table;

       But a drop or two, well, that's no trial at all,

2045   To judge right what I need's a real mouthful.

ALTMAYER [*In an undertone*] They're from the Rhineland,[5] I would swear.

MEPHISTO   Let's have an auger, please.

BRANDER   What for?

       Don't tell me you've barrels piled outside the door!

ALTMAYER   There's a basket of tools—look, over there.

MEPHISTO [*Picking out an auger, to* FROSCH]

2050   Now gentlemen—name what you'll have, please?

FROSCH   What do you mean? We have a choice?

MEPHISTO   Whatever you wish, I'll produce.

ALTMAYER [*To* FROSCH]   Licking his lips already, he is!

FROSCH   Fine, fine! For me—a Rhine wine any day,

2055   The best stuff's from the Fatherland, I say.

MEPHISTO [*Boring a hole in the table edge at* FROSCH's *place*]

       Some wax to stop the holes with, quick!

ALTMAYER   Hell, it's just a sideshow trick.

MEPHISTO [*To* BRANDER]

       And you?

BRANDER   The best champagne you have, friend, please,

       With lots of sparkle, lots of fizz.

       [MEPHISTOPHELES *goes round the table boring holes at all the places,*

       which one of the drinkers stops with bungs made of wax.]

2060 You can't always avoid what's foreign;

       About pleasure I'm nonpartisan.

       A man who's a true German can't stand Frenchmen,

       But he can stand their wine, oh how he can!

SIEBEL [*As* MEPHISTOPHELES *reaches his place*]

       I confess your dry wines don't

---

5. The region near the river Rhine in western Germany, long known for its production of wine.

2065   Please my palate, I'll take sweet.
         MEPHISTO   Tokay[6] for you! Coming up shortly!
         ALTMAYER   No, gentlemen! Look at me honestly,
         The whole thing's meant to make fools of us.
         MEPHISTO   Come on, my friend, I'm not so obtuse!
2070   Trying something like that on you would be risky.
         So what's your pleasure, I'm waiting—speak!
         ALTMAYER   Whatever you like, just don't take all week.
         MEPHISTO [All the holes are now bored and stopped; gesturing grotesquely]
                 Grapes grow on the vine,
                 Horns on the head of the goat,
2075   O vinestock of hard wood,
                 O juice of the tender grape!
                 And a wooden table shall,
                 When summoned, yield wine as well!
                 O depths of Nature, mysterious, secret,
2080   Here is a miracle—if you believe it!
         Now pull the plugs, all, drink and be merry!
         ALL [Drawing the bungs and the wine each drinker asked for gushing into
            his glass]
         Sweet fountain, flowing for us only!
         MEPHISTO   But take good care you don't spill any.
                 [They drink glass after glass.]
         ALL [Singing]
                 How lovely everything is, I'm dreaming!
2085   Like cannibals having a feast,
                 Like pigs in a pen full of slops!
         MEPHISTO   They feel so free, what a time they're having!
         FAUST   I'd like to go now—nincompoops!
         MEPHISTO   Before we do, you must admire
2090   Their swinishness in its full splendor.
         SIEBEL [Spilling wine on the floor, where it bursts into flame]
         All Hell's afire, I burn, I burn!
         MEPHISTO [Conjuring the flame]
         Peace, my own element, down, down!
                 [To the drinkers]
         Only a pinch, for the present, of the purgatorial fire.
         SIEBEL   What's going on here? For this you'll pay dear!
2095   You don't seem to know the kind of men you have here.
         FROSCH   Once is enough for that kind of business!
         ALTMAYER   Throw him out on his ear, but quietly, no fuss!
         SIEBEL   You've got your nerve, trying out
         Stuff like that—damned hocus-pocus!
2100   MEPHISTO   Quiet, you tub of guts!
         SIEBEL   Bean pole, you!
         Now he insults us. I know what to do.
         BRANDER   A taste of our fists is what: one-two, one-two.
         ALTMAYER [Drawing a bung and flames shooting out at him]

         6. A sweet Hungarian wine.

I'm on fire, I'm on fire!

SIEBEL   It's witchcraft, no mistaking!

Stick him, the rogue, he's free for the taking!

   [*They draw their knives and fall on* MEPHISTOPHELES.]

MEPHISTO [*Gesturing solemnly*]

2105   False words, false shapes

Addle wits, muddle senses!

Let here and otherwheres

Change their places!

   [*All stand astonished and gape at each other.*]

ALTMAYER   Where am I? What a lovely country!

2110 FROSCH   Such vineyards! Do my eyes deceive me?

SIEBEL   And grapes you only need to reach for!

BRANDER   Just look inside this green arbor!

What vines, what grapes! Cluster on cluster!

   [*He seizes* SIEBEL *by the nose. The others do the same to each other and
   raise their knives.*]

MEPHISTO   Unspell, illusion, eyes and ears!

2115   —Take note the Devil's a jester, my dears!

   [*He vanishes with* FAUST; *the drinkers recoil from each other.*]

SIEBEL   What's happened?

ALTMAYER   What?

FROSCH   Was that your nose?

BRANDER [*To* SIEBEL]   And I'm still holding on to yours!

ALTMAYER   The shock I felt—in every limb!

Get me a chair, I'm caving in.

2120 FROSCH   But what the devil was it, tell me.

SIEBEL   If I ever catch that scoundrel,

He won't go home alive, believe me!

ALTMAYER   I saw him, horsed upon a barrel,

Vault straight out through the cellar door—

2125   My feet feel leaden, so unnatural.

   [*Turning toward the table*]

Well—maybe some wine's still trickling here.

SIEBEL   Lies, all, lies! Oh how they duped us.

FROSCH   I was drinking wine, I'd swear.

BRANDER   And all those grapes—I know what a grape is!

2130 ALTMAYER   Now try and tell me, you know-it-alls,

There's no such thing as miracles!

Witch's Kitchen

   [*A low hearth, and on the fire a large cauldron. In the steam rising up
   from it, various figures can be glimpsed. A* SHE-APE *is seated by the cauldron, skimming it to keep it from boiling over. The* MALE *with their
   young crouches close by, warming himself. Hanging on the walls and
   from the ceiling are all sorts of strange objects, the household gear of a
   witch.*]

FAUST, MEPHISTOPHELES.

FAUST   Why, it's revolting, all this crazy witchery!

Are you telling me I'll learn to be a new man
Stumbling around in this lunatic confusion?
2135 Is an ancient hag the doctor who will cure me?
And that stuff that beast's stirring, that's the remedy
To cancel thirty years, unbow my back?
If you can do no better, the outlook's black
For me, the hopes I nursed are dead already.
2140 Hasn't man's venturesome mind, instructed by Nature,
Discovered some sort of potent elixer?
MEPHISTO   Now you're speaking sensibly!
There *is* a natural way to recover your youth;
But that's another business entirely
2145 And not your sort of thing, is my belief.
FAUST   No, no, come on, I want to hear it.
MEPHISTO   All right. It's simple: you don't need to worry
About money, doctors, necromancy.
Go out into the fields right now, this minute,
2150 Start digging and hoeing with never a stop or a respite.
Confine yourself and your thoughts to the narrowest sphere,
Eat nothing but the plainest kind of fare,
Live with the cattle as cattle, don't think it too low
To spread your own dung on the fields that you plow.
2155 So there you have it, the sane way, the healthy,
To keep yourself young till the age of eighty!
FAUST   Yes, not my sort of thing, I'm afraid,
Humbling myself to work with a spade;
So straitened a life would never suit me.
2160 MEPHISTO   So it's back to the witch, my friend, are we?
FAUST   That horrible hag—no one else will do?
Why can't *you* concoct the brew?
MEPHISTO   A nice thing that, to waste the time of the Devil
When his every moment is claimed by the business of evil!
2165 Please understand. Not only skill and science
Are called for here, but also patience:
A mind must keep at it for years, very quietly,
Only time can supply the mixture its potency.
Such a deal of stuff goes into the process,
2170 All very strange, all so secret.
The Devil, it's true, taught her how to do it,
But it's no business of his to brew it.
                [*Seeing the* APES]
See here, those creatures, aren't they pretty!
That one's the housemaid, that one's the flunkey.
                [*To the* APES]
2175 Madam is not at home, it seems?
APES
                Flew straight up the chimney
                To dine out with friends.
MEPHISTO   And her feasting, how long does it usually take her?
APES   As long as we warm our paws by the fire.

2180 MEPHISTO [*To* FAUST] What do you think of this elegant troupe?

FAUST Nauseating—make me want to throw up.

MEPHISTO Well, just this sort of causerie[7]
  Is what I find most pleases me.
    [*To the* APES]
  Tell me, you ugly things, oh do,
2185 What's that you're stirring there, that brew?

APES Beggars' soup, it's thin stuff, goes down easy.

MEPHISTO Your public's assured—they like what's wishy-washy.

HE-APE [*Sidling up to* MEPHISTOPHELES *fawningly*]
  Oh let the dice roll,
  I need money, and quick,
2190 Let me win, make me rich,
  I'm so down on my luck.
  With a purse full of thaler,[8]
  An ape passes for clever.

MEPHISTO How very happy that monkey would be
2195 If he could buy chances in the lottery.
    [*Meanwhile the young* APES *have been rolling around a big ball to which
    they now give a push forward.*]

HE-APE
  The world, sirs, behold it!
  The up side goes down,
  The down side goes up,
  And there's never a respite.
2200 Touch it, it'll ring,
  It's like glass, fractures easily.
  When all's said and done,
  A hollow, void thing.
  Here it shines brightly,
2205 And brighter here—tinsel!
  —Oops, ain't I nimble!
  But you, son, take care
  And keep a safe distance,
  Or surely you'll die.
2210 The thing's made of clay,
  A knock, and it's fragments.

MEPHISTO What is that sieve for?

HE-APE [*Taking it down*]
  If you came here to thieve,
  It would be my informer.[9]
    [*He scampers across to the* SHE-APE *and has her look through it.*]
2215 Look through the sieve!
  Now say, do you know him?
  Or you don't dare name him?

MEPHISTO [*Approaching the fire*] And this pot over here?

---

7. Informal chat (French).
8. Large silver coins, issued by various German states from the 15th through the 19th centuries.
9. According to German folklore, a thief can be recognized if viewed through a sieve.

APES

   Oh, you're a blockhead, sir—

   Don't know what a pot's for!

2220 Nor a kettle neither.

MEPHISTO What a rude creature!

HE-APE

   Here, take this duster,

   Sit down in the armchair.

    [*Presses* MEPHISTOPHELES *down in the chair*]

FAUST [*Who meanwhile has been standing in front of a mirror, going forward
   to peer into it from close up and then stepping back*]

   What do I see? What a marvellous vision

2225 Shows itself in this magic glass!

   Love, lend me your wings, your swiftest, to pass

   Through the air to he heaven she must dwell in!

   Oh dear, unless I stay fixed to this spot,

   If I dare to move nearer even a bit,

2230 Mist blurs the vision and obscures her quite.

   Woman unrivaled, beauty absolute!

   Can such things be, a creature so lovely?

   The body so indolently stretched out there

   Surely epitomizes all that is heavenly.

2235 Can such a marvel inhabit down here?

MEPHISTO Of course when a god's sweated six whole days,

   And himself cries bravo in his works[1] praise,

   You can be certain the results are first class;

   Look all you want now in the glass,

2240 But I can find you just such a prize,

   And lucky the man, his bliss is assured,

   Who can bring home such a beauty to his bed and board.

    [FAUST *continues to stare into the mirror, while* MEPHISTOPHELES, *lean-
    ing back comfortably in the armchair and toying with the feather duster,
    talks on.*]

   Here I sit like a king on a throne,

   Scepter in hand, all I'm lacking's my crown.

APES [*Who have been performing all sorts of queer, involved movements,
   with loud cries bring* MEPHISTOPHELES *a crown*]

2245 Here, your majesty,

   If you would,

   Glue up the crown

   With sweat and blood!

    [*Their clumsy handling of the crown causes it to break in two, and they
    cavort around with the pieces*]

   Oh, oh, now it's broken!

2250 We look and we listen,

   We chatter, scream curses,

   And make up our verses—

1. See Genesis 1.31–2.3.

FAUST [*Still gazing raptly into the mirror*]
    Good God, how my mind reels, it's going to snap!
MEPHISTO [*Nodding toward the* APES]
    My own head's starting to spin like a top.
APES
2255   And if by some fluke
        The words happen to suit
        Then the rhyme makes a thought!
FAUST [*As above*]   I feel like my insides are on fire!
    Let's go, we've got to get out of here.
2260 MEPHISTO [*Keeping his seat*]   They tell the truth, these poets do,
    You've got to give the creatures their due.
       [*The cauldron, neglected by the* SHE-APE, *starts to boil over, causing a
       great tongue of flame to shoot up in the chimney.* THE WITCH *comes in
       riding down the flame, shrieking hideously.*]
THE WITCH   It hurts, it hurts!
    Monkeys, apes, incompetent brutes!
    Forgetting the pot and singeing your mistress—
2265   The servants I have! Utterly useless!
       [*Catching sight of* FAUST *and* MEPHISTOPHELES]
    What's this? What's this?
    Who are you? Explain!
    What's your business?
    Got in by chicane!
2270   Hellfires parch and make
    Your bones crack and break!
       [*She plunges the spoon into the cauldron and scatters fire over* FAUST,
       MEPHISTOPHELES *and the* APES. *The apes whine.*]
MEPHISTOPHELES [*Turning the duster upside down and hitting out violently
    among the glasses and jars with the butt end*]
        In pieces, in pieces,
        Soup spilt, smashed the dishes!
        It's all in fun, really—
2275   Beating time, you old carcass,
        To your melody.
       [THE WITCH *starts back in rage and fear.*]
    Can't recognize me, rattlebones, old donkey you?
    Can't recognize your lord and master?
    Why I don't chop up you and your monkey crew
2280   Into the littlest bits and pieces is a wonder!
    No respect at all for my red doublet?
    And my cock's feather means nothing to you, beldam?
    Is my face masked, or can you plainly see it?
    Must I tell *you* of all people who I am?
2285 THE WITCH   Oh sir, forgive my discourteous salute!
    But I look in vain for your cloven foot,
    And your two ravens, where are they?[2]

---

2. In folk belief, the devil was thought to have cloven feet like a goat's and to be accompanied by
ravens.

MEPHISTO   All right, this time you're let off—I remember,
It's been so long since we've seen each other.
2290   Also, the world's grown so cultured today,
Even the Devil's been swept up in it;
The northern bogey has made his departure,
No horns now, no tail, to make people shiver;
And as for my hoof, though I can't do without it,
2295   Socially it would raise too many eyebrows,
So like a lot of other young fellows,
I've padded my calves to try and conceal it.
THE WITCH [*Dancing with glee*]
I'm out of my mind with delight, I swear!
My lord Satan's dropped out of the air.
2300   MEPHISTO   Woman, that name—I forbid you to use it.
THE WITCH   Why not? Whyever now refuse it?
MEPHISTO   Since God knows when, it belongs to mythology,
But that's hardly improved the morals of humanity.
The Evil One's no more, evil ones more than ever.
2305   Address me as Baron, that will do,
A gentleman of rank like any other.
And if you doubt my blood is blue,
See, here's my house's arms, the noblest ever!
        [*He makes an indecent gesture.*]
THE WITCH [*Laughing excessively*]
Ha, ha! It's you, I see now, it's clear—
2310   The same old rascal you always were!
MEPHISTO [*To* FAUST]   Observe, friend, my diplomacy
And learn the art of witch-mastery.
THE WITCH   Gentlemen, now what's your pleasure?
MEPHISTO   A generous glass of your famous liquor.
2315   But please, let it be from your oldest supply;
It doubles in strength as the years multiply.
THE WITCH   At once! Here I've got, as it happens, a bottle
From which I myself every now and then tipple,
And what is more, it's lost all its stink.
2320   I'll gladly pour you out a cup.
        [*Under her breath*]
But if the fellow's unprepared, the drink
Might kill him, you know, before an hour's up.
MEPHISTO   I know the man well, he'll thrive up on it.
I wish him the best your kitchen affords.
2325   Now draw your circle, say the words,
And pour him out a brimming goblet.
        [*Making bizarre gestures,* THE WITCH *draws a circle and sets down an
        assortment of strange objects inside it. All the glasses start to ring and the
        pots to resound, providing a kind of musical accompaniment. Last of all,
        she brings out a great tome and stands the* APES *in the circle to serve as a
        lectern and to hold up the torches. Then she signals* FAUST *to approach.*]
FAUST [*To* MEPHISTOPHELES]
What's to be hoped from this, would you tell me?

That junk of hers, and her waving her arms crazily,
All the crude deceptions that she's practicing—
2330   I know them too well, I find them disgusting.
MEPHISTO   Nonsense, friend, it's not all that serious;
Really, you're being much too difficult.
Of course she employs hocus-pocus, she's a sorceress—
How else can her mixture produce a result?

[*He presses* FAUST *inside the circle.*]

THE WITCH [*Declaiming from the book, with great emphasis*]
2335   Listen and learn!
From one make ten,
And let two go,
And add three in,
And you are rich.
2340   Now cancel four!
From five and six,
So says the witch,
Make seven and eight—
Thus all's complete.
2345   And nine is one,
And ten is none,
And that's the witch's one-times-one.
FAUST   I think the old woman's throwing a fit.
MEPHISTO   We're nowhere near the end of it.
2350   I know the book, it's all like that.
The time I've wasted over it!
For a thoroughgoing paradox is what
Bemuses fools and wise men equally.
The trick's old as the hills yet it's still going strong:
2355   With Three-in-One and One-in-Three[3]
Lies are sown broadcast, truth may go hang.
Who questions professors about the claptrap they teach—
Who wants to debate and dispute with a fool?
People dutifully think, hearing floods of fine speech,
2360   It can't be such big words mean nothing at all.
THE WITCH [*Continuing*]
The power of science
From the whole world kept hidden!
Who don't have a thought,
To them it is given
2365   Unbidden, unsought
It's theirs without sweat.
FAUST   Did you hear that, my God, what nonsense,
It's giving me a headache, phew!
It makes me think I'm listening to
2370   A hundred thousand fools in chorus.
MEPHISTO   Enough, enough, O excellent Sibyl![4]

---

3. Allusions to the Holy Trinity (see note to   4. One of several female prophets in the clas-
line 1105).   sical world.

Bring on the potion, fill the stoup,
Your drink won't give my friend here trouble,
He's earned his Ph.D. in many a bout.

> [THE WITCH *very ceremoniously pours the potion into a bowl;*
> *when* FAUST *raises it to his lips, a low flame plays over it.*]

2375   Drink, now drink, no need to diddle,
It'll put you into a fine glow.
When you've got a sidekick in the Devil,
Why should some fire frighten you so?

> [THE WITCH *breaks the circle and* FAUST *steps out.*]

Now let's be off, you mustn't dally.
2380 THE WITCH   I hope that little nip, sir, hits the spot!
MEPHISTO [*To* THE WITCH]   Madam, thanks. If I can help *you* out,
Don't fail, upon Walpurgis Night,[5] to ask me.
THE WITCH [*To* FAUST]   Here is a song, sir, carol it now and then,
You'll find it assists the medicine.
2385 MEPHISTO   Come away quick! You must do as I say.
To soak up the potion body and soul,
A man's got to sweat a bucketful.
And after, I'll teach you the gentleman's way
Of wasting your time expensively.
2390   Soon yours the delight outdelights all things—
Boy Cupid astir in you, stretching his wings.
FAUST   One more look in the mirror, let me—
That woman was inexpressibly lovely!
MEPHISTO   No, no, soon enough, before you, vis-à-vis,
2395   Yours the fairest of fair women, I guarantee.
[*Aside.*] With that stuff in him, old Jack will
Soon see a Helen[6] in every Jill.

A Street

> [FAUST. MARGARETE *passing by.*]

FAUST   Pretty lady, here's my arm,
Would you allow me to see you home?
2400 MARGARETE   I'm neither pretty nor a lady,
And I can find my way unaided.

> [*She escapes his arm and passes by.*]

FAUST   By God, what a lovely girl,
I've never seen her like, a pearl!
A good girl, too, and quick-witted,
2405   Her behavior modest and yet spirited,
Those glowing cheeks, lips red as roses,
Will haunt me till my life closes!
The way she looked down shamefastly

---

5. April 30, the traditional German witches'
sabbath, celebrated on the Brocken mountain (see note to line 1902); this pagan holiday became associated with Saint Walburga
(ca. 710–779), whose feast day is May 1.

6. That is, Helen of Troy, in classical mythology the most beautiful woman in the world;
apparently it is her likeness that Faust sees in
the mirror.

Touched my heart, everlastingly;
2410 And bringing me up short, quite speechless—
Oh that was charming, that was priceless!

[*Enter* MEPHISTOPHELES]

FAUST Get me that girl, do you hear, you must!

MEPHISTO   What girl?

FAUST   The one who just went past.

MEPHISTO   Oh, her. She's just been to confession
2415 To be absolved of all her sins.
I sidled near the box to listen:
She could have spared herself her pains,
She is the soul of innocence
And has no reason, none at all,
2420 To visit the confessional.
Her kind is too much for me.

FAUST She's over fourteen, isn't she?

MEPHISTO   Well, listen to him, the lady-killer,
Eager to pluck every flower he sees,
2425 Who's quite convinced that every favor
Is his to have, hand it over, please.
But it doesn't go so easy always.

FAUST Dear Doctor of What's Right and Proper,
Spare me your lectures, I can do without.
2430 Let me tell you it straight out:
If I don't hold that darling creature
Tight in my arms this very night,
We're through, we two, come twelve midnight.

MEPHISTO   Impossible! That's out of the question!
2435 I must have two weeks at least
To spy out a propitious occasion.

FAUST With several hours or so, at the most,
I could seduce her handily—
Don't need the Devil to pimp for me.

2440 MEPHISTO   You're talking like a Frenchman now.
Calm down, there's no cause for vexation.
You'll find that instant gratification
Disappoints; if you allow
For compliments and billets doux,
2445 Whisperings and rendezvous,
The pleasure's felt so much more keenly.
Italian novels teach you exactly.

FAUST I've no use for your slow-paced courting;
My appetite needs no whetting.

2450 MEPHISTO   Please, I'm being serious.
With such a pretty little miss
You mustn't be impetuous
And assault the fortress frontally.
What's called for here is strategy.

2455 FAUST Something of hers, do you hear, I require!
Come, show me the way to the room she sleeps in,

Get me a scarf, a glove, a ribbon,
A garter with which to feed my desire!

MEPHISTO   To prove to you my earnest intention

2460   By every means to further your passion,
Not losing a minute, without delay
I'll take you to her room today.

FAUST   I'll see her, yes? And have her?

MEPHISTO   No!
She'll be at a neighbor's—you *must* go slow!

2465   Meanwhile alone there, in her room,
You'll breathe in her surrounding's perfume
And dream of the delights to come.

FAUST   Can we start now?

MEPHISTO   Too soon! Be patient!

FAUST   Then find me a pretty thing for a present.

                                            [*Exit*]

2470   MEPHISTO   Presents already? The man's proving a lover!
Now for his gift. I know there's treasure
Buried in many an out-of-the-way corner.
Off I go to reconnoiter!

Evening

[*A small room, very neat and clean.*]

MARGARETE [*As she braids her hair and puts it up*]
Who was he, I wonder, that gentleman,

2475   Who spoke to me this afternoon?
I wish I knew. He seemed very nice.
I'm sure he's noble, from some great house;
His look and manner told you that plainly,
Who else would possess such effrontery?

                                            [*Exit*]

[MEPHISTOPHELES, FAUST.]

2480   MEPHISTO   Come in now, in!—but take care, softly.

FAUST [*After a silent interval*]   Leave, please leave, I'd like
to be alone.

MEPHISTO [*Sniffing around*]   Not every girl keeps things so clean.

                                            [*Exit*]

FAUST   Welcome, evening's twilight gloom,
Stealing through this holy room.

2485   Possess my heart, O love's sweet anguish,
That lives in hope, in hope must languish.
Stillness reigns here, breathing quietly
Peace, good order and contentment—
What riches in this poverty,

2490   What bliss there is in this confinement!

[*He flings himself into a leather armchair by the bed.*]

Receive me as in generations past
You received the happy and distressed,
How often, I know, children crowded around

This chair where their grandsire sat enthrouned.
2495 Perhaps my darling too, a round-cheeked child,
Grateful for her Christmas present, kissed
Reverentially his shrunken hand.
I feel, dear girl, where you are all is comfort,
Where you are order, goodness all abound;
2500 Maternally instructed by your spirit,
Daily you spread the clean cloth on the table,
Sprinkle the sand on the floor so very neatly—
O lovely hand! Celestial!
That's made of this place something heavenly.
2505 And here—!
           [*He lifts a bed curtain.*]
                I tremble, frightened, with delight!
Here I could linger hour after hour.
Here the dear creature, gently dreaming, slept,
Her angel substance slowly shaped by Nature.
Here warm life in her tender bosom swelled,
2510 Here by a pure and holy weaving
Of the strands, there was revealed
The celestial being.

But me? What is it brought me here?
See how shaken I am, how nervous!
2515 What do I want? Why is my heart so anxious?
Poor Faust, I hardly know you any more.

Has this room put a spell on me?
I came here burning up with lust,
And melt with love now, helplessly.
2520 Are we blown about by every gust?

And if she came in now, this minute,
How I would pay dear, I would, for it.
The big talker, Herr Professor,
Would dwindle to nothing, grovel before her.
2525 MEPHISTO [*Entering*]   Hurry! I saw her, she's coming up.
  FAUST   Hurry indeed, I'll never come here again!
  MEPHISTO   Here's a jewel box I snatched up
When I—but who cares how or when.
Put it in the closet there,
2530 She'll jump for joy when she comes on it.
It's got a number of choice things in it,
Meant for another—but I declare,
Girls are girls, they're all the same,
The only thing that matters is the game.
2535 FAUST   Should I, I wonder?
  MEPHISTO   *Should* you, you say!
Do you mean to keep it for yourself?
If what you're after's treasure, pelf,

Then I have wasted my whole day,
Been put to a lot of needless bother.
2540   I hope you aren't some awful miser—
After all my head-scratching, scheming, labor!

      [*He puts the box in the closet and shuts it.*]

Come on, let's go!
Our aim? Your darling's favor,
So you may do with her as you'd like to do.
2545   And you do what?—only gape,
As if going into your lecture hall,
There before you in human shape
Stood physics and metaphysics, old and stale.

                             [*Exit*]

MARGARETE [*With a lamp*]   How close, oppressive it's in here.
      [*She opens the window.*]
2550   And yet outside it isn't warm.
I feel, I don't know why, so queer—
I wish Mother would come home.
I shivering so in every limb.
What a foolish, frightened girl I am!

      [*She sings as she undresses.*]

2555   There was a king in Thule,[7]
No truer man drank up,
To whom his mistress, dying,
Gave a golden cup.

Nothing he held dearer,
2560   And at the clamorous fête
Each time he raised the beaker
All saw his eyes were wet.

And when death knocked, he tallied
His towns and treasure up,
2565   Yielded his heirs all gladly,
All except the cup.

In the great hall of his fathers,
In the castle by the sea,
He and his knights sat down to
2570   Their last revelry.

Up stood the old carouser,
A last time knew wine's warmth,
Then pitched his beloved beaker
Down into the gulf.

---

7. In the classical world, the northernmost land of Europe; it became the name of legendary and
remote lands.

2575 He saw it fall and founder,
Beneath the waves it sank,
His eyes grew dim and never
Another drop he drank

[*She opens the closet to put her clothes away and sees the jewel box.*]

How did this pretty box get here?
2580 I locked the closet, I'm quite sure.
Whatever's in the box? Maybe
Mother took it in pledge[8] today.
And there's the little key on a ribbon.
I think I'd like to open it.
2585 —Look at all this, God in Heaven!
I've never seen the like of it!
Jewels! And *such* jewels, that a fine lady
Might wear on a great holiday.
How would the necklace look on me?
2590 Who is it owns these wonderful things?

[*She puts the jewelry on and stands in front of the mirror.*]

I wish they were mine, these lovely earrings!
When you put them on, you're changed completely.
What good's your pretty face, your youth?
Fine to have but little worth.
2595 Men praise you, do it half in pity,
The thing on their mind is money, money.
Gold is their god, all,
Oh us poor people!

Out Walking

[FAUST *strolling up and down, thinking. To him* MEPHISTOPHELES.]

MEPHISTO   By true love cruelly scorned! By Hellfire fierce and fiery!
2600 If only I could think of worse to swear by!
FAUST   What's eating you, now what's the trouble?
Such a face I've not seen till today.
MEPHISTO   The Devil take me, that's what I would say,
If it didn't so happen I'm the Devil.
2605 FAUST   Are you in your right mind—behaving
Like a madman, wildly raving?
MEPHISTO   The jewels I got for Gretchen, just imagine—
Every piece a damned priest's stolen!
The minute her mother saw them, she
2610 Began to tremble fearfully.
The woman has a nose! It's stuck
Forever in her prayerbook;
She knows right off, by the smell alone,
If something's sacred or profane;
2615 One whiff of the jewelry was enough
To tell her something's wrong with the stuff.

8. That is, in pledge for an unpaid debt.

My child—she cried—and listen well to me,
All property obtained unlawfully
Does body and soul a mortal injury.
2620　These jewels we'll consecrate to the Blessed Virgin,
And for reward have showers of manna⁹ from Heaven.
Our little Margaret pouted, loath—
Why look a gift horse in the mouth?
And surely the one to whom they owe it
2625　Wasn't wicked for practising charity on the quiet.
Her mother sent for the priest, and he,
When he saw how the land lay,
Was mightily pleased. You've done, he said,
Just as you should, mother and maid;
2630　Who overcometh, is repaid.
The Church's stomach's very capacious,
Gobbles up whole realms, anything precious,
Nor once suffers qualms, not even belches.
The Church alone, dear sister, God has named
2635　Receiver of goods unlawfully obtained.
FAUST　That's the way the whole world over,
From a king to a Jew,¹ so all do, ever.
MEPHISTO　So then he pockets brooches, chains and rings
As if they were quite ordinary things,
2640　And gives the women as much of a thank-you
As a body gets for a mouldy potato,
In Heaven, he says, you'll be compensated—
And makes off leaving them feeling elevated.
FAUST　And Gretchen?
MEPHISTO　　　　　　　　Sits there restlessly,
2645　Her mind confused, her will uncertain,
Thinks about jewels night and day,
Even more about her unknown patron.
FAUST　I can't bear that she should suffer.
Find her new ones immediately!
2650　Poor stuff, those others, anyway.
MEPHISTO　Oh yes indeed! With a snap of the fingers!
FAUST　Do what I say, march, man—how he lingers!
Insinuate yourself with her neighbor!
Damn it, devil, you move so sluggishly!
2655　Fetch Gretchen new and better jewelry!
MEPHISTO　Yes, yes, just as you wish, Your Majesty.

　　　　　　　　　　　　　　　　　　　[*Exit* FAUST]

A lovesick fool! To amuse his girl he'd blow up
Sun, moon, stars, the whole damn shop.

---

9. The food said to have miraculously fallen
from heaven for the hungry Israelites when
they wandered in the wilderness (Exodus 16).
1. Forbidden to Christians, moneylending

was one of the few occupations open to Jews
in the Middle Ages and Renaissance; hence
they were stereotyped as greedy usurers.

The Neighbor's House

MARTHE [*Alone*]   May God forgive that man of mine,
2660   He's done me wrong—disappeared
Into the night without a word
And left me here to sleep alone.
I never gave him cause for grief
But loved him as a faithful wife.
        [*She weeps*]
2665   Suppose he's dead—oh I feel hopeless!
If only I had an official notice.
        [*Enter* MARGARETE]

MARGARETE   Frau Marthe!

MARTHE   Gretel, what's wrong, tell me!

MARGARETE   I feel so weak I'm near collapse!
Just now I found another box
2670   Inside my closet. Ebony,
And such things in it, much more splendid
Than the first ones, I'm dumbfounded!

MARTHE   Never a word to your mother about it,
Or the priest will have all the next minute.

2675 MARGARETE   Just look at this, and this, and this here!

MARTHE [*Decking her out in the jewels.*]
Oh, what a lucky girl you are!

MARGARETE   But I mustn't be seen in the streets with such jewelry,
And never in church. Oh, it's too cruel!

MARTHE   Come over to me whenever you're able,
2680   Here you can wear them without any worry,
March back and forth in front of the mirror—
Won't we enjoy ourselves together!
And when it's a holiday, some such occasion,
You can start wearing them, with discretion.
2685   First a necklace, then a pearl earring,
Your mother'll never notice a thing.
And if she does we'll think of something.

MARGARETE   Who put the jewelry in my closet?
There's something that's not right about it.
        [*A knock*]
2690   Dear God above, can that be Mother?

MARTHE [*Peeping through the curtain*]
Please come in!—No, it's a stranger.
        [*Enter* MEPHISTOPHELES]

MEPHISTO   With your permission, my good women!
I beg you to excuse the intrusion.
        [*Steps back deferentially from* MARGARETE]
I'm looking for Frau[2] Marthe Schwerdtlein.

2695 MARTHE   I'm her. And what have you to say, sir?

2. Mrs. (German).

MEPHISTO [*Under his breath to her*]
    Now I know who you are, that's enough.
    You have a lady under your roof,
    I'll go away and come back later.
    MARTHE [*Aloud*]   Goodness, child, you won't believe me,
2700 What the gentleman thinks is, you're a lady!
    MARGARETE   A poor girl's what I am, no more.
    The gentleman's kind—I thank you, sir.
    These jewels don't belong to me.
    MEPHISTO   Ah, it's not just the jewelry,
2705 It's the Fräulein[3] herself, so clear-eyed, serene.
    —So delighted I'm allowed to remain.
    MARTHE   Why are you here, if you'll pardon the question?
    MEPHISTO   I wish my news were pleasanter.
    Don't blame me, the messenger:
2710 Your husband's dead. He sent his affection.
    MARTHE   The good man's dead, gone, departed?
    Then I'll die too. Oh, I'm broken-hearted!
    MARGARETE   Marthe dear, it's too violent, your sorrow!
    MEPHISTO   Hear the sad story I've come to tell you.
2715 MARGARETE   As long as I live I'll never love, no,
    It would kill me with grief to lose my man so.
    MEPHISTO   Joy's latter end is sorrow—and sorrow's joy.
    MARTHE   Tell me how the dear man died.
    MEPHISTO   He's buried in Padua, beside
2720 The blessed saint, sweet Anthony,[4]
    In hallowed ground where he can lie
    In rest eternal, quietly.
    MARTHE   And nothing else, sir, that is all?
    MEPHISTO   A last request. He enjoins you solemnly:
2725 Let three hundred masses be sung for his soul!
    As for anything else, my pocket's empty.
    MARTHE   What! No gold coin, jewel, souvenir,
    Such as every journeyman keeps in his wallet,
    And would sooner go hungry and beg than sell it?
2730 MEPHISTO   Nothing, I'm sorry to say, Madam dear.
    However—he never squandered his money,
    And he sincerely regretted his sins,
    Regretted even more he was so unlucky.
    MARGARETE   Why must so many be so unhappy!
2735 I'll pray for him often, say requiems.
    MEPHISTO   What a lovable creature, there's none dearer!
    What you should have now, right away,
    Is a good husband. It's true what I say.
    MARGARETE   Oh no, it's not time yet, that must come later.
2740 MEPHISTO   If not now a husband, meanwhile a lover.

---

3. Miss (German), the courtesy title given an unmarried woman.
4. A Portuguese Franciscan (1195–1231) who preached and taught in Italy; he was renowned as a miracle worker.

What blessing from Heaven, which one of life's charms
Rivals holding a dear thing like you in one's arms.
MARGARETE   With us people here it isn't the custom.
MEPHISTO   Custom or not, it's what's done and by more than some.
2745 MARTHE   Go on with your story, sir, go on!
MEPHISTO   He lay on a bed of half-rotten straw,
Better at least than a dunghill; and there
He died as a Christian, knowing well
Much remained outstanding on his bill.
2750 "Oh how," he cried, "I hate myself!
To abandon my trade, desert my wife!
It kills me even to think of it.
If only she would forgive and forget!"
MARTHE [*Weeping*]   I did, long ago! He's forgiven, dear man.
2755 MEPHISTO   "But she's more to blame, God knows, than I am."
MARTHE   Liar! How shameless! At death's very door!
MEPHISTO   His mind wandered as the end drew near,
If I'm anything of a connoisseur here.
"No pleasure," he said, "no good times, nor anything nice;
2760 First getting children, then getting them fed,
By fed meaning lots more things than bread,
With never a moment for having my bite in peace."
MARTHE   How could he forget my love and loyalty,
My hard work day and night, the drudgery!
2765 MEPHISTO   He didn't forget, he remembered all tenderly.
"When we set sail from Malta's port," he said,
"For wife and children fervently I prayed.
And Heaven, hearing, smiled down kindly,
For we captured a Turkish vessel, stuffed
2770 With the Sultan's treasure. How we rejoiced!
Our courage being recompensed,
I left the ship with a fatter purse
Than ever I'd owned before in my life."
MARTHE   Treasure! Do you think he buried it?
2775 MEPHISTO   Who knows what's become of it?
In Naples, where he wandered about,
A pretty miss with a kind heart
Showed the stranger such good will
Till the day he died he felt it still.
2780 MARTHE   The villain! Robbing his children, his wife!
And for all his misery, dire need,
He would never give up his scandalous life.
MEPHISTO   Well, he's been paid, the man is dead.
If I were in your shoes, my dear,
2785 I'd mourn him decently a year
And meanwhile keep an eye out for another.
MARTHE   Dear God, I'm sure it won't be easy
To find, on this earth, his successor;
So full of jokes he was, so jolly!
2790 But he was restless, always straying,

Loved foreign women, foreign wine,
And how he loved, drat him, dice-playing!

MEPHISTO   Oh well, I'm sure things worked out fine
If he was equally forgiving.

2795   With such an arrangement, why, I swear
I'd marry you myself, my dear!

MARTHE   Oh sir, you would? You're joking, I'm sure!

MEPHISTO [*Aside*]   Time to leave! This one's an ogress,
She'd sue the Devil for breach of promise!

[*To* GRETCHEN]

2800   And what's your love life like, my charmer?

MARGARETE   What do you mean?

MEPHISTO [*Aside*]   Oh you good girl,
All innocence! [*Aloud*] And now farewell.

MARGARETE   Farewell.

MARTHE   Quick, one last matter,
If you would. I want to know

2805   If I might have some proof to show
How and when my husband died
And where the poor man now is laid?
I like to have things right and proper,
With a notice published in the paper.

2810   MEPHISTO   Madam, yes. To attest the truth,
Two witnesses must swear an oath.
I know someone, a good man; we
Will go before the notary.
I'll introduce you to him.

MARTHE   Do.

2815   MEPHISTO   And she'll be here, your young friend, too?—
A very fine fellow who's been all over,
So polite to ladies, so urbane his behavior.

MARGARETE   I'd blush for shame before the gentleman.

MEPHISTO   No, not before a king or any man!

2820   MARTHE   We'll wait for you tonight, the two of us,
Inside my garden, just behind the house.

A Street

[FAUST, MEPHISTOPHELES]

FAUST   Well? What's doing? When am I going to have her?

MEPHISTO   Bravo, bravo, I can see you're all on fire!
Very shortly Gretchen will be all yours.

2825   This evening you will meet her at her neighbor's.
Oh, that's a woman made to order
To play the bawd, our Mistress Marthe.

FAUST   Good work.

MEPHISTO   There's something we must do for her, however.

FAUST   One good turn deserves another.

2830   MEPHISTO   All it is is swear an oath
Her husband's buried in the earth,

Interred in consecrated ground at Padua.

FAUST   So that means we must make a trip there—very clever!

MEPHISTO   Sancta simplicitas![5] Whoever said that?

2835   Just swear an oath; that's all there's to it.

FAUST   If that's your scheme, keep it, I'm through.

MEPHISTO   The saintly fellow! Just like you!
   Declaring falsely—Heaven forbid!—
   Is something Faustus never did.

2840   Haven't you pontificated
   About God and the world, undisconcerted,
   About man, man's mind and heart and being,
   As bold as brass, without blushing?
   Look at it closely and what's the truth?

2845   You know as much about those things
   As you know about Herr Schwerdtlein's death.

FAUST   You always were a sophist and a liar.

MEPHISTO   Indeed, indeed. If we look ahead a little further,
   To tomorrow, what do we see?

2850   You swearing, oh so honorably,
   Your soul is Gretchen's—cajoling and deceiving her.

FAUST   My soul, and all my heart as well.

MEPHISTO   Oh wonderful!
   You'll swear undying faith and love eternal,
   Go on about desire unique and irresistible,

2855   About longing, boundless, infinite:
   That, too, with all your heart—I'll bet!

FAUST   With all my heart! And now enough.
   What I feel, an emotion of such depth,
   Such turbulence—when I try to find

2860   A name for it and nothing comes to mind,
   And cast about, search heaven and earth
   For words to express its transcendent worth,
   And call the fire in which I burn
   Eternal, yes, eternal, never dying,

2865   Do you really mean to tell me
   That's just devil's doing, deception, lying?

MEPHISTO   Say what you please, I'm right.

FAUST   One word more, one only,
   And then I'll save my breath. A man who is unyielding,
   Sure, absolutely, he's right, and has a tongue in his mouth—

2870   Is right. So come, I'm sick of arguing.
   You're right, and the reason's simple enough:
   I must do what I must, can't help myself.

A Garden

[MARGARETE *with* FAUST, *her arm linked with his;* MARTHE *with*
MEPHISTOPHELES. *The two couples stroll up and down.*]

MARGARETE   You are too kind, sir, I am sure it's meant

5. Holy simplicity (Latin).

To spare a simple girl embarrassment.
2875 A traveler finds whatever amusement he can,
You've been all over, you're a gentleman—
How can anything I say
Interest you in any way?

FAUST   To me one word of yours, one look,
2880 'S worth more than all the wisdom in the great world's book.

[*He kisses her hand.*]

MARGARETE   No, no, sir, please, you mustn't! How could you kiss
A hand so ugly—red and coarse?
You can't imagine all the work I have to do;
My mother must have things just so.

[*They walk on.*]

2885 MARTHE   And you, sir, I believe, you constantly travel?

MEPHISTO   Business, business! It is so demanding!
Leaving a place you like can be so painful,
But there's no help for it, you have to keep on going.

MARTHE   How fine, how free, when you're young and full of ginger,
2890 To travel the world, see all that's doing.
But soon enough worse times arrive and worser;
Where's the one can find it to his liking
To crawl to his grave a lonely bachelor.

MEPHISTO   When I look at what's ahead, I tremble.

2895 MARTHE   Then, sir, bethink yourself while you're still able.

[*They walk on.*]

MARGARETE   Yes, out of sight is out of mind.
It's second nature with you, gallantry;
But you have heaps and heaps of friends
Cleverer by far, oh much, than me.

2900 FAUST   Dear girl, believe me, what's called cleverness
Is mostly shallowness and vanity.

MARGARETE   What do you mean?

FAUST   God, isn't it a pity
That unspoiled innocence and simpleness
Should never know itself and its own worth,
2905 That meekness, lowliness, those highest gifts
Kindly Nature endows us with—

MARGARETE   You'll think of me for a moment or two,
I'll have hours enough to think of you.

FAUST   You're alone a good deal, are you?

2910 MARGARETE   Our family's very small, it's true,
But still it has to be looked to.
We have no maid, I sweep the floors, I cook and knit
And sew, do all the errands, morning and night;
Mother's very careful about money,
2915 All's accounted for to the last penny.
Not that she really needs to pinch and save;
We could afford much more than others have.
My father left us a good bit,

With a small dwelling added to it,
2920   And a garden just outside the city.
But lately I've lived quietly.
My brother is a soldier. My little sister died.
The trouble that she cost me, the poor child!
But I loved her very much, I'd gladly do
2925   It all again.

FAUST   An angel, if at all like you.

MARGARETE   All the care of her was mine,
And she was very fond of her sister.
My father died before she was born,
And Mother, well, we nearly lost her;
2930   It took so long, oh many months, till she got better.
It was out of the question she should nurse
The poor little crying thing herself,
So I nursed her, on milk and water.
I felt she was my own daughter.
2935   In my arms, upon my lap,
She smiled and kicked, grew round and plump.

FAUST   The happiness it must have given you!

MARGARETE   But it was hard on me so often, too.
Her crib stood at my bedside, near my head,
2940   A slightest movement, cradle's creak,
And instantly I was awake;
I'd give her a bottle, or take her into my bed;
If still she fretted, up I'd raise,
Walk up and down with her, swaying and crooning,
2945   And be at the washtub early the next morning;
To market after that, and getting the hearth to blaze,
And so it went, day after day, always.
Home's not always cheerful, be it said;
But still—how good your supper, good your bed.

              [*They walk on.*]

2950   MARTHE   It's very hard on us poor women;
You bachelors don't listen, you're so stubborn!

MEPHISTO   What's needed are more charmers like yourself
To bring us bachelors down from off the shelf.

MARTHE   There's never, sir, been anyone? Confess!
2955   You've never lost your heart to one of us?

MEPHISTO   How does the proverb go? A loving wife,
And one's own hearthside, are more worth
Than all the gold that's hidden in the earth.

MARTHE   I mean, you've had no wish, yourself?

2960   MEPHISTO   Oh, everywhere I've been received politely.

MARTHE   No, what I mean is, hasn't there been somebody
Who ever made your heart beat? Seriously?

MEPHISTO   It's never a joking matter with women, believe me.

MARTHE   Oh, you don't understand!

MEPHISTO   So sorry! Still,

2965   I can see that you are—amiable.

                [*They walk on.*]

FAUST   You recognized me, angel, instantly
    When I came through the gate into the garden?

MARGARETE   I dropped my eyes. Didn't you see?

FAUST   And you'll forgive the liberty, you'll pardon

2970   My swaggering up in that insulting fashion
    When you came out of the church door?

MARGARETE   I was bewildered. Never before
    Had I been spoken to in that way.
    I'm a good girl. Who would dare

2975   To say a bad thing, ever, about me?
    Did he, I wondered, see a suggestion
    Of something flaunting in my look?
    There's a creature, he seemed to think,
    With whom a man might strike a bargain

2980   On the spot. But I'll confess,
    Something there was, I don't know what,
    Spoke in your favor, here in my breast.
    And oh how vexed I felt with myself
    To find I wasn't vexed with you in the least.

2985 FAUST   Dear girl!

MARGARETE   Just wait.

       [*Picking a daisy and plucking the petals one by one*]

FAUST   What is it for, a bouquet?

MARGARETE   Only a little game of ours.

FAUST   A game, is it?

MARGARETE   Never mind. I'm afraid you'll laugh at me.

       [*Murmuring to herself as she plucks the petals*]

FAUST   What are you saying?

MARGARETE [*Under her breath*]

                Loves me—loves me not—

FAUST   Oh, what a creature, heavenly!

2990 MARGARETE [*Continuing*]   He loves me—not—he loves me—not—

       [*Plucking the last petal and crying out delightedly*]

    He loves me.

FAUST   Dearest, yes! Yes, let the flower be
    The oracle by which the truth is said.
    He loves you! Do you understand?
    He loves you! Let me take your hand.

       [*He takes her hands in his.*]

2995 MARGARETE   I'm afraid!

FAUST   No, no, never! Read the look
    On my face, feel my hands gripping yours—
    They tell you what's impossible
    Ever to put in words:

3000   Utter surrender, and such rapture
    As must never end, must last forever!
    Yes, forever. An end—it would betoken

Utter despair, a heart forever broken!
No—no end! No end!

> [MARGARETE *squeezes his hands, frees herself and runs away.*
> *He doesn't move for a moment, thinking, then follows her.*]

3005 MARTHE   It's getting dark.

MEPHISTO   That's right. We have to go.

MARTHE   Please forgive me if I don't invite
You in. But ours is such a nasty-minded street,
You'd think people had no more to do
Than watch their neighbors' every coming and going.
3010 The gossip that goes on here, about nothing!
But where are they, our little couple?

MEPHISTO   Flew.
Up that path like butterflies.

MARTHE   He seems to like her.

MEPHISTO   And she him. Which is the way the world wags ever.

A Summerhouse

> [GRETCHEN *runs in and hides behind the door, putting her*
> *fingertips to her lips and peeping through a crack.*]

MARGARETE   Here he comes!

FAUST   You're teasing me, are you?
3015 I've got you now. [*Kisses her*]

MARGARETE [*Holding him around and returning the kiss*]
                                  I love you, yes, I do!

> [MEPHISTOPHELES *knocks*]

FAUST [*Stamping his foot*]
Who's there?

MEPHISTO   A friend.

FAUST   A fiend!

MEPHISTO   We must be on our way.

MARTHE [*Coming up.*]   Yes, sir, it's late.

FAUST   I'd like to walk you home.

MARGARETE   My mother, I'm afraid. . . . Goodbye!

FAUST   So we must say

Goodbye? Goodbye!

MARGARETE   I hope I'll see you soon.

> [*Exit* FAUST *and* MEPHISTOPHELES]

3020 Good God, the thoughts that fill the head
Of such a man, oh it's astounding!
I stand there dumbly, my face red,
And stammer yes to everything.
I don't understand. What in the world
3025 Does he see in me, an ignorant child?

A Cavern in the Forest

FAUST [*Alone*]   Sublime Spirit, all that I asked for, all,
You gave me. Not for nothing was it,
The face you showed me, all ablaze with fire.

You gave me glorious Nature for my kingdom,
3030   With the power to feel, to delight in her—nor as
A spectator only, coolly admiring her wonders,
But letting me see deep into her bosom
As a man sees deep into a dear friend's heart.
Before me you make pass all living things,
3035   From high to low, and teach me how to know
My brother creatures in the silent woods, the streams, the air.
And when the shrieking storm winds make the forest
Groan, toppling the giant fir whose fall
Bears nearby branches down with it and crushes
3040   Neighboring trees so that the hill returns
A hollow thunder—oh, then you lead me to
The shelter of this cave, lay bare my being to myself,
And all the mysteries hidden in my depths
Unfold themselves and open to the day.
3045   And when I see the moon ascend the sky,
Shedding a pure, assuaging light, out
Of the walls of rock, the dripping bushes, drift
Silvery figures from the ancient world
And temper meditation's austere joy.

3050   That nothing perfect's ever ours, oh but
I know it now. Together with the rapture
That I owe you, by which I am exalted
Nearer and still nearer to the gods, you gave me
A familiar, a creature whom already I
3055   Can't do without, though he's a cold
And shameless devil who drags me down
In my own eyes and with a whispered word
Makes all you granted me to be as nothing.
The longing that I feel for that enchanting
3060   Image of a woman, he busily blows up
Into a leaping flame. And so desire
Whips me, stumbling on, to seize enjoyment,
And once enjoyed, I languish for desire.
           [*Enter* MEPHISTOPHELES]
      MEPHISTO   Aren't you fed up with it by now,
3065   This mooning about? How can it still
Amuse you? You do it for a while,
All right; but enough's enough, on to the new!
      FAUST   Why, when I'm feeling a bit better,
Do you badger me with your insidious chatter?
3070   MEPHISTO   All right, all right, a little breather, have it.
But don't speak so, as if you really mean it—
I wouldn't shed tears, losing a companion
Who is so mad, so rude, so sullen.
I have my hands full every minute—
3075   Impossible to tell what pleases you or doesn't.
      FAUST   Why, that's just perfect, isn't it?

He bores me stiff and wants praise for it.

MEPHISTO   You poor earthly creature, would
You ever have managed at all without me?
3080   Whom do you have to thank for being cured
Of your mad ideas, your feverish frenzy?
If not for me you would have disappeared
From off the face of earth already.
What kind of life do you call it, dully fretting
3085   Owl-like in caves, or toad-like feeding
On oozing moss and dripping stone?
That's a way to spend your time? Go on!
You're still living in your head—I have to say so;
Only the old Dr. Faust would carry on so.

3090   FAUST   Try to understand: my life's renewed
When I wander, musing, in wild Nature.
But even if you could, I know you would
Begrudge me, Devil that you are, my rapture.

MEPHISTO   For sure, your rapture, spiritual, sublime!
3095   Sprawled on a mountain at night in the damp dewfall
And blissfully clasping heaven and earth to your bosom,
A god no less, so great you've grown, so swollen,
Penetrating the core of earth
By sheer force of intuition,
3100   Feeling the six creation days unfold inside yourself,
In your pride of strength delighting in—what, I can't imagine,
On the point of amorously over flowing the universe,
The earthly creature transcended and forgotten—
And how will it end, all your exalted insight?
           [Making a gesture]
3105   I forbid myself to say, it's not polite.

FAUST   For shame!

MEPHISTO   So that's not to your taste at all, sir?
You're right, "shame"'s right, the moral comment called for.
Never a word, when chaste ears are about,
Of what chaste hearts can't do without
3110   I mean, feel free to fool yourself
As and when it pleases you.
Yet you can't keep on doing as you do,
You look a wreck again already;
And if you do keep on, the time's not far
3115   When you'll go mad with horror, fear.
Enough, I say! Your sweetheart sits down there
And all's a dismal prison for her.
You haunt her mind continually,
She's mad about you, oh completely.
3120   At first your passion, like a freshet,
Swollen with melted snow, overthrowing
All barriers, engulfed a soul unknowing;
But now the flood's thinned to a streamlet.
Instead of playing monarch of the wood,

3125   My opinion is the Herr Professor
       Should make the silly little creature
       Some return, in gratitude.
       For her the hours creep along,
       She stands at the window, watching the clouds
3130   Pass slowly over the old town walls,
       "Lend me, sweet bird, your wings,"[6] is the song
       She sings all day and half the night.
       Sometimes she's cheerful, mostly she's downhearted,
       Sometimes she cries as if brokenhearted,
3135   Then she's calm again and seems all right,
       And heart-sick always.
    FAUST   Serpent! Snake!
    MEPHISTO [*Aside*]   I'll have you yet!
    FAUST   Get away from me, you fiend!
3140   Don't mention her, so beautiful, to me!
       Don't make my half-crazed senses crave again
       The sweetness of that lovely body!
    MEPHISTO   Then what? She thinks you've taken flight,
       And I must say, the girl's half right.
3145 FAUST   However far I wander, I am near her,
       I can't forget her for a minute.
       I even envy the Lord's body
       Her pressing her lips in church to it.[7]
    MEPHISTO I understand. I've often envied *you*
3150   Her pair of does that feed among the lilies.[8]
    FAUST Pimp, you! I won't hear your blasphemies!
    MEPHISTO   Fine! Insult me! And I laugh at you.
       The God that made you girls and boys
       Himself was first to recognize,
3155   And practice, what's the noblest calling,
       The furnishing of opportunities.
       Away! A crying shame this, never linger!
       You act as if hard fate were dragging
       You to death, not to your true love's chamber.
3160 FAUST   Heaven's out-heavened when she holds me tight,
       I'm warmed to life upon her bosom—
       But it doesn't matter, still I feel her plight.
       A fugitive is what I am, a beast
       That's houseless, restless, purposeless,
3165   A furious, impatient cataract
       That plunges down from rock to rock toward the abyss.
       And there she was, half grown up into womanhood,
       In her quiet cottage on the Alpine meadow,
       Her life the same unchanging quietude
3170   Within a little world where fell no shadow.

---

6. An old German folksong.
7. That is, while taking Communion, the sacrament that represents the blood and body of
Christ.
8. That is, her breasts (see Song of Solomon
4.5).

And I, abhorred by God,
Was not content to batter
Rocks to bits, I had
To undermine her peace and overwhelm her!
3175   This sacrifice you claimed, Hell, as your due!
Help me, Devil, please, to shorten
The anxious time I must go through!
Let happen quick what has to happen!
Let her fate fall on me, too, crushingly,
3180   And both together perish, her and me!

MEPHISTO   All worked up again, all in a sweat!
On your way, you fool, and comfort her.
When blockheads think there's no way out,
They give up instantly, they're done for.
3185   Long live the man who keeps on undeterred!
I'd rate your progress as a devil pretty fair;
But tell me, what is there that's more absurd
Than a moping devil, mewling in despair?

Gretchen's Room

GRETCHEN [*Alone at her spinning wheel*]
        My heart is sore,
3190   My peace is gone,
        Gone, gone forever
        And evermore.

        Him gone, all's grief,
        All's death, the grave;
3195   The whole world
        Gone sour, spoiled.

        My poor poor head,
        I tremble, nervous,
        I think I'm mad,
3200   My mind's a chaos.

        My heart is sore,
        My peace is gone,
        Gone, gone forever
        And evermore.

3205   I peer out the window,
        Walk out the door,
        It's him, only him,
        I look for.

        His bold brave walk,
3210   His princely person,
        His laughing look,
        His eyes' persuasion,

And his speech's grace—
Magicalness!
His hand's caress
And oh, his kiss!

My heart is sore,
My peace is gone,
Gone, gone forever
And evermore.

With blood and flesh
I strain toward him,
My only wish,
To have and hold him,

And kiss and kiss him,
Never ceasing,
Though I die in
His arms kissing.

Marthe's Garden

[MARGARETE, FAUST]

MARGARETE   Heinrich, the truth—I have to insist!
FAUST   As far as I'm able.
MARGARETE   Well, tell me, you must,
  About your religion—how do you feel?
  You're such a good man, kind and intelligent,
  But I suspect you are indifferent.
FAUST   Enough of that, my child. You know quite well
  I cherish you so very dearly,
  For those I love I'd give my life up gladly,
  And I never interfere with people's faith.
MARGARETE   That isn't right, you've got to have belief!
FAUST   You do?
MARGARETE   I know you think I am a dunce!
  You don't respect the sacraments.
FAUST   I do respect them.
MARGARETE   Not enough to go to mass.
  And tell me when you last went to confess?
  Do you believe in God?
FAUST   Who, my dear,
  Can say, I believe in God?
  Ask any priest, philosopher,
  And what you get by way of answer
  Sounds like a joke, pure mockery.
MARGARETE   So you don't believe in him?
FAUST   Don't misunderstand me, sweet.
  Who is there dares to give him a name
  And affirm,
  "I believe"? Who, feeling doubt,

Ventures to say right out,
"I don't believe"?

3255 The All-embracing,
All-sustaining
Sustains and embraces
You, me, himself.
The sky it arches overhead,

3260 The earth lies firm beneath our feet,
And the friendly shining stars, don't they
Mount aloft eternally?
Don't my eyes, seeking your eyes, meet?
And all that there is, doesn't it press

3265 Close on your mind and heart,
In eternal secrecy working,
Visibly, invisibly about you?
Fill heart with it to overflowing
In an ecstasy of blissful feeling,

3270 Which then call what you would:
Happiness! Heart! Love! Call it God!—
Don't ask me his name, how should I know?
Feeling is all,
Names sound and smoke,

3275 Obscuring heaven's glow.

MARGARETE I guess what you say is all right,
The priest speaks so, or pretty near,
Except his language isn't yours, not quite.

FAUST I speak as all speak here below,

3280 All souls beneath the sun of heaven,
They use the language that they know,
And I use mine. Are all mistaken?

MARGARETE It sounds fine the way you put it,
But something's wrong, there's still a question;

3285 The truth is, you are not a Christian.

FAUST Now darling!

MARGARETE   It is so upsetting, I can't bear it,
To see the company you keep.

FAUST Company?

MARGARETE That man you always have with you,

3290 I loathe him, oh how much I do;
In all my life I can't remember
Anything that's made me shiver
More than his face has, so horrid, hateful!

FAUST Silly thing, don't be so fearful.

3295 MARGARETE His presence puts my blood into a turmoil.
I like people, most of them indeed;
But even as I long for you,
I think of him with secret dread—
And he's a scoundrel, he is too!

3300 If I'm unjust, forgive me, Lord.

FAUST It takes all kinds to make a world.

MARGARETE   I wouldn't want to have his kind around me!
  His lips curl so sarcastically,
  Half angrily,
3305 When he pokes his head inside the door;
  You can see there's nothing he cares for;
  It's written on his face as plain as day
  He loves no one, we're all his enemy.
  I'm so happy with your arms around me,
3310 I'm yours, and feel so warm, so free, so easy,
  But when he's here it knots up so inside me.
FAUST   You angel, you, atremble with foreboding!
MARGARETE   What I feel's so strong, so overwhelming,
  That let him join us anywhere
3315 And right away I almost fear
  I don't love you anymore.
  And when he's near, my lips refuse to pray,
  Which causes me such agony.
  Don't you feel the same way too?
3320 FAUST   It's just that you dislike him so.
MARGARETE   I must go now.
FAUST   Shall we never
  Pass a quiet time alone together,
  Bosom pressed to bosom, two souls one?
MARGARETE   Oh, if I only slept alone!
3325 I'd draw the bolt for you tonight, yes, gladly;
  But my mother sleeps so lightly,
  And if we were surprised by her
  I know I'd die right then and there.
FAUST   Angel, there's no need to worry.
3330 Here's a vial—three drops only
  In her cup will subdue nature
  And lull her into pleasant slumber.
MARGARETE   What is there that I'd say no to
  When you ask?
3335 It won't harm her, though,
  There is no risk?
FAUST   If there was anything to fear,
  Would I suggest you give it her?
MARGARETE   Let me only look at you
3340 And I don't know, I have to do
  Your least wish.
  I have gone so far already,
  How much farther's left for me to go?

                [Exit]

  [Enter MEPHISTOPHELES]

MEPHISTO   The girl's a goose! I hope she's gone.
3345 FAUST   Spying around, are you, again?
MEPHISTO   I heard it all, yes, every bit of it,
  How she put the Doctor through his catechism,
  From which he'll have, I trust, much benefit.

Does a fellow stick to the old, the true religion?—
3350   That's what all the girls are keen to know.
  If he minds there, they think, then he'll mind us too.
FAUST   Monster, lacking the least comprehension
  How such a soul, so loving, pure,
  Whose faith is all in all to her,
3355   The sole means to obtain salvation,
  Should be tormented by the fear
  The one she loves is damned forever!
MEPHISTO   You transcendental, hot and sensual Romeo,
  See how a little skirt's got you in tow.
3360 FAUST   You misbegotten thing of filth and fire!
MEPHISTO   And she's an expert, too, in physiognomy.
  When I come in, she feels—what, she's not sure;
  This face I wear hides a dark mystery;
  I am genius of some kind, a bad one,
3365   About that she is absolutely certain,
  Even the Devil, very possibly.
  Now about tonight—?
FAUST   What's that to you?
MEPHISTO   I get my fun out of it too.

At the Well

[GRETCHEN *and* LIESCHEN *carrying pitchers.*]

LIESCHEN   You've heard about that Barbara, have you?
3370 GRETCHEN   No, not a word. I hardly see a soul.
LIESCHEN   Sybil told me; yes, the whole thing's true.
  She's gone and done it now, the little fool.
  You see what comes of being so stuck up!
GRETCHEN   What comes?
LIESCHEN   Oh, it smells bad, I tell you, phew!—
3375   When she eats now, she's feeding two.
GRETCHEN   Oh dear!
LIESCHEN   Serves her right, if you ask me.
  How she kept after him, without a letup
  Gadding about, the pair, and gallivanting
  Off to the village for the music, dancing,
3380   She had to be first always, everywhere,
  While he with wine and sweet cakes courted her.
  She thought her beauty echoed famously,
  Accepted his gifts shamelessly.
  They kissed and fondled by the hour,
3385   Till it was goodbye to her little flower.
GRETCHEN   The poor thing!
LIESCHEN   Poor thing, you say!
  While we two sat home spinning the whole day
  And our mothers wouldn't let us out at night,
  That one was outside, hugging her sweetheart
3390   On a bench, or up a dark alley,
  And never found an hour passed too slowly.

Well, now she's got to pay for it—
Shiver in church, in her sinner's shirt.
GRETCHEN   He'll marry her, oh I feel certain.
3395   LIESCHEN   Not him, he's too smart, is that one.
Elsewhere he'll find girls just as cordial.
In fact he's gone.
GRETCHEN   But that's not right, it's shameful!
LIESCHEN   And if he does, she'll rue the day,
The boys will snatch her bridal wreath away
3400   And we'll throw dirty straw down in her doorway.
                                                        [Exit]

GRETCHEN [Turning to go home]
How full of blame I used to be, how scornful
Of any girl who got herself in trouble!
I couldn't find words enough to express
My disgust for others' sinfulness.
3405   Black as all their misdeeds seemed to be,
I blackened them still more, so cruelly,
And still they weren't black enough for me.
I blessed myself, was smug and proud
To think I was so very good,
3410   And who's the sinner now? Me, me, oh God!
Yet everything that brought me to it,
God, was so good, oh, was so sweet!

The City Wall

[In a niche in the wall, an image of the Mater Dolorosa⁹
at the foot of the cross, with pots of flowers before it.]

GRETCHEN [Putting fresh flowers in the pots]
Incline, o
Thou sorrow-rich Lady,
3415   Thy countenance kindly on me!

With the sword in your heart,
Your torment, your hurt,
To your dying son upwards you gaze.

Up to the Father
3420   Your sighs race each other,
For his ordeal, your ordeal pleading.

Who's there knows
How it gnaws
Deep inside me, the pain?
3425   The heart-anguish I suffer,
Fright, tremblings, desire?
You only know, you alone!

---

9. Sorrowful Mother (Latin); that is, the Virgin Mary, grieving at the crucifixion of Jesus, a traditional image in Christian iconography.

I go no matter where,
The pain goes with me there,
3430   Aching, aching, aching!
No sooner I'm alone
I moan, I moan, I moan—
Mary, my heart is breaking!

From the box outside my window,
3435   Dropping tears like dew,
Leaning into the dawning,
I picked these flowers for you.

Into my room early
The bright sun put his head,
3440   Found me bolt upright sitting
Miserably on my bed.

Help! Save me from shame and death!
Incline, o
Thou sorrow-rich Lady,
3445   Thy countenance kindly on me!

Night

[*The street outside* GRETCHEN's *door.*]

VALENTINE [*A soldier,* GRETCHEN's *brother*]
Whenever at a bout the boys
Would fill the tavern with the noise
Of their loud bragging, swearing Mattie,
Handsome Kate or blushing Mary
3450   The finest girl in all the country,
Confirming what they said by drinking
Many a bumper, I'd say nothing,
My elbows on the table propped
Till all their boasting at last stopped;
3455   And then I'd stroke my beard and smiling,
Say there was no point to quarreling
About taste; but tell me where
There was one who could compare,
A virgin who could hold a candle
3460   To my beloved sister, Gretel?
Clink, clank, you heard the tankards rattle
All around and voices shout
He's right, he is, she gets our vote,
Among all her sex she has no equal!
3465   Which stopped those others cold. But now!—
I could tear my hair out, all,
Run right up the side of the wall!
All the drunks are free to crow
Over me, to needle, sneer,
3470   And I'm condemned to sitting there

Like a man with debts unpaid
Who sweats in fear what might be said.
I itch to smash them all, those beggars,
But still that wouldn't make them liars.

3475 Who's sneaking up here? Who is that?
There's two! And one I bet's that rat.
When I lay my hands on him
He won't be going home again!

[FAUST, MEPHISTOPHELES]

FAUST   How through the window of the vestry, look,
3480 The flickering altar lamp that's always lit,
Upward throws its light, while dim and weak,
By darkness choked, a gleam dies at our feet.
Just so all's night and gloom within my soul.

MEPHISTO   And me, I'm itching like a tomcat on his prowls,
3485 That slinks past fire escapes, hugs building walls.
An honest devil I am, after all;
It's nothing serious, the little thievery
I have in mind, the little lechery—
It merely shows Walpurgis Night's already
3490 Spooking up and down inside me.
Still another night of waiting, then
The glorious season's here again
When a fellow finds out waking beats
Sleeping life away between the sheets.

3495 FAUST   That flickering light I see, is that
Buried treasure rising, what?

MEPHISTO   Very soon you'll have the pleasure
Of lifting out a pot of treasure.
The other day I stole a look—
3500 Such lovely coins, oh you're in luck!

FAUST   No necklace, bracelet, some such thing
My darling can put on, a ring?

MEPHISTO   I think I glimpsed a string of pearls—
Just the thing to please the girls.

3505 FAUST   Good, good. It makes me feel unhappy
When I turn up with my hands empty.

MEPHISTO   Why should you mind it if you can
Enjoy a drink on the house now and then?
Look up, how the heavens sparkle, star full,
3510 Time for a song, a cunning one, artful:
I'll sing her a ballad that's moral, proper,
So as to delude the baggage the better.

[Sings to the guitar]

What business have you there,
Before your darling's door,
3515 O Katherine, my dear,
In dawning's chill?
You pretty child, beware,
The maid that enters there,

Out she shall come ne'er
3520   A maiden still.[1]

Girls, listen, trust no one,
Or when all's said and done,
You'll find you are *undone*
        And smart for it.
3525   Of your good selves take care,
Yield nothing though he swear,
Until your finger wear
        A ring on it.

VALENTINE [*Advancing*]
What's going on here with that braying?
3530   Abominable ratcatcher![2]
The devil take that thing you're playing,
And then take you, foul serenader!

MEPHISTO   Smashed my guitar! Now it's no good at all.

VALENTINE   What I'll smash next is your thick skull.

3535 MEPHISTO [*To* FAUST.]   Hold your ground, Professor! At the ready!
Stick close to me, I'll show you how.
Out with your pigsticker now!
You do the thrusting, I will parry.

VALENTINE   Parry that!

MEPHISTO   Why not?

VALENTINE   And this one too!

3540 MEPHISTO   So delighted, I am, to oblige you.

VALENTINE   It's the Devil I think I'm fighting!
What's this? My hand is feeling feeble.

MEPHISTO [*To* FAUST.]   Stick him!

VALENTINE [*Falling.*]   Oh!

MEPHISTO   See how the lout's turned civil.
What's called for now is legwork. Off and running!
3545 In no time they will raise a hue and cry.
I can manage sheriffs without trouble,
But not the High Judiciary.

[*Exeunt*[3]]

MARTHE [*Leaning out of the window*]
Neighbors, help!

GRETCHEN [*Leaning out of her window*]
        A light, a light!

MARTHE   They curse and brawl, they scream and fight.

3550 CROWD   Here's one on the ground. He's dead.

MARTHE [*Coming out*]   Where are the murderers? All fled?

GRETCHEN [*Coming out*]
Who's lying here?

CROWD   Your mother's son.

---

1. An echo of Ophelia's song in Shakespeare's *Hamlet* (ca. 1600–01), 4.5.53–54.
2. A figure of German legend who when the townspeople of Hamelin refused to pay him as promised for ridding them of rats lured away their children.
3. They exit (Latin).

GRETCHEN   My God, the misery! On and on!
VALENTINE   I'm dying! Well, it's soon said, that,
3555   And sooner done. You women, don't
          Stand there blubbering away.
          Come here, I've something I must say.
                    [All gather around him.]
          Gretchen, look here, you're young yet,
          A green girl, not so smart about
3560   Managing her business.
          We know it, don't we, you and me,
          You're a whore on the q.t.[4]—
          Go public, don't be shy, miss.
GRETCHEN   My brother! God! What wretchedness!
3565 VALENTINE   You can leave God out of this.
          What's done can't ever be undone.
          And as things went, so they'll go on.
          You let in one at the back door,
          Soon there'll be others, more and more—
3570   A whole dozen, hot for pleasure,
          And then the whole town for good measure.

          Shame is born in hugger-mugger,
          The lying-in veiled in black night,
          And she is swaddled up so tight
3575   In hopes the ugly thing will smother.
          But as she thrives, grows bigger, bolder,
          The hussy's eager to step out,
          Though she has grown no prettier.
          The more she's hateful to the sight,
3580   The more the creature seeks the light.

          I look ahead and I see what?
          The honest people of this place
          Standing back from you, you slut,
          As from a plague-infected corpse.
3585   When they look you in the face
          You'll cringe with shame, pierced to the heart.
          In church they'll drive you from the altar,
          No wearing gold chains any more,
          No putting on a fine lace collar
3590   For skipping round on the dance floor.
          You'll hide in dark and dirty corners
          With limping cripples, lousy beggars.
          God may pardon you at last,
          But here on earth you stand accurst!
3595 MARTHE   Look up to God and ask his mercy!
          Don't add to all your other sins
          Sacrilege and blasphemy.

---

4. Secretly; confidentially (slang).

VALENTINE   If I could only lay my hands
    On your scrawny, dried-up body,
3600   Vile panderer, repulsive bawd,
    Then I might hope to find forgiveness
    Ten times over from the Lord!
GRETCHEN   My brother! Oh, what hellish anguish!
VALENTINE   Stop your bawling, all your to-do.
3605   When you said goodbye to honor,
    That is what gave me the worst blow.
    And now I go down in the earth,
    Passing through the sleep of death
    To God—who in his life was a brave soldier.

                                  [*Dies*]

The Cathedral

[*Requiem mass, organ music, singing.* GRETCHEN *among
a crowd of worshippers. Behind her an* EVIL SPIRIT.]

3610 EVIL SPIRIT   Oh, it was different,
    Wasn't it, Gretchen,
    When you then, an innocent,
    Used to come here
    To the altar and kneeling,
3615   Prattle out prayers
    From the worn little prayer book,
    Half childish playing,
    Half God adoring,
    Gretchen!
3620   In your heart's hidden
    What horrid sin?

    Do you pray for the soul of your mother,
    Who by your contriving slept on,
    On into unending pain?
3625   That blood on your doorstep, whose is it?
    And under your heart, that faint stirring,
    A quickening in you, what is it?—
    Affrighting both you and itself
    With its foreboding presence.
3630 GRETCHEN   Misery! Misery!
    To be rid of these thoughts
    That go round and around in me,
    Accusing, accusing!
CHOIR   *Dies irae, dies illa*
3635   *Solvet saeclum in favilla.*[5]

                [*Organ music*]

---

5. Day of wrath, that day / Will dissolve the world in glowing ashes (Latin); the opening lines from a hymn used in the traditional Requiem Mass. The other Latin verse in this scene, sung by the choir, is from the same hymn.

EVIL SPIRIT   The wrath of God grips you!
    The trumpet is sounding,
    The sepulchers quaking,
    And your heart,
3640   From its ashen peace waking,
    Trembles upwards in flames
    Of burning qualms!
GRETCHEN   To be out of here, gone!
    I feel as if drowning
3645   In the organ's sound,
    Dissolving into nothing
    In the singing's profound.
CHOIR   *Judex ergo cum sedebit,*
    Quidquid latet apparebit,
3650   *Nil inultum remanebit.*[6]
GRETCHEN   I feel so oppressed here!
    The pillars imprison me!
    The vaulting presses
    Down on me! Air!
3655 EVIL SPIRIT   Hide yourself, try! Sin and shame
    Never stay hidden.
    Air! Light!
    Poor thing that you are!
CHOIR   *Quid sum miser tunc dicturus?*
3660   *Quem patronum rogaturus,*
    Cum vix justus sit securus?[7]
EVIL SPIRIT   The blessed avert
    Their faces from you.
    Pure souls snatch back
3665   Hands once offered you.
    Poor thing!
CHOIR   *Quid sum miser tunc dicturus?*
GRETCHEN   Neighbor, your smelling salts!
        [*She swoons.*]

Walpurgis Night

[*The Harz Mountains, near Schierke and Elend.*[8] FAUST,
MEPHISTOPHELES.]

MEPHISTO   What you would like now is a broomstick, right?
3670   Myself, give me a tough old billy goat.
    We've got a ways to go, still, on this route.
FAUST   While legs hold up and breath comes freely,
    This knotty blackthorn's all I want.
    Hastening our journey, what's the point?
3675   To loiter through each winding valley,

6. Thus when the judge will sit, / Whatever is hidden will appear, / Nothing will remain unavenged.
7. What am I, a wretch, then going to say? / Whom will I beg to be my patron, / When scarcely will the just man be safe?
8. Two villages; the highest peak of the Harz range is the Brocken.

Then clamber up this rocky slope
Down which that stream there tumbles ceaselessly—
That's what gives the pleasure to our tramp.
The spring has laid her finger on the birch,
3680   Even the fir tree feels her touch,
Then mustn't our limbs feel new energy?

MEPHISTO   Must they? I don't feel that way, not me.
My season's strictly wintertime,
I'd much prefer we went through ice and snow.
3685   The waning moon, making its tardy climb
Up the sky, gives off a reddish glow
So sad and dim, at every step you run
Into a tree or stumble on a stone.
You won't mind me, will you, begging help
3690   Of some quick-flitting will-o'-the-wisp?[9]
I see one yonder, shining merrily.
—Hello there, friend, we'd like your company!
Why blaze away so uselessly, for nothing?
Do us a favor, light up this path we're climbing.

3695 WILL-O'-THE-WISP   I hope the deep respect I hold you in, sir,
Will keep in check my all-too-skittish temper;
The way we go is zigzag, that's our nature.

MEPHISTO   Trying to ape mankind, poor silly flame.
Now listen to me: fly straight, in the Devil's name,
3700   Or I will blow your feeble flickering out!

WILL-O'-THE-WISP   Yes, yes, you give the orders here, all right;
I'll do what you require, eagerly.
But don't forget, the mountain on this night
Is mad with magic, witchcraft, sorcery,
3705   And if Jack-o'-Lantern[1] is your guide,
Don't expect more than he can provide.

FAUST, MEPHISTOPHELES, WILL-O'-THE-WISP [*Singing in turn*]
We have entered, as it seems,
Realm of magic, realm of dreams.
Lead us well and win the honor
3710   His to have, bright-shining creature,
By whose flicker we may hasten
Forward through this wide, waste region!

See the trees, one then another,
Spinning past us fast and faster,
3715   And the cliffs impending over,
And the jutting crags, like noses
Winds blow through with snoring noises!

Over stones and through the heather
Rills and runnels downwards hasten.

9. Here a nature spirit (literally, a light that appears over marshy ground, usually from the   burning of decomposing matter).
1. Another name for a will-o'-the-wisp.

3720 Is that water splashing, listen,
 Is it singing, that soft murmur,
 Is it love's sweet voice, lamenting
 For the days when all was heaven?
 How our hearts hoped, loving, yearning!
3725 And like a tale, an old, familiar,
 Echo once more tells it over.

 Whoo-oo! owl's hoot's heard nearer,
 Cry of cuckoo and of plover—
 Still not nested, still awake?
3730 Are those lizards in the brake?
 Straggle-legged, big of belly!
 And roots, winding every which way
 In the rock and sand, send far out
 Shoots to snare and make us cry out;
3735 Tree warts, swollen, gross excrescents,
 Send their tentacles like serpents
 Out to catch us. And mice scamper
 In great packs of every color
 Through the moss and through the heather.
3740 And the glowworms swarm around us
 In dense clouds and only lead us
 Hither, thither, to confuse us.

 Tell me, are we standing still, or
 Still advancing, climbing higher?
3745 Everything spins round us wildly,
 Rocks and trees grin at us madly,
 And the will-o'-the-wisps swell bigger
 In their size and in their number.

MEPHISTO Seize hold of my coattails, quick,
3750 We're coming to a middling peak
 Where you'll marvel at the sight
 Of Mammon's mountain, burning bright.
FAUST How strange that light is, there, far down,
 Dim and reddish, like the dawn.
3755 Its faint luminescence reaches
 Deep into the yawning gorges.
 Mist rises here and streams away there,
 Penetrated by pale fire.
 Now the fire curls and winds in
3760 A gold thread, now like a fountain
 Overflows, and spreading out
 In branching veins, pours through the valley,
 Or squeezed into a narrow gully,
 Collects into a pool of light.
3765 Sparks fly about as if a hand
 Were scattering golden grains of sand.
 And look there, how from base to top

The whole cliffside is lit up.

MEPHISTO   At holiday time Lord Mammon stages

3770   Quite a show, don't you agree?

Oh, you're a lucky man to see this.

And here the guests come—not so quietly!

FAUST   What a gale of wind is blowing,

Buffeting my back and shoulders!

3775   MEPHISTO   Clutch with your fingers that outcropping

Or you'll fall to your death among the boulders.

The mist is making it darker than ever.

Hear how the trees are pitching and tossing!

Frightened, the owls fly up in a flutter.

3780   The evergreen palace's pillars are creaking

And cracking, boughs snapping and breaking,

As down the trunks thunder

With a shriek of roots tearing,

Piling up on each other

3785   In a fearful disorder!

And through the wreckage-strewn ravines

The hurtling storm blast howls and keens.

And hear those voices in the air,

Some far off and others near?

3790   That's the witches' wizard singing,

Along the mountain shrilly ringing.

CHORUS OF WITCHES

The witches ride up to the Brocken,

Stubble's yellow, new grain green.

The great host meets upon the peak and

3795   There Urian[2] mounts his throne.

So over stock and stone go stumping,

Witches farting, billy goats stinking!

VOICE   Here comes Mother Baubo[3] now,

Riding on an old brood sow.

CHORUS

3800   Honor to whom honor is due![4]

Old Baubo to the head of the queue!

A fat pig and a fat frau[5] on her,

And all the witches following after!

VOICE   How did you come?

VOICE   Ilsenstein way.[6]

3805   I peeked in an owl's nest, passing by,

Oh how it stared!

VOICE   Oh go to hell, all!

Why such a rush, such a mad scramble?

VOICE   Too fast, too fast, my bottom's skinned sore!

2. A name for the devil.

3. In Greek mythology, an old woman who made bawdy jokes to console Demeter after Persephone, her daughter, was carried off by Hades, lord of the underworld.

4. A parodic quotation of Romans 13.7.

5. Woman; wife (German).

6. That is, by way of the Ilsenstein, a mountain in the Harz range.

Oh my wounds! Look here and here!

CHORUS OF WITCHES

3810 Broad the way and long the road,[7]
What a bumbling, stumbling crowd!
Broomstraw scratches, pitchfork pokes,
Mother's ripped and baby chokes.

HALF-CHORUS OF WARLOCKS

We crawl like snails lugging their whorled shell,
3815 The women have got a good mile's lead.
When where you're going's to the Devil,
It's woman knows how to get up speed.

OTHER HALF-CHORUS

A mile or so, why should we care?
Women may get the start of us,
3820 But for all of their forehandedness,
One jump carries a man right there.

VOICE [*Above*]   Come along with us, you down at the lake.
VOICE [*From below*]   Is there anything better we would like?
We scrub ourselves clean as a whistle,
3825 But it's no use, still we're infertile.

BOTH CHORUSES

The wind is still, the stars are fled,
The moon's relieved to hide her head.
With a rush and a roar a magic chorus
Scatters sparks by the thousands around us.

3830 VOICE [*From below*]   Wait, please wait, only a minute!
VOICE [*Above*]   From that crevice a voice, did y' hear it?
VOICE [*From below*]   Take me along, don't forget me!
For three hundred years I've tried to climb
Up to the summit—all in vain.
3835 I long for creatures who are like me.

BOTH CHORUSES

Straddle a broomstick, a pitchfork's fine too,
Get up on a goat, a plain stick will do.
Who can't make it up today
Forever is done for, and so bye-bye.

3840 HALF-WITCH [*From below*]   I trot breathlessly, and yet
How far ahead the rest have got.
No peace at all at home, and here
It's no better. Dear, oh dear!

CHORUS OF WITCHES

The unction gives us hags a lift,[8]
3845 A bit of rag will do for a sail,
Any tub's a fine sky boat—
Don't fly now and you never will.

BOTH CHORUSES

And when we've gained the very top,

---

7. That is, the road to destruction (see Matthew 7.13).
8. According to folklore, witches could fly by smearing their broomsticks with an ointment ("unction") made from the fat of unbaptized babies.

            Light down, swooping, to a stop.
3850   We'll darken the heath entirely
            With all our swarming witchery.
                [They alight.]

MEPHISTO   What a crowding and shoving, rushing and clattering,
            Hissing and shrieking, pushing and chattering,
            Burning and sparking, stinking and kicking!
3855   We're among witches, no mistaking!
            Stick close to me or we'll lose each other.
            But where are you?

FAUST   Here, over here!

MEPHISTO   Already swept away so far!
            I must show this mob who's master.
3860   Out of the way of Voland[9] the Devil,
            Out of the way, you charming rabble!
            Doctor, hang on, we'll make a quick dash
            And get ourselves out of this terrible crush—
            Even for me it's too much to endure.
3865   Yonder's a light has a strange lure,
            Those bushes, I don't know why, attract me,
            Quick now, dive in that shrubbery!

FAUST   Spirit of Contradiction! However,
            Lead the way!—He's clever, my devil:
3870   Walpurgis Night up the Brocken we scramble
            So as to do what? Hide ourselves in a corner!

MEPHISTO   Just look at that fire there, shining brightly,
            Clubmen are meeting, how nice all looks, sprightly.
            When the company's few, the feeling's jollier.

3875 FAUST   But I would feel much happier
            To be on the summit. I can make out
            A red glow and black smoke swirling,
            Satanwards a great crowd's toiling,
            And there, I don't have any doubt,
3880   Many a riddle's at last resolved.

MEPHISTO   And many another riddle revealed.
            Let the great world rush on crazily,
            We'll pass the time here cozily;
            And doing what has been for a long time the thing done,
3885   Inside that great world make us a little one.
            Look there, young witches, all stark naked,
            And old ones wisely petticoated.
            Don't sulk, be nice, if only to please me;
            Much fun at small cost, really it's easy.
3890   I hear music, a damned racket!
            You must learn not to mind it.
            No backing out now, in with me!
            You'll meet a distinguished company
            And again be much obliged to me.

9. A German nickname for Satan (evil fiend).

3895   —Now what do you think of this place, my friend?
        Our eyes can hardly see to its end.
        A hundred fires, in a row burning,
        People around them dancing, carousing,
        Talking and making love—oh, what a show!
3900   Where's anything better, I'd like to know.
      FAUST And when we enter into the revel,
        What part will you play, magician or devil?
      MEPHISTO I travel incognito normally,
        But when it comes to celebrations
3905   A man must show his decorations.
        The Garter's[1] never been awarded me,
        But in these parts the split hoof's much respected.
        That snail there, do you see it, creeping forwards,
        Its face pushing this way, that way, toward us?
3910   Already I've been smelt out, I'm detected.
        Even if deception was my aim,
        Here there's no denying who I am.
        Come on, we'll go along from fire to fire,
        Me the introducer, you the suitor.
          [*Addressing several figures huddled around a fading fire*]
3915   Old sirs, you keep apart, you're hardly merry,
        You'd please me better if you joined the party.
        You ought to be carousing with the youngsters,
        At home we're all alone enough, we oldsters.
      GENERAL Put no trust in nations, for the people,
3920   In spite of all you've done, are never grateful.
        It's with them always as it is with women,
        The young come first, and we—ignored, forgotten.
      MINISTER OF STATE The world has got completely off the track.
        Oh, they were men, the older generation!
3925   When we held every high position,
        That was the golden age, and no mistake.
      PARVENU We were no simpletons ourselves, we weren't,
        And often did the things we shouldn't.
        But everything's turned topsy-turvy, now
3930   That we are foursquare with the status quo.
      AUTHOR Who wants, today, to read a book
        With a modicum of sense or wit?
        And as for our younger folk,
        I've never seen such rude conceit.
      MEPHISTO [*Suddenly transformed into an old man*]
3935   For Judgment Day all now are ripe and ready
        Since I shan't ever again climb Brocken's top;
        And considering, too, my wine of life is running cloudy,
        The world also is coming to a stop.
      JUNK-DEALER WITCH Good sirs, don't pass me unawares,

---

1. That is, the Order of the Garter, the oldest and most prestigious British award of knighthood.

3940 Don't miss this opportunity!
Look here, will you, at my wares,
What richness, what variety!
Yet there is not a single item
Hasn't served to claim a victim,
3945 Nowhere on earth will you find such a stall!
No dagger here but it has drunk hot blood,
No cup but from it deadly poison's flowed
To waste a body once robust and hale,
No gem but has seduced a loving girl,
3950 No sword but has betrayed an ally or a friend,
Or struck an adversary from behind.

MEPHISTO   Auntie, think about the times you live in—
What's past is done! Done and gone![2]
The new, the latest, that's what you should deal in;
3955 The nouveau only, turns us on.

FAUST   Am I me, I wonder, I'm so giddy.
This is a fair to beat all fairs, believe me!

MEPHISTO   The scrambling mob climbs upwards, jostling rushed,
You think you're pushing and you're being pushed.

3960 FAUST   Who's that there?

MEPHISTO   Take a good look.
Lilith.

FAUST   Lilith? Who is that?

MEPHISTO   Adam's wife,[3] his first. Beware of her.
Her beauty's one boast is her dangerous hair.
When Lilith winds it tight around young men
3965 She doesn't soon let go of them again.

FAUST   Look, one old witch, one young one, there they sit—
They've waltzed around a lot already, I will bet!

MEPHISTO   Tonight's no night for resting but for fun,
Let's join the dance, a new one's just begun.

FAUST [Dancing with the YOUNG WITCH]
3970 A lovely dream I dreamt one day:
I saw a green-leaved apple tree,
Two apples swayed upon a stem,
So tempting! I climbed up for them.

THE PRETTY WITCH   Ever since the days of Eden
3975 Apples have been man's desire.
How overjoyed I am to think, sir,
Apples grow, too, in my garden.

MEPHISTO [Dancing with the OLD WITCH]
A naughty dream I one day:
I saw a tree split up the middle—
3980 A huge cleft, phenomenal!
And yet it pleased me every way.

2. Out of date; anachronistic.
3. Lilith, originally a Mesopotamian storm
demon, became in the Talmudic tradition the

incarnation of lust and in Jewish folklore the
first wife of Adam.

THE OLD WITCH   Welcome, welcome, to you, sire,
   Cloven-footed cavalier!
   Stand to with a proper stopper,
3985   Unless you fear to come a cropper.
PROCTOPHANTASMIST[4]   Accursed tribe, so bold, presumptuous!
   Hasn't it been proven past disputing
   Spirits all are footless, they lack standing?
   And here you're footing like the rest of us!
THE PRETTY WITCH [*Dancing*]
3990   What's he doing here, at our party?
FAUST [*Dancing*]
   Him? You find him everywhere, that killjoy;
   We others dance, he does the criticizing.
   Every step one takes requires analyzing;
   Until it's jawed about, it hasn't yet occurred.
3995   He can't stand how we go forward undeterred;
   If you keep going around in the same old circle,
   As he plods year in, year out on his treadmill,
   You might be favored with his good opinion,
   Provided you most humbly beg it of him.
4000 PROCTOPHANTASMIST   Still here, are you? It's an outrage!
   Vanish, ours is the Enlightened Age—
   You devils, no respect for rule and regulation.
   We've grown so wise, yet ghosts still walk in Tegel.[5]
   How long I've toiled to banish superstition,
4005   Yet it lives on. The whole thing is a scandal!
THE PRETTY WITCH   Stop, stop, how boring, all your gabble!
PROCTOPHANTASMIST   I tell you to your face you ghostly freaks,
   I'll not endure this tyranny of spooks—
   My spirit finds you spirits much too spiritual!
      [*They go on dancing.*]
4010   I see I'm getting nowhere with these devils,
   Still, it will add a chapter to my travels,
   And I hope, before my sands of life run out,
   To put foul fiends and poets all to rout.
MEPHISTO   He'll go and plump himself down in a puddle—
4015   It solaces him for all his ghostly trouble—
   And purge away his spirit and these other spirits
   By having leeches feed on where the M'sieur sits.
      [*To* FAUST, *who has broken off dancing and withdrawn*]
   What's this? You've left your partner in the lurch
   As she was sweetly singing, pretty witch.
4020 FAUST   Ugh! From her mouth a red mouse sprung
   In the middle of her song.

---

4. That is, "Anus Haunter" (Goethe's coinage)—a parodic allusion to Friedrich Nicolai (1733–1811), an Enlightenment author hostile to Goethe and to superstitious beliefs (he wrote of how hallucinations that he suffered were cured when leeches were applied to his buttocks).
5. A small town near Berlin; ghosts were reported there in 1799, but the story was later exposed as a hoax.

MEPHISTO   Is that anything to fuss about?
   And anyway it wasn't gray, was it?
   To take on so, to me, seems simply rudeness
4025   When you are sporting with your Phyllis.[6]
FAUST   And then I saw—
MEPHISTO   Saw what?
FAUST   Look there, Mephisto,
   At that lovely child, so pale, so wistful,
   Standing by herself. How painfully
   She makes her way along, how lifelessly,
4030   As if her feet were chained. To me,
   I must confess, it looks like Gretchen.
MEPHISTO   Let it be!
   It's bad, that thing, a lifeless shape, a wraith
   No man ever wants to meet up with.
   Your blood freezes under her dead stare,
4035   Almost turned to stone, you are.
   Medusa,[7] did you ever hear of her?
FAUST   Yes, yes, those are a corpse's eyes
   No loving hand was by to close.
   That's Gretchen's breast, which she so often
4040   Gave to me to rest my head on,
   That shape her dear, her lovely body
   She gave to me to enjoy freely.
MEPHISTO   It's all magic, hocus-pocus, idiot!
   Her power is, each thinks she is his sweetheart.
4045 FAUST   What rapture! And what suffering!
   I stand here spellbound by her look.
   How strange, that bit of scarlet string
   That ornaments her lovely neck,
   No thicker than a knife blade's back.
4050 MEPHISTO   Right you are. I see it, too.
   She's also perfectly able to
   Tuck her head beneath her arm
   And stroll about. Perseus[8]—remember him?—
   He was the one who hacked it off.
4055   —Man, I'd think you'd have enough of
   The mad ideas your head is stuffed with!
   Come, we'll climb this little hill where
   All's as lively as inside the Prater.[9]
   And unless somebody has bewitched me,
4060   The thing I see there is a theater.

---

6. That is, dallying with your lover. Phyllis is a conventional name of a shepherdess in pastoral poetry, used first in Theocritus's Greek *Idylls* (ca. 275 B.C.E.) and borrowed by Virgil for his Latin *Eclogues* (37 B.C.E.).
7. In Greek mythology, one of three snake-haired sisters called the Gorgons, the sight of whom turned all who looked at them to stone.
8. The mythological Greek hero who killed Medusa, looking only at her reflection in his bronze shield as he cut off her head.
9. A large public park in Vienna, opened in 1766.

What's happening?

SERVIBILIS   A play, a new one, starting shortly,
Last of seven. With us here it's customary
To offer a full repertory.
The playwright's a rank amateur,

4065   Amateurs, too, the whole company.
Well, I must hurry off now, please excuse me,
I need to raise the curtain—amateurishly!

MEPHISTO   How right it is that I should find you here, sirs;
The Blocksberg's[1] just the place for amateurs.

Walpurgis Night's Dream;
or
Oberon and Titania's Golden Wedding[2]

Intermezzo

4070   STAGE MANAGER [*To crew*]   Today we'll put by paint and canvas,
Mieding's brave sons,[3] all.
Nature paints the scene for us:
Gray steep and mist-filled vale.

HERALD   For the wedding to be golden,

4075   Years must pass, full fifty;
But if the quarrel is made up, then
It is golden truly.

OBERON   Spirits hovering all around,
Appear, dear imps, to me here!

4080   King and Queen are once more bound
Lovingly together.

PUCK   Here's Puck,[4] my lord, who spins and whirls
And cuts a merry caper,
A hundred follow at his heels,

4085   Skipping to the measure.

ARIEL   Ariel[5] strikes up his song,
The notes as pure as silver;
Philistines[6] all around him throng,
But those, too, with true culture.

4090   OBERON   Wives and husbands, learn from us
How two hearts unite:
To find connubial happiness,
Only separate.

TITANIA   If Master sulks and Mistress pouts,

---

1. That is, the Brocken.
2. In folklore, Oberon and Titania are king and queen of the fairies, as depicted in Shakespeare's comedy *A Midsummer Night's Dream* (ca. 1595).
3. That is, scene builders; Johann Martin Mieding (d. 1782) was a master carpenter for the amateur theater at the ducal court of Weimar, where Goethe was employed by the duke as privy councillor.

4. In folklore, a mischievous spirit or demon; he has a significant role in Shakespeare's *A Midsummer Night's Dream*.
5. A spirit in Shakespeare's *The Tempest* (ca. 1611).
6. Literally, biblical enemies of the Israelites; the name was applied by German students to those not at a university (and therefore unenlightened and uncultured).

4095   Here's the remedy:
        Send her on a trip down south,
        Send him the other way.

FULL ORCHESTRA [*Fortissimo*[7]]   Buzzing fly and humming gnat
        And all their consanguinity,
4100   Frog's hoarse croak, cicada's chirp
        Compose our symphony.

SOLO   Here I come, the bagpipes, who's
        Only a soap bubble.
        Hear me through my stumpy nose
4105   Go tootle-doodle-doodle.

A BUDDING IMAGINATION   A spider's foot, a green toad's gut,
        Two winglets—though a travesty
        Devoid of life and nature, yet
        It does as nonsense poetry.

4110 A YOUNG COUPLE   Short steps, smart leaps, all done neatly
        On the scented lawn—
        I grant you foot it very featly,[8]
        Yet we remain un-airborne.

AN INQUIRING TRAVELER   Can it be a fairground fraud,
4115   The shape at which I'm looking?
        Oberon the handsome god
        Still alive and kicking?

A PIOUS BELIEVER   I don't see claws, nor any tail,
        And yet it's indisputable:
4120   Like Greece's gods, his dishabille
        Shows he's a pagan devil.

AN ARTIST OF THE NORTH[9]   Here everything I undertake
        Is weak, is thin, is sketchy;
        But I'm preparing soon to make
4125   My Italian journey.

A STICKLER FOR DECORUM   I'm here, and most unhappily,
        Where all's impure, improper;
        Among this riotous witchery
        There's only two wear powder.

4130 A YOUNG WITCH   Powder, like a petticoat,
        Is right for wives with gray hair;
        But I'll sit naked on my goat,
        Show off my strapping figure.

A MATRON   We are too well bred by far
4135   To bandy words about:
        But may you, young thing that you are,
        Drop dead, and soon, cheap tart.

THE CONDUCTOR   Don't crowd so round the naked charmer,
        On with the concerto!

7. Very loud (Italian); a common musical
direction.
8. Nimbly; elegantly.
9. A character who represents Goethe him-

self; the journals he wrote while traveling in
Italy in the 1780s were published as *Italian
Journeys* (1816–17).

4140   Frog and blowfly, gnat, cicada—
    Mind you keep the tempo.
  A WEATHERCOCK [*Pointing one way*]
    No better company than maids
    Like these, kind and complaisant,
    And bachelors to match, old boys
4145   Agog all, all impatient!
  WEATHERCOCK [*Pointing the other way*]
    And if the earth don't open up
    And swallow this lewd rabble,
    Off I'll race at a great clip,
    Myself go to the Devil.
4150 SATIRICAL EPIGRAMS [XENIEN][1] We are gadflies, plant our sting
    In hides highborn and bourgeois,
    By so doing honoring
    Great Satan, our dear dada.
  HENNINGS[2] Look there at the pack of them,
4155   Like schoolboys jeering meanly.
    Next, I'm sure, they all will claim
    It's all in fun, friends, really.
  MUSAGET ["LEADER OF THE MUSES"]
    If I joined these witches here,
    I'm sure I'd not repine;
4160   I know I'd find it easier
    To lead them than the Nine.
  [A JOURNAL] FORMERLY [ENTITLED] "THE SPIRIT OF THE AGE"
    What counts is knowing the right people,
    With me, sir, you'll go places;
    The Blocksberg's got a place for all,
4165   Like Germany's Parnassus.[3]
  THE INQUIRING TRAVELER Who's that fellow who's so stiff
    And marches so majestical?
    He sniffs away for all he's worth
    "Pursuing things Jesuitical."
4170 A CRANE An earnest fisherman I am
    In clear and muddy waters,
    And thus it is a pious man
    'S seen hobnobbing with devils.
  A CHILD OF THIS WORLD All occasions serve the godly
4175   In their work. Atop
    The Blocksberg, even there, they
    Set up religious shop.

---

1. In 1796 Goethe and his fellow poet Friedrich Schiller (1759–1805) collaborated on *The Xenia* (in German, *Die Xenien*), a collection of epigrams satirizing the literary criticism of the era.

2. August Friedrich Hennings (1746–1826), editor of two journals whose names Goethe also borrows: *Musaget* (from the Greek *Mousēgetēs*, or "Leader of the Muses," an epithet of the god Apollo; 1798–99) and *Der Genius der Zeit* (*The Spirit of the Age*; 1794–1800), in which he attacked Goethe and Schiller.

3. A mountain in central Greece sacred to Apollo and the nine Muses and therefore associated with poetry.

A DANCER   What's that drumming, a new bunch
    Of musicians coming?
4180   No, no, they're bitterns in the marsh
    In *unisono* booming.
THE DANCING MASTER   How cautiously each lifts a foot,
    All the hard steps ducking,
    The crippled hop, they jump the stout,
4185   Heedless how they're looking.
THE FIDDLER   This riffraff's so hate-filled, each lusts
    To slit the other's throat;
    Orpheus with his lute tamed beasts.[4]
    These march to the bagpipes' note.
4190 A DOGMATIST   You can't rattle me by all,
    Your questionings and quibbles;
    The Devil is perfectly evil, hence real—
    For perfection entails existence: so devils.
AN IDEALIST   The mind's creative faculty
4195   This time has gone too far.
    If everything I see is me,
    I'm crazy, that's for sure.
A REALIST   It's pandemonium, it's mad,
    Oh, I feel so cast down;
4200   This is the first time I have stood
    On such shaky ground.
A SUPERNATURALIST   The presence of these devils here
    For me's reassuring evidence;
    From the demonical I infer
4205   The angelical's existence.
A SKEPTIC   They see a flickering light and gloat,
    There's treasure there, oh surely;
    Devil's a word that pairs with doubt,[5]
    This is a place that suits me.
4210 CONDUCTOR   Buzzing fly and humming gnat—
    What damned amateurs!
    Frog's hoarse croak, cicada's chirp—
    They call themselves performers!
THE SMART ONES   Sans all souci[6] we are, shift
4215   About with lightning speed;
    When walking on the feet is out,
    We walk upon the head.
THE NOT-SO-SMART ONES   At court we sat down to free dinners,
    And now, dear God, there's naught!
4220   We've worn out our dancing slippers
    And limp along barefoot.
WILL-O'-THE-WISPS   We're from the bottom lands, the swamps,
    Such is our lowly origin;

---

4. Orpheus (see note to line 140) had the
power to move animals, trees, and stones
with his music.
5. The German word *Teufel* (devil) has a par-

tial rhyme with *Zweifel* (doubt).
6. A play on the French expression *sans souci*,
"without worry."

4225

But now we sparkle as gallants
And dance in the cotillion.

A SHOOTING STAR   I shot across the sky's expanse,
A meteor, blazing bright.
Now fallen, I sprawl in the grass—
Who'll help me to my feet?

4230   THE BRUISERS   Look out, look out, we're coming through,
Trampling your lawn.
We're spirits too, but spirits who
Have lots of beef and brawn.

PUCK   Don't tramp like that, so heavily,

4235   Like young elephants.
Let robust Puck's own stamp today
Be the heaviest.

ARIEL   If you have wings, gift from kind Nature,
Or gift you owe the spirit,

4240   As I fly, fly close after,
Up to the rose hill's summit.

ORCHESTRA [*Pianissimo*[7]]
The shrouding mists and thick-massed clouds
Lighten in the dawn,
The breeze stirs leaves, wind rattles reeds,

4245   And all is scattered, gone.

An Overcast Day. A Field

[FAUST *and* MEPHISTOPHELES.]

FAUST   In misery! In despair! Stumbling about pitifully over the earth for so
long, and now a prisoner! A condemned criminal, shut up in a dungeon
and suffering horrible torments, the poor unfortunate child! It's come to
this, to this! And not a word about it breathed to me, you treacherous, odi-

4250   ous spirit! Stand there rolling your Devil's eyes around in rage, oh do! Brazen
it out with your intolerable presence! A prisoner! In misery, irremediable
misery! Delivered up to evil spirits and the stony-hearted justice of mankind!
And meanwhile you distract me with your insipid entertainments, keep
her situation, more desperate every day, from me, and leave her to perish

4255   helplessly!

MEPHISTO   She's[8] not the first.

FAUST   You dog, you monster! Change him, O you infinite Spirit, change the
worm back into a dog, give it back the shape it wore those evenings when it
liked to trot ahead of me and roll under the feet of some innocent wayfarer,

4260   tripping him up and leaping on him as he fell. Give it back its favorite
shape so it can crawl on its belly in the sand before me, and I can kick it as
it deserves, the abomination!—Not the first!—Such misery, such misery!
It's inconceivable, humanly inconceivable, that more than one creature
should ever have plumbed such depths of misery, that the first who did,

4265   writhing in her last agony under the eyes of the Eternal Forgiveness,
shouldn't have expiated the guilt of all the others who came after! I am cut

---

7. Very soft (Italian); a common musical
direction.

8. That is, Margarete (Gretchen).

to the quick, pierced to the marrow, by the suffering of this one being—you grin indifferently at the fate of thousands!

MEPHISTO   So once again we're at our wits' end, are we—reached the point where you fellows start feeling your brain is about to explode? Why did you ever throw in with us if you can't see the thing through? You'd like to fly but don't like heights. Did we force ourselves on you or you on us?

FAUST   Don't snarl at me that way with those wolfish fangs of yours, it sickens me!—Great and glorious Spirit, Spirit who vouchsafed to appear to me, who knows me in my heart and soul, why did you fasten me to this scoundrel who diets on destruction, delights to hurt?

MEPHISTO   Finished yet?

FAUST   Save her or you'll pay for it! With a curse on you, the dreadfulest there is, for thousands of years to come!

MEPHISTO   I'm powerless to strike off the Great Avenger's chains or draw his bolts.—Save her indeed!—Who's the one who ruined her, I would like to know—you or me?

[FAUST *looks around wildly.*]

Looking for a thunderbolt,[9] are you? A good thing you wretched mortals weren't given them. That's the tyrant's way of getting out of difficulties— strike down any innocent person who makes an objection, gets in his way.

FAUST   Take me to where she is, you hear? She's got to be set free.

MEPHISTO   In spite of the risk you would run? There's blood guilt on the town because of what you did. Where murder was, there the avenging spirits hover, waiting for the murderer to return.

FAUST   That from you, that too? Death and destruction, a world's worth, on your head, you monster! Take me there, I say, and set her free!

MEPHISTO   All right, all right, I'll carry you there. But hear what I can do—do you think all the powers of heaven and earth are mine? I'll muddle the turnkey's senses, then you seize his keys and lead her out. Only a human hand can do it. I'll keep watch. The spirit horses are ready. Off I'll carry both of you. That's what I can do.

FAUST   Very well. Let's go!

Night. Open Country

[FAUST *and* MEPHISTOPHELES *going by on black horses at a furious gallop.*]

FAUST   What's going on there, at the ravenstone?

MEPHISTO   Cooking up, getting up, something, who cares?

FAUST   Now here, now there, hovering, bowing, genuflecting.

MEPHISTO   A pack of witches.

FAUST   Hands strewing, consecrating.

MEPHISTO   Keep going, keep going!

A Prison

FAUST [*With a bunch of keys and carrying a lamp, at a narrow iron door*]
    I shudder as I haven't for so long—
    It overcomes me, all of mankind's misery!
    She's shut up inside these dank walls, poor thing,

9. In classical mythology, the weapon of the king of the gods, Zeus (Greek) or Jupiter (Roman).

And all her crime was love, the brave, the illusory.
You're hanging back from going in!
You're afraid of meeting her eyes again!

4310 In, in, your hesitation's her death, hurry!

[*He puts the key in the lock.*]

SINGING [*From within*]
My mother, the whore,
She's the one slew me!
My father, the knave,
He's the one ate me!

4315 My sister, wee thing,
Heaped up my bones
Underneath stones.
Then I became a pretty woodbird—
Fly away, fly away!

4320 FAUST [*Unlocking the door*] She doesn't dream her lover's listening.
Hears her chains rattle, the straw rustling.

[*He enters.*]

MARGARETE [*Cowering on her paillasse*]
They're coming, they're coming! How bitter, death, bitter!
FAUST [*Whispering*] Hush, dear girl, hush! You'll soon be free.
MARGARETE [*Groveling before him*]
If your heart's human, think how I suffer.

4325 FAUST   You'll wake the guards. Speak quietly.

[*Taking hold of the chains to unlock them*]

MARGARETE   [*On her knees*] Headsman, so early, it isn't right.
Have mercy on me! Too soon, too soon!
You come for me in the dead of night—
Isn't it time enough at dawn?

[*Stands up*]

4330 I'm still so young, too young surely—
Still I must die.
How pretty I was, that's what undid me.
He held me so close, now he's far away,
My wreath pulled apart, the flowers scattered.

4335 Don't grip me so hard, please, won't you spare me?
What did I ever do to you?
Don't let me beg in vain for mercy,
I never before laid eyes on you.
FAUST   It's unendurable, her misery,

4340 MARGARETE   What can I do, I'm in your power.
Only let me nurse my baby first,
All night long I hugged the dear creature;
How mean they were, snatched it from my breast,
And now they say I murdered it.

4345 And I'll never be happy, no, never again.
They sing songs about me in the street;
It's wicked of them.
There's an old fairy tale ends that way—
What has it got to do with me?

4350 FAUST [*Falling at her feet*]   It's me here who loves you, me, at your feet,
     To rescue you from this miserable fate.
     MARGARETE [*Kneeling beside him*]
     We'll kneel down, that's right, and pray to the saints.
     Look, under those steps,
     Below the doorsill,
4355 All Hell's a-boil!
     The Evil One
     In his horrible rage
     Makes such a noise.
     FAUST [*Crying out*]   Gretchen! Gretchen!
4360 MARGARETE [*Listening*]   That was my darling's own dear voice!
          [*She jumps up, the chains fall away.*]
     I heard him call. Where can he be?
     No one may stop me now, I'm free!
     Into his arms I'll run so fast,
     Lie on his breast at last, at last.
4365 Gretchen, he called, from there on the sill.
     Through all the howlings and gnashings of Hell,
     Through the furious, devilish sneering and scorn,
     I heard a dear voice, its sound so well known.
     FAUST   It's me!
4370 MARGARETE   It's you! Oh, say it again.
          [*Catching hold of him*]
     It's him! Where is the torture now, it's him!
     Where's my fear of the prison, the chains they put on me,
     It's you, it's you, you've come here to save me!
     I'm saved!
4375 —I see it before me, so very clear,
     The street I saw you the first time on,
     I see Marthe and me where we waited for you
     In the sunlit garden.
     FAUST [*Pulling her toward the door*]
     Come along, come!
     MARGARETE   Don't go, stay here!
4380 I love it so being wherever you are.
          [*Caressing him*]
     FAUST   Hurry!
     If you don't hurry,
     The price we will pay!
     MARGARETE   What? Don't know how to kiss anymore?
4385 Parted from me a short time only
     And quite forgotten what lips are for?
     Why am I frightened with your arms around me?
     Time was, at a word or a look from you,
     Straight to heaven I was transported
4390 And you kissed me as if you'd devour me.
     Kiss me, kiss me!
     Or I'll kiss you!
          [*She embraces him.*]

What cold lips you have,
You don't speak, look dumbly.
4395   What's become of your love?
Who took it from me?

[*She turns away from him.*]

FAUST   Come, follow me! Darling, be brave!
Oh, the kisses I'll give you, my love—
Only come now, we'll slip through that door.

MARGARETE [*Turning back to him*]
4400   Is it really you? Can I be sure?

FAUST   Yes, it's me—you must come!

MARGARETE   You strike off my chains,
Take me into your arms.
How is it you don't shrink away from me?
Have you any idea who you're letting go free?

4405 FAUST   Hurry, hurry! The night's almost over.

MARGARETE   I murdered my mother,
Drowned my infant,
Weren't both of us given it, you too its parent,
Given you, too? It's you, I can hardly believe it.
4410   Give me your hand. No, I haven't dreamt it.
Your dear hand!—But your hand is wet!
Wipe it off, there's blood on it!
My God, my God, what did you do?
Put away your sword,
4415   I beg you to!

FAUST   What's past is done, forget it all.
You're killing me.

MARGARETE   No, live on still.
I'll tell you how the graves should be;
4420   Tomorrow you must see to it.
Give my mother the best spot,
My brother put alongside her,
Me, put me some distance off,
Yet not too far,
4425   And at my right breast put my baby.
Nobody else shall lie beside me.
When I used to press up close to you,
How sweet it was, pure happiness,
But now I can't, it's over, all such bliss—
4430   I feel it as an effort I must make,
That I must force myself on you,
And you, I feel, resist me, push me back.
And yet it's you, with your good, kind look.

FAUST   If it's me, then come, we mustn't stay.

4435 MARGARETE   Out there?

FAUST   Out there, away!

MARGARETE   If the grave's out there, death waiting for me,
Come, yes, come! The two of us together!
But only to the last place, there, no other.

—You're going now?

4440   I'd go too if I could, Heinrich, believe me!

FAUST   You can! All you need is the will. Come on!
       The way is clear.

MARGARETE   No, I mayn't, for me all hope is gone.
       It's useless, flight. They'd keep, I'm sure,

4445   A sharp watch out. I'd find it dreadful
       To have to beg my bread of people,
       Beg with a bad conscience, too;
       Dreadful to have to wander about
       Where all is strange and new,

4450   Only to end up getting caught.

FAUST   But I'll stick to you!

MARGARETE   Quick, be quick!
       Save your child, run!
       Keep to the path

4455   That goes up by the brook,
       Over the bridge,
       Into the wood,
       Left where the plank is,
       There, in the pool—

4460   Reach down and catch it!
       It wants to come up,
       It's struggling still!
       Save it, save it!

FAUST   Get hold of yourself!

4465   One step and you're free, dear girl!

MARGARETE   If only we were well past the hill!
       On the rock over there Mother's sitting—
       I'm shaking with fear, I'm cold, feel a chill.
       She sits on the rock, her head heavy, nodding,

4470   Doesn't look, doesn't wave, can't hold it up straight,
       Her sleep was so long she will never wake.
       She slept so we might have our pleasure—
       The happy hours we passed together!

FAUST   If all my persuading is no use,

4475   I'll have to carry you off by force.

MARGARETE   Let go, let go, how dare you compel me!
       You're gripping me so brutally!
       I always did what you wanted, once.

FAUST   Soon day will be breaking! Darling, darling!

4480 MARGARETE   Day? Yes, day, my last one, dawning,
       My wedding day it should have been.
       Not a word to a soul, you've already been with your Gretchen.
       My poor wreath!
       Well, everything's finished, it's done.

4485   We'll see one another again,
       But not to go dancing.
       The crowd's collecting, silent, numb,
       The square and the streets lack enough room.

There goes the bell, now the staff shatters,
4490 They seize hold of me, fasten the fetters
And drag me bound to the block.
How it twitches, the skin on each neck,
As the axe-blade's about to strike mine.
Dumb lies the world as the grave.

4495 FAUST   I wish I had never been born!

MEPHISTOPHELES [*Appearing outside*]
Unless you come you are lost, now come on!
Shilly-shallying, debating, jabbering!
My horses are trembling.
A minute or two and it's day.

4500 MARGARETE   Who's that rising up out of the ground?
It's him, him, oh drive him away!
It's holy here, what does he want?
Me, he wants me!

FAUST   Live, I say!—live!

MARGARETE   It's the judgment of God! I submit!

4505 MEPHISTO   Die both of you, I have to leave.

MARGARETE   In your hands, our Father! oh, save me!
You angelical hosts, stand about me,
Draw up in your ranks to protect me!
I'm afraid of you, Heinrich, afraid!

4510 MEPHISTO   She's condemned.

VOICE [*From above*]

                                    She is saved!

MEPHISTO [*To* FAUST, *peremptorily*]
Now come on, I tell you, with me!
[*He disappears with* FAUST.]

VOICE   [*From within, dying away*]
Heinrich! Heinrich!

AESCHYLUS

Critical commentary on *Agamemnon* begins with the comic playwright Aristophanes, in *The Frogs* (405 B.C.E.), and also includes the first philosophical commentator on drama, Aristotle. As was true of other Greek playwrights, Aeschylus's plays survived through a series of historical accidents, including the actions of scribes at the Library of Alexandria, Roman scholars and teachers, and finally Renaissance humanists who excavated his largely forgotten texts after centuries of oblivion. Of all the Greek tragedians, Aeschylus is the most difficult to translate, owing to his dense poetic language. The translation selected for this anthology, by Robert Fagles (1975), is the most readable, while retaining much of the visual richness of the original. Students interested in the play may also want to consult the translation by Richmond Lattimore (1947), which stays closer to the syntax and language of the original. A more fluid translation is by Peter Meineck, an edition that also contains a particularly good introduction by Helene Foley (1998). One of the main interests of the critical literature devoted to Aeschylus has been the question of the origin of Greek tragedy. A classic in the field is George Thomson's *Aeschylus and Athens: A Study in the Social Origins of Drama* (1941). An excellent book on Aeschylus's language is Anne Lebeck's *The Oresteia: A Study in Language and Structure* (1971). Another insightful study of Aeschylus is Alan Sommer-

stein's *Aeschylean Tragedy* (1996). Froma Zeitlin's *Playing the Other: Gender and Society in Classical Greek Literature* (1996) contains a particularly good reading of the *Oresteia* from a gender perspective. Thomas G. Rosenmeyer's *The Art of Aeschylus* (1982) also pays close attention to language, including meter and rhythm, as part of an extensive close reading and discussion of the playwright and his craft. Rosenmeyer also analyzes the development of the theater, a topic more fully explored in David Wiles's *Tragedy in Athens: Performance Space and Theatrical Meaning* (1997) and in Sir Arthur Pickard-Cambridge's classic, *The Dramatic Festivals of Athens* (1953; 2nd ed., 1968). Eric Csapo and William J. Slater's *The Context of Ancient Drama* (1994) provides further valuable primary resources on all aspects of classical theater in production. Representative essays on the *Oresteia* can be found in Harold Bloom's collection *Aeschylus's "The Oresteia"* (1988). A good general introduction to all aspects of Greek tragedy is *The Cambridge Companion to Greek Tragedy* (1997), edited by P. E. Easterling, as well as Simon Goldhill's *Reading Greek Tragedy* (1986).

ARISTOPHANES

For a detailed description of the competitions and how they were staged, see Sir Arthur Pickard-Cambridge, *The Dramatic Festivals of Athens* (2nd ed., 1968). Eric Csapo and William

J. Slater's *The Context of Ancient Drama* (1994) provides further valuable primary resources on all aspects of classical theater in production. Useful overviews of the work of Aristophanes include K. J. Dover, *Aristophanic Comedy* (1972); A. M. Bowie, *Aristophanes: Myth, Ritual and Comedy* (1993); David Konstan, *Greek Comedy and Ideology* (1995) and James Robson, *Aristophanes: An Introduction* (2009). Two thematic studies with particular relevance to *Lysistrata* are Jeffrey Henderson, *The Maculate Muse: Obscene Language in Attic Comedy* (1975; 2nd ed., 1991), and Lauren K. Taaffe, *Aristophanes and Women* (1993). John Vaio's "The Manipulation of Theme and Action in Aristophanes' *Lysistrata*" (1973) and Jeffrey Henderson's "*Lysistrata*: The Play and Its Themes" (1980) provide excellent, detailed readings of the play, while Niall Slater's "Making the Aristophanic Audience" (1999) offers hypotheses about classic comedies in performance. The scholarly translations by Alan H. Sommerstein (2002), Jeffrey Henderson (1996), and Stephen Halliwell (1997) all offer detailed introductions and textual analysis of this complex and challenging text.

APHRA BEHN

Maureen Duffy, *The Passionate Shepherdess: Aphra Behn, 1640–89* (1977); Angeline Goreau, *Reconstructing Aphra: A Social Biography of Aphra Behn* (1980); George Woodcock, *Aphra Behn: The English Sappho* (1989); and Janet Todd, *The Secret Life of Aphra Behn* (1996) are the most recent and authoritative of a series of biographical studies. Todd's *The Sign of Angellica: Women, Writing, and Fiction, 1660–1800* (1989) documents the increasing presence and impact of women writers in England. Todd's edited volume, *Aphra Behn Studies* (1996), provides additional recent perspectives on Behn's work as a dramatist, poet, and fiction writer and further augments the Behn biographies, as does her volume edition with Derek Hughes, *The Cambridge Companion to Aphra Behn* (2004). Heidi Hutner's edited volume, *Rereading Aphra Behn: History, Theory, and Criticism* (1993), contributes other important essays on Behn's writing in all major genres. Individual essays on her work from a range of critical perspectives abound. For comparisons of *The Rover* and *Thomaso*, see especially Jones DeRitter, "The Gypsy, *The Rover*, and the Wanderer: Aphra Behn's Revision of Thomas Killigrew" (1986), and Elaine Hobby,

"No Stolen Object, but Her Own: Aphra Behn's *Rover* and Thomas Killigrew's *Thomaso*" (1999). For studies of the setting of the play, see Linda R. Payne, "The Carnivalesque Regeneration of Corrupt Economies in *The Rover*" (1998), and Dagny Boebel, "In the Carnival World of Adam's Garden: Roving and Rape in Behn's *Rover*," in *Broken Boundaries: Women and Feminism in Restoration Drama,* ed. Katherine M. Quinsey (1996). Readings that incorporate important considerations of staging and performance include Elin Diamond, "*Gestus* and Signature in Aphra Behn's *The Rover*" (1989), and John Franceschina, "Shadow and Substance in Aphra Behn's *The Rover*: The Semiotics of Restoration Performance" (1995). Mary Anne O'Donnell has compiled the useful reference volume *Aphra Behn: An Annotated Bibliography of Primary and Secondary Sources* (1986; 2nd ed., 2004). Among the growing body of historical and critical writings on Restoration drama and theater practice, see Robert D. Hume, *The Development of English Drama in the Late Seventeenth Century* (1976) and his *Rakish Stage: Studies in English Drama, 1660–1800* (1983); J. Douglas Canfield and Deborah C. Payne, eds., *Cultural Readings of Restoration and Eighteenth-Century English Theater* (1995); Laura Brown, *English Dramatic Form, 1660–1760: An Essay in Generic History* (1981); J. L. Styan, *Restoration Comedy in Performance* (1986); Mary Anne Schofield and Cecilia Macheski, eds., *Curtain Calls: British and American Women and Theater, 1660–1820* (1991); Jocelyn Powell, *Restoration Theatre Production* (1984); and Deborah Payne Fisk, ed., *The Cambridge Companion to English Restoration Theatre* (2000), which also contains a very useful bibliography. The definitive reference work for documenting performances of the period remains William Van Lennep et al., eds., *The London Stage, 1660–1800: A Calendar of Plays, Entertainments, and Afterpieces, together with Casts, Box-Receipts, and Contemporary Comment,* 5 vols. (1960–68).

PEDRO CALDERÓN DE LA BARCA

There is a growing body of scholarship in English relevant to the Spanish Golden Age and the works of Calderón. N. D. Shergold's *A History of the Spanish Stage: From Medieval Times Until the End of the Seventeenth Century* (1967) remains the standard source for the stage history of this period. Mary Parker's edited volume, *Spanish Dramatists of the Golden Age: A*

Bio-bibliographical Sourcebook (1998), provides a useful starting point for research on Calderón and his contemporaries. Don W. Cruickshank's *Don Pedro Calderón* (2009) is the first comprehensive biography in English. Bruce W. Wardropper edited a collection, *Critical Essays on the Theatre of Calderón* (1965), that includes much of the foundational scholarship that shaped the field. Alexander A. Parker's *The Mind and Art of Calderón: Essays on the Comedias* (1988) provides detailed readings. Dian Fox, *Kings in Calderón: A Study in Characterization and Political Theory* (1986), and Stephen Rupp, *Allegories of Kingship* (1996), both take up the central issue of leadership, while Fox considers these and other issues further in her *Refiguring the Hero: From Peasant to Noble in Lope de Vega and Calderón* (1991). Frederick A. de Armas and Manuel Delgado Morales have each edited cogent collections of criticism, *The Prince in the Tower: Perceptions of "La vida es sueño"* (1993) and *The Calderónian Stage: Body and Soul* (1997), respectively. The concluding chapter of Jackson I. Cope's *The Theater and the Dream: From Metaphor to Form in Renaissance Drama* (1973) explores some of the philosophical traditions that informed the play. Alan K. G. Paterson's "The Traffic of the Stage in Calderón's *La vida es sueño*" (1971) considers the relationship between staging and interpretation. C. Christopher Soufas and Teresa Scott Soufas, in "*La vida es sueño* and Post-Modern Sensibilities: Towards a New 'Method of Analysis and Interpretation,'" in *Studies in Honor of Bruce W. Wardropper*, ed. Dian Fox (1989), provide a balanced and articulate overview of some of the conflicting threads in Calderón criticism.

SOR JUANA INÉS DE LA CRUZ

There is no English translation of Sor Juana's complete works. Volumes of selected writings appeared in Spanish as early as 1676, but the definitive four-volume collection, edited by Alfonso Méndez Plancarte, was not published until 1951–57. The *loa* to *The Divine Narcissus* exists in three English translations, by Willis K. Jones (1966), Margaret Sayers Peden (1985), and Patricia A. Peters (1998); the Peden and Peters volumes also contain very useful critical introductions. The major critical biography of Sor Juana in English remains that of Octavio Paz, *Sor Juana; or, The Traps of Faith*, translated by Peden (1982; trans. 1988). The critical introductions to Peden's translation of Sor Juana's prose,

A Woman of Genius: The Intellectual Autobiography of Sor Juana Inés de la Cruz (1982), and to Electa Arenal and Amanda Powell's translation of *La Respuesta* (1994), provide further insights. Gerald Flynn's volume for the Twayne series, *Sor Juana Inés de la Cruz* (1971), contains a helpful, if limited, overview of her life and works. George H. Tavard's *Juana Inés de la Cruz and the Theology of Beauty: The First Mexican Theology* (1991) considers her primarily as a religious writer, while Pamela Kirk's *Sor Juana Inés de la Cruz: Religion, Art, and Feminism* (1998) examines in her work the interrelated elements named in the subtitle. Stephanie Merrim's *Early Modern Women's Writing and Sor Juana Inés de la Cruz* (1999) and her edited collection, *Feminist Perspectives on Sor Juana Inés de la Cruz* (1991), are the primary studies for feminist considerations of Sor Juana. The essay collections *A Reader in Latina Feminist Theology: Religion and Justice*, eds. María Pilar Aquino, Daisy L. Machado, and Jeanette Rodríguez (2002), and *Women, Culture, and Politics in Latin America*, by Emilie Bergmann et al. (1990), both contain useful pieces on Sor Juana in the context of Latin American studies. Comparatively little critical attention has focused on Sor Juana's *loas* with the exception of Lee A. Daniel's *The Loa of Sor Juana Inés de la Cruz* (1994). To gain an understanding of the *loa* and the *auto sacramental* in theater history, see Melveena McKendrick, *Theatre in Spain, 1490–1700* (1989).

EURIPIDES
Medea

Donald J. Mastronarde provides a helpful overview of Euripides' dramas in *The Art of Euripides: Dramatic Technique and Social Context* (2010). Other useful sources include the collection of essays *Greek Tragedy*, volume XXV of the *Yale Classical Studies* series, eds. T. F. Gould and C. J. Herington (1977), with essays by B. M. W. Knox ("The *Medea* of Euripides") and P. E. Easterling ("The Infanticide in Euripides' *Medea*). Some of the most significant research on *Medea* has appeared in scholarly journals. Anne Burnett's "*Medea* and the Tragedy of Revenge," published in *Classical Philology* (1973), has been particularly influential. Helene Foley's "Medea's Divided Self," which appeared in *Classical Antiquity* (1989), and Judith Fletcher's "Women and Oaths in Euripides," published in a special issue of *Theatre Journal* devoted to ancient theater (1983), are both worthwhile. Froma Zeitlin's *Playing the Other: Gender and Society in Classical Greek Literature* (1996) is a major study using feminist critical techniques. Anton Powell's edited volume *Euripides, Women, and Sexuality* (1990) also provides analyses of gender and sexuality in a select group of plays; Margaret Williamson's essay "A Woman's Place in Euripides' *Medea*" is an especially valuable contribution. Nancy Sorkin Rabinowitz, *Anxiety Veiled: Euripides and the Traffic in Women* (2003), offers a particularly insightful reading of Medea's character in the context of Euripidean dramaturgy. Several recent English-language translations of *Medea* include highly useful scholarly introductions. Foremost among these are Peter D. Arnott's *Three Greek Plays for the Theatre* (1961), John Harrison's *Medea* (2000), J. Michael Walton and Marianne McDonald's introduction to Walton's *Medea* (2002), and Robin Mitchell-Boysak's introduction to Diane Arnson Svarlien's *Euripides: Alcestis, Medea, Hippolytus* (2007), the source of the translation selected for this anthology. Emma Griffith's *Medea* (2006) offers a historical overview of this mythic figure, while *Medea in Performance, 1500–2000* (2000), ed. Edith Hall, Fiona Macintosh, and Oliver Taplin, provides a comprehensive study of the global appearance and influence of this character in the performing arts. Taplin's *Pots and Plays: Interactions between Tragedy and Greek Vase-Painting of the Fourth Century* (2007) makes a case for the use of vase imagery to understand both the influence of Greek drama on other art forms and its possible staging.

The Bacchae

Preserved through a series of historical accidents, the text of *The Bacchae* contains some omissions toward the end of the play and poses other intricate problems for those trying to establish an authoritative text. Classic studies of the playwright and the play are R. P. Winnington-Ingram's *Euripides and Dionysus: An Interpretation of the "Bacchae"* (1948) and H. D. F. Kitto's *Greek Tragedy: A Literary Study* (1939). Especially attuned to intricate construction of the play is Charles Segal's *Dionysiac Poetics and Euripides' "Bacchae"* (1982), which is informed by recent trends in philosophy and literary theory. Given the play's central concern with ritual and sacrifice, many commentators have mined the play for clues about the origin of Greek tragedy. Anthropology has been an especially

important influence on such studies: for example, see *Myth and Tragedy in Ancient Greece* (1972, trans. 1988) by Jean-Pierre Vernant and Pierre Vidal-Naquet. René Girard's *Violence and the Sacred* (1972, trans. 1977) uses the structural analysis of myth by the French theorist Claude Lévi-Strauss to illuminate the play. Also influenced by these theorists is Helene P. Foley's excellent *Ritual Irony: Poetry and Sacrifice in Euripides* (1985), which pays particular attention to gender. Richard Seaford's *Reciprocity and Ritual: Homer and Tragedy in the Developing City-State* (1994) relates tragedy to the political history of Athens. For information about the Dionysus festival of Athens, consult David Wiles's *Tragedy in Athens: Performing Space and Theatrical Meaning* (1997) and Sir Arthur Pickard-Cambridge's *The Dramatic Festivals of Athens* (1953; 2nd ed., 1968). Erica Csapo and William J. Slater's *The Context of Ancient Drama* (1994) provides further valuable primary resources on all aspects of classical theater in production. Good general introductions to all aspects of Greek tragedy are provided by *The Cambridge Companion to Greek Tragedy* (1997), edited by P. E. Easterling, and Simon Goldhill's *Reading Greek Tragedy* (1986).

EVERYMAN

A. C. Cawley's 1961 *Everyman* is the most widely cited text of the play; Cawley's introduction to this edition gives valuable background information. A more recent edition of *Everyman* can be found in Douglas Bruster and Eric Rasmussen, eds., *Everyman and Mankind* (2009), which appears in the Arden Early Modern Drama series. *The Mirror of Everyman's Salvation: A Prose Translation of the Original Everyman*, eds. John Conley, Guido de Baere, H. J. C. Schaap, and W. H. Toppen (1985), includes both the text of *Everyman* and a translation of the Dutch *Elckerlijc*. Important critical studies of *Everyman* include Lawrence V. Ryan, "Doctrine and Dramatic Structure in *Everyman*" (1957); Thomas F. Van Laan, "*Everyman*: A Structural Analysis" (1963); V. A. Kolve, "*Everyman* and the Parable of the Talents" (1972); C. J. Wortham, "*Everyman* and the Reformation" (1981); Carolynn Van Dyke, "The Intangible and Its Image: Allegorical Discourse and the Cast of *Everyman*" (1982); Donald F. Duclow, "*Everyman* and the *Ars moriendi*: Fifteenth-Century Ceremonies of Dying" (1983); Phoebe S. Spinrad, "The Last Temptation of Everyman" (1985); Stanton

B. Garner, Jr., "Theatricality in *Mankind* and *Everyman*" (1987); Jacqueline Vanhoutte, "When Elckerlijc Becomes Everyman: Translating Dutch to English, Performance to Print" (1995); David Mills, "The Theaters of *Everyman*" (1995); Elizabeth Harper and Britt Mize, "Material Economy, Spiritual Economy, and Social Critique in *Everyman*" (2006); and Julie Paulson, "Death's Arrival and Everyman's Separation" (2007). Robert Potter's *The English Morality Play: Origins, History and Influence of a Dramatic Tradition* (1975) discusses the influential 1901 revival of *Everyman* and the play's twentieth-century reputation.

JOHANN WOLFGANG VON GOETHE

Not surprisingly, given Goethe's early and lasting fame and the many fields of his intellectual activity, the critical literature in English alone is both rich and overwhelming. George Henry Lewes, the life partner of George Eliot, wrote the first, and still immensely readable, biography of Goethe in English (2 vols., 1855). Nicholas Boyle's *Goethe: The Poet and the Age*, 2 vols. (1991), is the most recent and one of the most extensive and informative biographies of Goethe and his work. More compact is John R. William's *The Life of Goethe: A Critical Biography* (1998), which is divided by genre and thus provides a good and concise overview of Goethe's dramatic work. A classic study of *Faust* in English is Stuart Atkins's *Goethe's Faust: A Literary Analysis* (1958), a close textual analysis of the play in the tradition of the New Critics. John R. William's *Goethe's Faust* (1987) is more varied in its method and includes a useful discussion of the different sources, versions, and revisions that led to the final text. Most attuned to literary form is Benjamin Bennett's *Goethe's Theory of Poetry: Faust and the Regeneration of Language* (1986), which discusses Goethe's use and interruption of the traditional tragic plot as well as other stylistic devices. The most compelling discussion of *Faust* in terms of genre is found in Franco Moretti's *Modern Epic: The World-System from Goethe to García Márquez* (1994; trans. 1996).

The scholarship on Goethe and theater history is much less extensive. One fortunate exception is Marvin Carlson's *Goethe and the Weimar Theatre* (1978), which details Goethe's involvement with the theater, his theory of acting, and his vision of the stage. A far briefer overview of Goethe's engagement with the stage is offered in a chapter of Michael Patterson's *The First German Theatre: Schiller, Goethe, Kleist, and Büchner in Performance* (1990). Goethe's *Faust* has also attracted the attention of philosophers and cultural critics. A mid-twentieth-century example was the Marxist critic Georg Lukács, whose *Goethe and His Age* (1947; trans. 1968) places Goethe within the history of political and social upheaval and argues against a simple denunciation of Goethe as a political reactionary. This line of interpretation was later taken up by Marshall Berman, whose powerful *All That Is Solid Melts into Air: The Experience of Modernity* (1982) reads *Faust* alongside Marx and Engels's *Communist Manifesto* (1848), written some fifteen years after Goethe's death, as an expression of modernist upheaval and productivity. Peter Sloterdijk's *Critique of Cynical Reason* (1983; trans. 1987), which takes its title from Immanuel Kant's *Critique of Pure Reason* (1781), understands Mephistopheles as the ambivalent figure of modern rationality and critical thought.

GUAN HANQING

The Yuan text of *Dou E Yuan* has been preserved in a collection of *zaju* plays published three centuries after Guan's lifetime, but there is no single authoritative written version that defines how the play has been experienced by audiences throughout China over the centuries. Like most Chinese drama, *zaju* plays present a traditional core that survives and proliferates in performance. Each *zaju* play has been excerpted, expanded, modified, and appropriated many times throughout the past seven hundred years. No *zaju* play, *Dou E Yuan* included, has a "definitive" text. For example, Ye Xianzu (1566–1641) adapted the third act of the Yuan text of *Dou E Yuan* as part of his play *Story of the Golden Lock*, which was written in the Ming dynasty form known as *chuanqi*. This play in turn has been adapted into numerous forms—song, storytelling, puppetry, and live theater—all of which, at some level, recognizably derive from Guan's creation. Chinese artists and audiences favor appropriating and transforming famous plays, for doing so presents old stories to contemporary audiences. These strategies are seen not as a violation of the playwright's intentions but rather as a means of keeping the text alive. Although Yang Xianyi and Gladys Yang's 1979 translation of *Dou E Yuan* included in this anthology is a nearly complete version based on the Yuan original, its title, *Snow in Midsummer*

(*Liuyue xue*), is taken from that given to a number of adaptations of a single act of *Dou E Yuan*. Other versions of Guan's play can be found in *Six Yuan Plays*, trans. Jung-en Liu (1972); *Injustice to Tou O (Tou O Yuan): A Study and Translation*, trans. Chung-wen Shih (1972); and *Monks, Bandits, Lovers, and Immortals: Eleven Early Chinese Plays*, ed. and trans. Stephen H. West and Wilt L. Idema (2010).

Criticism in English on Yuan drama, and more specifically on Guan Hanqing and *Dou E Yuan*, is fairly meager. Stephen H. West's article "A Study in Appropriation: Zang Maoxun's Injustice to Dou E" (1991) contains valuable information regarding the differences between the three published versions of the play. Ching-Hsi Perng's *Double Jeopardy: A Critique of Seven Yüan Courtroom Dramas* (1978) compares the play to others in its genre. Haiping Yan's "Theatricality in Classical Chinese Drama," in *Theatricality*, eds. Tracy C. Davis and Thomas Postlewait (2003), discusses the theatrical aspects of Guan's play. Wu-chi Liu's article "Kuan Han-Ch'ing: The Man and His Life" (1990–92) sorts through the scarce evidence on the life of the playwright. J. I. Crump's *Chinese Theater in the Days of Kublai Khan* (1980) describes the performance conventions and historical context of Yuan drama. Faye Chunfang Fei's *Chinese Theories of Theater and Performance from Confucius to the Present* (1999) contains important excerpts of Chinese dramatic theory relating to Guan Hanqing and Yuan drama in general.

HROTSVIT OF GANDERSHEIM

Major studies of the medieval theater include E. K. Chambers, *The Mediaeval Stage*, 2 vols. (1903); Karl Young, *The Drama of the Medieval Church* (1933); and O. B. Hardison Jr., *Christian Rite and Christian Drama in the Middle Ages: Essays in the Origin and Early History of Modern Drama* (1965). Anne Lyon Haight edited a useful bibliographical volume, *Hroswitha of Gandersheim: Her Life, Time, Works, and a Comprehensive Bibliography* (1965), that includes information on translations, productions, and scholarship. Among the most influential English translations of Hrotsvit are Christopher St. John, *The Plays of Roswitha* (1923); Larissa Bonfante, *The Plays of Hrotswitha of Gandersheim* (1979); and Katharina M. Wilson, *The Plays of Hrotsvit of Gandersheim* (1989), the last of which pro-

vides the text used in this anthology. Sister Mary Marguerite Butler's *Hrotsvitha: The Theatricality of Her Plays* (1960) cogently argues for the performative potential of the dramas. Bert Nagel, "The Dramas of Hrotsvit von Gandersheim" (1970), and Kenneth DeLuca, "Hrotsvit's 'Imitation' of Terence" (1974), are both significant additions to the scholarship. The chapter on Hrotsvit in Peter Dronke's *Women Writers of the Middle Ages: A Critical Study of Texts from Perpetua (d. 203) to Marguerite Porete (d. 1310)* (1984) has proven extremely influential. Feminist approaches to the dramatist include Sue-Ellen Case, "Re-Viewing Hrotsvit" (1983); M. R. Sperberg-McQueen, "Whose Body Is It? Chaste Strategies and the Reinforcement of Patriarchy in Three Plays by Hrotswitha von Gandersheim" (1993); and Patricia Demers, "*In virginea forma*: The Salvific Feminine in the Plays of Hrotsvitha of Gandersheim and Hildegard of Bingen" (1993). Among his many publications on the dramatist, Sandro Sticca's "Sacred Drama and Comic Realism in the Plays of Hrotswitha of Gandersheim" (1979) and "Hrotswitha's 'Dulcitius' and Christian Symbolism" (1970) are particularly valuable. In addition to her fine translation, Katharina M. Wilson has published two other notable volumes, *Hrotsvit of Gandersheim: The Ethics of Authorial Stance* (1988), and another collection of the nun's dramatic and nondramatic writings, *Hrotsvit of Gandersheim: A Florilegium of Her Works* (1998); she also co-edited the volume *Hrotsvit of Gandersheim: Contexts, Identities, Affinities, and Performances* (2004) with Phyllis R. Brown and Linda A. McMillin.

BEN JONSON

For much of the past century the standard edition of Ben Jonson's works has been *Ben Jonson* (1925–52), edited in eleven volumes by C. H. Herford and Percy and Evelyn Simpson. *The Cambridge Edition of the Works of Ben Jonson* provides an updated edition of the Jonson canon in print and electronic formats. A number of recent biographies of Jonson are available, including David Riggs, *Ben Jonson: A Life* (1989); W. David Kay, *Ben Jonson: A Literary Life* (1995); and Ian Donaldson, *Ben Jonson: A Life* (2011). The following books and essay collections are valuable introductions to *Volpone* and to Jonson's drama as a whole: Edward B. Partridge, *The Broken Compass: A Study of the Major Comedies of Ben Jonson* (1958); Jonas A.

Barish, ed., *Jonson, Volpone: A Casebook* (1972); Alexander Leggatt, *Ben Jonson: His Vision and His Art* (1981); Anne Barton, *Ben Jonson, Dramatist* (1984); Arnold P. Hinchliffe, *Volpone: Text and Performance* (1985); John Gordon Sweeney III, *Jonson and the Psychology of Public Theater: To Coin the Spirit, Spend the Soul* (1985); Richard Allen Cave, *Ben Jonson* (1991); Ian Donaldson, *Jonson's Magic Houses: Essays in Interpretation* (1997); Robert N. Watson, ed., *Critical Essays on Ben Jonson* (1997); Claude J. Summers and Ted-Larry Pebworth, *Ben Jonson Revised* (1999); Richard Harp and Stanley Stewart, eds., *The Cambridge Companion to Ben Jonson* (2000); Julie Sanders, ed., *Ben Jonson in Context* (2010); and Matthew Steggle, ed., *Volpone: A Critical Guide* (2011). In *Shakespeare, Jonson, and the Myth of Venice* (1990), David C. McPherson discusses English attitudes toward Venice during the Elizabethan and Jacobean period.

THOMAS KYD

F. S. Boas's *Works of Thomas Kyd* (1901) remains essential for its introductory biographical materials and extensive notes on Kyd's classical borrowings. J. R. Mulryne's edition of *The Spanish Tragedy* (1989; 2nd ed., New Mermaid series) is very useful. The definitive critical biography of Kyd remains Arthur Freeman's *Thomas Kyd: Facts and Problems* (1967). More recently, Lukas Erne has attempted a revision of the Kyd corpus in *Beyond "The Spanish Tragedy": A Study of the Works of Thomas Kyd* (2001).

Important discussions of *The Spanish Tragedy* occur in specific articles and chapters devoted to the play as well as in broader studies of revenge. These include Fredson Bowers, *Elizabethan Revenge Tragedy, 1587–1642* (1940); Jonas Barish, "The Spanish Tragedy, or The Pleasures and Perils of Rhetoric" (1966); Donna Hamilton, "The Spanish Tragedy: A Speaking Picture" (1974); Ronald Broude, "Revenge and Revenge Tragedy in Renaissance England" (1975); Michael Hattaway, *Elizabethan Popular Theatre: Plays in Performance* (1982); Gordon Braden, *Renaissance Tragedy and the Senecan Tradition: Anger's Privilege* (1985); James Shapiro, "'Tragedies naturally performed': Kyd's Representation of Violence, The Spanish Tragedy (c. 1592)" (1991); Frank Ardolino, *Apocalypse & Armada in Kyd's "Spanish Tragedy"* (1995); John Kerrigan, *Revenge Tragedy: Aeschylus to Armageddon* (1996); Frank

Whigham, *Seizures of the Will in Early Modern English Drama* (1996); Carla Mazzio, "Staging the Vernacular: Language and Nation in Thomas Kyd's The Spanish Tragedy" (1998); and Alexander Leggatt, "'A membrane has broken': Returning from the Dead in The Spanish Tragedy," in *Renaissance Go-Betweens: Cultural Exchange in Early Modern Europe*, eds. Andreas Höfele and Werner von Koppenfels (2005).

GEORGE LILLO

While *The Dramatic Works of George Lillo*, ed. James L. Steffensen (1993), is the authoritative edition of Lillo's collected plays, William H. McBurney's 1965 edition of *The London Merchant* still provides the most complete and informative introduction to Lillo's best-known drama. Among the wealth of recent criticism on *The London Merchant*, the following works are particularly useful: Stephan P. Flores, "Mastering the Self: The Ideological Incorporation of Desire in Lillo's The London Merchant" (1987); David Wallace, "Bourgeois Tragedy or Sentimental Melodrama? The Significance of George Lillo's The London Merchant" (1991–92); Tejumola Olaniyan, "The Ethics and Poetics of a 'Civilizing Mission': Some Notes on Lillo's The London Merchant" (1992); Lucinda Cole, "The London Merchant and the Institution of Apprenticeship" (1995); Lisa A. Freeman, "Tragic Flaws: Genre and Ideology in Lillo's London Merchant" (1999); and Peter Hynes, "Exchange and Excess in Lillo's London Merchant" (2003). Lincoln B. Faller's *The Popularity of Addison's "Cato" and Lillo's "The London Merchant," 1700–1776* (1988) discusses Lillo's play in relation to its audience, while Ralph Cohen's "Literary History and the Ballad of George Barnwel," in *Augustan Studies: Essays in Honor of Irvin Ehrenpreis*, eds. Douglas Lane Patey and Timothy Keegan (1985), examines the history of the seventeenth-century ballad on which *The London Merchant* is based.

CHRISTOPHER MARLOWE

Readers who are curious about the competing texts of *Doctor Faustus* would do well to consult *Doctor Faustus, 1604–1616: Parallel Texts*, ed. W. W. Greg (1950), and Michael Warren's authoritative essay "Doctor Faustus: The Old Man and the Text" (1981). The closest approximation to a standard scholarly text of the play is by Roma

Gill (2nd ed., 1989). A modern edition of *The English Faust Book* has been produced by John Henry Jones (1994). Among the classic book-length studies of Marlowe that include excellent discussions of *Doctor Faustus* are Harry Levin, *The Overreacher: A Study of Christopher Marlowe* (1952); Wilbur Sanders, *The Dramatist and the Received Idea: Studies in the Plays of Marlowe and Shakespeare* (1968); and J. B. Steane, *Marlowe: A Critical Study* (1964). More provocative approaches to Marlowe and *Doctor Faustus* can be found in Michael Goldman's "Marlowe and the Histrionics of Ravishment," Stephen J. Greenblatt's "Marlowe and Renaissance Self-Fashioning," and especially Edward A. Snow's "Marlowe's *Doctor Faustus* and the Ends of Desire," all of which appear in *Two Renaissance Mythmakers: Christopher Marlowe and Ben Jonson*, a remarkable collection of essays edited by Alvin Kernan (1977). Lawrence Danson's "Marlowe: The Questioner" (1982) also has special pertinence to *Doctor Faustus*. One of the more controversial and inventive scholarly engagements with *Doctor Faustus* is William Empson's posthumously published *Faustus and the Censor: The English Faust-book and Marlowe's "Doctor Faustus"* (1987). Readers looking for a similar blend of historical scholarship and high-wire speculation in a life of Marlowe should consult Charles Nicholl's *The Reckoning: The Murder of Christopher Marlowe* (1992; rev. ed., 2002). Those in search of a more traditional biography need look no further than David Riggs's *The World of Christopher Marlowe* (2004). *The Cambridge Introduction to Christopher Marlowe*, ed. Tom Rutter (2012), provides a useful overview of Marlowe's life and work, while *Christopher Marlowe the Craftsman: Lives, Stage, and Page*, eds. Sarah K. Scott and M. L. Stapleton (2010), is a valuable collection of essays on Marlowe the working artist.

MOLIÈRE (JEAN-BAPTISTE POQUELIN)

There is, to date, no definitive, complete edition of Molière's works in English, though his plays have regularly been translated into this and many other languages. Among English translations, those of the poet Richard Wilbur have long been admired; others, such as those of Maya Slater, attempt to capture more exactly the form of the French originals. The translation by Haskell M. Block (1985) includes the preface and letters to Louis XIV quoted above. The version of *Tartuffe* created for *The Norton Anthology of Drama* is by the playwright Constance Congdon, who based it on the scholarly translation of Virginia Scott. Scott's biography *Molière: A Theatrical Life* (2000) offers an accessible and balanced portrait of the artist and provides reasoned conjectures about many of the contested and unprovable details of his career. Congdon and Scott's co-edited Norton Critical Edition of the play, *Tartuffe: A New Verse Translation* (2008), provides valuable contextual materials. Useful introductions to seventeenth-century drama and theater include Henry Carrington Lancaster, *The Period of Molière, 1652–1672*, part 3 of *A History of French Dramatic Literature in the Seventeenth Century* (1936); Peter D. Arnott, *An Introduction to the French Theatre* (1977); John Lough, *Seventeenth-Century French Drama: The Background* (1979); Nicholas Hammond, *Creative Tensions: An Introduction to Seventeenth-Century French Literature* (1997); and Gerry McCarthy, *The Theatres of Molière* (2002). *The Molière Encyclopedia* (2002), edited by James F. Gaines, contains a wealth of useful and succinct information on the dramatist and his works. Richard Parish's edition of the play in French (1994) also includes an informative introduction and notes in English.

Full-length critical studies of Molière abound. Those with particularly helpful discussions for a consideration of *Tartuffe* include David Bradby and Andrew Calder's *Cambridge Companion to Moliere* (2006); James F. Gaines, *Social Structures in Molière's Theater* (1984); Nathan Gross, *From Gesture to Idea—Esthetics and Ethics in Molière's Comedy* (1982); W. D. Howarth, *Molière: A Playwright and His Audience* (1982); J. D. Hubert, *Molière & the Comedy of Intellect* (1962); Michael S. Koppisch, *Rivalry and the Disruption of Order in Molière's Theater* (2004); Gertrud Mander, *Molière* (1967, trans. 1973); and Martin Turnell, *The Classical Moment: Studies of Corneille, Molière and Racine* (1947). Jerry Lewis Kasparek's *Molière's "Tartuffe" and the Traditions of Roman Satire* (1977) explores sources and influences, and John Cairncross's *New Light on Molière: "Tartuffe"; "Elomire hypocondre"* (1956) establishes the arguments for the 1664 performance text accepted by many scholars as definitive. Albert Bermel's *Molière's Theatrical Bounty: A New View of the Plays* (1990) considers some of the more recent, influential productions of *Tartuffe*. Christopher Braider's chapter on *Tartuffe* in his study of French drama, *Indiscernible Counterparts: The Invention of the Text in French Classical Drama*

(2002), provides a most elegant and insightful contemporary reading of the play.

TITUS MACCIUS PLAUTUS

George E. Duckworth's *The Nature of Roman Comedy: A Study in Popular Entertainment* (1952; 2nd ed., 1994) has long been considered the foundational scholarly work in the field in English. *The Cambridge History of Classical Literature*, vol. 2, *Latin Literature*, ed. E. J. Kenney (1982), and *Ancient Writers: Greece and Rome*, ed. T. James Luce, vol. 1, *Homer to Caesar* (1982), also provide useful overviews. Several helpful bibliographies of criticism include J. A. Hanson's "Scholarship on Plautus since 1950" (1965), W. Geoffrey Arnott's *Menander, Plautus, Terence* (1975), J. David Hughes's *A Bibliography of Scholarship on Plautus* (1975), and Erich Segal's "Scholarship on Plautus, 1965–1976" (1981). Additional landmark studies include Erich Segal, *Roman Laughter: The Comedy of Plautus* (1968; 2nd ed., 1987); David Konstan, *Roman Comedy* (1983); Niall W. Slater, *Plautus in Performance: The Theatre of the Mind* (1985); William S. Anderson, *Barbarian Play: Plautus' Roman Comedy* (1993); and Kathleen McCarthy, *Slaves, Masters, and the Art of Authority in Plautine Comedy* (2000). Three collections of critical essays provide other useful examples of the range of critical approaches to Roman comedy: T. A. Dorey and Donald R. Dudley, eds., *Roman Drama* (1965); Ruth Scodel, ed., *Theater and Society in the Classical World* (1993); and especially Erich Segal, ed., *Oxford Readings in Menander, Plautus, and Terence* (2001), which contains A. R. Sharrock's 1996 essay "The Art of Deceit: Pseudolus and the Nature of Reading" and other recent scholarship. John Wright's widely cited essay "The Transformations of Pseudolus" (1975) focuses on the important relationship between language and character.

JEAN RACINE

Although most of the criticism on Racine is written in French, a number of useful studies are available in English. Geoffrey Brereton's *Jean Racine, a Critical Biography* (1951) is the fullest biography of Racine in English, while Claude Abraham's *Jean Racine* (1977) and Ronald W. Tobin's *Jean Racine Revisited* (1999) provide valuable (and more recent) introductions to Racine's life and work. Martin Turnell's excellent *Jean Racine—Dramatist* (1972) explores the dramatic foundations of Racine's plays, with particular attention to their life in performance; David Maskell's *Racine: A Theatrical Reading* (1991) offers a similar theatrical emphasis. Other studies of Racinian tragedy include Eugène Vinaver, *Racine and Poetic Tragedy* (1951; trans. 1955); John C. Lapp, *Aspects of Racinian Tragedy* (1955); Bernard Weinberg, *The Art of Jean Racine* (1963); Odette de Mourgues, *Racine, or, The Triumph of Relevance* (1967); P. J. Yarrow, *Racine* (1978); Richard E. Goodkin, *The Tragic Middle: Racine, Aristotle, Euripides* (1991); Richard Parish, *Racine: The Limits of Tragedy* (1993); John Campbell, *Questioning Racinian Tragedy* (2005); and Roland Racevskis, *Tragic Passages: Jean Racine's Art of the Threshold* (2008). Peter France, *Racine's Rhetoric* (1965), and Michael Hawcroft, *Word as Action: Racine, Rhetoric, and Theatrical Language* (1992), study the influence of classical rhetoric on Racine's drama. Jules Brody's "Freud, Racine, and the Epistemology of Tragedy" (1990) offers a psychological interpretation of *Phaedra*, while Nathan Edelman's splendid article "The Central Image in *Phèdre*," in his *The Eye of the Beholder: Essays in French Literature* (1974), explores the motif of light and darkness in Racine's final tragedy.

Two influential French studies have been translated into English: Lucien Goldmann, *The Hidden God: A Study of Tragic Vision in the Pensées of Pascal and the Tragedies of Racine* (1956; trans. 1964), is a sociological reading of Racine's drama, and Roland Barthes, *On Racine* (1960; trans. 1964), is a provocative collection of essays on Racine and the critical tradition that surrounds his plays. R. C. Knight, ed., *Racine* (1969), is a collection of mid-twentieth-century criticism on Racine, including many essays translated from French.

LUCIUS ANNAEUS SENECA

Although more facts are certain about Seneca than about many other authors of the period, many events and developments in his life and work, including the dates of all of his tragedies, remain unknown. The historically significant *Thyestes* translation of 1560 by Jasper Heywood has been made available by Josst Daaler (1982); the other historical edition, by Thomas Newton (1581), with its famous foreword by T. S. Eliot (1927), has been reprinted many times. The best general account of Seneca's astonishing life and work, with a good introduction to Roman culture and politics, is Villy Sørensen's *Seneca: The Humanist at the Court of Nero* (1976, trans. 1984). Norman T. Pratt's *Seneca's Drama* (1983) is the best general introduction to Seneca's dramatic art, a subject also addressed in Anna Lydia Motto and John R. Clark's *Senecan Tragedy* (1988). Particularly commendable is Alessandro Schiesaro's *The Passions in Play: "Thyestes" and the Dynamics of Senecan Drama* (2003), while the short *Seneca: Thyestes*, by P. J. Davis (2003), provides useful commentary, including a history of the play's performances in the twentieth century. A collection of essays edited by George W. M. Harrison, *Seneca in Performance* (2000), discusses the controversial question of performance from a variety of perspectives. Further readings on Seneca's drama can be found in two collections of essays, C. D. N. Costa's *Seneca* (1974) and Anna Lydia Motto and John R. Clark's *Essays on Seneca* (1993).

WILLIAM SHAKESPEARE

S. Schoenbaum's *William Shakespeare: A Compact Documentary Life* (1977; rev. ed., 1987) and Stephen Greenblatt's *Will in the World: How Shakespeare Became Shakespeare* (2004) are excellent places to learn more about Shakespeare's life and career. A very useful introduction to early modern culture and theatrical practices is Russ McDonald's *Bedford Companion to Shakespeare: An Introduction with Documents* (1996; 2nd ed., 2001).

Hamlet

A. C. Bradley's classic *Shakespearean Tragedy* (1904; 3rd ed., 1992) and Bert O. States's *Hamlet and the Concept of Character* (1992) are very different but equally outstanding investigations of Hamlet as a character. Harold Bloom's *Shakespeare: The Invention of the Human* (1998) offers an accessible and in-depth discussion of the complex and self-reflective nature of the mind of Hamlet. Ernest Jones's *Hamlet and Oedipus* (1949) is a landmark psychoanalytic work that offers a comprehensive explanation for Hamlet's delay. Arthur Kinney's recent edited volume *Hamlet: New Critical Essays* (2002) includes a number of useful articles. Janet Adelman's *Suffocating Mothers: Fantasies of Maternal Origin in Shakespeare's Plays, "Hamlet" to*

"The Tempest" (1992) combines feminist concerns with a psychological approach. Jacqueline Rose's "Hamlet—The Mona Lisa of Literature," originally published in 1986 and anthologized in *Shakespeare and Gender: A History*, eds. Deborah Barker and Ivo Kamps (1995), analyzes the influence of gender in interpretations of *Hamlet*.

Michael Cohen's *Hamlet in My Mind's Eye* (1989) offers a sustained, book-length reading of the play with a keen eye to performance possibilities. Stephen Greenblatt's *Hamlet in Purgatory* (2001) is a masterful treatment of the role of religious energies in the play.

Those interested in Shakespeare's representation of madness and its connection to political subversion can turn to Karin S. Coddon's "'Such Strange Designs': Madness, Subjectivity, and Treason in Hamlet and Elizabethan Culture," in *Shakespeare's Tragedies*, ed. Susan Zimmerman (1998). Carol Thomas Neely writes on madness in *Twelfth Night* and *Hamlet* in her historically informed essay "'Documents in Madness': Reading Madness and Gender in Shakespeare's Tragedies and Early Modern Culture" (1991). *Marxist Shakespeares* (2001), edited by Jean E. Howard and Scott Cutler Shershow, includes intriguing Marxist readings of *Hamlet*. Gary Taylor's "Hamlet in Africa 1607" in *Travel Knowledge: European "Discoveries" in the Early Modern Period*, eds. Ivo Kamps and Jyotsna G. Singh (2001), provides a fascinating account of the first non-European performance of *Hamlet* aboard a ship in Sierra Leone. Tony Howard's fascinating *Women as Hamlet: Performance and Interpretation in Theatre, Film, and Fiction* (2007) discusses the extensive tradition of women actors performing the role of Hamlet. Another excellent study, Margreta de Grazia's *"Hamlet" without Hamlet* (2007), considers Hamlet within the physical and metaphysical worlds he inhabits.

Twelfth Night

For a discussion of Shakespeare's comedies as a form influenced by popular Elizabethan festivals, see C. L. Barber's *Shakespeare's Festive Comedy: A Study of Dramatic Form and Its Relation to Social Custom* (1959). For details of Coleridge's famous interpretations, see Terence Hawkes's collection of them, *Coleridge's Writings on Shakespeare* (1959). Harold Bloom's *Shakespeare: The Invention of the Human* (1998) provides detailed characterological analyses.

Bruce Smith's *Twelfth Night, or, What You Will: Text and Contexts* (2001) offers a number of relevant texts and documents contemporaneous with the play. Jean Howard analyzes the practice of boy actors in female roles in "Cross-Dressing, the Theatre and Gender Struggle in Early Modern England" (1988), reprinted in *The Routledge Reader in Gender and Performance*, ed. Lizbeth Goodman with Jane de Gau (1998). A number of outstanding essays take up questions of gender and sexuality in *Twelfth Night*, including Dympna Callaghan's "'And All Is Semblative a Woman's Part': Body Politics and *Twelfth Night*" (1993); Stephen Greenblatt's "Fiction and Friction," in *Shakespearean Negotiations: The Circulation of Social Energy in Renaissance England* (1988); and Joseph Pequigney's "The Two Antonios and Same-Sex Love in *Twelfth Night* and *The Merchant of Venice*," in *Shakespeare and Gender: A History*, eds. Deborah Barker and Ivo Kamps (1995). Barbara Correll's "Malvolio at Malfi: Managing Desire in Shakespeare and Webster" (2007) offers a compelling study of this darker plotline, while M. J. Kietzmann's "Will Personified: Viola as Actor-Author in *Twelfth Night*" (2012) considers the performative dimensions of the comedy. *Twentieth Century Interpretations of "Twelfth Night": A Collection of Critical Essays*, ed. Walter N. King (1968), contains a number of classic assessments of the play, while James Schiffer's *Twelfth Night: New Critical Essays* (2011) offers more recent insights.

RICHARD BRINSLEY SHERIDAN

Cecil Price's two-volume *The Dramatic Works of Richard Brinsley Sheridan* (1973) is the authoritative edition of Sheridan's plays. The two most extensive biographies of Sheridan remain Thomas Moore, *Memoirs of the Life of the Right Honorable Richard Brinsley Sheridan* (1825), and Walter Sichel, *Sheridan: From New and Original Material, Including a Manuscript Diary by Georgiana, Duchess of Devonshire*, 2 vols. (1909). Later biographies of note include R. Crompton Rhodes, *Harlequin Sheridan: The Man and the Legends* (1933); Stanley Ayling, *A Portrait of Sheridan* (1985); and Fintan O'Toole, *A Traitor's Kiss: The Life of Richard Brinsley Sheridan* (1997). E. H. Mikhail, ed., *Sheridan: Interviews and Recollections* (1989), is a sourcebook of reminiscences by those who knew Sheridan. Useful overviews of Sheridan's life and writings include Jack D. Durant, *Richard Brinsley Sheridan*

(1975), and James Morwood, *The Life and Works of Richard Brinsley Sheridan* (1985). Discussions of Sheridan's plays can be found in Louis Kronenberger, *The Thread of Laughter: Chapters on English Stage Comedy from Jonson to Maugham* (1952); John Loftis, *Sheridan and the Drama of Georgian England* (1976); Mark S. Auburn, *Sheridan's Comedies: Their Contexts and Achievements* (1977); and Katharine Worth, *Sheridan and Goldsmith* (1992). David Francis Taylor, *Theatres of Opposition: Empire, Revolution, and Richard Brinsley Sheridan* (2012), examines Sheridan's theatrical practice in light of his career as a politician. *Sheridan: Comedies*, ed. Peter Davison (1986), contains reviews and critical essays on the major plays.

Important discussions of *The School for Scandal* include Andrew Schiller, "The School for Scandal: The Restoration Unrestored" (1956); Christian Deelman, "The Original Cast of *The School for Scandal*" (1962); Leonard J. Leff, "The Disguise Motif in Sheridan's *The School for Scandal*" (1970); Joseph Roach, "Gossip Girls: Lady Teazle, Nora Helmer, and Invisible-Hand Drama" (2010); and two essays in *Sheridan Studies*, eds. James Morwood and David Crane (1995): Eric Rump, "Sheridan, Congreve, and *The School for Scandal*," and James Morwood, "Sheridan, Molière, and the Idea of the School in *The School for Scandal*."

SHUDRAKA

In addition to the translation by Chatterjee used in this anthology, other relatively recent translations of *The Little Clay Cart* are by J. A. B. van Buitenen, available in *Two Plays of Ancient India: The Little Clay Cart, The Minister's Seal* (1968), and A. L. Basham, in *The Little Clay Cart: An English Translation of the Mṛcchakaṭika of Śūdraka*, ed. Arvind Sharma (1994). Both editions include useful introductions to the play. John P. Harrington, *The Life of the Neighborhood Playhouse on Grand Street* (2007), includes a fascinating discussion (with photographs) of the important 1924–25 New York production of *The Little Clay Cart*. Farley P. Richmond offers detailed discussions of Sanskrit theater and drama in the first two chapters of a collection edited by him, Darius L. Swann, and Phillip B. Zarrilli, *Indian Theatre: Traditions of Performance* (1990), and in James R. Brandon, ed., *The Cambridge Guide to Asian Theatre* (1993). Other useful studies include Henry H. Wells,

The Classical Drama of India: Studies in Its Values for the Literature and Theatre of the World (1963), and Rachel Van M. Baumer and James R. Brandon, eds., Sanskrit Drama in Performance (1981). In Rasa: Performing the Divine in India (2004), Susan L. Schwartz provides a valuable discussion of Indian theatrical aesthetics.

SOPHOCLES

Like all classical Greek tragedies, Sophocles' plays survived through a series of accidents. Generations of scholars have tried to approximate the original text, distorted by scribes, commentators, and adaptors. The recent scholarship on the playwright is extensive; it draws on newly discovered fragments of other plays, new archaeological evidence, and new insights into Greek society and culture. The French scholars Jean-Pierre Vernan and Pierre Vidal-Naquet have been especially successful, for example, in using new anthropological theories in their commentaries on the play. Their essays are collected in Myth and Tragedy in Ancient Greece (1972, trans. 1988). The best general introduction to Sophocles is R. P. Winnington-Ingram's Sophocles: An Interpretation (1980). An older classic, H. D. Kitto's Greek Tragedy: A Literary Study (1939), contains a good discussion of both plays as well as comments on the philosophical outlook of the playwright. However, Mary Whitlock Blundell's Helping Friends and Harming Enemies: A Study in Sophocles and Greek Ethics (1989) is a much more searching and sophisticated analysis of Sophocles in the context of Greek ethics and philosophy. The city of Thebes in Greek tragedy, with particular attention to Antigone and King Oedipus, is discussed by Froma Zeitlin in her essay in Zeitlin and John J. Winkler, eds., Nothing to Do with Dionysus (1990). The political dimensions of the two plays are particularly difficult to understand for modern readers and are explained in Michael Vickers, Sophocles and Alcibiades: Athenian Politics in Ancient Greek Literature (2008). Charles Segal's Oedipus Tyrannus: Tragic Heroism and the Limits of Knowledge (1993) also places Oedipus the King in the context of theories of knowledge, while David Seale, in his Vision and Stagecraft in Sophocles (1982), emphasizes the metaphor and role of vision and blindness in the play. Particularly influential has been Charles Segal's Tragedy and Civilization: An Interpretation of Sophocles (1981), which uses Sophocles to explore the relation of kinship and ritual in Greek society and culture. Both

plays have also been important for philosophers, from Aristotle, in his Poetics (ca. 330 B.C.E.), through G. W. F. Hegel, in his Lectures on Aesthetics (1835–38). Oedipus the King was central in the formulation of psychoanalysis, in Sigmund Freud's Interpretation of Dreams (1900). For information on Greek theater, Sir Arthur Pickard-Cambridge's The Dramatic Festivals of Athens (1968) is still a classic, and Eric Scapo and William J. Slater have made many fragments about Greek theater available in translation in their The Context of Ancient Drama (1995). Both plays have been adapted in many different ways for the modern stage; one important example is Seamus Heaney's version of Antigone, set in Northern Ireland, The Burial at Thebes (2004).

LOPE DE VEGA

Information on the life, times, and theater of Lope de Vega can be found in Heinz Gerstinger, Lope de Vega and Spanish Drama (1968; trans. 1974); Henryk Ziomek, A History of Spanish Golden Age Drama (1984); Malveena McKendrick, Theatre in Spain, 1490–1700 (1989) and in Alexander Samson and Jonathan Tucker, eds., A Companion to Lope de Vega (2008). Unfortunately, only a small fraction of Lope's works have been translated to date. Recent English versions of Fuenteovejuna, including those by Gwynne Edwards (1999) and Stanley Appelbaum (2002), also contain useful overviews of Lope's biography and the play's critical reception. Lope's The New Art of Writing Plays was translated by William T. Brewster and published with commentary by Brander Matthews in 1914; this remains the only English-language edition. A number of full-length studies of Spanish Golden Age literature generally, and the work of Lope de Vega specifically, contain helpful discussions of Fuenteovejuna; see especially Anthony J. Cascardi's Ideologies of History in the Spanish Golden Age (1997); Donald Gilbert-Santamaría's Writers on the Market: Consuming Literature in Early Seventeenth-Century Spain (2005); Donald R. Larson's The Honor Plays of Lope de Vega (1977); and Malveena McKendrick's Playing the King: Lope de Vega and the Limits of Conformity (2000). Essays providing insightful readings of the play from a number of critical perspectives include Paul Allatson, "Confounding Convention: 'Women' in Three Golden Age Plays" (1996); William R. Blue, "The Politics of Lope's Fuenteovejuna" (1991); Chad M. Gasta, "The

Politics of Agriculture: Dramatizing Agrarian Plight in Lope's *Fuenteovejuna*" (2003); Javier Herrero, "The New Monarchy: A Structural Reinterpretation of *Fuenteovejuna*" (1970–71); Paul E. Larson, "*Fuente Ovejuna*: History, Historiography, and Literary History" (2001); and A. Robert Lauer, "The Recovery of the Repressed: A Neo-Historical Reading of *Fuenteovejuna*," in *New Historicism and the Comedia: Poetics, Politics, and Praxis*, ed. José Antonio Madrigal (1997).

THE WAKEFIELD MASTER

The authoritative text of *The Second Shepherds' Play* can be found in Martin Stevens and A. C. Cawley, eds., *The Towneley Plays* (1994). Stevens and Cawley have also written the introduction to the published facsimile of the Towneley manuscript, *The Towneley Cycle: A Facsimile of the Huntington MS HM 1* (1976). Book-length studies of the Towneley Cycle and the plays of the Wakefield Master include Walter E. Meyers, *A Figure Given: Typology in the Wakefield Plays* (1969); John Gardner, *The Construction of the Wakefield Cycle* (1974); Jeffrey Helterman, *Symbolic Action in the Plays of the Wakefield Master* (1981); Martin Stevens, *Four Middle English Mystery Cycles: Textual, Contextual, and Critical Interpretations* (1987); Liam O. Purdon, *The Wakefield Master's Dramatic Art: A Drama of Spiritual Understanding* (2003); Warren Edminster, *The Preaching Fox: Festive Subversion in the Plays of the Wakefield Master* (2005); and Peter Happé, *The Towneley Cycle: Unity and Diversity* (2007). The introductions to A. C. Cawley, ed., *The Wakefield Pageants in the Towneley Cycle* (1958), and Martial Rose, ed., *The Wakefield Mystery Plays* (1961), contain valuable information on the Wakefield plays as a group, as does Peter Meredith's chapter on the Towneley cycle in *The Cambridge Companion to Medieval English Theatre*, eds. Richard Beadle and Alan J. Fletcher (1994; 2nd ed., 2008). Important articles include Claude Chidamian, "Mak and the Tossing in the Blanket" (1947); William M. Manly, "Shepherds and Prophets: Religious Unity in the Towneley *Secunda Pastorum*" (1963); Margery M. Morgan, "'High Fraud': Paradox and Double-Plot in the English Shepherds' Plays" (1964); Lawrence J. Ross, "Symbol and Structure in the *Secunda Pastorum*" (1967); Maynard Mack Jr., "The *Second Shepherds' Play*: A Reconsideration" (1978); Regula Meyer Evitt, "Musical Structure in the *Second Shepherds'*

Play" (1988–89); and Lisa J. Kiser, "'Mak's Heirs': Sheep and Humans in the Pastoral Ecology of the Towneley *First* and *Second Shepherds' Plays*" (2009). Rosemary Woolf, *The English Mystery Plays* (1972), is one of the finest general studies of the English Corpus Christi cycles.

JOHN WEBSTER

F. L. Lucas's *The Complete Works of John Webster*, 4 vols. (1927), remains the standard edition of the dramatist's works. Elizabeth M. Brennan's updated edition of *The Duchess of Malfi* (3rd ed., 1993) for New Mermaids is very useful, as is the Oxford *The Duchess of Malfi and Other Plays*, ed. René Weis (1996; 1998). The definitive critical biography of Webster is Charles Forker's *Skull beneath the Skin: The Achievement of John Webster* (1986). Muriel Bradbrook provides a stimulating approach to Webster's biography and works in *John Webster, Citizen and Dramatist* (1980).

The *Duchess* has been served well by earlier criticism and has received fresh, exciting attention in the past twenty years. R. W. Dent's *John Webster's Borrowing* (1960) remains crucial reading for an understanding of Webster's use of sources. Gunnar Boklund's "*The Duchess of Malfi*": *Sources, Themes, Characters* (1962) offers detailed background and analysis. There are several collections of essays on Webster and the *Duchess*, including *John Webster: A Critical Anthology*, eds. G. K. and S. K. Hunter (1969), and *Webster: "The White Devil" and "The Duchess of Malfi*," ed. R. V. Holdsworth (1975). Dympna Callaghan provides a more recent collection of essays, informed by feminist perspectives, in her anthology *The Duchess of Malfi: John Webster* (2000). "*The Duchess of Malfi*": *A Critical Guide* (2011), ed. Christina Luckyj, is another excellent collection of essays. Kate Aughterson's *Webster: The Tragedies* (2001) is a helpful reader's guide. Lee Bliss's *The World's Perspective: John Webster and the Jacobean Drama* (1983) offers an excellent overview of Webster's themes and conventions. Useful chapters in books include Frank Whigham, "Incest and Ideology: *The Duchess of Malfi* (1614)," in *Staging the Renaissance: Reinterpretations of Elizabethan and Jacobean Drama*, eds. David Scott Kastan and Peter Stallybrass (1991); Lynn Enterline, "'Hairy on the Inside': *The Duchess of Malfi* and the Body of Lycanthropy," in her *Tears of Narcissus: Melancholia and Masculinity in Early Modern Writing*

(1995); Ellen Caldwell, "Invasive Procedures in Webster's *The Duchess of Malfi*," in *Women, Violence, and English Renaissance Literature: Essays Honoring Paul Jorgensen*, eds. Linda Woodbridge and Sharon Beehler (2003); Eileen Allman, "The Duchess of Malfi," in her *Jacobean Revenge Tragedy and the Politics of Virtue* (1999); and Dympna Callaghan, "The Duchess of Malfi and Early Modern Widows," in *Early Modern English Drama: A Critical Companion*, eds. Garrett A. Sullivan Jr., Patrick Cheney, and Andrew Hadfield (2006).

WILLIAM WYCHERLEY

Scholars consider B. Eugene McCarthy's *William Wycherley: A Biography* (1979) the most authoritative, full-length study of the playwright's life to date. Numerous versions of Wycherley's plays, dating as far back as 1713, have been published; though no one text is authoritative, scholars often look to the editions by Leigh Hunt (1840) and Montague Summers (1924) as reputable. Later editions of *The Country Wife* by Thomas H. Fujimura (1965), Gerald Weales (1966), David Cook and John Swannell (1975), James Ogden (1991), and Peter Dixon (1996) are all considered trustworthy; Scott McMillin's (1973) has been included here. For information on theatrical productions of the time, historians rely on the reference work edited by William Van Lennep et al., *The London Stage, 1660–1800: A Calendar of Plays, Entertainments and Afterpieces, together with Casts, Box-receipts, and Contemporary Comment*, 5 vols. (1960–68). Robert D. Hume's edited volume *The London Theatre World, 1660–1800* (1980), along with his *The Development of English Drama in the Late Seventeenth Century* (1976), provides important overviews of the theater and drama of the era. Similarly useful volumes include John Loftis et al., *The "Revels" History of Drama in English*, general eds. Clifford Leech and T. W. Craik, vol. 5, *1660–1750* (1976); Frances M. Kavenik, *British Drama, 1660–1779: A Critical History* (1995); and Deborah Payne Fisk, ed., *The Cambridge Companion to English Restoration Theatre* (2000). For information on *The Country Wife* in production, see Jocelyn Powell, *Restoration Theatre Production* (1984); J. L. Styan, *Restoration Comedy in Performance* (1986); and Judith Milhous and Robert D. Hume, *Producible Interpretation: Eight English Plays, 1675–1707* (1985). Important studies of Restoration comedy include Thomas H. Fujimura, *The Restoration*

Comedy of Wit (1952); John Loftis, ed., *Restoration Drama: Modern Essays in Criticism* (1966); Robert D. Hume, *The Rakish Stage: Studies in English Drama, 1660–1800* (1983); Harold Weber, *The Restoration Rake-Hero: Transformation in Sexual Understanding in Seventeenth-Century England* (1986); Edward Burns, *Restoration Comedy: Crises of Desire and Identity* (1987); Robert Markley, *Two-Edg'd Weapons: Style and Ideology in the Comedies of Etherege, Wycherley, and Congreve* (1988); Pat Gill, *Interpreting Ladies: Women, Wit, and Morality in the Restoration Comedy of Manners* (1994); and Susan J. Owen, *Perspectives on Restoration Drama* (2002). B. Eugene McCarthy's *William Wycherley: A Reference Guide* (1985) presents a useful overview of scholarship on the dramatist. Full-length studies of note include Rose A. Zimbardo, *Wycherley's Drama* (1965); W. R. Chadwick, *The Four Plays of William Wycherley: A Link in the Development of English Satire* (1975); and James Thompson, *Language in Wycherley's Plays: Seventeeth-Century Language Theory and Drama* (1984). Eve Kosofsky Sedgwick's *Between Men: English Literature and Male Homosocial Desire* (1985) includes a noteworthy essay on *The Country Wife*.

ZEAMI MOTOKIYO

Although Zeami mentions *Atsumori* in his treatises, the earliest extant text is from the early sixteenth century. As a result, it is not possible to pinpoint the date of this play or to know if the text we have has been revised from Zeami's version. *Atsumori* was translated into French by Arthur Arrivet in 1895 but became well known in the West only in 1921 with the translation of Arthur Waley, which has been reprinted in *Masterpieces of the Orient*, ed. G. L. Anderson (1961; enlarged ed., 1977). The translation in Karen Brazell, ed., *Traditional Japanese Theater: An Anthology of Plays* (1997), has fuller stage directions than the version included here and is illustrated. That anthology also includes selections from other plays based on the Atsumori story and general information about Japanese theater. Royall Tyler's translation in *Japanese Nō Dramas* (1992) is also recommended. Zeami's treatises may be found in J. Thomas Rimer and Yamazaki Masakazu, trans., *On the Art of the Noh Drama: The Major Treatises of Zeami* (1984), and Tom Hare, trans., *Zeami: Performance Notes* (2008). Benito Ortolani, *The Japanese Theatre: From Shamanistic Ritual to Contemporary Pluralism*

(1990; rev. ed., 1995), is an authoritative history of noh and other Japanese theater traditions, while Kunio Konparu, *The Noh Theatre: Principles and Perspectives* (trans. 1983), contains a useful introductory discussion of noh theater. Thomas Blenham Hare's *Zeami's Style: The Noh Plays of Zeami Motokiyo* (1986) discusses Zeami's dramatic work as a whole; Shelley Fenno Quinn's *Developing Zeami: the Noh Actor's Attunement in Practice* (2005) explores Zeami's dramatic and theatrical writings with a particular emphasis on his theory of acting. *In the Artistry of Aeschylus and Zeami: A Comparative Study of Greek Tragedy and Nō* (1989), Mae J. Smethurst presents interesting similarities in and differences between the genres.

PERMISSIONS ACKNOWLEDGMENTS

TEXT

Plautus: *Pseudolus,* from SIX PLAYS OF PLAUTUS, translated by Lionel Casson. Translation copyright © 1963 by Lionel Casson. Used by permission of Doubleday, a division of Random House, Inc. Any third party use of this material, outside of this publication, is prohibited. Interested parties must apply directly to Random House, Inc. for permission.

Racine, Jean: *Phèdre,* by Jean Racine, translated by Ted Hughes. Translation copyright © 1998 by Ted Hughes. Reprinted by permission of Farrar, Straus and Giroux, LLC, and Faber and Faber Ltd.

The Second Shepherds' Play: from THE TOWNELEY PLAYS, volume 1, edited by Martin Stevens and A. C. Cawley. Copyright © 1994 by Oxford University Press. Used by permission of Oxford University Press.

Seneca: *Thyestes* from SENECA: SIX TRAGEDIES, translated by Emily Wilson. Copyright © 2010 by Emily Wilson. Reprinted by permission of Oxford University Press.

Shakespeare, William: *Hamlet* from HAMLET: A NORTON CRITICAL EDITION, edited by Robert S. Miola. Copyright © 2011 by W. W. Norton & Company, Inc.

Shudraka: *The Little Clay Cart,* translated by Sudipto Chatterjee. Copyright © 2006 Sudipto Chatterjee. Published by W. W. Norton & Company.

Sophocles: *Oedipus the King* from THREE THEBAN PLAYS by Sophocles, translated by Robert Fagles. Copyright © 1982 by Robert Fagles. Used by permission of Viking Penguin, a division of Penguin Group (USA), Inc. *Antigone* from THE COMPLETE PLAYS OF SOPHOCLES, translated by Robert Bagg and James Scully. Copyright © 2011 by Robert Bagg and James Scully. Reprinted by permission of HarperCollins Publishers.

Webster, John: *The Duchess of Malfi* from ENGLISH RENAISSANCE DRAMA: A NORTON ANTHOLOGY, edited by David Bevington et al. Copyright © 2002 by W. W. Norton & Company, Inc. Used by permission of W. W. Norton & Company, Inc.

Zeami Motokiyo: *Atsumori* from TRADITIONAL JAPANESE THEATRE: AN ANTHOLOGY OF PLAYS, edited and translated by Karen Brazell. Copyright © 1998 Columbia University Press. Reprinted with permission of the publisher.

ILLUSTRATIONS

3: Marty Nordstrom c/o the Guthrie Theater; **5:** Erich Lessing/Art Resource, NY; **7:** The Granger Collection, New York; **9:** Theatre and Playhouse by Richard and Helen Leacroft, Methuen Publishing, Ltd.; **11:** Vanni/Art Resource, NY; **12:** Museo Capitolino, Rome, Italy/ Ancient Art and Architecture Collection Ltd./The Bridgeman Art Library; **13:** Scala/Art Resource, NY; **15:** Kings Visualization Lab; **17:** ART; **18:** The Philadelphia Museum of Art/Art Resource, NY; **21:** Princeton University Press, 1976; **23:** AFP/Getty Images; **25:** ART; **26:** Theatre and Playhouse by Richard and Helen Leacroft, Methuen Publishing, Ltd.; **28:** Merridew: Coventry, 1825; **30:** Wikipedia Commons; **33:** Wikipedia Commons; **35:** Musee de la Ville de Paris, Musee Carnavalet, Paris, France/ Giraudon/The Bridgeman Art Library; **37:** Lebrecht Authors; **39:** The Art Archive; **42:** Lebrecht Authors; **43:** Kevin George/Alamy; **46:** akg-images; **47:** Lebrecht Authors; **49:** Private Collection/ The Bridgeman Art Library; **51:** Tate, London/Art Resource, NY; **54:** akg-images; **55** (top): akg-images; **55** (bottom): V&A Images, London/Art Resource, NY; **57:** Lebrecht Authors; **59:** Picture Collection, The Branch Libraries, The New York Public Library, Astor, Lenox and Tilden Foundations; **61:** Lebrecht Authors; **63:** Snark/Art Resource, NY; **64:** Lipnitzki/Roger Viollet/Getty Images; **65:** Kurt Weill Foundation/Lebrecht Music & Arts; **66:** The New York Public Library, Astor, Lenox and Tilden Foundations; **68:** Franklin D. Roosevelt Library; **71:** Lipnitzki/Roger Viollet/Getty Images; **72:** Hulton-Deutsch Collection/Corbis; **73:** W. Eugene Smith/Time & Life/Getty Images; **74:** Bettmann/Corbis; **76:** Julio Donoso/Corbis; **79:** Nobby Clark/Hulton Archive/Getty Images; **89:** Araldo de Luca/Corbis; **92:** Craig Schwartz/© 2008 J. Paul Getty Trust; **138:** Bettmann/Corbis; **140:** *Antigone* of Sophocles's Greek-Director Irene Papas.Teatro Siracusa.2005-AFI-Archive Foundation INDA Syracuse; **141:** Geraint Lewis; **223:** Museo Pio Clementino, Vatican Museums/Scala/ Art Resource, NY; **226:** Geraint Lewis; **228:** Kimball Art Museum, Fort Worth, Texas/Art Resource,

Index